W9-DBK-101

EDITORIAL BOARD

2003–2004 Edition

Federal Income Tax

Code and Regulations
Selected Sections

As of June 1, 2003

Edited by

MARTIN B. DICKINSON

Robert A. Schroeder Professor of Law
University of Kansas

CCH INCORPORATED
Chicago
A WoltersKluwer Company

ISBN 0-8080-0974-5

©2003, **CCH** INCORPORATED

4025 W. Peterson Ave.
Chicago, IL 60646-6085
1 800 248 3248
http://tax.cchgroup.com

Preface

This volume provides a selection of the Internal Revenue Code and Treasury Regulations provisions relating to the income tax. The selection reflects the collective judgment of the eight tax teachers who constitute the Editorial Board.

This edition is current through June 1, 2003, and fully reflects all changes in the Code and Regulations through that date, including the Jobs and Growth Tax Relief Reconciliation Act of 2003. The Jobs and Growth Tax Relief Reconciliation Act of 2003 and the Economic Growth and Tax Relief Reconciliation Act of 2001 provide that certain provisions of those acts are to have no effect after December 31, 2008, or December 31, 2010. The provisions that would be affected have not been indicated in this volume.

The CPI-adjusted dollar amounts for 2003 are provided at the outset of the volume, and a caution note precedes each Code section affected by CPI adjustment. A simplified corporation tax rate schedule and the most commonly used depreciation schedules are provided as well.

Caution notes precede many sections of the Regulations that do not reflect later changes in the Code. For example, the note preceding Reg. § 1.331-1 explains that Reg. § 1.331-1, last amended in 1968, does not reflect the 1982 amendments to Section 331 that deleted references to partial liquidations. No effort has been made to flag all such inconsistencies; only the most significant are noted. Proposed regulations are included in numeric order with final and temporary regulations.

The volume provides thorough coverage of the provisions most commonly addressed in income tax courses, together with limited coverage of many provisions of less general interest. Space limitations, however, have required exclusion of narrow provisions, such as those affecting only specialized businesses, *e.g.,* insurance. Virtually all provisions relating to foreign income and foreign taxpayers have been omitted; they are provided in a separate volume published by **CCH** INCORPORATED. Many provisions have been edited to remove obsolete items and material of marginal importance. Ellipsis marks are provided wherever material is omitted within a Code or Regulation section.

The volume is intended only for instructional use, and practitioners will of course need to consult the full, current text of the law.

The popularity of this volume is a tribute to the hard work of the editorial staff at **CCH** INCORPORATED, whose diligence and perfectionism continue to assure a volume that is both current and correct. Special thanks go to Joseph Gornick, Larry Norris, and Mary Ellen Guth.

We want this volume to meet the needs of as many tax teachers as possible, and we appreciate all suggestions toward that end. Communications should be sent to the undersigned at the School of Law, University of Kansas, 1535 W. 15th St., Lawrence, KS 66045-7577, or mbd@ku.edu.

Martin B. Dickinson

June 2003

Contents

CONSUMER PRICE INDEX ADJUSTMENTS FOR 2003

Certain dollar amounts stated in the Internal Revenue Code are adjusted for inflation each year, based on changes in the Consumer Price Index for all-urban consumers (CPI), published by the Department of Labor.

The adjusted amounts applicable to taxable years beginning in 2003 are set forth in certain revenue procedures, relevant portions of which are reproduced below. Each adjusted dollar amount is to be substituted for the amount stated in the Code for all purposes relating to taxable years beginning in 2003.

The Treasury is expected to issue new tables setting forth tax rates and brackets for taxable years beginning in 2003. These tables will incorporate both CPI adjustments and the rate reductions mandated by Code Section 1(i) as amended by the Jobs and Growth Tax Relief Reconciliation Act of 2003. CCH has provided unofficial projections below.

A caution note precedes each Code section or subsection subject to CPI adjustment.

CCH Projected 2003 Tax Rate Tables

TABLE 1—Section 1(a).—MARRIED INDIVIDUALS FILING JOINT RETURNS AND SURVIVING SPOUSES

If Taxable Income Is:	The Tax Is:
Not Over $14,000	10% of the taxable income
Over $14,000 but not over $56,800	$1,400.00 plus 15% of the excess over $14,000
Over $56,800 but not over $114,650	$7,820.00 plus 25% of the excess over $56,800
Over $114,650 but not over $174,700	$22,282.50 plus 28% of the excess over $114,650
Over $174,700 but not over $311,950	$39,096.50 plus 33% of the excess over $174,700
Over $311,950	$84,389.00 plus 35% of the excess over $311,950

TABLE 2—Section 1(b).—HEADS OF HOUSEHOLDS

If Taxable Income Is:	The Tax Is:
Not Over $10,000	10% of the taxable income
Over $10,000 but not over $38,050	$1,000.00 plus 15% of the excess over $10,000
Over $38,050 but not over $98,250	$5,207.50 plus 25% of the excess over $38,050
Over $98,250 but not over $159,100	$20,257.50 plus 28% of the excess over $98,250
Over $159,100 but not over $311,950	$37,295.50 plus 33% of the excess over $159,100
Over $311,950	$87,736.00 plus 35% of the excess over $311,950

TABLE 3—Section 1(c).—UNMARRIED INDIVIDUALS (OTHER THAN SURVIVING SPOUSES AND HEADS OF HOUSEHOLDS)

If Taxable Income Is:	The Tax Is:
Not Over $7,000	10% of the taxable income
Over $7,000 but not over $28,400	$700.00 plus 15% of the excess over $7,000
Over $28,400 but not over $68,800	$3,910.00 plus 25% of the excess over $28,400
Over $68,800 but not over $143,500	$14,010.00 plus 28% of the excess over $68,800
Over $143,500 but not over $311,950	$34,926.00 plus 33% of the excess over $143,500
Over $311,950	$90,514.50 plus 35% of the excess over $311,950

TABLE 4—Section 1(d).—MARRIED INDIVIDUALS FILING SEPARATE RETURNS

If Taxable Income Is:	The Tax Is:
Not Over $7,000	10% of the taxable income
Over $7,000 but not over $28,400	$700.00 plus 15% of the excess over $7,000
Over $28,400 but not over $57,325	$3,910.00 plus 25% of the excess over $28,400
Over $57,325 but not over $87,350	$11,141.25 plus 28% of the excess over $57,325
Over $87,350 but not over $155,975	$19,548.25 plus 33% of the excess over $87,350
Over $155,975	$42,194.50 plus 35% of the excess over $155,975

TABLE 5—Section 1(e).—ESTATES AND TRUSTS

If Taxable Income Is:	The Tax Is:
Not Over $1,900	15% of the taxable income
Over $1,900 but not over $4,500	$285.00 plus 25% of the excess over $1,900
Over $4,500 but not over $6,850	$935.00 plus 28% of the excess over $4,500
Over $6,850 but not over $9,350	$1,593.00 plus 33% of the excess over $6,850
Over $9,350	$2,418.00 plus 35% of the excess over $9,350

Revenue Procedure 2002-70, 2002-46 IRB 845

SECTION 1. PURPOSE

This revenue procedure sets forth inflation adjusted items for 2003.

* * *

SECTION 3. 2003 ADJUSTED ITEMS

* * *

.02 *Unearned Income of Minor Children Taxed as if Parent's Income (the "Kiddie Tax")*. For taxable years beginning in 2003, the amount in § 1(g)(4)(A)(ii)(I), which is used to reduce the net unearned income reported on the child's return that is subject to the "kiddie tax," is $750. (This amount is the same as the $750 standard deduction amount provided in section 3.09(2) of this revenue procedure.) The same $750 amount is used for purposes of § 1(g)(7) (that is, in determining whether a parent may elect to include a child's gross income in the parent's gross income and for calculating the "kiddie tax"). For example, one of the requirements for the parental election is that a child's gross income is more than the amount referenced in § 1(g)(4)(A)(ii)(I) but less than 10 times such amount; thus, a child's gross income for 2003 must be more than $750 but less than $7,500 to satisfy that requirement.

.03 *Adoption Credit*. For taxable years beginning in 2003, under § 23(a)(3) the maximum credit allowed in the case of an adoption of a child with special needs is $10,160. For taxable years beginning in 2003, under § 23(b)(1) the maximum credit allowed with regard to other adoptions is the amount of qualified adoption expenses up to

$10,160. The available adoption credit begins to phase out under § 23(b)(2)(A) for taxpayers with modified adjusted gross income in excess of $152,390 and is completely phased out for taxpayers with modified adjusted gross income of $192,390.

.04 *Child Tax Credit*. For taxable years beginning in 2003, the value used in § 24(d)(1)(B)(i) in determining the amount of credit under § 24 that may be refundable is $10,500.

.05 *Hope and Lifetime Learning Credits*.

(1) For taxable years beginning in 2003, 100 percent of qualified tuition and related expenses not in excess of $1,000 and 50 percent of such expenses in excess of $1,000 are taken into account in determining the amount of the Hope Scholarship Credit under § 25A(b)(1).

(2) For taxable years beginning in 2003, a taxpayer's modified adjusted gross income in excess of $41,000 ($83,000 in the case of a joint return) is taken into account in determining the reduction under § 25A(d)(2)(A)(ii) in the amount of the Hope Scholarship and Lifetime Learning Credits otherwise allowable under § 25A(a).

.06 *Earned Income Credit*.

(1) *In general*. For taxable years beginning in 2003, the following amounts are used to determine the earned income credit under § 32(b). The "earned income amount" is the amount of earned income at or above which the maximum amount of the earned income credit is allowed. The "threshold phaseout amount" is the amount of adjusted gross income (or, if greater, earned in-

come) above which the maximum amount of the credit begins to phase out. The "completed phaseout amount" is the amount of adjusted gross

income (or if greater, earned income) at or above which no credit is allowed.

Item	Number of Qualifying Children		
	One	Two or More	None
Earned Income Amount	$ 7,490	$10,510	$ 4,990
Maximum Amount of Credit	$ 2,547	$ 4,204	$ 382
Threshold Phaseout Amount.....................	$13,730	$13,730	$ 6,240
Completed Phaseout Amount	$29,666	$33,692	$11,230
Threshold Phaseout Amount (Married Filing Jointly)	$14,730	$14,730	$ 7,240
Completed Phaseout Amount (Married Filing Jointly)	$30,666	$34,692	$12,230

The instructions for the Form 1040 series provide tables showing the amount of the earned income credit for each type of taxpayer.

(2) *Excessive investment income.* For taxable years beginning in 2003, the earned income tax credit is denied under § 32(i) if the aggregate amount of certain investment income exceeds $2,600.

* * *

.08 *Alternative Minimum Tax Exemption for a Child Subject to the "Kiddie Tax."* For taxable years beginning in 2003, in the case of a child to whom the § 1(g) "kiddie tax" applies, the exemption amount under § § 55 and 59(j) for purposes of the alternative minimum tax under § 55 may not exceed the sum of (A) such child's earned income for the taxable year, plus (B) $5,600.

.09 *Standard Deduction.*

(1) *In general.* For taxable years beginning in 2003, the standard deduction amounts under § 63(c)(2) are as follows:

Filing Status	Standard Deduction
MARRIED INDIVIDUALS FILING JOINT RETURNS AND SURVIVING SPOUSES (§ 1(a))	$7,950
HEADS OF HOUSEHOLDS (§ 1(b))	$7,000
UNMARRIED INDIVIDUALS (OTHER THAN SURVIVING SPOUSES AND HEADS OF HOUSEHOLDS) (§ 1(c))	$4,750
MARRIED INDIVIDUALS FILING SEPARATE RETURNS (§ 1(d))........	$3,975

(2) *Dependent.* For taxable years beginning in 2003, the standard deduction amount under § 63(c)(5) for an individual who may be claimed as a dependent by another taxpayer may not exceed the greater of $750 or the sum of $250 and the individual's earned income.

(3) *Aged and blind.* For taxable years beginning in 2003, the additional standard deduction amounts under § 63(f) for the aged and for the blind are $950 for each. These amounts are increased to $1,150 if the individual is also unmarried and not a surviving spouse.

.10 *Overall Limitation on Itemized Deductions.* For taxable years beginning in 2003, the "applicable amount" of adjusted gross income under § 68(b), above which the amount of otherwise allowable itemized deductions is reduced under § 68, is $139,500 (or $69,750 for a separate return filed by a married individual).

.11 *Qualified Transportation Fringe.* For taxable years beginning in 2003, the monthly limitation under § 132(f)(2)(A), regarding the aggregate fringe benefit exclusion amount for transportation in a commuter highway vehicle and any transit pass, is $100. The monthly limitation under § 132(f)(2)(B) regarding the fringe benefit exclusion amount for qualified parking is $190.

.12 *Income from United States Savings Bonds for Taxpayers Who Pay Qualified Higher Education Expenses.* For taxable years beginning in 2003, the exclusion under § 135, regarding income from United States savings bonds for taxpayers who pay qualified higher education expenses, begins to phase out for modified adjusted gross income above $87,750 for joint returns and $58,500 for other returns. This exclusion completely phases out for modified adjusted gross income of $117,750 or more for joint returns and $73,500 or more for other returns.

* * *

.14 *Private Activity Bonds Volume Cap.* For calendar years beginning in 2003, the amounts used under § 146(d)(1) to calculate the State ceiling for the volume cap for private activity bonds is the greater of $75 multiplied by the State population or $228,580,000.

.15 *Personal Exemption.*

(1) *Exemption amount.* For taxable years beginning in 2003, the personal exemption amount under § 151(d) is $3,050.

(2) *Phase out.* For taxable years beginning in 2003, the personal exemption amount begins to phase out at, and is completely phased out after, the following adjusted gross income amounts:

Filing Status	AGI—Beginning of Phaseout	AGI Above Which Exemption Fully Phased Out
Code § 1(a)	$209,250	$331,750
Code § 1(b)	$174,400	$296,900
Code § 1(c)......	$139,500	$262,000
Code § 1(d)	$104,625	$165,875

.16 *Eligible Long-Term Care Premiums.* For taxable years beginning in 2003, the limitations under § 213(d)(10), regarding eligible long-term care premiums includible in the term "medical care," are as follows:

Attained age before the close of the taxable year:	Limitation on premiums:
40 or less......................	$ 250
More than 40 but not more than 50 ...	$ 470
More than 50 but not more than 60 ...	$ 940
More than 60 but not more than 70 ...	$2,510
More than 70	$3,130

* * *

.18 *Interest on Education Loans.* For taxable years beginning in 2003, the $2,500 maximum deduction for interest paid on qualified education loans under § 221 is reduced under § 221(b)(2)(B)

when modified adjusted gross income exceeds $50,000 ($100,000 for joint returns), and is completely eliminated when modified adjusted gross income is $65,000 ($130,000 for joint returns).

* * *

.30 *Property Exempt from Levy.* For calendar year 2003, the value of property exempt from levy under § 6334(a)(2) (fuel, provisions, furniture, and other household personal effects, as well as arms for personal use, livestock, and poultry) may not exceed $6,890. The value of property exempt from levy under § 6334(a)(3) (books and tools necessary for the trade, business, or profession of the taxpayer) may not exceed $3,440.

* * *

SECTION 4. EFFECTIVE DATE

.01 *General Rule.* Except as provided in section 4.02, this revenue procedure applies to taxable years beginning in 2003.

* * *

Revenue Ruling 2002-79, 2002-48 IRB 909

Table 1

Inflation-Adjusted Amounts Under Section 1274A

Calendar Year of Sale or Exchange	1274A(b) Amount (qualified debt instrument)	1274A(c)(2)(A) Amount (cash method debt instrument)
1990	$2,933,200	$2,095,100
1991	$3,079,600	$2,199,700
1992	$3,234,900	$2,310,600
1993	$3,332,400	$2,380,300
1994	$3,433,500	$2,452,500
1995	$3,523,600	$2,516,900
1996	$3,622,500	$2,587,500
1997	$3,723,800	$2,659,900
1998	$3,823,100	$2,730,800
1999	$3,885,500	$2,775,400
2000	$3,960,100	$2,828,700
2001	$4,085,900	$2,918,500
2002	$4,217,500	$3,012,500
2003	$4,280,800	$3,057,700

CORPORATION TAX RATE SCHEDULE

The table below provides a simplified method of determining the income tax imposed on most corporations pursuant to Section 11(b)(1).

CORPORATIONS

Taxable Income Over	Taxable Income Not Over	Pay	+ Tax Rate % ×	Excess Over
$ 0	$ 50,000	$ 0	15	$ 0
50,000	75,000	7,500	25	50,000
75,000	100,000	13,750	34	75,000
100,000	335,000	22,250	39	100,000
335,000	10,000,000	0	34	0
10,000,000	15,000,000	3,400,000	35	10,000,000
15,000,000	18,333,333	5,150,000	38	15,000,000
18,333,333	. . . .	0	35	0

CAPITAL GAIN TRANSITIONAL RULE FOR 2003

Section 301(c) of the Jobs and Growth Tax Relief Reconciliation Act of 2003 provides as follows:

(c) TRANSITIONAL RULES FOR TAXABLE YEARS WHICH INCLUDE MAY 6, 2003.—For purposes of applying section 1(h) of the Internal Revenue Code of 1986 in the case of a taxable year which includes May 6, 2003—

(1) The amount of tax determined under subparagraph (B) of section 1(h)(1) of such Code shall be the sum of—

(A) 5 percent of the lesser of—

(i) the net capital gain determined by taking into account only gain or loss properly taken into account for the portion of the taxable year on or after May 6, 2003 (determined without regard to collectibles gain or loss, gain described in section 1(h)(6)(A)(i) of such Code, and section 1202 gain), or

(ii) the amount on which a tax is determined under such subparagraph (without regard to this subsection),

(B) 8 percent of the lesser of—

(i) the qualified 5-year gain (as defined in section 1(h)(9) of the Internal Revenue Code of 1986, as in effect on the day before the date of the enactment of this Act) properly taken into account for the portion of the taxable year before May 6, 2003, or

(ii) the excess (if any) of—

(I) the amount on which a tax is determined under such subparagraph (without regard to this subsection), over

(II) the amount on which a tax is determined under subparagraph (A), plus

(C) 10 percent of the excess (if any) of—

(i) the amount on which a tax is determined under such subparagraph (without regard to this subsection), over

(ii) the sum of the amounts on which a tax is determined under subparagraphs (A) and (B).

(2) The amount of tax determined under subparagraph (C) of section (1)(h)(1) of such Code shall be the sum of—

(A) 15 percent of the lesser of—

(i) the excess (if any) of the amount of net capital gain determined under subparagraph (A)(i) of paragraph (1) of this subsection over the amount on which a tax is determined under subparagraph (A) of paragraph (1) of this subsection, or

(ii) the amount on which a tax is determined under such subparagraph (C) (without regard to this subsection), plus

(B) 20 percent of the excess (if any) of—

(i) the amount on which a tax is determined under such subparagraph (C) (without regard to this subsection), over

(ii) the amount on which a tax is determined under subparagraph (A) of this paragraph.

(3) For purposes of applying section 55(b)(3) of such Code, rules similar to the rules of paragraphs (1) and (2) of this subsection shall apply.

(4) In applying this subsection with respect to any pass-thru entity, the determination of when gains and losses are properly taken into account shall be made at the entity level.

(5) For purposes of applying section 1(h)(11) of such Code, as added by section 302 of this Act, to this subsection, dividends which are qualified dividend income shall be treated as gain properly taken into account for the portion of the taxable year on or after May 6, 2003.

(6) Terms used in this subsection which are also used in section 1(h) of such Code shall have the respective meanings that such terms have in such section.

DEPRECIATION TABLES

The Commissioner of Internal Revenue has promulgated tables that may, at the election of the taxpayer, be used in implementing the Accelerated Cost Recovery System of depreciation provided by Section 168. The most frequently used tables are reproduced below. Table 1 covers most personal property, and Table 6 covers residential rental property. Both are from Rev. Proc. 87-57, 1987-2 CB 687. Table A-7a, taken from IRS Publication 946, covers nonresidential real property placed in service on or after May 13, 1993. Tables for other circumstances, including the mid-quarter convention and the Section 168(g) alternative depreciation system, may be found in Rev. Proc. 87-57 and IRS Publication 946.

In the case of Table 1, the depreciation percentages reflect the 200 percent declining balance method, switching to straight line method, for property with applicable recovery periods of 3, 5, 7, or 10 years and the 150 percent declining balance method, switching to straight line method, for property with applicable recovery periods of 15 or 20 years.

The tables below set forth the percentages to be applied against the basis of the asset, after reducing the basis to reflect (1) any deduction available under Section 179 and (2) the special 30% or 50% depreciation deduction available for certain assets, pursuant to Section 168(k). The percentage set forth in the table is applied each year to the basis remaining after application of Sections 179 and 168(k), without any reduction for prior depreciation deductions under Section 168(a). For example, assume that the taxpayer purchases an asset subject to a 5-year recovery period, and that after reducing the basis to reflect deductions available under Sections 179 and 168(k), the remaining basis is $100,000. Under Table 1 below, the first-year depreciation (over and above that allowed under Section 168(k)) is $20,000, the second-year depreciation is $32,000, the third-year depreciation is $19,200, and so on.

Table 1. General Depreciation System
  Applicable Depreciation Method: 200 or 150 Percent
  Declining Balance Switching to Straight Line
  Applicable Recovery Periods: 3, 5, 7, 10, 15, 20 years
  Applicable Convention: Half-year

If the Recovery Year is:	3-year	5-year	7-year	10-year	15-year	20-year
1	33.33	20.00	14.29	10.00	5.00	3.750
2	44.45	32.00	24.49	18.00	9.50	7.219
3	14.81	19.20	17.49	14.40	8.55	6.677
4	7.41	11.52	12.49	11.52	7.70	6.177
5		11.52	8.93	9.22	6.93	5.713
6		5.76	8.92	7.37	6.23	5.285
7			8.93	6.55	5.90	4.888
8			4.46	6.55	5.90	4.522
9				6.56	5.91	4.462
10				6.55	5.90	4.461
11				3.28	5.91	4.462
12					5.90	4.461
13					5.91	4.462
14					5.90	4.461
15					5.91	4.462
16					2.95	4.461
17						4.462
18						4.461
19						4.462
20						4.461
21						2.231

Table 6. General Depreciation System
    Applicable Depreciation Method: Straight Line
    Applicable Recovery Period: 27.5 years
    Applicable Convention: Mid-month

If the Recovery Year is:	And the Month in the First Recovery Year the Property is Placed in Service is: the Depreciation Rate is:											
	1	2	3	4	5	6	7	8	9	10	11	12
1	3.485	3.182	2.879	2.576	2.273	1.970	1.667	1.364	1.061	0.758	0.455	0.152
2	3.636	3.636	3.636	3.636	3.636	3.636	3.636	3.636	3.636	3.636	3.636	3.636
3	3.636	3.636	3.636	3.636	3.636	3.636	3.636	3.636	3.636	3.636	3.636	3.636
4	3.636	3.636	3.636	3.636	3.636	3.636	3.636	3.636	3.636	3.636	3.636	3.636
5	3.636	3.636	3.636	3.636	3.636	3.636	3.636	3.636	3.636	3.636	3.636	3.636
6	3.636	3.636	3.636	3.636	3.636	3.636	3.636	3.636	3.636	3.636	3.636	3.636
7	3.636	3.636	3.636	3.636	3.636	3.636	3.636	3.636	3.636	3.636	3.636	3.636
8	3.636	3.636	3.636	3.636	3.636	3.636	3.636	3.636	3.636	3.636	3.636	3.636
9	3.636	3.636	3.636	3.636	3.636	3.636	3.636	3.636	3.636	3.636	3.636	3.636
10	3.637	3.637	3.637	3.637	3.637	3.637	3.636	3.636	3.636	3.636	3.636	3.636
11	3.636	3.636	3.636	3.636	3.636	3.636	3.637	3.637	3.637	3.637	3.637	3.637
12	3.637	3.637	3.637	3.637	3.637	3.637	3.636	3.636	3.636	3.636	3.636	3.636
13	3.636	3.636	3.636	3.636	3.636	3.636	3.637	3.637	3.637	3.637	3.637	3.637
14	3.637	3.637	3.637	3.637	3.637	3.637	3.636	3.636	3.636	3.636	3.636	3.636
15	3.636	3.636	3.636	3.636	3.636	3.636	3.637	3.637	3.637	3.637	3.637	3.637
16	3.637	3.637	3.637	3.637	3.637	3.637	3.636	3.636	3.636	3.636	3.636	3.636
17	3.636	3.636	3.636	3.636	3.636	3.636	3.637	3.637	3.637	3.637	3.637	3.637
18	3.637	3.637	3.637	3.637	3.637	3.637	3.636	3.636	3.636	3.636	3.636	3.636
19	3.636	3.636	3.636	3.636	3.636	3.636	3.637	3.637	3.637	3.637	3.637	3.637
20	3.637	3.637	3.637	3.637	3.637	3.637	3.636	3.636	3.636	3.636	3.636	3.636
21	3.636	3.636	3.636	3.636	3.636	3.636	3.637	3.637	3.637	3.637	3.637	3.637
22	3.637	3.637	3.637	3.637	3.637	3.637	3.636	3.636	3.636	3.636	3.636	3.636
23	3.636	3.636	3.636	3.636	3.636	3.636	3.637	3.637	3.637	3.637	3.637	3.637
24	3.637	3.637	3.637	3.637	3.637	3.637	3.636	3.636	3.636	3.636	3.636	3.636
25	3.636	3.636	3.636	3.636	3.636	3.636	3.637	3.637	3.637	3.637	3.637	3.637
26	3.637	3.637	3.637	3.637	3.637	3.637	3.636	3.636	3.636	3.636	3.636	3.636
27	3.636	3.636	3.636	3.636	3.636	3.636	3.637	3.637	3.637	3.637	3.637	3.637
28	1.970	2.273	2.576	2.879	3.182	3.485	3.636	3.636	3.636	3.636	3.636	3.636
29	0.000	0.000	0.000	0.000	0.000	0.000	0.152	0.455	0.758	1.061	1.364	1.667

Table A-7a. Nonresidential Real Property
Applicable Depreciation Method: Straight Line
Applicable Recovery Period: 39 years
Applicable Convention: Mid-month

If the Recovery Year is:	And the Month in the First Recovery Year the Property is Placed in Service is: the Depreciation Rate is:											
	1	2	3	4	5	6	7	8	9	10	11	12
1	2.461	2.247	2.033	1.819	1.605	1.391	1.177	0.963	0.749	0.535	0.321	0.107
2—39	2.564	2.564	2.564	2.564	2.564	2.564	2.564	2.564	2.564	2.564	2.564	2.564
40	0.107	0.321	0.535	0.749	0.963	1.177	1.391	1.605	1.819	2.033	2.247	2.461

Table of Code and Regulations Sections

Internal Revenue Code and Regulations Selected Sections

* Code provision or regulation not reproduced.

---

* Code provision or regulation not reproduced.

* Code provision or regulation not reproduced.

* Code provision or regulation not reproduced.

---

* Code provision or regulation not reproduced.

* Code provision or regulation not reproduced.

* Code provision or regulation not reproduced.

---

* Code provision or regulation not reproduced.

---

* Code provision or regulation not reproduced.

---

* Code provision or regulation not reproduced.

---

* Code provision or regulation not reproduced.

* Code provision or regulation not reproduced.

* Code provision or regulation not reproduced.

* Code provision or regulation not reproduced.

---

* Code provision or regulation not reproduced.

---

* Code provision or regulation not reproduced.

---

* Code provision or regulation not reproduced.

---

* Code provision or regulation not reproduced.

---

* Code provision or regulation not reproduced.

---

* Code provision or regulation not reproduced.

Internal Revenue Code

INTERNAL REVENUE CODE OF 1986

Subtitle A—Income Taxes

CHAPTER 1—NORMAL TAXES AND SURTAXES

Subchapter A—Determination of Tax Liability

PART I—TAX ON INDIVIDUALS

[Caution: Pursuant to Section 1(f), certain of the income brackets in Section 1(a), (b), (c), (d) and (e) are adjusted for taxable years beginning after 1993 to reflect increases in the Consumer Price Index. Pursuant to Section 1(i), the tax amounts for 2001 and later years are to reflect the rate reductions mandated by Section 1(i). The adjusted amounts applicable to taxable years beginning in 2003 are provided beginning at page ix.]

[Sec. 1]

SECTION 1. TAX IMPOSED.

[Sec. 1(a)]

(a) MARRIED INDIVIDUALS FILING JOINT RETURNS AND SURVIVING SPOUSES.—There is hereby imposed on the taxable income of—

> (1) every married individual (as defined in section 7703) who makes a single return jointly with his spouse under section 6013, and

> (2) every surviving spouse (as defined in section 2(a)),

a tax determined in accordance with the following table:

If taxable income is:	The tax is:
Not over $36,900	15% of taxable income.
Over $36,900 but not over $89,150	$5,535, plus 28% of the excess over $36,900.
Over $89,150 but not over $140,000	$20,165, plus 31% of the excess over $89,150.
Over $140,000 but not over $250,000	$35,928.50, plus 36% of the excess over $140,000.
Over $250,000	$75,528.50, plus 39.6% of the excess over $250,000.

[Sec. 1(b)]

(b) HEADS OF HOUSEHOLDS.—There is hereby imposed on the taxable income of every head of a household (as defined in section 2(b)) a tax determined in accordance with the following table:

If taxable income is:	The tax is:
Not over $29,600	15% of taxable income.
Over $29,600 but not over $76,400	$4,440, plus 28% of the excess over $29,600.
Over $76,400 but not over $127,500	$17,544, plus 31% of the excess over $76,400.
Over $127,500 but not over $250,000	$33,385, plus 36% of the excess over $127,500.
Over $250,000	$77,485, plus 39.6% of the excess over $250,000.

[Sec. 1(c)]

(c) UNMARRIED INDIVIDUALS (OTHER THAN SURVIVING SPOUSES AND HEADS OF HOUSEHOLDS).—There is hereby imposed on the taxable income of every individual (other than a surviving spouse as defined in section 2(a) or the head of a household as defined in section 2(b)) who is not a married individual (as defined in section 7703) a tax determined in accordance with the following table:

If taxable income is:	The tax is:
Not over $22,100	15% of taxable income.
Over $22,100 but not over $53,500	$3,315, plus 28% of the excess over $22,100.
Over $53,500 but not over $115,000	$12,107, plus 31% of the excess over $53,500.
Over $115,000 but not over $250,000	$31,172, plus 36% of the excess over $115,000.
Over $250,000	$79,772, plus 39.6% of the excess over $250,000.

[Sec. 1(d)]

(d) MARRIED INDIVIDUALS FILING SEPARATE RETURNS.—There is hereby imposed on the taxable income of every married individual (as defined in section 7703) who does not make a single return jointly with his spouse under section 6013, a tax determined in accordance with the following table:

If taxable income is:	The tax is:
Not over $18,450	15% of taxable income.
Over $18,450 but not over $44,575	$2,767.50, plus 28% of the excess over $18,450.
Over $44,575 but not over $70,000	$10,082.50, plus 31% of the excess over $44,575.
Over $70,000 but not over $125,000	$17,964.25, plus 36% of the excess over $70,000.
Over $125,000	$37,764.25, plus 39.6% of the excess over $125,000.

[Sec. 1(e)]

(e) ESTATES AND TRUSTS.—There is hereby imposed on the taxable income of—

(1) every estate, and

(2) every trust,

taxable under this subsection a tax determined in accordance with the following table:

If taxable income is:	The tax is:
Not over $1,500	15% of taxable income.
Over $1,500 but not over $3,500	$225, plus 28% of the excess over $1,500.
Over $3,500 but not over $5,500	$785, plus 31% of the excess over $3,500.
Over $5,500 but not over $7,500	$1,405, plus 36% of the excess over $5,500.
Over $7,500	$2,125, plus 39.6% of the excess over $7,500.

[Sec. 1(f)]

(f) PHASEOUT OF MARRIAGE PENALTY IN 15-PERCENT BRACKET; ADJUSTMENTS IN TAX TABLES SO THAT INFLATION WILL NOT RESULT IN TAX INCREASES.—

(1) IN GENERAL.—Not later than December 15 of 1993, and each subsequent calendar year, the Secretary shall prescribe tables which shall apply in lieu of the tables contained in subsections (a), (b), (c), (d), and (e) with respect to taxable years beginning in the succeeding calendar year.

(2) METHOD OF PRESCRIBING TABLES.—The table which under paragraph (1) is to apply in lieu of the table contained in subsection (a), (b), (c), (d), or (e), as the case may be, with respect to taxable years beginning in any calendar year shall be prescribed—

(A) except as provided in paragraph (8), by increasing the minimum and maximum dollar amounts for each rate bracket for which a tax is imposed under such table by the cost-of-living adjustment for such calendar year,

(B) by not changing the rate applicable to any rate bracket as adjusted under subparagraph (A), and

(C) by adjusting the amounts setting forth the tax to the extent necessary to reflect the adjustments in the rate brackets.

(3) COST-OF-LIVING ADJUSTMENT.—For purposes of paragraph (2), the cost-of-living adjustment for any calendar year is the percentage (if any) by which—

(A) the CPI for the preceding calendar year, exceeds

(B) the CPI for calendar year 1992.

(4) CPI FOR ANY CALENDAR YEAR.—For purposes of paragraph (3), the CPI for any calendar year is the average of the Consumer Price Index as of the close of the 12-month period ending on August 31 of such calendar year.

(5) CONSUMER PRICE INDEX.—For purposes of paragraph (4), the term "Consumer Price Index" means the last Consumer Price Index for all-urban consumers published by the Department of Labor. For purposes of the preceding sentence, the revision of the Consumer Price Index which is most consistent with the Consumer Price Index for calendar year 1986 shall be used.

(6) ROUNDING.—

(A) IN GENERAL.—If any increase determined under paragraph (2)(A), section 63(c)(4), section 68(b)(2) or section 151(d)(4) is not a multiple of $50, such increase shall be rounded to the next lowest multiple of $50.

(B) TABLE FOR MARRIED INDIVIDUALS FILING SEPARATELY.—In the case of a married individual filing a separate return, subparagraph (A) (other than with respect to sections 63(c)(4) and 151(d)(3)(A)) shall be applied by substituting "$25" for "$50" each place it appears.

(7) SPECIAL RULE FOR CERTAIN BRACKETS.—

(A) CALENDAR YEAR 1994.—In prescribing the tables under paragraph (1) which apply with respect to taxable years beginning in calendar year 1994, the Secretary shall make no adjustment to the dollar amounts at which the 36 percent rate bracket begins or at which the 39.6 percent rate begins under any table contained in subsection (a), (b), (c), (d), or (e).

(B) LATER CALENDAR YEARS.—In prescribing tables under paragraph (1) which apply with respect to taxable years beginning in a calendar year after 1994, the cost-of-living adjustment used in making adjustments to the dollar amounts referred to in subparagraph (A) shall be determined under paragraph (3) by substituting "1993" for "1992".

(8) PHASEOUT OF MARRIAGE PENALTY IN 15-PERCENT BRACKET.—

(A) IN GENERAL.—With respect to taxable years beginning after December 31, 2002, in prescribing the tables under paragraph (1)—

(i) the maximum taxable income in the 15-percent rate bracket in the table contained in subsection (a) (and the minimum taxable income in the next higher taxable income bracket in such table) shall be the applicable percentage of the maximum taxable income in the 15-percent rate bracket in the table contained in subsection (c) (after any other adjustment under this subsection), and

(ii) the comparable taxable income amounts in the table contained in subsection (d) shall be 1/2 of the amounts determined under clause (i).

(B) APPLICABLE PERCENTAGE.—For purposes of subparagraph (A), the applicable percentage shall be determined in accordance with the following table:

For taxable years beginning in calendar year—	The applicable percentage is—
2003 and 2004	200
2005	180
2006	187
2007	193
2008 and thereafter	200

(C) ROUNDING.—If any amount determined under subparagraph (A)(i) is not a multiple of $50, such amount shall be rounded to the next lowest multiple of $50.

[Sec. 1(g)]

(g) CERTAIN UNEARNED INCOME OF MINOR CHILDREN TAXED AS IF PARENT'S INCOME.—

(1) IN GENERAL.—In the case of any child to whom this subsection applies, the tax imposed by this section shall be equal to the greater of—

(A) the tax imposed by this section without regard to this subsection, or

(B) the sum of—

(i) the tax which would be imposed by this section if the taxable income of such child for the taxable year were reduced by the net unearned income of such child, plus

(ii) such child's share of the allocable parental tax.

(2) CHILD TO WHOM SUBSECTION APPLIES.—This subsection shall apply to any child for any taxable year if—

(A) such child has not attained age 14 before the close of the taxable year, and

(B) either parent of such child is alive at the close of the taxable year.

(3) ALLOCABLE PARENTAL TAX.—For purposes of this subsection—

(A) IN GENERAL.—The term "allocable parental tax" means the excess of—

(i) the tax which would be imposed by this section on the parent's taxable income if such income included the net unearned income of all children of the parent to whom this subsection applies, over

Sec. 1(g)

(ii) the tax imposed by this section on the parent without regard to this subsection.

For purposes of clause (i), net unearned income of all children of the parent shall not be taken into account in computing any exclusion, deduction, or credit of the parent.

(B) CHILD'S SHARE.—A child's share of any allocable parental tax of a parent shall be equal to an amount which bears the same ratio to the total allocable parental tax as the child's net unearned income bears to the aggregate net unearned income of all children of such parent to whom this subsection applies.

(C) SPECIAL RULE WHERE PARENT HAS DIFFERENT TAXABLE YEAR.—Except as provided in regulations, if the parent does not have the same taxable year as the child, the allocable parental tax shall be determined on the basis of the taxable year of the parent ending in the child's taxable year.

(4) NET UNEARNED INCOME.—For purposes of this subsection—

(A) IN GENERAL.—The term "net unearned income" means the excess of—

(i) the portion of the adjusted gross income for the taxable year which is not attributable to earned income (as defined in section 911(d)(2)), over

(ii) the sum of—

(I) the amount in effect for the taxable year under section 63(c)(5)(A) (relating to limitation on standard deduction in the case of certain dependents), plus

(II) The greater of the amount described in subclause (I) or, if the child itemizes his deductions for the taxable year, the amount of the itemized deductions allowed by this chapter for the taxable year which are directly connected with the production of the portion of adjusted gross income referred to in clause (i).

(B) LIMITATION BASED ON TAXABLE INCOME.—The amount of the net unearned income for any taxable year shall not exceed the individual's taxable income for such taxable year.

(5) SPECIAL RULES FOR DETERMINING PARENT TO WHOM SUBSECTION APPLIES.—For purposes of this subsection, the parent whose taxable income shall be taken into account shall be—

(A) in the case of parents who are not married (within the meaning of section 7703), the custodial parent (within the meaning of section 152(e)) of the child, and

(B) in the case of married individuals filing separately, the individual with the greater taxable income.

(6) PROVIDING OF PARENT'S TIN.—The parent of any child to whom this subsection applies for any taxable year shall provide the TIN of such parent to such child and such child shall include such TIN on the child's return of tax imposed by this section for such taxable year.

(7) ELECTION TO CLAIM CERTAIN UNEARNED INCOME OF CHILD ON PARENT'S RETURN.—

(A) IN GENERAL.—If—

(i) any child to whom this subsection applies has gross income for the taxable year only from interest and dividends (including Alaska Permanent Fund dividends),

(ii) such gross income is more than the amount described in paragraph (4)(A)(ii)(I) and less than 10 times the amount so described,

(iii) no estimated tax payments for such year are made in the name and TIN of such child, and no amount has been deducted and withheld under section 3406, and

(iv) the parent of such child (as determined under paragraph (5)) elects the application of subparagraph (B),

such child shall be treated (other than [for] purposes of this paragraph) as having no gross income for such year and shall not be required to file a return under section 6012.

(B) INCOME INCLUDED ON PARENT'S RETURN.—In the case of a parent making the election under this paragraph—

(i) the gross income of each child to whom such election applies (to the extent the gross income of such child exceeds twice the amount described in paragraph (4)(A)(ii)(I)) shall be included in such parent's gross income for the taxable year,

(ii) the tax imposed by this section for such year with respect to such parent shall be the amount equal to the sum of—

Sec. 1(g)

(I) the amount determined under this section after the application of clause (i), plus

(II) for each such child, 10 percent of the lesser of the amount described in paragraph (4)(A)(ii)(I) or the excess of the gross income of such child over the amount so described, and

(iii) any interest which is an item of tax preference under section 57(a)(5) of the child shall be treated as an item of tax preference of such parent (and not of such child).

(C) REGULATIONS.—The Secretary shall prescribe such regulations as may be necessary or appropriate to carry out the purposes of this paragraph.

[Caution: Section 301(c) of the Jobs and Growth Tax Relief Reconciliation Act of 2003 provides a transition rule for application of Code Sec. 1(h) to taxable years that include May 6, 2003. Section 301(c) is set forth on page xiv.]

[Sec. 1(h)]

(h) MAXIMUM CAPITAL GAINS RATE.—

(1) IN GENERAL.—If a taxpayer has a net capital gain for any taxable year, the tax imposed by this section for such taxable year shall not exceed the sum of—

(A) a tax computed at the rates and in the same manner as if this subsection had not been enacted on the greater of—

(i) taxable income reduced by the net capital gain, or

(ii) the lesser of—

(I) the amount of taxable income taxed at a rate below 25 percent; or

(II) taxable income reduced by the adjusted net capital gain;

(B) 5 percent (0 percent in the case of taxable years beginning after 2007) of so much of the adjusted net capital gain (or, if less, taxable income) as does not exceed the excess (if any) of—

(i) the amount of taxable income which would (without regard to this paragraph) be taxed at a rate below 25 percent, over

(ii) the taxable income reduced by the adjusted net capital gain;

(C) 15 percent of the adjusted net capital gain (or, if less, taxable income) in excess of the amount on which a tax is determined under subparagraph (B);

(D) 25 percent of the excess (if any) of—

(i) the unrecaptured section 1250 gain (or, if less, the net capital gain), over

(ii) the excess (if any) of—

(I) the sum of the amount on which tax is determined under subparagraph (A) plus the net capital gain, over

(II) taxable income; and

(E) 28 percent of the amount of taxable income in excess of the sum of the amounts on which tax is determined under the preceding subparagraphs of this paragraph.

(2) NET CAPITAL GAIN TAKEN INTO ACCOUNT AS INVESTMENT INCOME.—For purposes of this subsection, the net capital gain for any taxable year shall be reduced (but not below zero) by the amount which the taxpayer takes into account as investment income under section 163(d)(4)(B)(iii).

(3) ADJUSTED NET CAPITAL GAIN.—For purposes of this subsection, the term "adjusted net capital gain" means the sum of—

(A) net capital gain (determined without regard to paragraph (11)) reduced (but not below zero) by the sum of—

(i) unrecaptured section 1250 gain, and

(ii) 28-percent rate gain, plus

(B) qualified dividend income (as defined in paragraph (11)).

(4) 28-PERCENT RATE GAIN.—For purposes of this subsection, the term "28-percent rate gain" means the excess (if any) of—

Sec. 1(h)

(A) the sum of—

    (i) collectibles gain; and

    (ii) section 1202 gain, over

(B) the sum of—

    (i) collectibles loss;

    (ii) the net short-term capital loss, and

    (iii) the amount of long-term capital loss carried under section 1212(b)(1)(B) to the taxable year.

(5) COLLECTIBLES GAIN AND LOSS.—For purposes of this subsection—

    (A) IN GENERAL.—The terms "collectibles gain" and "collectibles loss" mean gain or loss (respectively) from the sale or exchange of a collectible (as defined in section 408(m) without regard to paragraph (3) thereof) which is a capital asset held for more than 1 year but only to the extent such gain is taken into account in computing gross income and such loss is taken into account in computing taxable income.

    (B) PARTNERSHIPS, ETC.—For purposes of subparagraph (A), any gain from the sale of an interest in a partnership, S corporation, or trust which is attributable to unrealized appreciation in the value of collectibles shall be treated as gain from the sale or exchange of a collectible. Rules similar to the rules of section 751 shall apply for purposes of the preceding sentence.

(6) UNRECAPTURED SECTION 1250 GAIN.—For purposes of this subsection—

    (A) IN GENERAL.—The term "unrecaptured section 1250 gain" means the excess (if any) of—

    (i) the amount of long-term capital gain (not otherwise treated as ordinary income) which would be treated as ordinary income if section 1250(b)(1) included all depreciation and the applicable percentage under section 1250(a) were 100 percent, over

    (ii) the excess (if any) of—

        (I) the amount described in paragraph (5)(B); over

        (II) the amount described in paragraph (5)(A).

    (B) LIMITATION WITH RESPECT TO SECTION 1231 PROPERTY.—The amount described in subparagraph (A)(i) from sales, exchanges, and conversions described in section 1231(a)(3)(A) for any taxable year shall not exceed the net section 1231 gain (as defined in section 1231(c)(3)) for such year.

(7) SECTION 1202 GAIN.—For purposes of this subsection, the term "section 1202 gain" means the excess of—

    (A) the gain which would be excluded from gross income under section 1202 but for the percentage limitation in section 1202(a), over

    (B) the gain excluded from gross income under section 1202.

(8) COORDINATION WITH RECAPTURE OF NET ORDINARY LOSSES UNDER SECTION 1231.—If any amount is treated as ordinary income under section 1231(c), such amount shall be allocated among the separate categories of net section 1231 gain (as defined in section 1231(c)(3)) in such manner as the Secretary may by forms or regulations prescribe.

(9) REGULATIONS.—The Secretary may prescribe such regulations as are appropriate (including regulations requiring reporting) to apply this subsection in the case of sales and exchanges by pass-thru entities and of interests in such entities.

(10) PASS-THRU ENTITY DEFINED.—For purposes of this subsection, the term "pass-thru entity" means—

    (A) a regulated investment company;

    (B) a real estate investment trust;

    (C) an S corporation;

    (D) a partnership;

    (E) an estate or trust;

    (F) a common trust fund;

(G) a foreign investment company which is described in section 1246(b)(1) and for which an election is in effect under section 1247; and

(H) a qualified electing fund (as defined in section 1295).

(11) DIVIDENDS TAXED AS NET CAPITAL GAIN.—

(A) IN GENERAL.—For purposes of this subsection, the term "net capital gain" means net capital gain (determined without regard to this paragraph) increased by qualified dividend income.

(B) QUALIFIED DIVIDEND INCOME.—For purposes of this paragraph—

(i) IN GENERAL.—The term "qualified dividend income" means dividends received during the taxable year from—

(I) domestic corporations, and

(II) qualified foreign corporations.

(ii) CERTAIN DIVIDENDS EXCLUDED.—Such term shall not include—

(I) any dividend from a corporation which for the taxable year of the corporation in which the distribution is made, or the preceding taxable year, is a corporation exempt from tax under section 501 or 521,

(II) any amount allowed as a deduction under section 591 (relating to deduction for dividends paid by mutual savings banks, etc.), and

(III) any dividend described in section 404(k).

(iii) COORDINATION WITH SECTION 246(C).—Such term shall not include any dividend on any share of stock—

(I) with respect to which the holding period requirements of section 246(c) are not met (determined by substituting in section 246(c)(1) "60 days" for "45 days" each place it appears and by substituting "120-day period" for "90-day period"), or

(II) to the extent that the taxpayer is under an obligation (whether pursuant to a short sale or otherwise) to make related payments with respect to positions in substantially similar or related property.

(C) QUALIFIED FOREIGN CORPORATIONS.—

(i) IN GENERAL.—Except as otherwise provided in this paragraph, the term "qualified foreign corporation" means any foreign corporation if—

(I) such corporation is incorporated in a possession of the United States, or

(II) such corporation is eligible for benefits of a comprehensive income tax treaty with the United States which the Secretary determines is satisfactory for purposes of this paragraph and which includes an exchange of information program.

(ii) DIVIDENDS ON STOCK READILY TRADABLE ON UNITED STATES SECURITIES MARKET.—A foreign corporation not otherwise treated as a qualified foreign corporation under clause (i) shall be so treated with respect to any dividend paid by such corporation if the stock with respect to which such dividend is paid is readily tradable on an established securities market in the United States.

(iii) EXCLUSION OF DIVIDENDS OF CERTAIN FOREIGN CORPORATIONS.—Such term shall not include any foreign corporation which for the taxable year of the corporation in which the dividend was paid, or the preceding taxable year, is a foreign personal holding company (as defined in section 552), a foreign investment company (as defined in section 1246(b)), or a passive foreign investment company (as defined in section 1297).

(iv) COORDINATION WITH FOREIGN TAX CREDIT LIMITATION.—Rules similar to the rules of section 904(b)(2)(B) shall apply with respect to the dividend rate differential under this paragraph.

(D) SPECIAL RULES.—

(i) AMOUNTS TAKEN INTO ACCOUNT AS INVESTMENT INCOME.—Qualified dividend income shall not include any amount which the taxpayer takes into account as investment income under section 163(d)(4)(B).

(ii) EXTRAORDINARY DIVIDENDS.—If an individual receives, with respect to any share of stock, qualified dividend income from 1 or more dividends which are extraordinary dividends (within the meaning of section 1059(c)), any loss on the sale or exchange of such share shall, to the extent of such dividends, be treated as long-term capital loss.

Sec. 1(h)

(iii) TREATMENT OF DIVIDENDS FROM REGULATED INVESTMENT COMPANIES AND REAL ESTATE INVESTMENT TRUSTS.—A dividend received from a regulated investment company or a real estate investment trust shall be subject to the limitations prescribed in sections 854 and 857.

[Sec. 1(i)]

(i) RATE REDUCTIONS AFTER 2000.—

(1) 10-PERCENT RATE BRACKET.—

(A) IN GENERAL.—In the case of taxable years beginning after December 31, 2000—

(i) the rate of tax under subsections (a), (b), (c), and (d) on taxable income not over the initial bracket amount shall be 10 percent, and

(ii) the 15 percent rate of tax shall apply only to taxable income over the initial bracket amount but not over the maximum dollar amount for the 15-percent rate bracket.

(B) INITIAL BRACKET AMOUNT.—For purposes of this paragraph, the initial bracket amount is—

(i) $14,000 ($12,000 in the case of taxable years beginning after December 31, 2004, and before January 1, 2008) in the case of subsection (a),

(ii) $10,000 in the case of subsection (b), and

(iii) ½ the amount applicable under clause (i) (after adjustment, if any, under subparagraph (C)) in the case of subsections (c) and (d).

(C) INFLATION ADJUSTEMT.—In prescribing the tables under subsection (f) which apply with respect to taxable years beginning in calendar years after 2000—

(i) except as provided in clause (ii), the Secretary shall make no adjustment to the initial bracket amounts for any taxable year beginning before January 1, 2009,

(ii) there shall be an adjustment under subsection (f) of such amounts which shall apply only to taxable years beginning in 2004, and such adjustment shall be determined under subsection (f)(3) by substituting "2002" for "1992" in subparagraph (B) thereof,

(iii) the cost-of-living adjustment used in making adjustments to the initial bracket amounts for any taxable year beginning after December 31, 2008, shall be determined under subsection (f)(3) by substituting "2007" for "1992" in subparagraph (B) thereof, and

(iv) the adjustments under clauses (ii) and (iii) shall not apply to the amount referred to in subparagraph (B)(iii).

If any amount after adjustment under the preceding sentence is not a multiple of $50, such amount shall be rounded to the next lowest multiple of $50.

(D) COORDINATION WITH ACCELERATION OF 10 PERCENT RATE BRACKET BENEFIT FOR 2001.— This paragraph shall not apply to any taxable year to which section 6428 applies.

(2) REDUCTIONS IN RATES AFTER JUNE 30, 2001.—In the case of taxable years beginning in a calendar year after 2000, the corresponding percentage specified for such calendar year in the following table shall be substituted for the otherwise applicable tax rate in the tables under subsections (a), (b), (c), (d), and (e).

In the case of taxable years beginning during calendar year:	The corresponding percentages shall be substituted for the following percentages:			
	28%	*31%*	*36%*	*39.6%*
2001	27.5%	30.5%	35.5%	39.1%
2002	27.0%	30.0%	35.0%	38.6%
2003 and thereafter	25.0%	28.0%	33.0%	35.0%

(3) ADJUSTMENT OF TABLES.—The Secretary shall adjust the tables prescribed under subsection (f) to carry out this subsection.

[Sec. 2]

SEC. 2. DEFINITIONS AND SPECIAL RULES.

[Sec. 2(a)]

(a) DEFINITION OF SURVIVING SPOUSE.—

(1) IN GENERAL.—For purposes of section 1, the term "surviving spouse" means a taxpayer—

(A) whose spouse died during either of his two taxable years immediately preceding the taxable year, and

(B) who maintains as his home a household which constitutes for the taxable year the principal place of abode (as a member of such household) of a dependent (i) who (within the meaning of section 152) is a son, stepson, daughter, or stepdaughter of the taxpayer, and (ii) with respect to whom the taxpayer is entitled to a deduction for the taxable year under section 151.

For purposes of this paragraph, an individual shall be considered as maintaining a household only if over half of the cost of maintaining the household during the taxable year is furnished by such individual.

(2) LIMITATIONS.—Notwithstanding paragraph (1), for purposes of section 1 a taxpayer shall not be considered to be a surviving spouse—

(A) if the taxpayer has remarried at any time before the close of the taxable year, or

(B) unless, for the taxpayer's taxable year during which his spouse died, a joint return could have been made under the provisions of section 6013 (without regard to subsection (a)(3) thereof).

* * *

[Sec. 2(b)]

(b) DEFINITION OF HEAD OF HOUSEHOLD.—

(1) IN GENERAL.—For purposes of this subtitle, an individual shall be considered a head of a household if, and only if, such individual is not married at the close of his taxable year, is not a surviving spouse (as defined in subsection (a)), and either—

(A) maintains as his home a household which constitutes for more than one-half of such taxable year the principal place of abode, as a member of such household, of—

(i) a son, stepson, daughter, or stepdaughter of the taxpayer, or a descendant of a son or daughter of the taxpayer, but if such son, stepson, daughter, stepdaughter, or descendant is married at the close of the taxpayer's taxable year, only if the taxpayer is entitled to a deduction for the taxable year for such person under section 151 (or would be so entitled but for paragraph (2) or (4) of section 152(e)), or

(ii) any other person who is a dependent of the taxpayer, if the taxpayer is entitled to a deduction for the taxable year for such person under section 151, or

(B) maintains a household which constitutes for such taxable year the principal place of abode of the father or mother of the taxpayer, if the taxpayer is entitled to a deduction for the taxable year for such father or mother under section 151.

For purposes of this paragraph, an individual shall be considered as maintaining a household only if over half of the cost of maintaining the household during the taxable year is furnished by such individual.

(2) DETERMINATION OF STATUS.—For purposes of this subsection—

(A) a legally adopted child of a person shall be considered a child of such person by blood;

(B) an individual who is legally separated from his spouse under a decree of divorce or of separate maintenance shall not be considered as married;

(C) a taxpayer shall be considered as not married at the close of his taxable year if at any time during the taxable year his spouse is a nonresident alien; and

(D) a taxpayer shall be considered as married at the close of his taxable year if his spouse (other than a spouse described in subparagraph (C)) died during the taxable year.

Sec. 2(b)

(3) LIMITATIONS.—Notwithstanding paragraph (1), for purposes of this subtitle a taxpayer shall not be considered to be a head of a household—

(A) if at any time during the taxable year he is a nonresident alien; or

(B) by reason of an individual who would not be a dependent for the taxable year but for—

(i) paragraph (9) of section 152(a), or

(ii) subsection (c) of section 152.

[Sec. 2(c)]

(c) CERTAIN MARRIED INDIVIDUALS LIVING APART.—For purposes of this part, an individual shall be treated as not married at the close of the taxable year if such individual is so treated under the provisions of section 7703(b).

[Sec. 2(d)]

(d) NONRESIDENT ALIENS.—In the case of a nonresident alien individual, the taxes imposed by sections 1 and 55 shall apply only as provided by section 871 or 877.

[Sec. 2(e)]

(e) CROSS REFERENCE.—

For definition of taxable income, see section 63.

[Sec. 3]

SEC. 3. TAX TABLES FOR INDIVIDUALS.

[Sec. 3(a)]

(a) IMPOSITION OF TAX TABLE TAX.—

(1) IN GENERAL.—In lieu of the tax imposed by section 1, there is hereby imposed for each taxable year on the taxable income of every individual—

(A) who does not itemize his deductions for the taxable year, and

(B) whose taxable income for such taxable year does not exceed the ceiling amount,

a tax determined under tables, applicable to such taxable year, which shall be prescribed by the Secretary and which shall be in such form as he determines appropriate. In the table so prescribed, the amounts of the tax shall be computed on the basis of the rates prescribed by section 1.

(2) CEILING AMOUNT DEFINED.—For purposes of paragraph (1), the term "ceiling amount" means, with respect to any taxpayer, the amount (not less than $20,000) determined by the Secretary for the tax rate category in which such taxpayer falls.

(3) AUTHORITY TO PRESCRIBE TABLES FOR TAXPAYERS WHO ITEMIZE DEDUCTIONS.—The Secretary may provide that this section shall apply also for any taxable year to individuals who itemize their deductions. Any tables prescribed under the preceding sentence shall be on the basis of taxable income.

[Sec. 3(b)]

(b) SECTION INAPPLICABLE TO CERTAIN INDIVIDUALS.—This section shall not apply to—

(1) an individual making a return under section 443(a)(1) for a period of less than 12 months on account of a change in annual accounting period, and

(2) an estate or trust.

* * *

PART II—TAX ON CORPORATIONS

[Note: A tax rate schedule setting forth a simplified method of determining the tax imposed on a corporation pursuant to Section 11(b)(1) is provided at page xiii.]

[Sec. 11]

SEC. 11. TAX IMPOSED.

[Sec. 11(a)]

(a) CORPORATIONS IN GENERAL.—A tax is hereby imposed for each taxable year on the taxable income of every corporation.

[Sec. 11(b)]

(b) AMOUNT OF TAX.—

(1) IN GENERAL.—The amount of the tax imposed by subsection (a) shall be the sum of—

(A) 15 percent of so much of the taxable income as does not exceed $50,000,

(B) 25 percent of so much of the taxable income as exceeds $50,000 but does not exceed $75,000,

(C) 34 percent of so much of the taxable income as exceeds $75,000 but does not exceed $10,000,000, and

(D) 35 percent of so much of the taxable income as exceeds $10,000,000.

In the case of a corporation which has taxable income in excess of $100,000 for any taxable year, the amount of tax determined under the preceding sentence for such taxable year shall be increased by the lesser of (i) 5 percent of such excess, or (ii) $11,750. In the case of a corporation which has taxable income in excess of $15,000,000, the amount of the tax determined under the foregoing provisions of this paragraph shall be increased by an additional amount equal to the lesser of (i) 3 percent of such excess, or (ii) $100,000.

(2) CERTAIN PERSONAL SERVICE CORPORATIONS NOT ELIGIBLE FOR GRADUATED RATES.—Notwithstanding paragraph (1), the amount of the tax imposed by subsection (a) on the taxable income of a qualified personal service corporation (as defined in section 448(d)(2)) shall be equal to 35 percent of the taxable income.

[Sec. 11(c)]

(c) EXCEPTIONS.—Subsection (a) shall not apply to a corporation subject to a tax imposed by—

(1) section 594 (relating to mutual savings banks conducting life insurance business),

(2) subchapter L (sec. 801 and following, relating to insurance companies), or

(3) subchapter M (sec. 851 and following, relating to regulated investment companies and real estate investment trusts).

[Sec. 11(d)]

(d) FOREIGN CORPORATIONS.—In the case of a foreign corporation, the taxes imposed by subsection (a) and section 55 shall apply only as provided by section 882.

PART IV—CREDITS AGAINST TAX

Subpart A—Nonrefundable Personal Credits

[Sec. 21]

SEC. 21. EXPENSES FOR HOUSEHOLD AND DEPENDENT CARE SERVICES NECESSARY FOR GAINFUL EMPLOYMENT.

[Sec. 21(a)]

(a) ALLOWANCE OF CREDIT.—

(1) IN GENERAL.—In the case of an individual who maintains a household which includes as a member one or more qualifying individuals (as defined in subsection (b)(1)), there shall be allowed as a credit against the tax imposed by this chapter for the taxable year an amount equal to the

applicable percentage of the employment-related expenses (as defined in subsection (b)(2)) paid by such individual during the taxable year.

(2) Applicable percentage defined.—For purposes of paragraph (1), the term "applicable percentage" means 35 percent reduced (but not below 20 percent) by 1 percentage point for each $2,000 (or fraction thereof) by which the taxpayer's adjusted gross income for the taxable year exceeds $15,000.

[Sec. 21(b)]

(b) Definitions of Qualifying Individual and Employment-Related Expenses.—For purposes of this section—

(1) Qualifying individual.—The term "qualifying individual" means—

(A) a dependent of the taxpayer who is under the age of 13 and with respect to whom the taxpayer is entitled to a deduction under section 151(c),

(B) a dependent of the taxpayer who is physically or mentally incapable of caring for himself, or

(C) the spouse of the taxpayer, if he is physically or mentally incapable of caring for himself.

(2) Employment-related expenses.—

(A) In general.—The term "employment-related expenses" means amounts paid for the following expenses, but only if such expenses are incurred to enable the taxpayer to be gainfully employed for any period for which there are 1 or more qualifying individuals with respect to the taxpayer:

(i) expenses for household services, and

(ii) expenses for the care of a qualifying individual.

Such term shall not include any amount paid for services outside the taxpayer's household at a camp where the qualifying individual stays overnight.

(B) Exception.—Employment-related expenses described in subparagraph (A) which are incurred for services outside the taxpayer's household shall be taken into account only if incurred for the care of—

(i) a qualifying individual described in paragraph (1)(A), or

(ii) a qualifying individual (not described in paragraph (1)(A)) who regularly spends at least 8 hours each day in the taxpayer's household.

(C) Dependent care centers.—Employment-related expenses described in subparagraph (A) which are incurred for services provided outside the taxpayer's household by a dependent care center (as defined in subparagraph (D)) shall be taken into account only if—

(i) such center complies with all applicable laws and regulations of a State or unit of local government, and

(ii) the requirements of subparagraph (B) are met.

(D) Dependent care center defined.—For purposes of this paragraph, the term "dependent care center" means any facility which—

(i) provides care for more than six individuals (other than individuals who reside at the facility), and

(ii) receives a fee, payment, or grant for providing services for any of the individuals (regardless of whether such facility is operated for profit).

[Sec. 21(c)]

(c) Dollar Limit on Amount Creditable.—The amount of the employment-related expenses incurred during any taxable year which may be taken into account under subsection (a) shall not exceed—

(1) $3,000 if there is 1 qualifying individual with respect to the taxpayer for such taxable year, or

(2) $6,000 if there are 2 or more qualifying individuals with respect to the taxpayer for such taxable year.

The amount determined under paragraph (1) or (2) (whichever is applicable) shall be reduced by the aggregate amount excludable from gross income under section 129 for the taxable year.

(d) EARNED INCOME LIMITATION.—

(1) IN GENERAL.—Except as otherwise provided in this subsection, the amount of the employment-related expenses incurred during any taxable year which may be taken into account under subsection (a) shall not exceed—

(A) in the case of an individual who is not married at the close of such year, such individual's earned income for such year, or

(B) in the case of an individual who is married at the close of such year, the lesser of such individual's earned income or the earned income of his spouse for such year.

(2) SPECIAL RULE FOR SPOUSE WHO IS A STUDENT OR INCAPABLE OF CARING FOR HIMSELF.—In the case of a spouse who is a student or a qualified individual described in subsection (b)(1)(C), for purposes of paragraph (1), such spouse shall be deemed for each month during which such spouse is a full-time student at an educational institution, or is such a qualifying individual, to be gainfully employed and to have earned income of not less than—

(A) $250 if subsection (c)(1) applies for the taxable year, or

(B) $500 if subsection (c)(2) applies for the taxable year.

In the case of any husband and wife, this paragraph shall apply with respect to only one spouse for any one month.

(e) SPECIAL RULES.—For purposes of this section—

(1) MAINTAINING HOUSEHOLD.—An individual shall be treated as maintaining a household for any period only if over half the cost of maintaining the household for such period is furnished by such individual (or, if such individual is married during such period, is furnished by such individual and his spouse).

(2) MARRIED COUPLES MUST FILE JOINT RETURN.—If the taxpayer is married at the close of the taxable year, the credit shall be allowed under subsection (a) only if the taxpayer and his spouse file a joint return for the taxable year.

(3) MARITAL STATUS.—An individual legally separated from his spouse under a decree of divorce or of separate maintenance shall not be considered as married.

(4) CERTAIN MARRIED INDIVIDUALS LIVING APART.—If—

(A) an individual who is married and who files a separate return—

(i) maintains as his home a household which constitutes for more than one-half of the taxable year the principal place of abode of a qualifying individual, and

(ii) furnishes over half of the cost of maintaining such household during the taxable year, and

(B) during the last 6 months of such taxable year such individual's spouse is not a member of such household,

such individual shall not be considered as married.

(5) SPECIAL DEPENDENCY TEST IN CASE OF DIVORCED PARENTS, ETC.—If—

(A) paragraph (2) or (4) of section 152(e) applies to any child with respect to any calendar year, and

(B) such child is under the age of 13 or is physically or mentally incapable of caring for himself,

in the case of any taxable year beginning in such calendar year, such child shall be treated as a qualifying individual described in subparagraph (A) or (B) of subsection (b)(1) (whichever is appropriate) with respect to the custodial parent (within the meaning of section 152(e)(1)), and shall not be treated as a qualifying individual with respect to the noncustodial parent.

(6) PAYMENTS TO RELATED INDIVIDUALS.—No credit shall be allowed under subsection (a) for any amount paid by the taxpayer to an individual—

(A) with respect to whom, for the taxable year, a deduction under section 151(c) (relating to deduction for personal exemptions for dependents) is allowable either to the taxpayer or his spouse, or

(B) who is a child of the taxpayer (within the meaning of section 151(c)(3)) who has not attained the age of 19 at the close of the taxable year.

For purposes of this paragraph, the term "taxable year" means the taxable year of the taxpayer in which the service is performed.

(7) STUDENT.—The term "student" means an individual who during each of 5 calendar months during the taxable year is a full-time student at an educational organization.

(8) EDUCATIONAL ORGANIZATION.—The term "educational organization" means an educational organization described in section 170(b)(1)(A)(ii).

(9) IDENTIFYING INFORMATION REQUIRED WITH RESPECT TO SERVICE PROVIDER.—No credit shall be allowed under subsection (a) for any amount paid to any person unless—

(A) the name, address, and taxpayer identification number of such person are included on the return claiming the credit, or

(B) if such person is an organization described in section 501(c)(3) and exempt from tax under section 501(a), the name and address of such person are included on the return claiming the credit.

In the case of a failure to provide the information required under the preceding sentence, the preceding sentence shall not apply if it is shown that the taxpayer exercised due diligence in attempting to provide the information so required.

(10) IDENTIFYING INFORMATION REQUIRED WITH RESPECT TO QUALIFYING INDIVIDUALS.—No credit shall be allowed under this section with respect to any qualifying individual unless the TIN of such individual is included on the return claiming the credit.

[Sec. 21(f)]

(f) REGULATIONS.—The Secretary shall prescribe such regulations as may be necessary to carry out the purposes of this section.

[Sec. 22]

SEC. 22. CREDIT FOR THE ELDERLY AND THE PERMANENTLY AND TOTALLY DISABLED.

[Sec. 22(a)]

(a) GENERAL RULE.—In the case of a qualified individual, there shall be allowed as a credit against the tax imposed by this chapter for the taxable year an amount equal to 15 percent of such individual's section 22 amount for such taxable year.

[Sec. 22(b)]

(b) QUALIFIED INDIVIDUAL.—For purposes of this section, the term "qualified individual" means any individual—

(1) who has attained age 65 before the close of the taxable year, or

(2) who retired on disability before the close of the taxable year and who, when he retired, was permanently and totally disabled.

[Sec. 22(c)]

(c) SECTION 22 AMOUNT.—For purposes of subsection (a)—

(1) IN GENERAL.—An individual's section 22 amount for the taxable year shall be the applicable initial amount determined under paragraph (2), reduced as provided in paragraph (3) and in subsection (d).

(2) INITIAL AMOUNT—

(A) IN GENERAL.—Except as provided in subparagraph (B), the initial amount shall be—

(i) $5,000 in the case of a single individual, or a joint return where only one spouse is a qualified individual,

(ii) $7,500 in the case of a joint return where both spouses are qualified individuals, or

(iii) $3,750 in the case of a married individual filing a separate return.

(B) LIMITATION IN CASE OF INDIVIDUALS WHO HAVE NOT ATTAINED AGE 65.—

(i) IN GENERAL.—In the case of a qualified individual who has not attained age 65 before the close of the taxable year, except as provided in clause (ii), the initial amount shall not exceed the disability income for the taxable year.

(ii) SPECIAL RULES IN CASE OF JOINT RETURN.—In the case of a joint return where both spouses are qualified individuals and at least one spouse has not attained age 65 before the close of the taxable year—

(I) if both spouses have not attained age 65 before the close of the taxable year, the initial amount shall not exceed the sum of such spouses' disability income, or

(II) if one spouse has attained age 65 before the close of the taxable year, the initial amount shall not exceed the sum of $5,000 plus the disability income for the taxable year of the spouse who has not attained age 65 before the close of the taxable year.

(iii) DISABILITY INCOME.—For purposes of this subparagraph, the term "disability income" means the aggregate amount includable in the gross income of the individual for the taxable year under section 72 or 105(a) to the extent such amount constitutes wages (or payments in lieu of wages) for the period during which the individual is absent from work on account of permanent and total disability.

(3) REDUCTION.—

(A) IN GENERAL.—The reduction under this paragraph is an amount equal to the sum of the amounts received by the individual (or, in the case of a joint return, by either spouse) as a pension or annuity or as a disability benefit—

(i) which is excluded from gross income and payable under—

(I) title II of the Social Security Act,

(II) the Railroad Retirement Act of 1974, or

(III) a law administered by the Veterans' Administration, or

(ii) which is excluded from gross income under any provision of law not contained in this title.

No reduction shall be made under clause (i)(III) for any amount described in section 104(a)(4).

(B) TREATMENT OF CERTAIN WORKMEN'S COMPENSATION BENEFITS.—For purposes of subparagraph (A), any amount treated as a social security benefit under section 86(d)(3) shall be treated as a disability benefit received under title II of the Social Security Act.

[Sec. 22(d)]

(d) ADJUSTED GROSS INCOME LIMITATION.—If the adjusted gross income of the taxpayer exceeds—

(1) $7,500 in the case of a single individual,

(2) $10,000 in the case of a joint return, or

(3) $5,000 in the case of a married individual filing a separate return,

the section 22 amount shall be reduced by one-half of the excess of the adjusted gross income over $7,500, $10,000, or $5,000, as the case may be.

[Sec. 22(e)]

(e) DEFINITIONS AND SPECIAL RULES.—For purposes of this section—

(1) MARRIED COUPLE MUST FILE JOINT RETURN.—Except in the case of a husband and wife who live apart at all times during the taxable year, if the taxpayer is married at the close of the taxable year, the credit provided by this section shall be allowed only if the taxpayer and his spouse file a joint return for the taxable year.

(2) MARITAL STATUS.—Marital status shall be determined under section 7703.

(3) PERMANENT AND TOTAL DISABILITY DEFINED.—An individual is permanently and totally disabled if he is unable to engage in any substantial gainful activity by reason of any medically determinable physical or mental impairment which can be expected to result in death or which has lasted or can be expected to last for a continuous period of not less than 12 months. An individual shall not be considered to be permanently and totally disabled unless he furnishes proof of the existence thereof in such form and manner, and at such times, as the Secretary may require.

* * *

Sec. 22(e)

[Caution: As provided in Section 23(h), the dollar amounts set forth in Section 23(a)(3), 23(b)(1), and 23(b)(2)(A)(i) are adjusted for taxable years after 2002 to reflect increases in the Consumer Price Index. The adjusted amounts applicable to taxable years beginning in 2003 are provided beginning at page ix.]

[Sec. 23]

SEC. 23. ADOPTION EXPENSES.

[Sec. 23(a)]

(a) ALLOWANCE OF CREDIT.—

(1) IN GENERAL.—In the case of an individual, there shall be allowed as a credit against the tax imposed by this chapter the amount of the qualified adoption expenses paid or incurred by the taxpayer.

(2) YEAR CREDIT ALLOWED.—The credit under paragraph (1) with respect to any expense shall be allowed—

(A) in the case of any expense paid or incurred before the taxable year in which such adoption becomes final, for the taxable year following the taxable year during which such expense is paid or incurred, and

(B) in the case of an expense paid or incurred during or after the taxable year in which such adoption becomes final, for the taxable year in which such expense is paid or incurred.

(3) $10,000 CREDIT FOR ADOPTION OF CHILD WITH SPECIAL NEEDS REGARDLESS OF EXPENSES.—In the case of an adoption of a child with special needs which becomes final during a taxable year, the taxpayer shall be treated as having paid during such year qualified adoption expenses with respect to such adoption in an amount equal to the excess (if any) of $10,000 over the aggregate qualified adoption expenses actually paid or incurred by the taxpayer with respect to such adoption during such taxable year and all prior taxable years.

[Sec. 23(b)]

(b) LIMITATIONS.—

(1) DOLLAR LIMITATION.—The aggregate amount of qualified adoption expenses which may be taken into account under subsection (a) for all taxable years with respect to the adoption of a child by the taxpayer shall not exceed $10,000.

(2) INCOME LIMITATION.—

(A) IN GENERAL.—The amount allowable as a credit under subsection (a) for any taxable year (determined without regard to subsection (c)) shall be reduced (but not below zero) by an amount which bears the same ratio to the amount so allowable (determined without regard to this paragraph but with regard to paragraph (1)) as—

(i) the amount (if any) by which the taxpayer's adjusted gross income exceeds $150,000, bears to

(ii) $40,000.

(B) DETERMINATION OF ADJUSTED GROSS INCOME.—For purposes of subparagraph (A), adjusted gross income shall be determined without regard to sections 911, 931, and 933.

(3) DENIAL OF DOUBLE BENEFIT.—

(A) IN GENERAL.—No credit shall be allowed under subsection (a) for any expense for which a deduction or credit is allowed under any other provision of this chapter.

(B) GRANTS.—No credit shall be allowed under subsection (a) for any expense to the extent that funds for such expense are received under any Federal, State, or local program.

[Caution: Code Sec. 23(b)(4), below, as added by P.L. 107-16, and as provided by P.L. 107-147, Act Sec. 601(b)(2), applies to tax years beginning after December 31, 2003.]

(4) LIMITATION BASED ON AMOUNT OF TAX.—The credit allowed under subsection (a) for any taxable year shall not exceed the excess of—

(A) the sum of the regular tax liability (as defined in section 26(b)) plus the tax imposed by section 55, over

(B) the sum of the credits allowable under this subpart (other than this section) and section 27 for the taxable year.

[Sec. 23(c)]

[Caution: Code Sec. 23(c), below, prior to amendment by P.L. 107-16, and as provided by P.L. 107-147, Act Sec. 601(b)(2), applies to tax years beginning on or before December 31, 2003.]

(c) CARRYFORWARDS OF UNUSED CREDIT.—If the credit allowable under subsection (a) for any taxable year exceeds the limitation imposed by section 26(a) for such taxable year reduced by the sum of the credits allowable under this subpart (other than this section and section 1400C), such excess shall be carried to the succeeding taxable year and added to the credit allowable under subsection (a) for such taxable year. No credit may be carried forward under this subsection to any taxable year following the fifth taxable year after the taxable year in which the credit arose. For purposes of the preceding sentence, credits shall be treated as used on a first-in first-out basis.

[Caution: Code Sec. 23(c), below, as amended by P.L. 107-16, and as provided by P.L. 107-147, Act Sec. 601(b)(2), applies to tax years beginning after December 31, 2003.]

(c) CARRYFORWARDS OF UNUSED CREDIT.—If the credit allowable under subsection (a) for any taxable year exceeds the limitation imposed by subsection (b)(4) for such taxable year, such excess shall be carried to the succeeding taxable year and added to the credit allowable under subsection (a) for such taxable year. No credit may be carried forward under this subsection to any taxable year following the fifth taxable year after the taxable year in which the credit arose. For purposes of the preceding sentence, credits shall be treated as used on a first-in first-out basis.

[Sec. 23(d)]

(d) DEFINITIONS.—For purposes of this section—

(1) QUALIFIED ADOPTION EXPENSES.—The term "qualified adoption expenses" means reasonable and necessary adoption fees, court costs, attorney fees, and other expenses—

(A) which are directly related to, and the principal purpose of which is for, the legal adoption of an eligible child by the taxpayer,

(B) which are not incurred in violation of State or Federal law or in carrying out any surrogate parenting arrangement,

(C) which are not expenses in connection with the adoption by an individual of a child who is the child of such individual's spouse, and

(D) which are not reimbursed under an employer program or otherwise.

(2) ELIGIBLE CHILD.—The term "eligible child" means any individual who—

(A) has not attained age 18, or

(B) is physically or mentally incapable of caring for himself.

(3) CHILD WITH SPECIAL NEEDS.—The term "child with special needs" means any child if—

(A) a State has determined that the child cannot or should not be returned to the home of his parents,

(B) such State has determined that there exists with respect to the child a specific factor or condition (such as his ethnic background, age, or membership in a minority or sibling group, or the presence of factors such as medical conditions or physical, mental, or emotional handicaps) because of which it is reasonable to conclude that such child cannot be placed with adoptive parents without providing adoption assistance, and

(C) such child is a citizen or resident of the United States (as defined in section 217(h)(3)).

[Sec. 23(e)]

(e) SPECIAL RULES FOR FOREIGN ADOPTIONS.—In the case of an adoption of a child who is not a citizen or resident of the United States (as defined in section 217(h)(3))—

(1) subsection (a) shall not apply to any qualified adoption expense with respect to such adoption unless such adoption becomes final, and

Sec. 23(e)

(2) any such expense which is paid or incurred before the taxable year in which such adoption becomes final shall be taken into account under this section as if such expense were paid or incurred during such year.

[Sec. 23(f)]

(f) FILING REQUIREMENTS.—

(1) MARRIED COUPLES MUST FILE JOINT RETURNS.—Rules similar to the rules of paragraphs (2), (3), and (4) of section 21(e) shall apply for purposes of this section.

(2) TAXPAYER MUST INCLUDE TIN.—

(A) IN GENERAL.—No credit shall be allowed under this section with respect to any eligible child unless the taxpayer includes (if known) the name, age, and TIN of such child on the return of tax for the taxable year.

(B) OTHER METHODS.—The Secretary may, in lieu of the information referred to in subparagraph (A), require other information meeting the purposes of subparagraph (A), including identification of an agent assisting with the adoption.

[Sec. 23(g)]

(g) BASIS ADJUSTMENTS.—For purposes of this subtitle, if a credit is allowed under this section for any expenditure with respect to any property, the increase in the basis of such property which would (but for this subsection) result from such expenditure shall be reduced by the amount of the credit so allowed.

[Sec. 23(h)]

(h) ADJUSTMENTS FOR INFLATION.—In the case of a taxable year beginning after December 31, 2002, each of the dollar amounts in subsection (a)(3) and paragraphs (1) and (2)(A)(i) of subsection (b) shall be increased by an amount equal to—

(1) such dollar amount, multiplied by

(2) the cost-of-living adjustment determined under section 1(f)(3) for the calendar year in which the taxable year begins, determined by substituting "calendar year 2001" for "calendar year 1992" in subparagraph (B) thereof.

If any amount as increased under the preceding sentence is not a multiple of $10, such amount shall be rounded to the nearest multiple of $10.

[Sec. 23(i)]

(i) REGULATIONS.—The Secretary shall prescribe such regulations as may be appropriate to carry out this section and section 137, including regulations which treat unmarried individuals who pay or incur qualified adoption expenses with respect to the same child as 1 taxpayer for purposes of applying the dollar amounts in subsections (a)(3) and (b)(1) of this section and in section 137(b)(1).

[Caution: As provided in Section 24(d)(3), the amount provided in Section 24(d)(1)(B) is adjusted for taxable years after 2001 to reflect increases in the Consumer Price Index. The adjusted amount applicable to taxable years beginning in 2003 is provided beginning at page ix.]

[Sec. 24]

SEC. 24. CHILD TAX CREDIT.

[Sec. 24(a)]

(a) ALLOWANCE OF CREDIT.—

(1) IN GENERAL.—There shall be allowed as a credit against the tax imposed by this chapter for the taxable year with respect to each qualifying child of the taxpayer an amount equal to the per child amount.

(2) PER CHILD AMOUNT.—For purposes of paragraph (1), the per child amount shall be determined as follows:

In the case of any taxable year beginning in—	The per child amount is—
2003 or 2004	$1,000
2005, 2006, 2007, or 2008	700
2009	800
2010 or thereafter	1,000

[Sec. 24(b)]

[Caution: Code Sec. 24(b), below, prior to amendment by P.L. 107-16, and as provided by P.L. 107-147, Act Sec. 601(b)(2), applies to tax years beginning on or before December 31, 2003.]

(b) LIMITATION BASED ON ADJUSTED GROSS INCOME.—

(1) IN GENERAL.—The amount of the credit allowable under subsection (a) shall be reduced (but not below zero) by $50 for each $1,000 (or fraction thereof) by which the taxpayer's modified adjusted gross income exceeds the threshold amount. For purposes of the preceding sentence, the term "modified adjusted gross income" means adjusted gross income increased by any amount excluded from gross income under section 911, 931, or 933.

(2) THRESHOLD AMOUNT.—For purposes of paragraph (1), the term "threshold amount" means—

(A) $110,000 in the case of a joint return,

(B) $75,000 in the case of an individual who is not married, and

(C) $55,000 in the case of a married individual filing a separate return.

For purposes of this paragraph, marital status shall be determined under section 7703.

[Caution: Code Sec. 24(b), below, as amended by P.L. 107-16, and as provided by P.L. 107-147, Act Sec. 601(b)(2), applies to tax years beginning after December 31, 2003.]

(b) LIMITATIONS.—

(1) LIMITATION BASED ON ADJUSTED GROSS INCOME.—The amount of the credit allowable under subsection (a) shall be reduced (but not below zero) by $50 for each $1,000 (or fraction thereof) by which the taxpayer's modified adjusted gross income exceeds the threshold amount. For purposes of the preceding sentence, the term "modified adjusted gross income" means adjusted gross income increased by any amount excluded from gross income under section 911, 931, or 933.

(2) THRESHOLD AMOUNT.—For purposes of paragraph (1), the term "threshold amount" means—

(A) $110,000 in the case of a joint return,

(B) $75,000 in the case of an individual who is not married, and

(C) $55,000 in the case of a married individual filing a separate return.

For purposes of this paragraph, marital status shall be determined under section 7703.

(3) LIMITATION BASED ON AMOUNT OF TAX.—The credit allowed under subsection (a) for any taxable year shall not exceed the excess of—

(A) the sum of the regular tax liability (as defined in section 26(b)) plus the tax imposed by section 55, over

(B) the sum of the credits allowable under this subpart (other than this section and sections 23 and 25B) and section 27 for the taxable year.

[Sec. 24(c)]

(c) QUALIFYING CHILD.—For purposes of this section—

(1) IN GENERAL.—The term "qualifying child" means any individual if—

(A) the taxpayer is allowed a deduction under section 151 with respect to such individual for the taxable year,

(B) such individual has not attained the age of 17 as of the close of the calendar year in which the taxable year of the taxpayer begins, and

(C) such individual bears a relationship to the taxpayer described in section 32(c)(3)(B).

(2) EXCEPTION FOR CERTAIN NONCITIZENS.—The term "qualifying child" shall not include any individual who would not be a dependent if the first sentence of section 152(b)(3) were applied without regard to all that follows "resident of the United States".

[Sec. 24(d)]

(d) PORTION OF CREDIT REFUNDABLE.—

[Caution: Code Sec. 24(d)(1), below, as amended by P.L. 107-16, Act Sec. 201(c)(1), but prior to amendment by Act Sec. 201(b)(2)(C)(i)-(ii), and as provided by P.L. 107-147, Act Sec. 601(b)(2), applies to tax years beginning on or before December 31, 2003.]

(1) IN GENERAL.—The aggregate credits allowed to a taxpayer under subpart C shall be increased by the lesser of—

(A) the credit which would be allowed under this section without regard to this subsection and the limitation under section 26(a), or

(B) the amount by which the aggregate amount of credits allowed by this subpart (determined without regard to this subsection) would increase if the limitation imposed by section 26(a) were increased by the greater of—

(i) 15 percent (10 percent in the case of taxable years beginning before January 1, 2005) of so much of the taxpayer's earned income (within the meaning of section 32) which is taken into account in computing taxable income for the taxable year as exceeds $10,000, or

(ii) in the case of a taxpayer with 3 or more qualifying children, the excess (if any) of—

(I) the taxpayer's social security taxes for the taxable year, over

(II) the credit allowed under section 32 for the taxable year.

The amount of the credit allowed under this subsection shall not be treated as a credit allowed under this subpart and shall reduce the amount of credit otherwise allowable under subsection (a) without regard to section 26(a).

[Caution: Code Sec. 24(d)(1), below, as amended by P.L. 107-16, Act Secs. 201(b)(2)(C)(i)-(ii) and 201(c)(1), and as provided by P.L. 107-147, Act Sec. 601(b)(2), applies to tax years beginning after December 31, 2003.]

(1) IN GENERAL.—The aggregate credits allowed to a taxpayer under subpart C shall be increased by the lesser of—

(A) the credit which would be allowed under this section without regard to this subsection and the limitation under subsection (b)(3), or

(B) the amount by which the aggregate amount of credits allowed by this subpart (determined without regard to this subsection) would increase if the limitation imposed by subsection (b)(3) were increased by the greater of—

(i) 15 percent (10 percent in the case of taxable years beginning before January 1, 2005) of so much of the taxpayer's earned income (within the meaning of section 32) which is taken into account in computing taxable income for the taxable year as exceeds $10,000, or

(ii) in the case of a taxpayer with 3 or more qualifying children, the excess (if any) of—

(I) the taxpayer's social security taxes for the taxable year, over

(II) the credit allowed under section 32 for the taxable year.

The amount of the credit allowed under this subsection shall not be treated as a credit allowed under this subpart and shall reduce the amount of credit otherwise allowable under subsection (a) without regard to subsection (b)(3).

(2) SOCIAL SECURITY TAXES.—For purposes of paragraph (1)—

(A) IN GENERAL.—The term "social security taxes" means, with respect to any taxpayer for any taxable year—

(i) the amount of the taxes imposed by sections 3101 and 3201(a) on amounts received by the taxpayer during the calendar year in which the taxable year begins,

(ii) 50 percent of the taxes imposed by section 1401 on the self-employment income of the taxpayer for the taxable year, and

(iii) 50 percent of the taxes imposed by section 3211(a) on amounts received by the taxpayer during the calendar year in which the taxable year begins.

(B) COORDINATION WITH SPECIAL REFUND OF SOCIAL SECURITY TAXES.—The term "social security taxes" shall not include any taxes to the extent the taxpayer is entitled to a special refund of such taxes under section 6413(c).

(C) SPECIAL RULE.—Any amounts paid pursuant to an agreement under section 3121(l) (relating to agreements entered into by American employers with respect to foreign affiliates) which are equivalent to the taxes referred to in subparagraph (A)(i) shall be treated as taxes referred to in such subparagraph.

(3) INFLATION ADJUSTMENT.—In the case of any taxable year beginning in a calendar year after 2001, the $10,000 amount contained in paragraph (1)(B) shall be increased by an amount equal to—

(A) such dollar amount, multiplied by

(B) the cost-of-living adjustment determined under section 1(f)(3) for the calendar year in which the taxable year begins, determined by substituting "calendar year 2000" for "calendar year 1992" in subparagraph (B) thereof.

Any increase determined under the preceding sentence shall be rounded to the nearest multiple of $50.

[Sec. 24(e)]

(e) IDENTIFICATION REQUIREMENT.—No credit shall be allowed under this section to a taxpayer with respect to any qualifying child unless the taxpayer includes the name and taxpayer identification number of such qualifying child on the return of tax for the taxable year.

[Sec. 24(f)]

(f) TAXABLE YEAR MUST BE FULL TAXABLE YEAR.—Except in the case of a taxable year closed by reason of the death of the taxpayer, no credit shall be allowable under this section in the case of a taxable year covering a period of less than 12 months.

[Caution: As provided in Section 25A(h), the amounts provided in Sections 25A(b)(1) and 25A(d)(2) are adjusted for taxable years after 2001 to reflect increases in the Consumer Price Index. The adjusted amounts applicable to taxable years beginning in 2003 are provided beginning at page ix.]

[Sec. 25A]

SEC. 25A. HOPE AND LIFETIME LEARNING CREDITS.

[Sec. 25A(a)]

(a) ALLOWANCE OF CREDIT.—In the case of an individual, there shall be allowed as a credit against the tax imposed by this chapter for the taxable year the amount equal to the sum of—

(1) the Hope Scholarship Credit, plus

(2) the Lifetime Learning Credit.

[Sec. 25A(b)]

(b) HOPE SCHOLARSHIP CREDIT.—

(1) PER STUDENT CREDIT.—In the case of any eligible student for whom an election is in effect under this section for any taxable year, the Hope Scholarship Credit is an amount equal to the sum of—

(A) 100 percent of so much of the qualified tuition and related expenses paid by the taxpayer during the taxable year (for education furnished to the eligible student during any academic period beginning in such taxable year) as does not exceed $1,000, plus

(B) 50 percent of such expenses so paid as exceeds $1,000 but does not exceed the applicable limit.

Sec. 25A(b)

(2) LIMITATIONS APPLICABLE TO HOPE SCHOLARSHIP CREDIT.—

(A) CREDIT ALLOWED ONLY FOR 2 TAXABLE YEARS.—An election to have this section apply with respect to any eligible student for purposes of the Hope Scholarship Credit under subsection (a)(1) may not be made for any taxable year if such an election (by the taxpayer or any other individual) is in effect with respect to such student for any 2 prior taxable years.

(B) CREDIT ALLOWED FOR YEAR ONLY IF INDIVIDUAL IS AT LEAST $1/2$ TIME STUDENT FOR PORTION OF YEAR.—The Hope Scholarship Credit under subsection (a)(1) shall not be allowed for a taxable year with respect to the qualified tuition and related expenses of an individual unless such individual is an eligible student for at least one academic period which begins during such year.

(C) CREDIT ALLOWED ONLY FOR FIRST 2 YEARS OF POSTSECONDARY EDUCATION.—The Hope Scholarship Credit under subsection (a)(1) shall not be allowed for a taxable year with respect to the qualified tuition and related expenses of an eligible student if the student has completed (before the beginning of such taxable year) the first 2 years of postsecondary education at an eligible educational institution.

(D) DENIAL OF CREDIT IF STUDENT CONVICTED OF A FELONY DRUG OFFENSE.—The Hope Scholarship Credit under subsection (a)(1) shall not be allowed for qualified tuition and related expenses for the enrollment or attendance of a student for any academic period if such student has been convicted of a Federal or State felony offense consisting of the possession or distribution of a controlled substance before the end of the taxable year with or within which such period ends.

(3) ELIGIBLE STUDENT.—For purposes of this subsection, the term "eligible student" means, with respect to any academic period, a student who—

(A) meets the requirements of section 484(a)(1) of the Higher Education Act of 1965 (20 U.S.C. 1091(a)(1)), as in effect on the date of the enactment of this section, and

(B) is carrying at least $1/2$ the normal full-time work load for the course of study the student is pursuing.

(4) APPLICABLE LIMIT.—For purposes of paragraph (1)(B), the applicable limit for any taxable year is an amount equal to 2 times the dollar amount in effect under paragraph (1)(A) for such taxable year.

[Sec. 25A(c)]

(c) LIFETIME LEARNING CREDIT.—

(1) PER TAXPAYER CREDIT.—The Lifetime Learning Credit for any taxpayer for any taxable year is an amount equal to 20 percent of so much of the qualified tuition and related expenses paid by the taxpayer during the taxable year (for education furnished during any academic period beginning in such taxable year) as does not exceed $10,000 ($5,000 in the case of taxable years beginning before January 1, 2003).

(2) SPECIAL RULES FOR DETERMINING EXPENSES.—

(A) COORDINATION WITH HOPE SCHOLARSHIP.—The qualified tuition and related expenses with respect to an individual who is an eligible student for whom a Hope Scholarship Credit under subsection (a)(1) is allowed for the taxable year shall not be taken into account under this subsection.

(B) EXPENSES ELIGIBLE FOR LIFETIME LEARNING CREDIT.—For purposes of paragraph (1), qualified tuition and related expenses shall include expenses described in subsection (f)(1) with respect to any course of instruction at an eligible educational institution to acquire or improve job skills of the individual.

[Sec. 25A(d)]

(d) LIMITATION BASED ON MODIFIED ADJUSTED GROSS INCOME.—

(1) IN GENERAL.—The amount which would (but for this subsection) be taken into account under subsection (a) for the taxable year shall be reduced (but not below zero) by the amount determined under paragraph (2).

(2) AMOUNT OF REDUCTION.—The amount determined under this paragraph is the amount which bears the same ratio to the amount which would be so taken into account as—

(A) the excess of—

(i) the taxpayer's modified adjusted gross income for such taxable year, over

(ii) $40,000 ($80,000 in the case of a joint return), bears to

(B) $10,000 ($20,000 in the case of a joint return).

(3) MODIFIED ADJUSTED GROSS INCOME.—The term "modified adjusted gross income" means the adjusted gross income of the taxpayer for the taxable year increased by any amount excluded from gross income under section 911, 931, or 933.

[Sec. 25A(e)]

(e) ELECTION NOT TO HAVE SECTION APPLY.—A taxpayer may elect not to have this section apply with respect to the qualified tuition and related expenses of an individual for any taxable year.

[Sec. 25A(f)]

(f) DEFINITIONS.—For purposes of this section—

(1) QUALIFIED TUITION AND RELATED EXPENSES.—

(A) IN GENERAL.—The term "qualified tuition and related expenses" means tuition and fees required for the enrollment or attendance of—

(i) the taxpayer,

(ii) the taxpayer's spouse, or

(iii) any dependent of the taxpayer with respect to whom the taxpayer is allowed a deduction under section 151, at an eligible educational institution for courses of instruction of such individual at such institution.

(B) EXCEPTION FOR EDUCATION INVOLVING SPORTS, ETC.—Such term does not include expenses with respect to any course or other education involving sports, games, or hobbies, unless such course or other education is part of the individual's degree program.

(C) EXCEPTION FOR NONACADEMIC FEES.—Such term does not include student activity fees, athletic fees, insurance expenses, or other expenses unrelated to an individual's academic course of instruction.

(2) ELIGIBLE EDUCATIONAL INSTITUTION.—The term "eligible educational institution" means an institution—

(A) which is described in section 481 of the Higher Education Act of 1965 (20 U.S.C. 1088), as in effect on the date of the enactment of this section, and

(B) which is eligible to participate in a program under title IV of such Act.

[Sec. 25A(g)]

(g) SPECIAL RULES.—

(1) IDENTIFICATION REQUIREMENT.—No credit shall be allowed under subsection (a) to a taxpayer with respect to the qualified tuition and related expenses of an individual unless the taxpayer includes the name and taxpayer identification number of such individual on the return of tax for the taxable year.

(2) ADJUSTMENT FOR CERTAIN SCHOLARSHIPS, ETC.—The amount of qualified tuition and related expenses otherwise taken into account under subsection (a) with respect to an individual for an academic period shall be reduced (before the application of subsections (b), (c), and (d)) by the sum of any amounts paid for the benefit of such individual which are allocable to such period as—

(A) a qualified scholarship which is excludable from gross income under section 117,

(B) an educational assistance allowance under chapter 30, 31, 32, 34, or 35 of title 38, United States Code, or under chapter 1606 of title 10, United States Code, and

(C) a payment (other than a gift, bequest, devise, or inheritance within the meaning of section 102(a)) for such individual's educational expenses, or attributable to such individual's enrollment at an eligible educational institution, which is excludable from gross income under any law of the United States.

(3) TREATMENT OF EXPENSES PAID BY DEPENDENT.—If a deduction under section 151 with respect to an individual is allowed to another taxpayer for a taxable year beginning in the calendar year in which such individual's taxable year begins—

(A) no credit shall be allowed under subsection (a) to such individual for such individual's taxable year, and

(B) qualified tuition and related expenses paid by such individual during such individual's taxable year shall be treated for purposes of this section as paid by such other taxpayer.

(4) TREATMENT OF CERTAIN PREPAYMENTS.—If qualified tuition and related expenses are paid by the taxpayer during a taxable year for an academic period which begins during the first 3 months following such taxable year, such academic period shall be treated for purposes of this section as beginning during such taxable year.

(5) DENIAL OF DOUBLE BENEFIT.—No credit shall be allowed under this section for any expense for which a deduction is allowed under any other provision of this chapter.

(6) NO CREDIT FOR MARRIED INDIVIDUALS FILING SEPARATE RETURNS.—If the taxpayer is a married individual (within the meaning of section 7703), this section shall apply only if the taxpayer and the taxpayer's spouse file a joint return for the taxable year.

(7) NONRESIDENT ALIENS.—If the taxpayer is a nonresident alien individual for any portion of the taxable year, this section shall apply only if such individual is treated as a resident alien of the United States for purposes of this chapter by reason of an election under subsection (g) or (h) of section 6013.

[Sec. 25A(h)]

(h) INFLATION ADJUSTMENTS.—

(1) DOLLAR LIMITATION ON AMOUNT OF CREDIT.—

(A) IN GENERAL.—In the case of a taxable year beginning after 2001, each of the $1,000 amounts under subsection (b)(1) shall be increased by an amount equal to—

(i) such dollar amount, multiplied by

(ii) the cost-of-living adjustment determined under section 1(f)(3) for the calendar year in which the taxable year begins, determined by substituting "calendar year 2000" for "calendar year 1992" in subparagraph (B) thereof.

(B) ROUNDING.—If any amount as adjusted under subparagraph (A) is not a multiple of $100, such amount shall be rounded to the next lowest multiple of $100.

(2) INCOME LIMITS.—

(A) IN GENERAL.—In the case of a taxable year beginning after 2001, the $40,000 and $80,000 amounts in subsection (d)(2) shall each be increased by an amount equal to—

(i) such dollar amount, multiplied by

(ii) the cost-of-living adjustment determined under section 1(f)(3) for the calendar year in which the taxable year begins, determined by substituting "calendar year 2000" for "calendar year 1992" in subparagraph (B) thereof.

(B) ROUNDING.—If any amount as adjusted under subparagraph (A) is not a multiple of $1,000, such amount shall be rounded to the next lowest multiple of $1,000.

[Sec. 25A(i)]

(i) REGULATIONS.—The Secretary may prescribe such regulations as may be necessary or appropriate to carry out this section, including regulations providing for a recapture of the credit allowed under this section in cases where there is a refund in a subsequent taxable year of any amount which was taken into account in determining the amount of such credit.

[Sec. 25B]

SEC. 25B. ELECTIVE DEFERRALS AND IRA CONTRIBUTIONS BY CERTAIN INDIVIDUALS.

[Sec. 25B(a)]

(a) ALLOWANCE OF CREDIT.—In the case of an eligible individual, there shall be allowed as a credit against the tax imposed by this subtitle for the taxable year an amount equal to the applicable percentage of so much of the qualified retirement savings contributions of the eligible individual for the taxable year as do not exceed $2,000.

[Sec. 25B(b)]

(b) APPLICABLE PERCENTAGE.—For purposes of this section, the applicable percentage is the percentage determined in accordance with the following table:

Adjusted Gross Income

Joint return		Head of a household		All other cases		Applicable
Over	Not over	Over	Not over	Over	Not over	percentage
	$30,000		$22,500		$15,000	50
30,000	32,500	22,500	24,375	15,000	16,250	20
32,500	50,000	24,375	37,500	16,250	25,000	10
50,000		37,500		25,000		0

[Sec. 25B(c)]

(c) ELIGIBLE INDIVIDUAL.—For purposes of this section—

(1) IN GENERAL.—The term "eligible individual" means any individual if such individual has attained the age of 18 as of the close of the taxable year.

(2) DEPENDENTS AND FULL-TIME STUDENTS NOT ELIGIBLE.—The term "eligible individual" shall not include—

(A) any individual with respect to whom a deduction under section 151 is allowed to another taxpayer for a taxable year beginning in the calendar year in which such individual's taxable year begins, and

(B) any individual who is a student (as defined in section 151(c)(4)).

[Sec. 25B(d)]

(d) QUALIFIED RETIREMENT SAVINGS CONTRIBUTIONS.—For purposes of this section—

(1) IN GENERAL.—The term "qualified retirement savings contributions" means, with respect to any taxable year, the sum of—

(A) the amount of the qualified retirement contributions (as defined in section 219(e)) made by the eligible individual,

(B) the amount of—

(i) any elective deferrals (as defined in section 402(g)(3)) of such individual, and

(ii) any elective deferral of compensation by such individual under an eligible deferred compensation plan (as defined in section 457(b)) of an eligible employer described in section 457(e)(1)(A), and

(C) the amount of voluntary employee contributions by such individual to any qualified retirement plan (as defined in section 4974(c)).

(2) REDUCTION FOR CERTAIN DISTRIBUTIONS.—

(A) IN GENERAL.—The qualified retirement savings contributions determined under paragraph (1) shall be reduced (but not below zero) by the aggregate distributions received by the individual during the testing period from any entity of a type to which contributions under paragraph (1) may be made. The preceding sentence shall not apply to the portion of any distribution which is not includible in gross income by reason of a trustee-to-trustee transfer or a rollover distribution.

(B) TESTING PERIOD.—For purposes of subparagraph (A), the testing period, with respect to a taxable year, is the period which includes—

(i) such taxable year,

(ii) the 2 preceding taxable years, and

(iii) the period after such taxable year and before the due date (including extensions) for filing the return of tax for such taxable year.

(C) EXCEPTED DISTRIBUTIONS.—There shall not be taken into account under subparagraph (A)—

(i) any distribution referred to in section 72(p), 401(k)(8), 401(m)(6), 402(g)(2), 404(k), or 408(d)(4), and

(ii) any distribution to which section 408A(d)(3) applies.

(D) TREATMENT OF DISTRIBUTIONS RECEIVED BY SPOUSE OF INDIVIDUAL.—For purposes of determining distributions received by an individual under subparagraph (A) for any taxable year, any distribution received by the spouse of such individual shall be treated as received by such individual if such individual and spouse file a joint return for such taxable year and for the taxable year during which the spouse receives the distribution.

[Sec. 25B(e)]

(e) ADJUSTED GROSS INCOME.—For purposes of this section, adjusted gross income shall be determined without regard to sections 911, 931, and 933.

[Sec. 25B(f)]

(f) INVESTMENT IN THE CONTRACT.—Notwithstanding any other provision of law, a qualified retirement savings contribution shall not fail to be included in determining the investment in the contract for purposes of section 72 by reason of the credit under this section.

[Caution: Code Sec. 25B(g), below, was added by P.L. 107-16. However, P.L. 107-147, Act Sec. 601(b)(2), provides that this amendment does not apply to tax years beginning during 2002 and 2003.]

[Sec. 25B(g)]

(g) LIMITATION BASED ON AMOUNT OF TAX.—The credit allowed under subsection (a) for the taxable year shall not exceed the excess of—

(1) the sum of the regular tax liability (as defined in section 26(b)) plus the tax imposed by section 55, over

(2) the sum of the credits allowable under this subpart (other than this section and section 23) and section 27 for the taxable year.

[Sec. 25B(h)]

(h) TERMINATION.—This section shall not apply to taxable years beginning after December 31, 2006.

[Sec. 26]

SEC. 26. LIMITATION BASED ON TAX LIABILITY; DEFINITION OF TAX LIABILITY.

[Sec. 26(a)]

(a) LIMITATION BASED ON AMOUNT OF TAX.—

[Caution: Code Sec. 26(a)(1), below, prior to amendment by P.L. 107-16, and as provided by P.L. 107-147, Act Sec. 601(b)(2), applies to tax years beginning on or before December 31, 2003.]

(1) IN GENERAL.—The aggregate amount of credits allowed by this subpart for the taxable year shall not exceed the excess (if any) of—

(A) the taxpayer's regular tax liability for the taxable year, over

(B) the tentative minimum tax for the taxable year (determined without regard to the alternative minimum tax foreign tax credit).

For purposes of subparagraph (B), the taxpayer's tentative minimum tax for any taxable year beginning during 1999 shall be treated as being zero.

[Caution: Code Sec. 26(a)(1), below, as amended by P.L. 107-16, and as provided by P.L. 107-147, Act Sec. 601(b)(2), applies to tax years beginning after December 31, 2003.]

(1) IN GENERAL.—The aggregate amount of credits allowed by this subpart (other than sections 23, 24, and 25B) for the taxable year shall not exceed the excess (if any) of—

(A) the taxpayer's regular tax liability for the taxable year, over

(B) the tentative minimum tax for the taxable year (determined without regard to the alternative minimum tax foreign tax credit).

For purposes of subparagraph (B), the taxpayer's tentative minimum tax for any taxable year beginning during 1999 shall be treated as being zero.

(2) SPECIAL RULE FOR 2000, 2001, 2002, AND 2003.—For purposes of any taxable year beginning during 2000, 2001, 2002, or 2003, the aggregate amount of credits allowed by this subpart for the taxable year shall not exceed the sum of—

(A) the taxpayer's regular tax liability for the taxable year reduced by the foreign tax credit allowable under section 27(a), and

(B) the tax imposed by section 55(a) for the taxable year.

[Sec. 26(b)]

(b) REGULAR TAX LIABILITY.—For purposes of this part—

(1) IN GENERAL.—The term "regular tax liability" means the tax imposed by this chapter for the taxable year.

(2) EXCEPTION FOR CERTAIN TAXES.—For purposes of paragraph (1), any tax imposed by any of the following provisions shall not be treated as tax imposed by this chapter:

(A) section 55 (relating to minimum tax),

(B) section 59A (relating to environmental tax),

(C) subsection (m)(5)(B), (q), (t), or (v) of section 72 (relating to additional taxes on certain distributions),

(D) section 143(m) (relating to recapture of proration of Federal subsidy from use of mortgage bonds and mortgage credit certificates),

(E) section 530(d)(3) (relating to additional tax on certain distributions from Coverdell education savings accounts),

(F) section 531 (relating to accumulated earnings tax),

(G) section 541 (relating to personal holding company tax),

(H) section 1351(d)(1) (relating to recoveries of foreign expropriation losses),

(I) section 1374 (relating to tax on certain certain built-in gains of S corporations),

(J) section 1375 (relating to tax imposed when passive investment income of corporation having subchapter C earnings and profits exceeds 25 percent of gross receipts),

(K) subparagraph (A) of section 7518(g)(6) (relating to nonqualified withdrawals from capital construction funds taxed at highest marginal rate),

(L) sections 871(a) and 881 (relating to certain income of nonresident aliens and foreign corporations),

(M) section 860E(e) (relating to taxes with respect to certain residual interests),

(N) section 884 (relating to branch profits tax),

(O) sections 453(l)(3) and 453A(c) (relating to interest on certain deferred tax liabilities),

(P) section 860K (relating to treatment of transfers of high-yield interests to disqualified holders),

(Q) section 220(f)(4) (relating to additional tax on Archer MSA distributions not used for qualified medical expenses), and

(R) section 138(c)(2) (relating to penalty for distributions from Medicare+Choice MSA not used for qualified medical expenses if minimum balance not maintained).

[Sec. 26(c)]

(c) TENTATIVE MINIMUM TAX.—For purposes of this part, the term "tentative minimum tax" means the amount determined under section 55(b)(1).

Subpart C—Refundable Credits

SEC. 31. TAX WITHHELD ON WAGES.

(a) WAGE WITHHOLDING FOR INCOME TAX PURPOSES.—

(1) IN GENERAL.—The amount withheld as tax under chapter 24 shall be allowed to the recipient of the income as a credit against the tax imposed by this subtitle.

(2) YEAR OF CREDIT.—The amount so withheld during any calendar year shall be allowed as a credit for the taxable year beginning in such calendar year. If more than one taxable year begins in a calendar year, such amount shall be allowed as a credit for the last taxable year so beginning.

* * *

[Caution: As provided in Section 32(j), the dollar amounts set forth in Sections 32(b)(2) and 32(i)(1) are adjusted for taxable years after 1996 to reflect increases in the Consumer Price Index. The adjusted amounts applicable to taxable years beginning in 2003 are provided beginning at page ix.]

SEC. 32. EARNED INCOME.

(a) ALLOWANCE OF CREDIT.—

(1) IN GENERAL.—In the case of an eligible individual, there shall be allowed as a credit against the tax imposed by this subtitle for the taxable year an amount equal to the credit percentage of so much of the taxpayer's earned income for the taxable year as does not exceed the earned income amount.

(2) LIMITATION.—The amount of the credit allowable to a taxpayer under paragraph (1) for any taxable year shall not exceed the excess (if any) of—

(A) the credit percentage of the earned income amount, over

(B) the phaseout percentage of so much of the adjusted gross income (or, if greater, the earned income) of the taxpayer for the taxable year as exceeds the phaseout amount.

(b) PERCENTAGES AND AMOUNTS.—For purposes of subsection (a)—

(1) PERCENTAGES.—The credit percentage and the phaseout percentage shall be determined as follows:

(A) IN GENERAL.—In the case of taxable years beginning after 1995:

In the case of an eligible individual with:	The credit percentage is:	The phaseout percentage is:
1 qualifying child	34	15.98
2 or more qualifying children	40	21.06
No qualifying children	7.65	7.65

* * *

(2) AMOUNTS.—

(A) IN GENERAL.—Subject to subparagraph (B), the earned income amount and the phaseout amount shall be determined as follows:

In the case of an eligible individual with:	The earned income amount is:	The phaseout amount is:
1 qualifying child	$6,330	$11,610
2 or more qualifying children	$8,890	$11,610
No qualifying children	$4,220	$ 5,280

(B) JOINT RETURNS.—In the case of a joint return filed by an eligible individual and such individual's spouse, the phaseout amount determined under subparagraph (A) shall be increased by—

(i) $1,000 in the case of taxable years beginning in 2002, 2003, and 2004,

(ii) $2,000 in the case of taxable years beginning in 2005, 2006, and 2007, and

(iii) $3,000 in the case of taxable years beginning after 2007.

[Sec. 32(c)]

(c) DEFINITIONS AND SPECIAL RULES.—For purposes of this section—

(1) ELIGIBLE INDIVIDUAL.—

(A) IN GENERAL.—The term "eligible individual" means—

(i) any individual who has a qualifying child for the taxable year, or

(ii) any other individual who does not have a qualifying child for the taxable year, if—

(I) such individual's principal place of abode is in the United States for more than one-half of such taxable year,

(II) such individual (or, if the individual is married, either the individual or the individual's spouse) has attained age 25 but not attained age 65 before the close of the taxable year, and

(III) such individual is not a dependent for whom a deduction is allowable under section 151 to another taxpayer for any taxable year beginning in the same calendar year as such taxable year.

For purposes of preceding sentence, marital status shall be determined under section 7703.

(B) QUALIFYING CHILD INELIGIBLE.—If an individual is the qualifying child of a taxpayer for any taxable year of such taxpayer beginning in a calendar year, such individual shall not be treated as an eligible individual for any taxable year of such individual beginning in such calendar year.

(C) 2 OR MORE CLAIMING QUALIFYING CHILD.—

(i) IN GENERAL.—Except as provided in clause (ii), if (but for this paragraph) an individual may be claimed, and is claimed, as a qualifying child by 2 or more taxpayers for a taxable year beginning in the same calendar year, such individual shall be treated as the qualifying child of the taxpayer who is—

(I) a parent of the individual, or

(II) if subclause (I) does not apply, the taxpayer with the highest adjusted gross income for such taxable year.

(ii) MORE THAN 1 CLAIMING CREDIT.—If the parents claiming the credit with respect to any qualifying child do not file a joint return together, such child shall be treated as the qualifying child of—

(I) the parent with whom the child resided for the longest period of time during the taxable year, or

(II) if the child resides with both parents for the same amount of time during such taxable year, the parent with the highest adjusted gross income.

(D) EXCEPTION FOR INDIVIDUAL CLAIMING BENEFITS UNDER SECTION 911.—The term "eligible individual" does not include any individual who claims the benefits of section 911 (relating to citizens or residents living abroad) for the taxable year.

(E) LIMITATION ON ELIGIBILITY OF NONRESIDENT ALIENS.—The term "eligible individual" shall not include any individual who is a nonresident alien individual for any portion of the taxable year unless such individual is treated for such taxable year as a resident of the United States for purposes of this chapter by reason of an election under subsection (g) or (h) of section 6013.

(F) IDENTIFICATION NUMBER REQUIREMENT.—No credit shall be allowed under this section to an eligible individual who does not include on the return of tax for the taxable year—

(i) such individual's taxpayer identification number, and

(ii) if the individual is married (within the meaning of section 7703), the taxpayer identification number of such individual's spouse.

(G) INDIVIDUALS WHO DO NOT INCLUDE TIN, ETC., OF ANY QUALIFYING CHILD.—No credit shall be allowed under this section to any eligible individual who has one or more qualifying children if no qualifying child of such individual is taken into account under subsection (b) by reason of paragraph (3)(D).

(2) EARNED INCOME.—

(A) The term "earned income" means—

(i) wages, salaries, tips, and other employee compensation, but only if such amounts are includible in gross income for the taxable year, plus

(ii) the amount of the taxpayer's net earnings from self-employment for the taxable year (within the meaning of section 1402(a)), but such net earnings shall be determined with regard to the deduction allowed to the taxpayer by section 164(f).

(B) For purposes of subparagraph (A)—

(i) the earned income of an individual shall be computed without regard to any community property laws,

(ii) no amount received as a pension or annuity shall be taken into account,

(iii) no amount to which section 871(a) applies (relating to income of nonresident alien individuals not connected with United States business) shall be taken into account,

(iv) no amount received for services provided by an individual while the individual is an inmate at a penal institution shall be taken into account, and

(v) no amount described in subparagraph (A) received for service performed in work activities as defined in paragraph (4) or (7) of section 407(d) of the Social Security Act to which the taxpayer is assigned under any State program under part A of title IV of such Act shall be taken into account, but only to the extent such amount is subsidized under such State program.

(3) QUALIFYING CHILD.—

(A) IN GENERAL.—The term "qualifying child" means, with respect to any taxpayer for any taxable year, an individual—

(i) who bears a relationship to the taxpayer described in subparagraph (B),

(ii) who has the same principal place of abode as the taxpayer for more than one-half of such taxable year, and

(iii) who meets the age requirements of subparagraph (C).

(B) RELATIONSHIP TEST.—

(i) IN GENERAL.—An individual bears a relationship to the taxpayer described in this subparagraph if such individual is—

(I) a son, daughter, stepson, or stepdaughter, or a descendant of any such individual,

(II) a brother, sister, stepbrother, or stepsister, or a descendant of any such individual, who the taxpayer cares for as the taxpayer's own child, or

(III) an eligible foster child of the taxpayer.

(ii) MARRIED CHILDREN.—Clause (i) shall not apply to any individual who is married as of the close of the taxpayer's taxable year unless the taxpayer is entitled to a deduction under section 151 for such taxable year with respect to such individual (or would be so entitled but for paragraph (2) or (4) of section 152(e)).

(iii) ELIGIBLE FOSTER CHILD.—For purposes of clause (i), the term "eligible foster child" means an individual not described in subclause (I) or (II) of clause (i) who—

(I) is placed with the taxpayer by an authorized placement agency, and

(II) the taxpayer cares for as the taxpayer's own child.

(iv) ADOPTION.—For purposes of this subparagraph, a child who is legally adopted, or who is placed with the taxpayer by an authorized placement agency for adoption by the taxpayer, shall be treated as a child by blood.

(C) AGE REQUIREMENTS.—An individual meets the requirements of this subparagraph if such individual—

(i) has not attained the age of 19 as of the close of the calendar year in which the taxable year of the taxpayer begins,

(ii) is a student (as defined in section 151(c)(4)) who has not attained the age of 24 as of the close of such calendar year, or

(iii) is permanently and totally disabled (as defined in section 22(e)(3)) at any time during the taxable year.

(D) IDENTIFICATION REQUIREMENTS.—

(i) IN GENERAL.—A qualifying child shall not be taken into account under subsection (b) unless the taxpayer includes the name, age, and TIN of the qualifying child on the return of tax for the taxable year.

(ii) OTHER METHODS.—The Secretary may prescribe other methods for providing the information described in clause (i).

(E) ABODE MUST BE IN THE UNITED STATES.—The requirements of subparagraph (A)(ii) shall be met only if the principal place of abode is in the United States.

(4) TREATMENT OF MILITARY PERSONNEL STATIONED OUTSIDE THE UNITED STATES.—For purposes of paragraphs (1)(A)(ii)(I) and (3)(E), the principal place of abode of a member of the Armed Forces of the United States shall be treated as in the United States during any period during which such member is stationed outside the United States while serving on extended active duty with the Armed Forces of the United States. For purposes of the preceding sentence, the term "extended active duty" means any period of active duty pursuant to a call or order to such duty for a period in excess of 90 days or for an indefinite period.

[Sec. 32(d)]

(d) MARRIED INDIVIDUALS.—In the case of an individual who is married (within the meaning of section 7703), this section shall apply only if a joint return is filed for the taxable year under section 6013.

[Sec. 32(e)]

(e) TAXABLE YEAR MUST BE FULL TAXABLE YEAR.—Except in the case of a taxable year closed by reason of the death of the taxpayer, no credit shall be allowable under this section in the case of a taxable year covering a period of less than 12 months.

[Sec. 32(f)]

(f) AMOUNT OF CREDIT TO BE DETERMINED UNDER TABLES.—

(1) IN GENERAL.—The amount of the credit allowed by this section shall be determined under tables prescribed by the Secretary.

(2) REQUIREMENTS FOR TABLES.—The tables prescribed under paragraph (1) shall reflect the provisions of subsections (a) and (b) and shall have income brackets of not greater than $50 each—

(A) for earned income between $0 and the amount of earned income at which the credit is phased out under subsection (b), and

(B) for adjusted gross income between the dollar amount at which the phaseout begins under subsection (b) and the amount of adjusted gross income at which the credit is phased out under subsection (b).

[Sec. 32(g)]

(g) COORDINATION WITH ADVANCE PAYMENTS OF EARNED INCOME CREDIT.—

(1) RECAPTURE OF EXCESS ADVANCE PAYMENTS.—If any payment is made to the individual by an employer under section 3507 during any calendar year, then the tax imposed by this chapter for the individual's last taxable year beginning in such calendar year shall be increased by the aggregate amount of such payments.

(2) RECONCILIATION OF PAYMENTS ADVANCED AND CREDIT ALLOWED.—Any increase in tax under paragraph (1) shall not be treated as tax imposed by this chapter for purposes of determining the amount of any credit (other than the credit allowed by subsection (a)) allowable under this part.

[Sec. 32(h)—Repealed]

[Sec. 32(i)]

(i) DENIAL OF CREDIT FOR INDIVIDUALS HAVING EXCESSIVE INVESTMENT INCOME.—

(1) IN GENERAL.—No credit shall be allowed under subsection (a) for the taxable year if the aggregate amount of disqualified income of the taxpayer for the taxable year exceeds $2,200.

(2) DISQUALIFIED INCOME.—For purposes of paragraph (1), the term "disqualified income" means—

(A) interest or dividends to the extent includible in gross income for the taxable year,

(B) interest received or accrued during the taxable year which is exempt from tax imposed by this chapter,

(C) the excess (if any) of—

(i) gross income from rents or royalties not derived in the ordinary course of a trade or business, over

(ii) the sum of—

(I) the deductions (other than interest) which are clearly and directly allocable to such gross income, plus

(II) interest deductions properly allocable to such gross income,

(D) the capital gain net income (as defined in section 1222) of the taxpayer for such taxable year, and

(E) the excess (if any) of—

(i) the aggregate income from all passive activities for the taxable year (determined without regard to any amount included in earned income under subsection (c)(2) or described in a preceding subparagraph), over

(ii) the aggregate losses from all passive activities for the taxable year (as so determined).

For purposes of subparagraph (E), the term "passive activity" has the meaning given such term by section 469.

[Sec. 32(j)]

(j) INFLATION ADJUSTMENTS.—

(1) IN GENERAL.—In the case of any taxable year beginning after 1996, each of the dollar amounts in subsections (b)(2) and (i)(1) shall be increased by an amount equal to—

(A) such dollar amount, multiplied by

(B) the cost-of-living adjustment determined under section 1(f)(3) for the calendar year in which the taxable year begins, determined—

(i) in the case of amounts in subsections (b)(2)(A) and (i)(1), by substituting "calendar year 1995" for "calendar year 1992" in subparagraph (B) thereof, and

(ii) in the case of the $3,000 amount in subsection (b)(2)(B)(iii), by substituting "calendar year 2007" for "calendar year 1992" in subparagraph (B) of such section 1.

(2) ROUNDING.—

(A) IN GENERAL.—If any dollar amount in subsection (b)(2)(A) (after being increased under subparagraph (B) thereof), after being increased under paragraph (1), is not a multiple of $10, such dollar amount shall be rounded to the nearest multiple of $10.

(B) DISQUALIFIED INCOME THRESHOLD AMOUNT.—If the dollar amount in subsection (i)(1), after being increased under paragraph (1), is not a multiple of $50, such amount shall be rounded to the next lowest multiple of $50.

[Sec. 32(k)]

(k) Restrictions on Taxpayers Who Improperly Claimed Credit in Prior Year.—

(1) Taxpayers making prior fraudulent or reckless claims.—

(A) In general.—No credit shall be allowed under this section for any taxable year in the disallowance period.

(B) Disallowance period.—For purposes of paragraph (1), the disallowance period is—

(i) the period of 10 taxable years after the most recent taxable year for which there was a final determination that the taxpayer's claim of credit under this section was due to fraud, and

(ii) the period of 2 taxable years after the most recent taxable year for which there was a final determination that the taxpayer's claim of credit under this section was due to reckless or intentional disregard of rules and regulations (but not due to fraud).

(2) Taxpayers making improper prior claims.—In the case of a taxpayer who is denied credit under this section for any taxable year as a result of the deficiency procedures under subchapter B of chapter 63, no credit shall be allowed under this section for any subsequent taxable year unless the taxpayer provides such information as the Secretary may require to demonstrate eligibility for such credit.

* * *

Subpart E—Rules for Computing Investment Credit

[Sec. 49]

SEC. 49. AT-RISK RULES.

[Sec. 49(a)]

(a) General Rule.—

(1) Certain nonrecourse financing excluded from credit base.—

* * *

(D) Nonqualified nonrecourse financing.—

* * *

(iv) Qualified person.—For purposes of this paragraph, the term "qualified person" means any person which is actively and regularly engaged in the business of lending money and which is not—

(I) a related person with respect to the taxpayer,

(II) a person from which the taxpayer acquired the property (or a related person to such person), or

(III) a person who receives a fee with respect to the taxpayer's investment in the property (or a related person to such person).

(v) Related person.—For purposes of this subparagraph, the term "related person" has the meaning given such term by section 465(b)(3)(C). Except as otherwise provided in regulations prescribed by the Secretary, the determination of whether a person is a related person shall be made as of the close of the taxable year in which the property is placed in service.

* * *

Subpart G—Credit Against Regular Tax for Prior Year Minimum Tax Liability

[Sec. 53]

SEC. 53. CREDIT FOR PRIOR YEAR MINIMUM TAX LIABILITY.

[Sec. 53(a)]

(a) Allowance of Credit.—There shall be allowed as a credit against the tax imposed by this chapter for any taxable year an amount equal to the minimum tax credit for such taxable year.

[Sec. 53(b)]

(b) MINIMUM TAX CREDIT.—For purposes of subsection (a), the minimum tax credit for any taxable year is the excess (if any) of—

(1) the adjusted net minimum tax imposed for all prior taxable years beginning after 1986, over

(2) the amount allowable as a credit under subsection (a) for such prior taxable years.

[Sec. 53(c)]

(c) LIMITATION.—The credit allowable under subsection (a) for any taxable year shall not exceed the excess (if any) of—

(1) The regular tax liability of the taxpayer for such taxable year reduced by the sum of the credits allowable under subparts A, B, D, E, and F of this part, over

(2) the tentative minimum tax for the taxable year.

[Sec. 53(d)]

(d) DEFINITIONS.—For purposes of this section—

(1) Net minimum tax.—

(A) IN GENERAL.—The term "net minimum tax" means the tax imposed by section 55.

(B) CREDIT NOT ALLOWED FOR EXCLUSION PREFERENCES.—

(i) ADJUSTED NET MINIMUM TAX.—The adjusted net minimum tax for any taxable year is—

(I) the amount of the net minimum tax for such taxable year, reduced by

(II) the amount which would be the net minimum tax for such taxable year if the only adjustments and items of tax preference taken into account were those specified in clause (ii) and if section 59(a)(2) did not apply.

(ii) SPECIFIED ITEMS.—The following are specified in this clause—

(I) the adjustments provided for in subsection (b)(1) of section 56, and

(II) the items of tax preference described in paragraphs (1), (5), and (7) of section 57(a).

(iii) SPECIAL RULE.—The adjusted net minimum tax for the taxable year shall be increased by the amount of the credit not allowed under section 29 (relating to credit for producing fuel from a nonconventional source) solely by reason of the application of section 29(b)(6)(B) or not allowed under section 30 solely by reason of the application of section 30(b)(3)(B).

(iv) CREDIT ALLOWABLE FOR EXCLUSION PREFERENCES OF CORPORATIONS.—In the case of a corporation—

(I) the preceding provisions of this subparagraph shall not apply, and

(II) the adjusted net minimum tax for any taxable year is the amount of the net minimum tax for such year increased in the manner provided in clause (iii).

(2) TENTATIVE MINIMUM TAX.—The term "tentative minimum tax" has the meaning given to such term by section 55(b).

PART VI—ALTERNATIVE MINIMUM TAX

[Sec. 55]

SEC. 55. ALTERNATIVE MINIMUM TAX IMPOSED.

[Sec. 55(a)]

(a) GENERAL RULE.—There is hereby imposed (in addition to any other tax imposed by this subtitle) a tax equal to the excess (if any) of—

(1) the tentative minimum tax for the taxable year, over

(2) the regular tax for the taxable year.

[Sec. 55(b)]

(b) TENTATIVE MINIMUM TAX.—For purposes of this part—

(1) AMOUNT OF TENTATIVE TAX.—

(A) NONCORPORATE TAXPAYERS.—

(i) IN GENERAL.—In the case of a taxpayer other than a corporation, the tentative minimum tax for the taxable year is the sum of—

(I) 26 percent of so much of the taxable excess as does not exceed $175,000, plus

(II) 28 percent of so much of the taxable excess as exceeds $175,000.

The amount determined under the preceding sentence shall be reduced by the alternative minimum tax foreign tax credit for the taxable year.

(ii) TAXABLE EXCESS.—For purposes of this subsection, the term "taxable excess" means so much of the alternative minimum taxable income for the taxable year as exceeds the exemption amount.

(iii) MARRIED INDIVIDUAL FILING SEPARATE RETURN.—In the case of a married individual filing a separate return, clause (i) shall be applied by substituting "$87,500" for "$175,000" each place it appears. For purposes of the preceding sentence, marital status shall be determined under section 7703.

(B) CORPORATIONS.—In the case of a corporation, the tentative minimum tax for the taxable year is—

(i) 20 percent of so much of the alternative minimum taxable income for the taxable year as exceeds the exemption amount, reduced by

(ii) the alternative minimum tax foreign tax credit for the taxable year.

(2) ALTERNATIVE MINIMUM TAXABLE INCOME.—The term "alternative minimum taxable income" means the taxable income of the taxpayer for the taxable year—

(A) determined with the adjustments provided in section 56 and section 58, and

(B) increased by the amount of the items of tax preference described in section 57.

If a taxpayer is subject to the regular tax, such taxpayer shall be subject to the tax imposed by this section (and, if the regular tax is determined by reference to an amount other than taxable income, such amount shall be treated as the taxable income of such taxpayer for purposes of the preceding sentence).

(3) MAXIMUM RATE OF TAX ON NET CAPITAL GAIN OF NONCORPORATE TAXPAYERS.—The amount determined under the first sentence of paragraph (1)(A)(i) shall not exceed the sum of—

(A) the amount determined under such first sentence computed at the rates and in the same manner as if this paragraph had not been enacted on the taxable excess reduced by the lesser of—

(i) the net capital gain; or

(ii) the sum of—

(I) the adjusted net capital gain, plus

(II) the unrecaptured section 1250 gain, plus

(B) 5 percent (0 percent in the case of taxable years beginning after 2007) of so much of the adjusted net capital gain (or, if less, taxable excess) as does not exceed the amount on which a tax is determined under section 1(h)(1)(B), plus

(C) 15 percent of the adjusted net capital gain (or, if less, taxable excess) in excess of the amount on which tax is determined under subparagraph (B), plus

(D) 25 percent of the amount of taxable excess in excess of the sum of the amounts on which tax is determined under the preceding subparagraphs of this paragraph.

Terms used in this paragraph which are also used in section 1(h) shall have the respective meanings given such terms by section 1(h) but computed with the adjustments under this part.

Sec. 55(b)

[Sec. 55(c)]

(c) REGULAR TAX.—

(1) IN GENERAL.—For purposes of this section, the term "regular tax" means the regular tax liability for the taxable year (as defined in section 26(b)) reduced by the foreign tax credit allowable under section 27(a), the section 936 credit allowable under section 27(b), and the Puerto Rico economic activity credit under section 30A. Such terms shall not include any increase in tax under section 49(b) or 50(a) or subsection (j) or (k) of section 42.

(2) CROSS REFERENCES.—

For provisions providing that certain credits are not allowable against the tax imposed by this section, see sections 26(a), 29(b)(6), 30(b)(3), and 38(c).

[Sec. 55(d)]

(d) EXEMPTION AMOUNT.—For purposes of this section—

(1) EXEMPTION AMOUNT FOR TAXPAYERS OTHER THAN CORPORATIONS.—In the case of a taxpayer other than a corporation, the term "exemption amount" means—

(A) $45,000 ($58,000 in the case of taxable years beginning in 2003 and 2004) in the case of—

(i) a joint return, or

(ii) a surviving spouse,

(B) $33,750 ($40,250 in the case of taxable years beginning in 2003 and 2004) in the case of an individual who—

(i) is not a married individual, and

(ii) is not a surviving spouse,

(C) 50 percent of the dollar amount applicable under paragraph (1)(A) in the case of a married individual who files a separate return, and

(D) $22,500 in the case of an estate or trust.

For purposes of this paragraph, the term "surviving spouse" has the meaning given to such term by section 2(a), and marital status shall be determined under section 7703.

(2) CORPORATIONS.—In the case of a corporation, the term "exemption amount" means $40,000.

(3) PHASE-OUT OF EXEMPTION AMOUNT.—The exemption amount of any taxpayers shall be reduced (but not below zero) by an amount equal to 25 percent of the amount by which the alternative minimum taxable income of the taxpayer exceeds—

(A) $150,000 in the case of a taxpayer described in paragraph (1)(A) or (2),

(B) $112,500 in the case of a taxpayer described in paragraph (1)(B), and

(C) $75,000 in the case of a taxpayer described in subparagraph (C) or (D) of paragraph (1).

In the case of a taxpayer described in paragraph (1)(C), alternative minimum taxable income shall be increased by the lesser of (i) 25 percent of the excess of alternative minimum taxable income (determined without regard to this sentence) over the minimum amount of such income (as so determined) for which the exemption amount under paragraph (1)(C) is zero, or (ii) such exemption amount (determined without regard to this paragraph).

[Sec. 55(e)]

(e) EXEMPTION FOR SMALL CORPORATIONS.—

(1) IN GENERAL.—

(A) $7,500,000 GROSS RECEIPTS TEST.—The tentative minimum tax of a corporation shall be zero for any taxable year if the corporation's average annual gross receipts for all 3-taxable-year periods ending before such taxable year does not exceed $7,500,000. For purposes of the preceding sentence, only taxable years beginning after December 31, 1993, shall be taken into account.

(B) $5,000,000 GROSS RECEIPTS TEST FOR FIRST 3-YEAR PERIOD.—Subparagraph (A) shall be applied by substituting "$5,000,000" for "$7,500,000" for the first 3-taxable-year period (or portion thereof) of the corporation which is taken into account under subparagraph (A).

(C) FIRST TAXABLE YEAR CORPORATION IN EXISTENCE.—If such taxable year is the first taxable year that such corporation is in existence, the tentative minimum tax of such corporation for such year shall be zero.

(D) SPECIAL RULES.—For purposes of this paragraph, the rules of paragraphs (2) and (3) of section 448(c) shall apply.

(2) PROSPECTIVE APPLICATION OF MINIMUM TAX IF SMALL CORPORATION CEASES TO BE SMALL.—In the case of a corporation whose tentative minimum tax is zero for any prior taxable year by reason of paragraph (1), the application of this part for taxable years beginning with the first taxable year such corporation ceases to be described in paragraph (1) shall be determined with the following modifications:

(A) Section 56(a)(1) (relating to depreciation) and section 56(a)(5) (relating to pollution control facilities) shall apply only to property placed in service on or after the change date.

(B) Section 56(a)(2) (relating to mining exploration and development costs) shall apply only to costs paid or incurred on or after the change date.

(C) Section 56(a)(3) (relating to treatment of long-term contracts) shall apply only to contracts entered into on or after the change date.

(D) Section 56(a)(4) (relating to alternative net operating loss deduction) shall apply in the same manner as if, in section 56(d)(2), the change date were substituted for "January 1, 1987" and the day before the change date were substituted for "December 31, 1986" each place it appears.

(E) Section 56(g)(2)(B) (relating to limitation on allowance of negative adjustments based on adjusted current earnings) shall apply only to prior taxable years beginning on or after the change date.

(F) Section 56(g)(4)(A) (relating to adjustment for depreciation to adjusted current earnings) shall not apply.

(G) Subparagraphs (D) and (F) of section 56(g)(4) (relating to other earnings and profits adjustments and depletion) shall apply in the same manner as if the day before the change date were substituted for "December 31, 1989" each place it appears therein.

(3) EXCEPTION.—The modifications in paragraph (2) shall not apply to—

(A) any item acquired by the corporation in a transaction to which section 381 applies, and

(B) any property the basis of which in the hands of the corporation is determined by reference to the basis of the property in the hands of the transferor, if such item or property was subject to any provision referred to in paragraph (2) while held by the transferor.

(4) CHANGE DATE.—For purposes of paragraph (2), the change date is the first day of the first taxable year for which the taxpayer ceases to be described in paragraph (1).

(5) LIMITATION ON USE OF CREDIT FOR PRIOR YEAR MINIMUM TAX LIABILITY.—In the case of a taxpayer whose tentative minimum tax for any taxable year is zero by reason of paragraph (1), section 53(c) shall be applied for such year by reducing the amount otherwise taken into account under section 53(c)(1) by 25 percent of so much of such amount as exceeds $25,000. Rules similar to the rules of section 38(c)(3)(B) shall apply for purposes of the preceding sentence.

[Sec. 56]

SEC. 56. ADJUSTMENTS IN COMPUTING ALTERNATIVE MINIMUM TAXABLE INCOME.

[Sec. 56(a)]

(a) ADJUSTMENTS APPLICABLE TO ALL TAXPAYERS.—In determining the amount of the alternative minimum taxable income for any taxable year the following treatment shall apply (in lieu of the treatment applicable for purposes of computing the regular tax):

(1) DEPRECIATION.—

(A) IN GENERAL.—

(i) PROPERTY OTHER THAN CERTAIN PERSONAL PROPERTY.—Except as provided in clause (ii), the depreciation deduction allowable under section 167 with respect to any tangible property placed in service after December 31, 1986, shall be determined under the alternative system of section 168(g). In the case of property placed in service after December 31, 1998, the preceding sentence shall not apply but clause (ii) shall continue to apply.

(ii) 150-PERCENT DECLINING BALANCE METHOD FOR CERTAIN PROPERTY.—The method of depreciation used shall be—

(I) the 150 percent declining balance method,

(II) switching to the straight line method for the 1st taxable year for which using the straight line method with respect to the adjusted basis as of the beginning of the year will yield a higher allowance.

The preceding sentence shall not apply to any section 1250 property (as defined in section 1250(c)) (and the straight line method shall be used for such section 1250 property) or to any other property if the depreciation deduction determined under section 168 with respect to such other property for purposes of the regular tax is determined by using the straight line method.

(B) EXCEPTION FOR CERTAIN PROPERTY.—This paragraph shall not apply to property described in paragraph (1), (2), (3), or (4) of section 168(f).

(C) COORDINATION WITH TRANSITIONAL RULES.—

(i) IN GENERAL.—This paragraph shall not apply to property placed in service after December 31, 1986, to which the amendments made by section 201 of the Tax Reform Act of 1986 do not apply by reason of section 203, 204, or 251(d) of such Act.

(ii) TREATMENT OF CERTAIN PROPERTY PLACED IN SERVICE BEFORE 1987.—This paragraph shall apply to any property to which the amendments made by section 201 of the Tax Reform Act of 1986 apply by reason of an election under section 203(a)(1)(B) of such Act without regard to the requirement of subparagraph (A) that the property be placed in service after December 31, 1986.

(D) NORMALIZATION RULES.—With respect to public utility property described in section 168(i)(10), the Secretary shall prescribe the requirements of a normalization method of accounting for this section.

(2) MINING EXPLORATION AND DEVELOPMENT COSTS.—

(A) IN GENERAL.—With respect to each mine or other natural deposit (other than an oil, gas, or geothermal well) of the taxpayer, the amount allowable as a deduction under section 616(a) or 617(a) (determined without regard to section 291(b)) in computing the regular tax for costs paid or incurred after December 31, 1986, shall be capitalized and amortized ratably over the 10-year period beginning with the taxable year in which the expenditures were made.

(B) LOSS ALLOWED.—If a loss is sustained with respect to any property described in subparagraph (A), a deduction shall be allowed for the expenditures described in subparagraph (A) for the taxable year in which such loss is sustained in an amount equal to the lesser of—

(i) the amount allowable under section 165(a) for the expenditures if they had remained capitalized, or

(ii) the amount of such expenditures which have not previously been amortized under subparagraph (A).

(3) TREATMENT OF CERTAIN LONG-TERM CONTRACTS.—In the case of any long-term contract entered into by the taxpayer on or after March 1, 1986, the taxable income from such contract shall be determined under the percentage of completion method of accounting (as modified by section 460(b)). For purposes of the preceding sentence, in the case of a contract described in section 460(e)(1), the percentage of the contract completed shall be determined under section 460(b)(1) by using the simplified procedures for allocation of costs prescribed under section 460(b)(3). The first sentence of this paragraph shall not apply to any home construction contract (as defined in section 460(e)(6)).

(4) ALTERNATIVE TAX NET OPERATING LOSS DEDUCTION.—The alternative tax net operating loss dedution shall be allowed in lieu of the net operating loss deduction allowed under section 172.

(5) POLLUTION CONTROL FACILITIES.—In the case of any certified pollution control facility placed in service after December 31, 1986, the deduction allowable under section 169 (without regard to section 291) shall be determined under the alternative system of section 168(g). In the case of such a facility placed in service after December 31, 1998, such deduction shall be determined under section 168 using the straight line method.

(6) ADJUSTED BASIS.—The adjusted basis of any property to which paragraph (1) or (5) applies (or with respect to which there are any expenditures to which paragraph (2) or subsection (b)(2)

applies) shall be determined on the basis of the treatment prescribed in paragraph (1), (2), or (5), or subsection (b)(2), whichever applies.

(7) SECTION 87 NOT APPLICABLE.—Section 87 (relating to alcohol fuel credit) shall not apply.

[Sec. 56(b)]

(b) ADJUSTMENTS APPLICABLE TO INDIVIDUALS.—In determining the amount of the alternative minimum taxable income of any taxpayer (other than a corporation), the following treatment shall apply (in lieu of the treatment applicable for purposes of computing the regular tax):

(1) LIMITATION ON DEDUCTIONS.—

(A) IN GENERAL.—No deduction shall be allowed—

(i) for any miscellaneous itemized deduction (as defined in section 67(b)), or

(ii) for any taxes described in paragraph (1), (2), or (3), of section 164(a).

Clause (ii) shall not apply to any amount allowable in computing adjusted gross income.

(B) MEDICAL EXPENSES.—In determining the amount allowable as a deduction under section 213, subsection (a) of section 213 shall be applied by substituting "10 percent" for "7.5 percent".

(C) INTEREST.—In determining the amount allowable as a deduction for interest, subsections (d) and (h) of section 163 shall apply, except that—

(i) in lieu of the exception under section 163(h)(2)(D), the term "personal interest" shall not include any qualified housing interest (as defined in subsection (e)),

(ii) sections 163(d)(6) and 163(h)(5) (relating to phase-ins) shall not apply,

(iii) interest on any specified private activity bond (and any amount treated as interest on a specified private activity bond under section 57(a)(5)(B)) and any deduction referred to in section 57(a)(5)(A), shall be treated as includible in gross income (or as deductible) for purposes of applying section 163(d),

(iv) in lieu of the exception under section 163(d)(3)(B)(i), the term "investment interest" shall not include any qualified housing interest (as defined in subsection (e)), and

(v) the adjustments of this section and sections 57 and 58 shall apply in determining net investment income under section 163(d).

(D) TREATMENT OF CERTAIN RECOVERIES.—No recovery of any tax to which subparagraph (A)(ii) applied shall be included in gross income for purposes of determining alternative minimum taxable income.

(E) STANDARD DEDUCTION AND DEDUCTION FOR PERSONAL EXEMPTIONS NOT ALLOWED.—The standard deduction under section 63(c), the deduction for personal exemptions under section 151, and the deduction under section 642(b) shall not be allowed.

(F) SECTION 68 NOT APPLICABLE.—Section 68 shall not apply.

(2) CIRCULATION AND RESEARCH AND EXPERIMENTAL EXPENDITURES.—

(A) IN GENERAL.—The amount allowable as a deduction under section 173 or 174(a) in computing the regular tax for amounts paid or incurred after December 31, 1986, shall be capitalized and—

(i) in the case of circulation expenditures described in section 173, shall be amortized ratably over the 3-year period beginning with the taxable year in which the expenditures were made, or

(ii) in the case of research and experimental expenditures described in section 174(a), shall be amortized ratably over the 10-year period beginning with the taxable year in which the expenditures were made.

(B) LOSS ALLOWED.—If a loss is sustained with respect to any property described in subparagraph (A), a deduction shall be allowed for the expenditures described in subparagraph (A) for the taxable year in which such loss is sustained in an amount equal to the lesser of—

(i) the amount allowable under section 165(a) for the expenditures if they had remained capitalized, or

(ii) the amount of such expenditures which have not previously been amortized under subparagraph (A).

Sec. 56(b)

(C) SPECIAL RULE FOR PERSONAL HOLDING COMPANIES.—In the case of circulation expenditures described in section 173, the adjustments provided in this paragraph shall apply also to a personal holding company (as defined in section 542).

(D) EXCEPTION FOR CERTAIN RESEARCH AND EXPERIMENTAL EXPENDITURES.—If the taxpayer materially participates (within the meaning of section 469(h)) in an activity, this paragraph shall not apply to any amount allowable as deduction under section 174(a) for expenditures paid or incurred in connection with such activity.

(3) TREATMENT OF INCENTIVE STOCK OPTIONS.—Section 421 shall not apply to the transfer of stock acquired pursuant to the exercise of an incentive stock option (as defined in section 422). Section 422(c)(2) shall apply in any case where the disposition and the inclusion for purposes of this part are within the same taxable year and such section shall not apply in any other case. The adjusted basis of any stock so acquired shall be determined on the basis of the treatment prescribed by this paragraph.

[Sec. 56(c)]

(c) ADJUSTMENTS APPLICABLE TO CORPORATIONS.—In determining the amount of the alternative minimum taxable income of a corporation, the following treatment shall apply:

(1) ADJUSTMENT FOR ADJUSTED CURRENT EARNINGS.—Alternative minimum taxable income shall be adjusted as provided in subsection (g).

(2) MERCHANT MARINE CAPITAL CONSTRUCTION FUNDS.—In the case of a capital construction fund established under section 607 of the Merchant Marine Act, 1936 (46 U.S.C. 1177)—

(A) subparagraphs (A), (B), and (C) of section 7518(c)(1) (and the corresponding provisions of such section 607) shall not apply to—

(i) any amount deposited in such fund after after December 31, 1986, or

(ii) any earnings (including gains and losses) after December 31, 1986, on amounts in such fund, and

(B) no reduction in basis shall be made under section 7518(f) (or the corresponding provisions of such section 607) with respect to the withdrawal from the fund of any amount to which subparagraph (A) applies.

For purposes of this paragraph, any withdrawal of deposits or earnings from the fund shall be treated as allocable first to deposits made before (and earnings received or accrued before) January 1, 1987.

(3) SPECIAL DEDUCTION FOR CERTAIN ORGANIZATIONS NOT ALLOWED.—The deduction determined under section 833(b) shall not be allowed.

[Sec. 56(d)]

(d) ALTERNATIVE TAX NET OPERATING LOSS DEDUCTION DEFINED.—

(1) IN GENERAL.—For purposes of subsection (a)(4), the term "alternative tax net operating loss deduction" means the net operating loss deduction allowable for the taxable year under section 172, except that—

(A) the amount of such deduction shall not exceed the sum of—

(i) the lesser of—

(I) the amount of such deduction attributable to net operating losses (other than the deduction attributable to carryovers described in clause (ii)(I)), or

(II) 90 percent of alternative minimum taxable income determined without regard to such deduction, plus

(ii) the lesser of—

(I) the amount of such deduction attributable to the sum of carrybacks of net operating losses for taxable years ending during 2001 or 2002 and carryforwards of net operating losses to taxable years ending during 2001 and 2002, or

(II) alternative minimum taxable income determined without regard to such deduction reduced by the amount determined under clause (i), and

(B) in determining the amount of such deduction—

(i) the net operating loss (within the meaning of section 172(c)) for any loss year shall be adjusted as provided in paragraph (2), and

(ii) appropriate adjustments in the application of section 172(b)(2) shall be made to take into account the limitation of subparagraph (A).

(2) ADJUSTMENTS TO NET OPERATING LOSS COMPUTATION.—

(A) POST-1986 LOSS YEARS.—In the case of a loss year beginning after December 31, 1986, the net operating loss for such year under section 172(c) shall—

(i) be determined with the adustments provided in this section and section 58, and

(ii) be reduced by the items of tax preference determined under section 57 for such year.

An item of tax preference shall be taken into account under clause (ii) only to the extent such item increased the amount of the net operating loss for the taxable year under section 172(c).

(B) PRE-1987 YEARS.—In the case of loss years beginning before January 1, 1987, the amount of the net operating loss which may be carried over to taxable years beginning after December 31, 1986, for purposes of paragraph (2), shall be equal to the amount which may be carried from the loss year to the first taxable year of the taxpayer beginning after December 31, 1986.

[Sec. 56(e)]

(e) QUALIFIED HOUSING INTEREST.—For purposes of this part—

(1) IN GENERAL.—The term "qualified housing interest" means interest which is qualified residence interest (as defined in section 163(h)(3)) and is paid or accrued during the taxable year on indebtedness which is incurred in acquiring, constructing, or substantially improving any property which—

(A) is the principal residence (within the meaning of section 121) of the taxpayer at the time such interest accrues, or

(B) is a qualified dwelling which is a qualified residence (within the meaning of section 163(h)(4)).

Such term also includes interest on any indebtedness resulting from the refinancing of indebtedness meeting the requirements of the preceding sentence; but only to the extent that the amount of the indebtedness resulting from such refinancing does not exceed the amount of the refinanced indebtedness immediately before the refinancing.

(2) QUALIFIED DWELLING.—The term "qualified dwelling" means any—

(A) house,

(B) apartment,

(C) condominium, or

(D) mobile home not used on a transient basis (within the meaning of section 7701(a)(19)(C)(v)),

including all structures or other property appurtenant thereto.

(3) SPECIAL RULE FOR INDEBTEDNESS INCURRED BEFORE JULY 1, 1982.—The term "qualified housing interest" includes interest which is qualified residence interest (as defined in section 163(h)(3)) and is paid or accrued on indebtedness which—

(A) was incurred by the taxpayer before July 1, 1982, and

(B) is secured by property which, at the time such indebtedness was incurred, was—

(i) the principal residence (within the meaning of section 121) of the taxpayer, or

(ii) a qualified dwelling used by the taxpayer (or any member of his family (within the meaning of section 267(c)(4))).

[Sec. 56(f)—Repealed]

[Sec. 56(g)]

(g) ADJUSTMENTS BASED ON ADJUSTED CURRENT EARNINGS.—

(1) IN GENERAL.—The alternative minimum taxable income of any corporation for any taxable year shall be increased by 75 percent of the excess (if any) of—

(A) the adjusted current earnings of the corporation, over

(B) the alternative minimum taxable income (determined without regard to this subsection and the alternative tax net operating loss deduction).

(2) ALLOWANCE OF NEGATIVE ADJUSTMENTS.—

(A) IN GENERAL.—The alternative minimum taxable income for any corporation of any taxable year shall be reduced by 75 percent of the excess (if any) of—

(i) the amount referred to in subparagraph (B) of paragraph (1), over

(ii) the amount referred to in subparagraph (A) of paragraph (1).

(B) LIMITATION.—The reduction under subparagraph (A) for any taxable year shall not exceed the excess (if any) of—

(i) the aggregate increases in alternative minimum taxable income under paragraph (1) for prior taxable years, over

(ii) the aggregate reductions under subparagraph (A) of this paragraph for prior taxable years.

(3) ADJUSTED CURRENT EARNINGS.—For purposes of this subsection, the term "adjusted current earnings" means the alternative minimum taxable income for the taxable year—

(A) determined with the adjustments provided in paragraph (4), and

(B) determined without regard to this subsection and the alternative tax net operating loss deduction.

(4) ADJUSTMENTS.—In determining adjusted current earnings, the following adjustments shall apply:

(A) DEPRECIATION.—

(i) PROPERTY PLACED IN SERVICE AFTER 1989.—The depreciation deduction with respect to any property placed in service in a taxable year beginning after 1989 shall be determined under the alternative system of section 168(g). The preceding sentence shall not apply to any property placed in service after December 31, 1993, and the depreciation deduction with respect to such property shall be determined under the rules of subsection (a)(1)(A).

(ii) PROPERTY TO WHICH NEW ACRS SYSTEM APPLIES.—In the case of any property to which the amendments made by section 201 of the Tax Reform Act of 1986 apply and which is placed in service in a taxable year beginning before 1990, the depreciation deduction shall be determined—

(I) by taking into account the adjusted basis of such property (as determined for purposes of computing alternative minimum taxable income) as of the close of the last taxable year beginning before January 1, 1990, and

(II) by using the straight-line method over the remainder of the recovery period applicable to such property under the alternative system of section 168(g).

(iii) PROPERTY TO WHICH ORIGINAL ACRS SYSTEM APPLIES.—In the case of any property to which section 168 (as in effect on the day before the date of the enactment of the Tax Reform Act of 1986 and without regard to subsection (d)(1)(A)(ii) thereof) applies and which is placed in service in a taxable year beginning before 1990, the depreciation deduction shall be determined—

(I) by taking into account the adjusted basis of such property (as determined for purposes of computing the regular tax) as of the close of the last taxable year beginning before January 1, 1990, and

(II) by using the straight line method over the remainder of the recovery period which would apply to such property under the alternative system of section 168(g).

(iv) PROPERTY PLACED IN SERVICE BEFORE 1981.—In the case of any property not described in clause (i), (ii), or (iii), the amount allowable as depreciation or amortization with respect to such property shall be determined in the same manner as for purposes of computing taxable income.

(v) SPECIAL RULE FOR CERTAIN PROPERTY.—In the case of any property described in paragraph (1), (2), (3), or (4) of section 168(f), the amount of depreciation allowable for purposes of the regular tax shall be treated as the amount allowable under the alternative system of section 168(g).

Sec. 56(g)

(B) INCLUSION OF ITEMS INCLUDED FOR PURPOSES OF COMPUTING EARNINGS AND PROFITS.—

(i) IN GENERAL.—In the case of any amount which is excluded from gross income for purposes of computing alternative minimum taxable income but is taken into account in determining the amount of earnings and profits—

(I) such amount shall be included in income in the same manner as if such amount were includible in gross income for purposes of computing alternative minimum taxable income, and

(II) the amount of such income shall be reduced by any deduction which would have been allowable in computing alternative minimum taxable income if such amount were includible in gross income.

The preceding sentence shall not apply in the case of any amount excluded from gross income under section 108 (or the corresponding provisions of prior law) or under section 114. In the case of any insurance company taxable under section 831(b), this clause shall not apply to any amount not described in section 834(b).

(ii) INCLUSION OF BUILDUP IN LIFE INSURANCE CONTRACTS.—In the case of any life insurance contract—

(I) the income on such contract (as determined under section 7702(g)) for any taxable year shall be treated as includible in gross income for such year, and

(II) there shall be allowed as a deduction that portion of any premium which is attributable to insurance coverage.

(iii) [Repealed.]

(C) DISALLOWANCE OF ITEMS NOT DEDUCTIBLE IN COMPUTING EARNINGS AND PROFITS.—

(i) IN GENERAL.—A deduction shall not be allowed for any item if such item would not be deductible for any taxable year for purposes of computing earnings and profits.

(ii) SPECIAL RULE FOR CERTAIN DIVIDENDS.—

(I) IN GENERAL.—Clause (i) shall not apply to any deduction allowable under section 243 or 245 for any dividend which is a 100-percent dividend or which is received from a 20-percent owned corporation (as defined in section 243(c)(2)), but only to the extent such dividend is attributable to income of the paying corporation which is subject to tax under this chapter (determined after the application of sections 30A, 936 (including subsections (a)(4), (i), and (j) thereof) and 921).

(II) 100-PERCENT DIVIDEND.—For purposes of subclause (I), the term "100 percent dividend" means any dividend if the percentage used for purposes of determining the amount allowable as a deduction under section 243 or 245 with respect to such dividend is 100 percent.

* * *

(iv) SPECIAL RULE FOR CERTAIN DIVIDENDS RECEIVED BY CERTAIN COOPERATIVES.—In the case of a cooperative described in section 927(a)(4), clause (i) shall not apply to any amount allowable as a deduction under section 245(c).

(D) CERTAIN OTHER EARNINGS AND PROFITS ADJUSTMENTS.—

(i) INTANGIBLE DRILLING COSTS.—The adjustments provided in section 312(n)(2)(A) shall apply in the case of amounts paid or incurred in taxable years beginning after December 31, 1989. In the case of a taxpayer other than an integrated oil company (as defined in section 291(b)(4)), in the case of any oil or gas well, this clause shall not apply in the case of amounts paid or incurred in taxable years beginning after December 31, 1992.

(ii) CERTAIN AMORTIZATION PROVISIONS NOT TO APPLY.—Sections 173 and 248 shall not apply to expenditures paid or incurred in taxable years beginning after December 31, 1989.

(iii) LIFO INVENTORY ADJUSTMENTS.—The adjustments provided in section 312(n)(4) shall apply, but only with respect to taxable years beginning after December 31, 1989.

(iv) INSTALLMENT SALES.—In the case of any installment sale in a taxable year beginning after December 31, 1989, adjusted current earnings shall be computed as if the corporation did not use the installment method. The preceding sentence shall not apply to the applicable percentage (as determined under section 453A) of the gain from any installment sale with respect to which section 453A(a)(1) applies.

Sec. 56(g)

(E) DISALLOWANCE OF LOSS ON EXCHANGE OF DEBT POOLS.—No loss shall be recognized on the exchange of any pool of debt obligations for another pool of debt obligations having substantially the same effective interest rates and maturities.

(F) DEPLETION.—

(i) IN GENERAL.—The allowance for depletion with respect to any property placed in service in a taxable year beginning after December 31, 1989, shall be cost depletion determined under section 611.

(ii) EXCEPTION FOR INDEPENDENT OIL AND GAS PRODUCERS AND ROYALTY OWNERS.—In the case of any taxable year beginning after December 31, 1992, clause (i) (and subparagraph (C)(i)) shall not apply to any deduction for depletion computed in accordance with section 613A(c).

(G) TREATMENT OF CERTAIN OWNERSHIP CHANGES.—If—

(i) there is an ownership change (within the meaning of section 382) in a taxable year beginning after 1989 with respect to any corporation, and

(ii) there is a net unrealized built-in loss (within the meaning of section 382(h)) with respect to such corporation,

then the adjusted basis of each asset of such corporation (immediately after the ownership change) shall be its proportionate share (determined on the basis of respective fair market values) of the fair market value of the assets of such corporation (determined under section 382(h)) immediately before the ownership change.

(H) ADJUSTED BASIS.—The adjusted basis of any property with respect to which an adjustment under this paragraph applies shall be determined by applying the treatment prescribed in this paragraph.

(I) TREATMENT OF CHARITABLE CONTRIBUTIONS.—Notwithstanding subparagraphs (B) and (C), no adjustment related to the earnings and profits effects of any charitable contribution shall be made in computing adjusted current earnings.

(5) OTHER DEFINITIONS.—For purposes of paragraph (4)—

(A) EARNINGS AND PROFITS.—The term "earnings and profits" means earnings and profits computed for purposes of subchapter C.

(B) TREATMENT OF ALTERNATIVE MINIMUM TAXABLE INCOME.—The treatment of any item for purposes of computing alternative minimum taxable income shall be determined without regard to this subsection.

(6) EXCEPTION FOR CERTAIN CORPORATIONS.—This subsection shall not apply to any S corporation, regulated investment company, real estate investment trust, REMIC, or FASIT.

[Sec. 57]

SEC. 57. ITEMS OF TAX PREFERENCE.

[Sec. 57(a)]

(a) GENERAL RULE.—For purposes of this part, the items of tax preference determined under this section are—

(1) DEPLETION.—With respect to each property (as defined in section 614), the excess of the deduction for depletion allowable under section 611 for the taxable year over the adjusted basis of the property at the end of the taxable year (determined without regard to the depletion deduction for the taxable year). Effective with respect to tax years beginning after December 31, 1992, this paragraph shall not apply to any deduction for depletion computed in accordance with section 613A(c).

(2) INTANGIBLE DRILLING COSTS.—

(A) IN GENERAL.—With respect to all oil, gas, and geothermal properties of the taxpayer, the amount (if any) by which the amount of the excess intangible drilling costs arising in the taxable year is greater than 65 percent of the net income of the taxpayer from oil, gas, and geothermal properties for the taxable year.

(B) EXCESS INTANGIBLE DRILLING COSTS.—For purposes of subparagraph (A), the amount of the excess intangible drilling costs arising in the taxable year is the excess of—

(i) the intangible drilling and development costs paid or incurred in connection with oil, gas, and geothermal wells (other than costs incurred in drilling a nonproductive well) allowable under section 263(c) or 291(b) for the taxable year, over

(ii) the amount which would have been allowable for the taxable year if such costs had been capitalized and straight line recovery of intangibles (as defined in subsection (b)) had been used with respect to such costs.

(C) NET INCOME FROM OIL, GAS, AND GEOTHERMAL PROPERTIES.—For purposes of subparagraph (A), the amount of the net income of the taxpayer from oil, gas, and geothermal properties for the taxable year is the excess of—

(i) the aggregate amount of gross income (within the meaning of section 613(a)) from all oil, gas, and geothermal properties of the taxpayer received or accrued by the taxpayer during the taxable year, over

(ii) the amount of any deductions allocable to such properties reduced by the excess described in subparagraph (B) for such taxable year.

(D) PARAGRAPH APPLIED SEPARATELY WITH RESPECT TO GEOTHERMAL PROPERTIES AND OIL AND GAS PROPERTIES.—This paragraph shall be applied separately with respect to—

(i) all oil and gas properties which are not described in clause (ii), and

(ii) all properties which are geothermal deposits (as defined in section 613(e)(2)).

(E) EXCEPTION FOR INDEPENDENT PRODUCERS.—In the case of any oil or gas well—

(i) IN GENERAL.—In the case of any taxable year beginning after December 31, 1992, this paragraph shall not apply to any taxpayer which is not an integrated oil company (as defined in section 291(b)(4)).

(ii) LIMITATION ON BENEFIT.—The reduction in alternative minimum taxable income by reason of clause (i) for any taxable year shall not exceed 40 percent (30 percent in case of taxable years beginning in 1993) of the alternative minimum taxable income for such year determined without regard to clause (i) and the alternative tax net operating loss deduction under section 56(a)(4).

(3) [Repealed.]

(4) [Stricken.]

(5) TAX-EXEMPT INTEREST.—

(A) IN GENERAL.—Interest on specified private activity bonds reduced by any deduction (not allowable in computing the regular tax) which would have been allowable if such interest were includible in gross income.

(B) TREATMENT OF EXEMPT-INTEREST DIVIDENDS.—Under regulations prescribed by the Secretary, any exempt-interest dividend (as defined in section 852(b)(5)(A)) shall be treated as interest on a specified private activity bond to the extent of its proportionate share of the interest on such bonds received by the company paying such dividend.

(C) SPECIFIED PRIVATE ACTIVITY BONDS.—

(i) IN GENERAL.—For purposes of this part, the term "specified private activity bond" means any private activity bond (as defined in section 141) which is issued after August 7, 1986, and the interest on which is not includible in gross income under section 103.

(ii) EXCEPTION FOR QUALIFIED 501(c)(3) BONDS.—For purposes of clause (i), the term "private activity bond" shall not include any qualified 501(c)(3) bond (as defined in section 145).

(iii) EXCEPTION FOR REFUNDINGS.—For purposes of clause (i), the term "private activity bond" shall not include any refunding bond (whether a current or advance refunding) if the refunded bond (or in the case of a series of refundings, the original bond) was issued before August 8, 1986.

(iv) CERTAIN BONDS ISSUED BEFORE SEPTEMBER 1, 1986.—For purposes of this subparagraph, a bond issued before September 1, 1986, shall be treated as issued before August 8, 1986, unless such bond would be a private activity bond if—

(I) paragraphs (1) and (2) of section 141(b) were applied by substituting "25 percent" for "10 percent" each place it appears,

(II) paragraphs (3), (4), and (5) of section 141(b) did not apply, and

(III) subparagraph (B) of section 141(c)(1) did not apply.

Sec. 57(a)

(6) ACCELERATED DEPRECIATION OR AMORTIZATION ON CERTAIN PROPERTY PLACED IN SERVICE BEFORE JANUARY 1, 1987.—The amounts which would be treated as items of tax preference with respect to the taxpayer under paragraphs (2), (3), (4), and (12) of this subsection (as in effect on the day before the date of the enactment of the Tax Reform Act of 1986). The preceding sentence shall not apply to any property to which section 56(a)(1) or (5) applies.

(7) EXCLUSION FOR GAINS ON SALE OF CERTAIN SMALL BUSINESS STOCK.—An amount equal to 7 percent of the amount excluded from gross income for the taxable year under section 1202.

[Sec. 57(b)]

(b) STRAIGHT LINE RECOVERY OF INTANGIBLES DEFINED.—For purposes of paragraph (2) of subsection (a)—

(1) IN GENERAL.—The term "straight line recovery of intangibles", when used with respect to intangible drilling and development costs for any well, means (except in the case of an election under paragraph (2)) ratable amortization of such costs over the 120-month period beginning with the month in which production from such well begins.

(2) ELECTION.—If the taxpayer elects with respect to the intangible drilling and development costs for any well, the term "straight line recovery of intangibles" means any method which would be permitted for purposes of determining cost depletion with respect to such well and which is selected by the taxpayer for purposes of subsection (a)(2).

[Sec. 58]

SEC. 58. DENIAL OF CERTAIN LOSSES.

[Sec. 58(a)]

(a) DENIAL OF FARM LOSS.—

(1) IN GENERAL.—For purposes of computing the amount of the alternative minimum taxable income for any taxable year of a taxpayer other than a corporation—

(A) DISALLOWANCE OF FARM LOSS.—No loss of the taxpayer for such taxable year from any tax shelter farm activity shall be allowed.

(B) DEDUCTION IN SUCCEEDING TAXABLE YEAR.—Any loss from a tax shelter farm activity disallowed under subparagraph (A) shall be treated as a deduction allocable to such activity in the 1st succeeding taxable year.

(2) TAX SHELTER FARM ACTIVITY.—For purposes of this subsection, the term "tax shelter farm activity" means—

(A) any farming syndicate as defined in section 464(c) and

(B) any other activity consisting of farming which is a passive activity (within the meaning of section 469(c)).

(3) APPLICATION TO PERSONAL SERVICE CORPORATIONS.—For purposes of paragraph (1), a personal service corporation (within the meaning of section 469(j)(2)) shall be treated as a taxpayer other than a corporation.

(4) DETERMINATION OF LOSS.—In determining the amount of the loss from any tax shelter farm activity, the adjustments of sections 56 and 57 shall apply.

[Sec. 58(b)]

(b) DISALLOWANCE OF PASSIVE ACTIVITY LOSS.—In computing the alternative minimum taxable income of the taxpayer for any taxable year, section 469 shall apply, except that in applying section 469—

(1) the adjustments of sections 56 and 57 shall apply,

(2) the provisions of section 469(m) (relating to phase-in of disallowance) shall not apply, and

(3) in lieu of applying section 469(j)(7), the passive activity loss of a taxpayer shall be computed without regard to qualified housing interest (as defined in section 56(e)).

[Sec. 58(c)]

(c) SPECIAL RULES.—For purposes of this section—

(1) SPECIAL RULE FOR INSOLVENT TAXPAYERS.—

(A) IN GENERAL.—The amount of losses to which subsection (a) or (b) applies shall be reduced by the amount (if any) by which the taxpayer is insolvent as of the close of the taxable year.

(B) INSOLVENT.—For purposes of this paragraph, the term "insolvent" means the excess of liabilities over the fair market value of assets.

(2) LOSS ALLOWED FOR YEAR OF DISPOSITION OF FARM SHELTER ACTIVITY.—If the taxpayer disposes of his entire interest in any tax shelter farm activity during any taxable year, the amount of the loss attributable to such activity (determined after carryovers under subsection (a)(1)(B)) shall (to the extent otherwise allowable) be allowed for such taxable year in computing alternative minimum taxable income and not treated as a loss from a tax shelter farm activity.

[Caution: As provided in Section 59(j)(2), the dollar amount set forth in Section 59(j)(1)(B) is adjusted for taxable years after 1998 to reflect increases in the Consumer Price Index. The adjusted amount for taxable years beginning in 2003 is provided beginning at page ix.]

[Sec. 59]

SEC. 59. OTHER DEFINITIONS AND SPECIAL RULES.

* * *

[Sec. 59(c)]

(c) TREATMENT OF ESTATES AND TRUSTS.—In the case of any estate or trust, the alternative minimum taxable income of such estate or trust and any beneficiary thereof shall be determined by applying part I of subchapter J with the adjustments provided in this part.

[Sec. 59(d)]

(d) APPORTIONMENT OF DIFFERENTLY TREATED ITEMS IN CASE OF CERTAIN ENTITIES.—

(1) IN GENERAL.—The differently treated items for the taxable year shall be apportioned (in accordance with regulations prescribed by the Secretary)—

(A) REGULATED INVESTMENT COMPANIES AND REAL ESTATE INVESTMENT TRUSTS.—In the case of a regulated investment company to which part I of subchapter M applies or a real estate investment company to which part II of subchapter M applies, between such company or trust and shareholders and holders of beneficial interest in such company or trust.

(B) COMMON TRUST FUNDS.—In the case of a common trust fund (as defined in section 584(a)), pro rata among the participants of such fund.

(2) DIFFERENTLY TREATED ITEMS.—For purposes of this section, the term "differently treated item" means any item of tax preference or any other item which is treated differently for purposes of this part than for purposes of computing the regular tax.

[Sec. 59(e)]

(e) OPTIONAL 10-YEAR WRITEOFF OF CERTAIN TAX PREFERENCES.—

(1) IN GENERAL.—For purposes of this title, any qualified expenditure to which an election under this paragraph applies shall be allowed as a deduction ratably over the 10-year period (3-year period in the case of circulation expenditures described in section 173) beginning with the taxable year in which such expenditure was made (or, in the case of a qualified expenditure described in paragraph (2)(C), over the 60-month period beginning with the month in which such expenditure was paid or incurred).

(2) QUALIFIED EXPENDITURE.—For purposes of this subsection, the term "qualified expenditure" means any amount which, but for an election under this subsection, would have been allowable as a deduction (determined without regard to section 291) for the taxable year in which paid or incurred under,

(A) section 173 (relating to circulation expenditures),

(B) section 174(a) (relating to research and experimental expenditures),

Sec. 59(e)

(C) section 263(c) (relating to intangible drilling and development expenditures),

(D) section 616(a) (relating to development expenditures), or

(E) section 617(a) (relating to mining exploration expenditures).

(3) OTHER SECTIONS NOT APPLICABLE.—Except as provided in this subsection, no deduction shall be allowed under any other section for any qualified expenditure to which an election under this subsection applies.

(4) Election.—

(A) IN GENERAL.—An election may be made under paragraph (1) with respect to any portion of any qualified expenditure.

(B) REVOCABLE ONLY WITH CONSENT.—Any election under this subsection may be revoked only with the consent of the Secretary.

(C) PARTNERS AND SHAREHOLDERS OF S CORPORATIONS.—In the case of a partnership, any election under paragraph (1) shall be made separately by each partner with respect to the partner's allocable share of any qualified expenditure. A similar rule shall apply in the case of an S corporation and its shareholders.

(5) DISPOSITIONS.—

(A) APPLICATION OF SECTION 1254.—In the case of any disposition of property to which section 1254 applies (determined without regard to this section), any deduction under paragraph (1) with respect to amounts which are allocable to such property shall, for purposes of section 1254, be treated as a deduction allowable under section 263(c), 616(a), or 617(a), whichever is appropriate.

(B) APPLICATION OF SECTION 617(d).—In the case of any disposition of mining property to which section 617(d) applies (determined without regard to this subsection), any deduction under paragraph (1) with respect to amounts which are allocable to such property shall, for purposes of section 617(d), be treated as a deduction allowable under section 617(a).

(6) AMOUNTS TO WHICH ELECTION APPLY NOT TREATED AS TAX PREFERENCE.—Any portion of any qualified expenditure to which an election under paragraph (1) applies shall not be treated as an item of tax preference under section 57(a) and section 56 shall not apply to such expenditure.

[Sec. 59(f)]

(f) COORDINATION WITH SECTION 291.—Except as otherwise provided in this part, section 291 (relating to cutback of corporate preferences) shall apply before the application of this part.

[Sec. 59(g)]

(g) TAX BENEFIT RULE.—The Secretary may prescribe regulations under which differently treated items shall be properly adjusted where the tax treatment giving rise to such items will not result in the reduction of the taxpayer's regular tax for the taxable year for which item is taken into account or for any other taxable year.

[Sec. 59(h)]

(h) COORDINATION WITH CERTAIN LIMITATIONS.—The limitations of sections 704(d), 465, and 1366(d) (and such other provisions as may be specified in regulations) shall be applied for purposes of computing the alternative minimum taxable income of the taxpayer for the taxable year with the adjustments of sections 56, 57, and 58.

[Sec. 59(i)]

(i) SPECIAL RULE FOR AMOUNTS TREATED AS TAX PREFERENCE.—For purposes of this subtitle (other than this part), any amount shall not fail to be treated as wholly exempt from tax imposed by this subtitle solely by reason of being included in alternative minimum taxable income.

[Sec. 59(j)]

(j) TREATMENT OF UNEARNED INCOME OF MINOR CHILDREN.—

(1) IN GENERAL.—In the case of a child to whom section 1(g) applies, the exemption amount for purposes of section 55 shall not exceed the sum of—

(A) such child's earned income (as defined in section 911(d)(2)) for the taxable year, plus

(B) $5,000.

Sec. 59(f)

(2) INFLATION ADJUSTMENT.—In the case of any taxable year beginning in a calendar year after 1998, the dollar amount in paragraph (1)(B) shall be increased by an amount equal to the product of—

(A) such dollar amount, and

(B) the cost-of-living adjustment determined under section 1(f)(3) for the calendar year in which the taxable year begins, determined by substituting "1997" for "1992" in subparagraph (B) thereof.

If any increase determined under the preceding sentence is not a multiple of $50, such increase shall be rounded to the nearest multiple of $50.

PART VII—ENVIRONMENTAL TAX

[Sec. 59A]

SEC. 59A. ENVIRONMENTAL TAX.

[Sec. 59A(a)]

(a) IMPOSITION OF TAX.—In the case of a corporation, there is hereby imposed (in addition to any other tax imposed by this subtitle) a tax equal to 0.12 percent of the excess of—

(1) the modified alternative minimum taxable income of such corporation for the taxable year, over

(2) $2,000,000.

[Sec. 59A(b)]

(b) MODIFIED ALTERNATIVE MINIMUM TAXABLE INCOME.—For purposes of this section, the term "modified alternative minimum taxable income" means alternative minimum taxable income (as defined in section 55(b)(2)) but determined without regard to—

(1) the alternative tax net operating loss deduction (as defined in section 56(d)), and

(2) the deduction allowed under 164(a)(5).

* * *

Subchapter B—Computation of Taxable Income

PART I—DEFINITION OF GROSS INCOME, ADJUSTED GROSS INCOME, TAXABLE INCOME, ETC.

[Sec. 61]

SEC. 61. GROSS INCOME DEFINED.

[Sec. 61(a)]

(a) GENERAL DEFINITION.—Except as otherwise provided in this subtitle, gross income means all income from whatever source derived, including (but not limited to) the following items:

(1) Compensation for services, including fees, commissions, fringe benefits, and similar items;

(2) Gross income derived from business;

(3) Gains derived from dealings in property;

(4) Interest;

(5) Rents;

(6) Royalties;

(7) Dividends;

(8) Alimony and separate maintenance payments;

(9) Annuities;

(10) Income from life insurance and endowment contracts;

(11) Pensions;

(12) Income from discharge of indebtedness;

(13) Distributive share of partnership gross income;

(14) Income in respect of a decedent; and

(15) Income from an interest in an estate or trust.

[Sec. 61(b)]

(b) CROSS REFERENCES.—

For items specifically included in gross income, see part II (sec. 71 and following). For items specifically excluded from gross income, see part III (sec. 101 and following).

[Sec. 62]

SEC. 62. ADJUSTED GROSS INCOME DEFINED.

[Sec. 62(a)]

(a) GENERAL RULE.—For purposes of this subtitle, the term "adjusted gross income" means, in the case of an individual, gross income minus the following deductions:

(1) TRADE AND BUSINESS DEDUCTIONS.—The deductions allowed by this chapter (other than by part VII of this subchapter) which are attributable to a trade or business carried on by the taxpayer, if such trade or business does not consist of the performance of services by the taxpayer as an employee.

(2) CERTAIN TRADE AND BUSINESS DEDUCTIONS OF EMPLOYEES.—

(A) REIMBURSED EXPENSES OF EMPLOYEES.—The deductions allowed by part VI (section 161 and following) which consist of expenses paid or incurred by the taxpayer, in connection with the performance by him of services as an employee, under a reimbursement or other expense allowance arrangement with his employer. The fact that the reimbursement may be provided by a third party shall not be determinative of whether or not the preceding sentence applies.

(B) CERTAIN EXPENSES OF PERFORMING ARTISTS.—The deductions allowed by section 162 which consist of expenses paid or incurred by a qualified performing artist in connection with the performances by him of services in the performing arts as an employee.

(C) CERTAIN EXPENSES OF OFFICIALS.—The deductions allowed by section 162 which consist of expenses paid or incurred with respect to services performed by an official as an employee of a State or a political subdivision thereof in a position compensated in whole or in part on a fee basis.

(D) CERTAIN EXPENSES OF ELEMENTARY AND SECONDARY SCHOOL TEACHERS.—In the case of taxable years beginning during 2002 or 2003, the deductions allowed by section 162 which consist of expenses, not in excess of $250, paid or incurred by an eligible educator in connection with books, supplies (other than nonathletic supplies for courses of instruction in health or physical education), computer equipment (including related software and services) and other equipment, and supplementary materials used by the eligible educator in the classroom.

(3) LOSSES FROM SALE OR EXCHANGE OF PROPERTY.—The deductions allowed by part VI (sec. 161 and following) as losses from the sale or exchange of property.

(4) DEDUCTIONS ATTRIBUTABLE TO RENTS AND ROYALTIES.—The deductions allowed by part VI (sec. 161 and following), by section 212 (relating to expenses for production of income), and by section 611 (relating to depletion) which are attributable to property held for the production of rents or royalties.

(5) CERTAIN DEDUCTIONS OF LIFE TENANTS AND INCOME BENEFICIARIES OF PROPERTY.—In the case of a life tenant of property, or an income beneficiary of property held in trust, or an heir, legatee, or devisee of an estate, the deduction for depreciation allowed by section 167 and the deduction allowed by section 611.

(6) PENSION, PROFIT-SHARING AND ANNUITY PLANS OF SELF-EMPLOYED INDIVIDUALS.—In the case of an individual who is an employee within the meaning of section 401(c)(1), the deduction allowed by section 404.

(7) RETIREMENT SAVINGS.—The deduction allowed by section 219 (relating to deduction for certain retirement savings).

(8) [Repealed.]

(9) PENALTIES FORFEITED BECAUSE OF PREMATURE WITHDRAWAL OF FUNDS FROM TIME SAVINGS ACCOUNTS OR DEPOSITS.—The deductions allowed by section 165 for losses incurred in any transaction entered into for profit, though not connected with a trade or business to the extent that such losses include amounts forfeited to a bank, mutual savings bank, savings and loan association, building and loan association, cooperative bank or homestead association as a penalty for premature withdrawal of funds from a time savings account, certificate of deposit, or similar class of deposit.

(10) ALIMONY.—The deduction allowed by section 215.

(11) REFORESTATION EXPENSES.—The deduction allowed by section 194.

(12) CERTAIN REQUIRED REPAYMENTS OF SUPPLEMENTAL UNEMPLOYMENT COMPENSATION BENEFITS.—The deduction allowed by section 165 for the repayment to a trust described in paragraph (9) or (17) of section 501(c) of supplemental unemployment compensation benefits received from such trust if such repayment is required because of the receipt of trade readjustment allowances under section 231 or 232 of the Trade Act of 1974 (19 U.S.C. 2291 and 2292).

(13) JURY DUTY PAY REMITTED TO EMPLOYER.—Any deduction allowable under this chapter by reason of an individual remitting any portion of any jury pay to such individual's employer in exchange for payment by the employer of compensation for the period such individual was performing jury duty. For purposes of the preceding sentence, the term "jury pay" means any payment received by the individual for the discharge of jury duty.

(14) DEDUCTION FOR CLEAN-FUEL VEHICLES AND CERTAIN REFUELING PROPERTY.—The deduction allowed by section 179A.

(15) MOVING EXPENSES.—The deduction allowed by section 217.

(16) ARCHER MSAS.—The deduction allowed by section 220.

(17) INTEREST ON EDUCATION LOANS.—The deduction allowed by section 221.

(18) HIGHER EDUCATION EXPENSES.—The deduction allowed by section 222.

Nothing in this section shall permit the same item to be deducted more than once.

[Sec. 62(b)]

(b) QUALIFIED PERFORMING ARTIST.—

(1) IN GENERAL.—For purposes of subsection (a)(2)(B), the term "qualfied performing artist" means, with respect to any taxable year, any individual if—

(A) such individual performed services in the performing arts as an employee during the taxable year for at least 2 employers,

(B) the aggregate amount allowable as a deduction under section 162 in connection with the performance of such services exceeds 10 percent of such individual's gross income attributable to the performance of such services, and

(C) the adjusted gross income of such individual for the taxable year (determined without regard to subsection (a)(2)(B)) does not exceed $16,000.

(2) NOMINAL EMPLOYER NOT TAKEN INTO ACCOUNT.—An individual shall not be treated as performing services in the performing arts as an employee for any employer during any taxable year unless the amount received by such individual from such employer for the performance of such services during the taxable year equals or exceeds $200.

(3) SPECIAL RULES FOR MARRIED COUPLES.—

(A) IN GENERAL.—Except in the case of a husband and wife who lived apart at all times during the taxable year, if the taxpayer is married at the close of the taxable year, subsection (a)(2)(B) shall apply only if the taxpayer and his spouse file a joint return for the taxable year.

(B) APPLICATION OF PARAGRAPH (1).—In the case of a joint return—

(i) paragraph (1) (other than subparagraph (C) thereof) shall be applied separately with respect to each spouse, but

(ii) paragraph (1)(C) shall be applied with respect to their combined adjusted gross income.

(C) Determination of Marital Status.—For purposes of this subsection, marital status shall be determined under section 7703(a).

(D) Joint Return.—For purposes of this subsection, the term "joint return" means the joint return of a husband and wife made under section 6013.

[Sec. 62(c)]

(c) Certain Arrangements Not Treated as Reimbursement Arrangements.—For purposes of subsection (a)(2)(A), an arrangement shall in no event be treated as a reimbursement or other expense allowance arrangement if—

(1) such arrangement does not require the employee to substantiate the expenses covered by the arrangement to the person providing the reimbursement, or

(2) such arrangement provides the employee the right to retain any amount in excess of the substantiated expenses covered under the arrangement.

The substantiation requirements of the preceding sentence shall not apply to any expense to the extent that substantiation is not required under section 274(d) for such expense by reason of the regulations prescribed under the 2nd sentence thereof.

[Sec. 62(d)]

(d) Definition; Special Rules.—

(1) Eligible Educator.—

(A) In general.—For purposes of subsection (a)(2)(D), the term "eligible educator" means, with respect to any taxable year, an individual who is a kindergarten through grade 12 teacher, instructor, counselor, principal, or aide in a school for at least 900 hours during a school year.

(B) School.—The term "school" means any school which provides elementary education or secondary education (kindergarten through grade 12), as determined under State law.

(2) Coordination with exclusions.—A deduction shall be allowed under subsection (a)(2)(D) for expenses only to the extent the amount of such expenses exceeds the amount excludable under section 135, 529(c)(1), or 530(d)(2) for the taxable year.

[Caution: As provided in Section 63(c)(4), the dollar amounts set forth in Section 63(c)(2), 63(c)(5)(A), and 63(f) are adjusted for taxable years after 1988 to reflect increases in the Consumer Price Index. The Section 63(c)(2), 63(c)(5)(A), and 63(f) amounts applicable to taxable years beginning in 2003 are provided beginning at page ix.]

[Sec. 63]

SEC. 63. TAXABLE INCOME DEFINED.

[Sec. 63(a)]

(a) In General.—Except as provided in subsection (b), for purposes of this subtitle, the term "taxable income" means gross income minus the deductions allowed by this chapter (other than the standard deduction).

[Sec. 63(b)]

(b) Individuals Who Do Not Itemize Their Deductions.—In the case of an individual who does not elect to itemize his deductions for the taxable year, for purposes of this subtitle, the term "taxable income" means adjusted gross income, minus—

(1) the standard deduction, and

(2) the deduction for personal exemptions provided in section 151.

[Sec. 63(c)]

(c) Standard Deduction.—For purposes of this subtitle—

(1) In general.—Except as otherwise provided in this subsection, the term "standard deduction" means the sum of—

(A) the basic standard deduction, and

(B) the additional standard deduction.

(2) BASIC STANDARD DEDUCTION.—For purposes of paragraph (1), the basic standard deduction is—

(A) the applicable percentage of the dollar amount in effect under subparagraph (D) for the taxable year in the case of—

(i) a joint return, or

(ii) a surviving spouse (as defined in section 2(a)),

(B) $4,400 in the case of a head of household (as defined in section 2(b)),

(C) one-half of the amount in effect under subparagraph (A) in the case of a married individual filing a separate return, or

(D) $3,000 in any other case.

If any amount determined under subparagraph (A) is not a multiple of $50, such amount shall be rounded to the next lowest multiple of $50.

(3) ADDITIONAL STANDARD DEDUCTION FOR AGED AND BLIND.—For purposes of paragraph (1), the additional standard deduction is the sum of each additional amount to which the taxpayer is entitled under subsection (f).

(4) ADJUSTMENTS FOR INFLATION.—In the case of any taxable year beginning in a calendar year after 1988, each dollar amount contained in paragraph (2)(B), (2)(D), or (5) or subsection (f) shall be increased by an amount equal to—

(A) such dollar amount, multiplied by

(B) the cost-of-living adjustment determined under section 1(f)(3) for the calendar year in which the taxable year begins, by substituting for "calendar year 1992" in subparagraph (B) thereof—

(i) "calendar year 1987" in the case of the dollar amounts contained in paragraph (2)(B), (2)(D), or (5)(A) or subsection (f), and

(ii) "calendar year 1997" in the case of the dollar amount contained in paragraph (5)(B).

(5) LIMITATION ON BASIC STANDARD DEDUCTION IN THE CASE OF CERTAIN DEPENDENTS.—In the case of an individual with respect to whom a deduction under section 151 is allowable to another taxpayer for a taxable year beginning in the calendar year in which the individual's taxable year begins, the basic standard deduction applicable to such individual for such individual's taxable year shall not exceed the greater of—

(A) $500, or

(B) the sum of $250 and such individual's earned income.

(6) CERTAIN INDIVIDUALS, ETC., NOT ELIGIBLE FOR STANDARD DEDUCTION.—In the case of—

(A) a married individual filing a separate return where either spouse itemizes deductions,

(B) a nonresident alien individual,

(C) an individual making a return under section 443(a)(1) for a period of less than 12 months on account of a change in his annual accounting period, or

(D) an estate or trust, common trust fund, or partnership,

the standard deduction shall be zero.

(7) APPLICABLE PERCENTAGE.—For purposes of paragraph (2), the applicable percentage shall be determined in accordance with the following table:

For taxable years beginning in calendar year—	The applicable percentage is—
2003 and 2004	200
2005	174
2006	184
2007	187
2008	190
2009 and thereafter	200

Sec. 63(c)

[Sec. 63(d)]

(d) ITEMIZED DEDUCTIONS.—For purposes of this subtitle, the term "itemized deductions" means the deductions allowable under this chapter other than—

(1) the deductions allowable in arriving at adjusted gross income, and

(2) the deduction for personal exemptions provided by section 151.

[Sec. 63(e)]

(e) ELECTION TO ITEMIZE.—

(1) IN GENERAL.—Unless an individual makes an election under this subsection for the taxable year, no itemized deduction shall be allowed for the taxable year. For purposes of this subtitle, the determination of whether a deduction is allowable under this chapter shall be made without regard to the preceding sentence.

(2) TIME AND MANNER OF ELECTION.—Any election under this subsection shall be made on the taxpayer's return, and the Secretary shall prescribe the manner of signifying such election on the return.

(3) CHANGE OF ELECTION.—Under regulations prescribed by the Secretary, a change of election with respect to itemized deductions for any taxable year may be made after the filing of the return for such year. If the spouse of the taxpayer filed a separate return for any taxable year corresponding to the taxable year of the taxpayer, the change shall not be allowed unless, in accordance with such regulations—

(A) the spouse makes a change of election with respect to itemized deductions, for the taxable year covered in such separate return, consistent with the change of treatment sought by the taxpayer, and

(B) the taxpayer and his spouse consent in writing to the assessment (within such period as may be agreed on with the Secretary) of any deficiency, to the extent attributable to such change of election, even though at the time of the filing of such consent the assessment of such deficiency would otherwise be prevented by the operation of any law or rule of law.

This paragraph shall not apply if the tax liability of the taxpayer's spouse for the taxable year corresponding to the taxable year of the taxpayer has been compromised under section 7122.

[Sec. 63(f)]

(f) AGED OR BLIND ADDITIONAL AMOUNTS.—

(1) ADDITIONAL AMOUNTS FOR THE AGED.—The taxpayer shall be entitled to an additional amount of $600—

(A) for himself if he has attained age 65 before the close of his taxable year, and

(B) for the spouse of the taxpayer if the spouse has attained age 65 before the close of the taxable year and an additional exemption is allowable to the taxpayer for such spouse under section 151(b).

(2) ADDITIONAL AMOUNT FOR BLIND.—The taxpayer shall be entitled to an additional amount of $600—

(A) for himself if he is blind at the close of the taxable year, and

(B) for the spouse of the taxpayer if the spouse is blind as of the close of the taxable year and an additional exemption is allowable to the taxpayer for such spouse under section 151(b).

For purposes of subparagraph (B), if the spouse dies during the taxable year the determination of whether such spouse is blind shall be made as of the time of such death.

(3) HIGHER AMOUNT FOR CERTAIN UNMARRIED INDIVIDUALS.—In the case of an individual who is not married and is not a surviving spouse, paragraphs (1) and (2) shall be applied by substituting "$750" for "$600".

(4) BLINDNESS DEFINED.—For purposes of this subsection, an individual is blind only if his central visual acuity does not exceed 20/200 in the better eye with correcting lenses, or if his visual acuity is greater than 20/200 but is accompanied by a limitation in the fields of vision such that the widest diameter of the visual field subtends an angle no greater than 20 degrees.

Sec. 63(d)

(g) MARITAL STATUS.—For purposes of this section, marital status shall be determined under section 7703.

[Sec. 64]

SEC. 64. ORDINARY INCOME DEFINED.

For purposes of this subtitle, the term "ordinary income" includes any gain from the sale or exchange of property which is neither a capital asset nor property described in section 1231(b). Any gain from the sale or exchange of property which is treated or considered, under other provisions of this subtitle, as "ordinary income" shall be treated as gain from the sale or exchange of property which is neither a capital asset nor property described in section 1231(b).

[Sec. 65]

SEC. 65. ORDINARY LOSS DEFINED.

For purposes of this subtitle, the term "ordinary loss" includes any loss from the sale or exchange of property which is not a capital asset. Any loss from the sale or exchange of property which is treated or considered, under other provisions of this subtitle, as "ordinary loss" shall be treated as loss from the sale or exchange of property which is not a capital asset.

[Sec. 66]

SEC. 66. TREATMENT OF COMMUNITY INCOME.

[Sec. 66(a)]

(a) TREATMENT OF COMMUNITY INCOME WHERE SPOUSES LIVE APART.—If—

(1) 2 individuals are married to each other at any time during a calendar year;

(2) such individuals—

(A) live apart at all times during the calendar year, and

(B) do not file a joint return under section 6013 with each other for a taxable year beginning or ending in the calendar year;

(3) one or both of such individuals have earned income for the calendar year which is community income; and

(4) no portion of such earned income is transferred (directly or indirectly) between such individuals before the close of the calendar year,

then, for purposes of this title, any community income of such individuals for the calendar year shall be treated in accordance with the rules provided by section 879(a).

[Sec. 66(b)]

(b) SECRETARY MAY DISREGARD COMMUNITY PROPERTY LAWS WHERE SPOUSE NOT NOTIFIED OF COMMUNITY INCOME.—The Secretary may disallow the benefits of any community property law to any taxpayer with respect to any income if such taxpayer acted as if solely entitled to such income and failed to notify the taxpayer's spouse before the due date (including extensions) for filing the return for the taxable year in which the income was derived of the nature and amount of such income.

[Sec. 66(c)]

(c) SPOUSE RELIEVED OF LIABILITY IN CERTAIN OTHER CASES.—Under regulations prescribed by the Secretary, if—

(1) an individual does not file a joint return for any taxable year,

(2) such individual does not include in gross income for such taxable year an item of community income properly includible therein which, in accordance with the rules contained in section 879(a), would be treated as the income of the other spouse,

(3) the individual establishes that he or she did not know of, and had no reason to know of, such item of community income, and

(4) taking into account all facts and circumstances, it is inequitable to include such item of community income in such individual's gross income,

then, for purposes of this title, such item of community income shall be included in the gross income of the other spouse (and not in the gross income of the individual). Under procedures prescribed by the

Secretary, if, taking into account all the facts and circumstances, it is inequitable to hold the individual liable for any unpaid tax or any deficiency (or any portion of either) attributable to any item for which relief is not available under the preceding sentence, the Secretary may relieve such individual of such liability.

[Sec. 66(d)]

(d) DEFINITIONS.—For purposes of this section—

(1) EARNED INCOME.—The term "earned income" has the meaning given to such term by section 911(d)(2).

(2) COMMUNITY INCOME.—The term "community income" means income which, under applicable community property laws, is treated as community income.

(3) COMMUNITY PROPERTY LAWS.—The term "community property laws" means the community property laws of a State, a foreign country, or a possession of the United States.

[Sec. 67]

SEC. 67. 2-PERCENT FLOOR ON MISCELLANEOUS ITEMIZED DEDUCTIONS.

[Sec. 67(a)]

(a) GENERAL RULE.—In the case of an individual, the miscellaneous itemized deductions for any taxable year shall be allowed only to the extent that the aggregate of such deductions exceeds 2 percent of adjusted gross income.

[Sec. 67(b)]

(b) MISCELLANEOUS ITEMIZED DEDUCTIONS.—For purposes of this section, the term "miscellaneous itemized deductions" means the itemized deductions other than—

(1) the deduction under section 163 (relating to interest),

(2) the deduction under section 164 (relating to taxes),

(3) the deduction under section 165(a) for casualty or theft losses described in paragraph (2) or (3) of section 165(c) or for losses described in section 165(d),

(4) the deductions under section 170 (relating to charitable, etc., contributions and gifts) and section 642(c) (relating to deduction for amounts paid or permanently set aside for a charitable purpose),

(5) the deduction under section 213 (relating to medical, dental, etc., expenses),

(6) any deduction allowable for impairment-related work expenses,

(7) the deduction under section 691(c) (relating to deduction for estate tax in case of income in respect of the decedent),

(8) any deduction allowable in connection with personal property used in a short sale,

(9) the deduction under section 1341 (relating to computation of tax where taxpayer restores substantial amount held under claim of right),

(10) the deduction under section 72(b)(3) (relating to deduction where annuity payments cease before investment recovered),

(11) the deduction under section 171 (relating to deduction for amortizable bond premium), and

(12) the deduction under section 216 (relating to deductions in connection with cooperative housing corporations).

* * *

[Sec. 67(d)]

(d) IMPAIRMENT-RELATED WORK EXPENSES.—For purposes of this section, the term "impairment-related work expenses" means expenses—

(1) of a handicapped individual (as defined in section 190(b)(3)) for attendant care services at the individual's place of employment and other expenses in connection with such place of employment which are necessary for such individual to be able to work, and

(2) with respect to which a deduction is allowable under section 162 (determined without regard to this section).

(e) DETERMINATION OF ADJUSTED GROSS INCOME IN CASE OF ESTATES AND TRUSTS.—For purposes of this section, the adjusted gross income of an estate or trust shall be computed in the same manner as in the case of an individual, except that—

(1) the deductions for costs which are paid or incurred in connection with the administration of the estate or trust and which would not have been incurred if the property were not held in such trust or estate, and

(2) the deductions allowable under sections 642(b), 651, and 661,

shall be treated as allowable in arriving at adjusted gross income. Under regulations, appropriate adjustments shall be made in the application of part I of subchapter J of this chapter to take into account the provisions of this section.

(f) COORDINATION WITH OTHER LIMITATION.—This section shall be applied before the application of the dollar limitation of the second sentence of section 162(a) (relating to trade or business expenses).

[Caution: As provided in Section 68(b)(2), the dollar amounts set forth in Section 68(b)(1) are adjusted for taxable years after 1991 to reflect increases in the Consumer Price Index. The adjusted amounts applicable to taxable years beginning in 2003 are provided beginning at page ix.]

SEC. 68. OVERALL LIMITATION ON ITEMIZED DEDUCTIONS.

(a) GENERAL RULE.—In the case of an individual whose adjusted gross income exceeds the applicable amount, the amount of the itemized deductions otherwise allowable for the taxable year shall be reduced by the lesser of—

(1) 3 percent of the excess of adjusted gross income over the applicable amount, or

(2) 80 percent of the amount of the itemized deductions otherwise allowable for such taxable year.

(b) APPLICABLE AMOUNT.—

(1) IN GENERAL.—For purposes of this section, the term "applicable amount" means $100,000 ($50,000 in the case of a separate return by a married individual within the meaning of section 7703).

(2) INFLATION ADJUSTMENTS.—In the case of any taxable year beginning in a calendar year after 1991, each dollar amount contained in paragraph (1) shall be increased by an amount equal to—

(A) such dollar amount, multiplied by

(B) the cost-of-living adjustment determined under section 1(f)(3) for the calendar year in which the taxable year begins, by substituting "calendar year 1990" for "calendar year 1992 " in subparagraph (B) thereof.

(c) EXCEPTION FOR CERTAIN ITEMIZED DEDUCTIONS.—For purposes of this section, the term "itemized deductions" does not include—

(1) the deduction under section 213 (relating to medical, etc. expenses),

(2) any deduction for investment interest (as defined in section 163(d)), and

(3) the deduction under section 165(a) for casualty or theft losses described in paragraph (2) or (3) of section 165(c) or for losses described in section 165(d).

[Sec. 68(d)]

(d) COORDINATION WITH OTHER LIMITATIONS.—This section shall be applied after the application of any other limitation on the allowance of any itemized deduction.

[Sec. 68(e)]

(e) EXCEPTION FOR ESTATES AND TRUSTS.—This section shall not apply to any estate or trust.

[Caution: Code Sec. 68(f), below, as added by P.L. 107-16, applies to tax years beginning after December 31, 2005.]

[Sec. 68(f)]

(f) PHASEOUT OF LIMITATION.—

(1) IN GENERAL.—In the case of taxable years beginning after December 31, 2005, and before January 1, 2010, the reduction under subsection (a) shall be equal to the applicable fraction of the amount which would (but for this subsection) be the amount of such reduction.

(2) APPLICABLE FRACTION.—For purposes of paragraph (1), the applicable fraction shall be determined in accordance with the following table:

For taxable years beginning in calendar year—	The applicable fraction is—
2006 and 2007	2/3
2008 and 2009	1/3

[Caution: Code Sec. 68(g), below, as added by P.L. 107-16, applies to tax years beginning after December 31, 2005.]

[Sec. 68(g)]

(g) TERMINATION.—This section shall not apply to any taxable year beginning after December 31, 2009.

PART II—ITEMS SPECIFICALLY INCLUDED IN GROSS INCOME

[Sec. 71]

SEC. 71. ALIMONY AND SEPARATE MAINTENANCE PAYMENTS.

[Sec. 71(a)]

(a) GENERAL RULE.—Gross income includes amounts received as alimony or separate maintenance payments.

[Sec. 71(b)]

(b) ALIMONY OR SEPARATE MAINTENANCE PAYMENTS DEFINED.—For purposes of this section—

(1) IN GENERAL.—The term "alimony or separate maintenance payment" means any payment in cash if—

(A) such payment is received by (or on behalf of) a spouse under a divorce or separation instrument,

(B) the divorce or separation instrument does not designate such payment as a payment which is not includible in gross income under this section and not allowable as a deduction under section 215,

(C) in the case of an individual legally separated from his spouse under a decree of divorce or of separate maintenance, the payee spouse and the payor spouse are not members of the same household at the time such payment is made, and

(D) there is no liability to make any such payment for any period after the death of the payee spouse and there is no liability to make any payment (in cash or property) as a substitute for such payments after the death of the payee spouse.

(2) DIVORCE OR SEPARATION INSTRUMENT.—The term "divorce or separation instrument" means—

Sec. 68(d)

(A) a decree of divorce or separate maintenance or a written instrument incident to such a decree,

(B) a written separation agreement, or

(C) a decree (not described in subparagraph (A)) requiring a spouse to make payments for the support or maintenance of the other spouse.

[Sec. 71(c)]

(c) PAYMENTS TO SUPPORT CHILDREN.—

(1) IN GENERAL.—Subsection (a) shall not apply to that part of any payment which the terms of the divorce or separation instrument fix (in terms of an amount of money or a part of the payment) as a sum which is payable for the support of children of the payor spouse.

(2) TREATMENT OF CERTAIN REDUCTIONS RELATED TO CONTINGENCIES INVOLVING CHILD.—For purposes of paragraph (1), if any amount specified in the instrument will be reduced—

(A) on the happening of a contingency specified in the instrument relating to a child (such as attaining a specified age, marrying, dying, leaving school, or a similar contingency), or

(B) at a time which can clearly be associated with a contingency of a kind specified in subparagraph (A),

an amount equal to the amount of such reduction will be treated as an amount fixed as payable for the support of children of the payor spouse.

(3) SPECIAL RULE WHERE PAYMENT IS LESS THAN AMOUNT SPECIFIED IN INSTRUMENT.—For purposes of this subsection, if any payment is less than the amount specified in the instrument, then so much of such payment as does not exceed the sum payable for support shall be considered a payment for such support.

[Sec. 71(d)]

(d) SPOUSE.—For purposes of this section, the term "spouse" includes a former spouse.

[Sec. 71(e)]

(e) EXCEPTION FOR JOINT RETURNS.—This section and section 215 shall not apply if the spouses make a joint return with each other.

[Sec. 71(f)]

(f) RECOMPUTATION WHERE EXCESS FRONT-LOADING OF ALIMONY PAYMENTS.—

(1) IN GENERAL.—If there are excess alimony payments—

(A) the payor spouse shall include the amount of such excess payments in gross income for the payor spouse's taxable year beginning in the 3rd post-separation year, and

(B) the payee spouse shall be allowed a deduction in computing adjusted gross income for the amount of such excess payments for the payee's taxable year beginning in the 3rd post-separation year.

(2) EXCESS ALIMONY PAYMENTS.—For purposes of this subsection, the term "excess alimony payments" mean the sum of—

(A) the excess payments for the 1st post-separation year, and

(B) the excess payments for the 2nd post-separation year.

(3) EXCESS PAYMENTS FOR 1ST POST-SEPARATION YEAR.—For purposes of this subsection, the amount of the excess payments for the 1st post-separation year is the excess (if any) of—

(A) the amount of the alimony or separate maintenance payments paid by the payor spouse during the 1st post-separation year, over

(B) the sum of—

(i) the average of—

(I) the alimony or separate maintenance payments paid by the payor spouse during the 2nd post-separation year, reduced by the excess payments for the 2nd post-separation year, and

(II) the alimony or separate maintenance payments paid by the payor spouse during the 3rd post-separation year, plus

(ii) $15,000.

(4) EXCESS PAYMENTS FOR 2ND POST-SEPARATION YEAR.—For purposes of this subsection, the amount of the excess payments for the 2nd post-separation year is the excess (if any) of—

(A) the amount of the alimony or separate maintenance payments paid by the payor spouse during the 2nd post-separation year, over

(B) the sum of—

(i) the amount of the alimony or separate maintenance payments paid by the payor spouse during the 3rd post-separation year, plus

(ii) $15,000.

(5) EXCEPTIONS.—

(A) WHERE PAYMENT CEASES BY REASON OF DEATH OR REMARRIAGE.—Paragraph (1) shall not apply if—

(i) either spouse dies before the close of the 3rd post-separation year, or the payee spouse remarries before the close of the 3rd post-separation year, and

(ii) the alimony or separate maintenance payments cease by reason of such death or remarriage.

(B) SUPPORT PAYMENTS.—For purposes of this subsection, the term "alimony or separate maintenance payment" shall not include any payment received under a decree described in subsection (b)(2)(C).

(C) FLUCTUATING PAYMENTS NOT WITHIN CONTROL OF PAYOR SPOUSE.—For purposes of this subsection, the term "alimony or separate maintenance payment" shall not include any payment to the extent it is made pursuant to a continuing liability (over a period of not less than 3 years) to pay a fixed portion or portions of the income from a business or property or from compensation for employment or self-employment.

(6) POST-SEPARATION YEARS.—For purposes of this subsection, the term "1st post-separation years" means the 1st calendar year in which the payor spouse paid to the payee spouse alimony or separate maintenance payments to which this section applies. The 2nd and 3rd post-separation years shall be the 1st and 2nd succeeding calendar years, respectively.

[Sec. 71(g)]

(g) CROSS REFERENCES.—

(1) For deduction of alimony or separate maintenance payments, see section 215.

(2) For taxable status of income of an estate or trust in the case of divorce, etc., see section 682.

[Sec. 72]

SEC. 72. ANNUITIES; CERTAIN PROCEEDS OF ENDOWMENT AND LIFE INSURANCE CONTRACTS.

[Sec. 72(a)]

(a) GENERAL RULE FOR ANNUITIES.—Except as otherwise provided in this chapter, gross income includes any amount received as an annuity (whether for a period certain or during one or more lives) under an annuity, endowment, or life insurance contract.

[Sec. 72(b)]

(b) EXCLUSION RATIO.—

(1) IN GENERAL.—Gross income does not include that part of any amount received as an annuity under an annuity, endowment, or life insurance contract which bears the same ratio to such amount as the investment in the contract (as of the annuity starting date) bears to the expected return under the contract (as of such date).

(2) EXCLUSION LIMITED TO INVESTMENT.—The portion of any amount received as an annuity which is excluded from gross income under paragraph (1) shall not exceed the unrecovered investment in the contract immediately before the receipt of such amount.

(3) DEDUCTION WHERE ANNUITY PAYMENTS CEASE BEFORE ENTIRE INVESTMENT RECOVERED.—

(A) IN GENERAL.—If—

(i) after the annuity starting date, payments as an annuity under the contract cease by reason of the death of an annuitant, and

(ii) as of the date of such cessation, there is unrecovered investment in the contract,

the amount of such unrecovered investment (in excess of any amount specified in subsection (e)(5) which was not included in gross income) shall be allowed as a deduction to the annuitant for his last taxable year.

(B) PAYMENTS TO OTHER PERSONS.—In the case of any contract which provides for payments meeting the requirements of subparagraphs (B) and (C) of subsection (c)(2), the deduction under subparagraph (A) shall be allowed to the person entitled to such payments for the taxable year in which such payments are received.

(C) NET OPERATING LOSS DEDUCTIONS PROVIDED.—For purposes of section 172, a deduction allowed under this paragraph shall be treated as if it were attributable to a trade or business of the taxpayer.

(4) UNRECOVERED INVESTMENT.—For purposes of this subsection, the unrecovered investment in the contract as of any date is—

(A) the investment in the contract (determined without regard to subsection (c)(2)) as of the annuity starting date, reduced by

(B) the aggregate amount received under the contract on or after such annuity starting date and before the date as of which the determination is being made, to the extent such amount was excludable from gross income under this subtitle.

[Sec. 72(c)]

(c) DEFINITIONS.—

(1) INVESTMENT IN THE CONTRACT.—For purposes of subsection (b), the investment in the contract as of the annuity starting date is—

(A) the aggregate amount of premiums or other consideration paid for the contract, minus

(B) the aggregate amount received under the contract before such date, to the extent that such amount was excludable from gross income under this subtitle or prior income tax laws.

(2) ADJUSTMENT IN INVESTMENT WHERE THERE IS REFUND FEATURE.—If—

(A) the expected return under the contract depends in whole or in part on the life expectancy of one or more individuals;

(B) the contract provides for payments to be made to a beneficiary (or to the estate of an annuitant) on or after the death of the annuitant or annuitants; and

(C) such payments are in the nature of a refund of the consideration paid,

then the value (computed without discount for interest) of such payments on the annuity starting date shall be subtracted from the amount determined under paragraph (1). Such value shall be computed in accordance with actuarial tables prescribed by the Secretary. For purposes of this paragraph and of subsection (e) (2) (A), the term "refund of the consideration paid" includes amounts payable after the death of an annuitant by reason of a provision in the contract for a life annuity with minimum period of payments certain, but (if part of the consideration was contributed by an employer) does not include that part of any payment to a beneficiary (or to the estate of the annuitant) which is not attributable to the consideration paid by the employee for the contract as determined under paragraph (1) (A).

(3) EXPECTED RETURN.—For purposes of subsection (b), the expected return under the contract shall be determined as follows:

(A) LIFE EXPECTANCY.—If the expected return under the contract, for the period on and after the annuity starting date, depends in whole or in part on the life expectancy of one or more individuals, the expected return shall be computed with reference to actuarial tables prescribed by the Secretary.

(B) INSTALLMENT PAYMENTS.—If subparagraph (A) does not apply, the expected return is the aggregate of the amounts receivable under the contract as an annuity.

Sec. 72(c)

(4) ANNUITY STARTING DATE.—For purposes of this section, the annuity starting date in the case of any contract is the first day of the first period for which an amount is received as an annuity under the contract; except that if such date was before January 1, 1954, then the annuity starting date is January 1, 1954.

* * *

[Sec. 72(e)]

(e) AMOUNTS NOT RECEIVED AS ANNUITIES.—

(1) APPLICATION OF SUBSECTION.—

(A) IN GENERAL.—This subsection shall apply to any amount which—

(i) is received under an annuity, endowment, or life insurance contract, and

(ii) is not received as an annuity, if no provision of this subtitle (other than this subsection) applies with respect to such amount.

(B) DIVIDENDS.—For purposes of this section, any amount received which is in the nature of a dividend or similar distribution shall be treated as an amount not received as an annuity.

(2) GENERAL RULE.—Any amount to which this subsection applies—

(A) if received on or after the annuity starting date, shall be included in gross income, or

(B) if received before the annuity starting date—

(i) shall be included in gross income to the extent allocable to income on the contract, and

(ii) shall not be included in gross income to the extent allocable to the investment in the contract.

(3) ALLOCATION OF AMOUNTS TO INCOME AND INVESTMENT.—For purposes of paragraph (2)(B)—

(A) ALLOCATION TO INCOME.—Any amount to which this subsection applies shall be treated as allocable to income on the contract to the extent that such amount does not exceed the excess (if any) of—

(i) the cash value of the contract (determined without regard to any surrender charge) immediately before the amount is received, over

(ii) the investment in the contract at such time.

(B) ALLOCATION TO INVESTMENT.—Any amount to which this subsection applies shall be treated as allocable to investment in the contract to the extent that such amount is not allocated to income under subparagraph (A).

(4) SPECIAL RULES FOR APPLICATION OF PARAGRAPH (2)(B).—For purposes of paragraph (2)(B)—

(A) LOANS TREATED AS DISTRIBUTIONS.—If, during any taxable year, an individual—

(i) receives (directly or indirectly) any amount as a loan under any contract to which this subsection applies, or

(ii) assigns or pledges (or agrees to assign or pledge) any portion of the value of any such contract,

such amount or portion shall be treated as received under the contract as an amount not received as an annuity. The preceding sentence shall not apply for purposes of determining investment in the contract, except that the investment in the contract shall be increased by any amount included in gross income by reason of the amount treated as received under the preceding sentence.

(B) TREATMENT OF POLICYHOLDER DIVIDENDS.—Any amount described in paragraph (1)(B) shall not be included in gross income under paragraph (2)(B)(i) to the extent such amount is retained by the insurer as a premium or other consideration paid for the contract.

(C) TREATMENT OF TRANSFERS WITHOUT ADEQUATE CONSIDERATION.—

(i) IN GENERAL.—If an individual who holds an annuity contract transfers it without full and adequate consideration, such individual shall be treated as receiving an amount equal to the excess of—

(I) the cash surrender value of such contract at the time of transfer, over

(II) the investment in such contract at such time,

under the contract as an amount not received as an annuity.

(ii) EXCEPTION FOR CERTAIN TRANSFERS BETWEEN SPOUSES OR FORMER SPOUSES.—Clause (i) shall not apply to any transfer to which section 1041(a) (relating to transfers of property between spouses or incident to divorce) applies.

(iii) ADJUSTMENT TO INVESTMENT IN CONTRACT OF TRANSFEREE.—If under clause (i) an amount is included in the gross income of the transferor of an annuity contract, the investment in the contract of the transferee in such contract shall be increased by the amount so included.

(5) RETENTION OF EXISTING RULES IN CERTAIN CASES.—

(A) IN GENERAL.—In any case to which this paragraph applies—

(i) paragraphs (2)(B) and (4)(A) shall not apply, and

(ii) if paragraph (2)(A) does not apply,

the amount shall be included in gross income, but only to the extent it exceeds the investment in the contract.

(B) EXISTING CONTRACTS.—This paragraph shall apply to contracts entered into before August 14, 1982. Any amount allocable to investment in the contract after August 13, 1982, shall be treated as from a contract entered into after such date.

(C) CERTAIN LIFE INSURANCE AND ENDOWMENT CONTRACTS.—Except as provided in paragraph (10) and except to the extent prescribed by the Secretary by regulations, this paragraph shall apply to any amount not received as an annuity which is received under a life insurance or endowment contract.

(D) CONTRACTS UNDER QUALIFIED PLANS.—Except as provided in paragraph (8), this paragraph shall apply to any amount received—

(i) from a trust described in section 401(a) which is exempt from tax under section 501(a),

(ii) from a contract—

(I) purchased by a trust described in clause (i),

(II) purchased as part of a plan described in section 403(a),

(III) described in section 403(b), or

(IV) provided for employees of a life insurance company under a plan described in section 818(a)(3), or

(iii) from an individual retirement account or an individual retirement annuity.

Any dividend described in section 404(k) which is received by a participant or beneficiary shall, for purposes of this subparagraph, be treated as paid under a separate contract to which clause (ii)(I) applies.

(E) FULL REFUNDS, SURRENDERS, REDEMPTIONS, AND MATURITIES.—This paragraph shall apply to—

(i) any amount received, whether in a single sum or otherwise, under a contract in full discharge of the obligation under the contract which is in the nature of a refund of the consideration paid for the contract, and

(ii) any amount received under a contract on its complete surrender, redemption, or maturity.

In the case of any amount to which the preceding sentence applies, the rule of paragraph (2)(A) shall not apply.

(6) INVESTMENT IN THE CONTRACT.—For purposes of this subsection, the investment in the contract as of any date is—

(A) the aggregate amount of premiums or other consideration paid for the contract before such date, minus

(B) the aggregate amount received under the contract before such date, to the extent that such amount was excludable from gross income under this subtitle or prior income tax laws.

* * *

Sec. 72(e)

(10) TREATMENT OF MODIFIED ENDOWMENT CONTRACTS.—

(A) IN GENERAL.—Notwithstanding paragraph (5)(C), in the case of any modified endowment contract (as defined in section 7702A)—

(i) paragraphs (2)(B) and (4)(A) shall apply, and

(ii) in applying paragraph (4)(A), "any person" shall be substituted for "an individual".

(B) TREATMENT OF CERTAIN BURIAL CONTRACTS.—Notwithstanding subparagraph (A), paragraph (4)(A) shall not apply to any assignment (or pledge) of a modified endowment contract if such assignment (or pledge) is solely to cover the payment of expenses referred to in section 7702(e)(2)(C)(iii) and if the maximum death benefit under such contract does not exceed $25,000.

(11) ANTI-ABUSE RULES.—

(A) IN GENERAL.—For purposes of determining the amount includible in gross income under this subsection—

(i) all modified endowment contracts issued by the same company to the same policyholder during any calendar year shall be treated as 1 modified endowment contract, and

(ii) all annuity contracts issued by the same company to the same policyholder during any calendar year shall be treated as 1 annuity contract.

The preceding sentence shall not apply to any contract described in paragraph (5)(D).

(B) REGULATORY AUTHORITY.—The Secretary may by regulations prescribe such additional rules as may be necessary or appropriate to prevent avoidance of the purposes of this subsection through serial purchases of contracts or otherwise.

[Sec. 72(f)]

(f) SPECIAL RULES FOR COMPUTING EMPLOYEES' CONTRIBUTIONS.—In computing, for purposes of subsection (c)(1)(A), the aggregate amount of premiums or other consideration paid for the contract, and for purposes of subsection (e)(6), the aggregate premiums or other consideration paid, amounts contributed by the employer shall be included, but only to the extent that—

(1) such amounts were includible in the gross income of the employee under this subtitle or prior income tax laws; or

(2) if such amounts had been paid directly to the employee at the time they were contributed, they would not have been includible in the gross income of the employee under the law applicable at the time of such contribution.

Paragraph (2) shall not apply to amounts which were contributed by the employer after December 31, 1962, and which would not have been includible in the gross income of the employee by reason of the application of section 911 if such amounts had been paid directly to the employee at the time of contribution. The preceding sentence shall not apply to amounts which were contributed by the employer, as determined under regulations prescribed by the Secretary, to provide pension or annuity credits, to the extent such credits are attributable to services performed before January 1, 1963, and are provided pursuant to pension or annuity plan provisions in existence on March 12, 1962, and on that date applicable to such services, or to the extent such credits are attributable to services performed as a foreign missionary (within the meaning of section 403(b)(2)(D)(iii), as in effect before the enactment of the Economic Growth and Tax Relief Reconciliation Act of 2001[)].

[Sec. 72(g)]

(g) RULES FOR TRANSFEREE WHERE TRANSFER WAS FOR VALUE.—Where any contract (or any interest therein) is transferred (by assignment or otherwise) for a valuable consideration, to the extent that the contract (or interest therein) does not, in the hands of the transferee, have a basis which is determined by reference to the basis in the hands of the transferor, then—

(1) for purposes of this section, only the actual value of such consideration, plus the amount of the premiums and other consideration paid by the transferee after the transfer, shall be taken into account in computing the aggregate amount of the premiums or other consideration paid for the contract;

(2) for purposes of subsection (c) (1) (B), there shall be taken into account only the aggregate amount received under the contract by the transferee before the annuity starting date, to the extent that such amount was excludable from gross income under this subtitle or prior income tax laws; and

(3) the annuity starting date is January 1, 1954, or the first day of the first period for which the transferee received an amount under the contract as an annuity, whichever is the later.

For purposes of this subsection, the term "transferee" includes a beneficiary of, or the estate of, the transferee.

[Sec. 72(h)]

(h) OPTION TO RECEIVE ANNUITY IN LIEU OF LUMP SUM.—If—

(1) a contract provides for payment of a lump sum in full discharge of an obligation under the contract, subject to an option to receive an annuity in lieu of such lump sum;

(2) the option is exercised within 60 days after the day on which such lump sum first became payable; and

(3) part or all of such lump sum would (but for this subsection) be includible in gross income by reason of subsection (e) (1),

then, for purposes of this subtitle, no part of such lump sum shall be considered as includible in gross income at the time such lump sum first became payable.

[Sec. 72(j)]

(j) INTEREST.—Notwithstanding any other provision of this section, if any amount is held under an agreement to pay interest thereon, the interest payments shall be included in gross income.

* * *

[Sec. 72(q)]

(q) 10-PERCENT PENALTY FOR PREMATURE DISTRIBUTIONS FROM ANNUITY CONTRACTS.—

(1) IMPOSITION OF PENALTY.—If any taxpayer receives any amount under an annuity contract, the taxpayer's tax under this chapter for the taxable year in which such amount is received shall be increased by an amount equal to 10 percent of the portion of such amount which is includible in gross income.

(2) SUBSECTION NOT TO APPLY TO CERTAIN DISTRIBUTIONS.—Paragraph (1) shall not apply to any distribution—

(A) made on or after the date on which the taxpayer attains age 59½,

(B) made on or after the death of the holder (or, where the holder is not an individual, the death of the primary annuitant (as defined in subsection (s)(6)(B))),

(C) attributable to the taxpayer's becoming disabled within the meaning of subsection (m)(7),

(D) which is a part of a series of substantially equal periodic payments (not less frequently than annually) made for the life (or life expectancy) of the taxpayer or the joint lives (or joint life expectancies) of such taxpayer and his designated beneficiary,

(E) from a plan, contract, account, trust, or annuity described in subsection (e)(5)(D),

(F) allocable to investment in the contract before August 14, 1982,

(G) under a qualified funding asset (within the meaning of section 130(d), but without regard to whether there is a qualified assignment,

(H) to which subsection (t) applies (without regard to paragraph (2) thereof),

(I) under an immediate annuity contract (within the meaning of section 72(u)(4)), or

(J) which is purchased by an employer upon the termination of a plan described in section 401(a) or 403(a) and which is held by the employer until such time as the employee separates from service.

(3) CHANGE IN SUBSTANTIALLY EQUAL PAYMENTS.—If—

(A) paragraph (1) does not apply to a distribution by reason of paragraph (2)(D), and

(B) the series of payments under such paragraph are subsequently modified (other than by reason of death or disability—

(i) before the close of the 5-year period beginning on the date of the first payment and after the taxpayer attains age 59½, or

(ii) before the taxpayer attains age 59½,

Sec. 72(q)

the taxpayer's tax for the 1st taxable year in which such modification occurs shall be increased by an amount, determined under regulations, equal to the tax which (but for paragraph (2)(D)) would have been imposed, plus interest for the deferral period (within the meaning of subsection (t)(4)(B)).

* * *

[Sec. 73]

SEC. 73. SERVICES OF CHILD.

[Sec. 73(a)]

(a) TREATMENT OF AMOUNTS RECEIVED.—Amounts received in respect of the services of a child shall be included in his gross income and not in the gross income of the parent, even though such amounts are not received by the child.

[Sec. 73(b)]

(b) TREATMENT OF EXPENDITURES.—All expenditures by the parent or the child attributable to amounts which are includible in the gross income of the child (and not of the parent) solely by reason of subsection (a) shall be treated as paid or incurred by the child.

[Sec. 73(c)]

(c) PARENT DEFINED.—For purposes of this section, the term "parent" includes an individual who is entitled to the services of a child by reason of having parental rights and duties in respect of the child.

* * *

[Sec. 74]

SEC. 74. PRIZES AND AWARDS.

[Sec. 74(a)]

(a) GENERAL RULE.—Except as otherwise provided in this section or in section 117 (relating to qualified scholarships), gross income includes amounts received as prizes and awards.

[Sec. 74(b)]

(b) EXCEPTION FOR CERTAIN PRIZES AND AWARDS TRANSFERRED TO CHARITIES.—Gross income does not include amounts received as prizes and awards made primarily in recognition of religious, charitable, scientific, educational, artistic, literary, or civic achievement, but only if—

(1) the recipient was selected without any action on his part to enter the contest or proceeding;

(2) the recipient is not required to render substantial future services as a condition to receiving the prize or award; and

(3) the prize or award is transferred by the payor to a governmental unit or organization described in paragraph (1) or (2) of section 170(c) pursuant to a designation made by the recipient.

[Sec. 74(c)]

(c) EXCEPTIONS FOR CERTAIN EMPLOYEE ACHIEVEMENT AWARDS.—

(1) IN GENERAL.—Gross income shall not include the value of an employee achievement award (as defined in section 274(j)) received by the taxpayer if the cost to the employer of the employee achievement award does not exceed the amount allowable as a deduction to the employer for the cost of the employee achievement award.

(2) EXCESS DEDUCTION AWARD.—If the cost to the employer of the employee achievement award received by the taxpayer exceeds the amount allowable as a deduction to the employer, then gross income includes the greater of—

(A) an amount equal to the portion of the cost to the employer of the award that is not allowable as a deduction to the employer (but not in excess of the value of the award), or

(B) the amount by which the value of the award exceeds the amount allowable as a deduction to the employer.

The remaining portion of the value of such award shall not be included in the gross income of the recipient.

(3) TREATMENT OF TAX-EXEMPT EMPLOYERS.—In the case of an employer exempt from taxation under this subtitle, any reference in this subsection to the amount allowable as a deduction to the employer shall be treated as a reference to the amount which would be allowable as a deduction to the employer if the employer were not exempt from taxation under this subtitle.

(4) CROSS REFERENCE.—

For provisions excluding certain de minimis fringes from gross income, see section 132(e).

[Sec. 77]

SEC. 77. COMMODITY CREDIT LOANS.

[Sec. 77(a)]

(a) ELECTION TO INCLUDE LOANS IN INCOME.—Amounts received as loans from the Commodity Credit Corporation shall, at the election of the taxpayer, be considered as income and shall be included in gross income for the taxable year in which received.

[Sec. 77(b)]

(b) EFFECT OF ELECTION ON ADJUSTMENTS FOR SUBSEQUENT YEARS.—If a taxpayer exercises the election provided for in subsection (a) for any taxable year, then the method of computing income so adopted shall be adhered to with respect to all subsequent taxable years unless with the approval of the Secretary a change to a different method is authorized.

[Sec. 79]

SEC. 79. GROUP-TERM LIFE INSURANCE PURCHASED FOR EMPLOYEES.

[Sec. 79(a)]

(a) GENERAL RULE.—There shall be included in the gross income of an employee for the taxable year an amount equal to the cost of group-term life insurance on his life provided for part or all of such year under a policy (or policies) carried directly or indirectly by his employer (or employers); but only to the extent that such cost exceeds the sum of—

(1) the cost of $50,000 of such insurance, and

(2) the amount (if any) paid by the employee toward the purchase of such insurance.

[Sec. 79(b)]

(b) EXCEPTIONS.—Subsection (a) shall not apply to—

(1) the cost of group-term life insurance on the life of an individual which is provided under a policy carried directly or indirectly by an employer after such individual has terminated his employment with such employer and is disabled (within the meaning of section 72(m)(7)),

(2) the cost of any portion of the group-term life insurance on the life of an employee provided during part or all of the taxable year of the employee under which—

(A) the employer is directly or indirectly the beneficiary, or

(B) a person described in section 170(c) is the sole beneficiary,

for the entire period during such taxable year for which the employee receives such insurance, and

(3) the cost of any group-term life insurance which is provided under a contract to which section 72(m)(3) applies.

[Sec. 79(c)]

(c) DETERMINATION OF COST OF INSURANCE.—For purposes of this section and section 6052, the cost of group-term insurance on the life of an employee provided during any period shall be determined on the basis of uniform premiums (computed on the basis of 5-year age brackets) prescribed by regulations by the Secretary.

[Sec. 79(d)]

(d) NONDISCRIMINATION REQUIREMENTS.—

(1) IN GENERAL.—In the case of a discriminatory group-term life insurance plan—

(A) subsection (a)(1) shall not apply with respect to any key employee, and

(B) the cost of group-term life insurance on the life of any key employee shall be the greater of—

(i) such cost determined without regard to subsection (c), or

(ii) such cost determined with regard to subsection (c).

(2) DISCRIMINATORY GROUP-TERM LIFE INSURANCE PLAN.—For purposes of this subsection, the term "discriminatory group-term life insurance plan" means any plan of an employer for providing group-term life insurance unless—

(A) the plan does not discriminate in favor of key employees as to eligibility to participate, and

(B) the type and amount of benefits available under the plan do not discriminate in favor of participants who are key employees.

(3) NONDISCRIMINATORY ELIGIBILITY CLASSIFICATION.—

(A) IN GENERAL.—A plan does not meet requirements of subparagraph (A) of paragraph (2) unless—

(i) such plan benefits 70 percent or more of all employees of the employer,

(ii) at least 85 percent of all employees who are participants under the plan are not key employees,

(iii) such plan benefits such employees as qualify under a classification set up by the employer and found by the Secretary not to be discriminatory in favor of key employees, or

(iv) in the case of a plan which is part of a cafeteria plan, the requirements of section 125 are met.

(B) EXCLUSION OF CERTAIN EMPLOYEES.—For purposes of subparagraph (A), there may be excluded from consideration—

(i) employees who have not completed 3 years of service;

(ii) part-time or seasonal employees;

(iii) employees not included in the plan who are included in a unit of employees covered by an agreement between employee representatives and one or more employers which the Secretary finds to be a collective bargaining agreement, if the benefits provided under the plan were the subject of good faith bargaining between such employee representatives and such employer or employers; and

(iv) employees who are nonresident aliens and who receive no earned income (within the meaning of section 911(d)(2)) from the employer which constitutes income from sources within the United States (within the meaning of section 861(a)(3)).

(4) NONDISCRIMINATORY BENEFITS.—A plan does not meet the requirements of paragraph (2)(B) unless all benefits available to participants who are key employees are available to all other participants.

(5) SPECIAL RULE.—A plan shall not fail to meet the requirements of paragraph (2)(B) merely because the amount of life insurance on behalf of the employees under the plan bears a uniform relationship to the total compensation or the basic or regular rate of compensation of such employees.

(6) KEY EMPLOYEE DEFINED.—For purposes of this subsection, the term "key employee" has the meaning given to such term by paragraph (1) of section 416(i). Such term also includes any former employee if such employee when he retired or separated from service was a key employee.

(7) EXEMPTION FOR CHURCH PLANS.—

(A) IN GENERAL.—This subsection shall not apply to a church plan maintained for church employees.

(B) DEFINITIONS.—For purposes of subparagraph (A), the terms "church plan" and "church employee" have the meaning given such terms by paragraphs (1) and (3)(B) of section 414(e), respectively, except that—

(i) section 414(e) shall be applied by substituting "section 501(c)(3)" for "section 501" each place it appears, and

(ii) the term "church employee" shall not include an employee of—

(I) an organization described in section 170(b)(1)(A)(ii) above the secondary school level (other than a school for religious training),

Sec. 79(d)

(II) an organization described in section 170(b)(1)(A)(iii), and

(III) an organization described in section 501(c)(3), the basis of the exemption for which is substantially similar to the basis for exemption of an organization described in subclause (II).

(8) TREATMENT OF FORMER EMPLOYEES.—To the extent provided in regulations, this subsection shall be applied separately with respect to former employees.

[Sec. 79(e)]

(e) EMPLOYEE INCLUDES FORMER EMPLOYEE.—For purposes of this section, the term "employee" includes a former employee.

[Sec. 82]

SEC. 82. REIMBURSEMENT FOR EXPENSES OF MOVING.

Except as provided in section 132(a)(6), there shall be included in gross income (as compensation for services) any amount received or accrued, directly or indirectly, by an individual as a payment for or reimbursement of expenses of moving from one residence to another residence which is attributable to employment or self-employment.

[Sec. 83]

SEC. 83. PROPERTY TRANSFERRED IN CONNECTION WITH PERFORMANCE OF SERVICES.

[Sec. 83(a)]

(a) GENERAL RULE.—If, in connection with the performance of services, property is transferred to any person other than the person for whom such services are performed, the excess of—

(1) the fair market value of such property (determined without regard to any restriction other than a restriction which by its terms will never lapse) at the first time the rights of the person having the beneficial interest in such property are transferable or are not subject to a substantial risk of forfeiture, whichever occurs earlier, over

(2) the amount (if any) paid for such property,

shall be included in the gross income of the person who performed such services in the first taxable year in which the rights of the person having the beneficial interest in such property are transferable or are not subject to a substantial risk of forfeiture, whichever is applicable. The preceding sentence shall not apply if such person sells or otherwise disposes of such property in an arm's length transaction before his rights in such property become transferable or not subject to a substantial risk of forfeiture.

[Sec. 83(b)]

(b) ELECTION TO INCLUDE IN GROSS INCOME IN YEAR OF TRANSFER.—

(1) IN GENERAL.—Any person who performs services in connection with which property is transferred to any person may elect to include in his gross income, for the taxable year in which such property is transferred, the excess of—

(A) the fair market value of such property at the time of transfer (determined without regard to any restriction other than a restriction which by its terms will never lapse), over

(B) the amount (if any) paid for such property.

If such election is made, subsection (a) shall not apply with respect to the transfer of such property, and if such property is subsequently forfeited, no deduction shall be allowed in respect of such forfeiture.

(2) ELECTION.—An election under paragraph (1) with respect to any transfer of property shall be made in such manner as the Secretary prescribes and shall be made not later than 30 days after the date of such transfer. Such election may not be revoked except with the consent of the Secretary.

(c) SPECIAL RULES.—For purposes of this section—

(1) SUBSTANTIAL RISK OF FORFEITURE.—The rights of a person in property are subject to a substantial risk of forfeiture if such person's rights to full enjoyment of such property are conditioned upon the future performance of substantial services by any individual.

(2) TRANSFERABILITY OF PROPERTY.—The rights of a person in property are transferable only if the rights in such property of any transferee are not subject to a substantial risk of forfeiture.

(3) SALES WHICH MAY GIVE RISE TO SUIT UNDER SECTION 16(B) OF THE SECURITIES EXCHANGE ACT OF 1934.—So long as the sale of property at a profit could subject a person to suit under section 16(b) of the Securities Exchange Act of 1934, such person's rights in such property are—

(A) subject to a substantial risk of forfeiture, and

(B) not transferable.

(d) CERTAIN RESTRICTIONS WHICH WILL NEVER LAPSE.—

(1) VALUATION.—In the case of property subject to a restriction which by its terms will never lapse, and which allows the transferee to sell such property only at a price determined under a formula, the price so determined shall be deemed to be the fair market value of the property unless established to the contrary by the Secretary, and the burden of proof shall be on the Secretary with respect to such value.

(2) CANCELLATION.—If, in the case of property subject to a restriction which by its terms will never lapse, the restriction is cancelled, then, unless the taxpayer establishes—

(A) that such cancellation was not compensatory, and

(B) that the person, if any, who would be allowed a deduction if the cancellation were treated as compensatory, will treat the transaction as not compensatory, as evidenced in such manner as the Secretary shall prescribe by regulations,

the excess of the fair market value of the property (computed without regard to the restrictions) at the time of cancellation over the sum of—

(C) the fair market value of such property (computed by taking the restriction into account) immediately before the cancellation, and

(D) the amount, if any, paid for the cancellation,

shall be treated as compensation for the taxable year in which such cancellation occurs.

(e) APPLICABILITY OF SECTION.—This section shall not apply to—

(1) a transaction to which section 421 applies,

(2) a transfer to or from a trust described in section 401(a) or a transfer under an annuity plan which meets the requirements of section 404(a)(2),

(3) the transfer of an option without a readily ascertainable fair market value,

(4) the transfer of property pursuant to the exercise of an option with a readily ascertainable fair market value at the date of grant, or

(5) group-term life insurance to which section 79 applies.

(f) HOLDING PERIOD.—In determining the period for which the taxpayer has held property to which subsection (a) applies, there shall be included only the period beginning at the first time his rights in such property are transferable or are not subject to a substantial risk of forfeiture, whichever occurs earlier.

(g) CERTAIN EXCHANGES.—If property to which subsection (a) applies is exchanged for property subject to restrictions and conditions substantially similar to those to which the property given in such exchange was subject, and if section 354, 355, 356, or 1036 (or so much of section 1031 as relates to section 1036) applied to such exchange, or if such exchange was pursuant to the exercise of a conversion privilege—

(1) such exchange shall be disregarded for purposes of subsection (a), and

(2) the property received shall be treated as property to which subsection (a) applies.

[Sec. 83(h)]

(h) DEDUCTION BY EMPLOYER.—In the case of a transfer of property to which this section applies or a cancellation of a restriction described in subsection (d), there shall be allowed as a deduction under section 162, to the person for whom were performed the services in connection with which such property was transferred, an amount equal to the amount included under subsection (a), (b), or (d)(2) in the gross income of the person who performed such services. Such deduction shall be allowed for the taxable year of such person in which or with which ends the taxable year in which such amount is included in the gross income of the person who performed such services.

[Sec. 85]

SEC. 85. UNEMPLOYMENT COMPENSATION.

[Sec. 85(a)]

(a) GENERAL RULE.—In the case of an individual, gross income includes unemployment compensation.

[Sec. 85(b)]

(b) UNEMPLOYMENT COMPENSATION DEFINED.—For purposes of this section, the term "unemployment compensation" means any amount received under a law of the United States or of a State which is in the nature of unemployment compensation.

[Sec. 86]

SEC. 86. SOCIAL SECURITY AND TIER 1 RAILROAD RETIREMENT BENEFITS.

[Sec. 86(a)]

(a) IN GENERAL.—

(1) IN GENERAL.—Except as provided in paragraph (2), gross income for the taxable year of any taxpayer described in subsection (b) (notwithstanding section 207 of the Social Security Act) includes social security benefits in an amount equal to the lesser of—

(A) one-half of the social security benefits received during the taxable year, or

(B) one-half of the excess described in subsection (b)(1).

(2) ADDITIONAL AMOUNT.—In the case of a taxpayer with respect to whom the amount determined under subsection (b)(1)(A) exceeds the adjusted base amount, the amount included in gross income under this section shall be equal to the lesser of—

(A) the sum of—

(i) 85 percent of such excess, plus

(ii) the lesser of the amount determined under paragraph (1) or an amount equal to one-half of the difference between the adjusted base amount and the base amount of the taxpayer, or

(B) 85 percent of the social security benefits received during the taxable year.

[Sec. 86(b)]

(b) TAXPAYERS TO WHOM SUBSECTION (a) APPLIES.—

(1) IN GENERAL.—A taxpayer is described in this subsection if—

(A) the sum of—

(i) the modified adjusted gross income of the taxpayer for the taxable year, plus

(ii) one-half of the social security benefits received during the taxable year, exceeds

(B) the base amount.

(2) MODIFIED ADJUSTED GROSS INCOME.—For purposes of this subsection, the term "modified adjusted gross income" means adjusted gross income—

(A) determined without regard to this section and sections 135, 137, 221, 222, 911, 931, and 933, and

(B) increased by the amount of interest received or accrued by the taxpayer during the taxable year which is exempt from tax.

Sec. 86(b)

[Sec. 86(c)]

(c) BASE AMOUNT AND ADJUSTED BASE AMOUNT.—For purposes of this section—

(1) BASE AMOUNT.—The term "base amount" means—

(A) except as otherwise provided in this paragraph, $25,000,

(B) $32,000 in the case of a joint return, and

(C) zero in the case of a taxpayer who—

(i) is married as of the close of the taxable year (within the meaning of section 7703) but does not file a joint return for such year, and

(ii) does not live apart from his spouse at all times during the taxable year.

(2) ADJUSTED BASE AMOUNT.—The term "adjusted base amount" means—

(A) except as otherwise provided in this paragraph, $34,000,

(B) $44,000 in the case of a joint return, and

(C) zero in the case of a taxpayer described in paragraph (1)(C).

[Sec. 86(d)]

(d) SOCIAL SECURITY BENEFIT.—

(1) IN GENERAL.—For purposes of this section, the term "social security benefit" means any amount received by the taxpayer by reason of entitlement to—

(A) a monthly benefit under title II of the Social Security Act, or

(B) a tier 1 railroad retirement benefit.

(2) ADJUSTMENT FOR REPAYMENTS DURING YEAR.—

(A) IN GENERAL.—For purposes of this section, the amount of social security benefits received during any taxable year shall be reduced by any repayment made by the taxpayer during the taxable year of a social security benefit previously received by the taxpayer (whether or not such benefit was received during the taxable year).

(B) DENIAL OF DEDUCTION.—If (but for this subparagraph) any portion of the repayments referred to in subparagraph (A) would have been allowable as a deduction for the taxable year under section 165, such portion shall be allowable as a deduction only to the extent it exceeds the social security benefits received by the taxpayer during the taxable year (and not repaid during such taxable year).

(3) WORKMEN'S COMPENSATION BENEFITS SUBSTITUTED FOR SOCIAL SECURITY BENEFITS.—For purposes of this section, if, by reason of section 224 of the Social Security Act (or by reason of section 3(a)(1) of the Railroad Retirement Act of 1974), any social security benefit is reduced by reason of the receipt of a benefit under a workmen's compensation act, the term "social security benefit" includes that portion of such benefit received under the workmen's compensation act which equals such reduction.

(4) TIER 1 RAILROAD RETIREMENT BENEFIT.—For purposes of paragraph (1), the term "tier 1 railroad retirement benefit" means—

(A) the amount of the annuity under the Railroad Retirement Act of 1974 equal to the amount of the benefit to which the taxpayer would have been entitled under the Social Security Act if all of the service after December 31, 1936, of the employee (on whose employment record the annuity is being paid) had been included in the term "employment" as defined in the Social Security Act, and

(B) a monthly annuity amount under section 3(f)(3) of the Railroad Retirement Act of 1974.

(5) EFFECT OF EARLY DELIVERY OF BENEFIT CHECKS.—For purposes of subsection (a), in any case where section 708 of the Social Security Act causes social security benefit checks to be delivered before the end of the calendar month for which they are issued, the benefits involved shall be deemed to have been received in the succeeding calendar month.

* * *

Sec. 86(c)

PART III—ITEMS SPECIFICALLY EXCLUDED FROM GROSS INCOME

[Sec. 101]

SEC. 101. CERTAIN DEATH BENEFITS.

[Sec. 101(a)]

(a) PROCEEDS OF LIFE INSURANCE CONTRACTS PAYABLE BY REASON OF DEATH.—

(1) GENERAL RULE.—Except as otherwise provided in paragraph (2), subsection (d), and subsection (f), gross income does not include amounts received (whether in a single sum or otherwise) under a life insurance contract, if such amounts are paid by reason of the death of the insured.

(2) TRANSFER FOR VALUABLE CONSIDERATION.—In the case of a transfer for a valuable consideration, by assignment or otherwise, of a life insurance contract or any interest therein, the amount excluded from gross income by paragraph (1) shall not exceed an amount equal to the sum of the actual value of such consideration and the premiums and other amounts subsequently paid by the transferee. The preceding sentence shall not apply in the case of such a transfer—

(A) if such contract or interest therein has a basis for determining gain or loss in the hands of a transferee determined in whole or in part by reference to such basis of such contract or interest therein in the hands of the transferor, or

(B) if such transfer is to the insured, to a partner of the insured, to a partnership in which the insured is a partner, or to a corporation in which the insured is a shareholder or officer.

The term "other amounts" in the first sentence of this paragraph includes interest paid or accrued by the transferee on indebtedness with respect to such contract or any interest therein if such interest paid or accrued is not allowable as a deduction by reason of section 264(a)(4).

[Sec. 101(b)—Repealed]

[Sec. 101(c)]

(c) INTEREST.—If any amount excluded from gross income by subsection (a) is held under an agreement to pay interest thereon, the interest payments shall be included in gross income.

[Sec. 101(d)]

(d) PAYMENT OF LIFE INSURANCE PROCEEDS AT A DATE LATER THAN DEATH.—

(1) GENERAL RULE.—The amounts held by an insurer with respect to any beneficiary shall be prorated (in accordance with such regulations as may be prescribed by the Secretary) over the period or periods with respect to which such payments are to be made. There shall be excluded from the gross income of such beneficiary in the taxable year received any amount determined by such proration.

Gross income includes, to the extent not excluded by the preceding sentence, amounts received under agreements to which this subsection applies.

(2) AMOUNT HELD BY AN INSURER.—An amount held by an insurer with respect to any beneficiary shall mean an amount to which subsection (a) applies which is—

(A) held by any insurer under an agreement provided for in the life insurance contract, whether as an option or otherwise, to pay such amount on a date or dates later than the death of the insured, and

(B) is equal to the value of such agreement to such beneficiary

(i) as of the date of death of the insured (as if any option exercised under the life insurance contract were exercised at such time), and

(ii) as discounted on the basis of the interest rate used by the insurer in calculating payments under the agreement and mortality tables prescribed by the Secretary.

(3) APPLICATION OF SUBSECTION.—This subsection shall not apply to any amount to which subsection (c) is applicable.

* * *

Sec. 101(d)

[Sec. 101(g)]

(g) TREATMENT OF CERTAIN ACCELERATED DEATH BENEFITS.—

(1) IN GENERAL.—For purposes of this section, the following amounts shall be treated as an amount paid by reason of the death of an insured:

(A) Any amount received under a life insurance contract on the life of an insured who is a terminally ill individual.

(B) Any amount received under a life insurance contract on the life of an insured who is a chronically ill individual.

(2) TREATMENT OF VIATICAL SETTLEMENTS.—

(A) IN GENERAL.—If any portion of the death benefit under a life insurance contract on the life of an insured described in paragraph (1) is sold or assigned to a viatical settlement provider, the amount paid for the sale or assignment of such portion shall be treated as an amount paid under the life insurance contract by reason of the death of such insured.

(B) VIATICAL SETTLEMENT PROVIDER.—

(i) IN GENERAL.—The term "viatical settlement provider" means any person regularly engaged in the trade or business of purchasing, or taking assignments of, life insurance contracts on the lives of insureds described in paragraph (1) if—

(I) such person is licensed for such purposes (with respect to insureds described in the same subparagraph of paragraph (1) as the insured) in the State in which the insured resides, or

(II) in the case of an insured who resides in a State not requiring the licensing of such persons for such purposes with respect to such insured, such person meets the requirements of clause (ii) or (iii), whichever applies to such insured.

(ii) TERMINALLY ILL INSUREDS.—A person meets the requirements of this clause with respect to an insured who is a terminally ill individual if such person—

(I) meets the requirements of sections 8 and 9 of the Viatical Settlements Model Act of the National Association of Insurance Commissioners, and

(II) meets the requirements of the Model Regulations of the National Association of Insurance Commissioners (relating to standards for evaluation of reasonable payments) in determining amounts paid by such person in connection with such purchases or assignments.

(iii) CHRONICALLY ILL INSUREDS.—A person meets the requirements of this clause with respect to an insured who is a chronically ill individual if such person—

(I) meets requirements similar to the requirements referred to in clause (ii)(I), and

(II) meets the standards (if any) of the National Association of Insurance Commissioners for evaluating the reasonableness of amounts paid by such person in connection with such purchases or assignments with respect to chronically ill individuals.

(3) SPECIAL RULES FOR CHRONICALLY ILL INSUREDS.—In the case of an insured who is a chronically ill individual—

(A) IN GENERAL.—Paragraphs (1) and (2) shall not apply to any payment received for any period unless—

(i) such payment is for costs incurred by the payee (not compensated for by insurance or otherwise) for qualified long-term care services provided for the insured for such period, and

(ii) the terms of the contract giving rise to such payment satisfy—

(I) the requirements of section 7702B(b)(1)(B), and

(II) the requirements (if any) applicable under subparagraph (B).

For purposes of the preceding sentence, the rule of section 7702B(b)(2)(B) shall apply.

(B) OTHER REQUIREMENTS.—The requirements applicable under this subparagraph are—

(i) those requirements of section 7702B(g) and section 4980C which the Secretary specifies as applying to such a purchase, assignment, or other arrangement,

      (ii) standards adopted by the National Association of Insurance Commissioners which specifically apply to chronically ill individuals (and, if such standards are adopted, the analogous requirements specified under clause (i) shall cease to apply), and

      (iii) standards adopted by the State in which the policyholder resides (and if such standards are adopted, the analogous requirements specified under clause (i) and (subject to section 4980C(f)) standards under clause (ii), shall cease to apply).

      (C) PER DIEM PAYMENTS.—A payment shall not fail to be described in subparagraph (A) by reason of being made on a per diem or other periodic basis without regard to the expenses incurred during the period to which the payment relates.

      (D) LIMITATION ON EXCLUSION FOR PERIODIC PAYMENTS.—For limitation on amount of periodic payments which are treated as described in paragraph (1), see section 7702B(d).

    (4) DEFINITIONS.—For purposes of this subsection—

      (A) TERMINALLY ILL INDIVIDUAL.—The term "terminally ill individual" means an individual who has been certified by a physician as having an illness or physical condition which can reasonably be expected to result in death in 24 months or less after the date of the certification.

      (B) CHRONICALLY ILL INDIVIDUAL.—The term "chronically ill individual" has the meaning given such term by section 7702B(c)(2); except that such term shall not include a terminally ill individual.

      (C) QUALIFIED LONG-TERM CARE SERVICES.—The term "qualified long-term care services" has the meaning given such term by section 7702B(c).

      (D) PHYSICIAN.—The term "physician" has the meaning given to such term by section 1861(r)(1) of the Social Security Act (42 U.S.C. 1395x(r)(1)).

    (5) EXCEPTION FOR BUSINESS-RELATED POLICIES.—This subsection shall not apply in the case of any amount paid to any taxpayer other than the insured if such taxpayer has an insurable interest with respect to the life of the insured by reason of the insured being a director, officer, or employee of the taxpayer or by reason of the insured being financially interested in any trade or business carried on by the taxpayer.

* * *

[Sec. 102]

SEC. 102. GIFTS AND INHERITANCES.

[Sec. 102(a)]

    (a) GENERAL RULE.—Gross income does not include the value of property acquired by gift, bequest, devise, or inheritance.

[Sec. 102(b)]

    (b) INCOME.—Subsection (a) shall not exclude from gross income—

    (1) the income from any property referred to in subsection (a); or

    (2) where the gift, bequest, devise, or inheritance is of income from property, the amount of such income.

Where, under the terms of the gift, bequest, devise, or inheritance, the payment, crediting, or distribution thereof is to be made at intervals, then, to the extent that it is paid or credited or to be distributed out of income from property, it shall be treated for purposes of paragraph (2) as a gift, bequest, devise, or inheritance of income from property. Any amount included in the gross income of a beneficiary under subchapter J shall be treated for purposes of paragraph (2) as a gift, bequest, devise, or inheritance of income from property.

[Sec. 102(c)]

    (c) EMPLOYEE GIFTS.—

    (1) IN GENERAL.—Subsection (a) shall not exclude from gross income any amount transferred by or for an employer to, or for the benefit of, an employee.

Sec. 102(c)

(2) CROSS REFERENCES.—

For provisions excluding certain employee achievement awards from gross income, see section 74(c).

For provisions excluding certain de minimis fringes from gross income, see section 132(e).

[Sec. 103]

SEC. 103. INTEREST ON STATE AND LOCAL BONDS.

[Sec. 103(a)]

(a) EXCLUSION.—Except as provided in subsection (b), gross income does not include interest on any State or local bond.

[Sec. 103(b)]

(b) EXCEPTIONS.—Subsection (a) shall not apply to—

(1) PRIVATE ACTIVITY BOND WHICH IS NOT A QUALIFIED BOND.—Any private activity bond which is not a qualified bond (within the meaning of section 141).

(2) ARBITRAGE BOND.—Any arbitrage bond (within the meaning of section 148).

(3) BOND NOT IN REGISTERED FORM, ETC.—Any bond unless such bond meets the applicable requirements of section 149.

[Sec. 103(c)]

(c) DEFINITIONS.—For purposes of this section and part IV—

(1) STATE OR LOCAL BOND.—The term "State or local bond" means an obligation of a state or political subdivision thereof.

(2) STATE.—The term "State" includes the District of Columbia and any possession of the United States.

[Sec. 104]

SEC. 104. COMPENSATION FOR INJURIES OR SICKNESS.

[Sec. 104(a)]

(a) IN GENERAL.—Except in the case of amounts attributable to (and not in excess of) deductions allowed under section 213 (relating to medical, etc., expenses) for any prior taxable year, gross income does not include—

(1) amounts received under workmen's compensation acts as compensation for personal injuries or sickness;

(2) the amount of any damages (other than punitive damages) received (whether by suit or agreement and whether as lump sums or as periodic payments) on account of personal physical injuries or physical sickness;

(3) amounts received through accident or health insurance (or through an arrangement having the effect of accident or health insurance) for personal injuries or sickness (other than amounts received by an employee, to the extent such amounts (A) are attributable to contributions by the employer which were not includible in the gross income of the employee, or (B) are paid by the employer);

(4) amounts received as a pension, annuity, or similar allowance for personal injuries or sickness resulting from active service in the armed forces of any country or in the Coast and Geodetic Survey or the Public Health Service, or as a disability annuity payable under the provisions of section 808 of the Foreign Service Act of 1980; and

(5) amounts received by an individual as disability income attributable to injuries incurred as a direct result of a terroristic or military action (as defined in section 692(c)(2)).

For purposes of paragraph (3), in the case of an individual who is, or has been, an employee within the meaning of section 401(c)(1) (relating to self-employed individuals), contributions made on behalf of such individual while he was such an employee to a trust described in section 401(a) which is exempt from tax under section 501(a), or under a plan described in section 403(a), shall, to the extent allowed as deductions under section 404, be treated as contributions by the employer which were not includible in the gross income of the employee. For purposes of paragraph (2), emotional distress shall not be treated as a physical injury or physical sickness. The preceding sentence shall not apply to an amount of damages not in excess of the amount paid for medical care (described in subparagraph (A) or (B) of section 213(d)(1)) attributable to emotional distress.

* * *

[Sec. 104(d)]

(d) CROSS REFERENCES.—

(1) For exclusion from employee's gross income of employer contributions to accident and health plans, see section 106.

(2) For exclusion of part of disability retirement pay from the application of subsection (a)(4) of this section, see section 1403 of title 10, United States Code (relating to career compensation laws).

[Sec. 105]

SEC. 105. AMOUNTS RECEIVED UNDER ACCIDENT AND HEALTH PLANS.

[Sec. 105(a)]

(a) AMOUNTS ATTRIBUTABLE TO EMPLOYER CONTRIBUTIONS.—Except as otherwise provided in this section, amounts received by an employee through accident or health insurance for personal injuries or sickness shall be included in gross income to the extent such amounts (1) are attributable to contributions by the employer which were not includible in the gross income of the employee, or (2) are paid by the employer.

[Sec. 105(b)]

(b) AMOUNTS EXPENDED FOR MEDICAL CARE.—Except in the case of amounts attributable to (and not in excess of) deductions allowed under section 213 (relating to medical, etc., expenses) for any prior taxable year, gross income does not include amounts referred to in subsection (a) if such amounts are paid, directly or indirectly, to the taxpayer to reimburse the taxpayer for expenses incurred by him for the medical care (as defined in section 213 (d)) of the taxpayer, his spouse, and his dependents (as defined in section 152). Any child to whom section 152(e) applies shall be treated as a dependent of both parents for purposes of this subsection.

[Sec. 105(c)]

(c) PAYMENTS UNRELATED TO ABSENCE FROM WORK.—Gross income does not include amounts referred to in subsection (a) to the extent such amounts—

(1) constitute payment for the permanent loss or loss of use of a member or function of the body, or the permanent disfigurement, of the taxpayer, his spouse, or a dependent (as defined in section 152), and

(2) are computed with reference to the nature of the injury without regard to the period the employee is absent from work.

[Sec. 105(e)]

(e) ACCIDENT AND HEALTH PLANS.—For purposes of this section and section 104—

(1) amounts received under an accident or health plan for employees, and

(2) amounts received from a sickness and disability fund for employees maintained under the law of a State, or the District of Columbia,

shall be treated as amounts received through accident or health insurance.

[Sec. 105(f)]

(f) RULES FOR APPLICATION OF SECTION 213.—For purposes of section 213 (a) (relating to medical, dental, etc., expenses) amounts excluded from gross income under subsection (c) or (d) shall not be considered as compensation (by insurance or otherwise) for expenses paid for medical care.

[Sec. 105(g)]

(g) SELF-EMPLOYED INDIVIDUAL NOT CONSIDERED AN EMPLOYEE.—For purposes of this section, the term "employee" does not include an individual who is an employee within the meaning of section 401(c)(1) (relating to self-employed individuals).

Sec. 105(g)

[Sec. 105(h)]

(h) AMOUNT PAID TO HIGHLY COMPENSATED INDIVIDUALS UNDER A DISCRIMINATORY SELF-INSURED MEDICAL EXPENSE REIMBURSEMENT PLAN.—

(1) IN GENERAL.—In the case of amounts paid to a highly compensated individual under a self-insured medical reimbursement plan which does not satisfy the requirements of paragraph (2) for a plan year, subsection (b) shall not apply to such amounts to the extent they constitute an excess reimbursement of such highly compensated individual.

(2) PROHIBITION OF DISCRIMINATION.—A self-insured medical reimbursement plan satisfies the requirements of this paragraph only if—

(A) the plan does not discriminate in favor of highly compensated individuals as to eligibility to participate; and

(B) the benefits provided under the plan do not discriminate in favor of participants who are highly compensated individuals.

(3) NONDISCRIMINATORY ELIGIBILITY CLASSIFICATIONS.—

(A) IN GENERAL.—A self-insured medical reimbursement plan does not satisfy the requirements of subparagraph (A) of paragraph (2) unless such plan benefits—

(i) 70 percent or more of all employees, or 80 percent or more of all the employees who are eligible to benefit under the plan if 70 percent or more of all employees are eligible to benefit under the plan; or

(ii) such employees as qualify under a classification set up by the employer and found by the Secretary not to be discriminatory in favor of highly compensated individuals.

(B) EXCLUSION OF CERTAIN EMPLOYEES.—For purposes of subparagraph (A), there may be excluded from consideration—

(i) employees who have not completed 3 years of service;

(ii) employees who have not attained age 25;

(iii) part-time or seasonal employees;

(iv) employees not included in the plan who are included in a unit of employees covered by an agreement between employee representatives and one or more employers which the Secretary finds to be a collective bargaining agreement, if accident and health benefits were the subject of good faith bargaining between such employee representatives and such employer or employers; and

(v) employees who are nonresident aliens and who receive no earned income (within the meaning of section 911(d)(2)) from the employer which constitutes income from sources within the United States (within the meaning of section 861(a)(3)).

(4) NONDISCRIMINATORY BENEFITS.—A self-insured medical reimbursement plan does not meet the requirements of subparagraph (B) of paragraph (2) unless all benefits provided for participants who are highly compensated individuals are provided for all other participants.

(5) HIGHLY COMPENSATED INDIVIDUAL DEFINED.—For purposes of this subsection, the term "highly compensated individual" means an individual who is—

(A) one of the 5 highest paid officers,

(B) a shareholder who owns (with the application of section 318) more than 10 percent in value of the stock of the employer, or

(C) among the highest paid 25 percent of all employees (other than employees described in paragraph (3)(B) who are not participants).

(6) SELF-INSURED MEDICAL REIMBURSEMENT PLAN.—The term "self-insured medical reimbursement plan" means a plan of an employer to reimburse employees for expenses referred to in subsection (b) for which reimbursement is not provided under a policy of accident and health insurance.

(7) EXCESS REIMBURSEMENT OF HIGHLY COMPENSATED INDIVIDUAL.—For purposes of this section, the excess reimbursement of a highly compensated individual which is attributable to a self-insured medical reimbursement plan is—

(A) in the case of a benefit available to highly compensated individuals but not to all other participants (or which otherwise fails to satisfy the requirements of paragraph (2)(B)), the amount reimbursed under the plan to the employee with respect to such benefit, and

(B) in the case of benefits (other than benefits described in subparagraph (A) paid to a highly compensated individual by a plan which fails to satisfy the requirements of paragraph (2), the total amount reimbursed to the highly compensated individual for the plan year multiplied by a fraction—

(i) the numerator of which is the total amount reimbursed to all participants who are highly compensated individuals under the plan for the plan year, and

(ii) the denominator of which is the total amount reimbursed to all employees under the plan for such plan year.

In determining the fraction under subparagraph (B), there shall not be taken into account any reimbursement which is attributable to a benefit described in subparagraph (A).

(8) CERTAIN CONTROLLED GROUPS, ETC.—All employees who are treated as employed by a single employer under subsection (b), (c), or (m) of section 414 shall be treated as employed by a single employer for purposes of this section.

(9) REGULATIONS.—The Secretary shall prescribe such regulations as may be necessary to carry out the provisions of this section.

(10) TIME OF INCLUSION.—Any amount paid for a plan year that is included in income by reason of this subsection shall be treated as received or accrued in the taxable year of the participant in which the plan year ends.

* * *

[Sec. 106]

SEC. 106. CONTRIBUTIONS BY EMPLOYER TO ACCIDENT AND HEALTH PLANS.

(a) GENERAL RULE.—Except as otherwise provided in this section, gross income of an employee does not include employer-provided coverage under an accident or health plan.

* * *

[Sec. 107]

SEC. 107. RENTAL VALUE OF PARSONAGES.

In the case of a minister of the gospel, gross income does not include—

(1) the rental value of a home furnished to him as part of his compensation; or

(2) the rental allowance paid to him as part of his compensation, to the extent used by him to rent or provide a home and to the extent such allowance does not exceed the fair rental value of the home, including furnishings and appurtenances such as a garage, plus the cost of utilities.

[Sec. 108]

SEC. 108. INCOME FROM DISCHARGE OF INDEBTEDNESS.

[Sec. 108(a)]

(a) EXCLUSION FROM GROSS INCOME.—

(1) IN GENERAL.—Gross income does not include any amount which (but for this subsection) would be includible in gross income by reason of the discharge (in whole or in part) of indebtedness of the taxpayer if—

(A) the discharge occurs in a title 11 case, or

(B) the discharge occurs when the taxpayer is insolvent,

(C) the indebtedness discharged is qualified farm indebtedness, or

(D) in the case of a taxpayer other than a C corporation, the indebtedness discharged is qualified real property business indebtedness.

(2) COORDINATION OF EXCLUSIONS.—

(A) TITLE 11 EXCLUSION TAKES PRECEDENCE.—Subparagraphs (B), (C), and (D) of paragraph (1) shall not apply to a discharge which occurs in a title 11 case.

(B) INSOLVENCY EXCLUSION TAKES PRECEDENCE OVER QUALIFIED FARM EXCLUSION AND QUALIFIED REAL PROPERTY BUSINESS EXCLUSION.—Subparagraphs (C) and (D) of paragraph (1) shall not apply to a discharge to the extent the taxpayer is insolvent.

Sec. 108(a)

(3) INSOLVENCY EXCLUSION LIMITED TO AMOUNT OF INSOLVENCY.—In the case of a discharge to which paragraph (1)(B) applies, the amount excluded under paragraph (1)(B) shall not exceed the amount by which the taxpayer is insolvent.

[Sec. 108(b)]

(b) REDUCTION OF TAX ATTRIBUTES.—

(1) IN GENERAL.—The amount excluded from gross income under subparagraph (A), (B), or (C) of subsection (a)(1) shall be applied to reduce the tax attributes of the taxpayer as provided in paragraph (2).

(2) TAX ATTRIBUTES AFFECTED; ORDER OF REDUCTION.—Except as provided in paragraph (5), the reduction referred to in paragraph (1) shall be made in the following tax attributes in the following order:

(A) NOL.—Any net operating loss for the taxable year of the discharge, and any net operating loss carryover to such taxable year.

(B) GENERAL BUSINESS CREDIT.—Any carryover to or from the taxable year of a discharge of an amount for purposes for determining the amount allowable as a credit under section 38 (relating to general business credit).

(C) MINIMUM TAX CREDIT.—The amount of the minimum tax credit available under section 53(b) as of the beginning of the taxable year immediately following the taxable year of the discharge.

(D) CAPITAL LOSS CARRYOVERS.—Any net capital loss for the taxable year of the discharge, and any capital loss carryover to such taxable year under section 1212.

(E) BASIS REDUCTION.—

(i) IN GENERAL.—The basis of the property of the taxpayer.

(ii) CROSS REFERENCE.—

For provisions for making the reduction described in clause (i), see section 1017.

(F) PASSIVE ACTIVITY LOSS AND CREDIT CARRYOVERS.—Any passive activity loss or credit carryover of the taxpayer under section 469(b) from the taxable year of the discharge.

(G) FOREIGN TAX CREDIT CARRYOVERS.—Any carryover to or from the taxable year of the discharge for purposes of determining the amount of the credit allowable under section 27.

(3) AMOUNT OF REDUCTION.—

(A) IN GENERAL.—Except as provided in subparagraph (B), the reductions described in paragraph (2) shall be one dollar for each dollar excluded by subsection (a).

(B) CREDIT CARRYOVER REDUCTION.—The reductions described in subparagraphs (B), (C), and (G) shall be 33 1/3 cents for each dollar excluded by subsection (a). The reduction described in subparagraph (F) in any passive activity credit carryover shall be 33 1/3 cents for each dollar excluded by subsection (a).

(4) ORDERING RULES.—

(A) REDUCTIONS MADE AFTER DETERMINATION OF TAX FOR YEAR.—The reductions described in paragraph (2) shall be made after the determination of the tax imposed by this chapter for the taxable year of the discharge.

(B) REDUCTIONS UNDER SUBPARAGRAPH (A) OR (D) OF PARAGRAPH (2).—The reductions described in subparagraph (A) or (D) of paragraph (2) (as the case may be) shall be made first in the loss for the taxable year of the discharge and then in the carryovers to such taxable year in the order of the taxable years from which each such carryover arose.

(C) REDUCTIONS UNDER SUBPARAGRAPHS (B) AND (G) OF PARAGRAPH (2).—The reductions described in subparagraphs (B) and (G) of paragraph (2) shall be made in the order in which carryovers are taken into account under this chapter for the taxable year of the discharge.

(5) ELECTION TO APPLY REDUCTION FIRST AGAINST DEPRECIABLE PROPERTY.—

(A) IN GENERAL.—The taxpayer may elect to apply any portion of the reduction referred to in paragraph (1) to the reduction under section 1017 of the basis of the depreciable property of the taxpayer.

(B) LIMITATION.—The amount to which an election under subparagraph (A) applies shall not exceed the aggregate adjusted bases of the depreciable property held by the taxpayer as of the beginning of the taxable year following the taxable year in which the discharge occurs.

(C) OTHER TAX ATTRIBUTES NOT REDUCED.—Paragraph (2) shall not apply to any amount to which an election under this paragraph applies.

[Sec. 108(c)]

(c) TREATMENT OF DISCHARGE OF QUALIFIED REAL PROPERTY BUSINESS INDEBTEDNESS.—

(1) BASIS REDUCTION.—

(A) IN GENERAL.—The amount excluded from gross income under subparagraph (D) of subsection (a)(1) shall be applied to reduce the basis of the depreciable real property of the taxpayer.

(B) CROSS REFERENCE.—For provisions making the reduction described in subparagraph (A), see section 1017.

(2) LIMITATIONS.—

(A) INDEBTEDNESS IN EXCESS OF VALUE.—The amount excluded under subparagraph (D) of subsection (a)(1) with respect to any qualified real property business indebtedness shall not exceed the excess (if any) of—

(i) the outstanding principal amount of such indebtedness (immediately before the discharge), over

(ii) the fair market value of the real property described in paragraph (3)(A) (as of such time), reduced by the outstanding principal amount of any other qualified real property business indebtedness secured by such property (as of such time).

(B) OVERALL LIMITATION.—The amount excluded under subparagraph (D) of subsection (a)(1) shall not exceed the aggregate adjusted bases of depreciable real property (determined after any reductions under subsections (b) and (g)) held by the taxpayer immediately before the discharge (other than depreciable real property acquired in contemplation of such discharge).

(3) QUALIFIED REAL PROPERTY BUSINESS INDEBTEDNESS.—The term "qualified real property business indebtedness" means indebtedness which—

(A) was incurred or assumed by the taxpayer in connection with real property used in a trade or business and is secured by such real property,

(B) was incurred or assumed before January 1, 1993, or if incurred or assumed on or after such date, is qualified acquisition indebtedness, and

(C) with respect to which such taxpayer makes an election to have this paragraph apply.

Such term shall not include qualified farm indebtedness. Indebtedness under subparagraph (B) shall include indebtedness resulting from the refinancing of indebtedness under subparagraph (B) (or this sentence), but only to the extent it does not exceed the amount of the indebtedness being refinanced.

(4) QUALIFIED ACQUISITION INDEBTEDNESS.—For purposes of paragraph (3)(B), the term "qualified acquisition indebtedness" means, with respect to any real property described in paragraph (3)(A), indebtedness incurred or assumed to acquire, construct, reconstruct, or substantially improve such property.

(5) REGULATIONS.—The Secretary shall issue such regulations as are necessary to carry out this subsection, including regulations preventing the abuse of this subsection through cross-collateralization or other means.

[Sec. 108(d)]

(d) MEANING OF TERMS; SPECIAL RULES RELATING TO CERTAIN PROVISIONS.—

(1) INDEBTEDNESS OF TAXPAYER.—For purposes of this section, the term "indebtedness of the taxpayer" means any indebtedness—

(A) for which the taxpayer is liable, or

(B) subject to which the taxpayer holds property.

(2) TITLE 11 CASE.—For purposes of this section, the term "title 11 case" means a case under title 11 of the United States Code (relating to bankruptcy), but only if the taxpayer is under the

Sec. 108(d)

jurisdiction of the court in such case and the discharge of indebtedness is granted by the court or is pursuant to a plan approved by the court.

(3) INSOLVENT.—For purposes of this section, the term "insolvent" means the excess of liabilities over the fair market value of assets. With respect to any discharge, whether or not the taxpayer is insolvent, and the amount by which the taxpayer is insolvent, shall be determined on the basis of the taxpayer's assets and liabilities immediately before the discharge.

(4) [Stricken.]

(5) DEPRECIABLE PROPERTY.—The term "depreciable property" has the same meaning as when used in section 1017.

(6) CERTAIN PROVISIONS TO BE APPLIED AT PARTNER LEVEL.—In the case of a partnership, subsections (a), (b), (c), and (g) shall be applied at the partner level.

(7) SPECIAL RULES FOR S CORPORATION.—

(A) CERTAIN PROVISIONS TO BE APPLIED AT CORPORATE LEVEL.—In the case of an S corporation, subsections (a), (b), (c), and (g) shall be applied at the corporate level, including by not taking into account under section 1366(a) any amount excluded under subsection (a) of this section.

(B) REDUCTION IN CARRYOVER OF DISALLOWED LOSSES AND DEDUCTIONS.—In the case of an S corporation, for purposes of subparagraph (A) of subsection (b)(2), any loss or deduction which is disallowed for the taxable year of the discharge under section 1366(d)(1) shall be treated as a net operating loss for such taxable year. The preceding sentence shall not apply to any discharge to the extent that subsection (a)(1)(D) applies to such discharge.

(C) COORDINATION WITH BASIS ADJUSTMENTS UNDER SECTION 1367(b)(2).—For purposes of subsection (e)(6), a shareholder's adjusted basis in indebtedness of an S corporation shall be determined without regard to any adjustments made under section 1367(b)(2).

(8) REDUCTIONS OF TAX ATTRIBUTES IN TITLE 11 CASES OF INDIVIDUALS TO BE MADE BY ESTATE.—In any case under chapter 7 or 11 of title 11 of the United States Code to which section 1398 applies, for purposes of paragraphs (1) and (5) of subsection (b) the estate (and not the individual) shall be treated as the taxpayer. The preceding sentence shall not apply for purposes of applying section 1017 to property transferred by the estate to the individual.

(9) TIME FOR MAKING ELECTION, ETC.—

(A) TIME.—An election under paragraph (5) of subsection (b) or under paragraph (3)(C) of subsection (c) shall be made on the taxpayer's return for the taxable year in which the discharge occurs or at such other time as may be permitted in regulations prescribed by the Secretary.

(B) REVOCATION ONLY WITH CONSENT.—An election referred to in subparagraph (A), once made, may be revoked only with the consent of the Secretary.

(C) MANNER.—An election referred to in subparagraph (A) shall be made in such manner as the Secretary may by regulations prescribe.

(10) CROSS REFERENCE.—

For provision that no reduction is to be made in the basis of exempt property of an individual debtor, see section 1017(c)(1).

[Sec. 108(e)]

(e) GENERAL RULES FOR DISCHARGE OF INDEBTEDNESS (INCLUDING DISCHARGES NOT IN TITLE 11 CASES OR INSOLVENCY).—For purposes of this title—

(1) NO OTHER INSOLVENCY EXCEPTION.—Except as otherwise provided in this section, there shall be no insolvency exception from the general rule that gross income includes income from the discharge of indebtedness.

(2) INCOME NOT REALIZED TO EXTENT OF LOST DEDUCTIONS.—No income shall be realized from the discharge of indebtedness to the extent that payment of the liability would have given rise to a deduction.

(3) ADJUSTMENTS FOR UNAMORTIZED PREMIUM AND DISCOUNT.—The amount taken into account with respect to any discharge shall be properly adjusted for unamortized premium and unamortized discount with respect to the indebtedness discharged.

(4) ACQUISITION OF INDEBTEDNESS BY PERSON RELATED TO DEBTOR.—

(A) TREATED AS ACQUISITION BY DEBTOR.—For purposes of determining income of the debtor from discharge of indebtedness, to the extent provided in regulations prescribed by the Secretary, the acquisition of outstanding indebtedness by a person bearing a relationship to the debtor specified in section 267(b) or 707(b)(1) from a person who does not bear such a relationship to the debtor shall be treated as the acquisition of such indebtedness by the debtor. Such regulations shall provide for such adjustments in the treatment of any subsequent transactions involving the indebtedness as may be appropriate by reason of the application of the preceding sentence.

(B) MEMBERS OF FAMILY.—For purposes of this paragraph, sections 267(b) and 707(b)(1) shall be applied as if section 267(c)(4) provided that the family of an individual consists of the individual's spouse, the individual's children, grandchildren, and parents, and any spouse of the individual's children or grandchildren.

(C) ENTITIES UNDER COMMON CONTROL TREATED AS RELATED.—For purposes of this paragraph, two entities which are treated as a single employer under subsection (b) or (c) of section 414 shall be treated as bearing a relationship to each other which is described in section 267(b).

(5) PURCHASE-MONEY DEBT REDUCTION FOR SOLVENT DEBTOR TREATED AS PRICE REDUCTION.—If—

(A) the debt of a purchaser of property to the seller of such property which arose out of the purchase of such property is reduced,

(B) such reduction does not occur—

(i) in a title 11 case, or

(ii) when the purchaser is insolvent, and

(C) but for this paragraph, such reduction would be treated as income to the purchaser from the discharge of indebtedness,

then such reduction shall be treated as a purchase price adjustment.

(6) INDEBTEDNESS CONTRIBUTED TO CAPITAL.—Except as provided in regulations, for purposes of determining income of the debtor from discharge of indebtedness, if a debtor corporation acquires its indebtedness from a shareholder as a contribution to capital—

(A) section 118 shall not apply, but

(B) such corporation shall be treated as having satisfied the indebtedness with an amount of money equal to the shareholder's adjusted basis in the indebtedness.

(7) RECAPTURE OF GAIN ON SUBSEQUENT SALE OF STOCK.—

(A) IN GENERAL.—If a creditor acquires stock of a debtor corporation in satisfaction of such corporation's indebtedness, for purposes of section 1245—

(i) such stock (and any other property the basis of which is determined in whole or in part by reference to the adjusted basis of such stock) shall be treated as section 1245 property,

(ii) the aggregate amount allowed to the creditor—

(I) as deductions under subsection (a) or (b) of section 166 (by reason of the worthlessness or partial worthlessness of the indebtedness), or

(II) as an ordinary loss on the exchange,

shall be treated as an amount allowed as a deduction for depreciation, and

(iii) an exchange of such stock qualifying under section 354(a), 355(a), or 356(a) shall be treated as an exchange to which section 1245(b)(3) applies.

The amount determined under clause (ii) shall be reduced by the amount (if any) included in the creditor's gross income on the exchange.

(B) SPECIAL RULE FOR CASH BASIS TAXPAYERS.—In the case of any creditor who computes his taxable income under the cash receipts and disbursements method, proper adjustment shall be made in the amount taken into account under clause (ii) of subparagraph (A) for any amount which was not included in the creditor's gross income but which would have been included in such gross income if such indebtedness had been satisfied in full.

(C) STOCK OF PARENT CORPORATION.—For purposes of this paragraph, stock of a corporation in control (within the meaning of section 368(c)) of the debtor corporation shall be treated as stock of the debtor corporation.

Sec. 108(e)

(D) TREATMENT OF SUCCESSOR CORPORATION.—For purposes of this paragraph, the term "debtor corporation" includes a successor corporation.

(E) PARTNERSHIP RULE.—Under regulations prescribed by the Secretary, rules similar to the rules of the foregoing subparagraphs of this paragraph shall apply with respect to the indebtedness of a partnership.

(8) INDEBTEDNESS SATISFIED BY CORPORATION'S STOCK.—For purposes of determining income of a debtor from discharge of indebtedness, if a debtor corporation transfers stock to a creditor in satisfaction of its indebtedness, such corporation shall be treated as having satisfied the indebtedness with an amount of money equal to the fair market value of the stock.

(9) DISCHARGE OF INDEBTEDNESS INCOME NOT TAKEN INTO ACCOUNT IN DETERMINING WHETHER ENTITY MEETS REIT QUALIFICATIONS.—Any amount included in gross income by reason of the discharge of indebtedness shall not be taken into account for purposes of paragraphs (2) and (3) of section 856(c).

(10) INDEBTEDNESS SATISFIED BY ISSUANCE OF DEBT INSTRUMENT.—

(A) IN GENERAL.—For purposes of determining income of a debtor from discharge of indebtedness, if a debtor issues a debt instrument in satisfaction of indebtedness, such debtor shall be treated as having satisfied the indebtedness with an amount of money equal to the issue price of such debt instrument.

(B) ISSUE PRICE.—For purposes of subparagraph (A), the issue price of any debt instrument shall be determined under sections 1273 and 1274. For purposes of the preceding sentence, section 1273(b)(4) shall be applied by reducing the stated redemption price of any instrument by the portion of such stated redemption price which is treated as interest for purposes of this chapter.

[Sec. 108(f)]

(f) STUDENT LOANS.—

(1) IN GENERAL.—In the case of an individual, gross income does not include any amount which (but for this subsection) would be includible in gross income by reason of the discharge (in whole or in part) of any student loan if such discharge was pursuant to a provision of such loan under which all or part of the indebtedness of the individual would be discharged if the individual worked for a certain period of time in certain professions for any of a broad class of employers.

(2) STUDENT LOAN.—For purposes of this subsection, the term "student loan" means any loan to an individual to assist the individual in attending an educational organization described in section 170(b)(1)(A)(ii) made by—

(A) the United States, or an instrumentality or agency thereof,

(B) a State, territory, or possession of the United States, or the District of Columbia, or any political subdivision thereof,

(C) a public benefit corporation—

(i) which is exempt from taxation under section 501(c)(3),

(ii) which has assumed control over a State, county, or municipal hospital, and

(iii) whose employees have been deemed to be public employees under State law, or

(D) any educational organization described in section 170(b)(1)(A)(ii) if such loan is made—

(i) pursuant to an agreement with any entity described in subparagraph (A), (B), or (C) under which the funds from which the loan was made were provided to such educational organization, or

(ii) pursuant to a program of such educational organization which is designed to encourage its students to serve in occupations with unmet needs or in areas with unmet needs and under which the services provided by the students (or former students) are for or under the direction of a governmental unit or an organization described in section 501(c)(3) and exempt from tax under section 501(a).

The term "student loan" includes any loan made by an educational organization described in section 170(b)(1)(A)(ii) or by an organization exempt from tax under section 501(a) to refinance a loan to an individual to assist the individual in attending any such educational organization but only if the refinancing loan is pursuant to a program of the refinancing organization which is designed as described in subparagraph (D)(ii).

(3) EXCEPTION FOR DISCHARGES ON ACCOUNT OF SERVICES PERFORMED FOR CERTAIN LENDERS.— Paragraph (1) shall not apply to the discharge of a loan made by an organization described in paragraph (2)(D) if the discharge is on account of services performed for either such organization.

[Sec. 108(g)]

(g) SPECIAL RULES FOR DISCHARGE OF QUALIFIED FARM INDEBTEDNESS.—

(1) DISCHARGE MUST BE BY QUALIFIED PERSON.—

(A) IN GENERAL.—Subparagraph (C) of subsection (a)(1) shall apply only if the discharge is by a qualified person.

(B) QUALIFIED PERSON.—For purposes of subparagraph (A), the term "qualified person" has the meaning given to such term by section 49(a)(1)(D)(iv); except that such term shall include any Federal, State, or local government or agency or instrumentality thereof.

(2) QUALIFIED FARM INDEBTEDNESS.—For purposes of this section, indebtedness of a taxpayer shall be treated as qualified farm indebtedness if—

(A) such indebtedness was incurred directly in connection with the operation by the taxpayer of the trade or business of farming, and

(B) 50 percent or more of the aggregate gross receipts of the taxpayer for the 3 taxable years preceding the taxable year in which the discharge of such indebtedness occurs is attributable to the trade or business of farming.

(3) AMOUNT EXCLUDED CANNOT EXCEED SUM OF TAX ATTRIBUTES AND BUSINESS AND INVESTMENT ASSETS.—

(A) IN GENERAL.—The amount excluded under subparagraph (C) of subsection (a)(1) shall not exceed the sum of—

(i) the adjusted tax attributes of the taxpayer, and

(ii) the aggregate adjusted bases of qualified property held by the taxpayer as of the beginning of the taxable year following the taxable year in which the discharge occurs.

(B) ADJUSTED TAX ATTRIBUTES.—For purposes of subparagraph (A), the term "adjusted tax attributes" means the sum of the tax attributes described in subparagraphs (A), (B), (C), (D), (F), and (G) of subsection (b)(2) determined by taking into account $3 for each $1 of the attributes described in subparagraphs (B), (C), and (G) of subsection (b)(2) and the attribute described in subparagraph (F) of subsection (b)(2) to the extent attributable to any passive activity credit carryover.

(C) QUALIFIED PROPERTY.—For purposes of this paragraph, the term "qualified property" means any property which is used or is held for use in a trade or business or for the production of income.

(D) COORDINATION WITH INSOLVENCY EXCLUSION.—For purposes of this paragraph, the adjusted basis of any qualified property and the amount of the adjusted tax attributes shall be determined after any reduction under subsection (b) by reason of amounts excluded from gross income under subsection (a)(1)(B).

[Sec. 109]

SEC. 109. IMPROVEMENTS BY LESSEE ON LESSOR'S PROPERTY.

Gross income does not include income (other than rent) derived by a lessor of real property on the termination of a lease, representing the value of such property attributable to buildings erected or other improvements made by the lessee.

[Sec. 111]

SEC. 111. RECOVERY OF TAX BENEFIT ITEMS.

[Sec. 111(a)]

(a) DEDUCTIONS.—Gross income does not include income attributable to the recovery during the taxable year of any amount deducted in any prior taxable year to the extent such amount did not reduce the amount of tax imposed by this chapter.

(b) CREDITS.—

(1) IN GENERAL.—If—

(A) a credit was allowable with respect to any amount for any prior taxable year, and

(B) during the taxable year there is a downward price adjustment or similar adjustment,

the tax imposed by this chapter for the taxable year shall be increased by the amount of the credit attributable to the adjustment.

(2) EXCEPTION WHERE CREDIT DID NOT REDUCE TAX.—Paragraph (1) shall not apply to the extent that the credit allowable for the recovered amount did not reduce the amount of tax imposed by this chapter.

(3) EXCEPTION FOR INVESTMENT TAX CREDIT AND FOREIGN TAX CREDIT.—This subsection shall not apply with respect to the credit determined under section 46 and the foreign tax credit.

(c) TREATMENT OF CARRYOVERS.—For purposes of this section, an increase in a carryover which has not expired before the beginning of the taxable year in which the recovery or adjustment takes place shall be treated as reducing tax imposed by this chapter.

(d) SPECIAL RULES FOR ACCUMULATED EARNINGS TAX AND FOR PERSONAL HOLDING COMPANY TAX.—In applying subsection (a) for the purpose of determining the accumulated earnings tax under section 531 or the tax under section 541 (relating to personal holding companies)—

(1) any excluded amount under subsection (a) allowed for the purposes of this subtitle (other than section 531 or section 541) shall be allowed whether or not such amount resulted in a reduction of the tax under section 531 or the tax under section 541 for the prior taxable year; and

(2) where any excluded amount under subsection (a) was not allowable as a deduction for the prior taxable year for purposes of this subtitle other than of section 531 or section 541 but was allowable for the same taxable year under section 531 or section 541, then such excluded amount shall be allowable if it did not result in a reduction of the tax under section 531 or the tax under section 541.

SEC. 112. CERTAIN COMBAT ZONE COMPENSATION OF MEMBERS OF THE ARMED FORCES.

(a) ENLISTED PERSONNEL.—Gross income does not include compensation received for active service as a member below the grade of commissioned officer in the Armed Forces of the United States for any month during any part of which such member—

(1) served in a combat zone, or

(2) was hospitalized as a result of wounds, disease, or injury incurred while serving in a combat zone; but this paragraph shall not apply for any month beginning more than 2 years after the date of the termination of combatant activities in such zone.

With respect to service in the combat zone designated for purposes of the Vietnam conflict, paragraph (2) shall not apply to any month after January 1978.

(b) COMMISSIONED OFFICERS.—Gross income does not include so much of the compensation as does not exceed the maximum enlisted amount received for active service as a commissioned officer in the Armed Forces of the United States for any month during any part of which such officer—

(1) served in a combat zone, or

(2) was hospitalized as a result of wounds, disease, or injury incurred while serving in a combat zone; but this paragraph shall not apply for any month beginning more than 2 years after the date of the termination of combatant activities in such zone.

With respect to service in the combat zone designated for purposes of the Vietnam conflict, paragraph (2) shall not apply to any month after January 1978.

[Sec. 112(c)]

(c) DEFINITIONS.—For purposes of this section—

(1) The term "commissioned officer" does not include a commissioned warrant officer.

(2) The term "combat zone" means any area which the President of the United States by Executive Order designates, for purposes of this section or corresponding provisions of prior income tax laws, as an area in which Armed Forces of the United States are or have (after June 24, 1950) engaged in combat.

(3) Service is performed in a combat zone only if performed on or after the date designated by the President by Executive Order as the date of the commencing of combatant activities in such zone, and on or before the date designated by the President by Executive Order as the date of the termination of combatant activities in such zone; except that June 25, 1950, shall be considered the date of the commencing of combatant activities in the combat zone designated in Executive Order 10195.

(4) The term "compensation" does not include pensions and retirement pay.

(5) The term "maximum enlisted amount" means, for any month, the sum of—

(A) the highest rate of basic pay payable for such month to any enlisted member of the Armed Forces of the United States at the highest pay grade applicable to enlisted members, and

(B) in the case of an officer entitled to special pay under section 310 of title 37, United States Code, for such month, the amount of such special pay payable to such officer for such month.

[Sec. 112(d)]

(d) PRISONERS OF WAR, ETC.

(1) MEMBERS OF THE ARMED FORCES.—Gross income does not include compensation received for active service as a member of the Armed Forces of the United States for any month during any part of which such member is in a missing status (as defined in section 551(2) of title 37, United States Code) during the Vietnam conflict as a result of such conflict, other than a period with respect to which it is officially determined under section 552(c) of such title 37 that he is officially absent from his post of duty without authority.

(2) CIVILIAN EMPLOYEES.—Gross income does not include compensation received for active service as an employee for any month during any part of which such employee is in a missing status during the Vietnam conflict as a result of such conflict. For purposes of this paragraph, the terms "active service", "employee", and "missing status" have the respective meanings given to such terms by section 5561 of title 5 of the United States Code.

(3) PERIOD OF CONFLICT.—For purposes of this subsection, the Vietnam conflict began February 28, 1961, and ends on the date designated by the President by Executive order as the date of the termination of combatant activities in Vietnam. For purposes of this subsection, an individual is in a missing status as a result of the Vietnam conflict if immediately before such status began he was performing service in Vietnam or was performing service in Southeast Asia in direct support of military operations in Vietnam.

[Sec. 115]

SEC. 115. INCOME OF STATES, MUNICIPALITIES, ETC.

Gross income does not include—

(1) income derived from any public utility or the exercise of any essential governmental function and accruing to a State or any political subdivision thereof, or the District of Columbia; or

(2) income accruing to the government of any possession of the United States, or any political subdivision thereof.

Sec. 115

SEC. 117. QUALIFIED SCHOLARSHIPS.

(a) GENERAL RULE.—Gross income does not include any amount received as a qualified scholarship by an individual who is a candidate for a degree at an educational organization described in section 170(b)(1)(A)(ii).

(b) QUALIFIED SCHOLARSHIP.—For purposes of this section—

(1) IN GENERAL.—The term "qualified scholarship" means any amount received by an individual as a scholarship or fellowship grant to the extent the individual establishes that, in accordance with the conditions of the grant, such amount was used for qualified tuition and related expenses.

(2) QUALIFIED TUITION AND RELATED EXPENSES.—For purposes of paragraph (1), the term "qualified tuition and related expenses" means—

(A) tuition and fees required for the enrollment or attendance of a student at an educational organization described in section 170(b)(1)(A)(ii), and

(B) fees, books, supplies, and equipment required for courses of instruction at such an educational organization.

(c) LIMITATION.—

(1) IN GENERAL.—Except as provided in paragraph (2), subsections (a) and (d) shall not apply to that portion of any amount received which represents payment for teaching, research, or other services by the student required as a condition for receiving the qualified scholarship or qualified tuition reduction.

(2) EXCEPTIONS.—Paragraph (1) shall not apply to any amount received by an individual under—

(A) the National Health Service Corps Scholarship Program under section 338A(g)(1)(A) of the Public Health Service Act, or

(B) the Armed Forces Health Professions Scholarship and Financial Assistance program under subchapter I of chapter 105 of title 10, United States Code.

(d) QUALIFIED TUITION REDUCTION.—

(1) IN GENERAL.—Gross income shall not include any qualified tuition reduction.

(2) QUALIFIED TUITION REDUCTION.—For purposes of this subsection, the term "qualified tuition reduction" means the amount of any reduction in tuition provided to an employee of an organization described in section 170(b)(1)(A)(ii) for the education (below the graduate level) at such organization (or another organization described in section 170(b)(1)(A)(ii)) of—

(A) such employee, or

(B) any person treated as an employee (or whose use is treated as an employee use) under the rules of section 132(h).

(3) REDUCTION MUST NOT DISCRIMINATE IN FAVOR OF HIGHLY COMPENSATED, ETC.—Paragraph (1) shall apply with respect to any qualified tuition reduction provided with respect to any highly compensated employee only if such reduction is available on substantially the same terms to each member of a group of employees which is defined under a reasonable classification set up by the employer which does not discriminate in favor of highly compensated employees (within the meaning of section 414(q)). For purposes of this paragraph, the term "highly compensated employee" has the meaning given such term by section 414(q).

(5)[4] SPECIAL RULES FOR TEACHING AND RESEARCH ASSISTANTS.—In the case of the education of an individual who is a graduate student at an educational organization described in section 170(b)(1)(A)(ii) and who is engaged in teaching or research activities for such organization, paragraph (2) shall be applied as if it did not contain the phrase "(below the graduate level)".

[Sec. 118]

SEC. 118. CONTRIBUTIONS TO THE CAPITAL OF A CORPORATION.

[Sec. 118(a)]

(a) GENERAL RULE.—In the case of a corporation, gross income does not include any contribution to the capital of the taxpayer.

[Sec. 118(b)]

(b) CONTRIBUTIONS IN AID OF CONSTRUCTION ETC.—For purposes of subsection (a), except as provided in subsection (c), the term "contribution to the capital of the taxpayer" does not include any contribution in aid of construction or any other contribution as a customer or potential customer.

* * *

[Sec. 118(e)]

(e) CROSS REFERENCES.—

(1) For basis of property acquired by a corporation through a contribution to its capital, see section 362.

(2) For special rules in the case of contributions of indebtedness, see section 108(e)(6).

[Sec. 119]

SEC. 119. MEALS OR LODGING FURNISHED FOR THE CONVENIENCE OF THE EMPLOYER.

[Sec. 119(a)]

(a) MEALS AND LODGING FURNISHED TO EMPLOYEE, HIS SPOUSE, AND HIS DEPENDENTS, PURSUANT TO EMPLOYMENT.—There shall be excluded from gross income of an employee the value of any meals or lodging furnished to him, his spouse, or any of his dependents by or on behalf of his employer for the convenience of the employer, but only if—

(1) in the case of meals, the meals are furnished on the business premises of the employer, or

(2) in the case of lodging, the employee is required to accept such lodging on the business premises of his employer as a condition of his employment.

[Sec. 119(b)]

(b) SPECIAL RULES.—For purposes of subsection (a)—

(1) PROVISIONS OF EMPLOYMENT CONTRACT OR STATE STATUTE NOT TO BE DETERMINATIVE.—In determining whether meals or lodging are furnished for the convenience of the employer, the provisions of an employment contract or of a State statute fixing terms of employment shall not be determinative of whether the meals or lodging are intended as compensation.

(2) CERTAIN FACTORS NOT TAKEN INTO ACCOUNT WITH RESPECT TO MEALS.—In determining whether meals are furnished for the convenience of the employer, the fact that a charge is made for such meals, and the fact that the employee may accept or decline such meals, shall not be taken into account.

(3) CERTAIN FIXED CHARGES FOR MEALS.—

(A) IN GENERAL.—If—

(i) an employee is required to pay on a periodic basis a fixed charge for his meals, and

(ii) such meals are furnished by the employer for the convenience of the employer, there shall be excluded from the employee's gross income an amount equal to such fixed charge.

(B) APPLICATION OF SUBPARAGRAPH (A).—Subparagraph (A) shall apply—

(i) whether the employee pays the fixed charge out of his stated compensation or out of his own funds, and

(ii) only if the employee is required to make the payment whether he accepts or declines the meals.

Sec. 119(b)

(4) MEALS FURNISHED TO EMPLOYEES ON BUSINESS PREMISES WHERE MEALS OF MOST EMPLOYEES ARE OTHERWISE EXCLUDABLE.—All meals furnished on the business premises of an employer to such employer's employees shall be treated as furnished for the convenience of the employer if, without regard to this paragraph, more than half of the employees to whom such meals are furnished on such premises are furnished such meals for the convenience of the employer.

* * *

[Sec. 119(d)]

(d) LODGING FURNISHED BY CERTAIN EDUCATIONAL INSTITUTIONS TO EMPLOYEES.—

(1) IN GENERAL.—In the case of an employee of an educational institution, gross income shall not include the value of qualified campus lodging furnished to such employee during the taxable year.

(2) EXCEPTION IN CASES OF INADEQUATE RENT.—Paragraph (1) shall not apply to the extent of the excess of—

(A) the lesser of—

(i) 5 percent of the appraised value of the qualified campus lodging, or

(ii) the average of the rentals paid by individuals (other than employees or students of the educational institution) during such calendar year for lodging provided by the educational institution which is comparable to the qualified campus lodging provided to the employee, over

(B) the rent paid by the employee for the qualified campus lodging during such calendar year.

The appraised value under subparagraph (A)(i) shall be determined as of the close of the calendar year in which the taxable year begins, or, in the case of a rental period not greater than 1 year, at any time during the calendar year in which such period begins.

(3) QUALIFIED CAMPUS LODGING.—For purposes of this subsection, the term "qualified campus lodging" means lodging to which subsection (a) does not apply and which is—

(A) located on, or in the proximity of, a campus of the educational institution, and

(B) furnished to the employee, his spouse, and any of his dependents by or on behalf of such institution for use as a residence.

(4) EDUCATIONAL INSTITUTION, ETC.—For purposes of this subsection—

(A) IN GENERAL.—The term "educational institution" means—

(i) an institution described in section 170(b)(1)(A)(ii) (or an entity organized under State law and composed of public institutions so described), or

(ii) an academic health center.

(B) ACADEMIC HEALTH CENTER.—For purposes of subparagraph (A), the term "academic health center" means an entity—

(i) which is described in section 170(b)(1)(A)(iii),

(ii) which receives (during the calendar year in which the taxable year of the taxpayer begins) payments under subsection (d)(5)(B) or (h) of section 1886 of the Social Security Act (relating to graduate medical education), and

(iii) which has as one of its principal purposes or functions the providing and teaching of basic and clinical medical science and research with the entity's own faculty.

[Sec. 121]

SEC. 121. EXCLUSION OF GAIN FROM SALE OF PRINCIPAL RESIDENCE.

[Sec. 121(a)]

(a) EXCLUSION.—Gross income shall not include gain from the sale or exchange of property if, during the 5-year period ending on the date of the sale or exchange, such property has been owned and used by the taxpayer as the taxpayer's principal residence for periods aggregating 2 years or more.

[Sec. 121(b)]

(b) LIMITATIONS.—

(1) IN GENERAL.—The amount of gain excluded from gross income under subsection (a) with respect to any sale or exchange shall not exceed $250,000.

(2) SPECIAL RULES FOR JOINT RETURNS.—In the case of a husband and wife who make a joint return for the taxable year of the sale or exchange of the property—

(A) $500,000 LIMITATION FOR CERTAIN JOINT RETURNS.—Paragraph (1) shall be applied by substituting "$500,000" for "$250,000" if—

(i) either spouse meets the ownership requirements of subsection (a) with respect to such property;

(ii) both spouses meet the use requirements of subsection (a) with respect to such property; and

(iii) neither spouse is ineligible for the benefits of subsection (a) with respect to such property by reason of paragraph (3).

(B) OTHER JOINT RETURNS.—If such spouses do not meet the requirements of subparagraph (A), the limitation under paragraph (1) shall be the sum of the limitations under paragraph (1) to which each spouse would be entitled if such spouses had not been married. For purposes of the preceding sentence, each spouse shall be treated as owning the property during the period that either spouse owned the property.

(3) APPLICATION TO ONLY 1 SALE OR EXCHANGE EVERY 2 YEARS.—

(A) IN GENERAL.—Subsection (a) shall not apply to any sale or exchange by the taxpayer if, during the 2-year period ending on the date of such sale or exchange, there was any other sale or exchange by the taxpayer to which subsection (a) applied.

(B) PRE-MAY 7, 1997, SALES NOT TAKEN INTO ACCOUNT.—Subparagraph (A) shall be applied without regard to any sale or exchange before May 7, 1997.

[Sec. 121(c)]

(c) EXCLUSION FOR TAXPAYERS FAILING TO MEET CERTAIN REQUIREMENTS.—

(1) IN GENERAL.—In the case of a sale or exchange to which this subsection applies, the ownership and use requirements of subsection (a), and subsection (b)(3), shall not apply; but the dollar limitation under paragraph (1) or (2) of subsection (b), whichever is applicable, shall be equal to—

(A) the amount which bears the same ratio to such limitation (determined without regard to this paragraph) as

(B)(i) the shorter of—

(I) the aggregate periods, during the 5-year period ending on the date of such sale or exchange, such property has been owned and used by the taxpayer as the taxpayer's principal residence; or

(II) the period after the date of the most recent prior sale or exchange by the taxpayer to which subsection (a) applied and before the date of such sale or exchange, bears to

(ii) 2 years.

(2) SALES AND EXCHANGES TO WHICH SUBSECTION APPLIES.—This subsection shall apply to any sale or exchange if—

(A) subsection (a) would not (but for this subsection) apply to such sale or exchange by reason of—

(i) a failure to meet the ownership and use requirements of subsection (a), or

(ii) subsection (b)(3), and

(B) such sale or exchange is by reason of a change in place of employment, health, or, to the extent provided in regulations, unforeseen circumstances.

[Sec. 121(d)]

(d) SPECIAL RULES.—

(1) JOINT RETURNS.—If a husband and wife make a joint return for the taxable year of the sale or exchange of the property, subsections (a) and (c) shall apply if either spouse meets the ownership and use requirements of subsection (a) with respect to such property.

(2) PROPERTY OF DECEASED SPOUSE.—For purposes of this section, in the case of an unmarried individual whose spouse is deceased on the date of the sale or exchange of property, the period such unmarried individual owned and used such property shall include the period such deceased spouse owned and used such property before death.

(3) PROPERTY OWNED BY SPOUSE OR FORMER SPOUSE.—For purposes of this section—

(A) PROPERTY TRANSFERRED TO INDIVIDUAL FROM SPOUSE OR FORMER SPOUSE.—In the case of an individual holding property transferred to such individual in a transaction described in section 1041(a), the period such individual owns such property shall include the period the transferor owned the property.

(B) PROPERTY USED BY FORMER SPOUSE PURSUANT TO DIVORCE DECREE, ETC.—Solely for purposes of this section, an individual shall be treated as using property as such individual's principal residence during any period of ownership while such individual's spouse or former spouse is granted use of the property under a divorce or separation instrument (as defined in section 71(b)(2)).

(4) TENANT-STOCKHOLDER IN COOPERATIVE HOUSING CORPORATION.—For purposes of this section, if the taxpayer holds stock as a tenant-stockholder (as defined in section 216) in a cooperative housing corporation (as defined in such section), then—

(A) the holding requirements of subsection (a) shall be applied to the holding of such stock, and

(B) the use requirements of subsection (a) shall be applied to the house or apartment which the taxpayer was entitled to occupy as such stockholder.

(5) INVOLUNTARY CONVERSIONS.—

(A) IN GENERAL.—For purposes of this section, the destruction, theft, seizure, requisition, or condemnation of property shall be treated as the sale of such property.

(B) APPLICATION OF SECTION 1033.—In applying section 1033 (relating to involuntary conversions), the amount realized from the sale or exchange of property shall be treated as being the amount determined without regard to this section, reduced by the amount of gain not included in gross income pursuant to this section.

(C) PROPERTY ACQUIRED AFTER INVOLUNTARY CONVERSION.—If the basis of the property sold or exchanged is determined (in whole or in part) under section 1033(b) (relating to basis of property acquired through involuntary conversion), then the holding and use by the taxpayer of the converted property shall be treated as holding and use by the taxpayer of the property sold or exchanged.

(6) RECOGNITION OF GAIN ATTRIBUTABLE TO DEPRECIATION.—Subsection (a) shall not apply to so much of the gain from the sale of any property as does not exceed the portion of the depreciation adjustments (as defined in section 1250(b)(3)) attributable to periods after May 6, 1997, in respect of such property.

(7) DETERMINATION OF USE DURING PERIODS OF OUT-OF-RESIDENCE CARE.—In the case of a taxpayer who—

(A) becomes physically or mentally incapable of self-care, and

(B) owns property and uses such property as the taxpayer's principal residence during the 5-year period described in subsection (a) for periods aggregating at least 1 year, then the taxpayer shall be treated as using such property as the taxpayer's principal residence during any time during such 5-year period in which the taxpayer owns the property and resides in any facility (including a nursing home) licensed by a State or political subdivision to care for an individual in the taxpayer's condition.

(8) SALES OF REMAINDER INTERESTS.—For purposes of this section—

(A) IN GENERAL.—At the election of the taxpayer, this section shall not fail to apply to the sale or exchange of an interest in a principal residence by reason of such interest being a remainder interest in such residence, but this section shall not apply to any other interest in such residence which is sold or exchanged separately.

(B) EXCEPTION FOR SALES TO RELATED PARTIES.—Subparagraph (A) shall not apply to any sale to, or exchange with, any person who bears a relationship to the taxpayer which is described in section 267(b) or 707(b).

Sec. 121(d)

[Caution: Code Sec. 121(d)(9), below, as added by P.L. 107-16, applies to estates of decedents dying after December 31, 2009.]

(9) PROPERTY ACQUIRED FROM A DECEDENT.—The exclusion under this section shall apply to property sold by—

(A) the estate of a decedent,

(B) any individual who acquired such property from the decedent (within the meaning of section 1022), and

(C) a trust which, immediately before the death of the decedent, was a qualified revocable trust (as defined in section 645(b)(1)) established by the decedent,

determined by taking into account the ownership and use by the decedent.

[Sec. 121(e)]

(e) DENIAL OF EXCLUSION FOR EXPATRIATES.—This section shall not apply to any sale or exchange by an individual if the treatment provided by section 877(a)(1) applies to such individual.

[Sec. 121(f)]

(f) ELECTION TO HAVE SECTION NOT APPLY.—This section shall not apply to any sale or exchange with respect to which the taxpayer elects not to have this section apply.

[Sec. 121(g)]

(g) RESIDENCES ACQUIRED IN ROLLOVERS UNDER SECTION 1034.—For purposes of this section, in the case of property the acquisition of which by the taxpayer resulted under section 1034 (as in effect on the day before the date of the enactment of this section) in the nonrecognition of any part of the gain realized on the sale or exchange of another residence, in determining the period for which the taxpayer has owned and used such property as the taxpayer's principal residence, there shall be included the aggregate periods for which such other residence (and each prior residence taken into account under section 1223(7) in determining the holding period of such property) had been so owned and used.

[Sec. 125]

SEC. 125. CAFETERIA PLANS.

[Sec. 125(a)]

(a) IN GENERAL.—Except as provided in subsection (b), no amount shall be included in the gross income of a participant in a cafeteria plan solely because, under the plan, the participant may choose among the benefits of the plan.

[Sec. 125(b)]

(b) EXCEPTION FOR HIGHLY COMPENSATED PARTICIPANTS AND KEY EMPLOYEES.—

(1) HIGHLY COMPENSATED PARTICIPANTS.—In the case of a highly compensated participant, subsection (a) shall not apply to any benefit attributable to a plan year for which the plan discriminates in favor of—

(A) highly compensated individuals as to eligibility to participate, or

(B) highly compensated participants as to contributions and benefits.

(2) KEY EMPLOYEES.—In the case of a key employee (within the meaning of section 416(i)(1)), subsection (a) shall not apply to any benefit attributable to a plan [year] for which the statutory nontaxable benefits provided to key employees exceed 25 percent of the aggregate of such benefits provided for all employees under the plan. For purposes of the preceding sentence, statutory nontaxable benefits shall be determined without regard to the last sentence of subsection (f).

(3) YEAR OF INCLUSION.—For purposes of determining the taxable year of inclusion, any benefit described in paragraph (1) or (2) shall be treated as received or accrued in the taxable year of the participant or key employee in which the plan year ends.

[Sec. 125(c)]

(c) DISCRIMINATION AS TO BENEFITS OR CONTRIBUTIONS.—For purposes of subparagraph (B) of subsection (b)(1), a cafeteria plan does not discriminate where qualified benefits and total benefits (or employer contributions allocable to statutory nontaxable benefits and employer contributions for total benefits) do not discriminate in favor of highly compensated participants.

[Sec. 125(d)]

(d) CAFETERIA PLAN DEFINED.—For purposes of this section—

(1) IN GENERAL.—The term "cafeteria plan" means a written plan under which—

(A) all participants are employees, and

(B) the participants may choose among 2 or more benefits consisting of cash and qualified benefits.

(2) DEFERRED COMPENSATION PLANS EXCLUDED.—

(A) IN GENERAL.—The term "cafeteria plan" does not include any plan which provides for deferred compensation.

(B) EXCEPTION FOR CASH AND DEFERRED ARRANGEMENTS.—Subparagraph (A) shall not apply to a profit-sharing or stock bonus plan or rural cooperative plan (within the meaning of section 401(k)(7)) which includes a qualified cash or deferred arrangement (as defined in section 401(k)(2)) to the extent of amounts which a covered employee may elect to have the employer pay as contributions to a trust under such plan on behalf of the employee.

(C) EXCEPTION FOR CERTAIN PLANS MAINTAINED BY EDUCATIONAL INSTITUTIONS.—Subparagraph (A) shall not apply to a plan maintained by an educational organization described in section 170(b)(1)(A)(ii) to the extent of amounts which a covered employee may elect to have the employer pay as contributions for post-retirement group life insurance if—

(i) all contributions for such insurance must be made before retirement, and

(ii) such life insurance does not have a cash surrender value at any time.

For purposes of section 79, any life insurance described in the preceding sentence shall be treated as group-term life insurance.

[Sec. 125(e)]

(e) HIGHLY COMPENSATED PARTICIPANT AND INDIVIDUAL DEFINED.—For purposes of this section—

(1) HIGHLY COMPENSATED PARTICIPANT.—The term "highly compensated participant" means a participant who is—

(A) an officer,

(B) a shareholder owning more than 5 percent of the voting power or value of all classes of stock of the employer,

(C) highly compensated, or

(D) a spouse or dependent (within the meaning of section 152) of an individual described in subparagraph (A), (B), or (C).

(2) HIGHLY COMPENSATED INDIVIDUAL.—The term "highly compensated individual" means an individual who is described in subparagraph (A), (B), (C), or (D) of paragraph (1).

[Sec. 125(f)]

(f) QUALIFIED BENEFITS DEFINED.—For purposes of this section, the term "qualified benefit" means any benefit which, with the application of subsection (a), is not includible in the gross income of the employee by reason of an express provision of this chapter (other than section 106(b), 117, 127, or 132). Such term includes any group term life insurance which is includible in gross income only because it exceeds the dollar limitation of section 79 and such term includes any other benefit permitted under regulations. Such term shall not include any product which is advertised, marketed, or offered as long-term care insurance.

[Sec. 125(g)]

(g) SPECIAL RULES.—

(1) COLLECTIVELY BARGAINED PLAN NOT CONSIDERED DISCRIMINATORY.—For purposes of this section, a plan shall not be treated as discriminatory if the plan is maintained under an agreement which the Secretary finds to be a collective bargaining agreement between employee representatives and one or more employers.

(2) HEALTH BENEFITS.—For purposes of subparagraph (B) of subsection (b)(1), a cafeteria plan which provides health benefits shall not be treated as discriminatory if—

(A) contributions under the plan on behalf of each participant include an amount which—

(i) equals 100 percent of the cost of the health benefit coverage under the plan of the majority of the highly compensated participants similarly situated, or

(ii) equals or exceeds 75 percent of the cost of the health benefit coverage of the participant (similarly situated) having the highest cost health benefit coverage under the plan, and

(B) contributions or benefits under the plan in excess of those described in subparagraph (A) bear a uniform relationship to compensation.

(3) CERTAIN PARTICIPATION ELIGIBILITY RULES NOT TREATED AS DISCRIMINATORY.—For purposes of subparagraph (A) of subsection (b)(1), a classification shall not be treated as discriminatory if the plan—

(A) benefits a group of employees described in section 410(b)(2)(A)(i), and

(B) meets the requirements of clauses (i) and (ii):

(i) No employee is required to complete more than 3 years of employment with the employer or employers maintaining the plan as a condition of participation in the plan, and the employment requirement for each employee is the same.

(ii) Any employee who has satisfied the employment requirement of clause (i) and who is otherwise entitled to participate in the plan commences participation no later than the first day of the first plan year beginning after the date the employment requirement was satisfied unless the employee was separated from service before the first day of that plan year.

(4) CERTAIN CONTROLLED GROUPS, ETC.—All employees who are treated as employed by a single employer under subsection (b), (c), or (m) of section 414 shall be treated as employed by a single employer for purposes of this section.

* * *

[Sec. 125(i)]

(i) REGULATIONS.—The Secretary shall prescribe such regulations as may be necessary to carry out the provisions of this section.

[Sec. 127]

SEC. 127. EDUCATIONAL ASSISTANCE PROGRAMS.

[Sec. 127(a)]

(a) EXCLUSION FROM GROSS INCOME.—

(1) IN GENERAL.—Gross income of an employee does not include amounts paid or expenses incurred by the employer for educational assistance to the employee if the assistance is furnished pursuant to a program which is described in subsection (b).

(2) $5,250 MAXIMUM EXCLUSION.—If, but for this paragraph, this section would exclude from gross income more than $5,250 of educational assistance furnished to an individual during a calendar year, this section shall apply only to the first $5,250 of such assistance so furnished.

[Sec. 127(b)]

(b) EDUCATIONAL ASSISTANCE PROGRAM.—

(1) IN GENERAL.—For purposes of this section, an educational assistance program is a separate written plan of an employer for the exclusive benefit of his employees to provide such employees with educational assistance. The program must meet the requirements of paragraphs (2) through (6) of this subsection.

(2) ELIGIBILITY.—The program shall benefit employees who qualify under a classification set up by the employer and found by the Secretary not to be discriminatory in favor of employees who are highly compensated employees (within the meaning of section 414(q)) or their dependents. For purposes of this paragraph, there shall be excluded from consideration employees not included in the program who are included in a unit of employees covered by an agreement which the Secretary of

Labor finds to be a collective bargaining agreement between employee representatives and one or more employers, if there is evidence that educational assistance benefits were the subject of good faith bargaining between such employee representatives and such employer or employers.

(3) PRINCIPAL SHAREHOLDERS OR OWNERS.—Not more than 5 percent of the amounts paid or incurred by the employer for educational assistance during the year may be provided for the class of individuals who are shareholders or owners (or their spouses or dependents), each of whom (on any day of the year) owns more than 5 percent of the stock or of the capital or profits interest in the employer.

(4) OTHER BENEFITS AS AN ALTERNATIVE.—A program must not provide eligible employees with a choice between educational assistance and other remuneration includible in gross income. For purposes of this section, the business practices of the employer (as well as the written program) will be taken into account.

(5) NO FUNDING REQUIRED.—A program referred to in paragraph (1) is not required to be funded.

(6) NOTIFICATION OF EMPLOYEES.—Reasonable notification of the availability and terms of the program must be provided to eligible employees.

[Sec. 127(c)]

(c) DEFINITIONS; SPECIAL RULES.—For purposes of this section—

(1) EDUCATIONAL ASSISTANCE.—The term "educational assistance" means—

(A) the payment, by an employer, of expenses incurred by or on behalf of an employee for education of the employee (including, but not limited to, tuition, fees, and similar payments, books, supplies, and equipment), and

(B) the provision, by an employer, of courses of instruction for such employee (including books, supplies, and equipment),

but does not include payment for, or the provision of, tools or supplies which may be retained by the employee after completion of a course of instruction, or meals, lodging, or transportation. The term "educational assistance" also does not include any payment for, or the provision of any benefits with respect to, any course or other education involving sports, games, or hobbies.

(2) EMPLOYEE.—The term "employee" includes, for any year, an individual who is an employee within the meaning of section 401(c)(1) (relating to self-employed individuals).

(3) EMPLOYER.—An individual who owns the entire interest in an unincorporated trade or business shall be treated as his own employer. A partnership shall be treated as the employer of each partner who is an employee within the meaning of paragraph (2).

(4) ATTRIBUTION RULES.—

(A) OWNERSHIP OF STOCK.—Ownership of stock in a corporation shall be determined in accordance with the rules provided under subsections (d) and (e) of section 1563 (without regard to section 1563(e)(3)(C)).

(B) INTEREST IN UNINCORPORATED TRADE OR BUSINESS.—The interest of an employee in a trade or business which is not incorporated shall be determined in accordance with regulations prescribed by the Secretary, which shall be based on principles similar to the principles which apply in the case of subparagraph (A).

(5) CERTAIN TESTS NOT APPLICABLE.—An educational assistance program shall not be held or considered to fail to meet any requirements of subsection (b) merely because—

(A) of utilization rates for the different types of educational assistance made available under the program; or

(B) successful completion, or attaining a particular course grade, is required for or considered in determining reimbursement under the program.

(6) RELATIONSHIP TO CURRENT LAW.—This section shall not be construed to affect the deduction or inclusion in income of amounts (not within the exclusion under this section) which are paid or incurred, or received as reimbursement, for educational expenses under section 117, 162 or 212.

(7) DISALLOWANCE OF EXCLUDED AMOUNTS AS CREDIT OR DEDUCTION.—No deduction or credit shall be allowed to the employee under any other section of this chapter for any amount excluded from income by reason of this section.

* * *

Sec. 127(c)

[Sec. 129]

SEC. 129. DEPENDENT CARE ASSISTANCE PROGRAMS.

[Sec. 129(a)]

(a) EXCLUSION.—

(1) IN GENERAL.—Gross income of an employee does not include amounts paid or incurred by the employer for dependent care assistance provided to such employee if the assistance is furnished pursuant to a program which is described in subsection (d).

(2) LIMITATION OF EXCLUSION.—

(A) IN GENERAL.—The amount which may be excluded under paragraph (1) for dependent care assistance with respect to dependent care services provided during a taxable year shall not exceed $5,000 ($2,500 in the case of a separate return by a married individual).

(B) YEAR OF INCLUSION.—The amount of any excess under subparagraph (A) shall be included in gross income in the taxable year in which the dependent care services were provided (even if payment of dependent care assistance for such services occurs in a subsequent taxable year).

(C) MARITAL STATUS.—For purposes of this paragraph, marital status shall be determined under the rules of paragraphs (3) and (4) of section 21(e).

[Sec. 129(b)]

(b) EARNED INCOME LIMITATION.—

(1) IN GENERAL.—The amount excluded from the income of an employee under subsection (a) for any taxable year shall not exceed—

(A) in the case of an employee who is not married at the close of such taxable year, the earned income of such employee for such taxable year, or

(B) in the case of an employee who is married at the close of such taxable year, the lesser of—

(i) the earned income of such employee for such taxable year, or

(ii) the earned income of the spouse of such employee for such taxable year.

(2) SPECIAL RULE FOR CERTAIN SPOUSES.—For purposes of paragraph (1), the provisions of section 21(d)(2) shall apply in determining the earned income of a spouse who is a student or incapable of caring for himself.

[Sec. 129(c)]

(c) PAYMENTS TO RELATED INDIVIDUALS.—No amount paid or incurred during the taxable year of an employee by an employer in providing dependent care assistance to such employee shall be excluded under subsection (a) if such amount was paid or incurred to an individual—

(1) with respect to whom, for such taxable year, a deduction is allowable under section 151(c) (relating to personal exemptions for dependents) to such employee or the spouse of such employee, or

(2) who is a child of such employee (within the meaning of section 151(c)(3)) under the age of 19 at the close of such taxable year.

[Sec. 129(d)]

(d) DEPENDENT CARE ASSISTANCE PROGRAM.—

(1) IN GENERAL.—For purposes of this section a dependent care assistance program is a separate written plan of an employer for the exclusive benefit of his employees to provide such employees with dependent care assistance which meets the requirements of paragraphs (2) through (8) of this subsection. If any plan would qualify as a dependent care assistance program but for a failure to meet the requirements of this subsection, then, notwithstanding such failure, such plan shall be treated as a dependent care assistance program in the case of employees who are not highly compensated employees.

(2) DISCRIMINATION.—The contributions or benefits provided under the plan shall not discriminate in favor of employees who are highly compensated employees (within the meaning of section 414(q)) or their dependents.

Sec. 129(d)

(3) ELIGIBILITY.—The program shall benefit employees who qualify under a classification set up by the employer and found by the Secretary not to be discriminatory in favor of employees described in paragraph (2), or their dependents.

(4) PRINCIPAL SHAREHOLDERS OR OWNERS.—Not more than 25 percent of the amounts paid or incurred by the employer for dependent care assistance during the year may be provided for the class of individuals who are shareholders or owners (or their spouses or dependents), each of whom (on any day of the year) owns more than 5 percent of the stock or of the capital or profits interest in the employer.

(5) NO FUNDING REQUIRED.—A program referred to in paragraph (1) is not required to be funded.

(6) NOTIFICATION OF ELIGIBLE EMPLOYEES.—Reasonable notification of the availability and terms of the program shall be provided to eligible employees.

(7) STATEMENT OF EXPENSES.—The plan shall furnish to an employee, on or before January 31, a written statement showing the amounts paid or expenses incurred by the employer in providing dependent care assistance to such employee during the previous calendar year.

(8) BENEFITS.—

   (A) IN GENERAL.—A plan meets the requirements of this paragraph if the average benefits provided to employees who are not highly compensated employees under all plans of the employer is at least 55 percent of the average benefits provided to highly compensated employees under all plans of the employer.

   (B) SALARY REDUCTION AGREEMENTS.—For purposes of subparagraph (A), in the case of any benefits provided through a salary reduction agreement, a plan may disregard any employees whose compensation is less than $25,000. For purposes of this subparagraph, the term "compensation" has the meaning given such term by section 414(q)(4), except that, under rules prescribed by the Secretary, an employer may elect to determine compensation on any other basis which does not discriminate in favor of highly compensated employees.

(9) EXCLUDED EMPLOYEES.—For purposes of paragraphs (3) and (8), there shall be excluded from consideration—

   (A) subject to rules similar to the rules of section 410(b)(4), employees who have not attained the age of 21 and completed 1 year of service (as defined in section 410(a)(3)), and

   (B) employees not included in a dependent care assistance program who are included in a unit of employees covered by an agreement which the Secretary finds to be a collective bargaining agreement between employee representatives and 1 or more employees, if there is evidence that dependent care benefits were the subject of good faith bargaining between such employee representatives and such employer or employers.

[Sec. 129(e)]

(e) DEFINITIONS AND SPECIAL RULES.—For purposes of this section—

(1) DEPENDENT CARE ASSISTANCE.—The term "dependent care assistance" means the payment of, or provision of, those services which if paid for by the employee would be considered employment-related expenses under section 21(b)(2) (relating to expenses for household and dependent care services necessary for gainful employment).

(2) EARNED INCOME.—The term "earned income" shall have the meaning given such term in section 32(c)(2), but such term shall not include any amounts paid or incurred by an employer for dependent care assistance to an employee.

(3) EMPLOYEE.—The term "employee" includes, for any year, an individual who is an employee within the meaning of section 401(c)(1) (relating to self-employed individuals).

(4) EMPLOYER.—An individual who owns the entire interest in an unincorporated trade or business shall be treated as his own employer. A partnership shall be treated as the employer of each partner who is an employee within the meaning of paragraph (3).

(5) ATTRIBUTION RULES.—

   (A) OWNERSHIP OF STOCK.—Ownership of stock in a corporation shall be determined in accordance with the rules provided under subsections (d) and (e) of section 1563 (without regard to section 1563(e)(3)(C)).

   (B) INTEREST IN UNINCORPORATED TRADE OR BUSINESS.—The interest of an employee in a trade or business which is not incorporated shall be determined in accordance with regulations prescribed by the Secretary, which shall be based on principles similar to the principles which apply in the case of subparagraph (A).

(6) UTILIZATION TEST NOT APPLICABLE.—A dependent care assistance program shall not be held or considered to fail to meet any requirements of subsection (d) (other than paragraphs (4) and (8) thereof) merely because of utilization rates for the different types of assistance made available under the program.

(7) DISALLOWANCE OF EXCLUDED AMOUNTS AS CREDIT OR DEDUCTION.—No deduction or credit shall be allowed to the employee under any other section of this chapter for any amount excluded from the gross income of the employee by reason of this section.

(8) TREATMENT OF ONSITE FACILITIES.—In the case of an onsite facility maintained by an employer, except to the extent provided in regulations, the amount of dependent care assistance provided to an employee excluded with respect to any dependent shall be based on—

(A) utilization of the facility by a dependent of the employee, and

(B) the value of the services provided with respect to such dependent.

(9) IDENTIFYING INFORMATION REQUIRED WITH RESPECT TO SERVICE PROVIDER.—No amount paid or incurred by an employer for dependent care assistance provided to an employee shall be excluded from the gross income of such employee unless—

(A) the name, address, and taxpayer identification number of the person performing the services are included on the return to which the exclusion relates, or

(B) if such person is an organization described in section 501(c)(3) and exempt from tax under section 501(a), the name and address of such person are included on the return to which the exclusion relates.

In the case of a failure to provide the information required under the preceding sentence, the preceding sentence shall not apply if it is shown that the taxpayer exercised due diligence in attempting to provide the information so required.

[Sec. 130]

SEC. 130. CERTAIN PERSONAL INJURY LIABILITY ASSIGNMENTS.

[Sec. 130(a)]

(a) IN GENERAL.—Any amount received for agreeing to a qualified assignment shall not be included in gross income to the extent that such amount does not exceed the aggregate cost of any qualified funding assets.

[Sec. 130(b)]

(b) TREATMENT OF QUALIFIED FUNDING ASSET.—In the case of any qualified funding asset—

(1) the basis of such asset shall be reduced by the amount excluded from gross income under subsection (a) by reason of the purchase of such asset, and

(2) any gain recognized on a disposition of such asset shall be treated as ordinary income.

[Sec. 130(c)]

(c) QUALIFIED ASSIGNMENT.—For purposes of this section, the term "qualified assignment" means any assignment of a liability to make periodic payments as damages (whether by suit or agreement), or as compensation under any workmen's compensation act, on account of personal injury or sickness (in a case involving physical injury or physical sickness)—

(1) if the assignee assumes such liability from a person who is a party to the suit or agreement, or the workmen's compensation claim, and

(2) if—

(A) such periodic payments are fixed and determinable as to amount and time of payment,

(B) such periodic payments cannot be accelerated, deferred, increased, or decreased by the recipient of such payments,

(C) the assignee's obligation on account of the personal injuries or sickness is no greater than the obligation of the person who assigned the liability, and

(D) such periodic payments are excludable from the gross income of the recipient under paragraph (1) or (2) of section 104(a).

The determination for purposes of this chapter of when the recipient is treated as having received any payment with respect to which there has been a qualified assignment shall be made without regard to any provision of such assignment which grants the recipient rights as a creditor greater than those of a general creditor.

[Sec. 130(d)]

(d) QUALIFIED FUNDING ASSET.—For purposes of this section, the term "qualified funding asset" means any annuity contract issued by a company licensed to do business as an insurance company under the laws of any State, or any obligation of the United States, if—

(1) such annuity contract or obligation is used by the assignee to fund periodic payments under any qualified assignment,

(2) the periods of the payments under the annuity contract or obligation are reasonably related to the periodic payments under the qualified assignment, and the amount of any such payment under the contract or obligation does not exceed the periodic payment to which it relates,

(3) such annuity contract or obligation is designated by the taxpayer (in such manner as the Secretary shall by regulations prescribe) as being taken into account under this section with respect to such qualified assignment, and

(4) such annuity contract or obligation is purchased by the taxpayer not more than 60 days before the date of the qualified assignment and not later than 60 days after the date of such assignment.

[*Caution: Pursuant to Section 132(f)(6), the limitation amounts set forth in Section 132(f)(2) are adjusted for taxable years beginning after 1993 to reflect increases in the Consumer Price Index. The adjusted amounts applicable to taxable years beginning in 2003 are provided beginning at page ix.*]

[Sec. 132]

SEC. 132. CERTAIN FRINGE BENEFITS.

[Sec. 132(a)]

(a) EXCLUSION FROM GROSS INCOME.—Gross income shall not include any fringe benefit which qualifies as a—

(1) no-additional-cost service,

(2) qualified employee discount,

(3) working condition fringe,

(4) de minimis fringe[,]

(5) qualified transportation fringe,

(6) qualified moving expense reimbursement, or

(7) qualified retirement planning services.

[Sec. 132(b)]

(b) NO-ADDITIONAL-COST SERVICE DEFINED.—For purposes of this section, the term "no-additional-cost service" means any service provided by an employer to an employee for use by such employee if—

(1) such service is offered for sale to customers in the ordinary course of the line of business of the employer in which the employee is performing services, and

(2) the employer incurs no substantial additional cost (including forgone revenue) in providing such service to the employee (determined without regard to any amount paid by the employee for such service).

[Sec. 132(c)]

(c) QUALIFIED EMPLOYEE DISCOUNT DEFINED.—For purposes of this section—

(1) QUALIFIED EMPLOYEE DISCOUNT.—The term "qualified employee discount" means any employee discount with respect to qualified property or services to the extent such discount does not exceed—

(A) in the case of property, the gross profit percentage of the price at which the property is being offered by the employer to customers, or

(B) in the case of services, 20 percent of the price at which the services are being offered by the employer to customers.

(2) GROSS PROFIT PERCENTAGE.—

(A) IN GENERAL.—The term "gross profit percentage" means the percent which—

(i) the excess of the aggregate sales price of property sold by the employer to customers over the aggregate cost of such property to the employer, is of

(ii) the aggregate sale price of such property.

(B) DETERMINATION OF GROSS PROFIT PERCENTAGE.—Gross profit percentage shall be determined on the basis of—

(i) all property offered to customers in the ordinary course of the line of business of the employer in which the employee is performing services (or a reasonable classification of property selected by the employer), and

(ii) the employer's experience during a representative period.

(3) EMPLOYEE DISCOUNT DEFINED.—The term "employee discount" means the amount by which—

(A) the price at which the property or services are provided by the employer to an employee for use by such employee, is less than

(B) the price at which such property or services are being offered by the employer to customers.

(4) QUALIFIED PROPERTY OR SERVICES.—The term "qualified property or services" means any property (other than real property and other than personal property of a kind held for investment) or services which are offered for sale to customers in the ordinary course of the line of business of the employer in which the employee is performing services.

[Sec. 132(d)]

(d) WORKING CONDITION FRINGE DEFINED.—For purposes of this section, the term "working condition fringe" means any property or services provided to an employee of the employer to the extent that, if the employee paid for such property or services, such payment would be allowable as a deduction under section 162 or 167.

[Sec. 132(e)]

(e) DE MINIMIS FRINGE DEFINED.—For purposes of this section—

(1) IN GENERAL.—The term "de minimis fringe" means any property or service the value of which is (after taking into account the frequency with which similar fringes are provided by the employer to the employer's employees) so small as to make accounting for it unreasonable or administratively impracticable.

(2) TREATMENT OF CERTAIN EATING FACILITIES.—The operation by an employer of any eating facility for employees shall be treated as a de minimis fringe if—

(A) such facility is located on or near the business premises of the employer, and

(B) revenue derived from such facility normally equals or exceeds the direct operating costs of such facility.

The preceding sentence shall apply with respect to any highly compensated employee only if access to the facility is available on substantially the same terms to each member of a group of employees which is defined under a reasonable classification set up by the employer which does not discriminate in favor of highly compensated employees. For purposes of subparagraph (B), an employee entitled under section 119 to exclude the value of a meal provided at such facility shall be treated as having paid an amount for such meal equal to the direct operating costs of the facility attributable to such meal.

[Sec. 132(f)]

(f) QUALIFIED TRANSPORTATION FRINGE.—

(1) IN GENERAL.—For purposes of this section, the term "qualified transportation fringe" means any of the following provided by an employer to an employee:

(A) Transportation in a commuter highway vehicle if such transportation is in connection with travel between the employee's residence and place of employment.

(B) Any transit pass.

(C) Qualified parking.

(2) LIMITATION ON EXCLUSION.—The amount of the fringe benefits which are provided by an employer to any employee and which may be excluded from gross income under subsection (a)(5) shall not exceed—

(A) $100 per month in the case of the aggregate of the benefits described in subparagraphs (A) and (B) of paragraph (1), and

(B) $175 per month in the case of qualified parking.

(3) CASH REIMBURSEMENTS.—For purposes of this subsection, the term "qualified transportation fringe" includes a cash reimbursement by an employer to an employee for a benefit described in paragraph (1). The preceding sentence shall apply to a cash reimbursement for any transit pass only if a voucher or similar item which may be exchanged only for a transit pass is not readily available for direct distribution by the employer to the employee.

(4) NO CONSTRUCTIVE RECEIPT.—No amount shall be included in the gross income of an employee solely because the employee may choose between any qualified transportation fringe and compensation which would otherwise be includible in gross income of such employee.

(5) DEFINITIONS.—For purposes of this subsection—

(A) TRANSIT PASS.—The term "transit pass" means any pass, token, farecard, voucher, or similar item entitling a person to transportation (or transportation at a reduced price) if such transportation is—

(i) on mass transit facilities (whether or not publicly owned), or

(ii) provided by any person in the business of transporting persons for compensation or hire if such transportation is provided in a vehicle meeting the requirements of subparagraph (B)(i).

(B) COMMUTER HIGHWAY VEHICLE.—The term "commuter highway vehicle" means any highway vehicle—

(i) the seating capacity of which is at least 6 adults (not including the driver), and

(ii) at least 80 percent of the mileage use of which can reasonably be expected to be—

(I) for purposes of transporting employees in connection with travel between their residences and their place of employment, and

(II) on trips during which the number of employees transported for such purposes is at least 1/2 of the adult seating capacity of such vehicle (not including the driver).

(C) QUALIFIED PARKING.—The term "qualified parking" means parking provided to an employee on or near the business premises of the employer or on or near a location from which the employee commutes to work by transportation described in subparagraph (A), in a commuter highway vehicle, or by carpool. Such term shall not include any parking on or near property used by the employee for residential purposes.

(D) TRANSPORTATION PROVIDED BY EMPLOYER.—Transportation referred to in paragraph (1)(A) shall be considered to be provided by an employer if such transportation is furnished in a commuter highway vehicle operated by or for the employer.

(E) EMPLOYEE.—For purposes of this subsection, the term "employee" does not include an individual who is an employee within the meaning of section 401(c)(1).

(6) INFLATION ADJUSTMENT.—

(A) IN GENERAL.—In the case of any taxable year beginning in a calendar year after 1999, the dollar amounts contained in subparagraphs (A) and (B) of paragraph (2) shall be increased by an amount equal to—

(i) such dollar amount, multiplied by

(ii) the cost-of-living adjustment determined under section 1(f)(3) for the calendar year in which the taxable year begins, by substituting "calendar year 1998" for "calendar year 1992".

In the case of any taxable year beginning in a calendar year after 2002, clause (ii) shall be applied by substituting "calendar year 2001" for "calendar year 1998" for purposes of adjusting the dollar amount contained in paragraph (2)(A).

(B) ROUNDING.—If any increase determined under subparagraph (A) is not a multiple of $5, such increase shall be rounded to the next lowest multiple of $5.

(7) COORDINATION WITH OTHER PROVISIONS.—For purposes of this section, the terms "working condition fringe" and "de minimis fringe" shall not include any qualified transportation fringe (determined without regard to paragraph (2)).

[Sec. 132(g)]

(g) QUALIFIED MOVING EXPENSE REIMBURSEMENT.—For purposes of this section, the term 'qualified moving expense reimbursement' means any amount received (directly or indirectly) by an individual from an employer as a payment for (or a reimbursement of) expenses which would be deductible as moving expenses under section 217 if directly paid or incurred by the individual. Such term shall not include any payment for (or reimbursement of) an expense actually deducted by the individual in a prior taxable year.

[Sec. 132(h)]

(h) CERTAIN INDIVIDUALS TREATED AS EMPLOYEES FOR PURPOSES OF SUBSECTIONS (a)(1) AND (2).—For purposes of paragraphs (1) and (2) of subsection (a)—

(1) RETIRED AND DISABLED EMPLOYEES AND SURVIVING SPOUSE OF EMPLOYEE TREATED AS EMPLOYEE.—With respect to a line of business of an employer, the term "employee" includes—

(A) any individual who was formerly employed by such employer in such line of business and who separated from service with such employer in such line of business by reason of retirement or disability, and

(B) any widow or widower of any individual who died while employed by such employer in such line of business or while an employee within the meaning of subparagraph (A).

(2) SPOUSE AND DEPENDENT CHILDREN.—

(A) IN GENERAL.—Any use by the spouse or a dependent child of the employee shall be treated as use by the employee.

(B) DEPENDENT CHILD.—For purposes of subparagraph (A), the term "dependent child" means any child (as defined in section 151(c)(3)) of the employee—

(i) who is a dependent of the employee, or

(ii) both of whose parents are deceased and who has not attained age 25.

For purposes of the preceding sentence, any child to whom section 152(e) applies shall be treated as the dependent of both parents.

(3) SPECIAL RULE FOR PARENTS IN THE CASE OF AIR TRANSPORTATION.—Any use of air transportation by a parent of an employee (determined without regard to paragraph (1)(B)) shall be treated as use by the employee.

[Sec. 132(i)]

(i) RECIPROCAL AGREEMENTS.—For purposes of paragraph (1) of subsection (a), any service provided by an employer to an employee of another employer shall be treated as provided by the employer of such employee if—

(1) such service is provided pursuant to a written agreement between such employers, and

(2) neither of such employers incurs any substantial additional costs (including foregone revenue) in providing such service or pursuant to such agreement.

[Sec. 132(j)]

(j) SPECIAL RULES.—

(1) EXCLUSIONS UNDER SUBSECTION (a)(1) AND (2) APPLY TO HIGHLY COMPENSATED EMPLOYEES ONLY IF NO DISCRIMINATION.—Paragraphs (1) and (2) of subsection (a) shall apply with respect to any

fringe benefit described therein provided with respect to any highly compensated employee only if such fringe benefit is available on substantially the same terms to each member of a group of employees which is defined under a reasonable classification set up by the employer which does not discriminate in favor of highly compensated employees.

* * *

(4) ON-PREMISES GYMS AND OTHER ATHLETIC FACILITIES.—

(A) IN GENERAL.—Gross income shall not include the value of any on-premises athletic facility provided by an employer to his employees.

(B) ON-PREMISES ATHLETIC FACILITY.—For purposes of this paragraph, the term "on-premises athletic facility" means any gym or other athletic facility—

(i) which is located on the premises of the employer,

(ii) which is operated by the employer, and

(iii) substantially all the use of which is by employees of the employer, their spouses, and their dependent children (within the meaning of subsection (h)).

* * *

(6) HIGHLY COMPENSATED EMPLOYEE.—For purposes of this section, the term "highly compensated employee" has the meaning given such term by section 414(q).

(7) AIR CARGO.—For purposes of subsection (b), the transportation of cargo by air and the transportation of passengers by air shall be treated as the same service.

(8) APPLICATION OF SECTION TO OTHERWISE TAXABLE EDUCATIONAL OR TRAINING BENEFITS.—Amounts paid or expenses incurred by the employer for education or training provided to the employee which are not excludable from gross income under section 127 shall be excluded from gross income under this section if (and only if) such amounts or expenses are a working condition fringe.

[Sec. 132(k)]

(k) CUSTOMERS NOT TO INCLUDE EMPLOYEES.—For purposes of this section (other than subsection (c)(2)), the term "customers" shall only include customers who are not employees.

[Sec. 132(l)]

(l) SECTION NOT TO APPLY TO FRINGE BENEFITS EXPRESSLY PROVIDED FOR ELSEWHERE.—This section (other than subsections (e) and (g)) shall not apply to any fringe benefits of a type the tax treatment of which is expressly provided for in any other section of this chapter.

[Sec. 132(m)]

(m) QUALIFIED RETIREMENT PLANNING SERVICES.—

(1) IN GENERAL.—For purposes of this section, the term "qualified retirement planning services" means any retirement planning advice or information provided to an employee and his spouse by an employer maintaining a qualified employer plan.

(2) NONDISCRIMINATION RULE.—Subsection (a)(7) shall apply in the case of highly compensated employees only if such services are available on substantially the same terms to each member of the group of employees normally provided education and information regarding the employer's qualified employer plan.

(3) QUALIFIED EMPLOYER PLAN.—For purposes of this subsection, the term "qualified employer plan" means a plan, contract, pension, or account described in section 219(g)(5).

[Sec. 132(n)]

(n) REGULATIONS.—The Secretary shall prescribe such regulations as may be necessary or appropriate to carry out the purposes of this section.

Sec. 132(k)

[Caution: Pursuant to Section 135(b)(2)(B), the modified adjusted gross income amounts stated in Section 135(b)(2)(A) are adjusted for taxable years beginning after 1990 to reflect increases in the Consumer Price Index. The adjusted amounts applicable to taxable years beginning in 2003 are provided beginning at page ix.]

[Sec. 135]

SEC. 135. INCOME FROM UNITED STATES SAVINGS BONDS USED TO PAY HIGHER EDUCATION TUITION AND FEES.

[Sec. 135(a)]

(a) GENERAL RULE.—In the case of an individual who pays qualified higher education expenses during the taxable year, no amount shall be includible in gross income by reason of the redemption during such year of any qualified United States savings bond.

[Sec. 135(b)]

(b) LIMITATIONS.—

(1) LIMITATION WHERE REDEMPTION PROCEEDS EXCEED HIGHER EDUCATION EXPENSES.—

(A) IN GENERAL.—If—

(i) the aggregate proceeds of qualified United States savings bonds redeemed by the taxpayer during the taxable year exceed

(ii) the qualified higher education expenses paid by the taxpayer during such taxable year,

the amount excludable from gross income under subsection (a) shall not exceed the applicable fraction of the amount excludable from gross income under subsection (a) without regard to this subsection.

(B) APPLICABLE FRACTION.—For purposes of subparagraph (A), the term "applicable fraction" means the fraction the numerator of which is the amount described in subparagraph (A)(ii) and the denominator of which is the amount described in subparagraph (A)(i).

(2) LIMITATION BASED ON MODIFIED ADJUSTED GROSS INCOME.—

(A) IN GENERAL.—If the modified adjusted gross income of the taxpayer for the taxable year exceeds $40,000 ($60,000 in the case of a joint return), the amount which would (but for this paragraph) be excludable from gross income under subsection (a) shall be reduced (but not below zero) by the amount which bears the same ratio to the amount which would be so excludable as such excess bears to $15,000 ($30,000 in the case of a joint return).

(B) INFLATION ADJUSTMENT.—In the case of any taxable year beginning in a calendar year after 1990, the $40,000 and $60,000 amounts contained in subparagraph (A) shall be increased by an amount equal to—

(i) such dollar amount, multiplied by

(ii) the cost-of-living adjustment under section 1(f)(3) for the calendar year in which the taxable year begins, determined by substituting "calendar year 1989" for "calendar year 1992" in subparagraph (B) thereof.

(C) ROUNDING.—If any amount as adjusted under subparagraph (B) is not a multiple of $50, such amount shall be rounded to the nearest multiple of $50 (or if such amount is a multiple of $25, such amount shall be rounded to the next highest multiple of $50).

[Sec. 135(c)]

(c) DEFINITIONS.—For purposes of this section—

(1) QUALIFIED UNITED STATES SAVINGS BOND.—The term "qualified United States savings bond" means any United States savings bond issued—

(A) after December 31, 1989,

(B) to an individual who has attained age 24 before the date of issuance, and

(C) at discount under section 3105 of title 31, United States Code.

Sec. 135(c)

(2) QUALIFIED HIGHER EDUCATION EXPENSES.—

(A) IN GENERAL.—The term "qualified higher education expenses" means tuition and fees required for the enrollment or attendance of—

(i) the taxpayer,

(ii) the taxpayer's spouse, or

(iii) any dependent of the taxpayer with respect to whom the taxpayer is allowed a deduction under section 151,

at an eligible educational institution.

(B) EXCEPTION FOR EDUCATION INVOLVING SPORTS, ETC.—Such term shall not include expenses with respect to any course or other education involving sports, games, or hobbies other than as part of a degree program.

(C) CONTRIBUTIONS TO QUALIFIED TUITION PROGRAM AND COVERDELL EDUCATION SAVINGS ACCOUNTS.—Such term shall include any contribution to a qualified tuition program (as defined in section 529) on behalf of a designated beneficiary (as defined in such section), or to a Coverdell education savings account (as defined in section 530) on behalf of an account beneficiary, who is an individual described in subparagraph (A); but there shall be no increase in the investment in the contract for purposes of applying section 72 by reason of any portion of such contribution which is not includible in gross income by reason of this subparagraph.

(3) ELIGIBLE EDUCATIONAL INSTITUTION.—The term "eligible educational institution" has the meaning given such term by section 529(e)(5).

(4) MODIFIED ADJUSTED GROSS INCOME.—The term "modified adjusted gross income" means the adjusted gross income of the taxpayer for the taxable year determined—

(A) without regard to this section and sections 137, 221, 222, 911, 931, and 933, and

(B) after the application of sections 86, 469, and 219.

[Sec. 135(d)]

(d) SPECIAL RULES.—

(1) ADJUSTMENT FOR CERTAIN SCHOLARSHIPS AND VETERANS BENEFITS.—The amount of qualified higher education expenses otherwise taken into account under subsection (a) with respect to the education of an individual shall be reduced (before the application of subsection (b)) by the sum of the amounts received with respect to such individual for the taxable year as—

(A) a qualified scholarship which under section 117 is not includable in gross income,

(B) an educational assistance allowance under chapter 30, 31, 32, 34, or 35 of title 38, United States Code,

(C) a payment (other than a gift, bequest, devise, or inheritance within the meaning of section 102(a)) for educational expenses, or attributable to attendance at an eligible educational institution, which is exempt from income taxation by any law of the United States, or

(D) a payment, waiver, or reimbursement of qualified higher education expenses under a qualified tuition program (within the meaning of section 529(b)).

(2) COORDINATION WITH OTHER HIGHER EDUCATION BENEFITS.—The amount of the qualified higher education expenses otherwise taken into account under subsection (a) with respect to the education of an individual shall be reduced (before the application of subsection (b)) by—

(A) the amount of such expenses which are taken into account in determining the credit allowed to the taxpayer or any other person under section 25A with respect to such expenses; and

(B) the amount of such expenses which are taken into account in determining the exclusions under sections 529(c)(3)(B) and 530(d)(2).

(3) NO EXCLUSION FOR MARRIED INDIVIDUALS FILING SEPARATE RETURNS.—If the taxpayer is a married individual (within the meaning of section 7703), this section shall apply only if the taxpayer and his spouse file a joint return for the taxable year.

(4) REGULATIONS.—The Secretary may prescribe such regulations as may be necessary or appropriate to carry out this section, including regulations requiring record keeping and information reporting.

PART IV—TAX EXEMPTION REQUIREMENTS FOR STATE AND LOCAL BONDS

Subpart A—Private Activity Bonds

[Sec. 141]

SEC. 141. PRIVATE ACTIVITY BOND; QUALIFIED BOND.

[Sec. 141(a)]

(a) PRIVATE ACTIVITY BOND.—For purposes of this title, the term "private activity bond" means any bond issued as part of an issue—

(1) which meets—

(A) the private business use test of paragraph (1) of subsection (b), and

(B) the private security or payment test of paragraph (2) of subsection (b), or

(2) which meets the private loan financing test of subsection (c).

[Sec. 141(b)]

(b) PRIVATE BUSINESS TESTS.—

(1) PRIVATE BUSINESS USE TEST.—Except as otherwise provided in this subsection, an issue meets the test of this paragraph if more than 10 percent of the proceeds of the issue are to be used for any private business use.

(2) PRIVATE SECURITY OR PAYMENT TEST.—Except as otherwise provided in this subsection, an issue meets the test of this paragraph if the payment of the principal of, or the interest on, more than 10 percent of the proceeds of such issue is (under the terms of such issue or any underlying arrangement) directly or indirectly—

(A) secured by any interest in—

(i) property used or to be used for a private business use, or

(ii) payments in respect of such property, or

(B) to be derived from payments (whether or not to the issuer) in respect of property, or borrowed money, used or to be used for a private business use.

(3) 5 PERCENT TEST FOR PRIVATE BUSINESS USE NOT RELATED OR DISPROPORTIONATE TO GOVERNMENT USE FINANCED BY THE ISSUE.—

(A) IN GENERAL.—An issue shall be treated as meeting the tests of paragraphs (1) and (2) if such tests would be met if such paragraphs were applied—

(i) by substituting "5 percent" for "10 percent" each place it appears, and

(ii) by taking into account only—

(I) the proceeds of the issue which are to be used for any private business use which is not related to any government use of such proceeds,

(II) the disproportionate related business use proceeds of the issue, and

(III) payments, property, and borrowed money with respect to any use of proceeds described in subclause (I) or (II).

(B) DISPROPORTIONATE RELATED BUSINESS USE PROCEEDS.—For purposes of subparagraph (A), the disproportionate related business use proceeds of an issue is an amount equal to the aggregate of the excesses (determined under the following sentence) for each private business use of the proceeds of an issue which is related to a government use of such proceeds. The excess determined under this sentence is the excess of—

(i) the proceeds of the issue which are to be used for the private business use, over

(ii) the proceeds of the issue which are to be used for the government use to which such private business use relates.

(4) LOWER LIMITATION FOR CERTAIN OUTPUT FACILITIES.—An issue 5 percent or more of the proceeds of which are to be used with respect to any output facility (other than a facility for the

Sec. 141(b)

furnishing of water) shall be treated as meeting the tests of paragraphs (1) and (2) if the nonqualified amount with respect to such issue exceeds the excess of—

(A) $15,000,000, over

(B) the aggregate nonqualified amounts with respect to all prior tax-exempt issues 5 percent or more of the proceeds of which are or will be used with respect to such facility (or any other facility which is part of the same project).

There shall not be taken into account under subparagraph (B) any bond which is not outstanding at the time of the later issue or which is to be redeemed (other than in an advance refunding) from the net proceeds of the later issue.

(5) COORDINATION WITH VOLUME CAP WHERE NONQUALIFIED AMOUNT EXCEEDS $15,000,000.—If the nonqualified amount with respect to an issue—

(A) exceeds $15,000,000, but

(B) does not exceed the amount which would cause a bond which is part of such issue to be treated as a private activity bond without regard to this paragraph,

such bond shall nonetheless be treated as a private activity bond unless the issuer allocates a portion of its volume cap under section 146 to such issue in an amount equal to the excess of such nonqualified amount over $15,000,000.

(6) PRIVATE BUSINESS USE DEFINED.—

(A) IN GENERAL.—For purposes of this subsection, the term "private business use" means use (directly or indirectly) in a trade or business carried on by any person other than a governmental unit. For purposes of the preceding sentence, use as a member of the general public shall not be taken into account.

(B) CLARIFICATION OF TRADE OR BUSINESS.—For purposes of the 1st sentence of subparagraph (A), any activity carried on by a person other than a natural person shall be treated as a trade or business.

(7) GOVERNMENT USE.—The term "government use" means any use other than a private business use.

(8) NONQUALIFIED AMOUNT.—For purposes of this subsection, the term "nonqualified amount" means, with respect to an issue, the lesser of—

(A) the proceeds of such issue which are to be used for any private business use, or

(B) the proceeds of such issue with respect to which there are payments (or property or borrowed money) described in paragraph (2).

(9) EXCEPTION FOR QUALIFIED 501(C)(3) BONDS.—There shall not be taken into account under this subsection or subsection (c) the portion of the proceeds of an issue which (if issued as a separate issue) would be treated as a qualified 501(c)(3) bond if the issuer elects to treat such portion as a qualified 501(c)(3) bond.

[Sec. 141(c)]

(c) PRIVATE LOAN FINANCING TEST.—

(1) IN GENERAL.—An issue meets the test of this subsection if the amount of the proceeds of the issue which are to be used (directly or indirectly) to make or finance loans (other than loans described in paragraph (2)) to persons other than governmental units exceeds the lesser of—

(A) 5 percent of such proceeds, or

(B) $5,000,000.

(2) EXCEPTION FOR TAX ASSESSMENT, ETC., LOANS.—For purposes of paragraph (1), a loan is described in this paragraph if such loan—

(A) enables the borrower to finance any governmental tax or assessment of general application for a specific essential governmental function, or

(B) is a nonpurpose investment (within the meaning of section 148(f)(6)(A)).

* * *

[Sec. 141(e)]

(e) QUALIFIED BOND.—For purposes of this part, the term "qualified bond" means any private activity bond if—

(1) IN GENERAL.—Such bond is—

(A) an exempt facility bond,

(B) a qualified mortgage bond,

(C) a qualified veterans' mortgage bond,

(D) a qualified small issue bond,

(E) a qualified student loan bond,

(F) a qualified redevelopment bond, or

(G) a qualified 501(c)(3) bond.

(2) VOLUME CAP.—Such bond is issued as part of an issue which meets the applicable requirements of section 146, and

(3) OTHER REQUIREMENTS.—Such bond meets the applicable requirements of each subsection of section 147.

[Sec. 142]

SEC. 142. EXEMPT FACILITY BOND.

[Sec. 142(a)]

(a) GENERAL RULE.—For purposes of this part, the term "exempt facility bond" means any bond issued as part of an issue 95 percent or more of the net proceeds of which are to be used to provide—

(1) airports,

(2) docks and wharves,

(3) mass commuting facilities,

(4) facilities for the furnishing of water,

(5) sewage facilities,

(6) solid waste disposal facilities,

(7) qualified residential rental projects,

(8) facilities for the local furnishing of electric energy or gas,

(9) local district heating or cooling facilities,

(10) qualified hazardous waste facilities,

(11) high-speed intercity rail facilities,

(12) environmental enhancements of hydroelectric generating facilities, or

(13) qualified public educational facilities.

[Sec. 142(b)]

(b) SPECIAL EXEMPT FACILITY BOND RULES.—For purposes of subsection (a)—

(1) CERTAIN FACILITIES MUST BE GOVERNMENTALLY OWNED.—

(A) IN GENERAL.—A facility shall be treated as described in paragraph (1), (2), (3), or (12) of subsection (a) only if all of the property to be financed by the net proceeds of the issue is to be owned by a governmental unit.

(B) SAFE HARBOR FOR LEASES AND MANAGEMENT CONTRACTS.—For purposes of subparagraph (A), property leased by a governmental unit shall be treated as owned by such governmental unit if—

(i) the lessee makes an irrevocable election (binding on the lessee and all successors in interest under the lease) not to claim depreciation or an investment credit with respect to such property,

(ii) the lease term (as defined in section 168(i)(3)) is not more than 80 percent of the reasonably expected economic life of the property (as determined under section 147(b)), and

(iii) the lessee has no option to purchase the property other than at fair market value (as of the time such option is exercised).

Rules similar to the rules of the preceding sentence shall apply to management contracts and similar types of operating agreements.

(2) LIMITATION ON OFFICE SPACE.—An office shall not be treated as described in a paragraph of subsection (a) unless—

(A) the office is located on the premises of a facility described in such a paragraph, and

(B) not more than a de minimis amount of the functions to be performed at such office is not directly related to the day-to-day operations at such facility.

[Sec. 142(c)]

(c) AIRPORTS, DOCKS AND WHARVES, MASS COMMUTING FACILITIES AND HIGH-SPEED INTERCITY RAIL FACILITIES.—For purposes of subsection (a)—

(1) STORAGE AND TRAINING FACILITIES.—Storage or training facilities directly related to a facility described in paragraph (1), (2), (3) or (11) of subsection (a) shall be treated as described in the paragraph in which such facility is described.

(2) EXCEPTION FOR CERTAIN PRIVATE FACILITIES.—Property shall not be treated as described in paragraph (1), (2), (3) or (11) of subsection (a) if such property is described in any of the following subparagraphs and is to be used for any private business use (as defined in section 141(b)(6)).

(A) Any lodging facility.

(B) Any retail facility (including food and beverage facilities) in excess of a size necessary to serve passengers and employees at the exempt facility.

(C) Any retail facility (other than parking) for passengers or the general public located outside the exempt facility terminal.

(D) Any office building for individuals who are not employees of a governmental unit or of the operating authority for the exempt facility.

(E) Any industrial park or manufacturing facility.

[Sec. 142(d)]

(d) QUALIFIED RESIDENTIAL RENTAL PROJECT.—For purposes of this section—

(1) IN GENERAL.—The term "qualified residential rental project" means any project for residential rental property if, at all times during the qualified project period, such project meets the requirements of subparagraph (A) or (B), whichever is elected by the issuer at the time of the issuance of the issue with respect to such project:

(A) 20-50 TEST.—The project meets the requirements of this subparagraph if 20 percent or more of the residential units in such project are occupied by individuals whose income is 50 percent or less of area median gross income.

(B) 40-60 TEST.—The project meets the requirements of this subparagraph if 40 percent or more of the residential units in such project are occupied by individuals whose income is 60 percent or less of area median gross income.

For purposes of this paragraph, any property shall not be treated as failing to be residential rental property merely because part of the building in which such property is located is used for purposes other than residential rental purposes.

* * *

[Sec. 142(k)]

(k) QUALIFIED PUBLIC EDUCATIONAL FACILITIES.—

(1) IN GENERAL.—For purposes of subsection (a)(13), the term "qualified public educational facility" means any school facility which is—

(A) part of a public elementary school or a public secondary school, and

(B) owned by a private, for-profit corporation pursuant to a public-private partnership agreement with a State or local educational agency described in paragraph (2).

(2) PUBLIC-PRIVATE PARTNERSHIP AGREEMENT DESCRIBED.—A public-private partnership agreement is described in this paragraph if it is an agreement—

(A) under which the corporation agrees—

(i) to do 1 or more of the following: construct, rehabilitate, refurbish, or equip a school facility, and

(ii) at the end of the term of the agreement, to transfer the school facility to such agency for no additional consideration, and

(B) the term of which does not exceed the term of the issue to be used to provide the school facility.

(3) SCHOOL FACILITY.—For purposes of this subsection, the term "school facility" means—

(A) any school building,

(B) any functionally related and subordinate facility and land with respect to such building, including any stadium or other facility primarily used for school events, and

(C) any property, to which section 168 applies (or would apply but for section 179), for use in a facility described in subparagraph (A) or (B).

(4) PUBLIC SCHOOLS.—For purposes of this subsection, the terms "elementary school" and "secondary school" have the meanings given such terms by section 14101 of the Elementary and Secondary Education Act of 1965 (20 U.S.C. 8801), as in effect on the date of the enactment of this subsection.

(5) ANNUAL AGGREGATE FACE AMOUNT OF TAX-EXEMPT FINANCING.—

(A) IN GENERAL.—An issue shall not be treated as an issue described in subsection (a)(13) if the aggregate face amount of bonds issued by the State pursuant thereto (when added to the aggregate face amount of bonds previously so issued during the calendar year) exceeds an amount equal to the greater of—

(i) $10 multiplied by the State population, or

(ii) $5,000,000.

(B) ALLOCATION RULES.—

(i) IN GENERAL.—Except as otherwise provided in this subparagraph, the State may allocate the amount described in subparagraph (A) for any calendar year in such manner as the State determines appropriate.

(ii) RULES FOR CARRYFORWARD OF UNUSED LIMITATION.—A State may elect to carry forward an unused limitation for any calendar year for 3 calendar years following the calendar year in which the unused limitation arose under rules similar to the rules of section 146(f), except that the only purpose for which the carryforward may be elected is the issuance of exempt facility bonds described in subsection (a)(13).

[Sec. 144]

SEC. 144. QUALIFIED SMALL ISSUE BOND; QUALIFIED STUDENT LOAN BOND; QUALIFIED REDEVELOPMENT BOND.

[Sec. 144(a)]

(a) QUALIFIED SMALL ISSUE BOND.—

(1) IN GENERAL.—For purposes of this part, the term "qualified small issue bond" means any bond issued as part of an issue the aggregate authorized face amount of which is $1,000,000 or less and 95 percent or more of the net proceeds of which are to be used—

(A) for the acquisition, construction, reconstruction, or improvement of land or property of a character subject to the allowance for depreciation, or

(B) to redeem part or all of a prior issue which was issued for purposes described in subparagraph (A) or this subparagraph.

(2) CERTAIN PRIOR ISSUES TAKEN INTO ACCOUNT.—If—

(A) the proceeds of 2 or more issues of bonds (whether or not the issuer of each such issue is the same) are or will be used primarily with respect to facilities located in the same incorporated municipality or located in the same county (but not in any incorporated municipality),

(B) the principal user of such facilities is or will be the same person or 2 or more related persons, and

(C) but for this paragraph, paragraph (1) (or the corresponding provision of prior law) would apply to each such issue,

then, for purposes of paragraph (1), in determining the aggregate face amount of any later issue there shall be taken into account the aggregate face amount of tax-exempt bonds issued under all prior such issues and outstanding at the time of such later issue (not including as outstanding any bond which is to be redeemed (other than in an advance refunding) from the net proceeds of the later issue).

(3) RELATED PERSONS.—For purposes of this subsection, a person is a related person to another person if—

(A) the relationship between such persons would result in a disallowance of losses under section 267 or 707(b), or

(B) such persons are members of the same controlled group of corporations (as defined in section 1563(a), except that "more than 50 percent" shall be substituted for "at least 80 percent" each place it appears therein).

(4) $10,000,000 LIMIT IN CERTAIN CASES.—

(A) IN GENERAL.—At the election of the issuer with respect to any issue, this subsection shall be applied—

(i) by substituting "$10,000,000" for "$1,000,000" in paragraph (1), and

(ii) in determining the aggregate face amount of such issue, by taking into account not only the amount described in paragraph (2), but also the aggregate amount of capital expenditures with respect to facilities described in subparagraph (B) paid or incurred during the 6-year period beginning 3 years before the date of such issue and ending 3 years after such date (and financed otherwise than out of the proceeds of outstanding tax-exempt issues to which paragraph (1) (or the corresponding provision of prior law) applied), as if the aggregate amount of such capital expenditures constituted the face amount of a prior outstanding issue described in paragraph (2).

(B) FACILITIES TAKEN INTO ACCOUNT.—For purposes of subparagraph (A)(ii), the facilities described in this subparagraph are facilities—

(i) located in the same incorporated municipality or located in the same county (but not in any incorporated municipality), and

(ii) the principal user of which is or will be the same person or 2 or more related persons.

For purposes of clause (i), the determination of whether or not facilities are located in the same governmental unit shall be made as of the date of issue of the issue in question.

(C) CERTAIN CAPITAL EXPENDITURES NOT TAKEN INTO ACCOUNT.—For purposes of subparagraph (A)(ii), any capital expenditure—

(i) to replace property destroyed or damaged by fire, storm, or other casualty, to the extent of the fair market value of the property replaced,

(ii) required by a change made after the date of issue of the issue in question in a Federal or State law or local ordinance of general application or required by a change made after such date in rules and regulations of general application issued under such a law or ordinance,

(iii) required by circumstances which could not be reasonably foreseen on such date of issue or arising out of a mistake of law or fact (but the aggregate amount of expenditures not taken into account under this clause with respect to any issue shall not exceed $1,000,000), or

(iv) described in clause (i) or (ii) of section 41(b)(2)(A) for which a deduction was allowed under section 174(a),

shall not be taken into account.

(D) LIMITATION ON LOSS OF TAX EXEMPTION.—In applying subparagraph (A)(ii) with respect to capital expenditures made after the date of any issue, no bond issued as a part of such issue shall cease to be treated as a qualified small issue bond by reason of any such expenditure for any period before the date on which such expenditure is paid or incurred.

(E) CERTAIN REFINANCING ISSUES.—In the case of any issue described in paragraph (1)(B), an election may be made under subparagraph (A) of this paragraph only if all of the prior issues being redeemed are issues to which paragraph (1) (or the corresponding provision of prior law)

Sec. 144(a)

applied. In applying subparagraph (A)(ii) with respect to such a refinancing issue, capital expenditures shall be taken into account only for purposes of determining whether the prior issues being redeemed qualified (and would have continued to qualify) under paragraph (1) (or the corresponding provision of prior law).

(F) AGGREGATE AMOUNT OF CAPITAL EXPENDITURES WHERE THERE IS URBAN DEVELOPMENT ACTION GRANT.—In the case of any issue 95 percent or more of the net proceeds of which are to be used to provide facilities with respect to which an urban development action grant has been made under section 119 of the Housing and Community Development Act of 1974, capital expenditures of not to exceed $10,000,000 shall not be taken into account for purposes of applying subparagraph (A)(ii).

(5) ISSUES FOR RESIDENTIAL PURPOSES.—This subsection shall not apply to any bond issued as part of an issue 5 percent or more of the net proceeds of which are to be used directly or indirectly to provide residential real property for family units.

(6) LIMITATIONS ON TREATMENT OF BONDS AS PART OF THE SAME ISSUE.—

(A) IN GENERAL.—For purposes of this subsection, separate lots of bonds which (but for this subparagraph) would be treated as part of the same issue shall be treated as separate issues unless the proceeds of such lots are to be used with respect to 2 or more facilities—

(i) which are located in more than 1 State, or

(ii) which have, or will have, as the same principal user the same person or related persons.

(B) FRANCHISES.—For purposes of subparagraph (A), a person (other than a governmental unit) shall be considered a principal user of a facility if such person (or a group of related persons which includes such person)—

(i) guarantees, arranges, participates in, or assists with the issuance (or pays any portion of the cost of issuance) of any bond the proceeds of which are to be used to finance or refinance such facility, and

(ii) provides any property, or any franchise, trademark, or trade name (within the meaning of section 1253), which is to be used in connection with such facility.

(7) SUBSECTION NOT TO APPLY IF BONDS ISSUED WITH CERTAIN OTHER TAX-EXEMPT BONDS.—This subsection shall not apply to any bond issued as part of an issue (other than an issue to which paragraph (4) applies) if the interest on any other bond which is part of such issue is excluded from gross income under any provision of law other than this subsection.

(8) RESTRICTIONS ON FINANCING CERTAIN FACILITIES.—This subsection shall not apply to an issue if—

(A) more than 25 percent of the net proceeds of the issue are to be used to provide a facility the primary purpose of which is one of the following: retail food and beverage services, automobile sales or service, or the provision of recreation or entertainment; or

(B) any portion of the proceeds of the issue is to be used to provide the following: any private or commercial golf course, country club, massage parlor, tennis club, skating facility (including roller skating, skateboard, and ice skating), racquet sports facility (including any handball or racquetball court), hot tub facility, suntan facility, or racetrack.

(9) AGGREGATION OF ISSUES WITH RESPECT TO SINGLE PROJECT.—For purposes of this subsection, 2 or more issues part or all of the net proceeds of which are to be used with respect to a single building, an enclosed shopping mall, or a strip of offices, stores, or warehouses using substantial common facilities shall be treated as 1 issue (and any person who is a principal user with respect to any of such issues shall be treated as a principal user with respect to the aggregated issue).

(10) AGGREGATE LIMIT PER TAXPAYER.—

(A) IN GENERAL.—This subsection shall not apply to any issue if the aggregate authorized face amount of such issue allocated to any test-period beneficiary (when increased by the outstanding tax-exempt facility-related bonds of such beneficiary) exceeds $40,000,000.

(B) OUTSTANDING TAX-EXEMPT FACILITY-RELATED BONDS.—

(i) IN GENERAL.—For purposes of applying subparagraph (A) with respect to any issue, the outstanding tax-exempt facility-related bonds of any person who is a test-period beneficiary with respect to such issue is the aggregate amount of tax-exempt bonds referred to in clause (ii)—

(I) which are allocated to such beneficiary, and

(II) which are outstanding at the time of such later issue (not including as outstanding any bond which is to be redeemed (other than in an advance refunding) from the net proceeds of the later issue).

(ii) BONDS TAKEN INTO ACCOUNT.—For purposes of clause (i), the bonds referred to in this clause are—

(I) exempt facility bonds, qualified small issue bonds, and qualified redevelopment bonds, and

(II) industrial development bonds (as defined in section 103(b)(2), as in effect on the day before the date of the enactment of the Tax Reform Act of 1986) to which section 141(a) does not apply.

(C) ALLOCATION OF FACE AMOUNT OF ISSUE.—

(i) IN GENERAL.—Except as otherwise provided in regulations, the portion of the face amount of an issue allocated to any test-period beneficiary of a facility financed by the proceeds of such issue (other than an owner of such facility) is an amount which bears the same relationship to the entire face amount of such issue as the portion of such facility used by such beneficiary bears to the entire facility.

(ii) OWNERS.—Except as otherwise provided in regulations, the portion of the face amount of an issue allocated to any test-period beneficiary who is an owner of a facility financed by the proceeds of such issue is an amount which bears the same relationship to the entire face amount of such issue as the portion of such facility owned by such beneficiary bears to the entire facility.

(D) TEST-PERIOD BENEFICIARY.—For purposes of this paragraph, except as provided in regulations, the term "test-period beneficiary" means any person who is an owner or a principal user of facilities being financed by the issue at any time during the 3-year period beginning on the later of—

(i) the date such facilities were placed in service, or

(ii) the date of issue.

(E) TREATMENT OF RELATED PERSONS.—For purposes of this paragraph, all persons who are related (within the meaning of paragraph (3)) to each other shall be treated as 1 person.

(11) LIMITATION ON ACQUISITION OF DEPRECIABLE FARM PROPERTY.—

(A) IN GENERAL.—This subsection shall not apply to any issue if more than $250,000 of the net proceeds of such issue are to be used to provide depreciable farm property with respect to which the principal user is or will be the same person or 2 or more related persons.

(B) DEPRECIABLE FARM PROPERTY.—For purposes of this paragraph, the term "depreciable farm property" means property of a character subject to the allowance for depreciation which is to be used in a trade or business of farming.

(C) PRIOR ISSUES TAKEN INTO ACCOUNT.—In determining the amount of proceeds of an issue to be used as described in subparagraph (A), there shall be taken into account the aggregate amount of each prior issue to which paragraph (1) (or the corresponding provisions of prior law) applied which were or will be so used.

(12) TERMINATION DATES.—

(A) IN GENERAL.—This subsection shall not apply to—

(i) any bond (other than a bond described in clause (ii)) issued after December 31, 1986, or

(ii) any bond (or series of bonds) issued to refund a bond issued on or before such date unless—

(I) the average maturity date of the issue of which the refunding bond is a part is not later than the average maturity date of the bonds to be refunded by such issue,

(II) the amount of the refunding bond does not exceed the outstanding amount of the refunded bond, and

(III) the net proceeds of the refunding bond are used to redeem the refunded bond not later than 90 days after the date of the issuance of the refunding bond.

For purposes of clause (ii)(I), average maturity shall be determined in accordance with section 147(b)(2)(A).

(B) BONDS ISSUED TO FINANCE MANUFACTURING FACILITIES AND FARM PROPERTY.—Subparagraph (A) shall not apply to any bond issued as part of an issue 95 percent or more of the net proceeds of which are to be used to provide—

(i) any manufacturing facility, or

(ii) any land or property in accordance with section 147(c)(2).

(C) MANUFACTURING FACILITY.—For purposes of this paragraph, the term "manufacturing facility" means any facility which is used in the manufacturing or production of tangible personal property (including the processing resulting in a change in the condition of such property). A rule similar to the rule of section 142(b)(2) shall apply for purposes of the preceding sentence. For purposes of the 1st sentence of this subparagraph, the term "manufacturing facility" includes facilities which are directly related and ancillary to a manufacturing facility (determined without regard to this sentence) if—

(i) such facilities are located on the same site as the manufacturing facility, and

(ii) not more than 25 percent of the net proceeds of the issue are used to provide such facilities.

* * *

[Sec. 145]

SEC. 145. QUALIFIED 501(c)(3) BOND.

[Sec. 145(a)]

(a) IN GENERAL.—For purposes of this part, except as otherwise provided in this section, the term "qualified 501(c)(3) bond" means any private activity bond issued as part of an issue if—

(1) all property which is to be provided by the net proceeds of the issue is to be owned by a 501(c)(3) organization or a governmental unit, and

(2) such bond would not be a private activity bond if—

(A) 501(c)(3) organizations were treated as governmental units with respect to their activities which do not constitute unrelated trades or businesses, determined by applying section 513(a), and

(B) paragraphs (1) and (2) of section 141(b) were applied by substituting "5 percent" for "10 percent" each place it appears and by substituting "net proceeds" for "proceeds" each place it appears.

[Sec. 145(b)]

(b) $150,000,000 LIMITATION ON BONDS OTHER THAN HOSPITAL BONDS.—

(1) IN GENERAL.—A bond (other than a qualified hospital bond) shall not be treated as a qualified 501(c)(3) bond if the aggregate authorized face amount of the issue (of which such bond is a part) allocated to any 501(c)(3) organization which is a test-period beneficiary (when increased by the outstanding tax-exempt nonhospital bonds of such organization) exceeds $150,000,000.

* * *

[*Caution: As provided in Section 146(d)(2), the dollar amounts set forth in Section 146(d)(1) are adjusted for taxable years after 2002 to reflect increases in the Consumer Price Index. The adjusted amounts applicable to taxable years beginning in 2003 are provided beginning at page ix.*]

[Sec. 146]

SEC. 146. VOLUME CAP.

[Sec. 146(a)]

(a) GENERAL RULE.—A private activity bond issued as part of an issue meets the requirements of this section if the aggregate face amount of the private activity bonds issued pursuant to such issue, when added to the aggregate face amount of tax-exempt private activity bonds previously issued by the issuing authority during the calendar year, does not exceed such authority's volume cap for such calendar year.

(b) VOLUME CAP FOR STATE AGENCIES.—For purposes of this section—

(1) IN GENERAL.—The volume cap for any agency of the State authorized to issue tax-exempt private activity bonds for any calendar year shall be 50 percent of the State ceiling for such calendar year.

(2) SPECIAL RULE WHERE STATE HAS MORE THAN 1 AGENCY.—If more than 1 agency of the State is authorized to issue tax-exempt private activity bonds, all such agencies shall be treated as a single agency.

(c) VOLUME CAP FOR OTHER ISSUERS.—For purposes of this section—

(1) IN GENERAL.—The volume cap for any issuing authority (other than a State agency) for any calendar year shall be an amount which bears the same ratio to 50 percent of the State ceiling for such calendar year as—

(A) the population of the jurisdiction of such issuing authority, bears to

(B) the population of the entire State.

(2) OVERLAPPING JURISDICTIONS.—For purposes of paragraph (1)(A), if an area is within the jurisdiction of 2 or more governmental units, such area shall be treated as only within the jurisdiction of the unit having jurisdiction over the smallest geographical area unless such unit agrees to surrender all or part of such jurisdiction for such calendar year to the unit with overlapping jurisdiction which has the next smallest geographical area.

(d) STATE CEILING.—For purposes of this section.—

(1) IN GENERAL.—The State ceiling applicable to any State for any calendar year shall be the greater of—

(A) an amount equal to $75 ($62.50 in the case of calendar year 2001) multiplied by the State population, or

(B) $225,000,000 ($187,500,000 in the case of calendar year 2001).

(2) COST-OF-LIVING ADJUSTMENT.—In the case of a calendar year after 2002, each of the dollar amounts contained in paragraph (1) shall be increased by an amount equal to—

(A) such dollar amount, multiplied by

(B) the cost-of-living adjustment determined under section 1(f)(3) for such calendar year by substituting "calendar year 2001" for "calendar year 1992" in subparagraph (B) thereof.

If any increase determined under the preceding sentence is not a multiple of $5 ($5,000 in the case of the dollar amount in paragraph (1)(B)), such increase shall be rounded to the nearest multiple thereof.

(3) SPECIAL RULE FOR STATES WITH CONSTITUTIONAL HOME RULE CITIES.—For purposes of this section—

(A) IN GENERAL.—The volume cap for any constitutional home rule city for any calendar year shall be determined under paragraph (1) of subsection (c) by substituting "100 percent" for "50 percent".

(B) COORDINATION WITH OTHER ALLOCATIONS.—In the case of any State which contains 1 or more constitutional home rule cities, for purposes of applying subsections (b) and (c) with respect to issuing authorities in such State other than constitutional home rule cities, the State ceiling for any calendar year shall be reduced by the aggregate volume caps determined for such year for all constitutional home rule cities in such State.

(C) CONSTITUTIONAL HOME RULE CITY.—For purposes of this section, the term "constitutional home rule city" means, with respect to any calendar year, any political subdivision of a State which, under a State constitution which was adopted in 1970 and effective on July 1, 1971, had home rule powers on the 1st day of the calendar year.

* * *

[Sec. 146(e)]

(e) STATE MAY PROVIDE FOR DIFFERENT ALLOCATION.—For purposes of this section—

(1) IN GENERAL.—Except as provided in paragraph (3), a State may, by law provide a different formula for allocating the State ceiling among the governmental units (or other authorities) in such State having authority to issue tax-exempt private activity bonds.

(2) INTERIM AUTHORITY FOR GOVERNOR.—

(A) IN GENERAL.—Except as otherwise provided in paragraph (3), the Governor of any State may proclaim a different formula for allocating the State ceiling among the governmental units (or other authorities) in such State having authority to issue private activity bonds.

(B) TERMINATION OF AUTHORITY.—The authority provided in subparagraph (A) shall not apply to bonds issued after the earlier of—

(i) the last day of the 1st calendar year after 1986 during which the legislature of the State met in regular session, or

(ii) the effective date of any State legislation with respect to the allocation of the State ceiling.

(3) STATE MAY NOT ALTER ALLOCATION TO CONSTITUTIONAL HOME RULE CITIES.—Except as otherwise provided in a State constitutional amendment (or law changing the home rule provision adopted in the manner provided by the State constitution), the authority provided in this subsection shall not apply to that portion of the State ceiling which is allocated to any constitutional home rule city in the State unless such city agrees to such different allocation.

* * *

Subpart B—Requirements Applicable to All State and Local Bonds

[Sec. 148]

SEC. 148. ARBITRAGE.

[Sec. 148(a)]

(a) ARBITRAGE BOND DEFINED.—For purposes of section 103, the term "arbitrage bond" means any bond issued as part of an issue any portion of the proceeds of which are reasonably expected (at the time of issuance of the bond) to be used directly or indirectly—

(1) to acquire higher yielding investments, or

(2) to replace funds which were used directly or indirectly to acquire higher yielding investments.

For purposes of this subsection, a bond shall be treated as an arbitrage bond if the issuer intentionally uses any portion of the proceeds of the issue of which such bond is a part in a manner described in paragraph (1) or (2).

[Sec. 148(b)]

(b) HIGHER YIELDING INVESTMENTS.—For purposes of this section—

(1) IN GENERAL.—The term "higher yielding investments" means any investment property which produces a yield over the term of the issue which is materially higher than the yield on the issue.

(2) INVESTMENT PROPERTY.—The term "investment property" means—

(A) any security (within the meaning of section 165(g)(2)(A) or (B)),

(B) any obligation,

(C) any annuity contract,

(D) any investment-type property, or

(E) in the case of a bond other than a private activity bond, any residential rental property for family units which is not located within the jurisdiction of the issuer and which is not acquired to implement a court ordered or approved housing desegregation plan.

* * *

[Sec. 149]

SEC. 149. BONDS MUST BE REGISTERED TO BE TAX EXEMPT; OTHER REQUIREMENTS.

[Sec. 149(a)]

(a) BONDS MUST BE REGISTERED TO BE TAX EXEMPT.—

(1) GENERAL RULE.—Nothing in section 103(a) or in any other provision of law shall be construed to provide an exemption from Federal income tax for interest on any registration-required bond unless such bond is in registered form.

(2) REGISTRATION-REQUIRED BOND.—For purposes of paragraph (1), the term "registration-required bond" means any bond other than a bond which—

(A) is not of a type offered to the public,

(B) has a maturity (at issue) of not more than 1 year, or

(C) is described in section 163(f)(2)(B).

(3) SPECIAL RULES.—

(A) BOOK ENTRIES PERMITTED.—For purposes of paragraph (1), a book entry bond shall be treated as in registered form if the right to the principal of, and stated interest on, such bond may be transferred only through a book entry consistent with regulations prescribed by the Secretary.

(B) NOMINEES.—The Secretary shall prescribe such regulations as may be necessary to carry out the purpose of paragraph (1) where there is a nominee or chain of nominees.

* * *

Subpart C—Definitions and Special Rules

[Sec. 150]

SEC. 150. DEFINITIONS AND SPECIAL RULES.

[Sec. 150(a)]

(a) GENERAL RULE.—For purposes of this part—

(1) BOND.—The term "bond" includes any obligation.

(2) GOVERNMENTAL UNIT NOT TO INCLUDE FEDERAL GOVERNNMENT.—The term "governmental unit" does not include the United States or any agency or instrumentality thereof.

(3) NET PROCEEDS.—The term "net proceeds" means, with respect to any issue, the proceeds of such issue reduced by amounts in a reasonably required reserve or replacement fund.

(4) 501(c)(3) ORGANIZATION.—The term "501(c)(3) organization" means any organization described in section 501(c)(3) and exempt from tax under section 501(a).

(5) OWNERSHIP OF PROPERTY.—Property shall be treated as owned by a governmental unit if it is owned on behalf of such unit.

(6) TAX-EXEMPT BOND.—The term "tax-exempt" means, with respect to any bond (or issue), that the interest on such bond (or on the bonds issued as part of such issue) is excluded from gross income.

* * *

PART V—DEDUCTIONS FOR PERSONAL EXEMPTIONS

[Caution: Pursuant to Section 151(d)(4), the exemption amount provided in Section 151(d)(1) and the threshold amounts provided in Section 151(d)(3)(C) are adjusted for taxable years beginning after 1989 and 1991, respectively, to reflect increases in the Consumer Price Index. The amounts applicable to taxable years beginning in 2003 are provided beginning at page ix.]

[Sec. 151]

SEC. 151. ALLOWANCE OF DEDUCTIONS FOR PERSONAL EXEMPTIONS.

[Sec. 151(a)]

(a) ALLOWANCE OF DEDUCTIONS.—In the case of an individual, the exemptions provided by this section shall be allowed as deductions in computing taxable income.

[Sec. 151(b)]

(b) TAXPAYER AND SPOUSE.—An exemption of the exemption amount for the taxpayer; and an additional exemption of the exemption amount for the spouse of the taxpayer if a joint return is not made by the taxpayer and his spouse, and if the spouse, for the calendar year in which the taxable year of the taxpayer begins, has no gross income and is not the dependent of another taxpayer.

[Sec. 151(c)]

(c) ADDITIONAL EXEMPTION FOR DEPENDENTS.—

(1) IN GENERAL.—An exemption of the exemption amount for each dependent (as defined in section 152)—

(A) whose gross income for the calendar year in which the taxable year of the taxpayer begins is less than the exemption amount, or

(B) who is a child of the taxpayer and who (i) has not attained the age of 19 at the close of the calendar year in which the taxable year of the taxpayer begins, or (ii) is a student who has not attained the age of 24 at the close of such calendar year.

(2) EXEMPTION DENIED IN CASE OF CERTAIN MARRIED DEPENDENTS.—No exemption shall be allowed under this subsection for any dependent who has made a joint return with his spouse under section 6013 for the taxable year beginning in the calendar year in which the taxable year of the taxpayer begins.

(3) CHILD DEFINED.—For purposes of paragraph (1) (B), the term "child" means an individual who (within the meaning of section 152) is a son, stepson, daughter, or stepdaughter of the taxpayer.

(4) STUDENT DEFINED.—For purposes of paragraph (1) (B) (ii), the term "student" means an individual who during each of 5 calendar months during the calendar year in which the taxable year of the taxpayer begins—

(A) is a full-time student at an educational organization described in section 170(b)(1)(A)(ii); or

(B) is pursuing a full-time course of institutional on-farm training under the supervision of an accredited agent of an educational organization described in section 170(b)(1)(A)(ii) or of a State or political subdivision of a State.

(5) CERTAIN INCOME OF HANDICAPPED DEPENDENTS NOT TAKEN INTO ACCOUNT.—

(A) IN GENERAL.—For purposes of paragraph (1)(A), the gross income of an individual who is permanently and totally disabled shall not include income attributable to services performed by the individual at a sheltered workshop if—

(i) the availability of medical care at such workshop is the principal reason for his presence there, and

(ii) the income arises solely from activities at such workshop which are incident to such medical care.

(B) SHELTERED WORKSHOP DEFINED.—For purposes of subparagraph (A), the term "sheltered workshop" means a school—

(i) which provides special instruction or training designed to alleviate the disability of the individual, and

(ii) which is operated by—

Sec. 151(c)

(I) an organization described in section 501(c)(3) and exempt from tax under section 501(a), or

(II) a State, a possession of the United States, any political subdivision of any of the foregoing, the United States, or the District of Columbia.

(C) PERMANENT AND TOTAL DISABILITY DEFINED.—An individual shall be treated as permanently and totally disabled for purposes of this paragraph if such individual would be so treated under paragraph (3) of section 22(e).

(6) TREATMENT OF MISSING CHILDREN.—

(A) IN GENERAL.—Solely for the purposes referred to in subparagraph (B), a child of the taxpayer—

(i) who is presumed by law enforcement authorities to have been kidnapped by someone who is not a member of the family of such child or the taxpayer, and

(ii) who was (without regard to this paragraph) the dependent of the taxpayer for the portion of the taxable year before the date of the kidnapping,

shall be treated as a dependent of the taxpayer for all taxable years ending during the period that the child is kidnapped.

(B) PURPOSES.—Subparagraph (A) shall apply solely for purposes of determining—

(i) the deduction under this section,

(ii) the credit under section 24 (relating to child tax credit), and

(iii) whether an individual is a surviving spouse or a head of a household (as such terms are defined in section 2).

(C) COMPARABLE TREATMENT FOR PRINCIPAL PLACE OF ABODE REQUIREMENTS.—An individual—

(i) who is presumed by law enforcement authorities to have been kidnapped by someone who is not a member of the family of such individual or the taxpayer, and

(ii) who had, for the taxable year in which the kidnapping occurred, the same principal place of abode as the taxpayer for more than one-half of the portion of such year before the date of the kidnapping,

shall be treated as meeting the principal place of abode requirements of section 2(a)(1)(B), section 2(b)(1)(A), and section 32(c)(3)(A)(ii) with respect to a taxpayer for all taxable years ending during the period that the individual is kidnapped.

(D) TERMINATION OF TREATMENT.—Subparagraphs (A) and (C) shall cease to apply as of the first taxable year of the taxpayer beginning after the calendar year in which there is a determination that the child is dead (or, if earlier, in which the child would have attained age 18).

[Sec. 151(d)]

(d) EXEMPTION AMOUNT.—For purposes of this section—

(1) IN GENERAL.—Except as otherwise provided in this subsection, the term "exemption amount" means $2,000.

(2) EXEMPTION AMOUNT DISALLOWED IN CASE OF CERTAIN DEPENDENTS.—In the case of an individual with respect to whom a deduction under this section is allowable to another taxpayer for a taxable year beginning in the calendar year in which the individual's taxable year begins, the exemption amount applicable to such individual for such individual's taxable year shall be zero.

(3) PHASEOUT.—

(A) IN GENERAL.—In the case of any taxpayer whose adjusted gross income for the taxable year exceeds the threshold amount, the exemption amount shall be reduced by the applicable percentage.

(B) APPLICABLE PERCENTAGE.—For purposes of subparagraph (A), the term "applicable percentage" means 2 percentage points for each $2,500 (or fraction thereof) by which the taxpayer's adjusted gross income for the taxable year exceeds the threshold amount. In the case of a married individual filing a separate return, the preceding sentence shall be applied by substituting "$1,250" for "$2,500". In no event shall the applicable percentage exceed 100 percent.

Sec. 151(d)

(C) THRESHOLD AMOUNT.—For purposes of this paragraph, the term "threshold amount" means—

(i) $150,000 in the case of a joint return or a surviving spouse (as defined in section 2(a)),

(ii) $125,000 in the case of a head of a household (as defined in section 2(b),

(iii) $100,000 in the case of an individual who is not married and who is not a surviving spouse or head of a household, and

(iv) $75,000 in the case of a married individual filing a separate return.

For purposes of this paragraph, marital status shall be determined under section 7703.

(D) COORDINATION WITH OTHER PROVISIONS.—The provisions of this paragraph shall not apply for purposes of determining whether a deduction under this section with respect to any individual is allowable to another taxpayer for any taxable year.

[*Caution: Code Sec. 151(d)(3)(E)-(F), below, as added by P.L. 107-16, applies to tax years beginning after December 31, 2005.*]

(E) REDUCTION OF PHASEOUT.—

(i) IN GENERAL.—In the case of taxable years beginning after December 31, 2005, and before January 1, 2010, the reduction under subparagraph (A) shall be equal to the applicable fraction of the amount which would (but for this subparagraph) be the amount of such reduction.

(ii) APPLICABLE FRACTION.—For purposes of clause (i), the applicable fraction shall be determined in accordance with the following table:

For taxable years beginning in calendar year—	*The applicable fraction is—*
2006 and 2007	2/3
2008 and 2009	1/3

(F) TERMINATION.—This paragraph shall not apply to any taxable year beginning after December 31, 2009.

(4) INFLATION ADJUSTMENTS.—

(A) ADJUSTMENT TO BASIC AMOUNT OF EXEMPTION.—In the case of any taxable year beginning in a calendar year after 1989, the dollar amount contained in paragraph (1) shall be increased by an amount equal to—

(i) such dollar amount, multiplied by

(ii) the cost-of-living adjustment determined under section 1(f)(3) for the calendar year in which the taxable year begins, by substituting "calendar year 1988" for "calendar year 1992" in subparagraph (B) thereof.

(B) ADJUSTMENT TO THRESHOLD AMOUNTS FOR YEARS AFTER 1991.—In the case of any taxable year beginning in a calendar year after 1991, each dollar amount contained in paragraph (3)(C) shall be increased by an amount equal to—

(i) such dollar amount, multiplied by

(ii) the cost-of-living adjustment determined under section 1(f)(3) for the calendar year in which the taxable year begins, by substituting "calendar year 1990" for "calendar year 1992" in subparagraph (B) thereof.

[Sec. 151(e)]

(e) IDENTIFYING INFORMATION REQUIRED.—No exemption shall be allowed under this section with respect to any individual unless the TIN of such individual is included on the return claiming the exemption.

Sec. 151(e)

SEC. 152. DEPENDENT DEFINED.

[Sec. 152(a)]

(a) GENERAL DEFINITION.—For purposes of this subtitle, the term "dependent" means any of the following individuals over half of whose support, for the calendar year in which the taxable year of the taxpayer begins, was received from the taxpayer (or is treated under subsection (c) or (e) as received from the taxpayer):

(1) A son or daughter of the taxpayer, or a descendant of either,

(2) A stepson or stepdaughter of the taxpayer,

(3) A brother, sister, stepbrother, or stepsister of the taxpayer,

(4) The father or mother of the taxpayer, or an ancester of either,

(5) A stepfather or stepmother of the taxpayer,

(6) A son or daughter of a brother or sister of the taxpayer,

(7) A brother or sister of the father or mother of the taxpayer,

(8) A son-in-law, daughter-in-law, father-in-law, mother-in-law, brother-in-law, or sister-in-law of the taxpayer, or

(9) An individual (other than an individual who at any time during the taxable year was the spouse, determined without regard to section 7703, of the taxpayer) who, for the taxable year of the taxpayer, has as his principal place of abode the home of the taxpayer and is a member of the taxpayer's household.

[Sec. 152(b)]

(b) RULES RELATING TO GENERAL DEFINITION.—For purposes of this section—

(1) The terms "brother" and "sister" include a brother or sister by the halfblood.

(2) In determining whether any of the relationships specified in subsection (a) or paragraph (1) of this subsection exists, a legally adopted child of an individual (and a child who is a member of an individual's household, if placed with such individual by an authorized placement agency for legal adoption by such individual), or a foster child of an individual (if such child satisfies the requirements of subsection (a)(9) with respect to such individual), shall be treated as a child of such individual by blood.

(3) The term "dependent" does not include any individual who is not a citizen or national of the United States unless such individual is a resident of the United States or of a country contiguous to the United States. The preceding sentence shall not exclude from the definition of "dependent" any child of the taxpayer legally adopted by him, if, for the taxable year of the taxpayer, the child has as his principal place of abode the home of the taxpayer and is a member of the taxpayer's household, and if the taxpayer is a citizen or national of the United States.

(4) A payment to a wife which is includible in the gross income of the wife under section 71 or 682 shall not be treated as a payment by her husband for the support of any dependent.

(5) An individual is not a member of the taxpayer's household if at any time during the taxable year of the taxpayer the relationship between such individual and the taxpayer is in violation of local law.

[Sec. 152(c)]

(c) MULTIPLE SUPPORT AGREEMENTS.—For purposes of subsection (a), over half of the support of an individual for a calendar year shall be treated as received from the taxpayer if—

(1) no one person contributed over half of such support;

(2) over half of such support was received from persons each of whom, but for the fact that he did not contribute over half of such support, would have been entitled to claim such individual as a dependent for a taxable year beginning in such calendar year;

(3) the taxpayer contributed over 10 percent of such support; and

(4) each person described in paragraph (2) (other than the taxpayer) who contributed over 10 percent of such support files a written declaration (in such manner and form as the Secretary may by

regulations prescribe) that he will not claim such individual as a dependent for any taxable year beginning in such calendar year.

[Sec. 152(d)]

(d) SPECIAL SUPPORT TEST IN CASE OF STUDENTS.—For purposes of subsection (a), in the case of any individual who is—

(1) a son, stepson, daughter, or stepdaughter of the taxpayer (within the meaning of this section), and

(2) a student (within the meaning of section 151(c)(4)),

amounts received as scholarships for study at an educational organization described in section 170(b)(1)(A)(ii) shall not be taken into account in determining whether such individual received more than half of his support from the taxpayer.

[Sec. 152(e)]

(e) SUPPORT TEST IN CASE OF CHILD OF DIVORCED PARENTS, ETC.—

(1) CUSTODIAL PARENT GETS EXEMPTION.—Except as otherwise provided in this subsection, if—

(A) a child (as defined in section 151(c)(3)) receives over half of his support during the calendar year from his parents—

(i) who are divorced or legally separated under a decree of divorce or separate maintenance,

(ii) who are separated under a written separation agreement, or

(iii) who live apart at all times during the last 6 months of the calendar year, and

(B) such child is in the custody of one or both of his parents for more than one-half of the calendar year,

such child shall be treated, for purposes of subsection (a), as receiving over half of his support during the calendar year from the parent having custody for a greater portion of the calendar year (hereinafter in this subsection referred to as the "custodial parent").

(2) EXCEPTION WHERE CUSTODIAL PARENT RELEASES CLAIM TO EXEMPTION FOR THE YEAR.—A child of parents described in paragraph (1) shall be treated as having received over half of his support during a calendar year from the noncustodial parent if—

(A) the custodial parent signs a written declaration (in such manner and form as the Secretary may by regulations prescribe) that such custodial parent will not claim such child as a dependent for any taxable year beginning in such calendar year, and

(B) the noncustodial parent attaches such written declaration to the noncustodial parent's return for the taxable year beginning during such calendar year.

For purposes of this subsection, the term "noncustodial parent" means the parent who is not the custodial parent.

(3) EXCEPTION FOR MULTIPLE-SUPPORT AGREEMENT.—This subsection shall not apply in any case where over half of the support of the child is treated as having been received from a taxpayer under the provisions of subsection (c).

* * *

(5) SPECIAL RULE FOR SUPPORT RECEIVED FROM NEW SPOUSE OF PARENT.—For purposes of this subsection, in the case of the remarriage of a parent, support of a child received from the parent's spouse shall be treated as received from the parent.

(6) CROSS REFERENCE.—

For provision treating child as dependent of both parents for purposes of medical expense deduction, see section 213(d)(5).

Sec. 152(e)

PART VI—ITEMIZED DEDUCTIONS FOR INDIVIDUALS AND CORPORATIONS

[Sec. 161]

SEC. 161. ALLOWANCE OF DEDUCTIONS.

In computing taxable income under section 63, there shall be allowed as deductions the items specified in this part, subject to the exceptions provided in part IX (sec. 261 and following, relating to items not deductible).

[Sec. 162]

SEC. 162. TRADE OR BUSINESS EXPENSES.

[Sec. 162(a)]

(a) IN GENERAL.—There shall be allowed as a deduction all the ordinary and necessary expenses paid or incurred during the taxable year in carrying on any trade or business, including—

(1) a reasonable allowance for salaries or other compensation for personal services actually rendered;

(2) traveling expenses (including amounts expended for meals and lodging other than amounts which are lavish or extravagant under the circumstances) while away from home in the pursuit of a trade or business; and

(3) rentals or other payments required to be made as a condition to the continued use or possession, for purposes of the trade or business, of property to which the taxpayer has not taken or is not taking title or in which he has no equity.

For purposes of the preceding sentence, the place of residence of a Member of Congress (including any Delegate and Resident Commissioner) within the State, congressional district, or possession which he represents in Congress shall be considered his home, but amounts expended by such Members within each taxable year for living expenses shall not be deductible for income tax purposes in excess of $3,000. For purposes of paragraph (2), the taxpayer shall not be treated as being temporarily away from home during any period of employment if such period exceeds 1 year. The preceding sentence shall not apply to any Federal employee during any period for which such employee is certified by the Attorney General (or the designee thereof) as traveling on behalf of the United States in temporary duty status to investigate or prosecute, or provide support services for the investigation or prosecution of, a Federal crime.

[Sec. 162(b)]

(b) CHARITABLE CONTRIBUTIONS AND GIFTS EXCEPTED.—No deduction shall be allowed under subsection (a) for any contribution or gift which would be allowable as a deduction under section 170 were it not for the percentage limitations, the dollar limitations, or the requirements as to the time of payment, set forth in such section.

[Sec. 162(c)]

(c) ILLEGAL BRIBES, KICKBACKS, AND OTHER PAYMENTS.—

(1) ILLEGAL PAYMENTS TO GOVERNMENT OFFICIALS OR EMPLOYEES.—No deduction shall be allowed under subsection (a) for any payment made, directly or indirectly, to an official or employee of any government, or of any agency or instrumentality of any government, if the payment constitutes an illegal bribe or kickback or, if the payment is to an official or employee of a foreign government, the payment is unlawful under the Foreign Corrupt Practices Act of 1977. The burden of proof in respect of the issue, for the purposes of this paragraph, as to whether a payment constitutes an illegal bribe or kickback (or is unlawful under the Foreign Corrupt Practices Act of 1977) shall be upon the Secretary to the same extent as he bears the burden of proof under section 7454 (concerning the burden of proof when the issue relates to fraud).

(2) OTHER ILLEGAL PAYMENTS.—No deduction shall be allowed under subsection (a) for any payment (other than a payment described in paragraph (1)) made, directly or indirectly, to any person, if the payment constitutes an illegal bribe, illegal kickback, or other illegal payment under any law of the United States, or under any law of a State (but only if such State law is generally enforced), which subjects the payor to a criminal penalty or the loss of license or privilege to engage in a trade or business. For purposes of this paragraph, a kickback includes a payment in

consideration of the referral of a client, patient, or customer. The burden of proof in respect of the issue, for purposes of this paragraph, as to whether a payment constitutes an illegal bribe, illegal kickback, or other illegal payment shall be upon the Secretary to the same extent as he bears the burden of proof under section 7454 (concerning the burden of proof when the issue relates to fraud).

(3) KICKBACKS, REBATES, AND BRIBES UNDER MEDICARE AND MEDICAID.—No deduction shall be allowed under subsection (a) for any kickback, rebate, or bribe made by any provider of services, supplier, physician, or other person who furnishes items or services for which payment is or may be made under the Social Security Act, or in whole or in part out of Federal funds under a State plan approved under such Act, if such kickback, rebate, or bribe is made in connection with the furnishing of such items or services or the making or receipt of such payments. For purposes of this paragraph, a kickback includes a payment in consideration of the referral of a client, patient, or customer.

* * *

[Sec. 162(e)]

(e) DENIAL OF DEDUCTION FOR CERTAIN LOBBYING AND POLITICAL EXPENDITURES.—

(1) IN GENERAL.—No deduction shall be allowed under subsection (a) for any amount paid or incurred in connection with—

(A) influencing legislation,

(B) participation in, or intervention in, any political campaign on behalf of (or in opposition to) any candidate for public office,

(C) any attempt to influence the general public, or segments thereof, with respect to elections, legislative matters, or referendums, or

(D) any direct communication with a covered executive branch official in an attempt to influence the official actions or positions of such official.

(2) EXCEPTION FOR LOCAL LEGISLATION.—In the case of any legislation of any local council or similar governing body—

(A) paragraph (1)(A) shall not apply, and

(B) the deduction allowed by subsection (a) shall include all ordinary and necessary expenses (including, but not limited to, traveling expenses described in subsection (a)(2) and the cost of preparing testimony) paid or incurred during the taxable year in carrying on any trade or business—

(i) in direct connection with appearances before, submission of statements to, or sending communications to the committees, or individual members, of such council or body with respect to legislation or proposed legislation of direct interest to the taxpayer, or

(ii) in direct connection with communication of information between the taxpayer and an organization of which the taxpayer is a member with respect to any such legislation or proposed legislation which is of direct interest to the taxpayer and to such organization, and that portion of the dues so paid or incurred with respect to any organization of which the taxpayer is a member which is attributable to the expenses of the activities described in clauses (i) and (ii) carried on by such organization.

(3) APPLICATION TO DUES OF TAX-EXEMPT ORGANIZATIONS.—No deduction shall be allowed under subsection (a) for the portion of dues or other similar amounts paid by the taxpayer to an organization which is exempt from tax under this subtitle which the organization notifies the taxpayer under section 6033(e)(1)(A)(ii) is allocable to expenditures to which paragraph (1) applies.

(4) INFLUENCING LEGISLATION.—For purposes of this subsection—

(A) IN GENERAL.—The term "influencing legislation" means any attempt to influence any legislation through communication with any member or employee of a legislative body, or with any government official or employee who may participate in the formulation of legislation.

(B) LEGISLATION.—The term "legislation" has the meaning given such term by section 4911(e)(2).

(5) OTHER SPECIAL RULES.—

(A) EXCEPTION FOR CERTAIN TAXPAYERS.—In the case of any taxpayer engaged in the trade or business of conducting activities described in paragraph (1), paragraph (1) shall not apply to expenditures of the taxpayer in conducting such activities directly on behalf of another person (but shall apply to payments by such other person to the taxpayer for conducting such activities).

(B) DE MINIMIS EXCEPTION.—

(i) IN GENERAL.—Paragraph (1) shall not apply to any in-house expenditures for any taxable year if such expenditures do not exceed $2,000. In determining whether a taxpayer exceeds the $2,000 limit under this clause, there shall not be taken into account overhead costs otherwise allocable to activities described in paragraphs (1)(A) and (D).

(ii) IN-HOUSE EXPENDITURES.—For purposes of clause (i), the term "in-house expenditures" means expenditures described in paragraphs (1)(A) and (D) other than—

(I) payments by the taxpayer to a person engaged in the trade or business of conducting activities described in paragraph (1) for the conduct of such activities on behalf of the taxpayer, or

(II) dues or other similar amounts paid or incurred by the taxpayer which are allocable to activities described in paragraph (1).

(C) EXPENSES INCURRED IN CONNECTION WITH LOBBYING AND POLITICAL ACTIVITIES.—Any amount paid or incurred for research for, or preparation, planning, or coordination of, any activity described in paragraph (1) shall be treated as paid or incurred in connection with such activity.

(6) COVERED EXECUTIVE BRANCH OFFICIAL.—For purposes of this subsection, the term "covered executive branch official" means—

(A) the President,

(B) the Vice President,

(C) any officer or employee of the White House Office of the Executive Office of the President, and the 2 most senior level officers of each of the other agencies in such Executive Office, and

(D)(i) any individual serving in a position in level I of the Executive Schedule under section 5312 of title 5, United States Code, (ii) any other individual designated by the President as having Cabinet level status, and (iii) any immediate deputy of an individual described in clause (i) or (ii).

(7) SPECIAL RULE FOR INDIAN TRIBAL GOVERNMENTS.—For purposes of this subsection, an Indian tribal government shall be treated in the same manner as a local council or similar governing body.

(8) CROSS REFERENCE.—

For reporting requirements and alternative taxes related to this subsection, see section 6033(e).

[Sec. 162(f)]

(f) FINES AND PENALTIES.—No deduction shall be allowed under subsection (a) for any fine or similar penalty paid to a government for the violation of any law.

[Sec. 162(g)]

(g) TREBLE DAMAGE PAYMENTS UNDER THE ANTITRUST LAWS.—If in a criminal proceeding a taxpayer is convicted of a violation of the antitrust laws, or his plea of guilty or nolo contendere to an indictment or information charging such a violation is entered or accepted in such a proceeding, no deduction shall be allowed under subsection (a) for two-thirds of any amount paid or incurred—

(1) on any judgment for damages entered against the taxpayer under section 4 of the Act entitled "An Act to supplement existing laws against unlawful restraints and monopolies, and for other purposes", approved October 15, 1914 (commonly known as the Clayton Act), on account of such violation or any related violation of the antitrust laws which occurred prior to the date of the final judgment of such conviction, or

(2) in settlement of any action brought under such section 4 on account of such violation or related violation.

The preceding sentence shall not apply with respect to any conviction or plea before January 1, 1970, or to any conviction or plea on or after such date in a new trial following an appeal of a conviction before such date.

* * * *

Sec. 162(f)

[Sec. 162(k)]

(k) STOCK REACQUISITION EXPENSES.—

(1) IN GENERAL.—Except as provided in paragraph (2), no deduction otherwise allowable shall be allowed under this chapter for any amount paid or incurred by a corporation in connection with the reacquisition of its stock or of the stock of any related person (as defined in section 465(b)(3)(C)).

(2) EXCEPTIONS.—Paragraph (1) shall not apply to—

(A) CERTAIN SPECIFIC DEDUCTIONS.—Any—

(i) deduction allowable under section 163 (relating to interest),

(ii) deduction for amounts which are properly allocable to indebtedness and amortized over the term of such indebtedness, or

(iii) deduction for dividends paid (within the meaning of section 561).

(B) STOCK OF CERTAIN REGULATED INVESTMENT COMPANIES.—Any amount paid or incurred in connection with the redemption of any stock in a regulated investment company which issues only stock which is redeemable upon the demand of the shareholder.

[Sec. 162(l)]

(l) SPECIAL RULES FOR HEALTH INSURANCE COSTS OF SELF-EMPLOYED INDIVIDUALS.—

(1) ALLOWANCE OF DEDUCTION.—

(A) IN GENERAL.—In the case of an individual who is an employee within the meaning of section 401(c)(1), there shall be allowed as a deduction under this section an amount equal to the applicable percentage of the amount paid during the taxable year for insurance which constitutes medical care for the taxpayer, his spouse, and dependents.

(B) APPLICABLE PERCENTAGE.—For purposes of subparagraph (A), the applicable percentage shall be determined under the following table:

For taxable years beginning in calendar year—	The applicable percentage is—
1999 through 2001	60
2002	70
2003 and thereafter	100

(2) LIMITATIONS.—

(A) DOLLAR AMOUNT.—No deduction shall be allowed under paragraph (1) to the extent that the amount of such deduction exceeds the taxpayer's earned income (within the meaning of section 401(c)) derived by the taxpayer from the trade or business with respect to which the plan providing the medical care coverage is established.

(B) OTHER COVERAGE.—Paragraph (1) shall not apply to any taxpayer for any calendar month for which the taxpayer is eligible to participate in any subsidized health plan maintained by any employer of the taxpayer or of the spouse of the taxpayer. The preceding sentence shall be applied separately with respect to—

(i) plans which include coverage for qualified long-term care services (as defined in section 7702B(c)) or are qualified long-term care insurance contracts (as defined in section 7702B(b)), and

(ii) plans which do not include such coverage and are not such contracts.

(C) LONG-TERM CARE PREMIUMS.—In the case of a qualified long-term care insurance contract (as defined in section 7702B(b)), only eligible long-term care premiums (as defined in section 213(d)(10)) shall be taken into account under paragraph (1).

(3) COORDINATION WITH MEDICAL DEDUCTION.—Any amount paid by a taxpayer for insurance to which paragraph (1) applies shall not be taken into account in computing the amount allowable to the taxpayer as a deduction under section 213(a).

(4) DEDUCTION NOT ALLOWED FOR SELF-EMPLOYMENT TAX PURPOSES.—The deduction allowable by reason of this subsection shall not be taken into account in determining an individual's net earnings from self-employment (within the meaning of section 1402(a)) for purposes of chapter 2.

(5) TREATMENT OF CERTAIN S CORPORATION SHAREHOLDERS.—This subsection shall apply in the case of any individual treated as a partner under section 1372(a), except that—

(A) for purposes of this subsection, such individual's wages (as defined in section 3121) from the S corporation shall be treated as such individual's earned income (within the meaning of section 401(c)(1)), and

(B) there shall be such adjustments in the application of this subsection as the Secretary may by regulations prescribe.

[Sec. 162(m)]

(m) CERTAIN EXCESSIVE EMPLOYEE REMUNERATION.—

(1) IN GENERAL.—In the case of any publicly held corporation, no deduction shall be allowed under this chapter for applicable employee remuneration with respect to any covered employee to the extent that the amount of such remuneration for the taxable year with respect to such employee exceeds $1,000,000.

(2) PUBLICLY HELD CORPORATION.—For purposes of this subsection, the term "publicly held corporation" means any corporation issuing any class of common equity securities required to be registered under section 12 of the Securities Exchange Act of 1934.

(3) COVERED EMPLOYEE.—For purposes of this subsection, the term "covered employee" means any employee of the taxpayer if—

(A) as of the close of the taxable year, such employee is the chief executive officer of the taxpayer or is an individual acting in such a capacity, or

(B) the total compensation of such employee for the taxable year is required to be reported to shareholders under the Securities Exchange Act of 1934 by reason of such employee being among the 4 highest compensated officers for the taxable year (other than the chief executive officer).

(4) APPLICABLE EMPLOYEE REMUNERATION.—For purposes of this subsection—

(A) IN GENERAL.—Except as otherwise provided in this paragraph, the term "applicable employee remuneration" means, with respect to any covered employee for any taxable year, the aggregate amount allowable as a deduction under this chapter for such taxable year (determined without regard to this subsection) for remuneration for services performed by such employee (whether or not during the taxable year).

(B) EXCEPTION FOR REMUNERATION PAYABLE ON COMMISSION BASIS.—The term "applicable employee remuneration" shall not include any remuneration payable on a commission basis solely on account of income generated directly by the individual performance of the individual to whom such remuneration is payable.

(C) OTHER PERFORMANCE-BASED COMPENSATION.—The term "applicable employee remuneration" shall not include any remuneration payable solely on account of the attainment of one or more performance goals, but only if—

(i) the performance goals are determined by a compensation committee of the board of directors of the taxpayer which is comprised solely of 2 or more outside directors,

(ii) the material terms under which the remuneration is to be paid, including the performance goals, are disclosed to shareholders and approved by a majority of the vote in a separate shareholder vote before the payment of such remuneration, and

(iii) before any payment of such remuneration, the compensation committee referred to in clause (i) certifies that the performance goals and any other material terms were in fact satisfied.

(D) EXCEPTION FOR EXISTING BINDING CONTRACTS.—The term "applicable employee remuneration" shall not include any remuneration payable under a written binding contract which was in effect on February 17, 1993, and which was not modified thereafter in any material respect before such remuneration is paid.

(E) REMUNERATION.—For purposes of this paragraph, the term "remuneration" includes any remuneration (including benefits) in any medium other than cash, but shall not include—

(i) any payment referred to in so much of section 3121(a)(5) as precedes subparagraph (E) thereof, and

(ii) any benefit provided to or on behalf of an employee if at the time such benefit is provided it is reasonable to believe that the employee will be able to exclude such benefit from gross income under this chapter.

For purposes of clause (i), section 3121(a)(5) shall be applied without regard to section 3121(v)(1).

(F) COORDINATION WITH DISALLOWED GOLDEN PARACHUTE PAYMENTS.—The dollar limitation contained in paragraph (1) shall be reduced (but not below zero) by the amount (if any) which would have been included in the applicable employee remuneration of the covered employee for the taxable year but for being disallowed under section 280G.

* * *

[Sec. 163]

SEC. 163. INTEREST.

[Sec. 163(a)]

(a) GENERAL RULE.—There shall be allowed as a deduction all interest paid or accrued within the taxable year on indebtedness.

[Sec. 163(b)]

(b) INSTALLMENT PURCHASES WHERE INTEREST CHARGE IS NOT SEPARATELY STATED.—

(1) GENERAL RULE.—If personal property or educational services are purchased under a contract—

(A) which provides that payment of part or all of the purchase price is to be made in installments, and

(B) in which carrying charges are separately stated but the interest charge cannot be ascertained,

then the payments made during the taxable year under the contract shall be treated for purposes of this section as if they included interest equal to 6 percent of the average unpaid balance under the contract during the taxable year. For purposes of the preceding sentence, the average unpaid balance is the sum of the unpaid balance outstanding on the first day of each month beginning during the taxable year, divided by 12. For purposes of this paragraph, the term "educational services" means any service (including lodging) which is purchased from an educational organization described in section 170(b)(1)(A)(ii) and which is provided for a student of such organization.

(2) LIMITATION.—In the case of any contract to which paragraph (1) applies, the amount treated as interest for any taxable year shall not exceed the aggregate carrying charges which are properly attributable to such taxable year.

[Sec. 163(c)]

(c) REDEEMABLE GROUND RENTS.—For purposes of this subtitle, any annual or periodic rental under a redeemable ground rent (excluding amounts in redemption thereof) shall be treated as interest on an indebtedness secured by a mortgage.

[Sec. 163(d)]

(d) LIMITATION ON INVESTMENT INTEREST.—

(1) IN GENERAL.—In the case of a taxpayer other than a corporation, the amount allowed as a deduction under this chapter for investment interest for any taxable year shall not exceed the net investment income of the taxpayer for the taxable year.

(2) CARRYFORWARD OF DISALLOWED INTEREST.—The amount not allowed as a deduction for any taxable year by reason of paragraph (1) shall be treated as investment interest paid or accrued by the taxpayer in the succeeding taxable year.

(3) INVESTMENT INTEREST.—For purposes of this subsection—

(A) IN GENERAL.—The term "investment interest" means any interest allowable as a deduction under this chapter (determined without regard to paragraph (1)) which is paid or accrued on indebtedness properly allocable to property held for investment.

(B) EXCEPTIONS.—The term "investment interest" shall not include—

(i) any qualified residence interest (as defined in subsection (h)(3)), or

(ii) any interest which is taken into account under section 469 in computing income or loss from a passive activity of the taxpayer.

Sec. 163(d)

(C) PERSONAL PROPERTY USED IN SHORT SALE.—For purposes of this paragraph, the term "interest" includes any amount allowable as a deduction in connection with personal property used in a short sale.

(4) NET INVESTMENT INCOME.—For purposes of this subsection—

(A) IN GENERAL.—The term "net investment income" means the excess of—

(i) investment income, over

(ii) investment expenses.

(B) INVESTMENT INCOME.—The term "investment income" means the sum of—

(i) gross income from property held for investment (other than any gain taken into account under clause (ii)(I)),

(ii) the excess (if any) of—

(I) the net gain attributable to the disposition of property held for investment, over

(II) the net capital gain determined by only taking into account gains and losses from dispositions of property held for investment, plus

(iii) so much of the net capital gain referred to in clause (ii)(II) (or, if lesser, the net gain referred to in clause (ii)(I)) as the taxpayer elects to take into account under this clause.

Such term shall include qualified dividend income (as defined in section 1(h)(11)(B)) only to the extent the taxpayer elects to treat such income as investment income for purposes of this subsection.

(C) INVESTMENT EXPENSES.—The term "investment expenses" means the deductions allowed under this chapter (other than for interest) which are directly connected with the production of investment income.

(D) INCOME AND EXPENSES FROM PASSIVE ACTIVITIES.—Investment income and investment expenses shall not include any income or expenses taken into account under section 469 in computing income or loss from a passive activity.

(E) REDUCTION IN INVESTMENT INCOME DURING PHASE-IN OF PASSIVE LOSS RULES.—Investment income of the taxpayer for any taxable year shall be reduced by the amount of the passive activity loss to which section 469(a) does not apply for such taxable year by reason of section 469(m). The preceding sentence shall not apply to any portion of such passive activity loss which is attributable to a rental real estate activity with respect to which the taxpayer actively participates (within the meaning of section 469(i)(6)) during such taxable year.

(5) PROPERTY HELD FOR INVESTMENT.—For purposes of this subsection—

(A) IN GENERAL.—The term "property held for investment" shall include—

(i) any property which produces income of a type described in section 469(e)(1), and

(ii) any interest held by a taxpayer in an activity involving the conduct of a trade or business—

(I) which is not a passive activity, and

(II) with respect to which the taxpayer does not materially participate.

(B) INVESTMENT EXPENSES.—In the case of property described in subparagraph (A)(i), expenses shall be allocated to such property in the same manner as under section 469.

(C) TERMS.—For purposes of this paragraph, the terms "activity", "passive activity", and "materially participate" have the meanings given such terms by section 469.

* * *

[Sec. 163(e)]

(e) ORIGINAL ISSUE DISCOUNT.—

(1) IN GENERAL.—In the case of any debt instrument issued after July 1, 1982, the portion of the original issue discount with respect to such debt instrument which is allowable as a deduction to the issuer for any taxable year shall be equal to the aggregate daily portions of the original issue discount for days during such taxable year.

(2) DEFINITIONS AND SPECIAL RULES.—For purposes of this subsection—

(A) DEBT INSTRUMENT.—The term "debt instrument" has the meaning given such term by section 1275(a)(1).

(B) DAILY PORTIONS.—The daily portion of the original issue discount for any day shall be determined under section 1272(a) (without regard to paragraph (7) thereof and without regard to section 1273(a)(3)).

(C) SHORT-TERM OBLIGATIONS.—In the case of an obligor of a short-term obligation (as defined in section 1283(a)(1)(A)) who uses the cash receipts and disbursements method of accounting, the original issue discount (and any other interest payable) on such obligation shall be deductible only when paid.

(3) SPECIAL RULE FOR ORIGINAL ISSUE DISCOUNT ON OBLIGATION HELD BY RELATED FOREIGN PERSON.—

(A) IN GENERAL.—If any debt instrument having original issue discount is held by a related foreign person, any portion of such original issue discount shall not be allowable as a deduction to the issuer until paid. The preceding sentence shall not apply to the extent that the original issue discount is effectively connected with the conduct by such foreign related person of a trade or business within the United States unless such original issue discount is exempt from taxation (or is subject to a reduced rate of tax) pursuant to a treaty obligation of the United States.

(B) RELATED FOREIGN PERSON.—For purposes of subparagraph (A), the term "related foreign person" means any person—

(i) who is not a United States person, and

(ii) who is related (within the meaning of section 267(b)) to the issuer.

(4) EXCEPTIONS.—This subsection shall not apply to any debt instrument described in—

(A) subparagraph (D) of section 1272(a)(2) (relating to obligations issued by natural persons before March 2, 1984), and

(B) subparagraph (E) of section 1272(a)(2) (relating to loans between natural persons).

(5) SPECIAL RULES FOR ORIGINAL ISSUE DISCOUNT ON CERTAIN HIGH YIELD OBLIGATIONS.—

(A) IN GENERAL.—In the case of an applicable high yield discount obligation issued by a corporation—

(i) no deduction shall be allowed under this chapter for the disqualified portion of the original issue discount on such obligation, and

(ii) the remainder of such original issue discount shall not be allowable as a deduction until paid.

For purposes of this paragraph, rules similar to the rules of subsection (i)(3)(B) shall apply in determining the amount of the original issue discount and when the original issue discount is paid.

(B) DISQUALIFIED PORTION TREATED AS STOCK DISTRIBUTION FOR PURPOSES OF DIVIDEND RECEIVED DEDUCTION.—

(i) IN GENERAL.—Solely for purposes of sections 243, 245, 246, and 246A, the dividend equivalent portion of any amount includible in gross income of a corporation under section 1272(a) in respect of an applicable high yield discount obligation shall be treated as a dividend received by such corporation from the corporation issuing such obligation.

(ii) DIVIDEND EQUIVALENT PORTION.—For purposes of clause (i), the dividend equivalent portion of any amount includible in gross income under section 1272(a) in respect of an applicable high yield discount obligation is the portion of the amount so includible—

(I) which is attributable to the disqualified portion of the original issue discount on such obligation, and

(II) which would have been treated as a dividend if it had been a distribution made by the issuing corporation with respect to stock in such corporation.

(C) DISQUALIFIED PORTION.—

(i) IN GENERAL.—For purposes of this paragraph, the disqualified portion of the original issue discount on any applicable high yield discount obligation is the lesser of—

Sec. 163(e)

(I) the amount of such original issue discount, or

(II) the portion of the total return on such obligation which bears the same ratio to such total return as the disqualified yield on such obligation bears to the yield to maturity on such obligation.

(ii) DEFINITIONS.—For purposes of clause (i), the term "disqualified yield" means the excess of the yield to maturity on the obligation over the sum referred to subsection (i)(1)(B) plus 1 percentage point, and the term "total return" is the amount which would have been the original issue discount on the obligation if interest described in the parenthetical in section 1273(a)(2) were included in the stated redemption price at maturity.

(D) EXCEPTION FOR S CORPORATIONS.—This paragraph shall not apply to any obligation issued by any corporation for any period for which such corporation is an S corporation.

(E) EFFECT ON EARNINGS AND PROFITS.—This paragraph shall not apply for purposes of determining earnings and profits; except that, for purposes of determining the dividend equivalent portion of any amount includible in gross income under section 1272(a) in respect of an applicable high yield discount obligation, no reduction shall be made for any amount attributable to the disqualified portion of any original issue discount on such obligation.

(F) CROSS REFERENCE.—

For definition of applicable high yield discount obligation, see subsection (i).

(6) CROSS REFERENCES.—

For provision relating to deduction of original issue discount on tax-exempt obligation, see section 1288.

For special rules in the case of the borrower under certain loans for personal use, see section 1275(b).

[Sec. 163(f)]

(f) DENIAL OF DEDUCTION FOR INTEREST ON CERTAIN OBLIGATIONS NOT IN REGISTERED FORM.—

(1) IN GENERAL.—Nothing in subsection (a) or in any other provision of law shall be construed to provide a deduction for interest on any registration-required obligation unless such obligation is in registered form.

(2) REGISTRATION-REQUIRED OBLIGATION.—For purposes of this section—

(A) IN GENERAL.—The term "registration-required obligation" means any obligation (including any obligation issued by a governmental entity) other than an obligation which—

(i) is issued by a natural person,

(ii) is not of a type offered to the public,

(iii) has a maturity (at issue) of not more than 1 year, or

(iv) is described in subparagraph (B).

(B) CERTAIN OBLIGATIONS NOT INCLUDED.—An obligation is described in this subparagraph if—

(i) there are arrangements reasonably designed to ensure that such obligation will be sold (or resold in connection with the original issue) only to a person who is not a United States person, and

(ii) in the case of an obligation not in registered form—

(I) interest on such obligation is payable only outside the United States and its possessions, and

(II) on the face of such obligation there is a statement that any United States person who holds such obligation will be subject to limitations under the United States income tax laws.

(C) AUTHORITY TO INCLUDE OTHER OBLIGATIONS.—Clauses (ii) and (iii) of subparagraph (A), and subparagraph (B), shall not apply to any obligation if—

(i) in the case of—

(I) subparagraph (A), such obligation is of a type which the Secretary has determined by regulations to be used frequently in avoiding Federal taxes, or

(II) subparagraph (B), such obligation is of a type specified by the Secretary in regulations, and

(ii) such obligation is issued after the date on which the regulations referred to in clause (i) take effect.

(3) BOOK ENTRIES PERMITTED, ETC.—For purposes of this subsection, rules similar to the rules of section 149(a)(3) shall apply.

* * *

[Sec. 163(h)]

(h) DISALLOWANCE OF DEDUCTION FOR PERSONAL INTEREST.—

(1) IN GENERAL.—In the case of a taxpayer other than a corporation, no deduction shall be allowed under this chapter for personal interest paid or accrued during the taxable year.

(2) PERSONAL INTEREST.—For purposes of this subsection, the term "personal interest" means any interest allowable as a deduction under this chapter other than—

(A) interest paid or accrued on indebtedness properly allocable to a trade or business (other than the trade or business of performing services as an employee),

(B) any investment interest (within the meaning of subsection (d)),

(C) any interest which is taken into account under section 469 in computing income or loss from a passive activity of the taxpayer,

(D) any qualified residence interest (within the meaning of paragraph (3)),

(E) any interest payable under section 6601 on any unpaid portion of the tax imposed by section 2001 for the period during which an extension of time for payment of such tax is in effect under section 6163, and

(F) any interest allowable as a deduction under section 221 (relating to interest on educational loans).

(3) QUALIFIED RESIDENCE INTEREST.—For purposes of this subsection—

(A) IN GENERAL.—The term "qualified residence interest" means any interest which is paid or accrued during the taxable year on—

(i) acquisition indebtedness with respect to any qualified residence of the taxpayer, or

(ii) home equity indebtedness with respect to any qualified residence of the taxpayer.

For purposes of the preceding sentence, the determination of whether any property is a qualified residence of the taxpayer shall be made as of the time the interest is accrued.

(B) ACQUISITION INDEBTEDNESS.—

(i) IN GENERAL.—The term "acquisition indebtedness" means any indebtedness which—

(I) is incurred in acquiring, constructing, or substantially improving any qualified residence of the taxpayer, and

(II) is secured by such residence.

Such term also includes any indebtedness secured by such residence resulting from the refinancing of indebtedness meeting the requirements of the preceding sentence (or this sentence); but only to the extent the amount of the indebtedness resulting from such refinancing does not exceed the amount of the refinanced indebtedness.

(ii) $1,000,000 LIMITATION.—The aggregate amount treated as acquisition indebtedness for any period shall not exceed $1,000,000 ($500,000 in the case of a married individual filing a separate return).

(C) HOME EQUITY INDEBTEDNESS.—

(i) IN GENERAL.—The term "home equity indebtedness" means any indebtedness (other than acquisition indebtedness) secured by a qualified residence to the extent the aggregate amount of such indebtedness does not exceed—

(I) the fair market value of such qualified residence, reduced by

(II) the amount of acquisition indebtedness with respect to such residence.

(ii) LIMITATION—The aggregate amount treated as home equity indebtedness for any period shall not exceed $100,000 ($50,000 in the case of a separate return by a married individual).

* * *

(5) [(4)] OTHER DEFINITIONS AND SPECIAL RULES.—For purposes of this subsection—

(A) QUALIFIED RESIDENCE.—For purposes of this subsection—

(i) IN GENERAL.—The term "qualified residence" means—

(I) the principal residence (within the meaning of section 121) of the taxpayer, and

(II) 1 other residence of the taxpayer which is selected by the taxpayer for purposes of this subsection for the taxable year and which is used by the taxpayer as a residence (within the meaning of section 280A(d)(1)).

(ii) MARRIED INDIVIDUALS FILING SEPARATE RETURNS.—If a married couple does not file a joint return for the taxable year—

(I) such couple shall be treated as 1 taxpayer for purposes of clause (i), and

(II) each individual shall be entitled to take into account 1 residence unless both individuals consent in writing to 1 individual taking into account the principal residence and 1 other residence.

(iii) RESIDENCE NOT RENTED.—For purposes of clause (i)(II), notwithstanding section 280A(d)(1), if the taxpayer does not rent a dwelling unit at any time during a taxable year, such unit may be treated as a residence for such taxable year.

(B) SPECIAL RULE FOR COOPERATIVE HOUSING CORPORATIONS.—Any indebtedness secured by stock held by the taxpayer as a tenant-stockholder (as defined in section 216) in a cooperative housing corporation (as so defined) shall be treated as secured by the house or apartment which the taxpayer is entitled to occupy as such a tenant-stockholder. If stock described in the preceding sentence may not be used to secure indebtedness, indebtedness shall be treated as so secured if the taxpayer establishes to the satisfaction of the Secretary that such indebtedness was incurred to acquire such stock.

(C) UNENFORCEABLE SECURITY INTERESTS.—Indebtedness shall not fail to be treated as secured by any property solely because, under any applicable State or local homestead or other debtor protection law in effect on August 16, 1986, the security interest is ineffective or the enforceability of the security interest is restricted.

(D) SPECIAL RULES FOR ESTATES AND TRUSTS.—For purposes of determining whether any interest paid or accrued by an estate or trust is qualified residence interest, any residence held by such estate or trust shall be treated as a qualified residence of such estate or trust if such estate or trust establishes that such residence is a qualified residence of a beneficiary who has a present interest in such estate or trust or an interest in the residuary of such estate or trust.

* * *

[Sec. 163(j)]

(j) LIMITATION ON DEDUCTION FOR INTEREST ON CERTAIN INDEBTEDNESS.—

(1) LIMITATION.—

(A) IN GENERAL.—If this subsection applies to any corporation for any taxable year, no deduction shall be allowed under this chapter for disqualified interest paid or accrued by such corporation during such taxable year. The amount disallowed under the preceding sentence shall not exceed the corporation's excess interest expense for the taxable year.

(B) DISALLOWED AMOUNT CARRIED TO SUCCEEDING TAXABLE YEAR.—Any amount disallowed under subparagraph (A) for any taxable year shall be treated as disqualified interest paid or accrued in the succeeding taxable year (and clause (ii) of paragraph (2)(A) shall not apply for purposes of applying this subsection to the amount so treated).

(2) CORPORATIONS TO WHICH SUBSECTION APPLIES.—

(A) IN GENERAL.—This subsection shall apply to any corporation for any taxable year if—

(i) such corporation has excess interest expense for such taxable year, and

(ii) the ratio of debt to equity of such corporation as of the close of such taxable year (or on any other day during the taxable year as the Secretary may by regulations prescribe) exceeds 1.5 to 1.

(B) Excess interest expense.—

(i) In general.—For purposes of this subsection, the term "excess interest expense" means the excess (if any) of—

(I) the corporation's net interest expense, over

(II) the sum of 50 percent of the adjusted taxable income of the corporation plus any excess limitation carryforward under clause (ii).

(ii) Excess limitation carryforward.—If a corporation has an excess limitation for any taxable year, the amount of such excess limitation shall be an excess limitation carryforward to the 1st succeeding taxable year and to the 2nd and 3rd succeeding taxable years to the extent not previously taken into account under this clause. The amount of such a carryforward taken into account for any such succeeding taxable year shall not exceed the excess interest expense for such succeeding taxable year (determined without regard to the carryforward from the taxable year of such excess limitation).

(iii) Excess limitation.—For purposes of clause (ii), the term "excess limitation" means the excess (if any) of—

(I) 50 percent of the adjusted taxable income of the corporation, over

(II) the corporation's net interest expense.

(C) Ratio of debt to equity.—For purposes of this paragraph, the term "ratio of debt to equity" means the ratio which the total indebtedness of the corporation bears to the sum of its money and all other assets reduced (but not below zero) by such total indebtedness. For purposes of the preceding sentence—

(i) the amount taken into account with respect to any asset shall be the adjusted basis thereof for purposes of determining gain,

(ii) the amount taken into account with respect to any indebtedness with original issue discount shall be its issue price plus the portion of the original issue discount previously accrued as determined under the rules of section 1272 (determined without regard to subsection (a)(7) or (b)(4) thereof), and

(iii) there shall be such other adjustments as the Secretary may by regulations prescribe.

(3) Disqualified interest.—For purposes of this subsection, the term "disqualified interest" means—

(A) any interest paid or accrued by the taxpayer (directly or indirectly) to a related person if no tax is imposed by this subtitle with respect to such interest,

(B) any interest paid or accrued by the taxpayer with respect to any indebtedness to a person who is not a related person if—

(i) there is a disqualified guarantee of such indebtedness, and

(ii) no gross basis tax is imposed by this subtitle with respect to such interest, and

(C) any interest paid or accrued (directly or indirectly) by a taxable REIT subsidiary (as defined in section 856(l)) of a real estate investment trust to such trust.

(4) Related person.—For purposes of this subsection—

(A) In general.—Except as provided in subparagraph (B), the term "related person" means any person who is related (within the meaning of section 267(b) or 707(b)(1)) to the taxpayer.

(B) Special rule for certain partnerships.—

(i) In general.—Any interest paid or accrued to a partnership which (without regard to this subparagraph) is a related person shall not be treated as paid or accrued to a related person if less than 10 percent of the profits and capital interests in such partnership are held by persons with respect to whom no tax is imposed by this subtitle on such interest. The preceding sentence shall not apply to any interest allocable to any partner in such partnership who is a related person to the taxpayer.

Sec. 163(j)

(ii) SPECIAL RULE WHERE TREATY REDUCTION.—If any treaty between the United States and any foreign country reduces the rate of tax imposed by this subtitle on a partner's share of any interest paid or accrued to a partnership, such partner's interests in such partnership shall, for purposes of clause (i), be treated as held in part by a tax-exempt person and in part by a taxable person under rules similar to the rules of paragraph (5)(B).

(5) SPECIAL RULES FOR DETERMINING WHETHER INTEREST IS SUBJECT TO TAX.—

(A) TREATMENT OF PASS-THRU ENTITIES.—In the case of any interest paid or accrued to a partnership, the determination of whether any tax is imposed by this subtitle on such interest shall be made at the partner level. Rules similar to the rules of the preceding sentence shall apply in the case of any pass-thru entity other than a partnership and in the case of tiered partnerships and other entities.

(B) INTEREST TREATED AS TAX-EXEMPT TO EXTENT OF TREATY REDUCTION.—If any treaty between the United States and any foreign country reduces the rate of tax imposed by this subtitle on any interest paid or accrued by the taxpayer, such interest shall be treated as interest on which no tax is imposed by this subtitle to the extent of the same proportion of such interest as—

(i) the rate of tax imposed without regard to such treaty, reduced by the rate of tax imposed under the treaty, bears to

(ii) the rate of tax imposed without regard to the treaty.

(6) OTHER DEFINITIONS AND SPECIAL RULES.—For purposes of this subsection—

(A) ADJUSTED TAXABLE INCOME.—The term "adjusted taxable income" means the taxable income of the taxpayer—

(i) computed without regard to—

(I) any deduction allowable under this chapter for the net interest expense,

(II) the amount of any net operating loss deduction under section 172, and

(III) any deduction allowable for depreciation, amortization, or depletion, and

(ii) computed with such other adjustments as the Secretary may by regulations prescribe.

(B) NET INTEREST EXPENSE.—The term "net interest expense" means the excess (if any) of—

(i) the interest paid or accrued by the taxpayer during the taxable year, over

(ii) the amount of interest includible in the gross income of such taxpayer for such taxable year.

The Secretary may by regulations provide for adjustments in determining the amount of net interest expense.

(C) TREATMENT OF AFFILIATED GROUP.—All members of the same affiliated group (within the meaning of section 1504(a)) shall be treated as 1 taxpayer.

(D) DISQUALIFIED GUARANTEE.—

(i) IN GENERAL.—Except as provided in clause (ii), the term "disqualified guarantee" means any guarantee by a related person which is—

(I) an organization exempt from taxation under this subtitle, or

(II) a foreign person.

(ii) EXCEPTIONS.—The term "disqualified guarantee" shall not include a guarantee—

(I) in any circumstances identified by the Secretary by regulation, where the interest on the indebtedness would have been subject to a net basis tax if the interest had been paid to the guarantor, or

(II) if the taxpayer owns a controllng interest in the guarantor.

For purposes of subclause (II), except as provided in regulations, the term "a controlling interest" means direct or indirect ownership of at least 80 percent of the total voting power and value of all classes of stock of a corporation, or 80 percent of the profit and capital interests in any other entity. For purposes of the preceding sentence, the rules of paragraphs (1) and (5) of section 267(c) shall apply; except that such rules shall also apply to interest in entities other than corporations.

(iii) GUARANTEE.—Except as provided in regulations, the term "guarantee" includes any arrangement under which a person (directly or indirectly through an entity or otherwise) assures, on a conditional or unconditional basis, the payment of another person's obligation under any indebtedness.

(E) GROSS BASIS AND NET BASIS TAXATION.—

(i) GROSS BASIS TAX.—The term "gross basis tax" means any tax imposed by this subtitle which is determined by reference to the gross amount of any item of income without any reduction for any deduction allowed by this subtitle.

(ii) NET BASIS TAX.—The term "net basis tax" means any tax imposed by this subtitle which is not a gross basis tax.

(7) COORDINATION WITH PASSIVE LOSS RULES, ETC.—This subsection shall be applied before sections 465 and 469.

(8) REGULATIONS.—The Secretary shall prescribe such regulations as may be appropriate to carry out the purposes of this subsection, including—

(A) such regulations as may be appropriate to prevent the avoidance of the purposes of this subsection,

(B) regulations providing such adjustments in the case of corporations which are members of an affiliated group as may be appropriate to carry out the purposes of this subsection, and

(C) regulations for the coordination of this subsection with section 884.

* * *

[Sec. 163(l)]

(l) DISALLOWANCE OF DEDUCTION ON CERTAIN DEBT INSTRUMENTS OF CORPORATIONS.—

(1) IN GENERAL.—No deduction shall be allowed under this chapter for any interest paid or accrued on a disqualified debt instrument.

(2) DISQUALIFIED DEBT INSTRUMENT.—For purposes of this subsection, the term "disqualified debt instrument" means any indebtedness of a corporation which is payable in equity of the issuer or a related party.

(3) SPECIAL RULES FOR AMOUNTS PAYABLE IN EQUITY.—For purposes of paragraph (2), indebtedness shall be treated as payable in equity of the issuer or a related party only if—

(A) a substantial amount of the principal or interest is required to be paid or converted, or at the option of the issuer or a related party is payable in, or convertible into, such equity,

(B) a substantial amount of the principal or interest is required to be determined, or at the option of the issuer or a related party is determined, by reference to the value of such equity, or

(C) the indebtedness is part of an arrangement which is reasonably expected to result in a transaction described in subparagraph (A) or (B).

For purposes of this paragraph, principal or interest shall be treated as required to be so paid, converted, or determined if it may be required at the option of the holder or a related party and there is a substantial certainty the option will be exercised.

(4) RELATED PARTY.—For purposes of this subsection, a person is a related party with respect to another person if such person bears a relationship to such other person described in section 267(b) or 707(b).

(5) REGULATIONS.—The Secretary shall prescribe such regulations as may be necessary or appropriate to carry out the purposes of this subsection, including regulations preventing avoidance of this subsection through the use of an issuer other than a corporation.

[Sec. 163(m)]

(m) CROSS REFERENCES.—

(1) For disallowance of certain amounts paid in connection with insurance, endowment, or annuity contracts, see section 264.

(2) For disallowance of deduction for interest relating to tax-exempt income, see section 265(a)(2).

(3) For disallowance of deduction for carrying charges chargeable to capital account, see section 266.

(4) For disallowance of interest with respect to transactions between related taxpayers, see section 267.

(5) For treatment of redeemable ground rents and real property held subject to liabilities under redeemable ground rents, see section 1055.

[Sec. 164]

SEC. 164. TAXES.

[Sec. 164(a)]

(a) GENERAL RULE.—Except as otherwise provided in this section, the following taxes shall be allowed as a deduction for the taxable year within which paid or accrued:

(1) State and local, and foreign, real property taxes.

(2) State and local personal property taxes.

(3) State and local, and foreign, income, war profits, and excess profits taxes.

(4) The GST tax imposed on income distributions.

(5) The environmental tax imposed by section 59A.

In addition, there shall be allowed as a deduction State and local, and foreign, taxes not described in the preceding sentence which are paid or accrued within the taxable year in carrying on a trade or business or an activity described in section 212 (relating to expenses for production of income). Notwithstanding the preceding sentence, any tax (not described in the first sentence of this subsection) which is paid or accrued by the taxpayer in connection with an acquisition or disposition of property shall be treated as part of the cost of the acquired property or, in the case of a disposition, as a reduction in the amount realized on the disposition.

[Sec. 164(b)]

(b) DEFINITIONS AND SPECIAL RULES.—For purposes of this section—

(1) PERSONAL PROPERTY TAXES.—The term "personal property tax" means an ad valorem tax which is imposed on an annual basis in respect of personal property.

(2) STATE OR LOCAL TAXES.—A State or local tax includes only a tax imposed by a State, a possession of the United States, or a political subdivision of any of the foregoing, or by the District of Columbia.

(3) FOREIGN TAXES.—A foreign tax includes only a tax imposed by the authority of a foreign country.

(4) SPECIAL RULES FOR GST TAX.—

(A) IN GENERAL.—The GST tax imposed on income distributions is—

(i) the tax imposed by section 2601, and

(ii) any State tax described in section 2604,

but only to the extent such tax is imposed on a transfer which is included in the gross income of the distributee and to which section 666 does not apply.

(B) SPECIAL RULE FOR TAX PAID BEFORE DUE DATE.—Any tax referred to in subparagraph (A) imposed with respect to a transfer occurring during the taxable year of the distributee (or, in the case of a taxable termination, the trust) which is paid not later than the time prescribed by law (including extensions) for filing the return with respect to such transfer shall be treated as having been paid on the last day of the taxable year in which the transfer was made.

[Sec. 164(c)]

(c) DEDUCTION DENIED IN CASE OF CERTAIN TAXES.—No deduction shall be allowed for the following taxes:

(1) Taxes assessed against local benefits of a kind tending to increase the value of the property assessed; but this paragraph shall not prevent the deduction of so much of such taxes as is properly allocable to maintenance or interest charges.

(2) Taxes on real property, to the extent that subsection (d) requires such taxes to be treated as imposed on another taxpayer.

[Sec. 164(d)]

(d) APPORTIONMENT OF TAXES ON REAL PROPERTY BETWEEN SELLER AND PURCHASER.—

(1) GENERAL RULE.—For purposes of subsection (a), if real property is sold during any real property tax year, then—

(A) so much of the real property tax as is properly allocable to that part of such year which ends on the day before the date of the sale shall be treated as a tax imposed on the seller, and

(B) so much of such tax as is properly allocable to that part of such year which begins on the date of the sale shall be treated as a tax imposed on the purchaser.

(2) SPECIAL RULES.—

(A) In the case of any sale of real property, if—

(i) a taxpayer may not, by reason of his method of accounting, deduct any amount for taxes unless paid, and

(ii) the other party to the sale is (under the law imposing the real property tax) liable for the real property tax for the real property tax year,

then for purposes of subsection (a) the taxpayer shall be treated as having paid, on the date of the sale, so much of such tax as, under paragraph (1) of this subsection, is treated as imposed on the taxpayer. For purposes of the preceding sentence, if neither party is liable for the tax, then the party holding the property at the time the tax becomes a lien on the property shall be considered liable for the real property tax for the real property tax year.

(B) In the case of any sale of real property, if the taxpayer's taxable income for the taxable year during which the sale occurs is computed under an accrual method of accounting, and if no election under section 461 (c) (relating to the accrual of real property taxes) applies, then, for purposes of subsection (a), that portion of such tax which—

(i) is treated, under paragraph (1) of this subsection, as imposed on the taxpayer, and

(ii) may not, by reason of the taxpayer's method of accounting, be deducted by the taxpayer for any taxable year,

shall be treated as having accrued on the date of the sale.

[Sec. 164(e)]

(e) TAXES OF SHAREHOLDER PAID BY CORPORATION.—Where a corporation pays a tax imposed on a shareholder on his interest as a shareholder, and where the shareholder does not reimburse the corporation, then—

(1) the deduction allowed by subsection (a) shall be allowed to the corporation; and

(2) no deduction shall be allowed the shareholder for such tax.

[Sec. 164(f)]

(f) DEDUCTION FOR ONE-HALF OF SELF-EMPLOYMENT TAXES.—

(1) IN GENERAL.—In the case of an individual, in addition to the taxes described in subsection (a), there shall be allowed as a deduction for the taxable year an amount equal to one-half of the taxes imposed by section 1401 for such taxable year.

(2) DEDUCTION TREATED AS ATTRIBUTABLE TO TRADE OR BUSINESS.—For purposes of this chapter, the deduction allowed by paragraph (1) shall be treated as attributable to a trade or business carried on by the taxpayer which does not consist of the performance of services by the taxpayer as an employee.

* * *

[Sec. 165]

SEC. 165. LOSSES.

[Sec. 165(a)]

(a) GENERAL RULE.—There shall be allowed as a deduction any loss sustained during the taxable year and not compensated for by insurance or otherwise.

[Sec. 165(b)]

(b) AMOUNT OF DEDUCTION.—For purposes of subsection (a), the basis for determining the amount of the deduction for any loss shall be the adjusted basis provided in section 1011 for determining the loss from the sale or other disposition of property.

[Sec. 165(c)]

(c) LIMITATION ON LOSSES OF INDIVIDUALS.—In the case of an individual, the deduction under subsection (a) shall be limited to—

(1) losses incurred in a trade or business;

(2) losses incurred in any transaction entered into for profit, though not connected with a trade or business; and

(3) except as provided in subsection (h), losses of property not connected with a trade or business or a transaction entered into for profit, if such losses arise from fire, storm, shipwreck, or other casualty, or from theft.

[Sec. 165(d)]

(d) WAGERING LOSSES.—Losses from wagering transactions shall be allowed only to the extent of the gains from such transactions.

[Sec. 165(e)]

(e) THEFT LOSSES.—For purposes of subsection (a), any loss arising from theft shall be treated as sustained during the taxable year in which the taxpayer discovers such loss.

[Sec. 165(f)]

(f) CAPITAL LOSSES.—Losses from sales or exchanges of capital assets shall be allowed only to the extent allowed in sections 1211 and 1212.

[Sec. 165(g)]

(g) WORTHLESS SECURITIES.—

(1) GENERAL RULE.—If any security which is a capital asset becomes worthless during the taxable year, the loss resulting therefrom shall, for purposes of this subtitle, be treated as a loss from the sale or exchange, on the last day of the taxable year, of a capital asset.

(2) SECURITY DEFINED.—For purposes of this subsection, the term "security" means—

(A) a share of stock in a corporation;

(B) a right to subscribe for, or to receive, a share of stock in a corporation; or

(C) a bond, debenture, note, or certificate, or other evidence of indebtedness, issued by a corporation or by a government or political subdivision thereof, with interest coupons or in registered form.

(3) SECURITIES IN AFFILIATED CORPORATION.—For purposes of paragraph (1), any security in a corporation affiliated with a taxpayer which is a domestic corporation shall not be treated as a capital asset. For purposes of the preceding sentence, a corporation shall be treated as affiliated with the taxpayer only if—

(A) the taxpayer owns directly stock in such corporation meeting the requirements of section 1504(a)(2), and

(B) more than 90 percent of the aggregate of its gross receipts for all taxable years has been from sources other than royalties, rents (except rents derived from rental of properties to employees of the corporation in the ordinary course of its operating business), dividends, interest (except interest received on deferred purchase price of operating assets sold), annuities, and gains from sales or exchanges of stocks and securities.

In computing gross receipts for purposes of the preceding sentence, gross receipts from sales or exchanges of stocks and securities shall be taken into account only to the extent of gains therefrom.

[Sec. 165(h)]

(h) TREATMENT OF CASUALTY GAINS AND LOSSES.—

(1) $100 LIMITATION PER CASUALTY.—Any loss of an individual described in subsection (c)(3) shall be allowed only to the extent that the amount of the loss to such individual arising from each casualty, or from each theft, exceeds $100.

(2) NET CASUALTY LOSS ALLOWED ONLY TO THE EXTENT IT EXCEEDS 10 PERCENT OF ADJUSTED GROSS INCOME.—

(A) IN GENERAL.—If the personal casualty losses for any taxable year exceed the personal casualty gains for such taxable year, such losses shall be allowed for the taxable year only to the extent of the sum of—

(i) the amount of the personal casualty gains for the taxable year, plus

(ii) so much of such excess as exceeds 10 percent of the adjusted gross income of the individual.

(B) SPECIAL RULE WHERE PERSONAL CASUALTY GAINS EXCEED PERSONAL CASUALTY LOSSES.—If the personal casualty gains for any taxable year exceed the personal casualty losses for such taxable year—

(i) all such gains shall be treated as gains from sales or exchanges of capital assets, and

(ii) all such losses shall be treated as losses from sales or exchanges of capital assets.

(3) DEFINITIONS OF PERSONAL CASUALTY GAIN AND PERSONAL CASUALTY LOSS.—For purposes of this subsection—

(A) PERSONAL CASUALTY GAIN.—The term "personal casualty gain" means the recognized gain from any involuntary conversion of property, which is described in subsection (c)(3) arising from fire, storm, shipwreck, or other casualty, or from theft.

(B) PERSONAL CASUALTY LOSS.—The term "personal casualty loss" means any loss described in subsection (c)(3). For purposes of paragraph (2), the amount of any personal casualty loss shall be determined after the application of paragraph (1).

(4) SPECIAL RULES.—

(A) PERSONAL CASUALTY LOSSES ALLOWABLE IN COMPUTING ADJUSTED GROSS INCOME TO THE EXTENT OF PERSONAL CASUALTY GAINS.—In any case to which paragraph (2)(A) applies, the deduction for personal casualty losses for any taxable year shall be treated as a deduction allowable in computing adjusted gross income to the extent such losses do not exceed the personal casualty gains for the taxable year.

(B) JOINT RETURNS.—For purposes of this subsection, a husband and wife making a joint return for the taxable year shall be treated as 1 individual.

(C) DETERMINATION OF ADJUSTED GROSS INCOME IN CASE OF ESTATES AND TRUSTS.—For purposes of paragraph (2), the adjusted gross income of an estate or trust shall be computed in the same manner as in the case of an individual, except that the deductions for costs paid or incurred in connection with the administration of the estate or trust shall be treated as allowable in arriving at adjusted gross income.

(D) COORDINATION WITH ESTATE TAX.—No loss described in subsection (c)(3) shall be allowed if, at the time of filing the return, such loss has been claimed for estate tax purposes in the estate tax return.

(E) CLAIM REQUIRED TO BE FILED IN CERTAIN CASES.—Any loss of an individual described in subsection (c)(3) to the extent covered by insurance shall be taken into account under this section only if the individual files a timely insurance claim with respect to such loss.

[Sec. 165(i)]

(i) DISASTER LOSSES.—

(1) ELECTION TO TAKE DEDUCTION FOR PRECEDING YEAR.—Notwithstanding the provisions of subsection (a), any loss attributable to a disaster occurring in an area subsequently determined by the President of the United States to warrant assistance by the Federal Government under the Disaster Relief and Emergency Assistance Act may, at the election of the taxpayer, be taken into account for the taxable year immediately preceding the taxable year in which the disaster occurred.

(2) YEAR OF LOSS.—If an election is made under this subsection, the casualty resulting in the loss shall be treated for purposes of this title as having occurred in the taxable year for which the deduction is claimed.

Sec. 165(i)

(3) AMOUNT OF LOSS.—The amount of the loss taken into account in the preceding taxable year by reason of paragraph (1) shall not exceed the uncompensated amount determined on the basis of the facts existing at the date the taxpayer claims the loss.

(4) USE OF DISASTER LOAN APPRAISALS TO ESTABLISH AMOUNT OF LOSS.—Nothing in this title shall be construed to prohibit the Secretary from prescribing regulations or other guidance under which an appraisal for the purpose of obtaining a loan of Federal funds or a loan guarantee from the Federal Government as a result of a Presidentially declared disaster (as defined by section 1033(h)(3)) may be used to establish the amount of any loss described in paragraph (1) or (2).

* * *

[Sec. 166]

SEC. 166. BAD DEBTS.

[Sec. 166(a)]

(a) GENERAL RULE.—

(1) WHOLLY WORTHLESS DEBTS.—There shall be allowed as a deduction any debt which becomes worthless within the taxable year.

(2) PARTIALLY WORTHLESS DEBTS.—When satisfied that a debt is recoverable only in part, the Secretary may allow such debt, in an amount not in excess of the part charged off within the taxable year, as a deduction.

[Sec. 166(b)]

(b) AMOUNT OF DEDUCTION.—For purposes of subsection (a), the basis for determining the amount of the deduction for any bad debt shall be the adjusted basis provided in section 1011 for determining the loss from the sale or other disposition of property.

[Sec. 166(d)]

(d) NONBUSINESS DEBTS.—

(1) GENERAL RULE.—In the case of a taxpayer other than a corporation—

(A) subsection (a) shall not apply to any nonbusiness debt; and

(B) where any nonbusiness debt becomes worthless within the taxable year, the loss resulting therefrom shall be considered a loss from the sale or exchange, during the taxable year, of a capital asset held for not more than 1 year.

(2) NONBUSINESS DEBT DEFINED.—For purposes of paragraph (1), the term "nonbusiness debt" means a debt other than—

(A) a debt created or acquired (as the case may be) in connection with a trade or business of the taxpayer; or

(B) a debt the loss from the worthlessness of which is incurred in the taxpayer's trade or business.

[Sec. 166(e)]

(e) WORTHLESS SECURITIES.—This section shall not apply to a debt which is evidenced by a security as defined in section 165(g) (2) (C).

* * *

[Sec. 167]

SEC. 167. DEPRECIATION.

[Sec. 167(a)]

(a) GENERAL RULE.—There shall be allowed as a depreciation deduction a reasonable allowance for the exhaustion, wear and tear (including a reasonable allowance for obsolescence)—

(1) of property used in the trade or business, or

(2) of property held for the production of income.

(b) CROSS REFERENCE.—

For determination of depreciation deduction in case of property to which section 168 applies, see section 168.

(c) BASIS FOR DEPRECIATION.—

(1) IN GENERAL.—The basis on which exhaustion, wear and tear, and obsolescence are to be allowed in respect of any property shall be the adjusted basis provided in section 1011, for the purpose of determining the gain on the sale or other disposition of such property.

(2) SPECIAL RULE FOR PROPERTY SUBJECT TO LEASE.—If any property is acquired subject to a lease—

(A) no portion of the adjusted basis shall be allocated to the leasehold interest, and

(B) the entire adjusted basis shall be taken into account in determining the depreciation deduction (if any) with respect to the property subject to the lease.

(d) LIFE TENANTS AND BENEFICIARIES OF TRUSTS AND ESTATES.—In the case of property held by one person for life with remainder to another person, the deduction shall be computed as if the life tenant were the absolute owner of the property and shall be allowed to the life tenant. In the case of property held in trust, the allowable deduction shall be apportioned between the income beneficiaries and the trustee in accordance with the pertinent provisions of the instrument creating the trust, or, in the absence of such provisions, on the basis of the trust income allocable to each. In the case of an estate, the allowable deduction shall be apportioned between the estate and the heirs, legatees, and devisees on the basis of the income of the estate allocable to each.

(e) CERTAIN TERM INTERESTS NOT DEPRECIABLE.—

(1) IN GENERAL.—No depreciation deduction shall be allowed under this section (and no depreciation or amortization deduction shall be allowed under any other provision of this subtitle) to the taxpayer for any term interest in property for any period during which the remainder interest in such property is held (directly or indirectly) by a related person.

(2) COORDINATION WITH OTHER PROVISIONS.—

(A) SECTION 273.—This subsection shall not apply to any term interest to which section 273 applies.

(B) SECTION 305(e).—This subsection shall not apply to the holder of the dividend rights which were separated from any stripped preferred stock to which section 305(e)(1) applies.

(3) BASIS ADJUSTMENTS.—If, but for this subsection, a depreciation or amortization deduction would be allowable to the taxpayer with respect to any term interest in property—

(A) the taxpayer's basis in such property shall be reduced by any depreciation or amortization deductions disallowed under this subsection, and

(B) the basis of the remainder interest in such property shall be increased by the amount of such disallowed deductions (properly adjusted for any depreciation deductions allowable under subsection (d) to the taxpayer).

(4) SPECIAL RULES.—

(A) DENIAL OF INCREASE IN BASIS OF REMAINDERMAN.—No increase in the basis of the remainder interest shall be made under paragraph (3)(B) for any disallowed deductions attributable to periods during which the term interest was held—

(i) by an organization exempt from tax under this subtitle, or

(ii) by a nonresident alien individual or foreign corporation but only if income from the term interest is not effectively connected with the conduct of a trade or business in the United States.

(B) COORDINATION WITH SUBSECTION (d).—If, but for this subsection, a depreciation or amortization deduction would be allowable to any person with respect to any term interest in property, the principles of subsection (d) shall apply to such person with respect to such term interest.

(5) DEFINITIONS.—For purposes of this subsection—

(A) TERM INTEREST IN PROPERTY.—The term "term interest in property" has the meaning given such term by section 1001(e)(2).

(B) RELATED PERSON.—The term "related person" means any person bearing a relationship to the taxpayer described in subsection (b) or (e) of section 267.

(6) REGULATIONS.—The Secretary shall prescribe such regulations as may be necessary to carry out the purposes of this subsection, including regulations preventing avoidance of this subsection through cross-ownership arrangements or otherwise.

[Sec. 167(f)]

(f) TREATMENT OF CERTAIN PROPERTY EXCLUDED FROM SECTION 197.—

(1) COMPUTER SOFTWARE.—

(A) IN GENERAL.—If a depreciation deduction is allowable under subsection (a) with respect to any computer software, such deduction shall be computed by using the straight line method and a useful life of 36 months.

(B) COMPUTER SOFTWARE.—For purposes of this section, the term "computer software" has the meaning given to such term by section 197(e)(3)(B); except that such term shall not include any such software which is an amortizable section 197 intangible.

(2) CERTAIN INTERESTS OR RIGHTS ACQUIRED SEPARATELY.—If a depreciation deduction is allowable under subsection (a) with respect to any property described in subparagraph (B), (C), or (D) of section 197(e)(4), such deduction shall be computed in accordance with regulations prescribed by the Secretary.

(3) MORTGAGE SERVICING RIGHTS.—If a depreciation deduction is allowable under subsection (a) with respect to any right described in section 197(e)(7), such deduction shall be computed by using the straight line method and a useful life of 108 months.

* * *

[Sec. 167(h)]

(h) CROSS REFERENCES.—

(1) For additional rule applicable to depreciation of improvements in the case of mines, oil and gas wells, other natural deposits, and timber, see section 611.

(2) For amortization of goodwill and certain other intangibles, see section 197.

[Note: The Commissioner of Internal Revenue has promulgated optional tables for use by taxpayers in implementing the provisions of Section 168. The most important of the tables are reproduced beginning at page xv.]

[Sec. 168]

SEC. 168. ACCELERATED COST RECOVERY SYSTEM.

[Sec. 168(a)]

(a) GENERAL RULE.—Except as otherwise provided in this section, the depreciation deduction provided by section 167(a) for any tangible property shall be determined by using—

(1) the applicable depreciation method,

(2) the applicable recovery period, and

(3) the applicable convention.

[Sec. 168(b)]

(b) APPLICABLE DEPRECIATION METHOD.—For purposes of this section—

(1) IN GENERAL.—Except as provided in paragraphs (2) and (3), the applicable depreciation method is—

(A) the 200 percent declining balance method,

(B) switching to the straight line method for the 1st taxable year for which using the straight line method with respect to the adjusted basis as of the beginning of such year will yield a larger allowance.

(2) 150 PERCENT DECLINING BALANCE METHOD IN CERTAIN CASES.—Paragraph (1) shall be applied by substituting "150 percent" for "200 percent" in the case of—

(A) any 15-year or 20-year property,

(B) any property used in a farming business (within the meaning of section 263A(e)(4)), or

(C) any property (other than property described in paragraph (3)) with respect to which the taxpayer elects under paragraph (5) to have the provisions of this paragraph apply.

(3) PROPERTY TO WHICH STRAIGHT LINE METHOD APPLIES.—The applicable depreciation method shall be the straight line method in the case of the following property:

(A) Nonresidential real property.

(B) Residential rental property.

(C) Any railroad grading or tunnel bore.

(D) Property with respect to which the taxpayer elects under paragraph (5) to have the provisions of this paragraph apply.

(E) Property described in subsection (e)(3)(D)(ii).

(F) Water utility property described in subsection (e)(5).

(4) SALVAGE VALUE TREATED AS ZERO.—Salvage value shall be treated as zero.

(5) ELECTION.—An election under paragraph (2)(C) or (3)(D) may be made with respect to 1 or more classes of property for any taxable year and once made with respect to any class shall apply to all property in such class placed in service during such taxable year. Such an election, once made, shall be irrevocable.

[Sec. 168(c)]

(c) APPLICABLE RECOVERY PERIOD.—For purposes of this section, the applicable recovery period shall be determined in accordance with the following table:

In the case of:	The applicable recovery period is:
3-year property	3 years
5-year property	5 years
7-year property	7 years
10-year property	10 years
15-year property	15 years
20-year property	20 years
Water utility property	25 years
Residential rental property	27.5 years
Nonresidential real property	39 years
Any railroad grading or tunnel bore	50 years

[Sec. 168(d)]

(d) APPLICABLE CONVENTION.—For purposes of this section—

(1) IN GENERAL.—Except as otherwise provided in this subsection, the applicable convention is the half-year convention.

(2) REAL PROPERTY.—In the case of—

(A) nonresidential real property,

(B) residential rental property, and

(C) any railroad grading or tunnel bore,

the applicable convention is the mid-month convention.

(3) SPECIAL RULE WHERE SUBSTANTIAL PROPERTY PLACED IN SERVICE DURING LAST 3 MONTHS OF TAXABLE YEAR.—

(A) IN GENERAL.—Except as provided in regulations, if during any taxable year—

Sec. 168(d)

(i) the aggregate bases of property to which this section applies placed in service during the last 3 months of the taxable year, exceed

(ii) 40 percent of the aggregate bases of property to which this section applies placed in service during such taxable year,

the applicable convention for all property to which this section applies placed in service during such taxable year shall be the mid-quarter convention.

(B) CERTAIN PROPERTY NOT TAKEN INTO ACCOUNT.—For purposes of subparagraph (A), there shall not be taken into account—

(i) any nonresidential real property and residential rental property and railroad grading or tunnel bore, and

(ii) any other property placed in service and disposed of during the same taxable year.

(4) DEFINITIONS.—

(A) HALF-YEAR CONVENTION.—The half-year convention is a convention which treats all property placed in service during any taxable year (or disposed of during any taxable year) as placed in service (or disposed of) on the mid-point of such taxable year.

(B) MID-MONTH CONVENTION.—The mid-month convention is a convention which treats all property placed in service during any month (or disposed of during any month) as placed in service (or disposed of) on the mid-point of such month.

(C) MID-QUARTER CONVENTION.—The mid-quarter convention is a convention which treats all property placed in service during any quarter of a taxable year (or disposed of during any quarter of a taxable year) as placed in service (or disposed of) on the mid-point of such quarter.

[Sec. 168(e)]

(e) CLASSIFICATION OF PROPERTY.—For purposes of this section—

(1) IN GENERAL.—Except as otherwise provided in this subsection, property shall be classified under the following table:

Property shall be treated as:	If such property has a class life (in years) of:
3-year property	4 or less
5-year property	More than 4 but less than 10
7-year property	10 or more but less than 16
10-year property	16 or more but less than 20
15-year property	20 or more but less than 25
20-year property	25 or more.

(2) RESIDENTIAL RENTAL OR NONRESIDENTIAL REAL PROPERTY.—

(A) RESIDENTIAL RENTAL PROPERTY.—

(i) RESIDENTIAL RENTAL PROPERTY.—The term "residential rental property" means any building or structure if 80 percent or more of the gross rental income from such building or structure for the taxable year is rental income from dwelling units.

(ii) DEFINITIONS.—For purposes of clause (i)—

(I) the term "dwelling unit" means a house or apartment used to provide living accommodations in a building or structure, but does not include a unit in a hotel, motel, or other establishment more than one-half of the units in which are used on a transient basis, and

(II) if any portion of the building or structure is occupied by the taxpayer, the gross rental income from such building or structure shall include the rental value of the portion so occupied.

(B) NONRESIDENTIAL REAL PROPERTY.—The term "nonresidential real property" means section 1250 property which is not—

(i) residential rental property, or

(ii) property with a class life of less than 27.5 years.

Sec. 168(e)

(3) CLASSIFICATION OF CERTAIN PROPERTY.—

(A) 3-YEAR PROPERTY.—The term "3-year property" includes—

(i) any race horse which is more than 2 years old at the time it is placed in service,

(ii) any horse other than a race horse which is more than 12 years old at the time it is placed in service, and

(iii) any qualified rent-to-own property.

(B) 5-YEAR PROPERTY.—The term "5-year property" includes—

(i) any automobile or light general purpose truck,

(ii) any semi-conductor manufacturing equipment,

(iii) any computer-based telephone central office switching equipment,

(iv) any qualified technological equipment,

(v) any section 1245 property used in connection with research and experimentation, and

(vi) any property which—

(I) is described in subparagraph (A) of section 48(a)(3) (or would be so described if "solar and wind" were substituted for "solar" in clause (i) thereof,

(II) is described in paragraph (15) of section 48(l) (as in effect on the day before the date of the enactment of the Revenue Reconciliation Act of 1990) and is a qualifying small power production facility within the meaning of section 3(17)(C) of the Federal Power Act (16 U.S.C. 796(17)(C)), as in effect on September 1, 1986, or

(III) is described in section 48(l)(3)(A)(ix) (as in effect on the day before the date of the enactment of the Revenue Reconciliation Act of 1990).

Nothing in any provision of law shall be construed to treat property as not being described in clause (vi)(I) (or the corresponding provisions of prior law) by reason of being public utility property (within the meaning of section 48(a)(3)).

(C) 7-YEAR PROPERTY.—The term "7-year property" includes—

(i) any railroad track,

(ii) any property which—

(I) does not have a class life, and

(II) is not otherwise classified under paragraph (2) or this paragraph.

(D) 10-YEAR PROPERTY.—The term "10-year property" includes—

(i) any single purpose agricultural or horticultural structure (within the meaning of subsection (i)(13)), and

(ii) any tree or vine bearing fruit or nuts.

(E) 15-YEAR PROPERTY.—The term "15-year property" includes—

(i) any municipal wastewater treatment plant,

(ii) any telephone distribution plant and comparable equipment used for 2-way exchange of voice and data communications, and

(iii) any section 1250 property which is a retail motor fuels outlet (whether or not food or other convenience items are sold at the outlet).

(F) [Stricken.]

(4) RAILROAD GRADING OR TUNNEL BORE.—The term "railroad grading or tunnel bore" means all improvements resulting from excavations (including tunneling), construction of embankments, clearings, diversions of roads and streams, sodding of slopes, and from similar work necessary to provide, construct, reconstruct, alter, protect, improve, replace, or restore a roadbed or right-of-way for railroad track.

(5) WATER UTILITY PROPERTY.—The term "water utility property" means property—

(A) which is an integral part of the gathering, treatment, or commercial distribution of water, and which, without regard to this paragraph, would be 20-year property, and

(B) any municipal sewer.

Sec. 168(e)

(f) PROPERTY TO WHICH SECTION DOES NOT APPLY.—This section shall not apply to—

(1) CERTAIN METHODS OF DEPRECIATION.—Any property if—

(A) the taxpayer elects to exclude such property from the application of this section, and

(B) for the 1st taxable year for which a depreciation deduction would be allowable with respect to such property in the hands of the taxpayer, the property is properly depreciated under the unit-of-production method or any method of depreciation not expressed in a term of years (other than the retirement-replacement-betterment method or similar method).

(2) CERTAIN PUBLIC UTILITY PROPERTY.—Any public utility property (within the meaning of subsection (i)(10)) if the taxpayer does not use a normalization method of accounting.

(3) FILMS AND VIDEO TAPE.—Any motion picture film or video tape.

(4) SOUND RECORDINGS.—Any works which result from the fixation of a series of musical, spoken, or other sounds, regardless of the nature of the material (such as discs, tapes, or other phonorecordings) in which such sounds are embodied.

* * *

(g) ALTERNATIVE DEPRECIATION SYSTEM FOR CERTAIN PROPERTY.—

(1) IN GENERAL.—In the case of—

(A) any tangible property which during the taxable year is used predominantly outside the United States,

(B) any tax-exempt use property,

(C) any tax-exempt bond financed property,

(D) any imported property covered by an Executive order under paragraph (6), and

(E) any property to which an election under paragraph (7) applies,

the depreciation deduction provided by section 167(a) shall be determined under the alternative depreciation system.

(2) ALTERNATIVE DEPRECIATION SYSTEM.—For purposes of paragraph (1), the alternative depreciation system is depreciation determined by using—

(A) the straight line method (without regard to salvage value),

(B) the applicable convention determined under subsection (d), and

(C) a recovery period determined under the following table:

In the case of:	The recovery period shall be:
(i) Property not described in clause (ii) or (iii)	The class life.
(ii) Personal property with no class life	12 years.
(iii) Nonresidential real and residential rental property	40 years.
(iv) Any railroad grading or tunnel bore or water utility property	50 years.

(3) SPECIAL RULES FOR DETERMINING CLASS LIFE.—

(A) TAX-EXEMPT USE PROPERTY SUBJECT TO LEASE.—In the case of any tax-exempt use property subject to a lease, the recovery period used for purposes of paragraph (2) shall in no event be less than 125 percent of the lease term.

(B) SPECIAL RULE FOR CERTAIN PROPERTY ASSIGNED TO CLASSES.—For purposes of paragraph (2), in the case of property described in any of the following subparagraphs of subsection (e)(3), the class life shall be determined as follows:

If property is described in subparagraph:	The class life is:
(A)(iii)	4
(B)(ii)	5
(B)(iii)	9.5
(C)(i)	10
(D)(i)	15
(D)(ii)	20
(E)(i)	24
(E)(ii)	24
(E)(iii)	20

(C) QUALIFIED TECHNOLOGICAL EQUIPMENT.—In the case of any qualified technological equipment, the recovery period used for purposes of paragraph (2) shall be 5 years.

(D) AUTOMOBILES, ETC.—In the case of any automobile or light general purpose truck, the recovery period used for purposes of paragraph (2) shall be 5 years.

(E) CERTAIN REAL PROPERTY.—In the case of any section 1245 property which is real property with no class life, the recovery period used for purposes of paragraph (2) shall be 40 years.

(4) EXCEPTION FOR CERTAIN PROPERTY USED OUTSIDE UNITED STATES.—Subparagraph (A) of paragraph (1) shall not apply to—

(A) any aircraft which is registered by the Administrator of the Federal Aviation Agency and which is operated to and from the United States or is operated under contract with the United States;

(B) rolling stock which is used within and without the United States and which is—

(i) of a rail carrier subject to part A of subtitle IV of title 49, or

(ii) of a United States person (other than a corporation described in clause (i)) but only if the rolling stock is not leased to one or more foreign persons for periods aggregating more than 12 months in any 24-month period;

(C) any vessel documented under the laws of the United States which is operated in the foreign or domestic commerce of the United States;

(D) any motor vehicle of a United States person (as defined in section 7701(a)(30)) which is operated to and from the United States;

(E) any container of a United States person which is used in the transportation of property to and from the United States;

(F) any property (other than a vessel or an aircraft of a United States person which is used for the purpose of exploring for, developing, removing, or transporting resources from the outer Continental Shelf (within the meaning of section 2 of the Outer Continental Shelf Lands Act, as amended and supplemented; (43 U.S.C. 1331));

(G) any property which is owned by a domestic corporation (other than a corporation which has an election in effect under section 936) or by a United States citizen (other than a citizen entitled to the benefits of section 931 or 933) and which is used predominantly in a possession of the United States by such a corporation or such a citizen, or by a corporation created or organized in, or under the law of, a possession of the United States;

(H) any communications satellite (as defined in section 103(3) of the Communications Satellite Act of 1962, 47 U.S.C. 702(3)), or any interest therein, of a United States person;

(I) any cable, or any interest therein, of a domestic corporation engaged in furnishing telephone service to which section 168(i)(10)(C) applies (or of a wholly owned domestic subsidiary of such a corporation), if such cable is part of a submarine cable system which constitutes part of a communication link exclusively between the United States and one or more foreign countries;

(J) any property (other than a vessel or an aircraft) of a United States person which is used in international or territorial waters within the northern portion of the Western Hemisphere for the purpose of exploring for, developing, removing, or transporting resources from ocean waters or deposits under such waters;

(K) any property described in section 48(l)(3)(A)(ix) (as in effect on the day before the date of the enactment of the Revenue Reconciliation Act of 1990) which is owned by a United States person and which is used in international or territorial waters to generate energy for use in the United States; and

(L) any satellite (not described in subparagraph (H)) or other spacecraft (or any interest therein) held by a United States person if such satellite or other spacecraft was launched from within the United States.

For purposes of subparagraph (J), the term "northern portion of the Western Hemisphere" means the area lying west of the 30th meridian west of Greenwich, east of the international dateline, and north of the Equator, but not including any foreign country which is a country of South America.

(5) TAX-EXEMPT BOND FINANCED PROPERTY.—For purposes of this subsection—

(A) IN GENERAL.—Except as otherwise provided in this paragraph, the term "tax-exempt bond financed property" means any property to the extent such property is financed (directly or indirectly) by an obligation the interest on which is exempt from tax under section 103(a).

Sec. 168(g)

(B) ALLOCATION OF BOND PROCEEDS.—For purposes of subparagraph (A), the proceeds of any obligation shall be treated as used to finance property acquired in connection with the issuance of such obligation in the order in which such property is placed in service.

(C) QUALIFIED RESIDENTIAL RENTAL PROJECTS.—The term "tax-exempt bond financed property" shall not include any qualified residential rental project (within the meaning of section 142(a)(7)).

(6) IMPORTED PROPERTY.—

(A) COUNTRIES MAINTAINING TRADE RESTRICTIONS OR ENGAGING IN DISCRIMINATORY ACTS.—If the President determines that a foreign country—

(i) maintains nontariff trade restrictions, including variable import fees, which substantially burden United States commerce in a manner inconsistent with provisions of trade agreements, or

(ii) engages in discriminatory or other acts (including tolerance of international cartels) or policies unjustifiably restricting United States commerce,

the President may by Executive order provide for the application of paragraph (1)(D) to any article or class of articles manufactured or produced in such foreign country for such period as may be provided by such Executive order. Any period specified in the preceding sentence shall not apply to any property ordered before (or the construction, reconstruction, or erection of which began before) the date of the Executive order unless the President determines an earlier date to be in the public interest and specifies such date in the Executive order.

(B) IMPORTED PROPERTY.—For purposes of this subsection, the term "imported property" means any property if—

(i) such property was completed outside the United States, or

(ii) less than 50 percent of the basis of such property is attributable to value added within the United States.

For purposes of this subparagraph, the term "United States" includes the Commonwealth of Puerto Rico and the possessions of the United States.

(7) ELECTION TO USE ALTERNATIVE DEPRECIATION SYSTEM.—

(A) IN GENERAL.—If the taxpayer makes an election under this paragraph with respect to any class of property for any taxable year, the alternative depreciation system under this subsection shall apply to all property in such class placed in service during such taxable year. Notwithstanding the preceding sentence, in the case of nonresidential real property or residential rental property, such election may be made separately with respect to each property.

(B) ELECTION IRREVOCABLE.—An election under subparagraph (A), once made, shall be irrevocable.

* * *

[Sec. 168(i)]

(i) DEFINITIONS AND SPECIAL RULES.—For purposes of this section—

(1) CLASS LIFE.—Except as provided in this section, the term "class life" means the class life (if any) which would be applicable with respect to any property as of January 1, 1986, under subsection (m) of section 167 (determined without regard to paragraph (4) and as if the taxpayer had made an election under such subsection). The Secretary, through an office established in the Treasury, shall monitor and analyze actual experience with respect to all depreciable assets. The reference in this paragraph to subsection (m) of section 167 shall be treated as a reference to such subsection as in effect on the day before the date of the enactment of the Revenue Reconciliation Act of 1990.

(2) QUALIFIED TECHNOLOGICAL EQUIPMENT.—

(A) IN GENERAL.—The term "qualified technological equipment" means—

(i) any computer or peripheral equipment,

(ii) any high technology telephone station equipment installed on the customer's premises, and

(iii) any high technology medical equipment.

(B) COMPUTER OR PERIPHERAL EQUIPMENT DEFINED.—For purposes of this paragraph—

(i) IN GENERAL.—The term "computer or peripheral equipment" means—

(I) any computer, and

(II) any related peripheral equipment.

(ii) COMPUTER.—The term "computer" means a programmable electronically activated device which—

(I) is capable of accepting information, applying prescribed processes to the information, and supplying the results of these processes with or without human intervention, and

(II) consists of a central processing unit containing extensive storage, logic, arithmetic, and control capabilities.

(iii) RELATED PERIPHERAL EQUIPMENT.—The term "related peripheral equipment" means any auxiliary machine (whether on-line or off-line) which is designed to be placed under the control of the central processing unit of a computer.

(iv) EXCEPTIONS.—The term "computer or peripheral equipment" shall not include—

(I) any equipment which is an integral part of other property which is not a computer,

(II) typewriters, calculators, adding and accounting machines, copiers, duplicating equipment, and similar equipment, and

(III) equipment of a kind used primarily for amusement or entertainment of the user.

(C) HIGH TECHNOLOGY MEDICAL EQUIPMENT.—For purposes of this paragraph, the term "high technology medical equipment" means any electronic, electromechanical, or computer-based high technology equipment used in the screening, monitoring, observation, diagnosis, or treatment of patients in a laboratory, medical, or hospital environment.

(3) LEASE TERM.—

(A) IN GENERAL.—In determining a lease term—

(i) there shall be taken into account options to renew, and

(ii) 2 or more successive leases which are part of the same transaction (or a series of related transactions) with respect to the same or substantially similar property shall be treated as 1 lease.

(B) SPECIAL RULE FOR FAIR RENTAL OPTIONS ON NONRESIDENTIAL REAL PROPERTY OR RESIDENTIAL RENTAL PROPERTY.—For purposes of clause (i) of subparagraph (A), in the case of nonresidential real property or residential rental property, there shall not be taken into account any option to renew at fair market value, determined at the time of renewal.

(4) GENERAL ASSET ACCOUNTS.—Under regulations, a taxpayer may maintain 1 or more general asset accounts for any property to which this section applies. Except as provided in regulations, all proceeds realized on any disposition of property in a general asset account shall be included in income as ordinary income.

(5) CHANGES IN USE.—The Secretary shall, by regulations, provide for the method of determining the deduction allowable under section 167(a) with respect to any tangible property for any taxable year (and the succeeding taxable years) during which such property changes status under this section but continues to be held by the same person.

(6) TREATMENTS OF ADDITIONS OR IMPROVEMENTS TO PROPERTY.—In the case of any addition to (or improvement of) any property—

(A) any deduction under subsection (a) for such addition or improvement shall be computed in the same manner as the deduction of such property would be computed if such property had been placed in service at the same time as such addition or improvement, and

(B) the applicable recovery period for such addition or improvement shall begin on the later of—

(i) the date on which such addition (or improvement) is placed in service, or

(ii) the date on which the property with respect to which such addition (or improvement) was made is placed in service.

Sec. 168(i)

(7) TREATMENT OF CERTAIN TRANSFEREES.—

(A) IN GENERAL.—In the case of any property transferred in a transaction described in subparagraph (B), the transferee shall be treated as the transferor for purposes of computing the depreciation deduction determined under this section with respect to so much of the basis in the hands of the transferee as does not exceed the adjusted basis in the hands of the transferor. In any case where this section as in effect before the amendments made by section 201 of the Tax Reform Act of 1986 applied to the property in the hands of the transferor, the reference in the preceding sentence to this section shall be treated as a reference to this section as so in effect.

(B) TRANSACTIONS COVERED.—The transactions described in this subparagraph are—

(i) any transaction described in section 332, 351, 361, 721, or 731, and

(ii) any transaction between members of the same affiliated group during any taxable year for which a consolidated return is made by such group.

Subparagraph (A) shall not apply in the case of a termination of a partnership under section 708(b)(1)(B).

(C) PROPERTY REACQUIRED BY THE TAXPAYER.—Under regulations, property which is disposed of and then reacquired by the taxpayer shall be treated for purposes of computing the deduction allowable under subsection (a) as if such property had not been disposed of.

(D) [Repealed.]

(8) TREATMENT OF LEASEHOLD IMPROVEMENTS.—

(A) IN GENERAL.—In the case of any building erected (or improvements made) on leased property, if such building or improvement is property to which this section applies, the depreciation deduction shall be determined under the provisions of this section.

(B) TREATMENT OF LESSOR IMPROVEMENTS WHICH ARE ABANDONED AT TERMINATION OF LEASE.—An improvement—

(i) which is made by the lessor of leased property for the lessee of such property, and

(ii) which is irrevocably disposed of or abandoned by the lessor at the termination of the lease by such lessee,

shall be treated for purposes of determining gain or loss under this title as disposed of by the lessor when so disposed of or abandoned.

(C) CROSS REFERENCE.—

For treatment of qualified long-term real property constructed or improved in connection with cash or rent reduction from lessor to lessee, see section 110(b).

(9) NORMALIZATION RULES.—

(A) IN GENERAL.—In order to use a normalization method of accounting with respect to any public utility property for purposes of subsection (f)(2)—

(i) the taxpayer must, in computing its tax expense for purposes of establishing its cost of service for ratemaking purposes and reflecting operating results in its regulated books of account, use a method of depreciation with respect to such property that is the same as, and a depreciation period for such property that is no shorter than, the method and period used to compute its depreciation expense for such purposes; and

(ii) if the amount allowable as a deduction under this section with respect to such property differs from the amount that would be allowable as a deduction under section 167 using the method (including the period, first and last year convention, and salvage value) used to compute regulated tax expense under clause (i), the taxpayer must make adjustments to a reserve to reflect the deferral of taxes resulting from such difference.

(B) USE OF INCONSISTENT ESTIMATES AND PROJECTIONS, ETC.—

(i) IN GENERAL.—One way in which the requirements of subparagraph (A) are not met is if the taxpayer, for ratemaking purposes, uses a procedure or adjustment which is inconsistent with the requirements of subparagraph (A).

(ii) USE OF INCONSISTENT ESTIMATES AND PROJECTIONS.—The procedures and adjustments which are to be treated as inconsistent for purposes of clause (i) shall include any procedure or adjustment for ratemaking purposes which uses an estimate or projection of the taxpayer's tax expense, depreciation expense, or reserve for deferred taxes under subparagraph (A)(ii) unless such estimate or projection is also used, for ratemaking purposes, with respect to the other 2 such items and with respect to the rate base.

(iii) REGULATORY AUTHORITY.—The Secretary may by regulations prescribe procedures and adjustments (in addition to those specified in clause (ii)) which are to be treated as inconsistent for purposes of clause (i).

(C) PUBLIC UTILITY PROPERTY WHICH DOES NOT MEET NORMALIZATION RULES.—In the case of any public utility property to which this section does not apply by reason of subsection (f)(2), the allowance for depreciation under section 167(a) shall be an amount computed using the method and period referred to in subparagraph (A)(i).

(10) PUBLIC UTILITY PROPERTY.—The term "public utility property" means property used predominantly in the trade or business of the furnishing or sale of—

(A) electrical energy, water, or sewage disposal services,

(B) gas or steam through a local distribution system,

(C) telephone services, or other communication services if furnished or sold by the Communications Satellite Corporation for purposes authorized by the Communications Satellite Act of 1962 (47 U.S.C. 701), or

(D) transportation of gas or steam by pipeline,

if the rates for such furnishing or sale, as the case may be, have been established or approved by a State or political subdivision thereof, by any agency or instrumentality of the United States, or by a public service or public utility commission or other similar body of any State or political subdivision thereof.

(11) RESEARCH AND EXPERIMENTATION.—The term "research and experimentation" has the same meaning as the term research and experimental has under section 174.

(12) SECTION 1245 AND 1250 PROPERTY.—The terms "section 1245 property" and "section 1250 property" have the meanings given such terms by sections 1245(a)(3) and 1250(c), respectively.

(13) SINGLE PURPOSE AGRICULTURAL OR HORTICULTURAL STRUCTURE.—

(A) IN GENERAL.—The term "single purpose agricultural or horticultural structure" means—

(i) a single purpose livestock structure, and

(ii) a single purpose horticultural structure.

(B) DEFINITIONS.—For purposes of this paragraph—

(i) SINGLE PURPOSE LIVESTOCK STRUCTURE.—The term "single purpose livestock structure" means any enclosure or structure specifically designed, constructed, and used—

(I) for housing, raising, and feeding a particular type of livestock and their produce, and

(II) for housing the equipment (including any replacements) necessary for the housing, raising, and feeding referred to in subclause (I).

(ii) SINGLE PURPOSE HORTICULTURAL STRUCTURE.—The term "single purpose horticultural structure" means—

(I) a greenhouse specifically designed, constructed, and used for the commercial production of plants, and

(II) a structure specifically designed, constructed, and used for the commercial production of mushrooms.

(iii) STRUCTURES WHICH INCLUDE WORK SPACE.—An enclosure or structure which provides work space shall be treated as a single purpose agricultural or horticultural structure only if such work space is solely for—

(I) the stocking, caring for, or collecting of livestock or plants (as the case may be) or their produce,

(II) the maintenance of the enclosure or structure, and

(III) the maintenance or replacement of the equipment or stock enclosed or housed therein.

(iv) LIVESTOCK.—The term "livestock" includes poultry.

* * *

Sec. 168(i)

[Sec. 168(k)]

(k) Special Allowance for Certain Property Acquired After September 10, 2001, and Before January 1, 2005.—

(1) Additional allowance.—In the case of any qualified property—

(A) the depreciation deduction provided by section 167(a) for the taxable year in which such property is placed in service shall include an allowance equal to 30 percent of the adjusted basis of the qualified property, and

(B) the adjusted basis of the qualified property shall be reduced by the amount of such deduction before computing the amount otherwise allowable as a depreciation deduction under this chapter for such taxable year and any subsequent taxable year.

(2) Qualified property.—For purposes of this subsection—

(A) In general.—The term "qualified property" means property—

(i)(I) to which this section applies which has a recovery period of 20 years or less,

(II) which is computer software (as defined in section 167(f)(1)(B)) for which a deduction is allowable under section 167(a) without regard to this subsection,

(III) which is water utility property, or

(IV) which is qualified leasehold improvement property,

(ii) the original use of which commences with the taxpayer after September 10, 2001,

(iii) which is—

(I) acquired by the taxpayer after September 10, 2001, and before January 1, 2005, but only if no written binding contract for the acquisition was in effect before September 11, 2001, or

(II) acquired by the taxpayer pursuant to a written binding contract which was entered into after September 10, 2001, and before January 1, 2005, and

(iv) which is placed in service by the taxpayer before January 1, 2005, or, in the case of property described in subparagraph (B), before January 1, 2006.

(B) Certain property having longer production periods treated as qualified property.—

(i) In general.—The term "qualified property" includes property—

(I) which meets the requirements of clauses (i), (ii), and (iii) of subparagraph (A),

(II) which has a recovery period of at least 10 years or is transportation property, and

(III) which is subject to section 263A by reason of clause (ii) or (iii) of subsection (f)(1)(B) thereof.

(ii) Only pre-January 1, 2005, basis eligible for additional allowance.—In the case of property which is qualified property solely by reason of clause (i), paragraph (1) shall apply only to the extent of the adjusted basis thereof attributable to manufacture, construction, or production before January 1, 2005.

(iii) Transportation property.—For purposes of this subparagraph, the term "transportation property" means tangible personal property used in the trade or business of transporting persons or property.

(C) Exceptions.—

(i) Alternative depreciation property.—The term "qualified property" shall not include any property to which the alternative depreciation system under subsection (g) applies, determined—

(I) without regard to paragraph (7) of subsection (g) (relating to election to have system apply), and

(II) after application of section 280F(b) (relating to listed property with limited business use).

(ii) Qualified new york liberty zone leasehold improvement property.—The term "qualified property" shall not include any qualified New York Liberty Zone leasehold improvement property (as defined in section 1400L(c)(2)).

(iii) ELECTION OUT.—If a taxpayer makes an election under this clause with respect to any class of property for any taxable year, this subsection shall not apply to all property in such class placed in service during such taxable year. The preceding sentence shall be applied separately with respect to property treated as qualified property by paragraph (4) and other qualified property.

(D) SPECIAL RULES.—

(i) SELF-CONSTRUCTED PROPERTY.—In the case of a taxpayer manufacturing, constructing, or producing property for the taxpayer's own use, the requirements of clause (iii) of subparagraph (A) shall be treated as met if the taxpayer begins manufacturing, constructing, or producing the property after September 10, 2001, and before January 1, 2005.

(ii) SALE-LEASEBACKS.—For purposes of subparagraph (A)(ii), if property—

(I) is originally placed in service after September 10, 2001, by a person, and

(II) sold and leased back by such person within 3 months after the date such property was originally placed in service,

such property shall be treated as originally placed in service not earlier than the date on which such property is used under the leaseback referred to in subclause (II).

(E) COORDINATION WITH SECTION 280F.—For purposes of section 280F—

(i) AUTOMOBILES.—In the case of a passenger automobile (as defined in section 280F(d)(5)) which is qualified property, the Secretary shall increase the limitation under section 280F(a)(1)(A)(i) by $4,600.

(ii) LISTED PROPERTY.—The deduction allowable under paragraph (1) shall be taken into account in computing any recapture amount under section 280F(b)(2).

(F) DEDUCTION ALLOWED IN COMPUTING MINIUMUM [MINIMUM] TAX.—For purposes of determining alternative minimum taxable income under section 55, the deduction under subsection (a) for qualified property shall be determined under this section without regard to any adjustment under section 56.

(3) QUALIFIED LEASEHOLD IMPROVEMENT PROPERTY.—For purposes of this subsection—

(A) IN GENERAL.—The term "qualified leasehold improvement property" means any improvement to an interior portion of a building which is nonresidential real property if—

(i) such improvement is made under or pursuant to a lease (as defined in subsection (h)(7))—

(I) by the lessee (or any sublessee) of such portion, or

(II) by the lessor of such portion,

(ii) such portion is to be occupied exclusively by the lessee (or any sublessee) of such portion, and

(iii) such improvement is placed in service more than 3 years after the date the building was first placed in service.

(B) CERTAIN IMPROVEMENTS NOT INCLUDED.—Such term shall not include any improvement for which the expenditure is attributable to—

(i) the enlargement of the building,

(ii) any elevator or escalator,

(iii) any structural component benefiting a common area, and

(iv) the internal structural framework of the building.

(C) DEFINITIONS AND SPECIAL RULES.—For purposes of this paragraph—

(i) COMMITMENT TO LEASE TREATED AS LEASE.—A commitment to enter into a lease shall be treated as a lease, and the parties to such commitment shall be treated as lessor and lessee, respectively.

(ii) RELATED PERSONS.—A lease between related persons shall not be considered a lease. For purposes of the preceding sentence, the term "related persons" means—

(I) members of an affiliated group (as defined in section 1504), and

Sec. 168(k)

(II) persons having a relationship described in subsection (b) of section 267; except that, for purposes of this clause, the phrase "80 percent or more" shall be substituted for the phrase "more than 50 percent" each place it appears in such subsection.

(4) 50-PERCENT BONUS DEPRECIATION FOR CERTAIN PROPERTY.—

(A) IN GENERAL.—In the case of 50-percent bonus depreciation property—

(i) paragraph (1)(A) shall be applied by substituting "50 percent" for "30 percent", and

(ii) except as provided in paragraph (2)(C), such property shall be treated as qualified property for purposes of this subsection.

(B) 50-PERCENT BONUS DEPRECIATION PROPERTY.—For purposes of this subsection, the term "50-percent bonus depreciation property" means property described in paragraph (2)(A)(i)—

(i) the original use of which commences with the taxpayer after May 5, 2003,

(ii) which is acquired by the taxpayer after May 5, 2003, and before January 1, 2005, but only if no written binding contract for the acquisition was in effect before May 6, 2003, and

(iii) which is placed in service by the taxpayer before January 1, 2005, or, in the case of property described in paragraph (2)(B) (as modified by subparagraph (C) of this paragraph), before January 1, 2006.

(C) SPECIAL RULES.—Rules similar to the rules of subparagraphs (B) and (D) of paragraph (2) shall apply for purposes of this paragraph; except that references to September 10, 2001, shall be treated as references to May 5, 2003.

(D) AUTOMOBILES.—Paragraph (2)(E) shall be applied by substituting "$7,650" for "$4,600" in the case of 50-percent bonus depreciation property.

(E) ELECTION OF 30-PERCENT BONUS.—If a taxpayer makes an election under this subparagraph with respect to any class of property for any taxable year, subparagraph (A)(i) shall not apply to all property in such class placed in service during such taxable year.

[Sec. 169]

SEC. 169. AMORTIZATION OF POLLUTION CONTROL FACILITIES.

[Sec. 169(a)]

(a) ALLOWANCE OF DEDUCTION.—Every person, at his election, shall be entitled to a deduction with respect to the amortization of the amortizable basis of any certified pollution control facility (as defined in subsection (d)), based on a period of 60 months. Such amortization deduction shall be an amount, with respect to each month of such period within the taxable year, equal to the amortizable basis of the pollution control facility at the end of such month divided by the number of months (including the month for which the deduction is computed) remaining in the period. Such amortizable basis at the end of the month shall be computed without regard to the amortization deduction for such month. The amortization deduction provided by this section with respect to any month shall be in lieu of the depreciation deduction with respect to such pollution control facility for such month provided by section 167. The 60-month period shall begin, as to any pollution control facility, at the election of the taxpayer, with the month following the month in which such facility was completed or acquired, or with the succeeding taxable year.

[Sec. 169(b)]

(b) ELECTION OF AMORTIZATION.—The election of the taxpayer to take the amortization deduction and to begin the 60-month period with the month following the month in which the facility is completed or acquired, or with the taxable year succeeding the taxable year in which such facility is completed or acquired, shall be made by filing with the Secretary, in such manner, in such form, and within such time, as the Secretary may by regulations prescribe, a statement of such election.

[Sec. 169(c)]

(c) TERMINATION OF AMORTIZATION DEDUCTION.—A taxpayer which has elected under subsection (b) to take the amortization deduction provided in subsection (a) may, at any time after making such election, discontinue the amortization deduction with respect to the remainder of the amortization period, such discontinuance to begin as of the beginning of any month specified by the taxpayer in a notice in writing filed with the Secretary before the beginning of such month. The depreciation deduction provided under section 167 shall be allowed, beginning with the first month as to which the amortization deduction does not apply, and the taxpayer shall not be entitled to any further amortization deduction under this section with respect to such pollution control facility.

[Sec. 169(d)]

(d) DEFINITIONS.—For purposes of this section—

(1) CERTIFIED POLLUTION CONTROL FACILITY.—The term "certified pollution control facility" means a new identifiable treatment facility which is used, in connection with a plant or other property in operation before January 1, 1976, to abate or control water or atmospheric pollution or contamination by removing, altering, disposing, storing, or preventing the creation or emission of pollutants, contaminants, wastes, or heat and which—

(A) the State certifying authority having jurisdiction with respect to such facility has certified to the Federal certifying authority as having been constructed, reconstructed, erected, or acquired in conformity with the State program or requirements for abatement or control of water or atmospheric pollution or contamination;

(B) the Federal certifying authority has certified to the Secretary (i) as being in compliance with the applicable regulations of Federal agencies and (ii) as being in furtherance of the general policy of the United States for cooperation with the States in the prevention and abatement of water pollution under the Federal Water Pollution Control Act, as amended (33 U. S. C. 466 et seq.), or in the prevention and abatement of atmospheric pollution and contamination under the Clean Air Act, as amended (42 U.S.C. 1857 et seq.); and

(C) does not significantly—

(i) increase the output or capacity, extend the useful life, or reduce the total operating costs of such plant or other property (or any unit thereof), or

(ii) alter the nature of the manufacturing or production process or facility.

(2) STATE CERTIFYING AUTHORITY.—The term "State certifying authority" means, in the case of water pollution, the State water pollution control agency as defined in section 13(a) of the Federal Water Pollution Control Act and, in the case of air pollution, the air pollution control agency as defined in section 302(b) of the Clean Air Act. The term "State certifying authority" includes any interstate agency authorized to act in place of a certifying authority of the State.

(3) FEDERAL CERTIFYING AUTHORITY.—The term "Federal certifying authority" means, in the case of water pollution, the Secretary of the Interior and, in the case of air pollution, the Secretary of Health, Education, and Welfare.

(4) NEW IDENTIFIABLE TREATMENT FACILITY.—

(A) IN GENERAL.—For purposes of paragraph (1), the term "new identifiable treatment facility" includes only tangible property (not including a building and its structural components, other than a building which is exclusively a treatment facility) which is of a character subject to the allowance for depreciation provided in section 167, which is identifiable as a treatment facility, and which is property—

(i) the construction, reconstruction, or erection of which is completed by the taxpayer after December 31, 1968, or

(ii) acquired after December 31, 1968, if the original use of the property commences with the taxpayer and commences after such date.

In applying this section in the case of property described in clause (i) there shall be taken into account only that portion of the basis which is properly attributable to construction, reconstruction, or erection after December 31, 1968.

(B) CERTAIN PLANTS, ETC., PLACED IN OPERATION AFTER 1968.—In the case of any treatment facility used in connection with any plant or other property not in operation before January 1, 1969, the preceding sentence shall be applied by substituting December 31, 1975, for December 31, 1968.

[Sec. 169(e)]

(e) PROFITMAKING ABATEMENT WORKS, ETC.—The Federal certifying authority shall not certify any property under subsection (d)(1)(B) to the extent it appears that by reason of profits derived through the recovery of wastes or otherwise in the operation of such property, its costs will be recovered over its actual useful life.

Sec. 169(e)

[Sec. 169(f)]

(f) AMORTIZABLE BASIS.—

(1) DEFINED.—For purposes of this section, the term "amortizable basis" means that portion of the adjusted basis (for determining gain) of a certified pollution control facility which may be amortized under this section.

(2) SPECIAL RULES.—

(A) If a certified pollution control facility has a useful life (determined as of the first day of the first month for which a deduction is allowable under this section) in excess of 15 years, the amortizable basis of such facility shall be equal to an amount which bears the same ratio to the portion of the adjusted basis of such facility, which would be eligible for amortization but for the application of this subparagraph, as 15 bears to the number of years of useful life of such facility.

(B) The amortizable basis of a certified pollution control facility with respect to which an election under this section is in effect shall not be increased, for purposes of this section, for additions or improvements after the amortization period has begun.

[Sec. 169(g)]

(g) DEPRECIATION DEDUCTION.—The depreciation deduction provided by section 167 shall, despite the provisions of subsection (a), be allowed with respect to the portion of the adjusted basis which is not the amortizable basis.

[Sec. 169(i)]

(i) LIFE TENANT AND REMAINDERMAN.—In the case of property held by one person for life with remainder to another person, the deduction under this section shall be computed as if the life tenant were the absolute owner of the property and shall be allowable to the life tenant.

[Sec. 169(j)]

(j) CROSS REFERENCE.—For special rule with respect to certain gain derived from the disposition of property the adjusted basis of which is determined with regard to this section, see section 1245.

[Sec. 170]

SEC. 170. CHARITABLE, ETC., CONTRIBUTIONS AND GIFTS.

[Sec. 170(a)]

(a) ALLOWANCE OF DEDUCTION.—

(1) GENERAL RULE.—There shall be allowed as a deduction any charitable contribution (as defined in subsection (c)) payment of which is made within the taxable year. A charitable contribution shall be allowable as a deduction only if verified under regulations prescribed by the Secretary.

(2) CORPORATIONS ON ACCRUAL BASIS.—In the case of a corporation reporting its taxable income on the accrual basis, if—

(A) the board of directors authorizes a charitable contribution during any taxable year, and

(B) payment of such contribution is made after the close of such taxable year and on or before the 15th day of the third month following the close of such taxable year,

then the taxpayer may elect to treat such contribution as paid during such taxable year. The election may be made only at the time of the filing of the return for such taxable year, and shall be signified in such manner as the Secretary shall by regulations prescribe.

(3) FUTURE INTERESTS IN TANGIBLE PERSONAL PROPERTY.—For purposes of this section, payment of a charitable contribution which consists of a future interest in tangible personal property shall be treated as made only when all intervening interests in, and rights to the actual possession or enjoyment of, the property have expired or are held by persons other than the taxpayer or those standing in a relationship to the taxpayer described in section 267(b) or 707(b). For purposes of the preceding sentence, a fixture which is intended to be severed from the real property shall be treated as tangible personal property.

[Sec. 170(b)]

(b) PERCENTAGE LIMITATIONS.—

(1) INDIVIDUALS.—In the case of an individual, the deduction provided in subsection (a) shall be limited as provided in the succeeding subparagraphs.

(A) GENERAL RULE.—Any charitable contribution to—

(i) a church or a convention or association of churches,

(ii) an educational organization which normally maintains a regular faculty and curriculum and normally has a regularly enrolled body of pupils or students in attendance at the place where its educational activities are regularly carried on,

(iii) an organization the principal purpose or functions of which are the providing of medical or hospital care or medical education or medical research, if the organization is a hospital, or if the organization is a medical research organization directly engaged in the continuous active conduct of medical research in conjunction with a hospital, and during the calendar year in which the contribution is made such organization is committed to spend such contributions for such research before January 1 of the fifth calendar year which begins after the date such contribution is made,

(iv) an organization which normally receives a substantial part of its support (exclusive of income received in the exercise or performance by such organization of its charitable, educational, or other purpose or function constituting the basis for its exemption under section 501(a)) from the United States or any State or political subdivision thereof or from direct or indirect contributions from the general public, and which is organized and operated exclusively to receive, hold, invest, and administer property and to make expenditures to or for the benefit of a college or university which is an organization referred to in clause (ii) of this subparagraph and which is an agency or instrumentality of a State or political subdivision thereof, or which is owned or operated by a State or political subdivision thereof or by an agency or instrumentality of one or more States or political subdivisions,

(v) a governmental unit referred to in subsection (c)(1),

(vi) an organization referred to in subsection (c)(2) which normally receives a substantial part of its support (exclusive of income received in the exercise or performance by such organization of its charitable, educational, or other purpose or function constituting the basis for its exemption under section 501(a)) from a governmental unit referred to in subsection (c)(1) or from direct or indirect contributions from the general public,

(vii) a private foundation described in subparagraph (E), or

(viii) an organization described in section 509(a)(2) or (3),

shall be allowed to the extent that the aggregate of such contributions does not exceed 50 percent of the taxpayer's contribution base for the taxable year.

(B) OTHER CONTRIBUTIONS.—Any charitable contribution other than a charitable contribution to which subparagraph (A) applies shall be allowed to the extent that the aggregate of such contributions does not exceed the lesser of—

(i) 30 percent of the taxpayer's contribution base for the taxable year, or

(ii) the excess of 50 percent of the taxpayer's contribution base for the taxable year over the amount of charitable contributions allowable under subparagraph (A) (determined without regard to subparagraph (C)).

If the aggregate of such contributions exceeds the limitation of the preceding sentence, such excess shall be treated (in a manner consistent with the rules of subsection (d)(1)) as a charitable contribution (to which subparagraph (A) does not apply) in each of the 5 succeeding taxable years in order of time.

(C) SPECIAL LIMITATION WITH RESPECT TO CONTRIBUTIONS DESCRIBED IN SUBPARAGRAPH (A) OF CERTAIN CAPITAL GAIN PROPERTY.—

(i) In the case of charitable contributions described in subparagraph (A) of capital gain property to which subsection (e)(1)(B) does not apply, the total amount of contributions of such property which may be taken into account under subsection (a) for any taxable year shall not exceed 30 percent of the taxpayer's contribution base for such year. For purposes of this subsection, contributions of capital gain property to which this subparagraph applies shall be taken into account after all other charitable contributions (other than charitable contributions to which subparagraph (D) applies).

(ii) If charitable contributions described in subparagraph (A) of capital gain property to which clause (i) applies exceeds 30 percent of the taxpayer's contribution base for any taxable year, such excess shall be treated, in a manner consistent with the rules of subsection (d)(1), as a charitable contribution of capital gain property to which clause (i) applies in each of the 5 succeeding taxable years in order of time.

(iii) At the election of the taxpayer (made at such time and in such manner as the Secretary prescribes by regulations), subsection (e)(1) shall apply to all contributions of capital gain property (to which subsection (e)(1)(B) does not otherwise apply) made by the taxpayer during the taxable year. If such an election is made, clauses (i) and (ii) shall not apply to contributions of capital gain property made during the taxable year, and, in applying subsection (d)(1) for such taxable year with respect to contributions of capital gain property made in any prior contribution year for which an election was not made under this clause, such contributions shall be reduced as if subsection (e)(1) had applied to such contributions in the year in which made.

(iv) For purposes of this paragraph, the term "capital gain property" means, with respect to any contribution, any capital asset the sale of which at its fair market value at the time of the contribution would have resulted in gain which would have been long-term capital gain. For purposes of the preceding sentence, any property which is property used in the trade or business (as defined in section 1231(b)) shall be treated as a capital asset.

(D) SPECIAL LIMITATION WITH RESPECT TO CONTRIBUTIONS OF CAPITAL GAIN PROPERTY TO ORGANIZATIONS NOT DESCRIBED IN SUBPARAGRAPH (A).—

(i) IN GENERAL.—In the case of charitable contributions (other than charitable contributions to which subparagraph (A) applies) of capital gain property, the total amount of such contributions of such property taken into account under subsection (a) for any taxable year shall not exceed the lesser of—

(I) 20 percent of the taxpayer's contribution base for the taxable year, or

(II) the excess of 30 percent of the taxpayer's contribution base for the taxable year over the amount of the contributions of capital gain property to which subparagraph (C) applies.

For purposes of this subsection, contributions of capital gain property to which this subparagraph applies shall be taken into account after all other charitable contributions.

(ii) CARRYOVER.—If the aggregate amount of contributions described in clause (i) exceeds the limitation of clause (i), such excess shall be treated (in a manner consistent with the rules of subsection (d)(1)) as a charitable contribution of capital gain property to which clause (i) applies in each of the 5 succeeding taxable years in order of time.

(E) CERTAIN PRIVATE FOUNDATIONS.—The private foundations referred to in subparagraph (A)(vii) and subsection (e)(1)(B) are—

(i) a private operating foundation (as defined in section 4942(j)(3)),

(ii) any other private foundation (as defined in section 509(a)) which, not later than the 15th day of the third month after the close of the foundation's taxable year in which contributions are received, makes qualifying distributions (as defined in section 4942(g), without regard to paragraph (3) thereof), which are treated, after the application of section 4942(g)(3), as distributions out of corpus (in accordance with section 4942(h)) in an amount equal to 100 percent of such contributions, and with respect to which the taxpayer obtains adequate records or other sufficient evidence from the foundation showing that the foundation made such qualifying distributions, and

(iii) a private foundation all of the contributions to which are pooled in a common fund and which would be described in section 509(a)(3) but for the right of any substantial contributor (hereafter in this clause called "donor") or his spouse to designate annually the recipients, from among organizations described in paragraph (1) of section 509(a), of the income attributable to the donor's contribution to the fund and to direct (by deed or by will) the payment, to an organization described in such paragraph (1), of the corpus in the common fund attributable to the donor's contribution; but this clause shall apply only if all of the income of the common fund is required to be (and is) distributed to one or more organizations described in such paragraph (1) not later than the 15th day of the third month after the close of the taxable year in which the income is realized by the fund and only if all of the corpus attributable to any donor's contribution to the fund is required to be (and is) distributed to one or more of such organizations not later than one year after his death or after the death of his surviving spouse if she has the right to designate the recipients of such corpus.

(F) CONTRIBUTION BASE DEFINED.—For purposes of this section, the term "contribution base" means adjusted gross income (computed without regard to any net operating loss carryback to the taxable year under section 172).

(2) CORPORATIONS.—In the case of a corporation, the total deductions under subsection (a) for any taxable year shall not exceed 10 percent of the taxpayer's taxable income computed without regard to—

(A) this section,

(B) part VIII (except section 248),

(C) any net operating loss carryback to the taxable year under section 172, and

(D) any capital loss carryback to the taxable year under section 1212(a)(1).

[Sec. 170(c)]

(c) CHARITABLE CONTRIBUTION DEFINED.—For purposes of this section, the term "charitable contribution" means a contribution or gift to or for the use of—

(1) A State, a possession of the United States, or any political subdivision of any of the foregoing, or the United States or the District of Columbia, but only if the contribution or gift is made for exclusively public purposes.

(2) A corporation, trust, or community chest, fund, or foundation—

(A) created or organized in the United States or in any possession thereof, or under the law of the United States, any State, the District of Columbia, or any possession of the United States;

(B) organized and operated exclusively for religious, charitable, scientific, literary, or educational purposes, or to foster national or international amateur sports competition (but only if no part of its activities involve the provision of athletic facilities or equipment), or for the prevention of cruelty to children or animals;

(C) no part of the net earnings of which inures to the benefit of any private shareholder or individual; and

(D) which is not disqualified for tax exemption under section 501(c)(3) by reason of attempting to influence legislation, and which does not participate in, or intervene in (including the publishing or distributing of statements), any political campaign on behalf of (or in opposition to) any candidate for public office.

A contribution or gift by a corporation to a trust, chest, fund, or foundation shall be deductible by reason of this paragraph only if it is to be used within the United States or any of its possessions exclusively for purposes specified in subparagraph (B). Rules similar to the rules of section 501(j) shall apply for purposes of this paragraph.

(3) A post or organization of war veterans, or an auxiliary unit or society of, or trust or foundation for, any such post or organization—

(A) organized in the United States or any of its possessions, and

(B) no part of the net earnings of which inures to the benefit of any private shareholder or individual.

(4) In the case of a contribution or gift by an individual, a domestic fraternal society, order, or association, operating under the lodge system, but only if such contribution or gift is to be used exclusively for religious, charitable, scientific, literary, or educational purposes, or for the prevention of cruelty to children or animals.

(5) A cemetery company owned and operated exclusively for the benefit of its members, or any corporation chartered solely for burial purposes as a cemetery corporation and not permitted by its charter to engage in any business not necessarily incident to that purpose, if such company or corporation is not operated for profit and no part of the net earnings of such company or corporation inures to the benefit of any private shareholder or individual.

For purposes of this section, the term "charitable contribution" also means an amount treated under subsection (g) as paid for the use of an organization described in paragraph (2), (3), or (4).

Sec. 170(c)

[Sec. 170(d)]

(d) CARRYOVERS OF EXCESS CONTRIBUTIONS.—

(1) INDIVIDUALS.—

(A) IN GENERAL.—In the case of an individual, if the amount of charitable contributions described in subsection (b)(1)(A) payment of which is made within a taxable year (hereinafter in this paragraph referred to as the "contribution year") exceeds 50 percent of the taxpayer's contribution base for such year, such excess shall be treated as a charitable contribution described in subsection (b)(1)(A) paid in each of the 5 succeeding taxable years in order of time, but, with respect to any such succeeding taxable year, only to the extent of the lesser of the two following amounts:

(i) the amount by which 50 percent of the taxpayer's contribution base for such succeeding taxable year exceeds the sum of the charitable contributions described in subsection (b)(1)(A) payment of which is made by the taxpayer within such succeeding taxable year (determined without regard to this subparagraph) and the charitable contributions described in subsection (b)(1)(A) payment of which was made in taxable years before the contribution year which are treated under this subparagraph as having been paid in such succeeding taxable year; or

(ii) in the case of the first succeeding taxable year, the amount of such excess, and in the case of the second, third, fourth, or fifth succeeding taxable year, the portion of such excess not treated under this subparagraph as a charitable contribution described in subsection (b)(1)(A) paid in any taxable year intervening between the contribution year and such succeeding taxable year.

(B) SPECIAL RULE FOR NET OPERATING LOSS CARRYOVERS.—In applying subparagraph (A), the excess determined under subparagraph (A) for the contribution year shall be reduced to the extent that such excess reduces taxable income (as computed for purposes of the second sentence of section 172(b)(2)) and increases the net operating loss deduction for a taxable year succeeding the contribution year.

(2) CORPORATIONS.—

(A) IN GENERAL.—Any contribution made by a corporation in a taxable year (hereinafter in this paragraph referred to as the "contribution year") in excess of the amount deductible for such year under subsection (b)(2) shall be deductible for each of the 5 succeeding taxable years in order of time, but only to the extent of the lesser of the two following amounts: (i) the excess of the maximum amount deductible for such succeeding taxable year under subsection (b)(2) over the sum of the contributions made in such year plus the aggregate of the excess contributions which were made in taxable years before the contribution year and which are deductible under this subparagraph for such succeeding taxable year; or (ii) in the case of the first succeeding taxable year, the amount of such excess contribution, and in the case of the second, third, fourth, or fifth succeeding taxable year, the portion of such excess contribution not deductible under this subparagraph for any taxable year intervening between the contribution year and such succeeding taxable year.

(B) SPECIAL RULE FOR NET OPERATING LOSS CARRYOVERS.—For purposes of subparagraph (A), the excess of—

(i) the contributions made by a corporation in a taxable year to which this section applies, over

(ii) the amount deductible in such year under the limitation in subsection (b)(2),

shall be reduced to the extent that such excess reduces taxable income (as computed for purposes of the second sentence of section 172(b)(2)) and increases a net operating loss carryover under section 172 to a succeeding taxable year.

[Sec. 170(e)]

(e) CERTAIN CONTRIBUTIONS OF ORDINARY INCOME AND CAPITAL GAIN PROPERTY.—

(1) GENERAL RULE.—The amount of any charitable contribution of property otherwise taken into account under this section shall be reduced by the sum of—

(A) the amount of gain which would not have been long-term capital gain if the property contributed had been sold by the taxpayer at its fair market value (determined at the time of such contribution), and

Sec. 170(d)

(B) in the case of a charitable contribution—

(i) of tangible personal property, if the use by the donee is unrelated to the purpose or function constituting the basis for its exemption under section 501 (or, in the case of a governmental unit, to any purpose or function described in subsection (c)), or

(ii) to or for the use of a private foundation (as defined in section 509(a)), other than a private foundation described in subsection (b)(1)(E),

the amount of gain which would have been long-term capital gain if the property contributed had been sold by the taxpayer at its fair market value (determined at the time of such contribution).

[*Caution: The flush text of Code Sec. 170(e)(1), below, prior to amendment by P.L. 107-16, applies to estates of decedents dying on or before December 31, 2009.*]

For purposes of applying this paragraph (other than in the case of gain to which section 617(d)(1), 1245(a), 1250(a), 1252(a), or 1254(a) applies), property which is property used in the trade or business (as defined in section 1231(b)) shall be treated as a capital asset. For purposes of applying this paragraph in the case of a charitable contribution of stock in an S corporation, rules similar to the rules of section 751 shall apply in determining whether gain on such stock would have been long-term capital gain if such stock were sold by the taxpayer.

[*Caution: The flush text of Code Sec. 170(e)(1), below, as amended by P.L. 107-16, applies to estates of decedents dying after December 31, 2009.*]

For purposes of applying this paragraph (other than in the case of gain to which section 617(d)(1), 1245(a), 1250(a), 1252(a), or 1254(a) applies), property which is property used in the trade or business (as defined in section 1231(b)) shall be treated as a capital asset. For purposes of applying this paragraph in the case of a charitable contribution of stock in an S corporation, rules similar to the rules of section 751 shall apply in determining whether gain on such stock would have been long-term capital gain if such stock were sold by the taxpayer. For purposes of this paragraph, the determination of whether property is a capital asset shall be made without regard to the exception contained in section 1221(a)(3)(C) for basis determined under section 1022.

(2) ALLOCATION OF BASIS.—For purposes of paragraph (1), in the case of a charitable contribution of less than the taxpayer's entire interest in the property contributed, the taxpayer's adjusted basis in such property shall be allocated between the interest contributed and any interest not contributed in accordance with regulations prescribed by the Secretary.

(3) SPECIAL RULE FOR CERTAIN CONTRIBUTIONS OF INVENTORY AND OTHER PROPERTY.—

(A) QUALIFIED CONTRIBUTIONS.—For purposes of this paragraph, a qualified contribution shall mean a charitable contribution of property described in paragraph (1) or (2) of section 1221(a), by a corporation (other than a corporation which is an S corporation) to an organization which is described in section 501(c)(3) and is exempt under section 501(a) (other than a private foundation, as defined in section 509(a), which is not an operating foundation, as defined in section 4942(j)(3)), but only if—

(i) the use of the property by the donee is related to the purpose or function constituting the basis for its exemption under section 501 and the property is to be used by the donee solely for the care of the ill, the needy, or infants;

(ii) the property is not transferred by the donee in exchange for money, other property, or services;

(iii) the taxpayer receives from the donee a written statement representing that its use and disposition of the property will be in accordance with the provisions of clauses (i) and (ii); and

(iv) in the case where the property is subject to regulation under the Federal Food, Drug, and Cosmetic Act, as amended, such property must fully satisfy the applicable requirements of such Act and regulations promulgated thereunder on the date of transfer and for one hundred and eighty days prior thereto.

(B) AMOUNT OF REDUCTION.—The reduction under paragraph (1)(A) for any qualified contribution (as defined in subparagraph (A)) shall be no greater than the sum of—

(i) one-half of the amount computed under paragraph (1)(A) (computed without regard to this paragraph), and

(ii) the amount (if any) by which the charitable contribution deduction under this section for any qualified contribution (computed by taking into account the amount determined in clause (i), but without regard to this clause) exceeds twice the basis of such property.

(C) This paragraph shall not apply to so much of the amount of the gain described in paragraph (1)(A) which would be long-term capital gain but for the application of sections 617, 1245, 1250, or 1252.

(4) SPECIAL RULE FOR CONTRIBUTIONS OF SCIENTIFIC PROPERTY USED FOR RESEARCH.—

(A) LIMIT ON REDUCTION.—In the case of a qualified research contribution, the reduction under paragraph (1)(A) shall be no greater than the amount determined under paragraph (3)(B).

(B) QUALIFIED RESEARCH CONTRIBUTIONS.—For purposes of this paragraph, the term "qualified research contribution" means a charitable contribution by a corporation of tangible personal property described in paragraph (1) of section 1221(a), but only if—

(i) the contribution is to an organization described in subparagraph (A) or subparagraph (B) of section 41(e)(6),

(ii) the property is constructed by the taxpayer,

(iii) the contribution is made not later than 2 years after the date the construction of the property is substantially completed,

(iv) the original use of the property is by the donee,

(v) the property is scientific equipment or apparatus substantially all of the use of which by the donee is for research or experimentation (within the meaning of section 174), or for research training, in the United States in physical or biological sciences,

(vi) the property is not transferred by the donee in exchange for money, other property, or services, and

(vii) the taxpayer receives from the donee a written statement representing that its use and disposition of the property will be in accordance with the provisions of clauses (v) and (vi).

(C) CONSTRUCTION OF PROPERTY BY TAXPAYER.—For purposes of this paragraph, property shall be treated as constructed by the taxpayer only if the cost of the parts used in the construction of such property (other than parts manufactured by the taxpayer or a related person) do not exceed 50 percent of the taxpayer's basis in such property.

(D) CORPORATION.—For purposes of this paragraph, the term "corporation" shall not include—

(i) an S corporation,

(ii) a personal holding company (as defined in section 542), and

(iii) a service organization (as defined in section 414(m)(3)).

(5) SPECIAL RULE FOR CONTRIBUTIONS OF STOCK FOR WHICH MARKET QUOTATIONS ARE READILY AVAILABLE.—

(A) IN GENERAL.—Subparagraph (B)(ii) of paragraph (1) shall not apply to any contribution of qualified appreciated stock.

(B) QUALIFIED APPRECIATED STOCK.—Except as provided in subparagraph (C), for purposes of this paragraph, the term "qualified appreciated stock" means any stock of a corporation—

(i) for which (as of the date of the contribution) market quotations are readily available on an established securities market, and

(ii) which is capital gain property (as defined in subsection (b)(1)(C)(iv)).

(C) DONOR MAY NOT CONTRIBUTE MORE THAN 10 PERCENT OF STOCK OF CORPORATION.—

(i) IN GENERAL.—In the case of any donor, the term "qualified appreciated stock" shall not include any stock of a corporation contributed by the donor in a contribution to which paragraph (1)(B)(ii) applies (determined without regard to this paragraph) to the extent that the amount of the stock so contributed (when increased by the aggregate amount of all prior such contributions by the donor of stock in such corporation) exceeds 10 percent (in value) of all of the outstanding stock of such corporation.

(ii) SPECIAL RULE.—For purposes of clause (i), an individual shall be treated as making all contributions made by any member of his family (as defined in section 267(c)(4)).

(6) SPECIAL RULE FOR CONTRIBUTIONS OF COMPUTER TECHNOLOGY AND EQUIPMENT FOR EDUCATIONAL PURPOSES.—

(A) LIMIT ON REDUCTION.—In the case of a qualified computer contribution, the reduction under paragraph (1)(A) shall be no greater than the amount determined under paragraph (3)(B).

(B) QUALIFIED COMPUTER CONTRIBUTION.—For purposes of this paragraph, the term "qualified computer contribution" means a charitable contribution by a corporation of any computer technology or equipment, but only if—

(i) the contribution is to—

(I) an educational organization described in subsection (b)(1)(A)(ii),

(II) an entity described in section 501(c)(3) and exempt from tax under section 501(a) (other than an entity described in subclause (I)) that is organized primarily for purposes of supporting elementary and secondary education, or

(III) a public library (within the meaning of section 213(2)(A) of the Library Services and Technology Act (20 U.S.C. 9122(2)(A)), as in effect on the date of the enactment of the Community Renewal Tax Relief Act of 2000), established and maintained by an entity described in subsection (c)(1),

(ii) the contribution is made not later than 3 years after the date the taxpayer acquired the property (or in the case of property constructed by the taxpayer, the date the construction of the property is substantially completed),

(iii) the original use of the property is by the donor or the donee,

(iv) substantially all of the use of the property by the donee is for use within the United States for educational purposes that are related to the purpose or function of the donee,

(v) the property is not transferred by the donee in exchange for money, other property, or services, except for shipping, installation and transfer costs,

(vi) the property will fit productively into the donee's education plan,

(vii) the donee's use and disposition of the property will be in accordance with the provisions of clauses (iv) and (v), and

(viii) the property meets such standards, if any, as the Secretary may prescribe by regulation to assure that the property meets minimum functionality and suitability standards for educational purposes.

(C) CONTRIBUTION TO PRIVATE FOUNDATION.—A contribution by a corporation of any computer technology or equipment to a private foundation (as defined in section 509) shall be treated as a qualified computer contribution for purposes of this paragraph if—

(i) the contribution to the private foundation satisfies the requirements of clauses (ii) and (v) of subparagraph (B), and

(ii) within 30 days after such contribution, the private foundation—

(I) contributes the property to a donee described in clause (i) of subparagraph (B) that satisfies the requirements of clauses (iv) through (vii) of subparagraph (B), and

(II) notifies the donor of such contribution.

(D) DONATIONS OF PROPERTY REACQUIRED BY MANUFACTURER.—In the case of property which is reacquired by the person who constructed the property—

(i) subparagraph (B)(ii) shall be applied to a contribution of such property by such person by taking into account the date that the original construction of the property was substantially completed, and

(ii) subparagraph (B)(iii) shall not apply to such contribution.

(E) SPECIAL RULE RELATING TO CONSTRUCTION OF PROPERTY.—For the purposes of this paragraph, the rules of paragraph (4)(C) shall apply.

(F) DEFINITIONS.—For the purposes of this paragraph—

(i) COMPUTER TECHNOLOGY OR EQUIPMENT.—The term "computer technology or equipment" means computer software (as defined by section 197(e)(3)(B)), computer or

Sec. 170(e)

peripheral equipment (as defined by section 168(i)(2)(B)), and fiber optic cable related to computer use.

(ii) CORPORATION.—The term "corporation" has the meaning given to such term by paragraph (4)(D).

(G) TERMINATION.—This paragraph shall not apply to any contribution made during any taxable year beginning after December 31, 2003.

[Sec. 170(f)]

(f) DISALLOWANCE OF DEDUCTION IN CERTAIN CASES AND SPECIAL RULES.—

(1) IN GENERAL.—No deduction shall be allowed under this section for a contribution to or for the use of an organization or trust described in section 508(d) or 4948(c)(4) subject to the conditions specified in such sections.

(2) CONTRIBUTIONS OF PROPERTY PLACED IN TRUST.—

(A) REMAINDER INTEREST.—In the case of property transferred in trust, no deduction shall be allowed under this section for the value of a contribution of a remainder interest unless the trust is a charitable remainder annuity trust or a charitable remainder unitrust (described in section 664), or a pooled income fund (described in section 642(c)(5)).

(B) INCOME INTERESTS, ETC.—No deduction shall be allowed under this section for the value of any interest in property (other than a remainder interest) transferred in trust unless the interest is in the form of a guaranteed annuity or the trust instrument specifies that the interest is a fixed percentage distributed yearly of the fair market value of the trust property (to be determined yearly) and the grantor is treated as the owner of such interest for purposes of applying section 671. If the donor ceases to be treated as the owner of such an interest for purposes of applying section 671, at the time the donor ceases to be so treated, the donor shall for purposes of this chapter be considered as having received an amount of income equal to the amount of any deduction he received under this section for the contribution reduced by the discounted value of all amounts of income earned by the trust and taxable to him before the time at which he ceases to be treated as the owner of the interest. Such amounts of income shall be discounted to the date of the contribution. The Secretary shall prescribe such regulations as may be necessary to carry out the purposes of this subparagraph.

(C) DENIAL OF DEDUCTION IN CASE OF PAYMENTS BY CERTAIN TRUSTS.—In any case in which a deduction is allowed under this section for the value of an interest in property described in subparagraph (B), transferred in trust, no deduction shall be allowed under this section to the grantor or any other person for the amount of any contribution made by the trust with respect to such interest.

(D) EXCEPTION.—This paragraph shall not apply in a case in which the value of all interests in property transferred in trust are deductible under subsection (a).

(3) DENIAL OF DEDUCTION IN CASE OF CERTAIN CONTRIBUTIONS OF PARTIAL INTERESTS IN PROPERTY.—

(A) IN GENERAL.—In the case of a contribution (not made by a transfer in trust) of an interest in property which consists of less than the taxpayer's entire interest in such property, a deduction shall be allowed under this section only to the extent that the value of the interest contributed would be allowable as a deduction under this section if such interest had been transferred in trust. For purposes of this subparagraph, a contribution by a taxpayer of the right to use property shall be treated as a contribution of less than the taxpayer's entire interest in such property.

(B) EXCEPTIONS.—Subparagraph (A) shall not apply to—

(i) a contribution of a remainder interest in a personal residence or farm,

(ii) a contribution of an undivided portion of the taxpayer's entire interest in property, and

(iii) a qualified conservation contribution.

(4) VALUATION OF REMAINDER INTEREST IN REAL PROPERTY.—For purposes of this section, in determining the value of a remainder interest in real property, depreciation (computed on the straight line method) and depletion of such property shall be taken into account, and such value shall be discounted at a rate of 6 percent per annum, except that the Secretary may prescribe a different rate.

(5) REDUCTION FOR CERTAIN INTEREST.—If, in connection with any charitable contribution, a liability is assumed by the recipient or by any other person, or if a charitable contribution is of property which is subject to a liability, then, to the extent necessary to avoid the duplication of amounts, the amount taken into account for purposes of this section as the amount of the charitable contribution—

(A) shall be reduced for interest (i) which has been paid (or is to be paid) by the taxpayer, (ii) which is attributable to the liability, and (iii) which is attributable to any period after the making of the contribution, and

(B) in the case of a bond, shall be further reduced for interest (i) which has been paid (or is to be paid) by the taxpayer on indebtedness incurred or continued to purchase or carry such bond, and (ii) which is attributable to any period before the making of the contribution.

The reduction pursuant to subparagraph (B) shall not exceed the interest (including interest equivalent) on the bond which is attributable to any period before the making of the contribution and which is not (under the taxpayer's method of accounting) includible in the gross income of the taxpayer for any taxable year. For purposes of this paragraph, the term "bond" means any bond, debenture, note, or certificate or other evidence of indebtedness.

(6) DEDUCTIONS FOR OUT-OF-POCKET EXPENDITURES.—No deduction shall be allowed under this section for an out-of-pocket expenditure made by any person on behalf of an organization described in subsection (c) (other than an organization described in section 501(h)(5) (relating to churches, etc.)) if the expenditure is made for the purpose of influencing legislation (within the meaning of section 501(c)(3)).

(7) REFORMATIONS TO COMPLY WITH PARAGRAPH (2).—

(A) IN GENERAL.—A deduction shall be allowed under subsection (a) in respect of any qualified reformation (within the meaning of section 2055(e)(3)(B)).

(B) RULES SIMILAR TO SECTION 2055 (e)(3) TO APPLY.—For purposes of this paragraph, rules similar to the rules of section 2055(e)(3) shall apply.

(8) SUBSTANTIATION REQUIREMENT FOR CERTAIN CONTRIBUTIONS.—

(A) GENERAL RULE.—No deduction shall be allowed under subsection (a) for any contribution of $250 or more unless the taxpayer substantiates the contribution by a contemporaneous written acknowledgment of the contribution by the donee organization that meets the requirements of subparagraph (B).

(B) CONTENT OF ACKNOWLEDGEMENT.—An acknowledgement meets the requirements of this subparagraph if it includes the following information:

(i) The amount of cash and a description (but not value) of any property other than cash contributed.

(ii) Whether the donee organization provided any goods or services in consideration, in whole or in part, for any property described in clause (i).

(iii) A description and good faith estimate of the value of any goods or services referred to in clause (ii) or, if such goods or services consist solely of intangible religious benefits, a statement to that effect.

For purposes of this subparagraph, the term "intangible religious benefit" means any intangible religious benefit which is provided by an organization organized exclusively for religious purposes and which generally is not sold in a commercial transaction outside the donative context.

(C) CONTEMPORANEOUS.—For purposes of subparagraph (A), an acknowledgment shall be considered to be contemporaneous if the taxpayer obtains the acknowledgment on or before the earlier of—

(i) the date on which the taxpayer files a return for the taxable year in which the contribution was made, or

(ii) the due date (including extensions) for filing such return.

(D) SUBSTANTIATION NOT REQUIRED FOR CONTRIBUTIONS REPORTED BY THE DONEE ORGANIZATION.—Subparagraph (A) shall not apply to a contribution if the donee organization files a return, on such form and in accordance with such regulations as the Secretary may prescribe, which includes the information described in subparagraph (B) with respect to the contribution.

Sec. 170(f)

(E) REGULATIONS.—The Secretary shall prescribe such regulations as may be necessary or appropriate to carry out the purposes of this paragraph, including regulations that may provide that some or all of the requirements of this paragraph do not apply in appropriate cases.

(9) DENIAL OF DEDUCTION WHERE CONTRIBUTION FOR LOBBYING ACTIVITIES.—No deduction shall be allowed under this section for a contribution to an organization which conducts activities to which section 162(e)(1) applies on matters of direct financial interest to the donor's trade or business, if a principal purpose of the contribution was to avoid Federal income tax by securing a deduction for such activities under this section which would be disallowed by reason of section 162(e) if the donor had conducted such activities directly. No deduction shall be allowed under section 162(a) for any amount for which a deduction is disallowed under the preceding sentence.

* * *

[Sec. 170(g)]

(g) AMOUNTS PAID TO MAINTAIN CERTAIN STUDENTS AS MEMBERS OF TAXPAYER'S HOUSEHOLD.—

(1) IN GENERAL.—Subject to the limitations provided by paragraph (2), amounts paid by the taxpayer to maintain an individual (other than a dependent, as defined in section 152, or a relative of the taxpayer) as a member of his household during the period that such individual is—

(A) a member of the taxpayer's household under a written agreement between the taxpayer and an organization described in paragraph (2), (3), or (4) of subsection (c) to implement a program of the organization to provide educational opportunities for pupils or students in private homes, and

(B) a full-time pupil or student in the twelfth or any lower grade at an educational organization described in section 170(b)(1)(A)(ii) located in the United States,

shall be treated as amounts paid for the use of the organization.

(2) LIMITATIONS.—

(A) AMOUNT.—Paragraph (1) shall apply to amounts paid within the taxable year only to the extent that such amounts do not exceed $50 multiplied by the number of full calendar months during the taxable year which fall within the period described in paragraph (1). For purposes of the preceding sentence, if 15 or more days of a calendar month fall within such period such month shall be considered as a full calendar month.

(B) COMPENSATION OR REIMBURSEMENT.—Paragraph (1) shall not apply to any amount paid by the taxpayer within the taxable year if the taxpayer receives any money or other property as compensation or reimbursement for maintaining the individual in his household during the period described in paragraph (1).

(3) RELATIVE DEFINED.—For purposes of paragraph (1), the term "relative of the taxpayer" means an individual who, with respect to the taxpayer, bears any of the relationships described in paragraphs (1) through (8) of section 152(a).

(4) NO OTHER AMOUNT ALLOWED AS DEDUCTION.—No deduction shall be allowed under subsection (a) for any amount paid by a taxpayer to maintain an individual as a member of his household under a program described in paragraph (1)(A) except as provided in this subsection.

[Sec. 170(h)]

(h) QUALIFIED CONSERVATION CONTRIBUTION.—

(1) IN GENERAL.—For purposes of subsection (f)(3)(B)(iii), the term "qualified conservation contribution" means a contribution—

(A) of a qualified real property interest,

(B) to a qualified organization,

(C) exclusively for conservation purposes.

(2) QUALIFIED REAL PROPERTY INTEREST.—For purposes of this subsection, the term "qualified real property interest" means any of the following interests in real property:

(A) the entire interest of the donor other than a qualified mineral interest,

(B) a remainder interest, and

(C) a restriction (granted in perpetuity) on the use which may be made of the real property.

(3) QUALIFIED ORGANIZATION.—For purposes of paragraph (1), the term "qualified organization" means an organization which—

(A) is described in clause (v) or (vi) of subsection (b)(1)(A), or

(B) is described in section 501(c)(3) and—

(i) meets the requirements of section 509(a)(2), or

(ii) meets the requirements of section 509(a)(3) and is controlled by an organization described in subparagraph (A) or in clause (i) of this subparagraph.

(4) CONSERVATION PURPOSE DEFINED.—

(A) IN GENERAL.—For purposes of this subsection, the term "conservation purpose" means—

(i) the preservation of land areas for outdoor recreation by, or the education of, the general public,

(ii) the protection of a relatively natural habitat of fish, wildlife, or plants, or similar ecosystem,

(iii) the preservation of open space (including farmland and forest land) where such preservation is—

(I) for the scenic enjoyment of the general public, or

(II) pursuant to a clearly delineated Federal, State, or local governmental conservation policy,

and will yield a significant public benefit, or

(iv) the preservation of an historically important land area or a certified historic structure.

(B) CERTIFIED HISTORIC STRUCTURE.—For purposes of subparagraph (A)(iv), the term "certified historic structure" means any building, structure, or land area which—

(i) is listed in the National Register, or

(ii) is located in a registered historic district (as defined in section 47(c)(3)(B)) and is certified by the Secretary of the Interior to the Secretary as being of historic significance to the district.

A building, structure, or land area satisfies the preceding sentence if it satisfies such sentence either at the time of the transfer or on the due date (including extensions) for filing the transferor's return under this chapter for the taxable year in which the transfer is made.

(5) EXCLUSIVELY FOR CONSERVATION PURPOSES.—For purposes of this subsection—

(A) CONSERVATION PURPOSE MUST BE PROTECTED.—A contribution shall not be treated as exclusively for conservation purposes unless the conservation purpose is protected in perpetuity.

(B) NO SURFACE MINING PERMITTED.—

(i) IN GENERAL.—Except as provided in clause (ii), in the case of a contribution of any interest where there is a retention of a qualified mineral interest, subparagraph (A) shall not be treated as met if at any time there may be extraction or removal of minerals by any surface mining method.

(ii) SPECIAL RULE.—With respect to any contribution of property in which the ownership of the surface estate and mineral interests has been and remains separated, subparagraph (A) shall be treated as met if the probability of surface mining occurring on such property is so remote as to be negligible.

(6) QUALIFIED MINERAL INTEREST.—For purposes of this subsection, the term "qualified mineral interest" means—

(A) subsurface oil, gas or other minerals, and

(B) the right to access to such minerals.

[Sec. 170(i)]

(i) STANDARD MILEAGE RATE FOR USE OF PASSENGER AUTOMOBILE.—For purposes of computing the deduction under this section for use of a passenger automobile, the standard mileage rate shall be 14 cents per mile.

Sec. 170(i)

(j) DENIAL OF DEDUCTION FOR CERTAIN TRAVEL EXPENSES.—No deduction shall be allowed under this section for traveling expenses (including amounts expended for meals and lodging) while away from home, whether paid directly or by reimbursement, unless there is no significant element of personal pleasure, recreation, or vacation in such travel.

(k) DISALLOWANCE OF DEDUCTIONS IN CERTAIN CASES.—

For disallowance of deductions for contributions to or for the use of communist controlled organizations, see section 11(a) of the Internal Security Act of 1950 (50 U.S.C. 790).

(l) TREATMENT OF CERTAIN AMOUNTS PAID TO OR FOR THE BENEFIT OF INSTITUTIONS OF HIGHER EDUCATION.—

(1) IN GENERAL.—For purposes of this section, 80 percent of any amount described in paragraph (2) shall be treated as a charitable contribution.

(2) AMOUNT DESCRIBED.—For purposes of paragraph (1), an amount is described in this paragraph if—

(A) the amount is paid by the taxpayer to or for the benefit of an educational organization—

(i) which is described in subsection (b)(1)(A)(ii), and

(ii) which is an institution of higher education (as defined in section 3304(f)), and

(B) such amount would be allowable as a deduction under this section but for the fact that the taxpayer receives (directly or indirectly) as a result of paying such amount the right to purchase tickets for seating at an athletic event in an athletic stadium of such institution.

If any portion of a payment is for the purchase of such tickets, such portion and the remaining portion (if any) of such payment shall be treated as separate amounts for purposes of this subsection.

* * *

SEC. 171. AMORTIZABLE BOND PREMIUM.

(a) GENERAL RULE.—In the case of any bond, as defined in subsection (d), the following rules shall apply to the amortizable bond premium (determined under subsection (b)) on the bond:

(1) TAXABLE BONDS.—In the case of a bond (other than a bond the interest on which is excludable from gross income), the amount of the amortizable bond premium for the taxable year shall be allowed as a deduction.

(2) TAX-EXEMPT BONDS.—In the case of any bond the interest on which is excludable from gross income, no deduction shall be allowed for the amortizable bond premium for the taxable year.

(3) CROSS REFERENCE.—

For adjustment to basis on account of amortizable bond premium, see section 1016 (a) (5).

(b) AMORTIZABLE BOND PREMIUM.—

(1) AMOUNT OF BOND PREMIUM.—For purposes of paragraph (2), the amount of bond premium, in the case of the holder of any bond, shall be determined—

(A) with reference to the amount of the basis (for determining loss on sale or exchange) of such bond,

(B) (i) with reference to the amount payable on maturity or on earlier call date, in the case of any bond other than a bond to which clause (ii) applies, or

(ii) with reference to the amount payable on maturity (or if it results in a smaller amortizable bond premium attributable to the period of earlier call date, with reference to the amount payable on earlier call date), in the case of any bond described in subsection (a)(1) which is acquired after December 31, 1957, and

(C) with adjustments proper to reflect unamortized bond premium, with respect to the bond, for the period before the date as of which subsection (a) becomes applicable with respect to the taxpayer with respect to such bond.

In no case shall the amount of bond premium on a convertible bond include any amount attributable to the conversion features of the bond.

(2) AMOUNT AMORTIZABLE.—The amortizable bond premium of the taxable year shall be the amount of the bond premium attributable to such year. In the case of a bond to which paragraph (1)(B)(ii) applies and which has a call date, the amount of bond premium attributable to the taxable year in which the bond is called shall include an amount equal to the excess of the amount of the adjusted basis (for determining loss on sale or exchange) of such bond as of the beginning of the taxable year over the amount received on redemption of the bond or (if greater) the amount payable on maturity.

(3) METHOD OF DETERMINATION.—

(A) IN GENERAL.—Except as provided in regulations prescribed by the Secretary, the determinations required under paragraphs (1) and (2) shall be made on the basis of the taxpayer's yield to maturity determined by—

(i) using the taxpayer's basis (for purposes of determining loss on sale or exchange) of the obligation, and

(ii) compounding at the close of each accrual period (as defined in section 1272(a)(5)).

(B) SPECIAL RULE WHERE EARLIER CALL DATE IS USED.—For purposes of subparagraph (A), if the amount payable on an earlier call date is used under paragraph (1)(B)(ii) in determining the amortizable bond premium attributable to the period before the earlier call date, such bond shall be treated as maturing on such date for the amount so payable and then reissued on such date for the amount so payable.

(4) TREATMENT OF CERTAIN BONDS ACQUIRED IN EXCHANGE FOR OTHER PROPERTY.—

(A) IN GENERAL.—If—

(i) a bond is acquired by any person in exchange for other property, and

(ii) the basis of such bond is determined (in whole or in part) by reference to the basis of such other property,

for purposes of applying this subsection to such bond while held by such person, the basis of such bond shall not exceed its fair market value immediately after the exchange. A similar rule shall apply in the case of such bond while held by any other person whose basis is determined (in whole or in part) by reference to the basis in the hands of the person referred to in clause (i).

(B) SPECIAL RULE WHERE BOND EXCHANGED IN REORGANIZATION.—Subparagraph (A) shall not apply to an exchange by the taxpayer of a bond for another bond if such exchange is a part of a reorganization (as defined in section 368). If any portion of the basis of the taxpayer in a bond transferred in such an exchange is not taken into account in determining bond premium by reason of this paragraph, such portion shall not be taken into account in determining the amount of bond premium on any bond received in the exchange.

[Sec. 171(c)]

(c) ELECTION AS TO TAXABLE BONDS.—

(1) ELIGIBILITY TO ELECT; BONDS WITH RESPECT TO WHICH ELECTION PERMITTED.—In the case of bonds the interest on which is not excludable from gross income, this section shall apply only if the taxpayer has so elected.

(2) MANNER AND EFFECT OF ELECTION.—The election authorized under this subsection shall be made in accordance with such regulations as the Secretary shall prescribe. If such election is made with respect to any bond (described in paragraph (1)) of the taxpayer, it shall also apply to all such bonds held by the taxpayer at the beginning of the first taxable year to which the election applies and to all such bonds thereafter acquired by him and shall be binding for all subsequent taxable years with respect to all such bonds of the taxpayer, unless, on application by the taxpayer, the Secretary permits him, subject to such conditions as the Secretary deems necessary, to revoke such election. In the case of bonds held by a common trust fund, as defined in section 584 (a), or by a foreign personal holding company, as defined in section 552, the election authorized under this subsection shall be

exercisable with respect to such bonds only by the common trust fund or foreign personal holding company. In case of bonds held by an estate or trust, the election authorized under this subsection shall be exercisable with respect to such bonds only by the fiduciary.

[Sec. 171(d)]

(d) BOND DEFINED.—For purposes of this section, the term "bond" means any bond, debenture, note, or certificate or other evidence of indebtedness, but does not include any such obligation which constitutes stock in trade of the taxpayer or any such obligation of a kind which would properly be included in the inventory of the taxpayer if on hand at the close of the taxable year, or any such obligation held by the

[Sec. 171(e)]

(e) TREATMENT AS OFFSET TO INTEREST PAYMENTS.—Except as provided in regulations, in the case of any taxable bond—

(1) the amount of any bond premium shall be allocated among the interest payments on the bond under rules similar to the rules of subsection (b)(3), and

(2) in lieu of any deduction under subsection (a), the amount of any premium so allocated to any interest payment shall be applied against (and operate to reduce) the amount of such interest payment.

For purposes of the preceding sentence, the term "taxable bond" means any bond the interest of which is not excludable from gross income.

* * *

[Sec. 172]
SEC. 172. NET OPERATING LOSS DEDUCTION.

[Sec. 172(a)]

(a) DEDUCTION ALLOWED.—There shall be allowed as a deduction for the taxable year an amount equal to the aggregate of (1) the net operating loss carryovers to such year, plus (2) the net operating loss carrybacks to such year. For purposes of this subtitle, the term "net operating loss deduction" means the deduction allowed by this subsection.

[Sec. 172(b)]

(b) NET OPERATING LOSS CARRYBACKS AND CARRYOVERS.—

(1) YEARS TO WHICH LOSS MAY BE CARRIED.—

(A) GENERAL RULE.—Except as otherwise provided in this paragraph, a net operating loss for any taxable year—

(i) shall be a net operating loss carryback to each of the 2 taxable years preceding the taxable year of such loss, and

(ii) shall be a net operating loss carryover to each of the 20 taxable years following the taxable year of the loss.

(B) SPECIAL RULES FOR REIT'S.—

(i) IN GENERAL.—A net operating loss for a REIT year shall not be a net operating loss carryback to any taxable year preceding the taxable year of such loss.

(ii) SPECIAL RULE.—In the case of any net operating loss for a taxable year which is not a REIT year, such loss shall not be carried back to any taxable year which is a REIT year.

(iii) REIT YEAR.—For purposes of this subparagraph, the term "REIT year" means any taxable year for which the provisions of part II of subchapter M (relating to real estate investment trusts) apply to the taxpayer.

(C) SPECIFIED LIABILITY LOSSES.—In the case of a taxpayer which has a specified liability loss (as defined in subsection (f)) for a taxable year, such specified liability loss shall be a net operating loss carryback to each of the 10 taxable years preceding the taxable year of such loss.

(D) BAD DEBT LOSSES OF COMMERCIAL BANKS.—In the case of any bank (as defined in section 585(a)(2)), the portion of the net operating loss for any taxable year beginning after December 31, 1986, and before January 1, 1994, which is attributable to the deduction allowed under section 166(a) shall be a net operating loss carryback to each of the 10 taxable years preceding the taxable year of the loss and a net operating loss carryover to each of the 5 taxable years following the taxable year of such loss.

(E) EXCESS INTEREST LOSS.—

(i) IN GENERAL.—If—

(I) there is a corporate equity reduction transaction, and

(II) an applicable corporation has a corporate equity reduction interest loss for any loss limitation year ending after August 2, 1989,

then the corporate equity reduction interest loss shall be a net operating loss carryback and carryover to the taxable years described in subparagraph (A), except that such loss shall not be carried back to a taxable year preceding the taxable year in which the corporate equity reduction transaction occurs.

(ii) LOSS LIMITATION YEAR.—For purposes of clause (i) and subsection (h), the term "loss limitation year" means, with respect to any corporate equity reduction transaction, the taxable year in which such transaction occurs and each of the 2 succeeding taxable years.

(iii) APPLICABLE CORPORATION.—For purposes of clause (i), the term "applicable corporation" means—

(I) a C corporation which acquires stock, or the stock of which is acquired in a major stock acquisition,

(II) a C corporation making distributions with respect to, or redeeming, its stock in connection with an excess distribution, or

(III) a C corporation which is a successor of a corporation described in subclause (I) or (II).

(iv) OTHER DEFINITIONS.—

For definitions of terms used in this subparagraph, see subsection (h).

(F) RETENTION OF 3-YEAR CARRYBACK IN CERTAIN CASES.—

(i) IN GENERAL.—Subparagraph (A)(i) shall be applied by substituting "3 taxable years" for "2 taxable years" with respect to the portion of the net operating loss for the taxable year which is an eligible loss with respect to the taxpayer.

(ii) ELIGIBLE LOSS.—For purposes of clause (i), the term "eligible loss" means—

(I) in the case of an individual, losses of property arising from fire, storm, shipwreck, or other casualty, or from theft,

(II) in the case of a taxpayer which is a small business, net operating losses attributable to Presidentially declared disasters (as defined in section 1033(h)(3)), and

(III) in the case of a taxpayer engaged in the trade or business of farming (as defined in section 263A(e)(4)), net operating losses attributable to such Presidentially declared disasters.

Such term shall not include any farming loss (as defined in subsection (i)).

(iii) SMALL BUSINESS.—For purposes of this subparagraph, the term "small business" means a corporation or partnership which meets the gross receipts test of section 448(c) for the taxable year in which the loss arose (or, in the case of a sole proprietorship, which would meet such test if such proprietorship were a corporation).

(iv) COORDINATION WITH PARAGRAPH (2).—For purposes of applying paragraph (2), an eligible loss for any taxable year shall be treated in a manner similar to the manner in which a specified liability loss is treated.

(G) FARMING LOSSES.—In the case of a taxpayer which has a farming loss (as defined in subsection (i)) for a taxable year, such farming loss shall be a net operating loss carryback to each of the 5 taxable years preceding the taxable year of such loss.

(H) In the case of a taxpayer which has a net operating loss for any taxable year ending during 2001 or 2002, subparagraph (A)(i) shall be applied by substituting "5" for "2" and subparagraph (F) shall not apply.

(2) AMOUNT OF CARRYBACKS AND CARRYOVERS.—The entire amount of the net operating loss for any taxable year (hereinafter in this section referred to as the "loss year") shall be carried to the earliest of the taxable years to which (by reason of paragraph (1)) such loss may be carried. The

portion of such loss which shall be carried to each of the other taxable years shall be the excess, if any, of the amount of such loss over the sum of the taxable income for each of the prior taxable years to which such loss may be carried. For purposes of the preceding sentence, the taxable income for any such prior taxable year shall be computed—

      (A) with the modifications specified in subsection (d) other than paragraphs (1), (4), and (5) thereof, and

      (B) by determining the amount of the net operating loss deduction without regard to the net operating loss for the loss year or for any taxable year thereafter,

and the taxable income so computed shall not be considered to be less than zero.

    (3) ELECTION TO WAIVE CARRYBACK.—Any taxpayer entitled to a carryback period under paragraph (1) may elect to relinquish the entire carryback period with respect to a net operating loss for any taxable year. Such election shall be made in such manner as may be prescribed by the Secretary, and shall be made by the due date (including extensions of time) for filing the taxpayer's return for the taxable year of the net operating loss for which the election is to be in effect. Such election, once made for any taxable year, shall be irrevocable for such taxable year.

[Sec. 172(c)]

(c) NET OPERATING LOSS DEFINED.—For purposes of this section, the term "net operating loss" means the excess of the deductions allowed by this chapter over the gross income. Such excess shall be computed with the modifications specified in subsection (d).

[Sec. 172(d)]

(d) MODIFICATIONS.—The modifications referred to in this section are as follows:

    (1) NET OPERATING LOSS DEDUCTION.—No net operating loss deduction shall be allowed.

    (2) CAPITAL GAINS AND LOSSES OF TAXPAYERS OTHER THAN CORPORATONS.—In the case of a taxpayer other than a corporation—

      (A) the amount deductible on account of losses from sales or exchanges of capital assets shall not exceed the amount includable on account of gains from sales or exchanges of capital assets; and

      (B) the exclusion provided by section 1202 shall not be allowed.

    (3) DEDUCTION FOR PERSONAL EXEMPTIONS.—No deduction shall be allowed under section 151 (relating to personal exemptions). No deduction in lieu of any such deduction shall be allowed.

    (4) NONBUSINESS DEDUCTIONS OF TAXPAYERS OTHER THAN CORPORATIONS.—In the case of a taxpayer other than a corporation, the deductions allowable by this chapter which are not attributable to a taxpayer's trade or business shall be allowed only to the extent of the amount of the gross income not derived from such trade or business. For purposes of the preceding sentence—

      (A) any gain or loss from the sale or other disposition of—

        (i) property, used in the trade or business, of a character which is subject to the allowance for depreciation provided in section 167, or

        (ii) real property used in the trade or business,

shall be treated as attributable to the trade or business;

      (B) the modifications specified in paragraphs (1), (2)(B), and (3) shall be taken into account;

      (C) any deduction for casualty or theft losses allowable under paragraph (2) or (3) of section 165(c) shall be treated as attributable to the trade or business; and

      (D) any deduction allowed under section 404 to the extent attributable to contributions which are made on behalf of an individual who is an employee within the meaning of section 401(c)(1) shall not be treated as attributable to the trade or business of such individual.

    (5) COMPUTATION OF DEDUCTION FOR DIVIDENDS RECEIVED, ETC.—The deductions allowed by sections 243 (relating to dividends received by corporations), 244 (relating to dividends received on certain preferred stock of public utilities), and 245 (relating to dividends received from certain foreign corporations) shall be computed without regard to section 246 (b) (relating to limitation on aggregate amount of deductions); and the deduction allowed by section 247 (relating to dividends paid on certain preferred stock of public utilities) shall be computed without regard to subsection (a) (1) (B) of such section.

(6) MODIFICATIONS RELATED TO REAL ESTATE INVESTMENT TRUSTS.—In the case of any taxable year for which part II of subchapter M (relating to real estate investment trusts) applies to the taxpayer—

(A) the net operating loss for such taxable year shall be computed by taking into account the adjustments described in section 857(b)(2) (other than the deduction for dividends paid described in section 857(b)(2)(B)); and

(B) where such taxable year is a "prior taxable year" referred to in paragraph (2) of subsection (b), the term "taxable income" in such paragraph shall mean "real estate investment trust taxable income" (as defined in section 857(b)(2)).

[Sec. 172(e)]

(e) LAW APPLICABLE TO COMPUTATIONS.—In determining the amount of any net operating loss carryback or carryover to any taxable year, the necessary computations involving any other taxable year shall be made under the law applicable to such other taxable year.

* * *

[Sec. 172(h)]

(h) CORPORATE EQUITY REDUCTION INTEREST LOSSES.—For purposes of this section—

(1) IN GENERAL.—The term "corporate equity reduction interest loss" means, with respect to any loss limitation year, the excess (if any) of—

(A) the net operating loss for such taxable year, over

(B) the net operating loss for such taxable year determined without regard to any allocable interest deductions otherwise taken into account in computing such loss.

(2) ALLOCABLE INTEREST DEDUCTIONS.—

(A) IN GENERAL.—The term "allocable interest deductions" means deductions allowed under this chapter for interest on the portion of any indebtedness allocable to a corporate equity reduction transaction.

(B) METHOD OF ALLOCATION.—Except as provided in regulations and subparagraph (E), indebtedness shall be allocated to a corporate equity reduction transaction in the manner prescribed under clause (ii) of section 263A(f)(2)(A) (without regard to clause (i) thereof).

(C) ALLOCABLE DEDUCTIONS NOT TO EXCEED INTEREST INCREASES.—Allocable interest deductions for any loss limitation year shall not exceed the excess (if any) of—

(i) the amount allowable as a deduction for interest paid or accrued by the taxpayer during the loss limitation year, over

(ii) the average of such amounts for the 3 taxable years preceding the taxable year in which the corporate equity reduction transaction occurred.

(D) DE MINIMIS RULE.—A taxpayer shall be treated as having no allocable interest deductions for any taxable year if the amount of such deductions (without regard to this subparagraph) is less than $1,000,000.

(E) SPECIAL RULE FOR CERTAIN UNFORESEEABLE EVENTS.—If an unforeseeable extraordinary adverse event occurs during a loss limitation year but after the corporate equity reduction transaction—

(i) indebtedness shall be allocated in the manner described in subparagraph (B) to unreimbursed costs paid or incurred in connection with such event before being allocated to the corporate equity reduction transaction, and

(ii) the amount determined under subparagraph (C)(i) shall be reduced by the amount of interest on indebtedness described in clause (i).

(F) TRANSITION RULE.—If any of the 3 taxable years described in subparagraph (C)(ii) end on or before August 2, 1989, the taxpayer may substitute for the amount determined under such subparagraph an amount equal to the interest paid or accrued (determined on an annualized basis) during the taxpayer's taxable year which includes August 3, 1989, on indebtedness of the taxpayer outstanding on August 2, 1989.

(3) CORPORATE EQUITY REDUCTION TRANSACTION.—

(A) IN GENERAL.—The term "corporate equity reduction transaction" means—

Sec. 172(h)

(i) a major stock acquisition, or

(ii) an excess distribution.

(B) MAJOR STOCK ACQUISITION.—

(i) IN GENERAL.—The term "major stock acquisition" means the acquisition by a corporation pursuant to a plan of such corporation (or any group of persons acting in concert with such corporation) of stock in another corporation representing 50 percent or more (by vote or value) of the stock in such other corporation.

(ii) EXCEPTION.—The term "major stock acquisition" does not include a qualified stock purchase (within the meaning of section 338) to which an election under section 338 applies.

(C) EXCESS DISTRIBUTION.—The term "excess distribution" means the excess (if any) of—

(i) the aggregate distributions (including redemptions) made during a taxable year by a corporation with respect to its stock, over

(ii) the greater of—

(I) 150 percent of the average of such distributions during the 3 taxable years immediately preceding such taxable year, or

(II) 10 percent of the fair market value of the stock of such corporation as of the beginning of such taxable year.

(D) RULES FOR APPLYING SUBPARAGRAPH (B).—For purposes of subparagraph (B)—

(i) PLANS TO ACQUIRE STOCK.—All plans referred to in subparagraph (B) by any corporation (or group of persons acting in concert with such corporation) with respect to another corporation shall be treated as 1 plan.

(ii) ACQUISITION DURING 24-MONTH PERIOD.—All acquisitions during any 24-month period shall be treated as pursuant to 1 plan.

(E) RULES FOR APPLYING SUBPARAGRAPH (C).—For purposes of subparagraph (C)—

(i) CERTAIN PREFERRED STOCK DISREGARDED.—Stock described in section 1504(a)(4), and distributions (including redemptions) with respect to such stock, shall be disregarded.

(ii) ISSUANCE OF STOCK.—The amounts determined under clauses (i) and (ii)(I) of subparagraph (C) shall be reduced by the aggregate amount of stock issued by the corporation during the applicable period in exchange for money or property other than stock in the corporation.

(4) OTHER RULES.—

(A) ORDERING RULE.—For purposes of paragraph (1), in determining the allocable interest deductions taken into account in computing the net operating loss for any taxable year, taxable income for such taxable year shall be treated as having been computed by taking allocable interest deductions into account after all other deductions.

(B) COORDINATION WITH SUBSECTION (b)(2).—For purposes of subsection (b)(2)—

(i) a corporate equity reduction interest loss shall be treated in a manner similar to the manner in which a specified liability loss is treated, and

(ii) in determining the net operating loss deduction for any prior taxable year referred to in the 3rd sentence of subsection (b)(2), the portion of any net operating loss which may not be carried to such taxable year under subsection (b)(1)(E) shall not be taken into account.

(C) MEMBERS OF AFFILIATED GROUPS.—Except as provided by regulations, all members of an affiliated group filing a consolidated return under section 1501 shall be treated as 1 taxpayer for purposes of this subsection and subsection (b)(1)(E).

(5) REGULATIONS.—The Secretary shall prescribe such regulations as may be necessary to carry out the purposes of this subsection, including regulations—

(A) for applying this subsection to successor corporations and in cases where a taxpayer becomes, or ceases to be, a member of an affiliated group filing a consolidated return under section 1501,

(B) to prevent the avoidance of this subsection through related parties, pass-through entities, and intermediaries, and

(C) for applying this subsection where more than 1 corporation is involved in a corporate equity reduction transaction.

* * *

[Sec. 172(j)]

(j) ELECTION TO DISREGARD 5-YEAR CARRYBACK FOR CERTAIN NET OPERATING LOSSES.—Any taxpayer entitled to a 5-year carryback under subsection (b)(1)(H) from any loss year may elect to have the carryback period with respect to such loss year determined without regard to subsection (b)(1)(H). Such election shall be made in such manner as may be prescribed by the Secretary and shall be made by the due date (including extensions of time) for filing the taxpayer's return for the taxable year of the net operating loss. Such election, once made for any taxable year, shall be irrevocable for such taxable year.

* * *

[Sec. 174]

SEC. 174. RESEARCH AND EXPERIMENTAL EXPENDITURES.

[Sec. 174(a)]

(a) TREATMENT AS EXPENSES.—

(1) IN GENERAL.—A taxpayer may treat research or experimental expenditures which are paid or incurred by him during the taxable year in connection with his trade or business as expenses which are not chargeable to capital account. The expenditures so treated shall be allowed as a deduction.

(2) WHEN METHOD MAY BE ADOPTED.—

(A) WITHOUT CONSENT.—A taxpayer may, without the consent of the Secretary, adopt the method provided in this subsection for his first taxable year—

(i) which begins after December 31, 1953, and ends after August 16, 1954, and

(ii) for which expenditures described in paragraph (1) are paid or incurred.

(B) WITH CONSENT.—A taxpayer may, with the consent of the Secretary, adopt at any time the method provided in this subsection.

(3) SCOPE.—The method adopted under this subsection shall apply to all expenditures described in paragraph (1). The method adopted shall be adhered to in computing taxable income for the taxable year and for all subsequent taxable years unless, with the approval of the Secretary, a change to a different method is authorized with respect to part or all of such expenditures.

[Sec. 174(b)]

(b) AMORTIZATION OF CERTAIN RESEARCH AND EXPERIMENTAL EXPENDITURES.—

(1) IN GENERAL.—At the election of the taxpayer, made in accordance with regulations prescribed by the Secretary, research or experimental expenditures which are—

(A) paid or incurred by the taxpayer in connection with his trade or business,

(B) not treated as expenses under subsection (a), and

(C) chargeable to capital account but not chargeable to property of a character which is subject to the allowance under section 167 (relating to allowance for depreciation, etc.) or section 611 (relating to allowance for depletion),

may be treated as deferred expenses. In computing taxable income, such deferred expenses shall be allowed as a deduction ratably over such period of not less than 60 months as may be selected by the taxpayer (beginning with the month in which the taxpayer first realizes benefits from such expenditures). Such deferred expenses are expenditures properly chargeable to capital account for purposes of section 1016 (a) (1) (relating to adjustments to basis of property).

(2) TIME FOR AND SCOPE OF ELECTION.—The election provided by paragraph (1) may be made for any taxable year beginning after December 31, 1953, but only if made not later than the time prescribed by law for filing the return for such taxable year (including extensions thereof). The method so elected, and the period selected by the taxpayer, shall be adhered to in computing taxable income for the taxable year for which the election is made and for all subsequent taxable years unless, with the approval of the Secretary, a change to a different method (or to a different period) is authorized with respect to part or all of such expenditures. The election shall not apply to any

expenditure paid or incurred during any taxable year before the taxable year for which the taxpayer makes the election.

[Sec. 174(c)]

(c) LAND AND OTHER PROPERTY.—This section shall not apply to any expenditure for the acquisition or improvement of land, or for the acquisition or improvement of property to be used in connection with the research or experimentation and of a character which is subject to the allowance under section 167 (relating to allowance for depreciation, etc.) or section 611 (relating to allowance for depletion); but for purposes of this section allowances under section 167, and allowances under section 611, shall be considered as expenditures.

[Sec. 174(d)]

(d) EXPLORATION EXPENDITURES.—This section shall not apply to any expenditure paid or incurred for the purpose of ascertaining the existence, location, extent, or quality of any deposit of ore or other mineral (including oil and gas).

[Sec. 174(e)]

(e) ONLY REASONABLE RESEARCH EXPENDITURES ELIGIBLE.—This section shall apply to a research or experimental expenditure only to the extent that the amount thereof is reasonable under the circumstances.

[Sec. 174(f)]

(f) CROSS REFERENCES.—

(1) For adjustments to basis of property for amounts allowed as deductions as deferred expenses under subsection (b), see section 1016 (a) (14).

(2) For election of 10-year amortization of expenditures allowable as a deduction under subsection (a), see section 59(e).

[Sec. 178]

SEC. 178. AMORTIZATION OF COST OF ACQUIRING A LEASE.

[Sec. 178(a)]

(a) GENERAL RULE.—In determining the amount of the deduction allowable to a lessee for exhaustion, wear and tear, obsolescence, or amortization in respect of any cost of acquiring the lease, the term of the lease shall be treated as including all renewal options (and any other period for which the parties reasonably expect the lease to be renewed) if less than 75 percent of such cost is attributable to the period of the term of the lease remaining on the date of its acquisition.

[Sec. 178(b)]

(b) CERTAIN PERIODS EXCLUDED.—For purposes of subsection (a), in determining the period of the term of the lease remaining on the date of acquisition, there shall not be taken into account any period for which the lease may subsequently be renewed, extended, or continued pursuant to an option exercisable by the lessee.

[Sec. 179]

SEC. 179. ELECTION TO EXPENSE CERTAIN DEPRECIABLE BUSINESS ASSETS.

[Sec. 179(a)]

(a) TREATMENT AS EXPENSES.—A taxpayer may elect to treat the cost of any section 179 property as an expense which is not chargeable to capital account. Any cost so treated shall be allowed as a deduction for the taxable year in which the section 179 property is placed in service.

[Sec. 179(b)]

(b) LIMITATIONS.—

(1) DOLLAR LIMITATION.—The aggregate cost which may be taken into account under subsection (a) for any taxable year shall not exceed $25,000 ($100,000 in the case of taxable years beginning after 2002 and before 2006).

(2) REDUCTION IN LIMITATION.—The limitation under paragraph (1) for any taxable year shall be reduced (but not below zero) by the amount by which the cost of section 179 property placed in service during such taxable year exceeds $200,000 ($400,000 in the case of taxable years beginning after 2002 and before 2006).

(3) LIMITATION BASED ON INCOME FROM TRADE OR BUSINESS.—

(A) IN GENERAL.—The amount allowed as a deduction under subsection (a) for any taxable year (determined after the application of paragraphs (1) and (2)) shall not exceed the aggregate amount of taxable income of the taxpayer for such taxable year which is derived from the active conduct by the taxpayer of any trade or business during such taxable year.

(B) CARRYOVER OF DISALLOWED DEDUCTION.—The amount allowable as a deduction under subsection (a) for any taxable year shall be increased by the lesser of—

(i) the aggregate amount disallowed under subparagraph (A) for all prior taxable years (to the extent not previously allowed as a deduction by reason of this subparagraph), or

(ii) the excess (if any) of—

(I) the limitation of paragraphs (1) and (2) (or if lesser, the aggregate amount of taxable income referred to in subparagraph (A)), over

(II) the amount allowable as a deduction under subsection (a) for such taxable year without regard to this subparagraph.

(C) COMPUTATION OF TAXABLE INCOME.—For purposes of this paragraph, taxable income derived from the conduct of a trade or business shall be computed without regard to the deduction allowable under this section.

(4) MARRIED INDIVIDUALS FILING SEPARATELY.—In the case of a husband and wife filing separate returns for the taxable year—

(A) such individuals shall be treated as 1 taxpayer for purposes of paragraphs (1) and (2), and

(B) unless such individuals elect otherwise, 50 percent of the cost which may be taken into account under subsection (a) for such taxable year (before application of paragraph (3)) shall be allocated to each such individual.

(5) INFLATION ADJUSTMENTS.—

(A) IN GENERAL.—In the case of any taxable year beginning in a calendar year after 2003 and before 2006, the $100,000 and $400,000 amounts in paragraphs (1) and (2) shall each be increased by an amount equal to—

(i) such dollar amount, multiplied by

(ii) the cost-of-living adjustment determined under section 1(f)(3) for the calendar year in which the taxable year begins, by substituting "calendar year 2002" for "calendar year 1992" in subparagraph (B) thereof.

(B) ROUNDING.—

(i) DOLLAR LIMITATION.—If the amount in paragraph (1) as increased under subparagraph (A) is not a multiple of $1,000, such amount shall be rounded to the nearest multiple of $1,000.

(ii) PHASEOUT AMOUNT.—If the amount in paragraph (2) as increased under subparagraph (A) is not a multiple of $10,000, such amount shall be rounded to the nearest multiple of $10,000.

[Sec. 179(c)]

(c) ELECTION.—

(1) IN GENERAL.—An election under this section for any taxable year shall—

(A) specify the items of section 179 property to which the election applies and the portion of the cost of each of such items which is to be taken into account under subsection (a), and

(B) be made on the taxpayer's return of the tax imposed by this chapter for the taxable year.

Such election shall be made in such manner as the Secretary may by regulations prescribe.

(2) ELECTION IRREVOCABLE.—Any election made under this section, and any specification contained in any such election, may not be revoked except with the consent of the Secretary. Any such election or specification with respect to any taxable year beginning after 2002 and before 2006 may be revoked by the taxpayer with respect to any property, and such revocation, once made, shall be irrevocable.

[Sec. 179(d)]

(d) DEFINITIONS AND SPECIAL RULES.—

(1) SECTION 179 PROPERTY.—For purposes of this section, the term "section 179 property" means property—

(A) which is—

(i) tangible property (to which section 168 applies), or

(ii) computer software (as defined in section 197(e)(3)(B)) which is described in section 197(e)(3)(A)(i), to which section 167 applies, and which is placed in service in a taxable year beginning after 2002 and before 2006,

(B) which is section 1245 property (as defined in section 1245(a)(3)), and

(C) which is acquired by purchase for use in the active conduct of a trade or business.

Such term shall not include any property described in section 50(b) and shall not include air conditioning or heating units.

(2) PURCHASE DEFINED.—For purposes of paragraph (1), the term "purchase" means any acquisition of property, but only if—

(A) the property is not acquired from a person whose relationship to the person acquiring it would result in the disallowance of losses under section 267 or 707(b) (but, in applying section 267(b) and (c) for purposes of this section, paragraph (4) of section 267(c) shall be treated as providing that the family of an individual shall include only his spouse, ancestors, and lineal descendants),

(B) the property is not acquired by one component member of a controlled group from another component member of the same controlled group, and

(C) the basis of the property in the hands of the person acquiring it is not determined—

(i) in whole or in part by reference to the adjusted basis of such property in the hands of the person from whom acquired, or

(ii) under section 1014(a) (relating to property acquired from a decedent).

(3) COST.—For purposes of this section, the cost of property does not include so much of the basis of such property as is determined by reference to the basis of other property held at any time by the person acquiring such property.

(4) SECTION NOT TO APPLY TO ESTATES AND TRUSTS.—This section shall not apply to estates and trusts.

(5) SECTION NOT TO APPLY TO CERTAIN NONCORPORATE LESSORS.—This section shall not apply to any section 179 property which is purchased by a person who is not a corporation and with respect to which such person is the lessor unless—

(A) the property subject to the lease has been manufactured or produced by the lessor, or

(B) the term of the lease (taking into account options to renew) is less than 50 percent of the class life of the property (as defined in section 168(i)(1)), and for the period consisting of the first 12 months after the date on which the property is transferred to the lessee the sum of the deductions with respect to such property which are allowable to the lessor solely by reason of section 162 (other than rents and reimbursed amounts with respect to such property) exceeds 15 percent of the rental income produced by such property.

(6) DOLLAR LIMITATION OF CONTROLLED GROUP.—For purposes of subsection (b) of this section—

(A) all component members of a controlled group shall be treated as one taxpayer, and

(B) the Secretary shall apportion the dollar limitation contained in subsection (b)(1) among the component members of such controlled group in such manner as he shall by regulations prescribe.

(7) CONTROLLED GROUP DEFINED.—For purposes of paragraphs (2) and (6), the term "controlled group" has the meaning assigned to it by section 1563(a), except that, for such purposes, the phrase

"more than 50 percent" shall be substituted for the phrase "at least 80 percent" each place it appears in section 1563(a)(1).

(8) Treatment of partnerships and S corporations.—In the case of a partnership, the limitations of subsection (b) shall apply with respect to the partnership and with respect to each partner. A similar rule shall apply in the case of an S corporation and its shareholders.

(9) Coordination with section 38.—No credit shall be allowed under section 38 with respect to any amount for which a deduction is allowed under subsection (a).

(10) Recapture in certain cases.—The Secretary shall, by regulations, provide for recapturing the benefit under any deduction allowable under subsection (a) with respect to any property which is not used predominantly in a trade or business at any time.

[Sec. 183]

SEC. 183. ACTIVITIES NOT ENGAGED IN FOR PROFIT.

[Sec. 183(a)]

(a) General Rule.—In the case of an activity engaged in by an individual or an S corporation, if such activity is not engaged in for profit, no deduction attributable to such activity shall be allowed under this chapter except as provided in this section.

[Sec. 183(b)]

(b) Deductions Allowable.—In the case of an activity not engaged in for profit to which subsection (a) applies, there shall be allowed—

(1) the deductions which would be allowable under this chapter for the taxable year without regard to whether or not such activity is engaged in for profit, and

(2) a deduction equal to the amount of the deductions which would be allowable under this chapter for the taxable year only if such activity were engaged in for profit, but only to the extent that the gross income derived from such activity for the taxable year exceeds the deductions allowable by reason of paragraph (1).

[Sec. 183(c)]

(c) Activity Not Engaged in for Profit Defined.—For purposes of this section, the term "activity not engaged in for profit" means any activity other than one with respect to which deductions are allowable for the taxable year under section 162 or under paragraph (1) or (2) of section 212.

[Sec. 183(d)]

(d) Presumption.—If the gross income derived from an activity for 3 or more of the taxable years in the period of 5 consecutive taxable years which ends with the taxable year exceeds the deductions attributable to such activity (determined without regard to whether or not such activity is engaged in for profit), then, unless the Secretary establishes to the contrary, such activity shall be presumed for purposes of this chapter for such taxable year to be an activity engaged in for profit. In the case of an activity which consists in major part of the breeding, training, showing, or racing of horses, the preceding sentence shall be applied by substituting "2" for "3" and "7" for "5".

[Sec. 183(e)]

(e) Special Rule.—

(1) In general.—A determination as to whether the presumption provided by subsection (d) applies with respect to any activity shall, if the taxpayer so elects, not be made before the close of the fourth taxable year (sixth taxable year, in the case of an activity described in the last sentence of such subsection) following the taxable year in which the taxpayer first engages in the activity. For purposes of the preceding sentence, a taxpayer shall be treated as not having engaged in an activity during any taxable year beginning before January 1, 1970.

(2) Initial period.—If the taxpayer makes an election under paragraph (1), the presumption provided by subsection (d) shall apply to each taxable year in the 5-taxable year (or 7-taxable year) period beginning with the taxable year in which the taxpayer first engages in the activity, if the gross income derived from the activity for 3 (or 2 if applicable) or more of the taxable years in such period exceeds the deductions attributable to the activity (determined without regard to whether or not the activity is engaged in for profit).

Sec. 183(e)

(3) ELECTION.—An election under paragraph (1) shall be made at such time and manner, and subject to such terms and conditions, as the Secretary may prescribe.

(4) TIME FOR ASSESSING DEFICIENCY ATTRIBUTABLE TO ACTIVITY.—If a taxpayer makes an election under paragraph (1) with respect to an activity, the statutory period for the assessment of any deficiency attributable to such activity shall not expire before the expiration of 2 years after the date prescribed by law (determined without extensions) for filing the return of tax under chapter 1 for the last taxable year in the period of 5 taxable years (or 7 taxable years) to which the election relates. Such deficiency may be assessed notwithstanding the provisions of any law or rule of law which would otherwise prevent such an assessment.

[Sec. 186]

SEC. 186. RECOVERIES OF DAMAGES FOR ANTITRUST VIOLATIONS, ETC.

[Sec. 186(a)]

(a) ALLOWANCE OF DEDUCTION.—If a compensatory amount which is included in gross income is received or accrued during the taxable year for a compensable injury, there shall be allowed as a deduction for the taxable year an amount equal to the lesser of—

(1) the amount of such compensatory amount, or

(2) the amount of the unrecovered losses sustained as a result of such compensable injury.

[Sec. 186(b)]

(b) COMPENSABLE INJURY.—For purposes of this section, the term "compensable injury" means—

(1) injuries sustained as a result of an infringement of a patent issued by the United States,

(2) injuries sustained as a result of a breach of contract or a breach of fiduciary duty or relationship, or

(3) injuries sustained in business, or to property, by reason of any conduct forbidden in the antitrust laws for which a civil action may be brought under section 4 of the Act entitled "An Act to supplement existing laws against unlawful restraints and monopolies, and for other purposes", approved October 15, 1914 (commonly known as the Clayton Act).

[Sec. 186(c)]

(c) COMPENSATORY AMOUNT.—For purposes of this section, the term "compensatory amount" means the amount received or accrued during the taxable year as damages as a result of an award in, or in settlement of, a civil action for recovery for a compensable injury, reduced by any amounts paid or incurred in the taxable year in securing such award or settlement.

[Sec. 186(d)]

(d) UNRECOVERED LOSSES.—

(1) IN GENERAL.—For purposes of this section, the amount of any unrecovered loss sustained as a result of any compensable injury is—

(A) the sum of the amount of the net operating losses (as determined under section 172) for each taxable year in whole or in part within the injury period, to the extent that such net operating losses are attributable to such compensable injury, reduced by

(B) the sum of—

(i) the amount of the net operating losses described in subparagraph (A) which were allowed for any prior taxable year as a deduction under section 172 as a net operating loss carryback or carryover to such taxable year, and

(ii) the amounts allowed as a deduction under subsection (a) for any prior taxable year for prior recoveries of compensatory amounts for such compensable injury.

(2) INJURY PERIOD.—For purposes of paragraph (1), the injury period is—

(A) with respect to any infringement of a patent, the period in which such infringement occurred,

(B) with respect to a breach of contract or breach of fiduciary duty or relationship, the period during which amounts would have been received or accrued but for the breach of contract or breach of fiduciary duty or relationship, and

Sec. 186

(C) with respect to injuries sustained by reason of any conduct forbidden in the antitrust laws, the period in which such injuries were sustained.

(3) NET OPERATING LOSSES ATTRIBUTABLE TO COMPENSABLE INJURIES.—For purposes of paragraph (1)—

(A) a net operating loss for any taxable year shall be treated as attributable to a compensable injury to the extent of the compensable injury sustained during such taxable year, and

(B) if only a portion of a net operating loss for any taxable year is attributable to a compensable injury, such portion shall (in applying section 172 for purposes of this section) be considered to be a separate net operating loss for such year to be applied after the other portion of such net operating loss.

[Sec. 186(e)]

(e) EFFECT ON NET OPERATING LOSS CARRYOVERS.—If for the taxable year in which a compensatory amount is received or accrued any portion of a net operating loss carryover to such year is attributable to the compensable injury for which such amount is received or accrued, such portion of such net operating loss carryover shall be reduced by an amount equal to—

(1) the deduction allowed under subsection (a) with respect to such compensatory amount, reduced by

(2) any portion of the unrecovered losses sustained as a result of the compensable injury with respect to which the period for carryover under section 172 has expired.

[Sec. 195]

SEC. 195. START-UP EXPENDITURES.

[Sec. 195(a)]

(a) CAPITALIZATION OF EXPENDITURES.—Except as otherwise provided in this section, no deduction shall be allowed for start-up expenditures.

[Sec. 195(b)]

(b) ELECTION TO AMORTIZE.—

(1) IN GENERAL.—Start-up expenditures may, at the election of the taxpayer, be treated as deferred expenses. Such deferred expenses shall be allowed as a deduction prorated equally over such period of not less than 60 months as may be selected by the taxpayer (beginning with the month in which the active trade or business begins).

(2) DISPOSITIONS BEFORE CLOSE OF AMORTIZATION PERIOD.—In any case in which a trade or business is completely disposed of by the taxpayer before the end of the period to which paragraph (1) applies, any deferred expenses attributable to such trade or business which were not allowed as a deduction by reason of this section may be deducted to the extent allowable under section 165.

[Sec. 195(c)]

(c) DEFINITIONS.—For purposes of this section—

(1) START-UP EXPENDITURES.—The term "start-up expenditure" means any amount—

(A) paid or incurred in connection with—

(i) investigating the creation or acquisition of an active trade or business, or

(ii) creating an active trade or business, or

(iii) any activity engaged in for profit and for the production of income before the day on which the active trade or business begins, in anticipation of such activity becoming an active trade or business, and

(B) which, if paid or incurred in connection with the operation of an existing active trade or business (in the same field as the trade or business referred to in subparagraph (A)), would be allowable as a deduction for the taxable year in which paid or incurred.

The term "start-up expenditure" does not include any amount with respect to which a deduction is allowable under section 163(a), 164, or 174.

Sec. 195(c)

(2) BEGINNING OF TRADE OR BUSINESS.—

(A) IN GENERAL.—Except as provided in subparagraph (B), the determination of when an active trade or business begins shall be made in accordance with such regulations as the Secretary may prescribe.

(B) ACQUIRED TRADE OR BUSINESS.—An acquired active trade or business shall be treated as beginning when the taxpayer acquires it.

[Sec. 195(d)]

(d) ELECTION.—

(1) TIME FOR MAKING ELECTION.—An election under subsection (b) shall be made not later than the time prescribed by law for filing the return for the taxable year in which the trade or business begins (including extensions thereof).

(2) SCOPE OF ELECTION.—The period selected under subsection (b) shall be adhered to in computing taxable income for the taxable year for which the election is made and all subsequent taxable years.

[Sec. 197]

SEC. 197. AMORTIZATION OF GOODWILL AND CERTAIN OTHER INTANGIBLES.

[Sec. 197(a)]

(a) GENERAL RULE.—A taxpayer shall be entitled to an amortization deduction with respect to any amortizable section 197 intangible. The amount of such deduction shall be determined by amortizing the adjusted basis (for purposes of determining gain) of such intangible ratably over the 15-year period beginning with the month in which such intangible was acquired.

[Sec. 197(b)]

(b) NO OTHER DEPRECIATION OR AMORTIZATION DEDUCTION ALLOWABLE.—Except as provided in subsection (a), no depreciation or amortization deduction shall be allowable with respect to any amortizable section 197 intangible.

[Sec. 197(c)]

(c) AMORTIZABLE SECTION 197 INTANGIBLE.—For purposes of this section—

(1) IN GENERAL.—Except as otherwise provided in this section, the term "amortizable section 197 intangible" means any section 197 intangible—

(A) which is acquired by the taxpayer after the date of the enactment [August 10, 1993] of this section, and

(B) which is held in connection with the conduct of a trade or business or an activity described in section 212.

(2) EXCLUSION OF SELF-CREATED INTANGIBLES, ETC.—The term "amortizable section 197 intangible" shall not include any section 197 intangible—

(A) which is not described in subparagraph (D), (E), or (F) of subsection (d)(1), and

(B) which is created by the taxpayer.

This paragraph shall not apply if the intangible is created in connection with a transaction (or series of related transactions) involving the acquisition of assets constituting a trade or business or substantial portion thereof.

(3) ANTI-CHURNING RULES.—

For exclusion of intangibles acquired in certain transactions, see subsection (f)(9).

[Sec. 197(d)]

(d) SECTION 197 INTANGIBLE.—For purposes of this section—

(1) IN GENERAL.—Except as otherwise provided in this section, the term "section 197 intangible" means—

(A) goodwill,

(B) going concern value,

(C) any of the following intangible items:

(i) workforce in place including its composition and terms and conditions (contractual or otherwise) of its employment,

(ii) business books and records, operating systems, or any other information base (including lists or other information with respect to current or prospective customers),

(iii) any patent, copyright, formula, process, design, pattern, knowhow, format, or other similar item,

(iv) any customer-based intangible,

(v) any supplier-based intangible, and

(vi) any other similar item,

(D) any license, permit, or other right granted by a governmental unit or an agency or instrumentality thereof,

(E) any covenant not to compete (or other arrangement to the extent such arrangement has substantially the same effect as a covenant not to compete) entered into in connection with an acquisition (directly or indirectly) of an interest in a trade or business or substantial portion thereof, and

(F) any franchise, trademark, or trade name.

(2) CUSTOMER-BASED INTANGIBLE.—

(A) IN GENERAL.—The term "customer-based intangible" means—

(i) composition of market,

(ii) market share, and

(iii) any other value resulting from future provision of goods or services pursuant to relationships (contractual or otherwise) in the ordinary course of business with customers.

(B) SPECIAL RULE FOR FINANCIAL INSTITUTIONS.—In the case of a financial institution, the term "customer-based intangible" includes deposit base and similar items.

(3) SUPPLIER-BASED INTANGIBLE.—The term "supplier-based intangible" means any value resulting from future acquisitions of goods or services pursuant to relationships (contractual or otherwise) in the ordinary course of business with suppliers of goods or services to be used or sold by the taxpayer.

[Sec. 197(e)]

(e) EXCEPTIONS.—For purposes of this section, the term "section 197 intangible" shall not include any of the following:

(1) FINANCIAL INTERESTS.—Any interest—

(A) in a corporation, partnership, trust, or estate, or

(B) under an existing futures contract, foreign currency contract, notional principal contract, or other similar financial contract.

(2) LAND.—Any interest in land.

(3) COMPUTER SOFTWARE.—

(A) IN GENERAL.—Any—

(i) computer software which is readily available for purchase by the general public, is subject to a nonexclusive license, and has not been substantially modified, and

(ii) other computer software which is not acquired in a transaction (or series of related transactions) involving the acquisition of assets constituting a trade or business or substantial portion thereof.

(B) COMPUTER SOFTWARE DEFINED.—For purposes of subparagraph (A), the term "computer software" means any program designed to cause a computer to perform a desired function. Such term shall not include any data base or similar item unless the data base or item is in the public domain and is incidental to the operation of otherwise qualifying computer software.

(4) CERTAIN INTERESTS OR RIGHTS ACQUIRED SEPARATELY.—Any of the following not acquired in a transaction (or series of related transactions) involving the acquisition of assets constituting a trade business or substantial portion thereof:

(A) Any interest in a film, sound recording, video tape, book, or similar property.

(B) Any right to receive tangible property or services under a contract or granted by a governmental unit or agency or instrumentality thereof.

(C) Any interest in a patent or copyright.

(D) To the extent provided in regulations, any right under a contract (or granted by a governmental unit or an agency or instrumentality thereof) if such right—

(i) has a fixed duration of less than 15 years, or

(ii) is fixed as to amount and, without regard to this section, would be recoverable under a method similar to the unit-of-production method.

(5) INTERESTS UNDER LEASES AND DEBT INSTRUMENTS.—Any interest under—

(A) an existing lease of tangible property, or

(B) except as provided in subsection (d)(2)(B), any existing indebtedness.

(6) TREATMENT OF SPORTS FRANCHISES.—A franchise to engage in professional football, basketball, baseball, or other professional sport, and any item acquired in connection with such a franchise.

(7) MORTGAGE SERVICING.—Any right to service indebtedness which is secured by residential real property unless such right is acquired in a transaction (or series of related transactions) involving the acquisition of assests (other than rights described in this paragraph) constituting a trade or business or substantial portion thereof.

(8) CERTAIN TRANSACTION COSTS.—Any fees for professional services, and any transaction costs, incurred by parties to a transaction with respect to which any portion of the gain or loss is not recognized under part III of subchapter C.

[Sec. 197(f)]

(f) SPECIAL RULES.—

(1) TREATMENT OF CERTAIN DISPOSITIONS, ETC.—

(A) IN GENERAL.—If there is a disposition of any amortizable section 197 intangible acquired in a transaction or series of related transactions (or any such intangible becomes worthless) and one or more other amortizable section 197 intangibles acquired in such transaction or series of related transactions are retained—

(i) no loss shall be recognized by reason of such disposition (or such worthlessness), and

(ii) appropriate ajdustments to the adjusted bases of such retained intangibles shall be made for any loss not recognized under clause (i).

(B) SPECIAL RULE FOR COVENANTS NOT TO COMPETE.—In the case of any section 197 intangible which is a covenant not to compete (or other arrangement) described in subsection (d)(1)(E), in no event shall such covenant or other arrangement be treated as disposed of (or becoming worthless) before the disposition of the entire interest described in such subsection in connection with which such covenant (or other arrangement) was entered into.

(C) SPECIAL RULE.—All persons treated as a single taxpayer under section 41(f)(1) shall be so treated for purposes of this paragraph.

(2) TREATMENT OF CERTAIN TRANSFERS.—

(A) IN GENERAL.—In the case of any section 197 intangible transferred in a transaction described in subparagraph (B), the transferee shall be treated as the transferor for purposes of applying this section with respect to so much of the adjusted basis in the hands of the transferee as does not exceed the adjusted basis in the hands of the transferor.

(B) TRANSACTIONS COVERED.—The transactions described in this subparagraph are—

(i) any transaction described in section 332, 351, 361, 721, 731, 1031, or 1033, and

(ii) any transaction between members of the same affiliated group during any taxable year for which a consolidated return is made by such group.

(3) TREATMENT OF AMOUNTS PAID PURSUANT TO COVENANTS NOT TO COMPETE, ETC.—Any amount paid or incurred pursuant to a covenant or arrangement referred to in subsection (d)(1)(E) shall be treated as an amount chargeable to capital account.

Sec. 197(f)

(4) TREATMENT OF FRANCHISES, ETC.—

(A) FRANCHISE.—The term "franchise" has the meaning given to such term by section 1253(b)(1).

(B) TREATMENT OF RENEWALS.—Any renewal of a franchise, trademark, or trade name (or of a license, a permit, or other right referred to in subsection (d)(1)(D)) shall be treated as an acquisition. The preceding sentence shall only apply with respect to costs incurred in connection with such renewal.

(C) CERTAIN AMOUNTS NOT TAKEN INTO ACCOUNT.—Any amount to which section 1253(d)(1) applies shall not be taken into account under this section.

(5) TREATMENT OF CERTAIN REINSURANCE TRANSACTIONS.—In the case of any amortizable section 197 intangible resulting from an assumption reinsurance transaction, the amount taken into account as the adjusted basis of such intangible under this section shall be the excess of—

(A) the amount paid or incurred by the acquirer under the assumption reinsurance transaction, over

(B) the amount required to be capitalized under section 848 in connection with such transaction.

Subsection (b) shall not apply to any amount required to be capitalized under section 848.

(6) TREATMENT OF CERTAIN SUBLEASES.—For purposes of this section, a sublease shall be treated in the same manner as a lease of the underlying property involved.

(7) TREATMENT AS DEPRECIABLE.—For purposes of this chapter, any amortizable section 197 intangible shall be treated as property which is of a character subject to the allowance for depreciation provided in section 167.

(8) TREATMENT OF CERTAIN INCREMENTS IN VALUE.—This section shall not apply to any increment in value if, without regard to this section, such increment is properly taken into account in determining the cost of property which is not a section 197 intangible.

(9) ANTI-CHURNING RULES.—For purposes of this section—

(A) IN GENERAL.—The term "amortizable section 197 intangible" shall not include any section 197 intangible which is described in subparagraph (A) or (B) of subsection (d)(1) (or for which depreciation or amortization would not have been allowable but for this section) and which is acquired by the taxpayer after the date of the enactment of this section, if—

(i) the intangible was held or used at any time on or after July 25, 1991, and on or before such date of enactment by the taxpayer or a related person,

(ii) the intangible was acquired from a person who held such intangible at any time on or after July 25, 1991, and on or before such date of enactment, and, as part of the transaction, the user of such intangible does not change, or

(iii) the taxpayer grants the right to use such intangible to a person (or a person related to such person) who held or used such intangible at any time on or after July 25, 1991, and on or before such date of enactment.

For purposes of this subparagraph, the determination of whether the user of property changes as part of a transaction shall be determined in accordance with regulations prescribed by the Secretary. For purposes of this subparagraph, deductions allowable under section 1253(d) shall be treated as deductions allowable for amortization.

(B) EXCEPTION WHERE GAIN RECOGNIZED.—If—

(i) subparagraph (A) would not apply to an intangible acquired by the taxpayer but for the last sentence of subparagraph (C)(i), and

(ii) the person from whom the taxpayer acquired the intangible elects, notwithstanding any other provision of this title—

(I) to recognize gain on the disposition of the intangible, and

(II) to pay a tax on such gain which, when added to any other income tax on such gain under this title, equals such gain multiplied by the highest rate of income tax applicable to such person under this title,

then subparagraph (A) shall apply to the intangible only to the extent that the taxpayer's adjusted basis in the intangible exceeds the gain recognized under clause (ii)(I).

Sec. 197(f)

(C) RELATED PERSON DEFINED.—For purposes of this paragraph—

(i) RELATED PERSON.—A person (hereinafter in this paragraph referred to as the "related person") is related to any person if—

(I) the related person bears a relationship to such person specified in section 267(b) or section 707(b)(1), or

(II) the related person and such person are engaged in trades or businesses under common control (within the meaning of subparagraphs (A) and (B) of section 41(f)(1)).

For purposes of subclause (I), in applying section 267(b) or 707(b)(1), "20 percent" shall be substituted for "50 percent".

(ii) TIME FOR MAKING DETERMINATION.—A person shall be treated as related to another person if such relationship exists immediately before or immediately after the acquisition of the intangible involved.

(D) ACQUISITIONS BY REASON OF DEATH.—Subparagraph (A) shall not apply to the acquisition of any property by the taxpayer if the basis of the property in the hands of the taxpayer is determined under section 1014(a).

(E) SPECIAL RULE FOR PARTNERSHIPS.—With respect to any increase in the basis of partnership property under section 732, 734, or 743, determinations under this paragraph shall be made at the partner level and each partner shall be treated as having owned and used such partner's proportionate share of the partnership assets.

(F) ANTI-ABUSE RULES.—The term "amortizable section 197 intangible" does not include any section 197 intangible acquired in a transaction, one of the principal purposes of which is to avoid the requirement of subsection (c)(1) that the intangible be acquired after the date of the enactment of this section or to avoid the provisions of subparagraph (A).

[Sec. 197(g)]

(g) REGULATIONS.—The Secretary shall prescribe such regulations as may be appropriate to carry out the purposes of this section, including such regulations as may be appropriate to prevent avoidance of the purposes of this section through related persons or otherwise.

[Sec. 198]

SEC. 198. EXPENSING OF ENVIRONMENTAL REMEDIATION COSTS.

[Sec. 198(a)]

(a) IN GENERAL.—A taxpayer may elect to treat any qualified environmental remediation expenditure which is paid or incurred by the taxpayer as an expense which is not chargeable to capital account. Any expenditure which is so treated shall be allowed as a deduction for the taxable year in which it is paid or incurred.

[Sec. 198(b)]

(b) QUALIFIED ENVIRONMENTAL REMEDIATION EXPENDITURE.—For purposes of this section—

(1) IN GENERAL.—The term "qualified environmental remediation expenditure" means any expenditure—

(A) which is otherwise chargeable to capital account, and

(B) which is paid or incurred in connection with the abatement or control of hazardous substances at a qualified contaminated site.

(2) SPECIAL RULE FOR EXPENDITURES FOR DEPRECIABLE PROPERTY.—Such term shall not include any expenditure for the acquisition of property of a character subject to the allowance for depreciation which is used in connection with the abatement or control of hazardous substances at a qualified contaminated site; except that the portion of the allowance under section 167 for such property which is otherwise allocated to such site shall be treated as a qualified environmental remediation expenditure.

(c) QUALIFIED CONTAMINATED SITE.—For purposes of this section—

(1) IN GENERAL.—The term "qualified contaminated site" means any area—

(A) which is held by the taxpayer for use in a trade or business or for the production of income, or which is property described in section 1221(a)(1) in the hands of the taxpayer, and

(B) at or on which there has been a release (or threat of release) or disposal of any hazardous substance.

(2) NATIONAL PRIORITIES LISTED SITES NOT INCLUDED.—Such term shall not include any site which is on, or proposed for, the national priorities list under section 105(a)(8)(B) of the Comprehensive Environmental Response, Compensation, and Liability Act of 1980 (as in effect on the date of the enactment of this section).

(3) TAXPAYER MUST RECEIVE STATEMENT FROM STATE ENVIRONMENTAL AGENCY.—An area shall be treated as a qualified contaminated site with respect to expenditures paid or incurred during any taxable year only if the taxpayer receives a statement from the appropriate agency of the State in which such area is located that such area meets the requirement of paragraph (1)(B).

(4) APPROPRIATE STATE AGENCY.—For purposes of paragraph (3), the chief executive officer of each State may, in consultation with the Administrator of the Environmental Protection Agency, designate the appropriate State environmental agency within 60 days of the date of the enactment of this section. If the chief executive officer of a State has not designated an appropriate environmental agency within such 60-day period, the appropriate environmental agency for such State shall be designated by the Administrator of the Environmental Protection Agency.

[Sec. 198(d)]

(d) HAZARDOUS SUBSTANCE.—For purposes of this section—

(1) IN GENERAL.—The term "hazardous substance" means—

(A) any substance which is a hazardous substance as defined in section 101(14) of the Comprehensive Environmental Response, Compensation, and Liability Act of 1980, and

(B) any substance which is designated as a hazardous substance under section 102 of such Act.

(2) EXCEPTION.—Such term shall not include any substance with respect to which a removal or remedial action is not permitted under section 104 of such Act by reason of subsection (a)(3) thereof.

[Sec. 198(e)]

(e) DEDUCTION RECAPTURED AS ORDINARY INCOME ON SALE, ETC.—Solely for purposes of section 1245, in the case of property to which a qualified environmental remediation expenditure would have been capitalized but for this section—

(1) the deduction allowed by this section for such expenditure shall be treated as a deduction for depreciation, and

(2) such property (if not otherwise section 1245 property) shall be treated as section 1245 property solely for purposes of applying section 1245 to such deduction.

[Sec. 198(f)]

(f) COORDINATION WITH OTHER PROVISIONS.—Sections 280B and 468 shall not apply to amounts which are treated as expenses under this section.

[Sec. 198(g)]

(g) REGULATIONS.—The Secretary shall prescribe such regulations as may be necessary or appropriate to carry out the purposes of this section.

[Sec. 198(h)]

(h) TERMINATION.—This section shall not apply to expenditures paid or incurred after December 31, 2003.

PART VII—ADDITIONAL ITEMIZED DEDUCTIONS FOR INDIVIDUALS

[Sec. 211]

SEC. 211. ALLOWANCE OF DEDUCTIONS.

In computing taxable income under section 63, there shall be allowed as deductions the items specified in this part, subject to the exceptions provided in part IX (section 261 and following, relating to items not deductible).

[Sec. 212]

SEC. 212. EXPENSES FOR PRODUCTION OF INCOME.

In the case of an individual, there shall be allowed as a deduction all the ordinary and necessary expenses paid or incurred during the taxable year—

(1) for the production or collection of income;

(2) for the management, conservation, or maintenance of property held for the production of income; or

(3) in connection with the determination, collection, or refund of any tax.

[*Caution: Pursuant to Section 213(d)(10)(B), the dollar amounts specified in Section 213(d)(10)(A) are adjusted for taxable years beginning after 1997 to reflect increases in the Consumer Price Index. The adjusted amounts applicable to taxable years beginning in 2003 are provided beginning at page ix.*]

[Sec. 213]

SEC. 213. MEDICAL, DENTAL, ETC., EXPENSES.

[Sec. 213(a)]

(a) ALLOWANCE OF DEDUCTION.—There shall be allowed as a deduction the expenses paid during the taxable year, not compensated for by insurance or otherwise, for medical care of the taxpayer, his spouse, or a dependent (as defined in section 152), to the extent that such expenses exceed 7.5 percent of adjusted gross income.

[Sec. 213(b)]

(b) LIMITATION WITH RESPECT TO MEDICINE AND DRUGS.—An amount paid during the taxable year for medicine or a drug shall be taken into account under subsection (a) only if such medicine or drug is a prescribed drug or is insulin.

[Sec. 213(c)]

(c) SPECIAL RULE FOR DECEDENTS.—

(1) TREATMENT OF EXPENSES PAID AFTER DEATH.—For purposes of subsection (a), expenses for the medical care of the taxpayer which are paid out of his estate during the 1-year period beginning with the day after the date of his death shall be treated as paid by the taxpayer at the time incurred.

(2) LIMITATION.—Paragraph (1) shall not apply if the amount paid is allowable under section 2053 as a deduction in computing the taxable estate of the decedent, but this paragraph shall not apply if (within the time and in the manner and form prescribed by the Secretary) there is filed—

(A) a statement that such amount has not been allowed as a deduction under section 2053, and

(B) a waiver of the right to have such amount allowed at any time as a deduction under section 2053.

[Sec. 213(d)]

(d) DEFINITIONS.—For purposes of this section—

(1) The term "medical care" means amounts paid—

(A) for the diagnosis, cure, mitigation, treatment, or prevention of disease, or for the purpose of affecting any structure or function of the body,

Sec. 211

(B) for transportation primarily for and essential to medical care referred to in subparagraph (A),

(C) for qualified long-term care services (as defined in section 7702B(c)), or

(D) for insurance (including amounts paid as premiums under part B of title XVIII of the Social Security Act, relating to supplementary medical insurance for the aged) covering medical care referred to in subparagraphs (A) and (B) or for any qualified long-term care insurance contract (as defined in section 7702B(b)).

In the case of a qualified long-term care insurance contract (as defined in section 7702B(b)), only eligible long-term care premiums (as defined in paragraph (10)) shall be taken into account under subparagraph (D).

(2) AMOUNTS PAID FOR CERTAIN LODGING AWAY FROM HOME TREATED AS PAID FOR MEDICAL CARE.— Amounts paid for lodging (not lavish or extravagant under the circumstances) while away from home primarily for and essential to medical care referred to in paragraph (1)(A) shall be treated as amounts paid for medical care if—

(A) the medical care referred to in paragraph (1)(A) is provided by a physician in a licensed hospital (or in a medical care facility which is related to, or the equivalent of, a licensed hospital), and

(B) there is no significant element of personal pleasure, recreation, or vacation in the travel away from home.

The amount taken into account under the preceding sentence shall not exceed $50 for each night for each individual.

(3) PRESCRIBED DRUG.—The term "prescribed drug" means a drug or biological which requires a prescription of a physician for its use by an individual.

(4) PHYSICIAN.—The term "physician" has the meaning given to such term by section 1861(r) of the Social Security Act (42 U.S.C. 1395x(r)).

(5) SPECIAL RULE IN THE CASE OF CHILD OF DIVORCED PARENTS, ETC.—Any child to whom section 152(e) applies shall be treated as a dependent of both parents for purposes of this section.

(6) In the case of an insurance contract under which amounts are payable for other than medical care referred to in subparagraphs (A), (B), and (C) of paragraph (1)—

(A) no amount shall be treated as paid for insurance to which paragraph (1)(D) applies unless the charge for such insurance is either separately stated in the contract, or furnished to the policyholder by the insurance company in a separate statement,

(B) the amount taken into account as the amount paid for such insurance shall not exceed such charge, and

(C) no amount shall be treated as paid for such insurance if the amount specified in the contract (or furnished to the policyholder by the insurance company in a separate statement) as the charge for such insurance is unreasonably large in relation to the total charges under the contract.

(7) Subject to the limitations of paragraph (6) [(5) after 1984], premiums paid during the taxable year by a taxpayer before he attains the age of 65 for insurance covering medical care (within the meaning of subparagraphs (A), (B), and (C) of paragraph (1)) for the taxpayer, his spouse, or a dependent after the taxpayer attains the age of 65 shall be treated as expenses paid during the taxable year for insurance which constitutes medical care if premiums for such insurance are payable (on a level payment basis) under the contract for a period of 10 years or more or until the year in which the taxpayer attains the age of 65 (but in no case for a period of less than 5 years).

(8) The determination of whether an individual is married at any time during the taxable year shall be made in accordance with the provisions of section 6013(d) (relating to determination of status as husband and wife).

(9) COSMETIC SURGERY.—

(A) IN GENERAL.—The term "medical care" does not include cosmetic surgery or other similar procedures, unless the surgery or procedure is necessary to ameliorate a deformity arising from, or directly related to, a congenital abnormality, a personal injury resulting from an accident or trauma, or disfiguring disease.

Sec. 213(d)

(B) COSMETIC SURGERY DEFINED.—For purposes of this paragraph, the term "cosmetic surgery" means any procedure which is directed at improving the patient's appearance and does not meaningfully promote the proper function of the body or prevent or treat illness or disease.

(10) ELIGIBLE LONG-TERM CARE PREMIUMS.—

(A) IN GENERAL.—For purposes of this section, the term "eligible long-term care premiums" means the amount paid during a taxable year for any qualified long-term care insurance contract (as defined in section 7702B(b)) covering an individual, to the extent such amount does not exceed the limitation determined under the following table:

In the case of an individual with an attained age before the close of the taxable year of:	The limitation is:
40 or less	$ 200
More than 40 but not more than 50	375
More than 50 but not more than 60	750
More than 60 but not more than 70	2,000
More than 70	2,500

(B) INDEXING.—

(i) IN GENERAL.—In the case of any taxable year beginning in a calendar year after 1997, each dollar amount contained in subparagraph (A) shall be increased by the medical care cost adjustment of such amount for such calendar year. If any increase determined under the preceding sentence is not a multiple of $10, such increase shall be rounded to the nearest multiple of $10.

(ii) MEDICAL CARE COST ADJUSTMENT.—For purposes of clause (i), the medical care cost adjustment for any calendar year is the percentage (if any) by which—

(I) the medical care component of the Consumer Price Index (as defined in section 1(f)(5)) for August of the preceding calendar year, exceeds

(II) such component for August of 1996. The Secretary shall, in consultation with the Secretary of Health and Human Services, prescribe an adjustment which the Secretary determines is more appropriate for purposes of this paragraph than the adjustment described in the preceding sentence, and the adjustment so prescribed shall apply in lieu of the adjustment described in the preceding sentence.

(11) CERTAIN PAYMENTS TO RELATIVES TREATED AS NOT PAID FOR MEDICAL CARE.—An amount paid for a qualified long-term care service (as defined in section 7702B(c)) provided to an individual shall be treated as not paid for medical care if such service is provided—

(A) by the spouse of the individual or by a relative (directly or through a partnership, corporation, or other entity) unless the service is provided by a licensed professional with respect to such service, or

(B) by a corporation or partnership which is related (within the meaning of section 267(b) or 707(b)) to the individual.

For purposes of this paragraph, the term "relative" means an individual bearing a relationship to the individual which is described in any of paragraphs (1) through (8) of section 152(a). This paragraph shall not apply for purposes of section 105(b) with respect to reimbursements through insurance.

[Sec. 213(e)]

(e) EXCLUSION OF AMOUNTS ALLOWED FOR CARE OF CERTAIN DEPENDENTS.—Any expense allowed as a credit under section 21 shall not be treated as an expense paid for medical care.

[Sec. 215]

SEC. 215.   ALIMONY, ETC., PAYMENTS.

[Sec. 215(a)]

(a) GENERAL RULE.—In the case of an individual, there shall be allowed as a deduction an amount equal to the alimony or separate maintenance payments paid during such individual's taxable year.

[Sec. 215(b)]

(b) ALIMONY OR SEPARATE MAINTENANCE PAYMENTS DEFINED.—For purposes of this section, the term "alimony or separate maintenance payment" means any alimony or separate maintenance payment (as defined in section 71(b)) which is includible in the gross income of the recipient under section 71.

(c) REQUIREMENT OF IDENTIFICATION NUMBER.—The Secretary may prescribe regulations under which—

(1) any individual receiving alimony or separate maintenance payments is required to furnish such individual's taxpayer identification number to the individual making such payments, and

(2) the individual making such payments is required to include such taxpayer identification number on such individual's return for the taxable year in which such payments are made.

(d) COORDINATION WITH SECTION 682.—No deduction shall be allowed under this section with respect to any payment if, by reason of section 682 (relating to income of alimony trusts), the amount thereof is not includible in such individual's gross income.

SEC. 216. DEDUCTION OF TAXES, INTEREST, AND BUSINESS DEPRECIATION BY COOPERATIVE HOUSING CORPORATION TENANT-STOCKHOLDER.

(a) ALLOWANCE OF DEDUCTION.—In the case of a tenant-stockholder (as defined in subsection (b) (2)), there shall be allowed as a deduction amounts (not otherwise deductible) paid or accrued to a cooperative housing corporation within the taxable year, but only to the extent that such amounts represent the tenant-stockholder's proportionate share of—

(1) the real estate taxes allowable as a deduction to the corporation under section 164 which are paid or incurred by the corporation on the houses or apartment building and on the land on which such houses (or building) are situated, or

(2) the interest allowable as a deduction to the corporation under section 163 which is paid or incurred by the corporation on its indebtedness contracted—

(A) in the acquisition, construction, alteration, rehabilitation, or maintenance of the houses or apartment building, or

(B) in the acquisition of the land on which the houses (or apartment building) are situated.

(b) DEFINITIONS.—For purposes of this section—

(1) COOPERATIVE HOUSING CORPORATION.—The term "cooperative housing corporation" means a corporation—

(A) having one and only one class of stock outstanding,

(B) each of the stockholders of which is entitled, solely by reason of his ownership of stock in the corporation, to occupy for dwelling purposes a house, or an apartment in a building, owned or leased by such corporation,

(C) no stockholder of which is entitled (either conditionally or unconditionally) to receive any distribution not out of earnings and profits of the corporation except on a complete or partial liquidation of the corporation, and

(D) 80 percent or more of the gross income of which for the taxable year in which the taxes and interest described in subsection (a) are paid or incurred is derived from tenant-stockholders.

(2) TENANT-STOCKHOLDER.—The term "tenant-stockholder" means a person who is a stockholder in a cooperative housing corporation, and whose stock is fully paid-up in an amount not less than an amount shown to the satisfaction of the Secretary as bearing a reasonable relationship to the portion of the value of the corporation's equity in the houses or apartment building and the land on which situated which is attributable to the house or apartment which such person is entitled to occupy.

(3) TENANT-STOCKHOLDER'S PROPORTIONATE SHARE.—

(A) IN GENERAL.—Except as provided in subparagraph (B), the term "tenant-stockholder's proportionate share" means that proportion which the stock of the cooperative housing corporation owned by the tenant-stockholder is of the total outstanding stock of the corporation (including any stock held by the corporation).

(B) SPECIAL RULE WHERE ALLOCATION OF TAXES OR INTEREST REFLECT COST TO CORPORATION OF STOCKHOLDER'S UNIT.—

(i) IN GENERAL.—If, for any taxable year—

(I) each dwelling unit owned or leased by a cooperative housing corporation is separately allocated a share of such corporation's real estate taxes described in subsection (a)(1) or a share of such corporation's interest described in subsection (a)(2), and

(II) such allocations reasonably reflect the cost to such corporation of such taxes, or of such interest, attributable to the tenant-stockholder's dwelling unit (and such unit's share of the common areas),

then the term "tenant-stockholder's proportionate share" means the shares determined in accordance with the allocations described in subclause (II).

(ii) ELECTION BY CORPORATION REQUIRED.—Clause (i) shall apply with respect to any cooperative housing corporation only if such corporation elects its application. Such an election, once made, may be revoked only with the consent of the Secretary.

* * *

[Sec. 216(c)]

(c) TREATMENT AS PROPERTY SUBJECT TO DEPRECIATION.—

(1) IN GENERAL.—So much of the stock of a tenant-stockholder in a cooperative housing corporation as is allocable, under regulations prescribed by the Secretary, to a proprietary lease or right of tenancy in property subject to the allowance for depreciation under section 167(a) shall, to the extent such proprietary lease or right of tenancy is used by such tenant-stockholder in a trade or business or for the production of income, be treated as property subject to the allowance for depreciation under section 167(a). The preceding sentence shall not be construed to limit or deny a deduction for depreciation under section 167(a) by a cooperative housing corporation with respect to property owned by such a corporation and leased to tenant-stockholders.

(2) DEDUCTION LIMITED TO ADJUSTED BASIS IN STOCK.—

(A) IN GENERAL.—The amount of any deduction for depreciation allowable under section 167(a) to tenant-stockholder with respect to any stock for any taxable year by reason of paragraph (1) shall not exceed the adjusted basis of such stock as of the close of the taxable year of the tenant-stockholder in which such deduction was incurred.

(B) CARRYFORWARD OF DISALLOWED AMOUNT.—The amount of any deduction which is not allowed by reason of subparagraph (A) shall, subject to the provisions of subparagraph (A), be treated as a deduction allowable under section 167(a) in the succeeding taxable year.

* * *

[Sec. 216(e)]

(e) DISTRIBUTIONS BY COOPERATIVE HOUSING CORPORATIONS.—Except as provided in regulations, no gain or loss shall be recognized on the distribution by a cooperative housing corporation of a dwelling unit to a stockholder in such cooperation if such distribution is in exchange for the stockholder's stock in such corporation and such dwelling unit is used as his principal residence (within the meaning of section 121).

[Sec. 217]

SEC. 217. MOVING EXPENSES.

[Sec. 217(a)]

(a) DEDUCTION ALLOWED.—There shall be allowed as a deduction moving expenses paid or incurred during the taxable year in connection with the commencement of work by the taxpayer as an employee or as a self-employed individual at a new principal place of work.

[Sec. 217(b)]

(b) DEFINITION OF MOVING EXPENSES.—

(1) IN GENERAL.—For purposes of this section, the term "moving expenses" means only the reasonable expenses—

(A) of moving household goods and personal effects from the former residence to the new residence, and

(B) of traveling (including lodging) from the former residence to the new place of residence.

Such term shall not include any expenses for meals.

(2) INDIVIDUALS OTHER THAN TAXPAYER.—In the case of any individual other than the taxpayer, expenses referred to in paragraph (1) shall be taken into account only if such individual has both the former residence and the new residence as his principal place of abode and is a member of the taxpayer's household.

[Sec. 217(c)]

(c) CONDITIONS FOR ALLOWANCE.—No deduction shall be allowed under this section unless—

(1) the taxpayer's new principal place of work—

(A) is at least 50 miles farther from his former residence than was his former principal place of work, or

(B) if he had no former principal place of work, is at least 50 miles from his former residence, and

(2) either—

(A) during the 12-month period immediately following his arrival in the general location of his new principal place of work, the taxpayer is a full-time employee, in such general location, during at least 39 weeks, or

(B) during the 24-month period immediately following his arrival in the general location of his new principal place of work, the taxpayer is a full-time employee or performs services as a self-employed individual on a full-time basis, in such general location, during at least 78 weeks, of which not less than 39 weeks are during the 12-month period referred to in subparagraph (A).

For purposes of paragraph (1), the distance between two points shall be the shortest of the more commonly traveled routes between such two points.

[Sec. 217(d)]

(d) RULES FOR APPLICATION OF SUBSECTION (c)(2).—

(1) The condition of subsection (c)(2) shall not apply if the taxpayer is unable to satisfy such condition by reason of—

(A) death or disability, or

(B) involuntary separation (other than for willful misconduct) from the service of, or transfer for the benefit of, an employer after obtaining full-time employment in which the taxpayer could reasonably have been expected to satisfy such condition.

(2) If a taxpayer has not satisfied the condition of subsection(c)(2) before the time prescribed by law (including extensions thereof) for filing the return for the taxable year during which he paid or incurred moving expenses which would otherwise be deductible under this section, but may still satisfy such condition, then such expenses may (at the election of the taxpayer) be deducted for such taxable year notwithstanding subsection (c)(2).

(3) If—

(A) for any taxable year moving expenses have been deducted in accordance with the rule provided in paragraph (2), and

(B) the condition of subsection (c)(2) cannot be satisfied at the close of a subsequent taxable year,

then an amount equal to the expenses which were so deducted shall be included in gross income for the first such subsequent taxable year.

[Sec. 217(f)]

(f) SELF-EMPLOYED INDIVIDUAL.—For purposes of this section, the term "self-employed individual" means an individual who performs personal services—

(1) as the owner of the entire interest in an unincorporated trade or business, or

(2) as a partner in a partnership carrying on a trade or business.

[Sec. 217(g)]

(g) RULES FOR MEMBERS OF THE ARMED FORCES OF THE UNITED STATES.—In the case of a member of the Armed Forces of the United States on active duty who moves pursuant to a military order and incident to a permanent change of station—

(1) the limitations under subsection (c) shall not apply;

(2) any moving and storage expenses which are furnished in kind (or for which reimbursement or an allowance is provided, but only to the extent of the expenses paid or incurred) to such member, his spouse, or his dependents, shall not be includible in gross income, and no reporting with respect to such expenses shall be required by the Secretary of Defense or the Secretary of Transportation, as the case may be; and

(3) if moving and storage expenses are furnished in kind (or if reimbursement or an allowance for such expenses is provided) to such member's spouse and his dependents with regard to moving to a location other than the one to which such member moves (or from a location other than the one from which such member moves), this section shall apply with respect to the moving expenses of his spouse and dependents—

(A) as if his spouse commenced work as an employee at a new principal place of work at such location; and

(B) without regard to the limitations under subsection (c).

[Sec. 217(h)]

(h) SPECIAL RULES FOR FOREIGN MOVES.—

(1) ALLOWANCE OF CERTAIN STORAGE FEES.—In the case of a foreign move, for purposes of this section, the moving expenses described in subsection (b)(1)(A) include the reasonable expenses—

(A) of moving household goods and personal effects to and from storage, and

(B) of storing such goods and effects for part or all of the period during which the new place of work continues to be the taxpayer's principal place of work.

(2) FOREIGN MOVE.—For purposes of this subsection, the term "foreign move" means the commencement of work by the taxpayer at a new principal place of work located outside the United States.

(3) UNITED STATES DEFINED.—For purposes of this subsection and subsection (i), the term "United States" includes the possessions of the United States.

* * *

[Sec. 217(j)]

(j) REGULATIONS.—The Secretary or his delegate shall prescribe such regulations as may be necessary to carry out the purposes of this section.

[Sec. 219]

SEC. 219. RETIREMENT SAVINGS.

[Sec. 219(a)]

(a) ALLOWANCE OF DEDUCTION.—In the case of an individual, there shall be allowed as a deduction an amount equal to the qualified retirement contributions of the individual for the taxable year.

[Sec. 219(b)]

(b) MAXIMUM AMOUNT OF DEDUCTION—

(1) IN GENERAL.—The amount allowable as a deduction under subsection (a) to any individual for any taxable year shall not exceed the lesser of—

(A) the deductible amount, or

(B) an amount equal to the compensation includible in the individual's gross income for such taxable year.

(2) SPECIAL RULE FOR EMPLOYER CONTRIBUTIONS UNDER SIMPLIFIED EMPLOYEE PENSIONS.—This section shall not apply with respect to an employer contribution to a simplified employee pension.

(3) PLANS UNDER SECTION 501(c)(18).—Notwithstanding paragraph (1), the amount allowable as a deduction under subsection (a) with respect to any contributions on behalf of a employee to a plan described in section 501(c)(18) shall not exceed the lesser of—

(A) $7,000 or

(B) an amount equal to 25 percent of the compensation (as defined in section 415(c)(3)) includible in the individual's gross income for such taxable year.

(4) SPECIAL RULE FOR SIMPLE RETIREMENT ACCOUNTS.—This section shall not apply with respect to any amount contributed to a simple retirement account established under section 408(p).

(5) DEDUCTIBLE AMOUNT.—For purposes of paragraph (1)(A)—

(A) IN GENERAL.—The deductible amount shall be determined in accordance with the following table:

For taxable years beginning in:	The deductible amount is:
2002 through 2004	$3,000
2005 through 2007	$4,000
2008 and thereafter	$5,000

(B) CATCH-UP CONTRIBUTIONS FOR INDIVIDUALS 50 OR OLDER.—

(i) IN GENERAL.—In the case of an individual who has attained the age of 50 before the close of the taxable year, the deductible amount for such taxable year shall be increased by the applicable amount.

(ii) APPLICABLE AMOUNT.—For purposes of clause (i), the applicable amount shall be the amount determined in accordance with the following table:

For taxable years beginning in:	The applicable amount is:
2002 through 2005	$ 500
2006 and thereafter	$1,000

(C) COST-OF-LIVING ADJUSTMENT.—

(i) IN GENERAL.—In the case of any taxable year beginning in a calendar year after 2008, the $5,000 amount under subparagraph (A) shall be increased by an amount equal to—

(I) such dollar amount, multiplied by

(II) the cost-of-living adjustment determined under section 1(f)(3) for the calendar year in which the taxable year begins, determined by substituting "calendar year 2007" for "calendar year 1992" in subparagraph (B) thereof.

(ii) ROUNDING RULES.—If any amount after adjustment under clause (i) is not a multiple of $500, such amount shall be rounded to the next lower multiple of $500.

[Sec. 219(c)]

(c) SPECIAL RULES FOR CERTAIN MARRIED INDIVIDUALS.—

(1) IN GENERAL.—In the case of an individual to whom this paragraph applies for the taxable year, the limitation of paragraph (1) of subsection (b) shall be equal to the lesser of—

(A) the dollar amount in effect under subsection (b)(1)(A) for the taxable year, or

(B) the sum of—

(i) the compensation includible in such individual's gross income for the taxable year, plus

(ii) the compensation includible in the gross income of such individual's spouse for the taxable year reduced by—

(I) the amount allowed as a deduction under subsection (a) to such spouse for such taxable year,

(II) the amount of any designated nondeductible contribution (as defined in section 408(o)) on behalf of such spouse for such taxable year, and

(III) the amount of any contribution on behalf of such spouse to a Roth IRA under section 408A for such taxable year.

Sec. 219(c)

(2) INDIVIDUALS TO WHOM PARAGRAPH (1) APPLIES.—Paragraph (1) shall apply to any individual if—

(A) such individual files a joint return for the taxable year, and

(B) the amount of compensation (if any) includible in such individual's gross income for the taxable year is less than the compensation includible in the gross income of such individual's spouse for the taxable year.

[Sec. 219(d)]

(d) OTHER LIMITATIONS AND RESTRICTIONS.—

(1) BENEFICIARY MUST BE UNDER AGE 70½.—No deduction shall be allowed under this section with respect to any qualified retirement contribution for the benefit of an individual if such individual has attained age 70½ before the close of such individual's taxable year for which the contribution was made.

(2) RECONTRIBUTED AMOUNTS.—No deduction shall be allowed under this section with respect to a rollover contribution described in section 402(c), 403(a)(4), 403(b)(8), 408(d)(3), or 457(e)(16).

(3) AMOUNTS CONTRIBUTED UNDER ENDOWMENT CONTRACT.—In the case of an endowment contract described in section 408(b), no deduction shall be allowed under this section for that portion of the amounts paid under the contract for the taxable year which is properly allocable, under regulations prescribed by the Secretary, to the cost of life insurance.

(4) DENIAL OF DEDUCTION FOR AMOUNT CONTRIBUTED TO INHERITED ANNUITIES OR ACCOUNTS.—No deduction shall be allowed under this section with respect to any amount paid to an inherited individual retirement account or individual retirement annuity (within the meaning of section 408(d)(3)(C)(ii)).

[Sec. 219(e)]

(e) QUALIFIED RETIREMENT CONTRIBUTION.—For purposes of this section, the term "qualified retirement contribution" means—

(1) any amount paid in cash for the taxable year by or on behalf of an individual to an individual retirement plan for such individual's benefit, and

(2) any amount contributed on behalf of any individual to a plan described in section 501(c)(18).

[Sec. 219(f)]

(f) OTHER DEFINITIONS AND SPECIAL RULES.—

(1) COMPENSATION.—For purposes of this section, the term "compensation" includes earned income (as defined in section 401(c)(2)). The term "compensation" does not include any amount received as a pension or annuity and does not include any amount received as deferred compensation. The term "compensation" shall include any amount includible in the individual's gross income under section 71 with respect to a divorce or separation instrument described in subparagraph (A) of section 71(b)(2). For purposes of this paragraph, section 401(c)(2) shall be applied as if the term trade or business for purposes of section 1402 included service described in subsection (c)(6).

(2) MARRIED INDIVIDUALS.—The maximum deduction under subsection (b) shall be computed separately for each individual, and this section shall be applied without regard to any community property laws.

(3) TIME WHEN CONTRIBUTIONS DEEMED MADE.—For purposes of this section, a taxpayer shall be deemed to have made a contribution to an individual retirement plan on the last day of the preceding taxable year if the contribution is made on account of such taxable year and is made not later than the time prescribed by law for filing the return for such taxable year (not including extensions thereof).

(4) REPORTS.—The Secretary shall prescribe regulations which prescribe the time and the manner in which reports to the Secretary and plan participants shall be made by the plan administrator of a qualified employer or government plan receiving qualified voluntary employee contributions.

(5) EMPLOYER PAYMENTS.—For purposes of this title, any amount paid by an employer to an individual retirement plan shall be treated as payment of compensation to the employee (other than a self-employed individual who is an employee within the meaning of section 401(c)(1)) includible in

his gross income in the taxable year for which the amount was contributed, whether or not a deduction for such payment is allowable under this section to the employee.

(6) EXCESS CONTRIBUTIONS TREATED AS CONTRIBUTION MADE DURING SUBSEQUENT YEAR FOR WHICH THERE IS AN UNUSED LIMITATION.—

(A) IN GENERAL.—If for the taxable year the maximum amount allowable as a deduction under this section for contributions to an individual retirement plan exceeds the amount contributed, then the taxpayer shall be treated as having made an additional contribution for the taxable year in an amount equal to the lesser of—

(i) the amount of such excess, or

(ii) the amount of the excess contributions for such taxable year (determined under section 4973(b)(2) without regard to subparagraph (C) thereof).

(B) AMOUNT CONTRIBUTED.—For purposes of this paragraph, the amount contributed—

(i) shall be determined without regard to this paragraph, and

(ii) shall not include any rollover contribution.

(C) SPECIAL RULE WHERE EXCESS DEDUCTION WAS ALLOWED FOR CLOSED YEAR.—Proper reduction shall be made in the amount allowable as a deduction by reason of this paragraph for any amount allowed as a deduction under this section for a prior taxable year for which the period for assessing deficiency has expired if the amount so allowed exceeds the amount which should have been allowed for such prior taxable year.

(7) ELECTION NOT TO DEDUCT CONTRIBUTIONS.—

For election not to deduct contributions to individual retirement plans, see section 408(o)(2)(B)(ii).

[Sec. 219(g)]

(g) LIMITATION ON DEDUCTION FOR ACTIVE PARTICIPANTS IN CERTAIN PENSION PLANS.—

(1) IN GENERAL.—If (for any part of any plan year ending with or within a taxable year) an individual or the individual's spouse is an active participant, each of the dollar limitations contained in subsections (b)(1)(A) and (c)(1)(A) for such taxable year shall be reduced (but not below zero) by the amount determined under paragraph (2).

(2) AMOUNT OF REDUCTION.—

(A) IN GENERAL.—The amount determined under this paragraph with respect to any dollar limitation shall be the amount which bears the same ratio to such limitation as—

(i) the excess of—

(I) the taxpayer's adjusted gross income for such taxable year, over

(II) the applicable dollar amount, bears to

(ii) $10,000 ($20,000 in the case of a joint return for a taxable year beginning after December 31, 2006).

(B) NO REDUCTION BELOW $200 UNTIL COMPLETE PHASEOUT.—No dollar limitation shall be reduced below $200 under paragraph (1) unless (without regard to this subparagraph) such limitation is reduced to zero.

(C) ROUNDING.—Any amount determined under this paragraph which is not a multiple of $10 shall be rounded to the next lowest $10.

(3) ADJUSTED GROSS INCOME; APPLICABLE DOLLAR AMOUNT.—For purposes of this subsection—

(A) ADJUSTED GROSS INCOME.—Adjusted gross income of any taxpayer shall be determined—

(i) after application of sections 86 and 469, and

(ii) without regard to sections 135, 137, 221, 222, and 911 or the deduction allowable under this section.

(B) APPLICABLE DOLLAR AMOUNT.—The term "applicable dollar amount" means the following:

(i) In the case of a taxpayer filing a joint return:

For taxable years beginning in:	The applicable dollar amount is:
1998	$50,000
1999	$51,000
2000	$52,000
2001	$53,000
2002	$54,000
2003	$60,000
2004	$65,000
2005	$70,000
2006	$75,000
2007 and thereafter	$80,000

(ii) In the case of any other taxpayer (other than a married individual filing a separate return):

For taxable years beginning in:	The applicable dollar amount is:
1998	$30,000
1999	$31,000
2000	$32,000
2001	$33,000
2002	$34,000
2003	$40,000
2004	$45,000
2005 and thereafter	$50,000

(iii) In the case of a married individual filing a separate return, zero.

(4) SPECIAL RULE FOR MARRIED INDIVIDUALS FILING SEPARATELY AND LIVING APART.—A husband and wife who—

(A) file separate returns for any taxable year, and

(B) live apart at all times during such taxable year,

shall not be treated as married individuals for purposes of this subsection.

(5) ACTIVE PARTICIPANT.—For purposes of this subsection, the term "active participant" means, with respect to any plan year, an individual—

(A) who is an active participant in—

(i) a plan described in section 401(a) which includes a trust exempt from tax under section 501(a),

(ii) an annuity plan described in section 403(a),

(iii) a plan established for its employees by the United States, by a State or political subdivision thereof, or by an agency or instrumentality of any of the foregoing,

(iv) an annuity contract described in section 403(b),

(v) a simplified employee pension (within the meaning of section 408(k)), or

(vi) any simple retirement account (within the meaning of section 408(p)), or

(B) who makes deductible contributions to a trust described in section 501(c)(18).

The determination of whether an individual is an active participant shall be made without regard to whether or not such individual's rights under a plan, trust, or contract are nonforfeitable. An eligible deferred compensation plan (within the meaning of section 457(b)) shall not be treated as a plan described in subparagraph (A)(iii).

(6) CERTAIN INDIVIDUALS NOT TREATED AS ACTIVE PARTICIPANTS.—For purposes of this subsection, any individual described in any of the following subparagraphs shall not be treated as an active participant for any taxable year solely because of any participation so described:

(A) MEMBERS OF RESERVE COMPONENTS.—Participation in a plan described in subparagraph (A)(iii) of paragraph (5) by reason of service as a member of a reserve component of the Armed Forces (as defined in section 10101 of title 10), unless such individual has served in excess of 90 days on active duty (other than active duty for training) during the year.

(B) VOLUNTEER FIREFIGHTERS.—A volunteer firefighter—

(i) who is a participant in a plan described in subparagraph (A)(iii) of paragraph (5) based on his activity as a volunteer firefighter, and

Sec. 219(g)

(ii) whose accrued benefit as of the beginning of the taxable year is not more than an annual benefit of $1,800 (when expressed as a single life annuity commencing at age 65).

(7) SPECIAL RULE FOR SPOUSES WHO ARE NOT ACTIVE PARTICIPANTS.—If this subsection applies to an individual for any taxable year solely because their spouse is an active participant, then, in applying this subsection to the individual (but not their spouse)—

(A) the applicable dollar amount under paragraph (3)(B)(i) shall be $150,000; and

(B) the amount applicable under paragraph (2)(A)(ii) shall be $10,000.

* * *

[Caution: As provided in Section 221(f), the amounts provided in Section 221(b)(2) are adjusted for taxable years after 2002 to reflect increases in the Consumer Price Index. The adjusted amounts applicable to taxable years beginning in 2003 are provided beginning at page ix.]

[Sec. 221]

SEC. 221. INTEREST ON EDUCATION LOANS.

[Sec. 221(a)]

(a) ALLOWANCE OF DEDUCTION.—In the case of an individual, there shall be allowed as a deduction for the taxable year an amount equal to the interest paid by the taxpayer during the taxable year on any qualified education loan.

[Sec. 221(b)]

(b) MAXIMUM DEDUCTION.—

(1) IN GENERAL.—Except as provided in paragraph (2), the deduction allowed by subsection (a) for the taxable year shall not exceed the amount determined in accordance with the following table:

In the case of taxable years beginning in:	The dollar amount is:
1998	$1,000
1999	$1,500
2000	$2,000
2001 or thereafter	$2,500

(2) LIMITATION BASED ON MODIFIED ADJUSTED GROSS INCOME.—

(A) IN GENERAL.—The amount which would (but for this paragraph) be allowable as a deduction under this section shall be reduced (but not below zero) by the amount determined under subparagraph (B).

(B) AMOUNT OF REDUCTION.—The amount determined under this subparagraph is the amount which bears the same ratio to the amount which would be so taken into account as—

(i) the excess of—

(I) the taxpayer's modified adjusted gross income for such taxable year, over

(II) $50,000 ($100,000 in the case of a joint return), bears to

(ii) $15,000 ($30,000 in the case of a joint return).

(C) MODIFIED ADJUSTED GROSS INCOME.—The term "modified adjusted gross income" means adjusted gross income determined—

(i) without regard to this section and sections 222, 911, 931, and 933, and

(ii) after application of sections 86, 135, 137, 219, and 469.

[Sec. 221(c)]

(c) DEPENDENTS NOT ELIGIBLE FOR DEDUCTION.—No deduction shall be allowed by this section to an individual for the taxable year if a deduction under section 151 with respect to such individual is allowed to another taxpayer for the taxable year beginning in the calendar year in which such individual's taxable year begins.

Sec. 221(c)

[Sec. 221(d)]

(d) DEFINITIONS.—For purposes of this section—

(1) QUALIFIED EDUCATION LOAN.—The term "qualified education loan" means any indebtedness incurred by the taxpayer solely to pay qualified higher education expenses—

(A) which are incurred on behalf of the taxpayer, the taxpayer's spouse, or any dependent of the taxpayer as of the time the indebtedness was incurred,

(B) which are paid or incurred within a reasonable period of time before or after the indebtedness is incurred, and

(C) which are attributable to education furnished during a period during which the recipient was an eligible student.

Such term includes indebtedness used to refinance indebtedness which qualifies as a qualified education loan. The term "qualified education loan" shall not include any indebtedness owed to a person who is related (within the meaning of section 267(b) or 707(b)(1)) to the taxpayer or to any person by reason of a loan under any qualified employer plan (as defined in section 72(p)(4)) or under any contract referred to in section 72(p)(5).

(2) QUALIFIED HIGHER EDUCATION EXPENSES.—The term "qualified higher education expenses" means the cost of attendance (as defined in section 472 of the Higher Education Act of 1965, 20 U.S.C. 1087ll, as in effect on the day before the date of the enactment of this Act) at an eligible educational institution, reduced by the sum of—

(A) the amount excluded from gross income under section 127, 135, 529, or 530 by reason of such expenses, and

(B) the amount of any scholarship, allowance, or payment described in section 25A(g)(2).

For purposes of the preceding sentence, the term "eligible educational institution" has the same meaning given such term by section 25A(f)(2), except that such term shall also include an institution conducting an internship or residency program leading to a degree or certificate awarded by an institution of higher education, a hospital, or a health care facility which offers postgraduate training.

(3) ELIGIBLE STUDENT.—The term "eligible student" has the meaning given such term by section 25A(b)(3).

(4) DEPENDENT.—The term "dependent" has the meaning given such term by section 152.

[Sec. 221(e)]

(e) SPECIAL RULES.—

(1) DENIAL OF DOUBLE BENEFIT.—No deduction shall be allowed under this section for any amount for which a deduction is allowable under any other provision of this chapter.

(2) MARRIED COUPLES MUST FILE JOINT RETURN.—If the taxpayer is married at the close of the taxable year, the deduction shall be allowed under subsection (a) only if the taxpayer and the taxpayer's spouse file a joint return for the taxable year.

(3) MARITAL STATUS.—Marital status shall be determined in accordance with section 7703.

[Sec. 221(f)]

(f) INFLATION ADJUSTMENTS.—

(1) IN GENERAL.—In the case of a taxable year beginning after 2002, the $50,000 and $100,000 amounts in subsection (b)(2) shall each be increased by an amount equal to—

(A) such dollar amount, multiplied by

(B) the cost-of-living adjustment determined under section 1(f)(3) for the calendar year in which the taxable year begins, determined by substituting "calendar year 2001" for "calendar year 1992" in subparagraph (B) thereof.

(2) ROUNDING.—If any amount as adjusted under paragraph (1) is not a multiple of $5,000, such amount shall be rounded to the next lowest multiple of $5,000.

[Sec. 222]

SEC. 222. QUALIFIED TUITION AND RELATED EXPENSES.

[Sec. 222(a)]

(a) ALLOWANCE OF DEDUCTION.—In the case of an individual, there shall be allowed as a deduction an amount equal to the qualified tuition and related expenses paid by the taxpayer during the taxable year.

[Sec. 222(b)]

(b) DOLLAR LIMITATIONS.—

(1) IN GENERAL.—The amount allowed as a deduction under subsection (a) with respect to the taxpayer for any taxable year shall not exceed the applicable dollar limit.

(2) APPLICABLE DOLLAR LIMIT.—

(A) 2002 AND 2003.—In the case of a taxable year beginning in 2002 or 2003, the applicable dollar limit shall be equal to—

(i) in the case of a taxpayer whose adjusted gross income for the taxable year does not exceed $65,000 ($130,000 in the case of a joint return), $3,000, and—

(ii) in the case of any other taxpayer, zero.

(B) 2004 AND 2005.—In the case of a taxable year beginning in 2004 or 2005, the applicable dollar amount shall be equal to—

(i) in the case of a taxpayer whose adjusted gross income for the taxable year does not exceed $65,000 ($130,000 in the case of a joint return), $4,000,

(ii) in the case of a taxpayer not described in clause (i) whose adjusted gross income for the taxable year does not exceed $80,000 ($160,000 in the case of a joint return), $2,000, and

(iii) in the case of any other taxpayer, zero.

(C) ADJUSTED GROSS INCOME.—For purposes of this paragraph, adjusted gross income shall be determined—

(i) without regard to this section and sections 911, 931, and 933, and

(ii) after application of sections 86, 135, 137, 219, 221, and 469.

[Sec. 222(c)]

(c) NO DOUBLE BENEFIT.—

(1) IN GENERAL.—No deduction shall be allowed under subsection (a) for any expense for which a deduction is allowed to the taxpayer under any other provision of this chapter.

(2) COORDINATION WITH OTHER EDUCATION INCENTIVES.—

(A) DENIAL OF DEDUCTION IF CREDIT ELECTED.—No deduction shall be allowed under subsection (a) for a taxable year with respect to the qualified tuition and related expenses with respect to an individual if the taxpayer or any other person elects to have section 25A apply with respect to such individual for such year.

(B) COORDINATION WITH EXCLUSIONS.—The total amount of qualified tuition and related expenses shall be reduced by the amount of such expenses taken into account in determining any amount excluded under section 135, 529(c)(1), or 530(d)(2). For purposes of the preceding sentence, the amount taken into account in determining the amount excluded under section 529(c)(1) shall not include that portion of the distribution which represents a return of any contributions to the plan.

(3) DEPENDENTS.—No deduction shall be allowed under subsection (a) to any individual with respect to whom a deduction under section 151 is allowable to another taxpayer for a taxable year beginning in the calendar year in which such individual's taxable year begins.

[Sec. 222(d)]

(d) DEFINITIONS AND SPECIAL RULES.—For purposes of this section—

(1) QUALIFIED TUITION AND RELATED EXPENSES.—The term "qualified tuition and related expenses" has the meaning given such term by section 25A(f). Such expenses shall be reduced in the same manner as under section 25A(g)(2).

Sec. 222(d)

(2) IDENTIFICATION REQUIREMENT.—No deduction shall be allowed under subsection (a) to a taxpayer with respect to the qualified tuition and related expenses of an individual unless the taxpayer includes the name and taxpayer identification number of the individual on the return of tax for the taxable year.

(3) LIMITATION ON TAXABLE YEAR OF DEDUCTION.—

(A) IN GENERAL.—A deduction shall be allowed under subsection (a) for qualified tuition and related expenses for any taxable year only to the extent such expenses are in connection with enrollment at an institution of higher education during the taxable year.

(B) CERTAIN PREPAYMENTS ALLOWED.—Subparagraph (A) shall not apply to qualified tuition and related expenses paid during a taxable year if such expenses are in connection with an academic term beginning during such taxable year or during the first 3 months of the next taxable year.

(4) NO DEDUCTION FOR MARRIED INDIVIDUALS FILING SEPARATE RETURNS.—If the taxpayer is a married individual (within the meaning of section 7703), this section shall apply only if the taxpayer and the taxpayer's spouse file a joint return for the taxable year.

(5) NONRESIDENT ALIENS.—If the taxpayer is a nonresident alien individual for any portion of the taxable year, this section shall apply only if such individual is treated as a resident alien of the United States for purposes of this chapter by reason of an election under subsection (g) or (h) of section 6013.

(6) REGULATIONS.—The Secretary may prescribe such regulations as may be necessary or appropriate to carry out this section, including regulations requiring recordkeeping and information reporting.

[Sec. 222(e)]

(e) TERMINATION.—This section shall not apply to taxable years beginning after December 31, 2005.

PART VIII—SPECIAL DEDUCTIONS FOR CORPORATIONS

[Sec. 241]

SEC. 241. ALLOWANCE OF SPECIAL DEDUCTIONS.

In addition to the deductions provided in part VI (sec. 161 and following), there shall be allowed as deductions in computing taxable income the items specified in this part.

[Sec. 243]

SEC. 243. DIVIDENDS RECEIVED BY CORPORATIONS.

[Sec. 243(a)]

(a) GENERAL RULE.—In the case of a corporation, there shall be allowed as a deduction an amount equal to the following percentages of the amount received as dividends from a domestic corporation which is subject to taxation under this chapter:

(1) 70 percent, in the case of dividends other than dividends described in paragraph (2) or (3);

(2) 100 percent, in the case of dividends received by a small business investment company operating under the Small Business Investment Act of 1958 (15 U.S.C. 661 and following); and

(3) 100 percent, in the case of qualifying dividends (as defined in subsection (b)(1)).

[Sec. 243(b)]

(b) QUALIFYING DIVIDENDS.—

(1) IN GENERAL.—For purposes of this section, the term "qualifying dividend" means any dividend received by a corporation—

(A) if at the close of the day on which such dividend is received, such corporation is a member of the same affiliated group as the corporation distributing such dividend, and

(B) if—

(i) such dividend is distributed out of the earnings and profits of a taxable year of the distributing corporation which ends after December 31, 1963, for which an election under section 1562 was not in effect, and on each day of which the distributing corporation and the corporation receiving the dividend were members of such affiliated group, or

(ii) such dividend is paid by a corporation with respect to which an election under section 936 is in effect for the taxable year in which such dividend is paid.

(2) AFFILIATED GROUP.—For purposes of this subsection:

(A) IN GENERAL.—The term "affiliated group" has the meaning given such term by section 1504(a), except that for such purposes sections 1504(b)(2), 1504(b)(4), and 1504(c) shall not apply.

* * *

[Sec. 243(c)]

(c) RETENTION OF 80-PERCENT DIVIDENDS RECEIVED DEDUCTION FOR DIVIDENDS FROM 20-PERCENT OWNED CORPORATIONS.—

(1) IN GENERAL.—In the case of any dividend received from a 20-percent owned corporation—

(A) subsection (a)(1) of this section, and

(B) subsections (a)(3) and (b)(2) of section 244,

shall be applied by substituting "80 percent" for "70 percent".

(2) 20-PERCENT OWNED CORPORATION.—For purposes of this section, the term "20-percent owned corporation" means any corporation if 20 percent or more of the stock of such corporation (by vote and value) is owned by the taxpayer. For purposes of the preceding sentence, stock described in section 1504(a)(4) shall not be taken into account.

* * *

[Sec. 246]

SEC. 246. RULES APPLYING TO DEDUCTIONS FOR DIVIDENDS RECEIVED.

[Sec. 246(a)]

(a) DEDUCTION NOT ALLOWED FOR DIVIDENDS FROM CERTAIN CORPORATIONS.—

(1) IN GENERAL.—The deductions allowed by sections 243, 244, and 245 shall not apply to any dividend from a corporation which, for the taxable year of the corporation in which the distribution is made, or for the next preceding taxable year of the corporation, is a corporation exempt from tax under section 501 (relating to certain charitable, etc., organizations) or section 521 (relating to farmers' cooperative associations).

* * *

[Sec. 246(b)]

(b) LIMITATION ON AGGREGATE AMOUNT OF DEDUCTIONS.—

(1) GENERAL RULE.—Except as provided in paragraph (2), the aggregate amount of the deductions allowed by sections 243(a)(1), 244(a), and subsection (a) or (b) of section 245 shall not exceed the percentage determined under paragraph (3) of the taxable income computed without regard to the deductions allowed by sections 172, 243(a)(1), 244(a), subsection (a) or (b) of section 245, and 247, without regard to any adjustment under section 1059, and without regard to any capital loss carryback to the taxable year under section 1212(a)(1).

(2) EFFECT OF NET OPERATING LOSS.—Paragraph (1) shall not apply for any taxable year for which there is a net operating loss (as determined under section 172).

(3) SPECIAL RULES.—The provisions of paragraph (1) shall be applied—

(A) first separately with respect to dividends from 20-percent owned corporations (as defined in section 243(c)(2)) and the percentage determined under this paragraph shall be 80 percent, and

(B) then separately with respect to dividends not from 20-percent owned corporations and the percentage determined under this paragraph shall be 70 percent and the taxable income shall be reduced by the aggregate amount of dividends from 20-percent owned corporations (as so defined).

Sec. 246(b)

[Sec. 246(c)]

(c) EXCLUSION OF CERTAIN DIVIDENDS.—

(1) IN GENERAL.—No deduction shall be allowed under section 243, 244, or 245, in respect of any dividend on any share of stock—

(A) which is held by the taxpayer for 45 days or less during the 90-day period beginning on the date which is 45 days before the date on which such share becomes ex-dividend with respect to such dividend, or

(B) to the extent that the taxpayer is under an obligation (whether pursuant to a short sale or otherwise) to make related payments with respect to positions in substantially similar or related property.

(2) 90-DAY RULE IN THE CASE OF CERTAIN PREFERENCE DIVIDENDS.—In the case of stock having preference in dividends, if the taxpayer receives dividends with respect to such stock which are attributable to a period or periods aggregating in excess of 366 days, paragraph (1)(A) shall be applied—

(A) by substituting "90 days" for "45 days" each place it appears, and

(B) by substituting "180-day period" for "90-day period".

(3) DETERMINATION OF HOLDING PERIODS.—For purposes of this subsection, in determining the period for which the taxpayer has held any share of stock—

(A) the day of disposition, but not the day of acquisition, shall be taken into account, and

(B) paragraph (4) of section 1223 shall not apply.

(4) HOLDING PERIOD REDUCED FOR PERIODS WHERE RISK OF LOSS DIMINISHED.—The holding periods determined for purposes of this subsection shall be appropriately reduced (in the manner provided in regulations prescribed by the Secretary) for any period (during such periods) in which—

(A) the taxpayer has an option to sell, is under a contractual obligation to sell, or has made (and not closed) a short sale of, substantially identical stock or securities,

(B) the taxpayer is the grantor of an option to buy substantially identical stock or securities, or

(C) under regulations prescribed by the Secretary, a taxpayer has diminished his risk of loss by holding 1 or more other positions with respect to substantially similar or related property.

The preceding sentence shall not apply in the case of any qualified covered call (as defined in section 1092(c)(4) but without regard to the requirement that gain or loss with respect to the option not be ordinary income or loss).

* * *

[Sec. 246A]

SEC. 246A. DIVIDENDS RECEIVED DEDUCTION REDUCED WHERE PORTFOLIO STOCK IS DEBT FINANCED.

[Sec. 246A(a)]

(a) GENERAL RULE.—In the case of any dividend on debt-financed portfolio stock, there shall be substituted for the percentage which (but for this subsection) would be used in determining the amount of the deduction allowable under section 243, 244, or 245(a) a percentage equal to the product of—

(1) 70 percent (80 percent in the case of any dividend from a 20-percent owned corporation as defined in section 243(c)(2)), and

(2) 100 percent minus the average indebtedness percentage.

[Sec. 246A(b)]

(b) SECTION NOT TO APPLY TO DIVIDENDS FOR WHICH 100 PERCENT DIVIDENDS RECEIVED DEDUCTION ALLOWABLE.—Subsection (a) shall not apply to—

(1) qualifying dividends (as defined in section 243(b) without regard to section 243(c)(4)), and

(2) dividends received by a small business investment company operating under the Small Business Investment Act of 1958.

[Sec. 246A(c)]

(c) DEBT FINANCED PORTFOLIO STOCK.—For purposes of this section—

(1) IN GENERAL.—The term "debt financed portfolio stock" means any portfolio stock if at some time during the base period there is portfolio indebtedness with respect to such stock.

(2) PORTFOLIO STOCK.—The term "portfolio stock" means any stock of a corporation unless—

(A) as of the beginning of the ex-dividend date, the taxpayer owns stock of such corporation—

(i) possessing at least 50 percent of the total voting power of the stock of such corporation, and

(ii) having a value equal to at least 50 percent of the total value of the stock of such corporation, or

(B) as of the beginning of the ex-dividend date—

(i) the taxpayer owns stock of such corporation which would meet the requirements of subparagraph (A) if "20 percent" were substituted for "50 percent" each place it appears in such subparagraph, and

(ii) stock meeting the requirements of subparagraph (A) is owned by 5 or fewer corporate shareholders.

[Sec. 246A(d)]

(d) AVERAGE INDEBTEDNESS PERCENTAGE.—For purposes of this section—

(1) IN GENERAL.—Except as provided in paragraph (2), the term "average indebtedness percentage" means the percentage obtained by dividing—

(A) the average amount (determined under regulations prescribed by the Secretary) of the portfolio indebtedness with respect to the stock during the base period, by

(B) the average amount (determined under regulations prescribed by the Secretary) of the adjusted basis of the stock during the base period.

(2) SPECIAL RULE WHERE STOCK NOT HELD THROUGHOUT BASE PERIOD.—In the case of any stock which was not held by the taxpayer throughout the base period, paragraph (1) shall be applied as if the base period consisted only of that portion of the base period during which the stock was held by the taxpayer.

(3) PORTFOLIO INDEBTEDNESS.—

(A) IN GENERAL.—The term "portfolio indebtedness" means any indebtedness directly attributable to investment in the portfolio stock.

(B) CERTAIN AMOUNTS RECEIVED FROM SHORT SALE TREATED AS INDEBTEDNESS.—For purposes of subparagraph (A), any amount received from a short sale shall be treated as indebtedness for the period beginning on the day on which such amount is received and ending on the day the short sale is closed.

(4) BASE PERIOD.—The term "base period" means, with respect to any dividend, the shorter of—

(A) the period beginning on the ex-dividend date for the most recent previous dividend on the stock and ending on the day before the ex-dividend date for the dividend involved, or

(B) the 1-year period ending on the day before the ex-dividend date for the dividend involved.

[Sec. 246A(e)]

(e) REDUCTION IN DIVIDENDS RECEIVED DEDUCTION NOT TO EXCEED ALLOCABLE INTEREST.—Under regulations prescribed by the Secretary, any reduction under this section in the amount allowable as a deduction under section 243, 244, or 245 with respect to any dividend shall not exceed the amount of any interest deduction (including any deductible short sale expense) allocable to such dividend.

[Sec. 246A(f)]

(f) REGULATIONS.—The regulations prescribed for purposes of this section under section 7701(f) shall include regulations providing for the disallowance of interest deductions or other appropriate treatment (in lieu of reducing the dividend received deduction) where the obligor of the indebtedness is a person other than the person receiving the dividend.

Sec. 246A(f)

[Sec. 248]

SEC. 248. ORGANIZATIONAL EXPENDITURES.

[Sec. 248(a)]

(a) ELECTION TO AMORTIZE.—The organizational expenditures of a corporation may, at the election of the corporation (made in accordance with regulations prescribed by the Secretary), be treated as deferred expenses. In computing taxable income, such deferred expenses shall be allowed as a deduction ratably over such period of not less than 60 months as may be selected by the corporation (beginning with the month in which the corporation begins business).

[Sec. 248(b)]

(b) ORGANIZATIONAL EXPENDITURES DEFINED.—The term "organizational expenditures" means any expenditure which—

(1) is incident to the creation of the corporation;

(2) is chargeable to capital account; and

(3) is of a character which, if expended incident to the creation of a corporation having a limited life, would be amortizable over such life.

[Sec. 248(c)]

(c) TIME FOR AND SCOPE OF ELECTION.—The election provided by subsection (a) may be made for any taxable year beginning after December 31, 1953, but only if made not later than the time prescribed by law for filing the return for such taxable year (including extensions thereof). The period so elected shall be adhered to in computing the taxable income of the corporation for the taxable year for which the election is made and all subsequent taxable years. The election shall apply only with respect to expenditures paid or incurred on or after August 16, 1954.

PART IX—ITEMS NOT DEDUCTIBLE

[Sec. 261]

SEC. 261. GENERAL RULE FOR DISALLOWANCE OF DEDUCTIONS.

In computing taxable income no deduction shall in any case be allowed in respect of the items specified in this part.

[Sec. 262]

SEC. 262. PERSONAL, LIVING, AND FAMILY EXPENSES.

[Sec. 262(a)]

(a) GENERAL RULE.—Except as otherwise expressly provided in this chapter, no deduction shall be allowed for personal, living, or family expenses.

[Sec. 262(b)]

(b) TREATMENT OF CERTAIN PHONE EXPENSES.—For purposes of subsection (a), in the case of an individual, any charge (including taxes thereon) for basic local telephone service with respect to the 1st telephone line provided to any residence of the taxpayer shall be treated as a personal expense.

[Sec. 263]

SEC. 263. CAPITAL EXPENDITURES.

[Sec. 263(a)]

(a) GENERAL RULE.—No deduction shall be allowed for—

(1) Any amount paid out for new buildings or for permanent improvements or betterments made to increase the value of any property or estate. This paragraph shall not apply to—

(A) expenditures for the development of mines or deposits deductible under section 616,

(B) research and experimental expenditures deductible under section 174,

(C) soil and water conservation expenditures deductible under section 175,

(D) expenditures by farmers for fertilizer, etc., deductible under section 180,

(E) expenditures for removal of architectural and transportation barriers to the handicapped and elderly which the taxpayer elects to deduct under section 190,

(F) expenditures for tertiary injectants with respect to which a deduction is allowed under section 193;

(G) expenditures for which a deduction is allowed under section 179; or

(H) expenditures for which a deduction is allowed under section 179A.

(2) Any amount expended in restoring property or in making good the exhaustion thereof for which an allowance is or has been made.

[Sec. 263(b)—Repealed]

[Sec. 263(c)]

(c) INTANGIBLE DRILLING AND DEVELOPMENT COSTS IN THE CASE OF OIL AND GAS WELLS AND GEOTHERMAL WELLS.—Notwithstanding subsection (a), and except as provided in subsection (i), regulations shall be prescribed by the Secretary under this subtitle corresponding to the regulations which granted the option to deduct as expenses intangible drilling and development costs in the case of oil and gas wells and which were recognized and approved by the Congress in House Concurrent Resolution 50, Seventy-ninth Congress. Such regulations shall also grant the option to deduct as expenses intangible drilling and development costs in the case of wells drilled for any geothermal deposit (as defined in section 613(e)(2)) to the same extent and in the same manner as such expenses are deductible in the case of oil and gas wells. This subsection shall not apply with respect to any costs to which any deduction is allowed under section 59(e) or 291.

* * *

[Sec. 263A]

SEC. 263A. CAPITALIZATION AND INCLUSION IN INVENTORY COSTS OF CERTAIN EXPENSES.

[Sec. 263A(a)]

(a) NONDEDUCTIBILITY OF CERTAIN DIRECT AND INDIRECT COSTS.—

(1) IN GENERAL.—In the case of any property to which this section applies, any costs described in paragraph (2)—

(A) in the case of property which is inventory in the hands of the taxpayer, shall be included in inventory costs, and

(B) in the case of any other property, shall be capitalized.

(2) ALLOCABLE COSTS.—The costs described in this paragraph with respect to any property are—

(A) the direct costs of such property, and

(B) such property's proper share of those indirect costs (including taxes) part or all of which are allocable to such property.

Any cost which (but for this subsection) could not be taken into account in computing taxable income for any taxable year shall not be treated as a cost described in this paragraph.

[Sec. 263A(b)]

(b) PROPERTY TO WHICH SECTION APPLIES.—Except as otherwise provided in this section, this section shall apply to—

(1) PROPERTY PRODUCED BY TAXPAYER.—Real or tangible personal property produced by the taxpayer.

(2) PROPERTY ACQUIRED FOR RESALE.—

(A) IN GENERAL.—Real or personal property described in section 1221(a)(1) which is acquired by the taxpayer for resale.

(B) EXCEPTION FOR TAXPAYER WITH GROSS RECEIPTS OF $10,000,000 OR LESS.—Subparagraph (A) shall not apply to any personal property acquired during any taxable year by the taxpayer for resale if the average annual gross receipts of the taxpayer (or any predecessor) for the

3-taxable year period ending with the taxable year preceding such taxable year do not exceed $10,000,000.

      (C) AGGREGATION RULES, ETC.—For purposes of subparagraph (B), rules similar to the rules of paragraphs (2) and (3) of section 448(c) shall apply.

For purposes of paragraph (1), the term "tangible personal property" shall include a film, sound recording, video tape, book, or similar property.

[Sec. 263A(c)]

(c) GENERAL EXCEPTIONS.—

      (1) PERSONAL USE PROPERTY.—This section shall not apply to any property produced by the taxpayer for use by the taxpayer other than in a trade or business or an activity conducted for profit.

      (2) RESEARCH AND EXPERIMENTAL EXPENDIITURES.—This section shall not apply to any amount allowable as a deduction under section 174.

      (3) CERTAIN DEVELOPMENT AND OTHER COSTS OF OIL AND GAS WELLS OR OTHER MINERAL PROPERTY.—This section shall not apply to any cost allowable as a deduction under section 263(c), 263(i), 291(b)(2), 616, or 617.

      (4) COORDINATION WITH LONG-TERM CONTRACT RULES.—This section shall not apply to any property produced by the taxpayer pursuant to a long-term contract.

      (5) TIMBER AND CERTAIN ORNAMENTAL TREES.—This section shall not apply to—

          (A) trees raised, harvested, or grown by the taxpayer other than trees described in clause (ii) of subsection (e)(4)(B) (after application of the last sentence thereof), and

          (B) any real property underlying such trees.

      (6) COORDINATION WITH SECTION 59(e).—Paragraphs (2) and (3) shall apply to any amount allowable as a deduction under section 59(e) for qualified expenditures described in subparagraphs (B), (C), (D), and (E) of paragraph (2) thereof.

      * * *

[Sec. 263A(e)]

(e) DEFINITIONS AND SPECIAL RULES FOR PURPOSES OF SUBSECTION (d).—

(1) RECAPTURE OF EXPENSED AMOUNTS ON DISPOSITION.—

      (A) IN GENERAL.—In the case of any plant with respect to which amounts would have been capitalized under subsection (a) but for an election under subsection (d)(3)—

          (i) such plant (if not otherwise section 1245 property) shall be treated as section 1245 property, and

          (ii) for purposes of section 1245, the recapture amount shall be treated as a deduction allowed for depreciation with respect to such property.

      (B) RECAPTURE AMOUNT.—For purposes of subparagraph (A), the term "recapture amount" means any amount allowable as a deduction to the taxpayer which, but for an election under subsection (d)(3), would have been capitalized with respect to the plant.

(2) EFFECTS OF ELECTION ON DEPRECIATION.—

      (A) IN GENERAL.—If the taxpayer (or any related person) makes an election under subsection (d)(3), the provisions of section 168(g)(2) (relating to alternative depreciation) shall apply to all property of the taxpayer used predominantly in the farming business and placed in service in any taxable year during which any such election is in effect.

      (B) RELATED PERSON.—For purposes of subparagraph (A), the term "related person" means—

          (i) the taxpayer and members of the taxpayer's family,

          (ii) any corporation (including an S corporation) if 50 percent or more (in value) of the stock of such corporation is owned (directly or through the application of section 318) by the taxpayer or members of the taxpayer's family,

          (iii) a corporation and any other corporation which is a member of the same controlled group described in section 1563(a)(1), and

(iv) any partnership if 50 percent or more (in value) of the interests in such partnership is owned directly or indirectly by the taxpayer or members of the taxpayer's family.

(C) MEMBERS OF FAMILY.—For purposes of this paragraph, the term "family" means the taxpayer, the spouse of the taxpayer, and any of their children who have not attained age 18 before the close of the taxable year.

(3) PREPRODUCTIVE PERIOD.—

(A) IN GENERAL.—For purposes of this section, the term "preproductive period" means—

(i) in the case of a plant which will have more than 1 crop or yield, the period before the 1st marketable crop or yield from such plant, or

(ii) in the case of any other plant, the period before such plant is reasonably expected to be disposed of.

For purposes of this subparagraph, use by the taxpayer in a farming business of any supply produced in such business shall be treated as a disposition.

(B) RULE FOR DETERMINING PERIOD.—In the case of a plant grown in commercial quantities in the United States, the preproductive period for such plant if grown in the United States shall be based on the nationwide weighted average preproductive period for such plant.

(4) FARMING BUSINESS.—For purposes of this section—

(A) IN GENERAL.—The term "farming business" means the trade or business of farming.

(B) CERTAIN TRADES AND BUSINESSES INCLUDED.—The term "farming business" shall include the trade or business of—

(i) operating a nursery or sod farm, or

(ii) the raising or harvesting of trees bearing fruit, nuts, or other crops, or ornamental trees.

For purposes of clause (ii), an evergreen tree which is more than 6 years old at the time severed from the roots shall not be treated as an ornamental tree.

(5) CERTAIN INVENTORY VALUATION METHODS PERMITTED.—The Secretary shall by regulations permit the taxpayer to use reasonable inventory valuation methods to compute the amount required to be capitalized under subsection (a) in the case of any plant.

[Sec. 263A(f)]

(f) SPECIAL RULES FOR ALLOCATION OF INTEREST TO PROPERTY PRODUCED BY THE TAXPAYER.—

(1) INTEREST CAPITALIZED ONLY IN CERTAIN CASES.—Subsection (a) shall only apply to interest costs which are—

(A) paid or incurred during the production period, and

(B) allocable to property which is described in subsection (b)(1) and which has—

(i) a long useful life,

(ii) an estimated production period exceeding 2 years, or

(iii) an estimated production period exceeding 1 year and a cost exceeding $1,000,000.

(2) ALLOCATION RULES.—

(A) IN GENERAL.—In determining the amount of interest required to be capitalized under subsection (a) with respect to any property—

(i) interest on any indebtedness directly attributable to production expenditures with respect to such property shall be assigned to such property, and

(ii) interest on any other indebtedness shall be assigned to such property to the extent that the taxpayer's interest costs could have been reduced if production expenditures (not attributable to indebtedness described in clause (i)) had not been incurred.

(B) EXCEPTION FOR QUALIFIED RESIDENCE INTEREST.—Subparagraph (A) shall not apply to any qualified residence interest (within the meaning of section 163(h)).

(C) SPECIAL RULE FOR FLOW-THROUGH ENTITIES.—Except as provided in regulations, in the case of any flow-through entity, this paragraph shall be applied first at the entity level and then at the beneficiary level.

(3) INTEREST RELATING TO PROPERTY USED TO PRODUCE PROPERTY.—This subsection shall apply to any interest on indebtedness allocable (as determined under paragraph (2)) to and property used to produce property to which this subsection applies to the extent such interest is allocable (as so determined) to the produced property.

(4) DEFINITIONS.—For purposes of this subsection—

(A) LONG USEFUL LIFE.—Property has a long useful life if such property is—

(i) real property, or

(ii) property with a class life of 20 years or more (as determined under section 168).

(B) PRODUCTION PERIOD.—The term "production period" means, when used with respect to any property, the period—

(i) beginning on the date on which production of the property begins, and

(ii) ending on the date on which the property is ready to be placed in service or is ready to be held for sale.

(C) PRODUCTION EXPENDITURES.—The term "production expenditures" means the costs (whether or not incurred during the production period) required to be capitalized under subsection (a) with respect to the property.

[Sec. 263A(g)]

(g) PRODUCTION.—For purposes of this section—

(1) IN GENERAL.—The term "produce" includes construct, build, install, manufacture, develop, or improve.

(2) TREATMENT OF PROPERTY PRODUCED UNDER CONTRACT FOR THE TAXPAYER.—The taxpayer shall be treated as producing any property produced for the taxpayer under a contract with the taxpayer; except that only costs paid or incurred by the taxpayer (whether under such contract or otherwise) shall be taken into account in applying subsection (a) to the taxpayer.

[Sec. 263A(h)]

(h) EXEMPTION FOR FREE LANCE AUTHORS, PHOTOGRAPHERS, AND ARTISTS.—

(1) IN GENERAL.—Nothing in this section shall require the capitalization of any qualified creative expense.

(2) QUALIFIED CREATIVE EXPENSE.—For purposes of this subsection, the term "qualified creative expense" means any expense—

(A) which is paid or incurred by an individual in the trade or business of such individual (other than as an employee) of being a writer, photographer, or artist, and

(B) which, without regard to this section, would be allowable as a deduction for the taxable year.

Such term does not include any expense related to printing, photographic plates, motion picture films, video tapes, or similar items.

(3) DEFINITIONS.—For purposes of this subsection—

(A) WRITER.—The term "writer" means any individual if the personal efforts of such individual create (or may reasonably be expected to create) a literary manuscript, musical composition (including any accompanying words), or dance score.

(B) PHOTOGRAPHER.—The term "photographer" means any individual if the personal efforts of such individual create (or may reasonably be expected to create) a photograph or photographic negative or transparency.

(C) ARTIST.—

(i) IN GENERAL.—The term "artist" means any individual if the personal efforts of such individual create (or may reasonably be expected to create) a picture, painting, sculpture, statue, etching, drawing, cartoon, graphic design, or original print edition.

(ii) CRITERIA.—In determining whether any expense is paid or incurred in the trade or business of being an artist, the following criteria shall be taken into account:

(I) The originality and uniqueness of the item created (or to be created).

(II) The predominance of aesthetic value over utilitarian value of the item created (or to be created).

(D) TREATMENT OF CERTAIN CORPORATIONS.—

(i) IN GENERAL.—If—

(I) substantially all of the stock of a corporation is owned by a qualified employee-owner and members of his family (as defined in section 267(c)(4)), and

(II) the principal activity of such corporation is performance of personal services directly related to the activities of the qualified employee-owner and such services are substantially performed by the qualified employee-owner,

this subsection shall apply to any expense of such corporation which directly relates to the activities of such employee-owner in the same manner as if such expense were incurred by such employee-owner.

(ii) QUALIFIED EMPLOYEE-OWNER.—For purposes of this subparagraph, the term "qualified employee-owner" means any individual who is an employee-owner of the corporation (as defined in section 269A(b)(2)) and who is a writer, photographer, or artist.

[Sec. 263A(i)]

(i) REGULATIONS.—The Secretary shall prescribe such regulations as may be necessary or appropriate to carry out the purposes of this section, including—

(1) regulations to prevent the use of related parties, pass-thru entities, or intermediaries to avoid the application of this section, and

(2) regulations providing for simplified procedures for the application of this section in the case of property described in subsection (b)(2).

[Sec. 264]

SEC. 264. CERTAIN AMOUNTS PAID IN CONNECTION WITH INSURANCE CONTRACTS.

[Sec. 264(a)]

(a) GENERAL RULE.—No deduction shall be allowed for—

(1) Premiums on any life insurance policy, or endowment or annuity contract, if the taxpayer is directly or indirectly a beneficiary under the policy or contract.

(2) Any amount paid or accrued on indebtedness incurred or continued to purchase or carry a single premium life insurance, endowment, or annuity contract.

(3) Except as provided in subsection (d), any amount paid or accrued on indebtedness incurred or continued to purchase or carry a life insurance, endowment, or annuity contract (other than a single premium contract or a contract treated as a single premium contract) pursuant to a plan of purchase which contemplates the systematic direct or indirect borrowing of part or all of the increases in the cash value of such contract (either from the insurer or otherwise).

(4) Except as provided in subsection (e), any interest paid or accrued on any indebtedness with respect to 1 or more life insurance policies owned by the taxpayer covering the life of any individual, or any endowment or annuity contracts owned by the taxpayer covering any individual.

Paragraph (2) shall apply in respect of annuity contracts only as to contracts purchased after March 1, 1954. Paragraph (3) shall apply only in respect of contracts purchased after August 6, 1963. Paragraph (4) shall apply with respect to contracts purchased after June 20, 1986.

[Sec. 264(b)]

(b) EXCEPTIONS TO SUBSECTION (a)(1).—Subsection (a)(1) shall not apply to—

(1) any annuity contract described in section 72(s)(5), and

(2) any annuity contract to which section 72(u) applies.

[Sec. 264(c)]

(c) CONTRACTS TREATED AS SINGLE PREMIUM CONTRACTS.—For purposes of subsection (a) (2), a contract shall be treated as a single premium contract—

Sec. 264(c)

(1) if substantially all the premiums on the contract are paid within a period of 4 years from the date on which the contract is purchased, or

(2) if an amount is deposited after March 1, 1954, with the insurer for payment of a substantial number of future premiums on the contract.

[Sec. 264(d)]

(d) EXCEPTIONS.—Subsection (a)(3) shall not apply to any amount paid or accrued by a person during a taxable year on indebtedness incurred or continued as part of a plan referred to in subsection (a)(3)—

(1) if no part of 4 of the annual premiums due during the 7-year period (beginning with the date the first premium on the contract to which such plan relates was paid) is paid under such plan by means of indebtedness,

(2) if the total of the amounts paid or accrued by such person during such taxable year for which (without regard to this paragraph) no deduction would be allowable by reason of subsection (a)(3) does not exceed $100,

(3) if such amount was paid or accrued on indebtedness incurred because of an unforeseen substantial loss of income or unforeseen substantial increase in his financial obligations, or

(4) if such indebtedness was incurred in connection with his trade or business.

For purposes of applying paragraph (1), if there is a substantial increase in the premiums on a contract, a new 7-year period described in such paragraph with respect to such contract shall commence on the date the first such increased premium is paid.

[Sec. 264(e)]

(e) SPECIAL RULES FOR APPLICATION OF SUBSECTION (a)(4).—

(1) EXCEPTION FOR KEY PERSONS.—Subsection (a)(4) shall not apply to any interest paid or accrued on any indebtedness with respect to policies or contracts covering an individual who is a key person to the extent that the aggregate amount of such indebtedness with respect to policies and contracts covering such individual does not exceed $50,000.

* * *

(3) KEY PERSON.—For purposes of paragraph (1), the term "key person" means an officer or 20-percent owner, except that the number of individuals who may be treated as key persons with respect to any taxpayer shall not exceed the greater of—

(A) 5 individuals, or

(B) the lesser of 5 percent of the total officers and employees of the taxpayer or 20 individuals.

(4) 20-PERCENT OWNER.—For purposes of this subsection, the term "20-percent owner" means—

(A) if the taxpayer is a corporation, any person who owns directly 20 percent or more of the outstanding stock of the corporation or stock possessing 20 percent or more of the total combined voting power of all stock of the corporation, or

(B) if the taxpayer is not a corporation, any person who owns 20 percent or more of the capital or profits interest in the taxpayer.

(5) AGGREGATION RULES.—

(A) IN GENERAL.—For purposes of paragraph (4)(A) and applying the $50,000 limitation in paragraph (1)—

(i) all members of a controlled group shall be treated as 1 taxpayer, and

(ii) such limitation shall be allocated among the members of such group in such manner as the Secretary may prescribe.

(B) CONTROLLED GROUP.—For purposes of this paragraph, all persons treated as a single employer under subsection (a) or (b) of section 52 or subsection (m) or (o) of section 414 shall be treated as members of a controlled group.

* * *

[Sec. 265]

SEC. 265. EXPENSES AND INTEREST RELATING TO TAX-EXEMPT INCOME.

[Sec. 265(a)]

(a) GENERAL RULE.—No deduction shall be allowed for—

(1) EXPENSES.—Any amount otherwise allowable as a deduction which is allocable to one or more classes of income other than interest (whether or not any amount of income of that class or classes is received or accrued) wholly exempt from the taxes imposed by this subtitle, or any amount otherwise allowable under section 212 (relating to expenses for production of income) which is allocable to interest (whether or not any amount of such interest is received or accrued) wholly exempt from the taxes imposed by this subtitle.

(2) INTEREST.—Interest on indebtedness incurred or continued to purchase or carry obligations the interest on which is wholly exempt from the taxes imposed by this subtitle.

* * *

(6) SECTION NOT TO APPLY WITH RESPECT TO PARSONAGE AND MILITARY HOUSING ALLOWANCES.—No deduction shall be denied under this section for interest on a mortgage on, or real property taxes on, the home of the taxpayer by reason of the receipt of an amount as—

(A) a military housing allowance, or

(B) a parsonage allowance excludable from gross income under section 107.

* * *

[Sec. 266]

SEC. 266. CARRYING CHARGES.

No deduction shall be allowed for amounts paid or accrued for such taxes and carrying charges as, under regulations prescribed by the Secretary, are chargeable to capital account with respect to property, if the taxpayer elects, in accordance with such regulations, to treat such taxes or charges as so chargeable.

[Sec. 267]

SEC. 267. LOSSES, EXPENSES, AND INTEREST WITH RESPECT TO TRANSACTIONS BETWEEN RELATED TAXPAYERS.

[Sec. 267(a)]

(a) IN GENERAL.—

(1) DEDUCTION FOR LOSSES DISALLOWED.—No deduction shall be allowed in respect of any loss from the sale or exchange of property, directly or indirectly, between persons specified in any of the paragraphs of subsection (b). The preceding sentence shall not apply to any loss of the distributing corporation (or the distributee) in the case of a distribution in complete liquidation.

(2) MATCHING OF DEDUCTION AND PAYEE INCOME ITEM IN THE CASE OF EXPENSES AND INTEREST.—If—

(A) by reason of the method of accounting of the person to whom the payment is to be made, the amount thereof is not (unless paid) includible in the gross income of such person, and

(B) at the close of the taxable year of the taxpayer for which (but for this paragraph) the amount would be deductible under this chapter, both the taxpayer and the person to whom the payment is to be made are persons specified in any of the paragraphs of subsection (b),

then any deduction allowable under this chapter in respect of such amount shall be allowable as of the day as of which such amount is includible in the gross income of the person to whom the payment is made (or, if later, as of the day on which it would be so allowable but for this paragraph). For purposes of this paragraph, in the case of a personal service corporation (within the meaning of section 441(i)(2)), such corporation and any employee-owner (within the meaning of section 269A(b)(2), as modified by section 441(i)(2)) shall be treated as persons specified in subsection (b).

(3) PAYMENTS TO FOREIGN PERSONS. The Secretary shall by regulations apply the matching principle of paragraph (2) in cases in which the person to whom the payment is to be made is not a United States person.

Sec. 267(a)

[Sec. 267(b)]

(b) RELATIONSHIPS.—The persons referred to in subsection (a) are:

(1) Members of a family, as defined in subsection (c) (4);

(2) An individual and a corporation more than 50 percent in value of the outstanding stock of which is owned, directly or indirectly, by or for such individual;

(3) Two corporations which are members of the same controlled group (as defined in subsection (f));

(4) A grantor and a fiduciary of any trust;

(5) A fiduciary of a trust and a fiduciary of another trust, if the same person is a grantor of both trusts;

(6) A fiduciary of a trust and a beneficiary of such trust;

(7) A fiduciary of a trust and a beneficiary of another trust, if the same person is a grantor of both trusts;

(8) A fiduciary of a trust and a corporation more than 50 percent in value of the outstanding stock of which is owned, directly or indirectly, by or for the trust or by or for a person who is a grantor of the trust;

(9) A person and an organization to which section 501 (relating to certain educational and charitable organizations which are exempt from tax) applies and which is controlled directly or indirectly by such person or (if such person is an individual) by members of the family of such individual;

(10) A corporation and a partnership if the same persons own—

(A) more than 50 percent in value of the outstanding stock of the corporation, and

(B) more than 50 percent of the capital interest, or the profits interest, in the partnership;

(11) An S corporation and another S corporation if the same persons own more than 50 percent in value of the outstanding stock of each corporation;

(12) An S corporation and a C corporation, if the same persons own more than 50 percent in value of the outstanding stock of each corporation; or

(13) Except in the case of a sale or exchange in satisfaction of a pecuniary bequest, an executor of an estate and a beneficiary of such estate.

[Sec. 267(c)]

(c) CONSTRUCTIVE OWNERSHIP OF STOCK.—For purposes of determining, in applying subsection (b), the ownership of stock—

(1) Stock owned, directly or indirectly, by or for a corporation, partnership, estate, or trust shall be considered as being owned proportionately by or for its shareholders, partners, or beneficiaries;

(2) An individual shall be considered as owning the stock owned, directly or indirectly, by or for his family;

(3) An individual owning (otherwise than by the application of paragraph (2)) any stock in a corporation shall be considered as owning the stock owned, directly or indirectly, by or for his partner;

(4) The family of an individual shall include only his brothers and sisters (whether by the whole or half blood), spouse, ancestors, and lineal descendants; and

(5) Stock constructively owned by a person by reason of the application of paragraph (1) shall, for the purpose of applying paragraph (1), (2), or (3), be treated as actually owned by such person, but stock constructively owned by an individual by reason of the application of paragraph (2) or (3) shall not be treated as owned by him for the purpose of again applying either of such paragraphs in order to make another the constructive owner of such stock.

[Sec. 267(d)]

(d) AMOUNT OF GAIN WHERE LOSS PREVIOUSLY DISALLOWED.—If—

(1) in the case of a sale or exchange of property to the taxpayer a loss sustained by the transferor is not allowable to the transferor as a deduction by reason of subsection (a) (1) (or by reason of section 24 (b) of the Internal Revenue Code of 1939); and

(2) after December 31, 1953, the taxpayer sells or otherwise disposes of such property (or of other property the basis of which in his hands is determined directly or indirectly by reference to such property) at a gain,

then such gain shall be recognized only to the extent that it exceeds so much of such loss as is properly allocable to the property sold or otherwise disposed of by the taxpayer. This subsection applies with respect to taxable years ending after December 31, 1953. This subsection shall not apply if the loss sustained by the transferor is not allowable to the transferor as a deduction by reason of section 1091 (relating to wash sales) or by reason of section 118 of the Internal Revenue Code of 1939.

[Sec. 267(e)]

(e) SPECIAL RULES FOR PASS-THRU ENTITIES.—

(1) IN GENERAL.—In the case of any amount paid or incurred by, to, or on behalf of, a pass-thru entity, for purposes of applying subsection (a)(2)—

(A) such entity,

(B) in the case of—

(i) a partnership, any person who owns (directly or indirectly) any capital interest or profits interest of such partnership, or

(ii) an S corporation, any person who owns (directly or indirectly) any of the stock of such corporation,

(C) any person who owns (directly or indirectly) any capital interests or profits interest of a partnership in which such entity owns (directly or indirectly) any capital interest or profits interest, and

(D) any person related (within the meaning of subsection (b) of this section or section 707(b)(1) to a person described in subparagraph (B) or (C),

shall be treated as persons specified in a paragraph of subsection (b). Subparagraph (C) shall apply to a transaction only if such transaction is related either to the operations of the partnership described in such subparagraph or to an interest in such partnership.

(2) PASS-THRU ENTITY.—For purposes of this section, the term "pass-thru entity" means—

(A) a partnership, and

(B) an S corporation.3

(3) CONSTRUCTIVE OWNERSHIP IN THE CASE OF PARTNERSHIPS.—For purposes of determining ownership of a capital interest or profits interest of a partnership, the principles of subsection (c) shall apply, except that—

(A) paragraph (3) of subsection (c) shall not apply, and

(B) interests owned (directly or indirectly) by or for a C corporation shall be considered as owned by or for any shareholder only if such shareholder owns (directly or indirectly) 5 percent or more in value of the stock of such corporation.

(4) SUBSECTION (A)(2) NOT TO APPLY TO CERTAIN GUARANTEED PAYMENTS OF PARTNERSHIPS.—In the case of any amount paid or incurred by a partnership, subsection (a)(2) shall not apply to the extent that section 707(c) applies to such amount.

(5) EXCEPTION FOR CERTAIN EXPENSES AND INTEREST OF PARTNERSHIPS OWNING LOW-INCOME HOUSING.—

(A) IN GENERAL.—This subsection shall not apply with respect to qualified expenses and interest paid or incurred by a partnership owning low-income housing to—

(i) any qualified 5-percent or less partner of such partnership, or

(ii) any person related (within the meaning of subsection (b) of this section or section 707(b)(1)) to any qualified 5-percent or less partner of such partnership.

(B) QUALIFIED 5-PERCENT OR LESS PARTNER.—For purposes of this paragraph, the term "qualified 5-percent or less partner" means any partner who has (directly or indirectly) an interest of 5 percent or less in the aggregate capital and profits interests of the partnership but only if—

(i) such partner owned the low-income housing at all times during the 2-year period ending on the date such housing was transferred to the partnership, or

(ii) such partnership acquired the low-income housing pursuant to a purchase, assignment, or other transfer from the Department of Housing and Urban Development or any State or local housing authority.

For purposes of the preceding sentence, a partner shall be treated as holding any interest in the partnership which is held (directly or indirectly) by any person related (within the meaning of subsection (b) of this section or section 707(b)(1)) to such partner.

(C) QUALIFIED EXPENSES AND INTEREST.—For purpose of this paragraph, the term "qualified expenses and interest" means any expense or interest incurred by the partnership with respect to low-income housing held by the partnership but—

(i) only if the amount of such expense or interest (as the case may be) is unconditionally required to be paid by the partnership not later than 10 years after the date such amount was incurred, and

(ii) in the case of such interest, only if such interest is incurred at an annual rate not in excess of 12 percent.

(D) LOW-INCOME HOUSING.—For purposes of this paragraph, the term "low-income housing" means—

(i) any interest in property described in clause (i), (ii), (iii), or (iv) of section 1250(a)(1)(B), and

(ii) any interest in a partnership owning such property.

(6) CROSS REFERENCE.—

For additional rules relating to partnerships, see section 707(b).

[Sec. 267(f)]

(f) CONTROLLED GROUP DEFINED; SPECIAL RULES APPLICABLE TO CONTROLLED GROUPS.—

(1) CONTROLLED GROUP DEFINED.—For purposes of this section, the term "controlled group" has the meaning given to such term by section 1563(a), except that—

(A) "more than 50 percent" shall be substituted for "at least 80 percent" each place it appears in section 1563(a), and

(B) the determination shall be made without regard to subsections (a)(4) and (e)(3)(C) of section 1563.

(2) DEFERRAL (RATHER THAN DENIAL) OF LOSS FROM SALE OR EXCHANGE BETWEEN MEMBERS.—In the case of any loss from the sale or exchange of property which is between members of the same controlled group and to which subsection (a)(1) applies (determined without regard to this paragraph but with regard to paragraph (3))—

(A) subsections (a)(1) and (d) shall not apply to such loss, but

(B) such loss shall be deferred until the property is transferred outside such controlled group and there would be recognition of loss under consolidated return principles or until such other time as may be prescribed in regulations.

(3) LOSS DEFERRAL RULES NOT TO APPLY IN CERTAIN CASES.—

(A) TRANSFER TO DISC.—For purposes of applying subsection (a)(1), the term "controlled group" shall not include a DISC.

(B) CERTAIN SALES OF INVENTORY.—Except to the extent provided in regulations prescribed by the Secretary, subsection (a)(1) shall not apply to the sale or exchange of property between members of the same controlled group (or persons described in subsection (b)(10)) if—

(i) such property in the hands of the transferor is property described in section 1221(a)(1),

(ii) such sale or exchange is in the ordinary course of the transferor's trade or business,

(iii) such property in the hands of the transferee is property described in section 1221(a)(1), and

(iv) the transferee or the transferor is a foreign corporation.

(C) CERTAIN FOREIGN CURRENCY LOSSES.—To the extent povided in regulations, subsection (a)(1) shall not apply to any loss sustained by a member of a controlled group on the repayment of a loan made to another member of such group if such loan is payable in a foreign currency or is denominated in such a currency and such loss is attributable to a reduction in value of such foreign currency.

(4) DETERMINATION OF RELATIONSHIP RESULTING IN DISALLOWANCE OF LOSS, FOR PURPOSES OF OTHER PROVISIONS.—For purposes of any other section of this title which refers to a relationship which would result in a disallowance of losses under this section, deferral under paragraph (2) shall be treated as disallowance.

[Sec. 267(g)]

(g) COORDINATION WITH SECTION 1041.—Subsection (a)(1) shall not apply to any transfer described in section 1041(a) (relating to transfers of property between spouses or incident to divorce).

[Sec. 269]

SEC. 269. ACQUISITIONS MADE TO EVADE OR AVOID INCOME TAX.

[Sec. 269(a)]

(a) IN GENERAL.—If—

(1) any person or persons acquire, or acquired on or after October 8, 1940, directly or indirectly, control of a corporation, or

(2) any corporation acquires, or acquired on or after October 8, 1940, directly or indirectly, property of another corporation, not controlled, directly or indirectly, immediately before such acquisition, by such acquiring corporation or its stockholders, the basis of which property, in the hands of the acquiring corporation, is determined by reference to the basis in the hands of the transferor corporation,

and the principal purpose for which such acquisition was made is evasion or avoidance of Federal income tax by securing the benefit of a deduction, credit, or other allowance which such person or corporation would not otherwise enjoy, then the Secretary may disallow such deduction, credit, or other allowance. For purposes of paragraphs (1) and (2), control means the ownership of stock possessing at least 50 percent of the total combined voting power of all classes of stock entitled to vote or at least 50 percent of the total value of shares of all classes of stock of the corporation.

[Sec. 269(b)]

(b) CERTAIN LIQUIDATIONS AFTER QUALIFIED STOCK PURCHASES.—

(1) IN GENERAL.—If—

(A) there is a qualified stock purchase by a corporation of another corporation,

(B) an election is not made under section 338 with respect to such purchase,

(C) the acquired corporation is liquidated pursuant to a plan of liquidation adopted not more than 2 years after the acquisition date, and

(D) the principal purpose for such liquidation is the evasion or avoidance of Federal income tax by securing the benefit of a deduction, credit, or other allowance which the acquiring corporation would not otherwise enjoy,

then the Secretary may disallow such deduction, credit, or other allowance.

(2) MEANING OF TERMS.—For purposes of paragraph (1), the terms "qualified stock purchase" and "acquisition date" have the same respective meanings as when used in section 338.

[Sec. 269(c)]

(c) POWER OF SECRETARY TO ALLOW DEDUCTION, ETC., IN PART.—In any case to which subsection (a) or (b) applies the Secretary is authorized—

(1) to allow as a deduction, credit, or allowance any part of any amount disallowed by such subsection, if he determines that such allowance will not result in the evasion or avoidance of Federal income tax for which the acquisition was made; or

(2) to distribute, apportion, or allocate gross income, and distribute, apportion, or allocate the deductions, credits, or allowances the benefit of which was sought to be secured, between or among the corporations, or properties, or parts thereof, involved, and to allow such deductions, credits, or allowances so distributed, apportioned, or allocated, but to give effect to such allowance only to such

extent as he determines will not result in the evasion or avoidance of Federal income tax for which the acquisition was made; or

(3) to exercise his powers in part under paragraph (1) and in part under paragraph (2).

[Sec. 269A]

SEC. 269A. PERSONAL SERVICE CORPORATIONS FORMED OR AVAILED OF TO AVOID OR EVADE INCOME TAX.

[Sec. 269A(a)]

(a) GENERAL RULE.—If—

(1) substantially all of the services of a personal service corporation are performed for (or on behalf of) 1 other corporation, partnership, or other entity, and

(2) the principal purpose for forming, or availing of, such personal service corporation is the avoidance or evasion of Federal income tax by reducing the income of, or securing the benefit of any expense, deduction, credit, exclusion, or other allowance for, any employee-owner which would not otherwise be available,

then the Secretary may allocate all income, deductions, credits, exclusions, and other allowances between such personal service corporation and its employee-owners, if such allocation is necessary to prevent avoidance or evasion of Federal income tax or clearly to reflect the income of the personal service corporation or any of its employee-owners.

[Sec. 269A(b)]

(b) DEFINITIONS.—For purposes of this section—

(1) PERSONAL SERVICE CORPORATION.—The term "personal service corporation" means a corporation the principal activity of which is the performance of personal services and such services are substantially performed by employee-owners.

(2) EMPLOYEE-OWNER.—The term "employee-owner" means any employee who owns, on any day during the taxable year, more than 10 percent of the outstanding stock of the personal service corporation. For purposes of the preceding sentence, section 318 shall apply, except that "5 percent" shall be substituted for "50 percent" in section 318(a)(2)(C).

(3) RELATED PERSONS.—All related persons (within the meaning of section 144(a)(3)) shall be treated as 1 entity.

[Sec. 271]

SEC. 271. DEBTS OWED BY POLITICAL PARTIES, ETC.

[Sec. 271(a)]

(a) GENERAL RULE.—In the case of a taxpayer (other than a bank as defined in section 581) no deduction shall be allowed under section 166 (relating to bad debts) or under section 165 (g) (relating to worthlessness of securities) by reason of the worthlessness of any debt owed by a political party.

[Sec. 271(b)]

(b) DEFINITIONS.—

(1) POLITICAL PARTY.—For purposes of subsection (a), the term "political party" means—

(A) a political party;

(B) a national, State, or local committee of a political party; or

(C) a committee, association, or organization which accepts contributions or makes expenditures for the purpose of influencing or attempting to influence the election of presidential or vice-presidential electors or of any individual whose name is presented for election to any Federal, State, or local elective public office, whether or not such individual is elected.

(2) CONTRIBUTIONS.—For purposes of paragraph (1) (C), the term "contributions" includes a gift, subscription, loan, advance, or deposit, of money, or anything of value, and includes a contract, promise, or agreement to make a contribution, whether or not legally enforceable.

(3) EXPENDITURES.—For purposes of paragraph (1) (C), the term "expenditures" includes a payment, distribution, loan, advance, deposit, or gift, of money, or anything of value, and includes a contract, promise, or agreement to make an expenditure, whether or not legally enforceable.

[Sec. 271(c)]

(c) EXCEPTION.—In the case of a taxpayer who uses an accrual method of accounting, subsection (a) shall not apply to a debt which accrued as a receivable on a bona fide sale of goods or services in the ordinary course of a taxpayer's trade or business if—

(1) for the taxable year in which such receivable accrued, more than 30 percent of all receivables which accrued in the ordinary course of the trades and businesses of the taxpayer were due from political parties, and

(2) the taxpayer made substantial continuing efforts to collect on the debt.

[Sec. 273]

SEC. 273. HOLDERS OF LIFE OR TERMINABLE INTEREST.

Amounts paid under the laws of a State, the District of Columbia, a possession of the United States, or a foreign country as income to the holder of a life or terminable interest acquired by gift, bequest, or inheritance shall not be reduced or diminished by any deduction for shrinkage (by whatever name called) in the value of such interest due to the lapse of time.

[Sec. 274]

SEC. 274. DISALLOWANCE OF CERTAIN ENTERTAINMENT, ETC., EXPENSES.

[Sec. 274(a)]

(a) ENTERTAINMENT, AMUSEMENT, OR RECREATION.—

(1) IN GENERAL.—No deduction otherwise allowable under this chapter shall be allowed for any item—

(A) ACTIVITY.—With respect to an activity which is of a type generally considered to constitute entertainment, amusement, or recreation, unless the taxpayer establishes that the item was directly related to, or, in the case of an item directly preceding or following a substantial and bona fide business discussion (including business meetings at a convention or otherwise), that such item was associated with, the active conduct of the taxpayer's trade or business, or

(B) FACILITY.—With respect to a facility used in connection with an activity referred to in subparagraph (A).

In the case of an item described in subparagraph (A), the deduction shall in no event exceed the portion of such item which meets the requirements of subparagraph (A).

(2) SPECIAL RULES.—For purposes of applying paragraph (1)—

(A) Dues or fees to any social, athletic, or sporting club or organization shall be treated as items with respect to facilities.

(B) An activity described in section 212 shall be treated as a trade or business.

(C) In the case of a club, paragraph (1)(B) shall apply unless the taxpayer establishes that the facility was used primarily for the furtherance of the taxpayer's trade or business and that the item was directly related to the active conduct of such trade or business.

(3) DENIAL OF DEDUCTION FOR CLUB DUES.—Notwithstanding the preceding provisions of this subsection, no deduction shall be allowed under this chapter for amounts paid or incurred for membership in any club organized for business, pleasure, recreation, or other social purpose.

[Sec. 274(b)]

(b) GIFTS.—

(1) LIMITATION.—No deduction shall be allowed under section 162 or section 212 for any expense for gifts made directly or indirectly to any individual to the extent that such expense, when added to prior expenses of the taxpayer for gifts made to such individual during the same taxable year, exceeds $25. For purposes of this section, the term "gift" means any item excludable from gross income of the recipient under section 102 which is not excludable from his gross income under any other provision of this chapter, but such term does not include—

(A) an item having a cost to the taxpayer not in excess of $4.00 on which the name of the taxpayer is clearly and permanently imprinted and which is one of a number of identical items distributed generally by the taxpayer, or

(B) a sign, display rack, or other promotional material to be used on the business premises of the recipient.

(2) SPECIAL RULES.—

(A) In the case of a gift by a partnership, the limitation contained in paragraph (1) shall apply to the partnership as well as to each member thereof.

(B) For purposes of paragraph (1), a husband and wife shall be treated as one taxpayer.

[Sec. 274(c)]

(c) CERTAIN FOREIGN TRAVEL.—

(1) IN GENERAL.—In the case of any individual who travels outside the United States away from home in pursuit of a trade or business or in pursuit of an activity described in section 212, no deduction shall be allowed under section 162 or section 212 for that portion of the expenses of such travel otherwise allowable under such section which, under regulations prescribed by the Secretary, is not allocable to such trade or business or to such activity.

(2) EXCEPTION.—Paragraph (1) shall not apply to the expenses of any travel outside the United States away from home if—

(A) such travel does not exceed one week, or

(B) the portion of the time of travel outside the United States away from home which is not attributable to the pursuit of the taxpayer's trade or business or an activity described in section 212 is less than 25 percent of the total time on such travel.

(3) DOMESTIC TRAVEL EXCLUDED.—For purposes of this subsection, travel outside the United States does not include any travel from one point in the United States to another point in the United States.

[Sec. 274(d)]

(d) SUBSTANTIATION REQUIRED.—No deduction or credit shall be allowed—

(1) under section 162 or 212 for any traveling expense (including meals and lodging while away from home),

(2) for any item with respect to an activity which is of a type generally considered to constitute entertainment, amusement, or recreation, or with respect to a facility used in connection with such an activity,

(3) for any expense for gifts, or

(4) with respect to any listed property (as defined in section 280F(d)(4)),

unless the taxpayer substantiates by adequate records or by sufficient evidence corroborating the taxpayer's own statement (A) the amount of such expense or other item, (B) the time and place of the travel, entertainment, amusement, recreation, or use of the facility or property, or the date and description of the gift, (C) the business purpose of the expense or other item, and (D) the business relationship to the taxpayer of persons entertained, using the facility or property, or receiving the gift. The Secretary may by regulations provide that some or all of the requirements of the preceding sentence shall not apply in the case of an expense which does not exceed an amount prescribed pursuant to such regulations. This subsection shall not apply to any qualified nonpersonal use vehicle (as defined in subsection (i)).

[Sec. 274(e)]

(e) SPECIFIC EXCEPTIONS TO APPLICATION OF SUBSECTION (a).—Subsection (a) shall not apply to—

(1) FOOD AND BEVERAGES FOR EMPLOYEES.—Expenses for food and beverages (and facilities used in connection therewith) furnished on the business premises of the taxpayer primarily for his employees.

(2) EXPENSES TREATED AS COMPENSATION.—Expenses for goods, services, and facilities, to the extent that the expenses are treated by the taxpayer, with respect to the recipient of the entertainment, amusement, or recreation, as compensation to an employee on the taxpayer's return of tax under this chapter and as wages to such employee for purposes of chapter 24 (relating to withholding of income tax at source on wages).

Sec. 274(c)

(3) REIMBURSED EXPENSES.—Expenses paid or incurred by the taxpayer, in connection with the performance by him of services for another person (whether or not such other person is his employer), under a reimbursement or other expense allowance arrangement with such other person, but this paragraph shall apply—

(A) where the services are performed for an employer, only if the employer has not treated such expenses in the manner provided in paragraph (2), or

(B) where the services are performed for a person other than an employer, only if the taxpayer accounts (to the extent provided by subsection (d)) to such person.

(4) RECREATIONAL, ETC., EXPENSES FOR EMPLOYEES.—Expenses for recreational, social, or similar activities (including facilities therefor) primarily for the benefit of employees (other than employees who are highly compensated employees (within the meaning of section 414(q))). For purposes of this paragraph, an individual owning less than a 10-percent interest in the taxpayer's trade or business shall not be considered a shareholder or other owner, and for such purposes an individual shall be treated as owning any interest owned by a member of his family (within the meaning of section 267(c)(4)). This paragraph shall not apply for purposes of subsection (a)(3).

(5) EMPLOYEE, STOCKHOLDER, ETC., BUSINESS MEETINGS.—Expenses incurred by a taxpayer which are directly related to business meetings of his employees, stockholders, agents, or directors.

(6) MEETINGS OF BUSINESS LEAGUES, ETC.—Expenses directly related and necessary to attendance at a business meeting or convention of any organization described in section 501(c)(6) (relating to business leagues, chambers of commerce, real estate boards, and boards of trade) and exempt from taxation under section 501(a).

(7) ITEMS AVAILABLE TO PUBLIC.—Expenses for goods, services, and facilities made available by the taxpayer to the general public.

(8) ENTERTAINMENT SOLD TO CUSTOMERS.—Expenses for goods or services (including the use of facilities) which are sold by the taxpayer in a bona fide transaction for an adequate and full consideration in money or money's worth.

(9) EXPENSES INCLUDIBLE IN INCOME OF PERSONS WHO ARE NOT EMPLOYEES.—Expenses paid or incurred by the taxpayer for goods, services, and facilities to the extent that the expenses are includible in the gross income of a recipient of the entertainment, amusement, or recreation who is not an employee of the taxpayer as compensation for services rendered or as a prize or award under section 74. The preceding sentence shall not apply to any amount paid or incurred by the taxpayer if such amount is required to be included (or would be so required except that the amount is less than $600) in any information return filed by such taxpayer under part III of subchapter A of chapter 61 and is not so included.

For purposes of this subsection, any item referred to in subsection (a) shall be treated as an expense.

[Sec. 274(f)]

(f) INTEREST, TAXES, CASUALTY LOSSES, ETC.—This section shall not apply to any deduction allowable to the taxpayer without regard to its connection with his trade or business (or with his income-producing activity). In the case of a taxpayer which is not an individual, the preceding sentence shall be applied as if it were an individual.

[Sec. 274(g)]

(g) TREATMENT OF ENTERTAINMENT, ETC., TYPE FACILITY.—For purposes of this chapter, if deductions are disallowed under subsection (a) with respect to any portion of a facility, such portion shall be treated as an asset which is used for personal, living, and family purposes (and not as an asset used in the trade or business).

[Sec. 274(h)]

(h) ATTENDANCE AT CONVENTIONS, ETC.—

(1) IN GENERAL.—In the case of any individual who attends a convention, seminar, or similar meeting which is held outside the North American area, no deduction shall be allowed under section 162 for expenses allocable to such meeting unless the taxpayer establishes that the meeting is directly related to the active conduct of his trade or business and that, after taking into account in the manner provided by regulations prescribed by the Secretary—

(A) the purpose of such meeting and the activities taking place at such meeting,

(B) the purposes and activities of the sponsoring organizations or groups,

(C) the residences of the active members of the sponsoring organization and the places at which other meetings of the sponsoring organization or groups have been held or will be held, and

(D) such other relevant factors as the taxpayer may present,

it is as reasonable for the meeting to be held outside the North American area as within the North American area.

(2) CONVENTIONS ON CRUISE SHIPS.—In the case of any individual who attends a convention, seminar, or other meeting which is held on any cruise ship, no deduction shall be allowed under section 162 for expenses allocable to such meeting, unless the taxpayer meets the requirements of paragraph (5) and establishes that the meeting is directly related to the active conduct of his trade or business and that—

(A) the cruise ship is a vessel registered in the United States; and

(B) all ports of call of such cruise ship are located in the United States or in possessions of the United States.

With respect to cruises beginning in any calendar year, not more than $2,000 of the expenses attributable to an individual attending one or more meetings may be taken into account under section 162 by reason of the preceding sentence.

(3) DEFINITIONS.—For purposes of this subsection—

(A) NORTH AMERICAN AREA.—The term "North American area" means the United States, its possessions, and the Trust Territory of the Pacific Islands, and Canada and Mexico.

(B) CRUISE SHIP.—The term "cruise ship" means any vessel sailing within or without the territorial waters of the United States.

(4) SUBSECTION TO APPLY TO EMPLOYER AS WELL AS TO TRAVELER.—

(A) Except as provided in subparagraph (B), this subsection shall apply to deductions otherwise allowable under section 162 to any person, whether or not such person is the individual attending the convention, seminar, or similar meeting.

(B) This subsection shall not deny a deduction to any person other than the individual attending the convention, seminar, or similar meeting with respect to any amount paid by such person to or on behalf of such individual if includible in the gross income of such individual. The preceding sentence shall not apply if the amount is required to be included in any information return filed by such person under part III of subchapter A of chapter 61 and is not so included.

(5) REPORTING REQUIREMENTS.—No deduction shall be allowed under section 162 for expenses allocable to attendance at a convention, seminar, or similar meeting on any cruise ship unless the taxpayer claiming the deduction attaches to the return of tax on which the deduction is claimed—

(A) a written statement signed by the individual attending the meeting which includes—

(i) information with respect to the total days of the trip, excluding the days of transportation to and from the cruise ship port, and the number of hours of each day of the trip which such individual devoted to scheduled business activities,

(ii) a program of the scheduled business activities of the meeting, and

(iii) such other information as may be required in regulations prescribed by the Secretary; and

(B) a written statement signed by an officer of the organization or group sponsoring the meeting which includes—

(i) a schedule of business activities of each day of the meeting,

(ii) the number of hours which the individual attending the meeting attended such scheduled business activities, and

(iii) such other information as may be required in regulations prescribed by the Secretary.

* * *

(7) SEMINARS, ETC. FOR SECTION 212 PURPOSES.—No deduction shall be allowed under section 212 for expenses allocable to a convention, seminar, or similar meeting.

[Sec. 274(i)]

(i) QUALIFIED NONPERSONAL USE VEHICLE.—For purposes of subsection (d), the term "qualified nonpersonal use vehicle" means any vehicle which, by reason of its nature, is not likely to be used more than a de minimis amount for personal purposes.

Sec. 274(i)

[Sec. 274(j)]

(j) EMPLOYEE ACHIEVEMENT AWARDS.—

(1) GENERAL RULE.—No deduction shall be allowed under section 162 or section 212 for the cost of an employee achievement award except to the extent that such cost does not exceed the deduction limitations of paragraph (2).

(2) DEDUCTION LIMITATIONS.—The deduction for the cost of an employee achievement award made by an employer to an employee—

(A) which is not a qualified plan award, when added to the cost to the employer for all other employee achievement awards made to such employee during the taxable year which are not qualified plan awards, shall not exceed $400, and

(B) which is a qualified plan award, when added to the cost to the employer for all other employee achievement awards made to such employee during the taxable year (including employee achievement awards which are not qualified plan awards), shall not exceed $1,600.

(3) DEFINITIONS.—For purposes of this subsection—

(A) EMPLOYEE ACHIEVEMENT AWARD.—The term "employee achievement award" means an item of tangible personal property which is—

(i) transferred by an employer to an employee for length of service achievement or safety achievement,

(ii) awarded as part of a meaningful presentation, and

(iii) awarded under conditions and circumstances that do not create a significant likelihood of the payment of disguised compensation.

(B) QUALIFIED PLAN AWARD.—

(i) IN GENERAL.—The term "qualified plan award" means an employee achievement award awarded as part of an established written plan or program of the taxpayer which does not discriminate in favor of highly compensated employees (within the meaning of section 414(q)) as to eligibility or benefits.

(ii) LIMITATION.—An employee achievement award shall not be treated as a qualified plan award for any taxable year if the average cost of all employee achievement awards which are provided by the employer during the year, and which would be qualified plan awards but for this subparagraph, exceeds $400. For purposes of the preceding sentence, average cost shall be determined by including the entire cost of qualified plan awards, without taking into account employee achievement awards of nominal value.

(4) SPECIAL RULES.—For purposes of this subsection—

(A) PARTNERSHIPS.—In the case of an employee achievement award made by a partnership, the deduction limitations contained in paragraph (2) shall apply to the partnership as well as to each member thereof.

(B) LENGTH OF SERVICE AWARDS.—An item shall not be treated as having been provided for length of service achievement if the item is received during the recipient's 1st 5 years of employment or if the recipient received a length of service achievement award (other than an award excludable under section 132(e)(1)) during that year or any of the prior 4 years.

[Sec. 274(k)]

(k) BUSINESS MEALS.—

(1) IN GENERAL.—No deduction shall be allowed under this chapter for the expense of any food or beverages unless—

(A) such expense is not lavish or extravagant under the circumstances, and

(B) the taxpayer (or an employee of the taxpayer) is present at the furnishing of such food or beverages.

(2) EXCEPTIONS.—Paragraph (1) shall not apply to—

(A) any expense described in paragraph (2), (3), (4), (7), (8), or (9) of subsection (e), and

(B) any other expense to the extent provided in regulations.

Sec. 274(k)

[Sec. 274(l)]

(l) ADDITIONAL LIMITATIONS ON ENTERTAINMENT TICKETS.—

(1) ENTERTAINMENT TICKETS.—

(A) IN GENERAL.—In determining the amount allowable as a deduction under this chapter for any ticket for any activity or facility described in subsection (d)(2), the amount taken into account shall not exceed the face value of such ticket.

(B) EXCEPTION FOR CERTAIN CHARITABLE SPORTS EVENTS.—Subparagraph (A) shall not apply to any ticket for any sports event—

(i) which is organized for the primary purpose of benefiting an organization which is described in section 501(c)(3) and exempt from tax under section 501(a),

(ii) all of the net proceeds of which are contributed to such organization, and

(iii) which utilizes volunteers for substantially all of the work performed in carrying out such event.

(2) SKYBOXES, ETC.—In the case of a skybox or other private luxury box leased for more than 1 event, the amount allowable as a deduction under this chapter with respect to such events shall not exceed the sum of the face value of non-luxury box seat tickets for the seats in such box covered by the lease. For purposes of the preceding sentence, 2 or more related leases shall be treated as 1 lease.

[Sec. 274(m)]

(m) ADDITIONAL LIMITATIONS ON TRAVEL EXPENSES.—

(1) LUXURY WATER TRANSPORTATION.—

(A) IN GENERAL.—No deduction shall be allowed under this chapter for expenses incurred for transportation by water to the extent such expenses exceed twice the aggregate per diem amounts for days of such transportation. For purposes of the preceding sentence, the term "per diem amounts" means the highest amount generally allowable with respect to a day to employees of the executive branch of the Federal Government for per diem while away from home but serving in the United States.

(B) EXCEPTIONS.—Subparagraph (A) shall not apply to—

(i) any expense allocable to a convention, seminar, or other meeting which is held on any cruise ship, and

(ii) any expense described in paragraph (2), (3), (4), (7), (8), or (9) of subsection (e).

(2) TRAVEL AS FORM OF EDUCATION.—No deduction shall be allowed under this chapter for expenses for travel as a form of education.

(3) TRAVEL EXPENSES OF SPOUSE, DEPENDENT, OR OTHERS.—No deduction shall be allowed under this chapter (other than section 217) for travel expenses paid or incurred with respect to a spouse, dependent, or other individual accompanying the taxpayer (or an officer or employee of the taxpayer) on business travel, unless—

(A) the spouse, dependent, or other individual is an employee of the taxpayer,

(B) the travel of the spouse, dependent, or other individual is for a bona fide business purpose, and

(C) such expenses would otherwise be deductible by the spouse, dependent, or other individual.

[Sec. 274(n)]

(n) ONLY 50 PERCENT OF MEAL AND ENTERTAINMENT EXPENSES ALLOWED AS DEDUCTION.—

(1) IN GENERAL.—The amount allowable as a deduction under this chapter for—

(A) any expense for food or beverages, and

(B) any item with respect to an activity which is of a type generally considered to constitute entertainment, amusement, or recreation, or with respect to a facility used in connection with such activity,

shall not exceed 50 percent of the amount of such expense or item which would (but for this paragraph) be allowable as a deduction under this chapter.

(2) EXCEPTIONS.—Paragraph (1) shall not apply to any expense if—

(A) such expense is described in paragraph (2), (3), (4), (7), (8), or (9) of subsection (e).

(B) in the case of an expense for food or beverages, such expense is excludable from the gross income of the recipient under section 132 by reason of subsection (e) thereof (relating to de minimis fringes),

(C) such expense is covered by a package involving a ticket described in subsection (l)(1)(B),

(D) in the case of an employer who pays or reimburses moving expenses of an employee, such expenses are includible in the income of the employee under section 82, or

(E) such expense is for food or beverages—

(i) required by any Federal law to be provided to crew members of a commercial vessel,

(ii) provided to crew members of a commercial vessel—

(I) which is operating on the Great Lakes, the Saint Lawrence Seaway, or any inland waterway of the United States, and

(II) which is of a kind which would be required by Federal law to provide food and beverages to crew members if it were operated at sea,

(iii) provided on an oil or gas platform or drilling rig if the platform or rig is located offshore, or

(iv) provided on an oil or gas platform or drilling rig, or at a support camp which is in proximity and integral to such platform or rig, if the platform or rig is located in the United States north of 54 degrees north latitude.

Clauses (i) and (ii) of subparagraph (E) shall not apply to vessels primarily engaged in providing luxury water transportation (determined under the principles of subsection (m)). In the case of the employee, the exception of subparagraph (A) shall not apply to expenses described in subparagraph (D).

(3) SPECIAL RULE FOR INDIVIDUALS SUBJECT TO FEDERAL HOURS OF SERVICE.—

(A) IN GENERAL.—In the case of any expenses for food or beverages consumed while away from home (within the meaning of section 162(a)(2)) by an individual during, or incident to, the period of duty subject to the hours of service limitations of the Department of Transportation, paragraph (1) shall be applied by substituting "the applicable percentage" for "50 percent".

(B) APPLICABLE PERCENTAGE.—For purposes of this paragraph, the term "applicable percentage" means the percentage determined under the following table:

For taxable years beginning in calendar year—	The applicable percentage is—
1998 or 1999	55
2000 or 2001	60
2002 or 2003	65
2004 or 2005	70
2006 or 2007	75
2008 or thereafter	80

[Sec. 274(o)]

(o) REGULATORY AUTHORITY.—The Secretary shall prescribe such regulations as he may deem necessary to carry out the purposes of this section, including regulations prescribing whether subsection (a) or subsection (b) applies in cases where both such subsections would otherwise apply.

[Sec. 275]

SEC. 275. CERTAIN TAXES.

[Sec. 275(a)]

(a) GENERAL RULE.—No deduction shall be allowed for the following taxes:

(1) Federal income taxes, including—

(A) the tax imposed by section 3101 (relating to the tax on employees under the Federal Insurance Contributions Act);

(B) the taxes imposed by sections 3201 and 3211 (relating to the taxes on railroad employees and railroad employee representatives); and

(C) the tax withheld at source on wages under section 3402.

(2) Federal war profits and excess profits taxes.

(3) Estate, inheritance, legacy, succession, and gift taxes.

(4) Income, war profits, and excess profits taxes imposed by the authority of any foreign country or possession of the United States if—

(A) the taxpayer chooses to take to any extent the benefits of section 901,

(B) such taxes are paid or accrued with respect to foreign trade income (within the meaning of section 923(b)) of a FSC, or

(C) such taxes are paid or accrued with respect to qualifying foreign trade income (as defined in section 941).

(5) Taxes on real property, to the extent that section 164(d) requires such taxes to be treated as imposed on another taxpayer.

(6) Taxes imposed by chapters 41, 42, 43, 44, 46, and 54.

Paragraph (1) shall not apply to any taxes to the extent such taxes are allowable as a deduction under section 164(f). Paragraph (1) shall not apply to the tax imposed by section 59A.

[Sec. 275(b)]

(b) CROSS REFERENCE.—

For disallowance of certain other taxes, see section 164(c).

[Sec. 276]

SEC. 276. CERTAIN INDIRECT CONTRIBUTIONS TO POLITICAL PARTIES.

[Sec. 276(a)]

(a) DISALLOWANCE OF DEDUCTIONS.—No deduction otherwise allowable under this chapter shall be allowed for any amount paid or incurred for—

(1) advertising in a convention program of a political party, or in any other publication if any part of the proceeds of such publication directly or indirectly inures (or is intended to inure) to or for the use of a political party or a political candidate,

(2) admission to any dinner or program, if any part of the proceeds of such dinner or program directly or indirectly inures (or is intended to inure) to or for the use of a political party or a political candidate, or

(3) admission to an inaugural ball, inaugural gala, inaugural parade, or inaugural concert, or to any similar event which is identified with a political party or a political candidate.

[Sec. 276(b)]

(b) DEFINITIONS.—For purposes of this section—

(1) POLITICAL PARTY.—The term "political party" means—

(A) a political party;

(B) a National, State, or local committee of a political party; or

(C) a committee, association, or organization, whether incorporated or not, which directly or indirectly accepts contributions (as defined in section 271(b)(2)) or make[s] expenditures (as defined in section 271(b)(3)) for the purpose of influencing or attempting to influence the selection, nomination, or election of any individual to any Federal, State, or local elective public office, or the election of presidential and vice-presidential electors, whether or not such individual or electors are selected, nominated, or elected.

(2) PROCEEDS INURING TO OR FOR THE USE OF POLITICAL CANDIDATES.—Proceeds shall be treated as inuring to or for the use of a political candidate only if—

(A) such proceeds may be used directly or indirectly for the purpose of furthering his candidacy for selection, nomination, or election to any elective public office, and

(B) such proceeds are not received by such candidate in the ordinary course of a trade or business (other than the trade or business of holding elective public office).

[Sec. 276(c)]

(c) CROSS REFERENCE.—

For disallowance of certain entertainment, etc., expenses, see section 274.

[Sec. 279]

SEC. 279. INTEREST ON INDEBTEDNESS INCURRED BY CORPORATION TO ACQUIRE STOCK OR ASSETS OF ANOTHER CORPORATION.

[Sec. 279(a)]

(a) GENERAL RULE.—No deduction shall be allowed for any interest paid or incurred by a corporation during the taxable year with respect to its corporate acquisition indebtedness to the extent that such interest exceeds—

(1) $5,000,000, reduced by

(2) the amount of interest paid or incurred by such corporation during such year on obligations (A) issued after December 31, 1967, to provide consideration for an acquisition described in paragraph (1) of subsection (b), but (B) which are not corporate acquisition indebtedness.

[Sec. 279(b)]

(b) CORPORATE ACQUISITION INDEBTEDNESS.—For purposes of this section, the term "corporate acquisition indebtedness" means any obligation evidenced by a bond, debenture, note, or certificate or other evidence of indebtedness issued after October 9, 1969, by a corporation (hereinafter in this section referred to as "issuing corporation") if—

(1) such obligation is issued to provide consideration for the acquisition of—

(A) stock in another corporation (hereinafter in this section referred to as "acquired corporation"), or

(B) assets of another corporation (hereinafter in this section referred to as "acquired corporation") pursuant to a plan under which at least two-thirds (in value) of all the assets (excluding money) used in trades and businesses carried on by such corporation are acquired,

(2) such obligation is either—

(A) subordinated to the claims of trade creditors of the issuing corporation generally, or

(B) expressly subordinated in right of payment to the payment of any substantial amount of unsecured indebtedness, whether outstanding or subsequently issued, of the issuing corporation,

(3) the bond or other evidence of indebtedness is either—

(A) convertible directly or indirectly into stock of the issuing corporation, or

(B) part of an investment unit or other arrangement which includes, in addition to such bond or other evidence of indebtedness, an option to acquire, directly or indirectly, stock in the issuing corporation, and

(4) as of a day determined under subsection (c)(1), either—

(A) the ratio of debt to equity (as defined in subsection (c)(2)) of the issuing corporation exceeds 2 to 1, or

(B) the projected earnings (as defined in subsection (c)(3)) do not exceed 3 times the annual interest to be paid or incurred (determined under subsection (c)(4)).

[Sec. 279(c)]

(c) RULES FOR APPLICATION OF SUBSECTION (b)(4).—For purposes of subsection (b)(4)—

(1) TIME OF DETERMINATION.—Determinations are to be made as of the last day of any taxable year of the issuing corporation in which it issues any obligation to provide consideration for an acquisition described in subsection (b)(1) of stock in, or assets of, the acquired corporation.

(2) RATIO OF DEBT TO EQUITY.—The term "ratio of debt to equity" means the ratio which the total indebtedness of the issuing corporation bears to the sum of its money and all its other assets (in an amount equal to their adjusted basis for determining gain) less such total indebtedness.

(3) PROJECTED EARNINGS.—

(A) The term "projected earnings" means the "average annual earnings" (as defined in subparagraph (B)) of—

(i) the issuing corporation only, if clause (ii) does not apply, or

(ii) both the issuing corporation and the acquired corporation, in any case where the issuing corporation has acquired control (as defined in section 368(c)), or has acquired substantially all of the properties, of the acquired corporation.

(B) The average annual earnings referred to in subparagraph (A) is, for any corporation, the amount of its earnings and profits for any 3-year period ending with the last day of a taxable year of the issuing corporation described in paragraph (1), computed without reduction for—

(i) interest paid or incurred,

(ii) depreciation or amortization allowed under this chapter,

(iii) liability for tax under this chapter, and

(iv) distributions to which section 301(c)(1) applies (other than such distributions from the acquired to the issuing corporation),

and reduced to an annual average for such 3-year period pursuant to regulations prescribed by the Secretary. Such regulations shall include rules for cases where any corporation was not in existence for all of such 3-year period or such period includes only a portion of a taxable year of any corporation.

(4) ANNUAL INTEREST TO BE PAID OR INCURRED.—The term "annual interest to be paid or incurred" means—

(A) if subparagraph (B) does not apply, the annual interest to be paid or incurred by the issuing corporation only, determined by reference to its total indebtedness outstanding, or

(B) if projected earnings are determined under clause (ii) of paragraph (3)(A), the annual interest to be paid or incurred by both the issuing corporation and the acquired corporation, determined by reference to their combined total indebtedness outstanding.

(5) SPECIAL RULES FOR BANKS AND LENDING OR FINANCE COMPANIES.—With respect to any corporation which is a bank (as defined in section 581) or is primarily engaged in a lending or finance business—

(A) in determining under paragraph (2) the ratio of debt to equity of such corporation (or of the affiliated group of which such corporation is a member), the total indebtedness of such corporation (and the assets of such corporation) shall be reduced by an amount equal to the total indebtedness owed to such corporation which arises out of the banking business of such corporation, or out of the lending or finance business of such corporation, as the case may be;

(B) in determining under paragraph (4) the annual interest to be paid or incurred by such corporation (or by the issuing and acquired corporations referred to in paragraph (4)(B) or by the affiliated group of which such corporation is a member) the amount of such interest (determined without regard to this paragraph) shall be reduced by an amount which bears the same ratio to the amount of such interest as the amount of the reduction for the taxable year under subparagraph (A) bears to the total indebtedness of such corporation; and

(C) in determining under paragraph (3)(B) the average annual earnings, the amount of the earnings and profits for the 3-year period shall be reduced by the sum of the reductions under subparagraph (B) for such period.

For purposes of this paragraph, the term "lending or finance business" means a business of making loans or purchasing or discounting accounts receivable, notes, or installment obligations.

Sec. 279(c)

(d) TAXABLE YEARS TO WHICH APPLICABLE.—In applying this section—

(1) FIRST YEAR OF DISALLOWANCE.—The deduction of interest on any obligation shall not be disallowed under subsection (a) before the first taxable year of the issuing corporation as of the last day of which the application of either subparagraph (A) or subparagraph (B) of subsection (b)(4) results in such obligation being corporate acquisition indebtedness.

(2) GENERAL RULE FOR SUCCEEDING YEARS.—Except as provided in paragraphs (3), (4), and (5), if an obligation is determined to be corporate acquisition indebtedness as of the last day of any taxable year of the issuing corporation, it shall be corporate acquisition indebtedness for such taxable year and all subsequent taxable years.

(3) REDETERMINATION WHERE CONTROL, ETC., IS ACQUIRED.—If an obligation is determined to be corporate acquisition indebtedness as of the close of a taxable year of the issuing corporation in which clause (i) of subsection (c)(3)(A) applied, but would not be corporate acquisition indebtedness if the determination were made as of the close of the first taxable year of such corporation thereafter in which clause (ii) of subsection (c)(3)(A) could apply, such obligation shall be considered not to be corporate acquisition indebtedness for such later taxable year and all taxable years thereafter.

(4) SPECIAL 3-YEAR RULE.—If an obligation which has been determined to be corporate acquisition indebtedness for any taxable year would not be such indebtedness for each of any 3 consecutive taxable years thereafter if subsection (b)(4) were applied as of the close of each of such 3 years, then such obligation shall not be corporate acquisition indebtedness for all taxable years after such 3 consecutive taxable years.

(5) 5 PERCENT STOCK RULE.—In the case of obligations issued to provide consideration for the acquisition of stock in another corporation, such obligations shall be corporate acquisition indebtedness for a taxable year only if at some time after October 9, 1969, and before the close of such year the issuing corporation owns 5 percent or more of the total combined voting power of all classes of stock entitled to vote of such other corporation.

[Sec. 279(e)]

(e) CERTAIN NONTAXABLE TRANSACTIONS.—An acquisition of stock of a corporation of which the issuing corporation is in control (as defined in section 368 (c)) in a transaction in which gain or loss is not recognized shall be deemed an acquisition described in paragraph (1) of subsection (b) only if immediately before such transaction (1) the acquired corporation was in existence, and (2) the issuing corporation was not in control (as defined in section 368(c)) of such corporation.

* * *

[Sec. 279(g)]

(g) AFFILIATED GROUPS.—In any case in which the issuing corporation is a member of an affiliated group, the application of this section shall be determined, pursuant to regulations prescribed by the Secretary, by treating all of the members of the affiliated group in the aggregate as the issuing corporation, except that the ratio of debt to equity of, projected earnings of, and annual interest to be paid or incurred by any corporation (other than the issuing corporation determined without regard to this subsection) shall be included in the determinations required under subparagraphs (A) and (B) of subsection (b)(4) as of any day only if such corporation is a member of the affiliated group on such day, and, in determining projected earnings of such corporation under subsection (c)(3), there shall be taken into account only the earnings and profits of such corporation for the period during which it was a member of the affiliated group. For purposes of the preceding sentence, the term "affiliated group" has the meaning assigned to such term by section 1504(a), except that all corporations other than the acquired corporation shall be treated as includible corporations (without any exclusion under section 1504(b)) and the acquired corporation shall not be treated as an includible corporation.

[Sec. 279(h)]

(h) CHANGES IN OBLIGATION.—For purposes of this section—

(1) Any extension, renewal, or refinancing of an obligation evidencing a preexisting indebtedness shall not be deemed to be the issuance of a new obligation.

(2) Any obligation which is corporate acquisition indebtedness of the issuing corporation is also corporate acquisition indebtedness of any corporation which becomes liable for such obligation as guarantor, endorser, or indemnitor or which assumes liability for such obligation in any transaction.

* * *

[Sec. 279(j)]

(j) EFFECT ON OTHER PROVISIONS.—No inference shall be drawn from any provision in this section that any instrument designated as a bond, debenture, note, or certificate or other evidence of indebtedness by its issuer represents an obligation or indebtedness of such issuer in applying any other provision of this title.

[Sec. 280A]

SEC. 280A. DISALLOWANCE OF CERTAIN EXPENSES IN CONNECTION WITH BUSINESS USE OF HOME, RENTAL OF VACATION HOMES, ETC.

[Sec. 280A(a)]

(a) GENERAL RULE.—Except as otherwise provided in this section, in the case of a taxpayer who is an individual or an S corporation, no deduction otherwise allowable under this chapter shall be allowed with respect to the use of a dwelling unit which is used by the taxpayer during the taxable year as a residence.

[Sec. 280A(b)]

(b) EXCEPTION FOR INTEREST, TAXES, CASUALTY LOSSES, ETC.—Subsection (a) shall not apply to any deduction allowable to the taxpayer without regard to its connection with his trade or business (or with his income-producing activity).

[Sec. 280A(c)]

(c) EXCEPTIONS FOR CERTAIN BUSINESS OR RENTAL USE; LIMITATION ON DEDUCTIONS FOR SUCH USE.—

(1) CERTAIN BUSINESS USE.—Subsection (a) shall not apply to any item to the extent such item is allocable to a portion of the dwelling unit which is exclusively used on a regular basis—

(A) as the principal place of business for any trade or business of the taxpayer,

(B) as a place of business which is used by patients, clients, or customers in meeting or dealing with the taxpayer in the normal course of his trade or business, or

(C) in the case of a separate structure which is not attached to the dwelling unit, in connection with the taxpayer's trade or business.

In the case of an employee, the preceding sentence shall apply only if the exclusive use referred to in the preceding sentence is for the convenience of his employer. For purposes of subparagraph (A), the term "principal place of business" includes a place of business which is used by the taxpayer for the administrative or management activities of any trade or business of the taxpayer if there is no other fixed location of such trade or business where the taxpayer conducts substantial administrative or management activities of such trade or business.

(2) CERTAIN STORAGE USE.—Subsection (a) shall not apply to any item to the extent such item is allocable to space within the dwelling unit which is used on a regular basis as a storage unit for the inventory or product samples of the taxpayer held for use in the taxpayer's trade or business of selling products at retail or wholesale, but only if the dwelling unit is the sole fixed location of such trade or business.

(3) RENTAL USE.—Subsection (a) shall not apply to any item which is attributable to the rental of the dwelling unit or portion thereof (determined after the application of subsection (e)).

(4) USE IN PROVIDING DAY CARE SERVICES.-

(A) IN GENERAL.—Subsection (a) shall not apply to any item to the extent that such item is allocable to the use of any portion of the dwelling unit on a regular basis in the taxpayer's trade or business of providing day care for children, for individuals who have attained age 65, or for individuals who are physically or mentally incapable of caring for themselves.

(B) LICENSING, ETC., REQUIREMENT.—Subparagraph (A) shall apply to items accruing for a period only if the owner or operator of the trade or business referred to in subparagraph (A)—

(i) has applied for (and such application has not been rejected),

(ii) has been granted (and such granting has not been revoked), or

(iii) is exempt from having,

a license, certification, registration, or approval as a day care center or as a family or group day care home under the provisions of any applicable State law. This subparagraph shall apply only to items accruing in periods beginning on or after the first day of the first month which begins more than 90 days after the date of the enactment of the Tax Reduction and Simplification Act of 1977.

(C) ALLOCATION FORMULA.—If a portion of the taxpayer's dwelling unit used for the purposes described in subparagraph (A) is not used exclusively for those purposes, the amount of the expenses attributable to that portion shall not exceed an amount which bears the same ratio to the total amount of the items allocable to such portion as the number of hours the portion is used for such purposes bears to the number of hours the portion is available for use.

(5) LIMITATION ON DEDUCTIONS.—In the case of a use described in paragraph (1), (2), or (4), and in the case of a use described in paragraph (3) where the dwelling unit is used by the taxpayer during the taxable year as a residence, the deductions allowed under this chapter for the taxable year by reason of being attributed to such use shall not exceed the excess of—

(A) the gross income derived from such use for the taxable year, over

(B) the sum of—

(i) the deductions allocable to such use which are allowable under this chapter for the taxable year whether or not such unit (or portion thereof) was so used, and

(ii) the deductions allocable to the trade or business (or rental activity) in which such use occurs (but which are not allocable to such use) for such taxable year.

Any amount not allowable as a deduction under this chapter by reason of the preceding sentence shall be taken into account as a deduction (allocable to such use) under this chapter for the succeeding taxable year. Any amount taken into account for any taxable year under the preceding sentence shall be subject to the limitation of the 1st sentence of this paragraph whether or not the dwelling unit is used as a residence during such taxable year.

(6) TREATMENT OF RENTAL TO EMPLOYER.—Paragraphs (1) and (3) shall not apply to any item which is attributable to the rental of the dwelling unit (or any portion thereof) by the taxpayer to his employer during any period in which the taxpayer uses the dwelling unit (or portion) in performing services as an employee of the employer.

[Sec. 280A(d)]

(d) USE AS RESIDENCE.—

(1) IN GENERAL.—For purposes of this section, a taxpayer uses a dwelling unit during the taxable year as a residence if he uses such unit (or portion thereof) for personal purposes for a number of days which exceeds the greater of—

(A) 14 days, or

(B) 10 percent of the number of days during such year for which such unit is rented at a fair rental.

For purposes of subparagraph (B), a unit shall not be treated as rented at a fair rental for any day for which it is used for personal purposes.

(2) PERSONAL USE OF UNIT.—For purposes of this section, the taxpayer shall be deemed to have used a dwelling unit for personal purposes for a day if, for any part of such day, the unit is used—

(A) for personal purposes by the taxpayer or any other person who has an interest in such unit, or by any member of the family (as defined in section 267(c)(4)) of the taxpayer or such other person;

(B) by any individual who uses the unit under an arrangement which enables the taxpayer to use some other dwelling unit (whether or not a rental is charged for the use of such other unit); or

(C) by any individual (other than an employee with respect to whose use section 119 applies), unless for such day the dwelling unit is rented for a rental which, under the facts and circumstances, is fair rental.

The Secretary shall prescribe regulations with respect to the circumstances under which use of the unit for repairs and annual maintenance will not constitute personal use under this paragraph, except that if the taxpayer is engaged in repair and maintenance on a substantially full time basis for any day, such authority shall not allow the Secretary to treat a dwelling unit as being used for personal use by the taxpayer on such day merely because other individuals who are on the premises on such day are not so engaged.

(3) RENTAL TO FAMILY MEMBER, ETC., FOR USE AS PRINCIPAL RESIDENCE.—

(A) IN GENERAL.—A taxpayer shall not be treated as using a dwelling unit for personal purposes by reason of a rental arrangement for any period if for such period such dwelling unit is rented, at a fair rental, to any person for use as such person's principal residence.

(B) SPECIAL RULES FOR RENTAL TO PERSON HAVING INTEREST IN UNIT.—

(i) RENTAL MUST BE PURSUANT TO SHARED EQUITY FINANCING AGREEMENT.—Subparagraph (A) shall apply to a rental to a person who has an interest in the dwelling unit only if such rental is pursuant to a shared equity financing agreement.

(ii) DETERMINATION OF FAIR RENTAL.—In the case of a rental pursuant to a shared equity financing agreement, fair rental shall be determined as of the time the agreement is entered into and by taking into account the occupant's qualified ownership interest.

(C) SHARED EQUITY FINANCING AGREEMENT.—For purposes of this paragraph, the term "shared equity financing agreement" means an agreement under which—

(i) 2 or more persons acquire qualified ownership interests in a dwelling unit, and

(ii) the person (or persons) holding 1 or more of such interests—

(I) is entitled to occupy the dwelling unit for use as a principal residence, and

(II) is required to pay rent to 1 or more other persons holding qualified ownership interests in the dwelling unit.

(D) QUALIFIED OWNERSHIP INTEREST.—For purposes of this paragraph, the term "qualified ownership interest" means an undivided interest for more than 50 years in the entire dwelling unit and appurtenant land being acquired in the transaction to which the shared equity financing agreement relates.

(4) RENTAL OF PRINCIPAL RESIDENCE.—

(A) IN GENERAL.—For purposes of applying subsection (c)(5) to deductions allocable to a qualified rental period, a taxpayer shall not be considered to have used a dwelling unit for personal purposes for any day during the taxable year which occurs before or after a qualified rental period described in subparagraph (B)(i), or before a qualified rental period described in subparagraph (B)(ii), if with respect to such day such unit constitutes the principal residence (within the meaning of section 121) of the taxpayer.

(B) QUALIFIED RENTAL PERIOD.—For purposes of subparagraph (A), the term "qualified rental period" means a consecutive period of—

(i) 12 or more months which begins or ends in such taxable year, or

(ii) less than 12 months which begins in such taxable year and at the end of which such dwelling unit is sold or exchanged, and

for which such unit is rented, or is held for rental, at a fair rental.

[Sec. 280A(e)]

(e) EXPENSES ATTRIBUTABLE TO RENTAL.—

(1) IN GENERAL.—In any case where a taxpayer who is an individual or an S corporation uses a dwelling unit for personal purposes on any day during the taxable year (whether or not he is treated under this section as using such unit as a residence), the amount deductible under this chapter with respect to expenses attributable to the rental of the unit (or portion thereof) for the taxable year shall not exceed an amount which bears the same relationship to such expenses as the number of days during each year that the unit (or portion thereof) is rented at a fair rental bears to the total number of days during such year that the unit (or portion thereof) is used.

(2) EXCEPTION FOR DEDUCTIONS OTHERWISE ALLOWABLE.—This subsection shall not apply with respect to deductions which would be allowable under this chapter for the taxable year whether or not such unit (or portion thereof) was rented.

[Sec. 280A(f)]

(f) DEFINITIONS AND SPECIAL RULES.—

 (1) DWELLING UNIT DEFINED.—For purposes of this section—

  (A) IN GENERAL.—The term "dwelling unit" includes a house, apartment, condominium, mobile home, boat, or similar property, and all structures or other property appurtenant to such dwelling unit.

  (B) EXCEPTION.—The term "dwelling unit" does not include that portion of a unit which is used exclusively as a hotel, motel, inn, or similar establishment.

 (2) PERSONAL USE BY SHAREHOLDERS OF S CORPORATION.—In the case of an S corporation, subparagraphs (A) and (B) of subsection (d)(2) shall be applied by substituting "any shareholder of the S corporation" for "the taxpayer" each place it appears.

 (3) COORDINATION WITH SECTION 183.—If subsection (a) applies with respect to any dwelling unit (or portion thereof) for the taxable year—

  (A) section 183 (relating to activities not engaged in for profit) shall not apply to such unit (or portion thereof) for such year, but

  (B) such year shall be taken into account as a taxable year for purposes of applying subsection (d) of section 183 (relating to 5-year presumption).

 (4) COORDINATION WITH SECTION 162(a)(2).—Nothing in this section shall be construed to disallow any deduction allowable under section 162(a)(2) (or any deduction which meets the tests of section 162(a)(2) but is allowable under another provision of this title) by reason of the taxpayer's being away from home in the pursuit of a trade or business (other than the trade or business of renting dwelling units).

[Sec. 280A(g)]

(g) SPECIAL RULE FOR CERTAIN RENTAL USE.—Notwithstanding any other provision of this section or section 183, if a dwelling unit is used during the taxable year by the taxpayer as a residence and such dwelling unit is actually rented for less than 15 days during the taxable year, then—

 (1) no deduction otherwise allowable under this chapter because of the rental use of such dwelling unit shall be allowed, and

 (2) the income derived from such use for the taxable year shall not be included in the gross income of such taxpayer under section 61.

[Sec. 280B]

SEC. 280B. DEMOLITION OF STRUCTURES.

[Sec. 280B(a)]

(a) In the case of the demolition of any structure—

 (1) no deduction otherwise allowable under this chapter shall be allowed to the owner or lessee of such structure for—

  (A) any amount expended for such demolition, or

  (B) any loss sustained on account of such demolition; and

 (2) amounts described in paragraph (1) shall be treated as properly chargeable to capital account with respect to the land on which the demolished structure was located.

[Sec. 280E]

SEC. 280E. EXPENDITURES IN CONNECTION WITH THE ILLEGAL SALE OF DRUGS.

No deduction or credit shall be allowed for any amount paid or incurred during the taxable year in carrying on any trade or business if such trade or business (or the activities which comprise such trade or business) consists of trafficking in controlled substances (within the meaning of schedule I and II of the Controlled Substances Act) which is prohibited by Federal law or the law of any State in which such trade or business is conducted.

Sec. 280E

[Caution: As provided in Section 280F(d)(7), the dollar amounts set forth in Section 280F(a) are adjusted for taxable years after 1988 to reflect increases in the Consumer Price Index.]

[Sec. 280F]

SEC. 280F. LIMITATION ON DEPRECIATION FOR LUXURY AUTOMOBILES; LIMITATION WHERE CERTAIN PROPERTY USED FOR PERSONAL PURPOSES.

[Sec. 280F(a)]

(a) LIMITATION ON AMOUNT OF DEPRECIATION FOR LUXURY AUTOMOBILES.—

(1) DEPRECIATION.—

(A) LIMITATION.—The amount of the depreciation deduction for any taxable year for any passenger automobile shall not exceed—

(i) $2,560 for the 1st taxable year in the recovery period,

(ii) $4,100 for the 2nd taxable year in the recovery period,

(iii) $2,450 for the 3rd taxable year in the recovery period, and

(iv) $1,475 for each succeeding taxable year in the recovery period.

(B) DISALLOWED DEDUCTIONS ALLOWED FOR YEARS AFTER RECOVERY PERIOD.—

(i) IN GENERAL.—Except as provided in clause (ii), the unrecovered basis of any passenger automobile shall be treated as an expense for the 1st taxable year after the recovery period. Any excess of the unrecovered basis over the limitation of clause (ii) shall be treated as an expense in the succeeding taxable year.

(ii) $1,475 LIMITATION.—The amount treated as an expense under clause (i) for any taxable year shall not exceed $1,475.

(iii) PROPERTY MUST BE DEPRECIABLE.—No amount shall be allowable as a deduction by reason of this subparagraph with respect to any property for any taxable year unless a depreciation deduction would be allowable with respect to such property for such taxable year.

(iv) AMOUNT TREATED AS DEPRECIATION DEDUCTION.—For purposes of this subtitle, any amount allowable as a deduction by reason of this subparagraph shall be treated as a depreciation deduction allowable under section 168.

(C) SPECIAL RULE FOR CERTAIN CLEAN-FUEL PASSENGER AUTOMOBILES.—

(i) MODIFIED AUTOMOBILES.—In the case of a passenger automobile which is propelled by a fuel which is not a clean-burning fuel and to which is installed qualified clean-fuel vehicle property (as defined in section 179A(c)(1)(A)) for purposes of permitting such vehicle to be propelled by a clean burning fuel (as defined in section 179A(e)(1)), subparagraph (A) shall not apply to the cost of the installed qualified clean burning vehicle property.

(ii) PURPOSE BUILT PASSENGER VEHICLES.—In the case of a purpose built passenger vehicle (as defined in section 4001(a)(2)(C)(ii)), each of the annual limitations specified in subparagraphs (A) and (B) shall be tripled.

(iii) APPLICATION OF SUBPARAGRAPH.—This subparagraph shall apply to property placed in service after August 5, 1997, and before January 1, 2007.

(2) COORDINATION WITH REDUCTIONS IN AMOUNT ALLOWABLE BY REASON OF PERSONAL USE, ETC.— This subsection shall be applied before—

(A) the application of subsection (b), and

(B) the application of any other reduction in the amount of any depreciation deduction allowable under section 168 by reason of any use not qualifying the property for such credit or depreciation deduction.

Sec. 280F

[Sec. 280F(b)]

(b) LIMITATION WHERE BUSINESS USE OF LISTED PROPERTY NOT GREATER THAN 50 PERCENT.—

(1) DEPRECIATION.—If any listed property is not predominantly used in a qualified business use for any taxable year, the deduction allowed under section 168 with respect to such property for such taxable year and any subsequent taxable year shall be determined under section 168(g) (relating to alternative depreciation system).

(2) RECAPTURE.—

(A) WHERE BUSINESS USE PERCENTAGE DOES NOT EXCEED 50 PERCENT.—If—

(i) property is predominantly used in a qualified business use in a taxable year in which it is placed in service, and

(ii) such property is not predominantly used in a qualified business use for any subsequent taxable year,

then any excess depreciation shall be included in gross income for the taxable year referred to in clause (ii), and the depreciation deduction for the taxable year referred to in clause (ii) and any subsequent taxable years shall be determined under section 168(g) (relating to alternative depreciation system).

(B) EXCESS DEPRECIATION.—For purposes of subparagraph (A), the term "excess depreciation" means the excess (if any) of—

(i) the amount of the depreciation deductions allowable with respect to the property for taxable years before the 1st taxable year in which the property was not predominantly used in a qualified business use, over

(ii) the amount which would have been so allowable if the property had not been predominantly used in a qualified business use for the taxable year in which it was placed in service.

(3) PROPERTY PREDOMINANTLY USED IN QUALIFIED BUSINESS USE.—For purposes of this subsection, property shall be treated as predominantly used in a qualified business use for any taxable year if the business use percentage for such taxable year exceeds 50 percent.

[Sec. 280F(c)]

(c) TREATMENT OF LEASES.—

(1) LESSOR'S DEDUCTIONS NOT AFFECTED.—This section shall not apply to any listed property leased or held for leasing by any person regularly engaged in the business of leasing such property.

(2) LESSEE'S DEDUCTIONS REDUCED.—For purposes of determining the amount allowable as a deduction under this chapter for rentals or other payments under a lease for a period of 30 days or more of listed property, only the allowable percentage of such payments shall be taken into account.

(3) ALLOWABLE PERCENTAGE.—For purposes of paragraph (2), the allowable percentage shall be determined under tables prescribed by the Secretary. Such tables shall be prescribed so that the reduction in the deduction under paragraph (2) is substantially equivalent to the applicable restrictions contained in subsections (a) and (b).

(4) LEASE TERM.—In determining the term of any lease for purposes of paragraph (2), the rules of section 168(i)(3)(A) shall apply.

(5) LESSEE RECAPTURE.—Under regulations prescribed by the Secretary, rules similar to the rules of subsection (b)(3) shall apply to any lessee to which paragraph (2) applies.

[Sec. 280F(d)]

(d) DEFINITIONS AND SPECIAL RULES.—For purposes of this section—

(1) COORDINATION WITH SECTION 179.—Any deduction allowable under section 179 with respect to any listed property shall be subject to the limitations of subsections (a) and (b), and the limitation of paragraph (3) of this subsection, in the same manner as if it were a depreciation deduction allowable under section 168.

(2) SUBSEQUENT DEPRECIATION DEDUCTIONS REDUCED FOR DEDUCTIONS ALLOCABLE TO PERSONAL USE.—Solely for purposes of determining the amount of the depreciation deduction for subsequent taxable years, if less than 100 percent of the use of any listed property during any taxable year is used in a trade or business (including the holding for the production of income), all of the use of such property during such taxable year shall be treated as use so described.

(3) DEDUCTIONS OF EMPLOYEE.—

(A) IN GENERAL.—Any employee use of listed property shall not be treated as use in a trade or business for purposes of determining the amount of any depreciation deduction allowable to the employee (or the amount of any deduction allowable to the employee for rentals or other payments under a lease of listed property) unless such use is for the convenience of the employer and required as a condition of employment.

(B) EMPLOYEE USE.—For purposes of subparagraph (A), the term "employee use" means any use in connection with the performance of services as an employee.

(4) LISTED PROPERTY.—

(A) IN GENERAL.—Except as provided in subparagraph (B), the term "listed property" means—

(i) any passenger automobile,

(ii) any other property used as a means of transportation,

(iii) any property of a type generally used for purposes of entertainment, recreation, or amusement,

(iv) any computer or peripheral equipment (as defined in section 168(i)(2)(B)),

(v) any cellular telephone (or other similar telecommunications equipment), and

(vi) any other property of a type specified by the Secretary by regulations.

(B) EXCEPTION FOR CERTAIN COMPUTERS.—The term "listed property" shall not include any computer or peripheral equipment (as so defined) used exclusively at a regular business establishment and owned or leased by the person operating such establishment. For purposes of the preceding sentence, any portion of a dwelling unit shall be treated as a regular business establishment if (and only if) the requirements of section 280A(c)(1) are met with respect to such portion.

(C) EXCEPTION FOR PROPERTY USED IN BUSINESS OF TRANSPORTING PERSONS OR PROPERTY.—Except to the extent provided in regulations, clause (ii) of subparagraph (A) shall not apply to any property substantially all of the use of which is in a trade or business of providing to unrelated persons services consisting of the transportation of persons or property for compensation or hire.

(5) PASSENGER AUTOMOBILE.—

(A) IN GENERAL.—Except as provided in subparagraph (B), the term "passenger automobile" means any 4-wheeled vehicle—

(i) which is manufactured primarily for use on public streets, roads, and highways, and

(ii) which is rated at 6,000 pounds unloaded gross vehicle weight or less.

In the case of a truck or van, clause (ii) shall be applied by substituting "gross vehicle weight" for "unloaded gross vehicle weight."

(B) EXCEPTION FOR CERTAIN VEHICLES.—The term "passenger automobile" shall not include—

(i) any ambulance, hearse, or combination ambulance-hearse used by the taxpayer directly in a trade or business,

(ii) any vehicle used by the taxpayer directly in the trade or business of transporting persons or property for compensation or hire, and

(iii) under regulations, any truck or van.

(6) BUSINESS USE PERCENTAGE.—

(A) IN GENERAL.—The term "business use percentage" means the percentage of the use of any listed property during any taxable year which is a qualified business use.

(B) QUALIFIED BUSINESS USE.—Except as provided in subparagraph (C), the term "qualified business use" means any use in a trade or business of the taxpayer.

(C) EXCEPTION FOR CERTAIN USE BY 5-PERCENT OWNERS AND RELATED PERSONS.—

(i) IN GENERAL.—The term "qualified business use" shall not include—

(I) leasing property to any 5-percent owner or related person,

(II) use of property provided as compensation for the performance of services by a 5-percent owner or related person, or

Sec. 280F(d)

(III) use of property provided as compensation for the performance of services by any person not described in subclause (II) unless an amount is included in the gross income of such person with respect to such use, and, where required, there was withholding under chapter 24.

(ii) SPECIAL RULE FOR AIRCRAFT.—Clause (i) shall not apply with respect to any aircraft if at least 25 percent of the total use of the aircraft during the taxable year consists of qualified business use not described in clause (i).

(D) DEFINITIONS.—For purposes of this paragraph—

(i) 5-PERCENT OWNER.—The term "5-percent owner" means any person who is a 5-percent owner with respect to the taxpayer (as defined in section 416(i)(1)(B)(i)).

(ii) RELATED PERSON.—The term "related person" means any person related to the taxpayer (within the meaning of section 267(b)).

(7) AUTOMOBILE PRICE INFLATION ADJUSTMENT.—

(A) IN GENERAL.—In the case of any passenger automobile placed in service after 1988, subsection (a) shall be applied by increasing each dollar amount contained in such subsection by the automobile price inflation adjustment for the calendar year in which such automobile is placed in service. Any increase under the preceding sentence shall be rounded to the nearest multiple of $100 (or if the increase is a multiple of $50, such increase shall be increased to the next higher multiple of $100).

(B) AUTOMOBILE PRICE INFLATION ADJUSTMENT.—For purposes of this paragraph—

(i) IN GENERAL.—The automobile price inflation adjustment for any calendar year is the percentage (if any) by which—

(I) the CPI automobile component for October of the preceding calendar year, exceeds

(II) the CPI automobile component for October of 1987.

(ii) CPI AUTOMOBILE COMPONENT.—The term "CPI automobile component" means the automobile component of the Consumer Price Index for All Urban Consumers published by the Department of Labor.

(8) UNRECOVERED BASIS.—For purposes of subsection (a)(2), the term "unrecovered basis" means the adjusted basis of the passenger automobile determined after the application of subsection (a) and as if all use during the recovery period were use in a trade or business (including the holding of property for the production of income).

(9) ALL TAXPAYERS HOLDING INTERESTS IN PASSENGER AUTOMOBILE TREATED AS 1 TAXPAYER.—All taxpayers holding interests in any passenger automobile shall be treated as 1 taxpayer for purposes of applying subsection (a) to such automobile, and the limitations of subsection (a) shall be allocated among such taxpayers in proportion to their interests in such automobile.

(10) SPECIAL RULE FOR PROPERTY ACQUIRED IN NONRECOGNITION TRANSACTIONS.—For purposes of subsection (a)(2) any property acquired in a nonrecognition transaction shall be treated as a single property originally placed in service in the taxable year in which it was placed in service after being so acquired.

[Sec. 280F(e)]

(e) REGULATIONS.—The Secretary shall prescribe such regulations as may be necessary or appropriate to carry out the purposes of this section, including regulations with respect to items properly included in, or excluded from, the adjusted basis of any listed property.

[Sec. 280G]

SEC. 280G. GOLDEN PARACHUTE PAYMENTS.

[Sec. 280G(a)]

(a) GENERAL RULE.—No deduction shall be allowed under this chapter for any excess parachute payment.

[Sec. 280G(b)]

(b) EXCESS PARACHUTE PAYMENT.—For purposes of this section—

(1) IN GENERAL.—The term "excess parachute payment" means an amount equal to the excess of any parachute payment over the portion of the base amount allocated to such payment.

Sec. 280G(b)

(2) PARACHUTE PAYMENT DEFINED.—

(A) IN GENERAL.—The term "parachute payment" means any payment in the nature of compensation to (or for the benefit of) a disqualified individual if—

(i) such payment is contingent on a change—

(I) in the ownership or effective control of the corporation, or

(II) in the ownership of a substantial portion of the assets of the corporation, and

(ii) the aggregate present value of the payments in the nature of compensation to (or for the benefit of) such individual which are contingent on such change equals or exceeds an amount equal to 3 times the base amount.

For purposes of clause (ii), payments not treated as parachute payments under paragraph (4)(A), (5), or (6) shall not be taken into account.

(B) AGREEMENTS.—The term "parachute payment" shall also include any payment in the nature of compensation to (or for the benefit of) a disqualified individual if such payment is made pursuant to an agreement which violates any generally enforced securities laws or regulations. In any proceeding involving the issue of whether any payment made to a disqualified individual is a parachute payment on account of a violation of any generally enforced securities laws or regulations, the burden of proof with respect to establishing the occurrence of a violation of such a law or regulation shall be upon the Secretary.

(C) TREATMENT OF CERTAIN AGREEMENTS ENTERED INTO WITHIN 1 YEAR BEFORE CHANGE OF OWNERSHIP.—For purposes of subparagraph (A)(i), any payment pursuant to—

(i) an agreement entered into within 1 year before the change described in subparagraph (A)(i), or

(ii) an amendment made within such 1-year period of a previous agreement,

shall be presumed to be contingent on such change unless the contrary is established by clear and convincing evidence.

(3) BASE AMOUNT.—

(A) IN GENERAL.—The term "base amount" means the individual's annualized includible compensation for the base period.

(B) ALLOCATION.—The portion of the base amount allocated to any parachute payment shall be an amount which bears the same ratio to the base amount as—

(i) the present value of such payment, bears to

(ii) the aggregate present value of all such payments.

(4) TREATMENT OF AMOUNTS WHICH TAXPAYER ESTABLISHES AS REASONABLE COMPENSATION.—In the case of any payment described in paragraph (2)(A)—

(A) the amount treated as a parachute payment shall not include the portion of such payment which the taxpayer establishes by clear and convincing evidence is reasonable compensation for personal services to be rendered on or after the date of the change described in paragraph (2)(A)(i), and

(B) the amount treated as an excess parachute payment shall be reduced by the portion of such payment which the taxpayer establishes by clear and convincing evidence is reasonable compensation for personal services actually rendered before the date of the change described in paragraph (2)(A)(i).

For purposes of subparagraph (B), reasonable compensation for services actually rendered before the date of the change described in paragraph (2)(A)(i) shall be first offset against the base amount.

(5) EXEMPTION FOR SMALL BUSINESS CORPORATIONS, ETC.—

(A) IN GENERAL.—Notwithstanding paragraph (2), the term "parachute payment" does not include—

(i) any payment to a disqualified individual with respect to a corporation which (immediately before the change described in paragraph (2)(A)(i)) was a small business corporation (as defined in section 1361(b) but without regard to paragraph (1)(C) thereof), and

Sec. 280G(b)

(ii) any payment to a disqualified individual with respect to a corporation (other than a corporation described in clause (i)) if—

(I) immediately before the change described in paragraph (2)(A)(i), no stock in such corporation was readily tradeable on an established securities market or otherwise, and

(II) the shareholder approval requirements of subparagraph (B) are met with respect to such payment.

The Secretary may, by regulations, prescribe that the requirements of subclause (I) of clause (ii) are not met where a substantial portion of the assets of any entity consists (directly or indirectly) of stock in such corporation and interests in such other entity are readily tradeable on an established securities market, or otherwise. Stock described in section 1504(a)(4) shall not be taken into account under clause (ii)(I) if the payment does not adversely affect the shareholder's redemption and liquidation rights.

(B) SHAREHOLDER APPROVAL REQUIREMENTS.—The shareholder approval requirements of this subparagraph are met with respect to any payment if—

(i) such payment was approved by a vote of the persons who owned, immediately before the change described in paragraph (2)(A)(i), more than 75 percent of the voting power of all outstanding stock of the corporation, and

(ii) there was adequate disclosure to shareholders of all material facts concerning all payments which (but for this paragraph) would be parachute payments with respect to a disqualified individual.

The regulations prescribed under subsection (e) shall include regulations providing for the application of this subparagraph in the case of shareholders which are not individuals (including the treatment of nonvoting interests in an entity which is a shareholder) and where an entity holds a de minimis amount of stock in the corporation.

(6) EXEMPTION FOR PAYMENTS UNDER QUALIFIED PLANS.—Notwithstanding paragraph (2), the term "parachute payment" shall not include any payment to or from—

(A) a plan described in section 401(a) which includes a trust exempt from tax under section 501(a),

(B) an annuity plan described in section 403(a),

(C) a simplified employee pension (as defined in section 408(k)), or

(D) a simple retirement account described in section 408(p).

[Sec. 280G(c)]

(c) DISQUALIFIED INDIVIDUALS.—For purposes of this section, the term "disqualified individual" means any individual who is—

(1) an employee, independent contractor, or other person specified in regulations by the Secretary who performs personal services for any corporation, and

(2) is an officer, shareholder, or highly-compensated individual.

For purposes of this section, a personal service corporation (or similar entity) shall be treated as an individual. For purposes of paragraph (2), the term "highly-compensated individual" only includes an individual who is (or would be if the individual were an employee) a member of the group consisting of the highest paid 1 percent of the employees of the corporation or, if less, the highest paid 250 employees of the corporation.

[Sec. 280G(d)]

(d) OTHER DEFINITIONS AND SPECIAL RULES.—For purposes of this section—

(1) ANNUALIZED INCLUDIBLE COMPENSATION FOR BASE PERIOD.—The term "annualized includible compensation for the base period" means the average annual compensation which—

(A) was payable by the corporation with respect to which the change in ownership or control described in paragraph (2)(A) of subsection (b) occurs, and

(B) was includible in the gross income of the disqualified individual for taxable years in the base period.

(2) BASE PERIOD.—The term "base period" means the period consisting of the most recent 5 taxable years ending before the date on which the change in ownership or control described in paragraph (2)(A) of subsection (b) occurs (or such portion of such period during which the disqualified individual performed personal services for the corporation).

(3) PROPERTY TRANSFERS.—Any transfer of property—

(A) shall be treated as a payment, and

(B) shall be taken into account as its fair market value.

(4) PRESENT VALUE.—Present value shall be determined by using a discount rate equal to 120 percent of the applicable Federal rate (determined under section 1274(d)), compounded semiannually.

(5) TREATMENT OF AFFILIATED GROUPS.—Except as otherwise provided in regulations, all members of the same affiliated group (as defined in section 1504, determined without regard to section 1504(b)) shall be treated as 1 corporation for purposes of this section. Any person who is an officer of any member of such group shall be treated as an officer of such 1 corporation.

* * *

PART XI—SPECIAL RULES RELATING TO CORPORATE PREFERENCE ITEMS

[Sec. 291]

SEC. 291. SPECIAL RULES RELATING TO CORPORATE PREFERENCE ITEMS.

[Sec. 291(a)]

(a) REDUCTION IN CERTAIN PREFERENCE ITEMS, ETC.—For purposes of this subtitle, in the case of a corporation—

(1) SECTION 1250 CAPITAL GAIN TREATMENT.—In the case of section 1250 property which is disposed of during the taxable year, 20 percent of the excess (if any) of—

(A) the amount which would be treated as ordinary income if such property was section 1245 property, over

(B) the amount treated as ordinary income under section 1250 (determined without regard to this paragraph),

shall be treated as gain which is ordinary income under section 1250 and shall be recognized notwithstanding any other provision of this title. Under regulations prescribed by the Secretary, the provisions of this paragraph shall not apply to the disposition of any property to the extent section 1250(a) does not apply to such disposition by reason of section 1250(d).

(2) REDUCTION IN PERCENTAGE DEPLETION.—In the case of iron ore and coal (including lignite), the amount allowable as a deduction under section 613 with respect to any property (as defined in section 614) shall be reduced by 20 percent of the amount of the excess (if any) of—

(A) the amount of the deduction allowable under section 613 for the taxable year (determined without regard to this paragraph), over

(B) the adjusted basis of the property at the close of the taxable year (determined without regard to the depletion deduction for the taxable year).

(3) CERTAIN FINANCIAL INSTITUTION PREFERENCE ITEMS.—The amount allowable as a deduction under this chapter (determined without regard to this section) with respect to any financial institution preference item shall be reduced by 20 percent.

(4) CERTAIN FSC INCOME.—In the case of taxable years beginning after December 31, 1984, section 923(a) shall be applied with respect to any FSC by substituting—

(A) "30 percent" for "32 percent" in paragraph (2), and

(B) "15/23" for "16/23" in paragraph (3).

If all of the stock in the FSC is not held by 1 or more C corporations throughout the taxable year, under regulations, proper adjustments shall be made in the application of the preceding sentence to take into account stock held by persons other than C corporations.

Sec. 291

(5) AMORTIZATION OF POLLUTION CONTROL FACILITIES.—If an election is made under section 169 with respect to any certified pollution control facility, the amortizable basis of such facility for purposes of such section shall be reduced by 20 percent.

[Sec. 291(b)]

(b) SPECIAL RULES FOR TREATMENT OF INTANGIBLE DRILLING COSTS AND MINERAL EXPLORATION AND DEVELOPMENT COSTS.—For purposes of this subtitle, in the case of a corporation—

(1) IN GENERAL.—The amount allowable as a deduction for any taxable year (determined without regard to this section)—

(A) under section 263(c) in the case of an integrated oil company, or

(B) under section 616(a) or 617(a),

shall be reduced by 30 percent.

(2) AMORTIZATION OF AMOUNTS NOT ALLOWABLE AS DEDUCTIONS UNDER PARAGRAPH (1).—The amount not allowable as a deduction under section 263(c), 616(a), or 617(a) (as the case may be) for any taxable year by reason of paragraph (1) shall be allowable as a deduction ratably over the 60-month period beginning with the month in which the costs are paid or incurred.

(3) DISPOSITIONS.—For purposes of section 1254, any deduction under paragraph (2) shall be treated as a deduction allowable under section 263(c), 616(a), or 617(a) (whichever is appropriate).

(4) INTEGRATED OIL COMPANY DEFINED.—For purposes of this subsection, the term "integrated oil company" means, with respect to any taxable year, any producer of crude oil to whom subsection (c) of section 613A does not apply by reason of paragraph (2) or (4) of section 613A(d).

(5) COORDINATION WITH COST DEPLETION.—The portion of the adjusted basis of any property which is attributable to amounts to which paragraph (1) applied shall not be taken into account for purposes of determining depletion under section 611.

[Sec. 291(c)]

(c) SPECIAL RULES RELATING TO POLLUTION CONTROL FACILITIES.—For purposes of this subtitle—

(1) ACCELERATED COST RECOVERY DEDUCTION.—Section 168 shall apply with respect to that portion of the basis of any property not taken into account under section 169 by reason of subsection (a)(5).

(2) 1250 RECAPTURE.—Subsection (a)(1) shall not apply to any section 1250 property which is part of a certified pollution control facility (within the meaning of section 169(d)(1)) with respect to which an election under section 169 was made.

* * *

[Sec. 291(e)]

(e) DEFINITIONS.—For purposes of this section—

(1) FINANCIAL INSTITUTION PREFERENCE ITEM.—The term "financial institution preference item" includes the following:

(A) [Repealed.]

(B) INTEREST ON DEBT TO CARRY TAX-EXEMPT OBLIGATIONS ACQUIRED AFTER DECEMBER 31, 1982, AND BEFORE AUGUST 8, 1986.—

(i) IN GENERAL.—In the case of a financial institution which is a bank (as defined in section 585(a)(2)), the amount of interest on indebtedness incurred or continued to purchase or carry obligations acquired after December 31, 1982, and before August 8, 1986 the interest on which is exempt from taxes for the taxable year, to the extent that a deduction would (but for this paragraph or section 265(b)) be allowable with respect to such interest for such taxable year.

(ii) DETERMINATION OF INTEREST ALLOCABLE TO INDEBTEDNESS ON TAX-EXEMPT OBLIGATIONS.—Unless the taxpayer (under regulations prescribed by the Secretary) establishes otherwise, the amount determined under clause (i) shall be an amount which bears the same ratio to the aggregate amount allowable (determined without regard to this section and section 265(b)) to the taxpayer as a deduction for interest for the taxable year as—

(I) the taxpayer's average adjusted basis (within the meaning of section 1016) of obligations described in clause (i), bears to

(II) such average adjusted basis for all assets of the taxpayer.

(iii) INTEREST.—For purposes of this subparagraph, the term "interest" includes amounts (whether or not designated as interest) paid in respect of deposits, investment certificates, or withdrawable or repurchasable shares.

(iv) APPLICATION OF SUBPARAGRAPH TO CERTAIN OBLIGATIONS ISSUED AFTER AUGUST 7, 1986.—For application of this subparagraph to certain obligations issued after August 7, 1986, see section 265(b)(3).

(2) SECTION 1245 AND 1250 PROPERTY.—The terms "section 1245 property" and "section 1250 property" have the meanings given such terms by sections 1245(a)(3) and 1250(c), respectively.

Subchapter C—Corporate Distributions and Adjustments

PART I—DISTRIBUTIONS BY CORPORATIONS

Subpart A—Effects on Recipients

[Sec. 301]

SEC. 301. DISTRIBUTIONS OF PROPERTY.

[Sec. 301(a)]

(a) IN GENERAL.—Except as otherwise provided in this chapter, a distribution of property (as defined in section 317(a)) made by a corporation to a shareholder with respect to its stock shall be treated in the manner provided in subsection (c).

[Sec. 301(b)]

(b) AMOUNT DISTRIBUTED.—

(1) GENERAL RULE.—For purposes of this section, the amount of any distribution shall be the amount of money received, plus the fair market value of the other property received.

(2) REDUCTION FOR LIABILITIES.—The amount of any distribution determined under paragraph (1) shall be reduced (but not below zero) by—

(A) the amount of any liability of the corporation assumed by the shareholder in connection with the distribution, and

(B) the amount of any liability to which the property received by the shareholder is subject immediately before, and immediately after, the distribution.

(3) DETERMINATION OF FAIR MARKET VALUE.—For purposes of this section, fair market value shall be determined as of the date of the distribution.

[Sec. 301(c)]

(c) AMOUNT TAXABLE.—In the case of a distribution to which subsection (a) applies—

(1) AMOUNT CONSTITUTING DIVIDEND.—That portion of the distribution which is a dividend (as defined in section 316) shall be included in gross income.

(2) AMOUNT APPLIED AGAINST BASIS.—That portion of the distribution which is not a dividend shall be applied against and reduce the adjusted basis of the stock.

(3) AMOUNT IN EXCESS OF BASIS.—

(A) IN GENERAL.—Except as provided in subparagraph (B), that portion of the distribution which is not a dividend, to the extent that it exceeds the adjusted basis of the stock, shall be treated as gain from the sale or exchange of property.

(B) DISTRIBUTIONS OUT OF INCREASE IN VALUE ACCRUED BEFORE MARCH 1, 1913.—That portion of the distribution which is not a dividend, to the extent that it exceeds the adjusted basis of the stock and to the extent that it is out of increase in value accrued before March 1, 1913, shall be exempt from tax.

[Sec. 301(d)]

(d) Basis.—The basis of property received in a distribution to which subsection (a) applies shall be the fair market value of such property.

[Sec. 301(e)]

(e) Special Rule for Certain Distributions Received by 20 Percent Corporate Shareholder.—

(1) In general.—Except to the extent otherwise provided in regulations, solely for purposes of determining the taxable income of any 20 percent corporate shareholder (and its adjusted basis in the stock of the distributing corporation), section 312 shall be applied with respect to the distributing corporation as if it did not contain subsections (k) and (n) thereof.

(2) 20 percent corporate shareholder.—For purposes of this subsection, the term "20 percent corporate shareholder" means, with respect to any distribution, any corporation which owns (directly or through the application of section 318)—

(A) stock in the corporation making the distribution possessing at least 20 percent of the total combined voting power of all classes of stock entitled to vote, or

(B) at least 20 percent of the total value of all stock of the distributing corporation (except nonvoting stock which is limited and preferred as to dividends),

but only if, but for this subsection, the distributee corporation would be entitled to a deduction under section 243, 244, or 245 with respect to such distribution.

(3) Application of section 312(n)(7) not affected.—The reference in paragraph (1) to subsection (n) of section 312 shall be treated as not including a reference to paragraph (7) of such subsection.

(4) Regulations.—The Secretary shall prescribe such regulations as may be necessary or appropriate to carry out the purposes of this subsection.

[Sec. 301(f)]

(f) Special Rules.—

(1) For distributions in redemption of stock, see section 302.

(2) For distributions in complete liquidation, see part II (sec. 331 and following).

(3) For distributions in corporate organizations and reorganizations, see part III (sec. 351 and following).

(4) For taxation of dividends received by individuals at capital gain rates, see section 1(h)(11).

[Sec. 302]

SEC. 302. DISTRIBUTIONS IN REDEMPTION OF STOCK.

[Sec. 302(a)]

(a) General Rule.—If a corporation redeems its stock (within the meaning of section 317 (b)), and if paragraph (1), (2), (3), or (4) of subsection (b) applies, such redemption shall be treated as a distribution in part or full payment in exchange for the stock.

[Sec. 302(b)]

(b) Redemptions Treated as Exchanges.—

(1) Redemptions not equivalent to dividends.—Subsection (a) shall apply if the redemption is not essentially equivalent to a dividend.

(2) Substantially disproportionate redemption of stock.—

(A) In general.—Subsection (a) shall apply if the distribution is substantially disproportionate with respect to the shareholder.

(B) Limitation.—This paragraph shall not apply unless immediately after the redemption the shareholder owns less than 50 percent of the total combined voting power of all classes of stock entitled to vote.

(C) Definitions.—For purposes of this paragraph, the distribution is substantially disproportionate if—

(i) the ratio which the voting stock of the corporation owned by the shareholder immediately after the redemption bears to all of the voting stock of the corporation at such time,

is less than 80 percent of—

(ii) the ratio which the voting stock of the corporation owned by the shareholder immediately before the redemption bears to all of the voting stock of the corporation at such time.

For purposes of this paragraph, no distribution shall be treated as substantially disproportionate unless the shareholder's ownership of the common stock of the corporation (whether voting or nonvoting) after and before redemption also meets the 80 percent requirement of the preceding sentence. For purposes of the preceding sentence, if there is more than one class of common stock, the determinations shall be made by reference to fair market value.

(D) SERIES OF REDEMPTIONS.—This paragraph shall not apply to any redemption made pursuant to a plan the purpose or effect of which is a series of redemptions resulting in a distribution which (in the aggregate) is not substantially disproportionate with respect to the shareholder.

(3) TERMINATION OF SHAREHOLDER'S INTEREST.—Subsection (a) shall apply if the redemption is in complete redemption of all of the stock of the corporation owned by the shareholder.

(4) REDEMPTION FROM NONCORPORATE SHAREHOLDER IN PARTIAL LIQUIDATION.—Subsection (a) shall apply to a distribution if such distribution is—

(A) in redemption of stock held by a shareholder who is not a corporation, and

(B) in partial liquidation of the distributing corporation.

(5) APPLICATION OF PARAGRAPHS.—In determining whether a redemption meets the requirements of paragraph (1), the fact that such redemption fails to meet the requirements of paragraph (2), (3), or (4) shall not be taken into account. If a redemption meets the requirements of paragraph (3) and also the requirements of paragraph (1), (2), or (4), then so much of subsection (c) (2) as would (but for this sentence) apply in respect of the acquisition of an interest in the corporation within the 10-year period beginning on the date of the distribution shall not apply.

[Sec. 302(c)]

(c) CONSTRUCTIVE OWNERSHIP OF STOCK.—

(1) IN GENERAL.—Except as provided in paragraph (2) of this subsection, section 318 (a) shall apply in determining the ownership of stock for purposes of this section.

(2) FOR DETERMINING TERMINATION OF INTEREST.—

(A) In the case of a distribution described in subsection (b) (3), section 318 (a) (1) shall not apply if—

(i) immediately after the distribution the distributee has no interest in the corporation (including an interest as officer, director, or employee), other than an interest as a creditor,

(ii) the distributee does not acquire any such interest (other than stock acquired by bequest or inheritance) within 10 years from the date of such distribution, and

(iii) the distributee, at such time and in such manner as the Secretary by regulations prescribes, files an agreement to notify the Secretary of any acquisition described in clause (ii) and to retain such records as may be necessary for the application of this paragraph.

If the distributee acquires such an interest in the corporation (other than by bequest or inheritance) within 10 years from the date of the distribution, then the periods of limitation provided in sections 6501 and 6502 on the making of an assessment and the collection by levy or a proceeding in court shall, with respect to any deficiency (including interest and additions to the tax) resulting from such acquisition, include one year immediately following the date on which the distributee (in accordance with regulations prescribed by the Secretary) notifies the Secretary of such acquisition; and such assessment and collection may be made notwithstanding any provision of law or rule of law which otherwise would prevent such assessment and collection.

(B) Subparagraph (A) of this paragraph shall not apply if—

(i) any portion of the stock redeemed was acquired, directly or indirectly, within the 10-year period ending on the date of the distribution by the distributee from a person the ownership of whose stock would (at the time of distribution) be attributable to the distributee under section 318 (a), or

(ii) any person owns (at the time of the distribution) stock the ownership of which is attributable to the distributee under section 318 (a) and such person acquired any stock in the corporation, directly or indirectly, from the distributee within the 10-year period ending on the date of the distribution, unless such stock so acquired from the distributee is redeemed in the same transaction.

The preceding sentence shall not apply if the acquisition (or, in the case of clause (ii), the disposition) by the distributee did not have as one of its principal purposes the avoidance of Federal income tax.

(C) SPECIAL RULE FOR WAIVERS BY ENTITIES.—

(i) IN GENERAL.—Subparagraph (A) shall not apply to a distribution to any entity unless—

(I) such entity and each related person meet the requirements of clauses (i), (ii), and (iii) of subparagraph (A), and

(II) each related person agrees to be jointly and severally liable for any deficiency (including interest and additions to tax) resulting from an acquisition described in clause (ii) of subparagraph (A).

In any case to which the preceding sentence applies, the second sentence of subparagraph (A) and subparagraph (B)(ii) shall be applied by substituting "distributee or any related person" for "distributee" each place it appears.

(ii) DEFINITIONS.—For purposes of this subparagraph—

(I) the term "entity" means a partnership, estate, trust, or corporation; and

(II) the term "related person" means any person to whom ownership of stock in the corporation is (at the time of the distribution) attributable under section 318(a)(1) if such stock is further attributable to the entity under section 318(a)(3).

[Sec. 302(d)]

(d) REDEMPTIONS TREATED AS DISTRIBUTIONS OF PROPERTY.—Except as otherwise provided in this subchapter, if a corporation redeems its stock (within the meaning of section 317 (b)), and if subsection (a) of this section does not apply, such redemption shall be treated as a distribution of property to which section 301 applies.

[Sec. 302(e)]

(e) PARTIAL LIQUIDATION DEFINED.—

(1) IN GENERAL.—For purposes of subsection (b)(4), a distribution shall be treated as in partial liquidation of a corporation if—

(A) the distribution is not essentially equivalent to a dividend (determined at the corporate level rather than at the shareholder level), and

(B) the distribution is pursuant to a plan and occurs within the taxable year in which the plan is adopted or within the succeeding taxable year.

(2) TERMINATION OF BUSINESS.—The distributions which meet the requirements of paragraph (1)(A) shall include (but shall not be limited to) a distribution which meets the requirements of subparagraphs (A) and (B) of this paragraph:

(A) The distribution is attributable to the distributing corporation's ceasing to conduct, or consists of the assets of, a qualified trade or business.

(B) Immediately after the distribution, the distributing corporation is actively engaged in the conduct of a qualified trade or business.

(3) QUALIFIED TRADE OR BUSINESS.—For purposes of paragraph (2), the term "qualified trade or business" means any trade or business which—

(A) was actively conducted throughout the 5-year period ending on the date of the redemption, and

(B) was not acquired by the corporation within such period in a transaction in which gain or loss was recognized in whole or in part.

(4) REDEMPTION MAY BE PRO RATA.—Whether or not a redemption meets the requirements of subparagraphs (A) and (B) of paragraph (2) shall be determined without regard to whether or not the redemption is pro rata with respect to all of the shareholders of the corporation.

(5) TREATMENT OF CERTAIN PASS-THRU ENTITIES.—For purposes of determining under subsection (b)(4) whether any stock is held by a shareholder who is not a corporation, any stock held by a partnership, estate, or trust shall be treated as if it were actually held proportionately by its partners or beneficiaries.

[Sec. 302(f)]

(f) CROSS REFERENCES.—

For special rules relating to redemption—

(1) Death Taxes.—Of stock to pay death taxes, see section 303.

(2) Section 306 Stock.—Of section 306 stock, see section 306.

(3) Liquidations.—Of stock in complete liquidation, see section 331.

[Sec. 303]

SEC. 303. DISTRIBUTIONS IN REDEMPTION OF STOCK TO PAY DEATH TAXES.

[Sec. 303(a)]

(a) IN GENERAL.—A distribution of property to a shareholder by a corporation in redemption of part or all of the stock of such corporation which (for Federal estate tax purposes) is included in determining the gross estate of a decedent, to the extent that the amount of such distribution does not exceed the sum of—

(1) the estate, inheritance, legacy, and succession taxes (including any interest collected as a part of such taxes) imposed because of such decedent's death, and

(2) the amount of funeral and administration expenses allowable as deductions to the estate under section 2053 (or under section 2106 in the case of the estate of a decedent nonresident, not a citizen of the United States),

shall be treated as a distribution in full payment in exchange for the stock so redeemed.

[Sec. 303(b)]

(b) LIMITATIONS ON APPLICATION OF SUBSECTION (a).—

(1) PERIOD FOR DISTRIBUTION.—Subsection (a) shall apply only to amounts distributed after the death of the decedent and—

(A) within the period of limitations provided in section 6501 (a) for the assessment of the Federal estate tax (determined without the application of any provision other than section 6501 (a)), or within 90 days after the expiration of such period,

(B) if a petition for redetermination of a deficiency in such estate tax has been filed with the Tax Court within the time prescribed in section 6213, at any time before the expiration of 60 days after the decision of the Tax Court becomes final, or

(C) if an election has been made under section 6166 and if the time prescribed by this subparagraph expires at a later date than the time prescribed by subparagraph (B) of this paragraph, within the time determined under section 6166 for the payment of the installments.

(2) RELATIONSHIP OF STOCK TO DECEDENT'S ESTATE.—

(A) IN GENERAL.—Subsection (a) shall apply to a distribution by a corporation only if the value (for Federal estate tax purposes) of all of the stock of such corporation which is included in determining the value of the decedent's gross estate exceeds 35 percent of the excess of—

(i) the value of the gross estate of such decedent, over

(ii) the sum of the amounts allowable as a deduction under section 2053 or 2054.

(B) SPECIAL RULE FOR STOCK IN 2 OR MORE CORPORATIONS.—For purposes of subparagraph (A), stock of 2 or more corporations, with respect to each of which there is included in determining the value of the decedent's gross estate 20 percent or more in value of the outstanding stock, shall be treated as the stock of a single corporation. For purposes of the 20-percent requirement of the preceding sentence, stock which, at the decedent's death, represents the surviving spouse's interest in property held by the decedent and the surviving spouse as community property or as joint tenants, tenants by the entirety, or tenants in common shall be treated as having been included in determining the value of the decedent's gross estate.

(3) RELATIONSHIP OF SHAREHOLDER TO ESTATE TAX.—Subsection (a) shall apply to a distribution by a corporation only to the extent that the interest of the shareholder is reduced directly (or through a binding obligation to contribute) by any payment of an amount described in paragraph (1) or (2) of subsection (a).

(4) ADDITIONAL REQUIREMENTS FOR DISTRIBUTIONS MADE MORE THAN 4 YEARS AFTER DECEDENT'S DEATH.—In the case of amounts distributed more than 4 years after the date of the decedent's death, subsection (a) shall apply to a distribution by a corporation only to the extent of the lesser of—

(A) the aggregate of the amounts referred to in paragraph (1) or (2) of subsection (a) which remained unpaid immediately before the distribution, or

(B) the aggregate of the amounts referred to in paragraph (1) or (2) of subsection (a) which are paid during the 1-year period beginning on the date of such distribution.

[Sec. 303(c)]

(c) STOCK WITH SUBSTITUTED BASIS.—If—

(1) a shareholder owns stock of a corporation (referred to in this subsection as "new stock") the basis of which is determined by reference to the basis of stock of a corporation (referred to in this subsection as "old stock"),

(2) the old stock was included (for Federal estate tax purposes) in determining the gross estate of a decedent, and

(3) subsection (a) would apply to a distribution of property to such shareholder in redemption of the old stock,

then, subject to the limitations specified in subsection (b), subsection (a) shall apply in respect of a distribution in redemption of the new stock.

[Sec. 303(d)]

(d) SPECIAL RULES FOR GENERATION-SKIPPING TRANSFERS.—Where stock in a corporation is the subject of a generation-skipping transfer (within the meaning of section 2611(a)) occurring at the same time as and as a result of the death of an individual—

(1) the stock shall be deemed to be included in the gross estate of such individual;

(2) taxes of the kind referred to in subsection (a)(1) which are imposed because of the generation-skipping transfer shall be treated as imposed because of such individual's death (and for this purpose the tax imposed by section 2601 shall be treated as an estate tax);

(3) the period of distribution shall be measured from the date of the generation-skipping transfer; and

(4) the relationship of stock to the decedent's estate shall be measured with reference solely to the amount of the generation-skipping transfer.

[Sec. 304]

SEC. 304. REDEMPTION THROUGH USE OF RELATED CORPORATIONS.

[Sec. 304(a)]

(a) TREATMENT OF CERTAIN STOCK PURCHASES.—

(1) ACQUISITION BY RELATED CORPORATION (OTHER THAN SUBSIDIARY).—For purposes of sections 302 and 303, if—

(A) one or more persons are in control of each of two corporations, and

(B) in return for property, one of the corporations acquires stock in the other corporation from the person (or persons) so in control,

then (unless paragraph (2) applies) such property shall be treated as a distribution in redemption of the stock of the corporation acquiring such stock. To the extent that such distribution is treated as a distribution to which section 301 applies, the transferor and the acquiring corporation shall be treated in the same manner as if the transferor had transferred the stock so acquired to the acquiring corporation in exchange for stock of the acquiring corporation in a transaction to which section

Sec. 304(a)

351(a) applies, and then the acquiring corporation had redeemed the stock it was treated as issuing in such transaction.

(2) ACQUISITION BY SUBSIDIARY.—For purposes of sections 302 and 303, if—

(A) in return for property, one corporation acquires from a shareholder of another corporation stock in such other corporation, and

(B) the issuing corporation controls the acquiring corporation,

then such property shall be treated as a distribution in redemption of the stock of the issuing corporation.

[Sec. 304(b)]

(b) SPECIAL RULES FOR APPLICATION OF SUBSECTION (a).—

(1) RULE FOR DETERMINATIONS UNDER SECTION 302(b).—In the case of any acquisition of stock to which subsection (a) of this section applies, determinations as to whether the acquisition is, by reason of section 302 (b), to be treated as a distribution in part or full payment in exchange for the stock shall be made by reference to the stock of the issuing corporation. In applying section 318(a) (relating to constructive ownership of stock) with respect to section 302(b) for purposes of this paragraph, sections 318(a)(2)(C) and 318(a)(3)(C) shall be applied without regard to the 50 percent limitation contained therein.

(2) AMOUNT CONSTITUTING DIVIDEND.—In the case of any acquisition of stock to which subsection (a) applies, the determination of the amount which is a dividend (and the source thereof) shall be made as if the property were distributed—

(A) by the acquiring corporation to the extent of its earnings and profits, and

(B) then by the issuing corporation to the extent of its earnings and profits.

(3) COORDINATION WITH SECTION 351.—

(A) PROPERTY TREATED AS RECEIVED IN REDEMPTION.—Except as otherwise provided in this paragraph, subsection (a) (and not section 351 and not so much of sections 357 and 358 as relates to section 351) shall apply to any property received in a distribution described in subsection (a).

(B) CERTAIN ASSUMPTIONS OF LIABILITY, ETC.—

(i) IN GENERAL.—In the case of an acquisition described in section 351, subsection (a) shall not apply to any liability—

(I) assumed by the acquiring corporation, or

(II) to which the stock is subject,

if such liability was incurred by the transferor to acquire the stock. For purposes of the preceding sentence, the term "stock" means stock referred to in paragraph (1)(B) or (2)(A) of subsection (a).

(ii) EXTENSION OF OBLIGATIONS, ETC.—For purposes of clause (i), an extension, renewal, or refinancing of a libility which meets the requirements of clause (i) shall be treated as meeting such requirements.

(iii) CLAUSE (i) DOES NOT APPLY TO STOCK ACQUIRED FROM RELATED PERSON EXCEPT WHERE COMPLETE TERMINATION.—Clause (i) shall apply only to stock acquired by the transferor from a person—

(I) none of whose stock is attributable to the transferor under section 318(a) (other than paragraph (4) thereof), or

(II) who satisfies rules similar to the rules of section 302(c)(2) with respect to both the acquiring and the issuing corporations (determined as if such person were a distributee of each such corporation).

(C) DISTRIBUTIONS INCIDENT TO FORMATION OF BANK HOLDING COMPANIES.—If—

(i) pursuant to a plan, control of a bank is acquired and within 2 years after the date on which such control is acquired, stock constituting control of such bank is transferred to a BHC in connection with its formation,

(ii) incident to the formation of the BHC there is a distribution of property described in subsection (a), and

(iii) the shareholders of the BHC who receive distributions of such property do not have control of such BHC,

then, subsection (a) shall not apply to any securities received by a qualified minority shareholder incident to the formation of such BHC. For purposes of this subparagraph, any assumption of (or acquisition of stock subject to) a liability under subparagraph (B) shall not be treated as a distribution of property.

(D) DEFINITIONS AND SPECIAL RULE.—For purposes of subparagraph (C) and this subparagraph—

(i) QUALIFIED MINORITY SHAREHOLDER.—The term "qualified minority shareholder" means any shareholder who owns less than 10 percent (in value) of the stock of the BHC. For purposes of the preceding sentence, the rules of paragraph (3) of subsection (c) shall apply.

(ii) BHC.—The term "BHC" means a bank holding company (within the meaning of section 2(a) of the Bank Holding Company Act of 1956).

(iii) SPECIAL RULE IN CASE OF BHC'S FORMED BEFORE 1985.—In the case of a BHC which is formed before 1985, clause (i) of subparagraph (C) shall not apply.

(4) TREATMENT OF CERTAIN INTRAGROUP TRANSACTIONS.—

(A) IN GENERAL.—In the case of any transfer described in subsection (a) of stock from 1 member of an affiliated group to another member of such group, proper adjustments shall be made to—

(i) the adjusted basis of any intragroup stock, and

(ii) the earnings and profits of any member of such group,

to the extent necessary to carry out the purposes of this section.

(B) DEFINITIONS.—For purposes of this paragraph—

(i) AFFILIATED GROUP.—The term "affiliated group" has the meaning given such term by section 1504(a).

(ii) INTRAGROUP STOCK.—The term "intragroup stock" means any stock which—

(I) is in a corporation which is a member of an affiliated group, and

(II) is held by another member of such group.

* * *

(6) AVOIDANCE OF MULTIPLE INCLUSIONS, ETC.—In the case of any acquisition to which subsection (a) applies in which the acquiring corporation or the issuing corporation is a foreign corporation, the Secretary shall prescribe such regulations as are appropriate in order to eliminate a multiple inclusion of any item in income by reason of this subpart and to provide appropriate basis adjustments (including modifications to the application of sections 959 and 961).

[Sec. 304(c)]

(c) CONTROL.—

(1) IN GENERAL.—For purposes of this section, control means the ownership of stock possessing at least 50 percent of the total combined voting power of all classes of stock entitled to vote, or at least 50 percent of the total value of shares of all classes of stock. If a person (or persons) is in control (within the meaning of the preceding sentence) of a corporation which in turn owns at least 50 percent of the total combined voting power of all stock entitled to vote of another corporation, or owns at least 50 percent of the total value of the shares of all classes of stock of another corporation, then such person (or persons) shall be treated as in control of such other corporation.

(2) STOCK ACQUIRED IN THE TRANSACTION.—For purposes of subsection (a)(1)—

(A) GENERAL RULE.—Where 1 or more persons in control of the issuing corporation transfer stock of such corporation in exchange for stock of the acquiring corporation, the stock of the acquiring corporation received shall be taken into account in determining whether such person or persons are in control of the acquiring corporation.

(B) DEFINITION OF CONTROL GROUP.—Where 2 or more persons in control of the issuing corporation transfer stock of such corporation to acquiring corporation and, after the transfer, the transferors are in control of the acquiring corporation, the person or persons in control of each corporation shall include each of the persons who so transfer stock.

(3) CONSTRUCTIVE OWNERSHIP.—

(A) IN GENERAL.—Section 318(a) (relating to constructive ownership of stock) shall apply for purposes of determining control under this section.

(B) MODIFICATION OF 50-PERCENT LIMITATIONS IN SECTION 318.—For purposes of subparagraph (A)—

(i) paragraph (2)(C) of section 318(a) shall be applied by substituting "5 percent" for "50 percent", and

(ii) paragraph (3)(C) of section 318(a) shall be applied—

(I) by substituting "5 percent" for "50 percent", and

(II) in any case where such paragraph would not apply but for subclause (I), by considering a corporation as owning the stock (other than stock in such corporation) owned by or for any shareholder of such corporation in that proportion which the value of the stock which such shareholder owned in such corporation bears to the value of all stock in such corporation.

[Sec. 305]

SEC. 305. DISTRIBUTIONS OF STOCK AND STOCK RIGHTS.

[Sec. 305(a)]

(a) GENERAL RULE.—Except as otherwise provided in this section, gross income does not include the amount of any distribution of the stock of a corporation made by such corporation to its shareholders with respect to its stock.

[Sec. 305(b)]

(b) EXCEPTIONS.—Subsection (a) shall not apply to a distribution by a corporation of its stock, and the distribution shall be treated as a distribution of property to which section 301 applies—

(1) DISTRIBUTIONS IN LIEU OF MONEY.—If the distribution is, at the election of any of the shareholders (whether exercised before or after the declaration thereof), payable either—

(A) in its stock, or

(B) in property.

(2) DISPROPORTIONATE DISTRIBUTIONS.—If the distribution (or a series of distributions of which such distribution is one) has the result of—

(A) the receipt of property by some shareholders, and

(B) an increase in the proportionate interests of other shareholders in the assets or earnings and profits of the corporation.

(3) DISTRIBUTIONS OF COMMON AND PREFERRED STOCK.—If the distribution (or a series of distributions of which such distribution is one) has the result of—

(A) the receipt of preferred stock by some common shareholders, and

(B) the receipt of common stock by other common shareholders.

(4) DISTRIBUTIONS ON PREFERRED STOCK.—If the distribution is with respect to preferred stock, other than an increase in the conversion ratio of convertible preferred stock made solely to take account of a stock dividend or stock split with respect to the stock into which such convertible stock is convertible.

(5) DISTRIBUTIONS OF CONVERTIBLE PREFERRED STOCK.—If the distribution is of convertible preferred stock, unless it is established to the satisfaction of the Secretary that such distribution will not have the result described in paragraph (2).

[Sec. 305(c)]

(c) CERTAIN TRANSACTIONS TREATED AS DISTRIBUTIONS.—For purposes of this section and section 301, the Secretary shall prescribe regulations under which a change in conversion ratio, a change in redemption price, a difference between redemption price and issue price, a redemption which is treated as a distribution to which section 301 applies, or any transaction (including a recapitalization) having a similar effect on the interest of any shareholder shall be treated as a distribution with respect to any shareholder whose proportionate interest in the earnings and profits or assets of the corporation is

Sec. 305

increased by such change, difference, redemption, or similar transaction. Regulations prescribed under the preceding sentence shall provide that—

(1) where the issuer of stock is required to redeem the stock at a specified time or the holder of stock has the option to require the issuer to redeem the stock, a redemption premium resulting from such requirement or option shall be treated as reasonable only if the amount of such premium does not exceed the amount determined under the principles of section 1273(a)(3),

(2) a redemption of premium shall not fail to be treated as a distribution (or series of distributions) merely because the stock is callable, and

(3) in any case in which a redemption premium is treated as a distribution (or series of distributions), such premium shall be taken into account under principles similar to the principles of section 1272(a).

[Sec. 305(d)]

(d) DEFINITIONS.—

(1) RIGHTS TO ACQUIRE STOCK.—For purposes of this section, the term "stock" includes rights to acquire such stock.

(2) SHAREHOLDERS.—For purposes of subsections (b) and (c), the term "shareholder" includes a holder of rights or of convertible securities.

* * *

[Sec. 305(f)]

(f) CROSS REFERENCES.—

For special rules—

(1) Relating to the receipt of stock rights in corporate organizations and reorganizations, see part III (sec. 351 and following).

(2) In the case of a distribution which results in a gift, see section 2501 and following.

(3) In the case of a distribution which has the effect of the payment of compensation, see section 61 (a) (1).

[Sec. 306]

SEC. 306. DISPOSITIONS OF CERTAIN STOCK.

[Sec. 306(a)]

(a) GENERAL RULE.—If a shareholder sells or otherwise disposes of section 306 stock (as defined in subsection (c))—

(1) DISPOSITIONS OTHER THAN REDEMPTIONS.—If such disposition is not a redemption (within the meaning of section 317 (b))—

(A) The amount realized shall be treated as ordinary income. This subparagraph shall not apply to the extent that—

(i) the amount realized, exceeds

(ii) such stock's ratable share of the amount which would have been a dividend at the time of distribution if (in lieu of section 306 stock) the corporation had distributed money in an amount equal to the fair market value of the stock at the time of distribution.

(B) Any excess of the amount realized over the sum of—

(i) the amount treated under subparagraph (A) as ordinary income, plus

(ii) the adjusted basis of the stock,

shall be treated as gain from the sale of such stock.

(C) No loss shall be recognized.

(D) TREATMENT AS DIVIDEND.—For purposes of section 1(h)(11) and such other provisions as the Secretary may specify, any amount treated as ordinary income under this paragraph shall be treated as a dividend received from the corporation.

(2) REDEMPTION.—If the disposition is a redemption, the amount realized shall be treated as a distribution of property to which section 301 applies.

Sec. 306(a)

(b) EXCEPTIONS.—Subsection (a) shall not apply—

　　(1) TERMINATION OF SHAREHOLDER'S INTEREST, ETC.—

　　　　(A) NOT IN REDEMPTION.—If the disposition—

　　　　　　(i) is not a redemption;

　　　　　　(ii) is not, directly or indirectly, to a person the ownership of whose stock would (under section 318 (a)) be attributable to the shareholder; and

　　　　　　(iii) terminates the entire stock interest of the shareholder in the corporation (and for purposes of this clause, section 318 (a) shall apply).

　　　　(B) IN REDEMPTION.—If the disposition is a redemption and paragraph (3) or (4) of section 302(b) applies.

　　(2) LIQUIDATIONS.—If the section 306 stock is redeemed in a distribution in complete liquidation to which part II (sec. 331 and following) applies.

　　(3) WHERE GAIN OR LOSS IS NOT RECOGNIZED.—To the extent that, under any provision of this subtitle, gain or loss to the shareholder is not recognized with respect to the disposition of the section 306 stock.

　　(4) TRANSACTIONS NOT IN AVOIDANCE.—If it is established to the satisfaction of the Secretary—

　　　　(A) that the distribution, and the disposition or redemption, or

　　　　(B) in the case of a prior or simultaneous disposition (or redemption) of the stock with respect to which the section 306 stock disposed of (or redeemed) was issued, that the disposition (or redemption) of the section 306 stock,

was not in pursuance of a plan having as one of its principal purposes the avoidance of Federal income tax.

(c) SECTION 306 [STOCK] DEFINED.—

　　(1) IN GENERAL.—For purposes of this subchapter, the term "section 306 stock" means stock which meets the requirements of subparagraph (A), (B), or (C) of this paragraph.

　　　　(A) DISTRIBUTED TO SELLER.—Stock (other than common stock issued with respect to common stock) which was distributed to the shareholder selling or otherwise disposing of such stock if, by reason of section 305 (a), any part of such distribution was not includible in the gross income of the shareholder.

　　　　(B) RECEIVED IN A CORPORATE REORGANIZATION OR SEPARATION.—Stock which is not common stock and—

　　　　　　(i) which was received, by the shareholder selling or otherwise disposing of such stock, in pursuance of a plan of reorganization (within the meaning of section 368 (a)), or in a distribution or exchange to which section 355 (or so much of section 356 as relates to section 355) applied, and

　　　　　　(ii) with respect to the receipt of which gain or loss to the shareholder was to any extent not recognized by reason of part III, but only to the extent that either the effect of the transaction was substantially the same as the receipt of a stock dividend, or the stock was received in exchange for section 306 stock.

For purposes of this section, a receipt of stock to which the foregoing provisions of this subparagraph apply shall be treated as a distribution of stock.

　　　　(C) STOCK HAVING TRANSFERRED OR SUBSTITUTED BASIS.—Except as otherwise provided in subparagraph (B), stock the basis of which (in the hands of the shareholder selling or otherwise disposing of such stock) is determined by reference to the basis (in the hands of such shareholder or any other person) of section 306 stock.

　　(2) EXCEPTION WHERE NO EARNINGS AND PROFITS.—For purposes of this section, the term "section 306 stock" does not include any stock no part of the distribution of which would have been a dividend at the time of the distribution if money had been distributed in lieu of the stock.

　　(3) CERTAIN STOCK ACQUIRED IN SECTION 351 EXCHANGE.—The term "section 306 stock" also includes any stock which is not common stock acquired in an exchange to which section 351 applied if

receipt of money (in lieu of the stock) would have been treated as a dividend to any extent. Rules similar to the rules of section 304(b)(2) shall apply—

(A) for purposes of the preceding sentence, and

(B) for purposes of determining the application of this section to any subsequent disposition of stock which is section 306 stock by reason of an exchange described in the preceding sentence.

(4) APPLICATION OF ATTRIBUTION RULES FOR CERTAIN PURPOSES.—For purposes of paragraphs (1)(B)(ii) and (3), section 318(a) shall apply. For purposes of applying the preceding sentence to paragraph (3), the rules of section 304(c)(3)(B) shall apply.

[Sec. 306(d)]

(d) STOCK RIGHTS.—For purposes of this section—

(1) stock rights shall be treated as stock, and

(2) stock acquired through the exercise of stock rights shall be treated as stock distributed at the time of the distribution of the stock rights, to the extent of the fair market value of such rights at the time of the distribution.

[Sec. 306(e)]

(e) CONVERTIBLE STOCK.—For purposes of subsection (c)—

(1) if section 306 stock was issued with respect to common stock and later such section 306 stock is exchanged for common stock in the same corporation (whether or not such exchange is pursuant to a conversion privilege contained in the section 306 stock), then (except as provided in paragraph (2)) the common stock so received shall not be treated as section 306 stock; and

(2) common stock with respect to which there is a privilege of converting into stock other than common stock (or into property), whether or not the conversion privilege is contained in such stock, shall not be treated as common stock.

[Sec. 306(f)]

(f) SOURCE OF GAIN.—The amount treated under subsection (a)(1)(A) as ordinary income shall, for purposes of part I of subchapter N (sec. 861 and following, relating to determination of sources of income), be treated as derived from the same source as would have been the source if money had been received from the corporation as a dividend at the time of the distribution of such stock. If under the preceding sentence such amount is determined to be derived from sources within the United States, such amount shall be considered to be fixed or determinable annual or periodical gains, profits, and income within the meaning of section 871 (a) or section 881 (a), as the case may be.

[Sec. 306(g)]

(g) CHANGE IN TERMS AND CONDITIONS OF STOCK.—If a substantial change is made in the terms and conditions of any stock, then, for purposes of this section—

(1) the fair market value of such stock shall be the fair market value at the time of the distribution or at the time of such change, whichever such value is higher;

(2) such stock's ratable share of the amount which would have been a dividend if money had been distributed in lieu of stock shall be determined as of the time of distribution or as of the time of such change, whichever such ratable share is higher; and

(3) subsection (c) (2) shall not apply unless the stock meets the requirements of such subsection both at the time of such distribution and at the time of such change.

[Sec. 307]

SEC. 307. BASIS OF STOCK AND STOCK RIGHTS ACQUIRED IN DISTRIBUTIONS.

[Sec. 307(a)]

(a) GENERAL RULE.—If a shareholder in a corporation receives its stock or rights to acquire its stock (referred to in this subsection as "new stock") in a distribution to which section 305 (a) applies, then the basis of such new stock and of the stock with respect to which it is distributed (referred to in this section as "old stock"), respectively, shall, in the shareholder's hands, be determined by allocating between the old stock and the new stock the adjusted basis of the old stock. Such allocation shall be made under regulations prescribed by the Secretary.

[Sec. 307(b)]

(b) EXCEPTION FOR CERTAIN STOCK RIGHTS.—

(1) IN GENERAL.—If—

(A) a corporation distributes rights to acquire its stock to a shareholder in a distribution to which section 305 (a) applies, and

(B) the fair market value of such rights at the time of the distribution is less than 15 percent of the fair market value of the old stock at such time,

then subsection (a) shall not apply and the basis of such rights shall be zero, unless the taxpayer elects under paragraph (2) of this subsection to determine the basis of the old stock and of the stock rights under the method of allocation provided in subsection (a).

(2) ELECTION.—The election referred to in paragraph (1) shall be made in the return filed within the time prescribed by law (including extensions thereof) for the taxable year in which such rights were received. Such election shall be made in such manner as the Secretary may by regulations prescribe, and shall be irrevocable when made.

* * *

Subpart B—Effects on Corporation

[Sec. 311]

SEC. 311. TAXABILITY OF CORPORATION ON DISTRIBUTION.

[Sec. 311(a)]

(a) GENERAL RULE.—Except as provided in subsection (b), no gain or loss shall be recognized to a corporation on the distribution (not in complete liquidation) with respect to its stock of—

(1) its stock (or rights to acquire its stock), or

(2) property.

[Sec. 311(b)]

(b) DISTRIBUTIONS OF APPRECIATED PROPERTY.—

(1) IN GENERAL.—If—

(A) a corporation distributes property (other than an obligation of such corporation) to a shareholder in a distribution to which subpart A applies, and

(B) the fair market value of such property exceeds its adjusted basis (in the hands of the distributing corporation),

then gain shall be recognized to the distributing corporation as if such property were sold to the distributee at its fair market value.

(2) TREATMENT OF LIABILITIES.—Rules similar to the rules of section 336(b) shall apply for purposes of this subsection.

(3) SPECIAL RULE FOR CERTAIN DISTRIBUTIONS OF PARTNERSHIP OR TRUST INTERESTS.—If the property distributed consists of an interest in a partnership or trust, the Secretary may by regulations provide that the amount of the gain recognized under paragraph (1) shall be computed without regard to any loss attributable to property contributed to the partnership or trust for the principal purpose of recognizing such loss on the distribution.

[Sec. 312]

SEC. 312. EFFECT ON EARNINGS AND PROFITS.

[Sec. 312(a)]

(a) GENERAL RULE.—Except as otherwise provided in this section, on the distribution of property by a corporation with respect to its stock, the earnings and profits of the corporation (to the extent thereof) shall be decreased by the sum of—

(1) the amount of money,

(2) the principal amount of the obligations of such corporation (or, in the case of obligations having original issue discount, the aggregate issue price of such obligations), and

(3) the adjusted basis of the other property,

so distributed.

[Sec. 312(b)]

(b) DISTRIBUTIONS OF APPRECIATED PROPERTY.—On the distribution by a corporation, with respect to its stock, of any property (other than an obligation of such corporation) the fair market value of which exceeds the adjusted basis thereof—

(1) the earnings and profits of the corporation shall be increased by the amount of such excess, and

(2) subsection (a)(3) shall be applied by substituting "fair market value" for "adjusted basis". For purposes of this subsection and subsection (a), the adjusted basis of any property is its adjusted basis as determined for purposes of computing earnings and profits.

[Sec. 312(c)]

(c) ADJUSTMENTS FOR LIABILITIES.—In making the adjustments to the earnings and profits of a corporation under subsection (a) or (b), proper adjustment shall be made for—

(1) the amount of any liability to which the property distributed is subject, and

(2) the amount of any liability of the corporation assumed by a shareholder in connection with the distribution.

[Sec. 312(d)]

(d) CERTAIN DISTRIBUTIONS OF STOCK AND SECURITIES.—

(1) IN GENERAL.—The distribution to a distributee by or on behalf of a corporation of its stock or securities, of stock or securities in another corporation, or of property, in a distribution to which this title applies, shall not be considered a distribution of the earnings and profits of any corporation—

(A) if no gain to such distributee from the receipt of such stock or securities, or property, was recognized under this title, or

(B) if the distribution was not subject to tax in the hands of such distributee by reason of section 305 (a).

(2) PRIOR DISTRIBUTIONS.—In the case of a distribution of stock or securities, or property, to which section 115 (h) of the Internal Revenue Code of 1939 (or the corresponding provision of prior law) applied, the effect on earnings and profits of such distribution shall be determined under such section 115 (h), or the corresponding provision of prior law, as the case may be.

(3) STOCK OR SECURITIES.—For purposes of this subsection, the term "stock or securities" includes rights to acquire stock or securities.

[Sec. 312(e)—Repealed]

[Sec. 312(f)]

(f) EFFECT ON EARNINGS AND PROFITS OF GAIN OR LOSS AND OF RECEIPT OF TAX-FREE DISTRIBUTIONS.—

(1) EFFECT ON EARNINGS AND PROFITS OF GAIN OR LOSS.—The gain or loss realized from the sale or other disposition (after February 28, 1913) of property by a corporation—

(A) for the purpose of the computation of the earnings and profits of the corporation, shall (except as provided in subparagraph (B)) be determined by using as the adjusted basis the adjusted basis (under the law applicable to the year in which the sale or other disposition was made) for determining gain, except that no regard shall be had to the value of the property as of March 1, 1913; but

(B) for purposes of the computation of the earnings and profits of the corporation for any period beginning after February 28, 1913, shall be determined by using as the adjusted basis the adjusted basis (under the law applicable to the year in which the sale or other disposition was made) for determining gain.

Gain or loss so realized shall increase or decrease the earnings and profits to, but not beyond, the extent to which such a realized gain or loss was recognized in computing taxable income under the law applicable to the year in which such sale or disposition was made. Where, in determining the adjusted basis used in computing such realized gain or loss, the adjustment to the basis differs from the adjustment proper for the purpose of determining earnings and profits, then the latter adjustment shall be used in determining the increase or decrease above provided. For purposes of this subsection, a loss with respect to which a deduction is disallowed under section 1091 (relating to wash sales of stock or securities), or the corresponding provision of prior law, shall not be deemed to be recognized.

(2) EFFECT ON EARNINGS AND PROFITS OF RECEIPT OF TAX-FREE DISTRIBUTIONS.—Where a corporation receives (after February 28, 1913) a distribution from a second corporation which (under the law applicable to the year in which the distribution was made) was not a taxable dividend to the shareholders of the second corporation, the amount of such distribution shall not increase the earnings and profits of the first corporation in the following cases:

(A) no such increase shall be made in respect of the part of such distribution which (under such law) is directly applied in reduction of the basis of the stock in respect of which the distribution was made; and

(B) no such increase shall be made if (under such law) the distribution causes the basis of the stock in respect of which the distribution was made to be allocated between such stock and the property received (or such basis would, but for section 307 (b), be so allocated).

[Sec. 312(g)]

(g) EARNINGS AND PROFITS—INCREASE IN VALUE ACCRUED BEFORE MARCH 1, 1913.—

(1) If any increase or decrease in the earnings and profits for any period beginning after February 28, 1913, with respect to any matter would be different had the adjusted basis of the property involved been determined without regard to its March 1, 1913, value, then, except as provided in paragraph (2), an increase (properly reflecting such difference) shall be made in that part of the earnings and profits consisting of increase in value of property accrued before March 1, 1913.

(2) If the application of subsection (f) to a sale or other disposition after February 28, 1913, results in a loss which is to be applied in decrease of earnings and profits for any period beginning after February 28, 1913, then, notwithstanding subsection (f) and in lieu of the rule provided in paragraph (1) of this subsection, the amount of such loss so to be applied shall be reduced by the amount, if any, by which the adjusted basis of the property used in determining the loss exceeds the adjusted basis computed without regard to the value of the property on March 1, 1913, and if such amount so applied in reduction of the decrease exceeds such loss, the excess over such loss shall increase that part of the earnings and profits consisting of increase in value of property accrued before March 1, 1913.

[Sec. 312(h)]

(h) ALLOCATION IN CERTAIN CORPORATE SEPARATIONS AND REORGANIZATIONS.—

(1) SECTION 355.—In the case of a distribution or exchange to which section 355 (or so much of section 356 as relates to section 355) applies, proper allocation with respect to the earnings and profits of the distributing corporation and the controlled corporation (or corporations) shall be made under regulations prescribed by the Secretary.

(2) SECTION 368(a)(1)(C) OR (D).—In the case of a reorganization described in subparagraph (C) or (D) of section 368(a)(1), proper allocation with respect to the earnings and profits of the acquired corporation shall, under regulations prescribed by the Secretary, be made between the acquiring corporation and the acquired corporation (or any corporation which had control of the acquired corporation before the reorganization).

[Sec. 312(i)]

(i) DISTRIBUTION OF PROCEEDS OF LOAN INSURED BY THE UNITED STATES.—If a corporation distributes property with respect to its stock and if, at the time of distribution—

(1) there is outstanding a loan to such corporation which was made, guaranteed, or insured by the United States (or by any agency or instrumentality thereof), and

(2) the amount of such loan so outstanding exceeds the adjusted basis of the property constituting security for such loan,

then the earnings and profits of the corporation shall be increased by the amount of such excess, and (immediately after the distribution) shall be decreased by the amount of such excess. For purposes of paragraph (2), the adjusted basis of the property at the time of distribution shall be determined without regard to any adjustment under section 1016(a)(2) (relating to adjustment for depreciation, etc.). For purposes of this subsection, a commitment to make, guarantee, or insure a loan shall be treated as the making, guaranteeing, or insuring of a loan.

* * *

[Sec. 312(k)]

(k) EFFECT OF DEPRECIATION ON EARNINGS AND PROFITS.—

(1) GENERAL RULE.—For purposes of computing the earnings and profits of a corporation for any taxable year beginning after June 30, 1972, the allowance for depreciation (and amortization, if any) shall be deemed to be the amount which would be allowable for such year if the straight line method of depreciation had been used for each taxable year beginning after June 30, 1972.

(2) EXCEPTION.—If for any taxable year a method of depreciation was used by the taxpayer which the Secretary has determined results in a reasonable allowance under section 167(a) and which is the unit-of-production method or other method not expressed in a term of years, then the adjustment to earnings and profits for depreciation for such year shall be determined under the method so used (in lieu of the straight line method).

(3) EXCEPTION FOR TANGIBLE PROPERTY.—

(A) IN GENERAL.—Except as provided in subparagraph (B), in the case of tangible property to which section 168 applies, the adjustment to earnings and profits for depreciation for any taxable year shall be determined under the alternative depreciation system (within the meaning of section 168(g)(2)).

(B) TREATMENT OF AMOUNTS DEDUCTIBLE UNDER SECTION 179 OR 179A.—For purposes of computing the earnings and profits of a corporation, any amount deductible under section 179 or 179A shall be allowed as a deduction ratably over the period of 5 taxable years (beginning with the taxable year for which such amount is deductible under section 179 or 179A, as the case may be).

(4) CERTAIN FOREIGN CORPORATIONS.—The provisions of paragraph (1) shall not apply in computing the earnings and profits of a foreign corporation for any taxable year for which less than 20 percent of the gross income from all sources of such corporation is derived from sources within the United States.

(5) BASIS ADJUSTMENT NOT TAKEN INTO ACCOUNT.—In computing the earnings and profits of a corporation for any taxable year, the allowance for depreciation (and amortization, if any) shall be computed without regard to any basis adjustment under section 50(c).

[Sec. 312(l)]

(l) DISCHARGE OF INDEBTEDNESS INCOME.—

(1) DOES NOT INCREASE EARNINGS AND PROFITS IF APPLIED TO REDUCE BASIS.—The earnings and profits of a corporation shall not include income from the discharge of indebtedness to the extent of the amount applied to reduce basis under section 1017.

(2) REDUCTION OF DEFICIT IN EARNINGS AND PROFITS IN CERTAIN CASES.—If—

(A) the interest of any shareholder of a corporation is terminated or extinguished in a title 11 or similar case (within the meaning of section 368(a)(3)(A)), and

(B) there is a deficit in the earnings and profits of the corporation,

then such deficit shall be reduced by an amount equal to the paid-in capital which is allocable to the interest of the shareholder which is so terminated or extinguished.

[Sec. 312(m)]

(m) NO ADJUSTMENT FOR INTEREST PAID ON CERTAIN REGISTRATION-REQUIRED OBLIGATIONS NOT IN REGISTERED FORM.—The earnings and profits of any corporation shall not be decreased by any interest with respect to which a deduction is not or would not be allowable by reason of section 163(f), unless at the time of issuance the issuer is a foreign corporation that is not a controlled foreign corporation (within the meaning of section 957), a foreign investment company (within the meaning of section 1246(b)), or a foreign personal holding company (within the meaning of section 552) and the issuance did not have as a purpose the avoidance of section 163(f) of this subsection.

[Sec. 312(n)]

(n) ADJUSTMENTS TO EARNINGS AND PROFITS TO MORE ACCURATELY REFLECT ECONOMIC GAIN AND LOSS.—For purposes of computing the earnings and profits of a corporation, the following adjustments shall be made:

(1) CONSTRUCTION PERIOD CARRYING CHARGES.—

(A) IN GENERAL.—In the case of any amount paid or incurred for construction period carrying charges—

(i) no deduction shall be allowed with respect to such amount, and

(ii) the basis of the property with respect to which such charges are allocable shall be increased by such amount.

(B) CONSTRUCTION PERIOD CARRYING CHARGES DEFINED.—For purposes of this paragraph, the term "construction period carrying charges" means all—

(i) interest paid or accrued on indebtedness incurred or continued to acquire, construct, or carry property,

(ii) property taxes, and

(iii) similar carrying charges,

to the extent such interest, taxes, or charges are attributable to the construction period for such property and would be allowable as a deduction in determining taxable income under this chapter for the taxable year in which paid or incurred.

(C) CONSTRUCTION PERIOD.—The term "construction period" has the meaning given the term production period under section 263A(f)(4)(B).

(2) INTANGIBLE DRILLING COSTS AND MINERAL EXPLORATION AND DEVELOPMENT COSTS.—

(A) INTANGIBLE DRILLING COSTS.—Any amount allowable as a deduction under section 263(c) in determining taxable income (other than costs incurred in connection with a nonproductive well)—

(i) shall be capitalized, and

(ii) shall be allowed as a deduction ratably over the 60-month period beginning with the month in which such amount was paid or incurred.

(B) MINERAL EXPLORATION AND DEVELOPMENT COSTS.—Any amount allowable as a deduction under section 616(a) or 617 in determining taxable income—

(i) shall be capitalized, and

(ii) shall be allowed as a deduction ratably over the 120-month period beginning with the later of—

(I) the month in which production from the deposit begins, or

(II) the month in which such amount was paid or incurred.

(3) CERTAIN AMORTIZATION PROVISIONS NOT TO APPLY.—Sections 173 and 248 shall not apply.

(4) LIFO INVENTORY ADJUSTMENTS.—

(A) IN GENERAL.—Earnings and profits shall be increased or decreased by the amount of any increase or decrease in the LIFO recapture amount as of the close of each taxable year; except that any decrease below the LIFO recapture amount as of the close of the taxable year preceding the 1st taxable year to which this paragraph applies to the taxpayer shall be taken into account only to the extent provided in regulations prescribed by the Secretary.

(B) LIFO RECAPTURE AMOUNT.—For purposes of this paragraph, the term "LIFO recapture amount" means the amount (if any) by which—

(i) the inventory amount of the inventory assets under the first-in, first-out method authorized by section 471, exceeds

(ii) the inventory amount of such assets under the LIFO method.

(C) DEFINITIONS.—For purposes of this paragraph—

    (i) LIFO METHOD.—The term "LIFO method" means the method authorized by section 472 (relating to last-in, first-out inventories).

    (ii) INVENTORY ASSETS.—The term "inventory assets" means stock in trade of the corporation, or other property of a kind which would properly be included in the inventory of the corporation if on hand at the close of the taxable year.

    (iii) INVENTORY AMOUNT.—The inventory amount of assets under the first-in, first-out method authorized by section 471 shall be determined—

        (I) if the corporation uses the retail method of valuing inventories under section 472, by using such method, or

        (II) if subclause (I) does not apply, by using cost or market, whichever is lower.

(5) INSTALLMENT SALES.—In the case of any installment sale, earnings and profits shall be computed as if the corporation did not use the installment method.

(6) COMPLETED CONTRACT METHOD OF ACCOUNTING.—In the case of a taxpayer who uses the completed contract method of accounting, earnings and profits shall be computed as if such taxpayer used the percentage of completion method of accounting.

(7) REDEMPTIONS.—If a corporation distributes amounts in a redemption to which section 302(a) or 303 applies, the part of such distribution which is properly chargeable to earnings and profits shall be an amount which is not in excess of the ratable share of the earnings and profits of such corporation accumulated after February 28, 1913, attributable to the stock so redeemed.

* * *

Subpart C—Definitions; Constructive Ownership of Stock

[Sec. 316]

SEC. 316. DIVIDEND DEFINED.

[Sec. 316(a)]

(a) GENERAL RULE.—For purposes of this subtitle, the term "dividend" means any distribution of property made by a corporation to its shareholders—

(1) out of its earnings and profits accumulated after February 28, 1913, or

(2) out of its earnings and profits of the taxable year (computed as of the close of the taxable year without diminution by reason of any distributions made during the taxable year), without regard to the amount of the earnings and profits at the time the distribution was made.

Except as otherwise provided in this subtitle, every distribution is made out of earnings and profits to the extent thereof, and from the most recently accumulated earnings and profits. To the extent that any distribution is, under any provision of this subchapter, treated as a distribution of property to which section 301 applies, such distribution shall be treated as a distribution of property for purposes of this subsection.

* * *

[Sec. 317]

SEC. 317. OTHER DEFINITIONS.

[Sec. 317(a)]

(a) PROPERTY.—For purposes of this part, the term "property" means money, securities, and any other property; except that such term does not include stock in the corporation making the distribution (or rights to acquire such stock).

[Sec. 317(b)]

(b) REDEMPTION OF STOCK.—For purposes of this part, stock shall be treated as redeemed by a corporation if the corporation acquires its stock from a shareholder in exchange for property, whether or not the stock so acquired is cancelled, retired, or held as treasury stock.

[Sec. 318]

SEC. 318. CONSTRUCTIVE OWNERSHIP OF STOCK.

[Sec. 318(a)]

(a) GENERAL RULE.—For purposes of those provisions of this subchapter to which the rules contained in this section are expressly made applicable—

(1) MEMBERS OF FAMILY.—

(A) IN GENERAL.—An individual shall be considered as owning the stock owned, directly or indirectly, by or for—

(i) his spouse (other than a spouse who is legally separated from the individual under a decree of divorce or separate maintenance), and

(ii) his children, grandchildren, and parents.

(B) EFFECT OF ADOPTION.—For purposes of subparagraph (A) (ii), a legally adopted child of an individual shall be treated as a child of such individual by blood.

(2) ATTRIBUTION FROM PARTNERSHIPS, ESTATES, TRUSTS, AND CORPORATIONS.—

(A) FROM PARTNERSHIPS AND ESTATES.—Stock owned, directly or indirectly, by or for a partnership or estate shall be considered as owned proportionately by its partners or beneficiaries.

(B) FROM TRUSTS.—

(i) Stock owned, directly or indirectly, by or for a trust (other than an employees' trust described in section 401(a) which is exempt from tax under section 501(a)) shall be considered as owned by its beneficiaries in proportion to the actuarial interest of such beneficiaries in such trust.

(ii) Stock owned, directly or indirectly, by or for any portion of a trust of which a person is considered the owner under subpart E of part I of subchapter J (relating to grantors and others treated as substantial owners) shall be considered as owned by such person.

(C) FROM CORPORATIONS.—If 50 percent or more in value of the stock in a corporation is owned, directly or indirectly, by or for any person, such person shall be considered as owning the stock owned, directly or indirectly, by or for such corporation, in that proportion which the value of the stock which such person so owns bears to the value of all the stock in such corporation.

(3) ATTRIBUTION TO PARTNERSHIPS, ESTATES, TRUSTS, AND CORPORATIONS.—

(A) TO PARTNERSHIPS AND ESTATES.—Stock owned, directly or indirectly, by or for a partner or a beneficiary of an estate shall be considered as owned by the partnership or estate.

(B) TO TRUSTS.—

(i) Stock owned, directly or indirectly, by or for a beneficiary of a trust (other than an employees' trust described in section 401(a) which is exempt from tax under section 501 (a)) shall be considered as owned by the trust, unless such beneficiary's interest in the trust is a remote contingent interest. For purposes of this clause, a contingent interest of a beneficiary in a trust shall be considered remote if, under the maximum exercise of discretion by the trustee in favor of such beneficiary, the value of such interest, computed actuarially, is 5 percent or less of the value of the trust property.

(ii) Stock owned, directly or indirectly, by or for a person who is considered the owner of any portion of a trust under subpart E of part I of subchapter J (relating to grantors and others treated as substantial owners) shall be considered as owned by the trust.

(C) TO CORPORATIONS.—If 50 percent or more in value of the stock in a corporation is owned, directly or indirectly, by or for any person, such corporation shall be considered as owning the stock owned, directly or indirectly, by or for such person.

(4) OPTIONS.—If any person has an option to acquire stock, such stock shall be considered as owned by such person. For purposes of this paragraph, an option to acquire such an option, and each one of a series of such options, shall be considered as an option to acquire such stock.

(5) OPERATING RULES.—

(A) IN GENERAL.—Except as provided in subparagraphs (B) and (C), stock constructively owned by a person by reason of the application of paragraph (1), (2), (3), or (4), shall, for purposes of applying paragraphs (1), (2), (3), and (4), be considered as actually owned by such person.

(B) MEMBERS OF FAMILY.—Stock constructively owned by an individual by reason of the application of paragraph (1) shall not be considered as owned by him for purposes of again applying paragraph (1) in order to make another the constructive owner of such stock.

(C) PARTNERSHIPS, ESTATES, TRUSTS, AND CORPORATIONS.—Stock constructively owned by a partnership, estate, trust, or corporation by reason of the application of paragraph (3) shall not be considered as owned by it for purposes of applying paragraph (2) in order to make another the constructive owner of such stock.

(D) OPTION RULE IN LIEU OF FAMILY RULE.—For purposes of this paragraph, if stock may be considered as owned by an individual under paragraph (1) or (4), it shall be considered as owned by him under paragraph (4).

(E) S CORPORATION TREATED AS PARTNERSHIP.—For purposes of this subsection—

(i) an S corporation shall be treated as a partnership, and

(ii) any shareholder of the S corporation shall be treated as a partner of such partnership.

The preceding sentence shall not apply for purposes of determining whether stock in the S corporation is constructively owned by any person.

[Sec. 318(b)]

(b) CROSS REFERENCES.—

For provisions to which the rules contained in subsection (a) apply, see—

(1) section 302 (relating to redemption of stock);

(2) section 304 (relating to redemption by related corporations);

(3) section 306 (b) (1) (A) (relating to disposition of section 306 stock);

(4) section 338(h)(3) (defining purchase);

(5) section 382(l)(3) (relating to special limitations on net operating loss carryovers);

* * *

PART II—CORPORATE LIQUIDATIONS

Subpart A—Effects on Recipients

[Sec. 331]

SEC. 331. GAIN OR LOSS TO SHAREHOLDERS IN CORPORATE LIQUIDATIONS.

[Sec. 331(a)]

(a) DISTRIBUTIONS IN COMPLETE LIQUIDATION TREATED AS EXCHANGES.—Amounts received by a shareholder in a distribution in complete liquidation of a corporation shall be treated as in full payment in exchange for the stock.

[Sec. 331(b)]

(b) NONAPPLICATION OF SECTION 301.—Section 301 (relating to effects on shareholder of distributions of property) shall not apply to any distribution of property (other than a distribution referred to in paragraph (2)(B) of section 316(b)), in complete liquidation.

* * *

[Sec. 332]

SEC. 332. COMPLETE LIQUIDATIONS OF SUBSIDIARIES.

[Sec. 332(a)]

(a) GENERAL RULE.—No gain or loss shall be recognized on the receipt by a corporation of property distributed in complete liquidation of another corporation.

Sec. 332(a)

(b) LIQUIDATIONS TO WHICH SECTION APPLIES.—For purposes of this section, a distribution shall be considered to be in complete liquidation only if—

(1) the corporation receiving such property was, on the date of the adoption of the plan of liquidation, and has continued to be at all times until the receipt of the property, the owner of stock (in such other corporation) meeting the requirements of section 1504(a)(2); and either

(2) the distribution is by such other corporation in complete cancellation or redemption of all its stock, and the transfer of all the property occurs within the taxable year; in such case the adoption by the shareholders of the resolution under which is authorized the distribution of all the assets of such corporation in complete cancellation or redemption of all its stock shall be considered an adoption of a plan of liquidation, even though no time for the completion of the transfer of the property is specified in such resolution; or

(3) such distribution is one of a series of distributions by such other corporation in complete cancellation or redemption of all its stock in accordance with a plan of liquidation under which the transfer of all the property under the liquidation is to be completed within 3 years from the close of the taxable year during which is made the first of the series of distributions under the plan, except that if such transfer is not completed within such period, or if the taxpayer does not continue qualified under paragraph (1) until the completion of such transfer, no distribution under the plan shall be considered a distribution in complete liquidation.

If such transfer of all the property does not occur within the taxable year, the Secretary may require of the taxpayer such bond, or waiver of the statute of limitations on assessment and collection, or both, as he may deem necessary to insure, if the transfer of the property is not completed within such 3-year period, or if the taxpayer does not continue qualified under paragraph (1) until the completion of such transfer, the assessment and collection of all income taxes then imposed by law for such taxable year or subsequent taxable years, to the extent attributable to property so received. A distribution otherwise constituting a distribution in complete liquidation within the meaning of this subsection shall not be considered as not constituting such a distribution merely because it does not constitute a distribution or liquidation within the meaning of the corporate law under which the distribution is made; and for purposes of this subsection a transfer of property of such other corporation to the taxpayer shall not be considered as not constituting a distribution (or one of a series of distributions) in complete cancellation or redemption of all the stock of such other corporation, merely because the carrying out of the plan involves (A) the transfer under the plan to the taxpayer by such other corporation of property, not attributable to shares owned by the taxpayer, on an exchange described in section 361, and (B) the complete cancellation or redemption under the plan, as a result of exchanges described in section 354, of the shares not owned by the taxpayer.

(c) DEDUCTIBLE LIQUIDATING DISTRIBUTIONS OF REGULATED INVESTMENT COMPANIES AND REAL ESTATE INVESTMENT TRUSTS.—If a corporation receives a distribution from a regulated investment company or a real estate investment trust which is considered under subsection (b) as being in complete liquidation of such company or trust, then, notwithstanding any other provision of this chapter, such corporation shall recognize and treat as a dividend from such company or trust an amount equal to the deduction for dividends paid allowable to such company or trust by reason of such distribution.

SEC. 334. BASIS OF PROPERTY RECEIVED IN LIQUIDATIONS.

(a) GENERAL RULE.—If property is received in a distribution in complete liquidation, and if gain or loss is recognized on receipt of such property, then the basis of the property in the hands of the distributee shall be the fair market value of such property at the time of the distribution.

(b) LIQUIDATION OF SUBSIDIARY.—

(1) IN GENERAL.—If property is received by a corporate distributee in a distribution in a complete liquidation to which section 332 applies (or in a transfer described in section 337(b)(1)), the basis of such property in the hands of such distributee shall be the same as it would be in the hands of the transferor; except that, in any case in which gain or loss is recognized by the liquidating

corporation with respect to such property, the basis of such property in the hands of such distributee shall be the fair market value of the property at the time of the distribution.

(2) CORPORATE DISTRIBUTEE.—For purposes of this subsection, the term "corporate distributee" means only the corporation which meets the stock ownership requirements specified in section 332(b).

Subpart B—Effects on Corporation

[Sec. 336]

SEC. 336. GAIN OR LOSS RECOGNIZED ON PROPERTY DISTRIBUTED IN COMPLETE LIQUIDATION.

[Sec. 336(a)]

(a) GENERAL RULE.—Except as otherwise provided in this section or section 337, gain or loss shall be recognized to a liquidating corporation on the distribution of property in complete liquidation as if such property were sold to the distributee at its fair market value.

[Sec. 336(b)]

(b) TREATMENT OF LIABILITIES.—If any property distributed in the liquidation is subject to a liability or the shareholder assumes a liability of the liquidating corporation in connection with the distribution, for purposes of subsection (a) and section 337, the fair market value of such property shall be treated as not less than the amount of such liability.

[Sec. 336(c)]

(c) EXCEPTION FOR LIQUIDATIONS WHICH ARE PART OF A REORGANIZATION.—For provision providing that this subpart does not apply to distributions in pursuance of a plan of reorganization, see section 361(c)(4).

[Sec. 336(d)]

(d) LIMITATIONS ON RECOGNITION OF LOSS.—

(1) NO LOSS RECOGNIZED IN CERTAIN DISTRIBUTIONS TO RELATED PERSONS.—

(A) IN GENERAL.—No loss shall be recognized to a liquidating corporation on the distribution of any property to a related person (within the meaning of section 267) if—

(i) such distribution is not pro rata, or

(ii) such property is disqualified property.

(B) DISQUALIFIED PROPERTY.—For purposes of subparagraph (A), the term "disqualified property" means any property which is acquired by the liquidating corporation in a transaction to which section 351 applied, or as a contribution to capital, during the 5-year period ending on the date of the distribution. Such term includes any property if the adjusted basis of such property is determined (in whole or in part) by reference to the adjusted basis of property described in the preceding sentence.

(2) SPECIAL RULE FOR CERTAIN PROPERTY ACQUIRED IN CERTAIN CARRYOVER BASIS TRANSACTIONS.—

(A) IN GENERAL.—For purposes of determining the amount of loss recognized by any liquidating corporation on any sale, exchange, or distribution of property described in subparagraph (B), the adjusted basis of such property shall be reduced (but not below zero) by the excess (if any) of—

(i) the adjusted basis of such property immediately after its acquisition by such corporation, over

(ii) the fair market value of such property as of such time.

(B) DESCRIPTION OF PROPERTY.—

(i) IN GENERAL.—For purposes of subparagraph (A), property is described in this subparagraph if—

(I) such property is acquired by the liquidating corporation in a transaction to which section 351 applied or as a contribution to capital, and

Sec. 336(d)

(II) the acquisition of such property by the liquidating corporation was part of a plan a principal purpose of which was to recognize loss by the liquidating corporation with respect to such property in connection with the liquidation.

Other property shall be treated as so described if the adjusted basis of such other property is determined (in whole or in part) by reference to the adjusted basis of property described in the preceding sentence.

(ii) CERTAIN ACQUISITIONS TREATED AS PART OF PLAN.—For purposes of clause (i), any property described in clause (i)(I) acquired by the liquidated corporation after the date 2 years before the date of the adoption of the plan of complete liquidation shall, except as provided in regulations, be treated as acquired as part of a plan described in clause (i)(II).

(C) RECAPTURE IN LIEU OF DISALLOWANCE.—The Secretary may prescribe regulations under which, in lieu of disallowing a loss under subparagraph (A) for a prior taxable year, the gross income of the liquidating corporation for the taxable year in which the plan of complete liquidation is adopted shall be increased by the amount of the disallowed loss.

(3) SPECIAL RULE IN CASE OF LIQUIDATION TO WHICH SECTION 332 APPLIES.—In the case of any liquidation to which section 332 applies, no loss shall be recognized to the liquidating corporation on any distribution in such liquidation. The preceding sentence shall apply to any distribution to the 80-percent distributee only if subsection (a) or (b)(1) of section 337 applies to such distribution.

[Sec. 336(e)]

(e) CERTAIN STOCK SALES AND DISTRIBUTIONS MAY BE TREATED AS ASSET TRANSFERS.—Under regulations prescribed by the Secretary, if—

(1) a corporation owns stock in another corporation meeting the requirements of section 1504(a)(2), and

(2) such corporation sells, exchanges, or distributes all of such stock,

an election may be made to treat such sale, exchange, or distribution as a disposition of all of the assets of such other corporation, and no gain or loss shall be recognized on the sale, exchange, or distribution of such stock.

[Sec. 337]

SEC. 337. NONRECOGNITION FOR PROPERTY DISTRIBUTED TO PARENT IN COMPLETE LIQUIDATION OF SUBSIDIARY.

[Sec. 337(a)]

(a) IN GENERAL.—No gain or loss shall be recognized to the liquidating corporation on the distribution to the 80-percent distributee of any property in a complete liquidation to which section 332 applies.

[Sec. 337(b)]

(b) TREATMENT OF INDEBTEDNESS OF SUBSIDIARY, ETC.—

(1) INDEBTEDNESS OF SUBSIDIARY TO PARENT.—If—

(A) a corporation is liquidated in a liquidation to which section 332 applies, and

(B) on the date of the adoption of the plan of liquidation, such corporation was indebted to the 80-percent distributee.

for purposes of this section and section 336, any transfer of property to the 80-percent distributee in satisfaction of such indebtedness shall be treated as a distribution to such distributee in such liquidation.

* * *

[Sec. 337(c)]

(c) 80-PERCENT DISTRIBUTEE.—For purposes of this section, the term "80-percent distributee" means only the corporation which meets the 80-percent stock ownership requirements specified in section 332(b). For purposes of this section, the determination of whether any corporation is an 80-percent distributee shall be made without regard to any consolidated return regulation.

* * *

[Sec. 338]

SEC. 338. CERTAIN STOCK PURCHASES TREATED AS ASSET ACQUISITIONS.

[Sec. 338(a)]

(a) GENERAL RULE.—For purposes of this subtitle, if a purchasing corporation makes an election under this section (or is treated under subsection (e) as having made such an election), then, in the case of any qualified stock purchase, the target corporation—

(1) shall be treated as having sold all of its assets at the close of the acquisition date at fair market value in a single transaction, and

(2) shall be treated as a new corporation which purchased all of the assets referred to in paragraph (1) as of the beginning of the day after the acquisition date.

[Sec. 338(b)]

(b) BASIS OF ASSETS AFTER DEEMED PURCHASE.—

(1) IN GENERAL.—For purposes of subsection (a), the assets of the target corporation shall be treated as purchased for an amount equal to the sum of—

(A) the grossed-up basis of the purchasing corporation's recently purchased stock, and

(B) the basis of the purchasing corporation's nonrecently purchased stock.

(2) ADJUSTMENT FOR LIABILITIES AND OTHER RELEVANT ITEMS.—The amount described in paragraph (1) shall be adjusted under regulations prescribed by the Secretary for liabilities of the target corporation and other relevant items.

(3) ELECTION TO STEP-UP THE BASIS OF CERTAIN TARGET STOCK.—

(A) IN GENERAL.—Under regulations prescribed by the Secretary, the basis of the purchasing corporation's nonrecently purchased stock shall be the basis amount determined under subparagraph (B) of this paragraph if the purchasing corporation makes an election to recognize gain as if such stock were sold on the acquisition date for an amount equal to the basis amount determined under subparagraph (B).

(B) DETERMINATION OF BASIS AMOUNT.—For purposes of subparagraph (A), the basis amount determined under this subparagraph shall be an amount equal to the grossed-up basis determined under subparagraph (A) of paragraph (1) multiplied by a fraction—

(i) the numerator of which is the percentage of stock (by value) in the target corporation attributable to the purchasing corporation's nonrecently purchased stock, and

(ii) the denominator of which is 100 percent minus the percentage referred to in clause (i).

(4) GROSSED-UP BASIS.—For purposes of paragraph (1), the grossed-up basis shall be an amount equal to the basis of the corporation's recently purchased stock, multiplied by a fraction—

(A) the numerator of which is 100 percent, minus the percentage of stock (by value) in the target corporation attributable to the purchasing corporation's nonrecently purchased stock, and

(B) the denominator of which is the percentage of stock (by value) in the target corporation attributable to the purchasing corporation's recently purchased stock.

(5) ALLOCATION AMONG ASSETS.—The amount determined under paragraphs (1) and (2) shall be allocated among the assets of the target corporation under regulations prescribed by the Secretary.

(6) DEFINITIONS OF RECENTLY PURCHASED STOCK AND NONRECENTLY PURCHASED STOCK.—For purposes of this subsection—

(A) RECENTLY PURCHASED STOCK.—The term "recently purchased stock" means any stock in the target corporation which is held by the purchasing corporation on the acquisition date and which was purchased by such corporation during the 12-month acquisition period.

(B) NONRECENTLY PURCHASED STOCK.—The term "nonrecently purchased stock" means any stock in the target corporation which is held by the purchasing corporation on the acquisition date and which is not recently purchased stock.

Sec. 338(b)

(d) PURCHASING CORPORATION; TARGET CORPORATION; QUALIFIED STOCK PURCHASE.—For purposes of this section—

(1) PURCHASING CORPORATION.—The term "purchasing corporation" means any corporation which makes a qualified stock purchase of stock of another corporation.

(2) TARGET CORPORATION.—The term "target corporation" means any corporation the stock of which is acquired by another corporation in a qualified stock purchase.

(3) QUALIFIED STOCK PURCHASE.—The term "qualified stock purchase" means any transaction or series of transactions in which stock (meeting the requirements of section 1504(a)(2)) of 1 corporation is acquired by another corporation by purchase during the 12-month acquisition period.

(e) DEEMED ELECTION WHERE PURCHASING CORPORATION ACQUIRES ASSET OF TARGET CORPORATION.—

(1) IN GENERAL.—A purchasing corporation shall be treated as having made an election under this section with respect to any target corporation if, at any time during the consistency period, it acquires any asset of the target corporation (or a target affiliate).

(2) EXCEPTIONS.—Paragraph (1) shall not apply with respect to any acquisition by the purchasing corporation if—

(A) such acquisition is pursuant to a sale by the target corporation (or the target affiliate) in the ordinary course of its trade or business,

(B) the basis of the property acquired is determined (wholly) by reference to the adjusted basis of such property in the hands of the person from whom acquired,

(C) such acquisition was before September 1, 1982, or

(D) such acquisition is described in regulations prescribed by the Secretary and meets such conditions as such regulations may provide.

(3) ANTI-AVOIDANCE RULE.—Whenever necessary to carry out the purpose of this subsection and subsection (f), the Secretary may treat stock acquisitions which are pursuant to a plan and which meet the requirements of section 1504(a)(2) as qualified stock purchases.

(f) CONSISTENCY REQUIRED FOR ALL STOCK ACQUISITIONS FROM SAME AFFILIATED GROUP.—If a purchasing corporation makes qualified stock purchases with respect to the target corporation and 1 or more target affiliates during any consistency period, then (except as otherwise provided in subsection (e))—

(1) any election under this section with respect to the first such purchase shall apply to each other such purchase, and

(2) no election may be made under this section with respect to the second or subsequent such purchase if such an election was not made with respect to the first such purchase.

(g) ELECTION.—

(1) WHEN MADE.—Except as otherwise provided in regulations, an election under this section shall be made not later than the 15th day of the 9th month, beginning after the month in which the acquisition date occurs.

(2) MANNER.—An election by the purchasing corporation under this section shall be made in such manner as the Secretary shall by regulations prescribe.

(3) ELECTION IRREVOCABLE.—An election by a purchasing corporation under this section, once made, shall be irrevocable.

(h) DEFINITIONS AND SPECIAL RULES.—For purposes of this section—

(1) 12-MONTH ACQUISITION PERIOD.—The term "12-month acquisition period" means the 12-month period beginning with the date of the first acquisition by purchase of stock included in a qualified stock purchase (or, if any of such stock was acquired in an acquisition which is a purchase

by reason of subparagraph (C) of paragraph (3), the date on which the acquiring corporation is first considered under section 318(a) (other than paragraph (4) thereof) as owning stock owned by the corporation from which such acquisition was made).

(2) ACQUISITION DATE.—The term "acquisition date" means, with respect to any corporation, the first day on which there is a qualified stock purchase with respect to the stock of such corporation.

(3) PURCHASE.—

(A) IN GENERAL.—The term "purchase" means any acquisition of stock, but only if—

(i) the basis of the stock in the hands of the purchasing corporation is not determined (I) in whole or in part by reference to the adjusted basis of such stock in the hands of the person from whom acquired, or (II) under section 1014(a) (relating to property acquired from a decedent),

(ii) the stock is not acquired in an exchange to which section 351, 354, 355, or 356 applies and is not acquired in any other transaction described in regulations in which the transferor does not recognize the entire amount of the gain or loss realized on the transaction, and

(iii) the stock is not acquired from a person the ownership of whose stock would, under section 318(a) (other than paragraph (4) thereof), be attributed to the person acquiring such stock.

(B) DEEMED PURCHASE UNDER SUBSECTION (a).—The term "purchase" includes any deemed purchase under subsection (a)(2). The acquisition date for a corporation which is deemed purchased under subsection (a)(2) shall be determined under regulations prescribed by the Secretary. SM05 00 wrap is set at 60

(C) CERTAIN STOCK ACQUISITIONS FROM RELATED CORPORATIONS.—

(i) IN GENERAL.—Clause (iii) of subparagraph (A) shall not apply to an acquisition of stock from a related corporation if at least 50 percent in value of the stock of such related corporation was acquired by purchase (within the meaning of subparagraphs (A) and (B)).

(ii) CERTAIN DISTRIBUTIONS.—Clause (i) of subparagraph (A) shall not apply to an acquisition of stock described in clause (i) of this subparagraph if the corporation acquiring such stock—

(I) made a qualified stock purchase of stock of the related corporation, and

(II) made an election under this section (or is treated under subsection (e) as having made such an election) with respect to such qualified stock purchase.

(iii) RELATED CORPORATION DEFINED.—For purposes of this subparagraph, a corporation is a related corporation if stock owned by such corporation is treated (under section 318(a) other than paragraph (4) thereof) as owned by the corporation acquiring the stock.

(4) CONSISTENCY PERIOD.—

(A) IN GENERAL.—Except as provided in subparagraph (B), the term "consistency period" means the period consisting of—

(i) the 1-year period before the beginning of the 12-month acquisition period for the target corporation,

(ii) such acquisition period (up to and including the acquisition date), and

(iii) the 1-year period beginning on the day after the acquisition date.

(B) EXTENSION WHERE THERE IS PLAN.—The period referred to in subparagraph (A) shall also include any period during which the Secretary determines that there was in effect a plan to make a qualified stock purchase plus 1 or more other qualified stock purchases (or asset acquisitions described in subsection (e)) with respect to the target corporation or any target affiliate.

(5) AFFILIATED GROUP.—The term "affiliated group" has the meaning given to such term by section 1504(a) (determined without regard to the exceptions contained in section 1504(b)).

(6) TARGET AFFILIATE.—

(A) IN GENERAL.—A corporation shall be treated as a target affiliate of the target corporation if each of such corporations was, at any time during so much of the consistency

Sec. 338(h)

period as ends on the acquisition date of the target corporation, a member of an affiliated group which had the same common parent.

(B) CERTAIN FOREIGN CORPORATIONS, ETC.—Except as otherwise provided in regulations (and subject to such conditions as may be provided in regulations)—

(i) the term "target affiliate" does not include a foreign corporation, a DISC, or a corporation to which an election under section 936 applies, and

(ii) stock held by a target affiliate in a foreign corporation or a domestic corporation which is a DISC or described in section 1248(e) shall be excluded from the operation of this section.

(7) [Repealed.]

(8) ACQUISITIONS BY AFFILIATED GROUP TREATED AS MADE BY 1 CORPORATION.—Except as provided in regulations prescribed by the Secretary, stock and asset acquisitions made by members of the same affiliated group shall be treated as made by 1 corporation.

(9) TARGET NOT TREATED AS MEMBER OF AFFILIATED GROUP.—Except as otherwise provided in paragraph (10) or in regulations prescribed under this paragraph, the target corporation shall not be treated as a member of an affiliated group with respect to the sale described in subsection (a)(1).

(10) ELECTIVE RECOGNITION OF GAIN OR LOSS BY TARGET CORPORATION, TOGETHER WITH NONRECOGNITION OF GAIN OR LOSS ON STOCK SOLD BY SELLING CONSOLIDATED GROUP.—

(A) IN GENERAL.—Under regulations prescribed by the Secretary, an election may be made under which if—

(i) the target corporation was, before the transaction, a member of the selling consolidated group, and

(ii) the target corporation recognizes gain or loss with respect to the transaction as if it sold all of its assets in a single transaction,

then the target corporation shall be treated as a member of the selling consolidated group with respect to such sale, and (to the extent provided in regulations) no gain or loss will be recognized on stock sold or exchanged in the transaction by members of the selling consolidated group.

(B) SELLING CONSOLIDATED GROUP.—For purposes of subparagraph (A), the term "selling consolidated group" means any group of corporations which (for the taxable period which includes the transaction)—

(i) includes the target corporation, and

(ii) files a consolidated return.

To the extent provided in regulations, such term also includes any affiliated group of corporations which includes the target corporation (whether or not such group files a consolidated return).

(C) INFORMATION REQUIRED TO BE FURNISHED TO THE SECRETARY.—Under regulations, where an election is made under subparagraph (A), the purchasing corporation and the common parent of the selling consolidated group shall, at such times and in such manner as may be provided in regulations, furnish to the Secretary the following information:

(i) The amount allocated under subsection (b)(5) to goodwill or going concern value.

(ii) Any modification of the amount described in clause (i).

(iii) Any other information as the Secretary deems necessary to carry out the provisions of this paragraph.

(11) ELECTIVE FORMULA FOR DETERMINING FAIR MARKET VALUE.—For purposes of subsection (a)(1), fair market value may be determined on the basis of a formula provided in regulations prescribed by the Secretary which takes into account liabilities and other relevant items.

(12) [Repealed.]

(13) TAX ON DEEMED SALE NOT TAKEN INTO ACCOUNT FOR ESTIMATED TAX PURPOSES.—For purposes of section 6655, tax attributable to the sale described in subsection (a)(1) shall not be taken into account.

(14) [Stricken.]

(15) COMBINED DEEMED SALE RETURN.—Under regulations prescribed by the Secretary, a combined deemed sale return may be filed by all target corporations acquired by a purchasing

corporation on the same acquisition date if such target corporations were members of the same selling consolidated group (as defined in subparagraph (B) of paragraph (10)).

(16) COORDINATION WITH FOREIGN TAX CREDIT PROVISIONS.—Except as provided in regulations, this section shall not apply for purposes of determining the source or character of any item for purposes of subpart A of part III of subchapter N of this chapter (relating to foreign tax credit). The preceding sentence shall not apply to any gain to the extent such gain is includible in gross income as a dividend under section 1248 (determined without regard to any deemed sale under this section by a foreign corporation).

[Sec. 338(i)]

(i) REGULATIONS.—The Secretary shall prescribe such regulations as may be necessary or appropriate to carry out the purposes of this section, including—

(1) regulations to ensure that the purpose of this section to require consistency of treatment of stock and asset sales and purchases may not be circumvented through the use of any provision of law or regulations (including the consolidated return regulations) and

(2) regulations providing for the coordination of the provisions of this section with the provision of this title relating to foreign corporations and their shareholders.

Subpart D—Definition and Special Rule

[Sec. 346]

SEC. 346. DEFINITION AND SPECIAL RULE.

[Sec. 346(a)]

(a) COMPLETE LIQUIDATION.—For purposes of this subchapter, a distribution shall be treated as in complete liquidation of a corporation if the distribution is one of a series of distributions in redemption of all of the stock of the corporation pursuant to a plan.

[Sec. 346(b)]

(b) TRANSACTIONS WHICH MIGHT REACH SAME RESULT AS PARTIAL LIQUIDATIONS.—The Secretary shall prescribe such regulations as may be necessary to ensure that the purposes of subsections (a) and (b) of section 222 of the Tax Equity and Fiscal Responsibility Act of 1982 (which repeal the special tax treatment for partial liquidations) may not be circumvented through the use of section 355, 351, or any other provision of law or regulations (including the consolidated return regulations).

PART III—CORPORATE ORGANIZATIONS AND REORGANIZATIONS

Subpart A—Corporate Organizations

[Sec. 351]

SEC. 351. TRANSFER TO CORPORATION CONTROLLED BY TRANSFEROR.

[Sec. 351(a)]

(a) GENERAL RULE.—No gain or loss shall be recognized if property is transferred to a corporation by one or more persons solely in exchange for stock in such corporation and immediately after the exchange such person or persons are in control (as defined in section 368(c)) of the corporation.

[Sec. 351(b)]

(b) RECEIPT OF PROPERTY.—If subsection (a) would apply to an exchange but for the fact that there is received, in addition to the stock permitted to be received under subsection (a), other property or money, then—

(1) gain (if any) to such recipient shall be recognized, but not in excess of—

(A) the amount of money received, plus

(B) the fair market value of such other property received; and

(2) no loss to such recipient shall be recognized.

[Sec. 351(c)]

(c) SPECIAL RULES WHERE DISTRIBUTION TO SHAREHOLDERS.—

(1) IN GENERAL.—In determining control for purposes of this section, the fact that any corporate transferor distributes part or all of the stock in the corporation which it receives in the exchange to its shareholders shall not be taken into account.

(2) SPECIAL RULE FOR SECTION 355.—If the requirements of section 355 (or so much of section 356 as relates to section 355) are met with respect to a distribution described in paragraph (1), then, solely for purposes of determining the tax treatment of the transfers of property to the controlled corporation by the distributing corporation, the fact that the shareholders of the distributing corporation dispose of part or all of the distributed stock, or the fact that the corporation whose stock was distributed issues additional stock, shall not be taken into account in determining control for purposes of this section.

[Sec. 351(d)]

(d) SERVICES, CERTAIN INDEBTEDNESS, AND ACCRUED INTEREST NOT TREATED AS PROPERTY.—For purposes of this section, stock issued for—

(1) services,

(2) indebtedness of the transferee corporation which is not evidenced by a security, or

(3) interest on indebtedness of the transferee corporation which accrued on or after the beginning of the transferor's holding period for the debt,

shall not be considered as issued in return for property.

[Sec. 351(e)]

(e) EXCEPTIONS.—This section shall not apply to—

(1) TRANSFER OF PROPERTY TO AN INVESTMENT COMPANY.—A transfer of property to an investment company. For purposes of the preceding sentence, the determination of whether a company is an investment company shall be made—

(A) by taking into account all stock and securities held by the company, and

(B) by treating as stock and securities—

(i) money,

(ii) stocks and other equity interests in a corporation, evidences of indebtedness, options, forward or futures contracts, notional principal contracts and derivatives,

(iii) any foreign currency,

(iv) any interest in a real estate investment trust, a common trust fund, a regulated investment company, a publicly-traded partnership (as defined in section 7704(b)) or any other equity interest (other than in a corporation) which pursuant to its terms or any other arrangement is readily convertible into, or exchangeable for, any asset described in any preceding clause, this clause or clause (v) or (viii),

(v) except to the extent provided in regulations prescribed by the Secretary, any interest in a precious metal, unless such metal is used or held in the active conduct of a trade or business after the contribution,

(vi) except as otherwise provided in regulations prescribed by the Secretary, interests in any entity if substantially all of the assets of such entity consist (directly or indirectly) of any assets described in any preceding clause or clause (viii),

(vii) to the extent provided in regulations prescribed by the Secretary, any interest in any entity not described in clause (vi), but only to the extent of the value of such interest that is attributable to assets listed in clauses (i) through (v) or clause (viii), or

(viii) any other asset specified in regulations prescribed by the Secretary.

The Secretary may prescribe regulations that, under appropriate circumstances, treat any asset described in clauses (i) through (v) as not so listed.

(2) TITLE 11 OR SIMILAR CASE.—A transfer of property of a debtor pursuant to a plan while the debtor is under the jurisdiction of a court in a title 11 or similar case (within the meaning of section 368(a)(3)(A)), to the extent that the stock received in the exchange is used to satisfy the indebtedness of such debtor.

Sec. 351(c)

[Sec. 351(f)]

(f) TREATMENT OF CONTROLLED CORPORATION.—If—

(1) property is transferred to a corporation (hereinafter in this subsection referred to as the "controlled corporation") in an exchange with respect to which gain or loss is not recognized (in whole or in part) to the transferor under this section, and

(2) such exchange is not in pursuance of a plan of reorganization,

section 311 shall apply to any transfer in such exchange by the controlled corporation in the same manner as if such transfer were a distribution to which subpart A of part I applies.

[Sec. 351(g)]

(g) NONQUALIFIED PREFERRED STOCK NOT TREATED AS STOCK.—

(1) IN GENERAL.—In the case of a person who transfers property to a corporation and receives nonqualified preferred stock—

(A) subsection (a) shall not apply to such transferor, and

(B) if (and only if) the transferor receives stock other than nonqualified preferred stock—

(i) subsection (b) shall apply to such transferor; and

(ii) such nonqualified preferred stock shall be treated as other property for purposes of applying subsection (b).

(2) NONQUALIFIED PREFERRED STOCK.—For purposes of paragraph (1)—

(A) IN GENERAL.—The term "nonqualified preferred stock" means preferred stock if—

(i) the holder of such stock has the right to require the issuer or a related person to redeem or purchase the stock,

(ii) the issuer or a related person is required to redeem or purchase such stock,

(iii) the issuer or a related person has the right to redeem or purchase the stock and, as of the issue date, it is more likely than not that such right will be exercised, or

(iv) the dividend rate on such stock varies in whole or in part (directly or indirectly) with reference to interest rates, commodity prices, or other similar indices.

(B) LIMITATIONS.—Clauses (i), (ii), and (iii) of subparagraph (A) shall apply only if the right or obligation referred to therein may be exercised within the 20-year period beginning on the issue date of such stock and such right or obligation is not subject to a contingency which, as of the issue date, makes remote the likelihood of the redemption or purchase.

(C) EXCEPTIONS FOR CERTAIN RIGHTS OR OBLIGATIONS.—

(i) IN GENERAL.—A right or obligation shall not be treated as described in clause (i), (ii), or (iii) of subparagraph (A) if—

(I) it may be exercised only upon the death, disability, or mental incompetency of the holder, or

(II) in the case of a right or obligation to redeem or purchase stock transferred in connection with the performance of services for the issuer or a related person (and which represents reasonable compensation), it may be exercised only upon the holder's separation from service from the issuer or a related person.

(ii) EXCEPTION.—Clause (i)(I) shall not apply if the stock relinquished in the exchange, or the stock acquired in the exchange is in—

(I) a corporation if any class of stock in such corporation or a related party is readily tradable on an established securities market or otherwise, or

(II) any other corporation if such exchange is part of a transaction or series of transactions in which such corporation is to become a corporation described in subclause (I).

(3) DEFINITIONS.—For purposes of this subsection—

(A) PREFERRED STOCK.—The term "preferred stock" means stock which is limited and preferred as to dividends and does not participate in corporate growth to any significant extent.

(B) RELATED PERSON.—A person shall be treated as related to another person if they bear a relationship to such other person described in section 267(b) or 707(b).

(4) REGULATIONS.—The Secretary may prescribe such regulations as may be necessary or appropriate to carry out the purposes of this subsection and sections 354(a)(2)(C), 355(a)(3)(D), and 356(e). The Secretary may also prescribe regulations, consistent with the treatment under this subsection and such sections, for the treatment of nonqualified preferred stock under other provisions of this title.

[Sec. 351(h)]

(h) CROSS REFERENCES.—

(1) For special rule where another party to the exchange assumes a liability, see section 357.

(2) For the basis of stock or property received in an exchange to which this section applies, see sections 358 and 362.

(3) For special rule in the case of an exchange described in this section but which results in a gift, see section 2501 and following.

(4) For special rule in the case of an exchange described in this section but which has the effect of the payment of compensation by the corporation or by a transferor, see section 61(a)(1).

(5) For coordination of this section with section 304, see section 304(b)(3).

Subpart B—Effects on Shareholders and Security Holders

[Sec. 354]

SEC. 354. EXCHANGES OF STOCK AND SECURITIES IN CERTAIN REORGANIZATIONS.

[Sec. 354(a)]

(a) GENERAL RULE.—

(1) IN GENERAL.—No gain or loss shall be recognized if stock or securities in a corporation a party to a reorganization are, in pursuance of the plan of reorganization, exchanged solely for stock or securities in such corporation or in another corporation a party to the reorganization.

(2) LIMITATIONS.—

(A) EXCESS PRINCIPAL AMOUNT.—Paragraph (1) shall not apply if—

(i) the principal amount of any such securities received exceeds the principal amount of any such securities surrendered, or

(ii) any such securities are received and no such securities are surrendered.

(B) PROPERTY ATTRIBUTABLE TO ACCRUED INTEREST.—Neither paragraph (1) nor so much of section 356 as relates to paragraph (1) shall apply to the extent that any stock (including nonqualified preferred stock, as defined in section 351(g)(2)), securities, or other property received is attributable to interest which has accrued on securities on or after the beginning of the holder's holding period.

(C) NONQUALIFIED PREFERRED STOCK.—

(i) IN GENERAL.—Nonqualified preferred stock (as defined in section 351(g)(2)) received in exchange for stock other than nonqualified preferred stock (as so defined) shall not be treated as stock or securities.

(ii) RECAPITALIZATIONS OF FAMILY-OWNED CORPORATIONS.—

(I) IN GENERAL.—Clause (i) shall not apply in the case of a recapitalization under section 368(a)(1)(E) of a family-owned corporation.

(II) FAMILY-OWNED CORPORATION.—For purposes of this clause, except as provided in regulations, the term "family-owned corporation" means any corporation which is described in clause (i) of section 447(d)(2)(C) throughout the 8-year period beginning on the date which is 5 years before the date of the recapitalization. For purposes of the preceding sentence, stock shall not be treated as owned by a family member during any period described in section 355(d)(6)(B).

(III) EXTENSION OF STATUTE OF LIMITATIONS.—The statutory period for the assessment of any deficiency attributable to a corporation failing to be a family-owned corporation shall not expire before the expiration of 3 years after the date the Secretary is notified by the corporation (in such manner as the Secretary may prescribe) of such failure, and such deficiency may be assessed before the expiration of such 3-year period notwithstanding the provisions of any other law or rule of law which would otherwise prevent such assessment.

(3) CROSS REFERENCES.—

(A) For treatment of the exchange if any property is received which is not permitted to be received under this subsection (including nonqualified preferred stock and an excess principal amount of securities received over securities surrendered, but not including property to which paragraph (2)(B) applies), see section 356.

(B) For treatment of accrued interest in the case of an exchange described in paragraph (2)(B), see section 61.

[Sec. 354(b)]

(b) EXCEPTION.—

(1) IN GENERAL.—Subsection (a) shall not apply to an exchange in pursuance of a plan of reorganization within the meaning of subparagraph (D) or (G) of section 368(a)(1), unless—

(A) the corporation to which the assets are transferred acquires substantially all of the assets of the transferor of such assets; and

(B) the stock, securities, and other properties received by such transferor, as well as the other properties of such transferor, are distributed in pursuance of the plan of reorganization.

(2) CROSS REFERENCE.—

For special rules for certain exchanges in pursuance of plans of reorganization within the meaning of subparagraph (D) or (G) of section 368(a)(1), see section 355.

* * *

[Sec. 355]

SEC. 355. DISTRIBUTION OF STOCK AND SECURITIES OF A CONTROLLED CORPORATION.

[Sec. 355(a)]

(a) EFFECT ON DISTRIBUTEES.—

(1) GENERAL RULE.—If—

(A) a corporation (referred to in this section as the "distributing corporation")

(i) distributes to a shareholder, with respect to its stock, or

(ii) distributes to a security holder, in exchange for its securities,

solely stock or securities of a corporation (referred to in this section as "controlled corporation") which it controls immediately before the distribution,

(B) the transaction was not used principally as a device for the distribution of the earnings and profits of the distributing corporation or the controlled corporation or both (but the mere fact that subsequent to the distribution stock or securities in one or more of such corporations are sold or exchanged by all or some of the distributees (other than pursuant to an arrangement negotiated or agreed upon prior to such distribution) shall not be construed to mean that the transaction was used principally as such a device),

(C) the requirements of subsection (b) (relating to active businesses) are satisfied, and

(D) as part of the distribution, the distributing corporation distributes—

(i) all of the stock and securities in the controlled corporation held by it immediately before the distribution, or

(ii) an amount of stock in the controlled corporation constituting control within the meaning of section 368 (c), and it is established to the satisfaction of the Secretary that the retention by the distributing corporation of stock (or stock and securities) in the controlled corporation was not in pursuance of a plan having as one of its principal purposes the avoidance of Federal income tax,

then no gain or loss shall be recognized to (and no amount shall be includible in the income of) such shareholder or security holder on the receipt of such stock or securities.

(2) NON PRO RATA DISTRIBUTIONS, ETC.—Paragraph (1) shall be applied without regard to the following:

(A) whether or not the distribution is pro rata with respect to all of the shareholders of the distributing corporation,

(B) whether or not the shareholder surrenders stock in the distributing corporation, and

(C) whether or not the distribution is in pursuance of a plan of reorganization (within the meaning of section 368 (a) (1) (D)).

(3) LIMITATIONS.—

(A) EXCESS PRINCIPAL AMOUNT.—Paragraph (1) shall not apply if—

(i) the principal amount of the securities in the controlled corporation which are received exceeds the principal amount of the securities which are surrendered in connection with such distribution, or

(ii) securities in the controlled corporation are received and no securities are surrendered in connection with such distribution.

(B) STOCK ACQUIRED IN TAXABLE TRANSACTIONS WITHIN 5 YEARS TREATED AS BOOT.—For purposes of this section (other than paragraph (1)(D) of this subsection) and so much of section 356 as relates to this section, stock of a controlled corporation acquired by the distributing corporation by reason of any transaction—

(i) which occurs within 5 years of the distribution of such stock, and

(ii) in which gain or loss was recognized in whole or in part,

shall not be treated as stock of such controlled corporation, but as other property.

(C) PROPERTY ATTRIBUTABLE TO ACCRUED INTEREST.—Neither paragraph (1) nor so much of section 356 as relates to paragraph (1) shall apply to the extent that any stock (including nonqualified preferred stock, as defined in section 351(g)(2)), securities, or other property received is attributable to interest which has accrued on securities on or after the beginning of the holder's holding period.

(D) NONQUALIFIED PREFERRED STOCK.—Nonqualified preferred stock (as defined in section 351(g)(2)) received in a distribution with respect to stock other than nonqualified preferred stock (as so defined) shall not be treated as stock or securities.

(4) CROSS REFERENCES.—

(A) For treatment of the exchange if any property is received which is not permitted to be received under this subsection (including nonqualified preferred stock and an excess principal amount of securities received over securities surrendered, but not including property to which paragraph (3)(C) applies), see section 356.

(B) For treatment of accrued interest in the case of an exchange described in paragraph (3)(C), see section 61.

[Sec. 355(b)]

(b) REQUIREMENTS AS TO ACTIVE BUSINESS.—

(1) IN GENERAL.—Subsection (a) shall apply only if either—

(A) the distributing corporation, and the controlled corporation (or, if stock of more than one controlled corporation is distributed, each of such corporations), is engaged immediately after the distribution in the active conduct of a trade or business, or

(B) immediately before the distribution, the distributing corporation had no assets other than stock or securities in the controlled corporations and each of the controlled corporations is engaged immediately after the distribution in the active conduct of a trade or business.

(2) DEFINITION.—For purposes of paragraph (1), a corporation shall be treated as engaged in the active conduct of a trade or business if and only if—

(A) it is engaged in the active conduct of a trade or business, or substantially all of its assets consist of stock and securities of a corporation controlled by it (immediately after the distribution) which is so engaged,

(B) such trade or business has been actively conducted throughout the 5-year period ending on the date of the distribution,

(C) such trade or business was not acquired within the period described in subparagraph (B) in a transaction in which gain or loss was recognized in whole or in part, and

(D) control of a corporation which (at the time of acquisition of control) was conducting such trade or business—

(i) was not acquired by any distributee corporation directly (or through 1 or more corporations, whether through the distributing corporation or otherwise) within the period described in subparagraph (B) and was not acquired by the distributing corporation directly (or through 1 or more corporations) within such period, or

(ii) was so acquired by any such corporation within such period, but, in each case in which such control was so acquired, it was so acquired, only by reason of transactions in which gain or loss was not recognized in whole or in part, or only by reason of such transactions combined with acquisitions before the beginning of such period.

For purposes of subparagraph (D), all distributee corporations which are members of the same affiliated group (as defined in section 1504(a) without regard to section 1504(b)) shall be treated as 1 distributee corporation.

[Sec. 355(c)]

(c) Taxability of Corporation on Distribution.—

(1) In general.—Except as provided in paragraph (2), no gain or loss shall be recognized to a corporation on any distribution to which this section (or so much of section 356 as relates to this section) applies and which is not in pursuance of a plan of reorganization.

(2) Distribution of appreciated property.—

(A) In general.—If—

(i) in a distribution referred to in paragraph (1), the corporation distributes property other than qualified property, and

(ii) the fair market value of such property exceeds its adjusted basis (in the hands of the distributing corporation),

then gain shall be recognized to the distributing corporation as if such property were sold to the distributee at its fair market value.

(B) Qualified property.—For purposes of subparagraph (A), the term "qualified property" means any stock or securities in the controlled corporation.

(C) Treatment of liabilities.—If any property distributed in the distribution referred to in paragraph (1) is subject to a liability or the shareholder assumes a liability of the distributing corporation in connection with the distribution, then, for purposes of subparagraph (A), the fair market value of such property shall be treated as not less than the amount of such liability.

(3) Coordination with sections 311 and 336(a).—Sections 311 and 336(a) shall not apply to any distribution referred to in paragraph (1).

[Sec. 355(d)]

(d) Recognition of Gain on Certain Distributions of Stock or Securities in Controlled Corporation.—

(1) In general.—In the case of a disqualified distribution, any stock or securities in the controlled corporation shall not be treated as qualified property for purposes of subsection (c)(2) of this section or section 361(c)(2).

(2) Disqualified distribution.—For purposes of this subsection, the term "disqualified distribution" means any distribution to which this section (or so much of section 356 as relates to this section) applies if, immediately after the distribution—

(A) any person holds disqualified stock in the distributing corporation which constitutes a 50-percent or greater interest in such corporation, or

(B) any person holds disqualified stock in the controlled corporation (or, if stock of more than 1 controlled corporation is distributed, in any controlled corporation) which constitutes a 50-percent or greater interest in such corporation.

(3) Disqualified stock.—For purposes of this subsection, the term "disqualified stock" means—

(A) any stock in the distributing corporation acquired by purchase after October 9, 1990, and during the 5-year period ending on the date of the distribution, and

(B) any stock in any controlled corporation—

(i) acquired by purchase after October 9, 1990, and during the 5-year period ending on the date of the distribution, or

(ii) received in the distribution to the extent attributable to distributions on—

(I) stock described in subparagraph (A), or

(II) any securities in the distributing corporation acquired by purchase after October 9, 1990, and during the 5-year period ending on the date of the distribution.

(4) 50-PERCENT OR GREATER INTEREST.—For purposes of this subsection, the term "50-percent or greater interest" means stock possessing at least 50 percent of the total combined voting power of all classes of stock entitled to vote or at least 50 percent of the total value of shares of all classes of stock.

(5) PURCHASE.—For purposes of this subsection—

(A) IN GENERAL.—Except as otherwise provided in this paragraph, the term "purchase" means any acquisition but only if—

(i) the basis of the property acquired in the hands of the acquirer is not determined (I) in whole or in part by reference to the adjusted basis of such property in the hands of the person from whom acquired, or (II) under section 1014(a), and

(ii) the property is not acquired in an exchange to which section 351, 354, 355, or 356 applies.

(B) CERTAIN SECTION 351 EXCHANGES TREATED AS PURCHASES.—The term "purchase" includes any acquisition of property in an exchange to which section 351 applies to the extent such property is acquired in exchange for—

(i) any cash or cash item,

(ii) any marketable stock or security, or

(iii) any debt of the transferor.

(C) CARRYOVER BASIS TRANSACTIONS.—If—

(i) any person acquires property from another person who acquired such property by purchase (as determined under this paragraph with regard to this subparagraph), and

(ii) the adjusted basis of such property in the hands of such acquirer is determined in whole or in part by reference to the adjusted basis of such property in the hands of such other person,

such acquirer shall be treated as having acquired such property by purchase on the date it was so acquired by such other person.

(6) SPECIAL RULE WHERE SUBSTANTIAL DIMINUTION OF RISK.—

(A) IN GENERAL.—If this paragraph applies to any stock or securities for any period, the running of any 5-year period set forth in subparagraph (A) or (B) of paragraph (3) (whichever applies) shall be suspended during such period.

(B) PROPERTY TO WHICH SUSPENSION APPLIES.—This paragraph applies to any stock or securities for any period during which the holder's risk of loss with respect to such stock or securities, or with respect to any portion of the activities of the corporation, is (directly or indirectly) substantially diminished by—

(i) an option,

(ii) a short sale,

(iii) any special class of stock, or

(iv) any other device or transaction.

(7) AGGREGATION RULES.—

(A) IN GENERAL.—For purposes of this subsection, a person and all persons related to such person (within the meaning of section 267(b) or 707(b)(1)) shall be treated as one person.

(B) PERSONS ACTING PURSUANT TO PLANS OR ARRANGEMENTS.—If two or more persons act pursuant to a plan or arrangement with respect to acquisitions of stock or securities in the distributing corporation or controlled corporation, such persons shall be treated as one person for purposes of this subsection.

(8) ATTRIBUTION FROM ENTITIES.—

(A) IN GENERAL.—Paragraph (2) of section 318(a) shall apply in determining whether a person holds stock or securities in any corporation (determined by substituting "10 percent" for "50 percent" in subparagraph (C) of such paragraph (2) and by treating any reference to stock as including a reference to securities).

(B) DEEMED PURCHASE RULE.—If—

(i) any person acquires by purchase an interest in any entity, and

(ii) such person is treated under subparagraph (A) as holding any stock or securities by reason of holding such interest,

such stock or securities shall be treated as acquired by purchase by such person on the later of the date of the purchase of the interest in such entity or the date such stock or securities are acquired by purchase by such entity.

(9) REGULATIONS.—The Secretary shall prescribe such regulations as may be necessary to carry out the purposes of this subsection, including—

(A) regulations to prevent the avoidance of the purposes of this subsection through the use of related persons, intermediaries, pass-thru entities, options, or other arrangements, and

(B) regulations modifying the definition of the term "purchase".

[Sec. 355(e)]

(e) RECOGNITION OF GAIN ON CERTAIN DISTRIBUTIONS OF STOCK OR SECURITIES IN CONNECTION WITH ACQUISITIONS.—

(1) GENERAL RULE.—If there is a distribution to which this subsection applies, any stock or securities in the controlled corporation shall not be treated as qualified property for purposes of subsection (c)(2) of this section or section 361(c)(2).

(2) DISTRIBUTIONS TO WHICH SUBSECTION APPLIES.—

(A) IN GENERAL.—This subsection shall apply to any distribution—

(i) to which this section (or so much of section 356 as relates to this section) applies, and

(ii) which is part of a plan (or series of related transactions) pursuant to which 1 or more persons acquire directly or indirectly stock representing a 50-percent or greater interest in the distributing corporation or any controlled corporation.

(B) PLAN PRESUMED TO EXIST IN CERTAIN CASES.—If 1 or more persons acquire directly or indirectly stock representing a 50-percent or greater interest in the distributing corporation or any controlled corporation during the 4-year period beginning on the date which is 2 years before the date of the distribution, such acquisition shall be treated as pursuant to a plan described in subparagraph (A)(ii) unless it is established that the distribution and the acquisition are not pursuant to a plan or series of related transactions.

(C) CERTAIN PLANS DISREGARDED.—A plan (or series of related transactions) shall not be treated as described in subparagraph (A)(ii) if, immediately after the completion of such plan or transactions, the distributing corporation and all controlled corporations are members of a single affiliated group (as defined in section 1504 without regard to subsection (b) thereof).

(D) COORDINATION WITH SUBSECTION (d).—This subsection shall not apply to any distribution to which subsection (d) applies.

(3) SPECIAL RULES RELATING TO ACQUISITIONS.—

(A) CERTAIN ACQUISITIONS NOT TAKEN INTO ACCOUNT.—Except as provided in regulations, the following acquisitions shall not be taken into account in applying paragraph (2)(A)(ii):

(i) The acquisition of stock in any controlled corporation by the distributing corporation.

(ii) The acquisition by a person of stock in any controlled corporation by reason of holding stock or securities in the distributing corporation.

(iii) The acquisition by a person of stock in any successor corporation of the distributing corporation or any controlled corporation by reason of holding stock or securities in such distributing or controlled corporation.

Sec. 355(e)

(iv) The acquisition of stock in the distributing corporation or any controlled corporation to the extent that the percentage of stock owned directly or indirectly in such corporation by each person owning stock in such corporation immediately before the acquisition does not decrease.

This subparagraph shall not apply to any acquisition if the stock held before the acquisition was acquired pursuant to a plan (or series of related transactions) described in paragraph (2)(A)(ii).

(B) ASSET ACQUISITIONS.—Except as provided in regulations, for purposes of this subsection, if the assets of the distributing corporation or any controlled corporation are acquired by a successor corporation in a transaction described in subparagraph (A), (C), or (D) of section 368(a)(1) or any other transaction specified in regulations by the Secretary, the shareholders (immediately before the acquisition) of the corporation acquiring such assets shall be treated as acquiring stock in the corporation from which the assets were acquired.

(4) DEFINITION AND SPECIAL RULES.—For purposes of this subsection—

(A) 50-PERCENT OR GREATER INTEREST.—The term "50-percent or greater interest" has the meaning given such term by subsection (d)(4).

(B) DISTRIBUTIONS IN TITLE 11 OR SIMILAR CASE.—Paragraph (1) shall not apply to any distribution made in a title 11 or similar case (as defined in section 368(a)(3)).

(C) AGGREGATION AND ATTRIBUTION RULES.—

(i) AGGREGATION.—The rules of paragraph (7)(A) of subsection (d) shall apply.

(ii) ATTRIBUTION.—Section 318(a)(2) shall apply in determining whether a person holds stock or securities in any corporation. Except as provided in regulations, section 318(a)(2)(C) shall be applied without regard to the phrase "50 percent or more in value" for purposes of the preceding sentence.

(D) SUCCESSORS AND PREDECESSORS.—For purposes of this subsection, any reference to a controlled corporation or a distributing corporation shall include a reference to any predecessor or successor of such corporation.

(E) STATUTE OF LIMITATIONS.—If there is a distribution to which paragraph (1) applies—

(i) the statutory period for the assessment of any deficiency attributable to any part of the gain recognized under this subsection by reason of such distribution shall not expire before the expiration of 3 years from the date the Secretary is notified by the taxpayer (in such manner as the Secretary may by regulations prescribe) that such distribution occurred, and

(ii) such deficiency may be assessed before the expiration of such 3-year period notwithstanding the provisions of any other law or rule of law which would otherwise prevent such assessment.

(5) REGULATIONS.—The Secretary shall prescribe such regulations as may be necessary to carry out the purposes of this subsection, including regulations—

(A) providing for the application of this subsection where there is more than 1 controlled corporation,

(B) treating 2 or more distributions as 1 distribution where necessary to prevent the avoidance of such purposes, and

(C) providing for the application of rules similar to the rules of subsection (d)(6) where appropriate for purposes of paragraph (2)(B).

[Sec. 355(f)]

(f) SECTION NOT TO APPLY TO CERTAIN INTRAGROUP DISTRIBUTIONS.—Except as provided in regulations, this section (or so much of section 356 as relates to this section) shall not apply to the distribution of stock from 1 member of an affiliated group (as defined in section 1504(a)) to another member of such group if such distribution is part of a plan (or series of related transactions) described in subsection (e)(2)(A)(ii) (determined after the application of subsection (e)).

SEC. 356. RECEIPT OF ADDITIONAL CONSIDERATION.

[Sec. 356(a)]

(a) Gain on Exchanges.—

(1) Recognition of gain.—If—

(A) section 354 or 355 would apply to an exchange but for the fact that

(B) the property received in the exchange consists not only of property permitted by section 354 or 355 to be received without the recognition of gain but also of other property or money,

then the gain, if any, to the recipient shall be recognized, but in an amount not in excess of the sum of such money and the fair market value of such other property.

(2) Treatment as dividend.—If an exchange is described in paragraph (1) but has the effect of the distribution of a dividend (determined with the application of section 318(a)), then there shall be treated as a dividend to each distributee such an amount of the gain recognized under paragraph (1) as is not in excess of his ratable share of the undistributed earnings and profits of the corporation accumulated after February 28, 1913. The remainder, if any, of the gain recognized under paragraph (1) shall be treated as gain from the exchange of property.

[Sec. 356(b)]

(b) Additional Consideration Received in Certain Distributions.—If—

(1) section 355 would apply to a distribution but for the fact that

(2) the property received in the distribution consists not only of property permitted by section 355 to be received without the recognition of gain, but also of other property or money,

then an amount equal to the sum of such money and the fair market value of such other property shall be treated as a distribution of property to which section 301 applies.

[Sec. 356(c)]

(c) Loss.—If—

(1) section 354 would apply to an exchange, or section 355 would apply to an exchange or distribution, but for the fact that

(2) the property received in the exchange or distribution consists not only of property permitted by section 354 or 355 to be received without the recognition of gain or loss, but also of other property or money,

then no loss from the exchange or distribution shall be recognized.

[Sec. 356(d)]

(d) Securities as Other Property.—For purposes of this section—

(1) In general.—Except as provided in paragraph (2), the term "other property" includes securities.

(2) Exceptions.—

(A) Securities with respect to which nonrecognition of gain would be permitted.—The term "other property" does not include securities to the extent that, under section 354 or 355, such securities would be permitted to be received without the recognition of gain.

(B) Greater principal amount in section 354 exchange.—If—

(i) in an exchange described in section 354 (other than subsection (c) thereof), securities of a corporation a party to the reorganization are surrendered and securities of any corporation a party to the reorganization are received, and

(ii) the principal amount of such securities received exceeds the principal amount of such securities surrendered,

then, with respect to such securities received, the term "other property" means only the fair market value of such excess. For purposes of this subparagraph and subparagraph (C), if no securities are surrendered, the excess shall be the entire principal amount of the securities received.

Sec. 356(d)

(C) GREATER PRINCIPAL AMOUNT IN SECTION 355 TRANSACTION.—If, in an exchange or distribution described in section 355, the principal amount of the securities in the controlled corporation which are received exceeds the principal amount of the securities in the distributing corporation which are surrendered, then, with respect to such securities received, the term "other property" means only the fair market value of such excess.

[Sec. 356(e)]

(e) NONQUALIFIED PREFERRED STOCK TREATED AS OTHER PROPERTY.—For purposes of this section—

(1) IN GENERAL.—Except as provided in paragraph (2), the term "other property" includes nonqualified preferred stock (as defined in section 351(g)(2)).

(2) EXCEPTION.—The term "other property" does not include nonqualified preferred stock (as so defined) to the extent that, under section 354 or 355, such preferred stock would be permitted to be received without the recognition of gain.

[Sec. 356(f)]

(f) EXCHANGES FOR SECTION 306 STOCK.—Notwithstanding any other provision of this section, to the extent that any of the other property (or money) is received in exchange for section 306 stock, an amount equal to the fair market value of such other property (or the amount of such money) shall be treated as a distribution of property to which section 301 applies.

[Sec. 356(g)]

(g) TRANSACTIONS INVOLVING GIFT OR COMPENSATION.—

For special rules for a transaction described in section 354, 355, or this section, but which—

(1) results in a gift, see section 2501 and following, or

(2) has the effect of the payment of compensation, see section 61(a)(1).

[Sec. 357]

SEC. 357. ASSUMPTION OF LIABILITY.

[Sec. 357(a)]

(a) GENERAL RULE.—Except as provided in subsections (b) and (c), if—

(1) the taxpayer receives property which would be permitted to be received under section 351 or 361 without the recognition of gain if it were the sole consideration, and

(2) as part of the consideration, another party to the exchange assumes a liability of the taxpayer,

then such assumption shall not be treated as money or other property, and shall not prevent the exchange from being within the provisions of section 351 or 361, as the case may be.

[Sec. 357(b)]

(b) TAX AVOIDANCE PURPOSE.—

(1) IN GENERAL.—If, taking into consideration the nature of the liability and the circumstances in the light of which the arrangement for the assumption was made, it appears that the principal purpose of the taxpayer with respect to the assumption described in subsection (a)—

(A) was a purpose to avoid Federal income tax on the exchange, or

(B) if not such purpose, was not a bona fide business purpose,

then such assumption (in the total amount of the liability assumed pursuant to such exchange) shall, for purposes of section 351 or 361 (as the case may be), be considered as money received by the taxpayer on the exchange.

(2) BURDEN OF PROOF.—In any suit or proceeding where the burden is on the taxpayer to prove such assumption is not to be treated as money received by the taxpayer, such burden shall not be considered as sustained unless the taxpayer sustains such burden by the clear preponderance of the evidence.

(c) LIABILITIES IN EXCESS OF BASIS.—

(1) IN GENERAL.—In the case of an exchange—

(A) to which section 351 applies, or

(B) to which section 361 applies by reason of a plan of reorganization within the meaning of section 368(a)(1)(D),

if the sum of the amount of the liabilities assumed exceeds the total of the adjusted basis of the property transferred pursuant to such exchange, then such excess shall be considered as a gain from the sale or exchange of a capital asset or of property which is not a capital asset, as the case may be.

(2) EXCEPTIONS.—Paragraph (1) shall not apply to any exchange—

(A) to which subsection (b)(1) of this section applies, or

(B) which is pursuant to a plan of reorganization within the meaning of section 368(a)(1)(G) where no former shareholder of the transferor corporation receives any consideration for his stock.

(3) CERTAIN LIABILITIES EXCLUDED.—

(A) IN GENERAL.—If a taxpayer transfers, in an exchange to which section 351 applies, a liability the payment of which either—

(i) would give rise to a deduction, or

(ii) would be described in section 736(a),

then, for purposes of paragraph (1), the amount of such liability shall be excluded in determining the amount of liabilities assumed.

(B) EXCEPTION.—Subparagraph (A) shall not apply to any liability to the extent that the incurrence of the liability resulted in the creation of, or an increase in, the basis of any property.

(d) DETERMINATION OF AMOUNT OF LIABILITY ASSUMED.—

(1) IN GENERAL.—For purposes of this section, section 358(d), section 358(h), section 362(d), section 368(a)(1)(C), and section 368(a)(2)(B), except as provided in regulations—

(A) a recourse liability (or portion thereof) shall be treated as having been assumed if, as determined on the basis of all facts and circumstances, the transferee has agreed to, and is expected to, satisfy such liability (or portion), whether or not the transferor has been relieved of such liability; and

(B) except to the extent provided in paragraph (2), a nonrecourse liability shall be treated as having been assumed by the transferee of any asset subject to such liability.

(2) EXCEPTION FOR NONRECOURSE LIABILITY.—The amount of the nonrecourse liability treated as described in paragraph (1)(B) shall be reduced by the lesser of—

(A) the amount of such liability which an owner of other assets not transferred to the transferee and also subject to such liability has agreed with the transferee to, and is expected to, satisfy, or

(B) the fair market value of such other assets (determined without regard to section 7701(g)).

(3) REGULATIONS.—The Secretary shall prescribe such regulations as may be necessary to carry out the purposes of this subsection and section 362(d). The Secretary may also prescribe regulations which provide that the manner in which a liability is treated as assumed under this subsection is applied, where appropriate, elsewhere in this title.

SEC. 358. BASIS TO DISTRIBUTEES.

(a) GENERAL RULE.—In the case of an exchange to which section 351, 354, 355, 356, or 361 applies—

(1) NONRECOGNITION PROPERTY.—The basis of the property permitted to be received under such section without the recognition of gain or loss shall be the same as that of the property exchanged—

(A) decreased by—

(i) the fair market value of any other property (except money) received by the taxpayer,

(ii) the amount of any money received by the taxpayer, and

(iii) the amount of loss to the taxpayer which was recognized on such exchange, and

(B) increased by—

(i) the amount which was treated as a dividend, and

(ii) the amount of gain to the taxpayer which was recognized on such exchange (not including any portion of such gain which was treated as a dividend).

(2) OTHER PROPERTY.—The basis of any other property (except money) received by the taxpayer shall be its fair market value.

[Sec. 358(b)]

(b) ALLOCATION OF BASIS.—

(1) IN GENERAL.—Under regulations prescribed by the Secretary, the basis determined under subsection (a) (1) shall be allocated among the properties permitted to be received without the recognition of gain or loss.

(2) SPECIAL RULE FOR SECTION 355.—In the case of an exchange to which section 355 (or so much of section 356 as relates to section 355) applies, then in making the allocation under paragraph (1) of this subsection, there shall be taken into account not only the property so permitted to be received without the recognition of gain or loss, but also the stock or securities (if any) of the distributing corporation which are retained, and the allocation of basis shall be made among all such properties.

[Sec. 358(c)]

(c) SECTION 355 TRANSACTIONS WHICH ARE NOT EXCHANGES.—For purposes of this section, a distribution to which section 355 (or so much of section 356 as relates to section 355) applies shall be treated as an exchange, and for such purposes the stock and securities of the distributing corporation which are retained shall be treated as surrendered, and received back, in the exchange.

[Sec. 358(d)]

(d) ASSUMPTION OF LIABILITY.—

(1) IN GENERAL.—Where, as part of the consideration to the taxpayer, another party to the exchange assumed a liability of the taxpayer, such assumption shall, for purposes of this section, be treated as money received by the taxpayer on the exchange.

(2) EXCEPTION.—Paragraph (1) shall not apply to the amount of any liability excluded under section 357(c)(3).

[Sec. 358(e)]

(e) EXCEPTION.—This section shall not apply to property acquired by a corporation by the exchange of its stock or securities (or the stock or securities of a corporation which is in control of the acquiring corporation) as consideration in whole or in part for the transfer of the property to it.

[Sec. 358(f)]

(f) DEFINITION OF NONRECOGNITION PROPERTY IN CASE OF SECTION 361 EXCHANGE.—For purposes of this section, the property permitted to be received under section 361 without the recognition of gain or loss shall be treated as consisting only of stock or securities in another corporation a party to the reorganization.

[Sec. 358(g)]

(g) ADJUSTMENTS IN INTRAGROUP TRANSACTIONS INVOLVING SECTION 355.—In the case of a distribution to which section 355 (or so much of section 356 as relates to section 355) applies and which involves the distribution of stock from 1 member of an affiliated group (as defined in section 1504(a) without regard to subsection (b) thereof) to another member of such group, the Secretary may, notwithstanding any other provision of this section, provide adjustments to the adjusted basis of any stock which—

(1) is in a corporation which is a member of such group, and

(2) is held by another member of such group, to appropriately reflect the proper treatment of such distribution.

Sec. 358(b)

[Sec. 358(h)]

(h) SPECIAL RULES FOR ASSUMPTION OF LIABILITIES TO WHICH SUBSECTION (D) DOES NOT APPLY.—

(1) IN GENERAL.—If, after application of the other provisions of this section to an exchange or series of exchanges, the basis of property to which subsection (a)(1) applies exceeds the fair market value of such property, then such basis shall be reduced (but not below such fair market value) by the amount (determined as of the date of the exchange) of any liability—

(A) which is assumed by another person as part of the exchange, and

(B) with respect to which subsection (d)(1) does not apply to the assumption.

(2) EXCEPTIONS.—Except as provided by the Secretary, paragraph (1) shall not apply to any liability if—

(A) the trade or business with which the liability is associated is transferred to the person assuming the liability as part of the exchange, or

(B) substantially all of the assets with which the liability is associated are transferred to the person assuming the liability as part of the exchange.

(3) LIABILITY.—For purposes of this subsection, the term "liability" shall include any fixed or contingent obligation to make payment, without regard to whether the obligation is otherwise taken into account for purposes of this title.

Subpart C—Effects on Corporations

[Sec. 361]

SEC. 361. NONRECOGNITION OF GAIN OR LOSS TO CORPORATIONS; TREATMENT OF DISTRIBUTIONS.

[Sec. 361(a)]

(a) GENERAL RULE.—No gain or loss shall be recognized to a corporation if such corporation is a party to a reorganization and exchanges property, in pursuance of the plan of reorganization, solely for stock or securities in another corporation a party to the reorganization.

[Sec. 361(b)]

(b) EXCHANGES NOT SOLELY IN KIND.—

(1) GAIN.—If subsection (a) would apply to an exchange but for the fact that the property received in exchange consists not only of stock or securities permitted by subsection (a) to be received without the recognition of gain, but also of other property or money, then—

(A) PROPERTY DISTRIBUTED.—If the corporation receiving such other property or money distributes it in pursuance of the plan of reorganization, no gain to the corporation shall be recognized from the exchange, but

(B) PROPERTY NOT DISTRIBUTED.—If the corporation receiving such other property or money does not distribute it in pursuance of the plan of reorganization, the gain, if any, to the corporation shall be recognized.

The amount of gain recognized under subparagraph (B) shall not exceed the sum of the money and the fair market value of the other property so received which is not so distributed.

(2) LOSS.—If subsection (a) would apply to an exchange but for the fact that the property received in exchange consists not only of property permitted by subsection (a) to be received without the recognition of gain or loss, but also of other property or money, then no loss from the exchange shall be recognized.

(3) TREATMENT OF TRANSFERS TO CREDITORS.—For purposes of paragraph (1), any transfer of the other property or money received in the exchange by the corporation to its creditors in connection with the reorganization shall be treated as a distribution in pursuance of the plan of reorganization. The Secretary may prescribe such regulations as may be necessary to prevent avoidance of tax through abuse of the preceding sentence or subsection (c)(3).

[Sec. 361(c)]

(c) TREATMENT OF DISTRIBUTIONS.—

(1) IN GENERAL.—Except as provided in paragraph (2), no gain or loss shall be recognized to a corporation a party to a reorganization on the distribution to its shareholders of property in pursuance of the plan of reorganization.

(2) DISTRIBUTIONS OF APPRECIATED PROPERTY.—

(A) IN GENERAL.—If—

(i) in a distribution referred to in paragraph (1), the corporation distributes property other than qualified property, and

(ii) the fair market value of such property exceeds its adjusted basis (in the hands of the distributing corporation),

then gain shall be recognized to the distributing corporation as if such property were sold to the distributee at its fair market value.

(B) QUALIFIED PROPERTY.—For purposes of this subsection, the term "qualified property" means—

(i) any stock in (or right to acquire stock in) the distributing corporation or obligation of the distributing corporation, or

(ii) any stock in (or right to acquire stock in) another corporation which is a party to the reorganization or obligation of another corporation which is such a party if such stock (or right) or obligation is received by the distributing corporation in the exchange.

(C) TREATMENT OF LIABILITIES.—If any property distributed in the distribution referred to in paragraph (1) is subject to a liability or the shareholder assumes a liability of the distributing corporation in connection with the distribution, then, for purposes of subparagraph (A), the fair market value of such property shall be treated as not less than the amount of such liability.

(3) TREATMENT OF CERTAIN TRANSFERS TO CREDITORS.—For purposes of this subsection, any transfer of qualified property by the corporation to its creditors in connection with the reorganization shall be treated as a distribution to its shareholders pursuant to the plan of reorganization.

(4) COORDINATION WITH OTHER PROVISIONS.—Section 311 and subpart B of part II of this subchapter shall not apply to any distribution referred to in paragraph (1).

(5) CROSS REFERENCE.—

For provision providing for recognition of gain in certain distributions, see section 355(d).

[Sec. 362]

SEC. 362. BASIS TO CORPORATIONS.

[Sec. 362(a)]

(a) PROPERTY ACQUIRED BY ISSUANCE OF STOCK OR AS PAID-IN SURPLUS.—If property was acquired on or after June 22, 1954, by a corporation—

(1) in connection with a transaction to which section 351 (relating to transfer of property to corporation controlled by transferor) applies, or

(2) as paid-in surplus or as a contribution to capital,

then the basis shall be the same as it would be in the hands of the transferor, increased in the amount of gain recognized to the transferor on such transfer.

[Sec. 362(b)]

(b) TRANSFERS TO CORPORATIONS.—If property was acquired by a corporation in connection with a reorganization to which this part applies, then the basis shall be the same as it would be in the hands of the transferor, increased in the amount of gain recognized to the transferor on such transfer. This subsection shall not apply if the property acquired consists of stock or securities in a corporation a party to the reorganization, unless acquired by the exchange of stock or securities of the transferee (or of a corporation which is in control of the transferee) as the consideration in whole or in part for the transfer.

[Sec. 362(c)]

(c) SPECIAL RULE FOR CERTAIN CONTRIBUTIONS TO CAPITAL.—

(1) PROPERTY OTHER THAN MONEY.—Notwithstanding subsection (a)(2), if property other than money—

(A) is acquired by a corporation, on or after June 22, 1954, as a contribution to capital, and

(B) is not contributed by a shareholder as such,

then the basis of such property shall be zero.

(2) MONEY.—Notwithstanding subsection (a)(2), if money—

(A) is received by a corporation, on or after June 22, 1954, as a contribution to capital, and

(B) is not contributed by a shareholder as such,

then the basis of any property acquired with such money during the 12-month period beginning on the day the contribution is received shall be reduced by the amount of such contribution. The excess (if any) of the amount of such contribution over the amount of the reduction under the preceding sentence shall be applied to the reduction (as of the last day of the period specified in the preceding sentence) of the basis of any other property held by the taxpayer. The particular properties to which the reductions required by this paragraph shall be allocated shall be determined under regulations prescribed by the Secretary.

(3) [Repealed.]

[Sec. 362(d)]

(d) LIMITATION ON BASIS INCREASE ATTRIBUTABLE TO ASSUMPTION OF LIABILITY.—

(1) IN GENERAL.—In no event shall the basis of any property be increased under subsection (a) or (b) above the fair market value of such property (determined without regard to section 7701(g)) by reason of any gain recognized to the transferor as a result of the assumption of a liability.

(2) TREATMENT OF GAIN NOT SUBJECT TO TAX.—Except as provided in regulations, if—

(A) gain is recognized to the transferor as a result of an assumption of a nonrecourse liability by a transferee which is also secured by assets not transferred to such transferee; and

(B) no person is subject to tax under this title on such gain,

then, for purposes of determining basis under subsections (a) and (b), the amount of gain recognized by the transferor as a result of the assumption of the liability shall be determined as if the liability assumed by the transferee equaled such transferee's ratable portion of such liability determined on the basis of the relative fair market values (determined without regard to section 7701(g)) of all of the assets subject to such liability.

Subpart D—Special Rule; Definitions

[Sec. 368]

SEC. 368. DEFINITIONS RELATING TO CORPORATE REORGANIZATIONS.

[Sec. 368(a)]

(a) REORGANIZATION.—

(1) IN GENERAL.—For purposes of parts I and II and this part, the term "reorganization" means—

(A) a statutory merger or consolidation;

(B) the acquisition by one corporation, in exchange solely for all or a part of its voting stock (or in exchange solely for all or a part of the voting stock of a corporation which is in control of the acquiring corporation), of stock of another corporation if, immediately after the acquisition, the acquiring corporation has control of such other corporation (whether or not such acquiring corporation had control immediately before the acquisition);

(C) the acquisition by one corporation, in exchange solely for all or a part of its voting stock (or in exchange solely for all or a part of the voting stock of a corporation which is in control of the acquiring corporation), of substantially all of the properties of another corporation, but in determining whether the exchange is solely for stock the assumption by the acquiring corporation of a liability of the other shall be disregarded;

(D) a transfer by a corporation of all or a part of its assets to another corporation if immediately after the transfer the transferor, or one or more of its shareholders (including persons who were shareholders immediately before the transfer), or any combination thereof, is in control of the corporation to which the assets are transferred; but only if, in pursuance of the plan, stock or securities of the corporation to which the assets are transferred are distributed in a transaction which qualifies under section 354, 355, or 356;

(E) a recapitalization;

(F) a mere change in identity, form, or place of organization of one corporation, however effected; or

(G) a transfer by a corporation of all or part of its assets to another corporation in a title 11 or similar case; but only if, in pursuance of the plan, stock or securities of the corporation to which the assets are transferred are distributed in a transaction which qualifies under section 354, 355, or 356.

(2) SPECIAL RULES RELATING TO PARAGRAPH (1).—

(A) REORGANIZATIONS DESCRIBED IN BOTH PARAGRAPH (1) (C) AND PARAGRAPH (1) (D).—If a transaction is described in both paragraph (1) (C) and paragraph (1) (D), then, for purposes of this subchapter (other than for purposes of subparagraph (C)), such transaction shall be treated as described only in paragraph (1) (D).

(B) ADDITIONAL CONSIDERATION IN CERTAIN PARAGRAPH (1) (C) CASES.—If—

(i) one corporation acquires substantially all of the properties of another corporation,

(ii) the acquisition would qualify under paragraph (1) (C) but for the fact that the acquiring corporation exchanges money or other property in addition to voting stock, and

(iii) the acquiring corporation acquires, solely for voting stock described in paragraph (1) (C), property of the other corporation having a fair market value which is at least 80 percent of the fair market value of all of the property of the other corporation,

then such acquisition shall (subject to subparagraph (A) of this paragraph) be treated as qualifying under paragraph (1) (C). Solely for the purpose of determining whether clause (iii) of the preceding sentence applies, the amount of any liability assumed by the acquiring corporation shall be treated as money paid for the property.

(C) TRANSFERS OF ASSETS OR STOCK TO SUBSIDIARIES IN CERTAIN PARAGRAPH (1)(A), (1)(B), (1)(C), AND (1)(G) CASES.—A transaction otherwise qualifying under paragraph (1)(A), (1)(B), or (1)(C) shall not be disqualified by reason of the fact that part or all of the assets or stock which were acquired in the transaction are transferred to a corporation controlled by the corporation acquiring such assets or stock. A similar rule shall apply to a transaction otherwise qualifying under paragraph (1)(G) where the requirements of subparagraphs (A) and (B) of section 354(b)(1) are met with respect to the acquisition of the assets.

(D) USE OF STOCK OF CONTROLLING CORPORATION IN PARAGRAPH (1)(A) AND (1)(G) CASES.— The acquisition by one corporation, in exchange for stock of a corporation (referred to in this subparagraph as "controlling corporation") which is in control of the acquiring corporation, of substantially all of the properties of another corporation shall not disqualify a transaction under paragraph (1)(A) or (1)(G) if—

(i) no stock of the acquiring corporation is used in the transaction, and

(ii) in the case of a transaction under paragraph (1)(A), such transaction would have qualified under paragraph (1)(A) had the merger been into the controlling corporation.

(E) STATUTORY MERGER USING VOTING STOCK OF CORPORATION CONTROLLING MERGED CORPORATION.—A transaction otherwise qualifying under paragraph (1)(A) shall not be disqualified by reason of the fact that stock of a corporation (referred to in this subparagraph as the "controlling corporation") which before the merger was in control of the merged corporation is used in the transaction, if—

(i) after the transaction, the corporation surviving the merger holds substantially all of its properties and of the properties of the merged corporation (other than stock of the controlling corporation distributed in the transaction); and

Sec. 368(a)

(ii) in the transaction, former shareholders of the surviving corporation exchanged, for an amount of voting stock of the controlling corporation, an amount of stock in the surviving corporation which constitutes control of such corporation.

* * *

(G) DISTRIBUTION REQUIREMENT FOR PARAGRAPH (1)(C).—

(i) IN GENERAL.—A transaction shall fail to meet the requirements of paragraph (1)(C) unless the acquired corporation distributes the stock, securities, and other properties it receives, as well as its other properties, in pursuance of the plan of reorganization. For purposes of the preceding sentence, if the acquired corporation is liquidated pursuant to the plan of reorganization, any distribution to its creditors in connection with such liquidation shall be treated as pursuant to the plan of reorganization.

(ii) EXCEPTION.—The Secretary may waive the application of clause (i) to any transaction subject to any conditions the Secretary may prescribe.

(H) SPECIAL RULES FOR DETERMINING WHETHER CERTAIN TRANSACTIONS ARE QUALIFIED UNDER PARAGRAPH (1)(D).—For purposes of determining whether a transaction qualifies under paragraph (1)(D)—

(i) in the case of a transaction with respect to which the requirements of subparagraphs (A) and (B) of section 354(b)(1) are met, the term "control" has the meaning given such term by section 304(c), and

(ii) in the case of a transaction with respect to which the requirements of section 355 (or so much of section 356 as relates to section 355) are met, the fact that the shareholders of the distributing corporation dispose of part or all of the distributed stock, or the fact that the corporation whose stock was distributed issues additional stock, shall not be taken into account.

* * *

[Sec. 368(b)]

(b) PARTY TO A REORGANIZATION.—For purposes of this part, the term "a party to a reorganization" includes—

(1) a corporation resulting from a reorganization, and

(2) both corporations, in the case of a reorganization resulting from the acquisition by one corporation of stock or properties of another.

In the case of a reorganization qualifying under paragraph (1)(B) or (1)(C) of subsection (a), if the stock exchanged for the stock or properties is stock of a corporation which is in control of the acquiring corporation, the term "a party to a reorganization" includes the corporation so controlling the acquiring corporation. In the case of a reorganization qualifying under paragraph (1)(A), (1)(B), (1)(C), or (1)(G) of subsection (a) by reason of paragraph (2)(C) of subsection (a), the term "a party to a reorganization" includes the corporation controlling the corporation to which the acquired assets or stock are transferred. In the case of a reorganization qualifying under paragraph (1)(A) or (1)(G) of subsection (a) by reason of paragraph (2)(D) of that subsection, the term "a party to a reorganization" includes the controlling corporation referred to in such paragraph (2)(D). In the case of a reorganization qualifying under subsection (a)(1)(A) by reason of subsection (a)(2)(E), the term "party to a reorganization" includes the controlling corporation referred to in subsection (a)(2)(E).

[Sec. 368(c)]

(c) CONTROL DEFINED.—For purposes of part I (other than section 304), part II, this part, and part V, the term "control" means the ownership of stock possessing at least 80 percent of the total combined voting power of all classes of stock entitled to vote and at least 80 percent of the total number of shares of all other classes of stock of the corporation.

PART V—CARRYOVERS

[Sec. 381]

SEC. 381. CARRYOVERS IN CERTAIN CORPORATE ACQUISITIONS.

[Sec. 381(a)]

(a) GENERAL RULE.—In the case of the acquisition of assets of a corporation by another corporation—

(1) in a distribution to such other corporation to which section 332 (relating to liquidations of subsidiaries) applies; or

(2) in a transfer to which section 361 (relating to nonrecognition of gain or loss to corporations) applies, but only if the transfer is in connection with a reorganization described in subparagraph (A), (C), (D), (F), or (G) of section 368(a)(1),

the acquiring corporation shall succeed to and take into account, as of the close of the day of distribution or transfer, the items described in subsection (c) of the distributor or transferor corporation, subject to the conditions and limitations specified in subsections (b) and (c). For purposes of the preceding sentence, a reorganization shall be treated as meeting the requirements of subparagraph (D) or (G) of section 368(a)(1) only if the requirements of subparagraphs (A) and (B) of section 354(b)(1) are met.

[Sec. 381(b)]

(b) OPERATING RULES.—Except in the case of an acquisition in connection with a reorganization described in subparagraph (F) of section 368 (a) (1)—

(1) The taxable year of the distributor or transferor corporation shall end on the date of distribution or transfer.

(2) For purposes of this section, the date of distribution or transfer shall be the day on which the distribution or transfer is completed; except that, under regulations prescribed by the Secretary, the date when substantially all of the property has been distributed or transferred may be used if the distributor or transferor corporation ceases all operations, other than liquidating activities, after such date.

(3) The corporation acquiring property in a distribution or transfer described in subsection (a) shall not be entitled to carry back a net operating loss or a net capital loss for a taxable year ending after the date of distribution or transfer to a taxable year of the distributor or transferor corporation.

[Sec. 381(c)]

(c) ITEMS OF THE DISTRIBUTOR OR TRANSFEROR CORPORATION.—The items referred to in subsection (a) are:

(1) NET OPERATING LOSS CARRYOVERS.—The net operating loss carryovers determined under section 172, subject to the following conditions and limitations:

(A) The taxable year of the acquiring corporation to which the net operating loss carryovers of the distributor or transferor corporation are first carried shall be the first taxable year ending after the date of distribution or transfer.

(B) In determining the net operating loss deduction, the portion of such deduction attributable to the net operating loss carryovers of the distributor or transferor corporation to the first taxable year of the acquiring corporation ending after the date of distribution or transfer shall be limited to an amount which bears the same ratio to the taxable income (determined without regard to a net operating loss deduction) of the acquiring corporation in such taxable year as the number of days in the taxable year after the date of distribution or transfer bears to the total number of days in the taxable year.

(C) For the purpose of determining the amount of the net operating loss carryovers under section 172 (b) (2), a net operating loss for a taxable year (hereinafter in this subparagraph referred to as the "loss year") of a distributor or transferor corporation which ends on or before the end of a loss year of the acquiring corporation shall be considered to be a net operating loss for a year prior to such loss year of the acquiring corporation. For the same purpose, the taxable income for a "prior taxable year" (as the term is used in section 172 (b) (2)) shall be computed as provided in such section; except that, if the date of distribution or transfer is on a day other than the last day of a taxable year of the acquiring corporation—

(i) such taxable year shall (for the purpose of this subparagraph only) be considered to be 2 taxable years (hereinafter in this subparagraph referred to as the "pre-acquisition part year" and the "post-acquisition part year");

(ii) the pre-acquisition part year shall begin on the same day as such taxable year begins and shall end on the date of distribution or transfer;

(iii) the post-acquisition part year shall begin on the day following the date of distribution or transfer and shall end on the same day as the end of such taxable year;

(iv) the taxable income for such taxable year (computed with the modifications specified in section 172 (b) (2) (A) but without a net operating loss deduction) shall be divided between the pre-acquisition part year and the post-acquisition part year in proportion to the number of days in each;

(v) the net operating loss deduction for the pre-acquisition part year shall be determined as provided in section 172 (b) (2) (B), but without regard to a net operating loss year of the distributor or transferor corporation; and

(vi) the net operating loss deduction for the post-acquisition part year shall be determined as provided in section 172 (b) (2) (B).

(2) EARNINGS AND PROFITS.—In the case of a distribution or transfer described in subsection (a)—

(A) the earnings and profits or deficit in earnings and profits, as the case may be, of the distributor or transferor corporation shall, subject to subparagraph (B), be deemed to have been received or incurred by the acquiring corporation as of the close of the date of the distribution or transfer; and

(B) a deficit in earnings and profits of the distributor, transferor, or acquiring corporation shall be used only to offset earnings and profits accumulated after the date of transfer. For this purpose, the earnings and profits for the taxable year of the acquiring corporation in which the distribution or transfer occurs shall be deemed to have been accumulated after such distribution or transfer in an amount which bears the same ratio to the undistributed earnings and profits of the acquiring corporation for such taxable year (computed without regard to any earnings and profits received from the distributor or transferor corporation, as described in subparagraph (A) of this paragraph) as the number of days in the taxable year after the date of distribution or transfer bears to the total number of days in the taxable year.

(3) CAPITAL LOSS CARRYOVER.—The capital loss carryover determined under section 1212, subject to the following conditions and limitations:

(A) The taxable year of the acquiring corporation to which the capital loss carryover of the distributor or transferor corporation is first carried shall be the first taxable year ending after the date of distribution or transfer.

(B) The capital loss carryover shall be a short-term capital loss in the taxable year determined under subparagraph (A) but shall be limited to an amount which bears the same ratio to the capital gain net income (determined without regard to a short-term capital loss attributable to capital loss carryover), if any, of the acquiring corporation in such taxable year as the number of days in the taxable year after the date of distribution or transfer bears to the total number of days in the taxable year.

(C) For purposes of determining the amount of such capital loss carryover to taxable years following the taxable year determined under subparagraph (A), the capital gain net income in the taxable year determined under subparagraph (A) shall be considered to be an amount equal to the amount determined under subparagraph (B).

(4) METHOD OF ACCOUNTING.—The acquiring corporation shall use the method of accounting used by the distributor or transferor corporation on the date of distribution or transfer unless different methods were used by several distributor or transferor corporations or by a distributor or transferor corporation and the acquiring corporation. If different methods were used, the acquiring corporation shall use the method or combination of methods of computing taxable income adopted pursuant to regulations prescribed by the Secretary.

(5) INVENTORIES.—In any case in which inventories are received by the acquiring corporation, such inventories shall be taken by such corporation (in determining its income) on the same basis on which such inventories were taken by the distributor or transferor corporation, unless different methods were used by several distributor or transferor corporations or by a distributor or transferor corporation and the acquiring corporation. If different methods were used, the acquiring corporation

Sec. 381(c)

shall use the method or combination of methods of taking inventory adopted pursuant to regulations prescribed by the Secretary.

(6) METHOD OF COMPUTING DEPRECIATION ALLOWANCE.—The acquiring corporation shall be treated as the distributor or transferor corporation for purposes of computing the depreciation allowance under sections 167 and 168 on property acquired in a distribution or transfer with respect to so much of the basis in the hands of the acquiring corporation as does not exceed the adjusted basis in the hands of the distributor or transferor corporation.

(8) INSTALLMENT METHOD.—If the acquiring corporation acquires installment obligations (the income from which the distributor or transferor corporation reports on the installment basis under section 453) the acquiring corporation shall, for purposes of section 453, be treated as if it were the distributor or transferor corporation.

(9) AMORTIZATION OF BOND DISCOUNT OR PREMIUM.—If the acquiring corporation assumes liability for bonds of the distributor or transferor corporation issued at a discount or premium, the acquiring corporation shall be treated as the distributor or transferor corporation after the date of distribution or transfer for purposes of determining the amount of amortization allowable or includible with respect to such discount or premium.

(10) TREATMENT OF CERTAIN MINING DEVELOPMENT AND EXPLORATION EXPENSES OF DISTRIBUTOR OR TRANSFEROR CORPORATION.—The acquiring corporation shall be entitled to deduct, as if it were the distributor or transferor corporation, expenses deferred under section 616 (relating to certain development expenditures) if the distributor or transferor corporation has so elected.

(11) CONTRIBUTIONS TO PENSION PLANS, EMPLOYEES' ANNUITY PLANS, AND STOCK BONUS AND PROFIT-SHARING PLANS.—The acquiring corporation shall be considered to be the distributor or transferor corporation after the date of distribution or transfer for the purpose of determining the amounts deductible under section 404 with respect to pension plans, employees' annuity plans, and stock bonus and profit-sharing plans.

(12) RECOVERY OF TAX BENEFIT ITEMS.—If the acquiring corporation is entitled to the recovery of any amounts previously deducted by (or allowable as credits to) the distributor or transferor corporation, the acquiring corporation shall succeed to the treatment under section 111 which would apply to such amounts in the hands of the distributor or transferor corporation.

(13) INVOLUNTARY CONVERSIONS UNDER SECTION 1033.—The acquiring corporation shall be treated as the distributor or transferor corporation after the date of distribution or transfer for purposes of applying section 1033.

(14) DIVIDEND CARRYOVER TO PERSONAL HOLDING COMPANY.—The dividend carryover (described in section 564) to taxable years ending after the date of distribution or transfer.

(16) CERTAIN OBLIGATIONS OF DISTRIBUTOR OR TRANSFEROR CORPORATION.—If the acquiring corporation—

(A) assumes an obligation of the distributor or transferor corporation which, after the date of the distribution or transfer, gives rise to a liability, and

(B) such liability, if paid or accrued by the distributor or transferor corporation, would have been deductible in computing its taxable income,

the acquiring corporation shall be entitled to deduct such items when paid or accrued, as the case may be, as if such corporation were the distributor or transferor corporation. A corporation which would have been an acquiring corporation under this section if the date of distribution or transfer had occurred on or after the effective date of the provisions of this subchapter applicable to a liquidation or reorganization, as the case may be, shall be entitled, even though the date of distribution or transfer occurred before such effective date, to apply this paragraph with respect to amounts paid or accrued in taxable years beginning after December 31, 1953, on account of such obligations of the distributor or transferor corporation. This paragraph shall not apply if such obligations are reflected in the amount of stock, securities, or property transferred by the acquiring corporation to the transferor corporation for the property of the transferor corporation.

(17) DEFICIENCY DIVIDEND OF PERSONAL HOLDING COMPANY.—If the acquiring corporation pays a deficiency dividend (as defined in section 547 (d)) with respect to the distributor or transferor corporation, such distributor or transferor corporation shall, with respect to such payments, be entitled to the deficiency dividend deduction provided in section 547.

(18) PERCENTAGE DEPLETION ON EXTRACTION OF ORES OR MINERALS FROM THE WASTE OR RESIDUE OF PRIOR MINING.—The acquiring corporation shall be considered to be the distributor or transferor

corporation for the purpose of determining the applicability of section 613 (c) (3) (relating to extraction of ores or minerals from the ground).

(19) CHARITABLE CONTRIBUTIONS IN EXCESS OF PRIOR YEARS' LIMITATIONS.—Contributions made in the taxable year ending on the date of distribution or transfer and the 4 prior taxable years by the distributor or transferor corporation in excess of the amount deductible under section 170(b)(2) for such taxable years shall be deductible by the acquiring corporation for its taxable years which begin after the date of distribution or transfer, subject to the limitations imposed in section 170(b)(2). In applying the preceding sentence, each taxable year of the distributor or transferor corporation beginning on or before the date of distribution or transfer shall be treated as a prior taxable year with reference to the acquiring corporation's taxable years beginning after such date.

(22) SUCCESSOR INSURANCE COMPANY.—If the acquiring corporation is an insurance company taxable under subchapter L, there shall be taken into account (to the extent proper to carry out the purposes of this section and of subchapter L, and under such regulations as may be prescribed by the Secretary) the items required to be taken into account for purposes of subchapter L in respect of the distributor or transferor corporation.

(23) DEFICIENCY DIVIDEND OF REGULATED INVESTMENT COMPANY OR REAL ESTATE INVESTMENT TRUST.—If the acquiring corporation pays a deficiency dividend (as defined in section 860(f)) with respect to the distributor or transferor corporation, such distributor or transferor corporation shall, with respect to such payments, be entitled to the deficiency dividend deduction provided in section 860.

(24) CREDIT UNDER SECTION 38.—The acquiring corporation shall take into account (to the extent proper to carry out the purposes of this section and section 38, and under such regulations as may be prescribed by the Secretary) the items required to be taken into account for purposes of section 38 in respect of the distributor or transferor corporation.

(25) CREDIT UNDER SECTION 53.—The acquiring corporation shall take into account (to the extent proper to carry out the purposes of this section 53, and under such regulations as may be prescribed by the Secretary) the items required to be taken into account for purposes of section 53 in respect of the distributor or transferor corporation.

(26) ENTERPRISE ZONE PROVISIONS.—The acquiring corporation shall take into account (to the extent proper to carry out the purposes of this section and subchapter U, and under such regulations as may be prescribed by the Secretary) the items required to be taken into account for purposes of subchapter U in respect of the distributor or transferor corporation.

* * *

[Sec. 382]

SEC. 382. LIMITATION ON NET OPERATING LOSS CARRYFORWARDS AND CERTAIN BUILT-IN LOSSES FOLLOWING OWNERSHIP CHANGE.

[Sec. 382(a)]

(a) GENERAL RULE.—The amount of the taxable income of any new loss corporation for any post-change year which may be offset by pre-change losses shall not exceed the section 382 limitation for such year.

[Sec. 382(b)]

(b) SECTION 382 LIMITATION.—For purposes of this section—

(1) IN GENERAL.—Except as otherwise provided in this section, the section 382 limitation for any post-change year is an amount equal to—

(A) the value of the old loss corporation, multiplied by

(B) the long-term tax-exempt rate.

(2) CARRYFORWARD OF UNUSED LIMITATION.—If the section 382 limitation for any post-change year exceeds the taxable income of the new loss corporation for such year which was offset by pre-change losses, the section 382 limitation for the next post-change year shall be increased by the amount of such excess.

(3) SPECIAL RULE FOR POST-CHANGE YEAR WHICH INCLUDES CHANGE DATE.—In the case of any post-change year which includes the change date—

(A) LIMITATION DOES NOT APPLY TO TAXABLE INCOME BEFORE CHANGE.—Subsection (a) shall not apply to the portion of the taxable income for such year which is allocable to the period in such year on or before the change date. Except as provided in subsection (h)(5) and in regulations, taxable income shall be allocated ratably to each day in the year.

(B) LIMITATION FOR PERIOD AFTER CHANGE.—For purposes of applying the limitation of subsection (a) to the remainder of the taxable income for such year, the section 382 limitation shall be an amount which bears the same ratio to such limitation (determined without regard to this paragraph) as—

(i) the number of days in such year after the change date, bears to

(ii) the total number of days in such year.

[Sec. 382(c)]

(c) CARRYFORWARDS DISALLOWED IF CONTINUITY OF BUSINESS REQUIREMENTS NOT MET.—

(1) IN GENERAL.—Except as provided in paragraph (2), if the new loss corporation does not continue the business enterprise of the old loss corporation at all times during the 2-year period beginning on the change date, the section 382 limitation for any post-change year shall be zero.

(2) EXCEPTION FOR CERTAIN GAINS.—The section 382 limitation for any post-change year shall not be less than the sum of—

(A) any increase in such limitation under—

(i) subsection (h)(1)(A) for recognized built-in gains for such year, and

(ii) subsection (h)(1)(C) for gain recognized by reason of an election under section 338, plus

(B) any increase in such limitation under subsection (b)(2) for amounts described in subparagraph (A) which are carried forward to such year.

[Sec. 382(d)]

(d) PRE-CHANGE LOSS AND POST-CHANGE YEAR.—For purposes of this section—

(1) PRE-CHANGE LOSS.—The term "pre-change loss" means—

(A) any net operating loss carryforward of the old loss corporation to the taxable year ending with the ownership change or in which the change date occurs, and

(B) the net operating loss of the old loss corporation for the taxable year in which the ownership change occurs to the extent such loss is allocable to the period in such year on or before the change date.

Except as provided in subsection (h)(5) and in regulations, the net operating loss shall, for purposes of subparagraph (B), be allocated ratably to each day in the year.

(2) POST-CHANGE YEAR.—The term "post-change year" means any taxable year ending after the change date.

[Sec. 382(e)]

(e) VALUE OF OLD LOSS CORPORATION.—For purposes of this section—

(1) IN GENERAL.—Except as otherwise provided in this subsection, the value of the old loss corporation is the value of the stock of such corporation (including any stock described in section 1504(a)(4)) immediately before the ownership change.

(2) SPECIAL RULE IN THE CASE OF REDEMPTION OR OTHER CORPORATE CONTRACTION.—If a redemption or other corporate contraction occurs in connection with an ownership change, the value under paragraph (1) shall be determined after taking such redemption or other corporate contraction into account.

(3) TREATMENT OF FOREIGN CORPORATIONS.—Except as otherwise provided in regulations, in determining the value of any old loss corporation which is a foreign corporation, there shall be taken into account only items treated as connected with the conduct of a trade or business in the United States.

[Sec. 382(f)]

(f) LONG-TERM TAX-EXEMPT RATE.—For purposes of this section—

(1) IN GENERAL.—The long-term tax-exempt rate shall be the highest of the adjusted Federal long-term rates in effect for any month in the 3-calendar-month period ending with the calendar month in which the change date occurs.

(2) ADJUSTED FEDERAL LONG-TERM RATE.—For purposes of paragraph (1), the term "adjusted Federal long-term rate" means the Federal long-term rate determined under section 1274(d), except that—

(A) paragraphs (2) and (3) thereof shall not apply, and

(B) such rate shall be properly adjusted for differences between rates on long-term taxable and tax-exempt obligations.

[Sec. 382(g)]

(g) OWNERSHIP CHANGE.—For purposes of this section—

(1) IN GENERAL.—There is an ownership change if, immediately after any owner shift involving a 5-percent shareholder or any equity structure shift—

(A) the percentage of the stock of the loss corporation owned by 1 or more 5-percent shareholders has increased by more than 50 percentage points over

(B) the lowest percentage of stock of the loss corporation (or any predecessor corporation) owned by such shareholders at any time during the testing period.

(2) OWNER SHIFT INVOLVING 5-PERCENT SHAREHOLDER.—There is an owner shift involving a 5-percent shareholder if—

(A) there is any change in the respective ownership of stock of a corporation, and

(B) such change affects the percentage of stock of such corporation owned by any person who is a 5-percent shareholder before or after such change.

(3) EQUITY STRUCTURE SHIFT DEFINED.—

(A) IN GENERAL.—The term "equity structure shift" means any reorganization (within the meaning of section 368). Such term shall not include—

(i) any reorganization described in subparagraph (D) or (G) of section 368(a)(1) unless the requirements of section 354(b)(1) are met, and

(ii) any reorganization described in subparagraph (F) of section 368(a)(1).

(B) TAXABLE REORGANIZATION-TYPE TRANSACTIONS, ETC.—To the extent provided in regulations, the term "equity structure shift" includes taxable reorganization-type transactions, public offerings, and similar transactions.

(4) SPECIAL RULES FOR APPLICATION OF SUBSECTION.—

(A) TREATMENT OF LESS THAN 5-PERCENT SHAREHOLDERS.—Except as provided in subparagraphs (B)(i) and (C), in determining whether an ownership change has occurred, all stock owned by shareholders of a corporation who are not 5-percent shareholders of such corporation shall be treated as stock owned by 1 5-percent shareholder of such corporation.

(B) COORDINATION WITH EQUITY STRUCTURE SHIFTS.—For purposes of determining whether an equity structure shift (or subsequent transaction) is an ownership change—

(i) LESS THAN 5-PERCENT SHAREHOLDERS.—Subparagraph (A) shall be applied separately with respect to each group of shareholders (immediately before such equity structure shift) of each corporation which was a party to the reorganization involved in such equity structure shift.

(ii) ACQUISITIONS OF STOCK.—Unless a different proportion is established, acquisitions of stock after such equity structure shift shall be treated as being made proportionately from all shareholders immediately before such acquisition.

(C) COORDINATION WITH OTHER OWNER SHIFTS.—Except as provided in regulations, rules similar to the rules of subparagraph (B) shall apply in determining whether there has been an owner shift involving a 5-percent shareholder and whether such shift (or subsequent transaction) results in an ownership change.

(D) TREATMENT OF WORTHLESS STOCK.—If any stock held by a 50-percent shareholder is treated by such shareholder as becoming worthless during any taxable year of such shareholder

Sec. 382(g)

and such stock is held by such shareholder as of the close of such taxable year, for purposes of determining whether an ownership change occurs after the close of such taxable year, such shareholder—

(i) shall be treated as having acquired such stock on the 1st day of his 1st succeeding taxable year, and

(ii) shall not be treated as having owned such stock during any prior period.

For purposes of the preceding sentence, the term "50-percent shareholder" means any person owning 50 percent or more of the stock of the corporation at any time during the 3-year period ending on the last day of the taxable year with respect to which the stock was so treated.

[Sec. 382(h)]

(h) SPECIAL RULES FOR BUILT-IN GAINS AND LOSSES AND SECTION 338 GAINS.—For purposes of this section—

(1) IN GENERAL.—

(A) NET UNREALIZED BUILT-IN GAIN.—

(i) IN GENERAL.—If the old loss corporation has a net unrealized built-in gain, the section 382 limitation for any recognition period taxable year shall be increased by the recognized built-in gains for such taxable year.

(ii) LIMITATION.—The increase under clause (i) for any recognition period taxable year shall not exceed—

(I) the net unrealized built-in gain, reduced by

(II) recognized built-in gains for prior years ending in the recognition period.

(B) NET UNREALIZED BUILT-IN LOSS.—

(i) IN GENERAL.—If the old loss corporation has a net unrealized built-in loss, the recognized built-in loss for any recognition period taxable year shall be subject to limitation under this section in the same manner as if such loss were a pre-change loss.

(ii) LIMITATION.—Clause (i) shall apply to recognized built-in losses for any recognition period taxable year only to the extent such losses do not exceed—

(I) the net unrealized built-in loss, reduced by

(II) recognized built-in losses for prior taxable years ending in the recognition period.

(C) SPECIAL RULES FOR CERTAIN SECTION 338 GAINS.—If an election under section 338 is made in connection with an ownership change and the net unrealized built-in gain is zero by reason of paragraph (3)(B), then, with respect to such change, the section 382 limitation for the post-change year in which gain is recognized by reason of such election shall be increased by the lesser of—

(i) the recognized built-in gains by reason of such election, or

(ii) the net unrealized built-in gain (determined without regard to paragraph (3)(B)).

(2) RECOGNIZED BUILT-IN GAIN AND LOSS.—

(A) RECOGNIZED BUILT-IN GAIN.—The term "recognized built-in gain" means any gain recognized during the recognition period on the disposition of any asset to the extent the new loss corporation establishes that—

(i) such asset was held by the old loss corporation immediately before the change date, and

(ii) such gain does not exceed the excess of—

(I) the fair market value of such asset on the change date, over

(II) the adjusted basis of such asset on such date.

(B) RECOGNIZED BUILT-IN LOSS.—The term "recognized built-in loss" means any loss recognized during the recognition period on the disposition of any asset except to the extent the new loss corporation establishes that—

(i) such asset was not held by the old loss corporation immediately before the change date, or

(ii) such loss exceeds the excess of—

Sec. 382(h)

(I) the adjusted basis of such asset on the change date, over

(II) the fair market value of such asset on such date.

Such term includes any amount allowable as depreciation, amortization, or depletion for any period within the recognition period except to the extent the new loss corporation establishes that the amount so allowable is not attributable to the excess described in clause (ii).

(3) NET UNREALIZED BUILT-IN GAIN AND LOSS DEFINED.—

(A) NET UNREALIZED BUILT-IN GAIN AND LOSS.—

(i) IN GENERAL.—The terms "net unrealized built-in gain" and "net unrealized built-in loss" mean, with respect to any old loss corporation, the amount by which—

(I) the fair market value of the assets of such corporation immediately before an ownership change is more or less, respectively, than

(II) the aggregate adjusted basis of such assets at such time.

(ii) SPECIAL RULE FOR REDEMPTIONS OR OTHER CORPORATE CONTRACTIONS.—If a redemption or other corporate contraction occurs in connection with an ownership change, to the extent provided in regulations, determinations under clause (i) shall be made after taking such redemption or other corporate contractions into account.

(B) THRESHOLD REQUIREMENT.—

(i) IN GENERAL.—If the amount of the net unrealized built-in gain or net unrealized built-in loss (determined without regard to this subparagraph) of any old loss corporation is not greater than the lesser of—

(I) 15 percent of the amount determined for purposes of subparagraph (A)(i)(I), or

(II) $10,000,000,

the net unrealized built-in gain or net unrealized built-in loss shall be zero.

(ii) CASH AND CASH ITEMS NOT TAKEN INTO ACCOUNT.—In computing any net unrealized built-in gain or unrealized built-in loss under clause (i), except as provided in regulations, there shall not be taken into account—

(I) any cash or cash item, or

(II) any marketable security which has a value which does not substantially differ from adjusted basis.

(4) DISALLOWED LOSS ALLOWED AS A CARRYFORWARD.—If a deduction for any portion of a recognized built-in loss is disallowed for any post-change year, such portion—

(A) shall be carried forward to subsequent taxable years under rules similar to the rules for the carrying forward of net operating losses (or to the extent the amount so disallowed is attributable to capital losses, under rules similar to the rules for the carrying forward of net capital losses) but

(B) shall be subject to limitation under this section in the same manner as a pre-change loss.

(5) SPECIAL RULES FOR POST-CHANGE YEAR WHICH INCLUDES CHANGE DATE.—For purposes of subsection (b)(3)—

(A) in applying subparagraph (A) thereof, taxable income shall be computed without regard to recognized built-in gains to the extent such gains increased the section 382 limitation for the year (or recognized built-in losses to the extent such losses are treated as pre-change losses), and gain described in paragraph (1)(C), for the year, and

(B) in applying subparagraph (B) thereof, the section 382 limitation shall be computed without regard to recognized built-in gains, and gain described in paragraph (1)(C), for the year.

(6) TREATMENT OF CERTAIN BUILT-IN ITEMS.—

(A) INCOME ITEMS.—Any item of income which is properly taken into account during the recognition period but which is attributable to periods before the change date shall be treated as a recognized built-in gain for the taxable year in which it is properly taken into account.

(B) DEDUCTION ITEMS.—Any amount which is allowable as a deduction during the recognition period (determined without regard to any carryover) but which is attributable to periods before the change date shall be treated as a recogized built-in loss for the taxable year for which it is allowable as a deduction.

Sec. 382(h)

(C) ADJUSTMENTS.—The amount of the net unrealized built-in gain or loss shall be properly adjusted for amounts which would be treated as recognized built-in gains or losses under this paragraph if such amounts were properly taken into account (or allowable as a deduction) during the recognition period.

(7) RECOGNITION PERIOD, ETC.—

(A) RECOGNITION PERIOD.—The term "recognition period" means, with respect to any ownership change, the 5-year period beginning on the change date.

(B) RECOGNITION PERIOD TAXABLE YEAR.—The term "recognition period taxable year" means any taxable year any portion of which is in the recognition period.

(8) DETERMINATION OF FAIR MARKET VALUE IN CERTAIN CASES.—If 80 percent or more in value of the stock of a corporation is acquired in 1 transaction (or in a series of related transactions during any 12-month period), for purposes of determining the net unrealized built-in loss, the fair market value of the assets of such corporation shall not exceed the grossed up amount paid for such stock properly adjusted for indebtedness of the corporation and other relevent items.

(9) TAX-FREE EXCHANGES OR TRANSFERS.—The Secretary shall prescribe such regulations as may be necessary to carry out the purposes of this subsection where property held on the change date was acquired (or is subsequently transferred) in a transaction where gain or loss is not recognized (in whole or in part).

[Sec. 382(i)]

(i) TESTING PERIOD.—For purposes of this section—

(1) 3-YEAR PERIOD.—Except as otherwise provided in this section, the testing period is the 3-year period ending on the day of any owner shift involving a 5-percent shareholder or equity structure shift.

(2) SHORTER PERIOD WHERE THERE HAS BEEN RECENT OWNERSHIP CHANGE.—If there has been an ownership change under this section, the testing period for determining whether a 2nd ownership change has occurred shall not begin before the 1st day following the change date for such earlier ownership change.

(3) SHORTER PERIOD WHERE ALL LOSSES ARISE AFTER 3-YEAR PERIOD BEGINS.—The testing period shall not begin before the earlier of the 1st day of the 1st taxable year from which there is a carryforward of a loss or of an excess credit to the 1st post-change year or the taxable year in which the transaction being tested occurs. Except as provided in regulations, this paragraph shall not apply to any loss corporation which has a net unrealized built-in loss (determined after application of subsection (h)(3)(B)).

[Sec. 382(j)]

(j) CHANGE DATE.—For purposes of this section, the change date is—

(1) in the case where the last component of an ownership change is an owner shift involving a 5-percent shareholder, the date on which such shift occurs, and

(2) in the case where the last component of an ownership change is an equity structure, shift, the date of the reorganization.

[Sec. 382(k)]

(k) DEFINITIONS AND SPECIAL RULES.—For purposes of this section—

(1) LOSS CORPORATION.—The term "loss corporation" means a corporation entitled to use a net operating loss carryover or having a net operating loss for the taxable year in which the ownereship change occurs. Except to the extent provided in regulations, such term includes any corporation with a net unrealized built-in loss.

(2) OLD LOSS CORPORATION.—The term "old loss corporation" means any corporation—

(A) with respect to which there is an ownership change, and

(B) which (before the ownership change) was a loss corporation.

(3) NEW LOSS CORPORATION.—The term "new loss corporation" means a corporation which (after an ownership change) is a loss corporation. Nothing in this section shall be treated as implying that the same corporation may not be both the old loss corporation and the new loss corporation.

(4) TAXABLE INCOME.—Taxable income shall be computed with the modifications set forth in section 172(d).

(5) VALUE.—The term "value" means fair market value.

(6) RULES RELATING TO STOCK.—

(A) PREFERRED STOCK.—Except as provided in regulations and subsection (e), the term "stock" means stock other than stock described in section 1504(a)(4).

(B) TREATMENT OF CERTAIN RIGHTS, ETC.—The Secretary shall prescribe such regulations as may be necessary—

(i) to treat warrants, options, contracts to acquire stock, convertible debt interests, and other similar interests as stock, and

(ii) to treat stock as not stock.

(C) DETERMINATIONS ON BASIS OF VALUE.—Determinations of the percentage of stock of any corporation held by any person shall be made on the basis of value.

(7) 5-PERCENT SHAREHOLDER.—The term "5-percent shareholder" means any person holding 5 percent or more of the stock of the corporation at any time during the testing period.

[Sec. 382(l)]

(l) CERTAIN ADDITIONAL OPERATING RULES.—For purposes of this section—

(1) CERTAIN CAPITAL CONTRIBUTIONS NOT TAKEN INTO ACCOUNT.—

(A) IN GENERAL.—Any capital contribution received by an old loss corporation as part of a plan a principal purpose of which is to avoid or increase any limitation under this section shall not be taken into account for purposes of this section.

(B) CERTAIN CONTRIBUTIONS TREATED AS PART OF PLAN.—For purposes of subparagraph (A), any capital contribution made during the 2-year period ending on the change date shall, except as provided in regulations, be treated as part of a plan described in subparagraph (A).

(2) ORDERING RULES FOR APPLICATION OF SECTION.—

(A) COORDINATION WITH SECTION 172(b) CARRYOVER RULES.—In the case of any pre-change loss for any taxable year (hereinafter in this subparagraph referred to as the "loss year" subject to limitation under this section, for purposes of determining under the 2nd sentence of section 172(b)(2) the amount of such loss which may be carried to any taxable year, taxable income for any taxable year shall be treated as not greater than—

(i) the section 382 limitation for such taxable year, reduced by

(ii) the unused pre-change losses for taxable years preceding the loss year.

Similar rules shall apply in the case of any credit or loss subject to limitation under section 383.

(B) ORDERING RULE FOR LOSSES CARRIED FROM SAME TAXABLE YEAR.—In any case in which—

(i) a pre-change loss of a loss corporation for any taxable year is subject to a section 382 limitation, and

(ii) a net operating loss of such corporation from such taxable year is not subject to such limitation,

taxable income shall be treated as having been offset first by the loss subject to such limitation.

(3) OPERATING RULES RELATING TO OWNERSHIP OF STOCK.—

(A) CONSTRUCTIVE OWNERSHIP.—Section 318 (relating to constructive ownership of stock) shall apply in determining ownership of stock, except that—

(i) paragraphs (1) and (5)(B) of section 318(a) shall not apply and an individual and all members of his family described in paragraph (1) of section 318(a) shall be treated as 1 individual for purposes of applying this section,

(ii) paragraph (2) of section 318(a) shall be applied—

(I) without regard to the 50-percent limitation contained in subparagraph (C) thereof, and

(II) except as provided in regulations, by treating stock attributed thereunder as no longer being held by the entity from which attributed,

(iii) paragraph (3) of section 318(a) shall be applied only to the extent provided in regulations,

(iv) except to the extent provided in regulations, an option to acquire stock shall be treated as exercised if such exercise results in an ownership change, and

(v) in attributing stock from an entity under paragraph (2) of section 318(a), there shall not be taken into account—

(I) in the case of attribution from a corporation, stock which is not treated as stock for purposes of this section, or

(II) in the case of attribution from another entity, an interest in such entity similar to stock described in subclause (I).

A rule similar to the rule of clause (iv) shall apply in the case of any contingent purchase, warrant, convertible debt, put, stock subject to a risk of forfeiture, contract to acquire stock, or similar interests.

(B) STOCK ACQUIRED BY REASON OF DEATH, GIFT, DIVORCE, SEPARATION, ETC.—If—

(i) the basis of any stock in the hands of any person is determined—

(I) under section 1014 (relating to property acquired from a decedent),

(II) section 1015 (relating to property acquired by a gift or transfer in trust), or

(III) section 1041(b)(2) (relating to transfers of property between spouses or incident to divorce),

(ii) stock is received by any person in satisfaction of a right to receive a pecuniary bequest, or

(iii) stock is acquired by a person pursuant to any divorce or separation instrument (within the meaning of section 71(b)(2)),

such person shall be treated as owning such stock during the period such stock was owned by the person from whom it was acquired.

(C) CERTAIN CHANGES IN PERCENTAGE OWNERSHIP WHICH ARE ATTRIBUTABLE TO FLUCTUATIONS IN VALUE NOT TAKEN INTO ACCOUNT.—Except as provided in regulations, any change in proportionate ownership which is attributable solely to fluctuations in the relative fair market values of different classes of stock shall not be taken into account.

(4) REDUCTION IN VALUE WHERE SUBSTANTIAL NONBUSINESS ASSETS.—

(A) IN GENERAL.—If, immediately after an ownership change, the new loss corporation has substantial nonbusiness assets, the value of the old loss corporation shall be reduced by the excess (if any) of

(i) the fair market value of the nonbusiness assets of the old loss corporation, over

(ii) the nonbusiness asset share of indebtedness for which such corporation is liable.

(B) CORPORATION HAVING SUBSTANTIAL NONBUSINESS ASSETS.—For purposes of subparagraph (A)—

(i) IN GENERAL.—The old loss corporation shall be treated as having substantial nonbusiness assets if at least 1/3 of the value of the total assets of such corporation consists of nonbusiness assets.

(ii) EXCEPTION FOR CERTAIN INVESTMENT ENTITIES.—A regulated investment company to which part I of subchapter M applies, a real estate investment trust to which part II of subchapter M applies, a REMIC to which part IV of subchapter M applies, or a FASIT to which part V of subchapter M applies, shall not be treated as a new loss corporation having substantial nonbusiness assets.

(C) NONBUSINESS ASSETS.—For purposes of this paragraph, the term "nonbusiness assets" means assets held for investment.

(D) NONBUSINESS ASSET SHARE.—For purposes of this paragraph, the nonbusiness asset share of the indebtedness of the corporation is an amount which bears the same ratio to such indebtedness as—

(i) the fair market value of the nonbusiness assets of the corporation, bears to

(ii) the fair market value of all assets of such corporation.

Sec. 382(l)

(E) Treatment of subsidiaries.—For purposes of this paragraph, stock and securities in any subsidiary corporation shall be disregarded and the parent corporation shall be deemed to own its ratable share of the subsidiary's assets. For purposes of the preceding sentence, a corporation shall be treated as a subsidiary if the parent owns 50 percent or more of the combined voting power of all classes of stock entitled to vote, and 50 percent or more of the total value of shares of all classes of stock.

(5) Title 11 or similar case.—

(A) In general.—Subsection (a) shall not apply to any ownership change if—

(i) the old loss corporation is (immediately before such ownership change) under the jurisdiction of the court in a title 11 or similar case, and

(ii) the shareholders and creditors of the old loss corporation (determined immediately before such ownership change) own (after such ownership change and as a result of being shareholders or creditors immediately before such change) stock of the new loss corporation (or stock of a controlling corporation if also in bankruptcy) which meets the requirements of section 1504(a)(2) (determined by substituting "50 percent" for "80 percent" each place it appears).

(B) Reduction for interest payments to creditors becoming shareholders.—In any case to which subparagraph (A) applies, the pre-change losses and excess credits (within the meaning of section 383(a)(2)) which may be carried to a post-change year shall be computed as if no deduction was allowable under this chapter for the interest paid or accrued by the old loss corporation on indebtedness which was converted into stock pursuant to title 11 or similar case during—

(i) any taxable year ending during the 3-year period preceding the taxable year in which the ownership change occurs, and

(ii) the period of the taxable year in which ownership change occurs on or before the change date.

(C) Coordination with section 108.—In applying section 108(e)(8) to any case to which subparagraph (A) applies, there shall not be taken into account any indebtedness for interest described in subparagraph (B).

(D) Section 382 limitation zero if another change within 2 years.—If, during the 2-year period immediately following an ownership change to which this paragraph applies, an ownership change of the new loss corporation occurs, this paragraph shall not apply and the section 382 limitation with respect to the 2nd ownership change for any post-change year ending after the change date of the 2nd ownership change shall be zero.

(E) Only certain stock taken into account.—For purposes of subparagraph (A)(ii), stock transferred to a creditor shall be taken into account only to the extent such stock is transferred in satisfaction of indebtedness and only if such indebtedness—

(i) was held by the creditor at least 18 months before the date of the filing of the title 11 or similar case, or

(ii) arose in the ordinary course of the trade or business of the old loss corporation and is held by the person who at all times held the beneficial interest in such indebtedness.

(F) Special rule for certain financial institutions.—

(i) In general.—In the case of any ownership change to which this subparagraph applies, this paragraph shall be applied—

(I) by substituting "1504(a)(2)(B)" for "1504(a)(2)" and "20 percent" for "50 percent" in subparagraph (A)(ii), and

(II) without regard to subparagraphs (B) and (C).

(ii) Special rule for depositors.—For purposes of applying this paragraph to an ownership change to which this subparagraph applies—

(I) a depositor in the old loss corporation shall be treated as a stockholder in such loss corporation immediately before the change,

(II) deposits which, after the change, become deposits of the new loss corporation shall be treated as stock of the new loss corporation, and

Sec. 382(l)

(III) the fair market value of the outstanding stock of the new loss corporation shall include the amount of deposits in the new loss corporation immediately after the change.

(iii) CHANGES TO WHICH SUBPARAGRAPH APPLIES.—This subparagraph shall apply to—

(I) an equity structure shift which is a reorganization described in section 368 (a)(3)(D)(ii) (as modified by section 368(a)(3)(D)(iv)), or

(II) any other equity structure shift (or transaction to which section 351 applies) which occurs as an integral part of a transaction involving a change to which subclause (I) applies.

This subparagraph shall not apply to any equity structure shift or transaction occurring on or after May 10, 1989.

(G) TITLE 11 OR SIMILAR CASE.—For purposes of this paragraph, the term "title 11 or similar case" has the meaning given such term by section 368(a)(3)(A).

(H) ELECTION NOT TO HAVE PARAGRAPH APPLY.—A new loss corporation may elect, subject to such terms and conditions as the Secretary may prescribe, not to have the provisions of this paragraph apply.

(6) SPECIAL RULE FOR INSOLVENCY TRANSACTIONS.—If paragraph (5) does not apply to any reorganization described in subparagraph (G) of section 368(a)(1) or any exchange of debt for stock in a title 11 or similar case (as defined in section 368(a)(3)(A)), the value under subsection (e) shall reflect the increase (if any) in value of the old loss corporation resulting from any surrender or cancellation of creditors' claims in the transaction.

(7) COORDINATION WITH ALTERNATIVE MINIMUM TAX.—The Secretary shall by regulation provide for the application of this section to the alternative tax net operating loss deduction under section 56(d).

(8) PREDECESSOR AND SUCCESSOR ENTITIES.—Except as provided in regulations, any entity and any predecessor or successor entities of such entity shall be treated as 1 entity.

[Sec. 382(m)]

(m) REGULATIONS.—The Secretary shall prescribe such regulations as may be necessary or appropriate to carry out the purposes of this section and section 383, including (but not limited to) regulations—

(1) providing for the application of this section and section 383 where an ownership change with respect to the old loss corporation is followed by an ownership change with respect to the new loss corporation, and

(2) providing for the application of this section and section 383 in the case of a short taxable year,

(3) providing for such adjustments to the application of this section and section 383 as is necessary to prevent the avoidance of the purposes of this section and section 383, including the avoidance of such purposes through the use of related persons, pass-thru entities, or other intermediaries,

(4) providing for the application of subsection (g)(4) where there is only 1 corporation involved, and

(5) providing, in the case of any group of corporations described in section 1563(a) (determined by substituting "50 percent" for "80 percent" each place it appears and determined without regard to paragraph (4) thereof), appropriate adjustments to value, built-in gain or loss, and other items so that items are not omitted or taken into account more than once.

[Sec. 383]

SEC. 383. SPECIAL LIMITATIONS ON CERTAIN EXCESS CREDITS, ETC.

[SEC. 383(a)]

(a) EXCESS CREDITS.—

(1) IN GENERAL.—Under regulations, if an ownership change occurs with respect to a corporation, the amount of any excess credit for any taxable year which may be used in any post-change year shall be limited to an amount determined on the basis of the tax liability which is

attributable to so much of the taxable income as does not exceed the section 382 limitation for such post-change year to the extent available after the application of section 382 and subsections (b) and (c) of this section.

(2) EXCESS CREDIT.—For purposes of paragraph (1), the term "excess credit" means—

(A) any unused general business credit of the corporation under section 39, and

(B) any unused minimum tax credit of the corporation under section 53.

[Sec. 383(b)]

(b) LIMITATION ON NET CAPITAL LOSS.—If an ownership change occurs with respect to a corporation, the amount of any net capital loss under section 1212 for any taxable year before the 1st post-change year which may be used in any post-change year shall be limited under regulations which shall be based on the principles applicable under section 382. Such regulations shall provide that any such net capital loss used in a post-change year shall reduce the section 382 limitation which is applied to pre-change losses under section 382 for such year.

* * *

[Sec. 383(d)]

(d) PRO RATION RULES FOR YEAR WHICH INCLUDES CHANGE.—For purposes of this section, rules similar to the rules of subsections (b)(3) and (d)(1)(B) of section 382 shall apply.

[Sec. 383(e)]

(e) DEFINITIONS.—Terms used in this section shall have the same respective meanings as when used in section 382, except that appropriate adjustments shall be made to take into account that the limitations of this section apply to credits and net capital losses.

[Sec. 384]

SEC. 384. LIMITATION ON USE OF PREACQUISITION LOSSES TO OFFSET BUILT-IN GAINS.

[Sec. 384(a)]

(a) GENERAL RULE.—If—

(1)(A) a corporation acquires directly (or through 1 or more other corporations) control of another corporation, or

(B) the assets of a corporation are acquired by another corporation in a reorganization described in subparagraph (A), (C), or (D) of section 368(a)(1), and

(2) either of such corporations is a gain corporation,

income for any recognition period taxable year (to the extent attributable to recognized built-in gains) shall not be offset by any preacquisition loss (other than a preacquisition loss of the gain corporation).

[Sec. 384(b)]

(b) EXCEPTION WHERE CORPORATIONS UNDER COMMON CONTROL.—

(1) IN GENERAL.—Subsection (a) shall not apply to the preacquisition loss of any corporation if such corporation and the gain corporation were members of the same controlled group at all times during the 5-year period ending on the acquisition date.

(2) CONTROLLED GROUP.—For purposes of this subsection, the term "controlled group" means a controlled group of corporations (as defined in section 1563(a)); except that—

(A) "more than 50 percent" shall be substituted for "at least 80 percent" each place it appears,

(B) the ownership requirements of section 1563(a) must be met both with respect to voting power and value, and

(C) the determination shall be made without regard to subsection (a)(4) of section 1563.

(3) SHORTER PERIOD WHERE CORPORATIONS NOT IN EXISTENCE FOR 5 YEARS.—If either of the corporations referred to in paragraph (1) was not in existence throughout the 5-year period referred to in paragraph (1), the period during which such corporation was in existence (or if both, the shorter of such periods) shall be substituted for such 5-year period.

[Sec. 384(c)]

(c) DEFINITIONS.—For purposes of this section—

(1) RECOGNIZED BUILT-IN GAIN.—

(A) IN GENERAL.—The term "recognized built-in gain" means any gain recognized during the recognition period on the disposition of any asset except to the extent the gain corporation (or, in any case described in subsection (a)(1)(B), the acquiring corporation) establishes that—

(i) such asset was not held by the gain corporation on the acquisition date, or

(ii) such gain exceeds the excess (if any) of—

(I) the fair market value of such asset on the acquisition date, over

(II) the adjusted basis of such asset on such date.

(B) TREATMENT OF CERTAIN INCOME ITEMS.—Any item of income which is properly taken into account for any recognition period taxable year but which is attributable to periods before the acquisition date shall be treated as a recognized built-in gain for the taxable year in which it is properly taken into account and shall be taken into account in determining the amount of the net unrealized built-in gain.

(C) LIMITATION.—The amount of the recognized built-in gains for any recognition period taxable year shall not exceed—

(i) the net unrealized built-in gain, reduced by

(ii) the recognized built-in gains for prior years ending in the recognition period which (but for this section) would have been offset by preacquisition losses.

(2) ACQUISITION DATE..—The term "acquisition date" means—

(A) in any case described in subsection (a)(1)(A), the date on which the acquisition of control occurs, or

(B) in any case described in subsection (a)(1)(B), the date of the transfer in the reorganization.

(3) PREACQUISITION LOSS.—

(A) IN GENERAL.—The term "preacquisition loss" means—

(i) any net operating loss carryforward to the taxable year in which the acquisition date occurs, and

(ii) any net operating loss for the taxable year in which the acquisition date occurs to the extent such loss is allocable to the period in such year on or before the acquisition date.

Except as provided in regulations, the net operating loss shall, for purposes of clause (ii), be allocated ratably to each day in the year.

(B) TREATMENT OF RECOGNIZED BUILT-IN LOSS.—In the case of a corporation with a net unrealized built-in loss, the term "preacquisition loss" includes any recognized built-in loss.

(4) GAIN CORPORATION.—The term "gain corporation" means any corporation with a net unrealized built-in gain.

(5) CONTROL.—The term "control" means ownership of stock in a corporation which meets the requirements of section 1504(a)(2).

(6) TREATMENT OF MEMBERS OF SAME GROUP.—Except as provided in regulations and except for purposes of subsection (b), all corporations which are members of the same affiliated group immediately before the acquisition date shall be treated as 1 corporation. To the extent provided in regulations, section 1504 shall be applied without regard to subsection (b) thereof for purposes of the preceding sentence.

(7) TREATMENT OF PREDECESSORS AND SUCCESSORS.—Any reference in this section to a corporation shall include a reference to any predecessor or successor thereof.

(8) OTHER DEFINITIONS.—Except as provided in regulations, the terms "net unrealized built-in gain" "net unrealized built-in loss", "recognized built-in loss", "recognition period", and "recognition period taxable year", have the same respective meanings as when used in section 382(h), except that the acquisition date shall be taken into account in lieu of the change date.

Sec. 384(c)

[Sec. 384(d)]

(d) LIMITATION ALSO TO APPLY TO EXCESS CREDITS OR NET CAPITAL LOSSES.—Rules similar to the rules of subsection (a) shall also apply in the case of any excess credit (as defined in section 383(a)(2)) or net capital loss.

[Sec. 384(e)]

(e) ORDERING RULES FOR NET OPERATING LOSSES, ETC.—

(1) CARRYOVER RULES.—If any preacquisition loss may not offset a recognized built-in gain by reason of this section, such gain shall not be taken into account in determining under section 172(b)(2) the amount of such loss which may be carried to other taxable years. A similar rule shall apply in the case of any excess credit or net capital loss limited by reason of subsection (d).

(2) ORDERING RULE FOR LOSSES CARRIED FROM SAME TAXABLE YEAR.—In any case in which—

(A) a preacquisition loss for any taxable year is subject to limitation under subsection (a), and

(B) a net operating loss from such taxable year is not subject to such limitation, taxable income shall be treated as having been offset 1st by the loss subject to such limitation.

[Sec. 384(f)]

(f) REGULATIONS.—The Secretary shall prescribe such regulations as may be necessary to carry out the purposes of this section, including regulations to ensure that the purposes of this section may not be circumvented through—

(1) the use of any provision of law or regulations (including subchapter K of this chapter), or

(2) contributions of property to a corporation.

PART VI—TREATMENT OF CERTAIN CORPORATE INTERESTS AS STOCK OR INDEBTEDNESS

[Sec. 385]

SEC. 385. TREATMENT OF CERTAIN INTERESTS IN CORPORATIONS AS STOCK OR INDEBTEDNESS.

[Sec. 385(a)]

(a) AUTHORITY TO PRESCRIBE REGULATIONS.—The Secretary is authorized to prescribe such regulations as may be necessary or appropriate to determine whether an interest in a corporation is to be treated for purposes of this title as stock or indebtedness (or as in part stock and in part indebtedness).

[Sec. 385(b)]

(b) FACTORS.—The regulations prescribed under this section shall set forth factors which are to be taken into account in determining with respect to a particular factual situation whether a debtor-creditor relationship exists or a corporation-shareholder relationship exists. The factors so set forth in the regulations may include among other factors:

(1) whether there is a written unconditional promise to pay on demand or on a specified date a sum certain in money in return for an adequate consideration in money or money's worth, and to pay a fixed rate of interest,

(2) whether there is subordination to or preference over any indebtedness of the corporation,

(3) the ratio of debt to equity of the corporation,

(4) whether there is convertibility into the stock of the corporation, and

(5) the relationship between holdings of stock in the corporation and holdings of the interest in question.

[Sec. 385(c)]

(c) EFFECT OF CLASSIFICATION BY ISSUER.—

(1) IN GENERAL.—The characterization (as of the time of issuance) by the issuer as to whether an interest in a corporation is stock or indebtedness shall be binding on such issuer and on all holders of such interest (but shall not be binding on the Secretary).

(2) NOTIFICATION OF INCONSISTENT TREATMENT.—Except as provided in regulations, paragraph (1) shall not apply to any holder of an interest if such holder on his return discloses that he is treating such interest in a manner inconsistent with the characterization referred to in paragraph (1).

(3) REGULATIONS.—The Secretary is authorized to require such information as the Secretary determines to be necessary to carry out the provisions of this subsection.

Subchapter D—Deferred Compensation, Etc.

PART I—PENSION, PROFIT-SHARING, STOCK BONUS PLANS, ETC.

Subpart A—General Rule

[Sec. 401]

SEC. 401. QUALIFIED PENSION, PROFIT-SHARING, AND STOCK BONUS PLANS.

* * *

[Sec. 401(c)]

(c) DEFINITIONS AND RULES RELATING TO SELF-EMPLOYED INDIVIDUALS AND OWNER-EMPLOYEES.—For purposes of this section—

(1) SELF-EMPLOYED INDIVIDUAL TREATED AS EMPLOYEE.—

(A) IN GENERAL.—The term "employee" includes, for any taxable year, an individual who is a self-employed individual for such taxable year.

(B) SELF-EMPLOYED INDIVIDUAL.—The term "self-employed individual" means, with respect to any taxable year, an individual who has earned income (as defined in paragraph (2)) for such taxable year. To the extent provided in regulations prescribed by the Secretary, such term also includes, for any taxable year—

(i) an individual who would be a self-employed individual within the meaning of the preceding sentence but for the fact that the trade or business carried on by such individual did not have net profits for the taxable year, and

(ii) an individual who has been a self-employed individual within the meaning of the preceding sentence for any prior taxable year.

(2) EARNED INCOME.—

(A) IN GENERAL.—The term "earned income" means the net earnings from self-employment (as defined in section 1402(a)), but such net earnings shall be determined—

(i) only with respect to a trade or business in which personal services of the taxpayer are a material income-producing factor,

(ii) without regard to paragraphs (4) and (5) of section 1402(c),

(iii) in the case of any individual who is treated as an employee under sections 3121(d)(3)(A), (C), or (D), without regard to paragraph (2) of section 1402(c),

(iv) without regard to items which are not included in gross income for purposes of this chapter, and the deductions properly allocable to or chargeable against such items,

(v) with regard to the deductions allowed by section 404 to the taxpayer, and

(vi) with regard to the deduction allowed to the taxpayer by section 164(f).

For purposes of this subparagraph, section 1402, as in effect for a taxable year ending on December 31, 1962, shall be treated as having been in effect for all taxable years ending before such date. For purposes of this part only (other than sections 419 and 419A), this subparagraph shall be applied as if the term "trade or business" for purposes of section 1402 included service described in section 1402(c)(6).

(C)[B] INCOME FROM DISPOSITION OF CERTAIN PROPERTY.—For purposes of this section, the term "earned income" includes gains (other than any gain which is treated under any provision of this chapter as gain from the sale or exchange of a capital asset) and net earnings derived from the sale or other disposition of, the transfer of any interest in, or the licensing of the use of property (other than good will) by an individual whose personal efforts created such property.

* * *

[Sec. 408]
SEC. 408. INDIVIDUAL RETIREMENT ACCOUNTS.

[Sec. 408(a)]

(a) INDIVIDUAL RETIREMENT ACCOUNT.—For purposes of this section, the term "individual retirement account" means a trust created or organized in the United States for the exclusive benefit of an individual or his beneficiaries, but only if the written governing instrument creating the trust meets the following requirements:

(1) Except in the case of a rollover contribution described in subsection (d)(3), in section 402(c), 403(a)(4), 403(b)(8), or 457(e)(16), no contribution will be accepted unless it is in cash, and contributions will not be accepted for the taxable year on behalf of any individual in excess of the amount in effect for such taxable year under section 219(b)(1)(A).

(2) The trustee is a bank (as defined in subsection (n)) or such other person who demonstrates to the satisfaction of the Secretary that the manner in which such other person will administer the trust will be consistent with the requirements of this section.

(3) No part of the trust funds will be invested in life insurance contracts.

(4) The interest of an individual in the balance of his account is nonforfeitable.

(5) The assets of the trust will not be commingled with other property except in a common trust fund or common investment fund.

(6) Under regulations prescribed by the Secretary, rules similar to the rules of section 401(a)(9) and the incidental death benefit requirements of section 401(a) shall apply to the distribution of the entire interest of an individual for whose benefit the trust is maintained.

[Sec. 408(b)]

(b) INDIVIDUAL RETIREMENT ANNUITY.—For purposes of this section, the term "individual retirement annuity" means an annuity contract, or an endowment contract (as determined under regulations prescribed by the Secretary), issued by an insurance company which meets the following requirements:

(1) The contract is not transferable by the owner.

(2) Under the contract—

(A) the premiums are not fixed,

(B) the annual premium on behalf of any individual will not exceed the dollar amount in effect under section 219(b)(1)(A), and

(C) any refund of premiums will be applied before the close of the calendar year following the year of the refund toward the payment of future premiums or the purchase of additional benefits.

(3) Under regulations prescribed by the Secretary, rules similar to the rules of section 401(a)(9) and the incidental death benefit requirements of section 401(a) shall apply to the distribution of the entire interest of the owner.

(4) The entire interest of the owner is nonforfeitable.

Such term does not include such an annuity contract for any taxable year of the owner in which it is disqualified on the application of subsection (e) or for any subsequent taxable year. For purposes of this subsection, no contract shall be treated as an endowment contract if it matures later than the taxable year in which the individual in whose name such contract is purchased attains age 70½; if it is not for the exclusive benefit of the individual in whose name it is purchased or his beneficiaries; or if the aggregate annual premiums under all such contracts purchased in the name of such individual for any taxable year exceed the dollar amount in effect under section 219(b)(1)(A).

* * *

(d) TAX TREATMENT OF DISTRIBUTIONS.—

(1) IN GENERAL.—Except as otherwise provided in this subsection, any amount paid or distributed out of an individual retirement plan shall be included in gross income by the payee or distributee, as the case may be, in the manner provided under section 72.

(2) SPECIAL RULES FOR APPLYING SECTION 72.—For purposes of applying section 72 to any amount described in paragraph (1)—

(A) all individual retirement plans shall be treated as 1 contract,

(B) all distributions during any taxable year shall be treated as 1 distribution, and

(C) the value of the contract, income on the contract, and investment in the contract shall be computed as of the close of the calendar year in which the taxable year begins.

For purposes of subparagraph (C), the value of the contract shall be increased by the amount of any distributions during the calendar year.

(3) ROLLOVER CONTRIBUTION.—An amount is described in this paragraph as a rollover contribution if it meets the requirements of subparagraphs (A) and (B).

(A) IN GENERAL.—Paragraph (1) does not apply to any amount paid or distributed out of an individual retirement account or individual retirement annuity to the individual for whose benefit the account or annuity is maintained if—

(i) the entire amount received (including money and any other property) is paid into an individual retirement account or individual retirement annuity (other than an endowment contract) for the benefit of such individual not later than the 60th day after the day on which he receives the payment or distribution; or

(ii) the entire amount received (including money and any other property) is paid into an eligible retirement plan for the benefit of such individual not later than the 60th day after the date on which the payment or distribution is received, except that the maximum amount which may be paid into such plan may not exceed the portion of the amount received which is includible in gross income (determined without regard to this paragraph).

For purposes of clause (ii), the term "eligible retirement plan" means an eligible retirement plan described in clause (iii), (iv), (v), or (vi) of section 402(c)(8)(B).

(B) LIMITATION.—This paragraph does not apply to any amount described in subparagraph (A)(i) received by an individual from an individual retirement account or individual retirement annuity if at any time during the 1-year period ending on the day of such receipt such individual received any other amount described in that subparagraph from an individual retirement account or an individual retirement annuity which was not includible in his gross income because of the application of this paragraph.

(C) DENIAL OF ROLLOVER TREATMENT FOR INHERITED ACCOUNTS, ETC.—

(i) IN GENERAL.—In the case of an inherited individual retirement account or individual retirement annuity—

(I) this paragraph shall not apply to any amount received by an individual from such an account or annuity (and no amount transferred from such account or annuity to another individual retirement account or annuity shall be excluded from gross income by reason of such transfer), and

(II) such inherited account or annuity shall not be treated as an individual retirement account or annuity for purposes of determining whether any other amount is a rollover contribution.

(ii) INHERITED INDIVIDUAL RETIREMENT ACCOUNT OR ANNUITY.—An individual retirement account or individual retirement annuity shall be treated as inherited if—

(I) the individual for whose benefit the account or annuity is maintained acquired such account by reason of the death of another individual, and

(II) such individual was not the surviving spouse of such other individual.

(D) PARTIAL ROLLOVERS PERMITTED.—

(i) IN GENERAL.—If any amount paid or distributed out of an individual retirement account or individual retirement annuity would meet the requirements of subparagraph (A) but for the fact that the entire amount was not paid into an eligible plan as required by clause (i) or (ii) of subparagraph (A), such amount shall be treated as meeting the requirements of subparagraph (A) to the extent it is paid into an eligible plan referred to in such clause not later than the 60th day referred to in such clause.

(ii) ELIGIBLE PLAN.—For purposes of clause (i), the term "eligible plan" means any account, annuity, contract, or plan referred to in subparagraph (A).

(E) DENIAL OF ROLLOVER TREATMENT FOR REQUIRED DISTRIBUTIONS.—This paragraph shall not apply to any amount to the extent such amount is required to be distributed under subsection (a)(6) or (b)(3).

(F) FROZEN DEPOSITS.—For purposes of this paragraph, rules similar to the rules of section 402(c)(7) (relating to frozen deposits) shall apply.

(G) SIMPLE RETIREMENT ACCOUNTS.—In the case of any payment or distribution out of a simple retirement account (as defined in subsection (p)) to which section 72(t)(6) applies, this paragraph shall not apply unless such payment or distribution is paid into another simple retirement account.

(H) APPLICATION OF SECTION 72.—

(i) IN GENERAL.—If—

(I) a distribution is made from an individual retirement plan, and

(II) a rollover contribution is made to an eligible retirement plan described in section 402(c)(8)(B)(iii), (iv), (v), or (vi) with respect to all or part of such distribution,

then, notwithstanding paragraph (2), the rules of clause (ii) shall apply for purposes of applying section 72.

(ii) APPLICABLE RULES.—In the case of a distribution described in clause (i)—

(I) section 72 shall be applied separately to such distribution,

(II) notwithstanding the pro rata allocation of income on, and investment in, the contract to distributions under section 72, the portion of such distribution rolled over to an eligible retirement plan described in clause (i) shall be treated as from income on the contract (to the extent of the aggregate income on the contract from all individual retirement plans of the distributee), and

(III) appropriate adjustments shall be made in applying section 72 to other distributions in such taxable year and subsequent taxable years.

(I) WAIVER OF 60-DAY REQUIREMENT.—The Secretary may waive the 60-day requirement under subparagraphs (A) and (D) where the failure to waive such requirement would be against equity or good conscience, including casualty, disaster, or other events beyond the reasonable control of the individual subject to such requirement.

(4) CONTRIBUTIONS RETURNED BEFORE DUE DATE OF RETURN.—Paragraph (1) does not apply to the distribution of any contribution paid during a taxable year to an individual retirement account or for an individual retirement annuity if—

(A) such distribution is received on or before the day prescribed by law (including extensions of time) for filing such individual's return for such taxable year,

(B) no deduction is allowed under section 219 with respect to such contribution, and

(C) such distribution is accompanied by the amount of net income attributable to such contribution.

In the case of such a distribution, for purposes of section 61, any net income described in subparagraph (C) shall be deemed to have been earned and receivable in the taxable year in which such contribution is made.

(5) DISTRIBUTIONS OF EXCESS CONTRIBUTIONS AFTER DUE DATE FOR TAXABLE YEAR AND CERTAIN EXCESS ROLLOVER CONTRIBUTIONS.—

(A) IN GENERAL.—In the case of any individual, if the aggregate contributions (other than rollover contributions) paid for any taxable year to an individual retirement account or for an individual retirement annuity do not exceed the dollar amount in effect under section 219(b)(1)(A), paragraph (1) shall not apply to the distribution of any such contribution to the extent that such contribution exceeds the amount allowable as a deduction under section 219 for the taxable year for which the contribution was paid—

(i) if such distribution is received after the date described in paragraph (4),

(ii) but only to the extent that no deduction has been allowed under section 219 with respect to such excess contribution.

If employer contributions on behalf of the individual are paid for the taxable year to a simplified employee pension, the dollar limitation of the preceding sentence shall be increased by the lesser of the amount of such contributions or the dollar limitation in effect under section 415(c)(1)(A) for such taxable year.

(B) EXCESS ROLLOVER CONTRIBUTIONS ATTRIBUTABLE TO ERRONEOUS INFORMATION.—If—

(i) the taxpayer reasonably relies on information supplied pursuant to subtitle F for determining the amount of a rollover contribution, but

(ii) the information was erroneous,

subparagraph (A) shall be applied by increasing the dollar limit set forth therein by that portion of the excess contribution which was attributable to such information.

For purposes of this paragraph, the amount allowable as a deduction under section 219 shall be computed without regard to section 219(g).

(6) TRANSFER OF ACCOUNT INCIDENT TO DIVORCE.—The transfer of an individual's interest in an individual retirement account or an individual retirement annuity to his spouse or former spouse under a divorce or separation instrument described in subparagraph (A) of section 71(b)(2) is not to be considered a taxable transfer made by such individual notwithstanding any other provision of this subtitle, and such interest at the time of the transfer is to be treated as an individual retirement account of such spouse, and not of such individual. Thereafter such account or annuity for purposes of this subtitle is to be treated as maintained for the benefit of such spouse.

* * *

[Sec. 408(e)]

(e) TAX TREATMENT OF ACCOUNTS AND ANNUITIES.—

(1) EXEMPTION FROM TAX.—Any individual retirement account is exempt from taxation under this subtitle unless such account has ceased to be an individual retirement account by reason of paragraph (2) or (3). Notwithstanding the preceding sentence, any such account is subject to the taxes imposed by section 511 (relating to imposition of tax on unrelated business income of charitable, etc. organizations).

(2) LOSS OF EXEMPTION OF ACCOUNT WHERE EMPLOYEE ENGAGES IN PROHIBITED TRANSACTION.—

(A) IN GENERAL.—If, during any taxable year of the individual for whose benefit any individual retirement account is established, that individual or his beneficiary engages in any transaction prohibited by section 4975 with respect to such account, such account ceases to be an individual retirement account as of the first day of such taxable year. For purposes of this paragraph—

(i) the individual for whose benefit any account was established is treated as the creator of such account, and

(ii) the separate account for any individual within an individual retirement account maintained by an employer or association of employees is treated as a separate individual retirement account.

(B) ACCOUNT TREATED AS DISTRIBUTING ALL ITS ASSETS.—In any case in which any account ceases to be an individual retirement account by reason of subparagraph (A) as of the first day of any taxable year, paragraph (1) of subsection (d) applies as if there were a distribution on such first day in an amount equal to the fair market value (on such first day) of all assets in the account (on such first day).

(3) EFFECT OF BORROWING ON ANNUITY CONTRACT.—If during any taxable year the owner of an individual retirement annuity borrows any money under or by use of such contract, the contract ceases to be an individual retirement annuity as of the first day of such taxable year. Such owner shall include in gross income for such year an amount equal to the fair market value of such contract as of such first day.

(4) EFFECT OF PLEDGING ACCOUNT AS SECURITY.—If, during any taxable year of the individual for whose benefit an individual retirement account is established, that individual uses the account or any portion thereof as security for a loan, the portion so used is treated as distributed to that individual.

Sec. 408(e)

(5) Purchase of Endowment Contract by Individual Retirement Account.—If the assets of an individual retirement account or any part of such assets are used to purchase an endowment contract for the benefit of the individual for whose benefit the account is established—

(A) to the extent that the amount of the assets involved in the purchase are not attributable to the purchase of life insurance, the purchase is treated as a rollover contribution described in subsection (d)(3), and

(B) to the extent that the amount of the assets involved in the purchase are attributable to the purchase of life, health, accident, or other insurance such amounts are treated as distributed to that individual (but the provisions of subsection (f) do not apply).

(6) Commingling Individual Retirement Account Amounts in Certain Common Trust Funds and Common Investment Funds.—Any common trust fund or common investment fund of individual retirement account assets which is exempt from taxation under this subtitle does not cease to be exempt on account of the participation or inclusion of assets of a trust exempt from taxation under section 501(a) which is described in section 401(a).

* * *

[Sec. 408(m)]

(m) Investment in Collectibles Treated as Distributions.—

(1) In General.—The acquisition by an individual retirement account or by an individually-directed account under a plan described in section 401(a) of any collectible shall be treated (for purposes of this section and section 402) as a distribution from such account in an amount equal to the cost to such account of such collectible.

(2) Collectible Defined.—For purposes of this subsection, the term "collectible" means—

(A) any work of art,

(B) any rug or antique,

(C) any metal or gem,

(D) any stamp or coin,

(E) any alcoholic beverage, or

(F) any other tangible personal property specified by the Secretary for purposes of this subsection.

(3) Exception for Certain Coins and Bullion.—For purposes of this subsection, the term "collectible" shall not include—

(A) any coin which is—

(i) a gold coin described in paragraph (7), (8), (9), or (10) of section 5112(a) of title 31, United States Code,

(ii) a silver coin described in section 5112(e) of title 31, United States Code,

(iii) a platinum coin described in section 5112(k) of title 31, United States Code, or

(iv) a coin issued under the laws of any State, or

(B) any gold, silver, platinum, or palladium bullion of a fineness equal to or exceeding the minimum fineness that a contract market (as described in section 7 of the Commodity Exchange Act, 7 U.S.C. 7) requires for metals which may be delivered in satisfaction of a regulated futures contract,

if such bullion is in the physical possession of a trustee described under subsection (a) of this section.

* * *

[Sec. 408(o)]

(o) Definitions and Rules Relating to Nondeductible Contributions to Individual Retirement Plans.—

(1) In General.—Subject to the provisions of this subsection, designated nondeductible contributions may be made on behalf of an individual to an individual retirement plan.

Sec. 408(o)

(2) LIMITS ON AMOUNTS WHICH MAY BE CONTRIBUTED.—

(A) IN GENERAL.—The amount of the designated nondeductible contributions made on behalf of any individual for any taxable year shall not exceed the nondeductible limit for such taxable year.

(B) NONDEDUCTIBLE LIMIT.—For purposes of this paragraph—

(i) IN GENERAL.—The term "nondeductible limit" means the excess of—

(I) the amount allowable as a deduction under section 219 (determined without regard to section 219(g)), over

(II) the amount allowable as a deduction under section 219 (determined with regard to section 219(g)).

(ii) TAXPAYER MAY ELECT TO TREAT DEDUCTIBLE CONTRIBUTIONS AS NONDEDUCTIBLE.—If a taxpayer elects not to deduct an amount which (without regard to this clause) is allowable as a deduction under section 219 for any taxable year, the nondeductible limit for such taxable year shall be increased by such amount.

(C) DESIGNATED NONDEDUCTIBLE CONTRIBUTIONS.—

(i) IN GENERAL.—For purposes of this paragraph, the term "designated nondeductible contribution" means any contribution to an individual retirement plan for the taxable year which is designated (in such manner as the Secretary may prescribe) as a contribution for which a deduction is not allowable under section 219.

(ii) DESIGNATION.—Any designation under clause (i) shall be made on the return of tax imposed by chapter 1 for the taxable year.

(3) TIME WHEN CONTRIBUTIONS MADE.—In determining for which taxable year a designated nondeductible contribution is made, the rule of section 219(f)(3) shall apply.

(4) INDIVIDUAL REQUIRED TO REPORT AMOUNT OF DESIGNATED NONDEDUCTIBLE CONTRIBUTIONS.—

(A) IN GENERAL.—Any individual who—

(i) makes a designated nondeductible contribution to any individual retirement plan for any taxable year, or

(ii) receives any amount from any individual retirement plan for any taxable year,

shall include on his return of the tax imposed by chapter 1 for such taxable year and any succeeding taxable year (or on such other form as the Secretary may prescribe for any such taxable year) information described in subparagraph (B).

(B) INFORMATION REQUIRED TO BE SUPPLIED.—The following information is described in this subparagraph:

(i) The amount of designated nondeductible contributions for the taxable year.

(ii) The amount of distributions from individual retirement plans for the taxable year.

(iii) The excess (if any) of—

(I) the aggregate amount of designated nondeductible contributions for all preceding taxable years, over

(II) the aggregate amount of distributions from individual retirement plans which was excludable from gross income for such taxable years.

(iv) The aggregate balance of all individual retirement plans of the individual as of the close of the calendar year in which the taxable year begins.

(v) Such other information as the Secretary may prescribe.

(C) PENALTY FOR REPORTING CONTRIBUTIONS NOT MADE.—

For penalty where individual reports designated nondeductible contributions not made, see section 6693(b).

* * *

Sec. 408(o)

SEC. 408A. ROTH IRAS.

[Sec. 408A(a)]

(a) GENERAL RULE.—Except as provided in this section, a Roth IRA shall be treated for purposes of this title in the same manner as an individual retirement plan.

[Sec. 408A(b)]

(b) ROTH IRA.—For purposes of this title, the term "Roth IRA" means an individual retirement plan (as defined in section 7701(a)(37)) which is designated (in such manner as the Secretary may prescribe) at the time of establishment of the plan as a Roth IRA. Such designation shall be made in such manner as the Secretary may prescribe.

[Sec. 408A(c)]

(c) TREATMENT OF CONTRIBUTIONS.—

(1) NO DEDUCTION ALLOWED.—No deduction shall be allowed under section 219 for a contribution to a Roth IRA.

(2) CONTRIBUTION LIMIT.—The aggregate amount of contributions for any taxable year to all Roth IRAs maintained for the benefit of an individual shall not exceed the excess (if any) of—

(A) the maximum amount allowable as a deduction under section 219 with respect to such individual for such taxable year (computed without regard to subsection (d)(1) or (g) of such section), over

(B) the aggregate amount of contributions for such taxable year to all other individual retirement plans (other than Roth IRAs) maintained for the benefit of the individual.

(3) LIMITS BASED ON MODIFIED ADJUSTED GROSS INCOME.—

(A) DOLLAR LIMIT.—The amount determined under paragraph (2) for any taxable year shall not exceed an amount equal to the amount determined under paragraph (2)(A) for such taxable year, reduced (but not below zero) by the amount which bears the same ratio to such amount as—

(i) the excess of—

(I) the taxpayer's adjusted gross income for such taxable year, over

(II) the applicable dollar amount, bears to

(ii) $15,000 ($10,000 in the case of a joint return or a married individual filing a separate return).

The rules of subparagraphs (B) and (C) of section 219(g)(2) shall apply to any reduction under this subparagraph.

(B) ROLLOVER FROM IRA.—A taxpayer shall not be allowed to make a qualified rollover contribution to a Roth IRA from an individual retirement plan other than a Roth IRA during any taxable year if, for the taxable year of the distribution to which such contribution relates—

(i) the taxpayer's adjusted gross income exceeds $100,000, or

(ii) the taxpayer is a married individual filing a separate return.

(C) DEFINITIONS.—For purposes of this paragraph—

[Caution: Code Sec. 408A(c)(3)(C)(i), below, prior to amendment by P.L. 105-206 and P.L. 105-277, applies to tax years beginning on or before December 31, 2004.]

(i) adjusted gross income shall be determined in the same manner as under section 219(g)(3), except that any amount included in gross income under subsection (d)(3) shall not be taken into account, and

[*Caution: Code Sec. 408A(c)(3)(C)(i), below, as amended by P.L. 105-206 and P.L. 105-277, applies to tax years beginning after December 31, 2004.*]

(i) adjusted gross income shall be determined in the same manner as under section 219(g)(3), except that—

(I) any amount included in gross income under subsection (d)(3) shall not be taken into account; and

(II) any amount included in gross income by reason of a required distribution under a provision described in paragraph (5) shall not be taken into account for purposes of subparagraph (B)(i), and

(ii) the applicable dollar amount is—

(I) in the case of a taxpayer filing a joint return, $150,000,

(II) in the case of any other taxpayer (other than a married individual filing a separate return), $95,000, and

(III) in the case of a married individual filing a separate return, zero.

(D) MARITAL STATUS.—Section 219(g)(4) shall apply for purposes of this paragraph.

(4) CONTRIBUTIONS PERMITTED AFTER AGE 70½.—Contributions to a Roth IRA may be made even after the individual for whom the account is maintained has attained age 70½.

(5) MANDATORY DISTRIBUTION RULES NOT TO APPLY BEFORE DEATH.—Notwithstanding subsections (a)(6) and (b)(3) of section 408 (relating to required distributions), the following provisions shall not apply to any Roth IRA:

(A) Section 401(a)(9)(A).

(B) The incidental death benefit requirements of section 401(a).

(6) ROLLOVER CONTRIBUTIONS.—

(A) IN GENERAL.—No rollover contribution may be made to a Roth IRA unless it is a qualified rollover contribution.

(B) COORDINATION WITH LIMIT.—A qualified rollover contribution shall not be taken into account for purposes of paragraph (2).

(7) TIME WHEN CONTRIBUTIONS MADE.—For purposes of this section, the rule of section 219(f)(3) shall apply.

[Sec. 408A(d)]

(d) DISTRIBUTION RULES.—For purposes of this title—

(1) EXCLUSION.—Any qualified distribution from a Roth IRA shall not be includible in gross income.

(2) QUALIFIED DISTRIBUTION.—For purposes of this subsection—

(A) IN GENERAL.—The term "qualified distribution" means any payment or distribution—

(i) made on or after the date on which the individual attains age 59½,

(ii) made to a beneficiary (or to the estate of the individual) on or after the death of the individual,

(iii) attributable to the individual's being disabled (within the meaning of section 72(m)(7)), or

(iv) which is a qualified special purpose distribution.

(B) DISTRIBUTIONS WITHIN NONEXCLUSION PERIOD.—A payment or distribution from a Roth IRA shall not be treated as a qualified distribution under subparagraph (A) if such payment or distribution is made within the 5-taxable year period beginning with the 1st taxable year for which the individual made a contribution to a Roth IRA (or such individual's spouse made a contribution to a Roth IRA) established for such individual.

(C) DISTRIBUTIONS OF EXCESS CONTRIBUTIONS AND EARNINGS.—The term "qualified distribution" shall not include any distribution of any contribution described in section 408(d)(4) and any net income allocable to the contribution.

(3) ROLLOVERS FROM AN IRA OTHER THAN A ROTH IRA.—

(A) IN GENERAL.—Notwithstanding section 408(d)(3), in the case of any distribution to which this paragraph applies—

(i) there shall be included in gross income any amount which would be includible were it not part of a qualified rollover contribution,

(ii) section 72(t) shall not apply, and

(iii) unless the taxpayer elects not to have this clause apply for any taxable year, any amount required to be included in gross income for such taxable year by reason of this paragraph for any distribution before January 1, 1999, shall be so included ratably over the 4-taxable year period beginning with such taxable year.

Any election under clause (iii) for any distributions during a taxable year may not be changed after the due date for such taxable year.

(B) DISTRIBUTIONS TO WHICH PARAGRAPH APPLIES.—This paragraph shall apply to a distribution from an individual retirement plan (other than a Roth IRA) maintained for the benefit of an individual which is contributed to a Roth IRA maintained for the benefit of such individual in a qualified rollover contribution.

(C) CONVERSIONS.—The conversion of an individual retirement plan (other than a Roth IRA) to a Roth IRA shall be treated for purposes of this paragraph as a distribution to which this paragraph applies.

(D) ADDITIONAL REPORTING REQUIREMENTS.—Trustees of Roth IRAs, trustees of individual retirement plans, or both, whichever is appropriate, shall include such additional information in reports required under section 408(i) as the Secretary may require to ensure that amounts required to be included in gross income under subparagraph (A) are so included.

(E) SPECIAL RULES FOR CONTRIBUTIONS TO WHICH 4-YEAR AVERAGING APPLIES.—In the case of a qualified rollover contribution to a Roth IRA of a distribution to which subparagraph (A)(iii) applied, the following rules shall apply:

(i) ACCELERATION OF INCLUSION.—

(I) IN GENERAL.—The amount required to be included in gross income for each of the first 3 taxable years in the 4-year period under subparagraph (A)(iii) shall be increased by the aggregate distributions from Roth IRAs for such taxable year which are allocable under paragraph (4) to the portion of such qualified rollover contribution required to be included in gross income under subparagraph (A)(i).

(II) LIMITATION ON AGGREGATE AMOUNT INCLUDED.—The amount required to be included in gross income for any taxable year under subparagraph (A)(iii) shall not exceed the aggregate amount required to be included in gross income under subparagraph (A)(iii) for all taxable years in the 4-year period (without regard to subclause (I)) reduced by amounts included for all preceding taxable years.

(ii) DEATH OF DISTRIBUTEE.—

(I) IN GENERAL.—If the individual required to include amounts in gross income under such subparagraph dies before all of such amounts are included, all remaining amounts shall be included in gross income for the taxable year which includes the date of death.

(II) SPECIAL RULE FOR SURVIVING SPOUSE.—If the spouse of the individual described in subclause (I) acquires the individual's entire interest in any Roth IRA to which such qualified rollover contribution is properly allocable, the spouse may elect to treat the remaining amounts described in subclause (I) as includible in the spouse's gross income in the taxable years of the spouse ending with or within the taxable years of such individual in which such amounts would otherwise have been includible. Any such election may not be made or changed after the due date for the spouse's taxable year which includes the date of death.

(F) SPECIAL RULE FOR APPLYING SECTION 72.—

(i) IN GENERAL.—If—

(I) any portion of a distribution from a Roth IRA is properly allocable to a qualified rollover contribution described in this paragraph; and

Sec. 408A(d)

(II) such distribution is made within the 5-taxable year period beginning with the taxable year in which such contribution was made,

then section 72(t) shall be applied as if such portion were includible in gross income.

(ii) LIMITATION.—Clause (i) shall apply only to the extent of the amount of the qualified rollover contribution includible in gross income under subparagraph (A)(i).

(4) AGGREGATION AND ORDERING RULES.—

(A) AGGREGATION RULES.—Section 408(d)(2) shall be applied separately with respect to Roth IRAs and other individual retirement plans.

(B) ORDERING RULES.—For purposes of applying this section and section 72 to any distribution from a Roth IRA, such distribution shall be treated as made—

(i) from contributions to the extent that the amount of such distribution, when added to all previous distributions from the Roth IRA, does not exceed the aggregate contributions to the Roth IRA; and

(ii) from such contributions in the following order:

(I) Contributions other than qualified rollover contributions to which paragraph (3) applies.

(II) Qualified rollover contributions to which paragraph (3) applies on a first-in, first-out basis.

Any distribution allocated to a qualified rollover contribution under clause (ii)(II) shall be allocated first to the portion of such contribution required to be included in gross income.

(5) QUALIFIED SPECIAL PURPOSE DISTRIBUTION.—For purposes of this section, the term "qualified special purpose distribution" means any distribution to which subparagraph (F) of section 72(t)(2) applies.

(6) TAXPAYER MAY MAKE ADJUSTMENTS BEFORE DUE DATE.—

(A) IN GENERAL.—Except as provided by the Secretary, if, on or before the due date for any taxable year, a taxpayer transfers in a trustee-to-trustee transfer any contribution to an individual retirement plan made during such taxable year from such plan to any other individual retirement plan, then, for purposes of this chapter, such contribution shall be treated as having been made to the transferee plan (and not the transferor plan).

(B) SPECIAL RULES.—

(i) TRANSFER OF EARNINGS.—Subparagraph (A) shall not apply to the transfer of any contribution unless such transfer is accompanied by any net income allocable to such contribution.

(ii) NO DEDUCTION.—Subparagraph (A) shall apply to the transfer of any contribution only to the extent no deduction was allowed with respect to the contribution to the transferor plan.

(7) DUE DATE.—For purposes of this subsection, the due date for any taxable year is the date prescribed by law (including extensions of time) for filing the taxpayer's return for such taxable year.

[Sec. 408A(e)]

[*Caution: Code Sec. 408A(e), below, prior to amendment by P.L. 107-16, applies to tax years beginning on or before December 31, 2005.*]

(e) QUALIFIED ROLLOVER CONTRIBUTION.—For purposes of this section, the term "qualified rollover contribution" means a rollover contribution to a Roth IRA from another such account, or from an individual retirement plan, but only if such rollover contribution meets the requirements of section 408(d)(3). For purposes of section 408(d)(3)(B), there shall be disregarded any qualified rollover contribution from an individual retirement plan (other than a Roth IRA) to a Roth IRA.

[*Caution: Code Sec. 408A(e), below, as amended by P.L. 107-16, applies to tax years beginning after December 31, 2005.*]

(e) QUALIFIED ROLLOVER CONTRIBUTION.—For purposes of this section, the term "qualified rollover contribution" means a rollover contribution to a Roth IRA from another such account, or from an individual retirement plan, but only if such rollover contribution meets the requirements of section 408(d)(3). Such term includes a rollover contribution described in section 402A(c)(3)(A). For purposes of section 408(d)(3)(B), there shall be disregarded any qualified rollover contribution from an individual retirement plan (other than a Roth IRA) to a Roth IRA.

[Sec. 408A(f)]

(f) INDIVIDUAL RETIREMENT PLAN.—For purposes of this section—

(1) a simplified employee pension or a simple retirement account may not be designated as a Roth IRA; and

(2) contributions to any such pension or account shall not be taken into account for purposes of subsection (c)(2)(B).

PART II—CERTAIN STOCK OPTIONS

[Sec. 421]

SEC. 421. GENERAL RULES.

[Sec. 421(a)]

(a) EFFECT OF QUALIFYING TRANSFER.—If a share of stock is transferred to an individual in a transfer in respect of which the requirements of section 422(a) or 423(a) are met—

(1) no income shall result at the time of the transfer of such share to the individual upon his exercise of the option with respect to such share;

(2) no deduction under section 162 (relating to trade or business expenses) shall be allowable at any time to the employer corporation, a parent or subsidiary corporation of such corporation, or a corporation issuing or assuming a stock option in a transaction to which section 424(a) applies, with respect to the share so transferred; and

(3) no amount other than the price paid under the option shall be considered as received by any of such corporations for the share so transferred.

[Sec. 421(b)]

(b) Effect of Disqualifying Disposition.—If the transfer of a share of stock to an individual pursuant to his exercise of an option would otherwise meet the requirements of section 422(a) or 423(a) except that there is a failure to meet any of the holding period requirements of section 422(a)(1) or 423(a)(1), then any increase in the income of such individual or deduction from the income of his employer corporation for the taxable year in which such exercise occurred attributable to such disposition, shall be treated as an increase in income or a deduction from income in the taxable year of such individual or of such employer corporation in which such disposition occurred.

[Sec. 421(c)]

(c) EXERCISE BY ESTATE.—

(1) IN GENERAL.—If an option to which this part applies is exercised after the death of the employee by the estate of the decedent, or by a person who acquired the right to exercise such option by bequest or inheritance or by reason of the death of the decedent, the provisions of subsection (a) shall apply to the same extent as if the option had been exercised by the decedent, except that—

(A) the holding period and employment requirements of sections 422(a) and 423(a) shall not apply, and

(B) any transfer by the estate of stock acquired shall be considered a disposition of such stock for purposes of section 423(c).

(2) DEDUCTION FOR ESTATE TAX.—If an amount is required to be included under section 423(c) in gross income of the estate of the deceased employee or of a person described in paragraph (1), there shall be allowed to the estate or such person a deduction with respect to the estate tax attributable to the inclusion in the taxable estate of the deceased employee of the net value for estate tax purposes of the option. For this purpose, the deduction shall be determined under section 691(c) as if the option acquired from the deceased employee were an item of gross income in respect of the decedent under section 691 and as if the amount includible in gross income under section 423(c) were an amount included in gross income under section 691 in respect of such item of gross income.

(3) BASIS OF SHARES ACQUIRED.—In the case of a share of stock acquired by the exercise of an option to which paragraph (1) applies—

(A) the basis of such share shall include so much of the basis of the option as is attributable to such share; except that the basis of such share shall be reduced by the excess (if any) of (i) the amount which would have been includible in gross income under section 423(c) if the employee had exercised the option on the date of this death and had held the share acquired pursuant to such exercise at the time of his death, over (ii) the amount which is includible in gross income under such section; and

(B) the last sentence of section 423(c) shall apply only to the extent that the amount includible in gross income under such section exceeds so much of the basis of the option as is attributable to such share.

[Sec. 422]

SEC. 422. INCENTIVE STOCK OPTIONS.

[Sec. 422(a)]

(a) IN GENERAL.—Section 421(a) shall apply with respect to the transfer of a share of stock to an individual pursuant to his exercise of an incentive stock option if—

(1) no disposition of such share is made by him within 2 years from the date of the granting of the option nor within 1 year after the transfer of such share to him, and

(2) at all times during the period beginning on the date of the granting of the option and ending on the day 3 months before the date of such exercise, such individual was an employee of either the corporation granting such option, a parent or subsidiary corporation of such corporation, or a corporation or a parent or subsidiary corporation of such corporation issuing or assuming a stock option in a transaction to which section 424(a) applies.

[Sec. 422(b)]

(b) INCENTIVE STOCK OPTION.—For purposes of this part, the term "incentive stock option" means an option granted to an individual for any reason connected with his employment by a corporation, if granted by the employer corporation or its parent or subsidiary corporation, to purchase stock of any of such corporations, but only if—

(1) the option is granted pursuant to a plan which includes the aggregate number of shares which may be issued under options and the employees (or class of employees) eligible to receive options, and which is approved by the stockholders of the granting corporation within 12 months before or after the date such plan is adopted;

(2) such option is granted within 10 years from the date such plan is adopted, or the date such plan is approved by the stockholders, whichever is earlier;

(3) such option by its terms is not exercisable after the expiration of 10 years from the date such option is granted;

(4) the option price is not less than the fair market value of the stock at the time such option is granted;

(5) such option by its terms is not transferable by such individual otherwise than by will or the laws of descent and distribution, and is exercisable, during his lifetime, only by him; and

(6) such individual, at the time the option is granted, does not own stock possessing more than 10 percent of the total combined voting power of all classes of stock of the employer corporation or of its parent or subsidiary corporation.

Such term shall not include any option if (as of the time the option is granted) the terms of such option provide that it will not be treated as an incentive stock option.

[Sec. 422(c)]

(c) SPECIAL RULES.—

(1) GOOD FAITH EFFORTS TO VALUE STOCK.—If a share of stock is transferred pursuant to the exercise by an individual of an option which would fail to qualify as an incentive stock option under subsection (b) because there was a failure in an attempt, made in good faith, to meet the requirement of subsection (b)(4), the requirement of subsection (b)(4) shall be considered to have been met. To the extent provided in regulations by the Secretary, a similar rule shall apply for purposes of subsection (d).

(2) CERTAIN DISQUALIFYING DISPOSITIONS WHERE AMOUNT REALIZED IS LESS THAN VALUE AT EXERCISE.—If—

Sec. 422

(A) an individual who has acquired a share of stock by the exercise of an incentive stock option makes a disposition of such share within either of the periods described in subsection (a)(1), and

(B) such disposition is a sale or exchange with respect to which a loss (if sustained) would be recognized to such individual,

then the amount which is includible in the gross income of such individual, and the amount which is deductible from the income of his employer corporation, as compensation attributable to the exercise of such option shall not exceed the excess (if any) of the amount realized on such sale or exchange over the adjusted basis of such share.

(3) CERTAIN TRANSFERS BY INSOLVENT INDIVIDUALS.—If an insolvent individual holds a share of stock acquired pursuant to his exercise of an incentive stock option, and if such share is transferred to a trustee, receiver, or any other similar fiduciary in any proceeding under title 11 or any other similar insolvency proceeding, neither such transfer, nor any other transfer of such share for the benefit of his creditors in such proceeding, shall constitute a disposition of such share for purposes of subsection (a)(1).

(4) PERMISSIBLE PROVISIONS.—An option which meets the requirements of subsection (b) shall be treated as an incentive stock option even if—

(A) the employee may pay for the stock with stock of the corporation granting the option,

(B) the employee has a right to receive property at the time of exercise of the option, or

(C) the option is subject to any condition not inconsistent with the provisions of subsection (b).

Subparagraph (B) shall apply to a transfer of property (other than cash) only if section 83 applies to the property so transferred.

(5) 10-PERCENT SHAREHOLDER RULE.—Subsection (b)(6) shall not apply if at the time such option is granted the option price is at least 110 percent of the fair market value of the stock subject to the option and such option by its terms is not exercisable after the expiration of 5 years from the date such option is granted.

(6) SPECIAL RULE WHEN DISABLED.—For purposes of subsection (a)(2), in the case of an employee who is disabled (within the meaning of section 22(e)(3)), the 3-month period of subsection (a)(2) shall be 1 year.

(7) FAIR MARKET VALUE.—For purposes of this section, the fair market value of stock shall be determined without regard to any restriction other than a restriction which, by its terms, will never lapse.

[Sec. 422(d)]

(d) $100,000 PER YEAR LIMITATION.—

(1) IN GENERAL.—To the extent that the aggregate fair market value of stock with respect to which incentive stock options (determined without regard to this subsection) are exercisable for the 1st time by any individual during any calendar year (under all plans of the individual's employer corporation and its parent and subsidiary corporations) exceeds $100,000, such options shall be treated as options which are not incentive stock options.

(2) ORDERING RULE.—Paragraph (1) shall be applied by taking options into account in the order in which they were granted.

(3) DETERMINATION OF FAIR MARKET VALUE.—For purposes of paragraph (1), the fair market value of any stock shall be determined as of the time the option with respect to such stock is granted.

[Sec. 423]

SEC. 423. EMPLOYEE STOCK PURCHASE PLANS.

[Sec. 423(a)]

(a) GENERAL RULE.—Section 421(a) shall apply with respect to the transfer of a share of stock to an individual pursuant to his exercise of an option granted after December 31, 1963, under an employee stock purchase plan (as defined in subsection (b)) if—

(1) no disposition of such share is made by him within 2 years after the date of the granting of the option nor within 1 year after the transfer of such share to him; and

Sec. 423(a)

(2) at all times during the period beginning with the date of the granting of the option and ending on the day 3 months before the date of such exercise, he is an employee of the corporation granting such option, a parent or subsidiary corporation of such corporation, or a corporation or a parent or subsidiary corporation of such corporation issuing or assuming a stock option in a transaction to which section 424(a) applies.

[Sec. 423(b)]

(b) EMPLOYEE STOCK PURCHASE PLAN.—For purposes of this part, the term "employee stock purchase plan" means a plan which meets the following requirements:

(1) the plan provides that options are to be granted only to employees of the employer corporation or of its parent or subsidiary corporation to purchase stock in any such corporation;

(2) such plan is approved by the stockholders of the granting corporation within 12 months before or after the date such plan is adopted;

(3) under the terms of the plan, no employee can be granted an option if such employee, immediately after the option is granted, owns stock possessing 5 percent or more of the total combined voting power or value of all classes of stock of the employer corporation or of its parent or subsidiary corporation. For purposes of this paragraph, the rules of section 424(d) shall apply in determining the stock ownership of an individual, and stock which the employee may purchase under outstanding options shall be treated as stock owned by the employee;

(4) under the terms of the plan, options are to be granted to all employees of any corporation whose employees are granted any of such options by reason of their employment by such corporation, except that there may be excluded—

(A) employees who have been employed less than 2 years,

(B) employees whose customary employment is 20 hours or less per week,

(C) employees whose customary employment is for not more than 5 months in any calendar year, and

(D) highly compensated employees (within the meaning of section 414(q));

(5) under the terms of the plan, all employees granted such options shall have the same rights and privileges, except that the amount of stock which may be purchased by any employee under such option may bear a uniform relationship to the total compensation, or the basic or regular rate of compensation, of employees, and the plan may provide that no employee may purchase more than a maximum amount of stock fixed under the plan;

(6) under the terms of the plan, the option price is not less than the lesser of—

(A) an amount equal to 85 percent of the fair market value of the stock at the time such option is granted, or

(B) an amount which under the terms of the option may not be less than 85 percent of the fair market value of the stock at the time such option is exercised;

(7) under the terms of the plan, such option cannot be exercised after the expiration of—

(A) 5 years from the date such option is granted if, under the terms of such plan, the option price is to be not less than 85 percent of the fair market value of such stock at the time of the exercise of the option, or

(B) 27 months from the date such option is granted, if the option price is not determinable in the manner described in subparagraph (A);

(8) under the terms of the plan, no employee may be granted an option which permits his rights to purchase stock under all such plans of his employer corporation and its parent and subsidiary corporations to accrue at a rate which exceeds $25,000 of fair market value of such stock (determined at the time such option is granted) for each calendar year in which such option is outstanding at any time. For purposes of this paragraph—

(A) the right to purchase stock under an option accrues when the option (or any portion thereof) first becomes exercisable during the calendar year;

(B) the right to purchase stock under an option accrues at the rate provided in the option, but in no case may such rate exceed $25,000 of fair market value of such stock (determined at the time such option is granted) for any one calendar year; and

(C) a right to purchase stock which has accrued under one option granted pursuant to the plan may not be carried over to any other option; and

(9) under the terms of the plan, such option is not transferable by such individual otherwise than by will or the laws of descent and distribution, and is exercisable, during his lifetime, only by him.

For purposes of paragraphs (3) to (9), inclusive, where additional terms are contained in an offering made under a plan, such additional terms shall, with respect to options exercised under such offering, be treated as a part of the terms of such plan.

[Sec. 423(c)]

(c) SPECIAL RULE WHERE OPTION PRICE IS BETWEEN 85 PERCENT AND 100 PERCENT OF VALUE OF STOCK.—If the option price of a share of stock acquired by an individual pursuant to a transfer to which subsection (a) applies was less than 100 percent of the fair market value of such share at the time such option was granted, then, in the event of any disposition of such share by him which meets the holding period requirements of subsection (a), or in the event of his death (whenever occurring) while owning such share, there shall be included as compensation (and not as gain upon the sale or exchange of a capital asset) in his gross income, for the taxable year in which falls the date of such disposition or for the taxable year closing with his death, whichever applies, an amount equal to the lesser of—

(1) the excess of the fair market value of the share at the time of such disposition or death over the amount paid for the share under the option, or

(2) the excess of the fair market value of the share at the time the option was granted over the option price.

If the option price is not fixed or determinable at the time the option is granted, then for purposes of this subsection, the option price shall be determined as if the option were exercised at such time. In the case of the disposition of such share by the individual, the basis of the share in his hands at the time of such disposition shall be increased by an amount equal to the amount so includible in his gross income.

Subchapter E—Accounting Periods and Methods of Accounting

PART I—ACCOUNTING PERIODS

[Sec. 441]

SEC. 441. PERIOD FOR COMPUTATION OF TAXABLE INCOME.

[Sec. 441(a)]

(a) COMPUTATION OF TAXABLE INCOME.—Taxable income shall be computed on the basis of the taxpayer's taxable year.

[Sec. 441(b)]

(b) TAXABLE YEAR.—For purposes of this subtitle, the term "taxable year" means—

(1) the taxpayer's annual accounting period, if it is a calendar year or a fiscal year;

(2) the calendar year, if subsection (g) applies;

(3) the period for which the return is made, if a return is made for a period of less than 12 months; or

(4) in the case of a FSC or DISC filing a return for a period of at least 12 months, the period determined under subsection (h).

[Sec. 441(c)]

(c) ANNUAL ACCOUNTING PERIOD.—For purposes of this subtitle, the term "annual accounting period" means the annual period on the basis of which the taxpayer regularly computes his income in keeping his books.

[Sec. 441(d)]

(d) CALENDAR YEAR.—For purposes of this subtitle, the term "calendar year" means a period of 12 months ending on December 31.

[Sec. 441(e)]

(e) FISCAL YEAR.—For purposes of this subtitle, the term "fiscal year" means a period of 12 months ending on the last day of any month other than December. In the case of any taxpayer who has made the election provided by subsection (f), the term means the annual period (varying from 52 to 53 weeks) so elected.

[Sec. 441(f)]

(f) ELECTION OF YEAR CONSISTING OF 52-53 WEEKS.—

(1) GENERAL RULE.—A taxpayer who, in keeping his books, regularly computes his income on the basis of an annual period which varies from 52 to 53 weeks and ends always on the same day of the week and ends always—

(A) on whatever date such same day of the week last occurs in a calendar month, or

(B) on whatever date such same day of the week falls which is nearest to the last day of a calendar month,

may (in accordance with the regulations prescribed under paragraph (3)) elect to compute his taxable income for purposes of this subtitle on the basis of such annual period. This paragraph shall apply to taxable years ending after the date of the enactment of this title.

(2) SPECIAL RULES FOR 52-53-WEEK YEAR.—

(A) EFFECTIVE DATES.—In any case in which the effective date or the applicability of any provision of this title is expressed in terms of taxable years beginning, including, or ending with reference to a specified date which is the first or last day of a month, a taxable year described in paragraph (1) shall (except for purposes of the computation under section 15) be treated—

(i) as beginning with the first day of the calendar month beginning nearest to the first day of such taxable year, or

(ii) as ending with the last day of the calendar month ending nearest to the last day of such taxable year,

as the case may be.

(B) CHANGE IN ACCOUNTING PERIOD.—In the case of a change from or to a taxable year described in paragraph (1)—

(i) if such change results in a short period (within the meaning of section 443) of 359 days or more, or of less than 7 days, section 443 (b) (relating to alternative tax computation) shall not apply;

(ii) if such change results in a short period of less than 7 days, such short period shall, for purposes of this subtitle, be added to and deemed a part of the following taxable year; and

(iii) if such change results in a short period to which subsection (b) of section 443 applies, the taxable income for such short period shall be placed on an annual basis for purposes of such subsection by multiplying the gross income for such short period (minus the deductions allowed by this chapter for the short period, but only the adjusted amount of the deductions for personal exemptions as described in section 443(c)) by 365, by dividing the result by the number of days in the short period, and the tax shall be the same part of the tax computed on the annual basis as the number of days in the short period is of 365 days.

(3) SPECIAL RULE FOR PARTNERSHIPS, S CORPORATIONS, AND PERSONAL SERVICE CORPORATIONS.—The Secretary may by regulation provide terms and conditions for the application of this subsection to a partnership, S corporation, or personal service corporation (within the meaning of section 441(i)(2)).

(4) REGULATIONS.—The Secretary shall prescribe such regulations as he deems necessary for the application of this subsection.

[Sec. 441(g)]

(g) NO BOOKS KEPT; NO ACCOUNTING PERIOD.—Except as provided in section 443 (relating to returns for periods of less than 12 months), the taxpayer's taxable year shall be the calendar year if—

(1) the taxpayer keeps no books;

(2) the taxpayer does not have an annual accounting period; or

(3) the taxpayer has an annual accounting period, but such period does not qualify as a fiscal year.

* * *

Sec. 441(e)

[Sec. 441(i)]

(i) TAXABLE YEAR OF PERSONAL SERVICE CORPORATIONS.—

(1) IN GENERAL.—For purposes of this subtitle, the taxable year of any personal service corporation shall be the calendar year unless the corporation establishes, to the satisfaction of the Secretary, a business purpose for having a different period for its taxable year. For purposes of this paragraph, any deferral of income to shareholders shall not be treated as a business purpose.

(2) PERSONAL SERVICE CORPORATION.—For purposes of this subsection, the term "personal service corporation" has the meaning given such term by section 269A(b)(1), except that section 269A(b)(2) shall be applied—

(A) by substituting "any" for "more than 10 percent", and

(B) by substituting "any" for "50 percent or more in value" in section 318(a)(2)(C).

A corporation shall not be treated as a personal service corporation unless more than 10 percent of the stock (by value) in such corporation is held by employee-owners (within the meaning of section 269A(b)(2), as modified by the preceding sentence). If a corporation is a member of an affiliated group filing a consolidated return, all members of such group shall be taken into account in determining whether such corporation is a personal service corporation.

[Sec. 442]

SEC. 442. CHANGE OF ANNUAL ACCOUNTING PERIOD.

If a taxpayer changes his annual accounting period, the new accounting period shall become the taxpayer's taxable year only if the change is approved by the Secretary. For purposes of this subtitle, if a taxpayer to whom section 441 (g) applies adopts an annual accounting period (as defined in section 441 (c)) other than a calendar year, the taxpayer shall be treated as having changed his annual accounting period.

[Sec. 443]

SEC. 443. RETURNS FOR A PERIOD OF LESS THAN 12 MONTHS.

[Sec. 443(a)]

(a) RETURNS FOR SHORT PERIOD.—A return for a period of less than 12 months (referred to in this section as "short period") shall be made under any of the following circumstances:

(1) CHANGE OF ANNUAL ACCOUNTING PERIOD.—When the taxpayer, with the approval of the Secretary, changes his annual accounting period. In such a case, the return shall be made for the short period beginning on the day after the close of the former taxable year and ending at the close of the day before the day designated as the first day of the new taxable year.

(2) TAXPAYER NOT IN EXISTENCE FOR ENTIRE TAXABLE YEAR.—When the taxpayer is in existence during only part of what would otherwise be his taxable year.

[Sec. 443(b)]

(b) COMPUTATION OF TAX ON CHANGE OF ANNUAL ACCOUNTING PERIOD.—

(1) GENERAL RULE.—If a return is made under paragraph (1) of subsection (a), the taxable income for the short period shall be placed on an annual basis by multiplying the modified taxable income for such short period by 12, dividing the result by the number of months in the short period. The tax shall be the same part of the tax computed on the annual basis as the number of months in the short period is of 12 months.

(2) EXCEPTION.—

(A) COMPUTATION BASED ON 12-MONTH PERIOD.—If the taxpayer applies for the benefits of this paragraph and establishes the amount of his taxable income for the 12-month period described in subparagraph (B), computed as if that period were a taxable year and under the law applicable to that year, then the tax for the short period, computed under paragraph (1), shall be reduced to the greater of the following:

Sec. 443(b)

(i) an amount which bears the same ratio to the tax computed on the taxable income for the 12-month period as the modified taxable income computed on the basis of the short period bears to the modified taxable income for the 12-month period; or

(ii) the tax computed on the modified taxable income for the short period.

The taxpayer (other than a taxpayer to whom subparagraph (B) (ii) applies) shall compute the tax and file his return without the application of this paragraph.

(B) 12-MONTH PERIOD.—The 12-month period referred to in subparagraph (A) shall be—

(i) the period of 12 months beginning on the first day of the short period, or

(ii) the period of 12 months ending at the close of the last day of the short period, if at the end of the 12 months referred to in clause (i) the taxpayer is not in existence or (if a corporation) has theretofore disposed of substantially all of its assets.

(C) APPLICATION FOR BENEFITS.—Application for the benefits of this paragraph shall be made in such manner and at such time as the regulations prescribed under subparagraph (D) may require; except that the time so prescribed shall not be later than the time (including extensions) for filing the return for the first taxable year which ends on or after the day which is 12 months after the first day of the short period. Such application, in case the return was filed without regard to this paragraph, shall be considered a claim for credit or refund with respect to the amount by which the tax is reduced under this paragraph.

(D) REGULATIONS.—The Secretary shall prescribe such regulations as he deems necessary for the application of this paragraph.

(3) MODIFIED TAXABLE INCOME DEFINED.—For purposes of this subsection the term "modified taxable income" means, with respect to any period, the gross income for such period minus the deductions allowed by this chapter for such period (but, in the case of a short period, only the adjusted amount of the deductions for personal exemptions).

[Sec. 443(c)]

(c) ADJUSTMENT IN DEDUCTION FOR PERSONAL EXEMPTION.—In the case of a taxpayer other than a corporation, if a return is made for a short period by reason of subsection (a) (1) and if the tax is not computed under subsection (b) (2), then the exemptions allowed as a deduction under section 151 (and any deduction in lieu thereof) shall be reduced to amounts which bear the same ratio to the full exemptions as the number of months in the short period bears to 12.

[Sec. 443(d)]

(d) ADJUSTMENT IN COMPUTING MINIMUM TAX AND TAX PREFERENCES.—If a return is made for a short period by reason of subsection (a)—

(1) the alternative minimum taxable income for the short period shall be placed on an annual basis by multiplying such amount by 12 and dividing the result by the number of months in the short period, and

(2) the amount computed under paragraph (1) of section 55(a) shall bear the same relation to the tax computed on the annual basis as the number of months in the short period bears to 12.

[Sec. 443(e)]

(e) CROSS REFERENCES.—

For inapplicability of subsection (b) in computing—

(1) Accumulated earnings tax, see section 536.

(2) Personal holding company tax, see section 546.

(3) Undistributed foreign personal holding company income, see section 557.

(4) The taxable income of a regulated investment company, see section 852 (b) (2) (E).

(5) The taxable income of a real estate investment trust, see section 857(b)(2)(C).

For returns for a period of less than 12 months in the case of a debtor's election to terminate a taxable year, see section 1398(d)(2)(E).

Sec. 443(c)

SEC. 444. ELECTION OF TAXABLE YEAR OTHER THAN REQUIRED TAXABLE YEAR.

[Sec. 444(a)]

(a) GENERAL RULE.—Except as otherwise provided in this section, a partnership, S corporation, or personal service corporation may elect to have a taxable year other than the required taxable year.

[Sec. 444(b)]

(b) LIMITATIONS ON TAXABLE YEARS WHICH MAY BE ELECTED.—

(1) IN GENERAL.—Except as provided in paragraphs (2) and (3), an election may be made under subsection (a) only if the deferral period of the taxable year elected is not longer than 3 months.

(2) CHANGES IN TAXABLE YEAR.—Except as provided in paragraph (3), in the case of an entity changing a taxable year, an election may be made under subsection (a) only if the deferral period of the taxable year elected is not longer than the shorter of—

(A) 3 months, or

(B) the deferral period of the taxable year which is being changed.

(3) SPECIAL RULE FOR ENTITIES RETAINING 1986 TAXABLE YEARS.—In the case of an entity's 1st taxable year beginning after December 31, 1986, an entity may elect a taxable year under subsection (a) which is the same as the entity's last taxable year beginning in 1986.

(4) DEFERRAL PERIOD.—For purposes of this subsection, except as provided in regulations, the term "deferral period" means, with respect to any taxable year of the entity, the months between—

(A) the beginning of such year, and

(B) the close of the 1st required taxable year ending within such year.

[Sec. 444(c)]

(c) EFFECT OF ELECTION.—If an entity makes an election under subsection (a), then—

(1) in the case of a partnership or S corporation, such entity shall make the payments required by section 7519, and

(2) in the case of a personal service corporation, such corporation shall be subject to the deduction limitations of section 280H.

[Sec. 444(d)]

(d) ELECTIONS.—

(1) PERSON MAKING ELECTION.—An election under subsection (a) shall be made by the partnership, S corporation, or personal service corporation.

(2) PERIOD OF ELECTION.—

(A) IN GENERAL.—Any election under subsection (a) shall remain in effect until the partnership, S corporation, or personal service corporation changes its taxable year or otherwise terminates such election. Any change to a required taxable year may be made without the consent of the Secretary.

(B) NO FURTHER ELECTION.—If an election is terminated under subparagraph (A) or paragraph (3)(A), the partnership, S corporation, or personal service corporation may not make another election under subsection (a).

(3) TIERED STRUCTURES, ETC.—

(A) IN GENERAL.—Except as otherwise provided in this paragraph—

(i) no election may be under subsection (a) with respect to any entity which is part of a tiered structure, and

(ii) an election under subsection (a) with respect to any entity shall be terminated if such entity becomes part of a tiered structure.

(B) EXCEPTIONS FOR STRUCTURES CONSISTING OF CERTAIN ENTITIES WITH SAME TAXABLE YEAR.—Subparagraph (A) shall not apply to any tiered structure which consists only of partnerships or S corporations (or both) all of which have the same taxable year.

Sec. 444(d)

[Sec. 444(e)]

(e) REQUIRED TAXABLE YEAR.—For purposes of this section, the term "required taxable year" means the taxable year determined under section 706(b), 1378, or 441(i) without taking into account any taxable year which is allowable by reason of business purposes. Solely for purposes of the preceding sentence, sections 706(b), 1378, and 441(i) shall be treated as in effect for taxable years beginning before January 1, 1987.

[Sec. 444(f)]

(f) PERSONAL SERVICE CORPORATION.—For purposes of this section, the term "personal service corporation" has the meaning given to such term by section 441(i)(2).

* * *

PART II—METHODS OF ACCOUNTING

Subpart A—Methods of Accounting in General

[Sec. 446]

SEC. 446. GENERAL RULE FOR METHODS OF ACCOUNTING.

[Sec. 446(a)]

(a) GENERAL RULE.—Taxable income shall be computed under the method of accounting on the basis of which the taxpayer regularly computes his income in keeping his books.

[Sec. 446(b)]

(b) EXCEPTIONS.—If no method of accounting has been regularly used by the taxpayer, or if the method used does not clearly reflect income, the computation of taxable income shall be made under such method as, in the opinion of the Secretary, does clearly reflect income.

[Sec. 446(c)]

(c) PERMISSIBLE METHODS.—Subject to the provisions of subsections (a) and (b), a taxpayer may compute taxable income under any of the following methods of accounting—

(1) the cash receipts and disbursements method;

(2) an accrual method;

(3) any other method permitted by this chapter; or

(4) any combination of the foregoing methods permitted under regulations prescribed by the Secretary.

[Sec. 446(d)]

(d) TAXPAYER ENGAGED IN MORE THAN ONE BUSINESS.—A taxpayer engaged in more than one trade or business may, in computing taxable income, use a different method of accounting for each trade or business.

[Sec. 446(e)]

(e) REQUIREMENT RESPECTING CHANGE OF ACCOUNTING METHOD.—Except as otherwise expressly provided in this chapter, a taxpayer who changes the method of accounting on the basis of which he regularly computes his income in keeping his books shall, before computing his taxable income under the new method, secure the consent of the Secretary.

[Sec. 446(f)]

(f) FAILURE TO REQUEST CHANGE OF METHOD OF ACCOUNTING.—If the taxpayer does not file with the Secretary a request to change the method of accounting, the absence of the consent of the Secretary to a change in the method of accounting shall not be taken into account—

(1) to prevent the imposition of any penalty, or the addition of any amount to tax, under this title, or

(2) to diminish the amount of such penalty or addition to tax.

[Sec. 447]

SEC. 447. METHOD OF ACCOUNTING FOR CORPORATIONS ENGAGED IN FARMING.

* * *

[Sec. 447(d)]

(d) GROSS RECEIPTS REQUIREMENTS.—

* * *

(2) SPECIAL RULES FOR FAMILY CORPORATIONS.—

* * *

(C) FAMILY CORPORATION.—For purposes of this section, the term "family corporation" means—

(i) any corporation if at least 50 percent of the total combined voting power of all classes of stock entitled to vote, and at least 50 percent of all other classes of stock of the corporation, are owned by members of the same family * * *

* * *

[Sec. 447(e)]

(e) MEMBERS OF THE SAME FAMILY.—For purposes of subsection (d)—

(1) the members of the same family are an individual, such individual's brothers and sisters, the brothers and sisters of such individual's parents and grandparents, the ancestors and lineal descendants of any of the foregoing, a spouse of any of the foregoing, and the estate of any of the foregoing,

(2) stock owned, directly or indirectly, by or for a partnership or trust shall be treated as owned proportionately by its partners or beneficiaries, and

(3) if 50 percent or more in value of the stock in a corporation (hereinafter in this paragraph referred to as "first corporation") is owned, directly or through paragraph (2), by or for members of the same family, such members shall be considered as owning each class of stock in a second corporation (or a wholly owned subsidiary of such second corporation) owned, directly or indirectly, by or for the first corporation, in that proportion which the value of the stock in the first corporation which such members so own bears to the value of all the stock in the first corporation.

For purposes of paragraph (1), individuals related by the half blood or by legal adoption shall be treated as if they were related by the whole blood.

* * *

[Sec. 448]

SEC. 448. LIMITATION ON USE OF CASH METHOD OF ACCOUNTING.

[Sec. 448(a)]

(a) GENERAL RULE.—Except as otherwise provided in this section, in the case of a—

(1) C corporation,

(2) partnership which has a C corporation as a partner, or

(3) tax shelter,

taxable income shall not be computed under the cash receipts and disbursements method of accounting.

[Sec. 448(b)]

(b) EXCEPTIONS.—

(1) FARMING BUSINESS.—Paragraphs (1) and (2) of subsection (a) shall not apply to any farming business.

(2) QUALIFIED PERSONAL SERVICE CORPORATIONS.—Paragraphs (1) and (2) of subsection (a) shall not apply to a qualified personal service corporation, and such a corporation shall be treated as an individual for purposes of determining whether paragraph (2) of subsection (a) applies to any partnership.

Sec. 448(b)

(3) ENTITIES WITH GROSS RECEIPTS OF NOT MORE THAN $5,000,000.—Paragraphs (1) and (2) of subsection (a) shall not apply to any corporation or partnership for any taxable year if, for all prior taxable years beginning after December 31, 1985, such entity (or any predecessor) met the $5,000,000 gross receipts test of subsection (c).

[Sec. 448(c)]

(c) $5,000,000 GROSS RECEIPTS TEST.—For purposes of this section—

(1) IN GENERAL.—A corporation or partnership meets the $5,000,000 gross receipts test of this subsection for any prior taxable year if the average annual gross receipts of such entity for the 3-taxable-year period ending with such prior taxable year does not exceed $5,000,000.

(2) AGGREGATION RULES.—All persons treated as a single employer under subsection (a) or (b) of section 52 or subsection (m) or (o) of section 414 shall be treated as one person for purposes of paragraph (1).

(3) SPECIAL RULES.—For purposes of this subsection—

(A) NOT IN EXISTENCE FOR ENTIRE 3-YEAR PERIOD.—If the entity was not in existence for the entire 3-year period referred to in paragraph (1), such paragraph shall be applied on the basis of the period during which such entity (or trade or business) was in existence.

(B) SHORT TAXABLE YEARS.—Gross receipts for any taxable year of less than 12 months shall be annualized by multiplying the gross receipts for the short period by 12 and dividing the result by the number of months in the short period.

(C) GROSS RECEIPTS.—Gross receipts for any taxable year shall be reduced by returns and allowances made during such year.

(D) TREATMENT OF PREDECESSORS.—Any reference in this subsection to an entity shall include a reference to any predecessor of such entity.

[Sec. 448(d)]

(d) DEFINITIONS AND SPECIAL RULES.—For purposes of this section—

(1) FARMING BUSINESS.—

(A) IN GENERAL.—The term "farming business" means the trade or business of farming (within the meaning of section 263A(e)(4)).

(B) TIMBER AND ORNAMENTAL TREES.—The term "farming business" includes the raising, harvesting, or growing of trees to which section 263A(c)(5) applies.

(2) QUALIFIED PERSONAL SERVICE CORPORATION.—The term "qualified personal service corporation" means any corporation—

(A) substantially all of the activities of which involve the performance of services in the fields of health, law, engineering, architecture, accounting, actuarial science, performing arts, or consulting, and

(B) substantially all of the stock of which (by value) is held directly (or indirectly through 1 or more partnerships, S corporations, or qualified personal service corporations not described in paragraph (2) or (3) of subsection (a)) by—

(i) employees performing services for such corporation in connection with the activities involving a field referred to in subparagraph (A),

(ii) retired employees who had performed such services for such corporation,

(iii) the estate of any individual described in clause (i) or (ii), or

(iv) any other person who acquired such stock by reason of the death of an individual described in clause (i) or (ii) (but only for the 2-year period beginning on the date of the death of such individual).

To the extent provided in regulations which shall be prescribed by the Secretary, indirect holdings through a trust shall be taken into account under subparagraph (B).

(3) TAX SHELTER DEFINED.—The term "tax shelter" has the meaning given such term by section 461(i)(3) (determined after application of paragraph (4) thereof). An S corporation shall not be treated as a tax shelter for purposes of this section merely by reason of being required to file a notice of exemption from registration with a State agency described in section 461(i)(3)(A), but only if there is a requirement applicable to all corporations offering securities for sale in the State that to be exempt from such registration the corporation must file such a notice.

(4) SPECIAL RULES FOR APPLICATION OF PARAGRAPH (2).—For purposes of paragraph (2)—

(A) community property laws shall be disregarded,

(B) stock held by a plan described in section 401(a) which is exempt from tax under section 501(a) shall be treated as held by an employee described in paragraph (2)(B)(i), and

(C) at the election of the common parent of an affiliated group (within the meaning of section 1504(a)), all members of such group may be treated as 1 taxpayer for purposes of paragraph (2)(B) if 90 percent or more of the activities of such group involve the performance of services in the same field described in paragraph (2)(A).

(5) SPECIAL RULE FOR CERTAIN SERVICES.—

(A) IN GENERAL.—In the case of any person using an accrual method of accounting with respect to amounts to be received for the performance of services by such person, such person shall not be required to accrue any portion of such amounts which (on the basis of such person's experience) will not be collected if—

(i) such services are in fields referred to in paragraph (2)(A), or

(ii) such person meets the gross receipts test of subsection (c) for all prior taxable years.

(B) EXCEPTION.—This paragraph shall not apply to any amount if interest is required to be paid on such amount or there is any penalty for failure to timely pay such amount.

(C) REGULATIONS.—The Secretary shall prescribe regulations to permit taxpayers to determine amounts referred to in subparagraph (A) using computations or formulas which, based on experience, accurately reflect the amount of income that will not be collected by such person. A taxpayer may adopt, or request consent of the Secretary to change to, a computation or formula that clearly reflects the taxpayer's experience. A request under the preceding sentence shall be approved if such computation or formula clearly reflects the taxpayer's experience.

(6) TREATMENT OF CERTAIN TRUSTS SUBJECT TO TAX ON UNRELATED BUSINESS INCOME.—For purposes of this section, a trust subject to tax under section 511(b) shall be treated as a C corporation with respect to its activities constituting an unrelated trade or business.

(7) COORDINATION WITH SECTION 481.—In the case of any taxpayer required by this section to change its method of accounting for any taxable year—

(A) such change shall be treated as initiated by the taxpayer,

(B) such change shall be treated as made with the consent of the Secretary, and

(C) the period for taking into account the adjustments under section 481 by reason of such change—

(i) except as provided in clause (ii), shall not exceed 4 years, and

(ii) in the case of a hospital, shall be 10 years.

(8) USE OF RELATED PARTIES, ETC.—The Secretary shall prescribe such regulations as may be necessary to prevent the use of related parties, pass-thru entities, or intermediaries to avoid the application of this section.

Subpart B—Taxable Year for Which Items of Gross Income Included

[Sec. 451]
SEC. 451. GENERAL RULE FOR TAXABLE YEAR OF INCLUSION.

[Sec. 451(a)]

(a) GENERAL RULE.—The amount of any item of gross income shall be included in the gross income for the taxable year in which received by the taxpayer, unless, under the method of accounting used in computing taxable income, such amount is to be properly accounted for as of a different period.

[Sec. 451(b)]

(b) SPECIAL RULE IN CASE OF DEATH.—In the case of the death of a taxpayer whose taxable income is computed under an accrual method of accounting, any amount accrued only by reason of the death of the taxpayer shall not be included in computing taxable income for the period in which falls the date of the taxpayer's death.

[Sec. 451(c)]

(c) SPECIAL RULE FOR EMPLOYEE TIPS.—For purposes of subsection (a), tips included in a written statement furnished an employer by an employee pursuant to section 6053(a) shall be deemed to be received at the time the written statement including such tips is furnished to the employer.

* * *

[Sec. 453]

SEC. 453. INSTALLMENT METHOD.

[Sec. 453(a)]

(a) GENERAL RULE.—Except as otherwise provided in this section, income from an installment sale shall be taken into account for purposes of this title under the installment method.

[Sec. 453(b)]

(b) INSTALLMENT SALE DEFINED.—For purposes of this section—

(1) IN GENERAL.—The term "installment sale" means a disposition of property where at least 1 payment is to be received after the close of the taxable year in which the disposition occurs.

(2) EXCEPTIONS.—The term "installment sale" does not include—

(A) DEALER DISPOSITIONS.—Any dealer disposition (as defined in subsection (1)).

(B) INVENTORIES OF PERSONAL PROPERTY.—A disposition of personal property of a kind which is required to be included in the inventory of the taxpayer if on hand at the close of the taxable year.

[Sec. 453(c)]

(c) INSTALLMENT METHOD DEFINED.—For purposes of this section, the term "installment method" means a method under which the income recognized for any taxable year from a disposition is that proportion of the payments received in that year which the gross profit (realized or to be realized when payment is completed) bears to the total contract price.

[Sec. 453(d)]

(d) ELECTION OUT.—

(1) IN GENERAL.—Subsection (a) shall not apply to any disposition if the taxpayer elects to have subsection (a) not apply to such disposition.

(2) TIME AND MANNER FOR MAKING ELECTION.—Except as otherwise provided by regulations, an election under paragraph (1) with respect to a disposition may be made only on or before the due date prescribed by law (including extensions) for filing the taxpayer's return of the tax imposed by this chapter for the taxable year in which the disposition occurs. Such an election shall be made in the manner prescribed by regulations.

(3) ELECTION REVOCABLE ONLY WITH CONSENT.—An election under paragraph (1) with respect to any disposition may be revoked only with the consent of the Secretary.

[Sec. 453(e)]

(e) SECOND DISPOSITIONS BY RELATED PERSONS.—

(1) IN GENERAL.—If—

(A) Any person disposes of property to a related person (hereinafter in this subsection referred to as the "first disposition"), and

(B) before the person making the first disposition receives all payments with respect to such disposition, the related person disposes of the property (hereinafter in this subsection referred to as the "second disposition"),

then, for purposes of this section, the amount realized with respect to such second disposition shall be treated as received at the time of the second disposition by the person making the first disposition.

(2) 2-YEAR CUTOFF FOR PROPERTY OTHER THAN MARKETABLE SECURITIES.—

(A) IN GENERAL.—Except in the case of marketable securities, paragraph (1) shall apply only if the date of the second disposition is not more than 2 years after the date of the first disposition.

(B) SUBSTANTIAL DIMINISHING OF RISK OF OWNERSHIP.—The running of the 2-year period set forth in subparagraph (A) shall be suspended with respect to any property for any period during which the related person's risk of loss with respect to the property is substantially diminished by—

(i) the holding of a put with respect to such property (or similar property),

(ii) the holding by another person of a right to acquire the property, or

(iii) a short sale or any other transaction.

(3) LIMITATION ON AMOUNT TREATED AS RECEIVED.—The amount treated for any taxable year as received by the person making the first disposition by reason of paragraph (1) shall not exceed the excess of—

(A) the lesser of—

(i) the total amount realized with respect to any second disposition of the property occurring before the close of the taxable year, or

(ii) the total contract price for the first disposition, over

(B) the sum of—

(i) the aggregate amount of payments received with respect to the first disposition before the close of such year, plus

(ii) the aggregate amount treated as received with respect to the first disposition for prior taxable years by reason of this subsection.

(4) FAIR MARKET VALUE WHERE DISPOSITION IS NOT SALE OR EXCHANGE.—For purposes of this subsection, if the second disposition is not a sale or exchange, an amount equal to the fair market value of the property disposed of shall be substituted for the amount realized.

(5) LATER PAYMENTS TREATED AS RECEIPT OF TAX PAID AMOUNTS.—If paragraph (1) applies for any taxable year, payments received in subsequent taxable years by the person making the first disposition shall not be treated as the receipt of payments with respect to the first disposition to the extent that the aggregate of such payments does not exceed the amount treated as received by reason of paragraph (1).

(6) EXCEPTION FOR CERTAIN DISPOSITIONS.—For purposes of this subsection—

(A) REACQUISITIONS OF STOCK BY ISSUING CORPORATION NOT TREATED AS FIRST DISPOSITIONS.— Any sale or exchange of stock to the issuing corporation shall not be treated as a first disposition.

(B) INVOLUNTARY CONVERSIONS NOT TREATED AS SECOND DISPOSITIONS.—A compulsory or involuntary conversion (within the meaning of section 1033) and any transfer thereafter shall not be treated as a second disposition if the first disposition occurred before the threat or imminence of the conversion.

(C) DISPOSITIONS AFTER DEATH.—Any transfer after the earlier of—

(i) the death of the person making the first disposition, or

(ii) the death of the person acquiring the property in the first disposition,

and any transfer thereafter shall not be treated as a second disposition.

(7) EXCEPTION WHERE TAX AVOIDANCE NOT A PRINCIPAL PURPOSE.—This subsection shall not apply to a second disposition (and any transfer thereafter) if it is established to the satisfaction of the Secretary that neither the first disposition nor the second disposition had as one of its principal purposes the avoidance of Federal income tax.

(8) EXTENSION OF STATUTE OF LIMITATIONS.—The period for assessing a deficiency with respect to a first disposition (to the extent such deficiency is attributable to the application of this subsection) shall not expire before the day which is 2 years after the date on which the person making the first disposition furnishes (in such manner as the Secretary may by regulations prescribe) a notice that there was a second disposition of the property to which this subsection may have applied. Such deficiency may be assessed notwithstanding the provisions of any law or rule of law which would otherwise prevent such assessment.

Sec. 453(e)

[Sec. 453(f)]

(f) DEFINITIONS AND SPECIAL RULES.—For purposes of this section—

(1) RELATED PERSON.—Except for purposes of subsections (g) and (h), the term "related person" means—

(A) a person whose stock would be attributed under section 318(a) (other than paragraph (4) thereof) to the person first disposing of the property, or

(B) a person who bears a relationship described in section 267(b) to the person first disposing of the property.

(2) MARKETABLE SECURITIES.—The term "marketable securities" means any security for which, as of the date of the disposition, there was a market on an established securities market or otherwise.

(3) PAYMENT.—Except as provided in paragraph (4), the term "payment" does not include the receipt of evidences of indebtedness of the person acquiring the property (whether or not payment of such indebtedness is guaranteed by another person).

(4) PURCHASER EVIDENCES OF INDEBTEDNESS PAYABLE ON DEMAND OR READILY TRADABLE.—Receipt of a bond or other evidence of indebtedness which—

(A) is payable on demand, or

(B) is issued by a corporation or a government or political subdivision thereof and is readily tradable,

shall be treated as receipt of payment.

(5) READILY TRADABLE DEFINED.—For purposes of paragraph (4), the term "readily tradable" means a bond or other evidence of indebtedness which is issued—

(A) with interest coupons attached or in registered form (other than one in registered form which the taxpayer establishes will not be readily tradable in an established securities market), or

(B) in any other form designed to render such bond or other evidence of indebtedness readily tradable in an established securities market.

(6) LIKE-KIND EXCHANGES.—In the case of any exchange described in section 1031(b)—

(A) the total contract price shall be reduced to take into account the amount of any property permitted to be received in such exchange without recognition of gain,

(B) the gross profit from such exchange shall be reduced to take into account any amount not recognized by reason of section 1031(b), and

(C) the term "payment", when used in any provision of this section other than subsection (b)(1), shall not include any property permitted to be received in such exchange without recognition of gain.

Similar rules shall apply in the case of an exchange which is described in section 356(a) and is not treated as a dividend.

(7) DEPRECIABLE PROPERTY.—The term "depreciable property" means property of a character which (in the hands of the transferee) is subject to the allowance for depreciation provided in section 167.

(8) PAYMENTS TO BE RECEIVED DEFINED.—The term "payments to be received" includes—

(A) the aggregate amount of all payments which are not contingent as to amount, and

(B) the fair market value of any payments which are contingent as to amount.

[Sec. 453(g)]

(g) SALE OF DEPRECIABLE PROPERTY TO CONTROLLED ENTITY.—

(1) IN GENERAL.—In the case of an installment sale of depreciable property between related persons—

(A) subsection (a) shall not apply,

(B) for purposes of this title—

(i) except as provided in clause (ii), all payments to be received shall be treated as received in the year of the disposition, and

(ii) in the case of any payments which are contingent as to the amount but with respect to which the fair market value may not be reasonably ascertained, the basis shall be recovered ratably, and

(C) the purchaser may not increase the basis of any property acquired in such sale by any amount before the time such amount is includible in the gross income of the seller.

(2) EXCEPTION WHERE TAX AVOIDANCE NOT A PRINCIPAL PURPOSE.—Paragraph (1) shall not apply if it is established to the satisfaction of the Secretary that the disposition did not have as one of its principal purposes the avoidance of Federal income tax.

(3) RELATED PERSONS.—For purposes of this subsection, the term "related persons" has the meaning given to such term by section 1239(b), except that such term shall include 2 or more partnerships having a relationship to each other described in section 707(b)(1)(B).

[Sec. 453(h)]

(h) USE OF INSTALLMENT METHOD BY SHAREHOLDERS IN CERTAIN LIQUIDATIONS.—

(1) RECEIPT OF OBLIGATIONS NOT TREATED AS RECEIPT OF PAYMENT.—

(A) IN GENERAL.—If, in a liquidation to which section 331 applies, the shareholder receives (in exchange for the shareholder's stock) an installment obligation acquired in respect of a sale or exchange by the corporation during the 12-month period beginning on the date a plan of complete liquidation is adopted and the liquidation is completed during such 12-month period, then, for purposes of this section, the receipt of payments under such obligation (but not the receipt of such obligation) by the shareholder shall be treated as the receipt of payment for the stock.

(B) OBLIGATIONS ATTRIBUTABLE TO SALE OF INVENTORY MUST RESULT FROM BULK SALE.—Subparagraph (A) shall not apply to an installment obligation acquired in respect of a sale or exchange of—

(i) stock in trade of the corporation,

(ii) other property of a kind which would properly be included in the inventory of the corporation if on hand at the close of the taxable year, and

(iii) property held by the corporation primarily for sale to customers in the ordinary course of its trade or business,

unless such sale or exchange is to 1 person in 1 transaction and involves substantially all of such property attributable to a trade or business of the corporation.

(C) SPECIAL RULE WHERE OBLIGOR AND SHAREHOLDER ARE RELATED PERSONS.—If the obligor of any installment obligation and the shareholder are married to each other or are related persons (within the meaning of section 1239(b)), to the extent such installment obligation is attributable to the disposition by the corporation of depreciable property—

(i) subparagraph (A) shall not apply to such obligation, and

(ii) for purposes of this title, all payments to be received by the shareholder shall be deemed received in the year the shareholder receives the obligation.

(D) COORDINATION WITH SUBSECTION (e)(1)(A).—For purposes of subsection (e)(1)(A), disposition of property by the corporation shall be treated also as disposition of such property by the shareholder.

(E) SALES BY LIQUIDATING SUBSIDIARIES.—For purposes of subparagraph (A), in the case of controlling corporate shareholder (within the meaning of section 368(c)) of a selling corporation, an obligation acquired in respect of a sale or exchange by the selling corporation shall be treated as so acquired by such controlling corporate shareholder. The preceding sentence shall be applied successively to each controlling corporate shareholder above such controlling corporate shareholder.

(2) DISTRIBUTIONS RECEIVED IN MORE THAN 1 TAXABLE YEAR OF SHAREHOLDER.—If—

(A) paragraph (1) applies with respect to any installment obligation received by a shareholder from a corporation, and

(B) by reason of the liquidation such shareholder receives property in more than 1 taxable year,

Sec. 453(h)

then, on completion of the liquidation, basis previously allocated to property so received shall be reallocated for all such taxable years so that the shareholder's basis in the stock of the corporation is properly allocated among all property received by such shareholder in such liquidation.

[Sec. 453(i)]

(i) RECOGNITION OF RECAPTURE INCOME IN YEAR OF DISPOSITION.—

(1) IN GENERAL.—In the case of any installment sale of property to which subsection (a) applies—

(A) notwithstanding subsection (a), any recapture income shall be recognized in the year of the disposition, and

(B) any gain in excess of the recapture income shall be taken into account under the installment method.

(2) RECAPTURE INCOME.—For purposes of paragraph (1), the term "recapture income" means, with respect to any installment sale, the aggregate amount which would be treated as ordinary income under section 1245 or 1250 (or so much of section 751 as relates to section 1245 or 1250) for the taxable year of the disposition if all payments to be received were received in the taxable year of disposition.

[Sec. 453(j)]

(j) REGULATIONS.—

(1) IN GENERAL.—The Secretary shall prescribe such regulations as may be necessary or appropriate to carry out the provisions of this section.

(2) SELLING PRICE NOT READILY ASCERTAINABLE.—The regulations prescribed under paragraph (1) shall include regulations providing for ratable basis recovery in transactions where the gross profit or the total contract price (or both) cannot be readily ascertained.

[Sec. 453(k)]

(k) CURRENT INCLUSION IN CASE OF REVOLVING CREDIT PLANS, ETC.—In the case of—

(1) any disposition of personal property under a revolving credit plan, or

(2) any installment obligation arising out of a sale of—

(A) stock or securities which are traded on an established securities market, or

(B) to the extent provided in regulations, property (other than stock or securities) of a kind regularly traded on an established market,

subsection (a) shall not apply, and, for purposes of this title, all payments to be received shall be treated as received in the year of disposition. The Secretary may provide for the application of this subsection in whole or in part for transactions in which the rules of this subsection otherwise would be avoided through the use of related parties, pass-thru entities, or intermediaries.

[Sec. 453(l)]

(l) DEALER DISPOSITIONS.—For purposes of subsection (b)(2)(A)—

(1) IN GENERAL.—The term "dealer disposition" means any of the following dispositions:

(A) PERSONAL PROPERTY.—Any disposition of personal property by a person who regularly sells or otherwise disposes of personal property of the same type on the installment plan.

(B) REAL PROPERTY.—Any disposition of real property which is held by the taxpayer for sale to customers in the ordinary course of the taxpayer's trade or business.

(2) EXCEPTIONS.—The term "dealer disposition" does not include—

(A) FARM PROPERTY.—The disposition on the installment plan of any property used or produced in the trade or business of farming (within the meaning of section 2032A(e)(4) or (5)).

(B) TIMESHARES AND RESIDENTIAL LOTS.—

(i) IN GENERAL.—Any dispositions described in clause (ii) on the installment plan if the taxpayer elects to have paragraph (3) apply to any installment obligations which arise from such dispositions. An election under this paragraph shall not apply with respect to an installment obligation which is guaranteed by any person other than an individual.

Sec. 453(i)

(ii) Dispositions to which subparagraph applies.—A disposition is described in this clause if it is a disposition in the ordinary course of the taxpayer's trade or business to an individual of—

(I) a timeshare right to use or a timeshare ownership interest in residential real property for not more than 6 weeks per year, or a right to use specified campgrounds for recreational purposes, or

(II) any residential lot, but only if the taxpayer (or any related person) is not to make any improvements with respect to such lot.

For purposes of subclause (I), a timeshare right to use (or timeshare ownership interest in) property held by the spouse, children, grandchildren, or parents of an individual shall be treated as held by such individual.

(C) Carrying charges or interest.—Any carrying charges or interest with respect to a disposition described in subparagraph (A) or (B) which are added on the books of account of the seller to the established cash selling price of the property shall be included in the total contract price of the property and, if such charges or interest are not so included, any payments received shall be treated as applying first against such carrying charges or interest.

(3) Payment of interest on timeshares and residential lots.—

(A) In general.—In the case of any installment obligation to which paragraph (2)(B) applies, the tax imposed by this chapter for any taxable year for which payment is received on such obligation shall be increased by the amount of interest determined in the manner provided under subparagraph (B).

(B) Computation of interest.—

(i) In general.—The amount of interest referred to in subparagraph (A) for any taxable year shall be determined—

(I) on the amount of the tax for such taxable year which is attributable to the payments received during such taxable year on installment obligations to which this subsection applies.

(II) for the period beginning on the date of sale, and ending on the date such payment is received, and

(III) by using the applicable Federal rate under section 1274 (without regard to subsection (d)(2) thereof) in effect at the time of the sale compounded semiannually.

(ii) Interest not taken into account.—For purposes of clause (i), the portion of any tax attributable to the receipt of any payment shall be determined without regard to any interest imposed under subparagraph (A).

(iii) Taxable year of sale.—No interest shall be determined for any payment received in the taxable year of the disposition from which the installment obligation arises.

(C) Treatment as interest.—Any amount payable under this paragraph shall be taken into account in computing the amount of any deduction allowable to the taxpayer for interest paid or accrued during such taxable year.

[Sec. 453A]

SEC. 453A. SPECIAL RULES FOR NONDEALERS.

[Sec. 453A(a)]

(a) General Rule.—In the case of an installment obligation to which this section applies—

(1) interest shall be paid on the deferred tax liability with respect to such obligation in the manner provided under subsection (c), and

(2) the pledging rules under subsection (d) shall apply.

[Sec. 453A(b)]

(b) Installment Obligations to Which Section Applies.—

(1) In general.—This section shall apply to any obligation which arises from the disposition of any property under the installment method, but only if the sales price of such property exceeds $150,000.

(2) SPECIAL RULE FOR INTEREST PAYMENTS.—For purposes of subsection (a)(1), this section shall apply to an obligation described in paragraph (1) arising during a taxable year only if—

(A) such obligation is outstanding as of the close of such taxable year, and

(B) the face amount of all such obligations held by the taxpayer which arose during, and are outstanding as of the close of, such taxable year exceeds $5,000,000.

Except as provided in regulations, all persons treated as a single employer under subsection (a) or (b) of section 52 shall be treated as one person for purposes of this paragraph and subsection (c)(4).

(3) EXCEPTION FOR PERSONAL USE AND FARM PROPERTY.—An installment obligation shall not be treated as described in paragraph (1) if it arises from the disposition—

(A) by an individual of personal use property (within the meaning of section 1275(b)(3)), or

(B) of any property used or produced in the trade or business of farming (within the meaning of section 2032A(e)(4) or (5)).

(4) SPECIAL RULE FOR TIMESHARES AND RESIDENTIAL LOTS.—An installment obligation shall not be treated as described in paragraph (1) if it arises from a disposition described in section 453(1)(2)(B), but the provisions of section 453(1)(3) (relating to interest payments on timeshares and residential lots) shall apply to such obligation.

(5) SALES PRICE.—For purposes of paragraph (1), all sales or exchanges which are part of the same transaction (or a series of related transactions) shall be treated as 1 sale or exchange.

[Sec. 453A(c)]

(c) INTEREST ON DEFERRED TAX LIABILITY.—

(1) IN GENERAL.—If an obligation to which this section applies is outstanding as of the close of any taxable year, the tax imposed by this chapter for such taxable year shall be increased by the amount of interest determined in the manner provided under paragraph (2).

(2) COMPUTATION OF INTEREST.—For purposes of paragraph (1), the interest for any taxable year shall be an amount equal to the product of—

(A) the applicable percentage of the deferred tax liability with respect to such obligation, multiplied by

(B) the underpayment rate in effect under section 6621(a)(2) for the month with or within which the taxable year ends.

(3) DEFERRED TAX LIABILITY.—For purposes of this section, the term "deferred tax liability" means, with respect to any taxable year, the product of—

(A) the amount of gain with respect to an obligation which has not been recognized as of the close of such taxable year, multiplied by

(B) the maximum rate of tax in effect under section 1 or 11, whichever is appropriate, for such taxable year.

For purposes of applying the preceding sentence with respect to so much of the gain which, when recognized, will be treated as long-term capital gain, the maximum rate on net capital gain under section 1(h) or 1201 (whichever is appropriate) shall be taken into account.

(4) APPLICABLE PERCENTAGE.—For purposes of this subsection, the term "applicable percentage" means, with respect to obligations arising in any taxable year, the percentage determined by dividing—

(A) the portion of the aggregate face amount of such obligations outstanding as of the close of such taxable year in excess of $5,000,000, by

(B) the aggregate face amount of such obligations outstanding as of the close of such taxable year.

(5) TREATMENT AS INTEREST.—Any amount payable under this subsection shall be taken into account in computing the amount of any deduction allowable to the taxpayer for interest paid or accrued during the taxable year.

(6) REGULATIONS.—The Secretary shall prescribe such regulations as may be necessary to carry out the provisions of this subsection including regulations providing for the application of this subsection in the case of contingent payments, short taxable years, and pass-thru entities.

[Sec. 453A(d)]

(d) PLEDGES, ETC., OF INSTALLMENT OBLIGATIONS.—

(1) IN GENERAL.—For purposes of section 453, if any indebtedness (hereinafter in this subsection referred to as "secured indebtedness") is secured by an installment obligation to which this section applies, the net proceeds of the secured indebtedness shall be treated as a payment received on such installment obligation as of the later of—

(A) the time the indebtedness becomes secured indebtedness, or

(B) the time the proceeds of such indebtedness are received by the taxpayer.

(2) LIMITATION BASED ON TOTAL CONTRACT PRICE.—The amount treated as received under paragraph (1) by reason of any secured indebtedness shall not exceed the excess (if any) of—

(A) the total contract price, over

(B) any portion of the total contract price received under the contract before the later of the times referred to in subparagraph (A) or (B) of paragraph (1) (including amounts previously treated as received under paragraph (1) but not including amounts not taken into account by reason of paragraph (3)).

(3) LATER PAYMENTS TREATED AS RECEIPT OF TAX PAID AMOUNTS.—If any amount is treated as received under paragraph (1) with respect to any installment obligation, subsequent payments received on such obligation shall not be taken into account for purposes of section 453 to the extent that the aggregate of such subsequent payments does not exceed the aggregate amount treated as received under paragraph (1).

(4) SECURED INDEBTEDNESS.—For purposes of this subsection indebtedness is secured by an installment obligation to the extent that payment of principal or interest on such indebtedness is directly secured (under the terms of the indebtedness or any underlying arrangements) by any interest in such installment obligation. A payment shall be treated as directly secured by an interest in an installment obligation to the extent an arrangement allows the taxpayer to satisfy all or a portion of the indebtedness with the installment obligation.

[Sec. 453A(e)]

(e) REGULATIONS.—The Secretary shall prescribe such regulations as may be necessary to carry out the purposes of this section, including regulations—

(1) disallowing the use of the installment method in whole or in part for transactions in which the rules of this section otherwise would be avoided through the use of related persons, pass-thru entities, or intermediaries, and

(2) providing that the sale of an interest in a partnership or other pass-thru entity will be treated as a sale of the proportionate share of the assets of the partnership or other entity.

[Sec. 453B]

SEC. 453B. GAIN OR LOSS ON DISPOSITION OF INSTALLMENT OBLIGATIONS.

[Sec. 453B(a)]

(a) GENERAL RULE.—If an installment obligation is satisfied at other than its face value or distributed, transmitted, sold, or otherwise disposed of, gain or loss shall result to the extent of the difference between the basis of the obligation and—

(1) the amount realized, in the case of satisfaction at other than face value or a sale or exchange, or

(2) the fair market value of the obligation at the time of distribution, transmission, or disposition, in the case of the distribution, transmission, or disposition otherwise than by sale or exchange.

Any gain or loss so resulting shall be considered as resulting from the sale or exchange of the property in respect of which the installment obligation was received.

[Sec. 453B(b)]

(b) BASIS OF OBLIGATION.—The basis of an installment obligation shall be the excess of the face value of the obligation over an amount equal to the income which would be returnable were the obligation satisfied in full.

[Sec. 453B(c)]

(c) SPECIAL RULE FOR TRANSMISSION AT DEATH.—Except as provided in section 691 (relating to recipients of income in respect of decedents), this section shall not apply to the transmission of installment obligations at death.

[Sec. 453B(d)]

(d) EXCEPTION FOR DISTRIBUTIONS TO WHICH SECTION 337(A) APPLIES.—Subsection (a) shall not apply to any distribution to which section 337(a) applies.

* * *

[Sec. 453B(f)]

(f) OBLIGATION BECOMES UNENFORCEABLE.—For purposes of this section, if any installment obligation is canceled or otherwise becomes unenforceable—

(1) the obligation shall be treated as if it were disposed of in a transaction other than a sale or exchange, and

(2) if the obligor and obligee are related persons (within the meaning of section 453(f)(1)), the fair market value of the obligation shall be treated as not less than its face amount.

[Sec. 453B(g)]

(g) TRANSFERS BETWEEN SPOUSES OR INCIDENT TO DIVORCE.—In the case of any transfer described in subsection (a) of section 1041 (other than a transfer in trust)—

(1) subsection (a) of this section shall not apply, and

(2) the same tax treatment with respect to the transferred installment obligation shall apply to the transferee as would have applied to the transferor.

[Sec. 453B(h)]

(h) CERTAIN LIQUIDATING DISTRIBUTIONS BY S CORPORATIONS.—If—

(1) an installment obligation is distributed by an S corporation in a complete liquidation, and

(2) receipt of the obligation is not treated as payment for the stock by reason of section 453(h)(1).

then, except for purposes of any tax imposed by subchaper S, no gain or loss with respect to the distribution of the obligation shall be recognized by the distributing corporation. Under regulations prescribed by the Secretary, the character of the gain or loss to the shareholder shall be determined in accordance with the principles of section 1366(b).

[Sec. 454]

SEC. 454. OBLIGATIONS ISSUED AT DISCOUNT.

[Sec. 454(a)]

(a) NON-INTEREST-BEARING OBLIGATIONS ISSUED AT A DISCOUNT.—If, in the case of a taxpayer owning any non-interest-bearing obligation issued at a discount and redeemable for fixed amounts increasing at stated intervals or owning an obligation described in paragraph (2) of subsection (c), the increase in the redemption price of such obligation occurring in the taxable year does not (under the method of accounting used in computing his taxable income) constitute income to him in such year, such taxpayer may, at his election made in his return for any taxable year, treat such increase as income received in such taxable year. If any such election is made with respect to any such obligation, it shall apply also to all such obligations owned by the taxpayer at the beginning of the first taxable year to which it applies and to all such obligations thereafter acquired by him and shall be binding for all subsequent taxable years, unless on application by the taxpayer the Secretary permits him, subject to such conditions as the Secretary deems necessary, to change to a different method. In the case of any such obligations owned by the taxpayer at the beginning of the first taxable year to which his election applies, the increase in the redemption price of such obligations occurring between the date of acquisition (or, in the case of an obligation described in paragraph (2) of subsection (c), the date of acquisition of the series E bond involved) and the first day of such taxable year shall also be treated as income received in such taxable year.

(b) SHORT-TERM OBLIGATIONS ISSUED ON DISCOUNT BASIS.—In the case of any obligation—

(1) of the United States; or

(2) of a State, or a possession of the United States, or any political subdivision of any of the foregoing, or of the District of Columbia,

which is issued on a discount basis and payable without interest at a fixed maturity date not exceeding 1 year from the date of issue, the amount of discount at which such obligation is originally sold shall not be considered to accrue until the date on which such obligation is paid at maturity, sold, or otherwise disposed of.

(c) MATURED UNITED STATES SAVINGS BONDS.—In the case of a taxpayer who—

(1) holds a series E United States savings bond at the date of maturity, and

(2) pursuant to regulations prescribed under chapter 31 of title 31 (A) retains his investment in such series E bond in an obligation of the United States, other than a current income obligation, or (B) exchanges such series E bond for another nontransferable obligation of the United States in an exchange upon which gain or loss is not recognized because of section 1037 (or so much of section 1031 as relates to section 1037),

the increase in redemption value (to the extent not previously includible in gross income) in excess of the amount paid for such series E bond shall be includible in gross income in the taxable year in which the obligation is finally redeemed or in the taxable year of final maturity, whichever is earlier. This subsection shall not apply to a corporation, and shall not apply in the case of any taxable year for which the taxpayer's taxable income is computed under an accrual method of accounting or for which an election made by the taxpayer under subsection (a) applies.

SEC. 455. PREPAID SUBSCRIPTION INCOME.

(a) YEAR IN WHICH INCLUDED.—Prepaid subscription income to which this section applies shall be included in gross income for the taxable years during which the liability described in subsection (d) (2) exists.

(b) WHERE TAXPAYER'S LIABILITY CEASES.—In the case of any prepaid subscription income to which this section applies—

(1) If the liability described in subsection (d) (2) ends, then so much of such income as was not includible in gross income under subsection (a) for preceding taxable years shall be included in gross income for the taxable year in which the liability ends.

(2) If the taxpayer dies or ceases to exist, then so much of such income as was not includible in gross income under subsection (a) for preceding taxable years shall be included in gross income for the taxable year in which such death, or such cessation of existence, occurs.

(c) PREPAID SUBSCRIPTION INCOME TO WHICH THIS SECTION APPLIES.—

(1) ELECTION OF BENEFITS.—This section shall apply to prepaid subscription income if and only if the taxpayer makes an election under this section with respect to the trade or business in connection with which such income is received. The election shall be made in such manner as the Secretary may by regulations prescribe. No election may be made with respect to a trade or business if in computing taxable income the cash receipts and disbursements method of accounting is used with respect to such trade or business.

(2) SCOPE OF ELECTION.—An election made under this section shall apply to all prepaid subscription income received in connection with the trade or business with respect to which the taxpayer has made the election; except that the taxpayer may, to the extent permitted under regulations prescribed by the Secretary, include in gross income for the taxable year of receipt the entire amount of any prepaid subscription income if the liability from which it arose is to end within

12 months after the date of receipt. An election made under this section shall not apply to any prepaid subscription income received before the first taxable year for which the election is made.

(3) WHEN ELECTION MAY BE MADE.—

(A) WITH CONSENT.—A taxpayer may, with the consent of the Secretary, make an election under this section at any time.

(B) WITHOUT CONSENT.—A taxpayer may, without the consent of the Secretary, make an election under this section for his first taxable year in which he receives prepaid subscription income in the trade or business. Such election shall be made not later than the time prescribed by law for filing the return for the taxable year (including extensions thereof) with respect to which such election is made.

(4) PERIOD TO WHICH ELECTION APPLIES.—An election under this section shall be effective for the taxable year with respect to which it is first made and for all subsequent taxable years, unless the taxpayer secures the consent of the Secretary to the revocation of such election. For purposes of this title, the computation of taxable income under an election made under this section shall be treated as a method of accounting.

[Sec. 455(d)]

(d) DEFINITIONS.—For purposes of this section—

(1) PREPAID SUBSCRIPTION INCOME.—The term "prepaid subscription income" means any amount (includible in gross income) which is received in connection with, and is directly attributable to, a liability which extends beyond the close of the taxable year in which such amount is received, and which is income from a subscription to a newspaper, magazine, or other periodical.

(2) LIABILITY.—The term "liability" means a liability to furnish or deliver a newspaper, magazine, or other periodical.

(3) RECEIPT OF PREPAID SUBSCRIPTION INCOME.—Prepaid subscription income shall be treated as received during the taxable year for which it is includible in gross income under section 451 (without regard to this section).

[Sec. 455(e)]

(e) DEFERRAL OF INCOME UNDER ESTABLISHED ACCOUNTING PROCEDURES.—Notwithstanding the provisions of this section, any taxpayer who has, for taxable years prior to the first taxable year to which this section applies, reported his income under an established and consistent method or practice of accounting for prepaid subscription income (to which this section would apply if an election were made) may continue to report his income for taxable years to which this title applies in accordance with such method or practice.

Subpart C—Taxable Year for Which Deductions Taken

[Sec. 461]

SEC. 461. GENERAL RULE FOR TAXABLE YEAR OF DEDUCTION.

[Sec. 461(a)]

(a) GENERAL RULE.—The amount of any deduction or credit allowed by this subtitle shall be taken for the taxable year which is the proper taxable year under the method of accounting used in computing taxable income.

[Sec. 461(b)]

(b) SPECIAL RULE IN CASE OF DEATH.—In the case of the death of a taxpayer whose taxable income is computed under an accrual method of accounting, any amount accrued as a deduction or credit only by reason of the death of the taxpayer shall not be allowed in computing taxable income for the period in which falls the date of the taxpayer's death.

[Sec. 461(c)]

(c) ACCRUAL OF REAL PROPERTY TAXES.—

(1) IN GENERAL.—If the taxable income is computed under an accrual method of accounting, then, at the election of the taxpayer, any real property tax which is related to a definite period of time shall be accrued ratably over that period.

(2) WHEN ELECTION MAY BE MADE.—

(A) WITHOUT CONSENT.—A taxpayer may, without the consent of the Secretary, make an election under this subsection for his first taxable year in which he incurs real property taxes. Such an election shall be made not later than the time prescribed by law for filing the return for such year (including extensions thereof).

(B) WITH CONSENT.—A taxpayer may, with the consent of the Secretary, make an election under this subsection at any time.

[Sec. 461(d)]

(d) LIMITATION ON ACCELERATION OF ACCRUAL OF TAXES.—

(1) GENERAL RULE.—In the case of a taxpayer whose taxable income is computed under an accrual method of accounting, to the extent that the time for accruing taxes is earlier than it would be but for any action of any taxing jurisdiction taken after December 31, 1960, then, under regulations prescribed by the Secretary, such taxes shall be treated as accruing at the time they would have accrued but for such action by such taxing jurisdiction.

(2) LIMITATION.—Under regulations prescribed by the Secretary, paragraph (1) shall be inapplicable to any item of tax to the extent that its application would (but for this paragraph) prevent all persons (including successors in interest) from ever taking such item into account.

[Sec. 461(e)]

(e) DIVIDENDS OR INTEREST PAID ON CERTAIN DEPOSITS OR WITHDRAWABLE ACCOUNTS.—Except as provided in regulations prescribed by the Secretary, amounts paid to, or credited to the accounts of, depositors or holders of accounts as dividends or interest on their deposits or withdrawable accounts (if such amounts paid or credited are withdrawable on demand subject only to customary notice to withdraw) by a mutual savings bank not having capital stock represented by shares, a domestic building and loan association, or a cooperative bank shall not be allowed as a deduction for the taxable year to the extent such amounts are paid or credited for periods representing more than 12 months. Any such amount not allowed as a deduction as the result of the application of the preceding sentence shall be allowed as a deduction for such other taxable year as the Secretary determines to be consistent with the preceding sentence.

[Sec. 461(f)]

(f) CONTESTED LIABILITIES.—If—

(1) the taxpayer contests an asserted liability,

(2) the taxpayer transfers money or other property to provide for the satisfaction of the asserted liability,

(3) the contest with respect to the asserted liability exists after the time of the transfer, and

(4) but for the fact that the asserted liability is contested, a deduction would be allowed for the taxable year of the transfer (or for an earlier taxable year) determined after application of subsection (h),

then the deduction shall be allowed for the taxable year of the transfer. This subsection shall not apply in respect of the deduction for income, war profits, and excess profits taxes imposed by the authority of any foreign country or possession of the United States.

[Sec. 461(g)]

(g) PREPAID INTEREST.—

(1) IN GENERAL.—If the taxable income of the taxpayer is computed under the cash receipts and disbursements method of accounting, interest paid by the taxpayer which, under regulations prescribed by the Secretary, is properly allocable to any period—

(A) with respect to which the interest represents a charge for the use or forbearance of money, and

Sec. 461(g)

(B) which is after the close of the taxable year in which paid,

shall be charged to capital account and shall be treated as paid in the period to which so allocable.

(2) EXCEPTION.—This subsection shall not apply to points paid in respect of any indebtedness incurred in connection with the purchase or improvement of, and secured by, the principal residence of the taxpayer to the extent that, under regulations prescribed by the Secretary, such payment of points is an established business practice in the area in which such indebtedness is incurred, and the amount of such payment does not exceed the amount generally charged in such area.

[Sec. 461(h)]

(h) CERTAIN LIABILITIES NOT INCURRED BEFORE ECONOMIC PERFORMANCE.—

(1) IN GENERAL.—For purposes of this title, in determining whether an amount has been incurred with respect to any item during any taxable year, the all events test shall not be treated as met any earlier than when economic performance with respect to such item occurs.

(2) TIME WHEN ECONOMIC PERFORMANCE OCCURS.—Except as provided in regulations prescribed by the Secretary, the time when economic performance occurs shall be determined under the following principles:

(A) SERVICES AND PROPERTY PROVIDED TO THE TAXPAYER.—If the liability of the taxpayer arises out of—

(i) the providing of services to the taxpayer by another person, economic performance occurs as such person provides such services,

(ii) the providing of property to the taxpayer by another person, economic performance occurs as the person provides such property, or

(iii) the use of property by the taxpayer, economic performance occurs as the taxpayer uses such property.

(B) SERVICES AND PROPERTY PROVIDED BY THE TAXPAYER.—If the liability of the taxpayer requires the taxpayer to provide property or services, economic performance occurs as the taxpayer provides such property or services.

(C) WORKERS COMPENSATION AND TORT LIABILITIES OF THE TAXPAYER.—If the liability of the taxpayer requires a payment to another person and—

(i) arises under any workers compensation act, or

(ii) arises out of any tort,

economic performance occurs as the payments to such person are made. Subparagraphs (A) and (B) shall not apply to any liability described in the preceding sentence.

(D) OTHER ITEMS.—In the case of any other liability of the taxpayer, economic performance occurs at the time determined under regulations prescribed by the Secretary.

(3) EXCEPTION FOR CERTAIN RECURRING ITEMS.—

(A) IN GENERAL.—Notwithstanding paragraph (1) an item shall be treated as incurred during any taxable year if—

(i) the all events test with respect to such item is met during such taxable year (determined without regard to paragraph (1)),

(ii) economic performance with respect to such item occurs within the shorter of—

(I) a reasonable period after the close of such taxable year, or

(II) $8\frac{1}{2}$ months after the close of such taxable year,

(iii) such item is recurring in nature and the taxpayer consistently treats items of such kind as incurred in the taxable year in which the requirements of clause (i) are met, and

(iv) either—

(I) such item is not a material item, or

(II) the accrual of such item in the taxable year in which the requirements of clause (i) are met results in a more proper match against income than accruing such item in the taxable year in which economic performance occurs.

(B) FINANCIAL STATEMENTS CONSIDERED UNDER SUBPARAGRAPH (A)(iv).—In making a determination under subparagraph (A)(iv), the treatment of such item on financial statements shall be taken into account.

(C) PARAGRAPH NOT TO APPLY TO WORKERS COMPENSATION AND TORT LIABILITIES.—This paragraph shall not apply to any item described in subparagraph (C) of paragraph (2).

(4) ALL EVENTS TEST.—For purposes of this subsection, the all events test is met with respect to any item if all events have occurred which determine the fact of liability and the amount of such liability can be determined with reasonable accuracy.

(5) SUBSECTION NOT TO APPLY TO CERTAIN ITEMS.—This subsection shall not apply to any item for which a deduction is allowable under a provision of this title which specifically provides for a deduction for a reserve for estimated expenses.

[Sec. 461(i)]

(i) SPECIAL RULES FOR TAX SHELTERS.—

(1) RECURRING ITEM EXCEPTION NOT TO APPLY.—In the case of a tax shelter, economic performance shall be determined without regard to paragraph (3) of subsection (h).

(2) SPECIAL RULE FOR SPUDDING OF OIL OR GAS WELLS.—

(A) IN GENERAL.—In the case of a tax shelter, economic performance with respect to amounts paid during the taxable year for drilling an oil or gas well shall be treated as having occurred within a taxable year if drilling of the well commences before the close of the 90th day after the close of the taxable year.

(B) DEDUCTION LIMITED TO CASH BASIS.—

(i) TAX SHELTER PARTNERSHIPS.—In the case of a tax shelter which is a partnership, in applying section 704(d) to a deduction or loss for any taxable year attributable to an item which is deductible by reason of subparagraph (A), the term "cash basis" shall be substituted for the term "adjusted basis".

(ii) OTHER TAX SHELTERS.—Under regulations prescribed by the Secretary, in the case of a tax shelter other than a partnership, the aggregate amount of the deductions allowable by reason of subparagraph (A) for any taxable year shall be limited in a manner similar to the limitation under clause (i).

(C) CASH BASIS DEFINED.—For purposes of subparagraph (B), a partner's cash basis in a partnership shall be equal to the adjusted basis of such partner's interest in the partnership, determined without regard to—

(i) any liability of the partnership, and

(ii) any amount borrowed by the partner with respect to such partnership which—

(I) was arranged by the partnership or by any person who participated in the organization, sale, or management of the partnership (or any person related to such person within the meaning of section 465(b)(3)(C)), or

(II) was secured by any asset of the partnership.

(3) TAX SHELTER DEFINED.—For purposes of this subsection, the term "tax shelter" means—

(A) any enterprise (other than a C corporation) if at any time interests in such enterprise have been offered for sale in any offering required to be registered with any Federal or State agency having the authority to regulate the offering of securities for sale,

(B) any syndicate (within the meaning of section 1256(e)(3)(B)), and

(C) any tax shelter (as defined in section 6662(d)(2)(C)(iii)).

(4) SPECIAL RULES FOR FARMING.—In the case of the trade or business of farming (as defined in section 464(e)), in determining whether an entity is a tax shelter, the definition of farming syndicate in section 464(c) shall be substituted for subparagraphs (A) and (B) of paragraph (3).

(5) ECONOMIC PERFORMANCE.—For purposes of this subsection, the term "economic performance" has the meaning given such term by subsection (h).

[Sec. 465]

SEC. 465. DEDUCTIONS LIMITED TO AMOUNT AT RISK.

[Sec. 465(a)]

(a) LIMITATION TO AMOUNT AT RISK.—

(1) IN GENERAL.—In the case of—

(A) an individual, and

(B) a C corporation with respect to which the stock ownership requirement of paragraph (2) of section 542(a) is met,

engaged in an activity to which this section applies, any loss from such activity for the taxable year shall be allowed only to the extent of the aggregate amount with respect to which the taxpayer is at risk (within the meaning of subsection (b)) for such activity at the close of the taxable year.

(2) DEDUCTION IN SUCCEEDING YEAR.—Any loss from an activity to which this section applies not allowed under this section for the taxable year shall be treated as a deduction allocable to such activity in the first succeeding taxable year.

(3) SPECIAL RULES FOR APPLYING PARAGRAPH (1)(B).—For purposes of paragraph (1)(B)—

(A) section 544(a)(2) shall be applied as if such section did not contain the phrase "or by or for his partner"; and

(B) sections 544(a)(4)(A) and 544(b)(1) shall be applied by substituting "the corporation meet the stock ownership requirements of section 542(a)(2)" for "the corporation a personal holding company."

[Sec. 465(b)]

(b) AMOUNTS CONSIDERED AT RISK.—

(1) IN GENERAL.—For purposes of this section, a taxpayer shall be considered at risk for an activity with respect to amounts including—

(A) the amount of money and the adjusted basis of other property contributed by the taxpayer to the activity, and

(B) amounts borrowed with respect to such activity (as determined under paragraph (2)).

(2) BORROWED AMOUNTS.—For purposes of this section, a taxpayer shall be considered at risk with respect to amounts borrowed for use in an activity to the extent that he—

(A) is personally liable for the repayment of such amounts, or

(B) has pledged property, other than property used in such activity, as security for such borrowed amount (to the extent of the net fair market value of the taxpayer's interest in such property).

No property shall be taken into account as security if such property is directly or indirectly financed by indebtedness which is secured by property described in paragraph (1).

(3) CERTAIN BORROWED AMOUNTS EXCLUDED.—

(A) IN GENERAL.—Except to the extent provided in regulations, for purposes of paragraph (1)(B), amounts borrowed shall not be considered to be at risk with respect to an activity if such amounts are borrowed from any person who has an interest in such activity or from a related person to a person (other than the taxpayer) having such an interest.

(B) EXCEPTIONS.—

(i) INTEREST AS CREDITOR.—Subparagraph (A) shall not apply to an interest as a creditor in the activity.

(ii) INTEREST AS SHAREHOLDER WITH RESPECT TO AMOUNTS BORROWED BY CORPORATION.— In the case of amounts borrowed by a corporation from a shareholder, subparagraph (A) shall not apply to an interest as a shareholder.

(C) RELATED PERSON.—For purposes of this subsection, a person (herein after in this paragraph referred to as the "related person") is related to any person if—

(i) the related person bears a relationship to such person specified in section 267(b) or section 707(b)(1), or

(ii) the related person and such person are engaged in trades or business under common control (within the meaning of subsections (a) and (b) of section 52).

For purposes of clause (i), in applying section 267(b) or 707(b)(1), "10 percent" shall be substituted for "50 percent."

(4) EXCEPTION.—Notwithstanding any other provision of this section, a taxpayer shall not be considered at risk with respect to amounts protected against loss through nonrecourse financing, guarantees, stop loss agreements, or other similar arrangements.

Sec. 465(b)

(5) AMOUNTS AT RISK IN SUBSEQUENT YEARS.—If in any taxable year the taxpayer has a loss from an activity to which subsection (a) applies, the amount with respect to which a taxpayer is considered to be at risk (within the meaning of subsection (b)) in subsequent taxable years with respect to that activity shall be reduced by that portion of the loss which (after the application of subsection (a)) is allowable as a deduction.

(6) QUALIFIED NONRECOURSE FINANCING TREATED AS AMOUNT AT RISK.—For purposes of this section—

(A) IN GENERAL.—Notwithstanding any other provision of this subsection, in the case of an activity of holding real property, a taxpayer shall be considered at risk with respect to the taxpayer's share of any qualified nonrecourse financing which is secured by real property used in such activity.

(B) QUALIFIED NONRECOURSE FINANCING.—For purposes of this paragraph, the term "qualified nonrecourse financing" means any financing—

(i) which is borrowed by the taxpayer with respect to the activity of holding real property,

(ii) which is borrowed by the taxpayer from a qualified person or represents a loan from any Federal, State, or local government or instrumentality thereof, or is guaranteed by any Federal, State, or local government,

(iii) except to the extent provided in regulations, with respect to which no person is personally liable for repayment, and

(iv) which is not convertible debt.

(C) SPECIAL RULE FOR PARTNERSHIPS.—In the case of a partnership, a partner's share of any qualified nonrecourse financing of such partnership shall be determined on the basis of the partner's share of liabilities of such partnership incurred in connection with such financing (within the meaning of section 752).

(D) QUALIFIED PERSON DEFINED.—For purposes of this paragraph—

(i) IN GENERAL.—The term "qualified person" has the meaning given such term by section 49(a)(1)(D)(iv).

(ii) CERTAIN COMMERCIALLY REASONABLE FINANCING FROM RELATED PERSONS.—For purposes of clause (i), section 49(a)(1) D)(iv) shall be applied without regard to subclause (I) thereof (relating to financing from related persons) if the financing from the related person is commercially reasonable and on substantially the same terms as loans involving unrelated persons.

(E) ACTIVITY OF HOLDING REAL PROPERTY.—For purposes of this paragraph—

(i) INCIDENTAL PERSONAL PROPERTY AND SERVICES.—The activity of holding real property includes the holding of personal property and the providing of services which are incidental to making real property available as living accommodations.

(ii) MINERAL PROPERTY.—The activity of holding real property shall not include the holding of mineral property.

[Sec. 465(c)]

(c) ACTIVITIES TO WHICH SECTION APPLIES.—

(1) TYPES OF ACTIVITIES.—This section applies to any taxpayer engaged in the activity of—

(A) holding, producing, or distributing motion picture films or video tapes,

(B) farming (as defined in section 464(e)),

(C) leasing any section 1245 property (as defined in section 1245(a)(3)),

(D) exploring for, or exploiting, oil and gas resources, or

(E) exploring for, or exploiting, geothermal deposits (as defined in section 613(e)(2))

as a trade or business or for the production of income.

(2) SEPARATE ACTIVITIES.—For purposes of this section—

(A) IN GENERAL.—Except as provided in subparagraph (B), a taxpayer's activity with respect to each—

(i) film or video tape,

(ii) section 1245 property which is leased or held for leasing,

(iii) farm,

(iv) oil and gas property (as defined under section 614), or

(v) geothermal property (as defined under section 614),

shall be treated as a separate activity.

(B) AGGREGATION RULES.—

(i) SPECIAL RULE FOR LEASES OF SECTION 1245 PROPERTY BY PARTNERSHIPS OR S CORPORATIONS.—In the case of any partnership or S corporation, all activities with respect to section 1245 properties which—

(I) are leased or held for lease, and

(II) are placed in service in any taxable year of the partnership or S corporation,

shall be treated as a single activity.

(ii) OTHER AGGREGATION RULES.—Rules similar to the rules of subparagraphs (B) and (C) of paragraph (3) shall apply for purposes of this paragraph.

(3) EXTENSION TO OTHER ACTIVITIES.—

(A) IN GENERAL.—In the case of taxable years beginning after December 31, 1978, this section also applies to each activity—

(i) engaged in by the taxpayer in carrying on a trade or business or for the production of income, and

(ii) which is not described in paragraph (1).

(B) AGGREGATION OF ACTIVITIES WHERE TAXPAYER ACTIVELY PARTICIPATES IN MANAGEMENT OF TRADE OR BUSINESS.—Except as provided in subparagraph (C), for purposes of this section, activities described in subparagraph (A) which constitute a trade or business shall be treated as one activity if—

(i) the taxpayer actively participates in the management of such trade or business, or

(ii) such trade or business is carried on by a partnership or an S corporation and 65 percent or more of the losses for the taxable year is allocable to persons who actively participate in the management of the trade or business.

(C) AGGREGATION OR SEPARATION OF ACTIVITIES UNDER REGULATIONS.—The Secretary shall prescribe regulations under which activities described in subparagraph (A) shall be aggregated or treated as separate activities.

(D) APPLICATION OF SUBSECTION (b)(3).—In the case of an activity described in subparagraph (A), subsection (b)(3) shall apply only to the extent provided in regulations prescribed by the Secretary.

(4) EXCLUSION FOR CERTAIN EQUIPMENT LEASING BY CLOSELY-HELD CORPORATIONS.—

(A) IN GENERAL.—In the case of a corporation described in subsection (a)(1)(B) actively engaged in equipment leasing—

(i) the activity of equipment leasing shall be treated as a separate activity, and

(ii) subsection (a) shall not apply to losses from such activity.

(B) 50-PERCENT GROSS RECEIPTS TEST.—For purposes of subparagraph (A), a corporation shall not be considered to be actively engaged in equipment leasing unless 50 percent or more of the gross receipts of the corporation for the taxable year is attributable, under regulations prescribed by the Secretary, to equipment leasing.

(C) COMPONENT MEMBERS OF CONTROLLED GROUP TREATED AS A SINGLE CORPORATION.—For purposes of subparagraph (A), the component members of a controlled group of corporations shall be treated as a single corporation.

(5) WAIVER OF CONTROLLED GROUP RULE WHERE THERE IS SUBSTANTIAL LEASING ACTIVITY.—

(A) IN GENERAL.—In the case of the component members of a qualified leasing group, paragraph (4) shall be applied—

(i) by substituting "80 percent" for "50 percent" in subparagraph (B) thereof, and

(ii) as if paragraph (4) did not include subparagraph (C) thereof.

Sec. 465(c)

(B) QUALIFIED LEASING GROUP.—For purposes of this paragraph, the term "qualified leasing group" means a controlled group of corporations which, for the taxable year and each of the 2 immediately preceding taxable years, satisfied each of the following 3 requirements:

(i) AT LEAST 3 EMPLOYEES.—During the entire year, the group had at least 3 fulltime employees substantially all of the services of whom were services directly related to the equipment leasing activity of the qualified leasing members.

(ii) AT LEAST 5 SEPARATE LEASING TRANSACTIONS.—During the year, the qualified leasing members in the aggregate entered into at least 5 separate equipment leasing transactions.

(iii) AT LEAST $1,000,000 EQUIPMENT LEASING RECEIPTS.—During the year, the qualified leasing members in the aggregate had at least $1,000,000 in gross receipts from equipment leasing.

The term "qualified leasing group" does not include any controlled group of corporations to which, without regard to this paragraph, paragraph (4) applies.

(C) QUALIFIED LEASING MEMBER.—For purposes of this paragraph, a corporation shall be treated as a qualified leasing member for the taxable year only if for each of the taxable years referred to in subparagraph (B)—

(i) it is a component member of the controlled group of corporations, and

(ii) it meets the requirements of paragraph (4)(B) (as modified by subparagraph (A)(i) of this paragraph).

(6) DEFINITIONS RELATING TO PARAGRAPHS (4) AND (5)—.For purposes of paragraphs (4) and (5)—

(A) EQUIPMENT LEASING.—The term "equipment leasing" means—

(i) the leasing of equipment which is section 1245 property, and

(ii) the purchasing, servicing, and selling of such equipment.

(B) LEASING OF MASTER SOUND RECORDINGS, ETC., EXCLUDED.—The term "equipment leasing" does not include the leasing of master sound recordings, and other similar contractual arrangements with respect to tangible or intangible assets associated with literary, artistic, or musical properties.

(C) CONTROLLED GROUP OF CORPORATIONS; COMPONENT MEMBER.—The terms "controlled group of corporations" and "component member" have the same meanings as when used in section 1563. The determination of the taxable years taken into account with respect to any controlled group of corporations shall be made in a manner consistent with the manner set forth in section 1563.

(7) EXCLUSION OF ACTIVE BUSINESSES OF QUALIFIED C CORPORATIONS.—

(A) IN GENERAL.—In the case of a taxpayer which is a qualified C corporation—

(i) each qualifying business carried on by such taxpayer shall be treated as a separate activity, and

(ii) subsection (a) shall not apply to losses from such business.

(B) QUALIFIED C CORPORATION.—For purposes of subparagraph (A), the term "qualified C corporation" means any corporation described in subparagraph (B) of subsection (a)(1) which is not—

(i) a personal holding company (as defined in section 542(a)),

(ii) a foreign personal holding company (as defined in section 552(a)), or

(iii) a personal service corporation (as defined in section 269A(b) but determined by substituting "5 percent" for "10 percent" in section 269A(b)(2)).

(C) QUALIFYING BUSINESS.—For purposes of this paragraph, the term "qualifying business" means any active business if—

(i) during the entire 12-month period ending on the last day of the taxable year, such corporation had at least 1 full-time employee substantially all the services of whom were in the active management of such business,

(ii) during the entire 12-month period ending on the last day of the taxable year, such corporation had at least 3 full-time, nonowner employees substantially all of the services of whom were services directly related to such business,

Sec. 465(c)

(iii) the amount of the deductions attributable to such business which are allowable to the taxpayer solely by reason of sections 162 and 404 for the taxable year exceeds 15 percent of the gross income from such business for such year, and

(iv) such business is not an excluded business.

(D) SPECIAL RULES FOR APPLICATION OF SUBPARAGRAPH (C).—

(i) PARTNERSHIPS IN WHICH TAXPAYER IS A QUALIFIED CORPORATE PARTNER.—In the case of an active business of a partnership, if—

(I) the taxpayer is a qualified corporate partner in the partnership, and

(II) during the entire 12-month period ending on the last day of the partnership's taxable year, there was at least 1 full-time employee of the partnership (or of a qualified corporate partner) substantially all the services of whom were in the active management of such business,

then the taxpayer's proportionate share (determined on the basis of its profits interest) of the activities of the partnership in such business shall be treated as activities of the taxpayer (and clause (i) of subparagraph (C) shall not apply in determining whether such business is a qualifying business of the taxpayer).

(ii) QUALIFIED CORPORATE PARTNER.—For purposes of clause (i), the term "qualified corporate partner" means any corporation if—

(I) such corporation is a general partner in the partnership,

(II) such corporation has an interest of 10 percent or more in the profits and losses of the partnership, and

(III) such corporation has contributed property to the partnership in an amount not less than the lesser of $500,000 or 10 percent of the net worth of the corporation.

For purposes of subclause (III), and contribution of property other than money shall be taken into account at its fair market value.

(iii) DEDUCTION FOR OWNER EMPLOYEE CONPENSATION NOT TAKEN INTO ACCOUNT.—For purposes of clause (iii) of subparagraph (C), there shall not be taken into account any deduction in respect of compensation for personal services rendered by any employee (other than a non-owner employee) of the taxpayer or any member of such employee's family (within the meaning of section 318(a)(1)).

* * *

(E) DEFINITIONS.—For purposes of this paragraph—

(i) NON-OWNER EMPLOYEE.—The term "non-owner employee" means any employee who does not own, at any time during the taxable year, more than 5 percent in value of the outstanding stock of the taxpayer. For purposes of the preceding sentence, section 318 shall apply, except that "5 percent" shall be substituted for "50 percent" in section 318(a)(2)(C).

(ii) EXCLUDED BUSINESS.—The term "excluded business" means—

(I) equipment leasing (as defined in paragraph (6)), and

(II) any business involving the use, exploitation, sale, lease, or other disposition of master sound recordings, motion picture films, video tapes, or tangible or intangible assets associated with literary, artistic, musical, or similar properties.

(iii) SPECIAL RULES RELATING TO COMMUNICATIONS INDUSTRY, ETC.—

(I) BUSINESS NOT EXCLUDED WHERE TAXPAYER NOT COMPLETELY AT RISK.—A business involving the use, exploitation, sale, lease, or other disposition of property described in subclause (II) of clause (ii) shall not constitute an excluded business by reason of such subclause if the taxpayer is at risk with respect to all amounts paid or incurred (or chargeable to capital account) in such business.

(II) CERTAIN LICENSED BUSINESSES NOT EXCLUDED.—For purposes of subclause (II) of clause (ii), the provision of radio, television, cable television, or similar services pursuant to a license or franchise granted by the Federal Communications Commission or any other Federal, State, or local authority shall not constitute an excluded business by reason of such subclause.

(F) AFFILIATED GROUP TREATED AS 1 TAXPAYER.—For purposes of this paragraph—

(i) IN GENERAL.—Except as provided in subparagraph (G), the component members of an affiliated group of corporations shall be treated as a single taxpayer.

(ii) AFFILIATED GROUP OF CORPORATIONS.—The term "affiliated group of corporations" means an affiliated group (as defined in section 1504(a)) which files or is required to file consolidated income tax returns.

(iii) COMPONENT MEMBER.—The term "component member" means an includible corporation (as defined in section 1504) which is a member of the affiliated group.

(G) LOSS OF 1 MEMBER OF AFFILIATED GROUP MAY NOT OFFSET INCOME OF PERSONAL HOLDING COMPANY OR PERSONAL SERVICE CORPORATION.—Nothing in this paragraph shall permit any loss of a member of an affiliated group to be used as an offset against the income of any other member of such group which is a personal holding company (as defined in section 542(a)) or a personal service corporation (as defined in section 269A(b) but determined by substituting "5 percent" for "10 percent" in section 269A(b)(2)).

[Sec. 465(d)]

(d) DEFINITION OF LOSS.—For purposes of this section, the term "loss" means the excess of the deductions allowable under this chapter for the taxable year (determined without regard to the first sentence of subsection (a)) and allocable to an activity to which this section applies over the income received or accrued by the taxpayer during the taxable year from such activity (determined without regard to subsection (e)(1)(A)).

[Sec. 465(e)]

(e) RECAPTURE OF LOSSES WHERE AMOUNT AT RISK IS LESS THAN ZERO.—

(1) IN GENERAL.—If zero exceeds the amount for which the taxpayer is at risk in any activity at the close of any taxable year—

(A) the taxpayer shall include in his gross income for such taxable year (as income from such activity) an amount equal to such excess, and

(B) an amount equal to the amount so included in gross income shall be treated as a deduction allocable to such activity for the first succeeding taxable year.

(2) LIMITATION.—The excess referred to in paragraph (1) shall not exceed—

(A) the aggregate amount of the reductions required by subsection (b)(5) with respect to the activity by reason of losses for all prior taxable years beginning after December 31, 1978, reduced by

(B) the amounts previously included in gross income with respect to such activity under this subsection.

[Sec. 467]

SEC. 467. CERTAIN PAYMENTS FOR THE USE OF PROPERTY OR SERVICES.

[Sec. 467(a)]

(a) ACCRUAL METHOD ON PRESENT VALUE BASIS.—In the case of the lessor or lessee under any section 467 rental agreement, there shall be taken into account for purposes of this title for any taxable year the sum of—

(1) the amount of the rent which accrues during such taxable year as determined under subsection (b), and

(2) interest for the year on the amounts which were taken into account under this subsection for prior taxable years and which are unpaid.

[Sec. 467(b)]

(b) ACCRUAL OF RENTAL PAYMENTS.—

(1) ALLOCATION FOLLOWS AGREEMENT.—Except as provided in paragraph (2), the determination of the amount of the rent under any section 467 rental agreement which accrues during any taxable year shall be made—

(A) by allocating rents in accordance with the agreement, and

(B) by taking into account any rent to be paid after the close of the period in an amount determined under regulations which shall be based on present value concepts.

(2) CONSTANT RENTAL ACCRUAL IN CASE OF CERTAIN TAX AVOIDANCE TRANSACTIONS, ETC.—In the case of any section 467 rental agreement to which this paragraph applies, the portion of the rent which accrues during any taxable year shall be that portion of the constant rental amount with respect to such agreement which is allocable to such taxable year.

(3) AGREEMENTS TO WHICH PARAGRAPH (2) APPLIES.—Paragraph (2) applies to any rental payment agreement if—

(A) such agreement is a disqualified leaseback or long-term agreement, or

(B) such agreement does not provide for the allocation referred to in paragraph (1)(A).

(4) DISQUALIFIED LEASEBACK OR LONG-TERM AGREEMENT.—For purposes of this subsection, the term "disqualified leaseback or long-term agreement" means any section 467 rental agreement if—

(A) such agreement is part of a leaseback transaction or such agreement is for a term in excess of 75 percent of the statutory recovery period for the property, and

(B) a principal purpose for providing increasing rents under the agreement is the avoidance of tax imposed by this subtitle.

(5) EXCEPTIONS TO DISQUALIFICATION IN CERTAIN CASES.—The Secretary shall prescribe regulations setting forth circumstances under which agreements will not be treated as disqualified leaseback or long-term agreements, including circumstances relating to—

(A) changes in amounts paid determined by reference to price indices,

(B) rents based on a fixed percentage of lessee receipts or similar amounts,

(C) reasonable rent holidays, or

(D) changes in amounts paid to unrelated 3rd parties.

[Sec. 467(c)]

(c) RECAPTURE OF PRIOR UNDERSTATED INCLUSIONS UNDER LEASEBACK OR LONG-TERM AGREEMENTS.—

(1) IN GENERAL.—If—

(A) the lessor under any section 467 rental agreement disposes of any property subject to such agreement during the term of such agreement, and

(B) such agreement is a leaseback or long-term agreement to which paragraph (2) of subsection (b) did not apply,

the recapture amount shall be treated as ordinary income. Such gain shall be recognized notwithstanding any other provision of this subtitle.

(2) RECAPTURE AMOUNT.—For purposes of paragraph (1), the term "recapture amount" means the lesser of—

(A) the prior understated inclusions, or

(B) the excess of the amount realized (or in the case of a disposition other than a sale, exchange, or involuntary conversion, the fair market value of the property) over the adjusted basis of such property.

The amount determined under subparagraph (B) shall be reduced by the amount of any gain treated as ordinary income on the disposition under any other provision of this subtitle.

(3) PRIOR UNDERSTATED INCLUSIONS.—For purposes of this subsection, the term "prior understated inclusion" means the excess (if any) of—

(A) the amount which would have been taken into account by the lessor under subsection (a) for periods before the disposition if subsection (b)(2) had applied to the agreement, over

(B) the amount taken into account under subsection (a) by the lessor for periods before the disposition.

(4) LEASEBACK OR LONG-TERM AGREEMENT.—For purposes of this subsection, the term "leaseback or long-term agreement" means any agreement described in subsection (b)(4)(A).

(5) SPECIAL RULES.—Under regulations prescribed by the Secretary—

(A) exceptions similar to the exceptions applicable under section 1245 or 1250 (whichever is appropriate) shall apply for purposes of this subsection,

(B) any transferee in a disposition excepted by reason of subparagraph (A) who has a transferred basis in the property shall be treated in the same manner as the transferor, and

(C) for purposes of sections 170(e) and 751(c), amounts treated as ordinary income under this section shall be treated in the same manner as amounts treated as ordinary income under section 1245 or 1250.

[Sec. 467(d)]

(d) SECTION 467 RENTAL AGREEMENTS.—

(1) IN GENERAL.—Except as otherwise provided in this subsection, the term "section 467 rental agreements" means any rental agreement for the use of tangible property under which—

(A) there is at least one amount allocable to the use of property during a calendar year which is to be paid after the close of the calendar year following the calendar year in which such use occurs, or

(B) there are increases in the amount to be paid as rent under the agreement.

(2) SECTION NOT TO APPLY TO AGREEMENTS INVOLVING PAYMENTS OF $250,000 OR LESS.—This section shall not apply to any amount to be paid for the use of property if the sum of the following amounts does not exceed $250,000—

(A) the aggregate amount of payments received as consideration for such use of property, and

(B) the aggregate value of any other consideration to be received for such use of property.

For purposes of the preceding sentence, rules similar to the rules of clauses (ii) and (iii) of section 1274(c)(4)(C) shall apply.

[Sec. 467(e)]

(e) DEFINITIONS.—For purposes of this section—

(1) CONSTANT RENTAL AMOUNT.—The term "constant rental amount" means, with respect to any section 467 rental agreement, the amount which, if paid as of the close of each lease period under the agreement, would result in an aggregate present value equal to the present value of the aggregate payments required under the agreement.

(2) LEASEBACK TRANSACTION.—A transaction is a leaseback transaction if it involves a leaseback to any person who had an interest in such property at any time within 2 years before such leaseback (or to a related person).

(3) STATUTORY RECOVERY PERIOD.—

(A) IN GENERAL.—

In the case of:	The statutory recovery period is:
3-year property	3 years
5-year property	5 years
7-year property	7 years
10-year property	10 years
15-year and 20-year property	15 years
Residential rental property and nonresidential real property	19 years
Any railroad grading or tunnel bore	50 years.

(B) SPECIAL RULE FOR PROPERTY NOT DEPRECIABLE UNDER SECTION 168.—In the case of property to which section 168 does not apply, subparagraph (A) shall be applied as if section 168 applies to such property.

(4) DISCOUNT AND INTEREST RATE.—For purposes of computing present value and interest under subsection (a)(2), the rate used shall be equal to 110 percent of the applicable Federal rate determined under section 1274(d) (compounded semiannually) which is in effect at the time the agreement is entered into with respect to debt instruments having a maturity equal to the term of the agreement.

(5) RELATED PERSON.—The term "related person" has the meaning given to such term by section 465(b)[3](C).

Sec. 467(e)

(6) CERTAIN OPTIONS OF LESSEE TO RENEW NOT TAKEN INTO ACCOUNT.—Except as provided in regulations prescribed by the Secretary, there shall not be taken into account in computing the term of any agreement for purposes of this section any extension which is solely at the option of the lessee.

[Sec. 467(f)]

(f) COMPARABLE RULES WHERE AGREEMENT FOR DECREASING PAYMENTS.—Under regulations prescribed by the Secretary, rules comparable to the rules of this section shall also apply in the case of any agreement where the amount paid under the agreement for the use of property decreases during the term of the agreement.

[Sec. 467(g)]

(g) COMPARABLE RULES FOR SERVICES.—Under regulations prescribed by the Secretary, rules comparable to the rules of subsection (a)(2) shall also apply in the case of payments for services which meet requirements comparable to the requirements of subsection (d). The preceding sentence shall not apply to any amount to which section 404 or 404A (or any other provision specified in regulations) applies.

[Sec. 467(h)]

(h) REGULATIONS.—The Secretary shall prescribe such regulations as may be appropriate to carry out the purposes of this section, including regulations providing for the application of this section in the case of contingent payments.

[Sec. 469]

SEC. 469. PASSIVE ACTIVITY LOSSES AND CREDITS LIMITED.

[Sec. 469(a)]

(a) DISALLOWANCE.—

(1) IN GENERAL.—If for any taxable year the taxpayer is described in paragraph (2), neither—

(A) the passive activity loss, nor

(B) the passive activity credit,

for the taxable year shall be allowed.

(2) PERSONS DESCRIBED.—The following are described in this paragraph:

(A) any individual, estate, or trust,

(B) any closely held C corporation, and

(C) any personal service corporation.

[Sec. 469(b)]

(b) DISALLOWED LOSS OR CREDIT CARRIED TO NEXT YEAR.—Except as otherwise provided in this section, any loss or credit from an activity which is disallowed under subsection (a) shall be treated as a deduction or credit allocable to such activity in the next taxable year.

[Sec. 469(c)]

(c) PASSIVE ACTIVITY DEFINED.—For purposes of this section—

(1) IN GENERAL.—The term "passive activity" means any activity—

(A) which involves the conduct of any trade or business, and

(B) in which the taxpayer does not materially participate.

(2) PASSIVE ACTIVITY INCLUDES ANY RENTAL ACTIVITY.—Except as provided in paragraph (7), the term "passive activity" includes any rental activity.

(3) WORKING INTERESTS IN OIL AND GAS PROPERTY.—

(A) IN GENERAL.—The term "passive activity" shall not include any working interest in any oil or gas property which the taxpayer holds directly or through an entity which does not limit the liability of the taxpayer with respect to such interest.

(B) INCOME IN SUBSEQUENT YEARS.—If any taxpayer has any loss for any taxable year from a working interest in any oil or gas property which is treated as a loss which is not from a passive activity, then any net income from such property (or any property the basis of which is determined in whole or in part by reference to the basis of such property) for any succeeding taxable year shall be treated as income of the taxpayer which is not from a passive activity. If the preceding sentence applies to the net income from any property for any taxable year, any credits allowable under subpart B (other than section 27(a)) or D of part IV of subchapter A for such taxable year which are attributable to such property shall be treated as credits not from a passive activity to the extent the amount of such credits does not exceed the regular tax liability of the taxpayer for the taxable year which is allocable to such net income.

(4) MATERIAL PARTICIPATION NOT REQUIRED FOR PARAGRAPHS (2) AND (3).—Paragraphs (2) and (3) shall be applied without regard to whether or not the taxpayer materially participates in the activity.

(5) TRADE OR BUSINESS INCLUDES RESEARCH AND EXPERIMENTATION ACTIVITY.—For purposes of paragraph (1)(A), the term "trade or business" includes any activity involving research or experimentation (within the meaning of section 174).

(6) ACTIVITY IN CONNECTION WITH TRADE OR BUSINESS OR PRODUCTION OF INCOME.—To the extent provided in regulations, for purposes of paragraph (1)(A), the term "trade or business" includes—

(A) any activity in connection with a trade or business, or

(B) any activity with respect to which expenses are allowable as a deduction under section 212.

(7) SPECIAL RULES FOR TAXPAYERS IN REAL PROPERTY BUSINESS—

(A) IN GENERAL.—If this paragraph applies to any taxpayer for a taxable year—

(i) paragraph (2) shall not apply to any rental real estate activity of such taxpayer for such taxable year, and

(ii) this section shall be applied as if each interest of the taxpayer in rental real estate were a separate activity.

Notwithstanding clause (ii), a taxpayer may elect to treat all interests in rental real estate as one activity. Nothing in the preceding provisions of this subparagraph shall be construed as affecting the determination of whether the taxpayer materially participates with respect to any interest in a limited partnership as a limited partner.

(B) TAXPAYERS TO WHOM PARAGRAPH APPLIES.—This paragraph shall apply to a taxpayer for a taxable year if—

(i) more than one-half of the personal services performed in trades or businesses by the taxpayer during such taxable year are performed in real property trades or businesses in which the taxpayer materially participates, and

(ii) such taxpayer performs more than 750 hours of services during the taxable year in real property trades or businesses in which the taxpayer materially participates.

In the case of a joint return, the requirements of the preceding sentence are satisfied if and only if either spouse separately satisfied such requirements. For purposes of the preceding sentence, activities in which a spouse materially participates shall be determined under subsection (h).

(C) REAL PROPERTY TRADE OR BUSINESS.—For purposes of this paragraph, the term "real property trade or business" means any real property development, redevelopment, construction, reconstruction, acquisition, conversion, rental, operation, management, leasing, or brokerage trade or business.

(D) SPECIAL RULES FOR SUBPARAGRAPH (B).—

(i) CLOSELY HELD C CORPORATIONS.—In the case of a closely held C corporation, the requirements of subparagraph (B) shall be treated as met for any taxable year if more than 50 percent of the gross receipts of such corporation for such taxable year are derived from real property trades or businesses in which the corporation materially participates.

(ii) PERSONAL SERVICES AS AN EMPLOYEE.—For purposes of subparagraph (B), personal services performed as an employee shall not be treated as performed in real property trades or businesses. The preceding sentence shall not apply if such employee is a 5-percent owner (as defined in section 416(i)(1)(B)) in the employer.

[Sec. 469(d)]

(d) PASSIVE ACTIVITY LOSS AND CREDIT DEFINED.—For purposes of this section—

(1) PASSIVE ACTIVITY LOSS.—The term "passive activity loss" means the amount (if any) by which—

(A) the aggregate losses from all passive activities for the taxable year, exceed

(B) the aggregate income from all passive activities for such year.

(2) PASSIVE ACTIVITY CREDIT.—The term "passive activity credit" means the amount (if any) by which—

(A) the sum of the credits from all passive activities allowable for the taxable year under—

(i) subpart D of part IV of subchapter A, or

(ii) subpart B (other than section 27(a)) of such part IV, exceeds

(B) the regular tax liability of the taxpayer for the taxable year allocable to all passive activities.

[Sec. 469(e)]

(e) SPECIAL RULES FOR DETERMINING INCOME OR LOSS FROM A PASSIVE ACTIVITY.—For purposes of this section—

(1) CERTAIN INCOME NOT TREATED AS INCOME FROM PASSIVE ACTIVITY.—In determining the income or loss from any activity—

(A) IN GENERAL.—There shall not be taken into account—

(i) any—

(I) gross income from interest, dividends, annuities, or royalties not derived in the ordinary course of a trade or business,

(II) expenses (other than interest) which are clearly and directly allocable to such gross income, and

(III) interest expense properly allocable to such gross income, and

(ii) gain or loss not derived in the ordinary course of a trade or business which is attributable to the disposition of property—

(I) producing income of a type described in clause (i), or

(II) held for investment.

For purposes of clause (ii), any interest in a passive activity shall not be treated as property held for investment.

(B) RETURN ON WORKING CAPITAL.—For purposes of subparagraph (A), any income, gain, or loss which is attributable to an investment of working capital shall be treated as not derived in the ordinary course of a trade or business.

(2) PASSIVE LOSSES OF CERTAIN CLOSELY HELD CORPORATIONS MAY OFFSET ACTIVE INCOME.—

(A) IN GENERAL.—If a closely held C corporation (other than a personal service corporation) has net active income for any taxable year, the passive activity loss of such taxpayer for such taxable year (determined without regard to this paragraph)—

(i) shall be allowable as a deduction against net active income, and

(ii) shall not be taken into account under subsection (a) to the extent so allowable as a deduction.

A similar rule shall apply in the case of any passive activity credit of the taxpayer.

(B) NET ACTIVE INCOME.—For purposes of this paragraph, the term "net active income" means the taxable income of the taxpayer for the taxable year determined without regard to—

(i) any income or loss from a passive activity, and

(ii) any item of gross income, expense, gain, or loss described in paragraph (1)(A).

(3) COMPENSATION FOR PERSONAL SERVICES.—Earned income (within the meaning of section 911(d)(2)(A)) shall not be taken into account in computing the income or loss from a passive activity for any taxable year.

(4) DIVIDENDS REDUCED BY DIVIDENDS RECEIVED DEDUCTION.—For purposes of paragraphs (1) and (2), income from dividends shall be reduced by the amount of any dividends received deduction under section 243, 244 or 245.

Sec. 469(d)

[Sec. 469(f)]

(f) TREATMENT OF FORMER PASSIVE ACTIVITIES.—For purposes of this section—

(1) IN GENERAL.—If an activity is a former passive activity for any taxable year—

(A) any unused deduction allocable to such activity under subsection (b) shall be offset against the income from such activity for the taxable year,

(B) any unused credit allocable to such activity under subsection (b) shall be offset against the regular tax liability (computed after the application of paragraph (1)) allocable to such activity for the taxable year, and

(C) any such deduction or credit remaining after the application of subparagraphs (A) and (B) shall continue to be treated as arising from a passive activity.

(2) CHANGE IN STATUS OF CLOSELY HELD C CORPORATION OR PERSONAL CORPORATION.—If a taxpayer ceases for any taxable year to be a closely held C corporation or personal service corporation, this section shall continue to apply to losses and credits to which this section applied for any preceding taxable year in the same manner as if such taxpayer continued to be a closely held C corporation or personal service corporation, whichever is applicable.

(3) FORMER PASSIVE ACTIVITY.—The term "former passive activity" means any activity which, with respect to the taxpayer—

(A) is not a passive activity for the taxable year, but

(B) was a passive activity for any prior taxable year.

[Sec. 469(g)]

(g) DISPOSITIONS OF ENTIRE INTEREST IN PASSIVE ACTIVITY.—If during the taxable year a taxpayer disposes of his entire interest in any passive activity (or former passive activity), the following rules shall apply:

(1) FULLY TAXABLE TRANSACTION.—

(A) IN GENERAL.—If all gain or loss realized on such disposition is recognized, the excess of—

(i) any loss from such activity for such taxable year (determined after the application of subsection (b)), over

(ii) any net income or gain for such taxable year from all other passive activities (determined after the application of subsection (b)),

shall be treated as a loss which is not from a passive activity.

(B) SUBPARAGRAPH (A) NOT TO APPLY TO DISPOSITION INVOLVING RELATED PARTY.—If the taxpayer and the person acquiring the interest bear a relationship to each other described in section 267(b) or section 707(b)(1), then subparagraph (A) shall not apply to any loss of the taxpayer until the taxable year in which such interest is acquired (in a transaction described in subparagraph (A)) by another person who does not bear such a relationship to the taxpayer.

(C) INCOME FROM PRIOR YEARS.—To the extent provided in regulations, income or gain from the activity for preceding taxable years shall be taken into account under subparagraph (A)(ii) for the taxable year to the extent necessary to prevent the avoidance of this section.

(2) DISPOSITION BY DEATH.—If an interest in the activity is transferred by reason of the death of the taxpayer—

(A) paragraph (1)(A) shall apply to losses described in paragraph (1)(A) to the extent such losses are greater than the excess (if any) of—

(i) the basis of such property in the hands of the transferee, over

(ii) the adjusted basis of such property immediately before the death of the taxpayer, and

(B) any losses to the extent of the excess described in subparagraph (A) shall not be allowed as a deduction for any taxable year.

(3) INSTALLMENT SALE OF ENTIRE INTEREST.—In the case of an installment sale of an entire interest in an activity to which section 453 applies, paragraph (1) shall apply to the portion of such losses for each taxable year which bears the same ratio to all such losses as the gain recognized on such sale during such taxable year bears to the gross profit from such sale (realized or to be realized when payment is completed).

Sec. 469(g)

(h) MATERIAL PARTICIPATION DEFINED.—For purposes of this section—

(1) IN GENERAL.—A taxpayer shall be treated as materially participating in an activity only if the taxpayer is involved in the operations of the activity on a basis which is—

(A) regular,

(B) continuous, and

(C) substantial.

(2) INTERESTS IN LIMITED PARTNERSHIPS.—Except as provided in regulations, no interest in a limited partnership as a limited partner shall be treated as an interest with respect to which a taxpayer materially participates.

(3) TREATMENT OF CERTAIN RETIRED INDIVIDUALS AND SURVIVING SPOUSES.—A taxpayer shall be treated as materially participating in any farming activity for a taxable year if paragraph (4) or (5) of section 2032A(b) would cause the requirements of section 2032A(b)(1)(C)(ii) to be met with respect to real property used in such activity if such taxpayer had died during the taxable year.

(4) CERTAIN CLOSELY HELD C CORPORATIONS AND PERSONAL SERVICE CORPORATIONS.—A closely held C corporation or personal service corporation shall be treated as materially participating in an activity only if—

(A) 1 or more shareholders holding stock representing more than 50 percent (by value) of the outstanding stock of such corporation materially participate in such activity, or

(B) in the case of a closely held C corporation (other than a personal service corporation), the requirements of section 465(c)(7)(C) (without regard to clause (iv)) are met with respect to such activity.

(5) PARTICIPATION BY SPOUSE.—In determining whether a taxpayer materially participates, the participation of the spouse of the taxpayer shall be taken into account.

(i) $25,000 OFFSET FOR RENTAL REAL ESTATE ACTIVITIES.—

(1) IN GENERAL.—In the case of any natural person, subsection (a) shall not apply to that portion of the passive activity loss or the deduction equivalent (within the meaning of subsection (j)(5)) of the passive activity credit for any taxable year which is attributable to all rental real estate activities with respect to which such individual actively participated in such taxable year (and if any portion of such loss or credit arose in another taxable year, in such other taxable year).

(2) DOLLAR LIMITATION.—The aggregate amount to which paragraph (1) applies for any taxable year shall not exceed $25,000.

(3) PHASE-OUT OF EXEMPTION.—

(A) IN GENERAL.—In the case of any taxpayer, the $25,000 amount under paragraph (2) shall be reduced (but not below zero) by 50 percent of the amount by which the adjusted gross income of the taxpayer for the taxable year exceeds $100,000.

(B) SPECIAL PHASE-OUT OF REHABILITATION CREDIT.—In the case of any portion of the passive activity credit for any taxable year which is attributable to the rehabilitation credit determined under section 47, subparagraph (A) shall be applied by substituting "$200,000" for "$100,000".

(C) EXCEPTION FOR COMMERCIAL REVITALIZATION DEDUCTION.—Subparagraph (A) shall not apply to any portion of the passive activity loss for any taxable year which is attributable to the commercial revitalization deduction under section 1400I.

(D) EXCEPTION FOR LOW-INCOME HOUSING CREDIT.—Subparagraph (A) shall not apply to any portion of the passive activity credit for any taxable year which is attributable to any credit determined under section 42.

(E) ORDERING RULES TO REFLECT EXCEPTIONS AND SEPARATE PHASE-OUTS.—If subparagraph (B), (C), or (D) applies for a taxable year, paragraph (1) shall be applied—

(i) first to the portion of the passive activity loss to which subparagraph (C) does not apply,

(ii) second to the portion of such loss to which subparagraph (C) applies,

(iii) third to the portion of the passive activity credit to which subparagraph (B) or (D) does not apply,

(iv) fourth to the portion of such credit to which subparagraph (B) applies, and

(v) then to the portion of such credit to which subparagraph (D) applies.

(F) ADJUSTED GROSS INCOME.—For purposes of this paragraph, adjusted gross income shall be determined without regard to—

(i) any amount includible in gross income under section 86,

(ii) the amounts excludable from gross income under sections 135 and 137,

(iii) the amounts allowable as a deduction under sections 219, 221, and 222 and

(iv) any passive activity loss or any loss allowable by reason of subsection (c)(7).

(4) SPECIAL RULE FOR ESTATES.—

(A) IN GENERAL.—In the case of taxable years of an estate ending less than 2 years after the date of the death of the decedent, this subsection shall apply to all rental real estate activities with respect to which such decedent actively participated before his death.

(B) REDUCTION FOR SURVIVING SPOUSE'S EXEMPTION.—For purposes of subparagraph (A), the $25,000 amount under paragraph (2) shall be reduced by the amount of the exemption under paragraph (1) (without regard to paragraph (3)) allowable to the surviving spouse of the decedent for the taxable year ending with or within the taxable year of the estate.

(5) MARRIED INDIVIDUALS FILING SEPARATELY.—

(A) IN GENERAL.—Except as provided in subparagraph (B), in the case of any married individual filing a separate return, this subsection shall be applied by substituting—

(i) "$12,500" for "$25,000" each place it appears,

(ii) "$50,000" for "$100,000" in paragraph (3)(A), and

(iii) "$100,000" for "$200,000" in paragraph (3)(B).

(B) TAXPAYERS NOT LIVING APART.—This subsection shall not apply to a taxpayer who—

(i) is a married individual filing a separate return for any taxpayer year, and

(ii) does not live apart from his spouse at all times during such taxable year.

(6) ACTIVE PARTICIPATION.—

(A) IN GENERAL.—An individual shall not be treated as actively participating with respect to any interest in any rental real estate activity for any period if, at any time during such period, such interest (including any interest of the spouse of the individual) is less than 10 percent (by value) of all interests in such activity.

(B) NO PARTICIPATION REQUIREMENT FOR LOW-INCOME HOUSING, REHABILITATION CREDIT, OR COMMERCIAL REVITALIZATION DEDUCTION.—Paragraphs (1) and (4)(A) shall be applied without regard to the active participation requirement in the case of—

(i) any credit determined under section 42 for any taxable year,

(ii) any rehabilitation credit determined under section 47, or

(iii) any deduction under section 1400I (relating to commercial revitalization deduction).

(C) INTEREST AS A LIMITED PARTNER.—Except as provided in regulations, no interest as a limited partner in a limited partnership shall be treated as an interest with respect to which the taxpayer actively participates.

(D) PARTICIPATION BY SPOUSE.—In determining whether a taxpayer actively participates, the participation of the spouse of the taxpayer shall be taken into account.

[Sec. 469(j)]

(j) OTHER DEFINITIONS AND SPECIAL RULES.—For purposes of this section—

(1) CLOSELY HELD C CORPORATION.—The term "closely held C corporation" means any C corporation described in section 465(a)(1)(B).

(2) PERSONAL SERVICE CORPORATION.—The term "personal service corporation" has the meaning given such term by section 269A(b)(1), except that section 269A(b)(2) shall be applied—

(A) by substituting "any" for "more than 10 percent", and

(B) by substituting "any" for "50 percent or more in value" in section 318(a)(2)(C).

Sec. 469(j)

A corporation shall not be treated as a personal service corporation unless more than 10 percent of the stock (by value) in such corporation is held by employee-owners (within the meaning of section 269A(b)(2), as modified by the preceding sentence).

(3) REGULAR TAX LIABILITY.—The term "regular tax liability" has the meaning given such term by section 26(b).

(4) ALLOCATION OF PASSIVE ACTIVITY LOSS AND CREDIT.—The passive activity loss and the passive activity credit (and the $25,000 amount under subsection (i)) shall be allocated to activities, and within activities, on a pro rata basis in such manner as the Secretary may prescribe.

(5) DEDUCTION EQUIVALENT.—The deduction equivalent of credits from a passive activity for any taxable year is the amount which (if allowed as a deduction) would reduce the regular tax liability for such taxable year by an amount equal to such credits.

(6) SPECIAL RULE FOR GIFTS.—In the case of a disposition of any interest in a passive activity by gift—

(A) the basis of such interest immediately before the transfer shall be increased by the amount of any passive activity losses allocable to such interest with respect to which a deduction has not been allowed by reason of subsection (a), and

(B) such losses shall not be allowable as a deduction for any taxable year.

(7) QUALIFIED RESIDENCE INTEREST.—The passive activity loss of a taxpayer shall be computed without regard to qualified residence interest (within the meaning of section 163(h)(3)).

(8) RENTAL ACTIVITY.—The term "rental activity" means any activity where payments are principally for the use of tangible property.

(9) ELECTION TO INCREASE BASIS OF PROPERTY BY AMOUNT OF DISALLOWED CREDIT.—For purposes of determining gain or loss from a disposition of any property to which subsection (g)(1) applies, the transferor may elect to increase the basis of such property immediately before the transfer by an amount equal to the portion of any unused credit allowable under this chapter which reduced the basis of such property for the taxable year in which such credit arose. If the taxpayer elects the application of this paragraph, such portion of the passive activity credit of such taxpayer shall not be allowed for any taxable year.

(10) COORDINATION WITH SECTION 280A.—If a passive activity involves the use of a dwelling unit to which section 280A(c)(5) applies for any taxable year, any income, deduction, gain, or loss allocable to such use shall not be taken into account for purposes of this section for such taxable year.

(11) AGGREGATION OF MEMBERS OF AFFILIATED GROUPS.—Except as provided in regulations, all members of an affiliated group which files a consolidated return shall be treated as 1 corporation.

(12) SPECIAL RULE FOR DISTRIBUTIONS BY ESTATES OR TRUSTS.—If any interest in a passive activity is distributed by an estate or trust—

(A) the basis of such interest immediately before such distribution shall be increased by the amount of any passive activity losses allocable to such interest, and

(B) such losses shall not be allowable as a deduction for any taxable year.

[Sec. 469(k)]

(k) SEPARATE APPLICATION OF SECTION IN CASE OF PUBLICLY TRADED PARTNERSHIPS.—

(1) IN GENERAL.—This section shall be applied separately with respect to items attributable to each publicly traded partnership (and subsection (i) shall not apply with respect to items attributable to any such partnership). The preceding sentence shall not apply to any credit determined under section 42, or any rehabilitation credit determined under section 47, attributable to a publicly traded partnership to the extent the amount of any such credits exceeds the regular tax liability attributable to income from such partnership.

(2) PUBLICLY TRADED PARTNERSHIP.—For purposes of this section, the term "publicly traded partnership" means any partnership if—

(A) interests in such partnership are traded on an established securities market, or

(B) interests in such partnership are readily tradable on a secondary market (or the substantial equivalent thereof).

(3) COORDINATION WITH SUBSECTION (g).—For purposes of subsection (g), a taxpayer shall not be treated as having disposed of his entire interest in an activity of a publicly traded partnership until he disposes of his entire interest in such partnership.

Sec. 469(k)

[Sec. 469(l)]

(l) REGULATIONS.—The Secretary shall prescribe such regulations as may be necessary or appropriate to carry out provisions of this section, including regulations—

(1) which specify what constitutes an activity, material participation, or active participation for purposes of this section,

(2) which provide that certain items of gross income will not be taken into account in determining income or loss from any activity (and the treatment of expenses allocable to such income),

(3) requiring net income or gain from a limited partnership or other passive activity to be treated as not from a passive activity,

(4) which provide for the determination of the allocation of interest expense for purposes of this section, and

(5) which deal with changes in marital status and changes between joint returns and separate returns.

* * *

Subpart D—Inventories

[Sec. 471]

SEC. 471. GENERAL RULE FOR INVENTORIES.

[Sec. 471(a)]

(a) GENERAL RULE.—Whenever in the opinion of the Secretary the use of inventories is necessary in order clearly to determine the income of any taxpayer, inventories shall be taken by such taxpayer on such basis as the Secretary may prescribe as conforming as nearly as may be to the best accounting practice in the trade or business and as most clearly reflecting the income.

[Sec. 471(b)]

(b) ESTIMATES OF INVENTORY SHRINKAGE PERMITTED.—A method of determining inventories shall not be treated as failing to clearly reflect income solely because it utilizes estimates of inventory shrinkage that are confirmed by a physical count only after the last day of the taxable year if—

(1) the taxpayer normally does a physical count of inventories at each location on a regular and consistent basis, and

(2) the taxpayer makes proper adjustments to such inventories and to its estimating methods to the extent such estimates are greater than or less than the actual shrinkage.

[Sec. 471(c)]

(c) CROSS REFERENCE.—

For rules relating to capitalization of direct and indirect costs of property, see section 263A.

[Sec. 472]

SEC. 472. LAST-IN, FIRST-OUT INVENTORIES.

[Sec. 472(a)]

(a) AUTHORIZATION.—A taxpayer may use the method provided in subsection (b) (whether or not such method has been prescribed under section 471) in inventorying goods specified in an application to use such method filed at such time and in such manner as the Secretary may prescribe. The change to, and the use of, such method shall be in accordance with such regulations as the Secretary may prescribe as necessary in order that the use of such method may clearly reflect income.

[Sec. 472(b)]

(b) METHOD APPLICABLE.—In inventorying goods specified in the application described in subsection (a), the taxpayer shall:

(1) Treat those remaining on hand at the close of the taxable year as being: First, those included in the opening inventory of the taxable year (in the order of acquisition) to the extent thereof; and second, those acquired in the taxable year;

(2) Inventory them at cost; and

(3) Treat those included in the opening inventory of the taxable year in which such method is first used as having been acquired at the same time and determine their cost by the average cost method.

[Sec. 472(c)]

(c) CONDITION.—Subsection (a) shall apply only if the taxpayer establishes to the satisfaction of the Secretary that the taxpayer has used no procedure other than that specified in paragraphs (1) and (3) of subsection (b) in inventorying such goods to ascertain the income, profit, or loss of the first taxable year for which the method described in subsection (b) is to be used, for the purpose of a report or statement covering such taxable year—

(1) to shareholders, partners, or other proprietors, or to beneficiaries, or

(2) for credit purposes.

[Sec. 472(d)]

(d) 3-YEAR AVERAGING FOR INCREASES IN INVENTORY VALUE.—The beginning inventory for the first taxable year for which the method described in subsection (b) is used shall be valued at cost. Any change in the inventory amount resulting from the application of the preceding sentence shall be taken into account ratably in each of the 3 taxable years beginning with the first taxable year for which the method described in subsection (b) is first used.

[Sec. 472(e)]

(e) SUBSEQUENT INVENTORIES.—If a taxpayer, having complied with subsection (a), uses the method described in subsection (b) for any taxable year, then such method shall be used in all subsequent taxable years unless—

(1) with the approval of the Secretary a change to a different method is authorized; or,

(2) the Secretary determines that the taxpayer has used for any such subsequent taxable year some procedure other than that specified in paragraph (1) of subsection (b) in inventorying the goods specified in the application to ascertain the income, profit, or loss of such subsequent taxable year for the purpose of a report or statement covering such taxable year (A) to shareholders, partners, or other proprietors, or beneficiaries, or (B) for credit purposes; and requires a change to a method different from that prescribed in subsection (b) beginning with such subsequent taxable year or any taxable year thereafter.

If paragraph (1) or (2) of this subsection applies, the change to, and the use of, the different method shall be in accordance with such regulations as the Secretary may prescribe as necessary in order that the use of such method may clearly reflect income.

[Sec. 472(f)]

(f) USE OF GOVERNMENT PRICE INDEXES IN PRICING INVENTORY.—The Secretary shall prescribe regulations permitting the use of suitable published governmental indexes in such manner and circumstances as determined by the Secretary for purposes of the method described in subsection (b).

[Sec. 472(g)]

(g) CONFORMITY RULES APPLIED ON CONTROLLED GROUP BASIS.—

(1) IN GENERAL.—Except as otherwise provided in regulations, all members of the same group of financially related corporations shall be treated as 1 taxpayer for purposes of subsections (c) and (e)(2).

(2) GROUP OF FINANCIALLY RELATED CORPORATIONS.—For purposes of paragraph (1), the term "group of financially related corporations" means—

(A) any affiliated group as defined in section 1504 determined by substituting "50 percent" for "80 percent" each place it appears in section 1504(a) and without regard to section 1504(b), and

(B) any other group of corporations which consolidate or combine for purposes of financial statements.

[Sec. 474]

SEC. 474. SIMPLIFIED DOLLAR-VALUE LIFO METHOD FOR CERTAIN SMALL BUSINESSES.

[Sec. 474(a)]

(a) GENERAL RULE.—An eligible small business may elect to use the simplified dollar-value method of pricing inventories for purposes of the LIFO method.

[Sec. 474(b)]

(b) SIMPLIFIED DOLLAR-VALUE METHOD OF PRICING INVENTORIES.—For purposes of this section—

(1) IN GENERAL.—The simplified dollar-value method of pricing inventories is a dollar-value method of pricing inventories under which—

(A) the taxpayer maintains a separate inventory pool for items in each major category in the applicable Government price index, and

(B) the adjustment for each such separate pool is based on the change from the preceding taxable year in the component of such index for the major category.

(2) APPLICABLE GOVERNMENT PRICE INDEX.—The term "applicable Government price index" means—

(A) except as provided in subparagraph (B), the Producer Price Index published by the Bureau of Labor Statistics, or

(B) in the case of a retailer using the retail method, the Consumer Price Index published by the Bureau of Labor Statistics.

(3) MAJOR CATEGORY.—The term "major category" means—

(A) in the case of the Producer Price Index, any of the 2-digit standard industrial classifications in the Producer Prices Data Report, or

(B) in the case of the Consumer Price Index, any of the general expenditure categories in the Consumer Price Index Detailed Report.

[Sec. 474(c)]

(c) ELIGIBLE SMALL BUSINESS.—For purposes of this section, a taxpayer is an eligible small business for any taxable year if the average annual gross receipts of the taxpayer for the 3 preceding taxable years do not exceed $5,000,000. For purposes of the preceding sentence, rules similar to the rules of section 448(c)(3) shall apply.

[Sec. 474(d)]

(d) SPECIAL RULES.—For purposes of this section—

(1) CONTROLLED GROUPS.—

(A) IN GENERAL.—In the case of a taxpayer which is a member of a controlled group, all persons which are component members of such group shall be treated as 1 taxpayer for purposes of determining the gross receipts of the taxpayer.

(B) CONTROLLED GROUP DEFINED.—For purposes of subparagraph (A), persons shall be treated as being component members of a controlled group if such persons would be treated as a single employer under section 52.

(2) ELECTION.—

(A) IN GENERAL.—The election under this section may be made without the consent of the Secretary.

(B) PERIOD TO WHICH ELECTION APPLIES.—The election under this section shall apply—

(i) to the taxable year for which it is made, and

(ii) to all subsequent taxable years for which the taxpayer is an eligible small business, unless the taxpayer secures the consent of the Secretary to the revocation of such election.

(3) LIFO METHOD.—The term "LIFO method" means the method provided by section 472(b).

Sec. 474(d)

(4) TRANSITIONAL RULES.—

(A) IN GENERAL.—In the case of a year of change under this section—

(i) the inventory pools shall—

(I) in the case of the 1st taxable year to which such an election applies, be established in accordance with the major categories in the applicable Government price index, or

(II) in the case of the 1st taxable year after such election ceases to apply, be established in the manner provided by regulations under section 472;

(ii) the aggregate dollar amount of the taxpayer's inventory as of the beginning of the year of change shall be the same as the aggregate dollar value as of the close of the taxable year preceding the year of change, and

(iii) the year of change shall be treated as a new base year in accordance with procedures provided by regulations under section 472.

(B) YEAR OF CHANGE.—For purposes of this paragraph, the year of change under this section is—

(i) the 1st taxable year to which an election under this section applies, or

(ii) in the case of a cessation of such an election, the 1st taxable year after such election ceases to apply.

[Sec. 475]

SEC. 475. MARK TO MARKET ACCOUNTING METHOD FOR DEALERS IN SECURITIES.

[Sec. 475(a)]

(a) GENERAL RULE.—Notwithstanding any other provision of this subpart, the following rules shall apply to securities held by a dealer in securities:

(1) Any security which is inventory in the hands of the dealer shall be included in inventory at its fair market value.

(2) In the case of any security which is not inventory in the hands of the dealer and which is held at the close of any taxable year—

(A) the dealer shall recognize gain or loss as if such security were sold for its fair market value on the last business day of such taxable year, and

(B) any gain or loss shall be taken into account for such taxable year.

Proper adjustment shall be made in the amount of any gain or loss subsequently realized for gain or loss taken into account under the preceding sentence. The Secretary may provide by regulations for the application of this paragraph at times other than the times provided in this paragraph.

[Sec. 475(b)]

(b) EXCEPTIONS.—

(1) IN GENERAL.—Subsection (a) shall not apply to—

(A) any security held for investment,

(B)(i) any security described in subsection (c)(2)(C) which is acquired (including originated) by the taxpayer in the ordinary course of a trade or business of the taxpayer and which is not held for sale, and (ii) any obligation to acquire a security described in clause (i) if such obligation is entered into in the ordinary course of such trade or business and is not held for sale, and

(C) any security which is a hedge with respect to—

(i) a security to which subsection (a) does not apply, or

(ii) a position, right to income, or a liability which is not a security in the hands of the taxpayer.

To the extent provided in regulations, subparagraph (C) shall not apply to any security held by a person in its capacity as a dealer in securities.

Sec. 475

(2) IDENTIFICATION REQUIRED.—A security shall not be treated as described in subparagraph (A), (B), or (C) of paragraph (1), as the case may be, unless such security is clearly identified in the dealer's records as being described in such subparagraph before the close of the day on which it was acquired, originated, or entered into (or such other time as the Secretary may by regulations prescribe).

(3) SECURITIES SUBSEQUENTLY NOT EXEMPT.—If a security ceases to be described in paragraph (1) at any time after it was identified as such under paragraph (2), subsection (a) shall apply to any changes in value of the security occurring after the cessation.

(4) SPECIAL RULE FOR PROPERTY HELD FOR INVESTMENT.—To the extent provided in regulations, subparagraph (A) of paragraph (1) shall not apply to any security described in subparagraph (D) or (E) of subsection (c)(2) which is held by a dealer in such securities.

[Sec. 475(c)]

(c) DEFINITIONS.—For purposes of this section—

(1) DEALER IN SECURITIES DEFINED.—The term "dealer in securities" means a taxpayer who—

(A) regularly purchases securities from or sells securities to customers in the ordinary course of a trade or business; or

(B) regularly offers to enter into, assume, offset, assign or otherwise terminate positions in securities with customers in the ordinary course of a trade or business.

(2) SECURITY DEFINED.—The term "security" means any—

(A) share of stock in a corporation;

(B) partnership or beneficial ownership interest in a widely held or publicly traded partnership or trust;

(C) note, bond, debenture, or other evidence of indebtedness;

(D) interest rate, currency, or equity notional principal contract;

(E) evidence of an interest in, or a derivative financial instrument in, any security described in subparagraph (A), (B), (C), or (D), or any currency, including any option, forward contract, short position, and any similar financial instrument in such a security or currency; and

(F) position which—

(i) is not a security described in subparagraph (A), (B), (C), (D), or (E),

(ii) is a hedge with respect to such a security, and

(iii) is clearly identified in the dealer's records as being described in this subparagraph before the close of the day on which it was acquired or entered into (or such other time as the Secretary may by regulations prescribe).

Subparagraph (E) shall not include any contract to which section 1256(a) applies.

(3) HEDGE.—The term "hedge" means any position which manages the dealer's risk of interest rate or price changes or currency fluctuations, including any position which is reasonably expected to become a hedge within 60 days after the acquisition of the position.

(4) SPECIAL RULES FOR CERTAIN RECEIVABLES.—

(A) IN GENERAL.—Paragraph (2)(C) shall not include any nonfinancial customer paper.

(B) NONFINANCIAL CUSTOMER PAPER.— For purposes of subparagraph (A), the term "nonfinancial customer paper" means any receivable which—

(i) is a note, bond, debenture, or other evidence of indebtedness;

(ii) arises out of the sale of nonfinancial goods or services by a person the principal activity of which is the selling or providing of nonfinancial goods or services; and

(iii) is held by such person (or a person who bears a relationship to such person described in section 267(b) or 707(b)) at all times since issue.

[Sec. 475(d)]

(d) SPECIAL RULES.—For purposes of this section—

(1) COORDINATION WITH CERTAIN RULES.—The rules of sections 263(g), 263A, and 1256(a) shall not apply to securities to which subsection (a) applies, and section 1091 shall not apply (and section 1092 shall apply) to any loss recognized under subsection (a).

(2) IMPROPER IDENTIFICATION.—If a taxpayer—

(A) identifies any security under subsection (b)(2) as being described in subsection (b)(1) and such security is not so described, or

(B) fails under subsection (c)(2)(F)(iii) to identify any position which is described in subsection (c)(2)(F) (without regard to clause (iii) thereof) at the time such identification is required,

the provisions of subsection (a) shall apply to such security or position, except that any loss under this section prior to the disposition of the security or position shall be recognized only to the extent of gain previously recognized under this section (and not previously taken into account under this paragraph) with respect to such security or position.

(3) CHARACTER OF GAIN OR LOSS.—

(A) IN GENERAL.—Except as provided in subparagraph (B) or section 1236(b)—

(i) IN GENERAL.—Any gain or loss with respect to a security under subsection (a)(2) shall be treated as ordinary income or loss.

(ii) SPECIAL RULE FOR DISPOSITIONS.—If—

(I) gain or loss is recognized with respect to a security before the close of the taxable year, and

(II) subsection (a)(2) would have applied if the security were held as of the close of the taxable year, such gain or loss shall be treated as ordinary income or loss.

(B) EXCEPTION.—Subparagraph (A) shall not apply to any gain or loss which is allocable to a period during which—

(i) the security is described in subsection (b)(1)(C) (without regard to subsection (b)(2)),

(ii) the security is held by a person other than in connection with its activities as a dealer in securities, or

(iii) the security is improperly identified (within the meaning of subparagraph (A) or (B) of paragraph (2)).

[Sec. 475(e)]

(e) ELECTION OF MARK TO MARKET FOR DEALERS IN COMMODITIES.—

(1) IN GENERAL.—In the case of a dealer in commodities who elects the application of this subsection, this section shall apply to commodities held by such dealer in the same manner as this section applies to securities held by a dealer in securities.

(2) COMMODITY.—For purposes of this subsection and subsection (f), the term "commodity" means—

(A) any commodity which is actively traded (within the meaning of section 1092(d)(1));

(B) any notional principal contract with respect to any commodity described in subparagraph (A);

(C) any evidence of an interest in, or a derivative instrument in, any commodity described in subparagraph (A) or (B), including any option, forward contract, futures contract, short position, and any similar instrument in such a commodity; and

(D) any position which—

(i) is not a commodity described in subparagraph (A), (B), or (C),

(ii) is a hedge with respect to such a commodity, and

(iii) is clearly identified in the taxpayer's records as being described in this subparagraph before the close of the day on which it was acquired or entered into (or such other time as the Secretary may by regulations prescribe).

(3) ELECTION.—An election under this subsection may be made without the consent of the Secretary. Such an election, once made, shall apply to the taxable year for which made and all subsequent taxable years unless revoked with the consent of the Secretary.

Sec. 475(e)

[Sec. 475(f)]

(f) ELECTION OF MARK TO MARKET FOR TRADERS IN SECURITIES OR COMMODITIES.—

(1) TRADERS IN SECURITIES.—

(A) IN GENERAL.—In the case of a person who is engaged in a trade or business as a trader in securities and who elects to have this paragraph apply to such trade or business—

(i) such person shall recognize gain or loss on any security held in connection with such trade or business at the close of any taxable year as if such security were sold for its fair market value on the last business day of such taxable year, and

(ii) any gain or loss shall be taken into account for such taxable year.

Proper adjustment shall be made in the amount of any gain or loss subsequently realized for gain or loss taken into account under the preceding sentence. The Secretary may provide by regulations for the application of this subparagraph at times other than the times provided in this subparagraph.

(B) EXCEPTION.—Subparagraph (A) shall not apply to any security—

(i) which is established to the satisfaction of the Secretary as having no connection to the activities of such person as a trader, and

(ii) which is clearly identified in such person's records as being described in clause (i) before the close of the day on which it was acquired, originated, or entered into (or such other time as the Secretary may by regulations prescribe).

If a security ceases to be described in clause (i) at any time after it was identified as such under clause (ii), subparagraph (A) shall apply to any changes in value of the security occurring after the cessation.

(C) COORDINATION WITH SECTION 1259.—Any security to which subparagraph (A) applies and which was acquired in the normal course of the taxpayer's activities as a trader in securities shall not be taken into account in applying section 1259 to any position to which subparagraph (A) does not apply.

(D) OTHER RULES TO APPLY.—Rules similar to the rules of subsections (b)(4) and (d) shall apply to securities held by a person in any trade or business with respect to which an election under this paragraph is in effect. Subsection (d)(3) shall not apply under the preceding sentence for purposes of applying sections 1402 and 7704.

(2) TRADERS IN COMMODITIES.—In the case of a person who is engaged in a trade or business as a trader in commodities and who elects to have this paragraph apply to such trade or business, paragraph (1) shall apply to commodities held by such trader in connection with such trade or business in the same manner as paragraph (1) applies to securities held by a trader in securities.

(3) ELECTION.—The elections under paragraphs (1) and (2) may be made separately for each trade or business and without the consent of the Secretary. Such an election, once made, shall apply to the taxable year for which made and all subsequent taxable years unless revoked with the consent of the Secretary.

[Sec. 475(g)]

(g) REGULATORY AUTHORITY.—The Secretary shall prescribe such regulations as may be necessary or appropriate to carry out the purposes of this section, including rules—

(1) to prevent the use of year-end transfers, related parties, or other arrangements to avoid the provisions of this section,

(2) to provide for the application of this section to any security which is a hedge which cannot be identified with a specific security, position, right to income, or liability, and

(3) to prevent the use by taxpayers of subsection (c)(4) to avoid the application of this section to a receivable that is inventory in the hands of the taxpayer (or a person who bears a relationship to the taxpayer described in section 267(b) or 707(b)).

Sec. 475(g)

PART III—ADJUSTMENTS

[Sec. 481]

SEC. 481. ADJUSTMENTS REQUIRED BY CHANGES IN METHOD OF ACCOUNTING.

[Sec. 481(a)]

(a) GENERAL RULE.—In computing the taxpayer's taxable income for any taxable year (referred to in this section as the "year of the change")—

(1) if such computation is under a method of accounting different from the method under which the taxpayer's taxable income for the preceding taxable year was computed, then

(2) there shall be taken into account those adjustments which are determined to be necessary solely by reason of the change in order to prevent amounts from being duplicated or omitted, except there shall not be taken into account any adjustment in respect of any taxable year to which this section does not apply unless the adjustment is attributable to a change in the method of accounting initiated by the taxpayer.

[Sec. 481(b)]

(b) LIMITATION ON TAX WHERE ADJUSTMENTS ARE SUBSTANTIAL.—

(1) THREE YEAR ALLOCATION.—If—

(A) the method of accounting from which the change is made was used by the taxpayer in computing his taxable income for the 2 taxable years preceding the year of the change, and

(B) the increase in taxable income for the year of the change which results solely by reason of the adjustments required by subsection (a)(2) exceeds $3,000,

then the tax under this chapter attributable to such increase in taxable income shall not be greater than the aggregate increase in the taxes under this chapter (or under the corresponding provisions of prior revenue laws) which would result if one-third of such increase in taxable income were included in taxable income for the year of the change and one-third of such increase were included for each of the 2 preceding taxable years.

(2) ALLOCATION UNDER NEW METHOD OF ACCOUNTING.—If—

(A) the increase in taxable income for the year of the change which results solely by reason of the adjustments required by subsection (a)(2) exceeds $3,000, and

(B) the taxpayer establishes his taxable income (under the new method of accounting) for one or more taxable years consecutively preceding the taxable year of the change for which the taxpayer in computing taxable income used the method of accounting from which the change is made,

then the tax under this chapter attributable to such increase in taxable income shall not be greater than the net increase in the taxes under this chapter (or under the corresponding provisions of prior revenue laws) which would result if the adjustments required by subsection (a) (2) were allocated to the taxable year or years specified in subparagraph (B) to which they are properly allocable under the new method of accounting and the balance of the adjustments required by subsection (a) (2) was allocated to the taxable year of the change.

(3) SPECIAL RULES FOR COMPUTATIONS UNDER PARAGRAPHS (1) AND (2).—For purposes of this subsection—

(A) There shall be taken into account the increase or decrease in tax for any taxable year preceding the year of the change to which no adjustment is allocated under paragraph (1) or (2) but which is affected by a net operating loss (as defined in section 172) or by a capital loss carryback or carryover (as defined in section 1212), determined with reference to taxable years with respect to which adjustments under paragraph (1) or (2) are allocated.

(B) The increase or decrease in the tax for any taxable year for which an assessment of any deficiency, or a credit or refund of any overpayment, is prevented by any law or rule of law, shall be determined by reference to the tax previously determined (within the meaning of section 1314 (a)) for such year.

Sec. 481

(C) In applying section 7807 (b) (1), the provisions of chapter 1 (other than subchapter E, relating to self-employment income) and chapter 2 of the Internal Revenue Code of 1939 shall be treated as the corresponding provisions of the Internal Revenue Code of 1939 [1954].

[Sec. 481(c)]

(c) ADJUSTMENTS UNDER REGULATIONS.—In the case of any change described in subsection (a), the taxpayer may, in such manner and subject to such conditions as the Secretary may by regulations prescribe, take the adjustments required by subsection (a) (2) into account in computing the tax imposed by this chapter for the taxable year or years permitted under such regulations.

[Sec. 482]

SEC. 482. ALLOCATION OF INCOME AND DEDUCTIONS AMONG TAXPAYERS.

In any case of two or more organizations, trades, or businesses (whether or not incorporated, whether or not organized in the United States, and whether or not affiliated) owned or controlled directly or indirectly by the same interests, the Secretary may distribute, apportion, or allocate gross income, deductions, credits, or allowances between or among such organizations, trades, or businesses, if he determines that such distribution, apportionment, or allocation is necessary in order to prevent evasion of taxes or clearly to reflect the income of any of such organizations, trades, or businesses. In the case of any transfer (or license) of intangible property (within the meaning of section 936(h)(3)(B)), the income with respect to such transfer or license shall be commensurate with the income attributable to the intangible.

[Sec. 483]

SEC. 483. INTEREST ON CERTAIN DEFERRED PAYMENTS.

[Sec. 483(a)]

(a) AMOUNT CONSTITUTING INTEREST.—For purposes of this title, in the case of any payment—

(1) under any contract for the sale or exchange of any property, and

(2) to which this section applies,

there shall be treated as interest that portion of the total unstated interest under such contract which, as determined in a manner consistent with the method of computing interest under section 1272(a), is properly allocable to such payment.

[Sec. 483(b)]

(b) TOTAL UNSTATED INTEREST.—For purposes of this section, the term "total unstated interest" means, with respect to a contract for the sale or exchange of property, an amount equal to the excess of—

(1) the sum of the payments to which this section applies which are due under the contract, over

(2) the sum of the present values of such payments and the present values of any interest payments due under the contract.

For purposes of the preceding sentence, the present value of a payment shall be determined under the rules of section 1274(b)(2) using a discount rate equal to the applicable Federal rate determined under section 1274(d).

[Sec. 483(c)]

(c) PAYMENTS TO WHICH SUBSECTION (a) APPLIES.—

(1) IN GENERAL.—Except as provided in subsection (d), this section shall apply to any payment on account of the sale or exchange of property which constitutes part or all of the sales price and which is due more than 6 months after the date of such sale or exchange under a contract—

(A) under which some or all of the payments are due more than 1 year after the date of such sale or exchange, and

(B) under which there is total unstated interest.

(2) TREATMENT OF OTHER DEBT INSTRUMENTS.—For purposes of this section, a debt instrument of the purchaser which is given in consideration for the sale or exchange of property shall not be treated as a payment, and any payment due under such debt instrument shall be treated as due under the contract for the sale or exchange.

(3) DEBT INSTRUMENT DEFINED.—For purposes of this subsection, the term "debt instrument" has the meaning given such term by section 1275(a)(1).

[Sec. 483(d)]

(d) EXCEPTIONS AND LIMITATIONS.—

(1) COORDINATION WITH ORIGINAL ISSUE DISCOUNT RULES.—This section shall not apply to any debt instrument for which an issue price is determined under section 1273(b) (other than paragraph (4) thereof) or section 1274.

(2) SALES PRICES OF $3,000 OR LESS.—This section shall not apply to any payment on account of the sale or exchange of property if it can be determined at the time of such sale or exchange that the sales price cannot exceed $3,000.

(3) CARRYING CHARGES.—In the case of the purchaser, the tax treatment of amounts paid on account of the sale or exchange of property shall be made without regard to this section if any such amounts are treated under section 163(b) as if they included interest.

(4) CERTAIN SALES OF PATENTS.—In the case of any transfer described in section 1235(a) (relating to sale or exchange of patents), this section shall not apply to any amount contingent on the productivity, use, or disposition of the property transferred.

[Sec. 483(e)]

(e) MAXIMUM RATE OF INTEREST ON CERTAIN TRANSFERS OF LAND BETWEEN RELATED PARTIES.—

(1) IN GENERAL.—In the case of any qualified sale, the discount rate used in determining the total unstated interest rate under subsection (b) shall not exceed 6 percent, compounded semiannually.

(2) QUALIFIED SALE.—For purposes of this subsection, the term "qualified sale" means any sale or exchange of land by an individual to a member of such individual's family (within the meaning of section 267(c)(4)).

(3) $500,000 LIMITATION.—Paragraph (1) shall not apply to any qualified sale between individuals made during any calendar year to the extent that the sales price for such sale (when added to the aggregate sale price for prior qualified sales between such individuals during the calendar year) exceeds $500,000.

(4) NONRESIDENT ALIEN INDIVIDUALS.—Paragraph (1) shall not apply to any sale or exchange if any party to such sale or exchange is a nonresident alien individual.

[Sec. 483(f)]

(f) REGULATIONS.—The Secretary shall prescribe such regulations as may be necessary or appropriate to carry out the purposes of this section including regulations providing for the application of this section in the case of—

(1) any contract for the sale or exchange of property under which the liability for, or the amount or due date of, a payment cannot be determined at the time of the sale or exchange, or

(2) any change in the liability for, or the amount or due date of, any payment (including interest) under a contract for the sale or exchange of property.

[Sec. 483(g)]

(g) CROSS REFERENCES.—

(1) For treatment of assumptions, see section 1274(c)(4).

(2) For special rules for certain transactions where stated principal amount does not exceed $2,800,000, see section 1274A.

(3) For special rules in the case of the borrower under certain loans for personal use, see section 1275(b).

Sec. 483(d)

Subchapter F—Exempt Organizations

PART I—GENERAL RULE

[Sec. 501]

SEC. 501. EXEMPTION FROM TAX ON CORPORATIONS, CERTAIN TRUSTS, ETC.

[Sec. 501(a)]

(a) EXEMPTION FROM TAXATION.—An organization described in subsection (c) or (d) or section 401 (a) shall be exempt from taxation under this subtitle unless such exemption is denied under section 502 or 503.

[Sec. 501(b)]

(b) TAX ON UNRELATED BUSINESS INCOME AND CERTAIN OTHER ACTIVITIES.—An organization exempt from taxation under subsection (a) shall be subject to tax to the extent provided in parts II, III, and VI of this subchapter, but (notwithstanding parts II, III and VI of this subchapter) shall be considered an organization exempt from income taxes for the purpose of any law which refers to organizations exempt from income taxes.

[Sec. 501(c)]

(c) LIST OF EXEMPT ORGANIZATIONS.—The following organizations are referred to in subsection (a):

(1) Any corporation organized under Act of Congress which is an instrumentality of the United States but only if such corporation—

(A) is exempt from Federal income taxes—

(i) under such Act as amended and supplemented before July 18, 1984, or

(ii) under this title without regard to any provision of law which is not contained in this title and which is not contained in a revenue Act, or

(B) is described in subsection (l).

(2) Corporations organized for the exclusive purpose of holding title to property, collecting income therefrom, and turning over the entire amount thereof, less expenses, to an organization which itself is exempt under this section. Rules similar to the rules of subparagraph (G) of paragraph (25) shall apply for purposes of this paragraph.

(3) Corporations, and any community chest, fund, or foundation, organized and operated exclusively for religious, charitable, scientific, testing for public safety, literary, or educational purposes, or to foster national or international amateur sports competition (but only if no part of its activities involve the provision of athletic facilities or equipment), or for the prevention of cruelty to children or animals, no part of the net earnings of which inures to the benefit of any private shareholder or individual, no substantial part of the activities of which is carrying on propaganda, or otherwise attempting, to influence legislation, (except as otherwise provided in subsection (h)), and which does not participate in, or intervene in (including the publishing or distributing of statements), any political campaign on behalf of (or in opposition to) any candidate for public office.

(4)(A) Civic leagues or organizations not organized for profit but operated exclusively for the promotion of social welfare, or local associations of employees, the membership of which is limited to the employees of a designated person or persons in a particular municipality, and the net earnings of which are devoted exclusively to charitable, educational, or recreational purposes.

(B) Subparagraph (A) shall not apply to an entity unless no part of the net earnings of such entity inures to the benefit of any private shareholder or individual.

(5) Labor, agricultural, or horticultural organizations.

(6) Business leagues, chambers of commerce, real-estate boards, boards of trade, or professional football leagues (whether or not administering a pension fund for football players), not organized for profit and no part of the net earnings of which inures to the benefit of any private shareholder or individual.

(7) Clubs organized for pleasure, recreation, and other nonprofitable purposes, substantially all of the activities of which are for such purposes and no part of the net earnings of which inures to the benefit of any private shareholder.

(8) Fraternal beneficiary societies, orders, or associations—

(A) operating under the lodge system or for the exclusive benefit of the members of a fraternity itself operating under the lodge system, and

(B) providing for the payment of life, sick, accident, or other benefits to the members of such society, order, or association or their dependents.

(9) Voluntary employees' beneficiary associations providing for the payment of life, sick, accident, or other benefits to the members of such association or their dependents or designated beneficiaries, if no part of the net earnings of such association inures (other than through such payments) to the benefit of any private shareholder or individual.

(10) Domestic fraternal societies, orders, or associations, operating under the lodge system—

(A) the net earnings of which are devoted exclusively to religious, charitable, scientific, literary, educational, and fraternal purposes, and

(B) which do not provide for the payment of life, sick, accident, or other benefits.

(11) Teachers' retirement fund associations of a purely local character, if—

(A) no part of their net earnings inures (other than through payment of retirement benefits) to the benefit of any private shareholder or individual, and

(B) the income consists solely of amounts received from public taxation, amounts received from assessments on the teaching salaries of members, and income in respect of investments.

* * *

(13) Cemetery companies owned and operated exclusively for the benefit of their members or which are not operated for profit; and any corporation chartered solely for the purpose of the disposal of bodies by burial or cremation which is not permitted by its charter to engage in any business not necessarily incident to that purpose, no part of the net earnings of which inures to the benefit of any private shareholder or individual.

(14)(A) Credit unions without capital stock organized and operated for mutual purposes and without profit.

(B) Corporations or associations without capital stock organized before September 1, 1957, and operated for mutual purposes and without profit for the purpose of providing reserve funds for, and insurance of, shares or deposits in—

(i) domestic building and loan associations,

(ii) cooperative banks without capital stock organized and operated for mutual purposes and without profit,

(iii) mutual savings banks not having capital stock represented by shares, or

(iv) mutual savings banks described in section 591(b).

(C) Corporations or associations organized before September 1, 1957, and operated for mutual purposes and without profit for the purpose of providing reserve funds for associations or banks described in clause (i), (ii), or (iii) of subparagraph (B); but only if 85 percent or more of the income is attributable to providing such reserve funds and to investments. This subparagraph shall not apply to any corporation or association entitled to exemption under subparagraph (B).

* * *

(19) A post or organization of past or present members of the Armed Forces of the United States, or an auxiliary unit or society of, or a trust or foundation for, any such post or organization—

(A) organized in the United States or any of its possessions,

(B) at least 75 percent of the members of which are past or present members of the Armed Forces of the United States and substantially all of the other members of which are individuals who are cadets or are spouses, widows, or widowers of past or present members of the Armed Forces of the United States or of cadets, and

(C) no part of the net earnings of which inures to the benefit of any private shareholder or individual.

(20) An organization or trust created or organized in the United States, the exclusive function of which is to form part of a qualified group legal services plan or plans, within the meaning of section 120. An organization or trust which receives contributions because of section 120(c)(5)(C) shall not be prevented from qualifying as an organization described in this paragraph merely because it

Sec. 501(c)

provides legal services or indemnification against the cost of legal services unassociated with a qualified group legal services plan.

* * *

(23) Any association organized before 1880 more than 75 percent of the members of which are present or past members of the Armed Forces and a principal purpose of which is to provide insurance and other benefits to veterans or their dependents.

(24) A trust described in section 4049 of the Employee Retirement Income Security Act of 1974 (as in effect on the date of the enactment of the Single-Employer Pension Plan Amendments Act of 1986).

(25)(A) Any corporation or trust which—

(i) has no more than 35 shareholders or beneficiaries,

(ii) has only 1 class of stock or beneficial interest, and

(iii) is organized for the exclusive purposes of—

(I) acquiring real property and holding title to, and collecting income from, such property, and

(II) remitting the entire amount of income from such property (less expenses) to 1 or more organizations described in subparagraph (C) which are shareholders of such corporation or beneficiaries of such trust.

For purposes of clause (iii), the term "real property" shall not include any interest as a tenant in common (or similar interest) and shall not include any indirect interest.

(B) A corporation or trust shall be described in subparagraph (A) without regard to whether the corporation or trust is organized by 1 or more organizations described in subparagraph (C).

(C) An organization is described in this subparagraph if such organization is—

(i) a qualified pension, profit sharing, or stock bonus plan that meets the requirements of section 401(a),

(ii) a governmental plan (within the meaning of section 414(d)),

(iii) the United States, any State or political subdivision thereof, or any agency or instrumentality of any of the foregoing, or

(iv) any organization described in paragraph (3).

(D) A corporation or trust shall in no event be treated as described in subparagraph (A) unless such corporation or trust permits its shareholders or beneficiaries—

(i) to dismiss the corporation's or trust's investment adviser, following reasonable notice, upon a vote of the shareholders or beneficiaries holding a majority of interest in the corporation or trust, and

(ii) to terminate their interest in the corporation or trust by either, or both, of the following alternatives, as determined by the corporation or trust:

(I) by selling or exchanging their stock in the corporation or interest in the trust (subject to any Federal or State securities law) to any organization described in subparagraph (C) so long as the sale or exchange does not increase the number of shareholders or beneficiaries in such corporation or trust above 35, or

(II) by having their stock or interest redeemed by the corporation or trust after the shareholder or beneficiary has provided 90 days notice to such corporation or trust.

(E)(i) For purposes of this title—

(I) a corporation which is a qualified subsidiary shall not be treated as a separate corporation, and

(II) all assets, liabilities, and items of income, deduction, and credit of a qualified subsidiary shall be treated as assets, liabilities, and such items (as the case may be) of the corporation or trust described in subparagraph (A).

(ii) For purposes of this subparagraph, the term "qualified subsidiary" means any corporation if, at all times during the period such corporation was in existence, 100 percent of the stock of such corporation is held by the corporation or trust described in subparagraph (A).

Sec. 501(c)

(iii) For purposes of this subtitle, if any corporation which was a qualified subsidiary ceases to meet the requirements of clause (ii), such corporation shall be treated as a new corporation acquiring all of its assets (and assuming all of its liabilities) immediately before such cessation from the corporation or trust described in subparagraph (A) in exchange for its the stock.

(F) For purposes of subparagraph (A), the term "real property" includes any personal property which is leased under, or in connection with, a lease of real property, but only if the rent attributable to such personal property (determined under the rules of section 856(d)(1)) for the taxable year does not exceed 15 percent of the total rent for the taxable year attributable to both the real and personal property leased under, or in connection with, such lease.

(G)(i) An organization shall not be treated as failing to be described in this paragraph merely by reason of the receipt of any otherwise disqualifying income which is incidentally derived from the holding of real property.

(ii) Clause (i) shall not apply if the amount of gross income described in such clause exceeds 10 percent of the organization's gross income for the taxable year unless the organization establishes to the satisfaction of the Secretary that the receipt of gross income described in clause (i) in excess of such limitation was inadvertent and reasonable steps are being taken to correct the circumstances giving rise to such income.

* * *

[Sec. 501(d)]

(d) RELIGIOUS AND APOSTOLIC ORGANIZATIONS.—The following organizations are referred to in subsection (a): Religious or apostolic associations or corporations, if such associations or corporations have a common treasury or community treasury, even if such associations or corporations engage in business for the common benefit of the members, but only if the members thereof include (at the time of filing their returns) in their gross income their entire pro rata shares, whether distributed or not, of the taxable income of the association or corporation for such year. Any amount so included in the gross income of a member shall be treated as a dividend received.

* * *

[Sec. 501(f)]

(f) COOPERATIVE SERVICE ORGANIZATIONS OF OPERATING EDUCATIONAL ORGANIZATIONS.—For purposes of this title, if an organization is—

(1) organized and operated solely to hold, commingle, and collectively invest and reinvest (including arranging for and supervising the performance by independent contractors of investment services related thereto) in stocks and securities, the moneys contributed thereto by each of the members of such organization, and to collect income therefrom and turn over the entire amount thereof, less expenses, to such members,

(2) organized and controlled by one or more such members, and

(3) comprised solely of members that are organizations described in clause (ii) or (iv) of section 170(b)(1)(A)—

(A) which are exempt from taxation under subsection (a), or

(B) the income of which is excluded from taxation under section 115(a),

then such organization shall be treated as an organization organized and operated exclusively for charitable purposes.

[Sec. 501(g)]

(g) DEFINITION OF AGRICULTURAL.—For purposes of subsection (c)(5), the term "agricultural" includes the art or science of cultivating land, harvesting crops or aquatic resources, or raising livestock.

[Sec. 501(h)]

(h) EXPENDITURES BY PUBLIC CHARITIES TO INFLUENCE LEGISLATION.—

(1) GENERAL RULE.—In the case of an organization to which this subsection applies, exemption from taxation under subsection (a) shall be denied because a substantial part of the activities of such organization consists of carrying on propaganda, or otherwise attempting, to influence legislation, but only if such organization normally—

Sec. 501(d)

(A) makes lobbying expenditures in excess of the lobbying ceiling amount for such organization for each taxable year, or

(B) makes grass roots expenditures in excess of the grass roots ceiling amount for such organization for each taxable year.

(2) DEFINITIONS.—For purposes of this subsection—

(A) LOBBYING EXPENDITURES.—The term "lobbying expenditures" means expenditures for the purpose of influencing legislation (as defined in section 4911(d)).

(B) LOBBYING CEILING AMOUNT.—The lobbying ceiling amount for any organization for any taxable year is 150 percent of the lobbying nontaxable amount for such organization for such taxable year, determined under section 4911.

(C) GRASS ROOTS EXPENDITURES.—The term "grass roots expenditures" means expenditures for the purpose of influencing legislation (as defined in section 4911(d) without regard to paragraph (1)(B) thereof).

(D) GRASS ROOTS CEILING AMOUNT.—The grass roots ceiling amount for any organization for any taxable year is 150 percent of the grass roots nontaxable amount for such organization for such taxable year, determined under section 4911.

(3) ORGANIZATIONS TO WHICH THIS SUBSECTION APPLIES.—This subsection shall apply to any organization which has elected (in such manner and at such time as the Secretary may prescribe) to have the provisions of this subsection apply to such organization and which, for the taxable year which includes the date the election is made, is described in subsection (c)(3) and—

(A) is described in paragraph (4), and

(B) is not a disqualified organization under paragraph (5).

(4) ORGANIZATIONS PERMITTED TO ELECT TO HAVE THIS SUBSECTION APPLY.—An organization is described in this paragraph if it is described in—

(A) section 170(b)(1)(A)(ii) (relating to educational institutions),

(B) section 170(b)(1)(A)(iii) (relating to hospitals and medical research organizations),

(C) section 170(b)(1)(A)(iv) (relating to organizations supporting government schools),

(D) section 170(b)(1)(A)(vi) (relating to organizations publicly supported by charitable contributions),

(E) section 509(a)(2) (relating to organizations publicly supported by admissions, sales, etc.), or

(F) section 509(a)(3) (relating to organizations supporting certain types of public charities) except that for purposes of this subparagraph, section 509(a)(3) shall be applied without regard to the last sentence of section 509(a).

(5) DISQUALIFIED ORGANIZATIONS.—For purposes of paragraph (3) an organization is a disqualified organization if it is—

(A) described in section 170(b)(1)(A)(i) (relating to churches),

(B) an integrated auxiliary of a church or of a convention or association of churches, or

(C) a member of an affiliated group of organizations (within the meaning of section 4911(f)(2)) if one or more members of such group is described in subparagraph (A) or (B).

(6) YEARS FOR WHICH ELECTION IS EFFECTIVE.—An election by an organization under this subsection shall be effective for all taxable years of such organization which—

(A) end after the date the election is made, and

(B) begin before the date the election is revoked by such organization (under regulations prescribed by the Secretary).

(7) NO EFFECT ON CERTAIN ORGANIZATIONS.—With respect to any organization for a taxable year for which—

(A) such organization is a disqualified organization (within the meaning of paragraph (5)), or

(B) an election under this subsection is not in effect for such organization, nothing in this subsection or in section 4911 shall be construed to affect the interpretation of the phrase, "no substantial part of the activities of which is carrying on propaganda, or otherwise attempting, to influence legislation," under subsection (c)(3).

(8) AFFILIATED ORGANIZATIONS.—

For rules regarding affiliated organizations, see section 4911(f).

[Sec. 501(i)]

(i) PROHIBITION OF DISCRIMINATION BY CERTAIN SOCIAL CLUBS.—Notwithstanding subsection (a), an organization which is described in subsection (c)(7) shall not be exempt from taxation under subsection (a) for any taxable year if, at any time during such taxable year, the charter, bylaws, or other governing instrument, of such organization or any written policy statement of such organization contains a provision which provides for discrimination against any person on the basis of race, color, or religion. The preceding sentence to the extent it relates to discrimination on the basis of religion shall not apply to—

(1) an auxiliary of a fraternal beneficiary society if such society—

(A) is described in subsection (c)(8) and exempt from tax under subsection (a), and

(B) limits its membership to the members of a particular religion, or

(2) a club which in good faith limits its membership to the members of a particular religion in order to further the teachings or principles of that religion, and not to exclude individuals of a particular race or color.

[Sec. 501(j)]

(j) SPECIAL RULES FOR CERTAIN AMATEUR SPORTS ORGANIZATIONS.—

(1) IN GENERAL.—In the case of a qualified amateur sports organization—

(A) the requirement of subsection (c)(3) that no part of its activites involve the provision of athletic facilities or equipment shall not apply, and

(B) such organization shall not fail to meet the requirements of subsection (c)(3) merely because its membership is local or regional in nature.

(2) QUALIFIED AMATEUR SPORTS ORGANIZATION DEFINED.—For purposes of this subsection, the term "qualified amateur sports organization" means any organization organized and operated exclusively to foster national or international amateur sports competition if such organization is also organized and operated primarily to conduct national or international competition in sports or to support and develop amateur athletes for national or international competition in sports.

[Sec. 501(k)]

(k) TREATMENT OF CERTAIN ORGANIZATIONS PROVIDING CHILD CARE.—For purposes of subsection (c)(3) of this section and sections 170(c)(2), 2055(a)(2), and 2522(a)(2), the term "educational purposes" includes the providing of care of children away from their homes if—

(1) substantially all of the care provided by the organization is for purposes of enabling individuals to be gainfully employed, and

(2) the services provided by the organization are available to the general public.

* * *

[Sec. 501(m)]

(m) CERTAIN ORGANIZATIONS PROVIDING COMMERCIAL-TYPE INSURANCE NOT EXEMPT FROM TAX.—

(1) DENIAL OF TAX EXEMPTION WHERE PROVIDING COMMERCIAL-TYPE INSURANCE IS SUBSTANTIAL PART OF ACTIVITIES.—An organization described in paragraph (3) or (4) of subsection (c) shall be exempt from tax under subsection (a) only if no substantial part of its activities consists of providing commercial-type insurance.

(2) OTHER ORGANIZATIONS TAXED AS INSURANCE COMPANIES ON INSURANCE BUSINESS.—In the case of an organization described in paragraph (3) or (4) of subsection (c) which is exempt from tax under subsection (a) after the application of paragraph (1) of this subsection—

(A) the activity of providing commercial-type insurance shall be treated as an unrelated trade or business (as defined in section 513), and

(B) in lieu of the tax imposed by section 511 with respect to such activity, such organization shall be treated as an insurance company for purposes of applying subchapter L with respect to such activity.

(3) COMMERCIAL-TYPE INSURANCE.—For purposes of this subsection, the term "commercial-type insurance" shall not include—

(A) insurance provided at substantially below cost to a class of charitable recipients,

(B) incidental health insurance provided by a health maintenance organization of a kind customarily provided by such organizations,

(C) property or casualty insurance provided (directly or through an organization described in section 414(e)(3)(B)(ii)) by a church or convention or association of churches for such church or convention or association of churches,

(D) providing retirement or welfare benefits (or both) by a church or a convention or association of churches (directly or through an organization described in section 414(e)(3)(A) or 414(e)(3)(B)(ii)) for the employees (including employees described in section 414(e)(3)(B)) of such church or convention or association of churches or the beneficiaries of such employees, and

(E) charitable gift annuities.

(4) INSURANCE INCLUDES ANNUITIES.—For purposes of this subsection, the issuance of annuity contracts shall be treated as providing insurance.

(5) CHARITABLE GIFT ANNUITY.—For purposes of paragraph (3)(E), the term "charitable gift annuity" means an annuity if—

(A) a portion of the amount paid in connection with the issuance of the annuity is allowable as a deduction under section 170 or 2055, and

(B) the annuity is described in section 514(c)(5) (determined as if any amount paid in cash in connection with such issuance were property).

* * *

[Sec. 501(p)]

(p) CROSS REFERENCE.—

For nonexemption of Communist-controlled organizations, see section 11(b) of the Internal Security Act of 1950 (64 Stat. 997; 50 U. S. C. 790 (b)).

PART II—PRIVATE FOUNDATIONS

[Sec. 508]

SEC. 508. SPECIAL RULES WITH RESPECT TO SECTION 501(c)(3) ORGANIZATIONS.

[Sec. 508(a)]

(a) NEW ORGANIZATIONS MUST NOTIFY SECRETARY THAT THEY ARE APPLYING FOR RECOGNITION OF SECTION 501(c)(3) STATUS.—Except as provided in subsection (c), an organization organized after October 9, 1969, shall not be treated as an organization described in section 501(c)(3)—

(1) unless it has given notice to the Secretary, in such manner as the Secretary may by regulations prescribe, that it is applying for recognition of such status, or

(2) for any period before the giving of such notice, if such notice is given after the time prescribed by the Secretary by regulations for giving notice under this subsection.

[Sec. 508(b)]

(b) PRESUMPTION THAT ORGANIZATIONS ARE PRIVATE FOUNDATIONS.—Except as provided in subsection (c), any organization (including an organization in existence on October 9, 1969) which is described in section 501(c)(3) and which does not notify the Secretary, at such time and in such manner as the Secretary may by regulations prescribe, that it is not a private foundation shall be presumed to be a private foundation.

Sec. 508(b)

(c) EXCEPTIONS.—

(1) MANDATORY EXCEPTIONS.—Subsections (a) and (b) shall not apply to—

(A) churches, their integrated auxiliaries, and conventions or associations of churches, or

(B) any organization which is not a private foundation (as defined in section 509(a)) and the gross receipts of which in each taxable year are normally not more than $5,000.

(2) EXCEPTIONS BY REGULATIONS.—The Secretary may by regulations exempt (to the extent and subject to such conditions as may be prescribed in such regulations) from the provisions of subsection (a) or (b) or both—

(A) educational organizations described in section 170(b)(1)(A)(ii), and

(B) any other class of organizations with respect to which the Secretary determines that full compliance with the provisions of subsections (a) and (b) is not necessary to the efficient administration of the provisions of this title relating to private foundations.

* * *

[Sec. 509]

SEC. 509. PRIVATE FOUNDATION DEFINED.

[Sec. 509(a)]

(a) GENERAL RULE.—For purposes of this title, the term "private foundation" means a domestic or foreign organization described in section 501(c)(3) other than—

(1) an organization described in section 170(b)(1)(A) (other than in clauses (vii) and (viii));

(2) an organization which—

(A) normally receives more than one-third of its support in each taxable year from any combination of—

(i) gifts, grants, contributions, or membership fees, and

(ii) gross receipts from admissions, sales of merchandise, performance of services, or furnishing of facilities, in an activity which is not an unrelated trade or business (within the meaning of section 513), not including such receipts from any person, or from any bureau or similar agency of a governmental unit (as described in section 170(c)(1)), in any taxable year to the extent such receipts exceed the greater of $5,000 or 1 percent of the organization's support in such taxable year,

from persons other than disqualified persons (as defined in section 4946) with respect to the organization, from governmental units described in section 170(c)(1), or from organizations described in section 170(b)(1)(A) (other than in clauses (vii) and (viii)), and

(B) normally receives not more than one-third of its support in each taxable year from the sum of—

(i) gross investment income (as defined in subsection (e)) and

(ii) the excess (if any) of the amount of the unrelated business taxable income (as defined in section 512) over the amount of the tax imposed by section 511;

(3) an organization which—

(A) is organized, and at all times thereafter is operated, exclusively for the benefit of, to perform the functions of, or to carry out the purposes of one or more specified organizations described in paragraph (1) or (2),

(B) is operated, supervised, or controlled by or in connection with one or more organizations, described in paragraph (1) or (2), and

(C) is not controlled directly or indirectly by one or more disqualified persons (as defined in section 4946) other than foundation managers and other than one or more organizations described in paragraph (1) or (2); and

(4) an organization which is organized and operated exclusively for testing for public safety.

For purposes of paragraph (3), an organization described in paragraph (2) shall be deemed to include an organization described in section 501(c)(4), (5), or (6) which would be described in paragraph (2) if it were an organization described in section 501(c)(3).

* * *

[Sec. 509(d)]

(d) DEFINITION OF SUPPORT.—For purposes of this part and chapter 42, the term "support" includes (but is not limited to)—

(1) gifts, grants, contributions, or membership fees,

(2) gross receipts from admissions, sales of merchandise, performance of services, or furnishing of facilities in any activity which is not an unrelated trade or business (within the meaning of section 513),

(3) net income from unrelated business activities, whether or not such activities are carried on regularly as a trade or business,

(4) gross investment income (as defined in subsection (e)),

(5) tax revenues levied for the benefit of an organization and either paid to or expended on behalf of such organization, and

(6) the value of services or facilities (exclusive of services or facilities generally furnished to the public without charge) furnished by a governmental unit referred to in section 170(c)(1) to an organization without charge.

Such term does not include any gain from the sale or other disposition of property which would be considered as gain from the sale or exchange of a capital asset, or the value of exemption from any Federal, State, or local tax or any similar benefit.

[Sec. 509(e)]

(e) DEFINITION OF GROSS INVESTMENT INCOME.—For purposes of subsection (d), the term "gross investment income" means the gross amount of income from interest, dividends, payments with respect to securities loans (as defined in section 512(a)(5)), rents, and royalties, but not including any such income to the extent included in computing the tax imposed by section 511.

PART III—TAXATION OF BUSINESS INCOME OF CERTAIN EXEMPT ORGANIZATIONS

[Sec. 511]

SEC. 511. IMPOSITION OF TAX ON UNRELATED BUSINESS INCOME OF CHARITABLE, ETC., ORGANIZATIONS.

[Sec. 511(a)]

(a) CHARITABLE, ETC., ORGANIZATIONS TAXABLE AT CORPORATION RATES.—

(1) IMPOSITION OF TAX.—There is hereby imposed for each taxable year on the unrelated business taxable income (as defined in section 512) of every organization described in paragraph (2) a tax computed as provided in section 11. In making such computation for purposes of this section, the term "taxable income" as used in section 11 shall be read as "unrelated business taxable income".

(2) ORGANIZATIONS SUBJECT TO TAX.—

(A) ORGANIZATIONS DESCRIBED IN SECTIONS 401(a) AND 501(c).—The tax imposed by paragraph (1) shall apply in the case of any organization (other than a trust described in subsection (b) or an organization described in section 501(c)(1)) which is exempt, except as provided in this part or part II (relating to private foundations), from taxation under this subtitle by reason of section 501(a).

(B) STATE COLLEGES AND UNIVERSITIES.—The tax imposed by paragraph (1) shall apply in the case of any college or university which is an agency or instrumentality of any government or any political subdivision thereof, or which is owned or operated by a government or any political subdivision thereof, or by any agency or instrumentality of one or more governments or political subdivisions. Such tax shall also apply in the case of any corporation wholly owned by one or more such colleges or universities.

(b) TAX ON CHARITABLE, ETC., TRUSTS.—

(1) IMPOSITION OF TAX.—There is hereby imposed for each taxable year on the unrelated business taxable income of every trust described in paragraph (2) a tax computed as provided in section 1(e). In making such computation for purposes of this section, the term "taxable income" as used in section 1 shall be read as "unrelated business taxable income" as defined in section 512.

(2) CHARITABLE, ETC., TRUSTS SUBJECT TO TAX.—The tax imposed by paragraph (1) shall apply in the case of any trust which is exempt, except as provided in this part or part II (relating to private foundations), from taxation under this subtitle by reason of section 501(a) and which, if it were not for such exemption, would be subject to subchapter J (sec. 641 and following, relating to estates, trusts, beneficiaries, and decedents).

SEC. 512. UNRELATED BUSINESS TAXABLE INCOME.

(a) DEFINITION.—For purposes of this title—

(1) GENERAL RULE.—Except as otherwise provided in this subsection, the term "unrelated business taxable income" means the gross income derived by any organization from any unrelated trade or business (as defined in section 513) regularly carried on by it, less the deductions allowed by this chapter which are directly connected with the carrying on of such trade or business, both computed with the modifications provided in subsection (b).

* * *

(b) MODIFICATIONS.—The modifications referred to in subsection (a) are the following:

(1) There shall be excluded all dividends, interest, payments with respect to securities loans (as defined in section 512(a)(5)), amounts received or accrued as consideration for entering into agreements to make loans, and annuities, and all deductions directly connected with such income.

(2) There shall be excluded all royalties (including overriding royalties) whether measured by production or by gross or taxable income from the property, and all deductions directly connected with such income.

(3) In the case of rents—

(A) Except as provided in subparagraph (B), there shall be excluded—

(i) all rents from real property (including property described in section 1245(a)(3)(C)), and

(ii) all rents from personal property (including for purposes of this paragraph as personal property any property described in section 1245(a)(3)(B)) leased with such real property, if the rents attributable to such personal property are an incidental amount of the total rents received or accrued under the lease, determined at the time the personal property is placed in service.

(B) Subparagraph (A) shall not apply—

(i) if more than 50 percent of the total rent received or accrued under the lease is attributable to personal property described in Subparagraph (A)(ii), or

(ii) if the determination of the amount of such rent depends in whole or in part on the income or profits derived by any person from the property leased (other than an amount based on a fixed percentage or percentages of receipts or sales).

(C) There shall be excluded all deductions directly connected with rents excluded under subparagraph (A).

(4) Notwithstanding paragraph (1), (2), (3), or (5), in the case of debt-financed property (as defined in section 514) there shall be included, as an item of gross income derived from an unrelated trade or business, the amount ascertained under section 514(a)(1), and there shall be allowed, as a deduction, the amount ascertained under section 514(a)(2).

(5) There shall be excluded all gains or losses from the sale, exchange, or other disposition of property other than—

(A) stock in trade or other property of a kind which would properly be includible in inventory if on hand at the close of the taxable year, or

(B) property held primarily for sale to customers in the ordinary course of the trade or business.

There shall also be excluded all gains or losses recognized, in connection with the organization's investment activities, from the lapse or termination of options to buy or sell securities (as defined in section 1236(c)) or real property and all gains or losses from the forfeiture of good-faith deposits (that are consistent with established business practice) for the purchase, sale, or lease of real property in connection with the organization's investment activities.

(6) The net operating loss deduction provided in section 172 shall be allowed, except that—

(A) the net operating loss for any taxable year, the amount of the net operating loss carryback or carryover to any taxable year, and the net operating loss deduction for any taxable year shall be determined under section 172 without taking into account any amount of income or deduction which is excluded under this part in computing the unrelated business taxable income; and

(B) the terms "preceding taxable year" and "preceding taxable years" as used in section 172 shall not include any taxable year for which the organization was not subject to the provisions of this part.

(7) There shall be excluded all income derived from research for (A) the United States, or any of its agencies or instrumentalities, or (B) any State or political subdivision thereof; and there shall be excluded all deductions directly connected with such income.

(8) In the case of a college, university, or hospital, there shall be excluded all income derived from research performed for any person, and all deductions directly connected with such income.

(9) In the case of an organization operated primarily for purposes of carrying on fundamental research the results of which are freely available to the general public, there shall be excluded all income derived from research performed for any person, and all deductions directly connected with such income.

(10) In the case of any organization described in section 511 (a), the deduction allowed by section 170 (relating to charitable etc. contributions and gifts) shall be allowed (whether or not directly connected with the carrying on of the trade or business), but shall not exceed 10 percent of the unrelated business taxable income computed without the benefit of this paragraph.

(11) In the case of any trust described in section 511 (b), the deduction allowed by section 170 (relating to charitable etc. contributions and gifts) shall be allowed (whether or not directly connected with the carrying on of the trade or business), and for such purpose a distribution made by the trust to a beneficiary described in section 170 shall be considered as a gift or contribution. The deduction allowed by this paragraph shall be allowed with the limitations prescribed in section 170 (b) (1) (A) and (B) determined with reference to the unrelated business taxable income computed without the benefit of this paragraph (in lieu of with reference to adjusted gross income).

(12) Except for purposes of computing the net operating loss under section 172 and paragraph (6), there shall be allowed a specific deduction of $1,000. In the case of a diocese, province of a religious order, or a convention or association of churches, there shall also be allowed, with respect to each parish, individual church, district, or other local unit, a specific deduction equal to the lower of—

(A) $1,000, or

(B) the gross income derived from any unrelated trade or business regularly carried on by such local unit.

(13) SPECIAL RULES FOR CERTAIN AMOUNTS RECEIVED FROM CONTROLLED ENTITIES.—

(A) IN GENERAL.—If an organization (in this paragraph referred to as the "controlling organization") receives or accrues (directly or indirectly) a specified payment from another entity which it controls (in this paragraph referred to as the "controlled entity"), notwithstanding paragraphs (1), (2), and (3), the controlling organization shall include such payment as an item of gross income derived from an unrelated trade or business to the extent such payment reduces the net unrelated income of the controlled entity (or increases any net unrelated loss of the controlled entity). There shall be allowed all deductions of the controlling organization directly connected with amounts treated as derived from an unrelated trade or business under the preceding sentence.

(B) NET UNRELATED INCOME OR LOSS.—For purposes of this paragraph—

(i) NET UNRELATED INCOME.—The term "net unrelated income" means—

(I) in the case of a controlled entity which is not exempt from tax under section 501(a), the portion of such entity's taxable income which would be unrelated business taxable income if such entity were exempt from tax under section 501(a) and had the same exempt purposes as the controlling organization, or

(II) in the case of a controlled entity which is exempt from tax under section 501(a), the amount of the unrelated business taxable income of the controlled entity.

(ii) NET UNRELATED LOSS.—The term "net unrelated loss" means the net operating loss adjusted under rules similar to the rules of clause (i).

(C) SPECIFIED PAYMENT.—For purposes of this paragraph, the term "specified payment" means any interest, annuity, royalty, or rent.

(D) DEFINITION OF CONTROL.—For purposes of this paragraph—

(i) CONTROL.—The term "control" means—

(I) in the case of a corporation, ownership (by vote or value) of more than 50 percent of the stock in such corporation,

(II) in the case of a partnership, ownership of more than 50 percent of the profits interests or capital interests in such partnership, or

(III) in any other case, ownership of more than 50 percent of the beneficial interests in the entity.

(ii) CONSTRUCTIVE OWNERSHIP.—Section 318 (relating to constructive ownership of stock) shall apply for purposes of determining ownership of stock in a corporation. Similar principles shall apply for purposes of determining ownership of interests in any other entity.

(E) RELATED PERSONS.—The Secretary shall prescribe such rules as may be necessary or appropriate to prevent avoidance of the purposes of this paragraph through the use of related persons.

(14) [Repealed.]

(15) Except as provided in paragraph (4), in the case of a trade or business—

(A) which consists of providing services under license issued by a Federal regulatory agency,

(B) which is carried on by a religious order or by an educational organization described in section 170(b)(1)(A)(ii) maintained by such religious order, and which was so carried on before May 27, 1959, and

(C) less than 10 percent of the net income of which for each taxable year is used for activities which are not related to the purpose constituting the basis for the religious order's exemption,

there shall be excluded all gross income derived from such trade or business and all deductions directly connected with the carrying on of such trade or business, so long as it is established to the satisfaction of the Secretary that the rates or other charges for such services are competitive with rates or other charges charged for similar services by persons not exempt from taxation.

* * *

[Sec. 512(c)]

(c) SPECIAL RULES FOR PARTNERSHIPS.—

(1) IN GENERAL.—If a trade or business regularly carried on by a partnership of which an organization is a member is an unrelated trade or business with respect to such organization, such organization in computing its unrelated business taxable income shall, subject to the exceptions, additions, and limitations contained in subsection (b), include its share (whether or not distributed) of the gross income of the partnership from such unrelated trade or business and its share of the partnership deductions directly connected with such gross income.

(2) SPECIAL RULE WHERE PARTNERSHIP YEAR IS DIFFERENT FROM ORGANIZATION'S YEAR.—If the taxable year of the organization is different from that of the partnership, the amounts to be included or deducted in computing the unrelated business taxable income under paragraph (1) shall be based

upon the income and deductions of the partnership for any taxable year of the partnership ending within or with the taxable year of the organization.

* * *

[Sec. 512(e)]

(e) SPECIAL RULES APPLICABLE TO S CORPORATIONS.—

(1) IN GENERAL.—If an organization described in section 1361(c)(6) holds stock in an S corporation—

(A) such interest shall be treated as an interest in an unrelated trade or business; and

(B) notwithstanding any other provision of this part—

(i) all items of income, loss, or deduction taken into account under section 1366(a), and

(ii) any gain or loss on the disposition of the stock in the S corporation

shall be taken into account in computing the unrelated business taxable income of such organization.

(2) BASIS REDUCTION.—Except as provided in regulations, for purposes of paragraph (1), the basis of any stock acquired by purchase (as defined in section 1361(e)(1)(C)) shall be reduced by the amount of any dividends received by the organization with respect to the stock.

(3) EXCEPTION FOR ESOPs.—This subsection shall not apply to employer securities (within the meaning of section 409(l)) held by an employee stock ownership plan described in section 4975(e)(7).

[Sec. 513]

SEC. 513. UNRELATED TRADE OR BUSINESS.

[Sec. 513(a)]

(a) GENERAL RULE.—The term "unrelated trade or business" means, in the case of any organization subject to the tax imposed by section 511, any trade or business the conduct of which is not substantially related (aside from the need of such organization for income or funds or the use it makes of the profits derived) to the exercise or performance by such organization of its charitable, educational, or other purpose or function constituting the basis for its exemption under section 501 (or, in the case of an organization described in section 511 (a) (2) (B), to the exercise or performance of any purpose or function described in section 501 (c) (3)), except that such term does not include any trade or business—

(1) in which substantially all the work in carrying on such trade or business is performed for the organization without compensation; or

(2) which is carried on, in the case of an organization described in section 501 (c) (3) or in the case of a college or university described in section 511 (a) (2) (B), by the organization primarily for the convenience of its members, students, patients, officers, or employees, or, in the case of a local association of employees described in section 501(c)(4) organized before May 27, 1969, which is the selling by the organization of items of work-related clothes and equipment and items normally sold through vending machines, through food dispensing facilities, or by snack bars, for the convenience of its members at their usual places of employment; or

(3) which is the selling of merchandise, substantially all of which has been received by the organization as gifts or contributions.

[Sec. 513(b)]

(b) SPECIAL RULE FOR TRUSTS.—The term "unrelated trade or business" means, in the case of—

(1) a trust computing its unrelated business taxable income under section 512 for purposes of section 681; or

(2) a trust described in section 401(a), or section 501(c)(17), which is exempt from tax under section 501(a);

any trade or business regularly carried on by such trust or by a partnership of which it is a member.

[Sec. 513(c)]

(c) ADVERTISING, ETC., ACTIVITIES.—For purposes of this section, the term "trade or business" includes any activity which is carried on for the production of income from the sale of goods or the performance of services. For purposes of the preceding sentence, an activity does not lose identity as a trade or business merely because it is carried on within a larger aggregate of similar activities or within a larger complex of other endeavors which may, or may not, be related to the exempt purposes of the organization. Where an activity carried on for profit constitutes an unrelated trade or business, no part of such trade or business shall be excluded from such classification merely because it does not result in profit.

* * *

PART VIII—HIGHER EDUCATION SAVINGS ENTITIES

[Sec. 529]

SEC. 529. QUALIFIED TUITION PROGRAMS.

[Sec. 529(a)]

(a) GENERAL RULE.—A qualified tuition program shall be exempt from taxation under this subtitle. Notwithstanding the preceding sentence, such program shall be subject to the taxes imposed by section 511 (relating to imposition of tax on unrelated business income of charitable organizations).

[Sec. 529(b)]

(b) QUALIFIED TUITION PROGRAM.—For purposes of this section—

(1) IN GENERAL.—The term "qualified tuition program" means a program established and maintained by a State or agency or instrumentality thereof or by 1 or more eligible educational institutions—

(A) under which a person—

(i) may purchase tuition credits or certificates on behalf of a designated beneficiary which entitle the beneficiary to the waiver or payment of qualified higher education expenses of the beneficiary, or

(ii) in the case of a program established and maintained by a State or agency or instrumentality thereof, may make contributions to an account which is established for the purpose of meeting the qualified higher education expenses of the designated beneficiary of the account, and

(B) which meets the other requirements of this subsection.

Except to the extent provided in regulations, a program established and maintained by 1 or more eligible educational institutions shall not be treated as a qualified tuition program unless such program provides that amounts are held in a qualified trust and such program has received a ruling or determination that such program meets the applicable requirements for a qualified tuition program. For purposes of the preceding sentence, the term "qualified trust" means a trust which is created or organized in the United States for the exclusive benefit of designated beneficiaries and with respect to which the requirements of paragraphs (2) and (5) of section 408(a) are met.

(2) CASH CONTRIBUTIONS.—A program shall not be treated as a qualified tuition program unless it provides that purchases or contributions may only be made in cash.

(3) SEPARATE ACCOUNTING.—A program shall not be treated as a qualified tuition program unless it provides separate accounting for each designated beneficiary.

(4) NO INVESTMENT DIRECTION.—A program shall not be treated as a qualified tuition program unless it provides that any contributor to, or designated beneficiary under, such program may not directly or indirectly direct the investment of any contributions to the program (or any earnings thereon).

(5) NO PLEDGING OF INTEREST AS SECURITY.—A program shall not be treated as a qualified tuition program if it allows any interest in the program or any portion thereof to be used as security for a loan.

(6) PROHIBITION ON EXCESS CONTRIBUTIONS.—A program shall not be treated as a qualified tuition program unless it provides adequate safeguards to prevent contributions on behalf of a designated beneficiary in excess of those necessary to provide for the qualified higher education expenses of the beneficiary.

Sec. 529

[Sec. 529(c)]

(c) Tax Treatment of Designated Beneficiaries and Contributors.—

(1) In general.—Except as otherwise provided in this subsection, no amount shall be includible in gross income of—

(A) a designated beneficiary under a qualified tuition program, or

(B) a contributor to such program on behalf of a designated beneficiary,

with respect to any distribution or earnings under such program.

(2) Gift tax treatment of contributions.—For purposes of chapters 12 and 13—

(A) In general.—Any contribution to a qualified tuition program on behalf of any designated beneficiary—

(i) shall be treated as a completed gift to such beneficiary which is not a future interest in property, and

(ii) shall not be treated as a qualified transfer under section 2503(e).

(B) Treatment of excess contributions.—If the aggregate amount of contributions described in subparagraph (A) during the calendar year by a donor exceeds the limitation for such year under section 2503(b), such aggregate amount shall, at the election of the donor, be taken into account for purposes of such section ratably over the 5-year period beginning with such calendar year.

(3) Distributions.—

(A) In general.—Any distribution under a qualified tuition program shall be includible in the gross income of the distributee in the manner as provided under section 72 to the extent not excluded from gross income under any other provision of this chapter.

(B) Distributions for qualified higher education expenses.—For purposes of this paragraph—

(i) In-kind distributions.—No amount shall be includible in gross income under subparagraph (A) by reason of a distribution which consists of providing a benefit to the distributee which, if paid for by the distributee, would constitute payment of a qualified higher education expense.

(ii) Cash distributions.—In the case of distributions not described in clause (i), if—

(I) such distributions do not exceed the qualified higher education expenses (reduced by expenses described in clause (i)), no amount shall be includible in gross income, and

(II) in any other case, the amount otherwise includible in gross income shall be reduced by an amount which bears the same ratio to such amount as such expenses bear to such distributions.

(iii) Exception for institutional programs.—In the case of any taxable year beginning before January 1, 2004, clauses (i) and (ii) shall not apply with respect to any distribution during such taxable year under a qualified tuition program established and maintained by 1 or more eligible educational institutions.

(iv) Treatment as distributions.—Any benefit furnished to a designated beneficiary under a qualified tuition program shall be treated as a distribution to the beneficiary for purposes of this paragraph.

(v) Coordination with hope and lifetime learning credits.—The total amount of qualified higher education expenses with respect to an individual for the taxable year shall be reduced—

(I) as provided in section 25A(g)(2), and

(II) by the amount of such expenses which were taken into account in determining the credit allowed to the taxpayer or any other person under section 25A.

(vi) Coordination with coverdell education savings accounts.—If, with respect to an individual for any taxable year—

(I) the aggregate distributions to which clauses (i) and (ii) and section 530(d)(2)(A) apply, exceed

(II) the total amount of qualified higher education expenses otherwise taken into account under clauses (i) and (ii) (after the application of clause (v)) for such year,

the taxpayer shall allocate such expenses among such distributions for purposes of determining the amount of the exclusion under clauses (i) and (ii) and section 530(d)(2)(A).

(C) CHANGE IN BENEFICIARIES OR PROGRAMS.—

(i) ROLLOVERS.—Subparagraph (A) shall not apply to that portion of any distribution which, within 60 days of such distribution, is transferred—

(I) to another qualified tuition program for the benefit of the designated beneficiary, or

(II) to the credit of another designated beneficiary under a qualified tuition program who is a member of the family of the designated beneficiary with respect to which the distribution was made.

(ii) CHANGE IN DESIGNATED BENEFICIARIES.—Any change in the designated beneficiary of an interest in a qualified tuition program shall not be treated as a distribution for purposes of subparagraph (A) if the new beneficiary is a member of the family of the old beneficiary.

(iii) LIMITATION ON CERTAIN ROLLOVERS.—Clause (i)(I) shall not apply to any transfer if such transfer occurs within 12 months from the date of a previous transfer to any qualified tuition program for the benefit of the designated beneficiary.

(D) OPERATING RULES.—For purposes of applying section 72—

(i) to the extent provided by the Secretary, all qualified tuition programs of which an individual is a designated beneficiary shall be treated as one program,

(ii) except to the extent provided by the Secretary, all distributions during a taxable year shall be treated as one distribution, and

(iii) except to the extent provided by the Secretary, the value of the contract, income on the contract, and investment in the contract shall be computed as of the close of the calendar year in which the taxable year begins.

(4) ESTATE TAX TREATMENT.—

(A) IN GENERAL.—No amount shall be includible in the gross estate of any individual for purposes of chapter 11 by reason of an interest in a qualified tuition program.

(B) AMOUNTS INCLUDIBLE IN ESTATE OF DESIGNATED BENEFICIARY IN CERTAIN CASES.— Subparagraph (A) shall not apply to amounts distributed on account of the death of a beneficiary.

(C) AMOUNTS INCLUDIBLE IN ESTATE OF DONOR MAKING EXCESS CONTRIBUTIONS.—In the case of a donor who makes the election described in paragraph (2)(B) and who dies before the close of the 5-year period referred to in such paragraph, notwithstanding subparagraph (A), the gross estate of the donor shall include the portion of such contributions properly allocable to periods after the date of death of the donor.

(5) OTHER GIFT TAX RULES.—For purposes of chapters 12 and 13—

(A) TREATMENT OF DISTRIBUTIONS.—Except as provided in subparagraph (B), in no event shall a distribution from a qualified tuition program be treated as a taxable gift.

(B) TREATMENT OF DESIGNATION OF NEW BENEFICIARY.—The taxes imposed by chapters 12 and 13 shall apply to a transfer by reason of a change in the designated beneficiary under the program (or a rollover to the account of a new beneficiary) only if the new beneficiary is a generation below the generation of the old beneficiary (determined in accordance with section 2651).

(6) ADDITIONAL TAX.—The tax imposed by section 530(d)(4) shall apply to any payment or distribution from a qualified tuition program in the same manner as such tax applies to a payment or distribution from an education individual retirement account. This paragraph shall not apply to any payment or distribution in any taxable year beginning before January 1, 2004, which is includible in gross income but used for qualified higher education expenses of the designated beneficiary.

Sec. 529(c)

[Sec. 529(d)]

(d) Reports.—Each officer or employee having control of the qualified tuition program or their designee shall make such reports regarding such program to the Secretary and to designated beneficiaries with respect to contributions, distributions, and such other matters as the Secretary may require. The reports required by this subsection shall be filed at such time and in such manner and furnished to such individuals at such time and in such manner as may be required by the Secretary.

[Sec. 529(e)]

(e) Other Definitions and Special Rules.—For purposes of this section—

(1) Designated beneficiary.—The term "designated beneficiary" means—

(A) the individual designated at the commencement of participation in the qualified tuition program as the beneficiary of amounts paid (or to be paid) to the program,

(B) in the case of a change in beneficiaries described in subsection (c)(3)(C), the individual who is the new beneficiary, and

(C) in the case of an interest in a qualified tuition program purchased by a State or local government (or agency or instrumentality thereof) or an organization described in section 501(c)(3) and exempt from taxation under section 501(a) as part of a scholarship program operated by such government or organization, the individual receiving such interest as a scholarship.

(2) Member of family.—The term "member of the family" means, with respect to any designated beneficiary—

(A) the spouse of such beneficiary;

(B) an individual who bears a relationship to such beneficiary which is described in paragraphs (1) through (8) of section 152(a);

(C) the spouse of any individual described in subparagraph (B); and

(D) any first cousin of such beneficiary.

(3) Qualified higher education expenses.—

(A) In general.—The term "qualified higher education expenses" means—

(i) tuition, fees, books, supplies, and equipment required for the enrollment or attendance of a designated beneficiary at an eligible educational institution; and

(ii) expenses for special needs services in the case of a special needs beneficiary which are incurred in connection with such enrollment or attendance.

(B) Room and board included for students who are at least half-time.—

(i) In general.—In the case of an individual who is an eligible student (as defined in section 25A(b)(3)) for any academic period, such term shall also include reasonable costs for such period (as determined under the qualified tuition program) incurred by the designated beneficiary for room and board while attending such institution. For purposes of subsection (b)(6), a designated beneficiary shall be treated as meeting the requirements of this clause.

(ii) Limitation.—The amount treated as qualified higher education expenses by reason of clause (i) shall not exceed—

(I) the allowance (applicable to the student) for room and board included in the cost of attendance (as defined in section 472 of the Higher Education Act of 1965 (20 U.S.C. 1087ll), as in effect on the date of the enactment of the Economic Growth and Tax Relief Reconciliation Act of 2001) as determined by the eligible educational institution for such period, or

(II) if greater, the actual invoice amount the student residing in housing owned or operated by the eligible educational institution is charged by such institution for room and board costs for such period.

(4) Application of section 514.—An interest in a qualified tuition program shall not be treated as debt for purposes of section 514.

(5) Eligible educational institution.—The term "eligible educational institution" means an institution—

(A) which is described in section 481 of the Higher Education Act of 1965 (20 U.S.C. 1088), as in effect on the date of the enactment of this paragraph, and

(B) which is eligible to participate in a program under title IV of such Act.

Sec. 529(e)

[Sec. 530]

SEC. 530. COVERDELL EDUCATION SAVINGS ACCOUNTS.

[Sec. 530(a)]

(a) GENERAL RULE.—A Coverdell education savings account shall be exempt from taxation under this subtitle. Notwithstanding the preceding sentence, the Coverdell education savings account shall be subject to the taxes imposed by section 511 (relating to imposition of tax on unrelated business income of charitable organizations).

[Sec. 530(b)]

(b) DEFINITIONS AND SPECIAL RULES.—For purposes of this section—

(1) COVERDELL EDUCATION SAVINGS ACCOUNT.—The term "Coverdell education savings account" means a trust created or organized in the United States exclusively for the purpose of paying the qualified education expenses of an individual who is the designated beneficiary of the trust (and designated as a Coverdell education savings account at the time created or organized), but only if the written governing instrument creating the trust meets the following requirements:

(A) No contribution will be accepted—

(i) unless it is in cash,

(ii) after the date on which such beneficiary attains age 18, or

(iii) except in the case of rollover contributions, if such contribution would result in aggregate contributions for the taxable year exceeding $2,000.

(B) The trustee is a bank (as defined in section 408(n)) or another person who demonstrates to the satisfaction of the Secretary that the manner in which that person will administer the trust will be consistent with the requirements of this section or who has so demonstrated with respect to any individual retirement plan.

(C) No part of the trust assets will be invested in life insurance contracts.

(D) The assets of the trust shall not be commingled with other property except in a common trust fund or common investment fund.

(E) Except as provided in subsection (d)(7), any balance to the credit of the designated beneficiary on the date on which the beneficiary attains age 30 shall be distributed within 30 days after such date to the beneficiary or, if the beneficiary dies before attaining age 30, shall be distributed within 30 days after the date of death of such beneficiary.

The age limitations in subparagraphs (A)(ii) and (E), and paragraphs (5) and (6) of subsection (d), shall not apply to any designated beneficiary with special needs (as determined under regulations prescribed by the Secretary).

(2) QUALIFIED EDUCATION EXPENSES.—

(A) IN GENERAL.—The term "qualified education expenses" means—

(i) qualified higher education expenses (as defined in section 529(e)(3)), and

(ii) qualified elementary and secondary education expenses (as defined in paragraph (4)).

(B) QUALIFIED TUITION PROGRAMS.—Such term shall include any contribution to a qualified tuition program (as defined in section 529(b)) on behalf of the designated beneficiary (as defined in section 529(e)(1)); but there shall be no increase in the investment in the contract for purposes of applying section 72 by reason of any portion of such contribution which is not includible in gross income by reason of subsection (d)(2).

(3) ELIGIBLE EDUCATIONAL INSTITUTION.—The term "eligible educational institution" has the meaning given such term by section 529(e)(5).

(4) QUALIFIED ELEMENTARY AND SECONDARY EDUCATION EXPENSES.—

(A) IN GENERAL.—The term "qualified elementary and secondary education expenses" means—

(i) expenses for tuition, fees, academic tutoring, special needs services in the case of a special needs beneficiary, books, supplies, and other equipment which are incurred in connection with the enrollment or attendance of the designated beneficiary of the trust as an elementary or secondary school student at a public, private, or religious school,

Sec. 530

(ii) expenses for room and board, uniforms, transportation, and supplementary items and services (including extended day programs) which are required or provided by a public, private, or religious school in connection with such enrollment or attendance, and

(iii) expenses for the purchase of any computer technology or equipment (as defined in section 170(e)(6)(F)(i)) or Internet access and related services, if such technology, equipment, or services are to be used by the beneficiary and the beneficiary's family during any of the years the beneficiary is in school.

Clause (iii) shall not include expenses for computer software designed for sports, games, or hobbies unless the software is predominantly educational in nature.

(B) SCHOOL.—The term "school" means any school which provides elementary education or secondary education (kindergarten through grade 12), as determined under State law.

(5) TIME WHEN CONTRIBUTIONS DEEMED MADE.—An individual shall be deemed to have made a contribution to a Coverdell education savings account on the last day of the preceding taxable year if the contribution is made on account of such taxable year and is made not later than the time prescribed by law for filing the return for such taxable year (not including extensions thereof).

[Sec. 530(c)]

(c) REDUCTION IN PERMITTED CONTRIBUTIONS BASED ON ADJUSTED GROSS INCOME.—

(1) IN GENERAL.—In the case of a contributor who is an individual, the maximum amount the contributor could otherwise make to an account under this section shall be reduced by an amount which bears the same ratio to such maximum amount as—

(A) the excess of—

(i) the contributor's modified adjusted gross income for such taxable year, over

(ii) $95,000 ($190,000 in the case of a joint return), bears to

(B) $15,000 ($30,000 in the case of a joint return).

(2) MODIFIED ADJUSTED GROSS INCOME.—For purposes of paragraph (1), the term "modified adjusted gross income" means the adjusted gross income of the taxpayer for the taxable year increased by any amount excluded from gross income under section 911, 931, or 933.

[Sec. 530(d)]

(d) TAX TREATMENT OF DISTRIBUTIONS.—

(1) IN GENERAL.—Any distribution shall be includible in the gross income of the distributee in the manner as provided in section 72.

(2) DISTRIBUTIONS FOR QUALIFIED EDUCATION EXPENSES.—

(A) IN GENERAL.—No amount shall be includible in gross income under paragraph (1) if the qualified education expenses of the designated beneficiary during the taxable year are not less than the aggregate distributions during the taxable year.

(B) DISTRIBUTIONS IN EXCESS OF EXPENSES.—If such aggregate distributions exceed such expenses during the taxable year, the amount otherwise includible in gross income under paragraph (1) shall be reduced by the amount which bears the same ratio to the amount which would be includible in gross income under paragraph (1) (without regard to this subparagraph) as the qualified education expenses bear to such aggregate distributions.

(C) COORDINATION WITH HOPE AND LIFETIME LEARNING CREDITS AND QUALIFIED TUITION PROGRAMS.—For purposes of subparagraph (A)—

(i) CREDIT COORDINATION.—The total amount of qualified higher education expenses with respect to an individual for the taxable year shall be reduced—

(I) as provided in section 25A(g)(2), and

(II) by the amount of such expenses which were taken into account in determining the credit allowed to the taxpayer or any other person under section 25A.

(ii) COORDINATION WITH QUALIFIED TUITION PROGRAMS.—If, with respect to an individual for any taxable year—

(I) the aggregate distributions during such year to which subparagraph (A) and section 529(c)(3)(B) apply, exceed

(II) the total amount of qualified education expenses (after the application of clause (i)) for such year,

the taxpayer shall allocate such expenses among such distributions for purposes of determining the amount of the exclusion under subparagraph (A) and section 529(c)(3)(B).

(D) DISALLOWANCE OF EXCLUDED AMOUNTS AS DEDUCTION, CREDIT, OR EXCLUSION.—No deduction, credit, or exclusion shall be allowed to the taxpayer under any other section of this chapter for any qualified education expenses to the extent taken into account in determining the amount of the exclusion under this paragraph.

(3) SPECIAL RULES FOR APPLYING ESTATE AND GIFT TAXES WITH RESPECT TO ACCOUNT.—Rules similar to the rules of paragraphs (2), (4), and (5) of section 529(c) shall apply for purposes of this section.

(4) ADDITIONAL TAX FOR DISTRIBUTIONS NOT USED FOR EDUCATIONAL EXPENSES.—

(A) IN GENERAL.—The tax imposed by this chapter for any taxable year on any taxpayer who receives a payment or distribution from a Coverdell education savings account which is includible in gross income shall be increased by 10 percent of the amount which is so includible.

(B) EXCEPTIONS.—Subparagraph (A) shall not apply if the payment or distribution is—

(i) made to a beneficiary (or to the estate of the designated beneficiary) on or after the death of the designated beneficiary,

(ii) attributable to the designated beneficiary's being disabled (within the meaning of section 72(m)(7)),

(iii) made on account of a scholarship, allowance, or payment described in section 25A(g)(2) received by the account holder to the extent the amount of the payment or distribution does not exceed the amount of the scholarship, allowance, or payment, or

(iv) an amount which is includible in gross income solely by application of paragraph (2)(C)(i)(II) for the taxable year.

(C) CONTRIBUTIONS RETURNED BEFORE CERTAIN DATE.—Subparagraph (A) shall not apply to the distribution of any contribution made during a taxable year on behalf of the designated beneficiary if—

(i) such distribution is made before the first day of the sixth month of the taxable year following the taxable year, and

(ii) such distribution is accompanied by the amount of net income attributable to such excess contribution.

Any net income described in clause (ii) shall be included in gross income for the taxable year in which such excess contribution was made.

(5) ROLLOVER CONTRIBUTIONS.—Paragraph (1) shall not apply to any amount paid or distributed from a Coverdell education savings account to the extent that the amount received is paid, not later than the 60th day after the date of such payment or distribution, into another Coverdell education savings account for the benefit of the same beneficiary or a member of the family (within the meaning of section 529(e)(2)) of such beneficiary who has not attained age 30 as of such date. The preceding sentence shall not apply to any payment or distribution if it applied to any prior payment or distribution during the 12-month period ending on the date of the payment or distribution.

(6) CHANGE IN BENEFICIARY.—Any change in the beneficiary of a Coverdell education savings account shall not be treated as a distribution for purposes of paragraph (1) if the new beneficiary is a member of the family (as so defined) of the old beneficiary and has not attained age 30 as of the date of such change.

(7) SPECIAL RULES FOR DEATH AND DIVORCE.—Rules similar to the rules of paragraphs (7) and (8) of section 220(f) shall apply. In applying the preceding sentence, members of the family (as so defined) of the designated beneficiary shall be treated in the same manner as the spouse under such paragraph (8).

(8) DEEMED DISTRIBUTION ON REQUIRED DISTRIBUTION DATE.—In any case in which a distribution is required under subsection (b)(1)(E), any balance to the credit of a designated beneficiary as of the close of the 30-day period referred to in such subsection for making such distribution shall be deemed distributed at the close of such period.

Sec. 530(d)

[Sec. 530(e)]

(e) TAX TREATMENT OF ACCOUNTS.—Rules similar to the rules of paragraphs (2) and (4) of section 408(e) shall apply to any Coverdell education savings account.

[Sec. 530(f)]

(f) COMMUNITY PROPERTY LAWS.—This section shall be applied without regard to any community property laws.

[Sec. 530(g)]

(g) CUSTODIAL ACCOUNTS.—For purposes of this section, a custodial account shall be treated as a trust if the assets of such account are held by a bank (as defined in section 408(n)) or another person who demonstrates, to the satisfaction of the Secretary, that the manner in which he will administer the account will be consistent with the requirements of this section, and if the custodial account would, except for the fact that it is not a trust, constitute an account described in subsection (b)(1). For purposes of this title, in the case of a custodial account treated as a trust by reason of the preceding sentence, the custodian of such account shall be treated as the trustee thereof.

[Sec. 530(h)]

(h) REPORTS.—The trustee of a Coverdell education savings account shall make such reports regarding such account to the Secretary and to the beneficiary of the account with respect to contributions, distributions, and such other matters as the Secretary may require. The reports required by this subsection shall be filed at such time and in such manner and furnished to such individuals at such time and in such manner as may be required.

Subchapter G—Corporations Used to Avoid Income Tax on Shareholders

PART I—CORPORATIONS IMPROPERLY ACCUMULATING SURPLUS

[Sec. 531]

SEC. 531. IMPOSITION OF ACCUMULATED EARNINGS TAX.

In addition to other taxes imposed by this chapter, there is hereby imposed for each taxable year on the accumulated taxable income (as defined in section 535) of each corporation described in section 532, an accumulated earnings tax equal to 15 percent of the accumulated taxable income.

[Sec. 532]

SEC. 532. CORPORATIONS SUBJECT TO ACCUMULATED EARNINGS TAX.

[Sec. 532(a)]

(a) GENERAL RULE.—The accumulated earnings tax imposed by section 531 shall apply to every corporation (other than those described in subsection (b)) formed or availed of for the purpose of avoiding the income tax with respect to its shareholders or the shareholders of any other corporation, by permitting earnings and profits to accumulate instead of being divided or distributed.

[Sec. 532(b)]

(b) EXCEPTIONS.—The accumulated earnings tax imposed by section 531 shall not apply to—

(1) a personal holding company (as defined in section 542),

(2) a foreign personal holding company (as defined in section 552),

(3) a corporation exempt from tax under subchapter F (section 501 and following), or

(4) a passive foreign investment company (as defined in section 1297).

(c) APPLICATION DETERMINED WITHOUT REGARD TO NUMBER OF SHAREHOLDERS.—The application of this part to a corporation shall be determined without regard to the number of shareholders of such corporation.

Sec. 532(b)

[Sec. 533]

SEC. 533. EVIDENCE OF PURPOSE TO AVOID INCOME TAX.

[Sec. 533(a)]

(a) UNREASONABLE ACCUMULATION DETERMINATIVE OF PURPOSE.—For purposes of section 532, the fact that the earnings and profits of a corporation are permitted to accumulate beyond the reasonable needs of the business shall be determinative of the purpose to avoid the income tax with respect to shareholders, unless the corporation by the preponderance of the evidence shall prove to the contrary.

[Sec. 533(b)]

(b) HOLDING OR INVESTMENT COMPANY.—The fact that any corporation is a mere holding or investment company shall be prima facie evidence of the purpose to avoid the income tax with respect to shareholders.

[Sec. 534]

SEC. 534. BURDEN OF PROOF.

[Sec. 534(a)]

(a) GENERAL RULE.—In any proceeding before the Tax Court involving a notice of deficiency based in whole or in part on the allegation that all or any part of the earnings and profits have been permitted to accumulate beyond the reasonable needs of the business, the burden of proof with respect to such allegation shall—

(1) if notification has not been sent in accordance with subsection (b), be on the Secretary, or

(2) if the taxpayer has submitted the statement described in subsection (c), be on the Secretary with respect to the grounds set forth in such statement in accordance with the provisions of such subsection.

[Sec. 534(b)]

(b) NOTIFICATION BY SECRETARY.—Before mailing the notice of deficiency referred to in subsection (a), the Secretary may send by certified mail or registered mail a notification informing the taxpayer that the proposed notice of deficiency includes an amount with respect to the accumulated earnings tax imposed by section 531.

[Sec. 534(c)]

(c) STATEMENT BY TAXPAYER.—Within such time (but not less than 30 days) after the mailing of the notification described in subsection (b) as the Secretary may prescribe by regulations, the taxpayer may submit a statement of the grounds (together with facts sufficient to show the basis thereof) on which the taxpayer relies to establish that all or any part of the earnings and profits have not been permitted to accumulate beyond the reasonable needs of the business.

[Sec. 534(d)]

(d) JEOPARDY ASSESSMENT.—If pursuant to section 6861 (a) a jeopardy assessment is made before the mailing of the notice of deficiency referred to in subsection (a), for purposes of this section such notice of deficiency shall, to the extent that it informs the taxpayer that such deficiency includes the accumulated earnings tax imposed by section 531, constitute the notification described in subsection (b), and in that event the statement described in subsection (c) may be included in the taxpayer's petition to the Tax Court.

[Sec. 535]

SEC. 535. ACCUMULATED TAXABLE INCOME.

[Sec. 535(a)]

(a) DEFINITION.—For purposes of this subtitle, the term "accumulated taxable income" means the taxable income, adjusted in the manner provided in subsection (b), minus the sum of the dividends paid deduction (as defined in section 561) and the accumulated earnings credit (as defined in subsection (c)).

[Sec. 535(b)]

(b) ADJUSTMENTS TO TAXABLE INCOME.—For purposes of subsection (a), taxable income shall be adjusted as follows:

(1) TAXES.—There shall be allowed as a deduction Federal income and excess profits taxes and income, war profits, and excess profits taxes of foreign countries and possessions of the United States (to the extent not allowable as a deduction under section 275(a)(4)), accrued during the taxable year or deemed to be paid by a domestic corporation under section 902(a) or 960(a)(1) for the taxable year, but not including the accumulated earnings tax imposed by section 531, the personal holding company tax imposed by section 541, or the taxes imposed by corresponding sections of a prior income tax law.

(2) CHARITABLE CONTRIBUTIONS.—The deduction for charitable contributions provided under section 170 shall be allowed without regard to section 170(b)(2).

(3) SPECIAL DEDUCTIONS DISALLOWED.—The special deductions for corporations provided in part VIII (except section 248) of subchapter B (section 241 and following, relating to the deduction for dividends received by corporations, etc.) shall not be allowed.

(4) NET OPERATING LOSS.—The net operating loss deduction provided in section 172 shall not be allowed.

(5) CAPITAL LOSSES.—

(A) IN GENERAL.—Except as provided in subparagraph (B), there shall be allowed as a deduction an amount equal to the net capital loss for the taxable year (determined without regard to paragraph (7)(A)).

(B) RECAPTURE OF PREVIOUS DEDUCTIONS FOR CAPITAL GAINS.—The aggregate amount allowable as a deduction under subparagraph (A) for any taxable year shall be reduced by the lesser of—

(i) the nonrecaptured capital gains deductions, or

(ii) the amount of the accumulated earnings and profits of the corporation as of the close of the preceding taxable year.

(C) NONRECAPTURED CAPITAL GAINS DEDUCTIONS.—For purposes of subparagraph (B), the term "nonrecaptured capital gains deductions" means the excess of—

(i) the aggregate amount allowable as a deduction under paragraph (6) for preceding taxable years beginning after July 18, 1984, over

(ii) the aggregate of the reductions under subparagraph (B) for preceding taxable years.

(6) NET CAPITAL GAINS.—

(A) IN GENERAL.—There shall be allowed as a deduction—

(i) the net capital gain for the taxable year (determined with the application of paragraph (7)), reduced by

(ii) the taxes attributable to such net capital gain.

(B) ATTRIBUTABLE TAXES.—For purposes of subparagraph (A), the taxes attributable to the net capital gain shall be an amount equal to the difference between—

(i) the taxes imposed by this subtitle (except the tax imposed by this part) for the taxable year, and

(ii) such taxes computed for such year without including in taxable income the net capital gain for the taxable year (determined without the application of paragraph (7)).

(7) CAPITAL LOSS CARRYOVERS.—

(A) UNLIMITED CARRYFORWARD.—The net capital loss for any taxable year shall be treated as a short-term capital loss in the next taxable year.

(B) SECTION 1212 INAPPLICABLE.—No allowance shall be made for the capital loss carryback or carryforward provided in section 1212.

(8) SPECIAL RULES FOR MERE HOLDING OR INVESTMENT COMPANIES.—In the case of a mere holding or investment company—

(A) CAPITAL LOSS DEDUCTION, ETC., NOT ALLOWED.—Paragraphs (5) and (7)(A) shall not apply.

Sec. 535(b)

(B) DEDUCTION FOR CERTAIN OFFSETS.—There shall be allowed as a deduction the net short-term capital gain for the taxable year to the extent such gain does not exceed the amount of any capital loss carryover to such taxable year under section 1212 (determined without regard to paragraph (7)(B)).

(C) EARNINGS AND PROFITS.—For purposes of subchapter C, the accumulated earnings and profits at any time shall not be less than they would be if this subsection had applied to the computation of earnings and profits for all taxable years beginning after July 18, 1984.

(9) SPECIAL RULE FOR CAPITAL GAINS AND LOSSES OF FOREIGN CORPORATIONS.—In the case of a foreign corporation, paragraph (6) shall be applied by taking into account only gains and losses which are effectively connected with the conduct of a trade or business within the United States and are not exempt from tax under treaty.

[Sec. 535(c)]

(c) ACCUMULATED EARNINGS CREDIT.—

(1) GENERAL RULE.—For purposes of subsection (a), in the case of a corporation other than a mere holding or investment company the accumulated earnings credit is (A) an amount equal to such part of the earnings and profits for the taxable year as are retained for the reasonable needs of the business, minus (B) the deduction allowed by subsection (b)(6). For purposes of this paragraph, the amount of the earnings and profits for the taxable year which are retained is the amount by which the earnings and profits for the taxable year exceed the dividends paid deduction (as defined in section 561) for such year.

(2) MINIMUM CREDIT.—

(A) IN GENERAL.—The credit allowable under paragraph (1) shall in no case be less than the amount by which $250,000 exceeds the accumulated earnings and profits of the corporation at the close of the preceding taxable year.

(B) CERTAIN SERVICE CORPORATIONS.—In the case of a corporation the principal function of which is the performance of services in the field of health, law, engineering, architecture, accounting, actuarial science, performing arts, or consulting, subparagraph (A) shall be applied by substituting "$150,000" for "$250,000".

(3) HOLDING AND INVESTMENT COMPANIES.—In the case of a corporation which is a mere holding or investment company, the accumulated earnings credit is the amount (if any) by which $250,000 exceeds the accumulated earnings and profits of the corporation at the close of the preceding taxable year.

(4) ACCUMULATED EARNINGS AND PROFITS.—For purposes of paragraphs (2) and (3), the accumulated earnings and profits at the close of the preceding taxable year shall be reduced by the dividends which under section 563(a) (relating to dividends paid after the close of the taxable year) are considered as paid during such taxable year.

(5) CROSS REFERENCE.—

For denial of credit provided in paragraph (2) or (3) where multiple corporations are formed to avoid tax, see section 1551, and for limitation on such credit in the case of certain controlled corporations, see section 1561.

* * *

[Sec. 536]

SEC. 536. INCOME NOT PLACED ON ANNUAL BASIS.

Section 443(b) (relating to computation of tax on change of annual accounting period) shall not apply in the computation of the accumulated earnings tax imposed by section 531.

[Sec. 537]

SEC. 537. REASONABLE NEEDS OF THE BUSINESS.

[Sec. 537(a)]

(a) GENERAL RULE.—For purposes of this part, the term "reasonable needs of the business" includes—

(1) the reasonably anticipated needs of the business,

(2) the section 303 redemption needs of the business, and

(3) the excess business holdings redemption needs of the business.

Sec. 535(c)

[Sec. 537(b)]

(b) SPECIAL RULES.—For purposes of subsection (a)—

(1) SECTION 303 REDEMPTION NEEDS.—The term "section 303 redemption needs" means, with respect to the taxable year of the corporation in which a shareholder of the corporation died or any taxable year thereafter, the amount needed (or reasonably anticipated to be needed) to make a redemption of stock included in the gross estate of the decedent (but not in excess of the maximum amount of stock to which section 303(a) may apply).

(2) EXCESS BUSINESS HOLDINGS REDEMPTION NEEDS.—The term "excess business holdings redemption needs" means the amount needed (or reasonably anticipated to be needed) to redeem from a private foundation stock which—

(A) such foundation held on May 26, 1969 (or which was received by such foundation pursuant to a will or irrevocable trust to which section 4943(c)(5) applies), and

(B) constituted excess business holdings on May 26, 1969, or would have constituted excess business holdings as of such date if there were taken into account (i) stock received pursuant to a will or trust described in subparagraph (A), and (ii) the reduction in the total outstanding stock of the corporation which would have resulted solely from the redemption of stock held by the private foundation.

(3) OBLIGATIONS INCURRED TO MAKE REDEMPTIONS.—In applying paragraphs (1) and (2), the discharge of any obligation incurred to make a redemption described in such paragraphs shall be treated as the making of such redemption.

(4) PRODUCT LIABILITY LOSS RESERVES.—The accumulation of reasonable amounts for the payment of reasonably anticipated product liability losses (as defined in section 172(f)), as determined under regulations prescribed by the Secretary, shall be treated as accumulated for the reasonably anticipated needs of the business.

(5) NO INFERENCE AS TO PRIOR TAXABLE YEARS.—The application of this part to any taxable year before the first taxable year specified in paragraph (1) shall be made without regard to the fact that distributions in redemption coming within the terms of such paragraphs were subsequently made.

PART II—PERSONAL HOLDING COMPANIES

[Sec. 541]

SEC. 541. IMPOSITION OF PERSONAL HOLDING COMPANY TAX.

In addition to other taxes imposed by this chapter, there is hereby imposed for each taxable year on the undistributed personal holding company income (as defined in section 545) of every personal holding company (as defined in section 542) a personal holding company tax equal to 15 percent of the undistributed personal holding company income.

[Sec. 542]

SEC. 542. DEFINITION OF PERSONAL HOLDING COMPANY.

[Sec. 542(a)]

(a) GENERAL RULE.—For purposes of this subtitle, the term "personal holding company" means any corporation (other than a corporation described in subsection (c)) if—

(1) ADJUSTED ORDINARY GROSS INCOME REQUIREMENT.—At least 60 percent of its adjusted ordinary gross income (as defined in section 543(b)(2)) for the taxable year is personal holding company income (as defined in section 543(a)), and

(2) STOCK OWNERSHIP REQUIREMENT.—At any time during the last half of the taxable year more than 50 percent in value of its outstanding stock is owned, directly or indirectly, by or for not more than 5 individuals. For purposes of this paragraph, an organization described in section 401(a), 501(c)(17), or 509(a) or a portion of a trust permanently set aside or to be used exclusively for the purposes described in section 642(c) or a corresponding provision of a prior income tax law shall be considered an individual.

[Sec. 542(b)]

(b) CORPORATIONS FILING CONSOLIDATED RETURNS.—

(1) GENERAL RULE.—In the case of an affiliated group of corporations filing or required to file a consolidated return under section 1501 for any taxable year, the adjusted ordinary gross income requirement of subsection (a) (1) of this section shall, except as provided in paragraphs (2) and (3), be applied for such year with respect to the consolidated adjusted ordinary gross income and the consolidated personal holding company income of the affiliated group. No member of such an affiliated group shall be considered to meet such adjusted ordinary gross income requirement unless the affiliated group meets such requirement.

(2) INELIGIBLE AFFILIATED GROUP.—Paragraph (1) shall not apply to an affiliated group of corporations if—

(A) any member of the affiliated group of corporations (including the common parent corporation) derived 10 percent or more of its adjusted ordinary gross income for the taxable year from sources outside the affiliated group, and

(B) 80 percent or more of the amount described in subparagraph (A) consists of personal holding company income (as defined in section 543).

For purposes of this paragraph, section 543 shall be applied as if the amount described in subparagraph (A) were the adjusted ordinary gross income of the corporation.

(3) EXCLUDED CORPORATIONS.—Paragraph (1) shall not apply to an affiliated group of corporations if any member of the affiliated group (including the common parent corporation) is a corporation excluded from the definition of personal holding company under subsection (c).

(4) CERTAIN DIVIDEND INCOME RECEIVED BY A COMMON PARENT.—In applying paragraph (2) (A) and (B), personal holding company income and adjusted ordinary gross income shall not include dividends received by a common parent corporation from another corporation if—

(A) the common parent corporation owns, directly or indirectly, more than 50 percent of the outstanding voting stock of such other corporation, and

(B) such other corporation is not a personal holding company for the taxable year in which the dividends are paid.

* * *

[Sec. 542(c)]

(c) EXCEPTIONS.—The term "personal holding company" as defined in subsection (a) does not include—

(1) a corporation exempt from tax under subchapter F (sec. 501 and following);

(2) a bank as defined in section 581, or a domestic building and loan association within the meaning of section 7701(a)(19);

(3) a life insurance company;

(4) a surety company;

(5) a foreign personal holding company as defined in section 552;

(6) a lending or finance company if—

(A) 60 percent or more of its ordinary gross income (as defined in section 543(b)(1)) is derived directly from the active and regular conduct of a lending or finance business;

(B) the personal holding company income for the taxable year (computed without regard to income described in subsection (d)(3) and income derived directly from the active and regular conduct of a lending or finance business, and computed by including as personal holding company income the entire amount of the gross income from rents, royalties, produced film rents, and compensation for use of corporate property by shareholders) is not more than 20 percent of the ordinary gross income;

(C) the sum of the deductions which are directly allocable to the active and regular conduct of its lending or finance business equals or exceeds the sum of—

(i) 15 percent of so much of the ordinary gross income derived therefrom as does not exceed $500,000, plus

(ii) 5 percent of so much of the ordinary gross income derived therefrom as exceeds $500,000; and

(D) the loans to a person who is a shareholder in such company during the taxable year by or for whom 10 percent or more in value of its outstanding stock is owned directly or indirectly (including, in the case of an individual, stock owned by members of his family as defined in section 544(a)(2)), outstanding at any time during such year do not exceed $5,000 in principal amount;

(7) a foreign corporation (other than a corporation which has income to which section 543(a)(7) applies for the taxable year), if all of its stock outstanding during the last half of the taxable year is owned by nonresident alien individuals, whether directly or indirectly through foreign estates, foreign trusts, foreign partnerships, or other foreign corporations;

(8) a small business investment company which is licensed by the Small Business Administration and operating under the Small Business Investment Act of 1958 (15 U.S.C. 661 and following) and which is actively engaged in the business of providing funds to small business concerns under that Act. This paragraph shall not apply if any shareholder of the small business investment company owns at any time during the taxable year directly or indirectly (including, in the case of an individual, ownership by the members of his family as defined in section 544(a)(2)) a 5 per centum or more proprietary interest in a small business concern to which funds are provided by the investment company or 5 per centum or more in value of the outstanding stock of such concern;

(9) a corporation which is subject to the jurisdiction of the court in a title 11 or similar case (within the meaning of section 368(a)(3)(A)) unless a major purpose of instituting or continuing such case is the avoidance of the tax imposed by section 541; and

(10) a passive foreign investment company (as defined in section 1297).

* * *

[Sec. 543]

SEC. 543. PERSONAL HOLDING COMPANY INCOME.

[Sec. 543(a)]

(a) GENERAL RULE.—For purposes of this subtitle, the term "personal holding company income" means the portion of the adjusted ordinary gross income which consists of:

(1) DIVIDENDS, ETC.—Dividends, interest, royalties (other than mineral, oil, or gas royalties or copyright royalties), and annuities. This paragraph shall not apply to—

(A) interest constituting rent (as defined in subsection (b)(3)),

(B) interest on amounts set aside in a reserve fund under section 511 or 607 of the Merchant Marine Act, 1936 (46 U.S.C. App 1161 or 1177),

(C) active business computer software royalties (within the meaning of subsection (d)), and

(D) interest received by a broker or dealer (within the meaning of section 3(a)(4) or (5) of the Securities and Exchange Act of 1934) in connection with—

(i) any securities or money market instruments held as property described in section 1221(a)(1),

(ii) margin accounts, or

(iii) any financing for a customer secured by securities or money market instruments.

(2) RENTS.—The adjusted income from rents; except that such adjusted income shall not be included if—

(A) such adjusted income constitutes 50 percent or more of the adjusted ordinary gross income, and

(B) the sum of—

(i) the dividends paid during the taxable year (determined under section 562),

(ii) the dividends considered as paid on the last day of the taxable year under section 563(d) (as limited by the second sentence of section 563(b)), and

(iii) the consent dividends for the taxable year (determined under section 565),

equals or exceeds the amount, if any, by which the personal holding company income for the taxable year (computed without regard to this paragraph and paragraph (6), and computed by including as personal holding company income copyright royalties and the adjusted income from mineral, oil, and gas royalties) exceeds 10 percent of the ordinary gross income.

(3) MINERAL, OIL, AND GAS ROYALTIES.—The adjusted income from mineral, oil, and gas royalties; except that such adjusted income shall not be included if—

(A) such adjusted income constitutes 50 percent or more of the adjusted ordinary gross income,

(B) the personal holding company income for the taxable year (computed without regard to this paragraph, and computed by including as personal holding company income copyright royalties and the adjusted income from rents) is not more than 10 percent of the ordinary gross income, and

(C) the sum of the deductions which are allowable under section 162 (relating to trade or business expenses) other than—

(i) deductions for compensation for personal services rendered by the shareholders, and

(ii) deductions which are specifically allowable under sections other than section 162,

equals or exceeds 15 percent of the adjusted ordinary gross income.

(4) COPYRIGHT ROYALTIES.—Copyright royalties; except that copyright royalties shall not be included if—

(A) such royalties (exclusive of royalties received for the use of, or right to use, copyrights or interests in copyrights on works created in whole, or in part, by any shareholder) constitute 50 percent or more of the ordinary gross income,

(B) the personal holding company income for the taxable year computed—

(i) without regard to copyright royalties, other than royalties received for the use of, or right to use, copyrights or interests in copyrights in works created in whole, or in part, by any shareholder owning more than 10 percent of the total outstanding capital stock of the corporation,

(ii) without regard to dividends from any corporation in which the taxpayer owns at least 50 percent of all classes of stock entitled to vote and at least 50 percent of the total value of all classes of stock and which corporation meets the requirements of this subparagraph and subparagraphs (A) and (C), and

(iii) by including as personal holding company income the adjusted income from rents and the adjusted income from mineral, oil, and gas royalties,

is not more than 10 percent of the ordinary gross income, and

(C) the sum of the deductions which are properly allocable to such royalties and which are allowable under section 162, other than—

(i) deductions for compensation for personal services rendered by the shareholders,

(ii) deductions for royalties paid or accrued, and

(iii) deductions which are specifically allowable under sections other than section 162,

equals or exceeds 25 percent of the amount by which the ordinary gross income exceeds the sum of the royalties paid or accrued and the amounts allowable as deductions under section 167 (relating to depreciation) with respect to copyright royalties.

For purposes of this subsection, the term "copyright royalties" means compensation, however designated, for the use of, or the right to use, copyrights in works protected by copyright issued under title 17 of the United States Code and to which copyright protection is also extended by the laws of any country other than the United States of America by virtue of any international treaty, convention, or agreement, or interests in any such copyrighted works, and includes payments from any person for performing rights in any such copyrighted work and payments (other than produced film rents as defined in paragraph (5)(B)) received for the use of, or right to use, films. For purposes of this paragraph, the term "shareholder" shall include any person who owns stock within the meaning of section 544. This paragraph shall not apply to active business computer software royalties.

(5) PRODUCED FILM RENTS.—

(A) Produced film rents; except that such rents shall not be included if such rents constitute 50 percent or more of the ordinary gross income.

(B) For purposes of this section, the term "produced film rents" means payments received with respect to an interest in a film for the use of, or right to use, such film, but only to the extent that such interest was acquired before substantial completion of production of such film. In the

Sec. 543(a)

case of a producer who actively participates in the production of the film, such term includes an interest in the proceeds or profits from the film, but only to the extent such interest is attributable to such active participation.

(6) USE OF CORPORATE PROPERTY BY SHAREHOLDER.—

(A) Amounts received as compensation (however designated and from whomever received) for the use of, or the right to use, tangible property of the corporation in any case where, at any time during the taxable year, 25 percent or more in value of the outstanding stock of the corporation is owned, directly or indirectly, by or for an individual entitled to the use of the property (whether such right is obtained directly from the corporation or by means of a sublease or other arrangement).

(B) Subparagraph (A) shall apply only to a corporation which has personal holding company income in excess of 10 percent of its ordinary gross income.

(C) For purposes of the limitation in subparagraph (B), personal holding company income shall be computed—

(i) without regard to subparagraph (A) or paragraph (2),

(ii) by excluding amounts received as compensation for the use of (or right to use) intangible property (other than mineral, oil, or gas royalties or copyright royalties) if a substantial part of the tangible property used in connection with such intangible property is owned by the corporation and all such tangible and intangible property is used in the active conduct of a trade or business by an individual or individuals described in subparagraph (A), and

(iii) by including copyright royalties and adjusted income from mineral, oil, and gas royalties.

(7) PERSONAL SERVICE CONTRACTS.—

(A) Amounts received under a contract under which the corporation is to furnish personal services; if some person other than the corporation has the right to designate (by name or by description) the individual who is to perform the services, or if the individual who is to perform the services is designated (by name or by description) in the contract; and

(B) amounts received from the sale or other disposition of such a contract.

This paragraph shall apply with respect to amounts received for services under a particular contract only if at some time during the taxable year 25 percent or more in value of the outstanding stock of the corporation is owned, directly or indirectly, by or for the individual who has performed, is to perform, or may be designated (by name or by description) as the one to perform, such services.

(8) ESTATES AND TRUSTS.—Amounts includible in computing the taxable income of the corporation under part I of subchapter J (sec. 641 and following, relating to estates, trusts, and beneficiaries).

[Sec. 543(b)]

(b) DEFINITIONS.—For purposes of this part—

(1) ORDINARY GROSS INCOME.—The term "ordinary gross income" means the gross income determined by excluding—

(A) all gains from the sale or other disposition of capital assets,

(B) all gains (other than those referred to in subparagraph (A)) from the sale or other disposition of property described in section 1231(b), and

(C) in the case of a foreign corporation all of the outstanding stock of which during the last half of the taxable year is owned by nonresident alien individuals (whether directly or indirectly through foreign estates, foreign trusts, foreign partnerships, or other foreign corporations), all items of income which would, but for this subparagraph, constitute personal holding company income under any paragraph of subsection (a) other than paragraph (7) thereof.

(2) ADJUSTED ORDINARY GROSS INCOME.—The term "adjusted ordinary gross income" means the ordinary gross income adjusted as follows:

(A) RENTS.—From the gross income from rents (as defined in the second sentence of paragraph (3) of this subsection) subtract the amount allowable as deductions for—

(i) exhaustion, wear and tear, obsolescence, and amortization of property other than tangible personal property which is not customarily retained by any one lessee for more than three years,

(ii) property taxes,

(iii) interest, and

(iv) rent,

to the extent allocable, under regulations prescribed by the Secretary, to such gross income from rents. The amount subtracted under this subparagraph shall not exceed such gross income from rents.

(B) MINERAL ROYALTIES, ETC.—From the gross income from mineral, oil, and gas royalties described in paragraph (4), and from the gross income from working interests in an oil or gas well, subtract the amount allowable as deductions for—

(i) exhaustion, wear and tear, obsolescence, amortization, and depletion,

(ii) property and severance taxes,

(iii) interest, and

(iv) rent,

to the extent allocable, under regulations prescribed by the Secretary, to such gross income from royalties or such gross income from working interests in oil or gas wells. The amount subtracted under this subparagraph with respect to royalties shall not exceed the gross income from such royalties, and the amount subtracted under this subparagraph with respect to working interests shall not exceed the gross income from such working interests.

(C) INTEREST.—There shall be excluded—

(i) interest received on a direct obligation of the United States held for sale to customers in the ordinary course of trade or business by a regular dealer who is making a primary market in such obligations, and

(ii) interest on a condemnation award, a judgment, and a tax refund.

(D) CERTAIN EXCLUDED RENTS.—From the gross income consisting of compensation described in subparagraph (D) of paragraph (3) subtract the amount allowable as deductions for the items described in clauses (i), (ii), (iii), and (iv) of subparagraph (A) to the extent allocable, under regulations prescribed by the Secretary, to such gross income. The amount subtracted under this subparagraph shall not exceed such gross income.

(3) ADJUSTED INCOME FROM RENTS.—The term "adjusted income from rents" means the gross income from rents, reduced by the amount subtracted under paragraph (2)(A) of this subsection. For purposes of the preceding sentence, the term "rents" means compensation, however designated, for the use of, or right to use, property, and the interest on debts owed to the corporation, to the extent such debts represent the price for which real property held primarily for sale to customers in the ordinary course of its trade or business was sold or exchanged by the corporation; but such term does not include—

(A) amounts constituting personal holding company income under subsection (a)(6),

(B) copyright royalties (as defined in subsection (a)(4)),

(C) produced film rents (as defined in subsection (a)(5)(B)),

(D) compensation, however designated, for the use of, or the right to use, any tangible personal property manufactured or produced by the taxpayer, if during the taxable year the taxpayer is engaged in substantial manufacturing or production of tangible personal property of the same type, or

(E) active business computer software royalties (as defined in subsection (d)).

(4) ADJUSTED INCOME FROM MINERAL, OIL, AND GAS ROYALTIES.—The term "adjusted income from mineral, oil, and gas royalties" means the gross income from mineral, oil, and gas royalties (including production payments and overriding royalties), reduced by the amount subtracted under paragraph (2)(B) of this subsection in respect of such royalties.

* * *

Sec. 543(b)

[Sec. 544]

SEC. 544. RULES FOR DETERMINING STOCK OWNERSHIP.

[Sec. 544(a)]

(a) CONSTRUCTIVE OWNERSHIP.—For purposes of determining whether a corporation is a personal holding company, insofar as such determination is based on stock ownership under section 542(a)(2), section 543(a)(7), section 543(a)(6) or section 543(a)(4)—

(1) STOCK NOT OWNED BY INDIVIDUAL.—Stock owned, directly or indirectly, by or for a corporation, partnership, estate, or trust shall be considered as being owned proportionately by its shareholders, partners, or beneficiaries.

(2) FAMILY AND PARTNERSHIP OWNERSHIP.—An individual shall be considered as owning the stock owned, directly or indirectly, by or for his family or by or for his partner. For purposes of this paragraph, the family of an individual includes only his brothers and sisters (whether by the whole or half blood), spouse, ancestors, and lineal descendants.

(3) OPTIONS.—If any person has an option to acquire stock, such stock shall be considered as owned by such person. For purposes of this paragraph, an option to acquire such an option, and each one of a series of such options, shall be considered as an option to acquire such stock.

(4) APPLICATION OF FAMILY-PARTNERSHIP AND OPTION RULES.—Paragraphs (2) and (3) shall be applied—

(A) for purposes of the stock ownership requirement provided in section 542(a)(2), if, but only if, the effect is to make the corporation a personal holding company;

(B) for purposes of section 543(a)(7) (relating to personal service contracts), of section 543(a)(6) (relating to the use of property by shareholders), or of section 543(a)(4) (relating to copyright royalties), if, but only if, the effect is to make the amounts therein referred to includible under such paragraph as personal holding company income.

(5) CONSTRUCTIVE OWNERSHIP AS ACTUAL OWNERSHIP.—Stock constructively owned by a person by reason of the application of paragraph (1) or (3) shall, for purposes of applying paragraph (1) or (2), be treated as actually owned by such person; but stock constructively owned by an individual by reason of the application of paragraph (2) shall not be treated as owned by him for purposes of again applying such paragraph in order to make another the constructive owner of such stock.

(6) OPTION RULE IN LIEU OF FAMILY AND PARTNERSHIP RULE.—If stock may be considered as owned by an individual under either paragraph (2) or (3) it shall be considered as owned by him under paragraph (3).

[Sec. 544(b)]

(b) CONVERTIBLE SECURITIES.—Outstanding securities convertible into stock (whether or not convertible during the taxable year) shall be considered as outstanding stock—

(1) for purposes of the stock ownership requirement provided in section 542(a)(2), but only if the effect of the inclusion of all such securities is to make the corporation a personal holding company;

(2) for purposes of section 543(a)(7) (relating to personal service contracts), but only if the effect of the inclusion of all such securities is to make the amounts therein referred to includible under such paragraph as personal holding company income;

(3) for purposes of section 543(a)(6) (relating to the use of property by shareholders), but only if the effect of the inclusion of all such securities is to make the amounts therein referred to includible under such paragraph as personal holding company income; and

(4) for purposes of section 543(a)(4) (relating to copyright royalties), but only if the effect of the inclusion of all such securities is to make the amounts therein referred to includible under such paragraph as personal holding company income.

The requirement in paragraphs (1), (2), (3), and (4) that all convertible securities must be included if any are to be included shall be subject to the exception that, where some of the outstanding securities are convertible only after a later date than in the case of others, the class having the earlier conversion date may be included although the others are not included, but no convertible securities shall be included unless all outstanding securities having a prior conversion date are also included.

Sec. 544(b)

SEC. 545. UNDISTRIBUTED PERSONAL HOLDING COMPANY INCOME.

[Sec. 545(a)]

(a) DEFINITION.—For purposes of this part, the term "undistributed personal holding company income" means the taxable income of a personal holding company adjusted in the manner provided in subsections (b), (c), and (d), minus the dividends paid deduction as defined in section 561. In the case of a personal holding company which is a foreign corporation, not more than 10 percent in value of the outstanding stock of which is owned (within the meaning of section 958(a)) during the last half of the taxable year by United States persons, the term "undistributed personal holding company income" means the amount determined by multiplying the undistributed personal holding company income (determined without regard to this sentence) by the percentage in value of its outstanding stock which is the greatest percentage in value of its outstanding stock so owned by United States persons on any one day during such period.

[Sec. 545(b)]

(b) ADJUSTMENTS TO TAXABLE INCOME.—For the purposes of subsection (a), the taxable income shall be adjusted as follows:

(1) TAXES.—There shall be allowed as a deduction Federal income and excess profits taxes and income, war profits and excess profits taxes of foreign countries and possessions of the United States (to the extent not allowable as a deduction under section 275(a)(4)), accrued during the taxable year or deemed to be paid by a domestic corporation under section 902(a) or 960(a)(1) for the taxable year, but not including the accumulated earnings tax imposed by section 531, the personal holding company tax imposed by section 541, or the taxes imposed by corresponding sections of a prior income tax law.

(2) CHARITABLE CONTRIBUTIONS.—The deduction for charitable contributions provided under section 170 shall be allowed, but in computing such deduction the limitations in section 170(b)(1)(A), (B), and (D) shall apply, and section 170(b)(2) and (d)(1) shall not apply. For purposes of this paragraph, the term "contribution base" when used in section 170(b)(1) means the taxable income computed with the adjustments (other than the 10-percent limitation) provided in section 170(b)(2) and (d)(1) and without deduction of the amount disallowed under paragraph (6) of this subsection.

(3) SPECIAL DEDUCTIONS DISALLOWED.—The special deductions for corporations provided in part VIII (except section 248) of subchapter B (section 241 and following, relating to the deduction for dividends received by corporations, etc.) shall not be allowed.

(4) NET OPERATING LOSS.—The net operating loss deduction provided in section 172 shall not be allowed, but there shall be allowed as a deduction the amount of the net operating loss (as defined in section 172 (c)) for the preceding taxable year computed without the deductions provided in part VIII (except section 248) of subchapter B.

(5) NET CAPITAL GAINS.—There shall be allowed as a deduction the net capital gain for the taxable year, minus the taxes imposed by this subtitle attributable to such excess. The taxes attributable to such net capital gain shall be an amount equal to the difference between—

(A) the taxes imposed by this subtitle (except the tax imposed by this part) for such year, and

(B) such taxes computed for such year without including such net capital gain in taxable income.

(6) EXPENSES AND DEPRECIATION APPLICABLE TO PROPERTY OF THE TAXPAYER.—The aggregate of the deductions allowed under section 162 (relating to trade or business expenses) and section 167 (relating to depreciation), which are allocable to the operation and maintenance of property owned or operated by the corporation, shall be allowed only in an amount equal to the rent or other compensation received for the use of, or the right to use, the property, unless it is established (under regulations prescribed by the Secretary) to the satisfaction of the Secretary—

(A) that the rent or other compensation received was the highest obtainable, or, if none was received, that none was obtainable;

(B) that the property was held in the course of a business carried on bona fide for profit; and

Sec. 545

(C) either that there was reasonable expectation that the operation of the property would result in a profit, or that the property was necessary to the conduct of the business.

* * *

[Sec. 546]

SEC. 546. INCOME NOT PLACED ON ANNUAL BASIS.

Section 443 (b) (relating to computation of tax on change of annual accounting period) shall not apply in the computation of the personal holding company tax imposed by section 541.

[Sec. 547]

SEC. 547. DEDUCTION FOR DEFICIENCY DIVIDENDS.

[Sec. 547(a)]

(a) GENERAL RULE.—If a determination (as defined in subsection (c)) with respect to a taxpayer establishes liability for personal holding company tax imposed by section 541 (or by a corresponding provision of a prior income tax law) for any taxable year, a deduction shall be allowed to the taxpayer for the amount of deficiency dividends (as defined in subsection (d)) for the purpose of determining the personal holding company tax for such year, but not for the purpose of determining interest, additional amounts, or assessable penalties computed with respect to such personal holding company tax.

[Sec. 547(b)]

(b) RULES FOR APPLICATION OF SECTION.—

(1) ALLOWANCE OF DEDUCTION.—The deficiency dividend deduction shall be allowed as of the date the claim for the deficiency dividend deduction is filed.

(2) CREDIT OR REFUND.—If the allowance of a deficiency dividend deduction results in an overpayment of personal holding company tax for any taxable year, credit or refund with respect to such overpayment shall be made as if on the date of the determination 2 years remained before the expiration of the period of limitation on the filing of claim for refund for the taxable year to which the overpayment relates. No interest shall be allowed on a credit or refund arising from the application of this section.

[Sec. 547(c)]

(c) DETERMINATION.—For purposes of this section, the term "determination" means—

(1) a decision by the Tax Court or a judgment, decree, or other order by any court of competent jurisdiction, which has become final;

(2) a closing agreement made under section 7121; or

(3) under regulations prescribed by the Secretary, an agreement signed by the Secretary and by, or on behalf of, the taxpayer relating to the liability of such taxpayer for personal holding company tax.

[Sec. 547(d)]

(d) DEFICIENCY DIVIDENDS.—

(1) DEFINITION.—For purposes of this section, the term "deficiency dividends" means the amount of the dividends paid by the corporation on or after the date of the determination and before filing claim under subsection (e), which would have been includible in the computation of the deduction for dividends paid under section 561 for the taxable year with respect to which the liability for personal holding company tax exists, if distributed during such taxable year. No dividends shall be considered as deficiency dividends for purposes of subsection (a) unless distributed within 90 days after the determination.

(2) EFFECT ON DIVIDENDS PAID DEDUCTION.—

(A) FOR TAXABLE YEAR IN WHICH PAID.—Deficiency dividends paid in any taxable year (to the extent of the portion thereof taken into account under subsection (a) in determining personal holding company tax) shall not be included in the amount of dividends paid for such year for purposes of computing the dividends paid deduction for such year and succeeding years.

(B) FOR PRIOR TAXABLE YEAR.—Deficiency dividends paid in any taxable year (to the extent of the portion thereof taken into account under subsection (a) in determining personal holding company tax) shall not be allowed for purposes of section 563 (b) in the computation of the dividends paid deduction for the taxable year preceding the taxable year in which paid.

[Sec. 547(e)]

(e) CLAIM REQUIRED.—No deficiency dividend deduction shall be allowed under subsection (a) unless (under regulations prescribed by the Secretary) claim therefor is filed within 120 days after the determination.

[Sec. 547(f)]

(f) SUSPENSION OF STATUTE OF LIMITATIONS AND STAY OF COLLECTION.—

(1) SUSPENSION OF RUNNING OF STATUTE.—If the corporation files a claim, as provided in subsection (e), the running of the statute of limitations provided in section 6501 on the making of assessments, and the bringing of distraint or a proceeding in court for collection, in respect of the deficiency and all interest, additional amounts, or assessable penalties, shall be suspended for a period of 2 years after the date of the determination.

(2) STAY OF COLLECTION.—In the case of any deficiency with respect to the tax imposed by section 541 established by a determination under this section—

(A) the collection of the deficiency and all interest, additional amounts, and assessable penalties shall, except in cases of jeopardy, be stayed until the expiration of 120 days after the date of the determination, and

(B) if claim for deficiency dividend deduction is filed under subsection (e), the collection of such part of the deficiency as is not reduced by the deduction for deficiency dividends provided in subsection (a) shall be stayed until the date the claim is disallowed (in whole or in part), and if disallowed in part collection shall be made only with respect to the part disallowed.

No distraint or proceeding in court shall be begun for the collection of an amount the collection of which is stayed under subparagraph (A) or (B) during the period for which the collection of such amount is stayed.

[Sec. 547(g)]

(g) DEDUCTION DENIED IN CASE OF FRAUD, ETC.—No deficiency dividend deduction shall be allowed under subsection (a) if the determination contains a finding that any part of the deficiency is due to fraud with intent to evade tax, or to wilful failure to file an income tax return within the time prescribed by law or prescribed by the Secretary in pursuance of law.

PART IV—DEDUCTION FOR DIVIDENDS PAID

[Sec. 561]

SEC. 561. DEFINITION OF DEDUCTION FOR DIVIDENDS PAID.

[Sec. 561(a)]

(a) GENERAL RULE.—The deduction for dividends paid shall be the sum of—

(1) the dividends paid during the taxable year,

(2) the consent dividends for the taxable year (determined under section 565), and

(3) in the case of a personal holding company, the dividend carryover described in section 564.

[Sec. 561(b)]

(b) SPECIAL RULES APPLICABLE.—In determining the deduction for dividends paid, the rules provided in section 562 (relating to rules applicable in determining dividends eligible for dividends paid deduction) and section 563 (relating to dividends paid after the close of the taxable year) shall be applicable.

[Sec. 562]

SEC. 562. RULES APPLICABLE IN DETERMINING DIVIDENDS ELIGIBLE FOR DIVIDENDS PAID DEDUCTION.

[Sec. 562(a)]

(a) GENERAL RULE.—For purposes of this part, the term "dividend" shall, except as otherwise provided in this section, include only dividends described in section 316 (relating to definition of dividends for purposes of corporate distributions).

[Sec. 562(b)]

(b) DISTRIBUTIONS IN LIQUIDATION.—

(1) Except in the case of a personal holding company described in section 542 or a foreign personal holding company described in section 552—

(A) in the case of amounts distributed in liquidation, the part of such distribution which is properly chargeable to earnings and profits accumulated after February 28, 1913, shall be treated as a dividend for purposes of computing the dividends paid deduction, and

(B) in the case of a complete liquidation occurring within 24 months after the adoption of a plan of liquidation, any distribution within such period pursuant to such plan shall, to the extent of the earnings and profits (computed without regard to capital losses) of the corporation for the taxable year in which such distribution is made, be treated as a dividend for purposes of computing the dividends paid deduction.

For purposes of subparagraph (A), a liquidation includes a redemption of stock to which section 302 applies. Except to the extent provided in regulations, the preceding sentence shall not apply in the case of any mere holding or investment company which is not a regulated investment company.

(2) In the case of a complete liquidation of a personal holding company occurring within 24 months after the adoption of a plan of liquidation, the amount of any distribution within such period pursuant to such plan shall be treated as a dividend for purposes of computing the dividends paid deduction, to the extent that such amount is distributed to corporate distributees and represents such corporate distributees' allocable share of the undistributed personal holding company income for the taxable year of such distribution computed without regard to this paragraph and without regard to subparagraph (B) of section 316(b)(2).

[Sec. 562(c)]

(c) PREFERENTIAL DIVIDENDS.—The amount of any distribution shall not be considered as a dividend for purposes of computing the dividends paid deduction, unless such distribution is pro rata, with no preference to any share of stock as compared with other shares of the same class, and with no preference to one class of stock as compared with another class except to the extent that the former is entitled (without reference to waivers of their rights by shareholders) to such preference. In the case of a distribution by a regulated investment company to a shareholder who made an initial investment of at least $10,000,000 in such company, such distribution shall not be treated as not being pro rata or as being preferential solely by reason of an increase in the distribution by reason of reductions in administrative expenses of the company.

[Sec. 562(d)]

(d) DISTRIBUTIONS BY A MEMBER OF AN AFFILIATED GROUP.—In the case where a corporation which is a member of an affiliated group of corporations filing or required to file a consolidated return for a taxable year is required to file a separate personal holding company schedule for such taxable year, a distribution by such corporation to another member of the affiliated group shall be considered as a dividend for purposes of computing the dividends paid deduction if such distribution would constitute a dividend under the other provisions of this section to a recipient which is not a member of an affiliated group.

* * *

[Sec. 563]

SEC. 563. RULES RELATING TO DIVIDENDS PAID AFTER CLOSE OF TAXABLE YEAR.

[Sec. 563(a)]

(a) ACCUMULATED EARNINGS TAX.—In the determination of the dividends paid deduction for purposes of the accumulated earnings tax imposed by section 531, a dividend paid after the close of any taxable year and on or before the 15th day of the third month following the close of such taxable year shall be considered as paid during such taxable year.

[Sec. 563(b)]

(b) PERSONAL HOLDING COMPANY TAX.—In the determination of the dividends paid deduction for purposes of the personal holding company tax imposed by section 541, a dividend paid after the close of any taxable year and on or before the 15th day of the third month following the close of such taxable year shall, to the extent the taxpayer elects in its return for the taxable year, be considered as paid during such taxable year. The amount allowed as a dividend by reason of the application of this subsection with respect to any taxable year shall not exceed either—

(1) The undistributed personal holding company income of the corporation for the taxable year, computed without regard to this subsection, or

(2) 20 percent of the sum of the dividends paid during the taxable year, computed without regard to this subsection.

* * *

[Sec. 563(d)]

(d) DIVIDENDS CONSIDERED AS PAID ON LAST DAY OF TAXABLE YEAR.—For the purpose of applying section 562(a), with respect to distributions under subsection (a), (b), or (c) of this section, a distribution made after the close of a taxable year and on or before the 15th day of the third month following the close of the taxable year shall be considered as made on the last day of such taxable year.

[Sec. 564]

SEC. 564. DIVIDEND CARRYOVER.

[Sec. 564(a)]

(a) GENERAL RULE.—For purposes of computing the dividends paid deduction under section 561, in the case of a personal holding company the dividend carryover for any taxable year shall be the dividend carryover to such taxable year, computed as provided in subsection (b), from the two preceding taxable years.

[Sec. 564(b)]

(b) COMPUTATION OF DIVIDEND CARRYOVER.—The dividend carryover to the taxable year shall be determined as follows:

(1) For each of the 2 preceding taxable years there shall be determined the taxable income computed with the adjustments provided in section 545 (whether or not the taxpayer was a personal holding company for either of such preceding taxable years), and there shall also be determined for each such year the deduction for dividends paid during such year as provided in section 561 (but determined without regard to the dividend carryover to such year).

(2) There shall be determined for each such taxable year whether there is an excess of such taxable income over such deduction for dividends paid or an excess of such deduction for dividends paid over such taxable income, and the amount of each such excess.

(3) If there is an excess of such deductions for dividends paid over such taxable income for the first preceding taxable year, such excess shall be allowed as a dividend carryover to the taxable year.

(4) If there is an excess of such deduction for dividends paid over such taxable income for the second preceding taxable year, such excess shall be reduced by the amount determined in paragraph (5), and the remainder of such excess shall be allowed as a dividend carryover to the taxable year.

(5) The amount of the reduction specified in paragraph (4) shall be the amount of the excess of the taxable income, if any, for the first preceding taxable year over such deduction for dividends paid, if any, for the first preceding taxable year.

[Sec. 565]

SEC. 565. CONSENT DIVIDENDS.

[Sec. 565(a)]

(a) GENERAL RULE.—If any person owns consent stock (as defined in subsection (f)(1)) in a corporation on the last day of the taxable year of such corporation, and such person agrees, in a consent filed with the return of such corporation in accordance with regulations prescribed by the Secretary, to treat as a dividend the amount specified in such consent, the amount so specified shall, except as provided in subsection (b), constitute a consent dividend for purposes of section 561 (relating to the deduction for dividends paid).

[Sec. 565(b)]

(b) LIMITATIONS.—A consent dividend shall not include—

(1) an amount specified in a consent which, if distributed in money, would constitute, or be part of, a distribution which would be disqualified for purposes of the dividends paid deduction under section 562(c) (relating to preferential dividends), or

(2) an amount specified in a consent which would not constitute a dividend (as defined in section 316) if the total amounts specified in consents filed by the corporation had been distributed in money to shareholders on the last day of the taxable year of such corporation.

[Sec. 565(c)]

(c) EFFECT OF CONSENT.—The amount of a consent dividend shall be considered, for purposes of this title—

(1) as distributed in money by the corporation to the shareholder on the last day of the taxable year of the corporation, and

(2) as contributed to the capital of the corporation by the shareholder on such day.

[Sec. 565(d)]

(d) CONSENT DIVIDENDS AND OTHER DISTRIBUTIONS.—If a distribution by a corporation consists in part of money or other property, the entire amount specified in the consents and the amount of such money or other property shall be considered together for purposes of applying this title.

* * *

[Sec. 565(f)]

(f) DEFINITIONS.—

(1) CONSENT STOCK.—Consent stock, for purposes of this section, means the class or classes of stock entitled, after the payment of preferred dividends, to a share in the distribution (other than in complete or partial liquidation) within the taxable year of all the remaining earnings and profits, which share constitutes the same proportion of such distribution regardless of the amount of such distribution.

(2) PREFERRED DIVIDENDS.—Preferred dividends, for purposes of this section, means a distribution (other than in complete or partial liquidation), limited in amount, which must be made on any class of stock before a further distribution (other than in complete or partial liquidation) of earnings and profits may be made within the taxable year.

Sec. 565(f)

Subchapter I—Natural Resources

PART I—DEDUCTIONS

[Sec. 611]

SEC. 611. ALLOWANCE OF DEDUCTION FOR DEPLETION.

[Sec. 611(a)]

(a) GENERAL RULE.—In the case of mines, oil and gas wells, other natural deposits, and timber, there shall be allowed as a deduction in computing taxable income a reasonable allowance for depletion and for depreciation of improvements, according to the peculiar conditions in each case; such reasonable allowance in all cases to be made under regulations prescribed by Secretary. For purposes of this part, the term "mines" includes deposits of waste or residue, the extraction of ores or minerals from which is treated as mining under section 613 (c). In any case in which it is ascertained as a result of operations or of development work that the recoverable units are greater or less than the prior estimate thereof, then such prior estimate (but not the basis for depletion) shall be revised and the allowance under this section for subsequent taxable years shall be based on such revised estimate.

[Sec. 611(b)]

(b) SPECIAL RULES.—

(1) LEASES.—In the case of a lease, the deduction under this section shall be equitably apportioned between the lessor and lessee.

(2) LIFE TENANT AND REMAINDERMAN.—In the case of property held by one person for life with remainder to another person, the deduction under this section shall be computed as if the life tenant were the absolute owner of the property and shall be allowed to the life tenant.

(3) PROPERTY HELD IN TRUST.—In the case of property held in trust, the deduction under this section shall be apportioned between the income beneficiaries and the trustee in accordance with the pertinent provisions of the instrument creating the trust, or, in the absence of such provisions, on the basis of the trust income allocable to each.

(4) PROPERTY HELD BY ESTATE.—In the case of an estate, the deduction under this section shall be apportioned between the estate and the heirs, legatees, and devisees on the basis of the income of the estate allocable to each.

[Sec. 611(c)]

(c) CROSS REFERENCE.—

For other rules applicable to depreciation of improvements, see section 167.

[Sec. 612]

SEC. 612. BASIS FOR COST DEPLETION.

Except as otherwise provided in this subchapter, the basis on which depletion is to be allowed in respect of any property shall be the adjusted basis provided in section 1011 for the purpose of determining the gain upon the sale or other disposition of such property.

[Sec. 613]

SEC. 613. PERCENTAGE DEPLETION.

[Sec. 613(a)]

(a) GENERAL RULE.—In the case of the mines, wells, and other natural deposits listed in subsection (b), the allowance for depletion under section 611 shall be the percentage, specified in subsection (b), of the gross income from the property excluding from such gross income an amount equal to any rents or royalties paid or incurred by the taxpayer in respect of the property. Such allowance shall not exceed 50 percent (100 percent in the case of oil and gas properties) of the taxpayer's taxable income from the property (computed without allowances for depletion). For purposes of the preceding sentence, the allowable deductions taken into account with respect to expenses of mining in computing the taxable income from the property shall be decreased by an amount equal to so much of any gain which (1) is treated under section 1245 (relating to gain from disposition of certain depreciable property) as ordinary income, and (2) is properly allocable to the property. In no case shall the allowance for depletion under section 611 be less than it would be if computed without reference to this section.

[Sec. 613(b)]

(b) PERCENTAGE DEPLETION RATES.—The mines, wells, and other natural deposits, and the percentages, referred to in subsection (a) are as follows:

(1) 22 PERCENT—

(A) sulphur and uranium; and

(B) if from deposits in the United States—anorthosite, clay, laterite, and nephelite syenite (to the extent that alumina and aluminum compounds are extracted therefrom), asbestos, bauxite, celestite, chromite, corundum, fluorspar, graphite, ilmenite, kyanite, mica, olivine, quartz crystals (radio grade), rutile, block steatite talc, and zircon, and ores of the following metals: antimony, beryllium, bismuth, cadmium, cobalt, columbium, lead, lithium, manganese, mercury, molybdenum, nickel, platinum and platinum group metals, tantalum, thorium, tin, titanium, tungsten, vanadium, and zinc.

(2) 15 PERCENT—If from deposits in the United States—

(A) gold, silver, copper, and iron ore, and

(B) oil shale (except shale described in paragraph (5)).

(3) 14 PERCENT—

(A) metal mines (if paragraph (1)(B) or (2)(A) does not apply), rock asphalt, and vermiculite; and

(B) if paragraph (1)(B), (5), or (6)(B) does not apply, ball clay, bentonite, china clay, sagger clay, and clay used or sold for use for purposes dependent on its refractory properties.

(4) 10 PERCENT—asbestos (if paragraph (1)(B) does not apply), brucite, coal, lignite, perlite, sodium chloride, and wollastonite.

(5) 7½ PERCENT—clay and shale used or sold for use in the manufacture of sewer pipe or brick, and clay, shale, and slate used or sold for use as sintered or burned lightweight aggregates.

(6) 5 PERCENT—

(A) gravel, peat, pumice, sand, scoria, shale (except shale described in paragraph (2)(B) or (5)), and stone (except stone described in paragraph (7));

(B) clay used, or sold for use, in the manufacture of drainage and roofing tile, flower pots, and kindred products; and

(C) if from brine wells—bromine, calcium chloride, and magnesium chloride.

(7) 14 PERCENT— all other minerals, including, but not limited to, aplite, barite, borax, calcium carbonates, diatomaceous earth, dolomite, feldspar, fullers earth, garnet, gilsonite, granite, limestone, magnesite, magnesium carbonates, marble, mollusk shells (including clam shells and oyster shells), phosphate rock, potash, quartzite, slate, soapstone, stone (used or sold for use by the mine owner or operator as dimension stone or ornamental stone), thenardite, tripoli, trona, and (if paragraph (1)(B) does not apply) bauxite, flake graphite, fluorspar, lepidolite, mica, spodumene, and talc (including pyrophyllite), except that, unless sold on bid in direct competition with a bona fide bid to sell a mineral listed in paragraph (3), the percentage shall be 5 percent for any such other mineral (other than slate to which paragraph (5) applies) when used, or sold for use, by the mine owner or operator as rip rap, ballast, road material, rubble, concrete aggregates, or for similar purposes. For purposes of this paragraph, the term "all other minerals" does not include—

(A) soil, sod, dirt, turf, water, or mosses;

(B) minerals from sea water, the air, or similar inexhaustible sources or

(C) oil and gas wells.

For the purposes of this subsection, minerals (other than sodium chloride) extracted from brines pumped from a saline perennial lake within the United States shall not be considered minerals from an inexhaustible source.

Sec. 613(b)

[Sec. 613(c)]

(c) DEFINITION OF GROSS INCOME FROM PROPERTY.—For purposes of this section—

(1) GROSS INCOME FROM THE PROPERTY.—The term "gross income from the property" means, in the case of a property other than an oil or gas well and other than a geothermal deposit, the gross income from mining.

(2) MINING.—The term "mining" includes not merely the extraction of the ores or minerals from the ground but also the treatment processes considered as mining described in paragraph (4) (and the treatment processes necessary or incidental thereto), and so much of the transportation of ores or minerals (whether or not by common carrier) from the point of extraction from the ground to the plants or mills in which such treatment processes are applied thereto as is not in excess of 50 miles unless the Secretary finds that the physical and other requirements are such that the ore or mineral must be transported a greater distance to such plants or mills.

(3) EXTRACTION OF THE ORES OR MINERALS FROM THE GROUND.—The term "extraction of the ores or minerals from the ground" includes the extraction by mine owners or operators of ores or minerals from the waste or residue of prior mining. The preceding sentence shall not apply to any such extraction of the mineral or ore by a purchaser of such waste or residue or of the rights to extract ores or minerals therefrom.

(4) TREATMENT PROCESSES CONSIDERED AS MINING.—The following treatment processes where applied by the mine owner or operator shall be considered as mining to the extent they are applied to the ore or mineral in respect of which he is entitled to a deduction for depletion under section 611:

(A) In the case of coal—cleaning, breaking, sizing, dust allaying, treating to prevent freezing, and loading for shipment;

(B) in the case of sulfur recovered by the Frasch process—cleaning, pumping to vats, cooling, breaking, and loading for shipment;

(C) in the case of iron ore, bauxite, ball and sagger clay, rock asphalt, and ores or minerals which are customarily sold in the form of a crude mineral product—sorting, concentrating, sintering, and substantially equivalent processes to bring to shipping grade and form, and loading for shipment;

(D) in the case of lead, zinc, copper, gold, silver, uranium, or fluorspar ores, potash, and ores or minerals which are not customarily sold in the form of the crude mineral product—crushing, grinding, and beneficiation by concentration (gravity, flotation, amalgamation, electrostatic, or magnetic), cyanidation, leaching, crystallization, precipitation (but not including electrolytic deposition, roasting, thermal or electric smelting, or refining), or by substantially equivalent processes or combination of processes used in the separation or extraction of the product or products from the ore or the mineral or minerals from other material from the mine or other natural deposit;

(E) the pulverization of talc, the burning of magnesite, the sintering and nodulizing of phosphate rock, the decarbonation of trona, and the furnacing of quicksilver ores;

(F) in the case of calcium carbonates and other minerals when used in making cement—all processes (other than preheating of the kiln feed) applied prior to the introduction of the kiln feed into the kiln, but not including any subsequent process;

(G) in the case of clay to which paragraph (5) or (6)(B) of subsection (b) applies—crushing, grinding, and separating the mineral from waste, but not including any subsequent process;

(H) in the case of oil shale—extraction from the ground, crushing, loading into the retort, and retorting, but not hydrogenation, refining, or any other process subsequent to retorting; and

(I) any other treatment process provided for by regulations prescribed by the Secretary which, with respect to the particular ore or mineral, is not inconsistent with the preceding provisions of this paragraph.

(5) TREATMENT PROCESSES NOT CONSIDERED AS MINING.—Unless such processes are otherwise provided for in paragraph (4) (or are necessary or incidental to processes so provided for), the following processes shall not be considered as "mining": electrolytic deposition, roasting, calcining, thermal or electric smelting, refining, polishing, fine pulverization, blending with other materials, treatment effecting a chemical change, thermal action, and molding or shaping.

[Sec. 613(d)]

(d) DENIAL OF PERCENTAGE DEPLETION IN CASE OF OIL AND GAS WELLS.—Except as provided in Section 613A, in the case of any oil or gas well, the allowance for depletion shall be computed without reference to this section.

[Sec. 613(e)]

(e) PERCENTAGE DEPLETION FOR GEOTHERMAL DEPOSITS.—

(1) IN GENERAL.—In the case of geothermal deposits located in the United States or in a possession of the United States, for purposes of subsection (a)—

(A) such deposits shall be treated as listed in subsection (b), and

(B) 15 percent shall be deemed to be the percentage specified in subsection (b).

(2) GEOTHERMAL DEPOSIT DEFINED.—For purposes of paragraph (1), the term "geothermal deposit" means a geothermal reservoir consisting of natural heat which is stored in rocks or in an aqueous liquid or vapor (whether or not under pressure). Such a deposit shall in no case be treated as a gas well for purposes of this section or section 613A, and this section shall not apply to a geothermal deposit which is located outside the United States or its possessions.

(3) PERCENTAGE DEPLETION NOT TO INCLUDE LEASE BONUSES, ETC.—In the case of any geothermal deposit, the term "gross income from the property" shall, for purposes of this section, not include any amount described in section 613A(d)(5).

[Sec. 613A]

SEC. 613A. LIMITATIONS ON PERCENTAGE DEPLETION IN CASE OF OIL AND GAS WELLS.

[Sec. 613A(a)]

(a) GENERAL RULE.—Except as otherwise provided in this section, the allowance for depletion under section 611 with respect to any oil or gas well shall be computed without regard to section 613.

[Sec. 613A(b)]

(b) EXEMPTION FOR CERTAIN DOMESTIC GAS WELLS.—

(1) IN GENERAL.—The allowance for depletion under section 611 shall be computed in accordance with section 613 with respect to—

(A) regulated natural gas, and

(B) natural gas sold under a fixed contract,

and 22 percent shall be deemed to be specified in subsection (b) of section 613 for purposes of subsection (a) of that section.

(2) NATURAL GAS FROM GEOPRESSURED BRINE.—The allowance for depletion under section 611 shall be computed in accordance with section 613 with respect to any qualified natural gas from geopressured brine, and 10 percent shall be deemed to be specified in subsection (b) of section 613 for purposes of subsection (a) of such section.

(3) DEFINITIONS.—For purposes of this subsection—

(A) NATURAL GAS SOLD UNDER A FIXED CONTRACT.—The term "natural gas sold under a fixed contract" means domestic natural gas sold by the producer under a contract, in effect on February 1, 1975, and at all times thereafter before such sale, under which the price for such gas cannot be adjusted to reflect to any extent the increase in liabilities of the seller for tax under this chapter by reason of the repeal of percentage depletion for gas. Price increases after February 1, 1975, shall be presumed to take increases in tax liabilities into account unless the taxpayer demonstrates to the contrary by clear and convincing evidence.

(B) REGULATED NATURAL GAS.—The term "regulated natural gas" means domestic natural gas produced and sold by the producer, before July 1, 1976, subject to the jurisdiction of the Federal Power Commission, the price for which has not been adjusted to reflect to any extent the increase in liability of the seller for tax under this chapter by reason of the repeal of percentage depletion for gas. Price increases after February 1, 1975, shall be presumed to take increases in tax liabilities into account unless the taxpayer demonstrates the contrary by clear and convincing evidence.

(C) QUALIFIED NATURAL GAS FROM GEOPRESSURED BRINE.—The term "qualified natural gas from geopressured brine" means any natural gas—

(i) which is determined in accordance with section 503 of the Natural Gas Policy Act of 1978 to be produced from geopressured brine, and

(ii) which is produced from any well the drilling of which began after September 30, 1978, and before January 1, 1984.

[Sec. 613A(c)]

(c) EXEMPTION FOR INDEPENDENT PRODUCERS AND ROYALTY OWNERS.—

(1) IN GENERAL.—Except as provided in subsection (d), the allowance for depletion under section 611 shall be computed in accordance with section 613 with respect to—

(A) so much of the taxpayer's average daily production of domestic crude oil as does not exceed the taxpayer's depletable oil quantity; and

(B) so much of the taxpayer's average daily production of domestic natural gas as does not exceed the taxpayer's depletable natural gas quantity;

and 15 percent shall be deemed to be specified in subsection (b) of section 613 for purposes of subsection (a) of that section.

(2) AVERAGE DAILY PRODUCTION.—For purposes of paragraph (1)—

(A) the taxpayer's average daily production of domestic crude oil or natural gas for any taxable year, shall be determined by dividing his aggregate production of domestic crude oil or natural gas, as the case may be, during the taxable year by the number of days in such taxable year, and

(B) in the case of a taxpayer holding a partial interest in the production from any property (including an interest held in a partnership) such taxpayer's production shall be considered to be that amount of such production determined by multiplying the total production of such property by the taxpayer's percentage participation in the revenues from such property.

(3) DEPLETABLE OIL QUANTITY.—

(A) IN GENERAL.—For purposes of paragraph (1), the taxpayer's depletable oil quantity shall be equal to—

(i) the tentative quantity determined under subparagraph (B), reduced (but not below zero) by

(ii) except in the case of a taxpayer making an election under paragraph (6)(B), the taxpayer's average daily marginal production for the taxable year.

(B) Tentative quantity.—For purposes of subparagraph (A), the tentative quantity is 1,000 barrels.

(4) DAILY DEPLETABLE NATURAL GAS QUANTITY.—For purposes of paragraph (1), the depletable natural gas quantity of any taxpayer for any taxable year shall be equal to 6,000 cubic feet multiplied by the number of barrels of the taxpayer's depletable oil quantity to which the taxpayer elects to have this paragraph apply. The taxpayer's depletable oil quantity for any taxable year shall be reduced by the number of barrels with respect to which an election under this paragraph applies. Such election shall be made at such time and in such manner as the Secretary shall by regulations prescribe.

(6) OIL AND NATURAL GAS PRODUCED FROM MARGINAL PROPERTIES.—

(A) IN GENERAL.—Except as provided in subsection (d) and subparagraph (B), the allowance for depletion under section 611 shall be computed in accordance with section 613 with respect to—

(i) so much of the taxpayer's average daily marginal production of domestic crude oil as does not exceed the taxpayer's depletable oil quantity (determined without regard to paragraph (3)(A)(ii)), and

(ii) so much of the taxpayer's average daily marginal production of domestic natural gas as does not exceed the taxpayer's depletable natural gas quantity (determined without regard to paragraph (3)(A)(ii)),

and the applicable percentage shall be deemed to be specified in subsection (b) of section 613 for purposes of subsection (a) of that section.

(B) ELECTION TO HAVE PARAGRAPH APPLY TO PRO RATA PORTION OF MARGINAL PRODUCTION.—If the taxpayer elects to have this subparagraph apply for any taxable year, the rules of subparagraph (A) shall apply to the average daily marginal production of domestic crude oil or domestic natural gas of the taxpayer to which paragraph (1) would have applied without regard to this paragraph.

Sec. 613A(c)

(C) APPLICABLE PERCENTAGE.—For purposes of subparagraph (A), the term "applicable percentage" means the percentage (not greater than 25 percent) equal to the sum of—

(i) 15 percent, plus

(ii) 1 percentage point for each whole dollar by which $20 exceeds the reference price for crude oil for the calendar year preceding the calendar year in which the taxable year begins.

For purposes of this paragraph, the term "reference price" means, with respect to any calendar year, the reference price determined for such calendar year under section 29(d)(2)(C).

(D) MARGINAL PRODUCTION.—The term "marginal production" means domestic crude oil or domestic natural gas which is produced during any taxable year from a property which—

(i) is a stripper well property for the calendar year in which the taxable year begins, or

(ii) is a property substantially all of the production of which during such calendar year is heavy oil.

(E) STRIPPER WELL PROPERTY.—For purposes of this paragraph, the term "stripper well property" means, with respect to any calendar year, any property with respect to which the amount determined by dividing—

(i) the average daily production of domestic crude oil and domestic natural gas from producing wells on such property for such calendar year, by

(ii) the number of such wells, is 15 barrel equivalents or less.

(F) HEAVY OIL..—For purposes of this paragraph, the term "heavy oil" means domestic crude oil produced from any property if such crude oil had a weighted average gravity of 20 degrees API or less (corrected to 60 degrees Fahrenheit).

(G) AVERAGE DAILY MARGINAL PRODUCTION.—For purposes of this subsection—

(i) the taxpayer's average daily marginal production of domestic crude oil or natural gas for any taxable year shall be determined by dividing the taxpayer's aggregate marginal production of domestic crude oil or natural gas, as the case may be, during the taxable year by the number of days in such taxable year, and

(ii) in the case of a taxpayer holding a partial interest in the production from any property (including any interest held in any partnership), such taxpayer's production shall be considered to be that amount of such production determined by multiplying the total production of such property by the taxpayer's percentage participation in the revenues from such property.

(H) TEMPORARY SUSPENSION OF TAXABLE INCOME LIMIT WITH RESPECT TO MARGINAL PRODUCTION.—The second sentence of subsection (a) of section 613 shall not apply to so much of the allowance for depletion as is determined under subparagraph (A) for any taxable year beginning after December 31, 1997, and before January 1, 2004.

(7) SPECIAL RULES.—

(A) PRODUCTION OF CRUDE OIL IN EXCESS OF DEPLETABLE OIL QUANTITY.—If the taxpayer's average daily production of domestic crude oil exceeds his depletable oil quantity, the allowance under paragraph (1)(A) with respect to oil produced during the taxable year from each property in the United States shall be that amount which bears the same ratio to the amount of depletion which would have been allowable under section 613(a) for all of the taxpayer's oil produced from such property during the taxable year (computed as if section 613 applied to all of such production at the rate specified in paragraph (1) or (6), as the case may be) as his depletable oil quantity bears to the aggregate number of barrels representing the average daily production of domestic crude oil of the taxpayer for such year.

(B) PRODUCTION OF NATURAL GAS IN EXCESS OF DEPLETABLE NATURAL GAS QUANTITY.—If the taxpayer's average daily production of domestic natural gas exceeds his depletable natural gas quantity, the allowance under paragraph (1)(B) with respect to natural gas produced during the taxable year from each property in the United States shall be that amount which bears the same ratio to the amount of depletion which would have been allowable under section 613(a) for all of the taxpayers natural gas produced from such property during the taxable year (computed as if section 613 applied to all of such production at the rate specified in paragraph (1) or (6), as the case may be) as the amount of his depletable natural gas quantity in cubic feet bears to the aggregate number of cubic feet representing the average daily production of domestic natural gas of the taxpayer for such year.

Sec. 613A(c)

(C) Taxable income from the property.—If both oil and gas are produced from the property during the taxable year, for purposes of subparagraphs (A) and (B) the taxable income from the property, in applying the taxable income limitation in section 613(a), shall be allocated between the oil production and the gas production in proportion to the gross income during the taxable year from each.

(D) Partnerships.—In the case of a partnership, the depletion allowance shall be computed separately by the partners and not by the partnership. The partnership shall allocate to each partner his proportionate share of the adjusted basis of each partnership oil or gas property. The allocation is to be made as of the later of the date of acquisition of the oil or gas property by the partnership, or January 1, 1975. A partner's proportionate share of the adjusted basis of partnership property shall be determined in accordance with his interest in partnership capital or income and, in the case of property contributed to the partnership by a partner, section 704(c) (relating to contributed property) shall apply in determining such share. Each partner shall separately keep records of his share of the adjusted basis in each oil and gas property of the partnership, adjust such share of the adjusted basis for any depletion taken on such property, and use such adjusted basis each year in the computation of his cost depletion or in the computation of his gain or loss on the disposition of such property by the partnership. For purposes of section 732 (relating to basis of distributed property other than money), the partnership's adjusted basis in mineral property shall be an amount equal to the sum of the partners' adjusted bases in such property as determined under this paragraph.

(8) Businesses under common control; members of the same family.—

(A) Component members of controlled group treated as one taxpayer.—For purposes of this subsection, persons who are members of the same controlled group of corporations shall be treated as one taxpayer.

(B) Aggregation of business entities under common control.—If 50 percent or more of the beneficial interest in two or more corporations, trusts, or estates is owned by the same or related persons (taking into account only persons who own at least 5 percent of such beneficial interest), the tentative quantity determined under paragraph (3)(B) shall be allocated among all such entities in proportion to the respective production of domestic crude oil during the period in question by such entities.

(C) Allocation among members of the same family.—In the case of individuals who are members of the same family, the tentative quantity determined under paragraph (3)(B) shall be allocated among such individuals in proportion to the respective production of domestic crude oil during the period in question by such individuals.

(D) Definition and special rules.—For purposes of this paragraph—

(i) the term "controlled group of corporations" has the meaning given to such term by section 1563(a), except that section 1563(b)(2) shall not apply and except that "more than 50 percent" shall be substituted for "at least 80 percent" each place it appears in section 1563(a),

(ii) a person is a related person to another person if such persons are members of the same controlled group of corporations or if the relationship between such persons would result in a disallowance of losses under section 267 or 707(b), except that for this purpose the family of an individual includes only his spouse and minor children,

(iii) the family of an individual includes only his spouse and minor children, and

(iv) each 6,000 cubic feet of domestic natural gas shall be treated as 1 barrel of domestic crude oil.

(9) Special rule for fiscal year taxpayers.—In applying this subsection to a taxable year which is not a calendar year, each portion of such taxable year which occurs during a single calendar year shall be treated as if it were a short taxable year.

(10) Certain production not taken into account.—In applying this subsection, there shall not be taken into account the production of natural gas with respect to which subsection (b) applies.

(11) Subchapter s corporations.—

(A) Computation of depletion allowance at shareholder level.—In the case of an S corporation, the allowance for depletion with respect to any oil or gas property shall be computed separately by each shareholder.

(B) ALLOCATION OF BASIS.—The S corporation shall allocate to each shareholder his pro rata share of the adjusted basis of the S corporation in each oil or gas property held by the S corporation. The allocation shall be made as of the later of the date of acquisition of the property by the S corporation, or the first day of the first taxable year of the S corporation to which the Subchapter S Revison Act of 1982 applies. Each shareholder shall separately keep records of his share of the adjusted basis in each oil and gas property of the S corporation, adjust such share of the adjusted basis for any depletion taken on such property, and use such adjusted basis each year in the computation of his cost depletion or in the computation of his gain or loss on the disposition of such property by the S corporation. In the case of any distribution of oil or gas property to its shareholders by the S corporation, the corporation's adjusted basis in the property shall be an amount equal to the sum of the shareholders' adjusted bases in such property, as determined under this subparagraph.

[Sec. 613A(d)]

(d) LIMITATIONS ON APPLICATION OF SUBSECTION (c).—

(1) LIMITATION BASED ON TAXABLE INCOME.—The deduction for the taxable year attributable to the application of subsection (c) shall not exceed 65 percent of the taxpayer's taxable income for the year computed without regard to—

(A) any depletion on production from an oil or gas property which is subject to the provisions of subsection (c).

(B) any net operating loss carryback to the taxable year under section 172,

(C) any capital loss carryback to the taxable year under section 1212, and

(D) in the case of a trust, any distributions to its beneficiary, except in the case of any trust where any beneficiary of such trust is a member of the family (as defined in section 267(c)(4)) of a settlor who created inter vivos and testamentary trusts for members of the family and such settlor died within the last six days of the fifth month in 1970, and the law in the jurisdiction in which such trust was created requires all or a portion of the gross or net proceeds of any royalty or other interest in oil, gas, or other mineral representing any percentage depletion allowance to be allocated to the principal of the trust.

If an amount is disallowed as a deduction for the taxable year by reason of application of the preceding sentence, the disallowed amount shall be treated as an amount allowable as a deduction under subsection (c) for the following taxable year, subject to the application of the preceding sentence to such taxable year. For purposes of basis adjustments and determining whether cost depletion exceeds percentage depletion with respect to the production from a property, any amount disallowed as a deduction on the application of this paragraph shall be allocated to the respective properties from which the oil or gas was produced in proportion to the percentage depletion otherwise allowable to such properties under subsection (c).

(2) RETAILERS EXCLUDED.—Subsection (c) shall not apply in the case of any taxpayer who directly, or through a related person, sells oil or natural gas (excluding bulk sales of such items to commercial or industrial users), or any product derived from oil or natural gas (excluding bulk sales of aviation fuels to the Department of Defense)—

(A) through any retail outlet operated by the taxpayer or a related person, or

(B) to any person—

(i) obligated under an agreement or contract with the taxpayer or a related person to use a trademark, trade name, or service mark or name owned by such taxpayer or related persons, in marketing or distributing oil or natural gas or any product derived from oil or natural gas, or

(ii) given authority, pursuant to an agreement or contract with the taxpayer or a related person, to occupy any retail outlet owned, leased, or in any way controlled by the taxpayer or a related person.

Notwithstanding the preceding sentence this paragraph shall not apply in any case where the combined gross receipts from the sale of such oil, natural gas, or any product derived therefrom, for the taxable year of all retail outlets taken into account for purposes of this paragraph do not exceed $5,000,000. For purposes of this paragraph, sales of oil, natural gas, or any product derived from oil or natural gas shall not include sales made of such items outside the United States, if no domestic production of the taxpayer or a related person is exported during the taxable year or the immediately preceding taxable year.

(3) RELATED PERSON.—For purposes of this subsection, a person is a related person with respect to the taxpayer if a significant ownership interest in either the taxpayer or such person is held by the other, or if a third person has a significant ownership interest in both the taxpayer and such person. For purposes of the preceding sentence, the term "significant ownership interest" means—

    (A) with respect to any corporation, 5 percent or more in value of the outstanding stock of such corporation,

    (B) with respect to a partnership, 5 percent or more interest in the profits or capital of such partnership, and

    (C) with respect to an estate or trust, 5 percent or more of the beneficial interests in such estate or trust.

For purposes of determining significant ownership interest, an interest owned by or for a corporation, partnership, trust, or estate shall be considered as owned directly both by itself and proportionately by its shareholders, partners, or beneficiaries, as the case may be.

(4) CERTAIN REFINERS EXCLUDED.—If the taxpayer or a related person engages in the refining of crude oil, subsection (c) shall not apply to such taxpayer if on any day during the taxable year the refinery runs of the taxpayer and such person exceed 50,000 barrels.

(5) PERCENTAGE DEPLETION NOT ALLOWED FOR LEASE BONUSES, ETC.—In the case of any oil or gas property to which subsection (c) applies, for purposes of section 613, the term "gross income from the property" shall not include any lease bonus, advance royalty, or other amount payable without regard to production from property.

[Sec. 613A(e)]

(e) DEFINITIONS.—For purposes of this section—

(1) CRUDE OIL.—The term "crude oil" includes a natural gas liquid recovered from a gas well in lease separators or field facilities.

(2) NATURAL GAS.—The term "natural gas" means any product (other than crude oil) of an oil or gas well if a deduction for depletion is allowable under section 611 with respect to such product.

(3) DOMESTIC.—The term "domestic" refers to production from an oil or gas well located in the United States or in a possession of the United States.

(4) BARREL.—The term "barrel" means 42 United States gallons.

[Sec. 614]

SEC. 614. DEFINITION OF PROPERTY.

[Sec. 614(a)]

(a) GENERAL RULE.—For the purpose of computing the depletion allowance in the case of mines, wells, and other natural deposits, the term "property" means each separate interest owned by the taxpayer in each mineral deposit in each separate tract or parcel of land.

* * *

[Sec. 616]

SEC. 616. DEVELOPMENT EXPENDITURES.

[Sec. 616(a)]

(a) IN GENERAL.—Except as provided in subsections (b) and (d), there shall be allowed as a deduction in computing taxable income all expenditures paid or incurred during the taxable year for the development of a mine or other natural deposit (other than an oil or gas well) if paid or incurred after the existence of ores or minerals in commercially marketable quantities has been disclosed. This section shall not apply to expenditures for the acquisition or improvement of property of a character which is subject to the allowance for depreciation provided in section 167, but allowances for depreciation shall be considered, for purposes of this section, as expenditures.

[Sec. 616(b)]

(b) ELECTION OF TAXPAYER.—At the election of the taxpayer, made in accordance with regulations prescribed by the Secretary, expenditures described in subsection (a) paid or incurred during the taxable year shall be treated as deferred expenses and shall be deductible on a ratable basis as the units of produced ores or minerals benefited by such expenditures are sold. In the case of such expenditures paid or incurred during the development stage of the mine or deposit, the election shall apply only with respect to the excess of such expenditures during the taxable year over the net receipts during the taxable year from the ores or minerals produced from such mine or deposit. The election under this subsection, if made, must be for the total amount of such expenditures, or the total amount of such excess, as the case may be, with respect to the mine or deposit, and shall be binding for such taxable year.

[Sec. 616(c)]

(c) ADJUSTED BASIS OF MINE OR DEPOSIT.—The amount of expenditures which are treated under subsection (b) as deferred expenses shall be taken into account in computing the adjusted basis of the mine or deposit, except that such amount, and the adjustments to basis provided in section 1016 (a) (9), shall be disregarded in determining the adjusted basis of the property for the purpose of computing a deduction for depletion under section 611.

* * *

[Sec. 617]

SEC. 617. DEDUCTION AND RECAPTURE OF CERTAIN MINING EXPLORATION EXPENDITURES.

[Sec. 617(a)]

(a) ALLOWANCE OF DEDUCTION.—

(1) GENERAL RULE.—At the election of the taxpayer, expenditures paid or incurred during the taxable year for the purpose of ascertaining the existence, location, extent, or quality of any deposit of ore or other mineral, and paid or incurred before the beginning of the development stage of the mine, shall be allowed as a deduction in computing taxable income. This subsection shall apply only with respect to the amount of such expenditures which, but for this subsection, would not be allowable as a deduction for the taxable year. This subsection shall not apply to expenditures for the acquisition or improvement of property of a character which is subject to the allowance for depreciation provided in section 167, but allowances for depreciation shall be considered, for purposes of this subsection, as expenditures paid or incurred. In no case shall this subsection apply with respect to amounts paid or incurred for the purpose of ascertaining the existence, location, extent, or quality of any deposit of oil or gas or of any mineral with respect to which a deduction for percentage depletion is not allowable under section 613.

(2) ELECTIONS.—

(A) METHOD.—Any election under this subsection shall be made in such manner as the Secretary may by regulations prescribe.

(B) TIME AND SCOPE.—The election provided by paragraph (1) for the taxable year may be made at any time before the expiration of the period prescribed for making a claim for credit or refund of the tax imposed by this chapter for the taxable year. Such an election for the taxable year shall apply to all expenditures described in paragraph (1) paid or incurred by the taxpayer during the taxable year or during any subsequent taxable year. Such an election may not be revoked unless the Secretary consents to such revocation.

(C) DEFICIENCIES.—The statutory period for the assessment of any deficiency for any taxable year, to the extent such deficiency is attributable to an election or revocation of an election under this subsection, shall not expire before the last day of the 2-year period beginning on the day after the date on which such election or revocation of election is made; and such deficiency may be assessed at any time before the expiration of such 2-year period, notwithstanding any law or rule of law which would otherwise prevent such assessment.

[Sec. 617(b)]

(b) RECAPTURE ON REACHING PRODUCING STAGE.—

(1) RECAPTURE.—If, in any taxable year, any mine with respect to which expenditures were deducted pursuant to subsection (a) reaches the producing stage, then—

(A) If the taxpayer so elects with respect to all such mines reaching the producing stage during the taxable year, he shall include in gross income for the taxable year an amount equal to the adjusted exploration expenditures with respect to such mines, and the amount so included in income shall be treated for purposes of this subtitle as expenditures which (i) are paid or

Sec. 617(b)

incurred on the respective dates on which the mines reach the producing stage, and (ii) are properly chargeable to capital account.

(B) If subparagraph (A) does not apply with respect to any such mine, then the deduction for depletion under section 611 with respect to the property shall be disallowed until the amount of depletion which would be allowable but for this subparagraph equals the amount of the adjusted exploration expenditures with respect to such mine.

(2) ELECTIONS.—

(A) METHOD.—Any election under this subsection shall be made in such manner as the Secretary may by regulations prescribe.

(B) TIME AND SCOPE.—The election provided by paragraph (1) for any taxable year may be made or changed not later than the time prescribed by law for filing the return (including extensions thereof) for such taxable year.

[Sec. 617(c)]

(c) RECAPTURE IN CASE OF BONUS OR ROYALTY.—If an election has been made under subsection (a) with respect to expenditures relating to a mining property and the taxpayer receives or accrues a bonus or a royalty with respect to such property, then the deduction for depletion under section 611 with respect to the bonus or royalty shall be disallowed until the amount of depletion which would be allowable but for this subsection equals the amount of the adjusted exploration expenditures with respect to the property to which the bonus or royalty relates.

[Sec. 617(d)]

(d) GAIN FROM DISPOSITIONS OF CERTAIN MINING PROPERTY.—

(1) GENERAL RULE.—Except as otherwise provided in this subsection, if mining property is disposed of the lower of—

(A) the adjusted exploration expenditures with respect to such property, or

(B) the excess of—

(i) the amount realized (in the case of a sale, exchange, or involuntary conversion), or the fair market value (in the case of any other disposition), over

(ii) the adjusted basis of such property,

shall be treated as ordinary income. Such gain shall be recognized notwithstanding any other provision of this subtitle.

(2) DISPOSITION OF PORTION OF PROPERTY.—For purposes of paragraph (1)—

(A) In the case of the disposition of a portion of a mining property (other than an undivided interest), the entire amount of the adjusted exploration expenditures with respect to such property shall be treated as attributable to such portion to the extent of the amount of the gain to which paragraph (1) applies.

(B) In the case of the disposition of an undivided interest in a mining property (or a portion thereof), a proportionate part of the adjusted exploration expenditures with respect to such property shall be treated as attributable to such undivided interest to the extent of the amount of the gain to which paragraph (1) applies.

This paragraph shall not apply to any expenditure to the extent the taxpayer establishes to the satisfaction of the Secretary that such expenditure relates neither to the portion (or interest therein) disposed of nor to any mine, in the property held by the taxpayer before the disposition, which has reached the producing stage.

(3) EXCEPTIONS AND LIMITATIONS.—Paragraphs (1), (2), and (3) of section 1245(b) (relating to exceptions and limitations with respect to gain from disposition of certain depreciable property) shall apply in respect of this subsection in the same manner and with the same effect as if references in section 1245(b) to section 1245 or any provision thereof were references to this subsection or the corresponding provisions of this subsection and as if references to section 1245 property were references to mining property.

(4) APPLICATION OF SUBSECTION.—This subsection shall apply notwithstanding any other provision of this subtitle.

(5) COORDINATION WITH SECTION 1254.—This subsection shall not apply to any disposition to which section 1254 applies.

[Sec. 617(e)]

(e) BASIS OF PROPERTY.—

(1) BASIS.—The basis of any property shall not be reduced by the amount of any depletion which would be allowable but for the application of this section.

(2) ADJUSTMENTS.—The Secretary shall prescribe such regulations as he may deem necessary to provide for adjustments to the basis of property to reflect gain recognized under subsection (d)(1).

[Sec. 617(f)]

(f) DEFINITIONS.—For purposes of this section—

(1) ADJUSTED EXPLORATION EXPENDITURES.—The term "adjusted exploration expenditures" means, with respect to any property or mine—

(A) the amount of the expenditures allowed for the taxable year and all preceding taxable years as deductions under subsection (a) to the taxpayer or any other person which are properly chargeable to such property or mine and which (but for the election under subsection (a)) would be reflected in the adjusted basis of such property or mine, reduced by

(B) for the taxable year and for each preceding taxable year, the amount (if any) by which (i) the amount which would have been allowable for percentage depletion under section 613 but for the deduction of such expenditures, exceeds (ii) the amount allowable for depletion under section 611,

properly adjusted for any amounts included in gross income under subsection (b) or (c) and for any amounts of gain to which subsection (d) applied.

(2) MINING PROPERTY.—The term "mining property" means any property (within the meaning of section 614 after the application of subsections (c) and (e) thereof) with respect to which any expenditures allowed as a deduction under subsection (a)(1) are properly chargeable.

(3) DISPOSAL OF COAL OR DOMESTIC IRON ORE WITH A RETAINED ECONOMIC INTEREST.—A transaction which constitutes a disposal of coal or iron ore under section 631(c) shall be treated as a disposition. In such a case, the excess referred to in subsection (d)(1)(B) shall be treated as equal to the gain (if any) referred to in section 631(c).

[Sec. 617(g)]

(g) SPECIAL RULES RELATING TO PARTNERSHIP PROPERTY.—

(1) PROPERTY DISTRIBUTED TO PARTNER.—In the case of any property or mine received by the taxpayer in a distribution with respect to part or all of his interest in a partnership, the adjusted exploration expenditures with respect to such property or mine include the adjusted exploration expenditures (not otherwise included under subsection (f)(1)) with respect to such property or mine immediately prior to such distribution, but the adjusted exploration expenditures with respect to any such property or mine shall be reduced by the amount of gain to which section 751(b) applied realized by the partnership (as constituted after the distribution) on the distribution of such property or mine.

(2) PROPERTY RETAINED BY PARTNERSHIP.—In the case of any property or mine held by a partnership after a distribution to a partner to which section 751(b) applied, the adjusted exploration expenditures with respect to such property or mine shall, under regulations prescribed by the Secretary, be reduced by the amount of gain to which section 751(b) applied realized by such partner with respect to such distribution on account of such property or mine.

* * *

PART III—SALES AND EXCHANGES

[Sec. 631]

SEC. 631. GAIN OR LOSS IN THE CASE OF TIMBER, COAL, OR DOMESTIC IRON ORE.

[Sec. 631(a)]

(a) ELECTION TO CONSIDER CUTTING AS SALE OR EXCHANGE.—If the taxpayer so elects on his return for a taxable year, the cutting of timber (for sale or for use in the taxpayer's trade or business) during such

Sec. 631(a)

year by the taxpayer who owns, or has a contract right to cut, such timber (providing he has owned such timber or has held such contract right for a period of more than 1 year) shall be considered as a sale or exchange of such timber cut during such year. If such election has been made, gain or loss to the taxpayer shall be recognized in an amount equal to the difference between the fair market value of such timber, and the adjusted basis for depletion of such timber in the hands of the taxpayer. Such fair market value shall be the fair market value as of the first day of the taxable year in which such timber is cut, and shall thereafter be considered as the cost of such cut timber to the taxpayer for all purposes for which such cost is a necessary factor. If a taxpayer makes an election under this subsection, such election shall apply with respect to all timber which is owned by the taxpayer or which the taxpayer has a contract right to cut and shall be binding on the taxpayer for the taxable year for which the election is made and for all subsequent years, unless the Secretary, on showing of undue hardship, permits the taxpayer to revoke his election; such revocation, however, shall preclude any further elections under this subsection except with the consent of the Secretary. For purposes of this subsection and subsection (b), the term "timber" includes evergreen trees which are more than 6 years old at the time severed from the roots and are sold for ornamental purposes.

[Sec. 631(b)]

(b) DISPOSAL OF TIMBER WITH A RETAINED ECONOMIC INTEREST.—In the case of the disposal of timber held for more than 1 year before such disposal, by the owner thereof under any form or type of contract by virtue of which such owner retains an economic interest in such timber, the difference between the amount realized from the disposal of such timber and the adjusted depletion basis thereof, shall be considered as though it were a gain or loss, as the case may be, on the sale of such timber. In determining the gross income, the adjusted gross income, or the taxable income of the lessee, the deductions allowable with respect to rents and royalties shall be determined without regard to the provisions of this subsection. The date of disposal of such timber shall be deemed to be the date such timber is cut, but if payment is made to the owner under the contract before such timber is cut the owner may elect to treat the date of such payment as the date of disposal of such timber. For purposes of this subsection, the term "owner" means any person who owns an interest in such timber, including a sublessor and a holder of a contract to cut timber.

[Sec. 631(c)]

(c) DISPOSAL OF COAL OR DOMESTIC IRON ORE WITH A RETAINED ECONOMIC INTEREST.—In the case of the disposal of coal (including lignite), or iron ore mined in the United States, held for more than 1 year before such disposal, by the owner thereof under any form of contract by virtue of which such owner retains an economic interest in such coal or iron ore, the difference between the amount realized from the disposal of such coal or iron ore and the adjusted depletion basis thereof plus the deductions disallowed for the taxable year under section 272 shall be considered as though it were a gain or loss, as the case may be, on the sale of such coal or iron ore. If for the taxable year of such gain or loss the maximum rate of tax imposed by this chapter on any net capital gain is less than such maximum rate for ordinary income, such owner shall not be entitled to the allowance for percentage depletion provided in section 613 with respect to such coal or iron ore. This subsection shall not apply to income realized by any owner as a co-adventurer, partner, or principal in the mining of such coal or iron ore, and the word "owner" means any person who owns an economic interest in coal or iron ore in place, including a sublessor. The date of disposal of such coal or iron ore shall be deemed to be the date such coal or iron ore is mined. In determining the gross income, the adjusted gross income, or the taxable income of the lessee, the deductions allowable with respect to rents and royalties shall be determined without regard to the provisions of this subsection. This subsection shall have no application, for purposes of applying subchapter G, relating to corporations used to avoid income tax on shareholders (including the determinations of the amount of the deductions under section 535(b)(6) or section 545(b)(5)). This subsection shall not apply to any disposal of iron ore or coal—

    (1) to a person whose relationship to the person disposing of such iron ore or coal would result in the disallowance of losses under section 267 or 707(b), or

    (2) to a person owned or controlled directly or indirectly by the same interests which own or control the person disposing of such iron ore or coal.

PART IV—MINERAL PRODUCTION PAYMENTS

[Sec. 636]

SEC. 636. INCOME TAX TREATMENT OF MINERAL PRODUCTION PAYMENTS.

[Sec. 636(a)]

(a) CARVED-OUT PRODUCTION PAYMENT.—A production payment carved out of mineral property shall be treated, for purposes of this subtitle, as if it were a mortgage loan on the property, and shall not qualify as an economic interest in the mineral property. In the case of a production payment carved out for exploration or development of a mineral property, the preceding sentence shall apply only if and to the extent gross income from the property (for purposes of section 613) would be realized, in the absence of the application of such sentence, by the person creating the production payment.

[Sec. 636(b)]

(b) RETAINED PRODUCTION PAYMENT ON SALE OF MINERAL PROPERTY.—A production payment retained on the sale of a mineral property shall be treated, for purposes of this subtitle, as if it were a purchase money mortgage loan and shall not qualify as an economic interest in the mineral property.

[Sec. 636(c)]

(c) RETAINED PRODUCTION PAYMENT ON LEASE OF MINERAL PROPERTY.—A production payment retained in a mineral property by the lessor in a leasing transaction shall be treated, for purposes of this subtitle, insofar as the lessee (or his successors in interest) is concerned, as if it were a bonus granted by the lessee to the lessor payable in installments. The treatment of the production payment in the hands of the lessor shall be determined without regard to the provisions of this subsection.

[Sec. 636(d)]

(d) DEFINITION.—As used in this section, the term "mineral property" has the meaning assigned to the term "property" in section 614(a).

[Sec. 636(e)]

(e) REGULATIONS.—The Secretary shall prescribe such regulations as may be necessary to carry out the purposes of this section.

Subchapter J—Estates, Trusts, Beneficiaries, and Decedents

PART I—ESTATES, TRUSTS, AND BENEFICIARIES

Subpart A—General Rules for Taxation of Estates and Trusts

[Sec. 641]

SEC. 641. IMPOSITION OF TAX.

[Sec. 641(a)]

(a) APPLICATION OF TAX.—The tax imposed by section 1(e) shall apply to the taxable income of estates or of any kind of property held in trust, including—

(1) income accumulated in trust for the benefit of unborn or unascertained persons or persons with contingent interests, and income accumulated or held for future distribution under the terms of the will or trust;

(2) income which is to be distributed currently by the fiduciary to the beneficiaries, and income collected by a guardian of an infant which is to be held or distributed as the court may direct;

(3) income received by estates of deceased persons during the period of administration or settlement of the estate; and

(4) income which, in the discretion of the fiduciary, may be either distributed to the beneficiaries or accumulated.

Sec. 641(a)

(b) COMPUTATION AND PAYMENT.—The taxable income of an estate or trust shall be computed in the same manner as in the case of an individual, except as otherwise provided in this part. The tax shall be computed on such taxable income and shall be paid by the fiduciary. For purposes of this subsection, a foreign trust or foreign estate shall be treated as a nonresident alien individual who is not present in the United States at any time.

(c) SPECIAL RULES FOR TAXATION OF ELECTING SMALL BUSINESS TRUSTS.—

(1) IN GENERAL.—For purposes of this chapter—

(A) the portion of any electing small business trust which consists of stock in 1 or more S corporations shall be treated as a separate trust, and

(B) the amount of the tax imposed by this chapter on such separate trust shall be determined with the modifications of paragraph (2).

(2) MODIFICATIONS.—For purposes of paragraph (1), the modifications of this paragraph are the following:

(A) Except as provided in section 1(h), the amount of the tax imposed by section 1(e) shall be determined by using the highest rate of tax set forth in section 1(e).

(B) The exemption amount under section 55(d) shall be zero.

(C) The only items of income, loss, deduction, or credit to be taken into account are the following:

(i) The items required to be taken into account under section 1366.

(ii) Any gain or loss from the disposition of stock in an S corporation.

(iii) To the extent provided in regulations, State or local income taxes or administrative expenses to the extent allocable to items described in clauses (i) and (ii).

No deduction or credit shall be allowed for any amount not described in this paragraph, and no item described in this paragraph shall be apportioned to any beneficiary.

(D) No amount shall be allowed under paragraph (1) or (2) of section 1211(b).

(3) TREATMENT OF REMAINDER OF TRUST AND DISTRIBUTIONS.—For purposes of determining—

(A) the amount of the tax imposed by this chapter on the portion of any electing small business trust not treated as a separate trust under paragraph (1), and

(B) the distributable net income of the entire trust,

the items referred to in paragraph (2)(C) shall be excluded. Except as provided in the preceding sentence, this subsection shall not affect the taxation of any distribution from the trust.

(4) TREATMENT OF UNUSED DEDUCTIONS WHERE TERMINATION OF SEPARATE TRUST.—If a portion of an electing small business trust ceases to be treated as a separate trust under paragraph (1), any carryover or excess deduction of the separate trust which is referred to in section 642(h) shall be taken into account by the entire trust.

(5) ELECTING SMALL BUSINESS TRUST.—For purposes of this subsection, the term "electing small business trust" has the meaning given such term by section 1361(e)(1).

SEC. 642. SPECIAL RULES FOR CREDITS AND DEDUCTIONS.

(a) FOREIGN TAX CREDIT ALLOWED.—An estate or trust shall be allowed the credit against tax for taxes imposed by foreign countries and possessions of the United States, to the extent allowed by section 901, only in respect of so much of the taxes described in such section as is not properly allocable under such section to the beneficiaries.

(b) DEDUCTION FOR PERSONAL EXEMPTION.—

(1) ESTATES.—An estate shall be allowed a deduction of $600.

(2) TRUSTS.—

(A) IN GENERAL.—Except as otherwise provided in this paragraph, a trust shall be allowed a deduction of $100.

(B) TRUSTS DISTRIBUTING INCOME CURRENTLY.—A trust which, under its governing instrument, is required to distribute all of its income currently shall be allowed a deduction of $300.

(C) DISABILITY TRUSTS.—

(i) IN GENERAL.—A qualified disability trust shall be allowed a deduction equal to the exemption amount under section 151(d), determined—

(I) by treating such trust as an individual described in section 151(d)(3)(C)(iii), and

(II) by applying section 67(e) (without the reference to section 642(b)) for purposes of determining the adjusted gross income of the trust.

(ii) QUALIFIED DISABILITY TRUST.—For purposes of clause (i), the term "qualified disability trust" means any trust if—

(I) such trust is a disability trust described in subsection (c)(2)(B)(iv) of section 1917 of the Social Security Act (42 U.S.C. 1396p), and

(II) all of the beneficiaries of the trust as of the close of the taxable year are determined by the Commissioner of Social Security to have been disabled (within the meaning of section 1614(a)(3) of the Social Security Act, 42 U.S.C. 1382c(a)(3)) for some portion of such year.

A trust shall not fail to meet the requirements of subclause (II) merely because the corpus of the trust may revert to a person who is not so disabled after the trust ceases to have any beneficiary who is so disabled.

(3) DEDUCTIONS IN LIEU OF PERSONAL EXEMPTION.—The deductions allowed by this subsection shall be in lieu of the deductions allowed under section 151 (relating to deduction for personal exemption).

[Sec. 642(c)]

(c) DEDUCTION FOR AMOUNTS PAID OR PERMANENTLY SET ASIDE FOR A CHARITABLE PURPOSE.—

(1) GENERAL RULE.—In the case of an estate or trust (other than a trust meeting the specifications of subpart B), there shall be allowed as a deduction in computing its taxable income (in lieu of the deduction allowed by section 170(a), relating to deduction for charitable, etc., contributions and gifts) any amount of the gross income, without limitation, which pursuant to the terms of the governing instrument is, during the taxable year, paid for a purpose specified in section 170(c) (determined without regard to section 170(c)(2)(A)). If a charitable contribution is paid after the close of such taxable year and on or before the last day of the year following the close of such taxable year, then the trustee or administrator may elect to treat such contribution as paid during such taxable year. The election shall be made at such time and in such manner as the Secretary prescribes by regulations.

(2) AMOUNTS PERMANENTLY SET ASIDE.—In the case of an estate, and in the case of a trust (other than a trust meeting the specifications of subpart B) required by the terms of its governing instrument to set aside amounts which was—

(A) created on or before October 9, 1969, if—

(i) an irrevocable remainder interest is transferred to or for the use of an organization described in section 170(c), or

(ii) the grantor is at all times after October 9, 1969, under a mental disability to change the terms of the trust; or

(B) established by a will executed on or before October 9, 1969, if—

(i) the testator dies before October 9, 1972, without having republished the will after October 9, 1969, by codicil or otherwise,

(ii) the testator at no time after October 9, 1969, had the right to change the portions of the will which pertain to the trust, or

(iii) the will is not republished by codicil or otherwise before October 9, 1972, and the testator is on such date and at all times thereafter under a mental disability to republish the will by codicil or otherwise,

there shall also be allowed as a deduction in computing its taxable income any amount of the gross income, without limitation, which pursuant to the terms of the governing instrument is, during the taxable year, permanently set aside for a purpose specified in section 170(c), or is to be used exclusively for religious, charitable, scientific, literary, or educational purposes, or for the prevention of cruelty to children or animals, or for the establishment, acquisition, maintenance, or operation of a public cemetery not operated for profit. In the case of a trust, the preceding sentence shall apply only to gross income earned with respect to amounts transferred to the trust before October 9, 1969, or transferred under a will to which subparagraph (B) applies.

(3) POOLED INCOME FUNDS.—In the case of a pooled income fund (as defined in paragraph (5)), there shall also be allowed as a deduction in computing its taxable income any amount of the gross income attributable to gain from the sale of a capital asset held for more than 1 year, without limitation, which pursuant to the terms of the governing instrument is, during the taxable year, permanently set aside for a purpose specified in section 170(c).

(4) ADJUSTMENTS.—To the extent that the amount otherwise allowable as a deduction under this subsection consists of gain described in section 1202(a), proper adjustment shall be made for any exclusion allowable to the estate or trust under section 1202. In the case of a trust, the deduction allowed by this subsection shall be subject to section 681 (relating to unrelated business income).

(5) DEFINITION OF POOLED INCOME FUND.—For purposes of paragraph (3), a pooled income fund is a trust—

(A) to which each donor transfers property, contributing an irrevocable remainder interest in such property to or for the use of an organization described in section 170(b)(1)(A) (other than in clauses (vii) or (viii)), and retaining an income interest for the life of one or more beneficiaries (living at the time of such transfer),

(B) in which the property transferred by each donor is commingled with property transferred by other donors who have made or make similar transfers,

(C) which cannot have investments in securities which are exempt from taxes imposed by this subtitle,

(D) which includes only amounts received from transfers which meet the requirements of this paragraph,

(E) which is maintained by the organization to which the remainder interest is contributed and of which no donor or beneficiary of an income interest is a trustee, and

(F) from which each beneficiary of an income interest receives income, for each year for which he is entitled to receive the income interest referred to in subparagraph (A), determined by the rate of return earned by the trust for such year.

For purposes of determining the amount of any charitable contribution allowable by reason of a transfer of property to a pooled fund, the value of the income interest shall be determined on the basis of the highest rate of return earned by the fund for any of the 3 taxable years immediately preceding the taxable year of the fund in which the transfer is made. In the case of funds in existence less than 3 taxable years preceding the taxable year of the fund in which a transfer is made, the rate of return shall be deemed to be 6 percent per annum, except that the Secretary may prescribe a different rate of return.

(6) TAXABLE PRIVATE FOUNDATIONS.—In the case of a private foundation which is not exempt from taxation under section 501(a) for the taxable year, the provisions of this subsection shall not apply and the provisions of section 170 shall apply.

[Sec. 642(d)]

(d) NET OPERATING LOSS DEDUCTION.—The benefit of the deduction for net operating losses provided by section 172 shall be allowed to estates and trusts under regulations prescribed by the Secretary.

[Sec. 642(e)]

(e) DEDUCTION FOR DEPRECIATION AND DEPLETION.—An estate or trust shall be allowed the deduction for depreciation and depletion only to the extent not allowable to beneficiaries under sections 167(d) and 611(b).

Sec. 642(d)

[Sec. 642(f)]

(f) AMORTIZATION DEDUCTIONS.—The benefit of the deductions for amortization provided by sections 169 and 197 shall be allowed to estates and trusts in the same manner as in the case of an individual. The allowable deduction shall be apportioned between the income beneficiaries and the fiduciary under regulations prescribed by the Secretary.

[Sec. 642(g)]

(g) DISALLOWANCE OF DOUBLE DEDUCTIONS.—Amounts allowable under section 2053 or 2054 as a deduction in computing the taxable estate of a decedent shall not be allowed as a deduction (or as an offset against the sales price of property in determining gain or loss) in computing the taxable income of the estate or of any other person, unless there is filed, within the time and in the manner and form prescribed by the Secretary, a statement that the amounts have not been allowed as deductions under section 2053 or 2054 and a waiver of the right to have such amounts allowed at any time as deductions under section 2053 or 2054. Rules similar to the rules of the preceding sentence shall apply to amounts which may be taken into account under section 2621(a)(2) or 2622(b). This subsection shall not apply with respect to deductions allowed under part II (relating to income in respect of decedents).

[Sec. 642(h)]

(h) UNUSED LOSS CARRYOVERS AND EXCESS DEDUCTIONS ON TERMINATION AVAILABLE TO BENEFICIARIES.—If on the termination of an estate or trust, the estate or trust has—

    (1) a net operating loss carryover under section 172 or a capital loss carryover under section 1212, or

    (2) for the last taxable year of the estate or trust deductions (other than the deductions allowed under subsections (b) or (c)) in excess of gross income for such year,

then such carryover or such excess shall be allowed as a deduction, in accordance with regulations prescribed by the Secretary, to the beneficiaries succeeding to the property of the estate or trust.

* * *

[Sec. 643]

SEC. 643. DEFINITIONS APPLICABLE TO SUBPARTS A, B, C, AND D.

[Sec. 643(a)]

(a) DISTRIBUTABLE NET INCOME.—For purposes of this part, the term "distributable net income" means, with respect to any taxable year, the taxable income of the estate or trust computed with the following modifications—

    (1) DEDUCTION FOR DISTRIBUTIONS.—No deduction shall be taken under sections 651 and 661 (relating to additional deductions).

    (2) DEDUCTION FOR PERSONAL EXEMPTION.—No deduction shall be taken under section 642 (b) (relating to deduction for personal exemptions).

    (3) CAPITAL GAINS AND LOSSES.—Gains from the sale or exchange of capital assets shall be excluded to the extent that such gains are allocated to corpus and are not (A) paid, credited, or required to be distributed to any beneficiary during the taxable year, or (B) paid, permanently set aside, or to be used for the purposes specified in section 642 (c). Losses from the sale or exchange of capital assets shall be excluded, except to the extent such losses are taken into account in determining the amount of gains from the sale or exchange of capital assets which are paid, credited, or required to be distributed to any beneficiary during the taxable year. The exclusion under section 1202 shall not be taken into account.

    (4) EXTRAORDINARY DIVIDENDS AND TAXABLE STOCK DIVIDENDS.—For purposes only of subpart B (relating to trusts which distribute current income only), there shall be excluded those items of gross income constituting extraordinary dividends or taxable stock dividends which the fiduciary, acting in good faith, does not pay or credit to any beneficiary by reason of his determination that such dividends are allocable to corpus under the terms of the governing instrument and applicable local law.

Sec. 643(a)

(5) TAX-EXEMPT INTEREST.—There shall be included any tax-exempt interest to which section 103 applies, reduced by any amounts which would be deductible in respect of disbursements allocable to such interest but for the provisions of section 265 (relating to disallowance of certain deductions).

* * *

(7) ABUSIVE TRANSACTIONS.—The Secretary shall prescribe such regulations as may be necessary or appropriate to carry out the purposes of this part, including regulations to prevent avoidance of such purposes.

If the estate or trust is allowed a deduction under section 642 (c), the amount of the modifications specified in paragraphs (5) and (6) shall be reduced to the extent that the amount of income which is paid, permanently set aside, or to be used for the purposes specified in section 642 (c) is deemed to consist of items specified in those paragraphs. For this purpose, such amount shall (in the absence of specific provisions in the governing instrument) be deemed to consist of the same proportion of each class of items of income of the estate or trust as the total of each class bears to the total of all classes.

[Sec. 643(b)]

(b) INCOME.—For purposes of this subpart and subparts B, C, and D, the term "income", when not preceded by the words "taxable", "distributable net", "undistributed net", or "gross", means the amount of income of the estate or trust for the taxable year determined under the terms of the governing instrument and applicable local law. Items of gross income constituting extraordinary dividends or taxable stock dividends which the fiduciary, acting in good faith, determines to be allocable to corpus under the terms of the governing instrument and applicable local law shall not be considered income.

[Sec. 643(c)]

(c) BENEFICIARY.—For purposes of this part, the term "beneficiary" includes heir, legatee, devisee.

* * *

[Sec. 643(e)]

(e) TREATMENT OF PROPERTY DISTRIBUTED IN KIND.—

(1) BASIS OF BENEFICIARY.—The basis of any property received by a beneficiary in a distribution from an estate or trust shall be—

(A) the adjusted basis of such property in the hands of the estate or trust immediately before the distribution, adjusted for

(B) any gain or loss recognized to the estate or trust on the distribution.

(2) AMOUNT OF DISTRIBUTION.—In the case of any distribution of property (other than cash), the amount taken into account under sections 661(a)(2) and 662(a)(2) shall be the lesser of—

(A) the basis of such property in the hands of the beneficiary (as determined under paragraph (1)), or

(B) the fair market value of such property.

(3) ELECTION TO RECOGNIZE GAIN.—

(A) IN GENERAL.—In the case of any distribution of property (other than cash) to which an election under this paragraph applies—

(i) paragraph (2) shall not apply,

(ii) gain or loss shall be recognized by the estate or trust in the same manner as if such property had been sold to the distributee at its fair market value, and

(iii) the amount taken into account under sections 661(a)(2) and 662(a)(2) shall be the fair market value of such property.

(B) ELECTION.—Any election under this paragraph shall apply to all distributions made by the estate or trust during a taxable year and shall be made on the return of such estate or trust for such taxable year.

Any such election, once made, may be revoked only with the consent of the Secretary.

(4) EXCEPTION FOR DISTRIBUTIONS DESCRIBED IN SECTION 663(a).—This subsection shall not apply to any distribution described in section 663(a).

[Sec. 643(f)]

(f) TREATMENT OF MULTIPLE TRUSTS.—For purposes of this subchapter, under regulations prescribed by the Secretary, 2 or more trusts shall be treated as 1 trust if—

(1) such trusts have substantially the same grantor or grantors and substantially the same primary beneficiary or beneficiaries, and

(2) a principal purpose of such trusts is the avoidance of the tax imposed by this chapter.

For purposes of the preceding sentence, a husband and wife shall be treated as 1 person.

[Sec. 643(g)]

(g) CERTAIN PAYMENTS OF ESTIMATED TAX TREATED AS PAID BY BENEFICIARY.—

(1) IN GENERAL.—In the case of a trust—

(A) the trustee may elect to treat any portion of a payment of estimated tax made by such trust for any taxable year of the trust as a payment made by a beneficiary of such trust,

(B) any amount so treated shall be treated as paid or credited to the beneficiary on the last day of such taxable year, and

(C) for purposes of subtitle F, the amount so treated—

(i) shall not be treated as a payment of estimated tax made by the trust, but

(ii) shall be treated as a payment of estimated tax made by such beneficiary on January 15 following the taxable year.

(2) TIME FOR MAKING ELECTION.—An election under paragraph (1) shall be made on or before the 65th day after the close of the taxable year of the trust and in such manner as the Secretary may prescribe.

(3) EXTENSION TO LAST YEAR OF ESTATE.—In the case of a taxable year reasonably expected to be the last taxable year of an estate—

(A) any reference in this subsection to a trust shall be treated as including a reference to an estate, and

(B) the fiduciary of the estate shall be treated as the trustee.

* * *

[Sec. 644]

SEC. 644. TAXABLE YEAR OF TRUSTS.

[Sec. 644(a)]

(a) IN GENERAL.—For purposes of this subtitle, the taxable year of any trust shall be the calendar year.

[Sec. 644(b)]

(b) EXCEPTION FOR TRUSTS EXEMPT FROM TAX AND CHARITABLE TRUSTS.—Subsection (a) shall not apply to a trust exempt from taxation under section 501(a) or a trust described in section 4947(a)(1).

[Sec. 645]

SEC. 645. CERTAIN REVOCABLE TRUSTS TREATED AS PART OF ESTATE.

[Sec. 645(a)]

(a) GENERAL RULE.—For purposes of this subtitle, if both the executor (if any) of an estate and the trustee of a qualified revocable trust elect the treatment provided in this section, such trust shall be treated and taxed as part of such estate (and not as a separate trust) for all taxable years of the estate ending after the date of the decedent's death and before the applicable date.

[Sec. 645(b)]

(b) DEFINITIONS.—For purposes of subsection (a)—

(1) QUALIFIED REVOCABLE TRUST.—The term "qualified revocable trust" means any trust (or portion thereof) which was treated under section 676 as owned by the decedent of the estate referred to in subsection (a) by reason of a power in the grantor (determined without regard to section 672(e)).

Sec. 645(b)

(2) APPLICABLE DATE.—The term "applicable date" means—

(A) if no return of tax imposed by chapter 11 is required to be filed, the date which is 2 years after the date of the decedent's death, and

(B) if such a return is required to be filed, the date which is 6 months after the date of the final determination of the liability for tax imposed by chapter 11.

[Sec. 645(c)]

(c) ELECTION.—The election under subsection (a) shall be made not later than the time prescribed for filing the return of tax imposed by this chapter for the first taxable year of the estate (determined with regard to extensions) and, once made, shall be irrevocable.

Subpart B—Trusts Which Distribute Current Income Only

[Sec. 651]

SEC. 651. DEDUCTION FOR TRUSTS DISTRIBUTING CURRENT INCOME ONLY.

[Sec. 651(a)]

(a) DEDUCTION.—In the case of any trust the terms of which—

(1) provide that all of its income is required to be distributed currently, and

(2) do not provide that any amounts are to be paid, permanently set aside, or used for the purposes specified in section 642 (c) (relating to deduction for charitable, etc., purposes),

there shall be allowed as a deduction in computing the taxable income of the trust the amount of the income for the taxable year which is required to be distributed currently. This section shall not apply in any taxable year in which the trust distributes amounts other than amounts of income described in paragraph (1).

[Sec. 651(b)]

(b) LIMITATION ON DEDUCTION.—If the amount of income required to be distributed currently exceeds the distributable net income of the trust for the taxable year, the deduction shall be limited to the amount of the distributable net income. For this purpose, the computation of distributable net income shall not include items of income which are not included in the gross income of the trust and the deductions allocable thereto.

[Sec. 652]

SEC. 652. INCLUSION OF AMOUNTS IN GROSS INCOME OF BENEFICIARIES OF TRUSTS DISTRIBUTING CURRENT INCOME ONLY.

[Sec. 652(a)]

(a) INCLUSION.—Subject to subsection (b), the amount of income for the taxable year required to be distributed currently by a trust described in section 651 shall be included in the gross income of the beneficiaries to whom the income is required to be distributed, whether distributed or not. If such amount exceeds the distributable net income, there shall be included in the gross income of each beneficiary an amount which bears the same ratio to distributable net income as the amount of income required to be distributed to such beneficiary bears to the amount of income required to be distributed to all beneficiaries.

[Sec. 652(b)]

(b) CHARACTER OF AMOUNTS.—The amounts specified in subsection (a) shall have the same character in the hands of the beneficiary as in the hands of the trust. For this purpose, the amounts shall be treated as consisting of the same proportion of each class of items entering into the computation of distributable net income of the trust as the total of each class bears to the total distributable net income of the trust, unless the terms of the trust specifically allocate different classes of income to different beneficiaries. In the application of the preceding sentence, the items of deduction entering into the computation of distributable net income shall be allocated among the items of distributable net income in accordance with regulations prescribed by the Secretary.

Sec. 645(c)

[Sec. 652(c)]

(c) Different Taxable Years.—If the taxable year of a beneficiary is different from that of the trust, the amount which the beneficiary is required to include in gross income in accordance with the provisions of this section shall be based upon the amount of income of the trust for any taxable year or years of the trust ending within or with his taxable year.

Subpart C—Estates and Trusts Which May Accumulate Income or Which Distribute Corpus

[Sec. 661]

SEC. 661. DEDUCTION FOR ESTATES AND TRUSTS ACCUMULATING INCOME OR DISTRIBUTING CORPUS.

[Sec. 661(a)]

(a) Deduction.—In any taxable year there shall be allowed as a deduction in computing the taxable income of an estate or trust (other than a trust to which subpart B applies), the sum of—

(1) any amount of income for such taxable year required to be distributed currently (including any amount required to be distributed which may be paid out of income or corpus to the extent such amount is paid out of income for such taxable year); and

(2) any other amounts properly paid or credited or required to be distributed for such taxable year;

but such deduction shall not exceed the distributable net income of the estate or trust.

[Sec. 661(b)]

(b) Character of Amounts Distributed.—The amount determined under subsection (a) shall be treated as consisting of the same proportion of each class of items entering into the computation of distributable net income of the estate or trust as the total of each class bears to the total distributable net income of the estate or trust in the absence of the allocation of different classes of income under the specific terms of the governing instrument. In the application of the preceding sentence, the items of deduction entering into the computation of distributable net income (including the deduction allowed under section 642 (c)) shall be allocated among the items of distributable net income in accordance with regulations prescribed by the Secretary.

[Sec. 661(c)]

(c) Limitation on Deduction.—No deduction shall be allowed under subsection (a) in respect of any portion of the amount allowed as a deduction under that subsection (without regard to this subsection) which is treated under subsection (b) as consisting of any item of distributable net income which is not included in the gross income of the estate or trust.

[Sec. 662]

SEC. 662. INCLUSION OF AMOUNTS IN GROSS INCOME OF BENEFICIARIES OF ESTATES AND TRUSTS ACCUMULATING INCOME OR DISTRIBUTING CORPUS.

[Sec. 662(a)]

(a) Inclusion.—Subject to subsection (b), there shall be included in the gross income of a beneficiary to whom an amount specified in section 661 (a) is paid, credited, or required to be distributed (by an estate or trust described in section 661), the sum of the following amounts:

(1) Amounts required to be distributed currently.—The amount of income for the taxable year required to be distributed currently to such beneficiary, whether distributed or not. If the amount of income required to be distributed currently to all beneficiaries exceeds the distributable net income (computed without the deduction allowed by section 642 (c), relating to deduction for charitable, etc. purposes) of the estate or trust, then, in lieu of the amount provided in the preceding sentence, there shall be included in the gross income of the beneficiary an amount which bears the same ratio to distributable net income (as so computed) as the amount of income required to be distributed currently to such beneficiary bears to the amount required to be distributed currently to

Sec. 662(a)

all beneficiaries. For purposes of this section, the phrase "the amount of income for the taxable year required to be distributed currently" includes any amount required to be paid out of income or corpus to the extent such amount is paid out of income for such taxable year.

(2) OTHER AMOUNTS DISTRIBUTED.—All other amounts properly paid, credited, or required to be distributed to such beneficiary for the taxable year. If the sum of—

(A) the amount of income for the taxable year required to be distributed currently to all beneficiaries, and

(B) all other amounts properly paid, credited, or required to be distributed to all beneficiaries

exceeds the distributable net income of the estate or trust, then, in lieu of the amount provided in the preceding sentence, there shall be included in the gross income of the beneficiary an amount which bears the same ratio to distributable net income (reduced by the amounts specified in (A)) as the other amounts properly paid, credited or required to be distributed to the beneficiary bear to the other amounts properly paid, credited, or required to be distributed to all beneficiaries.

[Sec. 662(b)]

(b) CHARACTER OF AMOUNTS.—The amounts determined under subsection (a) shall have the same character in the hands of the beneficiary as in the hands of the estate or trust. For this purpose, the amounts shall be treated as consisting of the same proportion of each class of items entering into the computation of distributable net income as the total of each class bears to the total distributable net income of the estate or trust unless the terms of the governing instrument specifically allocate different classes of income to different beneficiaries. In the application of the preceding sentence, the items of deduction entering into the computation of distributable net income (including the deduction allowed under section 642 (c)) shall be allocated among the items of distributable net income in accordance with regulations prescribed by the Secretary. In the application of this subsection to the amount determined under paragraph (1) of subsection (a), distributable net income shall be computed without regard to any portion of the deduction under section 642 (c) which is not attributable to income of the taxable year.

[Sec. 662(c)]

(c) DIFFERENT TAXABLE YEARS.—If the taxable year of a beneficiary is different from that of the estate or trust, the amount to be included in the gross income of the beneficiary shall be based on the distributable net income of the estate or trust and the amounts properly paid, credited, or required to be distributed to the beneficiary during any taxable year or years of the estate or trust ending within or with his taxable year.

[Sec. 663]

SEC. 663. SPECIAL RULES APPLICABLE TO SECTIONS 661 AND 662.

[Sec. 663(a)]

(a) EXCLUSIONS.—There shall not be included as amounts falling within section 661(a) or 662(a)—

(1) GIFTS, BEQUESTS, ETC.—Any amount which, under the terms of the governing instrument, is properly paid or credited as a gift or bequest of a specific sum of money or of specific property and which is paid or credited all at once or in not more than 3 installments. For this purpose an amount which can be paid or credited only from the income of the estate or trust shall not be considered as a gift or bequest of a specific sum of money.

(2) CHARITABLE, ETC., DISTRIBUTIONS.—Any amount paid or permanently set aside or otherwise qualifying for the deduction provided in section 642(c) (computed without regard to sections 508(d), 681, and 4948(c)(4)).

(3) DENIAL OF DOUBLE DEDUCTION.—Any amount paid, credited, or distributed in the taxable year, if section 651 or section 661 applied to such amount for a preceding taxable year of an estate or trust because credited or required to be distributed in such preceding taxable year.

[Sec. 663(b)]

(b) DISTRIBUTIONS IN FIRST SIXTY-FIVE DAYS OF TAXABLE YEAR.—

(1) GENERAL RULE.—If within the first 65 days of any taxable year of an estate or a trust, an amount is properly paid or credited, such amount shall be considered paid or credited on the last day of the preceding taxable year.

(2) LIMITATION.—Paragraph (1) shall apply with respect to any taxable year of an estate or a trust only if the executor of such estate or the fiduciary of such trust (as the case may be) elects, in such manner and at such time as the Secretary prescribes by regulations, to have paragraph (1) apply for such taxable year.

[Sec. 663(c)]

(c) SEPARATE SHARES TREATED AS SEPARATE ESTATES OR TRUSTS.—For the sole purpose of determining the amount of distributable net income in the application of sections 661 and 662, in the case of a single trust having more than one beneficiary, substantially separate and independent shares of different beneficiaries in the trust shall be treated as separate trusts. Rules similar to the rules of the preceding provisions of this subsection shall apply to treat substantially separate and independent shares of different beneficiaries in an estate having more than 1 beneficiary as separate estates. The existence of such substantially separate and independent shares and the manner of treatment as separate trusts or estates, including the application of subpart D, shall be determined in accordance with regulations prescribed by the Secretary.

[Sec. 664]

SEC. 664. CHARITABLE REMAINDER TRUSTS.

[Sec. 664(a)]

(a) GENERAL RULE.—Notwithstanding any other provision of this subchapter, the provisions of this section shall, in accordance with regulations prescribed by the Secretary, apply in the case of a charitable remainder annuity trust and a charitable remainder unitrust.

[Sec. 664(b)]

(b) CHARACTER OF DISTRIBUTIONS.—Amounts distributed by a charitable remainder annuity trust or by a charitable remainder unitrust shall be considered as having the following characteristics in the hands of a beneficiary to whom is paid the annuity described in subsection (d)(1)(A) or the payment described in subsection (d)(2)(A):

(1) First, as amounts of income (other than gains, and amounts treated as gains, from the sale or other disposition of capital assets) includible in gross income to the extent of such income of the trust for the year and such undistributed income of the trust for prior years;

(2) Second, as a capital gain to the extent of the capital gain of the trust for the year and the undistributed capital gain of the trust for prior years;

(3) Third, as other income to the extent of such income of the trust for the year and such undistributed income of the trust for prior years; and

(4) Fourth, as a distribution of trust corpus.

For purposes of this section, the trust shall determine the amount of its undistributed capital gain on a cumulative net basis.

[Sec. 664(c)]

(c) EXEMPTION FROM INCOME TAXES.—A charitable remainder annuity trust and a charitable remainder unitrust shall, for any taxable year, not be subject to any tax imposed by this subtitle, unless such trust, for such year, has unrelated business taxable income (within the meaning of section 512, determined as if part III of subchapter F applied to such trust).

[Sec. 664(d)]

(d) DEFINITIONS.—

(1) CHARITABLE REMAINDER ANNUITY TRUST.—For purposes of this section, a charitable remainder annuity trust is a trust—

(A) from which a sum certain (which is not less than 5 percent nor more than 50 percent of the initial net fair market value of all property placed in trust) is to be paid, not less often than annually, to one or more persons (at least one of which is not an organization described in section 170(c) and, in the case of individuals, only to an individual who is living at the time of the creation of the trust) for a term of years (not in excess of 20 years) or for the life or lives of such individual or individuals,

(B) from which no amount other than the payments described in subparagraph (A) and other than qualified gratuitous transfers described in subparagraph (C) may be paid to or for the use of any person other than an organization described in section 170(c),

(C) following the termination of the payments described in subparagraph (A), the remainder interest in the trust is to be transferred to, or for the use of, an organization described in section 170(c) or is to be retained by the trust for such a use or, to the extent the remainder interest is in qualified employer securities (as defined in subsection (g)(4)), all or part of such securities are to be transferred to an employee stock ownership plan (as defined in section 4975(e)(7)) in a qualified gratuitous transfer (as defined by subsection (g)), and

(D) the value (determined under section 7520) of such remainder interest is at least 10 percent of the initial net fair market value of all property placed in the trust.

(2) CHARITABLE REMAINDER UNITRUST.—For purposes of this section, a charitable remainder unitrust is a trust—

(A) from which a fixed percentage (which is not less than 5 percent nor more than 50 percent) of the net fair market value of its assets, valued annually, is to be paid, not less often than annually, to one or more persons (at least one of which is not an organization described in section 170(c) and, in the case of individuals, only to an individual who is living at the time of the creation of the trust) for a term of years (not in excess of 20 years) or for the life or lives of such individual or individuals,

(B) from which no amount other than the payments described in subparagraph (A) and other than qualified gratuitous transfers described in subparagraph (C) may be paid to or for the use of any person other than an organization described in section 170(c),

(C) following the termination of the payments described in subparagraph (A), the remainder interest in the trust is to be transferred to, or for the use of, an organization described in section 170(c) or is to be retained by the trust for such a use or, to the extent the remainder interest is in qualified employer securities (as defined in subsection (g)(4)), all or part of such securities are to be transferred to an employee stock ownership plan (as defined in section 4975(e)(7)) in a qualified gratuitous transfer (as defined by subsection (g)), and

(D) with respect to each contribution of property to the trust, the value (determined under section 7520) of such remainder interest in such property is at least 10 percent of the net fair market value of such property as of the date such property is contributed to the trust.

(3) EXCEPTION.—Notwithstanding the provisions of paragraphs (2)(A) and (B), the trust instrument may provide that the trustee shall pay the income beneficiary for any year—

(A) the amount of the trust income, if such amount is less than the amount required to be distributed under paragraph (2)(A), and

(B) any amount of the trust income which is in excess of the amount required to be distributed under paragraph (2)(A), to the extent that (by reason of subparagraph (A)) the aggregate of the amounts paid in prior years was less than the aggregate of such required amounts.

(4) SEVERANCE OF CERTAIN ADDITIONAL CONTRIBUTIONS.—If—

(A) any contribution is made to a trust which before the contribution is a charitable remainder unitrust, and

(B) such contribution would (but for this paragraph) result in such trust ceasing to be a charitable unitrust by reason of paragraph (2)(D),

such contribution shall be treated as a transfer to a separate trust under regulations prescribed by the Secretary.

[Sec. 664(e)]

(e) VALUATION FOR PURPOSES OF CHARITABLE CONTRIBUTIONS.—For purposes of determining the amount of any charitable contribution, the remainder interest of a charitable remainder annuity trust or charitable remainder unitrust shall be computed on the basis that an amount equal to 5 percent of the net fair market value of its assets (or a greater amount, if required under the terms of the trust instrument) is to be distributed each year.

[Sec. 664(f)]

(f) CERTAIN CONTINGENCIES PERMITTED.—

(1) GENERAL RULE.—If a trust would, but for a qualified contingency, meet the requirements of paragraph (1)(A) or (2)(A) of subsection (d), such trust shall be treated as meeting such requirements.

(2) VALUE DETERMINED WITHOUT REGARD TO QUALIFIED CONTINGENCY.—For purposes of determining the amount of any charitable contribution (or the actuarial value of any interest), a qualified contingency shall not be taken into account.

(3) QUALIFIED CONTINGENCY.—For purposes of this subsection, the term "qualified contingency" means any provision of a trust which provides that, upon the happening of a contingency, the payments described in paragraph (1)(A) or (2)(A) of subsection (d) (as the case may be) will terminate not later than such payments would otherwise terminate under the trust.

* * *

Subpart E—Grantors and Others Treated as Substantial Owners

[Sec. 671]

SEC. 671. TRUST INCOME, DEDUCTIONS, AND CREDITS ATTRIBUTABLE TO GRANTORS AND OTHERS AS SUBSTANTIAL OWNERS.

Where it is specified in this subpart that the grantor or another person shall be treated as the owner of any portion of a trust, there shall then be included in computing the taxable income and credits of the grantor or the other person those items of income, deductions, and credits against tax of the trust which are attributable to that portion of the trust to the extent that such items would be taken into account under this chapter in computing taxable income or credits against the tax of an individual. Any remaining portion of the trust shall be subject to subparts A through D. No items of a trust shall be included in computing the taxable income and credits of the grantor or of any other person solely on the grounds of his dominion and control over the trust under section 61 (relating to definition of gross income) or any other provision of this title, except as specified in this subpart.

[Sec. 672]

SEC. 672. DEFINITIONS AND RULES.

[Sec. 672(a)]

(a) ADVERSE PARTY.—For purposes of this subpart, the term "adverse party" means any person having a substantial beneficial interest in the trust which would be adversely affected by the exercise or nonexercise of the power which he possesses respecting the trust. A person having a general power of appointment over the trust property shall be deemed to have a beneficial interest in the trust.

[Sec. 672(b)]

(b) NONADVERSE PARTY.—For purposes of this subpart, the term "nonadverse party" means any person who is not an adverse party.

[Sec. 672(c)]

(c) RELATED OR SUBORDINATE PARTY.—For purposes of this subpart, the term "related or subordinate party" means any nonadverse party who is—

(1) the grantor's spouse if living with the grantor;

(2) any one of the following: The grantor's father, mother, issue, brother or sister; an employee of the grantor; a corporation or any employee of a corporation in which the stock holdings of the grantor and the trust are significant from the viewpoint of voting control; a subordinate employee of a corporation in which the grantor is an executive.

For purposes of subsection (f) and sections 674 and 675, a related or subordinate party shall be presumed to be subservient to the grantor in respect of the exercise or nonexercise of the powers conferred on him unless such party is shown not to be subservient by a preponderance of the evidence.

[Sec. 672(d)]

(d) RULE WHERE POWER IS SUBJECT TO CONDITION PRECEDENT.—A person shall be considered to have a power described in this subpart even though the exercise of the power is subject to a precedent giving of notice or takes effect only on the expiration of a certain period after the exercise of the power.

Sec. 672(d)

[Sec. 672(e)]

(e) GRANTOR TREATED AS HOLDING ANY POWER OR INTEREST OF GRANTOR'S SPOUSE.—

(1) IN GENERAL.—For purposes of this subpart, a grantor shall be treated as holding any power or interest held by—

(A) any individual who was the spouse of the grantor at the time of the creation of such power or interest, or

(B) any individual who became the spouse of the grantor after the creation of such power or interest, but only with respect to periods after such individual became the spouse of the grantor.

(2) MARITAL STATUS.—For purposes of paragraph (1)(A), an individual legally separated from his spouse under a decree of divorce or of separate maintenance shall not be considered as married.

* * *

[Sec. 673]

SEC. 673. REVERSIONARY INTERESTS.

[Sec. 673(a)]

(a) GENERAL RULE.—The grantor shall be treated as the owner of any portion of a trust in which he has a reversionary interest in either the corpus or the income therefrom, if, as of the inception of that portion of the trust, the value of such interest exceeds 5 percent of the value of such portion.

[Sec. 673(b)]

(b) REVERSIONARY INTEREST TAKING EFFECT AT DEATH OF MINOR LINEAL DESCENDANT BENEFICIARY.—In the case of any beneficiary who—

(1) is a lineal descendant of the grantor, and

(2) holds all of the present interests in any portion of a trust, the grantor shall not be treated under subsection (a) as the owner of such portion solely by reason of a reversionary interest in such portion which takes effect upon the death of such beneficiary before such beneficiary attains age 21.

[Sec. 673(c)]

(c) SPECIAL RULE FOR DETERMINING VALUE OF REVERSIONARY INTEREST.—For purposes of subsection (a), the value of the grantor's reversionary interest shall be determined by assuming the maximum exercise of discretion in favor of the grantor.

[Sec. 673(d)]

(d) POSTPONEMENT OF DATE SPECIFIED FOR REACQUISITION.—Any postponement of the date specified for the reacquisition of possession or enjoyment of the reversionary interest shall be treated as a new transfer in trust commencing with the date on which the postponement is effective and terminating with the date prescribed by the postponement. However, income for any period shall not be included in the income of the grantor by reason of the preceding sentence if such income would not be so includible in the absence of such postponement.

[Sec. 674]

SEC. 674. POWER TO CONTROL BENEFICIAL ENJOYMENT.

[Sec. 674(a)]

(a) GENERAL RULE.—The grantor shall be treated as the owner of any portion of a trust in respect of which the beneficial enjoyment of the corpus or the income therefrom is subject to a power of disposition, exercisable by the grantor or a nonadverse party, or both, without the approval or consent of any adverse party.

[Sec. 674(b)]

(b) EXCEPTIONS FOR CERTAIN POWERS.—Subsection (a) shall not apply to the following powers regardless of by whom held:

(1) POWER TO APPLY INCOME TO SUPPORT OF A DEPENDENT.—A power described in section 677 (b) to the extent that the grantor would not be subject to tax under that section.

(2) POWER AFFECTING BENEFICIAL ENJOYMENT ONLY AFTER OCCURRENCE OF EVENT.—A power, the exercise of which can only affect the beneficial enjoyment of the income for a period commencing after the occurrence of an event such that a grantor would not be treated as the owner under section 673 if the power were a reversionary interest; but the grantor may be treated as the owner after the occurrence of the event unless the power is relinquished.

(3) POWER EXERCISABLE ONLY BY WILL.—A power exercisable only by will, other than a power in the grantor to appoint by will the income of the trust where the income is accumulated for such disposition by the grantor or may be so accumulated in the discretion of the grantor or a nonadverse party, or both, without the approval or consent of any adverse party.

(4) POWER TO ALLOCATE AMONG CHARITABLE BENEFICIARIES.—A power to determine the beneficial enjoyment of the corpus or the income therefrom if the corpus or income is irrevocably payable for a purpose specified in section 170(c) (relating to definition of charitable contributions) or to an employee stock ownership plan (as defined in section 4975(e)(7)) in a qualified gratuitous transfer (as defined in section 664(g)(1)).

(5) POWER TO DISTRIBUTE CORPUS.—A power to distribute corpus either—

(A) to or for a beneficiary or beneficiaries or to or for a class of beneficiaries (whether or not income beneficiaries) provided that the power is limited by a reasonably definite standard which is set forth in the trust instrument; or

(B) to or for any current income beneficiary, provided that the distribution of corpus must be chargeable against the proportionate share of corpus held in trust for the payment of income to the beneficiary as if the corpus constituted a separate trust.

A power does not fall within the powers described in this paragraph if any person has a power to add to the beneficiary or beneficiaries or to a class of beneficiaries designated to receive the income or corpus, except where such action is to provide for after-born or after-adopted children.

(6) POWER TO WITHHOLD INCOME TEMPORARILY.—A power to distribute or apply income to or for any current income beneficiary or to accumulate the income for him, provided that any accumulated income must ultimately be payable—

(A) to the beneficiary from whom distribution or application is withheld, to his estate, or to his appointees (or persons named as alternate takers in default of appointment) provided that such beneficiary possesses a power of appointment which does not exclude from the class of possible appointees any person other than the beneficiary, his estate, his creditors, or the creditors of his estate, or

(B) on termination of the trust, or in conjunction with a distribution of corpus which is augmented by such accumulated income, to the current income beneficiaries in shares which have been irrevocably specified in the trust instrument.

Accumulated income shall be considered so payable although it is provided that if any beneficiary does not survive a date of distribution which could reasonably have been expected to occur within the beneficiary's lifetime, the share of the deceased beneficiary is to be paid to his appointees or to one or more designated alternate takers (other than the grantor or the grantor's estate) whose shares have been irrevocably specified. A power does not fall within the powers described in this paragraph if any person has a power to add to the beneficiary or beneficiaries or to a class of beneficiaries designated to receive the income or corpus except where such action is to provide for after-born or after-adopted children.

(7) POWER TO WITHHOLD INCOME DURING DISABILITY OF A BENEFICIARY.—A power exercisable only during—

(A) the existence of a legal disability of any current income beneficiary, or

(B) the period during which any income beneficiary shall be under the age of 21 years,

to distribute or apply income to or for such beneficiary or to accumulate and add the income to corpus. A power does not fall within the powers described in this paragraph if any person has a power to add to the beneficiary or beneficiaries or to a class of beneficiaries designated to receive the income or corpus, except where such action is to provide for after-born or after-adopted children.

(8) POWER TO ALLOCATE BETWEEN CORPUS AND INCOME.—A power to allocate receipts and disbursements as between corpus and income, even though expressed in broad language.

Sec. 674(b)

[Sec. 674(c)]

(c) EXCEPTION FOR CERTAIN POWERS OF INDEPENDENT TRUSTEES.—Subsection (a) shall not apply to a power solely exercisable (without the approval or consent of any other person) by a trustee or trustees, none of whom is the grantor, and no more than half of whom are related or subordinate parties who are subservient to the wishes of the grantor—

(1) to distribute, apportion, or accumulate income to or for a beneficiary or beneficiaries, or to, for, or within a class of beneficiaries; or

(2) to pay out corpus to or for a beneficiary or beneficiaries or to or for a class of beneficiaries (whether or not income beneficiaries).

A power does not fall within the powers described in this subsection if any person has a power to add to the beneficiary or beneficiaries or to a class of beneficiaries designated to receive the income or corpus, except where such action is to provide for after-born or after-adopted children. For periods during which an individual is the spouse of the grantor (within the meaning of section 672(e)(2)), any reference in this subsection to the grantor shall be treated as including a reference to such individual.

[Sec. 674(d)]

(d) POWER TO ALLOCATE INCOME IF LIMITED BY A STANDARD.—Subsection (a) shall not apply to a power solely exercisable (without the approval or consent of any other person) by a trustee or trustees, none of whom is the grantor or spouse living with the grantor, to distribute, apportion, or accumulate income to or for a beneficiary or beneficiaries, or to, for, or within a class of beneficiaries, whether or not the conditions of paragraph (6) or (7) of subsection (b) are satisfied, if such power is limited by a reasonably definite external standard which is set forth in the trust instrument. A power does not fall within the powers described in this subsection if any person has a power to add to the beneficiary or beneficiaries or to a class of beneficiaries designated to receive the income or corpus except where such action is to provide for after-born or after-adopted children.

[Sec. 675]

SEC. 675. ADMINISTRATIVE POWERS.

The grantor shall be treated as the owner of any portion of a trust in respect of which—

(1) POWER TO DEAL FOR LESS THAN ADEQUATE AND FULL CONSIDERATION.—A power exercisable by the grantor or a nonadverse party, or both, without the approval or consent of any adverse party enables the grantor or any person to purchase, exchange, or otherwise deal with or dispose of the corpus or the income therefrom for less than an adequate consideration in money or money's worth.

(2) POWER TO BORROW WITHOUT ADEQUATE INTEREST OR SECURITY.—A power exercisable by the grantor or a nonadverse party, or both, enables the grantor to borrow the corpus or income, directly or indirectly, without adequate interest or without adequate security except where a trustee (other than the grantor) is authorized under a general lending power to make loans to any person without regard to interest or security.

(3) BORROWING OF THE TRUST FUNDS.—The grantor has directly or indirectly borrowed the corpus or income and has not completely repaid the loan, including any interest, before the beginning of the taxable year. The preceding sentence shall not apply to a loan which provides for adequate interest and adequate security, if such loan is made by a trustee other than the grantor and other than a related or subordinate trustee subservient to the grantor. For periods during which an individual is the spouse of the grantor (within the meaning of section 672(e)(2)), any reference in this paragraph to the grantor shall be treated as including a reference to such individual.

(4) GENERAL POWERS OF ADMINISTRATION.—A power of administration is exercisable in a nonfiduciary capacity by any person without the approval or consent of any person in a fiduciary capacity. For purposes of this paragraph, the term "power of administration" means any one or more of the following powers: (A) a power to vote or direct the voting of stock or other securities of a corporation in which the holdings of the grantor and the trust are significant from the viewpoint of voting control; (B) a power to control the investment of the trust funds either by directing investments or reinvestments, or by vetoing proposed investments or reinvestments, to the extent that the trust funds consist of stocks or securities of corporations in which the holdings of the grantor and the trust are significant from the viewpoint of voting control; or (C) a power to reacquire the trust corpus by substituting other property of an equivalent value.

[Sec. 676]

SEC. 676. POWER TO REVOKE.

[Sec. 676(a)]

(a) GENERAL RULE.—The grantor shall be treated as the owner of any portion of a trust, whether or not he is treated as such owner under any other provision of this part, where at any time the power to revest in the grantor title to such portion is exercisable by the grantor or a nonadverse party, or both.

[Sec. 676(b)]

(b) POWER AFFECTING BENEFICIAL ENJOYMENT ONLY AFTER OCCURRENCE OF EVENT.—Subsection (a) shall not apply to a power the exercise of which can only affect the beneficial enjoyment of the income for a period commencing after the occurrence of an event such that a grantor would not be treated as the owner under section 673 if the power were a reversionary interest. But the grantor may be treated as the owner after the occurrence of such event unless the power is relinquished.

[Sec. 677]

SEC. 677. INCOME FOR BENEFIT OF GRANTOR.

[Sec. 677(a)]

(a) GENERAL RULE.—The grantor shall be treated as the owner of any portion of a trust, whether or not he is treated as such owner under section 674, whose income without the approval or consent of any adverse party is, or, in the discretion of the grantor or a nonadverse party, or both, may be—

(1) distributed to the grantor or the grantor's spouse;

(2) held or accumulated for future distribution to the grantor or the grantor's spouse; or

(3) applied to the payment of premiums on policies of insurance on the life of the grantor or the grantor's spouse (except policies of insurance irrevocably payable for a purpose specified in section 170 (c) (relating to definition of charitable contributions)).

This subsection shall not apply to a power the exercise of which can only affect the beneficial enjoyment of the income for a period commencing after the occurrence of an event such that the grantor would not be treated as the owner under section 673 if the power were a reversionary interest; but the grantor may be treated as the owner after the occurrence of the event unless the power is relinquished.

[Sec. 677(b)]

(b) OBLIGATIONS OF SUPPORT.—Income of a trust shall not be considered taxable to the grantor under subsection (a) or any other provision of this chapter merely because such income in the discretion of another person, the trustee, or the grantor acting as trustee or co-trustee, may be applied or distributed for the support or maintenance of a beneficiary (other than the grantor's spouse) whom the grantor is legally obligated to support or maintain, except to the extent that such income is so applied or distributed. In cases where the amounts so applied or distributed are paid out of corpus or out of other than income for the taxable year, such amounts shall be considered to be an amount paid or credited within the meaning of paragraph (2) of section 661(a) and shall be taxed to the grantor under section 662.

[Sec. 678]

SEC. 678. PERSON OTHER THAN GRANTOR TREATED AS SUBSTANTIAL OWNER.

[Sec. 678(a)]

(a) GENERAL RULE.—A person other than the grantor shall be treated as the owner of any portion of a trust with respect to which:

(1) such person has a power exercisable solely by himself to vest the corpus or the income therefrom in himself, or

(2) such person has previously partially released or otherwise modified such a power and after the release or modification retains such control as would, within the principles of sections 671 to 677, inclusive, subject a grantor of a trust to treatment as the owner thereof.

Sec. 678(a)

(b) EXCEPTION WHERE GRANTOR IS TAXABLE.—Subsection (a) shall not apply with respect to a power over income, as originally granted or thereafter modified, if the grantor of the trust or a transferor (to whom section 679 applies) is otherwise treated as the owner under the provisions of this subpart other than this section.

(c) OBLIGATIONS OF SUPPORT.—Subsection (a) shall not apply to a power which enables such person, in the capacity of trustee or co-trustee, merely to apply the income of the trust to the support or maintenance of a person whom the holder of the power is obligated to support or maintain except to the extent that such income is so applied. In cases where the amounts so applied or distributed are paid out of corpus or out of other than income of the taxable year, such amounts shall be considered to be an amount paid or credited within the meaning of paragraph (2) of section 661 (a) and shall be taxed to the holder of the power under section 662.

(d) EFFECT OF RENUNCIATION OR DISCLAIMER.—Subsection (a) shall not apply with respect to a power which has been renounced or disclaimed within a reasonable time after the holder of the power first became aware of its existence.

(e) CROSS REFERENCE.—

For provision under which beneficiary of trust is treated as owner of the portion of the trust which consists of stock in an S corporation, see section 1361(d).

Subpart F—Miscellaneous

SEC. 682. INCOME OF AN ESTATE OR TRUST IN CASE OF DIVORCE, ETC.

(a) INCLUSION IN GROSS INCOME OF WIFE.—There shall be included in the gross income of a wife who is divorced or legally separated under a decree of divorce or of separate maintenance (or who is separated from her husband under a written separation agreement) the amount of the income of any trust which such wife is entitled to receive and which, except for this section, would be includible in the gross income of her husband, and such amount shall not, despite any other provision of this subtitle, be includible in the gross income of such husband. This subsection shall not apply to that part of any such income of the trust which the terms of the decree, written separation agreement, or trust instrument fix, in terms of an amount of money or a portion of such income, as a sum which is payable for the support of minor children of such husband. In case such income is less than the amount specified in the decree, agreement, or instrument, for the purpose of applying the preceding sentence, such income, to the extent of such sum payable for such support, shall be considered a payment for such support.

(b) WIFE CONSIDERED A BENEFICIARY.—For purposes of computing the taxable income of the estate or trust and the taxable income of a wife to whom subsection (a) applies, such wife shall be considered as the beneficiary specified in this part.

(c) CROSS REFERENCE.—

For definitions of "husband" and "wife", as used in this section, see section 7701 (a) (17).

[Sec. 683]

SEC. 683. USE OF TRUST AS AN EXCHANGE FUND.

[Sec. 683(a)]

(a) GENERAL RULE.—Except as provided in subsection (b), if property is transferred to a trust in exchange for an interest in other trust property and if the trust would be an investment company (within the meaning of section 351) if it were a corporation, then gain shall be recognized to the transferor.

[Sec. 683(b)]

(b) EXCEPTION FOR POOLED INCOME FUNDS.—Subsection (a) shall not apply to any transfer to a pooled income fund (within the meaning of section 642(c)(5)).

PART II—INCOME IN RESPECT OF DECEDENTS

[Sec. 691]

SEC. 691. RECIPIENTS OF INCOME IN RESPECT OF DECEDENTS.

[Sec. 691(a)]

(a) INCLUSION IN GROSS INCOME.—

(1) GENERAL RULE.—The amount of all items of gross income in respect of a decedent which are not properly includible in respect of the taxable period in which falls the date of his death or a prior period (including the amount of all items of gross income in respect of a prior decedent, if the right to receive such amount was acquired by reason of the death of the prior decedent or by bequest, devise, or inheritance from the prior decedent) shall be included in the gross income, for the taxable year when received, of:

(A) the estate of the decedent, if the right to receive the amount is acquired by the decedent's estate from the decedent;

(B) the person who, by reason of the death of the decedent, acquires the right to receive the amount, if the right to receive the amount is not acquired by the decedent's estate from the decedent; or

(C) the person who acquires from the decedent the right to receive the amount by bequest, devise, or inheritance, if the amount is received after a distribution by the decedent's estate of such right.

(2) INCOME IN CASE OF SALE, ETC.—If a right, described in paragraph (1), to receive an amount is transferred by the estate of the decedent or a person who received such right by reason of the death of the decedent or by bequest, devise, or inheritance from the decedent, there shall be included in the gross income of the estate or such person, as the case may be, for the taxable period in which the transfer occurs, the fair market value of such right at the time of such transfer plus the amount by which any consideration for the transfer exceeds such fair market value. For purposes of this paragraph, the term "transfer" includes sale, exchange, or other disposition, or the satisfaction of an installment obligation at other than face value, but does not include transmission at death to the estate of the decedent or a transfer to a person pursuant to the right of such person to receive such amount by reason of the death of the decedent or by bequest, devise, or inheritance from the decedent.

(3) CHARACTER OF INCOME DETERMINED BY REFERENCE TO DECEDENT.—The right, described in paragraph (1), to receive an amount shall be treated, in the hands of the estate of the decedent or any person who acquired such right by reason of the death of the decedent, or by bequest, devise, or inheritance from the decedent, as if it had been acquired by the estate or such person in the transaction in which the right to receive the income was originally derived and the amount includible in gross income under paragraph (1) or (2) shall be considered in the hands of the estate or such person to have the character which it would have had in the hands of the decedent if the decedent had lived and received such amount.

(4) INSTALLMENT OBLIGATIONS ACQUIRED FROM DECEDENT.—In the case of an installment obligation reportable by the decedent on the installment method under section 453, if such obligation is acquired by the decedent's estate from the decedent or by any person by reason of the death of the decedent or by bequest, devise, or inheritance from the decedent—

(A) an amount equal to the excess of the face amount of such obligation over the basis of the obligation in the hands of the decedent (determined under section 453B) shall, for the purpose of paragraph (1), be considered as an item of gross income in respect of the decedent; and

(B) such obligation shall, for purposes of paragraphs (2) and (3), be considered a right to receive an item of gross income in respect of the decedent, but the amount includible in gross income under paragraph (2) shall be reduced by an amount equal to the basis of the obligation in the hands of the decedent (determined under section 453B).

(5) OTHER RULES RELATING TO INSTALLMENT OBLIGATIONS.—

(A) IN GENERAL.—In the case of an installment obligation reportable by the decedent on the installment method under section 453, for purposes of paragraph (2)—

(i) the second sentence of paragraph (2) shall be applied by inserting "(other than the obligor)" after "or a transfer to a person,"

(ii) any cancellation of such an obligation shall be treated as a transfer, and

(iii) any cancellation of such an obligation occurring at the death of the decedent shall be treated as a transfer by the estate of the decedent (or, if held by a person other than the decedent before the death of the decedent, by such person).

(B) FACE AMOUNT TREATED AS FAIR MARKET VALUE IN CERTAIN CASES.—In any case to which the first sentence of paragraph (2) applies by reason of subparagraph (A), if the decedent and the obligor were related persons (within the meaning of section 453(f)(1)), the fair market value of the installment obligation shall be treated as not less than its face amount.

(C) CANCELLATION INCLUDES BECOMING UNENFORCEABLE.—For purposes of subparagraph (A), an installment obligation which becomes unenforceable shall be treated as if it were canceled.

[Sec. 691(b)]

(b) ALLOWANCE OF DEDUCTIONS AND CREDIT.—The amount of any deduction specified in section 162, 163, 164, 212, or 611 (relating to deductions for expenses, interest, taxes, and depletion) or credit specified in section 27 (relating to foreign tax credit), in respect of a decedent which is not properly allowable to the decedent in respect of the taxable period in which falls the date of his death, or a prior period, shall be allowed:

(1) EXPENSES, INTEREST, AND TAXES.—In the case of a deduction specified in section 162, 163, 164, or 212 and a credit specified in section 27, in the taxable year when paid—

(A) to the estate of the decedent; except that

(B) if the estate of the decedent is not liable to discharge the obligation to which the deduction or credit relates, to the person who, by reason of the death of the decedent of by bequest, devise, or inheritance acquires, subject to such obligation, from the decedent an interest in property of the decedent.

(2) DEPLETION.—In the case of the deduction specified in section 611, to the person described in subsection (a) (1) (A), (B), or (C) who, in the manner described therein, receives the income to which the deduction relates, in the taxable year when such income is received.

[Sec. 691(c)]

(c) DEDUCTION FOR ESTATE TAX.—

(1) ALLOWANCE OF DEDUCTION.—

(A) GENERAL RULE.—A person who includes an amount in gross income under subsection (a) shall be allowed, for the same taxable year, as a deduction an amount which bears the same ratio to the estate tax attributable to the net value for estate tax purposes of all the items described in subsection (a) (1) as the value for estate tax purposes of the items of gross income or portions thereof in respect of which such person included the amount in gross income (or the amount included in gross income, whichever is lower) bears to the value for estate tax purposes of all the items described in subsection (a) (1).

(B) ESTATES AND TRUSTS.—In the case of an estate or trust, the amount allowed as a deduction under subparagraph (A) shall be computed by excluding from the gross income of the estate or trust the portion (if any) of the items described in subsection (a) (1) which is properly paid, credited, or to be distributed to the beneficiaries during the taxable year.

(2) METHOD OF COMPUTING DEDUCTION.—For purposes of paragraph (1)—

(A) The term "estate tax" means the tax imposed on the estate of the decedent or any prior decedent under section 2001 or 2101, reduced by the credits against such tax.

(B) The net value for estate tax purposes of all the items described in subsection (a) (1) shall be the excess of the value for estate tax purposes of all the items described in subsection (a) (1) over the deductions from the gross estate in respect of claims which represent the deductions and credit described in subsection (b). Such net value shall be determined with respect to the provisions of section 421(c)(2), relating to the deduction for estate tax with respect to stock options to which part II of subchapter D applies.

(C) The estate tax attributable to such net value shall be an amount equal to the excess of the estate tax over the estate tax computed without including in the gross estate such net value.

(3) SPECIAL RULE FOR GENERATION-SKIPPING TRANSFERS.—In the case of any tax imposed by chapter 13 on a taxable termination or a direct skip occurring as a result of the death of the transferor, there shall be allowed a deduction (under principles similar to the principles of this subsection) for the portion of such tax attributable to items of gross income of the trust which were not properly includible in the gross income of the trust for periods before the date of such termination.

(4) COORDINATION WITH CAPITAL GAIN PROVISIONS.—For purposes of sections 1(h), 1201, 1202, and 1211, the amount of any gain taken into account with respect to any item described in subsection (a)(1) shall be reduced (but not below zero) by the amount of the deduction allowable under paragraph (1) of this subsection with respect to such item.

[Sec. 691(d)]

(d) AMOUNTS RECEIVED BY SURVIVING ANNUITANT UNDER JOINT AND SURVIVOR ANNUITY CONTRACT.—

(1) DEDUCTION FOR ESTATE TAX.—For purposes of computing the deduction under subsection (c) (1) (A), amounts received by a surviving annuitant—

(A) as an annuity under a joint and survivor annuity contract where the decedent annuitant died after December 31, 1953, and after the annuity starting date (as defined in section 72 (c) (4)), and

(B) during the surviving annuitant's life expectancy period,

shall, to the extent included in gross income under section 72, be considered as amounts included in gross income under subsection (a).

(2) NET VALUE FOR ESTATE TAX PURPOSES.—In determining the net value for estate tax purposes under subsection (c) (2) (B) for purposes of this subsection, the value for estate tax purposes of the items described in paragraph (1) of this subsection shall be computed—

(A) by determining the excess of the value of the annuity at the date of the death of the deceased annuitant over the total amount excludable from the gross income of the surviving annuitant under section 72 during the surviving annuitant's life expectancy period, and

(B) by multiplying the figure so obtained by the ratio which the value of the annuity for estate tax purposes bears to the value of the annuity at the date of the death of the deceased.

(3) DEFINITIONS.—For purposes of this subsection—

(A) The term "life expectancy period" means the period beginning with the first day of the first period for which an amount is received by the surviving annuitant under the contract and ending with the close of the taxable year with or in which falls the termination of the life expectancy of the surviving annuitant. For purposes of this subparagraph, the life expectancy of the surviving annuitant shall be determined, as of the date of the death of the deceased annuitant, with reference to actuarial tables prescribed by the Secretary.

(B) The surviving annuitant's expected return under the contract shall be computed, as of the death of the deceased annuitant, with reference to actuarial tables prescribed by the Secretary.

[Sec. 691(e)]

(e) CROSS REFERENCE.—

For application of this section to income in respect of a deceased partner, see section 753.

Sec. 691(e)

Subchapter K—Partners and Partnerships

PART I—DETERMINATION OF TAX LIABILITY

[Sec. 701]

SEC. 701. PARTNERS, NOT PARTNERSHIP, SUBJECT TO TAX.

A partnership as such shall not be subject to the income tax imposed by this chapter. Persons carrying on business as partners shall be liable for income tax only in their separate or individual capacities.

[Sec. 702]

SEC. 702. INCOME AND CREDITS OF PARTNER.

[Sec. 702(a)]

(a) GENERAL RULE.—In determining his income tax, each partner shall take into account separately his distributive share of the partnership's—

(1) gains and losses from sales or exchanges of capital assets held for not more than 1 year,

(2) gains and losses from sales or exchanges of capital assets held for more than 1 year,

(3) gains and losses from sales or exchanges of property described in section 1231 (relating to certain property used in a trade or business and involuntary conversions),

(4) charitable contributions (as defined in section 170 (c)),

(5) dividends with respect to which section 1(h)(11) or part VIII of subchapter B applies,

(6) taxes, described in section 901, paid or accrued to foreign countries and to possessions of the United States,

(7) other items of income, gain, loss, deduction, or credit, to the extent provided by regulations prescribed by the Secretary, and

(8) taxable income or loss, exclusive of items requiring separate computation under other paragraphs of this subsection.

[Sec. 702(b)]

(b) CHARACTER OF ITEMS CONSTITUTING DISTRIBUTIVE SHARE.—The character of any item of income, gain, loss, deduction, or credit included in a partner's distributive share under paragraphs (1) through (7) of subsection (a) shall be determined as if such item were realized directly from the source from which realized by the partnership, or incurred in the same manner as incurred by the partnership.

[Sec. 702(c)]

(c) GROSS INCOME OF A PARTNER.—In any case where it is necessary to determine the gross income of a partner for purposes of this title, such amount shall include his distributive share of the gross income of the partnership.

* * *

[Sec. 703]

SEC. 703. PARTNERSHIP COMPUTATIONS.

[Sec. 703(a)]

(a) INCOME AND DEDUCTIONS.—The taxable income of a partnership shall be computed in the same manner as in the case of an individual except that—

(1) the items described in section 702 (a) shall be separately stated, and

(2) the following deductions shall not be allowed to the partnership:

(A) the deductions for personal exemptions provided in section 151,

(B) the deduction for taxes provided in section 164 (a) with respect to taxes, described in section 901, paid or accrued to foreign countries and to possessions of the United States,

(C) the deduction for charitable contributions provided in section 170,

Sec. 701

(D) the net operating loss deduction provided in section 172,

(E) the additional itemized deductions for individuals provided in part VII of subchapter B (sec. 211 and following), and

(F) the deduction for depletion under section 611 with respect to oil and gas wells.

[Sec. 703(b)]

(b) ELECTIONS OF THE PARTNERSHIP.—Any election affecting the computation of taxable income derived from a partnership shall be made by the partnership, except that any election under—

(1) subsection (b)(5) or (c)(3) of section 108 (relating to income from discharge of indebtedness),

(2) section 617 (relating to deduction and recapture of certain mining exploration expenditures), or

(3) section 901 (relating to taxes of foreign countries and possessions of the United States),

shall be made by each partner separately.

[Sec. 704]

SEC. 704. PARTNER'S DISTRIBUTIVE SHARE.

[Sec. 704(a)]

(a) EFFECT OF PARTNERSHIP AGREEMENT.—A partner's distributive share of income, gain, loss, deduction, or credit shall, except as otherwise provided in this chapter, be determined by the partnership agreement.

[Sec. 704(b)]

(b) DETERMINATION OF DISTRIBUTIVE SHARE.—A partner's distributive share of income, gain, loss, deduction, or credit (or item thereof) shall be determined in accordance with the partner's interest in the partnership (determined by taking into account all facts and circumstances), if—

(1) the partnership agreement does not provide as to the partner's distributive share of income, gain, loss, deduction, or credit (or item thereof), or

(2) the allocation to a partner under the agreement of income, gain, loss, deduction, or credit (or item thereof) does not have substantial economic effect.

[Sec. 704(c)]

(c) CONTRIBUTED PROPERTY.—

(1) IN GENERAL.—Under regulations prescribed by the Secretary—

(A) income, gain, loss, and deduction with respect to property contributed to the partnership by a partner shall be shared among the partners so as to take account of the variation between the basis of the property to the partnership and its fair market value at the time of contribution, and

(B) if any property so contributed is distributed (directly or indirectly) by the partnership (other than to the contributing partner) within 7 years of being contributed—

(i) the contributing partner shall be treated as recognizing gain or loss (as the case may be) from the sale of such property in an amount equal to the gain or loss which would have been allocated to such partner under subparagraph (A) by reason of the variation described in subparagraph (A) if the property had been sold at its fair market value at the time of the distribution,

(ii) the character of such gain or loss shall be determined by reference to the character of the gain or loss which would have resulted if such property had been sold by the partnership to the distributee, and

(iii) appropriate adjustments shall be made to the adjusted basis of the contributing partner's interest in the partnership and to the adjusted basis of the property distributed to reflect any gain or loss recognized under this subparagraph.

(2) SPECIAL RULE FOR DISTRIBUTIONS WHERE GAIN OR LOSS WOULD NOT BE RECOGNIZED OUTSIDE PARTNERSHIPS.—Under regulations prescribed by the Secretary, if—

(A) property contributed by a partner (hereinafter referred to as the "contributing partner") is distributed by the partnership to another partner, and

(B) other property of a like kind (within the meaning of section 1031) is distributed by the partnership to the contributing partner not later than the earlier of—

(i) the 180th day after the date of the distribution described in subparagraph (A), or

(ii) the due date (determined with regard to extensions) for the contributing partner's return of the tax imposed by this chapter for the taxable year in which the distribution described in subparagraph (A) occurs,

then to the extent of the value of the property described in subparagraph (B), paragraph (1)(B) shall be applied as if the contributing partner had contributed to the partnership the property described in subparagraph (B).

(3) OTHER RULES.—Under regulations prescribed by the Secretary, rules similar to the rules of paragraph (1) shall apply to contributions by a partner (using the cash receipts and disbursements method of accounting) of accounts payable and other accrued but unpaid items. Any reference in paragraph (1) or (2) to the contributing partner shall be treated as including a reference to any successor of such partner.

[Sec. 704(d)]

(d) LIMITATION ON ALLOWANCE OF LOSSES.—A partner's distributive share of partnership loss (including capital loss) shall be allowed only to the extent of the adjusted basis of such partner's interest in the partnership at the end of the partnership year in which such loss occurred. Any excess of such loss over such basis shall be allowed as a deduction at the end of the partnership year in which such excess is repaid to the partnership.

[Sec. 704(e)]

(e) FAMILY PARTNERSHIPS.—

(1) RECOGNITION OF INTEREST CREATED BY PURCHASE OR GIFT.—A person shall be recognized as a partner for purposes of this subtitle if he owns a capital interest in a partnership in which capital is a material income-producing factor, whether or not such interest was derived by purchase or gift from any other person.

(2) DISTRIBUTIVE SHARE OF DONEE INCLUDIBLE IN GROSS INCOME.—In the case of any partnership interest created by gift, the distributive share of the donee under the partnership agreement shall be includible in his gross income, except to the extent that such share is determined without allowance of reasonable compensation for services rendered to the partnership by the donor, and except to the extent that the portion of such share attributable to donated capital is proportionately greater than the share of the donor attributable to the donor's capital. The distributive share of a partner in the earnings of the partnership shall not be diminished because of absence due to military service.

(3) PURCHASE OF INTEREST BY MEMBER OF FAMILY.—For purposes of this section, an interest purchased by one member of a family from another shall be considered to be created by gift from the seller, and the fair market value of the purchased interest shall be considered to be donated capital. The "family" of any individual shall include only his spouse, ancestors, and lineal descendants, and any trusts for the primary benefit of such persons.

[Sec. 704(f)]

(f) CROSS REFERENCE.—

For rules in the case of the sale, exchange, liquidation, or reduction of a partner's interest, see section 706(c)(2).

[Sec. 705]

SEC. 705. DETERMINATION OF BASIS OF PARTNER'S INTEREST.

[Sec. 705(a)]

(a) GENERAL RULE.—The adjusted basis of a partner's interest in a partnership shall, except as provided in subsection (b), be the basis of such interest determined under section 722 (relating to contributions to a partnership) or section 742 (relating to transfers of partnership interests)—

(1) increased by the sum of his distributive share for the taxable year and prior taxable years of—

(A) taxable income of the partnership as determined under section 703 (a),

(B) income of the partnership exempt from tax under this title, and

(C) the excess of the deductions for depletion over the basis of the property subject to depletion;

(2) decreased (but not below zero) by distributions by the partnership as provided in section 733 and by the sum of his distributive share for the taxable year and prior taxable years of—

(A) losses of the partnership, and

(B) expenditures of the partnership not deductible in computing its taxable income and not properly chargeable to capital account; and

(3) decreased (but not below zero) by the amount of the partner's deduction for depletion for any partnership oil and gas property to the extent such deduction does not exceed the proportionate share of the adjusted basis of such property allocated to such partner under section 613A(c)(7)(D).

[Sec. 705(b)]

(b) ALTERNATIVE RULE.—The Secretary shall prescribe by regulations the circumstances under which the adjusted basis of a partner's interest in a partnership may be determined by reference to his proportionate share of the adjusted basis of partnership property upon a termination of the partnership.

[Sec. 706]

SEC. 706. TAXABLE YEARS OF PARTNER AND PARTNERSHIP.

[Sec. 706(a)]

(a) YEAR IN WHICH PARTNERSHIP INCOME IS INCLUDIBLE.—In computing the taxable income of a partner for a taxable year, the inclusions required by section 702 and section 707 (c) with respect to a partnership shall be based on the income, gain, loss, deduction, or credit of the partnership for any taxable year of the partnership ending within or with the taxable year of the partner.

[Sec. 706(b)]

(b) TAXABLE YEAR.—

(1) PARTNERSHIP'S TAXABLE YEAR.—

(A) PARTNERSHIP TREATED AS TAXPAYER.—The taxable year of a partnership shall be determined as though the partnership were a taxpayer.

(B) TAXABLE YEAR DETERMINED BY REFERENCE TO PARTNERS.—Except as provided in subparagraph (C), a partnership shall not have a taxable year other than—

(i) the majority interest taxable year (as defined in paragraph (4)),

(ii) if there is no taxable year described in clause (i), the taxable year of all the principal partners of the partnership, or

(iii) if there is no taxable year described in clause (i) or (ii), the calendar year unless the Secretary by regulations prescribes another period.

(C) BUSINESS PURPOSE.—A partnership may have a taxable year not described in subparagraph (B) if it establishes, to the satisfaction of the Secretary, a business purpose therefor. For purposes of this subparagraph, any deferral of income to partners shall not be treated as a business purpose.

(2) PARTNER'S TAXABLE YEAR.—A partner may not change to a taxable year other than that of a partnership in which he is a principal partner unless he establishes, to the satisfaction of the Secretary, a business purpose therefor.

(3) PRINCIPAL PARTNER.—For the purpose of this subsection, a principal partner is a partner having an interest of 5 percent or more in partnership profits or capital.

(4) MAJORITY INTEREST TAXABLE YEAR; LIMITATION ON REQUIRED CHANGES.—

(A) MAJORITY INTEREST TAXABLE YEAR DEFINED.—For purposes of paragraph (1)(B)(i)—

(i) IN GENERAL.—The term "majority interest taxable year" means the taxable year (if any) which, on each testing day, constituted the taxable year of 1 or more partners having (on such day) an aggregate interest in partnership profits and capital of more than 50 percent.

(ii) TESTING DATE.—The testing days shall be—

(I) the 1st day of the partnership taxable year (determined without regard to clause (i)), or

(II) the days during such representative period as the Secretary may prescribe.

(B) FURTHER CHANGE NOT REQUIRED FOR 3 YEARS.—Except as provided in regulations necessary to prevent the avoidance of this section, if, by reason of paragraph (1)(B)(i), the taxable year of a partnership is changed, such partnership shall not be required to change to another taxable year for either of the 2 taxable years following the year of change.

(5) APPLICATION WITH OTHER SECTIONS.—Except as provided in regulations, for purposes of determining the taxable year to which a partnership is required to change by reason of this subsection, changes in taxable years of other persons required by this subsection, section 441(i), section 584(h), section 644, or section 1378(a) shall be taken into account.

[Sec. 706(c)]

(c) CLOSING OF PARTNERSHIP YEAR.—

(1) GENERAL RULE.—Except in the case of a termination of a partnership and except as provided in paragraph (2) of this subsection, the taxable year of a partnership shall not close as the result of the death of a partner, the entry of a new partner, the liquidation of a partner's interest in the partnership, or the sale or exchange of a partner's interest in the partnership.

(2) TREATMENT OF DISPOSITIONS.—

(A) DISPOSITION OF ENTIRE INTEREST.—The taxable year of a partnership shall close with respect to a partner whose entire interest in the partnership terminates (whether by reason of death, liquidation, or otherwise).

(B) DISPOSITION OF LESS THAN ENTIRE INTEREST.—The taxable year of a partnership shall not close (other than at the end of a partnership's taxable year as determined under subsection (b)(1)) with respect to a partner who sells or exchanges less than his entire interest in the partnership or with respect to a partner whose interest is reduced (whether by entry of a new partner, partial liquidation of a partner's interest, gift, or otherwise).

[Sec. 706(d)]

(d) DETERMINATION OF DISTRIBUTIVE SHARE WHEN PARTNER'S INTEREST CHANGES.—

(1) IN GENERAL.—Except as provided in paragraphs (2) and (3), if during any taxable year of the partnership there is a change in any partner's interest in the partnership, each partner's distributive share of any item of income, gain, loss, deduction, or credit of the partnership for such taxable year shall be determined by the use of any method prescribed by the Secretary by regulations which takes into account the varying interests of the partners in the partnership during such taxable year.

(2) CERTAIN CASH BASIS ITEMS PRORATED OVER PERIOD TO WHICH ATTRIBUTABLE.—

(A) IN GENERAL.—If during any taxable year of the partnership there is a change in any partner's interest in the partnership, then (except to the extent provided in regulations) each partner's distributive share of any allocable cash basis item shall be determined—

(i) by assigning the appropriate portion of such item to each day in the period to which it is attributable, and

(ii) by allocating the portion assigned to any such day among the partners in proportion to their interests in the partnership at the close of such day.

(B) ALLOCABLE CASH BASIS ITEM.—For purposes of this paragraph, the term "allocable cash basis item" means any of the following items with respect to which the partnership uses the cash receipts and disbursements method of accounting:

(i) Interest.

(ii) Taxes.

(iii) Payments for services or for the use of property.

(iv) Any other item of a kind specified in regulations prescribed by the Secretary as being an item with respect to which the application of this paragraph is appropriate to avoid significant misstatements of the income of the partners.

(C) ITEMS ATTRIBUTABLE TO PERIODS NOT WITHIN TAXABLE YEAR.—If any portion of any allocable cash basis item is attributable to—

(i) any period before the beginning of the taxable year, such portion shall be assigned under subparagraph (A)(i) to the first day of the taxable year, or

(ii) any period after the close of the taxable year, such portion shall be assigned under subparagraph (A)(i) to the last day of the taxable year.

(D) TREATMENT OF DEDUCTIBLE ITEMS ATTRIBUTABLE TO PRIOR PERIODS.—If any portion of a deductible cash basis item is assigned under subparagraph (C)(i) to the first day of any taxable year—

(i) such portion shall be allocated among persons who are partners in the partnership during the period to which such portion is attributable in accordance with their varying interests in the partnership during such period, and

(ii) any amount allocated under clause (i) to a person who is not a partner in the partnership on such first day shall be capitalized by the partnership and treated in the manner provided for in section 755.

(3) ITEMS ATTRIBUTABLE TO INTEREST IN LOWER TIER PARTNERSHIP PRORATED OVER ENTIRE TAXABLE YEAR.—If—

(A) during any taxable year of the partnership there is a change in any partner's interest in the partnership (hereinafter in this paragraph referred to as the "upper tier partnership"), and

(B) such partnership is a partner in another partnership (hereinafter in this paragraph referred to as the "lower tier partnership"),

then (except to the extent provided in regulations) each partner's distributive share of any item of the upper tier partnership attributable to the lower tier partnership shall be determined by assigning the appropriate portion (determined by applying principles similar to the principles of subparagraphs (C) and (D) of paragraph (2)) of each such item to the appropriate days during which the upper tier partnership is a partner in the lower tier partnership and by allocating the portion assigned to any such day among the partners in proportion to their interests in the upper tier partnership at the close of such day.

(4) TAXABLE YEAR DETERMINED WITHOUT REGARD TO SUBSECTION (C)(2)(A).—For purposes of this subsection, the taxable year of a partnership shall be determined without regard to subsection (c)(2)(A).

[Sec. 707]

SEC. 707. TRANSACTIONS BETWEEN PARTNER AND PARTNERSHIP.

[Sec. 707(a)]

(a) PARTNER NOT ACTING IN CAPACITY AS PARTNER.—

(1) IN GENERAL.—If a partner engages in a transaction with a partnership other than in his capacity as a member of such partnership, the transaction shall, except as otherwise provided in this section, be considered as occurring between the partnership and one who is not a partner.

(2) TREATMENT OF PAYMENTS TO PARTNERS FOR PROPERTY OR SERVICES.—Under regulations prescribed by the Secretary—

(A) TREATMENT OF CERTAIN SERVICES AND TRANSFERS OF PROPERTY.—If—

(i) a partner performs services for a partnership or transfers property to a partnership,

(ii) there is a related direct or indirect allocation and distribution to such partner, and

(iii) the performance of such services (or such transfer) and the allocation and distribution, when viewed together, are properly characterized as a transaction occurring between the partnership and a partner acting other than in his capacity as a member of the partnership,

such allocation and distribution shall be treated as a transaction described in paragraph (1).

Sec. 707(a)

(B) TREATMENT OF CERTAIN PROPERTY TRANSFERS.—If—

(i) there is a direct or indirect transfer of money or other property by a partner to a partnership,

(ii) there is a related direct or indirect transfer of money or other property by the partnership to such partner (or another partner), and

(iii) the transfers described in clauses (i) and (ii), when viewed together, are properly characterized as a sale or exchange of property,

such transfers shall be treated either as a transaction described in paragraph (1) or as a transaction between 2 or more partners acting other than in their capacity as members of the partnership.

[Sec. 707(b)]

(b) CERTAIN SALES OR EXCHANGES OF PROPERTY WITH RESPECT TO CONTROLLED PARTNERSHIPS.—

(1) LOSSES DISALLOWED.—No deduction shall be allowed in respect of losses from sales or exchanges of property (other than an interest in the partnership), directly or indirectly, between—

(A) a partnership and a person owning, directly or indirectly, more than 50 percent of the capital interest, or the profits interest, in such partnership, or

(B) two partnerships in which the same persons own, directly or indirectly, more than 50 percent of the capital interests or profits interests.

In the case of a subsequent sale or exchange by a transferee described in this paragraph, section 267(d) shall be applicable as if the loss were disallowed under section 267(a)(1). For purposes of section 267(a)(2), partnerships described in subparagraph (B) of this paragraph shall be treated as persons specified in section 267(b).

(2) GAINS TREATED AS ORDINARY INCOME.—In the case of a sale or exchange, directly or indirectly, of property, which, in the hands of the transferee, is property other than a capital asset as defined in section 1221—

(A) between a partnership and a person owning, directly or indirectly, more than 50 percent of the capital interest, or profits interest, in such partnership, or

(B) between two partnerships in which the same persons own, directly or indirectly, more than 50 percent of the capital interests or profits interests,

any gain recognized shall be considered as ordinary income.

(3) OWNERSHIP OF A CAPITAL OR PROFITS INTEREST.—For purposes of paragraphs (1) and (2) of this subsection, the ownership of a capital or profits interest in a partnership shall be determined in accordance with the rules for constructive ownership of stock provided in section 267 (c) other than paragraph (3) of such section.

[Sec. 707(c)]

(c) GUARANTEED PAYMENTS.—To the extent determined without regard to the income of the partnership, payments to a partner for services or the use of capital shall be considered as made to one who is not a member of the partnership, but only for the purposes of section 61 (a) (relating to gross income) and, subject to section 263, for purposes of section 162 (a) (relating to trade or business expenses).

[Sec. 708]

SEC. 708. CONTINUATION OF PARTNERSHIP.

[Sec. 708(a)]

(a) GENERAL RULE.—For purposes of this subchapter, an existing partnership shall be considered as continuing if it is not terminated.

[Sec. 708(b)]

(b) TERMINATION.—

(1) GENERAL RULE.—For purposes of subsection (a), a partnership shall be considered as terminated only if—

Actual (A) no part of any business, financial operation, or venture of the partnership continues to be carried on by any of its partners in a partnership, or

Sec. 707(b)

deemed (B) within a 12-month period there is a sale or exchange of 50 percent or more of the total interest in partnership capital and profits.

(2) SPECIAL RULES.—

(A) MERGER OR CONSOLIDATION.—In the case of the merger or consolidation of two or more partnerships, the resulting partnership shall, for purposes of this section, be considered the continuation of any merging or consolidating partnership whose members own an interest of more than 50 percent in the capital and profits of the resulting partnership.

(B) DIVISION OF A PARTNERSHIP.—In the case of a division of a partnership into two or more partnerships, the resulting partnerships (other than any resulting partnership the members of which had an interest of 50 percent or less in the capital and profits of the prior partnership) shall, for purposes of this section, be considered a continuation of the prior partnership.

[Sec. 709]

SEC. 709. TREATMENT OF ORGANIZATION AND SYNDICATION FEES.

[Sec. 709(a)]

(a) GENERAL RULE.—Except as provided in subsection (b), no deduction shall be allowed under this chapter to the partnership or to any partner for any amounts paid or incurred to organize a partnership or to promote the sale of (or to sell) an interest in such partnership.

[Sec. 709(b)]

(b) AMORTIZATION OF ORGANIZATION FEES.—

(1) DEDUCTION.—Amounts paid or incurred to organize a partnership may, at the election of the partnership (made in accordance with regulations prescribed by the Secretary), be treated as deferred expenses. Such deferred expenses shall be allowed as a deduction ratably over such period of not less than 60 months as may be selected by the partnership (beginning with the month in which the partnership begins business), or if the partnership is liquidated before the end of such 60-month period, such deferred expenses (to the extent not deducted under this section) may be deducted to the extent provided in section 165.

(2) ORGANIZATIONAL EXPENSES DEFINED.—The organizational expenses to which paragraph (1) applies, are expenditures which—

(A) are incident to the creation of the partnership;

(B) are chargeable to capital account; and

(C) are of a character which, if expended incident to the creation of a partnership having an ascertainable life, would be amortized over such life.

PART II—CONTRIBUTIONS, DISTRIBUTIONS, AND TRANSFERS

Subpart A—Contributions to a Partnership

[Sec. 721]

SEC. 721. NONRECOGNITION OF GAIN OR LOSS ON CONTRIBUTION.

[Sec. 721(a)]

(a) GENERAL RULE.—No gain or loss shall be recognized to a partnership or to any of its partners in the case of a contribution of property to the partnership in exchange for an interest in the partnership.

[Sec. 721(b)]

(b) SPECIAL RULE.—Subsection (a) shall not apply to gain realized on a transfer of property to a partnership which would be treated as an investment company (within the meaning of section 351) if the partnership were incorporated.

[Sec. 721(c)]

(c) REGULATIONS RELATING TO CERTAIN TRANSFERS TO PARTNERSHIPS.—The Secretary may provide by regulations that subsection (a) shall not apply to gain realized on the transfer of property to a partnership if such gain, when recognized, will be includible in the gross income of a person other than a United States person.

[Sec. 721(d)]

(d) TRANSFERS OF INTANGIBLES.—

For regulatory authority to treat intangibles transferred to a partnership as sold, see section 367(d)(3).

[Sec. 722]

SEC. 722. BASIS OF CONTRIBUTING PARTNER'S INTEREST.

The basis of an interest in a partnership acquired by a contribution of property, including money, to the partnership shall be the amount of such money and the adjusted basis of such property to the contributing partner at the time of the contribution increased by the amount (if any) of gain recognized under section 721(b) to the contributing partner at such time.

[Sec. 723]

SEC. 723. BASIS OF PROPERTY CONTRIBUTED TO PARTNERSHIP.

The basis of property contributed to a partnership by a partner shall be the adjusted basis of such property to the contributing partner at the time of the contribution increased by the amount (if any) of gain recognized under section 721(b) to the contributing partner at such time.

[Sec. 724]

SEC. 724. CHARACTER OF GAIN OR LOSS ON CONTRIBUTED UNREALIZED RECEIVABLES, INVENTORY ITEMS, AND CAPITAL LOSS PROPERTY.

[Sec. 724(a)]

(a) CONTRIBUTIONS OF UNREALIZED RECEIVABLES.—In the case of any property which—

(1) was contributed to the partnership by a partner, and

(2) was an unrealized receivable in the hands of such partner immediately before such contribution,

any gain or loss recognized by the partnership on the disposition of such property shall be treated as ordinary income or ordinary loss, as the case may be.

[Sec. 724(b)]

(b) CONTRIBUTIONS OF INVENTORY ITEMS.—In the case of any property which—

(1) was contributed to the partnership by a partner, and

(2) was an inventory item in the hands of such partner immediately before such contribution,

any gain or loss recognized by the partnership on the disposition of such property during the 5-year period beginning on the date of such contribution shall be treated as ordinary income or ordinary loss, as the case may be.

[Sec. 724(c)]

(c) CONTRIBUTIONS OF CAPITAL LOSS PROPERTY.—In the case of any property which—

(1) was contributed by a partner to the partnership, and

(2) was a capital asset in the hands of such partner immediately before such contribution,

any loss recognized by the partnership on the disposition of such property during the 5-year period beginning on the date of such contribution shall be treated as a loss from the sale of a capital asset to the extent that, immediately before such contribution, the adjusted basis of such property in the hands of the partner exceeded the fair market value of such property.

Sec. 721(c)

[Sec. 724(d)]

(d) DEFINITIONS.—For purposes of this section—

(1) UNREALIZED RECEIVABLE.—The term "unrealized receivable" has the meaning given such term by section 751(c) (determined by treating any reference to the partnership as referring to the partner).

(2) INVENTORY ITEM.—The term "inventory item" has the meaning given such term by section 751(d) (determined by treating any reference to the partnership as referring to the partner and by applying section 1231 without regard to any holding period therein provided).

(3) SUBSTITUTED BASIS PROPERTY.—

(A) IN GENERAL.—If any property described in subsection (a), (b), or (c) is disposed of in a nonrecognition transaction, the tax treatment which applies to such property under such subsection shall also apply to any substituted basis property resulting from such transaction. A similar rule shall also apply in the case of a series of non-recognition transactions.

(B) EXCEPTION FOR STOCK IN C CORPORATION.—Subparagraph (A) shall not apply to any stock in a C corporation received in an exchange described in section 351.

Subpart B—Distributions by a Partnership

[Sec. 731]

SEC. 731. EXTENT OF RECOGNITION OF GAIN OR LOSS ON DISTRIBUTION.

[Sec. 731(a)]

(a) PARTNERS.—In the case of a distribution by a partnership to a partner—

(1) gain shall not be recognized to such partner, except to the extent that any money distributed exceeds the adjusted basis of such partner's interest in the partnership immediately before the distribution, and

(2) loss shall not be recognized to such partner, except that upon a distribution in liquidation of a partner's interest in a partnership where no property other than that described in subparagraph (A) or (B) is distributed to such partner, loss shall be recognized to the extent of the excess of the adjusted basis of such partner's interest in the partnership over the sum of—

(A) any money distributed, and

(B) the basis to the distributee, as determined under section 732, of any unrealized receivables (as defined in section 751(c)) and inventory (as defined in section 751(d)).

Any gain or loss recognized under this subsection shall be considered as gain or loss from the sale or exchange of the partnership interest of the distributee partner.

[Sec. 731(b)]

(b) PARTNERSHIPS.—No gain or loss shall be recognized to a partnership on a distribution to a partner of property, including money.

[Sec. 731(c)]

(c) TREATMENT OF MARKETABLE SECURITIES.—

(1) IN GENERAL.—For purposes of subsection (a)(1) and section 737—

(A) the term "money" includes marketable securities, and

(B) such securities shall be taken into account at their fair market value as of the date of the distribution.

(2) MARKETABLE SECURITIES.—For purposes of this subsection:

(A) IN GENERAL.—The term "marketable securities" means financial instruments and foreign currencies which are, as of the date of the distribution, actively traded (within the meaning of section 1092(d)(1)).

(B) OTHER PROPERTY.—Such term includes—

(i) any interest in—

(I) a common trust fund, or

(II) a regulated investment company which is offering for sale or has outstanding any redeemable security (as defined in section 2(a)(32) of the Investment Company Act of 1940) of which it is the issuer,

(ii) any financial instrument which, pursuant to its terms or any other arrangement, is readily convertible into, or exchangeable for, money or marketable securities,

(iii) any financial instrument the value of which is determined substantially by reference to marketable securities,

(iv) except to the extent provided in regulations prescribed by the Secretary, any interest in a precious metal which, as of the date of the distribution, is actively traded (within the meaning of section 1092(d)(1)) unless such metal was produced, used, or held in the active conduct of a trade or business by the partnership,

(v) except as otherwise provided in regulations prescribed by the Secretary, interests in any entity if substantially all of the assets of such entity consist (directly or indirectly) of marketable securities, money, or both, and

(vi) to the extent provided in regulations prescribed by the Secretary, any interest in an entity not described in clause (v) but only to the extent of the value of such interest which is attributable to marketable securities, money, or both.

(C) FINANCIAL INSTRUMENT.—The term "financial instrument" includes stocks and other equity interests, evidences of indebtedness, options, forward or future contracts, notional principal contracts, and derivatives.

(3) EXCEPTIONS.—

(A) IN GENERAL.—Paragraph (1) shall not apply to the distribution from a partnership of a marketable security to a partner if—

(i) the security was contributed to the partnership by such partner, except to the extent that the value of the distributed security is attributable to marketable securities or money contributed (directly or indirectly) to the entity to which the distributed security relates,

(ii) to the extent provided in regulations prescribed by the Secretary, the property was not a marketable security when acquired by such partnership, or

(iii) such partnership is an investment partnership and such partner is an eligible partner thereof.

(B) LIMITATION ON GAIN RECOGNIZED.—In the case of a distribution of marketable securities to a partner, the amount taken into account under paragraph (1) shall be reduced (but not below zero) by the excess (if any) of—

(i) such partner's distributive share of the net gain which would be recognized if all of the marketable securities of the same class and issuer as the distributed securities held by the partnership were sold (immediately before the transaction to which the distribution relates) by the partnership for fair market value, over

(ii) such partner's distributive share of the net gain which is attributable to the marketable securities of the same class and issuer as the distributed securities held by the partnership immediately after the transaction, determined by using the same fair market value as used under clause (i).

Under regulations prescribed by the Secretary, all marketable securities held by the partnership may be treated as marketable securities of the same class and issuer as the distributed securities.

(C) DEFINITIONS RELATING TO INVESTMENT PARTNERSHIPS.—For purposes of subparagraph (A)(iii):

(i) INVESTMENT PARTNERSHIP.—The term "investment partnership" means any partnership which has never been engaged in a trade or business and substantially all of the assets (by value) of which have always consisted of—

(I) money,

(II) stock in a corporation,

(III) notes, bonds, debentures, or other evidences of indebtedness,

(IV) interest rate, currency, or equity notional principal contracts,

(V) foreign currencies,

(VI) interests in or derivative financial instruments (including options, forward or futures contracts, short positions, and similar financial instruments) in any asset

Sec. 731(c)

described in any other subclause of this clause or in any commodity traded on or subject to the rules of a board of trade or commodity exchange,

(VII) other assets specified in regulations prescribed by the Secretary, or

(VIII) any combination of the foregoing.

(ii) EXCEPTION FOR CERTAIN ACTIVITIES.—A partnership shall not be treated as engaged in a trade or business by reason of—

(I) any activity undertaken as an investor, trader, or dealer in any asset described in clause (i), or

(II) any other activity specified in regulations prescribed by the Secretary.

(iii) ELIGIBLE PARTNER.—

(I) IN GENERAL.—The term "eligible partner" means any partner who, before the date of the distribution, did not contribute to the partnership any property other than assets described in clause (i).

(II) EXCEPTION FOR CERTAIN NONRECOGNITION TRANSACTIONS.—The term "eligible partner" shall not include the transferor or transferee in a nonrecognition transaction involving a transfer of any portion of an interest in a partnership with respect to which the transferor was not an eligible partner.

(iv) LOOK-THRU OF PARTNERSHIP TIERS.—Except as otherwise provided in regulations prescribed by the Secretary—

(I) a partnership shall be treated as engaged in any trade or business engaged in by, and as holding (instead of a partnership interest) a proportionate share of the assets of, any other partnership in which the partnership holds a partnership interest, and

(II) a partner who contributes to a partnership an interest in another partnership shall be treated as contributing a proportionate share of the assets of the other partnership.

If the preceding sentence does not apply under such regulations with respect to any interest held by a partnership in another partnership, the interest in such other partnership shall be treated as if it were specified in a subclause of clause (i).

(4) BASIS OF SECURITIES DISTRIBUTED.—

(A) IN GENERAL.—The basis of marketable securities with respect to which gain is recognized by reason of this subsection shall be—

(i) their basis determined under section 732, increased by

(ii) the amount of such gain.

(B) ALLOCATION OF BASIS INCREASE.—Any increase in basis attributable to the gain described in subparagraph (A)(ii) shall be allocated to marketable securities in proportion to their respective amounts of unrealized appreciation before such increase.

(5) SUBSECTION DISREGARDED IN DETERMINING BASIS OF PARTNER'S INTEREST IN PARTNERSHIP AND OF BASIS OF PARTNERSHIP PROPERTY.—Sections 733 and 734 shall be applied as if no gain were recognized, and no adjustment were made to the basis of property, under this subsection.

(6) CHARACTER OF GAIN RECOGNIZED.—In the case of a distribution of a marketable security which is an unrealized receivable (as defined in section 751(c)) or an inventory item (as defined in section 751(c)) or an inventory item (as defined in section 751(d)), any gain recognized under this subsection shall be treated as ordinary income to the extent of any increase in the basis of such security attributable to the gain described in paragraph (4)(A)(ii).

(7) REGULATIONS.—The Secretary shall prescribe such regulations as may be necessary or appropriate to carry out the purposes of this subsection, including regulations to prevent the avoidance of such purposes.

[Sec. 731(d)]

(d) EXCEPTIONS.—This section shall not apply to the extent otherwise provided by section 736 (relating to payments to a retiring partner or a deceased partner's successor in interest), section 751 (relating to unrealized receivables and inventory items), and section 737 (relating to recognition of precontribution gain in case of certain distributions).

Sec. 731(d)

[Sec. 732]

SEC. 732. BASIS OF DISTRIBUTED PROPERTY OTHER THAN MONEY.

[Sec. 732(a)]

(a) DISTRIBUTIONS OTHER THAN IN LIQUIDATION OF A PARTNER'S INTEREST.—

(1) GENERAL RULE.—The basis of property (other than money) distributed by a partnership to a partner other than in liquidation of the partner's interest shall, except as provided in paragraph (2), be its adjusted basis to the partnership immediately before such distribution.

(2) LIMITATION.—The basis to the distributee partner of property to which paragraph (1) is applicable shall not exceed the adjusted basis of such partner's interest in the partnership reduced by any money distributed in the same transaction.

[Sec. 732(b)]

(b) DISTRIBUTIONS IN LIQUIDATION.—The basis of property (other than money) distributed by a partnership to a partner in liquidation of the partner's interest shall be an amount equal to the adjusted basis of such partner's interest in the partnership reduced by any money distributed in the same transaction.

[Sec. 732(c)]

(c) ALLOCATION OF BASIS.—

(1) IN GENERAL.—The basis of distributed properties to which subsection (a)(2) or (b) is applicable shall be allocated—

(A)(i) first to any unrealized receivables (as defined in section 751(c)) and inventory items (as defined in section 751(d)) in an amount equal to the adjusted basis of each such property to the partnership, and

(ii) if the basis to be allocated is less than the sum of the adjusted bases of such properties to the partnership, then, to the extent any decrease is required in order to have the adjusted bases of such properties equal the basis to be allocated, in the manner provided in paragraph (3), and

(B) to the extent of any basis remaining after the allocation under subparagraph (A), to other distributed properties—

(i) first by assigning to each such other property such other property's adjusted basis to the partnership, and

(ii) then, to the extent any increase or decrease in basis is required in order to have the adjusted bases of such other distributed properties equal such remaining basis, in the manner provided in paragraph (2) or (3), whichever is appropriate.

(2) METHOD OF ALLOCATING INCREASE.—Any increase required under paragraph (1)(B) shall be allocated among the properties—

(A) first to properties with unrealized appreciation in proportion to their respective amounts of unrealized appreciation before such increase (but only to the extent of each property's unrealized appreciation), and

(B) then, to the extent such increase is not allocated under subparagraph (A), in proportion to their respective fair market values.

(3) METHOD OF ALLOCATING DECREASE.—Any decrease required under paragraph (1)(A) or (1)(B) shall be allocated—

(A) first to properties with unrealized depreciation in proportion to their respective amounts of unrealized depreciation before such decrease (but only to the extent of each property's unrealized depreciation), and

(B) then, to the extent such decrease is not allocated under subparagraph (A), in proportion to their respective adjusted bases (as adjusted under subparagraph (A)).

Sec. 732

[Sec. 732(d)]

(d) SPECIAL PARTNERSHIP BASIS TO TRANSFEREE.—For purposes of subsections (a), (b), and (c), a partner who acquired all or part of his interest by a transfer with respect to which the election provided in section 754 is not in effect, and to whom a distribution of property (other than money) is made with respect to the transferred interest within 2 years after such transfer, may elect, under regulations prescribed by the Secretary, to treat as the adjusted partnership basis of such property the adjusted basis such property would have if the adjustment provided in section 743 (b) were in effect with respect to the partnership property. The Secretary may by regulations require the application of this subsection in the case of a distribution to a transferee partner, whether or not made within 2 years after the transfer, if at the time of the transfer the fair market value of the partnership property (other than money) exceeded 110 percent of its adjusted basis to the partnership.

[Sec. 732(e)]

(e) EXCEPTION.—This section shall not apply to the extent that a distribution is treated as a sale or exchange of property under section 751(b) (relating to unrealized receivables and inventory items).

[Sec. 732(f)]

(f) CORRESPONDING ADJUSTMENT TO BASIS OF ASSETS OF A DISTRIBUTED CORPORATION CONTROLLED BY A CORPORATE PARTNER.—

(1) IN GENERAL.—If—

(A) a corporation (hereafter in this subsection referred to as the "corporate partner") receives a distribution from a partnership of stock in another corporation (hereafter in this subsection referred to as the "distributed corporation"),

(B) the corporate partner has control of the distributed corporation immediately after the distribution or at any time thereafter, and

(C) the partnership's adjusted basis in such stock immediately before the distribution exceeded the corporate partner's adjusted basis in such stock immediately after the distribution,

then an amount equal to such excess shall be applied to reduce (in accordance with subsection (c)) the basis of property held by the distributed corporation at such time (or, if the corporate partner does not control the distributed corporation at such time, at the time the corporate partner first has such control).

(2) EXCEPTION FOR CERTAIN DISTRIBUTIONS BEFORE CONTROL ACQUIRED.—Paragraph (1) shall not apply to any distribution of stock in the distributed corporation if—

(A) the corporate partner does not have control of such corporation immediately after such distribution, and

(B) the corporate partner establishes to the satisfaction of the Secretary that such distribution was not part of a plan or arrangement to acquire control of the distributed corporation.

(3) LIMITATIONS ON BASIS REDUCTION.—

(A) IN GENERAL.—The amount of the reduction under paragraph (1) shall not exceed the amount by which the sum of the aggregate adjusted bases of the property and the amount of money of the distributed corporation exceeds the corporate partner's adjusted basis in the stock of the distributed corporation.

(B) REDUCTION NOT TO EXCEED ADJUSTED BASIS OF PROPERTY.—No reduction under paragraph (1) in the basis of any property shall exceed the adjusted basis of such property (determined without regard to such reduction).

(4) GAIN RECOGNITION WHERE REDUCTION LIMITED.—If the amount of any reduction under paragraph (1) (determined after the application of paragraph (3)(A)) exceeds the aggregate adjusted bases of the property of the distributed corporation—

(A) such excess shall be recognized by the corporate partner as long-term capital gain, and

(B) the corporate partner's adjusted basis in the stock of the distributed corporation shall be increased by such excess.

(5) CONTROL.—For purposes of this subsection, the term "control" means ownership of stock meeting the requirements of section 1504(a)(2).

Sec. 732(f)

(6) INDIRECT DISTRIBUTIONS.—For purposes of paragraph (1), if a corporation acquires (other than in a distribution from a partnership) stock the basis of which is determined (by reason of being distributed from a partnership) in whole or in part by reference to subsection (a)(2) or (b), the corporation shall be treated as receiving a distribution of such stock from a partnership.

(7) SPECIAL RULE FOR STOCK IN CONTROLLED CORPORATION.—If the property held by a distributed corporation is stock in a corporation which the distributed corporation controls, this subsection shall be applied to reduce the basis of the property of such controlled corporation. This subsection shall be reapplied to any property of any controlled corporation which is stock in a corporation which it controls.

(8) REGULATIONS.—The Secretary shall prescribe such regulations as may be necessary to carry out the purposes of this subsection, including regulations to avoid double counting and to prevent the abuse of such purposes.

[Sec. 733]

SEC. 733. BASIS OF DISTRIBUTEE PARTNER'S INTEREST.

In the case of a distribution by a partnership to a partner other than in liquidation of a partner's interest, the adjusted basis to such partner of his interest in the partnership shall be reduced (but not below zero) by—

(1) the amount of any money distributed to such partner, and

(2) the amount of the basis to such partner of distributed property other than money, as determined under section 732.

[Sec. 734]

SEC. 734. OPTIONAL ADJUSTMENT TO BASIS OF UNDISTRIBUTED PARTNERSHIP PROPERTY.

[Sec. 734(a)]

(a) GENERAL RULE.—The basis of partnership property shall not be adjusted as the result of a distribution of property to a partner unless the election, provided in section 754 (relating to optional adjustment to basis of partnership property), is in effect with respect to such partnership.

[Sec. 734(b)]

(b) METHOD OF ADJUSTMENT.—In the case of a distribution of property to a partner, a partnership, with respect to which the election provided in section 754 is in effect, shall—

(1) increase the adjusted basis of partnership property by—

(A) the amount of any gain recognized to the distributee partner with respect to such distribution under section 731(a)(1), and

(B) in the case of distributed property to which section 732(a)(2) or (b) applies, the excess of the adjusted basis of the distributed property to the partnership immediately before the distribution (as adjusted by section 732(d)) over the basis of the distributed property to the distributee, as determined under section 732, or

(2) decrease the adjusted basis of partnership property by—

(A) the amount of any loss recognized to the distributee partner with respect to such distribution under section 731(a)(2), and

(B) in the case of distributed property to which section 732(b) applies, the excess of the basis of the distributed property to the distributee, as determined under section 732, over the adjusted basis of the distributed property to the partnership immediately before such distribution (as adjusted by section 732(d)).

Paragraph (1)(B) shall not apply to any distributed property which is an interest in another partnership with respect to which the election provided in section 754 is not in effect.

[Sec. 734(c)]

(c) ALLOCATION OF BASIS.—The allocation of basis among partnership properties where subsection (b) is applicable shall be made in accordance with the rules provided in section 755.

Sec. 733

[Sec. 735]

SEC. 735. CHARACTER OF GAIN OR LOSS ON DISPOSITION OF DISTRIBUTED PROPERTY.

[Sec. 735(a)]

(a) SALE OR EXCHANGE OF CERTAIN DISTRIBUTED PROPERTY.—

(1) UNREALIZED RECEIVABLES.—Gain or loss on the disposition by a distributee partner of unrealized receivables (as defined in section 751(c)) distributed by a partnership, shall be considered as ordinary income or as ordinary loss, as the case may be.

(2) INVENTORY ITEMS.—Gain or loss on the sale or exchange by a distributee partner of inventory items (as defined in section 751(d)) distributed by a partnership shall, if sold or exchanged within 5 years from the date of the distribution, be considered as ordinary income or as ordinary loss, as the case may be.

[Sec. 735(b)]

(b) HOLDING PERIOD FOR DISTRIBUTED PROPERTY.—In determining the period for which a partner has held property received in a distribution from a partnership (other than for purposes of subsection (a)(2)), there shall be included the holding period of the partnership, as determined under section 1223, with respect to such property.

[Sec. 735(c)]

(c) SPECIAL RULES.—

(1) WAIVER OF HOLDING PERIODS CONTAINED IN SECTION 1231.—For purposes of this section, section 751(d) (defining inventory item) shall be applied without regard to any holding period in section 1231(b).

(2) SUBSTITUTED BASIS PROPERTY.—

(A) IN GENERAL.—If any property described in subsection (a) is disposed of in a nonrecognition transaction, the tax treatment which applies to such property under such subsection shall also apply to any substituted basis property resulting from such transaction. A similar rule shall also apply in the case of a series of nonrecognition transactions.

(B) EXCEPTION FOR STOCK IN C CORPORATION.—Subparagraph (A) shall not apply to any stock in a C corporation received in an exchange described in section 351.

[Sec. 736]

SEC. 736. PAYMENTS TO A RETIRING PARTNER OR A DECEASED PARTNER'S SUCCESSOR IN INTEREST.

[Sec. 736(a)]

(a) PAYMENTS CONSIDERED AS DISTRIBUTIVE SHARE OR GUARANTEED PAYMENT.—Payments made in liquidation of the interest of a retiring partner or a deceased partner shall, except as provided in subsection (b), be considered—

(1) as a distributive share to the recipient of partnership income if the amount thereof is determined with regard to the income of the partnership, or

(2) as a guaranteed payment described in section 707(c) if the amount thereof is determined without regard to the income of the partnership.

[Sec. 736(b)]

(b) PAYMENTS FOR INTEREST IN PARTNERSHIP.—

(1) GENERAL RULE.—Payments made in liquidation of the interest of a retiring partner or a deceased partner shall, to the extent such payments (other than payments described in paragraph (2)) are determined, under regulations prescribed by the Secretary, to be made in exchange for the interest of such partner in partnership property, be considered as a distribution by the partnership and not as a distributive share or guaranteed payment under subsection (a).

(2) SPECIAL RULES.—For purposes of this subsection, payments in exchange for an interest in partnership property shall not include amounts paid for—

(A) unrealized receivables of the partnership (as defined in section 751(c)), or

(B) good will of the partnership, except to the extent that the partnership agreement provides for a payment with respect to good will.

(3) LIMITATION ON APPLICATION OF PARAGRAPH (2).—Paragraph (2) shall apply only if—

(A) capital is not a material income-producing factor for the partnership, and

(B) the retiring or deceased partner was a general partner in the partnership.

[Sec. 737]

SEC. 737. RECOGNITION OF PRECONTRIBUTION GAIN IN CASE OF CERTAIN DISTRIBUTIONS TO CONTRIBUTING PARTNER.

[Sec. 737(a)]

(a) GENERAL RULE.—In the case of any distribution by a partnership to a partner, such partner shall be treated as recognizing gain in an amount equal to the lesser of—

(1) the excess (if any) of (A) the fair market value of property (other than money) received in the distribution over (B) the adjusted basis of such partner's interest in the partnership immediately before the distribution reduced (but not below zero) by the amount of money received in the distribution, or

(2) the net precontribution gain of the partner.

Gain recognized under the preceding sentence shall be in addition to any gain recognized under section 731. The character of such gain shall be determined by reference to the proportionate character of the net precontribution gain.

[Sec. 737(b)]

(b) NET PRECONTRIBUTION GAIN.—For purposes of this seciton, the term "net precontribution gain" means the net gain (if any) which would have been recognized by the distributee partner under section 704(c)(1)(B) if all property which—

(1) had been contributed to the partnership by the distributee partner within 7 years of the distribution, and

(2) is held by such partnership immediately before the distribution,

had been distributed by such partnership to another partner.

[Sec. 737(c)]

(c) BASIS RULES.—

(1) PARTNER'S INTEREST.—The adjusted basis of a partner's interest in a partnership shall be increased by the amount of any gain recognized by such partner under subsection (a). For purposes of determining the basis of the distributed property (other than money) such increase shall be treated as occurring immediately before the distribution.

(2) PARTNERSHIP'S BASIS IN CONTRIBUTED PROPERTY.—Appropriate adjustments shall be made to the adjusted basis of the partnership in the contributed property referred to in subsection (b) to reflect gain recognized under subsection (a).

[Sec. 737(d)]

(d) EXCEPTIONS.—

(1) DISTRIBUTIONS OF PREVIOUSLY CONTRIBUTED PROPERTY.—If any portion of the property distributed consists of property which had been contributed by the distributee partner to the partnership, such property shall not be taken into account under subsection (a)(1) and shall not be taken into account in determining the amount of the net precontribution gain. If the property distributed consists of an interest in an entity, the preceding sentence shall not apply to the extent that the value of such interest is attributable to property contributed to such entity after such interest had been contributed to the partnership.

(2) COORDINATION WITH SECTION 751.—This section shall not apply to the extent section 751(b) applies to such distribution.

Sec. 737

(e) Marketable Securities Treated as Money.—For treatment of marketable securities as money for purposes of this section, see section 731(c).

Subpart C—Transfers of Interests in a Partnership

[Sec. 741]

SEC. 741. RECOGNITION AND CHARACTER OF GAIN OR LOSS ON SALE OR EXCHANGE.

In the case of a sale or exchange of an interest in a partnership, gain or loss shall be recognized to the transferor partner. Such gain or loss shall be considered as gain or loss from the sale or exchange of a capital asset, except as otherwise provided in section 751 (relating to unrealized receivables and inventory items).

[Sec. 742]

SEC. 742. BASIS OF TRANFEREE PARTNER'S INTEREST.

The basis of an interest in a partnership acquired other than by contribution shall be determined under part II of subchapter O (sec. 1011 and following).

[Sec. 743]

SEC. 743. OPTIONAL ADJUSTMENT TO BASIS OF PARTNERSHIP PROPERTY.

[Sec. 743(a)]

(a) General Rule.—The basis of partnership property shall not be adjusted as the result of a transfer of an interest in a partnership by sale or exchange or on the death of a partner unless the election provided by section 754 (relating to optional adjustment to basis of partnership property) is in effect with respect to such partnership.

[Sec. 743(b)]

(b) Adjustment to Basis of Partnership Property.—In the case of a transfer of an interest in a partnership by sale or exchange or upon the death of a partner, a partnership with respect to which the election provided in section 754 is in effect shall—

(1) increase the adjusted basis of the partnership property by the excess of the basis to the transferee partner of his interest in the partnership over his proportionate share of the adjusted basis of the partnership property, or

(2) decrease the adjusted basis of the partnership property by the excess of the transferee partner's proportionate share of the adjusted basis of the partnership property over the basis of his interest in the partnership.

Under regulations prescribed by the Secretary, such increase or decrease shall constitute an adjustment to the basis of partnership property with respect to the transferee partner only. A partner's proportionate share of the adjusted basis of partnership property shall be determined in accordance with his interest in partnership capital and, in the case of property contributed to the partnership by a partner, section 704(c) (relating to contributed property) shall apply in determining such share. In the case of an adjustment under this subsection to the basis of partnership property subject to depletion, any depletion allowable shall be determined separately for the transferee partner with respect to his interest in such property.

[Sec. 743(c)]

(c) Allocation of Basis.—The allocation of basis among partnership properties where subsection (b) is applicable shall be made in accordance with the rules provided in section 755.

Subpart D—Provisions Common to Other Subparts

[Sec. 751]

SEC. 751. UNREALIZED RECEIVABLES AND INVENTORY ITEMS.

[Sec. 751(a)]

(a) SALE OR EXCHANGE OF INTEREST IN PARTNERSHIP.—The amount of any money, or the fair market value of any property, received by a transferor partner in exchange for all or a part of his interest in the partnership attributable to—

(1) unrealized receivables of the partnership, or

(2) inventory items of the partnership,

shall be considered as an amount realized from the sale or exchange of property other than a capital asset.

[Sec. 751(b)]

(b) CERTAIN DISTRIBUTIONS TREATED AS SALES OR EXCHANGES.—

(1) GENERAL RULE.—To the extent a partner receives in a distribution—

(A) partnership property which is—

(i) unrealized receivables, or

(ii) inventory items which have appreciated substantially in value,

in exchange for all or a part of his interest in other partnership property (including money), or

(B) partnership property (including money) other than property described in subparagraph (A)(i) or (ii) in exchange for all or a part of his interest in partnership property described in subparagraph (A)(i) or (ii),

such transactions shall, under regulations prescribed by the Secretary, be considered as a sale or exchange of such property between the distributee and the partnership (as constituted after the distribution).

(2) EXCEPTIONS.—Paragraph (1) shall not apply to—

(A) a distribution of property which the distributee contributed to the partnership, or

(B) payments, described in section 736 (a), to a retiring partner or successor in interest of a deceased partner.

(3) SUBSTANTIAL APPRECIATION.—For purposes of paragraph (1)—

(A) IN GENERAL.—Inventory items of the partnership shall be considered to have appreciated substantially in value if their fair market value exceeds 120 percent of the adjusted basis to the partnership of such property.

(B) CERTAIN PROPERTY EXCLUDED.—For purposes of subparagraph (A), there shall be excluded any inventory property if a principal purpose for acquiring such property was to avoid the provisions of this subsection relating to inventory items.

[Sec. 751(c)]

(c) UNREALIZED RECEIVABLES.—For purposes of this subchapter, the term "unrealized receivables" includes, to the extent not previously includible in income under the method of accounting used by the partnership, any rights (contractual or otherwise) to payment for—

(1) goods delivered, or to be delivered, to the extent the proceeds therefrom would be treated as amounts received from the sale or exchange of property other than a capital asset, or

(2) services rendered, or to be rendered.

For purposes of this section and, sections 731, 732, and 741 (but not for purposes of section 736), such term also includes mining property (as defined in section 617(f)(2)), stock in a DISC (as described in section 992(a)), section 1245 property (as defined in section 1245(a)(3)), stock in certain foreign corporations (as described in section 1248), section 1250 property (as defined in section 1250(c)), farm land (as defined in section 1252(a)), franchises, trademarks, or trade names (referred to in section 1253(a)), and an oil, gas, or geothermal property (described in section 1254) but only to the extent of the amount which would be treated as gain to which section 617(d)(1),995(c),1245(a),1248(a), 1250(a), 1252(a), 1253(a) or 1254(a) would apply if (at the time of the transaction described in this section or

Sec. 751

section 731, 732, or 741, as the case may be) such property had been sold by the partnership at its fair market value. For purposes of this section and, sections 731, 732, and 741 (but not for purposes of section 736), such term also includes any market discount bond (as defined in section 1278) and any short-term obligation (as defined in section 1283) but only to the extent of the amount which would be treated as ordinary income if (at the time of the transaction described in this section or section 731, 732, or 741, as the case may be) such property had been sold by the partnership.

[Sec. 751(d)]

(d) INVENTORY ITEMS.—For purposes of this subchapter, the term "inventory items" means—

(1) property of the partnership of the kind described in section 1221(a)(1),

(2) any other property of the partnership which, on sale or exchange by the partnership, would be considered property other than a capital asset and other than property described in section 1231,

(3) any other property of the partnership which, if sold or exchanged by the partnership, would result in a gain taxable under subsection (a) of section 1246 (relating to gain on foreign investment company stock), and

(4) any other property held by the partnership which, if held by the selling or distributee partner, would be considered property of the type described in paragraph (1), (2), or (3).

* * *

[Sec. 751(f)]

(f) SPECIAL RULES IN THE CASE OF TIERED PARTNERSHIPS, ETC.—In determining whether property of a partnership is—

(1) an unrealized receivable, or

(2) an inventory item,

such partnership shall be treated as owning its proportionate share of the property of any other partnership in which it is a partner. Under regulations, rules similar to the rules of the preceding sentence shall also apply in the case of interests in trusts.

[Sec. 752]

SEC. 752. TREATMENT OF CERTAIN LIABILITIES.

[Sec. 752(a)]

(a) INCREASE IN PARTNER'S LIABILITIES.—Any increase in a partner's share of the liabilities of a partnership, or any increase in a partner's individual liabilities by reason of the assumption by such partner of partnership liabilities, shall be considered as a contribution of money by such partner to the partnership.

[Sec. 752(b)]

(b) DECREASE IN PARTNER'S LIABILITIES.—Any decrease in a partner's share of the liabilities of a partnership, or any decrease in a partner's individual liabilities by reason of the assumption by the partnership of such individual liabilities, shall be considered as a distribution of money to the partner by the partnership.

[Sec. 752(c)]

(c) LIABILITY TO WHICH PROPERTY IS SUBJECT.—For purposes of this section, a liability to which property is subject shall, to the extent of the fair market value of such property, be considered as a liability of the owner of the property.

[Sec. 752(d)]

(d) SALE OR EXCHANGE OF AN INTEREST.—In the case of a sale or exchange of an interest in a partnership, liabilities shall be treated in the same manner as liabilities in connection with the sale or exchange of property not associated with partnerships.

Sec. 752(d)

[Sec. 753]

SEC. 753. PARTNER RECEIVING INCOME IN RESPECT OF DECEDENT.

The amount includible in the gross income of a successor in interest of a deceased partner under section 736 (a) shall be considered income in respect of a decedent under section 691.

[Sec. 754]

SEC. 754. MANNER OF ELECTING OPTIONAL ADJUSTMENT TO BASIS OF PARTNERSHIP PROPERTY.

If a partnership files an election, in accordance with regulations prescribed by the Secretary, the basis of partnership property shall be adjusted, in the case of a distribution of property, in the manner provided in section 734 and, in the case of a transfer of a partnership interest, in the manner provided in section 743. Such an election shall apply with respect to all distributions of property by the partnership and to all transfers of interests in the partnership during the taxable year with respect to which such election was filed and all subsequent taxable years. Such election may be revoked by the partnership, subject to such limitations as may be provided by regulations prescribed by the Secretary.

[Sec. 755]

SEC. 755. RULES FOR ALLOCATION OF BASIS.

[Sec. 755(a)]

(a) GENERAL RULE.—Any increase or decrease in the adjusted basis of partnership property under section 734 (b) (relating to the optional adjustment to the basis of undistributed partnership property) or section 743 (b) (relating to the optional adjustment to the basis of partnership property in the case of a transfer of an interest in a partnership) shall, except as provided in subsection (b), be allocated—

(1) in a manner which has the effect of reducing the difference between the fair market value and the adjusted basis of partnership properties, or

(2) in any other manner permitted by regulations prescribed by the Secretary.

[Sec. 755(b)]

(b) SPECIAL RULE.—In applying the allocation rules provided in subsection (a), increases or decreases in the adjusted basis of partnership property arising from a distribution of, or a transfer of an interest attributable to, property consisting of—

(1) capital assets and property described in section 1231 (b), or

(2) any other property of the partnership,

shall be allocated to partnership property of a like character except that the basis of any such partnership property shall not be reduced below zero. If, in the case of a distribution, the adjustment to basis of property described in paragraph (1) or (2) is prevented by the absence of such property or by insufficient adjusted basis for such property, such adjustment shall be applied to subsequently acquired property of a like character in accordance with regulations prescribed by the Secretary.

PART III—DEFINITIONS

[Sec. 761]

SEC. 761. TERMS DEFINED.

[Sec. 761(a)]

(a) PARTNERSHIP.—For purposes of this subtitle, the term "partnership" includes a syndicate, group, pool, joint venture or other unincorporated organization through or by means of which any business, financial operation, or venture is carried on, and which is not, within the meaning of this title [subtitle], a corporation or a trust or estate. Under regulations the Secretary may, at the election of all the members of an unincorporated organization, exclude such organization from the application of all or part of this subchapter, if it is availed of—

(1) for investment purposes only and not for the active conduct of a business,

(2) for the joint production, extraction, or use of property, but not for the purpose of selling services or property produced or extracted, or

Sec. 753

(3) by dealers in securities for a short period for the purpose of underwriting, selling, or distributing a particular issue of securities,

if the income of the members of the organization may be adequately determined without the computation of partnership taxable income.

[Sec. 761(b)]

(b) PARTNER.—For purposes of this subtitle, the term "partner" means a member of a partnership.

[Sec. 761(c)]

(c) PARTNERSHIP AGREEMENT.—For purposes of this subchapter, a partnership agreement includes any modifications of the partnership agreement made prior to, or at, the time prescribed by law for the filing of the partnership return for the taxable year (not including extensions) which are agreed to by all the partners, or which are adopted in such other manner as may be provided by the partnership agreement.

[Sec. 761(d)]

(d) LIQUIDATION OF A PARTNER'S INTEREST.—For purposes of this subchapter, the term "liquidation of a partner's interest" means the termination of a partner's entire interest in a partnership by means of a distribution, or a series of distributions, to the partner by the partnership.

[Sec. 761(e)]

(e) DISTRIBUTIONS OF PARTNERSHIP INTERESTS TREATED AS EXCHANGES.—Except as otherwise provided in regulations, for purposes of—

(1) section 708 (relating to continuation of partnership),

(2) section 743 (relating to optional adjustment to basis of partnership property), and

(3) any other provision of this subchapter specified in regulations prescribed by the Secretary, any distribution of an interest in a partnership (not otherwise treated as an exchange) shall be treated as an exchange.

[Sec. 761(f)]

(f) CROSS REFERENCE.—For rules in the case of the sale, exchange, liquidation, or reduction of a partner's interest, see sections 704(b) and 706(c)(2).

PART IV—SPECIAL RULES FOR ELECTING LARGE PARTNERSHIPS

[Sec. 771]

SEC. 771. APPLICATION OF SUBCHAPTER TO ELECTING LARGE PARTNERSHIPS.

The preceding provisions of this subchapter to the extent inconsistent with the provisions of this part shall not apply to an electing large partnership and its partners.

[Sec. 772]

SEC. 772. SIMPLIFIED FLOW-THROUGH.

[Sec. 772(a)]

(a) GENERAL RULE.—In determining the income tax of a partner of an electing large partnership, such partner shall take into account separately such partner's distributive share of the partnership's—

(1) taxable income or loss from passive loss limitation activities,

(2) taxable income or loss from other activities,

(3) net capital gain (or net capital loss)—

(A) to the extent allocable to passive loss limitation activities, and

(B) to the extent allocable to other activities,

(4) tax-exempt interest,

Sec. 772(a)

(5) applicable net AMT adjustment separately computed for—

   (A) passive loss limitation activities, and

   (B) other activities,

(6) general credits,

(7) low-income housing credit determined under section 42,

(8) rehabilitation credit determined under section 47,

(9) foreign income taxes,

(10) the credit allowable under section 29, and

(11) other items to the extent that the Secretary determines that the separate treatment of such items is appropriate.

[Sec. 772(b)]

(b) SEPARATE COMPUTATIONS.—In determining the amounts required under subsection (a) to be separately taken into account by any partner, this section and section 773 shall be applied separately with respect to such partner by taking into account such partner's distributive share of the items of income, gain, loss, deduction, or credit of the partnership.

[Sec. 772(c)]

(c) TREATMENT AT PARTNER LEVEL.—

   (1) IN GENERAL.—Except as provided in this subsection, rules similar to the rules of section 702(b) shall apply to any partner's distributive share of the amounts referred to in subsection (a).

   (2) INCOME OR LOSS FROM PASSIVE LOSS LIMITATION ACTIVITIES.—For purposes of this chapter, any partner's distributive share of any income or loss described in subsection (a)(1) shall be treated as an item of income or loss (as the case may be) from the conduct of a trade or business which is a single passive activity (as defined in section 469). A similar rule shall apply to a partner's distributive share of amounts referred to in paragraphs (3)(A) and (5)(A) of subsection (a).

   (3) INCOME OR LOSS FROM OTHER ACTIVITIES.—

      (A) IN GENERAL.—For purposes of this chapter, any partner's distributive share of any income or loss described in subsection (a)(2) shall be treated as an item of income or expense (as the case may be) with respect to property held for investment.

      (B) DEDUCTIONS FOR LOSS NOT SUBJECT TO SECTION 67.—The deduction under section 212 for any loss described in subparagraph (A) shall not be treated as a miscellaneous itemized deduction for purposes of section 67.

   (4) TREATMENT OF NET CAPITAL GAIN OR LOSS.—For purposes of this chapter, any partner's distributive share of any gain or loss described in subsection (a)(3) shall be treated as a long-term capital gain or loss, as the case may be.

   (5) MINIMUM TAX TREATMENT.—In determining the alternative minimum taxable income of any partner, such partner's distributive share of any applicable net AMT adjustment shall be taken into account in lieu of making the separate adjustments provided in sections 56, 57, and 58 with respect to the items of the partnership. Except as provided in regulations, the applicable net AMT adjustment shall be treated, for purposes of section 53, as an adjustment or item of tax preference not specified in section 53(d)(1)(B)(ii).

   (6) GENERAL CREDITS.—A partner's distributive share of the amount referred to in paragraph (6) of subsection (a) shall be taken into account as a current year business credit.

[Sec. 772(d)]

(d) OPERATING RULES.—For purposes of this section—

   (1) PASSIVE LOSS LIMITATION ACTIVITY.—The term "passive loss limitation activity" means—

      (A) any activity which involves the conduct of a trade or business, and

      (B) any rental activity.

For purposes of the preceding sentence, the term "trade or business" includes any activity treated as a trade or business under paragraph (5) or (6) of section 469(c).

Sec. 772(b)

(2) TAX-EXEMPT INTEREST.—The term "tax-exempt interest" means interest excludable from gross income under section 103.

(3) APPLICABLE NET AMT ADJUSTMENT.—

(A) IN GENERAL.—The applicable net AMT adjustment is—

(i) with respect to taxpayers other than corporations, the net adjustment determined by using the adjustments applicable to individuals, and

(ii) with respect to corporations, the net adjustment determined by using the adjustments applicable to corporations.

(B) NET ADJUSTMENT.—The term "net adjustment" means the net adjustment in the items attributable to passive loss activities or other activities (as the case may be) which would result if such items were determined with the adjustments of sections 56, 57, and 58.

(4) TREATMENT OF CERTAIN SEPARATELY STATED ITEMS.—

(A) EXCLUSION FOR CERTAIN PURPOSES.—In determining the amounts referred to in paragraphs (1) and (2) of subsection (a), any net capital gain or net capital loss (as the case may be), and any item referred to in subsection (a)(11), shall be excluded.

(B) ALLOCATION RULES.—The net capital gain shall be treated—

(i) as allocable to passive loss limitation activities to the extent the net capital gain does not exceed the net capital gain determined by only taking into account gains and losses from sales and exchanges of property used in connection with such activities, and

(ii) as allocable to other activities to the extent such gain exceeds the amount allocated under clause (i).

A similar rule shall apply for purposes of allocating any net capital loss.

(C) NET CAPITAL LOSS.—The term "net capital loss" means the excess of the losses from sales or exchanges of capital assets over the gains from sales or exchange of capital assets.

(5) GENERAL CREDITS.—The term "general credits" means any credit other than the low-income housing credit, the rehabilitation credit, the foreign tax credit, and the credit allowable under section 29.

(6) FOREIGN INCOME TAXES.—The term "foreign income taxes" means taxes described in section 901 which are paid or accrued to foreign countries and to possessions of the United States.

[Sec. 772(e)]

(e) SPECIAL RULE FOR UNRELATED BUSINESS TAX.—In the case of a partner which is an organization subject to tax under section 511, such partner's distributive share of any items shall be taken into account separately to the extent necessary to comply with the provisions of section 512(c)(1).

[Sec. 772(f)]

(f) SPECIAL RULES FOR APPLYING PASSIVE LOSS LIMITATIONS.—If any person holds an interest in an electing large partnership other than as a limited partner—

(1) paragraph (2) of subsection (c) shall not apply to such partner, and

(2) such partner's distributive share of the partnership items allocable to passive loss limitation activities shall be taken into account separately to the extent necessary to comply with the provisions of section 469.

The preceding sentence shall not apply to any items allocable to an interest held as a limited partner.

[Sec. 773]

SEC. 773. COMPUTATIONS AT PARTNERSHIP LEVEL.

[Sec. 773(a)]

(a) GENERAL RULE.—

(1) TAXABLE INCOME.—The taxable income of an electing large partnership shall be computed in the same manner as in the case of an individual except that—

(A) the items described in section 772(a) shall be separately stated, and

(B) the modifications of subsection (b) shall apply.

(2) ELECTIONS.—All elections affecting the computation of the taxable income of an electing large partnership or the computation of any credit of an electing large partnership shall be made by the partnership; except that the election under section 901, and any election under section 108, shall be made by each partner separately.

(3) LIMITATIONS, ETC.—

(A) IN GENERAL.—Except as provided in subparagraph (B), all limitations and other provisions affecting the computation of the taxable income of an electing large partnership or the computation of any credit of an electing large partnership shall be applied at the partnership level (and not at the partner level).

(B) CERTAIN LIMITATIONS APPLIED AT PARTNER LEVEL.—The following provisions shall be applied at the partner level (and not at the partnership level):

(i) Section 68 (relating to overall limitation on itemized deductions).

(ii) Sections 49 and 465 (relating to at risk limitations).

(iii) Section 469 (relating to limitation on passive activity losses and credits).

(iv) Any other provision specified in regulations.

(4) COORDINATION WITH OTHER PROVISIONS.—Paragraphs (2) and (3) shall apply notwithstanding any other provision of this chapter other than this part.

[Sec. 773(b)]

(b) MODIFICATIONS TO DETERMINATION OF TAXABLE INCOME.—In determining the taxable income of an electing large partnership—

(1) CERTAIN DEDUCTIONS NOT ALLOWED.—The following deductions shall not be allowed:

(A) The deduction for personal exemptions provided in section 151.

(B) The net operating loss deduction provided in section 172.

(C) The additional itemized deductions for individuals provided in part VII of subchapter B (other than section 212 thereof).

(2) CHARITABLE DEDUCTIONS.—In determining the amount allowable under section 170, the limitation of section 170(b)(2) shall apply.

(3) COORDINATION WITH SECTION 67.—In lieu of applying section 67, 70 percent of the amount of the miscellaneous itemized deductions shall be disallowed.

[Sec. 773(c)]

(c) SPECIAL RULES FOR INCOME FROM DISCHARGE OF INDEBTEDNESS.—If an electing large partnership has income from the discharge of any indebtedness—

(1) such income shall be excluded in determining the amounts referred to in section 772(a), and

(2) in determining the income tax of any partner of such partnership—

(A) such income shall be treated as an item required to be separately taken into account under section 772(a), and

(B) the provisions of section 108 shall be applied without regard to this part.

[Sec. 774]

SEC. 774. OTHER MODIFICATIONS.

[Sec. 774(a)]

(a) TREATMENT OF CERTAIN OPTIONAL ADJUSTMENTS, ETC.—In the case of an electing large partnership—

(1) computations under section 773 shall be made without regard to any adjustment under section 743(b) or 108(b), but

(2) a partner's distributive share of any amount referred to in section 772(a) shall be appropriately adjusted to take into account any adjustment under section 743(b) or 108(b) with respect to such partner.

[Sec. 774(b)]

(b) CREDIT RECAPTURE DETERMINED AT PARTNERSHIP LEVEL.—

(1) IN GENERAL.—In the case of an electing large partnership—

(A) any credit recapture shall be taken into account by the partnership, and

(B) the amount of such recapture shall be determined as if the credit with respect to which the recapture is made had been fully utilized to reduce tax.

(2) METHOD OF TAKING RECAPTURE INTO ACCOUNT.—An electing large partnership shall take into account a credit recapture by reducing the amount of the appropriate current year credit to the extent thereof, and if such recapture exceeds the amount of such current year credit, the partnership shall be liable to pay such excess.

(3) DISPOSITIONS NOT TO TRIGGER RECAPTURE.—No credit recapture shall be required by reason of any transfer of an interest in an electing large partnership.

(4) CREDIT RECAPTURE.—For purposes of this subsection, the term "credit recapture" means any increase in tax under section 42(j) or 50(a).

[Sec. 774(c)]

(c) PARTNERSHIP NOT TERMINATED BY REASON OF CHANGE IN OWNERSHIP.—Subparagraph (B) of section 708(b)(1) shall not apply to an electing large partnership.

[Sec. 774(d)]

(d) PARTNERSHIP ENTITLED TO CERTAIN CREDITS.—The following shall be allowed to an electing large partnership and shall not be taken into account by the partners of such partnership:

(1) The credit provided by section 34.

(2) Any credit or refund under section 852(b)(3)(D) or 857(b)(3)(D).

[Sec. 774(e)]

(e) TREATMENT OF REMIC RESIDUALS.—For purposes of applying section 860E(e)(6) to any electing large partnership—

(1) all interests in such partnership shall be treated as held by disqualified organizations,

(2) in lieu of applying subparagraph (C) of section 860E(e)(6), the amount subject to tax under section 860E(e)(6) shall be excluded from the gross income of such partnership, and

(3) subparagraph (D) of section 860E(e)(6) shall not apply.

[Sec. 774(f)]

(f) SPECIAL RULES FOR APPLYING CERTAIN INSTALLMENT SALE RULES.—In the case of an electing large partnership—

(1) the provisions of sections 453(l)(3) and 453A shall be applied at the partnership level, and

(2) in determining the amount of interest payable under such sections, such partnership shall be treated as subject to tax under this chapter at the highest rate of tax in effect under section 1 or 11.

[Sec. 775]

SEC. 775. ELECTING LARGE PARTNERSHIP DEFINED.

[Sec. 775(a)]

(a) GENERAL RULE.—For purposes of this part—

(1) IN GENERAL.—The term "electing large partnership" means, with respect to any partnership taxable year, any partnership if—

(A) the number of persons who were partners in such partnership in the preceding partnership taxable year equaled or exceeded 100, and

(B) such partnership elects the application of this part.

To the extent provided in regulations, a partnership shall cease to be treated as an electing large partnership for any partnership taxable year if in such taxable year fewer than 100 persons were partners in such partnership.

Sec. 775(a)

(2) ELECTION.—The election under this subsection shall apply to the taxable year for which made and all subsequent taxable years unless revoked with the consent of the Secretary.

[Sec. 775(b)]

(b) SPECIAL RULES FOR CERTAIN SERVICE PARTNERSHIPS.—

(1) CERTAIN PARTNERS NOT COUNTED.—For purposes of this section, the term "partner" does not include any individual performing substantial services in connection with the activities of the partnership and holding an interest in such partnership, or an individual who formerly performed substantial services in connection with such activities and who held an interest in such partnership at the time the individual performed such services.

(2) EXCLUSION.—For purposes of this part, an election under subsection (a) shall not be effective with respect to any partnership if substantially all the partners of such partnership—

(A) are individuals performing substantial services in connection with the activities of such partnership or are personal service corporations (as defined in section 269A(b)) the owner-employees (as defined in section 269A(b)) of which perform such substantial services,

(B) are retired partners who had performed such substantial services, or

(C) are spouses of partners who are performing (or had previously performed) such substantial services.

(3) SPECIAL RULE FOR LOWER TIER PARTNERSHIPS.—For purposes of this subsection, the activities of a partnership shall include the activities of any other partnership in which the partnership owns directly an interest in the capital and profits of at least 80 percent.

[Sec. 775(c)]

(c) EXCLUSION OF COMMODITY POOLS.—For purposes of this part, an election under subsection (a) shall not be effective with respect to any partnership the principal activity of which is the buying and selling of commodities (not described in section 1221(a)(1)), or options, futures, or forwards with respect to such commodities.

[Sec. 775(d)]

(d) SECRETARY MAY RELY ON TREATMENT ON RETURN.—If, on the partnership return of any partnership, such partnership is treated as an electing large partnership, such treatment shall be binding on such partnership and all partners of such partnership but not on the Secretary.

[Sec. 776]

SEC. 776. SPECIAL RULES FOR PARTNERSHIPS HOLDING OIL AND GAS PROPERTIES.

[Sec. 776(a)]

(a) COMPUTATION OF PERCENTAGE DEPLETION.—In the case of an electing large partnership, except as provided in subsection (b)—

(1) the allowance for depletion under section 611 with respect to any partnership oil or gas property shall be computed at the partnership level without regard to any provision of section 613A requiring such allowance to be computed separately by each partner,

(2) such allowance shall be determined without regard to the provisions of section 613A(c) limiting the amount of production for which percentage depletion is allowable and without regard to paragraph (1) of section 613A(d), and

(3) paragraph (3) of section 705(a) shall not apply.

[Sec. 776(b)]

(b) TREATMENT OF CERTAIN PARTNERS.—

(1) IN GENERAL.—In the case of a disqualified person, the treatment under this chapter of such person's distributive share of any item of income, gain, loss, deduction, or credit attributable to any partnership oil or gas property shall be determined without regard to this part. Such person's distributive share of any such items shall be excluded for purposes of making determinations under sections 772 and 773.

Sec. 775(b)

(2) DISQUALIFIED PERSON.—For purposes of paragraph (1), the term "disqualified person" means, with respect to any partnership taxable year—

(A) any person referred to in paragraph (2) or (4) of section 613A(d) for such person's taxable year in which such partnership taxable year ends, and

(B) any other person if such person's average daily production of domestic crude oil and natural gas for such person's taxable year in which such partnership taxable year ends exceeds 500 barrels.

(3) AVERAGE DAILY PRODUCTION.—For purposes of paragraph (2), a person's average daily production of domestic crude oil and natural gas for any taxable year shall be computed as provided in section 613A(c)(2)—

(A) by taking into account all production of domestic crude oil and natural gas (including such person's proportionate share of any production of a partnership),

(B) by treating 6,000 cubic feet of natural gas as a barrel of crude oil, and

(C) by treating as 1 person all persons treated as 1 taxpayer under section 613A(c)(8) or among whom allocations are required under such section.

[Sec. 777]

SEC. 777. REGULATIONS.

The Secretary shall prescribe such regulations as may be appropriate to carry out the purposes of this part.

Subchapter M—Regulated Investment Companies and Real Estate Investment Trusts

PART I—REGULATED INVESTMENT COMPANIES

[Sec. 851]

SEC. 851. DEFINITION OF REGULATED INVESTMENT COMPANY.

[Sec. 851(a)]

(a) GENERAL RULE.—For purposes of this subtitle, the term "regulated investment company" means any domestic corporation—

(1) which, at all times during the taxable year—

(A) is registered under the Investment Company Act of 1940, as amended (15 U.S.C. 80a-1 to 80b-2) as a management company or unit investment trust, or

(B) has in effect an election under such Act to be treated as a business development company, or

(2) which is a common trust fund or similar fund excluded by section 3 (c) (3) of such Act (15 U. S. C. 80 a-3 (c)) from the definition of "investment company" and is not included in the definition of "common trust fund" by section 584(a).

* * *

Subchapter N—Tax Based on Income From Sources Within or Without the United States

PART III—INCOME FROM SOURCES WITHOUT THE UNITED STATES

Subpart B—Earned Income of Citizens or Residents of United States

[Sec. 911]

SEC. 911. CITIZENS OR RESIDENTS OF THE UNITED STATES LIVING ABROAD.

* * *

[Sec. 911(d)]

(d) DEFINITIONS AND SPECIAL RULES.—For purposes of this section—

* * *

(2) EARNED INCOME.—

(A) IN GENERAL.—The term "earned income" means wages, salaries, or professional fees, and other amounts received as compensation for personal services actually rendered, but does not include that part of the compensation derived by the taxpayer for personal services rendered by him to a corporation which represents a distribution of earnings or profits rather than a reasonable allowance as compensation for the personal services actually rendered.

(B) TAXPAYER ENGAGED IN TRADE OR BUSINESS.—In the case of a taxpayer engaged in a trade or business in which both personal services and capital are material income-producing factors, under regulations prescribed by the Secretary, a reasonable allowance as compensation for the personal services rendered by the taxpayer, not in excess of 30 percent of his share of the net profits of such trade or business, shall be considered as earned income.

* * *

Subchapter O—Gain or Loss on Disposition of Property

PART I—DETERMINATION OF AMOUNT OF AND RECOGNITION OF GAIN OR LOSS

[Sec. 1001]

SEC. 1001. DETERMINATION OF AMOUNT OF AND RECOGNITION OF GAIN OR LOSS.

[Sec. 1001(a)]

(a) COMPUTATION OF GAIN OR LOSS.—The gain from the sale or other disposition of property shall be the excess of the amount realized therefrom over the adjusted basis provided in section 1011 for determining gain, and the loss shall be the excess of the adjusted basis provided in such section for determining loss over the amount realized.

[Sec. 1001(b)]

(b) AMOUNT REALIZED.—The amount realized from the sale or other disposition of property shall be the sum of any money received plus the fair market value of the property (other than money) received. In determining the amount realized—

(1) there shall not be taken into account any amount received as reimbursement for real property taxes which are treated under section 164(d) as imposed on the purchaser, and

(2) there shall be taken into account amounts representing real property taxes which are treated under section 164(d) as imposed on the taxpayer if such taxes are to be paid by the purchaser.

Sec. 911

[Sec. 1001(c)]

(c) RECOGNITION OF GAIN OR LOSS.—Except as otherwise provided in this subtitle, the entire amount of the gain or loss, determined under this section, on the sale or exchange of property shall be recognized.

[Sec. 1001(d)]

(d) INSTALLMENT SALES.—Nothing in this section shall be construed to prevent (in the case of property sold under contract providing for payment in installments) the taxation of that portion of any installment payment representing gain or profit in the year in which such payment is received.

[Sec. 1001(e)]

(e) CERTAIN TERM INTERESTS.—

(1) IN GENERAL.—In determining gain or loss from the sale or other disposition of a term interest in property, that portion of the adjusted basis of such interest which is determined pursuant to section 1014, 1015, or 1041 (to the extent that such adjusted basis is a portion of the entire adjusted basis of the property) shall be disregarded.

(2) TERM INTEREST IN PROPERTY DEFINED.—For purposes of paragraph (1), the term "term interest in property" means—

(A) a life interest in property,

(B) an interest in property for a term of years, or

(C) an income interest in a trust.

(3) EXCEPTION.—Paragraph (1) shall not apply to a sale or other disposition which is a part of a transaction in which the entire interest in property is transferred to any person or persons.

PART II—BASIS RULES OF GENERAL APPLICATION

[Sec. 1011]

SEC. 1011. ADJUSTED BASIS FOR DETERMINING GAIN OR LOSS.

[Sec. 1011(a)]

(a) GENERAL RULE.—The adjusted basis for determining the gain or loss from the sale or other disposition of property, whenever acquired, shall be the basis (determined under section 1012 or other applicable sections of this subchapter and subchapters C (relating to corporate distributions and adjustments), K (relating to partners and partnerships), and P (relating to capital gains and losses)), adjusted as provided in section 1016.

[Sec. 1011(b)]

(b) BARGAIN SALE TO A CHARITABLE ORGANIZATION.—If a deduction is allowable under section 170 (relating to charitable contributions) by reason of a sale, then the adjusted basis for determining the gain from such sale shall be that portion of the adjusted basis which bears the same ratio to the adjusted basis as the amount realized bears to the fair market value of the property.

[Sec. 1012]

SEC. 1012. BASIS OF PROPERTY—COST.

The basis of property shall be the cost of such property, except as otherwise provided in this subchapter and subchapters C (relating to corporate distributions and adjustments), K (relating to partners and partnerships), and P (relating to capital gains and losses). The cost of real property shall not include any amount in respect of real property taxes which are treated under section 164(d) as imposed on the taxpayer.

[Sec. 1013]

SEC. 1013. BASIS OF PROPERTY INCLUDED IN INVENTORY.

If the property should have been included in the last inventory, the basis shall be the last inventory value thereof.

[Sec. 1014]

SEC. 1014. BASIS OF PROPERTY ACQUIRED FROM A DECEDENT.

[Sec. 1014(a)]

(a) IN GENERAL.—Except as otherwise provided in this section, the basis of property in the hands of a person acquiring the property from a decedent or to whom the property passed from a decedent shall, if not sold, exchanged, or otherwise disposed of before the decedent's death by such person, be—

(1) the fair market value of the property at the date of the decedent's death,

(2) in the case of an election under either section 2032 or section 811(j) of the Internal Revenue Code of 1939 where the decedent died after October 21, 1942, its value at the applicable valuation date prescribed by those sections,

(3) in the case of an election under section 2032A, its value determined under such section, or

(4) to the extent of the applicability of the exclusion described in section 2031(c), the basis in the hands of the decedent.

[Sec. 1014(b)]

(b) PROPERTY ACQUIRED FROM THE DECEDENT.—For purposes of subsection (a), the following property shall be considered to have been acquired from or to have passed from the decedent:

(1) Property acquired by bequest, devise, or inheritance, or by the decedent's estate from the decedent;

(2) Property transferred by the decedent during his lifetime in trust to pay the income for life to or on the order or direction of the decedent, with the right reserved to the decedent at all times before his death to revoke the trust;

(3) In the case of decedents dying after December 31, 1951, property transferred by the decedent during his lifetime in trust to pay the income for life to or on the order or direction of the decedent with the right reserved to the decedent at all times before his death to make any change in the enjoyment thereof through the exercise of a power to alter, amend, or terminate the trust;

(4) Property passing without full and adequate consideration under a general power of appointment exercised by the decedent by will;

* * *

(6) In the case of decedents dying after December 31, 1947, property which represents the surviving spouse's one-half share of community property held by the decedent and the surviving spouse under the community property laws of any State, or possession of the United States or any foreign country, if at least one-half of the whole of the community interest in such property was includible in determining the value of the decedent's gross estate under chapter 11 of subtitle B (section 2001 and following, relating to estate tax) or section 811 of the Internal Revenue Code of 1939;

* * *

(9) In the case of decedents dying after December 31, 1953, property acquired from the decedent by reason of death, form of ownership, or other conditions (including property acquired through the exercise or non-exercise of a power of appointment), if by reason thereof the property is required to be included in determining the value of the decedent's gross estate under chapter 11 of subtitle B or under the Internal Revenue Code of 1939. In such case, if the property is acquired before the death of the decedent, the basis shall be the amount determined under subsection (a) reduced by the amount allowed to the taxpayer as deductions in computing taxable income under this subtitle or prior income tax laws for exhaustion, wear and tear, obsolescence, amortization, and depletion on such property before the death of the decedent. Such basis shall be applicable to the property commencing on the death of the decedent. This paragraph shall not apply to—

(A) annuities described in section 72;

(B) property to which paragraph (5) would apply if the property had been acquired by bequest; and

(C) property described in any other paragraph of this subsection.

(10) Property includible in the gross estate of the decedent under section 2044 (relating to certain property for which marital deduction was previously allowed). In any such case, the last 3 sentences of paragraph (9) shall apply as if such property were described in the first sentence of paragraph (9).

Sec. 1014

[Sec. 1014(c)]

(c) PROPERTY REPRESENTING INCOME IN RESPECT OF A DECEDENT.—This section shall not apply to property which constitutes a right to receive an item of income in respect of a decedent under section 691.

* * *

[Sec. 1014(e)]

(e) APPRECIATED PROPERTY ACQUIRED BY DECEDENT BY GIFT WITHIN 1 YEAR OF DEATH.—

(1) IN GENERAL.—In the case of a decedent dying after December 31, 1981, if—

(A) appreciated property was acquired by the decedent by gift during the 1-year period ending on the date of the decedent's death, and

(B) such property is acquired from the decedent by (or passes from the decedent to) the donor of such property (or the spouse of such donor),

the basis of such property in the hands of such donor (or spouse) shall be the adjusted basis of such property in the hands of the decedent immediately before the death of the decedent.

(2) DEFINITIONS.—For purposes of paragraph (1)—

(A) APPRECIATED PROPERTY.—The term "appreciated property" means any property if the fair market value of such property on the day it was transferred to the decedent by gift exceeds its adjusted basis.

(B) TREATMENT OF CERTAIN PROPERTY SOLD BY ESTATE.—In the case of any appreciated property described in subparagraph (A) of paragraph (1) sold by the estate of the decedent or by a trust of which the decedent was the grantor, rules similar to the rules of paragraph (1) shall apply to the extent the donor of such property (or the spouse of such donor) is entitled to the proceeds from such sale.

[Sec. 1014(f)]

(f) TERMINATION.—This section shall not apply with respect to decedents dying after December 31, 2009.

[Sec. 1015]

SEC. 1015. BASIS OF PROPERTY ACQUIRED BY GIFTS AND TRANSFERS IN TRUST.

[Sec. 1015(a)]

(a) GIFTS AFTER DECEMBER 31, 1920.—If the property was acquired by gift after December 31, 1920, the basis shall be the same as it would be in the hands of the donor or the last preceding owner by whom it was not acquired by gift, except that if such basis (adjusted for the period before the date of the gift as provided in section 1016) is greater than the fair market value of the property at the time of the gift, then for the purpose of determining loss the basis shall be such fair market value. If the facts necessary to determine the basis in the hands of the donor or the last preceding owner are unknown to the donee, the Secretary shall, if possible, obtain such facts from such donor or last preceding owner, or any other person cognizant thereof. If the Secretary finds it impossible to obtain such facts, the basis in the hands of such donor or last preceding owner shall be the fair market value of such property as found by the Secretary as of the date or approximate date at which, according to the best information that the Secretary is able to obtain, such property was acquired by such donor or last preceding owner.

[Sec. 1015(b)]

(b) TRANSFER IN TRUST AFTER DECEMBER 31, 1920.—If the property was acquired after December 31, 1920, by a transfer in trust (other than by a transfer in trust by a gift, bequest, or devise), the basis shall be the same as it would be in the hands of the grantor increased in the amount of gain or decreased in the amount of loss recognized to the grantor on such transfer under the law applicable to the year in which the transfer was made.

(c) GIFT OR TRANSFER IN TRUST BEFORE JANUARY 1, 1921.—If the property was acquired by gift or transfer in trust on or before December 31, 1920, the basis shall be the fair market value of such property at the time of such acquisition.

(d) INCREASED BASIS FOR GIFT TAX PAID.—

(1) IN GENERAL.—If—

(A) the property is acquired by gift on or after September 2, 1958, the basis shall be the basis determined under subsection (a), increased (but not above the fair market value of the property at the time of the gift) by the amount of gift tax paid with respect to such gift, or

(B) the property was acquired by gift before September 2, 1958, and has not been sold, exchanged, or otherwise disposed of before such date, the basis of the property shall be increased on such date by the amount of gift tax paid with respect to such gift, but such increase shall not exceed an amount equal to the amount by which the fair market value of the property at the time of the gift exceeded the basis of the property in the hands of the donor at the time of the gift.

(2) AMOUNT OF TAX PAID WITH RESPECT TO GIFT.—For purposes of paragraph (1), the amount of gift tax paid with respect to any gift is an amount which bears the same ratio to the amount of gift tax paid under chapter 12 with respect to all gifts made by the donor for the calendar year (or preceding calendar period) in which such gift is made as the amount of such gift bears to the taxable gifts (as defined in section 2503(a) but computed without the deduction allowed by section 2521) made by the donor during such calendar year or period. For purposes of the preceding sentence, the amount of any gift shall be the amount included with respect to such gift in determining (for the purposes of section 2503(a)) the total amount of gifts made during the calendar year or period, reduced by the amount of any deduction allowed with respect to such gift under section 2522 (relating to charitable deduction) or under section 2523 (relating to marital deduction).

(3) GIFTS TREATED AS MADE ONE-HALF BY EACH SPOUSE.—For purposes of paragraph (1), where the donor and his spouse elected, under section 2513 to have the gift considered as made one-half by each, the amount of gift tax paid with respect to such gift under chapter 12 shall be the sum of the amounts of tax paid with respect to each half of such gift (computed in the manner provided in paragraph (2)).

(4) TREATMENT AS ADJUSTMENT TO BASIS.—For purposes of section 1016(b), an increase in basis under paragraph (1) shall be treated as an adjustment under section 1016(a).

(5) APPLICATION TO GIFTS BEFORE 1955.—With respect to any property acquired by gift before 1955, references in this subsection to any provision of this title shall be deemed to refer to the corresponding provision of the Internal Revenue Code of 1939 or prior revenue laws which was effective for the year in which such gift was made.

(6) SPECIAL RULE FOR GIFTS MADE AFTER DECEMBER 31, 1976.—

(A) IN GENERAL.—In the case of any gift made after December 31, 1976, the increase in basis provided by this subsection with respect to any gift for the gift tax paid under chapter 12 shall be an amount (not in excess of the amount of tax so paid) which bears the same ratio to the amount of tax so paid as—

(i) the net appreciation in value of the gift, bears to

(ii) the amount of the gift.

(B) NET APPRECIATION.—For purposes of paragraph (1), the net appreciation in value of any gift is the amount by which the fair market value of the gift exceeds the donor's adjusted basis immediately before the gift.

(e) GIFTS BETWEEN SPOUSES.—In the case of any property acquired by gift in a transfer described in section 1041(a), the basis of such property in the hands of the transferee shall be determined under section 1041(b)(2) and not this section.

[Sec. 1016]

SEC. 1016. ADJUSTMENTS TO BASIS.

[Sec. 1016(a)]

(a) GENERAL RULE.—Proper adjustment in respect of the property shall in all cases be made—

(1) for expenditures, receipts, losses, or other items, properly chargeable to capital account, but no such adjustment shall be made—

(A) for taxes or other carrying charges described in section 266, or

(B) for expenditures described in section 173 (relating to circulation expenditures),

for which deductions have been taken by the taxpayer in determining taxable income for the taxable year or prior taxable years;

(2) in respect of any period since February 28, 1913, for exhaustion, wear and tear, obsolescence, amortization, and depletion, to the extent of the amount—

(A) allowed as deductions in computing taxable income under this subtitle or prior income tax laws, and

(B) resulting (by reason of the deductions so allowed) in a reduction for any taxable year of the taxpayer's taxes under this subtitle (other than chapter 2, relating to tax on self-employment income), or prior income, war-profits, or excess-profits tax laws,

but not less than the amount allowable under this subtitle or prior income tax laws. Where no method has been adopted under section 167 (relating to depreciation deduction), the amount allowable shall be determined under the straight line method. Subparagraph (B) of this paragraph shall not apply in respect of any period since February 28, 1913, and before January 1, 1952, unless an election has been made under section 1020 (as in effect before the date of the enactment of the Tax Reform Act of 1976). Where for any taxable year before the taxable year 1932 the depletion allowance was based on discovery value or a percentage of income, then the adjustment for depletion for such year shall be based on the depletion which would have been allowable for such year if computed without reference to discovery value or a percentage of income;

* * *

(7) in the case of a residence the acquisition of which resulted, under section 1034 (as in effect on the day before the date of the enactment of the Taxpayer Relief Act of 1997), in the nonrecognition of any part of the gain realized on the sale, exchange, or involuntary conversion of another residence, to the extent provided in section 1034(e) (as so in effect);

(8) in the case of property pledged to the Commodity Credit Corporation, to the extent of the amount received as a loan from the Commodity Credit Corporation and treated by the taxpayer as income for the year in which received pursuant to section 77, and to the extent of any deficiency on such loan with respect to which the taxpayer has been relieved from liability;

(9) for amounts allowed as deductions as deferred expenses under section 616(b) (relating to certain expenditures in the development of mines) and resulting in a reduction of the taxpayer's taxes under this subtitle, but not less than the amounts allowable under such section for the taxable year and prior years;

(11) for deductions to the extent disallowed under section 268 (relating to sale of land with unharvested crops), notwithstanding the provisions of any other paragraph of this subsection;

* * *

(14) for amounts allowed as deductions as deferred expenses under section 174(b)(1) (relating to research and experimental expenditures) and resulting in a reduction of the taxpayers' taxes under this subtitle, but not less than the amounts allowable under such section for the taxable year and prior years;

* * *

(17) to the extent provided in section 1367 in the case of stock of, and indebtedness owed to, shareholders of an S corporation;

* * *

(20) for amounts allowed as deductions under section 59(e) (relating to optional 10-year writeoff of certain tax preferences);

Sec. 1016(a)

(21) to the extent provided in section 1059 (relating to reduction in basis for extraordinary dividends);

* * *

(23) in the case of property the acquisition of which resulted under section 1043, 1044, 1045, or 1397B in the nonrecognition of any part of the gain realized on the sale of other property, to the extent provided in section 1043(c), 1044(d), 1045(b)(4), or 1397B(b)(4), as the case may be,

* * *

[Sec. 1016(b)]

(b) SUBSTITUTED BASIS.—Whenever it appears that the basis of property in the hands of the taxpayer is a substituted basis, then the adjustments provided in subsection (a) shall be made after first making in respect of such substituted basis proper adjustments of a similar nature in respect of the period during which the property was held by the transferor, donor, or grantor, or during which the other property was held by the person for whom the basis is to be determined. A similar rule shall be applied in the case of a series of substituted bases.

* * *

[Sec. 1017]

SEC. 1017. DISCHARGE OF INDEBTEDNESS.

[Sec. 1017(a)]

(a) GENERAL RULE.—If—

(1) an amount is excluded from gross income under subsection (a) of section 108 (relating to discharge of indebtedness), and

(2) under subsection (b)(2)(E), (b)(5), or (c)(1) of section 108, any portion of such amount is to be applied to reduce basis,

then such portion shall be applied in reduction of the basis of any property held by the taxpayer at the beginning of the taxable year following the taxable year in which the discharge occurs.

[Sec. 1017(b)]

(b) AMOUNT AND PROPERTIES DETERMINED UNDER REGULATIONS.—

(1) IN GENERAL.—The amount of reduction to be applied under subsection (a) (not in excess of the portion referred to in subsection (a)), and the particular properties the bases of which are to be reduced, shall be determined under regulations prescribed by the Secretary.

(2) LIMITATION IN TITLE 11 CASE OR INSOLVENCY.—In the case of a discharge to which subparagraph (A) or (B) of section 108(a)(1) applies, the reduction in basis under subsection (a) of this section shall not exceed the excess of—

(A) the aggregate of the bases of the property held by the taxpayer immediately after the discharge, over

(B) the aggregate of the liabilities of the taxpayer immediately after the discharge.

The preceding sentence shall not apply to any reduction in basis by reason of an election under section 108(b)(5).

(3) CERTAIN REDUCTIONS MAY ONLY BE MADE IN THE BASIS OF DEPRECIABLE PROPERTY.—

(A) IN GENERAL.—Any amount which under subsection (b)(5) or (c)(1) of section 108 is to be applied to reduce basis shall be applied only to reduce the basis of depreciable property held by the taxpayer.

(B) DEPRECIABLE PROPERTY.—For purposes of this section, the term "depreciable property" means any property of a character subject to the allowance for depreciation, but only if a basis reduction under subsection (a) will reduce the amount of depreciation or amortization which otherwise would be allowable for the period immediately following such reduction.

Sec. 1016(b)

(C) SPECIAL RULE FOR PARTNERSHIP INTERESTS.—For purposes of this section, any interest of a partner in a partnership shall be treated as depreciable property to the extent of such partner's proportionate interest in the depreciable property held by such partnership. The preceding sentence shall apply only if there is a corresponding reduction in the partnership's basis in depreciable property with respect to such partner.

(D) SPECIAL RULE IN CASE OF AFFILIATED GROUP.—For purposes of this section, if—

(i) a corporation holds stock in another corporation (hereinafter in this subparagraph referred to as the "subsidiary"), and

(ii) such corporations are members of the same affiliated group which file a consolidated return under section 1501 for the taxable year in which the discharge occurs,

then such stock shall be treated as depreciable property to the extent that such subsidiary consents to a corresponding reduction in the basis of its depreciable property.

(E) ELECTION TO TREAT CERTAIN INVENTORY AS DEPRECIABLE PROPERTY.—

(i) IN GENERAL.—At the election of the taxpayer, for purposes of this section, the term "depreciable property" includes any real property which is described in section 1221(a)(1).

(ii) ELECTION.—An election under clause (i) shall be made on the taxpayer's return for the taxable year in which the discharge occurs or at such other time as may be permitted in regulations prescribed by the Secretary. Such an election, once made, may be revoked only with the consent of the Secretary.

(F) SPECIAL RULES FOR QUALIFIED REAL PROPERTY BUSINESS INDEBTEDNESS.—In the case of any amount which under section 108(c)(1) is to be applied to reduce basis—

(i) depreciable property shall only include depreciable real property for purposes of subparagraphs (A) and (C),

(ii) subparagraph (E) shall not apply, and

(iii) in the case of property taken into account under section 108(c)(2)(B), the reduction with respect to such property shall be made as of the time immediately before disposition if earlier than the time under subsection (a).

(4) SPECIAL RULES FOR QUALIFIED FARM INDEBTEDNESS.—

(A) IN GENERAL.—Any amount which under subsection (b)(2)(E) of section 108 is to be applied to reduce basis and which is attributable to an amount excluded under subsection (a)(1)(C) of section 108—

(i) shall be applied only to reduce the basis of qualified property held by the taxpayer, and

(ii) shall be applied to reduce the basis of qualified property in the following order:

(I) First the basis of qualified property which is depreciable property.

(II) Second the basis of qualified property which is land used or held for use in the trade or business of farming.

(III) Then the basis of other qualified property.

(B) QUALIFIED PROPERTY.—For purposes of this paragraph, the term "qualified property" has the meaning given to such term by section 108(g)(3)(C).

(C) CERTAIN RULES MADE APPLICABLE.—Rules similar to the rules of subparagraphs (C), (D), and (E) of paragraph (3) shall apply for purposes of this paragraph and section 108(g).

[Sec. 1017(c)]

(c) SPECIAL RULES.—

(1) REDUCTION NOT TO BE MADE IN EXEMPT PROPERTY.—In the case of an amount excluded from gross income under section 108(a)(1)(A), no reduction in basis shall be made under this section in the basis of property which the debtor treats as exempt property under section 522 of title 11 of the United States Code.

(2) REDUCTIONS IN BASIS NOT TREATED AS DISPOSITIONS.—For purposes of this title, a reduction in basis under this section shall not be treated as a disposition.

(d) RECAPTURE OF REDUCTIONS.—

(1) IN GENERAL.—For purposes of sections 1245 and 1250—

(A) any property the basis of which is reduced under this section and which is neither section 1245 property nor section 1250 property shall be treated as section 1245 property, and

(B) any reduction under this section shall be treated as a deduction allowed for depreciation.

(2) SPECIAL RULE FOR SECTION 1250.—For purposes of section 1250(b), the determination of what would have been the depreciation adjustments under the straight line method shall be made as if there had been no reduction under this section.

[Sec. 1019]

SEC. 1019. PROPERTY ON WHICH LESSEE HAS MADE IMPROVEMENTS.

Neither the basis nor the adjusted basis of any portion of real property shall, in the case of the lessor of such property, be increased or diminished on account of income derived by the lessor in respect of such property and excludable from gross income under section 109 (relating to improvements by lessee on lessor's property). If an amount representing any part of the value of real property attributable to buildings erected or other improvements made by a lessee in respect of such property was included in gross income of the lessor for any taxable year beginning before January 1, 1942, the basis of each portion of such property shall be properly adjusted for the amount so included in gross income.

[Caution: Code Sec. 1022, below, as added by P.L. 107-16, applies to estates of decedents dying after December 31, 2009.]

[Sec. 1022]

SEC. 1022. TREATMENT OF PROPERTY ACQUIRED FROM A DECEDENT DYING AFTER DECEMBER 31, 2009.

[Sec. 1022(a)]

(a) IN GENERAL.—Except as otherwise provided in this section—

(1) property acquired from a decedent dying after December 31, 2009, shall be treated for purposes of this subtitle as transferred by gift, and

(2) the basis of the person acquiring property from such a decedent shall be the lesser of—

(A) the adjusted basis of the decedent, or

(B) the fair market value of the property at the date of the decedent's death.

[Sec. 1022(b)]

(b) BASIS INCREASE FOR CERTAIN PROPERTY.—

(1) IN GENERAL.—In the case of property to which this subsection applies, the basis of such property under subsection (a) shall be increased by its basis increase under this subsection.

(2) BASIS INCREASE.—For purposes of this subsection—

(A) IN GENERAL.—The basis increase under this subsection for any property is the portion of the aggregate basis increase which is allocated to the property pursuant to this section.

(B) AGGREGATE BASIS INCREASE.—In the case of any estate, the aggregate basis increase under this subsection is $1,300,000.

(C) LIMIT INCREASED BY UNUSED BUILT-IN LOSSES AND LOSS CARRYOVERS.—The limitation under subparagraph (B) shall be increased by—

(i) the sum of the amount of any capital loss carryover under section 1212(b), and the amount of any net operating loss carryover under section 172, which would (but for the decedent's death) be carried from the decedent's last taxable year to a later taxable year of the decedent, plus

(ii) the sum of the amount of any losses that would have been allowable under section 165 if the property acquired from the decedent had been sold at fair market value immediately before the decedent's death.

(3) DECEDENT NONRESIDENTS WHO ARE NOT CITIZENS OF THE UNITED STATES.—In the case of a decedent nonresident not a citizen of the United States—

(A) paragraph (2)(B) shall be applied by substituting "$60,000" for "$1,300,000", and

(B) paragraph (2)(C) shall not apply.

[Sec. 1022(c)]

(c) ADDITIONAL BASIS INCREASE FOR PROPERTY ACQUIRED BY SURVIVING SPOUSE.—

(1) IN GENERAL.—In the case of property to which this subsection applies and which is qualified spousal property, the basis of such property under subsection (a) (as increased under subsection (b)) shall be increased by its spousal property basis increase.

(2) SPOUSAL PROPERTY BASIS INCREASE.—For purposes of this subsection—

(A) IN GENERAL.—The spousal property basis increase for property referred to in paragraph (1) is the portion of the aggregate spousal property basis increase which is allocated to the property pursuant to this section.

(B) AGGREGATE SPOUSAL PROPERTY BASIS INCREASE.—In the case of any estate, the aggregate spousal property basis increase is $3,000,000.

(3) QUALIFIED SPOUSAL PROPERTY.—For purposes of this subsection, the term "qualified spousal property" means—

(A) outright transfer property, and

(B) qualified terminable interest property.

(4) OUTRIGHT TRANSFER PROPERTY.—For purposes of this subsection—

(A) IN GENERAL.—The term "outright transfer property" means any interest in property acquired from the decedent by the decedent's surviving spouse.

(B) EXCEPTION.—Subparagraph (A) shall not apply where, on the lapse of time, on the occurrence of an event or contingency, or on the failure of an event or contingency to occur, an interest passing to the surviving spouse will terminate or fail—

(i)(I) if an interest in such property passes or has passed (for less than an adequate and full consideration in money or money's worth) from the decedent to any person other than such surviving spouse (or the estate of such spouse), and

(II) if by reason of such passing such person (or his heirs or assigns) may possess or enjoy any part of such property after such termination or failure of the interest so passing to the surviving spouse, or

(ii) if such interest is to be acquired for the surviving spouse, pursuant to directions of the decedent, by his executor or by the trustee of a trust.

For purposes of this subparagraph, an interest shall not be considered as an interest which will terminate or fail merely because it is the ownership of a bond, note, or similar contractual obligation, the discharge of which would not have the effect of an annuity for life or for a term.

(C) INTEREST OF SPOUSE CONDITIONAL ON SURVIVAL FOR LIMITED PERIOD.—For purposes of this paragraph, an interest passing to the surviving spouse shall not be considered as an interest which will terminate or fail on the death of such spouse if—

(i) such death will cause a termination or failure of such interest only if it occurs within a period not exceeding 6 months after the decedent's death, or only if it occurs as a result of a common disaster resulting in the death of the decedent and the surviving spouse, or only if it occurs in the case of either such event, and

(ii) such termination or failure does not in fact occur.

(5) QUALIFIED TERMINABLE INTEREST PROPERTY.—For purposes of this subsection—

(A) IN GENERAL.—The term "qualified terminable interest property" means property—

(i) which passes from the decedent, and

(ii) in which the surviving spouse has a qualifying income interest for life.

(B) QUALIFYING INCOME INTEREST FOR LIFE.—The surviving spouse has a qualifying income interest for life if—

(i) the surviving spouse is entitled to all the income from the property, payable annually or at more frequent intervals, or has a usufruct interest for life in the property, and

(ii) no person has a power to appoint any part of the property to any person other than the surviving spouse.

Clause (ii) shall not apply to a power exercisable only at or after the death of the surviving spouse. To the extent provided in regulations, an annuity shall be treated in a manner similar to an income interest in property (regardless of whether the property from which the annuity is payable can be separately identified).

(C) PROPERTY INCLUDES INTEREST THEREIN.—The term "property" includes an interest in property.

(D) SPECIFIC PORTION TREATED AS SEPARATE PROPERTY.—A specific portion of property shall be treated as separate property. For purposes of the preceding sentence, the term "specific portion" only includes a portion determined on a fractional or percentage basis.

[Sec. 1022(d)]

(d) DEFINITIONS AND SPECIAL RULES FOR APPLICATION OF SUBSECTIONS (B) AND (C).—

(1) PROPERTY TO WHICH SUBSECTIONS (B) AND (C) APPLY.—

(A) IN GENERAL.—The basis of property acquired from a decedent may be increased under subsection (b) or (c) only if the property was owned by the decedent at the time of death.

(B) RULES RELATING TO OWNERSHIP.—

(i) JOINTLY HELD PROPERTY.—In the case of property which was owned by the decedent and another person as joint tenants with right of survivorship or tenants by the entirety—

(I) if the only such other person is the surviving spouse, the decedent shall be treated as the owner of only 50 percent of the property,

(II) in any case (to which subclause (I) does not apply) in which the decedent furnished consideration for the acquisition of the property, the decedent shall be treated as the owner to the extent of the portion of the property which is proportionate to such consideration, and

(III) in any case (to which subclause (I) does not apply) in which the property has been acquired by gift, bequest, devise, or inheritance by the decedent and any other person as joint tenants with right of survivorship and their interests are not otherwise specified or fixed by law, the decedent shall be treated as the owner to the extent of the value of a fractional part to be determined by dividing the value of the property by the number of joint tenants with right of survivorship.

(ii) REVOCABLE TRUSTS.—The decedent shall be treated as owning property transferred by the decedent during life to a qualified revocable trust (as defined in section 645(b)(1)).

(iii) POWERS OF APPOINTMENT.—The decedent shall not be treated as owning any property by reason of holding a power of appointment with respect to such property.

(iv) COMMUNITY PROPERTY.—Property which represents the surviving spouse's one-half share of community property held by the decedent and the surviving spouse under the community property laws of any State or possession of the United States or any foreign country shall be treated for purposes of this section as owned by, and acquired from, the decedent if at least one-half of the whole of the community interest in such property is treated as owned by, and acquired from, the decedent without regard to this clause.

(C) PROPERTY ACQUIRED BY DECEDENT BY GIFT WITHIN 3 YEARS OF DEATH.—

(i) IN GENERAL.—Subsections (b) and (c) shall not apply to property acquired by the decedent by gift or by inter vivos transfer for less than adequate and full consideration in money or money's worth during the 3-year period ending on the date of the decedent's death.

(ii) EXCEPTION FOR CERTAIN GIFTS FROM SPOUSE.—Clause (i) shall not apply to property acquired by the decedent from the decedent's spouse unless, during such 3-year period, such spouse acquired the property in whole or in part by gift or by inter vivos transfer for less than adequate and full consideration in money or money's worth.

(D) STOCK OF CERTAIN ENTITIES.—Subsections (b) and (c) shall not apply to—

(i) stock or securities of a foreign personal holding company,

(ii) stock of a DISC or former DISC,

(iii) stock of a foreign investment company, or

(iv) stock of a passive foreign investment company unless such company is a qualified electing fund (as defined in section 1295) with respect to the decedent.

(2) FAIR MARKET VALUE LIMITATION.—The adjustments under subsections (b) and (c) shall not increase the basis of any interest in property acquired from the decedent above its fair market value in the hands of the decedent as of the date of the decedent's death.

(3) ALLOCATION RULES.—

(A) IN GENERAL.—The executor shall allocate the adjustments under subsections (b) and (c) on the return required by section 6018.

(B) CHANGES IN ALLOCATION.—Any allocation made pursuant to subparagraph (A) may be changed only as provided by the Secretary.

(4) INFLATION ADJUSTMENT OF BASIS ADJUSTMENT AMOUNTS.—

(A) IN GENERAL.—In the case of decedents dying in a calendar year after 2010, the $1,300,000, $60,000, and $3,000,000 dollar amounts in subsections (b) and (c)(2)(B) shall each be increased by an amount equal to the product of—

(i) such dollar amount, and

(ii) the cost-of-living adjustment determined under section 1(f)(3) for such calendar year, determined by substituting "2009" for "1992" in subparagraph (B) thereof.

(B) ROUNDING.—If any increase determined under subparagraph (A) is not a multiple of—

(i) $100,000 in the case of the $1,300,000 amount,

(ii) $5,000 in the case of the $60,000 amount, and

(iii) $250,000 in the case of the $3,000,000 amount,

such increase shall be rounded to the next lowest multiple thereof.

[Sec. 1022(e)]

(e) PROPERTY ACQUIRED FROM THE DECEDENT.—For purposes of this section, the following property shall be considered to have been acquired from the decedent:

(1) Property acquired by bequest, devise, or inheritance, or by the decedent's estate from the decedent.

(2) Property transferred by the decedent during his lifetime—

(A) to a qualified revocable trust (as defined in section 645(b)(1)), or

(B) to any other trust with respect to which the decedent reserved the right to make any change in the enjoyment thereof through the exercise of a power to alter, amend, or terminate the trust.

(3) Any other property passing from the decedent by reason of death to the extent that such property passed without consideration.

[Sec. 1022(f)]

(f) COORDINATION WITH SECTION 691.—This section shall not apply to property which constitutes a right to receive an item of income in respect of a decedent under section 691.

[Sec. 1022(g)]

(g) CERTAIN LIABILITIES DISREGARDED.—

(1) IN GENERAL.—In determining whether gain is recognized on the acquisition of property—

(A) from a decedent by a decedent's estate or any beneficiary other than a tax-exempt beneficiary, and

(B) from the decedent's estate by any beneficiary other than a tax-exempt beneficiary,

and in determining the adjusted basis of such property, liabilities in excess of basis shall be disregarded.

Sec. 1022(g)

(2) TAX-EXEMPT BENEFICIARY.—For purposes of paragraph (1), the term "tax-exempt beneficiary" means—

(A) the United States, any State or political subdivision thereof, any possession of the United States, any Indian tribal government (within the meaning of section 7871), or any agency or instrumentality of any of the foregoing,

(B) an organization (other than a cooperative described in section 521) which is exempt from tax imposed by chapter 1,

(C) any foreign person or entity (within the meaning of section 168(h)(2)), and

(D) to the extent provided in regulations, any person to whom property is transferred for the principal purpose of tax avoidance.

[Sec. 1022(h)]

(h) REGULATIONS.—The Secretary shall prescribe such regulations as may be necessary to carry out the purposes of this section.

PART III—COMMON NONTAXABLE EXCHANGES

[Sec. 1031]

SEC. 1031. EXCHANGE OF PROPERTY HELD FOR PRODUCTIVE USE OR INVESTMENT.

[Sec. 1031(a)]

(a) NONRECOGNITION OF GAIN OR LOSS FROM EXCHANGES SOLELY IN KIND.—

(1) IN GENERAL.—No gain or loss shall be recognized on the exchange of property held for productive use in a trade or business or for investment if such property is exchanged solely for property of like kind which is to be held either for productive use in a trade or business or for investment.

(2) EXCEPTION.—This subsection shall not apply to any exchange of—

(A) stock in trade or other property held primarily for sale,

(B) stocks, bonds, or notes,

(C) other securities or evidences of indebtedness or interest,

(D) interests in a partnership,

(E) certificates of trust or beneficial interests, or

(F) choses in action.

For purposes of this section, an interest in a partnership which has in effect a valid election under section 761(a) to be excluded from the application of all of subchapter K shall be treated as an interest in each of the assets of such partnership and not as an interest in a partnership.

(3) REQUIREMENT THAT PROPERTY BE IDENTIFIED AND THAT EXCHANGE BE COMPLETED NOT MORE THAN 180 DAYS AFTER TRANSFER OF EXCHANGED PROPERTY.—For purposes of this subsection, any property received by the taxpayer shall be treated as property which is not like-kind property if—

(A) such property is not identified as property to be received in the exchange on or before the day which is 45 days after the date on which the taxpayer transfers the property relinquished in the exchange, or

(B) such property is received after the earlier of—

(i) the day which is 180 days after the date on which the taxpayer transfers the property relinquished in the exchange, or

(ii) the due date (determined with regard to extension) for the transferor's return of the tax imposed by this chapter for the taxable year in which the transfer of the relinquished property occurs.

[Sec. 1031(b)]

(b) GAIN FROM EXCHANGES NOT SOLELY IN KIND.—If an exchange would be within the provisions of subsection (a), of section 1035(a), of section 1036(a), or of section 1037(a), if it were not for the fact that the property received in exchange consists not only of property permitted by such provisions to be received without the recognition of gain, but also of other property or money, then the gain, if any, to the recipient shall be recognized, but in an amount not in excess of the sum of such money and the fair market value of such other property.

[Sec. 1031(c)]

(c) Loss From Exchanges Not Solely In Kind.—If an exchange would be within the provisions of subsection (a), of section 1035(a), of section 1036(a), or of section 1037(a), if it were not for the fact that the property received in exchange consists not only of property permitted by such provisions to be received without the recognition of gain or loss, but also of other property or money, then no loss from the exchange shall be recognized.

[Sec. 1031(d)]

(d) Basis.—If property was acquired on an exchange described in this section, section 1035(a), section 1036(a), or section 1037(a), then the basis shall be the same as that of the property exchanged, decreased in the amount of any money received by the taxpayer and increased in the amount of gain or decreased in the amount of loss to the taxpayer that was recognized on such exchange. If the property so acquired consisted in part of the type of property permitted by this section, section 1035(a), section 1036(a), or section 1037(a), to be received without the recognition of gain or loss, and in part of other property, the basis provided in this subsection shall be allocated between the properties (other than money) received, and for the purpose of the allocation there shall be assigned to such other property an amount equivalent to its fair market value at the date of the exchange. For purposes of this section, section 1035(a), and section 1036(a), where as part of the consideration to the taxpayer another party to the exchange assumed (as determined under section 357(d)) a liability of the taxpayer, such assumption shall be considered as money received by the taxpayer on the exchange.

[Sec. 1031(e)]

(e) Exchanges of Livestock of Different Sexes.—For purposes of this section, livestock of different sexes are not property of a like kind.

[Sec. 1031(f)]

(f) Special Rules for Exchanges Between Related Persons.—

(1) In general.—If—

(A) a taxpayer exchanges property with a related person,

(B) there is nonrecognition of gain or loss to the taxpayer under this section with respect to the exchange of such property (determined without regard to this subsection), and

(C) before the date 2 years after the date of the last transfer which was part of such exchange—

(i) the related person disposes of such property, or

(ii) the taxpayer disposes of the property received in the exchange from the related person which was of like kind to the property transferred by the taxpayer,

there shall be no nonrecognition of gain or loss under this section to the taxpayer with respect to such exchange; except that any gain or loss recognized by the taxpayer by reason of this subsection shall be taken into account as of the date on which the disposition referred to in subparagraph (C) occurs.

(2) Certain dispositions not taken into account.—For purposes of paragraph (1)(C), there shall not be taken into account any disposition—

(A) after the earlier of the death of the taxpayer or the death of the related person,

(B) in a compulsory or involuntary conversion (within the meaning of section 1033) if the exchange occurred before the threat or imminence of such conversion, or

(C) with respect to which it is established to the satisfaction of the Secretary that neither the exchange nor such disposition had as one of its principal purposes the avoidance of Federal income tax.

(3) Related person.—For purposes of this subsection, the term "related person" means any person bearing a relationship to the taxpayer described in section 267(b) or 707(b)(1).

(4) Treatment of certain transactions.—This section shall not apply to any exchange which is part of a transaction (or series of transactions) structured to avoid the purposes of this subsection.

[Sec. 1031(g)]

(g) SPECIAL RULE WHERE SUBSTANTIAL DIMINUTION OF RISK.—

(1) IN GENERAL.—If paragraph (2) applies to any property for any period, the running of the period set forth in subsection (f)(1)(C) with respect to such property shall be suspended during such period.

(2) PROPERTY TO WHICH SUBSECTION APPLIES.—This paragraph shall apply to any property for any period during which the holder's risk of loss with respect to the property is substantially diminished by—

(A) the holding of a put with respect to such property,

(B) the holding by another person of a right to acquire such property, or

(C) a short sale or any other transaction.

* * *

[Sec. 1032]

SEC. 1032. EXCHANGE OF STOCK FOR PROPERTY.

[Sec. 1032(a)]

(a) NONRECOGNITION OF GAIN OR LOSS.—No gain or loss shall be recognized to a corporation on the receipt of money or other property in exchange for stock (including treasury stock) of such corporation. No gain or loss shall be recognized by a corporation with respect to any lapse or acquisition of an option, or with respect to a securities futures contract (as defined in section 1234B), to buy or sell its stock (including treasury stock).

[Sec. 1032(b)]

(b) BASIS.—

For basis of property acquired by a corporation in certain exchanges for its stock, see section 362.

[Sec. 1033]

SEC. 1033. INVOLUNTARY CONVERSIONS.

[Sec. 1033(a)]

(a) GENERAL RULE.—If property (as a result of its destruction in whole or in part, theft, seizure, or requisition or condemnation or threat or imminence thereof) is compulsorily or involuntarily converted—

(1) CONVERSION INTO SIMILAR PROPERTY.—Into property similar or related in service or use to the property so converted, no gain shall be recognized.

(2) CONVERSION INTO MONEY.—Into money or into property not similar or related in service or use to the converted property, the gain (if any) shall be recognized except to the extent hereinafter provided in this paragraph:

(A) NONRECOGNITION OF GAIN.—If the taxpayer during the period specified in subparagraph (B), for the purpose of replacing the property so converted, purchases other property similar or related in service or use to the property so converted, or purchases stock in the acquisition of control of a corporation owning such other property, at the election of the taxpayer the gain shall be recognized only to the extent that the amount realized upon such conversion (regardless of whether such amount is received in one or more taxable years) exceeds the cost of such other property or such stock. Such election shall be made at such time and in such manner as the Secretary may by regulations prescribe. For purposes of this paragraph—

(i) no property or stock acquired before the disposition of the converted property shall be considered to have been acquired for the purpose of replacing such converted property unless held by the taxpayer on the date of such disposition; and

(ii) the taxpayer shall be considered to have purchased property or stock only if, but for the provisions of subsection (b) of this section, the unadjusted basis of such property or stock would be its cost within the meaning of section 1012.

(B) PERIOD WITHIN WHICH PROPERTY MUST BE REPLACED.—The period referred to in subparagraph (A) shall be the period beginning with the date of the disposition of the converted property, or the earliest date of the threat or imminence of requisition or condemnation of the converted property, whichever is the earlier, and ending—

(i) 2 years after the close of the first taxable year in which any part of the gain upon the conversion is realized, or

(ii) subject to such terms and conditions as may be specified by the Secretary, at the close of such later date as the Secretary may designate on application by the taxpayer. Such application shall be made at such time and in such manner as the Secretary may by regulations prescribe.

(C) TIME FOR ASSESSMENT OF DEFICIENCY ATTRIBUTABLE TO GAIN UPON CONVERSION.—If a taxpayer has made the election provided in subparagraph (A), then—

(i) the statutory period for the assessment of any deficiency, for any taxable year in which any part of the gain on such conversion is realized, attributable to such gain shall not expire prior to the expiration of 3 years from the date the Secretary is notified by the taxpayer (in such manner as the Secretary may by regulations prescribe) of the replacement of the converted property or of an intention not to replace, and

(ii) such deficiency may be assessed before the expiration of such 3-year period notwithstanding the provisions of section 6212 (c) or the provisions of any other law or rule of law which would otherwise prevent such assessment.

(D) TIME FOR ASSESSMENT OF OTHER DEFICIENCIES ATTRIBUTABLE TO ELECTION.—If the election provided in subparagraph (A) is made by the taxpayer and such other property or such stock was purchased before the beginning of the last taxable year in which any part of the gain upon such conversion is realized, any deficiency, to the extent resulting from such election, for any taxable year ending before such last taxable year may be assessed (notwithstanding the provisions of section 6212 (c) or 6501 or the provisions of any other law or rule of law which would otherwise prevent such assessment) at any time before the expiration of the period within which a deficiency for such last taxable year may be assessed.

(E) DEFINITIONS.—For purposes of this paragraph—

(i) CONTROL.—The term "control" means the ownership of stock possessing at least 80 percent of the total combined voting power of all classes of stock entitled to vote and at least 80 percent of the total number of shares of all other classes of stock of the corporation.

(ii) DISPOSITION OF THE CONVERTED PROPERTY.—The term "disposition of the converted property" means the destruction, theft, seizure, requisition, or condemnation of the converted property, or the sale or exchange of such property under threat or imminence of requisition or condemnation.

[Sec. 1033(b)]

(b) BASIS OF PROPERTY ACQUIRED THROUGH INVOLUNTARY CONVERSION.—

(1) CONVERSIONS DESCRIBED IN SUBSECTION (a)(1).—If the property was acquired as the result of a compulsory or involuntary conversion described in subsection (a)(1), the basis shall be the same as in the case of the property so converted—

(A) decreased in the amount of any money received by the taxpayer which was not expended in accordance with the provisions of law (applicable to the year in which such conversion was made) determining the taxable status of the gain or loss upon such conversion, and

(B) increased in the amount of gain or decreased in the amount of loss to the taxpayer recognized upon such conversion under the law applicable to the year in which such conversion was made.

(2) CONVERSIONS DESCRIBED IN SUBSECTION (a)(2).—In the case of property purchased by the taxpayer in a transaction described in subsection (a)(2) which resulted in the nonrecognition of any part of the gain realized as the result of a compulsory or involuntary conversion, the basis shall be the cost of such property decreased in the amount of the gain not so recognized; and if the property purchased consists of more than 1 piece of property, the basis determined under this sentence shall be allocated to the purchased properties in proportion to their respective costs.

(3) PROPERTY HELD BY CORPORATION THE STOCK OF WHICH IS REPLACEMENT PROPERTY.—

(A) IN GENERAL.—If the basis of stock in a corporation is decreased under paragraph (2), an amount equal to such decrease shall also be applied to reduce the basis of property held by the corporation at the time the taxpayer acquired control (as defined in subsection (a)(2)(E)) of such corporation.

Sec. 1033(b)

(B) LIMITATION.—Subparagraph (A) shall not apply to the extent that it would (but for this subparagraph) require a reduction in the aggregate adjusted bases of the property of the corporation below the taxpayer's adjusted basis of the stock in the corporation (determined immediately after such basis is decreased under paragraph (2)).

(C) ALLOCATION OF BASIS REDUCTION.—The decrease required under subparagraph (A) shall be allocated—

(i) first to property which is similar or related in service or use to the converted property,

(ii) second to depreciable property (as defined in section 1017(b)(3)(B)) not described in clause (i), and

(iii) then to other property.

(D) SPECIAL RULES.—

(i) REDUCTION NOT TO EXCEED ADJUSTED BASIS OF PROPERTY.—No reduction in the basis of any property under this paragraph shall exceed the adjusted basis of such property (determined without regard to such reduction).

(ii) ALLOCATION OF REDUCTION AMONG PROPERTIES.—If more than 1 property is described in a clause of subparagraph (C), the reduction under this paragraph shall be allocated among such property in proportion to the adjusted bases of such property (as so determined).

[Sec. 1033(c)]

(c) PROPERTY SOLD PURSUANT TO RECLAMATION LAWS.—For purposes of this subtitle, if property lying within an irrigation project is sold or otherwise disposed of in order to conform to the acreage limitation provisions of Federal reclamation laws, such sale or disposition shall be treated as an involuntary conversion to which this section applies.

* * *

[Sec. 1033(g)]

(g) CONDEMNATION OF REAL PROPERTY HELD FOR PRODUCTIVE USE IN TRADE OR BUSINESS OR FOR INVESTMENT.—

(1) SPECIAL RULE.—For purposes of subsection (a), if real property (not including stock in trade or other property held primarily for sale) held for productive use in trade or business or for investment is (as the result of its seizure, requisition, or condemnation, or threat or imminence thereof) compulsorily or involuntarily converted, property of a like kind to be held either for productive use in trade or business or for investment shall be treated as property similar or related in service or use to the property so converted.

(2) LIMITATION.—Paragraph (1) shall not apply to the purchase of stock in the acquisition of control of a corporation described in subsection (a)(2)(A).

(3) ELECTION TO TREAT OUTDOOR ADVERTISING DISPLAYS AS REAL PROPERTY.—

(A) IN GENERAL.—A taxpayer may elect, at such time and in such manner as the Secretary may prescribe, to treat property which constitutes an outdoor advertising display as real property for purposes of this chapter. The election provided by this subparagraph may not be made with respect to any property with respect to which an election under section 179(a) (relating to election to expense certain depreciable business assets) is in effect.

(B) ELECTION.—An election made under subparagraph (A) may not be revoked without the consent of the Secretary.

(C) OUTDOOR ADVERTISING DISPLAY.—For purposes of this paragraph, the term "outdoor advertising display" means a rigidly assembled sign, display, or device permanently affixed to the ground or permanently attached to a building or other inherently permanent structure constituting, or used for the display of, a commercial or other advertisement to the public.

(D) CHARACTER OF REPLACEMENT PROPERTY.—For purposes of this subsection, an interest in real property purchased as replacement property for a compulsorily or involuntarily converted outdoor advertising display defined in subparagraph (C) (and treated by the taxpayer as real property) shall be considered property of a like kind as the property converted without regard to whether the taxpayer's interest in the replacement property is the same kind of interest the taxpayer held in the converted property.

(4) Special rule.—In the case of a compulsory or involuntary conversion described in paragraph (1), subsection (a)(2)(B)(i) shall be applied by substituting "3 years" for "2 years".

[Sec. 1033(h)]

(h) Special Rules for Property Damaged by Presidentially Declared Disasters.—

(1) Principal residences.—If the taxpayer's principal residence or any of its contents is compulsorily or involuntarily converted as a result of a Presidentially declared disaster—

(A) Treatment of insurance proceeds.—

(i) Exclusion for unscheduled personal property.—No gain shall be recognized by reason of the receipt of any insurance proceeds for personal property which was part of such contents and which was not scheduled property for purposes of such insurance.

(ii) Other proceeds treated as common fund.—In the case of any insurance proceeds (not described in clause (i)) for such residence or contents—

(I) such proceeds shall be treated as received for the conversion of a single item of property, and

(II) any property which is similar or related in service or use to the residence so converted (or contents thereof) shall be treated for purposes of subsection (a)(2) as property similar or related in service or use to such single item of property.

(B) Extension of replacement period.—Subsection (a)(2)(B) shall be applied with respect to any property so converted by substituting "4 years" for "2 years".

(2) Trade or business and investment property.—If a taxpayer's property held for productive use in a trade or business or for investment is compulsorily or involuntarily converted as a result of a Presidentially declared disaster, tangible property of a type held for productive use in a trade or business shall be treated for purposes of subsection (a) as property similar or related in service or use to the property so converted.

(3) Presidentially declared disaster.—For purposes of this subsection, the term "Presidentially declared disaster" means any disaster which, with respect to the area in which the property is located, resulted in a subsequent determination by the President that such area warrants assistance by the Federal Government under the Disaster Relief and Emergency Assistance Act.

(4) Principal residence.—For purposes of this subsection, the term "principal residence" has the same meaning as when used in section 121, except that such term shall include a residence not treated as a principal residence solely because the taxpayer does not own the residence.

[Sec. 1033(i)]

(i) Replacement Property Must Be Acquired From Unrelated Person in Certain Cases.—

(1) In general.—If the property which is involuntarily converted is held by a taxpayer to which this subsection applies, subsection (a) shall not apply if the replacement property or stock is acquired from a related person. The preceding sentence shall not apply to the extent that the related person acquired the replacement property or stock from an unrelated person during the period applicable under subsection (a)(2)(B).

(2) Taxpayers to which subsection applies.—This subsection shall apply to—

(A) a C corporation,

(B) a partnership in which 1 or more C corporations own, directly or indirectly (determined in accordance with section 707(b)(3)), more than 50 percent of the capital interest, or profits interest, in such partnership at the time of the involuntary conversion, and

(C) any other taxpayer if, with respect to property which is involuntarily converted during the taxable year, the aggregate of the amount of realized gain on such property on which there is realized gain exceeds $100,000.

In the case of a partnership, subparagraph (C) shall apply with respect to the partnership and with respect to each partner. A similar rule shall apply in the case of an S corporation and its shareholders.

(3) Related person.—For purposes of this subsection, a person is related to another person if the person bears a relationship to the other person described in section 267(b) or 707(b)(1).

* * *

SEC. 1035. CERTAIN EXCHANGES OF INSURANCE POLICIES.

(a) GENERAL RULES.—No gain or loss shall be recognized on the exchange of—

(1) a contract of life insurance for another contract of life insurance or for an endowment or annuity contract; or

(2) a contract of endowment insurance (A) for another contract of endowment insurance which provides for regular payments beginning at a date not later than the date payments would have begun under the contract exchanged, or (B) for an annuity contract; or

(3) an annuity contract for an annuity contract.

(b) DEFINITIONS.—For the purpose of this section—

(1) ENDOWMENT CONTRACT.—A contract of endowment insurance is a contract with an insurance company which depends in part on the life expectancy of the insured, but which may be payable in full in a single payment during his life.

(2) ANNUITY CONTRACT.—An annuity contract is a contract to which paragraph (1) applies but which may be payable during the life of the annuitant only in installments.

(3) LIFE INSURANCE CONTRACT.—A contract of life insurance is a contract to which paragraph (1) applies but which is not ordinarily payable in full during the life of the insured.

(c) EXCHANGES INVOLVING FOREIGN PERSONS.—To the extent provided in regulations, subsection (a) shall not apply to any exchange having the effect of transferring property to any person other than a United States person.

(d) CROSS REFERENCES.—

(1) For rules relating to recognition of gain or loss where an exchange is not solely in kind, see subsections (b) and (c) of section 1031.

(2) For rules relating to the basis of property acquired in an exchange described in subsection (a), see subsection (d) of section 1031.

SEC. 1036. STOCK FOR STOCK OF SAME CORPORATION.

(a) GENERAL RULE.—No gain or loss shall be recognized if common stock in a corporation is exchanged solely for common stock in the same corporation, or if preferred stock in a corporation is exchanged solely for preferred stock in the same corporation.

(b) NONQUALIFIED PREFERRED STOCK NOT TREATED AS STOCK.—For purposes of this section, nonqualified preferred stock (as defined in section 351(g)(2)) shall be treated as property other than stock.

(c) CROSS REFERENCES.—

(1) For rules relating to recognition of gain or loss where an exchange is not solely in kind, see subsections (b) and (c) of section 1031.

(2) For rules relating to the basis of property acquired in an exchange described in subsection (a), see subsection (d) of section 1031.

[Sec. 1038]

SEC. 1038. CERTAIN REACQUISITIONS OF REAL PROPERTY.

[Sec. 1038(a)]

(a) GENERAL RULE.—If—

(1) a sale of real property gives rise to indebtedness to the seller which is secured by the real property sold, and

(2) the seller of such property reacquires such property in partial or full satisfaction of such indebtedness,

then, except as provided in subsections (b) and (d), no gain or loss shall result to the seller from such reacquisition, and no debt shall become worthless or partially worthless as a result of such reacquisition.

[Sec. 1038(b)]

(b) AMOUNT OF GAIN RESULTING.—

(1) IN GENERAL.—In the case of a reacquisition of real property to which subsection (a) applies, gain shall result from such reacquisition to the extent that—

(A) the amount of money and the fair market value of other property (other than obligations of the purchaser) received, prior to such reacquisition, with respect to the sale of such property, exceeds

(B) the amount of the gain on the sale of such property returned as income for periods prior to such reacquisition.

(2) LIMITATION.—The amount of gain determined under paragraph (1) resulting from a reacquisition during any taxable year beginning after the date of the enactment of this section shall not exceed the amount by which the price at which the real property was sold exceeded its adjusted basis, reduced by the sum of—

(A) the amount of the gain on the sale of such property returned as income for periods prior to the reacquisition of such property, and

(B) the amount of money and the fair market value of other property (other than obligations of the purchaser received with respect to the sale of such property) paid or transferred by the seller in connection with the reacquisition of such property.

For purposes of this paragraph, the price at which real property is sold is the gross sales price reduced by the selling commissions, legal fees, and other expenses incident to the sale of such property which are properly taken into account in determining gain or loss on such sale.

(3) GAIN RECOGNIZED.—Except as provided in this section, the gain determined under this subsection resulting from a reacquisition to which subsection (a) applies shall be recognized, notwithstanding any other provision of this subtitle.

[Sec. 1038(c)]

(c) BASIS OF REACQUIRED REAL PROPERTY.—If subsection (a) applies to the reacquisition of any real property, the basis of such property upon such reacquisition shall be the adjusted basis of the indebtedness to the seller secured by such property (determined as of the date of reacquisition), increased by the sum of—

(1) the amount of the gain determined under subsection (b) resulting from such reacquisition, and

(2) the amount described in subsection (b)(2)(B).

If any indebtedness to the seller secured by such property is not discharged upon the reacquisition of such property, the basis of such indebtedness shall be zero.

[Sec. 1038(d)]

(d) INDEBTEDNESS TREATED AS WORTHLESS PRIOR TO REACQUISITION.—If, prior to a reacquisition of real property to which subsection (a) applies, the seller has treated indebtedness secured by such property as having become worthless or partially worthless—

(1) such seller shall be considered as receiving, upon the reacquisition of such property, an amount equal to the amount of such indebtedness treated by him as having become worthless, and

(2) the adjusted basis of such indebtedness shall be increased (as of the date of reacquisition) by an amount equal to the amount so considered as received by such seller.

[Sec. 1038(e)]

(e) PRINCIPAL RESIDENCES.—If—

(1) subsection (a) applies to a reacquisition of real property with respect to the sale of which gain was not recognized under section 121 (relating to gain on sale of principal residence); and

(2) within 1 year after the date of the reacquisition of such property by the seller, such property is resold by him,

then, under regulations prescribed by the Secretary, subsections (b), (c), and (d) of this section shall not apply to the reacquisition of such property and, for purposes of applying section 121, the resale of such property shall be treated as a part of the transaction constituting the original sale of such property.

[Sec. 1038(f)—Stricken]

[Sec. 1038(g)]

(g) ACQUISITION BY ESTATE, ETC., OF SELLER.—Under regulations prescribed by the Secretary, if an installment obligation is indebtedness to the seller which is described in subsection (a), and if such obligation is, in the hands of the taxpayer, an obligation with respect to which section 691(a)(4)(B) applies, then—

(1) for purposes of subsection (a), acquisition of real property by the taxpayer shall be treated as reacquisition by the seller, and

(2) the basis of the real property acquired by the taxpayer shall be increased by an amount equal to the deduction under section 691(c) which would (but for this subsection) have been allowable to the taxpayer with respect to the gain on the exchange of the obligation for the real property.

[Sec. 1041]

SEC. 1041. TRANSFERS OF PROPERTY BETWEEN SPOUSES OR INCIDENT TO DIVORCE.

[Sec. 1041(a)]

(a) GENERAL RULE.—No gain or loss shall be recognized on a transfer of property from an individual to (or in trust for the benefit of)—

(1) a spouse, or

(2) a former spouse, but only if the transfer is incident to the divorce.

[Sec. 1041(b)]

(b) TRANSFER TREATED AS GIFT; TRANSFEREE HAS TRANSFEROR'S BASIS.—In the case of any transfer of property described in subsection (a)—

(1) for purposes of this subtitle, the property shall be treated as acquired by the transferee by gift, and

(2) the basis of the transferee in the property shall be the adjusted basis of the transferor.

[Sec. 1041(c)]

(c) INCIDENT TO DIVORCE.—For purposes of subsection (a)(2), a transfer of property is incident to the divorce if such transfer—

(1) occurs within 1 year after the date on which the marriage ceases, or

(2) is related to the cessation of the marriage.

[Sec. 1041(d)]

(d) SPECIAL RULE WHERE SPOUSE IS NONRESIDENT ALIEN.—Subsection (a) shall not apply if the spouse (or former spouse) of the individual making the transfer is a nonresident alien.

[Sec. 1041(e)]

(e) TRANSFERS IN TRUST WHERE LIABILITY EXCEEDS BASIS.—Subsection (a) shall not apply to the transfer of property in trust to the extent that—

(1) the sum of the amount of the liabilities assumed, plus the amount of the liabilities to which the property is subject, exceeds

(2) the total of the adjusted basis of the property transferred.

Proper adjustment shall be made under subsection (b) in the basis of the transferee in such property to take into account gain recognized by reason of the preceding sentence.

[Sec. 1044]

SEC. 1044. ROLLOVER OF PUBLICLY TRADED SECURITIES GAIN INTO SPECIALIZED SMALL BUSINESS INVESTMENT COMPANIES.

[Sec. 1044(a)]

(a) NONRECOGNITION OF GAIN.—In the case of the sale of any publicly traded securities with respect to which the taxpayer elects the application of this section, gain from such sale shall be recognized only to the extent that the amount realized on such sale exceeds.—

(1) the cost of any common stock or partnership interest in a specialized small business investment company purchased by the taxpayer during the 60-day period beginning on the date of such sale, reduced by

(2) any portion of such cost previously taken into account under this section.

This section shall not apply to any gain which is treated as ordinary income for purposes of this subtitle.

[Sec. 1044(b)]

(b) LIMITATIONS.—

(1) LIMITATION ON INDIVIDUALS.—In the case of an individual, the amount of gain which may be excluded under subsection (a) for any taxable year shall not exceed the lesser of—

(A) $50,000, or

(B) $500,000, reduced by the amount of gain excluded under subsection (a) for all preceding taxable years.

(2) LIMITATION ON C CORPORATIONS.—In the case of a C corporation, the amount of gain which may be excluded under subsection (a) for any taxable year shall not exceed the lesser of—

(A) $250,000, or

(B) $1,000,000, reduced by the amount of gain excluded under subsection (a) for all preceding taxable years.

(3) SPECIAL RULES FOR MARRIED INDIVIDUALS.—For purposes of this subsection—

(A) SEPARATE RETURNS.—In the case of a separate return by a married individual, paragraph (1) shall be applied by substituting "$25,000" for "$50,000" and "$250,000" for "$500,000".

(B) ALLOCATION OF GAIN.—In the case of any joint return, the amount of gain excluded under subsection (a) for any taxable year shall be allocated equally between the spouses for purposes of applying this subsection to subsequent taxable years.

(C) MARITAL STATUS.—For purposes of this subsection, marital status shall be determined under section 7703.

(4) SPECIAL RULES FOR C CORPORATION.—For purposes of this subsection—

(A) all corporations which are members of the same controlled group of corporations (within the meaning of section 52(a)) shall be treated as 1 taxpayer, and

(B) any gain excluded under subsection (a) by a predecessor of any C corporation shall be treated as having been excluded by such C corporation.

Sec. 1044(b)

[Sec. 1044(c)]

(c) DEFINITIONS AND SPECIAL RULES.—For purposes of this section—

(1) PUBLICLY TRADED SECURITIES.—The term "publicly traded securities" means securities which are traded on an established securities market.

(2) PURCHASE.—The taxpayer shall be considered to have purchased any property if, but for subsection (d), the unadjusted basis of such property would be its cost within the meaning of section 1012.

(3) SPECIALIZED SMALL BUSINESS INVESTMENT COMPANY.—The term "specialized small business investment company" means any partnership or corporation which is licensed by the Small Business Administration under section 301(d) of the Small Business Investment Act of 1958 (as in effect on May 13, 1993).

(4) CERTAIN ENTITIES NOT ELIGIBLE.—This section shall not apply to any estate, trust, partnership, or S corporation.

[Sec. 1044(d)]

(d) BASIS ADJUSTMENTS.—If gain from any sale is not recognized by reason of subsection (a), such gain shall be applied to reduce (in the order acquired) the basis for determining gain or loss of any common stock or partnership interest in any specialized small business investment company which is purchased by the taxpayer during the 60-day period described in subsection (a). This subsection shall not apply for purposes of section 1202.

[Sec. 1045]

SEC. 1045. ROLLOVER OF GAIN FROM QUALIFIED SMALL BUSINESS STOCK TO ANOTHER QUALIFIED SMALL BUSINESS STOCK.

[Sec. 1045(a)]

(a) NONRECOGNITION OF GAIN.—In the case of any sale of qualified small business stock held by a taxpayer other than a corporation for more than 6 months and with respect to which such taxpayer elects the application of this section, gain from such sale shall be recognized only to the extent that the amount realized on such sale exceeds—

(1) the cost of any qualified small business stock purchased by the taxpayer during the 60-day period beginning on the date of such sale, reduced by

(2) any portion of such cost previously taken into account under this section.

This section shall not apply to any gain which is treated as ordinary income for purposes of this title.

[Sec. 1045(b)]

(b) DEFINITIONS AND SPECIAL RULES.—For purposes of this section—

(1) QUALIFIED SMALL BUSINESS STOCK.—The term "qualified small business stock" has the meaning given such term by section 1202(c).

(2) PURCHASE.—A taxpayer shall be treated as having purchased any property if, but for paragraph (3), the unadjusted basis of such property in the hands of the taxpayer would be its cost (within the meaning of section 1012).

(3) BASIS ADJUSTMENTS.—If gain from any sale is not recognized by reason of subsection (a), such gain shall be applied to reduce (in the order acquired) the basis for determining gain or loss of any qualified small business stock which is purchased by the taxpayer during the 60-day period described in subsection (a).

(4) HOLDING PERIOD.—For purposes of determining whether the nonrecognition of gain under subsection (a) applies to stock which is sold—

(A) the taxpayer's holding period for such stock and the stock referred to in subsection (a)(1) shall be determined without regard to section 1223, and

(B) only the first 6 months of the taxpayer's holding period for the stock referred to in subsection (a)(1) shall be taken into account for purposes of applying section 1202(c)(2).

(5) CERTAIN RULES TO APPLY.—Rules similar to the rules of subsections (f), (g), (h), (i), (j), and (k) of section 1202 shall apply.

Sec. 1044(c)

PART IV—SPECIAL RULES

[Sec. 1059]

SEC. 1059. CORPORATE SHAREHOLDER'S BASIS IN STOCK REDUCED BY NONTAXED PORTION OF EXTRAORDINARY DIVIDENDS.

[Sec. 1059(a)]

(a) GENERAL RULE.—If any corporation receives any extraordinary dividend with respect to any share of stock and such corporation has not held such stock for more than 2 years before the dividend announcement date—

(1) REDUCTION IN BASIS.—The basis of such corporation in such stock shall be reduced (but not below zero) by the nontaxed portion of such dividends.

(2) AMOUNTS IN EXCESS OF BASIS.—If the nontaxed portion of such dividends exceeds such basis, such excess shall be treated as gain from the sale or exchange of such stock for the taxable year in which the extraordinary dividend is received.

[Sec. 1059(b)]

(b) NONTAXED PORTION.—For purposes of this section—

(1) IN GENERAL.—The nontaxed portion of any dividend is the excess (if any) of—

(A) the amount of such dividend, over

(B) the taxable portion of such dividend.

(2) TAXABLE PORTION.—The taxable portion of any dividend is—

(A) the portion of such dividend includible in gross income, reduced by

(B) the amount of any deduction allowable with respect to such dividend under section 243, 244, or 245.

[Sec. 1059(c)]

(c) EXTRAORDINARY DIVIDEND DEFINED.—For purposes of this section—

(1) IN GENERAL.—The term "extraordinary dividend" means any dividend with respect to a share of stock if the amount of such dividend equals or exceeds the threshold percentage of the taxpayer's adjusted basis in such share of stock.

(2) THRESHOLD PERCENTAGE.—The term "theshold percentage" means—

(A) 5 percent in the case of stock which is preferred as to dividends, and

(B) 10 percent in the case of any other stock.

(3) AGGREGATION OF DIVIDENDS.—

(A) AGGREGATION WITHIN 85-DAY PERIOD.—All dividends—

(i) which are received by the taxpayer (or a person described in subparagraph (C)) with respect to any share of stock, and

(ii) which have ex-dividend dates within the same period of 85 consecutive days,

shall be treated as 1 dividend.

(B) AGGREGATION WITHIN 1 YEAR WHERE DIVIDENDS EXCEED 20 PERCENT OF ADJUSTED BASIS.— All dividends—

(i) which are received by the taxpayer (or a person described in subparagraph (C)) with respect to any share of stock, and

(ii) which have ex-dividend dates during the same period of 365 consecutive days,

shall be treated as extraordinary dividends if the aggregate of such dividends exceeds 20 percent of the taxpayer's adjusted basis in such stock (determined without regard to this section).

(C) SUBSTITUTED BASIS TRANSACTIONS.—In the case of any stock, a person is described in this subparagraph if—

(i) the basis of such stock in the hands of such person is determined in whole or in part by reference to the basis of such stock in the hands of the taxpayer, or

Sec. 1059(c)

(ii) the basis of such stock in the hands of the taxpayer is determined in whole or in part by reference to the basis of such stock in the hands of such person.

(4) FAIR MARKET VALUE DETERMINATION.—If the taxpayer establishes to the satisfaction of the Secretary the fair market value of any share of stock as of the day before the ex-dividend date, the taxpayer may elect to apply paragraphs (1) and (3) by substituting such value for the taxpayer's adjusted basis.

[Sec. 1059(d)]

(d) SPECIAL RULES.—For purposes of this section—

(1) TIME FOR REDUCTION.—Any reduction in basis under subsection (a)(1) shall be treated as occurring at the beginning of the ex-dividend date of the extraordinary dividend to which the reduction relates.

(2) DISTRIBUTIONS IN KIND.—To the extent any dividend consists of property other than cash, the amount of such dividend shall be treated as the fair market value of such property (as of the date of the distribution) reduced as provided in section 301(b)(2).

(3) DETERMINATION OF HOLDING PERIOD.—For purposes of determining the holding period of stock under subsection (a), rules similar to the rules of paragraphs (3) and (4) of section 246(c) shall apply; except that "2 years" shall be substituted for the number of days specified in subparagraph (B) of section 246(c)(3).

(4) EX-DIVIDEND DATE.—The term "ex-dividend date" means the date on which the share of stock becomes ex-dividend.

(5) DIVIDEND ANNOUNCEMENT DATE.—The term "dividend announcement date" means, with respect to any dividend, the date on which the corporation declares, announces, or agrees to, the amount or payment of such dividend, whichever is the earliest.

(6) EXCEPTION WHERE STOCK HELD DURING ENTIRE EXISTENCE OF CORPORATION.—

(A) IN GENERAL.—Subsection (a) shall not apply to any extraordinary dividend with respect to any share of stock of a corporation if—

(i) such stock was held by the taxpayer during the entire period such corporation was in existence, and

(ii) except as provided in regulations, no earnings and profits of such corporation were attributable to transfers of property from (or earnings and profits of) a corporation which is not a qualified corporation.

(B) QUALIFIED CORPORATION.—For purposes of subparagraph (A), the term "qualified corporation" means any corporation (including a predecessor corporation)—

(i) with respect to which the taxpayer holds directly or indirectly during the entire period of such corporation's existence at least the same ownership interest as the taxpayer holds in the corporation distributing the extraordinary dividend, and

(ii) which has no earnings and profits—

(I) which were earned by, or

(II) which are attributable to gain on property which accrued during a period the corporation holding the property was,

a corporation not described in clause (i).

(C) APPLICATION OF PARAGRAPH.—This paragraph shall not apply to any extraordinary dividend to the extent such application is inconsistent with the purposes of this section.

[Sec. 1059(e)]

(e) SPECIAL RULES FOR CERTAIN DISTRIBUTIONS.—

(1) TREATMENT OF PARTIAL LIQUIDATIONS AND CERTAIN REDEMPTIONS.—Except as otherwise provided in regulations—

(A) REDEMPTIONS.—In the case of any redemption of stock—

(i) which is part of a partial liquidation (within the meaning of section 302(e)) of the redeeming corporation,

(ii) which is not pro rata as to all shareholders, or

Sec. 1059(d)

(iii) which would not have been treated (in whole or in part) as a dividend if—

(I) any options had not been taken into account under section 318(a)(4), or

(II) section 304(a) had not applied,

any amount treated as a dividend with respect to such redemption shall be treated as an extraordinary dividend to which paragraphs (1) and (2) of subsection (a) apply without regard to the period the taxpayer held such stock. In the case of a redemption described in clause (iii), only the basis in the stock redeemed shall be taken into account under subsection (a).

(B) REORGANIZATIONS, ETC.—An exchange described in section 356 which is treated as a dividend shall be treated as a redemption of stock for purposes of applying subparagraph (A).

(2) QUALIFYING DIVIDENDS.—

(A) IN GENERAL.—Except as provided in regulations, the term "extraordinary dividend" does not include any qualifying dividend (within the meaning of section 243).

(B) EXCEPTION.—Subparagraph (A) shall not apply to any portion of a dividend which is attributable to earnings and profits which—

(i) were earned by a corporation during a period it was not a member of the affiliated group, or

(ii) are attributable to gain on property which accrued during a period the corporation holding the property was not a member of the affiliated group.

(3) QUALIFIED PREFERRED DIVIDENDS.—

(A) IN GENERAL.—In the case of 1 or more qualified preferred dividends with respect to any share of stock—

(i) this section shall not apply to such dividends if the taxpayer holds such stock for more than 5 years, and

(ii) if the taxpayer disposes of such stock before it has been held for more than 5 years, the aggregate reduction under subsection (a)(1) with respect to such dividends shall not be greater than the excess (if any) of—

(I) the qualified preferred dividends paid with respect to such stock during the period the taxpayer held such stock, over

(II) the qualified preferred dividends which would have been paid during such period on the basis of the stated rate of return.

(B) RATE OF RETURN.—For the purposes of this paragraph—

(i) ACTUAL RATE OF RETURN.—The actual rate of return shall be the rate of return for the period for which the taxpayer held the stock, determined—

(I) by only taking into account dividends during such period, and

(II) by using the lesser of the adjusted basis of the taxpayer in such stock or the liquidation preference of such stock.

(ii) STATED RATE OF RETURN.—The stated rate of return shall be the annual rate of the qualified preferred dividend payable with respect to any share of stock (expressed as a percentage of the amount described in clause (i)(II)).

(C) DEFINITIONS AND SPECIAL RULES.—For purposes of this paragraph—

(i) QUALIFIED PREFERRED DIVIDEND.—The term "qualified preferred dividend" means any fixed dividend payable with respect to any share of stock which—

(I) provides for fixed preferred dividends payable not less frequently than annually, and

(II) is not in arrears as to dividends at the time the taxpayer acquires the stock.

Such term shall not include any dividend payable with respect to any share of stock if the actual rate of return on such stock exceeds 15 percent.

(ii) HOLDING PERIOD.—In determining the holding period for purposes of subparagraph (A)(ii), subsection (d)(3) shall be applied by substituting "5 years" for "2 years".

Sec. 1059(e)

[Sec. 1059(f)]

(f) TREATMENT OF DIVIDENDS ON CERTAIN PREFERRED STOCK.—

(1) IN GENERAL.—Any dividend with respect to disqualified preferred stock shall be treated as an extraordinary dividend to which paragraphs (1) and (2) of subsection (a) apply without regard to the period the taxpayer held the stock.

(2) DISQUALIFIED PREFERRED STOCK.—For purposes of this subsection, the term "disqualified preferred stock" means any stock which is preferred as to dividends if—

(A) when issued, such stock has a dividend rate which declines (or can reasonably be expected to decline) in the future,

(B) the issue price of such stock exceeds its liquidation rights or its stated redemption price, or

(C) such stock is otherwise structured—

(i) to avoid the other provisions of this section, and

(ii) to enable corporate shareholders to reduce tax through a combination of dividend received deductions and loss on the disposition of the stock.

[Sec. 1059(g)]

(g) REGULATIONS.—The Secretary shall prescribe such regulations as may be appropriate to carry out the purposes of this section, including regulations—

(1) providing for the application of this section in the case of stock dividends, stock splits, reorganizations, and other similar transactions, in the case of stock held by pass-thru entities, and in the case of consolidated groups, and

(2) providing that the rules of subsection (f) shall apply in the case of stock which is not preferred as to dividends in cases where stock is structured to avoid the purposes of this section.

[Sec. 1060]

SEC. 1060. SPECIAL ALLOCATION RULES FOR CERTAIN ASSET ACQUISITIONS.

[Sec. 1060(a)]

(a) GENERAL RULE.—In the case of any applicable asset acquisition, for purposes of determining both—

(1) the transferee's basis in such assets, and

(2) the gain or loss of the transferor with respect to such acquisition,

the consideration received for such assets shall be allocated among such assets acquired in such acquisition in the same manner as amounts are allocated to assets under section 338(b)(5). If in connection with an applicable asset acquisition, the transferee and transferor agree in writing as to the allocation of any consideration, or as to the fair market value of any of the assets, such agreement shall be binding on both the transferee and transferor unless the Secretary determines that such allocation (or fair market value) is not appropriate.

[Sec. 1060(b)]

(b) INFORMATION REQUIRED TO BE FURNISHED TO SECRETARY.—Under regulations, the transferor and transferee in an applicable asset acquisition shall, at such times and in such manner as may be provided in such regulations, furnish to the Secretary the following information:

(1) The amount of the consideration received for the assets which is allocated to Section 197 intangibles.

(2) Any modification of the amount described in paragraph (1).

(3) Any other information with respect to other assets transferred in such acquisition as the Secretary deems necessary to carry out the provisions of this section.

[Sec. 1060(c)]

(c) APPLICABLE ASSET ACQUISITION.—For purposes of this section, the term "applicable asset acquisition" means any transfer (whether directly or indirectly)—

(1) of assets which constitute a trade or business, and

(2) with respect to which the transferee's basis in such assets is determined wholly by reference to the consideration paid for such assets.

A transfer shall not be treated as failing to be an applicable asset acquisition merely because section 1031 applies to a portion of the assets transferred.

[Sec. 1060(d)]

(d) TREATMENT OF CERTAIN PARTNERSHIP TRANSACTIONS.—In the case of a distribution of partnership property or a transfer of an interest in a partnership—

(1) the rules of subsection (a) shall apply but only for purposes of determining the value of section 197 intangibles for purposes of applying section 755, and

(2) if section 755 applies, such distribution or transfer (as the case may be) shall be treated as an applicable asset acquisition for purposes of subsection (b).

[Sec. 1060(e)]

(e) INFORMATION REQUIRED IN CASE OF CERTAIN TRANSFERS OF INTERESTS IN ENTITIES.—

(1) IN GENERAL.—If—

(A) a person who is a 10-percent owner with respect to any entity transfers an interest in such entity, and

(B) in connection with such transfer, such owner (or a related person) enters into an employment contract, covenant not to compete, royalty or lease agreement, or other agreement with the transferee,

such owner and the transferee shall, at such time and in such manner as the Secretary may prescribe, furnish such information as the Secretary may require.

(2) 10-PERCENT OWNER.—For purposes of this subsection—

(A) IN GENERAL.—The term "10-percent owner" means, with respect to any entity, any person who holds 10 percent or more (by value) of the interests in such entity immediately before the transfer.

(B) CONSTRUCTIVE OWNERSHIP.—Section 318 shall apply in determining ownership of stock in a corporation. Similar principles shall apply in determining the ownership of interests in any other entity.

(3) RELATED PERSON.—For purposes of this subsection, the term "related person" means any person who is related (within the meaning of section 267(b) or 707(b)(1)) to the 10-percent owner.

* * *

PART VII—WASH SALES; STRADDLES

[Sec. 1091]

SEC. 1091. LOSS FROM WASH SALES OF STOCK OR SECURITIES.

[Sec. 1091(a)]

(a) DISALLOWANCE OF LOSS DEDUCTION.—In the case of any loss claimed to have been sustained from any sale or other disposition of shares of stock or securities where it appears that, within a period beginning 30 days before the date of such sale or disposition and ending 30 days after such date, the taxpayer has acquired (by purchase or by an exchange on which the entire amount of gain or loss was recognized by law), or has entered into a contract or option so to acquire, substantially identical stock or securities, then no deduction shall be allowed under section 165 unless the taxpayer is a dealer in stock or securities and the loss is sustained in a transaction made in the ordinary course of such business. For purposes of this section, the term "stock or securities" shall, except as provided in regulations, include contracts or options to acquire or sell stock or securities.

[Sec. 1091(b)]

(b) STOCK ACQUIRED LESS THAN STOCK SOLD.—If the amount of stock or securities acquired (or covered by the contract or option to acquire) is less than the amount of stock or securities sold or otherwise disposed of, then the particular shares of stock or securities the loss from the sale or other disposition of which is not deductible shall be determined under regulations prescribed by the Secretary.

Sec. 1091(b)

[Sec. 1091(c)]

(c) STOCK ACQUIRED NOT LESS THAN STOCK SOLD.—If the amount of stock or securities acquired (or covered by the contract or option to acquire) is not less than the amount of stock or securities sold or otherwise disposed of, then the particular shares of stock or securities the acquisition of which (or the contract or option to acquire which) resulted in the nondeductibility of the loss shall be determined under regulations prescribed by the Secretary.

[Sec. 1091(d)]

(d) UNADJUSTED BASIS IN CASE OF WASH SALE OF STOCK.—If the property consists of stock or securities the acquisition of which (or the contract or option to acquire which) resulted in the nondeductibility (under this section or corresponding provisions of prior internal revenue laws) of the loss from the sale or other disposition of substantially identical stock or securities, then the basis shall be the basis of the stock or securities so sold or disposed of, increased or decreased, as the case may be, by the difference, if any, between the price at which the property was acquired and the price at which such substantially identical stock or securities were sold or otherwise disposed of.

[Sec. 1091(e)]

(e) CERTAIN SHORT SALES OF STOCK OR SECURITIES AND SECURITIES FUTURES CONTRACTS TO SELL.— Rules similar to the rules of subsection (a) shall apply to any loss realized on the closing of a short sale of (or the sale, exchange, or termination of a securities futures contract to sell) stock or securities if, within a period beginning 30 days before the date of such closing and ending 30 days after such date—

    (1) substantially identical stock or securities were sold, or

    (2) another short sale of (or securities futures contracts to sell) substantially identical stock or securities was entered into.

For purposes of this subsection, the term "securities futures contract" has the meaning provided by section 1234B(c).

[Sec. 1091(f)]

(f) CASH SETTLEMENT.—This section shall not fail to apply to a contract or option to acquire or sell stock or securities solely by reason of the fact that the contract or option settles in (or could be settled in) cash or property other than such stock or securities.

[Sec. 1092]

SEC. 1092. STRADDLES.

[Sec. 1092(a)]

(a) RECOGNITION OF LOSS IN CASE OF STRADDLES, ETC.—

    (1) LIMITATION ON RECOGNITION OF LOSS.—

        (A) IN GENERAL.—Any loss with respect to 1 or more positions shall be taken into account for any taxable year only to the extent that the amount of such loss exceeds the unrecognized gain (if any) with respect to 1 or more positions which were offsetting positions with respect to 1 or more positions from which the loss arose.

        (B) CARRYOVER OF LOSS.—Any loss which may not be taken into account under subparagraph (A) for any taxable year shall, subject to the limitations under subparagraph (A), be treated as sustained in the succeeding taxable year.

    (2) SPECIAL RULE FOR IDENTIFIED STRADDLES.—

        (A) IN GENERAL.—In the case of any straddle which is an identified straddle as of the close of any taxable year—

            (i) paragraph (1) shall not apply for such taxable year, and

            (ii) any loss with respect to such straddle shall be treated as sustained not earlier than the day on which all of the positions making up the straddle are disposed of.

        (B) IDENTIFIED STRADDLE.—The term "identified straddle" means any straddle—

            (i) which is clearly identified on the taxpayer's records as an identified straddle before the earlier of—

                (I) the close of the day on which the straddle is acquired, or

                (II) such time as the Secretary may prescribe by regulations.

(ii) all of the original positions of which (as identified by the taxpayer) are acquired on the same day and with respect to which—

(I) all of such positions are disposed of on the same day during the taxable year, or

(II) none of such positions has been disposed of as of the close of the taxable year, and

(iii) which is not part of a larger straddle.

(3) UNRECOGNIZED GAIN.—For purposes of this subsection—

(A) IN GENERAL.—The term "unrecognized gain" means—

(i) in the case of any position held by the taxpayer as of the close of the taxable year, the amount of gain which would be taken into account with respect to such position if such position were sold on the last business day of such taxable year at its fair market value, and

(ii) in the case of any position with respect to which, as of the close of the taxable year, gain has been realized but not recognized, the amount of gain so realized.

(B) REPORTING OF GAIN.—

(i) IN GENERAL.—Each taxpayer shall disclose to the Secretary, at such time and in such manner and form as the Secretary may prescribe by regulations—

(I) each position (whether or not part of a straddle) with respect to which, as of the close of the taxable year, there is unrecognized gain, and

(II) the amount of such unrecognized gain.

(ii) REPORTS NOT REQUIRED IN CERTAIN CASES.—Clause (i) shall not apply—

(I) to any position which is part of an identified straddle,

(II) to any position which, with respect to the taxpayer, is property described in paragraph (1) or (2) of section 1221(a) or to any position which is part of a hedging transaction (as defined in section 1256(e)), or

(III) with respect to any taxable year if no loss on a position (including a regulated futures contract) has been sustained during such taxable year or if the only loss sustained on such position is a loss described in subclause (II).

* * *

[Sec. 1092(c)]

(c) STRADDLE DEFINED.—For purposes of this section—

(1) IN GENERAL.—The term "straddle" means offsetting positions with respect to personal property.

(2) OFFSETTING POSITIONS.—

(A) IN GENERAL.—A taxpayer holds offsetting positions with respect to personal property if there is a substantial diminution of the taxpayer's risk of loss from holding any position with respect to personal property by reason of his holding 1 or more other positions with respect to personal property (whether or not of the same kind).

(B) ONE SIDE LARGER THAN OTHER SIDE.—If 1 or more positions offset only a portion of 1 or more other positions, the Secretary shall by regulations prescribe the method for determining the portion of such other positions which is to be taken into account for purposes of this section.

(C) SPECIAL RULE FOR IDENTIFIED STRADDLES.—In the case of any position which is not part of an identified straddle (within the meaning of subsection (a)(2)(B)), such position shall not be treated as offsetting with respect to any position which is part of an identifed straddle.

(3) PRESUMPTION.—

(A) IN GENERAL.—For purposes of paragraph (2), 2 or more positions shall be presumed to be offsetting if—

(i) the positions are in the same personal property (whether established in such property or a contract for such property),

(ii) the positions are in the same personal property, even though such property may be in a substantially altered form,

(iii) the positions are in debt instruments of a similar maturity or other debt instruments described in regulations prescribed by the Secretary,

(iv) the positions are sold or marketed as offsetting positions (whether or not such positions are called a straddle, spread, butterfly, or any similar name),

(v) the aggregate margin requirement for such positions is lower than the sum of the margin requirements for each such position (if held separately), or

(vi) there are such other factors (or satisfaction of subjective or objective tests) as the Secretary may by regulations prescribe as indicating that such positions are offsetting.

For purposes of the preceding sentence, 2 or more positions shall be treated as described in clause (i), (ii), (iii), or (vi) only if the value of 1 or more of such positions ordinarily varies inversely with the value of 1 or more other such positions.

(B) PRESUMPTION MAY BE REBUTTED.—Any presumption established pursuant to subparagraph (A) may be rebutted.

(4) EXCEPTION FOR CERTAIN STRADDLES CONSISTING OF QUALIFIED COVERED CALL OPTIONS AND THE OPTIONED STOCK.—

(A) IN GENERAL.—If—

(i) all the offsetting positions making up any straddle consist of 1 or more qualified covered call options and the stock to be purchased from the taxpayer under such options, and

(ii) such straddle is not part of a larger straddle,

such straddle shall not be treated as a straddle for purposes of this section and section 263(g).

(B) QUALIFIED COVERED CALL OPTION DEFINED.—For purposes of subparagraph (A), the term "qualified covered call option" means any option granted by the taxpayer to purchase stock held by the taxpayer (or stock acquired by the taxpayer in connection with the granting of the option) but only if—

(i) such option is traded on a national securities exchange which is registered with the Securities and Exchange Commission or other market which the Secretary determines has rules adequate to carry out the purposes of this paragraph,

(ii) such option is granted more than 30 days before the day on which the option expires,

(iii) such option is not a deep-in-the-money option,

(iv) such option is not granted by an options dealer (within the meaning of section 1256(g)(8)) in connection with his activity of dealing in options, and

(v) gain or loss with respect to such option is not ordinary income or loss.

(C) DEEP-IN-THE-MONEY OPTION.—For purposes of subparagraph (B), the term "deep-in-the-money option" means an option having a strike price lower than the lowest qualified bench mark.

(D) LOWEST QUALIFIED BENCH MARK.—

(i) IN GENERAL.—Except as otherwise provided in this subparagraph, for purposes of subparagraph (C), the term "lowest qualified bench mark" means the highest available strike price which is less than the applicable stock price.

(ii) SPECIAL RULE WHERE OPTION IS FOR PERIOD MORE THAN 90 DAYS AND STRIKE PRICE EXCEEDS $50.—In the case of an option—

(I) which is granted more than 90 days before the date on which such option expires, and

(II) with respect to which the strike price is more than $50,

the lowest qualified bench mark is the second highest available strike price which is less than the applicable stock price.

(iii) 85 PERCENT RULE WHERE APPLICABLE STOCK PRICE $25 OR LESS.—If—

(I) the applicable stock price is $25 or less, and

(II) but for this clause, the lowest qualified bench mark would be less than 85 percent of the applicable stock price,

the lowest qualified bench mark shall be treated as equal to 85 percent of the applicable stock price.

Sec. 1092(c)

      (iv) LIMITATION WHERE APPLICABLE STOCK PRICE $150 OR LESS.—If—

         (I) the applicable stock price is $150 or less, and

         (II) but for this clause, the lowest qualified bench mark would be less than the applicable stock price reduced by $10,

the lowest qualified bench mark shall be treated as equal to the applicable stock price reduced by $10.

      (E) SPECIAL YEAR-END RULE.—Subparagraph (A) shall not apply to any straddle for purposes of section 1092(a) if—

         (i) the qualified covered call options referred to in such subparagraph are closed or the stock is disposed of at a loss during any taxable year,

         (ii) gain on disposition of the stock to be purchased from the taxpayer under such options or gains on such options are includible in gross income for a later taxable year, and

         (iii) such stock or option was not held by the taxpayer for 30 days or more after the closing of such options or the disposition of such stock.

For purposes of the preceding sentence, the rules of paragraphs (3) (other than subparagraph (B) thereof) and (4) of section 246(c) shall apply in determining the period for which the taxpayer holds the stock.

      (F) STRIKE PRICE.—For purposes of this paragraph, the term "strike price" means the price at which the option is exercisable.

      (G) APPLICABLE STOCK PRICE.—For purposes of subparagraph (D), the term "applicable stock price" means, with respect to any stock for which an option has been granted—

         (i) the closing price of such stock on the most recent day on which such stock was traded before the date on which such option was granted, or

         (ii) the opening price of such stock on the day on which such option was granted, but only if such price is greater than 110 percent of the price determined under clause (i).

      (H) REGULATIONS.—The Secretary shall prescribe such regulations as may be necessary or appropriate to carry out the purposes of this paragraph. Such regulations may include modifications to the provisions of this paragraph which are appropriate to take account of changes in the practices of option exchanges or to prevent the use of options for tax avoidance purposes.

[Sec. 1092(d)]

(d) DEFINITIONS AND SPECIAL RULES.—For purposes of this section—

    (1) PERSONAL PROPERTY.—The term "personal property" means any personal property of a type which is actively traded.

    (2) POSITION.—The term "position" means an interest (including a futures or forward contract or option) in personal property.

    (3) SPECIAL RULES FOR STOCK.—For purposes of paragraph (1)—

      (A) IN GENERAL.—Except as provided in subparagraph (B), the term "personal property" does not include stock. The preceding sentence shall not apply to any interest in stock.

      (B) EXCEPTIONS.—The term "personal property" includes—

         (i) any stock which is part of a straddle at least 1 of the offsetting positions of which is—

         (I) an option with respect to such stock or substantially identical stock or securities,

         (II) a securities futures contract (as defined in section 1234B) with respect to such stock or substantially identical stock or securities, or

         (III) under regulations, a position with respect to substantially similar or related property (other than stock), and

         (ii) any stock of a corporation formed or availed of to take positions in personal property which offset positions taken by any shareholder.

      (C) SPECIAL RULES.—

         (i) For purposes of subparagraph (B), subsection (c) and paragraph (4) shall be applied as if stock described in clause (i) or (ii) of subparagraph (B) were personal property.

(ii) For purposes of determining whether subsection (e) applies to any transaction with respect to stock described in clause (ii) of subparagraph (B), all includible corporations of an affiliated group (within the meaning of section 1504(a)) shall be treated as 1 taxpayer.

(4) POSITIONS HELD BY RELATED PERSONS, ETC.—

(A) IN GENERAL.—In determining whether 2 or more positions are offsetting, the taxpayer shall be treated as holding any position held by a related person.

(B) RELATED PERSON.—For purposes of subparagraph (A), a person is a related person to the taxpayer if with respect to any period during which a position is held by such person, such person—

(i) is the spouse of the taxpayer, or

(ii) files a consolidated return (within the meaning of section 1501) with the taxpayer for any taxable year which includes a portion of such period.

(C) CERTAIN FLOWTHROUGH ENTITIES.—If part or all of the gain or loss with respect to a position held by a partnership, trust, or other entity would properly be taken into account for purposes of this chapter by a taxpayer, then, except to the extent otherwise provided in regulations, such position shall be treated as held by the taxpayer.

(5) SPECIAL RULE FOR SECTION 1256 CONTRACTS.—

(A) GENERAL RULE.—In the case of a straddle at least 1 (but not all) of the positions of which are section 1256 contracts, the provisions of this section shall apply to any section 1256 contract and any other position making up such straddle.

(B) SPECIAL RULE FOR IDENTIFIED STRADDLES.—For purposes of subsection (a)(2) (relating to identified straddles), subparagraph (A) and section 1256(a)(4) shall not apply to a straddle all of the offsetting positions of which consist of section 1256 contracts.

(6) SECTION 1256 CONTRACT.—The term "section 1256 contract" has the meaning given such term by section 1256(b).

(7) SPECIAL RULES FOR FOREIGN CURRENCY.—

(A) POSITION TO INCLUDE INTEREST IN CERTAIN DEBT.—For purposes of paragraph (2), an obligor's interest in a nonfunctional currency denominated debt obligation is treated as a position in the nonfunctional currency.

(B) ACTIVELY TRADED REQUIREMENT.—For purposes of paragraph (1), foreign currency for which there is an active interbank market is presumed to be actively traded.

[Sec. 1092(e)]

(e) EXCEPTION FOR HEDGING TRANSACTIONS.—This section shall not apply in the case of any hedging transaction (as defined in section 1256(e)).

[Sec. 1092(f)]

(f) TREATMENT OF GAIN OR LOSS AND SUSPENSION OF HOLDING PERIOD WHERE TAXPAYER GRANTOR OF QUALIFIED COVERED CALL OPTION.—If a taxpayer holds any stock and grants a qualified covered call option to purchase such stock with a strike price less than the applicable stock price—

(1) TREATMENT OF LOSS.—Any loss with respect to such option shall be treated as long-term capital loss if, at the time such loss is realized, gain on the sale or exchange of such stock would be treated as long-term capital gain.

(2) SUSPENSION OF HOLDING PERIOD.—The holding period of such stock shall not include any period during which the taxpayer is the grantor of such option.

* * *

Sec. 1092(e)

Subchapter P—Capital Gains and Losses

PART I—TREATMENT OF CAPITAL GAINS

[Sec. 1201]

SEC. 1201. ALTERNATIVE TAX FOR CORPORATIONS.

[Sec. 1201(a)]

(a) GENERAL RULE.—If for any taxable year a corporation has a net capital gain and any rate of tax imposed by section 11, 511, or 831(a) or (b) (whichever is applicable) exceeds 35 percent (determined without regard to the last 2 sentences of section 11(b)(1)), then, in lieu of any such tax, there is hereby imposed a tax (if such tax is less than the tax imposed by such sections) which shall consist of the sum of—

(1) a tax computed on the taxable income reduced by the amount of the net capital gain, at the rates and in the manner as if this subsection had not been enacted, plus

(2) a tax of 35 percent of the net capital gain (or, if less, taxable income).

* * *

[Sec. 1202]

SEC. 1202. PARTIAL EXCLUSION FOR GAIN FROM CERTAIN SMALL BUSINESS STOCK.

[Sec. 1202(a)]

(a) EXCLUSION.—

(1) IN GENERAL.—In the case of a taxpayer other than a corporation, gross income shall not include 50 percent of any gain from the sale or exchange of qualified small business stock held for more than 5 years.

(2) EMPOWERMENT ZONE BUSINESSES.—

(A) IN GENERAL.—In the case of qualified small business stock acquired after the date of the enactment of this paragraph in a corporation which is a qualified business entity (as defined in section 1397C(b)) during substantially all of the taxpayer's holding period for such stock, paragraph (1) shall be applied by substituting "60 percent" for "50 percent".

(B) CERTAIN RULES TO APPLY.—Rules similar to the rules of paragraphs (5) and (7) of section 1400B(b) shall apply for purposes of this paragraph.

(C) GAIN AFTER 2014 NOT QUALIFIED.—Subparagraph (A) shall not apply to gain attributable to periods after December 31, 2014.

(D) TREATMENT OF DC ZONE.—The District of Columbia Enterprise Zone shall not be treated as an empowerment zone for purposes of this paragraph.

[Sec. 1202(b)]

(b) PER-ISSUER LIMITATION ON TAXPAYER'S ELIGIBLE GAIN.—

(1) IN GENERAL.—If the taxpayer has eligible gain for the taxable year from 1 or more dispositions of stock issued by any corporation, the aggregate amount of such gain from dispositions of stock issued by such corporation which may be taken into account under subsection (a) for the taxable year shall not exceed the greater of—

(A) $10,000,000 reduced by the aggregate amount of eligible gain taken into account by the taxpayer under subsection (a) for prior taxable years attributable to dispositions of stock issued by such corporation, or

(B) 10 times the aggregate adjusted bases of qualified small business stock issued by such corporation and disposed of by the taxpayer during the taxable year.

For purposes of subparagraph (B), the adjusted basis of any stock shall be determined without regard to any addition to basis after the date on which such stock was originally issued.

(2) ELIGIBLE GAIN.—For purposes of this subsection, the term "eligible gain" means any gain from the sale or exchange of qualified small business stock held for more than 5 years.

(3) TREATMENT OF MARRIED INDIVIDUALS.—

(A) SEPARATE RETURNS.—In the case of a separate return by a married individual, paragraph (1)(A) shall be applied by substituting "$5,000,000" for "$10,000,000".

(B) ALLOCATION OF EXCLUSION.—In the case of any joint return, the amount of gain taken into account under subsection (a) shall be allocated equally between the spouses for purposes of applying this subsection to subsequent taxable years.

(C) MARITAL STATUS.—For purposes of this subsection, marital status shall be determined under section 7703.

[Sec. 1202(c)]

(c) QUALIFIED SMALL BUSINESS STOCK.—For purposes of this section—

(1) IN GENERAL.—Except as otherwise provided in this section, the term "qualified small business stock" means any stock in a C corporation which is originally issued after the date of the enactment of the Revenue Reconciliation Act of 1993, if—

(A) as of the date of issuance, such corporation is a qualified small business, and

(B) except as provided in subsections (f) and (h), such stock is acquired by the taxpayer at its original issue (directly or through an underwriter)—

(i) in exchange for money or other property (not including stock), or

(ii) as compensation for services provided to such corporation (other than services performed as an underwriter of such stock).

(2) ACTIVE BUSINESS REQUIREMENTS; ETC.—

(A) IN GENERAL.—Stock in a corporation shall not be treated as qualified small business stock unless, during substantially all of the taxpayer's holding period for such stock, such corporation meets the active business requirements of subsection (e) and such corporation is a C corporation.

(B) SPECIAL RULE FOR CERTAIN SMALL BUSINESS INVESTMENT COMPANIES.—

(i) WAIVER OF ACTIVE BUSINESS REQUIREMENT.—Notwithstanding any provision of subsection (e), a corporation shall be treated as meeting the active business requirements of such subsection for any period during which such corporation qualifies as a specialized small business investment company.

(ii) SPECIALIZED SMALL BUSINESS INVESTMENT COMPANY.—For purposes of clause (i), the term "specialized small business investment company" means any eligible corporation (as defined in subsection (e)(4)) which is licensed to operate under section 301(d) of the Small Business Investment Act of 1958 (as in effect on May 13, 1993).

(3) CERTAIN PURCHASES BY CORPORATION OF ITS OWN STOCK.—

(A) REDEMPTIONS FROM TAXPAYER OR RELATED PERSON.—Stock acquired by the taxpayer shall not be treated as qualified small busienss stock if, at any time during the 4-year period beginning on the date 2 years before the issuance of such stock, the corporation issuing such stock purchased (directly or indirectly) any of its stock from the taxpayer or from a person related (within the meaning of section 267(b) or 707(b)) to the taxpayer.

(B) SIGNIFICANT REDEMPTIONS.—Stock issued by a corporation shall not be treated as qualified business stock if, during the 2-year period beginning on the date 1 year before the issuance of such stock, such corporation made 1 or more purchases of its stock with an aggregate value (as of the time of the respective purchases) exceeding 5 percent of the aggregate value of all of its stock as of the beginning of such 2-year period.

(C) TREATMENT OF CERTAIN TRANSACTIONS.—If any transaction is treated under section 304(a) as a distribution in redemption of the stock of any corporation, for purposes of subparagraphs (A) and (B), such corporation shall be treated as purchasing an amount of its stock equal to the amount treated as such a distribution under section 304(a).

[Sec. 1202(d)]

(d) QUALIFIED SMALL BUSINESS.—For purposes of this section—

(1) IN GENERAL.—The term 'qualified small business' means any domestic corporation which is a C corporation if—

(A) the aggregate gross assets of such corporation (or any predecessor thereof) at all times on or after the date of the enactment of the Revenue Reconciliation Act of 1993 and before the issuance did not exceed $50,000,000,

(B) the aggregate gross assets of such corporation immediately after the issuance (determined by taking into account amounts received in the issuance) do not exceed $50,000,000, and

(C) such corporation agrees to submit such reports to the Secretary and to shareholders as the Secretary may require to carry out the purposes of this section.

(2) AGGREGATE GROSS ASSETS.—

(A) IN GENERAL.—For purposes of paragraph (1), the term "aggregate gross assets" means the amount of cash and the aggregate adjusted bases of other property held by the corporation.

(B) TREATMENT OF CONTRIBUTED PROPERTY.—For purposes of subparagraph (A), the adjusted basis of any property contributed to the corporation (or other property with a basis determined in whole or in part by reference to the adjusted basis of property so contributed) shall be determined as if the basis of the property contributed to the corporation (immediately after such contribution) were equal to its fair market value as of the time of such contribution.

(3) AGGREGATION RULES.—

(A) IN GENERAL.—All corporations which are members of the same parent-subsidiary controlled group shall be treated as 1 corporation for purposes of this subsection.

(B) PARENT-SUBSIDIARY CONTROLLED GROUP.—For purposes of subparagraph (A), the term "parent-subsidiary controlled group" means any controlled group of corporations as defined in section 1563(a)(1), except that—

(i) "more than 50 percent" shall be substituted for "at least 80 percent" each place it appears in section 1563(a)(1), and

(ii) section 1563(a)(4) shall not apply.

[Sec. 1202(e)]

(e) ACTIVE BUSINESS REQUIREMENT.—

(1) IN GENERAL.—For purposes of subsection (c)(2), the requirements of this subsection are met by a corporation for any period if during such period—

(A) at least 80 percent (by value) of the assets of such corporation are used by such corporation in the active conduct of 1 or more qualified trades or businesses, and

(B) such corporation is an eligible corporation.

(2) SPECIAL RULE FOR CERTAIN ACTIVITIES.—For purposes of paragraph (1), if, in connection with any future qualified trade or business, a corporation is engaged in—

(A) start-up activities described in section 195(c)(1)(A),

(B) activities resulting in the payment or incurring of expenditures which may be treated as research and experimental expenditures under section 174, or

(C) activities with respect to in-house research expenses described in section 41(b)(4),

assets used in such activities shall be treated as used in the active conduct of a qualified trade or business. Any determination under this paragraph shall be made without regard to whether a corporation has any gross income from such activities at the time of the determination.

(3) QUALIFIED TRADE OR BUSINESS.—For purposes of this subsection, the term "qualified trade or business" means any trade or business other than—

(A) any trade or business involving the performance of services in the fields of health, law, engineering, architecture, accounting, actuarial science, performing arts, consulting, athletics, financial services, brokerage services, or any trade or business where the principal asset of such trade or business is the reputation or skill of 1 or more of its employees,

(B) any banking, insurance, financing, leasing, investing, or similar business,

(C) any farming business (including the business of raising or harvesting trees),

(D) any business involving the production or extraction of products of a character with respect to which a deduction is allowable under section 613 or 613A, and

(E) any business of operating a hotel, motel, restaurant, or similar business.

(4) ELIGIBLE CORPORATION.—For purposes of this subsection, the term 'eligible corporation' means any domestic corporation; except that such term shall not include—

(A) a DISC or former DISC,

(B) a corporation with respect to which an election under section 936 is in effect or which has a direct or indirect subsidiary with respect to which such an election is in effect,

(C) a regulated investment company, real estate investment trust, REMIC, or FASIT, and

(D) a cooperative.

(5) STOCK IN OTHER CORPORATIONS.—

(A) LOOK-THRU IN CASE OF SUBSIDIARIES.—For purposes of this subsection, stock and debt in any subsidiary corporation shall be disregarded and the parent corporation shall be deemed to own its ratable share of the subsidiary's assets, and to conduct its ratable share of the subsidiary's activities.

(B) PORTFOLIO STOCK OR SECURITIES.—A corporation shall be treated as failing to meet the requirements of paragraph (1) for any period during which more than 10 percent of the value of its assets (in excess of liabilities) consists of stock or securities in other corporations which are not subsidiaries of such corporation (other than assets described in paragraph (6)).

(C) SUBSIDIARY.—For purposes of this paragraph, a corporation shall be considered a subsidiary if the parent owns more than 50 percent of the combined voting power of all classes of stock entitled to vote, or more than 50 percent in value of all outstanding stock, of such corporation.

(6) WORKING CAPITAL.—For purposes of paragraph (1)(A), any assets which—

(A) are held as a part of the reasonably required working capital needs of a qualified trade or business of the corporation, or

(B) are held for investment and are reasonably expected to be used within 2 years to finance research and experimentation in a qualified trade or business or increases in working capital needs of a qualified trade or business,

shall be treated as used in the active conduct of a qualified trade or business. For periods after the corporation has been in existence for at least 2 years, in no event may more than 50 percent of the assets of the corporation qualify as used in the active conduct of a qualified trade or business by reason of this paragraph.

(7) MAXIMUM REAL ESTATE HOLDINGS.—A corporation shall not be treated as meeting the requirements of paragraph (1) for any period during which more than 10 percent of the total value of its assets consists of real property which is not used in the active conduct of a qualified trade or business. For purposes of the preceding sentence, the ownership of, dealing in, or renting of real property shall not be treated as the active conduct of a qualified trade or business.

(8) COMPUTER SOFTWARE ROYALTIES.—For purposes of paragraph (1), rights to computer software which produces active business computer software royalties (within the meaning of section 543(d)(1)) shall be treated as an asset used in the active conduct of a trade or business.

[Sec. 1202(f)]

(f) STOCK ACQUIRED ON CONVERSION OF OTHER STOCK.—If any stock in a corporation is acquired solely through the conversion of other stock in such corporation which is qualified small business stock in the hands of the taxpayer—

(1) the stock so acquired shall be treated as qualified small business stock in the hands of the taxpayer, and

(2) the stock so acquired shall be treated as having been held during the period during which the converted stock was held.

[Sec. 1202(g)]

(g) TREATMENT OF PASS-THRU ENTITIES.—

(1) IN GENERAL.—If any amount included in gross income by reason of holding an interest in a pass-thru entity meets the requirements of paragraph (2)—

(A) such amount shall be treated as gain described in subsection (a), and

Sec. 1202(f)

(B) for purposes of applying subsection (b), such amount shall be treated as gain from a disposition of stock in the corporation issuing the stock disposed of by the pass-thru entity and the taxpayer's proportionate share of the adjusted basis of the pass-thru entity in such stock shall be taken into account.

(2) REQUIREMENTS.—An amount meets the requirements of this paragraph if—

(A) such amount is attributable to gain on the sale or exchange by the pass-thru entity of stock which is qualified small business stock in the hands of such entity (determined by treating such entity as an individual) and which was held by such entity for more than 5 years, and

(B) such amount is includible in the gross income of the taxpayer by reason of the holding of an interest in such entity which was held by the taxpayer on the date on which such pass-thru entity acquired such stock and at all times thereafter before the disposition of such stock by such pass-thru entity.

(3) LIMITATION BASED ON INTEREST ORIGINALLY HELD BY TAXPAYER.—Paragraph (1) shall not apply to any amount to the extent such amount exceeds the amount to which paragraph (1) would have applied if such amount were determined by reference to the interest the taxpayer held in the pass-thru entity on the date the qualified small business stock was acquired.

(4) PASS-THRU ENTITY.—For purposes of this subsection, the term "pass-thru entity" means—

(A) any partnership,

(B) any S corporation,

(C) any regulated investment company, and

(D) any common trust fund.

[Sec. 1202(h)]

(h) CERTAIN TAX-FREE AND OTHER TRANSFERS.—For purposes of this section—

(1) IN GENERAL.—In the case of a transfer described in paragraph (2), the transferee shall be treated as—

(A) having acquired such stock in the same manner as the transferor, and

(B) having held such stock during any continuous period immediately preceding the transfer during which it was held (or treated as held under this subsection) by the transferor.

(2) DESCRIPTION OF TRANSFERS.—A transfer is described in this subsection if such transfer is—

(A) by gift,

(B) at death, or

(C) from a partnership to a partner of stock with respect to which requirements similar to the requirements of subsection (g) are met at the time of the transfer (without regard to the 5-year holding period requirement).

(3) CERTAIN RULES MADE APPLICABLE.—Rules similar to the rules of section 1244(d)(2) shall apply for purposes of this section.

(4) INCORPORATIONS AND REORGANIZATIONS INVOLVING NONQUALIFIED STOCK.—

(A) IN GENERAL.—In the case of a transaction described in section 351 or a reorganization described in section 368, if qualified small business stock is exchanged for other stock which would not qualify as qualified small business stock but for this subparagraph, such other stock shall be treated as qualified small business stock acquired on the date on which the exchanged stock was acquired.

(B) LIMITATION.—This section shall apply to gain from the sale or exchange of stock treated as qualifed small business stock by reason of subparagraph (A) only to the extent of the gain which would have been recognized at the time of the transfer described in subparagraph (A) if section 351 or 368 had not applied at such time. The preceding sentence shall not apply if the stock which is treated as qualified small business stock by reason of subparagraph (A) is issued by a corporation which (as of the time of the transfer described in subparagraph (A)) is a qualified small business.

(C) SUCCESSIVE APPLICATION.—For purposes of this paragraph, stock treated as qualified small business stock under subparagraph (A) shall be so treated for subsequent transactions or reorganizations, except that the limitation of subparagraph (B) shall be applied as of the time of the first transfer to which such limitation applied (determined after the application of the second sentence of subparagraph (B)).

(D) CONTROL TEST.—In the case of a transaction described in section 351, this paragraph shall apply only if, immediately after the transaction, the corporation issuing the stock owns directly or indirectly stock representing control (within the meaning of section 368(c)) of the corporation whose stock was exchanged.

[Sec. 1202(i)]

(i) BASIS RULES.—For purposes of this section—

(1) STOCK EXCHANGED FOR PROPERTY.—In the case where the taxpayer transfers property (other than money or stock) to a corporation in exchange for stock in such corporation—

(A) such stock shall be treated as having been acquired by the taxpayer on the date of such exchange, and

(B) the basis of such stock in the hands of the taxpayer shall in no event be less than the fair market value of the property exchanged.

(2) TREATMENT OF CONTRIBUTIONS TO CAPITAL.—If the adjusted basis of any qualified small business stock is adjusted by reason of any contribution to capital after the date on which such stock was originally issued, in determining the amount of the adjustment by reason of such contribution, the basis of the contributed property shall in no event be treated as less than its fair market value on the date of the contribution.

* * *

[Sec. 1202(k)]

(k) REGULATIONS.—The Secretary shall prescribe such regulations as may be appropriate to carry out the purposes of this section, including regulations to prevent the avoidance of the purposes of this section through split-ups, shell corporations, partnerships, or otherwise.

PART II—TREATMENT OF CAPITAL LOSSES

[Sec. 1211]
SEC. 1211. LIMITATION ON CAPITAL LOSSES.

[Sec. 1211(a)]

(a) CORPORATIONS.—In the case of a corporation, losses from sales or exchanges of capital assets shall be allowed only to the extent of gains from such sales or exchanges.

[Sec. 1211(b)]

(b) OTHER TAXPAYERS.—In the case of a taxpayer other than a corporation, losses from sales or exchanges of capital assets shall be allowed only to the extent of the gains from such sales or exchanges, plus (if such losses exceed such gains) the lower of—

(1) $3,000 ($1,500 in the case of a married individual filing a separate return), or

(2) the excess of such losses over such gains.

[Sec. 1212]
SEC. 1212. CAPITAL LOSS CARRYBACKS AND CARRYOVERS.

[Sec. 1212(a)]

(a) CORPORATIONS.—

(1) IN GENERAL.—If a corporation has a net capital loss for any taxable year (hereinafter in this paragraph referred to as the "loss year"), the amount thereof shall be—

(A) a capital loss carryback to each of the 3 taxable years preceding the loss year, but only to the extent—

(i) such loss is not attributable to a foreign expropriation capital loss, and

Sec. 1202(i)

(ii) the carryback of such loss does not increase or produce a net operating loss (as defined in section 172(c)) for the taxable year to which it is being carried back;

(B) except as provided in subparagraph (C), a capital loss carryover to each of the 5 taxable years succeeding the loss year; and

(C) a capital loss carryover—

(i) in the case of a regulated investment company (as defined in section 851) to each of the 8 taxable years succeeding the loss year, and

(ii) to the extent such loss is attributable to a foreign expropriation capital loss, to each of the 10 taxable years succeeding the loss year,

and shall be treated as a short-term capital loss in each such taxable year. The entire amount of the net capital loss for any taxable year shall be carried to the earliest of the taxable years to which such loss may be carried, and the portion of such loss which shall be carried to each of the other taxable years to which such loss may be carried shall be the excess, if any, of such loss over the total of the capital gain net income for each of the prior taxable years to which such loss may be carried. For purposes of the preceding sentence, the capital gain net income for any such prior taxable year shall be computed without regard to the net capital loss for the loss year or for any taxable year thereafter. In the case of any net capital loss which cannot be carried back in full to a preceding taxable year by reason of clause (ii) of subparagraph (A), the capital gain net income for such prior taxable year shall in no case be treated as greater than the amount of such loss which can be carried back to such preceding taxable year upon the application of such clause (ii).

* * *

(3) SPECIAL RULES ON CARRYBACKS.—A net capital loss of a corporation shall not be carried back under paragraph (1)(A) to a taxable year—

(A) for which it is a foreign personal holding company (as defined in section 552);

(B) for which it is a regulated investment company (as defined in section 851);

(C) for which it is a real estate investment trust (as defined in section 856); or

(D) for which an election made by it under section 1247 is applicable (relating to election by foreign investment companies to distribute income currently).

[Sec. 1212(b)]

(b) OTHER TAXPAYERS.—

(1) IN GENERAL.—If a taxpayer other than a corporation has a net capital loss for any taxable year—

(A) the excess of the net short-term capital loss over the net long-term capital gain for such year shall be a short-term capital loss in the succeeding taxable year, and

(B) the excess of the net long-term capital loss over the net short-term capital gain for such year shall be a long-term capital loss in the succeeding taxable year.

(2) TREATMENT OF AMOUNTS ALLOWED UNDER SECTION 1211(b)(1) OR (2).—

(A) IN GENERAL.—For purposes of determining the excess referred to in subparagraph (A) or (B) of paragraph (1), there shall be treated as a short-term capital gain in the taxable year an amount equal to the lesser of—

(i) the amount allowed for the taxable year under paragraph (1) or (2) of section 1211(b), or

(ii) the adjusted taxable income for such taxable year.

(B) ADJUSTED TAXABLE INCOME.—For purposes of subparagraph (A), the term "adjusted taxable income" means taxable income increased by the sum of—

(i) the amount allowed for the taxable year under paragraph (1) or (2) of section 1211(b), and

(ii) the deduction allowed for such year under section 151 or any deduction in lieu thereof.

For purposes of the preceding sentence, any excess of the deductions allowed for the taxable year over the gross income for such year shall be taken into account as negative taxable income.

[Sec. 1212(c)]

(c) CARRYBACK OF LOSSES FROM SECTION 1256 CONTRACTS TO OFFSET PRIOR GAINS FROM SUCH Contracts.—

(1) IN GENERAL.—If a taxpayer (other than a corporation) has a net section 1256 contracts loss for the taxable year and elects to have this subsection apply to such taxable year, the amount of such net section 1256 contracts loss—

(A) shall be a carryback to each of the 3 taxable years preceding the loss year, and

(B) to the extent that, after the application of paragraphs (2) and (3), such loss is allowed as a carryback to any such preceding taxable year—

(i) 40 percent of the amount so allowed shall be treated as a short-term capital loss from section 1256 contracts, and

(ii) 60 percent of the amount so allowed shall be treated as a long-term capital loss from section 1256 contracts.

(2) AMOUNT CARRIED TO EACH TAXABLE YEAR.—The entire amount of the net section 1256 contracts loss for any taxable year shall be carried to the earliest of the taxable years to which such loss may be carried back under paragraph (1). The portion of such loss which shall be carried to each of the 2 other taxable years to which such loss may be carried back shall be the excess (if any) of such loss over the portion of such loss which, after the application of paragraph (3), was allowed as a carryback for any prior taxable year.

(3) AMOUNT WHICH MAY BE USED IN ANY PRIOR TAXABLE YEAR.—An amount shall be allowed as a carryback under paragraph (1) to any prior taxable year only to the extent—

(A) such amount does not exceed the net section 1256 contract gain for such year, and

(B) the allowance of such carryback does not increase or produce a net operating loss (as defined in section 172(c)) for such year.

(4) NET SECTION 1256 CONTRACTS LOSS.—For purposes of paragraph (1), the term "net section 1256 contracts loss" means the lesser of—

(A) the net capital loss for the taxable year determined by taking into account only gains and losses from section 1256 contracts, or

(B) the sum of the amounts which, but for paragraph (6)(A), would be treated as capital losses in the succeeding taxable year under subparagraphs (A) and (B) of subsection (b)(1).

(5) NET SECTION 1256 CONTRACT GAIN.—For purposes of paragraph (1)—

(A) IN GENERAL.—The term "net section 1256 contract gain" means the lesser of—

(i) the capital gain net income for the taxable year determined by taking into account only gains and losses from section 1256 contracts, or

(ii) the capital gain net income for the taxable year.

(B) SPECIAL RULE.—The net section 1256 contract gain for any taxable year before the loss year shall be computed without regard to the net section 1256 contracts loss for the loss year or for any taxable year thereafter.

(6) COORDINATION WITH CARRYFORWARD PROVISIONS OF SUBSECTION (b)(1).—

(A) CARRYFORWARD AMOUNT REDUCED BY AMOUNT USED AS CARRYBACK.—For purposes of applying subsection (b)(1), if any portion of the net section 1256 contracts loss for any taxable year is allowed as a carryback under paragraph (1) to any preceding taxable year—

(i) 40 percent of the amount allowed as a carryback shall be treated as a short-term capital gain for the loss year, and

(ii) 60 percent of the amount allowed as a carryback shall be treated as a long-term capital gain for the loss year.

(B) CARRYOVER LOSS RETAINS CHARACTER AS ATTRIBUTABLE TO SECTION 1256 CONTRACT.—Any amount carried forward as a short-term or long-term capital loss to any taxable year under subsection (b)(1) (after the application of subparagraph (A)) shall, to the extent attributable to losses from section 1256 contracts, be treated as loss from section 1256 contracts for such taxable year.

Sec. 1212(c)

(7) OTHER DEFINITIONS AND SPECIAL RULES.—For purposes of this subsection—

(A) SECTION 1256 CONTRACT.—The term "section 1256 contract" means any section 1256 contract (as defined in section 1256(b)) to which section 1256 applies.

(B) EXCLUSION FOR ESTATES AND TRUSTS.—This subsection shall not apply to any estate or trust.

PART III—GENERAL RULES FOR DETERMINING CAPITAL GAINS AND LOSSES

[Sec. 1221]

SEC. 1221. CAPITAL ASSET DEFINED.

[Sec. 1221(a)]

(a) IN GENERAL.—For purposes of this subtitle, the term "capital asset" means property held by the taxpayer (whether or not connected with his trade or business), but does not include—

(1) stock in trade of the taxpayer or other property of a kind which would properly be included in the inventory of the taxpayer if on hand at the close of the taxable year, or property held by the taxpayer primarily for sale to customers in the ordinary course of his trade or business;

(2) property, used in his trade or business, of a character which is subject to the allowance for depreciation provided in section 167, or real property used in his trade or business;

(3) a copyright, a literary, musical, or artistic composition, a letter or memorandum, or similar property, held by—

(A) a taxpayer whose personal efforts created such property,

(B) in the case of a letter, memorandum, or similar property, a taxpayer for whom such property was prepared or produced, or

[*Caution: Code Sec. 1221(a)(3)(C), below, prior to amendment by P.L. 107-16, applies to estates of decedents dying on or before December 31, 2009.*]

(C) a taxpayer in whose hands the basis of such property is determined, for purposes of determining gain from a sale or exchange, in whole or part by reference to the basis of such property in the hands of a taxpayer described in subparagraph (A) or (B);

[*Caution: Code Sec. 1221(a)(3)(C), below, as amended by P.L. 107-16, applies to estates of decedents dying after December 31, 2009.*]

(C) a taxpayer in whose hands the basis of such property is determined (other than by reason of section 1022), for purposes of determining gain from a sale or exchange, in whole or part by reference to the basis of such property in the hands of a taxpayer described in subparagraph (A) or (B);

(4) accounts or notes receivable acquired in the ordinary course of trade or business for services rendered or from the sale of property described in paragraph (1);

(5) a publication of the United States Government (including the Congressional Record) which is received from the United States Government or any agency thereof, other than by purchase at the price at which it is offered for sale to the public, and which is held by—

(A) a taxpayer who so received such publication, or

(B) a taxpayer in whose hands the basis of such publication is determined, for purposes of determining gain from a sale or exchange, in whole or in part by reference to the basis of such publication in the hands of a taxpayer described in subparagraph (A);

(6) any commodities derivative financial instrument held by a commodities derivatives dealer, unless—

(A) it is established to the satisfaction of the Secretary that such instrument has no connection to the activities of such dealer as a dealer, and

(B) such instrument is clearly identified in such dealer's records as being described in subparagraph (A) before the close of the day on which it was acquired, originated, or entered into (or such other time as the Secretary may by regulations prescribe);

Sec. 1221(a)

(7) any hedging transaction which is clearly identified as such before the close of the day on which it was acquired, originated, or entered into (or such other time as the Secretary may by regulations prescribe); or

(8) supplies of a type regularly used or consumed by the taxpayer in the ordinary course of a trade or business of the taxpayer.

[Sec. 1221(b)]

(b) DEFINITIONS AND SPECIAL RULES.—

(1) COMMODITIES DERIVATIVE FINANCIAL INSTRUMENTS.—For purposes of subsection (a)(6)—

(A) COMMODITIES DERIVATIVES DEALER.—The term "commodities derivatives dealer" means a person which regularly offers to enter into, assume, offset, assign, or terminate positions in commodities derivative financial instruments with customers in the ordinary course of a trade or business.

(B) COMMODITIES DERIVATIVE FINANCIAL INSTRUMENT.—

(i) IN GENERAL.—The term "commodities derivative financial instrument" means any contract or financial instrument with respect to commodities (other than a share of stock in a corporation, a beneficial interest in a partnership or trust, a note, bond, debenture, or other evidence of indebtedness, or a section 1256 contract (as defined in section 1256(b))), the value or settlement price of which is calculated by or determined by reference to a specified index.

(ii) SPECIFIED INDEX.—The term "specified index" means any one or more or any combination of—

(I) a fixed rate, price, or amount, or

(II) a variable rate, price, or amount,

which is based on any current, objectively determinable financial or economic information with respect to commodities which is not within the control of any of the parties to the contract or instrument and is not unique to any of the parties' circumstances.

(2) HEDGING TRANSACTION.—

(A) IN GENERAL.—For purposes of this section, the term "hedging transaction" means any transaction entered into by the taxpayer in the normal course of the taxpayer's trade or business primarily—

(i) to manage risk of price changes or currency fluctuations with respect to ordinary property which is held or to be held by the taxpayer,

(ii) to manage risk of interest rate or price changes or currency fluctuations with respect to borrowings made or to be made, or ordinary obligations incurred or to be incurred, by the taxpayer, or

(iii) to manage such other risks as the Secretary may prescribe in regulations.

(B) TREATMENT OF NONIDENTIFICATION OR IMPROPER IDENTIFICATION OF HEDGING TRANSACTIONS.—Notwithstanding subsection (a)(7), the Secretary shall prescribe regulations to properly characterize any income, gain, expense, or loss arising from a transaction—

(i) which is a hedging transaction but which was not identified as such in accordance with subsection (a)(7), or

(ii) which was so identified but is not a hedging transaction.

(3) REGULATIONS.—The Secretary shall prescribe such regulations as are appropriate to carry out the purposes of paragraph (6) and (7) of subsection (a) in the case of transactions involving related parties.

[Sec. 1222]

SEC. 1222. OTHER TERMS RELATING TO CAPITAL GAINS AND LOSSES.

For purposes of this subtitle—

(1) SHORT-TERM CAPITAL GAIN.—The term "short-term capital gain" means gain from the sale or exchange of a capital asset held for not more than 1 year, if and to the extent such gain is taken into account in computing gross income.

Sec. 1221(b)

(2) SHORT-TERM CAPITAL LOSS.—The term "short-term capital loss" means loss from the sale or exchange of a capital asset held for not more than 1 year, if and to the extent that such loss is taken into account in computing taxable income.

(3) LONG-TERM CAPITAL GAIN.—The term "long-term capital gain" means gain from the sale or exchange of a capital asset held for more than 1 year, if and to the extent such gain is taken into account in computing gross income.

(4) LONG-TERM CAPITAL LOSS.—The term "long-term capital loss" means loss from the sale or exchange of a capital asset held for more than 1 year, if and to the extent that such loss is taken into account in computing taxable income.

(5) NET SHORT-TERM CAPITAL GAIN.—The term "net short-term capital gain" means the excess of short-term capital gains for the taxable year over the short-term capital losses for such year.

(6) NET SHORT-TERM CAPITAL LOSS.—The term "net short-term capital loss" means the excess of short-term capital losses for the taxable year over the short-term capital gains for such year.

(7) NET LONG-TERM CAPITAL GAIN.—The term "net long-term capital gain" means the excess of long-term capital gains for the taxable year over the long-term capital losses for such year.

(8) NET LONG-TERM CAPITAL LOSS.—The term "net long-term capital loss" means the excess of long-term capital losses for the taxable year over the long-term capital gains for such year.

(9) CAPITAL GAIN NET INCOME.—The term "capital gain net income" means the excess of the gains from sales or exchanges of capital assets over the losses from such sales or exchanges.

(10) NET CAPITAL LOSS.—The term "net capital loss" means the excess of the losses from sales or exchanges of capital assets over the sum allowed under section 1211. In the case of a corporation, for the purpose of determining losses under this paragraph, amounts which are short-term capital losses under section 1212 shall be excluded.

(11) NET CAPITAL GAIN.—The term "net capital gain" means the excess of the net long-term capital gain for the taxable year over the net short-term capital loss for such year.

For purposes of this subtitle, in the case of futures transactions in any commodity subject to the rules of a board of trade or commodity exchange, the length of the holding period taken into account under this section or under any other section amended by section 1402 of the Tax Reform Act of 1976 shall be determined without regard to the amendments made by subsections (a) and (b) of such section 1402.

[Sec. 1223]

SEC. 1223. HOLDING PERIOD OF PROPERTY.

For purposes of this subtitle—

(1) In determining the period for which the taxpayer has held property received in an exchange, there shall be included the period for which he held the property exchanged if, under this chapter, the property has, for the purpose of determining gain or loss from a sale or exchange, the same basis in whole or in part in his hands as the property exchanged, and, in the case of such exchanges after March 1, 1954, the property exchanged at the time of such exchange was a capital asset as defined in section 1221 or property described in section 1231. For purposes of this paragraph—

(A) an involuntary conversion described in section 1033 shall be considered an exchange of the property converted for the property acquired, and

(B) a distribution to which section 355 (or so much of section 356 as relates to section 355) applies shall be treated as an exchange.

(2) In determining the period for which the taxpayer has held property however acquired there shall be included the period for which such property was held by any other person, if under this chapter such property has, for the purpose of determining gain or loss from a sale or exchange, the same basis in whole or in part in his hands as it would have in the hands of such other person.

(3) In determining the period for which the taxpayer has held stock or securities received upon a distribution where no gain was recognized to the distributee under section 1081 (c) (or under section 112 (g) of the Revenue Act of 1928, 45 Stat. 818, or the Revenue Act of 1932, 48 Stat. 705), there shall be included the period for which he held the stock or securities in the distributing corporation before the receipt of the stock or securities on such distribution.

(4) In determining the period for which the taxpayer has held stock or securities the acquisition of which (or the contract or option to acquire which) resulted in the nondeductibility (under section 1091 relating to wash sales) of the loss from the sale or other disposition of substantially identical

stock or securities, there shall be included the period for which he held the stock or securities the loss from the sale or other disposition of which was not deductible.

(5) In determining the period for which the taxpayer has held stock or rights to acquire stock received on a distribution, if the basis of such stock or rights is determined under section 307 (or under so much of section 1052 (c) as refers to section 113 (a) (23) of the Internal Revenue Code of 1939), there shall (under regulations prescribed by the Secretary) be included the period for which he held the stock in the distributing corporation before the receipt of such stock or rights upon such distribution.

(6) In determining the period for which the taxpayer has held stock or securities acquired from a corporation by the exercise of rights to acquire such stock or securities, there shall be included only the period beginning with the date on which the right to acquire was exercised.

(7) In determining the period for which the taxpayer has held a residence, the acquisition of which resulted under section 1034 (as in effect on the day before the date of the enactment of the Taxpayer Relief Act of 1997) in the nonrecognition of any part of the gain realized on the sale or exchange of another residence, there shall be included the period for which such other residence had been held as of the date of such sale or exchange. For purposes of this paragraph, the term "sale or exchange" includes an involuntary conversion occurring after December 31, 1950, and before January 1, 1954.

(8) In determining the period for which the taxpayer has held a commodity acquired in satisfaction of a commodity futures contract (other than a commodity futures contract to which section 1256 applies) there shall be included the period for which he held the commodity futures contract if such commodity futures contract was a capital asset in his hands.

(9) Any reference in this section to a provision of this title shall, where applicable, be deemed a reference to the corresponding provision of the Internal Revenue Code of 1939, or prior internal revenue laws.

(10) In determining the period for which the taxpayer has held trust certificates of a trust to which subsection (d) of section 1246 applies, or the period for which the taxpayer has held stock in a corporation to which subsection (d) of section 1246 applies, there shall be included the period for which the trust or corporation (as the case may be) held the stock of foreign investment companies.

(11) In the case of a person acquiring property from a decedent or to whom property passed from a decedent (within the meaning of section 1014(b)), if—

(A) the basis of such property in the hands of such person is determined under section 1014, and

(B) such property is sold or otherwise disposed of by such person within 1 year after the decedent's death,

then such person shall be considered to have held such property for more than 1 year.

(12) If—

(A) property is acquired by any person in a transfer to which section 1040 applies,

(B) such property is sold or otherwise disposed of by such person within 1 year after the decedent's death, and

(C) such sale or disposition is to a person who is a qualified heir (as defined in section 2032A(e)(1)) with respect to the decedent,

then the person making such sale or other disposition shall be considered to have held such property for more than 1 year.

(13) In determining the period for which the taxpayer has held qualified replacement property (within the meaning of section 1042(b)) the acquisition of which resulted under section 1042 in the nonrecognition of any part of the gain realized on the sale of qualified securities (within the meaning of section 1042(b)), there shall be included the period for which such qualified securities had been held by the taxpayer.

(14) In determining the period for which the taxpayer has held property the acquisition of which resulted under section 1043 in the nonrecognition of any part of the gain realized on the sale of other property, there shall be included the period for which such other property had been held as of the date of such sale.

(15) Except for purposes of sections 1202(a)(2), 1202(c)(2)(A), 1400B(b),and1400F(b), in determining the period for which the taxpayer has held property the acquisition of which resulted

Sec. 1223

under section 1045 or 1397B in the nonrecognition of any part of the gain realized on the sale of other property, there shall be included the period for which such other property has been held as of the date of such sale.

(16) If the security to which a securities futures contract (as defined in section 1234B) relates (other than a contract to which section 1256 applies) is acquired in satisfaction of such contract, in determining the period for which the taxpayer has held such security, there shall be included the period for which the taxpayer held such contract if such contract was a capital asset in the hands of the taxpayer.

(17) CROSS REFERENCE.—

For special holding period provision relating to certain partnership distributions, see section 735(b).

PART IV—SPECIAL RULES FOR DETERMINING CAPITAL GAINS AND LOSSES

[Sec. 1231]

SEC. 1231. PROPERTY USED IN THE TRADE OR BUSINESS AND INVOLUNTARY CONVERSIONS.

[Sec. 1231(a)]

(a) GENERAL RULE.—

(1) GAINS EXCEED LOSSES.—If—

(A) the section 1231 gains for any taxable year, exceed

(B) the section 1231 losses for such taxable year,

such gains and losses shall be treated as long-term capital gains or long-term capital losses, as the case may be.

(2) GAINS DO NOT EXCEED LOSSES.—If—

(A) the section 1231 gains for any taxable year, do not exceed

(B) the section 1231 losses for such taxable year,

such gains and losses shall not be treated as gains and losses from sales or exchanges of capital assets.

(3) SECTION 1231 GAINS AND LOSSES.—For purposes of this subsection—

(A) SECTION 1231 GAIN.—The term "section 1231 gain" means—

(i) any recognized gain on the sale or exchange of property used in the trade or business, and

(ii) any recognized gain from the compulsory or involuntary conversion (as a result of destruction in whole or in part, theft or seizure, or an exercise of the power of requisition or condemnation or the threat or imminence thereof) into other property or money of—

(I) property used in the trade or business, or

(II) any capital asset which is held for more than 1 year and is held in connection with a trade or business or a transaction entered into for profit.

(B) SECTION 1231 LOSS.—The term "section 1231 loss" means any recognized loss from a sale or exchange or conversion described in subparagraph (A).

(4) SPECIAL RULES.—For purposes of this subsection—

(A) In determining under this subsection whether gains exceed losses—

(i) the section 1231 gains shall be included only if and to the extent taken into account in computing gross income, and

(ii) the section 1231 losses shall be included only if and to the extent taken into account in computing taxable income, except that section 1211 shall not apply.

(B) Losses (including losses not compensated for by insurance or otherwise) on the destruction, in whole or in part, theft or seizure, or requisition or condemnation of—

(i) property used in the trade or business, or

(ii) capital assets which are held for more than 1 year and are held in connection with a trade or business or a transaction entered into for profit,

shall be treated as losses from a compulsory or involuntary conversion.

(C) In the case of any involuntary conversion (subject to the provisions of this subsection but for this sentence) arising from fire, storm, shipwreck, or other casualty, or from theft, of any—

(i) property used in the trade or business, or

(ii) any capital asset which is held for more than 1 year and is held in connection with a trade or business or a transaction entered into for profit,

this subsection shall not apply to such conversion (whether resulting in gain or loss) if during the taxable year the recognized losses from such conversions exceed the recognized gains from such conversions.

[Sec. 1231(b)]

(b) DEFINITION OF PROPERTY USED IN THE TRADE OR BUSINESS.—For purposes of this section—

(1) GENERAL RULE.—The term "property used in the trade or business" means property used in the trade or business, of a character which is subject to the allowance for depreciation provided in section 167, held for more than 1 year, and real property used in the trade or business, held for more than 1 year, which is not—

(A) property of a kind which would properly be includible in the inventory of the taxpayer if on hand at the close of the taxable year,

(B) property held by the taxpayer primarily for sale to customers in the ordinary course of his trade or business,

(C) a copyright, a literary, musical, or artistic composition, a letter or memorandum, or similar property, held by a taxpayer described in paragraph (3) of section 1221(a), or

(D) a publication of the United States Government (including the Congressional Record) which is received from the United States Government, or any agency thereof, other than by purchase at the price at which it is offered for sale to the public, and which is held by a taxpayer described in paragraph (5) of section 1221(a).

(2) TIMBER, COAL, OR DOMESTIC IRON ORE.—Such term includes timber, coal, and iron ore with respect to which section 631 applies.

(3) LIVESTOCK.—Such term includes—

(A) cattle and horses, regardless of age, held by the taxpayer for draft, breeding, dairy, or sporting purposes, and held by him for 24 months or more from the date of acquisition, and

(B) other livestock, regardless of age, held by the taxpayer for draft, breeding, dairy, or sporting purposes, and held by him for 12 months or more from the date of acquisition.

Such term does not include poultry.

(4) UNHARVESTED CROP.—In the case of an unharvested crop on land used in the trade or business and held for more than 1 year, if the crop and the land are sold or exchanged (or compulsorily or involuntarily converted) at the same time and to the same person, the crop shall be considered as "property used in the trade or business."

[Sec. 1231(c)]

(c) RECAPTURE OF NET ORDINARY LOSSES.—

(1) IN GENERAL.—The net section 1231 gain for any taxable year shall be treated as ordinary income to the extent such gain does not exceed the non-recaptured net section 1231 losses.

(2) NON-RECAPTURED NET SECTION 1231 LOSSES.—For purposes of this subsection, the term "non-recaptured net section 1231 losses" means the excess of—

(A) the aggregate amount of the net section 1231 losses for the 5 most recent preceding taxable years beginning after December 31, 1981, over

(B) the portion of such losses taken into account under paragraph (1) for such preceding taxable years.

(3) NET SECTION 1231 GAIN.—For purposes of this subsection, the term "net section 1231 gain" means the excess of—

Sec. 1231(b)

(A) the section 1231 gains, over

(B) the section 1231 losses.

(4) NET SECTION 1231 LOSS.—For purposes of this subsection, the term "net section 1231 loss" means the excess of—

(A) the section 1231 losses, over

(B) the section 1231 gains.

(5) SPECIAL RULES.—For purposes of determining the amount of the net section 1231 gain or loss for any taxable year, the rules of paragraph (4) of subsection (a) shall apply.

[Sec. 1234]

SEC. 1234. OPTIONS TO BUY OR SELL.

[Sec. 1234(a)]

(a) TREATMENT OF GAIN OR LOSS IN THE CASE OF THE PURCHASER.—

(1) GENERAL RULE.—Gain or loss attributable to the sale or exchange of, or loss attributable to failure to exercise, an option to buy or sell property shall be considered gain or loss from the sale or exchange of property which has the same character as the property to which the option relates has in the hands of the taxpayer (or would have in the hands of the taxpayer if acquired by him).

(2) SPECIAL RULE FOR LOSS ATTRIBUTABLE TO FAILURE TO EXERCISE OPTION.—For purposes of paragraph (1), if loss is attributable to failure to exercise an option, the option shall be deemed to have been sold or exchanged on the day it expired.

(3) NONAPPLICATION OF SUBSECTION.—This subsection shall not apply to—

(A) an option which constitutes property described in paragraph (1) of section 1221(a);

(B) in the case of gain attributable to the sale or exchange of an option, any income derived in connection with such option which, without regard to this subsection, is treated as other than gain from the sale or exchange of a capital asset; and

(C) a loss attributable to failure to exercise an option described in section 1233(c).

[Sec. 1234(b)]

(b) TREATMENT OF GRANTOR OF OPTION IN THE CASE OF STOCK, SECURITIES, OR COMMODITIES.—

(1) GENERAL RULE.—In the case of the grantor of the option, gain or loss from any closing transaction with respect to, and gain on lapse of, an option in property shall be treated as a gain or loss from the sale or exchange of a capital asset held not more than 1 year.

(2) DEFINITIONS.—For purposes of this subsection—

(A) CLOSING TRANSACTION.—The term "closing transaction" means any termination of the taxpayer's obligation under an option in property other than through the exercise or lapse of the option.

(B) PROPERTY.—The term "property" means stocks and securities (including stocks and securities dealt with on a "when issued" basis), commodities, and commodity futures.

(3) NONAPPLICATION OF SUBSECTION.—This subsection shall not apply to any option granted in the ordinary course of the taxpayer's trade or business of granting options.

[Sec. 1234(c)]

(c) TREATMENT OF OPTIONS ON SECTION 1256 CONTRACTS AND CASH SETTLEMENT OPTIONS.—

(1) SECTION 1256 CONTRACTS.—Gain or loss shall be recognized on the exercise of an option on a section 1256 contract (within the meaning of section 1256(b)).

(2) TREATMENT OF CASH SETTLEMENT OPTIONS.—

(A) IN GENERAL.—For purposes of subsections (a) and (b), a cash settlement option shall be treated as an option to buy or sell property.

(B) CASH SETTLEMENT OPTION.—For purposes of subparagraph (A), the term "cash settlement option" means any option which on exercise settles in (or could be settled in) cash or property other than the underlying property.

SEC. 1234A. GAINS OR LOSSES FROM CERTAIN TERMINATIONS.

Gain or loss attributable to the cancellation, lapse, expiration, or other termination of—

(1) a right or obligation (other than a securities contract, as defined in section 1234B) with respect to property which is (or on acquisition would be) a capital asset in the hands of the taxpayer, or

(2) a section 1256 contract (as defined in section 1256) not described in paragraph (1) which is a capital asset in the hands of the taxpayer,

shall be treated as gain or loss from the sale of a capital asset. The preceding sentence shall not apply to the retirement of any debt instrument (whether or not through a trust or other participation arrangement).

SEC. 1234B. GAINS OR LOSSES FROM SECURITIES FUTURES CONTRACTS.

(a) TREATMENT OF GAIN OR LOSS.—

(1) IN GENERAL.—Gain or loss attributable to the sale, exchange, or termination of a securities futures contract shall be considered gain or loss from the sale or exchange of property which has the same character as the property to which the contract relates has in the hands of the taxpayer (or would have in the hands of the taxpayer if acquired by the taxpayer).

(2) NONAPPLICATION OF SUBSECTION.—This subsection shall not apply to—

(A) a contract which constitutes property described in paragraph (1) or (7) of section 1221(a), and

(B) any income derived in connection with a contract which, without regard to this subsection, is treated as other than gain from the sale or exchange of a capital asset.

(b) SHORT-TERM GAINS AND LOSSES.—Except as provided in the regulations under section 1092(b) or this section, or in section 1233, if gain or loss on the sale, exchange, or termination of a securities futures contract to sell property is considered as gain or loss from the sale or exchange of a capital asset, such gain or loss shall be treated as short-term capital gain or loss.

(c) SECURITIES FUTURES CONTRACT.—For purposes of this section, the term "securities futures contract" means any security future (as defined in section 3(a)(55)(A) of the Securities Exchange Act of 1934, as in effect on the date of the enactment of this section).

(d) CONTRACTS NOT TREATED AS COMMODITY FUTURES CONTRACTS.—For purposes of this title, a securities futures contract shall not be treated as a commodity futures contract.

(e) REGULATIONS.—The Secretary shall prescribe such regulations as may be appropriate to provide for the proper treatment of securities futures contracts under this title.

(f) CROSS REFERENCE.—

For special rules relating to dealer securities futures contracts, see section 1256.

SEC. 1235. SALE OR EXCHANGE OF PATENTS.

[Sec. 1235(a)]

(a) GENERAL.—A transfer (other than by gift, inheritance, or devise) of property consisting of all substantial rights to a patent, or an undivided interest therein which includes a part of all such rights, by any holder shall be considered the sale or exchange of a capital asset held for more than 1 year, regardless of whether or not payments in consideration of such transfer are—

(1) payable periodically over a period generally coterminous with the transferee's use of the patent, or

(2) contingent on the productivity, use, or disposition of the property transferred.

[Sec. 1235(b)]

(b) "HOLDER" DEFINED.—For purposes of this section, the term "holder" means—

(1) any individual whose efforts created such property, or

(2) any other individual who has acquired his interest in such property in exchange for consideration in money or money's worth paid to such creator prior to actual reduction to practice of the invention covered by the patent, if such individual is neither—

(A) the employer of such creator, nor

(B) related to such creator (within the meaning of subsection (d)).

[Sec. 1235(c)]

(c) EFFECTIVE DATE.—This section shall be applicable with regard to any amounts received, or payments made, pursuant to a transfer described in subsection (a) in any taxable year to which this subtitle applies, regardless of the taxable year in which such transfer occurred.

[Sec. 1235(d)]

(d) RELATED PERSONS.—Subsection (a) shall not apply to any transfer, directly or indirectly, between persons specified within any one of the paragraphs of section 267(b) or persons described in section 707(b); except that, in applying section 267(b) and (c) and section 707(b) for purposes of this section—

(1) the phrase "25 percent or more" shall be substituted for the phrase "more than 50 percent" each place it appears in section 267(b) or 707(b), and

(2) paragraph (4) of section 267(c) shall be treated as providing that the family of an individual shall include only his spouse, ancestors, and lineal descendants.

* * *

[Sec. 1236]

SEC. 1236. DEALERS IN SECURITIES.

[Sec. 1236(a)]

(a) CAPITAL GAINS.—Gain by a dealer in securities from the sale or exchange of any security shall in no event be considered as gain from the sale or exchange of a capital asset unless—

(1) the security was, before the close of the day on which it was acquired (or such earlier time as the Secretary may prescribe by regulations), clearly identified in the dealer's records as a security held for investment; and

(2) the security was not, at any time after the close of such day (or such earlier time), held by such dealer primarily for sale to customers in the ordinary course of his trade or business.

[Sec. 1236(b)]

(b) ORDINARY LOSSES.—Loss by a dealer in securities from the sale or exchange of any security shall, except as otherwise provided in section 582 (c) (relating to bond, etc., losses of banks), in no event be considered as an ordinary loss if at any time after November 19, 1951, the security was clearly identified in the dealer's records as a security held for investment.

[Sec. 1236(c)]

(c) DEFINITION OF SECURITY.—For purposes of this section, the term "security" means any share of stock in any corporation, certificate of stock or interest in any corporation, note, bond, debenture, or evidence of indebtedness, or any evidence of an interest in or right to subscribe to or purchase any of the foregoing.

* * *

[Sec. 1236(e)]

(e) SPECIAL RULE FOR OPTIONS.—For purposes of subsection (a), any security acquired by a dealer pursuant to an option held by such dealer may be treated as held for investment only if the dealer, before the close of the day on which the option was acquired, clearly identified the option on his records as held for investment. For purposes of the preceding sentence, the term "option" includes the right to subscribe to or purchase any security.

[Sec. 1237]

SEC. 1237. REAL PROPERTY SUBDIVIDED FOR SALE.

[Sec. 1237(a)]

(a) GENERAL.—Any lot or parcel which is part of a tract of real property in the hands of a taxpayer other than a C corporation shall not be deemed to be held primarily for sale to customers in the ordinary course of trade or business at the time of sale solely because of the taxpayer having subdivided such tract for purposes of sale or because of any activity incident to such subdivision or sale, if—

(1) such tract, or any lot or parcel thereof, had not previously been held by such taxpayer primarily for sale to customers in the ordinary course of trade or business (unless such tract at such previous time would have been covered by this section) and, in the same taxable year in which the sale occurs, such taxpayer does not so hold any other real property; and

(2) no substantial improvement that substantially enhances the value of the lot or parcel sold is made by the taxpayer on such tract while held by the taxpayer or is made pursuant to a contract of sale entered into between the taxpayer and the buyer. For purposes of this paragraph, an improvement shall be deemed to be made by the taxpayer if such improvement was made by—

(A) the taxpayer or members of his family (as defined in section 267(c)(4)), by a corporation controlled by the taxpayer, an S corporation which included the taxpayer as a shareholder, or by a partnership which included the taxpayer as a partner; or

(B) a lessee, but only if the improvement constitutes income to the taxpayer; or

(C) Federal, State, or local government, or political subdivision thereof, but only if the improvement constitutes an addition to basis for the taxpayer; and

(3) such lot or parcel, except in the case of real property acquired by inheritance or devise, is held by the taxpayer for a period of 5 years.

[Sec. 1237(b)]

(b) SPECIAL RULES FOR APPLICATION OF SECTION.—

(1) GAINS.—If more than 5 lots or parcels contained in the same tract of real property are sold or exchanged, gain from any sale or exchange (which occurs in or after the taxable year in which the sixth lot or parcel is sold or exchanged) of any lot or parcel which comes within the provisions of paragraphs (1), (2) and (3) of subsection (a) of this section shall be deemed to be gain from the sale of property held primarily for sale to customers in the ordinary course of the trade or business to the extent of 5 percent of the selling price.

(2) EXPENDITURES OF SALE.—For the purpose of computing gain under paragraph (1) of this subsection, expenditures incurred in connection with the sale or exchange of any lot or parcel shall neither be allowed as a deduction in computing taxable income, nor treated as reducing the amount realized on such sale or exchange; but so much of such expenditures as does not exceed the portion of gain deemed under paragraph (1) of this subsection to be gain from the sale of property held primarily for sale to customers in the ordinary course of trade or business shall be so allowed as a deduction, and the remainder, if any, shall be treated as reducing the amount realized on such sale or exchange.

(3) NECESSARY IMPROVEMENTS.—No improvement shall be deemed a substantial improvement for purposes of subsection (a) if the lot or parcel is held by the taxpayer for a period of 10 years and if—

(A) such improvement is the building or installation of water, sewer, or drainage facilities or roads (if such improvement would except for this paragraph constitute a substantial improvement);

(B) it is shown to the satisfaction of the Secretary that the lot or parcel, the value of which was substantially enhanced by such improvement, would not have been marketable at the prevailing local price for similar building sites without such improvement; and

(C) the taxpayer elects, in accordance with regulations prescribed by the Secretary, to make no adjustment to basis of the lot or parcel, or of any other property owned by the taxpayer, on account of the expenditures for such improvements. Such election shall not make any item deductible which would not otherwise be deductible.

[Sec. 1237(c)]

(c) TRACT DEFINED.—For purposes of this section, the term "tract of real property" means a single piece of real property, except that 2 or more pieces of real property shall be considered a tract if at any time they were contiguous in the hands of the taxpayer or if they would be contiguous except for the interposition of a road, street, railroad, stream, or similar property. If, following the sale or exchange of any lot or parcel from a tract of real property, no further sales or exchanges of any other lots or parcels from the remainder of such tract are made for a period of 5 years, such remainder shall be deemed a tract.

[Sec. 1239]

SEC. 1239. GAIN FROM SALE OF DEPRECIABLE PROPERTY BETWEEN CERTAIN RELATED TAXPAYERS.

[Sec. 1239(a)]

(a) TREATMENT OF GAIN AS ORDINARY INCOME.—In the case of a sale or exchange of property, directly or indirectly, between related persons, any gain recognized to the transferor shall be treated as ordinary income if such property is, in the hands of the transferee, of a character which is subject to the allowance for depreciation provided in section 167.

[Sec. 1239(b)]

(b) RELATED PERSONS.—For purposes of subsection (a), the term "related persons" means—

(1) a person and all entities which are controlled entities with respect to such person,

(2) a taxpayer and any trust in which such taxpayer (or his spouse) is a beneficiary, unless such beneficiary's interest in the trust is a remote contingent interest (within the meaning of section 318(a)(3)(B)(i)), and

(3) except in the case of a sale or exchange in satisfaction of a pecuniary bequest, an executor of an estate and a beneficiary of such estate.

[Sec. 1239(c)]

(c) CONTROLLED ENTITY DEFINED.—

(1) GENERAL RULE.—For purposes of this section, the term "controlled entity" means, with respect to any person—

(A) a corporation more than 50 percent of the value of the outstanding stock of which is owned (directly or indirectly) by or for such person,

(B) a partnership more than 50 percent of the capital interest or profits interest in which is owned (directly or indirectly) by or for such person, and

(C) any entity which is a related person to such person under paragraph (3), (10), (11), or (12) of section 267(b).

(2) CONSTRUCTIVE OWNERSHIP.—For purposes of this section, ownership shall be determined in accordance with rules similar to the rules under section 267(c) (other than paragraph (3) thereof).

Sec. 1239(c)

[Sec. 1239(d)]

(d) EMPLOYER AND RELATED EMPLOYEE ASSOCIATION.—For purposes of subsection (a), the term "related person" also includes—

(1) an employer and any person related to the employer (within the meaning of subsection (b)), and

(2) a welfare benefit fund (within the meaning of section 419(e)) which is controlled directly or indirectly by persons referred to in paragraph (1).

[Sec. 1239(e)]

(e) PATENT APPLICATIONS TREATED AS DEPRECIABLE PROPERTY.—For purposes of this section, a patent application shall be treated as property which, in the hands of the transferee, is of a character which is subject to the allowance for depreciation provided in section 167.

[Sec. 1241]

SEC. 1241. CANCELLATION OF LEASE OR DISTRIBUTOR'S AGREEMENT.

Amounts received by a lessee for the cancellation of a lease, or by a distributor of goods for the cancellation of a distributor's agreement (if the distributor has a substantial capital investment in the distributorship), shall be considered as amounts received in exchange for such lease or agreement.

[Sec. 1244]

SEC. 1244. LOSSES ON SMALL BUSINESS STOCK.

[Sec. 1244(a)]

(a) GENERAL RULE.—In the case of an individual, a loss on section 1244 stock issued to such individual or to a partnership which would (but for this section) be treated as a loss from the sale or exchange of a capital asset shall, to the extent provided in this section, be treated as an ordinary loss.

[Sec. 1244(b)]

(b) MAXIMUM AMOUNT FOR ANY TAXABLE YEAR.—For any taxable year the aggregate amount treated by the taxpayer by reason of this section as an ordinary loss shall not exceed—

(1) $50,000, or

(2) $100,000, in the case of a husband and wife filing a joint return for such year under section 6013.

[Sec. 1244(c)]

(c) SECTION 1244 STOCK DEFINED.—

(1) IN GENERAL.—For purposes of this section, the term "section 1244 stock" means stock in a domestic corporation if—

(A) at the time such stock is issued, such corporation was a small business corporation,

(B) such stock was issued by such corporation for money or other property (other than stock and securities), and

(C) such corporation, during the period of its 5 most recent taxable years ending before the date the loss on such stock was sustained, derived more than 50 percent of its aggregate gross receipts from sources other than royalties, rents, dividends, interests, annuities, and sales or exchanges of stocks or securities.

(2) RULES FOR APPLICATION OF PARAGRAPH (1)(C).—

(A) PERIOD TAKEN INTO ACCOUNT WITH RESPECT TO NEW CORPORATIONS.—For purposes of paragraph (1)(C), if the corporation has not been in existence for 5 taxable years ending before the date the loss on the stock was sustained, there shall be substituted for such 5-year period—

(i) the period of the corporation's taxable years ending before such date, or

(ii) if the corporation has not been in existence for 1 taxable year ending before such date, the period such corporation has been in existence before such date.

(B) GROSS RECEIPTS FROM SALES OF SECURITIES.—For purposes of paragraph (1)(C), gross receipts from the sales or exchanges of stock or securities shall be taken into account only to the extent of gains therefrom.

(C) NONAPPLICATION WHERE DEDUCTIONS EXCEED GROSS INCOME.—Paragraph (1)(C) shall not apply with respect to any corporation if, for the period taken into account for purposes of paragraph (1)(C), the amount of the deductions allowed by this chapter (other than by sections 172, 243, 244, and 245) exceeds the amount of gross income.

(3) SMALL BUSINESS CORPORATION DEFINED.—

(A) IN GENERAL.—For purposes of this section, a corporation shall be treated as a small business corporation if the aggregate amount of money and other property received by the corporation for stock, as a contribution to capital, and as paid-in surplus, does not exceed $1,000,000. The determination under the preceding sentence shall be made as of the time of the issuance of the stock in question but shall include amounts received for such stock and for all stock theretofore issued.

(B) AMOUNT TAKEN INTO ACCOUNT WITH RESPECT TO PROPERTY.—For purposes of subparagraph (A), the amount taken into account with respect to any property other than money shall be the amount equal to the adjusted basis to the corporation of such property for determining gain, reduced by any liability to which the property was subject or which was assumed by the corporation. The determination under the preceding sentence shall be made as of the time the property was received by the corporation.

[Sec. 1244(d)]

(d) SPECIAL RULES.—

(1) LIMITATIONS ON AMOUNT OF ORDINARY LOSS.—

(A) CONTRIBUTIONS OF PROPERTY HAVING BASIS IN EXCESS OF VALUE.—If—

(i) section 1244 stock was issued in exchange for property,

(ii) the basis of such stock in the hands of the taxpayer is determined by reference to the basis in his hands of such property, and

(iii) the adjusted basis (for determining loss) of such property immediately before the exchange exceeded its fair market value at such time,

then in computing the amount of the loss on such stock for purposes of this section the basis of such stock shall be reduced by an amount equal to the excess described in clause (iii).

(B) INCREASES IN BASIS.—In computing the amount of the loss on stock for purposes of this section, any increase in the basis of such stock (through contributions to the capital of the corporation, or otherwise) shall be treated as allocable to stock which is not section 1244 stock.

(2) RECAPITALIZATIONS, CHANGES IN NAME, ETC.—To the extent provided in regulations prescribed by the Secretary, stock in a corporation, the basis of which (in the hands of a taxpayer) is determined in whole or in part by reference to the basis in his hands of stock in such corporation which meets the requirements of subsection (c)(1) (other than subparagraph (C) thereof), or which is received in a reorganization described in section 368(a)(1)(F) in exchange for stock which meets such requirements, shall be treated as meeting such requirements. For purposes of paragraphs (1)(C) and (3)(A) of subsection (c), a successor corporation in a reorganization described in section 368(a)(1)(F) shall be treated as the same corporation as its predecessor.

(3) RELATIONSHIP TO NET OPERATING LOSS DEDUCTION.—For purposes of section 172 (relating to the net operating loss deduction), any amount of loss treated by reason of this section as an ordinary loss shall be treated as attributable to a trade or business of the taxpayer.

(4) INDIVIDUAL DEFINED.—For purposes of this section, the term "individual" does not include a trust or estate.

[Sec. 1244(e)]

(e) REGULATIONS.—The Secretary shall prescribe such regulations as may be necessary to carry out the purposes of this section.

Sec. 1244(e)

[Sec. 1245]

SEC. 1245. GAIN FROM DISPOSITIONS OF CERTAIN DEPRECIABLE PROPERTY.

[Sec. 1245(a)]

(a) GENERAL RULE.—

(1) ORDINARY INCOME.—Except as otherwise provided in this section, if section 1245 property is disposed of the amount by which the lower of—

(A) the recomputed basis of the property, or

(B)(i) in the case of a sale, exchange, or involuntary conversion, the amount realized, or

(ii) in the case of any other disposition, the fair market value of such property,

exceeds the adjusted basis of such property shall be treated as ordinary income. Such gain shall be recognized notwithstanding any other provision of this subtitle.

(2) RECOMPUTED BASIS.—For purposes of this section—

(A) IN GENERAL.—The term "recomputed basis" means, with respect to any property, its adjusted basis recomputed by adding thereto all adjustments reflected in such adjusted basis on account of deductions (whether in respect of the same or other property) allowed or allowable to the taxpayer or to any other person for depreciation or amortization.

(B) TAXPAYER MAY ESTABLISH AMOUNT ALLOWED.—For purposes of subparagraph (A), if the taxpayer can establish by adequate records or other sufficient evidence that the amount allowed for depreciation or amortization for any period was less than the amount allowable, the amount added for such period shall be the amount allowed.

(C) CERTAIN DEDUCTIONS TREATED AS AMORTIZATION.—Any deduction allowable under section 179, 179A, 190, or 193 shall be treated as if it were a deduction allowable for amortization.

(3) SECTION 1245 PROPERTY.—For purposes of this section, the term "section 1245 property" means any property which is or has been property of a character subject to the allowance for depreciation provided in section 167 and is either—

(A) personal property,

(B) other property (not including a building or its structural components) but only if such other property is tangible and has an adjusted basis in which there are reflected adjustments described in paragraph (2) for a period in which such property (or other property)—

(i) was used as an integral part of manufacturing, production, or extraction or of furnishing transportation, communications, electrical energy, gas, water, or sewage disposal services, or

(ii) constituted a research facility used in connection with any of the activities referred to in clause (i), or

(iii) constituted a facility used in connection with any of the activities referred to in clause (i) for the bulk storage of fungible commodities (including commodities in a liquid or gaseous state),

(C) so much of any real property (other than any property described in subparagraph B)) which has an adjusted basis in which there are reflected adjustments for amortization under section 169, 179, 179A, 185, 188 (as in effect before its repeal by the Revenue Reconciliation Act of 1990), 190, 193, or 194,

(D) a single purpose agricultural or horticultural structure (as defined in section 168(i)(13),

(E) a storage facility (not including a building or its structural components) used in connection with the distribution of petroleum or any primary product of petroleum, or

(F) any railroad grading or tunnel bore (as defined in section 168(e)(4)).

(4) SPECIAL RULE FOR PLAYER CONTRACTS.—

(A) IN GENERAL.—For purposes of this section, if a franchise to conduct any sports enterprise is sold or exchanged, and if, in connection with such sale or exchange, there is a transfer of any player contracts, the recomputed basis of such player contracts in the hands of the transferor shall be the adjusted basis of such contracts increased by the greater of—

Sec. 1245

(i) the previously unrecaptured depreciation with respect to player contracts acquired by the transferor at the time of acquisition of such franchise, or

(ii) the previously unrecaptured depreciation with respect to the player contracts involved in such transfer.

(B) PREVIOUSLY UNRECAPTURED DEPRECIATION WITH RESPECT TO INITIAL CONTRACTS.—For purposes of subparagraph (A)(i), the term "previously unrecaptured depreciation" means the excess (if any) of—

(i) the sum of the deduction allowed or allowable to the taxpayer transferor for the depreciation attributable to periods after December 31, 1975, of any player contracts acquired by him at the time of acquisition of such franchise, plus the deduction allowed or allowable for losses incurred after December 31, 1975, with respect to such player contracts acquired at the time of such acquisition, over

(ii) the aggregate of the amounts described in clause (i) treated as ordinary income by reason of this section with respect to prior dispositions of such player contracts acquired upon acquisition of the franchise.

(C) PREVIOUSLY UNRECAPTURED DEPRECIATION WITH RESPECT TO CONTRACTS TRANSFERRED.— For purposes of subparagraph (A)(ii), the term "previously unrecaptured depreciation" means the amount of any deduction allowed or allowable to the taxpayer transferor for the depreciation of any contracts involved in such transfer.

(D) PLAYER CONTRACT.—For purposes of this paragraph, the term "player contract" means any contract for the services of an athlete which, in the hands of the taxpayer, is of a character subject to the allowance for depreciation provided in section 167.

[Sec. 1245(b)]

(b) EXCEPTIONS AND LIMITATIONS.—

(1) GIFTS.—Subsection (a) shall not apply to a disposition by gift.

(2) TRANSFERS AT DEATH.—Except as provided in section 691 (relating to income in respect of a decedent), subsection (a) shall not apply to a transfer at death.

(3) CERTAIN TAX-FREE TRANSACTIONS.—If the basis of property in the hands of a transferee is determined by reference to its basis in the hands of the transferor by reason of the application of section 332, 351, 361, 721, or 731, then the amount of gain taken into account by the transferor under subsection (a)(1) shall not exceed the amount of gain recognized to the transferor on the transfer of such property (determined without regard to this section). Except as provided in paragraph (7), this paragraph shall not apply to a disposition to an organization (other than a cooperative described in section 521) which is exempt from the tax imposed by this chapter.

(4) LIKE KIND EXCHANGES; INVOLUNTARY CONVERSIONS, ETC.—If property is disposed of and gain (determined without regard to this section) is not recognized in whole or in part under section 1031 or 1033, then the amount of gain taken into account by the transferor under subsection (a)(1) shall not exceed the sum of—

(A) the amount of gain recognized on such disposition (determined without regard to this section), plus

(B) the fair market value of property acquired which is not section 1245 property and which is not taken into account under subparagraph (A).

(5) SECTION 1081 TRANSACTIONS.—Under regulations prescribed by the Secretary, rules consistent with paragraphs (3) and (4) of this subsection shall apply in the case of transactions described in section 1081 (relating to exchanges in obedience to SEC orders).

(6) PROPERTY DISTRIBUTED BY A PARTNERSHIP TO A PARTNER.—

(A) IN GENERAL.—For purposes of this section, the basis of section 1245 property distributed by a partnership to a partner shall be deemed to be determined by reference to the adjusted basis of such property to the partnership.

(B) ADJUSTMENTS ADDED BACK.—In the case of any property described in subparagraph (A), for purposes of computing the recomputed basis of such property the amount of the adjustments added back for periods before the distribution by the partnership shall be—

(i) the amount of the gain to which subsection (a) would have applied if such property had been sold by the partnership immediately before the distribution at its fair market value at such time, reduced by

(ii) the amount of such gain to which section 751(b) applied.

(7) TRANSFERS TO TAX-EXEMPT ORGANIZATION WHERE PROPERTY WILL BE USED IN UNRELATED BUSINESS.—

(A) IN GENERAL.—The second sentence of paragraph (3) shall not apply to a disposition of section 1245 property to an organization described in section 511(a)(2) or 511(b)(2) if, immediately after such disposition, such organization uses such property in an unrelated trade or business (as defined in section 513).

(B) LATER CHANGE IN USE.—If any property with respect to the disposition of which gain is not recognized by reason of subparagraph (A) ceases to be used in an unrelated trade or business of the organization acquiring such property, such organization shall be treated for purposes of this section as having disposed of such property on the date of such cessation.

(8) TIMBER PROPERTY.—In determining, under subsection (a)(2), the recomputed basis of property with respect to which a deduction under section 194 was allowed for any taxable year, the taxpayer shall not take into account adjustments under section 194 to the extent such adjustments are attributable to the amortizable basis of the taxpayer acquired before the 10th taxable year preceding the taxable year in which gain with respect to the property is recognized.

[Sec. 1245(c)]

(c) ADJUSTMENTS TO BASIS.—The Secretary shall prescribe such regulations as he may deem necessary to provide for adjustments to the basis of property to reflect gain recognized under subsection (a).

[Sec. 1245(d)]

(d) APPLICATION OF SECTION.—This section shall apply notwithstanding any other provision of this subtitle.

[Sec. 1250]

SEC. 1250. GAIN FROM DISPOSITIONS OF CERTAIN DEPRECIABLE REALTY.

[Sec. 1250(a)]

(a) GENERAL RULE.—Except as otherwise provided in this section—

(1) ADDITIONAL DEPRECIATION AFTER DECEMBER 31, 1975.—

(A) IN GENERAL.—If section 1250 property is disposed of after December 31, 1975, then the applicable percentage of the lower of—

(i) that portion of the additional depreciation (as defined in subsection (b)(1) or (4)) attributable to periods after December 31, 1975, in respect of the property, or

(ii) the excess of the amount realized (in the case of a sale, exchange, or involuntary conversion), or the fair market value of such property (in the case of any other disposition), over the adjusted basis of such property,

shall be treated as gain which is ordinary income. Such gain shall be recognized notwithstanding any other provision of this subtitle.

(B) APPLICABLE PERCENTAGE.—For purposes of subparagraph (A), the term "applicable percentage" means—

(i) in the case of section 1250 property with respect to which a mortgage is insured under section 221(d)(3) or 236 of the National Housing Act, or housing financed or assisted by direct loan or tax abatement under similar provisions of State or local laws and with respect to which the owner is subject to the restrictions described in section 1039(b)(1)(B), (as in effect on the day before the date of the enactment of the Revenue Reconciliation Act of 1990), 100 percent minus 1 percentage point for each full month the property was held after the date the property was held 100 full months;

(ii) in the case of dwelling units which, on the average, were held for occupancy by families or individuals eligible to receive subsidies under section 8 of the United States Housing Act of 1937, as amended, or under the provisions of State or local law authorizing similar levels of subsidy for lower-income families, 100 percent minus 1 percentage point for each full month the property was held after the date the property was held 100 full months;

(iii) in the case of section 1250 property with respect to which a depreciation deduction for rehabilitation expenditures was allowed under section 167(k), 100 percent minus 1 percentage point for each full month in excess of 100 full months after the date on which such property was placed in service;

(iv) in the case of section 1250 property with respect to which a loan is made or insured under title V of the Housing Act of 1949, 100 percent minus 1 percentage point for each full month the property was held after the date the property was held 100 full months; and

(v) in the case of all other section 1250 property, 100 percent.

In the case of a building (or a portion of a building devoted to dwelling units), if, on the average, 85 percent or more of the dwelling units contained in such building (or portion thereof) are units described in clause (ii), such building (or portion thereof) shall be treated as property described in clause (ii). Clauses (i), (ii), and (iv) shall not apply with respect to the additional depreciation described in subsection (b)(4) which was allowed under section 167(k).

* * *

[Sec. 1250(b)]

(b) ADDITIONAL DEPRECIATION DEFINED.—For purposes of this section—

(1) IN GENERAL.—The term "additional depreciation" means, in the case of any property, the depreciation adjustments in respect of such property; except that, in the case of property held more than one year, it means such adjustments only to the extent that they exceed the amount of the depreciation adjustments which would have resulted if such adjustments had been determined for each taxable year under the straight line method of adjustment.

(2) PROPERTY HELD BY LESSEE.—In the case of a lessee, in determining the depreciation adjustments which would have resulted in respect of any building erected (or other improvement made) on the leased property, or in respect of any cost of acquiring the lease, the lease period shall be treated as including all renewal periods. For purposes of the preceding sentence—

(A) the term "renewal period" means any period for which the lease may be renewed, extended, or continued pursuant to an option exercisable by the lessee, but

(B) the inclusion of renewal periods shall not extend the period taken into account by more than 2/3 of the period on the basis of which the depreciation adjustments were allowed.

(3) DEPRECIATION ADJUSTMENTS.—The term "depreciation adjustments" means, in respect of any property, all adjustments attributable to periods after December 31, 1963, reflected in the adjusted basis of such property on account of deductions (whether in respect of the same or other property) allowed or allowable to the taxpayer or to any other person for exhaustion, wear and tear, obsolescence, or amortization (other than amortization under section 168 (as in effect before its repeal by the Tax Reform Act of 1976), 169, 185 (as in effect before its repeal by the Tax Reform Act of 1986), 188 (as in effect before its repeal by the Revenue Reconciliation Act of 1990), 190, or 193). For purposes of the preceding sentence, if the taxpayer can establish by adequate records or other sufficient evidence that the amount allowed as a deduction for any period was less than the amount allowable, the amount taken into account for such period shall be the amount allowed.

(4) ADDITIONAL DEPRECIATION ATTRIBUTABLE TO REHABILITATION EXPENDITURES.—The term "additional depreciation" also means, in the case of section 1250 property with respect to which a depreciation or amortization deduction for rehabilitation expenditures was allowed under section 167(k) (as in effect on the day before the date of the enactment of the Revenue Reconciliation Act of 1990) or 191 (as in effect before its repeal by the Economic Recovery Tax Act of 1981), the depreciation or amortization adjustments allowed under such section to the extent attributable to such property, except that, in the case of such property held for more than one year after the rehabilitation expenditures so allowed were incurred, it means such adjustments only to the extent that they exceed the amount of the depreciation adjustments which would have resulted if such adjustments had been determined under the straight line method of adjustment without regard to the useful life permitted under section 167(k) (as in effect on the day before the date of the enactment of the Revenue Reconciliation Act of 1990) or 191 (as in effect before its repeal by the Economic Recovery Tax Act of 1981).

(5) METHOD OF COMPUTING STRAIGHT LINE ADJUSTMENTS.—For purposes of paragraph (1), the depreciation adjustments which would have resulted for any taxable year under the straight line method shall be determined—

(A) in the case of property to which section 168 applies, by determining the adjustments which would have resulted for such year if the taxpayer had elected the straight line method for such year using the recovery period applicable to such property, and

(B) in the case of any property to which section 168 does not apply, if a useful life (or salvage value) was used in determining the amount allowable as a deduction for any taxable year, by using such life (or value).

[Sec. 1250(c)]

(c) SECTION 1250 PROPERTY.—For purposes of this section, the term "section 1250 property" means any real property (other than section 1245 property, as defined in section 1245(a)(3)) which is or has been property of a character subject to the allowance for depreciation provided in section 167.

[Sec. 1250(d)]

(d) EXCEPTIONS AND LIMITATIONS.—

(1) GIFTS.—Subsection (a) shall not apply to a disposition by gift.

(2) TRANSFERS AT DEATH.—Except as provided in section 691 (relating to income in respect of a decedent), subsection (a) shall not apply to a transfer at death.

(3) CERTAIN TAX-FREE TRANSACTIONS.—If the basis of property in the hands of a transferee is determined by reference to its basis in the hands of the transferor by reason of the application of section 332, 351, 361, 721, or 731, then the amount of gain taken into account by the transferor under subsection (a) shall not exceed the amount of gain recognized to the transferor on the transfer of such property (determined without regard to this section). Except as provided in paragraph (9), this paragraph shall not apply to a disposition to an organization (other than a cooperative described in section 521) which is exempt from the tax imposed by this chapter.

(4) LIKE KIND EXCHANGES; INVOLUNTARY CONVERSIONS, ETC.—

(A) RECOGNITION LIMIT.—If property is disposed of and gain (determined without regard to this section) is not recognized in whole or in part under section 1031 or 1033, then the amount of gain taken into account by the transferor under subsection (a) shall not exceed the greater of the following:

(i) the amount of gain recognized on the disposition (determined without regard to this section), increased as provided in subparagraph (B), or

(ii) the amount determined under subparagraph (C).

(B) INCREASE FOR CERTAIN STOCK.—With respect to any transaction, the increase provided by this subparagraph is the amount equal to the fair market value of any stock purchased in a corporation which (but for this paragraph) would result in nonrecognition of gain under section 1033(a)(2)(A).

(C) ADJUSTMENT WHERE INSUFFICIENT SECTION 1250 PROPERTY IS ACQUIRED.—With respect to any transaction, the amount determined under this subparagraph shall be the excess of—

(i) the amount of gain which would (but for this paragraph) be taken into account under subsection (a), over

(ii) the fair market value (or cost in the case of a transaction described in section 1033(a)(2)) of the section 1250 property acquired in the transaction.

(D) BASIS OF PROPERTY ACQUIRED.—In the case of property purchased by the taxpayer in a transaction described in section 1033(a)(2), in applying [the last sentence of] section 1033(b)(2), such sentence shall be applied—

(i) first solely to section 1250 properties and to the amount of gain not taken into account under subsection (a) by reason of this paragraph, and

(ii) then to all purchased properties to which such sentence applies and to the remaining gain not recognized on the transaction as if the cost of the section 1250 properties were the basis of such properties computed under clause (i).

In the case of property acquired in any other transaction to which this paragraph applies, rules consistent with the preceding sentence shall be applied under regulations prescribed by the Secretary.

(E) ADDITIONAL DEPRECIATION WITH RESPECT TO PROPERTY DISPOSED OF.—In the case of any transaction described in section 1031 or 1033, the additional depreciation in respect of the section 1250 property acquired which is attributable to the section 1250 property disposed of shall be an amount equal to the amount of the gain which was not taken into account under subsection (a) by reason of the application of this paragraph.

* * *

(6) PROPERTY DISTRIBUTED BY A PARTNERSHIP TO A PARTNER.—

(A) IN GENERAL.—For purposes of this section, the basis of section 1250 property distributed by a partnership to a partner shall be deemed to be determined by reference to the adjusted basis of such property to the partnership.

(B) ADDITIONAL DEPRECIATION.—In respect of any property described in subparagraph (A), the additional depreciation attributable to periods before the distribution by the partnership shall be—

(i) the amount of the gain to which subsection (a) would have applied if such property had been sold by the partnership immediately before the distribution at its fair market value at such time and the applicable percentage for the property had been 100 percent, reduced by

(ii) if section 751(b) applied to any part of such gain, the amount of such gain to which section 751(b) would have applied if the applicable percentage for the property had been 100 percent.

(7) TRANSFERS TO TAX-EXEMPT ORGANIZATION WHERE PROPERTY WILL BE USED IN UNRELATED BUSINESS.—

(A) IN GENERAL.—The second sentence of paragraph (3) shall not apply to a disposition of section 1250 property to an organization described in section 511(a)(2) or 511(b)(2) if, immediately after such disposition, such organization uses such property in an unrelated trade or business (as defined in section 513),

(B) LATER CHANGE IN USE.—If any property with respect to the disposition of which gain is not recognized by reason of subparagraph (A) ceases to be used in an unrelated trade or business of the organization acquiring such property, such organization shall be treated for purposes of this section as having disposed of such property on the date of such cessation.

(8) FORECLOSURE DISPOSITIONS.—If any section 1250 property is disposed of by the taxpayer pursuant to a bid for such property at foreclosure or by operation of an agreement or of process of law after there was a default on indebtedness which such property secured, the applicable percentage referred to in paragraph (1)(B), (2)(B), or (3)(B) of subsection (a), as the case may be, shall be determined as if the taxpayer ceased to hold such property on the date of the beginning of the proceedings pursuant to which the disposition occurred, or, in the event there are no proceedings, such percentage shall be determined as if the taxpayer ceased to hold such property on the date, determined under regulations prescribed by the Secretary, on which such operation of an agreement or process of law, pursuant to which the disposition occurred, began.

[Sec. 1250(e)]

(e) HOLDING PERIOD.—For purposes of determining the applicable percentage under this section, the provisions of section 1223 shall not apply, and the holding period of section 1250 property shall be determined under the following rules:

(1) BEGINNING OF HOLDING PERIOD.—The holding period of section 1250 property shall be deemed to begin—

(A) in the case of property acquired by the taxpayer, on the day after the date of acquisition, or

(B) in the case of property constructed, reconstructed, or erected by the taxpayer, on the first day of the month during which the property is placed in service.

(2) PROPERTY WITH TRANSFERRED BASIS.—If the basis of property acquired in a transaction described in paragraph (1), (2), (3), or (5) of subsection (d) is determined by reference to its basis in

the hands of the transferor, then the holding period of the property in the hands of the transferee shall include the holding period of the property in the hands of the transferor.

[Sec. 1250(f)]

(f) SPECIAL RULES FOR PROPERTY WHICH IS SUBSTANTIALLY IMPROVED.—

(1) AMOUNT TREATED AS ORDINARY INCOME.—If, in the case of a disposition of section 1250 property, the property is treated as consisting of more than one element by reason of paragraph (3), then the amount taken into account under subsection (a) in respect of such section 1250 property as ordinary income shall be the sum of the amounts determined under paragraph (2).

(2) ORDINARY INCOME ATTRIBUTABLE TO AN ELEMENT.—For purposes of paragraph (1), the amount taken into account for any element shall be the sum of a series of amounts determined for the periods set forth in subsection (a), with the amount for any such period being determined by multiplying—

(A) the amount which bears the same ratio to the lower of the amounts specified in clause (i) or (ii) of subsection (a)(1)(A), in clause (i) or (ii) of subsection (a)(2)(A), or in clause (i) or (ii) of subsection (a)(3)(A), as the case may be, for the section 1250 property as the additional depreciation for such element attributable to such period bears to the sum of the additional depreciation for all elements attributable to such period, by

(B) the applicable percentage for such element for such period.

For purposes of this paragraph, determinations with respect to any element shall be made as if it were a separate property.

(3) PROPERTY CONSISTING OF MORE THAN ONE ELEMENT.—In applying this subsection in the case of any section 1250 property, there shall be treated as a separate element—

(A) each separate improvement,

(B) if, before completion of section 1250 property, units thereof (as distinguished from improvements) were placed in service, each such unit of section 1250 property, and

(C) the remaining property which is not taken into account under subparagraphs (A) and (B).

(4) PROPERTY WHICH IS SUBSTANTIALLY IMPROVED.—For purposes of this subsection—

(A) IN GENERAL.—The term "separate improvement" means each improvement added during the 36-month period ending on the last day of any taxable year to the capital account for the property, but only if the sum of the amounts added to such account during such period exceeds the greatest of—

(i) 25 percent of the adjusted basis of the property,

(ii) 10 percent of the adjusted basis of the property, determined without regard to the adjustments provided in paragraphs (2) and (3) of section 1016(a), or

(iii) $5,000.

For purposes of clauses (i) and (ii), the adjusted basis of the property shall be determined as of the beginning of the first day of such 36-month period, or of the holding period of the property (within the meaning of subsection (e)), whichever is the later.

(B) EXCEPTION.—Improvements in any taxable year shall be taken into account for purposes of subparagraph (A) only if the sum of the amounts added to the capital account for the property for such taxable year exceeds the greater of—

(i) $2,000, or

(ii) one percent of the adjusted basis referred to in subparagraph (A)(ii), determined, however, as of the beginning of such taxable year.

For purposes of this section, if the amount added to the capital account for any separate improvement does not exceed the greater of clause (i) or (ii), such improvement shall be treated as placed in service on the first day, of a calendar month, which is closest to the middle of the taxable year.

(C) IMPROVEMENT.—The term "improvement" means, in the case of any section 1250 property, any addition to capital account for such property after the initial acquisition or after completion of the property.

Sec. 1250(f)

(g) ADJUSTMENTS TO BASIS.—The Secretary shall prescribe such regulations as he may deem necessary to provide for adjustments to the basis of property to reflect gain recognized under subsection (a).

(h) APPLICATION OF SECTION.—This section shall apply notwithstanding any other provision of this subtitle.

SEC. 1253. TRANSFERS OF FRANCHISES, TRADEMARKS, AND TRADE NAMES.

(a) GENERAL RULE.—A transfer of a franchise, trademark, or trade name shall not be treated as a sale or exchange of a capital asset if the transferor retains any significant power, right, or continuing interest with respect to the subject matter of the franchise, trademark, or trade name.

(b) DEFINITIONS.—For purposes of this section—

(1) FRANCHISE.—The term "franchise" includes an agreement which gives one of the parties to the agreement the right to distribute, sell, or provide goods, services, or facilities, within a specified area.

(2) SIGNIFICANT POWER, RIGHT, OR CONTINUING INTEREST.—The term "significant power, right, or continuing interest" includes, but is not limited to, the following rights with respect to the interest transferred:

(A) A right to disapprove any assignment of such interest, or any part thereof.

(B) A right to terminate at will.

(C) A right to prescribe the standards of quality of products used or sold, or of services furnished, and of the equipment and facilities used to promote such products or services.

(D) A right to require that the transferee sell or advertise only products or services of the transferor.

(E) A right to require that the transferee purchase substantially all of his supplies and equipment from the transferor.

(F) A right to payments contingent on the productivity, use, or disposition of the subject matter of the interest transferred, if such payments constitute a substantial element under the transfer agreement.

(3) TRANSFER.—The term "transfer" includes the renewal of a franchise, trademark, or trade name.

(c) TREATMENT OF CONTINGENT PAYMENTS BY TRANSFEROR.—Amounts received or accrued on account of a transfer, sale, or other disposition of a franchise, trademark, or trade name which are contingent on the productivity, use, or disposition of the franchise, trademark, or trade name transferred shall be treated as amounts received or accrued from the sale or other disposition of property which is not a capital asset.

(d) TREATMENT OF PAYMENTS BY TRANSFEREE.—

(1) CONTINGENT SERIAL PAYMENTS.—

(A) IN GENERAL.—Any amount described in subparagraph (B) which is paid or incurred during the taxable year on account of a transfer, sale, or other disposition of a franchise, trademark, or trade name shall be allowed as a deduction under section 162(a) (relating to trade or business expenses).

(B) AMOUNTS TO WHICH PARAGRAPH APPLIES.—An amount is described in this subparagraph if it—

(i) is contingent on the productivity, use, or disposition of the franchise, trademark, or trade name, and

(ii) is paid as part of a series of payments—

(I) which are payable not less frequently than annually throughout the entire term of the transfer agreement, and

(II) which are substantially equal in amount (or payable under a fixed formula).

(2) OTHER PAYMENTS.—Any amount paid or incurred on account of a transfer, sale, or other disposition of a franchise, trademark, or trade name to which paragraph (1) does not apply shall be treated as an amount chargeable to capital account.

(3) RENEWALS, ETC.—For purposes of determining the term of a transfer agreement under this section, there shall be taken into account all renewal options (and any other period for which the parties reasonably expect the agreement to be renewed).

[Sec. 1253(e)]

(e) EXCEPTION.—This section shall not apply to the transfer of a franchise to engage in professional football, basketball, baseball, or other professional sport.

[Sec. 1254]

SEC. 1254. GAIN FROM DISPOSITION OF INTEREST IN OIL, GAS, GEOTHERMAL, OR OTHER MINERAL PROPERTIES.

[Sec. 1254(a)]

(a) GENERAL RULE.—

(1) ORDINARY INCOME.—If any section 1254 property is disposed of, the lesser of—

(A) the aggregate amount of—

(i) expenditures which have been deducted by the taxpayer or any person under section 263, 616, or 617 with respect to such property and which, but for such deduction, would have been included in the adjusted basis of such property, and

(ii) the deductions for depletion under section 611 which reduced the adjusted basis of such property, or

(B) the excess of—

(i) in the case of—

(I) a sale, exchange, or involuntary conversion, the amount realized, or

(II) in the case of any other disposition, the fair market value of such property, over

(ii) the adjusted basis of such property,

shall be treated as gain which is ordinary income. Such gain shall be recognized notwithstanding any other provision of this subtitle.

(2) DISPOSITION OF PORTION OF PROPERTY.—For purposes of paragraph (1)—

(A) In the case of the disposition of a portion of section 1254 property (other than an undivided interest), the entire amount of the aggregate expenditures or deductions described in paragraph (1)(A) with respect to such property shall be treated as allocable to such portion to the extent of the amount of the gain to which paragraph (1) applies.

(B) In the case of the disposition of an undivided interest in a section 1254 property (or a portion thereof), a proportionate part of the expenditures or deductions described in paragraph (1)(A) with respect to such property shall be treated as allocable to such undivided interest to the extent of the amount of the gain to which paragraph (1) applies.

This paragraph shall not apply to any expenditures to the extent the taxpayer establishes to the satisfaction of the Secretary that such expenditures do not relate to the portion (or interest therein) disposed of.

(3) SECTION 1254 PROPERTY.—The term "section 1254 property" means any property (within the meaning of section 614) if—

(A) any expenditures described in paragraph (1)(A) are properly chargeable to such property, or

(B) the adjusted basis of such property includes adjustments for deductions for depletion under section 611.

(4) ADJUSTMENT FOR AMOUNTS INCLUDED IN GROSS INCOME UNDER SECTION 617(b)(1)(A).—The amount of the expenditures referred to in paragraph (1)(A)(i) shall be properly adjusted for amounts included in gross income under section 617(b)(1)(A).

* * *

[Sec. 1256]
SEC. 1256. SECTION 1256 CONTRACTS MARKED TO MARKET.

[Sec. 1256(a)]

(a) GENERAL RULE.—For purposes of this subtitle—

(1) each section 1256 contract held by the taxpayer at the close of the taxable year shall be treated as sold for its fair market value on the last business day of such taxable year (and any gain or loss shall be taken into account for the taxable year),

(2) proper adjustment shall be made in the amount of any gain or loss subsequently realized for gain or loss taken into account by reason of paragraph (1),

(3) any gain or loss with respect to a section 1256 contract shall be treated as—

(A) short-term capital gain or loss, to the extent of 40 percent of such gain or loss, and

(B) long-term capital gain or loss, to the extent of 60 percent of such gain or loss, and

(4) if all the offsetting positions making up any straddle consist of section 1256 contracts to which this section applies (and such straddle is not part of a larger straddle), sections 1092 and 263(g) shall not apply with respect to such straddle.

[Sec. 1256(b)]

(b) SECTION 1256 CONTRACT DEFINED.—For purposes of this section, the term "section 1256 contract" means—

(1) any regulated futures contract,

(2) any foreign currency contract,

(3) any nonequity option,

(4) any dealer equity option, and

(5) any dealer securities futures contract.

The term "section 1256 contract" shall not include any securities futures contract or option on such a contract unless such contract or option is a dealer securities futures contract.

[Sec. 1256(c)]

(c) TERMINATIONS, ETC.—

(1) IN GENERAL.—The rules of paragraphs (1), (2), and (3) of subsection (a) shall also apply to the termination (or transfer) during the taxable year of the taxpayer's obligation (or rights) with respect to a section 1256 contract by offsetting, by taking or making delivery, by exercise or being exercised, by assignment or being assigned, by lapse, or otherwise.

(2) SPECIAL RULE WHERE TAXPAYER TAKES DELIVERY ON OR EXERCISES PART OF STRADDLE.—If—

(A) 2 or more section 1256 contracts are part of a straddle (as defined in section 1092(c)), and

(B) the taxpayer takes delivery under or exercises any of such contracts,

then, for purposes of this section, each of the other such contracts shall be treated as terminated on the day on which the taxpayer took delivery.

(3) FAIR MARKET VALUE TAKEN INTO ACCOUNT.—For purposes of this subsection, fair market value at the time of the termination (or transfer) shall be taken into account.

(d) ELECTIONS WITH RESPECT TO MIXED STRADDLES.—

(1) ELECTION.—The taxpayer may elect to have this section not to apply to all section 1256 contracts which are part of a mixed straddle.

(2) TIME AND MANNER.—An election under paragraph (1) shall be made at such time and in such manner as the Secretary may by regulations prescribe.

(3) ELECTION REVOCABLE ONLY WITH CONSENT.—An election under paragraph (1) shall apply to the taxpayer's taxable year for which made and to all subsequent taxable years, unless the Secretary consents to a revocation of such election.

(4) MIXED STRADDLE.—For purposes of this subsection, the term "mixed straddle" means any straddle (as defined in section 1092(c))—

(A) at least 1 (but not all) of the positions of which are section 1256 contracts, and

(B) with respect to which each position forming part of such straddle is clearly identified, before the close of the day on which the first section 1256 contract forming part of the straddle is acquired (or such earlier time as the Secretary may prescribe by regulations), as being part of such straddle.

(e) MARK TO MARKET NOT TO APPLY TO HEDGING TRANSACTIONS.—

(1) SECTION NOT TO APPLY.—Subsection (a) shall not apply in the case of a hedging transaction.

(2) DEFINITION OF HEDGING TRANSACTION.—For purposes of this subsection, the term "hedging transaction" means any hedging transaction (as defined in section 1221(b)(2)(A)) if, before the close of the day on which such transaction was entered into (or such earlier time as the Secretary may prescribe by regulations), the taxpayer clearly identifies such transaction as being a hedging transaction.

(3) SPECIAL RULE FOR SYNDICATES.—

(A) IN GENERAL.—Notwithstanding paragraph (2), the term "hedging transaction" shall not include any transaction entered into by or for a syndicate.

(B) SYNDICATE DEFINED.—For purposes of subparagraph (A), the term "syndicate" means any partnership or other entity (other than a corporation which is not an S corporation) if more than 35 percent of the losses of such entity during the taxable year are allocable to limited partners or limited entrepreneurs (within the meaning of section 464(e)(2)).

(C) HOLDINGS ATTRIBUTABLE TO ACTIVE MANAGEMENT.—For purposes of subparagraph (B), an interest in an entity shall not be treated as held by a limited partner or a limited entrepreneur (within the meaning of section 464(e)(2))—

(i) for any period if during such period such interest is held by an individual who actively participates at all times during such period in the management of such entity,

(ii) for any period if during such period such interest is held by the spouse, children, grandchildren, and parents of an individual who actively participates at all times during such period in the management of such entity,

(iii) if such interest is held by an individual who actively participated in the management of such entity for a period of not less than 5 years,

(iv) if such interest is held by the estate of an individual who actively participated in the management of such entity or is held by the estate of an individual if with respect to such individual such interest was at any time described in clause (ii), or

(v) if the Secretary determines (by regulations or otherwise) that such interest should be treated as held by an individual who actively participates in the management of such entity, and that such entity and such interest are not used (or to be used) for tax-avoidance purposes.

For purposes of this subparagraph, a legally adopted child of an individual shall be treated as a child of such individual by blood.

(4) LIMITATION ON LOSSES FROM HEDGING TRANSACTIONS.—

(A) IN GENERAL.—

(i) LIMITATION.—Any hedging loss for a taxable year which is allocable to any limited partner or limited entrepreneur (within the meaning of paragraph (3)) shall be allowed only to the extent of the taxable income of such limited partner or entrepreneur for such taxable year attributable to the trade or business in which the hedging transactions were entered into. For purposes of the preceding sentence, taxable income shall be determined by not taking into account items attributable to hedging transactions.

(ii) CARRYOVER OF DISALLOWED LOSS.—Any hedging loss disallowed under clause (i) shall be treated as a deduction attributable to a hedging transaction allowable in the first succeeding taxable year.

(B) EXCEPTION WHERE ECONOMIC LOSS.—Subparagraph (A)(i) shall not apply to any hedging loss to the extent that such loss exceeds the aggregate unrecognized gains from hedging transactions as of the close of the taxable year attributable to the trade or business in which the hedging transactions were entered into.

(C) EXCEPTION FOR CERTAIN HEDGING TRANSACTIONS.—In the case of any hedging transaction relating to property other than stock or securities, this paragraph shall apply only in the case of a taxpayer described in section 465(a)(1).

(D) HEDGING LOSS.—The term "hedging loss" means the excess of—

(i) the deductions allowable under this chapter for the taxable year attributable to hedging transactions (determined without regard to subparagraph (A)(i)), over

(ii) income received or accrued by the taxpayer during such taxable year from such transactions.

(E) UNRECOGNIZED GAIN.—The term "unrecognized gain" has the meaning given to such term by section 1092(a)(3).

[Sec. 1256(f)]

(f) SPECIAL RULES.—

(1) DENIAL OF CAPITAL GAINS TREATMENT FOR PROPERTY IDENTIFIED AS PART OF A HEDGING TRANSACTION.—For purposes of this title, gain from any property shall in no event be considered as gain from the sale or exchange of a capital asset if such property was at any time personal property (as defined in section 1092(d)(1)) identified under subsection (e)(2)(C) by the taxpayer as being part of a hedging transaction.

(2) SUBSECTION (a)(3) NOT TO APPLY TO ORDINARY INCOME PROPERTY.—Paragraph (3) of subsection (a) shall not apply to any gain or loss which, but for such paragraph, would be ordinary income or loss.

(3) CAPITAL GAIN TREATMENT FOR TRADERS IN SECTION 1256 CONTRACTS.—

(A) IN GENERAL.—For purposes of this title, gain or loss from trading of section 1256 contracts shall be treated as gain or loss from the sale or exchange of a capital asset.

(B) EXCEPTION FOR CERTAIN HEDGING TRANSACTIONS.—Subparagraph (A) shall not apply to any section 1256 contract to the extent such contract is held for purposes of hedging property if any loss with respect to such property in the hands of the taxpayer would be ordinary loss.

(C) TREATMENT OF UNDERLYING PROPERTY.—For purposes of determining whether gain or loss with respect to any property is ordinary income or loss, the fact that the taxpayer is actively engaged in dealing in or trading section 1256 contracts related to such property shall not be taken into account.

(4) SPECIAL RULE FOR DEALER EQUITY OPTIONS AND DEALER SECURITIES FUTURES CONTRACTS OF LIMITED PARTNERS OR LIMITED ENTREPRENEURS.—In the case of any gain or loss with respect to dealer equity options, or dealer securities futures contracts, which are allocable to limited partners or limited entrepreneurs (within the meaning of subsection (e)(3))—

(A) paragraph (3) of subsection (a) shall not apply to any such gain or loss, and

(B) all such gains or losses shall be treated as short-term capital gains or losses, as the case may be.

(5) SPECIAL RULE RELATED TO LOSSES.—Section 1091 (relating to loss from wash sales of stock or securities) shall not apply to any loss taken into account by reason of paragraph (1) of subsection (a).

[Sec. 1256(g)]

(g) DEFINITIONS.—For purposes of this section—

(1) REGULATED FUTURES CONTRACTS DEFINED.—The term "regulated futures contract" means a contract—

(A) with respect to which the amount required to be deposited and the amount which may be withdrawn depends on a system of marking to market, and

(B) which is traded on or subject to the rules of a qualified board or exchange.

(2) FOREIGN CURRENCY CONTRACT DEFINED.—

(A) FOREIGN CURRENCY CONTRACT.—The term "foreign currency contract" means a contract—

(i) which requires delivery of, or the settlement of which depends on the value of, a foreign currency which is a currency in which positions are also traded through regulated futures contracts,

(ii) which is traded in the interbank market, and

(iii) which is entered into at arm's length at a price determined by reference to the price in the interbank market.

(B) REGULATIONS.—The Secretary shall prescribe such regulations as may be necessary or appropriate to carry out the purposes of subparagraph (A), including regulations excluding from the application of subparagraph (A) any contract (or type of contract) if its application thereto would be inconsistent with such purposes.

(3) NONEQUITY OPTION.—The term "nonequity option" means any listed option which is not an equity option.

(4) DEALER EQUITY OPTION.—The term "dealer equity option" means, with respect to an options dealer, any listed option which—

(A) is an equity option,

(B) is purchased or granted by such options dealer in the normal course of his activity of dealing in options, and

(C) is listed on the qualified board or exchange on which such options dealer is registered.

(5) LISTED OPTION.—The term "listed option" means any option (other than a right to acquire stock from the issuer) which is traded on (or subject to the rules of) a qualified board or exchange.

(6) EQUITY OPTION.—The term "equity option" means any option—

(A) to buy or sell stock, or

(B) the value of which is determined directly or indirectly by reference to any stock or any narrow-based security index (as defined in section 3(a)(55) of the Securities Exchange Act of 1934, as in effect on the date of the enactment of this paragraph).

The term "equity option" includes such an option on a group of stocks only if such group meets the requirements for a narrow-based security index (as so defined).

(7) QUALIFIED BOARD OR EXCHANGE.—The term "qualified board or exchange" means—

(A) a national securities exchange which is registered with the Securities and Exchange Commission,

(B) a domestic board of trade designated as a contract market by the Commodity Futures Trading Commission, or

(C) any other exchange, board of trade, or other market which the Secretary determines has rules adequate to carry out the purposes of this section.

(8) OPTIONS DEALER.—

(A) IN GENERAL.—The term "options dealer" means any person registered with an appropriate national securities exchange as a market maker or specialist in listed options.

(B) PERSONS TRADING IN OTHER MARKETS.—In any case in which the Secretary makes a determination under subparagraph (C) of paragraph (7), the term "options dealer" also includes any person whom the Secretary determines performs functions similar to the persons described in subparagraph (A). Such determinations shall be made to the extent appropriate to carry out the purposes of this section.

(9) DEALER SECURITIES FUTURES CONTRACT.—

(A) IN GENERAL.—The term "dealer securities futures contract" means, with respect to any dealer, any securities futures contract, and any option on such a contract, which—

Sec. 1256(g)

(i) is entered into by such dealer (or, in the case of an option, is purchased or granted by such dealer) in the normal course of his activity of dealing in such contracts or options, as the case may be, and

(ii) is traded on a qualified board or exchange.

(B) DEALER.—For purposes of subparagraph (A), a person shall be treated as a dealer in securities futures contracts or options on such contracts if the Secretary determines that such person performs, with respect to such contracts or options, as the case may be, functions similar to the functions performed by persons described in paragraph (8)(A). Such determination shall be made to the extent appropriate to carry out the purposes of this section.

(C) SECURITIES FUTURES CONTRACT.—The term "securities futures contract" has the meaning given to such term by section 1234B.

[Sec. 1258]

SEC. 1258. RECHARACTERIZATION OF GAIN FROM CERTAIN FINANCIAL TRANSACTIONS.

[Sec. 1258(a)]

(a) GENERAL RULE.—In the case of any gain—

(1) which (but for this section) would be treated as gain from the sale or exchange of a capital asset, and

(2) which is recognized on the disposition or other termination of any position which was held as part of a conversion transaction,

such gain (to the extent such gain does not exceed the applicable imputed income amount) shall be treated as ordinary income.

[Sec. 1258(b)]

(b) APPLICABLE IMPUTED INCOME AMOUNT.—For purposes of subsection (a), the term "applicable imputed income amount" means, with respect to any disposition or other termination referred to in subsection (a), an amount equal to—

(1) the amount of interest which would have accrued on the taxpayer's net investment in the conversion transaction for the period ending on the date of such disposition or other termination (or, if earlier, the date on which the requirements of subsection (c) ceased to be satisfied) at a rate equal to 120 percent of the applicable rate, reduced by

(2) the amount treated as ordinary income under subsection (a) with respect to any prior disposition or other termination of a position which was held as a part of such transaction.

The Secretary shall by regulations provide for such reductions in the applicable imputed income amount as may be appropriate by reason of amounts capitalized under section 263(g), ordinary income received, or otherwise.

[Sec. 1258(c)]

(c) CONVERSION TRANSACTION.—For purposes of this section, the term "conversion transaction" means any transaction—

(1) substantially all of the taxpayer's expected return from which is attributable to the time value of the taxpayer's net investment in such transaction, and

(2) which is—

(A) the holding of any property (whether or not actively traded), and the entering into a contract to sell such property (or substantially identical property) at a price determined in accordance with such contract, but only if such property was acquired and such contract was entered into on a substantially contemporaneous basis,

(B) an applicable straddle,

(C) any other transaction which is marketed or sold as producing capital gains from a transaction described in paragraph (1), or

(D) any other transaction specified in regulations prescribed by the Secretary.

Sec. 1258(c)

[Sec. 1258(d)]

(d) DEFINITIONS AND SPECIAL RULES.—For purposes of this section—

(1) APPLICABLE STRADDLE.—The term "applicable straddle" means any straddle (within the meaning of section 1092(c)); except that the term "personal property" shall include stock.

(2) APPLICABLE RATE.—The term "applicable rate" means—

(A) the applicable Federal rate determined under section 1274(d) (compounded semiannually) as if the conversion transaction were a debt instrument, or

(B) if the term of the conversion transaction is indefinite, the Federal short-term rates in effect under section 6621(b) during the period of the conversion transaction (compounded daily).

(3) TREATMENT OF BUILT-IN LOSSES.—

(A) IN GENERAL.—If any position with a built-in loss becomes part of a conversion transaction—

(i) for purposes of applying this subtitle to such position for periods after such position becomes part of such transaction, such position shall be taken into account at its fair market value as of the time it became part of such transaction, except that

(ii) upon the disposition or other termination of such position in a transaction in which gain or loss is recognized, such built-in loss shall be recognized and shall have a character determined without regard to this section.

(B) BUILT-IN LOSS.—For purposes of subparagraph (A), the term "built-in loss" means the loss (if any) which would have been realized if the position had been disposed of or otherwise terminated at its fair market value as of the time such position became part of the conversion transaction.

(4) POSITION TAKEN INTO ACCOUNT AT FAIR MARKET VALUE.—In determining the taxpayer's net investment in any conversion transaction, there shall be included the fair market value of any position which becomes part of such transaction (determined as of the time such position became part of such transaction).

(5) SPECIAL RULE FOR OPTIONS DEALERS AND COMMODITIES TRADERS.—

(A) IN GENERAL.—Subsection (a) shall not apply to transactions—

(i) of an options dealer in the normal course of the dealer's trade or business of dealing in options, or

(ii) of a commodities trader in the normal course of the trader's trade or business of trading section 1256 contracts.

(B) DEFINITIONS.—For purposes of this paragraph—

(i) OPTIONS DEALER.—The term "options dealer" has the meaning given such term by section 1256(g)(8).

(ii) COMMODITIES TRADER.—The term "commodities trader" means any person who is a member (or, except as otherwise provided in regulations, is entitled to trade as a member) of a domestic board of trade which is designated as a contract market by the Commodity Futures Trading Commission.

(C) LIMITED PARTNERS AND LIMITED ENTREPRENEURS.—In the case of any gain from a transaction recognized by an entity which is allocable to a limited partner or limited entrepreneur (within the meaning of section 464(e)(2)), subparagraph (A) shall not apply if—

(i) substantially all of the limited partner's (or limited entrepreneur's) expected return from the entity is attributable to the time value of the partner's (or entrepreneur's) net investment in such entity,

(ii) the transaction (or the interest in the entity) was marketed or sold as producing capital gains treatment from a transaction described in subsection (c)(1), or

(iii) the transaction (or the interest in the entity) is a transaction (or interest) specified in regulations prescribed by the Secretary.

[Sec. 1259]

SEC. 1259. CONSTRUCTIVE SALES TREATMENT FOR APPRECIATED FINANCIAL POSITIONS.

[Sec. 1259(a)]

(a) IN GENERAL.—If there is a constructive sale of an appreciated financial position—

(1) the taxpayer shall recognize gain as if such position were sold, assigned, or otherwise terminated at its fair market value on the date of such constructive sale (and any gain shall be taken into account for the taxable year which includes such date), and

(2) for purposes of applying this title for periods after the constructive sale—

(A) proper adjustment shall be made in the amount of any gain or loss subsequently realized with respect to such position for any gain taken into account by reason of paragraph (1), and

(B) the holding period of such position shall be determined as if such position were originally acquired on the date of such constructive sale.

[Sec. 1259(b)]

(b) APPRECIATED FINANCIAL POSITION.—For purposes of this section—

(1) IN GENERAL.—Except as provided in paragraph (2), the term "appreciated financial position" means any position with respect to any stock, debt instrument, or partnership interest if there would be gain were such position sold, assigned, or otherwise terminated at its fair market value.

(2) EXCEPTIONS.—The term "appreciated financial position" shall not include—

(A) any position with respect to debt if—

(i) the position unconditionally entitles the holder to receive a specified principal amount,

(ii) the interest payments (or other similar amounts) with respect to such position meet the requirements of clause (i) of section 860G(a)(1)(B), and

(iii) such position is not convertible (directly or indirectly) into stock of the issuer or any related person,

(B) any hedge with respect to a position described in subparagraph (A), and

(C) any position which is marked to market under any provision of this title or the regulations thereunder.

(3) POSITION.—The term "position" means an interest, including a futures or forward contract, short sale, or option.

[Sec. 1259(c)]

(c) CONSTRUCTIVE SALE.—For purposes of this section—

(1) IN GENERAL.—A taxpayer shall be treated as having made a constructive sale of an appreciated financial position if the taxpayer (or a related person)—

(A) enters into a short sale of the same or substantially identical property,

(B) enters into an offsetting notional principal contract with respect to the same or substantially identical property,

(C) enters into a futures or forward contract to deliver the same or substantially identical property,

(D) in the case of an appreciated financial position that is a short sale or a contract described in subparagraph (B) or (C) with respect to any property, acquires the same or substantially identical property, or

(E) to the extent prescribed by the Secretary in regulations, enters into 1 or more other transactions (or acquires 1 or more positions) that have substantially the same effect as a transaction described in any of the preceding subparagraphs.

(2) EXCEPTION FOR SALES OF NONPUBLICLY TRADED PROPERTY.—The term "constructive sale" shall not include any contract for sale of any stock, debt instrument, or partnership interest which is

Sec. 1259(c)

not a marketable security (as defined in section 453(f)) if the contract settles within 1 year after the date such contract is entered into.

(3) EXCEPTION FOR CERTAIN CLOSED TRANSACTIONS.—

(A) IN GENERAL.—In applying this section, there shall be disregarded any transaction (which would otherwise be treated as a constructive sale) during the taxable year if—

(i) such transaction is closed before the end of the 30th day after the close of such taxable year,

(ii) the taxpayer holds the appreciated financial position throughout the 60-day period beginning on the date such transaction is closed, and

(iii) at no time during such 60-day period is the taxpayer's risk of loss with respect to such position reduced by reason of a circumstance which would be described in section 246(c)(4) if references to stock included references to such position.

(B) TREATMENT OF POSITIONS WHICH ARE REESTABLISHED.—If—

(i) a transaction, which would otherwise be treated as a constructive sale of an appreciated financial position, is closed during the taxable year or during the 30 days thereafter, and

(ii) another substantially similar transaction is entered into during the 60-day period beginning on the date the transaction referred to in clause (i) is closed—

(I) which also would otherwise be treated as a constructive sale of such position,

(II) which is closed before the 30th day after the close of the taxable year in which the transaction referred to in clause (i) occurs, and

(III) which meets the requirements of clauses (ii) and (iii) of subparagraph (A),

the transaction referred to in clause (ii) shall be disregarded for purposes of determining whether the requirements of subparagraph (A)(iii) are met with respect to the transaction described in clause (i).

(4) RELATED PERSON.—A person is related to another person with respect to a transaction if—

(A) the relationship is described in section 267(b) or 707(b), and

(B) such transaction is entered into with a view toward avoiding the purposes of this section.

[Sec. 1259(d)]

(d) OTHER DEFINITIONS.—For purposes of this section—

(1) FORWARD CONTRACT.—The term "forward contract" means a contract to deliver a substantially fixed amount of property (including cash) for a substantially fixed price.

(2) OFFSETTING NOTIONAL PRINCIPAL CONTRACT.—The term "offsetting notional principal contract" means, with respect to any property, an agreement which includes—

(A) a requirement to pay (or provide credit for) all or substantially all of the investment yield (including appreciation) on such property for a specified period, and

(B) a right to be reimbursed for (or receive credit for) all or substantially all of any decline in the value of such property.

[Sec. 1259(e)]

(e) SPECIAL RULES.—

(1) TREATMENT OF SUBSEQUENT SALE OF POSITION WHICH WAS DEEMED SOLD.—If—

(A) there is a constructive sale of any appreciated financial position,

(B) such position is subsequently disposed of, and

(C) at the time of such disposition, the transaction resulting in the constructive sale of such position is open with respect to the taxpayer or any related person,

solely for purposes of determining whether the taxpayer has entered into a constructive sale of any other appreciated financial position held by the taxpayer, the taxpayer shall be treated as entering into such transaction immediately after such disposition. For purposes of the preceding sentence, an assignment or other termination shall be treated as a disposition.

Sec. 1259(d)

(2) CERTAIN TRUST INSTRUMENTS TREATED AS STOCK.—For purposes of this section, an interest in a trust which is actively traded (within the meaning of section 1092(d)(1)) shall be treated as stock unless substantially all (by value) of the property held by the trust is debt described in subsection (b)(2)(A).

(3) MULTIPLE POSITIONS IN PROPERTY.—If a taxpayer holds multiple positions in property, the determination of whether a specific transaction is a constructive sale and, if so, which appreciated financial position is deemed sold shall be made in the same manner as actual sales.

[Sec. 1259(f)]

(f) REGULATIONS.—The Secretary shall prescribe such regulations as may be necessary or appropriate to carry out the purposes of this section.

PART V—SPECIAL RULES FOR BONDS AND OTHER DEBT INSTRUMENTS

Subpart A—Original Issue Discount

[Sec. 1271]

SEC. 1271. TREATMENT OF AMOUNTS RECEIVED ON RETIREMENT OR SALE OR EXCHANGE OF DEBT INSTRUMENTS.

[Sec. 1271(a)]

(a) GENERAL RULE.—For purposes of this title—

(1) RETIREMENT.—Amounts received by the holder on retirement of any debt instrument shall be considered as amounts received in exchange therefor.

(2) ORDINARY INCOME ON SALE OR EXCHANGE WHERE INTENTION TO CALL BEFORE MATURITY.—

(A) IN GENERAL.—If at the time of original issue there was an intention to call a debt instrument before maturity, any gain realized on the sale or exchange thereof which does not exceed an amount equal to—

(i) the original issue discount, reduced by

(ii) the portion of original issue discount previously includible in the gross income of any holder (without regard to subsection (a)(7) or (b)(4) of section 1272 (or the corresponding provisions of prior law)),

shall be treated as ordinary income.

(B) EXCEPTIONS.—This paragraph (and paragraph (2) of subsection (c)) shall not apply to—

(i) any tax-exempt obligation, or

(ii) any holder who has purchased the debt instrument at a premium.

(3) CERTAIN SHORT-TERM GOVERNMENT OBLIGATIONS.—

(A) IN GENERAL.—On the sale or exchange of any short-term Government obligation, any gain realized which does not exceed an amount equal to the ratable share of the acquisition discount shall be treated as ordinary income.

(B) SHORT-TERM GOVERNMENT OBLIGATION.—For purposes of this paragraph, the term "short-term Government obligation" means any obligation of the United States or any of its possessions, or of a State or any political subdivision thereof, or of the District of Columbia, which has a fixed maturity date not more than 1 year from the date of issue. Such term does not include any tax-exempt obligation.

(C) ACQUISITION DISCOUNT.—For purposes of this paragraph, the term "acquisition discount" means the excess of the stated redemption price at maturity over the taxpayer's basis for the obligation.

(D) RATABLE SHARE.—For purposes of this paragraph, except as provided in subparagraph (E) the ratable share of the acquisition discount is an amount which bears the same ratio to such discount as—

(i) the number of days which the taxpayer held the obligation, bears to

(ii) the number of days after the date the taxpayer acquired the obligation and up to (and including) the date of its maturity.

(E) ELECTION OF ACCRUAL ON BASIS OF CONSTANT INTEREST RATE.—At the election of the taxpayer with respect to any obligation, the ratable share of the aquisition discount is the portion of the acquisition discount accruing while the taxpayer held the obligation determined (under regulations prescribed by the Secretary) on the basis of—

(i) the taxpayer's yield to maturity based on the taxpayer's cost of acquiring the obligation, and

(ii) compounding daily.

An election under this subparagraph, once made with respect to any obligation, shall be irrevocable.

(4) CERTAIN SHORT-TERM NONGOVERNMENT OBLIGATIONS.—

(A) IN GENERAL.—On the sale or exchange of any short-term nongovernment obligation, any gain realized which does not exceed an amount equal to the ratable share of the original issue discount shall be treated as ordinary income.

(B) SHORT-TERM NONGOVERNMENT OBLIGATION.—For purposes of this paragraph, the term "short-term nongovernment obligation" means any obligation which—

(i) has a fixed maturity date not more than 1 year from the date of the issue, and

(ii) is not a short-term Government obligation (as defined in paragraph (3)(B) without regard to the last sentence thereof).

(C) RATABLE SHARE.—For purposes of this paragraph, except as provided in subparagraph (D), the ratable share of the original issue discount is an amount which bears the same ratio to such discount as—

(i) the number of days which the taxpayer held the obligation, bears to

(ii) the number of days after the date of original issue and up to (and including) the date of its maturity.

(D) ELECTION OF ACCRUAL ON BASIS OF CONSTANT INTEREST RATE.—At the election of the taxpayer with respect to any obligation, the ratable share of the original issue discount is the portion of the original issue discount accruing while the taxpayer held the obligation determined (under regulations prescribed by the Secretary) on the basis of—

(i) the yield to maturity based on the issue price of the obligation, and

(ii) compounding daily.

Any election under this subparagraph, once made with respect to any obligation, shall be irrevocable.

[Sec. 1271(b)]

(b) EXCEPTION FOR CERTAIN OBLIGATIONS.—

(1) IN GENERAL.—This section shall not apply to—

(A) any obligation issued by a natural person before June 9, 1997, and

(B) any obligation issued before July 2, 1982, by an issuer which is not a corporation and is not a government or political subdivision thereof.

(2) TERMINATION.—Paragraph (1) shall not apply to any obligation purchased (within the meaning of section 1272(d)(1)) after June 8, 1997.

* * *

[Sec. 1271(d)]

(d) DOUBLE INCLUSION IN INCOME NOT REQUIRED.—This section and sections 1272 and 1286 shall not require the inclusion of any amount previously includible in gross income.

Sec. 1271(b)

[Sec. 1272]

SEC. 1272. CURRENT INCLUSION IN INCOME OF ORIGINAL ISSUE DISCOUNT.

[Sec. 1272(a)]

(a) ORIGINAL ISSUE DISCOUNT ON DEBT INSTRUMENTS ISSUED AFTER JULY 1, 1982, INCLUDED IN INCOME ON BASIS OF CONSTANT INTEREST RATE.—

(1) GENERAL RULE.—For purposes of this title, there shall be included in the gross income of the holder of any debt instrument having original issue discount issued after July 1, 1982, an amount equal to the sum of the daily portions of the original issue discount for each day during the taxable year on which such holder held such debt instrument.

(2) EXCEPTIONS.—Paragraph (1) shall not apply to—

(A) TAX-EXEMPT OBLIGATIONS.—Any tax-exempt obligation.

(B) UNITED STATES SAVINGS BONDS.—Any United States savings bond.

(C) SHORT-TERM OBLIGATIONS.—Any debt instrument which has a fixed maturity date not more than 1 year from the date of issue.

(D) OBLIGATIONS ISSUED BY NATURAL PERSONS BEFORE MARCH 2, 1984.—Any obligation issued by a natural person before March 2, 1984.

(E) LOANS BETWEEN NATURAL PERSONS.—

(i) IN GENERAL.—Any loan made by a natural person to another natural person if—

(I) such loan is not made in the course of a trade or business of the lender, and

(II) the amount of such loan (when increased by the outstanding amount of prior loans by such natural person to such other natural person) does not exceed $10,000.

(ii) CLAUSE (i) NOT TO APPLY WHERE TAX AVOIDANCE A PRINCIPAL PURPOSE.—Clause (i) shall not apply if the loan has as 1 of its principal purposes the avoidance of any Federal tax.

(iii) TREATMENT OF HUSBAND AND WIFE.—For purposes of this subparagraph, a husband and wife shall be treated as 1 person. The preceding sentence shall not apply where the spouses lived apart at all times during the taxable year in which the loan is made.

(3) DETERMINATION OF DAILY PORTIONS.—For purposes of paragraph (1), the daily portion of the original issue discount on any debt instrument shall be determined by allocating to each day in any accrual period its ratable portion of the increase during such accrual period in the adjusted issue price of the debt instrument. For purposes of the preceding sentence, the increase in the adjusted issue price for any accrual period shall be an amount equal to the excess (if any) of—

(A) the product of—

(i) the adjusted issue price of the debt instrument at the beginning of such accrual period, and

(ii) the yield to maturity (determined on the basis of compounding at the close of each accrual period and properly adjusted for the length of the accrual period), over

(B) the sum of the amounts payable as interest on such debt instrument during such accrual period.

(4) ADJUSTED ISSUE PRICE.—For purposes of this subsection, the adjusted issue price of any debt instrument at the beginning of any accrual period is the sum of—

(A) the issue price of such debt instrument, plus

(B) the adjustments under this subsection to such issue price for all periods before the first day of such accrual period.

(5) ACCRUAL PERIOD.—Except as otherwise provided in regulations prescribed by the Secretary, the term "accrual period" means a 6-month period (or shorter period from the date of original issue of the debt instrument) which ends on a day in the calendar year corresponding to the maturity date of the debt instrument or the date 6 months before such maturity date.

(6) DETERMINATION OF DAILY PORTIONS WHERE PRINCIPAL SUBJECT TO ACCELERATION.—

(A) IN GENERAL.—In the case of any debt instrument to which this paragraph applies, the daily portion of the original issue discount shall be determined by allocating to each day in any accrual period its ratable portion of the excess (if any) of—

Sec. 1272(a)

(i) the sum of (I) the present value determined under subparagraph (B) of all remaining payments under the debt instrument as of the close of such period, and (II) the payments during the accrual period of amounts included in the stated redemption price of the debt instrument, over

(ii) the adjusted issue price of such debt instrument at the beginning of such period.

(B) DETERMINION OF PRESENT VALUE—For purposes of subparagraph (A), the present value shall be determined on the basis of—

(i) the original yield to maturity (determined on the basis of compounding at the close of each accrual period and properly adjusted for the length of the accrual period),

(ii) events which have occurred before the close of the accrual period, and

(iii) a prepayment assumption determined in the manner prescribed by regulations.

(C) DEBT INSTRUMENTS TO WHICH PARAGRAPH APPLIES.—This paragraph applies to—

(i) any regular interest in a REMIC or qualified mortgage held by a REMIC,

(ii) any other debt instrument if payments under such debt instrument may be accelerated by reason of prepayments of other obligations securing such debt instrument (or, to the extent provided in regulations, by reason of other events), or

(iii) any pool of debt instruments the yield on which may be affected by reason of prepayments (or to the extent provided in regulations, by reason of other events).

To the extent provided in regulations prescribed by the Secretary, in the case of a small business engaged in the trade or business of selling tangible personal property at retail, clause (iii) shall not apply to debt instruments incurred in the ordinary course of such trade or business while held by such business.

(7) REDUCTION WHERE SUBSEQUENT HOLDER PAYS ACQUISITION PREMIUM.—

(A) REDUCTION.—For purposes of this subsection, in the case of any purchase after its original issue of a debt instrument to which this subsection applies, the daily portion for any day shall be reduced by an amount equal to the amount which would be the daily portion for such day (without regard to this paragraph) multiplied by the fraction determined under subparagraph (B).

(B) DETERMINATION OF FRACTION.—For purposes of subparagraph (A), the fraction determined under this subparagraph is a fraction—

(i) the numerator of which is the excess (if any) of—

(I) the cost of such debt instrument incurred by the purchaser, over

(II) the issue price of such debt instrument, increased by the portion of original issue discount previously includible in the gross income of any holder (computed without regard to this paragraph), and

(ii) the denominator of which is the sum of the daily portions for such debt instrument for all days after the date of such purchase and ending on the stated maturity date (computed without regard to this paragraph).

* * *

[Sec. 1272(c)]

(c) EXCEPTIONS.—This section shall not apply to any holder—

(1) who has purchased the debt instrument at a premium, or

(2) which is a life insurance company to which section 811(b) applies.

[Sec. 1272(d)]

(d) DEFINITION AND SPECIAL RULE.—

(1) PURCHASE DEFINED.—For purposes of this section, the term "purchase" means—

(A) any acquisition of a debt instrument, where

(B) the basis of the debt instrument is not determined in whole or in part by reference to the adjusted basis of such debt instrument in the hands of the person from whom acquired.

(2) BASIS ADJUSTMENT.—The basis of any debt instrument in the hands of the holder thereof shall be increased by the amount included in his gross income pursuant to this section.

Sec. 1272(c)

[Sec. 1273]

SEC. 1273. DETERMINATION OF AMOUNT OF ORIGINAL ISSUE DISCOUNT.

[Sec. 1273(a)]

(a) GENERAL RULE.—for purposes of this subpart—

(1) IN GENERAL.—The term "original issue discount" means the excess (if any) of—

(A) the stated redemption price at maturity, over

(B) the issue price.

(2) STATED REDEMPTION PRICE AT MATURITY.—The term "stated redemption price at maturity" means the amount fixed by the last modification of the purchase agreement and includes interest and other amounts payable at that time (other than any interest based on a fixed rate, and payable unconditionally at fixed periodic intervals of 1 year or less during the entire term of the debt instrument).

(3) ¼ OF 1 PERCENT DE MINIMIS RULE.—If the original issue discount determined under paragraph (1) is less than—

(A) ¼ of 1 percent of the stated redemption price at maturity, multiplied by

(B) the number of complete years to maturity,

then the original issue discount shall be treated as zero.

[Sec. 1273(b)]

(b) ISSUE PRICE.—For purposes of this subpart—

(1) PUBLICLY OFFERED DEBT INSTRUMENTS NOT ISSUED FOR PROPERTY.—In the case of any issue of debt instruments—

(A) publicly offered, and

(B) not issued for property,

the issue price is the initial offering price to the public (excluding bond houses and brokers) at which price a substantial amount of such debt instruments was sold.

(2) OTHER DEBT INSTRUMENTS NOT ISSUED FOR PROPERTY.—In the case of any isssue of debt instruments not issued for property and not publicly offered, the issue price of each such instrument is the price paid by the first buyer of such debt instrument.

(3) DEBT INSTRUMENTS ISSUED FOR PROPERTY WHERE THERE IS PUBLIC TRADING.—In the case of a debt instrument which is issued for property and which—

(A) is part of an issue a portion of which is traded on an established securities market, or

(B)(i) is issued for stock or securities which are traded on an established securities market, or

(ii) to the extent provided in regulations, is issued for property (other than stock or securities) of a kind regularly traded on an established market,

the issue price of such debt instrument shall be the fair market value of such property.

(4) OTHER CASES.—Except in any case—

(A) to which paragraph (1), (2), or (3) of this subsection applies, or

(B) to which section 1274 applies,

the issue price of a debt instrument which is issued for property shall be the stated redemption price at maturity.

(5) PROPERTY.—In applying this subsection, the term "property" includes services and the right to use property, but such term does not include money.

[Sec. 1273(c)]

(c) SPECIAL RULES FOR APPLYING SUBSECTION (b).—for purposes of subsection (b)—

(1) INITIAL OFFERING PRICE; PRICE PAID BY THE FIRST BUYER.—The terms "initial offering price" and "price paid by the first buyer" include the aggregate payments made by the purchaser under the purchase agreement, including modifications thereof.

Sec. 1273(c)

(2) TREATMENT OF INVESTMENT UNITS.—In the case of any debt instrument and an option, security, or other property issued together as an investment unit—

(A) the issue price for such unit shall be determined in accordance with the rules of this subsection and subsection (b) as if it were a debt instrument,

(B) the issue price determined for such unit shall be allocated to each element of such unit on the basis of the relationship of the fair market value of such element to the fair market value of all elements in such unit, and

(C) the issue price of any debt instrument included in such unit shall be the portion of the issue price of the unit allocated to the debt instrument under subparagraph (B).

[Sec. 1274]

SEC 1274. DETERMINATION OF ISSUE PRICE IN THE CASE OF CERTAIN DEBT INSTRUMENTS ISSUED FOR PROPERTY.

[Sec. 1274(a)]

(a) IN GENERAL.—In the case of any debt instrument to which this section applies, for purposes of this subpart, the issue price shall be—

(1) where there is adequate stated interest, the stated principal amount, or

(2) in any other case, the imputed principal amount.

[Sec. 1274(b)]

(b) IMPUTED PRINCIPAL AMOUNT.—For purposes of this section—

(1) IN GENERAL.—Except as provided in paragraph (3), the imputed principal amount of any debt instrument shall be equal to the sum of the present values of all payments due under such debt instrument.

(2) DETERMINATION OF PRESENT VALUE.—For purposes of paragraph (1), the present value of a payment shall be determined in the manner provided by regulations prescribed by the Secretary—

(A) as of the date of the sale or exchange, and

(B) by using a discount rate equal to the applicable Federal rate, compounded semiannually.

(3) FAIR MARKET VALUE RULE IN POTENTIALLY ABUSIVE SITUATIONS.—

(A) IN GENERAL.—In the case of any potentially abusive situation, the imputed principal amount of any debt instrument received in exchange for property shall be the fair market value of such property adjusted to take into account other consideration involved in the transaction.

(B) POTENTIALLY ABUSIVE SITUATION DEFINED.—For purposes of subparagraph (A), the term "potentially abusive situation" means—

(i) a tax shelter (as defined in section 6662(d)(2)(C)(iii), and

(ii) any other situation which, by reason of—

(I) recent sales transactions,

(II) nonrecourse financing,

(III) financing with a term in excess of the economic life of the property, or

(IV) other circumstances,

is of a type which the Secretary specifies by regulations as having potential for tax avoidance.

[Sec. 1274(c)]

(c) DEBT INSTRUMENTS TO WHICH SECTION APPLIES.—

(1) IN GENERAL.—Except as otherwise provided in this subsection, this section shall apply to any debt instrument given in consideration for the sale or exchange of property if—

(A) the stated redemption price at maturity for such debt instrument exceeds—

(i) where there is adequate stated interest, the stated principal amount, or

Sec. 1274

(ii) in any other case, the imputed principal amount of such debt instrument determined under subsection (b), and

(B) some or all of the payments due under such debt instrument are due more than 6 months after the date of such sale or exchange.

(2) ADEQUATE STATED INTEREST.—For purposes of this section, there is adequate stated interest with respect to any debt instrument if the stated principal amount for such debt instrument is less than or equal to the imputed principal amount of such debt instrument determined under subsection (b).

(3) EXCEPTIONS.—This section shall not apply to—

(A) SALES FOR $1,000,000 OR LESS OF FARMS BY INDIVIDUALS OR SMALL BUSINESSES.—

(i) IN GENERAL.—Any debt instrument arising from the sale or exchange of a farm (within the meaning of section 6420(c)(2))—

(I) by an individual, estate, or testamentary trust,

(II) by a corporation which as of the date of the sale or exchange is a small business corporation (as defined in section 1244(c)(3)), or

(III) by a partnership which as of the date of the sale or exchange meets requirements similar to those of section 1244(c)(3).

(ii) $1,000,000 LIMITATION.—Clause (i) shall apply only if it can be determined at the time of the sale or exchange that the sales price cannot exceed $1,000,000. For purposes of the preceding sentence, all sales and exchanges which are part of the same transaction (or a series of related transactions) shall be treated as 1 sale or exchange.

(B) SALES OF PRINCIPAL RESIDENCES.—Any debt instrument arising from the sale or exchange by an individual of his principal residence (within the meaning of section 121).

(C) SALES INVOLVING TOTAL PAYMENTS OF $250,000 OR LESS.—

(i) IN GENERAL.—Any debt instrument arising from the sale or exchange of property if the sum of the following amounts does not exceed $250,000:

(I) the aggregate amount of the payments due under such debt instrument and all other debt instruments received as consideration for the sale or exchange, and

(II) the aggregate amount of any other consideration to be received for the sale or exchange.

(ii) CONSIDERATION OTHER THAN DEBT INSTRUMENT TAKEN INTO ACCOUNT AT FAIR MARKET VALUE.—For purposes of clause (i), any consideration (other than a debt instrument) shall be taken into account at its fair market value.

(iii) AGGREGATION OF TRANSACTIONS.—For purposes of this subparagraph, all sales and exchanges which are part of the same transaction (or a series of related transactions) shall be treated as 1 sale or exchange.

(D) DEBT INSTRUMENTS WHICH ARE PUBLICLY TRADED OR ISSUED FOR PUBLICLY TRADED PROPERTY.—Any debt instrument to which section 1273(b)(3) applies.

(E) CERTAIN SALES OF PATENTS.—In the case of any transfer described in section 1235(a) (relating to sale or exchange of patents), any amount contingent on the productivity, use, or disposition of the property transferred.

(F) SALES OR EXCHANGES TO WHICH SECTION 483(e) APPLIES.—Any debt instrument to the extent section 483(e) (relating to certain land transfers between related persons) applies to such instrument.

(4) EXCEPTION FOR ASSUMPTIONS.—If any person—

(A) in connection with the sale or exchange of property, assumes any debt instrument, or

(B) acquires any property subject to any debt instrument,

in determining whether this section or section 483 applies to such debt instrument, such assumption (or such acquisition) shall not be taken into account unless the terms and conditions of such debt instrument are modified (or the nature of the transaction is changed) in connection with the assumption (or acquisition).

Sec. 1274(c)

(d) DETERMINATION OF APPLICABLE FEDERAL RATE.—For purposes of this section—

(1) APPLICABLE FEDERAL RATE.—

(A) IN GENERAL.—

In the case of a debt instrument with a term of:	The applicable Federal rate is:
Not over 3 years	The Federal short-term rate.
Over 3 years but not over 9 years	The Federal mid-term rate.
Over 9 years	The Federal long-term rate.

(B) DETERMINATION OF RATES.—During each calendar month, the Secretary shall determine the Federal short-term rate, mid-term rate, and long-term rate which shall apply during the following calendar month.

(C) FEDERAL RATE FOR ANY CALENDAR MONTH.—For purposes of this paragraph—

(i) FEDERAL SHORT-TERM RATE.—The Federal short-term rate shall be the rate determined by the Secretary based on the average market yield (during any 1-month period selected by the Secretary and ending in the calendar month in which the determination is made) on outstanding marketable obligations of the United States with remaining periods to maturity of 3 years or less.

(ii) FEDERAL MID-TERM AND LONG-TERM RATES.—The Federal mid-term and long-term rate shall be determined in accordance with the principles of clause (i).

(D) LOWER RATE PERMITTED IN CERTAIN CASES.—The Secretary may by regulations permit a rate to be used with respect to any debt instrument which is lower than the applicable Federal rate if the taxpayer establishes to the satisfaction of the Secretary that such lower rate is based on the same principles as the applicable Federal rate and is appropriate for the term of such instrument.

(2) LOWEST 3-MONTH RATE APPLICABLE TO ANY SALE OR EXCHANGE.—

(A) IN GENERAL.—In the case of any sale or exchange, the applicable Federal rate shall be the lowest 3-month rate.

(B) LOWEST 3-MONTH RATE.—For purposes of subparagraph (A), the term "lowest 3-month rate" means the lowest of the applicable Federal rates in effect for any month in the 3-calendar-month period ending with the 1st calendar month in which there is a binding contract in writing for such sale or exchange.

(3) TERM OF DEBT INSTRUMENT.—In determining the term of a debt instrument for purposes of this subsection, under regulations prescribed by the Secretary, there shall be taken into account options to renew or extend.

[Sec. 1274(e)]

(e) 110 PERCENT RATE WHERE SALE-LEASEBACK INVOLVED.—

(1) IN GENERAL.—In the case of any debt instrument to which this subsection applies, the discount rate used under subsection (b)(2)(B) or section 483(b) shall be 110 percent of the applicable Federal rate, compounded semiannually.

(2) LOWER DISCOUNT RATES SHALL NOT APPLY.—Section 1274A shall not apply to any debt instrument to which this subsection applies.

(3) DEBT INSTRUMENTS TO WHICH THIS SUBSECTION APPLIES.—This subsection shall apply to any debt instrument given in consideration for the sale or exchange of any property if, pursuant to a plan, the transferor or any related person leases a portion of such property after such sale or exchange.

[*Caution: Pursuant to Section 1274A(d)(2), each dollar amount in Section 1274A is adjusted for taxable years beginning after 1989 to reflect increases in the Consumer Price Index. The adjusted amounts applicable to taxable years beginning in 2003 are provided at page xii.*]

[Sec. 1274A]

SEC. 1274A. SPECIAL RULES FOR CERTAIN TRANSACTIONS WHERE STATED PRINCIPAL AMOUNT DOES NOT EXCEED $2,800,000.

[Sec. 1274A(a)]

(a) LOWER DISCOUNT RATE.—In the case of any qualified debt instrument, the discount rate used for purposes of sections 483 and 1274 shall not exceed 9 percent, compounded semiannually.

[Sec. 1274A(b)]

(b) QUALIFIED DEBT INSTRUMENT DEFINED.—For purposes of this section, the term "qualified debt instrument" means any debt instrument given in consideration for the sale or exchange of property (other than new section 38 property within the meaning of section 48(b), as in effect on the day before the date of enactment of the Revenue Reconciliation Act of 1990) if the stated principal amount of such instrument does not exceed $2,800,000.

[Sec. 1274A(c)]

(c) ELECTION TO USE CASH METHOD WHERE STATED PRINCIPAL AMOUNT DOES NOT EXCEED $2,000,000.—

(1) IN GENERAL.—In the case of any cash method debt instrument—

(A) section 1274 shall not apply, and

(B) interest on such debt instrument shall be taken into account by both the borrower and the lender under the cash receipts and disbursements method of accounting.

(2) CASH METHOD DEBT INSTRUMENT.—For purposes of paragraph (1), the term "cash method debt instrument" means any qualified debt instrument if—

(A) the stated principal amount does not exceed $2,000,000,

(B) the lender does not use an accrual method of accounting and is not a dealer with respect to the property sold or exchanged,

(C) section 1274 would have applied to such instrument but for an election under this subsection, and

(D) an election under this subsection is jointly made with respect to such debt instrument by the borrower and lender.

(3) SUCCESSORS BOUND BY ELECTION.—

(A) IN GENERAL.—Except as provided in subparagraph (B), paragraph (1) shall apply to any successor to the borrower or lender with respect to a cash method debt instrument.

(B) EXCEPTION WHERE LENDER TRANSFERS DEBT INSTRUMENT TO ACCRUAL METHOD TAXPAYER.—If the lender (or any successor) transfers any cash method debt instrument to a taxpayer who uses an accrual method of accounting, this paragraph shall not apply with respect to such instrument for periods after such transfer.

(4) FAIR MARKET VALUE RULE IN POTENTIALLY ABUSIVE SITUATIONS.—In the case of any cash method debt instrument, section 483 shall be applied as if it included provisions similar to the provisions of section 1274(b)(3).

[Sec. 1274A(d)]

(d) OTHER SPECIAL RULES.—

(1) AGGREGATION RULES.—For purposes of this section—

(A) all sales or exchanges which are part of the same transaction (or a series of related transactions) shall be treated as 1 sale or exchange, and

(B) all debt instruments arising from the same transaction (or a series of related transactions) shall be treated as 1 debt instrument.

Sec. 1274A(d)

(2) INFLATION ADJUSTMENTS.—

(A) IN GENERAL.—In the case of any debt instrument arising out of a sale or exchange during any calendar year after 1989, each dollar amount contained in the preceding provisions of this section shall be increased by the inflation adjustment for such calendar year. Any increase under the preceding sentence shall be rounded to the nearest multiple of $100 (or, if such increase is a multiple of $50, such increase shall be increased to the nearest multiple of $100).

(B) INFLATION ADJUSTMENT.—For purposes of subparagraph (A), the inflation adjustment for any calendar year is the percentage (if any) by which—

(i) the CPI for the preceding calendar year exceeds

(ii) the CPI for calendar year 1988.

For purposes of the preceding sentence, the CPI for any calendar year is the average of the Consumer Price Index as of the close of the 12-month period ending on September 30 of such calendar year.

[Sec. 1274A(e)]

(e) REGULATIONS.—The Secretary shall prescribe such regulations as may be necessary to carry out the purposes of this subsection, including—

(1) regulations coordinating the provisions of this section with other provisions of this title,

(2) regulations necessary to prevent the avoidance of tax through the abuse of the provisions of subsection (c), and

(3) regulations relating to the treatment of transfers of cash method debt instruments.

[Sec. 1275]
SEC. 1275. OTHER DEFINITIONS AND SPECIAL RULES.

[Sec. 1275(a)]

(a) DEFINITIONS.—For purposes of this subpart—

(1) DEBT INSTRUMENT.—

(A) IN GENERAL.—Except as provided in subparagraph (B), the term "debt instrument" means a bond, debenture, note, or certificate or other evidence of indebtedness.

(B) EXCEPTION FOR CERTAIN ANNUITY CONTRACTS.—The term "debt instrument" shall not include any annuity contract to which section 72 applies and which—

(i) depends (in whole or in substantial part) on the life expectancy of 1 or more individuals, or

(ii) is issued by an insurance company subject to tax under subchapter L (or by an entity described in section 501(c) and exempt from tax under section 501(a) which would be subject to tax under subchapter L were it not so exempt)—

(I) in a transaction in which there is no consideration other than cash or another annuity contract meeting the requirements of this clause,

(II) pursuant to the exercise of an election under an insurance contract by a beneficiary thereof on the death of the insured party under such contract, or

(III) in a transaction involving a qualified pension or employee benefit plan.

(2) ISSUE DATE.—

(A) PUBLICLY OFFERED DEBT INSTRUMENTS.—In the case of any debt instrument which is publicly offered, the term "date of original issue" means the date on which the issue was first issued to the public.

(B) ISSUES NOT PUBLICLY OFFERED AND NOT ISSUED FOR PROPERTY.—In the case of any debt instrument to which section 1273(b)(2) applies, the term "date of original issue" means the date on which the debt instrument was sold by the issuer.

(C) OTHER DEBT INSTRUMENTS.—In the case of any debt instrument not described in subparagraph (A) or (B), the term "date of original issue" means the date on which the debt instrument was issued in a sale or exchange.

(3) TAX-EXEMPT OBLIGATION.—The term "tax-exempt obligation" means any obligation if—

(A) the interest on such obligation is not includible in gross income under section 103, or

(B) the interest on such obligation is exempt from tax (without regard to the identity of the holder) under any other provision of law.

(4) TREATMENT OF OBLIGATIONS DISTRIBUTED BY CORPORATIONS.—Any debt obligation of a corporation distributed by such corporation with respect to its stock shall be treated as if it had been issued by such corporation for property.

[Sec. 1275(b)]

(b) TREATMENT OF BORROWER IN THE CASE OF CERTAIN LOANS FOR PERSONAL USE.—

(1) SECTIONS 1274 AND 483 NOT TO APPLY.—In the case of the obligor under any debt instrument given in consideration for the sale or exchange of property, sections 1274 and 483 shall not apply if such property is personal use property.

(2) ORIGINAL ISSUE DISCOUNT DEDUCTED ON CASH BASIS IN CERTAIN CASES.—In the case of any debt instrument, if—

(A) such instrument—

(i) is incurred in connection with the acquisition or carrying of personal use property, and

(ii) has original issue discount (determined after the application of paragraph (1)), and

(B) the obligor under such instrument uses the cash receipts and disbursements method of accounting,

notwithstanding section 163(e), the original issue discount on such instrument shall be deductible only when paid.

(3) PERSONAL USE PROPERTY.—For purposes of this subsection, the term "personal use property" means any property substantially all of the use of which by the taxpayer is not in connection with a trade or business of the taxpayer or an activity described in section 212. The determination of whether property is described in the preceding sentence shall be made as of the time of issuance of the debt instrument.

[Sec. 1275(c)]

(c) INFORMATION REQUIREMENTS.—

(1) INFORMATION REQUIRED TO BE SET FORTH ON INSTRUMENT.—

(A) IN GENERAL.—In the case of any debt instrument having original issue discount, the Secretary may by regulations require that—

(i) the amount of the original issue discount, and

(ii) the issue date,

be set forth on such instrument.

(B) SPECIAL RULE FOR INSTRUMENTS NOT PUBLICLY OFFERED.—In the case of any issue of debt instruments not publicly offered, the regulations prescribed under subparagraph (A) shall not require the information to be set forth on the debt instrument before any disposition of such instrument by the first buyer.

(2) INFORMATION REQUIRED TO BE SUBMITTED TO SECRETARY.—In the case of any issue of publicly offered debt instruments having original issue discount, the issuer shall (at such time and in such manner as the Secretary shall by regulation prescribe) furnish the Secretary the following information:

(A) The amount of the original issue discount.

(B) The issue date.

(C) Such other information with respect to the issue as the Secretary may by regulations require.

For purposes of the preceding sentence, any person who makes a public offering of stripped bonds (or stripped coupons) shall be treated as the issuer of a publicly offered debt instrument having original issue discount.

(3) EXCEPTIONS.—This subsection shall not apply to any obligation referred to in section 1272(a)(2) (relating to exceptions from current inclusion of original issue discount).

(4) CROSS REFERENCE.—

For civil penalty for failure to meet requirements of this subsection, see section 6706.

Sec. 1275(c)

[Sec. 1275(d)]

(d) REGULATION AUTHORITY.—The Secretary may prescribe regulations providing that where, by reason of varying rates of interest, put or call options, indefinite maturities, contingent payments, assumptions of debt instruments, or other circumstances, the tax treatment under this subpart (or section 163(e)) does not carry out the purposes of this subpart (or section 163(e)), such treatment shall be modified to the extent appropriate to carry out the purposes of this subpart (or section 163(e)).

Subpart B—Market Discount on Bonds

[Sec. 1276]

SEC. 1276. DISPOSITION GAIN REPRESENTING ACCRUED MARKET DISCOUNT TREATED AS ORDINARY INCOME.

[Sec. 1276(a)]

(a) ORDINARY INCOME.—

(1) IN GENERAL.—Except as otherwise provided in this section, gain on the disposition of any market discount bond shall be treated as ordinary income to the extent it does not exceed the accrued market discount on such bond. Such gain shall be recognized notwithstanding any other provision of this subtitle.

(2) DISPOSITIONS OTHER THAN SALES, ETC.—For purposes of paragraph (1), a person disposing of any market discount bond in any transaction other than a sale, exchange, or involuntary conversion shall be treated as realizing an amount equal to the fair market value of the bond.

(3) TREATMENT OF PARTIAL PRINCIPAL PAYMENTS.—

(A) IN GENERAL.—Any partial principal payment on a market discount bond shall be included in gross income as ordinary income to the extent such payment does not exceed the accrued market discount on such bond.

(B) ADJUSTMENT.—If subparagraph (A) applies to any partial principal payment on any market discount bond, for purposes of applying this section to any disposition of (or subsequent partial principal payment on) such bond, the amount of accrued market discount shall be reduced by the amount of such partial principal payment included in gross income under subparagraph (A).

(4) GAIN TREATED AS INTEREST FOR CERTAIN PURPOSES.—Except for purposes of sections 103, 871(a), 881, 1441, 1442, and 6049 (and such other provisions as may be specified in regulations), any amount treated as ordinary income under paragraph (1) or (3) shall be treated as interest for purposes of this title.

[Sec. 1276(b)]

(b) ACCRUED MARKET DISCOUNT.—For purposes of this section—

(1) RATABLE ACCRUAL.—Except as otherwise provided in this subsection or subsection (c), the accrued market discount on any bond shall be an amount which bears the same ratio to the market discount on such bond as—

(A) the number of days which the taxpayer held the bond, bears to

(B) the number of days after the date the taxpayer acquired the bond and up to (and including) the date of its maturity.

(2) ELECTION OF ACCRUAL ON BASIS OF CONSTANT INTEREST RATE (IN LIEU OF RATABLE ACCRUAL).—

(A) IN GENERAL.—At the election of the taxpayer with respect to any bond, the accrued market discount on such bond shall be the aggregate amount which would have been includible in the gross income of the taxpayer under section 1272(a) (determined without regard to paragraph (2) thereof) with respect to such bond for all periods during which the bond was held by the taxpayer if such bond had been—

(i) originally issued on the date on which such bond was acquired by the taxpayer,

(ii) for an issue price equal to the basis of the taxpayer in such bond immediately after its acquisition.

(B) COORDINATION WHERE BOND HAS ORIGINAL ISSUE DISCOUNT.—In the case of any bond having original issue discount, for purposes of applying subparagraph (A)—

(i) the stated redemption price at maturity of such bond shall be treated as equal to its revised issue price, and

(ii) the determination of the portion of the original issue discount which would have been includible in the gross income of the taxpayer under section 1272(a) shall be made under regulations prescribed by the Secretary.

(C) ELECTION IRREVOCABLE.—An election under subparagraph (A), once made with respect to any bond, shall be irrevocable.

(3) SPECIAL RULE WHERE PARTIAL PRINCIPAL PAYMENTS.—In the case of a bond the principal of which may be paid in 2 or more payments, the amount of accrued market discount shall be determined under regulations prescribed by the Secretary.

[Sec. 1276(c)]

(c) TREATMENT OF NONRECOGNITION TRANSACTIONS.—Under regulations prescribed by the Secretary—

(1) TRANSFERRED BASIS PROPERTY.—If a market discount bond is transferred in a nonrecognition transaction and such bond is transferred basis property in the hands of the transferee, for purposes of determining the amount of the accrued market discount with respect to the transferee—

(A) the transferee shall be treated as having acquired the bond on the date on which it was acquired by the transferor for an amount equal to the basis of the transferor, and

(B) proper adjustments shall be made for gain recognized by the transferor on such transfer (and for any original issue discount or market discount included in the gross income of the transferor).

(2) EXCHANGED BASIS PROPERTY.—If any market discount bond is disposed of by the taxpayer in a nonrecognition transaction and paragraph (1) does not apply to such transaction, any accrued market discount determined with respect to the property disposed of to the extent not theretofore treated as ordinary income under subsection (a)—

(A) shall be treated as accrued market discount with respect to the exchanged basis property received by the taxpayer in such transaction if such property is a market discount bond, and

(B) shall be treated as ordinary income on the disposition of the exchanged basis property received by the taxpayer in such exchange if such property is not a market discount bond.

(3) PARAGRAPH (1) TO APPLY TO CERTAIN DISTRIBUTIONS BY CORPORATIONS OR PARTNERSHIPS.—For purposes of paragraph (1), if the basis of any market discount bond in the hands of a transferee is determined under section 732(a), or 732(b), such property shall be treated as transferred basis property in the hands of such transferee.

[Sec. 1276(d)]

(d) SPECIAL RULES.—Under regulations prescribed by the Secretary—

(1) rules similar to the rules of subsection (b) of section 1245 shall apply for purposes of this section; except that—

(A) paragraph (1) of such subsection shall not apply,

(B) an exchange qualifying under section 354(a), 355(a), or 356(a) (determined without regard to subsection (a) of this section) shall be treated as an exchange described in paragraph (3) of such subsection, and

(C) paragraph (3) of section 1245(b) shall be applied as if it did not contain a reference to section 351, and

(2) appropriate adjustments shall be made to the basis of any property to reflect gain recognized under subsection (a).

[Sec. 1277]

SEC. 1277. DEFERRAL OF INTEREST DEDUCTION ALLOCABLE TO ACCRUED MARKET DISCOUNT.

[Sec. 1277(a)]

(a) GENERAL RULE.—Except as otherwise provided in this section, the net direct interest expense with respect to any market discount bond shall be allowed as a deduction for the taxable year only to the

Sec. 1277(a)

extent that such expense exceeds the portion of the market discount allocable to the days during the taxable year on which such bond was held by the taxpayer (as determined under the rules of section 1276(b)).

[Sec. 1277(b)]

(b) DISALLOWED DEDUCTION ALLOWED FOR LATER YEARS.—

(1) ELECTION TO TAKE INTO ACCOUNT IN LATER YEAR WHERE NET INTEREST INCOME FROM BOND.—

(A) IN GENERAL.—If—

(i) there is net interest income for any taxable year with respect to any market discount bond, and

(ii) the taxpayer makes an election under this subparagraph with respect to such bond,

any disallowed interest expense with respect to such bond shall be treated as interest paid or accrued by the taxpayer during such taxable year to the extent such disallowed interest expense does not exceed the net interest income with respect to such bond.

(B) DETERMINATION OF DISALLOWED INTEREST EXPENSE.—For purposes of subparagraph (A), the amount of the disallowed interest expense—

(i) shall be determined as of the close of the preceding taxable year, and

(ii) shall not include any amount previously taken into account under subparagraph (A).

(C) NET INTEREST INCOME.—For purposes of this paragraph, the term "net interest income" means the excess of the amount determined under paragraph (2) of subsection (c) over the amount determined under paragraph (1) of subsection (c).

(2) REMAINDER OF DISALLOWED INTEREST EXPENSE ALLOWED FOR YEAR OF DISPOSITION.—

(A) IN GENERAL.—Except as otherwise provided in this paragraph, the amount of the disallowed interest expense with respect to any market discount bond shall be treated as interest paid or accrued by the taxpayer in the taxable year in which such bond is disposed of.

(B) NONRECOGNITION TRANSACTIONS.—If any market discount bond is disposed of in a nonrecognition transaction—

(i) the disallowed interest expense with respect to such bond shall be treated as interest paid or accrued in the year of disposition only to the extent of the amount of gain recognized on such disposition, and

(ii) the disallowed interest expense with respect to such property (to the extent not so treated) shall be treated as disallowed interest expense—

(I) in the case of a transaction described in section 1276(c)(1), of the transferee with respect to the transferred basis property, or

(II) in the case of a transaction described in section 1276(c)(2), with respect to the exchanged basis property.

(C) DISALLOWED INTEREST EXPENSE REDUCED FOR AMOUNTS PREVIOUSLY TAKEN INTO ACCOUNT UNDER PARAGRAPH (1).—For purposes of this paragraph, the amount of the disallowed interest expense shall not include any amount previously taken into account under paragraph (1).

(3) DISALLOWED INTEREST EXPENSE.—For purposes of this subsection, the term "disallowed interest expense" means the aggregate amount disallowed under subsection (a) with respect to the market discount bond.

[Sec. 1277(c)]

(c) NET DIRECT INTEREST EXPENSE.—For purposes of this section, the term "net direct interest expense" means, with respect to any market discount bond, the excess (if any) of—

(1) the amount of interest paid or accrued during the taxable year on indebtedness which is incurred or continued to purchase or carry such bond, over

(2) the aggregate amount of interest (including original issue discount) includible in gross income for the taxable year with respect to such bond.

In the case of any financial institution which is a bank (as defined in section 585(a)(2)), the determination of whether interest is described in paragraph (1) shall be made under principles similar to the principles of

Sec. 1277(b)

section 291(e)(1)(B)(ii). Under rules similar to the rules of section 265(a)(5), short sale expenses shall be treated as interest for purposes of determining net direct interest expense.

SEC. 1278. DEFINITIONS AND SPECIAL RULES.

(a) IN GENERAL.—For purposes of this part—

(1) MARKET DISCOUNT BOND.—

(A) IN GENERAL.—Except as provided in subparagraph (B), the term "market discount bond" means any bond having market discount.

(B) EXCEPTIONS.—The term "market discount bond" shall not include—

(i) SHORT-TERM OBLIGATIONS.—Any obligation with a fixed maturity date not exceeding 1 year from the date of issue.

(ii) UNITED STATES SAVINGS BONDS.—Any United States savings bond.

(iii) INSTALLMENT OBLIGATIONS.—Any installment obligation to which section 453B applies.

(C) SECTION 1277 NOT APPLICABLE TO TAX-EXEMPT OBLIGATIONS.—For purposes of section 1277, the term "market discount bond" shall not include any tax-exempt obligation (as defined in section 1275(a)(3)).

(D) TREATMENT OF BONDS ACQUIRED AT ORIGINAL ISSUE.—

(i) IN GENERAL.—Except as otherwise provided in this subparagraph or in regulations, the term "market discount bond" shall not include any bond acquired by the taxpayer at its original issue.

(ii) TREATMENT OF BONDS ACQUIRED FOR LESS THAN ISSUE PRICE.—Clause (i) shall not apply to any bond if—

(I) the basis of the taxpayer in such bond is determined under section 1012, and

(II) such basis is less than the issue price of such bond determined under subpart A of this part.

(iii) BONDS ACQUIRED IN CERTAIN REORGANIZATIONS.—Clause (i) shall not apply to any bond issued pursuant to a plan of reorganization (within the meaning of section 368(a)(1)) in exchange for another bond having market discount. Solely for purposes of section 1276, the preceding sentence shall not apply if such other bond was issued on or before July 18, 1984 (the date of the enactment of section 1276) and if the bond issued pursuant to such plan of reorganization has the same term and the same interest rate as such other bond had.

(iv) TREATMENT OF CERTAIN TRANSFERRED BASIS PROPERTY.—For purposes of clause (i), if the adjusted basis of any bond in the hands of the taxpayer is determined by reference to the adjusted basis of such bond in the hands of a person who acquired such bond at its original issue, such bond shall be treated as acquired by the taxpayer at its original issue.

(2) MARKET DISCOUNT.—

(A) IN GENERAL.—The term "market discount" means the excess (if any) of—

(i) the stated redemption price of the bond at maturity, over

(ii) the basis of such bond immediately after its acquisition by the taxpayer.

(B) COORDINATION WHERE BOND HAS ORIGINAL ISSUE DISCOUNT.—In the case of any bond having original issue discount, for purposes of subparagraph (A), the stated redemption price of such bond at maturity shall be treated as equal to its revised issue price.

(C) DE MINIMIS RULE.—If the market discount is less than 1/4 of 1 percent of the stated redemption price of the bond at maturity multiplied by the number of complete years to maturity (after the taxpayer acquired the bond), then the market discount shall be considered to be zero.

(3) BOND.—The term "bond" means any bond, debenture, note, certificate, or other evidence of indebtedness.

(4) REVISED ISSUE PRICE.—The term "revised issue price" means the sum of—

(A) the issue price of the bond, and

(B) the aggregate amount of the original issue discount includible in the gross income of all holders for periods before the acquisition of the bond by the taxpayer (determined without regard to section 1272(a)(7) or (b)(4)) or, in the case of a tax-exempt obligation, the aggregate amount of the original issue discount which accrued in the manner provided by section 1272(a) (determined without regard to paragraph (7) thereof) during periods before the acquisition of the bond by the taxpayer.

(5) ORIGINAL ISSUE DISCOUNT, ETC.—The terms "original issue discount", "stated redemption price at maturity", and "issue price" have the respective meanings given such terms by subpart A of this part.

[Sec. 1278(b)]

(b) ELECTION TO INCLUDE MARKET DISCOUNT CURRENTLY.—

(1) IN GENERAL.—If the taxpayer makes an election under this subsection—

(A) sections 1276 and 1277 shall not apply, and

(B) market discount on any market discount bond shall be included in the gross income of the taxpayer for the taxable years to which it is attributable (as determined under the rules of subsection (b) of section 1276).

Except for purposes of sections 103, 871(a), 881, 1441, 1442, and 6049 (and such other provisions as may be specified in regulations), any amount included in gross income under subparagraph (B) shall be treated as interest for purposes of this title.

(2) SCOPE OF ELECTION.—An election under this subsection shall apply to all market discount bonds acquired by the taxpayer on or after the 1st day of the 1st taxable year to which such election applies.

(3) PERIOD TO WHICH ELECTION APPLIES.—An election under this subsection shall apply to the taxable year for which is it made and for all subsequent taxable years, unless the taxpayer secures the consent of the Secretary to the revocation of such election.

(4) BASIS ADJUSTMENT.—The basis of any bond in the hands of the taxpayer shall be increased by the amount included in gross income pursuant to this subsection.

[Sec. 1278(c)]

(c) REGULATIONS.—The Secretary shall prescribe such regulations as may be necessary to carry out the purposes of this subpart, including regulations providing proper adjustments in the case of a bond the principal of which may be paid in 2 or more payments.

Subpart C—Discount on Short-Term Obligations

[Sec. 1281]

SEC. 1281. CURRENT INCLUSION IN INCOME OF DISCOUNT ON CERTAIN SHORT-TERM OBLIGATIONS.

[Sec. 1281(a)]

(a) GENERAL RULE.—In the case of any short-term obligation to which this section applies, for purposes of this title—

(1) there shall be included in the gross income of the holder an amount equal to the sum of the daily portions of the acquisition discount for each day during the taxable year on which such holder held such obligation, and

(2) any interest payable on the obligation (other than interest taken into account in determining the amount of the acquisition discount) shall be included in gross income as it accrues.

[Sec. 1281(b)]

(b) SHORT-TERM OBLIGATIONS TO WHICH SECTION APPLIES.—

(1) IN GENERAL.—This section shall apply to any short-term obligation which—

(A) is held by a taxpayer using an accrual method of accounting,

Sec. 1278(b)

(B) is held primarily for sale to customers in the ordinary course of the taxpayer's trade or business,

(C) is held by a bank (as defined in section 581),

(D) is held by a regulated investment company or a common trust fund,

(E) is identified by the taxpayer under section 1256(e)(2) as being part of a hedging transaction, or

(F) is a stripped bond or stripped coupon held by the person who stripped the bond or coupon (or by any other person whose basis is determined by reference to the basis in the hands of such person).

(2) TREATMENT OF OBLIGATIONS HELD BY PASS-THRU ENTITIES.—

(A) IN GENERAL.—This section shall apply also to—

(i) any short-term obligation which is held by a pass-thru entity which is formed or availed of for purposes of avoiding the provisions of this section, and

(ii) any short-term obligation which is acquired by a pass-thru entity (not described in clause (i)) during the required accrual period.

(B) REQUIRED ACCRUAL PERIOD.—For purposes of subparagraph (A), the term "required accrual period" means the period—

(i) which begins with the first taxable year for which the ownership test of subparagraph (C) is met with respect to the pass-thru entity (or a predecessor), and

(ii) which ends with the first taxable year after the taxable year referred to in clause (i) for which the ownership test of subparagraph (C) is not met and with respect to which the Secretary consents to the termination of the required accrual period.

(C) OWNERSHIP TEST.—The ownership test of this subparagraph is met for any taxable year if, on at least 90 days during the taxable year, 20 percent or more of the value of the interests in the pass-thru entity are held by persons described in paragraph (1) or by other pass-thru entities to which subparagraph (A) applies.

(D) PASS-THRU ENTITY.—The term "pass-thru entity" means any partnership, S corporation, trust, or other pass-thru entity.

[Sec. 1281(c)]

(c) CROSS REFERENCE.—

For special rules limiting the application of this section to original issue discount in the case of nongovernmental obligations, see section 1283(c).

[Sec. 1282]

SEC. 1282. DEFERRAL OF INTEREST DEDUCTION ALLOCABLE TO ACCRUED DISCOUNT.

[Sec. 1282(a)]

(a) GENERAL RULE.—Except as otherwise provided in this section, the net direct interest expense with respect to any short-term obligation shall be allowed as a deduction for the taxable year only to the extent such expense exceeds the sum of—

(1) the daily portions of the acquisition discount for each day during the taxable year on which the taxpayer held such obligation, and

(2) the amount of any interest payable on the obligation (other than interest taken into account in determining the amount of the acquisition discount) which accrues during the taxable year while the taxpayer held such obligation (and is not included in the gross income of the taxpayer for such taxable year by reason of the taxpayer's method of accounting).

[Sec. 1282(b)]

(b) SECTION NOT TO APPLY TO OBLIGATIONS TO WHICH SECTION 1281 APPLIES.—

(1) IN GENERAL.—This section shall not apply to any short-term obligation to which section 1281 applies.

(2) ELECTION TO HAVE SECTION 1281 APPLY TO ALL OBLIGATIONS.—

(A) IN GENERAL.—A taxpayer may make an election under this paragraph to have section 1281 apply to all short-term obligations acquired by the taxpayer on or after the 1st day of the 1st taxable year to which such election applies.

(B) PERIOD TO WHICH ELECTION APPLIES.—An election under this paragraph shall apply to the taxable year for which it is made and for all subsequent taxable years, unless the taxpayer secures the consent of the Secretary to the revocation of such election.

[Sec. 1282(c)]

(c) CERTAIN RULES MADE APPLICABLE.—Rules similar to the rules of subsections (b) and (c) of section 1277 shall apply for purposes of this section.

[Sec. 1282(d)]

(d) CROSS REFERENCE.—

For special rules limiting the application of this section to original issue discount in the case of nongovernmental obligations, see section 1283(c).

[Sec. 1283]

SEC. 1283. DEFINITIONS AND SPECIAL RULES.

[Sec. 1283(a)]

(a) DEFINITIONS.—For purposes of this subpart—

(1) SHORT-TERM OBLIGATION.—

(A) IN GENERAL.—Except as provided in subparagraph (B), the term "short-term obligation" means any bond, debenture, note, certificate, or other evidence of indebtedness which has a fixed maturity date not more than 1 year from the date of issue.

(B) EXCEPTIONS FOR TAX-EXEMPT OBLIGATIONS.—The term "short-term obligation" shall not include any tax-exempt obligation (as defined in section 1275(a)(3)).

(2) ACQUISITION DISCOUNT.—The term "acquisition discount" means the excess of—

(A) the stated redemption price at maturity (as defined in section 1273), over

(B) the taxpayer's basis for the obligation.

[Sec. 1283(b)]

(b) DAILY PORTION.—For purposes of this subpart—

(1) RATABLE ACCRUAL.—Except as otherwise provided in this subsection, the daily portion of the acquisition discount is an amount equal to—

(A) the amount of such discount, divided by

(B) the number of days after the day on which the taxpayer acquired the obligation and up to (and including) the day of its maturity.

(2) ELECTION OF ACCRUAL ON BASIS OF CONSTANT INTEREST RATE (IN LIEU OF RATABLE ACCRUAL).—

(A) IN GENERAL.—At the election of the taxpayer with respect to any obligation, the daily portion of the acquisition discount for any day is the portion of the acquisition discount accruing on such day determined (under regulations prescribed by the Secretary) on the basis of—

(i) the taxpayer's yield to maturity based on the taxpayer's cost of acquiring the obligation, and

(ii) compounding daily.

(B) ELECTION IRREVOCABLE.—An election under subparagraph (A), once made with respect to any obligation, shall be irrevocable.

[Sec. 1283(c)]

(c) SPECIAL RULES FOR NONGOVERNMENTAL OBLIGATIONS.—

(1) IN GENERAL.—In the case of any short-term obligation which is not a short-term Government obligation (as defined in section 1271(a)(3)(B))—

(A) sections 1281 and 1282 shall be applied by taking into account original issue discount in lieu of acquisition discount, and

(B) appropriate adjustments shall be made in the application of subsection (b) of this section.

(2) ELECTION TO HAVE PARAGRAPH (1) NOT APPLY.—

(A) IN GENERAL.—A taxpayer may make an election under this paragraph to have paragraph (1) not apply to all obligations acquired by the taxpayer on or after the first day of the first taxable year to which such election applies.

(B) PERIOD TO WHICH ELECTION APPLIES.—An election under this paragraph shall apply to the taxable year for which it is made and for all subsequent taxable years, unless the taxpayer secures the consent of the Secretary to the revocation of such election.

[Sec. 1283(d)]

(d) OTHER SPECIAL RULES.—

(1) BASIS ADJUSTMENTS.—The basis of any short-term obligation in the hands of the holder thereof shall be increased by the amount included in his gross income pursuant to section 1281.

(2) DOUBLE INCLUSION IN INCOME NOT REQUIRED.—Section 1281 shall not require the inclusion of any amount previously includible in gross income.

(3) COORDINATION WITH OTHER PROVISIONS.—Section 454(b) and paragraphs (3) and (4) of section 1271(a) shall not apply to any short-term obligation to which section 1281 applies.

Subpart D—Miscellaneous Provisions

[Sec. 1286]

SEC. 1286. TAX TREATMENT OF STRIPPED BONDS.

[Sec. 1286(a)]

(a) INCLUSION IN INCOME AS IF BOND AND COUPONS WERE ORIGINAL ISSUE DISCOUNT BONDS.—If any person purchases after July 1, 1982, a stripped bond or stripped coupon, then such bond or coupon while held by such purchaser (or by any other person whose basis is determined by reference to the basis in the hands of such purchaser) shall be treated for purposes of this part as a bond originally issued on the purchase date and having an original issue discount equal to the excess (if any) of—

(1) the stated redemption price at maturity (or, in the case of coupon, the amount payable on the due date of such coupon), over

(2) such bond's or coupon's ratable share of the purchase price.

For purposes of paragraph (2), ratable shares shall be determined on the basis of their respective fair market values on the date of purchase.

[Sec. 1286(b)]

(b) TAX TREATMENT OF PERSON STRIPPING BOND.—For purposes of this subtitle, if any person strips 1 or more coupons from a bond and after July 1, 1982, disposes of the bond or such coupon—

(1) such person shall include in gross income an amount equal to the sum of—

(A) the interest accrued on such bond while held by such person and before the time such coupon or bond was disposed of (to the extent such interest has not theretofore been included in such person's gross income), and

(B) the accrued market discount on such bond determined as of the time such coupon or bond was disposed of (to the extent such discount has not theretofore been included in such person's gross income),

(2) the basis of the bond and coupons shall be increased by the amount included in gross income under paragraph (1),

(3) the basis of the bond and coupons immediately before the disposition (as adjusted pursuant to paragraph (2)) shall be allocated among the items retained by such person and the items disposed of by such person on the basis of their respective fair market values, and

Sec. 1286(b)

(4) for purposes of subsection (a), such person shall be treated as having purchased on the date of such disposition each such item which he retains for an amount equal to the basis allocated to such item under paragraph (3).

A rule similar to the rule of paragraph (4) shall apply in the case of any person whose basis in any bond or coupon is determined by reference to the basis of the person described in the preceding sentence.

* * *

[Sec. 1286(d)]

(d) SPECIAL RULES FOR TAX-EXEMPT OBLIGATIONS.—

(1) IN GENERAL.—In the case of any tax-exempt obligation (as defined in section 1275(a)(3)) from which 1 or more coupons have been stripped—

(A) the amount of the original issue discount determined under subsection (a) with respect to any stripped bond or stripped coupon—

(i) shall be treated as original issue discount on a tax-exempt obligation to the extent such discount does not exceed the tax-exempt portion of such discount, and

(ii) shall be treated as original issue discount on an obligation which is not a tax-exempt obligation to the extent such discount exceeds the tax-exempt portion of such discount,

(B) subsection (b)(1)(A) shall not apply, and

(C) subsection (b)(2) shall be applied by increasing the basis of the bond or coupon by the sum of—

(i) the interest accrued but not paid before such bond or coupon was disposed of (and not previously reflected in basis), plus

(ii) the amount included in gross income under subsection (b)(1)(B).

(2) TAX-EXEMPT PORTION.—For purposes of paragraph (1), the tax-exempt portion of the original issue discount determined under subsection (a) is the excess of—

(A) the amount referred to in subsection (a)(1), over

(B) an issue price which would produce a yield to maturity as of the purchase date equal to the lower of—

(i) the coupon rate of interest on the obligation from which the coupons were separated, or

(ii) the yield to maturity (on the basis of the purchase price) of the stripped obligation or coupon.

The purchaser of any stripped obligation or coupon may elect to apply clause (i) by substituting "original yield to maturity of" for "coupon rate of interest on".

[Sec. 1286(e)]

(e) DEFINITIONS AND SPECIAL RULES.—For purposes of this section—

(1) BOND.—The term "bond" means a bond, debenture, note, or certificate or other evidence of indebtedness.

(2) STRIPPED BOND.—The term "stripped bond" means a bond issued at any time with interest coupons where there is a separation in ownership between the bond and any coupon which has not yet become payable.

(3) STRIPPED COUPON.—The term "stripped coupon" means any coupon relating to a stripped bond.

(4) STATED REDEMPTION PRICE AT MATURITY.—The term "stated redemption price at maturity" has the meaning given such term by section 1273(a)(2).

(5) COUPON.—The term "coupon" includes any right to receive interest on a bond (whether or not evidenced by a coupon). This paragraph shall apply for purposes of subsection (c) only in the case of purchases after July 1, 1982.

(6) PURCHASE.—The term "purchase" has the meaning given such term by section 1272(d)(1).

[Sec. 1286(f)]

(f) REGULATION AUTHORITY.—The Secretary may prescribe regulations providing that where, by reason of varying rates of interest, put or call options, or other circumstances, the tax treatment under this section does not accurately reflect the income of the holder of a stripped coupon or stripped bond, or of the person disposing of such bond or coupon, as the case may be, for any period, such treatment shall be modified to require that the proper amount of income be included for such period.

[Sec. 1287]

SEC. 1287. DENIAL OF CAPITAL GAIN TREATMENT FOR GAINS ON CERTAIN OBLIGATIONS NOT IN REGISTERED FORM.

[Sec. 1287(a)]

(a) IN GENERAL.—If any registration-required obligation is not in registered form, any gain on the sale or other disposition of such obligation shall be treated as ordinary income (unless the issuance of such obligation was subject to tax under section 4701).

[Sec. 1287(b)]

(b) DEFINITIONS.—For purposes of subsection (a)—

(1) REGISTRATION-REQUIRED OBLIGATION.—The term "registration-required obligation" has the meaning given to such term by section 163(f)(2) except that clause (iv) of subparagraph (A), and subparagraph (B), of such section shall not apply.

(2) REGISTERED FORM.—the term "registered form" has the same meaning as when used in section 163(f).

[Sec. 1288]

SEC. 1288. TREATMENT OF ORIGINAL ISSUE DISCOUNT ON TAX-EXEMPT OBLIGATIONS.

[Sec. 1288(a)]

(a) GENERAL RULE.—Original issue discount on any tax-exempt obligation shall be treated as accruing—

(1) for purposes of section 163, in the manner provided by section 1272(a) (determined without regard to paragraph (7) thereof), and

(2) for purposes of determining the adjusted basis of the holder, in the manner provided by section 1272(a) (determined with regard to paragraph (7) thereof).

[Sec. 1288(b)]

(b) DEFINITIONS AND SPECIAL RULES.—For purposes of this section—

(1) ORIGINAL ISSUE DISCOUNT.—The term "original issue discount" has the meaning given to such term by section 1273(a) without regard to paragraph (3) thereof. In applying section 483 or 1274, under regulations prescribed by the Secretary, appropriate adjustments shall be made to the applicable Federal rate to take into account the tax exemption for interest on the obligation.

(2) TAX-EXEMPT OBLIGATION.—The term "tax-exempt obligation" has the meaning given to such term by section 1275(a)(3).

(3) SHORT-TERM OBLIGATION.—In applying this section to obligations with maturity of 1 year or less, rules similar to the rules of section 1283(b) shall apply.

Subchapter Q—Readjustment of Tax Between Years and Special Limitations

PART II—MITIGATION OF EFFECT OF LIMITATIONS AND OTHER PROVISIONS

[Sec. 1311]

SEC. 1311. CORRECTION OF ERROR.

[Sec. 1311(a)]

(a) GENERAL RULE.—If a determination (as defined in section 1313) is described in one or more of the paragraphs of section 1312 and, on the date of the determination, correction of the effect of the error referred to in the applicable paragraph of section 1312 is prevented by the operation of any law or rule of law, other than this part and other than section 7122 (relating to compromises), then the effect of the error shall be corrected by an adjustment made in the amount and in the manner specified in section 1314.

[Sec. 1311(b)]

(b) CONDITIONS NECESSARY FOR ADJUSTMENT.—

(1) MAINTENANCE OF AN INCONSISTENT POSITION.—Except in cases described in paragraphs (3) (B) and (4) of section 1312, an adjustment shall be made under this part only if—

(A) in case the amount of the adjustment would be credited or refunded in the same manner as an overpayment under section 1314, there is adopted in the determination a position maintained by the Secretary, or

(B) in case the amount of the adjustment would be assessed and collected in the same manner as a deficiency under section 1314, there is adopted in the determination a position maintained by the taxpayer with respect to whom the determination is made,

and the position maintained by the Secretary in the case described in subparagraph (A) or maintained by the taxpayer in the case described in subparagraph (B) is inconsistent with the erroneous inclusion, exclusion, omission, allowance, disallowance, recognition, or nonrecognition, as the case may be.

(2) CORRECTION NOT BARRED AT TIME OF ERRONEOUS ACTION.—

(A) DETERMINATION DESCRIBED IN SECTION 1312 (3) (B).—In the case of a determination described in section 1312 (3) (B) (relating to certain exclusions from income), adjustment shall be made under this part only if assessment of a deficiency for the taxable year in which the item is includible or against the related taxpayer was not barred, by any law or rule of law, at the time the Secretary first maintained, in a notice of deficiency sent pursuant to section 6212 or before the Tax Court, that the item described in section 1312 (3) (B) should be included in the gross income of the taxpayer for the taxable year to which the determination relates.

(B) DETERMINATION DESCRIBED IN SECTION 1312 (4).—In the case of a determination described in section 1312 (4) (relating to disallowance of certain deductions and credits), adjustment shall be made under this part only if credit or refund of the overpayment attributable to the deduction or credit described in such section which should have been allowed to the taxpayer or related taxpayer was not barred, by any law or rule of law, at the time the taxpayer first maintained before the Secretary or before the Tax Court, in writing, that he was entitled to such deduction or credit for the taxable year to which the determination relates.

(3) EXISTENCE OF RELATIONSHIP.—In case the amount of the adjustment would be assessed and collected in the same manner as a deficiency (except for cases described in section 1312 (3) (B)), the adjustment shall not be made with respect to a related taxpayer unless he stands in such relationship to the taxpayer at the time the latter first maintains the inconsistent position in a return, claim for refund, or petition (or amended petition) to the Tax Court for the taxable year with respect to which the determination is made, or if such position is not so maintained, then at the time of the determination.

Sec. 1311

[Sec. 1312]

SEC. 1312. CIRCUMSTANCES OF ADJUSTMENT.

The circumstances under which the adjustment provided in section 1311 is authorized are as follows:

(1) DOUBLE INCLUSION OF AN ITEM OF GROSS INCOME.—The determination requires the inclusion in gross income of an item which was erroneously included in the gross income of the taxpayer for another taxable year or in the gross income of a related taxpayer.

(2) DOUBLE ALLOWANCE OF A DEDUCTION OR CREDIT.—The determination allows a deduction or credit which was erroneously allowed to the taxpayer for another taxable year or to a related taxpayer.

(3) DOUBLE EXCLUSION OF AN ITEM OF GROSS INCOME.—

(A) ITEMS INCLUDED IN INCOME.—The determination requires the exclusion from gross income of an item included in a return filed by the taxpayer or with respect to which tax was paid and which was erroneously excluded or omitted from the gross income of the taxpayer for another taxable year, or from the gross income of a related taxpayer; or

(B) ITEMS NOT INCLUDED IN INCOME.—The determination requires the exclusion from gross income of an item not included in a return filed by the taxpayer and with respect to which the tax was not paid but which is includible in the gross income of the taxpayer for another taxable year or in the gross income of a related taxpayer.

(4) DOUBLE DISALLOWANCE OF A DEDUCTION OR CREDIT.—The determination disallows a deduction or credit which should have been allowed to, but was not allowed to, the taxpayer for another taxable year, or to a related taxpayer.

(5) CORRELATIVE DEDUCTIONS AND INCLUSIONS FOR TRUSTS OR ESTATES AND LEGATEES, BENEFICIARIES, OR HEIRS.—The determination allows or disallows any of the additional deductions allowable in computing the taxable income of estates or trusts, or requires or denies any of the inclusions in the computation of taxable income of beneficiaries, heirs, or legatees, specified in subparts A to E, inclusive (secs. 641 and following, relating to estates, trusts, and beneficiaries) of part I of subchapter J of this chapter, or corresponding provisions of prior internal revenue laws, and the correlative inclusion or deduction, as the case may be, has been erroneously excluded, omitted, or included, or disallowed, omitted, or allowed, as the case may be, in respect of the related taxpayer.

(6) CORRELATIVE DEDUCTIONS AND CREDITS FOR CERTAIN RELATED CORPORATIONS.—The determination allows or disallows a deduction (including a credit) in computing the taxable income (or, as the case may be, net income, normal tax net income, or surtax net income) of a corporation, and a correlative deduction or credit has been erroneously allowed, omitted, or disallowed, as the case may be, in respect of a related taxpayer described in section 1313(c)(7).

(7) BASIS OF PROPERTY AFTER ERRONEOUS TREATMENT OF A PRIOR TRANSACTION.—

(A) GENERAL RULE.—The determination determines the basis of property, and in respect of any transaction on which such basis depends, or in respect of any transaction which was erroneously treated as affecting such basis, there occurred, with respect to a taxpayer described in subparagraph (B) of this paragraph, any of the errors described in subparagraph (C) of this paragraph.

(B) TAXPAYERS WITH RESPECT TO WHOM THE ERRONEOUS TREATMENT OCCURRED.—The taxpayer with respect to whom the erroneous treatment occurred must be—

(i) the taxpayer with respect to whom the determination is made,

(ii) a taxpayer who acquired title to the property in the transaction and from whom, mediately or immediately, the taxpayer with respect to whom the determination is made derived title, or

(iii) a taxpayer who had title to the property at the time of the transaction and from whom, mediately or immediately, the taxpayer with respect to whom the determination is made derived title, if the basis of the property in the hands of the taxpayer with respect to whom the determination is made is determined under section 1015 (a) (relating to the basis of property acquired by gift).

(C) PRIOR ERRONEOUS TREATMENT.—With respect to a taxpayer described in subparagraph (B) of this paragraph—

(i) there was an erroneous inclusion in, or omission from, gross income,

(ii) there was an erroneous recognition, or nonrecognition, of gain or loss, or

(iii) there was an erroneous deduction of an item properly chargeable to capital account or an erroneous charge to capital account of an item properly deductible.

[Sec. 1313]

SEC. 1313. DEFINITIONS.

[Sec. 1313(a)]

(a) DETERMINATION.—For purposes of this part, the term "determination" means—

(1) a decision by the Tax Court or a judgment, decree, or other order by any court of competent jurisdiction, which has become final;

(2) a closing agreement made under section 7121;

(3) a final disposition by the Secretary of a claim for refund. For purposes of this part, a claim for refund shall be deemed finally disposed of by the Secretary—

(A) as to items with respect to which the claim was allowed, on the date of allowance of refund or credit or on the date of mailing notice of disallowance (by reason of offsetting items) of the claim for refund, and

(B) as to items with respect to which the claim was disallowed, in whole or in part, or as to items applied by the Secretary in reduction of the refund or credit, on expiration of the time for instituting suit with respect thereto (unless suit is instituted before the expiration of such time); or

(4) under regulations prescribed by the Secretary, an agreement for purposes of this part, signed by the Secretary and by any person, relating to the liability of such person (or the person for whom he acts) in respect of a tax under this subtitle for any taxable period.

[Sec. 1313(b)]

(b) TAXPAYER.—Notwithstanding section 7701 (a) (14), the term "taxpayer" means any person subject to a tax under the applicable revenue law.

[Sec. 1313(c)]

(c) RELATED TAXPAYER.—For purposes of this part, the term "related taxpayer" means a taxpayer who, with the taxpayer with respect to whom a determination is made, stood, in the taxable year with respect to which the erroneous inclusion, exclusion, omission, allowance, or disallowance was made, in one of the following relationships:

(1) husband and wife,

(2) grantor and fiduciary,

(3) grantor and beneficiary,

(4) fiduciary and beneficiary, legatee, or heir,

(5) decedent and decedent's estate,

(6) partner, or

(7) member of an affiliated group of corporations (as defined in section 1504).

[Sec. 1314]

SEC. 1314. AMOUNT AND METHOD OF ADJUSTMENT.

[Sec. 1314(a)]

(a) ASCERTAINMENT OF AMOUNT OF ADJUSTMENT.—In computing the amount of an adjustment under this part there shall first be ascertained the tax previously determined for the taxable year with respect to which the error was made. The amount of the tax previously determined shall be the excess of—

(1) the sum of—

(A) the amount shown as the tax by the taxpayer on his return (determined as provided in section 6211 (b) (1), (3), and (4), relating to the definition of deficiency), if a return was made by the taxpayer and an amount was shown as the tax by the taxpayer thereon, plus

(B) the amounts previously assessed (or collected without assessment) as a deficiency, over—

(2) the amount of rebates, as defined in section 6211 (b) (2), made.

There shall then be ascertained the increase or decrease in tax previously determined which results solely from the correct treatment of the item which was the subject of the error (with due regard given to the effect of the item in the computation of gross income, taxable income, and other matters under this subtitle). A similar computation shall be made for any other taxable year affected, or treated as affected, by a net operating loss deduction (as defined in section 172) or by a capital loss carryback or carryover (as defined in section 1212), determined with reference to the taxable year with respect to which the error was made. The amount so ascertained (together with any amounts wrongfully collected as additions to the tax or interest, as a result of such error) for each taxable year shall be the amount of the adjustment for that taxable year.

[Sec. 1314(b)]

(b) METHOD OF ADJUSTMENT.—The adjustment authorized in section 1311 (a) shall be made by assessing and collecting, or refunding or crediting, the amount thereof in the same manner as if it were a deficiency determined by the Secretary with respect to the taxpayer as to whom the error was made or an overpayment claimed by such taxpayer, as the case may be, for the taxable year or years with respect to which an amount is ascertained under subsection (a), and as if on the date of the determination one year remained before the expiration of the periods of limitation upon assessment or filing claim for refund for such taxable year or years. If, as a result of a determination described in section 1313(a) (4), an adjustment has been made by the assessment and collection of a deficiency or the refund or credit of an overpayment, and subsequently such determination is altered or revoked, the amount of the adjustment ascertained under subsection (a) of this section shall be redetermined on the basis of such alteration or revocation and any overpayment or deficiency resulting from such redetermination shall be refunded or credited, or assessed and collected, as the case may be, as an adjustment under this part. In the case of an adjustment resulting from an increase or decrease in a net operating loss or net capital loss which is carried back to the year of adjustment, interest shall not be collected or paid for any period prior to the close of the taxable year in which the net operating loss or net capital loss arises.

[Sec. 1314(c)]

(c) ADJUSTMENT UNAFFECTED BY OTHER ITEMS.—The amount to be assessed and collected in the same manner as a deficiency, or to be refunded or credited in the same manner as an overpayment, under this part, shall not be diminished by any credit or set-off based upon any item other than the one which was the subject of the adjustment. The amount of the adjustment under this part, if paid, shall not be recovered by a claim or suit for refund or suit for erroneous refund based upon any item other than the one which was the subject of the adjustment.

* * *

PART V—CLAIM OF RIGHT

[Sec. 1341]

SEC. 1341. COMPUTATION OF TAX WHERE TAXPAYER RESTORES SUBSTANTIAL AMOUNT HELD UNDER CLAIM OF RIGHT.

[Sec. 1341(a)]

(a) GENERAL RULE.—If—

(1) an item was included in gross income for a prior taxable year (or years) because it appeared that the taxpayer had an unrestricted right to such item;

(2) a deduction is allowable for the taxable year because it was established after the close of such prior taxable year (or years) that the taxpayer did not have an unrestricted right to such item or to a portion of such item; and

(3) the amount of such deduction exceeds $3,000,

Sec. 1341(a)

then the tax imposed by this chapter for the taxable year shall be the lesser of the following:

(4) the tax for the taxable year computed with such deduction; or

(5) an amount equal to—

(A) the tax for the taxable year computed without such deduction, minus

(B) the decrease in tax under this chapter (or the corresponding provisions of prior revenue laws) for the prior taxable year (or years) which would result solely from the exclusion of such item (or portion thereof) from gross income for such prior taxable year (or years).

For purposes of paragraph (5) (B), the corresponding provisions of the Internal Revenue Code of 1939 shall be chapter 1 of such code (other than subchapter E, relating to self-employment income) and subchapter E of chapter 2 of such code.

[Sec. 1341(b)]

(b) SPECIAL RULES.—

(1) If the decrease in tax ascertained under subsection (a) (5) (B) exceeds the tax imposed by this chapter for the taxable year (computed without the deduction) such excess shall be considered to be a payment of tax on the last day prescribed by law for the payment of tax for the taxable year, and shall be refunded or credited in the same manner as if it were an overpayment for such taxable year.

(2) Subsection (a) does not apply to any deduction allowable with respect to an item which was included in gross income by reason of the sale or other disposition of stock in trade of the taxpayer (or other property of a kind which would properly have been included in the inventory of the taxpayer if on hand at the close of the prior taxable year) or property held by the taxpayer primarily for sale to customers in the ordinary course of his trade or business. This paragraph shall not apply if the deduction arises out of refunds or repayments with respect to rates made by a regulated public utility (as defined in section 7701(a)(33) without regard to the limitation contained in the last two sentences thereof) if such refunds or repayments are required to be made by the Government, political subdivision, agency, or instrumentality referred to in such section, or by an order of a court, or are made in settlement of litigation or under threat or imminence of litigation.

(3) If the tax imposed by this chapter for the taxable year is the amount determined under subsection (a)(5), then the deduction referred to in subsection (a)(2) shall not be taken into account for any purpose of this subtitle other than this section.

(4) For purposes of determining whether paragraph (4) or paragraph (5) of subsection (a) applies—

(A) in any case where the deduction referred to in paragraph (4) of subsection (a) results in a net operating loss, such loss shall, for purposes of computing the tax for the taxable year under such paragraph (4), be carried back to the same extent and in the same manner as is provided under section 172; and

(B) in any case where the exclusion referred to in paragraph (5)(B) of subsection (a) results in a net operating loss or capital loss for the prior taxable year (or years), such loss shall, for purposes of computing the decrease in tax for the prior taxable year (or years) under such paragraph (5)(B), be carried back and carried over to the same extent and in the same manner as is provided under section 172 or section 1212, except that no carryover beyond the taxable year shall be taken into account.

(5) For purposes of this chapter, the net operating loss described in paragraph (4)(A) of this subsection, or the net operating loss or capital loss described in paragraph (4)(B) of this subsection, as the case may be, shall (after the application of paragraph (4) or (5)(B) of subsection (a) for the taxable year) be taken into account under section 172 or 1212 for taxable years after the taxable year to the same extent and in the same manner as—

(A) a net operating loss sustained for the taxable year, if paragraph (4) of subsection (a) applied, or

(B) a net operating loss or capital loss sustained for the prior taxable year (or years), if paragraph (5)(B) of subsection (a) applied.

Subchapter S—Tax Treatment of S Corporations and Their Shareholders

PART I—IN GENERAL

[Sec. 1361]

SEC. 1361. S CORPORATION DEFINED.

[Sec. 1361(a)]

(a) S CORPORATION DEFINED.—

(1) IN GENERAL.—For purposes of this title, the term "S corporation" means, with respect to any taxable year, a small business corporation for which an election under section 1362(a) is in effect for such year.

(2) C CORPORATION.—For purposes of this title, the term "C corporation" means, with respect to any taxable year, a corporation which is not an S corporation for such year.

[Sec. 1361(b)]

(b) SMALL BUSINESS CORPORATION.—

(1) IN GENERAL.—For purposes of this subchapter, the term "small business corporation" means a domestic corporation which is not an ineligible corporation and which does not—

(A) have more than 75 shareholders,

(B) have as a shareholder a person (other than an estate, a trust described in subsection (c)(2), or an organization described in subsection (c)(6)) who is not an individual,

(C) have a nonresident alien as a shareholder, and

(D) have more than 1 class of stock.

(2) INELIGIBLE CORPORATION DEFINED.—For purposes of paragraph (1), the term "ineligible corporation" means any corporation which is—

(A) a financial institution which uses the reserve method of accounting for bad debts described in section 585,

(B) an insurance company subject to tax under subchapter L,

(C) a corporation to which an election under section 936 applies, or

(D) a DISC or former DISC.

(3) TREATMENT OF CERTAIN WHOLLY OWNED SUBSIDIARIES.—

(A) IN GENERAL.—Except as provided in regulations prescribed by the Secretary, for purposes of this title—

(i) a corporation which is a qualified subchapter S subsidiary shall not be treated as a separate corporation, and

(ii) all assets, liabilities, and items of income, deduction, and credit of a qualified subchapter S subsidiary shall be treated as assets, liabilities, and such items (as the case may be) of the S corporation.

(B) QUALIFIED SUBCHAPTER S SUBSIDIARY.—For purposes of this paragraph, the term "qualified subchapter S subsidiary" means any domestic corporation which is not an ineligible corporation (as defined in paragraph (2)), if—

(i) 100 percent of the stock of such corporation is held by the S corporation, and

(ii) the S corporation elects to treat such corporation as a qualified subchapter S subsidiary.

(C) TREATMENT OF TERMINATIONS OF QUALIFIED SUBCHAPTER S SUBSIDIARY STATUS.—For purposes of this title, if any corporation which was a qualified subchapter S subsidiary ceases to meet the requirements of subparagraph (B), such corporation shall be treated as a new corporation acquiring all of its assets (and assuming all of its liabilities) immediately before such cessation from the S corporation in exchange for its stock.

Sec. 1361(b)

(D) ELECTION AFTER TERMINATION.—If a corporation's status as a qualified subchapter S subsidiary terminates, such corporation (and any successor corporation) shall not be eligible to make—

(i) an election under subparagraph (B)(ii) to be treated as a qualified subchapter S subsidiary, or

(ii) an election under section 1362(a) to be treated as an S corporation,

before its 5th taxable year which begins after the 1st taxable year for which such termination was effective, unless the Secretary consents to such election.

[Sec. 1361(c)]

(c) SPECIAL RULES FOR APPLYING SUBSECTION (b).—

(1) HUSBAND AND WIFE TREATED AS 1 SHAREHOLDER.—For purposes of subsection (b)(1)(A), a husband and wife (and their estates) shall be treated as 1 shareholder.

(2) CERTAIN TRUSTS PERMITTED AS SHAREHOLDERS.—

(A) IN GENERAL.—For purposes of subsection (b)(1)(B), the following trusts may be shareholders:

(i) A trust all of which is treated (under subpart E of part I of subchapter J of this chapter) as owned by an individual who is a citizen or resident of the United States.

(ii) A trust which was described in clause (i) immediately before the death of the deemed owner and which continues in existence after such death, but only for the 2-year period beginning on the day of the deemed owner's death.

(iii) A trust with respect to stock transferred to it pursuant to the terms of a will, but only for the 2-year period beginning on the day on which such stock is transferred to it.

(iv) A trust created primarily to exercise the voting power of stock transferred to it.

(v) An electing small business trust.

This subparagraph shall not apply to any foreign trust.

(B) TREATMENT AS SHAREHOLDERS.—For purposes of subsection (b)(1)—

(i) In the case of a trust described in clause (i) of subparagraph (A), the deemed owner shall be treated as the shareholder.

(ii) In the case of a trust described in clause (ii) of subparagraph (A), the estate of the deemed owner shall be treated as the shareholder.

(iii) In the case of a trust described in clause (iii) of subparagraph (A), the estate of the testator shall be treated as the shareholder.

(iv) In the case of a trust described in clause (iv) of subparagraph (A), each beneficiary of the trust shall be treated as a shareholder.

(v) In the case of a trust described in clause (v) of subparagraph (A), each potential current beneficiary of such trust shall be treated as a shareholder; except that, if for any period there is no potential current beneficiary of such trust, such trust shall be treated as the shareholder during such period.

(3) ESTATE OF INDIVIDUAL IN BANKRUPTCY MAY BE SHAREHOLDER.—For purposes of subsection (b)(1)(B), the term "estate" includes the estate of an individual in a case under title 11 of the United States Code.

(4) DIFFERENCES IN COMMON STOCK VOTING RIGHTS DISREGARDED.—For purposes of subsection (b)(1)(D), a corporation shall not be treated as having more than 1 class of stock solely because there are differences in voting rights among the shares of common stock.

(5) STRAIGHT DEBT SAFE HARBOR.—

(A) IN GENERAL.—For purposes of subsection (b)(1)(D), straight debt shall not be treated as a second class of stock.

(B) STRAIGHT DEBT DEFINED.—For purposes of this paragraph, the term "straight debt" means any written unconditional promise to pay on demand or on a specified date a sum certain in money if—

(i) the interest rate (and interest payment dates) are not contingent on profits, the borrower's discretion, or similar factors,

(ii) there is no convertibility (directly or indirectly) into stock, and

(iii) the creditor is an individual (other than a nonresident alien), an estate, a trust described in paragraph (2), or a person which is actively and regularly engaged in the business of lending money.

(C) REGULATIONS.—The Secretary shall prescribe such regulations as may be necessary or appropriate to provide for the proper treatment of straight debt under this subchapter and for the coordination of such treatment with other provisions of this title.

(6) CERTAIN EXEMPT ORGANIZATIONS PERMITTED AS SHAREHOLDERS.—For purposes of subsection (b)(1)(B), an organization which is—

(A) described in section 401(a) or 501(c)(3), and

(B) exempt from taxation under section 501(a),

may be a shareholder in an S corporation.

[Sec. 1361(d)]

(d) SPECIAL RULE FOR QUALIFIED SUBCHAPTER S TRUST.—

(1) IN GENERAL.—In the case of a qualified subchapter S trust with respect to which a beneficiary makes an election under paragraph (2)—

(A) such trust shall be treated as a trust described in subsection (c)(2)(A)(i), and

(B) for purposes of section 678(a), the beneficiary of such trust shall be treated as the owner of that portion of the trust which consists of stock in an S corporation with respect to which the election under paragraph (2) is made.

(2) ELECTION.—

(A) IN GENERAL.—A beneficiary of a qualified subchapter S trust (or his legal representative) may elect to have this subsection apply.

(B) MANNER AND TIME OF ELECTION.—

(i) SEPARATE ELECTION WITH RESPECT TO EACH CORPORATION.—An election under this paragraph shall be made separately with respect to each corporation the stock of which is held by the trust.

(ii) ELECTIONS WITH RESPECT TO SUCCESSIVE INCOME BENEFICIARIES.—If there is an election under this paragraph with respect to any beneficiary, an election under this paragraph shall be treated as made by each successive beneficiary unless such beneficiary affirmatively refuses to consent to such election.

(iii) TIME, MANNER, AND FORM OF ELECTION.—Any election, or refusal, under this paragraph shall be made in such manner and form, and at such time, as the Secretary may prescribe.

(C) ELECTION IRREVOCABLE.—An election under this paragraph, once made, may be revoked only with the consent of the Secretary.

(D) GRACE PERIOD.—An election under this paragraph shall be effective up to 15 days and 2 months before the date of the election.

(3) QUALIFIED SUBCHAPTER S TRUST.—For purposes of this subsection, the term "qualified subchapter S trust" means a trust—

(A) the terms of which require that—

(i) during the life of the current income beneficiary, there shall be only 1 income beneficiary of the trust,

(ii) any corpus distributed during the life of the current income beneficiary may be distributed only to such beneficiary,

(iii) the income interest of the current income beneficiary in the trust shall terminate on the earlier of such beneficiary's death or the termination of the trust, and

(iv) upon the termination of the trust during the life of the current income beneficiary, the trust shall distribute all of its assets to such beneficiary, and

(B) all of the income (within the meaning of section 643(b)) of which is distributed (or required to be distributed) currently to 1 individual who is a citizen or resident of the United States.

Sec. 1361(d)

A substantially separate and independent share of a trust within the meaning of 663(c) shall be treated as a separate trust for purposes of this subsection and subsection (c).

(4) TRUST CEASING TO BE QUALIFIED.—

(A) FAILURE TO MEET REQUIREMENTS OF PARAGRAPH (3)(A).—If a qualified subchapter S trust ceases to meet any requirement of paragraph (3)(A), the provisions of this subsection shall not apply to such trust as of the date it ceases to meet such requirement.

(B) FAILURE TO MEET REQUIREMENTS OF PARAGRAPH (3)(B).—If any qualified subchapter S trust ceases to meet any requirement of paragraph (3)(B) but continues to meet the requirements of paragraph (3)(A), the provisions of this subsection shall not apply to such trust as of the first day of the first taxable year beginning after the first taxable year for which it failed to meet the requirements of paragraph (3)(B).

[Sec. 1361(e)]

(e) ELECTING SMALL BUSINESS TRUST DEFINED.—

(1) ELECTING SMALL BUSINESS TRUST.—For purposes of this section—

(A) IN GENERAL.—Except as provided in subparagraph (B), the term "electing small business trust" means any trust if—

(i) such trust does not have as a beneficiary any person other than (I) an individual, (II) an estate, (III) an organization described in paragraph (2), (3), (4), or (5) of section 170(c), or (IV) an organization described in section 170(c)(1) which holds a contingent interest in such trust and is not a potential current beneficiary,

(ii) no interest in such trust was acquired by purchase, and

(iii) an election under this subsection applies to such trust.

(B) CERTAIN TRUSTS NOT ELIGIBLE.—The term "electing small business trust" shall not include—

(i) any qualified subchapter S trust (as defined in subsection (d)(3)) if an election under subsection (d)(2) applies to any corporation the stock of which is held by such trust,

(ii) any trust exempt from tax under this subtitle, and

(iii) any charitable remainder annuity trust or charitable remainder unitrust (as defined in section 664(d)).

(C) PURCHASE.—For purposes of subparagraph (A), the term "purchase" means any acquisition if the basis of the property acquired is determined under section 1012.

(2) POTENTIAL CURRENT BENEFICIARY.—For purposes of this section, the term "potential current beneficiary" means, with respect to any period, any person who at any time during such period is entitled to, or at the discretion of any person may receive, a distribution from the principal or income of the trust. If a trust disposes of all of the stock which it holds in an S corporation, then, with respect to such corporation, the term "potential current beneficiary" does not include any person who first met the requirements of the preceding sentence during the 60-day period ending on the date of such disposition.

(3) ELECTION.—An election under this subsection shall be made by the trustee. Any such election shall apply to the taxable year of the trust for which made and all subsequent taxable years of such trust unless revoked with the consent of the Secretary.

(4) CROSS REFERENCE.—For special treatment of electing small business trusts, see section 641(c).

[Sec. 1362]

SEC. 1362. ELECTION; REVOCATION; TERMINATION.

[Sec. 1362(a)]

(a) ELECTION.—

(1) IN GENERAL.—Except as provided in subsection (g), a small business corporation may elect, in accordance with the provisions of this section, to be an S corporation.

Sec. 1361(e)

(2) ALL SHAREHOLDERS MUST CONSENT TO ELECTION.—An election under this subsection shall be valid only if all persons who are shareholders in such corporation on the day on which such election is made consent to such election.

[Sec. 1362(b)]

(b) WHEN MADE.—

(1) IN GENERAL.—An election under subsection (a) may be made by a small business corporation for any taxable year—

(A) at any time during the preceding taxable year, or

(B) at any time during the taxable year and on or before the 15th day of the 3d month of the taxable year.

(2) CERTAIN ELECTIONS MADE DURING 1ST 2½ MONTHS TREATED AS MADE FOR NEXT TAXABLE YEAR.—If—

(A) an election under subsection (a) is made for any taxable year during such year and on or before the 15th day of the 3d month of such year, but

(B) either—

(i) on 1 or more days in such taxable year before the day on which the election was made the corporation did not meet the requirements of subsection (b) of section 1361, or

(ii) 1 or more of the persons who held stock in the corporation during such taxable year and before the election was made did not consent to the election,

then such election shall be treated as made for the following taxable year.

(3) ELECTION MADE AFTER 1ST 2½ MONTHS TREATED AS MADE FOR FOLLOWING TAXABLE YEAR.—If—

(A) a small business corporation makes an election under subsection (a) for any taxable year, and

(B) such election is made after the 15th day of the 3d month of the taxable year and on or before the 15th day of the 3rd month of the following taxable year,

then such election shall be treated as made for the following taxable year.

(4) TAXABLE YEARS OF 2½ MONTHS OR LESS.—For purposes of this subsection, an election for a taxable year made not later than 2 months and 15 days after the first day of the taxable year shall be treated as timely made during such year.

(5) AUTHORITY TO TREAT LATE ELECTIONS, ETC., AS TIMELY.—If—

(A) an election under subsection (a) is made for any taxable year (determined without regard to paragraph (3)) after the date prescribed by this subsection for making such election for such taxable year or no such election is made for any taxable year, and

(B) the Secretary determines that there was reasonable cause for the failure to timely make such election,

the Secretary may treat such an election as timely made for such taxable year (and paragraph (3) shall not apply).

[Sec. 1362(c)]

(c) YEARS FOR WHICH EFFECTIVE.—An election under subsection (a) shall be effective for the taxable year of the corporation for which it is made and for all succeeding taxable years of the corporation, until such election is terminated under subsection (d).

[Sec. 1362(d)]

(d) TERMINATION.—

(1) BY REVOCATION.—

(A) IN GENERAL.—An election under subsection (a) may be terminated by revocation.

(B) MORE THAN ONE-HALF OF SHARES MUST CONSENT TO REVOCATION.—An election may be revoked only if shareholders holding more than one-half of the shares of stock of the corporation on the day on which the revocation is made consent to the revocation.

(C) WHEN EFFECTIVE.—Except as provided in subparagraph (D)—

(i) a revocation made during the taxable year and on or before the 15th day of the 3d month thereof shall be effective on the 1st day of such taxable year, and

(ii) a revocation made during the taxable year but after such 15th day shall be effective on the 1st day of the following taxable year.

(D) REVOCATION MAY SPECIFY PROSPECTIVE DATE.—If the revocation specifies a date for revocation which is on or after the day on which the revocation is made, the revocation shall be effective on and after the date so specified.

(2) BY CORPORATION CEASING TO BE SMALL BUSINESS CORPORATION.—

(A) IN GENERAL.—An election under subsection (a) shall be terminated whenever (at any time on or after the 1st day of the 1st taxable year for which the corporation is an S corporation) such corporation ceases to be a small business corporation.

(B) WHEN EFFECTIVE.—Any termination under this paragraph shall be effective on and after the date of cessation.

(3) WHERE PASSIVE INVESTMENT INCOME EXCEEDS 25 PERCENT OF GROSS RECEIPTS FOR 3 CONSECUTIVE TAXABLE YEARS AND CORPORATION HAS ACCUMULATED EARNINGS AND PROFITS.—

(A) TERMINATION.—

(i) IN GENERAL.—An election under subsection (a) shall be terminated whenever the corporation—

(I) has accumulated earnings and profits at the close of each of 3 consecutive taxable years, and

(II) has gross receipts for each of such taxable years more than 25 percent of which are passive investment income.

(ii) WHEN EFFECTIVE.—Any termination under this paragraph shall be effective on and after the first day of the first taxable year beginning after the third consecutive taxable year referred to in clause (i).

(iii) YEARS TAKEN INTO ACCOUNT.—A prior taxable year shall not be taken into account under clause (i) unless—

(I) such taxable year began after December 31, 1981, and

(II) the corporation was an S corporation for such taxable year.

(B) GROSS RECEIPTS FROM SALES OF CAPITAL ASSETS (OTHER THAN STOCK AND SECURITIES).—For purposes of this paragraph, in the case of dispositions of capital assets (other than stock and securities), gross receipts from such dispositions shall be taken into account only to the extent of the capital gain net income therefrom.

(C) PASSIVE INVESTMENT INCOME DEFINED.—For purposes of this paragraph—

(i) IN GENERAL.—Except as otherwise provided in this subparagraph, the term "passive investment income" means gross receipts derived from royalties, rents, dividends, interest, annuities, and sales or exchanges of stock or securities (gross receipts from such sales or exchanges being taken into account for purposes of this paragraph only to the extent of gains therefrom).

(ii) EXCEPTION FOR INTEREST ON NOTES FROM SALES OF INVENTORY.—The term "passive investment income" shall not include interest on any obligation acquired in the ordinary course of the corporation's trade or business from its sale of property described in section 1221(a)(1).

(iii) TREATMENT OF CERTAIN LENDING OR FINANCE COMPANIES.—If the S corporation meets the requirements of section 542(c)(6) for the taxable year, the term "passive investment income" shall not include gross receipts for the taxable year which are derived directly from the active and regular conduct of a lending or finance business (as defined in section 542(d)(1)).

(iv) TREATMENT OF CERTAIN LIQUIDATIONS.—Gross receipts derived from sales or exchanges of stock or securities shall not include amounts received by an S corporation which are treated under section 331 (relating to corporate liquidations) as payments in exchange for stock where the S corporation owned more than 50 percent of each class of stock of the liquidating corporation.

Sec. 1362(d)

(D) SPECIAL RULE FOR OPTIONS AND COMMODITY DEALINGS.—

(i) IN GENERAL.—In the case of any options dealer or commodities dealer, passive investment income shall be determined by not taking into account any gain or loss (in the normal course of the taxpayer's activity of dealing in or trading section 1256 contracts) from any section 1256 contract or property related to such a contract.

(ii) DEFINITIONS.—For purposes of this subparagraph—

(I) OPTIONS DEALER.—The term "options dealer" has the meaning given such term by section 1256(g)(8).

(II) COMMODITIES DEALER.—The term "commodities dealer" means a person who is actively engaged in trading section 1256 contracts and is registered with a domestic board of trade which is designated as a contract market by the Commodities Futures Trading Commission.

(III) SECTION 1256 CONTRACT.—The term "section 1256 contract" has the meaning given to such term by section 1256(b).

(E) TREATMENT OF CERTAIN DIVIDENDS.—If an S corporation holds stock in a C corporation meeting the requirements of section 1504(a)(2), the term "passive investment income" shall not include dividends from such C corporation to the extent such dividends are attributable to the earnings and profits of such C corporation derived from the active conduct of a trade or business.

[Sec. 1362(e)]

(e) TREATMENT OF S TERMINATION YEAR.—

(1) IN GENERAL.—In the case of an S termination year, for purposes of this title—

(A) S SHORT YEAR.—The portion of such year ending before the 1st day for which the termination is effective shall be treated as a short taxable year for which the corporation is an S corporation.

(B) C SHORT YEAR.—The portion of such year beginning on such 1st day shall be treated as a short taxable year for which the corporation is a C corporation.

(2) PRO RATA ALLOCATION.—Except as provided in paragraph (3) and subparagraphs (C) and (D) of paragraph (6), the determination of which items are to be taken into account for each of the short taxable years referred to in paragraph (1) shall be made—

(A) first by determining for the S termination year—

(i) the amount of each of the items of income, loss, deduction, or credit described in section 1366(a)(1)(A), and

(ii) the amount of the nonseparately computed income or loss, and

(B) then by assigning an equal portion of each amount determined under subparagraph (A) to each day of the S termination year.

(3) ELECTION TO HAVE ITEMS ASSIGNED TO EACH SHORT TAXABLE YEAR UNDER NORMAL TAX ACCOUNTING RULES.—

(A) IN GENERAL.—A corporation may elect to have paragraph (2) not apply.

(B) SHAREHOLDERS MUST CONSENT TO ELECTION.—An election under this subsection shall be valid only if all persons who are shareholders in the corporation at any time during the S short year and all persons who are shareholders in the corporation on the first day of the C short year consent to such election.

(4) S TERMINATION YEAR.—For purposes of this subsection, the term "S termination year" means any taxable year of a corporation (determined without regard to this subsection) in which a termination of an election made under subsection (a) takes effect (other than on the 1st day thereof).

(5) TAX FOR C SHORT YEAR DETERMINED ON ANNUALIZED BASIS.—

(A) IN GENERAL.—The taxable income for the short year described in subparagraph (B) of paragraph (1) shall be placed on an annual basis by multiplying the taxable income for such short year by the number of days in the S termination year and by dividing the result by the number of days in the short year. The tax shall be the same part of the tax computed on the annual basis as the number of days in such short year is of the number of days in the S termination year.

(B) SECTION 443(d)(2) TO APPLY.—Subsection (d) of section 443 shall apply to the short taxable year described in subparagraph (B) of paragraph (1).

(6) OTHER SPECIAL RULES.—For purposes of this title—

(A) SHORT YEARS TREATED AS 1 YEAR FOR CARRYOVER PURPOSES.—The short taxable year described in subparagraph (A) of paragraph (1) shall not be taken into account for purposes of determining the number of taxable years to which any item may be carried back or carried forward by the corporation.

(B) DUE DATE FOR S YEAR.—The due date for filing the return for the short taxable year described in subparagraph (A) of paragraph (1) shall be the same as the due date for filing the return for the short taxable year described in subparagraph (B) of paragraph (1) (including extensions thereof).

(C) PARAGRAPH (2) NOT TO APPLY TO ITEMS RESULTING FROM SECTION 338.—Paragraph (2) shall not apply with respect to any item resulting from the application of section 338.

(D) PRO RATA ALLOCATION FOR S TERMINATION YEAR NOT TO APPLY IF 50-PERCENT CHANGE IN OWNERSHIP.—Paragraph (2) shall not apply to an S termination year if there is a sale or exchange of 50 percent or more of the stock in such corporation during such year.

[Sec. 1362(f)]

(f) INADVERTENT INVALID ELECTIONS OR TERMINATIONS.—If—

(1) an election under subsection (a) by any corporation—

(A) was not effective for the taxable year for which made (determined without regard to subsection (b)(2)) by reason of a failure to meet the requirements of section 1361(b) or to obtain shareholder consents, or

(B) was terminated under paragraph (2) or (3) of subsection (d),

(2) the Secretary determines that the circumstances resulting in such ineffectiveness or termination were inadvertent,

(3) no later than a reasonable period of time after discovery of the circumstances resulting in such ineffectiveness or termination, steps were taken—

(A) so that the corporation is a small business corporation, or

(B) to acquire the required shareholder consents, and

(4) the corporation, and each person who was a shareholder in the corporation at any time during the period specified pursuant to this subsection, agrees to make such adjustments (consistent with the treatment of the corporation as an S corporation) as may be required by the Secretary with respect to such period,

then, notwithstanding the circumstances resulting in such ineffectiveness or termination, such corporation shall be treated as an S corporation during the period specified by the Secretary.

[Sec. 1362(g)]

(g) ELECTION AFTER TERMINATION.—If a small business corporation has made an election under subsection (a) and if such election has been terminated under subsection (d), such corporation (and any successor corporation) shall not be eligible to make an election under subsection (a) for any taxable year before its 5th taxable year which begins after the 1st taxable year for which such termination is effective, unless the Secretary consents to such election.

[Sec. 1363]

SEC. 1363. EFFECT OF ELECTION ON CORPORATION.

[Sec. 1363(a)]

(a) GENERAL RULE.—Except as otherwise provided in this subchapter, an S corporation shall not be subject to the taxes imposed by this chapter.

[Sec. 1363(b)]

(b) COMPUTATION OF CORPORATION'S TAXABLE INCOME.—The taxable income of an S corporation shall be computed in the same manner as in the case of an individual, except that—

(1) the items described in section 1366(a)(1)(A) shall be separately stated,

(2) the deductions referred to in section 703(a)(2) shall not be allowed to the corporation,

(3) section 248 shall apply, and

(4) section 291 shall apply if the S corporation (or any predecessor) was a C corporation for any of the 3 immediately preceding taxable years.

[Sec. 1363(c)]

(c) ELECTIONS OF THE S CORPORATION.—

(1) IN GENERAL.—Except as provided in paragraph (2), any election affecting the computation of items derived from an S corporation shall be made by the corporation.

(2) EXCEPTIONS.—In the case of an S corporation, elections under the following provisions shall be made by each shareholder separately—

(A) section 617 (relating to deduction and recapture of certain mining exploration expenditures), and

(B) section 901 (relating to taxes of foreign countries and possessions of the United States).

[Sec. 1363(d)]

(d) RECAPTURE OF LIFO BENEFITS.—

(1) IN GENERAL.—If—

(A) an S corporation was a C corporation for the last taxable year before the first taxable year for which the election under section 1362(a) was effective, and

(B) the corporation inventoried goods under the LIFO method for such last taxable year,

the LIFO recapture amount shall be included in the gross income of the corporation for such last taxable year (and appropriate adjustments to the basis of inventory shall be made to take into account the amount included in gross income under this paragraph).

(2) ADDITIONAL TAX PAYABLE IN INSTALLMENTS.—

(A) IN GENERAL.—Any increase in the tax imposed by this chapter by reason of this subsection shall be payable in 4 equal installments.

PART II—TAX TREATMENT OF SHAREHOLDERS

[Sec. 1366]

SEC. 1366. PASS-THRU OF ITEMS TO SHAREHOLDERS.

[Sec. 1366(a)]

(a) DETERMINATION OF SHAREHOLDER'S TAX LIABILITY.—

(1) IN GENERAL.—In determining the tax under this chapter of a shareholder for the shareholder's taxable year in which the taxable year of the S corporation ends (or for the final taxable year of a shareholder who dies, or of a trust or estate which terminates, before the end of the corporation's taxable year), there shall be taken into account the shareholder's pro rata share of the corporation's—

(A) items of income (including tax-exempt income), loss, deduction, or credit the separate treatment of which could affect the liability for tax of any shareholder, and

(B) nonseparately computed income or loss.

For purposes of the preceding sentence, the items referred to in subparagraph (A) shall include amounts described in paragraph (4) or (6) of section 702(a).

(2) NONSEPARATELY COMPUTED INCOME OR LOSS DEFINED.—For purposes of this subchapter, the term "nonseparately computed income or loss" means gross income minus the deductions allowed to the corporation under this chapter, determined by excluding all items described in paragraph (1)(A).

[Sec. 1366(b)]

(b) CHARACTER PASSED THRU.—The character of any item included in a shareholder's pro rata share under paragraph (1) of subsection (a) shall be determined as if such item were realized directly from the source from which realized by the corporation, or incurred in the same manner as incurred by the corporation.

Sec. 1366(b)

(c) GROSS INCOME OF A SHAREHOLDER.—In any case where it is necessary to determine the gross income of a shareholder for purposes of this title, such gross income shall include the shareholder's pro rata share of the gross income of the corporation.

(d) SPECIAL RULES FOR LOSSES AND DEDUCTIONS.—

(1) CANNOT EXCEED SHAREHOLDER'S BASIS IN STOCK AND DEBT.—The aggregate amount of losses and deductions taken into account by a shareholder under subsection (a) for any taxable year shall not exceed the sum of—

(A) the adjusted basis of the shareholder's stock in the S corporation (determined with regard to paragraphs (1) and (2)(A) of section 1367(a) for the taxable year), and

(B) the shareholder's adjusted basis of any indebtedness of the S corporation to the shareholder (determined without regard to any adjustment under paragraph (2) of section 1367(b) for the taxable year).

(2) INDEFINITE CARRYOVER OF DISALLOWED LOSSES AND DEDUCTIONS.—Any loss or deduction which is disallowed for any taxable year by reason of paragraph (1) shall be treated as incurred by the corporation in the succeeding taxable year with respect to that shareholder.

(3) CARRYOVER OF DISALLOWED LOSSES AND DEDUCTIONS TO POST-TERMINATION TRANSITION PERIOD.—

(A) IN GENERAL.—If for the last taxable year of a corporation for which it was an S corporation a loss or deduction was disallowed by reason of paragraph (1), such loss or deduction shall be treated as incurred by the shareholder on the last day of any post-termination transition period.

(B) CANNOT EXCEED SHAREHOLDER'S BASIS IN STOCK.—The aggregate amount of losses and deductions taken into account by a shareholder under subparagraph (A) shall not exceed the adjusted basis of the shareholder's stock in the corporation (determined at the close of the last day of the post-termination transition period and without regard to this paragraph).

(C) ADJUSTMENT IN BASIS OF STOCK.—The shareholder's basis in the stock of the corporation shall be reduced by the amount allowed as a deduction by reason of this paragraph.

(D) AT-RISK LIMITATIONS.—To the extent that any increase in adjusted basis described in subparagraph (B) would have increased the shareholder's amount at risk under section 465 if such increase had occurred on the day preceding the commencement of the post-termination transition period, rules similar to the rules described in subparagraphs (A) through (C) shall apply to any losses disallowed by reason of section 465(a).

(e) TREATMENT OF FAMILY GROUP.—If an individual who is a member of the family (within the meaning of section 704(e)(3)) of one or more shareholders of an S corporation renders services for the corporation or furnishes capital to the corporation without receiving reasonable compensation therefor, the Secretary shall make such adjustments in the items taken into account by such individual and such shareholders as may be necessary in order to reflect the value of such services or capital.

(f) SPECIAL RULES.—

(1) SUBSECTION (a) NOT TO APPLY TO CREDIT ALLOWABLE UNDER SECTION 34.—Subsection (a) shall not apply with respect to any credit allowable under section 34 (relating to certain uses of gasoline and special fuels).

(2) TREATMENT OF TAX IMPOSED ON BUILT-IN GAINS.—If any tax is imposed under section 1374 for any taxable year on an S corporation, for purposes of subsection (a), the amount so imposed shall be treated as a loss sustained by the S corporation during such taxable year. The character of such loss shall be determined by allocating the loss proportionately among the recognized built-in gains giving rise to such tax.

(3) REDUCTION IN PASS-THRU FOR TAX IMPOSED ON EXCESS NET PASSIVE INCOME.—If any tax is imposed under section 1375 for any taxable year on an S corporation, for purposes of subsection (a),

each item of passive investment income shall be reduced by an amount which bears the same ratio to the amount of such tax as—

(A) the amount of such item, bears to

(B) the total passive investment income for the taxable year.

[Sec. 1367]
SEC. 1367. ADJUSTMENTS TO BASIS OF STOCK OF SHAREHOLDERS, ETC.

[Sec. 1367(a)]

(a) GENERAL RULE.—

(1) INCREASES IN BASIS.—The basis of each shareholder's stock in an S corporation shall be increased for any period by the sum of the following items determined with respect to that shareholder for such period:

(A) the items of income described in subparagraph (A) of section 1366(a)(1),

(B) any nonseparately computed income determined under subparagraph (B) of section 1366(a)(1), and

(C) the excess of the deductions for depletion over the basis of the property subject to depletion.

(2) DECREASES IN BASIS.—The basis of each shareholder's stock in an S corporation shall be decreased for any period (but not below zero) by the sum of the following items determined with respect to the shareholder for such period:

(A) distributions by the corporation which were not includible in the income of the shareholder by reason of section 1368,

(B) the items of loss and deduction described in subparagraph (A) of section 1366(a)(1),

(C) any nonseparately computed loss determined under subparagraph (B) of section 1366(a)(1),

(D) any expense of the corporation not deductible in computing its taxable income and not properly chargeable to capital account, and

(E) the amount of the shareholder's deduction for depletion for any oil and gas property held by the S corporation to the extent such deduction does not exceed the proportionate share of the adjusted basis of such property allocated to such shareholder under section 613A(c)(11)(B).

[Sec. 1367(b)]

(b) SPECIAL RULES.—

(1) INCOME ITEMS.—An amount which is required to be included in the gross income of a shareholder and shown on his return shall be taken into account under subparagraph (A) or (B) of subsection (a)(1) only to the extent such amount is included in the shareholder's gross income on his return, increased or decreased by any adjustment of such amount in a redetermination of the shareholder's tax liability.

(2) ADJUSTMENTS IN BASIS OF INDEBTEDNESS.—

(A) REDUCTION OF BASIS.—If for any taxable year the amounts specified in subparagraphs (B), (C), (D), and (E) of subsection (a)(2) exceed the amount which reduces the shareholder's basis to zero, such excess shall be applied to reduce (but not below zero) the shareholder's basis in any indebtedness of the S corporation to the shareholder.

(B) RESTORATION OF BASIS.—If for any taxable year beginning after December 31, 1982, there is a reduction under subparagraph (A) in the shareholder's basis in the indebtedness of an S corporation to a shareholder, any net increase (after the application of paragraphs (1) and (2) of subsection (a)) for any subsequent taxable year shall be applied to restore such reduction in basis before any of it may be used to increase the shareholder's basis in the stock of the S corporation.

(3) COORDINATION WITH SECTIONS 165(g) AND 166(d).—This section and section 1366 shall be applied before the application of sections 165(g) and 166(d) to any taxable year of the shareholder or the corporation in which the security or debt becomes worthless.

(4) ADJUSTMENTS IN CASE OF INHERITED STOCK.—

(A) IN GENERAL.—If any person acquires stock in an S corporation by reason of the death of a decedent or by bequest, devise, or inheritance, section 691 shall be applied with respect to any item of income of the S corporation in the same manner as if the decedent had held directly his pro rata share of such item.

(B) ADJUSTMENTS TO BASIS.—The basis determined under section 1014 of any stock in an S corporation shall be reduced by the portion of the value of the stock which is attributable to items constituting income in respect of the decedent.

[Sec. 1368]

SEC. 1368. DISTRIBUTIONS.

[Sec. 1368(a)]

(a) GENERAL RULE.—A distribution of property made by an S corporation with respect to its stock to which (but for this subsection) section 301(c) would apply shall be treated in the manner provided in subsection (b) or (c), whichever applies.

[Sec. 1368(b)]

(b) S CORPORATION HAVING NO EARNINGS AND PROFITS.—In the case of a distribution described in subsection (a) by an S corporation which has no accumulated earnings and profits—

(1) AMOUNT APPLIED AGAINST BASIS.—The distribution shall not be included in gross income to the extent that it does not exceed the adjusted basis of the stock.

(2) AMOUNT IN EXCESS OF BASIS.—If the amount of the distribution exceeds the adjusted basis of the stock, such excess shall be treated as gain from the sale or exchange of property.

[Sec. 1368(c)]

(c) S CORPORATION HAVING EARNINGS AND PROFITS.—In the case of a distribution described in subsection (a) by an S corporation which has accumulated earnings and profits—

(1) ACCUMULATED ADJUSTMENTS ACCOUNT.—That portion of the distribution which does not exceed the accumulated adjustments account shall be treated in the manner provided by subsection (b).

(2) DIVIDEND.—That portion of the distribution which remains after the application of paragraph (1) shall be treated as a dividend to the extent it does not exceed the accumulated earnings and profits of the S corporation.

(3) TREATMENT OF REMAINDER.—Any portion of the distribution remaining after the application of paragraph (2) of this subsection shall be treated in the manner provided by subsection (b).

Except to the extent provided in regulations, if the distributions during the taxable year exceed the amount in the accumulated adjustments account at the close of the taxable year, for purposes of this subsection, the balance of such account shall be allocated among such distributions in proportion to their respective sizes.

[Sec. 1368(d)]

(d) CERTAIN ADJUSTMENTS TAKEN INTO ACCOUNT.—Subsections (b) and (c) shall be applied by taking into account (to the extent proper)—

(1) the adjustments to the basis of the shareholder's stock described in section 1367, and

(2) the adjustments to the accumulated adjustments account which are required by subsection (e)(1).

In the case of any distribution made during any taxable year, the adjusted basis of the stock shall be determined with regard to the adjustments provided in paragraph (1) of section 1367(a) for the taxable year.

[Sec. 1368(e)]

(e) DEFINITIONS AND SPECIAL RULES.—For purposes of this section—

(1) ACCUMULATED ADJUSTMENTS ACCOUNT.—

(A) IN GENERAL.—Except as otherwise provided in this paragraph, the term "accumulated adjustments account" means an account of the S corporation which is adjusted for the S period in a manner similar to the adjustments under section 1367 (except that no adjustment shall be made for income (and related expenses) which is exempt from tax under this title and the phrase "(but not below zero)" shall be disregarded in section 1367(a)(2)) and no adjustment shall be made for Federal taxes attributable to any taxable year in which the corporation was a C corporation.

(B) AMOUNT OF ADJUSTMENT IN THE CASE OF REDEMPTIONS.—In the case of any redemption which is treated as an exchange under section 302(a) or 303(a), the adjustment in the accumulated adjustments account shall be an amount which bears the same ratio to the balance in such account as the number of shares redeemed in such redemption bears to the number of shares of stock in the corporation immediately before such redemption.

(C) NET LOSS FOR YEAR DISREGARDED.—

(i) IN GENERAL.—In applying this section to distributions made during any taxable year, the amount in the accumulated adjustments account as of the close of such taxable year shall be determined without regard to any net negative adjustment for such taxable year.

(ii) NET NEGATIVE ADJUSTMENT.—For purposes of clause (i), the term "net negative adjustment" means, with respect to any taxable year, the excess (if any) of—

(I) the reductions in the account for the taxable year (other than for distributions), over

(II) the increases in such account for such taxable year.

(2) S PERIOD.—The term "S period" means the most recent continuous period during which the corporation has been an S corporation. Such period shall not include any taxable year beginning before January 1, 1983.

(3) ELECTION TO DISTRIBUTE EARNINGS FIRST.—

(A) IN GENERAL.—An S corporation may, with the consent of all of its affected shareholders, elect to have paragraph (1) of subsection (c) not apply to all distributions made during the taxable year for which the election is made.

(B) AFFECTED SHAREHOLDER.—For purposes of subparagraph (A), the term "affected shareholder" means any shareholder to whom a distribution is made by the S corporation during the taxable year.

PART III—SPECIAL RULES

[Sec. 1371]

SEC. 1371. COORDINATION WITH SUBCHAPTER C.

[Sec. 1371(a)]

(a) APPLICATION OF SUBCHAPTER C RULES.—Except as otherwise provided in this title, and except to the extent inconsistent with this subchapter, subchapter C shall apply to an S corporation and its shareholders.

[Sec. 1371(b)]

(b) NO CARRYOVER BETWEEN C YEAR AND S YEAR.—

(1) FROM C YEAR TO S YEAR.—No carryforward, and no carryback, arising for a taxable year for which a corporation is a C corporation may be carried to a taxable year for which such corporation is an S corporation.

(2) NO CARRYOVER FROM S YEAR.—No carryforward, and no carryback, shall arise at the corporate level for a taxable year for which a corporation is an S corporation.

(3) TREATMENT OF S YEAR AS ELAPSED YEAR.—Nothing in paragraphs (1) and (2) shall prevent treating a taxable year for which a corporation is an S corporation as a taxable year for purposes of determining the number of taxable years to which an item may be carried back or carried forward.

[Sec. 1371(c)]

(c) EARNINGS AND PROFITS.—

(1) IN GENERAL.—Except as provided in paragraphs (2) and (3) and subsection (d)(3), no adjustment shall be made to the earnings and profits of an S corporation.

(2) ADJUSTMENTS FOR REDEMPTIONS, LIQUIDATIONS, REORGANIZATIONS, DIVISIVES, ETC.—In the case of any transaction involving the application of subchapter C to any S corporation, proper adjustment to any accumulated earnings and profits of the corporation shall be made.

(3) ADJUSTMENTS IN CASE OF DISTRIBUTIONS TREATED AS DIVIDENDS UNDER SECTION 1368(c)(2).— Paragraph (1) shall not apply with respect to that portion of a distribution which is treated as a dividend under section 1368(c)(2).

* * *

[Sec. 1371(e)]

(e) CASH DISTRIBUTIONS DURING POST-TERMINATION TRANSITION PERIOD.—

(1) IN GENERAL.—Any distribution of money by a corporation with respect to its stock during a post-termination transition period shall be applied against and reduce the adjusted basis of the stock, to the extent that the amount of the distribution does not exceed the accumulated adjustments account (within the meaning of section 1368(e)).

(2) ELECTION TO DISTRIBUTE EARNINGS FIRST.—An S corporation may elect to have paragraph (1) not apply to all distributions made during a post-termination transition period described in section 1377(b)(1)(A). Such election shall not be effective unless all shareholders of the S corporation to whom distributions are made by the S corporation during such post-termination transition period consent to such election.

[Sec. 1372]

SEC. 1372. PARTNERSHIP RULES TO APPLY FOR FRINGE BENEFIT PURPOSES.

[Sec. 1372(a)]

(a) GENERAL RULE.—For purposes of applying the provisions of this subtitle which relate to employee fringe benefits—

(1) the S corporation shall be treated as a partnership, and

(2) any 2-percent shareholder of the S corporation shall be treated as a partner of such partnership.

[Sec. 1372(b)]

(b) 2-PERCENT SHAREHOLDER DEFINED.—For purposes of this section, the term "2-percent shareholder" means any person who owns (or is considered as owning within the meaning of section 318) on any day during the taxable year of the S corporation more than 2 percent of the outstanding stock of such corporation or stock possessing more than 2 percent of the total combined voting power of all stock of such corporation.

[Sec. 1374]

SEC. 1374. TAX IMPOSED ON CERTAIN BUILT-IN GAINS.

[Sec. 1374(a)]

(a) GENERAL RULE.—If for any taxable year beginning in the recognition period an S corporation has a net recognized built-in gain, there is hereby imposed a tax (computed under subsection (b)) on the income of such corporation for such taxable year.

[Sec. 1374(b)]

(b) AMOUNT OF TAX.—

(1) IN GENERAL.—The amount of the tax imposed by subsection (a) shall be computed by applying the highest rate of tax specified in section 11(b) to the net recognized built-in gain of the S corporation for the taxable year.

(2) NET OPERATING LOSS CARRYFORWARDS FROM C YEARS ALLOWED.—Notwithstanding section 1371(b)(1), any net operating loss carryforward arising in a taxable year for which the corporation was a C corporation shall be allowed for purposes of this section as a deduction against the net recognized built-in gain of the S corporation for the taxable year. For purposes of determining the amount of any such loss which may be carried to subsequent taxable years, the amount of the net recognized built-in gain shall be treated as taxable income. Rules similar to the rules of the preceding

sentences of this paragraph shall apply in the case of a capital loss carryforward arising in a taxable year for which the corporation was a C corporation.

(3) CREDITS.—

(A) IN GENERAL.—Except as provided in subparagraph (B), no credit shall be allowable under part IV if subchapter A of this chapter (other than under section 34) against the tax imposed by subsection (a).

(B) BUSINESS CREDIT CARRYFORWARDS FROM C YEARS ALLOWED.—Notwithstanding section 1371(b)(1), any business credit carryforward under section 39 arising in a taxable year for which the corporation was a C corporation shall be allowed as a credit against the tax imposed by subsection (a) in the same manner as if it were imposed by section 11. A similar rule shall apply in the case of the minimum tax credit under section 53 to the extent attributable to taxable years for which the corporation was a C corporation.

(4) COORDINATION WITH SECTION 1201(a).—For purposes of section 1201(a)—

(A) the tax imposed by subsection (a) shall be treated as if it were imposed by section 11, and

(B) the amount of the net recognized built-in gain shall be treated as the taxable income.

[Sec. 1374(c)]

(c) LIMITATIONS.—

(1) CORPORATIONS WHICH WERE ALWAYS S CORPORATIONS.—Subsection (a) shall not apply to any corporation if an election under section 1362(a) has been in effect with respect to such corporation for each of its taxable years. Except as provided in regulations, an S corporation and any predecessor corporation shall be treated as 1 corporation for purposes of the preceding sentence.

(2) LIMITATION ON AMOUNT OF RECOGNIZED BUILT-IN GAINS.—The amount of the net recognized built-in gain taken into account under this section for any taxable year shall not exceed the excess (if any) of—

(A) the net unrealized built-in gain, over

(B) the net recognized built-in gain for prior taxable years beginning in the recognition period.

[Sec. 1374(d)]

(d) DEFINITIONS AND SPECIAL RULES.—For purposes of this section—

(1) NET UNREALIZED BUILT-IN GAIN.—The term "net unrealized built-in gain" means the amount (if any) by which—

(A) the fair market value of the assets of S corporation as of the beginning of its 1st taxable year for which an election under section 1362(a) is in effect, exceeds

(B) the aggregate adjusted bases of such assets at such time.

(2) NET RECOGNIZED BUILT-IN GAIN.—

(A) IN GENERAL.—The term "net recognized built-in gain" means, with respect to any taxable year in the recognition period, the lesser of—

(i) the amount which would be taxable income of the S corporation for such taxable year if only recognized built-in gains and recognized built-in losses were taken into account, or

(ii) such corporation's taxable income for such taxable year (determined as provided in section 1375(b)(1)(B)).

(B) CARRYOVER.—If, for any taxable year, the amount referred to in clause (i) of subparagraph (A) exceeds the amount referred to in clause (ii) of subparagraph (A), such excess shall be treated as a recognized built-in gain in the succeeding taxable year. The preceding sentence shall apply only in the case of a corporation treated as an S corporation by reason of an election made on or after March 31, 1988.

(3) RECOGNIZED BUILT-IN GAIN.—The term "recognized built-in gain" means any gain recognized during the recognition period on the disposition of any asset except to the extent that the S corporation establishes that—

(A) such asset was not held by the S corporation as of the beginning of the 1st taxable year for which it was an S corporation, or

(B) such gain exceeds the excess (if any) of—

(i) the fair market value of such asset as of the beginning of such 1st taxable year, over

(ii) the adjusted basis of the asset as of such time.

(4) RECOGNIZED BUILT-IN LOSSES.—The term "recognized built-in loss" means any loss recognized during the recognition period on the disposition of any asset to the extent that the S corporation establishes that—

(A) such asset was held by the S corporation as of the beginning of the 1st taxable year referred to in paragraph (3), and

(B) such loss does not exceed the excess of—

(i) the adjusted basis of such asset as of the beginning of such 1st taxable year, over

(ii) the fair market value of such asset as of such time.

(5) TREATMENT OF CERTAIN BUILT-IN ITEMS.—

(A) INCOME ITEMS.—Any item of income which is properly taken into account during the recognition period but which is attributable to periods before the 1st taxable year for which the corporation was an S corporation shall be treated as a recognized built-in gain for the taxable year in which it is properly taken into account.

(B) DEDUCTION ITEMS.—Any amount which is allowable as a deduction during the recognition period (determined without regard to any carryover) but which is attributable to periods before the 1st taxable year referred to in subparagraph (A) shall be treated as a recognized built-in loss for the taxable year for which it is allowable as a deduction.

(C) ADJUSTMENT TO NET UNREALIZED BUILT-IN GAIN.—The amount of the net unrealized built-in gain shall be properly adjusted for amounts which would be treated as recognized built-in gains or losses under this paragraph if such amounts were properly taken into account (or allowable as a deduction) during the recognition period.

(6) TREATMENT OF CERTAIN PROPERTY.—If the adjusted basis of any asset is determined (in whole or in part) by reference to the adjusted basis of any other asset held by the S corporation as of the beginning of the 1st taxable year referred to in paragraph (3)—

(A) such asset shall be treated as held by the S corporation as of the beginning of such 1st taxable year, and

(B) any determination under paragraph (3)(B) or (4)(B) with respect to such asset shall be made by reference to the fair market value and adjusted basis of such other asset as of the beginning of such 1st taxable year.

(7) RECOGNITION PERIOD.—The term "recognition period" means the 10-year period beginning with the 1st day of the 1st taxable year for which the corporation was an S corporation. For purposes of applying this section to any amount includible in income by reason of section 593(e), the preceding sentence shall be applied without regard to the phrase "10-year".

(8) TREATMENT OF TRANSFER OF ASSETS FROM C CORPORATION TO S CORPORATION.—

(A) IN GENERAL.—Except to the extent provided in regulations, if—

(i) an S corporation acquires any asset, and

(ii) the S corporation's basis in such asset is determined (in whole or in part) by reference to the basis of such asset (or any other property) in the hands of a C corporation,

then a tax is hereby imposed on any net recognized built-in gain attributable to any such assets for any taxable year beginning in the recognition period. The amount of such tax shall be determined under the rules of this section as modified by subparagraph (B).

(B) MODIFICATIONS.—For purposes of this paragraph, the modifications of this subparagraph are as follows:

(i) IN GENERAL.—The preceding paragraphs of this subsection shall be applied by taking into account the day on which the assets were acquired by the S corporation in lieu of the beginning of the 1st taxable year for which the corporation was an S corporation.

(ii) SUBSECTION (c)(1) NOT TO APPLY.—Subsection (c)(1) shall not apply.

Sec. 1374(d)

(9) REFERENCE TO 1ST TAXABLE YEAR.—Any reference in this section to the 1st taxable year for which the corporation was an S corporation shall be treated as a reference to the 1st taxable year for which the corporation was an S corporation pursuant to its most recent election under section 1362.

[Sec. 1374(e)]

(e) REGULATIONS.—The Secretary shall prescribe such regulations as may be necessary to carry out the purposes of this section including regulations providing for the appropriate treatment of successor corporations.

[Sec. 1375]

SEC. 1375. TAX IMPOSED WHEN PASSIVE INVESTMENT INCOME OF CORPORATION HAVING ACCUMULATED EARNINGS AND PROFITS EXCEEDS 25 PERCENT OF GROSS RECEIPTS.

[Sec. 1375(a)]

(a) GENERAL RULE.—If for the taxable year an S corporation has—

(1) accumulated earnings and profits at the close of such taxable year, and

(2) gross receipts more than 25 percent of which are passive investment income,

then there is hereby imposed a tax on the income of such corporation for such taxable year. Such tax shall be computed by multiplying the excess net passive income by the highest rate of tax specified in section 11(b).

[Sec. 1375(b)]

(b) DEFINITIONS.—For purposes of this section—

(1) EXCESS NET PASSIVE INCOME.—

(A) IN GENERAL.—Except as provided in subparagraph (B), the term "excess net passive income" means an amount which bears the same ratio to the net passive income for the taxable year as—

(i) the amount by which the passive investment income for the taxable year exceeds 25 percent of the gross receipts for the taxable year, bears to

(ii) the passive investment income for the taxable year.

(B) LIMITATION.—The amount of the excess net passive income for any taxable year shall not exceed the amount of the corporation's taxable income for such taxable year as determined under section 63(a)—

(i) without regard to the deductions allowed by part VIII of subchapter B (other than the deduction allowed by section 248, relating to organization expenditures), and

(ii) without regard to the deduction under section 172.

(2) NET PASSIVE INCOME.—The term "net passive income" means—

(A) passive investment income, reduced by

(B) the deductions allowable under this chapter which are directly connected with the production of such income (other than deductions allowable under section 172 and part VIII of subchapter B).

(3) PASSIVE INVESTMENT INCOME, ETC.—The terms "passive investment income" and "gross receipts" have the same respective meanings as when used in paragraph (3) of section 1362(d).

(4) COORDINATION WITH SECTION 1374.—Notwithstanding paragraph (3), the amount of passive investment income shall be determined by not taking into account any recognized built-in gain or loss of the S corporation for any taxable year in the recognition period. Terms used in the preceding sentence shall have the same respective meanings as when used in section 1374.

[Sec. 1375(c)]

(c) CREDITS NOT ALLOWABLE.—No credit shall be allowed under part IV of subchapter A of this chapter (other than section 34) against the tax imposed by subsection (a).

Sec. 1375(c)

[Sec. 1375(d)]

(d) WAIVER OF TAX IN CERTAIN CASES.—If the S corporation establishes to the satisfaction of the Secretary that—

(1) it determined in good faith that it had no subchapter C earnings and profits at the close of a taxable year, and

(2) during a reasonable period of time after it was determined that it did have subchapter C earnings and profits at the close of such taxable year such earnings and profits were distributed,

the Secretary may waive the tax imposed by subsection (a) for such taxable year.

PART IV—DEFINITIONS; MISCELLANEOUS

[Sec. 1377]

SEC. 1377. DEFINITIONS AND SPECIAL RULE.

[Sec. 1377(a)]

(a) PRO RATA SHARE.—For purposes of this subchapter—

(1) IN GENERAL.—Except as provided in paragraph (2), each shareholder's pro rata share of any item for any taxable year shall be the sum of the amounts determined with respect to the shareholder—

(A) by assigning an equal portion of such item to each day of the taxable year, and

(B) then by dividing that portion pro rata among the shares outstanding on such day.

(2) ELECTION TO TERMINATE YEAR.—

(A) IN GENERAL.—Under regulations prescribed by the Secretary, if any shareholder terminates the shareholder's interest in the corporation during the taxable year and all affected shareholders and the corporation agree to the application of this paragraph, paragraph (1) shall be applied to the affected shareholders as if the taxable year consisted of 2 taxable years the first of which ends on the date of the termination.

(B) AFFECTED SHAREHOLDERS.—For purposes of subparagraph (A), the term "affected shareholders" means the shareholder whose interest is terminated and all shareholders to whom such shareholder has transferred shares during the taxable year. If such shareholder has transferred shares to the corporation, the term "affected shareholders" shall include all persons who are shareholders during the taxable year.

[Sec. 1377(b)]

(b) POST-TERMINATION TRANSITION PERIOD.—

(1) IN GENERAL.—For purposes of this subchapter, the term "post-termination transition period" means—

(A) the period beginning on the day after the last day of the corporation's last taxable year as an S corporation and ending on the later of—

(i) the day which is 1 year after such last day, or

(ii) the due date for filing the return for such last year as an S corporation (including extensions),

(B) the 120-day period beginning on the date of any determination pursuant to an audit of the taxpayer which follows the termination of the corporation's election and which adjusts a subchapter S item of income, loss, or deduction of the corporation arising during the S period (as defined in section 1368(e)(2)), and

(C) the 120-day period beginning on the date of a determination that the corporation's election under section 1362(a) had terminated for a previous taxable year.

(2) DETERMINATION DEFINED.—For purposes of paragraph (1), the term "determination" means—

(A) a determination as defined in section 1313(a), or

(B) an agreement between the corporation and the Secretary that the corporation failed to qualify as an S corporation.

Sec. 1375(d)

(c) MANNER OF MAKING ELECTIONS, ETC.—Any election under this subchapter, and any revocation under section 1362(d)(1), shall be made in such manner as the Secretary shall by regulations prescribe.

[Sec. 1378]

SEC. 1378. TAXABLE YEAR OF S CORPORATION.

[Sec. 1378(a)]

(a) GENERAL RULE.—For purposes of this subtitle, the taxable year of an S corporation shall be a permitted year.

[Sec. 1378(b)]

(b) PERMITTED YEAR DEFINED.—For purposes of this section, the term "permitted year" means a taxable year which—

(1) is a year ending December 31, or

(2) is any other accounting period for which the corporation establishes a business purpose to the satisfaction of the Secretary.

For purposes of paragraph (2), any deferral of income to shareholders shall not be treated as a business purpose.

Subchapter V—Title 11 Cases

[Sec. 1398]

SEC. 1398. RULES RELATING TO INDIVIDUALS' TITLE 11 CASES.

[Sec. 1398(a)]

(a) CASES TO WHICH SECTION APPLIES.—Except as provided in subsection (b), this section shall apply to any case under chapter 7 (relating to liquidations) or chapter 11 (relating to reorganizations) of title 11 of the United States Code in which the debtor is an individual.

[Sec. 1398(b)]

(b) EXCEPTIONS WHERE CASE IS DISMISSED, ETC.—

(1) SECTION DOES NOT APPLY WHERE CASE IS DISMISSED.—This section shall not apply if the case under chapter 7 or 11 of title 11 of the United States Code is dismissed.

(2) SECTION DOES NOT APPLY AT PARTNERSHIP LEVEL.—For purposes of subsection (a), a partnership shall not be treated as an individual, but the interest in a partnership of a debtor who is an individual shall be taken into account under this section in the same manner as any other interest of the debtor.

[Sec. 1398(c)]

(c) COMPUTATION AND PAYMENT OF TAX; BASIC STANDARD DEDUCTION.—

(1) COMPUTATION AND PAYMENT OF TAX.—Except as otherwise provided in this section, the taxable income of the estate shall be computed in the same manner as for an individual. The tax shall be computed on such taxable income and shall be paid by the trustee.

(2) TAX RATES.—The tax on the taxable income of the estate shall be determined under subsection (d) of section 1.

(3) BASIC STANDARD DEDUCTION.—In the case of an estate which does not itemize deductions, the basic standard deduction for the estate for the taxable year shall be the same as for a married individual filing a separate return for such year.

[Sec. 1398(d)]

(d) TAXABLE YEAR OF DEBTORS.—

(1) GENERAL RULE.—Except as provided in paragraph (2), the taxable year of the debtor shall be determined without regard to the case under title 11 of the United States Code to which this section applies.

(2) ELECTION TO TERMINATE DEBTOR'S YEAR WHEN CASE COMMENCES.—

(A) IN GENERAL.—Notwithstanding section 442, the debtor may (without the approval of the Secretary) elect to treat the debtor's taxable year which includes the commencement date as 2 taxable years—

(i) the first of which ends on the day before the commencement date, and

(ii) the second of which begins on the commencement date.

(B) SPOUSE MAY JOIN IN ELECTION.—In the case of a married individual (within the meaning of section 7703), the spouse may elect to have the debtor's election under subparagraph (A) also apply to the spouse, but only if the debtor and the spouse file a joint return for the taxable year referred to in subparagraph (A)(i).

(C) NO ELECTION WHERE DEBTOR HAS NO ASSETS.—No election may be made under subparagraph (A) by a debtor who has no assets other than property which the debtor may treat as exempt property under section 522 of title 11 of the United States Code.

(D) TIME FOR MAKING ELECTION.—An election under subparagraph (A) or (B) may be made only on or before the due date for filing the return for the taxable year referred to in subparagraph (A)(i). Any such election, once made, shall be irrevocable.

(E) RETURNS.—A return shall be made for each of the taxable years specified in subparagraph (A).

(F) ANNUALIZATION.—For purposes of subsections (b), (c), and (d) of section 443, a return filed for either of the taxable years referred to in subparagraph (A) shall be treated as a return made under paragraph (1) of subsection (a) of section 443.

(3) COMMENCEMENT DATE DEFINED.—For purposes of this subsection, the term "commencement date" means the day on which the case under title 11 of the United States Code to which this section applies commences.

[Sec. 1398(e)]

(e) TREATMENT OF INCOME, DEDUCTIONS, AND CREDITS.—

(1) ESTATE'S SHARE OF DEBTOR'S INCOME.—The gross income of the estate for each taxable year shall include the gross income of the debtor to which the estate is entitled under title 11 of the United States Code. The preceding sentence shall not apply to any amount received or accrued by the debtor before the commencement date (as defined in subsection (d)(3)).

(2) DEBTOR'S SHARE OF DEBTOR'S INCOME.—The gross income of the debtor for any taxable year shall not include any item to the extent that such item is included in the gross income of the estate by reason of paragraph (1).

(3) RULE FOR MAKING DETERMINATIONS WITH RESPECT TO DEDUCTIONS, CREDITS, AND EMPLOYMENT TAXES.—Except as otherwise provided in this section, the determination of whether or not any amount paid or incurred by the estate—

(A) is allowable as a deduction or credit under this chapter, or

(B) is wages for purposes of subtitle C,

shall be made as if the amount were paid or incurred by the debtor and as if the debtor were still engaged in the trades and businesses, and in the activities, the debtor was engaged in before the commencement of the case.

[Sec. 1398(f)]

(f) TREATMENT OF TRANSFERS BETWEEN DEBTOR AND ESTATE.—

(1) TRANSFER TO ESTATE NOT TREATED AS DISPOSITION.—A transfer (other than by sale or exchange) of an asset from the debtor to the estate shall not be treated as a disposition for purposes of any provision of this title assigning tax consequences to a disposition, and the estate shall be treated as the debtor would be treated with respect to such asset.

(2) TRANSFER FROM ESTATE TO DEBTOR NOT TREATED AS DISPOSITION.—In the case of a termination of the estate, a transfer (other than by sale or exchange) of an asset from the estate to the debtor shall not be treated as a disposition for purposes of any provision of this title assigning tax consequences to a disposition, and the debtor shall be treated as the estate would be treated with respect to such asset.

(g) ESTATE SUCCEEDS TO TAX ATTRIBUTES OF DEBTOR.—The estate shall succeed to and take into account the following items (determined as of the first day of the debtor's taxable year in which the case commences) of the debtor—

(1) NET OPERATING LOSS CARRYOVERS.—The net operating loss carryovers determined under section 172.

(2) CHARITABLE CONTRIBUTIONS CARRYOVERS.—The carryover of excess charitable contributions determined under section 170(d)(1).

(3) RECOVERY OF TAX BENEFIT ITEMS.—Any amount to which section 111 (relating to recovery of tax benefit items) applies.

(4) CREDIT CARRYOVERS, ETC.—The carryovers of any credit, and all other items which, but for the commencement of the case, would be required to be taken into account by the debtor with respect to any credit.

(5) CAPITAL LOSS CARRYOVERS.—The capital loss carryover determined under section 1212.

(6) BASIS, HOLDING PERIOD, AND CHARACTER OF ASSETS.—In the case of any asset acquired (other than by sale or exchange) by the estate from the debtor, the basis, holding period, and character it had in the hands of the debtor.

(7) METHOD OF ACCOUNTING.—The method of accounting used by the debtor.

(8) OTHER ATTRIBUTES.—Other tax attributes of the debtor, to the extent provided in regulations prescribed by the Secretary as necessary or appropriate to carry out the purposes of this section.

(h) ADMINISTRATION, LIQUIDATION, AND REORGANIZATION EXPENSES; CARRYOVERS AND CARRYBACKS OF CERTAIN EXCESS EXPENSES.—

(1) ADMINISTRATION, LIQUIDATION, AND REORGANIZATION EXPENSES.—Any administrative expense allowed under section 503 of title 11 of the United States Code, and any fee or charge assessed against the estate under chapter 123 of title 28 of the United States Code, to the extent not disallowed under any other provision of this title, shall be allowed as a deduction.

(2) CARRYBACK AND CARRYOVER OF EXCESS ADMINISTRATIVE COSTS, ETC., TO ESTATE TAXABLE YEARS.—

(A) DEDUCTION ALLOWED.—There shall be allowed as a deduction for the taxable year an amount equal to the aggregate of (i) the administrative expense carryovers to such year, plus (ii) the administrative expense carrybacks to such year.

(B) ADMINISTRATIVE EXPENSE LOSS, ETC.—If a net operating loss would be created or increased for any estate taxable year if section 172(c) were applied without the modification contained in paragraph (4) of section 172(d), then the amount of the net operating loss so created (or the amount of the increase in the net operating loss) shall be an administrative expense loss for such taxable year which shall be an administrative expense carryback to each of the 3 preceding taxable years and an administrative expense carryover to each of the 7 succeeding taxable years.

(C) DETERMINATION OF AMOUNT CARRIED TO EACH TAXABLE YEAR.—The portion of any administrative expense loss which may be carried to any other taxable year shall be determined under section 172(b)(2), except that for each taxable year the computation under section 172(b)(2) with respect to the net operating loss shall be made before the computation under this paragraph.

(D) ADMINISTRATIVE EXPENSE DEDUCTIONS ALLOWED ONLY TO ESTATE.—The deductions allowable under this chapter solely by reason of paragraph (1), and the deduction provided by subparagraph (A) of this paragraph, shall be allowable only to the estate.

(i) DEBTOR SUCCEEDS TO TAX ATTRIBUTES OF ESTATE.—In the case of a termination of an estate, the debtor shall succeed to and take into account the items referred to in paragraphs (1), (2), (3), (4), (5), and (6) of subsection (g) in a manner similar to that provided in such paragraphs (but taking into account that the transfer is from the estate to the debtor instead of from the debtor to the estate). In addition, the debtor shall succeed to and take into account the other tax attributes of the estate, to the extent provided in regulations prescribed by the Secretary as necessary or appropriate to carry out the purposes of this section.

[Sec. 1398(j)]

(j) OTHER SPECIAL RULES.—

(1) CHANGE OF ACCOUNTING PERIOD WITHOUT APPROVAL.—Notwithstanding section 442, the estate may change its annual accounting period one time without the approval of the Secretary.

(2) TREATMENT OF CERTAIN CARRYBACKS.—

(A) CARRYBACKS FROM ESTATE.—If any carryback year of the estate is a taxable year before the estate's first taxable year, the carryback to such carryback year shall be taken into account for the debtor's taxable year corresponding to the carryback year.

(B) CARRYBACKS FROM DEBTOR'S ACTIVITIES.—The debtor may not carry back to a taxable year before the debtor's taxable year in which the case commences any carryback from a taxable year ending after the case commences.

(C) CARRYBACK AND CARRYBACK YEAR DEFINED.—For purposes of this paragraph—

(i) CARRYBACK.—The term "carryback" means a net operating loss carryback under section 172 or a carryback of any credit provided by part IV of subchapter A.

(ii) CARRYBACK YEAR.—The term "carryback year" means the taxable year to which a carryback is carried.

[Sec. 1399]

SEC. 1399. NO SEPARATE TAXABLE ENTITIES FOR PARTNERSHIPS, CORPORATIONS, ETC.

Except in any case to which section 1398 applies, no separate taxable entity shall result from the commencement of a case under title 11 of the United States Code.

CHAPTER 6—CONSOLIDATED RETURNS

Subchapter A—Returns and Payment of Tax

[Sec. 1501]

SEC. 1501. PRIVILEGE TO FILE CONSOLIDATED RETURNS.

An affiliated group of corporations shall, subject to the provisions of this chapter, have the privilege of making a consolidated return with respect to the income tax imposed by chapter 1 for the taxable year in lieu of separate returns. The making of a consolidated return shall be upon the condition that all corporations which at any time during the taxable year have been members of the affiliated group consent to all the consolidated return regulations prescribed under section 1502 prior to the last day prescribed by law for the filing of such return. The making of a consolidated return shall be considered as such consent. In the case of a corporation which is a member of the affiliated group for a fractional part of the year, the consolidated return shall include the income of such corporation for such part of the year as it is a member of the affiliated group.

[Sec. 1502]

SEC. 1502. REGULATIONS.

The Secretary shall prescribe such regulations as he may deem necessary in order that the tax liability of any affiliated group of corporations making a consolidated return and of each corporation in the group, both during and after the period of affiliation, may be returned, determined, computed, assessed, collected, and adjusted, in such manner as clearly to reflect the income tax liability and the various factors necessary for the determination of such liability, and in order to prevent avoidance of such tax liability.

[Sec. 1503]

SEC. 1503. COMPUTATION AND PAYMENT OF TAX.

[Sec. 1503(a)]

[(a) GENERAL RULE.—] In any case in which a consolidated return is made or is required to be made, the tax shall be determined, computed, assessed, collected, and adjusted in accordance with the regulations under section 1502 prescribed before the last day prescribed by law for the filing of such return.

* * *

[Sec. 1504]

SEC. 1504. DEFINITIONS.

[Sec. 1504(a)]

(a) AFFILIATED GROUP DEFINED.—For purposes of this subtitle—

(1) IN GENERAL.—The term "affiliated group" means—

(A) 1 or more chains of includible corporations connected through stock ownership with a common parent corporation which is an includible corporation, but only if—

(B)(i) the common parent owns directly stock meeting the requirements of paragraph (2) in at least 1 of the other includible corporations, and

(ii) stock meeting the requirements of paragraph (2) in each of the includible corporations (except the common parent) is owned directly by 1 or more of the other includible corporations.

(2) 80-PERCENT VOTING AND VALUE TEST.—The ownership of stock of any corporation meets the requirements of this paragraph if it—

(A) possesses at least 80 percent of the total voting power of the stock of such corporation, and

(B) has a value equal to at least 80 percent of the total value of the stock of such corporation.

(3) 5 YEARS MUST ELAPSE BEFORE RECONSOLIDATION.—

(A) IN GENERAL.—If—

(i) a corporation is included (or required to be included) in a consolidated return filed by an affiliated group for a taxable year which includes any period after December 31, 1984, and

(ii) such corporation ceases to be a member of such group in a taxable year beginning after December 31, 1984,

with respect to periods after such cessation, such corporation (and any successor of such corporation) may not be included in any consolidated return filed by the affiliated group (or by another affiliated group with the same common parent or a successor of such common parent) before the 61st month beginning after its first taxable year in which it ceased to be a member of such affiliated group.

(B) SECRETARY MAY WAIVE APPLICATION OF SUBPARAGRAPH (A).—The Secretary may waive the application of subparagraph (A) to any corporation for any period subject to such conditions as the Secretary may prescribe.

(4) STOCK NOT TO INCLUDE CERTAIN PREFERRED STOCK.—For purposes of this subsection, the term "stock" does not include any stock which—

(A) is not entitled to vote,

(B) is limited and preferred as to dividends and does not participate in corporate growth to any significant extent,

(C) has redemption and liquidation rights which do not exceed the issue price of such stock (except for a reasonable redemption or liquidation premium), and

(D) is not convertible into another class of stock.

Sec. 1504(a)

(5) REGULATIONS.—The Secretary shall prescribe such regulations as may be necessary or appropriate to carry out the purposes of this subsection, including (but not limited to) regulations—

(A) which treat warrants, obligations convertible into stock, and other similar interests as stock, and stock as not stock,

(B) which treat options to acquire or sell stock as having been exercised,

(C) which provide that the requirements of paragraph (2)(B) shall be treated as met if the affiliated group, in reliance on a good faith determination of value, treated such requirements as met,

(D) which disregard an inadvertent ceasing to meet the requirements of paragraph (2)(B) by reason of changes in relative values of different classes of stock,

(E) which provide that transfers of stock within the group shall not be taken into account in determining whether a corporation ceases to be a member of an affiliated group, and

(F) which disregard changes in voting power to the extent such changes are disproportionate to related changes in value.

[Sec. 1504(b)]

(b) DEFINITION OF "INCLUDIBLE CORPORATION".—As used in this chapter, the term "includible corporation" means any corporation except—

(1) Corporations exempt from taxation under section 501.

(2) Insurance companies subject to taxation under section 801.

(3) Foreign corporations.

(4) Corporations with respect to which an election under section 936 (relating to possession tax credit) is in effect for the taxable year.

(5) Corporations organized under the China Trade Act, 1922 [repealed for taxable years beginning after December 31, 1977].

(6) Regulated investment companies and real estate investment trusts subject to tax under subchapter M of chapter 1.

(7) A DISC (as defined in section 992(a)(1)).

(8) An S corporation.

* * *

Subchapter B—Related Rules

PART I—IN GENERAL

[Sec. 1551]

SEC. 1551. DISALLOWANCE OF THE BENEFITS OF THE GRADUATED CORPORATE RATES AND ACCUMULATED EARNINGS CREDIT.

[Sec. 1551(a)]

(a) IN GENERAL.—If—

(1) any corporation transfers, on or after January 1, 1951, and on or before June 12, 1963, all or part of its property (other than money) to a transferee corporation,

(2) any corporation transfers, directly or indirectly, after June 12, 1963, all or part of its property (other than money) to a transferee corporation, or

(3) five or fewer individuals who are in control of a corporation transfer, directly or indirectly, after June 12, 1963, property (other than money) to a transferee corporation,

and the transferee corporation was created for the purpose of acquiring such property or was not actively engaged in business at the time of such acquisition, and if after such transfer the transferor or transferors are in control of such transferee corporation during any part of the taxable year of such transferee corporation, then for such taxable year of such transferee corporation the Secretary may (except as may be otherwise determined under subsection (c)) disallow the benefits of the rates contained in section 11(b) which are lower than the highest rate specified in such section, or the accumulated earnings credit provided in paragraph (2) or (3) of section 535(c), unless such transferee corporation shall establish by the clear preponderance of the evidence that the securing of such benefits or credit was not a major purpose of such transfer.

[Sec. 1551(b)]

(b) CONTROL.—For purposes of subsection (a), the term "control" means—

(1) With respect to a transferee corporation described in subsection (a)(1) or (2), the ownership by the transferor corporation, its shareholders, or both, of stock possessing at least 80 percent of the total combined voting power of all classes of stock entitled to vote or at least 80 percent of the total value of shares of all classes of the stock; or

(2) With respect to each corporation described in subsection (a)(3), the ownership by the five or fewer individuals described in such subsection of stock possessing—

(A) at least 80 percent of the total combined voting power of all classes of stock entitled to vote or at least 80 percent of the total value of shares of all classes of the stock of each corporation, and

(B) more than 50 percent of the total combined voting power of all classes of stock entitled to vote or more than 50 percent of the total value of shares of all classes of stock of each corporation, taking into account the stock ownership of each such individual only to the extent such stock ownership is identical with respect to each such corporation.

For purposes of this subsection, section 1563(e) shall apply in determining the ownership of stock.

[Sec. 1551(c)]

(c) AUTHORITY OF THE SECRETARY UNDER THIS SECTION.—The provisions of section 269(c), and the authority of the Secretary under such section, shall, to the extent not inconsistent with the provisions of this section, be applicable to this section.

[Sec. 1552]

SEC. 1552. EARNINGS AND PROFITS.

[Sec. 1552(a)]

(a) GENERAL RULE.—Pursuant to regulations prescribed by the Secretary the earnings and profits of each member of an affiliated group required to be included in a consolidated return for such group filed for a taxable year shall be determined by allocating the tax liability of the group for such year among the members of the group in accord with whichever of the following methods the group shall elect in its first consolidated return filed for such a taxable year:

(1) The tax liability shall be apportioned among the members of the group in accordance with the ratio which that portion of the consolidated taxable income attributable to each member of the group having taxable income bears to the consolidated taxable income.

(2) The tax liability of the group shall be allocated to the several members of the group on the basis of the percentage of the total tax which the tax of such member if computed on a separate return would bear to the total amount of the taxes for all members of the group so computed.

(3) The tax liability of the group (excluding the tax increases arising from the consolidation) shall be allocated on the basis of the contribution of each member of the group to the consolidated taxable income of the group. Any tax increases arising from the consolidation shall be distributed to the several members in direct proportion to the reduction in tax liability resulting to such members from the filing of the consolidated return as measured by the difference between their tax liabilities determined on a separate return basis and their tax liabilities based on their contributions to the consolidated taxable income.

(4) The tax liability of the group shall be allocated in accord with any other method selected by the group with the approval of the Secretary.

[Sec. 1552(b)]

(b) FAILURE TO ELECT.—If no election is made in such first return, the tax liability shall be allocated among the several members of the group pursuant to the method prescribed in subsection (a)(1).

Sec. 1552(b)

PART II—CERTAIN CONTROLLED CORPORATIONS

[Sec. 1561]

SEC. 1561. LIMITATIONS ON CERTAIN MULTIPLE TAX BENEFITS IN THE CASE OF CERTAIN CONTROLLED CORPORATIONS.

[Sec. 1561(a)]

(a) GENERAL RULE.—The component members of a controlled group of corporations on a December 31 shall, for their taxable years which include such December 31, be limited for purposes of this subtitle to—

(1) amounts in each taxable income bracket in the tax table in section 11(b)(1) which do not aggregate more than the maximum amount in such bracket to which a corporation which is not a component member of a controlled group is entitled,

(2) one $250,000 ($150,000 if any component member is a corporation described in section 535(c)(2)(B)) amount for purposes of computing the accumulated earnings credit under section 535(c)(2) and (3),

(3) one $40,000 exemption amount for purposes of computing the amount of the minimum tax, and

(4) one $2,000,000 amount for purposes of computing the tax imposed by section 59A.

The amounts specified in paragraph (1), the amount specified in paragraph (3), and the amount specified in paragraph (4) shall be divided equally among the component members of such group on such December 31 unless all of such component members consent (at such time and in such manner as the Secretary shall by regulations prescribe) to an apportionment plan providing for an unequal allocation of such amounts. The amounts specified in paragraph (2) shall be divided equally among the component members of such group on such December 31 unless the Secretary prescribes regulations permitting an unequal allocation of such amounts. Notwithstanding paragraph (1), in applying the last 2 sentences of section 11(b)(1) to such component members, the taxable income of all such component members shall be taken into account and any increase in tax under such last 2 sentences shall be divided among such component members in the same manner as amounts under paragraph (1). In applying section 55(d)(3), the alternative minimum taxable income of all component members shall be taken into account and any decrease in the exemption amount shall be allocated to the component members in the same manner as under paragraph (3).

[Sec. 1561(b)]

(b) CERTAIN SHORT TAXABLE YEARS.—If a corporation has a short taxable year which does not include a December 31 and is a component member of a controlled group of corporations with respect to such taxable year, then for purposes of this subtitle—

(1) the amount in each taxable income bracket in the tax table in section 11(b), and

(2) the amount to be used in computing the accumulated earnings credit under section 535(c)(2) and (3),

of such corporation for such taxable year shall be the amount specified in subsection (a)(1) or (2), as the case may be, divided by the number of corporations which are component members of such group on the last day of such taxable year. For purposes of the preceding sentence, section 1563(b) shall be applied as if such last day were substituted for December 31.

[Sec. 1563]

SEC. 1563. DEFINITIONS AND SPECIAL RULES.

[Sec. 1563(a)]

(a) CONTROLLED GROUP OF CORPORATIONS.—For purposes of this part, the term "controlled group of corporations" means any group of—

(1) PARENT-SUBSIDIARY CONTROLLED GROUP.—One or more chains of corporations connected through stock ownership with a common parent corporation if—

(A) stock possessing at least 80 percent of the total combined voting power of all classes of stock entitled to vote or at least 80 percent of the total value of shares of all classes of stock of

Sec. 1561

each of the corporations, except the common parent corporation, is owned (within the meaning of subsection (d)(1)) by one or more of the other corporations; and

(B) the common parent corporation owns (within the meaning of subsection (d)(1)) stock possessing at least 80 percent of the total combined voting power of all classes of stock entitled to vote or at least 80 percent of the total value of shares of all classes of stock of at least one of the other corporations, excluding, in computing such voting power or value, stock owned directly by such other corporations.

(2) BROTHER-SISTER CONTROLLED GROUP.—Two or more corporations if 5 or fewer persons who are individuals, estates, or trusts own (within the meaning of subsection (d)(2)) stock possessing—

(A) at least 80 percent of the total combined voting power of all classes of stock entitled to vote or at least 80 percent of the total value of shares of all classes of the stock of each corporation, and

(B) more than 50 percent of the total combined voting power of all classes of stock entitled to vote or more than 50 percent of the total value of shares of all classes of stock of each corporation, taking into account the stock ownership of each such person only to the extent such stock ownership is identical with respect to each such corporation.

(3) COMBINED GROUP.—Three or more corporations each of which is a member of a group of corporations described in paragraph (1) or (2), and one of which—

(A) is a common parent corporation included in a group of corporations described in paragraph (1), and also

(B) is included in a group of corporations described in paragraph (2).

* * *

[Sec. 1563(b)]

(b) COMPONENT MEMBER.—

(1) GENERAL RULE.—For purposes of this part, a corporation is a component member of a controlled group of corporations on a December 31 of any taxable year (and with respect to the taxable year which includes such December 31) if such corporation—

(A) is a member of such controlled group of corporations on the December 31 included in such year and is not treated as an excluded member under paragraph (2), or

(B) is not a member of such controlled group of corporations on the December 31 included in such year but is treated as an additional member under paragraph (3).

(2) EXCLUDED MEMBERS.—A corporation which is a member of a controlled group of corporations on December 31 of any taxable year shall be treated as an excluded member of such group for the taxable year including such December 31 if such corporation—

(A) is a member of such group for less than one-half the number of days in such taxable year which precede such December 31,

(B) is exempt from taxation under section 501(a) (except a corporation which is subject to tax on its unrelated business taxable income under section 511) for such taxable year,

(C) is a foreign corporation subject to tax under section 881 for such taxable year,

(D) is an insurance company subject to taxation under section 801 (other than an insurance company which is a member of a controlled group described in subsection (a)(4)), or

(E) is a franchised corporation, as defined in subsection (f)(4).

(3) ADDITIONAL MEMBERS.—A corporation which—

(A) was a member of a controlled group of corporations at any time during a calendar year,

(B) is not a member of such group on December 31 of such calendar year, and

(C) is not described, with respect to such group, in subparagraph (B), (C), (D), or (E) of paragraph (2),

shall be treated as an additional member of such group on December 31 for its taxable year including such December 31 if it was a member of such group for one-half (or more) of the number of days in such taxable year which precede such December 31.

(4) OVERLAPPING GROUPS.—If a corporation is a component member of more than one controlled group of corporations with respect to any taxable year, such corporation shall be treated as a

Sec. 1563(b)

component member of only one controlled group. The determination as to the group of which such corporation is a component member shall be made under regulations prescribed by the Secretary which are consistent with the purposes of this part.

[Sec. 1563(c)]

(c) CERTAIN STOCK EXCLUDED.—

(1) GENERAL RULE.—For purposes of this part, the term "stock" does not include—

(A) nonvoting stock which is limited and preferred as to dividends,

(B) treasury stock, and

(C) stock which is treated as "excluded stock" under paragraph (2).

(2) STOCK TREATED AS "EXCLUDED STOCK".—

(A) PARENT-SUBSIDIARY CONTROLLED GROUP.—For purposes of subsection (a)(1), if a corporation (referred to in this paragraph as "parent corporation") owns (within the meaning of subsections (d)(1) and (e)(4)), 50 percent or more of the total combined voting power of all classes of stock entitled to vote or 50 percent or more of the total value of shares of all classes of stock in another corporation (referred to in this paragraph as "subsidiary corporation"), the following stock of the subsidiary corporation shall be treated as excluded stock—

(i) stock in the subsidiary corporation held by a trust which is part of a plan of deferred compensation for the benefit of the employees of the parent corporation or the subsidiary corporation,

(ii) stock in the subsidiary corporation owned by an individual (within the meaning of subsection (d)(2)) who is a principal stockholder or officer of the parent corporation. For purposes of this clause, the term "principal stockholder" of a corporation means an individual who owns (within the meaning of subsection (d)(2)) 5 percent or more of the total combined voting power of all classes of stock entitled to vote or 5 percent or more of the total value of shares of all classes of stock in such corporation,

(iii) stock in the subsidiary corporation owned (within the meaning of subsection (d)(2)) by an employee of the subsidiary corporation if such stock is subject to conditions which run in favor of such parent (or subsidiary) corporation and which substantially restrict or limit the employee's right (or if the employee constructively owns such stock, the direct owner's right) to dispose of such stock, or

(iv) stock in the subsidiary corporation owned (within the meaning of subsection (d)(2)) by an organization (other than the parent corporation) to which section 501 (relating to certain educational and charitable organizations which are exempt from tax) applies and which is controlled directly or indirectly by the parent corporation or subsidiary corporation, by an individual, estate, or trust that is a principal stockholder (within the meaning of clause (ii)) of the parent corporation, by an officer of the parent corporation, or by any combination thereof.

(B) BROTHER-SISTER CONTROLLED GROUP.—For purposes of subsection (a)(2), if 5 or fewer persons who are individuals, estates, or trusts (referred to in this subparagraph as "common owners") own (within the meaning of subsection (d)(2)), 50 percent or more of the total combined voting power of all classes of stock entitled to vote or 50 percent or more of the total value of shares of all classes of stock in a corporation, the following stock of such corporation shall be treated as excluded stock—

(i) stock in such corporation held by an employees' trust described in section 401(a) which is exempt from tax under section 501(a), if such trust is for the benefit of the employees of such corporation,

(ii) stock in such corporation owned (within the meaning of subsection (d)(2)) by an employee of the corporation if such stock is subject to conditions which run in favor of any of such common owners (or such corporation) and which substantially restrict or limit the employee's right (or if the employee constructively owns such stock, the direct owner's right) to dispose of such stock. If a condition which limits or restricts the employee's right (or the direct owner's right) to dispose of such stock also applies to the stock held by any of the common owners pursuant to a bona fide reciprocal stock purchase arrangement, such condition shall not be treated as one which restricts or limits the employee's right to dispose of such stock, or

(iii) stock in such corporation owned (within the meaning of subsection (d)(2)) by an organization to which section 501 (relating to certain educational and charitable organizations which are exempt from tax) applies and which is controlled directly or indirectly by such corporation, by an individual, estate, or trust that is a principal stockholder (within the meaning of subparagraph (A)(ii)) of such corporation, by an officer of such corporation, or by any combination thereof.

[Sec. 1563(d)]

(d) RULES FOR DETERMINING STOCK OWNERSHIP.—

(1) PARENT-SUBSIDIARY CONTROLLED GROUP.—For purposes of determining whether a corporation is a member of a parent-subsidiary controlled group of corporations (within the meaning of subsection (a)(1)), stock owned by a corporation means—

(A) stock owned directly by such corporation, and

(B) stock owned with the application of paragraphs (1), (2), and (3) of subsection (e).

(2) BROTHER-SISTER CONTROLLED GROUP.—For purposes of determining whether a corporation is a member of a brother-sister controlled group of corporations (within the meaning of subsection (a)(2)), stock owned by a person who is an individual, estate, or trust means—

(A) stock owned directly by such person, and

(B) stock owned with the application of subsection (e).

[Sec. 1563(e)]

(e) CONSTRUCTIVE OWNERSHIP.—

(1) OPTIONS.—If any person has an option to acquire stock, such stock shall be considered as owned by such person. For purposes of this paragraph, an option to acquire such an option, and each one of a series of such options, shall be considered as an option to acquire such stock.

(2) ATTRIBUTION FROM PARTNERSHIPS.—Stock owned, directly or indirectly, by or for a partnership shall be considered as owned by any partner having an interest of 5 percent or more in either the capital or profits of the partnership in proportion to his interest in capital or profits, whichever such proportion is the greater.

(3) ATTRIBUTION FROM ESTATES OR TRUSTS.—

(A) Stock owned, directly or indirectly, by or for an estate or trust shall be considered as owned by any beneficiary who has an actuarial interest of 5 percent or more in such stock, to the extent of such actuarial interest. For purposes of this subparagraph, the actuarial interest of each beneficiary shall be determined by assuming the maximum exercise of discretion by the fiduciary in favor of such beneficiary and the maximum use of such stock to satisfy his rights as a beneficiary.

(B) Stock owned, directly or indirectly, by or for any portion of a trust of which a person is considered the owner under subpart E of part I of subchapter J (relating to grantors and others treated as substantial owners) shall be considered as owned by such person.

(C) This paragraph shall not apply to stock owned by any employees' trust described in section 401(a) which is exempt from tax under section 501(a).

(4) ATTRIBUTION FROM CORPORATIONS.—Stock owned, directly or indirectly, by or for a corporation shall be considered as owned by any person who owns (within the meaning of subsection (d)) 5 percent or more in value of its stock in that proportion which the value of the stock which such person so owns bears to the value of all the stock in such corporation.

(5) SPOUSE.—An individual shall be considered as owning stock in a corporation owned, directly or indirectly, by or for his spouse (other than a spouse who is legally separated from the individual under a decree of divorce whether interlocutory or final, or a decree of separate maintenance), except in the case of a corporation with respect to which each of the following conditions is satisfied for its taxable year—

(A) The individual does not, at any time during such taxable year, own directly any stock in such corporation;

(B) The individual is not a director or employee and does not participate in the management of such corporation at any time during such taxable year;

Sec. 1563(e)

(C) Not more than 50 percent of such corporation's gross income for such taxable year was derived from royalties, rents, dividends, interest, and annuities; and

(D) Such stock in such corporation is not, at any time during such taxable year, subject to conditions which substantially restrict or limit the spouse's right to dispose of such stock and which run in favor of the individual or his children who have not attained the age of 21 years.

(6) CHILDREN, GRANDCHILDREN, PARENTS, AND GRANDPARENTS.—

(A) MINOR CHILDREN.—An individual shall be considered as owning stock owned, directly or indirectly, by or for his children who have not attained the age of 21 years, and, if the individual has not attained the age of 21 years, the stock owned, directly or indirectly, by or for his parents.

(B) ADULT CHILDREN AND GRANDCHILDREN.—An individual who owns (within the meaning of subsection (d)(2), but without regard to this subparagraph) more than 50 percent of the total combined voting power of all classes of stock entitled to vote or more than 50 percent of the total value of shares of all classes of stock in a corporation shall be considered as owning the stock in such corporation owned, directly or indirectly, by or for his parents, grandparents, grandchildren, and children who have attained the age of 21 years.

(C) ADOPTED CHILD.—For purposes of this section, a legally adopted child of an individual shall be treated as a child of such individual by blood.

[Sec. 1563(f)]

(f) OTHER DEFINITIONS AND RULES.—

(1) EMPLOYEE DEFINED.—For purposes of this section the term "employee" has the same meaning such term is given by paragraphs (1) and (2) of section 3121(d).

(2) OPERATING RULES.—

(A) IN GENERAL.—Except as provided in subparagraph (B), stock constructively owned by a person by reason of the application of paragraph (1), (2), (3), (4), (5), or (6) of subsection (e) shall, for purposes of applying such paragraphs, be treated as actually owned by such person.

(B) MEMBERS OF FAMILY.—Stock constructively owned by an individual by reason of the application of paragraph (5) or (6) of subsection (e) shall not be treated as owned by him for purposes of again applying such paragraphs in order to make another the constructive owner of such stock.

(3) SPECIAL RULES.—For purposes of this section—

(A) If stock may be considered as owned by a person under subsection (e)(1) and under any other paragraph of subsection (e), it shall be considered as owned by him under subsection (e)(1).

(B) If stock is owned (within the meaning of subsection (d)) by two or more persons, such stock shall be considered as owned by the person whose ownership of such stock results in the corporation being a component member of a controlled group. If by reason of the preceding sentence, a corporation would (but for this sentence) become a component member of two controlled groups, it shall be treated as a component member of one controlled group. The determination as to the group of which such corporation is a component member shall be made under regulations prescribed by the Secretary which are consistent with the purposes of this part.

(C) If stock is owned by a person within the meaning of subsection (d) and such ownership results in the corporation being a component member of a controlled group, such stock shall not be treated as excluded stock under subsection (c)(2), if by reason of treating such stock as excluded stock the result is that such corporation is not a component member of a controlled group of corporations.

* * *

Sec. 1563(f)

Subtitle C—Employment Taxes

CHAPTER 24—COLLECTION OF INCOME TAX AT SOURCE ON WAGES

Subchapter A—Withholding from Wages

[Sec. 3401]

SEC. 3401. DEFINITIONS.

[Sec. 3401(a)]

(a) WAGES.—For purposes of this chapter, the term "wages" means all remuneration (other than fees paid to a public official) for services performed by an employee for his employer, including the cash value of all remuneration (including benefits) paid in any medium other than cash; except that such term shall not include remuneration paid—

* * *

(3) for domestic service in a private home, local college club, or local chapter of a college fraternity or sorority; or

(4) for service not in the course of the employer's trade or business performed in any calendar quarter by an employee, unless the cash remuneration paid for such service is $50 or more and such service is performed by an individual who is regularly employed by such employer to perform such service. For purposes of this paragraph, an individual shall be deemed to be regularly employed by an employer during a calendar quarter only if—

(A) on each of some 24 days during such quarter such individual performs for such employer for some portion of the day service not in the course of the employer's trade or business; or

(B) such individual was regularly employed (as determined under subparagraph (A)) by such employer in the performance of such service during the preceding calendar quarter; or

* * *

(9) for services performed by a duly ordained, commissioned, or licensed minister of a church in the exercise of his ministry or by a member of a religious order in the exercise of duties required by such order; or

(10) (A) for services performed by an individual under the age of 18 in the delivery or distribution of newspapers or shopping news, not including delivery or distribution to any point for subsequent delivery or distribution; or

(B) for services performed by an individual in, and at the time of, the sale of newspapers or magazines to ultimate consumers, under an arrangement under which the newspapers or magazines are to be sold by him at a fixed price, his compensation being based on the retention of the excess of such price over the amount at which the newspapers or magazines are charged to him, whether or not he is guaranteed a minimum amount of compensation for such services, or is entitled to be credited with the unsold newspapers or magazines turned back; or

(11) for services not in the course of the employer's trade or business, to the extent paid in any medium other than cash; or

* * *

(13) pursuant to any provision of law other than section 5(c) or 6(1) of the Peace Corps Act, for service performed as a volunteer or volunteer leader within the meaning of such Act; or

(14) in the form of group-term life insurance on the life of an employee; or

(15) to or on behalf of an employee if (and to the extent that) at the time of the payment of such remuneration it is reasonable to believe that a corresponding deduction is allowable under section 217 (determined without regard to section 274(n)); or

Sec. 3401(a)

(16) (A) as tips in any medium other than cash;

(B) as cash tips to an employee in any calendar month in the course of his employment by an employer unless the amount of such cash tips is $20 or more;

* * *

(18) for any payment made, or benefit furnished, to or for the benefit of an employee if at the time of such payment or such furnishing it is reasonable to believe that the employee will be able to exclude such payment or benefit from income under section 127 or 129;

(19) for any benefit provided to or on behalf of an employee if at the time such benefit is provided it is reasonable to believe that the employee will be able to exclude such benefit from income under section 74(c), 117 or 132;

(20) for any medical care reimbursement made to or for the benefit of an employee under a self-insured medical reimbursement plan (within the meaning of section 105(h)(6)); or

(21) for any payment made to or for the benefit of an employee if at the time of such payment it is reasonable to believe that the employee will be able to exclude such payment from income under section 106(b).

* * *

[Sec. 3402]

SEC. 3402. INCOME TAX COLLECTED AT SOURCE.

[Sec. 3402(a)]

(a) REQUIREMENT OF WITHHOLDING.—

(1) IN GENERAL.—Except as otherwise provided in this section, every employer making payment of wages shall deduct and withhold upon such wages a tax determined in accordance with tables or computational procedures prescribed by the Secretary. Any tables or procedures prescribed under this paragraph shall—

(A) apply with respect to the amount of wages paid during such periods as the Secretary may prescribe, and

(B) be in such form, and provide for such amounts to be deducted and withheld, as the Secretary determines to be most appropriate to carry out the purposes of this chapter and to reflect the provisions of chapter 1 applicable to such periods.

(2) AMOUNT OF WAGES.—For purposes of applying tables or procedures prescribed under paragraph (1), the term "the amount of wages" means the amount by which the wages exceed the number of withholding exemptions claimed multiplied by the amount of one such exemption. The amount of each withholding exemption shall be equal to the amount of one personal exemption provided in section 151(b), prorated to the payroll period. The maximum number of withholding exemptions permitted shall be calculated in accordance with regulations prescribed by the Secretary under this section, taking into account any reduction in withholding to which an employee is entitled under this section.

* * *

[Sec. 3403]

SEC. 3403. LIABILITY FOR TAX.

The employer shall be liable for the payment of the tax required to be deducted and withheld under this chapter, and shall not be liable to any person for the amount of any such payment.

Subtitle D—Miscellaneous Excise Taxes

CHAPTER 46—GOLDEN PARACHUTE PAYMENTS

[Sec. 4999]

SEC. 4999. GOLDEN PARACHUTE PAYMENTS.

[Sec. 4999(a)]

(a) IMPOSITION OF TAX.—There is hereby imposed on any person who receives an excess parachute payment a tax equal to 20 percent of the amount of such payment.

[Sec. 4999(b)]

(b) EXCESS PARACHUTE PAYMENT DEFINED.—For purposes of this section, the term "Excess parachute payment" has the meaning given to such term by section 280G(b).

* * *

Subtitle F—Procedure and Administration

CHAPTER 61—INFORMATION AND RETURNS

Subchapter A—Returns and Records

PART I—RECORDS, STATEMENTS, AND SPECIAL RETURNS

[Sec. 6001]

SEC. 6001. NOTICE OR REGULATIONS REQUIRING RECORDS, STATEMENTS, AND SPECIAL RETURNS.

Every person liable for any tax imposed by this title, or for the collection thereof, shall keep such records, render such statements, make such returns, and comply with such rules and regulations as the Secretary may from time to time prescribe. Whenever in the judgment of the Secretary it is necessary, he may require any person, by notice served upon such person or by regulations, to make such returns, render such statements, or keep such records, as the Secretary deems sufficient to show whether or not such person is liable for tax under this title. The only records which an employer shall be required to keep under this section in connection with charged tips shall be charge receipts, records necessary to comply with section 6053(c), and copies of statements furnished by employees under section 6053(a).

PART II—TAX RETURNS OR STATEMENTS

Subpart B—Income Tax Returns

[Sec. 6012]

SEC. 6012. PERSONS REQUIRED TO MAKE RETURNS OF INCOME.

[Sec. 6012(a)]

(a) GENERAL RULE.—Returns with respect to income taxes under subtitle A shall be made by the following:

(1)(A) Every individual having for the taxable year gross income which equals or exceeds the exemption amount, except that a return shall not be required of an individual—

(i) who is not married (determined by applying section 7703), is not a surviving spouse (as defined in section 2(a)), is not a head of a household (as defined in section 2(b)), and for the taxable year has gross income of less than the sum of the exemption amount plus the basic standard deduction applicable to such an individual,

(ii) who is a head of a household (as so defined) and for the taxable year has gross income of less than the sum of the exemption amount plus the basic standard deduction applicable to such an individual,

Sec. 6012(a)

(iii) who is a surviving spouse (as so defined) and for the taxable year has gross income of less than the sum of the exemption amount plus the basic standard deduction applicable to such an individual, or

(iv) who is entitled to make a joint return and whose gross income, when combined with the gross income of his spouse, is, for the taxable year, less than the sum of twice the exemption amount plus the basic standard deduction applicable to a joint return, but only if such individual and his spouse, at the close of the taxable year, had the same household as their home.

Clause (iv) shall not apply if for the taxable year such spouse makes a separate return or any other taxpayer is entitled to an exemption for such spouse under section 151(c).

(B) The amount specified in clause (i), (ii), or (iii) of subparagraph (A) shall be increased by the amount of 1 additional standard deduction (within the meaning of section 63(c)(3)) in the case of an individual entitled to such deduction by reason of section 63(f)(1)(A) (relating to individuals age 65 or more), and the amount specified in clause (iv) of subparagraph (A) shall be increased by the amount of the additional standard deduction for each additional standard deduction to which the individual or his spouse is entitled by reason of section 63(f)(1).

(C) The exception under subparagraph (A) shall not apply to any individual—

(i) who is described in section 63(c)(5) and who has—

(I) income (other than earned income) in excess of the sum of the amount in effect under section 63(c)(5)(A) plus the additional standard deduction (if any) to which the individual is entitled, or

(II) total gross income in excess of the standard deduction, or

(ii) for whom the standard deduction is zero under section 63(c)(6).

(D) For purposes of this subsection—

(i) The terms "standard deduction", "basic standard deduction" and "additional standard deduction" have the respective meanings given such terms by section 63(c).

(ii) The term "exemption amount" has the meaning given such term by section 151(d). In the case of an individual described in section 151(d)(2), the exemption amount shall be zero.

(2) Every corporation subject to taxation under subtitle A;

(3) Every estate the gross income of which for the taxable year is $600 or more;

(4) Every trust having for the taxable year any taxable income, or having gross income of $600 or over, regardless of the amount of taxable income;

(5) Every estate or trust of which any beneficiary is a nonresident alien;

(6) Every political organization (within the meaning of section 527(e)(1)), and every fund treated under section 527(g) as if it constituted a political organization, which has political organization taxable income (within the meaning of section 527(c)(1)) for the taxable year; and

(7) Every homeowners association (within the meaning of section 528(c)(1)) which has homeowners association taxable income (within the meaning of section 528(d)) for the taxable year.

(8) Every individual who receives payments during the calendar year in which the taxable year begins under section 3507 (relating to advance payment of earned income credit).

(9) Every estate of an individual under chapter 7 or 11 of title 11 of the United States Code (relating to bankruptcy) the gross income of which for the taxable year is not less than the sum of the exemption amount plus the basic standard deduction under section 63(c)(2)(D).

except that subject to such conditions, limitations, and exceptions and under such regulations as may be prescribed by the Secretary, nonresident alien individuals subject to the tax imposed by section 871 and foreign corporations subject to the tax imposed by section 881 may be exempted from the requirement of making returns under this section.

[Sec. 6012(b)]

(b) RETURNS MADE BY FIDUCIARIES AND RECEIVERS.—

(1) RETURNS OF DECEDENTS.—If an individual is deceased, the return of such individual required under subsection (a) shall be made by his executor, administrator, or other person charged with the property of such decedent.

Sec. 6012(b)

(2) PERSONS UNDER A DISABILITY.—If an individual is unable to make a return required under subsection (a), the return of such individual shall be made by a duly authorized agent, his committee, guardian, fiduciary or other person charged with the care of the person or property of such individual. The preceding sentence shall not apply in the case of a receiver appointed by authority of law in possession of only a part of the property of an individual.

(3) RECEIVERS, TRUSTEES AND ASSIGNEES FOR CORPORATIONS.—In a case where a receiver, trustee in a case under title 11 of the United States Code or assignee, by order of a court of competent jurisdiction, by operation of law or otherwise, has possession of or holds title to all or substantially all the property or business of a corporation, whether or not such property or business is being operated, such receiver, trustee, or assignee shall make the return of income for such corporation in the same manner and form as corporations are required to make such returns.

(4) RETURNS OF ESTATES AND TRUSTS.—Returns of an estate, a trust, or an estate of an individual under chapter 7 or 11 of title 11 of the United States Code shall be made by the fiduciary thereof.

(5) JOINT FIDUCIARIES.—Under such regulations as the Secretary may prescribe, a return made by one of two or more joint fiduciaries shall be sufficient compliance with the requirements of this section. A return made pursuant to this paragraph shall contain a statement that the fiduciary has sufficient knowledge of the affairs of the person for whom the return is made to enable him to make the return, and that the return is, to the best of his knowledge and belief, true and correct.

(6) IRA SHARE OF PARTNERSHIP INCOME.—In the case of a trust which is exempt from taxation under section 408(e), for purposes of this section, the trust's distributive share of items of gross income and gain of any partnership to which subchapter C or D of chapter 63 applies shall be treated as equal to the trust's distributive share of the taxable income of such partnership.

[Sec. 6012(c)]

(c) CERTAIN INCOME EARNED ABROAD OR FROM SALE OF RESIDENCE.—For purposes of this section, gross income shall be computed without regard to the exclusion provided for in section 121 (relating to gain from sale of principal residence) and without regard to the exclusion provided for in section 911 (relating to citizens or residents of the United States living abroad).

[Sec. 6012(d)]

(d) TAX-EXEMPT INTEREST REQUIRED TO BE SHOWN ON RETURN.—Every person required to file a return under this section for the taxable year shall include on such return the amount of interest received or accrued during the taxable year which is exempt from the tax imposed by chapter 1.

[Sec. 6012(e)]

(e) CONSOLIDATED RETURNS.—

For provisions relating to consolidated returns by affiliated corporations, see chapter 6.

[Sec. 6013]

SEC. 6013. JOINT RETURNS OF INCOME TAX BY HUSBAND AND WIFE.

[Sec. 6013(a)]

(a) JOINT RETURNS.—A husband and wife may make a single return jointly of income taxes under subtitle A, even though one of the spouses has neither gross income nor deductions, except as provided below:

(1) no joint return shall be made if either the husband or wife at any time during the taxable year is a nonresident alien;

(2) no joint return shall be made if the husband and wife have different taxable years; except that if such taxable years begin on the same day and end on different days because of the death of either or both, then the joint return may be made with respect to the taxable year of each. The above exception shall not apply if the surviving spouse remarries before the close of his taxable year, nor if the taxable year of either spouse is a fractional part of a year under section 443 (a) (1);

(3) in the case of death of one spouse or both spouses the joint return with respect to the decedent may be made only by his executor or administrator; except that in the case of the death of one spouse the joint return may be made by the surviving spouse with respect to both himself and the decedent if no return for the taxable year has been made by the decedent, no executor or administrator has been appointed, and no executor or administrator is appointed before the last day prescribed by law for

Sec. 6013(a)

filing the return of the surviving spouse. If an executor or administrator of the decedent is appointed after the making of the joint return by the surviving spouse, the executor or administrator may disaffirm such joint return by making, within 1 year after the last day prescribed by law for filing the return of the surviving spouse, a separate return for the taxable year of the decedent with respect to which the joint return was made, in which case the return made by the survivor shall constitute his separate return.

[Sec. 6013(b)]

(b) JOINT RETURN AFTER FILING SEPARATE RETURN.—

(1) IN GENERAL.—Except as provided in paragraph (2), if an individual has filed a separate return for a taxable year for which a joint return could have been made by him and his spouse under subsection (a) and the time prescribed by law for filing the return for such taxable year has expired, such individual and his spouse may nevertheless make a joint return for such taxable year. A joint return filed by the husband and wife under this subsection shall constitute the return of the husband and wife for such taxable year, and all payments, credits, refunds, or other repayments made or allowed with respect to the separate return of either spouse for such taxable year shall be taken into account in determining the extent to which the tax based upon the joint return has been paid. If a joint return is made under this subsection, any election (other than the election to file a separate return) made by either spouse in his separate return for such taxable year with respect to the treatment of any income, deduction, or credit of such spouse shall not be changed in the making of the joint return where such election would have been irrevocable if the joint return had not been made. If a joint return is made under this subsection after the death of either spouse, such return with respect to the decedent can be made only by his executor or administrator.

(2) LIMITATIONS FOR MAKING OF ELECTION.—The election provided for in paragraph (1) may not be made—

(A) after the expiration of 3 years from the last date prescribed by law for filing the return for such taxable year (determined without regard to any extension of time granted to either spouse); or

(B) after there has been mailed to either spouse, with respect to such taxable year, a notice of deficiency under section 6212, if the spouse, as to such notice, files a petition with the Tax Court within the time prescribed in section 6213; or

(C) after either spouse has commenced a suit in any court for the recovery of any part of the tax for such taxable year; or

(D) after either spouse has entered into a closing agreement under section 7121 with respect to such taxable year, or after any civil or criminal case arising against either spouse with respect to such taxable year has been compromised under section 7122.

(3) WHEN RETURN DEEMED FILED.—

(A) Assessment and Collection.—For purposes of section 6501 (relating to periods of limitations on assessment and collection), and for purposes of section 6651 (relating to delinquent returns), a joint return made under this subsection shall be deemed to have been filed—

(i) Where both spouses filed separate returns prior to making the joint return—on the date the last separate return was filed (but not earlier than the last date prescribed by law for filing the return of either spouse);

(ii) Where only one spouse filed a separate return prior to the making of the joint return, and the other spouse had less than the exemption amount of gross income for such taxable year—on the date of the filing of such separate return (but not earlier than the last date prescribed by law for the filing of such separate return); or

(iii) Where only one spouse filed a separate return prior to the making of the joint return, and the other spouse had gross income of the exemption amount or more for such taxable year—on the date of the filing of such joint return.

For purposes of this subparagraph, the term "exemption amount" has the meaning given to such term by section 151(d). For purposes of clauses (ii) and (iii), if the spouse whose gross income is being compared to the exemption amount is 65 or over, such clauses shall be applied by substituting "the sum of the exemption amount and the additional standard deduction under section 63(c)(2) by reason of section 63(f)(1)(A) for "the exemption amount".

Sec. 6013(b)

(B) CREDIT OR REFUND.—For purposes of section 6511, a joint return made under this subsection shall be deemed to have been filed on the last date prescribed by law for filing the return for such taxable year (determined without regard to any extension of time granted to either spouse).

(4) ADDITIONAL TIME FOR ASSESSMENT.—If a joint return is made under this subsection, the periods of limitations provided in sections 6501 and 6502 on the making of assessments and the beginning of levy or a proceeding in court for collection shall with respect to such return include one year immediately after the date of the filing of such joint return (computed without regard to the provisions of paragraph (3)).

(5) ADDITIONS TO THE TAX AND PENALTIES.—

(A) COORDINATION WITH PART II OF SUBCHAPTER A OF CHAPTER 68.—For purposes of part II of subchapter A of chapter 68, where the sum of the amounts shown as tax on the separate returns of each spouse is less than the amount shown as tax on the joint return made under this subsection—

(i) such sum shall be treated as the amount shown on the joint return,

(ii) any negligence (or disregard of rules or regulations) on either separate return shall be treated as negligence (or such disregard) on the joint return, and

(iii) any fraud on either separate return shall be treated as fraud on the joint return.

(B) CRIMINAL PENALTY.—For purposes of section 7206(1) and (2) and section 7207 (relating to criminal penalties in the case of fraudulent returns) the term "return" includes a separate return filed by a spouse with respect to a taxable year for which a joint return is made under this subsection after the filing of such separate return.

[Sec. 6013(c)]

(c) TREATMENT OF JOINT RETURN AFTER DEATH OF EITHER SPOUSE.—For purposes of sections 15, 443, and 7851(a)(1)(A), where the husband and wife have different taxable years because of the death of either spouse, the joint return shall be treated as if the taxable years of both spouses ended on the date of the closing of the surviving spouse's taxable year.

[Sec. 6013(d)]

(d) SPECIAL RULES.—For purposes of this section—

(1) the status as husband and wife of two individuals having taxable years beginning on the same day shall be determined—

(A) if both have the same taxable year—as of the close of such year; or

(B) if one dies before the close of the taxable year of the other—as of the time of such death;

(2) an individual who is legally separated from his spouse under a decree of divorce or of separate maintenance shall not be considered as married; and

(3) if a joint return is made, the tax shall be computed on the aggregate income and the liability with respect to the tax shall be joint and several.

[Sec. 6013(e)]

(e) [Stricken.]

* * *

[Sec. 6015]

SEC. 6015. RELIEF FROM JOINT AND SEVERAL LIABILITY ON JOINT RETURN.

[Sec. 6015(a)]

(a) IN GENERAL.—Notwithstanding section 6013(d)(3)—

(1) an individual who has made a joint return may elect to seek relief under the procedures prescribed under subsection (b); and

(2) if such individual is eligible to elect the application of subsection (c), such individual may, in addition to any election under paragraph (1), elect to limit such individual's liability for any deficiency with respect to such joint return in the manner prescribed under subsection (c).

Any determination under this section shall be made without regard to community property laws.

[Sec. 6015(b)]

(b) PROCEDURES FOR RELIEF FROM LIABILITY APPLICABLE TO ALL JOINT FILERS.—

(1) IN GENERAL.—Under procedures prescribed by the Secretary, if—

(A) a joint return has been made for a taxable year;

(B) on such return there is an understatement of tax attributable to erroneous items of 1 individual filing the joint return;

(C) the other individual filing the joint return establishes that in signing the return he or she did not know, and had no reason to know, that there was such understatement;

(D) taking into account all the facts and circumstances, it is inequitable to hold the other individual liable for the deficiency in tax for such taxable year attributable to such understatement; and

(E) the other individual elects (in such form as the Secretary may prescribe) the benefits of this subsection not later than the date which is 2 years after the date the Secretary has begun collection activities with respect to the individual making the election,

then the other individual shall be relieved of liability for tax (including interest, penalties, and other amounts) for such taxable year to the extent such liability is attributable to such understatement.

(2) APPORTIONMENT OF RELIEF.—If an individual who, but for paragraph (1)(C), would be relieved of liability under paragraph (1), establishes that in signing the return such individual did not know, and had no reason to know, the extent of such understatement, then such individual shall be relieved of liability for tax (including interest, penalties, and other amounts) for such taxable year to the extent that such liability is attributable to the portion of such understatement of which such individual did not know and had no reason to know.

(3) UNDERSTATEMENT.—For purposes of this subsection, the term "understatement" has the meaning given to such term by section 6662(d)(2)(A).

[Sec. 6015(c)]

(c) PROCEDURES TO LIMIT LIABILITY FOR TAXPAYERS NO LONGER MARRIED OR TAXPAYERS LEGALLY SEPARATED OR NOT LIVING TOGETHER.—

(1) IN GENERAL.—Except as provided in this subsection, if an individual who has made a joint return for any taxable year elects the application of this subsection, the individual's liability for any deficiency which is assessed with respect to the return shall not exceed the portion of such deficiency properly allocable to the individual under subsection (d).

(2) BURDEN OF PROOF.—Except as provided in subparagraph (A)(ii) or (C) of paragraph (3), each individual who elects the application of this subsection shall have the burden of proof with respect to establishing the portion of any deficiency allocable to such individual.

(3) ELECTION.—

(A) INDIVIDUALS ELIGIBLE TO MAKE ELECTION.—

(i) IN GENERAL.—An individual shall only be eligible to elect the application of this subsection if—

(I) at the time such election is filed, such individual is no longer married to, or is legally separated from, the individual with whom such individual filed the joint return to which the election relates; or

(II) such individual was not a member of the same household as the individual with whom such joint return was filed at any time during the 12-month period ending on the date such election is filed.

(ii) CERTAIN TAXPAYERS INELIGIBLE TO ELECT.—If the Secretary demonstrates that assets were transferred between individuals filing a joint return as part of a fraudulent scheme by such individuals, an election under this subsection by either individual shall be invalid (and section 6013(d)(3) shall apply to the joint return).

(B) TIME FOR ELECTION.—An election under this subsection for any taxable year may be made at any time after a deficiency for such year is asserted but not later than 2 years after the date on which the Secretary has begun collection activities with respect to the individual making the election.

Sec. 6015(b)

(C) ELECTION NOT VALID WITH RESPECT TO CERTAIN DEFICIENCIES.—If the Secretary demonstrates that an individual making an election under this subsection had actual knowledge, at the time such individual signed the return, of any item giving rise to a deficiency (or portion thereof) which is not allocable to such individual under subsection (d), such election shall not apply to such deficiency (or portion). This subparagraph shall not apply where the individual with actual knowledge establishes that such individual signed the return under duress.

(4) LIABILITY INCREASED BY REASON OF TRANSFERS OF PROPERTY TO AVOID TAX.—

(A) IN GENERAL.—Notwithstanding any other provision of this subsection, the portion of the deficiency for which the individual electing the application of this subsection is liable (without regard to this paragraph) shall be increased by the value of any disqualified asset transferred to the individual.

(B) DISQUALIFIED ASSET.—For purposes of this paragraph—

(i) IN GENERAL.—The term "disqualified asset" means any property or right to property transferred to an individual making the election under this subsection with respect to a joint return by the other individual filing such joint return if the principal purpose of the transfer was the avoidance of tax or payment of tax.

(ii) PRESUMPTION.—

(I) In general.—For purposes of clause (i), except as provided in subclause (II), any transfer which is made after the date which is 1 year before the date on which the first letter of proposed deficiency which allows the taxpayer an opportunity for administrative review in the Internal Revenue Service Office of Appeals is sent shall be presumed to have as its principal purpose the avoidance of tax or payment of tax.

(II) Exceptions.—Subclause (I) shall not apply to any transfer pursuant to a decree of divorce or separate maintenance or a written instrument incident to such a decree or to any transfer which an individual establishes did not have as its principal purpose the avoidance of tax or payment of tax.

[Sec. 6015(d)]

(d) ALLOCATION OF DEFICIENCY.—For purposes of subsection (c)—

(1) IN GENERAL.—The portion of any deficiency on a joint return allocated to an individual shall be the amount which bears the same ratio to such deficiency as the net amount of items taken into account in computing the deficiency and allocable to the individual under paragraph (3) bears to the net amount of all items taken into account in computing the deficiency.

(2) SEPARATE TREATMENT OF CERTAIN ITEMS.—If a deficiency (or portion thereof) is attributable to—

(A) the disallowance of a credit; or

(B) any tax (other than tax imposed by section 1 or 55) required to be included with the joint return;

and such item is allocated to one individual under paragraph (3), such deficiency (or portion) shall be allocated to such individual. Any such item shall not be taken into account under paragraph (1).

(3) ALLOCATION OF ITEMS GIVING RISE TO THE DEFICIENCY.—For purposes of this subsection—

(A) IN GENERAL.—Except as provided in paragraphs (4) and (5), any item giving rise to a deficiency on a joint return shall be allocated to individuals filing the return in the same manner as it would have been allocated if the individuals had filed separate returns for the taxable year.

(B) EXCEPTION WHERE OTHER SPOUSE BENEFITS.—Under rules prescribed by the Secretary, an item otherwise allocable to an individual under subparagraph (A) shall be allocated to the other individual filing the joint return to the extent the item gave rise to a tax benefit on the joint return to the other individual.

(C) EXCEPTION FOR FRAUD.—The Secretary may provide for an allocation of any item in a manner not prescribed by subparagraph (A) if the Secretary establishes that such allocation is appropriate due to fraud of one or both individuals.

(4) LIMITATIONS ON SEPARATE RETURNS DISREGARDED.—If an item of deduction or credit is disallowed in its entirety solely because a separate return is filed, such disallowance shall be disregarded and the item shall be computed as if a joint return had been filed and then allocated between the spouses appropriately. A similar rule shall apply for purposes of section 86.

(5) CHILD'S LIABILITY.—If the liability of a child of a taxpayer is included on a joint return, such liability shall be disregarded in computing the separate liability of either spouse and such liability shall be allocated appropriately between the spouses.

[Sec. 6015(e)]

(e) PETITION FOR REVIEW BY TAX COURT.—

(1) IN GENERAL.—In the case of an individual against whom a deficiency has been asserted and who elects to have subsection (b) or (c) apply—

(A) IN GENERAL.—In addition to any other remedy provided by law, the individual may petition the Tax Court (and the Tax Court shall have jurisdiction) to determine the appropriate relief available to the individual under this section if such petition is filed—

(i) at any time after the earlier of—

(I) the date the Secretary mails, by certified or registered mail to the taxpayer's last known address, notice of the Secretary's final determination of relief available to the individual, or

(II) the date which is 6 months after the date such election is filed with the Secretary, and

(ii) not later than the close of the 90th day after the date described in clause (i)(I).

(B) RESTRICTIONS APPLICABLE TO COLLECTION OF ASSESSMENT.—

(i) IN GENERAL.—Except as otherwise provided in section 6851 or 6861, no levy or proceeding in court shall be made, begun, or prosecuted against the individual making an election under subsection (b) or (c) for collection of any assessment to which such election relates until the close of the 90th day referred to in subparagraph (A)(ii), or, if a petition has been filed with the Tax Court under subparagraph (A), until the decision of the Tax Court has become final. Rules similar to the rules of section 7485 shall apply with respect to the collection of such assessment.

(ii) AUTHORITY TO ENJOIN COLLECTION ACTIONS.—Notwithstanding the provisions of section 7421(a), the beginning of such levy or proceeding during the time the prohibition under clause (i) is in force may be enjoined by a proceeding in the proper court, including the Tax Court. The Tax Court shall have no jurisdiction under this subparagraph to enjoin any action or proceeding unless a timely petition has been filed under subparagraph (A) and then only in respect of the amount of the assessment to which the election under subsection (b) or (c) relates.

(2) SUSPENSION OF RUNNING OF PERIOD OF LIMITATIONS.—The running of the period of limitations in section 6502 on the collection of the assessment to which the petition under paragraph (1)(A) relates shall be suspended—

(A) for the period during which the Secretary is prohibited by paragraph (1)(B) from collecting by levy or a proceeding in court and for 60 days thereafter, and

(B) if a waiver under paragraph (5) is made, from the date the claim for relief was filed until 60 days after the waiver is filed with the Secretary.

(3) LIMITATION ON TAX COURT JURISDICTION.—If a suit for refund is begun by either individual filing the joint return pursuant to section 6532—

(A) the Tax Court shall lose jurisdiction of the individual's action under this section to whatever extent jurisdiction is acquired by the district court or the United States Court of Federal Claims over the taxable years that are the subject of the suit for refund, and

(B) the court acquiring jurisdiction shall have jurisdiction over the petition filed under this subsection.

(4) NOTICE TO OTHER SPOUSE.—The Tax Court shall establish rules which provide the individual filing a joint return but not making the election under subsection (b) or (c) with adequate notice and an opportunity to become a party to a proceeding under either such subsection.

(5) WAIVER.—An individual who elects the application of subsection (b) or (c) (and who agrees with the Secretary's determination of relief) may waive in writing at any time the restrictions in paragraph (1)(B) with respect to collection of the outstanding assessment (whether or not a notice of the Secretary's final determination of relief has been mailed).

(f) EQUITABLE RELIEF.—Under procedures prescribed by the Secretary, if—

(1) taking into account all the facts and circumstances, it is inequitable to hold the individual liable for any unpaid tax or any deficiency (or any portion of either); and

(2) relief is not available to such individual under subsection (b) or (c),

the Secretary may relieve such individual of such liability.

(g) CREDITS AND REFUNDS.—

(1) IN GENERAL.—Except as provided in paragraphs (2) and (3), notwithstanding any other law or rule of law (other than section 6511, 6512(b), 7121, or 7122), credit or refund shall be allowed or made to the extent attributable to the application of this section.

(2) RES JUDICATA.—In the case of any election under subsection (b) or (c), if a decision of a court in any prior proceeding for the same taxable year has become final, such decision shall be conclusive except with respect to the qualification of the individual for relief which was not an issue in such proceeding. The exception contained in the preceding sentence shall not apply if the court determines that the individual participated meaningfully in such prior proceeding.

(3) CREDIT AND REFUND NOT ALLOWED UNDER SUBSECTION (c).—No credit or refund shall be allowed as a result of an election under subsection (c).

(h) REGULATIONS.—The Secretary shall prescribe such regulations as are necessary to carry out the provisions of this section, including—

(1) regulations providing methods for allocation of items other than the methods under subsection (d)(3); and

(2) regulations providing the opportunity for an individual to have notice of, and an opportunity to participate in, any administrative proceeding with respect to an election made under subsection (b) or (c) by the other individual filing the joint return.

PART III—INFORMATION RETURNS

Subpart A—Information Concerning Persons Subject to Special Provisions

SEC. 6031. RETURN OF PARTNERSHIP INCOME.

(a) GENERAL RULE.—Every partnership (as defined in section 761(a)) shall make a return for each taxable year, stating specifically the items of its gross income and the deductions allowable by subtitle A, and such other information for the purpose of carrying out the provisions of subtitle A as the Secretary may by forms and regulations prescribe, and shall include in the return the names and addresses of the individuals who would be entitled to share in the taxable income if distributed and the amount of the distributive share of each individual.

(b) COPIES TO PARTNERS.—Each partnership required to file a return under subsection (a) for any partnership taxable year shall (on or before the day on which the return for such taxable year was required to be filed) furnish to each person who is a partner or who holds an interest in such partnership as a nominee for another person at any time during such taxable year a copy of such information required to be shown on such return as may be required by regulations. In the case of an electing large partnership (as defined in section 775), such information shall be furnished on or before the first March 15 following the close of such taxable year.

(c) NOMINEE REPORTING.—Any person who holds an interest in a partnership as a nominee for another person—

  (1) shall furnish to the partnership, in the manner prescribed by the Secretary, the name and address of such other person, and any other information for such taxable year as the Secretary may by form and regulation prescribe, and

  (2) shall furnish in the manner prescribed by the Secretary such other person the information provided by such partnership under subsection (b).

(d) SEPARATE STATEMENT OF ITEMS OF UNRELATED BUSINESS TAXABLE INCOME.—In the case of any partnership regularly carrying on a trade or business (within the meaning of section 512(c)(1)), the information required under subsection (b) to be furnished to its partners shall include such information as is necessary to enable each partner to compute its distributive share of partnership income or loss from such trade or business in accordance with section 512(a)(1), but without regard to the modifications described in paragraphs (8) through (15) of section 512(b).

(e) FOREIGN PARTNERSHIPS.—

  (1) EXCEPTION FOR FOREIGN PARTNERSHIP.—Except as provided in paragraph (2), the preceding provisions of this section shall not apply to a foreign partnership.

  (2) CERTAIN FOREIGN PARTNERSHIPS REQUIRED TO FILE RETURN.—Except as provided in regulations prescribed by the Secretary, this section shall apply to a foreign partnership for any taxable year if for such year, such partnership has—

    (A) gross income derived from sources within the United States, or

    (B) gross income which is effectively connected with the conduct of a trade or business within the United States.

The Secretary may provide simplified filing procedures for foreign partnerships to which this section applies.

SEC. 6037. RETURN OF S CORPORATION.

(a) In General.—Every S corporation shall make a return for each taxable year, stating specifically the items of its gross income and the deductions allowable by subtitle A, the names and addresses of all persons owning stock in the corporation at any time during the taxable year, the number of shares of stock owned by each shareholder at all times during the taxable year, the amount of money and other property distributed by the corporation during the taxable year to each shareholder, the date of each such distribution, each shareholder's pro rata share of each item of the corporation for the taxable year, and such other information, for the purpose of carrying out the provisions of subchapter S of chapter 1, as the Secretary may by forms and regulations prescribe. Any return filed pursuant to this section shall, for purposes of chapter 66 (relating to limitations), be treated as a return filed by the corporation under section 6012.

(b) COPIES TO SHAREHOLDERS.—Each S corporation required to file a return under subsection (a) for any taxable year shall (on or before the day on which the return for such taxable year was filed) furnish to each person who is a shareholder at any time during such taxable year a copy of such information shown on such return as may be required by regulations.

[Sec. 6037(c)]

(c) SHAREHOLDER'S RETURN MUST BE CONSISTENT WITH CORPORATE RETURN OR SECRETARY NOTIFIED OF INCONSISTENCY.—

(1) IN GENERAL.—A shareholder of an S corporation shall, on such shareholder's return, treat a subchapter S item in a manner which is consistent with the treatment of such item on the corporate return.

(2) NOTIFICATION OF INCONSISTENT TREATMENT.—

(A) IN GENERAL.—In the case of any subchapter S item, if—

(i)(I) the corporation has filed a return but the shareholder's treatment on his return is (or may be) inconsistent with the treatment of the item on the corporate return, or

(II) the corporation has not filed a return, and

(ii) the shareholder files with the Secretary a statement identifying the inconsistency,

paragraph (1) shall not apply to such item.

(B) SHAREHOLDER RECEIVING INCORRECT INFORMATION.—A shareholder shall be treated as having complied with clause (ii) of subparagraph (A) with respect to a subchapter S item if the shareholder—

(i) demonstrates to the satisfaction of the Secretary that the treatment of the subchapter S item on the shareholder's return is consistent with the treatment of the item on the schedule furnished to the shareholder by the corporation, and

(ii) elects to have this paragraph apply with respect to that item.

(3) EFFECT OF FAILURE TO NOTIFY.—In any case—

(A) described in subparagraph (A)(i)(I) of paragraph (2), and

(B) in which the shareholder does not comply with subparagraph (A)(ii) of paragraph (2),

any adjustment required to make the treatment of the items by such shareholder consistent with the treatment of the items on the corporate return shall be treated as arising out of mathematical or clerical errors and assessed according to section 6213(b)(1). Paragraph (2) of section 6213(b) shall not apply to any assessment referred to in the preceding sentence.

(4) SUBCHAPTER S ITEM.—For purposes of this subsection, the term "subchapter S item" means any item of an S corporation to the extent that regulations prescribed by the Secretary provide that, for purposes of this subtitle, such item is more appropriately determined at the corporation level than at the shareholder level.

(5) ADDITION TO TAX FOR FAILURE TO COMPLY WITH SECTION.—For addition to tax in the case of a shareholder's negligence in connection with, or disregard of, the requirements of this section, see part II of subchapter A of chapter 68.

Subpart B—Information Concerning Transactions With Other Persons

[Sec. 6041]

SEC. 6041. INFORMATION AT SOURCE.

[Sec. 6041(a)]

(a) PAYMENTS OF $600 OR MORE.—All persons engaged in a trade or business and making payment in the course of such trade or business to another person, of rent, salaries, wages, premiums, annuities, compensations, remunerations, emoluments, or other fixed or determinable gains, profits, and income (other than payments to which section 6042(a)(1), 6044(a)(1), 6047(e)[d], 6049(a), or 6050N(a) applies, and other than payments with respect to which a statement is required under the authority of section 6042(a)(2), 6044(a)(2), or 6045), of $600 or more in any taxable year, or, in the case of such payments made by the United States, the officers or employees of the United States having information as to such payments and required to make returns in regard thereto by the regulations hereinafter provided for, shall render a true and accurate return to the Secretary, under such regulations and in such form and manner and to such extent as may be prescribed by the Secretary, setting forth the amount of such gains, profits, and income, and the name and address of the recipient of such payment.

* * *

[Sec. 6042]

SEC. 6042. RETURNS REGARDING PAYMENTS OF DIVIDENDS AND CORPORATE EARNINGS AND PROFITS.

[Sec. 6042(a)]

(a) REQUIREMENT OF REPORTING.—

(1) IN GENERAL.—Every person—

(A) who makes payments of dividends aggregating $10 or more to any other person during any calendar year, or

(B) who receives payments of dividends as a nominee and who makes payments aggregating $10 or more during any calendar year to any other person with respect to the dividends so received,

shall make a return according to the forms or regulations prescribed by the Secretary, setting forth the aggregate amount of such payments and the name and address of the person to whom paid.

(2) RETURNS REQUIRED BY THE SECRETARY.—Every person who makes payments of dividends aggregating less than $10 to any other person during any calendar year shall, when required by the Secretary, make a return setting forth the aggregate amount of such payments, and the name and address of the person to whom paid.

* * *

[Sec. 6043]

SEC. 6043. LIQUIDATING, ETC., TRANSACTIONS.

[Sec. 6043(a)]

(a) CORPORATE LIQUIDATING, ETC., TRANSACTIONS.—Every corporation shall—

(1) Within 30 days after the adoption by the corporation of a resolution or plan for the dissolution of the corporation or for the liquidation of the whole or any part of its capital stock, make a return setting forth the terms of such resolution or plan and such other information as the Secretary shall by forms or regulations prescribe; and

(2) When required by the Secretary, make a return regarding its distributions in liquidation, stating the name and address of, the number and class of shares owned by, and the amount paid to, each shareholder, or, if the distribution is in property other than money, the fair market value (as of the date the distribution is made) of the property distributed to each shareholder.

* * *

[Sec. 6043(c)]

(c) CHANGES IN CONTROL AND RECAPITALIZATIONS.—If—

(1) control (as defined in section 304(c)(1)) of a corporation is acquired by any person (or group of persons) in a transaction (or series of related transactions), or

(2) there is a recapitalization of a corporation or other substantial change in the capital structure of a corporation,

when required by the Secretary, such corporation shall make a return (at such time and in such manner as the Secretary may prescribe) setting forth the identity of the parties to the transaction, the fees involved, the changes in the capital structure involved, and such other information as the Secretary may require with respect to such transaction.

* * *

[Sec. 6045]

SEC. 6045. RETURNS OF BROKERS.

* * *

[Sec. 6045(e)]

(e) RETURN REQUIRED IN THE CASE OF REAL ESTATE TRANSACTIONS.—

Sec. 6042

(1) IN GENERAL.—In the case of a real estate transaction, the real estate reporting person shall file a return under subsection (a) and a statement under subsection (b) with respect to such transaction.

(2) REAL ESTATE REPORTING PERSON.—For purposes of this subsection, the term "real estate reporting person" means any of the following persons involved in a real estate transaction in the following order:

(A) the person (including any attorney or title company) responsible for closing the transaction,

(B) the mortgage lender,

(C) the seller's broker,

(D) the buyer's broker, or

(E) such other person designated in regulations prescribed by the Secretary.

Any person treated as a real estate reporting person under the preceding sentence shall be treated as a broker for purposes of subsection (c)(1).

(3) PROHIBITION OF SEPARATE CHARGE FOR FILING RETURN.—It shall be unlawful for any real estate reporting person to separately charge any customer for complying with any requirement of paragraph (1). Nothing in this paragraph shall be construed to prohibit the real estate reporting person from taking into account its cost of complying with such requirement in establishing its charge (other than a separate charge for complying with such requirement) to any customer for performing services in the case of a real estate transaction.

(4) ADDITIONAL INFORMATION REQUIRED.—In the case of a real estate transaction involving a residence, the real estate reporting person shall include the following information on the return under subsection (a) and on the statement under subsection (b):

(A) The portion of any real property tax which is treated as a tax imposed on the purchaser by reason of section 164(d)(1)(B).

(B) Whether or not the financing (if any) of the seller was federally-subsidized indebtedness (as defined in section 143(m)(3)).

(5) EXCEPTION FOR SALES OR EXCHANGES OF CERTAIN PRINCIPAL RESIDENCES.—

(A) IN GENERAL.—Paragraph (1) shall not apply to any sale or exchange of a residence for $250,000 or less if the person referred to in paragraph (2) receives written assurance in a form acceptable to the Secretary from the seller that—

(i) such residence is the principal residence (within the meaning of section 121) of the seller,

(ii) if the Secretary requires the inclusion on the return under subsection (a) of information as to whether there is federally subsidized mortgage financing assistance with respect to the mortgage on residences, that there is no such assistance with respect to the mortgage on such residence, and

(iii) the full amount of the gain on such sale or exchange is excludable from gross income under section 121.

If such assurance includes an assurance that the seller is married, the preceding sentence shall be applied by substituting "$500,000" for "$250,000".

The Secretary may by regulation increase the dollar amounts under this subparagraph if the Secretary determines that such an increase will not materially reduce revenues to the Treasury.

(B) SELLER.—For purposes of this paragraph, the term "seller" includes the person relinquishing the residence in an exchange.

[Sec. 6045(f)]

(f) RETURN REQUIRED IN THE CASE OF PAYMENTS TO ATTORNEYS.—

(1) IN GENERAL.—Any person engaged in a trade or business and making a payment (in the course of such trade or business) to which this subsection applies shall file a return under subsection (a) and a statement under subsection (b) with respect to such payment.

(2) APPLICATION OF SUBSECTION.—

(A) IN GENERAL.—This subsection shall apply to any payment to an attorney in connection with legal services (whether or not such services are performed for the payor).

Sec. 6045(f)

(B) EXCEPTION.—This subsection shall not apply to the portion of any payment which is required to be reported under section 6041(a) (or would be so required but for the dollar limitation contained therein) or section 6051.

[Sec. 6049]

SEC. 6049. RETURNS REGARDING PAYMENTS OF INTEREST.

[Sec. 6049(a)]

(a) REQUIREMENT OF REPORTING.—Every person—

(1) who makes payments of interest (as defined in subsection (b)) aggregating $10 or more to any other person during any calendar year, or

(2) who receives payments of interest (as so defined) as a nominee and who makes payments aggregating $10 or more during any calendar year to any other person with respect to the interest so received,

shall make a return according to the forms or regulations prescribed by the Secretary, setting forth the aggregate amount of such payments and the name and address of the person to whom paid.

* * *

[Sec. 6050H]

SEC. 6050H. RETURNS RELATING TO MORTGAGE INTEREST RECEIVED IN TRADE OR BUSINESS FROM INDIVIDUALS.

[Sec. 6050H(a)]

(a) MORTGAGE INTEREST OF $600 OR MORE.—Any person—

(1) who is engaged in a trade or business, and

(2) who, in the course of such trade or business, receives from any individual interest aggregating $600 or more for any calendar year on any mortgage,

shall make the return described in subsection (b) with respect to each individual from whom such interest was received at such time as the Secretary may by regulations prescribe.

* * *

[Sec. 6050I]

SEC. 6050I. RETURNS RELATING TO CASH RECEIVED IN TRADE OR BUSINESS, ETC.

[Sec. 6050I(a)]

(a) CASH RECEIPTS OF MORE THAN $10,000.—Any person—

(1) who is engaged in a trade or business, and

(2) who, in the course of such trade or business, receives more than $10,000 in cash in 1 transaction (or 2 or more related transactions),

shall make the return described in subsection (b) with respect to such transaction (or related transactions) at such time as the Secretary may by regulations prescribe.

[Sec. 6050I(b)]

(b) FORM AND MANNER OF RETURNS.—A return is described in this subsection if such return—

(1) is in such form as the Secretary may prescribe,

(2) contains—

(A) the name, address, and TIN of the person from whom the cash was received,

(B) the amount of cash received,

(C) the date and nature of the transaction, and

(D) such other information as the Secretary may prescribe.

[Sec. 6050I(c)]

(c) EXCEPTIONS.—

(1) CASH RECEIVED BY FINANCIAL INSTITUTIONS.—Subsection (a) shall not apply to—

(A) cash received in a transaction reported under title 31, United States Code, if the Secretary determines that reporting under this section would duplicate the reporting to the Treasury under title 31, United States Code, or

(B) cash received by any financial institution (as defined in subparagraphs (A), (B), (C), (D), (E), (F), (G), (J), (K), (R), and (S) of section 5312(a)(2) of title 31, United States Code).

(2) TRANSACTIONS OCCURRING OUTSIDE THE UNITED STATES.—Except to the extent provided in regulations prescribed by the Secretary, subsection (a) shall not apply to any transaction if the entire transaction occurs outside the United States.

* * *

[Sec. 6050I(f)]

(f) STRUCTURING TRANSACTIONS TO EVADE REPORTING REQUIREMENTS PROHIBITED.—

(1) IN GENERAL.—No person shall for the purpose of evading the return requirements of this section—

(A) cause or attempt to cause a trade or business to fail to file a return required under this section,

(B) cause or attempt to cause a trade or business to file a return required under this section that contains a material omission or misstatement of fact, or

(C) structure or assist in structuring, or attempt to structure or assist in structuring, any transaction with one or more trades or businesses.

(2) PENALTIES.—A person violating paragraph (1) of this subsection shall be subject to the same civil and criminal sanctions applicable to a person which fails to file or completes a false or incorrect return under this section.

* * *

[Sec. 6050N]

SEC. 6050N. RETURNS REGARDING PAYMENTS OF ROYALTIES.

[Sec. 6050N(a)]

(a) REQUIREMENT OF REPORTING.—Every person—

(1) who makes payments of royalties (or similar amounts) aggregating $10 or more to any other person during any calendar year, or

(2) who receives payments of royalties (or similar amounts) as a nominee and who makes payments aggregating $10 or more during any calendar year to any other person with respect to the royalties (or similar amounts) so received,

shall make a return according to the forms or regulations prescribed by the Secretary, setting forth the aggregate amount of such payments and the name and address of the person to whom paid.

* * *

Subpart C—Information Regarding Wages Paid Employees

[Sec. 6053]

SEC. 6053. REPORTING OF TIPS.

[Sec. 6053(a)]

(a) REPORTS BY EMPLOYEES.—Every employee who, in the course of his employment by an employer, receives in any calendar month tips which are wages (as defined in section 3121(a) or section 3401(a)) or which are compensation (as defined in section 3231(e)) shall report all such tips in one or more written statements furnished to his employer on or before the 10th day following such month. Such statements shall be furnished by the employee under such regulations, at such other times before such 10th day, and in such form and manner, as may be prescribed by the Secretary.

* * *

PART V—TIME FOR FILING RETURNS AND OTHER DOCUMENTS

[Sec. 6072]
SEC. 6072. TIME FOR FILING INCOME TAX RETURNS.

[Sec. 6072(a)]

(a) GENERAL RULE.—In the case of returns under section 6012, 6013, 6017, or 6031 (relating to income tax under subtitle A), returns made on the basis of the calendar year shall be filed on or before the 15th day of April following the close of the calendar year and returns made on the basis of a fiscal year shall be filed on or before the 15th day of the fourth month following the close of the fiscal year, except as otherwise provided in the following subsections of this section.

[Sec. 6072(b)]

(b) RETURNS OF CORPORATIONS.—Returns of corporations under section 6012 made on the basis of the calendar year shall be filed on or before the 15th day of March following the close of the calendar year, and such returns made on the basis of a fiscal year shall be filed on or before the 15th day of the third month following the close of the fiscal year. Returns required for a taxable year by section 6011(c)(2) (relating to returns of a DISC) shall be filed on or before the fifteenth day of the ninth month following the close of the taxable year.

* * *

PART VI—EXTENSION OF TIME FOR FILING RETURNS

[Sec. 6081]
SEC. 6081. EXTENSION OF TIME FOR FILING RETURNS.

[Sec. 6081(a)]

(a) GENERAL RULE.—The Secretary may grant a reasonable extension of time for filing any return, declaration, statement, or other document required by this title or by regulations. Except in the case of taxpayers who are abroad, no such extension shall be for more than 6 months.

[Sec. 6081(b)]

(b) AUTOMATIC EXTENSION FOR CORPORATION INCOME TAX RETURNS.—An extension of 3 months for the filing of the return of income taxes imposed by subtitle A shall be allowed any corporation if, in such manner and at such time as the Secretary may by regulations prescribe, there is filed on behalf of such corporation the form prescribed by the Secretary, and if such corporation pays, on or before the date prescribed for payment of the tax, the amount properly estimated as its tax; but this extension may be terminated at any time by the Secretary by mailing to the taxpayer notice of such termination at least 10 days prior to the date for termination fixed in such notice.

* * *

Subchapter B—Miscellaneous Provisions

[Sec. 6107]
SEC. 6107. INCOME TAX RETURN PREPARER MUST FURNISH COPY OF RETURN TO TAXPAYER AND MUST RETAIN A COPY OR LIST.

[Sec. 6107(a)]

(a) FURNISHING COPY TO TAXPAYER.—Any person who is an income tax return preparer with respect to any return or claim for refund shall furnish a completed copy of such return or claim to the taxpayer not later than the time such return or claim is presented for such taxpayer's signature.

[Sec. 6107(b)]

(b) COPY OR LIST TO BE RETAINED BY INCOME TAX RETURN PREPARER.—Any person who is an income tax return preparer with respect to a return or claim for refund shall, for the period ending 3 years after the close of the return period—

(1) retain a completed copy of such return or claim, or retain, on a list, the name and taxpayer identification number of the taxpayer for whom such return or claim was prepared, and

(2) make such copy or list available for inspection upon request by the Secretary.

[Sec. 6107(c)]

(c) REGULATIONS.—The Secretary shall prescribe regulations under which, in cases where 2 or more persons are income tax return preparers with respect to the same return or claim for refund, compliance with the requirements of subsection (a) or (b), as the case may be, of one such person shall be deemed to be compliance with the requirements of such subsection by the other persons.

* * *

[Sec. 6113]

SEC. 6113. DISCLOSURE OF NONDEDUCTIBILITY OF CONTRIBUTIONS.

[Sec. 6113(a)]

(a) GENERAL RULE.—Each fundraising solicitation by (or on behalf of) an organization to which this section applies shall contain an express statement (in a conspicuous and easily recognizable format) that contributions or gifts to such organization are not deductible as charitable contributions for Federal income tax purposes.

[Sec. 6113(b)]

(b) ORGANIZATION TO WHICH SECTION APPLIES.—

(1) IN GENERAL.—Except as otherwise provided in this subsection, this section shall apply to any organization which is not described in section 170(c) and which—

(A) is described in subsection (c) (other than paragraph (1) thereof) or (d) of section 501 and exempt from taxation under section 501(a),

(B) is a political organization (as defined in section 527(e)), or

(C) was an organization described in subparagraph (A) or (B) at any time during the 5-year period ending on the date of the fundraising solicitation or is a successor to an organization so described at any time during such 5-year period.

(2) EXEMPTION FOR SMALL ORGANIZATIONS.—

(A) ANNUAL GROSS RECEIPTS DO NOT EXCEED $100,000.—This section shall not apply to any organization the gross receipts of which in each taxable year are normally not more than $100,000.

(B) MULTIPLE ORGANIZATION RULE.—The Secretary may treat any group of 2 or more organizations as 1 organization for purposes of subparagraph (A) where necessary or appropriate to prevent the avoidance of this section through the use of multiple organizations.

(3) SPECIAL RULE FOR CERTAIN FRATERNAL ORGANIZATIONS.—For purposes of paragraph (1), an organization described in section 170(c)(4) shall be treated as described in section 170(c) only with respect to solicitations for contributions or gifts which are to be used exclusively for purposes referred to in section 170(c)(4).

[Sec. 6113(c)]

(c) FUNDRAISING SOLICITATION.—For purposes of this section—

(1) IN GENERAL.—Except as provided in paragraph (2), the term "fundraising solicitation" means any solicitation of contributions or gifts which is made—

(A) in written or printed form,

(B) by television or radio, or

(C) by telephone.

(2) Exception for certain letters or calls.—The term "fundraising solicitation" shall not include any letter or telephone call if such letter or call is not part of a coordinated fundraising campaign soliciting more than 10 persons during the calendar year.

[Sec. 6115]

SEC. 6115. DISCLOSURE RELATED TO QUID PRO QUO CONTRIBUTIONS.

[Sec. 6115(a)]

(a) Disclosure Requirement.—If an organization described in section 170(c) (other than paragraph (1) thereof) receives a quid pro quo contribution in excess of $75, the organization shall, in connection with the solicitation or receipt of the contribution, provide a written statement which—

(1) informs the donor that the amount of the contribution that is deductible for Federal income tax purposes is limited to the excess of the amount of any money and the value of any property other than money contributed by the donor over the value of the goods or services provided by the organization, and

(2) provides the donor with a good faith estimate of the value of such goods or services.

[Sec. 6115(b)]

(b) Quid Pro Quo Contribution.—For purposes of this section, the term "quid pro quo contribution" means a payment made partly as a contribution and partly in consideration for goods or services provided to the payor by the donee organization. A quid pro quo contribution does not include any payment made to an organization, organized exclusively for religious purposes, in return for which the taxpayer receives solely an intangible religious benefit that generally is not sold in a commercial transaction outside the donative context.

CHAPTER 62—TIME AND PLACE FOR PAYING TAX

Subchapter A—Place and Due Date for Payment of Tax

[Sec. 6151]

SEC. 6151. TIME AND PLACE FOR PAYING TAX SHOWN ON RETURNS.

[Sec. 6151(a)]

(a) General Rule.—Except as otherwise provided in this subchapter, when a return of tax is required under this title or regulations, the person required to make such return shall, without assessment or notice and demand from the Secretary, pay such tax to the internal revenue officer with whom the return is filed, and shall pay such tax at the time and place fixed for filing the return (determined without regard to any extension of time for filing the return).

* * *

Subchapter B—Extensions of Time for Payment

[Sec. 6161]

SEC. 6161. EXTENSION OF TIME FOR PAYING TAX.

[Sec. 6161(a)]

(a) Amount Determined by Taxpayer on Return.—

(1) General rule.—The Secretary, except as otherwise provided in this title, may extend the time for payment of the amount of the tax shown, or required to be shown, on any return or declaration required under authority of this title (or any installment thereof), for a reasonable period not to exceed 6 months (12 months in the case of estate tax) from the date fixed for payment thereof. Such extension may exceed 6 months in the case of a taxpayer who is abroad.

* * *

CHAPTER 63—ASSESSMENT

Subchapter C—Tax Treatment of Partnership Items

[Sec. 6221]

SEC. 6221. TAX TREATMENT DETERMINED AT PARTNERSHIP LEVEL.

Except as otherwise provided in this subchapter, the tax treatment of any partnership item (and the applicability of any penalty, addition to tax, or additional amount which relates to an adjustment to a partnership item) shall be determined at the partnership level.

[Sec. 6222]

SEC. 6222. PARTNER'S RETURN MUST BE CONSISTENT WITH PARTNERSHIP RETURN OR SECRETARY NOTIFIED OF INCONSISTENCY.

[Sec. 6222(a)]

(a) IN GENERAL.—A partner shall, on the partner's return, treat a partnership item in a manner which is consistent with the treatment of such partnership item on the partnership return.

[Sec. 6222(b)]

(b) NOTIFICATION OF INCONSISTENT TREATMENT.—

(1) IN GENERAL.—In the case of any partnership item, if—

(A)(i) the partnership has filed a return but the partner's treatment on his return is (or may be) inconsistent with the treatment of the item on the partnership return, or

(ii) the partnership has not filed a return, and

(B) the partner files with the Secretary a statement identifying the inconsistency,

subsection (a) shall not apply to such item.

(2) PARTNER RECEIVING INCORRECT INFORMATION.—A partner shall be treated as having complied with subparagraph (B) of paragraph (1) with respect to a partnership item if the partner—

(A) demonstrates to the satisfaction of the Secretary that the treatment of the partnership item on the partner's return is consistent with the treatment of the item on the schedule furnished to the partner by the partnership, and

(B) elects to have this paragraph apply with respect to that item.

[Sec. 6222(c)]

(c) EFFECT OF FAILURE TO NOTIFY.—In any case—

(1) described in paragraph (1)(A)(i) of subsection (b), and

(2) in which the partner does not comply with paragraph (1)(B) of subsection (b),

section 6225 shall not apply to any part of a deficiency attributable to any computational adjustment required to make the treatment of the items by such partner consistent with the treatment of the items on the partnership return.

* * *

CHAPTER 64—COLLECTION

Subchapter A—General Provisions

[Sec. 6304]

SEC. 6304. FAIR TAX COLLECTION PRACTICES.

[Sec. 6304(a)]

(a) COMMUNICATION WITH THE TAXPAYER.—Without the prior consent of the taxpayer given directly to the Secretary or the express permission of a court of competent jurisdiction, the Secretary may not communicate with a taxpayer in connection with the collection of any unpaid tax—

Sec. 6304(a)

(1) at any unusual time or place or a time or place known or which should be known to be inconvenient to the taxpayer;

(2) if the Secretary knows the taxpayer is represented by any person authorized to practice before the Internal Revenue Service with respect to such unpaid tax and has knowledge of, or can readily ascertain, such person's name and address, unless such person fails to respond within a reasonable period of time to a communication from the Secretary or unless such person consents to direct communication with the taxpayer; or

(3) at the taxpayer's place of employment if the Secretary knows or has reason to know that the taxpayer's employer prohibits the taxpayer from receiving such communication.

In the absence of knowledge of circumstances to the contrary, the Secretary shall assume that the convenient time for communicating with a taxpayer is after 8 a.m. and before 9 p.m., local time at the taxpayer's location.

[Sec. 6304(b)]

(b) PROHIBITION OF HARASSMENT AND ABUSE.—The Secretary may not engage in any conduct the natural consequence of which is to harass, oppress, or abuse any person in connection with the collection of any unpaid tax. Without limiting the general application of the foregoing, the following conduct is a violation of this subsection:

(1) The use or threat of use of violence or other criminal means to harm the physical person, reputation, or property of any person.

(2) The use of obscene or profane language or language the natural consequence of which is to abuse the hearer or reader.

(3) Causing a telephone to ring or engaging any person in telephone conversation repeatedly or continuously with intent to annoy, abuse, or harass any person at the called number.

(4) Except as provided under rules similar to the rules in section 804 of the Fair Debt Collection Practices Act (15 U.S.C. 1692b), the placement of telephone calls without meaningful disclosure of the caller's identity.

* * *

Subchapter B—Receipt of Payment

[Sec. 6315]

SEC. 6315. PAYMENTS OF ESTIMATED INCOME TAX.

Payment of the estimated income tax, or any installment thereof, shall be considered payment on account of the income taxes imposed by subtitle A for the taxable year.

Subchapter C—Lien for Taxes

PART I—DUE PROCESS FOR LIENS

[Sec. 6320]

SEC. 6320. NOTICE AND OPPORTUNITY FOR HEARING UPON FILING OF NOTICE OF LIEN.

[Sec. 6320(a)]

(a) REQUIREMENT OF NOTICE.—

(1) IN GENERAL.—The Secretary shall notify in writing the person described in section 6321 of the filing of a notice of lien under section 6323.

(2) TIME AND METHOD FOR NOTICE.—The notice required under paragraph (1) shall be—

(A) given in person;

(B) left at the dwelling or usual place of business of such person; or

(C) sent by certified or registered mail to such person's last known address,

not more than 5 business days after the day of the filing of the notice of lien.

(3) INFORMATION INCLUDED WITH NOTICE.—The notice required under paragraph (1) shall include in simple and nontechnical terms—

(A) the amount of unpaid tax;

(B) the right of the person to request a hearing during the 30-day period beginning on the day after the 5-day period described in paragraph (2);

(C) the administrative appeals available to the taxpayer with respect to such lien and the procedures relating to such appeals; and

(D) the provisions of this title and procedures relating to the release of liens on property.

[Sec. 6320(b)]

(b) RIGHT TO FAIR HEARING.—

(1) IN GENERAL.—If the person requests a hearing under subsection (a)(3)(B), such hearing shall be held by the Internal Revenue Service Office of Appeals.

(2) ONE HEARING PER PERIOD.—A person shall be entitled to only one hearing under this section with respect to the taxable period to which the unpaid tax specified in subsection (a)(3)(A) relates.

(3) IMPARTIAL OFFICER.—The hearing under this subsection shall be conducted by an officer or employee who has had no prior involvement with respect to the unpaid tax specified in subsection (a)(3)(A) before the first hearing under this section or section 6330. A taxpayer may waive the requirement of this paragraph.

(4) COORDINATION WITH SECTION 6330.—To the extent practicable, a hearing under this section shall be held in conjunction with a hearing under section 6330.

[Sec. 6320(c)]

(c) CONDUCT OF HEARING; REVIEW; SUSPENSIONS.—For purposes of this section, subsections (c), (d) (other than paragraph (2)(B) thereof), and (e) of section 6330 shall apply.

PART II—LIENS

[Sec. 6321]

SEC. 6321. LIEN FOR TAXES.

If any person liable to pay any tax neglects or refuses to pay the same after demand, the amount (including any interest, additional amount, addition to tax, or assessable penalty, together with any costs that may accrue in addition thereto) shall be a lien in favor of the United States upon all property and rights to property, whether real or personal, belonging to such person.

[Sec. 6322]

SEC. 6322. PERIOD OF LIEN.

Unless another date is specifically fixed by law, the lien imposed by section 6321 shall arise at the time the assessment is made and shall continue until the liability for the amount so assessed (or a judgment against the taxpayer arising out of such liability) is satisfied or becomes unenforceable by reason of lapse of time.

Subchapter D—Seizure of Property for Collection of Taxes

PART I—DUE PROCESS FOR COLLECTIONS

[Sec. 6330]

SEC. 6330. NOTICE AND OPPORTUNITY FOR HEARING BEFORE LEVY.

[Sec. 6330(a)]

(a) REQUIREMENT OF NOTICE BEFORE LEVY.—

(1) IN GENERAL.—No levy may be made on any property or right to property of any person unless the Secretary has notified such person in writing of their right to a hearing under this section

before such levy is made. Such notice shall be required only once for the taxable period to which the unpaid tax specified in paragraph (3)(A) relates.

(2) TIME AND METHOD FOR NOTICE.—The notice required under paragraph (1) shall be—

(A) given in person;

(B) left at the dwelling or usual place of business of such person; or

(C) sent by certified or registered mail, return receipt requested, to such person's last known address,

not less than 30 days before the day of the first levy with respect to the amount of the unpaid tax for the taxable period.

(3) INFORMATION INCLUDED WITH NOTICE.—The notice required under paragraph (1) shall include in simple and nontechnical terms—

(A) the amount of unpaid tax;

(B) the right of the person to request a hearing during the 30-day period under paragraph (2); and

(C) the proposed action by the Secretary and the rights of the person with respect to such action, including a brief statement which sets forth—

(i) the provisions of this title relating to levy and sale of property;

(ii) the procedures applicable to the levy and sale of property under this title;

(iii) the administrative appeals available to the taxpayer with respect to such levy and sale and the procedures relating to such appeals;

(iv) the alternatives available to taxpayers which could prevent levy on property (including installment agreements under section 6159); and

(v) the provisions of this title and procedures relating to redemption of property and release of liens on property.

[Sec. 6330(b)]

(b) RIGHT TO FAIR HEARING.—

(1) IN GENERAL.—If the person requests a hearing under subsection (a)(3)(B), such hearing shall be held by the Internal Revenue Service Office of Appeals.

(2) ONE HEARING PER PERIOD.—A person shall be entitled to only one hearing under this section with respect to the taxable period to which the unpaid tax specified in subsection (a)(3)(A) relates.

(3) IMPARTIAL OFFICER.—The hearing under this subsection shall be conducted by an officer or employee who has had no prior involvement with respect to the unpaid tax specified in subsection (a)(3)(A) before the first hearing under this section or section 6320. A taxpayer may waive the requirement of this paragraph.

[Sec. 6330(c)]

(c) MATTERS CONSIDERED AT HEARING.—In the case of any hearing conducted under this section—

(1) REQUIREMENT OF INVESTIGATION.—The appeals officer shall at the hearing obtain verification from the Secretary that the requirements of any applicable law or administrative procedure have been met.

(2) ISSUES AT HEARING.—

(A) IN GENERAL.—The person may raise at the hearing any relevant issue relating to the unpaid tax or the proposed levy, including—

(i) appropriate spousal defenses;

(ii) challenges to the appropriateness of collection actions; and

(iii) offers of collection alternatives, which may include the posting of a bond, the substitution of other assets, an installment agreement, or an offer-in-compromise.

(B) UNDERLYING LIABILITY.—The person may also raise at the hearing challenges to the existence or amount of the underlying tax liability for any tax period if the person did not receive any statutory notice of deficiency for such tax liability or did not otherwise have an opportunity to dispute such tax liability.

Sec. 6330(b)

(3) BASIS FOR THE DETERMINATION.—The determination by an appeals officer under this subsection shall take into consideration—

(A) the verification presented under paragraph (1);

(B) the issues raised under paragraph (2); and

(C) whether any proposed collection action balances the need for the efficient collection of taxes with the legitimate concern of the person that any collection action be no more intrusive than necessary.

(4) CERTAIN ISSUES PRECLUDED.—An issue may not be raised at the hearing if—

(A) the issue was raised and considered at a previous hearing under section 6320 or in any other previous administrative or judicial proceeding; and

(B) the person seeking to raise the issue participated meaningfully in such hearing or proceeding.

This paragraph shall not apply to any issue with respect to which subsection (d)(2)(B) applies.

[Sec. 6330(d)]

(d) PROCEEDING AFTER HEARING.—

(1) JUDICIAL REVIEW OF DETERMINATION.—The person may, within 30 days of a determination under this section, appeal such determination—

(A) to the Tax Court (and the Tax Court shall have jurisdiction with respect to such matter); or

(B) if the Tax Court does not have jurisdiction of the underlying tax liability, to a district court of the United States.

If a court determines that the appeal was to an incorrect court, a person shall have 30 days after the court determination to file such appeal with the correct court.

(2) JURISDICTION RETAINED AT IRS OFFICE OF APPEALS.—The Internal Revenue Service Office of Appeals shall retain jurisdiction with respect to any determination made under this section, including subsequent hearings requested by the person who requested the original hearing on issues regarding—

(A) collection actions taken or proposed with respect to such determination; and

(B) after the person has exhausted all administrative remedies, a change in circumstances with respect to such person which affects such determination.

[Sec. 6330(e)]

(e) SUSPENSION OF COLLECTIONS AND STATUTE OF LIMITATIONS.—

(1) IN GENERAL.—Except as provided in paragraph (2), if a hearing is requested under subsection (a)(3)(B), the levy actions which are the subject of the requested hearing and the running of any period of limitations under section 6502 (relating to collection after assessment), section 6531 (relating to criminal prosecutions), or section 6532 (relating to other suits) shall be suspended for the period during which such hearing, and appeals therein, are pending. In no event shall any such period expire before the 90th day after the day on which there is a final determination in such hearing. Notwithstanding the provisions of section 7421(a), the beginning of a levy or proceeding during the time the suspension under this paragraph is in force may be enjoined by a proceeding in the proper court, including the Tax Court. The Tax Court shall have no jurisdiction under this paragraph to enjoin any action or proceeding unless a timely appeal has been filed under subsection (d)(1) and then only in respect of the unpaid tax or proposed levy to which the determination being appealed relates.

(2) LEVY UPON APPEAL.—Paragraph (1) shall not apply to a levy action while an appeal is pending if the underlying tax liability is not at issue in the appeal and the court determines that the Secretary has shown good cause not to suspend the levy.

[Sec. 6330(f)]

(f) JEOPARDY AND STATE REFUND COLLECTION.—If—

(1) the Secretary has made a finding under the last sentence of section 6331(a) that the collection of tax is in jeopardy; or

Sec. 6330(f)

(2) the Secretary has served a levy on a State to collect a Federal tax liability from a State tax refund,

this section shall not apply, except that the taxpayer shall be given the opportunity for the hearing described in this section within a reasonable period of time after the levy.

PART II—LEVY

[Sec. 6331]

SEC. 6331. LEVY AND DISTRAINT.

[Sec. 6331(a)]

(a) AUTHORITY OF SECRETARY.—If any person liable to pay any tax neglects or refuses to pay the same within 10 days after notice and demand, it shall be lawful for the Secretary to collect such tax (and such further sum as shall be sufficient to cover the expenses of the levy) by levy upon all property and rights to property (except such property as is exempt under section 6334) belonging to such person or on which there is a lien provided in this chapter for the payment of such tax. Levy may be made upon the accrued salary or wages of any officer, employee, or elected official, of the United States, the District of Columbia, or any agency or instrumentality of the United States or the District of Columbia, by serving a notice of levy on the employer (as defined in section 3401 (d)) of such officer, employee, or elected official. If the Secretary makes a finding that the collection of such tax is in jeopardy, notice and demand for immediate payment of such tax may be made by the Secretary and, upon failure or refusal to pay such tax, collection thereof by levy shall be lawful without regard to the 10-day period provided in this section.

[Sec. 6331(b)]

(b) SEIZURE AND SALE OF PROPERTY.—The term "levy" as used in this title includes the power of distraint and seizure by any means. Except as otherwise provided in subsection (e), a levy shall extend only to property possessed and obligations existing at the time thereof. In any case in which the Secretary may levy upon property or rights to property, he may seize and sell such property or rights to property (whether real or personal, tangible or intangible).

[Sec. 6331(c)]

(c) SUCCESSIVE SEIZURES.—Whenever any property or right to property upon which levy has been made by virtue of subsection (a) is not sufficient to satisfy the claim of the United States for which levy is made, the Secretary may, thereafter, and as often as may be necessary, proceed to levy in like manner upon any other property liable to levy of the person against whom such claim exists, until the amount due from him, together with all expenses, is fully paid.

[Sec. 6331(d)]

(d) REQUIREMENT OF NOTICE BEFORE LEVY.—

(1) IN GENERAL.—Levy may be made under subsection (a) upon the salary or wages or other property of any person with respect to any unpaid tax only after the Secretary has notified such person in writing of his intention to make such levy.

(2) 30-DAY REQUIREMENT.—The notice required under paragraph (1) shall be—

(A) given in person,

(B) left at the dwelling or usual place of business of such person, or

(C) sent by certified or registered mail to such person's last known address,

no less than 30 days before the day of the levy.

(3) JEOPARDY.—Paragraph (1) shall not apply to a levy if the Secretary has made a finding under the last sentence of subsection (a) that the collection of tax is in jeopardy.

(4) INFORMATION INCLUDED WITH NOTICE.—The notice required under paragraph (1) shall include a brief statement which sets forth in simple and nontechnical terms—

(A) the provisions of this title relating to levy and sale of property,

(B) the procedures applicable to the levy and sale of property under this title,

(C) the administrative appeals available to the taxpayer with respect to such levy and sale and the procedures relating to such appeals,

Sec. 6331

(D) the alternatives available to taxpayers which could prevent levy on the property (including installment agreements under section 6159),

(E) the provisions of this title relating to redemption of property and release of liens on property, and

(F) the procedures applicable to the redemption of property and the release of a lien on property under this title.

[Sec. 6331(e)]

(e) CONTINUING LEVY ON SALARY AND WAGES.—The effect of a levy on salary or wages payable to or received by a taxpayer shall be continuous from the date such levy is first made until such levy is released under section 6343.

* * *

[Sec. 6331(j)]

(j) NO LEVY BEFORE INVESTIGATION OF STATUS OF PROPERTY.—

(1) IN GENERAL.—For purposes of applying the provisions of this subchapter, no levy may be made on any property or right to property which is to be sold under section 6335 until a thorough investigation of the status of such property has been completed.

(2) ELEMENTS IN INVESTIGATION.—For purposes of paragraph (1), an investigation of the status of any property shall include—

(A) a verification of the taxpayer's liability;

(B) the completion of an analysis under subsection (f);

(C) the determination that the equity in such property is sufficient to yield net proceeds from the sale of such property to apply to such liability; and

(D) a thorough consideration of alternative collection methods.

[Sec. 6331(k)]

(k) NO LEVY WHILE CERTAIN OFFERS PENDING OR INSTALLMENT AGREEMENT PENDING OR IN EFFECT.—

(1) OFFER-IN-COMPROMISE PENDING.—No levy may be made under subsection (a) on the property or rights to property of any person with respect to any unpaid tax—

(A) during the period that an offer-in-compromise by such person under section 7122 of such unpaid tax is pending with the Secretary; and

(B) if such offer is rejected by the Secretary, during the 30 days thereafter (and, if an appeal of such rejection is filed within such 30 days, during the period that such appeal is pending).

For purposes of subparagraph (A), an offer is pending beginning on the date the Secretary accepts such offer for processing.

(2) INSTALLMENT AGREEMENTS.—No levy may be made under subsection (a) on the property or rights to property of any person with respect to any unpaid tax—

(A) during the period that an offer by such person for an installment agreement under section 6159 for payment of such unpaid tax is pending with the Secretary;

(B) if such offer is rejected by the Secretary, during the 30 days thereafter (and, if an appeal of such rejection is filed within such 30 days, during the period that such appeal is pending);

(C) during the period that such an installment agreement for payment of such unpaid tax is in effect; and

(D) if such agreement is terminated by the Secretary, during the 30 days thereafter (and, if an appeal of such termination is filed within such 30 days, during the period that such appeal is pending).

(3) CERTAIN RULES TO APPLY.—Rules similar to the rules of—

(A) paragraphs (3) and (4) of subsection (i), and

(B) except in the case of paragraph (2)(C), paragraph (5) of subsection (i),

shall apply for purposes of this subsection.

* * *

Sec. 6331(k)

[Caution: Pursuant to Section 6334(g), the amounts set forth in Sections 6334(a)(2) and (3) are adjusted for taxable years beginning after 1999 to reflect increases in the Consumer Price Index. The adjusted amounts applicable to taxable years beginning in 2003 are provided beginning at page ix.]

[Sec. 6334]

SEC. 6334. PROPERTY EXEMPT FROM LEVY.

[Sec. 6334(a)]

(a) ENUMERATION.—There shall be exempt from levy—

(1) WEARING APPAREL AND SCHOOL BOOKS.—Such items of wearing apparel and such school books as are necessary for the taxpayer or for members of his family;

(2) FUEL, PROVISIONS, FURNITURE, AND PERSONAL EFFECTS.—So much of the fuel, provisions, furniture, and personal effects in the taxpayer's household, and of the arms for personal use, livestock, and poultry of the taxpayer, as does not exceed $6,250 in value;

(3) BOOKS AND TOOLS OF A TRADE, BUSINESS, OR PROFESSION.—So many of the books and tools necessary for the trade, business, or profession of the taxpayer as do not exceed in the aggregate $3,125 in value.

(4) UNEMPLOYMENT BENEFITS.—Any amount payable to an individual with respect to his unemployment (including any portion thereof payable with respect to dependents) under an unemployment compensation law of the United States, of any State, or of the District of Columbia or of the Commonwealth of Puerto Rico.

(5) UNDELIVERED MAIL.—Mail, addressed to any person, which has not been delivered to the addressee.

(6) CERTAIN ANNUITY AND PENSION PAYMENTS.—Annuity or pension payments under the Railroad Retirement Act, benefits under the Railroad Unemployment Insurance Act, special pension payments received by a person whose name has been entered on the Army, Navy, Air Force, and Coast Guard Medal of Honor roll (38 U. S. C. 562), and annuities based on retired or retainer pay under chapter 73 of title 10 of the United States Code.

(7) WORKMEN'S COMPENSATION.—Any amount payable to an individual as workmen's compensation (including any portion thereof payable with respect to dependents) under a workmen's compensation law of the United States, any State, the District of Columbia, or the Commonwealth of Puerto Rico.

(8) JUDGMENTS FOR SUPPORT OF MINOR CHILDREN.—If the taxpayer is required by judgment of a court of competent jurisdiction, entered prior to the date of levy, to contribute to the support of his minor children, so much of his salary, wages, or other income as is necessary to comply with such judgment.

(9) MINIMUM EXEMPTION FOR WAGES, SALARY, AND OTHER INCOME.—Any amount payable to or received by an individual as wages or salary for personal services, or as income derived from other sources, during any period, to the extent that the total of such amounts payable to or received by him during such period does not exceed the applicable exempt amount determined under subsection (d).

(10) CERTAIN SERVICE-CONNECTED DISABILITY PAYMENTS.—Any amount payable to an individual as a service-connected (within the meaning of section 101(16) of title 38, United States Code) disability benefit under—

(A) subchapter II, III, IV, V, or VI of chapter 11 of such title 38, or

(B) chapter 13, 21, 23, 31, 32, 34, 35, 37, or 39 of such title 38.

(11) CERTAIN PUBLIC ASSISTANCE PAYMENTS.—Any amount payable to an individual as a recipient of public assistance under—

(A) title IV or title XVI (relating to supplemental security income for the aged, blind, and disabled) of the Social Security Act, or

(B) State or local government public assistance or public welfare programs for which eligibility is determined by a needs or income test.

(12) ASSISTANCE UNDER JOB TRAINING PARTNERSHIP ACT.—Any amount payable to a participant under the Job Training Partnership Act (29 U.S.C. 1501 et seq.) from funds appropriated pursuant to such Act.

Sec. 6334

(13) RESIDENCES EXEMPT IN SMALL DEFICIENCY CASES AND PRINCIPAL RESIDENCES AND CERTAIN BUSINESS ASSETS EXEMPT IN ABSENCE OF CERTAIN APPROVAL OR JEOPARDY.—

(A) RESIDENCES IN SMALL DEFICIENCY CASES.—If the amount of the levy does not exceed $5,000—

(i) any real property used as a residence by the taxpayer; or

(ii) any real property of the taxpayer (other than real property which is rented) used by any other individual as a residence.

(B) PRINCIPAL RESIDENCES AND CERTAIN BUSINESS ASSETS.—Except to the extent provided in subsection (e)—

(i) the principal residence of the taxpayer (within the meaning of section 121); and

(ii) tangible personal property or real property (other than real property which is rented) used in the trade or business of an individual taxpayer.

* * *

[Sec. 6334(c)]

(c) NO OTHER PROPERTY EXEMPT.—Notwithstanding any other law of the United States (including section 207 of the Social Security Act), no property or rights to property shall be exempt from levy other than the property specifically made exempt by subsection (a).

[Sec. 6334(d)]

(d) EXEMPT AMOUNT OF WAGES, SALARY, OR OTHER INCOME.—

(1) INDIVIDUALS ON WEEKLY BASIS.—In the case of an individual who is paid or receives all of his wages, salary, and other income on a weekly basis, the amount of the wages, salary, and other income payable to or received by him during any week which is exempt from levy under subsection (a)(9) shall be the exempt amount.

(2) EXEMPT AMOUNT.—For purposes of paragraph (1), the term "exempt amount" means an amount equal to—

(A) the sum of—

(i) the standard deduction, and

(ii) the aggregate amount of the deductions for personal exemptions allowed the taxpayer under section 151 in the taxable year in which such levy occurs, divided by

(B) 52.

Unless the taxpayer submits to the Secretary a written and properly verified statement specifying the facts necessary to determine the proper amount under subparagraph (A), subparagraph (A) shall be applied as if the taxpayer were a married individual filing a separate return with only 1 personal exemption.

(3) INDIVIDUALS ON BASIS OTHER THAN WEEKLY.—In the case of any individual not described in paragraph (1), the amount of the wages, salary, and other income payable to or received by him during any applicable pay period or other fiscal period (as determined under regulations prescribed by the Secretary) which is exempt from levy under subsection (a)(9) shall be an amount (determined under such regulations) which as nearly as possible will result in the same total exemption from levy for such individual over a period of time as he would have under paragraph (1) if (during such period of time) he were paid or received such wages, salary, and other income on a regular weekly basis.

[Sec. 6334(e)]

(e) LEVY ALLOWED ON PRINCIPAL RESIDENCES AND CERTAIN BUSINESS ASSETS IN CERTAIN CIRCUMSTANCES.—

(1) PRINCIPAL RESIDENCES.—

(A) APPROVAL REQUIRED.—A principal residence shall not be exempt from levy if a judge or magistrate of a district court of the United States approves (in writing) the levy of such residence.

(B) JURISDICTION.—The district courts of the United States shall have exclusive jurisdiction to approve a levy under subparagraph (A).

(2) CERTAIN BUSINESS ASSETS.—Property (other than a principal residence) described in subsection (a)(13)(B) shall not be exempt from levy if—

(A) a district director or assistant district director of the Internal Revenue Service personally approves (in writing) the levy of such property; or

(B) the Secretary finds that the collection of tax is in jeopardy.

An official may not approve a levy under subparagraph (A) unless the official determines that the taxpayer's other assets subject to collection are insufficient to pay the amount due, together with expenses of the proceedings.

[Sec. 6334(f)]

(f) LEVY ALLOWED ON CERTAIN SPECIFIED PAYMENTS.—Any payment described in subparagraph (B) or (C) of section 6331(h)(2) shall not be exempt from levy if the Secretary approves the levy thereon under section 6331(h).

[Sec. 6334(g)]

(g) INFLATION ADJUSTMENT.—

(1) IN GENERAL.—In the case of any calendar year beginning after 1999, each dollar amount referred to in paragraphs (2) and (3) of subsection (a) shall be increased by an amount equal to—

(A) such dollar amount, multiplied by

(B) the cost-of-living adjustment determined under section 1(f)(3) for such calendar year, by substituting "calendar year 1998" for "calendar year 1992" in subparagraph (B) thereof.

(2) ROUNDING.—If any dollar amount after being increased under paragraph (1) is not a multiple of $10, such dollar amount shall be rounded to the nearest multiple of $10.

CHAPTER 65—ABATEMENTS, CREDITS, AND REFUNDS

Subchapter B—Rules of Special Application

[Sec. 6429]

SEC. 6429. ADVANCE PAYMENT OF PORTION OF INCREASED CHILD CREDIT FOR 2003.

[Sec. 6429(a)]

(a) IN GENERAL.—Each taxpayer who was allowed a credit under section 24 on the return for the taxpayer's first taxable year beginning in 2002 shall be treated as having made a payment against the tax imposed by chapter 1 for such taxable year in an amount equal to the child tax credit refund amount (if any) for such taxable year.

[Sec. 6429(b)]

(b) CHILD TAX CREDIT REFUND AMOUNT.—For purposes of this section, the child tax credit refund amount is the amount by which the aggregate credits allowed under part IV of subchapter A of chapter 1 for such first taxable year would have been increased if—

(1) the per child amount under section 24(a)(2) for such year were $1,000,

(2) only qualifying children (as defined in section 24(c)) of the taxpayer for such year who had not attained age 17 as of December 31, 2003, were taken into account, and

(3) section 24(d)(1)(B)(ii) did not apply.

[Sec. 6429(c)]

(c) TIMING OF PAYMENTS.—In the case of any overpayment attributable to this section, the Secretary shall, subject to the provisions of this title, refund or credit such overpayment as rapidly as possible and, to the extent practicable, before October 1, 2003. No refund or credit shall be made or allowed under this section after December 31, 2003.

(d) COORDINATION WITH CHILD TAX CREDIT.—

(1) IN GENERAL.—The amount of credit which would (but for this subsection and section 26) be allowed under section 24 for the taxpayer's first taxable year beginning in 2003 shall be reduced (but not below zero) by the payments made to the taxpayer under this section. Any failure to so reduce the credit shall be treated as arising out of a mathematical or clerical error and assessed according to section 6213(b)(1).

(2) JOINT RETURNS.—In the case of a payment under this section with respect to a joint return, half of such payment shall be treated as having been made to each individual filing such return.

(e) NO INTEREST.—No interest shall be allowed on any overpayment attributable to this section.

CHAPTER 66—LIMITATIONS

Subchapter A—Limitations on Assessment and Collection

SEC. 6501. LIMITATIONS ON ASSESSMENT AND COLLECTION.

(a) GENERAL RULE.—Except as otherwise provided in this section, the amount of any tax imposed by this title shall be assessed within 3 years after the return was filed (whether or not such return was filed on or after the date prescribed) or, if the tax is payable by stamp, at any time after such tax became due and before the expiration of 3 years after the date on which any part of such tax was paid, and no proceeding in court without assessment for the collection of such tax shall be begun after the expiration of such period. For purposes of this chapter, the term "return" means the return required to be filed by the taxpayer (and does not include a return of any person from whom the taxpayer has received an item of income, gain, loss, deduction, or credit).

(b) TIME RETURN DEEMED FILED.—

(1) EARLY RETURN.—For purposes of this section, a return of tax imposed by this title, except tax imposed by chapter 3, 21, or 24, filed before the last day prescribed by law or by regulations promulgated pursuant to law for the filing thereof, shall be considered as filed on such last day.

(2) RETURN OF CERTAIN EMPLOYMENT TAXES AND TAX IMPOSED BY CHAPTER 3.—For purposes of this section, if a return of tax imposed by chapter 3, 21 or 24 for any period ending with or within a calendar year is filed before April 15 of the succeeding calendar year, such return shall be considered filed on April 15 of such calendar year.

(3) RETURN EXECUTED BY SECRETARY.—Notwithstanding the provisions of paragraph (2) of section 6020(b), the execution of a return by the Secretary pursuant to the authority conferred by such section shall not start the running of the period of limitations on assessment and collection.

(4) RETURN OF EXCISE TAXES.—For purposes of this section, the filing of a return for a specified period on which an entry has been made with respect to a tax imposed under a provision of subtitle D (including a return on which an entry has been made showing no liability for such tax for such period) shall constitute the filing of a return of all amounts of such tax which, if properly paid, would be required to be reported on such return for such period.

(c) EXCEPTIONS.—

(1) FALSE RETURN.—In the case of a false or fraudulent return with the intent to evade tax, the tax may be assessed, or a proceeding in court for collection of such tax may be begun without assessment, at any time.

(2) WILLFUL ATTEMPT TO EVADE TAX.—In case of a willful attempt in any manner to defeat or evade tax imposed by this title (other than tax imposed by subtitle A or B), the tax may be assessed, or a proceeding in court for the collection of such tax may be begun without assessment, at any time.

(3) NO RETURN.—In the case of failure to file a return, the tax may be assessed, or a proceeding in court for the collection of such tax may be begun without assessment, at any time.

(4) EXTENSION BY AGREEMENT.—

(A) IN GENERAL.—Where before the expiration of the time prescribed in this section for the assessment of any tax imposed by this title, except the estate tax provided in chapter 11, both the Secretary and the taxpayer have consented in writing to its assessment after such time, the tax may be assessed at any time prior to the expiration of the period agreed upon. The period so agreed upon may be extended by subsequent agreements in writing made before the expiration of the period previously agreed upon.

(B) NOTICE TO TAXPAYER OF RIGHT TO REFUSE OR LIMIT EXTENSION.—The Secretary shall notify the taxpayer of the taxpayer's right to refuse to extend the period of limitations, or to limit such extension to particular issues or to a particular period of time, on each occasion when the taxpayer is requested to provide such consent.

(5) TAX RESULTING FROM CHANGES IN CERTAIN INCOME TAX OR ESTATE TAX CREDITS.—

For special rules applicable in cases where the adjustment of certain taxes allowed as a credit against income taxes or estate taxes results in additional tax, see section 905(c) (relating to the foreign tax credit for income tax purposes) and section 2016 (relating to taxes of foreign countries, States, etc., claimed as credit against estate taxes).

(6) TERMINATION OF PRIVATE FOUNDATION STATUS.—In the case of a tax on termination of private foundation status under section 507, such tax may be assessed, or a proceeding in court for the collection of such tax may be begun without assessment, at any time.

(7) SPECIAL RULE FOR CERTAIN AMENDED RETURNS.—Where, within the 60-day period ending on the day on which the time prescribed in this section for the assessment of any tax imposed by subtitle A for any taxable year would otherwise expire, the Secretary receives a written document signed by the taxpayer showing that the taxpayer owes an additional amount of such tax for such taxable year, the period for the assessment of such additional amount shall not expire before the day 60 days after the day on which the Secretary receives such document.

(8) FAILURE TO NOTIFY SECRETARY OF CERTAIN FOREIGN TRANSFERS.—In the case of any information which is required to be reported to the Secretary under section 6038, 6038A, 6038B, 6046, 6046A, or 6048, the time for assessment of any tax imposed by this title with respect to any event or period to which such information relates shall not expire before the date which is 3 years after the date on which the Secretary is furnished the information required to be reported under such section.

* * *

[Sec. 6501(d)]

(d) REQUEST FOR PROMPT ASSESSMENT.—Except as otherwise provided in subsection (c), (e), or (f), in the case of any tax (other than the tax imposed by chapter 11 of subtitle B, relating to estate taxes) for which return is required in the case of a decedent, or by his estate during the period of administration, or by a corporation, the tax shall be assessed, and any proceeding in court without assessment for the collection of such tax shall be begun, within 18 months after written request therefor (filed after the return is made and filed in such manner and such form as may be prescribed by regulations of the Secretary) by the executor, administrator, or other fiduciary representing the estate of such decedent, or by the corporation, but not after the expiration of 3 years after the return was filed. This subsection shall not apply in the case of a corporation unless—

(1)(A) such written request notifies the Secretary that the corporation contemplates dissolution at or before the expiration of such 18-month period, (B) the dissolution is in good faith begun before the expiration of such 18-month period, and (C) the dissolution is completed;

(2)(A) such written request notifies the Secretary that a dissolution has in good faith been begun, and (B) the dissolution is completed; or

(3) a dissolution has been completed at the time such written request is made.

Sec. 6501(d)

[Sec. 6501(e)]

(e) SUBSTANTIAL OMISSION OF ITEMS.—Except as otherwise provided in subsection (c)—

(1) INCOME TAXES.—In the case of any tax imposed by subtitle A—

(A) GENERAL RULE.—If the taxpayer omits from gross income an amount properly includible therein which is in excess of 25 percent of the amount of gross income stated in the return, the tax may be assessed, or a proceeding in court for the collection of such tax may be begun without assessment, at any time within 6 years after the return was filed. For purposes of this subparagraph—

(i) In the case of a trade or business, the term "gross income" means the total of the amounts received or accrued from the sale of goods or services (if such amounts are required to be shown on the return) prior to diminution by the cost of such sales or services; and

(ii) In determining the amount omitted from gross income, there shall not be taken into account any amount which is omitted from gross income stated in the return if such amount is disclosed in the return, or in a statement attached to the return, in a manner adequate to apprise the Secretary of the nature and amount of such item.

(B) CONSTRUCTIVE DIVIDENDS.—If the taxpayer omits from gross income an amount properly includible therein under section 551(b) (relating to the inclusion in the gross income of United States shareholders of their distributive shares of the undistributed foreign personal holding company income), the tax may be assessed, or a proceeding in court for the collection of such tax may be begun without assessment, at any time within 6 years after the return was filed.

(2) ESTATE AND GIFT TAXES.—In the case of a return of estate tax under chapter 11 or a return of gift tax under chapter 12, if the taxpayer omits from the gross estate or from the total amount of the gifts made during the period for which the return was filed items includible in such gross estate or such total gifts, as the case may be, as exceed in amount 25 percent of the gross estate stated in the return or the total amount of gifts stated in the return, the tax may be assessed, or a proceeding in court for the collection of such tax may be begun without assessment, at any time within 6 years after the return was filed. In determining the items omitted from the gross estate or the total gifts, there shall not be taken into account any item which is omitted from the gross estate or from the total gifts stated in the return if such item is disclosed in the return, or in a statement attached to the return, in a manner adequate to apprise the Secretary of the nature and amount of such item.

(3) EXCISE TAXES.—In the case of a return of a tax imposed under a provision of subtitle D, if the return omits an amount of such tax properly includible thereon which exceeds 25 percent of the amount of such tax reported thereon, the tax may be assessed, or a proceeding in court for the collection of such tax may be begun without assessment, at any time within 6 years after the return is filed. In determining the amount of tax omitted on a return, there shall not be taken into account any amount of tax imposed by chapter 41, 42, 43, or 44 which is omitted from the return if the transaction giving rise to such tax is disclosed in the return, or in a statement attached to the return, in a manner adequate to apprise the Secretary of the existence and nature of such item.

[Sec. 6501(f)]

(f) PERSONAL HOLDING COMPANY TAX.—If a corporation which is a personal holding company for any taxable year fails to file with its return under chapter 1 for such year a schedule setting forth—

(1) the items of gross income and adjusted ordinary gross income, described in section 543, received by the corporation during such year, and

(2) the names and addresses of the individuals who owned, within the meaning of section 544 (relating to rules for determining stock ownership), at any time during the last half of such year more than 50 percent in value of the outstanding capital stock of the corporation,

the personal holding company tax for such year may be assessed, or a proceeding in court for the collection of such tax may be begun without assessment, at any time within 6 years after the return for such year was filed.

[Sec. 6501(g)]

(g) CERTAIN INCOME TAX RETURNS OF CORPORATIONS.—

(1) TRUSTS OR PARTNERSHIPS.—If a taxpayer determines in good faith that it is a trust or partnership and files a return as such under subtitle A, and if such taxpayer is thereafter held to be a corporation for the taxable year for which the return is filed, such return shall be deemed the return of the corporation for purposes of this section.

(2) EXEMPT ORGANIZATIONS.—If a taxpayer determines in good faith that it is an exempt organization and files a return as such under section 6033, and if such taxpayer is thereafter held to be a taxable organization for the taxable year for which the return is filed, such return shall be deemed the return of the organization for purposes of this section.

(3) DISC.—If a corporation determines in good faith that it is a DISC (as defined in section 992(a)) and files a return as such under section 6011(c)(2) and if such corporation is thereafter held to be a corporation which is not a DISC for the taxable year for which the return is filed, such return shall be deemed the return of a corporation which is not a DISC for purposes of this section.

[Sec. 6501(h)]

(h) NET OPERATING LOSS OR CAPITAL LOSS CARRYBACKS.—In the case of a deficiency attributable to the application to the taxpayer of a net operating loss carryback or a capital loss carryback (including deficiencies which may be assessed pursuant to the provisions of section 6213 (b)(3)), such deficiency may be assessed at any time before the expiration of the period within which a deficiency for the taxable year of the net operating loss or net capital loss which results in such carryback may be assessed.

* * *

Subchapter B—Limitations on Credit or Refund

[Sec. 6511]

SEC. 6511. LIMITATIONS ON CREDIT OR REFUND.

[Sec. 6511(a)]

(a) PERIOD OF LIMITATION ON FILING CLAIM.—Claim for credit or refund of an overpayment of any tax imposed by this title in respect of which tax the taxpayer is required to file a return shall be filed by the taxpayer within 3 years from the time the return was filed or 2 years from the time the tax was paid, whichever of such periods expires the later, or if no return was filed by the taxpayer, within 2 years from the time the tax was paid. Claim for credit or refund of an overpayment of any tax imposed by this title which is required to be paid by means of a stamp shall be filed by the taxpayer within 3 years from the time the tax was paid.

[Sec. 6511(b)]

(b) LIMITATION ON ALLOWANCE OF CREDITS AND REFUNDS.—

(1) FILING OF CLAIM WITHIN PRESCRIBED PERIOD.—No credit or refund shall be allowed or made after the expiration of the period of limitation prescribed in subsection (a) for the filing of a claim for credit or refund, unless a claim for credit or refund is filed by the taxpayer within such period.

(2) LIMIT ON AMOUNT OF CREDIT OR REFUND.—

(A) LIMIT WHERE CLAIM FILED WITHIN 3-YEAR PERIOD.—If the claim was filed by the taxpayer during the 3-year period prescribed in subsection (a), the amount of the credit or refund shall not exceed the portion of the tax paid within the period, immediately preceding the filing of the claim, equal to 3 years plus the period of any extension of time for filing the return. If the tax was required to be paid by means of a stamp, the amount of the credit or refund shall not exceed the portion of the tax paid within the 3 years immediately preceding the filing of the claim.

(B) LIMIT WHERE CLAIM NOT FILED WITHIN 3-YEAR PERIOD.—If the claim was not filed within such 3-year period, the amount of the credit or refund shall not exceed the portion of the tax paid during the 2 years immediately preceding the filing of the claim.

(C) LIMIT IF NO CLAIM FILED.—If no claim was filed, the credit or refund shall not exceed the amount which would be allowable under subparagraph (A) or (B), as the case may be, if claim was filed on the date the credit or refund is allowed.

* * *

[Sec. 6511(d)]

(d) SPECIAL RULES APPLICABLE TO INCOME TAXES.—

(1) SEVEN-YEAR PERIOD OF LIMITATION WITH RESPECT TO BAD DEBTS AND WORTHLESS SECURITIES.—If the claim for credit or refund relates to an overpayment of tax imposed by subtitle A on account of—

(A) The deductibility by the taxpayer, under section 166 or section 832(c), of a debt as a debt which became worthless, or, under section 165(g), of a loss from worthlessness of a security, or

(B) The effect that the deductibility of a debt or loss described in subparagraph (A) has on the application to the taxpayer of a carryover,

in lieu of the 3-year period of limitation prescribed in subsection (a), the period shall be 7 years from the date prescribed by law for filing the return for the year with respect to which the claim is made. If the claim for credit or refund relates to an overpayment on account of the effect that the deductibility of such a debt or loss has on the application to the taxpayer of a carryback, the period shall be either 7 years from the date prescribed by law for filing the return for the year of the net operating loss which results in such carryback or the period prescribed in paragaph (2) of this subsection, whichever expires the later. In the case of a claim described in this paragraph the amount of the credit or refund may exceed the portion of the tax paid within the period prescribed in subsection (b)(2) or (c), whichever is applicable, to the extent of the amount of the overpayment attributable to the deductibility of items described in this paragraph.

(2) SPECIAL PERIOD OF LIMITATION WITH RESPECT TO NET OPERATING LOSS OR CAPITAL LOSS CARRYBACKS.—

(A) PERIOD OF LIMITATION.—If the claim for credit or refund relates to an overpayment attributable to a net operating loss carryback or a capital loss carryback, in lieu of the 3-year period of limitation prescribed in subsection (a), the period shall be that period which ends 3 years after the time prescribed by law for filing the return (including extensions thereof) for the taxable year of the net operating loss or net capital loss which results in such carryback, or the period prescribed in subsection (c) in respect of such taxable year, whichever expires later.

In the case of such a claim, the amount of the credit or refund may exceed the portion of the tax paid within the period provided in subsection (b)(2) or (c), whichever is applicable, to the extent of the amount of the overpayment attributable to such carryback.

(B) APPLICABLE RULES.—

(i) IN GENERAL.—If the allowance of a credit or refund of an overpayment of tax attributable to a net operating loss carryback or a capital loss carryback is otherwise prevented by the operation of any law or rule of law other than section 7122 (relating to compromises), such credit or refund may be allowed or made, if claim therefor is filed within the period provided in subparagraph (A) of this paragraph.

(ii) TENTATIVE CARRYBACK ADJUSTMENTS.—If the allowance of an application, credit, or refund of a decrease in tax determined under section 6411(b) is otherwise prevented by the operation of any law or rule of law other than section 7122, such application, credit, or refund may be allowed or made if application for a tentative carryback adjustment is made within the period provided in section 6411(a).

(iii) DETERMINATIONS BY COURTS TO BE CONCLUSIVE.—In the case of any such claim for credit or refund or any such application for a tentative carryback adjustment, the determination by any court, including the Tax Court, in any proceeding in which the decision of the court has become final, shall be conclusive except with respect to—

(I) the net operating loss deduction and the effect of such deduction, and

(II) the determination of a short-term capital loss and the effect of such short-term capital loss, to the extent that such deduction or short-term capital loss is affected by a carryback which was not an issue in such proceeding.

* * *

[Sec. 6513]

SEC. 6513. TIME RETURN DEEMED FILED AND TAX CONSIDERED PAID.

[Sec. 6513(a)]

(a) EARLY RETURN OR ADVANCE PAYMENT OF TAX.—For purposes of section 6511, any return filed before the last day prescribed for the filing thereof shall be considered as filed on such last day. For purposes of section 6511(b)(2) and (c) and section 6512, payment of any portion of the tax made before the last day prescribed for the payment of the tax shall be considered made on such last day. For purposes of this subsection, the last day prescribed for filing the return or paying the tax shall be determined without regard to any extension of time granted the taxpayer and without regard to any election to pay the tax in installments.

[Sec. 6513(b)]

(b) PREPAID INCOME TAX.—For purposes of section 6511 or 6512—

(1) Any tax actually deducted and withheld at the source during any calendar year under chapter 24 shall, in respect of the recipient of the income, be deemed to have been paid by him on the 15th day of the fourth month following the close of his taxable year with respect to which such tax is allowable as a credit under section 31.

(2) Any amount paid as estimated income tax for any taxable year shall be deemed to have been paid on the last day prescribed for filing the return under section 6012 for such taxable year (determined without regard to any extension of time for filing such return).

(3) Any tax withheld at the source under chapter 3 shall, in respect of the recipient of the income, be deemed to have been paid by such recipient on the last day prescribed for filing the return under section 6012 for the taxable year (determined without regard to any extension of time for filing) with respect to which such tax is allowable as a credit under section 1462. For this purpose, any exemption granted under section 6012 from the requirement of filing a return shall be disregarded.

* * *

Subchapter D—Periods of Limitation in Judicial Proceedings

[Sec. 6531]

SEC. 6531. PERIODS OF LIMITATION ON CRIMINAL PROSECUTIONS.

No person shall be prosecuted, tried, or punished for any of the various offenses arising under the internal revenue laws unless the indictment is found or the information instituted within 3 years next after the commission of the offense, except that the period of limitation shall be 6 years—

(1) for offenses involving the defrauding or attempting to defraud the United States or any agency thereof, whether by conspiracy or not, and in any manner;

(2) for the offense of willfully attempting in any manner to evade or defeat any tax or the payment thereof;

(3) for the offense of willfully aiding or assisting in, or procuring, counseling, or advising, the preparation or presentation under, or in connection with any matter arising under, the internal revenue laws, of a false or fraudulent return, affidavit, claim, or document (whether or not such falsity or fraud is with the knowledge or consent of the person authorized or required to present such return, affidavit, claim, or document);

(4) for the offense of willfully failing to pay any tax, or make any return (other than a return required under authority of part III of subchapter A of chapter 61) at the time or times required by law or regulations;

(5) for offenses described in sections 7206 (1) and 7207 (relating to false statements and fraudulent documents);

(6) for the offense described in section 7212 (a) (relating to intimidation of officers and employees of the United States);

(7) for offenses described in section 7214 (a) committed by officers and employees of the United States; and

(8) for offenses arising under section 371 of Title 18 of the United States Code, where the object of the conspiracy is to attempt in any manner to evade or defeat any tax or the payment thereof.

The time during which the person committing any of the various offenses arising under the internal revenue laws is outside the United States or is a fugitive from justice within the meaning of section 3290 of Title 18 of the United States Code, shall not be taken as any part of the time limited by law for the commencement of such proceedings. (The preceding sentence shall also be deemed an amendment to section 3748 (a) of the Internal Revenue Code of 1939, and shall apply in lieu of the sentence in section 3748 (a) which relates to the time during which a person committing an offense is absent from the district wherein the same is committed, except that such amendment shall apply only if the period of limitations under section 3748 would, without the application of such amendment, expire more than 3 years after the date of enactment of this title, and except that such period shall not, with the application of this amendment, expire prior to the date which is 3 years after the date of enactment of this title.) Where a complaint is instituted before a commissioner of the United States within the period above limited, the time shall be extended until the date which is 9 months after the date of the making of the complaint before the commissioner of the United States. For the purpose of determining the periods of limitation on criminal prosecutions, the rules of section 6513 shall be applicable.

CHAPTER 67—INTEREST

Subchapter A—Interest on Underpayments

[Sec. 6601]

SEC. 6601. INTEREST ON UNDERPAYMENT, NONPAYMENT, OR EXTENSIONS OF TIME FOR PAYMENT, OF TAX.

[Sec. 6601(a)]

(a) GENERAL RULE.—If any amount of tax imposed by this title (whether required to be shown on a return, or to be paid by stamp or by some other method) is not paid on or before the last date prescribed for payment, interest on such amount at the underpayment rate established under section 6621 shall be paid for the period from such last date to the date paid.

[Sec. 6601(b)]

(b) LAST DATE PRESCRIBED FOR PAYMENT.—For purposes of this section, the last date prescribed for payment of the tax shall be determined under chapter 62 with the application of the following rules:

(1) EXTENSIONS OF TIME DISREGARDED.—The last date prescribed for payment shall be determined without regard to any extension of time for payment or any installment agreement entered into under section 6159.

(2) INSTALLMENT PAYMENTS.—In the case of an election under section 6156(a) to pay the tax in installments—

(A) The date prescribed for payment of each installment of the tax shown on the return shall be determined under section 6156(b), and

(B) The last date prescribed for payment of the first installment shall be deemed the last date prescribed for payment of any portion of the tax not shown on the return.

(3) JEOPARDY.—The last date prescribed for payment shall be determined without regard to any notice and demand for payment issued, by reason of jeopardy (as provided in chapter 70), prior to the last date otherwise prescribed for such payment.

(4) ACCUMULATED EARNINGS TAX.—In the case of the tax imposed by section 531 for any taxable year, the last date prescribed for payment shall be deemed to be the due date (without regard to extensions) for the return of tax imposed by subtitle A for such taxable year.

(5) LAST DATE FOR PAYMENT NOT OTHERWISE PRESCRIBED.—In the case of taxes payable by stamp and in all other cases in which the last date for payment is not otherwise prescribed, the last date for payment shall be deemed to be the date the liability for tax arises (and in no event shall be later than the date notice and demand for the tax is made by the Secretary).

* * *

[Sec. 6601(e)]

(e) APPLICABLE RULES.—Except as otherwise provided in this title—

(1) INTEREST TREATED AS TAX.—Interest prescribed under this section on any tax shall be paid upon notice and demand, and shall be assessed, collected, and paid in the same manner as taxes. Any reference in this title (except subchapter B of chapter 63, relating to deficiency procedures) to any tax imposed by this title shall be deemed also to refer to interest imposed by this section on such tax.

(2) INTEREST ON PENALTIES, ADDITIONAL AMOUNTS, OR ADDITIONS TO THE TAX.—

(A) IN GENERAL.—Interest shall be imposed under subsection (a) in respect of any assessable penalty, additional amount, or addition to the tax (other than an addition to tax imposed under section 6651(a)(1) or 6653 or under part II of subchapter A of chapter 68) only if

Sec. 6601(e)

such assessable penalty, additional amount, or addition to the tax is not paid within 21 calendar days from the date of notice and demand therefor (10 business days if the amount for which such notice and demand is made equals or exceeds $100,000), and in such case interest shall be imposed only for the period from the date of the notice and demand to the date of payment.

(B) INTEREST ON CERTAIN ADDITIONS TO TAX.—Interest shall be imposed under this section with respect to any addition to tax imposed by section 6651(a)(1) or 6653 or under part II of subchapter A of chapter 68 for the period which—

(i) begins on the date on which the return of the tax with respect to which such addition to tax is imposed is required to be filed (including any extensions), and

(ii) ends on the date of payment of such addition to tax.

(3) PAYMENTS MADE WITHIN SPECIFIED PERIOD AFTER NOTICE AND DEMAND.—If notice and demand is made for payment of any amount and if such amount is paid within 21 calendar days (10 business days if the amount for which such notice and demand is made equals or exceeds $100,000) after the date of such notice and demand, interest under this section on the amount so paid shall not be imposed for the period after the date of such notice and demand.

* * *

Subchapter B—Interest on Overpayments

[Sec. 6611]

SEC. 6611. INTEREST ON OVERPAYMENTS.

[Sec. 6611(a)]

(a) RATE.—Interest shall be allowed and paid upon any overpayment in respect of any internal revenue tax at the overpayment rate established under section 6621.

[Sec. 6611(b)]

(b) PERIOD.—Such interest shall be allowed and paid as follows:

(1) CREDITS.—In the case of a credit, from the date of the overpayment to the due date of the amount against which the credit is taken.

(2) REFUNDS.—In the case of a refund, from the date of the overpayment to a date (to be determined by the Secretary) preceding the date of the refund check by not more than 30 days, whether or not such refund check is accepted by the taxpayer after tender of such check to the taxpayer. The acceptance of such check shall be without prejudice to any right of the taxpayer to claim any additional overpayment and interest thereon.

(3) LATE RETURNS.—Notwithstanding paragraph (1) or (2) in the case of a return of tax which is filed after the last date prescribed for filing such return (determined with regard to extentions), no interest shall be allowed or paid for any day before the date on which the return is filed.

* * *

[Sec. 6611(f)]

(f) REFUND OF INCOME TAX CAUSED BY CARRYBACK OR ADJUSTMENT FOR CERTAIN UNUSED DEDUCTIONS.—

(1) NET OPERATING LOSS OR CAPITAL LOSS CARRYBACK.—For purposes of subsection (a), if any overpayment of tax imposed by subtitle A results from a carryback of a net operating loss or net capital loss, such overpayment shall be deemed not to have been made prior to the filing date for the taxable year in which such net operating loss or net capital loss arises.

* * *

Subchapter C—Determination of Interest Rate; Compounding of Interest

[Sec. 6621]

SEC. 6621. DETERMINATION OF RATE OF INTEREST.

[Sec. 6621(a)]

(a) GENERAL RULE.—

(1) OVERPAYMENT RATE.—The overpayment rate established under this section shall be the sum of—

(A) the Federal short-term rate determined under subsection (b), plus

(B) 3 percentage points (2 percentage points in the case of a corporation).

To the extent that an overpayment of tax by a corporation for any taxable period (as defined in subsection (c)(3), applied by substituting "overpayment" for "underpayment") exceeds $10,000, subparagraph (B) shall be applied by substituting "0.5 percentage point" for "2 percentage points".

(2) UNDERPAYMENT RATE.—The underpayment rate established under this section shall be the sum of—

(A) the Federal short-term rate determined under subsection (b), plus

(B) 3 percentage points.

[Sec. 6621(b)]

(b) FEDERAL SHORT-TERM RATE.—For purposes of this section—

(1) GENERAL RULE.—The Secretary shall determine the Federal short-term rate for the first month in each calendar quarter.

(2) PERIOD DURING WHICH RATE APPLIES.—

(A) IN GENERAL.—Except as provided in subparagraph (B), the Federal short-term rate determined under paragraph (1) for any month shall apply during the first calendar quarter beginning after such month.

(B) SPECIAL RULE FOR INDIVIDUAL ESTIMATED TAX.—In determining the addition to tax under section 6654 for failure to pay estimated tax for any taxable year, the Federal short-term rate which applies during the 3rd month following such taxable year shall also apply during the first 15 days of the 4th month following such taxable year.

(3) FEDERAL SHORT-TERM RATE.—The Federal short-term rate for any month shall be the Federal short-term rate determined during such month by the Secretary in accordance with section 1274(d). Any such rate shall be rounded to the nearest full percent (or, if a multiple of $\frac{1}{2}$ of 1 percent, such rate shall be increased to the next highest full percent).

[Sec. 6621(c)]

(c) INCREASE IN UNDERPAYMENT RATE FOR LARGE CORPORATE UNDERPAYMENTS.—

(1) IN GENERAL.—For purposes of determining the amount of interest payable under section 6601 on any large corporate underpayment for periods after the applicable date, paragraph (2) of subsection (a) shall be applied by substituting "5 percentage points" for "3 percentage points".

(2) APPLICABLE RATE.—For purposes of this subsection—

(A) IN GENERAL.—The applicable date is the 30th day after the earlier of—

(i) the date on which the 1st letter of proposed deficiency which allows the taxpayer an opportunity for administrative review in the Internal Revenue Service Office of Appeals is sent, or

(ii) the date on which the deficiency notice under section 6212 is sent.

The preceding sentence shall be applied without regard to any such letter or notice which is withdrawn by the Secretary.

Sec. 6621(c)

(B) SPECIAL RULES.—

(i) NONDEFICIENCY PROCEDURES.—In the case of any underpayment of any tax imposed by this title to which the deficiency procedures do not apply, subparagraph (A) shall be applied by taking into account any letter or notice provided by the Secretary which notifies the taxpayer of the assessment or proposed assessment of the tax.

(ii) EXCEPTION WHERE AMOUNTS PAID IN FULL.—For purposes of subparagraph (A), a letter or notice shall be disregarded if, during the 30-day period beginning on the day on which it was sent, the taxpayer makes a payment equal to the amount shown as due in such letter or notice, as the case may be.

(iii) EXCEPTION FOR LETTERS OR NOTICES INVOLVING SMALL AMOUNTS.—For purposes of this paragraph, any letter or notice shall be disregarded if the amount of the deficiency or proposed deficiency (or the assessment or proposed assessment) set forth in such letter or notice is not greater than $100,000 (determined by not taking into account any interest, penalties, or additions to tax).

(3) LARGE CORPORATE UNDERPAYMENT.—For purposes of this subsection—

(A) IN GENERAL.—The term "large corporate underpayment" means any underpayment of a tax by a C corporation for any taxable period if the amount of such underpayment for such period exceeds $100,000.

(B) TAXABLE PERIOD.—For purposes of subparagraph (A), the term "taxable period" means—

(i) in the case of any tax imposed by subtitle A, the taxable year, or

(ii) in the case of any other tax, the period to which the underpayment relates.

[Sec. 6621(d)]

(d) ELIMINATION OF INTEREST ON OVERLAPPING PERIODS OF TAX OVERPAYMENTS AND UNDERPAYMENTS.—To the extent that, for any period, interest is payable under subchapter A and allowable under subchapter B on equivalent underpayments and overpayments by the same taxpayer of tax imposed by this title, the net rate of interest under this section on such amounts shall be zero for such period.

[Sec. 6622]

SEC. 6622. INTEREST COMPOUNDED DAILY.

[Sec. 6622(a)]

(a) GENERAL RULE.—In computing the amount of any interest required to be paid under this title or sections 1961(c)(1) or 2411 of title 28, United States Code, by the Secretary or by the taxpayer, or any other amount determined by reference to such amount of interest, such interest and such amount shall be compounded daily.

[Sec. 6622(b)]

(b) EXCEPTION FOR PENALTY FOR FAILURE TO FILE ESTIMATED TAX.—Subsection (a) shall not apply for purposes of computing the amount of any addition to tax under section 6654 or 6655.

CHAPTER 68—ADDITIONS TO THE TAX, ADDITIONAL AMOUNTS, AND ASSESSABLE PENALTIES

Subchapter A—Additions to the Tax and Additional Amounts

PART I—GENERAL PROVISIONS

[Sec. 6651]

SEC. 6651. FAILURE TO FILE TAX RETURN OR TO PAY TAX.

[Sec. 6651(a)]

(a) ADDITION TO THE TAX.—In case of failure—

(1) to file any return required under authority of subchapter A of chapter 61 (other than part III thereof), subchapter A of chapter 51 (relating to distilled spirits, wines, and beer), or of subchapter A of chapter 52 (relating to tobacco, cigars, cigarettes, and cigarette papers and tubes) or of subchapter A of chapter 53 (relating to machine guns and certain other firearms), on the date prescribed therefor (determined with regard to any extension of time for filing), unless it is shown that such failure is due to reasonable cause and not due to willful neglect, there shall be added to the amount required to be shown as tax on such return 5 percent of the amount of such tax if the failure is for not more than 1 month, with an additional 5 percent for each additional month or fraction thereof during which such failure continues, not exceeding 25 percent in the aggregate;

(2) to pay the amount shown as tax on any return specified in paragraph (1) on or before the date prescribed for payment of such tax (determined with regard to any extension of time for payment), unless it is shown that such failure is due to reasonable cause and not due to willful neglect, there shall be added to the amount shown as tax on such return 0.5 percent of the amount of such tax if the failure is for not more than 1 month, with an additional 0.5 percent for each additional month or fraction thereof during which such failure continues, not exceeding 25 percent in the aggregate; or

(3) to pay any amount in respect of any tax required to be shown on a return specified in paragraph (1) which is not so shown (including an assessment made pursuant to section 6213(b)) within 21 calendar days from the date of notice and demand therefor (10 business days if the amount for which such notice and demand is made equals or exceeds $100,000), unless it is shown that such failure is due to reasonable cause and not due to willful neglect, there shall be added to the amount of tax stated in such notice and demand 0.5 percent of the amount of such tax if the failure is for not more than 1 month, with an additional 0.5 percent for each additional month or fraction thereof during which such failure continues, not exceeding 25 percent in the aggregate.

In the case of a failure to file a return of tax imposed by chapter 1 within 60 days of the date prescribed for filing of such return (determined with regard to any extensions of time for filing), unless it is shown that such failure is due to reasonable cause and not due to willful neglect, the addition to tax under paragraph (1) shall not be less than the lesser of $100 or 100 percent of the amount required to be shown as tax on such return.

* * *

[Sec. 6654]

SEC. 6654. FAILURE BY INDIVIDUAL TO PAY ESTIMATED INCOME TAX.

[Sec. 6654(a)]

(a) ADDITION TO THE TAX.—Except as otherwise provided in this section, in the case of any underpayment of estimated tax by an individual, there shall be added to the tax under chapter 1 and the tax under chapter 2 for the taxable year an amount determined by applying—

(1) the underpayment rate established under section 6621,

(2) to the amount of the underpayment,

(3) for the period of the underpayment.

[Sec. 6654(b)]

(b) AMOUNT OF UNDERPAYMENT; PERIOD OF UNDERPAYMENT.—For purposes of subsection (a)—

(1) AMOUNT.—The amount of the underpayment shall be the excess of—

(A) the required installment, over

(B) the amount (if any) of the installment paid on or before the due date for the installment.

(2) PERIOD OF UNDERPAYMENT.—The period of the underpayment shall run from the due date for the installment to whichever of the following dates is the earlier—

(A) the 15th day of the 4th month following the close of the taxable year, or

(B) with respect to any portion of the underpayment, the date on which such portion is paid.

(3) ORDER OF CREDITING PAYMENTS.—For purposes of paragraph (2)(B), a payment of estimated tax shall be credited against unpaid required installments in the order in which such installments are required to be paid.

[Sec. 6654(c)]

(c) NUMBER OF REQUIRED INSTALLMENTS; DUE DATES.—For purposes of this section—

(1) PAYABLE IN 4 INSTALLMENTS.—There shall be 4 required installments for each taxable year.

(2) TIME FOR PAYMENT OF INSTALLMENTS.—

In the case of the following required installments:	The due date is:
1st	April 15
2nd	June 15
3rd	September 15
4th	January 15 of the following taxable year.

[Sec. 6654(d)]

(d) AMOUNT OF REQUIRED INSTALLMENTS.—For purposes of this section—

(1) AMOUNT.—

(A) IN GENERAL.—Except as provided in paragraph (2), the amount of any required installment shall be 25 percent of the required annual payment.

(B) REQUIRED ANNUAL PAYMENT.—For purposes of subparagraph (A), the term "required annual payment" means the lesser of—

(i) 90 percent of the tax shown on the return for the taxable year (or, if no return is filed, 90 percent of the tax for such year), or

(ii) 100 percent of the tax shown on the return of the individual for the preceding taxable year.

Clause (ii) shall not apply if the preceding taxable year was not a taxable year of 12 months or if the individual did not file a return for such preceding taxable year.

(C) LIMITATION ON USE OF PRECEDING YEAR'S TAX.—

(i) IN GENERAL.—If the adjusted gross income shown on the return of the individual for the preceding taxable year beginning in any calendar year exceeds $150,000, clause (ii) of subparagraph (B) shall be applied by substituting the applicable percentage for "100 percent". For purposes of the preceding sentence, the applicable percentage shall be determined in accordance with the following table:

If the preceding taxable year begins in:	The applicable percentage is:
1998	105
1999	108.6
2000	110
2001	112
2002 or thereafter	110

This clause shall not apply in the case of a preceding taxable year beginning in calendar year 1997.

(ii) SEPARATE RETURNS.—In the case of a married individual (within the meaning of section 7703) who files a separate return for the taxable year for which the amount of the installment is being determined, clause (i) shall be applied by substituting "$75,000" for "$150,000".

(iii) SPECIAL RULE.—In the case of an estate or trust, adjusted gross income shall be determined as provided in section 67(e).

(2) LOWER REQUIRED INSTALLMENT WHERE ANNUALIZED INCOME INSTALLMENT IS LESS THAN AMOUNT DETERMINED UNDER PARAGRAPH (1).—

(A) IN GENERAL.—In the case of any required installment, if the individual establishes that the annualized income installment is less than the amount determined under paragraph (1)—

(i) the amount of such required installment shall be the annualized income installment, and

(ii) any reduction in a required installment resulting from the application of this subparagraph shall be recaptured by increasing the amount of the next required installment determined under paragraph (1) by the amount of such reduction (and by increasing subsequent required installments to the extent that the reduction has not previously been recaptured under this clause).

Sec. 6654(c)

(B) DETERMINATION OF ANNUALIZED INCOME INSTALLMENT.—In the case of any required installment, the annualized income installment is the excess (if any) of—

(i) an amount equal to the applicable percentage of the tax for the taxable year computed by placing on an annualized basis the taxable income, alternative minimum taxable income, and adjusted self-employment income for months in the taxable year ending before the due date for the installment, over

(ii) the aggregate amount of any prior required installments for the taxable year.

(C) SPECIAL RULES.—For purposes of this paragraph—

(i) ANNUALIZATION.—The taxable income, alternative minimum taxable income, and adjusted self-employment income shall be placed on an annualized basis under regulations prescribed by the Secretary.

(ii) APPLICABLE PERCENTAGE.—

In the case of the following required installments:	The applicable percentage is:
1st	22.5
2nd	45
3rd	67.5
4th	90

(iii) ADJUSTED SELF-EMPLOYMENT INCOME.—The term "adjusted self-employment income" means self-employment income (as defined in section 1402(b)); except that section 1402(b) shall be applied by placing wages (within the meaning of section 1402(b)) for months in the taxable year ending before the due date for the installment on an annualized basis consistent with clause (i).

* * *

[Sec. 6654(e)]

(e) EXCEPTIONS.—

(1) WHERE TAX IS SMALL AMOUNT.—No addition to tax shall be imposed under subsection (a) for any taxable year if the tax shown on the return for such taxable year (or, if no return is filed, the tax), reduced by the credit allowable under section 31, is less than $1,000.

(2) WHERE NO TAX LIABILITY FOR PRECEDING TAXABLE YEAR.—No addition to tax shall be imposed under subsection (a) for any taxable year if—

(A) the preceding taxable year was a taxable year of 12 months,

(B) the individual did not have any liability for tax for the preceding taxable year, and

(C) the individual was a citizen or resident of the United States throughout the preceding taxable year.

(3) WAIVER IN CERTAIN CASES.—

(A) IN GENERAL.—No addition to tax shall be imposed under subsection (a) with respect to any underpayment to the extent the Secretary determines that by reason of casualty, disaster, or other unusual circumstances the imposition of such addition to tax would be against equity and good conscience.

(B) NEWLY RETIRED OR DISABLED INDIVIDUALS.—No addition to tax shall be imposed under subsection (a) with respect to any underpayment if the Secretary determines that—

(i) the taxpayer—

(I) retired after having attained age 62, or

(II) became disabled,

in the taxable year for which estimated payments were required to be made or in the taxable year preceding such taxable year, and

(ii) such underpayment was due to reasonable cause and not to willful neglect.

[Sec. 6654(f)]

(f) TAX COMPUTED AFTER APPLICATION OF CREDITS AGAINST TAX.—For purposes of this section, the term "tax" means—

Sec. 6654(f)

(1) the tax imposed by chapter 1 (other than any increase in such tax by reason of section 143(m)), plus

(2) the tax imposed by chapter 2, minus

(3) the credits against tax provided by part IV of subchapter A of chapter 1, other than the credit against tax provided by section 31 (relating to tax withheld on wages).

[Sec. 6654(g)]

(g) APPLICATION OF SECTION IN CASE OF TAX WITHHELD ON WAGES.—

(1) IN GENERAL.—For purposes of applying this section, the amount of the credit allowed under section 31 for the taxable year shall be deemed a payment of estimated tax, and an equal part of such amount shall be deemed paid on each due date for such taxable year, unless the taxpayer establishes the dates on which all amounts were actually withheld, in which case the amounts so withheld shall be deemed payments of estimated tax on the dates on which such amounts were actually withheld.

(2) SEPARATE APPLICATION.—The taxpayer may apply paragraph (1) separately with respect to—

(A) wage withholding, and

(B) all other amounts withheld for which credit is allowed under section 31.

[Sec. 6654(h)]

(h) SPECIAL RULE WHERE RETURN FILED ON OR BEFORE JANUARY 31.—If, on or before January 31 of the following taxable year, the taxpayer files a return for the taxable year and pays in full the amount computed on the return as payable, then no addition to tax shall be imposed under subsection (a) with respect to any underpayment of the 4th required installment for the taxable year.

[Sec. 6654(i)]

(i) SPECIAL RULES FOR FARMERS AND FISHERMEN.—For purposes of this section—

(1) IN GENERAL.—If an individual is a farmer or fisherman for any taxable year—

(A) there shall be only 1 required installment for the taxable year,

(B) the due date for such installment shall be January 15 of the following taxable year,

(C) the amount of such installment shall be equal to the required annual payment determined under subsection (d)(1)(B) by substituting "66⅔ percent" for "90 percent" and without regard to subparagraph (C) of subsection (d)(1), and

(D) subsection (h) shall be applied—

(i) by substituting "March 1" for "January 31", and

(ii) by treating the required installment described in subparagraph (A) of this paragraph as the 4th required installment.

(2) FARMER OR FISHERMAN DEFINED.—An individual is a farmer or fisherman for any taxable year if—

(A) the individual's gross income from farming or fishing (including oyster farming) for the taxable year is at least 66⅔ percent of the total gross income from all sources for the taxable year, or

(B) such individual's gross income from farming or fishing (including oyster farming) shown on the return of the individual for the preceding taxable year is at least 66⅔ percent of the total gross income from all sources shown on such return.

* * *

[Sec. 6655]

SEC. 6655. FAILURE BY CORPORATION TO PAY ESTIMATED INCOME TAX.

[Sec. 6655(a)]

(a) ADDITION TO TAX.—Except as otherwise provided in this section, in the case of any underpayment of estimated tax by a corporation, there shall be added to the tax under chapter 1 for the taxable year an amount determined by applying—

(1) the underpayment rate established under section 6621,

(2) to the amount of the underpayment,

(3) for the period of the underpayment.

[Sec. 6655(b)]

(b) AMOUNT OF UNDERPAYMENT; PERIOD OF UNDERPAYMENT.—For purposes of subsection (a)—

(1) AMOUNT.—The amount of the underpayment shall be the excess of

(A) the required installment, over

(B) the amount (if any) of the installment paid on or before the due date for the installment.

(2) PERIOD OF UNDERPAYMENT.—The period of the underpayment shall run from the due date for the installment to whichever of the following dates is the earlier—

(A) the 15th day of the 3rd month following the close of the taxable year, or

(B) with respect to any portion of the underpayment, the date on which such portion is paid.

(3) ORDER OF CREDITING PAYMENTS.—For purposes of paragraph (2)(B), a payment of estimated tax shall be credited against unpaid required installments in the order in which such installments are required to be paid.

[Sec. 6655(c)]

(c) NUMBER OF REQUIRED INSTALLMENTS; DUE DATES.—For purposes of this section—

(1) PAYABLE IN 4 INSTALLMENTS.—There shall be 4 required installments for each taxable year.

(2) TIME FOR PAYMENT OF INSTALLMENTS.—

In the case of the following required installments:	The due date is:
1st	April 15
2nd	June 15
3rd	September 15
4th	December 15.

[Sec. 6655(d)]

(d) AMOUNT OF REQUIRED INSTALLMENTS.—For purposes of this section—

(1) AMOUNT.—

(A) IN GENERAL.—Except as otherwise provided in this section, the amount of any required installment shall be 25 percent of the required annual payment.

(B) REQUIRED ANNUAL PAYMENT.—Except as otherwise provided in this subsection, the term "required annual payment" means the lesser of—

(i) 100 percent of the tax shown on the return for the taxable year (or, if no return is filed, 100 percent of the tax for such year), or

(ii) 100 percent of the tax shown on the return of the corporation for the preceding taxable year.

Clause (ii) shall not apply if the preceding taxable year was not a taxable year of 12 months, or the corporation did not file a return for such preceding taxable year showing a liability for tax.

(2) LARGE CORPORATIONS REQUIRED TO PAY 100 PERCENT OF CURRENT YEAR TAX.—

(A) IN GENERAL.—Except as provided in subparagraph (B), clause (ii) of paragraph (1)(B) shall not apply in the case of a large corporation.

(B) MAY USE LAST YEAR'S TAX FOR 1ST INSTALLMENT.—Subparagraph (A) shall not apply for purposes of determining the amount of the 1st required installment for any taxable year. Any reduction in such 1st installment by reason of the preceding sentence shall be recaptured by increasing the amount of the next required installment determined under paragraph (1) by the amount of such reduction.

Sec. 6655(d)

[Sec. 6655(e)]

(e) LOWER REQUIRED INSTALLMENT WHERE ANNUALIZED INCOME INSTALLMENT OR ADJUSTED SEASONAL INSTALLMENT IS LESS THAN AMOUNT DETERMINED UNDER SUBSECTION (d).—

(1) IN GENERAL.—In the case of any required installment, if the corporation establishes that the annualized income installment or the adjusted seasonal installment is less than the amount determined under subsection (d)(1) (as modified by paragraphs (2) and (3) of subsection (d))—

(A) the amount of such required installment shall be the annualized income installment (or, if lesser, the adjusted seasonal installment), and

(B) any reduction in a required installment resulting from the application of this paragraph shall be recaptured by increasing the amount of the next required installment determined under subsection (d)(1) (as so modified) by the amount of such reduction (and by increasing subsequent required installments to the extent that the reduction has not previously been recaptured under this subparagraph).

(2) DETERMINATION OF ANNUALIZED INCOME INSTALLMENT.—

(A) IN GENERAL.—In the case of any required installment, the annualized income installment is the excess (if any) of—

(i) an amount equal to the applicable percentage of the tax for the taxable year computed by placing on an annualized basis the taxable income, alternative minimum taxable income, and modified alternative minimum taxable income—

(I) for the first 3 months of the taxable year, in the case of the 1st required installment,

(II) for the first 3 months of the taxable year, in the case of the 2nd required installment,

(III) for the first 6 months of the taxable year in the case of the 3rd required installment, and

(IV) for the first 9 months of the taxable year, in the case of the 4th required installment, over

(ii) the aggregate amount of any prior required installments for the taxable year.

(B) SPECIAL RULES.—For purposes of this paragraph—

(i) Annualization.—The taxable income, alternative minimum taxable income, and modified alternative minimum taxable income shall be placed on an annualized basis under regulations prescribed by the Secretary.

(ii) Applicable Percentage.—

In the case of the following required installments:	The applicable percentage is:
1st	.25
2nd	.50
3rd	.75
4th	100.

(iii) Modified Alternative Minimum Taxable Income.—The term "modified alternative minimum taxable income" has the meaning given to such term by section 59A(b).

(C) ELECTION FOR DIFFERENT ANNUALIZATION PERIODS.—

(i) If the taxpayer makes an election under this clause—

(I) subclause (I) of subparagraph (A)(i) shall be applied by substituting "2 months" for "3 months",

(II) subclause (II) of subparagraph (A)(i) shall be applied by substituting "4 months" for "3 months",

(III) subclause (III) of subparagraph (A)(i) shall be applied by substituting "7 months" for "6 months", and

(IV) subclause (IV) of subparagraph (A)(i) shall be applied by substituting "10 months" for "9 months".

(ii) If the taxpayer makes an election under this clause—

(I) subclause (II) of subparagraph (A)(i) shall be applied by substituting "5 months" for "3 months",

(II) subclause (III) of subparagraph (A)(i) shall be applied by substituting "8 months" for "6 months",

Sec. 6655(e)

(III) subclause (IV) of subparagraph (A)(i) shall be applied by substituting "11 months" for "9 months".

(iii) An election under clause (i) or (ii) shall apply to the taxable year for which made and such an election shall be effective only if made on or before the date required for the payment of the first required installment for such taxable year.

(3) DETERMINATION OF ADJUSTED SEASONAL INSTALLMENT.—

(A) IN GENERAL.—In the case of any required installment, the amount of the adjusted seasonal installment is the excess (if any) of—

(i) 100 percent of the amount determined under subparagraph (C), over

(ii) the aggregate amount of all prior required installments for the taxable year.

(B) LIMITATION ON APPLICATION OF PARAGRAPH.—This paragraph shall apply only if the base period percentage for any 6 consecutive months of the taxable year equals or exceeds 70 percent.

(C) DETERMINATION OF AMOUNT.—The amount determined under this subparagraph for any installment shall be determined in the following manner—

(i) take the taxable income for all months during the taxable year preceding the filing month,

(ii) divide such amount by the base period percentage for all months during the taxable year preceding the filing month,

(iii) determine the tax on the amount determined under clause (ii), and

(iv) multiply the tax computed under clause (iii) by the base period percentage for the filing month and all months during the taxable year preceding the filing month.

(D) DEFINITIONS AND SPECIAL RULES.—For purposes of this paragraph—

(i) BASE PERIOD PERCENTAGE.—The base period percentage for any period of months shall be the average percent which the taxable income for the corresponding months in each of the 3 preceding taxable years bears to the taxable income for the 3 preceding taxable years.

(ii) FILING MONTH.—The term "filing month" means the month in which the installment is required to be paid.

(iii) REORGANIZATION, ETC.—The Secretary may by regulations provide for the determination of the base period percentage in the case of reorganizations, new corporations, and other similar circumstances.

* * *

[Sec. 6655(f)]

(f) EXCEPTION WHERE TAX IS SMALL AMOUNT.—No addition to tax shall be imposed under subsection (a) for any taxable year if the tax shown on the return for such taxable year (or, if no return is filed, the tax) is less than $500.

[Sec. 6655(g)]

(g) DEFINITIONS AND SPECIAL RULES.—

(1) TAX.—For purposes of this section, the term "tax" means the excess of—

(A) the sum of—

(i) the tax imposed by section 11 or 1201(a), or subchapter L of chapter 1, whichever applies,

(ii) the tax imposed by section 55,

(iii) the tax imposed by section 59A, plus

(iv) the tax imposed by section 887, over

(B) the credits against tax provided by part IV of subchapter A of chapter 1.

For purposes of the preceding sentence, in the case of a foreign corporation subject to taxation under section 11 or 1201(a), or under subchapter L of chapter 1, the tax imposed by section 881 shall be treated as a tax imposed by section 11.

Sec. 6655(g)

(2) LARGE CORPORATION.—

(A) IN GENERAL.—For purposes of this section, the term "large corporation" means any corporation if such corporation (or any predecessor corporation) had taxable income of $1,000,000 or more for any taxable year during the testing period.

(B) RULES FOR APPLYING SUBPARAGRAPH (A).—

(i) TESTING PERIOD.—For purposes of subparagraph (A), the term "testing period" means the 3 taxable years immediately preceding the taxable year involved.

(ii) MEMBERS OF CONTROLLED GROUP.—For purposes of applying subparagraph (A) to any taxable year in the testing period with respect to corporations which are component members of a controlled group of corporations for such taxable year, the $1,000,000 amount specified in subparagraph (A) shall be divided among such members under rules similar to the rules of section 1561.

(iii) CERTAIN CARRYBACKS AND CARRYOVERS NOT TAKEN INTO ACCOUNT.—For purposes of subparagraph (A), taxable income shall be determined without regard to any amount carried to the taxable year under section 172 or 1212(a).

(3) CERTAIN TAX-EXEMPT ORGANIZATIONS.—For purposes of this section—

(A) Any organization subject to the tax imposed by section 511, and any private foundation, shall be treated as a corporation subject to tax under section 11.

(B) Any tax imposed by section 511, and any tax imposed by section 1 or 4940 on a private foundation, shall be treated as a tax imposed by section 11.

(C) Any reference to taxable income shall be treated as including a reference to unrelated business taxable income or net investment income (as the case may be).

In the case of any organization described in subparagraph (A), subsection (b)(2)(A) shall be applied by substituting "5th month" for "3rd month", subsection (e)(2)(A) shall be applied by substituting "2 months" for "3 months" in clause (i)(I), the election under clause (i) of subsection (e)(2)(C) may be made separately for each installment, and clause (ii) of subsection (e)(2)(C) shall not apply. In the case of a private foundation, subsection (c)(2) shall be applied by substituting "May 15" for "April 15".

(4) APPLICATION OF SECTION TO CERTAIN TAXES IMPOSED ON S CORPORATIONS.—In the case of an S corporation, for purposes of this section—

(A) The following taxes shall be treated as imposed by section 11:

(i) The tax imposed by section 1374(a) (or the corresponding provisions of prior law).

(ii) The tax imposed by section 1375(a).

(iii) Any tax for which the S corporation is liable by reason of section 1371(d)(2).

(B) Paragraph (2) of subsection (d) shall not apply.

(C) Clause (ii) of subsection (d)(1)(B) shall be applied as if it read as follows:

"(ii) the sum of—

"(I) the amount determined under clause (i) by only taking into account the taxes referred to in clauses (i) and (iii) of subsection (g)(4)(A), and

"(II) 100 percent of the tax imposed by section 1375(a) which was shown on the return of the corporation for the preceding taxable year."

(D) The requirement in the last sentence of subsection (d)(1)(B) that the return for the preceding taxable year show a liability for tax shall not apply.

(E) Any reference in subsection (e) to taxable income shall be treated as including a reference to the net recognized built-in gain or the excess passive income (as the case may be).

* * *

Sec. 6655(g)

PART II—ACCURACY AND FRAUD-RELATED PENALTIES

[Sec. 6662]
SEC. 6662. IMPOSITION OF ACCURACY-RELATED PENALTY.

[Sec. 6662(a)]

(a) IMPOSITION OF PENALTY.—If this section applies to any portion of an underpayment of tax required to be shown on a return, there shall be added to the tax an amount equal to 20 percent of the portion of the underpayment to which this section applies.

[Sec. 6662(b)]

(b) PORTION OF UNDERPAYMENT TO WHICH SECTION APPLIES.—This section shall apply to the portion of any underpayment which is attributable to 1 or more of the following:

(1) Negligence or disregard of rules or regulations.

(2) Any substantial understatement of income tax.

(3) Any substantial valuation misstatement under chapter 1.

(4) Any substantial overstatement of pension liabilities.

(5) Any substantial estate or gift tax valuation understatement.

This section shall not apply to any portion of an underpayment on which a penalty is imposed under section 6663.

[Sec. 6662(c)]

(c) NEGLIGENCE.—For purposes of this section, the term "negligence" includes any failure to make a reasonable attempt to comply with the provisions of this title, and the term "disregard" includes any careless, reckless, or intentional disregard.

[Sec. 6662(d)]

(d) SUBSTANTIAL UNDERSTATEMENT OF INCOME TAX.—

(1) SUBSTANTIAL UNDERSTATEMENT.—

(A) IN GENERAL.—For purposes of this section, there is a substantial understatement of income tax for any taxable year if the amount of the understatement for the taxable year exceeds the greater of—

(i) 10 percent of the tax required to be shown on the return for the taxable year, or

(ii) $5,000.

(B) SPECIAL RULE FOR CORPORATIONS.—In the case of a corporation other than an S corporation or a personal holding company (as defined in section 542), paragraph (1) shall be applied by substituting "$10,000" for "$5,000".

(2) UNDERSTATEMENT.—

(A) IN GENERAL.—For purposes of paragraph (1), the term "understatement" means the excess of—

(i) the amount of the tax required to be shown on the return for the taxable year, over

(ii) the amount of the tax imposed which is shown on the return, reduced by any rebate (within the meaning of section 6211(b)(2)).

(B) REDUCTION FOR UNDERSTATEMENT DUE TO POSITION OF TAXPAYER OR DISCLOSED ITEM.—The amount of the understatement under subparagraph (A) shall be reduced by that portion of the understatement which is attributable to—

(i) the tax treatment of any item by the taxpayer if there is or was substantial authority for such treatment, or

(ii) any item if—

(I) the relevant facts affecting the item's tax treatment are adequately disclosed in the return or in a statement attached to the return, and

(II) there is a reasonable basis for the tax treatment of such item by the taxpayer.

Sec. 6662(d)

For purposes of clause (ii)(II), in no event shall a corporation be treated as having a reasonable basis for its tax treatment of an item attributable to a multiple-party financing transaction if such treatment does not clearly reflect the income of the corporation.

(C) SPECIAL RULES IN CASES INVOLVING TAX SHELTERS.—

(i) IN GENERAL.—In the case of any item of a taxpayer other than a corporation which is attributable to a tax shelter—

(I) subparagraph (B)(ii) shall not apply, and

(II) subparagraph (B)(i) shall not apply unless (in addition to meeting the requirements of such subparagraph) the taxpayer reasonably believed that the tax treatment of such item by the taxpayer was more likely than not the proper treatment.

(ii) SUBPARAGRAPH (B) NOT TO APPLY TO CORPORATIONS.—Subparagraph (B) shall not apply to any item of a corporation which is attributable to a tax shelter.

(iii) TAX SHELTER.—For purposes of this subparagraph, the term "tax shelter" means—

(I) a partnership or other entity,

(II) any investment plan or arrangement, or

(III) any other plan or arrangement,

if a significant purpose of such partnership, entity, plan, or arrangement is the avoidance or evasion of Federal income tax.

(D) SECRETARIAL LIST.—The Secretary shall prescribe (and revise not less frequently than annually) a list of positions—

(i) for which the Secretary believes there is not substantial authority, and

(ii) which affect a significant number of taxpayers.

Such list (and any revision thereof) shall be published in the Federal Register.

[Sec. 6662(e)]

(e) SUBSTANTIAL VALUATION MISSTATEMENT UNDER CHAPTER 1.—

(1) IN GENERAL.—For purposes of this section, there is a substantial valuation misstatement under chapter 1 if—

(A) the value of any property (or the adjusted basis of any property) claimed on any return of tax imposed by chapter 1 is 200 percent or more of the amount determined to be the correct amount of such valuation or adjusted basis (as the case may be), or

(B)(i) the price for any property or services (or for the use of property) claimed on any such return in connection with any transaction between persons described in section 482 is 200 percent or more (or 50 percent or less) of the amount determined under section 482 to be the correct amount of such price, or

(ii) the net section 482 transfer price adjustment for the taxable year exceeds the lesser of $5,000,000 or 10 percent of the taxpayer's gross receipts.

(2) LIMITATION.—No penalty shall be imposed by reason of subsection (b)(3) unless the portion of the underpayment for the taxable year attributable to substantial valuation misstatements under chapter 1 exceeds $5,000 ($10,000 in the case of a corporation other than an S corporation or a personal holding company (as defined in section 542)).

(3) NET SECTION 482 TRANSFER PRICE ADJUSTMENT.—For purposes of this subsection—

(A) IN GENERAL.—The term "net section 482 transfer price adjustment" means, with respect to any taxable year, the net increase in taxable income for the taxable year (determined without regard to any amount carried to such taxable year from another taxable year) resulting from adjustments under section 482 in the price for any property or services (or for the use of property).

(B) CERTAIN ADJUSTMENTS EXCLUDED IN DETERMINING THRESHOLD.—For purposes of determining whether the threshold requirements of paragraph (1)(B)(ii) are met, the following shall be excluded:

(i) Any portion of the net increase in taxable income referred to in subparagraph (A) which is attributable to any redetermination of a price if—

(I) it is established that the taxpayer determined such price in accordance with a specific pricing method set forth in the regulations prescribed under section 482 and that the taxpayer's use of such method was reasonable,

(II) the taxpayer has documentation (which was in existence as of the time of filing the return) which sets forth the determination of such price in accordance with such a method and which establishes that the use of such method was reasonable, and

(III) the taxpayer provides such documentation to the Secretary within 30 days of a request for such documentation.

(ii) Any portion of the net increase in taxable income referred to in subparagraph (A) which is attributable to a redetermination of price where such price was not determined in accordance with such a specific pricing method if—

(I) the taxpayer establishes that none of such pricing methods was likely to result in a price that would clearly reflect income, the taxpayer used another pricing method to determine such price, and such other pricing method was likely to result in a price that would clearly reflect income,

(II) the taxpayer has documentation (which was in existence as of the time of filing the return) which sets forth the determination of such price in accordance with such other method and which establishes that the requirements of subclause (I) were satisfied, and

(III) the taxpayer provides such documentation to the Secretary within 30 days of a request for such documentation.

(iii) Any portion of such net increase which is attributable to any transaction solely between foreign corporations unless, in the case of any such corporations, the treatment of such transaction affects the determination of income from sources within the United States or taxable income effectively connected with the conduct of a trade or business within the United States.

(C) SPECIAL RULE.—If the regular tax (as defined in section 55(c)) imposed by chapter 1 on the taxpayer is determined by reference to an amount other than taxable income, such amount shall be treated as the taxable income of such taxpayer for purposes of this paragraph.

* * *

[Sec. 6662(h)]

(h) INCREASE IN PENALTY IN CASE OF GROSS VALUATION MISSTATEMENTS.—

(1) IN GENERAL.—To the extent that a portion of the underpayment to which this section applies is attributable to one or more gross valuation misstatements, subsection (a) shall be applied with respect to such portion by substituting "40 percent" for "20 percent".

(2) GROSS VALUATION MISSTATEMENTS.—The term "gross valuation misstatements" means—

(A) any substantial valuation misstatement under chapter 1 as determined under subsection (e) by substituting—

(i) "400 percent" for "200 percent" each place it appears,

(ii) "25 percent" for "50 percent", and

(iii) in paragraph (1)(B)(ii)—

(I) "$20,000,000" for "$5,000,000", and

(II) "20 percent" for "10 percent".

(B) any substantial overstatement of pension liabilities as determined under subsection (f) by substituting "400 percent" for "200 percent", and

(C) any substantial estate or gift tax valuation understatement as determined under subsection (g) by substituting "25 percent" for "50 percent".

[Sec. 6663]

SEC. 6663. IMPOSITION OF FRAUD PENALTY.

[Sec. 6663(a)]

(a) IMPOSITION OF PENALTY.—If any part of any underpayment of tax required to be shown on a return is due to fraud, there shall be added to the tax an amount equal to 75 percent of the portion of the underpayment which is attributable to fraud.

[Sec. 6663(b)]

(b) DETERMINATION OF PORTION ATTRIBUTABLE TO FRAUD.—If the Secretary establishes that any portion of an underpayment is attributable to fraud, the entire underpayment shall be treated as attributable to fraud, except with respect to any portion of the underpayment which the taxpayer establishes (by a preponderance of the evidence) is not attributable to fraud.

[Sec. 6663(c)]

(c) SPECIAL RULE FOR JOINT RETURNS.—In the case of a joint return, this section shall not apply with respect to a spouse unless some part of the underpayment is due to the fraud of such spouse.

[Sec. 6664]

SEC 6664. DEFINITIONS AND SPECIAL RULES.

[Sec. 6664(a)]

(a) UNDERPAYMENT.—For purposes of this part, the term "underpayment" means the amount by which any tax imposed by this title exceeds the excess of—

(1) the sum of—

(A) the amount shown as the tax by the taxpayer on his return, plus

(B) amounts not so shown previously assessed (or collected without assessment), over

(2) the amount of rebates made.

For purposes of paragraph (2), the term "rebate" means so much of an abatement, credit, refund, or other repayment, as was made on the ground that tax imposed was less than the excess of the amount specified in paragraph (1) over the rebates previously made.

[Sec. 6664(b)]

(b) PENALTIES APPLICABLE ONLY WHERE RETURN FILED.—The penalties provided in this part shall apply only in cases where a return of tax is filed (other than a return prepared by the Secretary under the authority of section 6020(b)).

[Sec. 6664(c)]

(c) REASONABLE CAUSE EXCEPTION.—

(1) IN GENERAL.—No penalty shall be imposed under this part with respect to any portion of an underpayment if it is shown that there was a reasonable cause for such portion and that the taxpayer acted in good faith with respect to such portion.

(2) SPECIAL RULE FOR CERTAIN VALUATION OVERSTATEMENTS.—In the case of any underpayment attributable to a substantial or gross valuation over statement under chapter 1 with respect to charitable deduction property, paragraph (1) shall not apply unless—

(A) the claimed value of the property was based on a qualified appraisal made by a qualified appraiser, and

(B) in addition to obtaining such appraisal, the taxpayer made a good faith investigation of the value of the contributed property.

(3) DEFINITIONS.—For purposes of this subsection—

(A) CHARITABLE DEDUCTION PROPERTY.—The term "charitable deduction property" means any property contributed by the taxpayer in a contribution for which a deduction was claimed under section 170. For purposes of paragraph (2), such term shall not include any securities for which (as of the date of the contribution) market quotations are readily available on an established securities market.

Sec. 6663

(B) QUALIFIED APPRAISER.—The term "qualified appraiser" means any appraiser meeting the requirements of the regulations prescribed under section 170(a)(1).

(C) QUALIFIED APPRAISAL.—The term "qualified appraisal" means any appraisal meeting the requirements of the regulations prescribed under section 170(a)(1).

PART III—APPLICABLE RULES

[Sec. 6665]

SEC. 6665. APPLICABLE RULES.

[Sec. 6665(a)]

(a) ADDITIONS TREATED AS TAX.—Except as otherwise provided in this title—

(1) the additions to the tax, additional amounts, and penalties provided by this chapter shall be paid upon notice and demand and shall be assessed, collected, and paid in the same manner as taxes; and

(2) any reference in this title to "tax" imposed by this title shall be deemed also to refer to the additions to the tax, additional amounts, and penalties provided by this chapter.

[Sec. 6665(b)]

(b) PROCEDURE FOR ASSESSING CERTAIN ADDITIONS TO TAX.—For purposes of subchapter B of chapter 63 (relating to deficiency procedures for income, estate, gift, and certain excise taxes), subsection (a) shall not apply to any addition to tax under section 6651, 6654, 6655; except that it shall apply—

(1) in the case of an addition described in section 6651, to that portion of such addition which is attributable to a deficiency in tax described in section 6211; or

(2) to an addition described in section 6654 or 6655, if no return is filed for the taxable year.

Subchapter B—Assessable Penalties

PART I—GENERAL PROVISIONS

[Sec. 6672]

SEC. 6672. FAILURE TO COLLECT AND PAY OVER TAX, OR ATTEMPT TO EVADE OR DEFEAT TAX.

[Sec. 6672(a)]

(a) GENERAL RULE.—Any person required to collect, truthfully account for, and pay over any tax imposed by this title who willfully fails to collect such tax, or truthfully account for and pay over such tax, or willfully attempts in any manner to evade or defeat any such tax or the payment thereof, shall, in addition to other penalties provided by law, be liable to a penalty equal to the total amount of the tax evaded, or not collected, or not accounted for and paid over. No penalty shall be imposed under section 6653 or part II of subchapter A of chapter 68 for any offense to which this section is applicable.

* * *

[Sec. 6674]

SEC. 6674. FRAUDULENT STATEMENT OR FAILURE TO FURNISH STATEMENT TO EMPLOYEE.

In addition to the criminal penalty provided by section 7204, any person required under the provisions of section 6051 or 6053(b) to furnish a statement to an employee who willfully furnishes a false or fraudulent statement, or who willfully fails to furnish a statement in the manner, at the time, and showing the information required under section 6051 or 6053(b), or regulations prescribed thereunder, shall for each such failure be subject to a penalty under this subchapter of $50, which shall be assessed and collected in the same manner as the tax on employers imposed by section 3111.

[Sec. 6682]

SEC. 6682.   FALSE INFORMATION WITH RESPECT TO WITHHOLDING.

[Sec. 6682(a)]

(a) CIVIL PENALTY.—In addition to any criminal penalty provided by law, if—

(1) any individual makes a statement under section 3402 or section 3406 which results in a decrease in the amounts deducted and withheld under chapter 24, and

(2) as of the time such statement was made, there was no reasonable basis for such statement,

such individual shall pay a penalty of $500 for such statement.

[Sec. 6682(b)]

(b) EXCEPTION.—The Secretary may waive (in whole or in part) the penalty imposed under subsection (a) if the taxes imposed with respect to the individual under subtitle A for the taxable year are equal to or less than the sum of—

(1) the credits against such taxes allowed by part IV of subchapter A of chapter 1, and

(2) the payments of estimated tax which are considered payments on account of such taxes.

* * *

[Sec. 6694]

SEC. 6694. UNDERSTATEMENT OF TAXPAYER'S LIABILITY BY INCOME TAX RETURN PREPARER.

[Sec. 6694(a)]

(a) UNDERSTATEMENTS DUE TO UNREALISTIC POSITIONS.—If—

(1) any part of any understatement of liability with respect to any return or claim for refund is due to a position for which there was not a realistic possibility of being sustained on its merits,

(2) any person who is an income tax return preparer with respect to such return or claim knew (or reasonably should have known) of such position, and

(3) such position was not disclosed as provided in section 6662(d)(2)(B)(ii) or was frivolous,

such person shall pay a penalty of $250 with respect to such return or claim unless it is shown that there is reasonable cause for the understatement and such person acted in good faith.

[Sec. 6694(b)]

(b) WILLFUL OR RECKLESS CONDUCT.—If any part of any understatement of liability with respect to any return or claim for refund is due—

(1) to a willful attempt in any manner to understate the liability for tax by a person who is an income tax return preparer with respect to such return or claim, or

(2) to any reckless or intentional disregard of rules or regulations by any such person,

such person shall pay a penalty of $1,000 with respect to such return or claim. With respect to any return or claim, the amount of the penalty payable by any person by reason of this subsection shall be reduced by the amount of the penalty paid by such person by reason of subsection (a).

* * *

[Sec. 6695]

SEC. 6695. OTHER ASSESSABLE PENALTIES WITH RESPECT TO THE PREPARATION OF INCOME TAX RETURNS FOR OTHER PERSONS.

[Sec. 6695(a)]

(a) FAILURE TO FURNISH COPY TO TAXPAYER.—Any person who is an income tax return preparer with respect to any return or claim for refund who fails to comply with section 6107(a) with respect to such return or claim shall pay a penalty of $50 for such failure, unless it is shown that such failure is due to reasonable cause and not due to willful neglect. The maximum penalty imposed under this subsection on any person with respect to documents filed during any calendar year shall not exceed $25,000.

[Sec. 6695(b)]

(b) FAILURE TO SIGN RETURN.—Any person who is an income tax return preparer with respect to any return or claim for refund, who is required by regulations prescribed by the Secretary to sign such return or claim, and who fails to comply with such regulations with respect to such return or claim shall pay a penalty of $50 for such failure, unless it is shown that such failure is due to reasonable cause and not due to willful neglect. The maximum penalty imposed under this subsection on any person with respect to documents filed during any calendar year shall not exceed $25,000.

[Sec. 6695(c)]

(c) FAILURE TO FURNISH IDENTIFYING NUMBER.—Any person who is an income tax return preparer with respect to any return or claim for refund and who fails to comply with section 6109(a)(4) with respect to such return or claim shall pay a penalty of $50 for such failure, unless it is shown that such failure is due to reasonable cause and not due to willful neglect. The maximum penalty imposed under this subsection on any person with respect to documents filed during any calendar year shall not exceed $25,000.

[Sec. 6695(d)]

(d) FAILURE TO RETAIN COPY OR LIST.—Any person who is an income tax return preparer with respect to any return or claim for refund who fails to comply with section 6107(b) with respect to such return or claim shall pay a penalty of $50 for each such failure, unless it is shown that such failure is due to reasonable cause and not due to willful neglect. The maximum penalty imposed under this subsection on any person with respect to any return period shall not exceed $25,000.

[Sec. 6695(e)]

(e) FAILURE TO FILE CORRECT INFORMATION RETURNS.—Any person required to make a return under section 6060 who fails to comply with the requirements of such section shall pay a penalty of $50 for—

(1) each failure to file a return as required under such section, and

(2) each failure to set forth an item in the return as required under [such] section,

unless it is shown that such failure is due to reasonable cause and not due to willful neglect. The maximum penalty imposed under this subsection on any person with respect to any return period shall not exceed $25,000.

[Sec. 6695(f)]

(f) NEGOTIATION OF CHECK.—Any person who is an income tax return preparer who endorses or otherwise negotiates (directly or through an agent) any check made in respect of the taxes imposed by subtitle A which is issued to a taxpayer (other than the income tax return preparer) shall pay a penalty of $500 with respect to each such check. The preceding sentence shall not apply with respect to the deposit by a bank (within the meaning of section 581) of the full amount of the check in the taxpayer's account in such bank for the benefit of the taxpayer.

[Sec. 6695(g)]

(g) FAILURE TO BE DILIGENT IN DETERMINING ELIGIBILITY FOR EARNED INCOME CREDIT.—Any person who is an income tax return preparer with respect to any return or claim for refund who fails to comply with due diligence requirements imposed by the Secretary by regulations with respect to determining eligibility for, or the amount of, the credit allowable by section 32 shall pay a penalty of $100 for each such failure.

[Sec. 6701]

SEC. 6701. PENALTIES FOR AIDING AND ABETTING UNDERSTATEMENT OF TAX LIABILITY.

[Sec. 6701(a)]

(a) IMPOSITION OF PENALTY.—Any person—

(1) who aids or assists in, procures, or advises with respect to, the preparation or presentation of any portion of a return, affidavit, claim, or other document,

(2) who knows (or has reason to believe) that such portion will be used in connection with any material matter arising under the internal revenue laws, and

Sec. 6701(a)

(3) who knows that such portion (if so used) would result in an understatement of the liability for tax of another person,

shall pay a penalty with respect to each such document in the amount determined under subsection (b).

[Sec. 6701(b)]

(b) AMOUNT OF PENALTY.—

(1) IN GENERAL.—Except as provided in paragraph (2), the amount of the penalty imposed by subsection (a) shall be $1,000.

(2) CORPORATIONS.—If the return, affidavit, claim, or other document relates to the tax liability of a corporation, the amount of the penalty imposed by subsection (a) shall be $10,000.

(3) ONLY 1 PENALTY PER PERSON PER PERIOD.—If any person is subject to a penalty under subsection (a) with respect to any document relating to any taxpayer for any taxable period (or where there is no taxable period, any taxable event), such person shall not be subject to a penalty under subsection (a) with respect to any other document relating to such taxpayer for such taxable period (or event).

* * *

[Sec. 6702]

SEC. 6702. FRIVOLOUS INCOME TAX RETURN.

[Sec. 6702(a)]

(a) CIVIL PENALTY.—If—

(1) any individual files what purports to be a return of the tax imposed by subtitle A but which—

(A) does not contain information on which the substantial correctness of the self-assessment may be judged, or

(B) contains information that on its face indicates that the self-assessment is substantially incorrect; and

(2) the conduct referred to in paragraph (1) is due to—

(A) a position which is frivolous, or

(B) a desire (which appears on the purported return) to delay or impede the administration of Federal income tax laws,

then such individual shall pay a penalty of $500.

* * *

CHAPTER 71—TRANSFEREES AND FIDUCIARIES

[Sec. 6901]

SEC. 6901. TRANSFERRED ASSETS.

[Sec. 6901(a)]

(a) METHOD OF COLLECTION.—The amounts of the following liabilities shall, except as hereinafter in this section provided, be assessed, paid, and collected in the same manner and subject to the same provisions and limitations as in the case of the taxes with respect to which the liabilities were incurred:

(1) INCOME, ESTATE, AND GIFT TAXES.—

(A) TRANSFEREES.—The liability, at law or in equity, of a transferee of property—

(i) of a taxpayer in the case of a tax imposed by subtitle A (relating to income taxes),

(ii) of a decedent in the case of a tax imposed by chapter 11 (relating to estate taxes), or

(iii) of a donor in the case of a tax imposed by chapter 12 (relating to gift taxes),

in respect of the tax imposed by subtitle A or B.

(B) FIDUCIARIES.—The liability of a fiduciary under section 3713(b) of title 31, United States Code in respect of the payment of any tax described in subparagraph (A) from the estate of the taxpayer, the decedent, or the donor, as the case may be.

(2) OTHER TAXES.—The liability, at law or in equity of a transferee of property of any person liable in respect of any tax imposed by this title (other than a tax imposed by subtitle A or B), but only if such liability arises on the liquidation of a partnership or corporation, or on a reorganization within the meaning of section 368(a).

[Sec. 6901(b)]

(b) LIABILITY.—Any liability referred to in subsection (a) may be either as to the amount of tax shown on a return or as to any deficiency or underpayment of any tax.

* * *

[Sec. 6901(h)]

(h) DEFINITION OF TRANSFEREE.—As used in this section, the term "transferee" includes donee, heir, legatee, devisee, and distributee, and with respect to estate taxes, also includes any person who, under section 6324 (a) (2), is personally liable for any part of such tax.

* * *

CHAPTER 75—CRIMES, OTHER OFFENSES, AND FORFEITURES

Subchapter A—Crimes

PART I—GENERAL PROVISIONS

[Caution: See 18 U.S.C. § 3571, under which a larger fine may be imposed with respect to Section 7201.]

[Sec. 7201]

SEC. 7201. ATTEMPT TO EVADE OR DEFEAT TAX.

Any person who willfully attempts in any manner to evade or defeat any tax imposed by this title or the payment thereof shall, in addition to other penalties provided by law, be guilty of a felony and, upon conviction thereof, shall be fined not more than $100,000 ($500,000 in the case of a corporation), or imprisoned not more than 5 years, or both, together with the costs of prosecution.

[Caution: See 18 U.S.C. § 3571, under which a larger fine may be imposed with respect to Section 7202.]

[Sec. 7202]

SEC. 7202. WILLFUL FAILURE TO COLLECT OR PAY OVER TAX.

Any person required under this title to collect, account for, and pay over any tax imposed by this title who willfully fails to collect or truthfully account for and pay over such tax shall, in addition to other penalties provided by law, be guilty of a felony and, upon conviction thereof, shall be fined not more than $10,000, or imprisoned not more than 5 years, or both, together with the costs of prosecution.

[Sec. 7203]

SEC. 7203. WILLFUL FAILURE TO FILE RETURN, SUPPLY INFORMATION, OR PAY TAX.

Any person required under this title to pay any estimated tax or tax, or required by this title or by regulations made under authority thereof to make a return, keep any records, or supply any information, who willfully fails to pay such estimated tax or tax, make such return, keep such records, or supply such information, at the time or times required by law or regulations, shall, in addition to other penalties provided by law, be guilty of a misdemeanor and, upon conviction thereof, shall be fined not more than $25,000 ($100,000 in the case of a corporation), or imprisoned not more than 1 year, or both, together with the costs of prosecution. In the case of any person with respect to whom there is a failure to pay any estimated tax, this section shall not apply to such person with respect to such failure if there is no addition to tax under section 6654 or 6655 with respect to such failure. In the case of a willful violation of any provision of section 6050 I, the first sentence of this section shall be applied by substituting "felony" for "misdemeanor" and "5 years" for "1 year".

Sec. 7203

[Sec. 7205]

SEC. 7205. FRAUDULENT WITHHOLDING EXEMPTION CERTIFICATE OR FAILURE TO SUPPLY INFORMATION.

[Sec. 7205(a)]

(a) WITHHOLDING ON WAGES.—Any individual required to supply information to his employer under section 3402 who willfully supplies false or fraudulent information, or who willfully fails to supply information thereunder which would require an increase in the tax to be withheld under section 3402, shall, in addition to any other penalty provided by law, upon conviction thereof, be fined not more than $1,000, or imprisoned not more than 1 year, or both.

[Sec. 7205(b)]

(b) BACKUP WITHHOLDING ON INTEREST AND DIVIDENDS.—If any individual willfully makes a false certification under paragraph (1) or (2)(C) of section 3406(d), then such individual shall, in addition to any other penalty provided by law, upon conviction thereof, be fined not more than $1,000, or imprisoned not more than 1 year, or both.

[*Caution: See 18 U.S.C. § 3571, under which a larger fine may be imposed with respect to Section 7206.*]

[Sec. 7206]

SEC. 7206. FRAUD AND FALSE STATEMENTS.

Any person who—

(1) DECLARATION UNDER PENALTIES OF PERJURY.—Willfully makes and subscribes any return, statement, or other document, which contains or is verified by a written declaration that it is made under the penalties of perjury, and which he does not believe to be true and correct as to every material matter; or

(2) AID OR ASSISTANCE.—Willfully aids or assists in, or procures, counsels, or advises the preparation or presentation under, or in connection with any matter arising under, the internal revenue laws, of a return, affidavit, claim, or other document, which is fraudulent or is false as to any material matter, whether or not such falsity or fraud is with the knowledge or consent of the person authorized or required to present such return, affidavit, claim, or document; or

(3) FRAUDULENT BONDS, PERMITS, AND ENTRIES.—Simulates or falsely or fraudulently executes or signs any bond, permit, entry, or other document required by the provisions of the internal revenue laws, or by any regulation made in pursuance thereof, or procures the same to be falsely or fraudulently executed or advises, aids in, or connives at such execution thereof; or

(4) REMOVAL OR CONCEALMENT WITH INTENT TO DEFRAUD.—Removes, deposits, or conceals, or is concerned in removing, depositing, or concealing, any goods or commodities for or in respect whereof any tax is or shall be imposed, or any property upon which levy is authorized by section 6331, with intent to evade or defeat the assessment or collection of any tax imposed by this title; or

(5) COMPROMISES AND CLOSING AGREEMENTS.—In connection with any compromise under section 7122, or offer of such compromise, or in connection with any closing agreement under section 7121, or offer to enter into any such agreement, willfully—

(A) CONCEALMENT OF PROPERTY.—Conceals from any officer or employee of the United States any property belonging to the estate of a taxpayer or other person liable in respect of the tax, or

(B) WITHHOLDING, FALSIFYING, AND DESTROYING RECORDS.—Receives, withholds, destroys, mutilates, or falsifies any book, document, or record, or makes any false statement, relating to the estate or financial condition of the taxpayer or other person liable in respect of the tax;

shall be guilty of a felony and, upon conviction thereof, shall be fined not more than $100,000 ($500,000 in the case of a corporation) or imprisoned not more than 3 years, or both, together with the costs of prosecution.

CHAPTER 76—JUDICIAL PROCEEDINGS

Subchapter B—Proceedings by Taxpayers and Third Parties

[Sec. 7421]

SEC. 7421. PROHIBITION OF SUITS TO RESTRAIN ASSESSMENT OR COLLECTION.

[Sec. 7421(a)]

(a) TAX.—Except as provided in sections 6015(e), 6212(a) and (c), 6213(a), 6225(b), 6246(b), 6330(e)(1), 6331(i), 6672(c), 6694(c), 7426(a) and (b)(1), 7429(b), and 7436, no suit for the purpose of restraining the assessment or collection of any tax shall be maintained in any court by any person, whether or not such person is the person against whom such tax was assessed.

[Sec. 7421(b)]

(b) LIABILITY OF TRANSFEREE OR FIDUCIARY.—No suit shall be maintained in any court for the purpose of restraining the assessment or collection (pursuant to the provisions of chapter 71) of—

(1) the amount of the liability, at law or in equity, of a transferee of property of a taxpayer in respect of any internal revenue tax, or

(2) the amount of the liability of a fiduciary under section 3713(b) of title 31, United States Code in respect of any such tax.

[Sec. 7422]

SEC. 7422. CIVIL ACTIONS FOR REFUND.

[Sec. 7422(a)]

(a) NO SUIT PRIOR TO FILING CLAIM FOR REFUND.—No suit or proceeding shall be maintained in any court for the recovery of any internal revenue tax alleged to have been erroneously or illegally assessed or collected, or of any penalty claimed to have been collected without authority, or of any sum alleged to have been excessive or in any manner wrongfully collected, until a claim for refund or credit has been duly filed with the Secretary, according to the provisions of law in that regard, and the regulations of the Secretary established in pursuance thereof.

[Sec. 7422(b)]

(b) PROTEST OR DURESS.—Such suit or proceeding may be maintained whether or not such tax, penalty or sum has been paid under protest or duress.

* * *

[Sec. 7430]

SEC. 7430. AWARDING OF COSTS AND CERTAIN FEES.

[Sec. 7430(a)]

(a) IN GENERAL.—In any administrative or court proceeding which is brought by or against the United States in connection with the determination, collection, or refund of any tax, interest, or penalty under this title, the prevailing party may be awarded a judgment or a settlement for—

(1) reasonable administrative costs incurred in connection with such administrative proceeding within the Internal Revenue Service, and

(2) reasonable litigation costs incurred in connection with such court proceeding.

[Sec. 7430(b)]

(b) LIMITATIONS.—

(1) REQUIREMENT THAT ADMINISTRATIVE REMEDIES BE EXHAUSTED.—A judgment for reasonable litigation costs shall not be awarded under subsection (a) in any court proceeding unless the court determines that the prevailing party has exhausted the administrative remedies available to such party within the Internal Revenue Service. Any failure to agree to an extension of the time for the

Sec. 7430(b)

assessment of any tax shall not be taken into account for purposes of determining whether the prevailing party meets the requirements of the preceding sentence.

(2) ONLY COSTS ALLOCABLE TO THE UNITED STATES.—An award under subsection (a) shall be made only for reasonable litigation and administrative costs which are allocable to the United States and not to any other party.

(3) COSTS DENIED WHERE PARTY PREVAILING PROTRACTS PROCEEDINGS.—No award for reasonable litigation and administrative costs may be made under subsection (a) with respect to any portion of the administrative or court proceeding during which the prevailing party has unreasonably protracted such proceeding.

(4) PERIOD FOR APPLYING TO IRS FOR ADMINISTRATIVE COSTS.—An award may be made under subsection (a) by the Internal Revenue Service for reasonable administrative costs only if the prevailing party files an application with the Internal Revenue Service for such costs before the 91st day after the date on which the final decision of the Internal Revenue Service as to the determination of the tax, interest, or penalty is mailed to such party.

[Sec. 7430(c)]

(c) DEFINITIONS.—For purposes of this section—

(1) REASONABLE LITIGATION COSTS.—The term "reasonable litigation costs" includes—

(A) reasonable court costs, and

(B) based upon prevailing market rates for the kind or quality of services furnished—

(i) the reasonable expenses of expert witnesses in connection with a court proceeding, except that no expert witness shall be compensated at a rate in excess of the highest rate of compensation for expert witnesses paid by the United States,

(ii) the reasonable cost of any study, analysis, engineering report, test, or project which is found by the court to be necessary for the preparation of the party's case, and

(iii) reasonable fees paid or incurred for the services of attorneys in connection with the court proceeding, except that such fees shall not be in excess of $125 per hour unless the court determines that an increase in the cost of living or a special factor, such as the limited availability of qualified attorneys for such proceeding, the difficulty of the issues presented in the case, or the local availability of tax expertise, justifies a higher rate.

In the case of any calendar year beginning after 1996, the dollar amount referred to in clause (iii) shall be increased by an amount equal to such dollar amount multiplied by the cost-of-living adjustment determined under section 1(f)(3) for such calendar year, by substituting "calendar year 1995" for "calendar year 1992" in subparagraph (B) thereof. If any dollar amount after being increased under the preceding sentence is not a multiple of $10, such dollar amount shall be rounded to the nearest multiple of $10.

(2) REASONABLE ADMINISTRATIVE COSTS.—The term "reasonable administrative costs" means—

(A) any administrative fees or similar charges imposed by the Internal Revenue Service, and

(B) expenses, costs, and fees described in paragraph (1)(B), except that any determination made by the court under clause (ii) or (iii) thereof shall be made by the Internal Revenue Service in cases where the determination under paragraph (4)(C) of the awarding of reasonable administrative costs is made by the Internal Revenue Service.

Such term shall only include costs incurred on or after whichever of the following is the earliest: (i) the date of the receipt by the taxpayer of the notice of the decision of the Internal Revenue Service Office of Appeals; (ii) the date of the notice of deficiency; or (iii) the date on which the 1st letter of proposed deficiency which allows the taxpayer an opportunity for administrative review in the Internal Revenue Service Office of Appeals is sent.

(3) ATTORNEYS' FEES.—

(A) IN GENERAL.—For purposes of paragraphs (1) and (2), fees for the services of an individual (whether or not an attorney) who is authorized to practice before the Tax Court or before the Internal Revenue Service shall be treated as fees for the services of an attorney.

(B) PRO BONO SERVICES.—The court may award reasonable attorneys' fees under subsection (a) in excess of the attorneys' fees paid or incurred if such fees are less than the reasonable attorneys' fees because an individual is representing the prevailing party for no fee or for a fee which (taking into account all the facts and circumstances) is no more than a nominal fee. This subparagraph shall apply only if such award is paid to such individual or such individual's employer.

(4) PREVAILING PARTY.—

(A) IN GENERAL.—The term "prevailing party" means any party in any proceeding to which subsection (a) applies (other than the United States or any creditor of the taxpayer involved)—

(i) which—

(I) has substantially prevailed with respect to the amount in controversy, or

(II) has substantially prevailed with respect to the most significant issue or set of issues presented, and

(ii) which meets the requirements of the 1st sentence of section 2412(d)(1)(B) of title 28, United States Code (as in effect on October 22, 1986) except to the extent differing procedures are established by rule of court and meets the requirements of section 2412(d)(2)(B) of such title 28 (as so in effect).

(B) EXCEPTION IF UNITED STATES ESTABLISHES THAT ITS POSITION WAS SUBSTANTIALLY JUSTIFIED.—

(i) GENERAL RULE.—A party shall not be treated as the prevailing party in a proceeding to which subsection (a) applies if the United States establishes that the position of the United States in the proceeding was substantially justified.

(ii) PRESUMPTION OF NO JUSTIFICATION IF INTERNAL REVENUE SERVICE DID NOT FOLLOW CERTAIN PUBLISHED GUIDANCE.—For purposes of clause (i), the position of the United States shall be presumed not to be substantially justified if the Internal Revenue Service did not follow its applicable published guidance in the administrative proceeding. Such presumption may be rebutted.

(iii) EFFECT OF LOSING ON SUBSTANTIALLY SIMILAR ISSUES.—In determining for purposes of clause (i) whether the position of the United States was substantially justified, the court shall take into account whether the United States has lost in courts of appeal for other circuits on substantially similar issues.

(iv) APPLICABLE PUBLISHED GUIDANCE.—For purposes of clause (ii), the term "applicable published guidance" means—

(I) regulations, revenue rulings, revenue procedures, information releases, notices, and announcements, and

(II) any of the following which are issued to the taxpayer: private letter rulings, technical advice memoranda, and determination letters.

(C) DETERMINATION AS TO PREVAILING PARTY.—Any determination under this paragraph as to whether a party is a prevailing party shall be made by agreement of the parties or—

(i) in the case where the final determination with respect to the tax, interest, or penalty is made at the administrative level, by the Internal Revenue Service, or

(ii) in the case where such final determination is made by a court, the court.

(D) SPECIAL RULES FOR APPLYING NET WORTH REQUIREMENT.—In applying the requirements of section 2412(d)(2)(B) of title 28, United States Code, for purposes of subparagraph (A)(ii) of this paragraph—

(i) the net worth limitation in clause (i) of such section shall apply to—

(I) an estate but shall be determined as of the date of the decedent's death, and

(II) a trust but shall be determined as of the last day of the taxable year involved in the proceeding, and

(ii) individuals filing a joint return shall be treated as separate individuals for purposes of clause (i) of such section.

(E) SPECIAL RULES WHERE JUDGMENT LESS THAN TAXPAYER'S OFFER.—

(i) IN GENERAL.—A party to a court proceeding meeting the requirements of subparagraph (A)(ii) shall be treated as the prevailing party if the liability of the taxpayer pursuant to the judgment in the proceeding (determined without regard to interest) is equal to or less than the liability of the taxpayer which would have been so determined if the United States had accepted a qualified offer of the party under subsection (g).

(ii) EXCEPTIONS.—This subparagraph shall not apply to—

(I) any judgment issued pursuant to a settlement; or

(II) any proceeding in which the amount of tax liability is not in issue, including any declaratory judgment proceeding, any proceeding to enforce or quash any summons issued pursuant to this title, and any action to restrain disclosure under section 6110(f).

(iii) SPECIAL RULES.—If this subparagraph applies to any court proceeding—

(I) the determination under clause (i) shall be made by reference to the last qualified offer made with respect to the tax liability at issue in the proceeding; and

(II) reasonable administrative and litigation costs shall only include costs incurred on and after the date of such offer.

(iv) COORDINATION.—This subparagraph shall not apply to a party which is a prevailing party under any other provision of this paragraph.

(5) ADMINISTRATIVE PROCEEDINGS.—The term "administrative proceeding" means any procedure or other action before the Internal Revenue Service.

(6) COURT PROCEEDINGS.—The term "court proceeding" means any civil action brought in a court of the United States (including the Tax Court and the United States Claims Court).

(7) POSITION OF UNITED STATES.—The term "position of the United States" means—

(A) the position taken by the United States in a judicial proceeding to which subsection (a) applies, and

(B) the position taken in an administrative proceeding to which subsection (a) applies as of the earlier of—

(i) the date of the receipt by the taxpayer of the notice of the decision of the Internal Revenue Service Office of Appeals, or

(ii) the date of the notice of deficiency.

* * *

Subchapter E—Burden of Proof

[Sec. 7491]

SEC. 7491. BURDEN OF PROOF.

[Sec. 7491(a)]

(a) BURDEN SHIFTS WHERE TAXPAYER PRODUCES CREDIBLE EVIDENCE.—

(1) GENERAL RULE.—If, in any court proceeding, a taxpayer introduces credible evidence with respect to any factual issue relevant to ascertaining the liability of the taxpayer for any tax imposed by subtitle A or B, the Secretary shall have the burden of proof with respect to such issue.

(2) LIMITATIONS.—Paragraph (1) shall apply with respect to an issue only if—

(A) the taxpayer has complied with the requirements under this title to substantiate any item;

(B) the taxpayer has maintained all records required under this title and has cooperated with reasonable requests by the Secretary for witnesses, information, documents, meetings, and interviews; and

(C) in the case of a partnership, corporation, or trust, the taxpayer is described in section 7430(c)(4)(A)(ii).

Subparagraph (C) shall not apply to any qualified revocable trust (as defined in section 645(b)(1)) with respect to liability for tax for any taxable year ending after the date of the decedent's death and before the applicable date (as defined in section 645(b)(2)).

(3) COORDINATION.—Paragraph (1) shall not apply to any issue if any other provision of this title provides for a specific burden of proof with respect to such issue.

[Sec. 7491(b)]

(b) USE OF STATISTICAL INFORMATION ON UNRELATED TAXPAYERS.—In the case of an individual taxpayer, the Secretary shall have the burden of proof in any court proceeding with respect to any item of income which was reconstructed by the Secretary solely through the use of statistical information on unrelated taxpayers.

[Sec. 7491(c)]

(c) PENALTIES.—Notwithstanding any other provision of this title, the Secretary shall have the burden of production in any court proceeding with respect to the liability of any individual for any penalty, addition to tax, or additional amount imposed by this title.

CHAPTER 77—MISCELLANEOUS PROVISIONS

[Sec. 7502]

SEC. 7502.   TIMELY MAILING TREATED AS TIMELY FILING AND PAYING.

[Sec. 7502(a)]

(a) GENERAL RULE.—

(1) DATE OF DELIVERY.—If any return, claim, statement, or other document required to be filed, or any payment required to be made, within a prescribed period or on or before a prescribed date under authority of any provision of the internal revenue laws is, after such period or such date, delivered by United States mail to the agency, officer, or office with which such return, claim, statement, or other document is required to be filed, or to which such payment is required to be made, the date of the United States postmark stamped on the cover in which such return, claim, statement, or other document, or payment, is mailed shall be deemed to be the date of delivery or the date of payment, as the case may be.

(2) MAILING REQUIREMENTS.—This subsection shall apply only if—

(A) the postmark date falls within the prescribed period or on or before the prescribed date—

(i) for the filing (including any extension granted for such filing) of the return, claim, statement, or other document, or

(ii) for making the payment (including any extension granted for making such payment), and

(B) the return, claim, statement, or other document, or payment was, within the time prescribed in subparagraph (A), deposited in the mail in the United States in an envelope or other appropriate wrapper, postage prepaid, properly addressed to the agency, officer, or office with which the return, claim, statement, or other document is required to be filed, or to which such payment is required to be made.

[Sec. 7502(b)]

(b) POSTMARKS.—This section shall apply in the case of postmarks not made by the United States Postal Service only if and to the extent provided by regulations prescribed by the Secretary.

Source: New.

[Sec. 7502(c)]

(c) REGISTERED AND CERTIFIED MAILING; ELECTRONIC FILING.—

(1) REGISTERED MAIL.—For purposes of this section, if any return, claim, statement, or other document, or payment, is sent by United States registered mail—

(A) such registration shall be prima facie evidence that the return, claim, statement, or other document was delivered to the agency, officer, or office to which addressed; and

(B) the date of registration shall be deemed the postmark date.

(2) CERTIFIED MAIL; ELECTRONIC FILING.—The Secretary is authorized to provide by regulations the extent to which the provisions of paragraph (1) with respect to prima facie evidence of delivery and the postmark date shall apply to certified mail and electronic filing.

Sec. 7502(c)

[Sec. 7502(d)]

(d) Exceptions.—This section shall not apply with respect to—

(1) the filing of a document in, or the making of a payment to, any court other than the Tax Court,

(2) currency or other medium of payment unless actually received and accounted for, or

(3) returns, claims, statements, or other documents, or payments, which are required under any provision of the internal revenue laws or the regulations thereunder to be delivered by any method other than by mailing.

* * *

[Sec. 7502(f)]

(f) Treatment of Private Delivery Services.—

(1) In general.—Any reference in this section to the United States mail shall be treated as including a reference to any designated delivery service, and any reference in this section to a postmark by the United States Postal Service shall be treated as including a reference to any date recorded or marked as described in paragraph (2)(C) by any designated delivery service.

(2) Designated delivery service.—For purposes of this subsection, the term "designated delivery service" means any delivery service provided by a trade or business if such service is designated by the Secretary for purposes of this section. The Secretary may designate a delivery service under the preceding sentence only if the Secretary determines that such service—

(A) is available to the general public,

(B) is at least as timely and reliable on a regular basis as the United States mail,

(C) records electronically to its data base, kept in the regular course of its business, or marks on the cover in which any item referred to in this section is to be delivered, the date on which such item was given to such trade or business for delivery, and

(D) meets such other criteria as the Secretary may prescribe.

(3) Equivalents of registered and certified mail.—The Secretary may provide a rule similar to the rule of paragraph (1) with respect to any service provided by a designated delivery service which is substantially equivalent to United States registered or certified mail.

[Sec. 7519]

SEC. 7519. REQUIRED PAYMENTS FOR ENTITIES ELECTING NOT TO HAVE REQUIRED TAXABLE YEAR.

[Sec. 7519(a)]

(a) General Rule.—This section applies to a partnership or S corporation for any taxable year, if—

(1) an election under section 444 is in effect for the taxable year, and

(2) the required payment determined under subsection (b) for such taxable year (or any preceding taxable year) exceeds $500.

[Sec. 7519(b)]

(b) Required Payment.—For purposes of this section, the term "required payment" means, with respect to any applicable election year of a partnership or S corporation, an amount equal to—

(1) the excess of the product of—

(A) the applicable percentage of the adjusted highest section 1 rate, multiplied by

(B) the net base year income of the entity, over

(2) the net required payment balance.

For purposes of paragraph (1)(A), the term "adjusted highest section 1 rate" means the highest rate of tax in effect under section 1 as of the end of the base year plus 1 percentage point (or, in the case of applicable election years beginning in 1987, 36 percent).

(c) REFUND OF PAYMENTS.—

(1) IN GENERAL.—If, for any applicable election year, the amount determined under subsection (b)(2) exceeds the amount determined under subsection (b)(1), the entity shall be entitled to a refund of such excess for such year.

(2) TERMINATION OF ELECTIONS, ETC.—If—

(A) an election under section 444 is terminated effective with respect to any year, or

(B) the entity is liquidated during any year, the entity shall be entitled to a refund of the net required payment balance.

(3) DATE ON WHICH REFUND PAYABLE.—Any refund under this subsection shall be payable on the later of—

(A) April 15 of the calendar year following—

(i) in the case of the year referred to in paragraph (1), the calendar year in which it begins,

(ii) in the case of the year referred to in paragraph (2), the calendar year in which it ends, or

(B) the day 90 days after the day on which claim therefor is filed with the Secretary.

(d) NET BASE YEAR INCOME.—For purposes of this section—

(1) IN GENERAL.—An entity's net base year income shall be equal to the sum of—

(A) the deferral ratio multiplied by the entity's net income for the base year, plus

(B) the excess (if any) of—

(i) the deferral ratio multiplied by the aggregate amount of applicable payments made by the entity during the base year, over

(ii) the aggregate amount of such applicable payments made during the deferral period of the base year.

For purposes of this paragraph, the term "deferral ratio" means the ratio which the number of months in the deferral period of the base year bears to the number of months in the partnership's or S corporation's taxable year.

(2) NET INCOME.—Net income is determined by taking into account the aggregate amount of the following items—

(A) PARTNERSHIPS.—In the case of a partnership, net income shall be the amount (not below zero) determined by taking into account the aggregate amount of the partnership's items described in section 702(a) (other than credits and tax-exempt income).

(B) S CORPORATIONS.—In the case of an S corporation, net income shall be the amount (not below zero) determined by taking into account the aggregate amount of the S corporation's items described in section 1366(a) (other than credits and tax-exempt income). If the S corporation was a C corporation for the base year, its taxable income for such year shall be treated as its net income for such year (and such corporation shall be treated as an S corporation for such taxable year for purposes of paragraph (3)).

(C) CERTAIN LIMITATIONS DISREGARDED.—For purposes of subparagraph (A) or (B), any limitation on the amount of any item described in either such paragraph which may be taken into account for purposes of computing the taxable income of a partner or shareholder shall be disregarded.

(3) APPLICABLE PAYMENTS.—

(A) IN GENERAL.—The term "applicable payment" means amounts paid by a partnership or S corporation which are includible in gross income of a partner or shareholder.

(B) EXCEPTIONS.—The term "applicable payment" shall not include any—

(i) gain from the sale or exchange of property between the partner or shareholder and the partnership or S corporation, and

(ii) dividend paid by the S corporation.

(4) APPLICABLE PERCENTAGE.—The applicable percentage is the percentage determined in accordance with the following table:

If the applicable election year of the partnership or S corporation begins during:	The applicable percentage is:
1987	25
1988	50
1989	75
1990 or thereafter	100

Notwithstanding the preceding provisions of this paragraph, the applicable percentage for any partnership or S corporation shall be 100 percent unless more than 50 percent of such entity's net income for the short taxable year which would have resulted if the entity had not made an election under section 444 would have been allocated to partners or shareholders who would have been entitled to the benefits of section 806(e)(2)(C) of the Tax Reform Act of 1986 with respect to such income.

(5) TREATMENT OF GUARANTEED PAYMENTS.—

(A) IN GENERAL.—Any guaranteed payment by a partnership shall not be treated as an applicable payment, and the amount of the net income of the partnership shall be determined by not taking such guaranteed payment into account.

(B) GUARANTEED PAYMENT.—For purposes of subparagraph (A), the term "guaranteed payment" means any payment referred to in section 707(c).

[Sec. 7519(e)]

(e) OTHER DEFINITIONS AND SPECIAL RULES.—For purposes of this section—

(1) DEFERRAL PERIOD.—The term "deferral period" has the meaning given to such term by section 444(b)(4).

(2) YEARS.—

(A) BASE YEAR.—The term "base year" means, with respect to any applicable election year, the taxable year of the partnership or S corporation preceding such applicable election year.

(B) APPLICABLE ELECTION YEAR.—The term "applicable election year" means any taxable year of a partnership or S corporation with respect to which an election is in effect under section 444.

(3) REQUIREMENT OF REPORTING.—Each partnership or S corporation which makes an election under section 444 shall include on any required return or statement such information as the Secretary shall prescribe as is necessary to carry out the provisions of this section.

(4) NET REQUIRED PAYMENT BALANCE.—The term "net required payment balance" means the excess (if any) of—

(A) the aggregate of the required payments under this section for all preceding applicable election years, over

(B) the aggregate amount allowable as a refund to the entity under subsection (c) for all preceding applicable election years.

[Sec. 7519(f)]

(f) ADMINISTRATIVE PROVISIONS.—

(1) IN GENERAL.—Except as otherwise provided in this subsection or in regulations prescribed by the Secretary, any payment required by this section shall be assessed and collected in the same manner as if it were a tax imposed by subtitle C.

(2) DUE DATE.—The amount of any payment required by this section shall be paid on or before April 15 of the calendar year following the calendar year in which the applicable election year begins (or such later date as may be prescribed by the Secretary).

(3) INTEREST.—For purposes of determining interest, any payment required by this section shall be treated as a tax; except that no interest shall be allowed with respect to any refund of a payment made under this section.

(4) PENALTIES.—

(A) IN GENERAL.—In the case of any failure by any person to pay on the date prescribed therefor any amount required by this section, there shall be imposed on such person a penalty of 10 percent of the underpayment. For purposes of the preceding sentence, the term

Sec. 7519(e)

"underpayment" means the excess of the amount of the payment required under this section over the amount (if any) of such payment paid on or before the date prescribed therefor. No penalty shall be imposed under this subparagraph on any failure which is shown to be due to reasonable cause and not willful neglect.

(B) NEGLIGENCE AND FRAUD PENALTIES MADE APPLICABLE.—For purposes of part II of subchapter A of chapter 68, any payment required by this section shall be treated as a tax.

(C) WILLFULL FAILURE.—If any partnership or S corporation willfully fails to comply with the requirements of this section, section 444 shall cease to apply with respect to such partnership or S corporation.

[Sec. 7519(g)]

(g) REGULATIONS.—The Secretary shall prescribe such regulations as may be necessary or appropriate to carry out the provisions of this section and section 280H, including regulations providing for appropriate adjustments in the application of this section and sections 280H and 444 in cases where—

(1) 2 or more applicable election years begin in the same calendar year, or

(2) the base year is a taxable year of less than 12 months.

[Sec. 7520]

SEC. 7520. VALUATION TABLES.

[Sec. 7520(a)]

(a) GENERAL RULE.—For purposes of this title, the value of any annuity, any interest for life or a term of years, or any remainder or reversionary interest shall be determined—

(1) under tables prescribed by the Secretary, and

(2) by using an interest rate (rounded to the nearest $2/10$ths of 1 percent) equal to 120 percent of the Federal midterm rate in effect under section 1274(d)(1) for the month in which the valuation date falls.

If an income, estate, or gift tax charitable contribution is allowable for any part of the property transferred, the taxpayer may elect to use such Federal midterm rate for either of the 2 months preceding the month in which the valuation date falls for purposes of paragraph (2). In the case of transfers of more than 1 interest in the same property with respect to which the taxpayer may use the same rate under paragraph (2), the taxpayer shall use the same rate with respect to each such interest.

[Sec. 7520(b)]

(b) SECTION NOT TO APPLY FOR CERTAIN PURPOSES.—This section shall not apply for purposes of part I of subchapter D of chapter 1 or any other provision specified in regulations.

[Sec. 7520(c)]

(c) TABLES.—

(1) IN GENERAL.—The tables prescribed by the Secretary for purposes of subsection (a) shall contain valuation factors for a series of interest rate categories.

(2) INITIAL TABLE.—Not later than the day 3 months after the date of the enactment of this section, the Secretary shall prescribe initial tables for purposes of subsection (a). Such tables may be based on the same mortality experience as used for purposes of section 2031 on the date of the enactment of this section.

(3) REVISION FOR RECENT MORTALITY CHARGES.—Not later than December 31, 1989, the Secretary shall revise the initial tables prescribed for purposes of subsection (a) to take into account the most recent mortality experience available as of the time of such revision. Such tables shall be revised not less frequently than once each 10 years thereafter to take into account the most recent mortality experience available as of the time of the revision.

[Sec. 7520(d)]

(d) VALUATION DATE.—For purposes of this section, the term "valuation date" means the date as of which the valuation is made.

[Sec. 7520(e)]

(e) TABLES TO INCLUDE FORMULAS.—For purposes of this section, the term "tables" includes formulas.

[Sec. 7525]

SEC. 7525. CONFIDENTIALITY PRIVILEGES RELATING TO TAXPAYER COMMUNICATIONS.

[Sec. 7525(a)]

(a) UNIFORM APPLICATION TO TAXPAYER COMMUNICATIONS WITH FEDERALLY AUTHORIZED PRACTITIONERS.—

(1) GENERAL RULE.—With respect to tax advice, the same common law protections of confidentiality which apply to a communication between a taxpayer and an attorney shall also apply to a communication between a taxpayer and any federally authorized tax practitioner to the extent the communication would be considered a privileged communication if it were between a taxpayer and an attorney.

(2) LIMITATIONS.—Paragraph (1) may only be asserted in—

(A) any noncriminal tax matter before the Internal Revenue Service; and

(B) any noncriminal tax proceeding in Federal court brought by or against the United States.

(3) DEFINITIONS.—For purposes of this subsection—

(A) FEDERALLY AUTHORIZED TAX PRACTITIONER.—The term "federally authorized tax practitioner" means any individual who is authorized under Federal law to practice before the Internal Revenue Service if such practice is subject to Federal regulation under section 330 of title 31, United States Code.

(B) TAX ADVICE.—The term "tax advice" means advice given by an individual with respect to a matter which is within the scope of the individual's authority to practice described in subparagraph (A).

[Sec. 7525(b)]

(b) SECTION NOT TO APPLY TO COMMUNICATIONS REGARDING CORPORATE TAX SHELTERS.—The privilege under subsection (a) shall not apply to any written communication between a federally authorized tax practitioner and a director, shareholder, officer, or employee, agent, or representative of a corporation in connection with the promotion of the direct or indirect participation of such corporation in any tax shelter (as defined in section 6662(d)(2)(C)(iii)).

CHAPTER 79—DEFINITIONS

[Sec. 7701]

SEC. 7701. DEFINITIONS.

[Sec. 7701(a)]

(a) When used in this title, where not otherwise distinctly expressed or manifestly incompatible with the intent thereof—

(1) PERSON.—The term "person" shall be construed to mean and include an individual, a trust, estate, partnership, association, company or corporation.

(2) PARTNERSHIP AND PARTNER.—The term "partnership" includes a syndicate, group, pool, joint venture, or other unincorporated organization, through or by means of which any business, financial operation, or venture is carried on, and which is not, within the meaning of this title, a trust or estate or a corporation; and the term "partner" includes a member in such a syndicate, group, pool, joint venture, or organization.

(3) CORPORATION.—The term "corporation" includes associations, joint-stock companies, and insurance companies.

(4) DOMESTIC.—The term "domestic" when applied to a corporation or partnership means created or organized in the United States or under the law of the United States or of any State unless, in the case of a partnership, the Secretary provides otherwise by regulations.

(5) FOREIGN.—The term "foreign" when applied to a corporation or partnership means a corporation or partnership which is not domestic.

(6) FIDUCIARY.—The term "fiduciary" means a guardian, trustee, executor, administrator, receiver, conservator, or any person acting in any fiduciary capacity for any person.

(7) STOCK.—The term "stock" includes shares in an association, joint-stock company, or insurance company.

(8) SHAREHOLDER.—The term "shareholder" includes a member in an association, joint-stock company, or insurance company.

(9) UNITED STATES.—The term "United States" when used in a geographical sense includes only the States and the District of Columbia.

(10) STATE.—The term "State" shall be construed to include the District of Columbia, where such construction is necessary to carry out provisions of this title.

(11) SECRETARY OF THE TREASURY AND SECRETARY.—

(A) SECRETARY OF THE TREASURY.—The term "Secretary of the Treasury" means the Secretary of the Treasury, personally, and shall not include any delegate of his.

(B) SECRETARY.—The term "Secretary" means the Secretary of the Treasury or his delegate.

(12) DELEGATE.—

(A) IN GENERAL.—The term "or his delegate"—

(i) when used with reference to the Secretary of the Treasury, means any officer, employee, or agency of the Treasury Department duly authorized by the Secretary of the Treasury directly, or indirectly by one or more redelegations of authority, to perform the function mentioned or described in the context; and

(ii) when used with reference to any other official of the United States, shall be similarly construed.

* * *

(13) COMMISSIONER.—The term "Commissioner" means the Commissioner of Internal Revenue.

(14) TAXPAYER.—The term "taxpayer" means any person subject to any internal revenue tax.

(15) MILITARY OR NAVAL FORCES AND ARMED FORCES OF THE UNITED STATES.—The term "military or naval forces of the United States" and the term "Armed Forces of the United States" each includes all regular and reserve components of the uniformed services which are subject to the jurisdiction of the Secretary of Defense, the Secretary of the Army, the Secretary of the Navy, or the Secretary of the Air Force, and each term also includes the Coast Guard. The members of such forces include commissioned officers and personnel below the grade of commissioned officers in such forces.

(16) WITHHOLDING AGENT.—The term "withholding agent" means any person required to deduct and withhold any tax under the provisions of section 1441, 1442, 1443, or 1461.

(17) HUSBAND AND WIFE.—As used in sections 152(b)(4), 682, and 2516, if the husband and wife therein referred to are divorced, wherever appropriate to the meaning of such sections, the term "wife" shall be read "former wife" and the term "husband" shall be read "former husband"; and, if the payments described in such sections are made by or on behalf of the wife or former wife to the husband or former husband instead of vice versa, wherever appropriate to the meaning of such sections, the term "husband" shall be read "wife" and the term "wife" shall be read "husband."

* * *

(20) EMPLOYEE.—For the purpose of applying the provisions of section 79 with respect to group-term life insurance purchased for employees, for the purpose of applying the provisions of sections 104, 105, and 106 with respect to accident and health insurance or accident and health plans, and for the purpose of applying the provisions of subtitle A with respect to contributions to or under a stock bonus, pension, profit-sharing, or annuity plan, and with respect to distributions under such a plan, or by a trust forming part of such a plan, and for purposes of applying section 125 with respect to cafeteria plans, the term "employee" shall include a full-time life insurance salesman who is considered an employee for the purpose of chapter 21, or in the case of services performed before January 1, 1951, who would be considered an employee if his services were performed during 1951.

(21) LEVY.—The term "levy" includes the power of distraint and seizure by any means.

Sec. 7701(a)

(22) ATTORNEY GENERAL.—The term "Attorney General" means the Attorney General of the United States.

(23) TAXABLE YEAR.—The term "taxable year" means the calendar year, or the fiscal year ending during such calendar year, upon the basis of which the taxable income is computed under subtitle A. "Taxable year" means, in the case of a return made for a fractional part of a year under the provisions of subtitle A or under regulations prescribed by the Secretary, the period for which such return is made.

(24) FISCAL YEAR.—The term "fiscal year" means an accounting period of 12 months ending on the last day of any month other than December.

(25) PAID OR INCURRED, PAID OR ACCRUED.—The terms "paid or incurred" and "paid or accrued" shall be construed according to the method of accounting upon the basis of which the taxable income is computed under subtitle A.

(26) TRADE OR BUSINESS.—The term "trade or business" includes the performance of the functions of a public office.

(27) TAX COURT.—The term "Tax Court" means the United States Tax Court.

(28) OTHER TERMS.—Any term used in this subtitle with respect to the application of, or in connection with, the provisions of any other subtitle of this title shall have the same meaning as in such provisions.

(29) INTERNAL REVENUE CODE.—The term "Internal Revenue Code of 1986" means this title, and the term "Internal Revenue Code of 1939" means the Internal Revenue Code enacted February 10, 1939, as amended.

(30) UNITED STATES PERSON.—The term "United States person" means—

(A) a citizen or resident of the United States,

(B) a domestic partnership,

(C) a domestic corporation,

(D) any estate (other than a foreign estate, within the meaning of paragraph (31)), and

(E) any trust if—

(i) a court within the United States is able to exercise primary supervision over the administration of the trust, and

(ii) one or more United States persons have the authority to control all substantial decisions of the trust.

* * *

(36) INCOME TAX RETURN PREPARER.—

(A) IN GENERAL.—The term "income tax return preparer" means any person who prepares for compensation, or who employs one or more persons to prepare for compensation, any return of tax imposed by subtitle A or any claim for refund of tax imposed by subtitle A. For purposes of the preceding sentence, the preparation of a substantial portion of a return or claim for refund shall be treated as if it were the preparation of such return or claim for refund.

(B) EXCEPTIONS.—A person shall not be an "income tax return preparer" merely because such person—

(i) furnishes typing, reproducing, or other mechanical assistance,

(ii) prepares a return or claim for refund of the employer (or of an officer or employee of the employer) by whom he is regularly and continuously employed,

(iii) prepares as a fiduciary a return or claim for refund for any person, or

(iv) prepares a claim for refund for a taxpayer in response to any notice of deficiency issued to such taxpayer or in response to any waiver of restriction after the commencement of an audit of such taxpayer or another taxpayer if a determination in such audit of such other taxpayer directly or indirectly affects the tax liability of such taxpayer.

(37) INDIVIDUAL RETIREMENT PLAN.—The term "individual retirement plan" means—

(A) an individual retirement account described in section 408(a), and

(B) an individual retirement annuity described in section 408(b).

Sec. 7701(a)

(38) JOINT RETURN.—The term "joint return" means a single return made jointly under section 6013 by a husband and wife.

* * *

(41) TIN.—The term "TIN" means the identifying number assigned to a person under section 6109.

(42) SUBSTITUTED BASIS PROPERTY.—The term "substituted basis property" means property which is—

(A) transferred basis property, or

(B) exchanged basis property.

(43) TRANSFERRED BASIS PROPERTY.—The term "transferred basis property" means property having a basis determined under any provision of subtitle A (or under any corresponding provision of prior income tax law) providing that the basis shall be determined in whole or in part by reference to the basis in the hands of the donor, grantor, or other transferor.

(44) EXCHANGED BASIS PROPERTY.—The term "exchanged basis property" means property having a basis determined under any provision of subtitle A (or under any corresponding provision of prior income tax law) providing that the basis shall be determined in whole or in part by reference to other property held at any time by the person for whom the basis is to be determined.

(45) NONRECOGNITION TRANSACTION.—The term "nonrecognition transaction" means any disposition of property in a transaction in which gain or loss is not recognized in whole or in part for purposes of subtitle A.

* * *

[Caution: Code Sec. 7701(a)(47), below, as added by P.L. 107-16, applies to estates of decedents dying after December 31, 2009.]

(47) EXECUTOR.—The term "executor" means the executor or administrator of the decedent, or, if there is no executor or administrator appointed, qualified, and acting within the United States, then any person in actual or constructive possession of any property of the decedent.

* * *

[Sec. 7701(c)]

(c) INCLUDES AND INCLUDING.—The terms "includes" and "including" when used in a definition contained in this title shall not be deemed to exclude other things otherwise within the meaning of the term defined.

* * *

[Sec. 7701(g)]

(g) CLARIFICATION OF FAIR MARKET VALUE IN THE CASE OF NONRECOURSE INDEBTEDNESS.—For purposes of subtitle A, in determining the amount of gain or loss (or deemed gain or loss) with respect to any property, the fair market value of such property shall be treated as being not less than the amount of any nonrecourse indebtedness to which such property is subject.

* * *

[Sec. 7703]

SEC. 7703. DETERMINATION OF MARITAL STATUS.

[Sec. 7703(a)]

(a) GENERAL RULE.—For purposes of part v of subchapter B of chapter 1 and those provisions of this title which refer to this subsection—

(1) the determination of whether an individual is married shall be made as of the close of his taxable year; except that if his spouse dies during his taxable year such determination shall be made as of the time of such death; and

(2) an individual legally separated from his spouse under a decree of divorce or of separate maintenance shall not be considered as married.

Sec. 7703(a)

[Sec. 7703(b)]

(b) CERTAIN MARRIED INDIVIDUALS LIVING APART.—For purposes of those provisions of this title which refer to this subsection, if—

(1) an individual who is married (within the meaning of subsection (a)) and who files a separate return maintains as his home a household which constitutes for more than one-half of the taxable year the principal place of abode of a child (within the meaning of section 151(c)(3)) with respect to whom such individual is entitled to a deduction for the taxable year under section 151 (or would be so entitled but for paragraph (2) or (4) of section 152(e)),

(2) such individual furnishes over one-half of the cost of maintaining such household during the taxable year, and

(3) during the last 6 months of the taxable year, such individual's spouse is not a member of such household,

such individual shall not be considered as married.

[Sec. 7704]

SEC. 7704. CERTAIN PUBLICLY TRADED PARTNERSHIPS TREATED AS CORPORATIONS.

[Sec. 7704(a)]

(a) GENERAL RULE.—For purposes of this title, except as provided in subsection (c), a publicly traded partnership shall be treated as a corporation.

[Sec. 7704(b)]

(b) PUBLICLY TRADED PARTNERSHIP.—For purposes of this section, the term "publicly traded partnership" means any partnership if—

(1) interests in such partnership are traded on an established securities market, or

(2) interests in such partnership are readily tradable on a secondary market (or the substantial equivalent thereof).

[Sec. 7704(c)]

(c) EXCEPTION FOR PARTNERSHIPS WITH PASSIVE-TYPE INCOME.—

(1) IN GENERAL.—Subsection (a) shall not apply to any publicly traded partnership for any taxable year if such partnership met the gross income requirements of paragraph (2) for such taxable year and each preceding taxable year beginning after December 31, 1987, during which the partnership (or any predecessor) was in existence. For purposes of the preceding sentence, a partnership shall not be treated as being in existence during any period before the 1st taxable year in which such partnership (or a predecessor) was a publicly traded partnership.

(2) GROSS INCOME REQUIREMENTS.—A partnership meets the gross income requirements of this paragraph for any taxable year if 90 percent or more of the gross income of such partnership for such taxable year consists of qualifying income.

(3) EXCEPTION NOT TO APPLY TO CERTAIN PARTNERSHIPS WHICH COULD QUALIFY AS REGULATED INVESTMENT COMPANIES.—This subsection shall not apply to any partnership which would be described in section 851(a) if such partnership were a domestic corporation. To the extent provided in regulations, the preceding sentence shall not apply to any partnership a principal activity of which is the buying and selling of commodities (not described in section 1221(a)(1)), or options, futures, or forwards with respect to commodities.

[Sec. 7704(d)]

(d) QUALIFYING INCOME.—For purposes of this section—

(1) IN GENERAL.—Except as otherwise provided in this subsection, the term "qualifying income" means—

(A) interest,

(B) dividends,

(C) real property rents,

(D) gain from the sale or other disposition of real property (including property described in section 1221(a)(1)),

(E) income and gains derived from the exploration, development, mining or production, processing, refining, transportation (including pipelines transporting gas, oil, or products thereof), or the marketing of any mineral or natural resource (including fertilizer, geothermal energy, and timber),

(F) any gain from the sale or disposition of a capital asset (or property described in section 1231(b)) held for the production of income described in any of the foregoing subparagraphs of this paragraph, and

(G) in the case of a partnership described in the second sentence of subsection (c)(3), income and gains from commodities (not described in section 1221(a)(1)) or futures, forwards, and options with respect to commodities.

For purposes of subparagraph (E), the term "mineral or natural resource" means any product of a character with respect to which a deduction for depletion is allowable under section 611; except that such term shall not include any product described in subparagraph (A) or (B) of section 613(b)(7).

(2) CERTAIN INTEREST NOT QUALIFIED.—Interest shall not be treated as qualifying income if—

(A) such interest is derived in the conduct of a financial or insurance business, or

(B) such interest would be excluded from the term "interest" under section 856(f).

(3) REAL PROPERTY RENT.—The term "real property rent" means amounts which would qualify as rent from real property under section 856(d) if—

(A) such section were applied without regard to paragraph (2)(C) thereof (relating to independent contractor requirements), and

(B) stock owned, directly or indirectly, by or for a partner would not be considered as owned under section 318(a)(3)(A) by the partnership unless 5 percent or more (by value) of the interests in such partnership are owned, directly or indirectly, by or for such partner.

(4) CERTAIN INCOME QUALIFYING UNDER REGULATED INVESTMENT COMPANY OR REAL ESTATE TRUST PROVISIONS.—The term "qualifying income" also includes any income which would qualify under section 851(b)(2) or 856(c)(2).

(5) SPECIAL RULE FOR DETERMINING GROSS INCOME FROM CERTAIN REAL PROPERTY SALES.—In the case of the sale or other disposition of real property described in section 1221(a)(1), gross income shall not be reduced by inventory costs.

[Sec. 7704(e)]

(e) INADVERTENT TERMINATIONS.—If—

(1) A partnership fails to meet the gross income requirements of subsection (c)(2),

(2) the Secretary determines that such failure was inadvertent,

(3) no later than a reasonable time after the discovery of such failure, steps are taken so that such partnership once more meets such gross income requirements, and

(4) such partnership agrees to make such adjustments (including adjustments with respect to the partners) or to pay such amounts as may be required by the Secretary with respect to such period,

then, notwithstanding such failure, such entity shall be treated as continuing to meet such gross income requirements for such period.

[Sec. 7704(f)]

(f) EFFECT OF BECOMING CORPORATION.—As of the 1st day that a partnership is treated as a corporation under this section, for purposes of this title, such partnership shall be treated as—

(1) transferring all of its assets (subject to its liabilities) to a newly formed corporation in exchange for the stock of the corporation, and

(2) distributing such stock to its partners in liquidation of their interests in the partnership.

[Sec. 7704(g)]

(g) EXCEPTION FOR ELECTING 1987 PARTNERSHIPS.—

(1) IN GENERAL.—Subsection (a) shall not apply to an electing 1987 partnership.

Sec. 7704(g)

(2) ELECTING 1987 PARTNERSHIP.—For purposes of this subsection, the term "electing 1987 partnership" means any publicly traded partnership if—

(A) such partnership is an existing partnership (as defined in section 10211(c)(2) of the Revenue Reconciliation Act of 1987),

(B) subsection (a) has not applied (and without regard to subsection (c)(1) would not have applied) to such partnership for all prior taxable years beginning after December 31, 1987, and before January 1, 1998, and

(C) such partnership elects the application of this subsection, and consents to the application of the tax imposed by paragraph (3), for its first taxable year beginning after December 31, 1997.

A partnership which, but for this sentence, would be treated as an electing 1987 partnership shall cease to be so treated (and the election under subparagraph (C) shall cease to be in effect) as of the 1st day after December 31, 1997, on which there has been an addition of a substantial new line of business with respect to such partnership.

(3) ADDITIONAL TAX ON ELECTING PARTNERSHIPS.—

(A) IMPOSITION OF TAX.—There is hereby imposed for each taxable year on the income of each electing 1987 partnership a tax equal to 3.5 percent of such partnership's gross income for the taxable year from the active conduct of trades and businesses by the partnership.

(B) ADJUSTMENTS IN THE CASE OF TIERED PARTNERSHIPS.—For purposes of this paragraph, in the case of a partnership which is a partner in another partnership, the gross income referred to in subparagraph (A) shall include the partnership's distributive share of the gross income of such other partnership from the active conduct of trades and businesses of such other partnership. A similar rule shall apply in the case of lower-tiered partnerships.

(C) TREATMENT OF TAX.—For purposes of this title, the tax imposed by this paragraph shall be treated as imposed by chapter 1 other than for purposes of determining the amount of any credit allowable under chapter 1 and shall be paid by the partnership. Section 6655 shall be applied to such partnership with respect to such tax in the same manner as if the partnership were a corporation, such tax were imposed by section 11, and references in such section to taxable income were references to the gross income referred to in subparagraph (A).

(4) ELECTION.—An election and consent under this subsection shall apply to the taxable year for which made and all subsequent taxable years unless revoked by the partnership. Such revocation may be made without the consent of the Secretary, but, once so revoked, may not be reinstated.

CHAPTER 80—GENERAL RULES

Subchapter A—Application of Internal Revenue Laws

[Sec. 7805]

SEC. 7805. RULES AND REGULATIONS.

[Sec. 7805(a)]

(a) AUTHORIZATION.—Except where such authority is expressly given by this title to any person other than an officer or employee of the Treasury Department, the Secretary shall prescribe all needful rules and regulations for the enforcement of this title, including all rules and regulations as may be necessary by reason of any alteration of law in relation to internal revenue.

[Sec. 7805(b)]

(b) RETROACTIVITY OF REGULATIONS.—

(1) IN GENERAL.—Except as otherwise provided in this subsection, no temporary, proposed, or final regulation relating to the internal revenue laws shall apply to any taxable period ending before the earliest of the following dates:

(A) The date on which such regulation is filed with the Federal Register.

(B) In the case of any final regulation, the date on which any proposed or temporary regulation to which such final regulation relates was filed with the Federal Register.

(C) The date on which any notice substantially describing the expected contents of any temporary, proposed, or final regulation is issued to the public.

(2) EXCEPTION FOR PROMPTLY ISSUED REGULATIONS.—Paragraph (1) shall not apply to regulations filed or issued within 18 months of the date of the enactment of the statutory provision to which the regulation relates.

(3) PREVENTION OF ABUSE.—The Secretary may provide that any regulation may take effect or apply retroactively to prevent abuse.

(4) CORRECTION OF PROCEDURAL DEFECTS.—The Secretary may provide that any regulation may apply retroactively to correct a procedural defect in the issuance of any prior regulation.

(5) INTERNAL REGULATIONS.—The limitation of paragraph (1) shall not apply to any regulation relating to internal Treasury Department policies, practices, or procedures.

(6) CONGRESSIONAL AUTHORIZATION.—The limitation of paragraph (1) may be superseded by a legislative grant from Congress authorizing the Secretary to prescribe the effective date with respect to any regulation.

(7) ELECTION TO APPLY RETROACTIVELY.—The Secretary may provide for any taxpayer to elect to apply any regulation before the dates specified in paragraph (1).

(8) APPLICATION TO RULINGS.—The Secretary may prescribe the extent, if any, to which any ruling (including any judicial decision or any administrative determination other than by regulation) relating to the internal revenue laws shall be applied without retroactive effect.

* * *

[Sec. 7805(d)]

(d) MANNER OF MAKING ELECTIONS PRESCRIBED BY SECRETARY.—Except to the extent otherwise provided by this title, any election under this title shall be made at such time and in such manner as the Secretary shall prescribe.

[Sec. 7805(e)]

(e) TEMPORARY REGULATIONS.—

(1) ISSUANCE.—Any temporary regulation issued by the Secretary shall also be issued as a proposed regulation.

(2) 3-YEAR DURATION.—Any temporary regulation shall expire within 3 years after the date of issuance of such regulation.

* * *

[Sec. 7806]

SEC. 7806. CONSTRUCTION OF TITLE.

[Sec. 7806(a)]

(a) CROSS REFERENCES.—The cross references in this title to other portions of the title, or other provisions of law, where the word "see" is used, are made only for convenience, and shall be given no legal effect.

[Sec. 7806(b)]

(b) ARRANGEMENT AND CLASSIFICATION.—No inference, implication, or presumption of legislative construction shall be drawn or made by reason of the location or grouping of any particular section or provision or portion of this title, nor shall any table of contents, table of cross references, or similar outline, analysis, or descriptive matter relating to the contents of this title be given any legal effect. The preceding sentence also applies to the sidenotes and ancillary tables contained in the various prints of this Act before its enactment into law.

Sec. 7806(b)

Subchapter C—Provisions Affecting More than One Subtitle

[Sec. 7872]

SEC. 7872. TREATMENT OF LOANS WITH BELOW-MARKET INTEREST RATES.

[Sec. 7872(a)]

(a) TREATMENT OF GIFT LOANS AND DEMAND LOANS.—

(1) IN GENERAL.—For purposes of this title, in the case of any below-market loan to which this section applies and which is a gift loan or a demand loan, the forgone interest shall be treated as—

(A) transferred from the lender to the borrower, and

(B) retransferred by the borrower to the lender as interest.

(2) TIME WHEN TRANSFERS MADE.—Except as otherwise provided in regulations prescribed by the Secretary, any forgone interest attributable to periods during any calendar year shall be treated as transferred (and retransferred) under paragraph (1) on the last day of such calendar year.

[Sec. 7872(b)]

(b) TREATMENT OF OTHER BELOW-MARKET LOANS.—

(1) IN GENERAL.—For purposes of this title, in the case of any below-market loan to which this section applies and to which subsection (a)(1) does not apply, the lender shall be treated as having transferred on the date the loan was made (or, if later, on the first day on which this section applies to such loan), and the borrower shall be treated as having received on such date, cash in an amount equal to the excess of—

(A) the amount loaned, over

(B) the present value of all payments which are required to be made under the terms of the loan.

(2) OBLIGATION TREATED AS HAVING ORIGINAL ISSUE DISCOUNT.—For purposes of this title—

(A) IN GENERAL.—Any below-market loan to which paragraph (1) applies shall be treated as having original issue discount in an amount equal to the excess described in paragraph (1).

(B) AMOUNT IN ADDITION TO OTHER ORIGINAL ISSUE DISCOUNT.—Any original issue discount which a loan is treated as having by reason of subparagraph (A) shall be in addition to any other original issue discount on such loan (determined without regard to subparagraph (A)).

[Sec. 7872(c)]

(c) BELOW-MARKET LOANS TO WHICH SECTION APPLIES.—

(1) IN GENERAL.—Except as otherwise provided in this subsection and subsection (g), this section shall apply to—

(A) GIFTS.—Any below-market loan which is a gift loan.

(B) COMPENSATION-RELATED LOANS.—Any below-market loan directly or indirectly between—

(i) an employer and an employee, or

(ii) an independent contractor and a person for whom such independent contractor provides services.

(C) CORPORATION-SHAREHOLDER LOANS.—Any below-market loan directly or indirectly between a corporation and any shareholder of such corporation.

(D) TAX AVOIDANCE LOANS.—Any below-market loan 1 of the principal purposes of the interest arrangements of which is the avoidance of any Federal tax.

(E) OTHER BELOW-MARKET LOANS.—To the extent provided in regulations, any below-market loan which is not described in subparagraph (A), (B), (C), or (F) if the interest arrangements of such loan have a significant effect on any Federal tax liability of the lender or the borrower.

(F) LOANS TO QUALIFIED CONTINUING CARE FACILITIES.—Any loan to any qualified continuing care facility pursuant to a continuing care contract.

Sec. 7872

(2) $10,000 DE MINIMIS EXCEPTION FOR GIFT LOANS BETWEEN INDIVIDUALS.—

(A) IN GENERAL.—In the case of any gift loan directly between individuals, this section shall not apply to any day on which the aggregate outstanding amount of loans between such individuals does not exceed $10,000.

(B) DE MINIMIS EXCEPTION NOT TO APPLY TO LOANS ATTRIBUTABLE TO ACQUISITION OF INCOME-PRODUCING ASSETS.—Subparagraph (A) shall not apply to any gift loan directly attributable to the purchase or carrying of income-producing assets.

(C) CROSS REFERENCE.—

For limitation on amount treated as interest where loans do not exceed $100,000, see subsection (d)(1).

(3) $10,000 DE MINIMIS EXCEPTION FOR COMPENSATION-RELATED AND CORPORATE-SHAREHOLDER LOANS.—

(A) IN GENERAL.—In the case of any loan described in subparagraph (B) or (C) of paragraph (1), this section shall not apply to any day on which the aggregate outstanding amount of loans between the borrower and lender does not exceed $10,000.

(B) EXCEPTION NOT TO APPLY WHERE 1 OF PRINCIPAL PURPOSES IS TAX AVOIDANCE.—Subparagraph (A) shall not apply to any loan the interest arrangements of which have as 1 of their principal purposes the avoidance of any Federal tax.

[Sec. 7872(d)]

(d) SPECIAL RULES FOR GIFT LOANS.—

(1) LIMITATION ON INTEREST ACCRUAL FOR PURPOSES OF INCOME TAXES WHERE LOANS DO NOT EXCEED $100,000.—

(A) IN GENERAL.—For purposes of subtitle A, in the case of a gift loan directly between individuals, the amount treated as retransferred by the borrower to the lender as of the close of any year shall not exceed the borrower's net investment income for such year.

(B) LIMITATION NOT TO APPLY WHERE 1 OF PRINCIPAL PURPOSES IS TAX AVOIDANCE.—Subparagraph (A) shall not apply to any loan the interest arrangements of which have as 1 of their principal purposes the avoidance of any Federal tax.

(C) SPECIAL RULE WHERE MORE THAN 1 GIFT LOAN OUTSTANDING.—For purposes of subparagraph (A), in any case in which a borrower has outstanding more than 1 gift loan, the net investment income of such borrower shall be allocated among such loans in proportion to the respective amounts which would be treated as retransferred by the borrower without regard to this paragraph.

(D) LIMITATION NOT TO APPLY WHERE AGGREGATE AMOUNT OF LOANS EXCEED $100,000.—This paragraph shall not apply to any loan made by a lender to a borrower for any day on which the aggregate outstanding amount of loans between the borrower and lender exceeds $100,000.

(E) NET INVESTMENT INCOME.—For purposes of this paragraph—

(i) IN GENERAL.—The term "net investment income" has the meaning given such term by section 163(d)(4).

(ii) DE MINIMIS RULE.—If the net investment income of any borrower for any year does not exceed $1,000, the net investment income of such borrower for such year shall be treated as zero.

(iii) ADDITIONAL AMOUNTS TREATED AS INTEREST.—In determining the net investment income of a person for any year, any amount which would be included in the gross income of such person for such year by reason of section 1272 if such section applied to all deferred payment obligations shall be treated as interest received by such person for such year.

(iv) DEFERRED PAYMENT OBLIGATIONS.—The term "deferred payment obligation" includes any market discount bond, short-term obligation, United States savings bond, annuity, or similar obligation.

(2) SPECIAL RULE FOR GIFT TAX.—In the case of any gift loan which is a term loan, subsection (b)(1) (and not subsection (a)) shall apply for purposes of chapter 12.

Sec. 7872(d)

[Sec. 7872(e)]

(e) DEFINITIONS OF BELOW-MARKET LOAN AND FORGONE INTEREST.—For purposes of this section—

(1) BELOW-MARKET LOAN.—The term "below-market loan" means any loan if—

(A) in the case of a demand loan, interest is payable on the loan at a rate less than the applicable Federal rate, or

(B) in the case of a term loan, the amount loaned exceeds the present value of all payments due under the loan.

(2) FORGONE INTEREST.—The term "forgone interest" means, with respect to any period during which the loan is outstanding, the excess of—

(A) the amount of interest which would have been payable on the loan for the period if interest accrued on the loan at the applicable Federal rate and were payable annually on the day referred to in subsection (a)(2), over

(B) any interest payable on the loan properly allocable to such period.

[Sec. 7872(f)]

(f) OTHER DEFINITIONS AND SPECIAL RULES.—For purposes of this section—

(1) PRESENT VALUE.—The present value of any payment shall be determined in the manner provided by regulations prescribed by the Secretary—

(A) as of the date of the loan, and

(B) by using a discount rate equal to the applicable Federal rate.

(2) APPLICABLE FEDERAL RATE.—

(A) TERM LOANS.—In the case of any term loan, the applicable Federal rate shall be the applicable Federal rate in effect under section 1274(d) (as of the day on which the loan was made), compounded semiannually.

(B) DEMAND LOANS.—In the case of a demand loan, the applicable Federal rate shall be the Federal short-term rate in effect under section 1274(d) for the period for which the amount of forgone interest is being determined, compounded semiannually.

(3) GIFT LOAN.—The term "gift loan" means any below-market loan where the forgoing of interest is in the nature of a gift.

(4) AMOUNT LOANED.—The term "amount loaned" means the amount received by the borrower.

(5) DEMAND LOAN.—The term "demand loan" means any loan which is payable in full at any time on the demand of the lender. Such term also includes (for purposes other than determining the applicable Federal rate under paragraph (2)) any loan if the benefits of the interest arrangements of such loan are not transferable and are conditioned on the future performance of substantial services by an individual. To the extent provided in regulations, such term also includes any loan with an indefinite maturity.

(6) TERM LOAN.—The term "term loan" means any loan which is not a demand loan.

(7) HUSBAND AND WIFE TREATED AS 1 PERSON.—A husband and wife shall be treated as 1 person.

(8) LOANS TO WHICH SECTION 483, 643(i), OR 1274 APPLIES.—This section shall not apply to any loan to which section 483, 643(i), or 1274 applies.

* * *

(10) SPECIAL RULE FOR TERM LOANS.—If this section applies to any term loan on any day, this section shall continue to apply to such loan notwithstanding paragraphs (2) and (3) of subsection (c). In the case of a gift loan, the preceding sentence shall only apply for purposes of chapter 12.

* * *

[Sec. 7872(h)]

(h) REGULATIONS.—

(1) IN GENERAL.—The Secretary shall prescribe such regulations as may be necessary or appropriate to carry out the purposes of this section, including—

(A) regulations providing that where, by reason of varying rates of interest, conditional interest payments, waivers of interest, disposition of the lender's or borrower's interest in the loan, or other circumstances, the provisions of this section do not carry out the purposes of this section, adjustments to the provisions of this section will be made to the extent necessary to carry out the purposes of this section,

(B) regulations for the purpose of assuring that the positions of the borrower and lender are consistent as to the application (or nonapplication) of this section, and

(C) regulations exempting from the application of this section any class of transactions the interest arrangements of which have no significant effect on any Federal tax liability of the lender or the borrower.

Income Tax Regulations

Tax on Individuals

§ 1.1(h)-1. Capital gains look-through rule for sales or exchanges of interests in a partnership, S corporation, or trust.—(a) *In general.* When an interest in a partnership held for more than one year is sold or exchanged, the transferor may recognize ordinary income (e.g., under section 751(a)), collectibles gain, section 1250 capital gain, and residual long-term capital gain or loss. When stock in an S corporation held for more than one year is sold or exchanged, the transferor may recognize ordinary income (e.g., under sections 304, 306, 341, 1254), collectibles gain, and residual long-term capital gain or loss. When an interest in a trust held for more than one year is sold or exchanged, a transferor who is not treated as the owner of the portion of the trust attributable to the interest sold or exchanged (sections 673 through 679) (a non-grantor transferor) may recognize collectibles gain and residual long-term capital gain or loss.

(b) *Look-through capital gain*—(1) *In general.* Look-through capital gain is the share of collectibles gain allocable to an interest in a partnership, S corporation, or trust, plus the share of section 1250 capital gain allocable to an interest in a partnership, determined under paragraphs (b)(2) and (3) of this section.

(2) *Collectibles gain*—(i) *Definition.* For purposes of this section, *collectibles gain* shall be treated as gain from the sale or exchange of a collectible (as defined in section 408(m) without regard to section 408(m)(3)) that is a capital asset held for more than 1 year.

(ii) *Share of collectibles gain allocable to an interest in a partnership, S corporation, or a trust.* When an interest in a partnership, S corporation, or trust held for more than one year is sold or exchanged in a transaction in which all realized gain is recognized, the transferor shall recognize as collectibles gain the amount of net gain (but not net loss) that would be allocated to that partner (taking into account any remedial allocation under § 1.704-3(d)), shareholder, or beneficiary (to the extent attributable to the portion of the partnership interest, S corporation stock, or trust interest transferred that was held for more than one year) if the partnership, S corporation, or trust transferred all of its collectibles for cash equal to the fair market value of the assets in a fully taxable transaction immediately before the transfer of the interest in the partnership, S corporation, or trust. If less than all of the realized gain is recognized upon the sale or exchange of an interest in a partnership, S corporation, or trust, the same methodology shall apply to determine the collectibles gain recognized by the transferor, except that the partnership, S corporation, or

trust shall be treated as transferring only a proportionate amount of each of its collectibles determined as a fraction that is the amount of gain recognized in the sale or exchange over the amount of gain realized in the sale or exchange. With respect to the transfer of an interest in a trust, this paragraph (b)(2) applies only to transfers by non-grantor transferors (as defined in paragraph (a) of this section). This paragraph (b)(2) does not apply to a transaction that is treated, for Federal income tax purposes, as a redemption of an interest in a partnership, S corporation, or trust.

(3) *Section 1250 capital gain*—(i) *Definition.* For purposes of this section, *section 1250 capital gain* means the capital gain (not otherwise treated as ordinary income) that would be treated as ordinary income if section 1250(b)(1) included all depreciation and the applicable percentage under section 1250(a) were 100 percent.

(ii) *Share of section 1250 capital gain allocable to interest in partnership.* When an interest in a partnership held for more than one year is sold or exchanged in a transaction in which all realized gain is recognized, there shall be taken into account under section 1(h)(7)(A)(i) in determining the partner's unrecaptured section 1250 gain the amount of section 1250 capital gain that would be allocated (taking into account any remedial allocation under § 1.704-3(d)) to that partner (to the extent attributable to the portion of the partnership interest transferred that was held for more than one year) if the partnership transferred all of its section 1250 property in a fully taxable transaction for cash equal to the fair market value of the assets immediately before the transfer of the interest in the partnership. If less than all of the realized gain is recognized upon the sale or exchange of an interest in a partnership, the same methodology shall apply to determine the section 1250 capital gain recognized by the transferor, except that the partnership shall be treated as transferring only a proportionate amount of each section 1250 property determined as a fraction that is the amount of gain recognized in the sale or exchange over the amount of gain realized in the sale or exchange. This paragraph (b)(3) does not apply to a transaction that is treated, for Federal income tax purposes, as a redemption of a partnership interest.

(iii) *Limitation with respect to net section 1231 gain.* In determining a transferor partner's net section 1231 gain (as defined in section 1231(c)(3)) for purposes of section 1(h)(7)(B), the transferor partner's allocable share of section 1250 capital gain in partnership property shall not be treated as section 1231 gain, regardless of whether the partnership property is used in the trade or business (as defined in section 1231(b)).

(c) *Residual long-term capital gain or loss.* The amount of residual long-term capital gain or loss recognized by a partner, shareholder of an S corporation, or beneficiary of a trust on account of the sale or exchange of an interest in a partnership, S corporation, or trust shall equal the amount of long-term capital gain or loss that the partner would recognize under section 741, that the shareholder would recognize upon the sale or exchange of stock of an S corporation, or that the beneficiary would recognize upon the sale or exchange of an interest in a trust (pre-look-through long-term capital gain or loss) minus the amount of look-through capital gain determined under paragraph (b) of this section.

(d) *Special rule for tiered entities.* In determining whether a partnership, S corporation, or trust has gain from collectibles, such partnership, S corporation, or trust shall be treated as owning its proportionate share of the collectibles of any partnership, S corporation, or trust in which it owns an interest either directly or indirectly through a chain of such entities. In determining whether a partnership has section 1250 capital gain, such partnership shall be treated as owning its proportionate share of the section 1250 property of any partnership in which it owns an interest, either directly or indirectly through a chain of partnerships.

(e) *Notification requirements.* Reporting rules similar to those that apply to the partners and the partnership under section 751(a) shall apply in the case of sales or exchanges of interests in a partnership, S corporation, or trust that cause holders of such interests to recognize collectibles gain and in the case of sales or exchanges of interests in a partnership that cause holders of such interests to recognize section 1250 capital gain. See § 1.751-1(a)(3).

(f) *Examples.* The following examples illustrate the requirements of this section:

Example 1. Collectibles gain. (i) *A* and *B* are equal partners in a personal service partnership (*PRS*). *B* transfers *B*'s interest in *PRS* to *T* for $15,000 when *PRS*'s balance sheet (reflecting a cash receipts and disbursements method of accounting) is as follows:

ASSETS

	Adjusted Basis	Market Value
Cash	$ 3,000	$ 3,000
Loans Owed to Partnership	10,000	10,000
Collectibles	1,000	3,000
Other Capital Assets	6,000	2,000
Capital Assets	7,000	5,000
Unrealized Receivables	0	14,000
Total	$20,000	$32,000

LIABILITIES AND CAPITAL

	Adjusted Basis	Market Value
Liabilities	$ 2,000	$ 2,000
Capital:		
A	9,000	15,000
B	9,000	15,000
Total	$20,000	$32,000

(ii) At the time of the transfer, *B* has held the interest in *PRS* for more than one year, and *B*'s basis for the partnership interest is $10,000 ($9,000 plus $1,000, *B*'s share of partnership liabilities). None of the property owned by *PRS* is section 704(c) property. The total amount realized by *B* is $16,000, consisting of the cash received, $15,000, plus $1,000, *B*'s share of the partnership liabilities assumed by *T*. See section 752. *B*'s undivided one-half interest in *PRS* includes a one-half interest in the partnership's unrealized receivables and a one-half interest in the partnership's collectibles.

(iii) If *PRS* were to sell all of its section 751 property in a fully taxable transaction for cash equal to the fair market value of the assets immediately prior to the transfer of *B*'s partnership interest to *T*, *B* would be allocated $7,000 of ordinary income from the sale of *PRS*'s unrealized receivables. Therefore, *B* will recognize $7,000 of ordinary income with respect to the unrealized receivables. The difference between the amount of capital gain or loss that the partner would realize in the absence of section 751 ($6,000) and the amount of ordinary income or loss determined under § 1.751-1(a)(2) ($7,000) is the partner's capital gain or loss on the sale of the partnership interest under section 741. In this case, the transferor has a $1,000 pre-look-through long-term capital loss.

(iv) If *PRS* were to sell all of its collectibles in a fully taxable transaction for cash equal to the fair market value of the assets immediately prior to the transfer of *B*'s partnership interest to *T*, *B* would be allocated $1,000 of gain from the sale of the collectibles. Therefore, *B* will recognize $1,000 of collectibles gain on account of the collectibles held by *PRS*.

(v) The difference between the transferor's pre-look-through long-term capital gain or loss (−$1,000) and the look-through capital gain determined under this section ($1,000) is the transferor's residual long-term capital gain or loss on the sale of the partnership interest. Under these facts, *B* will recognize a $2,000 residual long-term capital loss on account of the sale or exchange of the interest in *PRS*.

Example 2. Special allocations. Assume the same facts as in *Example 1*, except that under the partnership agreement, all gain from the sale of the collectibles is specially allocated to *B*, and *B* transfers *B*'s interest to *T* for $16,000. All items of income, gain, loss, or deduction of *PRS*, other than the gain from the collectibles, are divided equally between *A* and *B*. Under these facts, *B*'s amount realized is $17,000, consisting of the cash received, $16,000, plus $1,000, *B*'s share of the partnership liabilities assumed by *T*. See section 752. *B* will recognize $7,000 of ordinary income with respect to the unrealized receivables (determined under § 1.751-1(a)(2)). Accordingly, *B*'s pre-look-through long-term capital gain would be $0. If *PRS* were to sell all of its collectibles in a fully taxable transaction for cash equal to the fair market value of the assets immediately prior to the transfer of *B*'s partnership interest to *T*, *B* would be allocated $2,000 of gain from the sale of the collectibles. Therefore, *B* will recognize $2,000 of collectibles gain on account of the collectibles held by *PRS*. *B* will recognize a $2,000 residual long-term capital loss on account of the sale of *B*'s interest in *PRS*.

Example 3. Net collectibles loss ignored. Assume the same facts as in *Example 1*, except that the collectibles held by *PRS* have an adjusted basis of $3,000 and a fair market value of $1,000, and the other capital assets have an adjusted basis of $4,000 and a fair market value of $4,000. (The total adjusted basis and fair market value of the partnership's capital assets are the same as in *Example 1*.) If *PRS* were to sell all of its collectibles in a fully taxable transaction for cash equal to the fair market value of the assets immediately prior to the transfer of *B*'s partnership

interest to *T*, *B* would be allocated $1,000 of loss from the sale of the collectibles. Because none of the gain from the sale of the interest in *PRS* is attributable to unrealized appreciation in the value of collectibles held by *PRS*, the net loss in collectibles held by *PRS* is not recognized at the time *B* transfers the interest in *PRS*. *B* will recognize $7,000 of ordinary income (determined under § 1.751-1(a)(2)) and a $1,000 long-term capital loss on account of the sale of *B*'s interest in *PRS*.

Example 4. Collectibles gain in an S corporation. (i) A corporation (*X*) has always been an S corporation and is owned by individuals *A*, *B*, and *C*. In 1996, *X* invested in antiques. Subsequent to their purchase, the antiques appreciated in value by $300. *A* owns one-third of the shares of *X* stock and has held that stock for more than one year. *A*'s adjusted basis in the *X* stock is $100. If *A* were to sell all of *A*'s *X* stock to *T* for $150, *A* would realize $50 of pre-look-through long-term capital gain.

(ii) If *X* were to sell its antiques in a fully taxable transaction for cash equal to the fair market value of the assets immediately before the transfer to *T*, *A* would be allocated $100 of gain on account of the sale. Therefore, *A* will recognize $100 of collectibles gain (look-through capital gain) on account of the collectibles held by *X*.

(iii) The difference between the transferor's pre-look-through long-term capital gain or loss ($50) and the look-through capital gain determined under this section ($100) is the transferor's residual long-term capital gain or loss on the sale of the S corporation stock. Under these facts, *A* will recognize $100 of collectibles gain and a $50 residual long-term capital loss on account of the sale of *A*'s interest in *X*.

Example 5. Sale or exchange of partnership interest where part of the interest has a short-term holding period. (i) *A*, *B*, and *C* form an equal partnership (*PRS*). In connection with the formation, *A* contributes $5,000 in cash and a capital asset with a fair market value of $5,000 and a basis of $2,000; *B* contributes $7,000 in cash and a collectible with a fair market value of $3,000 and a basis of $3,000; and *C* contributes $10,000 in cash. At the time of the contribution, *A* had held the contributed property for two years. Six months later, when *A*'s basis in *PRS* is $7,000, *A* transfers *A*'s interest in *PRS* to *T* for $14,000 at a time when *PRS*'s balance sheet (reflecting a cash receipts and disbursements method of accounting) is as follows:

ASSETS

	Adjusted Basis	Market Value
Cash	$22,000	$22,000
Unrealized Receivables	0	6,000
Capital Asset	2,000	5,000
Collectible	3,000	9,000
Capital Assets	5,000	14,000
Total	$27,000	$42,000

(ii) Although at the time of the transfer *A* has not held *A*'s interest in *PRS* for more than one year, 50 percent of the fair market value of *A*'s interest in *PRS* was received in exchange for a capital asset with a long-term holding period. Therefore, 50 percent of *A*'s interest in *PRS* has a long-term holding period. See § 1.1223-3(b)(1).

(iii) If *PRS* were to sell all of its section 751 property in a fully taxable transaction immediately before *A*'s transfer of the partnership interest, *A* would be allocated $2,000 of ordinary income. Accordingly, *A* will recognize $2,000 ordinary income and $5,000 ($7,000 − $2,000) of capital gain on account of the transfer to *T* of *A*'s interest in *PRS*. Fifty percent ($2,500) of that gain is long-term capital gain and 50 percent ($2,500) is short-term capital gain. See § 1.1223-3(c)(1).

(iv) If the collectible were sold or exchanged in a fully taxable transaction immediately before *A*'s transfer of the partnership interest, *A* would be allocated $2,000 of gain attributable to the collectible. The gain attributable to the collectible that is allocable to the portion of the transferred interest in *PRS* with a long-term holding period is $1,000 (50 percent of $2,000). Accordingly, *A* will recognize $1,000 of collectibles gain on account of the transfer of *A*'s interest in *PRS*.

(v) The difference between the amount of pre-look-through long-term capital gain or loss ($2,500) and the look-through capital gain ($1,000) is the amount of residual long-term capital gain or loss that *A* will recognize on account of the transfer of *A*'s interest in *PRS*. Under these facts, *A* will recognize a residual long-term capital gain of $1,500 and a short-term capital gain of $2,500.

(g) *Effective date.* This section applies to transfers of interests in partnerships, S corporations, and trusts that occur on or after September 21, 2000. [Reg. § 1.1(h)-1.]

☐ [*T.D.* 8902, 9-20-2000.]

[*Note: Section 1(i) as referred to in Reg. § 1.1(i)-1T was renumbered as Section 1(g) in 1990.*]

§ 1.1(i)-1T. Questions and answers relating to the tax on unearned income of certain minor children (Temporary).

In general.

Q-1. To whom does section 1(i) apply?

A-1. Section 1(i) applies to any child who is under 14 years of age at the close of the taxable year, who has at least one living parent at the close of the taxable year, and who recognizes over $1,000 of unearned income during the taxable year.

Q-2. What is the effective date of section 1(i)?

A-2. Section 1(i) applies to taxable years of the child beginning after December 31, 1986.

Computation of tax.

Q-3. What is the amount of tax imposed by section 1 on a child to whom section 1(i) applies?

A-3. In the case of a child to whom section 1(i) applies, the amount of tax imposed by section 1 equals the greater of (A) the tax imposed by section 1 without regard to section 1(i) or (B) the sum of the tax that would be imposed by section 1 if the child's taxable income was reduced by the child's net unearned income, plus the child's share of the allocable parental tax.

Q-4. What is the allocable parental tax?

A-4. The allocable parental tax is the excess of (A) the tax that would be imposed by section 1 on the sum of the parent's taxable income plus the net unearned income of all children of such parent to whom section 1(i) applies, over (B) the tax imposed by section 1 on the parent's taxable income. Thus, the allocable parental tax is not computed with reference to unearned income of a child over 14 or a child under 14 with less than $1,000 of unearned income. *See* A-10 through A-13 for rules regarding the determination of the parent(s) whose taxable income is taken into account under section 1(i). *See* A-14 for rules regarding the determination of children of the parent whose net unearned income is taken into account under section 1(i).

Q-5. What is the child's share of the allocable parental tax?

A-5. The child's share of the allocable parental tax is an amount that bears the same ratio to the total allocable parental tax as the child's net unearned income bears to the total net unearned income of all children of such parent to whom section 1(i) applies. See A-14.

Example (1). During 1988, D, a 12 year old, receives $5,000 of unearned income and no earned income. D has no itemized deductions and is not eligible for a personal exemption. D's parents have two other children, E, a 15 year old, and F, a

10 year old. E has $10,000 of unearned income and F has $100 of unearned income. D's parents file a joint return for 1988 and report taxable income of $70,000. Neither D's nor his parent's taxable income is attributable to net capital gain. D's tax liability for 1988, determined without regard to section 1(i), is $675 on $4,500 of taxable income ($5,000 less $500 allowable standard deduction). In applying section 1(i), D's tax would be equal to the sum of (A) the tax that would be imposed on D's taxable income if it were reduced by any net unearned income, plus (B) D's share of the allocable parental tax. Only D's unearned income is taken into account in determining the allocable parental tax because E is over 14 and F has less than $1,000 of unearned income. See A-4. D's net unearned income is $4,000 ($4,500 taxable unearned income less $500). The tax imposed on D's taxable income as reduced by D's net unearned income is $75 ($500 × 15%). The allocable parental tax is $1,225, the excess of $16,957.50 (the tax on $74,000, the parent's taxable income plus D's net unearned income) over $15,732.50 (the tax on $70,000, the parent's taxable income). See A-4. Thus, D's tax under section 1(i)(1)(B) is $1,300 ($1,225 + $75). Since this amount is greater than the amount of D's tax liability as determined without regard to section 1(i), the amount of tax imposed on D for 1988 is $1,300. See A-3.

Example (2). H and W have 3 children, A, B, and C, who are all under 14 years of age. For the taxable year 1988, H and W file a joint return and report taxable income of $129,750. The tax imposed by section 1 on H and W is $35,355. A has $5,000 of net unearned income and B and C each have $2,500 of net unearned income during 1988. The allocable parental tax imposed on A, B, and C's combined net unearned income of $10,000 is $3,300. This tax is the excess of $38,655, which is the tax imposed by section 1 on $139,750 ($129,750 + 10,000), over $35,355 (the tax imposed by section 1 on H and W's taxable income of $129,750). See A-4. Each child's share of the allocable parental tax is an amount that bears the same ratio to the total allocable parental tax as the child's net unearned income bears to the total net unearned income of A, B, and C. Thus, A's share of the allocable parental tax is $1,650

$$(\frac{5,000}{10,000} \times 3,300)$$

and B and C's share of the tax is $825

$$(\frac{2,500}{10,000} \times 3,300) \text{ each. See A-5.}$$

Definition of net unearned income.

Q-6. What is net unearned income?

A-6. Net unearned income is the excess of the portion of adjusted gross income for the taxable year that is not "earned income" as defined in

section 911(d)(2) (income that is not attributable to wages, salaries, or other amounts received as compensation for personal services), over the sum of the standard deduction amount provided for under section 63(c)(5)(A) ($500 for 1987 and 1988; adjusted for inflation thereafter), plus the greater of (A) $500 (adjusted for inflation after 1988) or (B) the amount of allowable itemized deductions that are directly connected with the production of unearned income. A child's net unearned income for any taxable year shall not exceed the child's taxable income for such year.

Example (3). A is a child who is under 14 years of age at the end of the taxable year 1987. Both of A's parents are alive at this time. During 1987, A receives $3,000 of interest from a bank savings account and earns $1,000 from a paper route and performing odd jobs. A has no itemized deductions for 1987. A's standard deduction is $1,000, which is an amount equal to A's earned income for 1987. Of this amount, $500 is applied against A's unearned income and the remaining $500 is applied against A's earned income. Thus, A's $500 of taxable earned income ($1,000 less the remaining $500 of the standard deduction) is taxed without regard to section 1(i); A has $2,500 of taxable unearned income ($3,000 gross unearned income less $500 of the standard deduction) of which $500 is taxed without regard to section 1(i). The remaining $2,000 of taxable unearned income is A's net unearned income and is taxed under section 1(i).

Example (4). B is a child who is subject to tax under section 1(i). B has $400 of earned income and $2,000 of unearned income. B has itemized deductions of $800 (net of the 2 percent of adjusted gross income (AGI) floor on miscellaneous itemized deductions under section 67) of which $200 are directly connected with the production of unearned income. The amount of itemized deductions that B may apply against unearned income is equal to the greater of $500 or the deductions directly connected with the production of unearned income. See A-6. Thus, $500 of B's itemized deductions are applied against the $2,000 of unearned income and the remaining $300 of deductions are applied against earned income. As a result, B has taxable earned income of $100 and taxable unearned income of $1,500. Of these amounts, all of the earned income and $500 of the unearned income are taxed without regard to section 1(i). The remaining $1,000 of unearned income is net unearned income and is taxed under section 1(i).

Unearned income subject to tax under section 1(i).

Q-7. Will a child be subject to tax under section 1(i) on net unearned income (as defined in section 1(i)(4) and A-6 of this section) that is attributable to property transferred to the child prior to 1987?

Reg. § 1.1(i)-1T

A-7. Yes. the tax imposed by section 1(i) on a child's net unearned income applies to any net unearned income of the child for taxable years beginning after December 31, 1986, regardless of when the underlying assets were transferred to the child.

Q-8. Will a child be subject to tax under section 1(i) on net unearned income that is attributable to gifts from persons other than the child's parents or attributable to assets resulting from the child's earned income?

A-8. Yes. The tax imposed by section 1(i) applies to all net unearned income of the child, regardless of the source of the assets that produced such income. Thus, the rules of section 1(i) apply to income attributable to gifts not only from the parents but also from any other source, such as the child's grandparents. Section 1(i) also applies to unearned income derived with respect to assets resulting from earned income of the child, such as interest earned on bank deposits.

Example (5). A is a child who is under 14 years of age at the end of the taxable year beginning on January 1, 1987. Both of A's parents are alive at the end of the taxable year. During 1987, A receives $2,000 in interest from his bank account and $1,500 from a paper route. Some of the interest earned by A from the bank account is attributable to A's paper route earnings that were deposited in the account. The balance of the account is attributable to cash gifts from A's parents and grandparents and interest earned prior to 1987. Some cash gifts were received by A prior to 1987. A has no itemized deductions and is eligible to be claimed as a dependent on his parent's return. Therefore, for the taxable year 1987, A's standard deduction is $1,500, the amount of A's earned income. Of this standard deduction amount, $500 is allocated against unearned income and $1,000 is allocated against earned income. A's taxable unearned income is $1,500 of which $500 is taxed without regard to section 1(i). The remaining taxable unearned income of $1,000 is net unearned income and is taxed under section 1(i). The fact that some of A's unearned income is attributable to interest on principal created by earned income and gifts from persons other than A's parents or that some of the unearned income is attributable to property transferred to A prior to 1987, will not affect the tax treatment of this income under section 1(i). *See* A-8.

Q-9. For purposes of section 1(i), does income which is not earned income (as defined in section 911(d)(2)) include social security benefits or pension benefits that are paid to the child?

A-9. Yes. For purposes of section 1(i), earned income (as defined in section 911(d)(2)) does not include any social security or pension benefits paid to the child. Thus, such amounts are included in unearned income to the extent they are includible in the child's gross income.

Determination of the parent's taxable income.

Q-10. If a child's parents file a joint return, what is the taxable income that must be taken into account by the child in determining tax liability under section 1(i)?

A-10. In the case of parents who file a joint return, the parental taxable income to be taken into account in determining the tax liability of a child is the total taxable income shown on the joint return.

Q-11. If a child's parents are married and file separate tax returns, which parent's taxable income must be taken into account by the child in determining tax liability under section 1(i)?

A-11. For purposes of determining the tax liability of a child under section 1(i), where such child's parents are married and file separate tax returns, the parent whose taxable income is the greater of the two for the taxable year shall be taken into account.

Q-12. If the parents of a child are divorced, legally separated, or treated as not married under section 7703(b), which parent's taxable income is taken into account in computing the child's tax liability?

A-12. If the child's parents are divorced, legally separated, or treated as not married under section 7703(b), the taxable income of the custodial parent (within the meaning of section 152(e)) of the child is taken into account under section 1(i) in determining the child's tax liability.

Q-13. If a parent whose taxable income must be taken into account in determining a child's tax liability under section 1(i) files a joint return with a spouse who is not a parent of the child, what taxable income must the child take into account?

A-13. The amount of a parent's taxable income that a child must take into account for purposes of section 1(i) where the parent files a joint return with a spouse who is not a parent of the child is the total taxable income shown on such joint return.

Children of the parent.

Q-14. In determining a child's share of the allocable parental tax, is the net unearned income of legally adopted children, children related to such child by half-blood, or children from a prior marriage of the spouse of such child's parent taken into account in addition to the natural children of such child's parent?

A-14. Yes. In determining a child's share of the allocable parental tax, the net unearned income of all children subject to tax under section 1(i) and who use the same parent's taxable income as such child to determine their tax liability under section 1(i) must be taken into account. Such children are taken into account regardless of whether they are adopted by the parent, related to such child by half-blood, or are children from a prior marriage of the spouse of such child's parent.

Rules regarding income from a trust or similar instrument.

Q-15. Will the unearned income of a child who is subject to section 1(i) that is attributable to gifts given to the child under the Uniform Gift to Minors Act (UGMA) be subject to tax under section 1(i)?

A-15. Yes. A gift under the UGMA vests legal title to the property in the child although an adult custodian is given certain rights to deal with the property until the child attains majority. Any unearned income attributable to such a gift is the child's unearned income and is subject to tax under section 1(i), whether distributed to the child or not.

Q-16. Will a child who is a beneficiary of a trust be required to take into account the income of a trust in determining the child's tax liability under section 1(i)?

A-16. The income of a trust must be taken into account for purposes of determining the tax liability of a beneficiary who is subject to section 1(i) only to the extent it is included in the child's gross income for the taxable year under sections 652(a) or 662(a). Thus, income from a trust for the fiscal taxable year of a trust ending during 1987, that is included in the gross income of a child who is subject to section 1(i) and who has a calendar taxable year, will be subject to tax under section 1(i) for the child's 1987 taxable year.

* * *

[Temporary Reg. § 1.1(i)-1T.]

☐ [*T.D.* 8158, 9-3-87.]

Credits Against Tax

[Note: In 1984 Section 44A was renumbered as Section 21. The regulations interpreting Section 21 may be found at § 1.44A-1.]

§ 1.25A-1. Calculation of education tax credit and general eligibility requirements.— (a) *Amount of education tax credit.* An individual taxpayer is allowed a nonrefundable education tax credit against income tax imposed by chapter 1 of the Internal Revenue Code for the taxable year. The amount of the education tax credit is the total of the Hope Scholarship Credit (as described in § 1.25A-3) plus the Lifetime Learning Credit (as described in § 1.25A-4). For limitations on the credits allowed by subpart A of part IV of subchapter A of chapter 1 of the Internal Revenue Code, see section 26.

(b) *Coordination of Hope Scholarship Credit and Lifetime Learning Credit*—(1) *In general.* In the same taxable year, a taxpayer may claim a Hope Scholarship Credit for each eligible student's qualified tuition and related expenses (as defined in § 1.25A-2(d)) and a Lifetime Learning Credit for one or more other students' qualified tuition and related expenses. However, a taxpayer may not claim both a Hope Scholarship Credit and a Lifetime Learning Credit with respect to the same student in the same taxable year.

(2) *Hope Scholarship Credit.* Subject to certain limitations, a Hope Scholarship Credit may be claimed for the qualified tuition and related expenses paid during a taxable year with respect to each eligible student (as defined in § 1.25A-3(d)). Qualified tuition and related expenses paid during a taxable year with respect to one student may not be taken into account in computing the amount of the Hope Scholarship

Credit with respect to any other student. In addition, qualified tuition and related expenses paid during a taxable year with respect to any student for whom a Hope Scholarship Credit is claimed may not be taken into account in computing the amount of the Lifetime Learning Credit.

(3) *Lifetime Learning Credit.* Subject to certain limitations, a Lifetime Learning Credit may be claimed for the aggregate amount of qualified tuition and related expenses paid during a taxable year with respect to students for whom no Hope Scholarship Credit is claimed.

(4) *Examples.* The following examples illustrate the rules of this paragraph (b):

Example 1. In 1999, Taxpayer A pays qualified tuition and related expenses for his dependent, B, to attend College Y during 1999. Assuming all other relevant requirements are met, Taxpayer A may claim either a Hope Scholarship Credit or a Lifetime Learning Credit with respect to dependent B, but not both. See § 1.25A-3(a) and § 1.25A-4(a).

Example 2. In 1999, Taxpayer C pays $2,000 in qualified tuition and related expenses for her dependent, D, to attend College Z during 1999. In 1999, Taxpayer C also pays $500 in qualified tuition and related expenses to attend a computer course during 1999 to improve Taxpayer C's job skills. Assuming all other relevant requirements are met, Taxpayer C may claim a Hope Scholarship Credit for the $2,000 of qualified tuition and related expenses attributable to dependent D (see § 1.25A-3(a)) and a Lifetime Learning Credit (see § 1.25A-4(a))for the $500 of qualified tuition and related expenses incurred to improve her job skills.

Example 3. The facts are the same as in *Example 2,* except that Taxpayer C pays $3,000 in qualified tuition and related expenses for her dependent, D, to attend College Z during 1999. Although a Hope Scholarship Credit is available only with respect to the first $2,000 of qualified tuition and related expenses paid with respect to D (see § 1.25A-3(a)), Taxpayer C may not add the $1,000 of excess expenses to her $500 of qualified tuition and related expenses in computing the amount of the Lifetime Learning Credit.

(c) *Limitation based on modified adjusted gross income*—(1) *In general.* The education tax credit that a taxpayer may otherwise claim is phased out ratably for taxpayers with modified adjusted gross income between $40,000 and $50,000 ($80,000 and $100,000 for married individuals who file a joint return). Thus, taxpayers with modified adjusted gross income above $50,000 (or $100,000 for joint filers) may not claim an education tax credit.

(2) *Modified adjusted gross income defined.* The term *modified adjusted gross income* means the adjusted gross income (as defined in section 62) of the taxpayer for the taxable year increased by any amount excluded from gross income under section 911, 931, or 933 (relating to income earned abroad or from certain U.S. possessions or Puerto Rico).

(3) *Inflation adjustment.* For taxable years beginning after 2001, the amounts in paragraph (c)(1) of this section will be increased for inflation occurring after 2000 in accordance with section 1(f)(3). If any amount adjusted under this paragraph (c)(3) is not a multiple of $1,000, the amount will be rounded to the next lowest multiple of $1,000.

(d) *Election.* No education tax credit is allowed unless a taxpayer elects to claim the credit on the taxpayer's federal income tax return for the taxable year in which the credit is claimed. The election is made by attaching Form 8863, "Education Credits (Hope and Lifetime Learning Credits)," to the Federal income tax return.

(e) *Identification requirement.* No education tax credit is allowed unless a taxpayer includes on the federal income tax return claiming the credit the name and the taxpayer identification number of the student for whom the credit is claimed. For rules relating to assessment for an omission of a correct taxpayer identification number, see section 6213(b) and (g)(2)(J).

(f) *Claiming the credit in the case of a dependent*—(1) *In general.* If a student is a claimed dependent of another taxpayer, only that taxpayer may claim the education tax credit for the student's qualified tuition and related expenses. However, if another taxpayer is eligible to, but does not, claim the student as a dependent, only the student may claim the education tax credit for the student's qualified tuition and related expenses.

(2) *Examples.* The following examples illustrate the rules of this paragraph (f):

Example 1. In 1999, Taxpayer A pays qualified tuition and related expenses for his dependent, B, to attend University Y during 1999. Taxpayer A claims B as a dependent on his federal income tax return. Therefore, assuming all other relevant requirements are met, Taxpayer A is allowed an education tax credit on his federal income tax return, and B is not allowed an education tax credit on B's federal income tax return. The result would be the same if B paid the qualified tuition and related expenses. See § 1.25A-5(a).

Example 2. In 1999, Taxpayer C has one dependent, D. In 1999, D pays qualified tuition and related expenses to attend University Z during 1999. Although Taxpayer C is eligible to claim D as a dependent on her federal income tax return, she does not do so. Therefore, assuming all other relevant requirements are met, D is allowed an education tax credit on D's federal income tax return, and Taxpayer C is not allowed an education tax credit on her federal income tax return, with respect to D's education expenses. The result would be the same if C paid the qualified tuition and related expenses on behalf of D. See § 1.25A-5(b).

(g) *Married taxpayers.* If a taxpayer is married (within the meaning of section 7703), no education tax credit is allowed to the taxpayer unless the taxpayer and the taxpayer's spouse file a joint Federal income tax return for the taxable year.

* * *

[Reg. § 1.25A-1.]

☐ [*T.D.* 9034, 12-24-2002.]

§ 1.25A-2. Definitions.—(a) *Claimed dependent.* A *claimed dependent* means a dependent (as defined in section 152) for whom a deduction under section 151 is allowed on a taxpayer's federal income tax return for the taxable year. Among other requirements under section 152, a nonresident alien student must be a resident of a country contiguous to the United States in order to be treated as a dependent.

(b) *Eligible educational institution*—(1) *In general.* In general, an *eligible educational institution* means a college, university, vocational school, or other postsecondary educational institution that is—

(i) Described in section 481 of the Higher Education Act of 1965 (20 U.S.C. 1088) as in effect on August 5, 1997, (generally all accredited public, nonprofit, and proprietary postsecondary institutions); and

(ii) Participating in a federal financial aid program under title IV of the Higher Education Act of 1965 or is certified by the Department of Education as eligible to participate in such a program but chooses not to participate.

(2) *Rules on federal financial aid programs.* For rules governing an educational institution's eligibility to participate in federal financial aid programs, see 20 U.S.C. 1070; 20 U.S.C. 1094; and 34 CFR 600 and 668.

(c) *Academic period. Academic period* means a quarter, semester, trimester, or other period of study as reasonably determined by an eligible educational institution. In the case of an eligible educational institution that uses credit hours or clock hours, and does not have academic terms, each payment period (as defined in 34 CFR 668.4, revised as of July 1, 2002) may be treated as an academic period.

(d) *Qualified tuition and related expenses—*(1) *In general. Qualified tuition and related expenses* means tuition and fees required for the enrollment or attendance of a student for courses of instruction at an eligible educational institution.

(2) *Required fees—*(i) *In general.* Except as provided in paragraph (d)(3) of this section, the test for determining whether any fee is a qualified tuition and related expense is whether the fee is required to be paid to the eligible educational institution as a condition of the student's enrollment or attendance at the institution.

(ii) *Books, supplies, and equipment.* Qualified tuition and related expenses include fees for books, supplies, and equipment used in a course of study only if the fees must be paid to the eligible educational institution for the enrollment or attendance of the student at the institution.

(iii) *Nonacademic fees.* Except as provided in paragraph (d)(3) of this section, qualified tuition and related expenses include fees charged by an eligible educational institution that are not used directly for, or allocated to, an academic course of instruction only if the fee must be paid to the eligible educational institution for the enrollment or attendance of the student at the institution.

(3) *Personal expenses.* Qualified tuition and related expenses do not include the costs of room and board, insurance, medical expenses (including student health fees), transportation, and similar personal, living, or family expenses, regardless of whether the fee must be paid to the eligible educational institution for the enrollment or attendance of the student at the institution.

(4) *Treatment of a comprehensive or bundled fee.* If a student is required to pay a fee (such as a comprehensive fee or a bundled fee) to an eligible educational institution that combines charges for qualified tuition and related expenses with charges for personal expenses described in paragraph (d)(3) of this section, the portion of the fee that is allocable to personal expenses is not included in qualified tuition and related expenses. The determination of what portion of the fee relates to qualified tuition and related expenses and what portion relates to personal expenses must be made by the institution using a reasonable method of allocation.

(5) *Hobby courses.* Qualified tuition and related expenses do not include expenses that relate to any course of instruction or other education that involves sports, games, or hobbies, or any noncredit course, unless the course or other education is part of the student's degree program, or in the case of the Lifetime Learning Credit, the student takes the course to acquire or improve job skills.

(6) *Examples.* The following examples illustrate the rules of this paragraph (d). In each example, assume that the institution is an eligible educational institution and that all other relevant requirements to claim an education tax credit are met. The examples are as follows:

Example 1. University V offers a degree program in dentistry. In addition to tuition, all students enrolled in the program are required to pay a fee to University V for the rental of dental equipment. Because the equipment rental fee must be paid to University V for enrollment and attendance, the tuition and the equipment rental fee are qualified tuition and related expenses.

Example 2. First-year students at College W are required to obtain books and other reading materials used in its mandatory first-year curriculum. The books and other reading materials are not required to be purchased from College W and may be borrowed from other students or purchased from off-campus bookstores, as well as from College W's bookstore. College W bills students for any books and materials purchased from College W's bookstore. The fee that College W charges for the first-year books and materials purchased at its bookstore is not a qualified tuition and related expense because the books and materials are not required to be purchased from College W for enrollment or attendance at the institution.

Example 3. All students who attend College X are required to pay a separate student activity fee in addition to their tuition. The student activity fee is used solely to fund on-campus organizations and activities run by students, such as the student newspaper and the student government

Reg. § 1.25A-2(d)(6)

(no portion of the fee covers personal expenses). Although labeled as a student activity fee, the fee is required for enrollment or attendance at College X. Therefore, the fee is a qualified tuition and related expense.

Example 4. The facts are the same as in *Example 3,* except that College X offers an optional athletic fee that students may pay to receive discounted tickets to sports events. The athletic fee is not required for enrollment or attendance at College X. Therefore, the fee is not a qualified tuition and related expense.

Example 5. College Y requires all students to live on campus. It charges a single comprehensive fee to cover tuition, required fees, and room and board. Based on College Y's reasonable allocation, sixty percent of the comprehensive fee is allocable to tuition and other required fees not allocable to personal expenses, and the remaining forty percent of the comprehensive fee is allocable to charges for room and board and other personal expenses. Therefore, only sixty percent of College Y's comprehensive fee is a qualified tuition and related expense.

Example 6. As a degree student at College Z, Student A is required to take a certain number of courses outside of her chosen major in Economics. To fulfill this requirement, Student A enrolls in a square dancing class offered by the Physical Education Department. Because Student A receives credit toward her degree program for the square dancing class, the tuition for the square dancing class is included in qualified tuition and related expenses.

[Reg. § 1.25A-2.]

☐ [*T.D.* 9034, 12-24-2002.]

§ 1.25A-3. Hope Scholarship Credit.—(a) *Amount of the credit*—(1) *In general.* Subject to the phaseout of the education tax credit described in § 1.25A-1(c), the Hope Scholarship Credit amount is the total of—

(i) 100 percent of the first $1,000 of qualified tuition and related expenses paid during the taxable year for education furnished to an eligible student (as defined in paragraph (d) of this section) who is the taxpayer, the taxpayer's spouse, or any claimed dependent during any academic period beginning in the taxable year (or treated as beginning in the taxable year, see § 1.25A-5(e)(2)); plus

(ii) 50 percent of the next $1,000 of such expenses paid with respect to that student.

(2) *Maximum credit.* For taxable years beginning before 2002, the maximum Hope Scholarship Credit allowed for each eligible student is $1,500. For taxable years beginning after 2001, the amounts used in paragraph (a)(1) of this sec-

tion to determine the maximum credit will be increased for inflation occurring after 2000 in accordance with section 1(f)(3). If any amount adjusted under this paragraph (a)(2) is not a multiple of $100, the amount will be rounded to the next lowest multiple of $100.

(b) *Per student credit*—(1) *In general.* A Hope Scholarship Credit may be claimed for the qualified tuition and related expenses of each eligible student (as defined in paragraph (d) of this section).

(2) *Example.* The following example illustrates the rule of this paragraph (b). In the example, assume that all the requirements to claim an education tax credit are met. The example is as follows:

Example. In 1999, Taxpayer A has two dependents, B and C, both of whom are eligible students. Taxpayer A pays $1,600 in qualified tuition and related expenses for dependent B to attend a community college. Taxpayer A pays $5,000 in qualified tuition and related expenses for dependent C to attend University X. Taxpayer A may claim a Hope Scholarship Credit of $1,300 ($1,000 + (.50 × $600)) for dependent B, and the maximum $1,500 Hope Scholarship Credit for dependent C, for a total Hope Scholarship Credit of $2,800.

(c) *Credit allowed for only two taxable years.* For each eligible student, the Hope Scholarship Credit may be claimed for no more than two taxable years.

(d) *Eligible student*—(1) *Eligible student defined.* For purposes of the Hope Scholarship Credit, the term *eligible student* means a student who satisfies all of the following requirements—

(i) *Degree requirement.* For at least one academic period that begins during the taxable year, the student enrolls at an eligible educational institution in a program leading toward a postsecondary degree, certificate, or other recognized postsecondary educational credential;

(ii) *Work load requirement.* For at least one academic period that begins during the taxable year, the student enrolls for at least one-half of the normal full-time work load for the course of study the student is pursuing. The standard for what is half of the normal full-time work load is determined by each eligible educational institution. However, the standard for half-time may not be lower than the applicable standard for half-time established by the Department of Education under the Higher Education Act of 1965 and set forth in 34 CFR 674.2(b) (revised as of July 1, 2002) for a half-time undergraduate student;

(iii) *Year of study requirement.* As of the beginning of the taxable year, the student has not completed the first two years of postsecondary education at an eligible educational institution. Whether a student has completed the first two years of postsecondary education at an eligible educational institution as of the beginning of a taxable year is determined based on whether the institution in which the student is enrolled in a degree program (as described in paragraph (d)(1)(i) of this section) awards the student two years of academic credit at that institution for postsecondary course work completed by the student prior to the beginning of the taxable year. Any academic credit awarded by the eligible educational institution solely on the basis of the student's performance on proficiency examinations is disregarded in determining whether the student has completed two years of postsecondary education; and

(iv) *No felony drug conviction.* The student has not been convicted of a federal or state felony offense for possession or distribution of a controlled substance as of the end of the taxable year for which the credit is claimed.

(2) *Examples.* The following examples illustrate the rules of this paragraph (d). In each example, assume that the student has not been convicted of a felony drug offense, that the institution is an eligible educational institution unless otherwise stated, that the qualified tuition and related expenses are paid during the same taxable year that the academic period begins, and that a Hope Scholarship Credit has not previously been claimed for the student (see paragraph (c) of this section). The examples are as follows:

Example 1. Student A graduates from high school in June 1998 and is enrolled in an undergraduate degree program at College U for the 1998 Fall semester on a full-time basis. For the 1999 Spring semester, Student A again is enrolled at College U on a full-time basis. For the 1999 Fall semester, Student A is enrolled in less than half the normal full-time course work for her degree program. Because Student A is enrolled in an undergraduate degree program on at least a half-time basis for at least one academic period that begins during 1998 and at least one academic period that begins during 1999, Student A is an eligible student for taxable years 1998 and 1999 (including the 1999 Fall semester when Student A enrolls at College U on less than a half-time basis).

Example 2. Prior to 1998, Student B attended college for several years on a full-time basis. Student B transfers to College V for the 1998 Spring semester. College V awards Student B credit for some (but not all) of the courses he previously completed, and College V classifies Student B as a first-semester sophomore. During both the Spring and Fall semesters of 1998, Student B is enrolled in at least one-half the normal full-time work load for his degree program at College V. Because College V does not classify Student B as having completed the first two years of postsecondary education as of the beginning of 1998, Student B is an eligible student for taxable year 1998.

Example 3. The facts are the same as in *Example 2.* After taking classes on a half-time basis for the 1998 Spring and Fall semesters, Student B is enrolled at College V for the 1999 Spring semester on a full-time basis. College V classifies Student B as a second-semester sophomore for the 1999 Spring semester and as a first-semester junior for the 1999 Fall semester. Because College V does not classify Student B as having completed the first two years of postsecondary education as of the beginning of 1999, Student B is an eligible student for taxable year 1999. Therefore, the qualified expenses and required fees paid for the 1999 Spring semester and the 1999 Fall semester are taken into account in calculating any Hope Scholarship Credit.

Example 4. Prior to 1998, Student C was not enrolled at another eligible educational institution. At the time that Student C enrolls in a degree program at College W for the 1998 Fall semester, Student C takes examinations to demonstrate her proficiency in several subjects. On the basis of Student C's performance on these examinations, College W classifies Student C as a second-semester sophomore as of the beginning of the 1998 Fall semester. Student C is enrolled at College W during the 1998 Fall semester and during the 1999 Spring and Fall semesters on a full-time basis and is classified as a first-semester junior as of the beginning of the 1999 Spring semester. Because Student C was not enrolled in a college or other eligible educational institution prior to 1998 (but rather was awarded three semesters of academic credit solely because of proficiency examinations), Student C is not treated as having completed the first two years of postsecondary education at an eligible educational institution as of the beginning of 1998 or as of the beginning of 1999. Therefore, Student C is an eligible student for both taxable years 1998 and 1999.

Example 5. During the 1998 Fall semester, Student D is a high school student who takes classes on a half-time basis at College X. Student D is not enrolled as part of a degree program at College X because College X does not admit students to a degree program unless the student has a high school diploma or equivalent. Because Student D is not enrolled in a degree program at College X during 1998, Student D is not an eligible student for taxable year 1998.

Reg. § 1.25A-3(d)(2)

Example 6. The facts are the same as in *Example 5.* In addition, during the 1999 Spring semester, Student D again attends College X but not as part of a degree program. Student D graduates from high school in June 1999. For the 1999 Fall semester, Student D enrolls in College X as part of a degree program, and College X awards Student D credit for her prior course work at College X. During the 1999 Fall semester, Student D is enrolled in more than one-half the normal full-time work load of courses for her degree program at College X. Because Student D is enrolled in a degree program at College X for the 1999 Fall term on at least a half-time basis, Student D is an eligible student for all of taxable year 1999. Therefore, the qualified tuition and required fees paid for classes taken at College X during both the 1999 Spring semester (during which Student D was not enrolled in a degree program) and the 1999 Fall semester are taken into account in computing any Hope Scholarship Credit.

Example 7. Student E completed two years of undergraduate study at College S. College S is not an eligible educational institution for purposes of the education tax credit. At the end of 1998, Student E enrolls in an undergraduate degree program at College Z, an eligible educational institution, for the 1999 Spring semester on a full-time basis. College Z awards Student E two years of academic credit for his previous course work at College S and classifies Student E as a first-semester junior for the 1999 Spring semester. Student E is treated as having completed the first two years of postsecondary education at an eligible educational institution as of the beginning of 1999. Therefore, Student E is not an eligible student for taxable year 1999.

Example 8. Student F received a degree in 1998 from College R. College R is not an eligible educational institution for purposes of the education tax credit. During 1999, Student F is enrolled in a graduate-degree program at College Y, an eligible educational institution, for the 1999 Fall semester on a full-time basis. By admitting Student F to its graduate degree program, College Y treats Student F as having completed the first two years of postsecondary education as of the beginning of 1999. Therefore, Student F is not an eligible student for taxable year 1999.

Example 9. Student G graduates from high school in June 2001. In January 2002, Student G is enrolled in a one-year postsecondary certificate program on a full-time basis to obtain a certificate as a travel agent. Student G completes the program in December 2002 and is awarded a certificate. In January 2003, Student G enrolls in a one-year postsecondary certificate program on a full-time basis to obtain a certificate as a computer programer. Student G meets the degree require-

ment, the work load requirement, and the year of study requirement for the taxable years 2002 and 2003. Therefore, Student G is an eligible student for both taxable years 2002 and 2003.

(e) *Academic period for prepayments*—(1) *In general.* For purposes of determining whether a student meets the requirements in paragraph (d) of this section for a taxable year, if qualified tuition and related expenses are paid during one taxable year for an academic period that begins during January, February or March of the next taxable year (for taxpayers on a fiscal taxable year, use the first three months of the next taxable year), the academic period is treated as beginning during the taxable year in which the payment is made.

(2) *Example.* The following example illustrates the rule of this paragraph (e). In the example, assume that all the requirements to claim a Hope Scholarship Credit are met. The example is as follows:

Example. Student G graduates from high school in June 1998. After graduation, Student G works full-time for several months to earn money for college. Student G is enrolled on a full-time basis in an undergraduate degree program at University W, an eligible educational institution, for the 1999 Spring semester, which begins in January 1999. Student G pays tuition to University W for the 1999 Spring semester in December 1998. Because the tuition paid by Student G in 1998 relates to an academic period that begins during the first three months of 1999, Student G's eligibility to claim a Hope Scholarship Credit in 1998 is determined as if the 1999 Spring semester began in 1998. Thus, assuming Student G has not been convicted of a felony drug offense as of December 31, 1998, Student G is an eligible student for 1998.

(f) *Effective date.* The Hope Scholarship Credit is applicable for qualified tuition and related expenses paid after December 31, 1997, for education furnished in academic periods beginning after December 31, 1997. [Reg. § 1.25A-3.]

☐ [T.D. 9034, 12-24-2002 (*corrected* 4-1-2003).]

§ 1.25A-4. Lifetime Learning Credit.—(a) *Amount of the credit*—(1) *Taxable years beginning before January 1, 2003.* Subject to the phaseout of the education tax credit described in § 1.25A-1(c), for taxable years beginning before 2003, the Lifetime Learning Credit amount is 20 percent of up to $5,000 of qualified tuition and related expenses paid during the taxable year for education furnished to the taxpayer, the taxpayer's spouse, and any claimed dependent during any academic period beginning in the taxable year (or treated as beginning in the taxable year, see § 1.25A-5(e)(2)).

(2) *Taxable years beginning after December 31, 2002.* Subject to the phaseout of the education tax credit described in § 1.25A-1(c), for taxable years beginning after 2002, the Lifetime Learning Credit amount is 20 percent of up to $10,000 of qualified tuition and related expenses paid during the taxable year for education furnished to the taxpayer, the taxpayer's spouse, and any claimed dependent during any academic period beginning in the taxable year (or treated as beginning in the taxable year, see § 1.25A-5(e)(2)).

(3) *Coordination with the Hope Scholarship Credit.* Expenses paid with respect to a student for whom the Hope Scholarship Credit is claimed are not eligible for the Lifetime Learning Credit.

(4) *Examples.* The following examples illustrate the rules of this paragraph (a). In each example, assume that all the requirements to claim a Lifetime Learning Credit or a Hope Scholarship Credit, as applicable, are met. The examples are as follows:

Example 1. In 1999, Taxpayer A pays qualified tuition and related expenses of $3,000 for dependent B to attend an eligible educational institution, and Taxpayer A pays qualified tuition and related expenses of $4,000 for dependent C to attend an eligible educational institution. Taxpayer A does not claim a Hope Scholarship Credit with respect to either B or C. Although Taxpayer A paid $7,000 of qualified tuition and related expenses during the taxable year, Taxpayer A may claim the Lifetime Learning Credit with respect to only $5,000 of such expenses. Therefore, the maximum Lifetime Learning Credit Taxpayer A may claim for 1999 is $1,000 (.20 × $5,000).

Example 2. In 1999, Taxpayer D pays $6,000 of qualified tuition and related expenses for dependent E, and $2,000 of qualified tuition and related expenses for dependent F, to attend eligible educational institutions. Dependent F has already completed the first two years of postsecondary education. For 1999, Taxpayer D claims the maximum $1,500 Hope Scholarship Credit with respect to dependent E. In computing the amount of the Lifetime Learning Credit, Taxpayer D may not include any of the $6,000 of qualified tuition and related expenses paid on behalf of dependent E but may include the $2,000 of qualified tuition and related expenses of dependent F.

(b) *Credit allowed for unlimited number of taxable years.* There is no limit to the number of taxable years that a taxpayer may claim a Lifetime Learning Credit with respect to any student.

(c) *Both degree and nondegree courses are eligible for the credit*—(1) *In general.* For purposes of the Lifetime Learning Credit, amounts paid for a course at an eligible educational institution are qualified tuition and related expenses if the course is either part of a postsecondary degree program or is not part of a postsecondary degree program but is taken by the student to acquire or improve job skills.

(2) *Examples.* The following examples illustrate the rule of this paragraph (c). In each example, assume that all the requirements to claim a Lifetime Learning Credit are met. The examples are as follows:

Example 1. Taxpayer A, a professional photographer, enrolls in an advanced photography course at a local community college. Although the course is not part of a degree program, Taxpayer A enrolls in the course to improve her job skills. The course fee paid by Taxpayer A is a qualified tuition and related expense for purposes of the Lifetime Learning Credit.

Example 2. Taxpayer B, a stockbroker, plans to travel abroad on a "photo-safari" for his next vacation. In preparation for the trip, Taxpayer B enrolls in a noncredit photography class at a local community college. Because Taxpayer B is not taking the photography course as part of a degree program or to acquire or improve his job skills, amounts paid by Taxpayer B for the course are not qualified tuition and related expenses for purposes of the Lifetime Learning Credit.

(d) *Effective date.* The Lifetime Learning Credit is applicable for qualified tuition and related expenses paid after June 30, 1998, for education furnished in academic periods beginning after June 30, 1998. [Reg. § 1.25A-4.]

□ [*T.D.* 9034, 12-24-2002.]

§ 1.25A-5. Special rules relating to characterization and timing of payments.—(a) *Educational expenses paid by claimed dependent.* For any taxable year for which the student is a claimed dependent of another taxpayer, qualified tuition and related expenses paid by the student are treated as paid by the taxpayer to whom the deduction under section 151 is allowed.

(b) *Educational expenses paid by a third party*—(1) *In general.* Solely for purposes of section 25A, if a third party (someone other than the taxpayer, the taxpayer's spouse if the taxpayer is treated as married within the meaning of section 7703, or a claimed dependent) makes a payment directly to an eligible educational institution to pay for a student's qualified tuition and related expenses, the student is treated as receiving the payment from the third party and, in turn, paying the qualified tuition and related expenses to the institution.

(2) *Special rule for tuition reduction included in gross income of employee.* Solely for purposes of section 25A, if an eligible educational institution provides a reduction in tuition to an employee of the institution (or to the spouse or dependent child of an employee, as described in section 132(h)(2)) and the amount of the tuition reduction is included in the employee's gross income, the employee is treated as receiving payment of an amount equal to the tuition reduction and, in turn, paying such amount to the institution.

(3) *Examples.* The following examples illustrate the rules of this paragraph (b). In each example, assume that all the requirements to claim an education tax credit are met. The examples are as follows:

Example 1. Grandparent D makes a direct payment to an eligible educational institution for Student E's qualified tuition and related expenses. Student E is not a claimed dependent in 1999. For purposes of claiming an education tax credit, Student E is treated as receiving the money from her grandparent and, in turn, paying her qualified tuition and related expenses.

Example 2. Under a court-approved divorce decree, Parent A is required to pay Student C's college tuition. Parent A makes a direct payment to an eligible educational institution for Student C's 1999 tuition. Under paragraph (b)(1) of this section, Student C is treated as receiving the money from Parent A and, in turn, paying the qualified tuition and related expenses. Under the divorce decree, Parent B has custody of Student C for 1999. Parent B properly claims Student C as a dependent on Parent B's 1999 federal income tax return. Under paragraph (a) of this section, expenses paid by Student C are treated as paid by Parent B. Thus, Parent B may claim an education tax credit for the qualified tuition and related expenses paid directly to the institution by Parent A.

Example 3. University A, an eligible educational institution, offers reduced tuition charges to its employees and their dependent children. F is an employee of University A. F's dependent child, G, enrolls in a graduate-level course at University A. Section 117(d) does not apply, because it is limited to tuition reductions provided for education below the graduate level. Therefore, the amount of the tuition reduction received by G is treated as additional compensation from University A to F and is included in F's gross income. For purposes of claiming a Lifetime Learning Credit, F is treated as receiving payment of an amount equal to the tuition reduction from University A and, in turn, paying such amount to University A on behalf of F's child, G.

(c) *Adjustment to qualified tuition and related expenses for certain excludable educational assistance*—(1) *In general.* In determining the amount of an education tax credit, qualified tuition and related expenses for any academic period must be reduced by the amount of any tax-free educational assistance allocable to such period. For this purpose, *tax-free educational assistance* means—

(i) A qualified scholarship that is excludable from income under section 117;

(ii) A veterans' or member of the armed forces' educational assistance allowance under chapter 30, 31, 32, 34 or 35 of title 38, United States Code, or under chapter 1606 of title 10, United States Code;

(iii) Employer-provided educational assistance that is excludable from income under section 127; or

(iv) Any other educational assistance that is excludable from gross income (other than as a gift, bequest, devise, or inheritance within the meaning of section 102(a)).

(2) *No adjustment for excludable educational assistance attributable to expenses paid in a prior year.* A reduction is not required under paragraph (c)(1) of this section if the amount of excludable educational assistance received during the taxable year is treated as a refund of qualified tuition and related expenses paid in a prior taxable year. See paragraph (f)(5) of this section.

(3) *Scholarships and fellowship grants.* For purposes of paragraph (c)(1)(i) of this section, a scholarship or fellowship grant is treated as a qualified scholarship excludable under section 117 except to the extent—

(i) The scholarship or fellowship grant (or any portion thereof) may be applied, by its terms, to expenses other than qualified tuition and related expenses within the meaning of section 117(b)(2) (such as room and board) and the student reports the grant (or the appropriate portion thereof) as income on the student's federal income tax return if the student is required to file a return; or

(ii) The scholarship or fellowship grant (or any portion thereof) must be applied, by its terms, to expenses other than qualified tuition and related expenses within the meaning of section 117(b)(2) (such as room and board) and the student reports the grant (or the appropriate portion thereof) as income on the student's federal income tax return if the student is required to file a return.

(4) *Examples.* The following examples illustrate the rules of this paragraph (c). In each example, assume that all the requirements to

Reg. § 1.25A-5(b)(2)

claim an education tax credit are met. The examples are as follows:

Example 1. University X charges Student A, who lives on University X's campus, $3,000 for tuition and $5,000 for room and board. University X awards Student A a $2,000 scholarship. The terms of the scholarship permit it to be used to pay any of a student's costs of attendance at University X, including tuition, room and board, and other incidental expenses. University X applies the $2,000 scholarship against Student A's $8,000 total bill, and Student A pays the $6,000 balance of her bill from University X with a combination of savings and amounts she earns from a summer job. University X does not require A to pay any additional fees beyond the $3,000 in tuition in order to enroll in or attend classes. Student A does not report any portion of the scholarship as income on her federal income tax return. Since Student A does not report the scholarship as income, the scholarship is treated under paragraph (c)(3) of this section as a qualified scholarship that is excludable under section 117. Therefore, for purposes of calculating an education tax credit, Student A is treated as having paid only $1,000 ($3,000 tuition − $2,000 scholarship) in qualified tuition and related expenses to University X.

Example 2. The facts are the same as in *Example 1*, except that Student A reports the entire scholarship as income on the student's federal income tax return. Since the full amount of the scholarship may be applied to expenses other than qualified expenses (room and board) and Student A reports the scholarship as income, the exception in paragraph (c)(3) of this section applies and the scholarship is not treated as a qualified scholarship excludable under section 117. Therefore, for purposes of calculating an education tax credit, Student A is treated as having paid $3,000 of qualified tuition and related expenses to University X.

Example 3. The facts are the same as in *Example 1*, except that the terms of the scholarship require it to be used to pay tuition. Under paragraph (c)(3) of this section, the scholarship is treated as a qualified scholarship excludable under section 117. Therefore, for purposes of calculating an education tax credit, Student A is treated as having paid only $1,000 ($3,000 tuition − $2,000 scholarship) in qualified tuition and related expenses to University X.

Example 4. The facts are the same as in *Example 1*, except that the terms of the scholarship require it to be used to pay tuition or room and board charged by University X, and the scholarship amount is $6,000. Under the terms of the scholarship, Student A may allocate the schol-arship between tuition and room and board in any manner. However, because room and board totals $5,000, that is the maximum amount that can be applied under the terms of the scholarship to expenses other than qualified expenses and at least $1,000 of the scholarship must be applied to tuition. Therefore, the maximum amount of the exception under paragraph (c)(3) of this section is $5,000 and at least $1,000 is treated as a qualified scholarship excludable under section 117 ($6,000 scholarship − $5,000 room and board). If Student A reports $5,000 of the scholarship as income on the student's federal income tax return, then Student A will be treated as having paid $2,000 ($3,000 tuition − $1,000 qualified scholarship excludable under section 117) in qualified tuition and related expenses to University X.

Example 5. The facts are the same as in *Example 1*, except that in addition to the scholarship that University X awards to Student A, University X also provides Student A with an education loan and pays Student A for working in a work/study job in the campus dining hall. The loan is not excludable educational assistance within the meaning of paragraph (c) of this section. In addition, wages paid to a student who is performing services for the payor are neither a qualified scholarship nor otherwise excludable from gross income. Therefore, Student A is not required to reduce her qualified tuition and related expenses by the amounts she receives from the student loan or as wages from her work/study job.

Example 6. In 1999, Student B pays University Y $1,000 in tuition for the 1999 Spring semester. University Y does not require Student B to pay any additional fees beyond the $1,000 in tuition in order to enroll in classes. Student B is an employee of Company Z. At the end of the academic period and during the same taxable year that Student B paid tuition to University Y, Student B provides Company Z with proof that he has satisfactorily completed his courses at University Y. Pursuant to an educational assistance program described in section 127(b), Company Z reimburses Student B for all of the tuition paid to University Y. Because the reimbursement from Company Z is employer-provided educational assistance that is excludable from Student B's gross income under section 127, the reimbursement reduces Student B's qualified tuition and related expenses. Therefore, for purposes of calculating an education tax credit, Student B is treated as having paid no qualified tuition and related expenses to University Y during 1999.

Example 7. The facts are the same as in *Example 6* except that the reimbursement from Company Z is not pursuant to an educational assistance program described in section 127(b), is

Reg. § 1.25A-5(c)(4)

not otherwise excludable from Student B's gross income, and is taxed as additional compensation to Student B. Because the reimbursement is not excludable educational assistance within the meaning of paragraph (c)(1) of this section, Student B is not required to reduce his qualified tuition and related expenses by the $1,000 reimbursement he received from his employer. Therefore, for purposes of calculating an education tax credit, Student B is treated as paying $1,000 in qualified tuition and related expenses to University Y during 1999.

(d) *No double benefit.* Qualified tuition and related expenses do not include any expense for which a deduction is allowed under section 162, section 222, or any other provision of chapter 1 of the Internal Revenue Code.

(e) *Timing rules*—(1) *In general.* Except as provided in paragraph (e)(2) of this section, an education tax credit is allowed only for payments of qualified tuition and related expenses for an academic period beginning in the same taxable year as the year the payment is made. Except for certain individuals who do not use the cash receipts and disbursements method of accounting, qualified tuition and related expenses are treated as paid in the year in which the expenses are actually paid. See § 1.461-1(a)(1).

(2) *Prepayment rule*—(i) *In general.* If qualified tuition and related expenses are paid during one taxable year for an academic period that begins during the first three months of the taxpayer's next taxable year (i.e., in January, February, or March of the next taxable year for calendar year taxpayers), an education tax credit is allowed with respect to the qualified tuition and related expenses only in the taxable year in which the expenses are paid.

(ii) *Example.* The following example illustrates the rule of this paragraph (e)(2). In the example, assume that all the requirements to claim an education tax credit are met. The example is as follows:

Example. In December 1998, Taxpayer A, a calendar year taxpayer, pays College Z $1,000 in qualified tuition and related expenses to attend classes during the 1999 Spring semester, which begins in January 1999. Taxpayer A may claim an education tax credit only in 1998 for payments made in 1998 for the 1999 Spring semester.

(3) *Expenses paid with loan proceeds.* An education tax credit may be claimed for qualified tuition and related expenses paid with the proceeds of a loan only in the taxable year in which the expenses are paid, and may not be claimed in the taxable year in which the loan is repaid. Loan proceeds disbursed directly to an eligible educational institution will be treated as paid on the date the institution credits the proceeds to the student's account. For example, in the case of any loan issued or guaranteed as part of a federal student loan program under Title IV of the Higher Education Act of 1965, loan proceeds will be treated as paid on the date of disbursement (as defined in 34 CFR 668.164(a), revised as of July 1, 2002) by the eligible educational institution. If a taxpayer does not know the date the institution credits the student's account, the taxpayer must treat the qualified tuition and related expenses as paid on the last date for payment prescribed by the institution.

(4) *Expenses paid through third party installment payment plans*—(i) *In general.* A taxpayer, an eligible educational institution, and a third party installment payment company may enter into an agreement in which the company agrees to collect installment payments of qualified tuition and related expenses from the taxpayer and to remit the installment payments to the institution. If the third party installment payment company is the taxpayer's agent for purposes of paying qualified tuition and related expenses to the eligible educational institution, the taxpayer is treated as paying the qualified expenses on the date the company pays the institution. However, if the third party installment payment company is the eligible educational institution's agent for purposes of collecting payments of qualified tuition and related expenses from the taxpayer, the taxpayer is treated as paying the qualified expenses on the date the taxpayer pays the company.

(ii) *Example.* The following example illustrates the rule of this paragraph (e)(4). The example is as follows:

Example. Student A, Company B, and College C enter into a written agreement in which Student A agrees to pay the tuition required to attend College C in 10 equal monthly installments to Company B. Under the written agreement, Student A is not relieved of her obligation to pay College C until Company B remits the payments to College C. Under the written agreement, Company B agrees to disburse the monthly installment payments to College C within 30 days of receipt. Because Company B acts as Student A's agent for purposes of paying qualified expenses to College C, Student A is treated as paying qualified expenses on the date Company B disburses payments to College C.

* * *

[Reg. § 1.25A-5.]

☐ [*T.D.* 9034, 12-24-2002 (*corrected* 4-1-2003).]

Reg. § 1.25A-5(d)

[*Note: In July of 1984 Section 44A was renumbered as Section 21.*]

§ 1.44A-1. Expenses for household and dependent care services necessary for gainful employment.—

* * *

(c) *Employment-related expenses*—(1) *Gainful employment*—(i) *In general.* Expenses are considered to be employment-related expenses only if they are incurred to enable the taxpayer to be gainfully employed and are paid for household services or for the care of one or more qualifying individuals. The expenses must be incurred while the taxpayer is gainfully employed or is in active search of gainful employment. The employment may consist of service either within or without the home of the taxpayer and may include self-employment. An expense is not considered to be employment-related merely because it is incurred while the taxpayer is gainfully employed. The purpose of the expense must be to enable the taxpayer to be gainfully employed. Volunteer work for a nominal salary does not constitute gainful employment. Whether the purpose of an expense is to enable the taxpayer to be gainfully employed depends upon the facts and circumstances of the particular case. Any tax required to be paid by the taxpayer under sections 3111 (relating to the Federal Insurance Contributions Act) and 3301 (relating to the Federal Unemployment Tax Act), or under similar State payroll taxes, in respect of any wages which otherwise constitute employment-related expenses is considered to be an employment-related expense.

(ii) *Determination of period of employment on a daily basis.* An allocation of expenses is required on a daily basis when the expenses cover any period during part of which the taxpayer is gainfully employed or is in active search of gainful employment and during the other part of which there is no employment or active search for gainful employment. Thus, for example, if a taxpayer incurs during each month of the taxable year $60 of expenses which would be employment-related if he or she were gainfully employed all year, and the taxpayer is gainfully employed, or in active search of gainful employment, for only 2 months and 10 days during such year, the amount of employment-related expenses is limited to $140.

(2) *Household services.* Expenses are considered to be paid for household services is they are paid for the performance in and about the taxpayer's home of ordinary and usual services necessary to the maintenance of the household. However, expenses are not considered as paid for household services unless the expenses are attributable in part to the care of the qualifying individual. Thus, amounts paid for the services of a domestic maid or cook are considered to be expenses paid for household services if a part of those services is provided to the qualifying individual. Amounts paid for the services of an individual who is employed as a chauffeur, bartender, or gardener, however, are not considered to be expenses paid for household services.

(3) *Care of qualifying individual.*—(i) *In general.* The primary purpose of expenses for the care of a qualifying individual must be to assure that individual's well-being and protection. Not all benefits bestowed upon a qualifying individual are considered as provided for the individual's care. Accordingly, amounts paid to provide food, clothing, or education are not expenses paid for the care of a qualifying individual. However, where the manner of providing care is such that the expense which is incurred includes expenses for other benefits which are incident to and inseparably a part of the care, the full amount of the expense is considered to be incurred for care. Thus, for example, the full amount paid to a nursery school in which a qualifying child is enrolled is considered as being for the care of the child, even though the school also furnishes lunch and educational services. Educational expenses incurred for a child in the first or higher grade level are not expenses incurred for the care of a qualifying individual. Expenses incurred for transportation of a qualifying individual described in paragraph (b)(1)(i) of this section between the taxpayer's household and a place outside the taxpayer's household where services for the care of the qualifying individual are provided are not incurred for the care of a qualifying individual.

(ii) *Manner of providing care.* The manner of providing the care need not be the least expensive alternative available to the taxpayer. For example, the taxpayer's mother may reside at the taxpayer's home and be available to provide adequate care at no cost for the taxpayer's wife who is physically or mentally incapable of caring for herself. Nevertheless, the expenses incurred in providing a nurse for the wife may be an expense for the care of the wife. See paragraph (c)(1)(i) of this section with respect to the requirement that the expense must be for the purpose of permitting the taxpayer to be gainfully employed.

(4) *Services outside the taxpayer's household.* The credit is allowed under section 44A with respect to employment-related expenses incurred for services performed outside the taxpayer's household only if those expenses are incurred for the care of—

(i) One or more qualifying individuals who are described in paragraph (b)(1)(i) of this section; or

(ii) One or more qualifying individuals (as to expenses incurred for taxable years beginning after December 31, 1981) who are described in paragraph (b)(1)(ii) or (iii) of this section and who regularly spend at least 8 hours each day in the taxpayer's household.

(5) *Dependent care centers.* The credit is allowed under section 44A with respect to employment-related expenses incurred in taxable years beginning after December 31, 1981, for services provided outside the taxpayer's household by a dependent care center only if—

(i) The center complies with all applicable laws and regulations of a State or unit of local government (*e.g.,* State or local requirements for licensing, if applicable, and building and fire Code regulations); and

(ii) The requirement provided in paragraph (c)(4)(i) or (ii) of this section is met.

The term "dependent care center" means any facility that provides full-time or part-time care for more than six individuals (other than residents of the facility) on a regular basis during the taxpayer's taxable year, and receives a fee, payment, or grant for providing services for any such individuals (regardless of whether such facility is operated for profit). For purposes of the preceding sentence, a facility will be presumed to provide full-time or part-time care for six or less individuals on a regular basis during the taxpayer's taxable year if the facility has six or less individuals (including the qualifying individual) enrolled for full-time or part-time care on the day the qualifying individual is enrolled in the facility (or on the first day of the taxable year the qualifying individual attends the facility in the case where the individual was enrolled in the facility in the preceding taxable year) unless the Internal Revenue Service demonstrates that the facility provides full-time or part-time care for more than six individuals on a regular basis during the taxpayer's taxable year.

(6) *Allocation of expenses.* Where a portion of an expense is for household services or for the care of a qualifying individual and a portion of such expense is for other purposes, a reasonable allocation must be made and only the portion of the expense paid which is attributable to such household services or care is considered to be an employment-related expense. No allocation is required to be made, however, if the portion of expense for the other purpose is minimal or insignificant. An allocation must be made, for example, if a servant performs household duties, cares for the qualifying children of the taxpayer, and also performs social services for the taxpayer (for which a deduction is not allowable) or clerical

services in the office of the taxpayer outside the home (for which a deduction may be allowable under section 162). Employment-related expenses include household service expenses which are provided in conjunction with the care of a qualifying individual. Thus, if an expense is in part attributable to the care of a qualifying individual and in part to household services, no allocation is required.

(7) *Illustrations.* The application of this paragraph (c) may be illustrated by the following examples:

Example (1). The taxpayer lives with her mother who is physically incapable of caring for herself. In order to be gainfully employed the taxpayer hires a practical nurse whose sole duty consists of providing for the care of the mother in the home while the taxpayer is at work. All amounts spent for the services of the nurse are employment-related expenses.

Example (2). The taxpayer has a dependent child 10 years of age who has been attending public school. The taxpayer, who has been working part time, is offered a position involving full-time employment which she can accept only if the child is placed in a boarding school. The taxpayer accepts the position and the child is sent to a boarding school. The expenses paid to the school must be allocated between that part of the expenses which represents care for the child and that part which represents tuition for education. The part of the expense representing care of the child is incurred for the purpose of permitting the taxpayer to be gainfully employed.

Example (3). The taxpayer, in order to be gainfully employed, employs a full-time housekeeper who cares for the taxpayer's two children, aged 9 and 15 years, respectively, performs regular household services of cleaning and cooking, and chauffeurs the taxpayer to and from his place of employment. The chauffeuring service never requires more than 30 minutes out of the total period of employment each day. No allocation is required for purposes of determining the portion of the expense attributable to the chauffeuring (not a household service expense) since it is *de minimis*. Further, no allocation is required for the purpose of determining the portion of the expense attributable to the care of the 15 year old child (not a qualifying individual) since the household expense is in part attributable to the care of the 9 year old child, who is a qualifying individual. Accordingly, the entire expense of employing the housekeeper is an employment-related expense. However, the total amount of employment-related expenses taken into account would be limited to the amount allowable for one qualifying individual.

Reg. § 1.44A-1(c)(5)

(d) *Maintenance of a household*—(1) *In general.* An individual is considered to have maintained a household for the taxable year (or lesser period) only if the individual (and his or her spouse if the individual is married) have furnished over one-half of the cost incurred for such taxable year (or lesser period) in maintaining the household. The household must actually constitute for the taxable year the principal place of abode of the taxpayer and the qualifying individual or individuals described in paragraph (b) of this section. It is not sufficient that the taxpayer maintain the household without being its occupant. A physical change in the location of the home does not, however, prevent the home from constituting the principal place of abode of the taxpayer and a qualifying individual. The fact that an individual is born or dies during the taxable year does not prevent a home from constituting his or her principal place of abode for such year. An individual is not considered to have terminated a household as his or her principal place of abode merely by reason of temporary absences therefrom by reason of illness, education, business, vacation, military service, or a custody agreement.

(2) *Two or more families.* Solely for purposes of section 44A and this section, if two or more families occupy living quarters in common, each of the families is treated as constituting a separate household, and the taxpayer who provides more than one-half of the costs of maintaining such a separate household is treated as maintaining that household. Thus, for example, if two unrelated taxpayers each with children occupy living quarters in common and each taxpayer pays more than one-half of the household costs incurred by each respective family, each taxpayer will be treated as maintaining a separate household.

(3) *Costs of maintaining a household.* The costs of maintaining a household are the expenses incurred for the mutual benefit of the occupants thereof by reason of its operation as the principal place of abode of the occupants. The expenses of maintaining a household include property taxes, mortgage interest, rent, utility charges, upkeep and repairs, property insurance, and food consumed on the premises. These expenses do not include the cost of clothing, education, medical treatment, vacations, life insurance, or transportation or payments on mortgage principal or for the purchase, permanent improvement, betterment, or replacement of property. Further, the costs of maintaining a household do not include the value of services performed in the household by a qualifying individual described in paragraph (b) of this section. An expense incurred by a taxpayer which is paid or reimbursed by another is not considered as a cost of maintaining a household.

(4) *Monthly proration of annual costs.* In determining the cost incurred for a period of less than a taxable year in maintaining a household, the cost incurred during the entire taxable year must be prorated on the basis of the number of calendar months within such lesser period. For this purpose a period of less than a calendar month will be treated as a calendar month. Thus, for example, if the cost of maintaining a household for a taxable year is $6,600, and the period in respect of which a determination is being made under section 44A is from June 20 to December 31, the taxpayer must furnish more than $1,925 [$6,000 × 7/12] × 50%) in maintaining the household from June 1 to December 31.

(e) *Substantiation.* A taxpayer claiming a credit under paragraph (a) of this section for employment-related expenses must substantiate by adequate records or other sufficient evidence any credit taken under this section. For example, if requested, the taxpayer must furnish information as to the nature and period of the physical or mental incapacity of any dependent or spouse in respect of whom a credit is claimed, including necessary information from the attending physician as to the nature of the physical or mental incapacity. [Reg. § 1.44A-1.]

☐ [*T.D.* 7643, 8-27-79. *Amended by T.D.* 7951, 4-26-84.]

Alternative Minimum Tax

§ 1.55-1. Alternative minimum taxable income.—(a) *General rule for computing alternative minimum taxable income.* Except as otherwise provided by statute, regulations, or other published guidance issued by the Commissioner, all Internal Revenue Code provisions that apply in determining the regular taxable income of a taxpayer also apply in determining the alternative minimum taxable income of the taxpayer.

(b) *Items based on adjusted gross income or modified adjusted gross income.* In determining the alternative minimum taxable income of a taxpayer other than a corporation, all references to the taxpayer's adjusted gross income or modified adjusted gross income in determining the amount of items of income, exclusion, or deduction must be treated as references to the taxpayer's adjusted gross income or modified adjusted gross income as determined for regular tax purposes.

* * *

[Reg. § 1.55-1.]

☐ [*T.D.* 8569, 11-23-94.]

§ 1.56(g)-1. **Adjusted current earnings.**—(a) *Adjustment for adjusted current earnings*—(1) *Positive adjustment.* For taxable years beginning after December 31, 1989, the alternative minimum taxable income of any taxpayer described in paragraph (a)(4) of this section is increased by the adjustment for adjusted current earnings. The adjustment for adjusted current earnings is 75 percent of the excess, if any, of—

(i) The adjusted current earnings (as defined in paragraph (a)(6)(ii) of this section) of the inventories to compute adjusted current earnings.taxpayer for the taxable year over

(ii) The pre-adjustment alternative minimum taxable income (as defined in paragraph (a)(6)(i) of this section) of the taxpayer for the taxable year.

(2) *Negative adjustment*—(i) *In general.* For taxable years beginning after December 31, 1989, the alternative minimum taxable income of any taxpayer is decreased, subject to the limitation of paragraph (a)(2)(ii) of this section, by 75 percent of the excess, if any, of pre-adjustment alternative minimum taxable income (as defined in paragraph (a)(6)(i) of this section), over adjusted current earnings (as defined in paragraph (a)(6)(ii) of this section).

(ii) *Limitation on negative adjustments.* The amount of the negative adjustment for any taxable year is limited to the excess, if any, of —

(A) The aggregate increases in alternative minimum taxable income in prior years under paragraph (a)(1) of this section over

(B) The aggregate decreases in alternative minimum taxable income in prior years under this paragraph (a)(2).

Any excess of pre-adjustment alternative minimum taxable income over adjusted current earnings that is not allowed as a negative adjustment for the taxable year because of the limitation in this paragraph (a)(2)(ii) is not applied to reduce any positive adjustment in any other taxable year.

(iii) *Example.* The following example illustrates the provisions of this paragraph (a)(2):

(A) Corporation P is a calendar-year taxpayer and has pre-adjustment alternative minimum taxable income and adjusted current earnings in the following amounts for 1990 through 1993:

Year	Pre-adjustment alternative minimum taxable income	Adjusted current earnings
1990	$800,000	$700,000
1991	600,000	900,000
1992	500,000	400,000
1993	500,000	100,000

(B) Under these facts, corporation P has the following positive and negative adjustments for adjusted current earnings:

Year	Negative adjustment	Positive adjustment
1990	–0–	–0–
1991	–0–	$225,000
1992	$ 75,000	–0–
1993	150,000	–0–

(C) In 1990, P has a potential negative adjustment (before the cumulative limitation) of $75,000 (75 percent of the $100,000 excess of pre-adjustment alternative minimum taxable income over adjusted current earnings). Nonetheless, P is not permitted a negative adjustment because P had no prior increases in its alternative minimum taxable income due to an adjustment for adjusted current earnings.

(D) In 1991, P has a positive adjustment of $225,000 (75 percent of the $300,000 excess of adjusted current earnings over pre-adjustment alternative minimum taxable income). P is not allowed to use the prior year's excess of pre-adjustment alternative minimum taxable income over adjusted current earnings to reduce its 1991 positive adjustment.

(E) In 1992, P is permitted a negative adjustment of $75,000, the full amount of 75 percent of the $100,000 excess of pre-adjustment alternative minimum taxable income over adjusted current earnings for the taxable year. This is because P's prior cumulative increases in alternative minimum taxable income due to the positive adjustments for adjusted current earnings exceed the negative adjustment for the year.

(F) In 1993, P has a potential negative adjustment (before the cumulative limitation) of $300,000 (75 percent of the $400,000 excess of pre-adjustment alternative minimum taxable income over adjusted current earnings). P's net cumulative increases in alternative minimum taxable income due to the adjustment for adjusted current earnings are $150,000 ($225,000 increase in 1991, less $75,000 decrease in 1992). Thus, P's Positive adjustment negative adjustment in 1993 is limited to $150,000. P may not use the remaining portion ($150,000) of the negative adjustment for 1993 to reduce positive adjustments in other taxable years.

(3) *Negative amounts.* In determining whether an excess exists under paragraph (a)(1) or (a)(2) of this section, a positive amount exceeds a negative amount by the sum of the absolute numbers, and a smaller negative amount exceeds a larger negative amount by the difference between the absolute numbers. Thus, for example, a positive amount of adjusted current earnings of $30 exceeds a negative amount (or loss) of pre-adjustment AMTI of $10 by the sum of the abso-

Reg. § 1.56(g)-1(a)(1)

lute numbers, or $40 (30 + 10). Accordingly, the adjustment for adjusted current earnings would be 75 percent of $40, or $30. In contrast, a negative amount of adjusted current earnings of $10 exceeds a negative amount (or loss) of pre-adjustment alternative minimum taxable income of $30 by the difference between the absolute numbers, or $20 (30 − 10). Accordingly, the adjustment for adjusted current earnings would be 75 percent of $20, or $15.

(4) *Taxpayers subject to adjustment for adjusted current earnings.* The adjustment for adjusted current earnings applies to any corporation other than—

(i) An S corporation as defined in section 1361,

(ii) A regulated investment company as defined in section 851,

(iii) A real estate investment trust as defined in section 856, or

(iv) A real estate mortgage investment conduit as defined in section 860A.

(5) *General rule for applying Internal Revenue Code provisions in determining adjusted current earnings*—(i) *In general.* Except as otherwise provided by regulations or other guidance issued by the Internal Revenue Service, all Internal Revenue Code provisions that apply in determining the regular taxable income of a taxpayer also apply in determining adjusted current earnings. For example, the rules of part V of subchapter P (relating to original issue discount and similar matters) of the Code apply in determining the amount (and the timing) of any interest income included in adjusted current earnings under this section. In applying Code provisions, however, the adjustments of section 56(g) and this section are also taken into account. For example, in applying the capitalization provisions of section 263A, the amount of depreciation to be capitalized is based on the amount of depreciation allowed in computing adjusted current earnings.

(ii) *Example.* The following example illustrates the provisions of this paragraph (a)(5):

(A) Corporation N is a calendar year manufacturer of golf clubs. N places new manufacturing equipment in service in 1990. The regular tax depreciation allowable for this equipment is $80,000; the pre-adjustment alternative minimum taxable income depreciation is $60,000; and the adjusted current earnings depreciation is $40,000. All of the golf clubs N produces in 1990 are unsold and are in ending inventory.

(B) Pursuant to section 263A and § 1.263A-1(e)(3)(ii)(I), N must capitalize the depreciation allowed for the year for the new manufacturing equipment in the ending inventory of golf clubs. Thus, when N sells the golf clubs (or is deemed to have sold them under its normal method of accounting), the cost of goods sold attributable to the capitalized depreciation will be $80,000 in computing regular taxable income; $60,000 in computing pre-adjustment alternative minimum taxable income; and $40,000 in computing adjusted current earnings.

(6) *Definitions.* The following terms have the following meanings for purposes of this section.

(i) *Pre-adjustment alternative minimum taxable income.* Pre-adjustment alternative minimum taxable income is the alternative minimum taxable income of the taxpayer for the taxable year, determined under section 55(b)(2), but without the adjustment for adjusted current earnings under section 56(g) and this section, without the alternative tax net operating loss deduction under section 56(a)(4), and without the alternative tax energy preference deduction under section 56(h).

(ii) *Adjusted current earnings.* Adjusted current earnings is the pre-adjustment alternative minimum taxable income of the taxpayer for the taxable year, adjusted as provided in section 56(g) and this section. To the extent an amount is included (or deducted) in computing pre-adjustment alternative minimum taxable income for the taxable year (whether because an adjustment is made under section 56 or 58, because of a tax preference item under section 57, or because the item is reflected in taxable income), that amount is not again included (or deducted) in computing adjusted current earnings for the taxable year.

(iii) *Earnings and profits.* Earnings and profits means current earnings and profits within the meaning of section 316(a)(2), that is, earnings and profits for the taxable year computed as of the close of the taxable year of the corporation without diminution by reason of any distributions made during the taxable year.

(7) *Application to foreign corporations.* See paragraph (m) of this section for rules relating to the application of this section to foreign corporations.

(b) *Depreciation allowed.* The depreciation deduction allowed in computing adjusted current earnings is determined under the rules of this paragraph (b). Generally, the rules for computing the adjusted current earnings depreciation deduction differ depending on the taxable year in which the property is placed in service and the method used in computing the depreciation deduction for taxable income purposes. See § 1.168(i)-1(k) for an election to use general asset accounts.

(1) *Property placed in service after 1989.* The depreciation deduction for property placed in service in a taxable year beginning after December 31, 1989, is the amount determined by using

Reg. § 1.56(g)-1(b)(1)

the alternative depreciation system of section 168(g). This paragraph (b)(1) does not apply to property to which paragraph (b)(4) of this section applies (relating to certain property described in sections 168(f)(1) through (f)(4)).

(2) *Property subject to new ACRS*—(i) *In general*. This paragraph (b)(2) provides the rules for computing the depreciation deduction for property to which the amendments made by section 201 of the Tax Reform Act of 1986 (new ACRS) apply (generally property placed in service after December 31, 1986), and that is placed in service in a taxable year beginning before January 1, 1990. This paragraph (b)(2) does not apply to property described in paragraph (b)(4) of this section (relating to certain property described in sections 168(f)(1) through (f)(4)) or to property described in paragraph (b)(5)(i) of this section (relating to certain churning transactions described in section 168(f)(5)).

(ii) *Rules for computing the depreciation deduction*. The depreciation deduction for property described in this paragraph (b)(2) is the amount determined by using—

(A) The adjusted basis of the property as determined in computing alternative minimum taxable income as of the close of the last taxable year beginning before January 1, 1990,

(B) The straight-line method, and

(C) The recovery period that consists of the remainder of the recovery period applicable to the property under the alternative depreciation system of section 168(g). Thus, the recovery period begins on the first day of the first taxable year beginning after December 31, 1989, and ends on the last day of the recovery period that would have applied had the recovery period for the property originally been determined under section 168(g). In determining the recovery period that would have applied, the property is deemed placed in service on the date it was considered placed in service under the depreciation convention that would have applied to the property under section 168(d).

(iii) *Example*. The following example illustrates the provisions of this paragraph (b)(2).

Example. Corporation X, a calendar-year taxpayer, purchases and places in service on August 1, 1987, computer-based telephone central office switching equipment. This is the only item of depreciable property X places in service during 1987. Thus, the applicable convention under section 168(d) is the half-year convention. As of December 31, 1989, the adjusted basis of the property used in computing alternative minimum taxable income is $42,000. The recovery period that would have applied to the property under section 168(g)(2) is 9.5 years (from July 1, 1987 to

December 31, 1996). Thus, the recovery period for computing adjusted current earnings under section 56(g)(4)(A)(ii) and this paragraph (b)(2) begins on January 1, 1990, and ends on December 31, 1996. X's 1990 depreciation deduction for computing adjusted current earnings is $6,000, determined under the straight-line method by dividing $42,000 (adjusted basis) by 7 (recovery period).

(3) *Property subject to original ACRS*—(i) *In general*. This paragraph (b)(3) provides the rules for computing the depreciation deduction for property to which section 168 as in effect on the day before the date of enactment of the Tax Reform Act of 1986 (original ACRS) applies and that is placed in service in a taxable year beginning before January 1, 1990 (generally property that was placed in service after December 31, 1980 and before January 1, 1987). In determining whether original ACRS applies to property, the fact that the unadjusted basis of the property is reduced or eliminated under section 168(d)(4)(A)(i) of original ACRS is not taken into account. This paragraph (b)(3) does not apply to property described in paragraph (b)(4) or (b)(5)(i) of this section (relating to certain section 168(f) property).

(ii) *Rules for computing the depreciation deduction*. The depreciation deduction for property described in this paragraph (b)(3) is the amount determined by using—

(A) The adjusted basis of the property as determined in computing taxable income as of the close of the last taxable year beginning before January 1, 1990,

(B) The straight-line method, and

(C) The recovery period that consists of the remainder of the recovery period applicable to the property under the alternative depreciation system of section 168(g). Thus, the recovery period begins on the first day of the first taxable year beginning after December 31, 1989, and ends on the last day of the recovery period that would have applied had the recovery period for the property originally been determined under section 168(g)(2). In determining the recovery period that would have applied, the property is deemed placed in service on the date it was considered placed in service under the depreciation convention that would have applied to the property under section 168(d) (without regard to section 168(d)(3)).

(iii) *Example*. The following example illustrates the provisions of this paragraph (b)(3).

Example. Corporation Y, a calendar-year taxpayer, purchases and places in service on December 1, 1986, computer-based telephone central office switching equipment. The depreciation convention that would have applied to this property under section 168(d) (without regard to section 168(d)(3)) is the half-year convention. As of December 31, 1989, the adjusted basis of the property used in computing taxable income is $21,000. The recovery period for the property under section 168(g)(2) is 9.5 years (from July 1, 1986 to December 31, 1995). Thus, the recovery period for computing adjusted current earnings under section 56(g)(4)(A)(iii) and this paragraph (b)(3) begins on January 1, 1990, and ends on December 31, 1995. Y's 1990 depreciation deduction for computing adjusted current earnings is $3,500, determined under the straight-line method by dividing $21,000 (adjusted basis) by 6 (recovery period).

(4) *Special rule for certain section 168(f) property.* The depreciation or amortization deduction for property described in section 168(f)(1) through (4) is determined in the same manner as used in computing taxable income, without regard to when the property is placed in service.

(5) *Certain property not subject to ACRS.* The depreciation or amortization deduction for property not described in paragraphs (b)(1) through (4) of this section is determined in the same manner as used in computing taxable income. Thus, this paragraph (b)(5) applies to—

(i) Property placed in service after December 31, 1980, in a taxable year beginning before January 1, 1990, and that is excluded from the application of original ACRS or new ACRS by section 168(e)(4) of original ACRS or section 168(f)(5)(A)(i) of new ACRS, and

(ii) Property placed in service before January 1, 1981.

(c) *Inclusion in adjusted current earnings of items included in earnings and profits*—(1) *In general.* Except as otherwise provided in paragraph (c)(4) of this section, adjusted current earnings includes all income items that are permanently excluded from (*i.e.,* not taken into account in determining) pre-adjustment alternative minimum taxable income but that are taken into account in determining earnings and profits. An income item is considered taken into account in determining pre-adjustment alternative minimum taxable income without regard to the timing of its inclusion. Thus, this paragraph (c)(1) does not apply to any income item that is, has been, or will be included in pre-adjustment alternative minimum taxable income. For example, a taxpayer eligible to use the completed contract method of accounting for long-term construction contracts does not take income (or expenses) into account in determining pre-adjustment alternative minimum taxable income for taxable years before the taxable year the contract is completed.

The taxpayer is required under section 312(n)(6) to include income (and expenses) in earnings and profits throughout the term of the contract under the percentage of completion method. This paragraph (c)(1) does not require the income on the contract to be included in adjusted current earnings, however, because the income will be taken into account in the taxable year the contract is completed and therefore is considered to be taken into account in determining pre-adjustment alternative minimum taxable income.

(2) *Certain amounts not taken into account in determining whether an item is permanently excluded.* The fact that proceeds from an income item may eventually be reflected in pre-adjustment alternative minimum taxable income of another taxpayer on the liquidation or disposal of a business, or similar circumstances, is not taken into account in determining whether the item is permanently excluded from pre-adjustment alternative minimum taxable income. Thus, for example, a corporation's adjusted current earnings include interest excluded from pre-adjustment alternative minimum taxable income under section 103 even though the interest might eventually be reflected in the pre-adjustment alternative minimum taxable income of a corporate shareholder as gain on the liquidation of the corporation.

(3) *Allowance of offsetting deductions.* In determining adjusted current earnings under this paragraph (c), a deduction is allowed for all items that relate to income required to be included in adjusted current earnings under this paragraph (c) and that would be deductible in computing pre-adjustment alternative minimum taxable income if the income items to which the items of deduction relate were included in pre-adjustment alternative minimum taxable income for any taxable year. For example, deductions disallowed under section 265(a)(2) for the costs of carrying tax-exempt obligations, the interest on which is excluded from pre-adjustment alternative minimum taxable income under section 103 but is included in adjusted current earnings under this paragraph (c), are generally allowed as deductions in computing adjusted current earnings. Amounts deductible under this paragraph (c)(3) are taken into account using the taxpayer's method of accounting and are subject to any provisions or limitations of the Code that would have applied if the amounts had been deductible in determining pre-adjustment alternative minimum taxable income. For example, section 267(a)(2) may affect the timing of a deduction otherwise disallowed under section 265(a)(2).

(4) *Special rules.* Adjusted current earnings does not include the following amounts.

(i) *Income from the discharge of indebtedness.* Amounts that are excluded from gross income under section 108 of the Internal Revenue Code of 1986 or any corresponding provision of prior law (including the Bankruptcy Tax Act of 1980, case law, income tax regulations and administrative pronouncements).

(ii) *Federal income tax refunds.* Refunds of federal income taxes.

(iii) *Income earned on behalf of states and municipalities.* Amounts that are excluded from gross income under section 115.

* * *

(6) *Partial list of income items excluded from gross income but included in earnings and profits.* The following is a partial list of items that are permanently excluded from pre-adjustment alternative minimum taxable income but that are included in earnings and profits, and are therefore included in adjusted current earnings under this paragraph (c).

(i) Proceeds of life insurance contracts that are excluded under section 101, to the extent provided in paragraph (c)(5)(v) or (c)(5)(vi) of this section.

(ii) Interest that is excluded under section 103.

(iii) Amounts received as compensation for injuries or sickness that are excluded under section 104.

(iv) Income taxes of a lessor of property that are paid by a lessee and are excluded under section 110.

(v) Income attributable to the recovery of an item deducted in computing earnings and profits in a prior year that is excluded under section 111.

(vi) Amounts received as proceeds from sports programs that are excluded under section 114.

(vii) Cost-sharing payments that are excluded under section 126, to the extent section 126(e) does not apply.

(viii) Interest on loans used to acquire employer securities that is excluded under section 133.

(ix) Financial assistance that is excluded under section 597.

(x) Amounts that are excluded from pre-adjustment alternative minimum taxable income as a result of an election under section 831(b) (allowing certain insurance companies to compute their pre-adjustment alternative minimum taxable income using only their investment income).

Items described in paragraph (c)(1) of this section must be included in earnings and profits (and therefore in adjusted current earnings) even if they are not identified in this paragraph (c)(6). The Commissioner may identify additional items described in paragraph (c)(1) in other published guidance.

(7) *Partial list of items excluded from both pre-adjustment alternative minimum taxable income and adjusted current earnings.* The following is a partial list of items that are excluded from both pre-adjustment alternative minimum taxable income and adjusted current earnings, and for which no adjustment is allowed under this section.

(i) The value of improvements made by a lessee to a lessor's property that is excluded from the lessor's income under section 109.

(ii) Contributions to the capital of a corporation by a non-shareholder that are excluded from the corporation's income under section 118.

The Commissioner may identify additional items described in this paragraph (c)(7) in other published guidance.

(d) *Disallowance of items not deductible in computing earnings and profits—(1) In general.* Except as otherwise provided in this paragraph (d), no deduction is allowed in computing adjusted current earnings for any items that are not taken into account in determining earnings and profits for any taxable year, even if the items are taken into account in determining pre-adjustment alternative minimum taxable income. These items therefore increase adjusted current earnings to the extent they are deducted in computing pre-adjustment alternative minimum taxable income. An item of deduction is considered taken into account without regard to the timing of its deductibility in computing earnings and profits. Thus, to the extent an item is, has been, or will be deducted for purposes of determining earnings and profits, it does not increase adjusted current earnings in the taxable year in which it is deducted for purposes of determining pre-adjustment alternative minimum taxable income. For example, a deduction allowed (in determining pre-adjustment alternative minimum taxable income) under section 196 for unused research credits allowable under section 41 is taken into account in computing earnings and profits because the costs that gave rise to the credit were deductible in computing earnings and profits when incurred. Therefore, the deduction does not increase adjusted current earnings. As a further example, payments by a United States parent corporation with respect to employees of certain foreign subsidiaries, which are deductible under section 176, are considered contributions to the capital of the foreign subsidiary for purposes of computing earnings and profits. Although the payments are not deductible in computing the earnings and profits of the United

Reg. § 1.56(g)-1(c)(6)

States parent corporation in the year incurred, the payments do increase the parent's basis in its stock in the foreign subsidiary. This basis increase will reduce any gain the parent may later realize for purposes of computing earnings and profits on the disposition of the stock of the foreign subsidiary. Therefore, the amount of the payment by the parent is considered taken into account in computing the earnings and profits of the parent and does not increase adjusted current earnings. Thus, only deduction items that are never taken into account in computing earnings and profits are disallowed in computing adjusted current earnings under this paragraph (d).

(2) *Deductions for certain dividends received*—(i) *Certain amounts deducted under sections 243 and 245.* Paragraph (d)(1) of this section does not apply to, and adjusted current earnings therefore are not increased by, amounts deducted under sections 243 and 245 that qualify as 100-percent deductible dividends under sections 243(a), 245(b) or 245(c), or to any dividend received from a 20-percent owned corporation (as defined in section 243(c)(2)), to the extent that the dividend giving rise to the deductions is attributable to earnings of the paying corporation that are subject to federal income tax. Earnings are considered subject to federal income tax if the earnings are included on the federal income tax return (that is filed or, if not, that should be filed) of an entity subject to United States taxation, even if there is no resulting United States tax liability (*e.g.*, because of net operating losses or tax credits, other than the credit provided for in section 936).

* * *

(3) *Partial list of items not deductible in computing earnings and profits.* The following is a partial list of items that are not taken into account in computing earnings and profits and thus are not deductible in computing adjusted current earnings.

(i) Unrecovered losses attributable to certain damages that are deductible under section 186, to the extent those damages were previously deducted in computing earnings and profits.

(ii) The deduction for small life insurance companies allowed under section 806.

(iii) Dividends deductible under the following sections of the Code:

(A) Dividends received by corporations that are deductible under section 243, to the extent paragraph (d)(2)(i) of this section does not apply.

(B) Dividends received on certain preferred stock that are deductible under section 244.

(C) Dividends received from certain foreign corporations that are deductible under section 245, to the extent neither paragraph (d)(2)(i) nor (d)(2)(iii) of this section applies.

(D) Dividends paid on certain preferred stock of public utilities that are deductible under section 247.

(E) Dividends paid to an employee stock ownership plan that are deductible under section 404(k).

(F) Non-patronage dividends that are paid and deductible under section 1382(c)(1).

Items described in paragraph (d)(1) of this section are not taken into account in computing earnings and profits (and thus are not deductible in computing adjusted current earnings) even if they are not identified in this paragraph (d)(3). The Commissioner may identify additional items described in paragraph (d)(1) of this section in other published guidance.

(4) *Partial list of items deductible for purposes of computing both pre-adjustment alternative minimum taxable income and adjusted current earnings.* The following is a partial list of items that are deductible for purposes of computing both pre-adjustment alternative minimum taxable income and adjusted current earnings, and for which no adjustment is allowed under this section.

(i) Payments by a United States corporation with respect to employees of certain foreign corporations that are deductible under section 176.

(ii) Dividends paid on deposits by thrift institutions that are deductible under section 591.

(iii) Life insurance policyholder dividends that are deductible under section 808.

(iv) Dividends paid by cooperatives that are deductible under sections 1382(b) or 1382(c)(2) and that are not paid with respect to stock.

The Commissioner may identify additional items described in this paragraph (d)(4) in other published guidance.

(e) *Treatment of income items included, and deduction items not allowed, in computing pre-adjustment alternative minimum taxable income.* Adjusted current earnings includes any income item that is included in pre-adjustment alternative minimum taxable income, even if that income item is not included in earnings and profits for the taxable year. Except as specifically provided in paragraph (c)(3) or (c)(5) of this section, no deduction is allowed for an item in computing adjusted current earnings if the item is not deductible in computing pre-adjustment alternative minimum taxable income for the taxable year, even if the item is deductible in computing earnings and profits for the year. Thus, for example, capital losses in excess of capital gains for the taxable year are not deductible in computing adjusted current earnings for the taxable year.

(f) *Certain other earnings and profits adjustments*—(1) *Intangible drilling costs.* For purposes of computing adjusted current earnings, the amount allowable as a deduction for intangible drilling costs (as defined in section 263(c)) for amounts paid or incurred in taxable years beginning after December 31, 1989, is determined as provided in section 312(n)(2)(A). See section 56(h) for an additional adjustment to alternative minimum taxable income based on energy preferences for taxable years beginning after 1990.

(2) *Certain amortization provisions do not apply.* For purposes of computing adjusted current earnings, sections 173 (relating to circulation expenditures) and 248 (relating to organizational expenditures) do not apply to amounts paid or incurred in taxable years beginning after December 31, 1989. If an election is made under section 59(e) to amortize circulation expenditures described in section 173 over a three-year period, the expenditures to which the election applies are deducted ratably over the three-year period for purposes of computing taxable income, pre-adjustment alternative minimum taxable income, and adjusted current earnings.

* * *

(q) *Treatment of distributions of property to shareholders*—(1) *In general.* If a distribution of an item of property by a corporation with respect to its stock gives rise to more than one adjustment to earnings and profits under section 312, all of the adjustments with respect to that item of property (including the adjustment described in section 312(c) with respect to liabilities to which the item is subject or which are assumed in connection with the distribution) are combined for purposes of determining the corporation's adjusted current earnings for the taxable year. If the amount included in pre-adjustment alternative minimum taxable income with respect to a distribution of an item of property exceeds the net increase in earnings and profits caused by the distribution, pre-adjustment alternative minimum taxable income is not reduced in computing adjusted current earnings. If the net increase in earnings and profits caused by a distribution of an item of property exceeds the amount included in pre-adjustment alternative minimum taxable income with respect

to the distribution, that excess is added to pre-adjustment alternative minimum taxable income in computing adjusted current earnings.

(2) *Examples.* The following examples illustrate the provisions of this paragraph (q).

(i) *Example 1.* K corporation distributes property with a fair market value of $150 and an adjusted basis of $100. The adjusted basis is the same for purposes of computing taxable income, pre-adjustment alternative minimum taxable income, adjusted current earnings, and earnings and profits. Under section 312(a)(3), as modified by section 312(b)(2), K decreases its earnings and profits by the fair market value of the property, or $150. Under section 312(b)(1), K increases its earnings and profits by the excess of the fair market value of the property over its adjusted basis, or $50. As a result of the distribution, there is a net decrease in K's earnings and profits of $100. K recognizes $50 of gain under section 311(b) as a result of the distribution as if K sold the property for $150. K thus has no amount permanently excluded from pre-adjustment alternative minimum taxable income that is taken into account in determining current earnings and profits, and thus has no adjustment under paragraph (c)(1) of this section.

(ii) *Example 2.* The facts are the same as in example 1, except that the distributee shareholder assumes a $190 liability in connection with the distribution. Under section 312(c)(1), K must adjust the adjustments to its earnings and profits under section 312(a) and (b) to account for the liability the shareholder assumes. K adjusts the $100 net decrease in its earnings and profits to reflect the $190 liability, resulting in an increase in its earnings and profits of $90. Because section 311(b)(2) makes the rules of section 336(b) apply, the fair market value of the property is not less than the amount of the liability, or $190. K therefore is treated as if it sold the property for $190, recognizing $90 of gain. K thus has no amount permanently excluded from pre-adjustment alternative minimum taxable income that is taken into account in determining current earnings and profits, and thus has no adjustment under paragraph (c)(1) of this section.

* * *

[Reg. § 1.56(g)-1.]

☐ [*T.D.* 8340, 3-14-91. *Amended by T.D.* 8352, 6-26-91; *T.D.* 8454, 12-18-92; *T.D.* 8482, 8-6-93; *T.D.* 8566, 10-7-94; *T.D.* 8858, 1-5-2000 *and T.D.* 8940, 2-12-2001.]

Definition of Gross Income, Taxable Income, Etc.

§ 1.61-1. Gross income.—(a) *General definition.* Gross income means all income from whatever source derived, unless excluded by law. Gross income includes income realized in any form, whether in money, property, or services. Income may be realized, therefore, in the form of services, meals, accommodations, stock, or other property, as well as in cash. Section 61 lists the more common items of gross income for purposes of illustration. For purposes of further illustration, § 1.61-14 mentions several miscellaneous items of gross income not listed specifically in section 61. Gross income, however, is not limited to the items so enumerated.

(b) *Cross references.* Cross references to other provisions of the Code are to be found throughout the regulations under section 61. The purpose of these cross references is to direct attention to the more common items which are included in or excluded from gross income entirely, or treated in some special manner. To the extent that another section of the Code or of the regulations thereunder, provides specific treatment for any item of income, such other provision shall apply notwithstanding section 61 and the regulations thereunder. The cross references do not cover all possible items.

(1) For examples of items specifically included in gross income, see part II (section 71 and following), subchapter B, chapter 1 of the Code.

(2) For examples of items specifically excluded from gross income, see part III (section 101 and following), subchapter B, chapter 1 of the Code.

(3) For general rules as to the taxable year for which an item is to be included in gross income, see section 451 and the regulations thereunder. [Reg. § 1.61-1.]

☐ [*T.D.* 6272, 11-25-57.]

§ 1.61-2. Compensation for services, including fees, commissions, and similar items.—(a) *In general.* (1) Wages, salaries, commissions paid salesmen, compensation for services on the basis of a percentage of profits, commissions on insurance premiums, tips, bonuses (including Christmas bonuses), termination or severance pay, rewards, jury fees, marriage fees and other contributions received by a clergyman for services, pay of persons in the military or naval forces of the United States, retired pay of employees, pensions, and retirement allowances are income to the recipients unless excluded by law. Several special rules apply to members of the Armed Forces, National Oceanic and Atmospheric Administration, and Public Health Service of the United States; see paragraph (b) of this section.

(2) The Internal Revenue Code provides special rules including the following items in gross income:

(i) Distributions from employees' trusts, see sections 72, 402, and 403, and the regulations thereunder;

(ii) Compensation for child's services (in child's gross income), see section 73 and the regulations thereunder;

(iii) Prizes and awards, see section 74 and the regulations thereunder.

(3) Similarly, the Code provides special rules excluding the following items from gross income in whole or in part:

(i) Gifts, see section 102 and the regulations thereunder;

(ii) Compensation for injuries or sickness, see section 104 and the regulations thereunder;

(iii) Amounts received under accident and health plans, see section 105 and the regulations thereunder;

(iv) Scholarship and fellowship grants, see section 117 and the regulations thereunder;

(v) Miscellaneous items, see section 122.

(b) *Members of the Armed Forces, National Oceanic and Atmospheric Administration, and Public Health Service.* (1) Subsistence and uniform allowances granted commissioned officers, chief warrant officers, warrant officers, and enlisted personnel of the Armed Forces, National Oceanic and Atmospheric Administration, and Public Health Service of the United States, and amounts received by them as commutation of quarters, are excluded from gross income. Similarly, the value of quarters or subsistence furnished to such persons is excluded from gross income.

(2) For purposes of this section, quarters or subsistence includes the following allowances for expenses incurred after December 31, 1993, by members of the Armed Forces, members of the commissioned corps of the National Oceanic and Atmospheric Administration, and members of the commissioned corps of the Public Health Service, to the extent that the allowances are not otherwise excluded from gross income under another provision of the Internal Revenue Code: a dislocation allowance, authorized by 37 U.S.C. 407; a temporary lodging allowance, authorized by 37 U.S.C. 405; a temporary lodging expense, authorized by 37 U.S.C. 404a; and a move-in housing allowance, authorized by 37 U.S.C. 405. No deduction is allowed under this chapter for any expenses reimbursed by such excluded allowances. For the exclusion from gross income of—

Reg. § 1.61-2(b)(2)

(i) Disability pensions, see section 104(a)(4) and the regulations thereunder;

(ii) Miscellaneous items, see section 122.

(3) The per diem or actual expense allowance, the monetary allowance in lieu of transportation, and the mileage allowance received by members of the Armed Forces, National Oceanic and Atmospheric Administration, and the Public Health Service, while in a travel status or on temporary duty fron their permanent stations, are included in their gross income except to the extent excluded under the accountable plan provisions of § 1.62-2.

(c) *Payment to charitable, etc., organization on behalf of person rendering services.* The value of services is not includible in gross income when such services are rendered directly and gratuitously to an organization described in section 170(c). Where, however, pursuant to an agreement or understanding, services are rendered to a person for the benefit of an organization described in section 170(c) and an amount for such services is paid to such organization by the person to whom the services are rendered, the amount so paid constitutes income to the person performing the services.

(d) *Compensation paid other than in cash* —(1) *In general.* Except as otherwise provided in paragraph (d)(6)(i) of this section (relating to certain property transferred after June 30, 1969), if services are paid for in property, the fair market value of the property taken in payment must be included in income as compensation. If services are paid for in exchange for other services, the fair market value of such other services taken in payment must be included in income as compensation. If the services are rendered at a stipulated price, such price will be presumed to be the fair market value of the compensation received in the absence of evidence to the contrary. For special rules relating to certain options received as compensation, see §§ 1.61-15, 1.83-7, and section 421 and the regulations thereunder. For special rules relating to premiums paid by an employer for an annuity contract which is not subject to section 403(a), see section 403(c) and the regulations thereunder and § 1.83-8(a). For special rules relating to contributions made to an employees' trust which is not exempt under section 501, see section 402(b) and the regulations thereunder and § 1.83-8(a).

(2) *Property transferred to employee or independent contractor.* (i) Except as otherwise provided in section 421 and the regulations thereunder and § 1.61-15 (relating to stock options), and paragraph (d)(6)(i) of this section, if property is transferred by an employer to an employee or if property is transferred to an independent contractor, as compensation for services, for an amount less than its fair market value, then regardless of whether the transfer is in the form of a sale or exchange, the difference between the amount paid for the property and the amount of its fair market value at the time of the transfer is compensation and shall be included in the gross income of the employee or independent contractor. In computing the gain or loss from the subsequent sale of such property, its basis shall be the amount paid for the property increased by the amount of such difference included in gross income.

(ii)(a) *Cost of life insurance on the life of the employee.* Generally, life insurance premiums paid by an employer on the life of his employee where the proceeds of such insurance are payable to the beneficiary of such employee are part of the gross income of the employee. However, the amount includible in the employee's gross income is determined with regard to the provisions of section 403 and the regulations thereunder in the case of an individual contract issued after December 31, 1962, or a group contract, which provides incidental life insurance protection and which satisfies the requirements of section 401(g) and § 1.401-9, relating to the nontransferability of annuity contracts. For the special rules relating to the includibility in an employee's gross income of an amount equal to the cost of certain group-term life insurance on the employee's life which is carried directly or indirectly by his employer, see section 79 and the regulations thereunder. For special rules relating to the exclusion of contributions by an employer to accident and health plans for the employees, see section 106 and the regulations thereunder.

(b) *Cost of group-term life insurance on the life of an individual other than an employee.* The cost (determined under paragraph (d)(2) of § 1.79-3) of group-term life insurance on the life of an individual other than an employee (such as the spouse or dependent of the employee) provided in connection with the performance of services by the employee is includible in the gross income of the employee.

(3) *Meals and living quarters.* The value of living quarters or meals which an employee receives in addition to his salary constitutes gross income unless they are furnished for the convenience of the employer and meet the conditions specified in section 119 and the regulations thereunder. For the treatment of rental value of parsonages or rental allowance paid to ministers, see section 107 and the regulations thereunder; for the treatment of statutory subsistence allowances received by police, see section 120 and the regulations thereunder.

(4) *Stock and notes transferred to employee or independent contractor.* Except as otherwise provided by section 421 and the regulations thereunder and § 1.61-15 (relating to stock options),

and paragraph (d)(6)(i) of this section, if a corporation transfers its own stock to an employee or independent contractor as compensation for services, the fair market value of the stock at the time of transfer shall be included in the gross income of the employee or independent contractor. Notes or other evidences of indebtedness received in payment for services constitute income in the amount of their fair market value at the time of the transfer. A taxpayer receiving as compensation a note regarded as good for its face value at maturity, but not bearing interest, shall treat as income as of the time of receipts its fair discounted value computed at the prevailing rate. As payments are received on such a note, there shall be included in income that portion of each payment which represents the proportionate part of the discount originally taken on the entire note.

* * *

(6) *Certain property transferred, premiums paid, and contributions made in connection with the performance of services after June 30, 1969—* (i) *Exception.* Paragraph (d)(1), (2), (4), and (5) of this section and § 1.61-15 do not apply to the transfer of property (as defined in § 1.83-3(e)) after June 30, 1969, unless § 1.83-8 (relating to the applicability of section 83 and transitional rules) applies. If section 83 applies to a transfer of property, and the property is not subject to a restriction that has a significant effect on the fair market value of such property, then the rules contained in paragraph (d)(1), (2), and (4) of this section and § 1.61-15 shall apply to such transfer to the extent such rules are not inconsistent with section 83.

* * *

[Reg. § 1.61-2.]

□ [*T.D. 6272, 11-25-57. Amended by T.D. 6416, 9-24-59; T.D. 6696, 12-11-63; T.D. 6856, 10-19-65; T.D. 6888, 7-5-66; T.D. 7554, 7-21-78; T.D. 7623, 5-14-79; T.D. 8256, 7-5-89 and T.D. 8607, 8-4-95.*]

§ 1.61-3. Gross income derived from business.—(a) *In general.* In a manufacturing, merchandising, or mining business, "gross income" means the total sales, less the cost of goods sold, plus any income from investments and from incidental or outside operations or sources. Gross income is determined without subtraction of depletion allowances based on a percentage of income to the extent that it exceeds cost depletion which may be required to be included in the amount of inventoriable costs as provided in § 1.471-11 and without subtraction of selling expenses, losses or other items not ordinarily used in computing costs of goods sold or amounts which are of a type for which a deduction would be disallowed under section 162(c), (f), or (g) in the

case of a business expense. The cost of goods sold should be determined in accordance with the method of accounting consistently used by the taxpayer. Thus, for example, an amount cannot be taken into account in the computation of cost of goods sold any earlier than the taxable year in which economic performance occurs with respect to the amount (see § 1.446-1(c)(1)(ii)).

(b) *State contracts.* The profit from a contract with a State or policitcal subdivision thereof must be included in gross income. If warrants are issued by a city, town, or other political subdivision of a State, and are accepted by the contractor in payment for public work done, the fair market value of such warrants should be returned as income. If, upon conversion of the warrants into cash, the contractor does not receive and cannot recover the full value of the warrants so returned, he may deduct any loss sustained from his gross income for the year in which the warrants are so converted. If, however, he realizes more than the value of the warrants so returned, he must include the excess in his gross income for the year in which realized. [Reg. § 1.61-3.]

□ [*T.D. 6272, 11-25-57. Amended by T.D. 7207, 10-3-72; T.D. 7285, 9-14-73 and T.D. 8408, 4-9-92.*]

§ 1.61-4. Gross income of farmers.—(a) *Farmers using the cash method of accounting.* A farmer using the cash receipts and disbursements method of accounting shall include in his gross income for the taxable year—

(1) The amount of cash and the value of merchandise or other property received during the taxable year from the sale of livestock and produce which he raised,

(2) The profits from the sale of any livestock or other items which were purchased,

(3) All amounts received from breeding fees, fees from rent of teams, machinery, or land, and other incidental farm income,

(4) All subsidy and conservation payments received which must be considered as income, and

(5) Gross income from all other sources.

The profit from the sale of livestock or other items which were purchased is to be ascertained by deducting the cost from the sales price in the year in which the sale occurs, except that in the case of the sale of purchased animals held for draft, breeding, or dairy purposes, the profits shall be the amount of any excess of the sales price over the amount representing the difference between the cost and the depreciation allowed or allowable (determined in accordance with the rules applicable under section 1016(a) and the regulations thereunder). However, see section 162 and the regulations thereunder with respect of the computation of taxable income on other than the crop method where the cost of seeds or young plants purchased for further development and cultivation prior to the sale is involved. Crop shares (whether or not considered rent under State law) shall be included in gross income as of the year in which the crop shares are reduced to money or the equivalent of money. See section 263A for rules regarding costs that are required to be capitalized.

(b) *Farmers using an accrual method of accounting.* A farmer using an accrual method of accounting must use inventories to determine his gross income. His gross income on an accrual method is determined by adding the total of the items described in subparagraphs (1) through (5) of this paragraph and subtracting therefrom the total of the items described in subparagraphs (6) and (7) of this paragraph. These items are as follows:

(1) The sales price of all livestock and other products held for sale and sold during the year;

(2) The inventory value of livestock and products on hand and not sold at the end of the year;

(3) All miscellaneous items of income, such as breeding fees, fees from the rent of teams, machinery, or land, or other incidental farm income;

(4) Any subsidy or conservation payments which must be considered as income;

(5) Gross income from all other sources;

(6) The inventory value of the livestock and products on hand and not sold at the beginning of the year; and

(7) The cost of any livestock or products purchased during the year (except livestock held for draft, dairy, or breeding purposes, unless included in inventory).

All livestock raised or purchased for sale shall be added in the inventory at their proper valuation determined in accordance with the method authorized and adopted for the purpose. Livestock acquired for draft, breeding, or dairy purposes and not for sale may be included in the inventory (see subparagraphs (2), (6), and (7) of this paragraph) instead of being treated as capital assets subject to depreciation, provided such practice is followed consistently from year to year by the taxpayer. When any livestock included in an inventory are sold, their cost must not be taken as an additional deduction in computing taxable income, because such deduction is reflected in the inventory. See the regulations under section 471. See section 263A for rules regarding costs that are required to be capitalized. Crop shares (whether or not considered rent under State law) shall be included in gross income as of the year in which

the crop shares are reduced to money or the equivalent of money.

(c) *Special rules for certain receipts.* In the case of the sale of machinery, farm equipment, or any other property (except stock in trade of the taxpayer, or property of a kind which would properly be included in the inventory of the taxpayer if on hand at the close of the taxable year, or property held by the taxpayer primarily for sale to customers in the ordinary course of his trade or business), any excess of the proceeds of the sale over the adjusted basis of such property shall be included in the taxpayer's gross income for the taxable year in which such sale is made. See, however, section 453 and the regulations thereunder for special rules relating to certain installment sales. If farm produce is exchanged for merchandise, groceries, or the like, the market value of the article received in exchange is to be included in gross income. Proceeds of insurance, such as hail or fire insurance on growing crops, should be included in gross income to the extent of the amount received in cash or its equivalent for the crop injured or destroyed. See section 451(d) for special rule relating to election to include crop insurance proceeds in income for taxable year following taxable year of destruction. For taxable years beginning after July 12, 1972, where a farmer is engaged in producing crops and the process of gathering and disposing of such crops is not completed within the taxable year in which such crops are planted, the income therefrom may, with the consent of the Commissioner (see section 446 and the regulations thereunder), be computed upon the crop method. For taxable years beginning on or before July 12, 1972, where a farmer is engaged in producing crops which take more than a year from the time of planting to the time of gathering and disposing, the income therefrom may, with the consent of the Commissioner (see section 446 and the regulations thereunder), be computed upon the crop method. In any case in which the crop method is used, the entire cost of producing the crop must be taken as a deduction for the year in which the gross income from the crop is realized, and not earlier.

(d) *Definition of "farm".* As used in this section, the term "farm" embraces the farm in the ordinarily accepted sense, and includes stock, dairy, poultry, fruit, and truck farms; also plantations, ranches, and all land used for farming operations. All individuals, partnerships, or corporations that cultivate, operate, or manage farms for gain or profit, either as owners or tenants, are designated as farmers. For more detailed rules with respect to the determination of whether or not an individual is engaged in farming, see § 1.175-3. For rules applicable to persons cultivating or operating a farm for recreation or pleasure, see sections 162 and 165, and the regulations thereunder.

(e) *Cross references.* (1) For election to include Commodity Credit Corporation loans as income, see section 77 and regulations thereunder.

(2) For definition of gross income derived from farming for purposes of limiting deductibility of soil and water conservation expenditures, see section 175 and regulations thereunder.

(3) For definition of gross income from farming in connection with declarations of estimated income tax, see section 6073 and regulations thereunder. [Reg. § 1.61-4.]

☐ [T.D. 6272, 11-25-57. *Amended by T.D. 7198, 7-12-72 and T.D. 8729, 8-21-97.*]

§ 1.61-6. Gains derived from dealings in property.—(a) *In general.* Gain realized on the sale or exchange of property is included in gross income, unless excluded by law. For this purpose property includes tangible items, such as a building, and intangible items, such as goodwill. Generally, the gain is the excess of the amount realized over the unrecovered cost or other basis for the property sold or exchanged. The specific rules for computing the amount of gain or loss are contained in section 1001 and the regulations thereunder. When a part of a larger property is sold, the cost or other basis of the entire property shall be equitably apportioned among the several parts, and the gain realized or loss sustained on the part of the entire property sold is the difference between the selling price and the cost or other basis allocated to such part. The sale of each part is treated as a separate transaction and gain or loss shall be computed separately on each part. Thus, gain or loss shall be determined at the time of sale of each part and not deferred until the entire property has been disposed of. This rule may be illustrated by the following examples:

Example (1). A, a dealer in real estate, acquires a 10-acre tract for $10,000, which he divides into 20 lots. The $10,000 cost must be equitably apportioned among the lots so that on the sale of each A can determine his taxable gain or deductible loss.

Example (2). B purchases for $25,000 property consisting of a used car lot and adjoining filling station. At the time, the fair market value of the filling station is $15,000 and the fair market value of the used car lot is $10,000. Five years later B sells the filling station for $20,000 at a time when $2,000 has been properly allowed as depreciation thereon. B's gain on this sale is $7,000, since $7,000 is the amount by which the selling price of the filling station exceeds the portion of the cost equitably allocable to the filling station at the time of purchase reduced by the depreciation properly allowed.

(b) *Nontaxable exchanges.* Certain realized gains or losses on the sale or exchange of property are not "recognized", that is, are not included in or deducted from gross income at the time the transaction occurs. Gain or loss from such sales or exchanges is generally recognized at some later time. Examples of such sales or exchanges are the following:

(1) Certain formations, reorganizations, and liquidations of corporations, see sections 331, 333, 337, 351, 354, 355, and 361;

(2) Certain formations and distributions of partnerships, see sections 721 and 731;

(3) Exchange of certain property held for productive use or investment for property of like kind, see section 1031;

(4) A corporation's exchange of its stock for property, see section 1032;

(5) Certain involuntary conversions of property if replaced, see section 1033;

(6) Sale or exchange of residence if replaced, see section 1034;

(7) Certain exchanges of insurance policies and annuity contracts, see section 1035; and

(8) Certain exchanges of stock for stock in the same corporation, see section 1036.

(c) *Character of recognized gain.* Under subchapter P, chapter 1 of the Code, relating to capital gains and losses, certain gains derived from dealings in property are treated specially, and under certain circumstances the maximum rate of tax on such gains is 25 percent, as provided in section 1201. Generally, the property subject to this treatment is a "capital asset," or treated as a "capital asset". For definition of such assets, see sections 1221 and 1231, and the regulations thereunder. For some of the rules either granting or denying this special treatment, see the following sections and the regulations thereunder:

(1) Transactions between partner and partnership, section 707;

(2) Sale or exchange of property used in the trade or business and involuntary conversions, section 1231;

(3) Payment of bonds and other evidences of indebtedness, section 1232;

(4) Gains and losses from short sales, section 1233;

(5) Options to buy or sell, section 1234;

(6) Sale or exchange of patents, section 1235;

(7) Securities sold by dealers in securities, section 1236;

(8) Real property subdivided for sale, section 1237;

Reg. § 1.61-6(c)(8)

(9) Amortization in excess of depreciation, section 1238;

(10) Gain from sale for certain property between spouses or between an individual and a controlled corporation, section 1239;

(11) Taxability to employee of termination payments, section 1240. [Reg. § 1.61-6.]

☐ [*T.D.* 6272, 11-25-57.]

§ 1.61-7. Interest.—(a) *In general.* As a general rule, interest received by or credited to the taxpayer constitutes gross income and is fully taxable. Interest income includes interest on savings or other bank deposits; interest on coupon bonds; interest on an open account, a promissory note, a mortgage, or a corporate bond or debenture; the interest portion of a condemnation award; usurious interest (unless by State law it is automatically converted to a payment on the principal); interest on legacies; interest on life insurance proceeds held under an agreement to pay interest thereon; and interest on refunds of Federal taxes. For rules determining the taxable year in which interest, including interest accrued or constructively received, is included in gross income, see section 451 and the regulations thereunder. For the inclusion of interest in income for the purpose of the retirement income credit, see section 37 and the regulations thereunder. For credit of tax withheld at source on interest on tax-free covenant bonds, see section 32 and the regulations thereunder. For rules relating to interest on certain deferred payments, see section 483 and the regulations thereunder.

* * *

[Reg. § 1.61-7.]

☐ [*T.D.* 6272, 11-25-57. *Amended by T.D.* 6723, 4-20-64; *and T.D.* 6873, 1-24-66.]

§ 1.61-8. Rents and royalties.—(a) *In general.* Gross income includes rentals received or accrued for the occupancy of real estate or the use of personal property. For the inclusion of rents in income for the purpose of the retirement income credit, see section 37 and the regulations thereunder. Gross income includes royalties. Royalties may be received from books, stories, plays, copyrights, trademarks, formulas, patents, and from the exploitation of natural resources, such as coal, gas, oil, copper, or timber. Payments received as a result of the transfer of patent rights may under some circumstances constitute capital gain instead of ordinary income. See section 1235 and the regulations thereunder. For special rules for certain income from natural resources, see subchapter I (611 and following), chapter 1 of the Code, and the regulations thereunder.

(b) *Advance rentals; cancellation payments.* Except as provided in section 467 and the regulations thereunder, gross income includes advance rentals, which must be included in income for the year of receipt regardless of the period covered or the method of accounting employed by the taxpayer. An amount received by a lessor from a lessee for cancelling a lease constitutes gross income for the year in which it is received, since it is essentially a substitute for rental payments. As to amounts received by a lessee for the cancellation of a lease, see section 1241 and the regulations thereunder.

(c) *Expenditures by lessee.* As a general rule, if a lessee pays any of the expenses of his lessor such payments are additional rental income of the lessor. If a lessee places improvements on real estate which constitute, in whole or in part, a substitute for rent, such improvements constitute rental income to the lessor. Whether or not improvements made by a lessee result in rental income to the lessor in a particular case depends upon the intention of the parties, which may be indicated either by the terms of the lease or by the surrounding circumstances. For the exclusion from gross income of income (other than rent) derived by a lessor of real property on the termination of a lease, representing the value of such property attributable to buildings erected or other improvements made by a lessee, see section 109 and the regulations thereunder. For the exclusion from gross income of a lessor corporation of certain of its income taxes on rental income paid by a lessee corporation under a lease entered into before January 1, 1954, see section 110 and the regulations thereunder. [Reg. § 1.61-8.]

☐ [*T.D.* 6272, 11-25-57. *Amended by T.D.* 8820, 5-17-99.]

§ 1.61-9. Dividends.—(a) *In general.* Except as otherwise specifically provided, dividends are included in gross income under sections 61 and 301. For the principal rules with respect to dividends includible in gross income, see section 316 and the regulations thereunder. As to distributions made or deemed to be made by regulated investment companies, see sections 851 through 855, and the regulations thereunder. As to distributions made by real estate investment trusts, see sections 856 through 858, and the regulations thereunder. See section 116 for the exclusion from gross income of $100 ($50 for dividends received in taxable years beginning before January 1, 1964) of dividends received by an individual, except those from certain corporations. Furthermore, dividends may give rise to a credit against tax under section 34, relating to dividends received by individuals (for dividends received on or before December 31, 1964), and under section 37, relating to retirement income.

(b) *Dividends in kind; stock dividends; stock redemptions.* Gross income includes dividends in property other than cash, as well as cash dividends. For amounts to be included in gross income when distributions of property are made, see section 301 and the regulations thereunder. A distribution of stock, or rights to acquire stock, in the corporation making the distribution is not a dividend except under the circumstances described in section 305(b). However, the term "dividend" includes a distribution of stock, or rights to acquire stock, in a corporation other than the corporation making the distribution. For determining when distributions in complete liquidation shall be treated as dividends, see section 333 and the regulations thereunder. For rules determining when amounts received in exchanges under section 354 or exchanges and distributions under section 355 shall be treated as dividends, see section 356 and the regulations thereunder.

(c) *Dividends on stock sold.* When stock is sold, and a dividend is both declared and paid after the sale, such dividend is not gross income to the seller. When stock is sold after the declaration of a dividend and after the date as of which the seller becomes entitled to the dividend, the dividend ordinarily is income to the seller. When stock is sold between the time of declaration and the time of payment of the dividend, and the sale takes place at such time that the purchaser becomes entitled to the dividend, the dividend ordinarily is income to him. The fact that the purchaser may have included the amount of the dividend in his purchase price in contemplation of receiving the dividend does not exempt him from tax. Nor can the purchaser deduct the added amount he advanced to the seller in anticipation of the dividend. That added amount is merely part of the purchase price of the stock. In some cases, however, the purchaser may be considered to be the recipient of the dividend even though he has not received the legal title to the stock itself and does not himself receive the dividend. For example, if the seller retains the legal title to the stock as trustee solely for the purpose of securing the payment of the purchase price, with the understanding that he is to apply the dividends received from time to time in reduction of the purchase price, the dividends are considered to be income to the purchaser. [Reg. § 1.61-9.]

☐ *[T.D. 6272, 11-25-57. Amended by T.D. 6598, 4-25-62; and T.D. 6777, 12-15-64.]*

§ 1.61-12. Income from discharge of indebtedness.—(a) *In general.* The discharge of indebtedness, in whole or in part, may result in the realization of income. If, for example, an individual performs services for a creditor, who in consideration thereof cancels the debt, the debtor realizes income in the amount of the debt as compensation for his services. A taxpayer may realize income by the payment or purchase of his obligations at less than their face value. In general, if a shareholder in a corporation which is indebted to him gratuitously forgives the debt, the transaction amounts to a contribution to the capital of the corporation to the extent of the principal of the debt.

* * *

[Reg. § 1.61-12.]

☐ *[T.D. 6272, 11-25-57. Amended by T.D. 6653, 5-22-63; T.D. 6984, 12-23-68; T.D. 7741, 12-11-80 and T.D. 8746, 12-30-97.]*

§ 1.61-14. Miscellaneous items of gross income.—(a) *In general.* In addition to the items enumerated in section 61(a), there are many other kinds of gross income. For example, punitive damages such as treble damages under the antitrust laws and exemplary damages for fraud are gross income. Another person's payment of the taxpayer's income taxes constitutes gross income to the taxpayer unless excluded by law. Illegal gains constitute gross income. Treasure trove, to the extent of its value in United States currency, constitutes gross income for the taxable year in which it is reduced to undisputed possession.

(b) *Cross references.* (1) Prizes and awards, see section 74 and regulations thereunder;

(2) Damages for personal injury or sickness, see section 104 and the regulations thereunder;

(3) Income taxes paid by lessee corporation, see section 110 and regulations thereunder;

(4) Scholarships and fellowship grants, see section 117 and regulations thereunder;

(5) Miscellaneous exemptions under other Acts of Congress, see section 122;

(6) Tax-free covenant bonds, see section 1451 and regulations thereunder.

(7) Notional principal contracts, see § 1.446-3. [Reg. § 1.61-14.]

☐ *[T.D. 6272, 11-25-57. Amended by T.D. 6856, 10-19-65 and T.D. 8491, 10-8-93.]*

§ 1.61-21. Taxation of fringe benefits.—(a) *Fringe benefits*—(1) *In general.* Section 61(a)(1) provides that, except as otherwise provided in subtitle A of the Internal Revenue Code of 1986, gross income includes compensation for services, including fees, commissions, fringe benefits, and similar items. For an outline of the regulations under this section relating to fringe benefits, see paragraph (a)(7) of this section. Examples of fringe benefits include: an employer-provided automobile, a flight on an employer-provided aircraft, an employer-provided free or discounted commercial airline flight, an employer-provided vacation, an employer-provided discount on property or services, an employer-provided membership in a country club or other social club, and an employer-provided ticket to an entertainment or sporting event.

(2) *Fringe benefits excluded from income.* To the extent that a particular fringe benefit is specifically excluded from gross income pursuant to another section of subtitle A of the Internal Revenue Code of 1986, that section shall govern the treatment of that fringe benefit. Thus, if the requirements of the governing section are satisfied, the fringe benefits may be excludable from gross income. Examples of excludable fringe benefits include qualified tuition reductions provided to an employee (section 117(d)); meals or lodging furnished to an employee for the convenience of the employer (section 119); benefits provided under a dependent care assistance program (section 129); and no-additional-cost services, qualified employee discounts, working condition fringes, and de minimis fringes (section 132). Similarly, the value of the use by an employee of an employer-provided vehicle or a flight provided to an employee on an employer-provided aircraft may be excludable from income under section 105 (because, for example, the transportation is provided for medical reasons) if and to the extent that the requirements of that section are satisfied. Section 134 excludes from gross income "qualified military benefits." An example of a benefit that is not a qualified military benefit is the personal use of an employer-provided vehicle. The fact that another section of subtitle A of the Internal Revenue Code addresses the taxation of a particular fringe benefit will not preclude section 61 and the regulations thereunder from applying, to the extent that they are not inconsistent with such other section. For example, many fringe benefits specifically addressed in other sections of subtitle A of the Internal Revenue Code are excluded from gross income only to the extent that they do not exceed specific dollar or percentage limits, or only if certain other requirements are met. If the limits are exceeded or the requirements are not met, some or all of the fringe benefit may be includible in gross income pursuant to section 61. See paragraph (b)(3) of this section.

(3) *Compensation for services.* A fringe benefit provided in connection with the performance of services shall be considered to have been provided as compensation for such services. Refraining from the performance of services (such as pursuant to a covenant not to compete) is deemed to be the performance of services for purposes of this section.

(4) *Person to whom fringe benefit is taxable—(i) In general.* A taxable fringe benefit is included in the income of the person performing the services in connection with which the fringe benefit is furnished. Thus, a fringe benefit may be taxable to a person even though that person did not actually receive the fringe benefit. If a fringe benefit is furnished to someone other than the service provider such benefit is considered in this section as furnished to the service provider, and use by the other person is considered use by the service provider. For example, the provision of an automobile by an employer to an employee's spouse in connection with the performance of services by the employee is taxable to the employee. The automobile is considered available to the employee and use by the employee's spouse is considered use by the employee.

(ii) *All persons to whom benefits are taxable referred to as employees.* The person to whom a fringe benefit is taxable need not be an employee of the provider of the fringe benefit, but may be, for example, a partner, director, or an independent contractor. For convenience, the term "employee" includes any person performing services in connection with which a fringe benefit is furnished, unless otherwise specifically provided in this section.

(5) *Provider of a fringe benefit referred to as an employer.* The "provider" of a fringe benefit is that person for whom the services are performed, regardless of whether that person actually provides the fringe benefit to the recipient. The provider of a fringe benefit need not be the employer of the recipient of the fringe benefit, but may be, for example, a client or customer of the employer or of an independent contractor. For convenience, the term "employer" includes any provider of a fringe benefit in connection with payment for the performance of services, unless otherwise specifically provided in this section.

* * *

(b) *Valuation of fringe benefits—(1) In general.* An employee must include in gross income the amount by which the fair market value of the fringe benefit exceeds the sum of—

(i) The amount, if any, paid for the benefit by or on behalf of the recipient, and

(ii) The amount, if any, specifically excluded from gross income by some other section of subtitle A of the Internal Revenue Code of 1986.

Therefore, for example, if the employee pays fair market value for what is received, no amount is includible in the gross income of the employee. In general, the determination of the fair market value of a fringe benefit must be made before subtracting out the amount, if any, paid for the benefit and the amount, if any, specifically excluded from gross income by another section of subtitle A. See paragraphs (d)(2)(ii) and (e)(1)(iii) of this section.

Reg. § 1.61-21(a)(2)

(2) *Fair market value.* In general, fair market value is determined on the basis of all the facts and circumstances. Specifically, the fair market value of a fringe benefit is the amount that an individual would have to pay for the particular fringe benefit in an arm's-length transaction. Thus, for example, the effect of any special relationship that may exist between the employer and the employee must be disregarded. Similarly, an employee's subjective perception of the value of a fringe benefit is not relevant to the determination of the fringe benefit's fair market value nor is the cost incurred by the employer determinative of its fair market value. For special rules relating to the valuation of certain fringe benefits, see paragraph (c) of this section.

(3) *Exclusion from income based on cost.* If a statutory exclusion phrased in terms of cost applies to the provision of a fringe benefit, section 61 does not require the inclusion in the recipient's gross income of the difference between the fair market value and the excludable cost of that fringe benefit. For example, section 129 provides an exclusion from an employee's gross income for amounts contributed by an employer to a dependent care assistance program for employees. Even if the fair market value of the dependent care assistance exceeds the employer's cost, the excess is not subject to inclusion under section 61 and this section. However, if the statutory cost exclusion is a limited amount, the fair market value of the fringe benefit attributable to any excess cost is subject to inclusion. This would be the case, for example, where an employer pays or incurs a cost of more than $5,000 to provide dependent care assistance to an employee.

* * *

[Reg. § 1.61-21.]

☐ [*T.D. 8256, 7-5-89. Amended by T.D. 8389, 1-15-92 and T.D. 8457, 12-29-92.*]

§ 1.62-1T. Adjusted gross income (temporary).—(a) *Basis for determining the amount of certain deductions.* The term "adjusted gross income" means the gross income computed under section 61 minus such of the deductions allowed by chapter 1 of the Code as are specified in section 62(a). Adjusted gross income is used as the basis for determining the following:

(1) The limitation on the amount of miscellaneous itemized deductions (under section 67).

(2) The limitation on the amount of the deduction for casualty losses (under section 165(h)(2)),

(3) The limitation on the amount of the deduction for charitable contributions (under section 170(b)(1)),

(4) The limitation on the amount of the deduction for medical and dental expenses (under section 213),

(5) The limitation on the amount of the deduction for qualified retirement contributions for active participants in certain pension plans (under section 219(g)), and

(6) The phase-out of the exemption from the disallowance of passive activity losses and credits (under section 469(i)(3)).

(b) *Double deduction not permitted.* Section 62(a) merely specifies which of the deductions provided in chapter 1 of the Code shall be allowed in computing adjusted gross income. It does not create any new deductions. The fact that a particular item may be described in more than one of the paragraphs under section 62(a) does not permit the item to be deducted twice in computing adjusted gross income or taxable income.

(c) *Deductions allowable in computing adjusted gross income.* The deductions specified in section 62(a) for purposes of computing adjusted gross income are:

(1) Deductions allowable under chapter 1 of the Code (other than by part VII (section 211 and following), subchapter B of such chapter) that are attributable to a trade or business carried on by the taxpayer not consisting of services performed as an employee;

(2) [Reserved]

(3) For taxable years beginning after December 31, 1986, deductions allowable under section 162 that consist of expenses paid or incurred by a qualified performing artist (as defined in section 62 (b)) in connection with the performance by him or her of services in the performing arts as an employee;

(4) Deductions allowable under part VI as losses from the sale or exchange of property;

(5) Deductions allowable under part VI, section 212, or section 611 that are attributable to property held for the production of rents or royalties;

(6) Deductions for depreciation or depletion allowable under sections 167 or 611 to a life tenant of property or to an income beneficiary of property held in trust or to an heir, legatee, or devisee of an estate;

(7) Deductions allowed by section 404 for contributions on behalf of a self-employed individual;

(8) Deductions allowed by section 219 for contributions to an individual retirement account described in section 408(a), or for an individual retirement annuity described in section 408(b);

Reg. § 1.62-1T(c)(8)

(9) Deductions allowed by section 402(e)(3) with respect to a lump-sum distribution;

(10) For taxable years beginning after December 31, 1972, deductions allowed by section 165 for losses incurred in any transaction entered into for profit though not connected with a trade or business, to the extent that such losses include amounts forfeited to a bank, mutual savings bank, savings and loan association, building and loan association, cooperative bank or homestead association as a penalty for premature withdrawal of funds from a time savings account, certificate of deposit, or similar class of deposit;

(11) For taxable years beginning after December 31, 1976, deductions for alimony and separate maintenance payments allowed by section 215;

(12) Deductions allowed by section 194 for the amortization of reforestation expenditures; and

(13) Deductions allowed by section 165 for the repayment (made in a taxable year beginning after December 28, 1980) to a trust described in paragraph (9) or (17) of section 501(c) of supplemental unemployment compensation benefits received from such trust if such repayment is required because of the receipt of trade readjustment allowances under section 231 or 232 of the Trade Act of 1974 (19 U.S.C. 2291 and 2292).

(d) *Expenses directly related to a trade or business.* For the purpose of the deductions specified in section 62, the performance of personal services as an employee does not constitute the carrying on of a trade or business, except as otherwise expressly provided. The practice of a profession, not as an employee, is considered the conduct of a trade or business within the meaning of such section. To be deductible for the purposes of determining adjusted gross income, expenses must be those directly, and not those merely remotely, connected with the conduct of a trade or business. For example, taxes are deductible in arriving at adjusted gross income only if they constitute expenditures directly attributable to a trade or business or to property from which rents or royalties are derived. Thus, property taxes paid or incurred on real property used in a trade or business are deductible, but state taxes on net income are not deductible even though the taxpayer's income is derived from the conduct of a trade or business.

(e) *Reimbursed and unreimbursed employee expenses*—(1) *In general.* Expenses paid or incurred by an employee that are deductible from gross income under part VI in computing taxable income (determined without regard to section 67) and for which the employee is reimbursed by the employer, its agent, or third party (for whom the employee performs a benefit as an employee of the employer) under an express agreement for reimbursement or pursuant to an *express* expense allowance arrangement may be deducted from gross income in computing adjusted gross income. Except as provided in paragraph (e)(2) and (e)(4) of this section, for taxable years beginning after December 31, 1986, if the amount of a reimbursement made by an employer, its agent, or third party to an employee is less than the total amount of the business expenses paid or incurred by the employee, the determination of to which of the employee's business expenses the reimbursement applies and the amount of each expense that is covered by the reimbursement is made on the basis of all of the facts and circumstances of the particular case.

(2) *Facts and circumstances unclear on business expenses for meals and entertainment.* If—

(i) The facts and circumstances do not make clear—

(A) That a reimbursement does not apply to business expenses for meals or entertainment, or

(B) The amount of business expenses for meals or entertainment that is covered by the reimbursement, and

(ii) the employee pays or incurs business expenses for meals or entertainment,

the amount of the reimbursement that applies to such expenses (or portion thereof with respect to which the facts and circumstances are unclear) shall be determined by multiplying the amount of the employee's business expenses for meals and entertainment (or portion thereof with respect to which the facts and circumstances are unclear) by a fraction, the numerator of which is the total amount of the reimbursement (or portion thereof with respect to which the facts and circumstances are unclear) and the denominator of which is the aggregate amount of all the business expenses of the employee (or portion thereof with respect to which the facts and circumstances are unclear).

(3) *Deductibility of unreimbursed expenses.* The amount of expenses that is determined not to be reimbursed pursuant to paragraph (e)(1) or (2) of this section is deductible from adjusted gross income in determining the employee's taxable income subject to the limitations applicable to such expenses (*e.g.,* the 2-percent floor of section 67 and the 80-percent limitation on meal and entertainment expenses provided for in section 274(n)).

* * *

(5) *Expenses paid directly by an employer, its agent, or third party.* In the case of an employer, its agent, or a third party who provides property or services to an employee or who pays

an employee's expenses directly instead of reimbursing the employee, see section 132 and the regulations thereunder for the income tax treatment of such expenses.

(6) *Examples.* The provisions of this paragraph (e) may be illustrated by the following examples:

Example (1). During 1987, A, an employee, while on business trips away form home pays $300 for travel fares, $200 for lodging and $100 for meals. In addition, A pays $50 for business meals in the area of his place of employment ("local meals"), $250 for continuing education courses, and $100 for business-related entertainment (other than meals). The total amount of the reimbursements received by A for his employee expenses from his employer is $750, and it is assumed that A's expenses meet the deductibility requirements of sections 162 and 274. A includes the amount of the reimbursement in his gross income. A's employer designates the reimbursement to cover in full A's expenses for travel fares, lodging, and meals while away from home, local meals, and entertainment, and no facts or circumstances indicate a contrary intention of the employer. Because the facts and circumstances make clear the amount of A's business expenses for meals and entertainment that is covered by the reimbursement, the reimbursement will be allocated to these expenses. In determining his adjusted gross income under section 62, A may deduct the full amount of the reimbursement for travel fares, lodging, and meals while away from home, local meals, and entertainment. In determining his taxable income under section 63, A may deduct his expenses for continuing education courses to the extent allowable by sections 67 and 162.

Example (2). Assume the facts are the same as in example (1) except that the facts and circumstances make clear that the reimbursement covers all types of deductible expenses but they do not make clear the amount of each type of expense that is covered by the reimbursement. The amount of the reimbursement that is allocated to A's business expenses for meals and entertainment is $187.50. This amount is determined by multiplying the total amount of A's business expenses for meals and entertainment ($250) by the ratio of A's total reimbursement to A's total business expenses ($750/$1,000). The remaining amount of the reimbursement, $562.50 ($750 − $187.50), is allocated to A's business expenses other than meal and entertainment expenses. Therefore, in determining his adjusted gross income under section 62, A may deduct $750 for reimbursed business expenses (including meals and entertainment). In determining his taxable income under section 63, A may deduct (subject

to the limitations and conditions of sections 67, 162, and 274) the unreimbursed portion of his expenses for meals and entertainment ($62.50 ($250 − $187.50)), and other employee business expenses ($187.50 ($750 − $562.50)).

Example (3). Assume the facts are the same as in example (1) except that the amount of the reimbursement is $500. Assume further that the facts and circumstances make clear that the reimbursement covers $100 of expenses for meals and that the remaining $400 of the reimbursement covers all types of deductible expenses (including any expenses for meals in excess of the $100 already designated) other than expenses for entertainment. The amount of the reimbursement that is allocated to A's business expenses for meals and entertainment is $125. This amount is equal to the sum of the amount of the reimbursement that clearly applies to meals ($100) and the amount of the reimbursement with respect to which the facts are unclear that is allocated to meals ($25). The latter amount is determined by multiplying the total amount of A's business expenses for meals and entertainment with respect to which the facts are unclear ($50) by the ratio of A's total reimbursement with respect to which the facts are unclear to A's total business expenses with respect to which the facts are unclear ($400/$800). The remaining amount of the reimbursement, $375 ($500 − $125) is allocated to A's business expenses other than meals and entertainment. Therefore, in determining his adjusted gross income under section 62, A may deduct $500 for reimbursed business expenses (including meals). In determining his taxable income under section 63, A may deduct (subject to the limitations and conditions of sections 67, 162, and 274) the unreimbursed portion of his expenses for meals ($25 ($150 − $125)), entertainment ($100), and other employee business expenses ($375 ($750 − $375)).

Example (4). During 1987 B, a research scientist, is employed by Corporation X. B gives a speech before members of Association Y, a professional organization of scientists, describing her most recent research findings. Pursuant to a reimbursement arrangement, Y reimburses B for the full amount of her travel fares to the site of the speech and for the full amount of her expenses for lodging and meals while there. B includes the amount of the reimbursement in her gross income. B may deduct the full amount of her travel expenses pursuant to section 62(a)(2)(A) in computing her adjusted gross income.

(f) [Reserved]

(g) *Moving expenses.* For taxable years beginning after December 31, 1986, a taxpayer described in section 217(a) shall not take into

Reg. § 1.62-1T(g)

account the deduction described in section 217 relating to moving expenses in computing adjusted gross income under section 62 even if the taxpayer is reimbursed for his or her moving expenses. Such a taxpayer shall include the amount of any reimbursement for moving expenses in income pursuant to section 82. The deduction described in section 217 shall be taken into account in computing the taxable income of the taxpayer under section 63. Pursuant to section 67(b)(6), the 2-percent floor described in section 67(a) does not apply to moving expenses.

* * *

[Temporary Reg. § 1.62-1T.]

☐ [*T.D. 8189*, 3-25-88. *Amended by T.D. 8276*, 12-7-89; *T.D. 8324*, 12-14-90 *and T.D. 8451*, 12-4-92.]

§ 1.62-2. Reimbursements and other expense allowance arrangements.—

* * *

(b) *Scope.* For purposes of determining "adjusted gross income," section 62(a)(2)(A) allows an employee a deduction for expenses allowed by Part VI (section 161 and following), subchapter B, chapter 1 of the Code, paid by the employee, in connection with the performance of services as an employee of the employer, under a reimbursement or other expense allowance arrangement with a payor (the employer, its agent, or a third party). Section 62(c) provides that an arrangement will not be treated as a reimbursement or other expense allowance arrangement for purposes of section 62(a)(2)(A) if (1) such arrangement does not require the employee to substantiate the expenses covered by the arrangement to the payor, or (2) such arrangement provides the employee the right to retain any amount in excess of the substantiated expenses covered under the arrangement. This section prescribes rules relating to the requirements of section 62(c).

(c) *Reimbursement or other expense allowance arrangement*—(1) *Defined.* For purposes of §§ 1.62-1, 1.62-1T and 1.62-2, the phrase "reimbursement or other expense allowance arrangement" means an arrangement that meets the requirements of paragraphs (d) (business connection), (e) (substantiation), and (f) (returning amounts in excess of expenses) of this section. A payor may have more than one arrangement with respect to a particular employee, depending on the facts and circumstances. See paragraph (d)(2) of this section (payor treated as having two arrangements under certain circumstances).

(2) *Accountable plans*—(i) *In general.* Except as provided in paragraph (c)(2)(ii) of this section, if an arrangement meets the requirements of paragraphs (d), (e), and (f) of this sec-

tion, all amounts paid under the arrangement are treated as paid under an "accountable plan."

(ii) *Special rule for failure to return excess.* If an arrangement meets the requirements of paragraphs (d), (e), and (f) of this section, but the employee fails to return, within a reasonable period of time, any amount in excess of the amount of the expenses substantiated in accordance with paragraph (e) of this section, only the amounts paid under the arrangement that are not in excess of the substantiated expenses are treated as paid under an accountable plan.

(3) *Nonaccountable plans*—(i) *In general.* If an arrangement does not satisfy one or more of the requirements of paragraphs (d), (e), or (f) of this section, all amounts paid under the arrangement are treated as paid under a "nonaccountable plan." If a payor provides a nonaccountable plan, an employee who receives payments under the plan cannot compel the payor to treat the payments as paid under an accountable plan by voluntarily substantiating the expenses and returning any excess to the payor.

(ii) *Special rule for failure to return excess.* If an arrangement meets the requirements of paragraphs (d), (e), and (f) of this section, but the employee fails to return, within a reasonable period of time, any amount in excess of the amount of the expenses substantiated in accordance with paragraph (e) of this section, the amounts paid under the arrangement that are in excess of the substantiated expenses are treated as paid under a nonaccountable plan.

(4) *Treatment of payments under accountable plans.* Amounts treated as paid under an accountable plan are excluded from the employee's gross income, are not reported as wages or other compensation on the employee's Form W-2, and are exempt from the withholding and payment of employment taxes (Federal Insurance Contributions Act (FICA), Federal Unemployment Tax Act (FUTA), Railroad Retirement Tax Act (RRTA), Railroad Unemployment Repayment Tax (RURT), and income tax). See paragraph (l) of this section for cross references.

(5) *Treatment of payments under nonaccountable plans.* Amounts treated as paid under a nonaccountable plan are included in the employee's gross income, must be reported as wages or other compensation on the employee's Form W-2, and are subject to withholding and payment of employment taxes (FICA, FUTA, RRTA, RURT, and income tax). See paragraph (h) of this section. Expenses attributable to amounts included in the employee's gross income may be deducted, provided the employee can substantiate the full amount of his or her expenses (i.e., the amount of the expenses, if any, the reimburse-

ment for which is treated as paid under an accountable plan as well as those for which the employee is claiming the deduction) in accordance with § 1.274-5T and 1.274(d)-1 or § 1.162-17, but only as a miscellaneous itemized deduction subject to the limitations applicable to such expenses (e.g., the 80-percent limitation on meal and entertainment expenses provided in section 274(n) and the 2-percent floor provided in section 67).

(d) *Business connection*—(1) *In general.* Except as provided in paragraphs (d)(2) and (d)(3) of this section, an arrangement meets the requirements of this paragraph (d) if it provides advances, allowances (including per diem allowances, allowances only for meals and incidental expenses, and mileage allowances), or reimbursements only for business expenses that are allowable as deductions by Part VI (section 161 and the following), subchapter B, chapter 1 of the Code, and that are paid or incurred by the employee in connection with the performance of services as an employee of the employer. The payment may be actually received from the employer, its agent, or a third party for whom the employee performs a service as an employee of the employer, and may include amounts charged directly or indirectly to the payor through credit card systems or otherwise. In addition, if both wages and the reimbursement or other expense allowance are combined in a single payment, the reimbursement or other expense allowance must be identified either by making a separate payment or by specifically identifying the amount of the reimbursement or other expense allowance.

(2) *Other bona fide expenses.* If an arrangement provides advances, allowances, or reimbursements for business expenses described in paragraph (d)(1) of this section (i.e., deductible employee business expenses) and for other bona fide expenses related to the employer's business (e.g., travel that is not away from home) that are not deductible under Part VI (section 161 and the following), subchapter B, chapter 1 of the Code, the payor is treated as maintaining two arrangements. The portion of the arrangement that provides payments for the deductible employee business expenses is treated as one arrangement that satisfies this paragraph (d). The portion of the arrangement that provides payments for the nondeductible employee expenses is treated as a second arrangement that does not satisfy this paragraph (d) and all amounts paid under this second arrangement will be treated as paid under a nonaccountable plan. See paragraphs (c)(5) and (h) of this section.

(3) *Reimbursement requirement*—(i) *In general.* If a payor arranges to pay an amount to an employee regardless of whether the employee incurs (or is reasonably expected to incur) business expenses of a type described in paragraph (d)(1) or (d)(2) of this section, the arrangement does not satisfy this paragraph (d) and all amounts paid under the arrangement are treated as paid under a nonaccountable plan. See paragraphs (c)(5) and (h) of this section.

(ii) *Per diem allowances.* An arrangement providing a per diem allowance for travel expenses of a type described in paragraph (d)(1) or (d)(2) of this section that is computed on a basis similar to that used in computing the employee's wages or other compensation (e.g., the number of hours worked, miles traveled, or pieces produced) meets the requirements of this paragraph (d) only if, on December 12, 1989, the per diem allowance was identified by the payor either by making a separate payment or by specifically identifying the amount of the per diem allowance, or a per diem allowance computed on that basis was commonly used in the industry in which the employee is employed. See section 274(d) and § 1.274(d)-1. A per diem allowance described in this paragraph (d)(3)(ii) may be adjusted in a manner that reasonably reflects actual increases in employee business expenses occurring after December 12, 1989.

(e) *Substantiation*—(1) *In general.* An arrangement meets the requirements of this paragraph (e) if it requires each business expense to be substantiated to the payor in accordance with paragraph (e)(2) or (e)(3) of this section, whichever is applicable, within a reasonable period of time. See § 1.274-5T or § 1.162-17.

(2) *Expenses governed by section 274(d).* An arrangement that reimburses travel, entertainment, use of a passenger automobile or other listed property, or other business expenses governed by section 274(d) meets the requirements of this paragraph (e)(2) if information sufficient to satisfy the substantiation requirements of section 274(d) and the regulations thereunder is submitted to the payor. See § 1.274-5. Under section 274(d), information sufficient to substantiate the requisite elements of each expenditure or use must be submitted to the payor. For example, with respect to travel away from home, § 1.274-5(b)(2) requires that information sufficient to substantiate the amount, time, place, and business purpose of the expense must be submitted to the payor. Similarly, with respect to use of a passenger automobile or other listed property, § 1.274-5(b)(6) requires that information sufficient to substantiate the amount, time, use, and business purpose of the expense must be submitted to the payor. See § 1.274-5(g), however, which grants the Commissioner authority to prescribe rules permitting the amount of certain expenses to be deemed substantiated to the payor (in lieu of substantiating the actual amount of such expenses) by means of per diem or mileage rates for

Reg. § 1.62-2(e)(2)

travel away from home or transportation expenses. See also § 1.274-5(j)(1), which grants the Commissioner the authority to establish a method under which a taxpayer may use a specified amount for meals while traveling away from home in lieu of substantiating the actual cost of meals, and § 1.274-5(j)(2), which grants the Commissioner the authority to establish a method under which a taxpayer may use mileage rates to determine the amount of the ordinary and necessary expenses of using a vehicle for local transportation and transportation to, from, and at the destination while traveling away from home in lieu of substantiating the actual costs. Substantiation of the amount of a business expense in accordance with rules prescribed pursuant to the authority granted by § 1.274-5(g) or (j) will be treated as substantiation of the amount of such expense for purposes of this section.

(3) *Expenses not governed by section 274(d)*. An arrangement that reimburses business expenses not governed by section 274(d) meets the requirements of this paragraph (e)(3) if information is submitted to the payor sufficient to enable the payor to identify the specific nature of each expense and to conclude that the expense is attributable to the payor's business activities. Therefore, each of the elements of an expenditure or use must be substantiated to the payor. It is not sufficient if an employee merely aggregates expenses into broad categories (such as "travel") or reports individual expenses through the use of vague, nondescriptive terms (such as "miscellaneous business expenses"). See § 1.162-17(b).

* * *

[Reg. § 1.62-2.]

☐ [*T.D.* 8324, 12-14-90. *Amended by T.D.* 8451, 12-4-92; *T.D.* 8666, 5-29-96; *T.D.* 8784, 9-30-98 *and T.D.* 8864, 1-21-2000.]

§ 1.67-1T. 2-percent floor on miscellaneous itemized deductions (temporary).—(a) *Type of expenses subject to the floor*—(1) *In general*. With respect to individuals, section 67 disallows deductions for miscellaneous itemized deductions (as defined in paragraph (b) of this section) in computing taxable income (*i.e.*, so-called "below-the-line" deductions) to the extent that such otherwise allowable deductions do not exceed 2 percent of the individual's adjusted gross income (as defined in section 62 and the regulations thereunder). Examples of expenses that, if otherwise deductible, are subject to the 2-percent floor include but are not limited to—

(i) Unreimbursed employee expenses, such as expenses for transportation, travel fares and lodging while away from home, business meals and entertainment, continuing education courses, subscriptions to professional journals, union or professional dues, professional uniforms, job hunting, and the business use of the employee's home,

(ii) Expenses for the production or collection of income for which a deduction is otherwise allowable under section 212(1) and (2), such as investment advisory fees, subscriptions to investment advisory publications, certain attorneys' fees, and the cost of safe deposit boxes,

(iii) Expenses for the determination of any tax for which a deduction is otherwise allowable under section 212(3), such as tax counsel fees and appraisal fees, and

(iv) Expenses for an activity for which a deduction is otherwise allowable under section 183.

See section 62 with respect to deductions that are allowable in computing adjusted gross income (*i.e.*, so-called "above-the-line" deductions).

(2) *Other limitations.* Except as otherwise provided in paragraph (d) of this section, to the extent that any limitation or restriction is placed on the amount of a miscellaneous itemized deduction, that limitation shall apply prior to the application of the 2-percent floor. For example, in the case of an expense for food or beverages, only 80 percent of which is allowable as a deduction because of the limitations provided in section 274(n), the otherwise deductible 80 percent of the expense is treated as a miscellaneous itemized deduction and is subject to the 2-percent limitation of section 67.

(b) *Definition of miscellaneous itemized deductions.* For purposes of this section, the term "miscellaneous itemized deductions" means the deductions allowable from adjusted gross income in determining taxable income, as defined in section 63, other than—

(1) The standard deduction as defined in section 63(c),

(2) Any deduction allowable for impairment-related work expenses as defined in section 67(d),

(3) The deduction under section 72(b)(3) (relating to deductions if annuity payments cease before the investment is recovered),

(4) The deductions allowable under section 151 for personal exemptions,

(5) The deduction under section 163 (relating to interest),

(6) The deduction under section 164 (relating to taxes),

(7) The deduction under section 165(a) for losses described in subsection (c)(3) or (d) of section 165,

(8) The deduction under section 170 (relating to charitable contributions and gifts),

(9) The deduction under section 171 (relating to deductions for amortizable bond premiums),

(10) The deduction under section 213 (relating to medical and dental expenses),

(11) The deduction under section 216 (relating to deductions in connection with cooperative housing corporations),

(12) The deduction under section 217 (relating to moving expenses),

(13) The deduction under section 691(c) (relating to the deduction for estate taxes in the case of income in respect of the decedent),

(14) The deduction under 1341 (relating to the computation of tax if a taxpayer restores a substantial amount held under claim of right), and

(15) Any deduction allowable in connection with personal property used in a short sale.

(c) *Allocation of expenses.* If a taxpayer incurs expenses that relate to both a trade or business activity (within the meaning of section 162) and a production of income or tax preparation activity (within the meaning of section 212), the taxpayer shall allocate such expenses between the activities on a reasonable basis.

* * *

[Temporary Reg. § 1.67-1T.]

☐ [*T.D.* 8189, 3-25-88.]

Items Specifically Included in Gross Income

§ 1.71-1T. Alimony and separate maintenance payments (temporary).—(a) *In general.*

Q-1. What is the income tax treatment of alimony or separate maintenance payments?

A-1. Alimony or separate maintenance payments are, under section 71, included in the gross income of the payee spouse and, under section 215, allowed as a deduction from the gross income of the payor spouse.

Q-2. What is an alimony or separate maintenance payment?

A-2. An alimony or separate maintenance payment is any payment received by or on behalf of a spouse (which for this purpose includes a former spouse) of the payor under a divorce or separation instrument that meets all of the following requirements:

(a) The payment is in cash (see A-5).

(b) The payment is not designated as a payment which is excludible from the gross income of the payee and nondeductible by the payor (see A-8).

(c) In the case of spouses legally separated under a decree of divorce or separate maintenance, the spouses are not members of the same household at the time the payment is made (see A-9).

(d) The payor has no liability to continue to make any payment after the death of the payee (or to make any payment as a substitute for such payment) and the divorce or separation instrument states that there is no such liability (see A-10).

(e) The payment is not treated as child support (see A-15).

(f) To the extent that one or more annual payments exceed $10,000 during any of the 6-post-separation years, the payor is obligated to make annual payments in each of the post-separation years (see A-19).

Q-3. In order to be treated as alimony or separate maintenance payments, must the payments be "periodic" as that term was defined prior to enactment of the Tax Reform Act of 1984 or be made in discharge of a legal obligation of the payor to support the payee arising out of a marital or family relationship?

A-3. No. The Tax Reform Act of 1984 replaces the old requirements with the requirements described in A-2 above. Thus, the requirements that alimony or separate maintenance payments be "periodic" and be made in discharge of a legal obligation to support arising out of a marital or family relationship have been eliminated.

Q-4. Are the instruments described in section 71(a) of prior law the same as divorce or separation instruments described in section 71, as amended by the Tax Reform Act of 1984?

A-4. Yes.

(b) *Specific requirements.*

Q-5. May alimony or separate maintenance payments be made in a form other than cash?

A-5. No. Only cash payments (including checks and money orders payable on demand) qualify as alimony or separate maintenance payments. Transfers of services or property (including a debt instrument of a third party or an annuity contract), execution of a debt instrument by the payor, or the use of property of the payor do not qualify as alimony or separate maintenance payments.

Q-6. May payments of cash to a third party on behalf of a spouse qualify as alimony or separate maintenance payments if the payments are pursuant to the terms of a divorce or separation instrument?

A-6. Yes. Assuming all other requirements are satisfied, a payment of cash by the payor spouse to a third party under the terms of the divorce or separation instrument will qualify as a payment of cash which is received "on behalf of a spouse".

For example, cash payments of rent, mortgage, tax, or tuition liabilities of the payee spouse made under the terms of the divorce or separation instrument will qualify as alimony or separate maintenance payments. Any payments to maintain property owned by the payor spouse and used by the payee spouse (including mortgage payments, real estate taxes and insurance premiums) are not payments on behalf of a spouse even if those payments are made pursuant to the terms of the divorce or separation instrument. Premiums paid by the payor spouse for term or whole life insurance on the payor's life made under the terms of the divorce or separation instrument will qualify as payments on behalf of the payee spouse to the extent that the payee spouse is the owner of the policy.

Q-7. May payments of cash to a third party on behalf of a spouse qualify as alimony or separate maintenance payments if the payments are made to the third party at the written request of the payee spouse?

A-7. Yes. For example, instead of making an alimony or separate maintenance payment directly to the payee, the payor spouse may make a cash payment to a charitable organization if such payment is pursuant to the written request, consent or ratification of the payee spouse. Such request, consent or ratification must state that the parties intend the payment to be treated as an alimony or separate maintenance payment to the payee spouse subject to the rules of section 71, and must be received by the payor spouse prior to the date of filing of the payor's first return of tax for the taxable year in which the payment was made.

Q-8. How may spouses designate that payments otherwise qualifying as alimony or separate maintenance payments shall be excludible from the gross income of the payee and nondeductible by the payor?

A-8. The spouses may designate that payments otherwise qualifying as alimony or separate maintenance payments shall be nondeductible by the payor and excludible from gross income by the payee by so providing in a divorce or separation instrument (as defined in section 71(b)(2)). If the spouses have executed a written separation agreement (as described in section 71(b)(2)(B)), any writing signed by both spouses which designates otherwise qualifying alimony or separate maintenance payments as nondeductible and excludible and which refers to the written separation agreement will be treated as a written separation agreement (and thus a divorce or separation instrument) for purposes of the preceding sentence. If the spouses are subject to temporary support orders (as described in section 71(b)(2)(C)), the designation of otherwise qualifying alimony or separate payments as nondeductible and excludible must be made in the original or a subsequent temporary support order. A copy of the instrument containing the designation of payments as not alimony or separate maintenance payments must be attached to the payee's first filed return of tax (Form 1040) for each year in which the designation applies.

Q-9. What are the consequences if, at the time a payment is made, the payor and payee spouses are members of the same household?

A-9. Generally, a payment made at the time when the payor and payee spouses are members of the same household cannot qualify as an alimony or separate maintenance payment if the spouses are legally separated under a decree of divorce or of separate maintenance. For purposes of the preceding sentence, a dwelling unit formerly shared by both spouses shall not be considered two separate households even if the spouses physically separate themselves within the dwelling unit. The spouses will not be treated as members of the same household if one spouse is preparing to depart from the household of the other spouse, and does depart not more than one month after the date the payment is made. If the spouses are not legally separated under a decree of divorce or separate maintenance, a payment under a written separation agreement or a decree described in section 71(b)(2)(C) may qualify as an alimony or separate maintenance payment notwithstanding that the payor and payee are members of the same household at the time the payment is made.

Q-10. Assuming all other requirements relating to the qualification of certain payments as alimony or separate maintenance payments are met, what are the consequences if the payor spouse is required to continue to make the payments after the death of the payee spouse?

A-10. None of the payments before (or after) the death of the payee spouse qualify as alimony or separate maintenance payments.

* * *

Q-13. What are the consequences if the payor spouse is required to make one or more payments (in cash or property) after the death of the payee spouse as a substitute for the continuation of pre-death payments which would otherwise qualify as alimony or separate maintenance payments?

A-13. If the payor spouse is required to make any such substitute payments, none of the otherwise qualifying payments will qualify as alimony or separate maintenance payments. The divorce or separation instrument need not state, however, that there is no liability to make any such substitute payment.

Reg. § 1.71-1T(b)

Q-14. Under what circumstances will one or more payments (in cash or property) which are to occur after the death of the payee spouse be treated as a substitute for a continuation of payments which would otherwise qualify as alimony or separate maintenance payments?

A-14. To the extent that one or more payments are to begin to be made, increase in amount, or become accelerated in time as a result of the death of the payee spouse, such payments may be treated as a substitute for the continuation of payments terminating on the death of the payee spouse which would otherwise qualify as alimony or separate maintenance payments. The determination of whether or not such payments are a substitute for the continuation of payments which would otherwise qualify as alimony or separate maintenance payments, and of the amount of the otherwise qualifying alimony or separate maintenance payments for which any such payments are a substitute, will depend on all of the facts and circumstances.

Example (1). Under the terms of a divorce decree, A is obligated to make annual alimony payments to B of $30,000, terminating on the earlier of the expiration of 6 years or the death of B. B maintains custody of the minor children of A and B. The decree provides that at the death of B, if there are minor children of A and B remaining, A will be obligated to make annual payments of $10,000 to a trust, the income and corpus of which are to be used for the benefit of the children until the youngest child attains the age of majority. These facts indicate that A's liability to make annual $10,000 payments in trust for the benefit of his minor children upon the death of B is a substitute for $10,000 of the $30,000 annual payments to B. Accordingly, $10,000 of each of the $30,000 annual payments to B will not qualify as alimony or separate maintenance payments.

Example (2). Under the terms of a divorce decree, A is obligated to make annual alimony payments to B of $30,000, terminating on the earlier of the expiration of 15 years or the death of B. The divorce decree provides that if B dies before the expiration of the 15 year period, A will pay to B's estate the difference between the total amount that A would have paid had B survived, minus the amount actually paid. For example, if B dies at the end of the 10th year in which payments are made, A will pay to B's estate $150,000 ($450,000 − $300,000). These facts indicate that A's liability to make a lump sum payment to B's estate upon the death of B is a substitute for the full amount of each of the annual $30,000 payments to B. Accordingly, none of the annual $30,000 payments to B will qualify as alimony or separate maintenance payments. The result would be the same if the lump sum payable

at B's death were discounted by an appropriate interest factor to account for the prepayment.

(c) *Child support payments.*

Q-15. What are the consequences of a payment which the terms of the divorce or separation instrument fix as payable for the support of a child of the payor spouse?

A-15. A payment which under the terms of the divorce or separation instrument is fixed (or treated as fixed) as payable for the support of a child of the payor spouse does not qualify as an alimony or separate maintenance payment. Thus, such a payment is not deductible by the payor spouse or includible in the income of the payee spouse.

Q-16. When is a payment fixed (or treated as fixed) as payable for the support of a child of the payor spouse?

A-16. A payment is fixed as payable for the support of a child of the payor spouse if the divorce or separation instrument specifically designates some sum or portion (which sum or portion may fluctuate) as payable for the support of a child of the payor spouse. A payment will be treated as fixed as payable for the support of a child of the payor spouse if the payment is reduced (a) on the happening of a contingency relating to a child of the payor, or (b) at a time which can clearly be associated with such a contingency. A payment may be treated as fixed as payable for the support of a child of the payor spouse even if other separate payments specifically are designated as payable for the support of a child of the payor spouse.

Q-17. When does a contingency relate to a child of the payor?

A-17. For this purpose, a contingency relates to a child of the payor if it depends on any event relating to that child, regardless of whether such event is certain or likely to occur. Events that relate to a child of the payor include the following: the child's attaining a specified age or income level, dying, marrying, leaving school, leaving the spouse's household, or gaining employment.

Q-18. When will a payment be treated as to be reduced at a time which can clearly be associated with the happening of a contingency relating to a child of the payor?

A-18. There are two situations, described below, in which payments which would otherwise qualify as alimony or separate maintenance payments will be presumed to be reduced at a time clearly associated with the happening of a contingency relating to a child of the payor. In all other situations, reductions in payments will not be treated as clearly associated with the happening of a contingency relating to a child of the payor.

The first situation referred to above is where the payments are to be reduced not more than 6 months before or after the date the child is to attain the age of 18, 21, or local age of majority. The second situation is where the payments are to be reduced on two or more occasions which occur not more than one year before or after a different child of the payor spouse attains a certain age between the ages of 18 and 24, inclusive. The certain age referred to in the preceding sentence must be the same for each such child, but need not be a whole number of years.

The presumption in the two situations described above that payments are to be reduced at a time clearly associated with the happening of a contingency relating to a child of the payor may be rebutted (either by the Service or by taxpayers) by showing that the time at which the payments are to be reduced was determined independently of any contingencies relating to the children of the payor. The presumption in the first situation will be rebutted conclusively if the reduction is a complete cessation of alimony or separate maintenance payments during the sixth post-separation year (described in A-21) or upon the expiration of a 72-month period. The presumption may also be rebutted in other circumstances, for example, by showing that alimony payments are to be made for a period customarily provided in the local jurisdiction, such as a period equal to one-half the duration of the marriage.

Example: A and B are divorced on July 1, 1985, when their children, C (born July 15, 1970) and D (born September 23, 1972), are 14 and 12, respectively. Under the divorce decree, A is to make alimony payments to B of $2,000 per month. Such payments are to be reduced to $1,500 per month on January 1, 1991 and to $1,000 per month on January 1, 1995. On January 1, 1991, the date of the first reduction in payments, C will be 20 years 5 months and 17 days old. On January 1, 1995, the date of the second reduction in payments, D will be 22 years 3 months and 9 days old. Each of the reductions in payments is to occur not more than one year before or after a different child of A attains the age of 21 years and 4 months. (Actually, the reductions are to occur not more than one year before or after C and D attain *any* of the ages 21 years 3 months and 9 days through 21 years 5 months and 17 days.) Accordingly, the reductions will be presumed to clearly be associated with the happening of a contingency relating to C and D. Unless this presumption is rebutted, payments under the divorce decree equal to the sum of the reductions ($1,000 per month) will be treated as fixed for the support of the children of

A and therefore will not quaify as alimony or separate maintenance payments.

* * *

[Temporary Reg. § 1.71-1T.]

☐ [*T.D. 7973, 8-30-84.*]

§ 1.72-1. Introduction.—(a) *General principle.* Section 72 prescribes rules relating to the inclusion in gross income of amounts received under a life insurance, endowment, or annuity contract unless such amounts are specifically excluded from gross income under other provisions of chapter 1 of the Code. In general, these rules provide that amounts subject to the provisions of section 72 are includible in the gross income of the recipient except to the extent that they are considered to represent a reduction or return of premiums or other consideration paid.

(b) *Amounts to be considered as a return of premiums.* For the purpose of determining the extent to which amounts received represent a reduction or return of premiums or other consideration paid, the provisions of section 72 distinguish between "amounts received as an annuity" and "amounts not received as an annuity". In general, "amounts received as an annuity" are amounts which are payable at regular intervals over a period of more than one full year from the date on which they are deemed to begin, provided the total of the amounts so payable or the period for which they are to be paid can be determined as of that date. See paragraph (b)(2) and (3) of § 1.72.2. Any other amounts to which the provisions of section 72 apply are considered to be "amounts not received as an annuity." See § 1.72-11.

(c) *"Amounts received as an annuity."* (1) In the case of "amounts received as an annuity" (other than certain employees' annuities described in section 72(d) and in § 1.72-13), a proportionate part of each amount so received is considered to represent a return of premiums or other consideration paid. The proportionate part of each annuity payment which is thus excludable from gross income is determined by the ratio which the investment in the contract as of the date on which the annuity is deemed to begin bears to the expected return under the contract as of that date. See § 1.72-4.

(2) In the case of employees' annuities of the type described in section 72(d), no amount received as an annuity in a taxable year to which the Internal Revenue Code of 1954 applies is includible in the gross income of a recipient until the aggregate of all amounts received thereunder and excluded from gross income under the applicable income tax law exceeds the consideration contributed (or deemed contributed) by the employee under § 1.72-8. Thereafter, all amounts so

received are includible in the gross income of the recipient. See § 1.72-13.

(d) *"Amounts not received as an annuity"*. In the case of "amounts not received as an annuity", if such amounts are received after an annuity has begun and during its continuance, amounts so received are generally includible in the gross income of the recipient. Amounts not received as an annuity which are received at any other time are generally includible in the gross income of the recipient only to the extent that such amounts, when added to all amounts previously received under the contract which were excludable from the gross income of the recipient under the income tax law applicable at the time of receipt, exceed the premiums or other consideration paid (see § 1.72-11). However, if the aggregate of premiums or other consideration paid for the contract includes amounts for which a deduction was allowed under section 404 as contributions on behalf of an owner-employee, the amounts received under the circumstances of the preceding sentence shall be includible in gross income until the amount so included equals the amount for which the deduction was so allowed. See paragraph (b) of § 1.72-17.

(e) *Classification of recipients.* For the purpose of the regulations under section 72, a recipient shall be considered an "annuitant" if he receives amounts under an annuity contract during the period that the annuity payments are to continue, whether for a term certain or during the continuing life or lives of the person or persons whose lives measure the duration of such annuity. However, a recipient shall be considered a "beneficiary" rather than an "annuitant" if the amounts he receives under a contract are received after the term of the annuity for a life or lives has expired and such amounts are paid by reason of the fact that the contract guarantees that payments of some minimum amount or for some minimum period shall be made. For special rules with respect to beneficiaries, see paragraphs (a)(1)(ii) and (c) of § 1.72-11. [Reg. § 1.72-1.]

□ [*T.D.* 6211, 11-14-56. *Amended by T.D.* 6676, 9-16-63.]

§ 1.72-4. Exclusion ratio.—(a) *General rule.* (1)(i) To determine the proportionate part of the total amount received each year as an annuity which is excludable from the gross income of a recipient in the taxable year of receipt (other than amounts received under (*a*) certain employee annuities described in section 72(d) and § 1.72-13, or (*b*) certain annuities described in section 72(o) and § 1.122-1), an exclusion ratio is to be determined for each contract. In general, this ratio is determined by dividing the investment in the contract as found under § 1.72-6 by the expected return under such contract as found under § 1.72-5. Where a single consideration is given for a particular contract which provides for two or more annuity elements, an exclusion ratio shall be determined for the contract as a whole by dividing the investment in such contract by the aggregate of the expected returns under all the annuity elements provided thereunder. However, where the provisions of paragraph (b)(3) of § 1.72-2 apply to payments received under such a contract, see paragraph (b)(3) of § 1.72-6. In the case of a contract to which § 1.72-6(d) (relating to contracts in which amounts were invested both before July 1, 1986, and after June 30, 1986) applies, the exclusion ratio for purposes of this paragraph (a) is determined in accordance with § 1.72-6(d) and, in particular, § 1.72-6(d)(5)(i).

(ii) The exclusion ratio for the particular contract is then applied to the total amount received as an annuity during the taxable year by each recipient. See, however, paragraph (e)(3) of § 1.72-5. Any excess of the total amount received as an annuity during the taxable year over the amount determined by the application of the exclusion ratio to such total amount shall be included in the gross income of the recipient for the taxable year of receipt.

(2) The principles of subparagraph (1) may be illustrated by the following example:

Example. Taxpayer A purchased an annuity contract providing for payments of $100 per month for a consideration of $12,650. Assuming that the expected return under this contract is $16,000 the exclusion ratio to be used by A is $12,650 ÷ [$]16,000; or 79.1 percent (79.06 rounded to the nearest tenth). If 12 such monthly payments are received by A during his taxable year, the total amount he may exclude from his gross income in such year is $949.20 ($1,200 × 79.1 percent). The balance of $250.80 ($1,200 less $949.20) is the amount to be included in gross income. If A instead received only five such payments during the year, he should exclude $395.50 ([$]500 × 79.1 percent) of the total amounts received.

For examples of the computation of the exclusion ratio in cases where two annuity elements are acquired for a single consideration, see paragraph (b)(1) of § 1.72-6.

(3) The exclusion ratio shall be applied only to amounts received as an annuity within the meaning of that term under paragraph (b)(2) and (3) of § 1.72-2. Where the periodic payments increase in amount after the annuity starting date in a manner not provided by the terms of the contract at such date, the portion of such payments representing the increase is not an amount received as an annuity. For the treatment of

Reg. § 1.72-4(a)(3)

amounts not received as an annuity, see section 72(e) and § 1.72-11. For special rules where paragraph (b)(3) of § 1.72-2 applies to amounts received, see paragraph (d)(3) of this section.

(4) After an exclusion ratio has been determined for a particular contract, it shall be applied to any amounts received as an annuity thereunder unless or until one of the following occurs:

(i) The contract is assigned or transferred for a valuable consideration (see section 72(g) and paragraph (a) of § 1.72-10);

(ii) The contract matures or is surrendered, redeemed, or discharged in accordance with the provisions of paragraph (c) or (d) of § 1.72-11;

(iii) The contract is exchanged (or is considered to have been exchanged) in a manner described in paragraph (e) of § 1.72-11.

(b) *Annuity starting date.* (1) Except as provided in subparagraph (2) of this paragraph, the annuity starting date is the first day of the first period for which an amount is received as an annuity, except that if such date was before January 1, 1954, then the annuity starting date is January 1, 1954. The first day of the first period for which an amount is received as an annuity shall be whichever of the following is the later:

(i) The date upon which the obligations under the contract became fixed, or

(ii) The first day of the period (year, half-year, quarter, month, or otherwise, depending on whether payments are to be made annually, semi-annually, quarterly, monthly, or otherwise) which ends on the date of the first annuity payment.

(2) Notwithstanding the provisions of paragraph (b)(1) of this section, the annuity starting date shall be determined in accordance with whichever of the following provisions is appropriate:

(i) In the case of a joint and survivor annuity contract described in section 72(i) and paragraph (b)(3) of § 1.72-5, the annuity starting date is January 1, 1954, or the first day of the first period for which an amount is received as an annuity by the surviving annuitant, whichever is the later;

(ii) In the case of the transfer of an annuity contract for a valuable consideration, as de-

scribed in section 72(g) and paragraph (a) of § 1.72-10, the annuity starting date shall be January 1, 1954, or the first day of the first period for which the transferee received an amount as an annuity, whichever is the later;

(iii) If the provisions of paragraph (e) of § 1.72-11 apply to an exchange of one contract for another, or to a transaction deemed to be such an exchange, the annuity starting date of the contract received (or deemed received) in exchange shall be January 1, 1954, or the first day of the first period for which an amount is received as an annuity under such contract, whichever is the later; and

(iv) In the case of an employee who has retired from work because of personal injuries or sickness, and who is receiving amounts under a plan that is a wage continuation plan under section 105(d) and § 1.105-4, the annuity starting date shall be the date the employee reaches mandatory retirement age, as defined in § 1.105-4(a)(3)(i)(B). (See, also §§ 1.72-15 and 1.105-6 for transitional and other special rules.)

* * *

[Reg. § 1.72-4.]

☐ [*T.D.* 6211, 11-14-56. *Amended by T.D.* 7043, 6-1-70, *T.D.* 7352, 4-9-75, and *T.D.* 8115, 12-16-86.]

§ 1.72-5. Expected return.—(a) *Expected return for but one life.* (1) If a contract to which section 72 applies provides that one annuitant is to receive a fixed monthly income for life, the expected return is determined by multiplying the total of the annuity payments to be received annually by the multiple shown in Table I or V (whichever is applicable) of § 1.79-9 under the age (as of the annuity starting date) and, if applicable, sex of the measuring life (usually the annuitant's). Thus, where a male purchases a contract before July 1, 1986, providing for an immediate annuity of $100 per month for his life and, as of the annuity starting date (in this case the date of purchase), the annuitant's age at his nearest birthday is 66, the expected return is computed as follows:

Monthly payment of $100 × 12 months equals annual payment of	$ 1,200
Multiple shown in Table I, male, age 66	14.4
Expected return ($1,200 × 14.4)	17,280

If, however, the taxpayer had purchased the contract after June 30, 1986, the expected return would be $23,040, determined by multiplying 19.2 (multiple shown in Table V, age 66) by $1,200.

(b) *Expected return under joint and survivor and joint annuities.* (1) In the case of a joint and survivor annuity contract involving two annuitants which provides the first annuitant with a fixed monthly income for life and, after the death of the first annuitant, provides an identical

* * *

Reg. § 1.72-5(a)

monthly income for life to a second annuitant, the expected return shall be determined by multiplying the total amount of the payments to be received annually by the multiple obtained from Table II or VI (whichever is applicable) of § 1.72-9 under the ages (as of the annuity starting date) and, if applicable, sexes of the living annuitants. For example, a husband purchases a joint

and survivor annuity contract providing for payments of $100 per month for life and, after his death, for the same amount to his wife for the remainder of her life. As of the annuity starting date his age at his nearest birthday is 70 and that of his wife at her nearest birthday is 67. If there is no post-June 1986 investment in the contract, the expected return is computed as follows:

Monthly payments of $100 × 12 months equals annual payment of . . . . $ 1,200
Multiple shown in Table II (male, age 70, female, age 67) 19.7

Expected return ($1,200 × 19.7) $23,640

If the annuitants purchased the same contract after June 30, 1986, the expected return would be $26,400, computed as follows:

Monthly payments of $100 × 12 months equals annual payment of . . . . $ 1,200
Multiple shown in Table VI (ages 70, 67) 22.0

Expected return ($1,200 × 22.0) $26,400

If payments are to be made quarterly, semiannually, or annually, an appropriate adjustment of the multiple found in Table II or VI (whichever is applicable) should be made in accordance with paragraph (a)(2) of this section.

* * *

(c) *Expected return for term certain.* In the case of a contract providing for specific periodic payments which are to be paid for a term certain such as a fixed number of months or years, without regard to life expectancy, the expected return is determined by multiplying the fixed number of years or months for which payments are to be on or after the annuity starting date by the amount of the payment provided in the contract for each such period.

* * *

[Reg. § 1.72-5.]

□ [*T.D. 6211, 11-14-56. Amended by T.D. 8115, 12-16-86.*]

§ 1.72-6. Investment in the contract.—(a) *General rule.* (1) For the purpose of computing the "investment in the contract", it is first necessary to determine the "aggregate amount of premiums or other consideration paid" for such contract. See section 72(c)(1). This determination is made as of the later of the annuity starting date of the contract or the date on which an amount is first received thereunder as an annuity. The amount so found is then reduced by the sum of the following amounts in order to find the investment in the contract:

    (i) The total amount of any return of premiums or dividends received (including unrepaid loans or dividends applied against the principal or interest on such loans) on or before the date on which the foregoing determination is made, and

    (ii) The total of any other amounts received with respect to the contract on or before

such date which were excludable from the gross income for the recipient under the income tax law applicable at the time of receipt.

Amounts to which subdivision (ii) of this subparagraph applies shall include, for example, amounts considered to be return of premiums or other consideration paid under section 22(b)(2) of the Internal Revenue Code of 1939 and amounts considered to be an employer-provided death benefit under section 22(b)(1)(B) of such Code. For rules relating to the extent to which an employee or his beneficiary may include employer contributions in the aggregate amount of premiums or other consideration paid, see § 1.72-8. If the aggregate amount of premiums or other consideration paid for the contract includes amounts for which deductions were allowed under section 404 as contributions on behalf of a self-employed individual, such amounts shall not be included in the investment in the contract.

* * *

[Reg. § 1.72-6.]

□ [*T.D. 6211, 11-14-56. Amended by T.D. 6676, 9-16-63, T.D. 7311, 3-29-74 and T.D. 8115, 12-16-86.*]

§ 1.72-9. Tables.—The following tables are to be used in connection with computations under section 72 and the regulations thereunder. Tables I, II, IIA, III, and IV are to be used if the investment in the contract does not include a post-June 1986 investment in the contract (as defined in § 1.72-6(d)(3)). Tables V, VI, VIA, VII, and VIII are to be used if the investment in the contract includes a post-June 1986 investment in the contract (as defined in § 1.72-6(d)(3)).

In the case of a contract under which amounts are received as an annuity after June 30, 1986, a taxpayer receiving such amounts may elect to treat the entire investment in the contract as

Reg. § 1.72-9

post-June 1986 investment in the contract and thus apply Tables V through VIII. A taxpayer may make the election for any taxable year in which such amounts are received by attaching to the taxpayer's return for such taxable year a statement that the taxpayer is electing under § 1.72-9 to treat the entire investment in the contract as post-June 1986 investment in the contract. The statement must contain the taxpayer's name, address, and taxpayer identification number. The election is irrevocable and applies with respect to all amounts that the taxpayer receives as an annuity under the contract in the taxable year for which the election is made or in any subsequent taxable year. (Note that for purposes of the examples in § § 1.72-4 through 1.72-11 the election described in this section is disregarded, (i.e., it is assumed that the taxpayer does not make an election under this section).)

* * *

TABLE I.—ORDINARY LIFE ANNUITIES—ONE LIFE—
EXPECTED RETURN MULTIPLES

Ages		Multiples	Ages		Multiples	Ages		Multiples
Male	Female		Male	Female		Male	Female	
6	11	65.0	41	46	33.0	76	81	9.1
7	12	64.1	42	47	32.1	77	82	8.7
8	13	63.2	43	48	31.2	78	83	8.3
9	14	62.3	44	49	30.4	79	84	7.8
10	15	61.4	45	50	29.6	80	85	7.5
11	16	60.4	46	51	28.7	81	86	7.1
12	17	59.5	47	52	27.9	82	87	6.7
13	18	58.6	48	53	27.1	83	88	6.3
14	19	57.7	49	54	26.3	84	89	6.0
15	20	56.7	50	55	25.5	85	90	5.7
16	21	55.8	51	56	24.7	86	91	5.4
17	22	54.9	52	57	24.0	87	92	5.1
18	23	53.9	53	58	23.2	88	93	4.8
19	24	53.0	54	59	22.4	89	94	4.5
20	25	52.1	55	60	21.7	90	95	4.2
21	26	51.1	56	61	21.0	91	96	4.0
22	27	50.2	57	62	20.3	92	97	3.7
23	28	49.3	58	63	19.6	93	98	3.5
24	29	48.3	59	64	18.9	94	99	3.3
25	30	47.4	60	65	18.2	95	100	3.1
26	31	46.5	61	66	17.5	96	101	2.9
27	32	45.6	62	67	16.9	97	102	2.7
28	33	44.6	63	68	16.2	98	103	2.5
29	34	43.7	64	69	15.6	99	104	2.3
30	35	42.8	65	70	15.0	100	105	2.1
31	36	41.9	66	71	14.4	101	106	1.9
32	37	41.0	67	72	13.8	102	107	1.7
33	38	40.0	68	73	13.2	103	108	1.5
34	39	39.1	69	74	12.6	104	109	1.3
35	40	38.2	70	75	12.1	105	110	1.2
						106	111	1.0
36	41	37.3	71	76	11.6	107	112	.8
37	42	36.5	72	77	11.0	108	113	.7
38	43	35.6	73	78	10.5	109	114	.6
39	44	34.7	74	79	10.1	110	115	.5
40	45	33.8	75	80	9.6	111	116	0

* * *

Reg. § 1.72-9

TABLE V.—ORDINARY LIFE ANNUITIES; ONE LIFE—EXPECTED RETURN MULTIPLES

Age	Multiple	Age	Multiple
5	76.6	61	23.3
6	75.6	62	22.5
7	74.7	63	21.6
8	73.7	64	20.8
9	72.7	65	20.0
10	71.7	66	19.2
11	70.7	67	18.4
12	69.7	68	17.6
13	68.8	69	16.8
14	67.8	70	16.0
15	66.8	71	15.3
16	65.8	72	14.6
17	64.8	73	13.9
18	63.9	74	13.2
19	62.9	75	12.5
20	61.9	76	11.9
21	60.9	77	11.2
22	59.9	78	10.6
23	59.9	79	10.0
24	58.9	80	9.5
25	57.9	81	8.9
26	56.0	82	8.4
27	55.1	83	7.9
28	54.1	84	7.4
29	53.1	85	6.9
30	52.2	86	6.5
31	51.2	87	6.1
32	50.2	88	5.7
33	49.3	89	5.3
34	48.3	90	5.0
35	47.3	91	4.7
36	46.4	92	4.4
37	45.4	93	4.1
38	44.4	94	3.9
39	43.5	95	3.7
40	42.5	96	3.4
41	41.5	97	3.2
42	40.6	98	3.0
43	39.6	99	2.8
44	38.7	100	2.7
45	37.7	101	2.5
46	36.8	102	2.3
47	35.9	103	2.1
48	34.9	104	1.9
49	34.0	105	1.8
50	33.1	106	1.6
51	32.2	107	1.4
52	31.3	108	1.3
53	30.4	109	1.1
54	29.5	110	1.0
55	28.6	111	.9
56	27.7	112	.8
57	26.8	113	.7
58	25.9	114	.6
59	25.0	115	.5
60	24.2		

* * *

[Reg. § 1.72-9.]

□ [*T.D. 6211, 11-14-56. Amended by T.D. 6233, 5-14-57 and T.D. 8115, 12-16-86.*]

§ 1.73-1. Services of child.—(a) Compensation for personal services of a child shall, regardless of the provisions of State law relating to who is entitled to the earnings of the child, and regardless of whether the income is in fact received by the child, be deemed to be the gross income of the child and not the gross income of the parent of the child. Such compensation, therefore, shall be included in the gross income of the child and shall be reflected in the return rendered by or for such child. The income of a minor child is not required to be included in the gross income of the parent for income tax purposes. For requirements for making the return by such child, or for such child by his guardian, or other person charged with the care of his person or property, see section 6012.

(b) In the determination of taxable income or adjusted gross income, as the case may be, all expenditures made by the parent or the child attributable to amounts which are includible in the gross income of the child and not of the parent

Reg. § 1.73-1(b)

solely by reason of section 73 are deemed to have been paid or incurred by the child. In such determination, the child is entitled to take deductions not only for expenditures made on his behalf by his parent which would be commonly considered as business expenses, but also for other expenditures such as charitable contributions made by the parent in the name of the child and out of the child's earnings.

(c) For purposes of section 73, the term "parent" includes any individual who is entitled to the services of the child by reason of having parental rights and duties in respect of the child. See section 6201(c) and the regulations in Part 301 of this chapter (Regulations on Procedure and Administration) for assessment of tax against the parent in certain cases. [Reg. § 1.73-1.]

☐ [*T.D. 6211, 11-14-56.*]

[*Caution: Reg. § 1.82-1 does not reflect changes made in Section 217 by the Omnibus Budget Reconciliation Act of 1993.***]**

§ 1.82-1. Payments for or reimbursements of expenses of moving from one residence to another residence attributable to employment or self-employment.—(a) *Reimbursements in gross income*—(1) *In general.* Any amount received or accrued, directly or indirectly, by an individual as a payment for or reimbursement of expenses of moving from one residence to another residence attributable to employment or self-employment is includible in gross income under section 82 as compensation for services in the taxable year received or accrued. For rules relating to the year a deduction may be allowed for expenses of moving from one residence to another residence, see section 217 and the regulations thereunder.

(2) *Amounts received or accrued as reimbursement or payment.* For purposes of this section, amounts are considered as being received or accrued by an individual as reimbursement or payment whether received in the form of money, property, or services. A cash basis taxpayer will include amounts in gross income under section 82 when they are received or treated as received by him. Thus, for example, if an employer moves an employee's household goods and personal effects from the employee's old residence to his new residence using the employer's facilities, the employee is considered as having received a payment in the amount of the fair market value of the services furnished at the time the services are furnished by the employer. If the employer pays a mover for moving the employee's household goods and personal effects, the employee is considered as having received the payment at the time the employer pays the mover, rather than at the time the mover moves the employee's household goods and effects. Where an employee receives a loan or advance from an employer to enable him to pay his moving expenses, the employee will not be deemed to have received a reimbursement of moving expenses until such time as he accounts to his employer if he is not required to repay such loan or advance and if he makes such accounting within a reasonable time. Such loan or advance will be deemed to be a reimbursement of moving expenses at the time of such accounting to the extent used by the employee for such moving expenses.

(3) *Direct or indirect payments or reimbursements.* For purposes of this section amounts are considered as being received or accrued whether received directly (paid or provided to an individual by an employer, a client, a customer, or similar person) or indirectly (paid to a third party on behalf of an individual by an employer, a client, a customer, or similar person). Thus, if an employer pays a mover for the expenses of moving an employee's household goods and personal effects from one residence to another residence, the employee has indirectly received a payment which is includible in his gross income under section 82.

(4) *Expenses of moving from one residence to another residence.* An expense of moving from one residence to another residence is any expenditure, cost, loss, or similar item paid or incurred in connection with a move from one residence to another residence. Moving expenses include (but are not limited to) any expenditure, cost, loss, or similar item directly or indirectly resulting from the acquisition, sale, or exchange of property, the transportation of goods or property, or travel (by the taxpayer or any other person) in connection with a change in residence. Such expenses include items described in section 217(b) (relating to the definition of moving expenses), irrespective of the dollar limitations contained in section 217(b)(3) and the conditions contained in section 217(c), as well as items not described in section 217(b), such as a loss sustained on the sale or exchange of personal property, storage charges, taxes, or expenses of refitting rugs or draperies.

(5) *Attributable to employment or self-employment.* Any amount received or accrued from an employer, a client, a customer, or similar person in connection with the performance of services for such employer, client, customer, or similar person, is attributable to employment or self-employment. Thus, for example, if an employer reimburses an employee for a loss incurred on the sale of the employee's house, reimbursement is attributable to the performance of services if made because of the employer-employee relationship. Similarly, if an employer in order to prevent an employee's sustaining a loss on a sale of a house acquires the property from the employee at a price in excess of fair market value, the employee

is considered to have received a payment attributable to employment to the extent that such payment exceeds the fair market value of the property.

* * *

[Reg. § 1.82-1.]

□ [*T.D. 7195, 7-10-72. Amended by T.D. 7578, 12-19-78.*]

§ 1.83-1. Property transferred in connection with the performance of services.—(a) *Inclusion in gross income*—(1) *General rule.* Section 83 provides rules for the taxation of property transferred to an employee or independent contractor (or beneficiary thereof) in connection with the performance of services by such employee or independent contractor. In general, such property is not taxable under section 83(a) until it has been transferred (as defined in § 1.83-3(a)) to such person and become substantially vested (as defined in § 1.83-3(b)) in such person. In that case, the excess of—

(i) The fair market value of such property (determined without regard to any lapse restriction, as defined in § 1.83-3(i)) at the time that the property becomes substantially vested, over

(ii) The amount (if any) paid for such property,

shall be included as compensation in the gross income of such employee or independent contractor for the taxable year in which the property becomes substantially vested. Until such property becomes substantially vested, the transferor shall be regarded as the owner of such property, and any income from such property received by the employee or independent contractor (or beneficiary thereof) or the right to the use of such property by the employee or independent contractor constitutes additional compensation and shall be included in the gross income of such employee or independent contractor for the taxable year in which such income is received or such use is made available. This paragraph applies to a transfer of property in connection with the performance of services even though the transferor is not the person for whom such services are performed.

(2) *Life insurance.* The cost of life insurance protection under a life insurance contract, retirement income contract, endowment contract, or other contract providing life insurance protection is taxable generally under section 61 and the regulations thereunder during the period such contract remains substantially nonvested (as defined in § 1.83-3(b)). The cost of such life insurance protection is the reasonable net premium cost, as determined by the Commissioner, of the current life insurance protection (as defined in § 1.72-16(b)(3)) provided by such contract.

(3) *Cross references.* For rules concerning the treatment of employers and other transferors of property in connection with the performance of services, see section 83(h) and § 1.83-6. For rules concerning the taxation of beneficiaries of an employees' trust that is not exempt under section 501(a), see section 402(b) and the regulations thereunder.

(b) *Subsequent sale, forfeiture, or other disposition of nonvested property.* (1) If substantially nonvested property (that has been transferred in connection with the performance of services) is subsequently sold or otherwise disposed of to a third party in an arm's length transaction while still substantially nonvested, the person who performed such services shall realize compensation in an amount equal to the excess of—

(i) The amount realized on such sale or other disposition, over

(ii) The amount (if any) paid for such property.

Such amount of compensation is includible in his gross income in accordance with his method of accounting. Two preceding sentences also apply when the person disposing of the property has received it in a non-arm's length transaction described in paragraph (c) of this section. In addition, section 83(a) and paragraph (a) of this section shall thereafter cease to apply with respect to such property.

(2) If substantially nonvested property that has been transferred in connection with the performance of services to the person performing such services is forfeited while still substantially nonvested and held by such person, the difference between the amount paid (if any) and the amount received upon forfeiture (if any) shall be treated as an ordinary gain or loss. This paragraph (b)(2) does not apply to property to which § 1.83-2(a) applies.

(3) This paragraph (b) shall not apply to, and no gain shall be recognized on, any sale, forfeiture, or other disposition described in this paragraph to the extent that any property received in exchange therefor is substantially nonvested. Instead, section 83 and this section shall apply with respect to such property received (as if it were substituted for the property disposed of).

(c) *Dispositions of nonvested property not at arm's length.* If substantially nonvested property (that has been transferred in connection with the performance of services) is disposed of in a transaction which is not at arm's length and the property remains substantially nonvested, the person who performed such services realizes compensation equal in amount to the sum of any money and the fair market value of any substantially

Reg. § 1.83-1(c)

vested property received in such disposition. Such amount of compensation is includible in his gross income in accordance with his method of accounting. However, such amount of compensation shall not exceed the fair market value of the property disposed of at the time of disposition (determined without regard to any lapse restriction), reduced by the amount paid for such property. In addition, section 83 and these regulations shall continue to apply with respect to such property, except that any amount previously includible in gross income under this paragraph (c) shall thereafter be treated as an amount paid for such property. For example, if in 1971 an employee pays $50 for a share of stock which has a fair market value of $100 and is substantially nonvested at that time and later in 1971 (at a time when the property still has a fair market value of $100 and is still substantially nonvested) the employee disposes of, in a transaction not at arm's length, the share of stock to his wife for $10, the employee realizes compensation of $10 in 1971. If in 1972, when the share of stock has a fair market value of $120, it becomes substantially vested, the employee realizes additional compensation in 1972 in the amount of $60 (the $120 fair market value of the stock less both the $50 price paid for the stock and the $10 taxed as compensation in 1971). For purposes of this paragraph, if substantially nonvested property has been transferred to a person other than the person who performed the services, and the transferee dies holding the property while the property is still substantially nonvested and while the person who performed the services is alive, the transfer which results by reason of the death of such transferee is a transfer not at arm's length.

(d) *Certain transfers upon death.* If substantially nonvested property has been transferred in connection with the performance of services and the person who performed such services dies while the property is still substantially nonvested, any income realized on or after such death with respect to such property under this section is income in respect of a decedent to which the rules of section 691 apply. In such a case the income in respect of such property shall be taxable under section 691 (except to the extent not includible under section 101(b)) to the estate or beneficiary of the person who performed the services, in accordance with section 83 and the regulations thereunder. However, if an item of income is realized upon such death before July 21, 1978, because the property became substantially vested upon death, the person responsible for filing decedent's income tax return for decedent's last taxable year may elect to treat such item as includible in gross income for decedent's last taxable year by including such item in gross income on the return or amended return filed for decedent's last taxable year.

(e) *Forfeiture after substantial vesting.* If a person is taxable under section 83(a) when the property transferred becomes substantially vested and thereafter the person's beneficial interest in such property is nevertheless forfeited pursuant to a lapse restriction, any loss incurred by such person (but not by a beneficiary of such person) upon such forfeiture shall be an ordinary loss to the extent the basis in such property has been increased as a result of the recognition of income by such person under section 83(a) with respect to such property.

(f) *Examples.* The provisions of this section may be illustrated by the following examples:

Example (1). On November 1, 1978, X corporation sells to E, an employee, 100 shares of X corporation stock at $10 per share. At the time of such sale the fair market value of the X corporation stock is $100 per share. Under the terms of the sale each share of stock is subject to a substantial risk of forfeiture which will not lapse until November 1, 1988. Evidence of this restriction is stamped on the face of E's stock certificates, which are therefore nontransferable (within the meaning of § 1.83-3(d)). Since in 1978 E's stock is substantially nonvested, E does not include any of such amount in his gross income as compensation in 1978. On November 1, 1988, the fair market value of the X corporation stock is $250 per share. Since the X corporation stock becomes substantially vested in 1988, E must include $24,000 (100 shares of X corporation stock × $250 fair market value per share less $10 price paid by E for each share) as compensation for 1988. Dividends paid by X to E on E's stock after it was transferred to E on November 1, 1973, are taxable to E as additional compensation during the period E's stock is substantially nonvested and are deductible as such by X.

Example (2). Assume the facts are the same as in example (1), except that on November 1, 1985, each share of stock of X corporation in E's hands could as a matter of law be transferred to a bona fide purchaser who would not be required to forfeit the stock if the risk of forfeiture materialized. In the event, however, that the risk materializes, E would be liable in damages to X. On November 1, 1985, the fair market value of the X corporation stock is $230 per share. Since E's stock is transferable within the meaning of § 1.83-3(d) in 1985, the stock is substantially vested and E must include $22,000 (100 shares of X corporation stock × $230 fair market value per share less $10 price paid by E for each share) as compensation for 1985.

Reg. § 1.83-1(d)

Example (3). Assume the facts are the same as in example (1) except that, in 1984 E sells his 100 shares of X corporation stock in an arm's length sale to I, an investment company, for $120 per share. At the time of this sale each share of X corporation's stock has a fair market value of $200. Under paragraph (b) of this section, E must include $11,000 (100 shares of X corporation stock × $120 amount realized per share less $10 price paid by E per share) as compensation for 1984 notwithstanding that the stock remains non-transferable and is still subject to a substantial risk of forfeiture at the time of such sale. Under § 1.83-4(b)(2), I's basis in the X corporation stock is $120 per share. [Reg. § 1.83-1.]

☐ [*T.D.* 7554, 7-21-78.]

§ 1.83-2. Election to include in gross income in year of transfer.—(a) *In general.* If property is transferred (within the meaning of § 1.83-3(a)) in connection with the performance of services, the person performing such services may elect to include in gross income under section 83(b) the excess (if any) of the fair market value of the property at the time of transfer (determined without regard to any lapse restriction, as defined in § 1.83-3(i)) over the amount (if any) paid for such property, as compensation for services. The fact that the transferee has paid full value for the property transferred, realizing no bargain element in the transaction, does not preclude the use of the election as provided for in this section. If this election is made, the substantial vesting rules of section 83(a) and the regulations thereunder do not apply with respect to such property, and except as otherwise provided in section 83(d)(2) and the regulations thereunder (relating to the cancellation of a nonlapse restriction), any subsequent appreciation in the value of the property is not taxable as compensation to the person who performed the services. Thus, property with respect to which this election is made shall be includible in gross income as of the time of transfer, even though such property is substantially nonvested (as defined in § 1.83-3(b)) at the time of transfer, and no compensation will be includible in gross income when such property becomes substantially vested (as defined in § 1.83-3(b)). In computing the gain or loss from the subsequent sale or exchange of such property, its basis shall be the amount paid for the property increased by the amount included in gross income under section 83(b). If property for which a section 83(b) election is in effect is forfeited while substantially nonvested, such forfeiture shall be treated as a sale or exchange upon which there is realized a loss equal to the excess (if any) of—

(1) The amount paid (if any) for such property, over,

(2) The amount realized (if any) upon such forfeiture.

If such property is a capital asset in the hands of the taxpayer, such loss shall be a capital loss. A sale or other disposition of the property that is in substance a forfeiture, or is made in contemplation of a forfeiture, shall be treated as a forfeiture under the two immediately preceding sentences.

* * *

[Reg. § 1.83-2.]

☐ [*T.D.* 7554, 7-21-78.]

§ 1.83-3. Meaning and use of certain terms.—(a) *Transfer*—(1) *In general.* For purposes of section 83 and the regulations thereunder, a transfer of property occurs when a person acquires a beneficial ownership interest in such property (disregarding any lapse restriction, as defined in § 1.83-3(i)).

(2) *Option.* The grant of an option to purchase certain property does not constitute a transfer of such property. However, see § 1.83-7 for the extent to which the grant of the option itself is subject to section 83. In addition, if the amount paid for the transfer of property is an indebtedness secured by the transferred property, on which there is no personal liability to pay all or a substantial part of such indebtedness, such transaction may be in substance the same as the grant of an option. The determination of the substance of the transaction shall be based upon all the facts and circumstances. The factors to be taken into account include the type of property involved, the extent to which the risk that the property will decline in value has been transferred, and the likelihood that the purchase price will, in fact, be paid. See also § 1.83-4(c) for the treatment of forgiveness of indebtedness that has constituted an amount paid.

(3) *Requirement that property be returned.* Similarly, no transfer may have occurred where property is transferred under conditions that require its return upon the happening of an event that is certain to occur, such as the termination of employment. In such a case, whether there is, in fact, a transfer depends upon all the facts and circumstances. Factors which indicate that no transfer has occurred are described in paragraph (a)(4), (5) and (6) of this section.

(4) *Similarity to option.* An indication that no transfer has occurred is the extent to which the conditions relating to a transfer are similar to an option.

(5) *Relationship to fair market value.* An indication that no transfer has occurred is the extent to which the consideration to be paid the transferee upon surrendering the property does not approach the fair market value of the prop-

Reg. § 1.83-3(a)(5)

erty at the time of surrender. For purposes of paragraph (a)(5) and (6) of this section, fair market value includes fair market value determined under the rules of § 1.83-5(a)(1), relating to the valuation of property subject to nonlapse restrictions. Therefore, the existence of a nonlapse restriction referred to in § 1.83-5(a)(1) is not a factor indicating no transfer has occurred.

(6) *Risk of loss.* An indication that no transfer has occurred is the extent to which the transferee does not incur the risk of a beneficial owner that the value of the property at the time of transfer will decline substantially. Therefore, for purposes of this (6), risk of decline in property value is not limited to the risk that any amount paid for the property may be lost.

(7) *Examples.* The provisions of this paragraph may be illustrated by the following examples:

Example (1). On January 3, 1971, X corporation sells for $500 to S, a salesman of X, 10 shares of stock in X corporation with a fair market value of $1,000. The stock is nontransferable and subject to return to the corporation (for $500) if S's sales do not reach a certain level by December 31, 1971. Disregarding the restriction concerning S's sales (since the restriction is a lapse restriction), S's interest in the stock is that of a beneficial owner and therefore a transfer occurs on January 3, 1971.

Example (2). On November 17, 1972, W sells to E 100 shares of stock in W corporation with a fair market value of $10,000 in exchange for a $10,000 note without personal liability. The note requires E to make yearly payments of $2,000 commencing in 1973. E collects the dividends, votes the stock and pays the interest on the note. However, he makes no payments towards the face amount of the note. Because E has no personal liability on the note, and since E is making no payments towards the face amount of the note, the likelihood of E paying the full purchase price is in substantial doubt. As a result, E has not incurred the risks of a beneficial owner that the value of the stock will decline. Therefore, no transfer of the stock has occurred on November 17, 1972, but an option to purchase the stock has been granted to E.

Example (3). On January 3, 1971, X corporation purports to transfer to E, an employee, 100 shares of stock in X corporation. The X stock is subject to the sole restriction that E must sell such stock to X on termination of employment for any reason for an amount which is equal to the excess (if any) of the book value of the X stock at termination of employment over book value on January 3, 1971. The stock is not transferable by E and the restrictions on transfer are stamped on

the certificate. Under these facts and circumstances, there is no transfer of the X stock within the meaning of section 83.

Example (4). Assume the same facts as in example (3) except that E paid $3,000 for the stock and that the restriction required E upon termination of employment to sell the stock to M for the total amount of dividends that have been declared on the stock since September 2, 1971, or $3,000 whichever is higher. Again, under the facts and circumstances, no transfer of the X stock has occurred.

Example (5). On July 4, 1971, X corporation purports to transfer to G an employee, 100 shares of X stock. The stock is subject to the sole restriction that upon termination of employment G must sell the stock to X for the greater of its fair market value at such time or $100, the amount G paid for the stock. On July 4, 1971 the X stock has a fair market value of $100. Therefore, G does not incur the risk of a beneficial owner that the value of the stock at the time of transfer ($100) will decline substantially. Under these facts and circumstances, no transfer has occurred.

(b) *Substantially vested and substantially nonvested property.* For purposes of section 83 and the regulations thereunder, property is substantially nonvested when it is subject to a substantial risk of forfeiture, within the meaning of paragraph (c) of this section, and is nontransferable, within the meaning of paragraph (d) of this section. Property is substantially vested for such purposes when it is either transferable or not subject to a substantial risk of forfeiture.

(c) *Substantial risk of forfeiture*—(1) *In general.* For purposes of section 83 and the regulations thereunder, whether a risk of forfeiture is substantial or not depends upon the facts and circumstances. A substantial risk of forfeiture exists where rights in property that are transferred are conditioned, directly or indirectly, upon the future performance (or refraining from performance) of substantial services by any person, or the occurrence of a condition related to a purpose of the transfer, and the possibility of forfeiture is substantial if such condition is not satisfied. Property is not transferred subject to a substantial risk of forfeiture to the extent that the employer is required to pay the fair market value of a portion of such property to the employee upon the return of such property. The risk that the value of property will decline during a certain period of time does not constitute a substantial risk of forfeiture. A nonlapse restriction, standing by itself, will not result in a substantial risk of forfeiture.

(2) *Illustrations of substantial risks of forfeiture.* The regularity of the performance of services and the time spent in performing such services

tend to indicate whether services required by a condition are substantial. The fact that the person performing services has the right to decline to perform such services without forfeiture may tend to establish that services are insubstantial. Where stock is transferred to an underwriter prior to a public offering and the full enjoyment of such stock is expressly or impliedly conditioned upon the successful completion of the underwriting, the stock is subject to a substantial risk of forfeiture. Where an employee receives property from an employer subject to a requirement that it be returned if the total earnings of the employer do not increase, such property is subject to a substantial risk of forfeiture. On the other hand, requirements that the property be returned to the employer if the employee is discharged for cause or for committing a crime will not be considered to result in a substantial risk of forfeiture. An enforceable requirement that the property be returned to the employer if the employee accepts a job with a competing firm will not ordinarily be considered to result in a substantial risk of forfeiture unless the particular facts and circumstances indicate to the contrary. Factors which may be taken into account in determining whether a covenant not to compete constitutes a substantial risk of forfeiture are the age of the employee, the availability of alternative employment opportunities, the likelihood of the employee's obtaining such other employment, the degree of skill possessed by the employee, the employee's health, and the practice (if any) of the employer to enforce such covenants. Similarly, rights in property transferred to a retiring employee subject to the sole requirement that it be returned unless he renders consulting services upon the request of his former employer will not be considered subject to a substantial risk of forfeiture unless he is in fact expected to perform substantial services.

(3) *Enforcement of forfeiture condition.* In determining whether the possibility of forfeiture is substantial in the case of rights in property transferred to an employee of a corporation who owns a significant amount of the total combined voting power or value of all classes of stock of the employer corporation or of its parent corporation, there will be taken into account (i) the employee's relationship to other stockholders and the extent of their control, potential control and possible loss of control of the corporation, (ii) the position of the employee in the corporation and the extent to which he is subordinate to other employees, (iii) the employee's relationship to the officers and directors of the corporation, (iv) the person or persons who must approve the employee's discharge, and (v) past actions of the employer in enforcing the provisions of the restrictions. For example, if an employee would be considered as having received rights in property subject to a substantial risk of forfeiture, but for the fact that the employee owns 20 percent of the single class of stock in the transferor corporation, and if the remaining 80 percent of the class of stock is owned by an unrelated individual (or members of such an individual's family) so that the possibility of the corporation enforcing a restriction on such rights is substantial, then such rights are subject to a substantial risk of forfeiture. On the other hand, if 4 percent of the voting power of all the stock of a corporation is owned by the president of such corporation and the remaining stock is so diversely held by the public that the president, in effect, controls the corporation, then the possibility of the corporation enforcing a restriction on rights in property transferred to the president is not substantial, and such rights are not subject to a substantial risk of forfeiture.

(4) *Examples.* The rules contained in paragraph (c)(1) of this section may be illustrated by the following examples. In each example it is assumed that, if the conditions on transfer are not satisfied, the forfeiture provision will be enforced.

Example (1). On November 1, 1971, corporation X transfers in connection with the performance of services to E, an employee, 100 shares of corporation X stock for $90 per share. Under the terms of the transfer, E will be subject to a binding commitment to resell the stock to corporation X at $90 per share if he leaves the employment of corporation X for any reason prior to the expiration of a 2-year period from the date of such transfer. Since E must perform substantial services for corporation X and will not be paid more than $90 for the stock, regardless of its value, if he fails to perform such services during such 2-year period, E's rights in the stock are subject to a substantial risk of forfeiture during such period.

Example (2). On November 10, 1971, corporation X transfers in connection with the performance of services to a trust for the benefit of employees, $100x. Under the terms of the trust any child of an employee who is an enrolled full-time student at an accredited educational institution as a candidate for a degree will receive an annual grant of cash for each academic year the student completes as a student in good standing, up to a maximum of four years. E, an employee, has a child who is enrolled as a full-time student at an accredited college as a candidate for a degree. Therefore, E has a beneficial interest in the assets of the trust equalling the value of four cash grants. Since E's child must complete one year of college in order to receive a cash grant, E's interest in the trust assets are subject to a substantial risk of forfeiture to the extent E's child has not become entitled to any grants.

Reg. § 1.83-3(c)(4)

Example (3). On November 25, 1971, corporation X gives to E, an employee, in connection with his performance of services to corporation X, a bonus of 100 shares of corporation X stock. Under the terms of the bonus arrangement E is obligated to return the corporation X stock to corporation X if he terminates his employment for any reason. However, for each year occurring after November 25, 1971, during which E remains employed with corporation X, E ceases to be obligated to return 10 shares of the corporation X stock. Since in each year occurring after November 25, 1971, for which E remains employed he is not required to return 10 shares of corporation X's stock, E's rights in 10 shares each year for 10 years cease to be subject to a substantial risk of forfeiture for each year he remains so employed.

Example (4). (a) Assume the same facts as in example (3) except that for each year occurring after November 25, 1971, for which E remains employed with corporation X, X agrees to pay, in redemption of the bonus shares given to E if he terminates employment for any reason, 10 percent of the fair market value of each share of stock on the date of such termination of employment. Since corporation X will pay E 10 percent of the value of his bonus stock for each of the 10 years after November 25, 1971, in which he remains employed by X, and the risk of a decline in value is not a substantial risk of forfeiture, E's interest in 10 percent of such bonus stock becomes substantially vested in each of those years.

(b) The following chart illustrates the fair market value of the bonus stock and the fair market value of the portion of bonus stock that becomes substantially vested on November 25, for the following years:

| Year | | Fair market value of: | |
		(I) All stock	(II) Portion of stock that becomes vested
1972		$200	$20
1973		300	30
1974		150	15
1975		150	15
1976		100	10

If E terminates his employment on July 1, 1977, when the fair market value of the bonus stock is $100, E must return the bonus stock to X, and X must pay, in redemption of the bonus stock, $50 (50 percent of the value of the bonus stock on the date of termination of employment). E has recognized income under section 83(a) and § 1.83-1(a) with respect to 50 percent of the bonus stock, and E's basis in that portion of the stock equals the amount of income recognized, $90. Under § 1.83-1(e), the $40 loss E incurred upon forfeiture ($90 basis less $50 redemption payment) is an ordinary loss.

Example (5). On January 7, 1971, corporation X, a computer service company, transfers to E, 100 shares of coporation X stock for $50. E is a highly compensated salesman who sold X's products in a three-state area since 1960. At the time of transfer each share of X stock has a fair market value of $100. The stock is transferred to E in connection with his termination of employment with X. Each share of X stock is subject to the sole condition that E can keep such share only if he does not engage in competition with X for a 5-year period in the three-state area where E had previously sold X's products. E, who is 45 years old, has no intention of retiring from the work force. In order to earn a salary comparable to his current compensation, while preventing the risk of forfeiture from arising, E will have to expend a substantial amount of time and effort in another industry or market to establish the necessary business contacts. Thus, under these facts and circumstances E's rights in the stock are subject to a substantial risk of forfeiture.

(d) *Transferability of property.* For purposes of section 83 and the regulations thereunder, the rights of a person in property are transferable if such person can transfer any interest in the property to any person other than the transferor of the property, but only if the rights in such property of such transferee are not subject to a substantial risk of forfeiture. Accordingly, property is transferable if the person performing the services or receiving the property can sell, assign, or pledge (as collateral for a loan, or as security for the performance of an obligation, or for any other purpose) his interest in the property to any person other than the transferor of such property and if the transferee is not required to give up the property or its value in the event the substantial risk of forfeiture materializes. On the other hand, property is not considered to be transferable merely because the person performing the services or receiving the property may designate a beneficiary to receive the property in the event of his death.

(e) *Property.* For purposes of section 83 and the regulations thereunder, the term "property" includes real and personal property other than ei-

Reg. § 1.83-3(b)

ther money or an unfunded and unsecured promise to pay money or property in the future. The term also includes a beneficial interest in assets (including money) which are transferred or set aside from the claims of creditors of the transferor, for example, in a trust or escrow account. See, however, § 1.83-8(a) with respect to employee trusts and annuity plans subject to section 402(b) and section 403(c). In the case of a transfer of a life insurance contract, retirement income contract, endowment contract, or other contract providing life insurance protection, only the cash surrender value of the contract is considered to be property. Where rights in a contract providing life insurance protection are substantially nonvested, see § 1.83-1(a)(2) for rules relating to the taxation of the cost of life insurance protection.

(f) *Property transferred in connection with the performance of services.* Property transferred to an employee or an independent contractor (or beneficiary thereof) in recognition of the performance of, or the refraining from performance of, services is considered transferred in connection with the performance of services within the meaning of section 83. The existence of other persons entitled to buy stock on the same terms and conditions as an employee, whether pursuant to a public or private offering may, however, indicate that in such circumstances a transfer to the employee is not in recognition of the performance of, or the refraining from performance of, services. The transfer of property is subject to section 83 whether such transfer is in respect of past, present, or future services.

(g) *Amount paid.* For purposes of section 83 and the regulations thereunder, the term "amount paid" refers to the value of any money or property paid for the transfer of property to which section 83 applies, and does not refer to any amount paid for the right to use such property or to receive the income therefrom. Such value does not include any stated or unstated interest payments. For rules regarding the calculation of the amount of unstated interest payments, see § 1.483-1(c). When section 83 applies to the transfer of property pursuant to the exercise of an option, the term "amount paid" refers to any amount paid for the grant of the option plus any amount paid as the exercise price of the option. For rules regarding the forgiveness of indebtedness treated as an amount paid, see § 1.83-4(c).

(h) *Nonlapse restriction.* For purposes of section 83 and the regulations thereunder, a restriction which by its terms will never lapse (also referred to as a "nonlapse restriction") is a permanent limitation on the transferability of property—

(i) Which will require the transferee of the property to sell, or offer to sell, such property at a price determined under a formula, and

(ii) Which will continue to apply to and be enforced against the transferee or any subsequent holder (other than the transferor).

A limitation subjecting the property to a permanent right of first refusal in a particular person at a price determined under a formula is a permanent nonlapse restriction. Limitations imposed by registration requirements of State or Federal security laws or similar laws imposed with respect to sales or other dispositions of stock or securities are not nonlapse restrictions. An obligation to resell or to offer to sell property transferred in connection with the performance of services to a specific person or persons at its fair market value at the time of such sale is not a nonlapse restriction. See § 1.83-5(c) for examples of nonlapse restrictions.

(i) *Lapse restriction.* For purposes of section 83 and the regulations thereunder, the term "lapse restriction" means a restriction other than a nonlapse restriction as defined in paragraph (h) of this section, and includes (but is not limited to) a restriction that carries a substantial risk of forfeiture.

* * *

(k) *Special rule for certain accounting rules.* (1) For purposes of section 83 and the regulations thereunder, property is subject to substantial risk of forfeiture and is not transferable so long as the property is subject to a restriction on transfer to comply with the "Pooling-of-Interests Accounting" rules set forth in Accounting Series Release Numbered 130 ((10/5/72) 37 FR 20937; 17 CFR 211.130) and Accounting Series Release Numbered 135 ((1/18/73) 38 FR 1734; 17 CFR 211.135).

(2) *Effective date.* This paragraph applies to property transferred after December 31, 1981. [Reg. § 1.83-3.]

☐ [*T.D. 7554, 7-21-78. Amended by T.D. 8042, 8-5-85.*]

§ 1.83-4. Special rules.—(a) *Holding period.* Under section 83(f), the holding period of transferred property to which section 83(a) applies shall begin just after such property is substantially vested. However, if the person who has performed the services in connection with which property is transferred has made an election under section 83(b), the holding period of such property shall begin just after the date such property is transferred. If property to which section 83 and the regulations thereunder apply is transferred at arm's length, the holding period of such property in the hands of the transferee shall be determined in accordance with the rules provided in section 1223.

(b) *Basis.* (1) Except as provided in paragraph (b) (2) of this section, if property to which section 83 and the regulations thereunder apply is acquired by any person (including a person who acquires such property in a subsequent transfer which is not at arm's length), while such property is still substantially nonvested, such person's basis for the property shall reflect any amount paid for such property and any amount includible in the gross income of the person who performed the services (including any amount so includible as a result of a disposition by the person who acquired such property). Such basis shall also reflect any adjustments to basis provided under sections 1015 and 1016.

(2) If property to which § 1.83-1 applies is transferred at arm's length, the basis of the property in the hands of the transferee shall be determined under section 1012 and the regulations thereunder.

(c) *Forgiveness of indebtedness treated as an amount paid.* If an indebtedness that has been treated as an amount paid under § 1.83-1 (a) (1) (ii) is subsequently cancelled, forgiven or satisfied for an amount less than the amount of such indebtedness, the amount that is not, in fact, paid shall be includible in the gross income of the service provider in the taxable year in which such cancellation, forgiveness or satisfaction occurs. [Reg. § 1.83-4.]

□ [*T.D. 7554, 7-21-78.*]

§ 1.83-5. Restrictions that will never lapse.—(a) *Valuation.* For purposes of section 83 and the regulations thereunder, in the case of property subject to a nonlapse restriction (as defined in § 1.83-3(h)), the price determined under the formula price will be considered to be the fair market value of the property unless established to the contrary by the Commissioner, and the burden of proof shall be on the Commissioner with respect to such value. If stock in a corporation is subject to a nonlapse restriction which requires the transferee to sell such stock only at a formula price based on book value, a reasonable multiple of earnings or a reaasonable combination thereof, the price so determined will ordinarily be regarded as determinative of the fair market value of such property for purposes of section 83. However, in certain circumstances the formula price will not be considered to be the fair market value of property subject to such a formula price restriction, even though the formula price restriction is a substantial factor in determining such value. For example, where the formula price is the current book value of stock, the book value of the stock at some time in the future may be a more accurate

measure of the value of the stock than the current book value of the stock for purposes of determining the fair market value of the stock at the time the stock becomes substantially vested.

(b) *Cancellation*—(1) *In general.* Under section 83(d) (2), if a nonlapse restriction imposed on property that is subject to section 83 is cancelled, then, unless the taxpayer establishes—

(i) That such cancellation was not compensatory, and

(ii) That the person who would be allowed a deduction, if any, if the cancellation were treated as compensatory, will treat the transaction as not compensatory, as provided in paragraph (c) (2) of this section, the excess of the fair market value of such property (computed without regard to such restriction) at the time of cancellation, over the sum of—

(iii) The fair market value of such property (computed by taking the restriction into account) immediately before the cancellation, and

(iv) The amount, if any, paid for the cancellation,

shall be treated as compensation for the taxable year in which such cancellation occurs. Whether there has been a noncompensatory cancellation of a nonlapse restriction under section 83 (d) (2) depends upon the particular facts and circumstances. Ordinarily the fact that the employee or independent contractor is required to perform additional services or that the salary or payment of such a person is adjusted to take the cancellation into account indicates that such cancellation has a compensatory purpose. On the other hand, the fact that the original purpose of a restriction no longer exists may indicate that the purpose of such cancellation is noncompensatory. Thus, for example, if a so-called "buy-sell" restriction was imposed on a corporation's stock to limit ownership of such stock and is being cancelled in connection with a public offering of the stock, such cancellation will generally be regarded as noncompensatory. However, the mere fact that the employer is willing to forego a deduction under section 83(h) is insufficient evidence to establish a noncompensatory cancellation of a nonlapse restriction. The refusal by a corporation or shareholder to repurchase stock of the corporation which is subject to a permanent right of first refusal will generally be treated as a cancellation of a nonlapse restriction. The preceding sentence shall not apply where there is no nonlapse restriction, for example, where the price to be paid for the stock subject to the right of first refusal is the fair market value of the stock. Section 83 (d) (2) and this (1) do not apply where immediately after the cancellation of a nonlapse restriction the property is still substantially nonvested and no section

83 (b) election has been made with respect to such property. In such a case the rules of section 83 (a) and § 1.83-1 shall apply to such property.

(2) *Evidence of noncompensatory cancellation.* In addition to the information necessary to establish the factors described in paragraph (b) (1) of this section, the taxpayer shall request the employer to furnish the taxpayer with a written statement indicating that the employer will not treat the cancellation of the nonlapse restriction as a compensatory event, and that no deduction will be taken with respect to such cancellation. The taxpayer shall file such written statement with his income tax return for the taxable year in which or with which such cancellation occurs.

(c) *Examples.* The provisions of this section may be illustrated by the following examples:

Example (1). On November 1, 1971, X corporation whose shares are closely held and not regularly traded, transfers to E, an employee, 100 shares of X corporation stock subject to the condition that, if he desires to dispose of such stock during the period of his employment, he must resell the stock to his employer at its then existing book value. In addition, E or E's estate is obligated to offer to sell the stock at his retirement or death to his employer at its then existing book value. Under these facts and circumstances, the restriction to which the shares of X corporation stock are subject is a nonlapse restriction. Consequently, the fair market value of the X stock is includible in E's gross income as compensation for taxable year 1971. However, in determining the fair market value of the X stock, the book value formula price will ordinarily be regarded as being determinative of such value.

Example (2). Assume the facts are the same as in example (1), except that the X stock is subject to the condition that if E desires to dispose of the stock during the period of his employment he must resell the stock to his employer at a multiple of earnings per share that is in this case a reasonable approximation of value at the time of transfer to E. In addition, E or E's estate is obligated to offer to sell the stock at his retirement or death to his employer at the same multiple of earnings. Under these facts and circumstances, the restriction to which the X corporation stock is subject is a nonlapse restriction. Consequently, the fair market value of the X stock is includible in E's gross income for taxable year 1971. However, in determining the fair market value of the X stock, the multiple-of-earnings formula price will ordinarily be regarded as determinative of such value.

Example (3). On January 4, 1971, X corporation transfers to E, an employee, 100 shares of stock in X corporation. Each such share of stock is subject to an agreement between X and E

whereby E agrees that such shares are to be held solely for investment purposes and not for resale (a so-called investment letter restriction). E's rights in such stock are substantially vested upon transfer, causing the fair market value of each share of X corporation stock to be includible in E's gross income as compensation for taxable year 1971. Since such an investment letter restriction does not constitute a nonlapse restriction, in determining the fair market value of each share, the investment letter restriction is disregarded.

Example (4). On September 1, 1971, X corporation transfers to B, an independent contractor, 500 shares of common stock in X corporation in exchange for B's agreement to provide services in the construction of an office building on property owned by X corporation. X corporation has 100 shares of preferred stock outstanding and an additional 500 shares of common stock outstanding. The preferred stock has a liquidation value of $1,000x, which is equal to the value of all assets owned by X. Therefore, the book value of the common stock in X corporation is $0. Under the terms of the transfer, if B wishes to dispose of the stock, B must offer to sell the stock to X for 150 percent of the then existing book value of B's common stock. The stock is also subject to a substantial risk of forfeiture until B performs the agreed-upon services. B makes a timely election under section 83(b) to include the value of the stock in gross income in 1971. Under these facts and circumstances, the restriction to which the shares of X corporation common stock are subject is a nonlapse restriction. In determining the fair market value of the X common stock at the time of transfer, the book value formula price would ordinarily be regarded as determinative of such value. However, the fair market value of X common stock at the time of transfer, subject to the book value restriction, is greater than $0 since B was willing to agree to provide valuable personal services in exchange for the stock. In determining the fair market value of the stock, the expected book value after construction of the office building would be given great weight. The likelihood of completion of construction would be a factor in determining the expected book value after completion of construction. [Reg. § 1.83-5.]

☐ [*T.D.* 7554, 7-21-78.]

§ 1.83-6. Deduction by employer.—(a) *Allowance of deduction*—(1) *General rule.* In the case of a transfer of property in connection with the performance of services, or a compensatory cancellation of a nonlapse restriction described in section 83(d) and § 1.83-5, a deduction is allowable under section 162 or 212 to the person for whom the services were performed. The amount of the deduction is equal to the amount included as compensation in the gross income of the service provider under section 83(a), (b), or (d)(2), but only to the extent the amount meets the requirements of section 162 or 212 and the regulations thereunder. The deduction is allowed only for the taxable year of that person in which or with which ends the taxable year of the service provider in which the amount is included as compensation. For purposes of this paragraph, any amount excluded from gross income under section 79 or section 101(b) or subchapter N is considered to have been included in gross income.

(2) *Special rule.* For purposes of paragraph (a)(1) of this section, the service provider is deemed to have included the amount as compensation in gross income if the person for whom the services were performed satisfies in a timely manner all requirements of section 6041 or section 6041A, and the regulations thereunder, with respect to that amount of compensation. For purposes of the preceding sentence, whether a person for whom services were performed satisfies all requirements of section 6041 or section 6041A, and the regulations thereunder, is determined without regard to § 1.6041-3(c) (exception for payments to corporations). In the case of a disqualifying disposition of stock described in section 421(b), an employer that otherwise satisfies all requirements of section 6041 and the regulations thereunder will be considered to have done so timely for purposes of this paragraph (a)(2) if Form W-2 or Form W-2c, as appropriate, is furnished to the employee or former employee, and is filed with the federal government, on or before the date on which the employer files the tax return claiming the deduction relating to the disqualifying disposition.

(3) *Exceptions.* Where property is substantially vested upon transfer, the deduction shall be allowed to such person in accordance with his method of accounting (in conformity with sections 446 and 461). In the case of a transfer to an employee benefit plan described in § 1.162-10(a) or a transfer to an employees' trust or annuity plan described in section 404(a)(5) and the regulations thereunder, section 83(h) and this section do not apply.

(4) *Capital expenditure, etc.* No deduction is allowed under section 83(h) to the extent that the transfer of property constitutes a capital expenditure, an item of deferred expense, or an amount properly includible in the value of inventory items. In the case of a capital expenditure, for example, the basis of the property to which such capital expenditure relates shall be increased at the same time and to the same extent as any amount includible in the employee's gross income in respect of such transfer. Thus, for example, no deduction is allowed to a corporation in respect of a transfer of its stock to a promoter upon its

organization, notwithstanding that such promoter must include the value of such stock in his gross income in accordance with the rules under section 83.

(5) *Effective date.* Paragraphs (a)(1) and (2) of this section apply to deductions for taxable years beginning on or after January 1, 1995. However, taxpayers may also apply paragraphs (a)(1) and (2) of this section when claiming deductions for taxable years beginning before that date if the claims are not barred by the statute of limitations. Paragraphs (a)(3) and (4) of this section are effective as set forth in § 1.83-8(b).

(b) *Recognition of gain or loss.* Except as provided in section 1032, at the time of a transfer of property in connection with the performance of services the transferor recognizes gain to the extent that the transferor receives an amount that exceeds the transferor's basis in the property. In addition, at the time a deduction is allowed under section 83(h) and paragraph (a) of this section, gain or loss is recognized to the extent of the difference between (i) the sum of the amount paid plus the amount allowed as a deduction under section 83(h), and (ii) the sum of the taxpayer's basis in the property plus any amount recognized pursuant to the previous sentence.

(c) *Forfeitures.* If, under section 83(h) and paragraph (a) of this section, a deduction, an increase in basis, or a reduction of gross income was allowable (disregarding the reasonableness of the amount of compensation) in respect of a transfer of property and such property is subsequently forfeited, the amount of such deduction, increase in basis or reduction of gross income shall be includible in the gross income of the person to whom it was allowable for the taxable year of forfeiture. The basis of such property in the hands of the person to whom it is forfeited shall include any such amount includible in the gross income of such person, as well as any amount such person pays upon forfeiture.

(d) *Special rules for transfers by shareholders—* (1) *Transfers.* If a shareholder of a corporation transfers property to an employee of such corporation or to an independent contractor (or to a beneficiary thereof), in consideration of services performed for the corporation, the transaction shall be considered to be a contribution of such property to the capital of such corporation by the shareholder, and immediately thereafter a transfer of such property by the corporation to the employee or independent contractor under paragraphs (a) and (b) of this section. For purposes of this (1), such a transfer will be considered to be in consideration for services performed for the corporation if either the property transferred is substantially nonvested at the time of transfer or an amount is includible in the gross income of the employee or independent contractor at the time of transfer under § 1.83-1(a)(1) or § 1.83-2(a). In the case of such a transfer, any money or other property paid to the shareholder for such stock shall be considered to be paid to the corporation and transferred immediately thereafter by the corporation to the shareholder as a distribution to which section 302 applies. For special rules that may apply to a corporation's transfer of its own stock to any person in consideration of services performed for another corporation or partnership, see § 1.1032-3. The preceding sentence applies to transfers of stock and amounts paid for such stock occurring on or after May 16, 2000.

(2) *Forfeiture.* If, following a transaction described in paragraph (d)(1) of this section, the transferred property is forfeited to the shareholder, paragraph (c) of this section shall apply both with respect to the shareholder and with respect to the corporation. In addition, the corporation shall, in the taxable year of forfeiture be allowed a loss (or realize a gain) to offset any gain (or loss) realized under paragraph (b) of this section. For example, if a shareholder transfers property to an employee of the corporation as compensation, and as a result the shareholder's basis of $200x in such property is allocated to his stock in such corporation and such corporation recognizes a short-term capital gain of $800x, and is allowed a deduction of $1,000x on such transfer, upon a subsequent forfeiture of the property to the shareholder, the shareholder shall take $200x into gross income, and the corporation shall take $1,000x into gross income and be allowed a short-term capital loss of $800x.

* * *

[Reg. § 1.83-6.]

☐ [*T.D. 7554, 7-21-78. Amended by T.D. 8599, 7-18-95 and T.D. 8883, 5-11-2000.*]

§ 1.83-7. Taxation of nonqualified stock options.—(a) *In general.* If there is granted to an employee or independent contractor (or beneficiary thereof) in connection with the performance of services, an option to which section 421 (relating generally to certain qualified and other options) does not apply, section 83(a) shall apply to such grant if the option has a readily ascertainable fair market value (determined in accordance with paragraph (b) of this section) at the time the option is granted. The person who performed such services realizes compensation upon such grant at the time and in the amount determined under section 83(a). If section 83(a) does not apply to the grant of such an option because the option does not have a readily ascertainable fair market value at the time of grant, sections 83(a) and

83(b) shall apply at the time the option is exercised or otherwise disposed of, even though the fair market value of such option may have become readily ascertainable before such time. If the option is exercised, sections 83(a) and 83(b) apply to the transfer of property pursuant to such exercise, and the employee or independent contractor realizes compensation upon such transfer at the time and in the amount determined under section 83(a) or 83(b). If the option is sold or otherwise disposed of in an arm's length transaction, sections 83(a) and 83(b) apply to the transfer of money or other property received in the same manner as sections 83(a) and 83(b) would have applied to the transfer of property pursuant to an exercise of the option.

(b) *Readily ascertainable defined* —(1) *Actively traded on an established market.* Options have a value at the time they are granted, but that value is ordinarily not readily ascertainable unless the option is actively traded on an established market. If an option is actively traded on an established market, the fair market value of such option is readily ascertainable for purposes of this section by applying the rules of valuation set forth in § 20.2031-2.

(2) *Not actively traded on an established market.* When an option is not actively traded on an established market, it does not have a readily ascertainable fair market value unless its fair market value can otherwise be measured with reasonable accuracy. For purposes of this section, if an option is not actively traded on an established market, the option does not have a readily ascertainable fair market value when granted unless the taxpayer can show that all of the following conditions exist:

(i) The option is transferable by the optionee;

(ii) The option is exercisable immediately in full by the optionee;

(iii) The option or the property subject to the option is not subject to any restriction or condition (other than a lien or other condition to secure the payment of the purchase price) which has a significant effect upon the fair market value of the option; and

(iv) The fair market value of the option privilege is readily ascertainable in accordance with paragraph (b)(3) of this section.

(3) *Option privilege.* The option privilege in the case of an option to buy is the opportunity to benefit during the option's exercise period from any increase in the value of property subject to the option during such period, without risking any capital. Similarly, the option privilege in the case of an option to sell is the opportunity to benefit during the exercise period from a decrease in the

Reg. § 1.83-7(b)(3)

value of property subject to the option. For example, if at some time during the exercise period of an option to buy, the fair market value of the property subject to the option is greater than the option's exercise price, a profit may be realized by exercising the option and immediately selling the property so acquired for its higher fair market value. Irrespective of whether any such gain may be realized immediately at the time an option is granted, the fair market value of an option to buy includes the value of the right to benefit from any future increase in the value of the property subject to the option (relative to the option exercise price), without risking any capital. Therefore, the fair market value of an option is not merely the difference that may exist at a particular time between the option's exercise price and the value of the property subject to the option, but also includes the value of the option privilege for the remainder of the exercise period. Accordingly, for purposes of this section, in determining whether

the fair market value of an option is readily ascertainable, it is necessary to consider whether the value of the entire option privilege can be measured with reasonable accuracy. In determining whether the value of the option privilege is readily ascertainable, and in determining the amount of such value when such value is readily ascertainable, it is necessary to consider—

(i) Whether the value of the property subject to the option can be ascertained;

(ii) The probability of any ascertainable value of such property increasing or decreasing; and

(iii) The length of the period during which the option can be exercised.

(c) *Reporting requirements.* [Reserved]

[Reg. § 1.83-7.]

☐ [*T.D.* 7554, 7-21-78.]

Items Specifically Excluded from Gross Income

§ 1.101-1. **Exclusion from gross income of proceeds of life insurance contracts payable by reason of death.**—(a)(1) *In general.* Section 101(a)(1) states the general rule that the proceeds of life insurance policies, if paid by reason of the death of the insured, are excluded from the gross income of the recipient. Death benefit payments having the characteristics of life insurance proceeds payable by reason of death under contracts, such as workmen's compensation insurance contracts, endowment contracts, or accident and health insurance contracts, are covered by this provision. For provisions relating to death benefits paid by or on behalf of employers, see section 101(b) and § 1.101-2. The exclusion from gross income allowed by section 101(a) applies whether payment is made to the estate of the insured or to any beneficiary (individual, corporation, or partnership) and whether it is made directly or in trust. The extent to which this exclusion applies in cases where life insurance policies have been transferred for a valuable consideration is stated in section 101(a)(2) and in paragraph (b) of this section. In cases where the proceeds of a life insurance policy, payable by reason of the death of the insured, are paid other than in a single sum at the time of such death, the amounts to be excluded from gross income may be affected by the provisions of section 101(c) (relating to amounts held under agreements to pay interest) or section 101(d) (relating to amounts payable at a date later than death). See §§ 1.101-3 and 1.101-4. However, neither section 101(c) nor section 101(d) applies to a single sum payment which does not exceed the amount payable at the time of

death even though such amount is actually paid at a date later than death.

(2) *Cross references.* For rules governing the taxability of insurance proceeds constituting benefits payable on the death of an employee—

(i) Under pension, profit-sharing, or stock bonus plans described in section 401(a) and exempt from tax under section 501(a), or under annuity plans described in section 403(a), see section 72(m)(3) and paragraph (c) of § 1.72-16;

(ii) Under annuity contracts to which paragraph (a) or (b) of § 1.403(b)-1 applies, see paragraph (c)(3) of § 1.403(b)-1; or

(iii) Under eligible State deferred compensation plans described in section 457(b), see paragraph (c) of § 1.457-1.

For the definition of a life insurance company, see section 801.

(b) *Transfers of life insurance policies.* (1) In the case of a transfer, by assignment or otherwise, of a life insurance policy or any interest therein for a valuable consideration, the amount of the proceeds attributable to such policy or interest which is excludable from the transferee's gross income is generally limited to the sum of (i) the actual value of the consideration for such transfer, and (ii) the premiums and other amounts subsequently paid by the transferee (see section 101(a)(2) and example (1) of subparagraph (5) of this paragraph). However, this limitation on the amount excludable from the transferee's gross income does not apply (except in certain special cases involving a series of transfers), where the basis of the policy or interest transferred, for the purpose of determining gain or loss with respect to the transferee, is determinable, in whole or in part, by reference to the basis of such policy or interest in the hands of the transferor (see section 101(a)(2)(A) and examples (2) and (4) of subparagraph (5) of this paragraph). Neither does the limitation apply where the policy or interest therein is transferred to the insured, to a partner of the insured, to a partnership in which the insured is a partner, or to a corporation in which the insured is a shareholder or officer (See section 101(a)(2)(B)). For rules relating to gratuitous transfers, see subparagraph (2) of this paragraph. For special rules with respect to certain cases where a series of transfers is involved, see subparagraph (3) of this paragraph.

(2) In the case of a gratuitous transfer, by assignment or otherwise, of a life insurance policy or any interest therein, as a general rule the amount of the proceeds attributable to such policy or interest which is excludable from the transferee's gross income under section 101(a) is limited to the sum of (i) the amount which would have been excludable by the transferor (in accordance with this section) if no such transfer had taken place, and (ii) any premiums and other amounts subsequently paid by the transferee. See example (6) of subparagraph (5) of this paragraph. However, where the gratuitous transfer in question is made by or to the insured, a partner of the insured, a partnership in which the insured is a partner, or a corporation in which the insured is a shareholder or officer, the entire amount of the proceeds attributable to the policy or interest transferred shall be excludable from the transferee's gross income (see section 101(a)(2)(B) and example (7) of subparagraph (5) of this paragraph).

(3) In the case of a series of transfers, if the last transfer of a life insurance policy or an interest therein is for a valuable consideration—

(i) The general rule is that the final transferee shall exclude from gross income, with respect to the proceeds of such policy or interest therein, only the sum of—

(a) The actual value of the consideration paid by him, and

(b) The premiums and other amounts subsequently paid by him;

(ii) If the final transfer is to the insured, to a partner of the insured, to a partnership in which the insured is a partner, or to a corporation in which the insured is a shareholder or officer, the final transferee shall exclude the entire amount of the proceeds from gross income;

(iii) Except where subdivision (ii) of this subparagraph applies, if the basis of the policy or interest transferred, for the purpose of determining gain or loss with respect to the final transferee, is determinable, in whole or in part, by reference to the basis of such policy or interest therein in the hands of the transferor, the amount of the proceeds which is excludable by the final transferee is limited to the sum of—

(a) The amount which would have been excludable by his transferor if no such transfer had taken place, and

(b) Any premiums and other amounts subsequently paid by the final transferee himself.

(4) For the purposes of section 101(a)(2) and subparagraphs (1) and (3) of this paragraph, a "transfer for a valuable consideration" is any absolute transfer for value of a right to receive all or a part of the proceeds of a life insurance policy. Thus, the creation, for value, of an enforceable contractual right to receive all or a part of the proceeds of a policy may constitute a transfer for a valuable consideration of the policy or an interest therein. On the other hand, the pledging or assignment of a policy as collateral security is not a transfer for a valuable consideration of such policy or an interest therein, and section 101 is inapplicable to any amounts received by the pledgee or assignee.

(5) The application of this paragraph may be illustrated by the following examples:

Example (1). A pays premiums of $500 for an insurance policy in the face amount of $1,000 upon the life of B, and subsequently transfers the policy to C for $600. C receives the proceeds of $1,000 upon the death of B. The amount which C can exclude from his gross income is limited to $600 plus any premiums paid by C subsequent to the transfer.

Example (2). The X Corporation purchases for a single premium of $500 an insurance policy in the face amount of $1,000 upon the life of A, one of its employees, naming the X Corporation as beneficiary. The X Corporation transfers the policy to the Y Corporation in a tax-free reorganization (the policy having a basis for determining gain or loss in the hands of the Y Corporation determined by reference to its basis in the hands of the X Corporation). The Y Corporation receives the proceeds of $1,000 upon the death of A. The entire $1,000 is to be excluded from the gross income of the Y Corporation.

Example (3). The facts are the same as in example (2) except that, prior to the death of A, the Y Corporation transfers the policy to the Z Corporation for $600. The Z Corporation receives the proceeds of $1,000 upon the death of A. The amount which the Z Corporation can exclude from its gross income is limited to $600 plus any premiums paid by the Z Corporation subsequent to the transfer of the policy to it.

Reg. § 1.101-1(b)(5)

Example (4). The facts are the same as in example (3) except that, prior to the death of A, the Z Corporation transfers the policy to the M Corporation in a tax-free reorganization (the policy having a basis for determining gain or loss in the hands of the M Corporation determined by reference to its basis in the hands of the Z Corporation). The M Corporation receives the proceeds of $1,000 upon the death of A. The amount which the M Corporation can exclude from its gross income is limited to $600 plus any premiums paid by the Z Corporation and the M Corporation subsequent to the transfer of the policy to the Z Corporation.

Example (5). The facts are the same as in example (3) except that, prior to the death of A, the Z Corporation transfers the policy to the N Corporation, in which A is a shareholder. The N Corporation receives the proceeds of $1,000 upon the death of A. The entire $1,000 is to be excluded from the gross income of the N Corporation.

Example (6). A pays premiums of $500 for an insurance policy in the face amount of $1,000 upon his own life, and subsequently transfers the policy to his wife B for $600. B later transfers the policy without consideration to C, who is the son of A and B. C receives the proceeds of $1,000 upon the death of A. The amount which C can exclude from his gross income is limited to $600 plus any premiums paid by B and C subsequent to the transfer of the policy to B.

Example (7). The facts are the same as in example (6) except that, prior to the death of A, C transfers the policy without consideration to A, the insured. A's estate receives the proceeds of $1,000 upon the death of A. The entire $1,000 is to be excluded from the gross income of A's estate. [Reg. § 1.101-1.]

□ [*T.D. 6280, 12-16-57. Amended by T.D. 6783, 12-23-64 and T.D. 7836, 9-23-82.*]

§ 1.101-3. Interest payments.—(a) *Applicability of section 101(c).* Section 101(c) provides that if any amount excluded from gross income by section 101(a) (relating to life insurance proceeds) or section 101(b) (relating to employees' death benefits) is held under an agreement to pay interest thereon, the interest payments shall be included in gross income. This provision applies to payments made (either by an insurer or by or on behalf of an employer) of interest earned on any amount so excluded from gross income which is held without substantial diminution of the principal amount during the period when such interest payments are being made or credited to the beneficiaries or estate of the insured or the employee. For example, if a monthly payment is $100, of which $99 represents interest and $1 represents diminution of the principal amount, the principal

amount shall be considered held under an agreement to pay interest thereon and the interest payment shall be included in the gross income of the recipient. Section 101(c) applies whether the election to have an amount held under an agreement to pay interest thereon is made by the insured or employee or by his beneficiaries or estate, and whether or not an interest rate is explicitly stated in the agreement. Section 101(d), relating to the payment of life insurance proceeds at a date later than death, shall not apply to any amount to which section 101(c) applies. See section 101(d)(4). However, both section 101(c) and section 101(d) may apply to payments received under a single life insurance contract. For provisions relating to the application of this rule to payments received under a permanent life insurance policy with a family income rider attached, see paragraph (h) of § 1.101-4.

(b) *Determinations of "present value".* For the purpose of determining whether section 101(c) or section 101(d) applies, the present value (at the time of the insured's death) of any amount which is to be paid at a date later than death shall be determined by the use of the interest rate and mortality tables used by the insurer in determining the size of the payments to be made. [Reg. § 1.101-3.]

□ [*T.D. 6280, 12-16-57. Amended by T.D. 6577, 10-27-61.*]

§ 1.101-4. Payment of life insurance proceeds at a date later than death.—(a) *In general.* (1) (i) Section 101(d) states the provisions governing the exclusion from gross income of amounts (other than those to which section 101(c) applies) received under a life insurance contract and paid by reason of the death of the insured which are paid to a beneficiary on a date or dates later than the death of the insured. However, if the amounts payable as proceeds of life insurance to which section 101(a)(1) applies cannot in any event exceed the amount payable at the time of the insured's death, such amounts are fully excludable from the gross income of the recipient (or recipients) without regard to the actual time of payment and no further determination need be made under this section. Section 101(d)(1)(A) provides an exclusion from gross income of any amount determined by a proration, under applicable regulations, of "an amount held by an insurer with respect to any beneficiary". The quoted phrase is defined in section 101(d)(2). For the regulations governing the method of computation of this proration, see paragraphs (c) through (f) of this section. The prorated amounts are to be excluded from the gross income of the beneficiary regardless of the taxable year in which they are actually received (see example (2) of subparagraph (2) of this paragraph).

(ii) Section 101(d)(1)(B) provides an additional exclusion where life insurance proceeds are paid to the surviving spouse of an insured. For purposes of this exclusion, the term "surviving spouse" means the spouse of the insured as of the date of death, including a spouse legally separated, but not under a decree of absolute divorce (section 101(d)(3)). To the extent that the total payments, under one or more agreements, made in excess of the amounts determined by proration under section 101(d)(1)(A) do not exceed $1,000 in the taxable year of receipt, they shall be excluded from the gross income of the surviving spouse (whether or not payment of any part of such amounts is guaranteed by the insurer). Amounts excludable under section 101(d)(1)(B) are not "prorated" amounts.

(2) The principles of this paragraph may be illustrated by the following examples:

Example (1). A surviving spouse elects to receive all of the life insurance proceeds with respect to one insured, amounting to $150,000, in ten annual installments of $16,500 each, based on a certain guaranteed interest rate. The prorated amount is $15,000 ($150,000 ÷ 10). As the second payment, the insurer pays $17,850, which exceeds the guaranteed payment by $1,350 as the result of earnings of the insurer in excess of those required to pay the guaranteed installments. The surviving spouse shall include $1,850 in gross income and exclude $16,000—determined in the following manner:

Fixed payment (including guaranteed interest) ..	$16,500
Excess interest	1,350
Total payment	17,850
Prorated amount	15,000
Excess over prorated amount .	2,850
Annual excess over prorated amount excludable under section 101(d)(1)(B) ..	$ 1,000
Amount includible in gross income	1,850

Example (2). Assume the same facts as in example (1), except that the third and fourth annual installments, totalling $33,000 (2 × $16,500), are received in a single subsequent taxable year of the surviving spouse. The prorated amount of $15,000 of each annual installment, totalling $30,000, shall be excluded even though the spouse receives more than one annual installment in the single subsequent taxable year. However, the surviving spouse is entitled to only one exclusion of $1,000 under section 101(d)(1)(B) for each taxable year of receipt. The surviving spouse shall include $2,000 in her gross income for the taxable year with respect to the above installment payments ($33,000 less the sum of $30,000 plus $1,000).

Example (3). Assume the same facts as in example (1), except that the surviving spouse dies before receiving all ten annual installments and the remaining installments are paid to her estate or beneficiary. In such a case, $15,000 of each installment would continue to be excludable from the gross income of the recipient, but any amounts received in excess thereof would be fully includible.

(b) *Amount held by an insurer.* (1) For the purpose of the proration referred to in section 101(d)(1), an "amount held by an insurer with respect to any beneficiary" means an amount equal to the present value to such beneficiary (as of the date of death of the insured) of an agreement by the insurer under a life insurance policy (whether as an option or otherwise) to pay such beneficiary an amount or amounts at a date or dates later than the death of the insured (section 101(d)(2)). The present value of such agreement is to be computed as if the agreement under the life insurance policy had been entered into on the date of death of the insured, except that such value shall be determined by the use of the mortality table and interest rate used by the insurer in calculating payments to be made to the beneficiary under such agreement. Where an insurance policy provides an option for the payment of a specific amount upon the death of the insured in full discharge of the contract, such lump sum is the amount held by the insurer with respect to all beneficiaries (or their beneficiaries) under the contract. See, however, paragraph (e) of this section.

(2) In the case of two or more beneficiaries, the "amount held by the insurer" with respect to each beneficiary depends on the relationship of the different benefits payable to such beneficiaries. Where the amounts payable to two or more beneficiaries are independent of each other, the "amount held by the insurer with respect to each beneficiary" shall be determined and prorated over the periods involved independently. Thus, if a certain amount per month is to be paid to A for his life, and, concurrently, another amount per month is to be paid to B for his life, the "amount held by the insurer" shall be determined and prorated for both A and B independently, but the aggregate shall not exceed the total present value of such payments to both. On the other hand, if the obligation to pay B was contingent on his surviving A, the "amount held by the insurer" shall be considered an amount held with respect to both beneficiaries simultaneously. Furthermore, it is immaterial whether B is a named beneficiary or merely the ultimate recipient of payments for a term of years. For the special rules governing the computation of the proration of the "amount held by an insurer" in determining amounts excludable under the provi-

Reg. § 1.101-4(b)(2)

sions of section 101(d), see paragraphs (c) to (f), inclusive, of this section.

(3) Notwithstanding any other provision of this section, if the policy was transferred for a valuable consideration, the total "amount held by an insurer" cannot exceed the sum of the consideration paid plus any premiums or other consideration paid subsequent to the transfer if the provisions of section 101(a)(2) and paragraph (b) of § 1.101-1 limit the excludability of the proceeds to such total.

* * *

[Reg. § 1.101-4.]

☐ [*T.D. 6280, 12-16-57. Amended by T.D. 6577, 10-27-61.*]

§ 1.102-1. Gifts and inheritances.—(a) *General rule.* Property received as a gift, or received under a will or under statutes of descent and distribution, is not includible in gross income, although the income from such property is includible in gross income. An amount of principal paid under a marriage settlement is a gift. However, see section 71 and the regulations thereunder for rules relating to alimony or allowances paid upon divorce or separation. Section 102 does not apply to prizes and awards (see section 74 and § 1.74-1) nor to scholarships and fellowship grants (see section 117 and the regulations thereunder).

(b) *Income from gifts and inheritances.* The income from any property received as a gift, or under a will or statute of descent and distribution shall not be excluded from gross income under paragraph (a) of this section.

(c) *Gifts and inheritances of income.* If the gift, bequest, devise, or inheritance is of income from property, it shall not be excluded from gross income under paragraph (a) of this section. Section 102 provides a special rule for the treatment of certain gifts, bequests, devises, or inheritances which by their terms are to be paid, credited, or distributed at intervals. Except as provided in section 663(a)(1) and paragraph (d) of this section, to the extent any such gift, bequest, devise, or inheritance is paid, credited, or to be distributed out of income from property, it shall be considered a gift, bequest, devise, or inheritance of income from property. Section 102 provides the same treatment for amounts of income from property which is paid, credited, or to be distributed under a gift or bequest whether the gift or bequest is in terms of a right to payments at intervals (regardless of income) or is in terms of a right to income. To the extent the amounts in either case are paid, credited, or to be distributed at intervals out of income, they are not to be excluded under section 102 from the taxpayer's gross income.

(d) *Effect of subchapter J.* Any amount required to be included in the gross income of a beneficiary under sections 652, 662, or 668 shall be treated for purposes of this section as a gift, bequest, devise, or inheritance of income from property. On the other hand, any amount excluded from the gross income of a beneficiary under section 663(a)(1) shall be treated for purposes of this section as property acquired by gift, bequest, devise, or inheritance.

(e) *Income taxed to grantor or assignor.* Section 102 is not intended to tax a donee upon the same income which is taxed to the grantor of a trust or assignor of income under section 61 or sections 671 through 677, inclusive. [Reg. § 1.102-1.]

☐ [*T.D. 6220, 12-28-56.*]

Proposed Amendment to Regulation

§ 1.102-1. Gifts and inheritances.

* * *

(f) *Exclusions*—(1) *In general.* Section 102 does not apply to prizes and awards (including employee achievement awards) (see section 74); certain de minimis fringe benefits (see section 132); any amount transferred by or for an employer to, or for the benefit of, an employee (see section 102(c)); or to qualified scholarships (see section 117).

(2) *Employer/Employee transfers.* For purposes of section 102(c), extraordinary transfers to the natural objects of an employer's bounty will not be considered transfers to, or for the benefit of, an employee if the employee can show that the transfer was not made in recognition of the employee's employment. Accordingly, section 102(c) shall not apply to amounts transferred between related parties (*e.g.*, father and son) if the purpose of the transfer can be substantially attributed to the familial relationship of the parties and not to the circumstances of their employment. [Reg. § 1.102-1.]

[Proposed 1-9-89.]

[*Caution: Reg. § 1.104-1 does not reflect changes made in Section 104(a)(2) by the Small Business Job Protection Act of 1996.*]

§ 1.104-1. Compensation for injuries or sickness.—(a) *In general.*—Section 104(a) provides an exclusion from gross income with respect to certain amounts described in paragraphs (b), (c), (d) and (e) of this section, which are received for personal injuries or sickness, except to the extent that such amounts are attributable to (but not in excess of) deductions allowed under section 213 (relating to medical, etc., expenses) for any prior taxable year. See section 213 and the regulations thereunder.

(b) *Amounts received under workmen's compensation acts.*—Section 104(a)(1) excludes from gross income amounts which are received by an employee under a workmen's compensation act (such as the Longshoremen's and Harbor Workers' Compensation Act, 33 U.S.C., c. 18), or under a statute in the nature of a workmen's compensation act which provides compensation to employees for personal injuries or sickness incurred in the course of employment. Section 104(a)(1) also applies to compensation which is paid under a workmen's compensation act to the survivor or survivors of a deceased employee. However, section 104(a)(1) does not apply to a retirement pension or annuity to the extent that it is determined by reference to the employee's age or length of service, or the employee's prior contributions, even though the employee's retirement is occasioned by an occupational injury or sickness. Section 104(a)(1) also does not apply to amounts which are received as compensation for a nonoccupational injury or sickness nor to amounts received as compensation for an occupational injury or sickness to the extent that they are in excess of the amount provided in the applicable workmen's compensation act or acts. See, however, §§ 1.105-1 through 1.105-5 for rules relating to exclusion of such amounts from gross income.

(c) *Damages received on account of personal injuries or sickness.*—Section 104(a)(2) excludes from gross income the amount of any damages received (whether by suit or agreement) on account of personal injuries or sickness. The term "damages received (whether by suit or agreement)" means an amount received (other than workmen's compensation) through prosecution of a legal suit or action based upon tort or tort type rights, or through a settlement agreement entered into in lieu of such prosecution.

(d) *Accident or health insurance.*—Section 104(a)(3) excludes from gross income amounts received through accident or health insurance for personal injuries or sickness (other than amounts received by an employee, to the extent that such amounts (1) are attributable to contributions of the employer which were not includible in the gross income of the employee, or (2) are paid by the employer). Similar treatment is also accorded to amounts received under accident or health plans and amounts received from sickness or disability funds. See section 105(e) and § 1.105-5. If, therefore, an individual purchases a policy of accident or health insurance out of his own funds, amounts received thereunder for personal injuries or sickness are excludable from his gross income under section 104(a)(3). See, however, section 213 and the regulations thereunder as to the inclusion in gross income of amounts attributable to deductions allowed under section 213 for any prior

taxable year. Section 104(a)(3) also applies to amounts received by an employee for personal injuries or sickness from a fund which is maintained exclusively by employee contributions. Conversely, if an employer is either the sole contributor to such a fund, or is the sole purchaser of a policy of accident or health insurance for his employees (on either a group or individual basis), the exclusion provided under section 104(a)(3) does not apply to any amounts received by his employees through such fund or insurance. If the employer and his employees contribute to a fund or purchase insurance which pays accident or health benefits to employees, section 104(a)(3) does not apply to amounts received thereunder by employees to the extent that such amounts are attributable to the employer's contributions. See § 1.105-1 for rules relating to the determination of the amount attributable to employer contributions. Although amounts paid by or on behalf of an employer to an employee for personal injuries or sickness are not excludable from the employee's gross income under section 104(a)(3), they may be excludable therefrom under section 105. See §§ 1.105-1 through 1.105-5 , inclusive. For treatment of accident or health benefits paid to or on behalf of a self-employed individual by a trust described in section 401(a) which is exempt under section 501(a) or under a plan described in section 403(a), see paragraph (g) of § 1.72-15.

* * *

[Reg. § 1.104-1.]

□ [*T.D.* 6169, 4-13-56. *Amended by T.D.* 6722, 4-13-64 *and T.D.* 7043, 6-1-70.]

§ 1.105-2. **Amounts expended for medical care.**—Section 105(b) provides an exclusion from gross income with respect to the amounts referred to in section 105(a) (see § 1.105-1) which are paid, directly or indirectly, to the taxpayer to reimburse him for expenses incurred for the medical care (as defined in section 213(e)) of the taxpayer, his spouse, and his dependents (as defined in section 152). However, the exclusion does not apply to amounts which are attributable to (and not in excess of) deductions allowed under section 213 (relating to medical, etc., expenses) for any prior taxable year. See section 213 and the regulations thereunder. Section 105(b) applies only to amounts which are paid specifically to reimburse the taxpayer for expenses incurred by him for the prescribed medical care. Thus, section 105(b) does not apply to amounts which the taxpayer would be entitled to receive irrespective of whether or not he incurs expenses for medical care. For example, if under a wage continuation plan the taxpayer is entitled to regular wages during a period of absence from work due to sickness or injury, amounts received under such plan are not excludable from his gross income under section 105(b) even though the taxpayer may have incurred medical expenses during the period of illness. Such amounts may, however, be excludable from his gross income under section 105(d). See § 1.105-4. If the amounts are paid to the taxpayer solely to reimburse him for expenses which he incurred for the prescribed medical care, section 105(b) is applicable even though such amounts are paid without proof of the amount of the actual expenses incurred by the taxpayer, but section 105(b) is not applicable to the extent that such amounts exceed the amount of the actual expenses for such medical care. If the taxpayer incurs an obligation for medical care, payment to the obligee in discharge of such obligation shall constitute indirect payment to the taxpayer as reimbursement for medical care. Similarly, payment to or on behalf of the taxpayer's spouse or dependents shall constitute indirect payment to the taxpayer. [Reg. § 1.105-2.]

☐ [*T.D.* 6169, 4-13-56.]

§ 1.106-1. Contributions by employer to accident and health plans.—The gross income of an employee does not include contributions which his employer makes to an accident or health plan for compensation (through insurance or otherwise) to the employee for personal injuries or sickness incurred by him, his spouse, or his dependents, as defined in section 152. The employer may contribute to an accident or health plan either by paying the premium (or a portion of the premium) on a policy of accident or health insurance covering one or more of his employees, or by contributing to a separate trust or fund (including a fund referred to in section 105(e)) which provides accident or health benefits directly or through insurance to one or more of his employees. However, if such insurance policy, trust, or fund provides other benefits in addition to accident or health benefits, section 106 applies only to the portion of the employer's contribution which is allocable to accident or health benefits. See paragraph (d) of § 1.104-1 and § § 1.105-1 through 1.105-5, inclusive, for regulations relating to exclusion from an employee's gross income of amounts received through accident or health insurance and through accident or health plans. [Reg. § 1.106-1.]

☐ [*T.D.* 6169, 4-13-56.]

§ 1.109-1. Exclusion from gross income of lessor of real property of value of improvements erected by lessee.—(a) Income derived by a lessor of real property upon the termination, through forfeiture or otherwise, of the lease of such property and attributable to buildings erected or other improvements made by the lessee upon the leased property is excluded from gross income. However, where the facts disclose that such buildings or improvements represent in whole or in part a liquidation in kind of lease rentals, the exclusion from gross income shall not apply to the extent that such buildings or improvements represent such liquidation. The exclusion applies only with respect to the income realized by the lessor upon the termination of the lease and has no application to income, if any, in the form of rent, which may be derived by a lessor during the period of the lease and attributable to buildings erected or other improvements made by the lessee. It has no application to income which may be realized by the lessor upon the termination of the lease but not attributable to the value of such buildings or improvements. Neither does it apply to income derived by the lessor subsequent to the termination of the lease incident to the ownership of such buildings or improvements.

(b) The provisions of this section may be illustrated by the following example:

Example. The A Corporation leased in 1945 for a period of 50 years unimproved real property to the B Corporation under a lease providing that the B Corporation erect on the leased premises an office building costing $500,000, in addition to paying the A Corporation a lease rental of $10,000 per annum beginning on the date of completion of the improvements, the sum of $100,000 being placed in escrow for the payment of the rental. The building was completed on January 1, 1950. The lease provided that all improvements made by the lessee on the leased property would become the absolute property of the A Corporation on the termination of the lease by forfeiture or otherwise and that the lessor would become entitled on such termination to the remainder of the sum, if any, remaining in the escrow fund. The B Corporation forfeited its lease on January 1, 1955, when the improvements had a value of $100,000. Under the provisions of section 109, the $100,000 is excluded from gross income. The amount of $50,000 representing the remainder in the escrow fund is forfeited to the A Corporation and is included in the gross income of that taxpayer. As to the basis of the property in the hands of the A Corporation, see § 1.1019-1. [Reg. § 1.109-1.]

☐ [*T.D.* 6220, 12-28-56.]

Proposed Regulation

§ 1.117-6. Qualified scholarships.—* * *

(b) *Exclusion of qualified scholarships*—(1) Gross income does not include any amount received as a qualified scholarship by an individual who is a candidate for a degree at an educational organization described in section 170(b)(1)(A)(ii), subject to the rules set forth in paragraph (d) of this section. Generally, any amount of a scholarship or fellowship grant that is not excludable under section 117 is includable in the gross income of the recipient for the taxable year in which such amount is received, notwithstanding the provisions of section 102 (relating to exclusion from gross income of gifts). However, see section 127 and the regulations thereunder for rules permitting an exclusion from gross income for certain educational assistance payments. See also section 162 and the regulations thereunder for the deductibility as a trade or business expense of the educational expenses of an individual who is not a candidate for a degree.

(2) If the amount of a scholarship or fellowship grant eligible to be excluded as a qualified scholarship under this paragraph cannot be determined when the grant is received because expenditures for qualified tuition and related expenses have not yet been incurred, then that portion of any amount received as a scholarship or fellowship grant that is not used for qualified tuition and related expenses within the academic period to which the scholarship or fellowship grant applies must be included in the gross income of the recipient for the taxable year in which such academic period ends.

(c) *Definitions*—(1) *Qualified scholarship.* For purposes of this section, a qualified scholarship is any amount received by an individual as a scholarship or fellowship grant (as defined in paragraph (c)(3) of this section), to the extent the individual establishes that, in accordance with the conditions of the grant, such amount was used for qualified tuition and related expenses (as defined in paragraph (c)(2) of this section). To be considered a qualified scholarship, the terms of the scholarship or fellowship grant need not expressly require that the amounts received be used for tuition and related expenses. However, to the extent that the terms of the grant specify that any portion of the grant cannot be used for tuition and related expenses or designate any portion of the grant for purposes other than tuition and related expenses (such as for room and board, or for a meal allowance), such amounts are not amounts received as a qualified scholarship. See paragraph (e) of this section for rules relating to recordkeeping requirements for establishing amounts used for qualified tuition and related expenses.

(2) *Qualified tuition and related expenses.* For purposes of this section, qualified tuition and related expenses are—

(i) Tuition and fees required for the enrollment or attendance of a student at an educational organization described in section 170(b)(1)(A)(ii); and

(ii) Fees, books, supplies, and equipment required for courses of instruction at such an educational organization.

In order to be treated as related expenses under this section, the fees, books, supplies, and equipment must be required of all students in the particular course of instruction. Incidental expenses are not considered related expenses. Incidental expenses include expenses incurred for room and board, travel, research, clerical help, and equipment and other expenses that are not required for either enrollment or attendance at an educational organization, or in a course of instruction at such educational organization. See paragraph (c)(6), Example (1) of this section.

(3) *Scholarship or fellowship grant*—(i) *In general.* Generally, a scholarship or fellowship grant is a cash amount paid or allowed to, or for the benefit of, an individual to aid such individual in the pursuit of study or research. A scholarship or fellowship grant also may be in the form of a reduction in the amount owed by the recipient to an educational organization for tuition, room and board, or any other fee. A scholarship or fellowship grant may be funded by a governmental agency, college or university, charitable organization, business, or any other source. To be considered a scholarship or fellowship grant for purposes of this section, any amount received need not be formally designated as a scholarship. For example, an "allowance" is treated as a scholarship if it meets the definition set forth in this paragraph. However, a scholarship or fellowship grant does not include any amount provided by an individual to aid a relative, friend, or other individual in the pursuit of study or research if the grantor is motivated by family or philanthropic considerations.

(ii) *Items not considered as scholarships or fellowship grants.* The following payments or allowances are not considered to be amounts received as a scholarship or fellowship grant for purposes of section 117:

(A) Educational and training allowances to a veteran pursuant to section 400 of the Servicemen's Readjustment Act of 1944 (58 Stat. 287) or pursuant to 38 U.S.C. 1631 (formerly section 231 of the Veterans' Readjustment Assistance Act of 1952).

(B) Tuition and subsistence allowances to members of the Armed Forces of the United States who are students at an educational institution operated by the United States or approved by the United States for their education and training, such as the United States Naval Academy and the United States Military Academy.

(4) *Candidate for a degree.* For purposes of this section, a candidate for a degree is—

(i) A primary or secondary school student;

(ii) An undergraduate or graduate student at a college or university who is pursuing studies or conducting research to meet the requirement for an academic or professional degree; or

(iii) A full-time or part-time student at an educational organization described in section 170(b)(1)(A)(ii) that—

(A) Provides an educational program that is acceptable for full credit towards a bachelor's or higher degree, or offers a program of training to prepare students for gainful employment in a recognized occupation, and

(B) Is authorized under Federal or State law to provide such a program and is accredited by a nationally recognized accreditation agency.

The student may pursue studies or conduct research at an educational organization other than the one conferring the degree provided that such study or research meets the requirements of the educational organization granting the degree. See paragraph (c)(6), Examples (2) and (3) of this section.

(5) *Educational organization.* For purposes of this section, an educational organization is an organization described under section 170(b)(1)(A)(ii) and the regulations thereunder. An educational organization is described in section 170(b)(1)(A)(ii) if it has as its primary function the presentation of formal instruction, and it normally maintains a regular faculty and curriculum and normally has a regularly enrolled body of pupils or students in attendance at the place where its educational activities are regularly carried on. See paragraph (c)(6), Example (4) of this section.

(6) *Examples.* The provisions of this paragraph may be illustrated by the following examples:

Example (1). On September 1, 1987, A receives a scholarship from University U for academic year 1987-1988. A is enrolled in a writing course at U. Suggested supplies for the writing course in which A is enrolled include a word processor, but students in the course are not required to obtain a word processor. Any amount used for suggested supplies is not an amount used for qualified tuition and related expenses for purposes of this section. Thus, A may not include the cost of a word processor in determining the amount received by A as a qualified scholarship.

Example (2). B is a scholarship student during academic year 1987-1988 at Technical School V located in State W. B is enrolled in a program to train individuals to become data processors. V is authorized by State W to provide this program and is accredited by an appropriate accreditation agency. B is a candidate for a degree for purposes of this section. Thus, B may exclude from gross income any amount received as a qualified scholarship, subject to the rules set forth in paragraph (d) of this section.

Example (3). C holds a Ph.D. in chemistry. On January 31, 1988, Foundation X awards C a fellowship. During 1988 C pursues chemistry research at Research Foundation Y, supported by the fellowship grant from X. C is not an employee of either foundation. C is not a candidate for a degree for purposes of this section. Thus, the fellowship grant from X must be included in C's gross income.

Example (4). On July 1, 1987, D receives a $500 scholarship to take a correspondence course from School Z. D receives and returns all lessons to Z through the mail. No students are in attendance at Z's place of business. D is not attending an educational organization described in section 170(b)(1)(A)(ii) for purposes of this section. Thus, the $500 scholarship must be included in D's gross income.

(d) *Inclusion of qualified scholarships and qualified tuition reductions representing payment for services*—(1) *In general.* The exclusion from gross income under this section does not apply to that portion of any amount received as a qualified scholarship or qualified tuition reduction (as defined under section 117(d)) that represents payment for teaching, research, or other services by the student required as a condition to receiving the qualified scholarship or qualified tuition reduction, regardless of whether all candidates for the degree are required to perform such services. The provisions of this paragraph (d) apply not only to cash amounts received in return for such services, but also to amounts by which the tuition or related expenses of the person who performs services are reduced, whether or not pursuant to a tuition reduction plan described in section 117(d).

(2) *Payment for services.* For purposes of this section, a scholarship or fellowship grant represents payment for services when the grantor requires the recipient to perform services in return for the granting of the scholarship or fellowship. A requirement that the recipient pursue studies, research, or other activities primarily for the benefit of the grantor is treated as a requirement to perform services. A requirement that a recipient furnish periodic reports to the grantor for the purpose of keeping the grantor informed as to the general progress of the individual, however, does not constitute the performance of services. A scholarship or fellowship grant conditioned upon either past, present, or future teaching, research, or other services by the recipient represents payment for services under this section. See para-

graph (d)(5), Examples (1), (2), (3) and (4) of this section.

(3) *Determination of amount of scholarship or fellowship grant representing payment for services.* If only a portion of a scholarship or fellowship grant represents payment for services, the grantor must determine the amount of the scholarship or fellowship grant (including any reduction in tuition or related expenses) to be allocated to payment for services. Factors to be taken into account in making this allocation include, but are not limited to, compensation paid by—

(i) The grantor for similar services performed by students with qualifications comparable to those of the scholarship recipient, but who do not receive scholarship or fellowship grants;

(ii) The grantor for similar services performed by full-time or part-time employees of the grantor who are not students; and

(iii) Educational organizations, other than the grantor of the scholarship or fellowship, for similar services performed either by students or other employees.

If the recipient includes in gross income the amount allocated by the grantor to payment for services and such amount represents reasonable compensation for those services, then any additional amount of a scholarship or fellowship grant received from the same grantor that meets the requirements of paragraph (b) of this section is excludable from gross income. See paragraph (d)(5), Examples (5) and (6) of this section.

(4) *Characterization of scholarship or fellowship grants representing payment for services for purposes of the reporting and withholding requirements.* Any amount of a scholarship or fellowship grant that represents payment for services (as defined in paragraph (d)(2) of this section) is considered wages for purposes of sections 3401 and 3402 (relating to withholding for income taxes), section 6041 (relating to returns of information), and section 6051 (relating to reporting wages of employees). The application of sections 3101 and 3111 (relating to the Federal Insurance Contributions Act (FICA)), or section 3301 (relating to the Federal Unemployment Tax Act (FUTA)) depends upon the nature of the employment and the status of the organization. See sections 3121(b), 3306(c), and the regulations thereunder.

(5) *Examples.* The provisions of this paragraph may be illustrated by the following examples:

Example (1). On November 15, 1987, A receives a $5,000 qualified scholarship (as defined in paragraph (c)(1) of this section) for academic year 1988-1989 under a federal program requiring A's future service as a federal employee. The $5,000 scholarship represents payment for services for purposes of this section. Thus, the $5,000 must be included in A's gross income as wages.

Example (2). B receives a $10,000 scholarship from V Corporation on June 4, 1987, for academic year 1987-1988. As a condition to receiving the scholarship, B agrees to work for V after graduation. B has no previous relationship with V. The $10,000 scholarship represents payment for future services for purposes of this section. Thus, the $10,000 scholarship must be included in B's gross income as wages.

Example (3). On March 15, 1987, C is awarded a fellowship for academic year 1987-1988 to pursue a research project the nature of which is determined by the grantor, University W. C must submit a paper to W that describes the research results. The paper does not fulfill any course requirements. Under the terms of the grant, W may publish C's results, or otherwise use the results of C's research. C is treated as performing services for W. Thus, C's fellowship from W represents payment for services and must be included in C's gross income as wages.

Example (4). On September 27, 1987, D receives a qualified scholarship (as defined in paragraph (c)(1) of this section) from University X for academic year 1987-1988. As a condition to receiving the scholarship, D performs services as a teaching assistant for X. Such services are required of all candidates for a degree at X. The amount of D's scholarship from X is equal to the compensation paid by X to teaching assistants who are part-time employees and not students at X. D's scholarship from X represents payment for services. Thus, the entire amount of D's scholarship from X must be included in D's gross income as wages.

Example (5). On June 11, 1987, E receives a $6,000 scholarship for academic year 1987-1988 from University Y. As a condition to receiving the scholarship, E performs services as a researcher for Y. Other researchers who are not scholarship recipients receive $2,000 for similar services for the year. Therefore, Y allocates $2,000 of the scholarship amount to compensation for services performed by E. Thus, the portion of the scholarship that represents payment for services, $2,000, must be included in E's gross income as wages. However, if E establishes expenditures of $4,000 for qualified tuition and related expenses (as defined in paragraph (c)(2) of this section), then $4,000 of E's scholarship is excludable from E's gross income as a qualified scholarship.

Example (6). During 1987 F is employed as a research assistant to a faculty member at University Z. F receives a salary from Z that represents reasonable compensation for the position of research assistant. In addition to salary, F receives from Z a qualified tuition reduction (as defined in section 117(d)) to be used to enroll in an undergraduate course at Z. F includes the salary in gross income. Thus, the qualified tuition reduction does not represent payment for services and therefore, is not includable in F's gross income.

(e) *Recordkeeping requirements.* In order to be eligible to exclude from gross income any amount received as a qualified scholarship (as defined in paragraph (c)(1) of this section), the recipient must maintain records that establish amounts used for qualified tuition and related expenses (as defined in paragraph (c)(2) of this section) as well as the total amount of qualified tuition and related expenses. Such amounts may be established by providing to the Service, upon request, copies of relevant bills, receipts, cancelled checks, or other documentation or records that clearly reflect the use of the money. The recipient must also submit, upon request, documentation that establishes receipt of the grant, notification date of the grant, and the conditions and requirements of the particular grant. Subject to the rules set forth in paragraph (d) of this section, qualified scholarship amounts are excludable without the need to trace particular grant dollars to particular expenditures for qualified tuition and related expenses.

* * *

(h) *Characterization of scholarship or fellowship grants exceeding amounts permitted to be excluded from gross income for purposes of the standard deduction and filing requirements for dependents.* For purposes of section 63(c)(5) (relating to the standard deduction for dependents) and section 6012(a)(1)(C)(i) (relating to dependents required to make returns of income), any amount of a scholarship or fellowship grant in excess of the amount permitted to be excluded from gross income under paragraph (b) of this section is considered earned income. For example, on June 11, 1987, A, a student who has no other earned or unearned income for the year and can be claimed as a dependent on another taxpayer's return of tax, receives a $1,000 scholarship for room and board. The $1,000 must be included in A's gross income because it is not a qualified scholarship under paragraph (b) of this section. However, for purposes of sections 63(c)(5) and 6012(a)(1)(C)(i), the $1,000 is earned income. Accordingly, A is not required to file a return of tax for 1987 because A's gross income ($1,000) does not exceed A's standard deduction ($1,000) and A has no unearned income. [Reg. § 1.117-6.]

[Proposed 6-9-88.]

§ 1.118-1. Contributions to the capital of a corporation.—In the case of a corporation, section 118 provides an exclusion from gross income with respect to any contribution of money or property to the capital of the taxpayer. Thus, if a corporation requires additional funds for conducting its business and obtains such funds through voluntary pro rata payments by its shareholders, the amounts so received being credited to its surplus account or to a special account, such amounts do not constitute income, although there is no increase in the outstanding shares of stock of the corporation. In such a case the payments are in the nature of assessments upon, and represent an additional price paid for, the shares of stock held by the individual shareholders, and will be treated as an addition to and as a part of the operating capital of the company. Section 118 also applies to contributions to capital made by persons other than shareholders. For example, the exclusion applies to the value of land or other property contributed to a corporation by a governmental unit or by a civic group for the purpose of inducing the corporation to locate its business in a particular community, or for the purpose of enabling the corporation to expand its operating facilities. However, the exclusion does not apply to any money or property transferred to the corporation in consideration for goods or services rendered, or to subsidies paid for the purpose of inducing the taxpayer to limit production. See section 362 for the basis of property acquired by a corporation through a contribution to its capital by its stockholders or by nonstockholders. [Reg. § 1.118-1.]

☐ [*T.D.* 6220, 12-28-56.]

§ 1.119-1. Meals and lodging furnished for the convenience of the employer.—(a) *Meals*—(1) *In general.* The value of meals furnished to an employee by his employer shall be excluded from the employee's gross income if two tests are met: (i) The meals are furnished on the business premises of the employer, and (ii) the meals are furnished for the convenience of the employer. The question of whether meals are furnished for the convenience of the employer is one of fact to be determined by analysis of all the facts and circumstances in each case. If the tests described in subdivisions (i) and (ii) of this subparagraph are met, the exclusion shall apply irrespective of whether under an employment contract or a statute fixing the terms of employment such meals are furnished as compensation.

(2) *Meals furnished without a charge.* (i) Meals furnished by an employer without charge to the employee will be regarded as furnished for the convenience of the employer if such meals are furnished for a substantial noncompensatory business reason of the employer. If an employer furnishes meals as a means of providing additional compensation to his employee (and not for a sub-

stantial noncompensatory business reason of the employer), the meals so furnished will not be regarded as furnished for the convenience of the employer. Conversely, if the employer furnishes meals to his employee for a substantial noncompensatory business reason, the meals so furnished will be regarded as furnished for the convenience of the employer, even though such meals are also furnished for a compensatory reason. In determining the reason of an employer for furnishing meals, the mere declaration that meals are furnished for a noncompensatory business reason is not sufficient to prove that meals are furnished for the convenience of the employer, but such determination will be based upon an examination of all the surrounding facts and circumstances. In subdivision (ii) of this subparagraph, there are set forth some of the substantial noncompensatory business reasons which occur frequently and which justify the conclusion that meals furnished for such a reason are furnished for the convenience of the employer. In subdivision (iii) of this subparagraph, there are set forth some of the business reasons which are considered to be compensatory and which, in the absence of a substantial noncompensatory business reason, justify the conclusion that meals furnished for such a reason are not furnished for the convenience of the employer. Generally, meals furnished before or after the working hours of the employee will not be regarded as furnished for the convenience of the employer, but see subdivision (ii)(d) and (f) of this subparagraph for some exceptions to this general rule. Meals furnished on nonworking days do not qualify for the exclusion under section 119. If the employee is required to occupy living quarters on the business premises of his employer as a condition of his employment (as defined in paragraph (b) of this section), the exclusion applies to the value of any meal furnished without charge to the employee on such premises.

(ii) (a) Meals will be regarded as furnished for a substantial noncompensatory business reason of the employer when the meals are furnished to the employee during his working hours to have the employee available for emergency call during his meal period. In order to demonstrate that meals are furnished to the employee to have the employee available for emergency call during the meal period, it must be shown that emergencies have actually occurred, or can reasonably be expected to occur, in the employer's business which have resulted, or will result, in the employer calling on the employee to perform his job during his meal period.

(b) Meals will be regarded as furnished for a substantial noncompensatory business reason of the employer when the meals are furnished to the employee during his working hours because the employer's business is such that the employee must be restricted to a short meal period, such as 30 or 45 minutes, and because the employee could not be expected to eat elsewhere in such a short meal period. For example, meals may qualify under this subdivision when the employer is engaged in a business in which the peak workload occurs during the normal lunch hours. However, meals cannot qualify under this subdivision (b) when the reason for restricting the time of the meal period is so that the employee can be let off earlier in the day.

(c) Meals will be regarded as furnished for a substantial noncompensatory business reason of the employer when the meals are furnished to the employee during his working hours because the employee could not otherwise secure proper meals within a reasonable meal period. For example, meals may qualify under this subdivision (c) when there are insufficient eating facilities in the vicinity of the employer's premises.

(d) A meal furnished to a restaurant employee or other food service employee for each meal period in which the employee works will be regarded as furnished for a substantial noncompensatory business reason of the employer, irrespective of whether the meal is furnished during, immediately before, or immediately after the working hours of the employee.

(e) If the employer furnishes meals to employees at a place of business and the reason for furnishing the meals to each of substantially all of the employees who are furnished the meals is a substantial noncompensatory business reason of the employer, the meals furnished to each other employee will also be regarded as furnished for a substantial noncompensatory business reason of the employer.

(f) If an employer would have furnished a meal to an employee during his working hours for a substantial noncompensatory business reason, a meal furnished to such an employee immediately after his working hours because his duties prevented him from obtaining a meal during his working hours will be regarded as furnished for a substantial noncompensatory business reason.

(iii) Meals will be regarded as furnished for a compensatory business reason of the employer when the meals are furnished to the employee to promote the morale or goodwill of the employee, or to attract prospective employees.

(3) *Meals furnished with a charge.* (i) If an employer provides meals which an employee may or may not purchase, the meals will not be regarded as furnished for the convenience of the employer. Thus, meals for which a charge is made by the employer will not be regarded as furnished for the convenience of the employer if the em-

Reg. § 1.119-1(a)(3)

ployee has a choice of accepting the meals and paying for them or of not paying for them and providing his meals in another manner.

(ii) If an employer furnishes an employee meals for which the employee is charged an unvarying amount (for example, by subtraction from his stated compensation) irrespective of whether he accepts the meals, the amount of such flat charge made by the employer for such meals is not, as such, part of the compensation includible in the gross income of the employee; whether the value of the meals so furnished is excludable under section 119 is determined by applying the rules of subparagraph (2) of this paragraph. If meals furnished for an unvarying amount are not furnished for the convenience of the employer in accordance with the rules of subparagraph (2) of this paragraph, the employee shall include in gross income the value of the meals regardless of whether the value exceeds or is less than the amount charged for such meals. In the absence of evidence to the contrary, the value of the meals may be deemed to be equal to the amount charged for them.

(b) *Lodging.* The value of lodging furnished to an employee by the employer shall be excluded from the employee's gross income if three tests are met:

(1) The lodging is furnished on the business premises of the employer,

(2) The lodging is furnished for the convenience of the employer, and

(3) The employee is required to accept such lodging as a condition of his employment.

The requirement of subparagraph (3) of this paragraph that the employee is required to accept such lodging as a condition of his employment means that he be required to accept the lodging in order to enable him properly to perform the duties of his employment. Lodging will be regarded as furnished to enable the employee properly to perform the duties of his employment when, for example, the lodging is furnished because the employee is required to be available for duty at all times or because the employee could not perform the services required of him unless he is furnished such lodging. If the tests described in subparagraphs (1), (2), and (3) of this paragraph are met, the exclusion shall apply irrespective of whether a charge is made, or whether, under an employment contract or statute fixing the terms of employment, such lodging is furnished as compensation. If the employer furnishes the employee lodging for which the employee is charged an unvarying amount irrespective of whether he accepts the lodging, the amount of the charge made by the employer for such lodging is not, as such, part of the compensation includible in the gross

income of the employee; whether the value of the lodging is excludable from gross income under section 119 is determined by applying the other rules of this paragraph. If the tests described in subparagraphs (1), (2), and (3) of this paragraph are not met, the employee shall include in gross income the value of the lodging regardless of whether it exceeds or is less than the amount charged. In the absence of evidence to the contrary, the value of the lodging may be deemed to be equal to the amount charged.

(c) *Business premises of the employer—*(1) *In general.* For purposes of this section, the term "business premises of the employer" generally means the place of employment of the employee. For example, meals and lodging furnished in the employer's home to a domestic servant would constitute meals and lodging furnished on the business premises of the employer. Similarly, meals furnished to cowhands while herding their employer's cattle on leased land would be regarded as furnished on the business premises of the employer.

* * *

(e) *Rules.* The exclusion provided by section 119 applies only to meals and lodging furnished in kind by or on behalf of an employer to his employee. If the employee has an option to receive additional compensation in lieu of meals or lodging in kind, the value of such meals and lodging is not excludable from gross income under section 119. However, the mere fact that an employee, at his option, may decline to accept meals tendered in kind will not of itself require inclusion of the value thereof in gross income. Cash allowances for meals or lodging received by an employee are includible in gross income to the extent that such allowances constitute compensation.

(f) *Examples.* The provisions of section 119 may be illustrated by the following examples:

Example (1). A waitress who works from 7 a.m. to 4 p.m. is furnished without charge two meals a work day. The employer encourages the waitress to have her breakfast on his business premises before starting work, but does not require her to have breakfast there. She is required, however, to have her lunch on such premises. Since the waitress is a food service employee and works during the normal breakfast and lunch periods, the waitress is permitted to exclude from her gross income both the value of the breakfast and the value of the lunch.

Example (2). The waitress in example (1) is allowed to have meals on the employer's premises without charge on her days off. The waitress is not permitted to exclude the value of such meals from her gross income.

Reg. § 1.119-1(b)(1)

Example (3). A bank teller who works from 9 a.m. to 5 p.m. is furnished his lunch without charge in a cafeteria which the bank maintains on its premises. The bank furnishes the teller such meals in order to limit his lunch period to 30 minutes since the bank's peak work load occurs during the normal lunch period. If the teller had to obtain his lunch elsewhere, it would take him considerably longer than 30 minutes for lunch, and the bank strictly enforces the 30-minute time limit. The bank teller may exclude from his gross income the value of such meals obtained in the bank cafeteria.

Example (4). Assume the same facts as in example (3), except that the bank charges the bank teller an unvarying rate per meal regardless of whether he eats in the cafeteria. The bank teller is not required to include in gross income such flat amount charged as part of his compensation, and he is entitled to exclude from his gross income the value of the meals he receives for such flat charge.

Example (5). A Civil Service employee of a State is employed at an institution and is required by his employer to be available for duty at all times. The employer furnishes the employee with meals and lodging at the institution without charge. Under the applicable State statute, his meals and lodging are regarded as part of the employee's compensation. The employee would nevertheless be entitled to exclude the value of such meals and lodging from his gross income.

Example (6). An employee of an institution is given the choice of residing at the institution free of charge, or of residing elsewhere and receiving a cash allowance in addition to his regular salary. If he elects to reside at the institution, the value to the employee of the lodging furnished by the employer will be includible in the employee's gross income because his residence at the institution is not required in order for him to perform properly the duties of his employment.

Example (7). A construction worker is employed at a construction project at a remote job site in Alaska. Due to the inaccessibility of facilities for the employees who are working at the job site to obtain food and lodging and the prevailing weather conditions, the employer is required to furnish meals and lodging to the employee at the camp site in order to carry on the construction project. The employee is required to pay $40 a week for the meals and lodging. The weekly charge of $40 is not, as such, part of the compensation includible in the gross income of the employee, and under paragraphs (a) and (b) of this section the value of the meals and lodging is excludable from his gross income.

Example (8). A manufacturing company provides a cafeteria on its premises at which its employees can purchase their lunch. There is no other eating facility located near the company's premises, but the employee can furnish his own meal by bringing his lunch. The amount of compensation which any employee is required to include in gross income is not reduced by the amount charged for the meals, and the meals are not considered to be furnished for the convenience of the employer.

Example (9). A hospital maintains a cafeteria on its premises where all of its 230 employees may obtain a meal during their working hours. No charge is made for these meals. The hospital furnishes such meals in order to have each of 210 of the employees available for any emergencies that may occur, and it is shown that each such employee is at times called upon to perform services during his meal period. Although the hospital does not require such employees to remain on the premises during meal periods, they rarely leave the hospital during their meal period. Since the hospital furnishes meals to each of substantially all of its employees in order to have each of them available for emergency call during his meal period, all of the hospital employees who obtain their meals in the hospital cafeteria may exclude from their gross income the value of such meals. [Reg. § 1.119-1.]

☐ [*T.D.* 6220, 12-28-56. *Amended by T.D.* 6745, 7-8-64 *and T.D.* 8006, 1-17-85.]

§ 1.121-1. Exclusion of gain from sale or exchange of a principal residence.—(a) *In general.* Section 121 provides that, under certain circumstances, gross income does not include gain realized on the sale or exchange of property that was owned and used by a taxpayer as the taxpayer's principal residence. Subject to the other provisions of section 121, a taxpayer may exclude gain only if, during the 5-year period ending on the date of the sale or exchange, the taxpayer owned and used the property as the taxpayer's principal residence for periods aggregating 2 years or more.

(b) *Residence*—(1) *In general.* Whether property is used by the taxpayer as the taxpayer's residence depends upon all the facts and circumstances. A property used by the taxpayer as the taxpayer's residence may include a houseboat, a house trailer, or the house or apartment that the taxpayer is entitled to occupy as a tenant-stockholder in a cooperative housing corporation (as those terms are defined in section 216(b)(1) and (2)). Property used by the taxpayer as the taxpayer's residence does not include personal property that is not a fixture under local law.

(2) *Principal residence.* In the case of a taxpayer using more than one property as a residence, whether property is used by the taxpayer

as the taxpayer's principal residence depends upon all the facts and circumstances. If a taxpayer alternates between 2 properties, using each as a residence for successive periods of time, the property that the taxpayer uses a majority of the time during the year ordinarily will be considered the taxpayer's principal residence. In addition to the taxpayer's use of the property, relevant factors in determining a taxpayer's principal residence, include, but are not limited to—

(i) The taxpayer's place of employment;

(ii) The principal place of abode of the taxpayer's family members;

(iii) The address listed on the taxpayer's federal and state tax returns, driver's license, automobile registration, and voter registration card;

(iv) The taxpayer's mailing address for bills and correspondence;

(v) The location of the taxpayer's banks; and

(vi) The location of religious organizations and recreational clubs with which the taxpayer is affiliated.

(3) *Vacant land*—(i) *In general.* The sale or exchange of vacant land is not a sale or exchange of the taxpayer's principal residence unless—

(A) The vacant land is adjacent to land containing the dwelling unit of the taxpayer's principal residence;

(B) The taxpayer owned and used the vacant land as part of the taxpayer's principal residence;

(C) The taxpayer sells or exchanges the dwelling unit in a sale or exchange that meets the requirements of section 121 within 2 years before or 2 years after the date of the sale or exchange of the vacant land; and

(D) The requirements of section 121 have otherwise been met with respect to the vacant land.

(ii) *Limitations*—(A) *Maximum limitation amount.* For purposes of section 121(b)(1) and (2) (relating to the maximum limitation amount of the section 121 exclusion), the sale or exchange of the dwelling unit and the vacant land are treated as one sale or exchange. Therefore, only one maximum limitation amount of $250,000 ($500,000 for certain joint returns) applies to the combined sales or exchanges of vacant land and the dwelling unit. In applying the maximum limitation amount to sales or exchanges that occur in different taxable years, gain from the sale or exchange of the dwelling unit, up to the maximum limitation amount under section 121(b)(1) or (2), is excluded first and each spouse is treated as excluding one-half of the gain from a sale or exchange to which section 121(b)(2)(A) and

§ 1.121-2(a)(3)(i) (relating to the limitation for certain joint returns) apply.

(B) *Sale or exchange of more than one principal residence in 2-year period.* If a dwelling unit and vacant land are sold or exchanged in separate transactions that qualify for the section 121 exclusion under this paragraph (b)(3), each of the transactions is disregarded in applying section 121(b)(3) (restricting the application of section 121 to only 1 sale or exchange every 2 years) to the other transactions but is taken into account as a sale or exchange of a principal residence on the date of the transaction in applying section 121(b)(3) to that transaction and the sale or exchange of any other principal residence.

(C) *Sale or exchange of vacant land before dwelling unit.* If the sale or exchange of the dwelling unit occurs in a later taxable year than the sale or exchange of the vacant land and after the date prescribed by law (including extensions) for the filing of the return for the taxable year of the sale or exchange of the vacant land, any gain from the sale or exchange of the vacant land must be treated as taxable on the taxpayer's return for the taxable year of the sale or exchange of the vacant land. If the taxpayer has reported gain from the sale or exchange of the vacant land as taxable, after satisfying the requirements of this paragraph (b)(3) the taxpayer may claim the section 121 exclusion with regard to the sale or exchange of the vacant land (for any period for which the period of limitation under section 6511 has not expired) by filing an amended return.

(4) *Examples.* The provisions of this paragraph (b) are illustrated by the following examples:

Example 1. Taxpayer A owns 2 residences, one in New York and one in Florida. From 1999 through 2004, he lives in the New York residence for 7 months and the Florida residence for 5 months of each year. In the absence of facts and circumstances indicating otherwise, the New York residence is A's principal residence. A would be eligible for the section 121 exclusion of gain from the sale or exchange of the New York residence, but not the Florida residence.

Example 2. Taxpayer B owns 2 residences, one in Virginia and one in Maine. During 1999 and 2000, she lives in the Virginia residence. During 2001 and 2002, she lives in the Maine residence. During 2003, she lives in the Virginia residence. B's principal residence during 1999, 2000, and 2003 is the Virginia residence. B's principal residence during 2001 and 2002 is the Maine residence. B would be eligible for the 121 exclusion of gain from the sale or exchange of either residence (but not both) during 2003.

Reg. § 1.121-1(b)(3)

Example 3. In 1991 Taxpayer C buys property consisting of a house and 10 acres that she uses as her principal residence. In May 2005 C sells 8 acres of the land and realizes a gain of $110,000. C does not sell the dwelling unit before the due date for filing C's 2005 return, therefore C is not eligible to exclude the $110,000 of gain. In March 2007 C sells the house and remaining 2 acres realizing a gain of $180,000 from the sale of the house. C may exclude the $180,000 of gain. Because the sale of the 8 acres occurred within 2 years from the date of the sale of the dwelling unit, the sale of the 8 acres is treated as a sale of the taxpayer's principal residence under paragraph (b)(3) of this section. C may file an amended return for 2005 to claim an exclusion for $70,000 ($250,000 − $180,000 gain previously excluded) of the $110,000 gain from the sale of the 8 acres.

Example 4. In 1998 Taxpayer D buys a house and 1 acre that he uses as his principal residence. In 1999 D buys 29 acres adjacent to his house and uses the vacant land as part of his principal residence. In 2003 D sells the house and 1 acre and the 29 acres in 2 separate transactions. D sells the house and 1 acre at a loss of $25,000. D realizes $270,000 of gain from the sale of the 29 acres. D may exclude the $245,000 gain from the 2 sales.

(c) *Ownership and use requirements*—(1) *In general.* The requirements of ownership and use for periods aggregating 2 years or more may be satisfied by establishing ownership and use for 24 full months or for 730 days (365 × 2). The requirements of ownership and use may be satisfied during nonconcurrent periods if both the ownership and use tests are met during the 5-year period ending on the date of the sale or exchange.

(2) *Use*—(i) In establishing whether a taxpayer has satisfied the 2-year use requirement, occupancy of the residence is required. However, short temporary absences, such as for vacation or other seasonal absence (although accompanied with rental of the residence), are counted as periods of use.

(ii) *Determination of use during periods of out-of-residence care.* If a taxpayer has become physically or mentally incapable of self-care and the taxpayer sells or exchanges property that the taxpayer owned and used as the taxpayer's principal residence for periods aggregating at least 1 year during the 5-year period preceding the sale or exchange, the taxpayer is treated as using the property as the taxpayer's principal residence for any period of time during the 5-year period in which the taxpayer owns the property and resides in any facility (including a nursing home) licensed by a State or political subdivision to care for an individual in the taxpayer's condition.

(3) *Ownership*—(i) *Trusts.* If a residence is owned by a trust, for the period that a taxpayer is treated under sections 671 through 679 (relating to the treatment of grantors and others as substantial owners) as the owner of the trust or the portion of the trust that includes the residence, the taxpayer will be treated as owning the residence for purposes of satisfying the 2-year ownership requirement of section 121, and the sale or exchange by the trust will be treated as if made by the taxpayer.

(ii) *Certain single owner entities.* If a residence is owned by an eligible entity (within the meaning of § 301.7701-3(a) of this chapter) that has a single owner and is disregarded for federal tax purposes as an entity separate from its owner under § 301.7701-3 of this chapter, the owner will be treated as owning the residence for purposes of satisfying the 2-year ownership requirement of section 121, and the sale or exchange by the entity will be treated as if made by the owner.

(4) *Examples.* The provisions of this paragraph (c) are illustrated by the following examples. The examples assume that § 1.121-3 (relating to the reduced maximum exclusion) does not apply to the sale of the property. The examples are as follows:

Example 1. Taxpayer A has owned and used his house as his principal residence since 1986. On January 31, 1998, A moves to another state. A rents his house to tenants from that date until April 18, 2000, when he sells it. A is eligible for the section 121 exclusion because he has owned and used the house as his principal residence for at least 2 of the 5 years preceding the sale.

Example 2. Taxpayer B owns and uses a house as her principal residence from 1986 to the end of 1997. On January 4, 1998, B moves to another state and ceases to use the house. B's son moves into the house in March 1999 and uses the residence until it is sold on July 1, 2001. B may not exclude gain from the sale under section 121 because she did not use the property as her principal residence for at least 2 years out of the 5 years preceding the sale.

Example 3. Taxpayer C lives in a townhouse that he rents from 1993 through 1996. On January 18, 1997, he purchases the townhouse. On February 1, 1998, C moves into his daughter's home. On May 25, 2000, while still living in his daughter's home, C sells his townhouse. The section 121 exclusion will apply to gain from the sale because C owned the townhouse for at least 2 years out of the 5 years preceding the sale (from January 19, 1997 until May 25, 2000) and he used the townhouse as his principal residence for at least 2 years during the 5-year period preceding the sale (from May 25, 1995 until February 1, 1998).

Example 4. Taxpayer D, a college professor, purchases and moves into a house on May 1, 1997. He uses the house as his principal residence continuously until September 1, 1998, when he goes abroad for a 1-year sabbatical leave. On October 1, 1999, 1 month after returning from the leave, D sells the house. Because his leave is not considered to be a short temporary absence under paragraph (c)(2) of this section, the period of the sabbatical leave may not be included in determining whether D used the house for periods aggregating 2 years during the 5-year period ending on the date of the sale. Consequently, D is not entitled to exclude gain under section 121 because he did not use the residence for the requisite period.

Example 5. Taxpayer E purchases a house on February 1, 1998, that he uses as his principal residence. During 1998 and 1999, E leaves his residence for a 2-month summer vacation. E sells the house on March 1, 2000. Although, in the 5-year period preceding the date of sale, the total time E used his residence is less than 2 years (21 months), the section 121 exclusion will apply to gain from the sale of the residence because, under paragraph (c)(2) of this section, the 2-month vacations are short temporary absences and are counted as periods of use in determining whether E used the residence for the requisite period.

(d) *Depreciation taken after May 6, 1997*—(1) *In general.* The section 121 exclusion does not apply to so much of the gain from the sale or exchange of property as does not exceed the portion of the depreciation adjustments (as defined in section 1250(b)(3)) attributable to the property for periods after May 6, 1997. Depreciation adjustments allocable to any portion of the property to which the section 121 exclusion does not apply under paragraph (e) of this section are not taken into account for this purpose.

(2) *Example.* The provisions of this paragraph (d) are illustrated by the following example:

Example. On July 1, 1999, Taxpayer A moves into a house that he owns and had rented to tenants since July 1, 1997. A took depreciation deductions totaling $14,000 for the period that he rented the property. After using the residence as his principal residence for 2 full years, A sells the property on August 1, 2001. A's gain realized from the sale is $40,000. A has no other section 1231 or capital gains or losses for 2001. Only $26,000 ($40,000 gain realized − $14,000 depreciation deductions) may be excluded under section 121. Under section 121(d)(6) and paragraph (d)(1) of this section, A must recognize $14,000 of

the gain as unrecaptured section 1250 gain within the meaning of section 1(h).

* * *

[Reg. § 1.121-1.]

☐ [*T.D.* 6856, 10-19-65. *Amended by T.D.* 7614, 4-26-79 *and T.D.* 9030, 12-23-2002.]

§ 1.121-2. Limitations.—(a) *Dollar limitations*—(1) *In general.* A taxpayer may exclude from gross income up to $250,000 of gain from the sale or exchange of the taxpayer's principal residence. A taxpayer is eligible for only one maximum exclusion per principal residence.

(2) *Joint owners.* If taxpayers jointly own a principal residence but file separate returns, each taxpayer may exclude from gross income up to $250,000 of gain that is attributable to each taxpayer's interest in the property, if the requirements of section 121 have otherwise been met.

(3) *Special rules for joint returns*—(i) *In general.* A husband and wife who make a joint return for the year of the sale or exchange of a principal residence may exclude up to $500,000 of gain if—

(A) Either spouse meets the 2-year ownership requirements of § 1.121-1(a) and (c);

(B) Both spouses meet the 2-year use requirements of § 1.121-1(a) and (c); and

(C) Neither spouse excluded gain from a prior sale or exchange of property under section 121 within the last 2 years (as determined under paragraph (b) of this section).

(ii) *Other joint returns.* For taxpayers filing jointly, if either spouse fails to meet the requirements of paragraph (a)(3)(i) of this section, the maximum limitation amount to be claimed by the couple is the sum of each spouse's limitation amount determined on a separate basis as if they had not been married. For this purpose, each spouse is treated as owning the property during the period that either spouse owned the property.

(4) *Examples.* The provisions of this paragraph (a) are illustrated by the following examples. The examples assume that § 1.121-3 (relating to the reduced maximum exclusion) does not apply to the sale of the property. The examples are as follows:

Example 1. Unmarried Taxpayers A and B own a house as joint owners, each owning a 50 percent interest in the house. They sell the house after owning and using it as their principal residence for 2 full years. The gain realized from the sale is $256,000. A and B are each eligible to exclude $128,000 of gain because the amount of realized gain allocable to each of them from the sale does not exceed each taxpayer's available limitation amount of $250,000.

Example 2. The facts are the same as in *Example 1*, except that A and B are married taxpayers who file a joint return for the taxable year of the sale. A and B are eligible to exclude the entire amount of realized gain ($256,000) from gross income because the gain realized from the sale does not exceed the limitation amount of $500,000 available to A and B as taxpayers filing a joint return.

Example 3. During 1999, married Taxpayers H and W each sell a residence that each had separately owned and used as a principal residence before their marriage. Each spouse meets the ownership and use tests for his or her respective residence. Neither spouse meets the use requirement for the other spouse's residence. H and W file a joint return for the year of the sales. The gain realized from the sale of H's residence is $200,000. The gain realized from the sale of W's residence is $300,000. Because the ownership and use requirements are met for each residence by each respective spouse, H and W are each eligible to exclude up to $250,000 of gain from the sale of their individual residences. However, W may not use H's unused exclusion to exclude gain in excess of her limitation amount. Therefore, H and W must recognize $50,000 of the gain realized on the sale of W's residence.

Example 4. Married Taxpayers H and W sell their residence and file a joint return for the year of the sale. W, but not H, satisfies the requirements of section 121. They are eligible to exclude up to $250,000 of the gain from the sale of the residence because that is the sum of each spouse's dollar limitation amount determined on a separate basis as if they had not been married ($0 for H, $250,000 for W).

Example 5. Married Taxpayers H and W have owned and used their principal residence since 1998. On February 16, 2001, H dies. On September 24, 2001, W sells the residence and realizes a gain of $350,000. Pursuant to section 6013(a)(3), W and H's executor make a joint return for 2001. All $350,000 of the gain from the sale of the residence may be excluded.

Example 6. Assume the same facts as *Example 5*, except that W does not sell the residence until January 31, 2002. Because W's filing status for the taxable year of the sale is single, the special rules for joint returns under paragraph (a)(3) of this section do not apply and W may exclude only $250,000 of the gain.

(b) *Application of section 121 to only 1 sale or exchange every 2 years*—(1) *In general.* Except as otherwise provided in § 1.121-3 (relating to the reduced maximum exclusion), a taxpayer may not exclude from gross income gain from the sale or exchange of a principal residence if, during the 2-year period ending on the date of the sale or exchange, the taxpayer sold or exchanged other property for which gain was excluded under section 121. For purposes of this paragraph (b)(1), any sale or exchange before May 7, 1997, is disregarded.

(2) *Example.* The following example illustrates the rules of this paragraph (b). The example assumes that § 1.121-3 (relating to the reduced maximum exclusion) does not apply to the sale of the property. The example is as follows:

Example. Taxpayer A owns a townhouse that he uses as his principal residence for 2 full years, 1998 and 1999. A buys a house in 2000 that he owns and uses as his principal residence. A sells the townhouse in 2002 and excludes gain realized on its sale under section 121. A sells the house in 2003. Although A meets the 2-year ownership and use requirements of section 121, A is not eligible to exclude gain from the sale of the house because A excluded gain within the last 2 years under section 121 from the sale of the townhouse.

(c) *Effective date.* This section is applicable for sales and exchanges on or after December 24, 2002. For rules on electing to apply the provisions of this section retroactively, see § 1.121-4(j). [Reg. § 1.121-2.]

□ [*T.D.* 6856, 10-19-65. *Amended by T.D.* 7614, 4-26-79 *and T.D.* 9030, 12-23-2002.]

§ 1.121-3. Reduced maximum exclusion for taxpayers failing to meet certain requirements.—(a) *In general.* In lieu of the limitation under section 121(b) and § 1.121-2, a reduced maximum exclusion limitation may be available for a taxpayer who sells or exchanges property used as the taxpayer's principal residence but fails to satisfy the ownership and use requirements described in § 1.121-1(a) and (c) or the 2-year limitation described in § 1.121-2(b).

(b) through (f) [Reserved]. For further guidance, see § 1.121-3T(b) through (f).

(g) *Computation of reduced maximum exclusion*—(1) The reduced maximum exclusion is computed by multiplying the maximum dollar limitation of $250,000 ($500,000 for certain joint filers) by a fraction. The numerator of the fraction is the shortest of the period of time that the taxpayer owned the property during the 5-year period ending on the date of the sale or exchange; the period of time that the taxpayer used the property as the taxpayer's principal residence during the 5-year period ending on the date of the sale or exchange; or the period of time between the date of a prior sale or exchange of property for which the taxpayer excluded gain under section 121 and the date of the current sale or exchange. The numerator of the fraction may be expressed in days or months. The denominator of the fraction is 730 days or 24 months (depending on the measure of time used in the numerator).

(2) *Examples.* The following examples illustrate the rules of this paragraph (g):

Example 1. Taxpayer A purchases a house that she uses as her principal residence. Twelve months after the purchase, A sells the house due to a change in place of her employment. A has not excluded gain under section 121 on a prior sale or exchange of property within the last 2 years. A is eligible to exclude up to $125,000 of the gain from the sale of her house (12/24 × $250,000).

Example 2. (i) Taxpayer H owns a house that he has used as his principal residence since 1996. On January 15, 1999, H and W marry and W begins to use H's house as her principal residence. On January 15, 2000, H sells the house due to a change in W's place of employment. Neither H nor W has excluded gain under section 121 on a prior sale or exchange of property within the last 2 years.

(ii) Because H and W have not each used the house as their principal residence for at least 2 years during the 5-year period preceding its sale, the maximum dollar limitation amount that may be claimed by H and W will not be $500,000, but the sum of each spouse's limitation amount determined on a separate basis as if they had not been married. (See § 1.121-2(a)(3)(ii).)

(iii) H is eligible to exclude up to $250,000 of gain because he meets the requirements of section 121. W is not eligible to exclude the maximum dollar limitation amount. Instead, because the sale of the house is due to a change in place of employment, W is eligible to claim a reduced maximum exclusion of up to $125,000 of the gain (365/730 × $250,000). Therefore, H and W are eligible to exclude up to $375,000 of gain ($250,000 + $125,000) from the sale of the house.

(h) [Reserved]. For further guidance, see § 1.121-3T(h).

(i) through (k) [Reserved].

(l) *Effective date.* This section is applicable for sales and exchanges on or after December 24, 2002. For rules on electing to apply the provisions of this section retroactively, see § 1.121-4(j). [Reg. § 1.121-3.]

□ [*T.D.* 6856, 10-19-65. *Amended by T.D.* 7614, 4-26-79 *and T.D.* 9030, 12-23-2002.]

§ 1.121-3T. Reduced maximum exclusion for taxpayers failing to meet certain requirements (temporary).

* * *

(b) *Primary reason for sale or exchange.* In order for a taxpayer to claim a reduced maximum exclusion under section 121(c), the sale or exchange must be by reason of a change in place of employment, health, or unforeseen circumstances. A sale or exchange is by reason of a change in place of employment, health, or unforeseen circumstances only if the primary reason for the sale or exchange is a change in place of employment (within the meaning of paragraph (c) of this section), health (within the meaning of paragraph (d) of this section), or unforeseen circumstances (within the meaning of paragraph (e) of this section). Whether the requirements of this section are satisfied depends upon all the facts and circumstances. If the taxpayer qualifies for a safe harbor described in this section, the taxpayer's primary reason is deemed to be a change in place of employment, health, or unforeseen circumstances. If the taxpayer does not qualify for a safe harbor, factors that may be relevant in determining the taxpayer's primary reason for the sale or exchange include (but are not limited to) the extent to which—

(1) The sale or exchange and the circumstances giving rise to the sale or exchange are proximate in time;

(2) The suitability of the property as the taxpayer's principal residence materially changes;

(3) The taxpayer's financial ability to maintain the property materially changes;

(4) The taxpayer uses the property as the taxpayer's residence during the period of the taxpayer's ownership of the property;

(5) The circumstances giving rise to the sale or exchange are not reasonably foreseeable when the taxpayer begins using the property as the taxpayer's principal residence; and

(6) The circumstances giving rise to the sale or exchange occur during the period of the taxpayer's ownership and use of the property as the taxpayer's principal residence.

(c) *Sale or exchange by reason of a change in place of employment*—(1) *In general.* A sale or exchange is by reason of a change in place of employment if, in the case of a qualified individual described in paragraph (f) of this section, the primary reason for the sale or exchange is a change in the location of the individual's employment.

(2) *Distance safe harbor.* The primary reason for the sale or exchange is deemed to be a change in place of employment (within the meaning of paragraph (c)(1) of this section) if—

(i) The change in place of employment occurs during the period of the taxpayer's ownership and use of the property as the taxpayer's principal residence; and

(ii) The individual's new place of employment is at least 50 miles farther from the residence sold or exchanged than was the former

Reg. § 1.121-3T(b)(1)

place of employment, or, if there was no former place of employment, the distance between the individual's new place of employment and the residence sold or exchanged is at least 50 miles.

(3) *Employment*. For purposes of this paragraph (c), *employment* includes the commencement of employment with a new employer, the continuation of employment with the same employer, and the commencement or continuation of self-employment.

(4) *Examples*. The following examples illustrate the rules of this paragraph (c):

Example 1. A is unemployed and owns a townhouse that she has owned and used as her principal residence since 2002. In 2003 A obtains a job that is 54 miles from her townhouse, and she sells the townhouse. Because the distance between A's new place of employment and the townhouse is at least 50 miles, the sale is within the safe harbor of paragraph (c)(2) of this section and A is entitled to claim a reduced maximum exclusion under section 121(c)(2).

Example 2. B is an officer in the United States Air Force stationed in Florida. B purchases a house in Florida in 2001. In May 2002 B moves out of his house to take a 3-year assignment in Germany. B sells his house in January 2003. Because B's new place of employment in Germany is at least 50 miles farther from the residence sold than is B's former place of employment in Florida, the sale is within the safe harbor of paragraph (c)(2) of this section and B is entitled to claim a reduced maximum exclusion under section 121(c)(2).

Example 3. C is employed by Employer R at R's Philadelphia office. C purchases a house in February 2001 that is 35 miles from R's Philadelphia office. In May 2002 C begins a temporary assignment at R's Wilmington office that is 72 miles from C's house, and moves out of the house. In June 2004 C is assigned to work in R's London office, and as a result, sells her house in August 2004. The sale of the house is not within the safe harbor of paragraph (c)(2) of this section by reason of the change in place of employment from Philadelphia to Wilmington because the Wilmington office is not 50 miles farther from C's house than is the Philadelphia office. Furthermore, the sale is not within the safe harbor by reason of the change in place of employment to London because C is not using the house as her principal residence when she moves to London. However, C is entitled to claim a reduced maximum exclusion under section 121(c)(2) because, under the facts and circumstances, the primary reason for the sale is the change in C's place of employment.

Example 4. In July 2002 D buys a condominium that is 5 miles from her place of employment and uses it as her principal residence. In February 2003 D, who works as an emergency medicine physician, obtains a job that is located 51 miles from D's condominium. D may be called in to work unscheduled hours and, when called, must be able to arrive at work quickly. Therefore, D sells her condominium and buys a townhouse that is 4 miles from her new place of employment. Because D's new place of employment is only 46 miles farther from the condominium than is D's former place of employment, the sale is not within the safe harbor of paragraph (c)(2) of this section. However, D is entitled to claim a reduced maximum exclusion under section 121(c)(2) because, under the facts and circumstances, the primary reason for the sale is the change in D's place of employment.

(d) *Sale or exchange by reason of health*—(1) *In general*. A sale or exchange is by reason of health if the primary reason for the sale or exchange is to obtain, provide, or facilitate the diagnosis, cure, mitigation, or treatment of disease, illness, or injury of a qualified individual described in paragraph (f) of this section, or to obtain or provide medical or personal care for a qualified individual suffering from a disease, illness, or injury. A sale or exchange that is merely beneficial to the general health or well-being of the individual is not a sale or exchange by reason of health.

(2) *Physician's recommendation safe harbor.* The primary reason for the sale or exchange is deemed to be health if a physician (as defined in section 213(d)(4)) recommends a change of residence for reasons of health (as defined in paragraph (d)(1) of this section).

* * *

(e) *Sale or exchange by reason of unforeseen circumstances*—(1) *In general*. A sale or exchange is by reason of unforeseen circumstances if the primary reason for the sale or exchange is the occurrence of an event that the taxpayer does not anticipate before purchasing and occupying the residence.

(2) *Specific event safe harbors*. The primary reason for the sale or exchange is deemed to be unforeseen circumstances (within the meaning of paragraph (e)(1) of this section) if any of the events specified in paragraphs (e)(2)(i) through (iii) of this section occur during the period of the taxpayer's ownership and use of the residence as the taxpayer's principal residence—

(i) The involuntary conversion of the residence;

(ii) Natural or man-made disasters or acts of war or terrorism resulting in a casualty to the residence (without regard to deductibility under section 165(h));

Reg. § 1.121-3T(e)(2)

(iii) In the case of a qualified individual described in paragraph (f) of this section—

(A) Death;

(B) The cessation of employment as a result of which the individual is eligible for unemployment compensation (as defined in section 85(b));

(C) A change in employment or self-employment status that results in the taxpayer's inability to pay housing costs and reasonable basic living expenses for the taxpayer's household (including amounts for food, clothing, medical expenses, taxes, transportation, court-ordered payments, and expenses reasonably necessary to the production of income, but not for the maintenance of an affluent or luxurious standard of living);

(D) Divorce or legal separation under a decree of divorce or separate maintenance; or

(E) Multiple births resulting from the same pregnancy; or

(iv) An event determined by the Commissioner to be an unforeseen circumstance to the extent provided in published guidance of general applicability or in a ruling directed to a specific taxpayer.

* * *

(f) *Qualified individual.* For purposes of this section, *qualified individual* means—

(1) The taxpayer;

(2) The taxpayer's spouse;

(3) A co-owner of the residence;

(4) A person whose principal place of abode is in the same household as the taxpayer; or

(5) For purposes of paragraph (d) of this section, a person bearing a relationship specified in sections 152(a)(1) through 152(a)(8) (without regard to qualification as a dependent) to a qualified individual described in paragraphs (f)(1) through (4) of this section, or a descendant of the taxpayer's grandparent.

* * *

[Temporary Reg. § 1.121-3T.]

☐ [*T.D.* 9031, 12-23-2002.]

§ 1.121-4. Special rules.—(a) *Property of deceased spouse*—(1) *In general.* For purposes of satisfying the ownership and use requirements of section 121, a taxpayer is treated as owning and using property as the taxpayer's principal residence during any period that the taxpayer's deceased spouse owned and used the property as a principal residence before death if—

(i) The taxpayer's spouse is deceased on the date of the sale or exchange of the property; and

(ii) The taxpayer has not remarried at the time of the sale or exchange of the property.

(2) *Example.* The provisions of this paragraph (a) are illustrated by the following example. The example assumes that § 1.121-3 (relating to the reduced maximum exclusion) does not apply to the sale of the property. The example is as follows:

Example. Taxpayer H has owned and used a house as his principal residence since 1987. H and W marry on July 1, 1999 and from that date they use H's house as their principal residence. H dies on August 15, 2000, and W inherits the property. W sells the property on September 1, 2000, at which time she has not remarried. Although W has owned and used the house for less than 2 years, W will be considered to have satisfied the ownership and use requirements of section 121 because W's period of ownership and use includes the period that H owned and used the property before death.

(b) *Property owned by spouse or former spouse*—(1) *Property transferred to individual from spouse or former spouse.* If a taxpayer obtains property from a spouse or former spouse in a transaction described in section 1041(a), the period that the taxpayer owns the property will include the period that the spouse or former spouse owned the property.

(2) *Property used by spouse or former spouse.* A taxpayer is treated as using property as the taxpayer's principal residence for any period that the taxpayer has an ownership interest in the property and the taxpayer's spouse or former spouse is granted use of the property under a divorce or separation instrument (as defined in section 71(b)(2)), provided that the spouse or former spouse uses the property as his or her principal residence.

(c) *Tenant-stockholder in cooperative housing corporation.* A taxpayer who holds stock as a tenant-stockholder in a cooperative housing corporation (as those terms are defined in section 216(b)(1) and (2)) may be eligible to exclude gain under section 121 on the sale or exchange of the stock. In determining whether the taxpayer meets the requirements of section 121, the ownership requirements are applied to the holding of the stock and the use requirements are applied to the house or apartment that the taxpayer is entitled to occupy by reason of the taxpayer's stock ownership.

* * *

(g) *Election to have section not apply.* A taxpayer may elect to have the section 121 exclusion not apply to a sale or exchange of property. The taxpayer makes the election by filing a return for the taxable year of the sale or exchange that includes the gain from the sale or exchange of the taxpayer's principal residence in the taxpayer's gross income. A taxpayer may make an election under this paragraph (g) to have section 121 not apply (or revoke an election to have section 121 not apply) at any time before the expiration of a 3-year period beginning on the last date prescribed by law (determined without regard to extensions) for the filing of the return for the taxable year in which the sale or exchange occurred.

* * *

[Reg. § 1.121-4.]

□ [*T.D.* 6856, 10-19-65. *Amended by T.D.* 7614, 4-26-79; *T.D.* 7927, 12-15-83 *and T.D.* 9030, 12-23-2002 (*corrected 2-6-2003*).]

Proposed Regulation

§ 1.125-2. Miscellaneous Cafeteria Plan Questions and Answers.—* * *

* * *

Q-2: What does section 125 of the Code provide?

A-2: In general, an employee who has an election among nontaxable benefits and taxable benefits (including cash) must include in gross income any taxable benefits that the employee could have actually received pursuant to the employee's election. The amount of these benefits is included in the employee's income in the year in which the employee would have actually received the taxable benefits if the employee had elected such benefits. This generally is the result even if the employee's election between the nontaxable benefits and taxable benefits is made prior to the year in which the employee would have actually received the taxable benefits. However, section 125 provides that cash (including certain taxable benefits) provided under a nondiscriminatory cafeteria plan will not be included in a participant's gross income merely because the participant has the opportunity, before the cash becomes currently available to the participant, to choose among cash and the nontaxable benefits under the cafeteria plan.

Q-3: What is a cafeteria plan under section 125?

A-3: A cafeteria plan is a plan maintained by an employer for the benefit of its employees that satisfies the requirements of section 89(k), under which all participants are employees, and under which each participant has the opportunity to choose among cash and qualified benefits. Additionally, a cafeteria plan satisfies the written plan document requirement of clause (v) of Q&A-3 of § 1.125-1 only if the plan describes the maximum amount of elective contributions available to any employee under the plan either by stating the maximum dollar amount or maximum percentage of compensation that may be contributed as elective contributions under the plan by employees or by stating the method for determining the maximum amount or percentage of elective contributions that employees may make under the plan. The meaning of "elective contributions" under a cafeteria plan is the same as the meaning of "salary reduction contributions" under a cafeteria plan. See also paragraph (a)(2) of Q&A-8 of § 1.89(a)-1.

Q-4: What benefits constitute qualified benefits and what benefits constitute cash under a cafeteria plan?

A-4: (a) *Qualified benefits*—(1) *In general.* A benefit is a qualified benefit under a cafeteria plan if the benefit does not defer the receipt of compensation and the benefit is not includible in an employee's gross income by reason of an express provision of Chapter 1 of the Code. In the case of insurance-type benefits, such as benefits provided under accident or health plans (sections 106 and 105) and group-term life insurance plans (section 79), the benefit is the coverage under the plan.

(2) *Items that constitute qualified benefits*—(i) *Accident or health plans.* Coverage under an accident or health plan is a qualified benefit to the extent that such coverage is excludable from income under section 106. Thus, for example, coverage under a long-term disability plan and coverage under an accidental death and dismemberment policy may be qualified benefits.

(ii) *Group-term life insurance.* Group-term life insurance coverage that is excludable from gross income under section 79 and group-term life insurance coverage that is includible in gross income solely because the death benefit payable thereunder is in excess of the dollar limit of section 79 are qualified benefits.

(iii) *Certain discriminatory benefits.* Accident or health plan coverage, group-term life insurance coverage, and benefits under a dependent care assistance program do not fail to be qualified benefits under a cafeteria plan merely because they are includible in gross income solely because of section 89 or any other applicable nondiscrimination requirement (e.g., section 129(d)).

(iv) *Certain dependent care assistance benefits.* Benefits under a dependent care assistance program that would have been excludable from gross income under section 129 but for the elimination of overnight camp expenses from dependent care assistance under such section (effective January 1, 1988) or the reduction of the age limit on children qualifying as dependents under such section (effective January 1, 1989) do not fail to be qualified benefits merely because such changes in law cause such benefits to be taxable. However, the preceding sentence applies only if the benefits are provided under a program that otherwise qualifies as a dependent care assistance program under section 129, are taxable to the employee upon receipt, and are provided by the December 31 next following the effective date of the applicable change in law. After such date, such benefits will not constitute qualified benefits but may be treated as cash pursuant to paragraph (b) of this Q&A-4.

(b) *Currently taxable benefits treated as cash.* In general, a benefit is treated as cash if such benefit does not defer the receipt of compensation and an employee who receives such benefit purchases such benefit with after-tax employee contributions or is treated, for all purposes under the Code (including, for example, reporting and withholding purposes), as receiving, at the time that such benefit is received, cash compensation equal to the full value of such benefit at such time and then purchasing such benefit with after-tax employee contributions. Thus, for example, long-term disability coverage is treated as cash if the cafeteria plan provides that an employee may purchase the coverage under the plan with after-tax employee contributions, or provides that the employee receiving such coverage is treated as having received cash compensation equal to the value of the coverage and then as having purchased the coverage with after-tax employee contributions. Any taxable benefit that is not described in paragraph (a) of this Q&A-4 and is not treated as cash under this paragraph (b) may not be included in a cafeteria plan.

(c) *Qualified cash or deferred arrangements.* Elective contributions to a qualified cash or deferred arrangement (section 401(k)) are permitted under a cafeteria plan. In addition, after-tax employee contributions under a qualified plan subject to section 401(m) are permitted under a cafeteria plan. The right to make such contributions will not cause a plan to fail to be a cafeteria plan merely because, under the qualified plan, employer matching contributions are made with respect to elective or after-tax employee contributions.

(d) *Benefits that do not constitute qualified benefits or cash.* Benefits of the type described in section 117 or 132 do not constitute qualified benefits or cash and thus may not be included in a cafeteria plan regardless of whether any such benefit is purchased with after-tax employee contributions or on any other basis. Thus, for example, health diagnostic or examination plans are qualified benefits under a cafeteria plan because such plans are accident or health plans that are eligible for the exclusion under section 106 and are not, in any case, eligible for the exclusion under section 132.

Q-5: May a cafeteria plan include a benefit that defers the receipt of compensation?

A-5: (a) *In general.* A cafeteria plan may not include any plan that offers a benefit that defers the receipt of compensation. In addition, a cafeteria plan may not operate in a manner that enables employees to defer compensation. For example, a plan that permits employees to carry over unused elective contributions or plan benefits (e.g., accident or health plan coverage) from one plan year to another operates to defer compensation. This is the case regardless of how the contributions or benefits are used by the employee in the subsequent plan year (e.g., whether they are automatically or electively converted into another taxable or nontaxable benefit in the subsequent plan year or used to provide additional benefits of the same type). Similarly, a cafeteria plan operates to permit the deferral of compensation if the plan permits participants to use contributions for one plan year to purchase a benefit that will be provided in a subsequent plan year (e.g., life, health, disability, or long-term care insurance coverage with a savings or investment feature, such as whole life insurance). For example, a cafeteria plan operates to permit the deferral of compensation if the cafeteria plan includes a health plan that is a flexible spending arrangement (as defined in Q&A-7 of this section) and such health plan may reimburse participants' premium payments for other accident or health coverage extending beyond the end of the plan year. See Q&A-7 of this section for the treatment of experience gains under a health plan that is a flexible spending arrangement.

(b) *Exceptions.* A plan does not fail to be a cafeteria plan merely because the plan permits participants to make elective contributions under a qualified cash or deferred arrangement under section 401(k) or permits participants employed by certain educational institutions to purchase retiree group-term life insurance. Similarly, a cafeteria plan does not include a benefit that defers the receipt of compensation merely because the cafeteria plan provides the opportunity to make after-tax employee contributions subject to section 401(m) under a qualified plan. In addition, a cafeteria plan will not be treated as including a benefit that defers the receipt of compensation merely because, under the qualified plan, employer matching contributions (as defined in section 401(m)(4)(A)) are made with respect to such elective contributions or after-tax employee contributions. Finally, reasonable premium rebates or policy dividends paid with respect to benefits provided under a cafeteria plan do not constitute impermissible deferred compensation if such rebates or dividends are paid before the close of the

Reg. § 1.125-2

12-month period immediately following the plan year to which such rebates and dividends relate.

(c) *Treatment of paid vacation days under a cafeteria plan*—(1) *In general*. A cafeteria plan may include elective, paid vacation days by permitting participants to receive either additional or fewer paid vacation days than the employer otherwise provides to the employees on a nonelective basis, if the inclusion of elective vacation days under the plan does not operate to permit the deferral of compensation.

(2) *Ordering of elective and nonelective vacation days*. In determining whether a plan that provides for paid vacation days operates to permit the deferral of compensation, and thus fails to be a cafeteria plan, a participant is deemed to use nonelective vacation days (i.e., the vacation days with respect to which the employee had no election) before elective vacation days.

(3) *Cashing out unused elective vacation days*. A plan does not operate to permit the deferral of compensation merely because the plan permits a participant who has not used all elective, paid vacation days for a plan year to receive in cash the value of such unused days in exchange for such days if the participant receives the cash on or before the earlier of the last day of the plan year of the cafeteria plan or the last day of the employee's taxable year to which the elective contributions used to purchase the unused days relate.

(4) *Examples*. The following examples illustrate the rules of this paragraph (c):

Example 1. Assume that an employer provides an employee with 2 weeks of paid vacation for each calendar year and maintains a calendar year cafeteria plan that permits the employee to "purchase," with elective contributions, an additional week of paid vacation. Assume further that Employee A, with a calendar tax year, purchases 1 additional week of vacation. If Employee A uses only 2 weeks of vacation during the year, the employee is treated as having used the 2 nonelective weeks and as having retained the 1 elective week. If the 1 remaining week (i.e., the elective week) may be carried over to the next year (or the value thereof used for any other purpose in the next year), the plan operates to permit the deferral of compensation and thus is not a cafeteria plan. However, the cafeteria plan may permit the employee to receive the value of the unused elective vacation week in cash before the end of the applicable calendar year.

Example 2. The facts are the same as set forth in Example 1, except that Employee A uses only 1 week of vacation during the year. Thus, Employee A is treated as having used 1 nonelective week and as having retained 1 nonelective week as well as 1 elective week of vacation. Because the nonelective vacation days are not part of the cafeteria plan (i.e., the employer or plan does not permit participants to exchange regular vacation days for other benefits), Employee A may be permitted to carry over the 1 nonelective week of vacation to the next year. In addition, under the terms of the cafeteria plan, Employee A must either forfeit the remaining elective vacation week or receive in cash the value of such unused days before the end of the applicable calendar year.

* * *

[Reg. § 1.125-2.]

[Proposed 3-7-89 and amended 11-7-97, 3-23-2000 and 1-10-2001.]

§ 1.132-1. Exclusion from gross income for certain fringe benefits.—(a) *In general*. Gross income does not include any fringe benefit which qualifies as a—

(1) No-additional-cost service,

(2) Qualified employee discount,

(3) Working condition fringe, or

(4) De minimis fringe.

Special rules apply with respect to certain on-premises gyms and other athletic facilities (§ 1.132-1(e)), demonstration use of employer-provided automobiles by full-time automobile salesmen (§ 1.132-5(o)), parking provided to an employee on or near the business premises of the employer (§ 1.132-5(p)), and on-premises eating facilities (§ 1.132-7).

(b) *Definition of employee*—(1) *No-additional-cost services and qualified employee discounts*. For purposes of section 132(a)(1) (relating to no-additional-cost services) and section 132(a)(2) (relating to qualified employee discounts), the term "employee" (with respect to a line of business of an employer) means—

(i) Any individual who is currently employed by the employer in the line of business,

(ii) Any individual who was formerly employed by the employer in the line of business and who separated from service with the employer in the line of business by reason of retirement or disability, and

(iii) Any widow or widower of an individual who died while employed by the employer in the line of business or who separated from service with the employer in the line of business by reason of retirement or disability.

For purposes of this paragraph (b)(1), any partner who performs services for a partnership is considered employed by the partnership. In addition, any use by the spouse or dependent child (as defined in paragraph (b)(5) of this section) of the employee will be treated as use by the employee. For purposes of section 132(a)(1) (relating to no-additional-cost services), any use of air transportation by a parent of an employee (determined without regard to section 132(f)(1)(B) and paragraph (b)(1)(iii) of this section) will be treated as use by the employee.

(2) *Working condition fringes.* For purposes of section 132(a)(3) (relating to working condition fringes), the term "employee" means—

(i) Any individual who is currently employed by the employer,

(ii) Any partner who performs services for the partnership,

(iii) Any director of the employer, and

(iv) Any independent contractor who performs services for the employer.

Notwithstanding anything in this paragraph (b)(2) to the contrary, an independent contractor who performs services for the employer cannot exclude the value of parking or the use of consumer goods provided pursuant to a product testing program under § 1.132-5(n); in addition, any director of the employer cannot exclude the value of the use of consumer goods provided pursuant to a product testing program under § 1.132-5(n).

(3) *On-premises athletic facilities.* For purposes of section 132(h)(5) (relating to on-premises athletic facilities), the term "employee" means—

(i) Any individual who is currently employed by the employer,

(ii) Any individual who was formerly employed by the employer and who separated from service with the employer by reason of retirement or disability, and

(iii) Any widow or widower of an individual who died while employed by the employer or who separated from service with the employer by reason of retirement or disability.

For purposes of this paragraph (b)(3), any partner who performs services for a partnership is considered employed by the partnership. In addition, any use by the spouse or dependent child (as defined in paragraph (b)(5) of this section) of the employee will be treated as use by the employee.

(4) *De minimis fringes.* For purposes of section 132(a)(4) (relating to de minimis fringes), the term "employee" means any recipient of a fringe benefit.

(5) *Dependent child.* The term "dependent child" means any son, stepson, daughter, or stepdaughter of the employee who is a dependent of the employee, or both of whose parents are deceased and who has not attained age 25. Any child to whom section 152(e) applies will be treated as the dependent of both parents.

(c) *Special rules for employers—Effect of section 414.* All employees treated as employed by a single employer under section 414(b), (c), (m), or (o) will be treated as employed by a single employer for purposes of this section. Thus, employees of one corporation that is part of a controlled group of corporations may under certain circumstances be eligible to receive section 132 benefits from the other corporations that comprise the controlled group. However, the aggregation of employers described in this paragraph (c) does not change the other requirements for an exclusion, such as the line of business requirement. Thus, for example, if a controlled group of corporations consists of two corporations that operate in different lines of business, the corporations are not treated as operating in the same line of business even though the corporations are treated as one employer.

(d) *Customers not to include employees.* For purposes of section 132 and the regulations thereunder, the term "customer" means any customer who is not an employee. However, the preceding sentence does not apply to section 132(c)(2) (relating to the gross profit percentage for determining a qualified employee discount). Thus, an employer that provides employee discounts cannot exclude sales made to employees in determining the aggregate sales to customers.

(e) *Treatment of on-premises athletic facilities—*(1) *In general.* Gross income does not include the value of any on-premises athletic facility provided by an employer to its employees. For purposes of section 132(h)(5) and this paragraph (e), the term "on-premises athletic facility" means any gym or other athletic facility (such as a pool, tennis court, or golf course)—

(i) Which is located on the premises of the employer,

(ii) Which is operated by the employer, and

(iii) Substantially all of the use of which during the calendar year is by employees of the employer, their spouses, and their dependent children.

For purposes of paragraph (e)(1)(iii) of this section, the term "dependent children" has the same meaning as the plural of the term "dependent child" in paragraph (b)(5) of this section. The exclusion of this paragraph (e) does not apply to any athletic facility if access to the facility is made available to the general public through the sale of memberships, the rental of the facility, or a similar arrangement.

(2) *Premises of the employer.* The athletic facility need not be located on the employer's business premises. However, the athletic facility must be located on premises of the employer. The

Reg. § 1.132-1(b)(2)

exclusion provided in this paragraph (e) applies whether the premises are owned or leased by the employer; in addition, the exclusion is available even if the employer is not a named lessee on the lease so long as the employer pays reasonable rent. The exclusion provided in this paragraph (e) does not apply to any athletic facility that is a facility for residential use. Thus, for example, a resort with accompanying athletic facilities (such as tennis courts, pool, and gym) would not qualify for the exclusion provided in this paragraph (e). An athletic facility is considered to be located on the employer's premises if the facility is located on the premises of a voluntary employees' beneficiary association funded by the employer.

(3) *Application of rules to membership in an athletic facility.* The exclusion provided in this paragraph (e) does not apply to any membership in an athletic facility (including health clubs or country clubs) unless the facility is owned (or leased) and operated by the employer and substantially all the use of the facility is by employees of the employer, their spouses, and their dependent children. Therefore, membership in a health club or country club not meeting the rules provided in this paragraph (e) would not qualify for the exclusion.

(4) *Operation by the employer.* An employer is considered to operate the athletic facility if the employer operates the facility through its own employees, or if the employer contracts out to another to operate the athletic facility. For example, if an employer hires an independent contractor to operate the athletic facility for the employer's employees, the facility is considered to be operated by the employer. In addition, if an athletic facility is operated by more than one employer, it is considered to be operated by each employer. For purposes of paragraph (e)(1)(iii) of this section, substantially all of the use of a facility that is operated by more than one employer must be by employees of the various employers, their spouses, and their dependent children. Where the facility is operated by more than one employer, an employer that pays rent either directly to the owner of the premises or to a sublessor of the premises is eligible for the exclusion. If an athletic facility is operated by a voluntary employees' beneficiary association funded by an employer, the employer is considered to operate the facility.

(5) *Nonapplicability of nondiscrimination rules.* The nondiscrimination rules of section 132 and § 1.132-8 do not apply to on-premises athletic facilities.

(f) *Nonapplicability of section 132 in certain cases*—(1) *Tax treatment provided for in another section.* If the tax treatment of a particular fringe benefit is expressly provided for in another section of Chapter 1 of the Internal Revenue Code of 1986, section 132 and the applicable regulations (except for section 132(e) and the regulations thereunder) do not apply to such fringe benefit. For example, because section 129 provides an exclusion from gross income for amounts paid or incurred by an employer for dependent care assistance for an employee, the exclusions under section 132 and this section do not apply to the provision by an employer to an employee of dependent care assistance. Similarly, because section 117(d) applies to tuition reductions, the exclusions under section 132 do not apply to free or discounted tuition provided to an employee by an organization operated by the employer, whether the tuition is for study at or below the graduate level. Of course, if the amounts paid by the employer are for education relating to the employee's trade or business of being an employee of the employer so that, if the employee paid for the education, the amount paid could be deducted under section 162, the costs of the education may be eligible for exclusion as a working condition fringe.

(2) *Limited statutory exclusions.* If another section of Chapter 1 of the Internal Revenue Code of 1986 provides an exclusion from gross income based on the cost of the benefit provided to the employee and such exclusion is a limited amount, section 132 and the regulations thereunder may apply to the extent the cost of the benefit exceeds the statutory exclusion.

* * *

[Reg. § 1.132-1.]

☐ [*T.D. 8256, 7-5-89. Amended by T.D. 8457, 12-29-92.*]

§ 1.132-2. No-additional-cost services.—(a) *In general*—(1) *Definition.* Gross income does not include the value of a no-additional-cost service. A "no-additional-cost service" is any service provided by an employer to an employee for the employee's personal use if—

(i) The service is offered for sale by the employer to its customers in the ordinary course of the line of business of the employer in which the employee performs substantial services, and

(ii) The employer incurs no substantial additional cost in providing the service to the employee (including foregone revenue and excluding any amount paid by or on behalf of the employee for the service).

For rules relating to the line of business limitation, see § 1.132-4. For purposes of this section, a service will not be considered to be offered for sale by the employer to its customers if that service is

Reg. § 1.132-2(a)(1)

primarily provided to employees and not to the employer's customers.

(2) *Excess capacity services.* Services that are eligible for treatment as no-additional-cost services include excess capacity services such as hotel accommodations; transportation by aircraft, train, bus, subway, or cruise line; and telephone services. Services that are not eligible for treatment as no-additional-cost services are non-excess capacity services such as the facilitation by a stock brokerage firm of the purchase of stock. Employees who receive non-excess capacity services may, however, be eligible for a qualified employee discount of up to 20 percent of the value of the service provided. See § 1.132-3.

(3) *Cash rebates.* The exclusion for a no-additional-cost service applies whether the service is provided at no charge or at a reduced price. The exclusion also applies if the benefit is provided through a partial or total cash rebate of an amount paid for the service.

(4) *Applicability of nondiscrimination rules.* The exclusion for a no-additional-cost service applies to highly compensated employees only if the service is available on substantially the same terms to each member of a group of employees that is defined under a reasonable classification set up by the employer that does not discriminate in favor of highly compensated employees. See § 1.132-8.

(5) *No substantial additional cost*—(i) *In general.* The exclusion for a no-additional-cost service applies only if the employer does not incur substantial additional cost in providing the service to the employee. For purposes of the preceding sentence, the term "cost" includes revenue that is forgone because the service is provided to an employee rather than a nonemployee. (For purposes of determining whether any revenue is forgone, it is assumed that the employee would not have purchased the service unless it were available to the employee at the actual price charged to the employee.) Whether an employer incurs substantial additional cost must be determined without regard to any amount paid by the employee for the service. Thus, any reimbursement by the employee for the cost of providing the service does not affect the determination of whether the employer incurs substantial additional cost.

(ii) *Labor intensive services.* An employer must include the cost of labor incurred in providing services to employees when determining whether the employer has incurred substantial additional cost. An employer incurs substantial additional cost, whether [or not] non-labor costs are incurred, if a substantial amount of time is spent by the employer or its employees in provid-

ing the service to employees. This would be the result whether the time spent by the employer or its employees in providing the services would have been "idle," or if the services were provided outside normal business hours. An employer generally incurs no substantial additional cost, however, if the services provided to the employee are merely incidental to the primary service being provided by the employer. For example, the in-flight services of a flight attendant and the cost of in-flight meals provided to airline employees traveling on a space-available basis are merely incidental to the primary service being provided (i.e., air transportation). Similarly, maid service provided to hotel employees renting hotel rooms on a space-available basis is merely incidental to the primary service being provided (i.e., hotel accommodations).

(6) *Payments for telephone service.* Payment made by an entity subject to the modified final judgment (as defined in section 559(c)(5) of the Tax Reform Act of 1984) of all or part of the cost of local telephone service provided to an employee by a person other than an entity subject to the modified final judgment shall be treated as telephone service provided to the employee by the entity making the payment for purposes of this section. The preceding sentence also applies to a rebate of the amount paid by the employee for the service and a payment to the person providing the service. This paragraph (a)(6) applies only to services and employees described in § 1.132-4(c). For a special line of business rule relating to such services and employees, see § 1.132-4(c).

(b) *Reciprocal agreements.* For purposes of the exclusion from gross income for a no-additional-cost service, an exclusion is available to an employee of one employer for a no-additional-cost service provided by an unrelated employer only if all of the following requirements are satisfied—

(1) The service provided to such employee by the unrelated employer is the same type of service generally provided to nonemployee customers by both the line of business in which the employee works and the line of business in which the service is provided to such employee (so that the employee would be permitted to exclude from gross income the value of the service if such service were provided directly by the employee's employer);

(2) Both employers are parties to a written reciprocal agreement under which a group of employees of each employer, all of whom perform substantial services in the same line of business, may receive no-additional-cost services from the other employer; and

(3) Neither employer incurs any substantial additional cost (including forgone revenue) in pro-

Reg. § 1.132-2(a)(2)

viding such service to the employees of the other employer, or pursuant to such agreement. If one employer receives a substantial payment from the other employer with respect to the reciprocal agreement, the paying employer will be considered to have incurred a substantial additional cost pursuant to the agreement, and consequently services performed under the reciprocal agreement will not qualify for exclusion as no-additional-cost services.

(c) *Example.* The rules of this section are illustrated by the following example:

Example. Assume that a commercial airline permits its employees to take personal flights on the airline at no charge and receive reserved seating. Because the employer forgoes potential revenue by permitting the employees to reserve seats, employees receiving such free flights are not eligible for the no-additional-cost exclusion. [Reg. § 1.132-2.]

☐ [*T.D.* 8256, 7-5-89.]

§ 1.132-3. Qualified employee discounts.— (a) *In general*—(1) *Definition.* Gross income does not include the value of a qualified employee discount. A "qualified employee discount" is any employee discount with respect to qualified property or services provided by an employer to an employee for use by the employee to the extent the discount does not exceed—

(i) The gross profit percentage multiplied by the price at which the property is offered to customers in the ordinary course of the employer's line of business, for discounts on property, or

(ii) Twenty percent of the price at which the service is offered to customers, for discounts on services.

(2) *Qualified property or services*—(i) *In general.* The term "qualified property or services" means any property or services that are offered for sale to customers in the ordinary course of the line of business of the employer in which the employee performs substantial services. For rules relating to the line of business limitation, see § 1.132-4.

(ii) *Exception for certain property.* The term "qualified property" does not include real property and it does not include personal property (whether tangible or intangible) of a kind commonly held for investment. Thus, an employee may not exclude from gross income the amount of an employee discount provided on the purchase of securities, commodities, or currency, or of either residential or commercial real estate, whether or not the particular purchase is made for investment purposes.

(iii) *Property and services not offered in ordinary course of business.* The term "qualified property or services" does not include any property or services of a kind that is not offered for sale to customers in the ordinary course of the line of business of the employer. For example, employee discounts provided on property or services that are offered for sale primarily to employees and their families (such as merchandise sold at an employee store or through an employer-provided catalog service) may not be excluded from gross income. For rules relating to employer-operated eating facilities, see § 1.132-7, and for rules relating to employer-operated on-premises athletic facilities, see § 1.132-1(e).

(3) *No reciprocal agreement exception.* The exclusion for a qualified employee discount does not apply to property or services provided by another employer pursuant to a written reciprocal agreement that exists between employers to provide discounts on property and services to employees of the other employer.

(4) *Property or services provided without charge, at a reduced price, or by rebates.* The exclusion for a qualified employee discount applies whether the property or service is provided at no charge (in which case only part of the discount may be excludable as a qualified employee discount) or at a reduced price. The exclusion also applies if the benefit is provided through a partial or total cash rebate of an amount paid for the property or service.

(5) *Property or services provided directly by the employer or indirectly through a third party.* A qualified employee discount may be provided either directly by the employer or indirectly through a third party. For example, an employee of an appliance manufacturer may receive a qualified employee discount on the manufacturer's appliances purchased at a retail store that offers such appliances for sale to customers. The employee may exclude the amount of the qualified employee discount whether the employee is provided the appliance at no charge or purchases it at a reduced price, or whether the employee receives a partial or total cash rebate from either the employer-manufacturer or the retailer. If an employee receives additional rights associated with the property that are not provided by the employee's employer to customers in the ordinary course of the line of business in which the employee performs substantial services (such as the right to return or exchange the property or special warranty rights), the employee may only receive a qualified employee discount with respect to the property and not the additional rights. Receipt of such additional rights may occur, for example, when an employee of a manufacturer purchases property manufactured by the employee's employer at a retail outlet.

Reg. § 1.132-3(a)(5)

(6) *Applicability of nondiscrimination rules.* The exclusion for a qualified employee discount applies to highly compensated employees only if the discount is available on substantially the same terms to each member of a group of employees that is defined under a reasonable classification set up by the employer that does not discriminate in favor of highly compensated employees. See § 1.132-8.

(b) *Employee discount*—(1) *Definition.* The term "employee discount" means the excess of—

(i) The price at which the property or service is being offered by the employer for sale to customers, over

(ii) The price at which the property or service is provided by the employer to an employee for use by the employee. A transfer of property by an employee without consideration is treated as use by the employee for purposes of this section. Thus, for example, if an employee receives a discount on property offered for sale by his employer to customers and the employee makes a gift of the property to his parent, the property will be considered to be provided for use by the employee; thus, the discount will be eligible for exclusion as a qualified employee discount.

(2) *Price to customers*—(i) *Determined at time of sale.* In determining the amount of an employee discount, the price at which the property or service is being offered to customers at the time of the employee's purchase is controlling. For example, assume that an employer offers a product to customers for $20 during the first six months of a calendar year, but at the time the employee purchases the product at a discount, the price at which the product is being offered to customers is $25. In this case, the price from which the employee discount is measured is $25. Assume instead that, at the time the employee purchases the product at a discount, the price at which the product is being offered to customers is $15 and the price charged the employee is $12. The employee discount is measured from $15, the price at which the product is offered for sale to customers at the time of the employee purchase. Thus, the employee discount is $15 − $12, or $3.

(ii) *Quantity discount not reflected.* The price at which a property or service is being offered to customers cannot reflect any quantity discount unless the employee actually purchases the requisite quantity of the property or service.

(iii) *Price to employer's customers controls.* In determining the amount of an employee discount, the price at which a property or service is offered to customers of the employee's employer is controlling. Thus, the price at which the property is sold to the wholesale customers of a manufacturer will generally be lower than the price at which the same property is sold to the customers of a retailer. However, see paragraph (a)(5) of this section regarding the effect of a wholesaler providing to its employees additional rights not provided to customers of the wholesaler in the ordinary course of its business.

(iv) *Discounts to discrete customer or consumer groups.* Subject to paragraph (2)(ii) of this section, if an employer offers for sale property or services at one or more discounted prices to discrete customer or consumer groups, and sales at all such discounted prices comprise at least 35 percent of the employer's gross sales for a representative period, then in determining the amount of an employee discount, the price at which such property or service is being offered to customers for purposes of this section is a discounted price. The applicable discounted price is the current undiscounted price, reduced by the percentage discount at which the greatest percentage of the employer's discounted gross sales are made for such representative period. If sales at different percentage discounts equal the same percentage of the employer's gross sales, the price at which the property or service is being provided to customers may be reduced by the average of the discounts offered to each of the two groups. For purposes of this section, a representative period is the taxable year of the employer immediately preceding the taxable year in which the property or service is provided to the employee at a discount. If more than one employer would be aggregated under section 414(b), (c), (m), or (o), and not all of the employers have the same taxable year, the employers required to be aggregated must designate the 12-month period to be used in determining gross sales for a representative period. The 12-month period designated, however, must be used on a consistent basis.

(v) *Examples.* The rules provided in this paragraph (b)(2) are illustrated by the following examples:

Example (1). Assume that a wholesale employer offers property for sale to two discrete customer groups at differing prices. Assume further that during the prior taxable year of the employer, 70 percent of the employer's gross sales are made at a 15 percent discount and 30 percent at no discount. For purposes of this paragraph (b)(2), the current undiscounted price at which the property or service is being offered by the employer for sale to customers may be reduced by the 15 percent discount.

Example (2). Assume that a retail employer offers a 20 percent discount to members of the American Bar Association, a 15 percent discount to members of the American Medical Association, and a ten percent discount to employees of the Federal Government. Assume further that during the prior taxable year of the employer, sales to American Bar Association members equal 15 percent of the employer's gross sales, sales to American Medical Association members equal 20 percent of the employer's gross sales, and sales to Federal Government employees equal 25 percent of the employer's gross sales. For purposes of this paragraph (b)(2), the current undiscounted price at which the property or service is being offered by the employer for sale to customers may be reduced by the ten percent Federal Government discount.

(3) *Damaged, distressed, or returned goods.* If an employee pays at least fair market value for damaged, distressed, or returned property, such employee will not have income attributable to such purchase.

(c) *Gross profit percentage*—(1) *In general*—(i) *General rule.* An exclusion from gross income for an employee discount on qualified property is limited to the price at which the property is being offered to customers in the ordinary course of the employer's line of business, multiplied by the employer's gross profit percentage. The term "gross profit percentage" means the excess of the aggregate sales price of the property sold by the employer to customers (including employees) over the employer's aggregate cost of the property, then divided by the aggregate sales price.

(ii) *Calculation of gross profit percentage.* The gross profit percentage must be calculated separately for each line of business based on the aggregate sales price and aggregate cost of property in that line of business for a representative period. For purposes of this section, a representative period is the taxable year of the employer immediately preceding the taxable year in which the discount is available. For example, if the aggregate amount of sales of property in an employer's line of business for the prior taxable year was $800,000, and the aggregate cost of the property for the year was $600,000, the gross profit percentage would be 25 percent ($800,000 minus $600,000, then divided by $800,000). If two or more employers are required to aggregate under section 414(b), (c), (m), or (o) (aggregated employer), and if all of the aggregated employers do not share the same taxable year, then the aggregated employers must designate the 12-month period to be used in determining the gross profit percentage. The 12-month period designated, however, must be used on a consistent basis. If an employee performs substantial services in more than one line of business, the gross profit percentage of the line of business in which the property is sold determines the amount of the excludable employee discount.

(iii) *Special rule for employers in their first year of existence.* An employer in its first year of existence may estimate the gross profit percentage of a line of business based on its mark-up from cost. Alternatively, an employer in its first year of existence may determine the gross profit percentage by reference to an appropriate industry average.

(iv) *Redetermination of gross profit percentage.* If substantial changes in an employer's business indicate at any time that it is inappropriate for the prior year's gross profit percentage to be used for the current year, the employer must, within a reasonable period, redetermine the gross profit percentage for the remaining portion of the current year as if such portion of the year were the first year of the employer's existence.

(2) *Line of business.* In general, an employer must determine the gross profit percentage on the basis of all property offered to customers (including employees) in each separate line of business. An employer may instead select a classification of property that is narrower than the applicable line of business. However, the classification must be reasonable. For example, if an employer computes gross profit percentage according to the department in which products are sold, such classification is reasonable. Similarly, it is reasonable to compute gross profit percentage on the basis of the type of merchandise sold (such as high mark-up and low mark-up classifications). It is not reasonable, however, for an employer to classify certain low mark-up products preferred by certain employees (such as highly compensated employees) with high mark-up products or to classify certain high mark-up products preferred by other employees with low mark-up products.

(3) *Generally accepted accounting principles.* In general, the aggregate sales price of property must be determined in accordance with generally accepted accounting principles. An employer must compute the aggregate cost of property in the same manner in which it is computed for the employer's Federal income tax liability; thus, for example, section 263A and the regulations thereunder apply in determining the cost of property.

* * *

(e) *Excess discounts.* Unless excludable under a provision of the Internal Revenue Code of 1986 other than section 132(a)(2), an employee discount provided on property is excludable to the extent of the gross profit percentage multiplied by the price at which the property is being offered for sale to customers. If an employee discount exceeds the gross profit percentage, the excess discount is includible in the employee's income. For example, if the discount on employer-purchased property is 30 percent and the employer's

Reg. § 1.132-3(e)

gross profit percentage for the period in the relevant line of business is 25 percent, then 5 percent of the price at which the property is being offered for sale to customers is includible in the employee's income. With respect to services, an employee discount of up to 20 percent may be excludable. If an employee discount exceeds 20 percent, the excess discount is includible in the employee's income. For example, assume that a commercial airline provides a pass to each of its employees permitting the employees to obtain a free roundtrip coach ticket with a confirmed seat to any destination the airline services. Neither the exclusion of section 132(a)(1) (relating to no-additional-cost services) nor any other statutory exclusion applies to a flight taken primarily for personal purposes by an employee under this program. However, an employee discount of up to 20 percent may be excluded as a qualified employee discount. Thus, if the price charged to customers for the flight taken is $300 (under restrictions comparable to those actually placed on travel associated with the employee airline ticket), $60 is excludible from gross income as a qualified employee discount and $240 is includible in gross income. [Reg. § 1.132-3.]

☐ [*T.D. 8256, 7-5-89.*]

§ 1.132-4. Line of business limitation.—(a) *In general*—(1) *Applicability*—(i) *General rule.* A no-additional-cost service or a qualified employee discount provided to an employee is only available with respect to property or services that are offered for sale to customers in the ordinary course of the same line of business in which the employee receiving the property or service performs substantial services. Thus, an employee who does not perform substantial services in a particular line of business of the employer may not exclude from income under section 132(a)(1) or (a)(2) the value of services or employee discounts received on property or services in that line of business. For rules that relax the line of business requirement, see paragraphs (b) through (g) of this section.

(ii) *Property and services sold to employees rather than customers.* Because the property or services must be offered for sale to customers in the ordinary course of the same line of business in which the employee performs substantial services, the line of business limitation is not satisfied if the employer's products or services are sold primarily to employees of the employer, rather than to customers. Thus, for example, an employer in the banking line of business is not considered in the variety store line of business if the employer establishes an employee store that offers variety store items for sale to the employer's employees. See § 1.132-7 for rules relating to employer-operated eating facilities, and see § 1.132-1(e) for rules relating to employer-operated on-premises athletic facilities.

(iii) *Performance of substantial services in more than one line of business.* An employee who performs services in more than one of the employer's lines of business may only exclude no-additional-cost services and qualified employee discounts in the lines of business in which the employee performs substantial services.

(iv) *Performance of services that directly benefit more than one line of business—(A) In general.* An employee who performs substantial services that directly benefit more than one line of business of an employer is treated as performing substantial services in all such lines of business. For example, an employee who maintains accounting records for an employer's three lines of business may receive qualified employee discounts in all three lines of business. Similarly, if an employee of a minor line of business of an employer that is significantly interrelated with a major line of business of the employer performs substantial services that directly benefit both the major and the minor lines of business, the employee is treated as performing substantial services for both the major and the minor lines of business.

(B) *Examples.* The rules provided in this paragraph (a)(1)(iv) are illustrated by the following examples:

Example (1). Assume that employees of units of an employer provide repair or financing services, or sell by catalog, with respect to retail merchandise sold by the employer. Such employees may be considered to perform substantial services for the retail merchandise line of business under paragraph (a)(1)(iv)(A) of this section.

Example (2). Assume that an employer operates a hospital and a laundry service. Assume further that some of the gross receipts of the laundry service line of business are from laundry services sold to customers other than the hospital employer. Only the employees of the laundry service who perform substantial services which directly benefit the hospital line of business (through the provision of laundry services to the hospital) will be treated as performing substantial services for the hospital line of business. Other employees of the laundry service line of business will not be treated as employees of the hospital line of business.

Example (3). Assume the same facts as in example (2), except that the employer also operates a chain of dry cleaning stores. Employees who perform substantial services which directly benefit the dry cleaning stores but who do not perform substantial services that directly benefit the hospital line of business will not be treated as performing substantial services for the hospital line of business.

(2) *Definition*—(i) *In general.* An employer's line of business is determined by reference to the Enterprise Standard Industrial Classification Manual (ESIC Manual) prepared by the Statistical Policy Division of the U.S. Office of Management and Budget. An employer is considered to have more than one line of business if the employer offers for sale to customers property or services in more than one two-digit code classification referred to in the ESIC Manual.

(ii) *Examples.* Examples of two-digit classifications are general retail merchandise stores; hotels and other lodging places; auto repair, services, and garages; and food stores.

(3) *Aggregation of two-digit classifications.* If, pursuant to paragraph (a)(2) of this section, an employer has more than one line of business, such lines of business will be treated as a single line of business where and to the extent that one or more of the following aggregation rules apply:

(i) If it is uncommon in the industry of the employer for any of the separate lines of business of the employer to be operated without the others, the separate lines of business are treated as one line of business.

(ii) If it is common for a substantial number of employees (other than those employees who work at the headquarters or main office of the employer) to perform substantial services for more than one line of business of the employer, so that determination of which employees perform substantial services for which line or lines of business would be difficult, then the separate lines of business of the employer in which such employees perform substantial services are treated as one line of business. For example, assume that an employer operates a delicatessen with an attached service counter at which food is sold for consumption on the premises. Assume further that most but not all employees work both at the delicatessen and at the service counter. Under the aggregation rule of this paragraph (a)(3)(ii), the delicatessen and the service counter are treated as one line of business.

(iii) If the retail operations of an employer that are located on the same premises are in separate lines of business but would be considered to be within one line of business under paragraph (a)(2) of this section if the merchandise offered for sale in such lines of business were offered for sale at a department store, then the operations are treated as one line of business. For example, assume that on the same premises an employer sells both women's apparel and jewelry. Because, if sold together at a department store, the opera-

tions would be part of the same line of business, the operations are treated as one line of business.

* * *

(h) *Line of business requirement does not expand benefits eligible for exclusion.* The line of business requirement limits the benefits eligible for the no-additional-cost service and qualified employee discount exclusions to property or services provided by an employer to its customers in the ordinary course of the line of business of the employer in which the employee performs substantial services. The requirement is intended to ensure that employers do not offer, on a tax-free or reduced basis, property or services to employees that are not offered to the employer's customers, even if the property or services offered to the customers and the employees are within the same line of business (as defined in this section). [Reg. § 1.132-4.]

☐ [*T.D.* 8256, 7-5-89.]

§ **1.132-5. Working condition fringes.**—(a) *In general*—(1) *Definition.* Gross income does not include the value of a working condition fringe. A "working condition fringe" is any property or service provided to an employee of an employer to the extent that, if the employee paid for the property or service, the amount paid would be allowable as a deduction under section 162 or 167.

(i) A service or property offered by an employer in connection with a flexible spending account is not excludable from gross income as a working condition fringe. For purposes of the preceding sentence, a flexible spending account is an agreement (whether or not written) entered into between an employer and an employee that makes available to the employee over a time period a certain level of unspecified non-cash benefits with a pre-determined cash value.

(ii) If, under section 274 or any other section, certain substantiation requirements must be met in order for a deduction under section 162 or 167 to be allowable, then those substantiation requirements apply when determining whether a property or service is excludable as a working condition fringe.

(iii) An amount that would be deductible by the employee under a section other than section 162 or 167, such as section 212, is not a working condition fringe.

(iv) A physical examination program provided by the employer is not excludable as a working condition fringe even if the value of such program might be deductible to the employee under section 213. The previous sentence applies without regard to whether the employer makes the program mandatory to some or all employees.

Reg. § 1.132-5(a)(1)

(v) A cash payment made by an employer to an employee will not qualify as a working condition fringe unless the employer requires the employee to—

(A) Use the payment for expenses in connection with a specific or pre-arranged activity or undertaking for which a deduction is allowable under section 162 or 167,

(B) Verify that the payment is actually used for such expenses, and

(C) Return to the employer any part of the payment not so used.

(vi) The limitation of section 67(a) (relating to the two-percent floor on miscellaneous itemized deductions) is not considered when determining the amount of a working condition fringe. For example, assume that an employer provides a $1,000 cash advance to Employee A and that the conditions of paragraph (a)(1)(v) of this section are not satisfied. Even to the extent A uses the allowance for expenses for which a deduction is allowable under section 162 or 167, because such cash payment is not a working condition fringe, section 67(a) applies. The $1,000 payment is includible in A's gross income and subject to income and employment tax withholding. If, however, the conditions of paragraph (a)(1)(v) of this section are satisfied with respect to the payment, then the amount of A's working condition fringe is determined without regard to section 67(a). The $1,000 payment is excludible from A's gross income and not subject to income and employment tax reporting and withholding.

(2) *Trade or business of the employee*—(i) *General.* If the hypothetical payment for a property or service would be allowable as a deduction with respect to a trade or business of an employee other than the employee's trade or business of being an employee of the employer, it cannot be taken into account for purposes of determining the amount, if any, of the working condition fringe.

(ii) *Examples.* The rule of paragraph (a)(2)(i) of this section may be illustrated by the following examples:

Example (1). Assume that, unrelated to company X's trade or business and unrelated to employee A's trade or business of being an employee of company X, A is a member of the board of directors of company Y. Assume further that company X provides A with air transportation to a company Y board of director's meeting. A may not exclude from gross income the value of the air transportation to the meeting as a working condition fringe. A may, however, deduct such amount under section 162 if the section 162 requirements are satisfied. The result would be the same whether the air transportation was provided in the form of a flight on a commercial airline or a seat on a company X airplane.

Example (2). Assume the same facts as in example (1) except that A serves on the board of directors of company Z and company Z regularly purchases a significant amount of goods and services from company X. Because of the relationship between Company Z and A's employer, A's membership on Company Z's board of directors is related to A's trade or business of being an employee of Company X. Thus, A may exclude from gross income the value of air transportation to board meetings as a working condition fringe.

Example (3). Assume the same facts as in example (1) except that A serves on the board of directors of a charitable organization. Assume further that the service by A on the charity's board is substantially related to company X's trade or business. In this case, A may exclude from gross income the value of air transportation to board meetings as a working condition fringe.

Example (4). Assume the same facts as in example (3) except that company X also provides A with the use of a company X conference room which A uses for monthly meetings relating to the charitable organization. Also assume that A uses company X's copy machine and word processor each month in connection with functions of the charitable organization. Because of the substantial business benefit that company X derives from A's service on the board of the charity, A may exclude as a working condition fringe the value of the use of company X property in connection with the charitable organization.

* * *

(c) *Applicability of substantiation requirements of sections 162 and 274 (d)*—(1) *In general.* The value of property or services provided to an employee may not be excluded from the employee's gross income as a working condition fringe, by either the employer or the employee, unless the applicable substantiation requirements of either section 274 (d) or section 162 (whichever is applicable) and the regulations thereunder are satisfied. The substantiation requirements of section 274(d) apply to an employee even if the requirements of section 274 do not apply to the employee's employer for deduction purposes (such as when the employer is a tax-exempt organization or a governmental unit).

(2) *Section 274(d) requirements.* The substantiation requirements of section 274(d) are satisfied by "adequate records or sufficient evidence corroborating the [employee's] own statement". Therefore, such records or evidence provided by the employee, and relied upon by the employer to the extent permitted by the regulations promul-

Reg. § 1.132-5(a)(2)

gated under section 274(d), will be sufficient to substantiate a working condition fringe exclusion.

* * *

[Reg. § 1.132-5.]

☐ [*T.D. 8256, 7-5-89. Amended by T.D. 8451, 12-4-92; T.D. 8457, 12-29-92; T.D. 8666, 5-29-96 and T.D. 8933, 1-10-2001.*]

§ 1.132-6. De minimis fringes.—(a) *In general.* Gross income does not include the value of a de minimis fringe provided to an employee. The term "de minimis fringe" means any property or service the value of which is (after taking into account the frequency with which similar fringes are provided by the employer to the employer's employees) so small as to make accounting for it unreasonable or administratively impracticable.

(b) *Frequency*—(1) *Employee-measured frequency.* Generally, the frequency with which similar fringes are provided by the employer to the employer's employees is determined by reference to the frequency with which the employer provides the fringes to each individual employee. For example, if an employer provides a free meal in kind to one employee on a daily basis, but not to any other employee, the value of the meals is not de minimis with respect to that one employee even though with respect to the employer's entire workforce the meals are provided "infrequently."

(2) *Employer-measured frequency.* Notwithstanding the rule of paragraph (b)(1) of this section, except for purposes of applying the special rules of paragraph (d)(2) of this section, where it would be administratively difficult to determine frequency with respect to individual employees, the frequency with which similar fringes are provided by the employer to the employer's employees is determined by reference to the frequency with which the employer provides the fringes to the workforce as a whole. Therefore, under this rule, the frequency with which any individual employee receives such a fringe benefit is not relevant and in some circumstances, the de minimis fringe exclusion may apply with respect to a benefit even though a particular employee receives the benefit frequently. For example, if an employer exercises sufficient control and imposes significant restrictions on the personal use of a company copying machine so that at least 85 percent of the use of the machine is for business purposes, any personal use of the copying machine by particular employees is considered to be a de minimis fringe.

(c) *Administrability.* Unless excluded by a provision of chapter 1 of the Internal Revenue Code of 1986 other than section 132(a)(4), the value of any fringe benefit that would not be unreasonable or administratively impracticable to account for is includible in the employee's gross income. Thus,

except as provided in paragraph (d)(2) of this section, the provision of any cash fringe benefit is never excludable under section 132(a) as a de minimis fringe benefit. Similarly except as otherwise provided in paragraph (d) of this section, a cash equivalent fringe benefit (such as a fringe benefit provided to an employee through the use of a gift certificate or charge or credit card) is generally not excludable under § 132(a) even if the same property or service acquired (if provided in kind) would be excludable as a de minimis fringe benefit. For example, the provision of cash to an employee for a theatre ticket that would itself be excludable as a de minimis fringe (see paragraph (e)(1) of this section) is not excludable as a de minimis fringe.

(d) *Special rules*—* * *

(2) *Occasional meal money or local transportation fare*—(i) *General rule.* Meals, meal money or local transportation fare provided to an employee is excluded as a de minimis fringe benefit if the benefit provided is reasonable and is provided in a manner that satisfies the following three conditions:

(A) *Occasional basis.* The meals, meal money or local transportation fare is provided to the employee on an occasional basis. Whether meal money or local transportation fare is provided to an employee on an occasional basis will depend upon the frequency i.e. the availability of the benefit and regularity with which the benefit is provided by the employer to the employee. Thus, meals, meal money, or local transportation fare or a combination of such benefits provided to an employee on a regular or routine basis is not provided on an occasional basis.

(B) *Overtime.* The meals, meal money or local transportation fare is provided to an employee because overtime work necessitates an extension of the employee's normal work schedule. This condition does not fail to be satisfied merely because the circumstances giving rise to the need for overtime work are reasonably foreseeable.

(C) *Meal money.* In the case of a meal or meal money, the meal or meal money is provided to enable the employee to work overtime. Thus, for example, meals provided on the employer's premises that are consumed during the period that the employee works overtime or meal money provided for meals consumed during such period satisfy this condition.

In no event shall meal money or local transportation fare calculated on the basis of the number of hours worked (e.g., $1.00 per hour for each hour over eight hours) be considered a de minimis fringe benefit.

(ii) *Applicability of other exclusions for certain meals and for transportation provided for*

Reg. § 1.132-6(d)(2)

security concerns. The value of meals furnished to an employee, an employee's spouse, or any of the employee's dependents by or on behalf of the employee's employer for the convenience of the employer is excluded from the employee's gross income if the meals are furnished on the business premises of the employer (see section 119). (For purposes of the exclusion under section 119, the definitions of an employee under § 1.132-1(b) do not apply.) If, for a bona fide business-oriented security concern, an employer provides an employee vehicle transportation that is specially designed for security (for example, the vehicle is equipped with bulletproof glass and armor plating), and the conditions of § 1.132-5(m) are satisfied, the value of the special security design is excludable from gross income as a working condition fringe if the employee would not have had such special security design but for the bona fide business-oriented security concern.

(iii) *Special rule for employer-provided transportation provided in certain circumstances.*—(A) *Partial exclusion of value.* If an employer provides transportation (such as taxi fare) to an employee for use in commuting to and/or from work because of unusual circumstances and because, based on the facts and circumstances, it is unsafe for the employee to use other available means of transportation, the excess of the value of each one-way trip over $1.50 per one-way commute is excluded from gross income. The rule of this paragraph (d)(2)(iii) is not available to a control employee as defined in § 1.61-21(f)(5) and (6).

(B) *"Unusual circumstances".* Unusual circumstances are determined with respect to the employee receiving the transportation and are based on all facts and circumstances. An example of unusual circumstances would be when an employee is asked to work outside of his normal work hours (such as being called to the workplace at 1:00 am when the employee normally works from 8:00 am to 4:00 pm). Another example of unusual circumstances is a temporary change in the employee's work schedule (such as working from 12 midnight to 8:00 am rather than from 8:00 am to 4:00 pm for a two-week period).

(C) *"Unsafe conditions".* Factors indicating whether it is unsafe for an employee to use other available means of transportation are the history of crime in the geographic area surrounding the employee's workplace or residence and the time of day during which the employee must commute.

(3) *Use of special rules or examples to establish a general rule.* The special rules provided in this paragraph (d) or examples provided in paragraph (e) of this section may not be used to

establish any general rule permitting exclusion as a de minimis fringe. For example, the fact that $252 (i.e., $21 per month for 12 months) worth of public transit passes can be excluded from gross income as a de minimis fringe in 1992 does not mean that any fringe benefit with a value equal to or less than $252 may be excluded as a de minimis fringe. As another example, the fact that the commuting use of an employer-provided vehicle more than one day a month is an example of a benefit not excludable as a de minimis fringe (see paragraph (e)(2) of this section) does not mean that the commuting use of a vehicle up to 12 times per year is excludable from gross income as a de minimis fringe.

(4) *Benefits exceeding value and frequency limits.* If a benefit provided to an employee is not de minimis because either the value or frequency exceeds a limit provided in this paragraph (d), no amount of the benefit is considered to be a de minimis fringe. For example, if, in 1992, an employer provides a $50 monthly public transit pass, the entire $50 must be included in income, not just the excess value over $21.

(e) *Examples*—(1) *Benefits excludable from income.* Examples of de minimis fringe benefits are occasional typing of personal letters by a company secretary; occasional personal use of an employer's copying machine, provided that the employer exercises sufficient control and imposes significant restrictions on the personal use of the machine so that at least 85 percent of the use of the machine is for business purposes; occasional cocktail parties, group meals, or picnics for employees and their guests; traditional birthday or holiday gifts of property (not cash) with a low fair market value; occasional theater or sporting event tickets; coffee, doughnuts, and soft drinks; local telephone calls; and flowers, fruit, books, or similar property provided to employees under special circumstances (e.g., on account of illness, outstanding performance, or family crisis).

(2) *Benefits not excludable as de minimis fringes.* Examples of fringe benefits that are not excludable from gross income as de minimis fringes are: season tickets to sporting or theatrical events; the commuting use of an employer-provided automobile or other vehicle more than one day a month; membership in a private country club or athletic facility, regardless of the frequency with which the employee uses the facility; employer-provided group-term life insurance on the life of the spouse or child of an employee; and use of employer-owned or leased facilities (such as an apartment, hunting lodge, boat, etc.) for a weekend. Some amount of the value of certain of these fringe benefits may be excluded from income under other statutory provisions, such as the

Reg. § 1.132-6(d)(3)

exclusion for working condition fringes. See § 1.132-5.

(f) *Nonapplicability of nondiscrimination rules.* Except to the extent provided in § 1.132-7, the nondiscrimination rules of section 132(h)(1) and § 1.132-8 do not apply in determining the amount, if any, of a de minimis fringe. Thus, a fringe benefit may be excludable as a de minimis fringe even if the benefit is provided exclusively to highly compensated employees of the employer. [Reg. § 1.132-6.]

☐ [*T.D. 8256, 7-5-89. Amended by T.D. 8389, 1-15-92.*]

§ 1.132-8. Fringe benefit nondiscrimination rules.—(a) *Application of nondiscrimination rules*—(1) *General rule.* A highly compensated employee who receives a no-additional cost service, a qualified employee discount or a meal provided at an employer-operated eating facility for employees shall not be permitted to exclude such benefit from his or her income unless the benefit is available on substantially the same terms to:

(i) All employees of the employer; or

(ii) A group of employees of the employer which is defined under a reasonable classification set up by the employer that does not discriminate in favor of highly compensated employees. See paragraph (f) of this section for the definition of a highly compensated employee.

(2) *Consequences of discrimination*—(i) *In general.* If an employer maintains more than one fringe benefit program, i.e., either different fringe benefits being provided to the same group of employees, or different classifications of employees or the same fringe benefit being provided to two or more classifications of employees, the nondiscrimination requirements of section 132 will generally be applied separately to each such program. Thus, a determination that one fringe benefit program discriminates in favor of highly compensated employees generally will not cause other fringe benefit programs covering the same highly compensated employees to be treated as discriminatory. If the fringe benefits provided to a highly compensated individual do not satisfy the nondiscrimination rules provided in this section, such individual shall be unable to exclude from gross income any portion of the benefit. For example, if an employer offers a 20 percent discount (which otherwise satisfies the requirements for a qualified employee discount) to all non-highly compensated employees and a 35 percent discount to all highly compensated employees, the entire value of the 35 percent discount (not just the excess over 20 percent) is includible in the gross income and wages of the highly compensated employees who make purchases at a discount.

(ii) *Exception*—(A) *Related fringe benefit programs.* If one of a group of fringe benefit programs discriminates in favor of highly compensated employees, no related fringe benefit provided to such highly compensated employees under any other fringe benefit program may be excluded from the gross income of such highly compensated employees. For example, assume a department store provides a 20 percent merchandise discount to all employees under one fringe benefit program. Assume further that under a second fringe benefit program, the department store provides an additional 15 percent merchandise discount to a group of employees defined under a classification which discriminates in favor of highly compensated employees. Because the second fringe benefit program is discriminatory, the 15 percent merchandise discount provided to the highly compensated employees is not a qualified employee discount. In addition, because the 20 percent merchandise discount provided under the first fringe benefit program is related to the fringe benefit provided under the second fringe benefit program, the 20 percent merchandise discount provided the highly compensated employees is not a qualified employee discount. Thus, the entire 35 percent merchandise discount provided to the highly compensated employees is includible in such employees' gross incomes.

(B) *Employer-operated eating facilities for employees.* For purposes of paragraph (a)(2)(ii)(A) of this section, meals at different employer-operated eating facilities for employees are not related fringe benefits, so that a highly compensated employee may exclude from gross income the value of a meal at a nondiscriminatory facility even though any meals provided to him or her at a discriminatory facility cannot be excluded.

(3) *Scope of the nondiscrimination rules provided in this section.* The nondiscrimination rules provided in this section apply only to fringe benefits provided pursuant to section 132(a)(1), (a)(2), and (e)(2). These rules have no application to any other employee benefit that may be subject to nondiscrimination requirements under any other section of the Code.

* * *

(f) *Highly compensated employee*—(1) *Government and nongovernment employees.* A highly compensated employee of any employer is any employee who, during the year or the preceding year—

(i) Was a 5-percent owner,

(ii) Received compensation from the employer in excess of $75,000,

Reg. § 1.132-8(f)(1)

(iii) Received compensation from the employer in excess of $50,000 and was in the top-paid group of employees for such year, or

(iv) Was at any time an officer and received compensation greater than 150 percent of the amount in effect under section 415(c)(1)(A) for such year.

For purposes of determining whether an employee is a highly compensated employee, the rules of sections 414(q), (s), and (t) apply.

(2) *Former employees.* A former employee shall be treated as a highly compensated employee if—

(i) The employee was a highly compensated employee when the employee separated from service, or

(ii) The employee was a highly compensated employee at any time after attaining age 55. [Reg. § 1.132-8.]

☐ [*T.D.* 8256, 7-5-89.]

§ 1.132-9.   Qualified   transportation fringes.— * * *

* * *

(b) *Questions and answers.*

Q-1. What is a qualified transportation fringe?

A-1. (a) The following benefits are qualified transportation fringe benefits:

(1) Transportation in a commuter highway vehicle.

(2) Transit passes.

(3) Qualified parking.

(b) An employer may simultaneously provide an employee with any one or more these three benefits.

Q-2. What is transportation in a commuter highway vehicle?

A-2. Transportation in a commuter highway vehicle is transportation provided by an employer to an employee in connection with travel between the employee's residence and place of employment. A commuter highway vehicle is a highway vehicle with a seating capacity of at least 6 adults (excluding the driver) and with respect to which at least 80 percent of the vehicle's mileage for a year is reasonably expected to be—

(a) For transporting employees in connection with travel between their residences and their place of employment; and

(b) On trips during which the number of employees transported for commuting is at least one-half of the adult seating capacity of the vehicle (excluding the driver).

Q-3. What are transit passes?

A-3. A transit pass is any pass, token, farecard, voucher, or similar item (including an item ex-changeable for fare media) that entitles a person to transportation—

(a) On mass transit facilities (whether or not publicly owned); or

(b) Provided by any person in the business of transporting persons for compensation or hire in a highway vehicle with a seating capacity of at least 6 adults (excluding the driver).

Q-4. What is qualified parking?

A-4. (a) Qualified parking is parking provided to an employee by an employer—

(1) On or near the employer's business premises; or

(2) At a location from which the employee commutes to work (including commuting by carpool, commuter highway vehicle, mass transit facilities, or transportation provided by any person in the business of transporting persons for compensation or hire).

(b) For purposes of section 132(f), parking on or near the employer's business premises includes parking on or near a work location at which the employee provides services for the employer. However, qualified parking does not include—

(1) The value of parking provided to an employee that is excludable from gross income under section 132(a)(3) (as a working condition fringe), or

(2) Reimbursement paid to an employee for parking costs that is excludable from gross income as an amount treated as paid under an accountable plan. See § 1.62-2.

(c) However, parking on or near property used by the employee for residential purposes is not qualified parking.

(d) Parking is provided by an employer if—

(1) The parking is on property that the employer owns or leases;

(2) The employer pays for the parking; or

(3) The employer reimburses the employee for parking expenses (see Q/A-16 of this section for rules relating to cash reimbursements).

Q-5. May qualified transportation fringes be provided to individuals who are not employees?

A-5. An employer may provide qualified transportation fringes only to individuals who are currently employees of the employer at the time the qualified transportation fringe is provided. The term employee for purposes of qualified transportation fringes is defined in § 1.132-1(b)(2)(i). This term includes only common law employees and other statutory employees, such as officers of corporations. See Q/A-24 of this section for rules regarding partners, 2-percent shareholders, and independent contractors.

Q-6. Must a qualified transportation fringe benefit plan be in writing?

A-6. No. Section 132(f) does not require that a qualified transportation fringe benefit plan be in writing.

Q-7. Is there a limit on the value of qualified transportation fringes that may be excluded from an employee's gross income?

A-7. (a) *Transportation in a commuter highway vehicle and transit passes.* Before January 1, 2002, up to $65 per month is excludable from the gross income of an employee for transportation in a commuter highway vehicle and transit passes provided by an employer. On January 1, 2002, this amount is increased to $100 per month.

(b) *Parking.* Up to $175 per month is excludable from the gross income of an employee for qualified parking.

(c) *Combination.* An employer may provide qualified parking benefits in addition to transportation in a commuter highway vehicle and transit passes.

(d) *Cost-of-living adjustments.* The amounts in paragraphs (a) and (b) of this Q/A-7 are adjusted annually, beginning with 2000, to reflect cost-of-living. The adjusted figures are announced by the Service before the beginning of the year.

Q-8. What amount is includible in an employee's wages for income and employment tax purposes if the value of the qualified transportation fringe exceeds the applicable statutory monthly limit?

A-8. (a) Generally, an employee must include in gross income the amount by which the fair market value of the benefit exceeds the sum of the amount, if any, paid by the employee and any amount excluded from gross income under section 132(a)(5). Thus, assuming no other statutory exclusion applies, if an employer provides an employee with a qualified transportation fringe that exceeds the applicable statutory monthly limit and the employee does not make any payment, the value of the benefits provided in excess of the applicable statutory monthly limit is included in the employee's wages for income and employment tax purposes. See § 1.61-21(b)(1).

(b) The following examples illustrate the principles of this Q/A-8:

Example 1. (i) For each month in a year in which the statutory monthly transit pass limit is $100 (i.e., a year after 2001), Employer M provides a transit pass valued at $110 to Employee D, who does not pay any amount to Employer M for the transit pass.

(ii) In this *Example 1*, because the value of the monthly transit pass exceeds the statutory monthly limit by $10, $120 ($110 − $100, times

12 months) must be included in D's wages for income and employment tax purposes for the year with respect to the transit passes.

Example 2. (i) For each month in a year in which the statutory monthly qualified parking limit is $175, Employer M provides qualified parking valued at $195 to Employee E, who does not pay any amount to M for the parking.

(ii) In this *Example 2*, because the fair market value of the qualified parking exceeds the statutory monthly limit by $20, $240 ($195 − $175, times 12 months) must be included in Employee E's wages for income and employment tax purposes for the year with respect to the qualified parking.

Example 3. (i) For each month in a year in which the statutory monthly qualified parking limit is $175, Employer P provides qualified parking with a fair market value of $220 per month to its employees, but charges each employee $45 per month.

(ii) In this *Example 3*, because the sum of the amount paid by an employee ($45) plus the amount excludable for qualified parking ($175) is not less than the fair market value of the monthly benefit, no amount is includible in the employee's wages for income and employment tax purposes with respect to the qualified parking.

* * *

Q-16. How does section 132(f) apply to expense reimbursements?

A-16. (a) *In general.* The term qualified transportation fringe includes cash reimbursement by an employer to an employee for expenses incurred or paid by an employee for transportation in a commuter highway vehicle or qualified parking. The term qualified transportation fringe also includes cash reimbursement for transit passes made under a bona fide reimbursement arrangement, but, in accordance with section 132(f)(3), only if permitted under paragraph (b) of this Q/A-16. The reimbursement must be made under a bona fide reimbursement arrangement which meets the rules of paragraph (c) of this Q/A-16. A payment made before the date an expense has been incurred or paid is not a reimbursement. In addition, a bona fide reimbursement arrangement does not include an arrangement that is dependent solely upon an employee certifying in advance that the employee will incur expenses at some future date.

(b) *Special rule for transit passes*—(1) *In general.* The term *qualified transportation fringe* includes cash reimbursement for transit passes made under a bona fide reimbursement arrangement, but, in accordance with section 132(f)(3), only if no voucher or similar item that may be

Reg. § 1.132-9(b)

exchanged only for a transit pass is readily available for direct distribution by the employer to employees. If a voucher is readily available, the requirement that a voucher be distributed in-kind by the employer is satisfied if the voucher is distributed by the employer or by another person on behalf of the employer (for example, if a transit operator credits amounts to the employee's fare card as a result of payments made to the operator by the employer).

(2) *Voucher or similar item.* For purposes of the special rule in paragraph (b) of this Q/A-16, a transit system voucher is an instrument that may be purchased by employers from a voucher provider that is accepted by one or more mass transit operators (e.g., train, subway, and bus) in an area as fare media or in exchange for fare media. Thus, for example, a transit pass that may be purchased by employers directly from a voucher provider is a transit system voucher.

(3) *Voucher provider.* The term voucher provider means any person in the trade or business of selling transit system vouchers to employers, or any transit system or transit operator that sells vouchers to employers for the purpose of direct distribution to employees. Thus, a transit operator might or might not be a voucher provider. A voucher provider is not, for example, a third-party employee benefits administrator that administers a transit pass benefit program for an employer using vouchers that the employer could obtain directly.

(4) *Readily available.* For purposes of this paragraph (b), a voucher or similar item is readily available for direct distribution by the employer to employees if and only if an employer can obtain it from a voucher provider that—

(i) does not impose fare media charges that cause vouchers to not be readily available as described in paragraph (b)(5) of this section; and

(ii) does not impose other restrictions that cause vouchers to not be readily available as described in paragraph (b)(6) of this section.

→ *Caution: The last sentence of Reg. § 1.132-9(b), Q/A-16(b)(5), below, is applicable for employee tax years beginning after December 31, 2003.*←

(5) *Fare media charges.* For purposes of paragraph (b)(4) of this section, fare media charges relate only to fees paid by the employer to voucher providers for vouchers. The determination of whether obtaining a voucher would result in fare media charges that cause vouchers to not be readily available as described in this paragraph (b) is made with respect to each transit system voucher. If more than one transit system voucher is available for direct distribution to employees, the employer must consider the fees imposed for the lowest cost monthly voucher for purposes of determining whether the fees imposed by the voucher provider satisfy this paragraph. However, if transit system vouchers for multiple transit systems are required in an area to meet the transit needs of the individual employees in that area, the employer has the option of averaging the costs applied to each transit system voucher for purposes of determining whether the fare media charges for transit system vouchers satisfy this paragraph. Fare media charges are described in this paragraph (b)(5), and therefore cause vouchers to not be readily available, if and only if the average annual fare media charges that the employer reasonably expects to incur for transit system vouchers purchased from the voucher provider (disregarding reasonable and customary delivery charges imposed by the voucher provider, e.g., not in excess of $15) are more than 1 percent of the average annual value of the vouchers for a transit system.

(6) *Other restrictions.* For purposes of paragraph (b)(4) of this section, restrictions that cause vouchers to not be readily available are restrictions imposed by the voucher provider other than fare media charges that effectively prevent the employer from obtaining vouchers appropriate for distribution to employees. Examples of such restrictions include—

(i) *Advance purchase requirements.* Advance purchase requirements cause vouchers to not be readily available only if the voucher provider does not offer vouchers at regular intervals or fails to provide the voucher within a reasonable period after receiving payment for the voucher. For example, a requirement that vouchers may be purchased only once per year may effectively prevent an employer from obtaining vouchers for distribution to employees. An advance purchase requirement that vouchers be purchased not more frequently than monthly does not effectively prevent the employer from obtaining vouchers for distribution to employees.

(ii) *Purchase quantity requirements.* Purchase quantity requirements cause vouchers to not be readily available if the voucher provider does not offer vouchers in quantities that are reasonably appropriate to the number of the employer's employees who use mass transportation (for example, the voucher provider requires a $1,000 minimum purchase and the employer seeks to purchase only $200 of vouchers).

(iii) *Limitations on denominations of vouchers that are available.* If the voucher provider does not offer vouchers in denominations appropriate for distribution to the employer's employees, vouchers are not readily available. For example, vouchers provided in $5 increments up to the

Reg. § 1.132-9(b)

monthly limit are appropriate for distribution to employees, while vouchers available only in a denomination equal to the monthly limit are not appropriate for distribution to employees if the amount of the benefit provided to the employer's employees each month is normally less than the monthly limit.

(7) *Example.* The following example illustrates the principles of this paragraph (b):

Example. (i) Company C in City X sells mass transit vouchers to employers in the metropolitan area of X in various denominations appropriate for distribution to employees. Employers can purchase vouchers monthly in reasonably appropriate quantities. Several different bus, rail, van pool, and ferry operators service X, and a number of the operators accept the vouchers either as fare media or in exchange for fare media. To cover its operating expenses, C imposes on each voucher a 50 cents charge, plus a reasonable and customary $15 charge for delivery of each order of vouchers. Employer M disburses vouchers purchased from C to its employees who use operators that accept the vouchers and M reasonably expects that $55 is the average value of the voucher it will purchase from C for the next calendar year.

(ii) In this *Example*, vouchers for X are readily available for direct distribution by the employer to employees because the expected cost of the vouchers disbursed to M's employees for the next calendar year is not more than 1 percent of the value of the vouchers (50 cents divided by $55 equals 0.91 percent), the delivery charges are disregarded because they are reasonable and customary, and there are no other restrictions that cause the vouchers to not be readily available. Thus, any reimbursement of mass transportation costs in X would not be a qualified transportation fringe.

(c) *Substantiation requirements.* Employers that make cash reimbursements must establish a bona fide reimbursement arrangement to establish that their employees have, in fact, incurred expenses for transportation in a commuter highway vehicle, transit passes, or qualified parking. For purposes of section 132(f), whether cash reimbursements are made under a bona fide reimbursement arrangement may vary depending on the facts and circumstances, including the method or methods of payment utilized within the mass transit system. The employer must implement reasonable procedures to ensure that an amount equal to the reimbursement was incurred for transportation in a commuter highway vehicle, transit passes, or qualified parking. The expense must be substantiated within a reasonable period of time. An expense substantiated to the payor within 180 days after it has been paid will be treated as having been substantiated within a reasonable period of time. An employee certification at the time of reimbursement in either written or electronic form may be a reasonable reimbursement procedure depending on the facts and circumstances. Examples of reasonable reimbursement procedures are set forth in paragraph (d) of this Q/A-16.

(d) *Illustrations of reasonable reimbursement procedures.* The following are examples of reasonable reimbursement procedures for purposes of paragraph (c) of this Q/A-16. In each case, the reimbursement is made at or within a reasonable period after the end of the events described in paragraphs (d)(1) through (d)(3) of this section.

(1) An employee presents to the employer a parking expense receipt for parking on or near the employer's business premises, the employee certifies that the parking was used by the employee, and the employer has no reason to doubt the employee's certification.

(2) An employee either submits a used time-sensitive transit pass (such as a monthly pass) to the employer and certifies that he or she purchased it or presents an unused or used transit pass to the employer and certifies that he or she purchased it and the employee certifies that he or she has not previously been reimbursed for the transit pass. In both cases, the employer has no reason to doubt the employee's certification.

(3) If a receipt is not provided in the ordinary course of business (e.g., if the employee uses metered parking or if used transit passes cannot be returned to the user), the employee certifies to the employer the type and the amount of expenses incurred, and the employer has no reason to doubt the employee's certification.

* * *

Q-20. How is the value of parking determined?

A-20. Section 1.61-21(b)(2) applies for purposes of determining the value of parking.

* * *

Q-23. How does section 132(f) interact with other fringe benefit rules?

A-23. For purposes of section 132, the terms working condition fringe and de minimis fringe do not include any qualified transportation fringe under section 132(f). If, however, an employer provides local transportation other than transit passes (without any direct or indirect compensation reduction election), the value of the benefit may be excludable, either totally or partially, under fringe benefit rules other than the qualified transportation fringe rules under section 132(f). See § § 1.132-6(d)(2)(i) (occasional local transportation fare), 1.132-6(d)(2)(iii) (transportation provided under unusual circumstances), and

Reg. § 1.132-9(b)

1.61-21(k) (valuation of local transportation provided to qualified employees). See also Q/A-4(b) of this section.

Q-24. May qualified transportation fringes be provided to individuals who are partners, 2-percent shareholders of S-corporations, or independent contractors?

A-24. (a) *General rule.* Section 132(f)(5)(E) states that self-employed individuals who are employees within the meaning of section 401(c)(1) are not employees for purposes of section 132(f). Therefore, individuals who are partners, sole proprietors, or other independent contractors are not employees for purposes of section 132(f). In addition, under section 1372(a), 2-percent shareholders of S corporations are treated as partners for fringe benefit purposes. Thus, an individual who is both a 2-percent shareholder of an S corporation and a common law employee of that S corporation is not considered an employee for purposes of section 132(f). However, while section 132(f) does not apply to individuals who are partners, 2-percent shareholders of S corporations, or independent contractors, other exclusions for working condition and de minimis fringes may be available as described in paragraphs (b) and (c) of this Q/A-24. See §§ 1.132-1(b)(2) and 1.132-1(b)(4).

(b) *Transit passes.* The working condition and de minimis fringe exclusions under section 132(a)(3) and (4) are available for transit passes provided to individuals who are partners, 2-percent shareholders, and independent contractors. For example, tokens or farecards provided by a partnership to an individual who is a partner that enable the partner to commute on a public transit system (not including privately-operated van pools) are excludable from the partner's gross income if the value of the tokens and farecards in any month does not exceed the dollar amount specified in § 1.132-6(d)(1). However, if the value of a pass provided in a month exceeds the dollar amount specified in § 1.132-6(d)(1), the full value of the benefit provided (not merely the amount in excess of the dollar amount specified in § 1.132-6(d)(1)) is includible in gross income.

(c) *Parking.* The working condition fringe rules under section 132(d) do not apply to commuter parking. See § 1.132-5(a)(1). However, the de minimis fringe rules under section 132(e) are available for parking provided to individuals who are partners, 2-percent shareholders, or independent contractors that qualifies under the de minimis rules. See § 1.132-6(a) and (b).

(d) *Example.* The following example illustrates the principles of this Q/A-24:

Example. (i) Individual G is a partner in partnership P. Individual G commutes to and from G's office every day and parks free of charge in P's lot.

(ii) In this *Example*, the value of the parking is not excluded under section 132(f), but may be excluded under section 132(e) if the parking is a de minimis fringe under § 1.132-6.

Q-25. What is the effective date of this section?

A-25. (a) Except as provided in paragraph (b) of this Q/A-25, this section is applicable for employee taxable years beginning after December 31, 2001. For this purpose, an employer may assume that the employee taxable year is the calendar year.

(b) The last sentence of paragraph (b)(5) of Q/A-16 of this section (relating to whether transit system vouchers for transit passes are readily available) is applicable for employee taxable years beginning after December 31, 2003. For this purpose, an employer may assume that the employee taxable year is the calendar year.

[Reg. § 1.132-9.]

☐ [*T.D.* 8933, 1-10-2001 (*corrected* 4-5-2001).]

Deductions for Personal Exemptions

§ 1.151-1. Deductions for personal exemptions.—* * *

(b) *Exemptions for individual taxpayer and spouse (so-called personal exemptions).* Section 151(b) allows an exemption for the taxpayer and an additional exemption for the spouse of the taxpayer if a joint return is not made by the taxpayer and his spouse, and if the spouse, for the calendar year in which the taxable year of the taxpayer begins, has no gross income and is not the dependent of another taxpayer. Thus, a husband is not entitled to an exemption for his wife on his separate return for the taxable year beginning in a calendar year during which she has any gross income (though insufficient to require her to file a return). Since, in the case of a joint return, there are two taxpayers (although under section 6013 there is only one income for the two taxpayers on such return, *i.e.*, their aggregate income), two exemptions are allowed on such return, one for each taxpayer spouse. If in any case a joint return is made by the taxpayer and his spouse, no other person is allowed an exemption for such spouse even though such other person would have been entitled to claim an exemption for such spouse as a dependent if such joint return had not been made.

* * *

[Reg. § 1.151-1.]

☐ [*T.D.* 6231, 4-25-57. *Amended by T.D.* 7114, 5-17-71 *and T.D.* 7230, 12-21-72.]

Reg. § 1.151-1(b)

§ 1.152-1. General definition of a dependent.—(a)(1) For purposes of the income taxes imposed on individuals by chapter 1 of the Code, the term "dependent" means any individual described in paragraphs (1) through (10) of section 152(a) over half of whose support, for the calendar year in which the taxable year of the taxpayer begins, was received from the taxpayer.

(2)(i) For purposes of determining whether or not an individual received, for a given calendar year, over half of his support from the taxpayer, there shall be taken into account the amount of support received from the taxpayer as compared to the entire amount of support which the individual received from all sources, including support which the individual himself supplied. The term "support" includes food, shelter, clothing, medical and dental care, education, and the like. Generally, the amount of an item of support will be the amount of expense incurred by the one furnishing such item. If the item of support furnished an individual is in the form of property or lodging, it will be necessary to measure the amount of such item of support in terms of its fair market value.

(ii) In computing the amount which is contributed for the support of an individual, there must be included any amount which is contributed by such individual for his own support, including income which is ordinarily excludable from gross income, such as benefits received under the Social Security Act. For example, a father receives $800 social security benefits, $400 interest, and $1,000 from his son during 1955, all of which sums represent his sole support during that year. The fact that the social security benefits of $800 are not includible in the father's gross income does not prevent such amount from entering into the computation of the total amount contributed for the father's support. Consequently, since the son's contribution of $1,000 was less than one-half of the father's support ($2,200) he may not claim his father as a dependent.

(iii)(a) For purposes of determining the amount of support furnished for a child (or children) by a taxpayer for a given calendar year, an arrearage payment made in a year subsequent to a calendar year for which there is an unpaid liability shall not be treated as paid either during that calendar year or in the year of payment, but no amount shall be treated as an arrearage payment to the extent that there is an unpaid liability (determined without regard to such payment) with respect to the support of a child for the taxable year of payment; and

(b) Similarly, payments made prior to any calendar year (whether or not made in the form of a lump sum payment in settlement of the parent's liability for support) shall not be treated as made during such calendar year, but payments made during any calendar year from amounts set aside in trust by a parent in a prior year, shall be treated as made during the calendar year in which paid.

(b) Section 152(a)(9) applies to any individual (other than an individual who at any time during the taxable year was the spouse, determined without regard to section 153, of the taxpayer) who lives with the taxpayer and is a member of the taxpayer's household during the entire taxable year of the taxpayer. An individual is not a member of the taxpayer's household if at any time during the taxable year of the taxpayer the relationship between such individual and the taxpayer is in violation of local law. It is not necessary under section 152(a)(9) that the dependent be related to the taxpayer. For example, foster children may qualify as dependents. It is necessary, however, that the taxpayer both maintain and occupy the household. The taxpayer and dependent will be considered as occupying the household for such entire taxable year notwithstanding temporary absences from the household due to special circumstances. A nonpermanent failure to occupy the common abode by reason of illness, education, business, vacation, military service, or a custody agreement under which the dependent is absent for less than six months in the taxable year of the taxpayer, shall be considered temporary absence due to special circumstances. The fact that the dependent dies during the year shall not deprive the taxpayer of the deduction if the dependent lived in the household for the entire part of the year preceding his death. Likewise, the period during the taxable year preceding the birth of an individual shall not prevent such individual from qualifying as a dependent under section 152(a)(9). Moreover, a child who actually becomes a member of the taxpayer's household during the taxable year shall not be prevented from being considered a member of such household for the entire taxable year, if the child is required to remain in a hospital for a period following its birth, and if such child would otherwise have been a member of the taxpayer's household during such period.

* * *

[Reg. § 1.152-1.]

☐ [*T.D. 6231, 4-25-57. Amended by T.D. 6304, 8-22-58, T.D. 6441, 1-4-60, T.D. 6663, 7-10-63, T.D. 7099, 3-19-71 and T.D. 7114, 5-17-71.*]

§ 1.152-3. Multiple support agreements.—(a) Section 152(c) provides that a taxpayer shall be treated as having contributed over half of the support of an individual for the calendar year (in cases where two or more taxpayers contributed to the support of such individual) if:

(1) No one person contributed over half of the individual's support,

(2) Each member of the group which collectively contributed more than half of the support of the individual would have been entitled to claim the individual as a dependent but for the fact that he did not contribute more than one-half of such support,

(3) The member of the group claiming the individual as a dependent contributed more than 10 percent of the individual's support, and

(4) Each other person in the group who contributed more than 10 percent of such support furnishes to the taxpayer claiming the dependent a written declaration that such other person will not claim the individual as a dependent for any taxable year beginning in such calendar year.

(b) *Examples.* Application of the rule contained in paragraph (a) of this section may be illustrated by the following examples:

Example (1). During the taxable year, brothers A, B, C, and D contributed the entire support of their mother in the following percentages: A, 30 percent; B, 20 percent; C, 29 percent; and D, 21 percent. Any one of the brothers, except for the fact that he did not contribute more than half of her support, would have been entitled to claim his mother as a dependent. Consequently, any one of the brothers could claim a deduction for the exemption of the mother if he obtained a written declaration (as provided in paragraph (a)(4) of this section) from each of the other brothers. Even though A and D together contributed more than one-half the support of the mother, A, if he wished to claim his mother as a dependent, would be required to obtain written declarations from B, C, and D, since each of those three contributed more than 10 percent of the support and, but for the failure to contribute more than half of the mother's support, would have been entitled to claim his mother as a dependent.

Example (2). During the taxable year, E, an individual who resides with his son, S, received his entire support for that year as follows:

Source	Percentage of total
Social Security	25
N, an unrelated neighbor	11
B, a brother	14
D, a daughter	10
S, a son	40
Total received by E	100

B, D, and S are persons each of whom, but for the fact that none contributed more than half of E's support, could claim E as a dependent for the taxable year. The three together contributed 64 percent of E's support, and, thus, each is a member of the group to be considered for the purpose of section 152(c). B and S are the only members of such group who can meet all the requirements of section 152(c), and either one could claim E as a dependent for his taxable year if he obtained a written declaration (as provided in paragraph (a)(4) of this section) signed by the other, and furnished the other information required by the return with respect to all the contributions to E. Inasmuch as D did not contribute more than 10 percent of E's support, she is not entitled to claim E as a dependent for the taxable year nor is she required to furnish a written declaration with respect to her contributions to E. N contributed over 10 percent of the support of E, but, since he is an unrelated neighbor, he does not qualify as a member of the group for the purpose of the multiple support agreement under section 152(c).

(c)(1) The member of a group of contributors who claims an individual as a dependent for a taxable year beginning before January 1, 2002, under the multiple support agreement provisions of section 152(c) must attach to the member's income tax return for the year of the deduction a written declaration from each of the other persons who contributed more than 10 percent of the support of such individual and who, but for the failure to contribute more than half of the support of the individual, would have been entitled to claim the individual as a dependent.

(2) The taxpayer claiming an individual as a dependent for a taxable year beginning after December 31, 2001, under the multiple support agreement provisions of section 152(c) must provide with the income tax return for the year of the deduction—

(i) A statement identifying each of the other persons who contributed more than 10 percent of the support of the individual and who, but for the failure to contribute more than half of the support of the individual, would have been entitled to claim the individual as a dependent; and

(ii) A statement indicating that the taxpayer obtained a written declaration from each of the persons described in section 152(c)(2) waiving the right to claim the individual as a dependent.

(3) The taxpayer claiming the individual as a dependent for a taxable year beginning after December 31, 2001, must retain the waiver declarations and should be prepared to furnish the waiver declarations and any other information necessary to substantiate the claim, which may include a statement showing the names of all contributors (whether or not members of the group described in section 152(c)(2)) and the amount contributed by

Reg. § 1.152-3(a)(1)

each to the support of the claimed dependent. [Reg. § 1.152-3.]

☐ [*T.D. 6231, 4-25-57. Amended by T.D. 6663, 7-10-63; T.D. 8989, 4-23-2002 and T.D. 9040, 1-30-2003.*]

§ 1.152-4. Support test in case of child of divorced or separated parents.—* * *

* * *

(b) *Custody.* "Custody", for purposes of this section, will be determined by the terms of the most recent decree of divorce or separate mainte-nance, or subsequent custody decree, or, if none, a written separation agreement. In the event of so-called "split" custody, or if neither a decree or agreement establishes who has custody, or if the validity or continuing effect of such decree or agreement is uncertain by reason of proceedings pending on the last day of the calendar year, "custody" will be deemed to be with the parent who, as between both parents, has the physical custody of the child for the greater portion of the calendar year.

* * *

[Reg. § 1.152-4.]

☐ [*T.D. 7099, 3-19-71. Amended by T.D. 7145, 10-14-71 and T.D. 7639, 8-17-79.*]

§ 1.152-4T. Dependency exemption in the case of child of divorced parent, etc. (Tempo-rary).—(a) *In general.*—

Q-1. Which parent may claim the dependency exemption in the case of a child of divorced or separated parents?

A-1. Provided the parents together would have been entitled to the dependency exemption had they been married and filing a joint return, the parent having custody of a child for the greater portion of the year (the custodial parent) will generally be entitled to the dependency exemp-tion. This rule applies to parents not living to-gether during the last 6 months of the calendar year, as well as those divorced or separated under a separation agreement.

Q-2. Are there any exceptions to the general rule in A-1?

A-2. Yes, there are three exceptions. The gen-eral rule does not apply (i) if a multiple support agreement is in effect (see section 152(c)), (ii) if a decree or agreement executed prior to January 1, 1985 provides that the custodial parent has agreed to release his or her claim to the depen-dency exemption to the noncustodial parent and the noncustodial parent provides at least $600 of support to the child (see section 152(e)(4)), or (iii) if the custodial parent relinquishes the exemption in the manner described in A-3.

Q-3. How may the exemption for a dependent child be claimed by a noncustodial parent?

A-3. A noncustodial parent may claim the ex-emption for a dependent child only if the noncus-todial parent attaches to his/her income tax return for the year of the exemption a written declaration from the custodial parent stating that he/she will not claim the child as a dependent for the taxable year beginning in such calendar year. The written declaration may be made on a form to be provided by the Service for this purpose. Once the Service has released the form, any decla-ration made other than on the official form shall conform to the substance of such form.

Q-4. For what period may a custodial parent release to the noncustodial parent a claim to the exemption for a dependent child?

A-4. The exemption may be released for a single year, for a number of specified years (for example, alternate years), or for all future years, as speci-fied in the declaration. If the exemption is re-leased for more than one year, the original release must be attached to the return of the noncustodial spouse and a copy of such release must be at-tached to his/her return for each succeeding taxa-ble year for which he/she claims the dependency exemption.

Q-5. May only the custodial parent claim a deduction under section 213(d) for medical ex-penses paid by the parent or an income exclusion under section 105(b) for medical expenses paid by an employer for a dependent child?

A-5. No. Under the new rules, if a child receives over half of his support during the calendar year from his parents who are divorced or legally sepa-rated under a decree of divorce or separate main-tenance, or who are separated under a written separation agreement, that child will be treated as a dependent of both parents for purposes of sections 105(b) and 213(d). Thus, a parent can deduct medical expenses paid by that parent for a child even though a dependency exemption for the child is claimed by the other parent. The special rule of sections 105(b) and 213(d) does not apply where over half of the support of a child is treated as having been received from a person under the provisions of section 152(c) (relating to multiple support agreements).

Q-6. When does section 152(e), as amended by the Tax Reform Act of 1984, become effective?

A-6. Section 152(e), as amended, is effective with respect to dependency exemptions for taxa-ble years beginning after December 31, 1984. [Temporary Reg. § 1.152-4T.]

☐ [*T.D. 7973, 8-30-84.*]

Reg. § 1.152-4T(a)

Itemized Deductions for Individuals and Corporations

§ 1.162-1. Business expenses.—(a) *In general.* Business expenses deductible from gross income include the ordinary and necessary expenditures directly connected with or pertaining to the taxpayer's trade or business, except items which are used as the basis for a deduction or a credit under provisions of law other than section 162. The cost of goods purchased for resale, with proper adjustment for opening and closing inventories, is deducted from gross sales in computing gross income. See paragraph (a) of § 1.61-3. Among the items included in business expenses are management expenses, commissions (but see section 263 and the regulations thereunder), labor, supplies, incidental repairs, operating expenses of automobiles used in the trade or business, traveling expenses while away from home solely in the pursuit of a trade or business (see § 1.162-2), advertising and other selling expenses, together with insurance premiums against fire, storm, theft, accident, or other similar losses in the case of a business, and rental for the use of business property. No such item shall be included in business expenses, however, to the extent that it is used by the taxpayer in computing the cost of property included in its inventory or used in determining the gain or loss basis of its plant, equipment, or other property. See section 1054 and the regulations thereunder. A deduction for an expense paid or incurred after December 30, 1969, which would otherwise be allowable under section 162 shall not be denied on the grounds that allowance of such deduction would frustrate a sharply defined public policy. See section 162(c), (f), and (g) and the regulations thereunder. The full amount of the allowable deduction for ordinary and necessary expenses in carrying on a business is deductible, even though such expenses exceed the gross income derived during the taxable year from such business. In the case of any sports program to which section 114 (relating to sports programs conducted for the American National Red Cross) applies, expenses described in section 114(a)(2) shall be allowable as deductions under section 162(a) only to the extent that such expenses exceed the amount excluded from gross income under section 114(a).

(b) *Cross references.* (1) For charitable contributions by individuals and corporations not deductible under section 162, see § 1.162-15.

(2) For items not deductible, see sections 261-276, inclusive, and the regulations thereunder.

(3) For research and experimental expenditures, see section 174 and regulations thereunder.

(4) For soil and water conservation expenditures, see section 175 and regulations thereunder.

(5) For expenditures attributable to grant or loan by United States for encouragement of exploration for, or development or mining of, critical and strategic minerals or metals, see section 621 and regulations thereunder.

(6) For treatment of certain rental payments with respect to public utility property, see section 167(1) and § 1.167(1)-3.

(7) For limitations on the deductibility of miscellaneous itemized deductions, see section 67 and § § 1.67-1T through 1.67-4T.

(8) For the timing of deductions with respect to notional principal contracts, see § 1.446-3. [Reg. § 1.162-1.]

☐ [*T.D.* 6291, 4-3-58. *Amended by T.D.* 6690, 11-18-63; *T.D.* 6996, 1-17-69; *T.D.* 7315, 6-6-74; *T.D.* 7345, 2-19-75; *T.D.* 8189, 3-25-88 *and T.D.* 8491, 10-8-93.]

§ 1.162-2. Traveling expenses.—(a) Traveling expenses include travel fares, meals and lodging, and expenses incident to travel such as expenses for sample rooms, telephone and telegraph, public stenographers, etc. Only such traveling expenses as are reasonable and necessary in the conduct of the taxpayer's business and directly attributable to it may be deducted. If the trip is undertaken for other than business purposes, the travel fares and expenses incident to travel are personal expenses and the meals and lodging are living expenses. If the trip is solely on business, the reasonable and necessary traveling expenses, including travel fares, meals and lodging, and expenses incident to travel, are business expenses. For the allowance of traveling expenses as deductions in determining adjusted gross income, see section 62(2)(B) and the regulations thereunder.

(b)(1) If a taxpayer travels to a destination and while at such destination engages in both business and personal activities, traveling expenses to and from such destination are deductible only if the trip is related primarily to the taxpayer's trade or business. If the trip is primarily personal in nature, the traveling expenses to and from the destination are not deductible even though the taxpayer engages in business activities while at such destination. However, expenses while at the destination which are properly allocable to the taxpayer's trade or business are deductible even though the traveling expenses to and from the destination are not deductible.

(2) Whether a trip is related primarily to the taxpayer's trade or business or is primarily personal in nature depends on the facts and circumstances in each case. The amount of time during the period of the trip which is spent on personal activity compared to the amount of time spent on activities directly relating to the taxpayer's trade

or business is an important factor in determining whether the trip is primarily personal. If, for example, a taxpayer spends one week while at a destination on activities which are directly related to his trade or business and subsequently spends an additional five weeks for vacation or other personal activities, the trip will be considered primarily personal in nature in the absence of a clear showing to the contrary.

(c) Where a taxpayer's wife accompanies him on a business trip, expenses attributable to her travel are not deductible unless it can be adequately shown that the wife's presence on the trip has a bona fide business purpose. The wife's performance of some incidental service does not cause her expenses to qualify as deductible business expenses. The same rules apply to any other members of the taxpayer's family who accompany him on such a trip.

(d) Expenses paid or incurred by a taxpayer in attending a convention or other meeting may constitute an ordinary and necessary business expense under section 162 depending upon the facts and circumstances of each case. No distinction will be made between self-employed persons and employees. The fact that an employee uses vacation or leave time or that his attendance at the convention is voluntary will not necessarily prohibit the allowance of the deduction. The allowance of deductions for such expenses will depend upon whether there is a sufficient relationship between the taxpayer's trade or business and his attendance at the convention or other meeting so that he is benefiting or advancing the interests of his trade or business by such attendance. If the convention is for political, social or other purposes unrelated to the taxpayer's trade or business, the expenses are not deductible.

(e) Commuters' fares are not considered as business expenses and are not deductible.

(f) For rules with respect to the reporting and substantiation of traveling and other business expenses of employees for taxable years beginning after December 31, 1957, see § 1.162-17. [Reg. § 1.162-2.]

☐ [*T.D.* 6291, 4-3-58. *Amended by T.D.* 6306, 8-27-58.]

§ 1.162-3. Cost of materials.—Taxpayers carrying materials and supplies on hand should include in expenses the charges for materials and supplies only in the amount that they are actually consumed and used in operation during the taxable year for which the return is made, provided that the costs of such materials and supplies have not been deducted in determining the net income or loss or taxable income for any previous year. If a taxpayer carries incidental materials or supplies on hand for which no record of consumption is kept or of which physical inventories at the beginning and end of the year are not taken, it will be permissible for the taxpayer to include in his expenses and to deduct from gross income the total cost of such supplies and materials as were purchased during the taxable year for which the return is made, provided the taxable income is clearly reflected by this method. [Reg. § 1.162-3.]

☐ [*T.D.* 6291, 4-3-58.]

§ 1.162-4. Repairs.—The cost of incidental repairs which neither materially add to the value of the property nor appreciably prolong its life, but keep it in an ordinarily efficient operating condition, may be deducted as an expense, provided the cost of acquisition or production or the gain or loss basis of the taxpayer's plant, equipment, or other property, as the case may be, is not increased by the amount of such expenditures. Repairs in the nature of replacements, to the extent that they arrest deterioration and appreciably prolong the life of the property, shall either be capitalized and depreciated in accordance with section 167 or charged against the depreciation reserve if such an account is kept. [Reg. § 1.162-4.]

☐ [*T.D.* 6291, 4-3-58.]

§ 1.162-5. Expenses for education.—(a) *General rule.* Expenditures made by an individual for education (including research undertaken as part of his educational program) which are not expenditures of a type described in paragraph (b)(2) or (3) of this section are deductible as ordinary and necessary business expenses (even though the education may lead to a degree) if the education—

(1) Maintains or improves skills required by the individual in his employment or other trade or business, or

(2) Meets the express requirements of the individual's employer, or the requirements of applicable law or regulations, imposed as a condition to the retention by the individual of an established employment relationship, status, or rate of compensation.

(b) *Nondeductible educational expenditures*— (1) *In general.* Educational expenditures described in subparagraphs (2) and (3) of this paragraph are personal expenditures or constitute an inseparable aggregate of personal and capital expenditures and, therefore, are not deductible as ordinary and necessary business expenses even though the education may maintain or improve skills required by the individual in his employment or other trade or business or may meet the express requirements of the individual's employer or of applicable law or regulations.

(2) *Minimum educational requirements.* (i) The first category of nondeductible educational expenses within the scope of subparagraph (1) of this paragraph are expenditures made by an indi-

Reg. § 1.162-5(b)(2)

vidual for education which is required of him in order to meet the minimum educational requirements for qualification in his employment or other trade or business. The minimum education necessary to qualify for a position or other trade or business must be determined from a consideration of such factors as the requirements of the employer, the applicable law and regulations, and the standards of the profession, trade, or business involved. The fact that an individual is already performing service in an employment status does not establish that he has met the minimum educational requirements for qualification in that employment. Once an individual has met the minimum educational requirements for qualification in his employment or other trade or business (as in effect when he enters the employment or trade or business), he shall be treated as continuing to meet those requirements even though they are changed.

(ii) The minimum educational requirements for qualification of a particular individual in a position in an educational institution is the minimum level of education (in terms of aggregate college hours or degree) which under the applicable laws or regulations, in effect at the time this individual is first employed in such position, is normally required of an individual initially being employed in such a position. If there are no normal requirements as to the minimum level of education required for a position in an educational institution, then an individual in such a position shall be considered to have met the minimum educational requirements for qualification in that position when he becomes a member of the faculty of the educational institution. The determination of whether an individual is a member of the faculty of an educational institution must be made on the basis of the particular practices of the institution. However, an individual will ordinarily be considered to be a member of the faculty of an institution if (a) he has tenure or his years of service are being counted toward obtaining tenure; (b) the institution is making contributions to a retirement plan (other than Social Security or a similar program) in respect of his employment; or (c) he has a vote in faculty affairs.

(iii) The application of this subparagraph may be illustrated by the following examples:

Example (1). General facts: State X requires a bachelor's degree for beginning secondary school teachers which must include 30 credit hours of professional educational courses. In addition, in order to retain his position, a secondary school teacher must complete a fifth year of preparation within 10 years after beginning his employment. If an employing school official certifies to the State Department of Education that appli-

cants having a bachelor's degree and the required courses in professional education cannot be found, he may hire individuals as secondary school teachers if they have completed a minimum of 90 semester hours of college work. However, to be retained in his position, such an individual must obtain his bachelor's degree and complete the required professional educational courses within 3 years after his employment commences. Under these facts, a bachelor's degree, without regard to whether it includes 30 credit hours of professional educational courses, is considered to be the minimum educational requirement for qualification as a secondary school teacher in State X. This is the case notwithstanding the number of teachers who are actually hired without such a degree. The following are examples of the application of these facts in particular situations:

Situation 1. A, at the time he is employed as a secondary school teacher in State X, has a bachelor's degree including 30 credit hours of professional educational courses. After his employment, A completes a fifth college year of education and, as a result, is issued a standard certificate. The fifth college year of education undertaken by A is not education required to meet the minimum educational requirements for qualification as a secondary school teacher. Accordingly, the expenditures for such education are deductible unless the expenditures are for education which is part of a program of study being pursued by A which will lead to qualifying him in a new trade or business.

Situation 2. Because of a shortage of applicants meeting the stated requirements, B, who has a bachelor's degree, is employed as a secondary school teacher in State X even though he has only 20 credit hours of professional educational courses. After his employment, B takes an additional 10 credit hours of professional educational courses. Since these courses do not constitute education required to meet the minimum educational requirements for qualification as a secondary school teacher which is a bachelor's degree and will not lead to qualifying B in a new trade or business, the expenditures for such courses are deductible.

Situation 3. Because of a shortage of applicants meeting the requirements, C is employed as a secondary school teacher in State X although he has only 90 semester hours of college work towards his bachelor's degree. After his employment, C undertakes courses leading to a bachelor's degree. These courses (including any courses in professional education) constitute education required to meet the minimum educational requirements for qualification as a secondary school teacher. Accordingly, the expenditures for such education are not deductible.

Reg. § 1.162-5(b)(2)

Situation 4. Subsequent to the employment of A, B, and C, but before they have completed a fifth college year of education, State X changes its requirements affecting secondary school teachers to provide that beginning teachers must have completed 5 college years of preparation. In the cases of A, B, and C, a fifth college year of education is not considered to be education undertaken to meet the minimum educational requirements for qualification as a secondary school teacher. Accordingly, expenditures for a fifth year of college will be deductible unless the expenditures are for education which is part of a program being pursued by A, B, or C which will lead to qualifying him in a new trade or business.

Example (2). D, who holds a bachelor's degree, obtains temporary employment as an instructor at University Y and undertakes graduate courses as a candidate for a graduate degree. D may become a faculty member only if he obtains a graduate degree and may continue to hold a position as instructor only so long as he shows satisfactory progress towards obtaining this graduate degree. The graduate courses taken by D constitute education required to meet the minimum educational requirements for qualification in D's trade or business and, thus, the expenditures for such courses are not deductible.

Example (3). E, who has completed 2 years of a normal 3-year law school course leading to a bachelor of laws degree (LL.B.), is hired by a law firm to do legal research and perform other functions on a full-time basis. As a condition to continued employment, E is required to obtain an LL.B. and pass the State bar examination. E completes his law school education by attending night law school, and he takes a bar review course in order to prepare for the State bar examination. The law courses and bar review course constitute education required to meet the minimum educational requirements for qualification in E's trade or business and, thus, the expenditures for such courses are not deductible.

(3) *Qualification for new trade or business.* (i) The second category of nondeductible educational expenses within the scope of subparagraph (1) of this paragraph are expenditures made by an individual for education which is part of a program of study being pursued by him which will lead to qualifying him in a new trade or business. In the case of an employee, a change of duties does not constitute a new trade or business if the new duties involve the same general type of work as is involved in the individual's present employment. For this purpose, all teaching and related duties shall be considered to involve the same general type of work. The following are examples of changes in duties which do not constitute new trades or businesses:

(*a*) Elementary to secondary school classroom teacher.

(*b*) Classroom teacher in one subject (such as mathematics) to classroom teacher in another subject (such as science).

(*c*) Classroom teacher to guidance counselor.

(*d*) Classroom teacher to principal.

(ii) The application of this subparagraph to individuals other than teachers may be illustrated by the following examples:

Example (1). A, a self-employed individual practicing a profession other than law, for example, engineering, accounting, etc., attends law school at night and after completing his law school studies receives a bachelor of laws degree. The expenditures made by A in attending law school are nondeductible because this course of study qualifies him for a new trade or business.

Example (2). Assume the same facts as in example (1) except that A has the status of an employee rather than a self-employed individual, and that his employer requires him to obtain a bachelor of laws degree. A intends to continue practicing his nonlegal profession as an employee of such employer. Nevertheless, the expenditures made by A in attending law school are not deductible since this course of study qualifies him for a new trade or business.

Example (3). B, a general practitioner of medicine, takes a 2-week course reviewing new developments in several specialized fields of medicine. B's expenses for the course are deductible because the course maintains or improves skills required by him in his trade or business and does not qualify him for a new trade or business.

Example (4). C, while engaged in the private practice of psychiatry, undertakes a program of study and training at an accredited psychoanalytic institute which will lead to qualifying him to practice psychoanalysis. C's expenditures for such study and training are deductible because the study and training maintains or improves skills required by him in his trade or business and does not qualify him for a new trade or business.

(c) *Deductible educational expenditures*—(1) *Maintaining or improving skills.* The deduction under the category of expenditures for education which maintains or improves skills required by the individual in his employment or other trade or business includes refresher courses or courses dealing with current developments as well as academic or vocational courses provided the expenditures for the courses are not within either category of nondeductible expenditures described in paragraph (b) (2) or (3) of this section.

Reg. § 1.162-5(c)(1)

(2) Meeting requirements of employer. An individual is considered to have undertaken education in order to meet the express requirements of his employer, or the requirements of applicable law or regulations, imposed as a condition to the retention by the taxpayer of his established employment relationship, status, or rate of compensation only if such requirements are imposed for a bona fide business purpose of the individual's employer. Only the minimum education necessary to the retention by the individual of his established employment relationship, status, or rate of compensation may be considered as undertaken to meet the express requirements of the taxpayer's employer. However, education in excess of such minimum education may qualify as education undertaken in order to maintain or improve the skills required by the taxpayer in his employment or other trade or business (see subparagraph (1) of this paragraph). In no event, however, is a deduction allowable for expenditures for education which, even though for education required by the employer or applicable law or regulations, are within one of the categories of nondeductible expenditures described in paragraph (b)(2) and (3) of this section.

(d) *Travel as a form of education.* Subject to the provisions of paragraph (b) and (e) of this section, expenditures for travel (including travel while on sabbatical leave) as a form of education are deductible only to the extent such expenditures are attributable to a period of travel that is directly related to the duties of the individual in his employment or other trade or business. For this purpose, a period of travel shall be considered directly related to the duties of the individual in his employment or other trade or business only if the major portion of the activities during such period is of a nature which directly maintains or improves skills required by the individual in such employment or other trade or business. The approval of a travel program by an employer or the fact that travel is accepted by an employer in the fulfillment of its requirements for retention of rate of compensation, status or employment, is not determinative that the required relationship exists between the travel involved and the duties of the individual in his particular position.

(e) *Travel away from home.* (1) If an individual travels away from home primarily to obtain education the expenses of which are deductible under this section, his expenditures for travel, meals, and lodging while away from home are deductible. However, if as an incident of such trip the individual engages in some personal activity such as sightseeing, social visiting, or entertaining, or other recreation, the portion of the expenses attributable to such personal activity constitutes nondeductible personal or living expenses and is

not allowable as a deduction. If the individual's travel away from home is primarily personal, the individual's expenditures for travel, meals and lodging (other than meals and lodging during the time spent in participating in deductible educational pursuits) are not deductible. Whether a particular trip is primarily personal or primarily to obtain education the expenses of which are deductible under this section depends upon all the facts and circumstances of each case. An important factor to be taken into consideration in making the determination is the relative amount of time devoted to personal activity as compared with the time devoted to educational pursuits. The rules set forth in this paragraph are subject to the provisions of section 162(a)(2), relating to deductibility of certain traveling expenses, and section 274(c) and (d), relating to allocation of certain foreign travel expenses and substantiation required, respectively, and the regulations thereunder.

(2) *Examples.* The application of this subsection may be illustrated by the following examples:

Example (1). A, a self-employed tax practitioner, decides to take a 1-week course in new developments in taxation, which is offered in City X, 500 miles away from his home. His primary purpose in going to X is to take the course, but he also takes a side trip to City Y (50 miles from X) for 1 day, takes a sightseeing trip while in X, and entertains some personal friends. A's transportation expenses to City X and return to his home are deductible but his transportation expenses to City Y are not deductible. A's expenses for meals and lodging while away from home will be allocated between his educational pursuits and his personal activities. Those expenses which are entirely personal, such as sightseeing and entertaining friends, are not deductible to any extent.

Example (2). The facts are the same as in example (1) except that A's primary purpose in going to City X is to take a vacation. This purpose is indicated by several factors, one of which is the fact that he spends only 1 week attending the tax course and devotes 5 weeks entirely to personal activities. None of A's transportation expenses are deductible and his expenses for meals and lodging while away from home are not deductible to the extent attributable to personal activities. His expenses for meals and lodging allocable to the week attending the tax course are, however, deductible.

Example (3). B, a high school mathematics teacher in New York City, in the summertime travels to a university in California in order to take a mathematics course the expense of which is deductible under this section. B pursues only one-fourth of a full course of study and the remainder of her time is devoted to personal activities the

Reg. § 1.162-5(c)(2)

expense of which is not deductible. Absent a showing by B of a substantial nonpersonal reason for taking the course in the university in California, the trip is considered taken primarily for personal reasons and the cost of traveling from New York City to California and return would not be deductible. However, one-fourth of the cost of B's meals and lodging while attending the university in California may be considered properly allocable to deductible educational pursuits and, therefore, is deductible. [Reg. § 1.162-5.]

☐ [*T.D. 6291, 4-3-58. Amended by T.D. 6918, 5-1-67.*]

§ 1.162-6. **Professional expenses.**—A professional man may claim as deductions the cost of supplies used by him in the practice of his profession, expenses paid or accrued in the operation and repair of an automobile used in making professional calls, dues to professional societies and subscriptions to professional journals, the rent paid or accrued for office rooms, the cost of the fuel, light, water, telephone, etc., used in such offices, and the hire of office assistants. Amounts currently paid or accrued for books, furniture, and professional instruments and equipment, the useful life of which is short, may be deducted. [Reg. § 1.162-6.]

☐ [*T.D. 6291, 4-3-58.*]

§ 1.162-7. **Compensation for personal services.**—(a) There may be included among the ordinary and necessary expenses paid or incurred in carrying on any trade or business a reasonable allowance for salaries or other compensation for personal services actually rendered. The test of deductibility in the case of compensation payments is whether they are reasonable and are in fact payments purely for services.

(b) The test set forth in paragraph (a) of this section and its practical application may be further stated and illustrated as follows:

(1) Any amount paid in the form of compensation, but not in fact as the purchase price of services is not deductible. An ostensible salary paid by a corporation may be a distribution of a dividend on stock. This is likely to occur in the case of a corporation having few shareholders, practically all of whom draw salaries. If in such a case the salaries are in excess of those ordinarily paid for similar services and the excessive payments correspond or bear a close relationship to the stockholdings of the officers or employees, it would seem likely that the salaries are not paid wholly for services rendered, but that the excessive payments are a distribution of earnings upon the stock. An ostensible salary may be in part payment for property. This may occur, for example, where a partnership sells out to a corporation, the former partners agreeing to continue in the service of the corporation. In such a case it may be found that the salaries of the former partners are not merely for services, but in part constitute payment for the transfer of their business.

(2) The form or method of fixing compensation is not decisive as to deductibility. While any form of contingent compensation invites scrutiny as a possible distribution of earnings of the enterprise, it does not follow that payments on a contingent basis are to be treated fundamentally on any basis different from that applying to compensation at a flat rate. Generally speaking, if contingent compensation is paid pursuant to a free bargain between the employer and the individual made before the services are rendered, not influenced by any consideration on the part of the employer other than that of securing on fair and advantageous terms the services of the individual, it should be allowed as a deduction even though in the actual working out of the contract it may prove to be greater than the amount which would ordinarily be paid.

(3) In any event the allowance for the compensation paid may not exceed what is reasonable under all the circumstances. It is, in general, just to assume that reasonable and true compensation is only such amount as would ordinarily be paid for like services by like enterprises under like circumstances. The circumstances to be taken into consideration are those existing at the date when the contract for services was made, not those existing at the date when the contract is questioned.

(4) For disallowance of deduction in the case of certain transfers of stock pursuant to employees stock options, see section 421 and the regulations thereunder. [Reg. § 1.162-7.]

☐ [*T.D. 6291, 4-3-58.*]

§ 1.162-8. **Treatment of excessive compensation.**—The income tax liability of the recipient in respect of an amount ostensibly paid to him as compensation, but not allowed to be deducted as such by the payor, will depend upon the circumstances of each case. Thus, in the case of excessive payments by corporations, if such payments correspond or bear a close relationship to stockholders, and are found to be a distribution of earnings or profits, the excessive payments will be treated as a dividend. If such payments constitute payment for property, they should be treated by the payor as a capital expenditure and by the recipient as part of the purchase price. In the absence of evidence to justify other treatment, excessive payments for salaries or other compensation for personal services will be included in gross income of the recipient. [Reg. § 1.162-8.]

☐ [*T.D. 6291, 4-3-58.*]

Reg. § 1.162-8

§ 1.162-9. Bonuses to employees.—Bonuses to employees will constitute allowable deductions from gross income when such payments are made in good faith and as additional compensation for the services actually rendered by the employees, provided such payments, when added to the stipulated salaries, do not exceed a reasonable compensation for the services rendered. It is immaterial whether such bonuses are paid in cash or in kind or partly in cash and partly in kind. Donations made to employees and others, which do not have in them the element of compensation or which are in excess of reasonable compensation for services, are not deductible from gross income. [Reg. § 1.162-9.]

☐ [T.D. 6291, 4-3-58.]

§ 1.162-11. Rentals.—(a) *Acquisition of a leasehold.* If a leasehold is acquired for business purposes for a specified sum, the purchaser may take as a deduction in his return an aliquot part of such sum each year, based on the number of years the lease has to run. Taxes paid by a tenant to or for a landlord for business property are additional rent and constitute a deductible item to the tenant and taxable income to the landlord, the amount of the tax being deductible by the latter. For disallowance of deduction for income taxes paid by a lessee corporation pursuant to a lease arrangement with the lessor corporation, see section 110 and the regulations thereunder. See section 178 and the regulations thereunder for rules governing the effect to be given renewal options in amortizing the costs incurred after July 28, 1958, of acquiring a lease. See § 1.197-2 for rules governing the amortization of costs to acquire limited interests in section 197 intangibles.

(b) *Improvements by lessee on lessor's property.* (1) The cost to a lessee of erecting buildings or making permanent improvements on property of which he is the lessee is a capital investment, and is not deductible as a business expense. If the estimated useful life in the hands of the taxpayer of the building erected or of the improvements made, determined without regard to the terms of the lease, is longer than the remaining period of the lease, an annual deduction may be made from gross income of an amount equal to the total cost of such improvements divided by the number of years remaining in the term of the lease, and such deduction shall be in lieu of a deduction for depreciation. If, on the other hand, the useful life of such buildings or improvements in the hands of the taxpayer is equal to or shorter than the remaining period of the lease, this deduction shall be computed under the provisions of section 167 (relating to depreciation).

(2) If the lessee began improvements on leased property before July 28, 1958, or if the

lessee was on such date and at all times thereafter under a binding legal obligation to make such improvements, the matter of spreading the cost of erecting buildings or making permanent improvements over the term of the original lease, together with the renewal period or periods depends upon the facts in the particular case, including the presence or absence of an obligation of renewal and the relationship between the parties. As a general rule, unless the lease has been renewed or the facts show with reasonable certainty that the lease will be renewed, the cost or other basis of the lease, or the cost of improvements shall be spread only over the number of years the lease has to run without taking into account any right of renewal. The provisions of this subparagraph may be illustrated by the following examples:

Example (1). A subsidiary corporation leases land from its parent at a fair rental for a 25-year period. The subsidiary erects on the land valuable factory buildings having an estimated useful life of 50 years. These facts show with reasonable certainty that the lease will be renewed, even though the lease contains no option of renewal. Therefore, the cost of the buildings shall be depreciated over the estimated useful life of the buildings in accordance with section 167 and the regulations thereunder.

Example (2). A retail merchandising corporation leases land at a fair rental from an unrelated lessor for the longest period that the lessor is willing to lease the land (30 years). The lessee erects on the land a department store having an estimated useful life of 40 years. These facts do not show with reasonable certainty that the lease will be renewed. Therefore, the cost of the building shall be spread over the remaining term of the lease. An annual deduction may be made of an amount equal to the cost of the building divided by the number of years remaining in the term of the lease, and such deduction shall be in lieu of a deduction for depreciation.

(3) See section 178 and the regulations thereunder for rules governing the effect to be given renewal options where a lessee begins improvements on leased property after July 28, 1958, other than improvements which on such date and at all times thereafter, the lessee was under a binding legal obligation to make. [Reg. § 1.162-11.]

☐ [T.D. 6291, 4-3-58. Amended by T.D. 6520, 12-30-60 and T.D. 8865, 1-20-2000.]

§ 1.162-15. Contributions, dues, etc.—(a) *Contributions to organizations described in section 170—*(1) *In general.* No deduction is allowable under section 162(a) for a contribution or gift by an individual or a corporation if any part thereof is deductible under section 170. For example, if a taxpayer makes a contribution of $5,000 and only $4,000 of this amount is deductible under section 170(a) (whether because of the percentage limitation under either section 170(b)(1) or (2), the requirement as to time of payment, or both) no deduction is allowable under section 162(a) for the remaining $1,000.

(2) *Scope of limitations.* The limitations provided in section 162(b) and this paragraph apply only to payments which are in fact contributions or gifts to organizations described in section 170. For example, payments by a transit company to a local hospital (which is a charitable organization within the meaning of section 170) in consideration of a binding obligation on the part of the hospital to provide hospital services and facilities for the company's employees are not contributions or gifts within the meaning of section 170 and may be deductible under section 162(a) if the requirements of section 162(a) are otherwise satisfied.

(b) *Other contributions.* Donations to organizations other than those described in section 170 which bear a direct relationship to the taxpayer's business and are made with a reasonable expectation of a financial return commensurate with the amount of the donation may constitute allowable deductions as business expenses, provided the donation is not made for a purpose for which a deduction is not allowable by reason of the provisions of paragraph (b)(1)(i) or (c) of § 1.162-20. For example, a transit company may donate a sum of money to an organization (of a class not referred to in section 170) intending to hold a convention in the city in which it operates, with a reasonable expectation that the holding of such convention will augment its income through a greater number of people using its transportation facilities.

(c) *Dues.* Dues and other payments to an organization, such as a labor union or a trade association, which otherwise meet the requirements of the regulations under section 162, are deductible in full. For limitations on the deductibility of dues and other payments, see paragraph (b) and (c) of § 1.162-20.

(d) *Cross reference.* For provisions dealing with expenditures for institutional or "good will" advertising, see § 1.162-20. [Reg. § 1.162-15.]

☐ [*T.D.* 6291, 4-3-58. *Amended by T.D.* 6435, 12-28-59 *and T.D.* 6819, 4-19-65.]

§ 1.162-17. Reporting and substantiation of certain business expenses of employees.—(a) *Introductory.* The purpose of the regulations in this section is to provide rules for the reporting of information on income tax returns by taxpayers who pay or incur ordinary and necessary business expenses in connection with the performance of

services as an employee and to furnish guidance as to the type of records which will be useful in compiling such information and in its substantiation, if required. The rules prescribed in this section do not apply to expenses paid or incurred for incidentals, such as office supplies for the employer or local transportation in connection with an errand. Employees incurring such incidental expenses are not required to provide substantiation for such amounts. The term "ordinary and necessary business expenses" means only those expenses which are ordinary and necessary in the conduct of the taxpayer's business and are directly attributable to such business. The term does not include nondeductible personal, living or family expenses.

(b) *Expenses for which the employee is required to account to his employer—*(1) *Reimbursements equal to expenses.* The employee need not report on his tax return (either itemized or in total amount) expenses for travel, transportation, entertainment, and similar purposes paid or incurred by him solely for the benefit of his employer for which he is required to account and does account to his employer and which are charged directly or indirectly to the employer (for example, through credit cards) or for which the employee is paid through advances, reimbursements, or otherwise, provided the total amount of such advances, reimbursements, and charges is equal to such expenses. In such a case the taxpayer need only state in his return that the total of amounts charged directly or indirectly to his employer through credit cards or otherwise and received from the employer as advances or reimbursements did not exceed the ordinary and necessary business expenses paid or incurred by the employee.

(2) *Reimbursements in excess of expenses.* In case the total of amounts charged directly or indirectly to the employer and received from the employer as advances, reimbursements, or otherwise, exceeds the ordinary and necessary business expenses paid or incurred by the employee and the employee is required to and does account to his employer for such expenses, the taxpayer must include such excess in income and state on his return that he has done so.

(3) *Expenses in excess of reimbursements.* If the employee's ordinary and necessary business expenses exceed the total of the amounts charged directly or indirectly to the employer and received from the employer as advances, reimbursements, or otherwise, and the employee is required to and does account to his employer for such expenses, the taxpayer may make the statement in his return required by subparagraph (1) of this paragraph unless he wishes to claim a deduction for such excess. If, however, he wishes to secure a

deduction for such excess, he must submit a statement showing the following information as part of his tax return:

(i) The total of any charges paid or borne by the employer and of any other amounts received from the employer for payment of expenses, whether by means of advances, reimbursements or otherwise; and

(ii) The nature of his occupation, the number of days away from home on business, and the total amount of ordinary and necessary business expenses paid or incurred by him (including those charged directly or indirectly to the employer through credit cards or otherwise) broken down into such broad categories as transportation, meals and lodging while away from home overnight, entertainment expenses, and other business expenses.

(4) To "account" to his employer as used in this section means to submit an expense account or other required written statement to the employer showing the business nature and the amount of all the employee's expenses (including those charged directly or indirectly to the employer through credit cards or otherwise) broken down into such broad categories as transportation, meals and lodging while away from home overnight, entertainment expenses, and other business expenses. For this purpose, the Commissioner in his discretion may approve reasonable business practices under which mileage, per diem in lieu of subsistence, and similar allowances providing for ordinary and necessary business expenses in accordance with a fixed scale may be regarded as equivalent to an accounting to the employer.

(c) *Expenses for which the employee is not required to account to his employer.* If the employee is not required to account to his employer for his ordinary and necessary business expenses, e.g., travel, transportation, entertainment, and similar items, or, though required, fails to account for such expenses, he must submit, as a part of his tax return, a statement showing the following information:

(1) The total of all amounts received as advances or reimbursements from his employer in connection with the ordinary and necessary business expenses of the employee, including amounts charged directly or indirectly to the employer through credit cards or otherwise; and

(2) The nature of his occupation, the number of days away from home on business, and the total amount of ordinary and necessary business expenses paid or incurred by him (including those charged directly or indirectly to the employer through credit cards or otherwise) broken down into such broad categories as transportation, meals and lodging while away from home over-

night, entertainment expenses, and other business expenses.

(d) *Substantiation of items of expense.* (1) Although the Commissioner may require any taxpayer to substantiate such information concerning expense accounts as may appear to be pertinent in determining tax liability, taxpayers ordinarily will not be called upon to substantiate expense account information except those in the following categories:

(i) A taxpayer who is not required to account to his employer, or who does not account;

(ii) A taxpayer whose expenses exceed the total of amounts charged to his employer and amounts received through advances, reimbursements or otherwise and who claims a deduction on his return for such excess;

(iii) A taxpayer who is related to his employer within the meaning of section 267(b); and

(iv) Other taxpayers in cases where it is determined that the accounting procedures used by the employer for the reporting and substantiation of expenses by employees are not adequate.

(2) The Code contemplates that taxpayers keep such records as will be sufficient to enable the Commissioner to correctly determine income tax liability. Accordingly, it is to the advantage of taxpayers who may be called upon to substantiate expense account information to maintain as adequate and detailed records of travel, transportation, entertainment, and similar business expenses as practical since the burden of proof is upon the taxpayer to show that such expenses were not only paid or incurred but also that they constitute ordinary and necessary business expenses. One method for substantiating expenses incurred by an employee in connection with his employment is through the preparation of a daily diary or record of expenditures, maintained in sufficient detail to enable him to readily identify the amount and nature of any expenditure, and the preservation of supporting documents, especially in connection with large or exceptional expenditures. Nevertheless, it is recognized that by reason of the nature of certain expenses or the circumstances under which they are incurred, it is often difficult for an employee to maintain detailed records or to preserve supporting documents for all his expenses. Detailed records of small expenditures incurred in traveling or for transportation, as for example, tips, will not be required.

(3) Where records are incomplete or documentary proof is unavailable, it may be possible to establish the amount of the expenditures by approximations based upon reliable secondary sources of information and collateral evidence. For example, in connection with an item of traveling expense a taxpayer might establish that he

was in a travel status a certain number of days but that it was impracticable for him to establish the details of all his various items of travel expense. In such a case rail fares or plane fares can usually be ascertained with exactness and automobile costs approximated on the basis of mileage covered. A reasonable approximation of meals and lodging might be based upon receipted hotel bills or upon average daily rates for such accommodations and meals prevailing in the particular community for comparable accommodations. Since detailed records of incidental items are not required, deductions for these items may be based upon a reasonable approximation. In cases where a taxpayer is called upon to substantiate expense account information, the burden is on the taxpayer to establish that the amounts claimed as a deduction are reasonably accurate and constitute ordinary and necessary business expenses paid or incurred by him in connection with his trade or business. In connection with the determination of factual matters of this type, due consideration will be given to the reasonableness of the stated expenditures for the claimed purposes in relation to the taxpayer's circumstances (such as his income and the nature of his occupation), to the reliability and accuracy of records in connection with other items more readily lending themselves to detailed record-keeping, and to all of the facts and circumstances in the particular case.

(e) *Applicability.* (1) Except as provided in subparagraph (2) of this paragraph, the provisions of the regulations in this section are supplemental to existing regulations relating to information required to be submitted with income tax returns, and shall be applicable with respect to taxable years beginning after December 31, 1957, notwithstanding any existing regulation to the contrary.

(2) With respect to taxable years ending after December 31, 1962, but only in respect of periods after such date, the provisions of the regulations in this section are superseded by the regulations under section 274(d) to the extent inconsistent therewith. See § 1.274-5.

(3) For taxable years beginning on or after January 1, 1989, the provisions of this section are superseded by the regulations under section 62(c) to the extent this section is inconsistent with those regulations. See § 1.62-2. [Reg. § 1.162-17.]

□ [*T.D.* 6306, 8-27-58. *Amended by T.D.* 6630, 12-27-62; *T.D.* 8276, 12-7-89 *and T.D.* 8324, 12-14-90.]

§ 1.162-18. Illegal bribes and kickbacks.—(a) *Illegal payments to government officials or employees*—(1) *In general.* No deduction shall be allowed under section 162(a) for any amount paid or incurred, directly or indirectly, to an official or

employee of any government, or of any agency or other instrumentality of any government, if—

(i) In the case of a payment made to an official or employee of a government other than a foreign government described in subparagraph (3)(ii) or (iii) of this paragraph, the payment constitutes an illegal bribe or kickback, or

(ii) In the case of a payment made to an official or employee of a foreign government described in subparagraph (3)(ii) or (iii) of this paragraph, the making of the payment would be unlawful under the laws of the United States (if such laws were applicable to the payment and to the official or employee at the time the expenses were paid or incurred).

No deduction shall be allowed for an accrued expense if the eventual payment thereof would fall within the prohibition of this section. The place where the expenses are paid or incurred is immaterial. For purposes of subdivision (ii) of this subparagraph, lawfulness or unlawfulness of the payment under the laws of the foreign country is immaterial.

(2) *Indirect payment.* For purposes of this paragraph, an indirect payment to an individual shall include any payment which inures to his benefit or promotes his interests, regardless of the medium in which the payment is made and regardless of the identity of the immediate recipient or payor. Thus, for example, payment made to an agent, relative, or independent contractor of an official or employee, or even directly into the general treasury of a foreign country of which the beneficiary is an official or employee, may be treated as an indirect payment to the official or employee, if in fact such payment inures or will inure to his benefit or promotes or will promote his financial or other interests. A payment made by an agent or independent contractor of the taxpayer which benefits the taxpayer shall be treated as an indirect payment by the taxpayer to the official or employee.

(3) *Official or employee of a government.* Any individual officially connected with—

(i) The government of the United States, a State, a territory or possession of the United States, the District of Columbia, or the Commonwealth of Puerto Rico,

(ii) The government of a foreign country, or

(iii) A political subdivision of, or a corporation or other entity serving as an agency or instrumentality of, any of the above,

in whatever capacity, whether on a permanent or temporary basis, and whether or not serving for compensation, shall be included within the term "official or employee of a government", regardless

Reg. § 1.162-18(a)(3)

of the place of residence or post of duty of such individual. An independent contractor would not ordinarily be considered to be an official or employee. For purposes of section 162(c) and this paragraph, the term "foreign country" shall include any foreign nation, whether or not such nation has been accorded diplomatic recognition by the United States. Individuals who purport to act on behalf of or as the government of a foreign nation, or an agency or instrumentality thereof, shall be treated under this section as officials or employees of a foreign government, whether or not such individuals in fact control such foreign nation, agency, or instrumentality, and whether or not such individuals are accorded diplomatic recognition. Accordingly, a group in rebellion against an established government ment shall be treated as officials or employees of a foreign government, as shall officials or employees of the government against which the group is in rebellion.

(4) *Laws of the United States.* The term "laws of the United States", to which reference is made in paragraph (a)(1)(ii) of this section, shall be deemed to include only Federal statutes, including State laws which are assimilated into Federal law by Federal statute, and legislative and interpretative regulations thereunder. The term shall also be limited to statutes which prohibit some act or acts, for the violation of which there is a civil or criminal penalty.

(5) *Burden of proof.* In any proceeding involving the issue of whether, for purposes of section 162(c)(1), a payment made to a government official or employee constitutes an illegal bribe or kickback (or would be unlawful under the laws of the United States) the burden of proof in respect of such issue shall be upon the Commissioner to the same extent as he bears the burden of proof in civil fraud cases under section 7454 (*i.e.,* he must prove the illegality of the payment by clear and convincing evidence).

(6) *Example.* The application of this paragraph may be illustrated by the following example:

Example. X Corp. is in the business of selling hospital equipment in State Y. During 1970, X Corp. employed A who at the time was employed full time by State Y as Superintendent of Hospitals. The purpose of A's employment by X Corp. was to procure for it an improper advantage over other concerns in the making of sales to hospitals in respect of which A, as Superintendent, had authority. X Corp. paid A $5,000 during 1970. The making of this payment was illegal under the laws of State Y. Under section 162(c)(1), X Corp. is precluded from deducting as a trade or business expense the $5,000 paid to A.

(b) *Other illegal payments*—(1) *In general.* No deduction shall be allowed under section 162(a) for any payment (other than a payment described in paragraph (a) of this section) made, directly or indirectly, to any person, if the payment constitutes an illegal bribe, illegal kickback, or other illegal payment under the laws of the United States (as defined in paragraph (a)(4) of this section), or under any State law (but only if such State law is generally enforced), which subjects the payor to a criminal penalty or the loss (including a suspension) of license or privilege to engage in a trade or business (whether or not such penalty or loss is actually imposed upon the taxpayer). For purposes of this paragraph, a kickback includes a payment in consideration of the referral of a client, patient, or customer. This paragraph applies only to payments made after December 30, 1969.

(2) *State law.* For purposes of this paragraph, State law means a statute of a State or the District of Columbia.

(3) *Generally enforced.* For purposes of this paragraph, a State law shall be considered to be generally enforced unless it is never enforced or the only persons normally charged with violations thereof in the State (or the District of Columbia) enacting the law are infamous or those whose violations are extraordinarily flagrant. For example, a criminal statute of a State shall be considered to be generally enforced unless violations of the statute which are brought to the attention of appropriate enforcement authorities do not result in any enforcement action in the absence of unusual circumstances.

(4) *Burden of proof.* In any proceeding involving the issue of whether, for purposes of section 162(c)(2), a payment constitutes an illegal bribe, illegal kickback, or other illegal payment the burden of proof in respect of such issue shall be upon the Commissioner to the same extent as he bears the burden of proof in civil fraud cases under section 7454 (*i.e.,* he must prove the illegality of the payment by clear and convincing evidence).

(5) *Example.* The application of this paragraph may be illustrated by the following example:

Example. X Corp., a calendar-year taxpayer, is engaged in the ship repair business in State Y. During 1970, repairs on foreign ships accounted for a substantial part of its total business. It was X Corp.'s practice to kick back approximately 10 percent of the repair bill to the captain and chief engineer of all foreign-owned vessels, which kickbacks are illegal under a law of State Y (which is generally enforced) and potentially subject X Corp. to fines. During 1970, X Corp. paid $50,000

Reg. § 1.162-18(a)(4)

in such kickbacks. On X Corp.'s return for 1970, a deduction under section 162 was taken for the $50,000. The deduction of the $50,000 of illegal kickbacks during 1970 is disallowed under section 162(c)(2), whether or not X Corp. is prosecuted with respect to the kickbacks.

(c) *Kickbacks, rebates, and bribes under medicare and medicaid.* No deduction shall be allowed under section 162(a) for any kickback, rebate, or bribe (whether or not illegal) made on or after December 10, 1971, by any provider of services, supplier, physician, or other person who furnishes items or services for which payment is or may be made under the Social Security Act, as amended, or in whole or in part out of Federal funds under a State plan approved under such Act, if such kickback, rebate, or bribe is made in connection with the furnishing of such items or services or the making or receipt of such payments. For purposes of this paragraph, a kickback includes a payment in consideration of the referral of a client, patient, or customer. [Reg. § 1.162-18.]

☐ [*T.D.* 6448, 1-26-60. *Amended by T.D.* 7345, 2-19-75.]

§ 1.162-21. Fines and penalties.—(a) *In general.* No deduction shall be allowed under section 162(a) for any fine or similar penalty paid to—

(1) The government of the United States, a State, a territory or possession of the United States, the District of Columbia, or the Commonwealth of Puerto Rico;

(2) The government of a foreign country; or

(3) A political subdivision of, or

corporation or other entity serving as an agency or instrumentality of, any of the above.

(b) *Definition.* (1) For purposes of this section a fine or similar penalty includes an amount—

(i) Paid pursuant to conviction or a plea of guilty or *nolo contendere* for a crime (felony or misdemeanor) in a criminal proceeding;

(ii) Paid as a civil penalty imposed by Federal, State, or local law, including additions to tax and additional amounts and assessable penalties imposed by chapter 68 of the Internal Revenue Code of 1954;

(iii) Paid in settlement of the taxpayer's actual or potential liability for a fine or penalty (civil or criminal); or

(iv) Forfeited as collateral posted in connection with a proceeding which could result in imposition of such a fine or penalty.

(2) The amount of a fine or penalty does not include legal fees and related expenses paid or incurred in the defense of a prosecution or civil action arising from a violation of the law imposing the fine or civil penalty, nor court costs assessed against the taxpayer, or stenographic and printing charges. Compensatory damages (including damages under section 4A of the Clayton Act (15 U.S.C. 15a), as amended) paid to a government do not constitute a fine or penalty.

(c) *Examples.* The application of this section may be illustrated by the following examples:

Example (1). M Corp. was indicted under section 1 of the Sherman Anti-Trust Act (15 U.S.C. 1) for fixing and maintaining prices of certain electrical products. M Corp. was convicted and fined $50,000. The United States sued M Corp. under section 4A of the Clayton Act (15 U.S.C. 15a) for $100,000, the amount of the actual damages resulting from the price fixing of which M Corp. was convicted. Pursuant to a final judgment entered in the civil action, M Corp. paid the United States $100,000 in damages. Section 162(f) precludes M Corp. from deducting the fine of $50,000 as a trade or business expense. Section 162(f) does not preclude it from deducting the $100,000 paid to the United States as actual damages.

Example (2). N Corp. was found to have violated 33 U.S.C. 1321(b)(3) when a vessel it operated discharged oil in harmful quantities into the navigable waters of the United States. A civil penalty under 33 U.S.C. 1321(b)(6) of $5,000 was assessed against N Corp. with respect to the discharge. N Corp. paid $5,000 to the Coast Guard in payment of the civil penalty. Section 162(f) precludes N Corp. from deducting the $5,000 penalty.

Example (3). O Corp., a manufacturer of motor vehicles, was found to have violated 42 U.S.C. 1857f-2(a)(1) by selling a new motor vehicle which was not covered by the required certificate of conformity. Pursuant to 42 U.S.C. 1857f-4, O Corp. was required to pay, and did pay, a civil penalty of $10,000. In addition, pursuant to 42 U.S.C. 1857f-5a(c)(1), O Corp. was required to expend, and did expend, $500 in order to remedy the noncomformity of that motor vehicle. Section 162(f) precludes O Corp. from deducting the $10,000 penalty as a trade or business expense, but does not preclude it from deducting the $500 which it expended to remedy the nonconformity.

Example (4). P Corp. was the operator of a coal mine in which occurred a violation of a mandatory safety standard prescribed by the Federal Coal Mine Health and Safety Act of 1969 (30 U.S.C. 801 et seq.). Pursuant to 30 U.S.C. 819(a), a civil penalty of $10,000 was assessed against P Corp., and P Corp. paid the penalty. Section 162(f) precludes P Corp. from deducting the $10,000 penalty.

Example (5). Q Corp., a common carrier engaged in interstate commerce by railroad, hauled a railroad car which was not equipped with efficient hand brakes, in violation of 45 U.S.C. 11. Q Corp. was found to be liable for a penalty of $250 pursuant to 45 U.S.C. 13. Q Corp. paid that penalty. Section 162(f) precludes Q Corp. from deducting the $250 penalty.

Example (6). R Corp. owned and operated on the highways of State X a truck weighing in excess of the amount permitted under the law of State X. R Corp. was found to have violated the law and was assessed a fine of $85 which it paid to State X. Section 162(f) precludes R Corp. from deducting the amount so paid.

Example (7). S Corp. was found to have violated a law of State Y which prohibited the emission into the air of particulate matter in excess of a limit set forth in a regulation promulgated under that law. The Environmental Quality Hearing Board of State Y assessed a fine of $500 against S Corp. The fine was payable to State Y, and S Corp. paid it. Section 162(f) precludes S Corp. from deducting the $500 fine.

Example (8). T Corp. was found by a magistrate of City Z to be operating in such city an apartment building which did not conform to a provision of the city housing code requiring operable fire escapes on apartment buildings of that type. Upon the basis of the magistrate's finding, T Corp. was required to pay, and did pay, a fine of $200 to City Z. Section 162(f) precludes T Corp. from deducting the $200 fine. [Reg. § 1.162-21.]

□ [*T.D. 7345, 2-19-75. Amended by T.D. 7366, 7-10-75.*]

§ 1.162-25T. Deductions with respect to noncash fringe benefits (temporary).—(a) *Employer*. If an employer includes the value of a noncash fringe benefit in an employee's gross income, the employer may not deduct this amount as compensation for services, but rather may deduct only the costs incurred by the employer in providing the benefit to the employee. The employer may be allowed a cost recovery deduction under section 168 or a deduction under section 179 for an expense not chargeable to capital account, or, if the noncash fringe benefit is property leased by the employer, a deduction for the ordinary and necessary business expense of leasing the property.

(b) [Reserved]

(c) *Examples*. The following examples illustrate the provisions of this section.

Example (1). On January 1, 1986, X Company owns and provides the use of an automobile with a fair market value of $20,000 to E, an employee, for the entire calendar year. Both X and E compute taxable income on the basis of the calendar year. Seventy percent of the use of the automobile by E is in connection with X's trade or business. If X uses the special rule provided in § 1.61-2T for valuing the availability of the automobile and takes into account the amount excludable as a working condition fringe, X would include $1,680 ($5,600, the Annual Lease Value, less 70 percent of $5,600) in E's gross income for 1986. X may not deduct the amount included in E's income as compensation for services. X may, however, determine a cost recovery deduction under section 168, subject to the limitations under section 280F, for taxable year 1986.

Example (2). The facts are the same as in example (1), except that X includes $5,600 in E's gross income, the value of the noncash fringe benefit without taking into account the amount excludable as a working condition fringe. X may not deduct that amount as compensation for services, but may determine a cost recovery deduction under section 168, subject to the limitations under section 280F. For purposes of determining adjusted gross income, E may deduct $3,920 ($5,600 multiplied by the percent of business use). [Temporary Reg. § 1.162-25T.]

□ [*T.D. 8004, 1-2-85. Amended by T.D. 8061, 11-1-85; T.D. 8063, 12-18-85; T.D. 8276, 12-7-89 and T.D. 8451, 12-4-92.*]

§ 1.162-27. Certain employee remuneration in excess of $1,000,000.—(a) *Scope*. This section provides rules for the application of the $1 million deduction limit under section 162(m) of the Internal Revenue Code. Paragraph (b) of this section provides the general rule limiting deductions under section 162(m). Paragraph (c) of this section provides definitions of generally applicable terms. Paragraph (d) of this section provides an exception from the deduction limit for compensation payable on a commission basis. Paragraph (e) of this section provides an exception for qualified performance-based compensation. Paragraphs (f) and (g) of this section provide special rules for corporations that become publicly held corporations and payments that are subject to section 280G, respectively. Paragraph (h) of this section provides transition rules, including the rules for contracts that are grandfathered and not subject to section 162(m). Paragraph (j) of this section contains the effective date provisions. For rules concerning the deductibility of compensation for services that are not covered by section 162(m) and this section, see section 162(a)(1) and § 1.162-7. This section is not determinative as to whether compensation meets the requirements of section 162(a)(1).

(b) *Limitation on deduction*. Section 162(m) precludes a deduction under chapter 1 of the Internal Revenue Code by any publicly held corporation for compensation paid to any covered employee to the extent that the compensation for the taxable year exceeds $1,000,000.

(c) *Definitions*—(1) *Publicly held corporation*—(i) *General rule.* A *publicly held corporation* means any corporation issuing any class of common equity securities required to be registered under section 12 of the Exchange Act. A corporation is not considered publicly held if the registration of its equity securities is voluntary. For purposes of this section, whether a corporation is publicly held is determined based solely on whether, as of the last day of its taxable year, the corporation is subject to the reporting obligations of section 12 of the Exchange Act.

(ii) *Affiliated groups.* A publicly held corporation includes an affiliated group of corporations, as defined in section 1504 (determined without regard to section 1504(b)). For purposes of this section, however, an affiliated group of corporations does not include any subsidiary that is itself a publicly held corporation. Such a publicly held subsidiary, and its subsidiaries (if any), are separately subject to this section. If a covered employee is paid compensation in a taxable year by more than one member of an affiliated group, compensation paid by each member of the affiliated group is aggregated with compensation paid to the covered employee by all other members of the group. Any amount disallowed as a deduction by this section must be prorated among the payor corporations in proportion to the amount of compensation paid to the covered employee by each such corporation in the taxable year.

(2) *Covered employee*—(i) *General rule.* A *covered employee* means any individual who, on the last day of the taxable year, is—

(A) The chief executive officer of the corporation or is acting in such capacity; or

(B) Among the four highest compensated officers (other than the chief executive officer).

(ii) *Application of rules of the Securities and Exchange Commission.* Whether an individual is the chief executive officer described in paragraph (c)(2)(i)(A) of this section or an officer described in paragraph (c)(2)(i)(B) of this section is determined pursuant to the executive compensation disclosure rules under the Exchange Act.

(3) *Compensation*—(i) *In general.* For purposes of the deduction limitation described in paragraph (b) of this section, *compensation* means the aggregate amount allowable as a deduction under chapter 1 of the Internal Revenue Code for the taxable year (determined without regard to section 162(m)) for remuneration for services performed by a covered employee, whether or not the services were performed during the taxable year.

(ii) *Exceptions. Compensation* does not include—

(A) Remuneration covered in section 3121(a)(5)(A) through section 3121(a)(5)(D) (concerning remuneration that is not treated as *wages* for purposes of the Federal Insurance Contributions Act); and

(B) Remuneration consisting of any benefit provided to or on behalf of an employee if, at the time the benefit is provided, it is reasonable to believe that the employee will be able to exclude it from gross income. In addition, compensation does not include salary reduction contributions described in section 3121(v)(1).

(4) *Compensation Committee.* The *compensation committee* means the committee of directors (including any subcommittee of directors) of the publicly held corporation that has the authority to establish and administer performance goals described in paragraph (e)(2) of this section, and to certify that performance goals are attained, as described in paragraph (e)(5) of this section. A committee of directors is not treated as failing to have the authority to establish performance goals merely because the goals are ratified by the board of directors of the publicly held corporation or, if applicable, any other committee of the board of directors. See paragraph (e)(3) of this section for rules concerning the composition of the compensation committee.

(5) *Exchange Act.* The *Exchange Act* means the Securities Exchange Act of 1934.

(6) *Examples.* This paragraph (c) may be illustrated by the following examples:

Example 1. Corporation X is a publicly held corporation with a July 1 to June 30 fiscal year. For Corporation X's taxable year ending on June 30, 1995, Corporation X pays compensation of $2,000,000 to A, an employee. However, A's compensation is not required to be reported to shareholders under the executive compensation disclosure rules of the Exchange Act because A is neither the chief executive officer nor one of the four highest compensated officers employed on the last day of the taxable year. A's compensation is not subject to the deduction limitation of paragraph (b) of this section.

Example 2. C, a covered employee, performs services and receives compensation from Corporations X, Y, and Z, members of an affiliated group of corporations. Corporation X, the parent corporation, is a publicly held corporation. The total compensation paid to C from all affiliated group members is $3,000,000 for the taxable year, of which Corporation X pays $1,500,000; Corporation Y pays $900,000; and Corporation Z pays $600,000. Because the compensation paid by all affiliated group members is aggregated for pur-

Reg. § 1.162-27(c)(6)

poses of section 162(m), $2,000,000 of the aggregate compensation paid is nondeductible. Corporations X, Y, and Z each are treated as paying a ratable portion of the nondeductible compensation. Thus, two thirds of each corporation's payment will be nondeductible. Corporation X has a nondeductible compensation expense of $1,000,000 ($1,500,000 x $2,000,000/$3,000,000). Corporation Y has a nondeductible compensation expense of $600,000 ($900,000 x $2,000,000/$3,000,000). Corporation Z has a nondeductible compensation expense of $400,000 ($600,000 x $2,000,000/$3,000,000).

Example 3. Corporation W, a calendar year taxpayer, has total assets equal to or exceeding $5 million and a class of equity security held of record by 500 or more persons on December 31, 1994. However, under the Exchange Act, Corporation W is not required to file a registration statement with respect to that security until April 30, 1995. Thus, Corporation W is not a publicly held corporation on December 31, 1994, but is a publicly held corporation on December 31, 1995.

Example 4. The facts are the same as in *Example 3*, except that on December 15, 1996, Corporation W files with the Securities and Exchange Commission to disclose that Corporation W is no longer required to be registered under section 12 of the Exchange Act and to terminate its registration of securities under that provision. Because Corporation W is no longer subject to Exchange Act reporting obligations as of December 31, 1996, Corporation W is not a publicly held corporation for taxable year 1996, even though the registration of Corporation W's securities does not terminate until 90 days after Corporation W files with the Securities and Exchange Commission.

(d) *Exception for compensation paid on a commission basis.* The deduction limit in paragraph (b) of this section shall not apply to any compensation paid on a commission basis. For this purpose, compensation is paid on a commission basis if the facts and circumstances show that it is paid solely on account of income generated directly by the individual performance of the individual to whom the compensation is paid. Compensation does not fail to be attributable directly to the individual merely because support services, such as secretarial or research services, are utilized in generating the income. However, if compensation is paid on account of broader performance standards, such as income produced by a business unit of the corporation, the compensation does not qualify for the exception provided under this paragraph (d).

(e) *Exception for qualified performance-based compensation—*

(1) *In general.* The deduction limit in paragraph (b) of this section does not apply to qualified performance-based compensation. Qualified performance-based compensation is compensation that meets all of the requirements of paragraphs (e)(2) through (e)(5) of this section.

(2) *Performance goal requirement*—(i) *Preestablished goal.* Qualified performance-based compensation must be paid solely on account of the attainment of one or more preestablished, objective performance goals. A performance goal is considered preestablished if it is established in writing by the compensation committee not later than 90 days after the commencement of the period of service to which the performance goal relates, provided that the outcome is substantially uncertain at the time the compensation committee actually establishes the goal. However, in no event will a performance goal be considered to be preestablished if it is established after 25 percent of the period of service (as scheduled in good faith at the time the goal is established) has elapsed. A performance goal is objective if a third party having knowledge of the relevant facts could determine whether the goal is met. Performance goals can be based on one or more business criteria that apply to the individual, a business unit, or the corporation as a whole. Such business criteria could include, for example, stock price, market share, sales, earnings per share, return on equity, or costs. A performance goal need not, however, be based upon an increase or positive result under a business criterion and could include, for example, maintaining the status quo or limiting economic losses (measured, in each case, by reference to a specific business criterion). A performance goal does not include the mere continued employment of the covered employee. Thus, a vesting provision based solely on continued employment would not constitute a performance goal. See paragraph (e)(2)(vi) of this section for rules on compensation that is based on an increase in the price of stock.

(ii) *Objective compensation formula.* A preestablished performance goal must state, in terms of an objective formula or standard, the method for computing the amount of compensation payable to the employee if the goal is attained. A formula or standard is objective if a third party having knowledge of the relevant performance results could calculate the amount to be paid to the employee. In addition, a formula or standard must specify the individual employees or class of employees to which it applies.

(iii) *Discretion.*

(A) The terms of an objective formula or standard must preclude discretion to increase the amount of compensation payable that would otherwise be due upon attainment of the goal. A

Reg. § 1.162-27(d)

performance goal is not discretionary for purposes of this paragraph (e)(2)(iii) merely because the compensation committee reduces or eliminates the compensation or other economic benefit that was due upon attainment of the goal. However, the exercise of negative discretion with respect to one employee is not permitted to result in an increase in the amount payable to another employee. Thus, for example, in the case of a bonus pool, if the amount payable to each employee is stated in terms of a percentage of the pool, the sum of these individual percentages of the pool is not permitted to exceed 100 percent. If the terms of an objective formula or standard fail to preclude discretion to increase the amount of compensation merely because the amount of compensation to be paid upon attainment of the performance goal is based, in whole or in part, on a percentage of salary or base pay and the dollar amount of the salary or base pay is not fixed at the time the performance goal is established, then the objective formula or standard will not be considered discretionary for purposes of this paragraph (e)(2)(iii) if the maximum dollar amount to be paid is fixed at that time.

(B) If compensation is payable upon or after the attainment of a performance goal, and a change is made to accelerate the payment of compensation to an earlier date after the attainment of the goal, the change will be treated as an increase in the amount of compensation, unless the amount of compensation paid is discounted to reasonably reflect the time value of money. If compensation is payable upon or after the attainment of a performance goal, and a change is made to defer the payment of compensation to a later date, any amount paid in excess of the amount that was originally owed to the employee will not be treated as an increase in the amount of compensation if the additional amount is based either on a reasonable rate of interest or on one or more predetermined actual investments (whether or not assets associated with the amount originally owed are actually invested therein) such that the amount payable by the employer at the later date will be based on the actual rate of return of a specific investment (including any decrease as well as any increase in the value of an investment). If compensation is payable in the form of property, a change in the timing of the transfer of that property after the attainment of the goal will not be treated as an increase in the amount of compensation for purposes of this paragraph (e)(2)(iii). Thus, for example, if the terms of a stock grant provide for stock to be transferred after the attainment of a performance goal and the transfer of the stock also is subject to a vesting schedule, a change in the vesting schedule that either accelerates or defers the transfer of stock

will not be treated as an increase in the amount of compensation payable under the performance goal.

(C) Compensation attributable to a stock option, stock appreciation right, or other stock-based compensation does not fail to satisfy the requirements of this paragraph (e)(2) to the extent that a change in the grant or award is made to reflect a change in corporate capitalization, such as a stock split or dividend, or a corporate transaction, such as any merger of a corporation into another corporation, any consolidation of two or more corporations into another corporation, any separation of a corporation (including a spinoff or other distribution of stock or property by a corporation), any reorganization of a corporation (whether or not such reorganization comes within the definition of such term in section 368), or any partial or complete liquidation by a corporation.

(iv) *Grant-by-grant determination.* The determination of whether compensation satisfies the requirements of this paragraph (e)(2) generally shall be made on a grant-by-grant basis. Thus, for example, whether compensation attributable to a stock option grant satisfies the requirements of this paragraph (e)(2) generally is determined on the basis of the particular grant made and without regard to the terms of any other option grant, or other grant of compensation, to the same or another employee. As a further example, except as provided in paragraph (e)(2)(vi), whether a grant of restricted stock or other stock-based compensation satisfies the requirements of this paragraph (e)(2) is determined without regard to whether dividends, dividend equivalents, or other similar distributions with respect to stock, on such stock-based compensation are payable prior to the attainment of the performance goal. Dividends, dividend equivalents, or other similar distributions with respect to stock that are treated as separate grants under this paragraph (e)(2)(iv) are not performance-based compensation unless they separately satisfy the requirements of this paragraph (e)(2).

(v) *Compensation contingent upon attainment of performance goal.* Compensation does not satisfy the requirements of this paragraph (e)(2) if the facts and circumstances indicate that the employee would receive all or part of the compensation regardless of whether the performance goal is attained. Thus, if the payment of compensation under a grant or award is only nominally or partially contingent on attaining a performance goal, none of the compensation payable under the grant or award will be considered performance-based. For example, if an employee is entitled to a bonus under either of two arrangements, where payment

Reg. § 1.162-27(e)(2)

under a nonperformance-based arrangement is contingent upon the failure to attain the performance goals under an otherwise performance-based arrangement, then neither arrangement provides for compensation that satisfies the requirements of this paragraph (e)(2). Compensation does not fail to be qualified performance-based compensation merely because the plan allows the compensation to be payable upon death, disability, or change of ownership or control, although compensation actually paid on account of those events prior to the attainment of the performance goal would not satisfy the requirements of this paragraph (e)(2). As an exception to the general rule set forth in the first sentence of paragraph (e)(2)(iv) of this section, the facts-and-circumstances determination referred to in the first sentence of this paragraph (e)(2)(v) is made taking into account all plans, arrangements, and agreements that provide for compensation to the employee.

(vi) *Application of requirements to stock options and stock appreciation rights*—(A) *In general.* Compensation attributable to a stock option or a stock appreciation right is deemed to satisfy the requirements of this paragraph (e)(2) if the grant or award is made by the compensation committee; the plan under which the option or right is granted states the maximum number of shares with respect to which options or rights may be granted during a specified period to any employee; and, under the terms of the option or right, the amount of compensation the employee could receive is based solely on an increase in the value of the stock after the date of the grant or award. Conversely, if the amount of compensation the employee will receive under the grant or award is not based solely on an increase in the value of the stock after the date of grant or award (e.g., in the case of restricted stock, or an option that is granted with an exercise price that is less than the fair market value of the stock as of the date of grant), none of the compensation attributable to the grant or award is qualified performance-based compensation because it does not satisfy the requirement of this paragraph (e)(2)(vi)(A). Whether a stock option grant is based solely on an increase in the value of the stock after the date of grant is determined without regard to any dividend equivalent that may be payable, provided that payment of the dividend equivalent is not made contingent on the exercise of the option. The rule that the compensation attributable to a stock option or stock appreciation right must be based solely on an increase in the value of the stock after the date of grant or award does not apply if the grant or award is made on account of, or if the vesting or exercisability of the grant or award is contingent

on, the attainment of a performance goal that satisfies the requirements of this paragraph (e)(2).

(B) *Cancellation and repricing.* Compensation attributable to a stock option or stock appreciation right does not satisfy the requirements of this paragraph (e)(2) to the extent that the number of options granted exceeds the maximum number of shares for which options may be granted to the employee as specified in the plan. If an option is canceled, the canceled option continues to be counted against the maximum number of shares for which options may be granted to the employee under the plan. If, after grant, the exercise price of an option is reduced, the transaction is treated as a cancellation of the option and a grant of a new option. In such case, both the option that is deemed to be canceled and the option that is deemed to be granted reduce the maximum number of shares for which options may be granted to the employee under the plan. This paragraph (e)(2)(vi)(B) also applies in the case of a stock appreciation right where, after the award is made, the base amount on which stock appreciation is calculated is reduced to reflect a reduction in the fair market value of stock.

* * *

(3) *Outside directors*—(i) *General rule.* The performance goal under which compensation is paid must be established by a compensation committee comprised solely of two or more outside directors. A director is an outside director if the director—

(A) Is not a current employee of the publicly held corporation;

(B) Is not a former employee of the publicly held corporation who receives compensation for prior services (other than benefits under a tax-qualified retirement plan) during the taxable year;

(C) Has not been an officer of the publicly held corporation; and

(D) Does not receive remuneration from the publicly held corporation, either directly or indirectly, in any capacity other than as a director. For this purpose, remuneration includes any payment in exchange for goods or services.

(ii) *Remuneration received.* For purposes of this paragraph (e)(3), remuneration is received, directly or indirectly, by a director in each of the following circumstances:

(A) If remuneration is paid, directly or indirectly, to the director personally or to an entity in which the director has a beneficial ownership interest of greater than 50 percent. For this purpose, remuneration is considered paid when actually paid (and throughout the remainder of

Reg. § 1.162-27(e)(3)

that taxable year of the corporation) and, if earlier, throughout the period when a contract or agreement to pay remuneration is outstanding.

(B) If remuneration, other than de minimis remuneration, was paid by the publicly held corporation in its preceding taxable year to an entity in which the director has a beneficial ownership interest of at least 5 percent but not more than 50 percent. For this purpose, remuneration is considered paid when actually paid or, if earlier, when the publicly held corporation becomes liable to pay it.

(C) If remuneration, other than de minimis remuneration, was paid by the publicly held corporation in its preceding taxable year to an entity by which the director is employed or self-employed other than as a director. For this purpose, remuneration is considered paid when actually paid or, if earlier, when the publicly held corporation becomes liable to pay it.

(iii) *De minimis remuneration*—(A) *In general.* For purposes of paragraphs (e)(3)(ii)(B) and (C) of this section, remuneration that was paid by the publicly held corporation in its preceding taxable year to an entity is de minimis if payments to the entity did not exceed 5 percent of the gross revenue of the entity for its taxable year ending with or within that preceding taxable year of the publicly held corporation.

(B) *Remuneration for personal services and substantial owners.* Notwithstanding paragraph (e)(3)(iii)(A) of this section, remuneration in excess of $60,000 is not de minimis if the remuneration is paid to an entity described in paragraph (e)(3)(ii)(B) of this section, or is paid for personal services to an entity described in paragraph (e)(3)(ii)(C) of this section.

(iv) *Remuneration for personal services.* For purposes of paragraph (e)(3)(iii)(B) of this section, remuneration from a publicly held corporation is for personal services if—

(A) The remuneration is paid to an entity for personal or professional services, consisting of legal, accounting, investment banking, and management consulting services (and other similar services that may be specified by the Commissioner in revenue rulings, notices, or other guidance published in the Internal Revenue Bulletin), performed for the publicly held corporation, and the remuneration is not for services that are incidental to the purchase of goods or to the purchase of services that are not personal services; and

(B) The director performs significant services (whether or not as an employee) for the corporation, division, or similar organization (within the entity) that actually provides the services described in paragraph (e)(3)(iv)(A) of this section to the publicly held corporation, or more than 50 percent of the entity's gross revenues (for the entity's preceding taxable year) are derived from that corporation, subsidiary, or similar organization.

(v) *Entity defined.* For purposes of this paragraph (e)(3), entity means an organization that is a sole proprietorship, trust, estate, partnership, or corporation. The term also includes an affiliated group of corporations as defined in section 1504 (determined without regard to section 1504(b)) and a group of organizations that would be an affiliated group but for the fact that one or more of the organizations are not incorporated. However, the aggregation rules referred to in the preceding sentence do not apply for purposes of determining whether a director has a beneficial ownership interest of at least 5 percent or greater than 50 percent.

(vi) *Employees and former officers.* Whether a director is an employee or a former officer is determined on the basis of the facts at the time that the individual is serving as a director on the compensation committee. Thus, a director is not precluded from being an outside director solely because the director is a former officer of a corporation that previously was an affiliated corporation of the publicly held corporation. For example, a director of a parent corporation of an affiliated group is not precluded from being an outside director solely because that director is a former officer of an affiliated subsidiary that was spun off or liquidated. However, an outside director would no longer be an outside director if a corporation in which the director was previously an officer became an affiliated corporation of the publicly held corporation.

(vii) *Officer.* Solely for purposes of this paragraph (e)(3), *officer* means an administrative executive who is or was in regular and continued service. The term implies continuity of service and excludes those employed for a special and single transaction. An individual who merely has (or had) the title of officer but not the authority of an officer is not considered an officer. The determination of whether an individual is or was an officer is based on all the facts and circumstances in the particular case, including without limitation the source of the individual's authority, the term for which the individual is elected or appointed, and the nature and extent of the individual's duties.

(viii) *Members of affiliated groups.* For purposes of this paragraph (e)(3), the outside directors of the publicly held member of an affiliated group are treated as the outside directors of all members of the affiliated group.

* * *

Reg. § 1.162-27(e)(3)

(4) *Shareholder approval requirement*—(i) *General rule.* The material terms of the performance goal under which the compensation is to be paid must be disclosed to and subsequently approved by the shareholders of the publicly held corporation before the compensation is paid. The requirements of this paragraph (e)(4) are not satisfied if the compensation would be paid regardless of whether the material terms are approved by shareholders. The material terms include the employees eligible to receive compensation; a description of the business criteria on which the performance goal is based; and either the maximum amount of compensation that could be paid to any employee or the formula used to calculate the amount of compensation to be paid to the employee if the performance goal is attained (except that, in the case of a formula that fails to preclude discretion to increase the amount of compensation (as described in paragraph (e)(2)(iii)(A) of this section) merely because the amount of compensation to be paid is based, in whole or in part, on a percentage of salary or base pay and the dollar amount of the salary or base pay is not fixed at the time the performance goal is established, the maximum dollar amount of compensation that could be paid to the employee must be disclosed).

(ii) *Eligible employees.* Disclosure of the employees eligible to receive compensation need not be so specific as to identify the particular individuals by name. A general description of the class of eligible employees by title or class is sufficient, such as the chief executive officer and vice presidents, or all salaried employees, all executive officers, or all key employees.

(iii) *Description of business criteria*—(A) *In general.* Disclosure of the business criteria on which the performance goal is based need not include the specific targets that must be satisfied under the performance goal. For example, if a bonus plan provides that a bonus will be paid if earnings per share increase by 10 percent, the 10-percent figure is a target that need not be disclosed to shareholders. However, in that case, disclosure must be made that the bonus plan is based on an earnings-per-share business criterion. In the case of a plan under which employees may be granted stock options or stock appreciation rights, no specific description of the business criteria is required if the grants or awards are based on a stock price that is no less than current fair market value.

(B) *Disclosure of confidential information.* The requirements of this paragraph (e)(4) may be satisfied even though information that otherwise would be a material term of a performance goal is not disclosed to shareholders, provided that the compensation committee determines that the information is confidential commercial or business information, the disclosure of which would have an adverse effect on the publicly held corporation. Whether disclosure would adversely affect the corporation is determined on the basis of the facts and circumstances. If the compensation committee makes such a determination, the disclosure to shareholders must state the compensation committee's belief that the information is confidential commercial or business information, the disclosure of which would adversely affect the company. In addition, the ability not to disclose confidential information does not eliminate the requirement that disclosure be made of the maximum amount of compensation that is payable to an individual under a performance goal. Confidential information does not include the identity of an executive or the class of executives to which a performance goal applies or the amount of compensation that is payable if the goal is satisfied.

(iv) *Description of compensation.* Disclosure as to the compensation payable under a performance goal must be specific enough so that shareholders can determine the maximum amount of compensation that could be paid to any employee during a specified period. If the terms of the performance goal do not provide for a maximum dollar amount, the disclosure must include the formula under which the compensation would be calculated. Thus, for example, if compensation attributable to the exercise of stock options is equal to the difference in the exercise price and the current value of the stock, disclosure would be required of the maximum number of shares for which grants may be made to any employee and the exercise price of those options (*e.g.*, fair market value on date of grant). In that case, shareholders could calculate the maximum amount of compensation that would be attributable to the exercise of options on the basis of their assumptions as to the future stock price.

(v) *Disclosure requirements of the Securities and Exchange Commission.* To the extent not otherwise specifically provided in this paragraph (e)(4), whether the material terms of a performance goal are adequately disclosed to shareholders is determined under the same standards as apply under the Exchange Act.

(vi) *Frequency of disclosure.* Once the material terms of a performance goal are disclosed to and approved by shareholders, no additional disclosure or approval is required unless the compensation committee changes the material terms of the performance goal. If, however, the compensation committee has authority to change the targets under a performance goal after shareholder approval of the goal, material terms of the performance goal must be disclosed to and reap-

Reg. § 1.162-27(e)(4)

proved by shareholders no later than the first shareholder meeting that occurs in the fifth year following the year in which shareholders previously approved the performance goal.

(vii) *Shareholder vote.* For purposes of this paragraph (e)(4), the material terms of a performance goal are approved by shareholders if, in a separate vote, a majority of the votes cast on the issue (including abstentions to the extent abstentions are counted as voting under applicable state law) are cast in favor of approval.

(viii) *Members of affiliated group.* For purposes of this paragraph (e)(4), the shareholders of the publicly held member of the affiliated group are treated as the shareholders of all members of the affiliated group.

* * *

(5) *Compensation committee certification.* The compensation committee must certify in writing prior to payment of the compensation that the performance goals and any other material terms were in fact satisfied. For this purpose, approved minutes of the compensation committee meeting in which the certification is made are treated as a written certification. Certification by the compensation committee is not required for compensation that is attributable solely to the increase in the value of the stock of the publicly held corporation.

* * *

[Reg. § 1.162-27.]

☐ [*T.D.* 8650, 12-19-95.]

§ 1.162-29. Influencing legislation.—(a) *Scope.* This section provides rules for determining whether an activity is influencing legislation for purposes of section 162(e)(1)(A). This section does not apply for purposes of sections 4911 and 4945 and the regulations thereunder.

(b) *Definitions.* For purposes of this section—

(1) *Influencing legislation.* Influencing legislation means—

(i) Any attempt to influence any legislation through a lobbying communication; and

(ii) All activities, such as research, preparation, planning, and coordination, including deciding whether to make a lobbying communication, engaged in for a purpose of making or supporting a lobbying communication, even if not yet made. See paragraph (c) of this section for rules for determining the purposes for engaging in an activity.

(2) *Attempt to influence legislation.* An attempt to influence any legislation through a lobbying communication is making the lobbying communication.

(3) *Lobbying communication.* A lobbying communication is any communication (other than any communication compelled by subpoena, or otherwise compelled by Federal or State law) with any member or employee of a legislative body or any other government official or employee who may participate in the formulation of the legislation that—

(i) Refers to specific legislation and reflects a view on that legislation; or

(ii) Clarifies, amplifies, modifies, or provides support for views reflected in a prior lobbying communication.

(4) *Legislation.* Legislation includes any action with respect to Acts, bills, resolutions, or other similar items by a legislative body. Legislation includes a proposed treaty required to be submitted by the President to the Senate for its advice and consent from the time the President's representative begins to negotiate its position with the prospective parties to the proposed treaty.

(5) *Specific legislation.* Specific legislation includes a specific legislative proposal that has not been introduced in a legislative body.

(6) *Legislative bodies.* Legislative bodies are Congress, state legislatures, and other similar governing bodies, excluding local councils (and similar governing bodies), and executive, judicial, or administrative bodies. For this purpose, administrative bodies include school boards, housing authorities, sewer and water districts, zoning boards, and other similar Federal, State, or local special purpose bodies, whether elective or appointive.

(7) *Examples.* The provisions of this paragraph (b) are illustrated by the following examples.

Example 1. Taxpayer P's employee, A, is assigned to approach members of Congress to gain their support for a pending bill. A drafts and P prints a position letter on the bill. P distributes the letter to members of Congress. Additionally, A personally contacts several members of Congress or their staffs to seek support for P's position on the bill. The letter and the personal contacts are lobbying communications. Therefore, P is influencing legislation.

Example 2. Taxpayer R is invited to provide testimony at a congressional oversight hearing concerning the implementation of The Financial Institutions Reform, Recovery, and Enforcement Act of 1989. Specifically, the hearing concerns a proposed regulation increasing the threshold value of commercial and residential real estate transactions for which an appraisal by a state licensed or certified appraiser is required. In its testimony, R states that it is in favor of the proposed regulation. Because R does not refer to any specific legislation or reflect a view on any such legisla-

Reg. § 1.162-29(b)(7)

tion, R has not made a lobbying communication. Therefore, R is not influencing legislation.

Example 3. State X enacts a statute that requires the licensing of all day-care providers. Agency B in State X is charged with writing rules to implement the statute. After the enactment of the statute, Taxpayer S sends a letter to Agency B providing detailed proposed rules that S recommends Agency B adopt to implement the statute on licensing of day-care providers. Because the letter to Agency B neither refers to nor reflects a view on any specific legislation, it is not a lobbying communication. Therefore, S is not influencing legislation.

Example 4. Taxpayer T proposes to a State Park Authority that it purchase a particular tract of land for a new park. Even if T's proposal would necessarily require the State Park Authority eventually to seek appropriations to acquire the land and develop the new park, T has not made a lobbying communication because there has been no reference to, nor any view reflected on, any specific legislation. Therefore, T's proposal is not influencing legislation.

Example 5. (i) Taxpayer U prepares a paper that asserts that lack of new capital is hurting State X's economy. The paper indicates that State X residents either should invest more in local businesses or increase their savings so that funds will be available to others interested in making investments. U forwards a summary of the unpublished paper to legislators in State X with a cover letter that states in part:

You must take action to improve the availability of new capital in the state.

(ii) Because neither the summary nor the cover letter refers to any specific legislative proposal and no other facts or circumstances indicate that they refer to an existing legislative proposal, forwarding the summary to legislators in State X is not a lobbying communication. Therefore, U is not influencing legislation.

(iii) Q, a member of the legislature of State X, calls U to request a copy of the unpublished paper from which the summary was prepared. U forwards the paper with a cover letter that simply refers to the enclosed materials. Because U's letter to Q and the unpublished paper do not refer to any specific legislation or reflect a view on any such legislation, the letter is not a lobbying communication. Therefore, U is not influencing legislation.

Example 6. (i) Taxpayer V prepares a paper that asserts that lack of new capital is hurting the national economy. The paper indicates that lowering the capital gains rate would increase the availability of capital and increase tax receipts from the capital gains tax. V forwards the paper

to its representatives in Congress with a cover letter that says, in part:

I urge you to support a reduction in the capital gains tax rate.

(ii) V's communication is a lobbying communication because it refers to and reflects a view on a specific legislative proposal (i.e., lowering the capital gains rate). Therefore, V is influencing legislation.

Example 7. Taxpayer W, based in State A, notes in a letter to a legislator of State A that State X has passed a bill that accomplishes a stated purpose and then says that State A should pass such a bill. No such bill has been introduced into the State A legislature. The communication is a lobbying communication because it refers to and reflects a view on a specific legislative proposal. Therefore, W is influencing legislation.

Example 8. (i) Taxpayer Y represents citrus fruit growers. Y writes a letter to a United States senator discussing how pesticide O has benefited citrus fruit growers and disputing problems linked to its use. The letter discusses a bill pending in Congress and states in part:

This bill would prohibit the use of pesticide O. If citrus growers are unable to use this pesticide, their crop yields will be severely reduced, leading to higher prices for consumers and lower profits, even bankruptcy, for growers.

(ii) Y's views on the bill are reflected in this statement. Thus, the communication is a lobbying communication, and Y is influencing legislation.

Example 9. (i) B, the president of Taxpayer Z, an insurance company, meets with Q, who chairs the X state legislature's committee with jurisdiction over laws regulating insurance companies, to discuss the possibility of legislation to address current problems with surplus-line companies. B recommends that legislation be introduced that would create minimum capital and surplus requirements for surplus-line companies and create clearer guidelines concerning the risks that surplus-line companies can insure. B's discussion with Q is a lobbying communication because B refers to and reflects a view on a specific legislative proposal. Therefore, Z is influencing legislation.

(ii) Q is not convinced that the market for surplus-line companies is substantial enough to warrant such legislation and requests that B provide information on the amount and types of risks covered by surplus-line companies. After the meeting, B has employees of Z prepare estimates of the percentage of property and casualty insurance risks handled by surplus-line companies. B sends the estimates with a cover letter that simply refers to the enclosed materials. Although B's follow-up letter to Q does not refer to specific legislation or reflect a view on such legislation, B's letter supports the views reflected in the earlier communication. Therefore, the letter is a lobbying communication and Z is influencing legislation.

(c) *Purpose for engaging in an activity*—(1) *In general.* The purposes for engaging in an activity are determined based on all the facts and circumstances. Facts and circumstances include, but are not limited to—

(i) Whether the activity and the lobbying communication are proximate in time;

(ii) Whether the activity and the lobbying communication relate to similar subject matter;

(iii) Whether the activity is performed at the request of, under the direction of, or on behalf of a person making the lobbying communication;

(iv) Whether the results of the activity are also used for a nonlobbying purpose; and

(v) Whether, at the time the taxpayer engages in the activity, there is specific legislation to which the activity relates.

(2) *Multiple purposes.* If a taxpayer engages in an activity both for the purpose of making or supporting a lobbying communication and for some nonlobbying purpose, the taxpayer must treat the activity as engaged in partially for a lobbying purpose and partially for a nonlobbying purpose. This division of the activity must result in a reasonable allocation of costs to influencing legislation. See § 1.162-28 (allocation rules for certain expenditures to which section 162(e)(1) applies). A taxpayer's treatment of these multiple-purpose activities will, in general, not result in a reasonable allocation if it allocates to influencing legislation—

(i) Only the incremental amount of costs that would not have been incurred but for the lobbying purpose; or

(ii) An amount based solely on the number of purposes for engaging in that activity without regard to the relative importance of those purposes.

(3) *Activities treated as having no purpose to influence legislation.* A taxpayer that engages in any of the following activities is treated as having done so without a purpose of making or supporting a lobbying communication—

(i) Before evidencing a purpose to influence any specific legislation referred to in paragraph (c)(3)(i)(A) or (B) of this section (or similar legislation)—

(A) Determining the existence or procedural status of specific legislation, or the time, place, and subject of any hearing to be held by a legislative body with respect to specific legislation; or

(B) Preparing routine, brief summaries of the provisions of specific legislation;

(ii) Performing an activity for purposes of complying with the requirements of any law (for example, satisfying state or federal securities law filing requirements);

(iii) Reading any publications available to the general public or viewing or listening to other mass media communications; and

(iv) Merely attending a widely attended speech.

* * *

[Reg. § 1.162-29.]

☐ [*T.D.* 8602, 7-20-95.]

§ 1.163-1. Interest deduction in general.—(a) Except as otherwise provided in sections 264 to 267, inclusive, interest paid or accrued within the taxable year on indebtedness shall be allowed as a deduction in computing taxable income. For rules relating to interest on certain deferred payments, see section 483 and the regulations thereunder.

(b) Interest paid by the taxpayer on a mortgage upon real estate of which he is the legal or equitable owner, even though the taxpayer is not directly liable upon the bond or note secured by such mortgage, may be deducted as interest on his indebtedness. Pursuant to the provisions of section 163(c), any annual or periodic rental payment made by a taxpayer on or after January 1, 1962, under a redeemable ground rent, as defined in section 1055(c) and paragraph (b) of § 1.1055-1, is required to be treated as interest on an indebtedness secured by a mortgage and, accordingly, may be deducted by the taxpayer as interest on his indebtedness. Section 163(c) has no application in respect of any annual or periodic rental payment made prior to January 1, 1962, or pursuant to an arrangement which does not constitute a "redeemable ground rent" as defined in section 1055(c) and paragraph (b) of § 1.1055-1. Accordingly, annual or periodic payments of Pennsylvania ground rents made before, on, or after January 1, 1962, are deductible as interest if the ground rent is redeemable. An annual or periodic rental payment under a Maryland redeemable ground rent made prior to January 1, 1962, is deductible in accordance with the rules and regulations applicable at the time such payment was made. Any annual or periodic rental payment under a Maryland redeemable ground rent made by the taxpayer on or after January 1, 1962, is, pursuant to the provisions of section 163(c), treated as interest on an indebtedness secured by a mortgage and, accordingly, is deductible by the taxpayer as interest on his indebtedness. In any case where the ground rent is irredeemable, any annual or periodic ground rent payment shall be

Reg. § 1.163-1(b)

treated as rent and shall be deductible only to the extent that the payment constitutes a proper business expense. Amounts paid in redemption of a ground rent shall not be treated as interest. For treatment of redeemable ground rents and real property held subject to liabilities under redeemable ground rents, see section 1055 and the regulations thereunder.

(c) Interest calculated for costkeeping or other purposes on account of capital or surplus invested in the business which does not represent a charge arising under an interest-bearing obligation, is not an allowable deduction from gross income. Interest paid by a corporation on scrip dividends is an allowable deduction. So-called interest on preferred stock, which is in reality a dividend thereon, cannot be deducted in computing taxable income. (See, however, section 583). In case of banks and loan or trust companies, interest paid within the year on deposits, such as interest paid on moneys received for investment and secured by interest-bearing certificates of indebtedness issued by such bank or loan or trust company, may be deducted from gross income.

(d) To the extent of assistance payments made in respect of an indebtedness of the taxpayer during the taxable year by the Department of Housing and Urban Development under section 235 of the National Housing Act (12 U.S.C. § 1715z), as amended, no deduction shall be allowed under section 163 and this section for interest paid or accrued with respect to such indebtedness. However, such payments shall not affect the amount of any deduction under any section of the Code other than section 163. The provisions of this paragraph shall apply to taxable years beginning after December 31, 1974. [Reg. § 1.163-1.]

☐ [*T.D. 6223, 1-23-57. Amended by T.D. 6593, 2-28-62, T.D. 6821, 5-3-65, T.D. 6873, 1-24-66, and T.D. 7408, 3-4-76.*]

§ 1.163-7. Deduction for OID on certain debt instruments.—(a) *General rule.* Except as otherwise provided in paragraph (b) of this section, an issuer (including a transferee) determines the amount of OID that is deductible each year under section 163(e)(1) by using the constant yield method described in § 1.1272-1(b). This determination, however, is made without regard to section 1272(a)(7) (relating to acquisition premium) and § 1.1273-1(d) (relating to de minimis OID). An issuer is permitted a deduction under section 163(e)(1) only to the extent the issuer is primarily liable on the debt instrument. For certain limitations on the deductibility of OID, see sections 163(e) and 1275(b)(2). To determine the amount of interest (OID) that is deductible each

year on a debt instrument that provides for contingent payments, see § 1.1275-4.

* * *

[Reg. § 1.163-7.]

☐ [*T.D. 8517, 1-27-94. Amended by T.D. 8674, 6-11-96 and T.D. 8934, 1-11-2001.*]

§ 1.163-8T. Allocation of interest expense among expenditures (temporary).—(a) *In general*—(1) *Application.* This section prescribes rules for allocating interest expense for purposes of applying sections 469 (the "passive loss limitation") and 163(d) and (h) (the "nonbusiness interest limitations").

* * *

(3) *Manner of allocation.* In general, interest expense on a debt is allocated in the same manner as the debt to which such interest expense relates is allocated. Debt is allocated by tracing disbursements of the debt proceeds to specific expenditures. This section prescribes rules for tracing debt proceeds to specific expenditures.

(4) *Treatment of interest expense*—(i) *General rule.* Except as otherwise provided in paragraph (m) of this section (relating to limitations on interest expense other than the passive loss and nonbusiness interest limitations), interest expense allocated under the rules of this section is treated in the following manner:

(A) Interest expense allocated to a trade or business expenditure (as defined in paragraph (b)(7) of this section) is taken into account under section 163(h)(2)(A);

(B) Interest expense allocated to a passive activity expenditure (as defined in paragraph (b)(4) of this section) or a former passive activity expenditure (as defined in paragraph (b)(2) of this section) is taken into account for purposes of section 469 in determining the income or loss from the activity to which such expenditure relates;

(C) Interest expense allocated to an investment expenditure (as defined in paragraph (b)(3) of this section) is treated for purposes of section 163(d) as investment interest;

(D) Interest expense allocated to a personal expenditure (as defined in paragraph (b)(5) of this section) is treated for purposes of section 163(h) as personal interest; and

(E) Interest expense allocated to a portfolio expenditure (as defined in paragraph (b)(6) of this section) is treated for purposes of section 469(e)(2)(B)(ii) as interest expense described in section 469(e)(1)(A)(i)(III).

* * *

(c) *Allocation of debt and interest expense*—(1) *Allocation in accordance with use of proceeds.* Debt is allocated to expenditures in accordance

Reg. § 1.163-7(a)

with the use of the debt proceeds and, except as provided in paragraph (m) of this section, interest expense accruing on a debt during any period is allocated to expenditures in the same manner as the debt is allocated from time to time during such period. Except as provided in paragraph (m) of this section, debt proceeds and related interest expense are allocated solely by reference to the use of such proceeds, and the allocation is not affected by the use of an interest in any property to secure the repayment of such debt or interest. The following example illustrates the principles of this paragraph (c)(1):

Example. Taxpayer A, an individual, pledges corporate stock held for investment as security for a loan and uses the debt proceeds to purchase an automobile for personal use. Interest expense accruing on the debt is allocated to the personal expenditure to purchase the automobile even though the debt is secured by investment property.

* * *

(4) *Allocation of debt; proceeds deposited in borrower's account—(i) Treatment of deposit.* For purposes of this section, a deposit of debt proceeds in an account is treated as an investment expenditure, and amounts held in an account (whether or not interest bearing) are treated as property held for investment. Debt allocated to an account under this paragraph (c)(4)(i) must be reallocated as required by paragraph (j) of this section whenever debt proceeds held in the account are used for another expenditure. This paragraph (c)(4) provides rules for determining when debt proceeds are expended from the account. The following example illustrates the principles of this paragraph (c)(4)(i):

Example. Taxpayer C, a calendar year taxpayer, borrows $100,000 on January 1 and immediately uses the proceeds to open a noninterest-bearing checking account. No other amounts are deposited in the account during the year, and no portion of the principal amount of the debt is repaid during the year. On April 1, C uses $20,000 of the debt proceeds held in the account for a passive activity expenditure. On September 1, C uses an additional $40,000 of the debt proceeds held in the account for a personal expenditure. Under this paragraph (c)(4)(i), from January 1 through March 31 the entire $100,000 debt is allocated to an investment expenditure for the account. From April 1 through August 31, $20,000 of the debt is allocated to the passive activity expenditure, and $80,000 of the debt is allocated to the investment expenditure for the account. From September 1 through December 31, $40,000 of the debt is allocated to the personal expenditure, $20,000 is allocated to the passive

activity expenditure, and $40,000 is allocated to an investment expenditure for the account.

(ii) *Expenditures from account; general ordering rule.* Except as provided in paragraph (c)(4)(iii)(B) or (C) of this section, debt proceeds deposited in an account are treated as expended before—

(A) Any unborrowed amounts held in the account at the time such debt proceeds are deposited; and

(B) Any amounts (borrowed or unborrowed) that are deposited in the account after such debt proceeds are deposited.

The following example illustrates the application of this paragraph (c)(4)(ii):

Example. On January 10, taxpayer E opens a checking account, depositing $500 of proceeds of Debt A and $1,000 of unborrowed funds. The following chart summarizes the transactions which occur during the year with respect to the account:

Date		Transaction
January 10	$ 500	proceeds of Debt A and $1,000 unborrowed funds deposited
January 11	$ 500	proceeds of Debt B deposited
February 17	$ 800	personal expenditure
February 26	$ 700	passive activity expenditure
June 21	$1,000	proceeds of Debt C deposited
November 24	$ 800	investment expenditure
December 20	$ 600	personal expenditure

The $800 personal expenditure is treated as made from the $500 proceeds of Debt A and $300 of the proceeds of Debt B. The $700 passive activity expenditure is treated as made from the remaining $200 proceeds of Debt B and $500 of unborrowed funds. The $800 investment expenditure is treated as made entirely from the proceeds of Debt C. The $600 personal expenditure is treated as made from the remaining $200 proceeds of Debt C and $400 of unborrowed funds. Under paragraph (c)(4)(i) of this section, debt is allocated to an investment expenditure for periods during which debt proceeds are held in the account.

(iii) *Expenditures from account; supplemental ordering rules—(A) Checking or similar accounts.* Except as otherwise provided in this paragraph (c)(4)(iii), an expenditure from a checking or similar account is treated as made at the time the check is written on the account, provided the check is delivered or mailed to the payee within a reasonable period after the writing

Reg. § 1.163-8T(c)(4)

of the check. For this purpose, the taxpayer may treat checks written on the same day as written in any order. In the absence of evidence to the contrary, a check is presumed to be written on the date appearing on the check and to be delivered or mailed to the payee within a reasonable period thereafter. Evidence to the contrary may include the fact that a check does not clear within a reasonable period after the date appearing on the check.

(B) *Expenditures within 15 days after deposit of borrowed funds.* The taxpayer may treat any expenditure made from an account within 15 days after debt proceeds are deposited in such account as made from such proceeds to the extent thereof even if under paragraph (c)(4)(ii) of this section the debt proceeds would be treated as used to make one or more other expenditures. Any such expenditures and the debt proceeds from which such expenditures are treated as made are disregarded in applying paragraph (c)(4)(ii) of this section. The following examples illustrate the application of this paragraph (c)(4)(iii)(B):

Example (1). Taxpayer D incurs a $1,000 debt on June 5 and immediately deposits the proceeds in an account ("Account A"). On June 17, D transfers $2,000 from Account A to another account ("Account B"). On June 30, D writes a $1,500 check on Account B for a passive activity expenditure. In addition, numerous deposits of borrowed and unborrowed amounts and expenditures occur with respect to both accounts throughout the month of June. Notwithstanding these other transactions, D may treat $1,000 of the deposit to Account B on June 17 as an expenditure from the debt proceeds deposited in Account A on June 5. In addition, D may similarly treat $1,000 of the passive activity expenditure on June 30 as made from debt proceeds treated as deposited in Account B on June 17.

Example (2). The facts are the same as in the example in paragraph (c)(4)(ii) of this section, except that the proceeds of Debt B are deposited on February 11 rather than on January 11. Since the $700 passive activity expenditure occurs within 15 days after the proceeds of Debt B are deposited in the account, E may treat such expenditure as being made from the proceeds of Debt B to the extent thereof. If E treats the passive activity expenditure in this manner, the expenditures from the account are treated as follows: The $800 personal expenditure is treated as made from the $500 proceeds of Debt A and $300 of unborrowed funds. The $700 passive activity expenditure is treated as made from the $500 proceeds of Debt B and $200 of unborrowed funds. The remaining expenditures are treated as in the example in paragraph (c)(4)(ii) of this section.

(C) *Interest on segregated account.* In the case of an account consisting solely of the proceeds of a debt and interest earned on such account, the taxpayer may treat any expenditure from such account as made first from amounts constituting interest (rather than debt proceeds) to the extent of the balance of such interest in the account at the time of the expenditure, determined by applying the rules in this paragraph (c)(4). To the extent any expenditure is treated as made from interest under this paragraph (c)(4)(iii)(C), the expenditure is disregarded in applying paragraph (c)(4)(ii) of this section.

(iv) *Optional method for determining date of reallocation.* Solely for the purpose of determining the date on which debt allocated to an account under paragraph (c)(4)(i) of this section is reallocated, the taxpayer may treat all expenditures made during any calendar month from debt proceeds in the account as occurring on the later of the first day of such month or the date on which such debt proceeds are deposited in the account. This paragraph (c)(4)(iv) applies only if all expenditures from an account during the same calendar month are similarly treated. The following example illustrates the application of this paragraph (c)(4)(iv):

Example. On January 10, taxpayer G opens a checking account, depositing $500 of proceeds of Debt A and $1,000 of unborrowed funds. The following chart summarizes the transactions which occur during the year with respect to the account (note that these facts are the same as the facts of the example in paragraph (c)(4)(ii) of this section):

Date	Transaction
January 10	$500 proceeds of Debt A and $1,000 unborrowed funds deposited
January 11	$500 proceeds of Debt B deposited
February 17	$800 personal expenditure
February 26	$700 passive activity expenditure
June 21	$1,000 proceeds of Debt C deposited
November 24	$800 investment expenditure
December 20	$600 personal expenditure

Assume that G chooses to apply the optional rule of this paragraph (c)(4)(iv) to all expenditures. For purposes of determining the date on which debt is allocated to the $800 personal expenditure made on February 17, the $500 treated as made from the proceeds of Debt A and the $300 treated as made from the proceeds of Debt B are treated as expenditures occurring on February 1. Accordingly, Debt A is allocated to an investment expenditure for the account from January 10 through January 31 and to the personal expenditure from

Reg. § 1.163-8T(c)(4)

February 1 through December 31, and $300 of Debt B is allocated to an investment expenditure for the account from January 11 through January 31 and to the personal expenditure from February 1 through December 31. The remaining $200 of Debt B is allocated to an investment expenditure for the account from January 11 through January 31 and to the passive activity expenditure from February 1 through December 31. The $800 of Debt C used to make the investment expenditure on November 24 is allocated to an investment expenditure for the account from June 21 through October 31 and to an investment expenditure from November 1 through December 31. The remaining $200 of Debt C is allocated to an investment expenditure for the account from June 21 through November 30 and to a personal expenditure from December 1 through December 31.

(v) *Simultaneous deposits—(A) In general.* If the proceeds of two or more debts are deposited in an account simultaneously, such proceeds are treated for purposes of this paragraph (c)(4) as deposited in the order in which the debts were incurred.

(B) *Order in which debts incurred.* If two or more debts are incurred simultaneously or are treated under applicable law as incurred simultaneously, the debts are treated for purposes of this paragraph (c)(4)(v) as incurred in any order the taxpayer selects.

(C) *Borrowings on which interest accrues at different rates.* If interest does not accrue at the same fixed or variable rate on the entire amount of a borrowing, each portion of the borrowing on which interest accrues at a different fixed or variable rate is treated as a separate debt for purposes of this paragraph (c)(4)(v).

(vi) *Multiple accounts.* The rules in this paragraph (c)(4) apply separately to each account of a taxpayer.

* * *

(d) *Debt repayments—(1) General ordering rule.* If, at the time any portion of a debt is repaid, such debt is allocated to more than one expenditure, the debt is treated for purposes of this section as repaid in the following order:

(i) Amounts allocated to personal expenditures;

(ii) Amounts allocated to investment expenditures and passive activity expenditures (other than passive activity expenditures described in paragraph (d)(1)(iii) of this section).

(iii) Amounts allocated to passive activity expenditures in connection with a rental real estate activity with respect to which the taxpayer actively participates (within the meaning of section 469(i));

(iv) Amounts allocated to former passive activity expenditures; and

(v) Amounts allocated to trade or business expenditures and to expenditures described in the last sentence of paragraph (b)(4) of this section.

* * *

(m) *Coordination with other provisions—(1) Effect of other limitations—(i) In general.* All debt is allocated among expenditures pursuant to the rules in this section, without regard to any limitations on the deductibility of interest expense on such debt. The applicability of the passive loss and nonbusiness interest limitations to interest on such debt, however, may be affected by other limitations on the deductibility of interest expense.

(ii) *Disallowance provisions.* Interest expense that is not allowable as a deduction by reason of a disallowance provision (within the meaning of paragraph (m)(7)(ii) of this section) is not taken into account for any taxable year for purposes of applying the passive loss and nonbusiness interest limitations.

(iii) *Deferral provisions.* Interest expense that is not allowable as a deduction for the taxable year in which paid or accrued by reason of a deferral provision (within the meaning of paragraph (m)(7)(iii) of this section) is allocated in the same manner as the debt giving rise to the interest expense is allocated for such taxable year. Such interest expense is taken into account for purposes of applying the passive loss and nonbusiness interest limitations for the taxable year in which such interest expense is allowable under such deferral provision.

(iv) *Capitalization provisions.* Interest expense that is capitalized pursuant to a capitalization provision (within the meaning of paragraph (m)(7)(i) of this section) is not taken into account as interest for any taxable year for purposes of applying the passive loss and nonbusiness interest limitations.

(2) *Effect on other limitations—(i) General rule.* Except as provided in paragraph (m)(2)(ii) of this section, any limitation on the deductibility of an item (other than the passive loss and nonbusiness interest limitations) applies without regard to the manner in which debt is allocated under this section. Thus, for example, interest expense treated under section 265(a)(2) as interest on indebtedness incurred or continued to purchase or carry obligations the interest on which is wholly exempt from Federal income tax is not deductible regardless of the expenditure to which the underlying debt is allocated under this section.

Reg. § 1.163-8T(m)(2)

(ii) *Exception.* Capitalization provisions (within the meaning of paragraph (m)(7)(i) of this section) do not apply to interest expense allocated to any personal expenditure under the rules of this section.

(3) *Qualified residence interest.* Qualified residence interest (within the meaning of section 163 (h)(3)) is allowable as a deduction without regard to the manner in which such interest expense is allocated under the rules of this section. In addition, qualified residence interest is not taken into account in determining the income or loss from any activity for purposes of section 469 or in determining the amount of investment interest for purposes of section 163(d). The following example illustrates the rule in this paragraph (m)(3):

Example. Taxpayer E, an individual, incurs a $20,000 debt secured by a residence and immediately uses the proceeds to purchase an automobile exclusively for E's personal use. Under the rules in this section, the debt and interest expense on the debt are allocated to a personal expenditure. If, however, the interest on the debt is qualified residence interest within the meaning of section 163(h)(3), the interest is not treated as personal interest for purposes of section 163(h).

* * *

[Temporary Reg. § 1.163-8T.]

☐ [*T.D. 8145, 7-1-87.*]

§ 1.163-9T. Personal interest (temporary).— (a) *In general.* No deduction under any provision of Chapter 1 of the Internal Revenue Code shall be allowed for personal interest paid or accrued during the taxable year by a taxpayer other than a corporation.

(b) *Personal interest*—(1) *Definition.* For purposes of this section, personal interest is any interest expense other than—

(i) Interest paid or accrued on indebtedness properly allocable (within the meaning of § 1.163-8T) to the conduct of a trade or business (other than the trade or business of performing services as an employee),

(ii) Any investment interest (within the meaning of section 163(d)(3)),

(iii) Any interest that is taken into account under section 469 in computing income or loss from a passive activity of the taxpayer,

(iv) Any qualified residence interest (within the meaning of section 163(h)(3) and § 1.163-10T), and

(v) Any interest payable under section 6601 with respect to the unpaid portion of the tax imposed by section 2001 for the period during which an extension of time for payment of such tax is in effect under section 6163, 6166, or 6166A

(as in effect before its repeal by the Economic Recovery Tax Act of 1981).

(2) *Interest relating to taxes*—(i) *In general.* Except as provided in paragraph (b)(2)(iii) of this section, personal interest includes interest—

(A) Paid on underpayments of individual Federal, State or local income taxes and on indebtedness used to pay such taxes (within the meaning of § 1.163-8T), regardless of the source of the income generating the tax liability;

(B) Paid under section 453C(e)(4)(B) (interest on deferred tax resulting from certain installment sales) and section 1291(c) (interest on deferred tax attributable to passive foreign investment companies); or

(C) Paid by a trust, S corporation, or other pass-through entity on underpayments of State or local income taxes and on indebtedness used to pay such taxes.

(ii) *Example.* A, an individual, owns stock of an S corporation. On its return for 1987, the corporation underreports its taxable income. Consequently, A underreports A's share of that income on A's tax return. In 1989, A pays the resulting deficiency plus interest to the Internal Revenue Service. The interest paid by A in 1989 on the tax deficiency is personal interest, notwithstanding the fact that the additional tax liability may have arisen out of income from a trade or business. The result would be the same if A's business had been operated as a sole proprietorship.

(iii) *Certain other taxes.* Personal interest does not include interest—

(A) Paid with respect to sales, excise and similar taxes that are incurred in connection with a trade or business or an investment activity;

(B) Paid by an S corporation with respect to an underpayment of income tax from a year in which the S corporation was a C corporation or with respect to an underpayment of the taxes imposed by sections 1374 or 1375, or similar provision of State law; or

(C) Paid by a transferee under section 6901 (tax liability resulting from transferred assets), or a similar provision of State law, with respect to a C corporation's underpayment of income tax.

(3) *Cross references.* See § 1.163-8T for rules for determining the allocation of interest expense to various activities. See § 1.163-10T for rules concerning qualified residence interest.

* * *

[Temporary Reg. § 1.163-9T.]

☐ [*T.D. 8168, 12-21-87 (corrected 3-18-2003).*]

Reg. § 1.163-9T(a)

§ 1.163-10T. Qualified residence interest (temporary).— * * *

(b) *Treatment of qualified residence interest.* Except as provided below, qualified residence interest is deductible under section 163(a). Qualified residence interest is not subject to limitation or otherwise taken into account under section 163(d) (limitation on investment interest), section 163(h)(1) (disallowance of deduction for personal interest), section 263A (capitalization and inclusion in inventory costs of certain expenses) or section 469 (limitations on losses from passive activities). Qualified residence interest is subject to the limitation imposed by section 263(g) (certain interest in the case of straddles), section 264(a)(2) and (4) (interest paid in connection with certain insurance), section 265(a)(2) (interest relating to tax-exempt income), section 266 (carrying charges), section 267(a)(2) (interest with respect to transactions between related taxpayers), section 465 (deductions limited to amount at risk), section 1277 (deferral of interest deduction allocable to accrued market discount), and section 1282 (deferral of interest deduction allocable to accrued discount).

(c) *Determination of qualified residence interest when secured debt does not exceed adjusted purchase price—*(1) *In general.* If the sum of the average balances for the taxable year of all secured debts on a qualified residence does not exceed the adjusted purchase price (determined as of the end of the taxable year) of the qualified residence, all of the interest paid or accrued during the taxable year with respect to the secured debts is qualified residence interest. If the sum of the average balances for the taxable year of all secured debts exceeds the adjusted purchase price of the qualified residences (determined as of the end of the taxable year), the taxpayer must use either the simplified method (see paragraph (d) of this section) or the exact method (see paragraph (e) of this section) to determine the amount of interest that is qualified residence interest.

(2) *Examples.*

Example (1). T purchases a qualified residence in 1987 for $65,000. T pays $6,500 in cash and finances the remainder of the purchase with a mortgage of $58,500. In 1988, the average balance of the mortgage is $58,000. Because the average balance of the mortgage is less than the adjusted purchase price of the residence ($65,000), all of the interest paid or accrued during 1988 on the mortgage is qualified residence interest.

Example (2). The facts are the same as in example (1), except that T incurs a second mortgage on January 1, 1988, with an initial principal balance of $2,000. The average balance of the second mortgage in 1988 is $1,900. Because the sum of the average balance of the first and second mortgages ($59,900) is less than the adjusted purchase price of the residence ($65,000), all of the interest paid or accrued during 1988 on both the first and second mortgages is qualified residence interest.

Example (3). P borrows $50,000 on January 1, 1988 and secures the debt by a qualified residence. P pays the interest on the debt monthly, but makes no principal payments in 1988. There are no other debts secured by the residence during 1988. On December 31, 1988, the adjusted purchase price of the residence is $40,000. The average balance of the debt in 1988 is $50,000. Because the average balance of the debt exceeds the adjusted purchase price ($10,000), some of the interest on the debt is not qualified residence interest. The portion of the total interest that is qualified residence interest must be determined in accordance with the rules of paragraph (d) or paragraph (e) of this section.

(d) *Determination of qualified residence interest when secured debt exceeds adjusted purchase price—Simplified method—*(1) *In general.* Under the simplified method, the amount of qualified residence interest for the taxable year is equal to the total interest paid or accrued during the taxable year with respect to all secured debts multiplied by a fraction (not in excess of one), the numerator of which is the adjusted purchase price (determined as of the end of the taxable year) of the qualified residence and the denominator of which is the sum of the average balances of all secured debts.

(2) *Treatment of interest paid or accrued on secured debt that is not qualified residence interest.* Under the simplified method, the excess of the total interest paid or accrued during the taxable year with respect to all secured debts over the amount of qualified residence interest is personal interest.

(3) *Example.* R's principal residence has an adjusted purchase price on December 31, 1988, of $105,000. R has two debts secured by the residence, with the following average balances and interest payments:

Debt	Date Secured	Average Balance	Interest
Debt 1	June 1983	$ 80,000	$ 8,000
Debt 2	May 1987	$ 40,000	$ 4,800
Total		$120,000	$12,800

The amount of qualified residence interest is determined under the simplified method by multiplying the total interest ($12,800) by a fraction (expressed as a decimal amount) equal to the adjusted purchase price ($105,000) of the resi-

Reg. § 1.163-10T(d)(3)

dence divided by the combined average balances ($120,000). For 1988, this fraction is equal to 0.875 ($105,000/$120,000). Therefore, $11,200 ($12,800 × 0.875) of the total interest is qualified residence interest. The remaining $1,600 in interest ($12,800 − $11,200) is personal interest, even if (under the rules of § 1.163-8T) such remaining interest would be allocated to some other category of interest.

* * *

(o) *Secured debt*—(1) *In general.* For purposes of this section, the term "secured debt" means a debt that is on the security of any instrument (such as a mortgage, deed of trust, or land contract)—

(i) That makes the interest of the debtor in the qualified residence specific security for the payment of the debt,

(ii) Under which, in the event of default, the residence could be subjected to the satisfaction of the debt with the same priority as a mortgage or deed of trust in the jurisdiction in which the property is situated, and

(iii) That is recorded, where permitted, or is otherwise perfected in accordance with applicable State law.

A debt will not be considered to be secured by a qualified residence if it is secured solely by virtue of a lien upon the general assets of the taxpayer or by a security interest, such as a mechanic's lien or judgment lien, that attaches to the property without the consent of the debtor.

(2) *Special rule for debt in certain States.* Debt will not fail to be treated as secured solely because, under an applicable State or local homestead law or other debtor protection law in effect on August 16, 1986, the security interest is ineffective or the enforceability of the security interest is restricted.

(3) *Time at which debt is treated as secured.* For purposes of this section, a debt is treated as secured as of the date on which each of the requirements of paragraph (o)(1) of this section are satisfied, regardless of when amounts are actually borrowed with respect to the debt. For purposes of this paragraph (o)(3), if the instrument is recorded within a commercially reasonable time after the security interest is granted, the instrument will be treated as recorded on the date that the security interest was granted.

(4) *Partially secured debt*—(i) *In general.* If the security interest is limited to a prescribed maximum amount or portion of the residence, and the average balance of the debt exceeds such amount or the value of such portion, such excess shall not be treated as secured debt for purposes of this section.

(ii) *Example.* T borrows $80,000 on January 1, 1991. T secures the debt with a principal residence. The security in the residence for the debt, however, is limited to $20,000. T pays $8,000 in interest on the debt in 1991 and the average balance of the debt in that year is $80,000. Because the average balance of the debt exceeds the maximum amount of the security interest, such excess is not treated as secured debt. Therefore, for purposes of applying the limitation on qualified residence interest, the average balance of the secured debt is $20,000 (the maximum amount of the security interest) and the interest paid or accrued on the secured debt is $2,000 (the total interest paid on the debt multiplied by the ratio of the average balance of the secured debt ($20,000) and the average balance of the total debt ($80,000)).

(5) *Election to treat debt as not secured by a qualified residence*—(i) *In general.* For purposes of this section, a taxpayer may elect to treat any debt that is secured by a qualified residence as not secured by the qualified residence. An election made under this paragraph shall be effective for the taxable year for which the election is made and for all subsequent taxable years unless revoked with the consent of the Commissioner.

(ii) *Example.* T owns a principal residence with a fair market value of $75,000 and an adjusted purchase price of $40,000. In 1988, debt A, the proceeds of which were used to purchase the residence, has an average balance of $15,000. The proceeds of debt B, which is secured by a second mortgage on the property, are allocable to T's trade or business under § 1.163-8T and has an average balance of $25,000. In 1988, T incurs debt C, which is also secured by T's principal residence and which has an average balance in 1988 of $5,000. In the absence of an election to treat debt B as unsecured, the applicable debt limit for debt C in 1988 under paragraph (e) of this section would be zero dollars ($40,000 − $15,000 − $25,000) and none of the interest paid on debt C would be qualified residence interest. If, however, T makes or has previously made an election pursuant to paragraph (o)(5)(i) of this section to treat debt B as not secured by the residence, the applicable debt limit for debt C would be $25,000 ($40,000 − $15,000), and all of the interest paid on debt C during the taxable year would be qualified residence interest. Since the proceeds of debt B are allocable to T's trade or business under § 1.163-8T, interest on debt B may be deductible under other sections of the Internal Revenue Code.

(iii) *Allocation of debt secured by two qualified residences.* [Reserved.]

Reg. § 1.163-10T(o)(1)

(p) *Definition of qualified residence—*(1) *In general.* The term "qualified residence" means the taxpayer's principal residence (as defined in paragraph (p)(2) of this section), or the taxpayer's second residence (as defined in paragraph (p)(3) of this section).

(2) *Principal residence.* The term "principal residence" means the taxpayer's principal residence within the meaning of section 1034. For purposes of this section, a taxpayer cannot have more than one principal residence at any one time.

(3) *Second residence—*(i) *In general.* The term "second residence" means—

(A) A residence within the meaning of paragraph (p)(3)(ii) of this section,

(B) That the taxpayer uses as a residence within the meaning of paragraph (p)(3)(iii) of this section, and

(C) That the taxpayer elects to treat as a second residence pursuant to paragraph (p)(3)(iv) of this section.

A taxpayer cannot have more than one second residence at any time.

(ii) *Definition of residence.* Whether property is a residence shall be determined based on all the facts and circumstances, including the good faith of the taxpayer. A residence generally includes a house, condominium, mobile home, boat, or house trailer, that contains sleeping space and toilet and cooking facilities. A residence does not include personal property, such as furniture or a television, that, in accordance with the applicable local law, is not a fixture.

(iii) *Use as a residence.* If a residence is rented at any time during the taxable year, it is considered to be used as a residence only if the taxpayer uses it during the taxable year as a residence within the meaning of section 280A(d). If a residence is not rented at any time during the taxable year, it shall be considered to be used as a residence. For purposes of the preceding sentence, a residence will be deemed to be rented during any period that the taxpayer holds the residence out for rental or resale or repairs or renovates the residence with the intention of holding it out for rental or resale.

(iv) *Election of second residence.* A taxpayer may elect a different residence (other than the taxpayer's principal residence) to be the taxpayer's second residence for each taxable year. A taxpayer may not elect different residences as second residences at different times of the same taxable year except as provided below—

(A) If the taxpayer acquires a new residence during the taxable year, the taxpayer may elect the new residence as the taxpayer's second residence as of the date acquired;

(B) If property that was the taxpayer's principal residence during the taxable year ceases to qualify as the taxpayer's principal residence, the taxpayer may elect that property as the taxpayer's second residence as of the date that the property ceases to be the taxpayer's principal residence; or

(C) If property that was the taxpayer's second residence is sold during the taxable year or becomes the taxpayer's principal residence, the taxpayer may elect a new second residence as of such day.

(4) *Allocations between residence and other property—*(i) *In general.* For purposes of this section, the adjusted purchase price and fair market value of property must be allocated between the portion of the property that is a qualified residence and the portion that is not a qualified residence. Neither the average balance of the secured debt nor the interest paid or accrued on secured debt is so allocated. Property that is not used for residential purposes does not qualify as a residence. For example, if a portion of the property is used as an office in the taxpayer's trade or business, that portion of the property does not qualify as a residence.

(ii) *Special rule for rental of residence.* If a taxpayer rents a portion of his or her principal or second residence to another person (a "tenant"), such portion may be treated as used by the taxpayer for residential purposes if, but only if—

(A) Such rented portion is used by the tenant primarily for residential purposes,

(B) The rented portion is not a self-contained residential unit containing separate sleeping space and toilet and cooking facilities, and

(C) The total number of tenants renting (directly or by sublease) the same or different portions of the residence at any time during the taxable year does not exceed two. For this purpose, if two persons (and the dependents, as defined by section 152, of either of them) share the same sleeping quarters, they shall be treated as a single tenant.

(iii) *Examples—Example (1).* D, a dentist, uses a room in D's principal residence as an office which qualifies under section 280A(c)(1)(B) as a portion of the dwelling unit used exclusively on a regular basis as a place of business for meeting with patients in the normal course of D's trade or business. D's adjusted purchase price of the property is $65,000; $10,000 of which is allocable under paragraph (o)(4)(i) of this section to the room used as an office. For purposes of this section, D's residence does not include the room used as an office. The adjusted purchase price of the residence is, accordingly, $55,000. Similarly, the fair market value of D's residence must be allocated between the office and the remainder of the property.

Example (2). J rents out the basement of property that is otherwise used as J's principal residence. The basement is a self-contained residential unit, with sleeping space and toilet and cooking facilities. The adjusted purchase price of the property is $100,000; $15,000 of which is allocable under paragraph (o)(4)(i) of this section to the basement. For purposes of this section, J's residence does not include the basement and the adjusted purchase price of the residence is $85,000. Similarly, the fair market value of the residence must be allocated between the basement unit and the remainder of the property.

(5) *Residence under construction*—(i) *In general.* A taxpayer may treat a residence under construction as a qualified residence for a period of up to 24 months, but only if the residence becomes a qualified residence, without regard to this paragraph (p)(5)(i), as of the time that the residence is ready for occupancy.

(ii) *Example.* X owns a residential lot suitable for the construction of a vacation home. On April 20, 1987, X obtains a mortgage secured by the lot and any property to be constructed on the lot. On August 9, 1987, X begins construction of a residence on the lot. The residence is ready for occupancy on November 9, 1989. The residence is used as a residence within the meaning of paragraph (p)(3)(iii) of this section during 1989 and X elects to treat the residence as his second residence for the period November 9, 1989, through December 31, 1989. Since the residence under construction is a qualified residence as of the first day that the residence is ready for occupancy (November 9, 1987), X may treat the residence as his second residence under paragraph (p)(5)(i) of this section for up to 24 months of the period during which the residence is under construction, commencing on or after the date that construction is begun (August 9, 1987). If X treats the residence under construction as X's second residence beginning on August 9, 1987, the residence under construction would cease to qualify as a qualified residence under paragraph (p)(5)(i) on August 8, 1989. The residence's status as a qualified residence for future periods would be determined without regard to paragraph (p)(5)(i) of this section.

(6) *Special rule for time-sharing arrangements.* Property that is otherwise a qualified residence will not fail to qualify as such solely because the taxpayer's interest in or right to use the property is restricted by an arrangement whereby two or more persons with interests in the property agree to exercise control over the property for different periods during the taxable year. For purposes of determining the use of a residence under paragraph (p)(3)(iii) of this section, a taxpayer will not be considered to have used or rented a residence during any period that the taxpayer does not have the right to use the property or to receive any benefits from the rental of the property.

* * *

[Temporary Reg. § 1.163-10T.]

☐ [*T.D. 8168,* 12-21-87.]

§ 1.164-1. Deduction for taxes.—(a) *In general.* Only the following taxes shall be allowed as a deduction under this section for the taxable year within which paid or accrued, according to the method of accounting used in computing taxable income:

(1) State and local, and foreign, real property taxes.

(2) State and local personal property taxes.

(3) State and local, and foreign, income, war profits, and excess profits taxes.

* * *

(5) State and local taxes on the sale of gasoline, diesel fuel, and other motor fuels.

In addition, there shall be allowed as a deduction under this section State and local, and foreign, taxes not described in subparagraphs (1) through (5) of this paragraph which are paid or accrued within the taxable year in carrying on a trade or business or an activity described in section 212 (relating to expenses for production of income). For example, dealers or investors in securities and dealers or investors in real estate may deduct State stock transfer and real estate transfer taxes, respectively, under section 164, to the extent they are expenses incurred in carrying on a trade or business or an activity for the production of income. In general, taxes are deductible only by the person upon whom they are imposed. However, see § 1.164-5 in the case of certain taxes paid by the consumer. Also, in the case of a qualified State individual income tax (as defined in section 6362 and the regulations thereunder) which is determined by reference to a percentage of the Federal income tax (pursuant to section 6362(c)), an accrual method taxpayer shall use the cash receipts and disbursements method to compute the amount of his deduction therefor. Thus, the deduction under section 164 is in the amount actually paid with respect to the qualified tax, rather than the amount accrued with respect thereto, during the taxable year even though the taxpayer uses the accrual method of accounting for other purposes. In addition, see paragraph (f)(1) of § 301.6361-1 of this chapter (Regulations on Procedure and Administration) with respect to rules relating to allocation and reallocation of amounts collected on account of the Federal income tax and qualified taxes.

* * *

[Reg. § 1.164-1.]

□ [*T.D.* 6256, 10-7-57. *Amended by T.D.* 6406, 8-14-59, *T.D.* 6780, 12-21-64 *and T.D.* 7577, 12-19-78.]

§ 1.164-3. Definitions and special rules.—For purposes of section 164 and § 1.164-1 to § 1.164-8, inclusive—

(a) *State or local taxes.* A State or local tax includes only a tax imposed by a State, a possession of the United States, or a political subdivision of any of the foregoing, or by the District of Columbia.

(b) *Real property taxes.* The term "real property taxes" means taxes imposed on interests in real property and levied for the general public welfare, but it does not include taxes assessed against local benefits. See § 1.164-4.

(c) *Personal property taxes.* The term "personal property tax" means an ad valorem tax which is imposed on an annual basis in respect of personal property. To qualify as a personal property tax, a tax must meet the following three tests:

(1) The tax must be ad valorem—that is, substantially in proportion to the value of the personal property. A tax which is based on criteria other than value does not qualify as ad valorem. For example, a motor vehicle tax based on weight, model year, and horsepower, or any of these characteristics is not an ad valorem tax. However, a tax which is partly based on value and partly based on other criteria may qualify in part. For example, in the case of a motor vehicle tax of 1 per cent of value plus 40 cents per hundredweight, the part of the tax equal to 1 percent of value qualifies as an ad valorem tax and the balance does not qualify.

(2) The tax must be imposed on an annual basis, even if collected more frequently or less frequently.

(3) The tax must be imposed in respect of personal property. A tax may be considered to be imposed in respect of personal property even if in form it is imposed on the exercise of a privilege. Thus, for taxable years beginning after December 31, 1963, State and local taxes on the registration or licensing of highway motor vehicles are not deductible as personal property taxes unless and to the extent that the tests prescribed in this subparagraph are met. For example, an annual ad valorem tax qualifies as a personal property tax

although it is denominated a registration fee imposed for the privilege of registering motor vehicles or of using them on the highways.

(d) *Foreign taxes.* The term "foreign tax" includes only a tax imposed by the authority of a foreign country. A tax imposed by a political subdivision of a foreign country is considered to be imposed by the authority of that foreign country.

* * *

[Reg. § 1.164-3.]

□ [*T.D.* 6256, 10-7-57. *Amended by T.D.* 6780, 12-21-64.]

§ 1.164-4. Taxes for local benefits.—(a) So-called taxes for local benefits referred to in paragraph (g) of § 1.164-2 more properly assessments, paid for local benefits such as street, sidewalks, and other like improvements, imposed because of and measured by some benefit inuring directly to the property against which the assessment is levied are not deductible as taxes. A tax is considered assessed against local benefits when the property subject to the tax is limited to property benefited. Special assessments are not deductible, even though an incidental benefit may inure to the public welfare. The real property taxes deductible are those levied for the general public welfare by the proper taxing authorities at a like rate against all property in the territory over which such authorities have jurisdiction. Assessments under the statutes of California relating to irrigation, and of Iowa relating to drainage, and under certain statutes of Tennessee relating to levees, are limited to property benefited, and if the assessments are so limited, the amounts paid thereunder are not deductible as taxes. For treatment of assessments for local benefits as adjustments to the basis of property, see section 1016(a)(1) and the regulations thereunder.

(b) (1) Insofar as assessments against local benefits are made for the purpose of maintenance or repair or for the purpose of meeting interest charges with respect to such benefits, they are deductible. In such cases, the burden is on the taxpayer to show the allocation of the amounts assessed to the different purposes. If the allocation cannot be made, none of the amount so paid is deductible.

(2) Taxes levied by a special taxing district which was in existence on December 31, 1963, for the purpose of retiring indebtedness existing on such date, are deductible, to the extent levied for such purpose, if (i) the district covers the whole of at least one county, (ii) if at least 1,000 persons are subject to the taxes levied by the district, and (iii) if the district levies its assessments annually at a uniform rate on the same assessed value of real property, including improvements, as is used

Reg. § 1.164-4(b)(2)

for purposes of the real property tax generally. [Reg. § 1.164-4.]

☐ [*T.D.* 6256, 10-7-57. *Amended by T.D.* 6780, 12-21-64.]

§ 1.164-6. Apportionment of taxes on real property between seller and purchaser.—(a) *Scope.* Except as provided otherwise in section 164(f) and § 1.164-8, when real property is sold, section 164(d)(1) governs the deduction by the seller and the purchaser of current real property taxes. Section 164(d)(1) performs two functions: (1) It provides a method by which a portion of the taxes for the real property tax year in which the property is sold may be deducted by the seller and a portion by the purchaser; and (2) it limits the deduction of the seller and the purchaser to the portion of the taxes corresponding to the part of the real property tax year during which each was the owner of the property. These functions are accomplished by treating a portion of the taxes for the real property tax year in which the property is sold as imposed on the seller and a portion as imposed on the purchaser. To the extent that the taxes are treated as imposed on the seller and the purchaser, each shall be allowed a deduction, under section 164(a), in the taxable year such tax is paid or accrued, or treated as paid or accrued under section 164(d)(2)(A) or (D) and this section. No deduction is allowed for taxes on real property to the extent that they are imposed on another taxpayer, or are treated as imposed on another taxpayer under section 164(d). For the election to accrue real property taxes ratably see section 461(c) and the regulations thereunder.

(b) *Application of rule of apportionment.* (1)(i) For purposes of the deduction provided by section 164(a), if real property is sold during any real property tax year, the portion of the real property tax properly allocable to that part of the real property tax year which ends on the day before the date of the sale shall be treated as a tax imposed on the seller, and the portion of such tax properly allocable to that part of such real property tax year which begins on the date of the sale shall be treated as a tax imposed on the purchaser. For definition of "real property tax year" see paragraph (c) of this section. This rule shall apply whether or not the seller and the purchaser apportion such tax. The rule of apportionment contained in section 164(d)(1) applies even though the same real property is sold more than once during the real property tax year. (See paragraph (d)(5) of this section for rule requiring inclusion in gross income of excess deductions.)

* * *

(c) *Real property tax year.* As used in section 164(d), the term "real property tax year" refers to the period which, under the law imposing the tax,

is regarded as the period to which the tax imposed relates. Where the State and one or more local governmental units each imposes a tax on real property, the real property tax year for each tax must be determined for purposes of applying the rule of apportionment of section 164(d)(1) to each tax. The time when the tax rate is determined, the time when the assessment is made, the time when the tax becomes a lien, or the time when the tax becomes due or delinquent does not necessarily determine the real property tax year. The real property tax year may or may not correspond to the fiscal year of the governmental unit imposing the tax. In each case the State or local law determines what constitutes the real property tax year. Although the seller and the purchaser may or may not make an allocation of real property taxes, the meaning of "real property tax year" in section 164(d) and the application of section 164(d) do not depend upon what real property taxes were allocated nor the method of allocation used by the parties.

* * *

[Reg. § 1.164-6.]

☐ [*T.D.* 6256, 10-7-57. *Amended by T.D.* 6293, 5-20-58 *and T.D.* 6406, 8-14-59.]

§ 1.165-1. Losses.—(a) *Allowance of deduction.* Section 165(a) provides that, in computing taxable income under section 63, any loss actually sustained during the taxable year and not made good by insurance or some other form of compensation shall be allowed as a deduction subject to any provision of the internal revenue laws which prohibits or limits the amount of the deduction. This deduction for losses sustained shall be taken in accordance with section 165 and the regulations thereunder. For the disallowance of deductions for worthless securities issued by a political party, see § 1.271-1.

(b) *Nature of loss allowable.* To be allowable as a deduction under section 165(a), a loss must be evidenced by closed and completed transactions, fixed by identifiable events, and, except as otherwise provided in section 165(h) and § 1.165-11, relating to disaster losses, actually sustained during the taxable year. Only a bona fide loss is allowable. Substance and not mere form shall govern in determining a deductible loss.

(c) *Amount deductible.* (1) The amount of loss allowable as a deduction under section 165(a) shall not exceed the amount prescribed by § 1.1011-1 as the adjusted basis for determining the loss from the sale or other disposition of the property involved. In the case of each such deduction claimed, therefore, the basis of the property must be properly adjusted as prescribed by § 1.1011-1 for such items as expenditures, receipts, or losses, properly chargeable to capital account, and for such items as depreciation, obsolescence, amortization, and depletion, in order to determine the amount of loss allowable as a deduction. To determine the allowable loss in the case of property acquired before March 1, 1913, see also paragraph (b) of § 1.1053-1.

(2) The amount of loss recognized upon the sale or exchange of property shall be determined for purposes of section 165(a) in accordance with § 1.1002-1.

(3) A loss from the sale or exchange of a capital asset shall be allowed as a deduction under section 165(a) but only to the extent allowed in section 1211 (relating to limitation on capital losses) and section 1212 (relating to capital loss carrybacks and carryovers), and in the regulations under those sections.

(4) In determining the amount of loss actually sustained for purposes of section 165(a), proper adjustment shall be made for any salvage value and for any insurance or other compensation received.

(d) *Year of deduction.* (1) A loss shall be allowed as a deduction under section 165(a) only for the taxable year in which the loss is sustained. For this purpose, a loss shall be treated as sustained during the taxable year in which the loss occurs as evidenced by closed and completed transactions and as fixed by identifiable events occurring in such taxable year. For provisions relating to situations where a loss attributable to a disaster will be treated as sustained in the taxable year immediately preceding the taxable year in which the disaster actually occurred, see section 165(h) and § 1.165-11.

(2)(i) If a casualty or other event occurs which may result in a loss and, in the year of such casualty or event, there exists a claim for reimbursement with respect to which there is a reasonable prospect of recovery, no portion of the loss with respect to which reimbursement may be received is sustained, for purposes of section 165, until it can be ascertained with reasonable certainty whether or not such reimbursement will be received. Whether a reasonable prospect of recovery exists with respect to a claim for reimbursement of a loss is a question of fact to be determined upon an examination of all facts and circumstances. Whether or not such reimbursement will be received may be ascertained with reasonable certainty, for example, by a settlement of the claim, by an adjudication of the claim, or by an abandonment of the claim. When a taxpayer claims that the taxable year in which a loss is sustained is fixed by his abandonment of the claim for reimbursement, he must be able to produce objective evidence of his having abandoned the claim, such as the execution of a release.

(ii) If in the year of the casualty or other event a portion of the loss is not covered by a claim for reimbursement with respect to which there is a reasonable prospect of recovery, then such portion of the loss is sustained during the taxable year in which the casualty or other event occurs. For example, if property having an adjusted basis of $10,000 is completely destroyed by fire in 1961, and if the taxpayer's only claim for reimbursement consists of an insurance claim for $8,000 which is settled in 1962, the taxpayer sustains a loss of $2,000 in 1961. However, if the taxpayer's automobile is completely destroyed in 1961 as a result of the negligence of another person and there exists a reasonable prospect of recovery on a claim for the full value of the automobile against such person, the taxpayer does not sustain any loss until the taxable year in which the claim is adjudicated or otherwise settled. If the automobile had an adjusted basis of $5,000 and the taxpayer secures a judgment of $4,000 in 1962, $1,000 is deductible for the taxable year 1962. If in 1963 it becomes reasonably certain that only $3,500 can ever be collected on such judgment, $500 is deductible for the taxable year 1963.

(iii) If the taxpayer deducted a loss in accordance with the provisions of this paragraph and in a subsequent taxable year receives reimbursement for such loss, he does not recompute the tax for the taxable year in which the deduction was taken but includes the amount of such reimbursement in his gross income for the taxable year in which received, subject to the provisions of section 111, relating to recovery of amounts previously deducted.

(3) Any loss arising from theft shall be treated as sustained during the taxable year in which the taxpayer discovers the loss (see § 1.165-8, relating to theft losses). However, if in the year of discovery there exists a claim for reimbursement with respect to which there is a reasonable prospect of recovery, no portion of the loss with respect to which reimbursement may be received is sustained, for purposes of section 165, until the taxable year in which it can be ascertained with reasonable certainty whether or not such reimbursement will be received.

* * *

(e) *Limitation on losses of individuals.* In the case of an individual, the deduction for losses granted by section 165(a) shall, subject to the provisions of section 165(c) and paragraph (a) of this section, be limited to:

(1) Losses incurred in a trade or business;

(2) Losses incurred in any transaction entered into for profit, though not connected with a trade or business; and

Reg. § 1.165-1(e)(2)

(3) Losses of property not connected with a trade or business and not incurred in any transaction entered into for profit, if such losses arise from fire, storm, shipwreck, or other casualty, or from theft, and if the loss involved has not been allowed for estate tax purposes in the estate tax return. For additional provisions pertaining to the allowance of casualty and theft losses, see §§ 1.165-7 and 1.165-8, respectively. For special rules relating to an election by a taxpayer to deduct disaster losses in the taxable year immediately preceding the taxable year in which the disaster occurred, see section 165(h) and § 1.165-11. [Reg. § 1.165-1.]

□ [*T.D. 6445, 1-15-60. Amended by T.D. 6753, 5-18-64, T.D. 6996, 1-17-69, T.D. 7301, 1-3-74 and T.D. 7522, 12-15-77.*]

§ 1.165-2. Obsolescence of nondepreciable property.—(a) *Allowance of deduction.* A loss incurred in a business or in a transaction entered into for profit and arising from the sudden termination of the usefulness in such business or transaction of any nondepreciable property, in a case where such business or transaction is discontinued or where such property is permanently discarded from use therein, shall be allowed as a deduction under section 165(a) for the taxable year in which the loss is actually sustained. For this purpose, the taxable year in which the loss is sustained is not necessarily the taxable year in which the overt act of abandonment, or the loss of title to the property, occurs.

(b) *Exceptions.* This section does not apply to losses sustained upon the sale or exchange of property, losses sustained upon the obsolescence or worthlessness of depreciable property, casualty losses, or losses reflected in inventories required to be taken under section 471. The limitations contained in sections 1211 and 1212 upon losses from the sale or exchange of capital assets do not apply to losses allowable under this section.

(c) *Cross references.* For the allowance under section 165(a) of losses arising from the permanent withdrawal of depreciable property from use in the trade or business or in the production of income, see § 1.167(a)-8. For provisions respecting the obsolescence of depreciable property, see § 1.167(a)-9. For the allowance of casualty losses, see § 1.165-7. [Reg. § 1.165-2.]

□ [*T.D. 6445, 1-15-60.*]

§ 1.165-4. Decline in value of stock.—(a) *Deduction disallowed.* No deduction shall be allowed under section 165(a) solely on account of a decline in the value of stock owned by the taxpayer when the decline is due to a fluctuation in the market price of the stock or to other similar cause. A mere shrinkage in the value of stock owned by the taxpayer, even though extensive, does not give rise to a deduction under section 165(a) if the stock has any recognizable value on the date claimed as the date of loss. No loss for a decline in the value of stock owned by the taxpayer shall be allowed as a deduction under section 165(a) except insofar as the loss is recognized under § 1.1002-1 upon the sale or exchange of the stock and except as otherwise provided in § 1.165-5 with respect to stock which becomes worthless during the taxable year.

(b) *Stock owned by banks.* (1) In the regulation of banks and certain other corporations, Federal and State authorities may require that stock owned by such organizations be charged off as worthless or written down to a nominal value. If, in any such case, this requirement is premised upon the worthlessness of the stock, the charging off or writing down will be considered prima facie evidence of worthlessness for purposes of section 165(a); but, if the charging off or writing down is due to a fluctuation in the market price of the stock or if no reasonable attempt to determine the worthlessness of the stock has been made, then no deduction shall be allowed under section 165(a) for the amount so charged off or written down.

(2) This paragraph shall not be construed, however, to permit a deduction under section 165(a) unless the stock owned by the bank or other corporation actually becomes worthless in the taxable year. Such a taxpayer owning stock which becomes worthless during the taxable year is not precluded from deducting the loss under section 165(a) merely because, in obedience to the specific orders or general policy of such supervisory authorities, the value of the stock is written down to a nominal amount instead of being charged off completely.

(c) *Application to inventories.* This section does not apply to a decline in the value of corporate stock reflected in inventories required to be taken by a dealer in securities under section 471. See § 1.471-5.

(d) *Definition.* As used in this section, the term "stock" means a share of stock in a corporation or a right to subscribe for, or to receive, a share of stock in a corporation. [Reg. § 1.165-4.]

□ [*T.D. 6445, 1-15-60.*]

§ 1.165-5. Worthless securities.—(a) *Definition of security.* As used in section 165(g) and this section, the term "security" means:

(1) A share of stock in a corporation;

(2) A right to subscribe for, or to receive, a share of stock in a corporation; or

(3) A bond, debenture, note, or certificate, or other evidence of indebtedness to pay a fixed or determinable sum of money, which has been issued with interest coupons or in registered form

by a domestic or foreign corporation or by any government or political subdivision thereof.

(b) *Ordinary loss.* If any security which is not a capital asset becomes wholly worthless during the taxable year, the loss resulting therefrom may be deducted under section 165(a) as an ordinary loss.

(c) *Capital loss.* If any security which is a capital asset becomes wholly worthless at any time during the taxable year, the loss resulting therefrom may be deducted under section 165(a) but only as though it were a loss from a sale or exchange, on the last day of the taxable year, of a capital asset. See section 165(g)(1). The amount so allowed as a deduction shall be subject to the limitations upon capital losses described in paragraph (c)(3) of § 1.165-1.

(d) *Loss on worthless securities of an affiliated corporation* —(1) *Deductible as an ordinary loss.* If a taxpayer which is a domestic corporation owns any security of a domestic or foreign corporation which is affiliated with the taxpayer within the meaning of subparagraph (2) of this paragraph and such security becomes wholly worthless during the taxable year, the loss resulting therefrom may be deducted under section 165(a) as an ordinary loss in accordance with paragraph (b) of this section. The fact that the security is in fact a capital asset of the taxpayer is immaterial for this purpose, since section 165(g)(3) provides that such security shall be treated as though it were not a capital asset for the purposes of section 165(g)(1). A debt which becomes wholly worthless during the taxable year shall be allowed as an ordinary loss in accordance with the provisions of this subparagraph, to the extent that such debt is a security within the meaning of paragraph (a)(3) of this section.

(2) *Affiliated corporation defined.* For purposes of this paragraph, a corporation shall be treated as affiliated with the taxpayer owning the security if—

(i)(*a*) In the case of a taxable year beginning on or after January 1, 1970, the taxpayer owns directly—

(*1*) Stock possessing at least 80 percent of the voting power of all classes of such corporation's stock, and

(*2*) At least 80 percent of each class of such corporation's nonvoting stock

excluding for purposes of this subdivision (i)(*a*) nonvoting stock which is limited and preferred as to dividends (see section 1504(a)), or

(*b*) In the case of a taxable year beginning before January 1, 1970, the taxpayer owns directly at least 95 percent of each class of the stock of such corporation;

(ii) None of the stock of such corporation was acquired by the taxpayer solely for the purpose of converting a capital loss sustained by reason of the worthlessness of any such stock into an ordinary loss under section 165(g)(3), and

(iii) More than 90 percent of the aggregate of the gross receipts of such corporation for all the taxable years during which it has been in existence has been from sources other than royalties, rents (except rents derived from rental of properties to employees of such corporation in the ordinary course of its operating business), dividends, interest (except interest received on the deferred purchase price of operating assets sold), annuities and gains from sales or exchanges of stocks and securities. For this purpose, the term "gross receipts" means total receipts determined without any deduction for cost of goods sold, and gross receipts from sales or exchanges of stocks and securities shall be taken into account only to the extent of gains from such sales or exchanges.

(e) *Bonds issued by an insolvent corporation.* A bond of an insolvent corporation secured only by a mortgage from which nothing is realized for the bondholders on foreclosure shall be regarded as having become worthless not later than the year of the foreclosure sale, and no deduction in respect of the loss shall be allowed under section 165(a) in computing a bondholder's taxable income for a subsequent year. See also paragraph (d) of § 1.165-1.

(f) *Decline in market value.* A taxpayer possessing a security to which this section relates shall not be allowed any deduction under section 165(a) on account of mere market fluctuation in the value of such security. See also § 1.165-4.

(g) *Application to inventories.* This section does not apply to any loss upon the worthlessness of any security reflected in inventories required to be taken by a dealer in securities under section 471. See § 1.471-5.

(h) *Special rules for banks.* For special rules applicable under this section to worthless securities of a bank, including securities issued by an affiliated bank, see § 1.582-1.

(i) *Examples.* The provisions of this section may be illustrated by the following examples:

Example (1). (i) X Corporation, a domestic manufacturing corporation which makes its return on the basis of the calendar year, owns 100 percent of each class of the stock of Y Corporation; and, in addition, 19 percent of the common stock (the only class of stock) of Z Corporation, which it acquired in 1948. Y Corporation, a domestic manufacturing corporation which makes its return on the basis of the calendar year, owns 81 percent of the common stock of Z Corporation, which it acquired in 1946. It is established that

Reg. § 1.165-5(i)

the stock of Z Corporation, which has from its inception derived all its gross receipts from manufacturing operations, became worthless during 1971.

(ii) Since the stock of Z Corporation which is owned by X Corporation is a capital asset and since X Corporation does not directly own at least 80 percent of the stock of Z Corporation, any loss sustained by X Corporation upon the worthlessness of such stock shall be deducted under section 165(g)(1) and paragraph (c) of this section as a loss from a sale or exchange on December 31, 1971, of a capital asset. The loss so sustained by X Corporation shall be considered a long-term capital loss under the provisions of section 1222(4), since the stock was held by that corporation for more than 6 months.

(iii) Since Z Corporation is considered to be affiliated with Y Corporation under the provisions of paragraph (d)(2) of this section, any loss sustained by Y Corporation upon the worthlessness of the stock of Z Corporation shall be deducted in 1971 under section 165(g)(3) and paragraph (d)(1) of this section as an ordinary loss.

Example (2). (i) On January 1, 1971, X Corporation, a domestic manufacturing corporation which makes its return on the basis of the calendar year, owns 60 percent of each class of the stock of Y Corporation, a foreign corporation, which it acquired in 1950. Y Corporation has, from the date of its incorporation, derived all of its gross receipts from manufacturing operations. It is established that the stock of Y Corporation became worthless on June 30, 1971. On August 1, 1971, X Corporation acquires the balance of the stock of Y Corporation for the purpose of obtaining the benefit of section 165(g)(3) with respect to the loss it has sustained on the worthlessness of the stock of Y Corporation.

(ii) Since the stock of Y Corporation which is owned by X Corporation is a capital asset and since Y Corporation is not to be treated as affiliated with X Corporation under the provisions of paragraph (d)(2) of this section, notwithstanding the fact that, at the close of 1971, X Corporation owns 100 percent of each class of stock of Y Corporation, any loss sustained by X Corporation upon the worthlessness of such stock shall be deducted under the provisions of section 165(g)(1) and paragraph (c) of this section as a loss from a sale or exchange on December 31, 1971, of a capital asset.

Example (3). (i) X Corporation, a domestic manufacturing corporation which makes its return on the basis of the calendar year, owns 80 percent of each class of the stock of Y Corporation, which from its inception has derived all of its gross receipts from manufacturing operations. As

one of its capital assets, X Corporation owns $100,000 in registered bonds issued by Y Corporation payable at maturity on December 31, 1974. It is established that these bonds became worthless during 1971.

(ii) Since Y Corporation is considered to be affiliated with X Corporation under the provisions of paragraph (d)(2) of this section, any loss sustained by X Corporation upon the worthlessness of these bonds may be deducted in 1971 under section 165(g)(3) and paragraph (d)(1) of this section as an ordinary loss. The loss may not be deducted under section 166 as a bad debt. See section 166(e). [Reg. § 1.165-5.]

☐ [*T.D. 6445, 1-15-60. Amended by T.D. 7224, 12-5-72.*]

§ 1.165-6. **Farming losses.**—(a) *Allowance of losses.* (1) Except as otherwise provided in this section, any loss incurred in the operation of a farm as a trade or business shall be allowed as a deduction under section 165(a) or as a net operating loss deduction in accordance with the provisions of section 172. See § 1.172-1.

(2) If the taxpayer owns and operates a farm for profit in addition to being engaged in another trade or business, but sustains a loss from the operation of the farming business, then the amount of loss sustained in the operation of the farm may be deducted from gross income, if any, from all other sources.

(3) Loss incurred in the operation of a farm for recreation or pleasure shall not be allowed as a deduction from gross income. See § 1.162-12.

(b) *Loss from shrinkage.* If, in the course of the business of farming, farm products are held for a favorable market, no deduction shall be allowed under section 165(a) in respect of such products merely because of shrinkage in weight, decline in value, or deterioration in storage.

(c) *Loss of prospective crop.* The total loss by frost, storm, flood, or fire of a prospective crop being grown in the business of farming shall not be allowed as a deduction under section 165(a).

(d) *Loss of livestock* —(1) *Raised stock.* A taxpayer engaged in the business of raising and selling livestock, such as cattle, sheep, or horses, may not deduct as a loss under section 165(a) the value of animals that perish from among those which were raised on the farm.

(2) *Purchased stock.* The loss sustained upon the death by disease, exposure, or injury of any livestock purchased and used in the trade or business of farming shall be allowed as a deduction under section 165(a). See, also, paragraph (e) of this section.

(e) *Loss due to compliance with orders of governmental authority.* The loss sustained upon the destruction by order of the United States, a State, or any other governmental authority, of any livestock, or other property, purchased and used in the trade or business of farming shall be allowed as a deduction under section 165(a).

(f) *Amount deductible* —(1) *Expenses of operation.* The cost of any feed, pasture, or care which is allowed under section 162 as an expense of operating a farm for profit shall not be included as a part of the cost of livestock for purposes of determining the amount of loss deductible under section 165(a) and this section. For the deduction of farming expenses, see § 1.162-12.

(2) *Losses reflected in inventories.* If inventories are taken into account in determining the income from the trade or business of farming, no deduction shall be allowed under this section for losses sustained during the taxable year upon livestock or other products, whether purchased for resale or produced on the farm, to the extent such losses are reflected in the inventory on hand at the close of the taxable year. Nothing in this section shall be construed to disallow the deduction of any loss reflected in the inventories of the taxpayer. For provisions relating to inventories of farmers, see section 471 and the regulations thereunder.

(3) *Other limitations.* For other provisions relating to the amount deductible under this section, see paragraph (c) of § 1.165-1, relating to the amount deductible under section 165(a); § 1.165-7, relating to casualty losses; and § 1.1231-1, relating to gains and losses from the sale or exchange of certain property used in the trade or business.

(g) *Other provisions applicable to farmers.* For other provisions relating to farmers, see § 1.61-4, relating to gross income of farmers; paragraph (b) of § 1.167(a)-6, relating to depreciation in the case of farmers; and § 1.175-1, relating to soil and water conservation expenditures. [Reg. § 1.165-6.]

☐ [*T.D.* 6445, 1-15-60.]

[Note: Reg. §1.165-7 does not reflect the limitations imposed by Section 165(h)(2), added in 1984.]

§ 1.165-7. Casualty losses.—(a) *In general* —(1) *Allowance of deduction.* Except as otherwise provided in paragraphs (b)(4) and (c) of this section, any loss arising from fire, storm, shipwreck, or other casualty is allowable as a deduction under section 165(a) for the taxable year in which the loss is sustained. However, see § 1.165-6, relating to farming losses, and § 1.165-11, relating to an election by a taxpayer to deduct disaster losses in the taxable year immediately preceding the taxable year in which the disaster occurred. The manner of determining the amount of a casualty loss allowable as a deduction in computing taxable

income under section 63 is the same whether the loss has been incurred in a trade or business or in any transaction entered into for profit, or whether it has been a loss of property not connected with a trade or business and not incurred in any transaction entered into for profit. The amount of a casualty loss shall be determined in accordance with paragraph (b) of this section. For other rules relating to the treatment of deductible casualty losses, see § 1.1231-1, relating to the involuntary conversion of property.

(2) *Method of valuation.* (i) In determining the amount of loss deductible under this section, the fair market value of the property immediately before and immediately after the casualty shall generally be ascertained by competent appraisal. This appraisal must recognize the effects of any general market decline affecting undamaged as well as damaged property which may occur simultaneously with the casualty, in order that any deduction under this section shall be limited to the actual loss resulting from damage to the property.

(ii) The cost of repairs to the property damaged is acceptable as evidence of the loss of value if the taxpayer shows that (*a*) the repairs are necessary to restore the property to its condition immediately before the casualty, (*b*) the amount spent for such repairs is not excessive, (*c*) the repairs do not care for more than the damage suffered, and (*d*) the value of the property after the repairs does not as a result of the repairs exceed the value of the property immediately before the casualty.

(3) *Damage to automobiles.* An automobile owned by the taxpayer, whether used for business purposes or maintained for recreation or pleasure, may be the subject of a casualty loss, including those losses specifically referred to in subparagraph (1) of this paragraph. In addition, a casualty loss occurs when an automobile owned by the taxpayer is damaged and when:

(i) The damage results from the faulty driving of the taxpayer or other person operating the automobile but is not due to the willful act or willful negligence of the taxpayer or of one acting in his behalf, or

(ii) The damage results from the faulty driving of the operator of the vehicle with which the automobile of the taxpayer collides.

(4) *Application to inventories.* This section does not apply to a casualty loss reflected in the inventories of the taxpayer. For provisions relating to inventories, see section 471 and the regulations thereunder.

(5) *Property converted from personal use.* In the case of property which originally was not used in the trade or business or for income-producing

purposes and which is thereafter converted to either of such uses, the fair market value of the property on the date of conversion, if less than the adjusted basis of the property at such time, shall be used, after making proper adjustments in respect of basis, as the basis for determining the amount of loss under paragraph (b)(1) of this section. See paragraph (b) of § 1.165-9, and § 1.167(g)-1.

(6) *Theft losses.* A loss which arises from theft is not considered a casualty loss for purposes of this section. See § 1.165-8, relating to theft losses.

(b) *Amount deductible* —(1) *General rule.* In the case of any casualty loss whether or not incurred in a trade or business or in any transaction entered into for profit, the amount of loss to be taken into account for purposes of section 165(a) shall be the lesser of either—

(i) The amount which is equal to the fair market value of the property immediately before the casualty reduced by the fair market value of the property immediately after the casualty; or

(ii) The amount of the adjusted basis prescribed in § 1.1011-1 for determining the loss from the sale or other disposition of the property involved. However, if the property used in a trade or business or held for the production of income is totally destroyed by casualty, and if the fair market value of such property immediately before the casualty is less than the adjusted basis of such property, the amount of the adjusted basis of such property shall be treated as the amount of the loss for purposes of section 165(a).

(2) *Aggregation of property for computing loss.* (i) A loss incurred in a trade or business or in any transaction entered into for profit shall be determined under subparagraph (1) of this paragraph by reference to the single, identifiable property damaged or destroyed. Thus, for example, in determining the fair market value of the property before and after the casualty in a case where damage by casualty has occurred to a building and ornamental or fruit trees used in a trade or business, the decrease in value shall be measured by taking the building and trees into account separately, and not together as an integral part of the realty, and separate losses shall be determined for such building and trees.

(ii) In determining a casualty loss involving real property and improvements thereon not used in a trade or business or in any transaction entered into for profit, the improvements (such as buildings and ornamental trees and shrubbery) to the property damaged or destroyed shall be considered an integral part of the property, for purposes of subparagraph (1) of this paragraph, and no separate basis need by apportioned to such improvements.

(3) *Examples.* The application of this paragraph may be illustrated by the following examples:

Example (1). In 1956 B purchases for $3,600 an automobile which he uses for nonbusiness purposes. In 1959 the automobile is damaged in an accidental collision with another automobile. The fair market value of B's automobile is $2,000 immediately before the collision and $1,500 immediately after the collision. B receives insurance proceeds of $300 to cover the loss. The amount of the deduction allowable under section 165(a) for the taxable year 1959 is $200, computed as follows:

Value of automobile immediately before casualty	$2,000
Less: Value of automobile immediately after casualty	1,500
Value of property actually destroyed	500
Loss to be taken into account for purposes of section 165(a): Lesser amount of property actually destroyed ($500) or adjusted basis of property ($3,600) . .	$ 500
Less: Insurance received	300
Deduction allowable	200

Example (2). In 1958 A purchases land containing an office building for the lump sum of $90,000. The purchase price is allocated between the land ($18,000) and the building ($72,000) for purposes of determining basis. After the purchase A planted trees and ornamental shrubs on the grounds surrounding the building. In 1961 the land, building, trees, and shrubs are damaged by hurricane. At the time of the casualty the adjusted basis of the land is $18,000 and the adjusted basis of the building is $66,000. At that time the trees and shrubs have an adjusted basis of $1,200. The fair market value of the land and building immediately before the casualty is $18,000 and $70,000, respectively, and immediately after the casualty is $18,000 and $52,000, respectively. The fair market value of the trees and shrubs immediately before the casualty is $2,000 and immediately after the casualty is $400. In 1961 insurance of $5,000 is received to cover the loss to the building. A has no other gains or losses in 1961 subject to section 1231 and § 1.1231-1. The amount of the deduction allowable under section 165(a) with respect to the building for the taxable year 1961 is $13,000, computed as follows:

Reg. § 1.165-7(a)(6)

Value of property immediately before casualty	$70,000
Less: Value of property immediately after casualty	52,000
Value of property actually destroyed	18,000

Loss to be taken into account for purposes of section 165(a):	
Lesser amount of property actually destroyed ($18,000) or adjusted basis	
of property ($66,000)	$18,000
Less: Insurance received	5,000
Deduction allowable	13,000

The amount of the deduction allowable under section 165(a) with respect to the trees and shrubs for the taxable year 1961 is $1,200, computed as follows:

Value of property immediately before casualty	$2,000
Less: Value of property immediately after casualty	400
Value of property actually destroyed	1,600

Loss to be taken into account for purposes of section 165(a): Lesser amount of	
property actually destroyed ($1,600) or adjusted basis of property ($1,200) .	$1,200

Example (3). Assume the same facts as in example (2) except that A purchases land containing a house instead of an office building. The house is used as his private residence. Since the property is used for personal purposes, no allocation of the purchase price is necessary for the land and house. Likewise, no individual determination of the fair market values of the land, house, trees, and shrubs is necessary. The amount of the deduction allowable under section 165(a) with respect to the land, house, trees, and shrubs for the taxable year 1961 is $14,600, computed as follows:

Value of property immediately before casualty	$90,000
Less: Value of property immediately after casualty	70,400
Value of property actually destroyed	$19,600

Loss to be taken into account for purposes of section 165(a): Lesser amount of	
property actually destroyed ($19,600) or adjusted basis of property	
($91,200)	$19,600
Less: Insurance received	5,000
Deduction allowable	14,600

(4) *Limitation on certain losses sustained by individuals after December 31, 1963.* (i) Pursuant to section 165(c)(3), the deduction allowable under section 165(a) in respect of a loss sustained—

    (*a*) After December 31, 1963, in a taxable year ending after such date,

    (*b*) In respect of property not used in a trade or business or for income producing purposes, and

    (*c*) From a single casualty

shall be limited to that portion of the loss which is in excess of $100. The nondeductibility of the first $100 of loss applies to a loss sustained after December 31, 1963, without regard to when the casualty occurred. Thus, if property not used in a trade or business or for income producing purposes is damaged or destroyed by a casualty which occurred prior to January 1, 1964, and loss resulting therefrom is sustained after December 31, 1963, the $100 limitation applies.

(ii) The $100 limitation applies separately in respect of each casualty and applies to the entire loss sustained from each casualty. Thus, if as a result of a particular casualty occurring in 1964, a taxpayer sustains in 1964 a loss of $40 and in 1965 a loss of $250, no deduction is allowable for the loss sustained in 1964 and the loss sustained in 1965 must be reduced by $60 ($100 — $40). The determination of whether damage to, or destruction of, property resulted from a single casualty or from two or more separate casualties will be made upon the basis of the particular facts of each case. However, events which are closely related in origin generally give rise to a single casualty. For example, if a storm damages a taxpayer's residence and his automobile parked in his driveway, any loss sustained results from a single casualty. Similarly, if a hurricane causes high waves, all wind and flood damage to a taxpayer's property caused by the hurricane and the waves results from a single casualty.

(iii) Except as otherwise provided in this subdivision, the $100 limitation applies sepa-

Reg. § 1.165-7(b)(4)

rately to each individual taxpayer who sustains a loss even though the property damaged or destroyed is owned by two or more individuals. Thus, if a house occupied by two sisters and jointly owned by them is damaged or destroyed, the $100 limitation applies separately to each sister in respect of any loss sustained by her. However, for purposes of applying the $100 limitation, a husband and wife who file a joint return for the first taxable year in which the loss is allowable as a deduction are treated as one individual taxpayer. Accordingly, if property jointly owned by a husband and wife, or property separately owned by the husband or by the wife, is damaged or destroyed by a single casualty in 1964, and a loss is sustained in that year by either or both the husband or wife, only one $100 limitation applies if a joint return is filed for 1964. If, however, the husband and wife file separate returns for 1964, the $100 limitation applies separately in respect of any loss sustained by the husband and in respect of any loss sustained by the wife. Where losses from a single casualty are sustained in two or more separate tax years, the husband and wife shall, for purposes of applying the $100 limitation to such losses, be treated as one individual for all such years if they file a joint return for the first year in which a loss is sustained from the casualty; they shall be treated as separate individuals for all such years if they file separate returns for the first such year. If a joint return is filed in the first loss year but separate returns are filed in a subsequent year, any unused portion of the $100 limitation shall be allocated equally between the husband and wife in the latter year.

(iv) If a loss is sustained in respect of property used partially for business and partially for nonbusiness purposes, the $100 limitation applies only to that portion of the loss properly attributable to the nonbusiness use. For example, if a taxpayer sustains a $1,000 loss in respect of an automobile which he uses 60 percent for business and 40 percent for nonbusiness, the loss is allocated 60 percent to business use and 40 percent to nonbusiness use. The $100 limitation applies to the portion of the loss allocable to the nonbusiness loss.

(c) *Loss sustained by an estate.* A casualty loss of property not connected with a trade or business and not incurred in any transaction entered into for profit which is sustained during the settlement of an estate shall be allowed as a deduction under sections 165(a) and 641(b) in computing the taxable income of the estate if the loss has not been allowed under section 2054 in computing the taxable estate of the decedent and if the statement has been filed in accordance with § 1.642(g)-1. See section 165(c)(3).

(d) *Loss treated as though attributable to a trade or business.* For the rule treating a casualty loss not connected with a trade or business as though it were a deduction attributable to a trade or business for purposes of computing a net operating loss, see paragraph (a)(3)(iii) of § 1.172-3.

* * *

[Reg. § 1.165-7.]

☐ [*T.D.* 6445, 1-15-60. *Amended by T.D.* 6712, 3-23-64, *T.D.* 6735, 5-18-64, *T.D.* 6786, 12-28-64 *and T.D.* 7522, 12-15-77.]

§ 1.165-8. Theft losses.—(a) *Allowance of deduction.* (1) Except as otherwise provided in paragraphs (b) and (c) of this section, any loss arising from theft is allowable as a deduction under section 165(a) for the taxable year in which the loss is sustained. See section 165(c)(3).

(2) A loss arising from theft shall be treated under section 165(a) as sustained during the taxable year in which the taxpayer discovers the loss. See section 165(e). Thus, a theft loss is not deductible under section 165(a) for the taxable year in which the theft actually occurs unless that is also the year in which the taxpayer discovers the loss. However, if in the year of discovery there exists a claim for reimbursement with respect to which there is a reasonable prospect of recovery, see paragraph (d) of § 1.165-1.

(3) The same theft loss shall not be taken into account both in computing a tax under chapter 1, relating to the income tax, or chapter 2, relating to additional income taxes, of the Internal Revenue Code of 1939 and in computing the income tax under the Internal Revenue Code of 1954. See section 7852(c), relating to items not to be twice deducted from income.

(b) *Loss sustained by an estate.* A theft loss of property not connected with a trade or business and not incurred in any transaction entered into for profit which is discovered during the settlement of an estate, even though the theft actually occurred during a taxable year of the decedent, shall be allowed as a deduction under sections 165(a) and 641(b) in computing the taxable income of the estate if the loss has not been allowed under section 2054 in computing the taxable estate of the decedent and if the statement has been filed in accordance with § 1.642(g)-1. See section 165(c)(3). For purposes of determining the year of deduction, see paragraph (a)(2) of this section.

(c) *Amount deductible.* The amount deductible under this section in respect of a theft loss shall be determined consistently with the manner prescribed in § 1.165-7 for determining the amount of casualty loss allowable as a deduction under section 165(a). In applying the provisions of paragraph (b) of § 1.165-7 for this purpose, the fair

Reg. § 1.165-8(a)(2)

market value of the property immediately after the theft shall be considered to be zero. In the case of a loss sustained after December 31, 1963, in a taxable year ending after such date, in respect of property not used in a trade or business or for income producing purposes, the amount deductible shall be limited to that portion of the loss which is in excess of $100. For rules applicable in applying the $100 limitation, see subparagraph (b)(4) of § 1.165-7. For other rules relating to the treatment of deductible theft losses, see § 1.1231-1, relating to the involuntary conversion of property.

(d) *Definition.* For purposes of this section the term "theft" shall be deemed to include, but shall not necessarily be limited to, larceny, embezzlement, and robbery.

(e) *Application to inventories.* This section does not apply to a theft loss reflected in the inventories of the taxpayer. For provisions relating to inventories, see section 471 and the regulations thereunder.

(f) *Example.* The application of this section may be illustrated by the following example:

Example. In 1955 B, who makes her return on the basis of the calendar year, purchases for personal use a diamond brooch costing $4,000. On November 30, 1961, at which time it has a fair market value of $3,500, the brooch is stolen; but B does not discover the loss until January 1962. The brooch was fully insured against theft. A controversy develops with the insurance company over its liability in respect of the loss. However, in 1962, B has a reasonable prospect of recovery of the fair market value of the brooch from the insurance company. The controversy is settled in March 1963, at which time B receives $2,000 in insurance proceeds to cover the loss from theft. No deduction for the loss is allowable for 1961 or 1962; but the amount of the deduction allowable under section 165(a) for the taxable year 1963 is $1,500, computed as follows:

Value of property immediately before theft	$3,500
Less: Value of property immediately after the theft	0
Balance	$3,500
Loss to be taken into account for purposes of section 165(a): ($3,500 but not to exceed adjusted basis of $4,000 at time of theft)	$3,500
Less: Insurance received in 1963 .	2,000
Deduction allowable for 1963	$1,500

[Reg. § 1.165-8.]

☐ [*T.D.* 6445, 1-15-60. *Amended by T.D.* 6786, 12-28-64.]

§ 1.165-9. Sale of residential property.—(a) *Losses not allowed.* A loss sustained on the sale of residential property purchased or constructed by the taxpayer for use as his personal residence and so used by him up to the time of the sale is not deductible under section 165(a).

(b) *Property converted from personal use.* (1) If property purchased or constructed by the taxpayer for use as his personal residence is, prior to its sale, rented or otherwise appropriated to income-producing purposes and is used for such purposes up to the time of its sale, a loss sustained on the sale of the property shall be allowed as a deduction under section 165(a).

(2) The loss allowed under this paragraph upon the sale of the property shall be the excess of the adjusted basis prescribed in § 1.1011-1 for determining loss over the amount realized from the sale. For this purpose, the adjusted basis for determining loss shall be the lesser of either of the following amounts, adjusted as prescribed in § 1.1011-1 for the period subsequent to the conversion of the property to income-producing purposes:

(i) The fair market value of the property at the time of conversion, or

(ii) The adjusted basis for loss, at the time of conversion, determined under § 1.1011-1 but without reference to the fair market value.

(3) For rules relating to casualty losses of property converted from personal use, see paragraph (a)(5) of § 1.165-7. To determine the basis for depreciation in the case of such property, see § 1.167(g)-1. For limitations on the loss from the sale of a capital asset, see paragraph (c)(3) of § 1.165-1.

(c) *Examples.* The application of paragraph (b) of this section may be illustrated by the following examples:

Example (1). Residential property is purchased by the taxpayer in 1943 for use as his personal residence at a cost of $25,000, of which $15,000 is allocable to the building. The taxpayer uses the property as his personal residence until January 1, 1952, at which time its fair market value is $22,000, of which $12,000 is allocable to the building. The taxpayer rents the property from January 1, 1952, until January 1, 1955, at which time it is sold for $16,000. On January 1, 1952, the building has an estimated useful life of 20 years. It is assumed that the building has no estimated salvage value and that there are no adjustments in respect of basis other than depreciation, which is computed on the straight-line method. The loss to be taken into account for purposes of section 165(a) for the taxable year 1955 is $4,200, computed as follows:

Reg. § 1.165-9(c)

Basis of property at time of
conversion for purposes of this
section (that is, the lesser of
$25,000 cost or $22,000 fair
market value) $22,000
Less: Depreciation allowable from
January 1, 1952, to January 1,
1955 (3 years at 5 percent
based on $12,000, the value of
the building at time of
conversion, as prescribed by
§ 1.167(g)-1) .... $ 1,800

Adjusted basis prescribed in
§ 1.1011-1 for determining loss
on sale of the property $20,200
Less: Amount realized on sale .. 16,000

Loss to be taken into account for
purposes of section 165(a) ... $ 4,200

In this example the value of the building at the
time of conversion is used as the basis for computing depreciation. See example (2) of this paragraph wherein the adjusted basis of the building is
required to be used for such purpose.

Example (2). Residential property is purchased
by the taxpayer in 1940 for use as his personal
residence at a cost of $23,000, of which $10,000 is
allocable to the building. The taxpayer uses the
property as his personal residence until January
1, 1953, at which time its fair market value is
$20,000, of which $12,000 is allocable to the
building. The taxpayer rents the property from
January 1, 1953, until January 1, 1957, at which
time it is sold for $17,000. On January 1, 1953,
the building has an estimated useful life of 20
years. It is assumed that the building has no
estimated salvage value and that there are no
adjustments in respect of basis other than depreciation, which is computed on the straight-line
method. The loss to be taken into account for
purposes of section 165(a) for the taxable year
1957 is $1,000, computed as follows:

Basis of property at time of
conversion for purposes of this
section (that is, the lesser of
$23,000 cost or $20,000 fair
market value) $20,000
Less: Depreciation allowable from
January 1, 1953, to January 1,
1957 (4 years at 5% based on
$10,000, the cost of the
building, as prescribed by
§ 1.167(g)-1) 2,000

Adjusted basis prescribed in
§ 1.1011-1 for determining loss
on sale of the property $18,000
Less: Amount realized on sale .. 17,000

Loss to be taken into account for
purposes of section 165(a) ... $ 1,000

[Reg. § 1.165-9.]

☐ [*T.D.* 6445, 1-15-60. *Amended by T.D.* 6712,
3-23-64.]

§ 1.165-10. Wagering losses.—Losses sustained during the taxable year on wagering transactions shall be allowed as a deduction but only to
the extent of the gains during the taxable year
from such transactions. In the case of a husband
and wife making a joint return for the taxable
year, the combined losses of the spouses from
wagering transactions shall be allowed to the extent of the combined gains of the spouses from
wagering transactions. [Reg. § 1.165-10.]

☐ [*T.D.* 6445, 1-15-60.]

§ 1.166-1. Bad debts.—(a) *Allowance of deduction.* Section 166 provides that, in computing taxable income under section 63, a deduction shall be
allowed in respect of bad debts owed to the taxpayer. For this purpose, bad debts shall, subject to
the provisions of section 166 and the regulations
thereunder, be taken into account either as—

(1) A deduction in respect of debts which
become worthless in whole or in part; or as

(2) A deduction for a reasonable addition to a
reserve for bad debts.

(b) *Manner of selecting method.* (1) A taxpayer
filing a return of income for the first taxable year
for which he is entitled to a bad debt deduction
may select either of the two methods prescribed
by paragraph (a) of this section for treating bad
debts, but such selection is subject to the approval
of the district director upon examination of the
return. If the method so selected is approved, it
shall be used in returns for all subsequent taxable
years unless the Commissioner grants permission
to use the other method. A statement of facts
substantiating any deduction claimed under section 166 on account of bad debts shall accompany
each return of income.

(2) Taxpayers who have properly selected
one of the two methods for treating bad debts
under provisions of prior law corresponding to
section 166 shall continue to use that method for
all subsequent taxable years unless the Commissioner grants permission to use the other method.

(3)(i) For taxable years beginning after December 31, 1959, application for permission to
change the method of treating bad debts shall be
made in accordance with section 446(e) and paragraph (e)(3) of § 1.446-1.

(ii) For taxable years beginning before January 1, 1960, application for permission to change
the method of treating bad debts shall be made at
least 30 days before the close of the taxable year
for which the change is effective.

(4) Notwithstanding paragraph (b) (1), (2),
and (3) of this section, a dealer in property currently employing the accrual method of accounting and currently maintaining a reserve for bad
debts under section 166(c) (which may have in-

Reg. § 1.165-10

cluded guaranteed debt obligations described in section 166(f)(1)(A)) may establish a reserve for section 166(f)(1)(A) guaranteed debt obligations for a taxable year ending after October 21, 1965 under section 166(f) and § 1.166-10 by filing on or before April 17, 1986, an amended return indicating that such a reserve has been established. The establishment of such a reserve will not be considered a change in method of accounting for purposes of section 446(e). However, an election by a taxpayer to establish a reserve for bad debts under section 166(c) shall be treated as a change in method of accounting. See also § 1.166-4, relating to reserve for bad debts, and § 1.166-10, relating to reserve for guaranteed debt obligations.

(c) *Bona fide debt required.* Only a bona fide debt qualifies for purposes of section 166. A bona fide debt is a debt which arises from a debtor-creditor relationship based upon a valid and enforceable obligation to pay a fixed or determinable sum of money. A debt arising out of the receivables of an accrual method taxpayer is deemed to be an enforceable obligation for purposes of the preceding sentence to the extent that the income such debt represents has been included in the return of income for the year for which the deduction as a bad debt is claimed or for a prior taxable year. For example, a debt arising out of gambling receivables that are unenforceable under state or local law, which an accrual method taxpayer includes in income under section 61, is an enforceable obligation for purposes of this paragraph. A gift or contribution to capital shall not be considered a debt for purposes of section 166. The fact that a bad debt is not due at the time of deduction shall not of itself prevent its allowance under section 166. For the disallowance of deductions for bad debts owed by a political party, see § 1.271-1.

(d) *Amount deductible* —(1) *General rule.* Except in the case of a deduction for a reasonable addition to a reserve for bad debts, the basis for determining the amount of deduction under section 166 in respect of a bad debt shall be the same as the adjusted basis prescribed by § 1.1011-1 for determining the loss from the sale or other disposition of property. To determine the allowable deduction in the case of obligations acquired before March 1, 1913, see also paragraph (b) of § 1.1053-1.

(2) *Specific cases.* Subject to any provision of section 166 and the regulations thereunder which provides to the contrary, the following amounts are deductible as bad debts:

(i) *Notes or accounts receivable.*

(a) If, in computing taxable income, a taxpayer values his notes or accounts receivable at their fair market value when received, the amount deductible as a bad debt under section 166 in respect of such receivables shall be limited to such fair market value even though it is less than their face value.

(b) A purchaser of accounts receivable which become worthless during the taxable year shall be entitled under section 166 to a deduction which is based upon the price he paid for such receivables but not upon their face value.

(ii) *Bankruptcy claim.* Only the difference between the amount received in distribution of the assets of a bankrupt and the amount of the claim may be deducted under section 166 as a bad debt.

(iii) *Claim against decedent's estate.* The excess of the amount of the claim over the amount received by a creditor of a decedent in distribution of the assets of the decedent's estate may be considered a worthless debt under section 166.

(e) *Prior inclusion in income required.* Worthless debts arising from unpaid wages, salaries, fees, rents, and similar items of taxable income shall not be allowed as a deduction under section 166 unless the income such items represent has been included in the return of income for the year for which the deduction as a bad debt is claimed or for a prior taxable year.

(f) *Recovery of bad debts.* Any amount attributable to the recovery during the taxable year of a bad debt, or of a part of a bad debt, which was allowed as a deduction from gross income in a prior taxable year shall be included in gross income for the taxable year of recovery, except to the extent that the recovery is excluded from gross income under the provisions of § 1.111-1, relating to the recovery of certain items previously deducted or credited. This paragraph shall not apply, however, to a bad debt which was previously charged against a reserve by a taxpayer on the reserve method of treating bad debts.

(g) *Worthless securities.* (1) Section 166 and the regulations thereunder do not apply to a debt which is evidenced by a bond, debenture, note, or certificate, or other evidence of indebtedness, issued by a corporation, or by a government or political subdivision thereof, with interest coupons or in registered form. See section 166(e). For provisions allowing the deduction of a loss resulting from the worthlessness of such a debt, see § 1.165-5.

(2) The provisions of subparagraph (1) of this paragraph do not apply to any loss sustained by a bank and resulting from the worthlessness of a security described in section 165(g)(2)(C). See paragraph (a) of § 1.582-1. [Reg. § 1.166-1.]

Reg. § 1.166-1(g)(2)

☐ [*T.D. 6403*, 7-30-59. *Amended by T.D. 6996*, 1-17-69, *T.D. 7902*, 7-20-83 and *T.D. 8071*, 1-17-86.]

§ 1.166-2. **Evidence of worthlessness.**—(a) *General rule.* In determining whether a debt is worthless in whole or in part the district director will consider all pertinent evidence, including the value of the collateral, if any, securing the debt and the financial condition of the debtor.

(b) *Legal action not required.* Where the surrounding circumstances indicate that a debt is worthless and uncollectible and that legal action to enforce payment would in all probability not result in the satisfaction of execution on a judgment, a showing of these facts will be sufficient evidence of the worthlessness of the debt for purposes of the deduction under section 166.

(c) *Bankruptcy* —(1) *General rule.* Bankruptcy is generally an indication of the worthlessness of at least a part of an unsecured and unpreferred debt.

(2) *Year of deduction.* In bankruptcy cases a debt may become worthless before settlement in some instances; and in others, only when a settlement in bankruptcy has been reached. In either case, the mere fact that bankruptcy proceedings instituted against the debtor are terminated in a later year, thereby confirming the conclusion that the debt is worthless, shall not authorize the shifting of the deduction under section 166 to such later year.

(d) *Banks and other regulated corporations* — (1) *Worthlessness presumed in year of charge-off.* If a bank or other corporation which is subject to supervision by Federal authorities, or by State authorities maintaining substantially equivalent standards, charges off a debt in whole or in part, either—

(i) In obedience to the specific orders of such authorities, or

(ii) In accordance with established policies of such authorities, and, upon their first audit of the bank or other corporation subsequent to the charge-off, such authorities confirm in writing that the charge-off would have been subject to such specific orders if the audit had been made on the date of the charge-off,

then the debt shall, to the extent charged off during the taxable year, be conclusively presumed to have become worthless, or worthless only in part, as the case may be, during such taxable year. But no such debt shall be so conclusively presumed to be worthless, or worthless only in part, as the case may be, if the amount so charged off is not claimed as a deduction by the taxpayer at the time of filing the return for the taxable year in which the charge-off takes place.

(2) *Evidence of worthlessness in later taxable year.* If such a bank or other corporation does not claim a deduction for such a totally or partially worthless debt in its return for the taxable year in which the charge-off takes place, but claims the deduction for a later taxable year, then the charge-off in the prior taxable year shall be deemed to have been involuntary and the deduction under section 166 shall be allowed for the taxable year for which claimed, provided that the taxpayer produces sufficient evidence to show that—

(i) The debt became wholly worthless in the later taxable year, or became recoverable only in part subsequent to the taxable year of the involuntary charge-off, as the case may be; and,

(ii) To the extent that the deduction claimed in the later taxable year for a debt partially worthless was not involuntarily charged off in prior taxable years, it was charged off in the later taxable year.

(3) *Conformity election*—(i) *Eligibility for election.* In lieu of applying paragraphs (d)(1) and (2) of this section, a bank (as defined in paragraph (d)(4)(i) of this section) that is subject to supervision by Federal authorities, or by state authorities maintaining substantially equivalent standards, may elect under this paragraph (d)(3) to use a method of accounting that establishes a conclusive presumption of worthlessness for debts, provided that the bank meets the express determination requirement of paragraph (d)(3)(iii)(D) of this section for the taxable year of the election.

(ii) *Conclusive presumption*—(A) *In general.* If a bank satisfies the express determination requirement of paragraph (d)(3)(iii)(D) of this section and elects to use the method of accounting under this paragraph (d)(3)—

(*1*) Debts charged off, in whole or in part, for regulatory purposes during a taxable year are conclusively presumed to have become worthless, or worthless only in part, as the case may be, during that year, but only if the charge-off results from a specific order of the bank's supervisory authority or corresponds to the bank's classification of the debt, in whole or in part, as a loss asset, as described in paragraph (d)(3)(ii)(C) of this section; and

(*2*) A bad debt deduction for a debt that is subject to regulatory loss classification standards is allowed for a taxable year only to the extent that the debt is conclusively presumed to have become worthless under paragraph (d)(3)(ii)(A)(*1*) of this section during that year.

(B) *Charge-off should have been made in earlier year.* The conclusive presumption that a debt is worthless in the year that it is charged off for regulatory purposes applies even if the bank's

Reg. § 1.166-2(a)

supervisory authority determines in a subsequent year that the charge-off should have been made in an earlier year. A pattern of charge-offs in the wrong year, however, may result in revocation of the bank's election by the Commissioner pursuant to paragraph (d)(3)(iv)(D) of this section.

(C) *Loss asset defined.* A debt is classified as a loss asset by a bank if the bank assigns the debt to a class that corresponds to a loss asset classification under the standards set forth in the "Uniform Agreement on the Classification of Assets and Securities Held by Banks" (See Attachment to Comptroller of the Currency Banking Circular No. 127, Rev. 4-26-91, Comptroller of the Currency, Communications Department, Washington, DC 20219) or similar guidance issued by the Office of the Comptroller of the Currency, the Federal Deposit Insurance Corporation, the Board of Governors of the Federal Reserve, or the Farm Credit Administration; or for institutions under the supervision of the Office of Thrift Supervision, 12 CFR 563.160(b)(3).

* * *

[Reg. § 1.166-2.]

☐ [*T.D.* 6403, 7-30-59. *Amended by T.D.* 7254, 1-24-73; *T.D.* 8396, 2-21-92; *T.D.* 8441, 10-1-92 *and T.D.* 8492, 10-15-93.]

§ 1.166-3. Partial or total worthlessness.—(a) *Partial worthlessness*—(1) *Applicable to specific debts only.* A deduction under section 166 (a)(2) on account of partially worthless debts shall be allowed with respect to specific debts only.

(2) *Charge-off required.* (i) If, from all the surrounding and attending circumstances, the district director is satisfied that a debt is partially worthless, the amount which has become worthless shall be allowed as a deduction under section 166(a)(2) but only to the extent charged off during the taxable year.

(ii) If a taxpayer claims a deduction for a part of a debt for the taxable year within which that part of the debt is charged off and the deduction is disallowed for that taxable year, then, in a case where the debt becomes partially worthless after the close of that taxable year, a deduction under section 166(a)(2) shall be allowed for a subsequent taxable year but not in excess of the amount charged off in the prior taxable year plus any amount charged off in the subsequent taxable year. In such instance, the charge-off in the prior taxable year shall, if consistently maintained as such, be sufficient to that extent to meet the charge-off requirement of section 166(a)(2) with respect to the subsequent taxable year.

(iii) Before a taxpayer may deduct a debt in part, he must be able to demonstrate to the satisfaction of the district director the amount

thereof which is worthless and the part thereof which has been charged off.

(3) *Significantly modified debt*—(i) *Deemed charge-off.* If a significant modification of a debt instrument (within the meaning of § 1.1001-3) during a taxable year results in the recognition of gain by a taxpayer under § 1.1001-1(a), and if the requirements of paragraph (a)(3)(ii) of this section are met, there is a deemed charge-off of the debt during that taxable year in the amount specified in paragraph (a)(3)(iii) of this section.

(ii) *Requirements for deemed charge-off.* A debt is deemed to have been charged off only if—

(A) The taxpayer (or, in the case of a debt that constitutes transferred basis property within the meaning of section 7701(a)(43), a transferor taxpayer) has claimed a deduction for partial worthlessness of the debt in any prior taxable year; and

(B) Each prior charge-off and deduction for partial worthlessness satisfied the requirements of paragraphs (a)(1) and (2) of this section.

(iii) *Amount of deemed charge-off.* The amount of the deemed charge-off, if any, is the amount by which the tax basis of the debt exceeds the greater of the fair market value of the debt or the amount of the debt recorded on the taxpayer's books and records reduced as appropriate for a specific allowance for loan losses. The amount of the deemed charge-off, however, may not exceed the amount of recognized gain described in paragraph (a)(3)(i) of this section.

(iv) *Effective date.* This paragraph (a)(3) applies to significant modifications of debt instruments occurring on or after September 23, 1996.

(b) *Total worthlessness.* If a debt becomes wholly worthless during the taxable year, the amount thereof which has not been allowed as a deduction from gross income for any prior taxable year shall be allowed as a deduction for the current taxable year. [Reg. § 1.166-3.]

☐ [*T.D.* 6403, 7-30-59. *Amended by T.D.* 8763, 1-28-98.]

§ 1.166-5. Nonbusiness debts.—(a) *Allowance of deduction as capital loss.* (1) The loss resulting from any nonbusiness debt's becoming partially or wholly worthless within the taxable year shall not be allowed as a deduction under either section 166(a) or section 166(c) in determining the taxable income of a taxpayer other than a corporation. See section 166(d)(1)(A).

(2) If, in the case of a taxpayer other than a corporation, a non-business debt becomes wholly worthless within the taxable year, the loss resulting therefrom shall be treated as a loss from the sale or exchange, during the taxable year, of a capital asset held for not more than 1 year (6

Reg. § 1.166-5(a)(2)

months for taxable years beginning before 1977; 9 months for taxable years beginning in 1977). Such a loss is subject to the limitations provided in section 1211, relating to the limitation on capital losses, and section 1212, relating to the capital loss carryover, and in the regulations under those sections. A loss on a nonbusiness debt shall be treated as sustained only if and when the debt has become totally worthless, and no deduction shall be allowed for a nonbusiness debt which is recoverable in part during the taxable year.

(b) *Nonbusiness debt defined.* For purposes of section 166 and this section, a nonbusiness debt is any debt other than —

(1) A debt which is created, or acquired, in the course of a trade or business of the taxpayer, determined without regard to the relationship of the debt to a trade or business of the taxpayer at the time when the debt becomes worthless; or

(2) A debt the loss from the worthlessness of which is incurred in the taxpayer's trade or business.

The question whether a debt is a nonbusiness debt is a question of fact in each particular case. The determination of whether the loss on a debt's becoming worthless has been incurred in a trade or business of the taxpayer shall, for this pupose, be made in substantially the same manner for determining whether a loss has been incurred in a trade or business for purposes of section 165(c)(1). For purposes of subparagraph (2) of this paragraph, the character of the debt is to be determined by the relation which the loss resulting from the debt's becoming worthless bears to the trade or business of the taxpayer. If that relation is a proximate one in the conduct of the trade or business in which the taxpayer is engaged at the time the debt becomes worthless, the debt comes within the exception provided by that subparagraph. The use to which the borrowed funds are put by the debtor is of no consequence in making a determination under this paragraph. For purposes of section 166 and this section, a nonbusiness debt does not include a debt described in section 165(g)(2)(C). See § 1.165-5, relating to losses on worthless securities.

(c) *Guaranty of obligations.* For provisions treating a loss sustained by a guarantor of obligations as a loss resulting from the worthlessness of a debt, see § § 1.166-8 and 1.166-9.

(d) *Examples.* The application of this section may be illustrated by the following examples involving a case where A, an individual who is engaged in the grocery business and who makes his return on the basis of the calendar year, extends credit to B in 1955 on an open account:

Example (1). In 1956 A sells the business but retains the claim against B. The claim becomes worthless in A's hands in 1957. A's loss is not controlled by the nonbusiness debt provisions, since the original consideration has been advanced by A in his trade or business.

Example (2). In 1956 A sells the business to C but sells the claim against B to the taxpayer, D. The claim becomes worthless in D's hands in 1957. During 1956 and 1957, D is not engaged in any trade or business. D's loss is controlled by the nonbusiness debt provisions even though the original consideration has been advanced by A in his trade or business, since the debt has not been created or acquired in connection with a trade or business of D and since in 1957 D is not engaged in a trade or business incident to the conduct of which a loss from the worthlessness of such claims is a proximate result.

Example (3). In 1956 A dies, leaving the business, including the accounts receivable, to his son, C, the taxpayer. The claim against B becomes worthless in C's hands in 1957. C's loss is not controlled by the nonbusiness debt provisions. While C does not advance any consideration for the claim, or create or acquire it in connection with his trade or business, the loss is sustained as a proximate incident to the conduct of the trade or business in which he is engaged at the time the debt becomes worthless.

Example (4). In 1956 A dies, leaving the business to his son, C, but leaving the claim against B to his son, D, the taxpayer. The claim against B becomes worthless in D's hands in 1957. During 1956 and 1957, D is not engaged in any trade or business. D's loss is controlled by the nonbusiness debt provisions even though the original consideration has been advanced by A in his trade or business, since the debt has not been created or acquired in connection with a trade or business of D and since in 1957 D is not engaged in a trade or business incident to the conduct of which a loss from the worthlessness of such claims is a proximate result.

Example (5). In 1956 A dies, and, while his executor, C, is carrying on the business, the claim against B becomes worthless in 1957. The loss sustained by A's estate is not controlled by the nonbusiness debt provisions. While C does not advance any consideration for the claim on behalf of the estate, or create or acquire it in connection with a trade or business in which the estate is engaged, the loss is sustained as a proximate incident to the conduct of the trade or business in which the estate is engaged at the time the debt becomes worthless.

Example (6). In 1956, A, in liquidating the business, attempts to collect the claim against B but finds that it has become worthless. A's loss is not controlled by the nonbusiness debt provisions,

Reg. § 1.166-5(b)(1)

since the original consideration has been advanced by A in his trade or business and since a loss incurred in liquidating a trade or business is a proximate incident to the conduct thereof. [Reg. § 1.166-5.]

☐ [*T.D. 6403, 7-23-59. Amended by T.D. 7657,* 11-28-79 *and T.D. 7728, 10-31-80.*]

§ 1.166-6. Sale of mortgaged or pledged property.—(a) *Deficiency deductible as bad debts*—(1) *Principal amount.* If mortgaged or pledged property is lawfully sold (whether to the creditor or another purchaser) for less than the amount of the debt, and the portion of the indebtedness remaining unsatisfied after the sale is wholly or partially uncollectible, the mortgagee or pledgee may deduct such amount under section 166(a) (to the extent that it constitutes capital or represents an item the income from which has been returned by him) as a bad debt for the taxable year in which it becomes wholly worthless or is charged off as partially worthless. See § 1.166-3.

(2) *Accrued interest.* Accrued interest may be included as part of the deduction allowable under this paragraph, but only if it has previously been returned as income.

(b) *Realization of gain or loss*—(1) *Determination of amount.* If, in the case of a sale described in paragraph (a) of this section, the creditor buys in the mortgaged or pledged property, loss or gain is also realized, measured by the difference between the amount of those obligations of the debtor which are applied to the purchase or bid price of the property (to the extent that such obligations constitute capital or represent an item the income from which has been returned by the creditor) and the fair market value of the property.

(2) *Fair market value defined.* The fair market value of the property for this purpose shall, in the absence of clear and convincing proof to the contrary, be presumed to be the amount for which it is bid in by the taxpayer.

(c) *Basis of property purchased.* If the creditor subsequently sells the property so acquired, the basis for determining gain or loss upon the subsequent sale is the fair market value of the property at the date of its acquisition by the creditor.

(d) *Special rules applicable to certain banking organizations.* For special rules relating to the treatment of mortgaged or pledged property by certain mutual savings banks, domestic building and loan associations, and cooperative banks, see section 595 and the regulations thereunder.

(e) *Special rules applicable to certain reacquisitions of real property.* Notwithstanding this section, special rules apply for taxable years beginning after September 2, 1964 (and for certain taxable years beginning after December 31, 1957), to the gain or loss on certain reacquisitions of real property, to indebtedness remaining unsatisfied as a result of such reacquisitions, and to the basis of the reacquired real property. See §§ 1.1038 through 1.1038-3. [Reg. § 1.166-6.]

☐ [*T.D. 6403, 7-30-59. Amended by T.D. 6814,* 4-6-65 *and T.D. 6916, 4-12-67.*]

§ 1.167(a)-1. Depreciation in general.—(a) *Reasonable allowance.* Section 167(a) provides that a reasonable allowance for the exhaustion, wear and tear, and obsolescence of property used in the trade or business or of property held by the taxpayer for the production of income shall be allowed as a depreciation deduction. The allowance is that amount which should be set aside for the taxable year in accordance with a reasonably consistent plan (not necessarily at a uniform rate), so that the aggregate of the amounts set aside, plus the salvage value, will, at the end of the estimated useful life of the depreciable property, equal the cost or other basis of the property as provided in section 167(g) and § 1.167(g)-1. An asset shall not be depreciated below a reasonable salvage value under any method of computing depreciation. However, see section 167(f) and § 1.167(f)-1 for rules which permit a reduction in the amount of salvage value to be taken into account for certain personal property acquired after October 16, 1962. See also paragraph (c) of this section for definition of salvage. The allowance shall not reflect amounts representing a mere reduction in market value. See section 179 and § 1.179-1 for a further description of the term "reasonable allowance."

(b) *Useful life.* For the purpose of section 167 the estimated useful life of an asset is not necessarily the useful life inherent in the asset but is the period over which the asset may reasonably be expected to be useful to the taxpayer in his trade or business or in the production of his income. This period shall be determined by reference to his experience with similar property taking into account present conditions and probable future developments. Some of the factors to be considered in determining this period are (1) wear and tear and decay or decline from natural causes, (2) the normal progress of the art, economic changes, inventions, and current developments within the industry and the taxpayer's trade or business, (3) the climatic and other local conditions peculiar to the taxpayer's trade or business, and (4) the taxpayer's policy as to repairs, renewals, and replacements. Salvage value is not a factor for the purpose of determining useful life. If the taxpayer's experience is inadequate, the general experience in the industry may be used until such time as the taxpayer's own experience forms an adequate basis for making the determination. The estimated remaining useful life may be subject to modification by reason of conditions known to exist at the end of the taxable year and shall be redetermined when necessary regardless of the method of computing depreciation. However, estimated remaining useful life shall be redetermined only when the change in the useful life is significant and there is a clear and convincing basis for the redetermination. For rules covering agreements with respect to useful life, see section 167(d) and § 1.167(d)-1. If a taxpayer claims an investment credit with respect to an asset for a taxable year preceding the taxable year in which the asset is considered as placed in service under § 1.167(a)-10(b) or § 1.167(a)-11(e), the useful life of the asset under this paragraph shall be the same useful life assigned to the asset under § 1.46-3(e).

* * *

[Reg. § 1.167(a)-1.]

☐ [*T.D.* 6182, 6-11-56. *Amended by T.D.* 6507, 12-1-60, *T.D.* 6712, 3-23-64 *and T.D.* 7203, 8-24-72.]

§ 1.167(a)-2. Tangible property.—The depreciation allowance in the case of tangible property applies only to that part of the property which is subject to wear and tear, to decay or decline from natural causes, to exhaustion, and to obsolescence. The allowance does not apply to inventories or stock in trade, or to land apart from the improvements of physical development added to it. The allowance does not apply to natural resources which are subject to the allowance for depletion provided in section 611. No deduction for depreciation shall be allowed on automobiles or other vehicles used solely for pleasure, on a building used by the taxpayer solely as his residence, or on furniture or furnishings therein, personal effects, or clothing; but properties and costumes used exclusively in a business, such as a theatrical business, may be depreciated. [Reg. § 1.167(a)-2.]

☐ [*T.D.* 6182, 6-11-56.]

§ 1.167(a)-3. Intangibles.—If an intangible asset is known from experience or other factors to be of use in the business or in the production of income for only a limited period, the length of which can be estimated with reasonable accuracy, such an intangible asset may be the subject of a depreciation allowance. Examples are patents and copyrights. An intangible asset, the useful life of which is not limited, is not subject to the allowance for depreciation. No allowance will be permitted merely because, in the unsupported opinion of the taxpayer, the intangible asset has a limited useful life. No deduction for depreciation is allowable with respect to good will. For rules with respect to organizational expenditures, see

section 248 and the regulations thereunder. For rules with respect to trademark and trade name expenditures, see section 177 and the regulations thereunder. See sections 197 and 167(f) and, to the extent applicable, § § 1.197-2 and 1.167(a)-14 for amortization of goodwill and certain other intangibles acquired after August 10, 1993, or after July 25, 1991, if a valid retroactive election under § 1.197-1T has been made. [Reg. § 1.167(a)-3.]

☐ [*T.D.* 6182, 6-11-56. *Amended by T.D.* 6452, 2-3-60 *and T.D.* 8865, 1-20-2000.]

Proposed Amendment to Regulation

§ 1.167(a)-3. Intangibles.—(a) *In general.* * * *

(b) *Safe harbor amortization for certain intangible assets*—(1) *Amortization period.* For purposes of determining the depreciation allowance referred to in paragraph (a) of this section, a taxpayer may treat an intangible asset as having a useful life equal to 15 years unless—

(i) An amortization period for the intangible asset is specifically prescribed or prohibited by the Internal Revenue Code, regulations, or other published guidance;

(ii) The intangible asset is described in § 1.263(a)-4(c) (relating to intangibles acquired from another person) or § 1.263(a)-4(d)(2) (relating to created financial interests);

(iii) The intangible asset has a useful life that is readily ascertainable; or

(iv) The intangible asset is described in § 1.263(a)-4(d)(8) (relating to certain benefits arising from the provision, production, or improvement of real property), in which case the taxpayer may treat the intangible asset as having a useful life equal to 25 years.

(2) *Applicability to restructurings, reorganizations, and acquisitions of capital.* The safe harbor amortization period provided by paragraph (b)(1) of this section does not apply to an amount required to be capitalized by § 1.263(a)-4(b)(1)(iii) (relating to amounts paid to facilitate a restructuring, reorganization or transaction involving the acquisition of capital).

(3) *Depreciation method.* A taxpayer that determines its depreciation allowance for an intangible asset using the 15-year amortization period prescribed by paragraph (b)(1) of this section (or the 25-year amortization period in the case of an intangible asset described in § 1.263(a)-4(d)(8)) must determine the allowance by amortizing the basis of the intangible asset (as determined under section 167(c) and without regard to salvage value) ratably over the amortization period beginning on the first day of the month in which the intangible asset is placed in

service by the taxpayer. The intangible asset is not eligible for amortization in the month of disposition. [Reg. § 1.167(a)-3.]

[Proposed 12-19-2002.]

§ 1.167(a)-4. Leased property.—Capital expenditures made by a lessee for the erection of buildings or the construction of other permanent improvements on leased property are recoverable through allowances for depreciation or amortization. If the useful life of such improvements in the hands of the taxpayer is equal to or shorter than the remaining period of the lease, the allowances shall take the form of depreciation under section 167. See §§ 1.167(b)-0, 1.167(b)-1, 1.167(b)-2, 1.167(b)-3, and 1.167(b)-4 for methods of computing such depreciation allowances. If, on the other hand, the estimated useful life of such property in the hands of the taxpayer, determined without regard to the terms of the lease, would be longer than the remaining period of such lease, the allowances shall take the form of annual deductions from gross income in an amount equal to the unrecovered cost of such capital expenditures divided by the number of years remaining of the term of the lease. Such deductions shall be in lieu of allowances for depreciation. See section 162 and the regulations thereunder. See section 178 and the regulations thereunder for rules governing the effect to be given renewal options in determining whether the useful life of the improvement exceeds the remaining term of the lease where a lessee begins improvements on leased property after July 28, 1958, other than improvements which on such date and at all times thereafter, the lessee was under a binding legal obligation to make. Capital expenditures made by a lessor for the erection of buildings or other improvements shall, if subject to depreciation allowances, be recovered by him over the estimated life of the improvements without regard to the period of the lease. [Reg. § 1.167(a)-4.]

☐ [*T.D.* 6182, 6-11-56. *Amended by T.D.* 6520, 12-23-60.]

§ 1.167(a)-5. Apportionment of basis.—In the case of the acquisition on or after March 1, 1913, of a combination of depreciable and nondepreciable property for a lump sum, as for example, buildings and land, the basis for depreciation cannot exceed an amount which bears the same proportion to the lump sum as the value of the depreciable property at the time of acquisition bears to the value of the entire property at that time. In the case of property which is subject to both the allowance for depreciation and amortization, depreciation is allowable only with respect to the portion of the depreciable property which is not subject to the allowance for amortization and may be taken concurrently with the allowance for

amortization. After the close of the amortization period or after amortization deductions have been discontinued with respect to any such property, the unrecovered cost or other basis of the depreciable portion of such property will be subject to depreciation. For adjustments to basis, see section 1016 and other applicable provisions of law. For the adjustment to the basis of a structure in the case of a donation of a qualified conservation contribution under section 170(h), see § 1.170A-14(h)(3)(iii). [Reg. § 1.167(a)-5.]

☐ [*T.D.* 6182, 6-11-56. *Amended by T.D.* 8069, 1-13-86.]

§ 1.167(a)-9. Obsolescence.—The depreciation allowance includes an allowance for normal obsolescence which should be taken into account to the extent that the expected useful life of property will be shortened by reason thereof. Obsolescence may render an asset economically useless to the taxpayer regardless of its physical condition. Obsolescence is attributable to many causes, including technological improvements and reasonably foreseeable economic changes. Among these causes are normal progress of the arts and sciences, supersession or inadequacy brought about by developments in the industry, products, methods, markets, sources of supply, and other like changes, and legislative or regulatory action. In any case in which the taxpayer shows that the estimated useful life previously used should be shortened by reason of obsolescence greater than had been assumed in computing such estimated useful life, a change to a new and shorter estimated useful life computed in accordance with such showing will be permitted. No such change will be permitted merely because in the unsupported opinion of the taxpayer the property may become obsolete. For rules governing the allowance of a loss when the usefulness of depreciable property is suddenly terminated, see § 1.167(a)-8. If the estimated useful life and the depreciation rates have been the subject of a previous agreement, see section 167(d) and § 1.167(d)-1. [Reg. § 1.167(a)-9.]

☐ [*T.D.* 6182, 6-11-56. *Amended by T.D.* 6445, 1-15-60.]

§ 1.167(a)-10. When depreciation deduction is allowable.—(a) A taxpayer should deduct the proper depreciation allowance each year and may not increase his depreciation allowances in later years by reason of his failure to deduct any depreciation allowance or of his action in deducting an allowance plainly inadequate under the known facts in prior years. The inadequacy of the depreciation allowance for property in prior years shall be determined on the basis of the allowable method of depreciation used by the taxpayer for such property or under the straight line method if no allowance has ever been claimed for such property. The preceding sentence shall not be construed as precluding application of any method provided in section 167 (b) if taxpayer's failure to claim any allowance for depreciation was due solely to erroneously treating as a deductible expense an item properly chargeable to capital account. For rules relating to adjustments to basis, see section 1016 and the regulations thereunder.

* * *

[Reg. § 1.167(a)-10.]

   ☐ [*T.D.* 6182, 6-11-56.]

§ 1.167(a)-14. Treatment of certain intangible property excluded from section 197.—(a) *Overview.* This section provides rules for the amortization of certain intangibles that are excluded from section 197 (relating to the amortization of goodwill and certain other intangibles). These excluded intangibles are specifically described in § 1.197-2(c)(4), (6), (7), (11), and (13) and include certain computer software and certain other separately acquired rights, such as rights to receive tangible property or services, patents and copyrights, certain mortgage servicing rights, and rights of fixed duration or amount. Intangibles for which an amortization amount is determined under section 167(f) and intangibles otherwise excluded from section 197 are amortizable only if they qualify as property subject to the allowance for depreciation under section 167(a).

(b) *Computer software*—(1) *In general.* The amount of the deduction for computer software described in section 167(f)(1) and § 1.197-2(c)(4) is determined by amortizing the cost or other basis of the computer software using the straight line method described in § 1.167(b)-1 (except that its salvage value is treated as zero) and an amortization period of 36 months beginning on the first day of the month that the computer software is placed in service. If costs for developing computer software that the taxpayer properly elects to defer under section 174(b) result in the development of property subject to the allowance for depreciation under section 167, the rules of this paragraph (b) will apply to the unrecovered costs. In addition, this paragraph (b) applies to the cost of separately acquired computer software where these costs are separately stated and the costs are required to be capitalized under section 263(a).

(2) *Exceptions.* Paragraph (b)(1) of this section does not apply to the cost of computer software properly and consistently taken into account under § 1.162-11. The cost of acquiring an interest in computer software that is included, without being separately stated, in the cost of the hardware or other tangible property is treated as part of the cost of the hardware or other tangible property that is capitalized and depreciated

under other applicable sections of the Internal Revenue Code.

(3) *Additional rules.* Rules similar to those in § 1.197-2(f)(1)(iii), (f)(1)(iv), and (f)(2) (relating to the computation of amortization deductions and the treatment of contingent amounts) apply for purposes of this paragraph (b).

(c) *Certain interests or rights not acquired as part of a purchase of a trade or business*—(1) *Certain rights to receive tangible property or services.* The amount of the deduction for a right (other than a right acquired as part of a purchase of a trade or business) to receive tangible property or services under a contract or from a governmental unit (as specified in section 167(f)(2) and § 1.197-2(c)(6)) is determined as follows:

(i) *Amortization of fixed amounts.* The basis of a right to receive a fixed amount of tangible property or services is amortized for each taxable year by multiplying the basis of the right by a fraction, the numerator of which is the amount of tangible property or services received during the taxable year and the denominator of which is the total amount of tangible property or services received or to be received under the terms of the contract or governmental grant. For example, if a taxpayer acquires a favorable contract right to receive a fixed amount of raw materials during an unspecified period, the taxpayer must amortize the cost of acquiring the contract right by multiplying the total cost by a fraction, the numerator of which is the amount of raw materials received under the contract during the taxable year and the denominator of which is the total amount of raw materials received or to be received under the contract.

(ii) *Amortization of unspecified amount over fixed period.* The cost or other basis of a right to receive an unspecified amount of tangible property or services over a fixed period is amortized ratably over the period of the right. (See paragraph (c)(3) of this section regarding renewals).

(iii) *Amortization in other cases.* [Reserved]

(2) *Rights of fixed duration or amount.* The amount of the deduction for a right (other than a right acquired as part of a purchase of a trade or business) of fixed duration or amount received under a contract or granted by a governmental unit (specified in section 167(f)(2) and § 1.197-2(c)(13)) and not covered by paragraph (c)(1) of this section is determined as follows:

(i) *Rights to a fixed amount.* The basis of a right to a fixed amount is amortized for each taxable year by multiplying the basis by a fraction, the numerator of which is the amount received during the taxable year and the denominator of which is the total amount received

Reg. § 1.167(a)-14(a)

or to be received under the terms of the contract or governmental grant.

(ii) *Rights to an unspecified amount over fixed duration of less than 15 years.* The basis of a right to an unspecified amount over a fixed duration of less than 15 years is amortized ratably over the period of the right.

(3) *Application of renewals*—(i) For purposes of paragraphs (c)(1) and (2) of this section, the duration of a right under a contract (or granted by a governmental unit) includes any renewal period if, based on all of the facts and circumstances in existence at any time during the taxable year in which the right is acquired, the facts clearly indicate a reasonable expectancy of renewal.

(ii) The mere fact that a taxpayer will have the opportunity to renew a contract right or other right on the same terms as are available to others, in a competitive auction or similar process that is designed to reflect fair market value and in which the taxpayer is not contractually advantaged, will generally not be taken into account in determining the duration of such right provided that the bidding produces a fair market value price comparable to the price that would be obtained if the rights were purchased immediately after renewal from a person (other than the person granting the renewal) in an arm's-length transaction.

(iii) The cost of a renewal not included in the terms of the contract or governmental grant is treated as the acquisition of a separate intangible asset.

(4) *Patents and copyrights.* If the purchase price of a interest (other than an interest acquired as part of a purchase of a trade or business) in a patent or copyright described in section 167(f)(2) and § 1.197-2(c)(7) is payable on at least an annual basis as either a fixed amount per use or a fixed percentage of the revenue derived from the use of the patent or copyright, the depreciation deduction for a taxable year is equal to the amount of the purchase price paid or incurred during the year. Otherwise, the basis of such patent or copyright (or an interest therein) is depreciated either ratably over its remaining useful life or under section 167(g) (income forecast method). If a patent or copyright becomes valueless in any year before its legal expiration, the adjusted basis may be deducted in that year.

(5) *Additional rules.* The period of amortization under paragraphs (c)(1) through (4) of this section begins when the intangible is placed in service, and rules similar to those in § 1.197-2(f)(2) apply for purposes of this paragraph (c).

* * *

[Reg. § 1.167(a)-14.]

☐ [*T.D.* 8865, 1-20-2000.]

§ 1.167(b)-1. Straight line method.—(a) *Application of method.* Under the straight line method the cost or other basis of the property less its estimated salvage value is deductible in equal annual amounts over the period of the estimated useful life of the property. The allowance for depreciation for the taxable year is determined by dividing the adjusted basis of the property at the beginning of the taxable year, less salvage value, by the remaining useful life of the property at such time. For convenience, the allowance so determined may be reduced to a percentage or fraction. The straight line method may be used in determining a reasonable allowance for depreciation for any property which is subject to depreciation under section 167 and it shall be used in all cases where the taxpayer has not adopted a different acceptable method with respect to such property.

* * *

[Reg. § 1.167(b)-1.]

☐ [*T.D.* 6182, 6-11-56.]

§ 1.167(b)-2. Declining balance method.—(a) *Application of method.* Under the declining balance method a uniform rate is applied each year to the unrecovered cost or other basis of the property. The unrecovered cost or other basis is the basis provided by section 167(g), adjusted for depreciation previously allowed or allowable, and for all other adjustments provided by section 1016 and other applicable provisions of law. The declining balance rate may be determined without resort to formula. Such rate determined under section 167(b)(2) shall not exceed twice the appropriate straight line rate computed without adjustment for salvage. While salvage is not taken into account in determining the annual allowances under this method, in no event shall an asset (or an account) be depreciated below a reasonable salvage value. However, see section 167(f) and § 1.167(f)-1 for rules which permit a reduction in the amount of salvage value to be taken into account for certain personal property acquired after October 16, 1962. Also, see section 167(c) and § 1.167(c)-1 for restrictions on the use of the declining balance method.

(b) *Illustrations.* The declining balance method is illustrated by the following examples:

Example (1). A new asset having an estimated useful life of 20 years was purchased on January 1, 1954, for $1,000. The normal straight line rate (without adjustment for salvage) is 5 percent, and the declining balance rate at twice the normal straight line rate is 10 percent. The annual depreciation allowances for 1954, 1955, and 1956 are as follows:

Year	Basis	Declining balance rate (percent)	Depreciation allowance
1954	$1,000	10	$100
1955	900	10	90
1956	810	10	81

* * *

[Reg. § 1.167(b)-2.]

☐ [*T.D.* 6182, 6-11-56. *Amended by T.D.* 6712, 3-23-64.]

§ 1.167(g)-1. Basis for depreciation.—The basis upon which the allowance for depreciation is to be computed with respect to any property shall be the adjusted basis provided in section 1011 for the purpose of determining gain on the sale or other disposition of such property. In the case of property which has not been used in the trade or business or held for the production of income and which is thereafter converted to such use, the fair market value on the date of such conversion, if less than the adjusted basis of the property at that time, is the basis for computing depreciation. [Reg. § 1.167(g)-1.]

☐ [*T.D.* 6182, 6-11-56. *Amended by T.D.* 6712, 3-23-64.]

§ 1.167(h)-1. Life tenants and beneficiaries of trusts and estates.—(a) *Life tenants.* In the case of property held by one person for life with remainder to another person, the deduction for depreciation shall be computed as if the life tenant were the absolute owner of the property so that he will be entitled to the deduction during his life, and thereafter the deduction, if any, shall be allowed to the remainderman.

(b) *Trusts.* If property is held in trust, the allowable deduction is to be apportioned between the income beneficiaries and the trustee on the basis of the trust income allocable to each, unless the governing instrument (or local law) requires or permits the trustee to maintain a reserve for depreciation in any amount. In the latter case, the deduction is first allocated to the trustee to the extent that income is set aside for a depreciation reserve, and any part of the deduction in excess of the income set aside for the reserve shall be apportioned between the income beneficiaries and the trustee on the basis of the trust income (in excess of the income set aside for the reserve) allocable to each. For example:

(1) If under the trust instrument or local law the income of a trust computed without regard to depreciation is to be distributed to a named beneficiary, the beneficiary is entitled to the deduction to the exclusion of the trustee.

(2) If under the trust instrument or local law the income of a trust is to be distributed to a named beneficiary, but the trustee is directed to maintain a reserve for depreciation in any amount, the deduction is allowed to the trustee (except to the extent that income set aside for the reserve is less than the allowable deduction). The same result would follow if the trustee sets aside income for a depreciation reserve pursuant to discretionary authority to do so in the governing instrument.

No effect shall be given to any allocation of the depreciation deduction which gives any beneficiary or the trustee a share of such deduction greater than his pro rata share of the trust income, irrespective of any provisions in the trust instrument, except as otherwise provided in this paragraph when the trust instrument or local law requires or permits the trustee to maintain a reserve for depreciation.

(c) *Estates.* In the case of an estate, the allowable deduction shall be apportioned between the estate and the heirs, legatees, and devisees on the basis of income of the estate which is allocable to each. [Reg. § 1.167(h)-1.]

☐ [*T.D.* 6182, 6-11-56. *Amended by T.D.* 6712, 3-23-64.]

§ 1.168(d)-1. Applicable conventions—Half-year and mid-quarter conventions.—(a) *In general.* Under section 168(d), the half-year convention applies to depreciable property (other than certain real property described in section 168(d)(2)) placed in service during a taxable year, unless the mid-quarter convention applies to the property. Under section 168(d)(3)(A), the mid-quarter convention applies to depreciable property (other than certain real property described in section 168(d)(2)) placed in service during a taxable year if the aggregate basis of property placed in service during the last three months of the taxable year exceeds 40 percent of the aggregate basis of property placed in service during the taxable year ("the 40-percent test"). Thus, if the depreciable property is placed in service during a taxable year that consists of three months or less, the mid-quarter convention applies to the property. Under section 168(d)(3)(B)(i), the depreciable basis of nonresidential real property, residential rental property, and any railroad grading or tunnel bore is disregarded in applying the 40-percent test. For rules regarding property that is placed in service and disposed of in the same taxable year, see paragraph (b)(3) of this section. For the definition of "aggregate basis of property," see paragraph (b)(4) of this section.

(b) *Additional rules for determining whether the mid-quarter convention applies and for applying the applicable convention*—(1) *Property de-*

scribed in section 168(f). In determining whether the 40-percent test is satisfied for a taxable year, the depreciable basis of property described in section 168(f) (property to which section 168 does not apply) is not taken into account.

(2) *Listed property.* The depreciable basis of listed property (as defined in section 280F(d)(4) and the regulations thereunder) placed in service during a taxable year is taken into account (unless otherwise excluded) in applying the 40-percent test.

(3) *Property placed in service and disposed of in the same taxable year*—(i) Under section 168(d)(3)(B)(ii), the depreciable basis of property placed in service and disposed of in the same taxable year is not taken into account in determining whether the 40-percent test is satisfied. However, the depreciable basis of property placed in service, disposed of, subsequently reacquired, and again placed in service in the same taxable year must be taken into account in applying the 40-percent test, but the basis of the property is only taken into account on the later of the dates that the property is placed in service during the taxable year.

(ii) The applicable convention, as determined under this section, applies to all depreciable property (except nonresidential real property, residential rental property, and any railroad grading or tunnel bore) placed in service during the taxable year, excluding property placed in service and disposed of in the same taxable year. No depreciation deduction is allowed for property placed in service and disposed of during the same taxable year.

(iii) The provisions of this paragraph (b)(3) are illustrated by the following examples.

Example 1. During 1990, A, a calendar-year taxpayer, purchases a light general purpose truck costing $8,000, an office desk costing $500, a safe costing $1,000, and a computer costing $3,000. The truck is placed in service in January, the desk and safe in August, and the computer in November. These are the only items placed in service during 1990. In September, A sells the truck and the desk. Thus, the truck and the desk were placed in service and disposed of in the same taxable year. Therefore, the depreciable basis of the truck and the desk are not taken into account in determining whether the mid-quarter convention applies to depreciable property placed in service during 1990. Because the computer was placed in service during the last three months of the taxable year and its basis ($3,000) exceeds 40 percent of the aggregate basis of depreciable property placed in service during the taxable year (safe and computer with an aggregate basis of $4,000), the mid-quarter convention applies to the

safe and the computer. No depreciation is allowed with respect to the truck and desk because they were placed in service and disposed of in the same taxable year.

Example 2. The facts are the same as in *Example 1,* except that, in December, A reacquires the truck for $7,000. Thus, the truck is considered placed in service in December and its basis is included in determining whether the mid-quarter convention applies. The mid-quarter convention is applicable, because the computer ($3,000) and the truck ($7,000) are placed in service during the last three months of the taxable year and their aggregate basis ($10,000) exceeds 40 percent of the aggregate basis of property placed in service during the taxable year (safe, computer, and truck with an aggregate basis of $11,000).

(4) *Aggregate basis of property.* For purposes of the 40-percent test, the term "aggregate basis of property" means the sum of the depreciable bases of all items of depreciable property that are taken into account in applying the 40-percent test. "Depreciable basis" means the basis of depreciable property for purposes of determining gain under sections 1011 through 1024. The depreciable basis for the taxable year the property is placed in service reflects the reduction in basis for—

(i) Any portion of the basis the taxpayer properly elects to treat as an expense under section 179;

(ii) Any adjustment to basis under section 48(q); and

(iii) The percentage of the taxpayer's use of property for the taxable year other than in the taxpayer's trade or business (or for the production of income), but is determined before any reduction for depreciation under section 167(a) for that taxable year.

* * *

(6) *Special rule for partnerships and S corporations.* In the case of property placed in service by a partnership or an S corporation, the 40-percent test is generally applied at the partnership or corporate level. However, if a partnership or an S corporation is formed or availed of for the principal purpose of either avoiding the application of the mid-quarter convention or having the mid-quarter convention apply where it otherwise would not, the 40-percent test is applied at the partner, shareholder, or other appropriate level.

* * *

(c) *Disposition of property subject to the half-year or mid-quarter convention*—(1) *In general.* If depreciable property is subject to the half-year (or mid-quarter) convention in the taxable year in which it is placed in service, it also is subject to the half-year (or mid-quarter) convention in the taxable year in which it is disposed of.

(2) *Example.* The provisions of paragraph (c)(1) of this section are illustrated by the following example.

Example. In October 1991, B, a calendar-year taxpayer, purchases and places in service a light general purpose truck costing $10,000. B does not elect to expense any part of the cost of the truck, and this is the only item of depreciable property placed in service by B during 1991. The 40-percent test is satisfied and the mid-quarter convention applies, because the truck is placed in service during the last three months of the taxable year and no other assets are placed in service in that year. In April 1993 (prior to the end of the truck's recovery period), B sells the truck. The mid-quarter convention applies in determining the depreciation deduction for the truck in 1993, the year of disposition.

(d) *Effective date.* This section applies to depreciable property placed in service in taxable years ending after January 30, 1991. For depreciable property placed in service after December 31, 1986, in taxable years ending on or before January 30, 1991, a taxpayer may use a method other than the method provided in this section in applying the 40-percent test and the applicable convention, provided the method is reasonable and is consistently applied to the taxpayer's property. [Reg. § 1.168(d)-1.]

☐ [*T.D.* 8444, 10-28-92.]

§ 1.168(i)-1. General asset accounts.—(a) *Scope.* This section provides rules for general asset accounts under section 168(i)(4). The provisions of this section apply only to assets for which an election has been made under paragraph (k) of this section.

(b) *Definitions.* For purposes of this section, the following definitions apply:

(1) *Unadjusted depreciable basis* is the basis of an asset for purposes of section 1011 without regard to any adjustments described in sections 1016(a)(2) and (3).

(2) *Unadjusted depreciable basis of the general asset account* is the sum of the unadjusted depreciable bases of all assets included in the general asset account.

(3) *Adjusted depreciable basis of the general asset account* is the unadjusted depreciable basis of the general asset account less the adjustments to basis described in sections 1016(a)(2) and (3).

(4) *Expensed cost* is the amount of any allowable credit or deduction treated as a deduction allowable for depreciation or amortization for purposes of section 1245 (for example, a credit allow-

able under section 30 or a deduction allowable under section 179, 179A, or 190).

(c) *Establishment of general asset accounts*—(1) *Assets eligible for general asset accounts*—(i) *General rules.* Assets that are subject to either the general depreciation system of section 168(a) or the alternative depreciation system of section 168(g) may be accounted for in one or more general asset accounts. An asset may be included in a general asset account only to the extent of the asset's unadjusted depreciable basis (for example, if, in 1995, a taxpayer places in service an asset that costs $20,000 and elects under section 179 to expense $17,500 of that asset's cost, the unadjusted depreciable basis of the asset is $2,500 and, therefore, only $2,500 of the asset's cost may be included in a general asset account). However, an asset is not to be included in a general asset account if the asset is used both in a trade or business (or for the production of income) and in a personal activity at any time during the taxable year in which the asset is first placed in service by the taxpayer.

(ii) *Special rules for assets generating foreign source income*—(A) Assets that generate foreign source income, both United States and foreign source income, or combined gross income of a FSC (as defined in section 922), DISC (as defined in section 992(a)), or possessions corporation (as defined in section 936) and its related supplier, may be included in a general asset account if the requirements of paragraph (c)(2)(i) of this section are satisfied. If, however, the inclusion of these assets in a general asset account results in a substantial distortion of income, the Commissioner may disregard the general asset account election and make any reallocations of income or expense necessary to clearly reflect income.

(B) A general asset account shall be treated as a single asset for purposes of applying the rules in § 1.861-9T(g)(3) (relating to allocation and apportionment of interest expense under the asset method). A general asset account that generates income in more than one grouping of income (statutory and residual) is a multiple category asset (as defined in § 1.861-9T(g)(3)(ii)), and the income yield from the general asset account must be determined by applying the rules for multiple category assets as if the general asset account were a single asset.

(2) *Grouping assets in general asset accounts*—(i) *General rules.* If a taxpayer makes the election under paragraph (k) of this section, assets that are subject to the election are grouped into one or more general asset accounts. Assets that are eligible to be grouped into a single general asset account may be divided into more than one

general asset account. Each general asset account must include only assets that—

(A) Have the same asset class (for further guidance, see Rev. Proc. 87-56, 1987-2 C.B. 674, and § 601.601(d)(2)(ii)(*b*) of this chapter);

(B) Have the same applicable depreciation method;

(C) Have the same applicable recovery period;

(D) Have the same applicable convention; and

(E) Are placed in service by the taxpayer in the same taxable year.

(ii) *Special rules.* In addition to the general rules in paragraph (c)(2)(i) of this section, the following rules apply when establishing general asset accounts—

(A) Assets without an asset class, but with the same characteristics described in paragraphs (c)(2)(i)(B), (C), (D), and (E) of this section, may be grouped into a general asset account;

(B) Assets subject to the mid-quarter convention may only be grouped into a general asset account with assets that are placed in service in the same quarter of the taxable year;

(C) Assets subject to the mid-month convention may only be grouped into a general asset account with assets that are placed in service in the same month of the taxable year; and

(D) Passenger automobiles for which the depreciation allowance is limited under section 280F(a) must be grouped into a separate general asset account.

(d) *Determination of depreciation allowance*— (1) *In general.* Depreciation allowances are determined for each general asset account by using the applicable depreciation method, recovery period, and convention for the assets in the account. The depreciation allowances are recorded in a depreciation reserve account for each general asset account. The allowance for depreciation under this section constitutes the amount of depreciation allowable under section 167(a).

(2) *Special rule for passenger automobiles.* For purposes of applying section 280F(a), the depreciation allowance for a general asset account established for passenger automobiles is limited for each taxable year to the amount prescribed in section 280F(a) multiplied by the excess of the number of automobiles originally included in the account over the number of automobiles disposed of during the taxable year or in any prior taxable year in a transaction described in paragraph (e)(3)(iii) (disposition of an asset in a qualifying disposition), (e)(3)(iv) (transactions subject to section 168(i)(7)), (e)(3)(v) (anti-abuse rule), (g) (as-

sets subject to recapture), or (h)(1) (conversion to personal use) of this section.

(e) *Disposition of an asset from a general asset account*—(1) *Scope.* This paragraph (e) provides rules applicable to dispositions of assets included in a general asset account. For purposes of this paragraph (e), an asset in a general asset account is disposed of when ownership of the asset is transferred or when the asset is permanently withdrawn from use either in the taxpayer's trade or business or in the production of income. A disposition includes the sale, exchange, retirement, physical abandonment, or destruction of an asset. A disposition also occurs when an asset is transferred to a supplies, scrap, or similar account. A disposition does not include, however, the retirement of a structural component of real property.

(2) *General rules for a disposition*—(i) *No immediate recovery of basis.* Immediately before a disposition of any asset in a general asset account, the asset is treated as having an adjusted basis of zero for purposes of section 1011. Therefore, no loss is realized upon the disposition of an asset from the general asset account. Similarly, where an asset is disposed of by transfer to a supplies, scrap, or similar account, the basis of the asset in the supplies, scrap, or similar account will be zero.

(ii) *Treatment of amount realized.* Any amount realized on a disposition is recognized as ordinary income (notwithstanding any other provision of subtitle A of the Internal Revenue Code (Code)) to the extent the sum of the unadjusted depreciable basis of the general asset account and any expensed cost (as defined in paragraph (b)(4) of this section) for assets in the account exceeds any amounts previously recognized as ordinary income upon the disposition of other assets in the account. The recognition and character of any excess amount realized are determined under other applicable provisions of the Code (other than sections 1245 and 1250 or provisions of the Code that treat gain on a disposition as subject to section 1245 or 1250).

(iii) *Effect of disposition on a general asset account.* The unadjusted depreciable basis and the depreciation reserve of the general asset account are not affected as a result of a disposition of an asset from the general asset account.

(iv) *Coordination with nonrecognition provisions.* For purposes of determining the basis of an asset acquired in a transaction described in paragraph (e)(3)(iii)(B)(*4*) of this section (relating to certain nonrecognition provisions), the amount of ordinary income recognized under this paragraph (e)(2) is treated as the amount of gain recognized on the disposition.

Reg. § 1.168(i)-1(e)(2)

(v) *Examples.* The following examples illustrate the application of this paragraph (e)(2).

Example 1. (i) *R*, a calendar-year corporation, maintains one general asset account for ten machines. The machines cost a total of $10,000 and were placed in service in June 1995. Of the ten machines, one machine costs $8,200 and nine machines cost a total of $1,800. Assume this general asset account has a depreciation method of 200 percent declining balance, a recovery period of 5 years, and a half-year convention. *R* does not make a section 179 election for any of the machines. As of January 1, 1996, the depreciation reserve of the account is $2,000 [(($10,000 − $0) × 40%) / 2].

(ii) On February 8, 1996, *R* sells the machine that cost $8,200 to an unrelated party for $9,000. Under paragraph (e)(2)(i) of this section, this machine has an adjusted basis of zero.

(iii) On its 1996 tax return, *R* recognizes the amount realized of $9,000 as ordinary income because such amount does not exceed the unadjusted depreciable basis of the general asset account ($10,000), plus any expensed cost for assets in the account ($0), less amounts previously recognized as ordinary income ($0). Moreover, the unadjusted depreciable basis and depreciation reserve of the account are not affected by the disposition of the machine. Thus, the depreciation allowance for the account in 1996 is $3,200 (($10,000 − $2,000) × 40%).

Example 2. (i) The facts are the same as in *Example 1.* In addition, on June 4, 1997, *R* sells seven machines to an unrelated party for a total of $1,100. In accordance with paragraph (e)(2)(i) of this section, these machines have an adjusted basis of zero.

(ii) On its 1997 tax return, *R* recognizes $1,000 as ordinary income (the unadjusted depreciable basis of $10,000, plus the expensed cost of $0, less the amount of $9,000 previously recognized as ordinary income). The recognition and character of the excess amount realized of $100 ($1,100 − $1,000) are determined under applicable provisions of the Code other than section 1245 (such as section 1231). Moreover, the unadjusted depreciable basis and depreciation reserve of the account are not affected by the disposition of the machines. Thus, the depreciation allowance for the account in 1997 is $1,920 (($10,000 − $5,200) × 40%).

(3) *Special rules*—(i) *In general.* This paragraph (e)(3) provides the rules for terminating general asset account treatment upon certain dispositions. While the rules under paragraphs (e)(3)(ii) and (iii) of this section are optional rules, the rules under paragraphs (e)(3)(iv) and (v) of this section are mandatory rules. A taxpayer applies paragraph (e)(3)(ii) or (iii) of this section by reporting the gain, loss, or other deduction on the taxpayer's timely filed (including extensions) income tax return for the taxable year in which the disposition occurs. For purposes of applying paragraph (e)(3)(iii) through (v) of this section, see paragraph (i) of this section for identifying the unadjusted depreciable basis of a disposed asset.

(ii) *Disposition of all assets remaining in a general asset account*—(A) *Optional termination of a general asset account.* Upon the disposition of all of the assets, or the last asset, in a general asset account, a taxpayer may apply this paragraph (e)(3)(ii) to recover the adjusted depreciable basis of the general asset account (rather than having paragraph (e)(2) of this section apply). Under this paragraph (e)(3)(ii), the general asset account terminates and the amount of gain or loss for the general asset account is determined under section 1001(a) by taking into account the adjusted depreciable basis of the general asset account at the time of the disposition. The recognition and character of the gain or loss are determined under other applicable provisions of the Code, except that the amount of gain subject to section 1245 (or section 1250) is limited to the excess of the depreciation allowed or allowable for the general asset account, including any expensed cost (or the excess of the additional depreciation allowed or allowable for the general asset account), over any amounts previously recognized as ordinary income under paragraph (e)(2) of this section.

(B) *Example.* The following example illustrates the application of this paragraph (e)(3)(ii).

Example. (i) *T*, a calendar-year corporation, maintains a general asset account for 1,000 calculators. The calculators cost a total of $60,000 and were placed in service in 1995. Assume this general asset account has a depreciation method of 200 percent declining balance, a recovery period of 5 years, and a half-year convention. *T* does not make a section 179 election for any of the calculators. In 1996, *T* sells 200 of the calculators to an unrelated party for a total of $10,000 and recognizes the $10,000 as ordinary income in accordance with paragraph (e)(2) of this section.

(ii) On March 26, 1997, *T* sells the remaining calculators in the general asset account to an unrelated party for $35,000. *T* chooses to apply paragraph (e)(3)(ii) of this section. As a result, the account terminates and gain or loss is determined for the account.

(iii) On the date of disposition, the adjusted depreciable basis of the account is $23,040 (unadjusted depreciable basis of $60,000 less the depreciation allowed or allowable of $36,960).

Reg. § 1.168(i)-1(e)(3)

Thus, in 1997, T recognizes gain of $11,960 (amount realized of $35,000 less the adjusted depreciable basis of $23,040). The gain of $11,960 is subject to section 1245 to the extent of the depreciation allowed or allowable for the account (plus the expensed cost for assets in the account) less the amounts previously recognized as ordinary income ($36,960 + $0 − $10,000 = $26,960). As a result, the entire gain of $11,960 is subject to section 1245.

(iii) *Disposition of an asset in a qualifying disposition*—(A) *Optional determination of the amount of gain, loss, or other deduction.* In the case of a qualifying disposition of an asset (described in paragraph (e)(3)(iii)(B) of this section), a taxpayer may apply this paragraph (e)(3)(iii) (rather than having paragraph (e)(2) of this section apply). Under this paragraph (e)(3)(iii), general asset account treatment for the asset terminates as of the first day of the taxable year in which the qualifying disposition occurs, and the amount of gain, loss, or other deduction for the asset is determined by taking into account the asset's adjusted basis. The adjusted basis of the asset at the time of the disposition equals the unadjusted depreciable basis of the asset less the depreciation allowed or allowable for the asset, computed by using the depreciation method, recovery period, and convention applicable to the general asset account in which the asset was included. The recognition and character of the gain, loss, or other deduction are determined under other applicable provisions of the Code, except that the amount of gain subject to section 1245 (or section 1250) is limited to the lesser of—

(*1*) The depreciation allowed or allowable for the asset, including any expensed cost (or the additional depreciation allowed or allowable for the asset); or

(*2*) The excess of—

(*i*) The original unadjusted depreciable basis of the general asset account plus, in the case of section 1245 property originally included in the general asset account, any expensed cost; over

(*ii*) The cumulative amounts of gain previously recognized as ordinary income under either paragraph (e)(2) of this section or section 1245 (or section 1250).

(B) *Qualifying dispositions.* A qualifying disposition is a disposition that does not involve all the assets, or the last asset, remaining in a general asset account and that is—

(*1*) A direct result of a fire, storm, shipwreck, or other casualty, or from theft;

(*2*) A charitable contribution for which a deduction is allowable under section 170;

(*3*) A direct result of a cessation, termination, or disposition of a business, manufacturing or other income producing process, operation, facility, plant, or other unit (other than by transfer to a supplies, scrap, or similar account); or

(*4*) A transaction, other than a transaction described in paragraph (e)(3)(iv) of this section (pertaining to transactions subject to section 168(i)(7)), to which a nonrecognition section of the Code applies (determined without regard to this section), such as section 1031 or 1033.

(C) *Effect of a qualifying disposition on a general asset account.* If the taxpayer applies this paragraph (e)(3)(iii) to a qualifying disposition of an asset, then—

(*1*) The asset is removed from the general asset account as of the first day of the taxable year in which the qualifying disposition occurs;

(*2*) The unadjusted depreciable basis of the general asset account is reduced by the unadjusted depreciable basis of the asset as of the first day of the taxable year in which the disposition occurs;

(*3*) The depreciation reserve of the general asset account is reduced by the depreciation allowed or allowable for the asset as of the end of the taxable year immediately preceding the year of disposition, computed by using the depreciation method, recovery period, and convention applicable to the general asset account in which the asset was included; and

(*4*) For purposes of determining the amount of gain realized on subsequent dispositions that is subject to ordinary income treatment under paragraph (e)(2)(ii) of this section, the amount of any expensed cost with respect to the asset is disregarded.

(D) *Example.* The provisions of this paragraph (e)(3)(iii) are illustrated by the following example.

Example. (i) Z, a calendar-year corporation, maintains one general asset account for 12 machines. Each machine costs $15,000 and was placed in service in 1995. Of the 12 machines, nine machines that cost a total of $135,000 are used in Z's Kentucky plant, and three machines that cost a total of $45,000 are used in Z's Ohio plant. Assume this general asset account has a depreciation method of 200 percent declining balance, a recovery period of 5 years, and a half-year convention. Z does not make a section 179 election for any of the machines. As of January 1, 1997, the depreciation reserve for the account is $93,600.

Reg. § 1.168(i)-1(e)(3)

(ii) On May 27, 1997, Z sells its entire manufacturing plant in Ohio to an unrelated party. The sales proceeds allocated to each of the three machines at the Ohio plant is $5,000. Because this transaction is a qualifying disposition under paragraph (e)(3)(iii)(B)(*3*) of this section, Z chooses to apply paragraph (e)(3)(iii) of this section.

(iii) For Z's 1997 return, the depreciation allowance for the account is computed as follows. As of December 31, 1996, the depreciation allowed or allowable for the three machines at the Ohio plant is $23,400. Thus, as of January 1, 1997, the unadjusted depreciable basis of the account is reduced from $180,000 to $135,000 ($180,000 less the unadjusted depreciable basis of $45,000 for the three machines), and the depreciation reserve of the account is decreased from $93,600 to $70,200 ($93,600 less the depreciation allowed or allowable of $23,400 for the three machines as of December 31, 1996). Consequently, the depreciation allowance for the account in 1997 is $25,920 (($135,000 − $70,200) × 40%).

(iv) For Z's 1997 return, gain or loss for each of the three machines at the Ohio plant is determined as follows. The depreciation allowed or allowable in 1997 for each machine is $1,440 [(($15,000 − $7,800) × 40%) / 2]. Thus, the adjusted basis of each machine under section 1011 is $5,760 (the adjusted depreciable basis of $7,200 removed from the account less the depreciation allowed or allowable of $1,440 in 1997). As a result, the loss recognized in 1997 for each machine is $760 ($5,000 − $5,760), which is subject to section 1231.

(iv) *Transactions subject to section 168(i)(7)*. If an asset in a general asset account is transferred in a transaction described in section 168(i)(7)(B) (pertaining to treatment of transferees in certain nonrecognition transactions), the transferor must remove the transferred asset from the general asset account as of the first day of the taxable year in which the transaction occurs. In addition, the adjustments to the general asset account described in paragraph (e)(3)(iii)(C)(*2*) through (*4*) of this section must be made. The transferee is bound by the transferor's election under paragraph (k) of this section with respect to so much of the asset's basis in the hands of the transferee as does not exceed the asset's adjusted basis in the hands of the transferor. If all of the assets, or the last asset, in a general asset account are transferred, the transferee's basis in the assets or asset transferred is equal to the adjusted depreciable basis of the general asset account as of the beginning of the transferor's taxable year in which the transaction occurs, decreased by the amount of depreciation allocable to the transferor for the year of the transfer.

(v) *Anti-abuse rule*—(A) *In general.* If an asset in a general asset account is disposed of by a taxpayer in a transaction described in paragraph (e)(3)(v)(B) of this section, general asset account treatment for the asset terminates as of the first day of the taxable year in which the disposition occurs. Consequently, the taxpayer must determine the amount of gain, loss, or other deduction attributable to the disposition in the manner described in paragraph (e)(3)(iii)(A) of this section (notwithstanding that paragraph (e)(3)(iii)(A) of this section is an optional rule) and must make the adjustments to the general asset account described in paragraph (e)(3)(iii)(C)(*1*) through (*4*) of this section.

(B) *Abusive transactions.* A transaction is described in this paragraph (e)(3)(v)(B) if the transaction is not described in paragraph (e)(3)(iv) of this section and the transaction is entered into, or made, with a principal purpose of achieving a tax benefit or result that would not be available absent an election under this section. Examples of these types of transactions include—

(*1*) A transaction entered into with a principal purpose of shifting income or deductions among taxpayers in a manner that would not be possible absent an election under this section in order to take advantage of differing effective tax rates among the taxpayers; or

(*2*) An election made under this section with a principal purpose of disposing of an asset from a general asset account in order to utilize an expiring net operating loss or credit. The fact that a taxpayer with a net operating loss carryover or a credit carryover transfers an asset to a related person or transfers an asset pursuant to an arrangement where the asset continues to be used (or is available for use) by the taxpayer pursuant to a lease (or otherwise) indicates, absent strong evidence to the contrary, that the transaction is described in this paragraph (e)(3)(v)(B).

* * *

(g) *Assets subject to recapture.* If the basis of an asset in a general asset account is increased as a result of the recapture of any allowable credit or deduction (for example, the basis adjustment for the recapture amount under section 30(d)(2), 50(c)(2), 179(d)(10), or 179A(e)(4)), general asset account treatment for the asset terminates as of the first day of the taxable year in which the recapture event occurs. Consequently, the taxpayer must remove the asset from the general asset account as of that day and must make the adjustments to the general asset account described in paragraph (e)(3)(iii)(C)(*2*) through (*4*) of this section.

Reg. § 1.168(i)-1(g)

(h) *Changes in use*—(1) *Conversion to personal use.* An asset in a general asset account becomes ineligible for general asset account treatment if a taxpayer uses the asset in a personal activity during a taxable year. Upon a conversion to personal use, the taxpayer must remove the asset from the general asset account as of the first day of the taxable year in which the change in use occurs and must make the adjustments to the general asset account described in paragraph (e)(3)(iii)(C)(*2*) through (*4*) of this section.

(2) *Other changes in use.* [Reserved].

(i) *Identification of disposed or converted asset.* A taxpayer may use any reasonable method that is consistently applied to the taxpayer's general asset accounts for purposes of determining the unadjusted depreciable basis of a disposed or converted asset in a transaction described in paragraph (e)(3)(iii) (disposition of an asset in a qualifying disposition), (e)(3)(iv) (transactions subject to section 168(i)(7)), (e)(3)(v) (anti-abuse rule), (g) (assets subject to recapture), or (h)(1) (conversion to personal use) of this section.

(j) *Effect of adjustments on prior dispositions.* The adjustments to a general asset account under paragraph (e)(3)(iii), (e)(3)(iv), (e)(3)(v), (g), or (h)(1) of this section have no effect on the recognition and character of prior dispositions subject to paragraph (e)(2) of this section.

* * *

[Reg. § 1.168(i)-1.]

☐ [*T.D.* 8566, 10-7-94.]

§ 1.170A-1. Charitable, etc., contributions and gifts; allowance of deduction.—(a) *Allowance of deduction.* Any charitable contribution, as defined in section 170(c), actually paid during the taxable year is allowable as a deduction in computing taxable income irrespective of the method of accounting employed or of the date on which the contribution is pledged. However, charitable contributions by corporations may under certain circumstances be deductible even though not paid during the taxable year, as provided in section 170(a)(2) and § 1.170A-11. For rules relating to record keeping and return requirements in support of deductions for charitable contributions (whether by an itemizing or nonitemizing taxpayer) see § 1.170A-13. The deduction is subject to the limitations of section 170(b) and § 1.170A-8 or § 1.170A-11. Subject to the provisions of section 170(d) and §§ 1.170A-10 and 1.170A-11, certain excess charitable contributions made by individuals and corporations shall be treated as paid in certain succeeding taxable years. For provisions relating to direct charitable deductions under section 63 by nonitemizers, see section 63(b)(1)(C) and (i) and section 170(i). For rules relating to the determination of, and the deduction for, amounts paid to maintain certain students as members of the taxpayer's household and treated under section 170(g) as paid for the use of an organization described in section 170(c)(2), (3), or (4), see § 1.170A-2. For the reduction of any charitable contributions for interest on certain indebtedness, see section 170(f)(5) and § 1.170A-3. For a special rule relating to the computation of the amount of the deduction with respect to a charitable contribution of certain ordinary income or capital gain property, see section 170(e) and § 1.170A-4 and § 1.170A-4A. For rules for postponing the time for deduction of a charitable contribution of a future interest in tangible personal property, see section 170(a)(3) and § 1.170A-5. For rules with respect to transfers in trust and of partial interests in property, see section 170(e), section 170(f)(2) and (3), § 1.170A-4, § 1.170A-6, and § 1.170A-7. For definition of the term "section 170(b)(1)(A) organization," see § 1.170A-9. For valuation of a remainder interest in real property, see section 170(f)(4) and the regulations thereunder. The deduction for charitable contributions is subject to verification by the district director.

(b) *Time of making contribution.* Ordinarily, a contribution is made at the time delivery is effected. The unconditional delivery or mailing of a check which subsequently clears in due course will constitute an effective contribution on the date of delivery or mailing. If a taxpayer unconditionally delivers or mails a properly endorsed stock certificate to a charitable donee or the donee's agent, the gift is completed on the date of delivery or, if such certificate is received in the ordinary course of the mails, on the date of mailing. If the donor delivers the stock certificate to his bank or broker as the donor's agent, or to the issuing corporation or its agent, for transfer into the name of the donee, the gift is completed on the date the stock is transferred on the books of the corporation. For rules relating to the date of payment of a contribution consisting of a future interest in tangible personal property, see section 170(a)(3) and § 1.170A-5.

(c) *Value of a contribution in property.* (1) If a charitable contribution is made in property other than money, the amount of the contribution is the fair market value of the property at the time of the contribution reduced as provided in section 170(e)(1) and paragraph (a) of § 1.170A-4, or section 170(e)(3) and paragraph (c) of § 1.170A-4A.

(2) The fair market value is the price at which the property would change hands between a willing buyer and a willing seller, neither being under any compulsion to buy or sell and both having reasonable knowledge of relevant facts. If the contribution is made in property of a type which the taxpayer sells in the course of his business, the fair market value is the price which the

Reg. § 1.170A-1(c)(2)

taxpayer would have received if he had sold the contributed property in the usual market in which he customarily sells, at the time and place of the contribution and, in the case of a contribution of goods in quantity, in the quantity contributed. The usual market of a manufacturer or other producer consists of the wholesalers or other distributors to or through whom he customarily sells, but if he sells only at retail the usual market consists of his retail customers.

(3) If the donor makes a charitable contribution of property, such as stock in trade, at a time when he could not reasonably have been expected to realize its usual selling price, the value of the gift is not the usual selling price but is the amount for which the quantity of property contributed would have been sold by the donor at the time of the contribution.

(4) Any costs and expenses pertaining to the contributed property which were incurred in taxable years preceding the year of contribution and are properly reflected in the opening inventory for the year of contribution must be removed from inventory and are not a part of the cost of goods sold for purposes of determining gross income for the year of contribution. Any costs and expenses pertaining to the contributed property which are incurred in the year of contribution and would, under the method of accounting used, be properly reflected in the cost of goods sold for such year are to be treated as part of the cost of goods sold for such year. If costs and expenses incurred in producing or acquiring the contributed property are, under the method of accounting used, properly deducted under section 162 or other section of the Code, such costs and expenses will be allowed as deductions for the taxable year in which they are paid or incurred, whether or not such year is the year of the contribution. Any such costs and expenses which are treated as part of the cost of goods sold for the year of contribution, and any such costs and expenses which are properly deducted under section 162 or other section of the Code, are not to be treated under any section of the Code as resulting in any basis for the contributed property. Thus, for example, the contributed property has no basis for purposes of determining under section 170(e)(1)(A) and paragraph (a) of § 1.170A-4 the amount of gain which would have been recognized if such property had been sold by the donor at its fair market value at the time of its contribution. The amount of any charitable contribution for the taxable year is not to be reduced by the amount of any costs or expenses pertaining to the contributed property which was properly deducted under section 162 or other section of the Code for any taxable year preceding the year of the contribution. This subparagraph applies only to property which was held by the

taxpayer for sale in the course of a trade or business. The application of this subparagraph may be illustrated by the following examples:

Example (1). In 1970, A, an individual using the calendar year as the taxable year and the accrual method of accounting, contributed to a church property from inventory having a fair market value of $600. The closing inventory at the end of 1969 properly included $400 of costs attributable to the acquisition of such property, and in 1969 A properly deducted under section 162 $50 of administrative and other expenses attributable to such property. Under section 170(e)(1)(A) and paragraph (a) of § 1.170A-4, the amount of the charitable contribution allowed for 1970 is $400 ($600 − [$600 − $400]). Pursuant to this subparagraph, the cost of goods sold to be used in determining gross income for 1970 may not include the $400 which was included in opening inventory for that year.

Example (2). The facts are the same as in example (1) except that the contributed property was acquired in 1970 at a cost of $400. The $400 cost of the property is included in determining the cost of goods sold for 1970, and $50 is allowed as a deduction for that year under section 162. A is not allowed any deduction under section 170 for the contributed property, since under section 170(e)(1)(A) and paragraph (a) of § 1.170A-4 the amount of the charitable contribution is reduced to zero ($600 − [$600 − $0]).

Example (3). In 1970, B, an individual using the calendar year as the taxable year and the accrual method of accounting, contributed to a church property from inventory having a fair market value of $600. Under § 1.471-3(c), the closing inventory at the end of 1969 properly included $450 costs attributable to the production of such property, including $50 of administrative and other indirect expenses which, under his method of accounting, was properly added to inventory rather than deducted as a business expense. Under section 170(e)(1)(A) and paragraph (a) of § 1.170A-4, the amount of the charitable contribution allowed for 1970 is $450 ($600 − [$600 − $450]). Pursuant to this subparagraph, the cost of goods sold to be used in determining gross income for 1970 may not include the $450 which was included in opening inventory for that year.

Example (4). The facts are the same as in example (3) except that the contributed property was produced in 1970 at a cost of $450, including $50 of administrative and other indirect expenses. The $450 cost of the property is included in determining the cost of goods sold for 1970. B is not allowed any deduction under section 170 for the contributed property, since under section

Reg. § 1.170A-1(c)(3)

170(e)(1)(A) and paragraph (a) of § 1.170A-4 the amount of the charitable contribution is reduced to zero ($600 − [$600 − $0]).

Example (5). In 1970, C, a farmer using the cash method of accounting and the calendar year as the taxable year, contributed to a church a quantity of grain which he had raised having a fair market value of $600. In 1969, C paid expenses of $450 in raising the property which he properly deducted for such year under section 162. Under section 170(e)(1)(A) and paragraph (a) of § 1.170A-4, the amount of the charitable contribution in 1970 is reduced to zero ($600 − [$600 − $0]). Accordingly, C is not allowed any deduction under section 170 for the contributed property.

Example (6). The facts are the same as in example (5) except that the $450 expenses incurred in raising the contributed property were paid in 1970. The result is the same as in example (5), except the amount of $450 is deductible under section 162 for 1970.

(5) Transfers of property to an organization described in section 170(c) which bear a direct relationship to the taxpayer's trade or business and which are made with a reasonable expectation of financial return commensurate with the amount of the transfer may constitute allowable deductions as trade or business expenses rather than as charitable contributions. See section 162 and the regulations thereunder.

(d) *Purchase of an annuity.* (1) In the case of an annuity or portion thereof purchased from an organization described in section 170(c), there shall be allowed as a deduction the excess of the amount paid over the value at the time of purchase of the annuity or portion purchased.

(2) The value of the annuity or portion is the value of the annuity determined in accordance with paragraph (e)(1)(iii)(*b*)(*2*) of § 1.101-2.

(3) For determining gain on any such transaction constituting a bargain sale, see section 1011(b) and § 1.1011-2.

(e) *Transfers subject to a condition or power.* If as of the date of a gift a transfer for charitable purposes is dependent upon the performance of some act or the happening of a precedent event in order that it might become effective, no deduction is allowable unless the possibility that the charitable transfer will not become effective is so remote as to be negligible. If an interest in property passes to, or is vested in, charity on the date of the gift and the interest would be defeated by the subsequent performance of some act or the happening of some event, the possibility of occurrence of which appears on the date of the gift to be so remote as to be negligible, the deduction is allowable. For example, A transfers land to a city government for as long as the land is used by the city for a public park. If on the date of the gift the city does plan to use the land for a park and the possibility that the city will not use the land for a public park is so remote as to be negligible, A is entitled to a deduction under section 170 for his charitable contribution.

* * *

(g) *Contributions of services.* No deduction is allowable under section 170 for a contribution of services. However, unreimbursed expenditures made incident to the rendition of services to an organization contributions to which are deductible may constitute a deductible contribution. For example, the cost of a uniform without general utility which is required to be worn in performing donated services is deductible. Similarly, out-of-pocket transportation expenses necessarily incurred in performing donated services are deductible. Reasonable expenditures for meals and lodging necessarily incurred while away from home in the course of performing donated services also are deductible. For the purposes of this paragraph, the phrase "while away from home" has the same meaning as that phrase is used for purposes of section 162 and the regulations thereunder.

(h) *Payment in exchange for consideration—(1) Burden on taxpayer to show that all or part of payment is a charitable contribution or gift.* No part of a payment that a taxpayer makes to or for the use of an organization described in section 170(c) that is in consideration for (as defined in § 1.170A-13(f)(6)) goods or services (as defined in § 1.170A-13(f)(5)) is a contribution or gift within the meaning of section 170(c) unless the taxpayer—

(i) Intends to make a payment in an amount that exceeds the fair market value of the goods or services; and

(ii) Makes a payment in an amount that exceeds the fair market value of the goods or services.

(2) *Limitation on amount deductible—(i) In general.* The charitable contribution deduction under section 170(a) for a payment a taxpayer makes partly in consideration for goods or services may not exceed the excess of—

(A) The amount of any cash paid and the fair market value of any property (other than cash) transferred by the taxpayer to an organization described in section 170(c); over

(B) The fair market value of the goods or services the organization provides in return.

(ii) *Special rules.* For special limits on the deduction for charitable contributions of ordinary

Reg. § 1.170A-1(h)(2)

income and capital gain property, see section 170(e) and §§ 1.170A-4 and 1.170A-4A.

(3) *Certain goods or services disregarded.* For purposes of section 170(a) and paragraphs (h)(1) and (h)(2) of this section, goods or services described in § 1.170A-13(f)(8)(i) or § 1.170A-13(f)(9)(i) are disregarded.

(4) *Donee estimates of the value of goods or services may be treated as fair market value*—(i) *In general.* For purposes of section 170(a), a taxpayer may rely on either a contemporaneous written acknowledgment provided under section 170(f)(8) and § 1.170A-13(f) or a written disclosure statement provided under section 6115 for the fair market value of any goods or services provided to the taxpayer by the donee organization.

(ii) *Exception.* A taxpayer may not treat an estimate of the value of goods or services as their fair market value if the taxpayer knows, or has reason to know, that such treatment is unreasonable. For example, if a taxpayer knows, or has reason to know, that there is an error in an estimate provided by an organization described in section 170(c) pertaining to goods or services that have a readily ascertainable value, it is unreasonable for the taxpayer to treat the estimate as the fair market value of the goods or services. Similarly, if a taxpayer is a dealer in the type of goods or services provided in consideration for the taxpayer's payment and knows, or has reason to know, that the estimate is in error, it is unreasonable for the taxpayer to treat the estimate as the fair market value of the goods or services.

(5) *Examples.* The following examples illustrate the rules of this paragraph (h).

Example 1. Certain goods or services disregarded. Taxpayer makes a $50 payment to Charity *B*, an organization described in section 170(c), in exchange for a family membership. The family membership entitles Taxpayer and members of Taxpayer's family to certain benefits. These benefits include free admission to weekly poetry readings, discounts on merchandise sold by *B* in its gift shop or by mail order, and invitations to special events for members only, such as lectures or informal receptions. When *B* first offers its membership package for the year, *B* reasonably projects that each special event for members will have a cost to *B*, excluding any allocable overhead, of $5 or less per person attending the event. Because the family membership benefits are disregarded pursuant to § 1.170A-13(f)(8)(i), Taxpayer may treat the $50 payment as a contribution or gift within the meaning of section 170(c), regardless of Taxpayer's intent and whether or not the payment exceeds the fair market value of the goods or services. Furthermore, any charitable contribu-

tion deduction available to Taxpayer may be calculated without regard to the membership benefits.

Example 2. Treatment of good faith estimate at auction as the fair market value. Taxpayer attends an auction held by Charity *C*, an organization described in section 170(c). Prior to the auction, *C* publishes a catalog that meets the requirements for a written disclosure statement under section 6115(a) (including *C*'s good faith estimate of the value of items that will be available for bidding). A representative of *C* gives a copy of the catalog to each individual (including Taxpayer) who attends the auction. Taxpayer notes that in the catalog *C*'s estimate of the value of a vase is $100. Taxpayer has no reason to doubt the accuracy of this estimate. Taxpayer successfully bids and pays $500 for the vase. Because Taxpayer knew, prior to making her payment, that the estimate in the catalog was less than the amount of her payment, Taxpayer satisfies the requirement of paragraph (h)(1)(i) of this section. Because Taxpayer makes a payment in an amount that exceeds that estimate, Taxpayer satisfies the requirements of paragraph (h)(1)(ii) of this section. Taxpayer may treat *C*'s estimate of the value of the vase as its fair market value in determining the amount of her charitable contribution deduction.

Example 3. Good faith estimate not in error. Taxpayer makes a $200 payment to Charity *D*, an organization described in section 170(c). In return for Taxpayer's payment, *D* gives Taxpayer a book that Taxpayer could buy at retail prices typically ranging from $18 to $25. *D* provides Taxpayer with a good faith estimate, in a written disclosure statement under section 6115(a), of $20 for the value of the book. Because the estimate is within the range of typical retail prices for the book, the estimate contained in the written disclosure statement is not in error. Although Taxpayer knows that the book is sold for as much as $25, Taxpayer may treat the estimate of $20 as the fair market value of the book in determining the amount of his charitable contribution deduction.

(i) [Reserved]

(j) *Exceptions and other rules.* (1) The provisions of section 170 do not apply to contributions by an estate; nor do they apply to a trust unless the trust is a private foundation which, pursuant to section 642(c)(6) and § 1.642(c)-4, is allowed a deduction under section 170 subject to the provisions applicable to individuals.

(2) No deduction shall be allowed under section 170 for a charitable contribution to or for the use of an organization or trust described in section 508(d) or 4948(c)(4), subject to the conditions

specified in such sections and the regulations thereunder.

(3) For disallowance of deductions for contributions to or for the use of communist controlled organizations, see section 11(a) of the Internal Security Act of 1950, as amended (50 U.S.C. 790).

(4) For denial of deductions for charitable contributions as trade or business expenses and rules with respect to treatment of payments to organizations other than those described in section 170(c), see section 162 and the regulations thereunder.

(5) No deduction shall be allowed under section 170 for amounts paid to an organization:

(i) Which is disqualified for tax exemption under section 501(c)(3) by reason of attempting to influence legislation, or

(ii) Which participates in, or intervenes in (including the publishing or distributing of statements), any political campaign on behalf of or in opposition to any candidate for public office.

For purposes of determining whether an organization is attempting to influence legislation or is engaging in political activities, see sections 501(c)(3), 501(h), 4911 and the regulations thereunder.

(6) No deduction shall be allowed under section 170 for expenditures for lobbying purposes, the promotion or defeat of legislation, etc. See also the regulations under sections 162 and 4945.

(7) No deduction for charitable contributions is allowed in computing the taxable income of a common trust fund or of a partnership. See sections 584(d)(3) and 703(a)(2)(D). However, a partner's distributive share of charitable contributions actually paid by a partnership during its taxable year may be allowed as a deduction in the partner's separate return for his taxable year with or within which the taxable year of the partnership ends, to the extent that the aggregate of his share of the partnership contributions and his own contributions does not exceed the limitations in section 170(b).

(8) For charitable contributions paid by a nonresident alien individual or a foreign corporation, see § 1.170A-4(b)(5) and sections 873, 876, 877, and 882(c), and the regulations thereunder.

(9) For charitable contributions paid by a citizen of the United States or a domestic corporation entitled to the benefits of section 931 (relating to income from sources within possessions of the United States), see section 931(d) and the regulations thereunder.

(10) For carryover of excess charitable contributions in certain corporate acquisitions, see section 381(c)(19) and the regulations thereunder.

(11) No deduction shall be allowed under section 170 for out-of-pocket expenditures on behalf of an eligible organization (within the meaning of § 1.501(h)-2(b)(1)) if the expenditure is made in connection with influencing legislation (within the meaning of section 501(c)(3) or § 56.4911-2), or in connection with the payment of the organization's tax liability under section 4911. For the treatment of similar expenditures on behalf of other organizations see paragraph (h)(6) of this section.

(k) *Effective date.* In general this section applies to contributions made in taxable years beginning after December 31, 1969. Paragraph (j)(11) of this section, however, applies only to out-of-pocket expenditures made in taxable years beginning after December 31, 1976. In addition, paragraph (h) of this section applies only to payments made on or after December 16, 1996. However, taxpayers may rely on the rules of paragraph (h) of this section for payments made on or after January 1, 1994. [Reg. § 1.170A-1.]

☐ [*T.D. 7207, 10-3-72. Amended by T.D. 7340, 1-6-75; T.D. 7807, 1-29-82; T.D. 8002, 12-26-84; T.D. 8308, 8-30-90 and T.D. 8690, 12-13-96.*]

§ 1.170A-4. Reduction in amount of charitable contributions of certain appreciated property.—* * *

(b) *Definitions and other rules.* For purposes of this section—

(1) *Ordinary income property.* The term "ordinary income property" means property any portion of the gain on which would not have been long-term capital gain if the property had been sold by the donor at its fair market value at the time of its contribution to the charitable organization. Such term includes, for example, property held by the donor primarily for sale to customers in the ordinary course of his trade or business, a work of art created by the donor, a manuscript prepared by the donor, letters and memorandums prepared by or for the donor, a capital asset held by the donor for not more than 1 year (6 months for taxable years beginning before 1977; 9 months for taxable years beginning in 1977), and stock described in section 306(a), 341(a), or 1248(a) to the extent that, after applying such section, gain on its disposition would not have been long-term capital gain. The term does not include an income interest in respect of which a deduction is allowed under section 170(f)(2)(B) and paragraph (c) of § 1.170A-6.

(2) *Section 170(e) capital gain property.* The term "section 170(e) capital gain property" means property any portion of the gain on which would have been treated as long-term capital gain if the property had been sold by the donor at its

fair market value at the time of its contribution to the charitable organization and which—

(i) Is contributed to or for the use of a private foundation, as defined in section 509(a) and the regulations thereunder, other than a private foundation described in section 170(b)(1)(E),

(ii) Constitutes tangible personal property contributed to or for the use of a charitable organization, other than a private foundation to which subdivision (i) of this subparagraph applies, which is put to an unrelated use by the charitable organization within the meaning of subparagraph (3) of this paragraph, or

(iii) Constitutes property not described in subdivision (i) or (ii) of this subparagraph which is 30-percent capital gain property to which an election under paragraph (d)(2) of § 1.170A-8 applies.

For purposes of this subparagraph a fixture which is intended to be severed from real property shall be treated as tangible personal property.

(3) *Unrelated use*—(i) *In general.* The term "unrelated use" means a use which is unrelated to the purpose or function constituting the basis of the charitable organization's exemption under section 501 or, in the case of a contribution of property to a governmental unit, the use of such property by such unit for other than exclusively public purposes. For example, if a painting contributed to an educational institution is used by that organization for educational purposes by being placed in its library for display and study by art students, the use is not an unrelated use; but if the painting is sold and the proceeds used by the organization for educational purposes, the use of the property is an unrelated use. If furnishings contributed to a charitable organization are used by it in its offices and buildings in the course of carrying out its functions, the use of the property is not an unrelated use. If a set or collection of items of tangible personal property is contributed to a charitable organization or governmental unit, the use of the set or collection is not an unrelated use if the donee sells or otherwise disposes of only an insubstantial portion of the set or collection. The use by a trust of tangible personal property contributed to it for the benefit of a charitable organization is an unrelated use if the use by the trust is one which would have been unrelated if made by the charitable organization.

(ii) *Proof of use.* For purposes of applying subparagraph (2)(ii) of this paragraph, a taxpayer who makes a charitable contribution of tangible personal property to or for the use of a charitable organization or governmental unit may treat such property as not being put to an unrelated use by the donee if—

(a) He establishes that the property is not in fact put to an unrelated use by the donee, or

(b) At the time of the contribution or at the time the contribution is treated as made, it is reasonable to anticipate that the property will not be put to an unrelated use by the donee. In the case of a contribution of tangible personal property to or for the use of a museum, if the object donated is of a general type normally retained by such museum or other museums for museum purposes, it will be reasonable for the donor to anticipate, unless he has actual knowledge to the contrary, that the object will not be put to an unrelated use by the donee, whether or not the object is later sold or exchanged by the donee.

(4) *Property used in trade or business.* For purposes of applying subparagraphs (1) and (2) of this paragraph, property which is used in the trade or business, as defined in section 1231(b), shall be treated as a capital asset, except that any gain in respect of such property which would have been recognized if the property had been sold by the donor at its fair market value at the time of its contribution to the charitable organization shall be treated as ordinary income to the extent that such gain would have constituted ordinary income by reason of the application of section 617(d)(1), 1245(a), 1250(a), 1251(c), 1252(a), or 1254(a).

* * *

[Reg. § 1.170A-4.]

☐ [*T.D. 7207, 10-3-72. Amended by T.D. 7728, 10-31-80, T.D. 7807, 1-29-82, T.D. 8176, 2-24-88 and T.D. 8540, 6-9-94.*]

§ 1.170A-5. Future interests in tangible personal property.—(a) *In general.* (1) A contribution consisting of a transfer of a future interest in tangible personal property shall be treated as made only when all intervening interests in, and rights to the actual possession or enjoyment of, the property—

(i) Have expired, or

(ii) Are held by persons other than the taxpayer or those standing in a relationship to the taxpayer described in section 267(b) and the regulations thereunder, relating to losses, expenses, and interest with respect to transactions between related taxpayers.

(2) Section 170(a)(3) and this section have no application in respect of a transfer of an undivided present interest in property. For example, a contribution of an undivided one-quarter interest in a painting with respect to which the donee is entitled to possession during three months of each year shall be treated as made upon the receipt by the donee of a formally executed and acknowl-

edged deed of gift. However, the period of initial possession by the donee may not be deferred in time for more than one year.

(3) Section 170(a)(3) and this section have no application in respect of a transfer of a future interest in intangible personal property or in real property. However, a fixture which is intended to be severed from real property shall be treated as tangible personal property. For example, a contribution of a future interest in a chandelier which is attached to a building is considered a contribution which consists of a future interest in tangible personal property if the transferor intends that it be detached from the building at or prior to the time when the charitable organization's right to possession or enjoyment of the chandelier is to commence.

(4) For purposes of section 170(a)(3) and this section, the term "future interest" has generally the same meaning as it has when used in section 2503 and § 25.2503-3 of this chapter (Gift Tax Regulations); it includes reversions, remainders, and other interests or estates, whether vested or contingent, and whether or not supported by a particular interest or estate, which are limited to commence in use, possession, or enjoyment at some future date or time. The term "future interest" includes situations in which a donor purports to give tangible personal property to a charitable organization, but has an understanding, arrangement, agreement, etc., whether written or oral, with the charitable organization which has the effect of reserving to, or retaining in, such donor a right to the use, possession, or enjoyment of the property.

(5) In the case of a charitable contribution of a future interest to which section 170(a)(3) and this section apply, the other provisions of section 170 and the regulations thereunder are inapplicable to the contribution until such time as the contribution is treated as made under section 170(a)(3).

(b) *Illustrations.* The application of this section may be illustrated by the following examples:

Example (1). On December 31, 1970, A, an individual who reports his income on the calendar year basis, conveys by deed of gift to a museum title to a painting, but reserves to himself the right to use, possession, and enjoyment of the painting during his lifetime. It is assumed that there was no intention to avoid the application of section 170(f)(3)(A) by the conveyance. At the time of the gift the value of the painting is $90,000. Since the contribution consists of a future interest in tangible personal property in which the donor has retained an intervening interest, no contribution is considered to have been made in 1970.

Example (2). Assume the same facts as in example (1) except that on December 31, 1971, A relinquishes all of his right to the use, possession, and enjoyment of the painting and delivers the painting to the museum. Assuming that the value of the painting has increased to $95,000, A is treated as having made a charitable contribution of $95,000 in 1971 for which a deduction is allowable without regard to section 170(f)(3)(A).

Example (3). Assume the same facts as in example (1) except A dies without relinquishing his right to the use, possession, and enjoyment of the painting. Since A did not relinquish his right to the use, possession, and enjoyment of the property during his life, A is treated as not having made a charitable contribution of the painting for income tax purposes.

Example (4). Assume the same facts as in example (1) except A, on December 31, 1971, transfers his interest in the painting to his son, B, who reports his income on the calendar year basis. Since the relationship between A and B is one described in section 267(b), no contribution of the remainder interest in the painting is considered to have been made in 1971.

Example (5). Assume the same facts as in example (4). Also assume that on December 31, 1972, B conveys to the museum the interest measured by A's life. B has made a charitable contribution of the present interest in the painting conveyed to the museum. In addition, since all intervening interests in, and rights to the actual possession or enjoyment of the property, have expired, a charitable contribution of the remainder interest is treated as having been made by A in 1972 for which a deduction is allowable without regard to section 170(f)(3)(A). Such remainder interest is valued according to § 20.2031-7A(c) of this chapter (Estate Tax Regulations), determined by subtracting the value of B's interest measured by A's life expectancy in 1972, and B receives a deduction in 1972 for the life interest measured by A's life expectancy and valued according to Table A (1) in such section.

Example (6). On December 31, 1970, C, an individual who reports his income on the calendar year basis, transfers a valuable painting to a pooled income fund described in section 642(c)(5), which is maintained by a university. C retains for himself for life an income interest in the painting, the remainder interest in the painting being contributed to the university. Since the contribution consists of a future interest in tangible personal property in which the donor has retained an intervening interest, no charitable contribution is considered to have been made in 1970.

Example (7). On January 15, 1972, D, an individual who reports his income on the calendar

Reg. § 1.170A-5(b)

year basis, transfers a capital asset held for more than 6 months consisting of a valuable painting to a pooled income fund described in section 642(c)(5), which is maintained by a university, and creates an income interest in such painting for E for life. E is an individual not standing in a relationship to D described in section 267(b). The remainder interest in the property is contributed by D to the university. The trustee of the pooled income fund puts the painting to an unrelated use within the meaning of paragraph (b)(3) of § 1.170A-4. Accordingly, D is allowed a deduction under section 170 in 1972 for the present value of the remainder interest in the painting, after reducing such amount under section 170(e)(1)(B)(i) and paragraph (a)(2) of § 1.170A-4. This reduction in the amount of the contribution is required since under paragraph (b)(3) of that section the use by the pooled income fund of the painting is a use which would have been an unrelated use if it had been made by the university.

(c) *Effective date.* This section applies only to contributions paid in taxable years beginning after December 31, 1969. [Reg. § 1.170A-5.]

☐ [*T.D. 7207, 10-3-72. Amended by T.D. 8540, 6-9-94.*]

§ 1.170A-6. Charitable contributions in trust.—(a) *In general*—(1) No deduction is allowed under section 170 for the fair market value of a charitable contribution of any interest in property which is less than the donor's entire interest in the property and which is transferred in trust unless the transfer meets the requirements of paragraph (b) or (c) of this section. If the donor's entire interest in the property is transferred in trust and is contributed to a charitable organization described in section 170(c), a deduction is allowed under section 170. Thus, if on July 1, 1972, property is transferred in trust with the requirement that the income of the trust be paid for a term of 20 years to a church and thereafter the remainder be paid to an educational organization described in section 170(b)(1)(A), a deduction is allowed for the value of such property. See section 170(f)(2) and (3)(B), and paragraph (b)(1) of § 1.170A-7.

(2) A deduction is allowed without regard to this section for a contribution of a partial interest in property if such interest is the taxpayer's entire interest in the property, such as an income interest or a remainder interest. If, however, the property in which such partial interest exists was divided in order to create such interest and thus avoid section 170(f)(2), the deduction will not be allowed. Thus, for example, assume that a taxpayer desires to contribute to a charitable organization the reversionary interest in certain stocks and bonds which he owns. If the taxpayer trans-

fers such property in trust with the requirement that the income of the trust be paid to his son for life and that the reversionary interest be paid to himself and immediately after creating the trust contributes the reversionary interest to a charitable organization, no deduction will be allowed under section 170 for the contribution of the taxpayer's entire interest consisting of the reversionary interest in the trust.

(b) *Charitable contribution of a remainder interest in trust*—(1) *In general.* No deduction is allowed under section 170 for the fair market value of a charitable contribution of a remainder interest in property which is less than the donor's entire interest in the property and which the donor transfers in trust unless the trust is—

(i) A pooled income fund described in section 642(c)(5) and § 1.642(c)-5,

(ii) A charitable remainder annuity trust described in section 664(d)(1) and § 1.664-2, or

(iii) A charitable remainder unitrust described in section 664(d)(2) and § 1.664-3.

(2) *Value of a remainder interest.* The fair market value of a remainder interest in a pooled income fund shall be computed under § 1.642(c)-6. The fair market value of a remainder interest in a charitable remainder annuity trust shall be computed under § 1.664-2. The fair market value of a remainder interest in a charitable remainder unitrust shall be computed under § 1.664-4. However, in some cases a reduction in the amount of a charitable contribution of the remainder interest may be required. See section 170(e) and § 1.170A-4.

(c) *Charitable contribution of an income interest in trust*—(1) *In general.* No deduction is allowed under section 170 for the fair market value of a charitable contribution of an income interest in property which is less than the donor's entire interest in the property and which the donor transfers in trust unless the income interest is either a guaranteed annuity interest or a unitrust interest, as defined in paragraph (c) (2) of this section, and the grantor is treated as the owner of such interest for purposes of applying section 671, relating to grantors and others treated as substantial owners. See section 4947(a)(2) for the application to such income interests in trust of the provisions relating to private foundations and section 508(e) for rules relating to provisions required in the governing instruments.

(2) *Definitions.* For purposes of this paragraph—

(i) *Guaranteed annuity interest*—(A) An income interest is a "guaranteed annuity interest" only if it is an irrevocable right pursuant to the governing instrument of the trust to receive a guaranteed annuity. A guaranteed annuity is an arrangement under which a determinable amount is paid periodically, but not less often than annually, for a specified term of years or for the life or lives of certain individuals, each of whom must be living at the date of transfer and can be ascertained at such date. Only one or more of the following individuals may be used as measuring lives: the donor, the donor's spouse, and an individual who, with respect to all remainder beneficiaries (other than charitable organizations described in section 170, 2055, or 2522), is either a lineal ancestor or the spouse of a lineal ancestor of those beneficiaries. A trust will satisfy the requirement that all noncharitable remainder beneficiaries are lineal descendants of the individual who is the measuring life, or that individual's spouse, if there is less than a 15% probability that individuals who are not lineal descendants will receive any trust corpus. This probability must be computed, based on the current applicable Life Table contained in § 20.2031-7, at the time property is transferred to the trust taking into account the interests of all primary and contingent remainder beneficiaries who are living at that time. An interest payable for a specified term of years can qualify as a guaranteed annuity interest even if the governing instrument contains a savings clause intended to ensure compliance with a rule against perpetuities. The savings clause must utilize a period for vesting of 21 years after the deaths of measuring lives who are selected to maximize, rather than limit, the term of the trust. The rule in this paragraph that a charitable interest may be payable for the life or lives of only certain specified individuals does not apply in the case of a charitable guaranteed annuity interest payable under a charitable remainder trust described in section 664. An amount is determinable if the exact amount which must be paid under the conditions specified in the governing instrument of the trust can be ascertained as of the date of transfer. For example, the amount to be paid may be a stated sum for a term of years, or for the life of the donor, at the expiration of which it may be changed by a specified amount, but it may not be redetermined by reference to a fluctuating index such as the cost of living index. In further illustration, the amount to be paid may be expressed in terms of a fraction or percentage of the cost of living index on the date of transfer.

(B) An income interest is a guaranteed annuity interest only if it is a guaranteed annuity interest in every respect. For example, if the income interest is the right to receive from a trust each year a payment equal to the lesser of a sum certain or a fixed percentage of the net fair market value of the trust assets, determined annually, such interest is not a guaranteed annuity interest.

(C) Where a charitable interest is in the form of a guaranteed annuity interest, the governing instrument of the trust may provide that income of the trust which is in excess of the amount required to pay the guaranteed annuity interest shall be paid to or for the use of a charitable organization. Nevertheless, the amount of the deduction under section 170(f)(2)(B) shall be limited to the fair market value of the guaranteed annuity interest as determined under paragraph (c)(3) of this section. For a rule relating to treatment by the grantor of any contribution made by the trust in excess of the amount required to pay the guaranteed annuity interest, see paragraph (d)(2)(ii) of this section.

(D) If the present value on the date of transfer of all the income interests for a charitable purpose exceeds 60 percent of the aggregate fair market value of all amounts in the trust (after the payment of liabilities), the income interest will not be considered a guaranteed annuity interest unless the governing instrument of the trust prohibits both the acquisition and the retention of assets which would give rise to a tax under section 4944 if the trustee had acquired such assets. The requirement in this subdivision (D) for a prohibition in the governing instrument against the retention of assets which would give rise to a tax under section 4944 if the trustee had acquired the assets shall not apply to a transfer in trust made on or before May 21, 1972.

(E) An income interest consisting of an annuity transferred in trust after May 21, 1972, will not be considered a guaranteed annuity interest if any amount other than an amount in payment of a guaranteed annuity interest may be paid by the trust for a private purpose before the expiration of all the income interests for a charitable purpose, unless such amount for a private purpose is paid from a group of assets which, pursuant to the governing instrument of the trust, are devoted exclusively to private purposes and to which section 4947(a)(2) is inapplicable by reason of section 4947(a)(2)(B). The exception in the immediately preceding sentence with respect to any guaranteed annuity for a private purpose shall apply only if the obligation to pay the annuity for a charitable purpose begins as of the date of creation of the trust and the obligation to pay the guaranteed annuity for a private purpose does not precede in point of time the obligation to pay the annuity for a charitable purpose and only if the governing instrument of the trust does not provide for any preference or priority in respect of any payment of the guaranteed annuity for a private purpose as opposed to any payment of any annuity for a charitable purpose. For purposes of this subdivision (E), an amount is not paid for a private purpose if it is paid for an

Reg. § 1.170A-6(c)(2)

adequate and full consideration in money or money's worth. See § 53.4947-1(c) of this chapter (Foundation Excise Tax Regulations) for rules relating to the inapplicability of section 4947(a)(2) to segregated amounts in a split-interest trust.

Example. In 1975, E transfers $75,000 in trust with the requirement that an annuity of $5,000 a year, payable annually at the end of each year, be paid to B, an individual, for a period of 5 years and thereafter an annuity of $5,000 a year, payable annually at the end of each year, be paid to M Charity for a period of 5 years. The remainder is to be paid to C, an individual. No deduction is allowed under subparagraph (1) of this paragraph with respect to the charitable annuity because it is not a "guaranteed annuity interest" with the meaning of this subdivision.

(F) For rules relating to certain governing instrument requirements and to the imposition of certain excise taxes where the guaranteed annuity interest is in trust and for rules governing payment of private income interests by a split-interest trust, see section 4947(a)(2) and (b)(3)(A), and the regulations thereunder.

(ii) *Unitrust interest*—(A) An income interest is a "unitrust interest" only if it is an irrevocable right pursuant to the governing instrument of the trust to receive payment, not less often than annually, of a fixed percentage of the net fair market value of the trust assets, determined annually. In computing the net fair market value of the trust assets, all assets and liabilities shall be taken into account without regard to whether particular items are taken into account in determining the income of the trust. The net fair market value of the trust assets may be determined on any one date during the year or by taking the average of valuations made on more than one date during the year, provided that the same valuation date or dates and valuation methods are used each year. Where the governing instrument of the trust does not specify the valuation date or dates, the trustee shall select such date or dates and shall indicate his selection on the first return on Form 1041 which the trust is required to file. Payments under a unitrust interest may be paid for a specified term of years or for the life or lives of certain individuals, each of whom must be living at the date of transfer and can be ascertained at such date. Only one or more of the following individuals may be used as measuring lives: the donor, the donor's spouse, and an individual who, with respect to all remainder beneficiaries (other than charitable organizations described in section 170, 2055, or 2522), is either a lineal ancestor or the spouse of a lineal ancestor of those beneficiaries. A trust will satisfy the requirement that all noncharitable remainder beneficiaries are lineal descendants of the individual who is the measuring life, or that individual's spouse, if there is less than a 15% probability that individuals who are not lineal descendants will receive any trust corpus. This probability must be computed, based on the current applicable Life Table contained in § 20.2031-7, at the time property is transferred to the trust taking into account the interests of all primary and contingent remainder beneficiaries who are living at that time. An interest payable for a specified term of years can qualify as a unitrust interest even if the governing instrument contains a savings clause intended to ensure compliance with a rule against perpetuities. The savings clause must utilize a period for vesting of 21 years after the deaths of measuring lives who are selected to maximize, rather than limit, the term of the trust. The rule in this paragraph that a charitable interest may be payable for the life or lives of only certain specified individuals does not apply in the case of a charitable unitrust interest payable under a charitable remainder trust described in section 664.

(B) An income interest is a unitrust interest only if it is a unitrust interest in every respect. For example, if the income interest is the right to receive from a trust each year a payment equal to the lesser of a sum certain or a fixed percentage of the net fair market value of the trust assets, determined annually, such interest is not a unitrust interest.

(C) Where a charitable interest is in the form of a unitrust interest, the governing instrument of the trust may provide that income of the trust which is in excess of the amount required to pay the unitrust interest shall be paid to or for the use of a charitable organization. Nevertheless, the amount of the deduction under section 170(f)(2)(B) shall be limited to the fair market value of the unitrust interest as determined under paragraph (c)(3) of this section. For a rule relating to treatment by the grantor of any contribution made by the trust in excess of the amount required to pay the unitrust interest, see paragraph (d)(2)(ii) of this section.

(D) An income interest in the form of a unitrust interest will not be considered a unitrust interest if any amount other than an amount in payment of a unitrust interest may be paid by the trust for a private purpose before the expiration of all the income interests for a charitable purpose, unless such amount for a private purpose is paid from a group of assets which, pursuant to the governing instrument of the trust, are devoted exclusively to private purposes and to which section 4947(a)(2) is inapplicable by reason of section 4947(a)(2)(B). The exception in the immediately preceding sentence with respect to any unitrust interest for a private purpose shall

Reg. § 1.170A-6(c)(2)

apply only if the obligation to pay the unitrust interest for a charitable purpose begins as of the date of creation of the trust and the obligation to pay the unitrust interest for a private purpose does not precede in point of time the obligation to pay the unitrust interest for a charitable purpose and only if the governing instrument of the trust does not provide for any preference or priority in respect of any payment of the unitrust interest for a private purpose as opposed to any payments of any unitrust interest for a charitable purpose. For purposes of this subdivision (D), an amount is not paid for a private purpose if it is paid for an adequate and full consideration in money or money's worth. See § 53.4947-1(c) of this chapter (Foundation Excise Tax Regulations) for rules relating to the inapplicability of section 4947(a)(2) to segregated amounts in a split-interest trust.

(E) For rules relating to certain governing instrument requirements and to the imposition of certain excise taxes where the unitrust interest is in trust and for rules governing payment of private income interests by a split-interest trust, see section 4947(a)(2) and (b)(3)(A), and the regulations thereunder.

(3) *Valuation of income interest*—(i) The deduction allowed by section 170(f)(2)(B) for a charitable contribution of a guaranteed annuity interest is limited to the fair market value of such interest on the date of contribution, as computed under § 20.2031-7 or, for certain prior periods, § 20.2031-7A of this chapter (Estate Tax Regulations).

(ii) The deduction allowed under section 170(f)(2)(B) for a charitable contribution of a unitrust interest is limited to the fair market value of the unitrust interest on the date of contribution. The fair market value of the unitrust interest shall be determined by subtracting the present value of all interests in the transferred property other than the unitrust interest from the fair market value of the transferred property.

(iii) If by reason of all the conditions and circumstances surrounding a transfer of an income interest in property in trust it appears that the charity may not receive the beneficial enjoyment of the interest, a deduction will be allowed under paragraph (c) (1) of this section only for the minimum amount it is evident the charity will receive. The application of this subdivision may be illustrated by the following examples:

Example (1). In 1972, B transfers $20,000 in trust with the requirement that M Church be paid a guaranteed annuity interest (as defined in subparagraph (2)(i) of this paragraph) of $4,000, payable annually at the end of each year for 9 years, and that the residue revert to himself. Since the fair market value of an annuity of $4,000 a year for a period of 9 years, as determined under § 20.2031-7A(c) of this chapter, is $27,206.80 ($4,000 × 6.8017), it appears that M will not receive the beneficial enjoyment of the income interest. Accordingly, even though B is treated as the owner of the trust under section 673, he is allowed a deduction under subparagraph (1) of this paragraph for only $20,000, which is the minimum amount it is evident M will receive.

Example (2). In 1975, C transfers $40,000 in trust with the requirement that D, an individual, and X Charity be paid simultaneously guaranteed annuity interests (as defined in subparagraph (2)(i) of this paragraph) of $5,000 a year each, payable annually at the end of each year, for a period of 5 years and that the remainder be paid to C's children. The fair market value of two annuities of $5,000 each a year for a period of 5 years is $42,124 ([$5,000 × 4.2124] × 2), as determined under § 20.2031-7A(c) of this chapter. The trust instrument provides that in the event the trust fund is insufficient to pay both annuities in a given year, the trust fund will be evenly divided between the charitable and private annuitants. The deduction under subparagraph (1) of this paragraph with respect to the charitable annuity will be limited to $20,000, which is the minimum amount it is evident X will receive.

Example (3). In 1975, D transfers $65,000 in trust with the requirement that a guaranteed annuity interest (as defined in subparagraph (2)(i) of this paragraph) of $5,000 a year, payable annually at the end of each year, be paid to Y Charity for a period of 10 years and that a guaranteed annuity interest (as defined in subparagraph (2)(i) of this paragraph) of $5,000 a year, payable annually at the end of each year, be paid to W, his wife, aged 62, for 10 years or until her prior death. The annuities are to be paid simultaneously, and the remainder is to be paid to D's children. The fair market value of the private annuity is $33,877 ($5,000 × 6.7754), as determined pursuant to § 20.2031-7A(c) of this chapter and by the use of factors involving one life and a term of years as published in Publication 723A (12-70). The fair market value of the charitable annuity is $36,800.50 ($5,000 × 7.3601), as determined under § 20.2031-7A(c) of this chapter. It is not evident from the governing instrument of the trust or from local law that the trustee would be required to apportion the trust fund between the wife and charity in the event the fund were insufficient to pay both annuities in a given year. Accordingly, the deduction under subparagraph (1) of this paragraph with respect to the charitable annuity will be limited to $31,123 ($65,000 less $33,877 [the value of the private annuity]),

Reg. § 1.170A-6(c)(3)

which is the minimum amount it is evident Y will receive.

(iv) See paragraph (b)(1) of § 1.170A-4 for rule that the term "ordinary income property" for purposes of section 170(e) does not include an income interest in respect of which a deduction is allowed under section 170(f)(2)(B) and this paragraph.

* * *

[Reg. § 1.170A-6.]

☐ [*T.D. 7207, 10-3-72. Amended by T.D. 7340, 1-6-75; T.D. 7955, 5-10-84; T.D. 8540, 6-9-94; T.D. 8819, 4-29-99 (corrected 6-21-99) and T.D. 8923, 1-4-2001.*]

§ 1.170A-7. Contributions not in trust of partial interests in property.—(a) *In general*— (1) In the case of a charitable contribution, not made by a transfer in trust, of any interest in property which consists of less than the donor's entire interest in such property, no deduction is allowed under section 170 for the value of such interest unless the interest is an interest described in paragraph (b) of this section. See section 170(f)(3)(A). For purposes of this section, a contribution of the right to use property which the donor owns, for example, a rent-free lease, shall be treated as a contribution of less than the taxpayer's entire interest in property.

(2)(i) A deduction is allowed without regard to this section for a contribution of a partial interest in property if such interest is the taxpayer's entire interest in the property, such as an income interest or a remainder interest. Thus, if securities are given to A for life, with the remainder over to B, and B makes a charitable contribution of his remainder interest to an organization described in section 170(c), a deduction is allowed under section 170 for the present value of B's remainder interest in the securities. If, however, the property in which such partial interest exists was divided in order to create such interest and thus avoid section 170(f)(3)(A), the deduction will not be allowed. Thus, for example, assume that a taxpayer desires to contribute to a charitable organization an income interest in property held by him, which is not of a type described in paragraph (b)(2) of this section. If the taxpayer transfers the remainder interest in such property to his son and immediately thereafter contributes the income interest to a charitable organization, no deduction shall be allowed under section 170 for the contribution of the taxpayer's entire interest consisting of the retained income interest. In further illustration, assume that a taxpayer desires to contribute to a charitable organization the reversionary interest in certain stocks and bonds held by him, which is not of a type described in paragraph (b)(2) of this section. If the taxpayer grants a life estate in such property to his son and immediately thereafter contributes the reversionary interest to a charitable organization, no deduction will be allowed under section 170 for the contribution of the taxpayer's entire interest consisting of the reversionary interest.

(ii) A deduction is allowed without regard to this section for a contribution of a partial interest in property if such contribution constitutes part of a charitable contribution not in trust in which all interests of the taxpayer in the property are given to a charitable organization described in section 170(c). Thus, if on March 1, 1971, an income interest in property is given not in trust to a church and the remainder interest in the property is given not in trust to an educational organization described in section 170(b)(1)(A), a deduction is allowed for the value of such property.

(3) A deduction shall not be disallowed under section 170(f)(3)(A) and this section merely because the interest which passes to, or is vested in, the charity may be defeated by the performance of some act or the happening of some event, if on the date of the gift it appears that the possibility that such act or event will occur is so remote as to be negligible. See paragraph (e) of § 1.170A-1.

(b) *Contributions of certain partial interests in property for which a deduction is allowed.* A deduction is allowed under section 170 for a contribution not in trust of a partial interest which is less than the donor's entire interest in property and which qualifies under one of the following subparagraphs:

(1) *Undivided portion of donor's entire interest*—(i) A deduction is allowed under section 170 for the value of a charitable contribution not in trust of an undivided portion of a donor's entire interest in property. An undivided portion of a donor's entire interest in property must consist of a fraction or percentage or each and every substantial interest or right owned by the donor in such property and must extend over the entire term of the donor's interest in such property and in other property into which such property is converted. For example, assuming that in 1967 B has been given a life estate in an office building for the life of A and that B has no other interest in the office building, B will be allowed a deduction under section 170 for his contribution in 1972 to charity of a one-half interest in such life estate in a transfer which is not made in trust. Such contribution by B will be considered a contribution of an undivided portion of the donor's entire interest in property. In further illustration, assuming that in 1968 C has been given the remainder interest in a trust created under the will of his father and C has no other interest in the trust, C will be al-

lowed a deduction under section 170 for his contribution in 1972 to charity of a 20-percent interest in such remainder interest in a transfer which is not made in trust. Such contribution by C will be considered a contribution of an undivided portion of the donor's entire interest in property. If a taxpayer owns 100 acres of land and makes a contribution of 50 acres to a charitable organization, the charitable contribution is allowed as a deduction under section 170. A deduction is allowed under section 170 for a contribution of property to a charitable organization whereby such organization is given the right, as a tenant in common with the donor, to possession, dominion, and control of the property for a portion of each year appropriate to its interest in such property. However, for purposes of this subparagraph a charitable contribution in perpetuity of an interest in property not in trust where the donor transfers some specific rights and retains other substantial rights will not be considered a contribution of an undivided portion of the donor's entire interest in property to which section 170(f)(3)(A) does not apply. Thus, for example, a deduction is not allowable for the value of an immediate and perpetual gift not in trust of an interest in original historic motion picture films to a charitable organization where the donor retains the exclusive right to make reproductions of such films and to exploit such reproductions commercially.

* * *

(2) *Partial interests in property which would be deductible in trust.* A deduction is allowed under section 170 for the value of a charitable contribution not in trust of a partial interest in property which is less than the donor's entire interest in the property and which would be deductible under section 170(f)(2) and § 1.170A-6 if such interest had been transferred in trust.

(3) *Contribution of a remainder interest in a personal residence.* A deduction is allowed under section 170 for the value of a charitable contribution not in trust of an irrevocable remainder interest in a personal residence which is not the donor's entire interest in such property. Thus, for example, if a taxpayer contributes not in trust to an organization described in section 170(c) a remainder interest in a personal residence and retains an estate in such property for life or for a term of years, a deduction is allowed under section 170 for the value of such remainder interest not transferred in trust. For purposes of section 170(f)(3)(B)(i) and this subparagraph, the term "personal residence" means any property used by the taxpayer as his personal residence even though it is not used as his principal residence. For example, the taxpayer's vacation home may

be a personal residence for purposes of this subparagraph. The term "personal residence" also includes stock owned by a taxpayer as a tenant-stockholder in a cooperative housing corporation (as those terms are defined in section 216(b)(1) and (2)) if the dwelling which the taxpayer is entitled to occupy as such stockholder is used by him as his personal residence.

(4) *Contribution of a remainder interest in a farm.* A deduction is allowed under section 170 for the value of a charitable contribution not in trust of an irrevocable remainder interest in a farm which is not the donor's entire interest in such property. Thus, for example, if a taxpayer contributes not in trust to an organization described in section 170(c) a remainder interest in a farm and retains an estate in such farm for life or for a term of years, a deduction is allowed under section 170 for the value of such remainder interest not transferred in trust. For purposes of section 170(f)(3)(B)(i) and this subparagraph, the term "farm" means any land used by the taxpayer or his tenant for the production of crops, fruits, or other agricultural products or for the sustenance of livestock. The term "livestock" includes cattle, hogs, horses, mules, donkeys, sheep, goats, captive fur-bearing animals, chickens, turkeys, pigeons, and other poultry. A farm includes the improvements thereon.

(5) *Qualified conservation contribution.* A deduction is allowed under section 170 for the value of a qualified conservation contribution. For the definition of a qualified conservation contribution, see § 1.170A-14.

(c) *Valuation of a partial interest in property.* Except as provided in § 1.170A-14, the amount of the deduction under section 170 in the case of a charitable contribution of a partial interest in property to which paragraph (b) of this section applies is the fair market value of the partial interest at the time of the contribution. See § 1.170A-1(c). the fair market value of such partial interest must be determined in accordance with § 20.2031-7 of this chapter (Estate Tax Regulations), except that, in the case of a charitable contribution of a remainder interest in real property which is not transferred in trust, the fair market value of such interest must be determined in accordance with section 170(f)(4) and § 1.170A-12. In the case of a charitable contribution of a remainder interest in the form of a remainder interest in a pooled income fund, a charitable remainder annuity trust, or a charitable remainder unitrust, the fair market value of the remainder interest must be determined as provided in paragraph (b)(2) of § 1.170A-6. However, in some cases a reduction in the amount of a charitable contribution of the remainder interest

Reg. § 1.170A-7(c)

may be required. See section 170(e) and paragraph (a) of § 1.170A-4.

(d) *Illustrations.* The application of this section may be illustrated by the following examples:

Example (1). A, an individual owning a 10-story office building, donates the rent-free use of the top floor of the building for the year 1971 to a charitable organization. Since A's contribution consists of a partial interest to which section 170(f)(3)(A) applies, he is not entitled to a charitable contributions deduction for the contribution of such partial interest.

Example (2). In 1971, B contributes to a charitable organization an undivided one-half interest in 100 acres of land, whereby as tenants in common they share in the economic benefits from the property. The present value of the contributed property is $50,000. Since B's contribution consists of an undivided portion of his entire interest in the property to which section 170(f)(3)(B) applies, he is allowed a deduction in 1971 for his charitable contribution of $50,000.

Example (3). In 1971, D loans $10,000 in cash to a charitable organization and does not require the organization to pay any interest for the use of the money. Since D's contribution consists of a partial interest to which section 170(f)(3)(A) applies, he is not entitled to a charitable contributions deduction for the contribution of such partial interest.

* * *

[Reg. § 1.170A-7.]

☐ [*T.D. 7207, 10-3-72. Amended by T.D. 7955, 5-10-84; T.D. 8069, 1-14-86 and T.D. 8540, 6-9-94.*]

§ **1.170A-13. Recordkeeping and return requirements for deductions for charitable contributions.**—* * *

* * *

(f) *Substantiation of charitable contributions of $250 or more*—(1) *In general.* No deduction is allowed under section 170(a) for all or part of any contribution of $250 or more unless the taxpayer substantiates the contribution with a contemporaneous written acknowledgment from the donee organization. A taxpayer who makes more than one contribution of $250 or more to a donee organization in a taxable year may substantiate the contributions with one or more contemporaneous written acknowledgments. Section 170(f)(8) does not apply to a payment of $250 or more if the amount contributed (as determined under § 1.170A-1(h)) is less than $250. Separate contributions of less than $250 are not subject to the requirements of section 170(f)(8), regardless of whether the sum of the contributions made by a taxpayer to a donee organization during a taxable year equals $250 or more.

(2) *Written acknowledgment.* Except as otherwise provided in paragraphs (f)(8) through (f)(11) and (f)(13) of this section, a written acknowledgment from a donee organization must provide the following information—

(i) The amount of any cash the taxpayer paid and a description (but not necessarily the value) of any property other than cash the taxpayer transferred to the donee organization;

(ii) A statement of whether or not the donee organization provides any goods or services in consideration, in whole or in part, for any of the cash or other property transferred to the donee organization;

(iii) If the donee organization provides any goods or services other than intangible religious benefits (as described in section 170(f)(8)), a description and good faith estimate of the value of those goods or services; and

(iv) If the donee organization provides any intangible religious benefits, a statement to that effect.

(3) *Contemporaneous.* A written acknowledgment is contemporaneous if it is obtained by the taxpayer on or before the earlier of—

(i) The date the taxpayer files the original return for the taxable year in which the contribution was made; or

(ii) The due date (including extensions) for filing the taxpayer's original return for that year.

(4) *Donee organization.* For purposes of this paragraph (f), a donee organization is an organization described in section 170(c).

(5) *Goods or services.* Goods or services means cash, property, services, benefits, and privileges.

(6) *In consideration for.* A donee organization provides goods or services in consideration for a taxpayer's payment if, at the time the taxpayer makes the payment to the donee organization, the taxpayer receives or expects to receive goods or services in exchange for that payment. Goods or services a donee organization provides in consideration for a payment by a taxpayer include goods or services provided in a year other than the year in which the taxpayer makes the payment to the donee organization.

(7) *Good faith estimate.* For purposes of this section, good faith estimate means a donee organization's estimate of the fair market value of any goods or services, without regard to the manner in which the organization in fact made that estimate. See § 1.170A-1(h)(4) for rules regarding when a taxpayer may treat a donee organization's

estimate of the value of goods or services as the fair market value.

(8) *Certain goods or services disregarded*—(i) *In general.* For purposes of section 170(f)(8), the following goods or services are disregarded—

(A) Goods or services that have insubstantial value under the guidelines provided in Revenue Procedures 90-12, 1990-1 C.B. 471, 92-49, 1992-1 C.B. 987, and any successor documents. (See § 601.601(d)(2)(ii) of the Statement of Procedural Rules, 26 CFR part 601.); and

(B) Annual membership benefits offered to a taxpayer in exchange for a payment of $75 or less per year that consist of—

(*1*) Any rights or privileges, other than those described in section 170(l), that the taxpayer can exercise frequently during the membership period. Examples of such rights and privileges may include, but are not limited to, free or discounted admission to the organization's facilities or events, free or discounted parking, preferred access to goods or services, and discounts on the purchase of goods or services; and

(*2*) Admission to events during the membership period that are open only to members of a donee organization and for which the donee organization reasonably projects that the cost per person (excluding any allocable overhead) attending each such event is within the limits established for "low cost articles" under section 513(h)(2). The projected cost to the donee organization is determined at the time the organization first offers its membership package for the year (using section 3.07 of Revenue Procedure 90-12, or any successor documents, to determine the cost of any items or services that are donated).

(ii) *Examples.* The following examples illustrate the rules of this paragraph (f)(8).

Example 1. Membership benefits disregarded. Performing Arts Center *E* is an organization described in section 170(c). In return for a payment of $75, *E* offers a package of basic membership benefits that includes the right to purchase tickets to performances one week before they go on sale to the general public, free parking in *E*'s garage during evening and weekend performances, and a 10% discount on merchandise sold in *E*'s gift shop. In return for a payment of $150, *E* offers a package of preferred membership benefits that includes all of the benefits in the $75 package as well as a poster that is sold in *E*'s gift shop for $20. The basic membership and the preferred membership are each valid for twelve months, and there are approximately 50 performances of various productions at *E* during a twelve-month period. *E*'s gift shop is open for several hours each week and at performance times. *F*, a patron of the arts, is solicited by *E* to make a

contribution. *E* offers *F* the preferred membership benefits in return for a payment of $150 or more. *F* makes a payment of $300 to *E*. *F* can satisfy the substantiation requirement of section 170(f)(8) by obtaining a contemporaneous written acknowledgment from *E* that includes a description of the poster and a good faith estimate of its fair market value ($20) and disregards the remaining membership benefits.

Example 2. Contemporaneous written acknowledgment need not mention rights or privileges that can be disregarded. The facts are the same as in Example 1, except that *F* made a payment of $300 and received only a basic membership. *F* can satisfy the section 170(f)(8) substantiation requirement with a contemporaneous written acknowledgment stating that no goods or services were provided.

Example 3. Rights or privileges that cannot be exercised frequently. Community Theater Group *G* is an organization described in section 170(c). Every summer, *G* performs four different plays. Each play is performed two times. In return for a membership fee of $60, *G* offers its members free admission to any of its performances. Non-members may purchase tickets on a performance by performance basis for $15 a ticket. *H*, an individual who is a sponsor of the theater, is solicited by *G* to make a contribution. *G* tells *H* that the membership benefit will be provided in return for any payment of $60 or more. *H* chooses to make a payment of $350 to *G* and receives in return the membership benefit. *G*'s membership benefit of free admission is not described in paragraph (f)(8)(i)(B) of this section because it is not a privilege that can be exercised frequently (due to the limited number of performances offered by *G*). Therefore, to meet the requirements of section 170(f)(8), a contemporaneous written acknowledgment of *H*'s $350 payment must include a description of the free admission benefit and a good faith estimate of its value.

Example 4. Multiple memberships. In December of each year, *K*, an individual, gives each of her six grandchildren a junior membership in Dinosaur Museum, an organization described in section 170(c). Each junior membership costs $50, and *K* makes a single payment of $300 for all six memberships. A junior member is entitled to free admission to the museum and to weekly films, slide shows, and lectures about dinosaurs. In addition, each junior member receives a bi-monthly, non-commercial quality newsletter with information about dinosaurs and upcoming events. *K*'s contemporaneous written acknowledgment from Dinosaur Museum may state that no goods or services were provided in exchange for *K*'s payment.

Reg. § 1.170A-13(f)(8)

(9) *Goods or services provided to employees or partners of donors*—(i) *Certain goods or services disregarded.* For purposes of section 170(f)(8), goods or services provided by a donee organization to employees of a donor, or to partners of a partnership that is a donor, in return for a payment to the organization may be disregarded to the extent that the goods or services provided to each employee or partner are the same as those described in paragraph (f)(8)(i) of this section.

(ii) *No good faith estimate required for other goods or services.* If a taxpayer makes a contribution of $250 or more to a donee organization and, in return, the donee organization offers the taxpayer's employees or partners goods or services other than those described in paragraph (f)(9)(i) of this section, the contemporaneous written acknowledgment of the taxpayer's contribution is not required to include a good faith estimate of the value of such goods or services but must include a description of those goods or services.

(iii) *Example.* The following example illustrates the rules of this paragraph (f)(9).

Example. Museum *J* is an organization described in section 170(c). For a payment of $40, *J* offers a package of basic membership benefits that includes free admission and a 10% discount on merchandise sold in *J*'s gift shop. *J*'s other membership categories are for supporters who contribute $100 or more. Corporation *K* makes a payment of $50,000 to *J* and, in return, *J* offers *K*'s employees free admission for one year, a tee-shirt with *J*'s logo that costs *J* $4.50, and a gift shop discount of 25% for one year. The free admission for *K*'s employees is the same as the benefit made available to holders of the $40 membership and is otherwise described in paragraph (f)(8)(i)(B) of this section. The tee-shirt given to each of *K*'s employees is described in paragraph (f)(8)(i)(A) of this section. Therefore, the contemporaneous written acknowledgment of *K*'s payment is not required to include a description or good faith estimate of the value of the free admission or the tee-shirts. However, because the gift shop discount offered to *K*'s employees is different than that offered to those who purchase the $40 membership, the discount is not described in paragraph (f)(8)(i) of this section. Therefore, the contemporaneous written acknowledgment of *K*'s payment is required to include a description of the 25% discount offered to *K*'s employees.

(10) *Substantiation of out-of-pocket expenses.* A taxpayer who incurs unreimbursed expenditures incident to the rendition of services, within the meaning of § 1.170A-1(g), is treated as having obtained a contemporaneous written acknowledgment of those expenditures if the taxpayer—

(i) Has adequate records under paragraph (a) of this section to substantiate the amount of the expenditures; and

(ii) Obtains by the date prescribed in paragraph (f)(3) of this section a statement prepared by the donee organization containing—

(A) A description of the services provided by the taxpayer;

(B) A statement of whether or not the donee organization provides any goods or services in consideration, in whole or in part, for the unreimbursed expenditures; and

(C) The information required by paragraphs (f)(2)(iii) and (iv) of this section.

* * *

[Reg. § 1.170A-13.]

☐ [*T.D.* 8002, 12-26-84. *Amended by T.D.* 8003, 12-26-84; *T.D.* 8199, 5-4-88; *T.D.* 8623, 10-11-95 *and T.D.* 8690, 12-13-96.]

§ 1.172-1. Net operating loss deduction.—(a) *Allowance of deduction.* Section 172(a) allows as a deduction in computing taxable income for any taxable year subject to the Code the aggregate of the net operating loss carryovers and net operating loss carrybacks to such taxable year. This deduction is referred to as the net operating loss deduction. The net operating loss is the basis for the computation of the net operating loss carryovers and net operating loss carrybacks and ultimately for the net operating loss deduction itself. The net operating loss deduction shall not be disallowed for any taxable year merely because the taxpayer has no income from a trade or business for the taxable year.

(b) *Steps in computation of net operating loss deduction.* The three steps to be taken in the ascertainment of the net operating loss deduction for any taxable year subject to the Code are as follows:

(1) Compute the net operating loss for any preceding or succeeding taxable year from which a net operating loss may be carried over or carried back to such taxable year.

(2) Compute the net operating loss carryovers to such taxable year from such preceding taxable years and the net operating loss carrybacks to such taxable year from such succeeding taxable years.

(3) Add such net operating loss carryovers and carrybacks in order to determine the net operating loss deduction for such taxable year.

(c) *Statement with tax return.* Every taxpayer claiming a net operating loss deduction for any taxable year shall file with his return for such

Reg. § 1.172-1(a)

year a concise statement setting forth the amount of the net operating loss deduction claimed and all material and pertinent facts relative thereto, including a detailed schedule showing the computation of the net operating loss deduction.

(d) *Ascertainment of deduction dependent upon net operating loss carryback.* If the taxpayer is entitled in computing his net operating loss deduction to a carryback which he is not able to ascertain at the time his return is due, he shall compute the net operating loss deduction on his return without regard to such net operating loss carryback. When the taxpayer ascertains the net operating loss carryback, he may within the applicable period of limitations file a claim for credit or refund of the overpayment, if any, resulting from the failure to compute the net operating loss deduction for the taxable year with the inclusion of such carryback; or he may file an application under the provisions of section 6411 for a tentative carryback adjustment.

(e) *Law applicable to computations.* (1) In determining the amount of any net operating loss carryback or carryover to any taxable year, the necessary computations involving any other taxable year shall be made under the law applicable to such other taxable year.

(2) The net operating loss for any taxable year shall be determined under the law applicable to that year without regard to the year to which it is to be carried and in which, in effect, it is to be deducted as part of the net operating loss deduction.

(3) The amount of the net operating loss deduction which shall be allowed for any taxable year shall be determined under the law applicable to that year.

(f) *Electing small business corporations.* In determining the amount of the net operating loss deduction of any corporation, there shall be disregarded the net operating loss of such corporation for any taxable year for which such corporation was an electing small business corporation under subchapter S (section 1371 and following), chapter 1 of the Code. In applying section 172(b)(1) and (2) to a net operating loss sustained in a taxable year in which the corporation was not an electing small business corporation, a taxable year in which the corporation was an electing small business corporation is counted as a taxable year to which such net operating loss is carried back or over. However, the taxable income for such year as determined under section 172(b)(2) is treated as if it were zero for purposes of computing the balance of the loss available to the corporation as a carryback or carryover to other taxable years in which the corporation is not an electing small business corporation. See section 1374 and the

regulations thereunder for allowance of a deduction to shareholders for a net operating loss sustained by an electing small business corporation.

(g) *Husband and wife.* The net operating loss deduction of a husband and wife shall be determined in accordance with this section, but subject also to the provisions of § 1.172-7. [Reg. § 1.172-1.]

☐ [*T.D. 6192, 7-23-56. Amended by T.D. 6486, 8-12-60 and T.D. 8107, 12-1-86.*]

§ 1.172-3. Net operating loss in case of a taxpayer other than a corporation.—(a) *Modification of deductions.* A net operating loss is sustained by a taxpayer other than a corporation in any taxable year if and to the extent that, for such year, there is an excess of deductions allowed by chapter 1 of the Internal Revenue Code over gross income computed thereunder. In determining the excess of deductions over gross income for such purpose—

(1) *Items not deductible.* No deduction shall be allowed under—

(i) Section 151 for the personal exemptions or under any other section which grants a deduction in lieu of the deductions allowed by section 151,

(ii) Section 172 for the net operating loss deduction, and

(iii) Section 1202 in respect of net long-term capital gain.

(2) *Capital losses.* (i) The amount deductible on account of business capital losses shall not exceed the sum of the amount includible on account of business capital gains and that portion of nonbusiness capital gains which is computed in accordance with paragraph (c) of this section.

(ii) The amount deductible on account of nonbusiness capital losses shall not exceed the amount includible on account of nonbusiness capital gains.

(3) *Nonbusiness deductions*—(i) *Ordinary deductions.* Ordinary nonbusiness deductions shall be taken into account without regard to the amount of business deductions and shall be allowed in full to the extent, but not in excess, of that amount which is the sum of the ordinary nonbusiness gross income and the excess of nonbusiness capital gains over nonbusiness capital losses. See paragraph (c) of this section. For purposes of section 172, nonbusiness deductions and income are those deductions and that income which are not attributable to, or derived from, a taxpayer's trade or business. Wages and salary constitute income attributable to the taxpayer's trade or business for such purposes.

(ii) *Sale of business property.* Any gain or loss on the sale or other disposition of property

Reg. § 1.172-3(a)(3)

which is used in the taxpayer's trade or business and which is of a character that is subject to the allowance for depreciation provided in section 167, or of real property used in the taxpayer's trade or business, shall be considered, for purposes of section 172(d)(4), as attributable to, or derived from, the taxpayer's trade or business. Such gains and losses are to be taken into account fully in computing a net operating loss without regard to the limitation on nonbusiness deductions. Thus, a farmer who sells at a loss land used in the business of farming may, in computing a net operating loss, include in full the deduction otherwise allowable with respect to such loss, without regard to the amount of his nonbusiness income and without regard to whether he is engaged in the trade or business of selling farms. Similarly, an individual who sells at a loss machinery which is used in his trade or business and which is of a character that is subject to the allowance for depreciation may, in computing the net operating loss, include in full the deduction otherwise allowable with respect to such loss.

(iii) *Casualty losses.* Any deduction allowable under section 165(c)(3) for losses of property not connected with a trade or business shall not be considered, for purposes of section 172(d)(4), to be a nonbusiness deduction but shall be treated as a deduction attributable to the taxpayer's trade or business.

(iv) *Self-employed retirement plans.* Any deduction allowed under section 404, relating to contributions of an employer to an employees' trust or annuity plan, or under section 405(c), relating to contributions to a bond purchase plan, to the extent attributable to contributions made on behalf of an individual while he is an employee within the meaning of section 401(c)(1), shall not be treated, for purposes of section 172(d)(4), as attributable to, or derived from, the taxpayer's trade or business, but shall be treated as a nonbusiness deduction.

(v) *Limitation.* The provisions of this subparagraph shall not be construed to permit the deduction of items disallowed by subparagraph (1) of this paragraph.

(b) *Treatment of capital loss carryovers.* Because of the distinction between business and nonbusiness capital gains and losses, a taxpayer who has a capital loss carryover from a preceding taxable year, includible by virtue of section 1212 among the capital losses for the taxable year in issue, is required to determine how much of such capital loss carryover is a business capital loss and how much is a nonbusiness capital loss. In order to make this determination, the taxpayer shall first ascertain what proportion of the net capital loss for such preceding taxable year was attributable

to an excess of business capital losses over business capital gains for such year, and what proportion was attributable to an excess of nonbusiness capital losses over nonbusiness capital gains. The same proportion of the capital loss carryover from such preceding taxable year shall be treated as a business capital loss and a nonbusiness capital loss, respectively. In order to determine the composition (business—nonbusiness) of a net capital loss for a taxable year, for purposes of this paragraph, if such net capital loss is computed under paragraph (b) of § 1.1212-1 and takes into account a capital loss carryover from a preceding taxable year, the composition (business—nonbusiness) of the net capital loss for such preceding taxable year must also be determined. For purposes of this paragraph, the term "capital loss carryover" means the sum of the short-term and long-term capital loss carryovers from such year This paragraph may be illustrated by the following examples:

Example (1). (i) A, an individual, has $5,000 ordinary taxable income (computed without regard to the deductions for personal exemptions) for the calendar year 1954 and also has the following capital gains and losses for such year: Business capital gains of $2,000; business capital losses of $3,200; nonbusiness capital gains of $1,000; and nonbusiness capital losses of $1,200.

(ii) A's net capital loss for the taxable year 1954 is $400, computed as follows:

Capital losses	$4,400
Capital gains	3,000
Excess of capital losses over capital gains	$1,400
Less: $1,000 of such ordinary taxable income	1,000
Net capital loss for 1954	$ 400

(iii) A's capital losses for 1954 exceeded his capital gains for such year by $1,400. Since A's business capital losses for 1954 exceeded his business capital gains for such year by $1,200, 6/7ths ($1,200/$1,400) of A's net capital loss for 1954 is attributable to an excess of his business capital losses over his business capital gains for such year. Similarly, 1/7th of the net capital loss is attributable to the excess of nonbusiness capital losses over nonbusiness capital gains. Since the capital loss carryover for 1954 to 1955 is $400, 6/7ths of $400, or $342.86, shall be treated as a business capital loss in 1955; and 1/7th of $400, or $57.14, as a nonbusiness capital loss.

Example (2). (i) A, an individual who is computing a net operating loss for the calendar year 1966, has a capital loss carryover from 1965 of $8,000. In order to apply the provisions of this paragraph, A must determine what portion of the $8,000 carryover is attributable to the excess of business capital losses over business capital gains

Reg. § 1.172-3(b)

and what portion thereof is attributable to the excess of nonbusiness capital losses over nonbusiness capital gains. For 1965, A had $10,000 ordinary taxable income (computed without regard to the deductions for personal exemptions), and a short-term capital loss carryover of $6,000 from 1964. In order to determine the composition (business—nonbusiness) of the $8,000 carryover from 1965, A first determines that of the $6,000 carryover from 1964, $5,000 is a business capital loss and $1,000 is a nonbusiness capital loss. This must be done since, under paragraph (b) of § 1.1212-1, the net capital loss for 1965 is computed by taking into account the capital loss carryover from 1964. A's capital gains and losses for 1965 are as follows:

	1965	Carried over from 1964
Business capital gains	$2,000	
Business capital losses	3,000	$5,000
Nonbusiness capital gains	4,000	
Nonbusiness capital losses	6,000	1,000

(ii) A's net capital loss for the taxable year 1965 is $8,000, computed as follows:

Capital losses (including carryovers)	$15,000
Capital gains	6,000
Excess of capital losses over capital gains	$ 9,000
Less: $1,000 of such ordinary taxable income	1,000
Net capital loss for 1965	$ 8,000

(iii) A's capital losses, including carryovers, for 1965 exceeded his capital gains for such year by $9,000. Since A's business capital losses for 1965 exceeded his business capital gains for such year by $6,000, 2/3rds ($6,000/$9,000) of A's net capital loss for 1965 is attributable to an excess of his business capital losses over his business capital gains for such year. Similarly, 1/3rd of the net capital loss is attributable to the excess of nonbusiness capital losses over nonbusiness capital gains. Since the total capital loss carryover from 1965 to 1966 is $8,000, 2/3rds of $8,000, or $5,333.33, shall be treated as a business capital loss in 1966; and 1/3rd of $8,000, or $2,666.67, as a nonbusiness capital loss.

(c) *Determination of portion of nonbusiness capital gains available for the deduction of business capital losses.* In the computation of a net operating loss a taxpayer other than a corporation must use his nonbusiness capital gains for the deduction of his nonbusiness capital losses. Any amount not necessary for this purpose shall then be used for the deduction of any excess of ordinary nonbusiness deductions over ordinary nonbusiness gross income. The remainder, computed by applying the excess ordinary nonbusiness deductions against the excess nonbusiness capital gains, shall

be treated as nonbusiness capital gains and used for the purpose of determining the deductibility of business capital losses under paragraph (a)(2)(i) of this section. This principle may be illustrated by the following example:

Example. (1) A, an individual, has a total nonbusiness gross income of $20,500, computed as follows:

Ordinary gross income	$ 7,500
Capital gains	13,000
Total gross income	20,500

(2) A also has total nonbusiness deductions of $16,000, computed as follows:

Ordinary deductions	$ 9,000
Capital loss	7,000
Total deductions	16,000

(3) The portion of nonbusiness capital gains to be used for the purpose of determining the deductibility of business capital losses is $4,500, computed as follows:

Nonbusiness capital gains		$13,000
Less: Nonbusiness capital loss		7,000
Excess to be taken into account for purposes of paragraph (a)(3)(i) of this section		6,000
Ordinary nonbusiness deductions	$9,000	
Less: Ordinary nonbusiness gross income	7,500	1,500
Portion of nonbusiness capital gains to be used for purposes of paragraph (a)(2)(i) of this section		4,500

(d) *Joint net operating loss of husband and wife.* In the case of a husband and wife, the joint net operating loss for any taxable year for which a joint return is filed is to be computed on the basis of the combined income and deductions of both spouses, and the modifications prescribed in paragraph (a) of this section are to be computed as if the combined income and deductions of both spouses were the income and deductions of one individual.

(e) *Illustration of computation of net operating loss of a taxpayer other than a corporation*—(1) *Facts.* For the calendar year 1954, A, an individual, has gross income of $483,000 and allowable deductions of $540,000. The latter amount does not include the net operating loss deduction or any deduction on account of the sale or exchange of capital assets. Included in gross income are business capital gains of $50,000 and ordinary nonbusiness income of $10,000. Included among the deductions are ordinary nonbusiness deductions of $12,000 and a deduction of $600 for his personal exemption. A has a business capital loss of $60,000 in 1954. A has no other items of income or deductions to which section 172(d) applies.

Reg. § 1.172-3(e)(1)

(2) *Computation.* On the basis of these facts, A has a net operating loss for 1954 of $104,400, computed as follows:

Deductions for 1954 (as specified in first sentence of subparagraph (1)) ..		$540,000
Plus: Amount of business capital loss ($60,000) to extent such amount does not exceed business capital gains ($50,000)		50,000
Total		590,000
Less: Excess of ordinary nonbusiness deductions over ordinary nonbusiness gross income ($12,000 minus $10,000) $2,000		
Deduction for personal exemption................ 600		2,600
Deductions for 1954 adjusted as required by section 172(d)		587,400
Gross income for 1954		483,000
Net operating loss for 1954		104,400

[Reg. § 1.172-3.]

☐ [*T.D.* 6192, 7-23-56. *Amended by T.D.* 6828, 6-16-65, *T.D.* 6862, 11-17-65 *and T.D.* 8107, 12-1-86.]

§ 1.174-1. Research and experimental expenditures; in general.—Section 174 provides two methods for treating research or experimental expenditures paid or incurred by the taxpayer in connection with his trade or business. These expenditures may be treated as expenses not chargeable to capital account and deducted in the year in which they are paid or incurred (see § 1.174-3), or they may be deferred and amortized (see § 1.174-4). Research or experimental expenditures which are neither treated as expenses nor deferred and amortized under section 174 must be charged to capital account. The expenditures to which section 174 applies may relate either to a general research program or to a particular project. See § 1.174-2 for the definition of research and experimental expenditures. The term "paid or incurred", as used in section 174 and in § § 1.174-1 to 1.174-4, inclusive, is to be construed according to the method of accounting used by the taxpayer in computing taxable income. See section 7701(a)(25). [Reg. § 1.174-1.]

☐ [*T.D.* 6255, 10-3-57.]

§ 1.174-2. Definition of research and experimental expenditures.—(a) *In general.* (1) The term *research or experimental expenditures*, as used in section 174, means expenditures incurred in connection with the taxpayer's trade or business which represent research and development costs in the experimental or laboratory sense. The term generally includes all such costs incident to the development or improvement of a product. The term includes the costs of obtaining a patent, such as attorneys' fees expended in making and perfecting a patent application. Expenditures represent research and development costs in the experimental or laboratory sense if they are for activities intended to discover information that would eliminate uncertainty concerning the development or improvement of a product. Uncertainty exists if the information available to the taxpayer does not establish the capability or method for developing or improving the product or the appropriate design of the product. Whether expenditures qualify as research or experimental expenditures depends on the nature of the activity to which the expenditures relate, not the nature of the product or improvement being developed or the level of technological advancement the product or improvement represents.

(2) For purposes of this section, the term *product* includes any pilot model, process, formula, invention, technique, patent, or similar property, and includes products to be used by the taxpayer in its trade or business as well as products to be held for sale, lease, or license.

(3) The term *research or experimental expenditures* does not include expenditures for—

(i) The ordinary testing or inspection of materials or products for quality control (quality control testing);

(ii) Efficiency surveys;

(iii) Management studies;

(iv) Consumer surveys;

(v) Advertising or promotions;

(vi) The acquisition of another's patent, model, production or process; or

(vii) Research in connection with literary, historical, or similar projects.

(4) For purposes of paragraph (a)(3)(i) of this section, testing or inspection to determine whether particular units of materials or products conform to specified parameters is quality control testing. However, quality control testing does not include testing to determine if the design of the product is appropriate.

(5) See section 263A and the regulations thereunder for cost capitalization rules which apply to expenditures paid or incurred for research in connection with literary, historical, or similar projects involving the production of property, including the production of films, sound recordings, video tapes, books, or similar properties.

(6) Section 174 applies to a research or experimental expenditure only to the extent that the amount of the expenditure is reasonable under the circumstances. In general, the amount of an expenditure for research or experimental activities is reasonable if the amount would ordinarily be paid for like activities by like enterprises under like circumstances. Amounts supposedly paid for

research that are not reasonable under the circumstances may be characterized as disguised dividends, gifts, loans, or similar payments. The reasonableness requirement of this paragraph (a)(6) does not apply to the reasonableness of the type or nature of the activities themselves.

(7) This paragraph (a) applies to taxable years beginning after October 3, 1994.

(8) The provisions of this section apply not only to costs paid or incurred by the taxpayer for research or experimentation undertaken directly by him but also to expenditures paid or incurred for research or experimentation carried on in his behalf by another person or organization (such as a research institute, foundation, engineering company, or similar contractor). However, any expenditures for research or experimentation carried on in the taxpayer's behalf by another person are not expenditures to which section 174 relates, to the extent that they represent expenditures for the acquisition or improvement of land or depreciable property, used in connection with the research or experimentation, to which the taxpayer acquires rights of ownership.

(9) The application of subparagraph (2) of this paragraph may be illustrated by the following examples:

Example (1). A engages B to undertake research and experimental work in order to create a particular product. B will be paid annually a fixed sum plus an amount equivalent to his actual expenditures. In 1957, A pays to B in respect of the project the sum of $150,000 of which $25,000 represents an addition to B's laboratory and the balance represents charges for research and experimentation on the project. It is agreed between the parties that A will absorb the entire cost of this addition to B's laboratory which will be retained by B. A may treat the entire $150,000 as expenditures under section 174.

Example (2). X Corporation, a manufacturer of explosives, contracts with the Y research organization to attempt through research and experimentation the creation of a new process for making certain explosives. Because of the danger involved in such an undertaking, Y is compelled to acquire an isolated tract of land on which to conduct the research and experimentation. It is agreed that upon completion of the project Y will transfer this tract, including any improvements thereon, to X. Section 174 does not apply to the amount paid to Y representing the costs of the tract of land and improvements.

(b) *Certain expenditures with respect to land and other property*. (1) Expenditures by the taxpayer for the acquisition or improvement of land, or for the acquisition or improvement of property which is subject to an allowance for depreciation

under section 167 or depletion under section 611, are not deductible under section 174, irrespective of the fact that the property or improvements may be used by the taxpayer in connection with research or experimentation. However, allowances for depreciation or depletion of property are considered as research or experimental expenditures, for purposes of section 174, to the extent that the property to which the allowances relate is used in connection with research or experimentation. If any part of the cost of acquisition or improvement of depreciable property is attributable to research or experimentation (whether made by the taxpayer or another), see subparagraphs (2), (3), and (4) of this paragraph.

(2) Expenditures for research or experimentation which result, as an end product of the research or experimentation, in depreciable property to be used in the taxpayer's trade or business may, subject to the limitations of subparagraph (4) of this paragraph, be allowable as a current expense deduction under section 174(a). Such expenditures cannot be amortized under section 174(b) except to the extent provided in paragraph (a)(4) of § 1.174-4.

(3) If expenditures for research or experimentation are incurred in connection with the construction or manufacture of depreciable property by another, they are deductible under section 174(a) only if made upon the taxpayer's order and at his risk. No deduction will be allowed (i) if the taxpayer purchases another's product under a performance guarantee (whether express, implied, or imposed by local law) unless the guarantee is limited, to engineering specifications or otherwise, in such a way that economic utility is not taken into account; or (ii) for any part of the purchase price of a product in regular production. For example, if a taxpayer orders a specially-built automatic milling machine under a guarantee that the machine will be capable of producing a given number of units per hour, no portion of the expenditure is deductible since none of it is made at the taxpayer's risk. Similarly, no deductible expense is incurred if a taxpayer enters into a contract for the construction of a new type of chemical processing plant under a turn-key contract guaranteeing a given annual production and a given consumption of raw material and fuel per unit. On the other hand, if the contract contained no guarantee of quality of production and of quantity of units in relation to consumption of raw material and fuel, and if real doubt existed as to the capabilities of the process, expenses for research or experimentation under the contract are at the taxpayer's risk and are deductible under section 174(a). However, see subparagraph (4) of this paragraph.

Reg. § 1.174-2(b)(3)

(4) The deductions referred to in subparagraphs (2) and (3) of this paragraph for expenditures in connection with the acquisition or production of depreciable property to be used in the taxpayer's trade or business are limited to amounts expended for research or experimentation. For the purpose of the preceding sentence, amounts expended for research or experimentation do not include the costs of the component materials of the depreciable property, the costs of labor or other elements involved in its construction and installation, or costs attributable to the acquisition or improvement of the property. For example, a taxpayer undertakes to develop a new machine for use in his business. He expends $30,000 on the project of which $10,000 represents the actual costs of material, labor, etc., to construct the machine, and $20,000 represents research costs which are not attributable to the machine itself. Under section 174(a) the taxpayer would be permitted to deduct the $20,000 as expenses not chargeable to capital account, but the $10,000 must be charged to the asset account (the machine).

(c) *Exploration expenditures.* The provisions of section 174 are not applicable to any expenditures paid or incurred for the purpose of ascertaining the existence, location, extent, or quality of any deposit of ore, oil, gas or other mineral. See sections 617 and 263. [Reg. § 1.174-2.]

☐ [*T.D. 6255, 10-3-57. Amended by T.D. 8131, 3-24-87 and T.D. 8562, 9-30-94.*]

[*Note: Reg. § 1.179-1 does not reflect later increases in the Section 179(b)(1) dollar limitation.*]

§ 1.179-1. Election to expense certain depreciable assets.—(a) *In general.* Section 179(a) allows a taxpayer to elect to expense the cost (as defined in § 1.179-4(d)), or a portion of the cost, of section 179 property (as defined in § 1.179-4(a)) for the taxable year in which the property is placed in service (as defined in § 1.179-4(e)). The election is not available for trusts, estates, and certain noncorporate lessors. See paragraph (i)(2) of this section for rules concerning noncorporate lessors. However, section 179(b) provides certain limitations on the amount that a taxpayer may elect to expense in any one taxable year. See § § 1.179-2 and 1.179-3 for rules relating to the dollar and taxable income limitations and the carryover of disallowed deduction rules. For rules describing the time and manner of making an election under section 179, see § 1.179-5. For the effective date, see § 1.179-6.

(b) *Cost subject to expense.* The expense deduction under section 179 is allowed for the entire cost or a portion of the cost of one or more items of section 179 property. This expense deduction is subject to the limitations of section 179(b) and § 1.179-2. The taxpayer may select the properties that are subject to the election as well as the portion of each property's cost to expense.

(c) *Proration not required*—(1) *In general.* The expense deduction under section 179 is determined without any proration based on—

(i) The period of time the section 179 property has been in service during the taxable year; or

(ii) The length of the taxable year in which the property is placed in service.

(2) *Example.* The following example illustrates the provisions of paragraph (c)(1) of this section.

Example. On December 1, 1991, X, a calendar-year corporation, purchases and places in service section 179 property costing $20,000. For the taxable year ending December 31, 1991, X may elect to claim a section 179 expense deduction on the property (subject to the limitations imposed under section 179(b)) without proration of its cost for the number of days in 1991 during which the property was in service.

(d) *Partial business use*—(1) *In general.* If a taxpayer uses section 179 property for trade or business as well as other purposes, the portion of the cost of the property attributable to the trade or business use is eligible for expensing under section 179 provided that more than 50 percent of the property's use in the taxable year is for trade or business purposes. The limitations of section 179(b) and § 1.179-2 are applied to the portion of the cost attributable to the trade or business use.

(2) *Example.* The following example illustrates the provisions of paragraph (d)(1) of this section.

Example. A purchases section 179 property costing $10,000 in 1991 for which 80 percent of its use will be in A's trade or business. The cost of the property adjusted to reflect the business use of the property is $8,000 (80 percent × $10,000). Thus, A may elect to expense up to $8,000 of the cost of the property (subject to the limitations imposed under section 179(b) and § 1.179-2).

(3) *Additional rules that may apply.* If a section 179 election is made for "listed property" within the meaning of section 280F(d)(4) and there is personal use of the property, section 280F(d)(1), which provides rules that coordinate section 179 with the section 280F limitation on the amount of depreciation, may apply. If section 179 property is no longer predominantly used in the taxpayer's trade or business, paragraphs (e)(1) through (4) of this section, relating to recapture of the section 179 deduction, may apply.

Reg. § 1.179-1(a)

(e) *Change in use; recapture*—(1) *In general.* If a taxpayer's section 179 property is not used predominantly in a trade or business of the taxpayer at any time before the end of the property's recovery period, the taxpayer must recapture in the taxable year in which the section 179 property is not used predominantly in a trade or business any benefit derived from expensing such property. The benefit derived from expensing the property is equal to the excess of the amount expensed under this section over the total amount that would have been allowable for prior taxable years and the taxable year of recapture as a deduction under section 168 (had section 179 not been elected) for the portion of the cost of the property to which the expensing relates (regardless of whether such excess reduced the taxpayer's tax liability). For purposes of the preceding sentence, (i) the "amount expensed under this section" shall not include any amount that was not allowed as a deduction to a taxpayer because the taxpayer's aggregate amount of allowable section 179 expenses exceeded the section 179(b) dollar limitation, and (ii) in the case of an individual who does not elect to itemize deductions under section 63(g) in the taxable year of recapture, the amount allowable as a deduction under section 168 in the taxable year of recapture shall be determined by treating property used in the production of income other than rents or royalties as being property used for personal purposes. The amount to be recaptured shall be treated as ordinary income for the taxable year in which the property is no longer used predominantly in a trade or business of the taxpayer. For taxable years following the year of recapture, the taxpayer's deductions under section 168(a) shall be determined as if no section 179 election with respect to the property had been made. However, see section 280F(d)(1) relating to the coordination of section 179 with the limitation on the amount of depreciation for luxury automobiles and where certain property is used for personal purposes. If the recapture rules of both section 280F(b)(2) and this paragraph (e)(1) apply to an item of section 179 property, the amount of recapture for such property shall be determined only under the rules of section 280F(b)(2).

(2) *Predominant use.* Property will be treated as not used predominantly in a trade or business of the taxpayer if 50 percent or more of the use of such property during any taxable year within the recapture period is for a use other than in a trade or business of the taxpayer. If during any taxable year of the recapture period the taxpayer disposes of the property (other than in a disposition to which section 1245(a) applies) or ceases to use the property in a trade or business in a manner that had the taxpayer claimed a credit

under section 38 for such property such disposition or cessation in use would cause recapture under section 47, the property will be treated as not used in a trade or business of the taxpayer. However, for purposes of applying the recapture rules of section 47 pursuant to the preceding sentence, converting the use of the property from use in a trade or business to use in the production of income will be treated as a conversion to personal use.

(3) *Basis; application with section 1245.* The basis of property with respect to which there is recapture under paragraph (e)(1) of this section shall be increased immediately before the event resulting in such recapture by the amount recaptured. If section 1245(a) applies to a disposition of property, there is no recapture under paragraph (e)(1) of this section.

(4) *Carryover of disallowed deduction.* See § 1.179-3 for rules on applying the recapture provisions of this paragraph (e) when a taxpayer has a carryover of disallowed deduction.

(5) *Example.* The following example illustrates the provisions of paragraphs (e)(1) through (e)(4) of this section.

Example. A, a calendar-year taxpayer, purchases and places in service on January 1, 1991, section 179 property costing $15,000. The property is 5-year property for section 168 purposes and is the only item of depreciable property placed in service by A during 1991. A properly elects to expense $10,000 of the cost and elects under section 168(b)(5) to depreciate the remaining cost under the straight-line method. On January 1, 1992, A converts the property from use in A's business to use for the production of income, and A uses the property in the latter capacity for the entire year. A elects to itemize deductions for 1992. Because the property was not predominantly used in A's trade or business in 1992, A must recapture any benefit derived from expensing the property under section 179. Had A not elected to expense the $10,000 in 1991, A would have been entitled to deduct, under section 168, 10 percent of the $10,000 in 1991, and 20 percent of the $10,000 in 1992. Therefore, A must include $7,000 in ordinary income for the 1992 taxable year, the excess of $10,000 (the section 179 expense amount) over $3,000 (30 percent of $10,000).

(f) *Basis*—(1) *In general.* A taxpayer who elects to expense under section 179 must reduce the depreciable basis of the section 179 property by the amount of the section 179 expense deduction.

(2) *Special rules for partnerships and S Corporations.*—Generally the basis of a partnership or S corporation's section 179 property must be reduced to reflect the amount of section 179 ex-

Reg. § 1.179-1(f)(2)

pense elected by the partnership or S corporation. This reduction must be made in the basis of partnership or S corporation property even if the limitations of section 179(b) and § 1.179-2 prevent a partner in a partnership or a shareholder in an S corporation from deducting all or a portion of the amount of the section 179 expense allocated by the partnership or S corporation. See § 1.179-3 for rules on applying the basis provisions of this paragraph (f) when a person has a carryover of disallowed deduction.

(3) *Special rules with respect to trusts and estates which are partners or S corporation shareholders.* Since the section 179 election is not available for trusts or estates, a partner or S corporation shareholder that is a trust or estate, may not deduct its allocable share of the section 179 expense elected by the partnership or S corporation. The partnership or S corporation's basis in section 179 property shall not be reduced to reflect any portion of the section 179 expense that is allocable to the trust or estate. Accordingly, the partnership or S corporation may claim a depreciation deduction under section 168 or a section 38 credit (if available) with respect to any depreciable basis resulting from the trust or estate's inability to claim its allocable portion of the section 179 expense.

(g) *Disallowance of the section 38 credit.* If a taxpayer elects to expense under section 179, no section 38 credit is allowable for the portion of the cost expensed. In addition, no section 38 credit shall be allowed under section 48(d) to a lessee of property for the portion of the cost of the property that the lessor expensed under section 179.

(h) *Partnerships and S corporations.*—(1) *In general.* In the case of property purchased and placed in service by a partnership or an S corporation, the determination of whether the property is section 179 property is made at the partnership or S corporation level. The election to expense the cost of section 179 property is made by the partnership or the S corporation. See sections 703(b), 1363(c), 6221, 6231(a)(3), 6241, and 6245.

(2) *Example.* The following example illustrates the provisions of paragraph (h)(1) of this section.

Example. A owns certain residential rental property as an investment. A and others form ABC partnership whose function is to rent and manage such property. A and ABC partnership file their income tax returns on a calendar-year basis. In 1991, ABC partnership purchases and places in service office furniture costing $20,000 to be used in the active conduct of ABC's business. Although the office furniture is used with respect to an investment activity of A, the furniture is being used in the active conduct of ABC's trade or business. Therefore, because the determination of whether property is section 179 property is made at the partnership level, the office furniture is section 179 property and ABC may elect to expense a portion of its cost under section 179.

(i) *Leasing of section 179 property*—(1) *In general.* A lessor of section 179 property who is treated as the owner of the property for Federal tax purposes will be entitled to the section 179 expense deduction if the requirements of section 179 and the regulations thereunder are met. These requirements will not be met if the lessor merely holds the property for the production of income. For certain leases entered prior to January 1, 1984, the safe harbor provisions of section 168(f)(8) apply in determining whether an agreement is treated as a lease for Federal tax purposes.

(2) *Noncorporate lessor.* In determining the class of taxpayers (other than an estate or trust) for which section 179 is applicable, section 179(d)(5) provides that if a taxpayer is a noncorporate lessor (*i.e.,* a person who is not a corporation and is a lessor), the taxpayer shall not be entitled to claim a section 179 expense for section 179 property purchased and leased by the taxpayer unless the taxpayer has satisfied all of the requirements of section 179(d)(5)(A) or (B).

(j) *Application of sections 263 and 263A.* Under section 263(a)(1)(G), expenditures for which a deduction is allowed under section 179 and this section are excluded from capitalization under section 263(a). Under this paragraph (j), amounts allowed as a deduction under section 179 and this section are excluded from the application of the uniform capitalization rules of section 263A.

(k) *Cross references.* See section 453(i) and the regulations thereunder with respect to installment sales of section 179 property. See section 1033(g)(3) and the regulations thereunder relating to the condemnation of outdoor advertising displays. See section 1245(a) and the regulations thereunder with respect to recapture rules for section 179 property. [Reg. § 1.179-1.]

☐ [*T.D.* 8121, 1-5-87. *Amended by T.D.* 8455, 12-23-92.]

§ 1.183-1. Activities not engaged in for profit.—(a) *In general.* Section 183 provides rules relating to the allowance of deductions in the case of activities (whether active or passive in character) not engaged in for profit by individuals and electing small business corporations, creates a presumption that an activity is engaged in for profit if certain requirements are met, and permits the taxpayer to elect to postpone determination of whether such presumption applies until he has engaged in the activity for at least five taxable years, or, in certain cases, seven taxable years.

Whether an activity is engaged in for profit is determined under section 162 and section 212(1) and (2) except insofar as section 183(d) creates a presumption that the activity is engaged in for profit. If deductions are not allowable under sections 162 and 212(1) and (2), the deduction allowance rules of section 183(b) and this section apply. Pursuant to section 641(b), the taxable income of an estate or trust is computed in the same manner as in the case of an individual, with certain exceptions not here relevant. Accordingly, where an estate or trust engages in an activity or activities which are not for profit, the rules of section 183 and this section apply in computing the allowable deductions of such trust or estate. No inference is to be drawn from the provisions of section 183 and the regulations thereunder that any activity of a corporation (other than an electing small business corporation) is or is not a business or engaged in for profit. For rules relating to the deductions that may be taken into account by taxable membership organizations which are operated primarily to furnish services, facilities, or goods to members, see section 277 and the regulations thereunder. For the definition of an activity not engaged in for profit, see § 1.183-2. For rules relating to the election contained in section 183(e), see § 1.183-3.

(b) *Deductions allowable*—(1) *Manner and extent.* If an activity is not engaged in for profit, deductions are allowable under section 183(b) in the following order and only to the following extent:

(i) Amounts allowable as deductions during the taxable year under chapter 1 of the Code without regard to whether the activity giving rise to such amounts was engaged in for profit are allowable to the full extent allowed by the relevant sections of the Code, determined after taking into account any limitations or exceptions with respect to the allowability of such amounts. For example, the allowability-of-interest expenses incurred with respect to activities not engaged in for profit is limited by the rules contained in section 163(d).

(ii) Amounts otherwise allowable as deductions during the taxable year under chapter 1 of the Code, but only if such allowance does not result in an adjustment to the basis of property, determined as if the activity giving rise to such amounts was engaged in for profit, are allowed only to the extent the gross income attributable to such activity exceeds the deductions allowed or allowable under subdivision (i) of this subparagraph.

(iii) Amounts otherwise allowable as deductions for the taxable year under chapter 1 of the Code which result in (or if otherwise allowed would have resulted in) an adjustment to the basis of property, determined as if the activity giving rise to such deductions was engaged in for profit, are allowed only to the extent the gross income attributable to such activity exceeds the deductions allowed or allowable under subdivisions (i) and (ii) of this subparagraph. Deductions falling within this subdivision include such items as depreciation, partial losses with respect to property, partially worthless debts, amortization, and amortizable bond premium.

(2) *Rule for deductions involving basis adjustments*—(i) *In general.* If deductions are allowed under subparagraph, (1)(iii) of this paragraph, and such deductions are allowed with respect to more than one asset, the deduction allowed with respect to each asset shall be determined separately in accordance with the computation set forth in subdivision (ii) of this paragraph.

(ii) *Basis adjustment fraction.* The deduction allowed under subparagraph (1)(iii) of this paragraph is computed by multiplying the amount which would have been allowed, had the activity been engaged in for profit, as a deduction with respect to each particular asset which involves a basis adjustment, by the basis adjustment fraction—

(a) The numerator of which is the total of deductions allowable under subparagraph (1)(iii) of this paragraph, and

(b) The denominator of which is the total of deductions which involve basis adjustments which would have been allowed with respect to the activity had the activity been engaged in for profit.

The amount resulting from this computation is the deduction allowed under subparagraph (1)(iii) of this paragraph with respect to the particular asset. The basis of such asset is adjusted only to the extent of such deduction.

* * *

(5) *Cross reference.* For rules relating to section 183(e) which permits a taxpayer to elect to postpone determination of whether any activity shall be presumed to be "an activity engaged in for profit" by operation of the presumption described in section 183(d) and this paragraph until after the close of the fourth taxable year (sixth taxable year, in the case of activity which consists in major part of breeding, training, showing, or racing of horses) following the taxable year in which the taxpayer first engages in the activity, see § 1.183-3.

(d) *Activity defined*—(1) *Ascertainment of activity.* In order to determine whether, and to what extent, section 183 and the regulations thereunder apply, the activity or activities of the taxpayer

Reg. § 1.183-1(d)(1)

must be ascertained. For instance, where the taxpayer is engaged in several undertakings, each of these may be a separate activity, or several undertakings may constitute one activity. In ascertaining the activity or activities of the taxpayer, all the facts and circumstances of the case must be taken into account. Generally, the most significant facts and circumstances in making this determination are the degree of organizational and economic interrelationship of various undertakings, the business purpose which is (or might be) served by carrying on the various undertakings separately or together in a trade or business or in an investment setting, and the similarity of various undertakings. Generally, the Commissioner will accept the characterization by the taxpayer of several undertakings either as a single activity or as separate activities. The taxpayer's characterization will not be accepted, however, when it appears that his characterization is artificial and cannot be reasonably supported under the facts and circumstances of the case. If the taxpayer engages in two or more separate activities, deductions and income from each separate activity are not aggregated either in determining whether a particular activity is engaged in for profit or in applying section 183. Where land is purchased or held primarily with the intent to profit from increase in its value, and the taxpayer also engages in farming on such land, the farming and the holding of the land will ordinarily be considered a single activity only if the farming activity reduces the net cost of carrying the land for its appreciation in value. Thus, the farming and holding of the land will be considered a single activity only if the income derived from farming exceeds the deductions attributable to the farming activity which are not directly attributable to the holding of the land (that is, deductions other than those directly attributable to the holding of the land such as interest on a mortgage secured by the land, annual property taxes attributable to the land and improvements, and depreciation of improvements to the land).

(2) *Rules for allocation of expenses.* If the taxpayer is engaged in more than one activity, an item of deduction or income may be allocated between two or more of these activities. Where property is used in several activities, and one or more of such activities is determined not to be engaged in for profit, deductions relating to such property must be allocated between the various activities on a reasonable and consistently applied basis.

* * *

(e) *Gross income from activity not engaged in for profit defined.* For purposes of section 183 and the regulations thereunder, gross income derived

from an activity not engaged in for profit includes the total of all gains from the sale, exchange, or other disposition of property, and all other gross receipts derived from such activity. Such gross income shall include, for instance, capital gains, and rents received for the use of property which is held in connection with the activity. The taxpayer may determine gross income from any activity by subtracting the cost of goods sold from the gross receipts so long as he consistently does so and follows generally accepted methods of accounting in determining such gross income.

(f) *Rule for electing small business corporations.* Section 183 and this section shall be applied at the corporate level in determining the allowable deductions of an electing small business corporation. [Reg. § 1.183-1.]

□ [*T.D. 7198, 7-12-72.*]

§ 1.183-2. Activity not engaged in for profit defined.—(a) *In general.* For purposes of section 183 and the regulations thereunder, the term "activity not engaged in for profit" means any activity other than one with respect to which deductions are allowable for the taxable year under section 162 or under paragraph (1) or (2) of section 212. Deductions are allowable under section 162 for expenses of carrying on activities which constitute a trade or business of the taxpayer and under section 212 for expenses incurred in connection with activities engaged in for the production or collection of income or for the management, conservation, or maintenance of property held for the production of income. Except as provided in section 183 and § 1.183-1, no deductions are allowable for expenses incurred in connection with activities which are not engaged in for profit. Thus, for example, deductions are not allowable under section 162 or 212 for activities which are carried on primarily as a sport, hobby, or for recreation. The determination whether an activity is engaged in for profit is to be made by reference to objective standards, taking into account all of the facts and circumstances of each case. Although a reasonable expectation of profit is not required, the facts and circumstances must indicate that the taxpayer entered into the activity, or continued the activity, with the objective of making a profit. In determining whether such an objective exists, it may be sufficient that there is a small chance of making a large profit. Thus it may be found that an investor in a wildcat oil well who incurs very substantial expenditures is in the venture for profit even though the expectation of a profit might be considered unreasonable. In determining whether an activity is engaged in for profit, greater weight is given to objective facts than to the taxpayer's mere statement of his intent.

Reg. § 1.183-2(a)

(b) *Relevant factors.* In determining whether an activity is engaged in for profit, all facts and circumstances with respect to the activity are to be taken into account. No one factor is determinative in making this determination. In addition, it is not intended that only the factors described in this paragraph are to be taken into account in making the determination, or that a determination is to be made on the basis that the number of factors (whether or not listed in this paragraph) indicating a lack of profit objective exceeds the number of factors indicating a profit objective, or vice versa. Among the factors which should normally be taken into account are the following:

(1) *Manner in which the taxpayer carries on the activity.* The fact that the taxpayer carries on the activity in a businesslike manner and maintains complete and accurate books and records may indicate that the activity is engaged in for profit. Similarly, where an activity is carried on in a manner substantially similar to other activities of the same nature which are profitable, a profit motive may be indicated. A change of operating methods, adoption of new techniques or abandonment of unprofitable methods in a manner consistent with an intent to improve profitability may also indicate a profit motive.

(2) *The expertise of the taxpayer or his advisors.* Preparation for the activity by extensive study of its accepted business, economic, and scientific practices, or consultation with those who are expert therein, may indicate that the taxpayer has a profit motive where the taxpayer carries on the activity in accordance with such practices. Where a taxpayer has such preparation or procures such expert advice, but does not carry on the activity in accordance with such practices, a lack of intent to derive profit may be indicated unless it appears that the taxpayer is attempting to develop new or superior techniques which may result in profits from the activity.

(3) *The time and effort expended by the taxpayer in carrying on the activity.* The fact that the taxpayer devotes much of his personal time and effort to carrying on an activity, particularly if the activity does not have substantial personal or recreational aspects, may indicate an intention to derive a profit. A taxpayer's withdrawal from another occupation to devote most of his energies to the activity may also be evidence that the activity is engaged in for profit. The fact that the taxpayer devotes a limited amount of time to an activity does not necessarily indicate a lack of profit motive where the taxpayer employs competent and qualified persons to carry on such activity.

(4) *Expectation that assets used in activity may appreciate in value.* The term "profit" encompasses appreciation in the value of assets, such as land, used in the activity. Thus, the taxpayer may intend to derive a profit from the operation of the activity, and may also intend that, even if no profit from current operations is derived, an overall profit will result when appreciation in the value of land used in the activity is realized since income from the activity together with the appreciation of land will exceed expenses of operation. See, however, paragraph (d) of § 1.183-1 for definition of an activity in this connection.

(5) *The success of the taxpayer in carrying on other similar or dissimilar activities.* The fact that the taxpayer has engaged in similar activities in the past and converted them from unprofitable to profitable enterprises may indicate that he is engaged in the present activity for profit, even though the activity is presently unprofitable.

(6) *The taxpayer's history of income or losses with respect to the activity.* A series of losses during the initial or start-up stage of an activity may not necessarily be an indication that the activity is not engaged in for profit. However, where losses continue to be sustained beyond the period which customarily is necessary to bring the operation to profitable status such continued losses, if not explainable, as due to customary business risks or reverses, may be indicative that the activity is not being engaged in for profit. If losses are sustained because of unforeseen or fortuitous circumstances which are beyond the control of the taxpayer, such as drought, disease, fire, theft, weather damages, other involuntary conversions, or depressed market conditions, such losses would not be an indication that the activity is not engaged in for profit. A series of years in which net income was realized would of course be strong evidence that the activity is engaged in for profit.

(7) *The amount of occasional profits, if any, which are earned.* The amount of profits in relation to the amount of losses incurred, and in relation to the amount of the taxpayer's investment and the value of the assets used in the activity, may provide useful criteria in determining the taxpayer's intent. An occasional small profit from an activity generating large losses, or from an activity in which the taxpayer has made a large investment, would not generally be determinative that the activity is engaged in for profit. However, substantial profit, though only occasional, would generally be indicative that an activity is engaged in for profit, where the investment or losses are comparatively small. Moreover, an opportunity to earn a substantial ultimate profit in a highly speculative venture is ordinarily sufficient to indicate that the activity is engaged in for profit even though losses or only occasional small profits are actually generated.

Reg. § 1.183-2(b)(7)

(8) *The financial status of the taxpayer.* The fact that the taxpayer does not have substantial income or capital from sources other than the activity may indicate that an activity is engaged in for profit. Substantial income from sources other than the activity (particularly if the losses from the activity generate substantial tax benefits) may indicate that the activity is not engaged in for profit especially if there are personal or recreational elements involved.

(9) *Elements of personal pleasure or recreation.* The presence of personal motives in carrying on of an activity may indicate that the activity is not engaged in for profit, especially where there are recreational or personal elements involved. On the other hand, a profit motivation may be indicated where an activity lacks any appeal other than profit. It is not, however, necessary that an activity be engaged in with the exclusive intention of deriving a profit or with the intention of maximizing profits. For example, the availability of other investments which would yield a higher return, or which would be more likely to be profitable, is not evidence that an activity is not engaged in for profit. An activity will not be treated as not engaged in for profit merely because the taxpayer has purposes or motivations other than solely to make a profit. Also, the fact that the taxpayer derives personal pleasure from engaging in the activity is not sufficient to cause the activity to be classified as not engaged in for profit if the activity is in fact engaged in for profit as evidenced by other factors whether or not listed in this paragraph.

(c) *Examples.* The provisions of this section may be illustrated by the following examples:

Example (1). The taxpayer inherited a farm from her husband in an area which was becoming largely residential, and is now nearly all so. The farm had never made a profit before the taxpayer inherited it, and the farm has since had substantial losses in each year. The decedent from whom the taxpayer inherited the farm was a stockbroker, and he also left the taxpayer substantial stock holdings which yield large income from dividends. The taxpayer lives on an area of the farm which is set aside exclusively for living purposes. A farm manager is employed to operate the farm, but modern methods are not used in operating the farm. The taxpayer was born and raised on a farm, and expresses a strong preference for living on a farm. The taxpayer's activity of farming, based on all the facts and circumstances, could be found not to be engaged in for profit.

Example (2). The taxpayer is a wealthy individual who is greatly interested in philosophy. During the past thirty years he has written and published at his own expense several pamphlets,

and he has engaged in extensive lecturing activity, advocating and disseminating his ideas. He has made a profit from these activities in only occasional years, and the profits in those years were small in relation to the amounts of the losses in all other years. The taxpayer has very sizable income from securities (dividends and capital gains) which constitutes the principal source of his livelihood. The activity of lecturing, publishing pamphlets, and disseminating his ideas is not an activity engaged in by the taxpayer for profit.

Example (3). The taxpayer, very successful in the business of retailing soft drinks, raises dogs and horses. He began raising a particular breed of dogs many years ago in the belief that the breed was in danger of declining, and he has raised and sold the dogs in each year since. The taxpayer recently began raising and racing thoroughbred horses. The losses from the taxpayer's dog and horse activities have increased in magnitude over the years, and he has not made a profit on these operations during any of the last 15 years. The taxpayer generally sells the dogs only to friends, does not advertise the dogs for sale, and shows the dogs only infrequently. The taxpayer races his horses only at the "prestige" tracks at which he combines his racing activities with social and recreational activities. The horse and dog operations are conducted at a large residential property on which the taxpayer also lives, which includes substantial living quarters and attractive recreational facilities for the taxpayer and his family. Since (i) the activity of raising dogs and horses and racing the horses is of a sporting and recreational nature, (ii) the taxpayer has substantial income from his business activities of retailing soft drinks, (iii) the horse and dog operations are not conducted in a businesslike manner, and (iv) such operations have a continuous record of losses, it could be determined that the horse and dog activities of the taxpayer are not engaged in for profit.

Example (4). The taxpayer inherited a farm of 65 acres from his parents when they died 6 years ago. The taxpayer moved to the farm from his house in a small nearby town, and he operates it in the same manner as his parents operated the farm before they died. The taxpayer is employed as a skilled machine operator in a nearby factory, for which he is paid approximately $8,500 per year. The farm has not been profitable for the past 15 years because of rising costs of operating farms in general, and because of the decline in the price of the produce of this farm in particular. The taxpayer consults the local agent of the State agricultural service from time-to-time, and the suggestions of the agent have generally been followed. The manner in which the farm is operated by the taxpayer is substantially similar to the manner in which farms of similar size, and which grow similar crops in the area are operated. Many of these other farms do not make profits. The taxpayer does much of the required labor around the farm himself, such as fixing fences, planting crops, etc. The activity of farming could be found, based on all the facts and circumstances, to be engaged in by the taxpayer for profit.

Example (5). A, an independent oil and gas operator, frequently engages in the activity of searching for oil on undeveloped and unexplored land which is not near proven fields. He does so in a manner substantially similar to that of others who engage in the same activity. The chances, based on the experience of A and others who engaged in this activity, are strong that A will not find a commercially profitable oil deposit when he drills on land not established geologically to be proven oil bearing land. However, on the rare occasions that these activities do result in discovering a well, the operator generally realizes a very large return from such activity. Thus, there is a small chance that A will make a large profit from his oil exploration activity. Under these circumstances, A is engaged in the activity of oil drilling for profit.

Example (6). C, a chemist, is employed by a large chemical company and is engaged in a wide variety of basic research projects for his employer. Although he does no work for his employer with respect to the development of new plastics, he has always been interested in such development and has outfitted a workshop in his home at his own expense which he uses to experiment in the field. He has patented several developments at his own expense but as yet has realized no income from his inventions or from such patents. C conducts his research on a regular, systematic basis, incurs fees to secure consultation on his projects from time to time, and makes extensive efforts to "market" his developments. C has devoted substantial time and expense in an effort to develop a plastic sufficiently hard, durable, and malleable that it could be used in lieu of sheet steel in many major applications, such as automobile bodies. Although there may be only a small chance that C will invent new plastics, the return from any such development would be so large that it induces C to incur the costs of his experimental work. C is sufficiently qualified by his background that there is some reasonable basis for his experimental activities. C's experimental work does not involve substantial personal or recreational aspects and is conducted in an effort to find practical applications for his work. Under these circumstances, C may be found to be engaged in the experimental activities for profit. [Reg. § 1.183-2.]

☐ [*T.D. 7198, 7-12-72.*]

§ 1.197-2. Amortization of goodwill and certain other intangibles.—(a) *Overview*—(1) *In general.* Section 197 allows an amortization deduction for the capitalized costs of an amortizable section 197 intangible and prohibits any other depreciation or amortization with respect to that property. Paragraphs (b), (c), and (e) of this section provide rules and definitions for determining whether property is a section 197 intangible, and paragraphs (d) and (e) of this section provide rules and definitions for determining whether a section 197 intangible is an amortizable section 197 intangible. The amortization deduction under section 197 is determined by amortizing basis ratably over a 15-year period under the rules of paragraph (f) of this section. Section 197 also includes various special rules pertaining to the disposition of amortizable section 197 intangibles, nonrecognition transactions, anti-churning rules, and anti-abuse rules. Rules relating to these provisions are contained in paragraphs (g), (h), and (j) of this section. Examples demonstrating the application of these provisions are contained in paragraph (k) of this section. The effective date of the rules in this section is contained in paragraph (l) of this section.

(2) *Section 167(f) property.* Section 167(f) prescribes rules for computing the depreciation deduction for certain property to which section 197 does not apply. See § 1.167(a)-14 for rules under section 167(f) and paragraphs (c)(4), (6), (7), (11), and (13) of this section for a description of the property subject to section 167(f).

(3) *Amounts otherwise deductible.* Section 197 does not apply to amounts that are not chargeable to capital account under paragraph (f)(3) (relating to basis determinations for covenants not to compete and certain contracts for the use of section 197 intangibles) of this section and are otherwise currently deductible. For this purpose, an amount described in § 1.162-11 is not currently deductible if, without regard to § 1.162-11, such amount is properly chargeable to capital account.

(b) *Section 197 intangibles; in general.* Except as otherwise provided in paragraph (c) of this section, the term *section 197 intangible* means any property described in section 197(d)(1). The following rules and definitions provide guidance concerning property that is a section 197 intangible unless an exception applies:

(1) *Goodwill.* Section 197 intangibles include goodwill. Goodwill is the value of a trade or business attributable to the expectancy of continued customer patronage. This expectancy may be due to the name or reputation of a trade or business or any other factor.

Reg. § 1.197-2(b)(1)

(2) *Going concern value.* Section 197 intangibles include going concern value. Going concern value is the additional value that attaches to property by reason of its existence as an integral part of an ongoing business activity. Going concern value includes the value attributable to the ability of a trade or business (or a part of a trade or business) to continue functioning or generating income without interruption notwithstanding a change in ownership, but does not include any of the intangibles described in any other provision of this paragraph (b). It also includes the value that is attributable to the immediate use or availability of an acquired trade or business, such as, for example, the use of the revenues or net earnings that otherwise would not be received during any period if the acquired trade or business were not available or operational.

(3) *Workforce in place.* Section 197 intangibles include workforce in place. Workforce in place (sometimes referred to as agency force or assembled workforce) includes the composition of a workforce (for example, the experience, education, or training of a workforce), the terms and conditions of employment whether contractual or otherwise, and any other value placed on employees or any of their attributes. Thus, the amount paid or incurred for workforce in place includes, for example, any portion of the purchase price of an acquired trade or business attributable to the existence of a highly-skilled workforce, an existing employment contract (or contracts), or a relationship with employees or consultants (including, but not limited to, any key employee contract or relationship). Workforce in place does not include any covenant not to compete or other similar arrangement described in paragraph (b)(9) of this section.

(4) *Information base.* Section 197 intangibles include any information base, including a customer-related information base. For this purpose, an information base includes business books and records, operating systems, and any other information base (regardless of the method of recording the information) and a customer-related information base is any information base that includes lists or other information with respect to current or prospective customers. Thus, the amount paid or incurred for information base includes, for example, any portion of the purchase price of an acquired trade or business attributable to the intangible value of technical manuals, training manuals or programs, data files, and accounting or inventory control systems. Other examples include the cost of acquiring customer lists, subscription lists, insurance expirations, patient or client files, or lists of newspaper, magazine, radio, or television advertisers.

(5) *Know-how, etc.* Section 197 intangibles include any patent, copyright, formula, process,

design, pattern, know-how, format, package design, computer software (as defined in paragraph (c)(4)(iv) of this section), or interest in a film, sound recording, video tape, book, or other similar property. (See, however, the exceptions in paragraph (c) of this section.)

(6) *Customer-based intangibles.* Section 197 intangibles include any customer-based intangible. A customer-based intangible is any composition of market, market share, or other value resulting from the future provision of goods or services pursuant to contractual or other relationships in the ordinary course of business with customers. Thus, the amount paid or incurred for customer-based intangibles includes, for example, any portion of the purchase price of an acquired trade or business attributable to the existence of a customer base, a circulation base, an undeveloped market or market growth, insurance in force, the existence of a qualification to supply goods or services to a particular customer, a mortgage servicing contract (as defined in paragraph (c)(11) of this section), an investment management contract, or other relationship with customers involving the future provision of goods or services. (See, however, the exceptions in paragraph (c) of this section.) In addition, customer-based intangibles include the deposit base and any similar asset of a financial institution. Thus, the amount paid or incurred for customer-based intangibles also includes any portion of the purchase price of an acquired financial institution attributable to the value represented by existing checking accounts, savings accounts, escrow accounts, and other similar items of the financial institution. However, any portion of the purchase price of an acquired trade or business attributable to accounts receivable or other similar rights to income for goods or services provided to customers prior to the acquisition of a trade or business is not an amount paid or incurred for a customer-based intangible.

(7) *Supplier-based intangibles.* Section 197 intangibles include any supplier-based intangible. A supplier-based intangible is the value resulting from the future acquisition, pursuant to contractual or other relationships with suppliers in the ordinary course of business, of goods or services that will be sold or used by the taxpayer. Thus, the amount paid or incurred for supplier-based intangibles includes, for example, any portion of the purchase price of an acquired trade or business attributable to the existence of a favorable relationship with persons providing distribution services (such as favorable shelf or display space at a retail outlet), the existence of a favorable credit rating, or the existence of favorable supply contracts. The amount paid or incurred for supplier-based intangibles does not include any amount required to be paid for the goods or ser-

Reg. § 1.197-2(b)(2)

vices themselves pursuant to the terms of the agreement or other relationship. In addition, see the exceptions in paragraph (c) of this section, including the exception in paragraph (c)(6) of this section for certain rights to receive tangible property or services from another person.

(8) *Licenses, permits, and other rights granted by governmental units.* Section 197 intangibles include any license, permit, or other right granted by a governmental unit (including, for purposes of section 197, an agency or instrumentality thereof) even if the right is granted for an indefinite period or is reasonably expected to be renewed for an indefinite period. These rights include, for example, a liquor license, a taxi-cab medallion (or license), an airport landing or take-off right (sometimes referred to as a slot), a regulated airline route, or a television or radio broadcasting license. The issuance or renewal of a license, permit, or other right granted by a governmental unit is considered an acquisition of the license, permit, or other right. (See, however, the exceptions in paragraph (c) of this section, including the exceptions in paragraph (c)(3) of this section for an interest in land, paragraph (c)(6) of this section for certain rights to receive tangible property or services, paragraph (c)(8) of this section for an interest under a lease of tangible property, and paragraph (c)(13) of this section for certain rights granted by a governmental unit. See paragraph (b)(10) of this section for the treatment of franchises.)

(9) *Covenants not to compete and other similar arrangements.* Section 197 intangibles include any covenant not to compete, or agreement having substantially the same effect, entered into in connection with the direct or indirect acquisition of an interest in a trade or business or a substantial portion thereof. For purposes of this paragraph (b)(9), an acquisition may be made in the form of an asset acquisition (including a qualified stock purchase that is treated as a purchase of assets under section 338), a stock acquisition or redemption, and the acquisition or redemption of a partnership interest. An agreement requiring the performance of services for the acquiring taxpayer or the provision of property or its use to the acquiring taxpayer does not have substantially the same effect as a covenant not to compete to the extent that the amount paid under the agreement represents reasonable compensation for the services actually rendered or for the property or use of the property actually provided.

(10) *Franchises, trademarks, and trade names*—(i) Section 197 intangibles include any franchise, trademark, or trade name. The term *franchise* has the meaning given in section 1253(b)(1) and includes any agreement that provides one of the parties to the agreement with the

right to distribute, sell, or provide goods, services, or facilities, within a specified area. The term *trademark* includes any word, name, symbol, or device, or any combination thereof, adopted and used to identify goods or services and distinguish them from those provided by others. The term *trade name* includes any name used to identify or designate a particular trade or business or the name or title used by a person or organization engaged in a trade or business. A license, permit, or other right granted by a governmental unit is a franchise if it otherwise meets the definition of a franchise. A trademark or trade name includes any trademark or trade name arising under statute or applicable common law, and any similar right granted by contract. The renewal of a franchise, trademark, or trade name is treated as an acquisition of the franchise, trademark, or trade name.

(ii) Notwithstanding the definitions provided in paragraph (b)(10)(i) of this section, any amount that is paid or incurred on account of a transfer, sale, or other disposition of a franchise, trademark, or trade name and that is subject to section 1253(d)(1) is not included in the basis of a section 197 intangible. (See paragraph (g)(6) of this section.)

(11) *Contracts for the use of, and term interests in, section 197 intangibles.* Section 197 intangibles include any right under a license, contract, or other arrangement providing for the use of property that would be a section 197 intangible under any provision of this paragraph (b) (including this paragraph (b)(11)) after giving effect to all of the exceptions provided in paragraph (c) of this section. Section 197 intangibles also include any term interest (whether outright or in trust) in such property.

(12) *Other similar items.* Section 197 intangibles include any other intangible property that is similar in all material respects to the property specifically described in section 197(d)(1)(C)(i) through (v) and paragraphs (b)(3) through (7) of this section. (See paragraph (g)(5) of this section for special rules regarding certain reinsurance transactions.)

(c) *Section 197 intangibles; exceptions.* The term *section 197 intangible* does not include property described in section 197(e). The following rules and definitions provide guidance concerning property to which the exceptions apply:

(1) *Interests in a corporation, partnership, trust, or estate.* Section 197 intangibles do not include an interest in a corporation, partnership, trust, or estate. Thus, for example, amortization under section 197 is not available for the cost of acquiring stock, partnership interests, or interests in a trust or estate, whether or not the interests

Reg. § 1.197-2(c)(1)

are regularly traded on an established market. (See paragraph (g)(3) of this section for special rules applicable to property of a partnership when a section 754 election is in effect for the partnership.)

(2) *Interests under certain financial contracts.* Section 197 intangibles do not include an interest under an existing futures contract, foreign currency contract, notional principal contract, interest rate swap, or other similar financial contract, whether or not the interest is regularly traded on an established market. However, this exception does not apply to an interest under a mortgage servicing contract, credit card servicing contract, or other contract to service another person's indebtedness, or an interest under an assumption reinsurance contract. (See paragraph (g)(5) of this section for the treatment of assumption reinsurance contracts. See paragraph (c)(11) of this section and § 1.167(a)-14(d) for the treatment of mortgage servicing rights.)

(3) *Interests in land.* Section 197 intangibles do not include any interest in land. For this purpose, an interest in land includes a fee interest, life estate, remainder, easement, mineral right, timber right, grazing right, riparian right, air right, zoning variance, and any other similar right, such as a farm allotment, quota for farm commodities, or crop acreage base. An interest in land does not include an airport landing or takeoff right, a regulated airline route, or a franchise to provide cable television service. The cost of acquiring a license, permit, or other land improvement right, such as a building construction or use permit, is taken into account in the same manner as the underlying improvement.

(4) *Certain computer software*—(i) *Publicly available.* Section 197 intangibles do not include any interest in computer software that is (or has been) readily available to the general public on similar terms, is subject to a nonexclusive license, and has not been substantially modified. Computer software will be treated as readily available to the general public if the software may be obtained on substantially the same terms by a significant number of persons that would reasonably be expected to use the software. This requirement can be met even though the software is not available through a system of retail distribution. Computer software will not be considered to have been substantially modified if the cost of all modifications to the version of the software that is readily available to the general public does not exceed the greater of 25 percent of the price at which the unmodified version of the software is readily available to the general public or $2,000. For the purpose of determining whether computer software has been substantially modified—

(A) Integrated programs acquired in a package from a single source are treated as a single computer program; and

(B) Any cost incurred to install the computer software on a system is not treated as a cost of the software. However, the costs for customization, such as tailoring to a user's specifications (other than embedded programming options) are costs of modifying the software.

(ii) *Not acquired as part of trade or business.* Section 197 intangibles do not include an interest in computer software that is not acquired as part of a purchase of a trade or business.

(iii) *Other exceptions.* For other exceptions applicable to computer software, see paragraph (a)(3) of this section (relating to otherwise deductible amounts) and paragraph (g)(7) of this section (relating to amounts properly taken into account in determining the cost of property that is not a section 197 intangible).

(iv) *Computer software defined.* For purposes of this section, computer software is any program or routine (that is, any sequence of machine-readable code) that is designed to cause a computer to perform a desired function or set of functions, and the documentation required to describe and maintain that program or routine. It includes all forms and media in which the software is contained, whether written, magnetic, or otherwise. Computer programs of all classes, for example, operating systems, executive systems, monitors, compilers and translators, assembly routines, and utility programs as well as application programs, are included. Computer software also includes any incidental and ancillary rights that are necessary to effect the acquisition of the title to, the ownership of, or the right to use the computer software, and that are used only in connection with that specific computer software. Such incidental and ancillary rights are not included in the definition of trademark or trade name under paragraph (b)(10)(i) of this section. For example, a trademark or trade name that is ancillary to the ownership or use of a specific computer software program in the taxpayer's trade or business and is not acquired for the purpose of marketing the computer software is included in the definition of computer software and is not included in the definition of trademark or trade name. Computer software does not include any data or information base described in paragraph (b)(4) of this section unless the data base or item is in the public domain and is incidental to a computer program. For this purpose, a copyrighted or proprietary data or information base is treated as in the public domain if its availability through the computer program does not contribute significantly to the cost of the program. For example, if a word-processing program includes a dictionary feature used to spell-check a document or any portion thereof, the entire program (including the dictionary feature) is computer software regardless of the form in which the feature is maintained or stored.

(5) *Certain interests in films, sound recordings, video tapes, books, or other similar property.* Section 197 intangibles do not include any interest (including an interest as a licensee) in a film, sound recording, video tape, book, or other similar property (such as the right to broadcast or transmit a live event) if the interest is not acquired as part of a purchase of a trade or business. A film, sound recording, video tape, book, or other similar property includes any incidental and ancillary rights (such as a trademark or trade name) that are necessary to effect the acquisition of title to, the ownership of, or the right to use the property and are used only in connection with that property. Such incidental and ancillary rights are not included in the definition of trademark or trade name under paragraph (b)(10)(i) of this section. For purposes of this paragraph (c)(5), computer software (as defined in paragraph (c)(4)(iv) of this section) is not treated as other property similar to a film, sound recording, video tape, or book. (See section 167 for amortization of excluded intangible property or interests.)

(6) *Certain rights to receive tangible property or services.* Section 197 intangibles do not include any right to receive tangible property or services under a contract or from a governmental unit if the right is not acquired as part of a purchase of a trade or business. Any right that is described in the preceding sentence is not treated as a section 197 intangible even though the right is also described in section 197(d)(1)(D) and paragraph (b)(8) of this section (relating to certain governmental licenses, permits, and other rights) and even though the right fails to meet one or more of the requirements of paragraph (c)(13) of this section (relating to certain rights of fixed duration or amount). (See § 1.167(a)-14(c)(1) and (3) for applicable rules.)

(7) *Certain interests in patents or copyrights.* Section 197 intangibles do not include any interest (including an interest as a licensee) in a patent, patent application, or copyright that is not acquired as part of a purchase of a trade or business. A patent or copyright includes any incidental and ancillary rights (such as a trademark or trade name) that are necessary to effect the acquisition of title to, the ownership of, or the right to use the property and are used only in connection with that property. Such incidental and ancillary rights are not included in the definition of trademark or trade name under paragraph (b)(10)(i) of this section. (See § 1.167(a)-14(c)(4) for applicable rules.)

(8) *Interests under leases of tangible property*—(i) *Interest as a lessor.* Section 197 intangibles do not include any interest as a lessor under an existing lease or sublease of tangible real or personal property. In addition, the cost of acquiring an interest as a lessor in connection with the acquisition of tangible property is taken into account as part of the cost of the tangible property. For example, if a taxpayer acquires a shopping center that is leased to tenants operating retail stores, any portion of the purchase price attributable to favorable lease terms is taken into account as part of the basis of the shopping center and in determining the depreciation deduction allowed with respect to the shopping center. (See section 167(c)(2).)

(ii) *Interest as a lessee.* Section 197 intangibles do not include any interest as a lessee under an existing lease of tangible real or personal property. For this purpose, an airline lease of an airport passenger or cargo gate is a lease of tangible property. The cost of acquiring such an interest is taken into account under section 178 and § 1.162-11(a). If an interest as a lessee under a lease of tangible property is acquired in a transaction with any other intangible property, a portion of the total purchase price may be allocable to the interest as a lessee based on all of the relevant facts and circumstances.

(9) *Interests under indebtedness*—(i) *In general.* Section 197 intangibles do not include any interest (whether as a creditor or debtor) under an indebtedness in existence when the interest was acquired. Thus, for example, the value attributable to the assumption of an indebtedness with a below-market interest rate is not amortizable under section 197. In addition, the premium paid for acquiring a debt instrument with an above-market interest rate is not amortizable under section 197. See section 171 for rules concerning the treatment of amortizable bond premium.

(ii) *Exceptions.* For purposes of this paragraph (c)(9), an interest under an existing indebtedness does not include the deposit base (and other similar items) of a financial institution. An interest under an existing indebtedness includes mortgage servicing rights, however, to the extent the rights are stripped coupons under section 1286.

(10) *Professional sports franchises.* Section 197 intangibles do not include any franchise to engage in professional baseball, basketball, football, or any other professional sport, and any item (even though otherwise qualifying as a section 197 intangible) acquired in connection with such a franchise.

(11) *Mortgage servicing rights.* Section 197 intangibles do not include any right described in

Reg. § 1.197-2(c)(11)

section 197(e)(7) (concerning rights to service indebtedness secured by residential real property that are not acquired as part of a purchase of a trade or business). (See § 1.167(a)-14(d) for applicable rules.)

(12) *Certain transaction costs.* Section 197 intangibles do not include any fees for professional services and any transaction costs incurred by parties to a transaction in which all or any portion of the gain or loss is not recognized under part III of subchapter C of the Internal Revenue Code.

(13) *Rights of fixed duration or amount*—(i) Section 197 intangibles do not include any right under a contract or any license, permit, or other right granted by a governmental unit if the right—

(A) Is acquired in the ordinary course of a trade or business (or an activity described in section 212) and not as part of a purchase of a trade or business;

(B) Is not described in section 197(d)(1)(A), (B), (E), or (F);

(C) Is not a customer-based intangible, a customer-related information base, or any other similar item; and

(D) Either—

(1) Has a fixed duration of less than 15 years; or

(2) Is fixed as to amount and the adjusted basis thereof is properly recoverable (without regard to this section) under a method similar to the unit-of-production method.

(ii) See § 1.167(a)-14(c)(2) and (3) for applicable rules.

(d) *Amortizable section 197 intangibles*—(1) *Definition.* Except as otherwise provided in this paragraph (d), the term *amortizable section 197 intangible* means any section 197 intangible acquired after August 10, 1993 (or after July 25, 1991, if a valid retroactive election under § 1.197-1T has been made), and held in connection with the conduct of a trade or business or an activity described in section 212.

(2) *Exception for self-created intangibles*—(i) *In general.* Except as provided in paragraph (d)(2)(iii) of this section, amortizable section 197 intangibles do not include any section 197 intangible created by the taxpayer (a self-created intangible).

(ii) *Created by the taxpayer*—(A) *Defined.* A section 197 intangible is created by the taxpayer to the extent the taxpayer makes payments or otherwise incurs costs for its creation, production, development, or improvement, whether the actual work is performed by the taxpayer or by another person under a contract with the taxpayer entered into before the contracted creation,

production, development, or improvement occurs. For example, a technological process developed specifically for a taxpayer under an arrangement with another person pursuant to which the taxpayer retains all rights to the process is created by the taxpayer.

(B) *Contracts for the use of intangibles.* A section 197 intangible is not a self-created intangible to the extent that it results from the entry into (or renewal of) a contract for the use of an existing section 197 intangible. Thus, for example, the exception for self-created intangibles does not apply to capitalized costs, such as legal and other professional fees, incurred by a licensee in connection with the entry into (or renewal of) a contract for the use of know-how or similar property.

(C) *Improvements and modifications.* If an existing section 197 intangible is improved or otherwise modified by the taxpayer or by another person under a contract with the taxpayer, the existing intangible and the capitalized costs (if any) of the improvements or other modifications are each treated as a separate section 197 intangible for purposes of this paragraph (d).

(iii) *Exceptions*—(A) The exception for self-created intangibles does not apply to any section 197 intangible described in section 197(d)(1)(D) (relating to licenses, permits or other rights granted by a governmental unit), 197(d)(1)(E) (relating to covenants not to compete), or 197(d)(1)(F) (relating to franchises, trademarks, and trade names). Thus, for example, capitalized costs incurred in the development, registration, or defense of a trademark or trade name do not qualify for the exception and are amortized over 15 years under section 197.

(B) The exception for self-created intangibles does not apply to any section 197 intangible created in connection with the purchase of a trade or business (as defined in paragraph (e) of this section).

(C) If a taxpayer disposes of a self-created intangible and subsequently reacquires the intangible in an acquisition described in paragraph (h)(5)(ii) of this section, the exception for self-created intangibles does not apply to the reacquired intangible.

(3) *Exception for property subject to anti-churning rules.* Amortizable section 197 intangibles do not include any property to which the anti-churning rules of section 197(f)(9) and paragraph (h) of this section apply.

(e) *Purchase of a trade or business.* Several of the exceptions in section 197 apply only to property that is not acquired in (or created in connection with) a transaction or series of related transactions involving the acquisition of assets constituting a trade or business or a substantial portion thereof. Property acquired in (or created in connection with) such a transaction or series of related transactions is referred to in this section as property acquired as part of (or created in connection with) a purchase of a trade or business. For purposes of section 197 and this section, the applicability of the limitation is determined under the following rules:

(1) *Goodwill or going concern value.* An asset or group of assets constitutes a trade or business or a substantial portion thereof if their use would constitute a trade or business under section 1060 (that is, if goodwill or going concern value could under any circumstances attach to the assets). See § 1.1060-1(b)(2). For this purpose, all the facts and circumstances, including any employee relationships that continue (or covenants not to compete that are entered into) as part of the transfer of the assets, are taken into account in determining whether goodwill or going concern value could attach to the assets.

(2) *Franchise, trademark, or trade name*—(i) *In general.* The acquisition of a franchise, trademark, or trade name constitutes the acquisition of a trade or business or a substantial portion thereof.

(ii) *Exceptions.* For purposes of this paragraph (e)(2)—

(A) A trademark or trade name is disregarded if it is included in computer software under paragraph (c)(4) of this section or in an interest in a film, sound recording, video tape, book, or other similar property under paragraph (c)(5) of this section;

(B) A franchise, trademark, or trade name is disregarded if its value is nominal or the taxpayer irrevocably disposes of it immediately after its acquisition; and

(C) The acquisition of a right or interest in a trademark or trade name is disregarded if the grant of the right or interest is not, under the principles of section 1253, a transfer of all substantial rights to such property or of an undivided interest in all substantial rights to such property.

(3) *Acquisitions to be included.* The assets acquired in a transaction (or series of related transactions) include only assets (including a beneficial or other indirect interest in assets where the interest is of a type described in paragraph (c)(1) of this section) acquired by the taxpayer and persons related to the taxpayer from another person and persons related to that other person. For purposes of this paragraph (e)(3), persons are related only if their relationship is described in section 267(b) or 707(b) or they are engaged in trades or businesses under common control within the meaning of section 41(f)(1).

(4) *Substantial portion.* The determination of whether acquired assets constitute a substantial portion of a trade or business is to be based on all of the facts and circumstances, including the nature and the amount of the assets acquired as well as the nature and amount of the assets retained by the transferor. The value of the assets acquired relative to the value of the assets retained by the transferor is not determinative of whether the acquired assets constitute a substantial portion of a trade or business.

(5) *Deemed asset purchases under section 338.* A qualified stock purchase that is treated as a purchase of assets under section 338 is treated as a transaction involving the acquisition of assets constituting a trade or business only if the direct acquisition of the assets of the corporation would have been treated as the acquisition of assets constituting a trade or business or a substantial portion thereof.

(6) *Mortgage servicing rights.* Mortgage servicing rights acquired in a transaction or series of related transactions are disregarded in determining for purposes of paragraph (c)(11) of this section whether the assets acquired in the transaction or transactions constitute a trade or business or substantial portion thereof.

(7) *Computer software acquired for internal use.* Computer software acquired in a transaction or series of related transactions solely for internal use in an existing trade or business is disregarded in determining for purposes of paragraph (c)(4) of this section whether the assets acquired in the transaction or series of related transactions constitute a trade or business or substantial portion thereof.

(f) *Computation of amortization deduction*—(1) *In general.* Except as provided in paragraph (f)(2) of this section, the amortization deduction allowable under section 197(a) is computed as follows:

(i) The basis of an amortizable section 197 intangible is amortized ratably over the 15-year period beginning on the later of—

(A) The first day of the month in which the property is acquired; or

(B) In the case of property held in connection with the conduct of a trade or business or in an activity described in section 212, the first day of the month in which the conduct of the trade or business or the activity begins.

(ii) Except as otherwise provided in this section, basis is determined under section 1011 and salvage value is disregarded.

(iii) Property is not eligible for amortization in the month of disposition.

Reg. § 1.197-2(f)(1)

(iv) The amortization deduction for a short taxable year is based on the number of months in the short taxable year.

(2) *Treatment of contingent amounts*—(i) *Amounts added to basis during 15-year period.* Any amount that is properly included in the basis of an amortizable section 197 intangible after the first month of the 15-year period described in paragraph (f)(1)(i) of this section and before the expiration of that period is amortized ratably over the remainder of the 15-year period. For this purpose, the remainder of the 15-year period begins on the first day of the month in which the basis increase occurs.

(ii) *Amounts becoming fixed after expiration of 15-year period.* Any amount that is not properly included in the basis of an amortizable section 197 intangible until after the expiration of the 15-year period described in paragraph (f)(1)(i) of this section is amortized in full immediately upon the inclusion of the amount in the basis of the intangible.

(iii) *Rules for including amounts in basis.* See § § 1.1275-4(c)(4) and 1.483-4(a) for rules governing the extent to which contingent amounts payable under a debt instrument given in consideration for the sale or exchange of an amortizable section 197 intangible are treated as payments of principal and the time at which the amount treated as principal is included in basis. See § 1.461-1(a)(1) and (2) for rules governing the time at which other contingent amounts are taken into account in determining the basis of an amortizable section 197 intangible.

(3) *Basis determinations for certain assets*—(i) *Covenants not to compete.* In the case of a covenant not to compete or other similar arrangement described in paragraph (b)(9) of this section (a covenant), the amount chargeable to capital account includes, except as provided in this paragraph (f)(3), all amounts that are required to be paid pursuant to the covenant, whether or not any such amount would be deductible under section 162 if the covenant were not a section 197 intangible.

(ii) *Contracts for the use of section 197 intangibles; acquired as part of a trade or business*—(A) *In general.* Except as provided in this paragraph (f)(3), any amount paid or incurred by the transferee on account of the transfer of a right or term interest described in paragraph (b)(11) of this section (relating to contracts for the use of, and term interests in, section 197 intangibles) by the owner of the property to which such right or interest relates and as part of a purchase of a trade or business is chargeable to capital account, whether or not such amount would be deductible under section 162 if the property were not a section 197 intangible.

(B) *Know-how and certain information base.* The amount chargeable to capital account with respect to a right or term interest described in paragraph (b)(11) of this section is determined without regard to the rule in paragraph (f)(3)(ii)(A) of this section if the right or interest relates to property (other than a customer-related information base) described in paragraph (b)(4) or (5) of this section and the acquiring taxpayer establishes that—

(*1*) The transfer of the right or interest is not, under the principles of section 1235, a transfer of all substantial rights to such property or of an individed interest in all substantial rights to such property; and

(*2*) The right or interest was transferred for an arm's-length consideration.

(iii) *Contracts for the use of section 197 intangibles; not acquired as part of a trade or business.* The transfer of a right or term interest described in paragraph (b)(11) of this section by the owner of the property to which such right or interest relates but not as part of a purchase of a trade or business will be closely scrutinized under the principles of section 1235 for purposes of determining whether the transfer is a sale or exchange and, accordingly, whether amounts paid on account of the transfer are chargeable to capital account. If under the principles of section 1235 the transaction is not a sale or exchange, amounts paid on account of the transfer are not chargeable to capital account under this paragraph (f)(3).

(iv) *Applicable rules*—(A) *Franchises, trademarks, and trade names.* For purposes of this paragraph (f)(3), section 197 intangibles described in paragraph (b)(11) of this section do not include any property that is also described in paragraph (b)(10) of this section (relating to franchises, trademarks, and trade names).

(B) *Certain amounts treated as payable under a debt instrument*—(*1*) *In general.* For purposes of applying any provision of the Internal Revenue Code to a person making payments of amounts that are otherwise chargeable to capital account under this paragraph (f)(3) and are payable after the acquisition of the section 197 intangible to which they relate, such amounts are treated as payable under a debt instrument given in consideration for the sale or exchange of the section 197 intangible.

(*2*) *Rights granted by governmental units.* For purposes of applying any provision of the Internal Revenue Code to any amounts that are otherwise chargeable to capital account with respect to a license, permit, or other right described in paragraph (b)(8) of this section (relating to rights granted by a governmental unit or agency or instrumentality thereof) and are payable after the acquisition of the section 197 intangible to which they relate, such amounts are treated, except as provided in paragraph (f)(4)(i) of this section (relating to renewal transactions), as payable under a debt instrument given in consideration for the sale or exchange of the section 197 intangible.

(3) *Treatment of other parties to transaction.* No person shall be treated as having sold, exchanged, or otherwise disposed of property in a transaction for purposes of any provision of the Internal Revenue Code solely by reason of the application of this paragraph (f)(3) to any other party to the transaction.

(4) *Basis determinations in certain transactions*—(i) *Certain renewal transactions.* The costs paid or incurred for the renewal of a franchise, trademark, or trade name or any license, permit, or other right granted by a governmental unit or an agency or instrumentality thereof are amortized over the 15-year period that begins with the month of renewal. Any costs paid or incurred for the issuance, or earlier renewal, continue to be taken into account over the remaining portion of the amortization period that began at the time of the issuance, or earlier renewal. Any amount paid or incurred for the protection, expansion, or defense of a trademark or trade name and chargeable to capital account is treated as an amount paid or incurred for a renewal.

(ii) *Transactions subject to section 338 or 1060.* In the case of a section 197 intangible deemed to have been acquired as the result of a qualified stock purchase within the meaning of section 338(d)(3), the basis shall be determined pursuant to section 338(b)(5) and the regulations thereunder. In the case of a section 197 intangible acquired in an applicable asset acquisition within the meaning of section 1060(c), the basis shall be determined pursuant to section 1060(a) and the regulations thereunder.

(iii) *Certain reinsurance transactions.* See paragraph (g)(5)(ii) of this section for special rules regarding the adjusted basis of an insurance contract acquired through an assumption reinsurance transaction.

(g) *Special rules*—* * *

(8) *Treatment of amortizable section 197 intangibles as depreciable property.* An amortizable section 197 intangible is treated as property of a character subject to the allowance for depreciation under section 167. Thus, for example, an amortizable section 197 intangible is not a capital asset for purposes of section 1221, but if used in a

trade or business and held for more than one year, gain or loss on its disposition generally qualifies as section 1231 gain or loss. Also, an amortizable section 197 intangible is section 1245 property and section 1239 applies to any gain recognized upon its sale or exchange between related persons (as defined in section 1239(b)).

* * *

(k) *Examples.* The following examples illustrate the application of this section:

Example 1. Advertising costs. (i) Q manufactures and sells consumer products through a series of wholesalers and distributors. In order to increase sales of its products by encouraging consumer loyalty to its products and to enhance the value of the goodwill, trademarks, and trade names of the business, Q advertises its products to the consuming public. It regularly incurs costs to develop radio, television, and print advertisements. These costs generally consist of employee costs and amounts paid to independent advertising agencies. Q also incurs costs to run these advertisements in the various media for which they were developed.

(ii) The advertising costs are not chargeable to capital account under paragraph (f)(3) of this section (relating to costs incurred for covenants not to compete, rights granted by governmental units, and contracts for the use of section 197 intangibles) and are currently deductible as ordinary and necessary expenses under section 162. Accordingly, under paragraph (a)(3) of this section, section 197 does not apply to these costs.

Example 2. Computer software. (i) X purchases all of the assets of an existing trade or business from Y. One of the assets acquired is all of Y's rights in certain computer software previously used by Y under the terms of a nonexclusive license from the software developer. The software was developed for use by manufacturers to maintain a comprehensive accounting system, including general and subsidiary ledgers, payroll, accounts receivable and payable, cash receipts and disbursements, fixed asset accounting, and inventory cost accounting and controls. The developer modified the software for use by Y at a cost of $1,000 and Y made additional modifications at a cost of $500. The developer does not maintain wholesale or retail outlets but markets the software directly to ultimate users. Y's license of the software is limited to an entity that is actively engaged in business as a manufacturer.

(ii) Notwithstanding these limitations, the software is considered to be readily available to the general public for purposes of paragraph (c)(4)(i) of this section. In addition, the software is not substantially modified because the cost of the modifications by the developer and Y to the

Reg. § 1.197-2(k)

version of the software that is readily available to the general public does not exceed $2,000. Accordingly, the software is not a section 197 intangible.

Example 3. Acquisition of software for internal use. (i) B, the owner and operator of a worldwide package-delivery service, purchases from S all rights to software developed by S. The software will be used by B for the sole purpose of improving its package-tracking operations. B does not purchase any other assets in the transaction or any related transaction.

(ii) Because B acquired the software solely for internal use, it is disregarded in determining for purposes of paragraph (c)(4)(ii) of this section whether the assets acquired in the transaction or series of related transactions constitute a trade or business or substantial portion thereof. Since no other assets were acquired, the software is not acquired as part of a purchase of a trade or business and under paragraph (c)(4)(ii) of this section is not a section 197 intangible.

Example 4. Governmental rights of fixed duration. (i) City M operates a municipal water system. In order to induce X to locate a new manufacturing business in the city, M grants X the right to purchase water for 16 years at a specified price.

(ii) The right granted by M is a right to receive tangible property or services described in section 197(e)(4)(B) and paragraph (c)(6) of this section and, thus, is not a section 197 intangible. This exclusion applies even though the right does not qualify for exclusion as a right of fixed duration or amount under section 197(e)(4)(D) and paragraph (c)(13) of this section because the duration exceeds 15 years and the right is not fixed as to amount. It is also immaterial that the right would not qualify for exclusion as a self-created intangible under section 197(c)(2) and paragraph (d)(2) of this section because it is granted by a governmental unit.

Example 5. Separate acquisition of franchise. (i) S is a franchiser of retail outlets for specialty coffees. G enters into a franchise agreement (within the meaning of section 1253(b)(1)) with S pursuant to which G is permitted to acquire and operate a store using the S trademark and trade name at the location specified in the agreement. G agrees to pay S $100,000 upon execution of the agreement and also agrees to pay, throughout the term of the franchise, additional amounts that are deductible under section 1253(d)(1). The agreement contains detailed specifications for the construction and operation of the business, but G is not required to purchase from S any of the materials necessary to construct the improvements at the location specified in the franchise agreement.

(ii) The franchise is a section 197 intangible within the meaning of paragraph (b)(10) of this section. The franchise does not qualify for the exclusion relating to self-created intangibles described in section 197(c)(2) and paragraph (d)(2) of this section because the franchise is described in section 197(d)(1)(F). In addition, because the acquisition of the franchise constitutes the acquisition of an interest in a trade or business or a substantial portion thereof, the franchise may not be excluded under section 197(e)(4). Thus, the franchise is an amortizable section 197 intangible, the basis of which must be recovered over a 15-year period. However, the amounts that are deductible under section 1253(d)(1) are not subject to the provisions of section 197 by reason of section 197(f)(4)(C) and paragraph (b)(10)(ii) of this section.

Example 6. Acquisition and amortization of covenant not to compete. (i) As part of the acquisition of a trade or business from C, B and C enter into an agreement containing a covenant not to compete. Under this agreement, C agrees that it will not compete with the business acquired by B within a prescribed geographical territory for a period of three years after the date on which the business is sold to B. In exchange for this agreement, B agrees to pay C $90,000 per year for each year in the term of the agreement. The agreement further provides that, in the event of a breach by C of his obligations under the agreement, B may terminate the agreement, cease making any of the payments due thereafter, and pursue any other legal or equitable remedies available under applicable law. The amounts payable to C under the agreement are not contingent payments for purposes of § 1.1275-4. The present fair market value of B's rights under the agreement is $225,000. The aggregate consideration paid excluding any amount treated as interest or original issue discount under applicable provisions of the Internal Revenue Code, for all assets acquired in the transaction (including the covenant not to compete) exceeds the sum of the amount of Class I assets and the aggregate fair market value of all Class II, Class III, Class IV, Class V, and Class VI assets by $50,000. See § 1.338-6(b) for rules for determining the assets in each class.

(ii) Because the covenant is acquired in an applicable asset acquisition (within the meaning of section 1060(c)), paragraph (f)(4)(ii) of this section applies and the basis of B in the covenant is determined pursuant to section 1060(a) and the regulations thereunder. Under §§ 1.1060-1(c)(2) and 1.338-6(c)(1), B's basis in the covenant cannot exceed its fair market value. Thus, B's basis in the covenant immediately after the acquisition is $225,000. This basis is amortized ratably over the 15-year period beginning on the first day of the

Reg. § 1.197-2(k)

month in which the agreement is entered into. All of the remaining consideration after allocation to the covenant and other Class VI assets, ($50,000) is allocated to Class VII assets (goodwill and going concern value). See § § 1.1060-1(c)(2) and 1.338-6(b).

Example 7. Stand-alone license of technology. (i) X is a manufacturer of consumer goods that does business throughout the world through subsidiary corporations organized under the laws of each country in which business is conducted. X licenses to Y, its subsidiary organized and conducting business in Country K, all of the patents, formulas, designs, and know-how necessary for Y to manufacture the same products that X manufactures in the United States. Assume that the license is not considered a sale or exchange under the principles of section 1235. The license is for a term of 18 years, and there are no facts to indicate that the license does not have a fixed duration. Y agrees to pay X a royalty equal to a specified, fixed percentage of the revenues obtained from selling products manufactured using the licensed technology. Assume that the royalty is reasonable and is not subject to adjustment under section 482. The license is not entered into in connection with any other transaction. Y incurs capitalized costs in connection with entering into the license.

(ii) The license is a contract for the use of a section 197 intangible within the meaning of paragraph (b)(11) of this section. It does not qualify for the exception in section 197(e)(4)(D) and paragraph (c)(13) of this section (relating to rights of fixed duration or amount) because it does not have a term of less than 15 years, and the other exceptions in section 197(e) and paragraph (c) of this section are also inapplicable. Accordingly, the license is a section 197 intangible.

(iii) The license is not acquired as part of a purchase of a trade or business. Thus, under paragraph (f)(3)(iii) of this section, the license will be closely scrutinized under the principles of section 1235 for purposes of determining whether the transfer is a sale or exchange and, accordingly, whether the payments under the license are chargeable to capital account. Because the license

is not a sale or exchange under the principles of section 1235, the royalty payments are not chargeable to capital account for purposes section 197. The capitalized costs of entering into the license are not within the exception under paragraph (d)(2) of this section for self-created intangibles, and thus are amortized under section 197.

Example 8. License of technology and trademarks. (i) The facts are the same as in *Example 7,* except that the license also includes the use of the trademarks and trade names that X uses to manufacture and distribute its products in the United States. Assume that under the principles of section 1253 the transfer is not a sale or exchange of the trademarks and trade names or an undivided interest therein and that the royalty payments are described in section 1253(d)(1)(B).

(ii) As in *Example 7*, the license is a section 197 intangible. Although the license conveys an interest in X's trademarks and trade names to Y, the transfer of the interest is disregarded for purposes of paragraph (e)(2) of this section unless the transfer is considered a sale or exchange of the trademarks and trade names or an undivided interest therein. Accordingly, the licensing of the technology and the trademarks and trade names is not treated as part of a purchase of a trade or business under paragraph (e)(2) of this section.

(iii) Because the technology license is not part of the purchase of a trade or business, it is treated in the manner described in *Example 7*. The royalty payments for the use of the trademarks and trade names are deductible under section 1253(d)(1) and, under section 197(f)(4)(C) and paragraph (b)(10)(ii) of this section, are not chargeable to capital account for purposes of section 197. The capitalized costs of entering into the license are treated in the same manner as in example 7.

* * *

[Reg. § 1.197-2.]

☐ [*T.D.* 8865, 1-20-2000 (*corrected 3-27-2000 and* 10-11-2000). *Amended by T.D.* 8907, 11-17-2000 *and T.D.* 8940, 2-12-2001.]

Additional Itemized Deductions for Individuals

§ 1.212-1. Nontrade or nonbusiness expenses.—(a) An expense may be deducted under section 212 only if—

(1) It has been paid or incurred by the taxpayer during the taxable year (i) for the production or collection of income which, if and when realized, will be required to be included in income for Federal income tax purposes, or (ii) for the management, conservation, or maintenance of property held for the production of such income,

or (iii) in connection with the determination, collection, or refund of any tax; and

(2) It is an ordinary and necessary expense for any of the purposes stated in subparagraph (1) of this paragraph.

(b) The term "income" for the purpose of section 212 includes not merely income of the taxable year but also income which the taxpayer has realized in a prior taxable year or may realize in subsequent taxable years; and is not confined to recurring income but applies as well to gains from the disposition of property. For example, if defaulted bonds, the interest from which if received would be includible in income, are purchased with the expectation of realizing capital gain on their resale, even though no current yield thereon is anticipated, ordinary and necessary expenses thereafter paid or incurred in connection with such bonds are deductible. Similarly, ordinary and necessary expenses paid or incurred in the management, conservation, or maintenance of a building devoted to rental purposes are deductible notwithstanding that there is actually no income therefrom in the taxable year, and regardless of the manner in which or the purpose for which the property in question was acquired. Expenses paid or incurred in managing, conserving, or maintaining property held for investment may be deductible under section 212 even though the property is not currently productive and there is no likelihood that the property will be sold at a profit or will otherwise be productive of income and even though the property is held merely to minimize a loss with respect thereto.

(c) In the case of taxable years beginning before January 1, 1970, expenses of carrying on transactions which do not constitute a trade or business of the taxpayer and are not carried on for the production or collection of income or for the management, conservation, or maintenance of property held for the production of income, but which are carried on primarily as a sport, hobby, or recreation are not allowable as nontrade or nonbusiness expenses. The question whether or not a transaction is carried on primarily for the production of income or for the management, conservation, or maintenance of property held for the production or collection of income, rather than primarily as a sport, hobby, or recreation, is not to be determined solely from the intention of the taxpayer but rather from all the circumstances of the case. For example, consideration will be given to the record of prior gain or loss of the taxpayer in the activity, the relation between the type of activity and the principal occupation of the taxpayer, and the uses to which the property or what it produces is put by the taxpayer. For provisions relating to activities not engaged in for profit applicable to taxable years beginning after December 31, 1969, see section 183 and the regulations thereunder.

(d) Expenses, to be deductible under section 212, must be "ordinary and necessary". Thus, such expenses must be reasonable in amount and must bear a reasonable and proximate relation to the production or collection of taxable income or to the management, conservation, or maintenance of property held for the production of income.

(e) A deduction under section 212 is subject to the restrictions and limitations in part IX (section 261 and following), subchapter B, chapter 1 of the Code, relating to items not deductible. Thus, no deduction is allowable under section 212 for any amount allocable to the production or collection of one or more classes of income which are not includible in gross income, or for any amount allocable to the management, conservation, or maintenance of property held for the production of income which is not included in gross income. See section 265. Nor does section 212 allow the deduction of any expenses which are disallowed by any of the provisions of subtitle A of the Code, even though such expenses may be paid or incurred for one of the purposes specified in section 212.

(f) Among expenditures not allowable as deductions under section 212 are the following: Commuter's expenses; expenses of taking special courses or training; expenses for improving personal appearance; the cost of rental of a safe-deposit box for storing jewelry and other personal effects; expenses such as those paid or incurred in seeking employment or in placing oneself in a position to begin rendering personal services for compensation, campaign expenses of a candidate for public office, bar examination fees and other expenses paid or incurred in securing admission to the bar, and corresponding fees and expenses paid or incurred by physicians, dentists, accountants, and other taxpayers for securing the right to practice their respective professions. See, however, section 162 and the regulations thereunder.

(g) Fees for services of investment counsel, custodial fees, clerical help, office rent, and similar expenses paid or incurred by a taxpayer in connection with investments held by him are deductible under section 212 only if (1) they are paid or incurred by the taxpayer for the production or collection of income or for the management, conservation, or maintenance of investments held by him for the production of income; and (2) they are ordinary and necessary under all the circumstances, having regard to the type of investment and to the relation of the taxpayer to such investment.

(h) Ordinary and necessary expenses paid or incurred in connection with the management, conservation, or maintenance of property held for use as a residence by the taxpayer are not deductible. However, ordinary and necessary expenses paid or incurred in connection with the management, conservation, or maintenance of property held by the taxpayer as rental property are deductible even though such property was formerly held by the taxpayer for use as a home.

Reg. § 1.212-1(c)

(i) Reasonable amounts paid or incurred by the fiduciary of an estate or trust on account of administration expenses, including fiduciaries' fees and expenses of litigation, which are ordinary and necessary in connection with the performance of the duties of administration are deductible under section 212 notwithstanding that the estate or trust is not engaged in a trade or business, except to the extent that such expenses are allocable to the production or collection of tax-exempt income. But see section 642(g) and the regulations thereunder for disallowance of such deductions to an estate where such items are allowed as a deduction under section 2053 or 2054 in computing the net estate subject to the estate tax.

(j) Reasonable amounts paid or incurred for the services of a guardian or committee for a ward or minor, and other expenses of guardians and committees which are ordinary and necessary, in connection with the production or collection of income inuring to the ward or minor, or in connection with the management, conservation, or maintenance of property, held for the production of income, belonging to the ward or minor, are deductible.

(k) Expenses paid or incurred in defending or perfecting title to property, in recovering property (other than investment property and amounts of income which, if and when recovered, must be included in gross income), or in developing or improving property, constitute a part of the cost of the property and are not deductible expenses. Attorneys' fees paid in a suit to quiet title to lands are not deductible; but if the suit is also to collect accrued rents thereon, that portion of such fees is deductible which is properly allocable to the services rendered in collecting such rents. Expenses paid or incurred in protecting or asserting one's rights to property of a decedent as heir or legatee, or as beneficiary under a testamentary trust, are not deductible.

(l) Expenses paid or incurred by an individual in connection with the determination, collection, or refund of any tax, whether the taxing authority be Federal, State, or municipal, and whether the tax be income, estate, gift, property, or any other tax, are deductible. Thus, expenses paid or incurred by a taxpayer for tax counsel or expenses paid or incurred in connection with the preparation of his tax returns or in connection with any proceedings involved in determining the extent of tax liability or in contesting his tax liability are deductible.

(m) An expense (not otherwise deductible) paid or incurred by an individual in determining or contesting a liability asserted against him does not become deductible by reason of the fact that property held by him for the production of income may be required to be used or sold for the purpose of satisfying such liability.

(n) Capital expenditures are not allowable as nontrade or nonbusiness expenses. The deduction of an item otherwise allowable under section 212 will not be disallowed simply because the taxpayer was entitled under subtitle A of the Code to treat such item as a capital expenditure, rather than to deduct it as an expense. For example, see section 266. Where, however, the item may properly be treated only as a capital expenditure or where it was properly so treated under an option granted in subtitle A, no deduction is allowable under section 212; and this is true regardless of whether any basis adjustment is allowed under any other provision of the Code.

(o) The provisions of section 212 are not intended in any way to disallow expenses which would otherwise be allowable under section 162 and the regulations thereunder. Double deductions are not permitted. Amounts deducted under one provision of the Internal Revenue Code of 1954 cannot again be deducted under any other provision thereof.

(p) *Frustration of public policy.* The deduction of a payment will be disallowed under section 212 if the payment is of a type for which a deduction would be disallowed under section 162(c), (f), or (g) and the regulations thereunder in the case of a business expense. [Reg. § 1.212-1.]

☐ [*T.D. 6279, 12-13-57. Amended by T.D. 7198, 7-12-72 and T.D. 7345, 2-19-75.*]

§ 1.213-1. Medical, dental, etc., expenses.— (a) *Allowance of deduction.* (1) Section 213 permits a deduction of payments for certain medical expenses (including expenses for medicine and drugs). Except as provided in paragraph (d) of this section (relating to special rule for decedents) a deduction is allowable only to individuals and only with respect to medical expenses actually paid during the taxable year, regardless of when the incident or event which occasioned the expenses occurred and regardless of the method of accounting employed by the taxpayer in making his income tax return. Thus, if the medical expenses are incurred but not paid during the taxable year, no deduction for such expenses shall be allowed for such year.

* * *

(e) *Definitions*—(1) *General.* (i) The term "medical care" includes the diagnosis, cure, mitigation, treatment, or prevention of disease. Expenses paid for "medical care" shall include those paid for the purpose of affecting any structure or function of the body or for transportation primarily for and essential to medical care. See subparagraph (4) of this paragraph for provisions relating to medical insurance.

Reg. § 1.213-1(e)(1)

(ii) Amounts paid for operations or treatments affecting any portion of the body, including obstetrical expenses and expenses of therapy or X-ray treatments, are deemed to be for the purpose of affecting any structure or function of the body and are therefore paid for medical care. Amounts expended for illegal operations or treatments are not deductible. Deductions for expenditures for medical care allowable under section 213 will be confined strictly to expenses incurred primarily for the prevention or alleviation of a physical or mental defect or illness. Thus, payments for the following are payments for medical care: Hospital services, nursing services (including nurses' board where paid by the taxpayer), medical, laboratory, surgical, dental and other diagnostic and healing services, X-rays, medicine and drugs (as defined in subparagraph (2) of this paragraph, subject to the 1 percent limitation in paragraph (b) of this section), artificial teeth or limbs, and ambulance hire. However, an expenditure which is merely beneficial to the general health of an individual, such as an expenditure for a vacation, is not an expenditure for medical care.

(iii) Capital expenditures are generally not deductible for Federal income tax purposes. See section 263 and the regulations thereunder. However, an expenditure which otherwise qualifies as a medical expense under section 213 shall not be disqualified merely because it is a capital expenditure. For purposes of section 213 and this paragraph, a capital expenditure made by the taxpayer may qualify as a medical expense, if it has as its primary purpose the medical care (as defined in subdivisions (i) and (ii) of this subparagraph) of the taxpayer, his spouse, or his dependent. Thus, a capital expenditure which is related only to the sick person and is not related to permanent improvement or betterment of property, if it otherwise qualifies as an expenditure for medical care, shall be deductible; for example, an expenditure for eye glasses, a seeing eye dog, artificial teeth and limbs, a wheel chair, crutches, an inclinator or an air conditioner which is detachable from the property and purchased only for the use of a sick person, etc. Moreover, a capital expenditure for permanent improvement or betterment of property which would not ordinarily be for the purpose of medical care (within the meaning of this paragraph) may, nevertheless, qualify as a medical expense to the extent that the expenditure exceeds the increase in the value of the related property, if the particular expenditure is related directly to medical care. Such a situation could arise, for example, where a taxpayer is advised by a physician to install an elevator in his residence so that the taxpayer's wife who is afflicted with heart disease will not be required to climb stairs. If the cost of installing

the elevator is $1,000 and the increase in the value of the residence is determined to be only $700, the difference of $300, which is the amount in excess of the value enhancement, is deductible as a medical expense. If, however, by reason of this expenditure, it is determined that the value of the residence has not been increased, the entire cost of installing the elevator would qualify as a medical expense. Expenditures made for the operation or maintenance of a capital asset are likewise deductible medical expenses if they have as their primary purpose the medical care (as defined in subdivisions (i) and (ii) of this subparagraph) of the taxpayer, his spouse, or his dependent. Normally, if a capital expenditure qualifies as a medical expense, expenditures for the operation or maintenance of the capital asset would also qualify provided that the medical reason for the capital expenditure still exists. The entire amount of such operation and maintenance expenditures qualifies, even if none or only a portion of the original cost of the capital asset itself qualified.

(iv) Expenses paid for transportation primarily for and essential to the rendition of the medical care are expenses paid for medical care. However, an amount allowable as a deduction for "transportation primarily for and essential to medical care" shall not include the cost of any meals and lodging while away from home receiving medical treatment. For example, if a doctor prescribes that a taxpayer go to a warm climate in order to alleviate a specific chronic ailment, the cost of meals and lodging while there would not be deductible. On the other hand, if the travel is undertaken merely for the general improvement of a taxpayer's health, neither the cost of transportation nor the cost of meals and lodging would be deductible. If a doctor prescribes an operation or other medical care, and the taxpayer chooses for purely personal considerations to travel to another locality (such as a resort area) for the operation or the other medical care, neither the cost of transportation nor the cost of meals and lodging (except where paid as part of a hospital bill) is deductible.

(v) The cost of in-patient hospital care (including the cost of meals and lodging therein) is an expenditure for medical care. The extent to which expenses for care in an institution other than a hospital shall constitute medical care is primarily a question of fact which depends upon the condition of the individual and the nature of the services he receives (rather than the nature of the institution). A private establishment which is regularly engaged in providing the types of care or services outlined in this subdivision shall be considered an institution for purposes of the rules

Reg. § 1.213-1(e)(1)

provided herein. In general, the following rules will be applied:

(a) Where an individual is in an institution because his condition is such that the availability of medical care (as defined in subdivisions (i) and (ii) of this subparagraph) in such institution is a principal reason for his presence there, and meals and lodging are furnished as a necessary incident to such care, the entire cost of medical care and meals and lodging at the institution, which are furnished while the individual requires continual medical care, shall constitute an expense for medical care. For example, medical care includes the entire cost of institutional care for a person who is mentally ill and unsafe when left alone. While ordinary education is not medical care, the cost of medical care includes the cost of attending a special school for a mentally or physically handicapped individual, if his condition is such that the resources of the institution for alleviating such mental or physical handicap are a principal reason for his presence there. In such a case, the cost of attending such a special school will include the cost of meals and lodging, if supplied, and the cost of ordinary education furnished which is incidental to the special services furnished by the school. Thus, the cost of medical care includes the cost of attending a special school designed to compensate for or overcome a physical handicap, in order to qualify the individual for future normal education or for normal living, such as a school for the teaching of braille or lip reading. Similarly, the cost of care and supervision, or of treatment and training, of a mentally retarded or physically handicapped individual at an institution is within the meaning of the term "medical care."

(b) Where an individual is in an institution, and his condition is such that the availability of medical care in such institution is not a principal reason for his presence there, only that part of the cost of care in the institution as is attributable to medical care (as defined in subdivisions (i) and (ii) of this subparagraph) shall be considered as a cost of medical care; meals and lodging at the institution in such a case are not considered a cost of medical care for purposes of this section. For example, an individual is in a home for the aged for personal or family considerations and not because he requires medical or nursing attention. In such case, medical care consists only of that part of the cost for care in the home which is attributable to medical care or nursing attention furnished to him; his meals and lodging at the home are not considered a cost of medical care.

(c) It is immaterial for purposes of this subdivision whether the medical care is furnished in a Federal or State institution or in a private institution.

(vi) See section 262 and the regulations thereunder for disallowance of deduction for personal, living, and family expenses not falling within the definition of medical care.

* * *

[Reg. § 1.213-1.]

☐ [*T.D.* 6279, 12-13-57. *Amended by T.D.* 6451, 2-3-60; *T.D.* 6604, 7-23-62; *T.D.* 6661, 6-26-63; *T.D.* 6761, 9-28-64; *T.D.* 6946, 2-12-68; *T.D.* 6985, 12-26-68; *T.D.* 7114, 5-17-71; *T.D.* 7317, 6-27-74 and T.D. 7643, 8-27-79.]

§ 1.217-2. Deduction for moving expenses paid or incurred in taxable years beginning after December 31, 1969.—(a) *Allowance of deduction*—(1) *In general.* Section 217(a) allows a deduction from gross income for moving expenses paid or incurred by the taxpayer during the taxable year in connection with his commencement of work as an employee or as a self-employed individual at a new principal place of work. For purposes of this section, amounts are considered as being paid or incurred by an individual whether goods or services are furnished to the taxpayer directly (by an employer, a client, a customer, or similar person) or indirectly (paid to a third party on behalf of the taxpayer by an employer, a client, a customer, or similar person). A cash basis taxpayer will treat moving expenses as being paid for purposes of section 217 and this section in the year in which the taxpayer is considered to have received such payment under section 82 and § 1.82-1. No deduction is allowable under section 162 for any expenses incurred by the taxpayer in connection with moving from one residence to another residence unless such expenses are deductible under section 162 without regard to such change in residence. To qualify for the deduction under section 217 the expenses must meet the definition of the term "moving expenses" provided in section 217(b) and the taxpayer must meet the conditions set forth in section 217(c). The term "employee" as used in this section has the same meaning as in § 31.3401(c)-1 of this chapter (Employment Tax Regulations). The term "self-employed individual" as used in this section is defined in paragraph (f)(1) of this section.

(2) *Expenses paid in a taxable year other than the taxable year in which reimbursement representing such expenses is received.* In general, moving expenses are deductible in the year paid or incurred. If a taxpayer who uses the cash receipts and disbursements method of accounting receives reimbursement for a moving expense in a taxable year other than the taxable year the taxpayer pays such expense, he may elect to deduct

Reg. § 1.217-2(a)(2)

such expense in the taxable year that he receives such reimbursement, rather than the taxable year when he paid such expense in any case where—

(i) The expense is paid in a taxable year prior to the taxable year in which the reimbursement is received, or

(ii) The expense is paid in the taxable year immediately following the taxable year in which the reimbursement is received, provided that such expense is paid on or before the due date prescribed for filing the return (determined with regard to any extension of time for such filing) for the taxable year in which the reimbursement is received.

An election to deduct moving expenses in the taxable year that the reimbursement is received shall be made by claiming the deduction on the return, amended return, or claim for refund for the taxable year in which the reimbursement is received.

(3) *Commencement of work.* (i) To be deductible, the moving expenses must be paid or incurred by the taxpayer in connection with his commencement of work at a new principal place of work (see paragraph (c)(3) of this section for a discussion of the term "principal place of work"). Except for those expenses described in section 217(b)(1)(C) and (D) it is not necessary for the taxpayer to have made arrangements to work prior to his moving to a new location; however, a deduction is not allowable unless employment or self-employment actually does occur. The term "commencement" includes (*a*) the beginning of work by a taxpayer as an employee or as a self-employed individual for the first time or after a substantial period of unemployment or part-time employment, (*b*) the beginning of work by a taxpayer for a different employer or in the case of a self-employed individual in a new trade or business, or (*c*) the beginning of work by a taxpayer for the same employer or in the case of a self-employed individual in the same trade or business at a new location. To qualify as being in connection with the commencement of work, the move must bear a reasonable proximity both in time and place to such commencement at the new principal place of work. In general, moving expenses incurred within one year of the date of the commencement of work are considered to be reasonably proximate in time to such commencement. Moving expenses incurred after the 1-year period may be considered reasonably proximate in time if it can be shown that circumstances existed which prevented the taxpayer from incurring the expenses of moving within the 1-year period allowed. Whether circumstances existed which prevented the taxpayer from incurring the expenses of moving within the period allowed is dependent

upon the facts and circumstances of each case. The length of the delay and the fact that the taxpayer may have incurred part of the expenses of the move within the 1-year period allowed shall be taken into account in determining whether expenses incurred after such period are allowable. In general, a move is not considered to be reasonably proximate in place to the commencement of work at the new principal place of work where the distance between the taxpayer's new residence and his new principal place of work exceeds the distance between his former residence and his new principal place of work. A move to a new residence which does not satisfy this test may, however, be considered reasonably proximate in place to the commencement of work if the taxpayer can demonstrate, for example, that he is required to live at such residence as a condition of employment or that living at such residence will result in an actual decrease in commuting time or expense. For example, assume that in 1977 A is transferred by his employer to a new principal place of work and the distance between his former residence and his new principal place of work is 35 miles greater than was the distance between his former residence and his former principal place of work. However, the distance between his new residence and his new principal place of work is 10 miles greater than was the distance between his former residence and his new principal place of work. Although the minimum distance requirement of section 217(c)(1) is met the expenses of moving to the new residence are not considered as incurred in connection with A's commencement of work at his new principal place of work since the new residence is not proximate in place to the new place of work. If, however, A can demonstrate, for example, that he is required to live at such new residence as a condition of employment or if living at such new residence will result in an actual decrease in commuting time or expense, the expenses of the move may be considered as incurred in connection with A's commencement of work at his new principal place of work.

(ii) The provisions of subdivision (i) of this subparagraph may be illustrated by the following examples:

Example (1). Assume that A is transferred by his employer from Boston, Massachusetts, to Washington, D.C. A moves to a new residence in Washington, D.C., and commences to work on February 1, 1971. A's wife and his two children remain in Boston until June 1972 in order to allow A's children to complete their grade school education in Boston. On June 1, 1972, A sells his home in Boston and his wife and children move to the new residence in Washington, D.C. The expenses incurred on June 1, 1972, in selling the old residence and in moving A's family, their household

Reg. § 1.217-2(a)(3)

goods, and personal effects to the new residence in Washington are allowable as a deduction although they were incurred 16 months after the date of the commencement of work by A since A has moved to and established a new residence in Washington, D.C., and thus incurred part of the total expenses of the move prior to the expiration of the 1-year period.

Example (2). Assume that A is transferred by his employer from Washington, D.C., to Baltimore, Maryland. A commences work on January 1, 1971 in Baltimore. A commutes from his residence in Washington to his new principal place of work in Baltimore for a period of 18 months. On July 1, 1972, A decides to move to and establish a new residence in Baltimore. None of the moving expenses otherwise allowable under section 217 may be deducted since A neither incurred the expenses within 1 year nor has shown circumstances under which he was prevented from moving within such period.

(b) Definition of moving expenses— * * *

* * *

(3) Expenses of moving household goods and personal effects. Expenses of moving household goods and personal effects include expenses of transporting such goods and effects from the taxpayer's former residence to his new residence, and expenses of packing, crating, and in-transit storage and insurance for such goods and effects. Such expenses also include any costs of connecting or disconnecting utilities required because of the moving of household goods, appliances, or personal effects. Expenses of storing and insuring household goods and personal effects constitute in-transit expenses if incurred within any consecutive 30-day period after the day such goods and effects are moved from the taxpayer's former residence and prior to delivery at the taxpayer's new residence. Expenses paid or incurred in moving household goods and personal effects to the taxpayer's new residence from a place other than his former residence are allowable, but only to the extent that such expenses do not exceed the amount which would be allowable had such goods and effects been moved from the taxpayer's former residence. Expenses of moving household goods and personal effects do not include, for example, storage charges (other than in-transit), costs incurred in the acquisition of property, costs incurred and losses sustained in the disposition of property, penalties for breaking leases, mortgage penalties, expenses of refitting rugs or draperies, losses sustained on the disposal of memberships in clubs, tuition fees, and similar items. The above expenses may, however, be described in other provisions of section 217(b) and if so a deduction may

be allowed for them subject to the allowable dollar limitations.

(4) Expenses of traveling from the former residence to the new place of residence. Expenses of traveling from the former residence to the new place of residence include the cost of transportation and of meals and lodging en route (including the date of arrival) from the taxpayer's former residence to his new place of residence and lodging incurred in the general location of the former residence within 1 day after the former residence is no longer suitable for occupancy because of the removal of household goods and personal effects shall be considered as expenses of traveling for purposes of this subparagraph. The date of arrival is the day the taxpayer secures lodging at the new place of residence, even if on a temporary basis. Expenses of traveling from the taxpayer's former residence to his new place of residence do not include, for example, living or other expenses following the date of arrival at the new place of residence and while waiting to enter the new residence or waiting for household goods to arrive, expenses in connection with house or apartment hunting, living expenses preceding date of departure for the new place of residence (other than expenses of meals and lodging incurred within 1 day after the former residence is no longer suitable for occupancy), expenses of trips for purposes of selling property, expenses of trips to the former residence by the taxpayer pending the move by his family to the new place of residence, or any allowance for depreciation. The above expenses may, however, be described in other provisions of section 217(b) and if so a deduction may be allowed for them subject to the allowable dollar limitations. The deduction for traveling expenses from the former residence to the new place of residence is allowable for only one trip made by the taxpayer and members of his household; however, it is not necessary that the taxpayer and all members of his household travel together or at the same time.

* * *

(c) Conditions for allowance— * * *

* * *

(3) Principal place of work. (i) A taxpayer's "principal place of work" usually is the place where he spends most of his working time. The principal place of work of a taxpayer who performs services as an employee is his employer's plant, office, shop, store, or other property. The principal place of work of a taxpayer who is self-employed is the plant, office, shop, store, or other property which serves as the center of his business activities. However, a taxpayer may have a principal place of work even if there is no one place where he spends a substantial portion of his work-

ing time. In such case, the taxpayer's principal place of work is the place where his business activities are centered—for example, because he reports there for work, or is required either by his employer or the nature of his employment to "base" his employment there. Thus, while a member of a railroad crew may spend most of his working time aboard a train, his principal place of work is his home terminal, station, or other such central point where he reports in, checks out, or receives instructions. The principal place of work of a taxpayer who is employed by a number of employers on a relatively short-term basis and secures employment by means of a union hall system (such as a construction or building trades worker) would be the union hall.

(ii) Where a taxpayer has more than one employment (i.e., the taxpayer is employed by more than one employer, or is self-employed in more than one trade or business, or is an employee and is self-employed at any particular time) his principal place of work is determined with reference to his principal employment. The location of a taxpayer's principal place of work is a question of fact determined on the basis of the particular circumstances in each case. The more important factors to be considered in making this determination are (a) the total time ordinarily spent by the taxpayer at each place, (b) the degree of the taxpayer's business activity at each place, and (c) the relative significance of the financial return to the taxpayer from each place.

(iii) Where a taxpayer maintains inconsistent positions by claiming a deduction for expenses of meals and lodging while away from home (incurred in the general location of the new principal place of work) under section 162 (relating to trade or business expenses) and by claiming a deduction under this section for moving expenses incurred in connection with the commencement of work at such place of work, it will be a question of facts and circumstances as to whether such new place of work will be considered a principal place of work, and accordingly which category of deductions he will be allowed.

(4) *Minimum period of employment.* (i) Under section 217(c)(2) no deduction is allowed unless—

(a) Where a taxpayer is an employee, during the 12-month period immediately following his arrival in the general location of the new principal place of work, he is a full-time employee, in such general location, during at least 39 weeks, or

(b) Where a taxpayer is a self-employed individual (including a taxpayer who is also an employee, but is unable to satisfy the requirements of the 39-week test of (a) of this subdivision

(i)), during the 24-month period immediately following his arrival in the general location of the new principal place of work, he is a full-time employee or performs services as a self-employed individual on a full-time basis, in such general location, during at least 78 weeks, of which not less than 39 weeks are during the 12-month period referred to above.

Where a taxpayer works as an employee and at the same time performs services as a self-employed individual his principal employment (determined according to subdivision (i) of subparagraph (3) of this paragraph) governs whether the 39-week or 78-week test is applicable.

(ii) The 12-month period and the 39-week period set forth in subparagraph (A) of section 217(c)(2) and the 12- and 24-month periods as well as 39- and 78-week periods set forth in subparagraph (B) of such section are measured from the date of the taxpayer's arrival in the general location of the new principal place of work. Generally, date of arrival is the date of the termination of the last trip preceding the taxpayer's commencement of work on a regular basis and is not the date the taxpayer's family or household goods and effects arrive.

(iii) The taxpayer need not remain in the employ of the same employer or remain self-employed in the same trade or business for the required number of weeks. However, he must be employed in the same general location of the new principal place of work during such period. The "general location" of the new principal place of work refers to a general commutation area and is usually the same area as the "new place of residence"; see paragraph (b)(8) of this section.

(iv) Only those weeks during which the taxpayer is a full-time employee or during which he performs services as a self-employed individual on a full-time basis qualify as a week of work for purposes of the minimum period of employment condition of section 217(c)(2).

(a) Whether an employee is a full-time employee during any particular week depends upon the customary practices of the occupation in the geographic area in which the taxpayer works. Where employment is on a seasonal basis, weeks occurring in the off-season when no work is required or available may be counted as weeks of full-time employment only if the employee's contract or agreement of employment covers the off-season period and such period is less than 6 months. Thus, for example, a school teacher whose employment contract covers a 12-month period and who teaches on a full-time basis for more than 6 months is considered a full-time employee during the entire 12-month period. A taxpayer will be treated as a full-time employee during any week

Reg. § 1.217-2(c)(4)

of involuntary temporary absence from work because of illness, strikes, shutouts, layoffs, natural disasters, etc. A taxpayer will, also, be treated as a full-time employee during any week in which he voluntarily absents himself from work for leave or vacation provided for in his contract or agreement of employment.

(b) Whether a taxpayer performs services as a self-employed individual on a full-time basis during any particular week depends on the practices of the trade or business in the geographic area in which the taxpayer works. For example, a self-employed dentist maintaining office hours 4 days a week is considered to perform services as a self-employed individual on a full-time basis providing it is not unusual for other self-employed dentists in the geographic area in which the taxpayer works to maintain office hours only 4 days a week. Where a trade or business is seasonal, weeks occurring during the off-season when no work is required or available may be counted as weeks of performance of services on a full-time basis only if the off-season is less than 6 months and the taxpayer performs services on a full-time basis both before and after the off-season. For example, a taxpayer who owns and operates a motel at a beach resort is considered to perform services as a self-employed individual on a full-time basis if the motel is closed for a period not exceeding 6 months during the off-season and if he performs services on a full-time basis as the operator of a motel both before and after the off-season. A taxpayer will be treated as performing services as a self-employed individual on a full-time basis during any week of involuntary temporary absence from work because of illness, strikes, natural disasters, etc.

(v) Where taxpayers file a joint return, either spouse may satisfy the minimum period of employment condition. However, weeks worked by one spouse may not be added to weeks worked by the other spouse in order to satisfy such condition. The taxpayer seeking to satisfy the minimum period of employment condition must satisfy the condition applicable to him. Thus, if a taxpayer is subject to the 39-week condition and his spouse is subject to the 78-week condition and the taxpayer satisfies the 39-week condition, his spouse need not satisfy the 78-week condition. On the other hand, if the taxpayer does not satisfy the 39-week condition, his spouse in such case must satisfy the 78-week condition.

(vi) The application of this subparagraph may be illustrated by the following examples:

Example (1). A is an electrician residing in New York City. He moves himself, his family, and his household goods and personal effects, at his own expense, to Denver where he commences employment with the M Aircraft Corporation. After working full-time for 30 weeks he voluntarily leaves his job, and he subsequently moves to and commences employment in Los Angeles, California, which employment lasts for more than 39 weeks. Since A was not employed in the general location of his new principal place of employment in Denver for at least 39 weeks, no deduction is allowable for moving expenses paid or incurred between New York City and Denver. A will be allowed to deduct only those moving expenses attributable to his move from Denver to Los Angeles, assuming all other conditions of section 217 are met.

Example (2). Assume the same facts as in example (1), except that A's wife commences employment in Denver at the same time as A, and that she continues to work in Denver for at least 9 weeks after A's departure for Los Angeles. Since she has met the 39-week requirement in Denver, and assuming all other requirements of section 217 are met, the moving expenses paid by A attributable to the move from New York City to Denver will be allowed as a deduction, provided A and his wife file a joint return. If A and his wife file separate returns moving expenses paid by A's wife attributable to the move from New York City to Denver will be allowed as a deduction on A's wife's return.

Example (3). Assume the same facts as in example (1), except that A's wife commences employment in Denver on the same day that A departs for Los Angeles, and continues to work in Denver for 9 weeks thereafter. Since neither A (who has worked 30 weeks) nor his wife (who has worked 9 weeks) has independently satisfied the 39-week requirement, no deduction for moving expenses attributable to the move from New York City to Denver is allowable.

* * *

[Reg. § 1.217-2.]

☐ [*T.D.* 7195, 7-10-72. *Amended by T.D.* 7578, 12-19-78; *T.D.* 7605, 3-29-79; *T.D.* 7689, 3-28-80; *T.D.* 7810, 2-5-82 *and T.D.* 8607, 8-4-95.]

Proposed Regulation

§ 1.221-1. Deduction for interest on qualified education loans.—(a) *In general.* An individual taxpayer is allowed a deduction under section 221 from gross income for certain interest paid during the taxable year on a qualified education loan. The deduction is allowed only with respect to interest paid on a qualified education loan during the first 60 months that interest payments are required under the terms of the loan. See paragraph (e) of this section for rules relating to the 60-month rule.

Reg. § 1.221-1(a)

(b) *Eligibility*—(1) *Taxpayer must be legally obligated to make interest payments.* A taxpayer is allowed a deduction under section 221 only if the taxpayer is legally obligated to make interest payments under the terms of the qualified education loan.

(2) *Claimed dependents not eligible*—(i) *In general.* An individual is not allowed a deduction under section 221 for a taxable year if the individual is a dependent (as defined in section 152) for whom a deduction under section 151 is claimed on another taxpayer's federal income tax return for the same taxable year (or, in the case of a fiscal year taxpayer, the taxable year beginning in the same calendar year as the individual's taxable year).

(ii) *Examples.* The following examples illustrate the rules of this paragraph (b):

Example 1. Student not claimed as dependent. Student A pays $750 of interest on qualified education loans during 1998. Student A's parents do not claim her as a dependent for 1998. Assuming all other relevant requirements are met, Student A may deduct the $750 of interest paid in 1998 under section 221.

Example 2. Student claimed as dependent. Student B pays $750 of interest on qualified education loans during 1998. Only Student B is legally obligated to make the payments. Student B's parent claims him as a dependent and a deduction under section 151 is allowed with respect to Student B in computing the parent's 1998 federal income tax. Neither Student B nor Student B's parent may deduct the $750 of interest paid in 1998 under section 221.

(3) *Married taxpayers.* If a taxpayer is married as of the close of the taxable year, a deduction under this section is allowed only if the taxpayer and the taxpayer's spouse file a joint return for that taxable year.

(c) *Maximum deduction.* In any taxable year, the amount allowed as a deduction under section 221 may not exceed the amount determined in accordance with the following table:

Taxable year beginning in:	Maximum Deduction
1998	$1,000
1999	$1,500
2000	$2,000
2001 and thereafter	$2,500

(d) *Limitation based on modified adjusted gross income*—(1) *In general.* The deduction allowed under section 221 is phased out ratably for taxpayers with modified adjusted gross income between $40,000 and $55,000 ($60,000 and $75,000 for married individuals who file a joint return). Taxpayers with modified adjusted gross income of $55,000 or above (or $75,000 or above for joint filers) are not allowed a deduction under section 221.

(2) *Modified adjusted gross income defined.* The term *modified adjusted gross income* means the adjusted gross income (as defined in section 62) of the taxpayer for the taxable year increased by any amount excluded from gross income under section 911, 931, or 933 (relating to income earned abroad or from certain U.S. possessions or Puerto Rico). Adjusted gross income must be determined under this section after taking into account the exclusions, deductions and limitations provided for by sections 86 (social security and tier 1 railroad retirement benefits), 135 (redemption of qualified U.S. savings bonds), 137 (adoption assistance programs), 219 (deductible IRA contributions) and 469 (limitation on passive activity losses and credits).

(3) *Inflation adjustment.* For taxable years beginning after 2002, the amounts in paragraph (d)(1) of this section will be increased for inflation occurring after 2001 in accordance with section 1(f)(3). If any amount adjusted under this paragraph (d)(3) is not a multiple of $5,000, the amount will be rounded to the next lowest multiple of $5,000.

(e) *60-month rule*—(1) *General rule.* A deduction for interest paid on a qualified education loan is allowed only for payments made during the first 60 months that interest payments are required on the loan. The 60-month period begins on the date the qualified education loan first enters repayment status and ends 60 months later, unless the period is suspended for periods of deferment or forbearance within the meaning of paragraph (e)(3) of this section. The 60-month period continues to elapse regardless of whether the required interest payments are actually made. The date on which the qualified education loan first enters repayment status is determined under the terms of the loan agreement or, in the case of a loan issued or guaranteed under a federal post-secondary education loan program, under applicable federal regulations. For special rules relating to loan refinancings, consolidated loans, and collapsed loans, see paragraph (h)(1) of this section.

(2) *Loans that entered repayment status prior to January 1, 1998.* In the case of any qualified education loan that entered repayment status prior to January 1, 1998, no deduction is allowed under section 221 for interest paid during the portion of the 60-month period described in paragraph (e)(1) of this section that occurred prior to January 1, 1998. A deduction is allowed only for interest due and paid during that portion, if any, of the 60-month period remaining after December 31, 1997.

Reg. § 1.221-1(b)(1)

(3) *Periods of deferment or forbearance.* The 60-month period described in paragraph (e)(1) of this section is suspended for any period when interest payments are not required on a qualified education loan because the borrower has been granted deferment or forbearance (including postponement in anticipation of cancellation). However, in the case of a qualified education loan that is not issued or guaranteed under a federal postsecondary education loan program, the 60-month period will be suspended under this paragraph (e)(3) only if the borrower satisfies one of the conditions for deferment or forbearance established by the U.S. Department of Education for federal student loan programs under Title IV of the Higher Education Act of 1965, such as half-time study at a postsecondary educational institution, study in an approved graduate fellowship program or in an approved rehabilitation program for the disabled, inability to find full-time employment, economic hardship, or the performance of services in certain occupations or federal programs. The 60-month period is not suspended if, under the terms of the loan—

(i) Interest continues to accrue while the loan is in deferment or forbearance; and

(ii) The taxpayer has the option of paying the interest currently or requesting that the interest be capitalized, and the taxpayer elects to make current interest payments.

(4) *Late payments.* A deduction is allowed for a payment of interest that was required to be made in one month but that actually is made in a subsequent month prior to the expiration of the 60-month period. A deduction is not allowed for a payment of interest that was required to be made in one month but that actually is made in a subsequent month after the expiration of the 60-month period.

(5) *Examples.* The following examples illustrate the rules of this paragraph (e). In the examples, assume that the institution is an eligible educational institution, the loan is a qualified education loan, and the student is legally obligated to make interest payments under the terms of the loan:

Example 1. Payment prior to 60-month period. Student C obtains a loan to attend College V. The terms of the loan provide that interest accrues on the loan while C earns his undergraduate degree but that C is not required to begin making payments of interest until six full calendar months after he graduates. Nevertheless, C voluntarily pays interest on the loan while attending College V. C is not allowed a deduction for interest paid while attending College V because the payments were made during a month prior to the start of the 60-month period.

Example 2. Deferment option not exercised. The facts are the same as *Example 1,* except that Student C makes no payments on the loan while C is enrolled at College V. C graduates in June, 1999 and is required to begin making monthly payments of principal and interest on the loan in January, 2000. The 60-month period described in paragraph (e)(1) of this section begins in January, 2000. In August, 2000, C enrolls in graduate school on a full-time basis. Under the terms of the loan, C may apply for deferment of the loan payments while C is enrolled in graduate school. However, C elects not to apply for deferment and continues to make monthly payments on the loan during graduate school. Assuming all other relevant requirements are met, C may deduct interest paid on the loan during the 60-month period beginning in January, 2000, including interest paid while C was enrolled in graduate school, but elected not to defer payment.

Example 3. Late payment, within 60-month period. The facts are the same as *Example 2,* except that, after the loan enters repayment status in January, 2000, Student C makes no interest payments until March, 2000. In March, 2000, C pays interest required to be paid for the months of January, February, and March, 2000. Assuming all other relevant requirements are met, C is allowed a deduction for the interest paid in March for the months of January, February, and March because the interest payments were required under the terms of the loan and were paid within the 60-month period, even though the January and February interest payments may be late.

Example 4. Late payment during deferment but within 60-month period. The terms of Student D's qualified education loan require her to begin making monthly payments of interest on the loan in January, 2000. The 60-month period described in paragraph (e)(1) of this section begins in January, 2000. D fails to make the required interest payments for the months of November and December, 2000. In January, 2001, D enrolls in graduate school on a half-time basis. Under the terms of the loan, D is eligible for deferment of the loan payments due while D is enrolled in graduate school. The deferment is granted effective January 1, 2001. In March, 2001, while the loan is in deferment, D pays the interest due for the months of November and December, 2000. Assuming all other relevant requirements are met, D is allowed a deduction for interest paid in March, 2001 for the months of November and December, 2000 because the interest payments were made paid prior to the expiration of the 60-month period, even though the November and December interest payments were late and were made while the loan was in deferment.

Reg. § 1.221-1(e)(5)

Example 5. 60-month period. The facts are the same as *Example 4* except that Student D graduates from graduate school in December, 2004 and is required to begin making monthly payments of interest on the loan in June, 2005. As of January, 2001, when the loan entered deferment status, 12 months of the 60-month period had elapsed (January-December, 2000). As of June, 2005, when the loan re-enters repayment status, there are 48 months remaining in the 60-month period for that loan.

Example 6. 60-month period. The terms of Student E's qualified education loan require him to begin making monthly payments of interest on the loan in November, 1999. The 60-month period described in paragraph (e)(1) of this section begins in November, 1999. In January, 2000, E enrolls in graduate school on a half-time basis. As permitted under the terms of the loan, E applies for deferment of the loan payments due while E is enrolled in graduate school. While awaiting formal notification from the lender that his request for deferment has been granted, E pays interest due for the month of January, 2000. In February, 2000, E receives notification from the lender that deferment has been granted, effective as January 1, 2000. Assuming all other requirements are met, E is allowed a deduction for interest paid in January, 2000, prior to his receipt of the notification, even though the deferment was granted retroactive to January 1, 2000. As of February, 2000, there are 57 months remaining in the 60-month period for that loan.

Example 7. Reduction of 60-month period for months prior to January 1, 1998. The first payment on a qualified education loan is due on January 1, 1997. Thereafter, interest is required to be paid on a monthly basis. The 60-month period for this loan begins on January 1, 1997. However, no deduction is allowed for interest paid by the borrower prior to January 1, 1998, the effective date of section 221. Assuming all other relevant requirements are met, the borrower may deduct interest due and paid on the loan during the 48 months beginning on January 1, 1998 (unless such period is extended for periods of deferment or forbearance under paragraph (e)(3) of this section).

(f) *Definitions*—(1) *Eligible educational institution.* In general, an *eligible educational institution* means any college, university, vocational school or other post-secondary educational institution that is described in section 481 of the Higher Education Act of 1965 (20 U.S.C. 1088), as in effect on August 5, 1997, and is certified by the U.S. Department of Education to be eligible to participate in student aid programs administered by the Department, as described in section 25A(f)(2). In addition, for purposes of this section,

an eligible educational institution also includes an institution that conducts an internship or residency program leading to a degree or certificate awarded by an institution, a hospital, or a health care facility that offers postgraduate training.

(2) *Qualified higher education expenses*—(i) *In general.* Qualified higher education expenses means the cost of attendance (as defined in section 472 of the Higher Education Act of 1965, 20 U.S.C. 1087ll, as in effect on August 4, 1997), at an eligible educational institution, reduced by the amounts described in paragraph (f)(2)(ii) of this section. Consistent with section 472 of the Higher Education Act of 1965, 20 U.S.C. 1087ll, the cost of attendance is determined by the eligible educational institution and includes tuition and fees normally assessed a student carrying the same academic workload, an allowance for room and board, and an allowance for books, supplies, transportation and miscellaneous expenses of the student.

(ii) *Reductions.* Qualified higher education expenses must be reduced by any amount paid to or on behalf of a student with respect to such expenses that is—

(A) A qualified scholarship that is excludable from income under section 117;

(B) A veterans' or member of the armed forces' educational assistance allowance under chapter 30, 31, 32, 34 or 35 of title 38, United States Code, or under chapter 1606 of title 10, United States Code;

(C) Employer-provided educational assistance that is excludable from income under section 127;

(D) Any other educational assistance that is excludable from gross income (other than as a gift, bequest, devise, or inheritance within the meaning of section 102(a));

(E) Any amount excluded from gross income under section 135 (relating to the redemption of United States savings bonds); or

(F) Any amount distributed from an education individual retirement account described in section 530 and excluded from gross income.

(3) *Qualified education loan*—(i) *In general.* Qualified education loan means indebtedness incurred by a taxpayer solely to pay qualified higher education expenses that are—

(A) Incurred on behalf of a student who is the taxpayer, the taxpayer's spouse, or a dependent (as defined in section 151) of the taxpayer at the time the indebtedness is incurred;

(B) Paid or incurred within a reasonable period of time before or after the indebtedness is incurred. Qualified higher education expenses that are paid with the proceeds of education loans that are part of a federal postsecondary education loan program are deemed to meet this requirement. For other loans, except as provided in paragraph (f)(3)(ii) of this section, what constitutes a reasonable period of time is determined based on all the relevant facts and circumstances; and

(C) Attributable to education provided during an academic period, as described in section 25A and the regulations thereunder, when the student is an eligible student as defined in section 25A(b)(3) (requiring that the student be a degree candidate carrying at least one-half the normal full-time workload).

(ii) *Reasonable period safe harbor.* For purposes of paragraph (f)(3)(i)(B) of this section, qualified higher education expenses are treated as paid or incurred within a reasonable period of time before or after the indebtedness is incurred if the expenses relate to a particular academic period and the loan proceeds are disbursed within a period that begins 60 days prior to the start of that academic period and ends 60 days after the end of that academic period.

(iii) *Related party.* A loan made by a person who is related to the borrower, within the meaning of section 267(b) or 707(b)(1), is not a qualified education loan. For example, a parent or grandparent of the borrower is a related person. In addition, a loan made under any qualified employer plan as defined in section 72(p)(4) or under any contract referred to in section 72(p)(5) is not a qualified education loan.

(iv) *Not federally issued or guaranteed.* A loan does not have to be issued or guaranteed under a federal postsecondary education loan program to be a qualified education loan.

(4) *Examples.* The following examples illustrate the rules in this paragraph (f):

Example 1. Eligible educational institution. University Z is a postsecondary educational institution described in section 481 of the Higher Education Act of 1965. University Z has completed the necessary paperwork and has been certified by the U.S. Department of Education as eligible to participate in federal financial aid programs administered by the Department, although University Z chooses not to participate. University Z is an eligible educational institution.

Example 2. Qualified education loan. Student F borrows money from a commercial bank to pay qualified higher education expenses related to his enrollment on a half-time basis in a graduate program at an eligible educational institution. All the loan proceeds are used to pay qualified higher education expenses incurred within a reasonable period of time after the indebtedness is incurred. The loan is not federally guaranteed. The commercial bank is not related to Student F within

the meaning of section 267(b) or 707(b)(1). The fact that Student F's loan is not federally issued or guaranteed does not prevent the loan from being a qualified education loan within the meaning of section 221.

Example 3. Qualified higher education expenses. Student G receives a $3,000 qualified scholarship for the 1999 Fall semester, that is excludable from F's gross income under section 117. Student G receives no other forms of financial assistance with respect to the 1999 Fall semester. Student G's cost of attendance for the Fall semester, as determined by Student G's eligible educational institution for purposes of calculating a student's financial need in accordance with section 472 of the Higher Education Act, is $16,000. For the 1999 Fall semester, Student G has qualified higher education expenses of $13,000 (the cost of attendance as determined by the institution ($16,000) reduced by the qualified scholarship proceeds excludable from gross income ($3,000)).

Example 4. Qualified education loan. Student H signs a promissory note for a loan on August 15, 1999, to pay for qualified higher education expenses for the 1999 Fall and 2000 Spring semesters. On August 20, 1999, loan proceeds are disbursed by the lender to Student H's college and credited to H's account to pay qualified higher education expenses for the 1999 Fall semester, that begins on August 23, 1999. On January 25, 2000, additional loan proceeds are disbursed by the lender to Student H's college and credited to H's account to pay qualified higher education expenses for the 2000 Spring semester, that began on January 10, 2000. Student H's qualified higher education expenses for the two semesters are paid within a reasonable period of time, as the first loan disbursement was made within 60 days prior to the start of the Fall 1999 semester and the second loan disbursement was made during the Spring 2000 semester.

Example 5. Mixed-use loans. Student I signs a promissory note for a loan which is secured by I's personal residence. Part of the loan proceeds will be used to pay for certain improvements to I's residence and part of the loan proceeds will be used to pay qualified higher education expenses of I's spouse. Because the loan is not incurred by I solely to pay qualified higher education expenses, the loan is not a qualified education loan.

(g) *Denial of double benefit.* No deduction is allowed under this section for any amount for which a deduction is allowed under another provision of Chapter 1 of the Internal Revenue Code.

* * *

[Reg. § 1.221-1.]

[Proposed 1-21-99.]

Reg. § 1.221-1(g)

Special Deductions for Corporations

§ 1.248-1. **Election to amortize organizational expenditures.**—(a) *In general.* (1) Section 248(a) provides that a corporation may elect for any taxable year beginning after December 31, 1953, to treat its organizational expenditures, as defined in subsection (b) of section 248 and in paragraph (b) of this section, as deferred expenses. A corporation which exercises such election must, at the time it makes the election, select a period of not less than 60 months, beginning with the month in which it began business, over which it will amortize its organizational expenditures. The period selected by the corporation may be equal to or greater, but not less, than 60 months, but in any event it must begin with the month in which the corporation began business. The organizational expenditures of the corporation which are treated as deferred expenses under the provisions of section 248 and this section shall then be allowed as a deduction in computing taxable income ratably over the period selected by the taxpayer. The period selected by the taxpayer in making its election may not be subsequently changed but shall be adhered to in computing taxable income for the taxable year for which the election is made and all subsequent taxable years.

(2) If a corporation exercises the election provided in section 248(a), such election shall apply to all of its expenditures which are organizational expenditures within the meaning of subsection (b) of section 248 and paragraph (b) of this section. The election shall apply, however, only with respect to expenditures incurred before the end of the taxable year in which the corporation begins business (without regard to whether the corporation files its returns on the accrual or cash method of accounting or whether the expenditures are paid in the taxable year in which they are incurred), if such expenditures are paid or incurred on or after August 16, 1954 (the date of enactment of the Internal Revenue Code of 1954).

(3) The deduction allowed under section 248 must be spread over a period beginning with the month in which the corporation begins business. The determination of the date the corporation begins business presents a question of fact which must be determined in each case in light of all the circumstances of the particular case. The words "begins business," however, do not have the same meaning as "in existence." Ordinarily, a corporation begins business when it starts the business operations for which it was organized; a corporation comes into existence on the date of its incorporation. Mere organizational activities, such as the obtaining of the corporate charter, are not alone sufficient to show the beginning of business. If the activities of the corporation have advanced to the extent necessary to establish the nature of

its business operations, however, it will be deemed to have begun business. For example, the acquisition of operating assets which are necessary to the type of business contemplated may constitute the beginning of business.

(b) *Organizational expenditures defined.* (1) Section 248(b) defines the term "organization expenditures." Such expenditures for purposes of section 248 and this section, are those expenditures which are directly incident to the creation of the corporation. An expenditure, in order to qualify as an organizational expenditure, must be (i) incident to the creation of the corporation, (ii) chargeable to the capital account of the corporation, and (iii) of a character which, if expended incident to the creation of a corporation having a limited life, would be amortizable over such life. An expenditure which fails to meet each of these three tests may not be considered an organizational expenditure for purposes of section 248 and this section.

(2) The following are examples of organizational expenditures within the meaning of section 248 and this section: legal services incident to the organization of the corporation, such as drafting the corporate charter, by-laws, minutes of organizational meetings, terms of original stock certificates, and the like; necessary accounting services; expenses of temporary directors and of organizational meetings of directors or stockholders; and fees paid to State of incorporation.

(3) The following expenditures are not organizational expenditures within the meaning of section 248 and this section:

(i) Expenditures connected with issuing or selling shares of stock or other securities, such as commissions, professional fees, and printing costs. This is so even where the particular issue of stock to which the expenditures relate is for a fixed term of years;

(ii) Expenditures connected with the transfer of assets to a corporation.

(4) Expenditures connected with the reorganization of a corporation, unless directly incident to the creation of a corporation, are not organizational expenditures within the meaning of section 248 and this section.

(c) *Time and manner of making election.* The election provided by section 248(a) and paragraph (a) of this section shall be made in a statement attached to the taxpayer's return for the taxable year in which it begins business. Such taxable year must be one which begins after December 31, 1953. The return and statement must be filed not later than the date prescribed by law for filing the return (including any extensions of time) for the taxable year in which the taxpayer begins business. The statement shall set forth the description and amount of the expenditures involved, the date such expenditures were incurred, the month in which the corporation began business, and the number of months (not less than 60 and beginning with the month in which the taxpayer began business) over which such expenditures are to be deducted ratably. [Reg. § 1.248-1.]

☐ [*T.D.* 6183, 6-13-56.]

Items Not Deductible

§ 1.262-1. Personal, living, and family expenses.—(a) *In general.* In computing taxable income, no deduction shall be allowed, except as otherwise expressly provided in chapter 1 of the Code, for personal, living, and family expenses.

(b) *Examples of personal, living, and family expenses.* Personal, living, and family expenses are illustrated in the following examples:

(1) Premiums paid for life insurance by the insured are not deductible. See also section 264 and the regulations thereunder.

(2) The cost of insuring a dwelling owned and occupied by the taxpayer as a personal residence is not deductible.

(3) Expenses of maintaining a household, including amounts paid for rent, water, utilities, domestic service, and the like, are not deductible. A taxpayer who rents a property for residential purposes, but incidentally conducts business there (his place of business being elsewhere) shall not deduct any part of the rent. If, however, he uses part of the house as his place of business, such portion of the rent and other similar expenses as is properly attributable to such place of business is deductible as a business expense. [But see Code Sec. 280A.]

(4) Losses sustained by the taxpayer upon the sale or other disposition of property held for personal, living, and family purposes are not deductible. But see section 165 and the regulations thereunder for deduction of losses sustained to such property by reason of casualty, etc.

(5) Expenses incurred in traveling away from home (which include transportation expenses, meals, and lodging) and any other transportation expenses are not deductible unless they qualify as expenses deductible under section 162, § 1.162-2, and paragraph (d) of § 1.162-5 (relating to trade or business expenses), section 170 and paragraph (a)(2) of § 1.170-2 or paragraph (g) of § 1.170A-1 (relating to charitable contributions), section 212 and § 1.212-1 (relating to expenses for production of income), section 213(e) and paragraph (e) of § 1.213-1 (relating to medical expenses) or section 217(a) and paragraph (a) of § 1.217-1 (relating to moving expenses). The taxpayer's costs of commuting to his place of business or employment are personal expenses and do not qualify as deductible expenses. The costs of the taxpayer's lodging not incurred in traveling away from home are personal expenses and are not deductible unless they qualify as deductible expenses under section 217. Except as permitted under section 162, 212, or 217, the costs of the taxpayer's meals not incurred in traveling away from home are personal expenses.

(6) Amounts paid as damages for breach of promise to marry, and attorney's fees and other costs of suit to recover such damages, are not deductible.

(7) Generally, attorney's fees and other costs paid in connection with a divorce, separation, or decree for support are not deductible by either the husband or the wife. However, the part of an attorney's fee and the part of the other costs paid in connection with a divorce, legal separation, written separation agreement, or a decree for support, which are properly attributable to the production or collection of amounts includible in gross income under section 71 are deductible by the wife under section 212.

(8) The cost of equipment of a member of the armed services is deductible only to the extent that it exceeds nontaxable allowances received for such equipment and to the extent that such equipment is especially required by his profession and does not merely take the place of articles required in civilian life. For example, the cost of a sword is an allowable deduction in computing taxable income, but the cost of a uniform is not. However, amounts expended by a reservist for the purchase and maintenance of uniforms which may be worn only when on active duty for training for temporary periods, when attending service school courses, or when attending training assemblies are deductible except to the extent that nontaxable allowances are received for such amounts.

(9) Expenditures made by a taxpayer in obtaining an education or in furthering his education are not deductible unless they qualify under section 162 and § 1.162-5 (relating to trade or business expenses).

(c) *Cross references.* Certain items of a personal, living, or family nature are deductible to the extent expressly provided under the following sections, and the regulations under those sections:

(1) Section 163 (interest).

(2) Section 164 (taxes).

(3) Section 165 (losses).

(4) Section 166 (bad debts).

Reg. § 1.262-1(c)(4)

(5) Section 170 (charitable, etc., contributions and gifts).

(6) Section 213 (medical, dental, etc., expenses).

(7) Section 214 (expenses for care of certain dependents). [Now a credit under Code § 44A.]

(8) Section 215 (alimony, etc., payments).

(9) Section 216 (amounts representing taxes and interest paid to cooperative housing corporation).

(10) Section 217 (moving expenses). [Reg. § 1.262-1.]

☐ [*T.D.* 6313, 9-16-58. *Amended by T.D.* 6796, 1-29-65; *T.D.* 6918, 5-1-67 *and T.D.* 7207, 10-3-72.]

§ 1.263(a)-1. Capital expenditures; in general.—(a) Except as otherwise provided in chapter 1 of the Code, no deduction shall be allowed for—

(1) Any amount paid out for new buildings or for permanent improvements or betterments made to increase the value of any property or estate, or

(2) Any amount expended in restoring property or in making good the exhaustion thereof for which an allowance is or has been made in the form of a deduction for depreciation, amortization, or depletion.

(b) In general, the amounts referred to in paragraph (a) of this section include amounts paid or incurred (1) to add to the value, or substantially prolong the useful life, of property owned by the taxpayer, such as plant or equipment, or (2) to adapt property to a new or different use. Amounts paid or incurred for incidental repairs and maintenance of property are not capital expenditures within the meaning of subparagraphs (1) and (2) of this paragraph. See section 162 and § 1.162-4. See section 263A and the regulations thereunder for cost capitalization rules which apply to amounts referred to in paragraph (a) of this section with respect to the production of real and tangible personal property (as defined in section 1.263A-1T (a)(5)(iii)), including films, sound recordings, video tapes, books, or similar properties. An amount referred to in paragraph (a) of this section is a capital expenditure that is taken into account through inclusion in inventory costs or a charge to capital accounts or basis no earlier than the taxable year during which the amount is incurred within the meaning of § 1.446-1(c)(1)(ii). See section 263A and the regulations thereunder for cost capitalization rules that apply to amounts referred to in paragraph (a) of this section with respect to the production of real and tangible personal property (as defined in § 1.263A-2(a)(2)),

including films, sound recordings, video tapes, books, or similar properties.

(c) The provisions of paragraph (a)(1) of this section shall not apply to expenditures deductible under—

(1) Section 616 and §§ 1.616-1 through 1.616-3, relating to the development of mines or deposits,

(2) Section 174 and §§ 1.174-1 through 1.174-4, relating to research and experimentation,

(3) Section 175 and §§ 1.175-1 through 1.175-6, relating to soil and water conservation,

(4) Section 179 and §§ 1.179-1 through 1.179-5, relating to election to expense certain depreciable business assets,

(5) Section 180 and §§ 1.180-1 and 1.180-2, relating to expenditures by farmers for fertilizer, lime, etc., and

(6) Section 182 and §§ 1.182-1 through 1.182-6, relating to expenditures by farmers for clearing land. [Reg. § 1.263(a)-1.]

☐ [*T.D.* 6313, 9-16-58. *Amended by T.D.* 6548, 2-21-61; *T.D.* 6794, 1-25-65; *T.D.* 8121, 1-5-87; *T.D.* 8131, 3-24-87; *T.D.* 8408, 4-9-92 *and T.D.* 8482, 8-6-93.]

§ 1.263(a)-2. Examples of capital expenditures.—The following paragraphs include examples of capital expenditures:

(a) The cost of acquisition, construction, or erection of buildings, machinery and equipment, furniture and fixtures, and similar property having a useful life substantially beyond the taxable year.

(b) Amounts expended for securing a copyright and plates, which remain the property of the person making the payments. See section 263A and the regulations thereunder for capitalization rules which apply to amounts expended in securing and producing a copyright and plates in connection with the production of property, including films, sound recordings, video tapes, books, or similar properties.

(c) The cost of defending or perfecting title to property.

(d) The amount expended for architect's services.

(e) Commissions paid in purchasing securities. Commissions paid in selling securities are an offset against the selling price, except that in the case of dealers in securities such commissions may be treated as an ordinary and necessary business expense.

(f) Amounts assessed and paid under an agreement between bondholders or shareholders of a corporation to be used in a reorganization of the corporation or voluntary contributions by share-

Reg. § 1.263(a)-1(a)(1)

holders to the capital of the corporation for any corporate purpose. Such amounts are capital investments and are not deductible. See section 118 and § 1.118-1.

(g) A holding company which guarantees dividends at a specified rate on the stock of a subsidiary corporation for the purpose of securing new capital for the subsidiary and increasing the value of its stockholdings in the subsidiary shall not deduct amounts paid in carrying out this guaranty in computing its taxable income, but such payments are capital expenditures to be added to the cost of its stock in the subsidiary.

(h) The cost of good will in connection with the acquisition of the assets of a going concern is a capital expenditure. [Reg. § 1.263(a)-2.]

☐ [*T.D.* 6313, 9-16-58. *Amended by T.D.* 8131, 3-24-87.]

Proposed Regulation

§ 1.263(a)-4. Amounts paid to acquire, create, or enhance intangible assets.—(a) *Overview.* This section provides rules for applying section 263(a) to amounts paid to acquire, create, or enhance intangible assets. Except to the extent provided in paragraph (d)(8) of this section, the rules provided by this section do not apply to amounts paid to acquire, create, or enhance tangible assets. Paragraph (b) of this section provides a general principle of capitalization. Paragraphs (c) and (d) of this section identify intangibles for which capitalization is specifically required under the general principle. Paragraph (e) of this section provides rules for determining the extent to which taxpayers must capitalize transaction costs. Paragraph (f) of this section provides a 12-month rule intended to simplify the application of the general principle to certain payments that create benefits of a brief duration. Additional rules and examples relating to these provisions are provided in paragraphs (g) through (n) of this section. The applicability date of the rules in this section is provided in paragraph (o) of this section.

(b) *Capitalization of intangible assets*—(1) *In general.* Except as otherwise provided in chapter 1 of the Internal Revenue Code, a taxpayer must capitalize—

(i) An amount paid to acquire, create, or enhance an intangible asset (within the meaning of paragraph (b)(2) of this section);

(ii) An amount paid to facilitate (within the meaning of paragraph (e)(1) of this section) the acquisition, creation, or enhancement of an intangible asset; and

(iii) An amount paid to facilitate (within the meaning of paragraph (e)(1) of this section) a restructuring or reorganization of a business entity or a transaction involving the acquisition of

capital, including a stock issuance, borrowing, or recapitalization.

(2) *Intangible asset*—(i) *In general.* For purposes of this section, the term *intangible asset* means—

(A) An intangible described in paragraph (c) of this section (relating to acquired intangibles);

(B) An intangible described in paragraph (d) of this section (relating to certain created or enhanced intangibles);

(C) A separate and distinct intangible asset within the meaning of paragraph (b)(3) of this section; or

(D) A future benefit identified in published guidance in the Federal Register or in the Internal Revenue Bulletin (see § 601.601(d)(2)(ii)(*b*) of this chapter) as an intangible asset for which capitalization is required under this section.

(ii) *Published guidance.* Any published guidance identifying a future benefit as an intangible asset for which capitalization is required under paragraph (b)(2)(i)(D) of this section applies only to amounts paid on or after the date of publication of the guidance.

(3) *Separate and distinct intangible asset*—(i) *Definition.* The term *separate and distinct intangible asset* means a property interest of ascertainable and measurable value in money's worth that is subject to protection under applicable state or federal law and the possession and control of which is intrinsically capable of being sold, transferred, or pledged (ignoring any restrictions imposed on assignability). The determination of whether an amount is paid to acquire, create, or enhance a separate and distinct intangible asset is made as of the taxable year during which the payment is made.

(ii) *Creation or termination of contract rights.* Amounts paid to another party to create or originate an agreement with that party that produces rights or benefits for the taxpayer do not create a separate and distinct intangible asset within the meaning of this paragraph (b)(3). Further, amounts paid to another party to terminate an agreement with that party do not create a separate and distinct intangible asset within the meaning of this paragraph (b)(3). See paragraphs (d)(2), (6) and (7) of this section for rules that specifically require capitalization of amounts paid to create or terminate certain agreements. See paragraph (e)(1)(ii) of this section for rules relating to the treatment of certain termination payments that facilitate another transaction for which capitalization is required under this section.

Reg. § 1.263(a)-4(b)(3)

(c) *Acquired intangibles*—(1) *In general*. A taxpayer must capitalize amounts paid to another party to acquire an intangible from that party in a purchase or similar transaction. Intangibles within the scope of this paragraph (c) include, but are not limited to, the following (if acquired from another party in a purchase or similar transaction):

(i) An ownership interest in a corporation, partnership, trust, estate, limited liability company, or other similar entity.

(ii) A debt instrument, deposit, stripped bond, stripped coupon (including a servicing right treated for federal income tax purposes as a stripped coupon), regular interest in a REMIC or FASIT, or any other intangible treated as debt for federal income tax purposes.

(iii) A financial instrument, including, but not limited to—

(A) A letter of credit;

(B) A credit card agreement;

(C) A notional principal contract;

(D) A foreign currency contract;

(E) A futures contract;

(F) A forward contract (including an agreement under which the taxpayer has the right and obligation to provide or to acquire property (or to be compensated for such property));

(G) An option (including an agreement under which the taxpayer has the right to provide or to acquire property (or to be compensated for such property)); and

(H) Any other financial derivative.

(iv) An endowment contract, annuity contract, or insurance contract that has or may have cash value.

(v) Non-functional currency.

(vi) A lease contract.

(vii) A patent or copyright.

(viii) A franchise, trademark or tradename (as defined in § 1.197-2(b)(10)).

(ix) An assembled workforce (as defined in § 1.197-2(b)(3)).

(x) Goodwill (as defined in § 1.197-2(b)(1)) or going concern value (as defined in § 1.197-2(b)(2)).

(xi) A customer list.

(xii) A servicing right (for example, a mortgage servicing right).

(xiii) A customer-based intangible (as defined in § 1.197-2(b)(6)) or supplierbased intangible (as defined in § 1.197-2(b)(7)).

(xiv) Computer software.

(2) *Readily available software*. An amount paid to obtain a nonexclusive license for software that is (or has been) readily available to the general public on similar terms and has not been substantially modified (within the meaning of § 1.197-2(c)(4)) is treated for purposes of this paragraph (c) as an amount paid to another party to acquire an intangible from that party in a purchase or similar transaction.

(3) *Intangibles acquired from an employee*. Amounts paid to an employee to acquire an intangible from that employee are not required to be capitalized under this section if the amounts are treated as compensation for personal services includible in the employee's income under section 61 or 83. For purposes of this section, whether an individual is an employee is determined in accordance with the rules contained in section 3401(c) and the regulations thereunder.

* * *

(d) *Created intangibles*—(1) *In general*. Except as provided in paragraph (f) of this section (relating to the 12-month rule), a taxpayer must capitalize amounts paid to create or enhance an intangible described in this paragraph (d).

(2) *Financial interests*—(i) *In general*. A taxpayer must capitalize amounts paid to another party to create or originate with that party any of the following financial interests, whether or not the interest is regularly traded on an established market:

(A) An ownership interest in a corporation, partnership, trust, estate, limited liability company, or other similar entity.

(B) A debt instrument, deposit, stripped bond, stripped coupon (including a servicing right treated for federal income tax purposes as a stripped coupon), regular interest in a REMIC or FASIT, or any other intangible treated as debt for federal income tax purposes.

(C) A financial instrument, including, but not limited to—

(*1*) A letter of credit;

(*2*) A credit card agreement;

(*3*) A notional principal contract;

(*4*) A foreign currency contract;

(*5*) A futures contract;

(*6*) A forward contract (including an agreement under which the taxpayer has the right and obligation to provide or to acquire property (or to be compensated for such property));

(*7*) An option (including an agreement under which the taxpayer has the right to provide or to acquire property (or to be compensated for such property)); and

(*8*) Any other financial derivative.

Reg. § 1.263(a)-4(c)(1)

(D) An endowment contract, annuity contract, or insurance contract that has or may have cash value.

(E) Non-functional currency.

(ii) *Exception for current and prior sales.* An amount is not required to be capitalized under paragraph (d)(2)(i)(C)(*6*) or (*7*) of this section if the amount is allocable to property required to be provided or acquired by the taxpayer prior to the end of the taxable year in which the amount is paid.

(iii) *Coordination with other provisions of this paragraph (d).* An amount described in this paragraph (d)(2) that is also described elsewhere in paragraph (d) of this section is treated as described only in this paragraph (d)(2).

* * *

(3) *Prepaid expenses*—(i) *In general.* A taxpayer must capitalize amounts prepaid for benefits to be received in the future.

* * *

(4) *Certain memberships and privileges*—(i) *In general.* A taxpayer must capitalize amounts paid to an organization to obtain or renew a membership or privilege from that organization. A taxpayer is not required to capitalize under this paragraph (d)(4) an amount paid to obtain certification of the taxpayer's products, services, or business processes.

* * *

(5) *Certain rights obtained from a governmental agency*—(i) *In general.* A taxpayer must capitalize amounts paid to a governmental agency to obtain or renew a trademark, trade name, copyright, license, permit, franchise, or other similar right granted by that governmental agency.

* * *

(6) *Certain contract rights*—(i) *In general.* Except as otherwise provided in this paragraph (d)(6), a taxpayer must capitalize amounts paid to another party to induce that party to enter into, renew, or renegotiate—

(A) An agreement providing the taxpayer the right to use tangible or intangible property or the right to be compensated for the use of such property;

(B) An agreement providing the taxpayer the right to provide or to acquire services (or the right to be compensated for such services); or

(C) A covenant not to compete or an agreement having substantially the same effect as a covenant not to compete (except, in the case of an agreement that requires the performance of services, to the extent that the amount represents

reasonable compensation for services actually rendered).

* * *

(7) *Certain contract terminations*—(i) *In general.* A taxpayer must capitalize amounts paid to another party to terminate—

(A) A lease of real or tangible personal property between the taxpayer (as lessor) and that party (as lessee);

(B) An agreement that grants that party the exclusive right to acquire or use the taxpayer's property or services or to conduct the taxpayer's business; or

(C) An agreement that prohibits the taxpayer from competing with that party or from acquiring property or services from a competitor of that party.

* * *

(8) *Certain benefits arising from the provision, production, or improvement of real property*—(i) *In general.* A taxpayer must capitalize amounts paid for real property relinquished to another, or amounts paid to produce or improve real property owned by another, if the real property can reasonably be expected to produce significant economic benefits for the taxpayer.

(ii) *Exclusions.* A taxpayer is not required to capitalize an amount under paragraph (d)(8)(i) of this section to the extent the payment —

(A) Is part of a transaction involving the sale of the real property by the taxpayer;

(B) Is part of the sale of services by the taxpayer to produce or improve the real property;

(C) Is a payment by the taxpayer for some other property or service provided to the taxpayer; or

(D) Is a payment by the taxpayer to another party to create an intangible described in paragraph (d) of this section (other than in this paragraph (d)(8)).

(iii) *Real property.* For purposes of this paragraph (d)(8), real property includes property that is affixed to real property and that will ordinarily remain affixed for an indefinite period of time, such as roads, bridges, tunnels, pavements, wharves and docks, breakwaters and sea walls, elevators, power generation and transmission facilities, and pollution control facilities.

(iv) *Impact fees and dedicated improvements.* Paragraph (d)(8)(i) of this section does not apply to amounts paid to satisfy one-time charges imposed by a state or local government against new development (or expansion of existing development) to finance specific offsite capital improvements for general public use that are necessitated by the new or expanded develop-

Reg. § 1.263(a)-4(d)(8)

ment. In addition, paragraph (d)(8)(i) of this section does not apply to amounts paid for real property or improvements to real property constructed by the taxpayer where the real property or improvements benefit new development or expansion of existing development, are immediately transferred to a state or local government for dedication to the general public use, and are maintained by the state or local government. See section 263A and the regulations thereunder for capitalization rules that apply to amounts referred to in this paragraph (d)(8)(iv).

* * *

(9) *Defense or perfection of title to intangible property*—(i) *In general.* A taxpayer must capitalize amounts paid to another party to defend or perfect title to intangible property where that other party challenges the taxpayer's title to the intangible property.

* * *

(e) *Transaction costs*—(1) *Scope of facilitate*—(i) *In general.* An amount is paid to facilitate a transaction described in paragraph (b)(1)(ii) of this section (an acquisition, creation, or enhancement of an intangible asset) or to facilitate a transaction described in paragraph (b)(1)(iii) of this section (a restructuring or reorganization of a business entity or a transaction involving the acquisition of capital) if the amount is paid in the process of pursuing the transaction. Whether an amount is paid in the process of pursuing a transaction is determined based on all facts and circumstances. The fact that an amount would (or would not) have been paid but-for the transaction is not relevant in determining whether the amount is paid to facilitate the transaction.

(ii) *Treatment of termination payments in integrated transactions.* An amount paid to terminate (or facilitate the termination of) an existing agreement constitutes an amount paid to facilitate a transaction referred to in paragraph (e)(1)(i) of this section if the transaction is expressly conditioned on the termination of the existing agreement.

(iii) *Ordering rules.* An amount required to be capitalized under paragraph (b)(1)(i) of this section does not facilitate a transaction referred to in paragraph (e)(1)(i) of this section. In addition, an amount paid to facilitate a borrowing does not facilitate another transaction (other than the borrowing) referred to in paragraph (e)(1)(i) of this section.

(2) *Transaction.* For purposes of this section, the term *transaction* means all of the factual elements comprising an acquisition, creation, or enhancement of an intangible asset (or a restructuring, reorganization, or transaction involving

the acquisition of capital) and includes a series of steps carried out as part of a single plan. Thus, a transaction can involve more than one invoice and more than one intangible asset. For example, a purchase of intangible assets under one purchase agreement may constitute a single transaction, notwithstanding the fact that the acquisition involves multiple intangible assets and the amounts paid to facilitate the acquisition are capable of being allocated among the various intangible assets acquired.

(3) *Simplifying conventions*—(i) *In general.* For purposes of this paragraph (e), compensation paid to employees (including bonuses and commissions paid to employees), overhead, and de minimis costs (within the meaning of paragraph (e)(3)(ii) of this section) are treated as amounts that do not facilitate a transaction referred to in paragraph (e)(1)(i) of this section. For purposes of this section, whether an individual is an employee is determined in accordance with the rules contained in section 3401(c) and the regulations thereunder.

(ii) *De minimis costs*—(A) *In general.* Except as provided in paragraph (e)(3)(ii)(B) of this section, the term *de minimis costs* means amounts referred to in paragraph (e)(1)(i) of this section that are paid with respect to a transaction if, in the aggregate, the amounts do not exceed $5,000. If the amounts exceed $5,000, no portion of the amounts is a de minimis cost within the meaning of this paragraph (e)(3)(ii)(A). In determining the amount of transaction costs paid with respect to a transaction, a taxpayer generally must account for the actual costs paid with respect to the transaction. However, a taxpayer may elect to determine the amount of transaction costs paid with respect to a transaction using the average cost pooling method described in paragraph (e)(3)(ii)(C) of this section.

(B) *Treatment of commissions.* The term *de minimis costs* does not include commissions paid to facilitate the acquisition of an intangible described in paragraphs (c)(1)(i) through (v) of this section or to facilitate the creation or origination of an intangible described in paragraphs (d)(2)(i)(A) through (E) of this section.

(C) *Average cost pooling method.* A taxpayer may elect to establish one or more pools of similar transactions for purposes of determining the amount of transaction costs paid with respect to a transaction. Under this pooling method, the amount of transaction costs paid with respect to each transaction included in the pool is equal to the average transaction costs paid with respect to all transactions included in the pool. A taxpayer computes the average transaction costs paid with respect to all transactions included in the pool by dividing the sum of all transaction costs paid with respect to all transactions included in the pool by the number of transactions included in the pool. See paragraph (h) of this section for additional rules relating to pooling.

(4) *Special rules applicable to certain trade or business acquisition and reorganization transactions*—(i) *Acquisitive transactions*—(A) *In general.* Except as provided in paragraph (e)(4)(i)(B) of this section, in the case of an acquisition of a trade or business (whether structured as an acquisition of stock or of assets and whether the taxpayer is the acquirer in the acquisition or the target of the acquisition), an amount paid in the process of pursuing the acquisition facilitates the acquisition within the meaning of this paragraph (e) only if the amount relates to activities performed on or after the earlier of—

(*1*) The date on which the acquirer submits to the target a letter of intent, offer letter, or similar written communication proposing a merger, acquisition, or other business combination; or

(*2*) The date on which an acquisition proposal is approved by the taxpayer's Board of Directors (or committee of the Board of Directors) or, in the case of a taxpayer that is not a corporation, the date on which the acquisition proposal is approved by the appropriate governing officials of the taxpayer.

(B) *Inherently facilitative amounts.* An amount paid in the process of pursuing an acquisition facilitates that acquisition if the amount is inherently facilitative, regardless of whether the amount is paid for activities performed prior to the date determined under paragraph (e)(4)(i)(A) of this section. An amount is inherently facilitative if the amount is paid for activities performed in determining the value of the target, negotiating or structuring the transaction, preparing and reviewing transactional documents, preparing and reviewing regulatory filings required by the transaction, obtaining regulatory approval of the transaction, securing advice on the tax consequences of the transaction, securing an opinion as to the fairness of the transaction, obtaining shareholder approval of the transaction, or conveying property between the parties to the transaction.

(C) *Success-based fees.* An amount paid that is contingent on the successful closing of an acquisition is an amount paid to facilitate the acquisition except to the extent that evidence clearly demonstrates that some portion of the amount is allocable to activities that do not facilitate the acquisition.

(D) *Integration costs.* An amount paid to integrate the business operations of the acquirer and the target does not facilitate the acqui-

sition within the meaning of paragraph (e)(1)(i) of this section, regardless of when the integration activities occur.

(ii) *Divisive transactions*—(A) *Stock distributions.* An amount paid to facilitate a distribution of stock to the shareholders of a taxpayer is not required to be capitalized under this section if the divestiture is required by law, regulatory mandate, or court order unless the divestiture itself facilitates another transaction referred to in paragraph (e)(1)(i) of this section. For example, where a taxpayer, to comply with a new law requiring the taxpayer to divest itself of a particular trade or business, contributes that trade or business to a new subsidiary and distributes the stock of the subsidiary to the taxpayer's shareholders, amounts paid to facilitate the distribution do not facilitate a transaction referred to in paragraph (e)(1)(i) of this section and are not required to be capitalized under this section. Conversely, where a taxpayer, to secure regulatory approval for its proposed acquisition of a target corporation, complies with a government mandate to divest itself of a particular trade or business and contributes the trade or business to a new subsidiary and distributes the stock of the subsidiary to the taxpayer's shareholders, amounts paid to facilitate the divestiture are amounts paid to facilitate the acquisition of the target and must be capitalized under this section.

(B) *Taxable asset sales.* An amount paid to facilitate the sale of assets in a transaction not described in section 368 is not required to be capitalized under this section unless the sale is required by law, regulatory mandate, or court order and the sale itself facilitates another transaction referred to in paragraph (e)(1)(i) of this section. For example, where a target corporation, in preparation for a merger with an acquirer, sells assets that are not desired by the acquirer, amounts paid to facilitate the sale are not required to be capitalized as amounts paid to facilitate the merger. Conversely, where a taxpayer, in order to secure regulatory approval for its proposed acquisition of a target corporation, complies with a government mandate to divest itself of a particular trade or business and sells the assets of that trade or business in a taxable sale, amounts paid to facilitate the sale are amounts paid to facilitate the acquisition of the target and must be capitalized under this section.

(iii) *Defense against a hostile acquisition attempt*—(A) *In general.* An amount paid to defend against an acquisition of the taxpayer in a hostile acquisition attempt is not an amount paid to facilitate a transaction within the meaning of paragraph (e)(1)(i) of this section. In determining whether an acquisition attempt is hostile, all relevant facts and circumstances are taken into ac-

Reg. § 1.263(a)-4(e)(4)

count. The mere fact that the taxpayer receives an unsolicited offer from a potential acquirer, or rejects an initial offer from a potential acquirer, is not determinative of whether an acquisition attempt is hostile. On the other hand, the fact that the taxpayer implements defensive measures in response to the acquisition attempt is evidence that the acquisition attempt is hostile. Once an acquisition attempt ceases to be hostile, an amount paid by the taxpayer in the process of pursuing the acquisition of its stock by the acquirer is an amount paid to facilitate a transaction referred to in paragraph (e)(1)(i) of this section.

(B) *Exception for amounts paid to facilitate another capital transaction.* An amount paid to defend against an acquisition of the taxpayer in a hostile acquisition attempt does not include a payment that, while intended to thwart a hostile acquisition attempt by an acquirer, itself facilitates another transaction referred to in paragraph (e)(1)(i) of this section. Thus, for example, an amount paid to effect a recapitalization in an effort to defend against a hostile acquisition attempt is not an amount paid to defend against an acquisition of the taxpayer in a hostile acquisition attempt for purposes of paragraph (e)(4)(iii)(A) of this section.

(5) *Coordination with paragraph (d) of this section.* In the case of an amount paid to facilitate the creation or enhancement of an intangible described in paragraph (d) of this section, the provisions of this paragraph (e) apply regardless of whether a payment described in paragraph (d) is made.

* * *

(f) *12-month rule*—(1) *In general*—(i) *Amounts paid to create or enhance an intangible asset.* A taxpayer is not required to capitalize amounts paid to create or enhance an intangible asset if the amounts do not create or enhance any right or benefit for the taxpayer that extends beyond the earlier of—

(A) 12 months after the first date on which the taxpayer realizes the right or benefit; or

(B) The end of the taxable year following the taxable year in which the payment is made.

(ii) *Transaction costs.* A taxpayer is not required to capitalize amounts paid to facilitate the creation or enhancement of an intangible asset if, by reason of paragraph (f)(1)(i) of this section, capitalization would not be required for amounts paid to create or enhance that intangible asset.

(2) *Duration of benefit for contract terminations.* For purposes of this paragraph (f), amounts

paid to terminate a contract or other agreement described in paragraph (d)(7)(i) of this section prior to its expiration date (or amounts paid to facilitate such termination) create a benefit for the taxpayer equal to the unexpired term of the agreement as of the date of the termination.

(3) *Inapplicability to created financial interests and self-created amortizable section 197 intangibles.* Paragraph (f)(1) of this section does not apply to amounts paid to create or enhance an intangible described in paragraph (d)(2) of this section (relating to amounts paid to create or enhance financial interests) or to amounts paid to create or enhance an intangible asset that constitutes an amortizable section 197 intangible within the meaning of section 197(c).

(4) *Inapplicability to rights of indefinite duration.* Paragraph (f)(1) of this section does not apply to amounts paid to create or enhance a right of indefinite duration. A right has an indefinite duration if it has no period of duration fixed by agreement or by law, or if it is not based on a period of time, such as a right attributable to an agreement to provide or receive a fixed amount of goods or services. For example, a license granted by a governmental agency that permits the taxpayer to operate a business conveys a right of indefinite duration if the license may be revoked only upon the taxpayer's violation of the terms of the license.

* * *

(7) *Coordination with section 461.* In the case of a taxpayer using an accrual method of accounting, the rules of this paragraph (f) do not affect the determination of whether a liability is incurred during the taxable year, including the determination of whether economic performance has occurred with respect to the liability. See § 1.461-4(d) for rules relating to economic performance.

(8) *Examples.* The rules of this paragraph (f) are illustrated by the following examples, in which it is assumed (unless otherwise stated) that the taxpayer is a calendar year, accrual method taxpayer:

Example 1. Prepaid expenses. On December 1, 2002, N corporation pays a $10,000 insurance premium to obtain a property insurance policy with a 1-year term that begins on February 1, 2003. The amount paid by N is a prepaid expense described in paragraph (d)(3) of this section. Because the right or benefit attributable to the $10,000 payment extends beyond the end of the taxable year following the taxable year in which the payment is made, the 12-month rule provided by this paragraph (f) does not apply. N must capitalize the $10,000 payment.

Reg. § 1.263(a)-4(e)(5)

Example 2. Prepaid expenses. Assume the same facts as in *Example 1*, except that the policy has a term beginning on December 15, 2002. The 12-month rule of this paragraph (f) applies to the $10,000 payment because the right or benefit attributable to the payment neither extends more than 12 months beyond December 15, 2002 (the first date the benefit is realized by the taxpayer) nor beyond the taxable year following the year in which the payment is made. Accordingly, N is not required to capitalize the $10,000 payment.

Example 3. Financial interests. On October 1, 2002, X corporation makes a 9-month loan to B in the principal amount of $250,000. The principal amount of the loan paid to B constitutes an amount paid to create or originate a financial interest under paragraph (d)(2)(i)(B) of this section. The 9-month term of the loan does not extend beyond the period prescribed by paragraph (f)(1)(i) of this section. However, as provided by paragraph (f)(3) of this section, the rules of this paragraph (f) do not apply to intangibles described in paragraph (d)(2) of this section. Accordingly, X must capitalize the $250,000 loan amount.

Example 4. Financial interests. X corporation owns all of the outstanding stock of Z corporation. On December 1, Y corporation, a calendar year taxpayer, pays X $1,000,000 in exchange for X's grant of a 9-month call option to Y permitting Y to purchase all of the outstanding stock of Z. Y's payment to X constitutes an amount paid to create or originate an option with X under paragraph (d)(2)(i)(C)(7) of this section. The 9-month term of the option does not extend beyond the period prescribed by paragraph (f)(1)(i) of this section. However, as provided by paragraph (f)(3) of this section, the rules of this paragraph (f) do not apply to intangibles described in paragraph (d)(2) of this section. Accordingly, Y must capitalize the $1,000,000 payment.

Example 5. License. (i) On July 1, 2002, R corporation pays $10,000 to state X to obtain a license to operate a business in state X for a period of 5 years. The terms of the license require R to pay state X an annual fee of $500 due on July 1 of each of the succeeding four years. R pays the $500 fee on July 1 of each succeeding year as required by the license.

(ii) R's payment of $10,000 is an amount paid to a governmental agency for a license granted by that agency to which paragraph (d)(5) of this section applies. Because R's payment creates rights or benefits for R that extend beyond the end of 2003 (the taxable year following the taxable year in which the payment is made), the rules of this paragraph (f) do not apply to R's

payment. Accordingly, R must capitalize the $10,000 payment.

(iii) R's payment of each $500 annual fee is a prepaid expense described in paragraph (d)(3) of this section. R is not required to capitalize the $500 fee in each of the succeeding four taxable years. The rules of this paragraph (f) apply to each such payment because each payment provides a right or benefit to R that does not extend beyond 12 months after the first date on which R realizes the rights or benefits attributable to the payment and does not extend beyond the end of the taxable year following the taxable year in which the payment is made.

* * *

(g) *Treatment of capitalized transaction costs*—(1) *Costs described in paragraph (b)(1)(i) or (ii) of this section.* Except in the case of amounts paid by an acquirer to facilitate an acquisition of stock or assets in a transaction described in section 368, an amount required to be capitalized by paragraph (b)(1)(i) or (ii) of this section is capitalized to the basis of the intangible asset acquired, created, or enhanced.

(2) *Costs described in paragraph (b)(1)(iii) of this section*—(i) *Stock issuance or recapitalization.* An amount paid to facilitate a stock issuance or a recapitalization is not capitalized to the basis of an intangible asset but is treated as a reduction of the proceeds from the stock issuance or the recapitalization.

(ii) [Reserved].

* * *

(j) *Application to accrual method taxpayers.* For purposes of this section, the terms *amount paid* and *payment* mean, in the case of a taxpayer using an accrual method of accounting, a liability incurred (within the meaning of § 1.446-1(c)(1)(ii)). A liability may not be taken into account under this section prior to the taxable year during which the liability is incurred.

* * *

[Reg. § 1.263(a)-4.]

[Proposed 12-19-2002 (*corrected* 1-31-2003).]

§ 1.265-1. Expenses relating to tax-exempt income.—(a) *Nondeductibility of expenses allocable to exempt income.* (1) No amount shall be allowed as a deduction under any provision of the Internal Revenue Code of 1954 for any expense or amount which is otherwise allowable as a deduction and which is allocable to a class or classes of exempt income other than a class or classes of exempt interest income.

(2) No amount shall be allowed as a deduction under section 212 (relating to expenses for production of income) for any expense or amount

which is otherwise allowable as a deduction and which is allocable to a class or classes of exempt interest income.

(b) *Exempt income and nonexempt income.* (1) As used in this section, the term "class of exempt income" means any class of income (whether or not any amount of income of such class is received or accrued) wholly exempt from the taxes imposed by subtitle A of the Code. For purposes of this section, a class of income which is considered as wholly exempt from the taxes imposed by subtitle A includes any class of income which is—

(i) Wholly excluded from gross income under any provision of subtitle A, or

(ii) Wholly exempt from the taxes imposed by subtitle A under the provisions of any other law.

(2) As used in this section the term "nonexempt income" means any income which is required to be included in gross income.

(c) *Allocation of expenses to a class or classes of exempt income.* Expenses and amounts otherwise allowable which are directly allocable to any class or classes of exempt income shall be allocated thereto; and expenses and amounts directly allocable to any class or classes of nonexempt income shall be allocated thereto. If an expense or amount otherwise allowable is indirectly allocable to both a class of nonexempt income and a class of exempt income, a reasonable proportion thereof determined in the light of all the facts and circumstances in each case shall be allocated to each.

(d) *Statement of classes of exempt income; records.* (1) A taxpayer receiving any class of exempt income or holding any property or engaging in any activity the income from which is exempt shall submit with his return as a part thereof an itemized statement, in detail, showing (i) the amount of each class of exempt income, and (ii) the amount of expenses and amounts otherwise allowable allocated to each such class (the amount allocated by apportionment being shown separately) as required by paragraph (c) of this section. If an item is apportioned between a class of exempt income and a class of nonexempt income, the statement shall show the basis of the apportionment. Such statement shall also recite that each deduction claimed in the return is not in any way attributable to a class of exempt income.

(2) The taxpayer shall keep such records as will enable him to make the allocations required by this section. See section 6001 and the regulations thereunder. [Reg. § 1.265-1.]

☐ [*T.D.* 6313, 9-16-58.]

§ 1.266-1. Taxes and carrying charges chargeable to capital account and treated as capital items.—(a)(1) *In general.* In accordance

with section 266, items enumerated in paragraph (b)(1) of this section may be capitalized at the election of the taxpayer. Thus, taxes and carrying charges with respect to property of the type described in this section are chargeable to capital account at the election of the taxpayer, notwithstanding that they are otherwise expressly deductible under provisions of subtitle A of the Code. No deduction is allowable for any items so treated.

(2) See §§ 1.263A-8 through 1.263A-15 for rules regarding the requirement to capitalize interest, that apply prior to the application of this section. After applying §§ 1.263A-8 through 1.263A-15, a taxpayer may elect to capitalize interest under section 266 with respect to designated property within the meaning of § 1.263A-8(b), provided a computation under any provision of the Internal Revenue Code is not thereby materially distorted, including computations relating to the source of deductions.

(b) *Taxes and carrying charges.* (1) The taxpayer may elect, as provided in paragraph (c) of this section, to treat the items enumerated in this subparagraph which are otherwise expressly deductible under the provisions of subtitle A of the Code as chargeable to capital account either as a component of original cost or other basis, for the purposes of section 1012, or as an adjustment to basis, for the purpose of section 1016(a)(1). The items thus chargeable to capital account are—

(i) In the case of unimproved and unproductive real property: Annual taxes, interest on a mortgage, and other carrying charges.

(ii) In the case of real property, whether improved or unimproved and whether productive or unproductive:

(*a*) Interest on a loan (but not theoretical interest of a taxpayer using his own funds),

(*b*) Taxes of the owner of such real property measured by compensation paid to his employees,

(*c*) Taxes of such owner imposed on the purchase of materials, or on the storage, use, or other consumption of materials, and

(*d*) Other necessary expenditures,

paid or incurred for the development of the real property or for the construction of an improvement or additional improvement to such real property, up to the time the development or construction work has been completed. The development or construction work with respect to which such items are incurred may relate to unimproved and unproductive real estate whether the construction work will make the property productive of income subject to tax (as in the case of a factory) or not (as in the case of a personal residence), or may relate to property already im-

Reg. § 1.266-1(a)(2)

proved or productive (as in the case of a plant addition or improvement, such as the construction of another floor on a factory or the installation of insulation therein).

(iii) In the case of personal property:

(a) Taxes of an employer measured by compensation for services rendered in transporting machinery or other fixed assets to the plant or installing them therein,

(b) Interest on a loan to purchase such property or to pay for transporting or installing the same, and

(c) Taxes of the owner thereof imposed on the purchase of such property or on the storage, use, or other consumption of such property, paid or incurred up to the date of installation or the date when such property is first put into use by the taxpayer, whichever date is later.

(iv) Any other taxes and carrying charges with respect to property, otherwise deductible, which in the opinion of the Commissioner are, under sound accounting principles, chargeable to capital account.

(2) The sole effect of section 266 is to permit the items enumerated in subparagraph (1) of this paragraph to be chargeable to capital account notwithstanding that such items are otherwise expressly deductible under the provisions of subtitle A of the Code. An item not otherwise deductible may not be capitalized under section 266.

(3) In the absence of a provision in this section for treating a given item as a capital item, this section has no effect on the treatment otherwise accorded such item. Thus, items which are otherwise deductible are deductible notwithstanding the provisions of this section, and items which are otherwise treated as capital items are to be so treated. Similarly, an item not otherwise deductible is not made deductible by this section. Nor is the absence of a provision in this section for treating a given item as a capital item to be construed as withdrawing or modifying the right now given to the taxpayer under any other provisions of subtitle A of the Code, or of the regulations thereunder, to elect to capitalize or to deduct a given item.

(c) *Election to charge taxes and carrying charges to capital account.* (1) If for any taxable year there are two or more items of the type described in paragraph (b)(1) of this section, which relate to the same project to which the election is applicable, the taxpayer may elect to capitalize any one or more of such items even though he does not elect to capitalize the remaining items or to capitalize items of the same type relating to other projects. However, if expenditures for several items of the same type are in-

curred with respect to a single project, the election to capitalize must, if exercised, be exercised as to all items of that type. For purposes of this section, a "project" means, in the case of items described in paragraph (b)(1)(ii) of this section, a particular development of, or construction of an improvement to, real property, and in the case of items described in paragraph (b)(1)(iii) of this section, the transportation and installation of machinery or other fixed assets.

(2)(i) An election with respect to an item described in paragraph (b)(1)(i) of this section is effective only for the year for which it is made.

(ii) An election with respect to an item described in—

(a) Paragraph (b)(1)(ii) of this section is effective until the development or construction work described in that subdivision has been completed;

(b) Paragraph (b)(1)(iii) of this section is effective until the later of either the date of installation of the property described in that subdivision, or the date when such property is first put into use by the taxpayer;

(c) Paragraph (b)(1)(iv) of this section is effective as determined by the Commissioner.

Thus, an item chargeable to capital account under this section must continue to be capitalized for the entire period described in this subdivision applicable to such election although such period may consist of more than one taxable year.

(3) If the taxpayer elects to capitalize an item or items under this section, such election shall be exercised by filing with the original return for the year for which the election is made a statement indicating the item or items (whether with respect to the same project or to different projects) which the taxpayer elects to treat as chargeable to capital account. Elections filed for taxable years beginning before January 1, 1954, and for taxable years ending before August 17, 1954, under section 24(a)(7) of the Internal Revenue Code of 1939, and the regulations thereunder, shall have the same effect as if they were filed under this section. See section 7807(b)(2).

(d) The following examples are illustrative of the application of the provisions of this section:

Example (1). In 1956 and 1957 A pays annual taxes and interest on a mortgage on a piece of real property. During 1956, the property is vacant and unproductive, but throughout 1957 A operates the property as a parking lot. A may capitalize the taxes and mortgage interest paid in 1956, but not the taxes and mortgage interest paid in 1957.

Example (2). In February 1957, B began the erection of an office building for himself. B in

1957, in connection with the erection of the building, paid $6,000 social security taxes, which in his 1957 return he elected to capitalize. B must continue to capitalize the social security taxes paid in connection with the erection of the building until its completion.

Example (3). Assume the same facts as in example (2) except that in November 1957, B also begins to build a hotel. In 1957 B pays $3,000 social security taxes in connection with the erection of the hotel. B's election to capitalize the social security taxes paid in erecting the office building started in February 1957 does not bind him to capitalize the social security taxes paid in erecting the hotel; he may deduct the $3,000 social security taxes paid in erecting the hotel.

Example (4). In 1957, M Corporation began the erection of a building for itself, which will take three years to complete. M Corporation in 1957 paid $4,000 social security taxes and $8,000 interest on a building loan in connection with this building. M Corporation may elect to capitalize the social security taxes although it deducts the interest charges.

Example (5). C purchases machinery in 1957 for use in his factory. He pays social security taxes on the labor for transportation and installation of the machinery, as well as interest on a loan to obtain funds to pay for the machinery and for transportation and installation costs. C may capitalize either the social security taxes or the interest, or both, up to the date of installation or until the machinery is first put into use by him, whichever date is later.

(e) *Allocation.* If any tax or carrying charge with respect to property is in part a type of item described in paragraph (b) of this section and in part a type of item or items with respect to which no election to treat as a capital item is given, a reasonable proportion of such tax or carrying charge, determined in the light of all the facts and circumstances in each case, shall be allocated to each item. The rule of this paragraph may be illustrated by the following example:

Example. N Corporation, the owner of a factory in New York on which a new addition is under construction, in 1957 pays its general manager, B, a salary of $10,000 and also pays a New York State unemployment insurance tax of $81 on B's salary. B spends nine-tenths of his time in the general business of the firm and the remaining one-tenth in supervising the construction work. N Corporation treats as expenses $9,000 of B's salary, and charges the remaining $1,000 to capital account. N Corporation may elect to capitalize $8.10 of the $81 New York State unemployment insurance tax paid in 1957 since such tax is deductible under section 164. [Reg. § 1.266-1.]

Reg. § 1.267(a)-1(a)

☐ [*T.D. 6313, 9-16-58. Amended by T.D. 6380, 5-26-59 and T.D. 8584, 12-28-94.*]

§ 1.267(a)-1. **Deductions disallowed.**—(a) *Losses.* Except in cases of distributions in corporate liquidations, no deduction shall be allowed for losses arising from direct or indirect sales or exchanges of property between persons who, on the date of the sale or exchange, are within any one of the relationships specified in section 267(b). See § 1.267(b)-1.

* * *

(c) *Scope of section.* Section 267(a) requires that deductions for losses or unpaid expenses or interest described therein be disallowed even though the transaction in which such losses, expenses, or interest were incurred was a bona fide transaction. However, section 267 is not exclusive. No deduction for losses or unpaid expenses or interest arising in a transaction which is not bona fide will be allowed even though section 267 does not apply to the transaction. [Reg. § 1.267(a)-1.]

☐ [*T.D. 6312, 9-10-58.*]

§ 1.267(b)-1. **Relationships.**—(a) *In general.* (1) The persons referred to in section 267(a) and § 1.267(a)-1 are specified in section 267(b).

(2) Under section 267(b)(3), it is not necessary that either of the two corporations be a personal holding company or a foreign personal holding company for the taxable year in which the sale or exchange occurs or in which the expenses or interest are properly accruable, but either one of them must be such a company for the taxable year next preceding the taxable year in which the sale or exchange occurs or in which the expenses or interest are accrued.

(3) Under section 267(b)(9), the control of certain educational and charitable organizations exempt from tax under section 501 includes any kind of control, direct or indirect, by means of which a person in fact controls such an organization, whether or not the control is legally enforceable and regardless of the method by which the control is exercised or exercisable. In the case of an individual, control possessed by the individual's family, as defined in section 267(c)(4) and paragraph (a)(4) of § 1.267(c)-1, shall be taken into account.

(b) *Partnerships*—(1) Since section 267 does not include members of a partnership and the partnership as related persons, transactions between partners and partnerships do not come within the scope of section 267. Such transactions are governed by section 707 for the purposes of which the partnership is considered to be an entity separate from the partners. See section 707 and § 1.707-1. Any transaction described in section 267(a) between a partnership and a person other than a partner shall be considered as occurring between the other person and the members of the partnership separately. Therefore, if the other person and a partner are within any one of the relationships specified in section 267(b), no deductions with respect to such transactions between the other person and the partnership shall be allowed—

(i) To the related partner to the extent of his distributive share of partnership deductions for losses or unpaid expenses or interest resulting from such transactions, and

(ii) To the other person to the extent the related partner acquires an interest in any property sold to or exchanged with the partnership by such other person at a loss, or to the extent of the related partner's distributive share of the unpaid expenses or interest payable to the partnership by the other person as a result of such transaction.

(2) The provisions of this paragraph may be illustrated by the following examples:

Example (1). A, an equal partner in the ABC partnership, personally owns all the stock of M Corporation. B and C are not related to A. The partnership and all the partners use an accrual method of accounting, and are on a calendar year. M Corporation uses the cash receipts and disbursements method of accounting and is also on a calendar year. During 1956 the partnership borrowed money from M Corporation and also sold property to M Corporation, sustaining a loss on the sale. On December 31, 1956, the partnership accrued its interest liability to the M Corporation and on April 1, 1957 (more than 2½ months after the close of its taxable year), it paid the M Corporation the amount of such accrued interest. Applying the rules of this paragraph, the transactions are considered as occurring between M Corporation and the partners separately. The sale and interest transactions considered as occurring between A and the M Corporation fall within the scope of section 267(a) and (b), but the transactions considered as occurring between partners B and C and the M Corporation do not. The latter two partners may, therefore, deduct their distributive shares of partnership deductions for the loss and the accrued interest. However, no deduction shall be allowed to A for his distributive shares of these partnership deductions. Furthermore, A's adjusted basis for his partnership interest must be decreased by the amount of his distributive share of such deductions. See section 705(a)(2).

Example (2). Assume the same facts as in example (1) of this subparagraph except that the partnership and all the partners use the cash receipts and disbursements method of accounting, and that M Corporation uses an accrual method. Assume further, that during 1956 M Corporation

borrowed money from the partnership and that on a sale of property to the partnership during that year M Corporation sustained a loss. On December 31, 1956, the M Corporation accrued its interest liability on the borrowed money and on April 1, 1957 (more than 2½ months after the close of its taxable year) it paid the accrued interest to the partnership. The corporation's deduction for the accrued interest is not allowed to the extent of A's distributive share (one-third) of such interest income. M Corporation's deduction for the loss on the sale of the property to the partnership is not allowed to the extent of A's one-third interest in the purchased property. [Reg. § 1.267(b)-1.]

☐ [*T.D.* 6312, 9-10-58.]

§ 1.267(c)-1. **Constructive ownership of stock.**—(a) *In general.* (1) The determination of stock ownership for purposes of section 267(b) shall be in accordance with the rules in section 267(c).

(2) For an individual to be considered under section 267(c)(2) as constructively owning the stock of a corporation which is owned, directly or indirectly, by or for members of his family it is not necessary that he own stock in the corporation either directly or indirectly. On the other hand, for an individual to be considered under section 267(c)(3) as owning the stock of a corporation owned either actually, or constructively under section 267(c)(1), by or for his partner, such individual must himself actually own, or constructively own under section 267(c)(1), stock of such corporation.

(3) An individual's constructive ownership, under section 267(c)(2) or (3), of stock owned directly or indirectly by or for a member of his family, or by or for his partner, is not to be considered as actual ownership of such stock, and the individual's constructive ownership of the stock is not to be attributed to another member of his family or to another partner. However, an individual's constructive ownership, under section 267(c)(1), of stock owned directly or indirectly by or for a corporation, partnership, estate, or trust shall be considered as actual ownership of the stock, and the individual's ownership may be attributed to a member of his family or to his partner.

(4) The family of an individual shall include only his brothers and sisters, spouse, ancestors, and lineal descendants. In determining whether any of these relationships exist, full effect shall be given to a legal adoption. The term "ancestors" includes parents and grandparents, and the term "lineal descendants" includes children and grandchildren.

(b) *Examples.* The application of section 267(c) may be illustrated by the following examples:

Reg. § 1.267(c)-1(b)

Example (1). On July 1, 1957, A owned 75 percent, and AW, his wife, owned 25 percent, of the outstanding stock of the M Corporation. The M Corporation in turn owned 80 percent of the outstanding stock of the O Corporation. Under section 267(c)(1), A and AW are each considered as owning an amount of the O Corporation stock actually owned by M Corporation in proportion to their respective ownership of M Corporation stock. Therefore, A constructively owns 60 percent (75 percent of 80 percent) of the O Corporation stock and AW constructively owns 20 percent (25 percent of 80 percent) of such stock. Under the family ownership rule of section 267(c)(2), an individual is considered as constructively owning the stock actually owned by his spouse. A and AW, therefore, are each considered as constructively owning the M Corporation stock actually owned by the other. For the purpose of applying this family ownership rule, A's and AW's constructive ownership of O Corporation stock is considered as actual ownership under section 267(c)(5). Thus, A constructively owns the 20 percent of the O Corporation stock constructively owned by AW, and AW constructively owns the 60 percent of the O Corporation stock constructively owned by A. In addition, the family ownership rule may be applied to make AWF, AW's father, the constructive owner of the 25 percent of the M Corporation stock actually owned by AW. As noted above, AW's constructive ownership of 20 percent of the O Corporation stock is considered as actual ownership for purposes of applying the family ownership rule, and AWF is thereby considered the constructive owner of this stock also. However, AW's constructive ownership of the stock constructively and actually owned by A may not be considered as actual ownership for the purpose of again applying the family ownership rule to make AWF the constructive owner of these shares. The ownership of the stock in the M and O Corporations may be tabulated as follows:

Person	Stock ownership in M Corporation		Total under Section 267	Stock ownership in O Corporation		Total under Section 267
	Actual Percent	Constructive Percent	Percent	Actual Percent	Constructive Percent	Percent
A	75	25	100	None	$\begin{Bmatrix} 60 \\ 20 \end{Bmatrix}$	80
AW (A's wife)	25	75	100	None	$\begin{Bmatrix} 20 \\ 60 \end{Bmatrix}$	80
AWF (AW's father)	None	25	25	None	20	20
M Corporation	...	...	...	80	None	80
O Corporation	None	None	None	...	...	...

Assuming that the M Corporation and the O Corporation make their income tax returns for calendar years, and that there was no distribution in liquidation of the M or O Corporation, and further assuming that either corporation was a personal holding company under section 542 for the calendar year 1956, no deduction is allowable with respect to losses from sales or exchanges of property made on July 1, 1957, between the two corporations. Moreover, whether or not either corporation was a personal holding company, no loss would be allowable on a sale or exchange between A or AW and either corporation. A deduction would be allowed, however, for a loss sustained in an arm's length sale or exchange between A and AWF, and between AWF and the M or O Corporation.

Example (2). On June 15, 1957, all of the stock of the N Corporation was owned in equal proportions by A and his partner, AP. Except in the case of distributions in liquidation by the N Corporation, no deduction is allowable with respect to losses from sales or exchanges of property made on June 15, 1957, between A and the N Corporation or AP and the N Corporation since each partner is considered as owning the stock owned by the other; therefore, each is considered as owning more than 50 percent in value of the outstanding stock of the N Corporation.

Example (3). On June 7, 1957, A owned no stock in X Corporation, but his wife, AW, owned 20 percent in value of the outstanding stock of X, and A's partner, AP, owned 60 percent in value of the outstanding stock of X. The partnership firm of A and AP owned no stock in X Corporation. The ownership of AW's stock is attributed to A, but not that of AP since A does not own any X Corporation stock either actually, or constructively under section 267(c)(1). A's constructive ownership of AW's stock is not the ownership required for the attribution of AP's stock. Therefore, deductions for losses from sales or exchanges of property made on June 7, 1957, between X Corporation and A or AW are allowable since neither person owned more than 50 percent in value of the outstanding stock of X, but deductions for losses from sales or exchanges between X Corporation and AP would not be allowable by section 267(a) (except for distributions in liquidation of X Corporation). [Reg. § 1.267(c)-1.]

☐ [*T.D.* 6312, 9-10-58.]

§ 1.267(d)-1. Amount of gain where loss previously disallowed.—(a) *General rule.*—(1) If a taxpayer acquires property by purchase or exchange from a transferor who, on the transaction, sustained a loss not allowable as a deduction by reason of section 267(a)(1) (or by reason of section 24(b) of the Internal Revenue Code of 1939), then any gain realized by the taxpayer on a sale or other disposition of the property after December 31, 1953, shall be recognized only to the extent that the gain exceeds the amount of such loss as is properly allocable to the property sold or otherwise disposed of by the taxpayer.

(2) The general rule is also applicable to a sale or other disposition of property by a taxpayer when the basis of such property in the taxpayer's hands is determined directly or indirectly by reference to other property acquired by the taxpayer from a transferor through a sale or exchange in which a loss sustained by the transferor was not allowable. Therefore, section 267(d) applies to a sale or other disposition of property after a series of transactions if the basis of the property acquired in each transaction is determined by reference to the basis of the property transferred, and if the original property was acquired in a transaction in which a loss to a transferor was not allowable by reason of section 267(a)(1) (or by reason of section 24(b) of the Internal Revenue Code of 1939).

(3) The benefit of the general rule is available only to the original transferee but does not apply to any original transferee (e.g., a donee) who acquired the property in any manner other than by purchase or exchange.

(4) The application of the provisions of this paragraph may be illustrated by the following examples:

Example (1). He sells to his wife, W, for $500, certain corporate stock with an adjusted basis for determining loss to him of $800. The loss of $300 is not allowable to H by reason of section 267(a)(1) and paragraph (a) of § 1.267(a)-1. W later sells this stock for $1,000. Although W's realized gain is $500 ($1,000 minus $500, her basis), her recognized gain under section 267(d) is only $200, the excess of the realized gain of $500 over the loss of $300 not allowable to H. In determining capital gain or loss W's holding period commences on the date of the sale from H to W.

Example (2). Assume the same facts as in example (1) except that W later sells her stock for $300 instead of $1,000. Her recognized loss is $200 and not $500 since section 267(d) applies only to the nonrecognition of gain and does not affect basis.

Example (3). Assume the same facts as in example (1) except that W transfers her stock as a gift to X. The basis of the stock in the hands of X for the purpose of determining gain, under the provisions of section 1015, is the same as W's, or $500. If X later sells the stock for $1,000 the entire $500 gain is taxed to him.

Example (4). H sells to his wife, W, for $5,500, farmland, with an adjusted basis for determining loss to him of $8,000. The loss of $2,500 is not allowable to H by reason of section 267(a)(1) and paragraph (a) of § 1.267(a)-1. W exchanges the farmland, held for investment purposes, with S, an unrelated individual, for two city lots, also held for investment purposes. The basis of the city lots in the hands of W ($5,500) is a substituted basis determined under section 1031(d) by reference to the basis of the farmland. Later W sells the city lots for $10,000. Although W's realized gain is $4,500 ($10,000 minus $5,500), her recognized gain under section 267(d) is only $2,000, the excess of the realized gain of $4,500 over the loss of $2,500 not allowable to H.

* * *

(c) *Special rules.*—(1) Section 267(d) does not affect the basis of property for determining gain. Depreciation and other items which depend on such basis are also not affected.

(2) The provisions of section 267(d) shall not apply if the loss sustained by the transferor is not allowable to the transferor as a deduction by reason of section 1091, or section 118 of the Internal Revenue Code of 1939, which relate to losses from wash sales of stock or securities.

(3) In determining the holding period in the hands of the transferee of property received in an exchange with a transferor with respect to whom a loss on the exchange is not allowable by reason of section 267, section 1223(2) does not apply to include the period during which the property was held by the transferor. In determining such holding period, however, section 1223(1) may apply to include the period during which the transferee held the property which he exchanged where, for example, he exchanged a capital asset in a transaction which, as to him, was nontaxable under section 1031 and the property received in the exchange has the same basis as the property exchanged. [Reg. § 1.267(d)-1.]

☐ [*T.D.* 6312, 9-10-58.]

§ 1.269-1. Meaning and use of terms.—As used in section 269 and § § 1.269-2 through 1.269-7—

(a) *Allowance.* The term "allowance" refers to anything in the internal revenue laws which has the effect of diminishing tax liability. The term includes, among other things, a deduction, a credit, an adjustment, an exemption, or an exclusion.

(b) *Evasion or avoidance.* The phrase "evasion or avoidance" is not limited to cases involving criminal penalties, or civil penalties for fraud.

(c) *Control.* The term "control" means the ownership of stock possessing at least 50 percent of the total combined voting power of all classes of stock entitled to vote, or at least 50 percent of the total value of shares of all classes of stock of the corporation. For control to be "acquired on or after October 8, 1940", it is not necessary that all of such stock be acquired on or after October 8, 1940. Thus, if A, on October 7, 1940, and at all times thereafter, owns 40 percent of the stock of X Corporation and acquires on October 8, 1940, an additional 10 percent of such stock, an acquisition within the meaning of such phrase is made by A on October 8, 1940. Similarly, if B, on October 7, 1940, owns certain assets and transfers on October 8, 1940, such assets to a newly organized Y Corporation in exchange for all the stock of Y Corporation, an acquisition within the meaning of such phrase is made by B on October 8, 1940. If, under the facts stated in the preceding sentence, B is a corporation, all of whose stock is owned by Z Corporation, then an acquisition within the meaning of such phrase is also made by Z Corporation on October 8, 1940, as well as by the shareholders of Z Corporation taken as a group on such date, and by any of such shareholders if such shareholders as a group own 50 percent of the stock of Z on such date.

(d) *Person.* The term "person" includes an individual, a trust, an estate, a partnership, an association, a company, or a corporation. [Reg. § 1.269-1.]

☐ [*T.D.* 6595, 4-13-62. *Amended by T.D.* 8388, 12-31-91.]

§ 1.269-2. Purpose and scope of section 269.—(a) *General.* Section 269 is designed to prevent in the instances specified therein the use of the sections of the Internal Revenue Code providing deductions, credits, or allowances in evading or avoiding Federal income tax. See § 1.269-3.

(b) *Disallowance of deduction, credit, or other allowance.* Under the Code, an amount otherwise constituting a deduction, credit, or other allowance becomes unavailable as such under certain circumstances. Characteristic of such circumstances are those in which the effect of the deduction, credit, or other allowance would be to distort the liability of the particular taxpayer when the essential nature of the transaction or situation is examined in the light of the basic purpose or plan which the deduction, credit, or other allowance was designed by the Congress to effectuate. The distortion may be evidenced, for example, by the fact that the transaction was not undertaken for reasons germane to the conduct of the business of the taxpayer, by the unreal nature of the transaction such as its sham character, or by the unreal or unreasonable relation which the deduction, credit, or other allowance bears to the transaction. The principle of law making an amount unavailable as a deduction, credit, or other allowance in cases in which the effect of making an amount so available would be to distort the liability of the taxpayer has been judicially recognized and applied in several cases. Included in these cases are *Gregory v. Helvering* (1935) (293 U.S. 465; Ct. D. 911, C.B. XIV-1, 193); *Griffiths v. Helvering* (1939) (308 U.S. 355; Ct. D. 1431, C.B. 1940-1, 136); *Higgins v. Smith* (1940) (308 U.S. 473; Ct. D. 1434, C.B. 1940-1, 127); and *J.D. & A.B. Spreckels Co. v. Commissioner* (1940) (41 B.T.A. 370). In order to give effect to such principle, but not in limitation thereof, several provisions of the Code, for example, section 267 and section 270, specify with some particularity instances in which disallowance of the deduction, credit, or other allowance is required. Section 269 is also included in such provisions of the Code. The principle of law and the particular sections of the Code are not mutually exclusive and in appropriate circumstances they may operate together or they may operate separately. See, for example, § 1.269-6. [Reg. § 1.269-2.]

☐ [*T.D.* 6595, 4-13-62.]

§ 1.269-3. Instances in which section 269(a) disallows a deduction, credit, or other allowance.—(a) *Instances of disallowance.* Section 269 specifies two instances in which a deduction, credit, or other allowance is to be disallowed. These instances, described in paragraphs (1) and (2) of section 269(a), are those in which—

(1) Any person or persons acquire, or acquired on or after October 8, 1940, directly or indirectly, control of a corporation, or

(2) Any corporation acquires, or acquired on or after October 8, 1940, directly or indirectly, property of another corporation (not controlled, directly or indirectly, immediately before such acquisition by such acquiring corporation or its stockholders), the basis of which property in the hands of the acquiring corporation is determined by reference to the basis in the hands of the transferor corporation.

In either instance the principal purpose for which the acquisition was made must have been the evasion or avoidance of Federal income tax by securing the benefit of a deduction, credit, or other allowance which such other person, or persons, or corporation, would not otherwise enjoy. If this requirement is satisfied, it is immaterial by what method or by what conjunction of events the benefit was sought. Thus, an acquiring person or corporation can secure the benefit of a deduction,

Reg. § 1.269-2(a)

credit, or other allowance within the meaning of section 269 even though it is the acquired corporation that is entitled to such deduction, credit, or other allowance in the determination of its tax. If the purpose to evade or avoid Federal income tax exceeds in importance any other purpose, it is the principal purpose. This does not mean that only those acquisitions fall within the provisions of section 269 which would not have been made if the evasion or avoidance purpose was not present. The determination of the purpose for which an acquisition was made requires a scrutiny of the entire circumstances in which the transaction or course of conduct occurred, in connection with the tax result claimed to arise therefrom.

(b) *Acquisition of control; transactions indicative of purpose to evade or avoid tax.* If the requisite acquisition of control within the meaning of paragraph (1) of section 269(a) exists, the transactions set forth in the following subparagraphs are among those which, in the absence of additional evidence to the contrary, ordinarily are indicative that the principal purpose for acquiring control was evasion or avoidance of Federal income tax:

(1) A corporation or other business enterprise (or the interest controlling such corporation or enterprise) with large profits acquires control of a corporation with current, past, or prospective credits, deductions, net operating losses, or other allowances and the acquisition is followed by such transfers or other action as is necessary to bring the deduction, credit, or other allowance into conjunction with the income (see further § 1.259-6). This subparagraph may be illustrated by the following example:

Example. Individual A acquires all of the stock of L Corporation which has been engaged in the business of operating retail drug stores. At the time of the acquisition, L Corporation has net operating loss carryovers aggregating $100,000 and its net worth is $100,000. After the acquisition, L Corporation continues to engage in the business of operating retail drug stores but the profits attributable to such business after the acquisition are not sufficient to absorb any substantial portion of the net operating loss carryovers. Shortly after the acquisition, individual A causes to be transferred to L Corporation the assets of a hardware business previously controlled by A which business produces profits sufficient to absorb a substantial portion of L Corporation's net operating loss carryovers. The transfer of the profitable business, which has the effect of using net operating loss carryovers to offset gains of a business unrelated to that which produced the losses, indicates that the principal purpose for which the acquisition of control was made is evasion or avoidance of Federal income tax.

(2) A person or persons organize two or more corporations instead of a single corporation in order to secure the benefit of multiple surtax exemptions (see section 11(c)) or multiple minimum accumulated earnings credits (see section 535(c)(2) and (3)).

(3) A person or persons with high earning assets transfer them to a newly organized controlled corporation retaining assets producing net operating losses which are utilized in an attempt to secure refunds.

(c) *Acquisition of property; transactions indicative of purpose to evade or avoid tax.* If the requisite acquisition of property within the meaning of paragraph (2) of section 269(a) exists, the transactions set forth in the following subparagraphs are among those which, in the absence of additional evidence to the contrary, ordinarily are indicative that the principal purpose for acquiring such property was evasion or avoidance of Federal income tax:

(1) A corporation acquires property having in its hands an aggregate carryover basis which is materially greater than its aggregate fair market value at the time of such acquisition and utilizes the property to create tax-reducing losses or deductions.

(2) A subsidiary corporation, which has sustained large net operating losses in the operation of business X and which has filed separate returns for the taxable years in which the losses were sustained, acquires high earning assets, comprising business Y, from its parent corporation. The acquisition occurs at a time when the parent would not succeed to the net operating loss carryovers of the subsidiary if the subsidiary were liquidated, and the profits of business Y are sufficient to offset a substantial portion of the net operating loss carryovers attributable to business X (see further example (3) of § 1.269-6).

(d) *Ownership changes to which section 382(l)(5) applies; transactions indicative of purpose to evade or avoid tax—*(1) *In general.* Absent strong evidence to the contrary, a requisite acquisition of control or property in connection with an ownership change to which section 382(l)(5) applies is considered to be made for the principal purpose of evasion or avoidance of Federal income tax unless the corporation carries on more than an insignificant amount of an active trade or business during and subsequent to the title 11 or similar case (as defined in section 382(l)(5)(G)). The determination of whether the corporation carries on more than an insignificant amount of an active trade or business is made without regard to the continuity of business enterprise requirement set forth in § 1.368-1(d). The determination is based on all the facts and circumstances, includ-

Reg. § 1.269-3(d)

ing, for example, the amount of business assets that continue to be used, or the number of employees in the work force who continue employment, in an active trade or business (although not necessarily the historic trade or business). Where the corporation continues to utilize a significant amount of its business assets or work force, the requirement of carrying on more than an insignificant amount of an active trade or business may be met even though all trade or business activities temporarily cease for a period of time in order to address business exigencies.

(2) *Effective date.* The presumption under paragraph (d) of this section applies to acquisitions of control or property effected pursuant to a plan of reorganization confirmed by a court in a title 11 or similar case (within the meaning of section 368(a)(3)(A)) after August 14, 1990.

(e) *Relationship of section 269 to 11 U.S.C. 1129(d).* In determining for purposes of section 269 of the Internal Revenue Code whether an acquisition pursuant to a plan of reorganization in a case under title 11 of the United States Code was made for the principal purpose of evasion or avoidance of Federal income tax, the fact that a governmental unit did not seek a determination under 11 U.S.C. 1129(d) is not taken into account and any determination by a court under 11 U.S.C. 1129(d) that the principal purpose of the plan is not avoidance of taxes is not controlling. [Reg. § 1.269-3.]

□ [*T.D.* 6595, 4-13-62. *Amended by T.D.* 8388, 12-31-91.]

§ 1.269-5. Time of acquisition of control.— (a) *In general.* For purposes of section 269, an acquisition of control occurs when one or more persons acquire beneficial ownership of stock possessing at least 50 percent of the total combined voting power of all classes of stock entitled to vote or at least 50 percent of the total value of shares of all classes of stock of the corporation.

(b) *Application of general rule to certain creditor acquisitions*—(1) For purposes of section 269, creditors of an insolvent or bankrupt corporation (by themselves or in conjunction with other persons) acquire control of the corporation when they acquire beneficial ownership of the requisite amount of stock. Although insolvency or bankruptcy may cause the interests of creditors to predominate as a practical matter, creditor interests do not constitute beneficial ownership of the corporation's stock. Solely for purposes of section 269, creditors of a bankrupt corporation are treated as acquiring beneficial ownership of stock of the corporation no earlier than the time a bankruptcy court confirms a plan of reorganization.

(2) The provisions of this section are illustrated by the following example.

Example. Corporation *L* files a petition under chapter 11 of the Bankruptcy Code on January 5, 1987. A creditors' committee is formed. On February 22, 1987, and upon the request of the creditors, the bankruptcy court removes the debtor-in-possession from business management and operations and appoints a trustee. The trustee consults regularly with the creditors' committee in formulating both short-term and long-term management decisions. After three years, the creditors approve a plan of reorganization in which the outstanding stock of Corporation *L* is cancelled and its creditors receive shares of stock constituting all of the outstanding shares. The bankruptcy court confirms the plan of reorganization on March 23, 1990, and the plan is put into effect on May 25, 1990. For purposes of section 269, the creditors acquired control of Corporation *L* no earlier than March 23, 1990. Similarly, the determination of whether the creditors acquired control of Corporation *L* with the principal purpose of evasion or avoidance of Federal income tax is made by reference to the creditors' purposes as of no earlier than March 23, 1990. [Reg. § 1.269-5.]

□ [*T.D.* 6595, 4-13-62. *Amended by T.D.* 8388, 12-31-91.]

§ 1.269-7. Relationship of section 269 to sections 382 and 383 after the Tax Reform Act of 1986.—Section 269 and § § 1.269-1 through 1.269-5 may be applied to disallow a deduction, credit, or other allowance notwithstanding that the utilization or amount of a deduction, credit, or other allowance is limited or reduced under section 382 or 383 and the regulations thereunder. However, the fact that the amount of taxable income or tax that may be offset by a deduction, credit, or other allowance is limited under section 382(a) or 383 and the regulations thereunder is relevant to the determination of whether the principal purpose of an acquisition is the evasion or avoidance of Federal income tax. [Reg. § 1.269-7.]

□ [*T.D.* 8388, 12-31-91.]

§ 1.273-1. Life or terminable interests.— Amounts paid as income to the holder of a life or a terminable interest acquired by gift, bequest, or inheritance shall not be subject to any deduction for shrinkage (whether called by depreciation or any other name) in the value of such interest due to the lapse of time. In other words, the holder of such an interest so acquired may not set up the value of the expected future payments as corpus or principal and claim deduction for shrinkage or exhaustion thereof due to the passage of time. For the treatment generally of distributions to beneficiaries of an estate or trust, see subparts A, B, C, and D (section 641 and following), subchapter J, chapter 1 of the Code, and the regulations thereunder. For basis of property acquired from a decedent and by gifts and transfers in trust, see sections 1014 and 1015, and the regulation thereunder. [Reg. § 1.273-1.]

☐ [*T.D. 6313, 9-16-58.*]

§ 1.274-1. Disallowance of certain entertainment, gift and travel expenses.—Section 274 disallows in whole, or in part, certain expenditures for entertainment, gifts and travel which would otherwise be allowable under chapter 1 of the Code. The requirements imposed by section 274 are in addition to the requirements for deductibility imposed by other provisions of the Code. If a deduction is claimed for an expenditure for entertainment, gifts, or travel, the taxpayer must first establish that it is otherwise allowable as a deduction under chapter 1 of the Code before the provisions of section 274 become applicable. An expenditure for entertainment, to the extent it is lavish or extravagant, shall not be allowable as a deduction. The taxpayer should then substantiate such an expenditure in accordance with the rules under section 274(d). See § 1.274-5. Section 274 is a disallowance provision exclusively, and does not make deductible any expense which is disallowed under any other provision of the Code. Similarly, section 274 does not affect the includability of an item in, or the excludability of an item from, the gross income of any taxpayer. For specific provisions with respect to the deductibility of expenditures: for an activity of a type generally considered to constitute entertainment, amusement, or recreation, and for a facility used in connection with such an activity, as well as certain travel expenses of a spouse, etc., see § 1.274-2; for expenses for gifts, see § 1.274-3; for expenses for foreign travel, see § 1.274-4; for expenditures deductible without regard to business activity, see § 1.274-6; and for treatment of personal portion of entertainment facility, see § 1.274-7. [Reg. § 1.274-1.]

☐ [*T.D. 6659, 6-24-63. Amended by T.D. 8666, 5-29-96.*]

§ 1.274-2. Disallowance of deductions for certain expenses for entertainment, amusement, recreation, or travel.—(a) *General rules*—(1) *Entertainment activity.* Except as provided in this section, no deduction otherwise allowable under chapter 1 of the Code shall be allowed for any expenditure with respect to entertainment unless the taxpayer establishes—

(i) That the expenditure was directly related to the active conduct of the taxpayer's trade or business, or

(ii) In the case of an expenditure directly preceding or following a substantial and bona fide business discussion (including business meetings at a convention or otherwise), that the expenditure was associated with the active conduct of the taxpayer's trade or business.

Such deduction shall not exceed the portion of the expenditure directly related to (or in the case of an expenditure described in subdivision (ii) above, the portion of the expenditure associated with) the active conduct of the taxpayer's trade or business.

(2) *Entertainment facilities*—(i) *Expenditures paid or incurred after December 31, 1978, and not with respect to a club.* Except as provided in this section with respect to a club, no deduction otherwise allowable under chapter 1 of the Code shall be allowed for any expenditure paid or incurred after December 31, 1978, with respect to a facility used in connection with entertainment.

* * *

(iii) *Expenditures paid or incurred after December 31, 1993, with respect to a club*—(*a*) *In general.* No deduction otherwise allowable under chapter 1 of the Internal Revenue Code shall be allowed for amounts paid or incurred after December 31, 1993, for membership in any club organized for business, pleasure, recreation, or other social purpose. The purposes and activities of a club, and not its name, determine whether it is organized for business, pleasure, recreation, or other social purpose. Clubs organized for business, pleasure, recreation, or other social purpose include any membership organization if a principal purpose of the organization is to conduct entertainment activities for members of the organization or their guests or to provide members or their guests with access to entertainment facilities within the meaning of paragraph (e)(2) of this section. Clubs organized for business, pleasure, recreation, or other social purpose include, but are not limited to, country clubs, golf and athletic clubs, airline clubs, hotel clubs, and clubs operated to provide meals under circumstances generally considered to be conducive to business discussion.

(*b*) *Exceptions.* Unless a principal purpose of the organization is to conduct entertainment activities for members or their guests or to provide members or their guests with access to entertainment facilities, business leagues, trade associations, chambers of commerce, boards of trade, real estate boards, professional organizations (such as bar associations and medical associations), and civic or public service organizations will not be treated as clubs organized for business, pleasure, recreation, or other social purpose.

(3) *Cross references.* For definition of the term "entertainment," see paragraph (b)(1) of

this section. For the disallowance of deductions for the cost of admission to a dinner or program any part of the proceeds of which inures to the use of a political party or political candidate, and cost of admission to an inaugural event or similar event identified with any political party or political candidate, see § 1.276-1. For rules and definitions with respect to—

(i) "Directly related entertainment", see paragraph (c) of this section,

(ii) "Associated entertainment", see paragraph (d) of this section,

(iii) "Expenditures paid or incurred before January 1, 1979, with respect to entertainment facilities or before January 1, 1994, with respect to clubs", see paragraph (e) of this section, and

(iv) "Specific exceptions" to the disallowance rules of this section, see paragraph (f) of this section.

(b) *Definitions*—(1) *Entertainment defined* — (i) *In general.* For purposes of this section, the term "entertainment" means any activity which is of a type generally considered to constitute entertainment, amusement, or recreation, such as entertaining at night clubs, cocktail lounges, theaters, country clubs, golf and athletic clubs, sporting events, and on hunting, fishing, vacation and similar trips, including such activity relating solely to the taxpayer or the taxpayer's family. The term "entertainment" may include an activity, the cost of which is claimed as a business expense by the taxpayer, which satisfies the personal, living, or family needs of any individual, such as providing food and beverages, a hotel suite, or an automobile to a business customer or his family. The term "entertainment" does not include activities which, although satisfying personal, living, or family needs of an individual, are clearly not regarded as constituting entertainment, such as *(a)* supper money provided by an employer to his employee working overtime, *(b)* a hotel room maintained by an employer for lodging of his employees while in business travel status, or *(c)* an automobile used in the active conduct of trade or business even though used for routine personal purposes such as commuting to and from work. On the other hand, the providing of a hotel room or an automobile by an employer to his employee who is on vacation would constitute entertainment of the employee.

(ii) *Objective test.* An objective test shall be used to determine whether an activity is of a type generally considered to constitute entertainment. Thus, if an activity is generally considered to be entertainment, it will constitute entertainment for purposes of this section and section 274(a) regardless of whether the expenditure can also be described otherwise, and even though the expenditure relates to the taxpayer alone. This objective test precludes arguments such as that "entertainment" means only entertainment of others or that an expenditure for entertainment should be characterized as an expenditure for advertising or public relations. However, in applying this test the taxpayer's trade or business shall be considered. Thus, although attending a theatrical performance would generally be considered entertainment, it would not be so considered in the case of a professional theater critic, attending in his professional capacity. Similarly, if a manufacturer of dresses conducts a fashion show to introduce his products to a group of store buyers, the show would not be generally considered to constitute entertainment. However, if an appliance distributor conducts a fashion show for the wives of his retailers, the fashion show would be generally considered to constitute entertainment.

(iii) *Special definitional rules*—*(a) In general.* Except as otherwise provided in *(b)* or *(c)* of this subdivision, any expenditure which might generally be considered either for a gift or entertainment, or considered either for travel or entertainment, shall be considered an expenditure for entertainment rather than for a gift or travel.

(b) Expenditures deemed gifts. An expenditure described in *(a)* of this subdivision shall be deemed for a gift to which this section does not apply if it is:

(1) An expenditure for packaged food or beverages transferred directly or indirectly to another person intended for consumption at a later time.

(2) An expenditure for tickets of admission to a place of entertainment transferred to another person if the taxpayer does not accompany the recipient to the entertainment unless the taxpayer treats the expenditure as entertainment. The taxpayer may change his treatment of such an expenditure as either a gift or entertainment at any time within the period prescribed for assessment of tax as provided in section 6501 of the Code and the regulations thereunder.

(3) Such other specific classes of expenditure generally considered to be for a gift as the Commissioner, in his discretion, may prescribe.

(c) Expenditures deemed travel. An expenditure described in *(a)* of this subdivision shall be deemed for travel to which this section does not apply if it is:

(1) With respect to a transportation type facility (such as an automobile or an airplane), even though used on other occasions in connection with an activity of a type generally considered to constitute entertainment, to the extent the facility is used in pursuit of a trade or

Reg. § 1.274-2(b)(1)

business for purposes of transportation not in connection with entertainment. See also paragraph (e)(3)(iii)(*b*) of this section for provisions covering non-entertainment expenditures with respect to such facilities.

(2) Such other specific classes of expenditure generally considered to be for travel as the Commissioner, in his discretion, may prescribe.

(2) *Other definitions*—(i) *Expenditure.* The term "expenditure" as used in this section shall include expenses paid or incurred for goods, services, facilities, and items (including items such as losses and depreciation).

(ii) *Expenses for production of income.* For purposes of this section, any reference to "trade or business" shall include any activity described in section 212.

(iii) *Business associate.* The term "business associate" as used in this section means a person with whom the taxpayer could reasonably expect to engage or deal in the active conduct of the taxpayer's trade or business such as the taxpayer's customer, client, supplier, employee, agent, partner, or professional adviser, whether established or prospective.

(c) *Directly related entertainment* —(1) *In general.* Except as otherwise provided in paragraph (d) of this section (relating to associated entertainment) or under paragraph (f) of this section (relating to business meals and other specific exceptions), no deduction shall be allowed for any expenditure for entertainment unless the taxpayer establishes that the expenditure was directly related to the active conduct of his trade or business within the meaning of this paragraph.

(2) *Directly related entertainment defined.* Any expenditure for entertainment, if it is otherwise allowable as a deduction under chapter 1 of the Code, shall be considered directly related to the active conduct of the taxpayer's trade or business if it meets the requirements of any one of subparagraphs (3), (4), (5), or (6) of this paragraph.

(3) *Directly related in general.* Except as provided in subparagraph (7) of this paragraph, an expenditure for entertainment shall be considered directly related to the active conduct of the taxpayer's trade or business if it is established that it meets all of the requirements of subdivisions (i), (ii), (iii) and (iv) of this subparagraph.

(i) At the time the taxpayer made the entertainment expenditure (or committed himself to make the expenditure), the taxpayer had more than a general expectation of deriving some income or other specific trade or business benefit (other than the goodwill of the person or persons

entertained) at some indefinite future time from the making of the expenditure. A taxpayer, however, shall not be required to show that income or other business benefit actually resulted from each and every expenditure for which a deduction is claimed.

(ii) During the entertainment period to which the expenditure related, the taxpayer actively engaged in a business meeting, negotiation, discussion, or other bona fide business transaction, other than entertainment, for the purpose of obtaining such income or other specific trade or business benefit (or, at the time the taxpayer made the expenditure or committed himself to the expenditure, it was reasonable for the taxpayer to expect that he would have done so, although such was not the case solely for reasons beyond the taxpayer's control).

(iii) In light of all the facts and circumstances of the case, the principal character or aspect of the combined business and entertainment to which the expenditure related was the active conduct of the taxpayer's trade or business (or at the time the taxpayer made the expenditure or committed himself to the expenditure, it was reasonable for the taxpayer to expect that the active conduct of trade or business would have been the principal character or aspect of the entertainment, although such was not the case solely for reasons beyond the taxpayer's control). It is not necessary that more time be devoted to business than to entertainment to meet this requirement. The active conduct of trade or business is considered not to be the principal character or aspect of combined business and entertainment activity on hunting or fishing trips or on yachts and other pleasure boats unless the taxpayer clearly establishes to the contrary.

(iv) The expenditure was allocable to the taxpayer and a person or persons with whom the taxpayer engaged in the active conduct of trade or business during the entertainment or with whom the taxpayer establishes he would have engaged in such active conduct of trade or business if it were not for circumstances beyond the taxpayer's control. For expenditures closely connected with directly related entertainment, see paragraph (d)(4) of this section.

(4) *Expenditures in clear business setting.* An expenditure for entertainment shall be considered directly related to the active conduct of the taxpayer's trade or business if it is established that the expenditure was for entertainment occurring in a clear business setting directly in furtherance of the taxpayer's trade or business. Generally, entertainment shall not be considered to have occurred in a clear business setting unless the taxpayer clearly establishes that any recipient of

the entertainment would have reasonably known that the taxpayer had no significant motive, in incurring the expenditure, other than directly furthering his trade or business. Objective rather than subjective standards will be determinative. Thus, entertainment which occurred under any circumstances described in subparagraph (7)(ii) of this paragraph ordinarily will not be considered as occurring in a clear business setting. Such entertainment will generally be considered to be socially rather than commercially motivated. Expenditures made for the furtherance of a taxpayer's trade or business in providing a "hospitality room" at a convention (described in paragraph (d)(3)(i)(*b*) of this section) at which goodwill is created through display or discussion of the taxpayer's products, will, however, be treated as directly related. In addition, entertainment of a clear business nature which occurred under circumstances where there was no meaningful personal or social relationship between the taxpayer and the recipients of the entertainment may be considered to have occurred in a clear business setting. For example, entertainment of business representatives and civic leaders at the opening of a new hotel or theatrical production, where the clear purpose of the taxpayer is to obtain business publicity rather than to create or maintain the goodwill of the recipients of the entertainment, would generally be considered to be in a clear business setting. Also, entertainment which has the principal effect of a price rebate in connection with the sale of the taxpayer's products generally will be considered to have occurred in a clear business setting. Such would be the case, for example, if a taxpayer owning a hotel were to provide occasional free dinners at the hotel for a customer who patronized the hotel.

(5) *Expenditures for services performed.* An expenditure shall be considered directly related to the active conduct of the taxpayer's trade or business if it is established that the expenditure was made directly or indirectly by the taxpayer for the benefit of an individual (other than an employee), and if such expenditure was in the nature of compensation for services rendered or was paid as a prize or award which is required to be included in gross income under section 74 and the regulations thereunder. For example, if a manufacturer of products provides a vacation trip for retailers of his products who exceed sales quotas, as a prize or award includible in gross income, the expenditure will be considered directly related to the active conduct of the taxpayer's trade or business.

(6) *Club dues, etc., allocable to business meals.* An expenditure shall be considered directly related to the active conduct of the taxpayer's trade or business if it is established that the

expenditure was with respect to a facility (as described in paragraph (e) of this section) used by the taxpayer for the furnishing of food or beverages under circumstances described in paragraph (f)(2)(i) of this section (relating to business meals and similar expenditures), to the extent allocable to the furnishing of such food or beverages. This paragraph (c)(6) applies to club dues paid or incurred before January 1, 1987.

(7) *Expenditures generally considered not directly related.* Expenditures for entertainment, even if connected with the taxpayer's trade or business, will generally be considered not directly related to the active conduct of the taxpayer's trade or business, if the entertainment occurred under circumstances where there was little or no possibility of engaging in the active conduct of trade or business. The following circumstances will generally be considered circumstances where there was little or no possibility of engaging in the active conduct of a trade or business:

(i) The taxpayer was not present;

(ii) The distractions were substantial, such as—

(*a*) A meeting or discussion at night clubs, theaters, and sporting events, or during essentially social gatherings such as cocktail parties, or

(*b*) A meeting or discussion, if the taxpayer meets with a group which includes persons other than business associates, at places such as cocktail lounges, country clubs, golf and athletic clubs, or at vacation resorts.

An expenditure for entertainment in any such case is considered not to be directly related to the active conduct of the taxpayer's trade or business unless the taxpayer clearly establishes to the contrary.

(d) *Associated entertainment* —(1) *In general.* Except as provided in paragraph (f) of this section (relating to business meals and other specific exceptions) and subparagraph (4) of this paragraph (relating to expenditures closely connected with directly related entertainment), any expenditure for entertainment which is not directly related to the active conduct of the taxpayer's trade or business will not be allowable as a deduction unless—

(i) It was associated with the active conduct of trade or business as defined in subparagraph (2) of this paragraph, and

(ii) The entertainment directly preceded or followed a substantial and bona fide business discussion as defined in subparagraph (3) of this paragraph.

(2) *Associated entertainment defined.* Generally, any expenditure for entertainment, if it is otherwise allowable under chapter 1 of the Code,

shall be considered associated with the active conduct of the taxpayer's trade or business if the taxpayer establishes that he had a clear business purpose in making the expenditure, such as to obtain new business or to encourage the continuation of an existing business relationship. However, any portion of an expenditure allocable to a person who was not closely connected with a person who engaged in the substantial and bona fide business discussion (as defined in subparagraph (3)(i) of this paragraph) shall not be considered associated with the active conduct of the taxpayer's trade or business. The portion of an expenditure allocable to the spouse of a person who engaged in the discussion will, if it is otherwise allowable under chapter 1 of the Code, be considered associated with the active conduct of the taxpayer's trade or business.

(3) *Directly preceding or following a substantial and bona fide business discussion defined —* (i) *Substantial and bona fide business discussion—(a) In general.* Whether any meeting, negotiation or discussion constitutes a "substantial and bona fide business discussion" within the meaning of this section depends upon the facts and circumstances of each case. It must be established, however, that the taxpayer actively engaged in a business meeting, negotiation, discussion, or other bona fide business transaction, other than entertainment, for the purpose of obtaining income or other specific trade or business benefit. In addition, it must be established that such a business meeting, negotiation, discussion, or transaction was substantial in relation to the entertainment. This requirement will be satisfied if the principal character or aspect of the combined entertainment and business activity was the active conduct of business. However, it is not necessary that more time be devoted to business than to entertainment to meet this requirement.

(b) *Meetings at conventions, etc.* Any meeting officially scheduled in connection with a program at a convention or similar general assembly, or at a bona fide trade or business meeting sponsored and conducted by business or professional organizations, shall be considered to constitute a substantial and bona fide business discussion within the meaning of this section provided—

(1) *Expenses necessary to taxpayer's attendance.* The expenses necessary to the attendance of the taxpayer at the convention, general assembly, or trade or business meeting, were ordinary and necessary within the meaning of section 162 or 212;

(2) *Convention program.* The organization which sponsored the convention, or trade or business meeting had scheduled a program of business activities (including committee meetings or presentation of lectures, panel discussions, display of products, or other similar activities), and that such program was the principal activity of the convention, general assembly, or trade or business meeting.

(ii) *Directly preceding or following.* Entertainment which occurs on the same day as a substantial and bona fide business discussion (as defined in subdivision (i) of this subparagraph) will be considered to directly precede or follow such discussion. If the entertainment and the business discussion do not occur on the same day, the facts and circumstances of each case are to be considered, including the place, date and duration of the business discussion, whether the taxpayer or his business associates are from out of town, and, if so, the date of arrival and departure, and the reasons the entertainment did not take place on the day of the business discussion. For example, if a group of business associates comes from out of town to the taxpayer's place of business to hold a substantial business discussion, the entertainment of such business guests and their wives on the evening prior to, or on the evening of the day following, the business discussion would generally be regarded as directly preceding or following such discussion.

(4) *Expenses closely connected with directly related entertainment.* If any portion of an expenditure meets the requirements of paragraph (c)(3) of this section (relating to directly related entertainment in general), the remaining portion of the expenditure, if it is otherwise allowable under chapter 1 of the Code, shall be considered associated with the active conduct of the taxpayer's trade or business to the extent allocable to a person or persons closely connected with a person referred to in paragraph (c)(3)(iv) of this section. The spouse of a person referred to in paragraph (c)(3)(iv) of this section will be considered closely connected to such a person for purposes of this subparagraph. Thus, if a taxpayer and his wife entertain a business customer and the customer's wife under circumstances where the entertainment of the customer is considered directly related to the active conduct of the taxpayer's trade or business (within the meaning of paragraph (c)(3) of this section) the portion of the expenditure allocable to both wives will be considered associated with the active conduct of the taxpayer's trade or business under this subparagraph.

* * *

(f) *Specific exceptions to application of this section—(1) In general.* The provisions of paragraphs (a) through (e) of this section (imposing limitations on deductions for entertainment expenses) are not applicable in the case of expenditures set forth in subparagraph (2) of this paragraph. Such expenditures are deductible to the extent allowable under Chapter 1 of the Code. This paragraph shall not be construed to affect the allowability or nonallowability of a deduction under section 162 or 212 and the regulations thereunder. The fact that an expenditure is not covered by a specific exception provided for in this paragraph shall not be determinative of the allowability or nonallowability of the expenditure under paragraphs (a) through (e) of this section. Expenditures described in subparagraph (2) of this paragraph are subject to the substantiation requirements of section 274(d) to the extent provided in § 1.274-5.

(2) *Exceptions.* The expenditures referred to in subparagraph (1) of this paragraph are set forth in subdivisions (i) through (ix) of this subparagraph.

* * *

(ii) *Food and beverages for employees.* Any expenditure by a taxpayer for food and beverages (or for use of a facility in connection therewith) furnished on the taxpayer's business premises primarily for employees is not subject to the limitations on allowability of deductions provided for in paragraphs (a) through (e) of this section. This exception applies not only to expenditures for food or beverages furnished in a typical company cafeteria or an executive dining room, but also to expenditures with respect to the operation of such facilities. This exception applies even though guests are occasionally served in the cafeteria or dining room.

(iii) *Certain entertainment and travel expenses treated as compensation*—(A) *In general.* Any expenditure by a taxpayer for entertainment (or for use of a facility in connection therewith) or for travel described in section 274(m)(3), if an employee is the recipient of the entertainment or travel, is not subject to the limitations on allowability of deductions provided for in paragraphs (a) through (e) of this section to the extent that the expenditure is treated by the taxpayer—

(*1*) On the taxpayer's income tax return as originally filed, as compensation paid to the employee; and

(*2*) As wages to the employee for purposes of withholding under chapter 24 (relating to collection of income tax at source on wages).

(B) *Expenses includible in income of persons who are not employees.* Any expenditure by a taxpayer for entertainment (or for use of a facility in connection therewith), or for travel described in section 274(m)(3), is not subject to the limitations on allowability of deductions provided for in paragraphs (a) through (e) of this

section to the extent the expenditure is includible in gross income as compensation for services rendered, or as a prize or award under section 74, by a recipient of the expenditure who is not an employee of the taxpayer. The preceding sentence shall not apply to any amount paid or incurred by the taxpayer if such amount is required to be included (or would be so required except that the amount is less that $600) in any information return filed by such taxpayer under part III of subchapter A of chapter 61 and is not so included. See section 274(e)(9).

(C) *Example.* The following example illustrates the provisions this paragraph (f):

Example. If an employer rewards the employee (and the employee's spouse) with an expense paid vacation trip, the expense is deductible by the employer (if otherwise allowable under section 162 and the regulations thereunder) to the extent the employer treats the expenses as compensation and as wages. On the other hand, if a taxpayer owns a yacht which the taxpayer uses for the entertainment of business customers, the portion of salary paid to employee members of the crew which is allocable to use of the yacht for entertainment purposes (even though treated on the taxpayer's tax return as compensation and treated as wages for withholding tax purposes) would not come within this exception since the members of the crew were not recipients of the entertainment. If an expenditure of a type described in this subdivision properly constitutes a dividend paid to a shareholder or if it constitutes unreasonable compensation paid to an employee, nothing in this exception prevents disallowance of the expenditure to the taxpayer under other provisions of the Internal Revenue Code.

(iv) *Reimbursed entertainment expenses*—(*a*) *Introductory.* In the case of any expenditure for entertainment paid or incurred by one person in connection with the performance by him of services for another person (whether or not such other person is an employer) under a reimbursement or other expense allowance arrangement, the limitations on allowability of deductions provided for in paragraphs (a) through (e) of this section shall be applied only once, either (*1*) to the person who makes the expenditure or (*2*) to the person who actually bears the expense, but not to both. For purposes of this subdivision (iv), the term "reimbursement or other expense allowance arrangement" has the same meaning as it has in section 62(2)(A), but without regard to whether the taxpayer is the employee of a person for whom services are performed. If an expenditure of a type described in this subdivision properly constitutes a dividend paid to a shareholder, unreasonable compensation paid to an employee, or a personal, living or family expense, nothing in this exception prevents disallowance of the expenditure to the taxpayer under other provisions of the Code.

(b) *Reimbursement arrangements between employee and employer.* In the case of an expenditure for entertainment paid or incurred by an employee under a reimbursement or other expense allowance arrangement with his employer, the limitations on deductions provided for in paragraphs (a) through (e) of this section shall not apply—

(1) *Employees.* To the employee except to the extent his employer has treated the expenditure on the employer's income tax return as originally filed as compensation paid to the employee and as wages to such employee for purposes of withholding under chapter 24 (relating to collection of income tax at source on wages).

(2) *Employers.* To the employer to the extent he has treated the expenditure as compensation and wages paid to an employee in the manner provided in (b)(1) of this subdivision.

(c) *Reimbursement arrangements between independent contractors and clients or customers.* In the case of an expenditure for entertainment paid or incurred by one person (hereinafter termed "independent contractor") under a reimbursement or other expense allowance arrangement with another person other than an employer (hereinafter termed "client or customer"), the limitations on deductions provided for in paragraphs (a) through (e) of this section shall not apply—

(1) *Independent contractors.* To the independent contractor to the extent he accounts to his client or customer within the meaning of section 274(d) and the regulations thereunder. See § 1.274-5.

(2) *Clients or customers.* To the client or customer if the expenditure is disallowed to the independent contractor under paragraphs (a) through (e) of this section.

(v) *Recreational expenses for employees generally.* Any expenditure by a taxpayer for a recreational, social, or similar activity (or for use of a facility in connection therewith), primarily for the benefit of his employees generally, is not subject to the limitations on allowability of deductions provided for in paragraphs (a) through (e) of this section. This exception applies only to expenditures made primarily for the benefit of employees of the taxpayer other than employees who are officers, shareholders or other owners who own a 10-percent or greater interest in the business, or other highly compensated employees. For purposes of the preceding sentence, an employee shall be treated as owning any interest owned by a member of his family (within the meaning of

section 267(c)(4) and the regulations thereunder). Ordinarily, this exception applies to usual employee benefit programs such as expenses of a taxpayer (a) in holding Christmas parties, annual picnics, or summer outings, for his employees generally, or (b) of maintaining a swimming pool, baseball diamond, bowling alley, or golf course available to his employees generally. Any expenditure for an activity which is made under circumstances which discriminate in favor of employees who are officers, shareholders or other owners, or highly compensated employees shall not be considered made primarily for the benefit of employees generally. On the other hand, an expenditure for an activity will not be considered outside of this exception merely because, due to the large number of employees involved, the activity is intended to benefit only a limited number of such employees at one time, provided the activity does not discriminate in favor of officers, shareholders, other owners, or highly compensated employees.

(vi) *Employee, stockholder, etc., business meetings.* Any expenditure by a taxpayer for entertainment which is directly related to bona fide business meetings of the taxpayer's employees, stockholders, agents, or directors held principally for discussion of trade or business is not subject to the limitations on allowability of deductions provided for in paragraphs (a) through (e) of this section. For purposes of this exception, a partnership is to be considered a taxpayer and a member of a partnership is to be considered an agent. For example, an expenditure by a taxpayer to furnish refreshments to his employees at a bona fide meeting, sponsored by the taxpayer for the principal purpose of instructing them with respect to a new procedure for conducting his business, would be within the provisions of this exception. A similar expenditure made at a bona fide meeting of stockholders of the taxpayer for the election of directors and discussion of corporate affairs would also be within the provisions of this exception. While this exception will apply to bona fide business meetings even though some social activities are provided, it will not apply to meetings which are primarily for social or nonbusiness purposes rather than for the transaction of the taxpayer's business. A meeting under circumstances where there was little or no possibility of engaging in the active conduct of trade or business (as described in paragraph (c)(7) of this section) generally will not be considered a business meeting for purposes of this subdivision. This exception will not apply to a meeting or convention of employees or agents, or similar meeting for directors, partners or others for the principal purpose of rewarding them for their services to the taxpayer. However, such a meeting or convention of employees might come within the scope of subdivisions (iii) or (v) of this subparagraph.

(vii) *Meetings of business leagues, etc.* Any expenditure for entertainment directly related and necessary to attendance at bona fide business meetings or conventions of organizations exempt from taxation under section 501(c)(6) of the Code, such as business leagues, chambers of commerce, real estate boards, boards of trade, and certain professional associations, is not subject to the limitations on allowability of deductions provided in paragraphs (a) through (e) of this section.

(viii) *Items available to the public.* Any expenditure by a taxpayer for entertainment (or for a facility in connection therewith) to the extent the entertainment is made available to the general public is not subject to the limitations on allowability of deductions provided for in paragraphs (a) through (e) of this section. Expenditures for entertainment of the general public by means of television, radio, newspapers and the like, will come within this exception, as will expenditures for distributing samples to the general public. Similarly, expenditures for maintaining private parks, golf courses and similar facilities, to the extent that they are available for public use, will come within this exception. For example, if a corporation maintains a swimming pool which it makes available for a period of time each week to children participating in a local public recreational program, the portion of the expense relating to such public use of the pool will come within this exception.

(ix) *Entertainment sold to customers.* Any expenditure by a taxpayer for entertainment (or for use of a facility in connection therewith) to the extent the entertainment is sold to customers in a bona fide transaction for an adequate and full consideration in money or money's worth is not subject to the limitations on allowability of deductions provided for in paragraphs (a) through (e) of this section. Thus, the cost of producing night club entertainment (such as salaries paid to employees of night clubs and amounts paid to performers) for sale to customers or the cost of operating a pleasure cruise ship as a business will come within this exception.

(g) *Additional provisions of section 274—travel of spouse, dependent or others.* Section 274(m)(3) provides that no deduction shall be allowed under this chapter (except section 217) for travel expenses paid or incurred with respect to a spouse, dependent, or other individual accompanying the taxpayer (or an officer or employee of the taxpayer) on business travel, unless certain conditions are met. As provided in section 274(m)(3), the term *other individual* does not include a business associate (as defined in paragraph (b)(2)(iii)

of this section) who otherwise meets the requirements of sections 274(m)(3)(B) and (C). [Reg. § 1.274-2.]

☐ [*T.D. 6659*, 6-24-63. *Amended by T.D. 6996*, 1-17-69; *T.D. 8051*, 9-6-85; *T.D. 8601*, 7-18-95 and *T.D. 8666*, 5-29-96.]

§ 1.274-3. Disallowance of deduction for gifts.—(a) *In general.* No deduction shall be allowed under section 162 or 212 for any expense for a gift made directly or indirectly by a taxpayer to any individual to the extent that such expense, when added to prior expenses of the taxpayer for gifts made to such individual during the taxpayer's taxable year, exceeds $25.

(b) *Gift defined.*—(1) *In general.* Except as provided in subparagraph (2) of this paragraph the term "gift", for purposes of this section, means any item excludable from the gross income of the recipient under section 102 which is not excludable from his gross income under any other provision of chapter 1 of the Code. Thus, a payment by an employer to a deceased employee's widow is not a gift, for purposes of this section, to the extent the payment constitutes an employee's death benefit excludable by the recipient under section 101(b). Similarly, a scholarship which is excludable from a recipient's gross income under section 117, and a prize or award which is excludable from a recipient's gross income under section 74(b), are not subject to the provisions of this section.

(2) *Items not treated as gifts.* The term "gift", for purposes of this section, does not include the following:

(i) An item having a cost to the taxpayer not in excess of $4.00 on which the name of the taxpayer is clearly and permanently imprinted and which is one of a number of identical items distributed generally by such a taxpayer.

(ii) A sign, display rack, or other promotional material to be used on the business premises of the recipient, or

(iii) In the case of a taxable year of a taxpayer ending on or after August 13, 1981, an item of tangible personal property which is awarded before January 1, 1987, to an employee of the taxpayer by reason of the employee's length of service (including an award upon retirement), productivity, or safety achievement, but only to the extent that—

(A) The cost of the item to the taxpayer does not exceed $400; or

(B) The item is a qualified plan award (as defined in paragraph (d) of this section); or

(iv) In the case of a taxable year of a taxpayer ending before August 13, 1981, an item of tangible personal property having a cost to the taxpayer not in excess of $100 which is awarded to an employee of the taxpayer by reason of the employee's length of service (including an award upon retirement) or safety achievement. For purposes of paragraphs (b)(2) (iii) and (iv), the term "tangible personal property" does not include cash or any gift certificate other than a nonnegotiable gift certificate conferring only the right to receive tangible personal property. Thus, for example, if a nonnegotiable gift certificate entitles an employee to choose between selecting an item of merchandise or receiving cash or reducing the balance due on his account with the issuer of the gift certificate, the gift certificate is not tangible personal property for purposes of this section. To the extent that an item is not treated as a gift for purposes of this section, the deductibility of the expense of the item is not governed by this section, and the taxpayer need not take such item into account in determining whether the $25 limitation on gifts to any individual has been exceeded. For example, if an employee receives by reason of his length of service a gift of an item of tangible personal property that costs the employer $450, the deductibility of only $50 ($450 minus $400) is governed by this section, and the employer takes the $50 into account for purposes of the $25 limitation on gifts to that employee. The fact that an item is wholly or partially excepted from the applicability of this section has no effect in determining whether the value of the item is includible in the gross income of the recipient. For rules relating to the taxability to the recipient of any item described in this subparagraph, see sections 61, 74, and 102 and the regulations thereunder. For rules relating to the deductibility of employee achievement awards awarded after December 31, 1986, see section 274(j).

(c) *Expense for a gift.* For purposes of this section, the term "expense for a gift" means the cost of the gift to the taxpayer, other than incidental costs such as for customary engraving on jewelry, or for packaging, insurance, and mailing or other delivery. A related cost will be considered "incidental" only if it does not add substantial value to the gift. Although the cost of customary gift wrapping will be considered an incidental cost, the purchase of an ornamental basket for packaging fruit will not be considered an incidental cost of packaging if the basket has a value which is substantial in relation to the value of the fruit.

* * *

[Reg. § 1.274-3.]

☐ [*T.D. 6659, 6-24-63. Amended by T.D. 8230, 9-19-88.*]

§ **1.274-5. Substantiation requirements.**—(a) and (b) [Reserved]. For further guidance, see § 1.274-5T(a) and (b).

(c) *Rules of substantiation*—(1) [Reserved]. For further guidance, see § 1.274-5T(c)(1).

(2) *Substantiation by adequate records*—(i) and (ii) [Reserved]. For further guidance, see § 1.274-5T(c)(2)(i) and (ii).

(iii) *Documentary evidence*—(A) Except as provided in paragraph (c)(2)(iii)(B), documentary evidence, such as receipts, paid bills, or similar evidence sufficient to support an expenditure, is required for—

(*1*) Any expenditure for lodging while traveling away from home, and

(*2*) Any other expenditure of $75 or more except, for transportation charges, documentary evidence will not be required if not readily available.

(B) The Commissioner, in his or her discretion, may prescribe rules waiving the documentary evidence requirements in circumstances where it is impracticable for such documentary evidence to be required. Ordinarily, documentary evidence will be considered adequate to support an expenditure if it includes sufficient information to establish the amount, date, place, and the essential character of the expenditure. For example, a hotel receipt is sufficient to support expenditures for business travel if it contains the following: name, location, date, and separate amounts for charges such as for lodging, meals, and telephone. Similarly, a restaurant receipt is sufficient to support an expenditure for a business meal if it contains the following: name and location of the restaurant, the date and amount of the expenditure, the number of people served, and, if a charge is made for an item other than meals and beverages, an indication that such is the case. A document may be indicative of only one (or part of one) element of an expenditure. Thus, a cancelled check, together with a bill from the payee, ordinarily would establish the element of cost. In contrast, a cancelled check drawn payable to a named payee would not by itself support a business expenditure without other evidence showing that the check was used for a certain business purpose.

(iv) and (v) [Reserved]. For further guidance, see § 1.274-5T(c)(2)(iv) and (v).

(3) through (7) [Reserved]. For further guidance, see § 1.274-5T(c)(3) through (7).

(d) and (e) [Reserved]. For further guidance, see § 1.274-5T(d) and (e).

(f) *Reporting and substantiation of expenses of certain employees for travel, entertainment, gifts, and with' respect to listed property*—(1) through

Reg. § 1.274-5(f)

(3) [Reserved]. For further guidance, see § 1.274-5T(f)(1) through (3).

(4) *Definition of an adequate accounting to the employer*—(i) *In general*. For purposes of this paragraph (f) an *adequate accounting* means the submission to the employer of an account book, diary, log, statement of expense, trip sheet, or similar record maintained by the employee in which the information as to each element of an expenditure or use (described in paragraph (b) of this section) is recorded at or near the time of the expenditure or use, together with supporting documentary evidence, in a manner that conforms to all the adequate records requirements of paragraph (c)(2) of this section. An adequate accounting requires that the employee account for all amounts received from the employer during the taxable year as advances, reimbursements, or allowances (including those charged directly or indirectly to the employer through credit cards or otherwise) for travel, entertainment, gifts, and the use of listed property. The methods of substantiation allowed under paragraph (c)(4) or (c)(5) of this section also will be considered to be an adequate accounting if the employer accepts an employee's substantiation and establishes that such substantiation meets the requirements of paragraph (c)(4) or (c)(5). For purposes of an adequate accounting, the method of substantiation allowed under paragraph (c)(3) of this section will not be permitted.

(ii) *Procedures for adequate accounting without documentary evidence*. The Commissioner may, in his or her discretion, prescribe rules under which an employee may make an adequate accounting to an employer by submitting an account book, log, diary, etc., alone, without submitting documentary evidence.

(iii) *Employer*. For purposes of this section, the term *employer* includes an agent of the employer or a third party payor who pays amounts to an employee under a reimbursement or other expense allowance arrangement.

(5) [Reserved]. For further guidance, see § 1.274-5T(f)(5).

(g) *Substantiation by reimbursement arrangements or per diem, mileage, and other traveling allowances*—(1) *In general*. The Commissioner may, in his or her discretion, prescribe rules in pronouncements of general applicability under which allowances for expenses described in paragraph (g)(2) of this section will, if in accordance with reasonable business practice, be regarded as equivalent to substantiation by adequate records or other sufficient evidence, for purposes of paragraph (c) of this section, of the amount of the expenses and as satisfying, with respect to the amount of the expenses, the requirements of an adequate accounting to the employer for purposes of paragraph (f)(4) of this section. If the total allowance received exceeds the deductible expenses paid or incurred by the employee, such excess must be reported as income on the employee's return. See paragraph (j)(1) of this section relating to the substantiation of meal expenses while traveling away from home, and paragraph (j)(2) of this section relating to the substantiation of expenses for the business use of a vehicle.

(2) *Allowances for expenses described*. An allowance for expenses is described in this paragraph (g)(2) if it is a—

(i) Reimbursement arrangement covering ordinary and necessary expenses of traveling away from home (exclusive of transportation expenses to and from destination);

(ii) Per them allowance providing for ordinary and necessary expenses of traveling away from home (exclusive of transportation costs to and from destination); or,

(iii) Mileage allowance providing for ordinary and necessary expenses of local transportation and transportation to, from, and at the destination while traveling away from home.

(h) [Reserved]. For further guidance, see § 1.274-5T(h).

(i) [Reserved].

(j) *Authority for optional methods of computing certain expenses*—(1) *Meal expenses while traveling away from home*. The Commissioner may establish a method under which a taxpayer may use a specified amount or amounts for meals while traveling away from home in lieu of substantiating the actual cost of meals. The taxpayer will not be relieved of the requirement to substantiate the actual cost of other travel expenses as well as the time, place, and business purpose of the travel. See paragraphs (b)(2) and (c) of this section.

(2) *Use of mileage rates for vehicle expenses*. The Commissioner may establish a method under which a taxpayer may use mileage rates to determine the amount of the ordinary and necessary expenses of using a vehicle for local transportation and transportation to, from, and at the destination while traveling away from home in lieu of substantiating the actual costs. The method may include appropriate limitations and conditions in order to reflect more accurately vehicle expenses over the entire period of usage. The taxpayer will not be relieved of the requirement to substantiate the amount of each business use (i.e., the business mileage), or the time and business purpose of each use. See paragraphs (b)(2) and (c) of this section.

(3) [Reserved]. For further guidance, see § 1.274-5T(j)(3).

Reg. § 1.274-5(f)(4)

(k) and (l) [Reserved]. For further guidance, see § 1.274-5T(k) and (l).

(m) *Effective date.* This section applies to expenses paid or incurred after December 31, 1997. [Reg. § 1.274-5.]

☐ [*T.D.* 8864, 1-21-2000 (*corrected* 3-22-2000). *Amended by T.D.* 9020, 11-8-2002.]

§ 1.274-5T. Substantiation requirements (temporary).—(a) *In general.* For taxable years beginning on or after January 1, 1986, no deduction or credit shall be allowed with respect to—

(1) Traveling away from home (including meals and lodging),

(2) Any activity which is of a type generally considered to constitute entertainment, amusement, or recreation, or with respect to a facility used in connection with such an activity, including the items specified in section 274(e),

(3) Gifts defined in section 274(b), or

(4) Any listed property (as defined in section 280F(d)(4) and § 1.280F-6T(b)),

unless the taxpayer substantiates each element of the expenditure or use (as described in paragraph (b) of this section) in the manner provided in paragraph (c) of this section. This limitation supersedes the doctrine founded in *Cohan v. Commissioner,* 39 F.2d 540 (2d Cir. 1930). The decision held that, where the evidence indicated a taxpayer incurred deductible travel or entertainment expenses but the exact amount could not be determined, the court should make a close approximation and not disallow the deduction entirely. Section 274(d) contemplates that no deduction or credit shall be allowed a taxpayer on the basis of such approximations or unsupported testimony of the taxpayer. For purposes of this section, the term "entertainment" means entertainment, amusement, or recreation, and use of a facility therefor; and the term "expenditure" includes expenses and items (including items such as loss and depreciation).

(b) *Elements of an expenditure or use*—(1) *In general.* Section 274(d) and this section contemplate that no deduction or credit shall be allowed for travel, entertainment, a gift, or with respect to listed property unless the taxpayer substantiates the requisite elements of each expenditure or use as set forth in this paragraph (b).

(2) *Travel away from home.* The elements to be proved with respect to an expenditure for travel away from home are—

(i) *Amount.* Amount of each separate expenditure for traveling away from home, such as cost of transportation or lodging, except that the daily cost of the traveler's own breakfast, lunch, and dinner and of expenditures incidental to such travel may be aggregated, if set forth in reasona-

ble categories, such as for meals, for gasoline and oil, and for taxi fares;

(ii) *Time.* Dates of departure and return for each trip away from home, and number of days away from home spent on business;

(iii) *Place.* Destinations or locality of travel, described by name of city or town or other similar designation; and

(iv) *Business purpose.* Business reason for travel or nature of the business benefit derived or expected to be derived as a result of travel.

(3) *Entertainment in general.* The elements to be proved with respect to an expenditure for entertainment are—

(i) *Amount.* Amount of each separate expenditure for entertainment, except that such incidental items as taxi fares or telephone calls may be aggregated on a daily basis;

(ii) *Time.* Date of entertainment;

(iii) *Place.* Name, if any, address or location, and designation of type of entertainment, such as dinner or theater, if such information is not apparent from the designation of the place;

(iv) *Business purpose.* Business reason for the entertainment or nature of business benefit derived or expected to be derived as a result of the entertainment and, except in the case of business meals described in section 274(e)(1), the nature of any business discussion or activity;

(v) *Business relationship.* Occupation or other information relating to the person or persons entertained, including name, title, or other designation, sufficient to establish business relationship to the taxpayer.

(4) *Entertainment directly preceding or following a substantial and bona fide business discussion.* If a taxpayer claims a deduction for entertainment directly preceding or following a substantial and bona fide business discussion on the ground that such entertainment was associated with the active conduct of the taxpayer's trade or business, the elements to be proved with respect to such expenditure, in addition to those enumerated in paragraph (b)(3)(i), (ii), (iii), and (v) of this section are—

(i) *Time.* Date and duration of business discussion;

(ii) *Place.* Place of business discussion;

(iii) *Business purpose.* Nature of business discussion, and business reason for the entertainment or nature of business benefit derived or expected to be derived as the result of the entertainment;

(iv) *Business relationship.* Identification of those persons entertained who participated in the business discussion.

Reg. § 1.274-5T(b)(4)

(5) *Gifts.* The elements to be proved with respect to an expenditure for a gift are—

(i) *Amount.* Cost of the gift to the taxpayer;

(ii) *Time.* Date of the gift;

(iii) *Description.* Description of the gift;

(iv) *Business purpose.* Business reason for the gift or nature of business benefit derived or expected to be derived as a result of the gift; and

(v) *Business relationship.* Occupation or other information relating to the recipient of the gift, including name, title, or other designation, sufficient to establish business relationship to the taxpayer.

(6) *Listed property.* The elements to be proved with respect to any listed property are—

(i) *Amount*—(A) *Expenditures.* The amount of each separate expenditure with respect to an item of listed property, such as the cost of acquisition, the cost of capital improvements, lease payments, the cost of maintenance and repairs, or other expenditures, and

(B) *Uses.* The amount of each business/investment use (as defined in § 1.280F-6T(d)(3) and (e)), based on the appropriate measure (i.e., mileage for automobiles and other means of transportation and time for other listed property, unless the Commissioner approves an alternative method), and the total use of the listed property for the taxable period.

(ii) *Time.* Date of the expenditure or use with respect to listed property, and

(iii) *Business or investment purpose.* The business purpose for an expenditure or use with respect to any listed property (*see* § 1.274-5T(c)(6)(i)(B) and (C) for special rules for the aggregation of expenditures and business use and § 1.280F-6T(d)(2) for the distinction between qualified business use and business/investment use).

See also § 1.274-5T(e) relating to the substantiation of business use of employer-provided listed property and § 1.274-6T for special rules for substantiating the business/investment use of certain types of listed property.

(c) *Rules of substantiation*—(1) *In general.* Except as otherwise provided in this section and § 1.274-6T, a taxpayer must substantiate each element of an expenditure or use (described in paragraph (b) of this section) by adequate records or by sufficient evidence corroborating his own statement. Section 274(d) contemplates that a taxpayer will maintain and produce such substantiation as will constitute proof of each expenditure or use referred to in section 274. Written evidence has considerably more probative value than oral evidence alone. In addition, the probative value of

written evidence is greater the closer in time it relates to the expenditure or use. A contemporaneous log is not required, but a record of the elements of an expenditure or of a business use of listed property made at or near the time of the expenditure or use, supported by sufficient documentary evidence, has a high degree of credibility not present with respect to a statement prepared subsequent thereto when generally there is a lack of accurate recall. Thus, the corroborative evidence required to support a statement not made at or near the time of the expenditure or use must have a high degree of probative value to elevate such statement and evidence to the level of credibility reflected by a record made at or near the time of the expenditure or use supported by sufficient documentary evidence. The substantiation requirements of section 274(d) are designed to encourage taxpayers to maintain the records, together with documentary evidence, as provided in paragraph (c)(2) of this section.

(2) *Substantiation by adequate records*—(i) *In general.* To meet the "adequate records" requirements of section 274(d), a taxpayer shall maintain an account book, diary, log, statement of expense, trip sheets, or similar record (as provided in paragraph (c)(2)(ii) of this section), and documentary evidence (as provided in paragraph (c)(2)(iii) of this section) which, in combination, are sufficient to establish each element of an expenditure or use specified in paragraph (b) of this section. It is not necessary to record information in an account book, diary, log, statement of expense, trip sheet, or similar record which duplicates information reflected on a receipt so long as the account book, etc., and receipt complement each other in an orderly manner.

(ii) *Account book, diary, etc.* An account book, diary, log, statement of expense, trip sheet, or similar record must be prepared or maintained in such manner that each recording of an element of an expenditure or use is made at or near the time of the expenditure or use.

(A) *Made at or near the time of the expenditure or use.* For purposes of this section, the phrase "made at or near the time of the expenditure or use" means the elements of an expenditure or use are recorded at a time when, in relation to the use or making of an expenditure, the taxpayer has full present knowledge of each element of the expenditure or use, such as the amount, time, place, and business purpose of the expenditure and business relationship of the expenditure and business relationship of the expenditure and business relationship. An expense account statement which is a transcription of an account book, diary, log, or similar record prepared or maintained in accordance with the provisions of this paragraph (c)(2)(ii) shall be considered a record prepared or maintained in the manner prescribed in the preceding sentence if such expense account statement is submitted by an employee to his employer or by an independent contractor to his client or customer in the regular course of good business practice. For example, a log maintained on a weekly basis, which accounts for use during the week, shall be considered a record made at or near the time of such use.

(B) *Substantiation of business purpose.* In order to constitute an adequate record of business purpose within the meaning of section 274(d) and this paragraph (c)(2), a written statement of business purpose generally is required. However, the degree of substantiation necessary to establish business purpose will vary depending upon the facts and circumstances of each case. Where the business purpose is evident from the surrounding facts and circumstances, a written explanation of such business purpose will not be required. For example, in the case of a salesman calling on customers on an established sales route, a written explanation of the business purpose of such travel ordinarily will not be required. Similarly, in the case of a business meal described in section 274(e)(1), if the business purpose of such meal is evident from the business relationship to the taxpayer of the persons entertained and other surrounding circumstances, a written explanation of such business purpose will not be required.

(C) *Substantiation of business use of listed property—(1) Degree of substantiation.* In order to constitute an adequate record (within the meaning of section 274(d) and this paragraph (c)(2)(ii)), which substantiates business/investment use of listed property (as defined in § 1.280F-6T(d)(3)), the record must contain sufficient information as to each element of every business/investment use. However, the level of detail required in an adequate record to substantiate business/investment use may vary depending upon the facts and circumstances. For example, a taxpayer who uses a truck for both business and personal purposes and whose only business use of a truck is to make deliveries to customers on an established route may satisfy the adequate record requirement by recording the total number [of] miles driven during the taxable year, the length of the delivery route once, and the date of each trip at or near the time of the trips. Alternatively, the taxpayer may establish the date of each trip with a receipt, record of delivery, or other documentary evidence.

(2) *Written record.* Generally, an adequate record must be written. However, a record of the business use of listed property, such as a computer or automobile, prepared in a computer memory device with the aid of a logging program will constitute an adequate record.

* * *

(f) *Reporting and substantiation of expenses of certain employees for travel, entertainment, gifts, and with respect to listed property—(1) In general.* The purpose of this paragraph is to provide rules for reporting and substantiation of certain expenses paid or incurred by employees in connection with the performance of services as employees. For purposes of this paragraph, the term "business expenses" means ordinary and necessary expenses for travel, entertainment, gifts, or with respect to listed property which are deductible under section 162, and the regulations thereunder, to the extent not disallowed by sections 262, 274(c), and 280F. Thus, the term "business expenses" does not include personal, living, or family expenses disallowed by section 262, travel expenses disallowed by section 274(c), or cost recovery deductions and credits with respect to listed property disallowed by section 280F(d)(3) because the use of such property is not for the convenience of the employer and required as a condition of employment. Except as provided in paragraph (f)(2), advances, reimbursements, or allowances for such expenditures must be reported as income by the employee.

(2) *Reporting of expenses for which the employee is required to make an adequate accounting to his employer—(i) Reimbursements equal to expenses.* For purposes of computing tax liability, an employee need not report on his tax return business expenses for travel, transportation, entertainment, gifts, or with respect to listed property, paid or incurred by him solely for the benefit of his employer for which he is required to, and does, make an adequate accounting to his employer (as defined in paragraph (f)(4) of this section) and which are charged directly or indirectly to the employer (for example, through credit cards) or for which the employee is paid through advances, reimbursements, or otherwise, provided that the total amount of such advances, reimbursements, and charges is equal to such expenses.

(ii) *Reimbursements in excess of expenses.* In case the total of the amounts charged directly or indirectly to the employer or received from the employer as advances, reimbursements, or otherwise, exceeds the business expenses paid or incurred by the employee and the employee is required to, and does, make an adequate accounting to his employer for such expenses, the employee must include such excess (including amounts received for expenditures not deductible by him) in income.

(iii) *Expenses in excess of reimbursement.* If an employee incurs deductible business expenses on behalf of his employer which exceed the total of the amounts charged directly or indirectly to the employer and received from the employer

Reg. § 1.274-5T(f)(2)

as advances, reimbursements, or otherwise, and the employee makes an adequate accounting to his employer, the employee must be able to substantiate any deduction for such excess with such records and supporting evidence as will substantiate each element of an expenditure (described in paragraph (b) of this section) in accordance with paragraph (c) of this section.

(3) *Reporting of expenses for which the employee is not required to make an adequate accounting to his employer.* If the employee is not required to make an adequate accounting to his employer for his business expenses or, though required, fails to make an adequate accounting for such expenses, he must submit, as a part of his tax return, the appropriate form issued by the Internal Revenue Service for claiming deductions for employee business expenses (e.g., Form 2106, Employee Business Expenses, for 1985) and provide the information requested on that form, including the information required by paragraph (d)(2) and (3) of this section if the employee's business expenses are with respect to the use of listed property. In addition, the employee must maintain such records and supporting evidence as will substantiate each element of an expenditure or use (described in paragraph (b) of this section) in accordance with paragraph (c) of this section.

(4) [Reserved]. For further guidance, see § 1.274-5(f)(4).

(5) *Substantiation of expenditures by certain employees.* An employee who makes an adequate accounting to his employer within the meaning of this paragraph will not again be required to substantiate such expense account information except in the following cases:

(i) An employee whose business expenses exceed the total of amounts charged to his employer and amounts received through advances, reimbursements or otherwise and who claims a deduction on his return for such excess,

(ii) An employee who is related to his employer within the meaning of section 267(b), but for this purpose the percentage referred to in section 267(b)(2) shall be 10 percent, and

(iii) Employees in cases where it is determined that the accounting procedures used by the employer for the reporting and substantiation of expenses by such employees are not adequate, or where it cannot be determined that such procedures are adequate. The district director will determine whether the employer's accounting procedures are adequate by considering the facts and circumstances of each case, including the use of proper internal controls. For example, an employer should require that an expense account be verified and approved by a reasonable person other than the person incurring such expenses.

Accounting procedures will be considered inadequate to the extent that the employer does not require an adequate accounting from his employees as defined in paragraph (f)(4) of this section, or does not maintain such substantiation. To the extent an employer fails to maintain adequate accounting procedures he will thereby obligate his employees to substantiate separately their expense account information.

* * *

[Temporary Reg. § 1.274-5T.]

☐ [*T.D.* 8061, 10-31-85. *Amended by T.D.* 8063, 12-18-85; *T.D.* 8276, 12-7-89; *T.D.* 8451, 12-4-92; *T.D.* 8601, 7-18-95; *T.D.* 8715, 3-24-97; *T.D.* 8864, 1-21-2000 *and T.D.* 9020, 11-8-2002.]

§ 1.274-6. Expenditures deductible without regard to trade or business or other income producing activity.—The provisions of §§ 1.274-1 through 1.274-5, inclusive, do not apply to any deduction allowable to the taxpayer without regard to its connection with the taxpayer's trade or business or other income producing activity. Examples of such items are interest, taxes such as real property taxes, and casualty losses. Thus, if a taxpayer owned a fishing camp, the taxpayer could still deduct mortgage interest and real property taxes in full even if deductions for its use are not allowable under section 274(a) and § 1.274-2. In the case of a taxpayer which is not an individual, the provisions of this section shall be applied as if it were an individual. Thus, if a corporation sustains a casualty loss on an entertainment facility used in its trade or business, it could deduct the loss even though deductions for the use of the facility are not allowable. [Reg. § 1.274-6.]

☐ [*T.D.* 6659, 6-24-63. *Amended by T.D.* 8051, 9-6-85.]

§ 1.274-7. Treatment of certain expenditures with respect to entertainment-type facilities.—If deductions are disallowed under § 1.274-2 with respect to any portion of a facility, such portion shall be treated as an asset which is used for personal, living, and family purposes (and not as an asset used in a trade or business). Thus, the basis of such a facility will be adjusted for purposes of computing depreciation deductions and determining gain or loss on the sale of such facility in the same manner as other property (for example, a residence) which is regarded as used partly for business and partly for personal purposes. [Reg. § 1.274-7.]

☐ [*T.D.* 6659, 6-24-63.]

§ 1.279-1. General rule; purpose.—An obligation issued to provide a consideration directly or indirectly for a corporate acquisition, although constituting a debt under section 385, may have characteristics which make it more appropriate that the participation in the corporation which the obligation represents be treated for purposes of the deduction of interest as if it were a stockholder interest rather than a creditors interest. To deal with such cases, section 279 imposes certain limitations on the deductibility of interest paid or incurred on obligations which have certain equity characteristics and are classified as corporate acquisition indebtedness. Generally, section 279 provides that no deduction will be allowed for any interest paid or incurred by a corporation during the taxable year with respect to its corporate acquisition indebtedness to the extent such interest exceeds $5 million. However, the $5 million limitation is reduced by the amount of interest paid or incurred on obligations issued under the circumstances described in section 279(a)(2) but are not corporate acquisition indebtedness. Section 279(b) provides that an obligation will be corporate acquisition indebtedness if it was issued under certain circumstances and meets the four tests enumerated therein. Although an obligation may satisfy the conditions referred to in the preceding sentence, it may still escape classification as corporate acquisition indebtedness if the conditions are described in sections 279(d)(3), (4), and (5), 279(f), or 279(i) are present. However, no inference should be drawn from the rules of section 279 as to whether a particular instrument labeled a bond, debenture, note, or other evidence of indebtedness is in fact a debt. Before the determination as to whether the deduction for payments pursuant to an obligation as described in this section is to be disallowed, the obligation must first qualify as debt in accordance with section 385. If the obligation is not debt under section 385, it will be unnecessary to apply section 279 to any payments pursuant to such obligation. [Reg. § 1.279-1.]

☐ [*T.D. 7262, 3-2-73.*]

§ 1.279-2. Amount of disallowance of interest on corporate acquisition indebtedness.—(a) *In general.* Under section 279(a), no deduction is allowed for any interest paid or incurred by a corporation during the taxable year with respect to its corporate acquisition indebtedness to the extent that such interest exceeds—

(1) $5 million, reduced by

(2) The amount of interest paid or incurred by such corporation during such year on any obligation issued after December 31, 1967, to provide consideration directly or indirectly for an acquisition described in section 279(b)(1) but which is not corporate acquisition indebtedness. Such an obligation is not corporate acquisition indebtedness if it—

(i) Was issued prior to October 10, 1969, or

(ii) Was issued after October 9, 1969, but does not meet any one or more of the tests of section 279(b)(2), (3), or (4), or

(iii) Was originally deemed to be corporate acquisition indebtedness but is no longer so treated by virtue of the application of paragraphs (3) or (4) of section 279(d), or

(iv) Is specifically excluded from treatment as corporate acquisition indebtedness by virtue of sections 279(d)(5), (f), or (i).

The computation of the amount by which the $5 million limitation described in this paragraph is to be reduced with respect to any taxable year is to be made as of the last day of the taxable year in which an acquisition described in section 279(b)(1) occurs. In no case shall the $5 million limitation be reduced below zero.

(b) *Certain terms defined.* When used in section 279 and the regulations thereunder—

(1) The term "issued" includes the giving of a note or other evidence of indebtedness to a bank or other lender as well as an issuance of a bond or debenture. In the case of obligations which are registered with the Securities and Exchange Commission, the date of issue is the date on which the issue is first offered to the public. In the case of obligations which are not so registered, the date of issue is the date on which the obligation is sold to the first purchaser.

(2) The term "interest" includes both stated interest and unstated interest (such as original issue discount as defined in paragraph (a)(1) of § 1.163-4 and amounts treated as interest under section 483).

(3) The term "money" means cash and its equivalent.

(4) The term "control" shall have the meaning assigned to such term by section 368(c).

(5) The term "affiliated group" shall have the meaning assigned to such term by section 1504(a), except that all corporations other than the acquired corporation shall be treated as includible corporations (without any exclusion under section 1504(b)) and the acquired corporation shall not be treated as an includible corporation. This definition shall apply whether or not some or all of the members of the affiliated group file a consolidated return.

(c) *Examples.* The provisions of paragraph (a) of this section may be illustrated by the following examples:

Example (1). On March 4, 1973, X Corporation, a calendar year taxpayer, issues an obligation which satisfies the test of section 279(b)(1) but fails to satisfy either of the tests of section 279(b)(2) or (3). Since at least one of the tests of section 279(b) is not satisfied the obligation is not

Reg. § 1.279-2(c)

corporate acquisition indebtedness. However, since the test of section 279(b)(1) is satisfied, the interest on the obligation will reduce the $5 million limitation provided by section 279(a)(1).

Example (2). On January 1, 1969, X Corporation, a calendar year taxpayer, issues an obligation, which satisfies all the tests of section 279(b), requiring it to pay $3.5 million of interest each year. Since the obligation was issued before October 10, 1969, the obligation cannot be corporate acquisition indebtedness, and a deduction for the $3.5 million of interest attributable to such obligation is not subject to disallowance under section 279(a). However, since the obligation was issued after December 31, 1967, in an acquisition described in section 279(b)(1), under section 279(a)(2) the $3.5 million of interest attributable to such obligation reduces the $5 million limitation provided by section 279(a)(1) to $1.5 million.

Example (3). Assume the same facts as in example (2). Assume further that on January 11, 1970, X Corporation issues more obligations which are classified as corporate acquisition indebtedness and which require X Corporation to pay $4 million of interest each year. For 1970 the amount of interest paid or accrued on corporate acquisition indebtedness, which may be deducted is $1.5 million ($5 million maximum provided by section 279(a)(1) less $3.5 million, the reduction required under section 279(a)(2)). Thus, $2.5 million of the $4 million interest incurred on a corporate acquisition indebtedness is subject to disallowance under section 279(a) for the taxable year 1970.

Example (4). Assume the same facts as in example (3). Assume further that on the last day of each of the taxable years 1971, 1972, and 1973 of X Corporation neither of the conditions described in section 279(b)(4) was present.

Under these circumstances, such obligations for all taxable years after 1973 are not corporate acquisition indebtedness under section 279(d)(4). Therefore, the $2.5 million of interest previously not deductible is now deductible for all taxable years after 1973. Although such obligations are no longer treated as corporate acquisition indebtedness, the interest attributable thereto must be applied in further reduction of the $5 million limitation. The $5 million limitation of section 279(a)(1) is therefore reduced to zero. While the limitation is at the zero level any interest paid or incurred on corporate acquisition indebtedness will be disallowed. [Reg. § 1.279-2.]

☐ [*T.D.* 7262, 3-2-73.]

Distributions by Corporations

§ 1.301-1. **Rules applicable with respect to distributions of money and other property.**— (a) *General.* Section 301 provides the general rule for treatment of distributions on or after June 22, 1954, of property by a corporation to a shareholder with respect to its stock. The term "property" is defined in section 317(a). Such distributions, except as otherwise provided in this chapter, shall be treated as provided in section 301(c). Under section 301(c), distributions may be included in gross income, applied against and reduce the adjusted basis of the stock, treated as gain from the sale or exchange of property, or (in the case of certain distributions out of increase in value accrued before March 1, 1913) may be exempt from tax. The amount of the distributions to which section 301 applies is determined in accordance with the provisions of section 301(b). The basis of property received in a distribution to which section 301 applies is determined in accordance with the provisions of section 301(d). Accordingly, except as otherwise provided in this chapter, a distribution on or after June 22, 1954, of property by a corporation to a shareholder with respect to its stock shall be included in gross income to the extent the amount distributed is considered a dividend under section 316. For examples of distributions treated otherwise, see sections 116, 301(c)(2), 301(c)(3)(B), 301(e), 302(b), 303, and 305. See also Part II (relating to distri-butions in partial or complete liquidation), Part III (relating to corporate organizations and reorganizations), and Part IV (relating to insolvency reorganizations) subchapter C, chapter 1 of the Code.

(b) *Time of inclusion in gross income and of determination of fair market value.*—A distribution made by a corporation to its shareholders shall be included in the gross income of the distributees when the cash or other property is unqualifiedly made subject to their demands. However, if such distribution is a distribution other than in cash, the fair market value of the property shall be determined as of the date of distribution without regard to whether such date is the same as that on which the distribution is includible in gross income. For example, if a corporation distributes a taxable dividend in property (the adjusted basis of which exceeds its fair market value on December 31, 1955) on December 31, 1955, which is received by, or unqualifiedly made subject to the demand of, its shareholders on January 2, 1956, the amount to be included in the gross income of the shareholders will be the fair market value of such property on December 31, 1955, although such amount will not be includible in the gross income of the shareholders until January 2, 1956.

(c) *Application of section to shareholders.*— Section 301 is not applicable to an amount paid by a corporation to a shareholder unless the amount is paid to the shareholder in his capacity as such.

(d) *Distributions to corporate shareholders.* (1) If the shareholder is a corporation, the amount of any distribution to be taken into account under section 301(c) shall be:

(i) The amount of money distributed,

(ii) An amount equal to the fair market value of any property distributed which consists of any obligations of the distributing corporation, stock of the distributing corporation treated as property under section 305(b), or rights to acquire such stock treated as property under section 305(b), plus

(iii) In the case of a distribution not described in subdivision (iv) of this subparagraph, an amount equal to (*a*) the fair market value of any other property distributed or, if lesser, (*b*) the adjusted basis of such other property in the hands of the distributing corporation (determined immediately before the distribution and increased for any gain recognized to the distributing corporation under section 311(b), (c), or (d), or under section 341(f), 617(d), 1245(a), 1250(a), 1251(c), 1252(a), or 1254(a)), or

(iv) In the case of a distribution made after November 8, 1971, to a shareholder which is a foreign corporation, an amount equal to the fair market value of any other property distributed, but only if the distribution received by such shareholder is not effectively connected for the taxable year with the conduct of a trade or business in the United States by such shareholder.

(2) In the case of a distribution the amount of which is determined by reference to the adjusted basis described in subparagraph (1)(iii)(*b*) or this paragraph:

(i) That portion of the distribution which is a dividend under section 301(c)(1) may not exceed such adjusted basis, or

(ii) If the distribution is not out of earnings and profits, the amount of the reduction in basis of the shareholder's stock, and the amount of any gain resulting from such distribution, are to be determined by reference to such adjusted basis of the property which is distributed.

(3) Notwithstanding paragraph (d)(1)(iii), if a distribution of property described in such paragraph is made after December 31, 1962, by a foreign corporation to a shareholder which is a corporation, the amount of the distribution to be taken into account under section 301(c) shall be determined under section 301(b)(1)(C) and paragraph (n) of this section.

(e) *Adjusted basis.* In determining the adjusted basis of property distributed in the hands of the distributing corporation immediately before the distribution for purposes of section 301(b)(1)(B)(ii), (b)(1)(C)(i), and (d)(2)(B), the basis to be used shall be the basis for determining gain upon a sale or exchange.

(f) *Examples.* The application of this section (except paragraph (n)) may be illustrated by the following examples:

Example (1). On January 1, 1955, A, an individual owned all of the stock of Corporation M with an adjusted basis of $2,000. During 1955, A received distributions from Corporation M totaling $30,000, consisting of $10,000 in cash and listed securities having a basis in the hands of Corporation M and a fair market value on the date distributed of $20,000. Corporation M's taxable year is the calendar year. As of December 31, 1954, Corporation M had earnings and profits accumulated after February 28, 1913, in the amount of $26,000, and it had no earnings and profits and no deficit for 1955. Of the $30,000 received by A, $26,000 will be treated as an ordinary dividend; the remaining $4,000 will be applied against the adjusted basis of his stock; the $2,000 in excess of the adjusted basis of his stock will either be treated as gain from the sale or exchange of property (under section 301(c)(3)(A)) or, if out of increase in value accrued before March 1, 1913, will (under section 301(c)(3)(B)) be exempt from tax. If A subsequently sells his stock in Corporation M, the basis for determining gain or loss on the sale will be zero.

Example (2). The facts are the same as in *Example 1* with the exceptions that the sole shareholder of Corporation M is Corporation W and that the securities which were distributed had an adjusted basis to Corporation M of $15,000. The distribution received by Corporation W totals $25,000 consisting of $10,000 in cash and securities with an adjusted basis of $15,000. The total $25,000 will be treated as a dividend to Corporation W since the earnings and profits of Corporation M ($26,000) are in excess of the amount of the distribution.

Example (3). Corporation X owns timber land which it acquired prior to March 1, 1913, at a cost of $50,000 with $5,000 allocated as the separate cost of the land. On March 1, 1913, this property had a fair market value of $150,000 of which $135,000 was attributable to the timber and $15,000 to the land. All of the timber was cut prior to 1955 and the full appreciation in the value thereof, $90,000 ($135,000 − $45,000), realized through depletion allowances based on March 1, 1913, value. None of this surplus from realized appreciation had been distributed. In

1955, Corporation X sold the land for $20,000 thereby realizing a gain of $15,000. Of this gain, $10,000 is due to realized appreciation in value which accrued before March 1, 1913 ($15,000 − $5,000). Of the gain of $15,000, $5,000 is taxable. Therefore, at December 31, 1955, Corporation X had a surplus from realized appreciation in the amount of $100,000. It had no accumulated earnings and profits and no deficit at January 1, 1955. The net earnings for 1955 (including the $5,000 gain on the sale of the land) were $20,000. During 1955, Corporation X distributed $75,000 to its stockholders. Of this amount, $20,000 will be treated as a dividend. The remaining $55,000, which is a distribution of realized appreciation, will be applied against and reduce the adjusted basis of the shareholder's stock. If any part of the $55,000 is in excess of the adjusted basis of a shareholder's stock, such part will be exempt from tax.

(g) *Reduction for liabilities*—(1) *General rule*. For the purpose of section 301, no reduction shall be made for the amount of any liability, unless the liability is assumed by the shareholder within the meaning of section 357(d).

(2) *No reduction below zero*. Any reduction pursuant to paragraph (g)(1) of this section shall not cause the amount of the distribution to be reduced below zero.

(3) *Effective dates*—(i) *In general*. This paragraph (g) applies to distributions occurring after January 4, 2001.

(ii) *Retroactive application*. This paragraph (g) also applies to distributions made on or before January 4, 2001, if the distribution is made as part of a transaction described in, or substantially similar to, the transaction in Notice 99-59 (1999-2 C.B. 761), including transactions designed to reduce gain (see § 601.601(d)(2) of this chapter). For rules for distributions on or before January 4, 2001 (other than distributions on or before that date to which this paragraph (g) applies), see rules in effect on January 4, 2001 (see § 1.301-1(g) as contained in 26 CFR Part 1 revised April 1, 2001).

(h) *Basis*.—The basis of property received in the distribution to which section 301 applies shall be—

(1) If the shareholder is not a corporation, the fair market value of such property;

(2) If the shareholder is a corporation—

(i) In the case of a distribution of the obligations of the distributing corporation or of the stock of such corporation or rights to acquire such stock (if such stock or rights are treated as property under section 305(b)), the fair market value of such obligations, stock, or rights;

(ii) In the case of the distribution of any other property, except as provided in subdivision (iii) (relating to certain distributions by a foreign corporation) or subdivision (iv) (relating to certain distributions to foreign corporate distributees) of this subparagraph, whichever of the following is the lesser—

(a) The fair market value of such property; or

(b) The adjusted basis (in the hands of the distributing corporation immediately before the distribution) of such property increased in the amount of gain to the distributing corporation which is recognized under section 311(b) (relating to distributions of LIFO inventory), section 311(c) (relating to distributions of property subject to liabilities in excess of basis), section 311(d) (relating to appreciated property used to redeem stock), section 341(f) (relating to certain sales of stock of consenting corporations), section 617(d) (relating to gain from dispositions of certain mining property), section 1245(a) or 1250(a) (relating to gain from dispositions of certain depreciable property), section 1251(c) (relating to gain from disposition of farm recapture property), section 1252(a) (relating to gain from disposition of farm land), or section 1254(a) (relating to gain from disposition of interest in natural resource recapture property);

(iii) In the case of the distribution by a foreign corporation of any other property after December 31, 1962, in a distribution not described in subdivision (iv) of this subparagraph, the amount determined under paragraph (n) of this section;

(iv) In the case of the distribution of any other property made after November 8, 1971, to a shareholder which is a foreign corporation, the fair market value of such property, but only if the distribution received by such shareholder is not effectively connected for the taxable year with the conduct of a trade or business in the United States by such shareholder.

[There is no "(i)" in the official Regulations.—CCH.]

(j) *Transfers for less than fair market value*.— If property is transferred by a corporation to a shareholder which is not a corporation for an amount less than its fair market value in a sale or exchange, such shareholder shall be treated as having received a distribution to which section 301 applies. In such case, the amount of the distribution shall be the difference between the amount paid for the property and its fair market value. If property is transferred in a sale or exchange by a corporation to a shareholder which is a corporation, for an amount less than its fair market value and also less than its adjusted basis, such shareholder shall be treated as having received a distribution to which section 301 applies, and—

(1) Where the fair market value of the property equals or exceeds its adjusted basis in the hands of the distributing corporation the amount of the distribution shall be the excess of the adjusted basis (increased by the amount of gain recognized under section 311(b), (c), or (d), or under section 341(f), 617(d), 1245(a), 1250(a), 1251(c), 1252(a), or 1254(a) to the distributing corporation) over the amount paid for the property;

(2) Where the fair market value of the property is less than its adjusted basis in the hands of the distributing corporation, the amount of the distribution shall be the excess of such fair market value over the amount paid for the property.

* * *

(l) *Transactions treated as distributions.*—A distribution to shareholders with respect to their stock is within the terms of section 301 although it takes place at the same time as another transaction if the distribution is in substance a separate transaction whether or not connected in a formal sense. This is most likely to occur in the case of a recapitalization, a reincorporation, or a merger of a corporation with a newly organized corporation having substantially no property. For example, if a corporation having only common stock outstanding, exchanges one share of newly issued common stock and one bond in the principal amount of $10 for each share of outstanding common stock, the distribution of the bonds will be a distribution of property (to the extent of their fair market value) to which section 301 applies, even though the exchange of common stock for common stock may be pursuant to a plan of reorganization under the terms of section 368(a)(1)(E) (recapitalization) and even though the exchange of common stock for common stock may be tax free by virtue of section 354.

(m) *Cancellation of indebtedness.*—The cancellation of indebtedness of a shareholder by a corporation shall be treated as a distribution of property.

* * *

(p) *Cross references.*—For certain rules relating to adjustments to earnings and profits and for determining the extent to which a distribution is a dividend, see sections 312 and 316 and regulations thereunder. [Reg. § 1.301-1.]

☐ [*T.D.* 6152, 12-2-55. *Amended by T.D.* 6752, 9-8-64; *T.D.* 7084, 1-7-71; *T.D.* 7209, 10-3-72; *T.D.* 7283, 8-2-73; *T.D.* 7293, 11-27-73; *T.D.* 7587, 1-4-79; *T.D.* 8474, 4-26-93; *T.D.* 8586,

1-9-95; *T.D.* 8924, 1-3-2001 *and T.D.* 8964, 9-26-2001.]

[*Note: Reg. § 1.302-1 does not reflect the 1982 change in location of the partial liquidation rules. The partial liquidation provisions formerly embodied in Section 346 are now set forth, with some modification, in Sections 302(b)(4) and 302(e).*]

§ 1.302-1. General.—(a) Under section 302(d), unless otherwise provided in subchapter C, chapter 1 of the Code, a distribution in redemption of stock shall be treated as a distribution of property to which section 301 applies if the distribution is not within any of the provisions of section 302(b). A distribution in redemption of stock shall be considered a distribution in part or full payment in exchange for the stock under section 302(a) provided paragraph (1), (2), (3), or (4) of section 302(b) applies. Section 318(a) (relating to constructive ownership of stock) applies to all redemptions under section 302 except that in the termination of a shareholder's interest certain limitations are placed on the application of section 318(a)(1) by section 302(c)(2). The term "redemption of stock" is defined in section 317(b). Section 302 does not apply to that portion of any distribution which qualifies as a distribution in partial liquidation under section 346. For special rules relating to redemption of stock to pay death taxes see section 303. For special rules relating to redemption of section 306 stock see section 306. For special rules relating to redemption of stock in partial or complete liquidation see section 331.

* * *

[Reg. § 1.302-1.]

☐ [*T.D.* 6152, 12-2-55.]

§ 1.302-2. Redemptions not taxable as dividends.—(a) The fact that a redemption fails to meet the requirements of paragraph (2), (3) or (4) of section 302(b) shall not be taken into account in determining whether the redemption is not essentially equivalent to a dividend under section 302(b)(1). See, however, paragraph (b) of this section. For example, if a shareholder owns only nonvoting stock of a corporation which is not section 306 stock and which is limited and preferred as to dividends and in liquidation, and one-half of such stock is redeemed, the distribution will ordinarily meet the requirements of paragraph (1) of section 302(b) but will not meet the requirements of paragraph (2), (3) or (4) of such section. The determination of whether or not a distribution is within the phrase "essentially equivalent to a dividend" (that is, having the same effect as a distribution without any redemption of stock) shall be made without regard to the earnings and profits of the corporation at the time of the distribution. For example, if A owns all the stock of a corporation and the corporation redeems part of his stock at a time when it has no earnings and profits, the distribution shall be treated as a distribution under section 301 pursuant to section 302(d).

(b) The question whether a distribution in redemption of stock of a shareholder is not essentially equivalent to a dividend under section 302(b)(1) depends upon the facts and circumstances of each case. One of the facts to be considered in making this determination is the constructive stock ownership of such shareholder under section 318(a). All distributions in pro rata redemptions of a part of the stock of a corporation generally will be treated as distributions under section 301 if the corporation has only one class of stock outstanding. However, for distributions in partial liquidation, see section 346. The redemption of all of one class of stock (except section 306 stock) either at one time or in a series of redemptions generally will be considered as a distribution under section 301 if all classes of stock outstanding at the time of the redemption are held in the same proportion. Distributions in redemption of stock may be treated as distributions under section 301 regardless of the provisions of the stock certificate and regardless of whether all stock being redeemed was acquired by the stockholders from whom the stock was redeemed by purchase or otherwise. In every case in which a shareholder transfers stock to the corporation which issued such stock in exchange for property, the facts and circumstances shall be reported on his return except as provided in paragraph (d) of § 1.331-1. See sections 346(a) and 6043 for requirements relating to returns by corporations.

(c) In any case in which an amount received in redemption of stock is treated as a distribution of a dividend, proper adjustment of the basis of the remaining stock will be made with respect to the stock redeemed. (For adjustments to basis required for certain redemptions of corporate shareholders that are treated as extraordinary dividends, see section 1059 and the regulations thereunder.) The following examples illustrate the application of this rule:

Example (1). A, an individual, purchased all of the stock of Corporation X for $100,000. In 1955 the corporation redeems half of the stock for $150,000, and it is determined that this amount constitutes a dividend. The remaining stock of Corporation X held by A has a basis of $100,000.

Example (2). H and W, husband and wife, each own half of the stock of Corporation X. All of the stock was purchased by H for $100,000 cash. In 1950 H gave one-half of the stock to W, the stock transferred having a value in excess of $50,000. In 1955 all of the stock of H is redeemed for

$150,000, and it is determined that the distribution to H in redemption of his shares constitutes the distribution of a dividend. Immediately after the transaction, W holds the remaining stock of Corporation X with a basis of $100,000.

Example (3). The facts are the same as in Example (2) with the additional facts that the outstanding stock of Corporation X consists of 1,000 shares and all but 10 shares of the stock of H is redeemed. Immediately after the transaction, H holds 10 shares of the stock of Corporation X with a basis of $50,000, and W holds 500 shares with a basis of $50,000. [Reg. § 1.302-2.]

□ [*T.D.* 6152, 12-2-55. *Amended by T.D.* 8724, 7-15-97.]

§ 1.302-3. Substantially disproportionate redemption.—(a) Section 302(b)(2) provides for the treatment of an amount received in redemption of stock as an amount received in exchange for such stock if—

(1) Immediately after the redemption the shareholder owns less than 50 percent of the total combined voting power of all classes of stock as provided in section 302(b)(2)(B),

(2) The redemption is a substantially disproportionate redemption within the meaning of section 302(b)(2)(C), and

(3) The redemption is not pursuant to a plan described in section 302(b)(2)(D).

Section 318(a) (relating to constructive ownership of stock) shall apply both in making the disproportionate redemption test and in determining the percentage of stock ownership after the redemption. The requirements under section 302(b)(2) shall be applied to each shareholder separately and shall be applied only with respect to stock which is issued and outstanding in the hands of the shareholders. Section 302(b)(2) only applies to a redemption of voting stock or to a redemption of both voting stock and other stock. Section 302(b)(2) does not apply to the redemption solely of nonvoting stock (common or preferred). However, if a redemption is treated as an exchange to a particular shareholder under the terms of section 302(b)(2), such section will apply to the simultaneous redemption of nonvoting preferred stock (which is not section 306 stock) owned by such shareholder and such redemption will also be treated as an exchange. Generally, for purposes of this section, stock which does not have voting rights until the happening of an event, such as a default in the payment of dividends on preferred stock, is not voting stock until the happening of the specified event. Subsection 302(b)(2)(D) provides that a redemption will not be treated as substantially disproportionate if made pursuant to a plan the purpose or effect of which is a series of redemptions which result in

Reg. § 1.302-3(a)(1)

the aggregate in a distribution which is not substantially disproportionate. Whether or not such a plan exists will be determined from all the facts and circumstances.

(b) The application of paragraph (a) of this section is illustrated by the following example:

Example. Corporation M has outstanding 400 shares of common stock of which A, B, C and D each own 100 shares or 25 percent. No stock is considered constructively owned by A, B, C or D under section 318. Corporation M redeems 55 shares from A, 25 shares from B, and 20 shares from C. For the redemption to be disproportionate as to any shareholder, such shareholder must own after the redemptions less than 20 percent (80 percent of 25 percent) of the 300 shares of stock then outstanding. After the redemptions, A owns 45 shares (15 percent), B owns 75 shares (25 percent), and C owns 80 shares (26⅔ percent). The distribution is disproportionate only with respect to A. [Reg. § 1.302-3.]

☐ [*T.D.* 6152, 12-2-55.]

§ 1.302-4. Termination of shareholder's interest.—Section 302(b)(3) provides that a distribution in redemption of all of the stock of the corporation owned by a shareholder shall be treated as a distribution in part or full payment in exchange for the stock of such shareholder. In determining whether all of the stock of the shareholder has been redeemed, the general rule of section 302(c)(1) requires that the rules of constructive ownership provided in section 318(a) shall apply. Section 302(c)(2), however, provides that section 318(a)(1) (relating to constructive ownership of stock owned by members of a family) shall not apply where the specific requirements of section 302(c)(2) are met. The following rules shall be applicable in determining whether the specific requirements of section 302(c)(2) are met:

(a)(1) The agreement specified in section 302(c)(2)(A)(iii) shall be in the form of a separate statement in duplicate signed by the distributee and attached to the first return filed by the distributee for the taxable year in which the distribution described in section 302(b)(3) occurs. The agreement shall recite that the distributee has not acquired, other than by bequest or inheritance, any interest in the corporation (as described in section 302(c)(2)(A)(i)) since the distribution and that the distributee agrees to notify the district director for the internal revenue district in which the distributee resides of any acquisition, other than by bequest or inheritance, of such an interest in the corporation within 30 days after the acquisition, if the acquisition occurs within 10 years from the date of the distribution.

(2) If the distributee fails to file the agreement specified in section 302(c)(2)(A)(iii) at the time provided in subparagraph (1) of this paragraph, then the district director for the internal revenue district in which the distributee resided at the time of filing the first return for the taxable year in which the distribution occurred shall grant a reasonable extension of time for filing such agreement, provided (i) it is established to the satisfaction of the district director that there was reasonable cause for failure to file the agreement within the prescribed time, and (ii) a request for such extension is filed within such time as the district director considers reasonable under the circumstances.

(b) The distributee who files an agreement under section 302(c)(2)(A)(iii) shall retain copies of income tax returns and any other records indicating fully the amount of tax which would have been payable had the redemption been treated as a distribution subject to section 301.

(c) If stock of a parent corporation is redeemed, section 302(c)(2)(A), relating to acquisition of an interest in the corporation within 10 years after termination shall be applied with reference to an interest both in the parent corporation and any subsidiary of such parent corporation. If stock of a parent corporation is sold to a subsidiary in a transaction described in section 304, section 302(c)(2)(A) shall be applicable to the acquisition of an interest in such subsidiary corporation or in the parent corporation. If stock of a subsidiary corporation is redeemed, section 302(c)(2)(A) shall be applied with reference to an interest both in such subsidiary corporation and its parent. Section 302(c)(2)(A) shall also be applied with respect to an interest in a corporation which is a successor corporation to the corporation the interest in which has been terminated.

(d) For the purpose of section 302(c)(2)(A)(i), a person will be considered to be a creditor only if the rights of such person with respect to the corporation are not greater or broader in scope than necessary for the enforcement of his claim. Such claim must not in any sense be proprietary and must not be subordinate to the claims of general creditors. An obligation in the form of a debt may thus constitute a proprietary interest. For example, if under the terms of the instrument the corporation may discharge the principal amount of its obligation to a person by payments, the amount or certainty of which are dependent upon the earnings of the corporation, such a person is not a creditor of the corporation. Furthermore, if under the terms of the instrument the rate of purported interest is dependent upon earnings, the holder of such instrument may not, in some cases, be a creditor.

(e) In the case of a distributee to whom section 302(b)(3) is applicable, who is a creditor after such transaction, the acquisition of the assets of the corporation in the enforcement of the rights of such creditor shall not be considered an acquisition of an interest in the corporation for purposes of section 302(c)(2) unless stock of the corporation, its parent corporation, or, in the case of a redemption of stock of a parent corporation, of a subsidiary of such corporation is acquired.

(f) In determining whether an entire interest in the corporation has been terminated under section 302(b)(3), under all circumstances paragraphs (2), (3), (4), and (5) of section 318(a) (relating to constructive ownership of stock) shall be applicable.

(g) Section 302(c)(2)(B) provides that section 302(c)(2)(A) shall not apply—

(1) If any portion of the stock redeemed was acquired directly or indirectly within the 10-year period ending on the date of the distribution by the distributee from a person, the ownership of whose stock would (at the time of distribution) be attributable to the distributee under section 318(a), or

(2) If any person owns (at the time of the distribution) stock, the ownership of which is attributable to the distributee under section 318(a), such person acquired any stock in the corporation directly or indirectly from the distributee within the 10-year period ending on the date of the distribution, and such stock so acquired from the distributee is not redeemed in the same transaction,

unless the acquisition (described in (1) of this paragraph) or the disposition by the distributee (described in subparagraph (2)) did not have as one of its principal purposes the avoidance of Federal income tax. A transfer of stock by the transferor, within the 10-year period ending on the date of the distribution, to a person whose stock would be attributable to the transferor shall not be deemed to have as one of its principal purposes the avoidance of Federal income tax merely because the transferee is in a lower income tax bracket than the transferor. [Reg. § 1.302-4.]

☐ [*T.D. 6152, 12-2-55. Amended by T.D. 6969, 8-22-68 and T.D. 7535, 3-14-78.*]

Proposed Regulation

§ 1.302-5. Redemptions taxable as dividends.—(a) *In general.* In any case in which an amount received in redemption of stock is treated as a distribution of a dividend, an amount equal to the basis of the redeemed stock, after adjusting such basis to reflect the application of section 301(c)(2), 961(b), 1059, § 1.1502-32, or any other applicable provision of the Internal Revenue Code or regulations thereunder, is treated as a loss recognized on a disposition of redeemed stock

on the date of the redemption. The redeemed shareholder (as defined in paragraph (b)(1) of this section) shall be permitted to take such loss into account pursuant to the provisions of this section. Although such loss may be taken into account on a date later than the date of the redemption, the attributes (e.g., character and source) of such loss are determined on the date of the redemption of the stock that gave rise to such loss. See § 1.1502-19(b)(5) for rules that apply where an amount received in redemption of stock is treated as a dividend and such amount either increases or creates an excess loss account in the redeemed stock.

(b) *Definitions*—(1) *Redeemed shareholder.* Except as provided in paragraphs (d)(6), (7), and (8) of this section, the redeemed shareholder is the person whose stock is redeemed in a transaction in which a portion or all of the redemption proceeds are treated as a dividend. If the assets of the redeemed shareholder are acquired in a transaction described in section 381(a), the acquiring corporation (within the meaning of section 381) thereafter is treated as the redeemed shareholder. For rules concerning the person that is treated as the redeemed shareholder where the redeemed stock is held by a partnership or an S corporation at the time of the redemption, see paragraphs (d)(6) and (7) of this section. For rules concerning the person that is treated as the redeemed shareholder where the redeemed stock is held by an estate or a trust not treated as wholly owned by the grantor or another person at the time of the redemption and a loss attributable to the basis of such redeemed stock is distributed to a beneficiary of such estate or trust, see paragraph (d)(8) of this section.

(2) *Redeeming corporation.* Except as provided in paragraph (d)(5) of this section, the redeeming corporation is the corporation that issued the stock that is redeemed. For rules concerning the entity that is treated as the redeeming corporation where the redeeming corporation ceases to exist in a transaction described in section 381(a) or where the redeeming corporation distributes to its shareholders stock of one or more controlled corporations in a distribution described in section 355(a), see paragraph (d)(5) of this section.

(3) *Final inclusion date.* Except as otherwise provided in paragraphs (d)(5), (6), (7), and (8) of this section, the final inclusion date is the first date on which the redeemed shareholder would satisfy the criteria of section 302(b)(1), (2), or (3) if the facts and circumstances that exist at the end of such day had existed immediately after the redemption. In addition, a date is the final inclusion date if there is no later date on which the redeemed shareholder could take the loss into account. For purposes of the preceding sentence, the

existence or creation of a limitation under section 382 is not treated as preventing the loss from being taken into account. For example, if the redeemed shareholder is an individual, the final inclusion date includes the date of death of such individual. if the redeemed shareholder is a corporation, the final inclusion date includes the date such corporation transfers its assets in a liquidation described in section 331. If the redeemed shareholder is a foreign corporation, the final inclusion date includes the date such corporation transfers its assets to a domestic corporation either a liquidation described in section 332 or a reorganization described in section 368(a)(1) to which section 381 applies. If the redeemed shareholder is a foreign corporation that is not a controlled foreign corporation, within the meaning of section 957(a), on the date of the redemption, the term final inclusion date includes the date such corporation transfers its assets to a controlled foreign corporation in a liquidation described in section 332 or a reorganization described in section 368(a)(1) to which section 381 applies.

(4) *Accelerated loss inclusion date.* An accelerated loss inclusion date is a date other than the final inclusion date on which the redeemed shareholder must take into account gain from an actual or deemed sale or exchange of stock of the redeeming corporation. For example, the redeemed shareholder must take into account gain from an actual or deemed sale or exchange of stock of the redeeming corporation when such shareholder receives a distribution with respect to stock of the redeeming corporation to which section 301(c)(3) applies, recognizes gain on stock of the redeeming corporation as a result of the application of section 475, recognizes gain on a sale or exchange of stock of the redeeming corporation (even if such gain is characterized as a dividend under section 1248), recognizes gain in connection with a constructive sale of stock of the redeeming corporation within the meaning of section 1259, or is a partner of a partnership or a shareholder of an S corporation that is allocated, and must take into account, gain recognized on the partnership's or S corporation's sale or exchange of stock of the redeeming corporation.

(c) *Inclusion of loss attributable to basis of redeemed stock*—(1) *Amount taken into account on final inclusion date.* On the final inclusion date, the redeemed shareholder is permitted to take into account the loss attributable to the basis of redeemed stock, reduced by the amount of such loss that was previously taken into account pursuant to paragraph (c)(2) of this section.

(2) *Amount taken into account on accelerated loss inclusion date.* On an accelerated loss inclusion date, the redeemed shareholder is permitted to take into account the loss attributable

to the basis of redeemed stock in the amount of the lesser of—

(i) The amount of such loss reduced by the amount of such loss previously taken into account pursuant to this paragraph (c)(2); and

(ii) The amount of gain recognized with respect to stock of the redeeming corporation that must be taken into account by the redeemed shareholder on such accelerated loss inclusion date.

(d) *Special rules*—(1) *Treatment of loss attributable to basis of redeemed stock.* Except as otherwise provided in this section, for purposes of applying the provisions of the Internal Revenue Code and the regulations thereunder, any loss attributable to the basis of redeemed stock that has not been permitted to be taken into account shall be treated as a net operating loss carryforward or a capital loss carryforward, as applicable. For example, for purposes of determining under sections 382 and 383 whether the redeemed shareholder is a loss corporation that has an ownership change and whether the loss attributable to the basis of redeemed stock is a pre-change loss, any loss attributable to the basis of redeemed stock that the redeemed shareholder is not permitted to take into account before a testing date shall be treated as a net operating loss carryforward or a capital loss carryforward, as applicable, that arose in the taxable year in which the redemption that gave rise to such loss occurred and that can be carried forward to the taxable year that includes the testing date. If such loss is treated as a pre-change loss because of an ownership change on the testing date, it is subject to the section 382 limitation (and the other rules of section 382 or 383) for any post-change year in which it is taken into account under paragraph (c) of this section and any other post-change year to which it is carried pursuant to section 172 or 1212, as applicable, and paragraph (d)(2) of this section. The order in which the loss is absorbed (and in which it absorbs the section 382 limitation (see § 1.383-1(d)(2)), however is determined in a manner consistent with the principles of section 172 or section 1212, as applicable, and paragraph (d)(2) of this section.

(2) *Net operating loss deduction and capital loss carrybacks and carryovers.* For purposes of sections 172 and 1212, any portion of a loss attributable to the basis of redeemed stock shall be treated as occurring in the taxable year in which the redeemed shareholder is permitted to take such loss into account, not the taxable year of the redemption that gave rise to such loss. If an estate or trust terminates before it is permitted to take into account all of the loss attributable to the basis of redeemed stock, such loss that it has not

Reg. § 1.302-5(d)(2)

been permitted to take into account is treated as a loss under section 172 or 1212 for purposes of section 642(h), provided, however, that the identification of carryover years of the beneficiaries will be determined in accordance with the preceding sentence. Notwithstanding the preceding sentence, each beneficiary's interest in the loss distributed under section 642(h) shall be limited to the proportion of that loss that is equal to the proportion of the total amount of the distribution treated as a dividend that is represented by that beneficiary's beneficial interest in that dividend. If a deduction for any portion of such loss is disallowed by section 382 or 383 for the taxable year in which the redeemed shareholder is permitted to take such loss into account, such portion shall be carried forward to subsequent taxable years under rules similar to the rules for the carrying forward of net operating losses or capital losses, as applicable, but shall be subject to the section 382 limitation (and the other rules of sections 382 and 383) for any post-change year to which it is carried.

(3) *Expenses apportioned on the basis of assets.* For special rules regarding adjustments in the case of taxpayers apportioning expenses on the basis of the tax book value of assets, see § 1.861-12(c)(2)(vi).

(4) *Effect of loss attributable to basis of redeemed stock on earnings and profits.* if the redeemed shareholder is a corporation, any loss attributable to the basis of redeemed stock is not reflected in such corporation's earnings and profits before it is taken into account pursuant to the rules of paragraph (c) of this section. See, for example, § § 1.312-6(a), 1.312-7, and 1.1502-33(c)(2).

(5) *Successors to the redeeming corporation*—(i) *Acquisitive transactions.* If the assets of the redeeming corporation are acquired by another corporation in a transaction described in section 381(a), the determination of whether a particular date is the final inclusion date or an accelerated loss inclusion date is made by treating the facts and circumstances that exist at the end of such day (including the acquisition of the assets of the redeeming corporation) as existing immediately after the redemption and treating the acquiring corporation (within the meaning of section 381) as the redeeming corporation.

(ii) *Divisive transactions.* In general, if the redeeming corporation distributes to its shareholders the stock of one or more controlled corporations in a distribution to which section 355 (or so much of section 356 as relates to section 355) applies, the loss attributable to the basis of redeemed stock is allocated among the stock of the distributing and any controlled corporations that

the redeemed shareholder owns, actually and constructively pursuant to the rules of section 318, immediately after the distribution in proportion to the fair market value of the stock of the distributing corporation that the redeemed shareholder is treated as so owning and the distributed stock of the controlled corporation that the redeemed shareholder is treated as so owning. To the extent that such loss is allocated to the stock of the distributing corporation, the distributing corporation will be treated as the redeeming corporation for purposes of determining whether a particular date is the final inclusion date of an accelerated loss inclusion date with respect to such loss. To the extent that such loss is allocated to the stock of a controlled corporation, such controlled corporation will be treated as the redeeming corporation for purposes of determining whether a particular date is the final inclusion date or an accelerated loss inclusion date with respect to such loss. Where the controlled corporation was wholly owned by the distributing corporation and all of the stock of the controlled corporation was distributed to the shareholders of the distributing corporation in a distribution to which section 355 (or so much of section 356 as relates to section 355) applies, the determination of whether a particular date is the final inclusion date with respect to a loss that is allocated to a controlled corporation is made by treating the redeemed shareholder as owning a percentage of stock of the controlled corporation immediately prior to the redemption equal to the percentage of stock of the distributing corporation the redeemed shareholder actually and constructively owned immediately prior to the redemption. In all other cases, appropriate calculations shall apply to determine whether a particular date is the final inclusion date.

* * *

(f) *Examples.* For purposes of the examples in this section, each of corporation X, corporation Y, corporation Z, corporation D, and corporation C is a domestic corporation that files U.S. tax returns on a calendar-year basis. The principles of this section are illustrated by the following examples:

Example 1. (i) *Facts.* A and B, husband and wife, each own 100 shares (50 percent) of the stock of corporation X and hold the corporation X stock as a capital asset. A purchased his corporation X shares on February 1, Year 1, for $200. On December 31, Year 1, corporation X redeems all of A's 100 shares of its stock for $300. At the end of Year 1, corporation X has current and accumulated earnings and profits of $200. In connection with the redemption transaction, A does not file an agreement described in section 302(c)(2) waiving the application of the family attribution rules. The redemption proceeds, therefore, are treated

Reg. § 1.302-5(d)(3)

under section 301(c)(1) as a dividend to the extent of corporation X's earnings and profits of $200, and under section 301(c)(2) as a recovery of basis in the amount of $100. On July 1, Year 2, B sells all of her shares of corporation X stock to G, her mother.

(ii) *Analysis.* Under this section, an amount equal to A's basis in the corporation X stock ($100 after application of section 301(c)(2)) is treated as a loss recognized on a disposition of the redeemed stock on December 31, Year 1, the date of the redemption. When B sells her shares to G, A no longer owns, actually or constructively, any shares of corporation X stock. Thus, if the facts that existed at the end of July 1, Year 2, had existed immediately after the redemption, A would have been treated as having received a distribution in part or full payment in exchange for the redeemed stock pursuant to section 302(a). Under this section, therefore, July 1, Year 2, is the final inclusion date and, on that date, A is permitted to take into account the loss of $100 attributable to his basis in the redeemed stock. Because that loss is treated as having been recognized on a disposition of the redeemed stock on the date of the redemption, December 31 of Year 1, such loss is treated as a short-term capital loss.

Example 2. (i) *Facts.* The facts are the same as in *Example 1*, except that, instead of selling all of her 100 shares of corporation X stock to G on July 1, Year 2, B sells only 75 shares of corporation X stock to G on that date.

(ii) *Analysis.* As in *Example 1*, an amount equal to A's basis in the redeemed stock ($100 after application of section 301(c)(2)) is treated as a loss recognized on a disposition of the redeemed stock on December 31, Year 1, the date of the redemption. Immediately after B's sale of 75 shares of corporation X stock to G, A constructively owns 25 percent of the shares of corporation, X stock. Thus, if the facts that existed at the end of July 1, Year 2, had existed immediately after the redemption, A would have been treated as receiving a distribution in part or full payment in exchange for the redeemed stock pursuant to section 302(a). Under this section, therefore, July 1, Year 2, is the final inclusion date and, on that date, A is permitted to take into account the loss of $100 attributable to his basis in the redeemed stock. Because that loss is treated as having been recognized on a disposition of the redeemed stock on the redemption date, December 31 of Year 1, such loss is treated as a short-term capital loss.

Example 3. (i) *Facts.* Corporation Y has 200 shares of common stock outstanding. L, an individual, owns 150 shares of common stock in corporation Y and has owned these shares for several years. The remaining 50 shares are owned by K,

L's father. In Year 1, corporation Y redeems 50 shares of L's corporation Y stock, which have a basis of $75, for $200. At the end of Year 1, corporation Y's current and accumulated earnings and profits exceed $200. The redemption of L's stock is treated as a distribution to which section 301 applies. L recognizes dividend income in the amount of $200. In Year 4, L sells 25 of his remaining shares of corporation Y stock, which have a basis of $50, to K for $100 and recognizes $50 of long-term capital gain.

(ii) *Analysis.* Under this section, an amount equal to L's basis in the corporation Y stock that is redeemed, $75, is treated as a loss recognized on a disposition of the redeemed stock on the date of the redemption. The date on which L sells 25 shares of corporation Y stock to K is not the final inclusion date under paragraph (b)(3) of this section because L does not satisfy the criteria of section 302(b)(1), (2), or (3) at the end of such day. Under paragraph (b)(4) of this section, however, that date is an accelerated loss inclusion date because, on that date, L recognizes gain of $50 on a disposition of stock of corporation Y, the redeeming corporation. Thus, on that date, L is permitted to take into account $50 of the loss attributable to his basis in the redeemed stock. The remaining $25 of such loss is taken into account on the earlier of the final inclusion date or the next accelerated loss inclusion date (to the extent of gain recognized).

Example 4. (i) *Facts.* The facts are the same as in *Example 3*, except that L does not sell any shares of corporation Y stock to K in Year 4. Instead, in Year 4, corporation Y distributes $75 to L with respect to his remaining 100 shares of corporation Y stock. L's basis in these shares is only $30, and at the end of Year 4, corporation Y's current and accumulated earnings and profits are $20, instead of $200. Under section 301(c)(1), $20 of the distribution is treated as a dividend, under section 301(c)(2), $30 of the distribution is treated as a recovery of basis, and, under section 301(c)(3), $25 of the distribution is treated as gain from the sale or exchange of stock.

(ii) *Analysis.* As in *Example 3*, an amount equal to L's basis in the corporation Y stock redeemed in Year 1, $75, is treated as a loss recognized on a disposition of the redeemed stock on the date of the redemption. Because L recognizes gain under section 301(c)(3) upon the receipt of the Year 4 distribution, the date of that distribution is an accelerated loss inclusion date. Accordingly, on that date, L is permitted to take into account $25 of the loss attributable to the basis the redeemed stock. The remaining $50 of such loss is taken into account on the earlier of the final inclusion date or

Reg. § 1.302-5(f)

the next accelerated loss inclusion date (to the extent of gain recognized).

* * *

[Reg. § 1.302-5.]

[Proposed 10-18-2002 (*corrected* 12-26-2002).]

§ 1.303-1. General.—Section 303 provides that in certain cases a distribution in redemption of stock, the value of which is included in determining the value of the gross estate of a decedent, shall be treated as a distribution in full payment in exchange for the stock so redeemed. [Reg. § 1.303-1.]

□ [*T.D.* 6152, 12-2-55.]

[*Note: The alternative qualification requirement relating to "50 percent of the taxable estate" referred to in Reg. § 1.303-2 was deleted in 1976. The 75 percent stock ownership requirement relating to multiple corporations, also referred to in Reg. § 1.303-2, was reduced to 20 percent in 1981.*]

§ 1.303-2. Requirements.—(a) Section 303 applies only where the distribution is with respect to stock of a corporation the value of whose stock in the gross estate of the decedent for Federal estate tax purposes is an amount in excess of (1) 35 percent of the value of the gross estate of such decedent, or (2) 50 percent of the taxable estate of such decedent. For the purposes of such 35 percent and 50 percent requirements, stock of two or more corporations shall be treated as the stock of a single corporation if more than 75 percent in value of the outstanding stock of each such corporation is included in determining the value of the decedent's gross estate. For the purpose of the 75 percent requirement, stock which, at the decedent's death, represents the surviving spouse's interest in community property shall be considered as having been included in determining the value of the decedent's gross estate.

(b) For the purpose of section 303(b)(2)(A)(i), the term "gross estate" means the gross estate as computed in accordance with section 2031 (or, in the case of the estate of a decedent nonresident not a citizen of the United States, in accordance with section 2103). For the purpose of section 303(b)(2)(A)(ii), the term "taxable estate" means the taxable estate as computed in accordance with section 2051 (or, in the case of the estate of a decedent non-resident not a citizen of the United States, in accordance with section 2106). In case the value of an estate is determined for Federal estate tax purposes under section 2032 (relating to alternate valuation), then, for purposes of section 303(b)(2), the value of the gross estate, the taxable estate, and the stock shall each be determined on the applicable date prescribed in section 2032.

(c)(1) In determining whether the estate of the decedent is comprised of stock of a corporation of sufficient value to satisfy the percentage requirements of section 303(b)(2)(A) and section 303(b)(2)(B), the total value, in the aggregate, of all classes of stock of the corporation includible in determining the value of the gross estate is taken into account. A distribution under section 303(a) may be in redemption of the stock of the corporation includible in determining the value of the gross estate, without regard to the class of such stock.

(2) The above may be illustrated by the following example:

Example. The gross estate of the decedent has a value of $1,000,000, the taxable estate is $700,000, and the sum of the death taxes and funeral and administration expenses is $275,000. Included in determining the gross estate of the decedent is stock of three corporations which, for Federal estate tax purposes, is valued as follows:

Corporation A:
   Common stock $100,000
   Preferred stock 100,000
Corporation B:
   Common stock 50,000
   Preferred stock 350,000
Corporation C:
   Common stock 200,000

The stock of Corporation A and Corporation C included in the estate of the decedent constitutes all of the outstanding stock of both corporations. The stock of Corporation A and the stock of Corporation C, treated as the stock of a single corporation under section 303(b)(2)(B), has a value in excess of $350,000 (35 percent of the gross estate or 50 percent of the taxable estate). Likewise, the stock of Corporation B has a value in excess of $350,000. The distribution by one or more of the above corporations, within the period prescribed in section 303(b)(1), of amounts not exceeding, in the aggregate, $275,000, in redemption of preferred stock or common stock of such corporation or corporations, will be treated as in full payment in exchange for the stock so redeemed.

(d) If stock includible in determining the value of the gross estate of a decedent is exchanged for new stock, the basis of which is determined by reference to the basis of the old stock, the redemption of the new stock will be treated the same under section 303 as the redemption of the old stock would have been. Thus, section 303 shall apply with respect to a distribution in redemption of stock received by the estate of a decedent (1) in connection with a reorganization under section 368, (2) in a distribution or exchange under section 355 (or so much of section 356 as relates to section 355), (3) in an exchange under section

Reg. § 1.303-1

1036 or (4) in a distribution to which section 305(a) applies. Similarly, a distribution in redemption of stock will qualify under section 303, notwithstanding the fact that the stock redeemed is section 306 stock to the extent that the conditions of section 303 are met.

(e) Section 303 applies to distributions made after the death of the decedent and (1) before the expiration of the 3-year period of limitations for the assessment of estate tax provided in section 6501(a) (determined without the application of any provisions of law extending or suspending the running of such period of limitations), or within 90 days after the expiration of such period, or (2) if a petition for redetermination of a deficiency in such estate tax has been filed with the Tax Court within the time prescribed in section 6213, at any time before the expiration of 60 days after the decision of the Tax Court becomes final. The extension of the period of distribution provided in section 303(b)(1)(B) has reference solely to bona fide contests in the Tax Court and will not apply in the case of a petition for redetermination of a deficiency which is initiated solely for the purpose of extending the period within which section 303 would otherwise be applicable.

(f) While section 303 will most frequently have application in the case where stock is redeemed from the executor or administrator of an estate, the section is also applicable to distributions in redemption of stock included in the decedent's gross estate and held at the time of the redemption by any person who acquired the stock by any of the means comprehended by Part III, Subchapter A, Chapter 11 of the Code, including the heir, legatee, or donee of the decedent, a surviving joint tenant, surviving spouse, appointee, or taker in default of appointment, or a trustee of a trust created by the decedent. Thus, section 303 may apply with respect to a distribution in redemption of stock from a donee to whom the decedent has transferred stock in contemplation of death where the value of such stock is included in the decedent's gross estate under section 2035. Similarly, section 303 may apply to the redemption of stock from a beneficiary of the estate to whom an executor has distributed the stock pursuant to the terms of the will of the decedent. However, section 303 is not applicable to the case where stock is redeemed from a stockholder who has acquired the stock by gift or purchase from any person to whom such stock has passed from the decedent. Nor is section 303 applicable to the case where stock is redeemed from a stockholder who has acquired the stock from the executor in satisfaction of a specific monetary bequest.

(g)(1) The total amount of the distributions to which section 303 may apply with respect to redemptions of stock included in the gross estate of a decedent may not exceed the sum of the estate, inheritance, legacy, and succession taxes (including any interest collected as a part of such taxes) imposed because of the decedent's death and the amount of funeral and administration expenses allowable as deductions to the estate. Where there is more than one distribution in redemption of stock described in section 303(b)(2) during the period of time prescribed in section 303(b)(1), the distributions shall be applied against the total amount which qualifies for treatment under section 303 in the order in which the distributions are made. For this purpose, all distributions in redemption of such stock shall be taken into account, including distributions which under another provision of the Code are treated as in part or full payment in exchange for the stock redeemed.

(2) Subparagraph (1) of this paragraph may be illustrated by the following example:

Example. (i) The gross estate of the decedent has a value of $800,000, the taxable estate is $500,000, and the sum of the death taxes and funeral and administrative expenses is $225,000. Included in determining the gross estate of the decedent is the stock of a corporation which for Federal estate tax purposes is valued at $450,000. During the first year of administration, one-third of such stock is distributed to a legatee and shortly thereafter this stock is redeemed by the corporation for $150,000. During the second year of administration, another one-third of such stock includible in the estate is redeemed for $150,000.

(ii) The first distribution of $150,000 is applied against the amount that qualifies for treatment under section 303, regardless of whether the first distribution was treated as in payment in exchange for stock under section 302(a). Thus, only $75,000 of the second distribution may be treated as in full payment in exchange for stock under section 303. The tax treatment of the remaining $75,000 would be determined under other provisions of the Code.

(h) For the purpose of section 303, the Federal estate tax or any other estate, inheritance, legacy, or succession tax shall be ascertained after the allowance of any credit, relief, discount, refund, remission or reduction of tax. [Reg. § 1.303-2.]

☐ [*T.D. 6152, 12-2-55. Amended by T.D. 6724, 4-20-64 and T.D. 7346, 3-6-75.*]

§ 1.303-3. Application of other sections.—(a) The sole effect of section 303 is to exempt from tax as a dividend a distribution to which such section is applicable when made in redemption of stock includible in a decedent's gross estate. Such section does not, however, in any other manner affect the principles set forth in sections 302 and 306. Thus, if stock of a corporation is owned

Reg. § 1.303-3(a)

equally by A, B, and the C Estate, and the corporation redeems one-half of the stock of each shareholder, the determination of whether the distributions to A and B are essentially equivalent to dividends shall be made without regard to the effect which section 303 may have upon the taxability of the distribution to the C Estate.

(b) See section 304 relative to redemption of stock through the use of related corporations. [Reg. § 1.303-3.]

☐ [*T.D.* 6152, 12-2-55.]

§ 1.304-1. General.—(a) Except as provided in paragraph (b) of this section, section 304 is applicable where a shareholder sells stock of one corporation to a related corporation as defined in section 304. Sales to which section 304 is applicable shall be treated as redemptions subject to sections 302 and 303.

(b) In the case of—

(1) Any acquisition of stock described in section 304 which occurred before June 22, 1954, and

(2) Any acquisition of stock described in section 304 which occurred on or after June 22, 1954, and on or before December 31, 1958, pursuant to a contract entered into before June 22, 1954,

the extent to which the property received in return for such acquisition shall be treated as a dividend shall be determined as if the Internal Revenue Code of 1939 continued to apply in respect of such acquisition and as if the Internal Revenue Code of 1954 had not been enacted. See section 391. In cases to which this paragraph applies, the basis of the stock received by the acquiring corporation shall be determined as if the Internal Revenue Code of 1939 continued to apply in respect of such acquisition and as if the Internal Revenue Code of 1954 had not been enacted. [Reg. § 1.304-1.]

☐ [*T.D.* 6152, 12-2-55. *Amended by T.D.* 6533, 1-18-61.]

§ 1.304-2. Acquisition by related corporation (other than subsidiary).—(a) If a corporation, in return for property, acquires stock of another corporation from one or more persons, and the person or persons from whom the stock was acquired were in control of both such corporations before the acquisition, then such property shall be treated as received in redemption of stock of the acquiring corporation. The stock received by the acquiring corporation shall be treated as a contribution to the capital of such corporation. See section 362(a) for determination of the basis of such stock. The transferor's basis for his stock in the acquiring corporation shall be increased by the basis of stock surrendered by him. (But see below in this paragraph for subsequent reductions of basis in certain cases.) As to each person trans-

ferring stock, the amount received shall be treated as a distribution of property under section 302(d), unless as to such person such amount is to be treated as received in exchange for the stock under the terms of section 302(a) or section 303. In applying section 302(b), reference shall be had to the shareholder's ownership of stock in the issuing corporation and not to his ownership of stock in the acquiring corporation (except for purposes of applying section 318(a)). In determining control and applying section 302(b), section 318(a) (relating to the constructive ownership of stock) shall be applied without regard to the 50-percent limitation contained in section 318(a)(2)(C) and (3)(C). A series of redemptions referred to in section 302(b)(2)(D) shall include acquisitions by either of the corporations of stock of the other and stock redemptions by both corporations. If section 302(d) applies to the surrender of stock by a shareholder, his basis for his stock in the acquiring corporation after the transaction (increased as stated above in this paragraph) shall not be decreased except as provided in section 301. If section 302(d) does not apply, the property received shall be treated as received in a distribution in payment in exchange for stock of the acquiring corporation under section 302(a), which stock has a basis equal to the amount by which the shareholder's basis for his stock in the acquiring corporation was increased on account of the contribution to capital as provided for above in this paragraph. Accordingly, such amount shall be applied in reduction of the shareholder's basis for his stock in the acquiring corporation. Thus, the basis of each share of the shareholder's stock in the acquiring corporation will be the same as the basis of such share before the entire transaction. The holding period of the stock which is considered to have been redeemed shall be the same as the holding period of the stock actually surrendered.

(b) In any case in which two or more persons, in the aggregate, control two corporations, section 304(a)(1) will apply to sales by such persons of stock in either corporation to the other (whether or not made simultaneously) provided the sales by each of such persons are related to each other. The determination of whether the sales are related to each other shall be dependent upon the facts and circumstances surrounding all of the sales. For this purpose, the fact that the sales may occur during a period of one or more years (such as in the case of a series of sales by persons who together control each of such corporations immediately prior to the first of such sales and immediately subsequent to the last of such sales) shall be disregarded, provided the other facts and circumstances indicate related transactions.

Reg. § 1.304-1(a)

(c) The application of section 304(a)(1) may be illustrated by the following examples:

Example (1). Corporation X and corporation Y each have outstanding 200 shares of common stock. One-half of the stock of each corporation is owned by an individual, A, and one-half by another individual, B, who is unrelated to A. On or after August 31, 1964, A sells 30 shares of corporation X stock to corporation Y for $50,000, such stock having an adjusted basis of $10,000 to A. After the sale, A is considered as owning corporation X stock as follows: (i) 70 shares directly, and (ii) 15 shares constructively, since by virtue of his 50-percent ownership of Y he constructively owns 50 percent of the 30 shares owned directly by Y. Since A's percentage of ownership of X's voting stock after the sale (85 out of 200 shares, or 42.5%) is not less than 80 percent of his percentage of ownership of X's voting stock before the sale (100 out of 200 shares, or 50%), the transfer is not "substantially disproportionate" as to him as provided in section 302(b)(2). Under these facts, and assuming that section 302(b)(1) is not applicable, the entire $50,000 is treated as a dividend to A to the extent of the earnings and profits of corporation Y. The basis of the corporation X stock to corporation Y is $10,000, its adjusted basis to A. The amount of $10,000 is added to the basis of the stock of corporation Y in the hands of A.

Example (2). The facts are the same as in example (1) except that A sells 80 shares of corporation X stock to corporation Y, and the sale occurs before August 31, 1964. After the sale, A is considered as owning corporation X stock as follows: (i) 20 shares directly, and (ii) 90 shares indirectly, since by virtue of his 50-percent ownership of Y he constructively owns 50 percent of the 80 shares owned directly by Y and 50 percent of the 100 shares attributed to Y because they are owned by Y's stockholder, B. Since after the sale A owns a total of more than 50 percent of the voting power of all of the outstanding stock of X (110 out of 200 shares, or 55%), the transfer is not "substantially disproportionate" as to him as provided in section 302(b)(2).

Example (3). Corporation X and corporation Y each have outstanding 100 shares of common stock. A, an individual, owns one-half the stock of each corporation. B owns one-half the stock of corporation X, and C owns one-half the stock of corporation Y. A, B, and C are unrelated. A sells 30 shares of the stock of corporation X to corporation Y for $50,000, such stock having an adjusted basis of $10,000 to him. After the sale, A is considered as owning 35 shares of the stock of corporation X (20 shares directly and 15 constructively because one-half of the 30 shares owned by corporation Y are attributed to him). Since before the sale he owned 50 percent of the stock of corporation X and after the sale he owned directly and constructively only 35 percent of such stock, the redemption is substantially disproportionate as to him pursuant to the provisions of section 302(b)(2). He, therefore, realizes a gain of $40,000 ($50,000 minus $10,000). If the stock surrendered is a capital asset, such gain is long-term or short-term capital gain depending on the period of time that such stock was held. The basis to A for the stock of corporation Y is not changed as a result of the entire transaction. The basis to corporation Y for the stock of corporation X is $50,000, *i.e.,* the basis of the transferor ($10,000), increased in the amount of gain recognized to the transferor ($40,000) on the transfer.

Example (4). Corporation X and corporation Y each have outstanding 100 shares of common stock. H, an individual, W, his wife, S, his son, and G, his grandson, each own 25 shares of stock of each corporation. H sells all of his 25 shares of stock of corporation X to corporation Y. Since both before and after the transaction H owned directly and constructively 100 percent of the stock of corporation X, and assuming that section 302(b)(1) is not applicable, the amount received by him for his stock of corporation X is treated as a dividend to him to the extent of the earnings and profits of corporation Y. [Reg. § 1.304-2.]

  ☐ [*T.D.* 6152, 12-2-55. *Amended by T.D.* 6533, 1-18-61 *and T.D.* 6969, 8-22-68.]

Proposed Amendment to Regulation

§ 1.304-2. **Acquisition by related corporation (other than subsidiary).**—(a) *In general.*—(1) If a corporation (the acquiring corporation), in return for property, acquires stock of another corporation (the issuing corporation) from one or more persons, and the person or persons from whom the stock was acquired were in control of both such corporations, then such property shall be treated as received in redemption of stock of the acquiring corporation. As to each person transferring stock, the amount received shall be treated as a distribution to which section 301 applies if section 302(a) or 303 does not apply. For rules regarding the amount constituting a dividend in such cases, see § 1.304-6.

(2) In applying section 302(b), reference shall be had to the shareholder's ownership of stock in the issuing corporation and not to its ownership of stock in the acquiring corporation (except for purposes of applying section 318(a)), section 318(a) (relating to the constructive ownership of stock) shall be applied without regard to the 50 percent limitation contained in section 318(a)(2)(C) and (3)(C), and a series of redemptions referred to in section 302(b)(2)(D) shall include acquisitions by either of the corporations of

Reg. § 1.304-2(a)(2)

stock of the other and stock redemptions by both corporations.

(3) If, pursuant to section 302(d), section 301 applies to the property treated as received in redemption of stock of the acquiring corporation pursuant to paragraph (a)(1) of this section, the transferor and the acquiring corporation shall be treated, for all Federal income tax purposes, in the same manner as if the transferor had transferred the stock of the issuing corporation to the acquiring corporation in exchange for stock of the acquiring corporation in a transaction to which section 351(a) applies, and then the acquiring corporation had redeemed the stock it was treated as issuing in the transaction in exchange for the property. Accordingly, under section 362, the acquiring corporation's basis in the stock of the issuing corporation is equal to the basis the transferor had in that stock and, under section 358, the transferor's basis in the stock of the acquiring corporation deemed issued to the transferor in the deemed transaction to which section 351(a) applies is equal to the transferor's basis in the stock of the issuing corporation it surrendered. Section 1.302-5 applies to the transferor's unutilized basis, if any, in the stock of the acquiring corporation treated as redeemed in connection with an acquisition described in paragraph (a)(1) of this section by treating the acquiring corporation as the redeeming corporation and the transferor as the redeemed shareholder.

(4) If section 301 does not apply to the property treated as received in redemption of stock of the acquiring corporation pursuant to paragraph (a)(1) of this section, the property received by the transferor shall be treated as received in a distribution in full payment in exchange for stock of the acquiring corporation under section 302(a). The basis and holding period of the stock of the acquiring corporation that is treated as having been redeemed shall be the same as the basis and holding period of the stock of the issuing corporation actually surrendered. The acquiring corporation shall take a cost basis in the stock of the issuing corporation that it acquires. See section 1012.

* * *

(c) *Examples.* For purposes of the examples in this section, each of corporation X and corporation Y is a domestic corporation that files U.S. tax returns on a calendar-year basis. The principles of this section are illustrated by the following examples:

Example 1. (i) *Facts.* Corporation X and corporation Y each have outstanding 100 shares of common stock. A, an individual, owns one-half of the stock of each corporation, B owns one-half of the stock of corporation X, and C owns one-half of the stock of corporation Y. A, B, and C are unrelated. A sells 30 shares of the stock of corporation X, which have an adjusted basis of $10,000, to corporation Y for $50,000.

(ii) *Analysis.* Because before the sale A owns 50 percent of the stock of corporation X and after the sale A owns only 35 percent of such stock (20 shares directly and 15 constructively because one-half of the 30 shares owned by corporation Y are attributed to A), the redemption is substantially disproportionate as to A pursuant to the provisions of section 302(b)(2). A, therefore, realizes a gain of $40,000 ($50,000 minus $10,000). If the stock surrendered is a capital asset, such gain is long-term or short-term capital gain depending on the period of time that such stock was held. The basis to A for the stock of corporation Y is not changed as a result of the sale. Under section 1012, the basis that corporation Y takes in the acquired stock of corporation X is its cost of $50,000.

Example 2. (i) *Facts.* Corporation X and corporation Y each have outstanding 200 shares of common stock, all of which are owned by H, an individual. H has a basis in his corporation X stock of $60 and in his corporation Y stock of $30. Corporation X has $80 of current and accumulated earnings and profits and corporation Y has $80 of current and accumulated earnings and profits. H sells his 200 shares of corporation X stock to corporation Y for $150.

(ii) *Analysis.* Because H is in control of both corporation X and corporation Y and receives property from corporation Y in exchange for the corporation X stock, H's sale of 200 shares of corporation X stock to corporation Y is subject to section 304(a)(1). Accordingly, H is treated as receiving $150 as a distribution in redemption of corporation Y stock. Because H actually owns 100 percent of corporation X before the sale and is treated as owning 100 percent of corporation X after the sale, pursuant to section 302(d), section 302(a) does not apply to the deemed redemption distribution and the proceeds of the deemed redemption are treated as a distribution to which section 301 applies. Therefore, H is treated as transferring the corporation X stock to corporation Y in exchange for corporation Y stock in a transaction to which section 351(a) applies. Corporation Y's basis in the corporation X stock acquired is $60, the same basis that H had in the corporation X stock surrendered. H takes a basis of $60 in the corporation Y stock he is treated as receiving in the deemed section 351 exchange. That corporation Y stock is then treated as redeemed by corporation Y for $150. Under section 302, that redemption is treated as a distribution to which section 301 applies because H owns directly 100 percent of corporation Y both before and after the redemption of the corporation Y stock that was deemed issued. Thus, the deemed redemption proceeds are treated as a distribution to which section 301 applies. Pursuant to § 1.304-6(a), H is treated as receiving a dividend of $150 ($80 from) the current and accumulated earnings and profits of corporation Y and then $70 from the current and accumulated earnings and profits of corporation X). An amount equal to the basis in the corporation Y stock that H is deemed to receive and that is deemed redeemed, $60 is treated as a loss recognized on a disposition of the stock deemed redeemed on the date of the deemed redemption and is taken into account under rules set forth in § 1.302-5. H's basis in the 200 shares of corporation Y stock that H owned before the sale and continues to own immediately after the sale remains $30.

Example 3. (i) *Facts.* The facts are the same as in *Example 2*, except that corporation X has $5 of current and accumulated earnings and profits and corporation Y has $25 of current and accumulated earnings and profits.

(ii) *Analysis.* As in *Example 2*, H takes a basis of $60 in the corporation Y stock he is treated as receiving and $150 is treated as a distribution to which section 301 applies. Pursuant to § 1.304-6(a), H is treated as receiving a dividend of $30 ($25 from the current and accumulated earnings and profits of corporation Y and $5 from the current and accumulated earnings and profits of corporation X). In addition, $60 of the distribution is treated as a return of basis and $60 of the distribution is treated as gain from the sale or exchange of corporation Y stock. H's basis in the 200 shares of corporation Y stock that he owned before and continues to own immediately after the sale remains $30. Corporation Y's basis in the corporation X stock acquired is $60, the same basis that H had in the corporation X stock surrendered.

Example 4. (i) *Facts.* A, an individual, owns 100 shares of corporation X stock, which is all of the outstanding stock of corporation X. A has a basis of $1 in each share of his corporation X stock. B, the son of A, owns all the outstanding stock of corporation Y. A sells 25 shares of the stock of corporation X to corporation Y for $50. For that year, the current and accumulated earnings and profits of corporation Y exceed $50.

(ii) *Analysis.* Because A is in control of both corporation X and corporation Y (corporation X directly and corporation Y through attribution from B) and receives property in exchange for the corporation X stock, A's sale of corporation X stock to corporation Y is subject to section 304(a)(1). Consequently, A is treated as transferring the corporation X stock to corporation Y in exchange for corporation Y stock in a transaction to which section 351(a) applies. That corporation Y stock is then treated as redeemed by corporation Y for $50. Before the deemed redemption of the corporation Y stock, A owned 100 percent of corporation Y directly and constructively. After the deemed redemption, A owns 100 percent of corporation Y constructively by attribution from B. Accordingly, the redemption distribution is treated as a distribution to which section 301 applies. Because the earnings and profits of corporation Y exceed the amount of cash paid by corporation Y to A for the corporation X stock, pursuant to § 1.304-6(a), the entire amount is a dividend. An amount equal to the basis in the corporation Y stock that A was deemed to receive and that was then deemed redeemed, $25, is treated as a loss recognized on a disposition of the stock deemed redeemed on the date of the deemed redemption and is taken into account under rules set forth in § 1.302-5. A's basis in the 75 shares that he continues to hold remains $1 per share for an aggregate basis of $75.

(d) *Effective date.* This section, except for paragraph (b) of this section, applies to transactions occurring after the date these regulations are published as final regulations in the Federal Register. Paragraph (b) of this section applies on and after December 2, 1955. [Reg. § 1.304-2.]

[Proposed 10-18-2002 (*corrected* 12-26-2002).]

§ 1.304-3. Acquisition by a subsidiary.—(a) If a subsidiary acquires stock of its parent corporation from a shareholder of the parent corporation, the acquisition of such stock shall be treated as though the parent corporation had redeemed its own stock. For the purpose of this section, a corporation is a parent corporation if it meets the 50 percent ownership requirements of section 304(c). The determination whether the amount received shall be treated as an amount received in payment in exchange for the stock shall be made by applying section 303, or by applying section 302(b) with reference to the stock of the issuing parent corporation. If such distribution would have been treated as a distribution of property (pursuant to section 302(d) under section 301, the entire amount of the selling price of the stock shall be treated as a dividend to the seller to the extent of the earnings and profits of the parent corporation determined as if the distribution had been made to it of the property that the subsidiary exchanged for the stock. In such cases, the transferor's basis for his remaining stock in the parent corporation will be determined by including the amount of the basis of the stock of the parent corporation sold to the subsidiary.

(b) Section 304(a)(2) may be illustrated by the following example:

Example. Corporation M has outstanding 100 shares of common stock which are owned as follows: B, 75 shares, C, son of B, 20 shares, and D, daughter of B, 5 shares. Corporation M owns the stock of Corporation X. B sells his 75 shares of Corporation M stock to Corporation X. Under section 302(b)(3) this is a termination of B's entire interest in Corporation M and the full amount received from the sale of his stock will be treated as payment in exchange for this stock, provided he fulfills the requirements of section 302(c)(2) (relating to an acquisition of an interest in the corporations). [Reg. § 1.304-3.]

☐ [*T.D.* 6152, 12-2-55.]

§ 1.304-5. Control.—(a) *Control requirement in general.* Section 304(c)(1) provides that, for purposes of section 304, control means the ownership of stock possessing at least 50 percent of the total combined voting power of all classes of stock entitled to vote or at least 50 percent of the total value of shares of all classes of stock. Section 304(c)(3) makes section 318(a) (relating to constructive ownership of stock), as modified by section 304(c)(3)(B), applicable to section 304 for purposes of determining control under section 304(c)(1).

(b) *Effect of section 304(c)(2)(B)*—(1) *In general.* In determining whether the control test with respect to both the issuing and acquiring corporations is satisfied, section 304(a)(1) considers only the person or persons that—

    (i) Control the issuing corporation before the transaction;

    (ii) Transfer issuing corporation stock to the acquiring corporation for property; and

    (iii) Control the acquiring corporation thereafter.

    (2) *Application.* Section 317 defines property to include money, securities, and any other property except stock (or stock rights) in the distributing corporation. However, section 304(c)(2)(B) provides a special rule to extend the relevant group of persons to be tested for control of both the issuing and acquiring corporations to include the person or persons that do not acquire property, but rather solely stock from the acquiring corporation in the transaction. Section 304(c)(2)(B) provides that if two or more persons in control of the issuing corporation transfer stock of such corporation to the acquiring corporation, and if the transferors are in control of the acquiring corporation after the transfer, the person or persons in control of each corporation include each of those transferors. Because the purpose of section 304(c)(2)(B) is to include in the relevant control group the person or persons that retain or acquire acquiring corporation stock in the transaction, only the person or persons transferring stock of the issuing corporation that retain or acquire any proprietary interest in the acquiring corporation are taken into account for purposes of applying section 304(c)(2)(B).

(3) *Example.* This section may be illustrated by the following example.

    Example. (a) A, the owner of 20% of T's only class of stock, transfers that stock to P solely in exchange for all of the P stock. Pursuant to the same transaction, P, solely in exchange for cash, acquires the remaining 80% of the T stock from T's other shareholder, B, who is unrelated to A and P.

    (b) Although A and B together were in control of T (the issuing corporation) before the transaction and A and B each transferred T stock to P (the acquiring corporation), sections 304(a)(1) and (c)(2)(B) do not apply to B because B did not retain or acquire any proprietary interest in P in the transaction. Section 304(a)(1) also does not apply to A because A (or any control group of which A was a member) did not control T before the transaction and P after the transaction.

(c) *Effective date.* This section is effective January 20, 1994. [Reg. § 1.304-5.]

☐ [*T.D.* 8515, 1-12-94.]

§ 1.305-1. Stock dividends.—(a) *In general.* Under section 305, a distribution made by a corporation to its shareholders in its stock or in rights to acquire its stock is not included in gross income except as provided in section 305(b) and the regulations promulgated under the authority of section 305(c). A distribution made by a corporation to its shareholders in its stock or rights to acquire its stock which would not otherwise be included in gross income by reason of section 305 shall not be so included merely because such distribution was made out of Treasury stock or consisted of rights to acquire Treasury stock. See section 307 for rules as to basis of stock and stock rights acquired in a distribution.

(b) *Amount of distribution.* (1) In general, where a distribution of stock or rights to acquire stock of a corporation is treated as a distribution of property to which section 301 applies by reason of section 305(b), the amount of the distribution, in accordance with section 301(b) and § 1.301-1, is the fair market value of such stock or rights on the date of distribution. See example (1) of § 1.305-2(b).

(2) Where a corporation which regularly distributes its earnings and profits, such as a regulated investment company, declares a dividend pursuant to which the shareholders may elect to receive either money or stock of the distributing corporation of equivalent value, the amount of the distribution of the stock received by any share-

holder electing to receive stock will be considered to equal the amount of the money which could have been received instead. See example (2) of § 1.305-2(b).

(3) For rules for determining the amount of the distribution where certain transactions, such as changes in conversion ratios or periodic redemptions, are treated as distributions under section 305(c), see examples (6), (8), (9), and (15) of § 1.305-3(e).

(c) *Adjustment in purchase price.* A transfer of stock (or rights to acquire stock) or an increase or decrease in the conversion ratio or redemption price of stock which represents an adjustment of the price to be paid by the distributing corporation in acquiring property (within the meaning of section 317(a)) is not within the purview of section 305 because it is not a distribution with respect to its stock. For example, assume that on January 1, 1970, pursuant to a reorganization, corporation X acquires all the stock of corporation Y solely in exchange for its convertible preferred class B stock. Under the terms of the class B stock, its conversion ratio is to be adjusted in 1976 under a formula based upon the earnings of corporation Y over the 6-year period ending on December 31, 1975. Such an adjustment in 1976 is not covered by section 305.

(d) *Definitions.* (1) For purposes of this section and § § 1.305-2 through 1.305-7, the term "stock" includes rights or warrants to acquire such stock.

(2) For purposes of § § 1.305-2 through 1.305-7, the term "shareholder" includes a holder of rights or warrants or a holder of convertible securities. [Reg. § 1.305-1.]

☐ [*T.D.* 6152, 12-2-55. *Amended by T.D. 7281,* 7-11-73.]

§ 1.305-2. Distributions in lieu of money.— (a) *In general.* Under section 305(b)(1), if any shareholder has the right to an election or option with respect to whether a distribution shall be made either in money or any other property, or in stock or rights to acquire stock of the distributing corporation, then, with respect to all shareholders, the distribution of stock or rights to acquire stock is treated as a distribution of property to which section 301 applies regardless of—

(1) Whether the distribution is actually made in whole or in part in stock or in stock rights;

(2) Whether the election or option is exercised or exercisable before or after the declaration of the distribution;

(3) Whether the declaration of the distribution provides that the distribution will be made in one medium unless the shareholder specifically requests payment in the other;

(4) Whether the election governing the nature of the distribution is provided in the declaration of the distribution or in the corporate charter or arises from the circumstances of the distribution; or

(5) Whether all or part of the shareholders have the election.

(b) *Examples.* The application of section 305(b)(1) may be illustrated by the following examples:

Example (1). (i) Corporation X declared a dividend payable in additional shares of its common stock to the holders of its outstanding common stock on the basis of two additional shares for each share held on the record date but with the provision that, at the election of any shareholder made within a specified period prior to the distribution date, he may receive one additional share for each share held on the record date plus $12 principal amount of securities of corporation Y owned by corporation X. The fair market value of the stock of corporation X on the distribution date was $10 per share. The fair market value of $12 principal amount of securities of corporation Y on the distribution date was $11 but such securities had a cost basis to corporation X of $9.

(ii) The distribution to all shareholders of one additional share of stock of corporation X (with respect to which no election applies) for each share outstanding is not a distribution to which section 301 applies.

(iii) The distribution of the second share of stock of corporation X to those shareholders who do not elect to receive securities of corporation Y is a distribution of property to which section 301 applies, whether such shareholders are individuals or corporations. The amount of the distribution to which section 301 applies is $10 per share of stock of corporation X held on the record date (the fair market value of the stock of corporation X on the distribution date).

(iv) The distribution of securities of corporation Y in lieu of the second share of stock of corporation X to the shareholders of corporation X whether individuals or corporations, who elect to receive such securities, is also a distribution of property to which section 301 applies.

(v) In the case of the individual shareholders of corporation X who elect to receive such securities, the amount of the distribution to which section 301 applies is $11 per share of stock of corporation X held on the record date (the fair market value of the $12 principal amount of securities of corporation Y on the distribution date).

(vi) In the case of the corporate shareholders of corporation X electing to receive such securities, the amount of the distribution to which sec-

Reg. § 1.305-2(b)

tion 301 applies is $9 per share of stock of corporation X held on the record date (the basis of the securities of corporation Y in the hands of corporation X).

Example (2). On January 10, 1970, corporation X, a regulated investment company, declared a dividend of $1 per share on its common stock payable on February 11, 1970, in cash or in stock of corporation X of equivalent value determined as of January 22, 1970, at the election of the shareholder made on or before January 22, 1970. The amount of the distribution to which section 301 applies is $1 per share whether the shareholder elects to take cash or stock and whether the shareholder is an individual or a corporation. Such amount will also be used in determining the dividend paid deduction of corporation X and the reduction in earnings and profits of corporation X. [Reg. § 1.305-2.]

☐ [*T.D.* 6152, 12-2-55. *Amended by T.D.* 6476, 6-3-60; *T.D.* 6990, 1-10-69; *T.D.* 7004, 2-7-69 *and T.D.* 7281, 7-11-73.]

§ 1.305-3. Disproportionate distributions.— (a) *In general.* Under section 305(b)(2), a distribution (including a deemed distribution) by a corporation of its stock or rights to acquire its stock is treated as a distribution of property to which section 301 applies if the distribution (or a series of distributions of which such distribution is one) has the result of (1) the receipt of money or other property by some shareholders, and (2) an increase in the proportionate interests of other shareholders in the assets or earnings and profits of the corporation. Thus, if a corporation has two classes of common stock outstanding and cash dividends are paid on one class and stock dividends are paid on the other class, the stock dividends are treated as distributions to which section 301 applies.

(b) *Special rules.* (1) As used in section 305(b)(2), the term "a series of distributions" encompasses all distributions of stock made or deemed made by a corporation which have the result of a receipt of cash or property by some shareholders and an increase in the proportionate interests of other shareholders.

(2) In order for a distribution of stock to be considered as one of a series of distributions it is not necessary that such distribution be pursuant to a plan to distribute cash or property to some shareholders and to increase the proportionate interests of other shareholders. It is sufficient if there is an actual or deemed distribution of stock (of which such distribution is one) and as a result of such distribution or distributions some shareholders receive cash or property and other shareholders increase their proportionate interests. For example, if a corporation pays quarterly stock dividends to one class of common shareholders and annual cash dividends to another class of common shareholders the quarterly stock dividends constitute a series of distributions of stock having the result of the receipt of cash or property by some shareholders and an increase in the proportionate interests of other shareholders. This is so whether or not the stock distributions and the cash distributions are steps in an overall plan or are independent and unrelated. Accordingly, all the quarterly stock dividends are distributions to which section 301 applies.

(3) There is no requirement that both elements of section 305(b)(2) (*i.e.,* receipt of cash or property by some shareholders and an increase in proportionate interests of other shareholders) occur in the form of a distribution or series of distributions as long as the result of a distribution or distributions of stock is that some shareholders' proportionate interests increase and other shareholders in fact receive cash or property. Thus, there is no requirement that the shareholders receiving cash or property acquire the cash or property by way of a corporate distribution with respect to their shares, so long as they receive such cash or property in their capacity as shareholders, if there is a stock distribution which results in a change in the proportionate interests of some shareholders and other shareholders receive cash or property. However, in order for a distribution of property to meet the requirements of section 305(b)(2), such distribution must be made to a shareholder in his capacity as a shareholder, and must be a distribution to which section 301, 356(a)(2), 871(a)(1)(A), 881(a)(1), 852(b), or 857(b) applies. (Under section 305(d)(2), the payment of interest to a holder of a convertible debenture is treated as a distribution of property to a shareholder for purposes of section 305(b)(2).) For example if a corporation makes a stock distribution to its shareholders, and, pursuant to a prearranged plan with such corporation, a related corporation purchases such stock from those shareholders who want cash, in a transaction to which section 301 applies by virtue of section 304, the requirements of section 305(b)(2) are satisfied. In addition, a distribution of property incident to an isolated redemption of stock (for example, pursuant to a tender offer) will not cause section 305(b)(2) to apply even though the redemption distribution is treated as a distribution of property to which section 301, 871(a)(1)(A), 881(a)(1), or 356(a)(2) applies.

(4) Where the receipt of cash or property occurs more than 36 months following a distribution or series of distributions of stock, or where a distribution or series of distributions of stock is made more than 36 months following the receipt of cash or property, such distribution or distributions will be presumed not to result in the receipt

of cash or property by some shareholders and an increase in the proportionate interest of other shareholders, unless the receipt of cash or property and the distribution or series of distributions of stock are made pursuant to a plan. For example, if, pursuant to a plan, a corporation pays cash dividends to some shareholders on January 1, 1971 and increases the proportionate interests of other shareholders on March 1, 1974, such increases in proportionate interests are distributions to which section 301 applies.

(5) In determining whether a distribution or a series of distributions has the result of a disproportionate distribution, there shall be treated as outstanding stock of the distributing corporation (i) any right to acquire such stock (whether or not exercisable during the taxable year), and (ii) any security convertible into stock of the distributing corporation (whether or not convertible during the taxable year).

(6) In cases where there is more than one class of stock outstanding, each class of stock is to be considered separately in determining whether a shareholder has increased his proportionate interest in the assets or earnings and profits of a corporation. The individual shareholders of a class of stock will be deemed to have an increased interest if the class of stock as a whole has an increased interest in the corporation.

(c) *Distributions of cash in lieu of fractional shares.* (1) Section 305(b)(2) will not apply if—

(i) A corporation declares a dividend payable in stock of the corporation and distributes cash in lieu of fractional shares to which shareholders would otherwise be entitled, or

(ii) Upon a conversion of convertible stock or securities a corporation distributes cash in lieu of fractional shares to which shareholders would otherwise be entitled.

Provided the purpose of the distribution of cash is to save the corporation the trouble, expense, and inconvenience of issuing and transferring fractional shares (or scrip representing fractional shares), or issuing full shares representing the sum of fractional shares, and not to give any particular group of shareholders an increased interest in the asset or earnings and profits of the corporation. For purposes of paragraph (c)(1)(i) of this section, if the total amount of cash distributed in lieu of fractional shares is 5 percent or less of the total fair market value of the stock distributed (determined as of the date of declaration), the distribution shall be considered to be for such valid purpose.

(2) In a case to which subparagraph (1) of this paragraph applies, the transaction will be treated as though the fractional shares were distributed as part of the stock distribution and then

were redeemed by the corporation. The treatment of the cash received by a shareholder will be determined under section 302.

(d) *Adjustment in conversion ratio.* (1) (i) Except as provided in subparagraph (2) of this paragraph, if a corporation has convertible stock or convertible securities outstanding (upon which it pays or is deemed to pay dividends or interest in money or other property) and distributes a stock dividend (or rights to acquire such stock) with respect to the stock into which the convertible stock or securities are convertible, an increase in proportionate interest in the assets or earnings and profits of the corporation by reason of such stock dividend shall be considered to have occurred unless a full adjustment in the conversion ratio or conversion price to reflect such stock dividend is made. Under certain circumstances, however, the application of an adjustment formula which in effect provides for a "credit" where stock is issued for consideration in excess of the conversion price may not satisfy the requirement for a "full adjustment". Thus, if under a "conversion price" antidilution formula the formula provides for a "credit" where stock is issued for consideration in excess of the conversion price (in effect as an offset against any decrease in the conversion price which would otherwise be required when stock is subsequently issued for consideration below the conversion price) there may still be an increase in proportionate interest by reason of a stock dividend after application of the formula, since any downward adjustment of the conversion price that would otherwise be required to reflect the stock dividend may be offset, in whole or in part, by the effect of prior sales made at prices above the conversion price. On the other hand, if there were no prior sales of stock above the conversion price then a full adjustment would occur upon the application of such an adjustment formula and there would be no change in proportionate interest. Similarly, if consideration is to be received in connection with the issuance of stock, such as in the case of a rights offering or a distribution of warrants, the fact that such consideration is taken into account in making the antidilution adjustment will not preclude a full adjustment. See paragraph (b) of the example in this subparagraph for a case where the application of an adjustment formula with a cumulative feature does not result in a full adjustment and where a change in proportionate interest therefore occurs. See paragraph (c) for a case where the application of an adjustment formula with a cumulative feature does result in a full adjustment and where no change in proportionate interest therefore occurs. See paragraph (d) for an application of an antidilution formula in the case of a rights offering. See paragraph (e) for a case where the application of a noncumulative type adjust-

Reg. § 1.305-3(d)

ment formula will in all cases prevent a change in proportionate interest from occurring in the case of a stock dividend, because of the omission of the cumulative feature.

(ii) The principles of this subparagraph may be illustrated by the following example:

Example. (a) Corporation S has two classes of securities outstanding, convertible debentures and common stock. At the time of issuance of the debentures the corporation had 100 shares of common stock outstanding. Each debenture is interest-paying and is convertible into common stock at a conversion price of $2. The debenture's conversion price is subject to reduction pursuant to the following formula:

(Number of common shares outstanding at date of issue of debentures times initial conversion price)

plus

(Consideration received upon issuance of additional common shares)

divided by

(Number of common shares outstanding at date of issue of debentures)

plus

(Number of additional common shares issued)

Under the formula, common stock dividends are treated as an issue of common stock for zero consideration. If the computation results in a figure which is less than the existing conversion price the conversion price is reduced. However, under the formula, the existing conversion price is never increased. The formula works upon a cumulative basis since the numerator includes the consideration received upon the issuance of all common shares subsequent to the issuance of the debentures, and the reduction effected by the formula because of a sale or issuance of common stock below the existing conversion price is thus limited by any prior sales made above the existing conversion price.

(b) In 1972 corporation S sells 100 common shares at $3 per share. In 1973 the corporation declares a stock dividend of 20 shares to all holders of common stock. Under the antidilution formula no adjustment will be made to the conversion price of the debentures to reflect the stock dividend to common stockholders since the prior sale of common stock in excess of the conversion price in 1972 offsets the reduction in the conversion price which would otherwise result, as follows:

$$100 \times \$2 + \$300 \div 100 + 120 = \frac{\$500}{220} = \$2.27$$

Since $2.27 is greater than the existing conversion price of $2 no adjustment is required. As a result, there is an increase in proportionate interest of the common stockholders by reason of the stock dividend and the additional shares of common

stock will be treated, pursuant to section 305(b)(2), as a distribution of property to which section 301 applies.

(c) Assume the same facts as above, but instead of selling 100 common shares at $3 per share in 1972, assume corporation S sold no shares. Application of the antidilution formula would give rise to an adjustment in the conversion price as follows:

$$100 \times \$2 + \$0 \div 100 + 20 = \frac{\$200}{220} = \$1.67$$

The conversion price, being reduced from $2 to $1.67, fully reflects the stock dividend distributed to the common stockholders. Hence, the distribution of common stock is not treated under section 305(b)(2) as one to which section 301 applies because the distribution does not increase the proportionate interests of the common shareholders as a class.

(d) Corporation S distributes to its shareholders rights entitling the shareholders to purchase a total of 20 shares at $1 per share. Application of the antidilution formula would produce an adjustment in the conversion price as follows:

$$100 \times \$2 + 20 \times \$1 \div 100 + 20 = \frac{\$220}{120} = \$1.83$$

The conversion price, being reduced from $2 to $1.83, fully reflects the distribution of rights to purchase stock at a price lower than the conversion price. Hence, the distribution of the rights is not treated under section 305(b)(2) as one to which section 301 applies because the distribution does not increase the proportionate interests of the common shareholders as a class.

(e) Assume the same facts as in (b) above, but instead of using a "conversion price" antidilution formula which operates on a cumulative basis, assume corporation S has employed a formula which operates as follows with respect to all stock dividends: The conversion price in effect at the opening of business on the day following the dividend record date is reduced by multiplying such conversion price by a fraction the numerator of which is the number of shares of common stock outstanding at the close of business on the record date and the denominator of which is the sum of such shares so outstanding and the number of shares constituting the stock dividend. Under such a formula the following adjustment would be made to the conversion price upon the declaration of a stock dividend of 20 shares in 1973:

$$200 \div 200 + 20 = \frac{200}{220} \times \$2 = \$1.82$$

The conversion price, being reduced from $2 to $1.82, fully reflects the stock dividend distributed

Reg. § 1.305-3(d)

to the common stockholders. Hence, the distribution of common stock is not treated under section 305(b)(2) as one to which section 301 applies because the distribution does not increase the proportionate interests of the common shareholders as a class.

(2)(i) A distributing corporation either must make the adjustment required by subparagraph (1) of this paragraph as of the date of the distribution of the stock dividend, or must elect (in the manner provided in subdivision (iii) of this subparagraph) to make such adjustment within the time provided in subdivision (ii) of this subparagraph.

(ii) If the distributing corporation elects to make such adjustment, such adjustment must be made no later than the earlier of (a) 3 years after the date of the stock dividend, or (b) that date as of which the aggregate stock dividends for which adjustment of the conversion ratio has not previously been made total at least 3 percent of the issued and outstanding stock with respect to which such stock dividends were distributed.

(iii) The election provided by subdivision (ii) of this subparagraph shall be made by filing with the income tax return for the taxable year during which the stock dividend is distributed—

(a) A statement that an adjustment will be made as provided by that subdivision, and

(b) A description of the antidilution provisions under which the adjustment will be made.

(3) Notwithstanding the preceding subparagraph, if a distribution has been made before July 12, 1973, and the adjustment required by subparagraph (1) or the election to make such adjustment was not made before such date, the adjustment or the election to make such adjustment, as the case may be, shall be considered valid if made no later than 15 days following the date of the first annual meeting of the shareholders after July 12, 1973, or July 12, 1974, whichever is earlier. If the election is made within such period, and if the income tax return has been filed before the time of such election, the statement of adjustment and the description of the antidilution provisions required by subparagraph (2)(iii) shall be filed with the Internal Revenue Service Center with which the income tax return was filed.

(4) See § 1.305-7(b) for a discussion of antidilution adjustments in connection with the application of section 305(c) in conjunction with section 305(b).

(e) *Examples.* The application of section 305(b)(2) to distributions of stock and section 305(c) to deemed distributions of stock may be illustrated by the following examples:

Example 1. Corporation X is organized with two classes of common stock, class A and class B. Each share of stock is entitled to share equally in the assets and earnings and profits of the corporation. Dividends may be paid in stock or in cash on either class of stock without regard to the medium of payment of dividends on the other class. A dividend is declared on the class A stock payable in additional shares of class A stock and a dividend is declared on class B stock payable in cash. Since the class A shareholders as a class will have increased their proportionate interests in the assets and earnings and profits of the corporation and the class B shareholders will have received cash, the additional shares of class A stock are distributions of property to which section 301 applies. This is true even with respect to those shareholders who may own class A stock and class B stock in the same proportion.

Example 2. Corporation Y is organized with two classes of stock, class A common, and class B, which is nonconvertible and limited and preferred as to dividends. A dividend is declared upon the class A stock payable in additional shares of class A stock and a dividend is declared on the class B stock payable in cash. The distribution of class A stock is not one to which section 301 applies because the distribution does not increase the proportionate interests of the class A shareholders as a class.

Example 3. Corporation K is organized with two classes of stock, class A common, and class B, which is nonconvertible preferred stock. A dividend is declared upon the class A stock payable in shares of class B stock and a dividend is declared on the class B stock payable in cash. Since the class A shareholders as a class have an increased interest in the assets and earnings and profits of the corporation, the stock distribution is treated as a distribution to which section 301 applies. If, however, a dividend were declared upon the class A stock payable in a new class of preferred stock that is subordinated in all respects to the class B stock, the distribution would not increase the proportionate interests of the class A shareholders in the assets or earnings and profits of the corporation and would not be treated as a distribution to which section 301 applies.

Example 4. (i) Corporation W has one class of stock outstanding, class A common. The corporation also has outstanding interest paying securities convertible into class A common stock which have a fixed conversion ratio that is not subject to a full adjustment in the event stock dividends or

Reg. § 1.305-3(e)

rights are distributed to the class A shareholders. Corporation W distributes to the class A shareholders rights to acquire additional shares of class A stock. During the year, interest is paid on the convertible securities.

(ii) The stock rights and convertible securities are considered to be outstanding stock of the corporation and the distribution increases the proportionate interests of the class A shareholders in the assets and earnings and profits of the corporation. Therefore, the distribution is treated as a distribution to which section 301 applies. The same result would follow if, instead of convertible securities, the corporation had outstanding convertible stock. If, however, the conversion ratio of the securities or stock were fully adjusted to reflect the distribution of rights to the class A shareholders, the rights to acquire class A stock would not increase the proportionate interests of the class A shareholders in the assets or earnings and profits of the corporation and would not be treated as a distribution to which section 301 applies.

Example 5. (i) Corporation S is organized with two classes of stock, class A common and class B convertible preferred. The class B is fully protected against dilution in the event of a stock dividend or stock split with respect to the class A stock; however, no adjustment in the conversion ratio is required to be made until the stock dividends equal 3 percent of the common stock issued and outstanding on the date of the first such stock dividend except that such adjustment must be made no later than 3 years after the date of the stock dividend. Cash dividends are paid annually on the class B stock.

(ii) Corporation S pays a 1 percent stock dividend on the class A stock in 1973. In 1974, another 1 percent stock dividend is paid and in 1975 another 1 percent stock dividend is paid. The conversion ratio of the class B stock is increased in 1975 to reflect the three stock dividends paid on the class A stock. The distributions of class A stock are not distributions to which section 301 applies because they do not increase the proportionate interests of the class A shareholders in the assets or earnings and profits of the corporation.

Example 6. (i) Corporation M is organized with two classes of stock outstanding, class A and class B. Each class B share may be converted, at the option of the holder, into class A shares. During the first year, the conversion ratio is one share of class A stock for each share of class B stock. At the beginning of each subsequent year, the conversion ratio is increased by 0.05 share of class A stock for each share of class B stock. Thus, during the second year, the conversion ratio would be 1.05 shares of class A stock for each share of class B

stock, during the third year, the ratio would be 1.10 shares, etc.

(ii) M pays an annual cash dividend on the class A stock. At the beginning of the second year, when the conversion ratio is increased to 1.05 shares of class A stock for each share of class B stock, a distribution of 0.05 shares of class A stock is deemed made under section 305(c) with respect to each share of class B stock, since the proportionate interests of the class B shareholders in the assets or earnings and profits of M are increased and the transaction has the effect described in section 305(b)(2). Accordingly, sections 305(b)(2) and 301 apply to the transaction.

Example 7. (i) Corporation N has two classes of stock outstanding, class A and class B. Each class B share is convertible into class A stock. However, in accordance with a specified formula, the conversion ratio is decreased each time a cash dividend is paid on the class B stock to reflect the amount of the cash dividend. The conversion ratio is also adjusted in the event that cash dividends are paid on the class A stock to increase the number of class A shares into which the class B shares are convertible to compensate the class B shareholders for the cash dividend paid on the class A stock.

(ii) In 1972, a $1 cash dividend per share is declared and paid on the class B stock. On the date of payment, the conversion ratio of the class B stock is decreased. A distribution of stock is deemed made under section 305(c) to the class A shareholders, since the proportionate interest of the class A shareholders in the assets or earnings and profits of the corporation is increased and the transaction has the effect described in section 305(b)(2). Accordingly, sections 305(b)(2) and 301 apply to the transaction.

(iii) In the following year a cash dividend is paid on the class A stock and none is paid on the class B stock. The increase in conversion rights of the class B shares is deemed to be a distribution under section 305(c) to the class B shareholders since their proportionate interest in the assets or earnings and profits of the corporation is increased and since the transaction has the effect described in section 305(b)(2). Accordingly, sections 305(b)(2) and 301 apply to the transaction.

Example 8. Corporation T has 1,000 shares of stock outstanding. C owns 100 shares. Nine other shareholders each owns 100 shares. Pursuant to a plan for periodic redemptions, T redeems up to 5 percent of each shareholder's stock each year. During the year, each of the nine other shareholders has five shares of his stock redeemed for cash. Thus, C's proportionate interest in the assets and earnings and profits of T is increased. Assuming that the cash received by the nine other share-

Reg. § 1.305-3(e)

holders is taxable under section 301, C is deemed under section 305(c) to have received a distribution under section 305(b)(2) of 5.25 shares of T stock to which section 301 applies. The amount of C's distribution is measured by the fair market value of the number of shares which would have been distributed to C had the corporation sought to increase his interest by 0.47 percentage points (C owned 10 percent of the T stock immediately before the redemption and 10.47 percent immediately thereafter) and the other shareholders continued to hold 900 shares (*i.e.,*

(a) $\dfrac{100}{955} = 10.47\%$ (percent of C's ownership after redemption);

(b) $\dfrac{100 + X}{1000 + X} = 10.47\%$; X = 5.25 (additional shares considered to be distributed to C)).

Since in computing the amount of additional shares deemed to be distributed to C the redemption of shares is disregarded, the redemption of shares will be similarly disregarded in determining the value of the stock of the corporation which is deemed to be distributed. Thus, in the example, 1,005.25 shares of stock are considered as outstanding after the redemption. The value of each share deemed to be distributed to C is then determined by dividing the 1,005.25 shares into the aggregate fair market value of the actual shares outstanding (955) after the redemption.

Example 9. (i) Corporation O has a stock redemption program under which, instead of paying out earnings and profits to its shareholders in the form of dividends, it redeems the stock of its shareholders up to a stated amount which is determined by the earnings and profits of the corporation. If the stock tendered for redemption exceeds the stated amount, the corporation redeems the stock on a pro rata basis up to the stated amount.

(ii) During the year corporation O offers to distribute $10,000 in redemption of its stock. At the time of the offering, corporation O has 1,000 shares outstanding of which E and F each owns 150 shares and G and H each own 350 shares. The corporation redeems 15 shares from E and 35 shares from G. F and H continue to hold all of their stock.

(iii) F and H have increased their proportionate interests in the assets and earnings and profits of the corporation. Assuming that the cash E and G receive is taxable under section 301, F will be deemed under section 305(c) to have received a distribution under section 305(b)(2) of 16.66 shares of stock to which section 301 applies and H will be deemed under section 305(c) to have received a distribution under section 305(b)(2) of 38.86 shares of stock to which section 301 applies. The amount of the distribution to F and H is

measured by the number of shares which would have been distributed to F and H had the corporation sought to increase the interest of F by 0.79 percentage points (F owned 15 percent of the stock immediately before the redemption and 15.79 percent immediately thereafter) and the interest of H by 1.84 percentage points (H owned 35 percent of the stock immediately before the redemption and 36.84 percent immediately thereafter) and E and G had continued to hold 150 shares and 350 shares, respectively (*i.e.,*

(a) $\dfrac{150}{950} + \dfrac{350}{950} = 52.63\%$ (percent of F and H's ownership after redemption);

(b) $\dfrac{500 + y}{1000 + y} = 52.63\%$; y = 55.52 (additional shares considered to be distributed to F and H);

(c)(1) $\dfrac{150}{500} \times 55.52 = 16.66$ (shares considered to be distributed to F);

(2) $\dfrac{350}{500} \times 55.52 = 38.86$ (shares considered to be distributed to H)).

Since in computing the amount of additional shares deemed to be distributed to F and H the redemption of shares is disregarded, the redemption of shares will be similarly disregarded in determining the value of the stock of the corporation which is deemed to be distributed. Thus, in the example, 1,055.52 shares of stock are considered as outstanding after the redemption. The value of each share deemed to be distributed to F and H is then determined by dividing the 1,055.52 shares into the aggregate fair market value of the actual shares outstanding (950) after the redemption.

Example 10. Corporation P has 1,000 shares of stock outstanding. T owns 700 shares of the P stock and G owns 300 shares of the P stock. In a single and isolated redemption to which section 301 applies, the corporation redeems 150 shares of T's stock. Since this is an isolated redemption and is not a part of a periodic redemption plan, G is not treated as having received a deemed distribution under section 305(c) to which sections 305(b)(2) and 301 apply even though he has an increased proportionate interest in the assets and earnings and profits of the corporation.

Example 11. Corporation Q is a large corporation whose sole class of stock is widely held. However, the four largest shareholders are officers of the corporation and each owns 8 percent of the outstanding stock. In 1974, in a distribution to which section 301 applies, the corporation redeems 1.5 percent of the stock from each of the four largest shareholders in preparation for their retirement. From 1970 through 1974, the corporation distributes annual stock dividends to its

Reg. § 1.305-3(e)

shareholders. No other distributions were made to these shareholders. Since the 1974 redemptions are isolated and are not part of a plan for periodically redeeming the stock of the corporation, the shareholders receiving stock dividends will not be treated as having received a distribution under section 305(b)(2) even though they have an increased proportionate interest in the assets and earnings and profits of the corporation and whether or not the redemptions are treated as distributions to which section 301 applies.

Example 12. Corporation R has 2,000 shares of class A stock outstanding. Five shareholders own 300 shares each and five shareholders own 100 shares each. In preparation for the retirement of the five major shareholders, corporation R, in a single and isolated transaction, has a recapitalization in which each share of class A stock may be exchanged either for five shares of new class B nonconvertible preferred stock plus 0.4 share of new class C common stock, or for two shares of new class C common stock. As a result of the exchanges, each of the five major shareholders receives 1,500 shares of class B nonconvertible preferred stock and 120 shares of class C common stock. The remaining shareholders each receives 200 shares of class C common stock. None of the exchanges are within the purview of section 305.

Example 13. Corporation P is a widely-held company whose shares are listed for trading on a stock exchange. P distributes annual cash dividends to its shareholders. P purchases shares of its common stock directly from small stockholders (holders of record of 100 shares or less) or through brokers where the holders may not be known at the time of purchase. Where such purchases are made through brokers, they are pursuant to the rules and regulations of the Securities and Exchange Commission. The shares are purchased for the purpose of issuance to employee stock investment plans, to holders of convertible stock or debt, to holders of stock options, or for future acquisitions. Provided the purchases are not pursuant to a plan to increase the proportionate interest of some shareholders and distribute property to other shareholders, thus the remaining shareholders of P are not treated as having received a deemed distribution under section 305 to which section 305(b)(2) and 301 apply, even though they have an increased proportionate interest in the assets and earnings and profits of the corporation.

Example 14. Corporation U is a large manufacturing company whose products are sold through independent dealers. In order to assist individuals who lack capital to become dealers, the corporation has an established investment plan under which it provides 75 percent of the capital necessary to form a dealership corporation and the individual dealer provides the remaining 25 percent. Corporation U receives class A stock and a note representing its 75 percent interest. The individual dealer receives class B stock representing his 25 percent interest. The class B stock is nonvoting until all the class A shares are redeemed. At least 70 percent of the earnings and profits of the dealership corporation must be used each year to retire the note and to redeem the class A stock. The class A stock is redeemed at a fixed price. The individual dealer has no control over the redemption of stock and has no right to have his stock redeemed during the period the plan is in existence. U's investment is thus systematically eliminated and the individual becomes the sole owner of the dealership corporation. Since this type of plan is akin to a security arrangement, the redemptions of the class A stock will not be deemed under section 305(c) as distributions taxable under sections 305(b)(2) and 301 during the years in which the class A stock is redeemed.

Example 15. (i) *Facts.* Corporation V is organized with two classes of stock, class A common and class B convertible preferred. The class B stock is issued for $100 per share and is convertible at the holder's option into class A at a fixed ratio that is not subject to full adjustment in the event stock dividends or rights are distributed to the class A shareholders. The class B stock pays no dividends but it is mandatorily redeemable in 10 years for $200. Under sections 305(c) and 305(b)(4), the entire redemption premium (i.e., the excess of the redemption price over the issue price) is deemed to be a distribution of preferred stock on preferred stock which is taxable as a distribution of property under section 301. This amount is considered to be distributed over the 10-year period under principles similar to the principles of section 1272(a). During the year, the corporation declares a dividend on the class A stock payable in additional shares of class A stock.

(ii) *Analysis.* The distribution on the class A stock is a distribution to which sections 305(b)(2) and 301 apply since it increases the proportionate interests of the class A shareholders in the assets and earnings and profits of the corporation and the class B shareholders have received property (i.e., the constructive distribution described above). If, however, the conversion ratio of the class B stock were subject to full adjustment to reflect the distribution of stock to class A shareholders, the distribution of stock dividends on the class A stock would not increase the proportionate interest of the class A shareholders in the assets and earnings and profits of the corporation and such distribution would not be a distribution to which section 301 applies.

(iii) *Effective date.* This *Example 15* applies to stock issued on or after December 20, 1995. For previously issued stock, see § 1.305-3(e) *Example (15)* (as contained in the 26 CFR part 1 edition revised April 1, 1995). [Reg. § 1.305-3.]

☐ [*T.D.* 6152, 12/2/55. *Amended by T.D.* 6990, 1/10/69, *T.D.* 7004, 2-7-69, *T.D.* 7281, 7-11-73, *T.D.* 7329, 10-11-74 *and T.D.* 8643, 12-20-95.]

§ 1.305-4. Distributions of common and preferred stock.—(a) *In general.* Under section 305(b)(3), a distribution (or a series of distributions) by a corporation which results in the receipt of preferred stock (whether or not convertible into common stock) by some common shareholders and the receipt of common stock by other common shareholders is treated as a distribution of property to which section 301 applies. For the meaning of the term "a series of distributions", see subparagraphs (1) through (6) of § 1.305-3(b).

(b) *Examples.* The application of section 305(b)(3) may be illustrated by the following examples:

Example (1). Corporation X is organized with two classes of common stock, class A and class B. Dividends may be paid in stock or in cash on either class of stock without regard to the medium of payment of dividends on the other class. A dividend is declared on the class A stock payable in additional shares of class A stock and a dividend is declared on class B stock payable in newly authorized class C stock which is nonconvertible and limited and preferred as to dividends. Both the distribution of class A shares and the distribution of new class C shares are distributions to which section 301 applies.

Example (2). Corporation Y is organized with one class of stock, class A common. During the year the corporation declares a dividend on the class A stock payable in newly authorized class B preferred stock which is convertible into class A stock no later than 6 months from the date of distribution at a price that is only slightly higher than the market price of class A stock on the date of distribution. Taking into account the dividend rate, redemption provisions, the marketability of the convertible stock, and the conversion price, it is reasonable to anticipate that within a relatively short period of time some shareholders will exercise their conversion rights and some will not. Since the distribution can reasonably be expected to result in the receipt of preferred stock by some common shareholders and the receipt of common stock by other common shareholders, the distribution is a distribution of property to which section 301 applies. [Reg. § 1.305-4.]

☐ [*T.D.* 7281, 7-11-73.]

§ 1.305-5. Distributions on preferred stock.—(a) *In general.* Under section 305(b)(4), a distribution by a corporation of its stock (or rights to acquire its stock) made (or deemed made under section 305(c)) with respect to its preferred stock is treated as a distribution of property to which section 301 applies unless the distribution is made with respect to convertible preferred stock to take into account a stock dividend, stock split, or any similar event (such as the sale of stock at less than the fair market value pursuant to a rights offering) which would otherwise result in the dilution of the conversion right. For purposes of the preceding sentence, an adjustment in the conversion ratio of convertible preferred stock made solely to take into account the distribution by a closed-end regulated investment company of a capital gain dividend with respect to the stock into which such stock is convertible shall not be considered a "similar event". The term "preferred stock" generally refers to stock which, in relation to other classes of stock outstanding enjoys certain limited rights and privileges (generally associated with specified dividend and liquidation priorities) but does not participate in corporate growth to any significant extent. The distinguishing feature of "preferred stock" for the purposes of section 305(b)(4) is not its privileged position as such, but that such privileged position is limited and that such stock does not participate in corporate growth to any significant extent. However, a right to participate which lacks substance will not prevent a class of stock from being treated as preferred stock. Thus, stock which enjoys a priority as to dividends and on liquidation but which is entitled to participate, over and above such priority, with another less privileged class of stock in earnings and profits and upon liquidation, may nevertheless be treated as preferred stock for purposes of section 305 if, taking into account all the facts and circumstances, it is reasonable to anticipate at the time a distribution is made (or is deemed to have been made) with respect to such stock that there is little or no likelihood of such stock actually participating in current and anticipated earnings and upon liquidation beyond its preferred interest. Among the facts and circumstances to be considered are the prior and anticipated earnings per share, the cash dividends per share, the book value per share, the extent of preference and of participation of each class, both absolutely and relative to each other, and any other facts which indicate whether or not the stock has a real and meaningful probability of actually participating in the earnings and growth of the corporation. The determination of whether stock is preferred for purposes of section 305 shall be made without regard to any right to convert such stock into another class of stock of the corporation. The term "preferred stock", however, does not include convertible debentures.

Reg. § 1.305-5(a)

(b) *Redemption premium*—(1) *In general.* If a corporation issues preferred stock that may be redeemed under the circumstances described in this paragraph (b) at a price higher than the issue price, the difference (the redemption premium) is treated under section 305(c) as a constructive distribution (or series of constructive distributions) of additional stock on preferred stock that is taken into account under principles similar to the principles of section 1272(a). However, constructive distribution treatment does not result under this paragraph (b) if the redemption premium does not exceed a de minimis amount, as determined under the principles of section 1273(a)(3). For purposes of this paragraph (b), preferred stock that may be acquired by a person other than the issuer (the third person) is deemed to be redeemable under the circumstances described in this paragraph (b), and references to the issuer include the third person, if—

(i) this paragraph (b) would apply to the stock if the third person were the issuer; and

(ii) either—

(A) the acquisition of the stock by the third person would be treated as a redemption for federal income tax purposes (under section 304 or otherwise); or

(B) the third person and the issuer are members of the same affiliated group (having the meaning for this purpose given the term by section 1504(a), except that section 1504(b) shall not apply) and a principal purpose of the arrangement for the third person to acquire the stock is to avoid the application of section 305 and paragraph (b)(1) of this section.

(2) *Mandatory redemption or holder put.* Paragraph (b)(1) of this section applies to stock if the issuer is required to redeem the stock at a specified time or the holder has the option (whether or not currently exercisable) to require the issuer to redeem the stock. However, paragraph (b)(1) of this section will not apply if the issuer's obligation to redeem or the holder's ability to require the issuer to redeem is subject to a contingency that is beyond the legal or practical control of either the holder or the holders as a group (or through a related party within the meaning of section 267(b) or 707(b)), and that, based on all of the facts and circumstances as of the issue date, renders remote the likelihood of redemption. For purposes of this paragraph, a contingency does not include the possibility of default, insolvency, or similar circumstances, or that a redemption may be precluded by applicable law which requires that the issuer have a particular level of capital, surplus, or similar items. A contingency also does not include an issuer's option to require earlier redemption of the

stock. For rules applicable if stock may be redeemed at more than one time, see paragraph (b)(4) of this section.

(3) *Issuer call*—(i) *In general.* Paragraph (b)(1) of this section applies to stock by reason of the issuer's right to redeem the stock (even if the right is immediately exercisable), but only if, based on all of the facts and circumstances as of the issue date, redemption pursuant to that right is more likely than not to occur. However, even if redemption is more likely than not to occur, paragraph (b)(1) of this section does not apply if the redemption premium is solely in the nature of a penalty for premature redemption. A redemption premium is not a penalty for premature redemption unless it is a premium paid as a result of changes in economic or market conditions over which neither the issuer nor the holder has legal or practical control.

(ii) *Safe harbor.* For purposes of this paragraph (b)(3), redemption pursuant to an issuer's right to redeem is not treated as more likely than not to occur if—

(A) The issuer and the holder are not related within the meaning of section 267(b) or 707(b) (for purposes of applying sections 267(b) and 707(b) (including section 267(f)(1)), the phrase "20 percent" shall be substituted for the phrase "50 percent");

(B) There are no plans, arrangements, or agreements that effectively require or are intended to compel the issuer to redeem the stock (disregarding, for this purpose, a separate mandatory redemption obligation described in paragraph (b)(2) of this section); and

(C) Exercise of the right to redeem would not reduce the yield of the stock, as determined under principles similar to the principles of section 1272(a) and the regulations under sections 1271 through 1275.

(iii) *Effect of not satisfying safe harbor.* The fact that a redemption right is not described in paragraph (b)(3)(ii) of this section does not affect the determination of whether a redemption pursuant to the right to redeem is more likely than not to occur.

(4) *Coordination of multiple redemption provisions.* If stock may be redeemed at more than one time, the time and price at which redemption is most likely to occur must be determined based on all of the facts and circumstances as of the issue date. Any constructive distribution under paragraph (b)(1) of this section will result only with respect to the time and price identified in the preceding sentence. However, if redemption does not occur at that identified time, the amount of any additional premium payable on any later redemption date, to the extent not previously

treated as distributed, is treated as a constructive distribution over the period from the missed call or put date to that later date, to the extent required under the principles of this paragraph (b).

(5) *Consistency.* The issuer's determination as to whether there is a constructive distribution under this paragraph (b) is binding on all holders of the stock, other than a holder that explicitly discloses that its determination as to whether there is a constructive distribution under this paragraph (b) differs from that of the issuer. Unless otherwise prescribed by the Commissioner, the disclosure must be made on a statement attached to the holder's timely filed federal income tax return for the taxable year that includes the date the holder acquired the stock. The issuer must provide the relevant information to the holder in a reasonable manner. For example, the issuer may provide the name or title and either the address or telephone number of a representative of the issuer who will make available to holders upon request the information required for holders to comply with this provision of this paragraph (b).

* * *

[Reg. § 1.305-5.]

☐ [*T.D. 7281, 7-11-73. Amended by T.D. 7329, 10-11-74 and T.D. 8643, 12-20-95.*]

§ 1.305-6. Distributions of convertible preferred.—(a) *In general.* (1) Under section 305(b)(5), a distribution by a corporation of its convertible preferred stock or rights to acquire such stock made or considered as made with respect to its stock is treated as a distribution of property to which section 301 applies unless the corporation establishes that such distribution will not result in a disproportionate distribution as described in § 1.305-3.

(2) The distribution of convertible preferred stock is likely to result in a disproportionate distribution when both of the following conditions exist: (i) The conversion right must be exercised within a relatively short period of time after the date of distribution of the stock; and (ii) taking into account such factors as the dividend rate, the redemption provisions, the marketability of the convertible stock, and the conversion price, it may be anticipated that some shareholders will exercise their conversion rights and some will not. On the other hand, where the conversion right may be exercised over a period of many years and the dividend rate is consistent with market conditions at the time of distribution of the stock, there is no basis for predicting at what time and the extent to which the stock will be converted and it is unlikely that a disproportionate distribution will result.

(b) *Examples.* The application of section 305(b)(5) may be illustrated by the following examples:

Example (1). Corporation Z is organized with one class of stock, class A common. During the year the corporation declares a dividend on the class A stock payable in newly authorized class B preferred stock which is convertible into class A stock for a period of 20 years from the date of issuance. Assuming dividend rates are normal in light of existing conditions so that there is no basis for predicting the extent to which the stock will be converted, these circumstances will ordinarily be sufficient to establish that a disproportionate distribution will not result since it is impossible to predict the extent to which the class B stock will be converted into class A stock. Accordingly, the distribution of class B stock is not one to which section 301 applies.

Example (2). Corporation X is organized with one class of stock, class A common. During the year the corporation declares a dividend on the class A stock payable in newly authorized redeemable class C preferred stock which is convertible into class A common stock no later than 4 months from the date of distribution at a price slightly higher than the market price of class A stock on the date of distribution. By prearrangement with corporation X, corporation Y, an insurance company, agrees to purchase class C stock from any shareholder who does not wish to convert. By reason of this prearrangement, it is anticipated that the shareholders will either sell the class C stock to the insurance company (which expects to retain the shares for investment purposes) or will convert. As a result, some of the shareholders exercise their conversion privilege and receive additional shares of class A stock, while other shareholders sell their class C stock to corporation Y and receive cash. The distribution is a distribution to which section 301 applies since it results in the receipt of property by some shareholders and an increase in the proportionate interests of other shareholders. [Reg. § 1.305-6.]

☐ [*T.D. 7281, 7-11-73.*]

§ 1.305-7. Certain transactions treated as distributions.—(a) *In general.* Under section 305(c), a change in conversion ratio, a change in redemption price, a difference between redemption price and issue price, a redemption which is treated as a distribution to which section 301 applies, or any transaction (including a recapitalization) having a similar effect on the interest of any shareholder may be treated as a distribution with respect to any shareholder whose proportionate interest in the earnings and profits or assets of the corporation is increased by such change, difference, redemption, or similar transaction. In

Reg. § 1.305-7(a)

general, such change, difference, redemption, or similar transaction will be treated as a distribution to which sections 305(b) and 301 apply where—

(1) The proportionate interest of any shareholder in the earnings and profits or assets of the corporation deemed to have made such distribution is increased by such change, difference, redemption, or similar transaction; and

(2) Such distribution has the result described in paragraph (2), (3), (4), or (5) of section 305(b).

Where such change, difference, redemption, or similar transaction is treated as a distribution under the provisions of this section, such distribution will be deemed made with respect to any shareholder whose interest in the earnings and profits or assets of the distributing corporation is increased thereby. Such distribution will be deemed to be a distribution of the stock of such corporation made by the corporation to such shareholder with respect to his stock. Depending upon the facts presented, the distribution may be deemed to be made in common or preferred stock. For example, where a redemption premium exists with respect to a class of preferred stock under the circumstances described in § 1.305-5(b) and the other requirements of this section are also met, the distribution will be deemed made with respect to such preferred stock, in stock of the same class. Accordingly, the preferred shareholders are considered under sections 305(b)(4) and 305(c) to have received a distribution of preferred stock to which section 301 applies. See the examples in §§ 1.305-3(e) and 1.305-5(d) for further illustrations of the application of section 305(c).

(b) *Antidilution provisions.* (1) For purposes of applying section 305(c) in conjunction with section 305(b), a change in the conversion ratio or conversion price of convertible preferred stock (or securities), or in the exercise price of rights or warrants, made pursuant to a bona fide, reasonable, adjustment formula (including, but not limited to, either the so-called "market price" or "conversion price" type of formulas) which has the effect of preventing dilution of the interest of the holders of such stock (or securities) will not be considered to result in a deemed distribution of stock. An adjustment in the conversion ratio or price to compensate for cash or property distributions to other shareholders that are taxable under section 301, 356(a)(2), 871(a)(1)(A), 881(a)(1), 852(b), or 857(b) will not be considered as made pursuant to a bona fide adjustment formula.

(2) The principles of this paragraph may be illustrated by the following example:

Example. (i) Corporation U has two classes of stock outstanding, class A and class B. Each class

B share is convertible into class A stock. In accordance with a bona fide, reasonable, antidilution provision, the conversion price is adjusted if the corporation transfers class A stock to anyone for a consideration that is below the conversion price.

(ii) The corporation sells class A stock to the public at the current market price but below the conversion price. Pursuant to the antidilution provision, the conversion price is adjusted downward. Such a change in conversion price will not be deemed to be a distribution under section 305(c) for the purposes of section 305(b).

(c) *Recapitalizations.* (1) A recapitalization (whether or not an isolated transaction) will be deemed to result in a distribution to which section 305(c) and this section apply if—

(i) It is pursuant to a plan to periodically increase a shareholder's proportionate interest in the assets or earnings and profits of the corporation, or

(ii) A shareholder owning preferred stock with dividends in arrears exchanges his stock for other stock and, as a result, increases his proportionate interest in the assets or earnings and profits of the corporation. An increase in a preferred shareholder's proportionate interest occurs in any case where the fair market value or the liquidation preference, whichever is greater, of the stock received in the exchange (determined immediately following the recapitalization), exceeds the issue price of the preferred stock surrendered.

(2) In a case to which subparagraph (1)(ii) of this paragraph applies, the amount of the distribution deemed under section 305(c) to result from the recapitalization is the lesser of (i) the amount by which the fair market value or the liquidation preference, whichever is greater, of the stock received in the exchange (determined immediately following the recapitalization) exceeds the issue price of the preferred stock surrendered, or (ii) the amount of the dividends in arrears.

(3) For purposes of applying subparagraphs (1) and (2) of this paragraph with respect to stock issued before July 12, 1973, the term "issue price of the preferred stock surrendered" shall mean the greater of the issue price or the liquidation preference (not including dividends in arrears) of the stock surrendered.

(4) For an illustration of the application of this paragraph, see example (12) of § 1.305-3(e) and examples (1), (2), (3), and (6) of § 1.305-5(d).

(5) For rules relating to redemption premiums on preferred stock, see § 1.305-5(b) [Reg. § 1.305-7.]

☐ [*T.D. 7281, 7-11-73. Amended by T.D. 8643, 12-20-95.*]

Reg. § 1.305-7(a)(1)

§ 1.306-1. General.—(a) Section 306 provides, in general, that the proceeds from the sale or redemption of certain stock (referred to as "section 306 stock") shall be treated either as ordinary income or as a distribution of property to which section 301 applies. Section 306 stock is defined in section 306(c) and is usually preferred stock received either as a nontaxable dividend or in a transaction in which no gain or loss is recognized. Section 306(b) lists certain circumstances in which the special rules of section 306(a) shall not apply.

(b)(1) If a shareholder sells or otherwise disposes of section 306 stock (other than by redemption or within the exceptions listed in section 306(b)), the entire proceeds received from such disposition shall be treated as ordinary income to the extent that the fair market value of the stock sold, on the date distributed to the shareholder, would have been a dividend to such shareholder had the distributing corporation distributed cash in lieu of stock. Any excess of the amount received over the sum of the amount treated as ordinary income plus the adjusted basis of the stock disposed of shall be treated as gain from the sale of a capital asset or noncapital asset as the case may be. No loss shall be recognized. No reduction of earnings and profits results from any disposition of stock other than a redemption. The term "disposition" under section 306(a)(1) includes, among other things, pledges of stock under certain circumstances, particularly where the pledgee can look only to the stock itself as its security.

(2) Section 306(a)(1) may be illustrated by the following examples:

Example (1). On December 15, 1954, A and B owned equally all of the stock of Corporation X which files its income tax return on a calendar year basis. On that date Corporation X distributed pro rata 100 shares of preferred stock as a dividend on its outstanding common stock. On December 15, 1954, the preferred stock had a fair market value of $10,000. On December 31, 1954, the earnings and profits of Corporation X were $20,000. The 50 shares of preferred stock so distributed to A had an allocated basis to him of $10 per share or a total of $500 for the 50 shares. Such shares had a fair market value of $5,000 when issued. A sold the 50 shares of preferred stock on July 1, 1955, for $6,000. Of this amount $5,000 will be treated as ordinary income; $500 ($6,000 minus $5,500) will be treated as gain from the sale of a capital or noncapital asset as the case may be.

Example (2). The facts are the same as in example 1 except that A sold his 50 shares of preferred stock for $5,100. Of this amount $5,000 will be treated as ordinary income. No loss will be allowed. There will be added back to the basis of the common stock of Corporation X with respect to which the preferred stock was distributed, $400, the allocated basis of $500 reduced by the $100 received.

Example (3). The facts are the same as in example 1 except that A sold 25 of his shares of preferred stock for $2,600. Of this amount $2,500 will be treated as ordinary income. No loss will be allowed. There will be added back to the basis of the common stock of Corporation X with respect to which the preferred stock was distributed, $150, the allocated basis of $250 reduced by the $100 received.

(c) The entire amount received by a shareholder from the redemption of section 306 stock shall be treated as a distribution of property under section 301. See also section 303 (relating to distribution in redemption of stock to pay death taxes). [Reg. § 1.306-1.]

☐ [*T.D.* 6152, 12-2-55. *Amended by T.D.* 7556, 8-2-78.]

§ 1.306-2. Exceptions.—(a) If a shareholder terminates his entire stock interest in a corporation—

(1) By a sale or other disposition within the requirements of section 306(b)(1)(A), or

(2) By redemption under section 302(b)(3) (through the application of section 306(b)(1)(B)),

the amount received from such disposition shall be treated as an amount received in part or full payment for the stock sold or redeemed. In the case of a sale, only the stock interest need be terminated. In determining whether an entire stock interest has been terminated under section 306(b)(1)(A), all of the provisions of section 318(a) (relating to constructive ownership of stock) shall be applicable. In determining whether a shareholder has terminated his entire interest in a corporation by a redemption of his stock under section 302(b)(3), all of the provisions of section 318(a) shall be applicable unless the shareholder meets the requirements of section 302(c)(2) (relating to termination of all interest in the corporation). If the requirements of section 302(c)(2) are met, section 318(a)(1) (relating to members of a family) shall be inapplicable. Under all circumstances paragraphs (2), (3), (4), and (5) of section 318(a) shall be applicable.

(b) Section 306(a) does not apply to—

(1) Redemptions of section 306 stock pursuant to a partial or complete liquidation of a corporation to which part (section 331 and following), subchapter C, chapter 1 of the Code applies,

(2) Exchanges of section 306 stock solely for stock in connection with a reorganization or in an exchange under section 351, 355, or section 1036 (relating to exchanges of stock for stock in the same corporation) to the extent that gain or loss is

not recognized to the shareholder as the result of the exchange of the stock (see paragraph (d) of § 1.306-3 relative to the receipt of other property), and

(3) A disposition or redemption, if it is established to the satisfaction of the Commissioner that the distribution, and the disposition or redemption, was not in pursuance of a plan having as one of its principal purposes the avoidance of Federal income tax. However, in the case of a prior or simultaneous disposition (or redemption) of the stock with respect to which the section 306 stock disposed of (or redeemed) was issued, it is not necessary to establish that the distribution was not in pursuance of such a plan. For example, in the absence of such a plan and of any other facts the first sentence of this subparagraph would be applicable to the case of dividends and isolated dispositions of section 306 stock by minority shareholders. Similarly, in the absence of such a plan and of any other facts, if a shareholder received a distribution of 100 shares of section 306 stock on his holdings of 100 shares of voting common stock in a corporation and sells his voting common stock before he disposes of his section 306 stock, the subsequent disposition of his section 306 stock would not ordinarily be considered a disposition one of the principal purposes of which is the avoidance of Federal income tax. [Reg. § 1.306-2.]

☐ [*T.D.* 6152, 12-2-55. *Amended by T.D.* 6969, 8-22-68.]

§ 1.306-3. Section 306 stock defined.—(a) For the purpose of subchapter C, chapter 1 of the Code, the term "section 306 stock" means stock which meets the requirements of section 306(c)(1). Any class of stock distributed to a shareholder in a transaction in which no amount is includible in the income of the shareholder or no gain or loss is recognized may be section 306 stock, if a distribution of money by the distributing corporation in lieu of such stock would have been a dividend in whole or in part. However, except as provided in section 306(g), if no part of a distribution of money by the distributing corporation in lieu of such stock would have been a dividend, the stock distributed will not constitute section 306 stock.

(b) For the purpose of section 306, rights to acquire stock shall be treated as stock. Such rights shall not be section 306 stock if no part of the distribution would have been a dividend if money had been distributed in lieu of the rights. When stock is acquired by the exercise of rights which are treated as section 306 stock, the stock acquired is section 306 stock. Upon the disposition of such stock (other than by redemption or within

the exceptions listed in section 306(b)), the proceeds received from the disposition shall be treated as ordinary income to the extent that the fair market value of the stock rights, on the date distributed to the shareholder, would have been a dividend to the shareholder had the distributing corporation distributed cash in lieu of stock rights. Any excess of the amount realized over the sum of the amount treated as ordinary income plus the adjusted basis of the stock shall be treated as gain from the sale of the stock.

(c) Section 306(c)(1)(A) provides that section 306 stock is any stock (other than common issued with respect to common) distributed to the shareholder selling or otherwise disposing thereof if, under section 305(a) (relating to distributions of stock and stock rights) any part of the distribution was not included in the gross income of the distributee.

(d) Section 306(c)(1)(B) includes in the definition of section 306 stock any stock except common stock, which is received by a shareholder in connection with a reorganization under section 368 or in a distribution or exchange under section 355 (or so much of section 356 as relates to section 355) provided the effect of the transaction is substantially the same as the receipt of a stock dividend, or the stock is received in exchange for section 306 stock. If, in a transaction to which section 356 is applicable, a shareholder exchanges section 306 stock for stock and money or other property, the entire amount of such money and of the fair market value of the other property (not limited to the gain recognized) shall be treated as a distribution of property to which section 301 applies. Common stock received in exchange for section 306 stock in a recapitalization shall not be considered section 306 stock. Ordinarily, section 306 stock includes stock which is not common stock received in pursuance of a plan of reorganization (within the meaning of section 368(a)) or received in a distribution or exchange to which section 355 (or so much of section 356 as relates to section 355) applies if cash received in lieu of such stock would have been treated as a dividend under section 356(a)(2) or would have been treated as a distribution to which section 301 applies by virtue of section 356(b) or section 302(d). The application of the preceding sentence is illustrated by the following examples:

Example (1). Corporation A, having only common stock outstanding, is merged in a statutory merger (qualifying as a reorganization under section 368(a)) with Corporation B. Pursuant to such merger, the shareholders of Corporation A received both common and preferred stock in Corporation B. The preferred stock received by such shareholders is section 306 stock.

Example (2). X and Y each own one-half of the 2,000 outstanding shares of preferred stock and one-half of the 2,000 outstanding shares of common stock of Corporation C. Pursuant to a reorganization within the meaning of section 368(a)(1)(E) (recapitalization) each shareholder exchanges his preferred stock for preferred stock of a new issue which is not substantially different from the preferred stock previously held. Unless the preferred stock exchanged was itself section 306 stock the preferred stock received is not section 306 stock.

(e) Section 306(c)(1)(C) includes in the definition of section 306 stock any stock (except as provided in section 306(c)(1)(B)) the basis of which in the hands of the person disposing of such stock, is determined by reference to section 306 stock held by such shareholder or any other person. Under this paragraph common stock can be section 306 stock. Thus, if a person owning section 306 stock in Corporation A transfers it to Corporation B which is controlled by him in exchange for common stock of Corporation B in a transaction to which section 351 is applicable, the common stock so received by him would be section 306 stock and subject to the provisions of section 306(a) on its disposition. In addition, the section 306 stock transferred is section 306 stock in the hands of Corporation B, the transferee. Section 306 stock transferred by gift remains section 306 stock in the hands of the donee. Stock received in exchange for section 306 stock under section 1036(a) (relating to exchange of stock for stock in the same corporation) or under so much of section 1031(b) as relates to section 1036(a) becomes section 306 stock and acquires, for purposes of section 306, the characteristics of the section 306 stock exchanged. The entire amount of the fair market value of the other property received in such transaction shall be considered as received upon a disposition (other than a redemption) to which section 306(a) applies. Section 306 stock ceases to be so classified if the basis of such stock is determined by reference to its fair market value on the date of the decedent-stockholder's death or the optional valuation date under section 1014.

(f) If section 306 stock which was distributed with respect to common stock is exchanged for common stock in the same corporation (whether or not such exchange is pursuant to a conversion privilege contained in section 306 stock), such common stock shall not be section 306 stock. This paragraph applies to exchanges not coming within the purview of section 306(c)(1)(B). Common stock which is convertible into stock other than common stock or into property, shall not be considered common stock. It is immaterial whether the conversion privilege is contained in the stock or in some type of collateral agreement.

(g) If there is a substantial change in the terms and conditions of any stock, then, for the purpose of this section—

(1) The fair market value of such stock shall be the fair market value at the time of distribution or the fair market value at the time of such change, whichever is higher;

(2) Such stock's ratable share of the amount which would have been a dividend if money had been distributed in lieu of stock shall be determined by reference to the time of distribution or by reference to the time of such change, whichever ratable share is higher; and

(3) Section 306(c)(2) shall be inapplicable if there would have been a dividend to any extent if money had been distributed in lieu of the stock either at the time of the distribution or at the time of such change.

(h) When section 306 stock is disposed of, the amount treated under section 306(a)(1)(A) as ordinary income will, for the purposes of Part I, subchapter N, chapter 1 of the Code, be treated as derived from the same source as would have been the source if money had been received from the corporation as a dividend at the time of the distribution of such stock. If the amount is determined to be derived from sources within the United States, the amount shall be considered to be fixed or determinable annual or periodic gains, profits, and income within the meaning of section 871(a) or section 881(a), relating, respectively, to the tax on nonresident alien individuals and on foreign corporations not engaged in business in the United States.

(i) Section 306 shall be inapplicable to stock received before June 22, 1954, and to stock received on or after June 22, 1954, in transactions subject to the provisions of the Internal Revenue Code of 1939. [Reg. § 1.306-3.]

☐ [*T.D. 6152, 12-2-55. Amended by T.D. 7281, 7-11-73, and T.D. 7556, 8-2-78.*]

§ 1.307-1. General.—(a) If a shareholder receives stock or stock rights as a distribution on stock previously held and under section 305 such distribution is not includible in gross income then, except as provided in section 307(b) and § 1.307-2, the basis of the stock with respect to which the distribution was made shall be allocated between the old and new stocks or rights in proportion to the fair market values of each on the date of distribution. If a shareholder receives stock or stock rights as a distribution on stock previously held and pursuant to section 305 part of the distribution is not includible in gross income, then (except as provided in section 307(b) and § 1.307-2) the basis of the stock with respect to which the distribution is made shall be allocated between (1) the old stock and (2) that part of the new stock or rights which is not includible in gross income, in proportion to the fair market values of each on the date of distribution. The date of distribution in each case shall be the date the stock or the rights are distributed to the stockholder and not the record date. The general rule will apply with respect to stock rights only if such rights are exercised or sold.

(b) The application of paragraph (a) of this section is illustrated by the following example:

Example. A taxpayer in 1947 purchased 100 shares of common stock at $100 per share and in 1954 by reason of the ownership of such stock acquired 100 rights entitling him to subscribe to 100 additional shares of such stock at $90 a share. Immediately after the issuance of the rights, each of the shares of stock in respect of which the rights were acquired had a fair market value, ex-rights, of $110 and the rights had a fair market value of $19 each. The basis of the rights and the common stock for the purpose of determining the basis for gain or loss on a subsequent sale or exercise of the rights or a sale of the old stock is computed as follows:

100 (shares) × $100	= $10,000, cost of old stock (stock in respect of which the rights were acquired).
100 (shares) × $110	= $11,000, market value of old stock.
100 (rights) × $ 19	= $ 1,900, market value of rights.
11,000/12,900 of $10,000	= $ 8,527.13, cost of old stock apportioned to such stock.
1,900/12,900 of $10,000	= $ 1,472.87, cost of old stock apportioned to rights.

If the rights are sold, the basis for determining gain or loss will be $14.7287 per right. If the rights are exercised, the basis of the new stock acquired will be the subscription price paid therefor ($90) plus the basis of the rights exercised ($14.7287 each) or $104.7287 per share. The remaining basis of the old stock for the purpose of determining gain or loss on a subsequent sale will be $85.2713 per share. [Reg. § 1.307-1.]

☐ [*T.D.* 6152, 12-2-55.]

§ 1.307-2. Exception.—The basis of rights to buy stock which are excluded from gross income under section 305(a), shall be zero if the fair market value of such rights on the date of distribution is less than 15 percent of the fair market value of the old stock on that date, unless the shareholder elects to allocate part of the basis of the old stock to the rights as provided in paragraph (a) of § 1.307-1. The election shall be made by a shareholder with respect to all the rights received by him in a particular distribution in respect of all the stock of the same class owned by him in the issuing corporation at the time of such distribution. Such election to allocate basis to rights shall be in the form of a statement attached to the shareholder's return for the year in which the rights are received. This election, once made, shall be irrevocable with respect to the rights for which the election was made. Any shareholder making such an election shall retain a copy of the election and of the tax return with which it was filed, in order to substantiate the use of an allocated basis upon a subsequent disposition of the stock acquired by exercise. [Reg. § 1.307-2.]

☐ [*T.D.* 6152, 12-2-55.]

§ 1.312-1. Adjustment to earnings and profits reflecting distributions by corporations.— (a) In general, on the distribution of property by a corporation with respect to its stock, its earnings and profits (to the extent thereof) shall be decreased by—

(1) The amount of money,

(2) The principal amount of the obligations of such corporation issued in such distribution, and

(3) The adjusted basis of other property.

For special rule with respect to distributions to which section 312(e) applies, see § 1.312-5.

(b) The adjustment provided in section 312(a)(3) and paragraph (a)(3) of this section with respect to a distribution of property (other than money or its own obligations) shall be made notwithstanding the fact that such property has appreciated or depreciated in value since acquisition.

(c) The application of paragraphs (a) and (b) of this section may be illustrated by the following examples:

Example (1). Corporation A distributes to its sole shareholder property with a value of $10,000 and a basis of $5,000. It has $12,500 in earnings and profits. The reduction in earnings and profits by reason of such distribution is $5,000. Such is the reduction even though the amount of $10,000 is includible in the income of the shareholder (other than a corporation) as a dividend.

Example (2). The facts are the same as in example (1) above except that the property has a basis of $15,000 and the earnings and profits of the corporation are $20,000. The reduction in earnings and profits is $15,000. Such is the reduction even though only the amount of $10,000 is includible in the income of the shareholder as a dividend.

(d) In the case of a distribution of stock or rights to acquire stock a portion of which is includible in income by reason of section 305(b), the earnings and profits shall be reduced by the fair market value of such portion. No reduction shall be made if a distribution of stock or rights to acquire stock is not includible in income under the provisions of section 305.

(e) No adjustment shall be made in the amount of the earnings and profits of the issuing corporation upon a disposition of section 306 stock unless such disposition is a redemption. [Reg. § 1.312-1.]

☐ [*T.D.* 6152, 12-2-55.]

§ 1.312-2. Distributions of inventory assets.—Section 312(b) provides for the increase and the decrease of the earnings and profits of a corporation which distributes, with respect to its stock, inventory assets as defined in section 312(b)(2), where the fair market value of such assets exceeds their adjusted basis. The rules provided in section 312(b) (relating to distributions of certain inventory assets) shall be applicable without regard to the method used in computing inventories for the purpose of the computation of taxable income. Section 312(b) does not apply to distributions described in section 312(e). [Reg. § 1.312-2.]

☐ [*T.D.* 6152, 12-2-55.]

§ 1.312-3. Liabilities.—The amount of any reductions in earnings and profits described in section 312(a) or (b) shall be (a) reduced by the amount of any liability to which the property distributed was subject and by the amount of any other liability of the corporation assumed by the shareholder in connection with such distribution, and (b) increased by the amount of gain recognized to the corporation under section 311(b), (c), or (d), or under section 341(f), 617(d), 1245(a), 1250(a), 1251(c), 1252(a), or 1254(a). [Reg. § 1.312-3.]

☐ [*T.D.* 6152, 12-2-55. *Amended by T.D.* 6832, 7-6-65, *T.D.* 7084, 1-7-71; *T.D.* 7209, 10-3-72 *and T.D.* 8586, 1-9-95.]

§ 1.312-6. Earnings and profits.—(a) In determining the amount of earnings and profits (whether of the taxable year, or accumulated since February 28, 1913, or accumulated before March 1, 1913) due consideration must be given to the facts, and, while mere bookkeeping entries increasing or decreasing surplus will not be conclusive, the amount of the earnings and profits in any case will be dependent upon the method of accounting properly employed in computing taxable income (or net income, as the case may be). For instance, a corporation keeping its books and filing its income tax returns under subchapter E, chapter 1 of the Code, on the cash receipts and disbursements basis may not use the accrual basis in determining earnings and profits; a corporation computing income on the installment basis as provided in section 453 shall, with respect to the installment transactions, compute earnings and

profits on such basis; and an insurance company subject to taxation under section 831 shall exclude from earnings and profits that portion of any premium which is unearned under the provisions of section 832(b)(4) and which is segregated accordingly in the unearned premium reserve.

(b) Among the items entering into the computation of corporate earnings and profits for a particular period are all income exempted by statute, income not taxable by the Federal Government under the Constitution, as well as all items includible in gross income under section 61 or corresponding provisions of prior revenue acts. Gains and losses within the purview of section 1002 or corresponding provisions of prior revenue acts are brought into the earnings and profits at the time and to the extent such gains and losses are recognized under that section. Interest on State bonds and certain other obligations, although not taxable when received by a corporation, is taxable to the same extent as other dividends when distributed to shareholders in the form of dividends.

(c)(1) In the case of a corporation in which depletion or depreciation is a factor in the determination of income, the only depletion or depreciation deductions to be considered in the computation of the total earnings and profits are those based on cost or other basis without regard to March 1, 1913, value. In computing the earnings and profits for any period beginning after February 28, 1913, the only depletion or depreciation deductions to be considered are those based on (i) cost or other basis, if the depletable or depreciable asset was acquired subsequent to February 28, 1913, or (ii) adjusted cost or March 1, 1913, value, whichever is higher, if acquired before March 1, 1913. Thus, discovery or percentage depletion under all revenue acts for mines and oil and gas wells is not to be taken into consideration in computing the earnings and profits of a corporation. Similarly, where the basis of property in the hands of a corporation is a substituted basis, such basis, and not the fair market value of the property at the time of the acquisition by the corporation, is the basis for computing depletion and depreciation for the purpose of determining earnings and profits of the corporation.

(2) The application of subparagraph (1) of this paragraph may be illustrated by the following example:

Example. Oil producing property which A had acquired in 1949 at a cost of $28,000 was transferred to Corporation Y in December 1951, in exchange for all of its capital stock. The fair market value of the stock and of the property as of the date of the transfer was $247,000. Corporation Y, after four years' operation, effected in 1955 a cash distribution to A in the amount of

$165,000. In determining the extent to which the earnings and profits of Corporation Y available for dividend distributions have been increased as the result of production and sale of oil, the depletion to be taken into account is to be computed upon the basis of $28,000 established in the nontaxable exchange in 1951 regardless of the fair market value of the property or of the stock issued in exchange therefor.

(d) A loss sustained for a year before the taxable year does not affect the earnings and profits of the taxable year. However, in determining the earnings and profits accumulated since February 28, 1913, the excess of a loss sustained for a year subsequent to February 28, 1913, over the undistributed earnings and profits accumulated since February 28, 1913, and before the year for which the loss was sustained, reduces surplus as of March 1, 1913, to the extent of such excess. If the surplus as of March 1, 1913, was sufficient to absorb such excess, distributions to shareholders after the year of the loss are out of earnings and profits accumulated since the year of the loss to the extent of such earnings.

(e) With respect to the effect on the earnings and profits accumulated since February 28, 1913, of distributions made on or after January 1, 1916, and before August 6, 1917, out of earnings or profits accumulated before March 1, 1913, which distributions were specifically declared to be out of earnings and profits accumulated before March 1, 1913, see section 31(b) of the Revenue Act of 1916, as amended by section 1211 of the Revenue Act of 1917 (40 Stat. 336). [Reg. § 1.312-6.].

□ [*T.D.* 6152, 12-2-55.]

§ 1.312-7. Effect on earnings and profits of gain or loss realized after February 28, 1913.— (a) In order to determine the effect on earnings and profits of gain or loss realized from the sale or other disposition (after February 28, 1913) of property by a corporation, section 312(f)(1) prescribes certain rules for—

(1) The computation of the total earnings and profits of the corporation of most frequent application in determining invested capital; and

(2) The computation of earnings and profits of the corporation for any period beginning after February 28, 1913, of most frequent application in determining the source of dividend distributions.

Such rules are applicable whenever under any provision of subtitle A of the Code it is necessary to compute either the total earnings and profits of the corporation or the earnings and profits for any period beginning after February 28, 1913. For example, since the earnings and profits accumulated after February 28, 1913, or the earnings and profits of the taxable year, are earnings and prof-

its for a period beginning after February 28, 1913, the determination of either must be in accordance with the regulations prescribed by this section, for the ascertainment of earnings and profits for any period beginning after February 28, 1913. Under subparagraph (1) of this paragraph, such gain or loss is determined by using the adjusted basis (under the law applicable to the year in which the sale or other disposition was made) for determining gain, but disregarding value as of March 1, 1913. Under subparagraph (2) of this paragraph, there is used such adjusted basis for determining gain, giving effect to the value as of March 1, 1913, whenever applicable. In both cases the rules are the same as those governing depreciation and depletion in computing earnings and profits (see § 1.312-6). Under both subparagraphs (1) and (2) of this paragraph, the adjusted basis is subject to the limitations of the third sentence of section 312(f)(1) requiring the use of adjustments proper in determining earnings and profits. The proper adjustments may differ under section 312(f)(1)(A) and (B) depending upon the basis to which the adjustments are to be made. If the application of section 312(f)(1)(B) results in a loss and if the application of section 312(f)(1)(A) to the same transaction reaches a different result, then the loss under section 312(f)(1)(B) will be subject to the adjustment thereto required by section 312(g)(2). (See § 1.312-9.)

(b)(1) The gain or loss so realized increases or decreases the earnings and profits to, but not beyond, the extent to which such gain or loss was recognized in computing taxable income (or net income, as the case may be) under the law applicable to the year in which such sale or disposition was made. As used in this paragraph, the term "recognized" has reference to that kind of realized gain or loss which is recognized for income tax purposes by the statute applicable to the year in which the gain or loss was realized. For example, see section 356. A loss (other than a wash sale loss with respect to which a deduction is disallowed under the provisions of section 1091 or corresponding provisions of prior revenue laws) may be recognized though not allowed as a deduction (by reason, for example, of the operation of sections 267 and 1211 and corresponding provisions of prior revenue laws) but the mere fact that it is not allowed does not prevent decrease in earnings and profits by the amount of such disallowed loss. Wash sale losses, however, disallowed under section 1091 and corresponding provisions of prior revenue laws, are deemed nonrecognized losses and do not reduce earnings or profits. The "recognized" gain or loss for the purpose of computing earnings and profits is determined by applying the recognition provisions to the realized gain or loss computed under the provisions of section

312(f)(1) as distinguished from the realized gain or loss used in computing taxable income (or net income, as the case may be).

(2) The application of subparagraph (1) of this paragraph may be illustrated by the following examples:

Example (1). Corporation X on January 1, 1952, owned stock in Corporation Y which it had acquired from Corporation Y in December 1951, in an exchange transaction in which no gain or loss was recognized. The adjusted basis to Corporation X of the property exchanged by it for the stock in Corporation Y was $30,000. The fair market value of the stock in Corporation Y when received by Corporation X was $930,000. On April 9, 1955, Corporation X made a cash distribution of $900,000 and, except for the possible effect of the transaction in 1951, had no earnings or profits accumulated after February 28, 1913, and had no earnings or profits for the taxable year. The amount of $900,000 representing the excess of the fair market value of the stock of Corporation Y over the adjusted basis of the property exchanged therefor was not recognized gain to Corporation X under the provisions of section 112 of the Internal Revenue Code of 1939. Accordingly, the earnings and profits of Corporation X are not increased by $900,000, the amount of the gain realized but not recognized in the exchange, and the distribution was not a taxable dividend. The basis in the hands of Corporation Y of the property acquired by it from Corporation X is $30,000. If such property is thereafter sold by Corporation Y, gain or loss will be computed on such basis of $30,000, and earnings and profits will be increased or decreased accordingly.

Example (2). On January 2, 1910, Corporation M acquired nondepreciable property at a cost of $1,000. On March 1, 1913, the fair market value of such property in the hands of Corporation M was $2,200. On December 31, 1952, Corporation M transfers such property to Corporation N in exchange for $1,900 in cash and all Corporation N's stock, which has a fair market value of $1,100. For the purpose of computing the total earnings and profits of Corporation M, the gain on such transaction is $2,000 (the sum of $1,900 in cash and stock worth $1,100 minus $1,000, the adjusted basis for computing gain, determined

without regard to March 1, 1913, value), $1,900 of which is recognized under section 356, since this was the amount of money received, although for the purpose of computing net income the gain is only $800 (the sum of $1,900 in cash and stock worth $1,100, minus $2,200, the adjusted basis for computing gain determined by giving effect to March 1, 1913, value). Such earnings and profits will therefore be increased by $1,900. In computing the earnings and profits of Corporation M for any period beginning after February 28, 1913, however, the gain arising from the transaction, like the taxable gain, is only $800, all of which is recognized under section 112(c) of the Internal Revenue Code of 1939, the money received being in excess of such amount. Such earnings and profits will therefore be increased by only $800 as a result of the transaction. For increase in that part of the earnings and profits consisting of increase in value of property accrued before, but realized on or after March 1, 1913, see § 1.312-9.

Example (3). On July 31, 1955, Corporation R owned oil-producing property acquired after February 28, 1913, at a cost of $200,000, but having an adjusted basis (by reason of taking percentage depletion) of $100,000 for determining gain. However, the adjusted basis of such property to be used in computing gain or loss for the purpose of earnings and profits is, because of the provisions of the third sentence of section 312(f)(1), $150,000. On such day Corporation R transferred such property to Corporation S in exchange for $25,000 in cash and all of the stock of Corporation S, which had a fair market value of $100,000. For the purpose of computing taxable income, Corporation R has realized a gain of $25,000 as a result of this transaction, all of which is recognized under section 356. For the purpose of computing earnings and profits, however, Corporation R has realized a loss of $25,000, none of which is recognized owing to the provisions of section 356(c). The earnings and profits of Corporation R are therefore neither increased nor decreased as a result of the transaction. The adjusted basis of the Corporation S stock in the hands of Corporation R for purposes of computing earnings and profits, however, will be $125,000 (though only $100,000 for the purpose of computing taxable income), computed as follows:

Basis of property transferred	$200,000
Less money received on exchange	25,000
Plus gain or minus loss recognized on exchange	None
Basis of stock	$175,000
Less adjustments (same as those used in determining adjusted basis of property transferred)	$50,000
Adjusted basis of stock	$125,000

If, therefore, Corporation R should subsequently sell the Corporation S stock for $100,000, a loss of

$25,000 will again be realized for the purpose of computing earnings and profits, all of which will be recognized and will be applied to decrease the earnings and profits of Corporation R.

(c)(1) The third sentence of section 312(f)(1) provides for cases in which the adjustments, prescribed in section 1016, to the basis indicated in section 312(f)(1)(A) or (B), as the case may be, differ from the adjustments to such basis proper for the purpose of determining earnings or profits. The adjustments provided by such third sentence reflect the treatment provided by § § 1.312-6 and 1.312-15 relative to cases where the deductions for depletion and depreciation in computing taxable income (or net income, as the case may be) differ from the deductions proper for the purpose of computing earnings and profits.

(2) The effect of the third sentence of section 312(f)(1) may be illustrated by the following examples:

Example (1). Corporation X purchased on January 2, 1931, an oil lease at a cost of $10,000. The lease was operated only for the years 1931 and 1932. The deduction for depletion in each of the years 1931 and 1932 amounted to $2,750, of which amount $1,750 represented percentage depletion in excess of depletion based on cost. The lease was sold in 1955 for $15,000. Under section 1016(a)(2), in determining the gain or loss from the sale of the property, the basis must be adjusted for cost depletion of $1,000 in 1931 and percentage depletion of $2,750 in 1932. However, the adjustment of such basis, proper for the determination of earnings and profits, is $1,000 for each year, or $2,000. Hence, the cost is to be adjusted only to the extent of $2,000, leaving an adjusted basis of $8,000 and the earnings and profits will be increased by $7,000, and not by $8,750. The difference of $1,750 is equal to the amount by which the percentage depletion for the year 1932 ($2,750) exceeds the depletion on cost for that year ($1,000) and has already been applied in the computation of earnings and profits for the year 1932 by taking into account only $1,000 instead of $2,750 for depletion in the computation of such earnings and profits. (See § 1.316-1.)

Example (2). If, in example (1), above, the property, instead of being sold, is exchanged in a transaction described in section 1031 for like property having a fair market value of $7,750 and cash of $7,250, then the increase in earnings and profits amounts to $7,000, that is, $15,000 ($7,750 plus $7,250) minus the basis of $8,000. However, in computing taxable income of Corporation X, the gain is $8,750, that is, $15,000 minus $6,250 ($10,000 less depletion of $3,750), of which only $7,250 is recognized because the recognized gain cannot exceed the sum of money received in the transaction. See section 1031(b)

and the corresponding provisions of prior revenue laws. If, however, the cash received was only $2,250 and the value of the property received was $12,750, then the increase in earnings and profits would be $2,250, that amount being the gain recognized under section 1031.

Example (3). On January 1, 1973, corporation X purchased for $10,000 a depreciable asset with an estimated useful life of 20 years and no salvage value. In computing depreciation on the asset, corporation X used the declining balance method with a rate twice the straight line rate. On December 31, 1976, the asset was sold for $9,000. Under section 1016(a)(2), the basis of the asset is adjusted for depreciation allowed for the years 1973 through 1976, or a total of $3,439. Thus, X realizes a gain of $2,439 (the excess of the amount realized, $9,000, over the adjusted basis, $6,561). However, the proper adjustment to basis for the purpose of determining earnings and profits is only $2,000, i.e., the total amount which, under § 1.312-15, was applied in the computation of earnings and profits for the years 1973-76. Hence, upon sale of the asset, earnings and profits are increased by only $1,000, i.e., the excess of the amount realized, $9,000, over the adjusted basis for earnings and profits purposes, $8,000.

(d) For adjustment and allocation of the earnings and profits of the transferor as between the transferor and the transferee in cases where the transfer of property by one corporation to another corporation results in the nonrecognition in whole or in part of gain or loss, see § 1.312-10; and see section 381 for earnings and profits of successor corporations in certain transactions. [Reg. § 1.312-7.]

☐ [*T.D. 6152, 12-2-55. Amended by T.D. 7221, 11-20-72.*]

§ 1.312-8. Effect on earnings and profits of receipt of tax-free distributions requiring adjustment or allocation of basis of stock.—(a) In order to determine the effect on earnings and profits, where a corporation receives (after February 28, 1913) from a second corporation a distribution which (under the law applicable to the year in which the distribution was made) was not a taxable dividend to the shareholders of the second corporation, section 312(f) prescribes certain rules. It provides that the amount of such distribution shall not increase the earnings and profits of the first or receiving corporation in the following cases: (1) No such increase shall be made in respect of the part of such distribution which (under the law applicable to the year in which the distribution was made) is directly applied in reduction of the basis of the stock in respect of which the distribution was made and (2) no such increase shall be made if (under the law applicable to the year in which the distribution was made) the distribution causes the basis of the stock in respect of which the distribution was made to be allocated between such stock and the property received (or such basis would but for section 307(b) be so allocated). Where, therefore, the law (applicable to the year in which the distribution was made, as, for example, a distribution in 1934 from earnings and profits accumulated before March 1, 1913) requires that the amount of such distribution shall be applied against and reduce the basis of the stock with respect to which the distribution was made, there is no increase in the earnings and profits by reason of the receipt of such distribution. Similarly, where there is received by a corporation a distribution from another corporation in the form of a stock dividend and the law applicable to the year in which such distribution was made requires the allocation, as between the old stock and the stock received as a dividend, of the basis of the old stock (or such basis would but for section 307(b) be so allocated), then there is no increase in the earnings and profits by reason of the receipt of such stock dividend even though such stock dividend constitutes income within the meaning of the sixteenth amendment to the Constitution.

(b) The principles set forth in paragraph (a) of this section may be illustrated by the following examples:

Example (1). Corporation X in 1955 distributed to Corporation Y, one of its shareholders, $10,000 which was out of earnings or profits accumulated before March 1, 1913, and did not exceed the adjusted basis of the stock in respect of which the distribution was made. This amount of $10,000 was, therefore, a tax-free distribution and under the provisions of section 301(c)(2) must be applied against and reduce the adjusted basis of the stock in respect of which the distribution was made. The earnings and profits of Corporation Y are not increased by reason of the receipt of this distribution.

Example (2). Corporation Z in 1955 had outstanding common and preferred stock of which Corporation Y held 100 shares of the common and no preferred. The stock had a cost basis to Corporation Y of $100 per share, or a total cost of $10,000. In December of that year it received a dividend of 100 shares of the preferred stock of Corporation Z. Such distribution is a stock dividend which, under section 305, was not taxable and was accordingly not included in the gross income of Corporation Y. The original cost of $10,000 is allocated to the 200 shares of Corporation Z none of which has been sold or otherwise disposed of by Corporation Y. See section 307 and § 1.307-1. The earnings and profits of Corporation Y are not increased by reason of the receipt of such stock dividend. [Reg. § 1.312-8.]

☐ [*T.D.* 6152, 12-2-55.]

§ 1.312-10. Allocation of earnings in certain corporate separations.—(a) If one corporation transfers part of its assets constituting an active trade or business to another corporation in a transaction to which section 368(a)(1)(D) applies and immediately thereafter the stock and securities of the controlled corporation are distributed in a distribution or exchange to which section 355 (or so much of section 356 as relates to section 355) applies, the earnings and profits of the distributing corporation immediately before the transaction shall be allocated between the distributing corporation and the controlled corporation. In the case of a newly created controlled corporation, such allocation generally shall be made in proportion to the fair market value of the business or businesses (and interests in any other properties) retained by the distributing corporation and the business or businesses (and interests in any other properties) of the controlled corporation immediately after the transaction. In a proper case, allocation shall be made between the distributing corporation and the controlled corporation in proportion to the net basis of the assets transferred and of the assets retained or by such other method as may be appropriate under the facts and circumstances of the case. The term "net basis" means the basis of the assets less liabilities assumed or liabilities to which such assets are subject. The part of the earnings and profits of the taxable year of the distributing corporation in which the transaction occurs allocable to the controlled corporation shall be included in the computation of the earnings and profits of the first taxable year of the controlled corporation ending after the date of the transaction.

(b) If a distribution or exchange to which section 355 applies (or so much of section 356 as relates to section 355) is not in pursuance of a plan meeting the requirements of a reorganization as defined in section 368(a)(1)(D), the earnings and profits of the distributing corporation shall be decreased by the lesser of the following amounts:

(1) The amount by which the earnings and profits of the distributing corporation would have been decreased if it had transferred the stock of the controlled corporation to a new corporation in a reorganization to which section 368(a)(1)(D) applied and immediately thereafter distributed the stock of such new corporation or,

(2) The net worth of the controlled corporation. (For this purpose the term "net worth" means the sum of the bases of all of the properties plus cash minus all liabilities.)

Reg. § 1.312-10(b)(2)

If the earnings and profits of the controlled corporation immediately before the transaction are less than the amount of the decrease in earnings and profits of the distributing corporation (including a case in which the controlled corporation has a deficit) the earnings and profits of the controlled corporation, after the transaction, shall be equal to the amount of such decrease. If the earnings and profits of the controlled corporation immediately before the transaction are more than the amount of the decrease in the earnings and profits of the distributing corporation, they shall remain unchanged.

(c) In no case shall any part of a deficit of a distributing corporation within the meaning of section 355 be allocated to a controlled corporation. [Reg. § 1.312-10.]

☐ [*T.D.* 6152, 12-2-55.]

§ 1.312-11. Effect on earnings and profits of certain other tax-free exchanges, tax-free distributions, and tax-free transfers from one corporation to another.—(a) If property is transferred by one corporation to another, and, under the law applicable to the year in which the transfer was made, no gain or loss was recognized (or was recognized only to the extent of the property received other than that permitted by such law to be received without the recognition of gain), then proper adjustment and allocation of the earnings and profits of the transferor shall be made as between the transferor and the transferee. Transfers to which the preceding sentence applies include contributions to capital, transfers under section 351, transfers in connection with reorganizations under section 368, transfers in liquidations under section 332 and intercompany transfers during a period of affiliation. However, if, for example, property is transferred from one corporation to another in a transaction under section 351 or as a contribution to capital and the transfer is not followed or preceded by a reorganization, a transaction under section 302(a) involving a substantial part of the transferor's stock, or a total or partial liquidation, then ordinarily no allocation of the earnings and profits of the transferor shall be made. For specific rules as to allocation of earnings and profits in certain reorganizations under section 368 and in certain liquidations under section 332 see section 381 and the regulations thereunder. For allocation of earnings and profits in certain corporate separations see section 312(i) and § 1.312-10.

(b) The general rule provided in section 316 that every distribution is made out of earnings or profits to the extent thereof and from the most recently accumulated earnings or profits does not apply to:

(1) The distribution, in pursuance of a plan of reorganization, by or on behalf of a corporation a party to the reorganization, or in a transaction subject to section 355, to its shareholders—

(i) Of stock or securities in such corporation or in another corporation a party to the reorganization in any taxable year beginning before January 1, 1934, without the surrender by the distributees of stock or securities in such corporation (see section 112(g) of the Revenue Act of 1932 (47 Stat. 197)); or

(ii) Of stock (other than preferred stock) in another corporation which is a party to the reorganization without the surrender by the distributees of stock in the distributing corporation if the distribution occurs after October 20, 1951, and is subject to section 112(b)(11) of the Internal Revenue Code of 1939; or

(iii) Of stock or securities in such corporation or in another corporation a party to the reorganization in any taxable year beginning before January 1, 1939, or on or after such date, in exchange for its stock or securities in a transaction to which section 112(b)(3) of the Internal Revenue Code of 1939 was applicable; or

(iv) Of stock or securities in such corporation or in another corporation in exchange for its stock or securities in a transaction subject to section 354 or 355,

if no gain to the distributees from the receipt of such stock or securities was recognzied by law.

(2) The distribution in any taxable year (beginning before January 1, 1939, or on or after such date) of stock or securities, or other property or money, to a corporation in complete liquidation of another corporation, under the circumstances described in section 112(b)(6) of the Revenue Act of 1936 (49 Stat. 1679), the Revenue Act of 1938 (52 Stat. 485), of the Internal Revenue Code of 1939, or section 332 of the Internal Revenue Code of 1954.

(3) The distribution in any taxable year (beginning after December 31, 1939 [1938]), of stock or securities, or other property or money, in the case of an exchange or distribution described in section 371 of the Internal Revenue Code of 1939 or in section 1081 of the Internal Revenue Code of 1954 (relating to exchanges and distributions in obedience to orders of the Securities and Exchange Commission), if no gain to the distributee from the receipt of such stock, securities, or other property or money was recognized by law.

(4) A stock dividend which was not subject to tax in the hands of the distributee because either it did not constitute income to him within the meaning of the sixteenth amendment to the Constitution or because exempt to him under section

115(f) of the Revenue Act of 1934 (48 Stat. 712) or a corresponding provision of a prior revenue act, or section 305 of the Code.

(5) The distribution, in a taxable year of the distributee beginning after December 31, 1931, by or on behalf of an insolvent corporation, in connection with a section 112(b)(10) reorganization under the Internal Revenue Code of 1939, or in a transaction subject to section 371 of the Internal Revenue Code of 1954, of stock or securities in a corporation organized or made use of to effectuate the plan of reorganization, if under section 112(I) of the Internal Revenue Code of 1939 or sections 371 of the Internal Revenue Code of 1954 no gain to the distributee from the receipt of such stock or securities was recognized by law.

(c) A distribution described in paragraph (b) of this section does not diminish the earnings or profits of any corporation. In such cases, the earnings or profits remain intact and available for distribution as dividends by the corporation making such distribution, or by another corporation to which the earnings or profits are transferred upon such reorganization or other exchange. In the case, however, of amounts distributed in liquidation (other than a tax-free liquidation or reorganization described in paragraph (b)(1), (2), (3), or (5) of this section) the earnings or profits of the corporation making the distribution are diminished by the portion of such distribution properly chargeable to earnings or profits accumulated after February 28, 1913, after first deducting from the amount of such distribution the portion thereof allocable to capital account.

* * *

[Reg. § 1.312-11.]

☐ [*T.D. 6152, 12-2-55. Amended by T.D. 6476, 6-30-60.*]

§ 1.312-15. Effect of depreciation on earnings and profits.—(a) *Depreciation for taxable years beginning after June 30, 1972*—(1) *In general.* Except as provided in subparagraph (2) of this paragraph and paragraph (c) of this section, for purposes of computing the earnings and profits of a corporation (including a real estate investment trust as defined in section 856) for any taxable year beginning after June 30, 1972, the allowance for depreciation (and amortization, if any) shall be deemed to be the amount which would be allowable for such year if the straight line method of depreciation had been used for all property for which depreciation is allowable for each taxable year beginning after June 30, 1972. Thus, for taxable years beginning after June 30, 1972, in determining the earnings and profits of a corporation, depreciation must be computed under the straight line method, notwithstanding that in determining taxable income the corpora-

tion uses an accelerated method of depreciation described in subparagraph (A), (B), or (C) of section 312(m)(2) or elects to amortize the basis of property under section 169, 184, 187, or 188, or any similar provision.

(2) *Exception.* (i) If, for any taxable year beginning after June 30, 1972, a method of depreciation is used by a corporation in computing taxable income which the Secretary or his delegate has determined results in a reasonable allowance under section 167(a) and which is not a declining balance method of depreciation (described in § 1.167(b)-2), the sum of the years-digits methods (described in § 1.167(b)-3), or any other method allowed solely by reason of the application of subsection (b)(4) or (j)(1)(C) of section 167, then the adjustment to earnings and profits for depreciation for such year shall be determined under the method so used (in lieu of the straight line method).

(ii) The Commissioner has determined that the "unit of production" (see § 1.167(b)-0 (b)), and the "machine hour" methods of depreciation, when properly used under appropriate circumstances, meet the requirements of subdivision (i) of this subparagraph. Thus, the adjustment to earnings and profits for depreciation (for the taxable year for which either of such methods is properly used under appropriate circumstances) shall be determined under whichever of such methods is used to compute taxable income.

(3) *Determinations under straight line method.* (i) In the case of property with respect to which an allowance for depreciation is claimed in computing taxable income, the determination of the amount which would be allowable under the straight line method shall be based on the manner in which the corporation computes depreciation in determining taxable income. Thus, if an election under § 1.167(a)-11 is in effect with respect to the property, the amount of depreciation which would be allowable under the straight line method shall be determined under § 1.167(a)-11(g)(3). On the other hand, if property is not depreciated under the provisions of § 1.167(a)-11, the amount of depreciation which would be allowable under the straight line method shall be determined under § 1.167(b)-1. Any election made under section 167(f), with respect to reducing the amount of salvage value taken into account in computing the depreciation allowance for certain property, or any convention adopted under § 1.167(a)-10(b) or § 1.167(a)-11(c)(2), with respect to additions and retirements from multiple asset accounts, which is used in computing depreciation for taxable income shall be used in computing depreciation for earnings and profits purposes.

(ii) In the case of property with respect to which an election to amortize is in effect under section 169, 184, 187, or 188, or any similar provision, the amount which would be allowable under the straight line method of depreciation shall be determined under the provisions of § 1.167(b)-1. Thus, the cost or other basis of the property, less its estimated salvage value, is to be deducted in equal annual amounts over the period of the estimated useful life of the property. In computing the amount of depreciation for earnings and profits purposes, a taxpayer may utilize the provisions of section 167(f) (relating to the reduction in the amount of salvage value taken into account in computing the depreciation allowance for certain property) and any convention which could have been adopted for such property under § 1.167(a)-10(b) (relating to additions and retirements from multiple asset accounts).

* * *

(d) *Books and records.* Wherever different methods of depreciation are used for taxable income and earnings and profits purposes, records shall be maintained which show the depreciation taken for earnings and profits purposes each year and which will allow computation of the adjusted basis of the property in each account using the depreciation taken for earnings and profits purposes. [Reg. § 1.312-15.]

☐ [*T.D.* 7221, 11-20-72.]

§ 1.316-1. Dividends.—(a)(1) The term "dividend" for the purpose of subtitle A of the Code (except when used in subchapter L, chapter 1 of the Code, in any case where the reference is to dividends and similar distributions of insurance companies paid to policyholders as such) comprises any distribution of property as defined in section 317 in the ordinary course of business, even though extraordinary in amount, made by a domestic or foreign corporation to its shareholders out of either—

(i) Earnings and profits accumulated since February 28, 1913, or

(ii) Earnings and profits of the taxable year computed without regard to the amount of the earnings and profits (whether of such year or accumulated since February 28, 1913) at the time the distribution was made.

The earnings and profits of the taxable year shall be computed as of the close of such year, without diminution by reason of any distributions made during the taxable year. For the purpose of determining whether a distribution constitutes a dividend, it is unnecessary to ascertain the amount of the earnings and profits accumulated since February 28, 1913, if the earnings and profits of the taxable year are equal to or in excess of the total

amount of the distributions made within such year.

(2) Where a corporation distributes property to its shareholders on or after June 22, 1954, the amount of the distribution which is a dividend to them may not exceed the earnings and profits of the distributing corporation.

(3) The rule of (2) above may be illustrated by the following example:

Example. X and Y, individuals, each own one-half of the stock of Corporation A which has earnings and profits of $10,000. Corporation A distributes property having a basis of $6,000 and a fair market value of $16,000 to its shareholders, each shareholder receiving property with a basis of $3,000 and with a fair market value of $8,000 in a distribution to which section 301 applies. The amount taxable to each shareholder as a dividend under section 301(c) is $5,000.

* * *

(e) The application of section 316 may be illustrated by the following examples:

Example (1). At the beginning of the calendar year 1955, Corporation M had an operating deficit of $200,000 and the earnings and profits for the year amounted to $100,000. Beginning on March 16, 1955, the corporation made quarterly distributions of $25,000 during the taxable year to its shareholders. Each distribution is a taxable dividend in full, irrespective of the actual or the pro rata amount of the earnings and profits on hand at any of the dates of distribution, since the total distributions made during the year ($100,000) did not exceed the total earnings and profits of the year ($100,000).

* * *

[Reg. § 1.316-1.]

☐ [*T.D.* 6152, 12-2-55. *Amended by T.D.* 6625, 12-18-62, *T.D.* 6949, 4-8-68, *T.D.* 7767, 2-3-81 and *T.D.* 7936, 1-17-84.]

§ 1.316-2. Sources of distribution in general.—(a) For the purpose of income taxation every distribution made by a corporation is made out of earnings and profits to the extent thereof and from the most recently accumulated earnings and profits. In determining the source of a distribution, consideration should be given first, to the earnings and profits of the taxable year; second, to the earnings and profits accumulated since February 28, 1913, only in the case where, and to the extent that, the distributions made during the taxable year are not regarded as out of the earnings and profits of that year; third, to the earnings and profits accumulated before March 1, 1913, only after all the earnings and profits of the taxable year and all the earnings and profits accumulated since February 28, 1913, have been distributed; and, fourth, to sources other than earnings and profits only after the earnings and profits have been distributed.

(b) If the earnings and profits of the taxable year (computed as of the close of the year without diminution by reason of any distributions made during the year and without regard to the amount of earnings and profits at the time of the distribution) are sufficient in amount to cover all the distributions made during that year, then each distribution is a taxable dividend. See § 1.316-1. If the distributions made during the taxable year consist only of money and exceed the earnings and profits of such year, then that proportion of each distribution which the total of the earnings and profits of the year bears to the total distributions made during the year shall be regarded as out of the earnings and profits of that year. The portion of each such distribution which is not regarded as out of earnings and profits of the taxable year shall be considered a taxable dividend to the extent of the earnings and profits accumulated since February 28, 1913, and available on the date of the distribution. In any case in which it is necessary to determine the amount of earnings and profits accumulated since February 28, 1913, and the actual earnings and profits to the date of a

distribution within any taxable year (whether beginning before January 1, 1936, or, in the case of an operating deficit, on or after that date) cannot be shown, the earnings and profits for the year (or accounting period, if less than a year) in which the distribution was made shall be prorated to the date of the distribution not counting the date on which the distribution was made.

(c) The provisions of the section may be illustrated by the following example:

Example. At the beginning of the calendar year 1955, Corporation M had $12,000 in earnings and profits accumulated since February 28, 1913. Its earnings and profits for 1955 amounted to $30,000. During the year it made quarterly cash distributions of $15,000 each. Of each of the four distributions made, $7,500 (that portion of $15,000 which the amount of $30,000, the total earnings and profits of the taxable year, bears to $60,000, the total distributions made during the year) was paid out of the earnings and profits of the taxable year; and of the first and second distributions, $7,500 and $4,500, respectively, were paid out of the earnings and profits accumulated after February 28, 1913, and before the taxable year, as follows:

Distributions during 1955		Portion out of earnings and profits of the taxable year	Portion out of earnings accumulated since Feb. 28, 1913, and before the taxable year	Taxable amount of each distribution
Date	Amount			
March 10	$15,000	$7,500	$7,500	$15,000
June 10	15,000	7,500	4,500	12,000
September 10	15,000	7,500	....	7,500
December 10	15,000	7,500	....	7,500
Total amount taxable as dividends				42,000

(d) Any distribution by a corporation out of earnings and profits accumulated before March 1, 1913, or out of increase in value of property accrued before March 1, 1913 (whether or not realized by sale or other disposition, and, if realized, whether before, on, or after March 1, 1913), is not a dividend within the meaning of subtitle A of the Code.

(e) A reserve set up out of gross income by a corporation and maintained for the purpose of making good any loss of capital assets on account of depletion or depreciation is not a part of surplus out of which ordinary dividends may be paid. A distribution made from a depletion or a depreciation reserve based upon the cost or other basis of the property will not be considered as having been paid out of earnings and profits, but the amount thereof shall be applied against and reduce the cost or other basis of the stock upon which de-

clared. If such a distribution is in excess of the basis, the excess shall be taxed as a gain from the sale or other disposition of property as provided in section 301(c)(3)(A). A distribution from a depletion reserve based upon discovery value to the extent that such reserve represents the excess of the discovery value over the cost or other basis for determining gain or loss, is, when received by the shareholders, taxable as an ordinary dividend. The amount by which a corporation's percentage depletion allowance for any year exceeds depletion sustained on cost or other basis, that is, determined without regard to discovery or percentage depletion allowances for the year of distribution or prior years, constitutes a part of the corporation's "earnings and profits accumulated after February 28, 1913," within the meaning of section 316, and, upon distribution to shareholders, is taxable to them as a dividend. A distribu-

Reg. § 1.316-2(e)

tion made from that portion of a depletion reserve based upon a valuation as of March 1, 1913, which is in excess of the depletion reserve based upon cost, will not be considered as having been paid out of earnings and profits, but the amount of the distribution shall be applied against and reduce the cost or other basis of the stock upon which declared. See section 301. No distribution, however, can be made from such a reserve until all the earnings and profits of the corporation have first been distributed. [Reg. § 1.316-2.]

    ☐ [*T.D.* 6152, 12-2-55.]

§ 1.317-1. Property defined.—The term "property", for purposes of Part 1, subchapter C, chapter 1 of the Code, means any property (including money, securities, and indebtedness to the corporation) other than stock, or rights to acquire stock, in the corporation making the distribution. [Reg. § 1.317-1.]

    ☐ [*T.D.* 6152, 12-2-55.]

§ 1.318-1. Constructive ownership of stock; introduction.—(a) For the purposes of certain provisions of chapter 1 of the Code, section 318(a) provides that stock owned by a taxpayer includes stock constructively owned by such taxpayer under the rules set forth in such section. An individual is considered to own the stock owned, directly or indirectly, by or for his spouse (other than a spouse who is legally separated from the individual under a decree of divorce or separate maintenance), and by or for his children, grandchildren, and parents. Under section 318(a)(2) and (3), constructive ownership rules are established for partnerships and partners, estates and beneficiaries, trusts and beneficiaries, and corporations and stockholders. If any person has an option to acquire stock, such stock is considered as owned by such person. The term "option" includes an option to acquire such an option and each of a series of such options.

(b) In applying section 318(a) to determine the stock ownership of any person for any one purpose—(1) A corporation shall not be considered to own its own stock by reason of section 318(a)(3)(C);

    (2) In any case in which an amount of stock owned by any person may be included in the computation more than one time, such stock shall be included only once, in the manner in which it will impute to the person concerned the largest total stock ownership; and

    (3) In determining the 50-percent requirement of section 318(a)(2)(C) and (3)(C) all of the stock owned actually and constructively by the person concerned shall be aggregated. [Reg. § 1.318-1.]

    ☐ [*T.D.* 6152, 12-2-55. *Amended by T.D.* 6598, 4-25-62, *T.D.* 6621, 11-30-62 *and T.D.* 6969, 8-22-68.]

§ 1.318-2. Application of general rules.—(a) The application of paragraph (b) of § 1.318-1 may be illustrated by the following examples:

Example (1). H, an individual owns all of the stock of Corporation A. Corporationo A is not considered to own the stock owned by H in Corporation A.

Example (2). H, an individual, his wife, W, and his son, S, each own one-third of the stock of the Green Corporation. For purposes of determining the amount of stock owned by H, W, or S for the purpose of section 318(a)(2)(C) and (3)(C), the amount of stock held by the other members of the family shall be added pursuant to paragraph (b)(3) of § 1.318-1 in applying the 50-percent requirement of such section. H, W, or S, as the case may be, is for this purpose deemed to own 100 percent of the stock of the Green Corporation.

(b) The application of section 318(a)(1), relating to members of a family, may be illustrated by the following example:

Example. An individual, H, his wife, W, his son, S, and his grandson (S's son), G, own the 100 outstanding shares of stock of a corporation, each owning 25 shares. H, W, and S are each considered as owning 100 shares. G is considered as owning only 50 shares, that is, his own and his father's.

(c) The application of section 318(a)(2) and (3), relating to partnerships, trusts and corporations, may be illustrated by the following examples:

Example (1). A, an individual, has a 50 percent interest in a partnership. The partnership owns 50 of the 100 outstanding shares of stock of a corporation, the remaining 50 shares being owned by A. The partnership is considered as owning 100 shares. A is considered as owning 75 shares.

Example (2). A testamentary trust owns 25 of the outstanding 100 shares of stock of a corporation. A, an individual, who holds a vested remainder in the trust having a value, computed actuarially equal to 4 percent of the value of the trust property, owns the remaining 75 shares. Since the interest of A in the trust is a vested interest rather than a contingent interest (whether or not remote), the trust is considered as owning 100 shares. A is considered as owning 76 shares.

Example (3). The facts are the same as in (2), above, except that A's interest in the trust is a contingent remainder. A is considered as owning 76 shares. However, since A's interest in the trust is a remote contingent interest, the trust is not considered as owning any of the shares owned by A.

Example (4). A and B, unrelated individuals, own 70 percent and 30 percent, respectively, in value of the stock of Corporation M. Corporation M owns 50 of the 100 outstanding shares of stock of Corporation O, the remaining 50 shares being owned by A. Corporation M is considered as owning 100 shares of Corporation O, and A is considered as owning 85 shares.

Example (5). A and B, unrelated individuals, own 70 percent and 30 percent, respectively, of the stock of corporation M. A, B, and corporation M all own stock of corporation O. Since B owns less than 50 percent in value of the stock of corporation M, neither B nor corporation M constructively owns the stock of corporation O owned by the other. However, for purposes of certain sections of the Code, such as sections 304 and 856(d), the 50-percent limitation of section 318(a)(2)(C) and (3)(C) is disregarded or is reduced to less than 30 percent. For such purposes, B constructively owns his proportionate share of the stock of corporation O owned directly by corporation M, and corporation M constructively owns the stock of corporation O owned by B. [Reg. § 1.318-2.]

☐ [*T.D. 6152, 12-2-55. Amended by T.D. 6969, 8-22-68.*]

§ 1.318-3. Estates, trusts, and options.—(a) For the purpose of applying section 318(a), relating to estates, property of a decedent shall be considered as owned by his estate if such property is subject to administration by the executor or administrator for the purpose of paying claims against the estate and expenses of administration notwithstanding that, under local law, legal title to such property vests in the decedent's heirs, legatees or devisees immediately upon death. The term "beneficiary" includes any person entitled to receive property of a decedent pursuant to a will or pursuant to laws of descent and distribution. A person shall no longer be considered a beneficiary of an estate when all the property to which he is entitled has been received by him, when he no longer has a claim against the estate arising out of having been a beneficiary, and when there is only a remote possibility that it will be necessary for the estate to seek the return of property or to seek payment from him by contribution or otherwise to satisfy claims against the estate or expenses of administration. When, pursuant to the preceding sentence, a person ceases to be a beneficiary, stock owned by him shall not thereafter be considered owned by the estate, and stock owned by the estate shall not thereafter be considered owned by him. The application of section 318(a) relating to estates may be illustrated by the following examples:

Example (1). (a) A decedent's estate owns 50 of the 100 outstanding shares of stock of corporation X. The remaining shares are owned by three unrelated individuals, A, B, and C, who together own the entire interest in the estate. A owns 12 shares of stock of corporation X directly and is entitled to 50 percent of the estate. B owns 18 shares directly and has a life estate in the remaining 50 percent of the estate. C owns 20 shares directly and also owns the remainder interest after B's life estate.

(b) If section 318(a)(5)(C) applies (see paragraph (c)(3) of § 1.318-4), the stock of corporation X is considered to be owned as follows: the estate is considered as owning 80 shares, 50 shares directly, 12 shares constructively through A, and 18 shares constructively through B; A is considered as owning 37 shares, 12 shares directly, and 25 shares constructively (50 percent of the 50 shares owned directly by the estate); B is considered as owning 43 shares, 18 shares directly and 25 shares constructively (50 percent of the 50 shares owned directly by the estate); C is considered as owning 20 shares directly and no shares constructively. C is not considered a beneficiary of the estate under section 318(a) since he has no direct present interest in the property held by the estate nor in the income produced by such property.

(c) If section 318(a)(5)(C) does not apply, A is considered as owning nine additional shares (50 percent of the 18 shares owned constuctively by the estate through B), and B is considered as owning six additional shares (50 percent of the 12 shares owned constructively by the estate through A).

Example (2). Under the will of A, Blackacre is left to B for life, remainder to C, an unrelated individual. The residue of the estate consisting of stock of a corporation is left to D. B and D are beneficiaries of the estate under section 318(a). C is not considered a beneficiary since he has no direct present interest in Blackacre nor in the income produced by such property. The stock owned by the estate is considered as owned proportionately by B and D.

(b) For the purpose of section 318(a)(2)(B) stock owned by a trust will be considered as being owned by its beneficiaries only to the extent of the interest of such beneficiaries in the trust. Accordingly, the interest of income beneficiaries, remainder beneficiaries, and other beneficiaries will be computed on an actuarial basis. Thus, if a trust owns 100 percent of the stock of Corporation A, and if, on an actuarial basis, W's life interest in the trust is 15 percent, Y's life interest is 25 percent, and Z's remainder interest is 60 percent, under this provision W will be considered to be the owner of 15 percent of the stock of Corporation A, Y will be considered to be the owner of 25 percent of such stock, and Z will be considered to be the owner of 60 percent of such stock. The factors and methods prescribed in § 20.2031-7 of this chapter (Estate Tax Regulations) for use in ascertaining the value of an interest in property for estate tax purposes shall be used in determining a beneficiary's actuarial interest in a trust for purposes of this section. See § 20.2031-7 of this chapter (Estate Tax Regulations) for examples illustrating the use of these factors and methods.

(c) The application of section 318(a) relating to options may be illustrated by the following example:

Example. A and B, unrelated individuals, own all of the 100 outstanding shares of stock of a corporation, each owning 50 shares. A has an option to acquire 25 of B's shares and has an option to acquire a further option to acquire the remaining 25 of B's shares. A is considered as owning the entire 100 shares of stock of the corporation. [Reg. § 1.318-3.]

☐ [*T.D. 6152, 12-2-55. Amended by T.D. 6462, 5-5-60 and T.D. 6969, 8-22-68.*]

§ 1.318-4. Constructive ownership as actual ownership; exceptions.—(a) *In general.* Section 318(a)(5)(A) provides that, except as provided in section 318(a)(5)(B) and (C), stock constructively owned by a person by reason of the application of section 318(a)(1), (2), (3), or (4) shall be considered as actually owned by such person for purposes of applying section 318(a)(1), (2), (3), and (4). For example, if a trust owns 50 percent of the stock of corporation X, stock of corporation Y owned by corporation X which is attributed to the trust may be further attributed to the beneficiaries of the trust.

(b) *Constructive family ownership.* Section 318(a)(5)(B) provides that stock constructively owned by an individual by reason of ownership by a member of his family shall not be considered as owned by him for purposes of making another family member the constructive owner of such

stock under section 318(a)(1). For example, if F and his two sons, A and B, each own one-third of the stock of a corporation, under section 381(a)(1), A is treated as owning constructively the stock owned by his father but is not treated as owning the stock owned by B. Section 318(a)(5)(B) prevents the attribution of the stock of one brother through the father to the other brother, an attribution beyond the scope of section 318(a)(1) directly.

(c) *Reattribution.* (1) Section 318(a)(5)(C) provides that stock constructively owned by a partnership, estate, trust, or corporation by reason of the application of section 318(a)(3) shall not be considered as owned by it for purposes of applying section 318(a)(2) in order to make another the constructive owner of such stock. For example, if two unrelated individuals are beneficiaries of the same trust, stock held by one which is attributed to the trust under section 318(a)(3) is not reattributed from the trust to the other beneficiary. However, stock constructively owned by reason of section 318(a)(2) may be reattributed under section 318(a)(3). Thus, for example, if all the stock of corporations X and Y is owned by A, stock of corporation Z held by X is attributed to Y through A.

(2) Section 318(a)(5)(C) does not prevent reattribution under section 318(a)(2) of stock constructively owned by an entity under section 318(a)(3) if the stock is also constructively owned by the entity under section 318(a)(4). For example, if individuals A and B are beneficiaries of a trust and the trust has an option to buy stock from A, B is considered under section 318(a)(2)(B) as owning a proportionate part of such stock.

(3) Section 318(a)(5)(C) is effective on and after August 31, 1964, except that for purposes of sections 302 and 304 it does not apply with respect to distributions in payment for stock acquisitions or redemptions if such acquisitions or redemptions occurred before August 31, 1964. [Reg. § 1.318-4.]

☐ [*T.D. 6152, 12-2-55. Amended by T.D. 6969, 8-22-68.*]

Corporate Liquidations

[*Note: Reg. § 1.331-1 does not reflect the 1982 changes in Section 331 deleting all references to partial liquidations.*]

§ 1.331-1. Corporate liquidations.—(a) Section 331 contains rules governing the extent to which gain or loss is recognized to a shareholder receiving a distribution in complete or partial liquidation of a corporation. Under section 331(a)(1), it is provided that amounts distributed in complete liquidation of a corporation shall be treated as in full payment in exchange for the

stock. Under section 331(a)(2), it is provided that amounts distributed in partial liquidation of a corporation shall be treated as in full or part payment in exchange for the stock. For this purpose, the term "partial liquidation" shall have the meaning ascribed in section 346. If section 331 is applicable to the distribution of property by a corporation, section 301 (relating to the effects on a shareholder of distributions of property) has no application other than to a distribution in complete liquidation to which section 316(b)(2)(B) applies. See paragraph (b)(2) of § 1.316-1.

(b) The gain or loss to a shareholder from a distribution in partial or complete liquidation is to be determined under section 1001 by comparing the amount of the distribution with the cost or other basis of the stock. The gain or loss will be recognized to the extent provided in section 1002 and will be subject to the provisions of parts I, II, and III (section 1201 and following), subchapter P, chapter 1 of the Code.

(c) A liquidation which is followed by a transfer to another corporation of all or part of the assets of the liquidating corporation or which is preceded by such a transfer may, however, have the effect of the distribution of a dividend or of a transaction in which no loss is recognized and gain is recognized only to the extent of "other property." See sections 301 and 356.

(d) In every case in which a shareholder transfers stock in exchange for property to the corporation which issued such stock, the facts and circumstances shall be reported on his return unless the property is part of a distribution made pursuant to a corporate resolution reciting that the distribution is made in liquidation of the corporation and the corporation is completely liquidated and dissolved within one year after the distribution. See section 6043 for requirements relating to returns by corporations.

(e) The provisions of this section may be illustrated by the following example:

Example. A, an individual who makes his income tax returns on the calendar year basis, owns 20 shares of stock of the P Corporation, a domestic corporation, 10 shares of which were acquired in 1951 at a cost of $1,500 and the remainder of 10 shares in December 1954 at a cost of $2,900. He receives in April 1955 a distribution of $250 per share in complete liquidation, or $2,500 on the 10 shares acquired in 1951, and $2,500 on the 10 shares acquired in December 1954. The gain of $1,000 on the shares acquired in 1951 is a long-term capital gain to be treated as provided in parts I, II, and III (section 1201 and following), subchapter P, chapter 1 of the Code. The loss of $400 on the shares acquired in 1954 is a short-term capital loss to be treated as provided in parts I, II, and III (section 1201 and following), subchapter P, chapter 1 of the Code. [Reg. § 1.331-1.]

□ [*T.D.* 6152, 12-2-55. *Amended by T.D.* 6949, 4-8-68.]

§ **1.332-1. Distributions in liquidation of subsidiary corporation; general.**—Under the general rule prescribed by section 331 for the treatment of distributions in liquidation of a corporation, amounts received by one corporation in complete liquidation of another corporation are treated as in full payment in exchange for stock in such other corporation, and gain or loss from the receipt of such amounts is to be determined as provided in section 1001. Section 332 excepts from the general rule property received, under certain specifically described circumstances, by one corporation as a distribution in complete liquidation of the stock of another corporation and provides for the nonrecognition of gain or loss in those cases which meet the statutory requirements. Section 367 places a limitation on the application of section 332 in the case of foreign corporations. See section 334(b) for the basis for determining gain or loss from the subsequent sale of property received upon complete liquidations such as described in this section. See section 453(d)(4)(A) relative to distribution of installment obligations by subsidiary. [Reg. § 1.332-1.]

□ [*T.D.* 6152, 12-2-55.]

§ **1.332-2. Requirements for nonrecognition of gain or loss.**—(a) The nonrecognition of gain or loss is limited to the receipt of such property by a corporation which is the actual owner of stock (in the liquidating corporation) possessing at least 80 percent of the total combined voting power of all classes of stock entitled to vote and the owner of at least 80 percent of the total number of shares of all other classes of stock (except nonvoting stock which is limited and preferred as to dividends). The recipient corporation must have been the owner of the specified amount of such stock on the date of the adoption of the plan of liquidation and have continued so to be at all times until the receipt of the property. If the recipient corporation does not continue qualified with respect to the ownership of stock of the liquidating corporation and if the failure to continue qualified occurs at any time prior to the completion of the transfer of all the property, the provisions for the nonrecognition of gain or loss do not apply to any distribution received under the plan.

(b) Section 332 applies only to those cases in which the recipient corporation receives at least partial payment for the stock which it owns in the liquidating corporation. If section 332 is not applicable, see section 165(g) relative to allowance of losses on worthless securities.

(c) To constitute a distribution in complete liquidation within the meaning of section 332, the distribution must be (1) made by the liquidating corporation in complete cancellation or redemption of all of its stock in accordance with a plan of liquidation, or (2) one of a series of distributions in complete cancellation or redemption of all its stock in accordance with a plan of liquidation. Where there is more than one distribution, it is essential that a status of liquidation exist at the time the first distribution is made under the plan and that such status continue until the liquidation is completed. Liquidation is completed when the liquidating corporation and the receiver or trustees in liquidation are finally divested of all the property (both tangible and intangible). A status of liquidation exists when the corporation ceases to be a going concern and its activities are merely for the purpose of winding up its affairs, paying its debts and distributing any remaining balance to its shareholders. A liquidation may be completed prior to the actual dissolution of the liquidating corporation. However, legal dissolution of the corporation is not required. Nor will the mere retention of a nominal amount of assets for the sole purpose of preserving the corporation's legal existence disqualify the transaction. (See 26 CFR (1939) 39.22(a)-20 (Regulations 118).)

(d) If a transaction constitutes a distribution in complete liquidation within the meaning of the Internal Revenue Code of 1954 and satisfies the requirements of section 332, it is not material that it is otherwise described under the local law. If a liquidating corporation distributes all of its property in complete liquidation and if pursuant to the plan for such complete liquidation a corporation owning the specified amount of stock in the liquidating corporation receives property constituting amounts distributed in complete liquidation within the meaning of the Code and also receives other property attributable to shares not owned by it, the transfer of the property to the recipient corporation shall not be treated, by reason of the receipt of such other property, as not being a distribution (or one of a series of distributions) in complete cancellation or redemption of all of the stock of the liquidating corporation within the meaning of section 332, even though for purposes of those provisions relating to corporate reorganizations the amount received by the recipient corporation in excess of its ratable share is regarded as acquired upon the issuance of its stock or securities in a tax-free exchange as described in section 361 and the cancellation or redemption of the stock not owned by the recipient corporation is treated as occurring as a result of a tax-free exchange described in section 354.

(e) The application of these rules may be illustrated by the following example:

Example. On September 1, 1954, the M Corporation had outstanding capital stock consisting of 3,000 shares of common stock, par value $100 a share, and 1,000 shares of preferred stock, par value $100 a share, which preferred stock was limited and preferred as to dividends and had no voting rights. On that date, and thereafter until the date of dissolution of the M Corporation, the O Corporation owned 2,500 shares of common

stock of the M Corporation. By statutory merger consummated on October 1, 1954, pursuant to a plan of liquidation adopted on September 1, 1954, the M Corporation was merged into the O Corporation, the O Corporation under the plan issuing stock which was received by the other holders of the stock of the M Corporation. The receipt by the O Corporation of the properties of the M Corporation is a distribution received by the O Corporation in complete liquidation of the M Corporation within the meaning of section 332, and no gain or loss is recognized as the result of the receipt of such properties. [Reg. § 1.332-2.]

☐ [*T.D.* 6152, 12-2-55.]

§ 1.332-3. Liquidations completed within one taxable year.—If in a liquidation completed within one taxable year pursuant to a plan of complete liquidation, distributions in complete liquidation are received by a corporation which owns the specified amount of stock in the liquidating corporation and which continues qualified with respect to the ownership of such stock until the transfer of all the property within such year is completed (see paragraph (a) of § 1.332-2), then no gain or loss shall be recognized with respect to the distributions received by the recipient corporation. In such case no waiver or bond is required of the recipient corporation under section 332. [Reg. § 1.332-3.]

☐ [*T.D.* 6152, 12-2-55.]

§ 1.332-4. Liquidations covering more than one taxable year.—(a) If the plan of liquidation is consummated by a series of distributions extending over a period of more than one taxable year, the nonrecognition of gain or loss with respect to the distributions in liquidation shall, in addition to the requirements of § 1.332-2, be subject to the following requirements:

(1) In order for the distribution in liquidation to be brought within the exception provided in section 332 to the general rule for computing gain or loss with respect to amounts received in liquidation of a corporation, the entire property of the corporation shall be transferred in accordance with a plan of liquidation, which plan shall include a statement showing the period within which the transfer of the property of the liquidating corporation to the recipient corporation is to be completed. The transfer of all the property under the liquidation must be completed within three years from the close of the taxable year during which is made the first of the series of distributions under the plan.

(2) For each of the taxable years which falls wholly or partly within the period of liquidation, the recipient corporation shall, at the time of filing its return, file with the district director of internal revenue a waiver of the statute of limita-

Reg. § 1.332-3

tions on assessment. The waiver shall be executed on such form as may be prescribed by the Commissioner and shall extend the period of assessment of all income and profits taxes for each such year to a date not earlier than one year after the last date of the period for assessment of such taxes for the last taxable year in which the transfer of the property of such liquidating corporation to the controlling corporation may be completed in accordance with section 332. Such waiver shall also contain such other terms with respect to assessment as may be considered by the Commissioner to be necessary to insure the assessment and collection of the correct tax liability for each year within the period of liquidation.

(3) For each of the taxable years which falls wholly or partly within the period of liquidation, the recipient corporation may be required to file a bond, the amount of which shall be fixed by the district director. The bond shall contain all terms specified by the Commissioner, including provisions unequivocally assuring prompt payment of the excess of income and profits taxes (plus penalty, if any, and interest) as computed by the district director without regard to the provisions of sections 332 and 334(b) over such taxes computed with regard to such provisions, regardless of whether such excess may or may not be made the subject of a notice of deficiency under section 6212 and regardless of whether it may or may not be assessed. Any bond required under section 332 shall have such surety or sureties as the Commissioner may require. However, see 6 U.S.C.15, providing that where a bond is required by law or regulations, in lieu of surety or sureties there may be deposited bonds or notes of the United States. Only surety companies holding certificates of authority from the Secretary as acceptable sureties on Federal bonds will be approved as sureties. The bonds shall be executed in triplicate so that the Commissioner, the taxpayer, and the surety or the depository may each have a copy. On and after September 1, 1953, the functions of the Commissioner with respect to such bonds shall be performed by the district director for the internal revenue district in which the return was filed and any bond filed on or after such date shall be filed with such district director.

(b) Pending the completion of the liquidation, if there is a compliance with paragraph (a)(1), (2), and (3) of this section and § 1.332-2 with respect to the nonrecognition of gain or loss, the income and profits tax liability of the recipient corporation for each of the years covered in whole or in part by the liquidation shall be determined without the recognition of any gain or loss on account of the receipt of the distributions in liquidation. In such determination, the basis of the property or properties received by the recipient corporation

shall be determined in accordance with section 334(b). However, if the transfer of the property is not completed within the three-year period allowed by section 332 or if the recipient corporation does not continue qualified with respect to the ownership of stock of the liquidating corporation as required by that section, gain or loss shall be recognized with respect to each distribution and the tax liability for each of the years covered in whole or in part by the liquidation shall be recomputed without regard to the provisions of section 332 or section 334(b) and the amount of any additional tax due upon such recomputation shall be promptly paid. [Reg. § 1.332-4.]

☐ [*T.D.* 6152, 12-2-55.]

§ 1.332-5. Distributions in liquidation as affecting minority interests.—Upon the liquidation of a corporation in pursuance of a plan of complete liquidation, the gain or loss of minority shareholders shall be determined without regard to section 332, since it does not apply to that part of distributions in liquidation received by minority shareholders. [Reg. § 1.332-5.]

☐ [*T.D.* 6152, 12-2-55.]

§ 1.332-7. Indebtedness of subsidiary to parent.—If section 332(a) is applicable to the receipt of the subsidiary's property in complete liquidation, then no gain or loss shall be recognized to the subsidiary upon the transfer of such properties even though some of the properties are transferred in satisfaction of the subsidiary's indebtedness to its parent. However, any gain or loss realized by the parent corporation on such satisfaction of indebtedness, shall be recognized to the parent corporation at the time of the liquidation. For example, if the parent corporation purchased its subsidiary's bonds at a discount and upon liquidation of the subsidiary the parent corporation receives payment for the face amount of such bonds, gain shall be recognized to the parent corporation. Such gain shall be measured by the difference between the cost or other basis of the bonds to the parent and the amount received in payment of the bonds. [Reg. § 1.332-7.]

☐ [*T.D.* 6152, 12-2-55.]

§ 1.338-1. General principles; status of old target and new target.—(a) *In general*—(1) *Deemed transaction.* Elections are available under section 338 when a purchasing corporation acquires the stock of another corporation (the target) in a qualified stock purchase. One type of election, under section 338(g), is available to the purchasing corporation. Another type of election, under section 338(h)(10), is, in more limited circumstances, available jointly to the purchasing corporation and the sellers of the stock. (Rules concerning eligibility for these elections are contained in § § 1.338-2, 1.338-3, and 1.338(h)(10)-1.)

Reg. § 1.338-1(a)(1)

Although target is a single corporation under corporate law, if a section 338 election is made, then two separate corporations, old target and new target, generally are considered to exist for purposes of subtitle A of the Internal Revenue Code. Old target is treated as transferring all of its assets to an unrelated person in exchange for consideration that includes the discharge of its liabilities (see § 1.1001-2(a)), and new target is treated as acquiring all of its assets from an unrelated person in exchange for consideration that includes the assumption of those liabilities. (Such transaction is, without regard to its characterization for Federal income tax purposes, referred to as the deemed asset sale and the income tax consequences thereof as the deemed sale tax consequences.) If a section 338(h)(10) election is made, old target is deemed to liquidate following the deemed asset sale.

(2) *Application of other rules of law.* Other rules of law apply to determine the tax consequences to the parties as if they had actually engaged in the transactions deemed to occur under section 338 and the regulations thereunder except to the extent otherwise provided in those regulations. See also § 1.338-6(c)(2). Other rules of law may characterize the transaction as something other than or in addition to a sale and purchase of assets; however, the transaction between old and new target must be a taxable transaction. For example, if target is an insurance company for which a section 338 election is made, the deemed asset sale would be characterized and taxed as an assumption-reinsurance transaction under applicable Federal income tax law. See § 1.817-4(d).

(3) *Overview.* Definitions and special nomenclature and rules for making the section 338 election are provided in § 1.338-2. Qualification for the section 338 election is addressed in § 1.338-3. The amount for which old target is treated as selling all of its assets (the aggregate deemed sale price, or ADSP) is addressed in § 1.338-4. The amount for which new target is deemed to have purchased all its assets (the adjusted grossed-up basis, or AGUB) is addressed in § 1.338-5. Section 1.338-6 addresses allocation both of ADSP among the assets old target is deemed to have sold and of AGUB among the assets new target is deemed to have purchased. Section 1.338-7 addresses allocation of ADSP or AGUB when those amounts subsequently change. Asset and stock consistency are addressed in § 1.338-8. International aspects of section 338 are covered in § 1.338-9. Rules for the filing of returns are provided in § 1.338-10. Eligibility for and treatment of section 338(h)(10) elections is addressed in § 1.338(h)(10)-1.

(b) *Treatment of target under other provisions of the Internal Revenue Code*—(1) *General rule for subtitle A.* Except as provided in this section, new target is treated as a new corporation that is unrelated to old target for purposes of subtitle A of the Internal Revenue Code. Thus—

(i) New target is not considered related to old target for purposes of section 168 and may make new elections under section 168 without taking into account the elections made by old target; and

(ii) New target may adopt, without obtaining prior approval from the Commissioner, any taxable year that meets the requirements of section 441 and any method of accounting that meets the requirements of section 446. Notwithstanding § 1.441-1T(b)(2), a new target may adopt a taxable year on or before the last day for making the election under section 338 by filing its first return for the desired taxable year on or before that date.

(2) *Exceptions for subtitle A.* New target and old target are treated as the same corporation for purposes of—

(i) The rules applicable to employee benefit plans (including those plans described in sections 79, 104, 105, 106, 125, 127, 129, 132, 137, and 220), qualified pension, profit-sharing, stock bonus and annuity plans (sections 401(a) and 403(a)), simplified employee pensions (section 408(k)), tax qualified stock option plans (sections 422 and 423), welfare benefit funds (sections 419, 419A, 512(a)(3), and 4976), and voluntary employee benefit associations (section 501(a)(9) and the regulations thereunder);

(ii) Sections 1311 through 1314 (relating to the mitigation of the effect of limitations), if a section 338(h)(10) election is not made for target;

(iii) Section 108(e)(5) (relating to the reduction of purchase money debt);

(iv) Section 45A (relating to the Indian Employment Credit), section 51 (relating to the Work Opportunity Credit), section 51A (relating to the Welfare to Work Credit), and section 1396 (relating to the Empowerment Zone Act);

(v) Sections 401(h) and 420 (relating to medical benefits for retirees);

(vi) Section 414 (relating to definitions and special rules); and

(vii) Any other provision designated in the Internal Revenue Bulletin by the Internal Revenue Service. See § 601.601(d)(2)(ii) of this chapter. See, for example, § 1.1001-3(e)(4)(i)(F) providing that an election under section 338 does not result in the substitution of a new obligor on target's debt. See also, for example, § 1.1502-77(e)(4), providing that an election under section 338 does not result in a deemed termination of target's existence for purposes of

Reg. § 1.338-1(a)(2)

the rules applicable to the agent for a consolidated group.

(3) *General rule for other provisions of the Internal Revenue Code.* Except as provided in the regulations under section 338 or in the Internal Revenue Bulletin by the Internal Revenue Service (see § 601.601(d)(2)(ii) of this chapter), new target is treated as a continuation of old target for purposes other than subtitle A of the Internal Revenue Code. For example—

(i) New target is liable for old target's Federal income tax liabilities, including the tax liability for the deemed sale tax consequences and those tax liabilities of the other members of any consolidated group that included old target that are attributable to taxable years in which those corporations and old target joined in the same consolidated return (see § 1.1502-6(a));

(ii) Wages earned by the employees of old target are considered wages earned by such employees from new target for purposes of sections 3101 and 3111 (Federal Insurance Contributions Act) and section 3301 (Federal Unemployment Tax Act); and

(iii) Old target and new target must use the same employer identification number.

(c) *Anti-abuse rule—*(1) *In general.* The rules of this paragraph (c) apply for purposes of applying the residual method as provided for under the regulations under sections 338 and 1060. The Commissioner is authorized to treat any property (including cash) transferred by old target in connection with the transactions resulting in the application of the residual method (and not held by target at the close of the acquisition date) as, nonetheless, property of target at the close of the acquisition date if the property so transferred is, within 24 months after the deemed asset sale, owned by new target, or is owned, directly or indirectly, by a member of the affiliated group of which new target is a member and continues after the acquisition date to be held or used primarily in connection with one or more of the activities of new target. In addition, the Commissioner is authorized to treat any property (including cash) transferred to old target in connection with the transactions resulting in the application of the residual method (and held by target at the close of the acquisition date) as, nonetheless, not being property of target at the close of the acquisition date if the property so transferred is, within 24 months after the deemed asset sale, not owned by new target but owned, directly or indirectly, by a member of the affiliated group of which new target is a member, or owned by new target but held or used primarily in connection with an activity conducted, directly or indirectly, by another member of the affiliated group of which new tar-

get is a member in combination with other property retained by or acquired, directly or indirectly, from the transferor of the property (or a member of the same affiliated group) to old target. For purposes of this paragraph (c)(1), an interest in an entity is considered held or used in connection with an activity if property of the entity is so held or used. The authority of the Commissioner under this paragraph (c)(1) includes the making of any appropriate correlative adjustments (avoiding, to the extent possible, the duplication or omission of any item of income, gain, loss, deduction, or basis).

(2) *Examples.* The following examples illustrate this paragraph (c):

Example 1. Prior to a qualified stock purchase under section 338, target transfers one of its assets to a related party. The purchasing corporation then purchases the target stock and also purchases the transferred asset from the related party. After its purchase of target, the purchasing corporation and target are members of the same affiliated group. A section 338 election is made. Under an arrangement with the purchaser, the separately transferred asset is used primarily in connection with target's activities. Applying the anti-abuse rule of this paragraph (c), the Commissioner may consider target to own the transferred asset for purposes of applying the residual method under section 338.

Example 2. T owns all the stock of T1. T1 leases intellectual property to T, which T uses in connection with its own activities. P, a purchasing corporation, wishes to buy the T-T1 chain of corporations. P, in connection with its planned purchase of the T stock, contracts to consummate a purchase of all the stock of T1 on March 1 and of all the stock of T on March 2. Section 338 elections are thereafter made for both T and T1. Immediately after the purchases, P, T and T1 are members of the same affiliated group. T continues to lease the intellectual property from T1 and that is the primary use of the intellectual property. Thus, an asset of T, the T1 stock, was removed from T's own assets prior to the qualified stock purchase of the T stock, T1's own assets are used after the deemed asset sale in connection with T's own activities, and the T1 stock is after the deemed asset sale owned by P, a member of the same affiliated group of which T is a member. Applying the anti-abuse rule of this paragraph (c), the Commissioner may, for purposes of application of the residual method under section 338 both to T and to T1, consider P to have bought only the stock of T, with T at the time of the qualified stock purchases of both T and T1 (the qualified stock purchase of T1 being triggered by the deemed sale under section 338 of T's assets) owning T1. The Commissioner accordingly would

Reg. § 1.338-1(c)(2)

allocate consideration to T's assets as though the T1 stock were one of those assets, and then allocate consideration within T1 based on the amount allocated to the T1 stock at the T level.

(d) *Next day rule for post-closing transactions.* If a target corporation for which an election under section 338 is made engages in a transaction outside the ordinary course of business on the acquisition date after the event resulting in the qualified stock purchase of the target or a higher tier corporation, the target and all persons related thereto (either before or after the qualified stock purchase) under section 267(b) or section 707 must treat the transaction for all Federal income tax purposes as occurring at the beginning of the day following the transaction and after the deemed purchase by new target. [Reg. § 1.338-1.]

☐ [*T.D.* 8940, 2-12-2001. *Amended by T.D.* 9002, 6-27-2002.]

§ 1.338-2. Nomenclature and definitions; mechanics of the section 338 election.—(a) *Scope.* This section prescribes rules relating to elections under section 338.

(b) *Nomenclature.* For purposes of the regulations under section 338 (except as otherwise provided):

(1) T is a domestic target corporation that has only one class of stock outstanding. Old T refers to T for periods ending on or before the close of T's acquisition date; new T refers to T for subsequent periods.

(2) P is the purchasing corporation.

(3) The P group is an affiliated group of which P is a member.

(4) P1, P2, etc., are domestic corporations that are members of the P group.

(5) T1, T2, etc., are domestic corporations that are target affiliates of T. These corporations (T1, T2, etc.) have only one class of stock outstanding and may also be targets.

(6) S is a domestic corporation (unrelated to P and B) that owns T prior to the purchase of T by P. (S is referred to in cases in which it is appropriate to consider the effects of having all of the outstanding stock of T owned by a domestic corporation.)

(7) A, a U.S. citizen or resident, is an individual (unrelated to P and B) who owns T prior to the purchase of T by P. (A is referred to in cases in which it is appropriate to consider the effects of having all of the outstanding stock of T owned by an individual who is a U.S. citizen or resident. Ownership of T by A and ownership of T by S are mutually exclusive circumstances.)

(8) B, a U.S. citizen or resident, is an individual (unrelated to T, S, and A) who owns the stock of P.

(9) F, used as a prefix with the other terms in this paragraph (b), connotes foreign, rather than domestic, status. For example, FT is a foreign corporation (as defined in section 7701(a)(5)) and FA is an individual other than a U.S. citizen or resident.

(10) CFC, used as a prefix with the other terms in this paragraph (b) referring to a corporation, connotes a controlled foreign corporation (as defined in section 957, taking into account section 953(c)). A corporation identified with the prefix F may be a controlled foreign corporation. (The prefix CFC is used when the corporation's status as a controlled foreign corporation is significant.)

(c) *Definitions.* For purposes of the regulations under section 338 (except as otherwise provided):

(1) *Acquisition date.* The term *acquisition date* has the same meaning as in section 338(h)(2).

(2) *Acquisition date assets.* Acquisition date assets are the assets of the target held at the beginning of the day after the acquisition date (but see § 1.338-1(d) (regarding certain transactions on the acquisition date)).

(3) *Affiliated group.* The term *affiliated group* has the same meaning as in section 338(h)(5). Corporations are affiliated on any day they are members of the same affiliated group.

(4) *Common parent.* The term *common parent* has the same meaning as in section 1504.

(5) *Consistency period.* The *consistency period* is the period described in section 338(h)(4)(A) unless extended pursuant to § 1.338-8(j)(1).

(6) *Deemed asset sale.* The *deemed asset sale* is the transaction described in § 1.338-1(a)(1) that is deemed to occur for purposes of subtitle A of the Internal Revenue Code if a section 338 election is made.

(7) *Deemed sale tax consequences. Deemed sale tax consequences* refers to, in the aggregate, the Federal income tax consequences (generally, the income, gain, deduction, and loss) of the deemed asset sale. Deemed sale tax consequences also refers to the Federal income tax consequences of the transfer of a particular asset in the deemed asset sale.

(8) *Deemed sale return.* The *deemed sale return* is the return on which target's deemed sale tax consequences are reported that does not include any other items of target. Target files a deemed sale return when a section 338 election (but not a section 338(h)(10) election) is filed for target and target is a member of a selling group (defined in paragraph (c)(16) of this section) that files a consolidated return for the period that includes the acquisition date. See § 1.338-10. If target is an S corporation for the period that ends

on the day before the acquisition date and a section 338 election (but not a section 338(h)(10) election) is filed for target, see § 1.338-10(a)(3).

(9) *Domestic corporation.* A *domestic corporation* is a corporation—

(i) That is domestic within the meaning of section 7701(a)(4) or that is treated as domestic for purposes of subtitle A of the Internal Revenue Code (e.g., to which an election under section 953(d) or 1504(d) applies); and

(ii) That is not a DISC, a corporation described in section 1248(e), or a corporation to which an election under section 936 applies.

(10) *Old target's final return.* Old target's final return is the income tax return of old target for the taxable year ending at the close of the acquisition date that includes the deemed sale tax consequences. However, if a deemed sale return is filed for old target, the deemed sale return is considered old target's final return.

(11) *Purchasing corporation.* The term *purchasing corporation* has the same meaning as in section 338(d)(1). The purchasing corporation may also be referred to as purchaser. Unless otherwise provided, any reference to the purchasing corporation is a reference to all members of the affiliated group of which the purchasing corporation is a member. See sections 338(h)(5) and (8). Also, unless otherwise provided, any reference to the purchasing corporation is, with respect to a deemed purchase of stock under section 338(a)(2), a reference to new target with respect to its own deemed purchase of stock in another target.

(12) *Qualified stock purchase.* The term *qualified stock purchase* has the same meaning as in section 338(d)(3).

(13) *Related persons.* Two persons are related if stock in a corporation owned by one of the persons would be attributed under section 318(a) (other than section 318(a)(4)) to the other.

(14) *Section 338 election.* A *section 338 election* is an election to apply section 338(a) to target. A section 338 election is made by filing a statement of section 338 election pursuant to paragraph (d) of this section. The form on which this statement is filed is referred to in the regulations under section 338 as the Form 8023, "Elections Under Section 338 For Corporations Making Qualified Stock Purchases."

(15) *Section 338(h)(10) election.* A *section 338(h)(10) election* is an election to apply section 338(h)(10) to target. A section 338(h)(10) election is made by making a joint election for target under § 1.338(h)(10)-1 on Form 8023.

(16) *Selling group.* The *selling group* is the affiliated group (as defined in section 1504) eligible to file a consolidated return that includes

target for the taxable period in which the acquisition date occurs. However, a selling group is not an affiliated group of which target is the common parent on the acquisition date.

(17) *Target; old target; new target. Target* is the target corporation as defined in section 338(d)(2). *Old target* refers to target for periods ending on or before the close of target's acquisition date. *New target* refers to target for subsequent periods.

(18) *Target affiliate.* The term *target affiliate* has the same meaning as in section 338(h)(6) (applied without section 338(h)(6)(B)(i)). Thus, a corporation described in section 338(h)(6)(B)(i) is considered a target affiliate for all purposes of section 338. If a target affiliate is acquired in a qualified stock purchase, it is also a target.

(19) *12-month acquisition period.* The *12-month acquisition period* is the period described in section 338(h)(1), unless extended pursuant to § 1.338-8(j)(2).

(d) *Time and manner of making election.* The purchasing corporation makes a section 338 election for target by filing a statement of section 338 election on Form 8023 in accordance with the instructions to the form. The section 338 election must be made not later than the 15th day of the 9th month beginning after the month in which the acquisition date occurs. A section 338 election is irrevocable. See § 1.338(h)(10)-1(c)(2) for section 338(h)(10) elections.

* * *

[Reg. § 1.338-2.]

☐ [*T.D. 8940, 2-12-2001.*]

§ 1.338-3. Qualification for the section 338 election.—(a) *Scope.* This section provides rules on whether certain acquisitions of stock are qualified stock purchases and on other miscellaneous issues under section 338.

(b) *Rules relating to qualified stock purchases*—(1) *Purchasing corporation requirement.* An individual cannot make a qualified stock purchase of target. Section 338(d)(3) requires, as a condition of a qualified stock purchase, that a corporation purchase the stock of target. If an individual forms a corporation (new P) to acquire target stock, new P can make a qualified stock purchase of target if new P is considered for tax purposes to purchase the target stock. Facts that may indicate that new P does not purchase the target stock include new P's merging downstream into target, liquidating, or otherwise disposing of the target stock following the purported qualified stock purchase.

(2) *Purchase.* The term *purchase* has the same meaning as in section 338(h)(3). Stock in a target (or target affiliate) may be considered pur-

chased if, under general principles of tax law, the purchasing corporation is considered to own stock of the target (or target affiliate) meeting the requirements of section 1504(a)(2), notwithstanding that no amount may be paid for (or allocated to) the stock.

(3) *Acquisitions of stock from related corporations*—(i) *In general.* Stock acquired by a purchasing corporation from a related corporation (R) is generally not considered acquired by purchase. See section 338(h)(3)(A)(iii).

(ii) *Time for testing relationship.* For purposes of section 338(h)(3)(A)(iii), a purchasing corporation is treated as related to another person if the relationship specified in section 338(h)(3)(A)(iii) exists—

(A) In the case of a single transaction, immediately after the purchase of target stock;

(B) In the case of a series of acquisitions otherwise constituting a qualified stock purchase within the meaning of section 338(d)(3), immediately after the last acquisition in such series; and

(C) In the case of a series of transactions effected pursuant to an integrated plan to dispose of target stock, immediately after the last transaction in such series.

(iii) *Cases where section 338(h)(3)(C) applies—acquisitions treated as purchases.* If section 338(h)(3)(C) applies and the purchasing corporation is treated as acquiring stock by purchase from R, solely for purposes of determining when the stock is considered acquired, target stock acquired from R is considered to have been acquired by the purchasing corporation on the day on which the purchasing corporation is first considered to own that stock under section 318(a) (other than section 318(a)(4)).

(iv) *Examples.* The following examples illustrate this paragraph (b)(3):

Example 1. (i) S is the parent of a group of corporations that are engaged in various businesses. Prior to January 1, Year 1, S decided to discontinue its involvement in one line of business. To accomplish this, S forms a new corporation, Newco, with a nominal amount of cash. Shortly thereafter, on January 1, Year 1, S transfers all the stock of the subsidiary conducting the unwanted business (T) to Newco in exchange for 100 shares of Newco common stock and a Newco promissory note. Prior to January 1, Year 1, S and Underwriter (U) had entered into a binding agreement pursuant to which U would purchase 60 shares of Newco common stock from S and then sell those shares in an Initial Public Offering (IPO). On January 6, Year 1, the IPO closes.

(ii) Newco's acquisition of T stock is one of a series of transactions undertaken pursuant to

one integrated plan. The series of transactions ends with the closing of the IPO and the transfer of all the shares of stock in accordance with the agreements. Immediately after the last transaction effected pursuant to the plan, S owns 40 percent of Newco, which does not give rise to a relationship described in section 338(h)(3)(A)(iii). See § 1.338-3(b)(3)(ii)(C). Accordingly, S and Newco are not related for purposes of section 338(h)(3)(A)(iii).

(iii) Further, because Newco's basis in the T stock is not determined by reference to S's basis in the T stock and because the transaction is not an exchange to which section 351, 354, 355, or 356 applies, Newco's acquisition of the T stock is a purchase within the meaning of section 338(h)(3).

Example 2. (i) On January 1 of Year 1, P purchases 75 percent in value of the R stock. On that date, R owns 4 of the 100 shares of T stock. On June 1 of Year 1, R acquires an additional 16 shares of T stock. On December 1 of Year 1, P purchases 70 shares of T stock from an unrelated person and 12 of the 20 shares of T stock held by R.

(ii) Of the 12 shares of T stock purchased by P from R on December 1 of Year 1, 3 of those shares are deemed to have been acquired by P on January 1 of Year 1, the date on which 3 of the 4 shares of T stock held by R on that date were first considered owned by P under section 318(a)(2)(C) (i.e., 4 × .75). The remaining 9 shares of T stock purchased by P from R on December 1 of Year 1 are deemed to have been acquired by P on June 1 of Year 1, the date on which an additional 12 of the 20 shares of T stock owned by R on that date were first considered owned by P under section 318(a)(2)(C) (i.e., (20 × .75) − 3). Because stock acquisitions by P sufficient for a qualified stock purchase of T occur within a 12-month period (i.e., 3 shares constructively on January 1 of Year 1, 9 shares constructively on June 1 of Year 1, and 70 shares actually on December 1 of Year 1), a qualified stock purchase is made on December 1 of Year 1.

Example 3. (i) On February 1 of Year 1, P acquires 25 percent in value of the R stock from B (the sole shareholder of P). That R stock is not acquired by purchase. See section 338(h)(3)(A)(iii). On that date, R owns 4 of the 100 shares of T stock. On June 1 of Year 1, P purchases an additional 25 percent in value of the R stock, and on January 1 of Year 2, P purchases another 25 percent in value of the R stock. On June 1 of Year 2, R acquires an additional 16 shares of the T stock. On December 1 of Year 2, P purchases 68 shares of the T stock from an unrelated person and 12 of the 20 shares of the T stock held by R.

(ii) Of the 12 shares of the T stock purchased by P from R on December 1 of Year 2, 2 of those shares are deemed to have been acquired by P on June 1 of Year 1, the date on which 2 of the 4 shares of the T stock held by R on that date were first considered owned by P under section 318(a)(2)(C) (i.e., 4 × .5). For purposes of this attribution, the R stock need not be acquired by P by purchase. See section 338(h)(1). (By contrast, the acquisition of the T stock by P from R does not qualify as a purchase unless P has acquired at least 50 percent in value of the R stock by purchase. Section 338(h)(3)(C)(i).) Of the remaining 10 shares of the T stock purchased by P from R on December 1 of Year 2, 1 of those shares is deemed to have been acquired by P on January 1 of Year 2, the date on which an additional 1 share of the 4 shares of the T stock held by R on that date was first considered owned by P under section 318(a)(2)(C) (i.e., (4 × .75) − 2). The remaining 9 shares of the T stock purchased by P from R on December 1 of Year 2, are deemed to have been acquired by P on June 1 of Year 2, the date on which an additional 12 shares of the T stock held by R on that date were first considered owned by P under section 318(a)(2)(C) (i.e., (20 × .75) − 3). Because a qualified stock purchase of T by P is made on December 1 of Year 2 only if all 12 shares of the T stock purchased by P from R on that date are considered acquired during a 12-month period ending on that date (so that, in conjunction with the 68 shares of the T stock P purchased on that date from the unrelated person, 80 of T's 100 shares are acquired by P during a 12-month period) and because 2 of those 12 shares are considered to have been acquired by P more than 12 months before December 1 of Year 2 (i.e., on June 1 of Year 1), a qualified stock purchase is not made. (Under § 1.338-8(j)(2), for purposes of applying the consistency rules, P is treated as making a qualified stock purchase of T if, pursuant to an arrangement, P purchases T stock satisfying the requirements of section 1504(a)(2) over a period of more than 12 months.)

Example 4. Assume the same facts as in *Example 3,* except that on February 1 of Year 1, P acquires 25 percent in value of the R stock by purchase. The result is the same as in *Example 3.*

(4) *Acquisition date for tiered targets*—(i) *Stock sold in deemed asset sale.* If an election under section 338 is made for target, old target is deemed to sell target's assets and new target is deemed to acquire those assets. Under section 338(h)(3)(B), new target's deemed purchase of stock of another corporation is a purchase for purposes of section 338(d)(3) on the acquisition date of target. If new target's deemed purchase causes a qualified stock purchase of the other corporation and if a section 338 election is made for the other corporation, the acquisition date for the other corporation is the same as the acquisition date of target. However, the deemed sale and purchase of the other corporation's assets is considered to take place after the deemed sale and purchase of target's assets.

(ii) *Example.* The following example illustrates this paragraph (b)(4):

Example. A owns all of the T stock. T owns 50 of the 100 shares of X stock. The other 50 shares of X stock are owned by corporation Y, which is unrelated to A, T, or P. On January 1 of Year 1, P makes a qualified stock purchase of T from A and makes a section 338 election for T. On December 1 of Year 1, P purchases the 50 shares of X stock held by Y. A qualified stock purchase of X is made on December 1 of Year 1, because the deemed purchase of 50 shares of X stock by new T because of the section 338 election for T and the actual purchase of 50 shares of X stock by P are treated as purchases made by one corporation. Section 338(h)(8). For purposes of determining whether those purchases occur within a 12-month acquisition period as required by section 338(d)(3), T is deemed to purchase its X stock on T's acquisition date, i.e., January 1 of Year 1.

(5) *Effect of redemptions*—(i) *General rule.* Except as provided in this paragraph (b)(5), a qualified stock purchase is made on the first day on which the percentage ownership requirements of section 338(d)(3) are satisfied by reference to target stock that is both—

(A) Held on that day by the purchasing corporation; and

(B) Purchased by the purchasing corporation during the 12-month period ending on that day.

(ii) *Redemptions from persons unrelated to the purchasing corporation.* Target stock redemptions from persons unrelated to the purchasing corporation that occur during the 12-month acquisition period are taken into account as reductions in target's outstanding stock for purposes of determining whether target stock purchased by the purchasing corporation in the 12-month acquisition period satisfies the percentage ownership requirements of section 338(d)(3).

(iii) *Redemptions from the purchasing corporation or related persons during 12-month acquisition period*—(A) *General rule.* For purposes of the percentage ownership requirements of section 338(d)(3), a redemption of target stock during the 12-month acquisition period from the purchasing corporation or from any person related to the purchasing corporation is not taken into account as a reduction in target's outstanding stock.

Reg. § 1.338-3(b)(5)

(B) *Exception for certain redemptions from related corporations.* A redemption of target stock during the 12-month acquisition period from a corporation related to the purchasing corporation is taken into account as a reduction in target's outstanding stock to the extent that the redeemed stock would have been considered purchased by the purchasing corporation (because of section 338(h)(3)(C)) during the 12-month acquisition period if the redeemed stock had been acquired by the purchasing corporation from the related corporation On the day of the redemption. See paragraph (b)(3) of this section.

* * *

(c) *Effect of post-acquisition events on eligibility for section 338 election*—(1) *Post-acquisition elimination of target*—(i) The purchasing corporation may make an election under section 338 for target even though target is liquidated on or after the acquisition date. If target liquidates on the acquisition date, the liquidation is considered to occur on the following day and immediately after new target's deemed purchase of assets. The purchasing corporation may also make an election under section 338 for target even though target is merged into another corporation, or otherwise disposed of by the purchasing corporation provided that, under the facts and circumstances, the purchasing corporation is considered for tax purposes as the purchaser of the target stock.

(ii) The following examples illustrate this paragraph (c)(1):

Example 1. On January 1 of Year 1, P purchases 100 percent of the outstanding common stock of T. On June 1 of Year 1, P sells the T stock to an unrelated person. Assuming that P is considered for tax purposes as the purchaser of the T stock, P remains eligible, after June 1 of Year 1, to make a section 338 election for T that results in a deemed asset sale of T's assets on January 1 of Year 1.

Example 2. On January 1 of Year 1, P makes a qualified stock purchase of T. On that date, T owns the stock of T1. On March 1 of Year 1, T sells the T1 stock to an unrelated person. On April 1 of Year 1, P makes a section 338 election for T. Notwithstanding that the T1 stock was sold on March 1 of Year 1, the section 338 election for T on April 1 of Year 1 results in a qualified stock purchase by T of T1 on January 1 of Year 1. See paragraph (b)(4)(i) of this section.

(2) *Post-acquisition elimination of the purchasing corporation.* An election under section 338 may be made for target after the acquisition of assets of the purchasing corporation by another corporation in a transaction described in section 381(a), provided that the purchasing corporation is considered for tax purposes as the purchaser of

the target stock. The acquiring corporation in the section 381(a) transaction may make an election under section 338 for target.

(d) *Consequences of post-acquisition elimination of target where section 338 election not made*—(1) *Scope.* The rules of this paragraph (d) apply to the transfer of target assets to the purchasing corporation (or another member of the same affiliated group as the purchasing corporation) (the transferee) following a qualified stock purchase of target stock, if the purchasing corporation does not make a section 338 election for target. Notwithstanding the rules of this paragraph (d), section 354(a) (and so much of section 356 as relates to section 354) cannot apply to any person other than the purchasing corporation or another member of the same affiliated group as the purchasing corporation unless the transfer of target assets is pursuant to a reorganization as determined without regard to this paragraph (d).

(2) *Continuity of interest.* By virtue of section 338, in determining whether the continuity of interest requirement of § 1.368-1(b) is satisfied on the transfer of assets from target to the transferee, the purchasing corporation's target stock acquired in the qualified stock purchase represents an interest on the part of a person who was an owner of the target's business enterprise prior to the transfer that can be continued in a reorganization.

(3) *Control requirement.* By virtue of section 338, the acquisition of target stock in the qualified stock purchase will not prevent the purchasing corporation from qualifying as a shareholder of the target transferor for the purpose of determining whether, immediately after the transfer of target assets, a shareholder of the transferor is in control of the corporation to which the assets are transferred within the meaning of section 368(a)(1)(D).

(4) *Solely for voting stock requirement.* By virtue of section 338, the acquisition of target stock in the qualified stock purchase for consideration other than voting stock will not prevent the subsequent transfer of target assets from satisfying the solely for voting stock requirement for purposes of determining if the transfer of target assets qualifies as a reorganization under section 368(a)(1)(C).

(5) *Example.* The following example illustrates this paragraph (d):

Example. (i) *Facts.* P, T, and X are domestic corporations. T and X each operate a trade or business. A and K, individuals unrelated to P, own 85 and 15 percent, respectively, of the stock of T. P owns all of the stock of X. The total adjusted basis of T's property exceeds the sum of T's liabilities plus the amount of liabilities to

Reg. § 1.338-3(c)(1)

which T's property is subject. P purchases all of A's T stock for cash in a qualified stock purchase. P does not make an election under section 338(g) with respect to its acquisition of T stock. Shortly after the acquisition date, and as part of the same plan, T merges under applicable state law into X in a transaction that, but for the question of continuity of interest, satisfies all the requirements of section 368(a)(1)(A). In the merger, all of T's assets are transferred to X. P and K receive X stock in exchange for their T stock. P intends to retain the stock of X indefinitely.

(ii) *Status of transfer as a reorganization.* By virtue of section 338, for the purpose of determining whether the continuity of interest requirement of § 1.368-1(b) is satisfied, P's T stock acquired in the qualified stock purchase represents an interest on the part of a person who was an owner of T's business enterprise prior to the transfer that can be continued in a reorganization through P's continuing ownership of X. Thus, the continuity of interest requirement is satisfied and the merger of T into X is a reorganization within the meaning of section 368(a)(1)(A). Moreover, by virtue of section 338, the requirement of section 368(a)(1)(D) that a target shareholder control the transferee immediately after the transfer is satisfied because P controls X immediately after the transfer. In addition, all of T's assets are transferred to X in the merger and P and K receive the X stock exchanged therefor in pursuance of the plan of reorganization. Thus, the merger of T into X is also a reorganization within the meaning of section 368(a)(1)(D).

(iii) *Treatment of T and X.* Under section 361(a), T recognizes no gain or loss in the merger. Under section 362(b), X's basis in the assets received in the merger is the same as the basis of the assets in T's hands. X succeeds to and takes into account the items of T as provided in section 381.

(iv) *Treatment of P.* By virtue of section 338, the transfer of T assets to X is a reorganization. Pursuant to that reorganization, P exchanges its T stock solely for stock of X, a party to the reorganization. Because P is the purchasing corporation, section 354 applies to P's exchange of T stock for X stock in the merger of T into X. Thus, P recognizes no gain or loss on the exchange. Under section 358, P's basis in the X stock received in the exchange is the same as the basis of P's T stock exchanged therefor.

(v) *Treatment of K.* Because K is not the purchasing corporation (or an affiliate thereof), section 354 cannot apply to K's exchange of T stock for X stock in the merger of T into X unless the transfer of T's assets is pursuant to a reorganization as determined without regard to this para-

graph (d). Under general principles of tax law applicable to reorganizations, the continuity of interest requirement is not satisfied because P's stock purchase and the merger of T into X are pursuant to an integrated transaction in which A, the owner of 85 percent of the stock of T, received solely cash in exchange for A's T stock. See, e.g., § 1.368-1(e)(1)(i); *Yoc Heating v. Commissioner,* 61 T.C. 168 (1973); *Kass v. Commissioner,* 60 T.C. 218 (1973), aff'd, 491 F.2d 749 (3d Cir. 1974). Thus, the requisite continuity of interest under § 1.368-1(b) is lacking and section 354 does not apply to K's exchange of T stock for X stock. K recognizes gain or loss, if any, pursuant to section 1001(c) with respect to its T stock.

[Reg. § 1.338-3.]

☐ [*T.D.* 8940, 2-12-2001 (*corrected* 3-29-2001).]

§ 1.338-4. Aggregate deemed sale price; various aspects of taxation of the deemed asset sale.—(a) *Scope.* This section provides rules under section 338(a)(1) to determine the aggregate deemed sale price (ADSP) for target. ADSP is the amount for which old target is deemed to have sold all of its assets in the deemed asset sale. ADSP is allocated among target's assets in accordance with § 1.338-6 to determine the amount for which each asset is deemed to have been sold. When a subsequent increase or decrease is required under general principles of tax law with respect to an element of ADSP, the redetermined ADSP is allocated among target's assets in accordance with § 1.338-7. This § 1.338-4 also provides rules regarding the recognition of gain or loss on the deemed sale of target affiliate stock. Notwithstanding section 338(h)(6)(B)(ii), stock held by a target affiliate in a foreign corporation or in a corporation that is a DISC or that is described in section 1248(e) is not excluded from the operation of section 338.

(b) *Determination of ADSP*—(1) *General rule.* ADSP is the sum of—

(i) The grossed-up amount realized on the sale to the purchasing corporation of the purchasing corporation's recently purchased target stock (as defined in section 338(b)(6)(A)); and

(ii) The liabilities of old target.

(2) *Time and amount of ADSP*—(i) *Original termination.* ADSP is initially determined at the beginning of the day after the acquisition date of target. General principles of tax law apply in determining the timing and amount of the elements of ADSP.

(ii) *Redetermination of ADSP.* ADSP is redetermined at such time and in such amount as an increase or decrease would be required, under general principles of tax law, for the elements of

ADSP. For example, ADSP is redetermined because of an increase or decrease in the amount realized for recently purchased stock or because liabilities not originally taken into account in determining ADSP are subsequently taken into account. Increases or decreases with respect to the elements of ADSP result in the reallocation of ADSP among target's assets under § 1.338-7.

(iii) *Example.* The following example illustrates this paragraph (b)(2):

Example. In Year 1, T, a manufacturer, purchases a customized delivery truck from X with purchase money indebtedness having a stated principal amount of $100,000. P acquires all of the stock of T in Year 3 for $700,000 and makes a section 338 election for T. Assume T has no liabilities other than its purchase money indebtedness to X. In Year 4, when T is neither insolvent nor in a title 11 case, T and X agree to reduce the amount of the purchase money indebtedness to $80,000. Assume further that the reduction would be a purchase price reduction under section 108(e)(5). T and X's agreement to reduce the amount of the purchase money indebtedness would not, under general principles of tax law that would apply if the deemed asset sale had actually occurred, change the amount of liabilities of old target taken into account in determining its amount realized. Accordingly, ADSP is not redetermined at the time of the reduction. See § 1.338-5(b)(2)(iii) *Example 1* for the effect on AGUB.

(c) *Grossed-up amount realized on the sale to the purchasing corporation of the purchasing corporation's recently purchased target stock*—(1) *Determination of amount.* The grossed-up amount realized on the sale to the purchasing corporation of the purchasing corporation's recently purchased target stock is an amount equal to—

(i) The amount realized on the sale to the purchasing corporation of the purchasing corporation's recently purchased target stock determined as if the selling shareholder(s) were required to use old target's accounting methods and characteristics and the installment method were not available and determined without regard to the selling costs taken into account under paragraph (c)(1)(iii) of this section;

(ii) Divided by the percentage of target stock (by value, determined on the acquisition date) attributable to that recently purchased target stock;

(iii) Less the selling costs incurred by the selling shareholders in connection with the sale to the purchasing corporation of the purchasing corporation's recently purchased target stock that reduce their amount realized on the sale of the stock (e.g., brokerage commissions and any similar costs to sell the stock).

(2) *Example.* The following example illustrates this paragraph (c):

Example. T has two classes of stock outstanding, voting common stock and preferred stock described in section 1504(a)(4). On March 1 of Year 1, P purchases 40 percent of the outstanding T stock from S1 for $500, 20 percent of the outstanding T stock from S2 for $225, and 20 percent of the outstanding T stock from S3 for $275. On that date, the fair market value of all the T voting common stock is $1,250 and the preferred stock $750. S1, S2, and S3 incur $40, $35, and $25 respectively of selling costs. S1 continues to own the remaining 20 percent of the outstanding T stock. The grossed-up amount realized on the sale to P of P's recently purchased T stock is calculated as follows: The total amount realized (without regard to selling costs) is $1,000 (500 + 225 + 275). The percentage of T stock by value on the acquisition date attributable to the recently purchased T stock is 50% (1,000/(1,250 + 750)). The selling costs are $100 (40 + 35 + 25). The grossed-up amount realized is $1,900 (1,000/.5 − 100).

(d) *Liabilities of old target*—(1) *In general.* In general, the liabilities of old target are measured as of the beginning of the day after the acquisition date. (But see § 1.338-1(d) (regarding certain transactions on the acquisition date).) In order to be taken into account in ADSP, a liability must be a liability of target that is properly taken into account in amount realized under general principles of tax law that would apply if old target had sold its assets to an unrelated person for consideration that included the discharge of its liabilities. See § 1.1001-2(a). Such liabilities may include liabilities for the tax consequences resulting from the deemed sale.

(2) *Time and amount of liabilities.* The time for taking into account liabilities of old target in determining ADSP and the amount of the liabilities taken into account is determined as if old target had sold its assets to an unrelated person for consideration that included the discharge of the liabilities by the unrelated person. For example, if no amount of a target liability is properly taken into account in amount realized as of the beginning of the day after the acquisition date, the liability is not initially taken into account in determining ADSP (although it may be taken into account at some later date).

(e) *Deemed sale tax consequences.* Gain or loss on each asset in the deemed sale is computed by reference to the ADSP allocated to that asset. ADSP is allocated under the rules of § 1.338-6. Though deemed sale tax consequences may increase or decrease ADSP by creating or reducing a tax liability, the amount of the tax liability itself may be a function of the size of the deemed sale tax consequences. Thus, these determinations may require trial and error computations.

(f) *Other rules apply in determining ADSP.* ADSP may not be applied in such a way as to contravene other applicable rules. For example, a capital loss cannot be applied to reduce ordinary income in calculating the tax liability on the deemed sale for purposes of determining ADSP.

(g) *Examples.* The following examples illustrate this section. For purposes of the examples in this paragraph (g), unless otherwise stated, T is a calendar year taxpayer that files separate returns and that has no loss, tax credit, or other carry-overs to Year 1. Depreciation for Year 1 is not taken into account. T has no liabilities other than the Federal income tax liability resulting from the deemed asset sale, and the T shareholders have no selling costs. Assume that T's tax rate for any ordinary income or net capital gain resulting from the deemed sale of assets is 34 percent and that any capital loss is offset by capital gain. On July 1 of Year 1, P purchases all of the stock of T and makes a section 338 election for T. The examples are as follows:

Example 1. One class. (i) On July 1 of Year 1, T's only asset is an item of section 1245 property with an adjusted basis to T of $50,400, a recomputed basis of $80,000, and a fair market value of $100,000. P purchases all of the T stock for $75,000, which also equals the amount realized for the stock determined as if the selling share-holder(s) were required to use old target's ac-counting methods and characteristics.

(ii) ADSP is determined as follows (for purposes of this section (g), G is the grossed-up amount realized on the sale to P of P's recently purchased T stock, L is T's liabilities other than T's tax liability for the deemed sale tax consequences, T_R is the applicable tax rate, and B is the adjusted basis of the asset deemed sold):

$$ADSP = G + L + T_R \times (ADSP - B)$$

$$ADSP = (\$75,000/1) + \$0 + .34 \times (ADSP - \$50,400)$$

$$ADSP = \$75,000 + .34ADSP - \$17,136$$

$$.66ADSP = \$57,864$$

$$ADSP = \$87,672.72$$

(iii) Because ADSP for T ($87,672.72) does not exceed the fair market value of T's asset ($100,000), a Class V asset, T's entire ADSP is allocated to that asset. Thus, T's deemed sale results in $37,272.72 of taxable income (consisting of $29,600 of ordinary income and $7,672.72 of capital gain).

(iv) The facts are the same as in paragraph (i) of this *Example 1*, except that on July 1 of Year 1, P purchases only 80 of the 100 shares of T stock for $60,000. The grossed-up amount realized on the sale to P of P's recently purchased T stock (G) is $75,000 ($60,000/.8). Consequently, ADSP and the deemed sale tax consequences are the same as in paragraphs (ii) and (iii) of this *Example 1*.

(v) The facts are the same as in paragraph (i) of this *Example 1*, except that T also has goodwill (a Class VII asset) with an appraised value of $10,000. The results are the same as in paragraphs (ii) and (iii) of this *Example 1*. Be-cause ADSP does not exceed the fair market value of the Class V asset, no amount is allocated to the Class VII asset (goodwill).

Example 2. More than one class. (i) P purchases all of the T stock for $140,000, which also equals the amount realized for the stock determined as if the selling shareholder(s) were required to use old target's accounting methods and characteristics. On July 1 of Year 1, T has liabilities (not includ-ing the tax liability for the deemed sale tax conse-quences) of $50,000, cash (a Class I asset) of $10,000, actively traded securities (a Class II asset) with a basis of $4,000 and a fair market value of $10,000, goodwill (a Class VII asset) with a basis of $3,000, and the following Class V assets:

Asset	Basis	FMV	Ratio of asset FMV to total Class V FMV
Land	$ 5,000	$ 35,000	.14
Building	10,000	50,000	.20
Equipment A (Recomputed basis $80,000)	5,000	90,000	.36
Equipment B (Recomputed basis $20,000)	10,000	75,000	.30
Totals	$30,000	$250,000	1.00

(ii) ADSP exceeds $20,000. Thus, $10,000 of ADSP is allocated to the cash and $10,000 to the actively traded securities. The amount allocated to an asset (other than a Class VII asset) cannot exceed its fair market value (however, the fair market value of any property subject to nonre-course indebtedness is treated as being not less than the amount of such indebtedness; see § 1.338-6(a)(2)). See § 1.338-6(c)(1) (relating to fair market value limitation).

Reg. § 1.338-4(g)

(iii) The portion of ADSP allocable to the Class V assets is preliminarily determined as follows (in the formula, the amount allocated to the Class I assets is referred to as I and the amount allocated to the Class II assets as II):

$$\text{ADSP}_V = (G - (I + II)) + L + T_R \times [(II - B_{II}) + (\text{ADSP}_V - B_V)]$$

$$\text{ADSP}_V = (\$140,000 - (\$10,000 + \$10,000)) + \$50,000 + .34 \times [(\$10,000 - \$4,000) + (\text{ADSP}_V - (\$5,000 + \$10,000 + \$5,000 + \$10,000))]$$

$$\text{ADSP}_V = \$161,840 + .34\ \text{ADSP}_V$$

$$.66\ \text{ADSP}_V = \$161,840$$

$$\text{ADSP}_V = \$245,212.12$$

(iv) Because, under the preliminary calculations of ADSP, the amount to be allocated to the Class I, II, III, IV, V, and VI assets does not exceed their aggregate fair market value, no ADSP amount is allocated to goodwill. Accordingly, the deemed sale of the goodwill results in a capital loss of $3,000. The portion of ADSP allocable to the Class V assets is finally determined by taking into account this loss as follows:

$$\text{ADSP}_V = (G - (I + II)) + L + T_R \times [(II - B_{II}) + (\text{ADSP}_V - B_V) + (\text{ADSP}_{VII} - B_{VII})]$$

$$\text{ADSP}_V = (\$140,000 - (\$10,000 + \$10,000)) + \$50,000 + .34 \times [(\$10,000 - \$4,000) + (\text{ADSP}_V - \$30,000) + (\$0 - \$3,000)]$$

$$\text{ADSP}_V = \$160,820 + .34\ \text{ADSP}_V$$

$$.66\ \text{ADSP}_V = \$160,820$$

$$\text{ADSP}_V = \$243,666.67$$

(v) The allocation of ADSP_V among the Class V assets is in proportion to their fair market values, as follows:

Asset	ADSP	Gain
Land	$ 34,113.33	$29,113.33 (capital gain)
Building	48,733.34	38,733.34 (capital gain)
Equipment A	87,720.00	82,720.00 (75,000 ordinary income 7,720 capital gain)
Equipment B	73,100.00	63,100.00 (10,000 ordinary income 53,100 capital gain)
Totals	$243,666.67	$213,666.67

Example 3. More than one class. (i) The facts are the same as in *Example 2*, except that P purchases the T stock for $150,000, rather than $140,000. The amount realized for the stock determined as if the selling shareholder(s) were required to use old target's accounting methods and characteristics is also $150,000.

(ii) As in *Example 2*, ADSP exceeds $20,000. Thus, $10,000 of ADSP is allocated to the cash and $10,000 to the actively traded securities.

(iii) The portion of ADSP allocable to the Class V assets as preliminarily determined under the formula set forth in paragraph (iii) of *Example 2* is $260,363.64. The amount allocated to the Class V assets cannot exceed their aggregate fair market value ($250,000). Thus, preliminarily, the ADSP amount allocated to Class V assets is $250,000.

(iv) Based on the preliminary allocation, the ADSP is determined as follows (in the formula, the amount allocated to the Class I assets is referred to as I, the amount allocated to the Class II assets as II, and the amount allocated to the Class V assets as V):

$$\text{ADSP} = G + L + T_R \times [(II - B_{II}) + (V - B_V) + (\text{ADSP} - (I + II + V + B_{VII}))]$$

$$\text{ADSP} = \$150,000 + \$50,000 + .34 \times [(\$10,000 - \$4,000) + (\$250,000 - \$30,000) + (\text{ADSP} - (\$10,000 + \$10,000 + \$250,000 + \$3,000))]$$

$$\text{ADSP} = \$200,000 + .34\text{ADSP} - \$15,980$$

$$.66\text{ADSP} = \$184,020$$

$$\text{ADSP} = \$278,818.18$$

Reg. § 1.338-4(g)

(v) Because ADSP as determined exceeds the aggregate fair market value of the Class I, II, III, IV, V, and VI assets, the $250,000 amount preliminarily allocated to the Class V assets is appropriate. Thus, the amount of ADSP allocated to Class V assets equals their aggregate fair market value ($250,000), and the allocated ADSP amount for each Class V asset is its fair market value. Further, because there are no Class VI assets, the allocable ADSP amount for the Class VII asset (goodwill) is $8,818.18 (the excess of ADSP over the aggregate ADSP amounts for the Class I, II, III, IV, V and VI assets).

Example 4. Amount allocated to T1 stock. (i) The facts are the same as in *Example 2*, except that T owns all of the T1 stock (instead of the building), and T1's only asset is the building. The T1 stock and the building each have a fair market value of $50,000, and the building has a basis of $10,000. A section 338 election is made for T1 (as well as T), and T1 has no liabilities other than the tax liability for the deemed sale tax consequences. T is the common parent of a consolidated group filing a final consolidated return described in § 1.338-10(a)(1).

(ii) ADSP exceeds $20,000. Thus, $10,000 of ADSP is allocated to the cash and $10,000 to the actively traded securities.

(iii) Because T does not recognize any gain on the deemed sale of the T1 stock under paragraph (h)(2) of this section, appropriate adjustments must be made to reflect accurately the fair market value of the T and T1 assets in determining the allocation of ADSP among T's Class V assets (including the T1 stock). In preliminarily calculating ADSPv in this case, the T1 stock can be disregarded and, because T owns all of the T1 stock, the T1 asset can be treated as a T asset. Under this assumption, ADSPV is $243,666.67. See paragraph (iv) of *Example 2*.

(iv) Because the portion of the preliminary ADSP allocable to Class V assets ($243,666.67) does not exceed their fair market value ($250,000), no amount is allocated to Class VII assets for T. Further, this amount ($243,666.67) is allocated among T's Class V assets in proportion to their fair market values. See paragraph (v) of *Example 2*. Tentatively, $48,733.34 of this amount is allocated to the T1 stock.

(v) The amount tentatively allocated to the T1 stock, however, reflects the tax incurred on the deemed sale of the T1 asset equal to $13,169.34 (.34 × ($48,733.34 − $10,000)). Thus, the ADSP allocable to the Class V assets of T, and the ADSP allocable to the T1 stock, as preliminarily calcu-

lated, each must be reduced by $13,169.34. Consequently, these amounts, respectively, are $230,497.33 and $35,564.00. In determining ADSP for T1, the grossed-up amount realized on the deemed sale to new T of new T's recently purchased T1 stock is $35,564.00.

(vi) The facts are the same as in paragraph (i) of this *Example 4*, except that the T1 building has a $12,500 basis and a $62,500 value, all of the outstanding T1 stock has a $62,500 value, and T owns 80 percent of the T1 stock. In preliminarily calculating ADSP$_V$, the T1 stock can be disregarded but, because T owns only 80 percent of the T1 stock, only 80 percent of T1 asset basis and value should be taken into account in calculating T's ADSP. By taking into account 80 percent of these amounts, the remaining calculations and results are the same as in paragraphs (ii), (iii), (iv), and (v) of this *Example 4*, except that the grossed-up amount realized on the sale of the recently purchased T1 stock is $44,455.00 ($35,564.00/0.8).

(h) *Deemed sale of target affiliate stock*—(1) *Scope.* This paragraph (h) prescribes rules relating to the treatment of gain or loss realized on the deemed sale of stock of a target affiliate when a section 338 election (but not a section 338(h)(10) election) is made for the target affiliate. For purposes of this paragraph (h), the definition of domestic corporation in § 1.338-2(c)(9) is applied without the exclusion therein for DISCs, corporations described in section 1248(e), and corporations to which an election under section 936 applies.

(2) *In general.* Except as otherwise provided in this paragraph (h), if a section 338 election is made for target, target recognizes no gain or loss on the deemed sale of stock of a target affiliate having the same acquisition date and for which a section 338 election is made if—

(i) Target directly owns stock in the target affiliate satisfying the requirements of section 1504(a)(2);

(ii) Target and the target affiliate are members of a consolidated group filing a final consolidated return described in § 1.338-10(a)(1); or

(iii) Target and the target affiliate file a combined return under § 1.338-10(a)(4).

(3) *Deemed sale of foreign target affiliate by a domestic target.* A domestic target recognizes gain or loss on the deemed sale of stock of a foreign target affiliate. For the proper treatment of such gain or loss, see, e.g., sections 1246, 1248, 1291 et seq., and 338(h)(16) and § 1.338-9.

Reg. § 1.338-4(h)(3)

(4) *Deemed sale producing effectively connected income.* A foreign target recognizes gain or loss on the deemed sale of stock of a foreign target affiliate to the extent that such gain or loss is effectively connected (or treated as effectively connected) with the conduct of a trade or business in the United States.

(5) *Deemed sale of insurance company target affiliate electing under section 953(d).* A domestic target recognizes gain (but not loss) on the deemed sale of stock of a target affiliate that has in effect an election under section 953(d) in an amount equal to the lesser of the gain realized or the earnings and profits described in section 953(d)(4)(B).

(6) *Deemed sale of DISC target affiliate.* A foreign or domestic target recognizes gain (but not loss) on the deemed sale of stock of a target affiliate that is a DISC or a former DISC (as defined in section 992(a)) in an amount equal to the lesser of the gain realized or the amount of accumulated DISC income determined with respect to such stock under section 995(c). Such gain is included in gross income as a dividend as provided in sections 995(c)(2) and 996(g).

(7) *Anti-stuffing rule.* If an asset the adjusted basis of which exceeds its fair market value is contributed or transferred to a target affiliate as transferred basis property (within the meaning of section 7701(a)(43)) and a purpose of such transaction is to reduce the gain (or increase the loss) recognized on the deemed sale of such target affiliate's stock, the gain or loss recognized by target on the deemed sale of stock of the target affiliate is determined as if such asset had not been contributed or transferred.

(8) *Examples.* The following examples illustrate this paragraph (h):

Example 1. (i) P makes a qualified stock purchase of T and makes a section 338 election for T. T's sole asset, all of the T1 stock, has a basis of $50 and a fair market value of $150. T's deemed purchase of the T1 stock results in a qualified stock purchase of T1 and a section 338 election is made for T1. T1's assets have a basis of $50 and a fair market value of $150.

(ii) T realizes $100 of gain on the deemed sale of the T1 stock, but the gain is not recognized because T directly owns stock in T1 satisfying the requirements of section 1504(a)(2) and a section 338 election is made for T1.

(iii) T1 recognizes gain of $100 on the deemed sale of its assets.

Example 2. The facts are the same as in *Example 1*, except that P does not make a section 338 election for T1. Because a section 338 election

is not made for T1, the $100 gain realized by T on the deemed sale of the T1 stock is recognized.

Example 3. (i) P makes a qualified stock purchase of T and makes a section 338 election for T. T owns all of the stock of T1 and T2. T's deemed purchase of the T1 and T2 stock results in a qualified stock purchase of T1 and T2 and section 338 elections are made for T1 and T2. T1 and T2 each own 50 percent of the vote and value of T3 stock. The deemed purchases by T1 and T2 of the T3 stock result in a qualified stock purchase of T3 and a section 338 election is made for T3. T is the common parent of a consolidated group and all of the deemed asset sales are reported on the T group's final consolidated return. See § 1.338-10(a)(1).

(ii) Because T, T1, T2 and T3 are members of a consolidated group filing a final consolidated return, no gain or loss is recognized by T, T1 or T2 on their respective deemed sales of target affiliate stock.

Example 4. (i) T's sole asset, all of the FT1 stock, has a basis of $25 and a fair market value of $150. FT1's sole asset, all of the FT2 stock, has a basis of $75 and a fair market value of $150. FT1 and FT2 each have $50 of accumulated earnings and profits for purposes of section 1248(c) and (d). FT2's assets have a basis of $125 and a fair market value of $150, and their sale would not generate subpart F income under section 951. The sale of the FT2 stock or assets would not generate income effectively connected with the conduct of a trade or business within the United States. FT1 does not have an election in effect under section 953(d) and neither FT1 nor FT2 is a passive foreign investment company.

(ii) P makes a qualified stock purchase of T and makes a section 338 election for T. T's deemed purchase of the FT1 stock results in a qualified stock purchase of FT1 and a section 338 election is made for M. Similarly, FT1's deemed purchase of the FT2 stock results in a qualified stock purchase of FT2 and a section 338 election is made for FT2.

(iii) T recognizes $125 of gain on the deemed sale of the FT1 stock under paragraph (h)(3) of this section. FT1 does not recognize $75 of gain on the deemed sale of the FT2 stock under paragraph (h)(2) of this section. FT2 recognizes $25 of gain on the deemed sale of its assets. The $125 gain T recognizes on the deemed sale of the FT1 stock is included in T's income as a dividend under section 1248, because FT1 and FT2 have sufficient earnings and profits for full recharacterization ($50 of accumulated earnings and profits in FT1, $50 of accumulated earnings and profits in FT2, and $25 of deemed sale earnings and profits in FT2). Section 1.338-9(b). For purposes of sections 901 through 908, the source and foreign tax credit limitation basket of $25 of the recharacterized gain on the deemed sale of the FT1 stock is determined under section 338(h)(16).

[Reg. § 1.338-4.]

☐ [*T.D.* 8940, 2-12-2001.]

§ 1.338-5. Adjusted grossed-up basis.—(a) *Scope.* This section provides rules under section 338(b) to determine the adjusted grossed-up basis (AGUB) for target. AGUB is the amount for which new target is deemed to have purchased all of its assets in the deemed purchase under section 338(a)(2). AGUB is allocated among target's assets in accordance with § 1.338-6 to determine the price at which the assets are deemed to have been purchased. When a subsequent increase or decrease with respect to an element of AGUB is required under general principles of tax law, redetermined AGUB is allocated among target's assets in accordance with § 1.338-7.

(b) *Determination of AGUB*—(1) *General rule.* AGUB is the sum of—

(i) The grossed-up basis in the purchasing corporation's recently purchased target stock;

(ii) The purchasing corporation's basis in nonrecently purchased target stock; and

(iii) The liabilities of new target.

(2) *Time and amount of AGUB*—(i) *Original determination.* AGUB is initially determined at the beginning of the day after the acquisition date of target. General principles of tax law apply in determining the timing and amount of the elements of AGUB.

(ii) *Redetermination of AGUB.* AGUB is redetermined at such time and in such amount as an increase or decrease would be required, under general principles of tax law, with respect to an element of AGUB. For example, AGUB is redetermined because of an increase or decrease in the amount paid or incurred for recently purchased stock or nonrecently purchased stock or because liabilities not originally taken into account in determining AGUB are subsequently taken into account. An increase or decrease to one element of AGUB also may cause an increase or decrease to another element of AGUB. For example, if there is an increase in the amount paid or incurred for recently purchased stock after the acquisition date, any increase in the basis of nonrecently purchased stock because a gain recognition election was made is also taken into account when AGUB is redetermined. Increases or decreases with respect to the elements of AGUB result in the reallocation of AGUB among target's assets under § 1.338-7.

(iii) *Examples.* The following examples illustrate this paragraph (b)(2):

Example 1. In Year 1, T, a manufacturer, purchases a customized delivery truck from X with purchase money indebtedness having a stated principal amount of $100,000. P acquires all of the stock of T in Year 3 for $700,000 and makes a section 338 election for T. Assume T has no liabilities other than its purchase money indebtedness to X. In Year 4, when T is neither insolvent nor in a title 11 case, T and X agree to reduce the amount of the purchase money indebtedness to $80,000. Assume that the reduction would be a purchase price reduction under section 108(e)(5). T and X's agreement to reduce the amount of the purchase money indebtedness would, under general principles of tax law that would apply if the deemed asset sale had actually occurred, change the amount of liabilities of old target taken into account in determining its basis. Accordingly, AGUB is redetermined at the time of the reduction. See paragraph (e)(2) of this section. Thus the purchase price reduction affects the basis of the truck only indirectly, through the mechanism of §§ 1.338-6 and 1.338-7. See § 1.338-4(b)(2)(iii) *Example* for the effect on ADSP.

Example 2. T, an accrual basis taxpayer, is a chemical manufacturer. In Year 1, T is obligated to remediate environmental contamination at the site of one of its plants. Assume that all the events have occurred that establish the fact of the liability and the amount of the liability can be determined with reasonable accuracy but economic performance has not occurred with respect to the liability within the meaning of section 461(h). P acquires all of the stock of T in Year 1 and makes a section 338 election for T. Assume that, if a corporation unrelated to T had actually purchased T's assets and assumed T's obligation to remediate the contamination, the corporation would not satisfy the economic performance requirements until Year 5. Under section 461(h), the assumed liability would not be treated as incurred and taken into account in basis until that time. The incurrence of the liability in Year 5 under the economic performance rules is an increase in the amount of liabilities properly taken into account in basis and results in the redetermination of AGUB. (Respecting ADSP, compare § 1.461-4(d)(5), which provides that economic performance occurs for old T as the amount of the liability is properly taken into account in amount realized on the deemed asset sale. Thus ADSP is not redetermined when new T satisfies the economic performance requirements.)

(c) *Grossed-up basis of recently purchased stock.* The purchasing corporation's grossed-up basis of recently purchased target stock (as defined in section 338(b)(6)(A)) is an amount equal to—

Reg. § 1.338-5(c)

(1) The purchasing corporation's basis in recently purchased target stock at the beginning of the day after the acquisition date determined without regard to the acquisition costs taken into account in paragraph (c)(3) of this section;

(2) Multiplied by a fraction, the numerator of which is 100 minus the number that is the percentage of target stock (by value, determined on the acquisition date) attributable to the purchasing corporation's nonrecently purchased target stock, and the denominator of which is the number equal to the percentage of target stock (by value, determined on the acquisition date) attributable to the purchasing corporation's recently purchased target stock;

(3) Plus the acquisition costs the purchasing corporation incurred in connection with its purchase of the recently purchased stock that are capitalized in the basis of such stock (e.g., brokerage commissions and any similar costs incurred by the purchasing corporation to acquire the stock).

(d) *Basis of nonrecently purchased stock; gain recognition election*—(1) *No gain recognition election.* In the absence of a gain recognition election under section 338(b)(3) and this section, the purchasing corporation retains its basis in the nonrecently purchased stock.

(2) *Procedure for making gain recognition election.* A gain recognition election may be made for nonrecently purchased stock of target (or a target affiliate) only if a section 338 election is made for target (or the target affiliate). The gain recognition election is made by attaching a gain recognition statement to a timely filed Form 8023 for target. The gain recognition statement must contain the information specified in the form and its instructions. The gain recognition election is irrevocable. If a section 338(h)(10) election is made for target, see § 1.338(h)(10)-1(d)(1) (providing that the purchasing corporation is automatically deemed to have made a gain recognition election for its nonrecently purchased T stock).

(3) *Effect of gain recognition election*—(i) *In general.* If the purchasing corporation makes a gain recognition election, then for all purposes of the Internal Revenue Code—

(A) The purchasing corporation is treated as if it sold on the acquisition date the nonrecently purchased target stock for the basis amount determined under paragraph (d)(3)(ii) of this section; and

(B) The purchasing corporation's basis on the acquisition date in nonrecently purchased target stock immediately following the deemed sale in paragraph (d)(3)(i)(A) of this section is the basis amount.

(ii) *Basis amount.* The basis amount is equal to the amount in paragraph (c)(1) of this section (the purchasing corporation's basis in recently purchased target stock at the beginning of the day after the acquisition date determined without regard to the acquisition costs taken into account in paragraph (c)(3) of this section) multiplied by a fraction the numerator of which is the percentage of target stock (by value, determined on the acquisition date) attributable to the purchasing corporation's nonrecently purchased target stock and the denominator of which is 100 percent minus the numerator amount. Thus, if target has a single class of outstanding stock, the purchasing corporation's basis in each share of nonrecently purchased target stock after the gain recognition election is equal to the average price per share of the purchasing corporation's recently purchased target stock.

(iii) *Losses not recognized.* Only gains (unreduced by losses) on the nonrecently purchased target stock are recognized.

(iv) *Stock subject to election.* The gain recognition election applies to—

(A) All nonrecently purchased target stock; and

(B) Any nonrecently purchased stock in a target affiliate having the same acquisition date as target if such target affiliate stock is held by the purchasing corporation on such date.

(e) *Liabilities of new target*—(1) *In general.* The liabilities of new target are the liabilities of target as of the beginning of the day after the acquisition date (but see § 1.338-1(d)(regarding certain transactions on the acquisition date)). In order to be taken into account in AGUB, a liability must be a liability of target that is properly taken into account in basis under general principles of tax law that would apply if new target had acquired its assets from an unrelated person for consideration that included discharge of the liabilities of that unrelated person. Such liabilities may include liabilities for the tax consequences resulting from the deemed sale.

(2) *Time and amount of liabilities.* The time for taking into account liabilities of old target in determining AGUB and the amount of the liabilities taken into account is determined as if new target had acquired its assets from an unrelated person for consideration that included the discharge of its liabilities.

(3) *Interaction with deemed sale tax consequences.* In general, see § 1.338-4(e). Although ADSP and AGUB are not necessarily linked, if an increase in the amount realized for recently purchased stock of target is taken into account after the acquisition date, and if the tax on the deemed sale tax consequences is a liability of target, any

Reg. § 1.338-5(c)(1)

increase in that liability is also taken into account in redetermining AGUB.

(f) *Adjustments by the Internal Revenue Service.* In connection with the examination of a return, the Commissioner may increase (or decrease) AGUB under the authority of section 338(b)(2) and allocate such amounts to target's assets under the authority of section 338(b)(5) so that AGUB and the basis of target's assets properly reflect the cost to the purchasing corporation of its interest in target's assets. Such items may include distributions from target to the purchasing corporation, capital contributions from the purchasing corporation to target during the 12-month acquisition period, or acquisitions of target stock by the purchasing corporation after the acquisition date from minority shareholders. See also § 1.338-1(d) (regarding certain transactions on the acquisition date).

(g) *Examples.* The following examples illustrate this section. For purposes of the examples in this paragraph (g), T has no liabilities other than the tax liability for the deemed sale tax consequences, T shareholders incur no costs in selling the T stock, and P incurs no costs in acquiring the T stock. The examples are as follows:

Example 1. (i) Before July 1 of Year 1, P purchases 10 of the 100 shares of T stock for $5,000. On July 1 of Year 2, P purchases 80 shares of T stock for $60,000 and makes a section 338 election for T. As of July 1 of Year 2, T's only asset is raw land with an adjusted basis to T of $50,400 and a fair market value of $100,000. T has no loss or tax credit carryovers to Year 2. T's marginal tax rate for any ordinary income or net capital gain resulting from the deemed asset sale is 34 percent. The 10 shares purchased before July 1 of Year 1 constitute nonrecently purchased T stock with respect to P's qualified stock purchase of T stock on July 1 of Year 2.

(ii) The ADSP formula as applied to these facts is the same as in § 1.338-4(g) *Example 1.* Accordingly, the ADSP for T is $87,672.72. The existence of nonrecently purchased T stock is irrelevant for purposes of the ADSP formula, because that formula treats P's nonrecently purchased T stock in the same manner as T stock not held by P.

(iii) The total tax liability resulting from T's deemed asset sale, as calculated under the ADSP formula, is $12,672.72.

(iv) If P does not make a gain recognition election, the AGUB of new T's assets is $85,172.72, determined as follows (in the following formula below, GRP is the grossed-up basis in P's recently purchased T stock, BNP is P's basis in nonrecently purchased T stock, L is T's liabilities, and X is P's acquisition costs for the recently purchased T stock):

$$AGUB = GRP + BNP + L + X$$

$$AGUB = \$60,000 \times [(1 - .1)/.8] + \$5,000 + \$12,672.72 + 0$$

$$AGUB = \$85,172.72$$

(v) If P makes a gain recognition election, the AGUB of new T's assets is $87,672.72, determined as follows:

$$AGUB = \$60,000 \times [(1 - .1)/.8] + \$60,000 \times [(1 - .1)/.8] \times [.1/(1 - .1)] + \$12,672.72$$

$$AGUB = \$87,672.72$$

(vi) The calculation of AGUB if P makes a gain recognition election may be simplified as follows:

$$AGUB = \$60,000/.8 + \$12,672.72$$

$$AGUB = \$87,672.72$$

(vii) As a result of the gain recognition election, P's basis in its nonrecently purchased T stock is increased from $5,000 to $7,500 (i.e., $60,000 × [(1 − .1)/.8] × [.1/(1 − .1)]). Thus, P recognizes a gain in Year 2 with respect to its nonrecently purchased T stock of $2,500 (i.e., $7,500 − $5,000).

Example 2. On January 1 of Year 1, P purchases one-third of the T stock. On March 1 of Year 1, T distributes a dividend to all of its shareholders. On April 15 of Year 1, P purchases the remaining T stock and makes a section 338 election for T. In appropriate circumstances, the Commissioner may decrease the AGUB of T to take into account the payment of the dividend and properly reflect the fair market value of T's assets deemed purchased.

Example 3. (i) T's sole asset is a building worth $100,000. At this time, T has 100 shares of stock outstanding. On August 1 of Year 1, P purchases 10 of the 100 shares of T stock for $8,000. On June 1 of Year 2, P purchases 50 shares of T stock for $50,000. On June 15 of Year 2, P contributes a tract of land to the capital of T and receives 10 additional shares of T stock as a result of the contribution. Both the basis and fair market value of the land at that time are $10,800. On June 30 of Year 2, P purchases the remaining 40 shares of T stock for $40,000 and makes a section 338 election for T. The AGUB of T is $108,800.

(ii) To prevent the shifting of basis from the contributed property to other assets of T, the Commissioner may allocate $10,800 of the AGUB to the land, leaving $98,000 to be allocated to the building. See paragraph (f) of this section. Otherwise, applying the allocation rules of § 1.338-6 would, on these facts, result in an allocation to the recently contributed land of an amount less than its value of $10,800, with the difference being allocated to the building already held by T.

[Reg. § 1.338-5.]

☐ [*T.D.* 8940, 2-12-2001.]

Reg. § 1.338-5(g)

§1.338-6. **Allocation of ADSP and AGUB among target assets.**—(a) *Scope*—(1) *In general*. This section prescribes rules for allocating ADSP and AGUB among the acquisition date assets of a target for which a section 338 election is made.

(2) *Fair market value*—(i) *In general*. Generally, the fair market value of an asset is its gross fair market value (i.e., fair market value determined without regard to mortgages, liens, pledges, or other liabilities). However, for purposes of determining the amount of old target's deemed sale tax consequences, the fair market value of any property subject to a nonrecourse indebtedness will be treated as being not less than the amount of such indebtedness. (For purposes of the preceding sentence, a liability that was incurred because of the acquisition of the property is disregarded to the extent that such liability was not taken into account in determining old target's basis in such property.)

(ii) *Transaction costs*. Transaction costs are not taken into account in allocating ADSP or AGUB to assets in the deemed sale (except indirectly through their effect on the total ADSP or AGUB to be allocated).

(iii) *Internal Revenue Service authority*. In connection with the examination of a return, the Internal Revenue Service may challenge the taxpayers determination of the fair market value of any asset by any appropriate method and take into account all factors, including any lack of adverse tax interests between the parties.

(b) *General rule for allocating ADSP and AGUB*—(1) *Reduction in the amount of consideration for Class I assets*. Both ADSP and AGUB, in the respective allocation of each, are first reduced by the amount of Class I assets. Class I assets are cash and general deposit accounts (including savings and checking accounts) other than certificates of deposit held in banks, savings and loan associations, and other depository institutions. If the amount of Class I assets exceeds AGUB, new target will immediately realize ordinary income in an amount equal to such excess. The amount of ADSP or AGUB remaining after the reduction is to be allocated to the remaining acquisition date assets.

(2) *Other assets*—(i) *In general*. Subject to the limitations and other rules of paragraph (c) of this section, ADSP and AGUB (as reduced by the amount of Class I assets) are allocated among Class II acquisition date assets of target in proportion to the fair market values of such Class II assets at such time, then among Class III assets so held in such proportion, then among Class IV assets so held in such proportion, then among

Class V assets so held in such proportion, then among Class VI assets so held in such proportion, and finally to Class VII assets. If an asset is described below as includible in more than one class, then it is included in such class with the lower or lowest class number (for instance, Class III has a lower class number than Class IV).

(ii) *Class II assets*. Class II assets are actively traded personal property within the meaning of section 1092(d)(1) and §1.1092(d)-1 (determined without regard to section 1092(d)(3)). In addition, Class II assets include certificates of deposit and foreign currency even if they are not actively traded personal property. Class II assets do not include stock of target affiliates, whether or not of a class that is actively traded, other than actively traded stock described in section 1504(a)(4). Examples of Class II assets include U.S. government securities and publicly traded stock.

(iii) *Class III assets*. Class III assets are assets that the taxpayer marks to market at least annually for Federal income tax purposes and debt instruments (including accounts receivable). However, Class III assets do not include—

(A) Debt instruments issued by persons related at the beginning of the day following the acquisition date to the target under section 267(b) or 707;

(B) Contingent debt instruments subject to §1.1275-4, §1.483-4, or section 988, unless the instrument is subject to the non-contingent bond method of §1.1275-4(b) or is described in §1.988-2(b)(2)(i)(B)(*2*); and

(C) Debt instruments convertible into the stock of the issuer or other property.

(iv) *Class IV assets*. Class IV assets are stock in trade of the taxpayer or other property of a kind that would properly be included in the inventory of taxpayer if on hand at the close of the taxable year, or property held by the taxpayer primarily for sale to customers in the ordinary course of its trade or business.

(v) *Class V assets*. Class V assets are all assets other than Class I, II, III, IV, VI, and VII assets.

(vi) *Class VI assets*. Class VI assets are all section 197 intangibles, as defined in section 197, except goodwill and going concern value.

(vii) *Class VII assets*. Class VII assets are goodwill and going concern value (whether or not the goodwill or going concern value qualifies as a section 197 intangible).

(3) *Other items designated by the Internal Revenue Service*. Similar items may be added to any class described in this paragraph (b) by desig-

Reg. § 1.338-6(a)(1)

nation in the Internal Revenue Bulletin by the Internal Revenue Service (see § 601.601(d)(2) of this chapter).

(c) *Certain limitations and other rules for allocation to an asset*—(1) *Allocation not to exceed fair market value.* The amount of ADSP or AGUB allocated to an asset (other than Class VII assets) cannot exceed the fair market value of that asset at the beginning of the day after the acquisition date.

(2) *Allocation subject to other rules.* The amount of ADSP or AGUB allocated to an asset is subject to other provisions of the Internal Revenue Code or general principles of tax law in the same manner as if such asset were transferred to or acquired from an unrelated person in a sale or exchange. For example, if the deemed asset sale is a transaction described in section 1056(a) (relating to basis limitation for player contracts transferred in connection with the sale of a franchise), the amount of AGUB allocated to a contract for the services of an athlete cannot exceed the limitation imposed by that section. As another example, section 197(f)(5) applies in determining the amount of AGUB allocated to an amortizable section 197 intangible resulting from an assumption-reinsurance transaction.

(3) *Special rule for allocating AGUB when purchasing corporation has nonrecently purchased stock*—(i) *Scope.* This paragraph (c)(3) applies if at the beginning of the day after the acquisition date—

(A) The purchasing corporation holds nonrecently purchased stock for which a gain recognition election under section 338(b)(3) and § 1.338-5(d) is not made; and

(B) The hypothetical purchase price determined under paragraph (c)(3)(ii) of this section exceeds the AGUB determined under § 1.338-5(b).

(ii) *Determination of hypothetical purchase price.* Hypothetical purchase price is the AGUB that would result if a gain recognition election were made.

(iii) *Allocation of AGUB.* Subject to the limitations in paragraphs (c)(1) and (2) of this section, the portion of AGUB (after reduction by the amount of Class I assets) to be allocated to each Class II, III, IV, V, VI, and VII asset of target held at the beginning of the day after the acquisition date is determined by multiplying—

(A) The amount that would be allocated to such asset under the general rules of this section were AGUB equal to the hypothetical purchase price; by

(B) A fraction, the numerator of which is actual AGUB (after reduction by the amount of Class I assets) and the denominator of which is the hypothetical purchase price (after reduction by the amount of Class I assets).

(4) *Liabilities taken into account in determining amount realized on subsequent disposition.* In determining the amount realized on a subsequent sale or other disposition of property deemed purchased by new target, § 1.1001-2(a)(3) shall not apply to any liability that was taken into account in AGUB.

(d) *Examples.* The following examples illustrate §§ 1.338-4, 1.338-5, and this section:

Example 1. (i) T owns 90 percent of the outstanding T1 stock. P purchases 100 percent of the outstanding T stock for $2,000. There are no acquisition costs. P makes a section 338 election for T and, as a result, T1 is considered acquired in a qualified stock purchase. A section 338 election is made for T1. The grossed-up basis of the T stock is $2,000 (i.e., $2,000 × 1/1).

(ii) The liabilities of T as of the beginning of the day after the acquisition date (including the tax liability for the deemed sale tax consequences) that would, under general principles of tax law, properly be taken into account at that time, are as follows:

Liabilities (nonrecourse mortgage plus unsecured liabilities)......	$ 700
Taxes Payable	300
Total	$1,000

(iii) The AGUB of T is determined as follows:

Grossed-up basis	$2,000
Total liabilities	1,000
AGUB	$3,000

(iv) Assume that ADSP is also $3,000.

(v) Assume that, at the beginning of the day after the acquisition date, T's cash and the fair market values of T's Class II, III, IV, and V assets are as follows:

Reg. § 1.338-6(d)

Asset Class	Asset	Fair market value
I	Cash	$ 200[*]
II	Portfolio of actively traded securities	300
III	Accounts receivable	600
IV	Inventory	300
V	Building	800
V	Land	200
V	Investment in T1	450
	Total	$2,850

[*] Amount

(vi) Under paragraph (b)(1) of this section, the amount of ADSP and AGUB allocable to T's Class II, III, IV, and V assets is reduced by the amount of cash to $2,800, i.e., $3,000 − $200. $300 of ADSP and of AGUB is then allocated to actively traded securities. $600 of ADSP and of AGUB is then allocated to accounts receivable. $300 of ADSP and of AGUB is then allocated to the inventory. Since the remaining amount of ADSP and of AGUB is $1,600 (i.e., $3,000 − ($200 + $300 + $600 + $300)), an amount which exceeds the sum of the fair market values of T's Class V assets, the amount of ADSP and of AGUB allocated to each Class V asset is its fair market value:

Building	800
Land	200
Investment in T1	450
Total	$1,450

(vii) T has no Class VI assets. The amount of ADSP and of AGUB allocated to T's Class VII assets (goodwill and going concern value) is $150, i.e., $1,600 − $1,450.

(viii) The grossed-up basis of the T1 stock is $500, i.e., $450 × 1/.9.

(ix) The liabilities of T1 as of the beginning of the day after the acquisition date (including the tax liability for the deemed sale tax consequences) that would, under general principles of tax law, properly be taken into account at that time, are as follows:

General Liabilities	$100
Taxes Payable	20
Total	$120

(x) The AGUB of T1 is determined as follows:

Grossed-up basis of T1 Stock.......	$500
Liabilities	120
AGUB	$620

(xi) Assume that ADSP is also $620.

(xii) Assume that at the beginning of the day after the acquisition date, T1's cash and the fair market values of its Class IV and VI assets are as follows:

Asset Class	Asset	Fair Market Value
I	Cash	$ 50[*]
IV	Inventory	200
VI	Patent	350
	Total	$600

[*] Amount.

(xiii) The amount of ADSP and of AGUB allocable to T1's Class IV and VI assets is first reduced by the $50 of cash.

(xiv) Because the remaining amount of ADSP and of AGUB ($570) is an amount which exceeds the fair market value of T1's only Class IV asset, the inventory, the amount allocated to the inventory is its fair market value ($200). After that, the remaining amount of ADSP and of AGUB ($370) exceeds the fair market value of T1's only Class VI asset, the patent. Thus, the amount of ADSP and of AGUB allocated to the patent is its fair market value ($350).

Reg. § 1.338-6(d)

(xv) The amount of ADSP and of AGUB allocated to T1's Class VII assets (goodwill and going concern value) is $20, i.e., $570 − $550.

Example 2. (i) Assume that the facts are the same as in *Example 1* except that P has, for five years, owned 20 percent of T's stock, which has a basis in P's hands at the beginning of the day after the acquisition date of $100, and P purchases the remaining 80 percent of T's stock for $1,600. P does not make a gain recognition election under section 338(b)(3).

(ii) Under § 1.338-5(c), the grossed-up basis of recently purchased T stock is $1,600, i.e., $1,600 × (1 − .2)/.8.

(iii) The AGUB of T is determined as follows:

Grossed-up basis of recently purchased stock as determined under § 1.338-5(c) ($1,600 × (1 − .2)/.8)	$1,600
Basis of nonrecently purchased stock	100
Liabilities	1,000
AGUB	$2,700

(iv) Since P holds nonrecently purchased stock, the hypothetical purchase price of the T stock must be computed and is determined as follows:

Grossed-up basis of recently purchased stock as determined under § 1.338-5(c) ($1,600 × (1 − .2)/.8)	$1,600
Basis of nonrecently purchased stock as if the gain recognition election under § 1.338-5(d)(2) had been made ($1,600 × .2/(1 − .2))	400
Liabilities	1,000
Total	$3,000

(v) Since the hypothetical purchase price ($3,000) exceeds the AGUB ($2,700) and no gain recognition election is made under section 338(b)(3), AGUB is allocated under paragraph (c)(3) of this section.

(vi) First, an AGUB amount equal to the hypothetical purchase price ($3,000) is allocated among the assets under the general rules of this section. The allocation is set forth in the column below entitled *Original Allocation*. Next, the allocation to each asset in Class II through Class VII is multiplied by a fraction having a numerator equal to the actual AGUB reduced by the amount of Class I assets ($2,700 − $200 = $2,500) and a denominator equal to the hypothetical purchase price reduced by the amount of Class I assets ($3,000 − $200 = $2,800), or 2,500/2,800. This produces the *Final Allocation*:

Class	Asset	Original Allocation	Final Allocation
I	Cash	$ 200	$ 200
II	Portfolio of actively traded securities	300	268*
III	Accounts receivable	600	536
IV	Inventory	300	268
V	Building	800	714
V	Land	200	178
V	Investment in T1	450	402
VII	Goodwill and going concern value	150	134
	Total	$3,000	$2,700

* All numbers rounded for convenience.

[Reg. § 1.338-6.]

☐ [*T.D.* 8940, 2-12-2001 (*corrected* 3-29-2001).]

§ 1.338-7. Allocation of redetermined ADSP and AGUB among target assets.—(a) *Scope.* ADSP and AGUB are redetermined at such time and in such amount as an increase or decrease would be required under general principles of tax law for the elements of ADSP or AGUB. This section provides rules for allocating redetermined ADSP or AGUB.

(b) *Allocation of redetermined ADSP and AGUB.* When ADSP or AGUB is redetermined, a new allocation of ADSP or AGUB is made by

Reg. § 1.338-7(b)

allocating the redetermined ADSP or AGUB amount under the rules of § 1.338-6. If the allocation of the redetermined ADSP or AGUB amount under § 1.338-6 to a given asset is different from the original allocation to it, the difference is added to or subtracted from the original allocation to the asset, as appropriate. (See paragraph (d) of this section for new target's treatment of the amount so allocated.) Amounts allocable to an acquisition date asset (or with respect to a disposed-of acquisition date asset) are subject to all the asset allocation rules (for example, the fair market value limitation in § 1.338-6(c)(1)) as if the redetermined ADSP or AGUB were the ADSP or AGUB on the acquisition date.

(c) *Special rules for ADSP*—(1) *Increases or decreases in deemed sale tax consequences taxable notwithstanding old target ceases to exist.* To the extent general principles of tax law would require a seller in an actual asset sale to account for events relating to the sale that occur after the sale date, target must make such an accounting. Target is not precluded from realizing additional deemed sale tax consequences because the target is treated as a new corporation after the acquisition date.

(2) *Procedure for transactions in which section 338(h)(10) is not elected*—(i) *Deemed sale tax consequences included in new target's return.* If an election under section 338(h)(10) is not made, any additional deemed sale tax consequences of old target resulting from an increase or decrease in the ADSP are included in new target's income tax return for new target's taxable year in which the increase or decrease is taken into account. For example, if after the acquisition date there is an increase in the allocable ADSP of section 1245 property for which the recomputed basis (but not the adjusted basis) exceeds the portion of the ADSP allocable to that particular asset on the acquisition date, the additional gain is treated as ordinary income to the extent it does not exceed such excess amount. See paragraph (c)(2)(ii) of this section for the special treatment of old target's carryovers and carrybacks. Although included in new target's income tax return, the deemed sale tax consequences are separately accounted for as an item of old target and may not be offset by income, gain, deduction, loss, credit, or other amount of new target. The amount of tax on income of old target resulting from an increase or decrease in the ADSP is determined as if such deemed sale tax consequences had been recognized in old target's taxable year ending at the close of the acquisition date. However, because the income resulting from the increase or decrease in ADSP is reportable in new target's taxable year of the increase or decrease, not in old target's taxable year ending at

the close of the acquisition date, there is not a resulting underpayment of tax in that past taxable year of old target for purposes of calculation of interest due.

(ii) *Carryovers and carrybacks*—(A) *Loss carryovers to new target taxable years.* A net operating loss or net capital loss of old target may be carried forward to a taxable year of new target, under the principles of section 172 or 1212, as applicable, but is allowed as a deduction only to the extent of any recognized income of old target for such taxable year, as described in paragraph (c)(2)(i) of this section. For this purpose, however, taxable years of new target are not taken into account in applying the limitations in section 172(b)(1) or 1212(a)(1)(B) (or other similar limitations). In applying sections 172(b) and 1212(a)(1), only income, gain, loss, deduction, credit, and other amounts of old target are taken into account. Thus, if old target has an unexpired net operating loss at the close of its taxable year in which the deemed asset sale occurred that could be carried forward to a subsequent taxable year, such loss may be carried forward until it is absorbed by old target's income.

(B) *Loss carrybacks to taxable years of old target.* An ordinary loss or capital loss accounted for as a separate item of old target under paragraph (c)(2)(i) of this section may be carried back to a taxable year of old target under the principles of section 172 or 1212, as applicable. For this purpose, taxable years of new target are not taken into account in applying the limitations in section 172(b) or 1212(a) (or other similar limitations).

(C) *Credit carryovers and carrybacks.* The principles described in paragraphs (c)(2)(ii)(A) and (B) of this section apply to carryovers and carrybacks of amounts for purposes of determining the amount of a credit allowable under part IV, subchapter A, chapter 1 of the Internal Revenue Code. Thus, for example, credit carryovers of old target may offset only income tax attributable to items described in paragraph (c)(2)(i) of this section.

(3) *Procedure for transactions in which section 338(h)(10) is elected.* If an election under section 338(h)(10) is made, any changes in the deemed sale tax consequences caused by an increase or decrease in the ADSP are accounted for in determining the taxable income (or other amount) of the member of the selling consolidated group, the selling affiliate, or the S corporation shareholders to which such income, loss, or other amount is attributable for the taxable year in which such increase or decrease is taken into account.

(d) *Special rules for AGUB*—(1) *Effect of disposition or depreciation of acquisition date assets.*

Reg. § 1.338-7(c)(1)

If an acquisition date asset has been disposed of, depreciated, amortized, or depleted by new target before an amount is added to the original allocation to the asset, the increased amount otherwise allocable to such asset is taken into account under general principles of tax law that apply when part of the cost of an asset not previously taken into account in basis is paid or incurred after the asset has been disposed of, depreciated, amortized, or depleted. A similar rule applies when an amount is subtracted from the original allocation to the asset. For purposes of the preceding sentence, an asset is considered to have been disposed of to the extent that its allocable portion of the decrease in AGUB would reduce its basis below zero.

(2) *Section 38 property.* Section 1.47-2(c) applies to a reduction in basis of section 38 property under this section.

* * *

[Reg. § 1.338-7.]

☐ [*T.D.* 8940, 2-12-2001.]

§ 1.338-8. Asset and stock consistency.—(a) *Introduction*—(1) *Overview.* This section implements the consistency rules of sections 338(e) and (f). Under this section, no election under section 338 is deemed made or required with respect to target or any target affiliate. Instead, the person acquiring an asset may have a carryover basis in the asset.

(2) *General application.* The consistency rules generally apply if the purchasing corporation acquires an asset directly from target during the target consistency period and target is a subsidiary in a consolidated group. In such a case, gain from the sale of the asset is reflected under the investment adjustment provisions of the consolidated return regulations in the basis of target stock and may reduce gain from the sale of the stock. See § 1.1502-32 (investment adjustment provisions). Under the consistency rules, the purchasing corporation generally takes a carryover basis in the asset, unless a section 338 election is made for target. Similar rules apply if the purchasing corporation acquires an asset directly from a lower-tier target affiliate if gain from the sale is reflected under the investment adjustment provisions in the basis of target stock.

(3) *Extensions of the general rules.* If an arrangement exists, paragraph (f) of this section generally extends the carryover basis rule to certain cases in which the purchasing corporation acquires assets indirectly from target (or a lower-tier target affiliate). To prevent avoidance of the consistency rules, paragraph (j) of this section also may extend the consistency period or the 12-month acquisition period and may disregard the presence of conduits.

(4) *Application where certain dividends are paid.* Paragraph (g) of this section extends the carryover basis rule to certain cases in which dividends are paid to a corporation that is not a member of the same consolidated group as the distributing corporation. Generally, this rule applies where a 100 percent dividends received deduction is used in conjunction with asset dispositions to achieve an effect similar to that available under the investment adjustment provisions of the consolidated return regulations.

(5) *Application to foreign target affiliates.* Paragraph (h) of this section extends the carryover basis rule to certain cases involving target affiliates that are controlled foreign corporations.

(6) *Stock consistency.* This section limits the application of the stock consistency rules to cases in which the rules are necessary to prevent avoidance of the asset consistency rules. Following the general treatment of a section 338(h)(10) election, a sale of a corporation's stock is treated as a sale of the corporation's assets if a section 338(h)(10) election is made. Because gain from this asset sale may be reflected in the basis of the stock of a higher-tier target, the carryover basis rule may apply to the assets.

(b) *Consistency for direct acquisitions*—(1) *General rule.* The basis rules of paragraph (d) of this section apply to an asset if—

(i) The asset is disposed of during the target consistency period;

(ii) The basis of target stock, as of the target acquisition date, reflects gain from the disposition of the asset (see paragraph (c) of this section); and

(iii) The asset is owned, immediately after its acquisition and on the target acquisition date, by a corporation that acquires stock of target in the qualified stock purchase (or by an affiliate of an acquiring corporation).

(2) *Section 338(h)(10) elections.* For purposes of this section, if a section 338(h)(10) election is made for a corporation acquired in a qualified stock purchase—

(i) The acquisition is treated as an acquisition of the corporation's assets (see § 1.338(h)(10)-1); and

(ii) The corporation is not treated as target.

(c) *Gain from disposition reflected in basis of target stock.* For purposes of this section:

(1) *General rule.* Gain from the disposition of an asset is reflected in the basis of a corporation's stock if the gain is taken into account under § 1.1502-32, directly or indirectly, in determining the basis of the stock, after applying section 1503(e) and other provisions of the Internal Revenue Code.

(2) *Gain not reflected if section 338 election made for target.* Gain from the disposition of an asset that is otherwise reflected in the basis of target stock as of the target acquisition date is not considered reflected in the basis of target stock if a section 338 election is made for target.

(3) *Gain reflected by reason of distributions.* Gain from the disposition of an asset is not considered reflected in the basis of target stock merely by reason of the receipt of a distribution from a

Reg. § 1.338-8(c)(3)

target affiliate that is not a member of the same consolidated group as the distributee. See paragraph (g) of this section for the treatment of dividends eligible for a 100 percent dividends received deduction.

(4) *Controlled foreign corporations.* For a limitation applicable to gain of a target affiliate that is a controlled foreign corporation, *see* paragraph (h)(2) of this section.

(5) *Gain recognized outside the consolidated group.* Gain from the disposition of an asset by a person other than target or a target affiliate is not reflected in the basis of a corporation's stock unless the person is a conduit, as defined in paragraph (j)(4) of this section.

(d) *Basis of acquired assets*—(1) *Carryover basis rule.* If this paragraph (d) applies to an asset, the asset's basis immediately after its acquisition is, for all purposes of the Internal Revenue Code, its adjusted basis immediately before its disposition.

(2) *Exceptions to carryover basis rule for certain assets.* The carryover basis rule of paragraph (d)(1) of this section does not apply to the following assets—

(i) Any asset disposed of in the ordinary course of a trade or business (see section 338(e)(2)(A));

(ii) Any asset the basis of which is determined wholly by reference to the adjusted basis of the asset in the hands of the person that disposed of the asset (see section 338(e)(2)(B));

(iii) Any debt or equity instrument issued by target or a target affiliate (*see* paragraph (h)(3) of this section for an exception relating to the stock of a target affiliate that is a controlled foreign corporation);

(iv) Any asset the basis of which immediately after its acquisition would otherwise be less than its adjusted basis immediately before its disposition; and

(v) Any asset identified by the Internal Revenue Service in a revenue ruling or revenue procedure.

(3) *Exception to carryover basis rule for de minimis assets.* The carryover basis rules of this section do not apply to an asset if the asset is not disposed of as part of the same arrangement as the acquisition of target and the aggregate amount realized for all assets otherwise subject to the carryover basis rules of this section does not exceed $250,000.

(4) *Mitigation rule*—(i) *General rule.* If the carryover basis rules of this section apply to an asset and the asset is transferred to a domestic corporation in a transaction to which section 351 applies or as a contribution to capital and no gain

is recognized, the transferor's basis in the stock of the transferee (but not the transferee's basis in the asset) is determined without taking into account the carryover basis rules of this section.

(ii) *Time for transfer.* This paragraph (d)(4) applies only if the asset is transferred before the due date (including extensions) for the transferor's income tax return for the year that includes the last date for which a section 338 election may be made for target.

* * *

[Reg. § 1.338-8.]

☐ [*T.D. 8515, 1-12-94. Amended by T.D. 8597, 7-12-95 and T.D. 8710, 1-22-97. Redesignated by T.D. 8858, 1-5-2000. Amended by T.D. 8940, 2-12-2001.*]

§ 1.338(h)(10)-1. Deemed asset sale and liquidation.—(a) *Scope.* This section prescribes rules for qualification for a section 338(h)(10) election and for making a section 338(h)(10) election. This section also prescribes the consequences of such election. The rules of this section are in addition to the rules of §§ 1.338-1 through 1.338-10 and, in appropriate cases, apply instead of the rules of §§ 1.338-1 through 1.338-10.

(b) *Definitions*—(1) *Consolidated target.* A *consolidated target* is a target that is a member of a consolidated group within the meaning of § 1.1502-1(h) on the acquisition date and is not the common parent of the group on that date.

(2) *Selling consolidated group.* A *selling consolidated group* is the consolidated group of which the consolidated target is a member on the acquisition date.

(3) *Selling affiliate; affiliated target.* A *selling affiliate* is a domestic corporation that owns on the acquisition date an amount of stock in a domestic target, which amount of stock is described in section 1504(a)(2), and does not join in filing a consolidated return with the target. In such case, the target is an *affiliated target.*

(4) *S corporation target.* An *S corporation target* is a target that is an S corporation immediately before the acquisition date.

(5) *S corporation shareholders. S corporation shareholders* are the S corporation target's shareholders. Unless otherwise indicated, a reference to S corporation shareholders refers both to S corporation shareholders who do and those who do not sell their target stock.

(6) *Liquidation.* Any reference in this section to a liquidation is treated as a reference to the transfer described in paragraph (d)(4) of this section notwithstanding its ultimate characterization for Federal income tax purposes.

(c) *Section 338(h)(10) election*—(1) *In general.* A section 338(h)(10) election may be made for T if P acquires stock meeting the requirements of section 1504(a)(2) from a selling consolidated group, a selling affiliate, or the S corporation shareholders in a qualified stock purchase.

(2) *Simultaneous joint election requirement.* A section 338(h)(10) election is made jointly by P and the selling consolidated group (or the selling affiliate or the S corporation shareholders) on Form 8023 in accordance with the instructions to the form. S corporation shareholders who do not sell their stock must also consent to the election. The section 338(h)(10) election must be made not later than the 15th day of the 9th month beginning after the month in which the acquisition date occurs.

(3) *Irrevocability.* A section 338(h)(10) election is irrevocable. If a section 338(h)(10) election is made for T, a section 338 election is deemed made for T.

(4) *Effect of invalid election.* If a section 338(h)(10) election for T is not valid, the section 338 election for T is also not valid.

(d) *Certain consequences of section 338(h)(10) election.* For purposes of subtitle A of the Internal Revenue Code (except as provided in § 1.338-1(b)(2)), the consequences to the parties of making a section 338(h)(10) election for T are as follows:

(1) *P.* P is automatically deemed to have made a gain recognition election for its nonrecently purchased T stock, if any. The effect of a gain recognition election includes a taxable deemed sale by P on the acquisition date of any nonrecently purchased target stock. See § 1.338-5(d).

(2) *New T.* The AGUB for new T's assets is determined under § 1.338-5 and is allocated among the acquisition date assets under § § 1.338-6 and 1.338-7. Notwithstanding paragraph (d)(4) of this section (deemed liquidation of old T), new T remains liable for the tax liabilities of old T (including the tax liability for the deemed sale tax consequences). For example, new T remains liable for the tax liabilities of the members of any consolidated group that are attributable to taxable years in which those corporations and old T joined in the same consolidated return. See § 1.1502-6(a).

(3) *Old T—deemed sale—*(i) *In general.* Old T is treated as transferring all of its assets to an unrelated person in exchange for consideration that includes the discharge of its liabilities in a single transaction at the close of the acquisition date (but before the deemed liquidation). See § 1.338-1(a) regarding the tax characterization of the deemed asset sale. Except as provided in § 1.338(h)(10)-1(d)(8) (regarding the installment method), old T recognizes all of the gain realized

on the deemed transfer of its assets in consideration for the ADSP. ADSP for old T is determined under § 1.338-4 and allocated among the acquisition date assets under § § 1.338-6 and 1.338-7. Old T realizes the deemed sale tax consequences from the deemed asset sale before the close of the acquisition date while old T is a member of the selling consolidated group (or owned by the selling affiliate or owned by the S corporation shareholders). If T is an affiliated target, or an S corporation target, the principles of § § 1.338-2(c)(10) and 1.338-10(a)(1), (5), and (6)(i) apply to the return on which the deemed sale tax consequences are reported. When T is an S corporation target, T's S election continues in effect through the close of the acquisition date (including the time of the deemed asset sale and the deemed liquidation) notwithstanding section 1362(d)(2)(B). Also, when T is an S corporation target (but not a qualified subchapter S subsidiary), any direct and indirect subsidiaries of T which T has elected to treat as qualified subchapter S subsidiaries under section 1361(b)(3) remain qualified subchapter S subsidiaries through the close of the acquisition date.

(ii) *Tiered targets.* In the case of parent-subsidiary chains of corporations making elections under section 338(h)(10), the deemed asset sale of a parent corporation is considered to precede that of its subsidiary. See § 1.338-3(b)(4)(i).

(4) *Old T and selling consolidated group, selling affiliate, or S corporation shareholders—deemed liquidation; tax characterization—*(i) *In general.* Old T is treated as if, before the close of the acquisition date, after the deemed asset sale in paragraph (d)(3) of this section, and while old T is a member of the selling consolidated group (or owned by the selling affiliate or owned by the S corporation shareholders), it transferred all of its assets to members of the selling consolidated group, the selling affiliate, or S corporation shareholders and ceased to exist. The transfer from old T is characterized for Federal income tax purposes in the same manner as if the parties had actually engaged in the transactions deemed to occur because of this section and taking into account other transactions that actually occurred or are deemed to occur. For example, the transfer may be treated as a distribution in pursuance of a plan of reorganization, a distribution in complete cancellation or redemption of all its stock, one of a series of distributions in complete cancellation or redemption of all its stock in accordance with a plan of liquidation, or part of a circular flow of cash. In most cases, the transfer will be treated as a distribution in complete liquidation to which section 336 or 337 applies.

(ii) *Tiered targets.* In the case of parent-subsidiary chains of corporations making elections under section 338(h)(10), the deemed liquidation of a subsidiary corporation is considered to precede the deemed liquidation of its parent.

(5) *Selling consolidated group, selling affiliate, or S corporation shareholders*—(i) *In general.* If T is an S corporation target, S corporation shareholders (whether or not they sell their stock) take their pro rata share of the deemed sale tax consequences into account under section 1366 and increase or decrease their basis in T stock under section 1367. Members of the selling consolidated group, the selling affiliate, or S corporation shareholders are treated as if, after the deemed asset sale in paragraph (d)(3) of this section and before the close of the acquisition date, they received the assets transferred by old T in the transaction described in paragraph (d)(4)(i) of this section. In most cases, the transfer will be treated as a distribution in complete liquidation to which section 331 or 332 applies.

(ii) *Basis and holding period of T stock not acquired.* A member of the selling consolidated group (or the selling affiliate or an S corporation shareholder) retaining T stock is treated as acquiring the stock so retained on the day after the acquisition date for its fair market value. The holding period for the retained stock starts on the day after the acquisition date. For purposes of this paragraph, the fair market value of all of the T stock equals the grossed-up amount realized on the sale to P of P's recently purchased target stock. See § 1.338-4(c).

(iii) *T stock sale.* Members of the selling consolidated group (or the selling affiliate or S corporation shareholders) recognize no gain or loss on the sale or exchange of T stock included in the qualified stock purchase (although they may recognize gain or loss on the T stock in the deemed liquidation).

(6) *Nonselling minority shareholders other than nonselling S corporation shareholders*—(i) *In general.* This paragraph (d)(6) describes the treatment of shareholders of old T other than the following: members of the selling consolidated group, the selling affiliate, S corporation shareholders (whether or not they sell their stock), and P. For a description of the treatment of S corporation shareholders, see paragraph (d)(5) of this section. A shareholder to which this paragraph (d)(6) applies is called a minority shareholder.

(ii) *T stock sale.* A minority shareholder recognizes gain or loss on the shareholder's sale or exchange of T stock included in the qualified stock purchase.

(iii) *T stock not acquired.* A minority shareholder does not recognize gain or loss under this section with respect to shares of T stock retained by the shareholder. The shareholder's

basis and holding period for that T stock is not affected by the section 338(h)(10) election.

(7) *Consolidated return of selling consolidated group.* If P acquires T in a qualified stock purchase from a selling consolidated group—

(i) The selling consolidated group must file a consolidated return for the taxable period that includes the acquisition date;

(ii) A consolidated return for the selling consolidated group for that period may not be withdrawn on or after the day that a section 338(h)(10) election is made for T; and

(iii) Permission to discontinue filing consolidated returns cannot be granted for, and cannot apply to, that period or any of the immediately preceding taxable periods during which consolidated returns continuously have been filed.

(8) *Availability of the section 453 installment method.* Solely for purposes of applying sections 453, 453A, and 453B, and the regulations thereunder (the installment method) to determine the consequences to old T in the deemed asset sale and to old T (and its shareholders, if relevant) in the deemed liquidation, the rules in paragraphs (d)(1) through (7) of this section are modified as follows:

(i) *In deemed asset sale.* Old T is treated as receiving in the deemed asset sale new T installment obligations, the terms of which are identical (except as to the obligor) to P installment obligations issued in exchange for recently purchased stock of T. Old T is treated as receiving in cash all other consideration in the deemed asset sale other than the assumption of, or taking subject to, old T liabilities. For example, old T is treated as receiving in cash any amounts attributable to the grossing-up of amount realized under § 1.338-4(c). The amount realized for recently purchased stock taken into account in determining ADSP is adjusted (and, thus, ADSP is redetermined) to reflect the amounts paid under an installment obligation for the stock when the total payments under the installment obligation are greater or less than the amount realized.

(ii) *In deemed liquidation.* Old T is treated as distributing in the deemed liquidation the new T installment obligations that it is treated as receiving in the deemed asset sale. The members of the selling consolidated group, the selling affiliate, or the S corporation shareholders are treated as receiving in the deemed liquidation the new T installment obligations that correspond to the P installment obligations they actually received individually in exchange for their recently purchased stock. The new T installment obligations may be recharacterized under other rules. See for example § 1.453-11(a)(2) which, in certain circumstances, treats the new T installment obligations deemed distributed by old T as if they were issued by new T in exchange for the stock in old T owned by members of the selling consolidated group, the selling affiliate, or the S corporation shareholders. The members of the selling consolidated group, the selling affiliate, or the S corporation shareholders are treated as receiving all other consideration in the deemed liquidation in cash.

(9) *Treatment consistent with an actual asset sale.* No provision in section 338(h)(10) or this section shall produce a Federal income tax result under subtitle A of the Internal Revenue Code that would not occur if the parties had actually engaged in the transactions deemed to occur because of this section and taking into account other transactions that actually occurred or are deemed to occur. See, however, § 1.338-1(b)(2) for certain exceptions to this rule.

(e) *Examples.* The following examples illustrate the provisions of this section:

Example 1. (i) S1 owns all of the T stock and T owns all of the stock of T1 and T2. S1 is the common parent of a consolidated group that includes T, T1, and T2. P makes a qualified stock purchase of all of the T stock from S1. S1 joins with P in making a section 338(h)(10) election for T and for the deemed purchase of T1. A section 338 election is not made for T2.

(ii) S1 does not recognize gain or loss on the sale of the T stock and T does not recognize gain or loss on the sale of the T1 stock because section 338(h)(10) elections are made for T and T1. Thus, for example, gain or loss realized on the sale of the T or T1 stock is not taken into account in earnings and profits. However, because a section 338 election is not made for T2, T must recognize any gain or loss realized on the deemed sale of the T2 stock. See § 1.338-4(h).

(iii) The results would be the same if S1, T, T1, and T2 are not members of any consolidated group, because S1 and T are selling affiliates.

Example 2. (i) S and T are solvent corporations. S owns all of the outstanding stock of T. S and P agree to undertake the following transaction: T will distribute half its assets to S, and S will assume half of T's liabilities. Then, P will purchase the stock of T from S. S and P will jointly make a section 338(h)(10) election with respect to the sale of T. The corporations then complete the transaction as agreed.

(ii) Under section 338(a), the assets present in T at the close of the acquisition date are deemed sold by old T to new T. Under paragraph (d)(4) of this section, the transactions described in paragraph (d) of this section are treated in the same manner as if they had actually occurred. Because S and P had agreed that, after T's actual distribu-

tion to S of part of its assets, S would sell T to P pursuant to an election under section 338(h)(10), and because paragraph (d)(4) of this section deems T subsequently to have transferred all its assets to its shareholder, T is deemed to have adopted a plan of complete liquidation under section 332. T's actual transfer of assets to S is treated as a distribution pursuant to that plan of complete liquidation.

Example 3. (i) S1 owns all of the outstanding stock of both T and S2. All three are corporations. S1 and P agree to undertake the following transaction. T will transfer substantially all of its assets and liabilities to S2, with S2 issuing no stock in exchange therefor, and retaining its other assets and liabilities. Then, P will purchase the stock of T from S1. S1 and P will jointly make a section 338(h)(10) election with respect to the sale of T. The corporations then complete the transaction as agreed.

(ii) Under section 338(a), the remaining assets present in T at the close of the acquisition date are deemed sold by old T to new T. Under paragraph (d)(4) of this section, the transactions described in this section are treated in the same manner as if they had actually occurred. Because old T transferred substantially all of its assets to S2, and is deemed to have distributed all its remaining assets and gone out of existence, the transfer of assets to S2, taking into account the related transfers, deemed and actual, qualifies as a reorganization under section 368(a)(1)(D). Section 361(c)(1) and not section 332 applies to T's deemed liquidation.

Example 4. (i) T owns two assets: an actively traded security (Class II) with a fair market value of $100 and an adjusted basis of $100, and inventory (Class IV) with a fair market value of $100 and an adjusted basis of $100. T has no liabilities. S is negotiating to sell all the stock in T to P for $100 cash and contingent consideration. Assume that under generally applicable tax accounting rules, P's adjusted basis in the T stock immediately after the purchase would be $100, because the contingent consideration is not taken into account. Thus, under the rules of § 1.338-5, AGUB would be $100. Under the allocation rules of § 1.338-6, the entire $100 would be allocated to the Class II asset, the actively traded security, and no amount would be allocated to the inventory. P, however, plans immediately to cause T to sell the inventory, but not the actively traded security, so it requests that, prior to the stock sale, S cause T to create a new subsidiary, Newco, and contribute the actively traded security to the capital of Newco. Because the stock in Newco, which would not be actively traded, is a Class V asset, under the rules of § 1.338-6 $100 of AGUB would be allocated to the inventory and no

Reg. § 1.338(h)(10)-1(e)

amount of AGUB would be allocated to the Newco stock. Newco's own AGUB, $0 under the rules of § 1.338-5, would be allocated to the actively traded security. When P subsequently causes T to sell the inventory, T would realize no gain or loss instead of realizing gain of $100.

(ii) Assume that, if the T stock had not itself been sold but T had instead sold both its inventory and the Newco stock to P, T would for tax purposes be deemed instead to have sold both its inventory and actively traded security directly to P, with P deemed then to have created Newco and contributed the actively traded security to the capital of Newco. Section 338, if elected, generally recharacterizes a stock sale as a deemed sale of assets. However, paragraph (d)(9) of this section states, in general, that no provision of section 338(h)(10) or the regulations thereunder shall produce a Federal income tax result under subtitle A of the Internal Revenue Code that would not occur if the parties had actually engaged in the transactions deemed to occur by virtue of the section 338(h)(10) election, taking into account other transactions that actually occurred or are deemed to occur. Hence, the deemed sale of assets under section 338(h)(10) should be treated as one

of the inventory and actively traded security themselves, not of the inventory and Newco stock. The anti-abuse rule of § 1.338-1(c) does not apply, because the substance of the deemed sale of assets is a sale of the inventory and the actively traded security themselves, not of the inventory and the Newco stock. Otherwise, the anti-abuse rule might apply.

Example 5. (i) T, a member of a selling consolidated group, has only one class of stock, all of which is owned by S1. On March 1 of Year 2, S1 sells its T stock to P for $80,000, and joins with P in making a section 338(h)(10) election for T. There are no selling costs or acquisition costs. On March 1 of Year 2, T owns land with a $50,000 basis and $75,000 fair market value and equipment with a $30,000 adjusted basis, $70,000 recomputed basis, and $60,000 fair market value. T also has a $40,000 liability. Sl pays old T's allocable share of the selling group's consolidated tax liability for Year 2 including the tax liability for the deemed sale tax consequences (a total of $13,600).

(ii) ADSP of $120,000 ($80,000 + $40,000 + 0) is allocated to each asset as follows:

Assets	Basis	FMV	Fraction	Allocable ADSP
Land	$50,000	$75,000	5/9	$ 66,667
Equipment	30,000	60,000	4/9	53,333
Total	$80,000	$135,000	1	$120,000

(iii) Under paragraph (d)(3) of this section, old T has gain on the deemed sale of $40,000 (consisting of $16,667 of capital gain and $23,333 of ordinary income).

(iv) Under paragraph (d)(5)(iii) of this section, S1 recognizes no gain or loss upon its sale of the old T stock to P. S1 also recognizes no gain or loss upon the deemed liquidation of T. See paragraph (d)(4) of this section and section 332.

(v) P's basis in new T stock is P's cost for the stock, $80,000. See section 1012.

(vi) Under § 1.338-5, the AGUB for new T is $120,000, i.e., P's cost for the old T stock ($80,000) plus T's liability ($40,000). This AGUB is allocated as basis among the new T assets under §§ 1.338-6 and 1.338-7.

Example 6. (i) The facts are the same as in *Example 5*, except that S1 sells 80 percent of the old T stock to P for $64,000, rather than 100 percent of the old T stock for $80,000.

(ii) The consequences to P, T, and S1 are the same as in *Example 5*, except that:

(A) P's basis for its 80-percent interest in the new T stock is P's $64,000 cost for the stock. See section 1012.

(B) Under § 1.338-5, the AGUB for new T is $120,000 (i.e., $64,000/.8 + $40,000 + $0).

(C) Under paragraph (d)(4) of this section, S1 recognizes no gain or loss with respect to the retained stock in T. See section 332.

(D) Under paragraph (d)(5)(ii) of this section, the basis of the T stock retained by S1 is $16,000 (i.e., $120,000 − $40,000 (the ADSP amount for the old T assets over the sum of new T's liabilities immediately after the acquisition date) × .20 (the proportion of T stock retained by S1)).

Example 7. (i) The facts are the same as in *Example 6*, except that K, a shareholder unrelated to T or P, owns the 20 percent of the T stock that is not acquired by P in the qualified stock purchase. K's basis in its T stock is $5,000.

(ii) The consequences to P, T, and S1 are the same as in *Example 6*.

(iii) Under paragraph (d)(6)(iii) of this section, K recognizes no gain or loss, and K's basis in its T stock remains at $5,000.

Example 8. (i) The facts are the same as in *Example 5*, except that the equipment is held by T1, a wholly-owned subsidiary of T, and a section 338(h)(10) election is also made for T1. The T1

Reg. § 1.338(h)(10)-1(e)

stock has a fair market value of $60,000. T1 has no assets other than the equipment and no liabilities. S1 pays old T's and old T1's allocable shares of the selling group's consolidated tax liability for Year 2 including the tax liability for T and T1's deemed sale tax consequences.

(ii) ADSP for T is $120,000, allocated $66,667 to the land and $53,333 to the stock. Old T's deemed sale results in $16,667 of capital gain on its deemed sale of the land. Under paragraph (d)(5)(iii) of this section, old T does not recognize gain or loss on its deemed sale of the T1 stock. See section 332.

(iii) ADSP for T1 is $53,333 (i.e., $53,333 + $0 + $0). On the deemed sale of the equipment, T1 recognizes ordinary income of $23,333.

(iv) Under paragraph (d)(5)(iii) of this section, S1 does not recognize gain or loss upon its sale of the old T stock to P.

Example 9. (i) The facts are the same as in *Example 8*, except that P already owns 20 percent of the T stock, which is nonrecently purchased stock with a basis of $6,000, and that P purchases the remaining 80 percent of the T stock from S1 for $64,000.

(ii) The results are the same as in *Example 8*, except that under paragraph (d)(1) of this section and § 1.338-5(d), P is deemed to have made a gain recognition election for its nonrecently purchased T stock. As a result, P recognizes gain of $10,000 and its basis in the nonrecently purchased T stock is increased from $6,000 to $16,000. P's basis in all the T stock is $80,000 (i.e., $64,000 + $16,000). The computations are as follows:

(A) P's grossed-up basis for the recently purchased T stock is $64,000 (i.e., $64,000 (the basis of the recently purchased T stock) × (1 − .2)/(.8) (the fraction in section 338(b)(4))).

(B) P's basis amount for the nonrecently purchased T stock is $16,000 (i.e., $64,000 (the grossed-up basis in the recently purchased T stock) × (.2)/(1.0 − .2) (the fraction in section 338(b)(3)(B))).

(C) The gain recognized on the nonrecently purchased stock is $10,000 (i.e., $16,000 − $6,000).

Example 10. (i) T is an S corporation whose sole class of stock is owned 40 percent each by A and B and 20 percent by C. T, A, B, and C all use the cash method of accounting. A and B each has an adjusted basis of $10,000 in the stock. C has an adjusted basis of $5,000 in the stock. A, B, and C hold no installment obligations to which section 453A applies. On March 1 of Year 1, A sells its stock to P for $40,000 in cash and B sells its stock to P for a $25,000 note issued by P and real estate having a fair market value of $15,000. The

$25,000 note, due in full in Year 7, is not publicly traded and bears adequate stated interest. A and B have no selling expenses. T's sole asset is real estate, which has a value of $110,000 and an adjusted basis of $35,000. Also, T's real estate is encumbered by long-outstanding purchase-money indebtedness of $10,000. The real estate does not have built-in gain subject to section 1374. A, B, and C join with P in making a section 338(h)(10) election for T.

(ii) Solely for purposes of application of sections 453, 453A, and 453B, old T is considered in its deemed asset sale to receive back from new T the $25,000 note (considered issued by new T) and $75,000 of cash (total consideration of $80,000 paid for all the stock sold, which is then divided by .80 in the grossing-up, with the resulting figure of $100,000 then reduced by the amount of the installment note). Absent an election under section 453(d), gain is reported by old T under the installment method.

(iii) In applying the installment method to old T's deemed asset sale, the contract price for old T's assets deemed sold is $100,000, the $110,000 selling price reduced by the indebtedness of $10,000 to which the assets are subject. (The $110,000 selling price is itself the sum of the $80,000 grossed-up in paragraph (ii) above to $100,000 and the $10,000 liability.) Gross profit is $75,000 ($110,000 selling price − old T's basis of $35,000). Old T's gross profit ratio is 0.75 (gross profit of $75,000 ÷ $100,000 contract price). Thus, $56,250 (0.75 × the $75,000 cash old T is deemed to receive in Year 1) is Year 1 gain attributable to the sale, and $18,750 ($75,000 − $56,250) is recovery of basis.

(iv) In its liquidation, old T is deemed to distribute the $25,000 note to B, since B actually sold the stock partly for that consideration. To the extent of the remaining liquidating distribution to B, it is deemed to receive, along with A and C, the balance of old T's liquidating assets in the form of cash. Under section 453(h), B, unless it makes an election under section 453(d), is not required to treat the receipt of the note as a payment for the T stock; P's payment of the $25,000 note in Year 7 to B is a payment for the T stock. Because section 453(h) applies to B, old T's deemed liquidating distribution of the note is, under section 453B(h), not treated as a taxable disposition by old T.

(v) Under section .1366, A reports 40 percent, or $22,500, of old T's $56,250 gain recognized in Year 1. Under section 1367, this increases A's $10,000 adjusted basis in the T stock to $32,500. Next, in old T's deemed liquidation, A is considered to receive $40,000 for its old T shares, caus-

Reg. § 1.338(h)(10)-1(e)

ing it to recognize an additional $7,500 gain in Year 1.

(vi) Under section 1366, B reports 40 percent, or $22,500, of old T's $56,250 gain recognized in Year 1. Under section 1367, this increases B's $10,000 adjusted basis in its T stock to $32,500. Next, in old T's deemed liquidation, B is considered to receive the $25,000 note and $15,000 of other consideration. Applying section 453, including section 453(h), to the deemed liquidation, B's selling price and contract price are both $40,000. Gross profit is $7,500 ($40,000 selling price − B's basis of $32,500). B's gross profit ratio is 0.1875 (gross profit of $7,500 ÷ $40,000 contract price). Thus, $2,812.50 (0.1875 × $15,000) is Year 1 gain attributable to the deemed liquidation. In Year 7, when the $25,000 note is paid, B has $4,687.50 (0.1875 × $25,000) of additional gain.

(vii) Under section 1366, C reports 20 percent, or $11,250, of old T's $56,250 gain recognized in Year 1. Under section 1367, this increases C's $5,000 adjusted basis in its T stock to $16,250. Next, in old T's deemed liquidation, C is considered to receive $20,000 for its old T shares, causing it to recognize an additional $3,750 gain in Year 1. Finally, under paragraph (d)(5)(ii) of this section, C is considered to acquire its stock in T on the day after the acquisition date for $20,000 (fair market value = grossed-up amount realized of $100,000 × 20%). C's holding period in the stock deemed received in new T begins at that time.

(f) *Inapplicability of provisions.* The provisions of section 6043, § 1.331-1(d), and § 1.332-6 (relating to information returns and recordkeeping requirements for corporate liquidations) do not apply to the deemed liquidation of old T under paragraph (d)(4) of this section.

(g) *Required information.* The Commissioner may exercise the authority granted in section 338(h)(10)(C)(iii) to require provision of any information deemed necessary to carry out the provisions of section 338(h)(10) by requiring submission of information on any tax reporting form. [Reg. § 1.338(h)(10)-1.]

☐ [*T.D.* 8940, 2-12-2001.]

[*Note: Reg. § 1.346-1 was issued under the prior version of Section 346, which covered partial liquidations until 1982. The partial liquidation provisions formerly embodied in Section 346 are now set forth, with some modifications, in Sections 302(b)(4) and 302(e). No regulations have been issued under Sections 302(b)(4) and 302(e).*]

§ 1.346-1. Partial liquidation.—(a) *General.* This section defines a partial liquidation. If amounts are distributed in partial liquidation such amounts are treated under section 331(a)(2)

as received in part or full payment in exchange for the stock. A distribution is treated as in partial liquidation of a corporation if:

(1) The distribution is one of a series of distributions in redemption of all the stock of the corporation pursuant to a plan of complete liquidation or

(2) The distribution:

    (i) Is not essentially equivalent to a dividend,

    (ii) Is in redemption of a part of the stock of the corporation pursuant to a plan, and

    (iii) Occurs within the taxable year in which the plan is adopted or within the succeeding taxable year.

An example of a distribution which will qualify as a partial liquidation under subparagraph (2) of this paragraph and section 346(a) is a distribution resulting from a genuine contraction of the corporate business such as the distribution of unused insurance proceeds recovered as a result of a fire which destroyed part of the business causing a cessation of a part of its activities. On the other hand, the distribution of funds attributable to a reserve for an expansion program which has been abandoned does not qualify as a partial liquidation within the meaning of section 346(a). A distribution to which section 355 applies (or so much of section 356 as relates to section 355) is not a distribution in partial liquidation within the meaning of section 346(a).

(b) *Special requirements on termination of business.* A distribution which occurs within the taxable year in which the plan is adopted or within the succeeding taxable year and which meets the requirements of subsection (b) of section 346 falls within paragraph (a)(2) of this section and within section 346(a)(2). The requirements which a distribution must meet to fall within subsection (b) of section 346 are:

(1) Such distribution is attributable to the corporation's ceasing to conduct, or consists of assets of, a trade or business which has been actively conducted throughout the five-year period immediately before the distribution, which trade or business was not acquired by the corporation within such period in a transaction in which gain or loss was recognized in whole or in part, and

(2) Immediately after such distribution by the corporation it is actively engaged in the conduct of a trade or business, which trade or business was actively conducted throughout the five-year period ending on the date of such distribution and was not acquired by the corporation within such period in a transaction in which gain or loss was recognized in whole or in part.

A distribution shall be treated as having been made in partial liquidation pursuant to section 346(b) if it consists of the proceeds of the sale of the assets of a trade or business which has been actively conducted for the five-year period and has been terminated, or if it is a distribution in kind of the assets of such a business, or if it is a distribution in kind of some of the assets of such a business and of the proceeds of the sale of the remainder of the assets of such a business. In general, a distribution which will qualify under section 346(b) may consist of, *but is not limited to—*

(i) Assets (other than inventory or property described in subdivision (ii) of this subparagraph) used in the trade or business throughout the five-year period immediately before the distribution (for this purpose an asset shall be considered used in the trade or business during the period of time the asset which it replaced was so used), or

(ii) Proceeds from the sale of assets described in (i), and, in addition,

(iii) The inventory of such trade or business or property held primarily for sale to customers in the ordinary course of business, if:

(*a*) The items constituting such inventory or such property were substantially similar to the items constituting such inventory or property during the five-year period immediately before the distribution, and

(*b*) The quantity of such items on the date of distribution was not substantially in excess of the quantity of similar items regularly on hand in the conduct of such business during such five-year period, or

(iv) Proceeds from the sale of inventory or property described in subdivision (iii) of this subparagraph, if such inventory or property is sold in bulk in the course of termination of such trade or business and if with respect to such inventory the conditions of subdivision (iii)(*a*) and (*b*) of this subparagraph would have been met had such inventory or property been distributed on the date of such sale.

(c) *Active conduct of a trade or business.* For the purpose of section 346(b)(1), a corporation shall be deemed to have actively conducted a trade or business immediately before the distribution, if:

(1) In the case of a business the assets of which have been distributed in kind, the business was operated by such corporation until the date of distribution, or

(2) In the case of a business the proceeds of the sale of the assets of which are distributed, such business was actively conducted until the date of sale and the proceeds of such sale were distributed as soon thereafter as reasonably possible.

The term "active conduct of a trade or business" shall have the same meaning in this section as in paragraph (c) of § 1.355-1. [Reg. § 1.346-1.]

☐ [*T.D.* 6152, 12-2-55.]

Corporate Organizations and Reorganizations

[Caution: Reg. §§ 1.351-1 and 1.351-2 do not reflect changes made by the Revenue Reconciliation Act of 1989, which deleted the words "or securities" after the word "stock" throughout Section 351.]

§ 1.351-1. Transfer to corporation controlled by transferor.—(a)(1)

Section 351(a) provides, in general, for the nonrecognition of gain or loss upon the transfer by one or more persons of property to a corporation solely in exchange for stock or securities in such corporation if, immediately after the exchange, such person or persons are in control of the corporation to which the property was transferred. As used in section 351, the phrase "one or more persons" includes individuals, trusts, estates, partnerships, associations, companies, or corporations (see section 7701(a)(1)). To be in control of the transferee corporation, such person or persons must own immediately after the transfer stock possessing at least 80 percent of the total combined voting power of all classes of stock entitled to vote and at least 80 per cent of the total number of shares of all other classes of stock of such corporation (see section 368(c)). In determining control under this section, the fact that any corporate transferor distributes part or all of the stock which it receives in the exchange to its shareholders shall not be taken into account. The phrase "immediately after the exchange" does not necessarily require simultaneous exchanges by two or more persons, but comprehends a situation where the rights of the parties have been previously defined and the execution of the agreement proceeds with an expedition consistent with orderly procedure. For purposes of this section—

(i) stock or securities issued for services rendered or to be rendered to or for the benefit of the issuing corporation will not be treated as having been issued in return for property, and

(ii) stock or securities issued for property which is of relatively small value in comparison to the value of the stock and securities already owned (or to be received for services) by the person who transferred such property, shall not be treated as having been issued in return for property if the primary purpose of the transfer is to qualify under this section the exchanges of property by other persons transferring property.

For the purpose of section 351, stock rights or stock warrants are not included in the term "stock or securities."

(2) The application of section 351(a) is illustrated by the following examples:

Example (1). C owns a patent right worth $25,000 and D owns a manufacturing plant worth $75,000. C and D organize the R Corporation with an authorized capital stock of $100,000. C transfers his patent right to the R Corporation for $25,000 of its stock and D transfers his plant to the new corporation for $75,000 of its stock. No gain or loss to C or D is recognized.

Example (2). B owns certain real estate which cost him $50,000 in 1930, but which has a fair market value of $200,000 in 1955. He transfers the property to the N Corporation in 1955 for 78 percent of each class of stock of the corporation having a fair market value of $200,000, the remaining 22 percent of the stock of the corporation having been issued by the corporation in 1940 to other persons for cash. B realized a taxable gain of $150,000 on this transaction.

Example (3). E, an individual, owns property with a basis of $10,000 but which has a fair market value of $18,000. E also had rendered services valued at $2,000 to Corporation F. Corporation F has outstanding 100 shares of common stock all of which are held by G. Corporation F issues 400 shares of its common stock (having a fair market value of $20,000) to E in exchange for his property worth $18,000 and in compensation for the services he has rendered worth $2,000. Since immediately after the transaction, E owns 80 percent of the outstanding stock of Corporation F, no gain is recognized upon the exchange of the property for the stock. However, E realized $2,000 of ordinary income as compensation for services rendered to Corporation F.

(3) *Underwritings of stock*—(i) *In general.* For the purpose of section 351, if a person acquires stock of a corporation from an underwriter in exchange for cash in a qualified underwriting transaction, the person who acquires stock from the underwriter is treated as transferring cash directly to the corporation in exchange for stock of the corporation and the underwriter is disregarded. A qualified underwriting transaction is a transaction in which a corporation issues stock for cash in an underwriting in which either the underwriter is an agent of the corporation or the underwriter's ownership of the stock is transitory.

(ii) *Effective date.* This paragraph (a)(3) is effective for qualified underwriting transactions occurring on or after May 1, 1996.

(b)(1) Where property is transferred to a corporation by two or more persons in exchange for stock or securities, as described in paragraph (a) of this section, it is not required that the stock and securities received by each be substantially in proportion to his interest in the property immediately prior to the transfer. However, where the stock and securities received are received in disproportion to such interest, the entire transaction will be given tax effect in accordance with its true nature, and in appropriate cases the transaction may be treated as if the stock and securities had first been received in proportion and then some of such stock and securities had been used to make gifts (section 2501 and following), to pay compensation (section 61(a)(1)), or to satisfy obligations of the transferor of any kind.

(2) The application of paragraph (b)(1) of this section may be illustrated as follows:

Example (1). Individuals A and B, father and son, organize a corporation with 100 shares of common stock to which A transfers property worth $8,000 in exchange for 20 shares of stock, and B transfers property worth $2,000 in exchange for 80 shares of stock. No gain or loss will be recognized under section 351. However, if it is determined that A in fact made a gift to B, such gift will be subject to tax under section 2501 and following. Similarly, if B had rendered services to A (such services having no relation to the assets transferred or to the business of the corporation) and the disproportion in the amount of stock received constituted the payment of compensation by A to B, B will be taxable upon the fair market value of the 60 shares of stock received as compensation for services rendered, and A will realize gain or loss upon the difference between the basis to him of the 60 shares and their fair market value at the time of the exchange.

Example (2). Individuals C and D each transferred, to a newly organized corporation, property having a fair market value of $4,500 in exchange for the issuance by the corporation of 45 shares of its capital stock to each transferor. At the same time, the corporation issued to E, an individual, 10 shares of its capital stock in payment for organizational and promotional services rendered by E for the benefit of the corporation. E transferred no property to the corporation. C and D were under no obligation to pay for E's services. No gain or loss is recognized to C or D. E received compensation taxable as ordinary income to the extent of the fair market value of the 10 shares of stock received by him.

(c)(1) The general rule of section 351 does not apply, and consequently gain or loss will be recognized, where property is transferred to an investment company after June 30, 1967. A transfer of

Reg. § 1.351-1(a)(2)

property after June 30, 1967, will be considered to be a transfer to an investment company if—

(i) The transfer results, directly or indirectly, in diversification of the transferors' interests, and

(ii) The transferee is (a) a regulated investment company, (b) a real estate investment trust, or (c) a corporation more than 80 percent of the value of whose assets (excluding cash and nonconvertible debt obligations from consideration) are held for investment and are readily marketable stocks or securities, or interests in regulated investment companies or real estate investment trusts.

(2) The determination of whether a corporation is an investment company shall ordinarily be made by reference to the circumstances in existence immediately after the transfer in question. However, where circumstances change thereafter pursuant to a plan in existence at the time of the transfer, this determination shall be made by reference to the later circumstances.

(3) Stocks and securities will be considered readily marketable if (and only if) they are part of a class of stock or securities which is traded on a securities exchange or traded or quoted regularly in the over-the-counter market. For purposes of subparagraph (1)(ii)(c) of this paragraph, the term "readily marketable stocks or securities" includes convertible debentures, convertible preferred stock, warrants, and other stock rights if the stock for which they may be converted or exchanged is readily marketable. Stocks and securities will be considered to be held for investment unless they are (i) held primarily for sale to customers in the ordinary course of business, or (ii) used in the trade or business of banking, insurance, brokerage, or a similar trade or business.

(4) In making the determination required under subparagraph (1)(ii)(c) of this paragraph, stock and securities in subsidiary corporations shall be disregarded and the parent corporation shall be deemed to own its ratable share of its subsidiaries' assets. A corporation shall be considered a subsidiary if the parent owns 50 percent or more of (i) the combined voting power of all classes of stock entitled to vote, or (ii) the total value of shares of all classes of stock outstanding.

(5) A transfer ordinarily results in the diversification of the transferors' interests if two or more persons transfer nonidentical assets to a corporation in the exchange. For this purpose, if any transaction involves one or more transfers of nonidentical assets which, taken in the aggregate, constitute an insignificant portion of the total value of assets transferred, such transfers shall be disregarded in determining whether diversifica-

tion has occurred. If there is only one transferor (or two or more transferors of identical assets) to a newly organized corporation, the transfer will generally be treated as not resulting in diversification. If a transfer is part of a plan to achieve diversification without recognition of gain, such as a plan which contemplates a subsequent transfer, however delayed, of the corporate assets (or of the stock or securities received in the earlier exchange) to an investment company in a transaction purporting to qualify for nonrecognition treatment, the original transfer will be treated as resulting in diversification.

(6)(i) For purposes of paragraph (c)(5) of this section, a transfer of stocks and securities will not be treated as resulting in a diversification of the transferors' interests if each transferor transfers a diversified portfolio of stocks and securities. For purposes of this paragraph(c)(6), a portfolio of stocks and securities is diversified if it satisfies the 25 and 50-percent tests of section 368(a)(2)(F)(ii), applying the relevant provisions of section 368(a)(2)(F). However, Government securities are included in total assets for purposes of the denominator of the 25 and 50-percent tests (unless the Government securities are acquired to meet the 25 and 50-percent tests), but are not treated as securities of an issuer for purposes of the numerator of the 25 and 50-percent tests.

(ii) Paragraph (c)(6)(i) of this section is effective for transfers completed on or after May 2, 1996. Transfers of diversified (within the meaning of paragraph (c)(6)(i) of this section), but nonidentical, portfolios of stocks and securities completed before May 2, 1996, may be treated either—

(A) Consistent with paragraph (c)(6)(i) of this section; or

(B) As resulting in diversification of the transferors' interests.

(7) The application of subparagraph (5) of this paragraph may be illustrated as follows:

Example (1). Individuals A, B, and C organize a corporation with 101 shares of common stock. A and B each transfers to it $10,000 worth of the only class of stock of corporation X, listed on the New York Stock Exchange, in exchanges for 50 shares of stock. C transfers $200 worth of readily marketable securities in corporation Y for one share of stock. In determining whether or not diversification has occurred, C's participation in the transaction will be disregarded. There is, therefore, no diversification, and gain or loss will not be recognized.

Example (2). A, together with 50 other transferors, organizes a corporation with 100 shares of stock. A transfers $10,000 worth of stock in corporation X, listed on the New York Stock Exchange,

Reg. § 1.351-1(c)(7)

in exchange for 50 shares of stock. Each of the other 50 transferors transfers $200 worth of readily marketable securities in corporations other than X in exchange for one share of stock. In determining whether or not diversification has occurred, all transfers will be taken into account. Therefore, diversification is present, and gain or loss will be recognized. [Reg. § 1.351-1.]

□ [*T.D. 6152, 12-2-55. Amended by T.D. 6942, 12-28-67; T.D. 8663, 5-1-96 and T.D. 8665, 4-30-96.*]

§ 1.351-2. Receipt of property.—(a) If an exchange would be within the provisions of section 351(a) if it were not for the fact that the property received in exchange consists not only of property permitted by such subsection to be received without the recognition of gain, but also of other property or money, then the gain, if any, to the recipient shall be recognized, but in an amount not in excess of the sum of such money and the fair market value of such other property. No loss to the recipient shall be recognized.

(b) See section 357 and the regulations pertaining to that section for applicable rules as to the treatment of liabilities as "other property" in cases subject to section 351, where another party to the exchange assumes a liability, or acquires property subject to a liability.

(c) See sections 358 and 362 and the regulations pertaining to those sections for applicable rules with respect to the determination of the basis of stock, securities, or other property received in exchanges subject to section 351.

(d) See part 1 (section 301 and following), subchapter C, chapter 1 of the Code, and the regulations thereunder for applicable rules with respect to the taxation of dividends where a distribution by a corporation of its stock or securities in connection with an exchange subject to section 351(a) has the effect of the distribution of a taxable dividend.

(e) See § 1.356-7(a) for the applicability of the definition of nonqualified preferred stock in section 351(g)(2) for stock issued prior to June 9, 1997, and for stock issued in transactions occurring after June 8, 1997, that are described in section 1014(f)(2) of the Taxpayer Relief Act of 1997, Public Law 105-34 (111 Stat. 788, 921). See § 1.356-7(c) for the treatment of preferred stock received in certain exchanges for common or preferred stock described in section 351(g)(2)(C)(i)(II). [Reg. § 1.351-2.]

□ [*T.D. 6152, 12-2-55. Amended by T.D. 8904, 9-29-2000.*]

§ 1.354-1. Exchanges of stock and securities in certain reorganizations.—(a) Section 354 provides that under certain circumstances no gain

or loss is recognized to a shareholder who surrenders his stock in exchange for other stock or to a security holder who surrenders his securities in exchange for stock. Section 354 also provides that under certain circumstances a security holder may surrender securities and receive securities in the same principal amount or in a lesser principal amount without the recognition of gain or loss to him. The exchanges to which section 354 applies must be pursuant to a plan of reorganization as provided in section 368(a) and the stock and securities surrendered as well as the stock and securities received must be those of a corporation which is a party to the reorganization. Section 354 does not apply to exchanges pursuant to a reorganization described in section 368(a)(1)(D) unless the transferor corporation—

(1) Transfers all or substantially all of its assets to a single corporation, and

(2) Distributes all of its remaining properties (if any) and the stock, securities and other properties received in the exchange to its shareholders or security holders in pursuance of the plan of reorganization. The fact that properties retained by the transferor corporation, or received in exchange for the properties transferred in the reorganization, are used to satisfy existing liabilities not represented by securities and which were incurred in the ordinary course of business before the reorganization does not prevent the application of section 354 to an exchange pursuant to a plan of reorganization defined in section 368(a)(1)(D).

(b) Except as provided in section 354(c) and (d), section 354 is not applicable to an exchange of stock or securities if a greater principal amount of securities is received than the principal amount of securities the recipient surrenders, or if securities are received and the recipient surrenders no securities. See, however, section 356 and regulations pertaining to such section. See also section 306 with respect to the receipt of preferred stock in a transaction to which section 354 is applicable.

(c) An exchange of stock or securities shall be subject to section 354(a)(1) even though—

(1) Such exchange is not pursuant to a plan of reorganization described in section 368(a), and

(2) The principal amount of the securities received exceeds the principal amount of the securities surrendered or if securities are received and no securities are surrendered—

if such exchange is pursuant to a plan of reorganization for a railroad corporation as defined in section 77(m) of the Bankruptcy Act (11 U.S.C. 205(m)) and is approved by the Interstate Commerce Commission under section 77 of such Act or under section 20b of the Interstate Commerce Act (49 U.S.C. 20b) as being in the public interest. Section 354 is not applicable to such exchanges if there is received property other than stock or securities. See, however, section 356 and regulations pertaining to such section.

(d) The rules of section 354 may be illustrated by the following examples:

Example 1. Pursuant to a reorganization under section 368(a) to which Corporations T and W are parties, A, a shareholder in Corporation T, surrenders all his common stock in Corporation T in exchange for common stock of Corporation W. No gain or loss is recognized to A.

Example 2. Pursuant to a reorganization under section 368(a) to which Corporations X and Y (which are not railroad corporations) are parties, B, a shareholder in Corporation X, surrenders all his stock in X for stock and securities in Y. Section 354 does not apply to this exchange. See, however, section 356.

Example 3. C, a shareholder in Corporation Z (which is not a railroad corporation), surrenders all his stock in Corporation Z in exchange for securities in Corporation Z. Whether or not this exchange is in connection with a recapitalization under section 368(a)(1)(E), section 354 does not apply. See, however, section 302.

Example 4. The facts are the same as in *Example 3* of this paragraph (d), except that C receives solely rights to acquire stock in Corporation Z. Section 354 does not apply.

(e) Except as provided in § 1.356-6, for purposes of section 354, the term *securities* includes rights issued by a party to the reorganization to acquire its stock. For purposes of this section and section 356(d)(2)(B), a right to acquire stock has no principal amount. For this purpose, rights to acquire stock has the same meaning as it does under sections 305 and 317(a). Other Internal Revenue Code provisions governing the treatment of rights to acquire stock may also apply to certain exchanges occurring in connection with a reorganization. See, for example, sections 83 and 421 through 424 and the regulations thereunder. This paragraph (e) applies to exchanges occurring on or after March 9, 1998.

(f) See § 1.356-7(a) and (b) for the treatment of nonqualified preferred stock (as defined in section 351(g)(2)) received in certain exchanges for nonqualified preferred stock or preferred stock. See § 1.356-7(c) for the treatment of preferred stock received in certain exchanges for common or preferred stock described in section 351(g)(2)(C)(i)(II). [Reg. § 1.354-1.]

☐ [*T.D.* 6152, 12-2-55. *Amended by T.D.* 7616, 5-7-79; *T.D.* 8752, 1-5-98; *T.D.* 8882, 5-15-2000 *and T.D.* 8904, 9-29-2000.]

§ 1.355-1. Distribution of stock and securities of a controlled corporation.— * * *

(b) *Application of section.* Section 355 provides for the separation, without recognition of gain or loss to (or the inclusion in income of) the shareholders and security holders, of one or more existing businesses formerly operated, directly or indirectly, by a single corporation (the "distributing corporation"). It applies only to the separation of existing businesses that have been in active operation for at least five years (or a business that has been in active operation for at least five years into separate businesses), and which, in general, have been owned, directly or indirectly, for at least five years by the distributing corporation. A separation is achieved through the distribution by the distributing corporation of stock, or stock and securities, of one or more subsidiaries (the "controlled corporations") to its shareholders with respect to its stock or to its security holders in exchange for its securities. The controlled corporations may be preexisting or newly created subsidiaries. Throughout the regulations under section 355, the term "distribution" refers to a distribution by the distributing corporation of stock, or stock and securities, of one or more controlled corporations, unless the context indicates otherwise. Section 355 contemplates the continued operation of the business or businesses existing prior to the separation. See § 1.355-4 for types of distributions that may qualify under section 355, including pro-rata distributions and non-pro-rata distributions.

(c) *Stock rights.* Except as provided in § 1.356-6, for purposes of section 355, the term *securities* includes rights issued by the distributing corporation or the controlled corporation to acquire the stock of that corporation. For purposes of this section and section 356(d)(2)(B), a right to acquire stock has no principal amount. For this purpose, rights to acquire stock has the same meaning as it does under sections 305 and 317(a). Other Internal Revenue Code provisions governing the treatment of rights to acquire stock may also apply to certain distributions occurring in connection with a transaction described in section 355. See, for example, sections 83 and 421 through 424 and the regulations thereunder. This paragraph (c) applies to distributions occurring on or after March 9, 1998.

(d) *Nonqualified preferred stock.* See § 1.356-7(a) and (b) for the treatment of nonqualified preferred stock (as defined in section 351(g)(2)) received in certain exchanges for (or in certain distributions with respect to) nonqualified preferred stock or preferred stock. See § 1.356-7(c) for the treatment of the receipt of preferred stock in certain exchanges for (or in certain distributions with respect to) common or preferred stock

Reg. § 1.355-1(d)

described in section 351(g)(2)(C)(i)(II). [Reg. § 1.355-1.]

☐ [*T.D. 6152, 12-2-55. Amended by T.D. 8238, 1-4-89; T.D. 8752, 1-5-98; T.D. 8882, 5-15-2000 and T.D. 8904, 9-29-2000.*]

§ 1.355-2. Limitations.—(a) *Property distributed.* Section 355 applies to a distribution only if the property distributed consists solely of stock, or stock and securities, of a controlled corporation. If additional property (including an excess principal amount of securities received over securities surrendered) is received, see section 356.

(b) *Independent business purpose*—(1) *Independent business purpose requirement.* Section 355 applies to a transaction only if it is carried out for one or more corporate business purposes. A transaction is carried out for a corporate business purpose if it is motivated, in whole or substantial part, by one or more corporate business purposes. The potential for the avoidance of Federal taxes by the distributing or controlled corporations (or a corporation controlled by either) is relevant in determining the extent to which an existing corporate business purpose motivated the distribution. The principal reason for this business purpose requirement is to provide nonrecognition treatment only to distributions that are incident to readjustments of corporate structures required by business exigencies and that effect only readjustments of continuing interests in property under modified corporate forms. This business purpose requirement is independent of the other requirements under section 355.

(2) *Corporate business purpose.* A corporate business purpose is a real and substantial non-Federal tax purpose germane to the business of the distributing corporation, the controlled corporation, or the affiliated group (as defined in § 1.355-3(b)(4)(iv)) to which the distributing corporation belongs. A purpose of reducing non-Federal taxes is not a corporate business purpose if (i) the transaction will effect a reduction in both Federal and non-Federal taxes because of similarities between Federal tax law and the tax law of the other jurisdiction and (ii) the reduction of Federal taxes is greater than or substantially coextensive with the reduction of non-Federal taxes. See examples (7) and (8) of paragraph (b)(5) of this section. A shareholder purpose (for example, the personal planning purposes of a shareholder) is not a corporate business purpose. Depending upon the facts of a particular case, however, a shareholder purpose for a transaction may be so nearly coextensive with a corporate business purpose as to preclude any distinction between them. In such a case, the transaction is carried out for one or more corporate business purposes. See example (2) of paragraph (b)(5) of this section.

(3) *Business purpose for distribution.* The distribution must be carried out for one or more corporate business purposes. See example (3) of paragraph (b)(5) of this section. If a corporate business purpose can be achieved through a non-taxable transaction that does not involve the distribution of stock of a controlled corporation and which is neither impractical nor unduly expensive, then, for purposes of paragraph (b)(1) of this section, the separation is not carried out for that corporate business purpose. See examples (3) and (4) of paragraph (b)(5) of this section. For rules with respect to the requirement of a business purpose for a transfer of assets to a controlled corporation in connection with a reorganization described in section 368(a)(1)(D), see § 1.368-1(b).

(4) *Business purpose as evidence of nondevice.* The corporate business purpose or purposes for a transaction are evidence that the transaction was not used principally as a device for the distribution of earnings and profits within the meaning of section 355(a)(1)(B). See paragraph (d)(3)(ii) of this section.

(5) *Examples.* The provisions of this paragraph (b) may be illustrated by the following examples:

Example (1). Corporation X is engaged in the production, transportation, and refining of petroleum products. In 1985, X acquires all of the properties of corporation Z, which is also engaged in the production, transportation, and refining of petroleum products. In 1991, as a result of antitrust litigation, X is ordered to divest itself of all of the properties acquired from Z. X transfers those properties to new corporation Y and distributes the stock of Y pro rata to X's shareholders. In view of the divestiture order, the distribution is carried out for a corporate business purpose. See paragraph (b)(1) of this section.

Example (2). Corporation X is engaged in two businesses: the manufacture and sale of furniture and the sale of jewelry. The businesses are of equal value. The outstanding stock of X is owned equally by unrelated individuals A and B. A is more interested in the furniture business, while B is more interested in the jewelry business. A and B decide to split up the businesses and go their separate ways. A and B anticipate that the operations of each business will be enhanced by the separation because each shareholder will be able to devote his undivided attention to the business in which he is more interested and more proficient. Accordingly, X transfers the jewelry business to new corporation Y and distributes the stock of Y to B in exchange for all of B's stock in X. The distribution is carried out for a corporate business purpose, notwithstanding that it is also carried out in part for shareholder purposes. See paragraph (b)(2) of this section.

Example (3). Corporation X is engaged in the manufacture and sale of toys and the manufacture and sale of candy. The shareholders of X wish to protect the candy business from the risks and vicissitudes of the toy business. Accordingly, X transfers the toy business to new corporation Y and distributes the stock of Y to X's shareholders. Under applicable law, the purpose of protecting the candy business from the risks and vicissitudes of the toy business is achieved as soon as X transfers the toy business to Y. Therefore, the distribution is not carried out for a corporate business purpose. See paragraph (b)(3) of this section.

Example (4). Corporation X is engaged in a regulated business in State T. X owns all of the stock of corporation Y, a profitable corporation that is not engaged in a regulated business. Commission C sets the rates that X may charge its customers, based on its total income. C has recently adopted rules according to which the total income of a corporation includes the income of a business if, and only if, the business is operated, directly or indirectly, by the corporation. Total income, for this purpose, includes the income of a wholly owned subsidiary corporation but does not include the income of a parent or "brother/sister" corporation. Under C's new rule, X's total income includes the income of Y, with the result that X has suffered a reduction of the rates that it may charge its customers. It would not be impractical or unduly expensive to create in a nontaxable transaction (such as a transaction qualifying under section 351) a holding company to hold the stock of X and Y. X distributes the stock of Y to X's shareholders. The distribution is not carried out for the purpose of increasing the rates that X may charge its customers because that purpose could be achieved through a nontaxable transaction, the creation of a holding company, that does not involve the distribution of stock of a controlled corporation and which is neither impractical nor unduly expensive. See paragraph (b)(3) of this section.

Example (5). The facts are the same as in example (4), except that C has recently adopted rules according to which the total income of a corporation includes not only the income included in example (3), but also the income of any member of the affiliated group to which the corporation belongs. In order to avoid a reduction in the rates that it may charge its customers, X distributes the stock of Y to X's shareholders. The distribution is carried out for a corporate business purpose. See paragraph (b)(3) of this section.

Example (6). (i) Corporation X owns all of the one class of stock of corporation Y. X distributes the stock of Y pro rata to its five shareholders, all of whom are individuals, for the sole purpose of enabling X and/or Y to elect to become an S corporation. The distribution does not meet the corporate business purpose requirement. See paragraph (b)(1) and (2) of this section.

(ii) The facts are the same as in Example (6)(i), except that the business of Y is operated as a division of X. X transfers this division to new corporation Y and distributes the stock of Y pro rata to its shareholders, all of whom are individuals, for the sole purpose of enabling X and/or Y to elect to become an S corporation. The distribution does not meet the corporate business purpose requirement. See paragraph (b)(1) and (2) of this section.

Example (7). The facts are the same as in example (6)(i), except that the distribution is made to enable X to elect to become an S corporation both for Federal tax purposes and for purposes of the income tax imposed by State M. State M has tax law provisions similar to subchapter S of the Internal Revenue Code of 1986. An election to be an S corporation for Federal tax purposes will effect a substantial reduction in Federal taxes that is greater than the reduction of State M taxes pursuant to an election to be an S corporation for State M purposes. The purpose of reducing State M taxes is not a corporate business purpose. The distribution does not meet the corporate business purpose requirement. See paragraph (b)(1) and (2) of this section.

Example (8). The facts are the same as Example (7), except that the distribution also is made to enable *A*, a key employee of Y, to acquire stock of Y without investing in X. *A* is considered to be critical to the success of Y and he has indicated that he will seriously consider leaving the company if he is not given the opportunity to purchase a significant amount of stock of Y. As a matter of state law, Y could not issue stock to the employee while it was a subsidiary of X. As in Example (7), the purpose of reducing State M taxes is not a corporate business purpose. In order to determine whether the issuance of stock to the key employee, in fact, motivated the distribution of the Y stock, the potential avoidance of Federal taxes is a relevant factor to take into account. If the facts and circumstances establish that the distribution was substantially motivated by the need to issue stock to the employee, the distribution will meet the corporate business purpose requirement.

(c) *Continuity of interest requirement*—(1) *Requirement*. Section 355 applies to a separation that effects only a readjustment of continuing interests in the property of the distributing and controlled corporations. In this regard section 355 requires that one or more persons who, directly or indirectly, were the owners of the enterprise prior to the distribution or exchange own, in the aggregate, an amount of stock establishing a continuity of interest in each of the modified corporate forms in which the enterprise is conducted after the separation. This continuity of interest requirement is independent of the other requirements under section 355.

(2) *Examples.*

Example (1). For more than five years, corporation X has been engaged directly in one business, and indirectly in a different business through its wholly owned subsidiary, S. The businesses are equal in value. At all times, the outstanding stock of X has been owned equally by unrelated individuals A and B. For valid business reasons, A and B cause X to distribute all of the stock of S to B in exchange for all of B's stock in X. After the transaction, A owns all the stock of X and B owns all the stock of S. The continuity of interest requirement is met because one or more persons who were the owners of X prior to the distribution (A and B) own, in the aggregate, an amount of stock establishing a continuity of interest in each of X and S after the distribution.

Example (2). Assume the same facts as in Example (1), except that pursuant to a plan to acquire a stock interest in X without acquiring, directly or indirectly, an interest in S, C purchased one-half of the X stock owned by A and immediately thereafter X distributed all of the S stock to B in exchange for all of B's stock in X. After the transactions, A owns 50 percent of X and B owns 100 percent of S. The distribution by X of all of the stock of S to B in exchange for all of B's stock in X will satisfy the continuity of interest requirement for section 355 because one or more persons who were the owners of X prior to the distribution (A and B) own, in the aggregate, an amount of stock establishing a continuity of interest in each of X and S after the distribution.

Example (3). Assume the same facts as in Example (1) and (2), except that C purchased all of the X stock owned by A. After the transactions, neither A nor B own any of the stock of X, and B owns all the stock of S. The continuity of interest requirement is not met because the owners of X prior to the distribution (A and B) do not, in the aggregate, own an amount of stock establishing a continuity of interest in each of X and S after the distribution, *i.e.,* although A and B collectively have retained 50 percent of their equity interest in the former combined enterprise, they have failed to continue to own the minimum stock interest in the distributing corporation, X, that

would be required in order to meet the continuity of interest requirement.

Example (4). Assume the same facts as in Examples (1) and (2), except that C purchased 80 percent of the X stock owned by A. After the transactions, A owns 20 percent of the stock of X, B owns no X stock, and B owns 100 percent of the S stock. The continuity of interest requirement is not met because the owners of X prior to the distribution (A and B) do not, in the aggregate, have a continuity of interest in each of X and S after the distribution, *i.e.,* although A and B collectively have retained 60 percent of their equity interest in the former combined enterprise, the 20 percent interest of A in X is less than the minimum equity interest in the distributing corporation, X, that would be required in order to meet the continuity of interest requirement.

(d) *Device for distribution of earnings and profits*—(1) *In general.* Section 355 does not apply to a transaction used principally as a device for the distribution of the earnings and profits of the distributing corporation, the controlled corporation, or both (a "device"). Section 355 recognizes that a tax-free distribution of the stock of a controlled corporation presents a potential for tax avoidance by facilitating the avoidance of the dividend provisions of the Code through the subsequent sale or exchange of stock of one corporation and the retention of the stock of another corporation. A device can include a transaction that effects a recovery of basis. In this paragraph (d), "exchange" includes transactions, such as redemptions, treated as exchanges under the Code. Generally, the determination of whether a transaction was used principally as a device will be made from all of the facts and circumstances, including, but not limited to, the presence of the device factors specified in paragraph (d)(2) of this section ("evidence of device"), and the presence of the nondevice factors specified in paragraph (d)(3) of this section ("evidence of nondevice"). However, if a transaction is specified in paragraph (d)(5) of this section, then it is ordinarily considered not to have been used principally as a device.

(2) *Device factors*—(i) *In general.* The presence of any of the device factors specified in this subparagraph (2) is evidence of device. The strength of this evidence depends on the facts and circumstances.

(ii) *Pro rata distribution.* A distribution that is pro rata or substantially pro rata among the shareholders of the distributing corporation presents the greatest potential for the avoidance of the dividend provisions of the Code and, in contrast to other types of distributions, is more likely to be used principally as a device. Accord-

Reg. § 1.355-2(c)(2)

ingly, the fact that a distribution is pro rata or substantially pro rata is evidence of device.

(iii) *Subsequent sale or exchange of stock*—(A) *In general.* A sale or exchange of stock of the distributing or the controlled corporation after the distribution (a "subsequent sale or exchange") is evidence of device. Generally, the greater the percentage of the stock sold or exchanged after the distribution, the stronger the evidence of device. In addition, the shorter the period of time between the distribution and the sale or exchange, the stronger the evidence of device.

(B) *Sale or exchange negotiated or agreed upon before the distribution.* A subsequent sale or exchange pursuant to an arrangement negotiated or agreed upon before the distribution is substantial evidence of device.

(C) *Sale or exchange not negotiated or agreed upon before the distribution.* A subsequent sale or exchange not pursuant to an arrangement negotiated or agreed upon before the distribution is evidence of device.

(D) *Negotiated or agreed upon before the distribution.* For purposes of this subparagraph (2), a sale or exchange is always pursuant to an arrangement negotiated or agreed upon before the distribution if enforceable rights to buy or sell existed before the distribution. If a sale or exchange was discussed by the buyer and the seller before the distribution and was reasonably to be anticipated by both parties, then the sale or exchange will ordinarily be considered to be pursuant to an arrangement negotiated or agreed upon before the distribution.

(E) *Exchange in pursuance of a plan of reorganization.* For purposes of this subparagraph (2), if stock is exchanged for stock in pursuance of a plan of reorganization, and either no gain or loss or only an insubstantial amount of gain is recognized on the exchange, then the exchange is not treated as a subsequent sale or exchange, but the stock received in the exchange is treated as the stock surrendered in the exchange. For this purpose, gain treated as a dividend pursuant to sections 356(a)(2) and 316 shall be disregarded.

(iv) *Nature and use of assets*—(A) *In general.* The determination of whether a transaction was used principally as a device will take into account the nature, kind, amount, and use of the assets of the distributing and the controlled corporations (and corporations controlled by them) immediately after the transaction.

(B) *Assets not used in a trade or business meeting the requirement of section 355(b).* The existence of assets that are not used in a trade or business that satisfies the requirements of section 355(b) is evidence of device. For this purpose, assets that are not used in a trade or business that satisfies the requirements of section 355(b) include, but are not limited to, cash and other liquid assets that are not related to the reasonable needs of a business satisfying such section. The strength of the evidence of device depends on all the facts and circumstances, including, but not limited to, the ratio for each corporation of the value of assets not used in a trade or business that satisfies the requirements of section 355(b) to the value of its business that satisfies such requirements. A difference in the ratio described in the preceding sentence for the distributing and controlled corporation is ordinarily not evidence of device if the distribution is not pro rata among the shareholders of the distributing corporation and such difference is attributable to a need to equalize the value of the stock distributed and the value of the stock or securities exchanged by the distributees.

(C) *Related function.* There is evidence of device if a business of either the distributing or controlled corporation (or a corporation controlled by it) is (*1*) a "secondary business" that continues as a secondary business for a significant period after the separation, and (*2*) can be sold without adversely affecting the business of the other corporation (or a corporation controlled by it). A secondary business is a business of either the distributing or controlled corporation, if its principal function is to serve the business of the other corporation (or a corporation controlled by it). A secondary business can include a business transferred to a newly-created subsidiary or a business which serves a business transferred to a newly-created subsidiary. The activities of the secondary business may consist of providing property or performing services. Thus, in example (11) of § 1.355-3(c), evidence of device would be presented if the principal function of the coal mine (satisfying the requirements of the steel business) continued after the separation and the coal mine could be sold without adversely affecting the steel business. Similarly, in example (10) of § 1.355-3(c), evidence of device would be presented if the principal function of the sales operation after the separation is to sell the output from the manufacturing operation and the sales operation could be sold without adversely affecting the manufacturing operation.

(3) *Nondevice factors*—(i) *In general.* The presence of any of the nondevice factors specified in this subparagraph (3) is evidence of nondevice. The strength of this evidence depends on all of the facts and circumstances.

(ii) *Corporate business purpose.* The corporate business purpose for the transaction is evidence of nondevice. The stronger the evidence of device (such as the presence of the device factors

Reg. § 1.355-2(d)(3)

specified in paragraph (d)(2) of this section), the stronger the corporate business purpose required to prevent the determination that the transaction was used principally as a device. Evidence of device presented by the transfer or retention of assets not used in a trade or business that satisfies the requirements of section 355(b) can be outweighed by the existence of a corporate business purpose for those transfers or retentions. The assessment of the strength of a corporate business purpose will be based on all of the facts and circumstances, including, but not limited to, the following factors:

(A) The importance of achieving the purpose to the success of the business;

(B) The extent to which the transaction is prompted by a person not having a proprietary interest in either corporation, or by other outside factors beyond the control of the distributing corporation; and

(C) The immediacy of the conditions prompting the transaction.

(iii) *Distributing corporation publicly traded and widely held.* The fact that the distributing corporation is publicly traded and has no shareholder who is directly or indirectly the beneficial owner of more than five percent of any class of stock is evidence of nondevice.

(iv) *Distribution to domestic corporate shareholders.* The fact that the stock of the controlled corporation is distributed to one or more domestic corporations that, if section 355 did not apply, would be entitled to a deduction under section 243(a)(1) available to corporations meeting the stock ownership requirements of section 243(c), or a deduction under section 243(a)(2) or (3) or 245(b) is evidence of nondevice.

(4) *Examples.* The provisions of paragraph (d)(1) through (3) of this section may be illustrated by the following examples:

Example (1). Individual A owns all of the stock of corporation X, which is engaged in the warehousing business. X owns all of the stock of corporation Y, which is engaged in the transportation business. X employs individual B, who is extremely knowledgeable of the warehousing business in general and the operations of X in particular. B has informed A that he will seriously consider leaving the company if he is not given the opportunity to purchase a significant amount of stock of X. Because of his knowledge and experience, the loss of B would seriously damage the business of X. B cannot afford to purchase any significant amount of stock of X as long as X owns Y. Accordingly, X distributes the stock of Y to A and A subsequently sells a portion of his X stock to B. However, X could have issued additional shares to B sufficient to give B an equivalent ownership interest in X. There is no other evidence of device or evidence of nondevice. In light of the fact that X could have issued additional shares to B, the sale of X stock by A is substantial evidence of device. The transaction is considered to have been used principally as a device. See paragraph (d)(1), (2)(ii), (iii)(A), (B) and (D), and (3)(i) and (ii) of this section.

Example (2). Corporation X owns and operates a fast food restaurant in State M and owns all of the stock of corporation Y, which owns and operates a fast food restaurant in State N. X and Y operate their businesses under franchises granted by D and E, respectively. X owns cash and marketable securities that exceed the reasonable needs of its business but whose value is small relative to the value of its business. E has recently changed its franchise policy and will no longer grant or renew franchises to subsidiaries (or other members of the same affiliated group) of corporations operating businesses under franchises granted by its competitors. Thus, Y will lose its franchise if it remains a subsidiary of X. The franchise is about to expire. Accordingly, X distributes the stock of Y pro rata among X's shareholders. X retains its business and transfers cash and marketable securities to Y in an amount proportional to the value of Y's business. There is no other evidence of device or evidence of nondevice. The transfer by X to Y and the retention by X of cash and marketable securities is relatively weak evidence of device because after the transfer X and Y hold cash and marketable securities in amounts proportional to the values of their businesses. The fact that the distribution is pro rata is evidence of device. A strong corporate business purpose is relatively strong evidence of nondevice. Accordingly, the transaction is considered not to have been used principally as a device. See paragraph (d)(1), (2)(ii), (iv)(A), and (B) and (3)(i) and (ii)(A), (B), and (C) of this section.

Example (3). Corporation X is engaged in a regulated business in State M and owns all of the stock of corporation Y, which is not engaged in a regulated business in State M. State M has recently amended its laws to provide that affiliated corporations operating in M may not conduct both regulated and unregulated businesses. X transfers cash not related to the reasonable needs of the business of X or Y to Y and then distributes the stock of Y pro rata among X's shareholders. As a result of the transfer of cash, the ratio of the value of its assets not used in a trade or business that satisfies the requirements of section 355(b) to the value of its business is substantially greater for Y than for X. There is no other evidence of device or evidence of nondevice. The transfer of cash by X to Y is relatively strong evidence of device because after the transfer Y holds dispro-

Reg. § 1.355-2(d)(4)

portionately many assets that are not used in a trade or business that satisfies the requirements of section 355(b). The fact that the distribution is pro rata is evidence of device. The strong business purpose is relatively strong evidence of nondevice, but it does not pertain to the transfer. Accordingly, the transaction is considered to have been used principally as a device. See paragraph (d)(1), (2)(ii), (iv)(A) and (B), and (3)(i) and (ii) of this section.

Example (4). The facts are the same as in example (3), except that, instead of transferring cash to Y, X purchases operating assets unrelated to the business of Y and transfers them to Y prior to the distribution. There is no other evidence of device or evidence of nondevice. The transaction is considered to have been used principally as a device. See paragraph (d)(1), (2)(ii), (iv)(A) and (B), and (3)(i) and (ii) of this section.

(5) *Transactions ordinarily not considered as a device*—(i) *In general.* This subparagraph (5) specifies three distributions that ordinarily do not present the potential for tax avoidance described in paragraph (d)(1) of this section. Accordingly, such distributions are ordinarily considered not to have been used principally as a device, notwithstanding the presence of any of the device factors described in paragraph (d)(2) of this section. A transaction described in paragraph (d)(5)(iii) or (iv) of this section is not protected by this subparagraph (5) from a determination that it was used principally as a device if it involves the distribution of the stock of more than one controlled corporation and facilitates the avoidance of the dividend provisions of the Code through the subsequent sale or exchange of stock of one corporation and the retention of the stock of another corporation.

(ii) *Absence of earnings and profits.* A distribution is ordinarily considered not to have been used principally as a device if—

(A) The distributing and controlled corporations have no accumulated earnings and profits at the beginning of their respective taxable years,

(B) The distributing and controlled corporations have no current earnings and profits as of the date of the distribution, and

(C) No distribution of property by the distributing corporation immediately before the separation would require recognition of gain resulting in current earnings and profits for the taxable year of the distribution.

(iii) *Section 303(a) transactions.* A distribution is ordinarily considered not to have been used principally as a device if, in the absence of section 355, with respect to each shareholder dis-

tributee, the distribution would be a redemption to which section 303(a) applied.

(iv) *Section 302(a) transactions.* A distribution is ordinarily considered not to have been used principally as a device if, in the absence of section 355, with respect to each shareholder distributee, the distribution would be a redemption to which section 302(a) applied. For purposes of the preceding sentence, section 302(c)(2)(A)(ii) and (iii) shall not apply.

(v) *Examples.* The provisions of this subparagraph (5) may be illustrated by the following examples:

Example (1). The facts are the same as in example (3) of paragraph (d)(4) of this section, except that X and Y had no accumulated earnings and profits at the beginning of its taxable year, X and Y have no current earnings and profits as of the date of the distribution, and no distribution of property by X immediately before the separation would require recognition of gain that would result in earnings and profits for the taxable year of the distribution. The transaction is considered not to have been used principally as a device. See paragraph (d)(5)(i) and (ii) of this section.

Example (2). Corporation X is engaged in three businesses: a hotel business, a restaurant business, and a rental real estate business. Individuals A, B, and C own all of the stock of X. X transfers the restaurant business to new corporation Y and transfers the rental real estate business to new corporation Z. X then distributes the stock of Y and Z pro rata between B and C in exchange for all of their stock in X. In the absence of section 355, the distribution would be a redemption to which section 302(a) applied. Since this distribution involves the stock of more than one controlled corporation and facilitates the avoidance of the dividend provisions of the Code through the subsequent sale or exchange of stock in one corporation and the retention of the stock of another corporation, it is not protected by paragraph (d)(5)(i) and (iv) of this section from a determination that it was used principally as a device. Thus, the determination of whether the transaction was used principally as a device must be made from all the facts and circumstances, including the presence of the device factors and nondevice factors specified in paragraph (d)(2) and (3) of this section.

(e) *Stock and securities distributed*—(1) *In general.* Section 355 applies to a distribution only if the distributing corporation distributes—

(i) All of the stock and securities of the controlled corporation that it owns, or

(ii) At least an amount of the stock of the controlled corporation that constitutes control as defined in section 368(c). In such a case, all, or

Reg. § 1.355-2(e)(1)

any part, of the securities of the controlled corporation may be distributed, and paragraph (e)(2) of this section shall apply.

(2) *Additional rules.* Where a part of either the stock or the securities of the controlled corporation is retained under paragraph (e)(1)(ii) of this section, it must be established to the satisfaction of the Commissioner that the retention by the distributing corporation was not in pursuance of a plan having as one of its principal purposes the avoidance of Federal income tax. Ordinarily, the corporate business purpose or purposes for the distribution will require the distribution of all of the stock and securities of the controlled corporation. If the distribution of all of the stock and securities of a controlled corporation would be treated to any extent as a distribution of "other property" under section 356, this fact tends to establish that the retention of stock or securities is in pursuance of a plan having as one of its principal purposes the avoidance of Federal income tax.

(f) *Principal amount of securities*—(1) *Securities received.* Section 355 does not apply to a distribution if, with respect to any shareholder or security holder, the principal amount of securities received exceeds the principal amount of securities surrendered, or securities are received but no securities are surrendered. In such cases, see section 356.

(2) *Only stock received.* If only stock is received in a distribution to which section 355(a)(1)(A) applies, the principal amount of the securities surrendered, if any, and the par value or stated value of the stock surrendered, if any, are not relevant to the application of that section.

(g) *Period of ownership*—(1) *Other property.* For purposes of section 355(a)(1)(A), stock of a controlled corporation acquired in a transaction in which gain or loss was recognized in whole or in part (other than a transaction described in § 1.355-3(b)(4)(iii)) within the five-year period ending on the date of the distribution shall not be treated as stock of the controlled corporation but shall be treated as "other property." See section 356. However, for purposes of section 355(a)(1)(D), the stock so acquired is stock of the controlled corporation.

(2) *Example.* Paragraph (g)(1) of this section may be illustrated by the following example:

Example. Corporation X has held 85 of the 100 outstanding shares of the stock of corporation Y for more than five years on the date of the distribution. Six months before that date, X purchased ten more shares. If X distributes all of its 95 shares of the stock of Y, so much of section 356 may apply to the transaction and the ten newly acquired shares are treated as other property. On the other hand, if X retains

ten of the shares of the stock of Y then the application of paragraph (e) of this section must take into account all of the stock of Y, including the ten shares newly acquired by X and the five shares owned by others. Similarly, if, by the use of any agency, X acquired any of the stock of Y within the five-year period ending on the date of the distribution in a transaction in which gain or loss was recognized in whole or in part (for example, where another subsidiary of X purchased stock of Y), then that stock is treated as other property. If X had held only 75 of the 100 outstanding shares of the stock of Y for more than five years on the date of the distribution and had purchased the remaining 25 shares six months before that date, then neither section 355 nor section 356 would apply to the distribution.

(h) *Active conduct of a trade or business.* Section 355 applies to a distribution only if the requirements of § 1.355-3 (relating to the active conduct of a trade or business) are satisfied. [Reg. § 1.355-2.]

☐ [*T.D.* 6152, 12-2-55. *Amended by T.D.* 8238, 1-4-89.]

§ 1.355-3. Active conduct of a trade or business.—(a) *General requirements*—(1) *Application of section 355.* Under section 355(b)(1), a distribution of stock, or stock and securities, of a controlled corporation qualifies under section 355 only if—

(i) The distributing and the controlled corporations are each engaged in the active conduct of a trade or business immediately after the distribution (section 355(b)(1)(A)), or

(ii) Immediately before the distribution, the distributing corporation had no assets other than stock or securities of the controlled corporations, and each of the controlled corporations is engaged in the active conduct of a trade or business immediately after the distribution (section 355(b)(1)(B)). A *de minimis* amount of assets held by the distributing corporation shall be disregarded for purposes of this paragraph (a)(1)(ii).

(2) *Examples.* Paragraph (a)(1) of this section may be illustrated by the following examples:

Example (1). Prior to the distribution, corporation X is engaged in the active conduct of a trade or business and owns all of the stock of corporation Y, which also is engaged in the active conduct of a trade or business. X distributes all of the stock of Y to X's shareholders, and each corporation continues the active conduct of its trade or business. The active business requirement of section 355(b)(1)(A) is satisfied.

Example (2). The facts are the same as in example (1), except that X transfers all of its assets other than the stock of Y to a new corporation in exchange for all of the stock of the new corporation and then distributes the stock of both controlled corporations to X's shareholders. The active business requirement of section 355(b)(1)(B) is satisfied.

(b) *Active conduct of a trade or business defined*—(1) *In general*. Section 355(b)(2) provides rules for determining whether a corporation is treated as engaged in the active conduct of a trade or business for purposes of section 355(b)(1). Under section 355(b)(2)(A), a corporation is treated as engaged in the active conduct of a trade or business if it is itself engaged in the active conduct of a trade or business or if substantially all of its assets consist of the stock, or stock and securities, of a corporation or corporations controlled by it (immediately after the distribution) each of which is engaged in the active conduct of a trade or business.

(2) *Active conduct of a trade or business immediately after distribution*—(i) *In general*. For purposes of section 355(b), a corporation shall be treated as engaged in the "active conduct of a trade or business" immediately after the distribution if the assets and activities of the corporation satisfy the requirements and limitations described in paragraph (b)(2)(ii), (iii), and (iv) of this section.

(ii) *Trade or business*. A corporation shall be treated as engaged in a trade or business immediately after the distribution if a specific group of activities are being carried on by the corporation for the purpose of earning income or profit, and the activities included in such group include every operation that forms a part of, or a step in, the process of earning income or profit. Such group of activities ordinarily must include the collection of income and the payment of expenses.

(iii) *Active conduct*. For purposes of section 355(b), the determination whether a trade or business is actively conducted will be made from all of the facts and circumstances. Generally, the corporation is required itself to perform active and substantial management and operational functions. Generally, activities performed by the corporation itself do not include activities performed by persons outside the corporation, including independent contractors. A corporation may satisfy the requirements of this subdivision (iii) through the activities that it performs itself, even though some of its activities are performed by others. Separations of real property all or substantially all of which is occupied prior to the distribution by the distributing or the controlled corporation (or by any corporation controlled directly or indirectly by either of those corporations) will be carefully scrutinized with respect to

the requirements of section 355(b) and this § 1.355-3.

(iv) *Limitations*. The active conduct of a trade or business does not include—

(A) The holding for investment purposes of stock, securities, land, or other property, or

(B) The ownership and operation (including leasing) of real or personal property used in a trade or business, unless the owner performs significant services with respect to the operation and management of the property.

(3) *Active conduct for five-year period preceding distribution*. Under section 355(b)(2)(B), a trade or business that is relied upon to meet the requirements of section 355(b) must have been actively conducted throughout the five-year period ending on the date of the distribution. For purposes of this subparagraph (3)—

(i) activities which constitute a trade or business under the tests described in paragraph (b)(2) of this section shall be treated as meeting the requirement of the preceding sentence if such activities were actively conducted throughout the 5-year period ending on the date of distribution, and

(ii) the fact that a trade or business underwent change during the five-year period preceding the distribution (for example, by the addition of new or the dropping of old products, changes in production capacity, and the like) shall be disregarded, provided that the changes are not of such a character as to constitute the acquisition of a new or different business. In particular, if a corporation engaged in the active conduct of one trade or business during that five-year period purchased, created, or otherwise acquired another trade or business in the same line of business, then the acquisition of that other business is ordinarily treated as an expansion of the original business, all of which is treated as having been actively conducted during that five-year period, unless that purchase, creation, or other acquisition effects a change of such a character as to constitute the acquisition of a new or different business.

* * *

(c) *Examples*. The following examples illustrate section 355(b)(2)(A) and (B) and paragraph (b)(1), (2), and (3) of this section. However, a transaction that satisfies these active business requirements will qualify under section 355 only if it satisfies the other requirements of section 355(a) and (b).

Example (1). Corporation X is engaged in the manufacture and sale of soap and detergents and also owns investment securities. X transfers the investment securities to new subsidiary Y and distributes the stock of Y to X's shareholders. Y

Reg. § 1.355-3(c)

does not satisfy the requirements of section 355(b) because the holding of investment securities does not constitute the active conduct of a trade or business. See paragraph (b)(2)(iv)(A) of this section.

Example (2). Corporation X owns, manages, and derives rental income from an office building and also owns vacant land. X transfers the land to new subsidiary Y and distributes the stock of Y to X's shareholders. Y will subdivide the land, install streets and utilities, and sell the developed lots to various homebuilders. Y does not satisfy the requirements of section 355(b) because no significant development activities were conducted with respect to the land during the five-year period ending on the date of the distribution. See paragraph (b)(3) of this section.

Example (3). Corporation X owns land on which it conducts a ranching business. Oil has been discovered in the area, and it is apparent that oil may be found under the land on which the ranching business is conducted. X has engaged in no significant activities in connection with its mineral rights. X transfers its mineral rights to new subsidiary Y and distributes the stock of Y to X's shareholders. Y will actively pursue the development of the oil producing potential of the property. Y does not satisfy the requirements of section 355(b) because X engaged in no significant exploitation activities with respect to the mineral rights during the five-year period ending on the date of the distribution. See paragraph (b)(3) of this section.

Example (4). For more than five years, corporation X has conducted a single business of constructing sewage disposal plants and other facilities. X transfers one half of its assets to new subsidiary Y. These assets include a contract for the construction of a sewage disposal plant in State M, construction equipment, cash, and other tangible assets. X retains a contract for the construction of a sewage disposal plant in State N, construction equipment, cash, and other intangible assets. X then distributes the stock of Y to one of X's shareholders in exchange for all of his stock of X. X and Y both satisfy the requirements of section 355(b). See paragraph (b)(3)(i) of this section.

Example (5). For the past six years, corporation X has owned and operated two factories devoted to the production of edible pork skins. The entire output of one factory is sold to one customer, C, while the output of the second factory is sold to C and a number of other customers. To eliminate errors in packaging, X opens a new factory. Thereafter, orders from C are processed and packaged at the two original factories, while the new factory handles only orders from other customers.

Eight months after opening the new factory, X transfers it and related business assets to new subsidiary Y and distributes the stock of Y to X's shareholders. X and Y both satisfy the requirements of section 355(b). See paragraph (b)(3)(i) and (ii) of this section.

Example (6). Corporation X has owned and operated a men's retail clothing store in the downtown area of the City of G for nine years and has owned and operated another men's retail clothing store in a suburban area of G for seven years. X transfers the store building, fixtures, inventory, and other assets related to the operations of the suburban store to new subsidiary Y. X also transfers to Y the delivery trucks and delivery personnel that formerly served both stores. Henceforth, X will contract with a local public delivery service to make its deliveries. X retains the warehouses that formerly served both stores. Henceforth, Y will lease warehouse space from an unrelated public warehouse company. X then distributes the stock of Y to X's shareholders. X and Y both satisfy the requirements of section 355(b). See paragraph (b)(3)(i) of this section.

Example (7). For the past nine years, corporation X has owned and operated a department store in the downtown area of the City of G. Three years ago, X acquired a parcel of land in a suburban area of G and constructed a new department store on it. X transfers the suburban store and related business assets to new subsidiary Y and distributes the stock of Y to X's shareholders. After the distribution, each store has its own manager and is operated independently of the other store. X and Y both satisfy the requirements of section 355(b). See paragraph (b)(3)(i) and (ii) of this section.

Example (8). For the past six years, corporation X has owned and operated hardware stores in several states. Two years ago, X purchased all of the assets of a hardware store in State M, where X had not previously conducted business. X transfers the State M store and related business assets to new subsidiary Y and distributes the stock of Y to X's shareholders. After the distribution, the State M store has its own manager and is operated independently of the other stores. X and Y both satisfy the requirements of section 355(b). See paragraph (b)(3)(i) and (ii) of this section.

Example (9). For the past eight years, corporation X has engaged in the manufacture and sale of household products. Throughout this period, X has maintained a research department for use in connection with its manufacturing activities. The research department has 30 employees actively engaged in the development of new products. X transfers the research department to new subsidiary Y and distributes the stock of Y to X's share-

Reg. § 1.355-3(c)

holders. After the distribution, Y continues its research operations on a contractual basis with several corporations, including X. X and Y both satisfy the requirements of section 355(b). See paragraph (b)(3)(i) of this section. The result in this example is the same if, after the distribution, Y continues its research operations but furnishes its services only to X. See paragraph (b)(3)(i) of this section. However, see § 1.355-2(d)(2)(iv)(C) (related function device factor) for possible evidence of device.

Example (10). For the past six years, corporation X has processed and sold meat products. X derives income from no other source. X separates the sales function from the processing function by transferring the business assets related to the sales function and cash for working capital to new subsidiary Y. X then distributes the stock of Y to X's shareholders. After the distribution, Y purchases for resale the meat products processed by X. X and Y both satisfy the requirements of section 355(b). See paragraph (b)(3)(i) of this section. However, see § 1.355-2(d)(2)(iv)(C) (related function device factor) for possible evidence of device.

Example (11). For the past eight years, corporation X has been engaged in the manufacture and sale of steel and steel products. X owns all of the stock of corporation Y, which, for the past six years, has owned and operated a coal mine for the sole purpose of supplying X's coal requirements in the manufacture of steel. X distributes the stock of Y to X's shareholders. X and Y both satisfy the requirements of section 355(b). See paragraph (b)(3)(i) of this section. However, see § 1.355-2(d)(2)(iv)(C) (related function device factor) for possible evidence of device.

Example (12). For the past seven years, corporation X, a bank, has owned an eleven-story office building, the ground floor of which X has occupied in the conduct of its banking business. The remaining ten floors are rented to various tenants. Throughout this seven-year period, the building has been managed and maintained by employees of the bank. X transfers the building to new subsidiary Y and distributes the stock of Y to X's shareholders. Henceforth, Y will manage the building, negotiate leases, seek new tenants, and repair and maintain the building. X and Y both satisfy the requirements of section 355(b). See paragraph (b)(3) of this section.

Example (13). For the past nine years, corporation X, a bank, has owned a two-story building, the ground floor and one half of the second floor of which X has occupied in the conduct of its banking business. The other half of the second floor has been rented as storage space to a neighboring retail merchant. X transfers the building to new

subsidiary Y and distributes the stock of Y to X's shareholders. After the distribution, X leases from Y the space in the building that it formerly occupied. Under the lease, X will repair and maintain its portion of the building and pay property taxes and insurance. Y does not satisfy the requirements of section 355(b) because it is not engaged in the active conduct of a trade or business immediately after the distribution. See paragraph (b)(2)(iv)(A) of this section. This example does not address the question of whether the activities of X with respect to the building prior to the separation would constitute the active conduct of a trade or business. [Reg. § 1.355-3.]

☐ [*T.D.* 6152, 12-2-55. *Amended by T.D. 8238,* 1-5-89.]

§ 1.355-4. Non pro rata distributions, etc.— Section 355 provides for nonrecognition of gain or loss with respect to a distribution whether or not (a) the distribution is pro rata with respect to all of the shareholders of the distributing corporation, (b) the distribution is pursuant to a plan of reorganization within the meaning of section 368(a)(1)(D), or (c) the shareholder surrenders stock in the distributing corporation. Under section 355, the stock of a controlled corporation may consist of common stock or preferred stock. (See, however, section 306 and the regulations thereunder.) Section 355 does not apply, however, if the substance of a transaction is merely an exchange between shareholders or security holders of stock or securities in one corporation for stock or securities in another corporation. For example, if two individuals, A and B, each own directly 50 percent of the stock of corporation X and 50 percent of the stock of corporation Y, section 355 would not apply to a transaction in which A and B transfer all of their stock of X and Y to a new corporation Z, for all of the stock of Z, and Z then distributes the stock of X to A and the stock of Y to B. [Reg. § 1.355-4.]

☐ [*T.D.* 6152, 12-2-55. *Amended by T.D. 8238,* 1-4-89.]

§ 1.355-6. Recognition of gain on certain distributions of stock or securities in controlled corporation.—(a) *Conventions*—**(1)** *Examples.* For purposes of the examples in this section, unless otherwise stated, assume that P, S, T, X, Y, N, HC, D, D1, D2, D3, and C are corporations, A and B are individuals, shareholders are not treated as one person under section 355(d)(7), stock has been owned for more than five years and section 355(d)(6) and paragraph (e)(4) of this section do not apply, no election under section 338 (if available) is made, and all transactions described are respected under general tax principles, including the step transaction doctrine. No inference should be drawn from any example as to

Reg. § 1.355-6(a)(1)

whether any requirements of section 355 other than those of section 355(d), as specified, are satisfied.

(2) *Five-year period.* For purposes of this section, the term five-year period means the five-year period (determined after applying section 355(d)(6) and paragraph (e)(4) of this section) ending on the date of the distribution, but in no event beginning earlier than October 10, 1990.

(3) *Distributing securities.* For purposes of determining if stock of any controlled corporation received in the distribution is disqualified stock described in section 355(d)(3)(B)(ii)(II) (relating to a distribution of controlled corporation stock on any securities in the distributing corporation acquired by purchase during the five-year period), references in this section to stock of a corporation that is or becomes a distributing corporation includes securities of the corporation. Similarly, a reference to stock in paragraph (c)(4) of this section (relating to a plan or arrangement) includes securities.

(4) *Marketable securities.* Unless otherwise stated, any reference in this section to marketable stock includes marketable securities.

(b) *General rules and purposes of section 355(d)*—(1) *Disqualified distributions in general.* In the case of a disqualified distribution, any stock or securities in the controlled corporation shall not be treated as qualified property for purposes of section 355(c)(2) or 361(c)(2). In general, a disqualified distribution is any distribution to which section 355 (or so much of section 356 as relates thereto) applies if, immediately after the distribution—

(i) Any person holds disqualified stock in the distributing corporation that constitutes a 50 percent or greater interest in such corporation; or

(ii) Any person holds disqualified stock in the controlled corporation (or, if stock of more than one controlled corporation is distributed, in any controlled corporation) that constitutes a 50 percent or greater interest in such corporation.

(2) *Disqualified stock*—(i) *In general. Disqualified stock* is—

(A) Any stock in the distributing corporation acquired by purchase during the five-year period; and

(B) Any stock in any controlled corporation—

(*1*) Acquired by purchase during the five-year period; or

(*2*) Received in the distribution to the extent attributable to distributions on any stock in the distributing corporation acquired by purchase during the five-year period.

(ii) *Purchase.* For the definition of a purchase for purposes of section 355(d) and this section, see section 355(d)(5) and paragraph (d) of this section.

(iii) *Exceptions*—(A) *Purchase eliminated.* Stock (or an interest in another entity) that is acquired by purchase (including stock (or another interest) that is treated as acquired by purchase under paragraph (e)(2), (3), or (4) of this section) ceases to be acquired by that purchase if (and when) the basis resulting from the purchase is eliminated. For purposes of this paragraph (b)(2)(iii), basis resulting from the purchase is basis in the stock (or in an interest in another entity) that is directly purchased during the five-year period or that is treated as acquired by purchase during such period under paragraph (e)(2), (3), or (4) of this section.

(B) *Deemed purchase eliminated.* Stock (or an interest in another entity) that is deemed purchased under section 355(d)(8) or paragraph (e)(1) of this section shall cease to be treated as purchased if (and when) the basis resulting from the purchase that effects the deemed purchase is eliminated.

(C) *Elimination of basis*—(*1*) *General rule.* Basis in the stock of a corporation (or in an interest in another entity) is eliminated if (and when) it would no longer be taken into account by any person in determining gain or loss on a sale or exchange of any stock of such corporation (or an interest in the other entity). Basis is not eliminated, however, if it is allocated between stock of two corporations under § 1.358-2(a).

(*2*) *Special rule for transferred and exchanged basis property.* Basis of stock (or an interest in another entity) resulting from a purchase (the first purchase) is eliminated if (and when) such stock (or other interest) is subsequently transferred to another person in an exchange or other transfer to which paragraph (e)(2) or (3) of this section applies (the second purchase). The elimination of basis in stock (or in another interest) resulting from the first purchase, however, does not eliminate the basis resulting from the second purchase in the stock (or other interest) that is treated as acquired by purchase by the acquirer in a transaction to which paragraph (e)(2) of this section applies or by the person making the exchange in a transaction to which paragraph (e)(3) of this section applies.

(*3*) *Special rule for split-offs and split-ups.* Under section 355(d)(3)(B)(ii) and paragraph (b)(2)(i)(B)(*2*) of this section, disqualified stock includes controlled corporation stock received in exchange for distributing corporation stock acquired by purchase. Solely for purposes of determining whether controlled corporation stock received in a distribution in exchange for distributing corporation stock is disqualified stock described in that section and paragraph immediately after the distribution, paragraph (b)(2)(iii)(C)(*2*) of this section does not apply to the exchange to eliminate basis resulting from a purchase of that distributing corporation stock (notwithstanding that paragraph (e)(3) of this section applies to the exchange).

(D) *Special rule if basis allocated between two corporations.* If the shareholder of a distributing corporation, pursuant to § 1.358-2, allocates basis resulting from a purchase between the stock of two or more corporations then, following such allocation, the determination of whether such basis has been eliminated shall be made separately with respect to the stock of each such corporation.

(3) *Certain distributions not disqualified distributions because purposes of section 355(d) not violated*—(i) *In general.* Notwithstanding the provisions of section 355(d)(2) and this paragraph (b), a distribution is not a disqualified distribution if the distribution does not violate the purposes of section 355(d) as provided in this paragraph (b)(3). A distribution does not violate the purposes of section 355(d) if the effect of the distribution is neither—

(A) To increase ownership (combined direct and indirect) in the distributing corporation or any controlled corporation by a disqualified person; nor

(B) To provide a disqualified person with a purchased basis in the stock of any controlled corporation.

(ii) *Disqualified person.* A disqualified person is any person (taking into account section 355(d)(7) and paragraph (c)(4) of this section) that, immediately after a distribution, holds (directly or indirectly under section 355(d)(8) and paragraph (e)(1) of this section) disqualified stock in the distributing corporation or controlled corporation that—

(A) The person—

(*1*) Acquired by purchase under section 355(d)(5) or (8) and paragraphs (d) and (e) of this section during the five-year period, or

(*2*) Received in the distribution to the extent attributable to distributions on any stock in the distributing corporation acquired by purchase under section 355(d)(5) or (8) and paragraphs (d) and (e) of this section by that person during the five-year period; and

(B) Constitutes a 50 percent or greater interest in such corporation (under section 355(d)(4) and paragraph (c) of this section).

(iii) *Purchased basis.* In general, a purchased basis is basis in controlled corporation stock that is disqualified stock. However, basis in controlled corporation stock that is disqualified stock will not be treated as purchased basis if the controlled corporation stock and any distributing corporation stock with respect to which the controlled corporation stock is distributed are treated as acquired by purchase solely under the attribution rules of section 355(d)(8) and paragraph (e)(1) of this section. The prior sentence will not apply, however, if the distributing corporation stock is treated as acquired by purchase under the attribution rules as a result of the acquisition of an interest in a partnership (the purchased partnership), and following the distribution, the controlled corporation stock is directly held by the purchased partnership (or a chain of partnerships that includes the purchased partnership).

(iv) *Increase in interest because of payment of cash in lieu of fractional shares.* Any increase in direct or indirect ownership in the distributing corporation or any controlled corporation by a disqualified person because of a payment of cash in lieu of issuing fractional shares will be disregarded for purposes of paragraph (b)(3)(i)(A) of this section if the payment of the cash is solely to avoid the expense and inconvenience of issuing fractional share interests, and does not represent separately bargained for consideration.

(v) *Other exceptions.* The Commissioner may provide by guidance published in the Internal Revenue Bulletin that other distributions are not disqualified distributions because they do not violate the purposes of section 355(d).

(vi) *Examples.* The following examples illustrate this paragraph (b)(3):

Example 1. Stock distributed in spin-off; no purchased basis. D owns all of the stock of D1, and D1 owns all the stock of C. A purchases 60 percent of the D stock for cash. Within five years of A's purchase, D1 distributes the C stock to D. A is treated as having purchased 60 percent of the stock of both D1 and C on the date A purchases 60 percent of the D stock under the attribution rules of section 355(d)(8) and paragraph (e)(1) of this section. The C stock received by D is attributable to a distribution on purchased D1 stock under section 355(d)(3)(B)(ii). Accordingly, the D1 and C stock each is disqualified stock under section 355(d)(3) and paragraph (b)(2) of this section, and A is a disqualified person under paragraph (b)(3)(ii) of this section. However, the purposes of section 355(d) under paragraph (b)(3)(i) of this section are not violated. A did not increase direct or indirect ownership in D1 or C. In addition, D's basis in the C stock is not a purchased

Reg. § 1.355-6(b)(3)

basis under paragraph (b)(3)(iii) of this section because both the D1 and the C stock are treated as acquired by purchase solely under the attribution rules of section 355(d)(8) and paragraph (e)(1) of this section. Accordingly, D1's distribution of the C stock to D is not a disqualified distribution under section 355(d)(2) and paragraph (b)(1) of this section.

Example 2. Stock distributed in spin-off; purchased basis. The facts are the same as *Example 1*, except that D immediately further distributes the C stock to its shareholders (including A) pro rata. The D and C stock each is disqualified stock under section 355(d)(3) and paragraph (b)(2) of this section, and A is a disqualified person under paragraph (b)(3)(ii) of this section. The purposes of section 355(d) under paragraph (b)(3)(i) of this section are violated. A did not increase direct or indirect ownership in D or C. However, A's basis in the C stock is a purchased basis under paragraph (b)(3)(iii) of this section because the D stock is not treated as acquired by purchase solely under the attribution rules of section 355(d)(8) and paragraph (e)(1) of this section. Accordingly, the further distribution is a disqualified distribution under section 355(d)(2) and paragraph (b)(1) of this section.

Example 3. Stock distributed in split-off with ownership increase; purchased basis. The facts are the same as *Example 1*, except that D immediately further distributes the C stock to A in exchange for A's purchased stock in D. The C stock received by A is attributable to a distribution on purchased D stock under section 355(d)(3)(B)(ii), and A's basis in the C stock is determined by reference to the adjusted basis of A's purchased D stock under paragraph (e)(3) of this section. (Under paragraph (b)(2)(iii)(B)(*3*) of this section, the basis resulting from A's purchase of D stock is not eliminated solely for purposes of determining if the C stock acquired by A is disqualified stock immediately after the distribution, notwithstanding that paragraph (e)(3) of this section applies to the exchange.) Accordingly, the D stock and the C stock each is disqualified stock under section 355(d)(3) and paragraph (b)(2) of this section, and A is a disqualified person under paragraph (b)(3)(ii) of this section. The purposes of section 355(d) under paragraph (b)(3)(i) of this section are violated because A increased its ownership in C from a 60 percent indirect interest to a 100 percent direct interest, and because A's basis in the C stock is a purchased basis under paragraph (b)(3)(iii) of this section. Accordingly, the further distribution is a disqualified distribution under section 355(d)(2) and paragraph (b)(1) of this section.

Example 4. Stock distributed in spin-off; purchased basis. D1 owns all the stock of C. D purchases all of the stock of D1 for cash Within five years of D's purchase of D1, P acquires all of the stock of D1 from D in a section 368(a)(i)(B) reorganization that is not a reorganization under section 368(a)(1)(A) by reason of section 368(a)(2)(E), and D1 distributes all of its C stock to P. P is treated as having acquired the D1 stock by purchase on the date D acquired it under the transferred basis rule of section 355(d)(5)(C) and paragraph (e)(2) of this section. P is treated as having purchased all of the C stock on the date D purchased the D1 stock under the attribution rules of section 355(d)(8) and paragraph (e)(1) of this section, and the C stock received by P is attributable to a distribution on purchased D1 stock under section 355(d)(3)(B)(ii). Accordingly, the D1 and C stock each is disqualified stock under section 355(d)(3) and paragraph (b)(2) of this section, and P is a disqualified person under paragraph (b)(3)(ii) of this section. The purposes of section 355(d) under paragraph (b)(3)(i) of this section are violated. P did not increase direct or indirect ownership in D1 or C. However, P's basis in the C stock is a purchased basis under paragraph (b)(3)(iii) of this section because the D1 stock is not treated as acquired by purchase solely under the attribution rules of section 355(d)(8) and paragraph (e)(1) of this section. Accordingly, D1's distribution of the C stock to P is a disqualified distribution under section 355(d)(2) and paragraph (b)(1) of this section.

Example 5. Stock distributed in split-off with ownership increase; no purchased basis. P owns 50 percent of the stock of D, the remaining D stock is owned by unrelated persons, D owns all the stock of C, and A purchases all of the P stock from the P shareholders. Within five years of A's purchase, D distributes all of the C stock to P in exchange for P's D stock. A is treated as having purchased 50 percent of the stock of both D and C on the date A purchases the P stock under the attribution rules of section 355(d)(8) and paragraph (e)(1) of this section. The C stock received by P is attributable to a distribution on purchased D stock under section 355(d)(3)(B)(ii). Accordingly, the D stock and the C stock each is disqualified stock under section 355(d)(3) and paragraph (b)(2) of this section, and A is a disqualified person under paragraph (b)(3)(ii) of this section. The purposes of section 355(d) under paragraph (b)(3)(i) of this section are violated because, even though P's basis in the C stock is not a purchased basis under paragraph (b)(3)(iii) of this section, A increased its direct or indirect ownership in C from a 50 percent indirect interest to a 100 percent indirect interest. Accordingly, D's distribution of the C stock to P is a disqualified distribution under section 355(d)(2) and paragraph (b)(1) of this section.

Reg. § 1.355-6(b)(3)

Example 6. Stock distributed in split-off with no ownership increase; no purchased basis. A purchases all of the stock of T. T later merges into D in a section 368(a)(1)(A) reorganization and A exchanges its purchased T stock for 60 percent of the stock of D. D owns all of the stock of D1 and D2, D1 and D2 each owns 50 percent of the stock of D3, and D3 owns all of the stock of C. Within five years of A's purchase of the T stock, D3 distributes the C stock to D1 in exchange for all of D1's D3 stock. A is treated as having acquired 60 percent of the D stock by purchase on the date A purchases the T stock under paragraph (e)(3) of this section. A is treated as having purchased 60 percent of the stock of D1, D2, D3, and C on the date A purchases the T stock under the attribution rules of section 355(d)(8) and paragraph (e)(1) of this section. The C stock received by D1 is attributable to a distribution on purchased D3 stock under section 355(d)(3)(B)(ii). Accordingly, the D3 stock and the C stock each is disqualified stock under section 355(d)(3) and paragraph (b)(2) of this section, and A is a disqualified person under paragraph (b)(3)(ii) of this section. However, the purposes of section 355(d) under paragraph (b)(3)(i) of this section are not violated. A did not increase direct or indirect ownership in D3 or C, and D1's basis in the C stock is not a purchased basis under paragraph (b)(3)(iii) of this section because the D3 stock is treated as acquired by purchase solely under the attribution rules of section 355(d)(8) and paragraph (e)(1) of this section. Accordingly, D3's distribution of the C stock to D1 is not a disqualified distribution under section 355(d)(2) and paragraph (b)(1) of this section.

Example 7. Purchased basis eliminated by liquidation; stock distributed in spin-off. P owns 30 percent of the stock of D, D owns all of the stock of D1, and D1 owns all of the stock of C. P purchases the remaining 70 percent of the D stock for cash. Within five years of P's purchase, P liquidates D in a transaction qualifying under sections 332 and 337(a), and D1 then distributes the stock of C to P. Prior to the liquidation, P is treated as having purchased 70 percent of the stock of D1 and C on the date P purchases the D stock under the attribution rules of section 355(d)(8)(B) and paragraph (e)(1) of this section. After the liquidation, however, under paragraph (b)(2)(iii) of this section, P is not treated as having acquired by purchase the D1 or the C stock under section 355(d)(8)(B) and paragraph (e)(1) of this section because P's basis in the D stock is eliminated in the liquidation of D. Under section 334(b)(1), P's basis in the D1 stock is determined by reference to D's basis in the D1 stock and not by reference to P's basis in D. Paragraph (d)(2)(i)(B) of this section does not treat the D1

stock as newly purchased in P's hands because no gain or loss was recognized by D in the liquidation. Accordingly, neither the D1 stock nor the C stock is disqualified stock under section 355(d)(3) and paragraph (b)(2) of this section in P's hands, and the distribution is not a disqualified distribution under section 355(d)(2) and paragraph (b)(1) of this section.

Example 8. Purchased basis eliminated by upstream merger; stock distributed in spin-off. D owns all of the stock of D1, and D1 owns all of the stock of C. P purchases 60 percent of the D stock for cash. Within five years of P's purchase, D merges into P in a section 368(a)(1)(A) reorganization, with the D shareholders other than P receiving solely P stock in exchange for their D stock, and D1 then distributes the stock of C to P. Prior to the merger, P is treated as having purchased 60 percent of the stock of D1 and C on the date P purchases the D stock under the attribution rules of section 355(d)(8) and paragraph (e)(1) of this section. After the merger, however, under paragraph (b)(2)(iii) of this section, P is not treated as having acquired by purchase the D1 or the C stock under section 355(d)(8)(B) and paragraph (e)(1) of this section because P's basis in the D stock is eliminated in the merger. Under section 362(b), P's basis in the D1 stock is determined by reference to D's basis in the D1 stock and not by reference to P's basis in D. Paragraph (d)(2)(i)(B) of this section does not treat the D1 stock as newly purchased in P's hands because no gain or loss was recognized by D in the merger. Accordingly, neither the D1 stock nor the C stock is disqualified stock under section 355(d)(3) and paragraph (b)(2) of this section in P's hands, and the distribution is not a disqualified distribution under section 355(d)(2) and paragraph (b)(1) of this section.

Example 9. Purchased basis eliminated by distribution; stock distributed in spin-off. A purchases all the stock of C for cash on Date 1. D acquires all of the stock of C from A in a section 368(a)(1)(B) reorganization that is not a reorganization under section 368(a)(1)(A) by reason of section 368(A)(1)(E). A receives ten percent of the D stock in the transaction. The remaining D stock is owned by B. Within five years of A's purchase of the C stock, D distributes all the stock of C pro rata to A and B. Under the transferred basis rule of paragraph (e)(2) of this section, D is treated as having purchased all of the C stock on the date A acquired it. Under the exchanged basis rule of paragraph (e)(3) of this section, A is treated as having purchased its D stock on Date 1 and A is treated as having purchased ten percent of the C stock on Date 1 under the attribution rules of section 355(d)(8) and paragraph (e)(3) of this section. Moreover, under paragraph (b)(2)(iii)(C)

Reg. § 1.355-6(b)(3)

of this section, A's basis in the C stock resulting from A's Date 1 purchase of C stock is eliminated. After the distribution, A's and B's bases in their C stock are determined by reference to the bases of their D stock under § 1.358-2(a)(2) (and not by reference to D's basis in the C stock). D's basis in the stock of C resulting from its deemed purchase of that stock under paragraph (e)(2) of this section is eliminated by the distribution of the C stock because it would no longer be taken into account by any person in determining gain or loss on the sale of C stock. Therefore, the C stock distributed to A and B is not disqualified stock as a result of D's purchase of C. However, A's basis in its D stock resulting from its deemed purchase of that stock under paragraph (e)(3) of this section is not eliminated. Therefore, A's ten percent interest in the stock of D is disqualified stock. Furthermore, A's ten percent interest in the stock of C is disqualified stock because the distribution of the C stock is attributable to A's D stock that was acquired by purchase. However, there has not been a disqualified distribution because no person, immediately after the distribution, holds disqualified stock in either D or C that constitutes a 50 percent or greater interest in such corporation.

Example 10. Allocation of purchased basis analyzed separately. (i) P owns all the stock of D. D purchases all the stock of D1 for cash on Date 1. D1 owns all the stock of C (which owns all the stock of C1) and S. Within five years of Date 1, D1 distributes all the stock of C to D. The D1 and C stock each is disqualified stock under section 355(d)(3) and paragraph (b)(2) of this section, and D is a disqualified person under paragraph (b)(3)(ii) of this section. The purposes of section 355(d) under paragraph (b)(3)(i) of this section are violated. D did not increase direct or indirect ownership in D1 or C. However, D's basis in the C stock is a purchased basis under paragraph (b)(3)(iii) of this section because the D1 stock is not treated as acquired by purchase solely under the attribution rules of section 355(d)(8) and paragraph (e)(1) of this section. Accordingly, the distribution is a disqualified distribution under section 355(d) and paragraph (b)(1) of this section. D's basis in the D1 stock is allocated pursuant to § 1.358-2 between the D1 stock and the C stock. Therefore, under paragraph (e)(4) of this section, the C stock is deemed to be acquired by purchase on Date 1, the date D purchased all the stock of D1. If thereafter, and within five years of Date 1, C were to distribute all the stock of C1 to D, that distribution would also be a disqualified distribution because of D's deemed purchase of the stock of C.

(ii) Following the distribution of the stock of C by D1, and within five years of Date 1, D distributes all the stock of D1 to P. Under para-

graph (b)(2)(iii)(D) of this section, the determination of whether D's basis in D1 has been eliminated shall be made without regard to D's allocated basis in C. After the distribution, P's basis in the D1 stock is determined by reference to its basis in its D stock under § 1.358-2(a)(2) (and not by reference to D's basis in the D1 stock). D's basis in the D1 stock resulting from the purchase of that stock is eliminated by the distribution of the D1 stock because it would no longer be taken into account by any person in determining gain or loss on the sale of D1 stock. Therefore, the D1 stock distributed to P is not disqualified stock as a result of D's purchase of D1. Moreover, a subsequent distribution of the S stock by D1 to P would not be a disqualified distribution because both the D1 and S stock would cease to be treated as purchased when D's basis in D1 has been eliminated.

(4) *Anti-avoidance rule*—(i) *In general.* Notwithstanding any provision of section 355(d) or this section, the Commissioner may treat any distribution as a disqualified distribution under section 355(d)(2) and paragraph (b)(1) of this section if the distribution or another transaction or transactions are engaged in or structured with a principal purpose to avoid the purposes of section 355(d) or this section with respect to the distribution. Without limiting the preceding sentence, the Commissioner may determine that the existence of a related person, intermediary, pass-through entity, or similar person (an intermediary) should be disregarded, in whole or in part, if the intermediary is formed or availed of with a principal purpose to avoid the purposes of section 355(d) or this section.

(ii) *Example.* The following example illustrates this paragraph (b)(4):

Example. Post-distribution redemption. B wholly owns D, which wholly owns C. With a principal purpose to avoid the purposes of section 355(d), A, B, D, and C engage in the following transactions. A purchases 45 of 100 shares of the only class of D stock. Within five years after A's purchase, D distributes all of its 100 shares in C to A and B pro rata. D then redeems 20 shares of B's D stock, and C redeems 20 shares of B's C stock. After the redemption, A owns 45 shares and B owns 35 shares in each of D and C. Under paragraph (b)(4)(i) of this section, the Commissioner may treat A as owning disqualified stock in D and C that constitutes a 50 percent or greater interest in D and C immediately after the distribution. Under that treatment, the distribution is a disqualified distribution under section 355(d)(2) and paragraph (b)(1) of this section.

(c) *Whether a person holds a 50 percent or greater interest*—(1) *In general.* Under section

355(d)(4), 50 percent or greater interest means stock possessing at least 50 percent of the total combined voting power of all classes of stock entitled to vote or at least 50 percent of the total value of shares of all classes of stock.

(2) *Valuation.* For purposes of section 355(d)(4) and this section, all shares of stock within a single class are considered to have the same value. But see paragraph (c)(3)(vii)(A) of this section (determination of whether it is reasonably certain that an option will be exercised).

(3) *Effect of options, warrants, convertible obligations, and other similar interests*—(i) *Application.* This paragraph (c)(3) provides rules to determine when an option is treated as exercised for purposes of section 355(d) (other than section 355(d)(6)). Except as provided in this paragraph (c)(3), an option is not treated as exercised for purposes of section 355(d). This paragraph (c)(3) does not affect the determination of whether an instrument is an option or stock under general principles of tax law (such as substance over form).

(ii) *General rule.* In determining whether a person has acquired by purchase a 50 percent or greater interest under section 355(d)(4), an option to acquire stock (as described in paragraphs (c)(3)(v) and (vi) of this section) that has not been exercised when a distribution occurs is treated as exercised on the date it was issued or most recently transferred if—

(A) Its exercise (whether by itself or in conjunction with the deemed exercise of one or more other options) would cause a person to become a disqualified person; and

(B) Immediately after the distribution, it is reasonably certain (as described in paragraph (c)(3)(vii) of this section) that the option will be exercised.

(iii) *Options deemed newly issued and substituted options*—(A) *Exchange, adjustment, or alteration of existing option.* For purposes of this paragraph (c)(3), each of the following is treated as a new issuance or transfer of an existing option only if it materially increases the likelihood that an option will be exercised—

(*1*) An exchange of an option for another option or options;

(*2*) An adjustment to the terms of an option (including an adjustment pursuant to the terms of the option);

(*3*) An adjustment to the terms of the underlying stock (including an adjustment pursuant to the terms of the stock);

(*4*) A change to the capital structure of the issuing corporation; and

(*5*) An alteration to the fair market value of issuing corporation stock through an asset transfer (other than regular, ordinary dividends) or through any other means.

(B) *Certain compensatory options.* An option described in paragraph (c)(3)(vi)(B)(*2*) of this section is treated as issued on the date it becomes transferable.

(C) *Substituted options.* If an option (existing option) is exchanged for another option or options (substituted option or options) and paragraph (c)(3)(iii)(A) of this section does not apply to treat such exchange as a new issuance or transfer of the existing option, the substituted option or options will be treated as issued or most recently transferred on the date that the existing option was issued or most recently transferred.

(iv) *Effect of treating an option as exercised*—(A) *In general.* For purposes of section 355(d), an option that is treated as exercised under this paragraph (c)(3) is treated as exercised both for purposes of determining the percentage of the voting power of stock owned by the holder and for purposes of determining the percentage of the value of stock owned by the holder.

(B) *Stock purchase agreement or similar arrangement.* If a stock purchase agreement or similar arrangement is deemed exercised, the purchaser is treated as having purchased the stock under the terms of the agreement or arrangement as though all covenants had been satisfied and all contingencies met. The agreement or arrangement is deemed to have been exercised as of the date it is entered into or most recently assigned.

(v) *Instruments treated as options.* For purposes of this paragraph (c)(3), except to the extent provided in paragraph (c)(3)(vi) of this section, the following are treated as options: A call option, warrant, convertible obligation, the conversion feature of convertible stock, put option, redemption agreement (including a right to cause the redemption of stock), notional principal contract (as defined in § 1.446-3(c)) that provides for the payment of amounts in stock, stock purchase agreement or similar arrangement, or any other instrument that provides for the right to purchase, issue, redeem, or transfer stock (including an option on an option).

(vi) *Instruments generally not treated as options.* For purposes of this paragraph (c)(3), the following are not treated as options, unless issued, transferred, or listed with a principal purpose to avoid the application of section 355(d) or this section:

(A) *Escrow, pledge, or other security agreements.* An option that is part of a security arrangement in a typical lending transaction (including a purchase money loan), if the arrangement is subject to customary commercial conditions. For this purpose, a security arrangement includes, for example, an agreement for holding stock in escrow or under a pledge or other security agreement, or an option to acquire stock contingent upon a default under a loan.

(B) *Compensatory options*—(*1*) *General rule.* An option to acquire stock in a corporation with customary terms and conditions, provided to an employee, director, or independent contractor in connection with the performance of services for the corporation or a person related to it under section 355(d)(7)(A) (and that is not excessive by reference to the services performed) and that—

(*i*) Is nontransferable within the meaning of § 1.83-3(d); and

(*ii*) Does not have a readily ascertainable fair market value as defined in § 1.83-7(b).

(*2*) *Exception.* Paragraph (c)(3)(vi)(B)(*1*) of this section ceases to apply to an option that becomes transferable.

(C) *Certain stock conversion features.* The conversion feature of convertible stock, provided that—

(*1*) The stock is not convertible for at least five years after issuance or transfer; and

(*2*) The terms of the conversion feature do not require the tender of any consideration other than the stock being converted.

(D) *Options exercisable only upon death, disability, mental incompetency, or separation from service.* Any option entered into between stockholders of a corporation (or a stockholder and the corporation) with respect to the stock of either stockholder that is exercisable only upon the death, disability, mental incompetency of the stockholder, or, in the case of stock acquired in connection with the performance of services for the corporation or a person related to it under section 355(d)(7)(A) (and that is not excessive by reference to the services performed), the stockholder's separation from service.

(E) *Rights of first refusal.* A bona fide right of first refusal regarding the corporation's stock with customary terms, entered into between stockholders of a corporation (or between the corporation and a stockholder).

(F) *Other enumerated instruments.* Any other instruments specified in regulations, a revenue ruling, or a revenue procedure. See § 601.601(d)(2) of this chapter.

(vii) *Reasonably certain that the option will be exercised*—(A) *In general.* The determination of whether, immediately after the distribution, an option is reasonably certain to be exercised is based on all the facts and circum-

stances. In applying the previous sentence, the fair market value of stock underlying an option is determined by taking into account control premiums and minority and blockage discounts.

(B) *Stock purchase agreement or similar arrangement.* A stock purchase agreement or similar arrangement is treated as reasonably certain to be exercised if the parties' obligations to complete the transaction are subject only to reasonable closing conditions.

(viii) *Examples.* The following examples illustrate this paragraph (c)(3):

Example 1. D owns all of the stock of C. A purchases 40 percent of D's only class of stock and an option to purchase D stock from D, that if deemed exercised, would result in A owning a total of 60 percent of the stock of D. Assume that no control premium or minority or blockage discount applies to the D stock underlying the option. The option permits A to acquire the D stock at $30 per share, and D's stock has a fair market value of $27 per share on the date the option is issued. The option is subject to no contingencies or restrictive covenants, may be exercised within five years after its issuance, and is not described in paragraph (c)(3)(vi) of this section (regarding instruments generally not treated as options). Within five years of A's purchase of the D stock and option, D distributes the stock of its subsidiary C pro rata and A receives 40 percent of the C stock in the distribution. Immediately after the distribution, D's stock has a fair market value of $30 per share and C's stock has a fair market value of $15 per share. At the time of the distribution, A exchanges A's option for an option to purchase 20 percent of the D stock at $20 per share and an option to purchase 20 percent of the C stock at $10 per share. The exchange of the options in D for options in D and C did not materially increase the likelihood that the options would be exercised. Nonetheless, based on all the facts and circumstances, it is reasonably certain, immediately after the distribution, that A will exercise its options. Under paragraph (c)(3)(iii)(C) of this section, the substituted options are treated as issued on the date the original option was issued. Accordingly, the options are treated as exercised by A on the date that A purchased the original option. A is treated as owning 60 percent of the D stock and 60 percent of the C stock that is disqualified stock, and the distribution is a disqualified distribution under section 355(d)(2) and paragraph (b)(1) of this section.

Example 2. D owns all of the stock of C. A purchases 37 percent of D's only class of stock. B owns 38 percent of the D stock, and the remaining 25 percent is owned by 20 individuals, each of whom owns less than five percent of D's stock. A purchases an option to purchase an additional 14 percent of the D stock from shareholders other than B for $50 per share. The option is subject to no contingencies or restrictive covenants, may be exercised within five years after its issuance, and is not described in paragraph (c)(3)(vi) of this section. Within five years of A's purchase of the option and 37 percent interest in D, D distributes the stock of its subsidiary C pro rata and A receives 37 percent of the C stock in the distribution. At the time of the distribution, A exchanges its option for an option to purchase 14 percent of the D stock at $25 per share and an option to purchase 14 percent of the C stock at $25 per share. Assume that, although a shareholder that owned no D or C stock would pay only $20 per share for D or C stock immediately after the distribution, a shareholder in A's position would pay $30 per share for 14 percent of the stock of D or C because of the control premium which attaches to the shares. The control premium is taken into account under paragraph (c)(3)(vii)(A) of this section to determine whether A is reasonably certain to exercise the options. The exchange of the options in D for options in D and C did not materially increase the likelihood that the options would be exercised. Nonetheless, based on all the facts and circumstances, it is reasonably certain, immediately after the distribution, that A will exercise its options. Under paragraph (c)(3)(iii)(C) of this section, the substituted options are treated as issued on the date the original option was issued. Accordingly, the options are treated as exercised by A on the date that A purchased the original option. Under paragraph (c)(2) of this section, all shares of D and C are considered to have the same value to determine the amount of stock A is treated as purchasing under the options. A is treated as owning 51 percent of the D stock and 51 percent of the C stock that is disqualified stock, and the distribution is a disqualified distribution under section 355(d)(2).

(4) *Plan or arrangement*—(i) *In general.* Under section 355(d)(7)(B), if two or more persons act pursuant to a plan or arrangement with respect to acquisitions of stock in the distributing corporation or controlled corporation, those persons are treated as one person for purposes of section 355(d).

(ii) *Understanding.* For purposes of section 355(d)(7)(B), two or more persons who are (or will after an acquisition become) shareholders (or are treated as shareholders under paragraph (c)(3)(ii) of this section) act pursuant to a plan or arrangement with respect to an acquisition of stock only if they have a formal or informal understanding among themselves to make a coordinated acquisi-

tion of stock. A principal element in determining if such an understanding exists is whether the investment decision of each person is based on the investment decision of one or more other existing or prospective shareholders. However, the participation by creditors in formulating a plan for an insolvency workout or a reorganization in a title 11 or similar case (whether as members of a creditors' committee or otherwise) and the receipt of stock by creditors in satisfaction of indebtedness pursuant to the workout or reorganization do not cause the creditors to be considered as acting pursuant to a plan or arrangement.

(iii) *Examples.* The following examples illustrate paragraph (c)(4)(ii) of this section:

Example 1. D has 1,000 shares of common stock outstanding. A group of 20 unrelated individuals who previously owned no D stock (the Group) agree among themselves to acquire 50 percent or more of D's stock. The Group is not a person under section 7701(a)(1). Subsequently, pursuant to their understanding, the members of the Group purchase 600 shares of D common stock from the existing D shareholders (a total of 60 percent of the D stock), with each member purchasing 30 shares. Under paragraph (c)(4)(ii) of this section, the members of the Group have a formal or informal understanding among themselves to make a coordinated acquisition of stock. Their interests are therefore aggregated under section 355(d)(7)(B), and they are treated as one person that purchased 600 shares of D's stock for purposes of section 355(d).

Example 2. D has 1,000 shares of outstanding stock owned by unrelated individuals. D's management is concerned that D may become subject to a takeover bid. In separate meetings, D's management meets with potential investors who own no stock and are friendly to management to convince them to acquire D's stock based on an understanding that D will assemble a group that in the aggregate will acquire more than 50 percent of D's stock. Subsequently, 15 of these investors each purchases four percent of D's outstanding stock. Under paragraph (c)(4)(ii) of this section, the 15 investors have a formal or informal understanding among themselves to make a coordinated acquisition of stock. Their interests are therefore aggregated under section 355(d)(7)(B), and they are treated as one person that purchased 600 shares of D stock for purposes of section 355(d).

Example 3. (i) D has 1,000 shares of outstanding stock owned by unrelated individuals. An investment advisor advises its clients that it believes D's stock is undervalued and recommends that they acquire D stock. Acting on the investment advisor's recommendation, 20 unrelated in-

Reg. § 1.355-6(c)(4)

dividuals each purchases 30 shares of the outstanding D stock. Each client's decision was not based on the investment decisions made by one or more other clients. Because there is no formal or informal understanding among the clients to make a coordinated acquisition of D stock, their interests are not aggregated under section 355(d)(7)(B) and they are treated as making separate purchases.

(ii) The facts are the same as in paragraph (i) of this *Example 3*, except that the investment advisor is also the underwriter (without regard to whether it is a firm commitment or best efforts underwriting) for a primary or secondary offering of D stock. The result is the same.

(iii) The facts are the same as in paragraph (i) of this *Example 3*, except that, instead of an investment advisor recommending that clients purchase D stock, the trustee of several trusts qualified under section 401(a) sponsored by unrelated corporations causes each trust to purchase the D stock. The result is the same, provided that the trustee's investment decision made on behalf of each trust was not based on the investment decision made on behalf of one or more of the other trusts.

(iv) *Exception*—(A) *Subsequent disposition.* If two or more persons do not act pursuant to a plan or arrangement within the meaning of this paragraph (c)(4) with respect to an acquisition of stock in a corporation (the first corporation), a subsequent acquisition in which such persons exchange their stock in the first corporation for stock in another corporation (the second corporation) in a transaction in which the basis of the second corporation's stock in the hands of such persons is determined in whole or in part by reference to the basis of their stock in the first corporation, will not result in such persons being treated as one person, even if the acquisition of the second corporation's stock is pursuant to a plan or arrangement.

(B) *Example.* The following example illustrates this paragraph (c)(4)(iv):

Example. In an initial public offering of D stock on Date 1, 100 investors independently purchase one percent each of the D stock. Two years later, D merges into P (in a reorganization described in section 368(a)(1)(A)) and, pursuant to the plan of reorganization, the D shareholders exchange their D stock for 50 percent of the stock of P. The D shareholders approve the plan by a two-thirds vote, as required by state law. Under section 358(a), each shareholder's basis in its P stock is determined by reference to the basis of the D stock it purchased. Under paragraph (e)(3) of this section, the former D shareholders are treated as purchasing their P stock on Date 1.

The investors do not become a single person under paragraph (c)(4) of this section with respect to the deemed purchase of the P stock on Date 1 by virtue of their acquisition of the P stock pursuant to the merger on Date 2.

(d) *Purchase*—(1) *In general*—(i) *Definition of purchase under section 355(d)(5)(A).* Under section 355(d)(5)(A), except as otherwise provided in section 355(d)(5)(B) and (C), a *purchase* means any acquisition, but only if—

(A) The basis of the property acquired in the hands of the acquirer is not determined—

(*1*) In whole or in part by reference to the adjusted basis of such property in the hands of the person from whom acquired; or

(*2*) Under section 1014(a); and

(B) The property is not acquired in an exchange to which section 351, 354, 355, or 356 applies.

(ii) *Section 355 distributions.* Paragraph (d)(1)(i)(B) of this section includes all section 355 distributions, whether in exchange (in whole or in part) for stock or pro rata.

(iii) *Example.* The following example illustrates this paragraph (d)(1):

Example. Section 304(a)(1) acquisition. A, who owns all of the stock of P and T, sells the T stock to P for cash. The T stock is not marketable stock under section 355(d)(5)(B)(ii) and paragraph (d)(3)(ii) of this section. A is treated under section 304(a)(1) as receiving a distribution in redemption of the P stock. Under section 302(d). the deemed redemption is treated as a section 301 distribution. Assume that under sections 304(b)(2) and 301 (c)(1), all of the distribution is a dividend. A and P are treated in the same manner as if A had transferred the T stock to P in exchange for stock of P in a transaction to which section 351(a) applies, and P had then redeemed the stock P was treated as issuing in the transaction. Under section 362(a), P's basis in the T stock is determined by reference to A's adjusted basis in the T stock, and there is no basis increase in the T stock because A recognizes no gain on the deemed transfer. Accordingly, P's acquisition of the T stock from A is not a purchase by P under section 355(d)(5)(A)(i)(I) and paragraphs (d)(1)(i)(A)(*1*) and (d)(2)(i)(B) of this section.

(2) *Exceptions to definition of purchase under section 355(d)(5)(A).* The following acquisitions are not treated as purchases under section 355(d)(5)(A):

(i) *Acquisition of stock in a transaction which includes other property or money*—(A) *Transferors and shareholders of transferor or distributing corporations*—(*1*) *In general.* An acquisition of stock permitted to be received by a transferor of property without the recognition of gain under section 351(a), or permitted to be received without the recognition of gain under section 354, 355, or 356 is not a purchase to the extent section 358(a)(1) applies to determine the recipient's basis in the stock received, whether or not the recipient recognizes gain under section 351(b) or 356. But see paragraph (e)(3) of this section (interest received in exchange for purchased interest in exchanged basis transaction treated as purchased).

(2) *Exception.* To the extent there is received in the exchange or distribution, in addition to stock described in paragraph (d)(2)(i)(A)(*1*) of this section, stock that is other property under section 351(b) or 356(a)(1), the stock is treated as purchased on the date of the exchange or distribution for purposes of section 355(d).

(B) *Transferee corporations—*(*1*) *In general.* An acquisition of stock by a corporation is not a purchase to the extent section 334(b) or 362(a) or (b) applies to determine the corporation's basis in the stock received. But see section 355(d)(5)(C) and paragraph (e)(2) of this section (purchased property transferred in transferred basis transaction is treated as purchased by transferee).

(*2*) *Exception.* If a corporation acquires stock, the stock is treated as purchased on the date of the stock acquisition for purposes of section 355(d)—

(*i*) If the liquidating corporation recognizes gain or loss with respect to the transferred stock as described in section 334(b)(1); or

(*ii*) To the extent the basis of the transferred stock is increased through the recognition of gain by the transferor under section 362(a) or (b).

(C) *Examples.* The following examples illustrate this paragraph (d)(2)(i):

Example 1. (i) A owns all the stock of T. T merges into D in a transaction qualifying under section 368(a)(1)(A), with A exchanging all of the T stock for D stock and $100 cash. Under section 356(a)(1), A recognizes $100 of the realized gain on the transaction. Under section 358(a)(1), A's basis in the D stock equals A's basis in the T stock, decreased by the $100 received and increased by the gain recognized, also $100. Under paragraph (d)(2)(i)(A) of this section, A is not treated as having purchased the D stock for purposes of section 355(d)(5).

(ii) The facts are the same as in paragraph (i) of this *Example 1*, except that rather than D stock and $100 cash, A receives D stock and stock in C, a corporation not a party to the

reorganization, with a fair market value of $100. Under section 358(a)(2), A's basis in the C stock is its fair market value, or $100. Under paragraph (d)(2)(i)(A)(*2*) of this section, A is treated as having purchased the C stock, but not the D stock, for purposes of section 355(d)(5).

Example 2. A purchases all of the stock of D, which is not marketable stock, on Date 1 for $90. Within five years of A's purchase, on Date 2, A contributes the D stock to P in exchange for P stock worth $90 and $10 cash in a transaction qualifying under section 351. A recognizes a gain of $10 as a result of the transfer. Under section 362(a), P's basis in D is $100. P is treated as having purchased 90 percent ($90 worth) of the D stock on Date 1 under section 355(d)(5)(C) and paragraph (e)(2) of this section and as having purchased 10 percent ($10 worth) of the D stock on Date 2 under paragraph (d)(2)(i)(B)(*2*)(*ii*) of this section.

(ii) *Acquisition of stock in a distribution to which section 305(a) applies.* An acquisition of stock in a distribution qualifying under section 305(a) is not a purchase to the extent section 307(a) applies to determine the recipient's basis. However, to the extent the distribution is of rights to acquire stock, see paragraph (c)(3) of this section for rules regarding options, warrants, convertible obligations, and other similar interests.

(iii) *Section 1036(a) exchange.* An exchange of stock qualifying under section 1036(a) is not a purchase by either party to the exchange to the extent the basis of the property acquired equals that of the property exchanged under section 1031(d).

(iv) *Section 338 elections—*(A) *In general.* Stock acquired in a qualified stock purchase with respect to which a section 338 election (or a section 338(h)(10) election) is made is not treated as a purchase for purposes of section 355(d)(5)(A). However, any stock (or an interest in another entity) held by old target that is treated as purchased by new target is treated as acquired by purchase for purposes of section 355(d)(5)(A) unless a section 338 election or section 338(h)(10) election also is made for that stock. See § 1.338-2T(c) for the definitions of section 338 election, section 338(h)(10) election, old target, and new target.

(B) *Example.* The following example illustrates this paragraph (d)(2)(iv):

Example. T owns all of the stock of S and no other assets. X acquires all of the T stock from the T shareholders for cash and makes an election under section 338. Under section 338(a) and (b), T, as Old T, is treated as having sold all of its assets at fair market value and purchased the assets as a new corporation, New T, as of the

Reg. § 1.355-6(d)(2)

beginning of the day after the acquisition date. Under paragraph (d)(2)(iv)(A) of this section, X is not treated as having purchased the T stock. Absent a section 338 election or a section 338(h)(10) election with respect to S, New T is treated as having purchased all of the S stock under section 355(d)(5)(A).

(v) *Partnership distributions*—(A) *Section 732(b).* An acquisition of stock (or an interest in another entity) in a liquidation of a partner's interest in a partnership in which basis is determined pursuant to section 732(b) is a purchase at the time of the liquidation.

(B) *Section 734(b).* If the adjusted basis of stock (or an interest in another entity) held by a partnership is increased under section 734(b), a proportionate amount of the stock (or other interest) will be treated as purchased at the time of the basis adjustment, determined by reference to the amount of the basis adjustment (but not in excess of the fair market value of the stock (or other interest) at the time of the adjustment) over the fair market value of the stock (or other interest) at the time of the adjustment.

(3) *Certain section 351 exchanges treated as purchases*—(i) *In general*—(A) *Treatment of stock received by transferor.* Under section 355(d)(5)(B), a purchase includes any acquisition of property in an exchange to which section 351 applies to the extent the property is acquired in exchange for any cash or cash item, any marketable stock, or any debt of the transferor. The property treated as acquired by purchase is the property received by the transferor in the exchange.

(B) *Multiple classes of stock.* If the transferor in a transaction described in section 355(d)(5)(B) receives stock or securities of more than one class, or receives both stock and securities, then the amount of stock or securities purchased is determined in a manner that corresponds to the allocation of basis to the stock or securities under section 358. See § 1.358-2(b).

(ii) *Cash item, marketable stock.* For purposes of section 355(d)(5)(B) and this paragraph (d)(3), either or both of the terms cash item and marketable stock include personal property within the meaning of section 1092(d)(1) and § 1.1092(d)-1, without giving effect to section 1092(d)(3).

(iii) *Exception for certain acquisitions*—(A) *In general.* Except to the extent provided in paragraph (e)(3) of this section (interest received in exchange for purchased interest in exchanged basis transaction treated as purchased), an acquisition of stock in a corporation in a section 351 transaction by one or more persons in exchange for an amount of stock in another corporation (the

transferred corporation) that meets the requirements of section 1504(a)(2) is not a purchase by the transferor or transferors, regardless of whether the stock of the transferred corporation is marketable stock under section 355(d)(5)(B)(ii) and paragraph (d)(3)(ii) of this section.

(B) *Example.* The following example illustrates this paragraph (d)(3)(iii):

Example. D's two classes of stock, voting common and nonvoting preferred, are both widely held and publicly traded. The nonvoting preferred stock is stock described in section 1504(a)(4). Assume that all of the D stock is marketable stock under section 355(d)(5)(B)(ii) and paragraph (d)(3)(ii) of this section. D's board of directors proposes that, for valid business purposes, D's common stock should be held by a holding company, HC, but its preferred stock should not be transferred to HC. As proposed, the D common shareholders exchange their D stock solely for HC common stock in a section 351(a) transaction. The D preferred shareholders retain their stock. HC acquires an amount of D stock that meets the requirements of section 1504(a)(2). Although the D common stock was marketable stock in the hands of the D shareholders immediately before the transfer, and the D nonvoting preferred stock is marketable stock after the transfer, the D shareholders are not treated as having acquired the HC stock by purchase (except to the extent the exchanged basis rule of paragraph (e)(3) of this section may apply to treat HC stock as purchased on the date the exchanged D stock was purchased).

(iv) *Exception for assets transferred as part of an active trade or business*—(A) *In general.* Except to the extent provided in paragraph (e)(3) of this section, an acquisition not described in paragraph (d)(3)(iii) of this section of stock in exchange for any cash or cash item, any marketable stock, or any debt of the transferor in a section 351 transaction is not a purchase if—

(*1*) The transferor is engaged in the active conduct of a trade or business under paragraph (d)(3)(iv)(B) of this section and the transferred items (including debt incurred in the ordinary course of the trade or business) are used in the trade or business;

(*2*) The transferred items do not exceed the reasonable needs of the trade or business under paragraph (d)(3)(iv)(C) of this section;

(*3*) The transferor transfers the items as part of the trade or business; and

(*4*) The transferee continues the active conduct of the trade or business.

(B) *Active conduct of a trade or business.* For purposes of this paragraph (d)(3)(iv),

Reg. § 1.355-6(d)(3)

whether, with respect to the trade or business at issue, the transferor and transferee are engaged in the active conduct of a trade or business is determined under § 1.355-3(b)(2) and (3), except that—

(1) Conduct is tested before the transfer (with respect to the transferor) and after the transfer (with respect to the transferee) rather than immediately after a distribution; and

(2) The trade or business need not have been conducted for five years before its transfer, but it must have been conducted for a sufficient period of time to establish that it is a viable and ongoing trade or business.

(C) *Reasonable needs of the trade or business.* For purposes of this paragraph (d)(3)(iv), the reasonable needs of the trade or business include only the amount of cash or cash items, marketable stock, or debt of the transferor that a prudent business person apprised of all relevant facts would consider necessary for the present and reasonably anticipated future needs of the business. Transferred items may be considered necessary for reasonably anticipated future needs only if the transferor and transferee have specific, definite, and feasible plans for their use. Those plans must require that items intended for anticipated future needs rather than present needs be used as expeditiously as possible consistent with the business purpose for retention of the items. Future needs are not reasonably anticipated if they are uncertain or vague or where the execution of the plan for their use is substantially postponed. The reasonable needs of a trade or business are generally its needs at the time of the transfer of the business including the items. However, for purposes of applying section 355(d) to a distribution, events and conditions after the transfer and through the date immediately after the distribution (including whether plans for the use of transferred items have been consummated or substantially postponed) may be considered to determine whether at the time of the transfer the items were necessary for the present and reasonably anticipated future needs of the business.

(D) *Consideration of all facts and circumstances.* All facts and circumstances are considered in determining whether this paragraph (d)(3)(iv) applies.

(E) *Successive transfers.* A transfer of assets does not fail to meet the requirements of paragraph (d)(3)(iv)(A)(4) of this section solely because the transferee transfers the assets directly (or indirectly through other members) to another member of the transferee's affiliated group, as defined in § 1.355-3(b)(4)(iv) (the final transferee), if the requirements of paragraphs (d)(3)(iv)(A)(1), (2), (3) and (4) of this section

would be met if the transferor had transferred the assets directly to the final transferee.

(v) *Exception for transfer between members of the same affiliated group*—(A) *In general.* Except to the extent provided in paragraph (e)(3) of this section, an acquisition of stock (whether actual or constructive) not described in paragraphs (d)(3)(iii) and (iv) of this section in exchange for any cash or cash item, marketable stock, or debt of the transferor in a section 351 transaction is not a purchase if—

(1) The transferor corporation or corporations and the transferee corporation (whether formed in the transaction or already existing) are members of the same affiliated group as defined in section 1504(a) before the section 351 transaction (if the transferee corporation is in existence before the transaction);

(2) The cash or cash item, marketable stock or debt of the transferor are not included in assets that are acquired (or treated as acquired) by the transferor (or another member of the transferor's affiliated group) from a nonmember in a related transaction in which section 362(a) or (b) applies to determine the basis in the acquired assets; and

(3) The transferor corporation or corporations, the transferee corporation, and any distributed controlled corporation of the transferee corporation do not cease to be members of such affiliated group in any transaction pursuant to a plan that includes the section 351 transaction (including any distribution of a controlled corporation by the transferee corporation). But see paragraph (b)(4) of this section where the transfer is made for a principal purpose to avoid the purposes of section 355(d).

(B) *Examples.* The following examples illustrate this paragraph (d)(3)(v):

Example 1. Publicly traded P has wholly owned S since 1990. S is engaged in the telecommunications business and the business of computer software development. S is developing new software for use in the managed health care industry. Over a period of four years beginning on January 31, 2000, P contributes a substantial amount of cash to S solely for the purpose of funding the software development. On completion of the software in January of 2004, 60 percent of the value of the S stock is attributable to the cash contributions made within the last four years. The P group's primary lender requires that S separately incorporate the software and related assets and distribute the new subsidiary to P as a condition of providing required funding to market the Software. Accordingly, on February 1, 2004, S forms N, contributes the software and related assets to N, and distributes all of the N stock to P

Reg. § 1.355-6(d)(3)

in a transaction intended to qualify under section 355(a). P, S, and N will not leave the affiliated group in any transaction related to the cash contributions. Under paragraph (d)(3)(v)(A) of this section, P's cash contributions to S are not treated as purchases of additional S stock, and the distribution of N from S to P is not a disqualified distribution under section 355(d)(2) and paragraph (b)(1) of this section.

Example 2. On Date 1, P contributes cash to its subsidiary S with a principal purpose to increase its stock basis in S. Sixty percent of the value of P's S stock is attributable to the cash contribution. Under paragraph (b)(4) of this section (anti-avoidance rule), 60 percent of the S stock is treated as purchased under section 355(d)(5)(B), notwithstanding paragraph (d)(3)(v)(A) of this section. Accordingly, any distribution of a subsidiary of S to P within the five-year period after Date 1 will be a disqualified distribution, regardless of whether P, S, and any distributed S subsidiary remain affiliated after the distribution and any transactions related to the cash contribution.

(4) *Triangular asset reorganizations*—(i) *Definition.* A *triangular asset reorganization* is a reorganization that qualifies under—

(A) Section 368(a)(1)(A) or (G) by reason of section 368(a)(2)(D);

(B) Section 368(a)(1)(A) by reason of section 368(a)(2)(E) (regardless of whether section 368(a)(3)(E) applies), unless the transaction also qualifies as either a section 351 transfer or a reorganization under section 368(a)(1)(B); or

(C) Section 368(a)(1)(C), and stock of the controlling corporation rather than the acquiring corporation is exchanged for the acquired corporation's properties.

(ii) *Treatment.* Notwithstanding section 355(d)(5)(A), for purposes of section 355(d), the controlling corporation in a triangular asset reorganization is treated as having—

(A) Acquired the assets of the acquired corporation (and as having assumed any liabilities assumed by the controlling corporation's subsidiary corporation or to which the acquired corporation's assets were subject (the acquired liabilities)) in a transaction in which the controlling corporation's basis in the acquired corporation's assets was determined under section 362(b); and

(B) Transferred the acquired assets and acquired liabilities to its subsidiary corporation in a section 351 transfer.

(iii) *Example.* The following example illustrates this paragraph (d)(4):

Example. Forward triangular reorganization. P forms S with $25 of cash and T merges into S in a reorganization qualifying under section 368(a)(1)(A) by reason of section 368(a)(2)(D) in which the T shareholders receive $70 of P stock and $15 of cash in exchange for their T stock. T is not a common parent of a consolidated group of corporations. The remaining $10 of cash with which P formed S will not be used in the acquired business. T's assets consist only of assets part of and used in its business with a value of $80, and $5 of cash that is not part of or used in T's business. T has no liabilities. S will use T's business assets in T's business (which will become S's business), but will invest the $5 of cash in an unrelated passive investment. Under paragraph (d)(4)(ii) of this section, P is treated as acquiring the T assets in a transaction in which P's basis in the T assets was determined under section 362(b) and contributing them to S in a section 351 transfer. Under paragraph (d)(3)(v) of this section, $10 (of the total $25) of cash contributed by P to S upon S's formation is not treated as a purchase of S stock. The $15 (of the total $25) of cash contributed by P to S upon S's formation that is paid to T's shareholders is not treated as a purchase of S stock. The exception in paragraph (d)(3)(v) of this section does not apply to the $5 of cash from T's business because P is treated as having acquired T's assets in a related transaction in which section 362(b) applies to determine P's basis in such assets. Accordingly, P is treated under section 355(d)(5)(B) and paragraph (d)(3)(iv) of this section as having purchased $5 of the S stock, but is not deemed to have purchased the remaining $80 of the S stock.

(5) *Reverse triangular reorganizations other than triangular asset reorganizations*—(i) *In general.* Except as provided in paragraph (d)(5)(ii) of this section, if a transaction qualifies as a reorganization under section 368(a)(1)(A) by reason of section 368(a)(2)(E) and also as either a reorganization under section 368(a)(1)(B) or a section 351 transfer, then either section 355(d)(5)(B) (and paragraphs (d)(3)(i) through (iv) of this section) or 355(d)(5)(C) (and paragraph (e)(2) of this section) applies. Regardless of which method the controlling corporation employs to determine its basis in the surviving corporation stock under § 1.358-6(c)(2)(ii) or § 1.1502-30(b), the total amount of surviving corporation stock treated as purchased by the controlling corporation will equal the higher of—

(A) The amount of surviving corporation stock that would be treated as purchased (on the date of the deemed section 351 transfer) by the controlling corporation if the controlling corporation acquired the surviving corporation's assets and assumed its liabilities in a transaction in

Reg. § 1.355-6(d)(4)

which the controlling corporation's basis in the surviving corporation assets was determined under section 362(b), and then transferred the acquired assets and liabilities to the surviving corporation in a section 351 transfer (see §§ 1.358-6(c)(1) and (2)(ii)(A), and 1.1502-30(b)); or

(B) The amount of surviving corporation stock that would be treated as purchased (on the date the surviving corporation shareholders purchased their surviving corporation stock) if the controlling corporation acquired the stock of the surviving corporation in a transaction in which the basis in the surviving corporation's stock was determined under section 362(b) (see §§ 1.358-6(c)(2)(ii)(B) and 1.1502-30(b)).

(ii) *Letter ruling and closing agreement.* If a controlling corporation obtains a letter ruling and enters into a closing agreement under section 7121 in which it agrees to determine its basis in surviving corporation stock under § 1.358-6(c)(2)(ii)(A), or under § 1.1502-30(b) by applying § 1.358-6(c)(2)(ii)(A) (deemed asset acquisition and transfer by controlling corporation), then section 355(d)(5)(B) and paragraphs (d)(3)(i) through (iv) of this section apply, and section 355(d)(5)(C) and paragraph (e)(2) of this section do not apply. If a controlling corporation obtains a letter ruling and enters into a closing agreement under section 7121 under which it agrees to determine its basis in surviving corporation stock under § 1.358-6(c)(2)(ii)(B), or under § 1.1502-30(b) by applying § 1.358-6(c)(2)(ii)(B) (deemed stock acquisition), then section 355(d)(5)(C) and paragraph (e)(2) of this section apply, and section 355(d)(5)(B) and paragraphs (d)(3)(i) through (iv) of this section do not apply.

(iii) *Example.* The following example illustrates this paragraph (d)(5):

Example. Reverse triangular reorganization; purchase. (i) A purchases 60 percent of the stock of D on Date 1. D owns no cash items, marketable stock, or transferor debt, but holds cash that is not part of or used in D's trade or business under paragraph (d)(3)(iv) of this section and that represents 20 percent of D's value. On Date 2, P forms S, and S merges into D in a reorganization qualifying under section 368(a)(1)(B) and under section 368(a)(1)(A) by reason of section 368(a)(2)(E). In the reorganization, P acquires all of the D stock in exchange solely for P stock. After Date 2, and within five years after Date 1, D distributes its wholly owned subsidiary C to P. P does not obtain a letter ruling and enter into a closing agreement under paragraph (d)(5)(ii) of this section. P would acquire 20 percent of the D stock by purchase on Date 2 under paragraph (d)(5)(i)(A) of this section by

operation of section 355(d)(5)(B) and paragraph (d)(3)(iv) of this section. The exception in paragraph (d)(3)(v) of this section does not apply because D was not affiliated with P before the transaction in which the section 351 transfer is deemed to occur and D's assets are treated as acquired by P in a related transaction in which section 362(b) applies to determine P's basis in the D assets. P would acquire 60 percent of the D stock by purchase on Date 1 under paragraph (d)(5)(i)(B) of this section because, under the transferred basis rule of section 355(d)(5)(C) and paragraph (e)(2) of this section, P is treated as though P purchased the D stock on the date A purchased it. Accordingly, under paragraph (d)(5)(i) of this section, P is treated as acquiring the higher amount (60 percent) by purchase on Date 1. D's distribution of C to P is a disqualified distribution under section 355(d)(2) and paragraph (b)(1) of this section. In addition. A is treated as acquiring the P stock by purchase on Date 1 under paragraph (e)(3) of this section because A's basis in the P stock is determined by reference to A's basis in the D stock.

(ii) The facts are the same as in paragraph (i) of this *Example*, except that P obtains a letter ruling and enters into a closing agreement under which it agrees to determine its basis in the D stock under § 1.358-6(c)(2)(ii)(A). Under paragraph (d)(5)(ii) of this section, section 355(d)(5)(B) (and paragraphs (d)(3)(i) through (iv) of this section) applies, and section 355(d)(5)(C) (and paragraph (e)(2) of this section) does not apply. Accordingly, P is treated as acquiring only 20 percent of the D stock by purchase on Date 2. D's distribution of C to P is not a disqualified distribution under section 355(d)(2) and paragraph (b)(1) of this section.

(6) *Treatment of group structure changes—* (i) *In general.* Notwithstanding section 355(d)(5)(A), for purposes of section 355(d), if a corporation succeeds another corporation as the common parent of a consolidated group in a group structure change to which § 1.1502-31 applies, the new common parent is treated as having acquired the assets and assumed the liabilities of the former common parent in a transaction in which the new common parent's basis in the former common parent's assets was determined under section 362(b), and then transferred the acquired assets and liabilities to the former common parent (or, if the former common parent does not survive, to the new common parent's subsidiary) in a section 351 transfer, with the new common parent and former common parent being treated as not in the same affiliated group at the time of the transfer for purposes of applying paragraph (d)(3)(v) of this section (notwithstanding § 1.1502-31(c)(2)).

Reg. § 1.355-6(d)(6)

(ii) *Adjustments to basis of higher-tier members.* A higher-tier member that indirectly owns all or part of the former common parent's stock after a group structure change is treated as having purchased the stock of an immediate subsidiary to the extent that the higher-tier member's basis in the subsidiary is increased under § 1.1502-31(d)(4).

(iii) *Example.* The following example illustrates this paragraph (d)(6):

Example. P is the common parent of a consolidated group, and T is the common parent of another group. P has owned S for more than five years, and the fair market value of the S stock is $50. T's assets consist only of non-marketable stock of direct and indirect wholly owned subsidiaries with a value of $50, assets used in its business with a value of $50, and $50 of marketable stock that is not part of or used in T's business. T has no liabilities. T merges into S with the T shareholders receiving solely P stock with a value of $150 in exchange for their T stock in a section 368(a)(2)(D) reorganization. S will use T's business assets in T's business (which will become S's business), but will hold the $50 of marketable stock for investment purposes. Assume that the transaction is a reverse acquisition under § 1.1502-75(d)(3) because the T shareholders, as a result of owning T stock, own more than 50 percent of the value of P's stock immediately after the transaction. Thus, the transaction is a group structure change under § 1.1502-33(f)(1). Under paragraph (d)(6) of this section, P is treated as having acquired the assets of T in a transaction in which P's basis in the T assets was determined under section 362(b), and then transferred the acquired assets to S in a section 351 transfer, with P and T being treated as not in the same affiliated group at the time of the transfer solely for purposes of paragraph (d)(3)(v) of this section. The exception in paragraph (d)(3)(v) of this section (transfers within an affiliated group) does not apply. Accordingly, P is treated under section 355(d)(5)(B) and paragraph (d)(3)(iv) of this section as having purchased $50 of the S stock (attributable to the marketable stock), but is not deemed to have purchased the remaining $150 of the S stock.

(7) *Special rules for triangular asset reorganizations, other reverse triangular reorganizations, and group structure changes.* The amount of acquiring subsidiary, surviving corporation, or former common parent stock that is treated as purchased under paragraph (c)(4), (5)(i)(A), or (6) of this section (by operation of section 355(d)(5)(B) and paragraphs (d)(3)(i) through (iv) of this section) is adjusted to reflect any basis adjustment under—

(i) Section 1.358-6(c)(2)(i)(B) and (C) (reduction of basis adjustment in reverse triangular reorganization where controlling corporation acquires less than all of the surviving corporation stock), § 1.1502-30(b) (applying § 1.358-6(c)(2)(i)(B) and (C) to a consolidated group), and § 1.1502-31(d)(2)(ii) (reduction of basis adjustment in group structure change where new common parent acquires less than all of the former common parent stock); or

(ii) Section 1.358-6(d) (reduction of basis adjustment in any triangular reorganization to the extent controlling corporation does not provide consideration), § 1.1502-30(b) (applying § 1.358-6(d) (except § 1.358-6(d)(2)) to a consolidated group), and § 1.1502-31(d)(1) (reduction of basis adjustment in group structure change to the extent new common parent does not provide consideration).

(e) *Deemed purchase and timing rules*—(1) *Attribution and aggregation*—(i) *In general.* Under section 355(d)(8)(B), if any person acquires by purchase an interest in any entity, and the person is treated under section 355(d)(8)(A) as holding any stock by reason of holding the interest, the stock shall be treated as acquired by purchase on the later of the date of the purchase of the interest in the entity or the date the stock is acquired by purchase by such entity.

(ii) *Purchase of additional interest.* If a person and an entity are treated as a single person under section 355(d)(7), and the person later purchases an additional interest in the entity, the person is treated as purchasing on the date of the later purchase the amount of stock attributed from the entity to the person under section 355(d)(8)(A) as a result of the additional interest.

(iii) *Purchase between persons treated as one person.* If two persons are treated as one person under section 355(d)(7), and one later purchases stock from the other, the date of the later purchase is used for purposes of determining when the five-year period commences.

(iv) *Purchase by a person already treated as holding stock under section 355(d)(8)(A).* If a person who is already treated as holding stock under section 355(d)(8)(A) later directly purchases such stock, the date of the later direct purchase is used for purposes of determining when the five-year period commences.

(v) *Examples.* The following examples illustrate this paragraph (e)(1):

Example 1. On Date 1, A purchases 10 percent of the stock of P, which has held 100 percent of the stock of T for more than five years at the time of A's purchase. A is deemed to have purchased 10 percent of P's T stock on Date 1. If A later purchases an additional 41 percent of the

Reg. § 1.355-6(d)(7)

stock of P on Date 2, A is deemed to have purchased an additional 41 percent of P's T stock on Date 2. Because A and P are now related persons under section 267(b), they are treated as one person under section 355(d)(7)(A), and A is treated as owning all of P's T stock. A is treated as acquiring 51 percent of the T stock by purchase at the times of A's respective purchases of P stock on Date 1 and Date 2. The remaining 49 percent of T stock is treated as acquired when P acquired the T stock, more than five years before Date 1. If P distributes T after Date 2 and within five years after Date 1, the distribution will be a disqualified distribution under section 355(d)(2) and paragraph (b)(1) of this section.

Example 2. A has owned 60 percent of the stock of P for more than five years, and P has owned 40 percent of the stock of T for more than five years. A and P are treated as one person, and A is treated as owning 40 percent of the stock of T for more than five years. If P later purchases an additional 20 percent of the stock of T on Date 1, A is treated as acquiring by purchase the additional 20 percent of T stock on Date 1. If A then purchases an additional 10 percent of the stock of P on Date 2, under paragraph (e)(1)(i) of this section, A is deemed to have purchased on Date 2 an additional four percent of the T stock (10 percent of the 40 percent that P originally owned). In addition, even though A and P were already treated as one person under section 355(d)(7)(A), A also is deemed to have purchased two percent of the T stock on Date 2 (10 percent of the 20 percent of the T stock that it was treated as purchasing on Date 1). A is still treated as owning all 60 percent of the T stock owned by P. However, of the 60 percent, A is treated as having purchased 18 percent of the T stock on Date 1 and 6 percent of the T stock on Date 2, for a total of 24 percent purchased stock.

Example 3. A purchases a 20 percent interest in partnership M on Date 1. M has owned 30 percent of the stock and 25 percent of the securities of P for more than five years. P has owned 40 percent of the stock and 100 percent of the securities of T for more than five years. Under section 318(a)(2)(C) as modified by section 355(d)(8)(A), M is deemed to own 12 percent of the stock (30 percent of the 40 percent P owns) and 30 percent of the securities (30 percent of the 100 percent P owns) of T. Under sections 318(a)(2)(A) and 355(d)(8)(B), A is deemed to have purchased 2.4 percent of the stock (20 percent of the 12 percent M is deemed to own) and 6 percent of the securities (20 percent of the 30 percent M is deemed to own) of T on Date 1. Similarly, A is deemed to have purchased 6 percent of the stock (20 percent of the 30 percent M owns) and five percent of the securities (20 per-

cent of the 25 percent M owns) of P on Date 1. If M later purchases an additional 10 percent of P stock on Date 2, M is deemed to have purchased four percent of the stock (10 percent of the 40 percent P owns) and 10 percent of the securities (10 percent of the 100 percent. P owns) of T on Date 2. A is deemed to have purchased two percent of the stock of P on Date 2 (20 percent of the 10 percent M purchased). A is also deemed to have purchased 0.8 percent of the stock (20 percent of the four percent M is deemed to have purchased) and two percent of the securities (20 percent of the 10 percent M is deemed to have purchased) of T on Date 2.

Example 4. A and B are brother and sister. For more than five years, A has owned 75 percent of the stock of P, and B has owned 25 percent of the stock of P. A and B are treated as one person under section 267(b), and the stock of each is treated as purchased on the date it was purchased by A and B, respectively. If B later purchases 50 percent of the P stock from A on Date 1, A and B are still treated as one person. However, under paragraph (e)(3)(iii) of this section, the 50 percent of P stock that B purchased from A is treated as purchased on Date 1.

(2) *Transferred basis rule.* If any person acquires property from another person who acquired the property by purchase (determined with regard to section 355(d)(5) and paragraphs (d) and (e)(2), (3) and (4) of this section, but without regard to section 355(d)(8) and paragraph (e)(1) of this section), and the adjusted basis of the property in the hands of the acquirer is determined in whole or in part by reference to the adjusted basis of the property in the hands of the other person, the acquirer is treated as having acquired the property by purchase on the date it was so acquired by the other person. The rule in this paragraph (e)(2) applies, for example, where stock of a corporation acquired by purchase is subsequently acquired in a section 351 transfer or a reorganization qualifying under section 368(a)(1)(B), but does not apply if the stock of a former common parent is acquired in a group structure change to which § 1.1502-31 applies. But see paragraph (d)(2)(i)(B)(2) of this section for situations where the stock is treated as purchased on the date of a transfer.

(3) *Exchanged basis rule—(i) In general.* If any person acquires an interest in an entity (the first interest) by purchase (determined with regard to section 355(d)(5) and paragraphs (d) and (e)(2), (3) and (4) of this section, but without regard to section 355(d)(8) and paragraph (e)(1) of this section), and the first interest is exchanged for an interest in the same or another entity (the second interest) where the adjusted basis of the second interest is determined in whole or in part

by reference to the adjusted basis of the first interest, then the second interest is treated as having been purchased on the date the first interest was purchased. The rule in this paragraph (e)(3) applies only to exchanges that are not otherwise treated as purchases under section 355(d)(5) and paragraph (d) of this section. The rule in this paragraph (e)(3) applies, for example, where stock of a corporation acquired by purchase is subsequently exchanged for other stock in a section 351, 354, or 1036(a) exchange. But see paragraph (d)(2)(i)(A)(2) of this section for situations where the stock is treated as purchased on the date of an exchange or distribution.

(ii) *Example.* The following example illustrates this paragraph (e)(3):

Example. A purchases 50 percent of the stock of T on Date 1. On Date 2, T merges into D in a section 368(a)(1)(A) reorganization, with A exchanging all of the T stock solely for stock of D. Under section 358(a), A's basis in the D stock is determined by reference to the basis of the T stock it purchased. Accordingly, A is treated as having purchased the D stock on Date 1, and has a purchased basis in the D stock under paragraph (b)(3)(iii) of this section.

(4) *Certain section 355 or section 305 distributions—*(i) *Section 355.* If a distributing corporation distributes any stock of a controlled corporation with respect to recently purchased distributing stock in a distribution that qualifies under section 355 (or so much of section 356 as relates to section 355), such controlled corporation stock is deemed to be acquired by purchase by the distributee on the date the distributee acquired the recently purchased distributing stock. Recently purchased distributing stock is stock in the distributing corporation acquired by purchase (determined with regard to section 355(d)(5) and paragraphs (d) and (e)(2), (3), and (4) of this section, but without regard to section 355(d)(8) and paragraph (e)(1) of this section) by the distributee during the five-year period with respect to that distribution.

(ii) *Section 305.* If a corporation distributes its stock in a distribution that qualifies under section 305(a), the stock received in the distribution (to the extent section 307(a) applies to determine the recipient's basis) is deemed to be acquired by purchase by the recipient on the date (if any) that the recipient acquired by purchase (determined with regard to section 355(d)(5) and paragraphs (d) and (e)(2), (3), and (4) of this section), the stock with respect to which the distribution is made.

(5) *Substantial diminution of risk—*(i) *In general.* If section 355(d)(6) applies to any stock for any period, the running of any five-year period

set forth in section 355(d)(3) is suspended during such period.

(ii) *Property to which suspension applies.* Section 355(d)(6) applies to any stock for any period during which the holder's risk of loss with respect to such stock, or with respect to any portion of the activities of the corporation, is (directly or indirectly) substantially diminished by an option, a short sale, any special class of stock, or any other device or transaction.

(iii) *Risk of loss substantially diminished.* Whether a holder's risk of loss is substantially diminished under section 355(d)(6) and paragraph (e)(5)(ii) of this section will be determined based on all facts and circumstances relating to the stock, the corporate activities, and arrangements for holding the stock.

(iv) *Special class of stock.* For purposes of section 355(d)(6) and paragraph (e)(5)(ii) of this section, the term special class of stock includes a class of stock that grants particular rights to, or bears particular risks for, the holder or the issuer with respect to the earnings, assets, or attributes of less than all the assets or activities of a corporation or any of its subsidiaries. The term includes, for example, tracking stock and stock (or any related instruments or arrangements) the terms of which provide for the distribution (whether or not at the option of any party or in the event of any contingency) of any controlled corporation or other specified assets to the holder or to one or more persons other than the holder.

(f) *Duty to determine stockholders—*(1) *In general.* In determining whether section 355(d) applies to a distribution of controlled corporation stock, a distributing corporation must determine whether a disqualified person holds its stock or the stock of any distributed controlled corporation. This paragraph (f) provides rules regarding this determination and the extent to which a distributing corporation must investigate whether a disqualified person holds stock.

(2) *Deemed knowledge of contents of securities filings.* A distributing corporation is deemed to have knowledge of the existence and contents of all schedules, forms, and other documents filed with or under the rules of the Securities and Exchange Commission, including without limitation any Schedule 13D or 13G (or any similar schedules) and amendments, with respect to any relevant corporation.

(3) *Presumption as to securities filings.* Absent actual knowledge to the contrary, in determining whether section 355(d) applies to a distribution, a distributing corporation may presume, with respect to stock that is reporting stock (while such stock is reporting stock), that every shareholder or other person required to file a

schedule, form, or other document with or under the rules of the Securities and Exchange Commission as of a given date has filed the schedule, form, or other document as of that date and that the contents of filed schedules, forms, or other documents are accurate and complete. Reporting stock is stock that is described in Rule 13d-1(i) of Regulation 13D (17 CFR 240.13d-1(i)) (or any rule or regulation to generally the same effect) promulgated by the Securities and Exchange Commission under the Securities Exchange Act of 1934 (15 U.S.C. 78a et seq.).

(4) *Presumption as to less-than-five-percent shareholders.* Absent actual knowledge (or deemed knowledge under paragraph (f)(2) of this section) immediately after the distribution to the contrary with regard to a particular shareholder, a distributing corporation may presume that no less-than-five-percent shareholder of a corporation acquired stock or securities by purchase under section 355(d)(5) or (8) and paragraphs (d) and (e) of this section during the five-year period. For purposes of this paragraph (f), a less-than-five-percent shareholder is a person that, at no time during the five-year period, holds directly (or by application of paragraph (c)(3)(ii) of this section, but not by application of section 355(d)(7) or (8)) stock possessing five percent or more of the total combined voting power of all classes of stock entitled to vote or the total value of shares of all classes of stock of a corporation. However, this presumption does not apply to any less-than-five-percent shareholder that, at any time during the five-year period—

(i) Is related under section 355(d)(7)(A) to a shareholder in the corporation that is at any time during the five-year period, not a less-than-five-percent shareholder;

(ii) Acted pursuant to a plan or arrangement, with respect to acquisitions of the corporation's stock or securities under section 355(d)(7)(B) and paragraph (c)(4) of this section, with a shareholder in the corporation that is, at any time during the five-year period, not a less-than-five-percent shareholder; or

(iii) Holds stock or securities that is attributed under section 355(d)(8)(A) to a shareholder in the corporation that is, at any time during the five-year period, not a less-than-five-percent shareholder.

(5) *Examples.* The following examples illustrate this paragraph (f):

Example 1. Publicly traded corporation; no schedules filed. D is a widely held and publicly traded corporation with a single class of reporting stock and no other class of stock. Assume that applicable federal law requires any person that directly holds five percent or more of the D stock to file a schedule with the Securities and Ex-

change Commission within 10 days after an acquisition. D distributes its wholly owned subsidiary C pro rata. D determines that no schedule, form, or other document has been filed with respect to its stock or the stock of any other relevant corporation during the five-year period or within 10 days after the distribution. Immediately after the distribution, D has no knowledge that any of its shareholders are (or were at any time during the five-year period) not less-than-five-percent shareholders, or that any particular shareholder acquired D stock by purchase under section 355(d)(5) or (8) and paragraphs (d) and (e) of this section during the five-year period. Under paragraph (f)(3) of this section, D may presume it has no shareholder that is or was not a less-than-five-percent shareholder during the five-year period due to the absence of any filed schedules, forms, or other documents. Under paragraph (f)(4) of this section, D may presume that none of its less-than-five-percent shareholders acquired D's stock by purchase during the five-year period. Accordingly, D may presume that section 355(d) does not apply to the distribution of C.

Example 2. Publicly traded corporation; schedule filed. The facts are the same as those in *Example 1*, except that D determines that, as of 10 days after the distribution, only one schedule has been filed with respect to its stock. That schedule discloses that X acquired 15 percent of the D stock one year before the distribution. Absent contrary knowledge, D may rely on the presumptions in paragraph (f)(3) of this section and so may presume that X is its only shareholder that is or was not a less-than-five-percent shareholder during the five-year period. D may not rely on the presumption in paragraph (f)(4) of this section with respect to X. In addition, D may not rely on the presumption in paragraph (f)(4) of this section with respect to any less-than-five-percent shareholder that, at any time during the five-year period, is related to X under section 355(d)(7)(A), acted pursuant to a plan or arrangement with X under section 355(d)(7)(B) and paragraph (c)(4) of this section with respect to acquisitions of D stock, or holds stock that is attributed to X under section 355(d)(8)(A). Accordingly, under paragraph (f)(1) of this section, to determine whether section 355(d) applies, D must determine: whether X acquired its directly held D stock by purchase under section 355(d)(5) and paragraphs (d) and (e)(2) and (3) of this section during the five-year period; whether X is treated as having purchased any additional D stock under section 355(d)(8) and paragraph (e)(1) of this section during the five-year period; and whether X is related to, or acquired its D stock pursuant to a plan or arrangement with, one or more of D's other shareholders during the five-year period under section 355(d)(7)(A) or (B) and paragraph (c)(4) of this section, and if so, whether those shareholders acquired their D stock by purchase under section 355(d)(5) or (8) and paragraphs (d) and (e) of this section during the five-year period.

Example 3. Acquisition of publicly traded corporation. The facts are the same as those in *Example 1,* except that P acquires all of the D stock in a section 368(a)(1)(B) reorganization that is not also a reorganization under section 368(a)(1)(A) by reason of section 368(a)(2)(E), and D distributes C to P one year later. Because D was widely held, P applies statistical sampling procedures that involve less than 50% of D's outstanding shares, to estimate the basis of all shares acquired, instead of surveying each shareholder. Under the deemed purchase rule of section 355(d)(5)(C) and paragraph (e)(2) of this section, P is treated as having acquired the D stock by purchase on the date the D shareholders acquired the D stock by purchase. Even though D has no less-than-five-percent shareholder immediately after the distribution, D may rely on the presumptions in paragraphs (f)(3) and (4) of this section to determine whether and to what extent the D stock is treated as purchased during the five-year period in P's hands under the deemed purchase rule of section 355(d)(5)(C) and paragraph (e)(2) of this section. Accordingly, D may presume that section 355(d) does not apply to the distribution of C to P. This result would not change even if the statistical sampling that involves less than 50 percent of D's outstanding shares indicated that more than 50% of D's shares were acquired by purchase during the five-year period.

Example 4. Non-publicly traded corporation. D is owned by 20 shareholders and has a single class of stock that is not reporting stock. D knows that A owns 40 percent of the D stock, and D does not know that any other shareholder has owned as much as five percent of the D stock at any time during the five-year period. D may not rely on the presumption in paragraph (f)(3) of this section because its stock is not reporting stock. D may not rely on the presumption in paragraph (f)(4) of this section with respect to A. In addition, D may not rely on the presumption in paragraph (f)(4) of this section for any less-than-five-percent shareholder that, at any time during the five-year period, is related to A under section 355(d)(7)(A), acted pursuant to a plan or arrangement with A under section 355(d)(7)(B) and paragraph (c)(4) of this section with respect to acquisitions of D stock, or holds stock that is attributed to A under section 355(d)(8)(A). D may rely on the presumption in paragraph (f)(4) of this section for less-than-five-percent shareholders that during the five-year period are not related to A, did not act

pursuant to a plan or arrangement with A, and do not hold stock attributed to A. Accordingly, under paragraph (f)(1) of this section, to determine whether section 355(d) applies, D must determine: that A is its only shareholder that is (or was at any time during the five-year period) not a less-than-five-percent shareholder; whether A acquired its directly held D stock by purchase under section 355(d)(5) and paragraphs (d) and (e)(2) and (3) of this section during the five-year period; whether A is treated as having purchased any additional D stock under section 355(d)(8) and paragraph (e)(1) of this section during the five-year period; and whether A is related to, or acquired its D stock pursuant to a plan or arrangement with, one or more of D's other shareholders during the five-year period under section 355(d)(7)(A) or (B) and paragraph (c)(4) of this section, and if so, whether those shareholders acquired their D stock by purchase under section 355(d)(5) or (8) and paragraphs (d) and (e) of this section during the five-year period.

(g) *Effective date.* This section applies to distributions occurring after December 20, 2000, except that they do not apply to any distributions occurring pursuant to a written agreement which is (subject to customary conditions) binding on December 20, 2000, and at all times thereafter. [Reg. § 1.355-6.]

□ *[T.D. 8238, 1-5-89. Amended by T.D. 8913, 12-19-2000 (corrected 2-5-2001).]*

§ 1.355-7T. Recognition of gain on certain distributions of stock or securities in connection with an acquisition.—(a) *In general.* Except as provided in section 355(e) and in this section, section 355(e) applies to any distribution—

(1) To which section 355 (or so much of section 356 as relates to section 355) applies; and

(2) That is part of a plan (or series of related transactions) (hereinafter, plan) pursuant to which 1 or more persons acquire directly or indirectly stock representing a 50-percent or greater interest in the distributing corporation (Distributing) or any controlled corporation (Controlled).

(b) *Plan*—(1) *In general.* Whether a distribution and an acquisition are part of a plan is determined based on all the facts and circumstances. The facts and circumstances to be considered in demonstrating whether a distribution and an acquisition are part of a plan include, but are not limited to, the facts and circumstances set forth in paragraphs (b)(3) and (4) of this section. In general, the weight to be given each of the facts and circumstances depends on the particular case. Whether a distribution and an acquisition are part of a plan does not depend on the relative number of facts and circumstances set forth in paragraph (b)(3) that evidence that a distribution and an acquisition are part of a plan as compared to the relative number of facts and circumstances set forth in paragraph (b)(4) that evidence that a distribution and an acquisition are not part of a plan.

(2) *Certain post-distribution acquisitions.* In the case of an acquisition (other than involving a public offering) after a distribution, the distribution and the acquisition can be part of a plan only if there was an agreement, understanding, arrangement, or substantial negotiations regarding the acquisition or a similar acquisition at some time during the 2-year period ending on the date of the distribution. In the case of an acquisition (other than involving a public offering) after a distribution, the existence of an agreement, understanding, arrangement, or substantial negotiations regarding the acquisition or a similar acquisition at some time during the 2-year period ending on the date of the distribution tends to show that the distribution and the acquisition are part of a plan. See paragraph (b)(3)(i) of this section. However, all facts and circumstances must be considered to determine whether the distribution and the acquisition are part of a plan. For example, in the case of an acquisition (other than involving a public offering) after a distribution, if the distribution was motivated in whole or substantial part by a corporate business purpose (within the meaning of § 1.355-2(b)) other than a business purpose to facilitate the acquisition or a similar acquisition of Distributing or Controlled (see paragraph (b)(4)(v) of this section) and would have occurred at approximately the same time and in similar form regardless of whether the acquisition or a similar acquisition was effected (see paragraph (b)(4)(vi) of this section), the taxpayer may be able to establish that the distribution and the acquisition are not part of a plan.

(3) *Plan factors.* Among the facts and circumstances tending to show that a distribution and an acquisition are part of a plan are the following:

(i) In the case of an acquisition (other than involving a public offering) after a distribution, at some time during the 2-year period ending on the date of the distribution, there was an agreement, understanding, arrangement, or substantial negotiations regarding the acquisition or a similar acquisition. The weight to be accorded this fact depends on the nature, extent, and timing of the agreement, understanding, arrangement, or substantial negotiations. The existence of an agreement, understanding, or arrangement at the time of the distribution is given substantial weight.

(ii) In the case of an acquisition involving a public offering after a distribution, at some time during the 2-year period ending on the date of the distribution, there were discussions by Distributing or Controlled with an investment banker regarding the acquisition or a similar acquisition. The weight to be accorded this fact depends on the nature, extent, and timing of the discussions.

(iii) In the case of an acquisition (other than involving a public offering) before a distribution, at some time during the 2-year period ending on the date of the acquisition, there were discussions by Distributing or Controlled with the acquirer regarding a distribution. The weight to be accorded this fact depends on the nature, extent, and timing of the discussions. In addition, in the case of an acquisition (other than involving a public offering) before a distribution, a person other than Distributing or Controlled intended to cause a distribution and, as a result of the acquisition, can meaningfully participate in the decision regarding whether to make a distribution.

(iv) In the case of an acquisition involving a public offering before a distribution, at some time during the 2-year period ending on the date of the acquisition, there were discussions by Distributing or Controlled with an investment banker regarding a distribution. The weight to be accorded this fact depends on the nature, extent, and timing of the discussions.

(v) In the case of an acquisition either before or after a distribution, the distribution was motivated by a business purpose to facilitate the acquisition or a similar acquisition.

(4) *Non-plan factors.* Among the facts and circumstances tending to show that a distribution and an acquisition are not part of a plan are the following:

(i) In the case of an acquisition involving a public offering after a distribution, during the 2-year period ending on the date of the distribution, there were no discussions by Distributing or Controlled with an investment banker regarding the acquisition or a similar acquisition.

(ii) In the case of an acquisition after a distribution, there was an identifiable, unexpected change in market or business conditions occurring after the distribution that resulted in the acquisition that was otherwise unexpected at the time of the distribution.

(iii) In the case of an acquisition (other than involving a public offering) before a distribution, during the 2-year period ending on the date of the acquisition, there were no discussions by Distributing or Controlled with the acquirer regarding a distribution. This paragraph (b)(4)(iii) does not apply if the acquisition occurred after the date of the public announcement of the planned distribution. In addition, this paragraph (b)(4)(iii) does not apply in the case of an acquisition where a person other than Distributing or Controlled intends to cause a distribution and, as a result of the acquisition, can meaningfully participate in the decision regarding whether to make a distribution.

(iv) In the case of an acquisition before a distribution, there was an identifiable, unexpected change in market or business conditions occurring after the acquisition that resulted in a distribution that was otherwise unexpected.

(v) In the case of an acquisition either before or after a distribution, the distribution was motivated in whole or substantial part by a corporate business purpose (within the meaning of § 1.355-2(b)) other than a business purpose to facilitate the acquisition or a similar acquisition.

(vi) In the case of an acquisition either before or after a distribution, the distribution would have occurred at approximately the same time and in similar form regardless of the acquisition or a similar acquisition.

(c) *Operating rules.* The operating rules contained in this paragraph (c) apply for all purposes of this section.

(1) *Internal discussions and discussions with outside advisors evidence of business purpose.* Internal discussions and discussions with outside advisors by or on behalf of officers or directors of Distributing or Controlled may be indicative of one or more business purposes for the distribution and the relative importance of such purposes.

(2) *Takeover defense.* If Distributing engages in discussions with a potential acquirer regarding an acquisition of Distributing or Controlled and distributes Controlled stock intending, in whole or substantial part, to decrease the likelihood of the acquisition of Distributing or Controlled by separating it from another corporation that is likely to be acquired, Distributing will be treated as having a business purpose to facilitate the acquisition of the corporation that was likely to be acquired.

(3) *Effect of distribution on trading in stock.* The fact that the distribution made all or a part of the stock of Controlled available for trading or made Distributing's or Controlled's stock trade more actively is not taken into account in determining whether the distribution and an acquisition of Distributing or Controlled stock were part of a plan.

(4) *Consequences of section 355(e) disregarded for certain purposes.* For purposes of determining the intentions of the relevant parties under this section, the consequences of the application of section 355(e), and the existence of any contractual indemnity by Controlled for tax resulting from the application of section 355(e)

caused by an acquisition of Controlled, are disregarded.

(5) *Multiple acquisitions.* All acquisitions of stock of Distributing or Controlled that are considered to be part of a plan with a distribution pursuant to paragraph (b) of this section will be aggregated for purposes of the 50-percent test of paragraph (a)(2) of this section.

(d) *Safe harbors*—(1) *Safe Harbor I.* A distribution and an acquisition occurring after the distribution will not be considered part of a plan if—

(i) The distribution was motivated in whole or substantial part by a corporate business purpose (within the meaning of § 1.355-2(b)), other than a business purpose to facilitate an acquisition of the acquired corporation (Distributing or Controlled); and

(ii) The acquisition occurred more than 6 months after the distribution and there was no agreement, understanding, arrangement, or substantial negotiations concerning the acquisition or a similar acquisition during the period that begins 1 year before the distribution and ends 6 months thereafter.

(2) *Safe Harbor II.* (i) A distribution and an acquisition occurring after the distribution will not be considered part of a plan if—

(A) The distribution was not motivated by a business purpose to facilitate the acquisition or a similar acquisition;

(B) The acquisition occurred more than 6 months after the distribution and there was no agreement, understanding, arrangement, or substantial negotiations concerning the acquisition or a similar acquisition during the period that begins 1 year before the distribution and ends 6 months thereafter; and

(C) No more than 25 percent of the stock of the acquired corporation (Distributing or Controlled) was either acquired or the subject of an agreement, understanding, arrangement, or substantial negotiations during the period that begins 1 year before the distribution and ends 6 months thereafter.

(ii) For purposes of paragraph (d)(2)(i)(C) of this section, acquisitions of stock that are treated as not part of a plan pursuant to Safe Harbor V, Safe Harbor VI, or Safe Harbor VII are disregarded.

(3) *Safe Harbor III.* If an acquisition occurs after a distribution, there was no agreement, understanding, or arrangement concerning the acquisition or a similar acquisition at the time of the distribution, and there was no agreement, understanding, arrangement, or substantial negotiations concerning the acquisition or a similar acquisition within 1 year after the distribution,

the acquisition and the distribution will not be considered part of a plan.

(4) *Safe Harbor IV.* If a distribution occurs more than 2 years after an acquisition, and there was no agreement, understanding, arrangement, or substantial negotiations concerning the distribution at the time of the acquisition or within 6 months thereafter, the acquisition and the distribution will not be considered part of a plan.

(5) *Safe Harbor V*—(i) *In general.* An acquisition of Distributing or Controlled stock that is listed on an established market is not part of a plan if, immediately before or immediately after the transfer, none of the transferor, the transferee, and any coordinating group of which either the transferor or the transferee is a member is—

(A) the acquired corporation (Distributing or Controlled);

(B) a corporation that the acquired corporation (Distributing or Controlled) controls within the meaning of section 368(c);

(C) a member of a controlled group of corporations within the meaning of section 1563 of which the acquired corporation (Distributing or Controlled) is a member;

(D) an underwriter with respect to such acquisition;

(E) a controlling shareholder of the acquired corporation (Distributing or Controlled); or

(F) a 10-percent shareholder of the acquired corporation (Distributing or Controlled).

(ii) *Special rules.* (A) This paragraph (d)(5) does not apply to a transfer of stock by or to a person if the corporation the stock of which is being transferred knows, or has reason to know, that the person or a coordinating group of which such person is a member intends to become a controlling shareholder or a 10-percent shareholder of the acquired corporation (Distributing or Controlled) at any time after the acquisition and before the date that is 2 years after the distribution.

(B) If a transfer of stock to which this paragraph (d)(5) applies results immediately, or upon a subsequent event or the passage of time, in an indirect acquisition of voting power by a person other than the transferee, this paragraph (d)(5) does not prevent an acquisition of stock (with the voting power such stock represents after the transfer to which this paragraph (d)(5) applies) by such other person from being treated as part of a plan.

(6) *Safe Harbor VI*—(i) *In general.* If stock of Distributing or Controlled is acquired by a person in connection with such person's performance of services as an employee, director, or independent contractor for Distributing, Controlled,

or a person related to Distributing or Controlled under section 355(d)(7)(A) (and that is not excessive by reference to the services performed) in a transaction to which section 83 or section 421(a) applies, the acquisition and the distribution will not be considered part of a plan.

(ii) *Special rule.* This paragraph (d)(6) does not apply to a stock acquisition described in (d)(6)(i) if the acquirer or a coordinating group of which the acquirer is a member is a controlling shareholder or a 10-percent shareholder of the acquired corporation (Distributing or Controlled) immediately after the acquisition.

(7) *Safe Harbor VII*—(i) *In general.* If stock of Distributing or Controlled is acquired by a retirement plan of an employer that qualifies under section 401(a) or 403(a), the acquisition and the distribution will not be considered part of a plan.

(ii) *Special rule.* This paragraph (d)(7) does not apply to stock acquisitions described in (d)(7)(i) of this section to the extent that the stock acquired pursuant to such acquisitions by all of the qualified plans of the employer described in paragraph (d)(7)(i) of this section, and any other person treated as the same employer as that described in paragraph (d)(7)(i) of this section under section 414(b), (c), (m), or (o), during the 4-year period beginning 2 years before the distribution, in the aggregate, represents 10 percent or more of the total combined voting power of all classes of stock entitled to vote, or 10 percent or more of the total value of shares of all classes of stock, of the acquired corporation (Distributing or Controlled).

(e) *Stock acquired by exercise of options, warrants, convertible obligations, and other similar interests*—(1) *Treatment of options*—(i) *General rule.* For purposes of this section, if stock of Distributing or Controlled is acquired pursuant to an option, the option will be treated as an agreement, understanding, or arrangement to acquire the stock on the earliest of the following dates: the date that the option is written, if the option was more likely than not to be exercised as of such date; the date that the option is transferred, if the option was more likely than not to be exercised as of such date; and the date that the option is modified in a manner that materially increases the likelihood of exercise, if the option was more likely than not to be exercised as of such date; provided, however, if the writing, transfer, or modification had a principal purpose of avoiding section 355(e), the option will be treated as an agreement, understanding, arrangement, or substantial negotiations to acquire the stock on the date of the distribution. The determination of whether an option was more likely than not to be exercised is based on all the facts and circum-

Reg. § 1.355-7T(e)

stances, taking control premiums and minority and blockage discounts into account in determining the fair market value of stock underlying an option.

(ii) *Agreement, understanding, or arrangement to write an option.* If there is an agreement, understanding, or arrangement to write an option, the option will be treated as written on the date of the agreement, understanding, or arrangement.

(iii) *Substantial negotiations related to options.* If an option is treated as an agreement, understanding, or arrangement to acquire the stock on the date that the option is written, substantial negotiations to acquire the option will be treated as substantial negotiations to acquire the stock subject to such option. If an option is treated as an agreement, understanding, or arrangement to acquire the stock on the date that the option is transferred, substantial negotiations regarding the transfer of the option will be treated as substantial negotiations to acquire the stock subject to such option. If an option is treated as an agreement, understanding, or arrangement to acquire the stock on the date that the option is modified in a manner that materially increases the likelihood of exercise, substantial negotiations regarding such modifications to the option will be treated as substantial negotiations to acquire the stock subject to such option.

(2) *Instruments treated as options.* For purposes of this paragraph (e), except to the extent provided in paragraph (e)(3) of this section, call options, warrants, convertible obligations, the conversion feature of convertible stock, put options, redemption agreements (including rights to cause the redemption of stock), any other instruments that provide for the right or possibility to issue, redeem, or transfer stock (including an option on an option), or any other similar interests are treated as options.

(3) *Instruments generally not treated as options.* For purposes of this paragraph (e), the following are not treated as options unless (in the case of paragraphs (e)(3)(i), (iii), and (iv) of this section) written, transferred (directly or indirectly), modified, or listed with a principal purpose of avoiding the application of section 355(e) or this section.

(i) *Escrow, pledge, or other security agreements.* An option that is part of a security arrangement in a typical lending transaction (including a purchase money loan), if the arrangement is subject to customary commercial conditions. For this purpose, a security arrangement includes, for example, an agreement for holding stock in escrow or under a pledge or other security agreement, or an option to acquire stock contingent upon a default under a loan.

(ii) *Compensatory options.* An option to acquire stock in Distributing or Controlled with customary terms and conditions provided to a person in connection with such person's performance of services as an employee, director, or independent contractor for the corporation or a person related to it under section 355(d)(7)(A) (and that is not excessive by reference to the services performed), provided that—

(A) The transfer of stock pursuant to such option is described in section 421(a); or

(B) The option is nontransferable within the meaning of § 1.83-3(d) and does not have a readily ascertainable fair market value as defined in § 1.83-7(b).

(iii) *Options exercisable only upon death, disability, mental incompetency, or separation from service.* Any option entered into between shareholders of a corporation (or a shareholder and the corporation) that is exercisable only upon the death, disability, or mental incompetency of the shareholder, or, in the case of stock acquired in connection with the performance of services for the corporation or a person related to it under section 355(d)(7)(A) (and that is not excessive by reference to the services performed), the shareholder's separation from service.

(iv) *Rights of first refusal.* A bona fide right of first refusal regarding the corporation's stock with customary terms, entered into between shareholders of a corporation (or between the corporation and a shareholder).

(v) *Other enumerated instruments.* Any other instrument the Commissioner may designate in revenue procedures, notices, or other guidance published in the Internal Revenue Bulletin (see § 601.601(d)(2) of this chapter).

(f) *Multiple controlled corporations.* Only the stock or securities of a controlled corporation in which 1 or more persons acquire directly or indirectly stock representing a 50-percent or greater interest as part of a plan involving the distribution of that corporation will be treated as not qualified property under section 355(e)(1) if—

(1) The stock or securities of more than 1 controlled corporation are distributed in distributions to which section 355 (or so much of section 356 as relates to section 355) applies; and

(2) One or more persons do not acquire, directly or indirectly, stock representing a 50-percent or greater interest in Distributing pursuant to a plan involving any of those distributions.

(g) *Valuation.* Except as provided in paragraph (e)(1)(i) of this section, for purposes of section 355(e) and this section, all shares of stock within a single class are considered to have the same value. Thus, control premiums and minority and blockage discounts within a single class are not taken into account.

(h) *Definitions*—(1) *Agreement, understanding, arrangement, or substantial negotiations.* (i) Whether an agreement, understanding, or arrangement exists depends on the facts and circumstances. The parties do not necessarily have to have entered into a binding contract or have reached agreement on all significant economic terms to have an agreement, understanding, or arrangement. However, an agreement, understanding, or arrangement clearly exists if a binding contract to acquire stock exists.

(ii) Substantial negotiations in the case of an acquisition (other than involving a public offering) generally require discussions of significant economic terms, e.g., the exchange ratio in a reorganization, by one or more officers, directors, or controlling shareholders of Distributing or Controlled, or another person or persons with the implicit or explicit permission of one or more officers, directors, or controlling shareholders of Distributing or Controlled, with the acquirer or a person or persons with the implicit or explicit permission of the acquirer.

(iii) In the case of an acquisition involving a public offering by Distributing or Controlled, the existence of an agreement, understanding, arrangement, or substantial negotiations will be based on discussions by one or more officers, directors, or controlling shareholders of Distributing or Controlled, or another person or persons with the implicit or explicit permission of one or more officers, directors, or controlling shareholders of Distributing or Controlled, with an investment banker.

(2) *Controlled corporation.* For purposes of this section, a controlled corporation is a corporation the stock of which is distributed in a distribution to which section 355 (or so much of section 356 as relates to section 355) applies.

(3) *Controlling shareholder.* (i) A controlling shareholder of a corporation the stock of which is listed on an established market is a 5-percent shareholder who actively participates in the management or operation of the corporation. For purposes of this paragraph (h)(3)(i), a corporate director will be treated as actively participating in the management of the corporation.

(ii) A controlling shareholder of a corporation the stock of which is not listed on an established market is any person that owns, actually or constructively under the rules of section 318, stock possessing voting power representing a meaningful voice in the governance of the corporation.

(iii) For purposes of this section, a person is a controlling shareholder if that person meets the definition of controlling shareholder in this paragraph (h)(3) immediately before or immediately after the acquisition being tested.

(iv) If a distribution precedes an acquisition, Controlled's controlling shareholders immediately after the distribution and Distributing are included among Controlled's controlling shareholders at the time of the distribution.

(4) *Coordinating group.* A coordinating group includes 2 or more persons that, pursuant to a formal or informal understanding, join in one or more coordinated acquisitions or dispositions of stock of Distributing or Controlled. A principal element in determining if such an understanding exists is whether the investment decision of each person is based on the investment decision of one or more other existing or prospective shareholders. A coordinating group is treated as a single shareholder for purposes of determining whether the coordinating group is treated as a controlling shareholder or a 10-percent shareholder.

(5) *Discussions.* Discussions by Distributing or Controlled generally require discussions by one or more officers, directors, or controlling shareholders of Distributing or Controlled, or another person or persons with the implicit or explicit permission of one or more officers, directors, or controlling shareholders of Distributing or Controlled. Discussions with the acquirer generally require discussions with the acquirer or a person or persons with the implicit or explicit permission of the acquirer.

(6) *Established market.* An established market is—

(i) A national securities exchange registered under section 6 of the Securities Exchange Act of 1934 (15 U.S.C. 78f);

(ii) An interdealer quotation system sponsored by a national securities association registered under section 15A of the Securities Act of 1934 (15 U.S.C. 78o-3); or

(iii) Any additional market that the Commissioner may designate in revenue procedures, notices, or other guidance published in the Internal Revenue Bulletin (see § 601.601(d)(2) of this chapter).

(7) *Five-percent shareholder.* A person will be considered a 5-percent shareholder of a corporation the stock of which is listed on an established market if the person owns, actually or constructively under the rules of section 318, 5 percent or more of any class of stock of the corporation whose stock is transferred. A person is a 5-percent shareholder if the person meets the requirements described above immediately before or immediately after the transfer. All options owned by a person are treated as exercised for the purpose of deter-

Reg. § 1.355-7T(h)(7)

mining whether such person is a 5-percent shareholder. Absent actual knowledge that a person is a 5-percent shareholder, a corporation can rely on Schedules 13D and 13G (or any similar schedules) filed with the Securities and Exchange Commission to identify its 5-percent shareholders.

(8) *Similar acquisition.* In general, an actual acquisition (other than a public offering or other stock issuance for cash) is similar to another potential acquisition if the actual acquisition effects a direct or indirect combination of all or a significant portion of the same business operations as the combination that would have been effected by such other potential acquisition. Thus, an actual acquisition may be similar to another acquisition even if the timing or terms of the actual acquisition are different from the timing or terms of the other acquisition. For example, an actual acquisition of Distributing by shareholders of another corporation in connection with a merger of such other corporation with and into Distributing is similar to another acquisition of Distributing by merger into such other corporation or into a subsidiary of such other corporation. However, in general, an actual acquisition (other than a public offering or other stock issuance for cash) is not similar to another acquisition if the ultimate owners of the business operations with which Distributing or Controlled is combined in the actual acquisition are substantially different from the ultimate owners of the business operations with which Distributing or Controlled was to be combined in such other acquisition. In the case of a public offering or other stock issuance for cash, an actual acquisition may be similar to another acquisition, even though there are changes in the terms of the stock, the class of stock being offered, the size of the offering, the timing of the offering, the price of the stock, or the participants in the offering.

(9) *Ten-percent shareholder.* A person will be considered a 10-percent shareholder of a corporation the stock of which is listed on an established market if the person owns, actually or constructively under the rules of section 318, 10 percent or more of any class of stock of the corporation whose stock is transferred. A person will be considered a 10-percent shareholder of a corporation the stock of which is not listed on an established market if the person owns, actually or constructively under the rules of section 318, stock possessing 10 percent or more of the total voting power of the stock of the corporation whose stock is transferred or stock having a value equal to 10 percent or more of the total value of the stock of the corporation whose stock is transferred. A person is a 10-percent shareholder if the person meets the requirements described above immediately before or immediately after the transfer. All options owned

by a person are treated as exercised for the purpose of determining whether such person is a 10-percent shareholder. Absent actual knowledge that a person is a 10-percent shareholder, a corporation the stock of which is listed on an established market can rely on Schedules 13D and 13G (or any similar schedules) filed with the Securities and Exchange Commission to identify its 10-percent shareholders.

(i) [Reserved]

(j) *Examples.* The following examples illustrate paragraphs (a) through (h) of this section. Throughout these examples, assume that Distributing (D) owns all of the stock of Controlled (C). Assume further that D distributes the stock of C in a distribution to which section 355 applies and to which section 355(d) does not apply. Unless otherwise stated, assume the corporations do not have controlling shareholders. No inference should be drawn from any example concerning whether any requirements of section 355 other than those of section 355(e) are satisfied. The examples are as follows:

Example 1. Unwanted assets. (i) D is in business 1. C is in business 2. D is relatively small in its industry. D wants to combine with X, a larger corporation also engaged in business 1. X and D begin negotiating for X to acquire D, but X does not want to acquire C. To facilitate the acquisition of D by X, D agrees to distribute all the stock of C pro rata before the acquisition. Prior to the distribution, D and X enter into a contract for D to merge into X subject to several conditions. One month after D and X enter into the contract, D distributes C and, on the day after the distribution, D merges into X. As a result of the merger, D's former shareholders own less than 50 percent of the stock of X.

(ii) The issue is whether the distribution of C and the merger of D into X are part of a plan. No Safe Harbor applies to this acquisition. To determine whether the distribution of C and the merger of D into X are part of a plan, D must consider all the facts and circumstances, including those described in paragraph (b) of this section.

(iii) The following tends to show that the distribution of C and the merger of D into X are part of a plan: X and D had an agreement regarding the acquisition during the 2-year period ending on the date of the distribution (paragraph (b)(3)(i) of this section), and the distribution was motivated by a business purpose to facilitate the merger (paragraph (b)(3)(v) of this section). Because the merger was agreed to at the time of the distribution, the fact described in paragraph (b)(3)(i) of this section is given substantial weight.

(iv) None of the facts and circumstances listed in paragraph (b)(4) of this section, tending to show that a distribution and an acquisition are not part of a plan, exist in this case.

(v) The distribution of C and the merger of D into X are part of a plan under paragraph (b) of this section.

Example 2. Public offering. (i) D's managers, directors, and investment banker discuss the possibility of offering D stock to the public. They decide a public offering of 20 percent of D's stock with D as a stand alone corporation would be in D's best interest. One month later, to facilitate a stock offering by D of 20 percent of its stock, D distributes all the stock of C pro rata to D's shareholders. D issues new shares amounting to 20 percent of its stock to the public in a public offering 7 months after the distribution.

(ii) The issue is whether the distribution of C and the public offering by D are part of a plan. No Safe Harbor applies to this acquisition. Safe Harbor V, relating to public trading, does not apply to public offerings (see paragraph (d)(5)(i)(A) of this section). To determine whether the distribution of C and the public offering by D are part of a plan, D must consider all the facts and circumstances, including those described in paragraph (b) of this section.

(iii) The following tends to show that the distribution of C and the public offering by D are part of a plan: D discussed the public offering with its investment banker during the 2-year period ending on the date of the distribution (paragraph (b)(3)(ii) of this section), and the distribution was motivated by a business purpose to facilitate the public offering (paragraph (b)(3)(v) of this section).

(iv) None of the facts and circumstances listed in paragraph (b)(4) of this section, tending to show that a distribution and an acquisition are not part of a plan, exist in this case.

(v) The distribution of C and the public offering by D are part of a plan under paragraph (b) of this section.

Example 3. Hot market. (i) D is a widely-held corporation the stock of which is listed on an established market. D announces a distribution of C and distributes C pro rata to D's shareholders. By contract, C agrees to indemnify D for any imposition of tax under section 355(e) caused by the acts of C. The distribution is motivated by a desire to improve D's access to financing at preferred customer interest rates, which will be more readily available if D separates from C. At the time of the distribution, although neither D nor C has been approached by any potential acquirer of C, it is reasonably certain that soon after the distribution either an acquisition of C will occur or there will be an agreement, understanding, arrangement, or substantial negotiations regard-

ing an acquisition of C. Corporation Y acquires C in a merger described in section 368(a)(2)(E) within 6 months after the distribution. The C shareholders receive less than 50 percent of the stock of Y in the exchange.

(ii) The issue is whether the distribution of C and the acquisition of C by Y are part of a plan. No Safe Harbor applies to this acquisition. Under paragraph (b)(2) of this section, because prior to the distribution neither D nor C and Y had an agreement, understanding, arrangement, or substantial negotiations regarding the acquisition or a similar acquisition, the distribution of C by D and the acquisition of C by Y are not part of a plan under paragraph (b) of this section.

Example 4. Unexpected opportunity. (i) D, the stock of which is listed on an established market, announces that it will distribute all the stock of C pro rata to D's shareholders. At the time of the announcement, the distribution is motivated wholly by a corporate business purpose (within the meaning of § 1.355-2(b)) other than a business purpose to facilitate an acquisition. After the announcement but before the distribution, widely-held X becomes available as an acquisition target. There were no discussions between D or C and X before the announcement. D negotiates with and acquires X before the distribution. After the acquisition, X's former shareholders own 55 percent of D's stock. D distributes the stock of C pro rata within 6 months after the acquisition of X.

(ii) The issue is whether the acquisition of X by D and the distribution of C are part of a plan. No Safe Harbor applies to this acquisition. To determine whether the acquisition of X by D and the distribution of C are part of a plan, D must consider all the facts and circumstances, including those described in paragraph (b) of this section.

(iii) Depending on whether a person other than D or C intends to cause a distribution and, as a result of the acquisition, can meaningfully participate in the decision regarding whether to cause a distribution, the fact described in (b)(3)(iii) of this section, tending to show that a distribution and an acquisition are part of a plan, may exist in this case.

(iv) Under paragraph (b)(4) of this section, D would assert that the following tends to show that the distribution of C and the acquisition of X by D are not part of a plan: the distribution was motivated by a corporate business purpose (within the meaning of § 1.355-2(b)) other than a business purpose to facilitate the acquisition or a similar acquisition (paragraph (b)(4)(v) of this section), and the distribution would have occurred at approximately the same time and in similar form regardless of the acquisition or a similar acquisition (paragraph (b)(4)(vi) of this section).

Reg. § 1.355-7T(j)

That D decided to distribute C and announced that decision before it became aware of the opportunity to acquire X suggests that the distribution would have occurred at approximately the same time and in similar form regardless of D's acquisition of X or a similar acquisition. X's lack of participation in the decision to distribute C, even though the X shareholders may have been able to prevent a distribution of C, also helps establish that fact.

(v) In determining whether the distribution of C and the acquisition of X by D are part of a plan, one should consider the importance of D's business purpose for the distribution in light of D's opportunity to acquire X. If D can establish that the distribution continued to be motivated by the stated business purpose, and if D would have distributed C regardless of D's acquisition of X, then D's acquisition of X and D's distribution of C are not part of a plan under paragraph (b) of this section.

Example 5. Vote shifting transaction. (i) D is in business 1. C is in business 2. D wants to combine with X, a larger corporation also engaged in business 1. The stock of X is closely held. X and D begin negotiating for D to acquire X, but the X shareholders do not want to acquire an indirect interest in C. To facilitate the acquisition of X by D, D agrees to distribute all the stock of C pro rata before the acquisition of X. D and X enter into a contract for X to merge into D subject to several conditions. Among those conditions is that D will amend its corporate charter to provide for 2 classes of stock: Class A and Class B. Under all circumstances, each share of Class A stock will be entitled to 10 votes in the election of each director on D's board of directors. Upon issuance, each share of Class B stock will be entitled to 10 votes in the election of each director on D's board of directors; however, a disposition of such share by its original holder will result in such share being entitled to only 1 vote, rather than 10 votes, in the election of each director. Immediately after the merger, the Class B shares will be listed on an established market. One month after D and X enter into the contract, D distributes C. Immediately after the distribution, the shareholders of D exchange their D stock for the new Class B shares. On the day after the distribution, X merges into D. In the merger, the former shareholders of X exchange their X stock for Class A shares of D. Immediately after the merger, D's historic shareholders own stock of D representing 51 percent of the total combined voting power of all classes of stock of D entitled to vote. During the 30-day period following the merger, none of the Class A shares are transferred, but a number of D's historic shareholders sell their Class B stock of D in public trading with the result that, at the end of that 30-day period, the Class A shares owned by the former X shareholders represent 52 percent of the total combined voting power of all classes of stock of D entitled to vote.

(ii) *X acquisition.* (A) The issue is whether the distribution of C and the merger of X into D are part of a plan. No Safe Harbor applies to this acquisition. To determine whether the distribution of C and the merger of X into D are part of a plan, D must consider all the facts and circumstances, including those described in paragraph (b) of this section.

(B) The following tends to show that the distribution of C and the merger of X into D are part of a plan: X and D had an agreement regarding the acquisition during the 2-year period ending on the date of the distribution (paragraph (b)(3)(i) of this section), and the distribution was motivated by a business purpose to facilitate the merger (paragraph (b)(3)(v) of this section). Because the merger was agreed to at the time of the distribution, the fact described in paragraph (b)(3)(i) of this section is given substantial weight.

(C) None of the facts and circumstances listed in paragraph (b)(4) of this section, tending to show that a distribution and an acquisition are not part of a plan, exist in this case.

(D) The distribution of C and the merger of X into D are part of a plan under paragraph (b) of this section.

(iii) *Public trading of Class B shares.* (A) Assuming that each of the transferors and the transferees of the Class B stock of D in public trading is not one of the prohibited transferors or transferees listed in paragraph (d)(5)(i), Safe Harbor V will apply to the acquisitions of the Class B stock during the 30-day period following the merger such that the distribution and those acquisitions will not be treated as part of the plan. However, to the extent that those acquisitions result in an indirect acquisition of voting power by a person other than the acquirer of the transferred stock, Safe Harbor V does not prevent the acquisition of the D stock (with the voting power such stock represents after those acquisitions) by the former X shareholders from being treated as part of a plan.

(B) To the extent that the transfer of the Class B shares causes the voting power of D to shift to the Class A stock acquired by the former X shareholders, such shifted voting power will be treated as attributable to the stock acquired by the former X shareholders as part of the plan that includes the distribution and the X acquisition.

Example 6. Acquisition that is not similar. (i) D, X, and Y are each corporations the stock of which is publicly traded and widely held. Each of D, X, and Y are engaged in the manufacture and sale of trucks. C is engaged in the manufacture and sale of buses. D and X engage in substantial negotiations concerning X's acquisition of the stock of D from the D shareholders in exchange for stock of X. D and X do not reach an agreement regarding that acquisition. Three months after D and X first began negotiations regarding that acquisition, D distributes the stock of C pro rata to its shareholders. Three months after the distribution, Y acquires the stock of D from the D shareholders in exchange for stock of Y.

(ii) Although both X and Y engage in the manufacture and sale of trucks, X's truck business and Y's truck business are not the same business operations. Therefore, because Y's acquisition of D does not effect a combination of the same business operations as X's acquisition of D would have effected, Y's acquisition of D is not similar to X's potential acquisition of D that was the subject of earlier negotiations.

Example 7. Acquisition that is similar. (i) D is engaged in the business of writing custom software for several industries (industries 1 through 6). The software business of D related to industries 4, 5, and 6 is significant relative to the software business of D related to industries 3, 4, 5, and 6. X, an unrelated corporation, is engaged in the business of writing software and the business of manufacturing and selling hardware devices. X's business of writing software is significant relative to its total businesses. X and D engage in substantial negotiations regarding X's acquisition of D stock from the D shareholders in exchange for stock of X. Because X does not want to acquire the software businesses related to industries 1 and 2, these negotiations relate to an acquisition of D stock where D owns the software businesses related only to industries 3, 4, 5, and 6. Thereafter, D concludes that the intellectual property licenses central to the software business related to industries 1 and 2 are not transferable and that a separation of the software business related to industry 3 from the software business related to industry 2 is not desirable. One month after D begins negotiating with X, D contributes the software businesses related to industries 4, 5, and 6 to C, and distributes the stock of C pro rata to its shareholders. In addition, X sells its hardware businesses for cash. After the distribution, C and X negotiate for X's acquisition of the C stock from the C shareholders in exchange for X stock, and X acquires the stock of C.

(ii) Although D and C are different corporations, C does not own the custom software business related to industry 3, and X sold its hardware business prior to the acquisition of C, because X's acquisition of C involves a combination of a significant portion of the same business operations as the combination that would have been effected by the acquisition of D that was the subject of negotiations between D and X, X's acquisition of C is the same as or similar to X's potential acquisition of D that was the subject of earlier negotiations.

* * *

[Temporary Reg. § 1.355-7T.]

☐ [*T.D. 8960, 8-2-2001. Amended by T.D. 8988, 4-23-2002 (corrected 5-31-2002).*]

§ 1.356-1. Receipt of additional consideration in connection with an exchange.—(a) If in any exchange to which the provisions of section 354 or section 355 would apply except for the fact that there is received by the shareholders or the security holders other property (in addition to property permitted to be received without recognition of gain by such sections) or money, then—

(1) The gain, if any, to the taxpayer shall be recognized in an amount not in excess of the sum of the money and the fair market value of the other property, but,

(2) The loss, if any, to the taxpayer from the exchange or distribution shall not be recognized to any extent.

(b) If the distribution of such other property or money by or on behalf of a corporation has the effect of the distribution of a dividend, then there shall be chargeable to each distributee (either an individual or a corporation)—

(1) As a dividend, such an amount of the gain recognized as is not in excess of the distributee's ratable share of the undistributed earnings and profits of the corporation accumulated after February 28, 1913, and

(2) As a gain from the exchange of property, the remainder of the gain so recognized.

(c) The rules of this section may be illustrated by the following examples:

Example (1). In an exchange to which the provisions of section 356 apply and to which section 354 would apply but for the receipt of property not permitted to be received without the recognition of gain or loss, A (either an individual or a corporation) received the following in exchange for a share of stock having an adjusted basis to him of $85:

Reg. § 1.356-1(c)

One share of stock worth	$100
Cash	25
Other property (basis $25) fair market value	50
Total fair market value of consideration received	$175
Adjusted basis of stock surrendered in exchange	$ 85
Total gain	90
Gain to be recognized, limited to cash and other property received	$ 75
A's pro rata share of earnings and profits accumulated after February 28, 1913 (taxable dividend)	$ 30
Remainder to be treated as a gain from the exchange of property	45

Example (2). If, in example (1), A's stock had an adjusted basis to him of $200, he would have realized a loss of $25 on the exchange, which loss would not be recognized.

(d) Section 301(b)(1)(B) and section 301(d)(2) do not apply to a distribution of "other property" to a corporate shareholder if such distribution is within the provisions of section 356.

(e) See paragraph (1) of § 1.301-1 for certain transactions which are not within the scope of section 356. [Reg. § 1.356-1.]

☐ [*T.D.* 6152, 12-2-55.]

§ 1.356-2. Receipt of additional consideration not in connection with an exchange.—(a) If, in a transaction to which section 355 would apply except for the fact that a shareholder (individual or corporate) receives property permitted by section 355 to be received without the recognition of gain, together with other property or money, without the surrender of any stock or securities of the distributing corporation, then the sum of the money and the fair market value of the other property as of the date of the distribution shall be treated as a distribution of property to which the rules of section 301 (other than section 301(b) and section 301(d) apply. See section 358 for determination of basis of such other property.

(b) Paragraph (a) of this section may be illustrated by the following examples:

Example (1). Individuals A and B each own 50 of the 100 outstanding shares of common stock of Corporation X. Corporation X owns all of the stock of Corporation Y, 100 shares. Corporation X distributes to each shareholder 50 shares of the stock of Corporation Y plus $100 cash without requiring the surrender of any shares of its own stock. The $100 cash received by each is treated as a distribution of property to which the rules of section 301 apply.

Example (2). If, in the above example, Corporation X distributes 50 shares of stock of Corporation Y to A and 30 shares of such stock plus $100 cash to B without requiring the surrender of any of its own stock, the amount of cash received by B is treated as a distribution of property to which the rules of section 301 apply. [Reg. § 1.356-2.]

☐ [*T.D.* 6152, 12-2-55.]

§ 1.356-3. Rules for treatment of securities as "other property."—(a) As a general rule, for purposes of section 356, the term "other property" includes securities. However, it does not include securities permitted under section 354 or section 355 to be received tax free. Thus, when securities are surrendered in a transaction to which section 354 or section 355 is applicable, the characterization of the securities received as "other property" does not include securities received where the principal amount of such securities does not exceed the principal amount of securities surrendered in the transaction. If a greater principal amount of securities is received in an exchange described in section 354(other than subsection (c) or (d) thereof) or section 355 over the principal amount of securities surrendered, the term "other property" includes the fair market value of such excess principal amount as of the date of the exchange. If no securities are surrendered in exchange, the term "other property" includes the fair market value, as of the date of receipt, of the entire principal amount of the securities received.

(b) Except as provided in § 1.356-6, for purposes of this section, a right to acquire stock that is treated as a security for purposes of section 354 or 355 has no principal amount. Thus, such right is not *other property* when received in a transaction to which section 356 applies (regardless of whether securities are surrendered in the exchange). This paragraph (b) applies to transactions occurring on or after March 9, 1998.

(c) In the examples in this paragraph (c), *stock* means common stock and *warrants* means rights to acquire common stock. The following examples illustrate the rules of paragraph (a) of this section:—

Example 1. A, an individual, exchanged 100 shares of stock for 100 shares of stock and a security in the principal amount of $1,000 with a fair market value of $990. The amount of $990 is treated as "other property."

Example 2. B, an individual, exchanged 100 shares of stock and a security in the principal amount of $1,000 for 300 shares of stock and a security in the principal amount of $1,500. The security had a fair market value on the date of receipt of $1,575. The fair market value of the excess principal amount, or $525, is treated as "other property."

Example 3. C, an individual, exchanged a security in a principal amount of $1,000 for 100 shares of stock and a security in the principal amount of $900. No part of the security received is treated as "other property."

Example 4. D, an individual, exchanged a security in the principal amount of $1,000 for 100 shares of stock and a security in the principal amount of $1,200 with a fair market value of $1,100. The fair market value of the excess principal amount, or $183.33, is treated as "other property."

Example 5. E, an individual, exchanged a security in the principal amount of $1,000 for another security in the principal amount of $1,200 with a fair market value of $1,080. The fair market value of the excess principal amount, or $180, is treated as "other property."

Example 6. F, an individual, exchanged a security in the principal amount of $1,000 for two different securities each in the principal amount of $750. One of the securities had a fair market value of $750, the other had a fair market value of $600. One-third of the fair market value of each security ($250 and $200) is treated as "other property."

Example 7. G, an individual, exchanged stock for stock and a warrant. The warrant had no principal amount. Thus, G received no excess principal amount within the meaning of section 356(d).

Example 8. H, an individual, exchanged a warrant for stock and a warrant. The warrants had no principal amount. Thus, H received no excess principal amount within the meaning of section 356(d).

Example 9. I, an individual, exchanged a warrant for stock and a debt security. The warrant had no principal amount. The debt security had a $100 principal amount. I received $100 of excess principal amount within the meaning of section 356(d).

[Reg. § 1.356-3.]

□ [*T.D.* 6152, 12-2-55. *Amended by T.D.* 7616, 5-7-79; *T.D.* 8752, 1-5-98 *and T.D.* 8882, 5-15-2000.]

§ 1.356-4. Exchanges for section 306 stock.—If, in a transaction to which section 356 is applicable, other property or money is received in exchange for section 306 stock, an amount equal to the fair market value of the property plus the money, if any, shall be treated as a distribution of property to which section 301 is applicable. The determination of whether section 306 stock is surrendered for other property (including money) is a question of fact to be decided under all of the circumstances of each case. Ordinarily, the other property (including money) received will first be treated as received in exchange for any section 306 stock owned by a shareholder prior to such transaction. For example, if a shareholder who owns a share of common stock (having a basis to him of $100) and a share of preferred stock which is section 306 stock (having a basis to him of $100) surrenders both shares in a transaction to which section 356 is applicable for one share of common stock having a fair market value of $80 and one $100 bond having a fair market value of $100, the bond will be deemed received in exchange for the section 306 stock and it will be treated as a distribution to which section 301 is applicable to the extent of its entire fair market value ($100). [Reg. § 1.356-4.]

□ [*T.D.* 6152, 12-2-55.]

§ 1.356-5. Transactions involving gift or compensation.—With respect to transactions described in sections 354, 355, or 356, but which—

(a) Result in a gift, see section 2501 and following, and the regulations pertaining thereto, or

(b) Have the effect of the payment of compensation, see section 61(a)(1), and the regulations pertaining thereto. [Reg. § 1.356-5.]

□ [*T.D.* 6152, 12-2-55.]

§ 1.356-6. Rules for treatment of nonqualified preferred stock as other property.—(a) *In general.* For purposes of § § 1.354-1(e), 1.355-1(c), and 1.356-3(b), the terms *stock* and *securities* do not include—

(1) Nonqualified preferred stock, as defined in section 351(g)(2), received in exchange for (or in a distribution with respect to) stock, or a right to acquire stock, other than nonqualified preferred stock; or

(2) A right to acquire such nonqualified preferred stock, received in exchange for (or in a distribution with respect to) stock, or a right to acquire stock, other than nonqualified preferred stock.

(b) *Exceptions.* The following exceptions apply:

(1) *Certain recapitalizations.* Paragraph (a) of this section does not apply in the case of a recapitalization under section 368(a)(1)(E) of a family-owned corporation as described in section 354(a)(2)(C)(ii)(II).

(2) *Transition rule.* Paragraph (a) of this section does not apply to a transaction described in section 1014(f)(2) of the Taxpayer Relief Act of 1997 (111 Stat. 921).

Reg. § 1.356-6(b)(2)

(c) *Effective date.* This section applies to non-qualified preferred stock, or a right to acquire such stock, received in connection with a transaction occurring on or after March 9, 1998. [Reg. § 1.356-6.]

☐ [*T.D.* 8753, 1-5-98. *Redesignated by T.D.* 8882, 5-15-2000.]

§ 1.357-1. Assumption of liability.—(a) *General rule.* Section 357(a) does not affect the rule that liabilities assumed are to be taken into account for the purpose of computing the amount of gain or loss realized under section 1001 upon an exchange. Section 357(a) provides, subject to the exceptions and limitations specified in section 357(b) and (c), that:

(1) Liabilities assumed are not to be treated as "other property or money" for the purpose of determining the amount of realized gain which is to be recognized under section 351, 361, 371, or 374, if the transactions would, but for the receipt

of "other property or money" have been exchanges of the type described in any one of such sections; and

(2) If the only type of consideration received by the transferor in addition to that permitted to be received by section 351, 361, 371, or 374, consists of an assumption of liabilities, the transaction, if otherwise qualified, will be deemed to be within the provisions of section 351, 361, 371, or 374.

(b) *Application of general rule.* The application of paragraph (a) of this section may be illustrated by the following example:

Example. A, an individual, transfers to a controlled corporation property with an adjusted basis of $10,000 in exchange for stock of the corporation with a fair market value of $8,000, $3,000 cash, and the assumption by the corporation of indebtedness of A amounting to $4,000. A's gain is $5,000, computed as follows:

Stock received, fair market value	$ 8,000
Cash received	3,000
Liability assumed by transferee	4,000
Total consideration received	15,000
Less: Adjusted basis of property transferred	10,000
Gain realized	$ 5,000

Assuming that the exchange falls within section 351 as a transaction in which the gain to be recognized is limited to "other property or money" received, the gain recognized to A will be limited to the $3,000 cash received, since, under the general rule of section 357(a), the assumption of the $4,000 liability does not constitute "other property."

(c) *Tax avoidance purpose.* The benefits of section 357(a) do not extend to any exchange involving an assumption of liabilities where it appears that the principal purpose of the taxpayer with respect to such assumption was to avoid Federal income tax on the exchange, or, if not such purpose, was not a bona fide business purpose. In such cases, the total amount of liabilities assumed or acquired pursuant to such exchange (and not merely a particular liability with respect to which the tax avoidance purpose existed) shall, for the purpose of determining the amount of gain to be recognized upon the exchange in which the liabilities are assumed or acquired, be treated as money received by the taxpayer upon the exchange. Thus, if in the example set forth in paragraph (b) of this section, the principal purpose of the assumption of the $4,000 liability was to avoid tax on the exchange, or was not a bona fide business purpose, then the amount of gain recognized would be $5,000. In any suit or proceeding where the burden is on the taxpayer to prove that an assumption of liabilities is not to be treated as

"other property or money" under section 357, which is the case if the Commissioner determines that the taxpayer's purpose with respect thereto was a purpose to avoid Federal income tax on the exchange or was not a bona fide business purpose, and the taxpayer contests such determination by litigation, the taxpayer must sustain such burden by the clear preponderance of the evidence. Thus, the taxpayer must prove his case by such a clear preponderance of all the evidence that the absence of a purpose to avoid Federal income tax on the exchange, or the presence of a bona fide business purpose, is unmistakable. [Reg. § 1.357-1.]

☐ [*T.D.* 6152, 12-2-55. *Amended by T.D.* 6528, 1-18-61.]

§ 1.357-2. Liabilities in excess of basis.—(a) Section 357(c) provides in general that in an exchange to which section 351 (relating to a transfer to a corporation controlled by the transferor) is applicable, or to which section 361 (relating to the nonrecognition of gain or loss to corporations) is applicable by reason of a section 368(a)(1)(D) reorganization, if the sum of the amount of liabilities assumed plus the amount of liabilities to which the property is subject exceeds the total of the adjusted basis of the property transferred pursuant to such exchange, then such excess shall be considered as a gain from the sale or exchange of a capital asset or of property which is not a capital asset as the case may be. Thus, if an individual transfers, under section 351, properties having a total basis in his hands of $20,000, one of which has a basis of $10,000 but is subject to a mortgage of $30,000, to a corporation controlled by him, such individual will be subject to tax with respect to $10,000, the excess of the amount of the liability over the total adjusted basis of all the properties in his hands. The same result will follow whether or not the liability is assumed by the transferee. The determination of whether a gain resulting from the transfer of capital assets is long-term or short-term capital gain shall be made by reference to the holding period to the transferor of the assets transferred. An exception to the general rule of section 357(c) is made (1) for any exchange as to which under section 357(b) (relating to assumption of liabilities for tax-avoidance purposes) the entire amount of the liabilities is treated as money received and (2) for an exchange to which section 371 (relating to reorganizations in certain receivership and bankruptcy proceedings) or section 374 (relating to gain or loss not recognized in certain railroad reorganizations) is applicable.

(b) The application of paragraph (a) of this section may be illustrated by the following examples:

Example (1). If all such assets transferred are capital assets and if half the assets (ascertained by reference to their fair market value at the time of the transfer) have been held for less than 1 year (6 months for taxable years beginning before 1977; 9 months for taxable years beginning in 1977) and the remaining half for more than 1 year (6 months for taxable years beginning before 1977; 9 months for taxable years beginning in 1977), half the excess of the amount of the liability over the total of the adjusted basis of the property transferred pursuant to the exchange shall be treated as short-term capital gain, and the remaining half shall be treated as long-term capital gain.

Example (2). If half of the assets (ascertained by reference to their fair market value at the time of the transfer) transferred are capital assets and half are assets other than capital assets, then half of the excess of the amount of the liability over the total of the adjusted basis of the property transferred pursuant to the exchange shall be treated as capital gain, and the remaining half shall be treated as gain from the sale or exchange of assets other than capital assets. [Reg. § 1.357-2.]

☐ [*T.D.* 6152, 12-2-55. *Amended by T.D.* 6528, 1-18-61 *and by T.D.* 7728, 10-31-80.]

§ 1.358-1. Basis to distributees.—(a) In the case of an exchange or distribution to which section 354, 355, or 371(b) applies in which, under the law applicable to the year in which the ex-

change is made, only nonrecognition property is received, the sum of the basis of all of the stock and securities in the corporation whose stock and securities are exchanged or with respect to which the distribution is made, held immediately after the transaction, plus the basis of all stock and securities received in the transaction shall be the same as the basis of all the stock and securities in such corporation held immediately before the transaction allocated in the manner described in § 1.358-2. In the case of an exchange to which section 351, 361, or 374 applies in which, under the law applicable to the year in which the exchange was made, only nonrecognition property is received, the basis of all the stock and securities received in the exchange shall be the same as the basis of all property exchanged therefor. If [in] an exchange or distribution to which section 351, 356, 361, 371(b), or 374 applies both nonrecognition property and "other property" are received, the basis of all the property except "other property" held after the transaction shall be determined as described in the preceding two sentences decreased by the sum of the money and the fair market value of the "other property" (as of the date of the transaction) and increased by the sum of the amount treated as a dividend (if any) and the amount of the gain recognized on the exchange, but the term "gain" as here used does not include any portion of the recognized gain that was treated as a dividend. In any case in which a taxpayer transfers property with respect to which loss is recognized, such loss shall be reflected in determining the basis of the property received in the exchange. The basis of the "other property" is its fair market value as of the date of the transaction. See § 1.460-4(k)(3)(iv)(A) for rules relating to stock basis adjustments required where a contract accounted for using a long-term contract method of accounting is transferred in a transaction described in section 351 or a reorganization described in section 368(a)(1)(D) with respect to which the requirements of section 355 (or so much of section 356 as relates to section 355) are met.

(b) The application of paragraph (a) of this section may be illustrated by the following example:

Example. A purchased a share of stock in Corporation X in 1935 for $150. Since that date he has received distributions out of other than earnings and profits (as defined in section 316) totalling $60, so that his adjusted basis for the stock is $90. In a transaction qualifying under section 356, A exchanged this share for one share in Corporation Y, worth $100, cash in the amount of $10, and other property with a fair market value of $30. The exchange had the effect of the distribution of a dividend. A's ratable share of the earnings and profits of Corporation X accumu-

Reg. § 1.358-1(b)

lated after February 28, 1913, was $5. A realized a gain of $50 on the exchange, but the amount recognized is limited to $40, the sum of the cash received and the fair market value of the other property. Of the gain recognized, $5 is taxable as a dividend, and $35 as a gain from the exchange of property. The basis to A of the one share of stock of Corporation Y is $90, that is, the adjusted basis of the one share of stock of Corporation X ($90), decreased by the sum of the cash received ($10) and the fair market value of the other property received ($30) and increased by the sum of the amount treated as a dividend ($5) and the amount treated as a gain from the exchange of property ($35). The basis of the other property received is $30. [Reg. § 1.358-1.]

☐ [*T.D. 6152, 12-2-55. Amended by T.D. 6533, 1-18-61, T.D. 7616, 5-7-79 and T.D. 8995, 5-14-2002.*]

§ 1.358-2. Allocation of basis among nonrecognition property.—(a)(1) As used in this paragraph the term "stock" means stock which is not "other property" under section 356 or 371(b), stock with respect to which a distribution is made, and, in the case of a surrender of part of the stock of a particular class, the retained part of such stock. The term "securities" means securities (including, where appropriate, fractional parts of securities) which are not "other property" under section 356 or 371(b) and in the case of a surrender of part of the securities of a particular class, the retained part of such securities. Stock, or securities, as the case may be, which differ either because they are in different corporations or because the rights attributable to them differ (although they are in the same corporation) are considered different classes of stock or securities, as the case may be, for purposes of this section.

(2) If as the result of an exchange or distribution under the terms of section 354, 355, 356 or 371(b) a shareholder who owned stock of only one class before the transaction owns stock of two or more classes after the transaction, then the basis of all the stock held before the transaction (as adjusted under § 1.358-1) shall be allocated among the stock of all classes (whether or not such stock was received in the transaction) held immediately after the transaction in proportion to the fair market values of the stock of each class.

(3) If as the result of an exchange under the terms of section 354, 355, 356 or 371(b) a security holder who owned only securities, all of one class, before the transaction, owns securities or stock of more than one class, or owns both stock and securities, then the basis of all the securities held before the transaction (as adjusted under § 1.358-1) shall be allocated among all the stock and securities (whether or not received in the transaction) held immediately after the transaction in proportion to the fair market values of the stock of each class and the securities of each class.

(4) In every case in which, before the transactions, a person owned stock of more than one class or securities of more than one class or owned both stock and securities, a determination must be made, upon the basis of all the facts, of the stock or securities received with respect to stock and securities of each class held (whether or not surrendered). The allocation described in subparagraph (2) of this paragraph shall be separately made as to the stock of each class with respect to which there is an exchange or distribution and the allocation described in subparagraph (3) of this paragraph shall be separately made with respect to the securities of each class, part or all of which are surrendered in the exchange.

(5) Notwithstanding the provisions of subparagraphs (2), (3) and (4) of this paragraph, in any case in which a plan of recapitalization under section 368(a)(1)(E) provides that each holder of stock or securities of a particular class shall have an option to surrender some or none of such stock or securities in exchange for stock or securities, and a shareholder or security holder exchanges an identifiable part of his stock or securities, the basis of the part of the stock or securities retained shall remain unchanged and shall not be taken into account in determining the basis of the stock or securities received.

(b)(1) As used in this paragraph the term "stock" refers only to stock which is not "other property" under section 351, 361, or 374 and the term "securities" refers only to securities which are not "other property" under section 351, 361, or 374.

(2) If in an exchange to which section 351 or 361 applies property is transferred to a corporation and the transferor receives stock or securities of more than one class or receives both stock and securities, then the basis of the property transferred (as adjusted under § 1.358-1) shall be allocated among all of the stock and securities received in proportion to the fair market values of the stock of each class and the securities of each class.

(c) The application of paragraphs (a) and (b) of this section may be illustrated by the following examples:

Example (1). A, an individual, owns stock in Corporation X with an adjusted basis of $1,000. In a transaction qualifying under section 356 (so far as such section relates to section 354), he exchanged this stock for 20 shares of stock of Corporation Y worth $1,200 and securities of Corporation Y worth $400. A realizes a gain of $600 of which $400 is recognized. The adjusted basis in

Reg. § 1.358-2(a)(2)

A's hands of each share of the stock of Corporation Y is $50 determined by allocating the basis of the stock of Corporation X ratably to the stock of Corporation Y received in the exchange. The securities of Corporation Y have a basis in the hands of A of $400.

Example (2). B, an individual, owns a security in the principal amount of $10,000 with a basis of $5,000. In a transaction to which section 354 is applicable, he exchanges this security for four securities in the principal amount of $750 each, worth $800 each, four securities in the principal amount of $750 each, worth $600 each, class A common stock worth $1,000, and Class B common stock worth $400. B realizes a gain of $2,000 none of which is recognized. The basis of his original security, $5,000, will be allocated 32/70ths to the four securities worth $800, 24/70ths to the four securities worth $600, 10/70ths to the class A common stock, and 4/70ths to the class B common stock.

Example (3). C, an individual, owns stock of Corporation Y with a basis of $5,000 and owns a security issued by Corporation Y in the principal amount of $5,000 with a basis of $5,000. In a transaction to which section 354 is applicable, he exchanges the stock of Corporation Y for stock of Corporation Z with a value of $6,000, and he exchanges the security of Corporation Y for stock of Corporation Z worth $1,500 and a security of Corporation Z in the principal amount of $4,500 worth $4,500. No gain is recognized to C on either exchange. The basis of the stock of Corporation Z received for the stock of Corporation Y is $5,000. The bases of the stock and security of Corporation Z received in exchange for the security of Corporation Y are $1,250 and $3,750, respectively.

Example (4). D, an individual, owns stock in Corporation M with a basis of $15,000, worth $40,000, and owns a security issued by Corporation M in the principal amount of $5,000 with a basis of $4,000. In a transaction qualifying under section 356 (so far as such section relates to section 355), he exchanges the security of Corporation M for a security of Corporation O (a controlled corporation) in the principal amount of $5,000, worth $5,000, and exchanges one-half of his stock of Corporation M for stock of Corpora-

tion O worth $15,000 and a security of Corporation O in the principal amount of $5,000, worth $5,000. All of the stock and securities of Corporation O are distributed pursuant to the transaction. D realizes a gain of $12,500 on the exchange of the stock of Corporation M for the stock and security of Corporation O of which $5,000 is recognized. D also realizes a gain of $1,000 on the exchange of a security of Corporation M for a security of Corporation O, none of which is recognized. The basis of his stock of Corporation M held before the transaction is allocated 20/35ths to the stock of Corporation M held after the transaction and 15/35ths to the stock of Corporation O. The basis of the security of Corporation O received in exchange for his security of Corporation M is $4,000, the basis of the security of Corporation M exchanged. The basis of the security of Corporation O received with respect to D's stock of Corporation M is $5,000, its fair market value. [Reg. § 1.358-2.]

☐ [*T.D.* 6152, 12-2-55. *Amended by T.D.* 7616, 5-7-79 *and T.D.* 8648. 12-20-95.]

§ 1.358-3. Treatment of assumption of liabilities.—(a) For purposes of section 358, where a party to the exchange assumes a liability of a distributee or acquires from him property subject to a liability, the amount of such liability is to be treated as money received by the distributee upon the exchange, whether or not the assumption of liabilities resulted in a recognition of gain or loss to the taxpayer under the law applicable to the year in which the exchange was made.

(b) The application of paragraph (a) of this section may be illustrated by the following examples:

Example (1). A, an individual, owns property with an adjusted basis of $100,000 on which there is a purchase money mortgage of $25,000. On December 1, 1954, A organizes Corporation X to which he transfers the property in exchange for all the stock of Corporation X and the assumption by Corporation X of the mortgage. The capital stock of the Corporation X has a fair market value of $150,000. Under sections 351 and 357, no gain or loss is recognized to A. The basis in A's hands of the stock of Corporation X is $75,000, computed as follows:

Adjusted basis of property transferred	$100,000
Less: Amount of money received (amount of liabilities assumed)	25,000
Basis of Corporation X stock to A	$ 75,000

Example (2). A, an individual, owns property with an adjusted basis of $25,000 on which there is a mortgage of $50,000. On December 1, 1954, A organizes Corporation X to which he transfers the property in exchange for all the stock of Corporation X and the assumption by Corporation X of

the mortgage. The stock of Corporation X has a fair market value of $50,000. Under sections 351 and 357, gain is recognized to A in the amount of $25,000. The basis in A's hands of the stock of Corporation X is zero, computed as follows:

Reg. § 1.358-3(b)

Adjusted basis of property transferred	$ 25,000
Less: Amount of money received (amount of liabilities)	−50,000
Plus: Amount of gain recognized to taxpayer	$ 25,000
Basis of Corporation X stock to A	$ 0

[Reg. § 1.358-3.]

☐ [*T.D.* 6152, 12-2-55.]

§ 1.358-4. Exceptions.—(a) *Plan of reorganization adopted after October 22, 1968.* In the case of a plan or reorganization adopted after October 22, 1968, section 358 does not apply in determining the basis of property acquired by a corporation in connection with such reorganization by the exchange of its stock or securities (or by the exchange of stock or securities of a corporation which is in control of the acquiring corporation) as the consideration in whole or in part for the transfer of the property to it. See section 362 and the regulations pertaining to that section for rules relating to basis to corporations of property acquired in such cases.

* * *

[Reg. § 1.358-4.]

☐ [*T.D.* 6152, 12-2-55. *Amended by T.D.* 7422, 6-25-76.]

§ 1.358-6. Stock basis in certain triangular reorganizations.—(a) *Scope.* This section provides rules for computing the basis of a controlling corporation in the stock of a controlled corporation as the result of certain reorganizations involving the stock of the controlling corporation as described in paragraph (b) of this section. The rules of this section are in addition to rules under other provisions of the Internal Revenue Code and principles of law. See, e.g., section 1001 for the recognition of gain or loss by the controlled corporation on the exchange of property for the assets or stock of a target corporation in a reorganization described in section 368.

(b) *Triangular reorganizations*—(1) *Nomenclature.* For purposes of this section—

(i) *P* is a corporation—

(A) That is a party to a reorganization,

(B) That is in control (within the meaning of section 368(c)) of another party to the reorganization, and

(C) Whose stock is transferred pursuant to the reorganization.

(ii) *S* is a corporation—

(A) That is a party to the reorganization, and

(B) That is controlled by *P.*

(iii) *T* is a corporation that is another party to the reorganization.

(2) *Definitions of triangular reorganizations.* This section applies to the following reorganizations (which are referred to collectively as *triangular reorganizations*):

(i) *Forward triangular merger.* A forward triangular merger is a statutory merger of *T* and *S,* with *S* surviving, that qualifies as a reorganization under section 368(a)(1)(A) or (G) by reason of the application of section 368(a)(2)(D).

(ii) *Triangular C reorganization.* A triangular C reorganization is an acquisition by *S* of substantially all of *T*'s assets in exchange for *P* stock in a transaction that qualifies as a reorganization under section 368(a)(1)(C).

(iii) *Reverse triangular merger.* A reverse triangular merger is a statutory merger of *S* and *T,* with *T* surviving, that qualifies as a reorganization under section 368(a)(1)(A) by reason of the application of section 368(a)(2)(E).

(iv) *Triangular B reorganization.* A triangular B reorganization is an acquisition by *S* of *T* stock in exchange for *P* stock in a transaction that qualifies as a reorganization under section 368(a)(1)(B).

(c) *General rules.* Subject to the special rule provided in paragraph (d) of this section, *P*'s basis in the stock of *S* or *T,* as applicable, as a result of a triangular reorganization, is adjusted under the following rules—

(1) *Forward triangular merger or triangular C reorganization*—(i) *In general.* In a forward triangular merger or a triangular C reorganization *P*'s basis in its *S* stock is adjusted as if—

(A) *P* acquired the *T* assets acquired by *S* in the reorganization (and *P* assumed any liabilities which *S* assumed or to which the *T* assets acquired by *S* were subject) directly from *T* in a transaction in which *P*'s basis in the *T* assets was determined under section 362(b); and

(B) *P* transferred the *T* assets (and liabilities which *S* assumed or to which the *T* assets acquired by *S* were subject) to *S* in a transaction in which *P*'s basis in *S* stock was determined under section 358.

(ii) *Limitation.* If, in applying section 358, the amount of *T* liabilities assumed by *S* or to which the *T* assets acquired *by S* are subject equals or exceeds *T*'s aggregate adjusted basis in its assets, the amount of the adjustment under paragraph (c)(1)(i) of this section is zero. *P* recognizes no gain under section 357(c) as a result of a triangular reorganization.

(2) *Reverse triangular merger*—(i) *In general*—(A) *Treated as a forward triangular merger.* Except as otherwise provided in this paragraph

(c)(2), P's basis in its T stock acquired in a reverse triangular merger equals its basis in its S stock immediately before the transaction adjusted as if T had merged into S in a forward triangular merger to which paragraph (c)(1) of this section applies.

(B) *Allocable share.* If P acquires less than all of the T stock in the transaction, the basis adjustment described in paragraph (c)(2)(i)(A) of this section is reduced in proportion to the percentage of T stock not acquired in the transaction. The percentage of T stock not acquired in the transaction is determined by taking into account the fair market value of all classes of T stock.

(C) *Special rule if P owns T stock before the transaction.* Solely for purposes of paragraphs (c)(2)(i)(A) and (B) of this section, if P owns T stock before the transaction, P may treat that stock as acquired in the transaction or not, without regard to the form of the transaction.

(ii) *Reverse triangular merger that qualifies as a section 351 transfer or section 368(a)(1)(B) reorganization.* Notwithstanding paragraph (c)(2)(i) of this section, if a reorganization qualifies as both a reverse triangular merger and as a section 351 transfer or as both a reverse triangular merger and a reorganization under section 368(a)(1)(B), P can—

(A) Determine the basis in its T stock as if paragraph (c)(2)(i) of this section applies; or

(B) Determine the basis in the T stock acquired as if P acquired such stock from the former T shareholders in a transaction in which P's basis in the T stock was determined under section 362(b).

(3) *Triangular B reorganization.* In a triangular B reorganization P's basis in its S stock is adjusted as if—

(i) P acquired the T stock acquired by S in the reorganization directly from the T shareholders in a transaction in which P's basis in the T stock was determined under section 362(b); and

(ii) P transferred the T stock to S in a transaction in which P's basis in its S stock was determined under section 358.

(4) *Examples.* The rules of this paragraph (c) are illustrated by the following examples. For purposes of these examples, P, S, and T are domestic corporations, P and S do not file consolidated returns, P owns all of the only class of S stock, the P stock exchanged in the transaction satisfies the requirements of the applicable triangular reorganization provisions, and the facts set forth the only corporate activity.

Example 1. Forward triangular merger. (a) *Facts.* T has assets with an aggregate basis of $60 and fair market value of $100 and no liabilities.

Pursuant to a plan, P forms S with $5 cash (which S retains), and T merges into S. In the merger, the T shareholders receive P stock worth $100 in exchange for their T stock. The transaction is a reorganization to which sections 368(a)(1)(A) and (a)(2)(D) apply.

(b) *Basis adjustment.* Under § 1.358-6(c) (1), P's $5 basis in its S stock is adjusted as if P acquired the T assets acquired by S in the reorganization directly from T in a transaction in which P's basis in the T assets was determined under section 362(b). Under section 362(b), P would have an aggregate basis of $60 in the T assets. P is then treated as if it transferred the T assets to S in a transaction in which P's basis in the S stock was determined under section 358. Under section 358, P's $5 basis in its S stock would be increased by the $60 basis in the T assets deemed transferred. Consequently, P has a $65 basis in its S stock as a result of the reorganization.

(c) *Use of pre-existing S.* The facts are the same as paragraph (a) of this *Example 1,* except that S is an operating company with substantial assets that has been in existence for several years. P has a $110 basis in the S stock. Under § 1.358-6(c)(1), P's $110 basis in its S stock is increased by the $60 basis in the T assets deemed transferred. Consequently, P has a $170 basis in its S stock as a result of the reorganization.

(d) *Mixed consideration.* The facts are the same as paragraph (a) of this *Example 1,* except that the T shareholders receive P stock worth $80 and $20 cash from P. Under section 358, P's $5 basis in its S stock is increased by the $60 basis in the T assets deemed transferred. Consequently, P has a $65 basis in its S stock as a result of the reorganization.

(e) *Liabilities.* The facts are the same as paragraph (a) of this *Example 1,* except that T's assets are subject to $50 of liabilities, and the T shareholders receive $50 of P stock in exchange for their T stock. Under section 358, P's basis in its S stock is increased by the $60 basis in the T assets deemed transferred and decreased by the $50 of liabilities to which the T assets acquired by S are subject. Consequently, P has a net basis adjustment of $10, and a $15 basis in its S stock as a result of the reorganization.

(f) *Liabilities in excess of basis.* The facts are the same as in paragraph (a) of this *Example 1,* except that T's assets are subject to liabilities of $90, and the T shareholders receive $10 of P stock in exchange for their T stock in the reorganization. Under § 1.358-6(c)(1)(ii), the adjustment under § 1.358-6(c) is zero if the amount of the liabilities which S assumed or to which the T assets acquired by S are subject exceeds the aggre-

Reg. § 1.358-6(c)(4)

gate adjusted basis in T's assets. Consequently, P has no adjustment in its S stock, and P has a $5 basis in its S stock as a result of the reorganization.

Example 2. Reverse triangular merger. (a) *Facts.* T has assets with an aggregate basis of $60 and a fair market value of $100 and no liabilities. P has a $110 basis in its S stock. Pursuant to a plan, S merges into T with T surviving. In the merger, the T shareholders receive $10 cash from P and P stock worth $90 in exchange for their T stock. The transaction is a reorganization to which sections 368(a)(1)(A) and (a)(2)(E) apply.

(b) *Basis adjustment.* Under § 1.358-6(c)(2)(i)(A), P's basis in the T stock acquired is P's $110 basis in its S stock before the transaction, adjusted as if T had merged into S in a forward triangular merger to which § 1.358-6(c)(1) applies. In such a case, P's $110 basis in its S stock before the transaction would have been increased by the $60 basis of the T assets deemed transferred. Consequently, P has a $170 basis in its T stock immediately after the transaction.

(c) *Reverse triangular merger that also qualifies under section 368(a)(1)(B).* The facts relating to T are the same as in paragraph (a) of this *Example 2.* P, however, forms S pursuant to the plan of reorganization. The T shareholders receive $100 worth of P stock (and no cash) in exchange for their T stock. The T shareholders have an aggregate basis in their T stock of $85 immediately before the reorganization. The reorganization qualifies as both a reverse triangular merger and a reorganization under section 368(a)(1)(B). Under § 1.358-6(c)(2)(ii), P may determine its basis in its T stock either as if § 1.358-6(c)(2)(i) applied to the T stock acquired, or as if P acquired the T stock from the former T shareholders in a transaction in which P's basis in the T stock was determined under section 362(b). Accordingly, P may determine a basis in its T stock of $60 (T's net asset basis) or $85 (the T shareholders' aggregate basis in the T stock immediately before the reorganization).

(d) *Allocable share in a reverse triangular merger.* The facts are the same as in paragraph (a) of this *Example 2,* except that X, a 10% shareholder of T, does not participate in the transaction. The remaining T shareholders receive $10 cash from P and P stock worth $80 for their T stock. P owns 90% of the T stock after the transaction. Under § 1.358-6(c)(2)(i)(A), P's basis in its T stock is P's $110 basis in its S stock before the reorganization, adjusted as if T had merged into S in a forward triangular merger. In such a case, P's basis would have been adjusted by the $60 basis in the T assets deemed transferred. Under

§ 1.358-6(c)(2)(i)(B), however, the basis adjustment determined under § 1.358-6(c)(2)(i)(A) is reduced in proportion to the percentage of T stock not acquired by P in the transaction. The percentage of T stock not acquired in the transaction is 10%. Therefore, P reduces its $60 basis adjustment by 10%, resulting in a net basis adjustment of $54. Consequently, P has a $164 basis in its T stock as a result of the transaction.

(e) *P's ownership of T stock.* The facts are the same as in paragraph (a) of this *Example 2,* except that P owns 10% of the T stock before the transaction. P's basis in that T stock is $8. All the T shareholders other than P surrender their T stock for $10 cash from P and P stock worth $80. P does not surrender the stock in the transaction. Under § 1.358-6(c)(i)(C), P may treat its T stock owned before the transaction as acquired in the transaction or not. If P treats that T stock as acquired in the transaction, P's basis in that T stock and the T stock actually acquired in the transaction equals P's $110 basis in its S stock before the transaction, adjusted by the $60 basis of the T assets deemed transferred, for a total basis of $170. If P treats its T stock as not acquired, P retains its $8 pre-transaction basis in that stock. P's basis in its other T shares equals P's $110 basis in its S stock before the transaction, adjusted by $54 (the $60 basis in the T assets deemed transferred, reduced by 10%), for a total basis of $164 in those shares. See § 1.358-6(c)(2)(i)(A) and (B). Consequently, if P treats its T shares as not acquired, P's total basis in all of its T shares is $172.

Example 3. Triangular B reorganization. (a) *Facts.* T has assets with a fair market value of $100 and no liabilities. The T shareholders have an aggregate basis in their T stock of $85 immediately before the reorganization. Pursuant to a plan, P forms S with $5 cash and S acquires all of the T stock in exchange for $100 of P stock. The transaction is a reorganization to which section 368(a)(1)(B) applies.

(b) *Basis adjustment.* Under § 1.358-6(c)(3), P adjusts its $5 basis in its S stock by treating P as if it acquired the T stock acquired by S in the reorganization directly from the T shareholders in exchange for the P stock in a transaction in which P's basis in the T stock was determined under section 362(b). Under section 362(b), P would have an aggregate basis of $85 in the T stock received by S in the reorganization. P is then treated as if it transferred the T stock to S in a transaction in which P's basis in the S stock was determined under section 358. Under section 358, P's basis in its S stock would be increased by the $85 basis in the T stock deemed transferred. Consequently, P has a $90 basis in its S stock as a result of the reorganization.

* * *

[Reg. § 1.358-6.]

☐ [*T.D.* 8648, 12-20-95.]

§ 1.361-1. Nonrecognition of gain or loss to corporations.—Section 361 provides the general rule that no gain or loss shall be recognized if a corporation, a party to a reorganization, exchanges property in pursuance of the plan of reorganization solely for stock or securities in another corporation, a party to the reorganization. This provision includes only stock and securities received in connection with a reorganization defined in section 368(a). It also includes nonvoting stock and securities in a corporation, a party to a reorganization, received in a transaction to which section 368(a)(1)(C) is applicable only by reason of section 368(a)(2)(B). [Reg. § 1.361-1.]

☐ [*T.D.* 6152, 12-2-55.]

§ 1.362-1. Basis to corporations.—(a) *In general.* Section 362 provides, as a general rule, that if property was acquired on or after June 22, 1954, by a corporation (1) in connection with a transaction to which section 351 (relating to transfer of property to corporation controlled by transferor) applies, (2) as paid-in surplus or as a contribution to capital, or (3) in connection with a reorganization to which part III, subchapter C, chapter 1 of the Code applies, then the basis shall be the same as it would be in the hands of the transferor, increased in the amount of gain recognized to the transferor on such transfer. (See also § 1.362-2.) See § 1.460-4(k)(3)(iv)(B)(*2*) for rules relating to adjustments to the basis of certain contracts accounted for using a long-term contract method of accounting that are acquired in certain liquidations described in section 332.

(b) *Exceptions.* (1) In the case of a plan of reorganization adopted after October 22, 1968, section 362 does not apply if the property acquired in connection with such reorganization consists of stock or securities in a corporation a party to the reorganization, unless acquired by the exchange of stock or securities of the transferee (or of a corporation which is in control of the transferee) as the consideration in whole or in part for the transfer.

* * *

[Reg. § 1.362-1.]

☐ [*T.D.* 6152, 12-2-55. *Amended by T.D. 7422, 6-25-76 and T.D. 8995, 5-14-2002.*]

§ 1.362-2. Certain contributions to capital.— The following regulations shall be used in the application of section 362(c):

(a) Property deemed to be acquired with contributed money shall be that property, if any, the acquisition of which was the purpose motivating the contribution;

(b) In the case of an excess of the amount of money contributed over the cost of the property deemed to be acquired with such money (as defined in (a) above) such excess shall be applied to the reduction of the basis (but not below zero) of other properties held by the corporation, on the last day of the 12-month period beginning on the day the contribution is received, in the following order—

(1) All property of a character subject to an allowance for depreciation (not including any properties as to which a deduction for amortization is allowable),

(2) Property with respect to which a deduction for amortization is allowable,

(3) Property with respect to which a deduction for depletion is allowable under section 611 but not under section 613, and

(4) All other remaining properties.

The reduction of the basis of each of the properties within each of the above categories shall be made in proportion to the relative bases of such properties.

(c) With the consent of the Commissioner, the taxpayer may, however, have the basis of the various units of property within a particular category adjusted in a manner different from the general rule set forth in paragraph (b) of this section. Variations from such rule may, for example, involve adjusting the basis of only certain units of the taxpayer's property within a given category. A request for variations from the general rule should be filed by the taxpayer with its return for the taxable year for which the transfer of the property has occurred. [Reg. § 1.362-2.]

☐ [*T.D.* 6152, 12-2-55.]

§ 1.368-1. Purpose and scope of exception of reorganization exchanges.—(a) *Reorganizations.* As used in the regulations under parts I, II, and III (section 301 and following), subchapter C of the Code, the terms ''reorganization'' and ''party to a reorganization'' mean only a reorganization or a party to a reorganization as defined in subsections (a) and (b) of section 368. In determining whether a transaction qualifies as a reorganization under section 368(a), the transaction must be evaluated under relevant provisions of law, including the step transaction doctrine. But see §§ 1.368-2(f) and (k) and 1.338-3(d). The preceding two sentences apply to transactions occurring after January 28, 1998, except that they do not apply to any transaction occurring pursuant to a written agreement which is binding on Janu-

Reg. § 1.368-1(a)

ary 28, 1998, and at all times thereafter. With respect to insolvency reorganizations, see part IV of subchapter C, chapter 1 of the Code.

(b) *Purpose.* Under the general rule, upon the exchange of property, gain or loss must be accounted for if the new property differs in a material particular, either in kind or in extent, from the old property. The purpose of the reorganization provisions of the Code is to except from the general rule certain specifically described exchanges incident to such readjustments of corporate structures made in one of the particular ways specified in the Code, as are required by business exigencies and which effect only a readjustment of continuing interest in property under modified corporate forms. Requisite to a reorganization under the Internal Revenue Code are a continuity of the business enterprise through the issuing corporation under the modified corporate form as described in paragraph (d) of this section, and (except as provided in section 368(a)(1)(D)) a continuity of interest as described in paragraph (e) of this section. (For rules regarding the continuity of interest requirement under section 355, see § 1.355-2(c).) For purposes of this section, the term *issuing corporation* means the acquiring corporation (as that term is used in section 368(a)), except that, in determining whether a reorganization qualifies as a triangular reorganization (as defined in § 1.358-6(b)(2)), the issuing corporation means the corporation in control of the acquiring corporation. The preceding three sentences apply to transactions occurring after January 28, 1998, except that they do not apply to any transaction occurring pursuant to a written agreement which is binding on January 28, 1998, and at all times thereafter. The continuity of business enterprise requirement is described in paragraph (d) of this section. The Code recognizes as a reorganization the amalgamation (occurring in a specified way) of two corporate enterprises under a single corporate structure if there exists among the holders of the stock and securities of either of the old corporations the requisite continuity of interest in the new corporation, but there is not a reorganization if the holders of the stock and securities of the old corporation are merely the holders of short-term notes in the new corporation. In order to exclude transactions not intended to be included, the specifications of the reorganization provisions of the law are precise. Both the terms of the specifications and their underlying assumptions and purposes must be satisfied in order to entitle the taxpayer to the benefit of the exception from the general rule. Accordingly, under the Code, a short-term purchase money note is not a security of a party to a reorganization, an ordinary dividend is to be treated as an ordinary dividend, and a sale is nevertheless to be treated as a sale even though

the mechanics of a reorganization have been set up.

(c) *Scope.* The nonrecognition of gain or loss is prescribed for two specifically described types of exchanges, viz.: The exchange that is provided for in section 354(a)(1) in which stock or securities in a corporation, a party to a reorganization, are, in pursuance of a plan of reorganization, exchanged for the stock or securities in a corporation, a party to the same reorganization; and the exchange that is provided for in section 361(a) in which a corporation, a party to a reorganization, exchanges property, in pursuance of a plan of reorganization, for stock or securities in another corporation, a party to the same reorganization. Section 368(a)(1) limits the definition of the term "reorganization" to six kinds of transactions and excludes all others. From its context, the term "a party to a reorganization" can only mean a party to a transaction specifically defined as a reorganization by section 368(a). Certain rules respecting boot received in either of the two types of exchanges provided for in section 354(a)(1) and section 361(a) are prescribed in sections 356, 357, and 361(b). A special rule respecting a transfer of property with a liability in excess of its basis is prescribed in section 357(c). Under section 367 a limitation is placed on all these provisions by providing that except under specified conditions foreign corporations shall not be deemed within their scope. The provisions of the Code referred to in this paragraph are inapplicable unless there is a plan of reorganization. A plan of reorganization must contemplate the bona fide execution of one of the transactions specifically described as a reorganization in section 368(a) and for the bona fide consummation of each of the requisite acts under which nonrecognition of gain is claimed. Such transaction and such acts must be an ordinary and necessary incident of the conduct of the enterprise and must provide for a continuation of the enterprise. A scheme, which involves an abrupt departure from normal reorganization procedure in connection with a transaction on which the imposition of tax is imminent, such as a mere device that puts on the form of a corporate reorganization as a disguise for concealing its real character, and the object and accomplishment of which is the consummation of a preconceived plan having no business or corporate purpose, is not a plan of reorganization.

(d) *Continuity of business enterprise*—(1) *General rule.* Continuity of business enterprise (COBE) requires that the issuing corporation (P), as defined in paragraph (b) of this section, either continue the target corporation's (T's) historic business or use a significant portion of T's historic business assets in a business. The preceding sentence applies to transactions occurring after January 28, 1998, except that it does not apply to any transaction occurring pursuant to a written agreement which is binding on January 28, 1998, and at all times thereafter. The application of this general rule to certain transactions, such as mergers of holding companies, will depend on all facts and circumstances. The policy underlying this general rule, which is to ensure that reorganizations are limited to readjustments of continuing interests in property under modified corporate form, provides the guidance necessary to make these facts and circumstances determinations.

(2) *Business continuity.* (i) The continuity of business enterprise requirement is satisfied if *P* continues *T*'s historic business. The fact *P* is in the same line of business as *T* tends to establish the requisite continuity, but is not alone sufficient.

(ii) If *T* has more than one line of business, continuity of business enterprise requires only that *P* continue a significant line of business.

(iii) In general, a corporation's historic business is the business it has conducted most recently. However, a corporation's historic business is not one the corporation enters into as part of a plan of reorganization.

(iv) All facts and circumstances are considered in determining the time when the plan comes into existence and in determining whether a line of business is "significant".

(3) *Asset continuity.* (i) The continuity of business enterprise requirement is satisfied if *P* uses a significant portion of *T*'s historic business assets in a business.

(ii) A corporation's historic business assets are the assets used in its historic business. Business assets may include stock and securities and intangible operating assets such as good will, patents, and trademarks, whether or not they have a tax basis.

(iii) In general, the determination of the portion of a corporation's assets considered "significant" is based on the relative importance of the assets to operation of the business. However, all other facts and circumstances, such as the net fair market value of those assets, will be considered.

(4) *Acquired assets or stock held by members of the qualified group or partnerships.* The following rules apply in determining whether the COBE requirement of paragraph (d)(1) of this section is satisfied:

(i) *Businesses and assets of members of a qualified group.* The issuing corporation is treated as holding all of the businesses and assets of all of the members of the qualified group, as defined in paragraph (d)(4)(ii) of this section.

(ii) *Qualified group.* A qualified group is one or more chains of corporations connected through stock ownership with the issuing corporation, but only if the issuing corporation owns directly stock meeting the requirements of section 368(c) in at least one other corporation, and stock meeting the requirements of section 368(c) in each of the corporations (except the issuing corporation) is owned directly by one of the other corporations.

(iii) *Partnerships*—(A) *Partnership assets.* Each partner of a partnership will be treated as owning the T business assets used in a business of the partnership in accordance with that partner's interest in the partnership.

(B) *Partnership businesses.* The issuing corporation will be treated as conducting a business of a partnership if—

(*1*) Members of the qualified group, in the aggregate, own an interest in the partnership representing a significant interest in that partnership business; or

(*2*) One or more members of the qualified group have active and substantial management functions as a partner with respect to that partnership business.

(C) *Conduct of the historic T business in a partnership.* If a significant historic T business is conducted in a partnership, the fact that P is treated as conducting such T business under paragraph (d)(4)(iii)(B) of this section tends to establish the requisite continuity, but is not alone sufficient.

(iv) *Effective date.* This paragraph (d)(4) applies to transactions occurring after January 28, 1998, except that it does not apply to any transaction occurring pursuant to a written agreement which is binding on January 28, 1998, and at all times thereafter.

(5) *Examples.* The following examples illustrate this paragraph (d). All corporations have only one class of stock outstanding. The preceding sentence and paragraph (d)(5) *Example 6* through *Example 12* apply to transactions occurring after January 28, 1998, except that they do not apply to any transaction occurring pursuant to a written agreement which is binding on January 28, 1998, and at all times thereafter.

Example 1. T conducts three lines of business: manufacture of synthetic resins, manufacture of chemicals for the textile industry, and distribution of chemicals. The three lines of business are approximately equal in value. On July 1, 1981, T sells the synthetic resin and chemical distribution businesses to a third party for cash and marketable securities. On December 31, 1981, T transfers all of its assets to P solely for P voting stock. *P* continues the chemical manufacturing business without interruption. The continuity of business enterprise requirement is met. Continuity of business enterprise requires only that *P* continue one of *T*'s three significant lines of business.

Example 2. P manufactures computers and *T* manufactures components for computers. *T* sells all of its output to *P*. On January 1, 1981, *P* decides to buy imported components only. On March 1, 1981, *T* merges into *P*. *P* continues buying imported components but retains *T*'s equipment as a backup source of supply. The use of the equipment as a backup source of supply constitutes use of a significant portion of *T*'s historic business assets, thus establishing continuity of business enterprise. *P* is not required to continue *T*'s business.

Example 3. T is a manufacturer of boys' and men's trousers. On January 1, 1978, as part of a plan of reorganization, *T* sold all of its assets to a third party for cash and purchased a highly diversified portfolio of stocks and bonds. As part of the plan *T* operates an investment business until July 1, 1981. On that date, the plan of reorganization culminates in a transfer by *T* of all its assets to *P*, a regulated investment company, solely in exchange for *P* voting stock. The continuity of business enterprise requirement is not met. *T*'s investment activity is not its historic business, and the stocks and bonds are not *T*'s historic business assets.

Example 4. T manufactures children's toys and *P* distributes steel and allied products. On January 1, 1981, *T* sells all of its assets to a third party for $100,000 cash and $900,000 in notes. On March 1, 1981, *T* merges into *P*. Continuity of business enterprise is lacking. The use of the sales proceeds in *P*'s business is not sufficient.

Example 5. T manufactures farm machinery and *P* operates a lumber mill. *T* merges into *P*. *P* disposes of *T*'s assets immediately after the merger as part of the plan of reorganization. *P* does not continue *T*'s farm machinery manufacturing business. Continuity of business enterprise is lacking.

Example 6. Use of a significant portion of T's historic business assets by the qualified group. (i) *Facts.* T operates an auto parts distributorship. P owns 80 percent of the stock of a holding company (HC). HC owns 80 percent of the stock of ten subsidiaries, S-1 through S-10. S-1 through S-10 each separately operate a full service gas station. Pursuant to a plan of reorganization, T merges into P and the T shareholders receive solely P stock. As part of the plan of reorganization, P transfers T's assets to HC, which in turn transfers some of the T assets to each of the ten subsidiar-

ies. No one subsidiary receives a significant portion of T's historic business assets. Each of the subsidiaries will use the T assets in the operation of its full service gas station. No P subsidiary will be an auto parts distributor.

(ii) *Continuity of business enterprise.* Under paragraph (d)(4)(i) of this section, P is treated as conducting the ten gas station businesses of S-1 through S-10 and as holding the historic T assets used in those businesses. P is treated as holding all the assets and conducting the businesses of all of the members of the qualified group, which includes S-1 through S-10 (paragraphs (d)(4)(i) and (ii) of this section). No member of the qualified group continues T's historic distributorship business. However, subsidiaries S-1 through S-10 continue to use the historic T assets in a business. Even though no one corporation of the qualified group is using a significant portion of T's historic business assets in a business, the COBE requirement of paragraph (d)(1) of this section is satisfied because, in the aggregate, the qualified group is using a significant portion of T's historic business assets in a business.

Example 7. Continuation of the historic T business in a Partnership satisfies continuity of business enterprise. (i) *Facts.* T manufactures ski boots. P owns all of the stock of S-1. S-1 owns all of the stock of S-2, and S-2 owns all of the stock of S-3. T merges into P and the T shareholders receive consideration consisting of P stock and cash. The T ski boot business is to be continued and expanded. In anticipation of this expansion, P transfers all of the T assets to S-1, S-1 transfers all of the T assets to S-2, and S-2 transfers all of the T assets to S-3. S-3 and X (an unrelated party) form a new partnership (PRS). As part of the plan of reorganization, S-3 transfers all the T assets to PRS, and S-3, in its capacity as a partner, performs active and substantial management functions for the PRS ski boot business, including making significant business decisions and regularly participating in the overall supervision, direction, and control of the employees of the ski boot business. S-3 receives a 20 percent interest in PRS. X transfers cash in exchange for an 80 percent interest in PRS.

(ii) *Continuity of business enterprise.* Under paragraph (d)(4)(iii)(B)(*2*) of this section, P is treated as conducting T's historic business because S-3 performs active and substantial management functions for the ski boot business in S-3's capacity as a partner. P is treated as holding all the assets and conducting the businesses of all of the members of the qualified group, which includes S-3 (paragraphs (d)(4)(i) and (ii) of this section). The COBE requirement of paragraph (d)(1) of this section is satisfied.

Reg. § 1.368-1(d)(5)

Example 8. Continuation of the historic T business in a partnership does not satisfy continuity of business enterprise. (i) *Facts.* The facts are the same as *Example 7* except that S-3 transfers the historic T business to PRS in exchange for a 1 percent interest in PRS.

(ii) *Continuity of business enterprise.* Under paragraph (d)(4)(iii)(B)(*2*) of this section, P is treated as conducting T's historic business because S-3 performs active and substantial management functions for the ski boot business in S-3's capacity as a partner. The fact that a significant historic T business is conducted in PRS, and P is treated as conducting such T business under (d)(4)(iii)(B) tends to establish the requisite continuity, but is not alone sufficient (paragraph (d)(4)(iii)(C) of this section). The COBE requirement of paragraph (d)(1) of this section is not satisfied.

Example 9. Continuation of the T historic business in a partnership satisfies continuity of business enterprise. (i) *Facts.* The facts are the same as *Example 7* except that S-3 transfers the historic T business to PRS in exchange for a 33 1/3 percent interest in PRS, and no member of P's qualified group performs active and substantial management functions for the ski boot business operated in PRS.

(ii) *Continuity of business enterprise.* Under paragraph (d)(4)(iii)(B)(*1*) of this section, P is treated as conducting T's historic business because S-3 owns an interest in the partnership representing a significant interest in that partnership business. P is treated as holding all the assets and conducting the businesses of all of the members of the qualified group, which includes S-3 (paragraphs (d)(4)(i) and (ii) of this section). The COBE requirement of paragraph (d)(1) of this section is satisfied.

Example 10. Use of T's historic business assets in a partnership business. (i) *Facts.* T is a fabric distributor. P owns all of the stock of S-1. T merges into P and the T shareholders receive solely P stock. S-1 and X (an unrelated party) own interests in a partnership (PRS). As part of the plan of reorganization, P transfers all of the T assets to S-1, and S-1 transfers all the T assets to PRS, increasing S-1's percentage interest in PRS from 5 to 33 1/3 percent. After the transfer, X owns the remaining 66 2/3 percent interest in PRS. Almost all of the T assets consist of T's large inventory of fabric, which PRS uses to manufacture sportswear. All of the T assets are used in the sportswear business. No member of P's qualified group performs active and substantial management functions for the sportswear business operated in PRS.

(ii) *Continuity of business enterprise.* Under paragraph (d)(4)(iii)(A) of this section, S-1 is treated as owning 33 1/3 percent of the T assets used in the PRS sportswear manufacturing business. Under paragraph (d)(4)(iii)(B)(*1*) of this section, P is treated as conducting the sportswear manufacturing business because S-1 owns an interest in the partnership representing a significant interest in that partnership business. P is treated as holding all the assets and conducting the businesses of all of the members of the qualified group, which includes S-1 (paragraphs (d)(4)(i) and (ii) of this section). The COBE requirement of paragraph (d)(1) of this section is satisfied.

Example 11. Aggregation of partnership interests among members of the qualified group: use of T's historic business assets in a partnership business. (i) *Facts.* The facts are the same as *Example 10,* except that S-1 transfers all the T assets to PRS, and P and X each transfer cash to PRS in exchange for partnership interests. After the transfers, P owns 11 percent, S-1 owns 22 1/3 percent, and X owns 66 2/3 percent of PRS.

(ii) *Continuity of business enterprise.* Under paragraph (d)(4)(iii)(B)(*1*) of this section, P is treated as conducting the sportswear manufacturing business because members of the qualified group, in the aggregate, own an interest in the partnership representing a significant interest in that business. P is treated as owning 11 percent of the assets directly, and S-1 is treated as owning 22 1/3 percent of the assets, used in the PRS sportswear business (paragraph (d)(4)(iii)(A) of this section). P is treated as holding all the assets of all of the members of the qualified group, which includes S-1, and thus in the aggregate, P is treated as owning 33 1/3 of the T assets (paragraph (d)(4)(i) and (ii) of this section). The COBE requirement of paragraph (d)(1) of this section is satisfied because P is treated as using a significant portion of T's historic business assets in its sportswear manufacturing business.

Example 12. Tiered partnerships: use of T's historic business assets in a partnership business. (i) *Facts.* T owns and manages a commercial office building in state Z. Pursuant to a plan of reorganization, T merges into P, solely in exchange for P stock, which is distributed to the T shareholders. P transfers all of the T assets to a partnership, PRS-1, which owns and operates television stations nationwide. After the transfer, P owns a 50 percent interest in PRS-1. P does not have active and substantial management functions as a partner with respect to the PRS-1 business. X, not a member of P's qualified group, owns the remaining 50 percent interest in PRS-1. PRS-1, in an effort to expand its state Z television operation, enters into a joint venture with U, an unrelated party. As part of the plan of reorganization, PRS-1 transfers all the T assets and its state Z television station to PRS-2, in exchange for a 75 percent partnership interest. U contributes cash to PRS-2 in exchange for a 25 percent partnership interest and oversees the management of the state Z television operation. PRS-1 does not actively and substantially manage PRS-2's business. PRS-2's state Z operations are moved into the acquired T office building. All of the assets that P acquired from T are used in PRS-2's business.

(ii) *Continuity of business enterprise.* Under paragraph (d)(4)(iii)(A) of this section, PRS-1 is treated as owning 75 percent of the T assets used in PRS-2's business. P, in turn, is treated as owning 50 percent of PRS-1's interest the T assets. Thus, P is treated as owning 37 1/2 percent (50 percent×75 percent) of the T assets used in the PRS-2 business. Under paragraph (d)(4)(iii)(B)(1) of this section, P is treated as conducting PRS-2's business, the operation of the state Z television station, and under paragraph (d)(4)(iii)(A) of this section, P is treated as using 37 1/2 percent of the historic T business assets in that business. The COBE requirement of paragraph (d)(1) of this section is satisfied because P is treated as using a significant portion of T's historic business assets in its television business.

(e) *Continuity of interest*—(1) *General rule*—(i) The purpose of the continuity of interest requirement is to prevent transactions that resemble sales from qualifying for nonrecognition of gain or loss available to corporate reorganizations. Continuity of interest requires that in substance a substantial part of the value of the proprietary interests in the target corporation be preserved in the reorganization. A proprietary interest in the target corporation is preserved if, in a potential reorganization, it is exchanged for a proprietary interest in the issuing corporation (as defined in paragraph (b) of this section), it is exchanged by the acquiring corporation for a direct interest in the target corporation enterprise, or it otherwise continues as a proprietary interest in the target corporation. However, a proprietary interest in the target corporation is not preserved if, in connection with the potential reorganization, it is acquired by the issuing corporation for consideration other than stock of the issuing corporation, or stock of the issuing corporation furnished in exchange for a proprietary interest in the target corporation in the potential reorganization is redeemed. All facts and circumstances must be considered in determining whether, in substance, a proprietary interest in the target corporation is preserved. For purposes of the continuity of interest requirement, a mere disposition of stock of the target corporation prior to a potential reorganization to persons not related (as defined in paragraph (e)(3) of this section determined without regard to paragraph (e)(3)(i)(A) of this section) to the target corporation or to persons not related (as defined in paragraph (e)(3) of this section) to the issuing corporation is disregarded and a mere disposition of stock of the issuing corporation received in a potential reorganization to persons not related (as defined in paragraph (e)(3) of this section) to the issuing corporation is disregarded.

(ii) For purposes of paragraph (e)(1)(i) of this section, a proprietary interest in the target corporation (other than one held by the acquiring corporation) is not preserved to the extent that consideration received prior to a potential reorganization, either in a redemption of the target corporation stock or in a distribution with respect to the target corporation stock, is treated as other property or money received in the exchange for purposes of section 356, or would be so treated if the target shareholder also had received stock of the issuing corporation in exchange for stock owned by the shareholder in the target corporation.

(2) *Related person acquisitions.* A proprietary interest in the target corporation is not preserved if, in connection with a potential reorganization, a person related (as defined in paragraph (e)(3) of this section) to the issuing corporation acquires, with consideration other than a proprietary interest in the issuing corporation, stock of the target corporation or stock of the issuing corporation furnished in exchange for a proprietary interest in the target corporation in the potential reorganization, except to the extent those persons who were the direct or indirect owners of the target corporation prior to the potential reorganization maintain a direct or indirect proprietary interest in the issuing corporation.

(3) *Definition of related person*—(i) *In general.* For purposes of this paragraph (e), two corporations are related persons if either—

(A) The corporations are members of the same affiliated group as defined in section 1504 (determined without regard to section 1504(b)); or

(B) A purchase of the stock of one corporation by another corporation would be treated as a distribution in redemption of the stock of the first corporation under section 304(a)(2) (determined without regard to § 1.1502-80(b)).

(ii) *Special rules.* The following rules apply solely for purposes of this paragraph (e)(3):

(A) A corporation will be treated as related to another corporation if such relationship exists immediately before or immediately after the acquisition of the stock involved.

Reg. § 1.368-1(e)(1)

(B) A corporation, other than the target corporation or a person related (as defined in paragraph (e)(3) of this section determined without regard to paragraph (e)(3)(i)(A) of this section) to the target corporation, will be treated as related to the issuing corporation if the relationship is created in connection with the potential reorganization.

(4) *Acquisitions by partnerships.* For purposes of this paragraph (e), each partner of a partnership will be treated as owning or acquiring any stock owned or acquired, as the case may be, by the partnership in accordance with that partner's interest in the partnership. If a partner is treated as acquiring any stock by reason of the application of this paragraph (e)(4), the partner is also treated as having furnished its share of any consideration furnished by the partnership to acquire the stock in accordance with that partner's interest in the partnership.

(5) *Successors and predecessors.* For purposes of this paragraph (e), any reference to the issuing corporation or the target corporation includes a reference to any successor or predecessor of such corporation, except that the target corporation is not treated as a predecessor of the issuing corporation and the issuing corporation is not treated as a successor of the target corporation.

(6) *Examples.* For purposes of the examples in this paragraph (e)(6), P is the issuing corporation, T is the target corporation, S is a wholly owned subsidiary of P, all corporations have only one class of stock outstanding, A and B are individuals, PRS is a partnership, all reorganization requirements other than the continuity of interest requirement are satisfied, and the transaction is not otherwise subject to recharacterization. The following examples illustrate the application of this paragraph (e):

Example 1. Sale of stock to third party. (i) *Sale of issuing corporation stock after merger.* A owns all of the stock of T. T merges into P. In the merger, A receives P stock having a fair market value of $50x and cash of $50x. Immediately after the merger, and pursuant to a preexisting binding contract, A sells all of the P stock received by A in the merger to B. Assume that there are no facts and circumstances indicating that the cash used by B to purchase A's P stock was in substance exchanged by P for T stock. Under paragraphs (e)(1) and (2) of this section, the sale to B is disregarded because B is not a person related to P within the meaning of paragraph (e)(3) of this section. Thus, the transaction satisfies the continuity of interest requirement because 50 percent of A's T stock was exchanged for P stock, preserving a substantial part of the value of the proprietary interest in T.

(ii) *Sale of target corporation stock before merger.* The facts are the same as paragraph (i) of this *Example 1,* except that B buys A's T stock prior to the merger of T into P and then exchanges the T stock for P stock having a fair market value of $50x and cash of $50x. The sale by A is disregarded. The continuity of interest requirement is satisfied because B's T stock was exchanged for P stock, preserving a substantial part of the value of the proprietary interest in T.

Example 2. Relationship created in connection with potential reorganization. Corporation X owns 60 percent of the stock of P and 30 percent of the stock of T. A owns the remaining 70 percent of the stock of T. X buys A's T stock for cash in a transaction which is not a qualified stock purchase within the meaning of section 338. T then merges into P. In the merger, X exchanges all of its T stock for additional stock of P. As a result of the issuance of the additional stock to X in the merger, X's ownership interest in P increases from 60 to 80 percent of the stock of P. X is not a person related to P under paragraph (e)(3)(i)(B) of this section, because a purchase of stock of P by X would not be treated as a distribution in redemption of the stock of P under section 304(a)(2). However, X is a person related to P under paragraphs (e)(3)(i)(A) and (ii)(B) of this section, because X becomes affiliated with P in the merger. The continuity of interest requirement is not satisfied, because X acquired a proprietary interest in T for consideration other than P stock, and a substantial part of the value of the proprietary interest in T is not preserved. See paragraph (e)(2) of this section.

Example 3. Participation by issuing corporation in post-merger sale. A owns 80 percent of the T stock and none of the P stock, which is widely held. T merges into P. In the merger, A receives P stock. In addition, A obtains rights pursuant to an arrangement with P to have P register the P stock under the Securities Act of 1933, as amended. P registers A's stock, and A sells the stock shortly after the merger. No person who purchased the P stock from A is a person related to P within the meaning of paragraph (e)(3) of this section. Under paragraphs (e)(1) and (2) of this section, the sale of the P stock by A is disregarded because no person who purchased the P stock from A is a person related to P within the meaning of paragraph (e)(3) of this section. The transaction satisfies the continuity of interest requirement because A's T stock was exchanged for P stock, preserving a substantial part of the value of the proprietary interest in T.

Example 4. Redemptions and purchases by issuing corporation or related persons. (i) *Redemption by issuing corporation.* A owns 100 percent of the stock of T and none of the stock of P. T merges into S. In the merger, A receives P stock. In connection with the merger, P redeems all of the P stock received by A in the merger for cash. The continuity of interest requirement is not satisfied, because, in connection with the merger, P redeemed the stock exchanged for a proprietary interest in T, and a substantial part of the value of the proprietary interest in T is not preserved. See paragraph (e)(1) of this section.

(ii) *Purchase of target corporation stock by issuing corporation.* The facts are the same as paragraph (i) of this *Example 4*, except that, instead of P redeeming its stock, prior to and in connection with the merger of T into S, P purchases 90 percent of the T stock from A for cash. The continuity of interest requirement is not satisfied, because in connection with the merger, P acquired a proprietary interest in T for consideration other than P stock, and a substantial part of the value of the proprietary interest in T is not preserved. See paragraph (e)(1) of this section. However, see § 1.338-3(d) (which may change the result in this case by providing that, by virtue of section 338, continuity of interest is satisfied for certain parties after a qualified stock purchase).

(iii) *Purchase of issuing corporation stock by person related to issuing corporation.* The facts are the same as paragraph (i) of this *Example 4*, except that, instead of P redeeming its stock, S buys all of the P stock received by A in the merger for cash. S is a person related to P under paragraphs (e)(3)(i)(A) and (B) of this section. The continuity of interest requirement is not satisfied, because S acquired P stock issued in the merger, and a substantial part of the value of the proprietary interest in T is not preserved. See paragraph (e)(2) of this section.

Example 5. Redemption in substance by issuing corporation. A owns 100 percent of the stock of T and none of the stock of P. T merges into P. In the merger, A receives P stock. In connection with the merger, B buys all of the P stock received by A in the merger for cash. Shortly thereafter, in connection with the merger, P redeems the stock held by B for cash. Based on all the facts and circumstances, P in substance has exchanged solely cash for T stock in the merger. The continuity of interest requirement is not satisfied, because in substance P redeemed the stock exchanged for a proprietary interest in T, and a substantial part of the value of the proprietary interest in T is not preserved. See paragraph (e)(1) of this section.

Example 6. Purchase of issuing corporation stock through partnership. A owns 100 percent of the stock of T and none of the stock of P. S is an 85 percent partner in PRS. The other 15 percent of PRS is owned by unrelated persons. T merges into P. In the merger, A receives P stock. In connection with the merger, PRS purchases all of the P stock received by A in the merger for cash. Under paragraph (e)(4) of this section, S, as an 85 percent partner of PRS, is treated as having acquired 85 percent of the P stock exchanged for A's T stock in the merger, and as having furnished 85 percent of the cash paid by PRS to acquire the P stock. S is a person related to P under paragraphs (e)(3)(i)(A) and (B) of this section. The continuity of interest requirement is not satisfied, because S is treated as acquiring 85 percent of the P stock issued in the merger, and a substantial part of the value of the proprietary interest in T is not preserved. See paragraph (e)(2) of this section.

Example 7. Exchange by acquiring corporation for direct interest. A owns 30 percent of the stock of T. P owns 70 percent of the stock of T, which was not acquired by P in connection with the acquisition of T's assets. T merges into P. A receives cash in the merger. The continuity of interest requirement is satisfied, because P's 70 percent proprietary interest in T is exchanged by P for a direct interest in the assets of the target corporation enterprise.

Example 8. Maintenance of direct or indirect interest in issuing corporation. X, a corporation, owns all of the stock of each of corporations P and Z. Z owns all of the stock of T. T merges into P. Z receives P stock in the merger. Immediately thereafter and in connection with the merger, Z distributes the P stock received in the merger to X. X is a person related to P under paragraph (e)(3)(i)(A) of this section. The continuity of interest requirement is satisfied, because X was an indirect owner of T prior to the merger who maintains a direct or indirect proprietary interest in P, preserving a substantial part of the value of the proprietary interest in T. See paragraph (e)(2) of this section.

Example 9. Preacquisition redemption by target corporation. T has two shareholders, A and B. P expresses an interest in acquiring the stock of T. A does not wish to own P stock. T redeems A's shares in T in exchange for cash. No funds have been or will be provided by P for this purpose. P subsequently acquires all the outstanding stock of T from B solely in exchange for voting stock of P. The cash received by A in the prereorganization redemption is not treated as other property or money under section 356, and would not be so treated even if A had received some stock of P in exchange for his T stock. The prereorganization redemption by T does not affect continuity of interest, because B's proprietary interest in T is unaffected, and the value of the proprietary interest in T is preserved.

(7) *Effective date.* This paragraph (e) applies to transactions occurring after January 28, 1998, except that it does not apply to any transaction occurring pursuant to a written agreement which is binding on January 28, 1998, and at all times thereafter. Paragraph (e)(1)(ii) of this section, however, applies to transactions occurring after August 30, 2000, unless the transaction occurs pursuant to a written agreement that is (subject to customary conditions) binding on that date and at all times thereafter. Taxpayers who entered into a binding agreement on or after January 28, 1998, and before August 30, 2000, may request a private letter ruling permitting them to apply the final regulation to their transaction. A private letter ruling will not be issued unless the taxpayer establishes to the satisfaction of the IRS that there is not a significant risk of different parties to the transaction taking inconsistent positions, for Federal tax purposes, with respect to the applicability of the final regulations to the transaction. [Reg. § 1.368-1.]

☐ [*T.D. 6152, 12-2-55. Amended by T.D. 7745, 12-29-80; T.D. 8760, 1-23-98; T.D. 8783, 9-22-98; T.D. 8858, 1-5-2000; T.D. 8898, 8-30-2000 and T.D. 8940, 2-12-2001.*]

§ 1.368-2. **Definition of terms.**—(a) The application of the term "reorganization" is to be strictly limited to the specific transactions set forth in section 368(a). The term does not embrace the mere purchase by one corporation of the properties of another corporation. The preceding sentence applies to transactions occurring after January 28, 1998, except that it does not apply to any transaction occurring pursuant to a written agreement which is binding on January 28, 1998, and at all times thereafter. If the properties are transferred for cash and deferred payment obligations of the transferee evidenced by short-term notes, the transaction is a sale and not an exchange in which gain or loss is not recognized.

(b)(1) For rules regarding statutory mergers or consolidations on or after January 24, 2003, see § 1.368-2T(b)(1). For rules regarding statutory mergers or consolidations before January 24, 2003, see § 1.368-2(b)(1) as in effect before January 24, 2003 (See 26 CFR part 1, revised April 1, 2002).

(2) In order for the transaction to qualify under section 368(a)(1)(A) by reason of the application of section 368(a)(2)(D), one corporation (the acquiring corporation) must acquire substantially all of the properties of another corporation (the acquired corporation) partly or entirely in exchange for stock of a corporation which is in control of the acquiring corporation (the controlling corporation), provided that (i) the transaction would have qualified under section 368(a)(1)(A) if

the merger had been into the controlling corporation, and (ii) no stock of the acquiring corporation is used in the transaction. The foregoing test of whether the transaction would have qualified under section 368(a)(1)(A) if the merger had been into the controlling corporation means that the general requirements of a reorganization under section 368(a)(1)(A) (such as a business purpose, continuity of business enterprise, and continuity of interest) must be met in addition to the special requirements of section 368(a)(2)(D). Under this test, it is not relevant whether the merger into the controlling corporation could have been effected pursuant to State or Federal corporation law. The term "substantially all" has the same meaning as it has in section 368(a)(1)(C). Although no stock of the acquiring corporation can be used in the transaction, there is no prohibition (other than the continuity of interest requirement) against using other property, such as cash or securities, of either the acquiring corporation or the parent or both. In addition, the controlling corporation may assume liabilities of the acquired corporation without disqualifying the transaction under section 368(a)(2)(D), and for purposes of section 357(a) the controlling corporation is considered a party to the exchange. For example, if the controlling corporation agrees to substitute its stock for stock of the acquired corporation under an outstanding employee stock option agreement, this assumption of liability will not prevent the transaction from qualifying as a reorganization under section 368(a)(2)(D) and the assumption of liability is not treated as money or other property for purposes of section 361(b). Section 368(a)(2)(D) applies whether or not the controlling corporation (or the acquiring corporation) is formed immediately before the merger, in anticipation of the merger, or after preliminary steps have been taken to merge directly into the controlling corporation. Section 368(a)(2)(D) applies only to statutory mergers occurring after October 22, 1968.

(3) For regulations under section 368(a)(2)(E), see paragraph (j) of this section.

(c) In order to qualify as a "reorganization" under section 368(a)(1)(B), the acquisition by the acquiring corporation of stock of another corporation must be in exchange solely for all or a part of the voting stock of the acquiring corporation (or, in the case of transactions occurring after December 31, 1963, solely for all or a part of the voting stock of a corporation which is in control of the acquiring corporation), and the acquiring corporation must be in control of the other corporation immediately after the transaction. If, for example, corporation X in one transaction exchanges nonvoting preferred stock or bonds in addition to all or a part of its voting stock in the acquisition of stock of corporation Y, the transaction is not a

Reg. § 1.368-2(c)

reorganization under section 368(a)(1)(B). Nor is a transaction a reorganization described in section 368(a)(1)(B) if stock is acquired in exchange for voting stock both of the acquiring corporation and of a corporation which is in control of the acquiring corporation. The acquisition of the stock of another corporation by the acquiring corporation solely for its voting stock (or solely for voting stock of a corporation which is in control of the acquiring corporation) is permitted tax free even though the acquiring corporation already owns some of the stock of the other corporation. Such an acquisition is permitted tax free in a single transaction or in a series of transactions taking place over a relatively short period of time such as 12 months. For example, corporation A purchased 30 percent of the common stock of corporation W (the only class of stock outstanding) for cash in 1939. On March 1, 1955, corporation A offers to exchange its own voting stock for all the stock of corporation W tendered within 6 months from the date of the offer. Within the 6 months' period corporation A acquires an additional 60 percent of stock of corporation W solely for its own voting stock, so that it owns 90 percent of the stock of corporation W. No gain or loss is recognized with respect to the exchanges of stock of corporation A for stock of corporation W. For this purpose, it is immaterial whether such exchanges occurred before corporation A acquired control (80 percent) of corporation W or after such control was acquired. If corporation A had acquired 80 percent of the stock of corporation W for cash in 1939, it could likewise acquire some or all of the remainder of such stock solely in exchange for its own voting stock without recognition of gain or loss.

(d) In order to qualify as a reorganization under section 368(a)(1)(C), the transaction must be one described in subparagraph (1) or (2) of this paragraph:

(1) One corporation must acquire substantially all the properties of another corporation solely in exchange for all or a part of its own voting stock, or solely in exchange for all or a part of the voting stock of a corporation which is in control of the acquiring corporation. For example, Corporation P owns all the stock of Corporation A. All the properties of Corporation W are transferred to Corporation A either solely in exchange for voting stock of Corporation P or solely in exchange for less than 80 percent of the voting stock of Corporation A. Either of such transactions constitutes a reorganization under section 368(a)(1)(C). However, if the properties of Corporation W are acquired in exchange for voting stock of both Corporation P and Corporation A, the transaction will not constitute a reorganization under section 368(a)(1)(C). In determining whether the exchange meets the requirement of

"solely for voting stock", the assumption by the acquiring corporation of liabilities of the transferor corporation, or the fact that property acquired from the transferor corporation is subject to a liability, shall be disregarded. Though such an assumption does not prevent an exchange from being solely for voting stock for the purposes of the definition of a reorganization contained in section 368(a)(1)(C), it may in some cases, however, so alter the character of the transaction as to place the transaction outside the purposes and assumptions of the reorganization provisions. Section 368(a)(1)(C) does not prevent consideration of the effect of an assumption of liabilities on the general character of the transaction but merely provides that the requirement that the exchange be solely for voting stock is satisfied if the only additional consideration is an assumption of liabilities.

(2) One corporation—

(i) Must acquire substantially all of the properties of another corporation in such manner that the acquisition would qualify under (1) above, but for the fact that the acquiring corporation exchanges money, or other property in addition to such voting stock, and

(ii) Must acquire solely for voting stock (either of the acquiring corporation or of a corporation which is in control of the acquiring corporation) properties of the other corporation having a fair market value which is at least 80 percent of the fair market value of all the properties of the other corporation.

(3) For the purposes of subparagraph (2)(ii) only, a liability assumed or to which the properties are subject is considered money paid for the properties. For example, Corporation A has properties with a fair market value of $100,000 and liabilities of $10,000. In exchange for these properties, Corporation Y transfers its own voting stock, assumes the $10,000 liabilities, and pays $8,000 in cash. The transaction is a reorganization even though a part of the properties of Corporation A is acquired for cash. On the other hand, if the properties of Corporation A worth $100,000, were subject to $50,000 in liabilities, an acquisition of all the properties, subject to the liabilities, for any consideration other than solely voting stock would not qualify as a reorganization under this section since the liabilities alone are in excess of 20 percent of the fair market value of the properties. If the transaction would qualify under either subparagraph (1) or (2) of this paragraph and also under section 368(a)(1)(D), such transaction shall not be treated as a reorganization under section 368(a)(1)(C).

(4)(i) For purposes of paragraphs (d)(1) and (2)(ii) of this section, prior ownership of stock of the target corporation by an acquiring corporation will not by itself prevent the solely for voting stock requirement of such paragraphs from being satisfied. In a transaction in which the acquiring corporation has prior ownership of stock of the target corporation, the requirement of paragraph (d)(2)(ii) of this section is satisfied only if the sum of the money or other property that is distributed in pursuance of the plan of reorganization to the shareholders of the target corporation other than the acquiring corporation and to the creditors of the target corporation pursuant to section 361(b)(3), and all of the liabilities of the target corporation assumed by the acquiring corporation (including liabilities to which the properties of the target corporation are subject), does not exceed 20 percent of the value of all of the properties of the target corporation. If, in connection with a potential acquisition by an acquiring corporation of substantially all of a target corporation's properties, the acquiring corporation acquires the target corporation's stock for consideration other than the acquiring corporation's own voting stock (or voting stock of a corporation in control of the acquiring corporation if such stock is used in the acquisition of the target corporation's properties), whether from a shareholder of the target corporation or the target corporation itself, such consideration is treated, for purposes of paragraphs (d)(1) and (2) of this section, as money or other property exchanged by the acquiring corporation for the target corporation's properties. Accordingly, the transaction will not qualify under section 368(a)(1)(C) unless, treating such consideration as money or other property, the requirements of section 368(a)(2)(B) and paragraph (d)(2)(ii) of this section are met. The determination of whether there has been an acquisition in connection with a potential reorganization under section 368(a)(1)(C) of a target corporation's stock for consideration other than an acquiring corporation's own voting stock (or voting stock of a corporation in control of the acquiring corporation if such stock is used in the acquisition of the target corporation's properties) will be made on the basis of all of the facts and circumstances.

(ii) The following examples illustrate the principles of this paragraph (d)(4):

Example 1. Corporation P (P) holds 60 percent of the Corporation T (T) stock that P purchased several years ago in an unrelated transaction. T has 100 shares of stock outstanding. The other 40 percent of the T stock is owned by Corporation X (X), an unrelated corporation. T has properties with a fair market value of $110 and liabilities of $10. T transfers all of its properties to P. In exchange, P assumes the $10 of liabilities, and transfers to T $30 of P voting stock and $10 of cash. T distributes the P voting stock

and $10 of cash to X and liquidates. The transaction satisfies the solely for voting stock requirement of paragraph (d)(2)(ii) of this section because the sum of $10 of cash paid to X and the assumption by P of $10 of liabilities does not exceed 20% of the value of the properties of T.

Example 2. The facts are the same as in *Example 1* except that P purchased the 60 shares of T for $60 in cash in connection with the acquisition of T's assets. The transaction does not satisfy the solely for voting stock requirement of paragraph (d)(2)(ii) of this section because P is treated as having acquired all of the T assets for consideration consisting of $70 of cash, $10 of liability assumption and $30 of P voting stock, and the sum of $70 of cash and the assumption by P of $10 of liabilities exceeds 20% of the value of the properties of T.

(iii) This paragraph (d)(4) applies to transactions occurring after December 31, 1999, unless the transaction occurs pursuant to a written agreement that is (subject to customary conditions) binding on that date and at all times thereafter.

(e) A "recapitalization", and therefore a reorganization, takes place if, for example:

(1) A corporation with $200,000 par value of bonds outstanding, instead of paying them off in cash, discharges them by issuing preferred shares to the bondholders;

(2) There is surrendered to a corporation for cancellation 25 percent of its preferred stock in exchange for no par value common stock;

(3) A corporation issues preferred stock, previously authorized but unissued, for outstanding common stock;

(4) An exchange is made of a corporation's outstanding preferred stock, having certain priorities with reference to the amount and time of payment of dividends and the distribution of the corporate assets upon liquidation, for a new issue of such corporation's common stock having no such rights;

(5) An exchange is made of an amount of a corporation's outstanding preferred stock with dividends in arrears for other stock of the corporation. However, if pursuant to such an exchange there is an increase in the proportionate interest of the preferred shareholders in the assets or earnings and profits of the corporation, then under § 1.305-7(c)(2), an amount equal to the lesser of (i) the amount by which the fair market value or liquidation preference, whichever is greater, of the stock received in the exchange (determined immediately following the recapitalization) exceeds the issue price of the preferred stock surrendered, or (ii) the amount of the dividends in

Reg. § 1.368-2(e)(5)

arrears, shall be treated under section 305(c) as a deemed distribution to which sections 305(b)(4) and 301 apply.

(f) The term "a party to a reorganization" includes a corporation resulting from a reorganization, and both corporations in a transaction qualifying as a reorganization where one corporation acquires stock or properties of another corporation. If a transaction otherwise qualifies as a reorganization, a corporation remains a party to the reorganization even though stock or assets acquired in the reorganization are transferred in a transaction described in paragraph (k) of this section. If a transaction otherwise qualifies as a reorganization, a corporation shall not cease to be a party to the reorganization solely by reason of the fact that part or all of the assets acquired in the reorganization are transferred to a partnership in which the transferor is a partner if the continuity of business enterprise requirement is satisfied. See § 1.368-1(d). The preceding three sentences apply to transactions occurring after January 28, 1998, except that they do not apply to any transaction occurring pursuant to a written agreement which is binding on January 28, 1998, and at all times thereafter. A corporation controlling an acquiring corporation is a party to the reorganization when the stock of such controlling corporation is used in the acquisition of properties. Both corporations are parties to the reorganization if, under statutory authority, Corporation A is merged into Corporation B. All three of the corporations are parties to the reorganization if, pursuant to statutory authority, Corporation C and Corporation D are consolidated into Corporation E. Both corporations are parties to the reorganization if Corporation F transfers substantially all its assets to Corporation G in exchange for all or a part of the voting stock of Corporation G. All three corporations are parties to the reorganization if Corporation H transfers substantially all its assets to Corporation K in exchange for all or part of the voting stock of Corporation L, which is in control of Corporation K. Both corporations are parties to the reorganization if Corporation M transfers all or a part of its assets to Corporation N in exchange for all or a part of the stock and securities of Corporation N, but only if (1) immediately after such transfer, Corporation M, or one or more of its shareholders (including persons who were shareholders immediately before such transfer), or any combination thereof, is in control of Corporation N, and (2) in pursuance of the plan, the stock and securities of Corporation N are transferred or distributed by Corporation M in a transaction in which gain or loss is not recognized under section 354 or 355, or is recognized only to the extent provided in section 356. Both Corporation O and Corporation P,

but not Corporation S, are parties to the reorganization if Corporation O acquires stock of Corporation P from Corporation S in exchange solely for a part of the voting stock of Corporation O, if (1) the stock of Corporation P does not constitute substantially all of the assets of Corporation S, (2) Corporation S is not in control of Corporation O immediately after the acquisition, and (3) Corporation O is in control of Corporation P immediately after the acquisition.

(g) The term "plan of reorganization" has reference to a consummated transaction specifically defined as a reorganization under section 368(a). The term is not to be construed as broadening the definition of "reorganization" as set forth in section 368(a), but is to be taken as limiting the nonrecognition of gain or loss to such exchanges or distributions as are directly a part of the transaction specifically described as a reorganization in section 368(a). Moreover, the transaction, or series of transactions, embraced in a plan of reorganization must not only come within the specific language of section 368(a), but the readjustments involved in the exchanges or distributions effected in the consummation thereof must be undertaken for reasons germane to the continuance of the business of a corporation a party to the reorganization. Section 368(a) contemplates genuine corporate reorganizations which are designed to effect a readjustment of continuing interests under modified corporate forms.

(h) As used in section 368, as well as in other provisions of the Internal Revenue Code, if the context so requires, the conjunction "or" denotes both the conjunctive and the disjunctive, and the singular includes the plural. For example, the provisions of the statute are complied with if "stock and securities" are received in exchange as well as if "stock or securities" are received.

(i) [Reserved]

(j)(1) This paragraph (j) prescribes rules relating to the application of section 368(a)(2)(E).

(2) Section 368(a)(2)(E) does not apply to a consolidation.

(3) A transaction otherwise qualifying under section 368(a)(1)(A) is not disqualified by reason of the fact that stock of a corporation (the controlling corporation) which before the merger was in control of the merged corporation is used in the transaction, if the conditions of section 368(a)(2)(E) are satisfied. Those conditions are as follows:

(i) In the transaction, shareholders of the surviving corporation must surrender stock in exchange for voting stock of the controlling corporation. Further, the stock so surrendered must constitute control of the surviving corporation. Control is defined in section 368(c). The amount of stock constituting control is measured immediately before the transaction. For purposes of this subdivision (i), stock in the surviving corporation which is surrendered in the transaction (by any shareholder except the controlling corporation) in exchange for consideration furnished by the surviving corporation (and not by the controlling corporation or the merged corporation) is considered not to be outstanding immediately before the transaction. For effect on "substantially all" test of consideration furnished by the surviving corporation, see paragraph (j)(3)(iii) of this section.

(ii) Except as provided in paragraph (k)(2) of this section, the controlling corporation must control the surviving corporation immediately after the transaction.

(iii) After the transaction, except as provided in paragraph (k)(2) of this section, the surviving corporation must hold substantially all of its own properties and substantially all of the properties of the merged corporation (other than stock of the controlling corporation distributed in the transaction). The term "substantially all" has the same meaning as in section 368(a)(1)(C). The "substantially all" test applies separately to the merged corporation and to the surviving corporation. In applying the "substantially all" test to the surviving corporation, consideration furnished in the transaction by the surviving corporation in exchange for its stock is property of the surviving corporation which it does not hold after the transaction. In applying the "substantially all" test to the merged corporation, assets transferred from the controlling corporation to the merged corporation in pursuance of the plan of reorganization are not taken into account. Thus, for example, money transferred from the controlling corporation to the merged corporation to be used for the following purposes is not taken into account for purposes of the "substantially all" test:

(A) To pay additional consideration to shareholders of the surviving corporation;

(B) To pay dissenting shareholders of the surviving corporation;

(C) To pay creditors of the surviving corporation;

(D) To pay reorganization expenses; or

(E) To enable the merged corporation to satisfy state minimum capitalization requirements (where the money is returned to the controlling corporation as part of the transaction).

(iv) Paragraphs (j)(3)(ii) and (iii) of this section apply to transactions occurring after January 28, 1998, except that they do not apply to any transaction occurring pursuant to a written agreement which is binding on January 28, 1998, and at all times thereafter.

(4) The controlling corporation may assume liabilities of the surviving corporation without disqualifying the transaction under section 368(a)(2)(E). An assumption of liabilities of the surviving corporation by the controlling corporation is a contribution to capital by the controlling corporation to the surviving corporation. If, in pursuance of the plan of reorganization, securities of the surviving corporation are exchanged for securities of the controlling corporation, or for other securities of the surviving corporation, see sections 354 and 356.

(5) In applying section 368(a)(2)(E), it makes no difference if the merged corporation is an existing corporation, or is formed immediately before the merger, in anticipation of the merger, or after preliminary steps have been taken to otherwise acquire control of the surviving corporation.

(6) The following examples illustrate the application of this paragraph (j). In each of the examples, Corporation P owns all of the stock of Corporation S and, except as otherwise stated, Corporation T has outstanding 1,000 shares of common stock and no shares of any other class. In each of the examples, it is also assumed that the transaction qualifies under section 368(a)(1)(A) if the conditions of section 368(a)(2)(E) are satisfied.

Example 1. P owns no T stock. On January 1, 1981, S merges into T. In the merger, T's shareholders surrender 950 shares of common stock in exchange for P voting stock. The holders of the other 50 shares (who dissent from the merger) are paid in cash with funds supplied by P. After the transaction, T holds all of its own assets and all of S's assets. Based on these facts, the transaction qualifies under section 368(a)(1)(A) by reason of the application of section 368(a)(2)(E). In the transaction, former shareholders of T surrender, in exchange for P voting stock, an amount of T stock (950/1,000 shares or 95 percent) which constitutes control of T.

Example 2. The facts are the same as in example (1) except that holders of 100 shares in corporation T, who dissented from the merger, are paid in cash with funds supplied by T (and not by P or S) and, in the merger, T's remaining shareholders surrender 720 shares of common stock in exchange for P voting stock and 180 shares of common stock for cash supplied by P. The requirements of section 368(a)(2)(E)(ii) are satisfied since, in the transaction, former shareholders of T surrender, in exchange for P voting stock, an amount of T stock (720/900 shares or 80 percent) which constitutes control of T. The T stock surrendered in exchange for consideration furnished by T is not considered outstanding for purposes of

Reg. § 1.368-2(j)(6)

determining whether the amount of T stock surrendered by T shareholders for P stock constitutes control of T.

Example 3. T has outstanding 1,000 shares of common stock, 100 shares of nonvoting preferred stock, and no shares of any other class. On January 1, 1981, S merges into T. Prior to the merger, as part of the transaction, T distributes its own cash in redemption of the 100 shares of preferred stock. In the transaction, T's remaining shareholders surrender their 1,000 shares of common stock in exchange for P voting stock. The requirements of section 368(a)(2)(E)(ii) are satisfied since, in the transaction, former shareholders of T surrender, in exchange for P voting stock, an amount of T stock (1,000/1,000 shares or 100 percent) which constitutes control of T. The preferred stock surrendered in exchange for consideration furnished by T is not considered outstanding for purposes of determining whether the amount of T stock surrendered by T shareholders for P stock constitutes control of T. However, the consideration furnished by T for its stock is property of T which does not hold after the transaction for purposes of the substantially all test in paragraph (j)(3)(iii) of this section.

Example 4. On January 1, 1971, P purchased 201 shares of T's stock. On January 1, 1981, S merges into T. In the merger, T's shareholders (other than P) surrender 799 shares of T stock in exchange for P voting stock. Based on these facts, in the transaction, former shareholders of T do not surrender, in exchange for P voting stock, an amount of T stock which constitutes control of T (799/1,000 shares being less than 80 percent). Therefore, the transaction does not qualify under section 368(a)(1)(A). However, if S is a transitory corporation, formed solely for purposes of effectuating the transaction, the transaction may qualify as a reorganization described in section 368(a)(1)(B) provided all of the applicable requirements are satisfied.

Example 5. On January 1, 1971, P purchased 200 shares of T's stock. On January 1, 1981, S merges into T. Prior to the merger, as part of the transaction, T distributes its own cash in redemption of 1 share of T stock from a T shareholder other than P. In the merger, T's remaining shareholders (other than P) surrender 799 shares of T stock in exchange for P voting stock. Based on these facts, in the transaction, former shareholders of T do not surrender, in exchange for P voting stock, an amount of T stock which constitutes control of T (799/999 shares being less than 80 percent). Therefore, the transaction does not qualify under section 368(a)(1)(A). However, if S is a transitory corporation, formed for purposes of effectuating the transaction, the transaction may qualify as a reorganization described in section

368(a)(1)(B) provided all of the applicable requirements are satisfied.

Example 6. The stock of S has a value of $25,000. The stock of T has a value of $75,000. On January 1, 1984, S merges into T. In the merger, T's shareholders surrender all of their T stock in exchange for P voting stock. After the transaction, T holds all of its own assets and all of S's assets. Based on these facts, the transaction qualifies under section 368(a)(1)(A) by reason of the application of section 368(a)(2)(E). In the transaction, former shareholders of T surrender, in exchange for P voting stock, an amount of T stock (1,000/1,000 shares or 100 percent) which constitutes control of T. The stock of T received by P in exchange for P's prior interest in S is not taken into account for purposes of section 368(a)(2)(E)(ii) since the amount of T stock constituting control of T is measured before the transaction.

Example 7. The stock of T has a value of $75,000. On January 1, 1984, S merges into T. In the merger, T's shareholders surrender all of their T stock in exchange for P voting stock. As part of the transaction, P contributes $25,000 to T in exchange for new shares of T stock. None of the cash received by T is distributed or otherwise paid out to former T shareholders. After the transaction, T holds all of its own assets and all of S's assets. Based on these facts, the transaction qualifies under section 368(a)(1)(A) by reason of the application of section 368(a)(2)(E). In the transaction, former shareholders of T surrender, in exchange for P voting stock, an amount of T stock (1,000/1,000 shares or 100 percent) which constitutes control of T. The T stock received by P in exchange for its contribution to T is not taken into account for purposes of section 368(a)(2)(E)(ii) since the amount of T stock constituting control of T is measured before the transaction.

Example 8. The facts are the same as in example (7) except that, as part of the transaction, corporation R, instead of P, contributes $25,000 to T in exchange for T stock. Based on these facts, the transaction does not qualify under section 368(a)(1)(A) by reason of section 368(a)(2)(E) since P does not control T immediately after the transaction.

Example 9. T stock has a value of $75,000. P owns 500 shares (½) of that stock with a value of $37,500. The stock of S has a value of $125,000. On January 1, 1984, S merges into T. In the merger, T's shareholders (other than P) surrender their T stock in exchange for P voting stock. Based on these facts, in the transaction, former shareholders of T do not surrender, in exchange for P voting stock, an amount of T stock which constitutes control of T (500/1,000 shares being less than 80 percent). Therefore, the transaction does not qualify under section 368(a)(1)(A). The stock of T received by P in exchange for P's prior interest in S does not contribute to satisfaction of the requirement of section 368(a)(2)(E)(ii).

(k) *Transfer of assets or stock in section 368(a)(1)(A), (B), (C), or (G) reorganizations*—(1) *General rule for transfers to controlled corporations.* Except as otherwise provided in this section, a transaction otherwise qualifying under section 368(a)(1)(A), (B), (C), or (G) (where the requirements of sections 354(b)(1)(A) and (B) are met) shall not be disqualified by reason of the fact that part or all of the acquired assets or stock acquired in the transaction are transferred or successively transferred to one or more corporations controlled in each transfer by the transferor corporation. Control is defined under section 368(c).

(2) *Transfers following a reverse triangular merger.* A transaction qualifying under section 368(a)(1)(A) by reason of the application of section 368(a)(2)(E) is not disqualified by reason of the fact that part or all of the stock of the surviving corporation is transferred or successively transferred to one or more corporations controlled in each transfer by the transferor corporation, or because part or all of the assets of the surviving corporation or the merged corporation are transferred or successively transferred to one or more corporations controlled in each transfer by the transferor corporation.

(3) *Examples.* The following examples illustrate the application of this paragraph (k). P is the issuing corporation and T is the target corporation. P has only one class of stock outstanding. The examples are as follows:

Example 1. Transfers of acquired assets to controlled corporations. (i) *Facts.* T operates a bakery which supplies delectable pastries and cookies to local retail stores. The acquiring corporate group produces a variety of baked goods for nationwide distribution. P owns 80 percent of the stock of S-1. Pursuant to a plan of reorganization, T transfers all of its assets to S-1 solely in exchange for P stock, which T distributes to its shareholders. S-1 owns 80 percent of the stock of S-2; S-2 owns 80 percent of the stock of S-3, which also makes and supplies pastries and cookies. Pursuant to the plan of reorganization, S-1 transfers the T assets to S-2; S-2 transfers the T assets to S-3.

(ii) *Analysis.* Under this paragraph (k), the transaction, otherwise qualifying as a reorganization under section 368(a)(1)(C), is not disqualified by reason of the fact of the successive transfers of all of the acquired assets from S-1 to S-2, and from S-2 to S-3 because in each transfer, the transferee

corporation is controlled by the transferor corporation. Control is defined under section 368(c).

Example 2. Transfers of acquired stock to controlled corporations. (i) *Facts.* The facts are the same as *Example 1* except that S-1 acquires all of the T stock rather than the T assets, and as part of the plan of reorganization, S-1 transfers all of the T stock to S-2, and S-2 transfers all of the T stock to S-3.

(ii) *Analysis.* Under this paragraph (k), the transaction, otherwise qualifying as a reorganization under section 368(a)(1)(B), is not disqualified by reason of the fact of the successive transfers of all of the acquired stock from S-1 to S-2, and from S-2 to S-3 because in each transfer, the transferee corporation is controlled by the transferor corporation.

Example 3. Transfers of acquired stock to partnerships. (i) *Facts.* The facts are the same as in *Example 2.* However, as part of the plan of reorganization, S-2 and S-3 form a new partnership, PRS. Immediately thereafter, S-3 transfers all of the T stock to PRS in exchange for an 80 percent partnership interest, and S-2 transfers cash to PRS in exchange for a 20 percent partnership interest.

(ii) *Analysis.* This paragraph (k) describes the successive transfer of the T stock to S-3, but does not describe S-3's transfer of the T stock to PRS. Therefore, the characterization of this transaction must be determined under the relevant provisions of law, including the step transaction doctrine. See § 1.368-1(a). The transaction fails to meet the control requirement of a reorganization described in section 368(a)(1)(B) because immediately after the acquisition of the T stock, the acquiring corporation does not have control of T.

(4) This paragraph (k) applies to transactions occurring after January 28, 1998, except that it does not apply to any transaction occurring pursuant to a written agreement which is binding on January 28, 1998, and at all times thereafter. [Reg. § 1.368-2.]

□ [*T.D. 6152, 12-2-55. Amended by T.D. 7281, 7-11-73; T.D. 7422, 6-25-76; T.D. 8059, 10-21-85; T.D. 8760, 1-23-98; T.D. 8885, 5-18-2000 and T.D. 9038, 1-23-2003.*]

§ 1.368-2T. Definition of terms (temporary).—(a) [Reserved]. For further guidance, see § 1.368-2(a).

(b)(1)(i) *Definitions.* For purposes of this paragraph (b)(1), the following terms shall have the following meanings:

(A) *Disregarded entity.* A disregarded entity is a business entity (as defined in § 301.7701-2(a) of this chapter) that is disregarded as an entity separate from its owner for

Federal tax purposes. Examples of disregarded entities include a domestic single member limited liability company that does not elect to be classified as a corporation for Federal tax purposes, a corporation (as defined in § 301.7701-2(b) of this chapter) that is a qualified REIT subsidiary (within the meaning of section 856(i)(2)), and a corporation that is a qualified subchapter S subsidiary (within the meaning of section 1361(b)(3)(B)).

(B) *Combining entity.* A combining entity is a business entity that is a corporation (as defined in § 301.7701-2(b) of this chapter) that is not a disregarded entity.

(C) *Combining unit.* A combining unit is composed solely of a combining entity and all disregarded entities, if any, the assets of which are treated as owned by such combining entity for Federal tax purposes.

(ii) *Statutory merger or consolidation generally.* For purposes of section 368(a)(1)(A), a statutory merger or consolidation is a transaction effected pursuant to the laws of the United States or a State or the District of Columbia, in which, as a result of the operation of such laws, the following events occur simultaneously at the effective time of the transaction—

(A) All of the assets (other than those distributed in the transaction) and liabilities (except to the extent satisfied or discharged in the transaction) of each member of one or more combining units (each a transferor unit) become the assets and liabilities of one or more members of one other combining unit (the transferee unit); and

(B) The combining entity of each transferor unit ceases its separate legal existence for all purposes; provided, however, that this requirement will be satisfied even if, pursuant to the laws of the United States or a State or the District of Columbia, after the effective time of the transaction, the combining entity of the transferor unit (or its officers, directors, or agents) may act or be acted against, or a member of the transferee unit (or its officers, directors, or agents) may act or be acted against in the name of the combining entity of the transferor unit, provided that such actions relate to assets or obligations of the combining entity of the transferor unit that arose, or relate to activities engaged in by such entity, prior to the effective time of the transaction, and such actions are not inconsistent with the requirements of paragraph (b)(1)(ii)(A) of this section.

(iii) *Statutory merger or consolidation involving disregarded entities.* A transaction effected pursuant to the laws of the United States or a State or the District of Columbia in which any of the assets and liabilities of a combining

entity of a transferor unit become assets and liabilities of one or more disregarded entities of the transferee unit is not a statutory merger or consolidation within the meaning of section 368(a)(1)(A) and paragraph (b)(1)(ii) of this section unless such combining entity, the combining entity of the transferee unit, such disregarded entities other than entities that were disregarded entities of the transferor unit immediately prior to the transaction, and each business entity through which the combining entity of the transferee unit holds its interests in such disregarded entities is organized under the laws of the United States or a State or the District of Columbia.

(iv) *Examples.* The following examples illustrate the rules of paragraph (b)(1) of this section. In each of the examples, except as otherwise provided, each of V, Y, and Z is a domestic C corporation. X is a domestic limited liability company. Except as otherwise provided, X is wholly owned by Y and is disregarded as an entity separate from Y for Federal tax purposes. The examples are as follows:

Example 1. Divisive transaction pursuant to a merger statute. (i) Under State W law, Z transfers some of its assets and liabilities to Y, retains the remainder of its assets and liabilities, and remains in existence following the transaction. The transaction qualifies as a merger under State W corporate law. Prior to the transaction, Y is not treated as owning any assets of an entity that is disregarded as an entity separate from its owner for Federal tax purposes.

(ii) The transaction does not satisfy the requirements of paragraph (b)(1)(ii)(A) of this section because all of the assets and liabilities of Z, the combining entity of the transferor unit, do not become the assets and liabilities of Y, the combining entity and sole member of the transferee unit. In addition, the transaction does not satisfy the requirements of paragraph (b)(1)(ii)(B) of this section because the separate legal existence of Z does not cease for all purposes. Accordingly, the transaction does not qualify as a statutory merger or consolidation under section 368(a)(1)(A).

Example 2. Merger of a target corporation into a disregarded entity in exchange for stock of the owner. (i) Under State W law, Z merges into X. Pursuant to such law, the following events occur simultaneously at the effective time of the transaction: all of the assets and liabilities of Z become the assets and liabilities of X and Z's separate legal existence ceases for all purposes. In the merger, the Z shareholders exchange their stock of Z for stock of Y. Prior to the transaction, Z is not treated as owning any assets of an entity

Reg. § 1.368-2T(b)

that is disregarded as an entity separate from its owner for Federal tax purposes.

(ii) The transaction satisfies the requirements of paragraph (b)(1)(ii) of this section because the transaction is effected pursuant to State W law and the following events occur simultaneously at the effective time of the transaction: all of the assets and liabilities of Z, the combining entity and sole member of the transferor unit, become the assets and liabilities of one or more members of the transferee unit that is comprised of Y, the combining entity of the transferee unit, and X, a disregarded entity the assets of which Y is treated as owning for Federal tax purposes, and Z ceases its separate legal existence for all purposes. Paragraph (b)(1)(iii) of this section does not apply to prevent the transaction from qualifying as a statutory merger or consolidation for purposes of section 368(a)(1)(A) because each of Z, Y, and X is a domestic entity. Accordingly, the transaction qualifies as a statutory merger or consolidation for purposes of section 368(a)(1)(A). The result would be the same if Z were treated as owning assets of an entity that is disregarded as an entity separate from Z, regardless of whether such disregarded entity became an entity disregarded as an entity separate from Y as a result of the transaction, or merged into X or a domestic entity disregarded as an entity separate from Y.

* * *

Example 4. Triangular merger of a target corporation into a disregarded entity. (i) The facts are the same as in *Example 2*, except that V owns 100 percent of the outstanding stock of Y and, in the merger of Z into X, the Z shareholders exchange their stock of Z for stock of V. In the transaction, Z transfers substantially all of its properties to X.

(ii) The transaction is not prevented from qualifying as a statutory merger or consolidation

under section 368(a)(1)(A), provided the requirements of section 368(a)(2)(D) are satisfied. Because the assets of X are treated for Federal tax purposes as the assets of Y, Y will be treated as acquiring substantially all of the properties of Z in the merger for purposes of determining whether the merger satisfies the requirements of section 368(a)(2)(D). As a result, the Z shareholders that receive stock of V will be treated as receiving stock of a corporation that is in control of Y, the combining entity of the transferee unit that is the acquiring corporation for purposes of section 368(a)(2)(D). Accordingly, the merger will satisfy the requirements of section 368(a)(2)(D).

* * *

Example 6. Merger of a disregarded entity into a corporation. (i) Under State W law, X merges into Z. Pursuant to such law, the following events occur simultaneously at the effective time of the transaction: all of the assets and liabilities of X (but not the assets and liabilities of Y other than those of X) become the assets and liabilities of Z and X's separate legal existence ceases for all purposes.

(ii) The transaction does not satisfy the requirements of paragraph (b)(1)(ii)(A) of this section because all of the assets and liabilities of a transferor unit do not become the assets and liabilities of one or more members of the transferee unit. The transaction also does not satisfy the requirements of paragraph (b)(1)(ii)(B) of this section because X does not qualify as a combining entity. Accordingly, the transaction cannot qualify as a statutory merger or consolidation for purposes of section 368(a)(1)(A).

* * *

[Temporary Reg. § 1.368-2T.]

☐ [*T.D.* 9038, 1-23-2003.]

Carryovers

§ 1.381(a)-1. General rule relating to carryovers in certain corporate acquisitions.—(a) *Allowance of carryovers.* Section 381 provides that a corporation which acquires the assets of another corporation in certain liquidations and reorganizations shall succeed to, and take into account, as of the close of the date of distribution or transfer, the items described in section 381(c) of the distributor or transferor corporation. These items shall be taken into account by the acquiring corporation subject to the conditions and limitations specified in sections 381, 382(b) and 383 and the regulations thereunder.

(b) *Determination of transactions and items to which section 381 applies*—(1) *Qualified transactions.* Except to the extent provided in section

381(c)(20), relating to the carryover of unused pension trust deductions in certain liquidations, the items described in section 381(c) are required by section 381 to be carried over to the acquiring corporation (as defined in subparagraph (2) of this paragraph) only in the following liquidations and reorganizations:

(i) The complete liquidation of a subsidiary corporation upon which no gain or loss is recognized in accordance with the provisions of section 332, but only if the basis of the assets distributed to the acquiring corporation is not required by section 334(b)(2) to be the adjusted basis of the stock with respect to which the distribution is made;

Reg. § 1.381(a)-1(b)(1)

(ii) A statutory merger or consolidation qualifying under section 368(a)(1)(A) to which section 361 applies;

(iii) A reorganization qualifying under section 368(a)(1)(C);

(iv) A reorganization qualifying under section 368(a)(1)(D) if the requirements of section 354(b)(1)(A) and (B) are satisfied; and

(v) A mere change in identify, form, or place of organization qualifying under section 368(a)(1)(F).

(2) *Acquiring corporation defined.* (i) Only a single corporation may be an acquiring corporation for purposes of section 381 and the regulations thereunder. The corporation which acquires the assets of its subsidiary corporation in a complete liquidation to which section 381(a)(1) applies is the acquiring corporation for purposes of section 381. Generally, in a transaction to which section 381(a)(2) applies, the acquiring corporation is that corporation which, pursuant to the plan of reorganization, ultimately acquires, directly or indirectly, all of the assets transferred by the transferor corporation. If, in a transaction qualifying under section 381(a)(2), no one corporation ultimately acquires all of the assets transferred by the transferor corporation, that corporation which directly acquires the assets so transferred shall be the acquiring corporation for purposes of section 381 and the regulations thereunder, even though such corporation ultimately retains none of the assets so transferred. Whether a corporation has acquired all of the assets transferred by the transferor corporation is a question of fact to be determined on the basis of all the facts and circumstances.

(ii) The application of this subparagraph may be illustrated by the following examples:

Example (1). Y Corporation, a wholly-owned subsidiary of X Corporation, directly acquired all the assets of Z Corporation solely in exchange for voting stock of X Corporation in a transaction qualifying under section 368(a)(1)(C). Y Corporation is the acquiring corporation for purposes of section 381.

Example (2). X Corporation acquired all the assets of Z Corporation solely in exchange for voting stock of X Corporation in a transaction qualifying under section 368(a)(1)(C). Thereafter, pursuant to the plan of reorganization X Corporation transferred all the assets so acquired to Y Corporation, its wholly-owned subsidiary (see section 368(a)(2)(C)). Y Corporation is the acquiring corporation for purposes of section 381.

Example (3). X Corporation acquired all the assets of Z Corporation solely in exchange for the voting stock of X Corporation in a transaction

qualifying under section 368(a)(1)(C). Thereafter, pursuant to the plan of reorganization X Corporation transferred one-half of the assets so acquired to Y Corporation, its wholly-owned subsidiary, and retained the other half of such assets. X Corporation is the acquiring corporation for purposes of section 381.

Example (4). X Corporation acquired all the assets of Z Corporation solely in exchange for voting stock of X Corporation in a transaction qualifying under section 368(a)(1)(C). Thereafter, pursuant to the plan of reorganization X Corporation transferred one-half of the assets so acquired to Y Corporation, its wholly-owned subsidiary, and the other half of such assets to M Corporation, another wholly-owned subsidiary of X Corporation. X Corporation is the acquiring corporation for purposes of section 381.

(3) *Transactions and items not covered by section 381.* (i) Section 381 does not apply to partial liquidations, divisive reorganizations, or other transactions not described in subparagraph (1) of this paragraph. Moreover, section 381 does not apply to the carryover of an item or tax attribute not specified in subsection (c) thereof. In a case where section 381 does not apply to a transaction, item, or tax attribute by reason of either of the preceding sentences, no inference is to be drawn from the provisions of section 381 as to whether any item or tax attribute shall be taken into account by the successor corporation.

(ii) If, pursuant to the provisions of subparagraph (2) of this paragraph, a corporation is considered to be the acquiring corporation even though a part of the acquired assets is transferred to one or more corporations controlled by the acquiring corporation, or all the acquired assets are transferred to two or more corporations controlled by the acquiring corporation, then the carryover of any item described in section 381(c) to such controlled corporation or corporations shall be determined without regard to section 381. Thus, for example, if a parent corporation is the acquiring corporation for purposes of section 381 notwithstanding the fact that, pursuant to the plan of reorganization, it transferred to its wholly-owned subsidiary property acquired from the transferor corporation which the transferor corporation had elected to inventory under the last-in first-out method, then the question whether the subsidiary corporation shall continue to use the same method of inventorying with respect to that property shall be determined without regard to section 381.

* * *

[Reg. § 1.381(a)-1.]

□ [*T.D.* 6480, 7-12-60. *Amended by T.D.* 7343, 1-8-75.]

Reg. § 1.381(a)-1(b)(2)

§ 1.381(b)-1. Operating rules applicable to carryovers in certain corporate acquisitions.— (a) *Closing of taxable year*—(1) *In general.* Except in the case of certain reorganizations qualifying under section 368(a)(1)(F), the taxable year of the distributor or transferor corporation shall end with the close of the date of distribution or transfer. With regard to the closing of the taxable year of the transferor corporation in certain reorganizations under section 368(a)(1)(F) involving a foreign corporation after December 31, 1986, see §§ 1.367(a)-1T(e) and 1.367(b)-2(f).

(2) *Reorganizations under section 368(a)(1)(F).* In the case of a reorganization qualifying under section 368(a)(1)(F) (whether or not such reorganization also qualifies under any other provision of section 368(a)(1)), the acquiring corporation shall be treated (for purposes of section 381) just as the transferor corporation would have been treated if there had been no reorganization. Thus, the taxable year of the transferor corporation shall not end on the date of transfer merely because of the transfer; a net operating loss of the acquiring corporation for any taxable year ending after the date of transfer shall be carried back in accordance with section 172(b) in computing the taxable income of the transferor corporation for a taxable year ending before the date of transfer; and the tax attributes of the transferor corporation enumerated in section 381(c) shall be taken into account by the acquiring corporation as if there had been no reorganization.

(b) *Date of distribution or transfer.* (1) The date of distribution or transfer shall be that day on which are distributed or transferred all those properties of the distributor or transferor corporation which are to be distributed or transferred pursuant to a liquidation or reorganization described in paragraph (b)(1) of § 1.381(a)-1. If the distribution or transfer of all such properties is not made on one day, then, except as provided in subparagraph (2) of this paragraph, the date of distribution or transfer shall be that day on which the distribution or transfer of all such properties is completed.

(2) If the distributor or transferor and acquiring corporations file the statements described in subparagraph (3) of this paragraph, the date of distribution or transfer shall be that day as of which (i) substantially all of the properties to be distributed or transferred have been distributed or transferred, and (ii) the distributor or transferor corporation has ceased all operations (other than liquidating activities). Such day also shall be the date of distribution or transfer if the completion of the distribution or transfer is unreasonably postponed beyond the date as of which substantially all the properties to be distributed or transferred have been distributed or transferred and the distributor or transferor corporation has ceased all operations other than liquidating activities. A corporation shall be considered to have distributed or transferred substantially all of its properties to be distributed or transferred even though it retains money or other property in a reasonable amount to pay outstanding debts or preserve the corporation's legal existence. A corporation shall be considered to have ceased all operations, other than liquidating activities, when it ceases to be a going concern and its activities are merely for the purpose of winding up its affairs, paying its debts, and distributing any remaining balance of its money or other properties to its shareholders.

(3) The statements referred to in subparagraph (2) of this paragraph shall specify the day considered to be the date of distribution or transfer and shall specify, as of such date (i) the nature and amount of the total assets which were distributed or transferred and the dates so distributed or transferred, (ii) the nature and amount of the assets not distributed or transferred and the purpose for which they were retained, and (iii) the date on which the distributor or transferor corporation ceased all operations other than liquidating activities. Such statements shall be attached to the timely filed income tax return of the distributor or transferor corporation for its taxable year ending with such date of distribution or transfer and to the timely filed income tax return of the acquiring corporation for its first taxable year ending after such date, except that, with respect to any income tax return filed before October 11, 1960, any such statement shall be filed before October 11, 1960, with the district director with whom such return is filed.

(4) If—

(i) The last day of the acquiring corporation's taxable year is a Saturday, Sunday, or legal holiday, and

(ii) The day specified in subparagraph (1) and (2) of this paragraph as the date of distribution or transfer is the last business day before such Saturday, Sunday, or holiday,

then the last day of the acquiring corporation's taxable year shall be the date of distribution or transfer for purposes of section 381(b) and this section. For purposes of this subparagraph, the term "business day" means a day which is not a Saturday, Sunday, or legal holiday, and also means a Saturday, Sunday, or legal holiday if the date of distribution or transfer determined under subparagraph (1) or (2) of this paragraph is such Saturday, Sunday, or holiday.

(c) *Return of distributor or transferor corporation.* The distributor or transferor corporation shall file an income tax return for the taxable year

Reg. § 1.381(b)-1(c)

ending with the date of distribution or transfer described in paragraph (b) of this section. If the distributor or transferor corporation remains in existence after such date of distribution or transfer, it shall file an income tax return for the taxable year beginning on the day following the date of distribution or transfer and ending with the date on which the distributor or transferor corporation's taxable year would have ended if there had been no distribution or transfer.

(d) *Carryback of net operating losses.* For provisions relating to the carryback of net operating losses of the acquiring corporation, see paragraph (b) of § 1.381(c)(1)-1. [Reg. § 1.381(b)-1.]

□ [*T.D. 6480, 7-12-60. Amended by T.D. 8280, 1-12-90 and T.D. 8862, 1-21-2000.*]

§ 1.381(c)(2)-1. Earnings and profits.—(a) *In general.* (1) Section 381(c)(2) requires the acquiring corporation in a transaction to which section 381(a) applies to succeed to, and take into account, the earnings and profits, or deficit in earnings and profits, of the distributor or transferor corporation as of the close of the date of distribution or transfer. In determining the amount of such earnings and profits, or deficit, to be carried over, and the manner in which they are to be used by the acquiring corporation after such date, the provisions of section 381(c)(2) and this section shall apply. For purposes of section 381(c)(2) and this section, if the distributor or transferor corporation accumulates earnings and profits, or incurs a deficit in earnings and profits, after the date of distribution or transfer and before the completion of the reorganization or liquidation, such earnings and profits, or deficit, shall be deemed to have been accumulated or incurred as of the close of the date of distribution or transfer.

(2) If the distributor or transferor corporation has accumulated earnings and profits as of the close of the date of distribution or transfer, such earnings and profits shall (except as hereinafter provided in this section) be deemed to be received by, and to become a part of the accumulated earnings and profits of, the acquiring corporation as of such time. Similarly, if the distributor or transferor corporation has a deficit in accumulated earnings and profits as of the close of the date of distribution or transfer, such deficit shall (except as hereinafter provided in this section) be deemed to be incurred by the acquiring corporation as of such time. In no event, however, shall the accumulated earnings and profits, or deficit, of the distributor or transferor corporation be taken into account in determining earnings and profits of the acquiring corporation for the taxable year during which occurs the date of distribution or transfer.

(3) Any part of the accumulated earnings and profits, or deficit in accumulated earnings and profits, of the distributor or transferor corporation which consists of earnings and profits, or deficits, accumulated before March 1, 1913, shall be deemed to become earnings and profits, or deficits, of the acquiring corporation accumulated before March 1, 1913, and any part of the accumulated earnings and profits of the distributor or transferor corporation which consists of increase in value of property accrued before March 1, 1913, shall be deemed to become earnings and profits of the acquiring corporation consisting of increase in value of property accrued before March 1, 1913.

(4) If the acquiring corporation and each distributor or transferor corporation has accumulated earnings and profits as of the close of the date of distribution or transfer, or if each of such corporations has a deficit in accumulated earnings and profits as of such time, then the accumulated earnings and profits (or deficit) of each such corporation shall be consolidated as of the close of the date of distribution or transfer in the accumulated earnings and profits account of the acquiring corporation. See subparagraph (6) of this paragraph for determination of the accumulated earnings and profits (or deficit) of the acquiring corporation as of the close of the date of distribution or transfer.

(5) If (i) one or more corporations a party to a distribution or transfer has accumulated earnings and profits as of the close of the date of distribution or transfer, and (ii) one or more of such corporations has a deficit in accumulated earnings and profits as of such time, the total of any such deficits shall be used only to offset earnings and profits accumulated, or deemed to have been accumulated under subparagraph (6) of this paragraph, by the acquiring corporation after the date of distribution or transfer. In such instance, the acquiring corporation will be considered as maintaining two separate earnings and profits accounts after the date of distribution or transfer. The first such account shall contain the total of the accumulated earnings and profits as of the close of the date of distribution or transfer of each corporation which has accumulated earnings and profits as of such time, and the second such account shall contain the total of the deficits in accumulated earnings and profits of each corporation which has a deficit as of such time. The total deficit in the second account may not be used to reduce the accumulated earnings and profits in the first account (although such earnings and profits may be offset by deficits incurred, or deemed to have been incurred, after the date of distribution or transfer) but shall be used only to offset earnings and profits accumulated, or

Reg. § 1.381(c)(2)-1(a)(2)

deemed to have been accumulated under subparagraph (6) of this paragraph, by the acquiring corporation after the date of distribution or transfer.

(6) In any case in which it is necessary to compute the accumulated earnings and profits, or the deficit in accumulated earnings and profits, of the acquiring corporation as of the close of the date of distribution or transfer and such date is a day other than the last day of a taxable year of the acquiring corporation—

(i) If the acquiring corporation has earnings and profits for its taxable year during which occurs the date of distribution or transfer, such earnings and profits (a) shall be deemed to have accumulated as of the close of such date in an amount which bears the same ratio to the undistributed earnings and profits of such corporation for such year as the number of days in the taxable year preceding the date following the date of distribution or transfer bears to the total number of days in the taxable year, and (b) shall be deemed to have accumulated after the date of distribution or transfer in an amount which bears the same ratio to the undistributed earnings and profits of such corporation for such year as the number of days in the taxable year following such date bears to the total number of days in such taxable year. For purposes of the preceding sentence, the undistributed earnings and profits of the acquiring corporation for such taxable year shall be the earnings and profits for such taxable year reduced by any distributions made therefrom during such taxable year.

(ii) If the acquiring corporation has an operating deficit for its taxable year during which occurs the date of distribution or transfer, then, unless the actual accumulated earnings and profits, or deficit, as of such date can be shown, such operating deficit shall be deemed to have accumulated in a manner similar to that described in subdivision (i) of this subparagraph.

* * *

(c) *Distribution of earnings and profits pursuant to reorganization or liquidation.* (1) If, in a reorganization to which section 381(a)(2) applies, the transferor corporation pursuant to the plan of reorganization distributes to its stockholders property consisting not only of property permitted by section 354 to be received without recognition of gain, but also of other property or money, then the accumulated earnings and profits of the transferor corporation as of the close of the date of transfer shall be computed by taking into account the amount of earnings and profits properly applicable to the distribution, regardless of whether such distribution occurs before or after the close of the date of transfer.

(2) If, in a distribution to which section 381(a)(1) (relating to certain liquidations of subsidiaries) applies, the acquiring corporation receives less than 100 percent of the assets distributed by the distributor corporation, then the accumulated earnings and profits of the distributor corporation as of the close of the date of distribution shall be computed by taking into account the amount of earnings and profits properly applicable to the distributions to minority stockholders, regardless of whether such distributions occur before or after the close of the date of distribution.

(d) *Treatment of earnings and profits where assets are transferred to a corporation controlled by the acquiring corporation.* If, pursuant to the provisions of paragraph (b)(2) of § 1.381(a)-1, a corporation is considered to be the acquiring corporation even though a part of the acquired assets is transferred to one or more corporations controlled by the acquiring corporation, or all the acquired assets are transferred to two or more corporations controlled by the acquiring corporation, then whether any portion of the earnings and profits received by the acquiring corporation under section 381(c)(2) is allocable to such controlled corporation or corporations shall be determined without regard to section 381. See paragraph (a) of § 1.312-11. [Reg. § 1.381(c)(2)-1.]

☐ [*T.D.* 6586, 12-27-61. *Amended by T.D.* 6692, 12-2-63.]

§ 1.382-2. General rules for ownership change.—(a) *Certain definitions for purposes of sections 382 and 383 and the regulations thereunder.* The following definitions apply for purposes of sections 382 and 383 and the regulations thereunder.

(1) *Loss corporation*—(i) *In general.* The term "loss corporation" means a corporation which—

(A) is entitled to use a net operating loss carryforward, a capital loss carryover, a carryover of excess foreign taxes under section 904(c), a carryforward of a general business credit under section 39, or a carryover of a minimum tax credit under section 53,

(B) for the taxable year that includes a testing date, as defined in paragraph (a)(4) of this section or § 1.382-2T(a)(2)(i), whichever is applicable (determined for purposes of this paragraph (a)(1) without regard to whether the corporation is a loss corporation), has a net operating loss, a net capital loss, excess foreign taxes under section 904(c), unused general business credits under section 38, or an unused minimum tax credit under section 53, or

(C) has a net unrealized built-in loss (determined for purposes of this paragraph (a)(1) by treating the date on which such determination is made as the change date). See section 382(h)(3) for the definition of net unrealized built-in loss. See section 383 and § 1.383-1 for rules relating to a loss corporation that has an ownership change and has capital losses, excess foreign taxes, general business credits or minimum tax credits. Any predecessor or successor to a loss corporation described in this paragraph (a)(1) is also a loss corporation.

(ii) *Distributor or transferor loss corporation in a transaction under section 381.* Notwithstanding that a loss corporation ceases to exist under state law, if its net operating loss carryforwards, excess foreign taxes, or other items described in section 381(c) are succeeded to and taken into account by an acquiring corporation in a transaction described in section 381(a), such loss corporation shall be treated as continuing in existence until—

(A) any pre-change losses (excluding pre-change credits described in § 1.383-1(c)(3)), determined as if the date of such transaction were the change date, are fully utilized or expire under either section 172 or section 1212,

(B) any net unrealized built-in losses, determined as if the date of such transaction were the change date, may no longer be treated as pre-change losses, and

(C) any pre-change credits (described in § 1.383-1(c)(3)), determined as if the date of such transaction were the change date, are fully utilized or expire under sections 39, 53, or 904(c).

Following a transaction described in the preceding sentence, the stock of the acquiring corporation shall be treated as the stock of the loss corporation for purposes of determining whether an ownership change occurs with respect to the pre-change losses and net unrealized built-in losses that may be treated as pre-change losses of the distributor or transferor corporation.

(iii) *Separate accounting required for losses and credits of an acquiring corporation and a distributor or transferor loss corporation.* Except as provided in paragraph (a)(1)(iv) of this section, pre-change losses (determined as if the testing date were the change date and treating the amount of any net unrealized built-in loss as a pre-change loss), that are succeeded to and taken into account by an acquiring corporation in a transaction to which section 381(a) applies must be accounted for separately from losses and credits of the acquiring corporation for purposes of applying this section. See Example (2) of § 1.382-2T(e)(2)(iv).

(iv) *End of separate accounting for losses and credits of distributor or transferor loss corporation.* The separate tracking of owner shifts of the stock of an acquiring corporation required by paragraph (a)(1)(iii) of this section with respect to the net operating loss carryovers and other attributes described in paragraph (a)(1)(ii) of this section ends when a fold-in event occurs. A fold-in event is either an ownership change of the distributor or transferor corporation in connection with, or after, the transaction to which section 381(a) applies, or a period of 5 consecutive years following the section 381(a) transaction during which the distributor or transferor corporation has not had an ownership change. Starting on the day after the earlier of the change date (but not earlier than the day of the section 381(a) transaction) or the last day of the 5 consecutive year period, the losses and other attributes of the distributor or transferor corporation are treated as losses and attributes of the acquiring corporation for purposes of determining whether an ownership change occurs with respect to such losses. Also, for purposes of determining the beginning of the acquiring corporation's testing period, such losses are considered to arise either in a taxable year that begins not earlier than the later of the day following the change date or the day of the section 381(a) transaction, or in a taxable year that begins 3 years before the end of the 5 consecutive year period. Pre-change losses of a distributor or transferor corporation that are subject to a limitation under section 382 continue to be subject to the limitation notwithstanding the occurrence of a fold-in event. Any ownership change that occurs in connection with, or subsequent to, the section 381 transaction may result in an additional, lesser limitation with respect to such pre-change losses. This paragraph (a)(1)(iv) applies to any testing date occurring on or after January 29, 1991.

(v) *Application to other successor corporations.* This paragraph (a)(1) also applies, as the context may require, to successor corporations other than successors in section 381(a) transactions. For example, if a corporation receives assets from the loss corporation that have basis in excess of value, the recipient corporation's basis for the assets is determined, directly or indirectly, in whole or in part, by reference to the loss corporation's basis, and the amount by which basis exceeds value is material, the recipient corporation is a successor corporation subject to this paragraph (a)(1). This paragraph (a)(1)(v) applies to any testing date occurring on or after January 1, 1997.

(2) *Pre-change loss.* The term pre-change loss means—

(i) any net operating loss carryforward of the old loss corporation to the taxable year ending

Reg. § 1.382-2(a)(2)

on the change date or in which the change date occurs,

(ii) any net operating loss of the old loss corporation for the taxable year in which the ownership change occurs to the extent such loss is allocable to the period in such year on or before the change date,

(iii) any recognized built-in loss for any recognition period taxable year (within the meaning of section 382(h)),

(iv) any pre-change capital losses described in § 1.383-1(c)(2)(i) and (ii), and

(v) any pre-change credits described in § 1.383-1(c)(3).

(3) *Stock*—(i) *In general.* Except as provided in this paragraph (a)(3)(i) and § 1.382-2T(f)(18)(ii) and (iii), the term "stock" means stock other than stock described in section 1504(a)(4). Notwithstanding the preceding sentence, stock that is not described in section 1504(a)(4) solely because it is entitled to vote as a result of dividend arrearages shall be treated as so described and thus shall not be considered stock. Stock described in section 1504(a)(4), however, is not excluded for purposes of determining the value of the loss corporation under section 382(e). The determination of the percentage of stock of any corporation owned by any person shall be made on the basis of the relative fair market value of the stock owned by such person to the total fair market value of the outstanding stock of the corporation. Solely for purposes of determining the percentage of stock owned by a person, each share of all the outstanding shares of stock that have the same material terms is treated as having the same value. Thus, for example, a control premium or blockage discount is disregarded in determining the percentage of stock owned by any person. The previous two sentences of this paragraph (a)(3)(i) apply to any testing date occurring on or after January 29, 1991.

(ii) *Convertible stock.* The term "stock" includes any convertible stock. For rules regarding the treatment of certain convertible stock as an option, see § 1.382-4(d)(9)(ii).

(4) *Testing date*—(i) *In general.* Except as provided in paragraph (a)(4)(ii) of this section, a loss corporation is required to determine whether an ownership change has occurred immediately after any owner shift, or issuance or transfer (including an issuance or transfer described in § 1.382-4(d)(8)(i) or (ii)) of an option with respect to stock of the loss corporation that is treated as exercised under § 1.382-4(d)(2). Each date on which a loss corporation is required to make a determination of whether an ownership change has occurred is referred to as a testing date. All computations of increases in percentage owner-

ship are to be made as of the close of the testing date and any transactions described in this paragraph (a)(4) that occur on that date are treated as occurring simultaneously at the close of the testing date. See § 1.382-2T(e)(1) for the definition of owner shift. The term *option*, as used in this paragraph (a)(4), includes interests that are treated as options under § 1.382-4(d)(9). For rules regarding the determination of whether dates prior to November 5, 1992, are testing dates, see § 1.382-2T(a)(2)(i).

(ii) *Exceptions.* A loss corporation is not required to determine whether an ownership change has occurred immediately after—

(A) Any transfer of stock, or an option with respect to stock, of the loss corporation in any of the circumstances described in section 382(l)(3)(B) (death, gift, divorce, etc.); or

(B) The transfer of an option described in § 1.382-4(d)(11)(i) or (ii) (relating to transfers between persons who are not 5-percent shareholders or between members of certain public groups).

(5) *Successor corporation.* A successor corporation is a distributee or transferee corporation that succeeds to and takes into account items described in section 381(c) from a corporation as the result of an acquisition of assets described in section 381(a). A successor corporation also includes, as the context may require, a corporation which receives an asset or assets from another corporation if the corporation's basis for the asset(s) is determined, directly or indirectly, in whole or in part, by reference to the other corporation's basis and the amount by which basis differs from value is, in the aggregate, material. The previous sentence of this paragraph (a)(5) applies to any testing date occurring on or after January 1, 1997.

(6) *Predecessor corporation.* A predecessor corporation is a distributor or transferor corporation that distributes or transfers its assets to an acquiring corporation in a transaction described in section 381(a). A predecessor corporation also includes, as the context may require, a corporation which transfers an asset or assets to another corporation if the transferee's basis for the asset(s) is determined, directly or indirectly, in whole or in part, by reference to the corporation's basis and the amount by which basis differs from value is, in the aggregate, material. The previous sentence of this paragraph (a)(6) applies to any testing date occurring on or after January 1, 1997.

* * *

[Reg. § 1.382-2.]

□ [*T.D.* 8352, 6-26-91. *Amended by T.D.* 8405, 3-27-92, *T.D.* 8440, 10-2-92; *T.D.* 8531, 3-17-94; *T.D.* 8679, 6-26-96 *and T.D.* 8825, 6-25-99.]

Reg. § 1.382-2(a)(6)

§ 1.382-2T. Definition of ownership change under section 382, as amended by the Tax Reform Act of 1986 (temporary).—(a) *Ownership change*—(1) *In general.* A corporation is a new loss corporation and thus subject to limitation under section 382 only if an ownership change has occurred with respect to such corporation. An ownership change occurs with respect to a corporation if it is a loss corporation on a testing date and, immediately after the close of the testing date, the percentage of stock of the corporation owned by one or more 5-percent shareholders has increased by more than 50 percentage points over the lowest percentage of stock of such corporation owned by such shareholders at any time during the testing period. See (a)(2)(i) of this section for the definition of testing date. See paragraph (d) of this section for the definition of testing period. See paragraphs § 1.382-2(a)(1) and paragraph (f)(3) of this section for the respective definitions of loss corporation and new loss corporation. See paragraph (g) of this section for the definition of 5-percent shareholder. See section 383 and § 1.383-1 for rules relating to loss corporations that have an ownership change and have capital loss carryovers, excess foreign taxes carried over under section 904(c), carryovers of general business credits under section 39, or unused minimum tax credits under section 53.

* * *

(b) *Nomenclature and assumptions.* For purposes of the examples in this section—

(1) L is a loss corporation, and, if there is more than one loss corporation, they are designated as L_1, L_2, L_3, etc.

(2) P is a corporation that is not a loss corporation, and, if there is more than one such corporation, they are designated as P_1, P_2, P_3, etc.

(3) HC is a corporation whose assets consist solely of the stock of other corporations.

(4) E is an entity other than a corporation (e.g., a partnership), and, if there is more than one such entity, they are designated as E_1, E_2, E_3, etc.

(5) Unless otherwise stated—

(i) A, B, C, D, AA, BB, CC, and DD are unrelated individuals who own interests in corporations or other entities only to the extent expressly stated,

(ii) all corporations have one class of stock outstanding and each share of stock has the same fair market value as each other share,

(iii) the capital structure of the loss corporation and its business do not change over time, and

(iv) the rules of paragraphs (k)(2) and (4) of this section are not applicable.

(6) Public L represents a group of unrelated individuals and entities that own direct (and not indirect) stock ownership interests in loss corporation L, each of whom owns less than five percent of the stock of the loss corporation, and, if there is more than one loss corporation, such groups are designated as Public L_1, Public L_2, Public L_3, etc.

(7) Public P represents a group of unrelated individuals and entities that own direct (and not indirect) stock ownership interests in corporation P, each of whom owns less than five percent of the stock of the corporation, and, if there is more than one corporation, such groups are designated as Public P_1, Public P_2, Public P_3, etc.

(8) Public E represents a group of unrelated individuals and entities that own direct (and not indirect) ownership interests in entity E, each of whom owns less than five percent of the entity, and, if there is more than one entity, such groups are designated as Public E_1, Public E_2, Public E_3, etc.

(c) *Computing the amount of increases in percentage ownership*—(1) *In general.* In order to determine whether an ownership change has occurred on a testing date, the loss corporation must identify each 5-percent shareholder whose percentage of stock ownership in the loss corporation immediately after the close of the testing date has increased, compared to such shareholder's lowest percentage of stock ownership in such corporation at any time during the testing period. The amount of the increase in the percentage of stock ownership in the loss corporation of each 5-percent shareholder must be computed separately by comparing the percentage ownership of each such 5-percent shareholder immediately after the close of the testing date to such shareholder's lowest percentage ownership at any time during the testing period. Each such increase in the percentage ownership of a 5-percent shareholder is then added together with any other such increases of other 5-percent shareholders to determine whether an ownership change has occurred. Because only those 5-percent shareholders whose percentages of stock ownership have increased are taken into account, a 5-percent shareholder is disregarded if his percentage of stock ownership, immediately after the close of the testing date, has decreased (or has remained the same), compared to his lowest percentage ownership interest on any previous date during the testing period.

(2) *Example*—(i) A and B each own 40 percent of the outstanding L stock. The remaining 20 percent of the L stock is owned by 100 unrelated individuals, none of whom own as much as five percent of L stock ("Public L"). C negotiates with A and B to purchase all their stock in L.

(ii) The acquisitions from both A and B are completed on September 13, 1990. C's acquisition of 80 percent of L stock results in an ownership change because C's percentage ownership has increased by 80 percentage points as of the testing date, compared to his lowest percentage ownership in L at any time during the testing period (0 percent).

(3) *Related and unrelated increases in percentage stock ownership.* The determination whether an ownership change has occurred is made without regard to whether the changes in stock ownership of the loss corporation (by one or more 5-percent shareholders) result from related or unrelated events.

(4) *Example*—(i) L has outstanding 200 shares of common stock. A, B and C respectively own 100, 50 and 50 shares of the L stock. On January 2, 1988, A sells 60 shares of L stock to B. Thus, B's percentage ownership interest in L increases by 30 percentage points, from 50 shares to 110 shares. On January 1, 1989, A purchases C's entire interest in L. Thus, A's percentage ownership interest in L increases by 25 percentage points, compared to his lowest percentage ownership interest in L, from 40 shares immediately following the January 2, 1988 sale to B to 90 shares. Even though A's ownership interest in L as of January 1, 1989 has decreased, compared to his 50 percent ownership interest at the beginning of the testing period, A is a 5-percent shareholder who must be taken into account for purposes of the computation required under paragraph (c)(1) of this section because his interest in L on that testing date (45 percent) has increased, compared to his lowest percentage ownership interest in L at any time during the testing period (20 percent following the sale to B).

(ii) Accordingly, although A and B jointly have increased their aggregate total ownership interest in L between January 2, 1988 and January 1, 1989 by only 25 percentage points (*i.e.*, the total ownership interest in L held by A and B at all times is not less than a 75 percent interest), the total of their separate increases in the percentage stock ownership of L, compared to their respective lowest percentage ownership interests at any time during the testing period, is 55 percentage points. Thus, an ownership change occurs as a result of A's acquisition of L stock on January 1, 1989.

(d) *Testing period*—(1) *In general.* Except as otherwise provided in this paragraph (d) and paragraph (m) of this section, the testing period for any testing date is the three-year period ending on the testing date. See paragraph (a)(2)(i) of this section for the definition of testing date.

(2) *Effect of a prior ownership change.* Following an ownership change, the testing period for determining whether a subsequent ownership change has occurred shall begin no earlier than the first day following the change date of the most recent ownership change. See paragraph (f)(19) of this section for the definition of change date.

(3) *Commencement of the testing period*—(i) *In general.* Except as otherwise provided in paragraph (d)(3)(ii) of this section, the testing period for any loss corporation shall not begin before the earlier of the first day of either—

(A) the first taxable year from which there is a loss or excess credit carryforward to the first taxable year ending after the testing date, or

(B) the taxable year in which the testing date occurs.

(ii) *Exception for corporations with net unrealized built-in loss.* Paragraph (d)(3)(i) of this section shall not apply if the corporation has a net unrealized built-in loss (determined after application of section 382(h)(3)(B)) on the testing date, unless the loss corporation establishes the taxable year in which the net unrealized built-in loss first accrued. In that event, the testing period shall not begin before the earlier of—

(A) the first day of the taxable year in which the net unrealized built-in loss first accrued, or

(B) the day described in paragraph (d)(3)(i) of this section.

See section 382(h) for the definition of net unrealized built-in loss.

(4) *Disregarding testing dates.* Any testing date that occurs before the beginning of the testing period shall be disregarded for purposes of this section.

(5) *Example*—(i) A owns all 100 outstanding shares of L stock. A sells 40 shares to B on January 1, 1988. C purchases 20 shares of L stock from A on July 1, 1991. In determining if an ownership change occurs on the July 1, 1991 testing date, B's acquisition of L stock is disregarded because it occurred before the testing period that ends on such testing date. Thus, B's ownership interest in L does not increase during the testing period, and no ownership change results from C's acquisition.

(ii) The facts are the same as in (i), except that throughout the period during which B negotiated his stock purchase transaction with A, B knew that C intended to attempt to acquire a significant stock interest in L. Also, B and C have been partners in a number of significant business ventures. The result is the same as in (i).

(e) *Owner shift and equity structure shift*—(1) *Owner shift*—(i) *Defined.* For purposes of this section, an owner shift is any change in the owner-

Reg. § 1.382-2T(e)(1)

ship of the stock of a loss corporation that affects the percentage of such stock owned by any 5-percent shareholder. See paragraph (g) of this section for the definition of a 5-percent shareholder. An owner shift includes, but is not limited to, the following transactions:

(A) a purchase or disposition of loss corporation stock by a 5-percent shareholder,

(B) a section 351 exchange that affects the percentage of stock owned by a 5-percent shareholder,

(C) a redemption or a recapitalization that affects the percentage of stock owned by a 5-percent shareholder,

(D) an issuance of loss corporation stock that affects the percentage of stock owned by a 5-percent shareholder, and

(E) an equity structure shift that affects the percentage of stock owned by a 5-percent shareholder.

(ii) *Transactions between persons who are not 5-percent shareholders disregarded.* Transfers of loss corporation stock between persons who are not 5-percent shareholders of such corporation (and between members of separate public groups resulting from the application of the segregation rules of paragraphs (j)(2) and (3)(iii) of this section) are not owner shifts and thus are not taken into account. See paragraph (h)(4)(xi) of this section for a similar rule applicable to transfers of options.

(iii) *Examples—Example (1).* A has owned all 1000 shares of outstanding L stock for more than three years. On June 15, 1988, A sells 300 of his L shares to B. This transaction is an owner shift. No other 5-percent shareholder has increased his percentage ownership of L stock during the testing period. Thus, the owner shift resulting from B's acquisition does not result in an ownership change, because B has increased his stock ownership in L by only 30 percentage points.

Example (2). The facts are the same as in Example (1). In addition, on June 15, 1989, L issues 100 shares to each of C, D and AA. The stock issuance is an owner shift. The transaction, however, does not result in an ownership change, because B, C, D and AA (the 5-percent shareholders whose stock ownership has increased as of the testing date, compared to any other time during the testing period) have increased their percentage of stock ownership in L by a total of only 46.2 percentage points during the testing period (by 23.1 percentage points [300 shares/1300 shares] for B, and 7.7 percentage points [100 shares/1300 shares] for each of C, D and AA).

Example (3). All 1000 shares of L stock are owned by a group of 100 unrelated individuals, none of whom own as much as five percent of L stock ("Public L"). Several of the members of Public L sell their L stock, amounting to a 30 percent ownership interest in L, to B on June 15, 1988. The sale of stock to B is an owner shift. Between June 16, 1988 and June 15, 1989, each of the remaining individuals in Public L sells his stock to another person who is not a 5-percent shareholder. Under paragraph (e)(1)(ii) of this section, trading activity among the members of Public L is disregarded and does not result in an owner shift. On June 15, 1989, L issues 100 shares to each of C, D and AA. The only sale transactions by members of Public L that are taken into account in determining whether an ownership change occurs on June 15, 1989 are the sales to B on June 15, 1988. Because B, C, D and AA together have increased their percentage ownership of L stock as a result of B's purchase and the stock issuance by an amount not in excess of 50 percentage points during the testing period ending on June 15, 1988, an ownership change does not occur on that date.

Example (4). The facts are the same as in Example (2). In addition, on December 15, 1989, L redeems 200 of the L shares from A. The redemption is an owner shift that results in an ownership change, because B, C, D and AA are 5-percent shareholders whose percentage ownership of L increase by a total of 54.6 percentage points during the testing period (by 27.3 percentage points [300 shares/1100 shares] for B and 9.1 percentage points [100 shares/1100 shares] for each of C, D and AA).

Example (5). L is owned entirely by 10,000 unrelated shareholders, none of whom owns as much as five percent of the stock of L ("Public L"). Accordingly, Public L is L's only 5-percent shareholder. See paragraph (j)(1) of this section. There are one million shares of common stock outstanding. On December 1, 1988, L issues two million new shares of its common stock to members of the public, none of whom owned any L stock prior to the issuance. Following the public offering, no shareholder of L owns, directly or indirectly, five percent or more of L stock. Under paragraph (j)(2) of this section, however, all of the newly issued stock is treated as acquired by a 5-percent shareholder ("Public NL") that is unrelated to Public L. Therefore, the public offering constitutes an owner shift that results in an ownership change because Public NL's percentage of stock ownership in L increased by 66⅔ percentage points (two million shares acquired in the public offering/three million shares outstanding following the offering) over its lowest percentage

Reg. § 1.382-2T(e)(1)

ownership during the testing period (0 percent prior to the offering).

    Example (6). The facts are the same as in Example (5), except that L issues only 500,000 new shares of L stock on December 1, 1988, and Public NL's percentage ownership interest in L increases by only 33⅓ percentage points (500,000 shares acquired in the public offering/1.5 million shares outstanding following the offering). During the two years following December 2, 1988, 14 percent of the stock outstanding on that date is sold over a public stock exchange. On December 3, 1990, A purchases five percent of L stock (75,000 shares) over a public stock exchange. The purchase of five percent of L stock by A is an owner shift and is presumed to have been made proportionately from Public L and Public NL under paragraph (j)(2)(vi) of this section. Under paragraph (e)(1)(ii) of this section, transfers of L stock in transactions not involving A (*i.e.*, in transactions among or between members of separate public groups resulting from the application of paragraphs (j)(2) and (3) of this section) are not taken into account, and do not constitute owner shifts. (Transfers between members of Public NL and Public L, which are treated as separate 5-percent shareholders solely by virtue of paragraph (j)(2) of this section, are disregarded even if L has actual knowledge of any such transfers.) A and Public NL, the only 5-percent shareholders whose interests in L have increased during the testing period, have increased their respective stock ownership by only 36⅔ percentage points—five percentage points for A [75,000 shares/1.5 million shares outstanding] and 31⅔ percentage points for Public NL [((500,000 shares issued in the public offering) − (5 percent × 500,000 shares presumed to have been acquired by A))/1.5 million shares outstanding]. Accordingly, there is no ownership change with respect to L notwithstanding that, taking into account the public trading, a change of more than 50 percentage points in the ultimate beneficial ownership of L stock occurred during the three-year period ending on the December 3, 1990 testing date.

    Example (7). The facts are the same as in Example 6, except that five percent of the L stock has always been owned by P which, in turn, has always been owned by Public P. On December 6, 1990, P sells all of its L stock over a public stock exchange. Although the trading of P stock among persons that are not 5-percent shareholders (without regard to the segregation rules of paragraph (j) of this section) are disregarded under paragraph (e)(1)(ii) of this section, the disposition of the L stock by P is not disregarded because the L stock is transferred in a transaction that is subject to paragraph (j)(3)(i) of this section.

    (2) *Equity structure shift*—(i) *Tax-free reorganizations.* An equity structure shift is any reorganization within the meaning of section 368 with respect to which the loss corporation is a party to the reorganization, except that such term does not include a reorganization described in—

    (A) Section 368(a)(1)(D) or (G) unless the requirements of section 354(b)(1) are met, or

    (B) Section 368(a)(1)(F).

    (ii) *Transactions designated under section 382(g)(3)(B) treated as equity structure shifts.* [Reserved].

    (iii) *Overlap of owner shift and equity structure shift.* Any equity structure shift that affects the percentage of loss corporation stock owned by a 5-percent shareholder also constitutes an owner shift. See paragraph (e)(1)(i)(E) of this section.

    (iv) *Examples—Example (1).* A owns all of the stock of L and B owns all of the stock of P. On October 13, 1988, L merges into P in a reorganization described in section 368(a)(1)(A). As a result of the merger, A and B own 25 and 75 percent, respectively, of the stock of P. The merger is an equity structure shift (and, because it affects the percentage of L stock owned by 5-shareholders, it also constitutes an owner shift). On the October 13, 1988 testing date, B is a 5-percent shareholder whose stock ownership in the loss corporation following the merger has increased by 75 percentage points over his lowest percentage of stock ownership in L at any time during the testing period (0 percent prior to the merger). Accordingly, an ownership change occurs as a result of the merger. P is thus a new loss corporation and L's pre-change losses are subject to limitation under section 382.

    Example (2)—(i) A owns 100 percent of L_1 stock and B owns 100 percent of L_2 stock. On January 1, 1988, L_1 merges into L_2 in a reorganization described in section 368(a)(1)(A). Immediately after the merger, A and B own 40 percent and 60 percent, respectively, of the L_2 stock. There is an equity structure shift (as well as an owner shift) with respect to both L_1 and L_2 on January 1, 1988.

    (*ii*) Because the percentage of L_2 stock owned by B immediately after the merger (60 percent) increases by more than 50 percentage points over the lowest percentage of the stock of L_1 owned by B during the testing period (0 percent prior to the merger), there is an ownership change with respect to L_1. L_2 is a new loss corporation and thus, under § 1.382-2(a)(1)(iii) of this section, the pre-change losses of L_1 must be accounted for separately by L_2 from the losses of L_2 (immediately before the ownership change) and are subject to limitation under section 382. See § 1.382-2(a)(1)(iv) of this section for rules that

Reg. § 1.382-2T(e)(2)

end separate accounting for L_1's pre-change losses on any testing date occurring on or after January 29, 1991.

(*iii*) L_2 is a new loss corporation because it is a successor corporation to L. There is no ownership change with respect to L_2, however, because A's stock ownership in L_2 increased by only 40 percentage points (to 40 percent) over the amount owned by A prior to the merger (0 percent). Therefore, the pre-change losses of L_2 are not limited under section 382 as a result of the merger.

Example (3). The result in Example (2) would be the same if L_1 had survived the merger (*i.e.*, L_2 merged into L_1) with A and B owning 40 and 60 percent, respectively, of L_1 stock. L_1's pre-change losses would be accounted for separately and limited under section 382 and the pre-change losses of L_2 would be accounted for separately under § 1.382-2(a)(1)(iii) of this section; but would not be limited under section 382. See § 1.382-2(a)(1)(ii) for the treatment of L_2 following the transaction.

Example (4). The facts are the same as Example (2), except, instead of acquiring L_1 in a merger, L_2 acquires all of the L_1 stock from A on January 1, 1988, solely in exchange for stock representing a 40 percent interest in L_2, in a reorganization described in section 368(a)(1)(B). The acquisition of stock by L_2 is an equity structure shift (as well as an owner shift) with respect to L_1 that results in an ownership change with respect to L_1 because the percentage of L_1 stock owned by B immediately after the reorganization (60 percent, by virtue of B's ownership of L_2, through the operation of the constructive ownership rules of paragraph (h) of this section) increases by more than 50 percentage points over the lowest percentage of L_1 stock owned by B at any time during the testing period (0 percent prior to the reorganization). The acquisition also results in an equity structure shift and an owner shift with respect to L_2, but L_2 incurs no ownership change, because A's stock ownership in L_2 increased by only 40 percentage points over the percentage of L_2 stock owned by A prior to the reorganization (0 percent).

(f) *Definitions.* For purposes of this section—

(1) *Loss corporation.* See section 382 and § 1.382-2(a)(1) for the definition of a loss corporation.

(2) *Old loss corporation.* The term "old loss corporation" means any corporation with respect to which there is an ownership change and that was a loss corporation immediately before the ownership change.

(3) *New loss corporation.* The term "new loss corporation" means a corporation with respect to which there is an ownership change if, immediately after such change, it is a loss corporation. A successor corporation to the corporation described in the preceding sentence also is a new loss corporation.

(4) *Successor corporation.* See § 1.382-2(a)(5) for the definition of *successor corporation.*

(5) *Predecessor corporation.* See § 1.382-2(a)(6) for the definitions of *predecessor corporation.*

(6) *Shift.* As the context may require, a shift means an equity structure shift, an owner shift or both.

(7) *Entity.* See § 1.382-3(a)(1) for the definition of an entity.

(8) *Direct ownership interest.* A direct ownership interest means the interest a person owns in an entity, including a loss corporation, without regard to the constructive ownership rules of paragraph (h) of this section.

(9) *First tier entity.* A first tier entity is an entity that, at any time during the testing period, owns a five percent or more direct ownership interest in the loss corporation.

(10) *5-percent owner.* A 5-percent owner is any individual that, at any time during the testing period, owns a five percent or more direct ownership interest in a first tier entity or a higher tier entity. See paragraph (g) of this section for rules to determine whether, as a result of the constructive ownership rules of paragraph (h) of this section, a 5-percent owner is a 5-percent shareholder.

(11) *Public shareholder.* A public shareholder is any individual, entity, or other person with a direct ownership interest in a loss corporation of less than five percent at all times during the testing period.

(12) *Public owner.* A public owner is any individual, entity, or other person that, at all times during the testing period, owns less than a five percent direct ownership interest in a first tier entity or any higher tier entity.

(13) *Public group.* A public group is a group of individuals, entities, or other persons each of whom owns, directly or constructively, less than five percent of the loss corporation. See paragraphs (g) and (j) of this section for the rules applicable to identify public groups and to determine whether a public group is a 5-percent shareholder.

(14) *Higher tier entity.* A higher tier entity is any entity that, at any time during the testing period, owns a five percent or more direct ownership interest in a first tier entity or in any higher tier entity.

Reg. § 1.382-2T(f)(1)

(15) *Indirect ownership interest.* An indirect ownership interest is an interest a person owns in an entity determined solely as a result of the application of the constructive ownership rules of paragraph (h) of this section and without regard to any direct ownership interest (or other beneficial ownership interest) in the entity.

(16) *Highest tier entity.* A highest tier entity is a first tier entity or a higher tier entity that is not owned, in whole or in part, at any time during the testing period by a higher tier entity.

(17) *Next lower tier entity.* The next lower tier entity with respect to a first tier entity is the loss corporation. The next lower tier entity with respect to a higher tier entity is any first tier entity or other higher tier entity in which the higher tier entity owns, at any time during the testing period, a five percent or more direct ownership interest.

(18) *Stock*—(i) *In general.* For further guidance, see § 1.382-2(a)(3)(i).

(ii) *Treating stock as not stock.* Any ownership interest that otherwise would be treated as stock under paragraph (f)(18)(i) of this section shall not be treated as stock if—

(A) As of the time of its issuance or transfer to (or by) a 5-percent shareholder, the likely participation of such interest in future corporate growth is disproportionately small when compared to the value of such stock as a proportion of the total value of the outstanding stock of the corporation,

(B) Treating the interest as not constituting stock would result in an ownership change, and

(C) The amount of the pre-change loss (determined as if the testing date were the change date and treating the amount of any net unrealized built-in loss as a pre-change loss) is more than twice the amount determined by multiplying (*1*) the value of the loss corporation (as determined under section 382(e)) on the testing date, by (*2*) the long-term tax exempt rate (as defined in section 382(f)) for the calendar month in which the testing date occurs. Stock that is not treated as stock under this paragraph (f)(18)(ii), however, is taken into account for purposes of determining the value of the loss corporation under section 382(e).

(iii) *Treating interests not constituting stock as stock.* Any ownership interest that would not be treated as stock under paragraph (f)(18)(i) of this section (other than an option that is subject to paragraph (h)(4) of this section) shall be treated as constituting stock if—

(A) As of the time of its issuance or transfer to (or by) a 5-percent shareholder (or a person who would be a 5-percent shareholder if the interest not constituting stock were treated as stock), such interest offers a potential significant participation in the growth of the corporation,

(B) Treating the interest as constituting stock would result in an ownership change, and

(C) The amount of the pre-change losses (determined as if the testing date were the change date and treating the amount of any net unrealized built-in loss as a pre-change loss) is more than twice the amount determined by multiplying (*1*) the value of the loss corporation (as determined under section 382(e)) on the testing date, by (*2*) the long-term tax exempt rate (as defined in section 382(f)) for the calendar month in which the testing date occurs. An ownership interest that is treated as stock under this paragraph (f)(18)(iii) is taken into account for purposes of determining the value of the loss corporation under section 382(e).

See § 1.382-4(d)(12) for rules that apply with respect to options and this paragraph (f)(18)(iii).

(iv) *Stock of the loss corporation.* The stock of the loss corporation means stock of such corporation within the meaning of this paragraph (f)(18) and, as the context may require, includes any indirect ownership interest in the loss corporation.

(19) *Change date.* The change date means the date on which a shift (or any other transaction described in paragraph (a)(2)(i) of this section) that is the last component of an ownership change occurs.

(20) *Year.* A year, or any multiple thereof, means a 365-day period (or a 366-day period in the case of a leap year), or any multiple thereof, unless the year is specifically identified as a taxable year.

(21) *Old section 382.* Old section 382 means section 382, as in effect prior to the effective date of section 382 in the Tax Reform Act of 1986 (the "Act"), but taking into account section 621(f)(2) of the Act.

(22) *Pre-change loss.* See section 382 and § 1.382-2(a)(2) for the definition of pre-change loss.

(23) *Unrelated.* Any two persons are unrelated if the constructive ownership rules of paragraph (h) of this section do not apply to treat either person as owning stock that is owned, directly or constructively, by the other person.

(24) *Percentage ownership interest.* A person's percentage ownership interest in—

(i) a corporation shall be determined under the rules of this section that are applicable to the determination of a shareholder's percentage stock ownership interest in a loss corporation (see paragraphs (f)(18)(i) through (iii) of this section),

(ii) a partnership shall be equal to the relative fair market value of such person's partnership interest to the total fair market value of all outstanding partnership interests, determined without regard to any limited and preferred partnership interest that is described in paragraph (h)(2)(ii)(C) of this section,

(iii) a trust shall be determined in accordance with the principles of section 318(a)(2)(B) for determining the constructive ownership of stock,

(iv) an estate shall be determined in accordance with the principles of section 318(a)(2)(A) for determining the constructive ownership of stock, and

(v) all other entities shall be determined by reference to the person's relative economic interest in the entity, taking into account all of the relevant facts and circumstances.

(g) *5-percent shareholder*—(1) *In general.* Subject to the rules of paragraphs (k)(2) and (4) of this section, the term "5-percent shareholder" means—

(i) an individual that owns, at any time during the testing period, (A) a direct ownership interest in the stock of the loss corporation of five percent or more or (B) an indirect ownership interest in the stock of the loss corporation of five percent or more by virtue of an ownership interest in any one first tier entity or higher tier entity,

(ii) a public group, of either a first tier entity or a higher tier entity, identified as a 5-percent shareholder under paragraphs (j)(1)(iv)(A) or (B) of this section,

(iii) a public group of the loss corporation identified as a 5-percent shareholder under paragraph (j)(1)(iv)(C) of this section, and

(iv) a public group, of the loss corporation, a first tier entity or a higher tier entity, identified as a 5-percent shareholder under paragraphs (j)(2) or (3) of this section. An individual owning five percent or more of the stock of the loss corporation at any time during the testing period is a 5-percent shareholder notwithstanding that the individual may own less than five percent of the stock of the loss corporation on the testing date. See paragraph (g)(5)(i)(B) of this section for rules permitting a loss corporation to make an adjustment in cases described in the preceding sentence.

(2) *Determination of whether a person is a 5-percent shareholder.* Except as provided in paragraphs (k)(2) and (4) of this section, a person shall be treated as constructively owning stock of the loss corporation pursuant to paragraph (h)(2) of this section only if the loss corporation stock is attributed to such person in the person's capacity as a higher tier entity or a 5-percent owner of the first tier entity or higher tier entity from which such stock is attributed. See paragraph (k)(3) of this section for rules explaining the extent of the obligation of the loss corporation to determine the identity of its 5-percent shareholders. Nothing in this paragraph (g)(2), however, shall limit the attribution of loss corporation stock under section 318(a)(2) and paragraph (h) of this section to a public owner.

(3) *Determination of the percentage stock ownership interest of a 5-percent shareholder.* Subject to the rules of paragraphs (k)(2) and (4) of this section, in determining a 5-percent shareholder's percentage ownership interest in the loss corporation, the shareholder's direct ownership interest, if any, and each indirect ownership interest that he may have in the loss corporation in his capacity as a 5-percent owner of any one first tier entity or higher tier entity, if any, are required to be added together and taken into account with respect to such shareholder only to the extent that each such direct or indirect ownership interest constitutes five percent or more of the stock of the loss corporation.

(4) *Examples—Example (1)*—(i) Twenty percent of L stock is owned by A, 10 percent is owned by P_1, 20 percent is owned by E, a joint venture, and the remaining 50 percent of L stock is owned by Public L. P_1 is owned 15 percent by B and 85 percent by Public P_1. E is owned 30 percent by P_2 and 70 percent by P_3, which, in turn, are owned by Public P_2 and Public P_3, respectively.

(ii) The ownership structure of L is illustrated by the following chart:

(iii) P₁ and E, each of which has a direct ownership interest in L of five percent or more, are first tier entities. The shareholders with direct ownership interests in L who individually own less than five percent of L are public shareholders (Public L). B, who has a direct ownership interest of five percent or more in P₁, is a 5-percent owner of P₁. P₂ and P₃, each of which has a direct ownership interest in a first tier entity (E) of five percent or more, are higher tier entities with respect to L and, because neither entity is owned at any time during the testing period by a higher tier entity, they also are highest tier entities. The shareholders of P₂ and P₃ (Public P₂ and Public P₃, respectively) are public owners of such entities, because none of those shareholders own five percent or more of either entity at any time during the testing period.

(iv) A, who has a 20 percent direct ownership interest in L, is a 5-percent shareholder of L. Because, by application of the constructive owner-ship rules of paragraph (h) of this section, B owns only 1.5 percent of L stock in his capacity as a 5-percent owner of P₁ (15 percent ownership of P₁ × 10 percent ownership of L), B is not a 5-percent shareholder of L, even though he is a 5-percent owner of P₁. Under the rules of paragraph (j) of this section, therefore, B is treated as a member of Public P₁. See Example (3) of paragraph (j)(1)(vi) of this section for a determination of which public owners and public shareholders constitute public groups that are treated as 5-percent shareholders of L.

Example (2)—(i) The facts are the same as in Example (1), except that P₃ is owned 60 percent by C, 30 percent by P₄, and 10 percent by Public P₃. The stock of P₄ is owned by a group of persons (Public P₄), none of whom own five per-cent or more of the stock of P₄.

(ii) The ownership structure of L is illus-trated by the following chart:

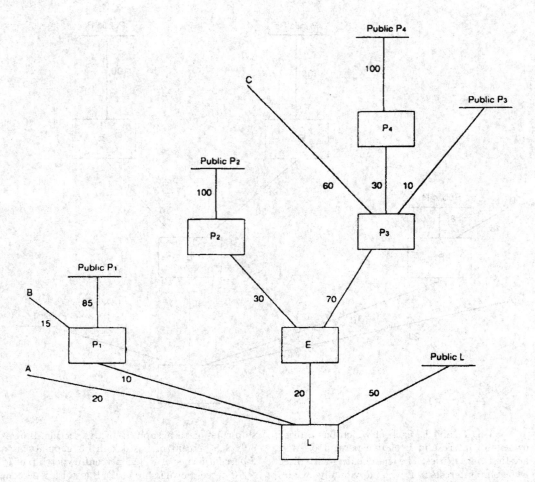

(iii) The defined terms are the same as in Example (1), except that P_3 is a higher tier entity, not a highest tier entity, because five percent or more of P_3 is, in turn, owned by another entity (P_4). P_4, which owns five percent or more of a higher tier entity (P_3), also is a higher tier entity and, because it is not owned at any time during any testing period by any entity that is also a higher tier entity, P_4 is a highest tier entity. All of the shareholders of P_4, none of which own a direct ownership interest of five percent or more in P_4, are public owners of P_4.

(iv) C is a 5-percent owner of P_3 and, under the constructive ownership rules of paragraph (h) of this section, C indirectly owns 8.4 percent of L ([60 percent ownership of P_3] × [70 percent ownership of E] × [20 percent ownership of L]), in his capacity as a 5-percent owner of P_3. B is a 5-percent owner of P_1 and, under the constructive ownership rules of paragraph (h) of this section, B owns 1.5 percent of L ([15 percent ownership of P_1] × [10 percent ownership of L]) in his capacity as a 5-percent owner of P_1. Therefore, C is a 5-percent shareholder of L, but B is not

a 5-percent shareholder of L, even though he is a 5-percent owner of P_1. See Example (4) of paragraph (j)(1)(vi) of this section for a determination of which public owners and public shareholders constitute public groups that are treated as separate 5-percent shareholders of L.

Example (3)—(i) L is owned 30 percent by A and 70 percent by P. A owns six percent of P stock and the balance (94 percent) is owned equally by 500 unrelated shareholders ("Public P").

(ii) A is a 5-percent shareholder because he directly owns 30 percent of L. Even though A is a 5-percent owner of P, A's 4.2 percent indirect ownership interest in L (six percent ownership interest in P × P's 70 percent ownership of L) is generally not taken into account in determining A's ownership interest, because such indirect ownership interest is less than five percent. Instead, A's 4.2 percent indirect interest is treated under paragraph (j)(1)(iv) of this section as owned by Public P. If, however, L has actual knowledge of A's less-than-five-percent indirect ownership interest in L and is thus subject to paragraph (k)(2) of this section, or paragraph (k)(4) of this section otherwise applies, L must take A's total 34.2 percent ownership interest into account in determining A's percentage ownership in L.

Example (4). The facts are the same as in Example (3), except that A owns ten percent of P's stock. Because A's indirect ownership interest in L in his capacity as a 5-percent owner of P is five percent or more, both A's 30 percent direct ownership interest in L and his seven percent indirect ownership interest in L (10 percent ownership interest in P × P's 70 percent ownership of L) are taken into account in determining his ownership interest in L, without regard to L's actual knowledge or whether paragraph (k)(4) of this section applies.

Example (5). See § 1.382-3(a)(1)(ii) for additional examples with respect to the definition of an entity.

(5) *Stock ownership presumptions in connection with certain acquisitions and dispositions of loss corporation stock*—(i) *In general.* For purposes of this section—

(A) if an individual owns less than five percent of the stock of a loss corporation during the testing period (excluding the testing date) and acquires an amount of such stock so that the individual becomes a 5-percent shareholder on the testing date, the loss corporation may treat any interest in the loss corporation owned by such individual prior to that acquisition as owned by a public group during the period of such individual's ownership of that interest and as not owned by the 5-percent shareholder during the same period, and

(B) if a 5-percent shareholder's percentage ownership interest in the loss corporation is reduced to less than five percent, the loss corporation may presume that the remaining stock owned by such 5-percent shareholder immediately after

such reduction is the stock owned by such shareholder for each subsequent testing date having a testing period that includes the date on which the reduction occurred as long as such shareholder continues to own less than five percent of the stock of the loss corporation. In that event, such ownership interest shall be treated as owned by a separate public group for purposes of the rules of paragraph (j)(2)(vi) of this section.

(ii) *Example.* L has 100,000 shares of stock outstanding. All of the L stock is owned equally by 40 unrelated, individual shareholders, including A (who owns 2.5 percent of L stock). Because no person owns as much as five percent of L stock, Public L is the only 5-percent shareholder of L. See paragraph (j)(1) of this section. A purchases 5,000 shares of L stock over a public stock exchange on June 8, 1989. The purchase is an owner shift. When added to his ownership interest before that date (the testing date), A owns 7,500 shares of L stock (7.5 percent). Under paragraph (g)(5)(i)(A) of this section, L may treat A and Public L as having owned 0 percent and 100 percent, respectively, at all times prior to June 8, 1989 (rather than having owned 2.5 percent by A and 97.5 percent by Public L, even if L has actual knowledge of A's less than five percent ownership interest). The increase in A's stock ownership of L as of June 8, 1989 thus would be 7.5 percentage points, rather than 5.0 percentage points, for purposes of determining whether an ownership change occurs on that testing date and any subsequent testing date.

* * *

[Temporary Reg. § 1.382-2T.]

☐ [*T.D. 8149, 8-5-87. Amended by T.D. 8264, 9-19-89; T.D. 8277, 12-22-89; T.D. 8352, 6-26-91; T.D. 8405, 3-27-92; T.D. 8407, 4-8-92; T.D. 8428, 8-21-92; T.D. 8440, 10-2-92; T.D. 8490, 10-1-93 T.D. 8531, 3-17-94; T.D. 8679, 6-26-96 and T.D. 8825, 6-25-99.*]

Pension, Profit-Sharing, Stock Bonus Plans, Etc.

§ 1.408A-1. Roth IRAs in general.—This section sets forth the following questions and answers that discuss the background and general features of Roth IRAs:

Q-1 What is a Roth IRA?

A-1. (a) A Roth IRA is a new type of individual retirement plan that individuals can use, beginning in 1998. Roth IRAs are described in section 408A, which was added by the Taxpayer Relief Act of 1997 (TRA 97), Public Law 105-34 (111 Stat. 788).

(b) Roth IRAs are treated like traditional IRAs except where the Internal Revenue Code specifies different treatment. For example, aggregate contributions (other than by a conversion or other

rollover) to all an individual's Roth IRAs are not permitted to exceed $2,000 for a taxable year. Further, income earned on funds held in a Roth IRA is generally not taxable. Similarly, the rules of section 408(e), such as the loss of exemption of the account where the owner engages in a prohibited transaction, apply to Roth IRAs in the same manner as to traditional IRAs.

Q-2. What are the significant differences between traditional IRAs and Roth IRAs?

A-2. There are several significant differences between traditional IRAs and Roth IRAs under the Internal Revenue Code. For example, eligibility to contribute to a Roth IRA is subject to special modified AGI (adjusted gross income) limits; contributions to a Roth IRA are never deductible; qualified distributions from a Roth IRA are not includible in gross income; the required minimum distribution rules under section 408(a)(6) and (b)(3) (which generally incorporate the provisions of section 401(a)(9)) do not apply to a Roth IRA during the lifetime of the owner; and contributions to a Roth IRA can be made after the owner has attained age 70 1/2.

[Reg. § 1.408A-1.]

☐ [*T.D.* 8816, 2-3-99.]

§ 1.408A-2. Establishing Roth IRAs.—This section sets forth the following questions and answers that provide rules applicable to establishing Roth IRAs:

Q-1. Who can establish a Roth IRA?

A-1. Except as provided in A-3 of this section, only an individual can establish a Roth IRA. In addition, in order to be eligible to contribute to a Roth IRA for a particular year, an individual must satisfy certain compensation requirements and adjusted gross income limits (see § 1.408A-3 A-3).

Q-2. How is a Roth IRA established?

A-2. A Roth IRA can be established with any bank, insurance company, or other person authorized in accordance with § 1.408-2(e) to serve as a trustee with respect to IRAs. The document establishing the Roth IRA must clearly designate the IRA as a Roth IRA, and this designation cannot be changed at a later date. Thus, an IRA that is designated as a Roth IRA cannot later be treated as a traditional IRA. However, see § 1.408A-4 A-1(b)(3) for certain rules for converting a traditional IRA to a Roth IRA with the same trustee by redesignating the traditional IRA as a Roth IRA, and see § 1.408A-5 for rules for recharacterizing certain IRA contributions.

Q-3. Can an employer or an association of employees establish a Roth IRA to hold contributions of employees or members?

A-3. Yes. Pursuant to section 408(c), an employer or an association of employees can establish a trust to hold contributions of employees or members made under a Roth IRA. Each employee's or member's account in the trust is treated as a separate Roth IRA that is subject to the generally applicable Roth IRA rules. The employer or association of employees may do certain acts otherwise required by an individual, for example, establishing and designating a trust as a Roth IRA.

Q-4. What is the effect of a surviving spouse of a Roth IRA owner treating an IRA as his or her own?

A-4. If the surviving spouse of a Roth IRA owner treats a Roth IRA as his or her own as of a date, the Roth IRA is treated from that date forward as though it were established for the benefit of the surviving spouse and not the original Roth IRA owner. Thus, for example, the surviving spouse is treated as the Roth IRA owner for purposes of applying the minimum distribution requirements under section 408(a)(6) and (b)(3). Similarly, the surviving spouse is treated as the Roth IRA owner rather than a beneficiary for purposes of determining the amount of any distribution from the Roth IRA that is includible in gross income and whether the distribution is subject to the 10-percent additional tax under section 72(t).

[Reg. § 1.408A-2.]

☐ [*T.D.* 8816, 2-3-99.]

§ 1.408A-3. Contributions to Roth IRAs.—This section sets forth the following questions and answers that provide rules regarding contributions to Roth IRAs:

Q-1. What types of contributions are permitted to be made to a Roth IRA?

A-1. There are two types of contributions that are permitted to be made to a Roth IRA: regular contributions and qualified rollover contributions (including conversion contributions). The term regular contributions means contributions other than qualified rollover contributions.

Q-2. When are contributions permitted to be made to a Roth IRA?

A-2. (a) The provisions of section 408A are effective for taxable years beginning on or after January 1, 1998. Thus, the first taxable year for which contributions are permitted to be made to a Roth IRA by an individual is the individual's taxable year beginning in 1998.

(b) Regular contributions for a particular taxable year must generally be contributed by the due date (not including extensions) for filing a Federal income tax return for that taxable year. (See § 1.408A-5 regarding recharacterization of certain contributions.)

Q-3. What is the maximum aggregate amount of regular contributions an individual is eligible to contribute to a Roth IRA for a taxable year?

A-3. (a) The maximum aggregate amount that an individual is eligible to contribute to all his or her Roth IRAs as a regular contribution for a taxable year is the same as the maximum for traditional IRAs: $2,000 or, if less, that individual's compensation for the year.

(b) For Roth IRAs, the maximum amount described in paragraph (a) of this A-3 is phased out between certain levels of modified AGI. For an individual who is not married, the dollar amount is phased out ratably between modified AGI of $95,000 and $110,000; for a married individual

Reg. § 1.408A-2

filing a joint return, between modified AGI of $150,000 and $160,000; and for a married individual filing separately, between modified AGI of $0 and $10,000. For this purpose, a married individual who has lived apart from his or her spouse for the entire taxable year and who files separately is treated as not married. Under section 408A(c)(3)(A), in applying the phase-out, the maximum amount is rounded up to the next higher multiple of $10 and is not reduced below $200 until completely phased out.

(c) If an individual makes regular contributions to both traditional IRAs and Roth IRAs for a taxable year, the maximum limit for the Roth IRA is the lesser of—

(1) The amount described in paragraph (a) of this A-3 reduced by the amount contributed to traditional IRAs for the taxable year; and

(2) The amount described in paragraph (b) of this A-3. Employer contributions, including elective deferrals, made under a SEP or SIMPLE IRA Plan on behalf of an individual (including a self-employed individual) do not reduce the amount of the individual's maximum regular contribution.

(d) The rules in this A-3 are illustrated by the following examples:

Example 1. In 1998, unmarried, calendar-year taxpayer B, age 60, has modified AGI of $40,000 and compensation of $5,000. For 1998, B can contribute a maximum of $2,000 to a traditional IRA, a Roth IRA or a combination of traditional and Roth IRAs.

Example 2. The facts are the same as in *Example 1.* However, assume that B violates the maximum regular contribution limit by contributing $2,000 to a traditional IRA and $2,000 to a Roth IRA for 1998. The $2,000 to B's Roth IRA would be an excess contribution to B's Roth IRA for 1998 because an individual's contributions are applied first to a traditional IRA, then to a Roth IRA.

Example 3. The facts are the same as in *Example 1,* except that B's compensation is $900. The maximum amount B can contribute to either a traditional IRA or a Roth (or a combination of the two) for 1998 is $900.

Example 4. In 1998, unmarried, calendar-year taxpayer C, age 60, has modified AGI of $100,000 and compensation of $5,000. For 1998, C contributes $800 to a traditional IRA and $1,200 to a Roth IRA. Because C's $1,200 Roth IRA contribution does not exceed the phased-out maximum Roth IRA contribution of $1,340 and because C's total IRA contributions do not exceed $2,000, C's Roth IRA contribution does not exceed the maximum permissible contribution.

Q-4. How is compensation defined for purposes of the Roth IRA contribution limit?

A-4. For purposes of the contribution limit described in A-3 of this section, an individual's compensation is the same as that used to determine the maximum contribution an individual can make to a traditional IRA. This amount is defined in section 219(f)(1) to include wages, commissions, professional fees, tips, and other amounts received for personal services, as well as taxable alimony and separate maintenance payments received under a decree of divorce or separate maintenance. Compensation also includes earned income as defined in section 401(c)(2), but does not include any amount received as a pension or annuity or as deferred compensation. In addition, under section 219(c), a married individual filing a joint return is permitted to make an IRA contribution by treating his or her spouse's higher compensation as his or her own, but only to the extent that the spouse's compensation is not being used for purposes of the spouse making a contribution to a Roth IRA or a deductible contribution to a traditional IRA.

Q-5. What is the significance of modified AGI and how is it determined?

A-5. Modified AGI is used for purposes of the phase-out rules described in A-3 of this section and for purposes of the $100,000 modified AGI limitation described in § 1.408A-4 A-2(a) (relating to eligibility for conversion). As defined in section 408A(c)(3)(C)(i), modified AGI is the same as adjusted gross income under section 219(g)(3)(A) (used to determine the amount of deductible contributions that can be made to a traditional IRA by an individual who is an active participant in an employer-sponsored retirement plan), except that any conversion is disregarded in determining modified AGI. For example, the deduction for contributions to an IRA is not taken into account for purposes of determining adjusted gross income under section 219 and thus does not apply in determining modified AGI for Roth IRA purposes.

Q-6. Is a required minimum distribution from an IRA for a year included in income for purposes of determining modified AGI?

A-6. (a) Yes. For taxable years beginning before January 1, 2005, any required minimum distribution from an IRA under section 408(a)(6) and (b)(3) (which generally incorporate the provisions of section 401(a)(9)) is included in income for purposes of determining modified AGI.

(b) For taxable years beginning after December 31, 2004, and solely for purposes of the $100,000 limitation applicable to conversions, modified AGI does not include any required minimum dis-

Reg. § 1.408A-3

tributions from an IRA under section 408(a)(6) and (b)(3).

Q-7. Does an excise tax apply if an individual exceeds the aggregate regular contribution limits for Roth IRAs?

A-7. Yes. Section 4973 imposes an annual 6-percent excise tax on aggregate amounts contributed to Roth IRAs that exceed the maximum contribution limits described in A-3 of this section. Any contribution that is distributed, together with net income, from a Roth IRA on or before the tax return due date (plus extensions) for the taxable year of the contribution is treated as not contributed. Net income described in the previous sentence is includible in gross income for the taxable year in which the contribution is made. Aggregate excess contributions that are not distributed from a Roth IRA on or before the tax return due date (with extensions) for the taxable year of the contributions are reduced as a deemed Roth IRA contribution for each subsequent taxable year to the extent that the Roth IRA owner does not actually make regular IRA contributions for such years. Section 4973 applies separately to an individual's Roth IRAs and other types of IRAs.

[Reg. § 1.408A-3.]

☐ [*T.D.* 8816, 2-3-99.]

§ 1.408A-4. Converting amounts to Roth IRAs.—This section sets forth the following questions and answers that provide rules applicable to Roth IRA conversions:

Q-1. Can an individual convert an amount in his or her traditional IRA to a Roth IRA?

A-1. (a) Yes. An amount in a traditional IRA may be converted to an amount in a Roth IRA if two requirements are satisfied. First, the IRA owner must satisfy the modified AGI limitation described in A-2(a) of this section and, if married, the joint filing requirement described in A-2(b) of this section. Second, the amount contributed to the Roth IRA must satisfy the definition of a qualified rollover contribution in section 408A(e) (i.e., it must satisfy the requirements for a rollover contribution as defined in section 408(d)(3), except that the one-rollover-per-year limitation in section 408(d)(3)(B) does not apply).

(b) An amount can be converted by any of three methods—

(1) An amount distributed from a traditional IRA is contributed (rolled over) to a Roth IRA within the 60-day period described in section 408(d)(3)(A)(i);

(2) An amount in a traditional IRA is transferred in a trustee-to-trustee transfer from the trustee of the traditional IRA to the trustee of the Roth IRA; or

(3) An amount in a traditional IRA is transferred to a Roth IRA maintained by the same trustee. For purposes of sections 408 and 408A, redesignating a traditional IRA as a Roth IRA is treated as a transfer of the entire account balance from a traditional IRA to a Roth IRA.

(c) Any converted amount is treated as a distribution from the traditional IRA and a qualified rollover contribution to the Roth IRA for purposes of section 408 and section 408A, even if the conversion is accomplished by means of a trustee-to-trustee transfer or a transfer between IRAs of the same trustee.

(d) A transaction that is treated as a failed conversion under § 1.408A-5 A-9(a)(1) is not a conversion.

Q-2. What are the modified AGI limitation and joint filing requirements for conversions?

A-2. (a) An individual with modified AGI in excess of $100,000 for a taxable year is not permitted to convert an amount to a Roth IRA during that taxable year. This $100,000 limitation applies to the taxable year that the funds are paid from the traditional IRA, rather than the year they are contributed to the Roth IRA.

(b) If the individual is married, he or she is permitted to convert an amount to a Roth IRA during a taxable year only if the individual and the individual's spouse file a joint return for the taxable year that the funds are paid from the traditional IRA. In this case, the modified AGI subject to the $100,000 limit is the modified AGI derived from the joint return using the couple's combined income. The only exception to this joint filing requirement is for an individual who has lived apart from his or her spouse for the entire taxable year. If the married individual has lived apart from his or her spouse for the entire taxable year, then such individual can treat himself or herself as not married for purposes of this paragraph, file a separate return and be subject to the $100,000 limit on his or her separate modified AGI. In all other cases, a married individual filing a separate return is not permitted to convert an amount to a Roth IRA, regardless of the individual's modified AGI.

Q-3. Is a remedy available to an individual who makes a failed conversion?

A-3. (a) Yes. See § 1.408A-5 for rules permitting a failed conversion amount to be recharacterized as a contribution to a traditional IRA. If the requirements in § 1.408A-5 are satisfied, the failed conversion amount will be treated as having been contributed to the traditional IRA and not to the Roth IRA.

(b) If the contribution is not recharacterized in accordance with § 1.408A-5, the contribution will

Reg. § 1.408A-4

be treated as a regular contribution to the Roth IRA and, thus, an excess contribution subject to the excise tax under section 4973 to the extent that it exceeds the individual's regular contribution limit. This is the result regardless of which of the three methods described in A-1(b) of this section applies to this transaction. Additionally, the distribution from the traditional IRA will not be eligible for the 4-year spread and will be subject to the additional tax under section 72(t) (unless an exception under that section applies).

Q-4. Do any special rules apply to a conversion of an amount in an individual's SEP IRA or SIMPLE IRA to a Roth IRA?

A-4. (a) An amount in an individual's SEP IRA can be converted to a Roth IRA on the same terms as an amount in any other traditional IRA.

(b) An amount in an individual's SIMPLE IRA can be converted to a Roth IRA on the same terms as a conversion from a traditional IRA, except that an amount distributed from a SIMPLE IRA during the 2-year period described in section 72(t)(6), which begins on the date that the individual first participated in any SIMPLE IRA Plan maintained by the individual's employer, cannot be converted to a Roth IRA. Pursuant to section 408(d)(3)(G), a distribution of an amount from an individual's SIMPLE IRA during this 2-year period is not eligible to be rolled over into an IRA that is not a SIMPLE IRA and thus cannot be a qualified rollover contribution. This 2-year period of section 408(d)(3)(G) applies separately to the contributions of each of an individual's employers maintaining a SIMPLE IRA Plan.

(c) Once an amount in a SEP IRA or SIMPLE IRA has been converted to a Roth IRA, it is treated as a contribution to a Roth IRA for all purposes. Future contributions under the SEP or under the SIMPLE IRA Plan may not be made to the Roth IRA.

Q-5. Can amounts in other kinds of retirement plans be converted to a Roth IRA?

A-5. No. Only amounts in another IRA can be converted to a Roth IRA. For example, amounts in a qualified plan or annuity plan described in section 401(a) or 403(a) cannot be converted directly to a Roth IRA. Also, amounts held in an annuity contract or account described in section 403(b) cannot be converted directly to a Roth IRA.

Q-6. Can an individual who has attained at least age 70 1/2 by the end of a calendar year convert an amount distributed from a traditional IRA during that year to a Roth IRA before receiving his or her required minimum distribution with respect to the traditional IRA for the year of the conversion?

A-6. (a) No. In order to be eligible for a conversion, an amount first must be eligible to be rolled over. Section 408(d)(3) prohibits the rollover of a required minimum distribution. If a minimum distribution is required for a year with respect to an IRA, the first dollars distributed during that year are treated as consisting of the required minimum distribution until an amount equal to the required minimum distribution for that year has been distributed.

(b) As provided in A-1(c) of this section, any amount converted is treated as a distribution from a traditional IRA and a rollover contribution to a Roth IRA and not as a trustee-to-trustee transfer for purposes of section 408 and section 408A. Thus, in a year for which a minimum distribution is required (including the calendar year in which the individual attains age 70 1/2), an individual may not convert the assets of an IRA (or any portion of those assets) to a Roth IRA to the extent that the required minimum distribution for the traditional IRA for the year has not been distributed.

(c) If a required minimum distribution is contributed to a Roth IRA, it is treated as having been distributed, subject to the normal rules under section 408(d)(1) and (2), and then contributed as a regular contribution to a Roth IRA. The amount of the required minimum distribution is not a conversion contribution.

Q-7. What are the tax consequences when an amount is converted to a Roth IRA?

A-7. (a) Any amount that is converted to a Roth IRA is includible in gross income as a distribution according to the rules of section 408(d)(1) and (2) for the taxable year in which the amount is distributed or transferred from the traditional IRA. Thus, any portion of the distribution or transfer that is treated as a return of basis under section 408(d)(1) and (2) is not includible in gross income as a result of the conversion.

(b) The 10-percent additional tax under section 72(t) generally does not apply to the taxable conversion amount. But see § 1.408A-6 A-5 for circumstances under which the taxable conversion amount would be subject to the additional tax under section 72(t).

(c) Pursuant to section 408A(e), a conversion is not treated as a rollover for purposes of the one-rollover-per-year rule of section 408(d)(3)(B).

Q-8. Is there an exception to the income-inclusion rule described in A-7 of this section for 1998 conversions?

A-8. Yes. In the case of a distribution (including a trustee-to-trustee transfer) from a traditional IRA on or before December 31, 1998, that is converted to a Roth IRA, instead of having the

Reg. § 1.408A-4

entire taxable conversion amount includible in income in 1998, an individual includes in gross income for 1998 only one quarter of that amount and one quarter of that amount for each of the next 3 years. This 4-year spread also applies if the conversion amount was distributed in 1998 and contributed to the Roth IRA within the 60-day period described in section 408(d)(3)(A)(i), but after December 31, 1998. However, see § 1.408A-6 A-6 for special rules requiring acceleration of inclusion if an amount subject to the 4-year spread is distributed from the Roth IRA before 2001.

Q-9. Is the taxable conversion amount included in income for all purposes?

A-9. Except as provided below, any taxable conversion amount includible in gross income for a year as a result of the conversion (regardless of whether the individual is using a 4-year spread) is included in income for all purposes. Thus, for example, it is counted for purposes of determining the taxable portion of social security payments under section 86 and for purposes of determining the phase-out of the $25,000 exemption under section 469(i) relating to the disallowance of passive activity losses from rental real estate activities. However, as provided in § 1.408A-3 A-5, the taxable conversion amount (and any resulting change in other elements of adjusted gross income) is disregarded for purposes of determining modified AGI for section 408A.

Q-10. Can an individual who makes a 1998 conversion elect not to have the 4-year spread apply and instead have the full taxable conversion amount includible in gross income for 1998?

A-10. Yes. Instead of having the taxable conversion amount for a 1998 conversion included over 4 years as provided under A-8 of this section, an individual can elect to include the full taxable conversion amount in income for 1998. The election is made on Form 8606 and cannot be made or changed after the due date (including extensions) for filing the 1998 Federal income tax return.

Q-11. What happens when an individual who is using the 4-year spread dies, files separately, or divorces before the full taxable conversion amount has been included in gross income?

A-11. (a) If an individual who is using the 4-year spread described in A-8 of this section dies before the full taxable conversion amount has been included in gross income, then the remainder must be included in the individual's gross income for the taxable year that includes the date of death.

(b) However, if the sole beneficiary of all the decedent's Roth IRAs is the decedent's spouse, then the spouse can elect to continue the 4-year spread. Thus, the spouse can elect to include in gross income the same amount that the decedent

would have included in each of the remaining years of the 4-year period. Where the spouse makes such an election, the amount includible under the 4-year spread for the taxable year that includes the date of the decedent's death remains includible in the decedent's gross income and is reported on the decedent's final Federal income tax return. The election is made on either Form 8606 or Form 1040, in accordance with the instructions to the applicable form, for the taxable year that includes the decedent's date of death and cannot be changed after the due date (including extensions) for filing the Federal income tax return for the spouse's taxable year that includes the decedent's date of death.

(c) If a Roth IRA owner who is using the 4-year spread and who was married in 1998 subsequently files separately or divorces before the full taxable conversion amount has been included in gross income, the remainder of the taxable conversion amount must be included in the Roth IRA owner's gross income over the remaining years in the 4-year period (unless accelerated because of distribution or death).

Q-12. Can an individual convert a traditional IRA to a Roth IRA if he or she is receiving substantially equal periodic payments within the meaning of section 72(t)(2)(A)(iv) from that traditional IRA?

A-12. Yes. Not only is the conversion amount itself not subject to the early distribution tax under section 72(t), but the conversion amount is also not treated as a distribution for purposes of determining whether a modification within the meaning of section 72(t)(4)(A) has occurred. Distributions from the Roth IRA that are part of the original series of substantially equal periodic payments will be nonqualified distributions from the Roth IRA until they meet the requirements for being a qualified distribution, described in § 1.408A-6 A-1(b). The additional 10-percent tax under section 72(t) will not apply to the extent that these nonqualified distributions are part of a series of substantially equal periodic payments. Nevertheless, to the extent that such distributions are allocable to a 1998 conversion contribution with respect to which the 4-year spread for the resultant income inclusion applies (see A-8 of this section) and are received during 1998, 1999, or 2000, the special acceleration rules of § 1.408A-6 A-6 apply. However, if the original series of substantially equal periodic payments does not continue to be distributed in substantially equal periodic payments from the Roth IRA after the conversion, the series of payments will have been modified and, if this modification occurs within 5 years of the first payment or prior to the individual becoming disabled or attaining age 59 1/2, the

Reg. § 1.408A-4

taxpayer will be subject to the recapture tax of section 72(t)(4)(A).

Q-13. Can a 1997 distribution from a traditional IRA be converted to a Roth IRA in 1998?

A-13. No. An amount distributed from a traditional IRA in 1997 that is contributed to a Roth IRA in 1998 would not be a conversion contribution. See A-3 of this section regarding the remedy for a failed conversion.

[Reg. § 1.408A-4.]

☐ [*T.D.* 8816, 2-3-99.]

§ 1.408A-6. Distributions.—This section sets forth the following questions and answers that provide rules regarding distributions from Roth IRAs:

Q-1. How are distributions from Roth IRAs taxed?

A-1. (a) The taxability of a distribution from a Roth IRA generally depends on whether or not the distribution is a qualified distribution. This A-1 provides rules for qualified distributions and certain other nontaxable distributions. A-4 of this section provides rules for the taxability of distributions that are not qualified distributions.

(b) A distribution from a Roth IRA is not includible in the owner's gross income if it is a qualified distribution or to the extent that it is a return of the owner's contributions to the Roth IRA (determined in accordance with A-8 of this section). A qualified distribution is one that is both—

(1) Made after a 5-taxable-year period (defined in A-2 of this section); and

(2) Made on or after the date on which the owner attains age 59 1/2, made to a beneficiary or the estate of the owner on or after the date of the owner's death, attributable to the owner's being disabled within the meaning of section 72(m)(7), or to which section 72(t)(2)(F) applies (exception for first-time home purchase).

(c) An amount distributed from a Roth IRA will not be included in gross income to the extent it is rolled over to another Roth IRA on a tax-free basis under the rules of sections 408(d)(3) and 408A(e).

(d) Contributions that are returned to the Roth IRA owner in accordance with section 408(d)(4) (corrective distributions) are not includible in gross income, but any net income required to be distributed under section 408(d)(4) together with the contributions is includible in gross income for the taxable year in which the contributions were made.

Q-2. When does the 5-taxable-year period described in A-1 of this section (relating to qualified distributions) begin and end?

A-2. The 5-taxable-year period described in A-1 of this section begins on the first day of the individual's taxable year for which the first regular contribution is made to any Roth IRA of the individual or, if earlier, the first day of the individual's taxable year in which the first conversion contribution is made to any Roth IRA of the individual. The 5-taxable-year period ends on the last day of the individual's fifth consecutive taxable year beginning with the taxable year described in the preceding sentence. For example, if an individual whose taxable year is the calendar year makes a first-time regular Roth IRA contribution any time between January 1, 1998, and April 15, 1999, for 1998, the 5-taxable-year period begins on January 1, 1998. Thus, each Roth IRA owner has only one 5-taxable-year period described in A-1 of this section for all the Roth IRAs of which he or she is the owner. Further, because of the requirement of the 5-taxable-year period, no qualified distributions can occur before taxable years beginning in 2003. For purposes of this A-2, the amount of any contribution distributed as a corrective distribution under A-1(d) of this section is treated as if it was never contributed.

Q-3. If a distribution is made to an individual who is the sole beneficiary of his or her deceased spouse's Roth IRA and the individual is treating the Roth IRA as his or her own, can the distribution be a qualified distribution based on being made to a beneficiary on or after the owner's death?

A-3. No. If a distribution is made to an individual who is the sole beneficiary of his or her deceased spouse's Roth IRA and the individual is treating the Roth IRA as his or her own, then, in accordance with § 1.408A-2 A-4, the distribution is treated as coming from the individual's own Roth IRA and not the deceased spouse's Roth IRA. Therefore, for purposes of determining whether the distribution is a qualified distribution, it is not treated as made to a beneficiary on or after the owner's death.

Q-4. How is a distribution from a Roth IRA taxed if it is not a qualified distribution?

A-4. A distribution that is not a qualified distribution, and is neither contributed to another Roth IRA in a qualified rollover contribution nor constitutes a corrective distribution, is includible in the owner's gross income to the extent that the amount of the distribution, when added to the amount of all prior distributions from the owner's Roth IRAs (whether or not they were qualified distributions) and reduced by the amount of those prior distributions previously includible in gross income, exceeds the owner's contributions to all his or her Roth IRAs. For purposes of this A-4,

Reg. § 1.408A-6

any amount distributed as a corrective distribution is treated as if it was never contributed.

Q-5. Will the additional tax under 72(t) apply to the amount of a distribution that is not a qualified distribution?

A-5. (a) The 10-percent additional tax under section 72(t) will apply (unless the distribution is excepted under section 72(t)) to any distribution from a Roth IRA includible in gross income.

(b) The 10-percent additional tax under section 72(t) also applies to a nonqualified distribution, even if it is not then includible in gross income, to the extent it is allocable to a conversion contribution, if the distribution is made within the 5-taxable-year period beginning with the first day of the individual's taxable year in which the conversion contribution was made. The 5-taxable-year period ends on the last day of the individual's fifth consecutive taxable year beginning with the taxable year described in the preceding sentence. For purposes of applying the tax, only the amount of the conversion contribution includible in gross income as a result of the conversion is taken into account. The exceptions under section 72(t) also apply to such a distribution.

(c) The 5-taxable-year period described in this A-5 for purposes of determining whether section 72(t) applies to a distribution allocable to a conversion contribution is separately determined for each conversion contribution, and need not be the same as the 5-taxable-year period used for purposes of determining whether a distribution is a qualified distribution under A-1(b) of this section. For example, if a calendar-year taxpayer who received a distribution from a traditional IRA on December 31, 1998, makes a conversion contribution by contributing the distributed amount to a Roth IRA on February 25, 1999 in a qualifying rollover contribution and makes a regular contribution for 1998 on the same date, the 5-taxable-year period for purposes of this A-5 begins on January 1, 1999, while the 5-taxable-year period for purposes of A-1(b) of this section begins on January 1, 1998.

Q-6. Is there a special rule for taxing distributions allocable to a 1998 conversion?

A-6. Yes. In the case of a distribution from a Roth IRA in 1998, 1999 or 2000 of amounts allocable to a 1998 conversion with respect to which the 4-year spread for the resultant income inclusion applies (see § 1.408A-4 A-8), any income deferred as a result of the election to years after the year of the distribution is accelerated so that it is includible in gross income in the year of the distribution up to the amount of the distribution allocable to the 1998 conversion (determined under A-8 of this section). This amount is in addition to the amount otherwise includible in the owner's gross income for that taxable year as a result of the conversion. However, this rule will not require the inclusion of any amount to the extent it exceeds the total amount of income required to be included over the 4-year period. The acceleration of income inclusion described in this A-6 applies in the case of a surviving spouse who elects to continue the 4-year spread in accordance with § 1.408A-4 A-11(b).

Q-7. Is the 5-taxable-year period described in A-1 of this section redetermined when a Roth IRA owner dies?

A-7. (a) No. The beginning of the 5-taxable-year period described in A-1 of this section is not redetermined when the Roth IRA owner dies. Thus, in determining the 5-taxable-year period, the period the Roth IRA is held in the name of a beneficiary, or in the name of a surviving spouse who treats the decedent's Roth IRA as his or her own, includes the period it was held by the decedent.

(b) The 5-taxable-year period for a Roth IRA held by an individual as a beneficiary of a deceased Roth IRA owner is determined independently of the 5-taxable-year period for the beneficiary's own Roth IRA. However, if a surviving spouse treats the Roth IRA as his or her own, the 5-taxable-year period with respect to any of the surviving spouse's Roth IRAs (including the one that the surviving spouse treats as his or her own) ends at the earlier of the end of either the 5-taxable-year period for the decedent or the 5-taxable-year period applicable to the spouse's own Roth IRAs.

* * *

Q-14. What minimum distribution rules apply to a Roth IRA?

A-14. (a) No minimum distributions are required to be made from a Roth IRA under section 408(a)(6) and (b)(3) (which generally incorporate the provisions of section 401(a)(9)) while the owner is alive. The post-death minimum distribution rules under section 401(a)(9)(B) that apply to traditional IRAs, with the exception of the at-least-as-rapidly rule described in section 401(a)(9)(B)(i), also apply to Roth IRAs.

(b) The minimum distribution rules apply to the Roth IRA as though the Roth IRA owner died before his or her required beginning date. Thus, generally, the entire interest in the Roth IRA must be distributed by the end of the fifth calendar year after the year of the owner's death unless the interest is payable to a designated beneficiary over a period not greater than that beneficiary's life expectancy and distribution commences before the end of the calendar year following the year of death. If the sole beneficiary is the decedent's spouse, such spouse may delay distributions

Reg. § 1.408A-6

until the decedent would have attained age 70 1/2 or may treat the Roth IRA as his or her own.

(c) Distributions to a beneficiary that are not qualified distributions will be includible in the beneficiary's gross income according to the rules in A-4 of this section.

Q-15. Does section 401(a)(9) apply separately to Roth IRAs and individual retirement plans that are not Roth IRAs?

A-15. Yes. An individual required to receive minimum distributions from his or her own traditional or SIMPLE IRA cannot choose to take the amount of the minimum distributions from any Roth IRA. Similarly, an individual required to receive minimum distributions from a Roth IRA cannot choose to take the amount of the minimum distributions from a traditional or SIMPLE IRA. In addition, an individual required to receive minimum distributions as a beneficiary under a Roth IRA can only satisfy the minimum distributions for one Roth IRA by distributing from another Roth IRA if the Roth IRAs were inherited from the same decedent.

Q-16. How is the basis of property distributed from a Roth IRA determined for purposes of a subsequent disposition?

A-16. The basis of property distributed from a Roth IRA is its fair market value (FMV) on the date of distribution, whether or not the distribution is a qualified distribution. Thus, for example, if a distribution consists of a share of stock in XYZ Corp. with an FMV of $40.00 on the date of distribution, for purposes of determining gain or loss on the subsequent sale of the share of XYZ Corp. stock, it has a basis of $40.00.

Q-17. What is the effect of distributing an amount from a Roth IRA and contributing it to another type of retirement plan other than a Roth IRA?

A-17. Any amount distributed from a Roth IRA and contributed to another type of retirement plan (other than a Roth IRA) is treated as a distribution from the Roth IRA that is neither a rollover contribution for purposes of section 408(d)(3) nor a qualified rollover contribution within the meaning of section 408A(e) to the other type of retirement plan. This treatment also applies to any amount transferred from a Roth IRA to any other type of retirement plan unless the transfer is a recharacterization described in § 1.408A-5.

Q-18. Can an amount be transferred directly from an education IRA to a Roth IRA (or distributed from an education IRA and rolled over to a Roth IRA)?

A-18. No amount may be transferred directly from an education IRA to a Roth IRA. A transfer of funds (or distribution and rollover) from an education IRA to a Roth IRA constitutes a distribution from the education IRA and a regular contribution to the Roth IRA (rather than a qualified rollover contribution to the Roth IRA).

Q-19. What are the Federal income tax consequences of a Roth IRA owner transferring his or her Roth IRA to another individual by gift?

A-19. A Roth IRA owner's transfer of his or her Roth IRA to another individual by gift constitutes an assignment of the owner's rights under the Roth IRA. At the time of the gift, the assets of the Roth IRA are deemed to be distributed to the owner and, accordingly, are treated as no longer held in a Roth IRA. In the case of any such gift of a Roth IRA made prior to October 1, 1998, if the entire interest in the Roth IRA is reconveyed to the Roth IRA owner prior to January 1, 1999, the Internal Revenue Service will treat the gift and reconveyance as never having occurred for estate tax, gift tax, and generation-skipping tax purposes and for purposes of this A-19.

[Reg. § 1.408A-6.]

☐ [*T.D.* 8816, 2-3-99.]

§ 1.408A-8. Definitions.—This section sets forth the following question and answer that provides definitions of terms used in the provisions of §§ 1.408A-1 through 1.408A-7 and this section:

Q-1. Are there any special definitions that govern in applying the provisions of §§ 1.408A-1 through 1.408A-7 and this section?

A-1. Yes, the following definitions govern in applying the provisions of §§ 1.408A-1 through 1.408A-7 and this section. Unless the context indicates otherwise, the use of a particular term excludes the use of the other terms.

(a) *Different types of IRAs*—(1) *IRA.* Sections 408(a) and (b), respectively, describe an individual retirement account and an individual retirement annuity. The term IRA means an IRA described in either section 408(a) or (b), including each IRA described in paragraphs (a)(2) through (5) of this A-1. However, the term IRA does not include an education IRA described in section 530.

(2) *Traditional IRA.* The term traditional IRA means an individual retirement account or individual retirement annuity described in section 408(a) or (b), respectively. This term includes a SEP IRA but does not include a SIMPLE IRA or a Roth IRA.

(3) *SEP IRA.* Section 408(k) describes a simplified employee pension (SEP) as an employer-sponsored plan under which an employer can make contributions to IRAs established for its employees. The term SEP IRA means an IRA that receives contributions made under a SEP. The term

Reg. § 1.408A-8

SEP includes a salary reduction SEP (SARSEP) described in section 408(k)(6).

(4) *SIMPLE IRA.* Section 408(p) describes a SIMPLE IRA Plan as an employer-sponsored plan under which an employer can make contributions to SIMPLE IRAs established for its employees. The term SIMPLE IRA means an IRA to which the only contributions that can be made are contributions under a SIMPLE IRA Plan or rollovers or transfers from another SIMPLE IRA.

(5) *Roth IRA.* The term Roth IRA means an IRA that meets the requirements of section 408A.

(b) *Other defined terms or phrases*—(1) *4-year spread.* The term 4-year spread is described in § 1.408A-4 A-8.

(2) *Conversion.* The term conversion means a transaction satisfying the requirements of § 1.408A-4 A-1.

(3) *Conversion amount or conversion contribution.* The term conversion amount or conversion contribution is the amount of a distribution and contribution with respect to which a conversion described in § 1.408A-4 A-1 is made.

(4) *Failed conversion.* The term failed conversion means a transaction in which an individual contributes to a Roth IRA an amount transferred or distributed from a traditional IRA or SIMPLE IRA (including a transfer by redesignation) in a transaction that does not constitute a conversion under § 1.408A-4 A-1.

(5) *Modified AGI.* The term modified AGI is defined in § 1.408A-3 A-5.

(6) *Recharacterization.* The term recharacterization means a transaction described in § 1.408A-5 A-1.

(7) *Recharacterized amount or recharacterized contribution.* The term recharacterized amount or recharacterized contribution means an amount or contribution treated as contributed to an IRA other than the one to which it was originally contributed pursuant to a recharacterization described in § 1.408A-5 A-1.

(8) *Taxable conversion amount.* The term taxable conversion amount means the portion of a conversion amount includible in income on account of a conversion, determined under the rules of section 408(d)(1) and (2).

(9) *Tax-free transfer.* The term tax-free transfer means a tax-free rollover described in section 402(c), 402(e)(6), 403(a)(4), 403(a)(5), 403(b)(8), 403(b)(10) or 408(d)(3), or a tax-free trustee-to-trustee transfer.

(10) *Treat an IRA as his or her own.* The phrase treat an IRA as his or her own means to treat an IRA for which a surviving spouse is the sole beneficiary as his or her own IRA after the death of the IRA owner in accordance with the terms of the IRA instrument or in the manner provided in the regulations under section 408(a)(6) or (b)(3).

(11) *Trustee.* The term trustee includes a custodian or issuer (in the case of an annuity) of an IRA (except where the context clearly indicates otherwise).

[Reg. § 1.408A-8.]

☐ [*T.D.* 8816, 2-3-99.]

Certain Stock Options

Proposed Regulation

[Note: In 1990 Section 422A was renumbered as Section 422.]

§ 1.422A-1. Incentive stock options—General rules.—(a) *Applicability of section 421(a).* (1)(i) Section 421(a) applies with respect to the transfer of a share of stock to an individual pursuant to the exercise of an incentive stock option if the following conditions are satisfied—

    (A) The individual makes no disposition of such share before the later of the expiration of the 2-year period beginning on the day of the grant of the option pursuant to which such share was transferred, or the expiration of the 1-year period beginning on the day of the transfer of such share, and

    (B) At all times during the period beginning on the day of the grant of the option and ending on the day 3 months before the date of such exercise, the individual was an employee of either the corporation granting the option, a related corporation of such corporation, or a corporation (or a related corporation of such corporation) issuing or assuming a stock option in a transaction to which section 425(a) applies.

    (ii) For rules relating to the disposition of shares of stock, see paragraph (c) of § 1.425-1. For rules relating to the requisite employment relationship, see paragraph (h) of § 1.421-7.

    (2)(i) The holding period requirement of section 422A(a)(1), set forth in paragraph (a)(1)(i)(A) of this section, does not apply to certain transfers by insolvent individuals. If an insolvent individual holds a share of stock acquired pursuant to the exercise of an incentive stock option, and if such share is transferred to a trustee, receiver, or other similar fiduciary in any proceeding under the Bankruptcy Act or any other similar insolvency proceeding, neither such transfer, nor any other transfer of such share for the benefit of the insolvent individual's creditors in such proceeding shall constitute a disposition of such share for the purpose of section 422A(a)(1). For the purpose of this paragraph (a)(2) an individual is an insolvent only if his liabilities exceed his assets, or if the individual is unable to satisfy his liabilities as they become due.

(ii) A transfer by the trustee or other fiduciary that is not treated as a disposition for the purpose of section 422A(a)(1) may be a sale or exchange for purposes of recognizing capital gain or loss with respect to the share transferred. For example, if the trustee transfers the share to a creditor in the insolvency proceeding in complete or partial satisfaction of such creditor's claim against the insolvent individual, capital gain or loss must be recognized by the insolvent individual to the extent of the difference between the amount realized from such transfer and the adjusted basis of such share. To the extent any transfer by the trustee or other fiduciary (other than a transfer back to the insolvent individual) is not for the exclusive benefit of the creditors in the insolvency proceeding, such transfer will be treated as a disposition for purposes of section 422A(a)(1). Similarly, if the trustee or other fiduciary transfers the share back to the insolvent individual, any subsequent disposition of the share which is not made in respect of the insolvency proceeding and for the exclusive benefit of the creditors in such proceeding will be treated as a disposition for purposes of section 422A(a)(1).

(3) If the employee exercising an option ceased employment because of permanent and total disability within the meaning of either section 37(e)(3) or section 105(d)(4), 1 year is substituted for 3 months in the employment period requirement of section 422A(a)(2) and paragraph (a)(1)(i)(B) of this section.

(b) *Failure to satisfy holding period requirement.* (1) A disqualifying disposition of a share of stock acquired by the exercise of an incentive stock option (*i.e.,* a disposition before the expiration of the holding periods as determined under section 422A(a)(1) and paragraph (a)(1)(i)(A) of this section) makes section 421(a) inapplicable to the transfer of such share. Pursuant to section 421(b), the income attributable to such transfer shall be treated by the individual as income received in the taxable year in which such disqualifying disposition occurs. Similarly, a deduction under section 162 attributable to the transfer of the share of stock pursuant to the exercise of the option shall be allowable for the taxable year in which such disqualifying disposition occurs to the employer corporation (or to a corporation issuing or assuming the option in a transaction to which section 425(a) applies). In such cases, no amount shall be treated as income, and no amount shall be allowed as a deduction, for any taxable year other than the taxable year in which the disqualifying disposition occurs. Except as provided by section 421(b) and paragraph (b) of this section, the effects of a disqualifying disposition shall be determined pursuant to section 83 and the regulations thereunder.

(2) If an individual makes a disqualifying disposition of a share of stock acquired by the exercise of an incentive stock option, and if such disposition is a sale or exchange with respect to which a loss (if sustained) would be recognized to the individual, then, under section 422A(c)(2), the amount includible in the gross income of such individual, and deductible from the income of employer corporation (or of a corporation issuing or assuming the option in a transaction to which section 425(a) applies) as compensation attributable to the exercise of such option, shall not exceed the excess (if any) of the amount realized on such sale or exchange over the adjusted basis of such share. Thus, the limitation does not apply when the disqualifying disposition is a sale described in section 1091 (relating to loss from wash sales of stock or securities), a gift, or a sale described in section 267(a)(1) (relating to sales between related persons), since a loss sustained in any such transaction would not be recognized. Subject to the limitation provided by section 422A(c)(2) and this paragraph (b)(2), the amount of compensation attributable to the exercise of the option is determined under § 1.83-7.

(3) The application of this paragraph may be illustrated by the following examples:

Example (1). On June 1, 1982, X Corporation grants an incentive stock option to A, an employee of X Corporation, entitling A to purchase one share of X Corporation stock. On August 1, 1982, A exercises the option and the share of X Corporation stock is transferred to A on that date. In order to meet the holding period requirements of section 422A(a)(1), A must not dispose of the share acquired by exercise of the incentive stock option before June 1, 1984.

Example (2). Assume the same facts as in example (1) except that A exercises the option on June 1, 1983, and the share of X Corporation stock is transferred to A on June 10, 1983. In order to meet the holding period requirements of section 422A(a)(1), A must not dispose of the share acquired by exercise of the incentive stock option before June 10, 1984.

* * *

(c) *Failure to satisfy employment requirement.* Section 421 does not apply to the transfer of a share of stock acquired by the exercise of an incentive stock option if the employment requirement as determined under section 422A(a)(2) and paragraph (a)(1)(i)(B) of this section is not met at the time of transfer. Consequently, the effects of such a transfer shall be determined pursuant to section 83 and the regulations thereunder. [Reg. § 1.422A-1.]

[Proposed 2-7-84.]

Reg. § 1.422A-1(c)

Accounting Periods

§ 1.441-1. Period for computation of taxable income.—(a) *Computation of taxable income*—(1) *In general.* Taxable income must be computed and a return must be made for a period known as the taxable year. For rules relating to methods of accounting, the taxable year for which items of gross income are included and deductions are taken, inventories, and adjustments, see parts II and III (section 446 and following), subchapter E, chapter 1 of the Internal Revenue Code, and the regulations thereunder.

(2) *Length of taxable year.* Except as otherwise provided in the Internal Revenue Code and the regulations thereunder (e.g., § 1.441-2 regarding 52-53-week taxable years), a taxable year may not cover a period of more than 12 calendar months.

(b) *General rules and definitions.* The general rules and definitions in this paragraph (b) apply for purposes of sections 441 and 442 and the regulations thereunder.

(1) *Taxable year. Taxable year* means—

(i) The period for which a return is made, if a return is made for a period of less than 12 months (short period). See section 443 and the regulations thereunder;

(ii) Except as provided in paragraph (b)(1)(i) of this section, the taxpayer's required taxable year (as defined in paragraph (b)(2) of this section), if applicable;

(iii) Except as provided in paragraphs (b)(1)(i) and (ii) of this section, the taxpayer's annual accounting period (as defined in paragraph (b)(3) of this section), if it is a calendar year or a fiscal year; or

(iv) Except as provided in paragraphs (b)(1)(i) and (ii) of this section, the calendar year, if the taxpayer keeps no books, does not have an annual accounting period, or has an annual accounting period that does not qualify as a fiscal year.

(2) *Required taxable year*—(i) *In general.* Certain taxpayers must use the particular taxable year that is required under the Internal Revenue Code and the regulations thereunder (the required taxable year). For example, the required taxable year is—

(A) In the case of a foreign sales corporation or domestic international sales corporation, the taxable year determined under section 441(h) and § 1.921-1T(a)(11), (b)(4), and (b)(6);

(B) In the case of a personal service corporation (PSC), the taxable year determined under section 441(i) and § 1.441-3;

(C) In the case of a nuclear decommissioning fund, the taxable year determined under § 1.468A-4(c)(1);

(D) In the case of a designated settlement fund or a qualified settlement fund, the taxable year determined under § 1.468B-2(j);

(E) In the case of a common trust fund, the taxable year determined under section 584(i);

(F) In the case of certain trusts, the taxable year determined under section 644;

(G) In the case of a partnership, the taxable year determined under section 706 and § 1.706-1;

(H) In the case of an insurance company, the taxable year determined under section 843 and § 1.1502-76(a)(2);

(I) In the case of a real estate investment trust, the taxable year determined under section 859;

(J) In the case of a real estate mortgage investment conduit, the taxable year determined under section 860D(a)(5) and § 1.860D-1(b)(6);

(K) In the case of a specified foreign corporation, the taxable year determined under section 898(c)(1)(A);

(L) In the case of an S corporation, the taxable year determined under section 1378 and § 1.1378-1; or

(M) In the case of a member of an affiliated group that makes a consolidated return, the taxable year determined under § 1.1502-76.

(ii) *Exceptions.* Notwithstanding paragraph (b)(2)(i) of this section, the following taxpayers may have a taxable year other than their required taxable year:

(A) *52-53-week taxable years.* Certain taxpayers may elect to use a 52-53-week taxable year that ends with reference to their required taxable year. See, for example, §§ 1.441-3 (PSCs), 1.706-1 (partnerships), 1.1378-1 (S corporations), and 1.1502-76(a)(1) (members of a consolidated group).

(B) *Partnerships, S corporations, and PSCs.* A partnership, S corporation, or PSC may use a taxable year other than its required taxable year if the taxpayer elects to use a taxable year other than its required taxable year under section 444, elects a 52-53-week taxable year that ends with reference to its required taxable year as provided in paragraph (b)(2)(ii)(A) of this section or to a taxable year elected under section 444, or establishes a business purpose to the satisfaction of the Commissioner under section 442 (such as a grandfathered fiscal year).

(C) *Specified foreign corporations.* A specified foreign corporation (as defined in section 898(b)) may use a taxable year other than its required taxable year if it elects a 52-53-week taxable year that ends with reference to its required taxable year as provided in paragraph (b)(2)(ii)(A) of this section or makes a one-month deferral election under section 898(c)(1)(B).

(3) *Annual accounting period. Annual accounting period* means the annual period (calendar year or fiscal year) on the basis of which the taxpayer regularly computes its income in keeping its books.

(4) *Calendar year. Calendar year* means a period of 12 consecutive months ending on December 31. A taxpayer who has not established a fiscal year must make its return on the basis of a calendar year.

(5) *Fiscal year*—(i) *Definition. Fiscal year* means—

(A) A period of 12 consecutive months ending on the last day of any month other than December; or

(B) A 52-53-week taxable year, if such period has been elected by the taxpayer. See § 1.441-2.

(ii) *Recognition.* A fiscal year will be recognized only if the books of the taxpayer are kept in accordance with such fiscal year.

(6) *Grandfathered fiscal year. Grandfathered fiscal year* means a fiscal year (other than a year that resulted in a three month or less deferral of income) that a partnership or an S corporation received permission to use on or after July 1, 1974, by a letter ruling (i.e., not by automatic approval).

(7) *Books. Books* include the taxpayer's regular books of account and such other records and data as may be necessary to support the entries on the taxpayer's books and on the taxpayer's return, as for example, a reconciliation of any difference between such books and the taxpayer's return. Records that are sufficient to reflect income adequately and clearly on the basis of an annual accounting period will be regarded as the keeping of books. See section 6001 and the regulations thereunder for rules relating to the keeping of books and records.

(8) *Taxpayer. Taxpayer* has the same meaning as the term *person* as defined in section 7701(a)(1) (*e.g.*, an individual, trust, estate, partnership, association, or corporation) rather than

the meaning of the term taxpayer as defined in section 7701(a)(14) (any person subject to tax).

(c) *Adoption of taxable year*—(1) *In general.* Except as provided in paragraph (c)(2) of this section, a new taxpayer may adopt any taxable year that satisfies the requirements of section 441 and the regulations thereunder without the approval of the Commissioner. A taxable year of a new taxpayer is adopted by filing its first Federal income tax return using that taxable year. The filing of an application for automatic extension of time to file a Federal income tax return (e.g., Form 7004, "Application for Automatic Extension of Time To File Corporation Income Tax Return"), the filing of an application for an employer identification number (i.e., Form SS-4, "Application for Employer Identification Number"), or the payment of estimated taxes, for a particular taxable year do not constitute an adoption of that taxable year.

(2) *Approval required*—(i) *Taxpayers with required taxable years.* A newly-formed partnership, S corporation, or PSC that wants to adopt a taxable year other than its required taxable year, a taxable year elected under section 444, or a 52-53-week taxable year that ends with reference to its required taxable year or a taxable year elected under section 444 must establish a business purpose and obtain the approval of the Commissioner under section 442.

(ii) *Taxpayers without books.* A taxpayer that must use a calendar year under section 441(g) and paragraph (f) of this section may not adopt a fiscal year without obtaining the approval of the Commissioner.

(d) *Retention of taxable year.* In certain cases, a partnership, S corporation, electing S corporation, or PSC will be required to change its taxable year unless it obtains the approval of the Commissioner under section 442, or makes an election under section 444, to retain its current taxable year. For example, a corporation using a June 30 fiscal year that either becomes a PSC or elects to be an S corporation and, as a result, is required to use the calendar year under section 441(i) or 1378, respectively, must obtain the approval of the Commissioner to retain its current fiscal year. Similarly, a partnership using a taxable year that corresponds to its required taxable year must obtain the approval of the Commissioner to retain such taxable year if its required taxable year changes as a result of a change in ownership. However, a partnership that previously established a business purpose to the satisfaction of the Commissioner to use a taxable year is not required to obtain the approval of the Commissioner if its required taxable year changes as a result of a change in ownership.

(e) *Change of taxable year.* Once a taxpayer has adopted a taxable year, such taxable year must be used in computing taxable income and making returns for all subsequent years unless the taxpayer obtains approval from the Commissioner to make a change or the taxpayer is otherwise authorized to change without the approval of the Commissioner under the Internal Revenue Code (e.g., section 444 or 859) or the regulations thereunder.

(f) *Obtaining approval of the Commissioner or making a section 444 election.* See § 1.442-1(b) for procedures for obtaining approval of the Commissioner (automatically or otherwise) to adopt, change, or retain an annual accounting period. See §§ 1.444-1T and 1.444-2T for qualifications, and 1.444-3T for procedures, for making an election under section 444. [Reg. § 1.441-1.]

☐ [*T.D.* 8996, 5-16-2002.]

§ 1.442-1. Change of annual accounting period.—(a) *Approval of the Commissioner.* A taxpayer that has adopted an annual accounting period (as defined in § 1.441-1(b)(3)) as its taxable year generally must continue to use that annual accounting period in computing its taxable income and for making its Federal income tax returns. If the taxpayer wants to change its annual accounting period and use a new taxable year, it must obtain the approval of the Commissioner, unless it is otherwise authorized to change without the approval of the Commissioner under either the Internal Revenue Code (e.g., section 444 and section 859) or the regulations thereunder (e.g., paragraph (c) of this section). In addition, as described in § 1.441-1(c) and (d), a partnership, S corporation, electing S corporation, or personal service corporation (PSC) generally is required to secure the approval of the Commissioner to adopt or retain an annual accounting period other than its required taxable year. The manner of obtaining approval from the Commissioner to adopt, change, or retain an annual accounting period is provided in paragraph (b) of this section. However, special rules for obtaining approval may be provided in other sections.

(b) *Obtaining approval*—(1) *Time and manner for requesting approval.* In order to secure the approval of the Commissioner to adopt, change, or retain an annual accounting period, a taxpayer must file an application, generally on Form 1128, "Application To Adopt, Change, or Retain a Tax Year," with the Commissioner within such time and in such manner as is provided in administrative procedures published by the Commissioner.

(2) *General requirements for approval.* An adoption, change, or retention in annual accounting period will be approved where the taxpayer establishes a business purpose for the requested

annual accounting period and agrees to the Commissioner's prescribed terms, conditions, and adjustments for effecting the adoption, change, or retention. In determining whether a taxpayer has established a business purpose and which terms, conditions, and adjustments will be required, consideration will be given to all the facts and circumstances relating to the adoption, change, or retention, including the tax consequences resulting therefrom. Generally, the requirement of a business purpose will be satisfied, and adjustments to neutralize any tax consequences will not be required, if the requested annual accounting period coincides with the taxpayer's required taxable year (as defined in § 1.441-1(b)(2)), ownership taxable year, or natural business year. In the case of a partnership, S corporation, electing S corporation, or PSC, deferral of income to partners, shareholders, or employee-owners will not be treated as a business purpose.

* * *

(d) *Special rule for newly married couples*—(1) A newly married husband or wife may obtain automatic approval under this paragraph (d) to change his or her annual accounting period in order to use the annual accounting period of the other spouse so that a joint return may be filed for the first or second taxable year of that spouse ending after the date of marriage. Such automatic approval will be granted only if the newly married husband or wife adopting the annual accounting period of the other spouse files a Federal income tax return for the short period required by that change on or before the 15th day of the 4th month following the close of the short period. See section 443 and the regulations thereunder. If the due date for any such short-period return occurs before the date of marriage, the first taxable year of the other spouse ending after the date of marriage cannot be adopted under this paragraph (d). The short-period return must contain a statement at the top of page one of the return that it is filed under the authority of this paragraph (d). The newly married husband or wife need not file Form 1128 with respect to a change described in this paragraph (d). For a change of annual accounting period by a husband or wife that does not qualify under this paragraph (d), see paragraph (b) of this section.

(2) The provisions of this paragraph (d) may be illustrated by the following example:

Example. H & W marry on September 25, 2001. H is on a fiscal year ending June 30, and W is on a calendar year. H wishes to change to a calendar year in order to file joint returns with W. W's first taxable year after marriage ends on December 31, 2001. H may not change to a calendar year for 2001 since, under this paragraph (d), he would have had to file a return for the short period from July 1 to December 31, 2000, by April 16, 2001. Since the date of marriage occurred subsequent to this due date, the return could not be filed under this paragraph (d). Therefore, H cannot change to a calendar year for 2001. However, H may change to a calendar year for 2002 by filing a return under this paragraph (d) by April 15, 2002, for the short period from July 1 to December 31, 2001. If H files such a return, H and W may file a joint return for calendar year 2002 (which is W's second taxable year ending after the date of marriage).

* * *

[Reg. § 1.442-1.]

☐ [*T.D. 6226, 2-27-57. Amended by T.D. 6432, 12-18-59, T.D. 6614, 10-12-62, T.D. 7235, 12-27-72, T.D. 7286, 9-26-73, T.D. 7323, 9-24-74, T.D. 7470, 2-28-77, T.D. 7767, 2-3-81, T.D. 7936, 1-17-84; T.D. 8123, 2-5-87 and T.D. 8996, 5-16-2002.*]

Methods of Accounting

§ 1.446-1. General rule for methods of accounting.—(a) *General rule*—(1) Section 446(a) provides that taxable income shall be computed under the method of accounting on the basis of which a taxpayer regularly computes his income in keeping his books. The term "method of accounting" includes not only the over-all method of accounting of the taxpayer but also the accounting treatment of any item. Examples of such over-all methods are the cash receipts and disbursements method, an accrual method, combinations of such methods, and combinations of the foregoing with various methods provided for the accounting treatment of special items. These methods of accounting for special items include the accounting treatment prescribed for research and experimental expenditures, soil and water conservation expenditures, depreciation, net operating losses, etc. Except for deviations permitted or required by such special accounting treatment, taxable income shall be computed under the method of accounting on the basis of which the taxpayer regularly computes his income in keeping his books. For requirement respecting the adoption or change of accounting method, see section 446(e) and paragraph (e) of this section.

(2) It is recognized that no uniform method of accounting can be prescribed for all taxpayers. Each taxpayer shall adopt such forms and systems as are, in his judgment, best suited to his needs. However, no method of accounting is acceptable unless, in the opinion of the Commissioner, it clearly reflects income. A method of accounting which reflects the consistent application of generally accepted accounting principles in a particular trade or business in accordance with accepted conditions or practices in that trade or business will ordinarily be regarded as clearly reflecting income, provided all items of gross income and expense are treated consistently from year to year.

(3) Items of gross income and expenditures which are elements in the computation of taxable income need not be in the form of cash. It is sufficient that such items can be valued in terms of money. For general rules relating to the taxable year for inclusion of income and for taking deductions, see sections 451 and 461, and the regulations thereunder.

(4) Each taxpayer is required to make a return of his taxable income for each taxable year and must maintain such accounting records as will enable him to file a correct return. See section 6001 and the regulations thereunder. Accounting records include the taxpayer's regular books of account and such other records and data as may be necessary to support the entries on his books of account and on his return, as for example, a reconciliation of any differences between such books and his return. The following are among the essential features that must be considered in maintaining such records:

(i) In all cases in which the production, purchase, or sale of merchandise of any kind in an income-producing factor, merchandise on hand (including finished goods, work in process, raw materials, and supplies) at the beginning and end of the year shall be taken into account in computing the taxable income of the year. (For rules relating to computation of inventories, see sections 263A, 471 and 472, and the regulations thereunder.)

(ii) Expenditures made during the year shall be properly classified as between capital and expense. For example, expenditures for such items as plant and equipment, which have a useful life extending substantially beyond the taxable year, shall be charged to a capital account and not to an expense account.

(iii) In any case in which there is allowable with respect to an asset a deduction for depreciation, amortization, or depletion, any expenditures (other than ordinary repairs) made to restore the asset or prolong its useful life shall be added to the asset account or charged against the appropriate reserve.

(b) *Exceptions*—(1) If the taxpayer does not regularly employ a method of accounting which clearly reflects his income, the computation of taxable income shall be made in a manner which, in the opinion of the Commissioner, does clearly reflect income.

(2) A taxpayer whose sole source of income is wages need not keep formal books in order to have an accounting method. Tax returns, copies thereof, or other records may be sufficient to establish the use of the method of accounting used in the preparation of the taxpayer's income tax returns.

(c) *Permissible methods*—(1) *In general.* Subject to the provisions of paragraphs (a) and (b) of this section, a taxpayer may compute his taxable income under any of the following methods of accounting:

(i) *Cash receipts and disbursements method.* Generally, under the cash receipts and disbursements method in the computation of taxable income, all items which constitute gross income (whether in the form of cash, property, or services) are to be included for the taxable year in which actually or constructively received. Expenditures are to be deducted for the taxable year in which actually made. For rules relating to constructive receipt, see § 1.451-2. For treatment of an expenditure attributable to more than one taxable year, see section 461(a) and paragraph (a)(1) of § 1.461-1.

(ii) *Accrual method*—(A) Generally, under an accrual method, income is to be included for the taxable year when all the events have occurred that fix the right to receive the income and the amount of the income can be determined with reasonable accuracy. Under such a method, a liability is incurred, and generally is taken into account for Federal income tax purposes, in the taxable year in which all the events have occurred that establish the fact of the liability, the amount of the liability can be determined with reasonable accuracy, and economic performance has occurred with respect to the liability. (See paragraph (a)(2)(iii)(A) of § 1.461-1 for examples of liabilities that may not be taken into account until after the taxable year incurred, and see § § 1.461-4 through 1.461-6 for rules relating to economic performance.) Applicable provisions of the Code, the Income Tax Regulations, and other guidance published by the Secretary prescribe the manner in which a liability that has been incurred is taken into account. For example, section 162 provides that a deductible liability generally is taken into account in the taxable year incurred through a deduction from gross income. As a further example, under section 263 or 263A, a liability that relates to the creation of an asset having a useful life extending substantially beyond the close of the taxable year is taken into account in the taxable year incurred through capitalization (within the meaning of § 1.263A-1(c)(3)), and

may later affect the computation of taxable income through depreciation or otherwise over a period including subsequent taxable years, in accordance with applicable Internal Revenue Code sections and related guidance.

(B) The term "liability" includes any item allowable as a deduction, cost, or expense for Federal income tax purposes. In addition to allowable deductions, the term includes any amount otherwise allowable as a capitalized cost, as a cost taken into account in computing cost of goods sold, as a cost allocable to a long-term contract, or as any other cost or expense. Thus, for example, an amount that a taxpayer expends or will expend for capital improvements to property must be incurred before the taxpayer may take the amount into account in computing its basis in the property. The term "liability" is not limited to items for which a legal obligation to pay exists at the time of payment. Thus, for example, amounts prepaid for goods or services and amounts paid without a legal obligation to do so may not be taken into account by an accrual basis taxpayer any earlier than the taxable year in which those amounts are incurred.

(C) No method of accounting is acceptable unless, in the opinion of the Commissioner, it clearly reflects income. The method used by the taxpayer in determining when income is to be accounted for will generally be acceptable if it accords with generally accepted accounting principles, is consistently used by the taxpayer from year to year, and is consistent with the Income Tax Regulations. For example, a taxpayer engaged in a manufacturing business may account for sales of the taxpayer's product when the goods are shipped, when the product is delivered or accepted, or when title to the goods passes to the customers, whether or not billed, depending on the method regularly employed in keeping the taxpayer's books.

(iii) *Other permissible methods.* Special methods of accounting are described elsewhere in chapter 1 of the Code and the regulations thereunder. For example, see the following sections and the regulations thereunder: Sections 61 and 162, relating to the crop method of accounting; section 453, relating to the installment method; section 460, relating to the long-term contract methods. In addition, special methods of accounting for particular items of income and expense are provided under other sections of chapter 1. For example, see section 174, relating to research and experimental expenditures, and section 175, relating to soil and water conservation expenditures.

(iv) *Combinations of the foregoing methods*—(a) In accordance with the following rules, any combination of the foregoing methods of accounting will be permitted in connection with a trade or business if such combination clearly reflects income and is consistently used. Where a combination of methods of accounting includes any special methods, such as those referred to in subdivision (iii) of this subparagraph, the taxpayer must comply with the requirements relating to such special methods. A taxpayer using an accrual method of accounting with respect to purchases and sales may use the cash method in computing all other items of income and expense. However, a taxpayer who uses the cash method of accounting in computing gross income from his trade or business shall use the cash method in computing expenses of such trade or business. Similarly, a taxpayer who uses an accrual method of accounting in computing business expenses shall use an accrual method in computing items affecting gross income from his trade or business.

(b) A taxpayer using one method of accounting in computing items of income and deductions of his trade or business may compute other items of income and deductions not connected with his trade or business under a different method of accounting.

(2) *Special rules*—(i) In any case in which it is necessary to use an inventory the accrual method of accounting must be used with regard to purchases and sales unless otherwise authorized under subdivision (ii) of this subparagraph.

(ii) No method of accounting will be regarded as clearly reflecting income unless all items of gross profit and deductions are treated with consistency from year to year. The Commissioner may authorize a taxpayer to adopt or change to a method of accounting permitted by this chapter although the method is not specifically described in this part if, in the opinion of the Commissioner, income is clearly reflected by the use of such method. Further, the Commissioner may authorize a taxpayer to continue the use of a method of accounting consistently used by the taxpayer, even though not specifically authorized by the regulations in this part, if, in the opinion of the Commissioner, income is clearly reflected by the use of such method. See section 446(a) and paragraph (a) of this section, which require that taxable income shall be computed under the method of accounting on the basis of which the taxpayer regularly computes his income in keeping his books, and section 446(e) and paragraph (e) of this section, which require the prior approval of the Commissioner in the case of changes in accounting method.

(iii) The timing rules of § 1.1502-13 are a method of accounting for intercompany transactions (as defined in § 1.1502-13(b)(1)(i)), to be applied by each member of a consolidated group

in addition to the member's other methods of accounting. See § 1.1502-13(a)(3)(i). This paragraph (c)(2)(iii) is applicable to consolidated return years beginning on or after November 7, 2001.

(d) *Taxpayer engaged in more than one business*—(1) Where a taxpayer has two or more separate and distinct trades or businesses, a different method of accounting may be used for each trade or business, provided the method used for each trade or business clearly reflects the income of that particular trade or business. For example, a taxpayer may account for the operations of a personal service business on the cash receipts and disbursements method and of a manufacturing business on an accrual method, provided such businesses are separate and distinct and the methods used for each clearly reflect income. The method first used in accounting for business income and deductions in connection with each trade or business, as evidenced in the taxpayer's income tax return in which such income or deductions are first reported, must be consistently followed thereafter.

(2) No trade or business will be considered separate and distinct for purposes of this paragraph unless a complete and separable set of books and records is kept for such trade or business.

(3) If, by reason of maintaining different methods of accounting, there is a creation or shifting of profits or losses between the trades or businesses of the taxpayer (for example, through inventory adjustments, sales, purchases, or expenses) so that income of the taxpayer is not clearly reflected, the trades or businesses of the taxpayer will not be considered to be separate and distinct.

(e) *Requirement respecting the adoption or change of accounting method*—(1) A taxpayer filing his first return may adopt any permissible method of accounting in computing taxable income for the taxable year covered by such return. See section 446(c) and paragraph (c) of this section for permissible methods. Moreover, a taxpayer may adopt any permissible method of accounting in connection with each separate and distinct trade or business, the income from which is reported for the first time. See section 446(d) and paragraph (d) of this section. See also section 446(a) and paragraph (a) of this section.

(2)(i) Except as otherwise expressly provided in chapter 1 of the Code and the regulations thereunder, a taxpayer who changes the method of accounting employed in keeping his books shall, before computing his income upon such new method for purposes of taxation, secure the consent of the Commissioner. Consent must be secured whether or not such method is proper or is permitted under the Internal Revenue Code or the regulations thereunder.

(ii)(*a*) A change in the method of accounting includes a change in the overall plan of accounting for gross income or deductions or a change in the treatment of any material item used in such overall plan. Although a method of accounting may exist under this definition without the necessity of a pattern of consistent treatment of an item, in most instances a method of accounting is not established for an item without such consistent treatment. A material item is any item which involves the proper time for the inclusion of the item in income or the taking of a deduction. Changes in method of accounting include a change from the cash receipts and disbursements method to an accrual method, or vice versa, a change involving the method or basis used in the valuation of inventories (see sections 471 and 472 and the regulations thereunder), a change from the cash or accrual method to a long-term contract method, or vice versa (see § 1.460-4), a change involving the adoption, use or discontinuance of any other specialized method of computing taxable income, such as the crop method, and a change where the Internal Revenue Code and regulations thereunder specifically require that the consent of the Commissioner must be obtained before adopting such a change.

(*b*) A change in method of accounting does not include correction of mathematical or posting errors, or errors in the computation of tax liability (such as errors in computation of the foreign tax credit, net operating loss, percentage depletion or investment credit). Also, a change in method of accounting does not include adjustment of any item of income or deduction which does not involve the proper time for the inclusion of the item of income or the taking of a deduction. For example, corrections of items that are deducted as interest or salary, but which are in fact payments of dividends, and of items that are deducted as business expenses, but which are in fact personal expenses, are not changes in method of accounting. In addition, a change in the method of accounting does not include an adjustment with respect to the addition to a reserve for bad debts or an adjustment in the useful life of a depreciable asset. Although such adjustments may involve the question of the proper time for the taking of a deduction, such items are traditionally corrected by adjustments in the current and future years. For the treatment of the adjustment of the addition to a bad debt reserve, see the regulations under section 166 of the Code; for the treatment of a change in the useful life of a depreciable asset, see the regulations under section 167(b) of the Code. A change in the method of accounting

also does not include a change in treatment resulting from a change in underlying facts. On the other hand, for example, a correction to require depreciation in lieu of a deduction for the cost of a class of depreciable assets which had been consistently treated as an expense in the year of purchase involves the question of the proper timing of an item, and is to be treated as a change in method of accounting.

(*c*) A change in an overall plan or system of identifying or valuing items in inventory is a change in method of accounting. Also a change in the treatment of any material item used in the overall plan for identifying or valuing items in inventory is a change in method of accounting.

(iii) A change in the method of accounting may be illustrated by the following examples:

Example (1). Although the sale of merchandise is an income producing factor, and therefore inventories are required, a taxpayer in the retail jewelry business reports his income on the cash receipts and disbursements method of accounting. A change from the cash receipts and disbursements method of accounting to the accrual method of accounting is a change in the overall plan of accounting and thus is a change in method of accounting.

Example (2). A taxpayer in the wholesale dry goods business computes its income and expenses on the accrual method of accounting and files its Federal income tax returns on such basis except for real estate taxes which have been reported on the cash receipts and disbursements method of accounting. A change in the treatment of real estate taxes from the cash receipts and disbursements method to the accrual method is a change in method of accounting because such change is a change in the treatment of a material item within his overall accounting practice.

Example (3). A taxpayer in the wholesale dry goods business computes its income and expenses on the accrual method of accounting and files its Federal income tax returns on such basis. Vacation pay has been deducted in the year in which paid because the taxpayer did not have a completely vested vacation pay plan, and, therefore, the liability for payment did not accrue until that year. Subsequently, the taxpayer adopts a completely vested vacation pay plan that changes its year for accruing the deduction from the year in which payment is made to the year in which the liability to make the payment now arises. The change for the year of deduction of the vacation pay plan is not a change in method of accounting but results, instead, because the underlying facts (that is, the type of vacation pay plan) have changed.

Reg. § 1.446-1(e)(2)

Example (4). From 1968 through 1970, a taxpayer has fairly allocated indirect overhead costs to the value of inventories on a fixed percentage of direct costs. If the ratio of indirect overhead costs to direct costs increases in 1971, a change in the underlying facts has occurred. Accordingly, an increase in the percentage in 1971 to fairly reflect the increase in the relative level of indirect overhead costs is not a change in method of accounting but is a change in treatment resulting from a change in the underlying facts.

Example (5). A taxpayer values inventories at cost. A change in the basis for valuation of inventories from cost to the lower of cost or market is a change in an overall practice of valuing items in inventory. The change, therefore, is a change of method of accounting for inventories.

Example (6). A taxpayer in the manufacturing business has for many taxable years valued its inventories at cost. However, cost has been improperly computed since no overhead costs have been included in valuing the inventories at cost. The failure to allocate an appropriate portion of overhead to the value of inventories is contrary to the requirement of the Internal Revenue Code and the regulations thereunder. A change requiring appropriate allocation of overhead is a change in method of accounting because it involves a change in the treatment of a material item used in the overall practice of identifying or valuing items in inventory.

Example (7). A taxpayer has for many taxable years valued certain inventories by a method which provides for deducting 20 percent of the cost of the inventory items in determining the final inventory valuation. The 20 percent adjustment is taken as a "reserve for price changes." Although this method is not a proper method of valuing inventories under the Internal Revenue Code or the regulations thereunder, it involves the treatment of a material item used in the overall practice of valuing inventory. A change in such practice or procedure is a change of method of accounting for inventories.

Example (8). A taxpayer has always used a base stock system of accounting for inventories. Under this system a constant price is applied to an assumed constant normal quantity of goods in stock. The base stock system is an overall plan of accounting for inventories which is not recognized as a proper method of accounting for inventories under the regulations. A change in this practice is, nevertheless, a change of method of accounting for inventories.

(3)(i) Except as otherwise provided under the authority of paragraph (e)(3)(ii) of this section, to secure the Commissioner's consent to a taxpayer's change in method of accounting the taxpayer must file an application on Form 3115 with the Commissioner during the taxable year in which the taxpayer desires to make the change in method of accounting. To the extent applicable, the taxpayer must furnish all information requested on the Form 3115. This information includes all classes of items that will be treated differently under the new method of accounting, any amounts that will be duplicated or omitted as a result of the proposed change, and the taxpayer's computation of any adjustments necessary to prevent such duplications or omissions. The Commissioner may require such other information as may be necessary to determine whether the proposed change will be permitted. Permission to change a taxpayer's method of accounting will not be granted unless the taxpayer agrees to the Commissioner's prescribed terms and conditions for effecting the change, including the taxable year or years in which any adjustment necessary to prevent amounts from being duplicated or omitted is to be taken into account. See section 481 and the regulations thereunder, relating to certain adjustments resulting from accounting method changes, and section 472 and the regulations thereunder, relating to adjustments for changes to and from the last-in, first-out inventory method. For any Form 3115 filed on or after May 15, 1997, see § 1.446-1T(e)(3)(i)(B).

(ii) Notwithstanding the provisions of paragraph (e)(3)(i) of this section, the Commissioner may prescribe administrative procedures under which taxpayers will be permitted to change their method of accounting. The administrative procedures shall prescribe those terms and conditions necessary to obtain the Commissioner's consent to effect the change and to prevent amounts from being duplicated or omitted. The terms and conditions that may be prescribed by the Commissioner may include terms and conditions that require the change in method of accounting to be effected on a cut-off basis or by an adjustment under section 481(a) to be taken into account in the taxable year or years prescribed by the Commissioner.

(iii) This paragraph (e)(3) applies to Forms 3115 filed on or after December 31, 1997. For other Forms 3115, see § 1.446-1(e)(3) in effect prior to December 31, 1997 (§ 1.446-1(e)(3) as contained in the 26 CFR part 1 edition revised as of April 1, 1997). [Reg. § 1.446-1.]

☐ [*T.D.* 6282, 12-24-57. *Amended by T.D.* 6584, 12-20-61; *T.D.* 7073, 11-17-70; *T.D.* 7285, 9-14-73; *T.D.* 8067, 12-30-85; *T.D.* 8131, 3-24-87; *T.D.* 8408, 4-9-92; *T.D.* 8482, 8-6-93; *T.D.* 8608, 8-4-95; *T.D.* 8719, 5-14-97; *T.D.* 8742, 12-30-97; *T.D.* 8929, 1-10-2001 *and T.D.* 9025, 12-13-2002.]

Reg. § 1.446-1(e)(3)

§ 1.446-2. Method of accounting for interest.—(a) *Applicability*—(1) *In general.* This section provides rules for determining the amount of interest that accrues during an accrual period (other than interest described in paragraph (a)(2) of this section) and for determining the portion of a payment that consists of accrued interest. For purposes of this section, interest includes original issue discount and amounts treated as interest (whether stated or unstated) any lending or deferred payment transaction. Accrued interest determined under this section is taken into account by a taxpayer under the taxpayer's regular method of accounting (e.g., an accrual method or the cash receipts and disbursements method). Application of an exception described in paragraph (a)(2) of this section to one party to a transaction does not affect the application of this section to any other party to the transaction.

(2) *Exceptions*—(i) *Interest included or deducted under certain other provisions.* This section does not apply to interest that is taken into account under—

(A) Sections 1272(a), 1275, and 163(e) (income and deductions relating to original issue discount);

(B) Section 467(a)(2) (certain payments for the use of property or services);

(C) Sections 1276 through 1278 (market discount);

(D) Sections 1281 through 1283 (discount on certain short-term obligations);

(E) Section 7872(a) (certain loans with below-market interest rates); or

(F) Section 1.1272-3 (an election by a holder to treat all interest on a debt instrument as original issue discount).

(ii) *De minimis original issue discount.* This section does not apply to de minimis original issue discount (other than de minimis original issue discount treated as qualified stated interest) as determined under § 1.1273-1(d). See § 1.163-7 for the treatment of de minimis.original issue discount by the issuer and §§ 1.1273-1(d) and 1.1272-3 for the treatment of de minimis original issue discount by the holder.

(b) *Accrual of qualified stated interest.* Qualified stated interest (as defined in § 1.1273-1(c)) accrues ratably over the accrual period (or periods) to which it is attributable and accrues at the stated rate for the period (or periods).

(c) *Accrual of interest other than qualified stated interest.* Subject to the modifications in paragraph (d) of this section, the amount of interest (other than qualified stated interest) that accrues for any accrual period is determined under rules similar to those in the regulations under sections 1272 and 1275 for the accrual of original issue discount. The preceding sentence applies regardless of any contrary formula agreed to by the parties.

(d) *Modifications*—(1) *Issue price.* The issue price of the loan or contract is equal to—

(i) In the case of a contract for the sale or exchange of property to which section 483 applies, the amount described in § 1.483-2(a)(1)(i) or (ii), whichever is applicable;

(ii) In the case of a contract for the sale or exchange of property to which section 483 does not apply, the stated principal amount; or

(iii) In any other case, the amount loaned.

(2) *Principal payments that are not deferred payments.* In the case of a contract to which section 483 applies, principal payments that are not deferred payments are ignored for purposes of determining yield and adjusted issue price.

(e) *Allocation of interest to payments*—(1) *In general.* Except as provided in paragraphs (e)(2), (e)(3), and (e)(4) of this section, each payment under a loan (other than payments of additional interest or similar charges provided with respect to amounts that are not paid when due) is treated as a payment of interest to the extent of the accrued and unpaid interest determined under paragraphs (b) and (c) of this section as of the date the payment becomes due.

(2) *Special rule for points deductible under section 461(g)(2).* If a payment of points is deductible by the borrower under section 461(g)(2), the payment is treated by the borrower as a payment of interest.

(3) *Allocation respected in certain small transactions.* [Reserved]

(4) *Pro rata prepayments.* Accrued but unpaid interest is allocated to a pro rata prepayment under rules similar to those for allocating accrued but unpaid original issue discount to a pro rata prepayment under § 1.1275-2(f). For purposes of the preceding sentence, a pro rata prepayment is a payment that is made prior to maturity that—

(i) Is not made pursuant to the contract's payment schedule; and

(ii) Results in a substantially pro rata reduction of each payment remaining to be paid on the contract.

(f) *Aggregation rule.* For purposes of this section, all contracts calling for deferred payments arising from the same transaction (or a series of related transactions) are treated as a single contract. This rule, however, generally only applies to contracts involving a single borrower and a single lender.

* * *

(h) *Example.* The following example illustrates the rules of this section.

Example. Allocation of unstated interest to deferred payments—(i) *Facts.* On July 1, 1996, A sells his personal residence to B for a stated purchase price of $1,297,143.66. The property is not personal use property (within the meaning of section 1275(b)(3)) in the hands of B. Under the loan agreement, B is required to make two installment payments of $648,571.83 each, the first due on June 30, 1998, and the second due on June 30, 2000. Both A and B use the cash receipts and disbursements method of accounting and use a calendar year for their taxable year.

(ii) *Amount of unstated interest.* Under section 483, the agreement does not provide for adequate stated interest. Thus, the loan's yield is the test rate of interest determined under § 1.483-3. Assume that both A and B use annual accrual periods and that the test rate of interest is 9.2 percent, compounded annually. Under § 1.483-2, the present value of the deferred payments is $1,000,000. Thus, the agreement has unstated interest of $297,143.66.

(iii) *First two accrual periods.* Under paragraph (d)(1) of this section, the issue price at the beginning of the first accrual period is $1,000,000 (the amount described in § 1.483-2(a)(1)(i)). Under paragraph (c) of this section, the amount of interest that accrues for the first accrual period is $92,000 ($1,000,000 × .092) and the amount of interest that accrues for the second accrual period is $100,464 ($1,092,000 × .092). Thus, $192,464 of interest has accrued as of the end of the second accrual period. Under paragraph (e)(1) of this section, the $648,571.83 payment made on June 30, 1998, is treated first as a payment of interest to the extent of $192,464. The remainder of the payment ($456,107.83) is treated as a payment of principal. Both A and B take the payment of interest ($192,464) into account in 1998.

(iv) *Second two accrual periods.* The adjusted issue price at the beginning of the third accrual period is $543,892.17 ($1,092,000 + $100,464 − $648,571.83). The amount of interest that accrues for the third accrual period is $50,038.08 ($543,892.17 × .092) and the amount of interest that accrues for the final accrual period is $54,641.58, the excess of the amount payable at maturity ($648,571.83), over the adjusted issue price at the beginning of the accrual period ($593,930.25). As of the date the second payment becomes due, $104,679.66 of interest has accrued. Thus, of the $648,571.83 payment made on June 30, 2000, $104,679.66 is treated as interest and $543,892.17 is treated as principal. Both A and B take the payment of interest ($104,679.66) into account in 2000.

* * *

[Reg. § 1.446-2.]

☐ [*T.D.* 8517, 1-27-94.]

§ 1.451-1. General rule for taxable year of inclusion.—(a) *General rule.* Gains, profits, and income are to be included in gross income for the taxable year in which they are actually or constructively received by the taxpayer unless includible for a different year in accordance with the taxpayer's method of accounting. Under an accrual method of accounting, income is includible in gross income when all the events have occurred which fix the right to receive such income and the amount thereof can be determined with reasonable accuracy. Therefore, under such a method of accounting if, in the case of compensation for services, no determination can be made as to the right to such compensation or the amount thereof until the services are completed, the amount of compensation is ordinarily income from the taxable year in which the determination can be made. Under the cash receipts and disbursements method of accounting, such an amount is includible in gross income when actually or constructively received. Where an amount of income is properly accrued on the basis of a reasonable estimate and the exact amount is subsequently determined, the difference, if any, shall be taken into account for the taxable year in which such determination is made. To the extent that income is attributable to the recovery of bad debts for accounts charged off in prior years, it is includible in the year of recovery in accordance with the taxpayer's method of accounting, regardless of the date when the amounts were charged off. For treatment of bad debts and bad debt recoveries, see sections 166 and 111 and the regulations thereunder. For rules relating to the treatment of amounts received in crop shares, see section 61 and the regulations thereunder. For the year in which a partner must include his distributive share of partnership income, see section 706(a) and paragraph (a) of § 1.706-1. If a taxpayer ascertains that an item should have been included in gross income in a prior taxable year, he should, if within the period of limitation, file an amended return and pay any additional tax due. Similarly, if a taxpayer ascertains that an item was improperly included in gross income in a prior taxable year, he should, if within the period of limitation, file claim for credit or refund of any overpayment of tax arising therefrom.

(b) *Special rule in case of death.* (1) A taxpayer's taxable year ends on the date of his death. See section 443(a)(2) and paragraph (a)(2) of § 1.443-1. In computing taxable income for such year, there shall be included only amounts properly includible under the method of accounting used by the taxpayer. However, if the taxpayer used an accrual method of accounting, amounts accrued only by reason of his death shall not be included in computing taxable income for such year. If the taxpayer uses no regular accounting method, only amounts actually or constructively received during such year shall be included. (For rules relating to the inclusion of partnership income in the return of a decedent partner, see subchapter K of chapter 1 of the Code and the regulations thereunder.)

(2) If the decedent owned an installment obligation the income from which was taxable to him under section 453, no income is required to be reported in the return of the decedent by reason of the transmission at death of such obligation. See section 453(d)(3). For the treatment of installment obligations acquired by the decedent's estate or by any person by bequest, devise, or inheritance from the decedent, see section 691(a)(4) and the regulations thereunder.

(c) *Special rule for employee tips.* Tips reported by an employee to his employer in a written statement furnished to the employer pursuant to section 6053(a) shall be included in gross income of the employee for the taxable year in which the written statement is furnished the employer. For provisions relating to the reporting of tips by an employee to his employer, see section 6053 and § 31.6053-1 of this chapter (Employment Tax Regulations).

(d) *Special rule for ratable inclusion of original issue discount.* For ratable inclusion of original issue discount in respect of certain corporate obligations issued after May 27, 1969, see section 1232(a)(3).

(e) *Special rule for inclusion of qualified tax refund effected by allocation.* For rules relating to the inclusion in income of an amount paid by a taxpayer in respect of his liability for a qualified State individual income tax and allocated or reallocated in such a manner as to apply it toward the taxpayer's liability for the Federal income tax, see paragraph (f)(1) of § 301.6361-1 of this chapter (Regulations on Procedure and Administration).

(f) *Timing of income from notional principal contracts.* For the timing of income with respect to notional principal contracts, see § 1.446-3.

(g) *Timing of income from section 467 rental agreements.* For the timing of income with respect to section 467 rental agreements, see section 467 and the regulations thereunder. [Reg. § 1.451-1.]

☐ [*T.D.* 6282, 12-24-57. *Amended by T.D.* 7001, 1-17-69; *T.D.* 7154, 12-27-71; *T.D.* 7577, 12-19-78; *T.D.* 8491, 10-8-93 *and T.D.* 8820, 5-17-99.]

§ 1.451-2. Constructive receipts of income.—
(a) *General rule.* Income although not actually reduced to a taxpayer's possession is constructively received by him in the taxable year during which it is credited to his account, set apart for him, or otherwise made available so that he may draw upon it at any time, or so that he could have drawn upon it during the taxable year if notice of intention to withdraw had been given. However, income is not constructively received if the taxpayer's control of its receipt is subject to substantial limitations or restrictions. Thus, if a corporation credits its employees with bonus stock, but the stock is not available to such employees until some future date, the mere crediting on the books of the corporation does not constitute receipt. In the case of interest, dividends, or other earnings (whether or not credited) payable in respect of any deposit or account in a bank, building and loan association, savings and loan association, or similar institution, the following are not substantial limitations or restrictions on the taxpayer's control over the receipt of such earnings:

(1) A requirement that the deposit or account, and the earnings thereon, must be withdrawn in multiples of even amounts;

(2) The fact that the taxpayer would, by withdrawing the earnings during the taxable year, receive earnings that are not substantially less in comparison with the earnings for the corresponding period to which the taxpayer would be entitled had he left the account on deposit until a later date (for example, if an amount equal to three months' interest must be forfeited upon withdrawal or redemption before maturity of a one year or less certificate of deposit, time deposit, bonus plan, or other deposit arrangement then the earnings payable on premature withdrawal or redemption would be substantially less when compared with the earnings available at maturity);

(3) A requirement that the earnings may be withdrawn only upon a withdrawal of all or part of the deposit or account. However, the mere fact that such institutions may pay earnings on withdrawals, total or partial, made during the last three business days of any calendar month ending a regular quarterly or semiannual earnings period at the applicable rate calculated to the end of such calendar month shall not constitute constructive receipt of income by any depositor or account holder in any such institution who has not made a withdrawal during such period;

(4) A requirement that a notice of intention to withdraw must be given in advance of the withdrawal. In any case when the rate of earnings payable in respect of such a deposit or account depends on the amount of notice of intention to withdraw that is given, earnings at the maximum

rate are constructively received during the taxable year regardless of how long the deposit or account was held during the year or whether, in fact, any notice of intention to withdraw is given during the year. However, if in the taxable year of withdrawal the depositor or account holder receives a lower rate of earnings because he failed to give the required notice of intention to withdraw, he shall be allowed an ordinary loss in such taxable year in an amount equal to the difference between the amount of earnings previously included in gross income and the amount of earnings actually received. See section 165 and the regulations thereunder.

(b) *Examples of constructive receipt.* Amounts payable with respect to interest coupons which have matured and are payable but which have not been cashed are constructively received in the taxable year during which the coupons mature, unless it can be shown that there are no funds available for payment of the interest during such year. Dividends on corporate stock are constructively received when unqualifiedly made subject to the demand of the shareholder. However, if a dividend is declared payable on December 31 and the corporation followed its usual practice of paying the dividends by checks mailed so that the shareholders would not receive them until January of the following year, such dividends are not considered to have been constructively received in December. Generally, the amount of dividends or interest credited on savings bank deposits or to shareholders of organizations such as building and loan associations or cooperative banks is income to the depositors or shareholders for the taxable year when credited. However, if any portion of such dividends or interest is not subject to withdrawal at the time credited, such portion is not constructively received and does not constitute income to the depositor or shareholder until the taxable year in which the portion first may be withdrawn. Accordingly, if, under a bonus or forfeiture plan, a portion of the dividends or interest is accumulated and may not be withdrawn until the maturity of the plan, the crediting of such portion to the account of the shareholder or depositor does not constitute constructive receipt. In this case, such credited portion is income to the depositor or shareholder in the year in which the plan matures. However, in the case of certain deposits made after December 31, 1970, in banks, domestic building and loan associations, and similar financial institutions, the ratable inclusion rules of section 1232(a)(3) apply. See § 1.1232-3A. Accrued interest on unwithdrawn insurance policy dividends is gross income to the taxpayer for the first taxable year during which such interest may be withdrawn by him. [Reg. § 1.451-2.]

□ [*T.D.* 6282, 12-24-57. *Amended by T.D.* 6723, 4-20-64; *T.D.* 7154, 12-27-71 and *T.D.* 7663, 12-21-79.]

§ 15A.453-1. Installment method reporting for sales of real property and casual sales of personal property (Temporary).—(a) *In general.* Unless the taxpayer otherwise elects in the manner prescribed in paragraph (d)(3) of this section, income from a sale of real property or a casual sale of personal property, where any payment is to be received in a taxable year after the year of sale, is to be reported on the installment method.

(b) *Installment sale defined* —(1) *In general.* The term "installment sale" means a disposition of property (except as provided in paragraph (b)(4) of this section) where at least one payment is to be received after the close of the taxable year in which the disposition occurs. The term "installment sale" includes dispositions from which payment is to be received in a lump sum in a taxable year subsequent to the year of sale. For purposes of this paragraph, the taxable year in which payments are to be received is to be determined without regard to section 453(e) (relating to related party sales), section (f)(3) (relating to the definition of a "payment") and section (g) (relating to sales of depreciable property to a spouse or 80-percent-owned entity).

(2) *Installment method defined* —(i) *In general.* Under the installment method, the amount of any payment which is income to the taxpayer is that portion of the installment payment received in that year which the gross profit realized or to be realized bears to the total contract price (the "gross profit ratio"). See paragraph (c) of this section for rules describing installment method reporting of contingent payment sales.

(ii) *Selling price defined.* The term "selling price" means the gross selling price without reduction to reflect any existing mortgage or other encumbrance on the property (whether assumed or taken subject to by the buyer) and, for installment sales in taxable years ending after October 19, 1980, without reduction to reflect any selling expenses. Neither interest, whether stated or unstated, nor original issue discount is considered to be a part of the selling price. See paragraph (c) of this section for rules describing installment method reporting of contingent payment sales.

(iii) *Contract price defined.* The term "contract price" means the total contract price equal to selling price reduced by that portion of any qualifying indebtedness (as defined in paragraph (b)(2)(iv) of this section), assumed or taken subject to by the buyer, which does not exceed the seller's basis in the property (adjusted, for installment sales in taxable years ending after October

Reg. § 15A.453-1(b)(2)

19, 1980, to reflect commissions and other selling expenses as provided in paragraph (b)(2)(v) of this section). See paragraph (c) of this section for rules describing installment method reporting of contingent payment sales.

(iv) *Qualifying indebtedness.* The term "qualifying indebtedness" means a mortgage or other indebtedness encumbering the property and indebtedness, not secured by the property but incurred or assumed by the purchaser incident to the purchaser's acquisition, holding, or operation in the ordinary course of business or investment, of the property. The term "qualifying indebtedness" does not include an obligation of the taxpayer incurred incident to the disposition of the property (*e.g.,* legal fees relating to the taxpayer's sale of the property) or an obligation functionally unrelated to the acquisition, holding, or operating of the property (*e.g.,* the taxpayer's medical bill). Any obligation created subsequent to the taxpayer's acquisition of the property and incurred or assumed by the taxpayer or placed as an encumbrance on the property in contemplation of disposition of the property is not qualifying indebtedness if the arrangement results in accelerating recovery of the taxpayer's basis in the installment sale.

(v) *Gross profit defined.* The term "gross profit" means the selling price less the adjusted basis as defined in section 1011 and the regulations thereunder. For sales in taxable years ending after October 19, 1980, in the case of sales of real property by a person other than a dealer and casual sales of personal property, commissions and other selling expenses shall be added to basis for purposes of determining the proportion of payments which is gross profit attributable to the disposition. Such additions to basis will not be deemed to affect the taxpayer's holding period in the transferred property.

(3) *Payment* —(i) *In general.* Except as provided in paragraph (e) of this section (relating to purchaser evidences of indebtedness payable on demand or readily tradable), the term "payment" does not include the receipt of evidences of indebtedness of the person acquiring the property ("installment obligation"), whether or not payment of such indebtedness is guaranteed by a third party (including a government agency). For special rules regarding the receipt of an evidence of indebtedness of a transferee of a qualified intermediary, see §§ 1.1031(b)-2(b) and 1.1031(k)-1(j)(2)(iii) of this chapter. A standby letter of credit (as defined in paragraph (b)(3)(iii) of this section) shall be treated as a third party guarantee. Payments include amounts actually or constructively received in the taxable year under an installment obligation. For a special rule regarding a transfer of property to a qualified inter-

mediary followed by the sale of such property by the qualified intermediary, see § 1.1031(k)-1(j)(2)(ii) of this chapter. Receipt of an evidence of indebtedness which is secured directly or indirectly by cash or a cash equivalent, such as a bank certificate of deposit or a treasury note, will be treated as the receipt of payment. For a special rule regarding a transfer of property in exchange for an obligation that is secured by cash or a cash equivalent held in a qualified escrow account or a qualified trust, see § 1.1031(k)-1(j)(2)(i) of this chapter. Payment may be received in cash or other property, including foreign currency, marketable securities, and evidences of indebtedness which are payable on demand or readily tradable. However, for special rules relating to the receipt of certain property with respect to which gain is not recognized, see paragraph (f) of this section (relating to transactions described in sections 351, 356(a) and 1031). Except as provided in § 15A.453-2 of these regulations (relating to distributions of installment obligations in corporate liquidations described in section 337), payment includes receipt of an evidence of indebtedness of a person other than the person acquiring the property from the taxpayer. For purposes of determining the amount of payment received in the taxable year, the amount of qualifying indebtedness (as defined in paragraph (b)(2)(iv) of this section) assumed or taken subject to by the person acquiring the property shall be included only to the extent that it exceeds the basis of the property (determined after adjustment to reflect selling expenses). For purposes of the preceding sentence, an arrangement under which the taxpayer's liability on qualifying indebtedness is eliminated incident to the disposition (*e.g.,* a novation) shall be treated as an assumption of the qualifying indebtedness. If the taxpayer sells property to a creditor of the taxpayer and indebtedness of the taxpayer is cancelled in consideration of the sale, such cancellation shall be treated as payment. To the extent that cancellation is not in consideration of the sale, see §§ 1.61-12(b)(1) and 1.1001-2(a)(2) relating to discharges of indebtedness. If the taxpayer sells property which is encumbered by a mortgage or other indebtedness on which the taxpayer is not personally liable, and the person acquiring the property is the obligee, the taxpayer shall be treated as having received payment in the amount of such indebtedness.

(ii) *Wrap-around mortgage.* This paragraph (b)(3)(ii) shall apply generally to any installment sale after March 4, 1981 unless the installment sale was completed before June 1, 1981 pursuant to a written obligation binding on the seller that was executed on or before March 4, 1981. A "wrap-around mortgage" means an agree-

Reg. § 15A.453-1(b)(3)

ment in which the buyer initially does not assume and purportedly does not take subject to part or all of the mortgage or other indebtedness encumbering the property ("wrapped indebtedness") and, instead, the buyer issues to the seller an installment obligation the principal amount of which reflects such wrapped indebtedness. Ordinarily, the seller will use payments received on the installment obligation to service the wrapped indebtedness. The wrapped indebtedness shall be deemed to have been taken subject to even though title to the property has not passed in the year of sale and even though the seller remains liable for payments on the wrapped indebtedness. In the hands of the seller, the wrap-around installment obligation shall have a basis equal to the seller's basis in the property which was the subject of the installment sale, increased by the amount of gain recognized in the year of sale, and decreased by the amount of cash and the fair market value of other nonqualifying property received in the year of sale. For purposes of this paragraph (b)(3)(ii), the amount of any indebtedness assumed or taken subject to by the buyer (other than wrapped indebtedness) is to be treated as cash received by the seller in the year of sale. Therefore, except as otherwise required by section 483 or 1232, the gross profit ratio with respect to the wrap-around installment obligation is a fraction, the numerator of which is the face value of the obligation less the taxpayer's basis in the obligation and the denominator of which is the face value of the obligation.

(iii) *Standby letter of credit.* The term "standby letter of credit" means a non-negotiable, nontransferable (except together with the evidence of indebtedness which it secures) letter of credit, issued by a bank or other financial institution, which serves as a guarantee of the evidence of indebtedness which is secured by the letter of credit. Whether or not the letter of credit explicitly states it is non-negotiable and nontransferable, it will be treated as non-negotiable and nontransferable if applicable local law so provides. The mere right of the secured party (under applicable local law) to transfer the proceeds of a letter of credit shall be disregarded in determining whether the instrument qualifies as a standby letter of credit. A letter of credit is not a standby letter of credit if it may be drawn upon in the absence of default in payment of the underlying evidence of indebtedness.

(4) *Exceptions.* The term "installment sale" does not include, and the provisions of section 453 do not apply to, dispositions of personal property on the installment plan by a person who regularly sells or otherwise disposes of personal property on the installment plan, or to dispositions of personal property of a kind which is required to be included in the inventory of the taxpayer if on hand

at the close of the taxable year. See section 453A and the regulations thereunder for rules relating to installment sales by dealers in personal property. A dealer in real property or a farmer who is not required under his method of accounting to maintain inventories may report the gain on the installment method under section 453.

(5) *Examples.* The following examples illustrate installment method reporting under this section:

Example (1). In 1980, A, a calendar year taxpayer, sells Blackacre, an unencumbered capital asset in A's hands, to B for $100,000: $10,000 down and the remainder payable in equal annual installments over the next 9 years, together with adequate stated interest. A's basis in Blackacre, exclusive of selling expenses, is $38,000. Selling expenses paid by A are $2,000. Therefore, the gross profit is $60,000 ($100,000 selling price − $40,000 basis inclusive of selling expenses). The gross profit ratio is 3/5 (gross profit of $60,000 divided by $100,000 contract price). Accordingly, $6,000 (3/5 of $10,000) of each $10,000 payment received is gain attributable to the sale and $4,000 ($10,000 − $6,000) is recovery of basis. The interest received in addition to principal is ordinary income to A.

Example (2). C sells Whiteacre to D for a selling price of $160,000. Whiteacre is encumbered by a longstanding mortgage in the principal amount of $60,000. D will assume or take subject to the $60,000 mortgage and pay the remaining $100,000 in 10 equal annual installments together with adequate stated interest. C's basis in Whiteacre is $90,000. There are no selling expenses. The contract price is $100,000, the $160,000 selling price reduced by the mortgage of $60,000 assumed or taken subject to. Gross profit is $70,000 ($160,000 selling price less C's basis of $90,000). C's gross profit ratio is 7/10 (gross profit of $70,000 divided by $100,000 contract price). Thus, $7,000 (7/10 of $10,000) of each $10,000 annual payment is gain attributable to the sale, and $3,000 ($10,000 − $7,000) is recovery of basis.

Example (3). The facts are the same as in example (2), except that C's basis in the land is $40,000. In the year of the sale C is deemed to have received payment of $20,000 ($60,000 − $40,000, the amount by which the mortgage D assumed or took subject to exceeds C's basis). Since basis is fully recovered in the year of sale, the gross profit ratio is 1 ($120,000/$120,000) and C will report 100% of the $20,000 deemed payment in the year of sale and each $10,000 annual payment as gain attributable to the sale.

Example (4). E sells Blackacre, an unencumbered capital gain property in E's hands, to F on

January 2, 1981. F makes a cash down payment of $500,000 and issues a note to E obliging F to pay an additional $500,000 on the fifth anniversary date. The note does not require a payment of interest. In determining selling price, section 483 will apply to recharacterize as interest a portion of the $500,000 future payment. Assume that under section 483 and the applicable regulations $193,045 is treated as total unstated interest, and the selling price is $806,955 ($1 million less unstated interest). Assuming E's basis (including selling expenses) in Blackacre is $200,000, gross profit is $606,955 ($806,955 − $200,000) and the gross profit ratio is 75.21547%. Accordingly, of the $500,000 cash down payment received by E in 1981, $376,077 (75.21547% of $500,000) is gain attributable to the sale and $123,923 is recovery of basis ($500,000 − $376,077).

Example (5). In 1982, G sells to H Blackacre, which is encumbered by a first mortgage with a principal amount of $500,000 and a second mortgage with a principal amount of $400,000, for a selling price of $2 million. G's basis in Blackacre is $700,000. Under the agreement between G and H, passage of title is deferred and H does not assume and purportedly does not take subject to either mortgage in the year of sale. H pays G $200,000 in cash and issues a wrap-around mortgage note with a principal amount of $1,800,000 bearing adequate stated interest. H is deemed to have acquired Blackacre subject to the first and second mortgages (wrapped indebtedness) totalling $900,000. The contract price is $1,300,000 (selling price of $2 million less $700,000 mortgages within the seller's basis assumed or taken subject to). Gross profit is also $1,300,000 (selling price of $2 million less $700,000 basis). Accordingly in the year of sale, the gross profit ratio is 1 ($1,300,000/$1,300,000). Payment in the year of sale is $400,000 ($200,000 cash received plus $200,000 mortgage in excess of basis ($900,000 − $700,000)). Therefore, G recognizes $400,000 gain in the year of sale ($400,000 × 1). In the hands of G the wrap-around installment obligation has a basis of $900,000, equal to G's basis in Blackacre ($700,000) increased by the gain recognized by G in the year of sale ($400,000) reduced by the cash received by G in the year of sale ($200,000). G's gross profit with respect to the note is $900,000 ($1,800,000 face amount less $900,000 basis in the note) and G's contract price with respect to the note is its face amount of $1,800,000. Therefore, the gross profit ratio with respect to the note is ½ ($900,000/$1,800,000).

Example (6). The facts are the same as example (5) except that under the terms of the agreement H assumes the $500,000 first mortgage on Blackacre. H does not assume and purportedly does not take subject to the $400,000 second mort-

gage on Blackacre. The wrap-around installment obligation issued by H to G has a face amount of $1,300,000. The tax results in the year of sale to G are the same as example (5) ($400,000 payment received and gain recognized). In the hands of G, basis in the wrap-around installment obligation is $400,000 ($700,000 basis in Blackacre plus $400,000 gain recognized in the year of sale minus $700,000 ($200,000 cash received and $500,000 treated as cash received as a result of H's assumption of the first mortgage)). G's gross profit with respect to the note is $900,000 ($1,300,000 face amount of the wrap-around installment obligation less $400,000 basis in that note) and G's contract price with respect to the note is its face value of $1,300,000. Therefore, the gross profit ratio with respect to the note is 9/13

$$\frac{(\$\ 900,000)}{(\$1,300,000)}.$$

Example (7). A sells the stock of X corporation to B for a $1 million installment obligation payable in equal annual installments over the next 10 years with adequate stated interest. The installment obligation is secured by a standby letter of credit (within the meaning of paragraph (b)(3)(iii) of this section) issued by M bank. Under the agreement between B and M bank, B is required to maintain a compensating balance in an account B maintains with M bank and is required by the M bank to post additional collateral, which may include cash or a cash equivalent, with M bank. Under neither the standby letter of credit nor any other agreement or arrangement is A granted a direct lien upon or other security interest in such cash or cash equivalent collateral. Receipt of B's installment obligation secured by the standby letter of credit will not be treated as the receipt of payment by A.

Example (8). The facts are the same as in example (7) except that the standby letter of credit is in the drawable sum of $600,000. To secure fully its $1 million note issued to A, B deposits in escrow $400,000 in cash and Treasury bills. Under the escrow agreement, upon default in payment of the note A may look directly to the escrowed collateral. Receipt of B's installment obligation will be treated as the receipt payment by A in the sum of $400,000.

(c) *Contingent payment sales*—(1) *In general.* Unless the taxpayer otherwise elects in the manner prescribed in paragraph (d)(3) of this section, contingent payment sales are to be reported on the installment method. As used in this section, the term "contingent payment sale" means a sale or other disposition of property in which the aggregate selling price cannot be determined by the close of the taxable year in which such sale or other disposition occurs.

Reg. § 15A.453-1(c)(1)

The term "contingent payment sale" does not include transactions with respect to which the installment obligation represents, under applicable principles of tax law, a retained interest in the property which is the subject of the transaction, an interest in a joint venture or a partnership, an equity interest in a corporation or similar transactions, regardless of the existence of a stated maximum selling price or a fixed payment term. See paragraph (c)(8) of this section, describing the extent to which the regulations under section 385 apply to the determination of whether an installment obligation represents an equity interest in a corporation.

This paragraph prescribes the rules to be applied in allocating the taxpayer's basis (including selling expenses except for selling expenses of dealers in real estate) to payments received and to be received in a contingent payment sale. The rules are designed appropriately to distinguish contingent payment sales for which a maximum selling price is determinable, sales for which a maximum selling price is not determinable but the time over which payments will be received is determinable, and sales for which neither a maximum selling price nor a definite payment term is determinable. In addition, rules are prescribed under which, in appropriate circumstances, the taxpayer will be permitted to recover basis under an income forecast computation.

(2) *Stated maximum selling price*—(i) *In general.* (A) A contingent payment sale will be treated as having a stated maximum selling price if, under the terms of the agreement, the maximum amount of sale proceeds that may be received by the taxpayer can be determined as of the end of the taxable year in which the sale or other disposition occurs. The stated maximum selling price shall be determined by assuming that all of the contingencies contemplated by the agreement are met or otherwise resolved in a manner that will maximize the selling price and accelerate payments to the earliest date or dates permitted under the agreement. Except as provided in paragraph (c)(2)(ii) and (7) of this section (relating to certain payment recomputations), the taxpayer's basis shall be allocated to payments received and to be received under a stated maximum selling price agreement by treating the stated maximum selling price as the selling price for purposes of paragraph (b) of this section. The stated maximum selling price, as initially determined, shall thereafter be treated as the selling price unless and until that maximum amount is reduced, whether pursuant to the terms of the original agreement, by subsequent amendment, by application of the payment recharacterization rule (described in paragraph (c)(2)(ii) of this section), or by a subsequent supervening

event such as bankruptcy of the obligor. When the maximum amount is subsequently reduced, the gross profit ratio will be recomputed with respect to payments received in or after the taxable year in which an event requiring reduction occurs. If, however, application of the foregoing rules in a particular case would substantially and inappropriately accelerate or defer recovery of the taxpayer's basis, a special rule will apply. See paragraph (c)(7) of this section.

(B) The following examples illustrate the provisions of paragraph (c)(2)(i) of this section. In each example, it is assumed that application of the rules illustrated will not substantially and inappropriately defer or accelerate recovery of the taxpayer's basis.

Example (1). A sells all of the stock of X corporation to B for $100,000 payable at closing plus an amount equal to 5% of the net profits of X for each of the next nine years, the contingent payments to be made annually together with adequate stated interest. The agreement provides that the maximum amount A may receive, inclusive of the $100,000 down payment but exclusive of interest, shall be $2,000,000. A's basis in the stock of X inclusive of selling expenses, is $200,000. Selling price and contract price are considered to be $2,000,000. Gross profit is $1,800,000, and the gross profit ratio is 9/10 ($1,800,000/$2,000,000). Accordingly, of the $100,000 received by A in the year of sale, $90,000 is reportable as gain attributable to the sale and $10,000 is recovery of basis.

Example (2). C owns Blackacre which is encumbered by a long-standing mortgage of $100,000. On January 15, 1981, C sells Blackacre to D under the following payment arrangement: $100,000 in cash on closing; nine equal annual installment payments of $100,000 commencing January 15, 1982; and nine annual payments (the first to be made on March 30, 1982) equal to 5% of the gross annual rental receipts from Blackacre generated during the preceding calendar year. The agreement provides that each deferred payment shall be accompanied by a payment of interest calculated at the rate of 12% per annum and that the maximum amount payable to C under the agreement (exclusive of interest) shall be $2,100,000. The agreement also specifies that D will assume the long-standing mortgage. C's basis (inclusive of selling expenses) in Blackacre is $300,000. Accordingly, selling price is $2,100,000 and contract price is $2,000,000 (selling price of $2,100,000 less the $100,000 mortgage). The gross profit ratio is 9/10 (gross profit of $1,800,000 divided by $2,000,000 contract price). Of the $100,000 cash payment received by C in 1981, $90,000 is gain attributable to the sale of Blackacre and $10,000 is recovery of basis.

Reg. § 15A.453-1(c)(2)

(ii) *Certain interest recomputations.* When interest is stated in the contingent price sale agreement at a rate equal to or greater than the applicable prescribed test rate referred to in § 1.483-1(d)(1)(ii) and such stated interest is payable in addition to the amounts otherwise payable under the agreement, such stated interest is not considered a part of the selling price. In other circumstances (i.e., section 483 is applicable because no interest is stated or interest is stated below the applicable test rate, or interest is stated under a payment recharacterization provision of the sale agreement), the special rule set forth in this (ii) shall be applied in the initial computation and subsequent recomputations of selling price, contract price, and gross profit ratio. The special rule is referred to in this section as the "price-interest recomputation rule." As used in this section, the term "payment recharacterization" refers to a contractual arrangement under which a computed amount otherwise payable as part of the selling price is denominated an interest payment. The amount of unstated interest determined under section 483 or (if section 483 is inapplicable in the particular case) the amount of interest determined under a payment recharacterization arrangement is collectively referred to in this section as "internal interest" amounts. The price-interest recomputation rule is applicable to any stated maximum selling price agreement which contemplates receipt of internal interest by the taxpayer. Under the rule, stated maximum selling price will be determined as of the end of the taxpayer's taxable year in which the sale or other disposition occurs, taking into account all events which have occurred and are subject to prompt subsequent calculation and verification and assuming that all amounts that may become payable under the agreement will be paid on the earliest date or dates permitted under the agreement. With respect to the year of sale, the amount (if any) of internal interest then shall be determined taking account of the respective components of that calculation. The maximum amount initially calculated, minus the internal interest so determined, is the initial stated maximum selling price under the price-interest recomputation rule. For each subsequent taxable year, stated maximum selling price (and thus selling price, contract price, and gross profit ratio) shall be recomputed, taking into account all events which have occurred and are subject to prompt subsequent calculation and verification and assuming that all amounts that may become payable under the agreement will be paid on the earliest date or dates permitted under the agreement. The redetermined gross profit ratio, adjusted to reflect payments received and gain recognized in prior

taxable years, shall be applied to payments received in that taxable year.

(iii) *Examples.* The following examples illustrate installment method reporting of a contingent payment sale under which there is a stated maximum selling price. In each example, it is assumed that application of the rules described will not substantially and inappropriately defer or accelerate recovery of the taxpayer's basis.

Example (1). A owns all of the stock of X corporation with a basis to A of $20 million. On July 1, 1981, A sells the stock of X to B under an agreement calling for fifteen annual payments respectively equal to 5% of the net profits of X earned in the immediately preceding fiscal year beginning with the fiscal year ending March 31, 1982. Each payment is to be made on the following June 15th, commencing June 15, 1982, together with adequate stated interest. The agreement specifies that the maximum amount (exclusive of interest) payable to A shall not exceed $60 million. Since stated interest is payable as an addition to the selling price and the specified rate is not below the section 483 test rate, there is no internal interest under the agreement. The stated maximum selling price is $60 million. The gross profit ratio is 2/3 (gross profit of $40 million divided by $60 million contract price). Thus, if on June 15, 1982, A receives a payment of $3 million (exclusive of interest) under the agreement, in that year A will report $2 million ($3 million × 2/3) as gain attributable to the sale, and $1 million as recovery of basis.

Example (2). (i) The facts are the same as in example (1) except that the agreement does not call for the payment of any stated interest but does provide for an initial cash payment of $3 million on July 1, 1981. The maximum amount payable, including the $3 million initial payment, remains $60 million. Since section 483 will apply to each payment received by A more than one year following the date of sale (section 483 is inapplicable to the contingent payment that will be received on June 15, 1982 since that date is within one year following the July 1, 1981 sale date), the agreement contemplates internal interest and the price-interest recomputation rule is applicable. Under the rule, an initial determination must be made for A's taxable year 1981. On December 31, 1981, the last day of the taxable year, no events with regard to the first fiscal year have occurred which are subject to prompt subsequent calculation and verification because that fiscal year will end March 31, 1982. Under the price-interest recomputation rule, on December 31, 1981 A is required to assume that the maximum amount subsequently payable under the agreement ($57 million, equal to $60 million less the $3 million initial cash payment received by A

Reg. § 15A.453-1(c)(2)

in 1981) will be paid on the earliest date permissible under the agreement, *i.e.*, on June 15, 1982. Since no part of a payment received on that date would be treated as interest under section 483, the initial stated maximum selling price, applicable to A's 1981 tax calculation, is deemed to be $60 million. Thus, the 1981 gross profit ratio is ⅔ and for the taxable year 1981 A will report $2 million as gain attributable to the sale.

(ii) The net profits of X for its fiscal year ending March 31, 1982 are $100 million. On June 15, 1982 A receives a payment from B equal to 5% of that amount, or $6 million. On December 31, 1982, A knows that the maximum amount he may subsequently receive under the agreement is $51 million, and A is required to assume that this amount will be paid to him on the earliest permissible date, June 15, 1983. Section 483 does not treat as interest any part of the $6 million received by A on June 15, 1982, but section 483 will treat as unstated interest a computed part of the $51 million it is assumed A will receive on June 15, 1983. Assuming that under the tables in the regulations under section 483, it is determined that the principal component of a payment received more than 21 months but less than 27 months after the date of sale is considered to be .82270, $41,957,700 of the presumed $51 million payment will be treated as principal. The balance of $9,042,300 is interest. Accordingly, in A's 1982 tax calculations stated maximum selling price will be $50,957,700, which amount is equal to the stated maximum selling price that was determined in the 1981 tax calculations ($60 million) reduced by the section 483 interest component of the $6 million payment received by A in 1982 ($0) and further reduced by the section 483 interest component of the $51 million presumed payment to be received by A on June 15, 1983 ($9,042,300). Similarly, in determining gross profit for 1982 tax calculations, the gross profit of $40 million determined in the 1981 tax calculations must be reduced by the same section 483 interest amounts, yielding a recomputed gross profit of $30,957,700 ($40,000,000 − $9,042,300). Further, since prior to 1982 A received payment under the agreement (1981 payment of $3 million of which $2 million was profit), the appropriate amounts must be subtracted in the 1982 tax calculation. The total previously received selling price payment of $3 million is subtracted from the recomputed maximum selling price of $50,957,700, yielding an adjusted selling price of $47,957,700. The total previously recognized gain of $2 million is subtracted from the recomputed maximum gross profit of $30,957,700, yielding an adjusted gross profit of $28,957,700. The gross profit percentage applicable to 1982 tax calculations thus is determined to be 60.38175%,

equal to the quotient of dividing the adjusted gross profit of $28,957,700 by the adjusted selling price of $47,957,700. Accordingly, of the $6 million received by A in 1982, no part of which is unstated interest under section 483, A will report $3,622,905 (60.38175% of $6 million) as gain attributable to the sale and $2,377,095 ($6,000,000 − $3,622,905) as recovery of basis.

(iii) The net profits of X for its fiscal year ending March 31, 1983 are $200 million. On June 15, 1983 A receives a payment from B equal to $10 million. On December 31, 1983, A knows that the maximum amount he may subsequently receive under the agreement is $41 million, and A is required to assume that this amount will be paid to him on the earliest permissible date, June 15, 1984. Assuming that under the tables in the regulations under section 483 it is determined that the principal component of a payment received more than 33 months but less than 39 months after the date of sale is .74622, $30,595,020 of the presumed $41 million ($51 million − $10 million) payment will be treated as principal and $10,404,980 is interest. Based upon the assumed factor for 21 months but less than 27 months (.82270) $8,227,000 of the $10 million payment is principal and $1,733,000 is interest. Accordingly, in A's 1983 tax calculations stated maximum selling price will be $47,822,020, which amount is equal to the stated maximum selling price determined in the 1981 calculation ($60 million) reduced by the section 483 interest component of the $6 million 1982 payment ($0), the section 483 interest component of the 1983 payment ($1,773,000) and by the section 483 interest component of the presumed $41 million payment to be received in 1984 ($10,404,980). The recomputed gross profit is $27,822,020 ($40 million − $10,404,980 − $1,773,000). The previously reported payments must be deducted for the 1983 calculation. Selling price is reduced to $38,822,020 by subtracting the $3 million 1981 payment and the $6 million 1982 payment ($47,822,020 − $9 million) and gross profit is reduced to $22,199,115 by subtracting the 1981 profit of $2 million and the 1982 profit of $3,622,905 ($27,822,020 − $5,622,905), yielding a gross profit percentage of 57.18176% ($22,199,115/$38,822,020). Accordingly, of the $10 million received in 1983, A will report $1,773,000 as interest under section 483, and of the remaining principal component of $8,227,000, $4,704,343 as gain attributable to the sale ($8,227,000 × 57.18176%) and $3,522,657 ($8,227,000 − $4,704,343) as recovery of basis.

Example (3). The facts are the same as in example (2) except that X is a collapsible corporation as defined in section 341(b)(1) and no limitation or exception under section 341(d), (e), or (f) is applicable. Under section 341(a), all of A's gain on the sale will be ordinary income. Accordingly, section 483 will not apply to treat as interest any part of the payments to be received by A under his agreement with B. See section 483(f)(3). Therefore, the price-interest recomputation rule is inapplicable and the tax results to A in each year in which payment is received will be determined in a manner consistent with example (1).

Example (4). The facts are the same as in example (2) (maximum amount payable under the agreement $60 million) except that the agreement between A and B contains the following "payment recharacterization" provision:

"Any payment made more than one year after the (July 1, 1981) date of sale shall be composed of an interest element and a principal element, the interest element being computed on the principal element at an interest rate of 9% per annum computed from the date of sale to the date of payment."

The results reached in example (2), with respect to the $3 million initial cash payment received by A in 1981 remain the same because, under the payment recharacterization formula, no amount received or assumed to be received prior to July 1, 1982 is treated as interest. The 1982 tax computation method described in example (2) is equally applicable to the $6 million payment received in 1982. However, the adjusted gross profit ratio determined in this example (4) will differ from the ratio determined in example (2). The difference is attributable to the difference between a 9% stated interest rate calculation (in this example (4)) and the compound rate of unstated interest required under section 483 and used in calculating the results in example (2).

Example (5). The facts are the same as in example (1). In 1992 X is adjudged a bankrupt and it is determined that, in and after 1992, B will not be required to make any further payments under the agreement, *i.e.,* B's contingent payment obligation held by A now has become worthless. Assume that A previously received aggregate payments (exclusive of interest) of $45 million and out of those payments recovered $15 million of A's total $20 million basis. For 1992 A will report a loss of $5 million attributable to the sale, taken at the time determined to be appropriate under the rules generally applicable to worthless debts.

Example (6). (i) C owns all of the stock of Z corporation, a calendar year taxpayer. On July 1, 1981, C sells the stock of Z to D under an agreement calling for payment, each year for the next ten years, of an amount equal to 10% of the net profits of Z earned in the immediately preceding calendar year beginning with the year ending December 31, 1981. Each payment is to be made on the following April 1st, commencing April 1, 1982. In addition, C is to receive a payment of $5 million on closing. The agreement specifies that the maximum amount payable to C, including the $5 million cash payment at closing, is $24 million. The agreement does not call for the payment of any stated interest. Since section 483 will apply to each payment received by C more than one year following the date of sale (section 483 is inapplicable to the payment that will be received on April 1, 1982, since that date is within one year following the July 1, 1981 sale date), the agreement contemplates internal interest and the price interest recomputation rule is applicable. Under that rule, C must make an initial determination for his taxable year 1981.

(ii) On December 31, 1981, the exact amount of Z's 1981 net profit is not known, since it normally takes a number of weeks to compile the relevant information. However, the events which will determine the amount of the payment C will receive on April 1, 1982 have already occurred, and the information (Z's 1981 financial statement) will be promptly calculated and verified and will be available prior to the time C's 1981 tax return is timely filed. On March 15, 1982, Z reports net income of $14 million, and on April 1, 1982 D pays C $1.4 million.

(iii) Under the price-interest recomputation rule, C is required to determine the gross profit ratio for the 1981 $5 million payment on the basis of the events which occurred by the close of that taxable year and which are verifiable before the due date of the 1981 return. Because at the end of C's 1981 taxable year all events which will determine the amount of the April 1, 1982 payment have occurred and because the actual facts are known prior to the due date of C's return, C will take those facts into account when calculating the gross profit ratio. Thus, because C knows that the 1982 payment is $1.4 million, C knows that the remaining amount to be recovered under the contract is $17.6 million ($24 million — ($5 million + $1.4 million)). For purposes of this paragraph C must assume that the entire $17.6 million will be paid on the earliest possible date, April 1, 1983. Because section 483 will apply to that payment, and assuming that under the tables in the regulations under section 483 the principal component of a payment received 21 months after the date of sale is considered to be .86384, $15,203,584 of the $17.6 million would be principal and $2,396,416 ($17,600,000 — $15,203,584) would be interest. Therefore C must assume, for purposes of reporting the $5 million payment received in 1981, that the selling price is $21,603,584 calculated as follows:

Reg. § 15A.453-1(c)(2)

$24,000,000	Total selling price
− 2,396,416	Interest component of the $17,600,000 payment which C must assume will be made April 1, 1983.
$21,603,584	Adjusted selling price to be used when reporting the 1981 payment.

(iv) Assume that on March 15, 1982, Z reports net income of $15 million for 1982 and that on April 1, 1983 D pays C $1.5 million. Because section 483 will apply to that payment, and assuming that under the tables in the regulations under section 483 the principal component of a payment received 21 months after the date of sale is considered to be .86384, $1,295,760 of the $1,500,000 payment will be principal and $204,240 ($1,500,000 − $1,295,760) will be interest. Because C knows the amount of the 1983 payment when filing the 1982 tax return, C must assume that the remaining amount to be received under the contract, $16.1 million ($24 million − ($5 million + $1.4 million + $1.5 million)), will be received as a lump sum on April 1, 1984. Because section 483 will again apply, and assuming that the principal component of a payment made 34 months after the date of the sale is .74622, $12,014,142 of the $16.1 million would be principal, and $4,085,858 ($16,100,000 − $12,014,142) would be interest. Therefore, C must assume, for purpose of reporting the $1.4 million payment made April 1, 1982, that the adjusted selling price (within the meaning of example (2)) is $14,709,902, calculated as follows:

$24,000,000	Total selling price
− 204,240	Interest component of the $1,500,000 payment made April 1, 1983.
− $ 4,085,858	Interest component of the $16,100,000 payment which C must assume will be made April 1, 1984.
− 5,000,000	Payment made in 1981.
$14,709,902	Adjusted selling price for calculations for reporting the 1982 payment.

(3) *Fixed period* —(i) *In general.* When a stated maximum selling price cannot be determined as of the close of the taxable year in which the sale or other disposition occurs, but the maximum period over which payments may be received under the contingent sale price agreement is fixed, the taxpayer's basis (inclusive of selling expenses) shall be allocated to the taxable years in which payment may be received under the agreement in equal annual increments. In making the allocation it is not relevant whether the buyer is required to pay adequate stated interest. However, if the terms of the agreement incorporate an arithmetic component that is not identical for all taxable years, basis shall be allocated among the taxable years to accord with that component unless, taking into account all of the payment terms of the agreement, it is inappropriate to presume that payments under the contract are likely to accord with the variable component. If in any taxable year no payment is received or the amount of payment received (exclusive of interest) is less than the basis allocated to that taxable year, no loss shall be allowed unless the taxable year is the final payment year under the agreement or unless it is otherwise determined in accordance with the rules generally applicable to worthless debts that the future payment obligation under the agreement has become worthless. When no loss is allowed, the unrecovered portion of the basis allocated to the taxable year shall be carried forward to the next succeeding taxable year. If application of the foregoing rules to a particular case would substantially and inappropriately defer or accelerate recovery of the taxpayer's basis, a special rule will apply. See paragraph (c)(7) of this section.

(ii) *Examples.* The following examples illustrate the rules for recovery of basis in a contingent payment sale in which stated maximum selling price cannot be determined but the period over which payments are to be received under the agreement is fixed. In each case, it is assumed that application of the described rules will not substantially and inappropriately defer or accelerate recovery of the taxpayer's basis.

Example (1). A sells Blackacre to B for 10 percent of Blackacre's gross yield for each of the next 5 years. A's basis in Blackacre is $5 million. Since the sales price is indefinite and the maximum selling price is not ascertainable from the terms of the contract, basis is recovered ratably over the period during which payment may be received under the contract. Thus, assuming A receives the payments (exclusive of interest) listed in the following table, A will report the following:

Year	Payment	Basis Recovered	Gain Attributable to the Sale
1	$1,300,000	$1,000,000	$ 300,000
2	$1,500,000	$1,000,000	$ 500,000
3	$1,400,000	$1,000,000	$ 400,000
4	$1,800,000	$1,000,000	$ 800,000
5	$2,100,000	$1,000,000	$1,100,000

Reg. § 15A.453-1(c)(3)

Example (2). The facts are the same as in example (1), except that the payment in year 1 is only $900,000. Since the installment payment is less than the amount of basis allocated to that year, the unrecovered basis, $100,000, is carried forward to year 2.

Year	Payment	Basis Recovered	Gain Attributable to the Sale
1........	$900,000	$900,000	—0—
2........	$1,500,000	$1,100,000	$ 400,000
3........	$1,400,000	$1,000,000	$ 400,000
4........	$1,800,000	$1,000,000	$ 800,000
5........	$2,100,000	$1,000,000	$1,100,000

Example (3). C owns all of the stock of X corporation with a basis of $100,000 (inclusive of selling expenses). D purchases the X stock from C and agrees to make four payments computed in accordance with the following formula: 40% of the net profits of X in year 1, 30% in year 2, 20% in year 3, and 10% in year 4. Accordingly, C's basis is allocated as follows: $40,000 to year 1, $30,000 to year 2, $20,000 to year 3, and $10,000 to year 4.

Example (4). The facts are the same as in example (3), but the agreement also requires that D make fixed installment payments in accordance with the following schedule: no payment in year 1, $100,000 in year 2, $200,000 in year 3, $300,000 in year 4, and $400,000 in year 5. Thus, while it is reasonable to project that the contingent component of the payments will decrease each year, the fixed component of the payments will increase each year. Accordingly, C is required to allocate $20,000 of basis to each of the taxable years 1 through 5.

(4) *Neither stated maximum selling price nor fixed period.* If the agreement neither specifies a maximum selling price nor limits payments to a fixed period, a question arises whether a sale realistically has occurred or whether, in economic effect, payments received under the agreement are in the nature of rent or royalty income. Arrangements of this sort will be closely scrutinized. If, taking into account all of the pertinent facts, including the nature of the property, the arrangement is determined to qualify as a sale, the taxpayer's basis (including selling expenses) shall be recovered in equal annual increments over a period of 15 years commencing with the date of sale. However, if in any taxable year no payment is received or the amount of payment received (exclusive of interest) is less than basis allocated to the year, no loss shall be allowed unless it is otherwise determined in accordance with the timing rules generally applicable to worthless debts that the future payment obligation under the agreement has become worthless; instead the excess basis shall be reallocated in level amounts over the balance of the 15-year term. Any basis not recovered at the end of the 15th year shall be carried forward to the next succeeding year, and to the extent unrecovered thereafter shall be carried forward from year to year until all basis has been recovered or the future payment obligation is determined to be worthless. The general rule requiring initial level allocation of basis over 15 years shall not apply if the taxpayer can establish to the satisfaction of the Internal Revenue Service that application of the general rule would substantially and inappropriately defer recovery of the taxpayer's basis. See paragraph (c)(7) of this section. If the Service determines that initially allocating basis in level amounts over the first 15 years will substantially and inappropriately accelerate recovery of the taxpayer's basis in early years of that 15-year term, the Service may require that basis be reallocated within the 15-year term but the Service will not require that basis initially be allocated over more than 15 years. See paragraph (c)(7) of this section.

* * *

(d) *Election not to report an installment sale on the installment method*—(1) *In general.* An installment sale is to be reported on the installment method unless the taxpayer elects otherwise in accordance with the rules set forth in paragraph (d)(3) of this section.

(2) *Treatment of an installment sale when a taxpayer elects not to report on the installment method*—(i) *In general.* A taxpayer who elects not to report an installment sale on the installment method must recognize gain on the sale in accordance with the taxpayer's method of accounting. The fair market value of an installment obligation shall be determined in accordance with paragraph (d)(2)(ii) and (iii) of this section. In making such determination, any provision of contract or local law restricting the transferability of the installment obligation shall be disregarded. Receipt of an installment obligation shall be treated as a receipt of property, in an amount equal to the fair market value of the installment obligation, whether or not such obligation is the equivalent of cash. An installment obligation is considered to be property and is subject to valuation, as provided in paragraph (d)(2)(ii) and (iii) of this section, without regard to whether the obligation is embodied in a note, an executory contract, or any other instrument, or is an oral promise enforceable under local law.

(ii) *Fixed amount obligations.* (A) A fixed amount obligation means an installment obligation the amount payable under which is fixed. Solely for the purpose of determining whether the amount payable under an installment obligation is fixed, the provisions of section 483 and any

Reg. § 15A.453-1(c)(4)

"payment recharacterization" arrangement (as defined in paragraph (c)(2)(ii) of this section) shall be disregarded. If the fixed amount payable is stated in identified, fungible units of property the value of which will or may vary over time in relation to the United States dollar (*e.g.,* foreign currency, ounces of gold, or bushels of wheat), such units shall be converted to United States dollars at the rate of exchange or dollar value on the date the installment sale is made. A taxpayer using the cash receipts and disbursements methods of accounting shall treat as an amount realized in the year of sale the fair market value of the installment obligation. In no event will the fair market value of the installment obligation be considered to be less than the fair market value of the property sold (minus any another consideration received by the taxpayer on the sale). A taxpayer using the accrual method of accounting shall treat as an amount realized in the year of sale the total amount payable under the installment obligation. For this purpose, neither interest (whether stated or unstated) nor original issue discount is considered to be part of the amount payable. If the amount payable is otherwise fixed, but because the time over which payments may be made is contingent, a portion of the fixed amount will or may be treated as internal interest (as defined in paragraph (c)(2)(ii) of this section), the amount payable shall be determined by applying the price interest recomputation rule (described in paragraph (c)(2)(ii) of this section). Under no circumstances will an installment sale for a fixed amount obligation be considered an "open" transaction. For purposes of this (ii) remote or incidental contingencies are not to be taken into account.

(B) The following examples illustrate the provisions of paragraph (d)(2) of this section.

Example (1). A, an accrual method taxpayer, owns all of the stock of X corporation with a basis of $20 million. On July 1, 1981, A sells the stock of X corporation to B for $60 million payable on June 15, 1992. The agreement also provides that, against this fixed amount, B shall make annual prepayments (on June 15) equal to 5% of the net profits of X earned in the immediately preceding fiscal year beginning with the fiscal year ending March 31, 1982. Thus, the first prepayment will be made on June 15, 1982. No stated interest is payable under the agreement and thus the unstated interest provisions of section 483 are applicable. Under section 483, no part of any payment made on June 15, 1982 (which is within one year following the July 1, 1981 sale date), will be treated as unstated interest. Under the price interest recomputation rule, it is presumed that the entire $60 million fixed amount will be paid on June 15, 1982. Accord-

ingly, if A elects not to report the transaction on the installment method, in 1981 A must report $60 million as the amount realized on the sale and must report $40 million as gain on the sale in that year.

Example (2). The facts are the same as in example (1) except that A uses the cash receipts and disbursements method of accounting. In 1981 A must report as an amount realized on the sale the fair market value of the installment obligation and must report as gain on the sale in 1981 the excess of that amount realized over A's basis of $20 million. In no event will the fair market value of the installment obligation be considered to be less than the fair market value of the stock of X. In determining the fair market value of the installment obligation, any contractual or legal restrictions on the transferability of the installment obligation, and any remote or incidental contingencies otherwise affecting the amount payable or time of payments under the installment obligation, shall be disregarded.

(iii) *Contingent payment obligations.* Any installment obligation which is not a fixed amount obligation (as defined in paragraph (d)(2)(ii) of this section) is a contingent payment obligation. If an installment obligation contains both a fixed amount component and a contingent payment component, the fixed amount component shall be treated under the rules of paragraph (d)(2)(ii) of this section and the contingent amount component shall be treated under the rules of this (iii). The fair market value of a contingent payment obligation shall be determined by disregarding any restrictions on transfer imposed by agreement or under local law. The fair market value of a contingent payment obligation may be ascertained from, and in no event shall be considered to be less than, the fair market value of the property sold (less the amount of any other consideration received in the sale). Only in those rare and extraordinary cases involving sales for a contingent payment obligation in which the fair market value of the obligation (determinable under the preceding sentences) cannot reasonably be ascertained will the taxpayer be entitled to assert that the transaction is "open." Any such transaction will be carefully scrutinized to determine whether a sale in fact has taken place. A taxpayer using the cash receipts and disbursements method of accounting must report as an amount realized in the year of sale the fair market value of the contingent payment obligation. A taxpayer using the accrual method of accounting must report an amount realized in the year of sale determined in accordance with that method of accounting, but in no event less than the fair market value of the contingent payment obligation.

Reg. § 15A.453-1(d)(2)

(3) *Time and manner for making election—*
(i) *In general.* An election under paragraph (d)(1) of this section must be made on or before the due date prescribed by law (including extensions) for filing the taxpayer's return for the taxable year in which the installment sale occurs. The election must be made in the manner prescribed by the appropriate forms for the taxpayer's return for the taxable year of the sale. A taxpayer who reports an amount realized equal to the selling price including the full face amount of any installment obligation on the tax return filed for the taxable year in which the installment sale occurs will be considered to have made an effective election under paragraph (d)(1) of this section. A cash method taxpayer receiving an obligation the fair market value of which is less than the face value must make the election in the manner prescribed by appropriate instructions for the return filed for the taxable year of the sale.

(ii) *Election made after the due date.* Elections after the time specified in paragraph (d)(3)(i) of this section will be permitted only in those rare circumstances when the Internal Revenue Service concludes that the taxpayer had good cause for failing to make a timely election. A recharacterization of a transaction as a sale in a taxable year subsequent to the taxable year in which the transaction occurred (*e.g.,* a transaction initially reported as a lease later is determined to have been an installment sale) will not justify a late election. No conditional elections will be permitted. For a special transitional rule relating to certain taxable years for which a return is filed prior to February 19, 1981, see paragraph (d)(5) of this section.

(4) *Revoking an election.* Generally, an election made under paragraph (d)(1) is irrevocable. An election may be revoked only with the consent of the Internal Revenue Service. A revocation is retroactive. A revocation will not be permitted when one of its purposes is the avoidance of federal income taxes, or when the taxable year in which any payment was received has closed. For a special transitional rule relating to certain taxable years for which a return is filed prior to February 19, 1981, see paragraph (d)(5) of this section.

* * *

(e) *Purchaser evidences of indebtedness payable on demand or readily tradable—*(1) *Treatment as payment.* (i) *In general.* A bond or other evidence of indebtedness (hereinafter in this section referred to as an obligation) issued by any person and payable on demand shall be treated as a payment in the year received, not as installment obligations payable in future years. In addition, an obligation issued by a corporation or a government or political subdivision thereof—

(A) With interest coupons attached (whether or not the obligation is readily tradable in an established securities market),

(B) In registered form (other than an obligation issued in registered form which the taxpayer establishes will not be readily tradable in an established securities market), or

(C) In any other form designed to render such obligation readily tradable in an established securities market,

shall be treated as a payment in the year received, not as an installment obligation payable in future years. For purposes of this paragraph, an obligation is to be considered in registered form if it is registered as to principal, interest, or both and if its transfer must be effected by the surrender of the old instrument and either the reissuance by the corporation of the old instrument to the new holder or the issuance by the corporation of a new instrument to the new holder.

(ii) *Examples.* The rules stated in this paragraph may be illustrated by the following examples:

Example (1). On July 1, 1981, A, an individual on the cash method of accounting reporting on a calendar year basis, transferred all of his stock in corporation X (traded on an established securities market and having a fair market value of $1,000,000) to corporation Y in exchange for 250 of Y's registered bonds (which are traded in an over-the-counter market) each with a principal amount and fair market value of $1,000 (with interest payable at the rate of 12 percent per year), and Y's unsecured promissory note with a principal amount of $750,000. At the time of such exchange A's basis in the X stock is $900,000. The promissory note is payable at the rate of $75,000 annually, due on July 1 of each year following 1981 until the principal balance is paid. The note provides for the payment of interest at the rate of 12 percent per year also payable on July 1 of each year. Under the rule stated in paragraph (e)(1)(i) of this section, the 250 registered bonds of Y are treated as a payment in 1981 in the amount of the value of the bonds, $250,000.

Example (2). Assume the same facts as in example (1). Assume further that on July 1, 1982, Y makes its first installment payment to A under the terms of the unsecured promissory note with 75 more of its $1,000 registered bonds. A must include $7,500 (*i.e.,* 10 percent gross profit percentage times $75,000), A's gross income for calendar year 1982. In addition, A includes the interest payment made by Y on July 1 in A's gross income for 1982.

(2) *Amounts treated as payment.* If under paragraph (e)(1) of this section an obligation is treated as a payment in the year received, the

amount realized by reason of such payment shall be determined in accordance with the taxpayer's method of accounting. If the taxpayer uses the cash receipts and disbursements method of accounting, the amount realized on such payment is the fair market value of the obligation. If the taxpayer uses the accrual method of accounting, the amount realized on receipt of an obligation payable on demand is the face amount of the obligation, and the amount realized on receipt of an obligation with coupons attached or a readily tradable obligation is the stated redemption price at maturity less any original issue discount (as defined in section 1232(b)(1)) or, if there is no original issue discount, the amount realized is the stated redemption price at maturity appropriately discounted to reflect total unstated interest (as defined in section 483(b)), if any.

(3) *Payable on demand.* An obligation shall be treated as payable on demand only if the obligation is treated as payable on demand under applicable state or local law.

(4) *Designed to be readily tradable in an established securities market* —(i) *In general.* Obligations issued by a corporation or government or political subdivision thereof will be deemed to be in a form designed to render such obligations readily tradable in an established securities market if—

(A) Steps necessary to create a market for them are taken at the time of issuance (or later, if taken pursuant to an expressed or implied agreement or understanding which existed at the time of issuance),

(B) If they are treated as readily tradable in an established securities market under paragraph (e)(4)(ii) of this section, or

(C) If they are convertible obligations to which paragraph (e)(5) of this section applies.

(ii) *Readily tradable in an established securities market.* An obligation will be treated as readily tradable in an established securities market if—

(A) The obligation is part of an issue or series of issues which are readily tradable in an established securities market, or

(B) The corporation issuing the obligation has other obligations of a comparable character which are described in paragraph (e)(4)(ii)(A) of this section.

For purposes of paragraph (e)(4)(ii)(B) of this section, the determination as to whether there exist obligations of a comparable character depends upon the particular facts and circumstances. Factors to be considered in making such determination include, but are not limited to, substantial similarity with respect to the presence and nature of security for the obligation, the number of obligations issued (or to be issued), the number of holders of such obligation, the principal amount of the obligation, and other relevant factors.

(iii) *Readily tradable.* For purposes of paragraph (e)(4)(ii)(A) of this section, an obligation shall be treated as readily tradable if it is regularly quoted by brokers or dealers making a market in such obligation or is part of an issue a portion of which is in fact traded in an established securities market.

(iv) *Established securities market.* For purposes of this paragraph, the term "established securities market" includes (A) a national securities exchange which is registered under section 6 of the Securities Exchange Act of 1934 (15 U.S.C. 78f), (B) an exchange which is exempted from registration under section 5 of the Securities Exchange Act of 1934 (15 U.S.C. 78e) because of its limited volume of transactions, and (C) any over-the-counter market. For purposes of this (iv), an over-the-counter market is reflected by the existence of an interdealer quotation system. An interdealer quotation system is any system of general circulation to brokers and dealers which regularly disseminates quotations of obligations by identified brokers or dealers, other than a quotation sheet prepared and distributed by a broker or dealer in the regular course of business and containing only quotations of such broker or dealer.

(v) *Examples.* The rules stated in this paragraph may be illustrated by the following examples:

Example (1). On June 1, 1982, 25 individuals owning equal interests in a tract of land with a fair market value of $1 million sell the land to corporation Y. The $1 million sales price is represented by 25 bonds issued by Y, each having a face value of $40,000. The bonds are not in registered form and do not have interest coupons attached, and, in addition, are payable in 120 equal installments, each due on the first business day of each month. In addition, the bonds are negotiable and may be assigned by the holder to any other person. However, the bonds are not quoted by any brokers or dealers who deal in corporate bonds, and, furthermore, there are no comparable obligations of Y (determined with reference to the characteristics set forth in paragraph (e)(2) of this section) which are so quoted. Therefore, the bonds are not treated as readily tradable in an established securities market. In addition, under the particular facts and circumstances stated, the bonds will not be considered to be in a form designed to render them readily tradable in an established securities market. The receipt of such

Reg. § 15A.453-1(e)(4)

bonds by the holder is not treated as a payment for purposes of section 453(f)(4), notwithstanding that they are freely assignable.

Example (2). On April 1, 1981, corporation M purchases in a casual sale of personal property a fleet of trucks from corporation N in exchange for M's negotiable notes, not in registered form and without coupons attached. The M notes are comparable to earlier notes issued by M, which notes are quoted in the Eastern Bond section of the National Daily Quotation Sheet, which is an interdealer quotation system. Both issues of notes are unsecured, held by more than 100 holders, have a maturity date of more than 5 years, and were issued for a comparable principle [sic] amount. On the basis of these similar characteristics it appears that the latest notes will also be readily tradable. Since an interdealer system reflects an over-the-counter market, the earlier notes are treated as readily tradable in an established securities market. Since the later notes are obligations comparable to the earlier ones, which are treated as readily tradable in an established securities market, the later notes are also treated as readily tradable in an established securities market (whether or not such notes are actually traded).

(5) *Special rule for convertible securities.* (i) *General rule.* If an obligation contains a right whereby the holder of such obligation may convert it directly or indirectly into another obligation which would be treated as a payment under paragraph (e)(1) of this section or may convert it directly or indirectly into stock which would be treated as readily tradable or designed to be readily tradable in an established securities market under paragraph (e)(4) of this section, the convertible obligation shall be considered to be in a form designed to render such obligation readily tradable in an established securities market unless such obligation is convertible only at a substantial discount. In determining whether the stock or obligation into which an obligation is convertible is readily tradable or designed to be readily tradable in an established securities market, the rules stated in paragraph (e)(4) of this section shall apply, and for purposes of such paragraph (e)(4) if such obligation is convertible into stock then the term "stock" shall be substituted for the term "obligation" wherever it appears in such paragraph (e)(4).

(ii) *Substantial discount rule.* Whether an obligation is convertible at a substantial discount depends upon the particular facts and circumstances. A substantial discount shall be considered to exist if at the time the convertible obligation is issued, the fair market value of the stock or obligation into which the obligation is convertible is less than 80 percent of the fair market value of the obligation (determined by taking into account all relevant factors, including proper discount to reflect the fact that the convertible obligation is not readily tradable in an established securities market and any additional consideration required to be paid by the taxpayer). Also, if a privilege to convert an obligation into stock or an obligation which is readily tradable in an established securities market may not be exercised within a period of one year from the date the obligation is issued, a substantial discount shall be considered to exist.

(6) *Effective date.* The provisions of this paragraph (e) shall apply to sales or other dispositions occurring after May 27, 1969, which are not made pursuant to a binding written contract entered into on or before such date. No inference shall be drawn from this section as to any questions of law concerning the application of section 453 to sales or other dispositions occurring on or before May 27, 1969. [Temporary Reg. § 15A.453-1.]

☐ [*T.D. 7768*, 1-30-81. *Amended by T.D. 7788*, 9-30-81 *and T.D. 8535*, 4-19-94.]

Proposed Amendment to Regulation
§ 1.453-1. Installment method reporting for sales of real property and casual sales of personal property.

* * *

(f) *Installment obligations received in certain nonrecognition exchanges—*(1) *Exchanges described in section 1031(b)—*(i) *In general.* The provisions of paragraph (f)(1) of this section apply to exchanges described in section 1031(b) ("section 1031(b) exchanges") in which the taxpayer receives as boot (property which is "other property" under section 1031(b)) an installment obligation issued by the other party to the exchange, as well as property with respect to which no gain or loss is recognized ("permitted property" for purposes of paragraph (f)(1) of this section). However, an exchange otherwise described in section 1036 in which the receipt of an installment obligation is treated as a dividend (or would be treated as a dividend if the issuing corporation had adequate earnings and profits) is not a section 1031(b) exchange for purposes of this section.

(ii) *Exclusion from payment.* Receipt of permitted property will not be considered payment for purposes of paragraph (c) of this section.

(iii) *Installment method determinations.* In a section 1031(b) exchange, the taxpayer's basis in the property transferred by the taxpayer, including nondeductible expenses of the exchange, will first be allocated to the permitted property received by the taxpayer up to, but not in excess of, the fair market value of such property. If the taxpayer's basis exceeds the fair market value of the permitted property, that excess amount of basis is "excess basis." In making all required installment method determinations, the exchange is treated as if the taxpayer had made an installment sale of appreciated property (with a basis equal to the amount of excess basis) in which the consideration received was the installment obligation and any other boot. In a section 1031(b) exchange, only net qualifying indebtedness is taken into account in determining the amount of qualifying indebtedness (as defined in § 1.453-1A(b)(2)(iv)). For this purpose, net qualifying indebtedness is the excess of—

(A) Liabilities of the taxpayer (or liabilities encumbering the property) assumed or taken subject to by the other party to the exchange as part of the consideration to the taxpayer, over

(B) The sum of any net cash paid (cash paid less any cash received) by the taxpayer in the exchange and any liability assumed or taken subject to by the taxpayer in the exchange.

Therefore, for purposes of installment method determinations, the selling price is the sum of the face value of the installment obligation (reduced by any portion of the obligation characterized as interest by section 483 or 1232), any net qualifying indebtedness, any cash received (in excess of any cash paid) by the taxpayer, and the fair market value of any other boot. The basis is the excess basis. The total contract price is the selling price less any net qualifying indebtedness that does not exceed the excess basis. Finally, payment in the year of exchange includes any net qualifying indebtedness that exceeds the excess basis.

(iv) *Examples.* The provisions of paragraph (f)(1) of this section are illustrated by the following examples:

Example (1). In 1981, A makes a section 1031(b) exchange of real property held for investment (basis $400,000) for permitted property worth $200,000, and an $800,000 installment obligation issued by the other party to the exchange bearing adequate stated interest. Neither the property transferred by A nor the property received in the exchange is mortgaged property. A's basis of $400,000 is allocated first to the permitted property received, up to the fair market value of $200,000. A's excess basis is $200,000 ($400,000 − $200,000). Since the installment obligation is the only boot received by A in the exchange, A's entire excess basis of $200,000 is allocable to it. Under the installment method, the selling price is $800,000 (the face amount of the installment obligation), and the contract price is also $800,000 (selling price less qualifying indebtedness, $800,000 − 0). The gross profit is $600,000 (selling price less excess basis allocated to the installment obligation, $800,000 −

$200,000), and the gross profit ratio is 75% ($600,000/$800,000). A recognizes no gain until payments are received on the installment obligation. As A receives payments (exclusive of interest) on the installment obligation, 75% of each payment will be gain attributable to the exchange and 25% of each payment will be recovery of basis. A will hold the permitted property received in the exchange with a basis of $200,000.

Example (2). The facts are the same as in example (1), except that in the exchange A receives permitted property worth $200,000, a $600,000 installment obligation, and $200,000 in cash. A is treated as having sold appreciated property (basis equal to the $200,000 excess basis) for $200,000 cash and a $600,000 installment obligation. As in example (1), the contract price and the selling price are $800,000, the gross profit is $600,000, and the gross profit ratio is 75%. Accordingly, A will recognize gain of $150,000 on receipt of the cash (75% of the $200,000 payment). A holds the permitted property with a basis of $200,000.

Example (3). The facts are the same as in example (2), except that A does not receive $200,000 in cash. Instead, the property transferred by A in the exchange was subject to a mortgage (meeting the definition of qualifying indebtedness) of $200,000 to which the other party to the exchange took subject. The permitted property received by A in the exchange was not subject to a mortgage. A is treated as having sold appreciated property (basis equal to $200,000 excess basis) for $600,000 cash and $200,000 net relief of mortgage liability. The mortgage liability of which A is deemed relieved ($200,000), reduced by any cash paid by A and any mortgage liability encumbering the like-kind property received by A in the simultaneous exchange ($0), is treated as qualifying indebtedness. Since the qualifying indebtedness ($200,000) does not exceed A's excess basis ($200,000), B's taking subject to such indebtedness does not constitute payment to A in the year of exchange. Under the installment method, the selling price is $800,000 and the total contract price is $600,000 (selling price of $800,000 less $200,000 of qualifying indebtedness that does not exceed A's excess basis). Gross profit is also $600,000 (800,000 selling price less $200,000 excess basis), and the gross profit ratio is 1 ($600,000/600,000). A recognizes no gain until payments are received on the installment obligation. As A receives payment (exclusive of interest) in the $600,000 installment obligation, the full amount received will be gain attributable to the exchange. A holds the permitted property with a basis of $200,000.

Example (4). The facts are the same as in example (2), except that A's basis in the property transferred by A was only $160,000. Since A's basis first must be allocated to permitted property received in the exchange up to the fair market value ($200,000) of that permitted property, there is no excess basis. Accordingly, A will recognize gain equal to the full amount of cash received ($200,000), and will hold the installment obligation at a basis of zero. A will hold the permitted property at a basis of $160,000.

(2) *Certain exchanges described in section 356(a)*—(i) *In general.* The provisions of paragraph (f)(2) of this section apply to exchanges described in section 356(a)(1) ("section 356(a)(1) exchanges") in which the taxpayer receives as boot (property which is "other property" under section 356(a)(1)(B)) an installment obligation issued by a qualifying corporation which is not treated as a dividend to the taxpayer. For purposes of section 453(f)(6) and paragraph (f)(2) of this section, any such section 356(a)(1) exchange shall be treated as a disposition of property by the taxpayer to the qualifying corporation and an acquisition of such property by the qualifying corporation from the taxpayer. If section 354 would apply to the exchange but for the receipt of boot, the term "qualifying corporation" means a corpoation the stock of which could be received by the taxpayer in the exchange without recognition of gain or loss. If section 355 would apply to the exchange but for the receipt of boot, the term "qualifying corporation" means the distributing corporation (referred to in section 355(a)(1)(A)). Receipt of an installment obligation is treated as a dividend if section 356(a)(2) applies (determined without regard to the presence or absence of accumulated earnings and profits), or if section 356(e) (relating to certain exchanges for section 306 stock) applies to the taxpayer's receipt of the installment obligation.

(ii) *Exclusion from payment.* Receipt of permitted property shall not be considered payment for purposes of paragraph (c) of this section. For purposes of paragraph (f)(1) of this section, "permitted property" means property, the receipt of which does not result in recognition of gain under section 356(a)(1) (i.e., stock of a qualifying corporation).

(iii) *Installment method determinations.* Installment method determinations with respect to an installment obligation received in an exchange to which paragraph (f)(2) of this section applies shall be made in accordance with the rules prescribed in paragraph (f)(1)(iii) of this section. In applying such rules, a section 356(a)(1) exchange shall be treated as a section 1031(b) exchange and permitted property shall mean permitted property described in paragraph (f)(2) of this section.

(iv) *Examples.* The provisions of paragraph (f)(2) of this section are illustrated by the following examples:

Example (1). T corporation and P corporation are unrelated closely held corporations. A owns 10% of the stock of T. A is not related to any other T stockholder or to any P stockholder. S corporation is a wholly-owned subsidiary of P. Pursuant to a plan of reorganization, T merges with and into S. In the merger, the T shares held by A are exchanged for shares of P worth $100,000 and a $300,000 installment obligation (bearing adequate interest) issued by P. In the merger the other stockholders of T exchange their T shares solely for P shares worth, in the aggregate, $3,600,000. The merger is a reorganization described in sections 368(a)(1)(A) and (a)(2)(D), and T, S, and P each is a party to the reorganization under section 368(b). P is a qualifying corporation and A is party to a section 356(a)(1) exchange in which receipt by A of the installment obligation will not be treated as a dividend to A. Because, for purposes of section 453(f)(6), this transaction is treated as a direct exchange between P and A, no gain or loss is recognized by S with respect to the P obligation. Assume A's basis in the T shares exchanged by A was $150,000. A's basis is allocated first to the permitted property (P shares) received, up to the fair market value of $100,000. A's excess basis is $50,000 ($150,000 − $100,000). Since the installment obligation is the only boot received by A in the exchange, the entire excess basis of $50,000 is allocable to it. Under the installment method, the contract price is $300,000 (face amount of the installment obligation), the gross profit is $250,000 (contract price less $50,000 excess basis allocated to the installment obligation), and the gross profit ratio is 5/6 ($250,000/$300,000). A recognizes no gain until payments are received on the installment obligation. As A receives payments (exclusive of interest) on the installment obligation, 5/6ths of each payment will be gain attributable to the exchange and 1/6th of each payment will be recovery of basis. A will hold the permitted property (P stock) received in the exchange at a basis of $100,000.

Example (2). The facts are the same as in exmaple (1). B, who also owns 10% of the stock of T directly and owns no other stock by T by attribution within the meaning of 318(a), exchanges the T shares in the merger for $400,000 installment obligation issued by P (bearing adequate interest). Although section 356(a)(1) will not apply to this exchange becasue B receives no P stock in the transaction and the character of the gain is determined under section 302(a), for purposes of section 453 and paragraph (a) of this section, B is treated as having sold the T shares to

Reg. § 1.453-1(f)(2)

P in exchange for P's installment obligation. B will report the installment sale on the installment method unless B elects under paragraph (e) of this section not to report the transaction on the installment method. If, by reason of constructive ownership of T shares under section 381(a) and failure to meet the requirements of section 302(c)(2), the character of the transaction as to B were determined under section 302(d), section 453 would not apply to the exchange by B.

Example (3). The facts are the same as in examples (1) and (2), except that the P stock is voting stock and S merges into T in a reorganization described in section 368(a)(2)(E). The results are the same as in examples (1) and (2).

Example (4) (i). T Corporation and larger P Corporation are unrelated public corporations the stock of each of which is widely held. A is a stockholder of T. S Corporation is a wholly owned subsidiary of P. On December 31, 1981, pursuant to a plan of reorganization which provides for a "note option" election, T merges with and into S. In the merger, A exercises the note option and the T shares held by A are exchanged for a $30,000 installment obligation (bearing adequate interest) issued by P, 1,000 P shares (worth $10 per share on the date of merger), and a non-negotiable certificate evidencing a right to receive (within 5 years from the date of merger) up to 1,000 additional P shares (plus adequate interest) if certain earnings conditions are satisfied. Neither the installment obligation nor the certificate evidencing the right to receive additional P shares is readily tradable within the meaning of § 1.453-1A(c)(4)(iv)(C). There is a valid business reason for not issuing all of the P shares immediately. Certain of the other T shareholders exercise the note option and exchange their T shares for a similar package. Other T shareholders do not exercise the note option and receive in the merger P shares plus a non-negotiable right to receive up to an equal number of additional P shares (plus adequate interest) within 5 years. In the aggregate, the total outstanding T shares are exchanged for 20% P installment obligations, 40% P shares, and rights to receive an equal number of additional P shares within 5 years. The merger of T into S qualifies as a reorganization under section 368(a)(1)(A) and (a)(2)(D). P is a qualifying corporation, the P shares received and which may subsequently be received by A are permitted property, and the exchange to which A is a party is a section 356(a)(1) exchange.

(ii) Assume A's basis in the T shares exchanged by A was $25,000. A's basis is allocated first to permitted property (P shares) up to fair market value. In the exchange A has received 1,000 P shares (worth $10,000) and may receive up to an additional 1,000 P shares in the future.

In allocating A's basis, it is assumed that all contingencies contemplated by the merger agreement will be met or otherwise resolved in a manner that will maximize the consideration A will receive. It is further assumed that each P share, when received, will have a fair market value equal to the fair market value ($10) of a P share at the date of merger. Accordingly, since A may receive a maximum of 2,000 P shares, $20,000 (2,000 × $10) of A's basis will be allocated to the 1,000 P shares A has received ($10 per share) and to A's right to receive up to an additional 1,000 P shares (at $10 per share). A's excess basis of $5,000 ($25,000 − $20,000) is allocated to the $30,000 P installment obligation.

(iii) In 1983 the earnings condition is fully satisfied and A receives an additional 1,000 P shares (plus adequate interest). Each P share held by A has a basis of $10.

(iv) Assume instead that the earnings condition is only partly satisfied and, by the close of 1986, A has received only an additional 600 P shares and is not entitled to receive any further P shares. Initially, each P share received by A was assigned a basis of $10. Of A's $25,000 basis in the T shares exchanged, $4,000 ($20,000 initially allocated to P shares received and to be received less $16,000 (1,600 P shares × $10)) now must be accounted for. The $4,000 of remaining basis will be assigned to the P shares than held by A. Thus, if A continues to hold all 1,600 P shares, A's basis in each P share will be increased by $2.50 ($4,000 divided by 1,600 P shares), If A previously sold 800 P shares and retains only 800 P shares, A's basis in each retained P share will be increased by $5 ($4,000 divided by 800 P shares). If A retains no P shares, and if all of the additional 600 P shares were issued to A and sold by A before the final year of the five year earn-out term (*i.e.,* by the end of 1985), A's remaining basis of $4,000 will be added to the basis at which A holds the unpaid portion of the P installment obligation (up to but not in excess of the maximum amount remaining payable under that obligation less A's remaining basis in the installment obligation determined immediately before the addition to basis). If A has previously disposed of the P installment obligation, so that A holds neither P shares nor the P installment obligation to which the remaining $4,000 of A's basis can be allocated, A will be allowed a $4,000 loss in 1986. Similarly, if A continues to hold the P installment obligation but the facts are such that the maximum amount thereafter payable under the obligation is only $3,000 in excess of A's basis in the obligation determined immediately before assignment of A's remaining $4,000 basis, $3,000 of that remaining basis would be assigned to the installment obligation and P would be allowed a $1,000 loss in 1986.

Reg. § 1.453-1(f)(2)

Example (5). Pursuant to a plan to acquire all the stock of T corporation, P purchases 90% of the T stock for cash. To acquire the remaining 10% of T stock P creates S corporation and transfers P stock and P's newly issued installment notes to S in exchange for all of S's stock. The P notes are not readily tradable. Thereafter S merges into T, and P stock and P's installment notes are distributed to the T minority shareholders, and the S stock held by P is automatically converted into T stock. Assume that for federal tax purposes the existence of S is disregarded and the transaction is treated as a sale of T stock to P in exchange for P stock and P's installment notes. The minority shareholders will report the gain realized on the receipt of the P installment notes on the installment method unless they elect otherwise. The receipt of P stock will be treated as a payment in the year of sale.

Example (6). The facts are the same as example (5) except P transferred only P's installment notes to S and only these notes were distributed to T minority shareholders. As in example (5) the transaction is treated as a sale of T stock to P in exchange for P's installment notes. Each minority shareholder realizing gain on the receipt of the installment notes will report the gain on the installment method unless electing otherwise.

(3) *Other partial recognition exchanges*—(i) *In general.* The provisions of paragraph (f)(3) of this section apply to exchanges not described in paragraph (f)(1) or (2) of this section in which a taxpayer, in exchange for appreciated property, receives both permitted property (*i.e.*, property with respect to which no gain or loss would be recognized but which, in the hands of the taxpayer, would have as basis for determining gain or loss the same basis in whole or in part as the property exchanged) and boot that includes an installment obligation issued by the other party to the exchange. Ordinarily, the installment method rules set forth in paragraph (f)(1)(ii) and (iii) of this section will apply to an exchange described in paragraph (f)(3) of this section subject to such variations, if any, as may be required under the applicable provisions of the Code.

(ii) *Exchanges to which section 351 applies.* If a taxpayer receives, in an exchange to which section 351(b) applies (a "section 351(b) exchange"), an installment obligation that is not a security within the meaning of section 351(a), the installment obligation is boot and the stock and securities (within the meaning of section 351(a)) are permitted property (within the meaning of paragraph (f)(1)(ii) of this section). The taxpayer will report the installment obligation on the installment method and any other boot received will be treated as a payment made in the year of the exchange. In applying the rules of paragraph

(f)(1)(iii) of this section to a section 351(b) exchange the excess basis is the amount, if any, by which the taxpayer's basis in the property transferred (plus any cash transferred) by the taxpayer exceeds the sum of the transferred liabilities which are not treated as money received under section 357 plus the fair market value of permitted property received by the taxpayer. In determining selling price and total contract price, transferred liabilities which are not treated as money received under section 357 shall be disregarded. For purposes of paragraph (f)(3)(ii) of this section, transferred liabilities are liabilities described in section 357(a)(2). Solely for the purpose of applying section 358(a)(1), the taxpayer shall be treated as if the taxpayer elected not to report receipt of the installment obligation on the installment method. Under section 362(a)(1) the corporation's basis in the property received from the taxpayer is the taxpayer's basis in the property increased by the gain recognized by the taxpayer at the time of the exchange. As the taxpayer recognizes gain on the installment method, the corporation will increase its basis in the property by an amount equal to the amount of gain recognized by the taxpayer.

(iii) *Examples.* The provisions of paragraph (f)(3) of this section are illustrated by the following examples. In each example, assume that adequate stated interest means both a reasonable rate of interest within the meaning of any applicable regulation promulgated under section 385 and a rate of interest not less than the test rate prescribed in the regulations under section 483, and that the debt to equity ratio of the issuing corporation is a permissible ratio under any applicable regulation promulgated under section 385.

Example (1). A owns Blackacre, unimproved real property, with a basis of $300,000. The fair market value of Blackacre is $700,000. Blackacre is encumbered by a longstanding mortgage of $200,000. A transfers Blackacre, subject to the mortgage, to a newly organized X corporation. A receives in exchange all of the stock of X, worth $400,000, and a $100,000 installment obligation (bearing adequate stated interest) issued by X. A realizes $400,000 of gain on the exchange. The installment obligation calls for a single payment of the full $100,000 face amount three years following the date of issue. The installment obligation is not a "security" within the meaning of section 351(a), and thus the exchange by A is a transaction described in section 351(b). The installment obligation is boot received by A in the exchange and the X stock is permitted property received by A in exchange. In applying the provisions of paragraph (f)(1)(ii) and (iii) of this section to a section 351(b) exchange, reference is required to section 357(a) under which the

Reg. § 1.453-1(f)(3)

$200,000 mortgage liability is not treated as money or other property received by A in the exchange, and to section 358(a)(1) under which the basis of the X stock in the hands of A will be determined. These rules apply as follows: Neither receipt of the X stock nor relief of the mortgage encumbrance is treated as payment to A and thus A will recognize no gain in the year of the exchange. A's basis of $300,000 in Blackacre is reduced by the $200,000 mortgage from which A is deemed relieved in the exchange. The remaining basis of $100,000 is allocated to the X stock (but not in excess of the fair market value of the X stock); since the fair market value of the X stock is $400,000, the basis of the X stock in the hands of A is $100,000. Accordingly, in A's hands the installment obligation has a basis of zero. In the hands of X, the initial basis of Blackacre, determined under section 362(a), is $300,000 (the basis of the property in the hands of A), increased by the amount of gain recognized by A at the time of the transfer ($0)). As A receives payments on the installment obligation and recognizes gain, X's basis in Blackacre will be increased, at that time, in an amount equal to the gain recognized by A. Thus, if the $100,000 installment obligation is paid in full on the third anniversary date, A will recognize gain of $100,000 (because A's basis in the installment obligation is zero) and X at that time will increase the basis at which it holds Blackacre by $100,000. If in the third year X had sold the property for cash before making payment on the installment obligation, X would recognize a loss of $100,000 when X paid the obligation in that amount to A on the third anniversary date.

Example (2). B owns Whiteacre, unencumbered, unimproved real property, with a basis of $250,000. The fair market value of Whiteacre is $300,000. A transfers Whiteacre to newly organized Y corporation in exchange for all of the stock of Y corporation (worth $200,000) and a $100,000 installment obligation (bearing adequate interest). The installment obligation is payable in full on the second anniversary of the date of issue. The installment obligation is not a "security" within the meaning of section 351(a), and thus the transaction is a section 351(b) exchange. Applying the rules summarized in example (1) to the facts of this case, receipt of the installment obligation is not treated as payment to A, $200,000 of A's basis of $250,000 in Whiteacre is allocated to the Y stock (equal to the fair market value of the Y stock), and the excess basis of $50,000 is allocated to the installment obligation. In the hands of Y, the basis of Whiteacre initially is $250,000, and will be increased by $50,000 when the installment obligation is paid and A recognizes gain of $50,000.

Example (3). D owns a machine which is unencumbered 5-year recovery property with an adjusted basis of $500,000. The recomputed basis (as defined in section 1245(a)(2)) of the machine in the hands of D is $1 million. The fair market value of the machine also is $1 million. D transfers the machine to newly organized X corporation, and E, an unrelated individual, simultaneously transfers property worth $1 million to X corporation. D receives in exchange 400 shares of X common stock worth $400,000, a $400,000 15-year debenture issued by X (worth its face amount), and a $200,000 installment obligation (bearing adequate interest) issed by X. The installment obligation calls for a single payment of the full $200,000 face amount two years following the date of issue. E receives in the exchange 1,000 shares of X common stock worth $1 million. D and E are in control (as defined in section 368(c)) of X immediately after the exchange. The debenture received by D is a "security" within the meaning of section 351(a), but the installment obligation received by D is not a "security" within the meaning of that section and thus the exchange by D is a transaction described in section 351(b). The installment obligation is boot received by D in the exchange and the X stock and X debenture are permitted property received by D in the exchange. Since the aggregate fair market value ($800,000) of X stock ($400,000) and the X debenture ($400,000) received by D exceeds D's $500,000 adjusted basis in the machine, all of that basis is allocated proportionately among the items of permitted property. Thus, D will hold the X stock with a basis of $250,000 and the X debenture with a basis of $250,000. Since there is no excess basis, in the hands of D the installment obligation has a basis of zero. In the hands of X, the adjusted basis of the machine remains $500,000. When D receives payment from X on the $200,000 installment obligation, D will recognize gain of $200,000, all of which gain will be treated as ordinary income. See sections 1245(a)(1) and 453B(a). At that time, X's adjusted basis in the machine will be increased in an amount equal to the $200,000 gain recognized by D.

Example (4). In 1976 H and W purchased Blackacre as their principal residence for $50,000. In 1981 H and W, both of whom are less than 55 years of age, sold Blackacre to A for $90,000: $15,000 cash, A's assumption of the $40,000 mortgage, and A's promise to pay H and W $7,000 (with adequate stated interest) in each of the next 5 years. Within 2 years of the sale of Blackacre, H and W acquire Whiteacre, an unencumbered property, which will be their principal residence, for $80,000. Of the $40,000 gain that H and W realized upon the sale of Whiteacre, $30,000 will

Reg. § 1.453-1(f)(3)

not be recognized pursuant to the provisions of section 1034. Unless H and W elect not to report the transaction on the installment method, they will treat the $10,000 gain to be recognized as the gross profit for purposes of calculating the gross profit ratio. Accordingly the gross profit ratio is 1/5 ($10,000 gross profit/$50,000 contract price) and H and W will report as gain $3,000 (1/5 × $15,000) in the year of the sale and $1,400 (1/5 × $7,000) in each of the next five years.

(4) *Installment obligations received as distributions in redemptions of stock pursuant to section 302(a).* If a corporation redeems its stock and the redemption is treated as a distribution in part or full payment in exchange for the stock under section 302(a), then an installment obligation which meets the requirements of section 453 and is distributed in the redemption shall be reported on the installment method unless the taxpayer elects otherwise.

Example. A owns 10% of the stock of X corporation and is not considered as owning (under section 318(a)) any other shares of X corporation. X redeems all of A's X shares and distributes its installment obligation to A in full payment. The reduction is treated as a sale of the X shares by A under section 302(b)(3). A will report any gain realized in the redemption on the installment method unless A elects otherwise.

* * *

[Reg. § 1.453-1.]

[Proposed 5-3-84.]

§ 1.453-11. Installment obligations received from a liquidating corporation.—(a) *In general*—(1) *Overview.* Except as provided in section 453(h)(1)(C) (relating to installment sales of depreciable property to certain closely related persons), a qualifying shareholder (as defined in paragraph (b) of this section) who receives a qualifying installment obligation (as defined in paragraph (c) of this section) in a liquidation that satisfies section 453(h)(1)(A) treats the receipt of payments in respect of the obligation, rather than the receipt of the obligation itself, as a receipt of payment for the shareholder's stock. The shareholder reports the payments received on the installment method unless the shareholder elects otherwise in accordance with § 15a.453-1(d) of this chapter.

(2) *Coordination with other provisions*—(i) *Deemed sale of stock for installment obligation.* Except as specifically provided in section 453(h)(1)(C), a qualifying shareholder treats a qualifying installment obligation, for all purposes of the Internal Revenue Code, as if the obligation is received by the shareholder from the person issuing the obligation in exchange for the shareholder's stock in the liquidating corporation. For

example, if the stock of a corporation that is liquidating is traded on an established securities market, an installment obligation distributed to a shareholder of the corporation in exchange for the shareholder's stock does not qualify for installment reporting pursuant to section 453(k)(2).

(ii) *Special rules to account for the qualifying installment obligation*—(A) *Issue price.* A qualifying installment obligation is treated by a qualifying shareholder as newly issued on the date of the distribution. The issue price of the qualifying installment obligation on that date is equal to the sum of the adjusted issue price of the obligation on the date of the distribution (as determined under § 1.1275-1(b)) and the amount of any qualified stated interest (as defined in § 1.1273-1(c)) that has accrued prior to the distribution but that is not payable until after the distribution. For purposes of the preceding sentence, if the qualifying installment obligation is subject to § 1.446-2 (e.g., a debt instrument that has unstated interest under section 483), the adjusted issue price of the obligation is determined under § 1.446-2(c) and (d).

(B) *Variable rate debt instrument.* If the qualifying installment obligation is a variable rate debt instrument (as defined in § 1.1275-5), the shareholder uses the equivalent fixed rate debt instrument (within the meaning of § 1.1275-5(e)(3)(ii)) constructed for the qualifying installment obligation as of the date the obligation was issued to the liquidating corporation to determine the accruals of original issue discount, if any, and interest on the obligation.

* * *

[Reg. § 1.453-11.]

☐ [*T.D. 8762, 1-27-98.*]

§ 1.461-1. General rule for taxable year of deduction.—(a) *General rule*—(1) *Taxpayer using cash receipts and disbursements method.* Under the cash receipts and disbursements method of accounting, amounts representing allowable deductions shall, as a general rule, be taken into account for the taxable year in which paid. Further, a taxpayer using this method may also be entitled to certain deductions in the computation of taxable income which do not involve cash disbursements during the taxable year, such as the deductions for depreciation, depletion, and losses under sections 167, 611, and 165, respectively. If an expenditure results in the creation of an asset having a useful life which extends substantially beyond the close of the taxable year, such an expenditure may not be deductible, or may be deductible only in part, for the taxable year in which made. An example is an expenditure for the construction of improvements by the lessee on leased property where the estimated life

Reg. § 1.453-11(a)(1)

of the improvements is in excess of the remaining period of the lease. In such a case, in lieu of the allowance for depreciation provided by section 167, the basis shall be amortized ratably over the remaining period of the lease. See section 178 and the regulations thereunder for rules governing the effect to be given renewal options in determining whether the useful life of the improvements exceeds the remaining term of the lease where a lessee begins improvements on leased property after July 28, 1958, other than improvements which on such date and at all times thereafter, the lessee was under a binding legal obligation to make. See section 263 and the regulations thereunder for rules relating to capital expenditures. See section 467 and the regulations thereunder for rules under which a liability arising out of the use of property pursuant to a section 467 rental agreement is taken into account.

(2) *Taxpayer using an accrual method*—(i) *In general.* Under an accrual method of accounting, a liability (as defined in § 1.446-1(c)(1)(ii)(B)) is incurred, and generally is taken into account for Federal income tax purposes, in the taxable year in which all the events have occurred that establish the fact of the liability, the amount of the liability can be determined with reasonable accuracy, and economic performance has occurred with respect to the liability. (See paragraph (a)(2)(iii)(A) of this section for examples of liabilities that may not be taken into account until a taxable year subsequent to the taxable year incurred, and see § § 1.461-4 through 1.461-6 for rules relating to economic performance.) Applicable provisions of the Code, the Income Tax Regulations, and other guidance published by the Secretary prescribe the manner in which a liability that has been incurred is taken into account. For example, section 162 provides that a deductible liability generally is taken into account in the taxable year incurred through a deduction from gross income. As a further example, under section 263 or 263A, a liability that relates to the creation of an asset having a useful life extending substantially beyond the close of the taxable year is taken into account in the taxable year incurred through capitalization (within the meaning of § 1.263A-1(c)(3)), and may later affect the computation of taxable income through depreciation or otherwise over a period including subsequent taxable years, in accordance with applicable Internal Revenue Code sections and guidance published by the Secretary. The principles of this paragraph (a)(2) also apply in the calculation of earnings and profits and accumulated earnings and profits.

(ii) *Uncertainty as to the amount of a liability.* While no liability shall be taken into account before economic performance and all of the events that fix the liability have occurred, the fact that the exact amount of the liability cannot be determined does not prevent a taxpayer from taking into account that portion of the amount of the liability which can be computed with reasonable accuracy within the taxable year. For example, A renders services to B during the taxable year for which A charges $10,000. B admits a liability to A for $6,000 but contests the remainder. B may take into account only $6,000 as an expense for the taxable year in which the services were rendered.

(iii) *Alternative timing rules.* (A) If any provision of the Code requires a liability to be taken into account in a taxable year later than the taxable year provided in paragraph (a)(2)(i) of this section, the liability is taken into account as prescribed in that Code provision. See, for example, section 267 (transactions between related parties) and section 464 (farming syndicates).

(B) If the liability of a taxpayer is subject to section 170 (charitable contributions), section 192 (black lung benefit trusts), section 194A (employer liability trusts), section 468 (mining and solid waste disposal reclamation and closing costs), or section 468A(a) (certain nuclear decommissioning costs), the liability is taken into account as determined under that section and not under section 461 or the regulations thereunder. For special rules relating to certain loss deductions, see sections 165(e), 165(i), and 165(l), relating to theft losses, disaster losses, and losses from certain deposits in qualified financial institutions.

(C) Section 461 and the regulations thereunder do not apply to any amount allowable under a provision of the Code as a deduction for a reserve for estimated expenses.

(D) Except as otherwise provided in any Internal Revenue regulation, revenue procedure, or revenue ruling, the economic performance requirement of section 461(h) and the regulations thereunder is satisfied to the extent that any amount is otherwise deductible under section 404 (employer contributions to a plan of deferred compensation), section 404A (certain foreign deferred compensation plans), or section 419 (welfare benefit funds). See § 1.461-4(d)(2)(iii).

(E) Except as otherwise provided by regulations or other published guidance issued by the Commissioner (See § 601.601(b)(2) of this chapter), in the case of a liability arising out of the use of property pursuant to a section 467 rental agreement, the all events test (including economic performance) is considered met in the taxable year in which the liability is to be taken into account under section 467 and the regulations thereunder.

(3) *Effect in current taxable year of improperly accounting for a liability in a prior taxable*

year. Each year's return should be complete in itself, and taxpayers shall ascertain the facts necessary to make a correct return. The expenses, liabilities, or loss of one year generally cannot be used to reduce the income of a subsequent year. A taxpayer may not take into account in a return for a subsequent taxable year liabilities that, under the taxpayer's method of accounting, should have been taken into account in a prior taxable year. If a taxpayer ascertains that a liability should have been taken into account in a prior taxable year, the taxpayer should, if within the period of limitation, file a claim for credit or refund of any overpayment of tax arising therefrom. Similarly, if a taxpayer ascertains that a liability was improperly taken into account in a prior taxable year, the taxpayer should, if within the period of limitation, file an amended return and pay any additional tax due. However, except as provided in section 905(c) and the regulations thereunder, if a liability is properly taken into account in an amount based on a computation made with reasonable accuracy and the exact amount of the liability is subsequently determined in a later taxable year, the difference, if any, between such amounts shall be taken into account for the later taxable year.

(4) *Deductions attributable to certain foreign income.* In any case in which, owing to monetary, exchange, or other restrictions imposed by a foreign country, an amount otherwise constituting gross income for the taxable year from sources without the United States is not includible in gross income of the taxpayer for that year, the deductions and credits properly chargeable against the amount so restricted shall not be deductible in such year but shall be deductible proportionately in any subsequent taxable year in which such amount or portion thereof is includible in gross income. See paragraph (b) of § 1.905-1 for rules relating to credit for foreign income taxes when foreign income is subject to exchange controls.

(b) *Special rule in case of death.* A taxpayer's taxable year ends on the date of his death. See section 443(a)(2) and paragraph (a)(2) of § 1.443-1. In computing taxable income for such year, there shall be deducted only amounts properly deductible under the method of accounting used by the taxpayer. However, if the taxpayer used an accrual method of accounting, no deduction shall be allowed for amounts accrued only by reason of his death. For rules relating to the inclusion of items of partnership deduction, loss, or credit in the return of a decedent partner, see subchapter K, chapter 1 of the Code, and the regulations thereunder.

* * *

Reg. § 1.461-2(a)(1)

[Reg. § 1.461-1.]

☐ [*T.D.* 6282, 12-24-57. *Amended by T.D.* 6520, 12-23-60; *T.D.* 6710, 3-17-64; *T.D.* 6735, 5-18-64; *T.D.* 6772, 11-23-64; *T.D.* 6917, 5-1-67; *T.D.* 8408, 4-9-92; *T.D.* 8482, 8-6-93; *T.D.* 8554, 7-13-94 *and T.D.* 8820, 5-17-99.]

§ 1.461-2. Contested liabilities.—(a) *General rule*—(1) *Taxable year of deduction.* If—

(i) The taxpayer contests an asserted liability,

(ii) The taxpayer transfers money or other property to provide for the satisfaction of the asserted liability,

(iii) The contest with respect to the asserted liability exists after the time of the transfer, and

(iv) But for the fact that the asserted liability is contested, a deduction would be allowed for the taxable year of the transfer (or, in the case of an accrual method taxpayer, for an earlier taxable year for which such amount would be accruable),

then the deduction with respect to the contested amount shall be allowed for the taxable year of the transfer.

(2) *Exception.* Subparagraph (1) of this paragraph shall not apply in respect of the deduction for income, war profits, and excess profits taxes imposed by the authority of any foreign country or possession of the United States, including a tax paid in lieu of a tax on income, war profits, or excess profits otherwise generally imposed by any foreign country or by any possession of the United States.

(3) *Refunds includible in gross income.* If any portion of the contested amount which is deducted under subparagraph (1) of this paragraph for the taxable year of transfer is refunded when the contest is settled, such portion is includible in gross income except as provided in § 1.111-1, relating to recovery of certain items previously deducted or credited. Such refunded amount is includible in gross income for the taxable year of receipt, or for an earlier taxable year if properly accruable for such earlier year.

(4) *Examples.* The provisions of this paragraph are illustrated by the following examples:

Example (1). X Corporation, which uses an accrual method of accounting, in 1964 contests $20 of a $100 asserted real property tax liability but pays the entire $100 to the taxing authority. In 1968, the contest is settled and X receives a refund of $5. X deducts $100 for the taxable year 1964, and includes $5 in gross income for the taxable year 1968 (assuming § 1.111-1 does not apply to such amount). If in 1964 X pays only $80 to the taxing authority, X deducts only $80 for 1964. The result would be the same if X Corporation used the cash method of accounting.

Example (2). Y Corporation makes its return on the basis of a calendar year and uses an accrual method of accounting. Y's real property taxes are assessed and become a lien on December 1, but are not payable until March 1 of the following year. On December 10, 1964, Y contests $20 of the $100 asserted real property tax which was assessed and became a lien on December 1, 1964. On March 1, 1965, Y pays the entire $100 to the taxing authority. In 1968, the contest is settled and Y receives a refund of $5. Y deducts $80 for the taxable year 1964, deducts $20 for the taxable year 1965, and includes $5 in gross income for the taxable year 1968 (assuming § 1.111-1 does not apply to such amount).

(5) *Liabilities described in paragraph (g) of § 1.461-4.* [Reserved]

(b) *Contest of asserted liability*—(1) *Asserted liability.* For purposes of paragraph (a)(1) of this section, the term "asserted liability" means an item with respect to which, but for the existence of any contest in respect of such item, a deduction would be allowable under an accrual method of accounting. For example, a notice of a local real estate tax assessment and a bill received for services may represent asserted liabilities.

(2) *Definition of the term "contest".* Any contest which would prevent accrual of a liability under section 461(a) shall be considered to be a contest in determining whether the taxpayer satisfies paragraph (a)(1)(i) of this section. A contest arises when there is a bona fide dispute as to the proper evaluation of the law or the facts necessary to determine the existence or correctness of the amount of an asserted liability. It is not necessary to institute suit in a court of law in order to contest an asserted liability. An affirmative act denying the validity or accuracy, or both, of an asserted liability to the person who is asserting such liability, such as including a written protest with payment of the asserted liability, is sufficient to commence a contest. Thus, lodging a protest in accordance with local law is sufficient to contest an asserted liability for taxes. It is not necessary that the affirmative act denying the validity or accuracy, or both, of an asserted liability be in writing if, upon examination of all the facts and circumstances, it can be established to the satisfaction of the Commissioner that a liability has been asserted and contested.

(3) *Example.* The provisions of this paragraph are illustrated by the following example:

Example: O Corporation makes its return on the basis of a calendar year and uses an accrual method of accounting. O receives a large shipment of typewriter ribbons from S Company on January 30, 1964, which O pays for in full on February 10, 1964. Subsequent to their receipt, several of the ribbons prove defective because of inferior materials used by the manufacturer. On August 9, 1964, O orally notifies S and demands refund of the full purchase price of the ribbons. After negotiations prove futile and a written demand is rejected by S, O institutes an action for the full purchase price. For purposes of paragraph (a)(1)(i) of this section, S has asserted a liability against O which O contests on August 9, 1964. O deducts the contested amount for 1964.

(c) *Transfer to provide for the satisfaction of an asserted liability*—(1) *In general.* A taxpayer may provide for the satisfaction of an asserted liability by transferring money or other property beyond his control (i) to the person who is asserting the liability, (ii) to an escrowee or trustee pursuant to a written agreement (among the escrowee or trustee, the taxpayer, and the person who is asserting the liability) that the money or other property be delivered in accordance with the settlement of the contest, or (iii) to an escrowee or trustee pursuant to an order of the United States, any State or political subdivision thereof, or any agency or instrumentality of the foregoing, or a court that the money or other property be delivered in accordance with the settlement of the contest. A taxpayer may also provide for the satisfaction of an asserted liability by transferring money or other property beyond his control to a court with jurisdiction over the contest. Purchasing a bond to guarantee payment of the asserted liability, an entry on the taxpayer's books of account, and a transfer to an account which is within the control of the taxpayer are not transfers to provide for the satisfaction of an asserted liability. In order for money or other property to be beyond the control of a taxpayer, the taxpayer must relinquish all authority over such money or other property.

(2) *Examples.* The provisions of this paragraph are illustrated by the following examples:

Example (1). M Corporation contests a $5,000 liability asserted against it by L Company for services rendered. To provide for the contingency that it might have to pay the liability, M establishes a separate bank account in its own name. M then transfers $5,000 from its general account to such separate account. Such transfer does not qualify as a transfer to provide for the satisfaction of an asserted liability because M has not transferred the money beyond its control.

Example (2). M Corporation contests a $5,000 liability asserted against it by L Company for services rendered. To provide for the contingency that it might have to pay the liability, M transfers $5,000 to an irrevocable trust pursuant to a written agreement among the trustee, M (the taxpayer), and L (the person who is asserting the liability) that the money shall be held until the contest is settled and then disbursed in accordance with the settlement. Such transfer qualifies as a transfer to provide for the satisfaction of an asserted liability.

(d) *Contest exists after transfer.* In order for a contest with respect to an asserted liability to exist after the time of transfer, such contest must be pursued subsequent to such time. Thus, the contest must have been neither settled nor abandoned at the time of the transfer. A contest may be settled by a decision, judgment, decree, or other order of any court of competent jurisdiction which has become final, or by written or oral agreement between the parties. For example, Z Corporation, which uses an accrual method of accounting, in 1964 contests a $100 asserted liability. In 1967 the contested liability is settled as being $80 which Z accrues and deducts for such year. In 1968 Z pays the $80. Section 461(f) does not apply to Z with respect to the transfer because a contest did not exist after the time of such transfer.

(e) *Deduction otherwise allowed* —(1) *In general.* The existence of the contest with respect to an asserted liability must prevent (without regard to section 461(f)) and be the only factor preventing a deduction for the taxable year of the transfer (or, in the case of an accrual method taxpayer, for an earlier taxable year for which such amount would be accruable) to provide for the satisfaction of such liability. Nothing in section 461(f) or this section shall be construed to give rise to a deduction since section 461(f) and this section relate only to the timing of deductions which are otherwise allowable under the Code.

(2) *Example.* The provisions of this paragraph are illustrated by the following example:

Example. A, an individual, makes a gift of certain property to B, an individual. A pays the entire amount of gift tax assessed against him but contests his liability for such tax. Section 275(a)(3) provides that gift taxes are not deductible. A does not satisfy the requirement of paragraph (a)(1)(iv) of this section since a deduction would not be allowed for the taxable year of the transfer even if A did not contest his liability to such tax.

* * *

[Reg. § 1.461-2.]

☐ [*T.D. 6772, 11-23-64. Amended by T.D. 8408, 4-9-92.*]

§ 1.461-4. Economic performance.—(a) *Introduction*—(1) *In general.* For purposes of determining whether an accrual basis taxpayer can treat the amount of any liability (as defined in § 1.446-1(c)(1)(ii)(B)) as incurred, the all events test is not treated as met any earlier than the taxable year in which economic performance occurs with respect to the liability.

(2) *Overview.* Paragraph (b) of this section lists exceptions to the economic performance requirement. Paragraph (c) of this section provides cross-references to the definitions of certain terms for purposes of section 461(h) and the regulations thereunder. Paragraphs (d) through (m) of this section and § 1.461-6 provide rules for determining when economic performance occurs. Section 1.461-5 provides rules relating to an exception under which certain recurring items may be incurred for the taxable year before the year during which economic performance occurs.

(b) *Exceptions to the economic performance requirement.* Paragraph (a)(2)(iii)(B) of § 1.461-1 provides examples of liabilities that are taken into account under rules that operate without regard to the all events test (including economic performance).

(c) *Definitions.* The following cross-references identify certain terms defined for purposes of section 461(h) and the regulations thereunder:

(1) *Liability.* See paragraph (c)(1)(ii)(B) of § 1.446-1 for the definition of "liability."

(2) *Payment.* See paragraph (g)(1)(ii) of this section for the definition of "payment."

(d) *Liabilities arising out of the provision of services, property, or the use of property*—(1) *In general.* The principles of this paragraph (d) determine when economic performance occurs with respect to liabilities arising out of the performance of services, the transfer of property, or the use of property. This paragraph (d) does not apply to liabilities described in paragraph (e) (relating to interest expense) or paragraph (g) (relating to breach of contract, workers compensation, tort, etc.) of this section. In addition, except as otherwise provided in Internal Revenue regulations, revenue procedures, or revenue rulings this paragraph (d) does not apply to amounts paid pursuant to a notional principal contract. The Commissioner may provide additional rules in regulations, revenue procedures, or revenue rulings concerning the time at which economic performance occurs for items described in this paragraph (d).

(2) *Services or property provided to the taxpayer*—(i) *In general.* Except as otherwise provided in paragraph (d)(5) of this section, if the liability of a taxpayer arises out of the providing of services or property to the taxpayer by another person, economic performance occurs as the services or property is provided.

Reg. § 1.461-4(a)(1)

(ii) *Long-term contracts.* In the case of any liability of a taxpayer described in paragraph (d)(2)(i) of this section that is an expense attributable to a long-term contract with respect to which the taxpayer uses the percentage of completion method, economic performance occurs—

(A) As the services or property is provided; or, if earlier,

(B) As the taxpayer makes payment (as defined in paragraph (g)(1)(ii) of this section) in satisfaction of the liability to the person providing the services or property. See paragraph (k)(2) of this section for the effective date of this paragraph (d)(2)(ii).

(iii) *Employee benefits*—(A) *In general.* Except as otherwise provided in any Internal Revenue regulation, revenue procedure, or revenue ruling, the economic performance requirement is satisfied to the extent that any amount is otherwise deductible under section 404 (employer contributions to a plan of deferred compensation), section 404A (certain foreign deferred compensation plans), and section 419 (welfare benefit funds). See § 1.461-1(a)(2)(iii)(D).

(B) *Property transferred in connection with performance of services.* [Reserved]

(iv) *Cross-references.* See *Examples 4 through 6* of paragraph (d)(7) of this section. See paragraph (d)(6) of this section for rules relating to when a taxpayer may treat services or property as provided to the taxpayer.

(3) *Use of property provided to the taxpayer*—(i) *In general.* Except as otherwise provided in this paragraph (d)(3) and paragraph (d)(5) of this section, if the liability of a taxpayer arises out of the use of property by the taxpayer, economic performance occurs ratably over the period of time the taxpayer is entitled to the use of the property (taking into account any reasonably expected renewal periods when necessary to carry out the purposes of section 461(h)). See *Examples 6 through 9* of paragraph (d)(7) of this section.

(ii) *Exceptions*—(A) *Volume, frequency of use, or income.* If the liability of a taxpayer arises out of the use of property by the taxpayer and all or a portion of the liability is determined by reference to the frequency or volume of use of the property or the income from the property, economic performance occurs for the portion of the liability determined by reference to the frequency or volume of use of the property or the income from the property as the taxpayer uses the property or includes income from the property. See *Examples 8* and *9* of paragraph (d)(7) of this section. This paragraph (d)(3)(ii) shall not apply if the District Director determines, that based on the substance of the transaction, the liability of the taxpayer for use of the property is more ap-

propriately measured ratably over the period of time the taxpayer is entitled to the use of the property.

(B) *Section 467 rental agreements.* In the case of a liability arising out of the use of property pursuant to a section 467 rental agreement, economic performance occurs as provided in § 1.461-1(a)(2)(iii)(E).

(4) *Services or property provided by the taxpayer*—(i) *In general.* Except as otherwise provided in paragraph (d)(5) of this section, if the liability of a taxpayer requires the taxpayer to provide services or property to another person, economic performance occurs as the taxpayer incurs costs (within the meaning of § 1.446-1(c)(1)(ii)) in connection with the satisfaction of the liability. See *Examples 1* through *3* of paragraph (d)(7) of this section.

(ii) *Barter transactions.* If the liability of a taxpayer requires the taxpayer to provide services, property, or the use of property, and arises out of the use of property by the taxpayer, or out of the provision of services or property to the taxpayer by another person, economic performance occurs to the extent of the lesser of—

(A) The cumulative extent to which the taxpayer incurs costs (within the meaning of § 1.446-1(c)(1)(ii)) in connection with its liability to provide the services or property; or

(B) The cumulative extent to which the services or property is provided to the taxpayer.

(5) *Liabilities that are assumed in connection with the sale of a trade or business*—(i) *In general.* If, in connection with the sale or exchange of a trade or business by a taxpayer, the purchaser expressly assumes a liability arising out of the trade or business that the taxpayer but for the economic performance requirement would have been entitled to incur as of the date of the sale, economic performance with respect to that liability occurs as the amount of the liability is properly included in the amount realized on the transaction by the taxpayer. See § 1.1001-2 for rules relating to the inclusion in amount realized from a discharge of liabilities resulting from a sale or exchange.

(ii) *Trade or business.* For purposes of this paragraph (d)(5), a trade or business is a specific group of activities carried on by the taxpayer for the purpose of earning income or profit if every operation that is necessary to the process of earning income or profit is included in the group. Thus, for example, the group of activities generally must include the collection of income and the payment of expenses.

(iii) *Tax avoidance.* This paragraph (d)(5) does not apply if the District Director determines

Reg. § 1.461-4(d)(5)

that tax avoidance is one of the taxpayer's principal purposes for the sale or exchange.

(6) *Rules relating to the provision of services or property to a taxpayer.* The following rules apply for purposes of this paragraph (d):

(i) Services or property provided to a taxpayer include services or property provided to another person at the direction of the taxpayer.

(ii) A taxpayer is permitted to treat services or property as provided to the taxpayer as the taxpayer makes payment to the person providing the services or property (as defined in paragraph (g)(1)(ii) of this section), if the taxpayer can reasonably expect the person to provide the services or property within 3 1/2 months after the date of payment.

(iii) A taxpayer is permitted to treat property as provided to the taxpayer when the property is delivered or accepted, or when title to the property passes. The method used by the taxpayer to determine when property is provided is a method of accounting that must comply with the rules of § 1.446-1(e). Thus, the method of determining when property is provided must be used consistently from year to year, and cannot be changed without the consent of the Commissioner.

(iv) If different services or items of property are required to be provided to a taxpayer under a single contract or agreement, economic performance generally occurs over the time each service is provided and as each item of property is provided. However, if a service or item of property to be provided to the taxpayer is incidental to other services or property to be provided under a contract or agreement, the taxpayer is not required to allocate any portion of the total contract price to the incidental service or property. For purposes of this paragraph (d)(6)(iv), services or property is treated as incidental only if—

(A) The cost of the services or property is treated on the taxpayer's books and records as part of the cost of the other services or property provided under the contract; and

(B) The aggregate cost of the services or property does not exceed 10 percent of the total contract price.

(7) *Examples.* The following examples illustrate the principles of this paragraph (d). For purposes of these examples, it is assumed that the requirements of the all events test other than economic performance have been met, and that the recurring item exception is not used. Assume further that the examples do not involve section 467 rental agreements and, therefore, section 467 is not applicable. The examples are as follows:

Example 1. Services or property provided by the taxpayer. (i) X corporation, a calendar year,

accrual method taxpayer, is an oil company. During March 1990, X enters into an oil and gas lease with Y. In November 1990, X installs a platform and commences drilling. The lease obligates X to remove its offshore platform and well fixtures upon abandonment of the well or termination of the lease. During 1998, X removes the platform and well fixtures at a cost of $200,000.

(ii) Under paragraph (d)(4)(i) of this section, economic performance with respect to X's liability to remove the offshore platform and well fixtures occurs as X incurs costs in connection with that liability. X incurs these costs in 1998 as, for example, X's employees provide X with removal services (see paragraph (d)(2) of this section). Consequently, X incurs $200,000 for the 1998 taxable year. Alternatively, assume that during 1990 X pays Z $130,000 to remove the platform and fixtures, and that Z performs these removal services in 1998. Under paragraph (d)(2) of this section, X does not incur this cost until Z performs the services. Thus, economic performance with respect to the $130,000 X pays Z occurs in 1998.

Example 2. Services or property provided by the taxpayer. (i) W corporation, a calendar year, accrual method taxpayer, sells tractors under a three-year warranty that obligates W to make any reasonable repairs to each tractor it sells. During 1990, W sells ten tractors. In 1992 W repairs, at a cost of $5,000, two tractors sold during 1990.

(ii) Under paragraph (d)(4)(i) of this section, economic performance with respect to W's liability to perform services under the warranty occurs as W incurs costs in connection with that liability. W incurs these costs in 1992 as, for example, replacement parts are provided to W (see paragraph (d)(2) of this section). Consequently, $5,000 is incurred by W for the 1992 taxable year.

Example 3. Services or property provided by the taxpayer; Long-term contracts. (i) W corporation, a calendar year, accrual method taxpayer, manufactures machine tool equipment. In November 1992, W contracts to provide X corporation with certain equipment. The contract is not a long-term contract under section 460 or § 1.451-3. In 1992, W pays Z corporation $50,000 to lease from Z, for the one-year period beginning on January 1, 1993, testing equipment to perform quality control tests required by the agreement with X. In 1992, pursuant to the terms of a contract, W pays Y corporation $100,000 for certain parts necessary to manufacture the equipment. The parts are provided to W in 1993. W's employees provide W with services necessary to manufacture the equipment during 1993, for which W pays $150,000 in 1993.

(ii) Under paragraph (d)(4) of this section, economic performance with respect to W's liability to provide the equipment to X occurs as W incurs costs in connection with that liability. W incurs these costs during 1993, as services, property, and the use of property necessary to manufacture the equipment are provided to W (see paragraphs (d)(2) and (d)(3) of this section). Thus, $300,000 is incurred by W for the 1993 taxable year. See section 263A and the regulations thereunder for rules relating to the capitalization and inclusion in inventory of these incurred costs.

(iii) Alternatively, assume that the agreement with X is a long-term contract as defined in section 460(f), and that W takes into account all items with respect to such contracts under the percentage of completion method as described in section 460 (b)(1). Under paragraph (d)(2)(ii) of this section, the $100,000 W pays in 1992 for parts is incurred for the 1992 taxable year, for purposes of determining the percentage of completion under section 460(b)(1)(A). W's other costs under the agreement are incurred for the 1993 taxable year for this purpose.

Example 4. Services or property provided to the taxpayer. (i) LP1, a calendar year, accrual method limited partnership, owns the working interest in a parcel of property containing oil and gas. During December 1990, LP1 enters into a turnkey contract with Z corporation pursuant to which LP1 pays Z $200,000 and Z is required to provide a completed well by the close of 1992. In May 1992, Z commences drilling the well, and, in December 1992, the well is completed.

(ii) Under paragraph (d)(2) of this section, economic performance with respect to LP1's liability for drilling and development services provided to LP1 by Z occurs as the services are provided. Consequently, $200,000 is incurred by LP1 for the 1992 taxable year.

Example 5. Services or property provided to the taxpayer. (i) X corporation, a calendar year, accrual method taxpayer, is an automobile dealer. On January 15, 1990, X agrees to pay an additional $10 to Y, the manufacturer of the automobiles, for each automobile purchased by X from Y. Y agrees to provide advertising and promotional activities to X.

(ii) During 1990, X purchases from Y 1,000 new automobiles and pays to Y an additional $10,000 as provided in the agreement. Y, in turn, uses this $10,000 to provide advertising and promotional activities during 1992.

(iii) Under paragraph (d)(2) of this section, economic performance with respect to X's liability for advertising and promotional services provided to X by Y occurs as the services are provided.

Consequently, $10,000 is incurred by X for the 1992 taxable year.

Example 6. Use of property provided to the taxpayer; services or property provided to the taxpayer. (i) V corporation, a calendar year, accrual method taxpayer, charters aircraft. On December 20, 1990, V leases a jet aircraft from L for the four-year period that begins on January 1, 1991. The lease obligates V to pay L a base rental of $500,000 per year. In addition, the lease requires V to pay $25 to an escrow account for each hour that the aircraft is flown. The escrow account funds are held by V and are to be used by L to make necessary repairs to the aircraft. Any amount remaining in the escrow account upon termination of the lease is payable to V. During 1991, the aircraft is flown 1,000 hours and V pays $25,000 to the escrow account. The aircraft is repaired by L in 1993. In 1994, $20,000 is released from the escrow account to pay L for the repairs.

(ii) Under paragraph (d)(3)(i) of this section, economic performance with respect to V's base rental liability occurs ratably over the period of time V is entitled to use the jet aircraft. Consequently, the $500,000 rent is incurred by V for the 1991 taxable year and for each of the next three taxable years. Under paragraph (d)(2) of this section, economic performance with respect to the liability to place amounts in escrow occurs as the aircraft is repaired. Consequently, V incurs $20,000 for the 1993 taxable year.

Example 7. Use of property provided to the taxpayer. (i) X corporation, a calendar year, accrual method taxpayer, manufactures and sells electronic circuitry. On November 15, 1990, X enters into a contract with Y that entitles X to the exclusive use of a product owned by Y for the five-year period beginning on January 1, 1991. Pursuant to the contract, X pays Y $100,000 on December 30, 1990.

(ii) Under paragraph (d)(3)(i) of this section, economic performance with respect to X's liability for the use of property occurs ratably over the period of time X is entitled to use the product. Consequently, $20,000 is incurred by X for 1991 and for each of the succeeding four taxable years.

Example 8. Use of property provided to the taxpayer. (i) Y corporation, a calendar year, accrual method taxpayer, enters into a five-year lease with Z for the use of a copy machine on July 1, 1991. Y also receives delivery of the copy machine on July 1, 1991. The lease obligates Y to pay Z a base rental payment of $6,000 per year at the beginning of each lease year and an additional charge of 5 cents per copy 30 days after the end of each lease year. The machine is used to make 50,000 copies during the first lease year: 20,000

Reg. § 1.461-4(d)(7)

copies in 1991 and 30,000 copies from January 1, 1992, to July 1, 1992. Y pays the $6,000 base rental payment to Z on July 1, 1991, and the $2,500 variable use payment on July 30, 1992.

(ii) Under paragraph (d)(3)(i) of this section, economic performance with respect to Y's base rental liability occurs ratably over the period of time Y is entitled to use the copy machine. Consequently, $3,000 rent is incurred by Y for the 1991 taxable year. Under paragraph (d)(3)(ii) of this section, economic performance with respect to Y's variable use portion of the liability occurs as Y uses the machine. Thus, the $1,000 of the $2,500 variable-use liability that relates to the 20,000 copies made in 1991 is incurred by Y for the 1991 taxable year.

Example 9. Use of property provided to the taxpayer. (i) X corporation, a calendar year, accrual method taxpayer, enters into a five-year product distribution agreement with Y, on January 1, 1992. The agreement provides for a payment of $100,000 on January 1, 1992, plus 10 percent of the gross profits earned by X from distribution of the product. The variable income portion of X's liability is payable on April 1 of each subsequent year. On January 1, 1992, X pays Y $100,000. On April 1, 1993, X pays Y $3 million representing 10 percent of X's gross profits from January 1 through December 31, 1992.

(ii) Under paragraph (d)(3)(i) of this section, economic performance with respect to X's $100,000 payment occurs ratably over the period of time X is entitled to use the product. Consequently, $20,000 is incurred by X for each year of the agreement beginning with 1992. Under paragraph (d)(3)(ii) of this section, economic performance with respect to X's variable income portion of the liability occurs as the income is earned by X. Thus, the $3 million variable-income liability is incurred by X for the 1992 taxable year.

(e) *Interest.* In the case of interest, economic performance occurs as the interest cost economically accrues, in accordance with the principles of relevant provisions of the Code.

(f) *Timing of deductions from notional principal contracts.* Economic performance on a notional principal contract occurs as provided under § 1.446-3.

(g) *Certain liabilities for which payment is economic performance—(1) In general—(i) Person to which payment must be made.* In the case of liabilities described in paragraphs (g)(2) through (7) of this section, economic performance occurs when, and to the extent that, payment is made to the person to which the liability is owed. Thus, except as otherwise provided in paragraph (g)(1)(iv) of this section and § 1.461-6, economic performance does not occur as a taxpayer makes

payments in connection with such a liability to any other person, including a trust, escrow account, court-administered fund, or any similar arrangement, unless the payments constitute payment to the person to which the liability is owed under paragraph (g)(1)(ii)(B) of this section. Instead, economic performance occurs as payments are made from that other person or fund to the person to which the liability is owed. The amount of economic performance that occurs as payment is made from the other person or fund to the person to which the liability is owed may not exceed the amount the taxpayer transferred to the other person or fund. For special rules relating to the taxation of amounts transferred to "qualified settlement funds," see section 468B and the regulations thereunder. The Commissioner may provide additional rules in regulations, revenue procedures, and revenue rulings concerning the time at which economic performance occurs for items described in this paragraph (g).

(ii) *Payment to person to which liability is owed.* Paragraph (d)(6) of this section provides that for purposes of paragraph (d) of this section (relating to the provision of services or property to the taxpayer) in certain cases a taxpayer may treat services or property as provided to the taxpayer as the taxpayer makes payments to the person providing the services or property. In addition, this paragraph (g) provides that in the case of certain liabilities of a taxpayer, economic performance occurs as the taxpayer makes payment to persons specified therein. For these and all other purposes of section 461(h) and the regulations thereunder:

(A) *Payment.* The term "payment" has the same meaning as is used when determining whether a taxpayer using the cash receipts and disbursements method of accounting has made a payment. Thus, for example, payment includes the furnishing of cash or cash equivalents and the netting of offsetting accounts. Payment does not include the furnishing of a note or other evidence of indebtedness of the taxpayer, whether or not the evidence is guaranteed by any other instrument (including a standby letter of credit) or by any third party (including a government agency). As a further example, payment does not include a promise of the taxpayer to provide services or property in the future (whether or not the promise is evidenced by a contract or other written agreement). In addition, payment does not include an amount transferred as a loan, refundable deposit, or contingent payment.

(B) *Person to which payment is made.* Payment to a particular person is accomplished if paragraph (g)(1)(ii)(A) of this section is satisfied and a cash basis taxpayer in the position of that person would be treated as having actually or constructively received the amount of the payment as gross income under the principles of section 451 (without regard to section 104(a) or any other provision that specifically excludes the amount from gross income). Thus, for example, the purchase of an annuity contract or any other asset generally does not constitute payment to the person to which a liability is owed unless the ownership of the contract or other asset is transferred to that person.

(C) *Liabilities that are assumed in connection with the sale of a trade or business.* Paragraph (d)(5) of this section provides rules that determine when economic performance occurs in the case of liabilities that are assumed in connection with the sale of a trade or business. The provisions of paragraph (d)(5) of this section also apply to any liability described in paragraph (g)(2) through (7) of this section that the purchaser expressly assumes in connection with the sale or exchange of a trade or business by a taxpayer, provided the taxpayer (but for the economic performance requirement) would have been entitled to incur the liability as of the date of the sale.

(iii) *Person.* For purposes of this paragraph (g), "person" has the same meaning as in section 7701(a)(1), except that it also includes any foreign state, the United States, any State or political subdivision thereof, any possession of the United States, and any agency or instrumentality of any of the foregoing.

(iv) *Assignments.* If a person that has a right to receive payment in satisfaction of a liability described in paragraphs (g)(2) through (7) of this section makes a valid assignment of that right to a second person, or if the right is assigned to the second person through operation of law, then payment to the second person in satisfaction of that liability constitutes payment to the person to which the liability is owed.

(2) *Liabilities arising under a workers compensation act or out of any tort, breach of contract, or violation of law.* If the liability of a taxpayer requires a payment or series of payments to another person and arises under any workers compensation act or out of any tort, breach of contract, or violation of law, economic performance occurs as payment is made to the person to which the liability is owed. See *Example 1* of paragraph (g)(8) of this section. For purposes of this paragraph (g)(2)—

(i) A liability to make payments for services, property, or other consideration provided under a contract is not a liability arising out of a breach of that contract unless the payments are in the nature of incidental, consequential, or liquidated damages; and

(ii) A liability arising out of a tort, breach of contract, or violation of law includes a liability arising out of the settlement of a dispute in which a tort, breach of contract, or violation of law, respectively, is alleged.

(3) *Rebates and refunds.* If the liability of a taxpayer is to pay a rebate, refund, or similar payment to another person (whether paid in property, money, or as a reduction in the price of goods or services to be provided in the future by the taxpayer), economic performance occurs as payment is made to the person to which the liability is owed. This paragraph (g)(3) applies to all rebates, refunds, and payments or transfers in the nature of a rebate or refund regardless of whether they are characterized as a deduction from gross income, an adjustment to gross receipts or total sales, or an adjustment or addition to cost of goods sold. In the case of a rebate or refund made as a reduction in the price of goods or services to be provided in the future by the taxpayer, "payment" is deemed to occur as the taxpayer would otherwise be required to recognize income resulting from a disposition at an unreduced price. See *Example 2* of paragraph (g)(8) of this section. For purposes of determining whether the recurring item exception of § 1.461-5 applies, a liability that arises out of a tort, breach of contract, or violation of law is not considered a rebate or refund.

(4) *Awards, prizes, and jackpots.* If the liability of a taxpayer is to provide an award, prize, jackpot, or other similar payment to another person, economic performance occurs as payment is made to the person to which the liability is owed. See *Examples 3* and *4* of paragraph (g)(8) of this section.

(5) *Insurance, warranty, and service contracts.* If the liability of a taxpayer arises out of the provision to the taxpayer of insurance, or a warranty or service contract, economic performance occurs as payment is made to the person to which the liability is owed. See *Examples 5* through *7* of paragraph (g)(8) of this section. For purposes of this paragraph (g)(5)—

(i) A warranty or service contract is a contract that a taxpayer enters into in connection with property bought or leased by the taxpayer, pursuant to which the other party to the contract promises to replace or repair the property under specified circumstances.

(ii) The term "insurance" has the same meaning as is used when determining the deductibility of amounts paid or incurred for insurance under section 162.

(6) Taxes—(i) *In general.* Except as otherwise provided in this paragraph (g)(6), if the liability of a taxpayer is to pay a tax, economic

performance occurs as the tax is paid to the governmental authority that imposed the tax. For purposes of this paragraph (g)(6), payment includes payments of estimated income tax and payments of tax where the taxpayer subsequently files a claim for credit or refund. In addition, for purposes of this paragraph (g)(6), a tax does not include a charge collected by a governmental authority for specific extraordinary services or property provided to a taxpayer by the governmental authority. Examples of such a charge include the purchase price of a parcel of land sold to a taxpayer by a governmental authority and a charge for labor engaged in by government employees to improve that parcel. In certain cases, a liability to pay a tax is permitted to be taken into account in the taxable year before the taxable year during which economic performance occurs under the recurring item exception of § 1.461-5. See *Example 8* of paragraph (g)(8) of this section.

(ii) *Licensing fees.* If the liability of a taxpayer is to pay a licensing or permit fee required by a governmental authority, economic performance occurs as the fee is paid to the governmental authority, or as payment is made to any other person at the direction of the governmental authority.

(iii) *Exceptions*—(A) *Real property taxes.* If a taxpayer has made a valid election under section 461(c), the taxpayer's accrual for real property taxes is determined under section 461(c). Otherwise, economic performance with respect to a property tax liability occurs as the tax is paid, as specified in paragraph (g)(6)(i) of this section.

(B) *Certain foreign taxes.* If the liability of a taxpayer is to pay an income, war profits, or excess profits tax that is imposed by the authority of any foreign country or possession of the United States and is creditable under section 901 (including a creditable tax described in section 903 that is paid in lieu of such a tax), economic performance occurs when the requirements of the all events test (as described in § 1.446-1(c)(1)(ii)) other than economic performance are met, whether or not the taxpayer elects to credit such taxes under section 901(a).

(7) *Other liabilities.* In the case of a taxpayer's liability for which economic performance rules are not provided elsewhere in this section or in any other Internal Revenue regulation, revenue ruling or revenue procedure, economic performance occurs as the taxpayer makes payments in satisfaction of the liability to the person to which the liability is owed. This paragraph (g)(7) applies only if the liability cannot properly be characterized as a liability covered by rules provided elsewhere in this section. If a liability may properly be characterized as, for example, a liability arising from the provision of services or property to, or by, a taxpayer, the determination as to when economic performance occurs with respect to that liability is made under paragraph (d) of this section and not under this paragraph (g)(7).

(8) *Examples.* The following examples illustrate the principles of this paragraph (g). For purposes of these examples, it is assumed that the requirements of the all events test other than economic performance have been met and, except as otherwise provided, that the recurring item exception is not used.

Example 1. Liabilities arising out of a tort. (i) During the period 1970 through 1975, Z corporation, a calendar year, accrual method taxpayer, manufactured and distributed industrial products that contained carcinogenic substances. In 1992, a number of lawsuits are filed against Z alleging damages due to exposure to these products. In settlement of a lawsuit maintained by A, Z agrees to purchase an annuity contract that will provide annual payments to A of $50,000 for a period of 25 years. On December 15, 1992, Z pays W, an unrelated life insurance company, $491,129 for such an annuity contract. Z retains ownership of the annuity contract.

(ii) Under paragraph (g)(2) of this section, economic performance with respect to Z's liability to A occurs as each payment is made to A. Consequently, $50,000 is incurred by Z for each taxable year that a payment is made to A under the annuity contract. (Z must also include in income a portion of amounts paid under the annuity, pursuant to section 72.) The result is the same if in 1992 Z secures its obligation with a standby letter of credit.

(iii) If Z later transfers ownership of the annuity contract to A, an amount equal to the fair market value of the annuity on the date of transfer is incurred by Z in the taxable year of the transfer (see paragraph (g)(1)(ii)(B) of this section). In addition, the transfer constitutes a transaction to which section 1001 applies.

Example 2. Rebates and refunds. (i) X corporation, a calendar year, accrual method taxpayer, manufactures and sells hardware products. X enters into agreements that entitle each of its distributors to a rebate (or discount on future purchases) from X based on the amount of purchases made by the distributor from X during any calendar year. During the 1992 calendar year, X becomes liable to pay a $2,000 rebate to distributor A. X pays A $1,200 of the rebate on January 15, 1993, and the remaining $800 on October 15, 1993. Assume the rebate is deductible (or allowable as an adjustment to gross receipts or cost of goods sold) when incurred.

Reg. § 1.461-4(g)(7)

(ii) If X does not adopt the recurring item exception described in § 1.461-5 with respect to rebates and refunds, then under paragraph (g)(3) of this section, economic performance with respect to the $2,000 rebate liability occurs in 1993. However, if X has made a proper election under § 1.461-5, and as of December 31, 1992, all events have occurred that determine the fact of the rebate liability, X incurs $1,200 for the 1992 taxable year. Because economic performance (payment) with respect to the remaining $800 does not occur until October 15, 1993 (more than 8½ months after the end of 1992), X cannot use the recurring item exception for this portion of the liability (see § 1.461-5). Thus, the $800 is not incurred by X until the 1993 taxable year. If, instead of making the cash payments to A during 1993, X adjusts the price of hardware purchased by A that is delivered to A during 1993, X's "payment" occurs as X would otherwise be required to recognize income resulting from a disposition at an unreduced price.

Example 3. Awards, prizes, and jackpots. (i) W corporation, a calendar year, accrual method taxpayer, produces and sells breakfast cereal. W conducts a contest pursuant to which the winner is entitled to $10,000 per year for a period of 20 years. On December 1, 1992, A is declared the winner of the contest and is paid $10,000 by W. In addition, on December 1 of each of the next nineteen years, W pays $10,000 to A.

(ii) Under paragraph (g)(4) of this section, economic performance with respect to the $200,000 contest liability occurs as each of the $10,000 payments is made by W to A. Consequently, $10,000 is incurred by W for the 1992 taxable year and for each of the succeeding nineteen taxable years.

Example 4. Awards, prizes, and jackpots. (i) Y corporation, a calendar year, accrual method taxpayer, owns a casino that contains progressive slot machines. A progressive slot machine provides a guaranteed jackpot amount that increases as money is gambled through the machine until the jackpot is won or until a maximum predetermined amount is reached. On July 1, 1993, the guaranteed jackpot amount on one of Y's slot machines reaches the maximum predetermined amount of $50,000. On October 1, 1994, the $50,000 jackpot is paid to B.

(ii) Under paragraph (g)(4) of this section, economic performance with respect to the $50,000 jackpot liability occurs on the date the jackpot is paid to B. Consequently, $50,000 is incurred by Y for the 1994 taxable year.

Example 5. Insurance, warranty, and service contracts. (i) V corporation, a calendar year, accrual method taxpayer, manufactures toys. V enters into a contract with W, an unrelated insurance company, on December 15, 1992. The contract obligates V to pay W a premium of $500,000 before the end of 1995. The contract obligates W to satisfy any liability of V resulting from claims made during 1993 or 1994 against V by any third party for damages attributable to defects in toys manufactured by V. Pursuant to the contract, V pays W a premium of $500,000 on October 1, 1995.

(ii) Assuming the arrangement constitutes insurance, under paragraph (g)(5) of this section economic performance occurs as the premium is paid. Thus, $500,000 is incurred by V for the 1995 taxable year.

Example 6. Insurance, warranty, and service contracts. (i) Y corporation, a calendar year, accrual method taxpayer, is a common carrier. On December 15, 1992, Y enters into a contract with Z, an unrelated insurance company, under which Z must satisfy any liability of Y that arises during the succeeding 5 years for damages under a workers compensation act or out of any tort, provided the event that causes the damages occurs during 1993 or 1994. Under the contract, Y pays $360,000 to Z on December 31, 1993.

(ii) Assuming the arrangement constitutes insurance, under paragraph (g)(5) of this section economic performance occurs as the premium is paid. Consequently, $360,000 is incurred by Y for the 1993 taxable year. The period for which the $360,000 amount is permitted to be taken into account is determined under the capitalization rules because the insurance contract is an asset having a useful life extending substantially beyond the close of the taxable year.

Example 7. Insurance, warranty, and service contracts. Assume the same facts as in *Example 6*, except that Y is obligated to pay the first $5,000 of any damages covered by the arrangement with Z. Y is, in effect, self-insured to the extent of this $5,000 "deductible." Thus, under paragraph (g)(2) of this section, economic performance with respect to the $5,000 liability does not occur until the amount is paid to the person to which the tort or workers compensation liability is owed.

Example 8. Taxes. (i) The laws of State A provide that every person owning personal property located in State A on the first day of January shall be liable for tax thereon and that a lien for the tax shall attach as of that date. In addition, the laws of State A provide that 60% of the tax is due on the first day of December following the lien date and the remaining 40% is due on the first day of July of the succeeding year. On January 1, 1992, X corporation, a calendar year, accrual method taxpayer, owns personal property

Reg. § 1.461-4(g)(8)

located in State A. State A imposes a $10,000 tax on X with respect to that property on January 1, 1992. X pays State A $6,000 of the tax on December 1, 1992, and the remaining $4,000 on July 1, 1993.

(ii) Under paragraph (g)(6) of this section, economic performance with respect to $6,000 of the tax liability occurs on December 1, 1992. Consequently, $6,000 is incurred by X for the 1992 taxable year. Economic performance with respect to the remaining $4,000 of the tax liability occurs on July 1, 1993. If X has adopted the recurring item exception described in § 1.461-5 as a method of accounting for taxes, and as of December 31, 1992, all events have occurred that determine the liability of X for the remaining $4,000, X also incurs $4,000 for the 1992 taxable year. If X does not adopt the recurring item exception method, the $4,000 is not incurred by X until the 1993 taxable year.

* * *

[Reg. § 1.461-4.]

□ [*T.D.* 8408, 4-9-92. *Amended by T.D.* 8491, 10-8-93; *T.D.* 8593, 4-7-95 *and T.D.* 8820, 5-17-99.]

Proposed Regulations

§ 1.465-1. General rules; limitation of deductions to amount at risk.—(a) *In general.* For taxable years beginning after December 31, 1975, section 465 generally limits the amount of any loss described in section 465(d) that is otherwise deductible in connection with an activity described in section 465(c)(1). Under section 465 the amount of the loss is allowed as a deduction only to the extent that the taxpayer is at risk with respect to the activity at the close of the taxable year. The determination of the amount the taxpayer is at risk in cases where the activity is engaged in by an entity separate from the taxpayer is made as of the close of the taxable year of the entity engaging in the activity (for example, a partnership). For the purposes of these regulations, in cases where the activity is engaged in by an entity separate from the taxpayer references to a taxable year shall apply to the taxable year of the entity unless otherwise stated. For rules determining the amount at risk and for more specific rules regarding the effective dates, see §§ 1.465-20 through 1.465-25 and 1.465-95.

(b) *Substance over form.* In applying section 465 and these regulations, substance will prevail over form. Regardless of the form a transaction may take, the taxpayer's amount at risk will not be increased if the transaction is inconsistent with normal commercial practices or is, in essence, a device to avoid section 465. See § 1.465-4 for rules regarding attempts to avoid the at risk provisions.

(c) *Activities.* See sections 465(c)(1)(A) through (D) and §§ 1.465-42 through 1.465-45 for the activities to which section 465 applies for taxable years beginning generally after December 31, 1975. These activities are holding, producing, or distributing movies and video tapes, farming, leasing of personal property, and exploring for or exploiting oil and gas resources. See section 465(c)(3) and section 465(c)(1)(E) for additional activities to which section 465 applies for taxable years beginning generally after December 31, 1978.

(d) *Taxpayers affected by at risk provisions.* (1) For taxable years beginning generally after December 31, 1975, section 465 applies to all noncorporate taxpayers, to electing small business corporations (as defined in section 1371(b)), and to personal holding companies (as defined in section 542). For special rules relating to electing small business corporations, see § 1.465-10.

(2) See section 465(a)(1)(C) for additional taxpayers to whom section 465 applies for taxable years beginning generally after December 31, 1978.

(e) *Basis.* The provisions of section 465 and the regulations thereunder are only intended to limit the extent to which certain losses in connection with covered activities may be deducted in a given year by a taxpayer. Section 465 does not apply for other purposes, such as determining adjusted basis. Thus, for example, the adjusted basis of a partner in a partnership interest is not affected by section 465. [Reg. § 1.465-1.]

[Proposed 6-5-79.]

§ 1.465-2. General rules; allowance of deductions.—(a) *In general.* In any taxable year, there are two ways in which deductions allocable to an activity to which section 465 applies will be allowable under section 465. First, deductions allocable to an activity and otherwise allowable will be allowable in a taxable year to the extent of income received or accrued from the activity in that taxable year. See the example at § 1.465-11(c)(2). Thus, to the extent there is income from the activity in a taxable year, deductions allocable to that activity will be allowable without regard to the amount at risk. Second, losses from the activity (that is, the excess of deductions allocable to the activity over the income received or accrued from the activity) will be allowable to the extent the taxpayer is at risk with respect to that activity at the close of the taxable year. See the example at § 1.465-11(a)(2). Also see §§ 1.465-11 through 1.465-13 for the definition of loss.

(b) *Carryover of loss.* A loss which is disallowed by reason of section 465(a) shall be treated as a deduction for the succeeding taxable year with respect to the same activity to which it is alloca-

Reg. § 1.465-1(a)

ble. In the succeeding taxable year there will again be two ways for the deduction to be allowable. There is no limit to the number of years to which a taxpayer may carry over a loss disallowed solely by reason of section 465(a). [Reg. § 1.465-2.]

[Proposed 6-5-79.]

§ 1.465-10. General rules; rules relating to subchapter S corporations and their shareholders.—(a) *In general.* In the case of electing small business corporations (as defined in section 1371(b)) the at risk rules of section 465 apply at both the corporate level and the shareholder level. Therefore, losses from an activity can be deducted by the corporation only to the extent that the corporation is at risk in the activity. In addition, each shareholder will be allowed a loss in the activity only to the extent that the shareholder is at risk in the activity.

(b) *Determination of corporation's amount at risk*—(1) *General rule.* Except as provided in paragraph (b)(2) of this section, an electing small business corporation's amount at risk in an activity is determined in the same manner as that of any other taxpayer.

(2) *Special rule for certain borrowed amounts.* Amounts borrowed by an electing small business corporation from one or more of its shareholders may increase the corporation's amount at risk, notwithstanding the fact that the shareholders have an interest in the activity other than that of a creditor.

(c) *Determination of shareholder's amount at risk.* The amount at risk of a shareholder of an electing small business corporation (as described in section 1371(b)) shall be adjusted to reflect any increase or decrease in the adjusted basis of any indebtedness of the corporation to the shareholder described in section 1374(c)(2)(B).

(d) *Example.* The provisions of this section may be illustrated by the following example:

Example. A is the single shareholder in X, an electing small business corporation engaged in an activity described in section 465(c)(1). A contributed $50,000 to X in exchange for its stock under section 351. In addition, A borrowed $40,000 for which A assumed personal liability A then loaned the entire amount to X for use in the activity. During its taxable year, X had a net operating loss of $75,000. At the close of the taxable year (without reduction for any losses of X) A's amount at risk is $90,000 ($50,000 + $40,000). However, it is also necessary to determine X's amount at risk in the activity. X is also at risk for the $40,000 borrowed from A and expended in the activity. Therefore, X's amount at risk in the activity is $90,000 ($50,000 + $40,000). Because X's amount at risk in the activity ($90,000) ex-

ceeds the net operating loss ($75,000), the entire loss is allowed to the corporation and allocated to A. Since A's amount at risk ($90,000) also exceeds the loss ($75,000) A will be allowed the entire loss deduction. [Reg. § 1.465-10.]

[Proposed 6-5-79.]

§ 1.465-24. Effect on amount at risk of loans for which borrower is personally liable for repayment.—(a) *Creation of loan*—(1) *General rule.* A taxpayer's amount at risk in an activity is increased by the amount of any liability incurred in the conduct of an activity for use in the activity to the extent the taxpayer is personally liable for repayment of the liability.

(2) *Partnerships*—(i) When a partnership incurs a liability in the conduct of an activity and under state law members of the partnership may be held personally liable for repayment of the liability, each partner's amount at risk is increased to the extent the partner is not protected against loss. To the extent the partner is protected against loss (such as through a right of contribution), the liability shall be treated in the same manner as amounts borrowed for which the taxpayer has no personal liability and for which no security is pledged. See § 1.465-25.

(ii) The application of this paragraph may be illustrated by the following example:

Example. A and B are equal general partners in partnership AB, which is engaged solely in an activity described in section 465(c)(1). AB borrows $25,000 from a bank to purchase equipment to be used in the activity. In addition to giving the bank a security interest in the newly purchased equipment, A and B each assumes personal liability for the loan. Although either A or B could be called upon by the bank to repay the entire $25,000, in such instance the partner who paid would be entitled to $12,500 from the other partner. Thus, although each is personally liable for $25,000, each is protected against loss in excess of $12,500. Accordingly, the loan increases the amount each is at risk with respect to the activity by $12,500.

(3) *Small business corporations.* The amount at risk of a shareholder of an electing small business corporation (as defined in section 1371(b)) shall not be increased by indebtedness incurred by the corporation from persons other than that shareholder. For treatment of indebtedness described in section 1374(c)(2)(B) (relating to loans by shareholders to electing small business corporations), see § 1.465-10(c).

* * *

[Reg. § 1.465-24.]

[Proposed 6-5-79.]

§ 1.465-27. Qualified nonrecourse financing.—(a) *In general*. Notwithstanding any provision of section 465(b) or the regulations under section 465(b), for an activity of holding real property, a taxpayer is considered at risk for the taxpayer's share of any qualified nonrecourse financing which is secured by real property used in such activity.

(b) *Qualified nonrecourse financing secured by real property*—(1) *In general*. For purposes of section 465(b)(6) and this section, the term *qualified nonrecourse financing* means any financing—

(i) Which is borrowed by the taxpayer with respect to the activity of holding real property;

(ii) Which is borrowed by the taxpayer from a qualified person or represents a loan from any federal, state, or local government or instrumentality thereof, or is guaranteed by any federal, state, or local government;

(iii) For which no person is personally liable for repayment, taking into account paragraphs (b)(3), (4), and (5) of this section; and

(iv) Which is not convertible debt.

(2) *Security for qualified nonrecourse financing*—(i) *Types of property*. For a taxpayer to be considered at risk under section 465(b)(6), qualified nonrecourse financing must be secured only by real property used in the activity of holding real property. For this purpose, however, property that is incidental to the activity of holding real property will be disregarded. In addition, for this purpose, property that is neither real property used in the activity of holding real property nor incidental property will be disregarded if the aggregate gross fair market value of such property is less than 10 percent of the aggregate gross fair market value of all the property securing the financing.

(ii) *Look-through rule for partnerships*. For purposes of paragraph (b)(2)(i) of this section, a borrower shall be treated as owning directly its proportional share of the assets in a partnership in which the borrower owns (directly or indirectly through a chain of partnerships) an equity interest.

(3) *Personal liability; partial liability*. If one or more persons are personally liable for repayment of a portion of a financing, the portion of the financing for which no person is personally liable may qualify as qualified nonrecourse financing.

(4) *Partnership liability*. For purposes of section 465(b)(6) and this paragraph (b), the personal liability of any partnership for repayment of a financing is disregarded and, provided the requirements contained in paragraphs (b)(1)(i), (ii), and (iv) of this section are satisfied, the financing

will be treated as qualified nonrecourse financing secured by real property if—

(i) The only persons personally liable to repay the financing are partnerships;

(ii) Each partnership with personal liability holds only property described in paragraph (b)(2)(i) of this section (applying the principles of paragraph (b)(2)(ii) of this section in determining the property held by each partnership); and

(iii) In exercising its remedies to collect on the financing in a default or default-like situation, the lender may proceed only against property that is described in paragraph (b)(2)(i) of this section and that is held by the partnership or partnerships (applying the principles of paragraph (b)(2)(ii) of this section in determining the property held by the partnership or partnerships).

(5) *Disregarded entities*. Principles similar to those described in paragraph (b)(4) of this section shall apply in determining whether a financing of an entity that is disregarded for federal tax purposes under § 301.7701-3 of this chapter is treated as qualified nonrecourse financing secured by real property.

(6) *Examples*. The following examples illustrate the rules of this section:

Example 1. Personal liability of a partnership; incidental property. (i) X is a limited liability company that is classified as a partnership for federal tax purposes. X engages only in the activity of holding real property. In addition to real property used in the activity of holding real property, X owns office equipment, a truck, and maintenance equipment that it uses to support the activity of holding real property. X borrows $500 to use in the activity. X is personally liable on the financing, but no member of X and no other person is liable for repayment of the financing under local law. The lender may proceed against all of X's assets if X defaults on the financing.

(ii) Under paragraph (b)(2)(i) of this section, the personal property is disregarded as incidental property used in the activity of holding real property. Under paragraph (b)(4) of this section, the personal liability of X for repayment of the financing is disregarded and, provided the requirements contained in paragraphs (b)(1)(i), (ii), and (iv) of this section are satisfied, the financing will be treated as qualified nonrecourse financing secured by real property.

Example 2. Bifurcation of a financing. The facts are the same as in *Example 1*, except that A, a member of X, is personally liable for repayment of $100 of the financing. If the requirements contained in paragraphs (b)(1)(i), (ii), and (iv) of this section are satisfied, then under paragraph (b)(3) of this section, the portion of the financing for

Reg. § 1.465-27(a)

which A is not personally liable for repayment ($400) will be treated as qualified nonrecourse financing secured by real property.

Example 3. Personal liability; tiered partnerships. (i) UTP1 and UTP2, both limited liability companies classified as partnerships, are the only general partners in Y, a limited partnership. Y borrows $500 with respect to the activity of holding real property. The financing is a general obligation of Y. UTP1 and UTP2, therefore, are personally liable to repay the financing. Under section 752, UTP1's share of the financing is $300, and UTP2's share is $200. No person other than Y, UTP1, and UTP2 is personally liable to repay the financing. Y, UTP1, and UTP2 each hold only real property.

(ii) Under paragraph (b)(4) of this section, the personal liability of Y, UTP1, and UTP2 to repay the financing is disregarded and, provided the requirements of paragraphs (b)(1)(i), (ii), and (iv) of this section are satisfied, UTP1's $300 share of the financing and UTP2's $200 share of the financing will be treated as qualified nonrecourse financing secured by real property.

Example 4. Personal liability; tiered partnerships. The facts are the same as in *Example 3,* except that Y's general partners are UTP1 and B, an individual. Because B, an individual, is also personally liable to repay the $500 financing, the entire financing fails to satisfy the requirement in paragraph (b)(1)(iii) of this section. Accordingly, UTP1's $300 share of the financing will not be treated as qualified nonrecourse financing secured by real property.

Example 5. Personal liability; tiered partnerships. The facts are the same as in *Example 3,* except that Y is a limited liability company and UTP1 and UTP2 are not personally liable for the debt. However, UTP1 and UTP2 each pledge property as security for the loan that is other than real property used in the activity of holding real property and other than property that is incidental to the activity of holding real property. The fair market value of the property pledged by UTP1 and UTP2 is greater than 10 percent of the sum of the aggregate gross fair market value of the property held by Y and the aggregate gross fair market value of the property pledged by UTP1 and UTP2. Accordingly, the financing fails to satisfy the requirement in paragraph (b)(1)(iii) of this section by virtue of its failure to satisfy paragraph (b)(4)(iii) of this section. Therefore, the financing is not qualified nonrecourse financing secured by real property.

Example 6. Personal liability; Disregarded entity. (i) X is a single member limited liability company that is disregarded as an entity separate from its owner for federal tax purposes under § 301.7701-3 of this chapter. X owns certain real property and property that is incidental to the activity of holding the real property. X does not own any other property. For federal tax purposes, A, the sole member of X, is considered to own all of the property held by X and is engaged in the activity of holding real property through X. X borrows $500 and uses the proceeds to purchase additional real property that is used in the activity of holding real property. X is personally liable to repay the financing, but A is not personally liable for repayment of the financing under local law. The lender may proceed against all of X's assets if X defaults on the financing.

(ii) X is disregarded so that the assets and liabilities of X are treated as the assets and liabilities of A. However, A is not personally liable for the $500 liability. Provided that the requirements contained in paragraphs (b)(1)(i), (ii), and (iv) of this section are satisfied, the financing will be treated as qualified nonrecourse financing secured by real property with respect to A.

(c) *Effective date.* This section is effective for any financing incurred on or after August 4, 1998. Taxpayers, however, may apply this section retroactively for financing incurred before August 4, 1998. [Reg. § 1.465-27.]

☐ [*T.D. 8777,* 8-3-98.]

§ 1.469-5T. Material participation (temporary).—(a) *In general.* Except as provided in paragraphs (e) and ((h)(2) of this section, an individual shall be treated, for purposes of section 469 and the regulations thereunder, as materially participating in an activity for the taxable year if and only if—

(1) The individual participates in the activity for more than 500 hours during such year;

(2) The individual's participation in the activity for the taxable year constitutes substantially all of the participation in such activity of all individuals (including individuals who are not owners of interests in the activity) for such year;

(3) The individual participates in the activity for more than 100 hours during the taxable year, and such individual's participation in the activity for the taxable year is not less than the participation in the activity of any other individual (including individuals who are not owners of interests in the activity) for such year;

(4) The activity is a significant participation activity (within the meaning of paragraph (c) of this section) for the taxable year, and the individual's aggregate participation in all significant participation activities during such year exceeds 500 hours;

(5) The individual materially participated in the activity (determined without regard to this

paragraph (a)(5)) for any five taxable years (whether or not consecutive) during the ten taxable years that immediately precede the taxable year;

(6) The activity is a personal service activity (within the meaning of paragraph (d) of this section), and the individual materially participated in the activity for any three taxable years (whether or not consecutive) preceding the taxable year; or

(7) Based on all of the facts and circumstances (taking into account the rules in paragraph (b) of this section), the individual participates in the activity on a regular, continuous, and substantial basis during such year.

(b) *Facts and circumstances*—(1) *In general.* [Reserved.]

(2) *Certain participation insufficient to constitute material participation under this paragraph (b)*—(i) *Participation satisfying standards not contained in section 469.* Except as provided in section 469(h)(3) and paragraph (h)(2) of this section (relating to certain retired individuals and surviving spouses in the case of farming activities), the fact that an individual satisfies the requirements of any participation standard (whether or not referred to as "material participation") under any provision (including sections 1402 and 2032A and the regulations thereunder) other than section 469 and the regulations thereunder shall not be taken into account in determining whether such individual materially participates in any activity for any taxable year for purposes of section 469 and the regulations thereunder.

(ii) *Certain management activities.* An individual's services performed in the management of an activity shall not be taken into account in determining whether such individual is treated as materially participating in such activity for the taxable year under paragraph (a)(7) of this section unless, for such taxable year—

(A) No person (other than such individual) who performs services in connection with the management of the activity receives compensation described in section 911(d)(2)(A) in consideration for such services; and

(B) No individual performs services in connection with the management of the activity that exceed (by hours) the amount of such services performed by such individual.

(iii) *Participation less than 100 hours.* If an individual participates in an activity for 100 hours or less during the taxable year, such individual shall not be treated as materially participating in such activity for the taxable year under paragraph (a)(7) of this section.

(c) *Significant participation activity*—(1) *In general.* For purposes of paragraph (a)(4) of this section, an activity is a significant participation activity of an individual if and only if such activity—

(i) Is a trade or business activity (within the meaning of § 1.469-1T(e)(2)) in which the individual significantly participates for the taxable year; and

(ii) Would be an activity in which the individual does not materially participate for the taxable year if material participation for such year were determined without regard to paragraph (a)(4) of this section.

(2) *Significant participation.* An individual is treated as significantly participating in an activity for a taxable year if and only if the individual participates in the activity for more than 100 hours during such year.

(d) *Personal service activity.* An activity constitutes a personal service activity for purposes of paragraph (a)(6) of this section if such activity involves the performance of personal services in—

(1) The fields of health, law, engineering, architecture, accounting, actuarial science, performing arts, or consulting; or

(2) Any other trade or business in which capital is not a material income-producing factor.

(e) *Treatment of limited partners*—(1) *General rule.* Except as otherwise provided in this paragraph (e), an individual shall not be treated as materially participating in any activity of a limited partnership for purposes of applying section 469 and the regulations thereunder to—

(i) The individual's share of any income, gain, loss, deduction, or credit from such activity that is attributable to a limited partnership interest in the partnership; and

(ii) Any gain or loss from such activity recognized upon a sale or exchange of such an interest.

(2) *Exceptions.* Paragraph (e)(1) of this section shall not apply to an individual's share of income, gain, loss, deduction, and credit for a taxable year from any activity in which the individual would be treated as materially participating for the taxable year under paragraph (a)(1), (5) or (6) of this section if the individual were not a limited partner for such taxable year.

(3) *Limited partnership interest*—(i) *In general.* Except as provided in paragraph (e)(3)(ii) of this section, for purposes of section 469(h)(2) and this paragraph (e), a partnership interest shall be treated as a limited partnership interest if—

(A) Such interest is designated a limited partnership interest in the limited partnership agreement or the certificate of limited partnership, without regard to whether the liability of the holder of such interest for obligations of the partnership is limited under the applicable State law; or

(B) The liability of the holder of such interest for obligations of the partnership is limited, under the law of the State in which the partnership is organized, to a determinable fixed amount (for example, the sum of the holder's capital contributions to the partnership and contractual obligations to make additional capital contributions to the partnership).

(ii) *Limited partner holding general partner interest.* A partnership interest of an individual shall not be treated as a limited partnership interest for the individual's taxable year if the individual is a general partner in the partnership at all times during the partnership's taxable year ending with or within the individual's taxable year (or portion of the partnership's taxable year during which the individual (directly or indirectly) owns such limited partnership interest).

(f) *Participation*—(1) [Reserved] See § 1.469-5(f)(1) for rules relating to this paragraph.

(2) *Exceptions*—(i) *Certain work not customarily done by owners.* Work done in connection with an activity shall not be treated as participation in the activity for purposes of this section if—

(A) Such work is not of a type that is customarily done by an owner of such an activity; and

(B) One of the principal purposes for the performance of such work is to avoid the disallowance, under section 469 and the regulations thereunder, of any loss or credit from such activity.

(ii) *Participation as an investor*—(A) *In general.* Work done by an individual in the individual's capacity as an investor in an activity shall not be treated as participation in the activity for purposes of this section unless the individual is directly involved in the day-to-day management or operations of the activity.

(B) *Work done in individual's capacity as an investor.* For purposes of this paragraph (f)(2)(ii), work done by an individual in the individual's capacity as an investor in an activity includes—

(1) Studying and reviewing financial statements or reports on operations of the activity;

(2) Preparing or compiling summaries or analyses of the finances or operations of the activity for the individual's own use; and

(3) Monitoring the finances or operations of the activity in a non-managerial capacity.

(3) *Participation of spouse.* In the case of any person who is a married individual (within the meaning of section 7703) for the taxable year, any participation by such person's spouse in the activity during the taxable year (without regard to whether the spouse owns an interest in the activity and without regard to whether the spouses file a joint return for the taxable year) shall be treated, for purposes of applying section 469 and the regulations thereunder to such person, as participation by such person in the activity during the taxable year.

(4) *Methods of proof.* The extent of an individual's participation in an activity may be established by any reasonable means. Contemporaneous daily time reports, logs, or similar documents are not required if the extent of such participation may be established by other reasonable means. Reasonable means for purposes of this paragraph may include but are not limited to the identification of services performed over a period of time and the approximate number of hours spent performing such services during such period, based on appointment books, calendars, or narrative summaries.

* * *

[Temporary Reg. § 1.469-5T.]

☐ [*T.D.* 8175, 2-19-88. *Amended by T.D.* 8253, 5-11-89 *and T.D.* 8417, 5-11-92.]

§ 1.471-1. Need for inventories.—In order to reflect taxable income correctly, inventories at the beginning and end of each taxable year are necessary in every case in which the production, purchase, or sale of merchandise is an income-producing factor. The inventory should include all finished or partly finished goods and, in the case of raw materials and supplies, only those which have been acquired for sale or which will physically become a part of merchandise intended for sale, in which class fall containers, such as kegs, bottles, and cases, whether returnable or not, if title thereto will pass to the purchaser of the product to be sold therein. Merchandise should be included in the inventory only if title thereto is vested in the taxpayer. Accordingly, the seller should include in his inventory goods under contract for sale but not yet segregated and applied to the contract and goods out upon consignment, but should exclude from inventory goods sold (including containers) title to which has passed to the purchaser. A purchaser should include in inventory merchandise purchased (including containers), title to which has passed to him, although such merchandise is in transit or for other reasons has not been reduced to physical possession, but should not include goods ordered for future delivery, transfer of title to which has

Reg. § 1.471-1

not yet been effected. (But see § 1.472-1.) [Reg. § 1.471-1.]

☐ [*T.D. 6336, 12-1-58.*]

§ **1.471-2. Valuation of inventories.**—(a) Section 471 provides two tests to which each inventory must conform:

(1) It must conform as nearly as may be to the best accounting practice in the trade or business, and

(2) It must clearly reflect the income.

(b) It follows, therefore, that inventory rules cannot be uniform but must give effect to trade customs which come within the scope of the best accounting practice in the particular trade or business. In order clearly to reflect income, the inventory practice of a taxpayer should be consistent from year to year, and greater weight is to be given to consistency than to any particular method of inventorying or basis of valuation so long as the method or basis used is in accord with §§ 1.471-1 through 1.471-11.

(c) The bases of valuation most commonly used by business concerns and which meet the requirements of section 471 are (1) cost and (2) cost or market, whichever is lower. (For inventories by dealers in securities, see § 1.471-5.) Any goods in an inventory which are unsalable at normal prices or unusable in the normal way because of damage, imperfections, shop wear, changes of style, odd or broken lots, or other similar causes, including secondhand goods taken in exchange, should be valued at bona fide selling prices less direct cost of disposition, whether subparagraph (1) or (2) of this paragraph is used, or if such goods consist of raw materials or partly finished goods held for use or consumption, they shall be valued upon a reasonable basis, taking into consideration the usability and the condition of the goods, but in no case shall such value be less than the scrap value. Bona fide selling price means actual offering of goods during a period ending not later than 30 days after inventory date. The burden of proof will rest upon the taxpayer to show that such exceptional goods as are valued upon such selling basis come within the classifications indicated above, and he shall maintain such records of the disposition of the goods as will enable a verification of the inventory to be made.

(d) In respect of normal goods, whichever method is adopted must be applied with reasonable consistency to the entire inventory of the taxpayer's trade or business except as to those goods inventoried under the last-in, first-out method authorized by section 472 or to animals inventoried under the elective unit-livestock-price-method authorized by § 1.471-6. See paragraph (d) of § 1.446-1 for rules permitting the use of different methods of accounting if the taxpayer has more than one trade or business. Where the taxpayer is engaged in more than one trade or business the Commissioner may require that the method of valuing inventories with respect to goods in one trade or business also be used with respect to similar goods in other trades or businesses if, in the opinion of the Commissioner, the use of such method with respect to such other goods is essential to a clear reflection of income. Taxpayers were given an option to adopt the basis of either (1) cost or (2) cost or market, whichever is lower, for their 1920 inventories. The basis properly adopted for that year or any subsequent year is controlling, and a change can now be made only after permission is secured from the Commissioner. Application for permission to change the basis of valuing inventories shall be made in writing and filed with the Commissioner as provided in paragraph (e) of § 1.446-1. Goods taken in the inventory which have been so intermingled that they cannot be identified with specific invoices will be deemed to be the goods most recently purchased or produced, and the cost thereof will be the actual cost of the goods purchased or produced during the period in which the quantity of goods in the inventory has been acquired. But see section 472 as to last-in, first-out inventories. Where the taxpayer maintains book inventories in accordance with a sound accounting system in which the respective inventory accounts are charged with the actual cost of the goods purchased or produced and credited with the value of goods used, transferred, or sold, calculated upon the basis of the actual cost of the goods acquired during the taxable year (including the inventory at the beginning of the year), the net value as shown by such inventory accounts will be deemed to be the cost of the goods on hand. The balances shown by such book inventories should be verified by physical inventories at reasonable intervals and adjusted to conform therewith.

(e) Inventories should be recorded in a legible manner, properly computed and summarized, and should be preserved as a part of the accounting records of the taxpayer. The inventories of taxpayers on whatever basis taken will be subject to investigation by the district director, and the taxpayer must satisfy the district director of the correctness of the prices adopted.

(f) The following methods, among others, are sometimes used in taking or valuing inventories, but are not in accord with the regulations in this part:

(1) Deducting from the inventory a reserve for price changes, or an estimated depreciation in the value thereof.

(2) Taking work in process, or other parts of the inventory, at a nominal price or at less than its proper value.

(3) Omitting portions of the stock on hand.

(4) Using a constant price or nominal value for so-called normal quantity of materials or goods in stock.

(5) Including stock in transit, shipped either to or from the taxpayer, the title to which is not vested in the taxpayer.

(6) Segregating indirect production costs into fixed and variable production cost classifications (as defined in § 1.471-11(b)(3)(ii)) and allocating only the variable costs to the cost of goods produced while treating fixed costs as period costs which are currently deductible. This method is commonly referred to as the "direct cost" method.

(7) Treating all or substantially all indirect production costs (whether classified as fixed or variable) as period costs which are currently deductible. This method is generally referred to as the "prime cost" method. [Reg. § 1.471-2.]

□ [*T.D.* 6336, 12-1-58. *Amended by T.D.* 7285, 9-14-73.]

§ 1.471-3. Inventories at cost.—Cost means:

(a) In the case of merchandise on hand at the beginning of the taxable year, the inventory price of such goods.

(b) In the case of merchandise purchased since the beginning of the taxable year, the invoice price less trade or other discounts, except strictly cash discounts approximating a fair interest rate, which may be deducted or not at the option of the taxpayer, provided a consistent course is followed. To this net invoice price should be added transportation or other necessary charges incurred in acquiring possession of the goods. For taxpayers acquiring merchandise for resale that are subject to the provisions of section 263A, see § § 1.263A-1 and 1.263A-3 for additional amounts that must be included in inventory costs.

(c) In the case of merchandise produced by the taxpayer since the beginning of the taxable year, (1) the cost of raw materials and supplies entering into or consumed in connection with the product, (2) expenditures for direct labor, and (3) indirect production costs incident to and necessary for the production of the particular article, including in such indirect production costs an appropriate portion of management expenses, but not including any cost of selling or return on capital, whether by way of interest or profit. See § § 1.263A-1 and 1.263A-2 for more specific rules regarding the treatment of production costs.

(d) In any industry in which the usual rules for computation of cost of production are inapplicable, costs may be approximated upon such basis as may be reasonable and in conformity with established trade practice in the particular industry. Among such cases are: (1) Farmers and raisers of livestock (see § 1.471-6); (2) miners and manufacturers who by a single process or uniform series of processes derive a product of two or more kinds, sizes, or grades, the unit cost of which is substantially alike (see § 1.471-7); and (3) retail merchants who use what is known as the "retail method" in ascertaining approximate cost (see § 1.471-8).

Notwithstanding the other rules of this section, cost shall not include an amount which is of a type for which a deduction would be disallowed under section 162(c), (f), or (g) and the regulations thereunder in the case of a business expense. [Reg. § 1.471-3.]

□ [*T.D.* 6336, 12-1-58. *Amended by T.D.* 7285, 9-14-73; *T.D.* 7345, 2-19-75; *T.D.* 8131, 3-24-87 *and T.D.* 8482, 8-6-93.]

§ 1.471-4. Inventories at cost or market, whichever is lower.—(a) *In general*—(1) *Market definition.* Under ordinary circumstances and for normal goods in an inventory, *market* means the aggregate of the current bid prices prevailing at the date of the inventory of the basic elements of cost reflected in inventories of goods purchased and on hand, goods in process of manufacture, and finished manufactured goods on hand. The basic elements of cost include direct materials, direct labor, and indirect costs required to be included in inventories by the taxpayer (e.g., under section 263A and its underlying regulations for taxpayers subject to that section). For taxpayers to which section 263A applies, for example, the basic elements of cost must reflect all direct costs and all indirect costs properly allocable to goods on hand at the inventory date at the current bid price of those costs, including but not limited to the cost of purchasing, handling, and storage activities conducted by the taxpayer, both prior to and subsequent to acquisition or production of the goods. The determination of the current bid price of the basic elements of costs reflected in goods on hand at the inventory date must be based on the usual volume of particular cost elements purchased (or incurred) by the taxpayer.

(2) *Fixed price contracts.* Paragraph (a)(1) of this section does not apply to any goods on hand or in process of manufacture for delivery upon firm sales contracts (i.e., those not legally subject to cancellation by either party) at fixed prices entered into before the date of the inventory, under which the taxpayer is protected against actual loss. Any such goods must be inventoried at cost.

Reg. § 1.471-4(a)(2)

(3) *Examples.* The valuation principles in paragraph (a)(1) of this section are illustrated by the following examples:

Example 1. (i) Taxpayer A manufactures tractors. A values its inventory using cost or mar-

Direct materials	$ 3,000
Direct labor	4,000
Indirect costs under section 263A	3,000
Total section 263A costs (cost)	$10,000

(ii) A determines that the aggregate of the current bid prices of the materials, labor, and overhead required to reproduce the tractor at the end of 1994 are as follows:

Direct materials	$ 3,100
Direct labor	4,100
Indirect costs under section 263A	3,100
Total section 263A costs (market)	$10,300

(iii) In determining the lower of cost or market value of the tractor, A compares the cost of the tractor, $10,000, with the market value of the tractor, $10,300, in accordance with paragraph (c) of this section. Thus, under this section, A values the tractor at $10,000.

Example 2. (i) Taxpayer B purchases and resells several lines of shoes and is subject to section 263A. B values its inventory using cost or market, whichever is lower, under paragraph (a)(1) of this section. At the end of 1994, the cost of one pair of shoes on hand is determined as follows:

Acquisition cost	$200
Indirect costs under section 263A	10
Total section 263A costs (cost)	$210

(ii) B determines the aggregate current bid prices prevailing at the end of 1994 for the elements of cost (both direct costs and indirect costs incurred prior and subsequent to acquisition of the shoes) based on the volume of the elements usually purchased (or incurred) by B as follows:

Acquisition cost	$178
Indirect costs under section 263A	12
Total [section] 263A costs (market)	$190

(iii) In determining the lower of cost or market value of the shoes, B compares the cost of the pair of shoes, $210, with the market value of the shoes, $190, in accordance with paragraph (c) of this section. Thus, under this section, B values the shoes at $190.

(b) *Inactive markets.* Where no open market exists or where quotations are nominal, due to inactive market conditions, the taxpayer must use such evidence of a fair market price at the date or dates nearest the inventory as may be available, such as specific purchases or sales by the taxpayer or others in reasonable volume and made in good faith, or compensation paid for cancellation of contracts for purchase commitments. Where the taxpayer in the regular course of business has offered for sale such merchandise at prices lower than the current price as above defined, the inventory may be valued at such prices less direct cost of disposition, and the correctness of such prices will be determined by reference to the actual sales of the taxpayer for a reasonable period before and after the date of the inventory. Prices which vary materially from the actual prices so ascertained will not be accepted as reflecting the market.

(c) *Comparison of cost and market.* Where the inventory is valued upon the basis of cost or market, whichever is lower, the market value of each article on hand at the inventory date shall be compared with the cost of the article, and the lower of such values shall be taken as the inventory value of the article.

* * *

[Reg. § 1.471-4.]

☐ [*T.D.* 6336, 12-1-58. *Amended by T.D.* 8482, 8-6-93.]

§ 1.471-5. **Inventories by dealers in securities.**—A dealer in securities who in his books of account regularly inventories unsold securities on hand either—

(a) At cost,

(b) At cost or market, whichever is lower, or

(c) At market value,

may make his return upon the basis upon which his accounts are kept, provided that a description of the method employed is included in or attached to the return, that all the securities are inventoried by the same method, and that such method is adhered to in subsequent years, unless another method is authorized by the Commissioner pursuant to a written application therefor filed as provided in paragraph (e) of § 1.446-1. A dealer in securities in whose books of account separate computations of the gain or loss from the sale of the various lots of securities sold are made on the basis of the cost of each lot shall be regarded, for the purposes of this section, as regularly inventorying his securities at cost. For the purposes of this section, a dealer in securities is a merchant of securities, whether an individual, partnership, or corporation, with an established place of business,

regularly engaged in the purchase of securities and their resale to customers; that is, one who as a merchant buys securities and sells them to customers with a view to the gains and profits that may be derived therefrom. If such business is simply a branch of the activities carried on by such person, the securities inventoried as provided in this section may include only those held for purposes of resale and not for investment. Taxpayers who buy and sell or hold securities for investment or speculation, irrespective of whether such buying or selling constitutes the carrying on of a trade or business, and officers of corporations and members of partnerships who in their individual capacities buy and sell securities, are not dealers in securities within the meaning of this section. See § § 1.263A-1 and 1.263A-3 for rules regarding the treatment of costs with respect to property acquired for resale. [Reg. § 1.471-5.]

☐ [*T.D. 6336, 12-1-58. Amended by T.D. 8131, 3-24-87 and T.D. 8482, 8-6-93.*]

Adjustments

§ 1.482-1. Allocation of income and deductions among taxpayers.—(a) *In general*—(1) *Purpose and scope.* The purpose of section 482 is to ensure that taxpayers clearly reflect income attributable to controlled transactions, and to prevent the avoidance of taxes with respect to such transactions. Section 482 places a controlled taxpayer on a tax parity with an uncontrolled taxpayer by determining the true taxable income of the controlled taxpayer. This § 1.482-1 sets forth general principles and guidelines to be followed under section 482. Section 1.482-2 provides rules for the determination of the true taxable income of controlled taxpayers in specific situations, including controlled transactions involving loans or advances, services, and property. Sections 1.482-3 through 1.482-6 elaborate on the rules that apply to controlled transactions involving property. Section 1.482-7T sets forth the cost sharing provisions. Finally, § 1.482-8 provides examples illustrating the application of the best method rule.

(2) *Authority to make allocations.* The district director may make allocations between or among the members of a controlled group if a controlled taxpayer has not reported its true taxable income. In such case, the district director may allocate income, deductions, credits, allowances, basis, or any other item or element affecting taxable income (referred to as allocations). The appropriate allocation may take the form of an increase or decrease in any relevant amount.

(3) *Taxpayer's use of section 482.* If necessary to reflect an arm's length result, a controlled taxpayer may report on a timely filed U.S. income

tax return (including extensions) the results of its controlled transactions based upon prices different from those actually charged. Except as provided in this paragraph, section 482 grants no other right to a controlled taxpayer to apply the provisions of section 482 at will or to compel the district director to apply such provisions. Therefore, no untimely or amended returns will be permitted to decrease taxable income based on allocations or other adjustments with respect to controlled transactions. See § 1.6662-6T(a)(2) or successor regulations.

(b) *Arm's length standard*—(1) *In general.* In determining the true taxable income of a controlled taxpayer, the standard to be applied in every case is that of a taxpayer dealing at arm's length with an uncontrolled taxpayer. A controlled transaction meets the arm's length standard if the results of the transaction are consistent with the results that would have been realized if uncontrolled taxpayers had engaged in the same transaction under the same circumstances (arm's length result). However, because identical transactions can rarely be located, whether a transaction produces an arm's length result generally will be determined by reference to the results of comparable transactions under comparable circumstances. See § 1.482-1(d)(2) (Standard of comparability). Evaluation of whether a controlled transaction produces an arm's length result is made pursuant to a method selected under the best method rule described in § 1.482-1(c).

(2) *Arm's length methods*—(i) *Methods.* Sections 1.482-2 through 1.482-6 provide specific

methods to be used to evaluate whether transactions between or among members of the controlled group satisfy the arm's length standard, and if they do not, to determine the arm's length result.

(ii) *Selection of category of method applicable to transaction.* The methods listed in § 1.482-2 apply to different types of transactions, such as transfers of property, services, loans or advances, and rentals. Accordingly, the method or methods most appropriate to the calculation of arm's length results for controlled transactions must be selected, and different methods may be applied to interrelated transactions if such transactions are most reliably evaluated on a separate basis. For example, if services are provided in connection with the transfer of property, it may be appropriate to separately apply the methods applicable to services and property in order to determine an arm's length result. But see § 1.482-1(f)(2)(i) (Aggregation of transactions). In addition, other applicable provisions of the Code may affect the characterization of a transaction, and therefore affect the methods applicable under section 482. See for example section 467.

(c) *Best method rule*—(1) *In general.* The arm's length result of a controlled transaction must be determined under the method that, under the facts and circumstances, provides the most reliable measure of an arm's length result. Thus, there is no strict priority of methods, and no method will invariably be considered to be more reliable than others. An arm's length result may be determined under any method without establishing the inapplicability of another method, but if another method subsequently is shown to produce a more reliable measure of an arm's length result, such other method must be used. Similarly, if two or more applications of a single method provide inconsistent results, the arm's length result must be determined under the application that, under the facts and circumstances, provides the most reliable measure of an arm's length result. See § 1.482-8 for examples of the application of the best method rule.

(2) *Determining the best method.* Data based on the results of transactions between unrelated parties provides the most objective basis for determining whether the results of a controlled transaction are arm's length. Thus, in determining which of two or more available methods (or applications of a single method) provides the most reliable measure of an arm's length result, the two primary factors to take into account are the degree of comparability between the controlled transaction (or taxpayer) and any uncontrolled comparables, and the quality of the data and assumptions used in the analysis. In addition, in certain circumstances, it also may be relevant to consider whether the results of an analysis are consistent with the results of an analysis under another method. These factors are explained in paragraphs (c)(2)(i), (ii), and (iii) of this section.

* * *

[Reg. § 1.482-1.]

☐ [*T.D.* 8552, 7-1-94.]

§ 1.483-1. Interest on certain deferred payments.—(a) *Amount constituting interest in certain deferred payment transactions*—(1) *In general.* Except as provided in paragraph (c) of this section, section 483 applies to a contract for the sale or exchange of property if the contract provides for one or more payments due more than 1 year after the date of the sale or exchange, and the contract does not provide for adequate stated interest. In general, a contract has adequate stated interest if the contract provides for a stated rate of interest that is at least equal to the test rate (determined under § 1.483-3) and the interest is paid or compounded at least annually. Section 483 may apply to a contract whether the contract is express (written or oral) or implied. For purposes of section 483, a sale or exchange is any transaction treated as a sale or exchange for tax purposes. In addition, for purposes of section 483, property includes debt instruments and investment units, but does not include money, services, or the right to use property. For the treatment of certain obligations given in exchange for services or the use of property, see sections 404 and 467. For purposes of this paragraph (a), money includes functional currency and, in certain circumstances, nonfunctional currency. See § 1.988-2(b)(2) for circumstances when nonfunctional currency is treated as money rather than as property.

(2) *Treatment of contracts to which section 483 applies*—(i) *Treatment of unstated interest.* If section 483 applies to a contract, unstated interest under the contract is treated as interest for tax purposes. Thus, for example, unstated interest is not treated as part of the amount realized from the sale or exchange of property (in the case of the seller), and is not included in the purchaser's basis in the property acquired in the sale or exchange.

(ii) *Method of accounting for interest on contracts subject to section 483.* Any stated or unstated interest on a contract subject to section 483 is taken into account by a taxpayer under the taxpayer's regular method of accounting (e.g., an accrual method or the cash receipts and disbursements method). See §§ 1.446-1, 1.451-1, and 1.461-1. For purposes of the preceding sentence, the amount of interest (including unstated interest) allocable to a payment under a contract to which section 483 applies is determined under § 1.446-2(e).

Reg. § 1.483-1(a)(1)

(b) *Definitions*—(1) *Deferred payments.* For purposes of the regulations under section 483, a deferred payment means any payment that constitutes all or a part of the sales price (as defined in paragraph (b)(2) of this section), and that is due more than 6 months after the date of the sale or exchange. Except as provided in section 483(c)(2) (relating to the treatment of a debt instrument of the purchaser), a payment may be made in the form of cash, stock or securities, or other property.

(2) *Sales price.* For purposes of section 483, the sales price for any sale or exchange is the sum of the amount due under the contract (other than stated interest) and the amount of any liability included in the amount realized from the sale or exchange. See § 1.1001-2. Thus, the sales price for any sale or exchange includes any amount of unstated interest under the contract.

(c) *Exceptions to and limitations on the application of section 483*—(1) *In general.* Sections 483(d), 1274(c)(4), and 1275(b) contain exceptions to and limitations on the application of section 483.

(2) *Sales price of $3,000 or less.* Section 483(d)(2) applies only if it can be determined at the time of the sale or exchange that the sales price cannot exceed $3,000, regardless of whether the sales price eventually paid for the property is less than $3,000.

(3) *Other exceptions and limitations*—(i) *Certain transfers subject to section 1041.* Section 483 does not apply to any transfer of property subject to section 1041 (relating to transfers of property between spouses or incident to divorce).

(ii) *Treatment of certain obligees.* Section 483 does not apply to an obligee under a contract for the sale or exchange of personal use property (within the meaning of section 1275(b)(3)) in the hands of the obligor and that evidences a below-market loan described in section 7872(c)(1).

(iii) *Transactions involving certain demand loans.* Section 483 does not apply to any payment under a contract that evidences a demand loan that is a below-market loan described in section 7872(c)(1).

(iv) *Transactions involving certain annuity contracts.* Section 483 does not apply to any payment under an annuity contract described in section 1275(a)(1)(B) (relating to annuity contracts excluded from the definition of debt instrument).

(v) *Options.* Section 483 does not apply to any payment under an option to buy or sell property.

(d) *Assumptions.* If a debt instrument is assumed, or property is taken subject to a debt instrument, in connection with a sale or exchange of property, the debt instrument is treated for purposes of section 483 in a manner consistent with the rules of § 1.1274-5.

(e) *Aggregation rule.* For purposes of section 483, all sales or exchanges that are part of the same transaction (or a series of related transactions) are treated as a single sale or exchange and all contracts calling for deferred payments arising from the same transaction (or a series of related transactions) are treated as a single contract. This rule, however, generally only applies to contracts and to sales or exchanges involving a single buyer and a single seller.

* * *

[Reg. § 1.483-1.]

☐ [*T.D.* 6873, 1-24-66. *Amended by T.D.* 7154, 12-27-71; *T.D.* 7394, 12-31-75; *T.D.* 7781, 7-1-81 and *T.D.* 8517, 1-27-94.]

§ 1.483-2. **Unstated interest.**—(a) *In general*—(1) *Adequate stated interest.* For purposes of section 483, a contract has unstated interest if the contract does not provide for adequate stated interest. A contract does not provide for adequate stated interest if the sum of the deferred payments exceeds—

(i) The sum of the present values of the deferred payments and the present values of any stated interest payments due under the contract; or

(ii) In the case of a cash method debt instrument (within the meaning of section 1274A(c)(2)) received in exchange for property in a potentially abusive situation (as defined in § 1.1274-3), the fair market value of the property reduced by the fair market value of any consideration other than the debt instrument, and reduced by the sum of all principal payments that are not deferred payments.

(2) *Amount of unstated interest.* For purposes of section 483, unstated interest means an amount equal to the excess of the sum of the deferred payments over the amount described in paragraph (a)(1)(i) or (a)(1)(ii) of this section, whichever is applicable.

(b) *Operational rules*—(1) *In general.* For purposes of paragraph (a) of this section, rules similar to those in § 1.1274-2 apply to determine whether a contract has adequate stated interest and the amount of unstated interest, if any, on the contract.

(2) *Present value.* For purposes of paragraph (a) of this section, the present value of any deferred payment or interest payment is determined by discounting the payment from the date it becomes due to the date of the sale or exchange at

Reg. § 1.483-2(b)(2)

the test rate of interest applicable to the contract in accordance with § 1.483-3.

(c) *Examples.* The following examples illustrate the rules of this section.

Example 1. Contract that does not have adequate stated interest. On January 1, 1995, A sells B nonpublicly traded property under a contract that calls for a $100,000 payment of principal on January 1, 2005, and 10 annual interest payments of $9,000 on January 1 of each year, beginning on January 1, 1996. Assume that the test rate of interest is 9.2 percent, compounded annually. The contract does not provide for adequate stated interest because it does not provide for interest equal to 9.2 percent, compounded annually. The present value of the deferred payments is $98,727.69. As a result, the contract has unstated interest of $1,272.31 ($100,000 − $98,727.69)

Example 2. Contract that does not have adequate stated interest; no interest for initial short period. On May 1, 1996, A sells B nonpublicly traded property under a contract that calls for B to make a principal payment of $200,000 on December 31, 1998, and semiannual interest payments of $9,000, payable on June 30 and December 31 of each year, beginning on December 31, 1996. Assume that the test rate of interest is 9 percent, compounded semiannually. Even though the contract calls for a stated rate of interest no lower than the test rate of interest, the contract does not provide for adequate stated interest because the stated rate of interest does not apply for the short period from May 1, 1996, through June 30, 1996.

Example 3. Potentially abusive situation—(i) *Facts.* In a potentially abusive situation, a contract for the sale of nonpublicly traded personal property calls for the issuance of a cash method debt instrument (as defined in section 1274A(c)(2)) with a stated principal amount of $700,000, payable in 5 years. No other consideration is given. The debt instrument calls for annual payments of interest over its entire term at a rate of 9.2 percent, compounded annually (the test rate of interest applicable to the debt instrument). Thus, the present value of the deferred payment and the interest payments is $700,000. Assume that the fair market value of the properly is $500,000.

(ii) *Amount of unstated interest.* A cash method debt instrument received in exchange for property in a potentially abusive situation provides for adequate stated interest only if the sum of the deferred payments under the instrument does not exceed the fair market value of the property. Because the deferred payment ($700,000) exceeds the fair market value of the property ($500,000), the debt instrument does not provide for adequate

stated interest. Therefore, the debt instrument has unstated interest of $200,000.

Example 4. Variable rate debt instrument with adequate stated interest; variable rate as of the issue date greater than the test rate—(i) *Facts.* A contract for the sale of nonpublicly traded property calls for the issuance of a debt instrument in the principal amount of $75,000 due in 10 years. The debt instrument calls for interest payable semiannually at a rate of 3 percentage points above the yield on 6-month Treasury bills at the mid-point of the semiannual period immediately preceding each interest payment date. Assume that the interest rate is a qualified floating rate and that the debt instrument is a variable rate debt instrument within the meaning of § 1.1275-5.

(ii) *Adequate stated interest.* Under paragraph (b)(1) of this section, rules similar to those in § 1.1274-2(f) apply to determine whether the debt instrument has adequate stated interest. Assume that the test rate of interest applicable to the debt instrument is 9 percent, compounded semiannually. Assume also that the yield on 6-month Treasury bills on the date of the sale is 8.89 percent, which is greater than the yield on 6-month Treasury bills on the first date on which there is a binding written contract that substantially sets forth the terms under which the sale is consummated. Under § 1.1274-2(f), the debt instrument is tested for adequate stated interest as if it provided for a stated rate of interest of 11.89 percent (3 percent plus 8.89 percent), compounded semiannually, payable over its entire term. Because the test rate of interest is 9 percent, compounded semiannually, and the debt instrument is treated as providing for stated interest of 11.89 percent, compounded semiannually, the debt instrument provides for adequate stated interest.

* * *

[Reg. § 1.483-2.]

☐ [*T.D.* 6873, 1-24-66. *Amended by T.D.* 8517, 1-27-94.]

§ 1.483-3. Test rate of interest applicable to a contract.—(a) *General rule.* For purposes of section 483, the test rate of interest for a contract is the same as the test rate that would apply under § 1.1274-4 if the contract were a debt instrument. Paragraph (b) of this section, however, provides for a lower test rate in the case of certain sales or exchanges of land between related individuals.

(b) *Lower rate for certain sales or exchanges of land between related individuals*—(1) *Test rate.* In the case of a qualified sale or exchange of land between related individuals (described in section 483(e)), the test rate is not greater than 6 percent, compounded semiannually, or an equivalent rate based on an appropriate compounding period.

Reg. § 1.483-3(a)

(2) *Special rules.* The following rules and definitions apply in determining whether a sale or exchange is a qualified sale under section 483(e):

(i) *Definition of family members.* The members of an individual's family are determined as of the date of the sale or exchange. The members of an individual's family include those individuals described in section 267(c)(4) and the spouses of those individuals. In addition, for purposes of section 267(c)(4), full effect is given to a legal adoption, ancestor means parents and grandparents, and lineal descendants means children and grandchildren.

(ii) *$500,000 limitation.* Section 483(e) does not apply to the extent that the stated principal amount of the debt instrument issued in the sale or exchange, when added to the aggregate stated principal amount of any other debt instruments to which section 483(e) applies that were issued in prior qualified sales between the same two individuals during the same calendar year, exceeds $500,000. See *Example 3* of paragraph (b)(3) of this section.

(iii) *Other limitations.* Section 483(e) does not apply if the parties to a contract include persons other than the related individuals and the parties enter into the contract with an intent to circumvent the purposes of section 483(e). In addition, if the property sold or exchanged includes any property other than land, section 483(e) applies only to the extent that the stated principal amount of the debt instrument issued in the sale or exchange is attributable to the land (based on the relative fair market values of the land and the other property).

(3) *Examples.* The following examples illustrate the rules of this paragraph (b).

Example 1. On January 1, 1995, A sells land to B, A's child, for $650,000. The contract for sale calls for B to make a $250,000 down payment and issue a debt instrument with a stated principal amount of $400,000. Because the stated principal amount of the debt instrument is less than $500,000, the sale is a qualified sale and section 483(e) applies to the debt instrument.

Example 2. The facts are the same as in *Example 1* of paragraph (b)(3) of this section, except that on June 1, 1995, A sells additional land to B under a contract that calls for B to issue a debt instrument with a stated principal amount of $100,000. The stated principal amount of this debt instrument ($100,000) when added to the stated principal amount of the prior debt instrument ($400,000) does not exceed $500,000. Thus, section 483(e) applies to both debt instruments.

Example 3. The facts are the same as in *Example 1* of paragraph (b)(3) of this section, except that on June 1, 1995, A sells additional land to B under a contract that calls for B to issue a debt instrument with a stated principal amount of $150,000. The stated principal amount of this debt instrument when added to the stated principal amount of the prior debt instrument ($400,000) exceeds $500,000. Thus, for purposes of section 483(e), the debt instrument issued in the sale of June 1, 1995, is treated as two separate debt instruments: a $100,000 debt instrument (to which section 483(e) applies) and a $50,000 debt instrument (to which section 1274, if otherwise applicable, applies).

* * *

[Reg. § 1.483-3.]

☐ [*T.D.* 8517, 1-27-94.]

Corporations Improperly Accumulating Surplus

§ 1.537-1. Reasonable needs of the business.—(a) *In general.* The term "reasonable needs of the business" includes (1) the reasonable anticipated needs of the business (including product liability loss reserves, as defined in paragraph (f) of this section), (2) the section 303 redemption needs of the business, as defined in paragraph (c) of this section, and (3) the excess business holdings redemption needs of the business as described in paragraph (d) of this section. See paragraph (e) of this section for additional rules relating to the section 303 redemption needs and the excess business holdings redemption needs of the business. An accumulation of the earnings and profits (including the undistributed earnings and profits of prior years) is in excess of the reasonable needs of the business if it exceeds the amount that a prudent businessman would consider appropriate for the present business purposes and for the reasonably anticipated future needs of the business. The need to retain earnings and profits must be directly connected with the needs of the corporation itself and must be for bona fide business purposes. For purposes of this paragraph the section 303 redemption needs of the business and the excess business holdings redemption needs of the business are deemed to be directly connected with the needs of the business and for a bona fide business purpose. See § 1.537-3 for a discussion of what constitutes the business of the corporation. The extent to which earnings and profits have been distributed by the corporation may be taken into account in determining whether or not retained earnings and profits exceed the reasonable needs of the business. See § 1.537-2, relating to grounds for accumulation of earnings and profits.

(b) *Reasonably anticipated needs.* (1) In order for a corporation to justify an accumulation of earnings and profits for reasonably anticipated future needs, there must be an indication that the future needs of the business require such accumulation, and the corporation must have specific, definite, and feasible plans for the use of such accumulation. Such an accumulation need not be used immediately, nor must the plans for its use be consummated within a short period after the close of the taxable year, provided that such accumulation will be used within a reasonable time depending upon all the facts and circumstances relating to the future needs of the business. Where the future needs of the business are uncertain or vague, where the plans for the future use of an accumulation are not specific, definite, and feasible, or where the execution of such a plan is postponed indefinitely, an accumulation cannot be justified on the grounds of reasonably anticipated needs of the business.

(2) Consideration shall be given to reasonably anticipated needs as they exist on the basis of the facts at the close of the taxable year. Thus, subsequent events shall not be used for the purpose of showing that the retention of earnings or profits was unreasonable at the close of the taxable year if all the elements of reasonable anticipation are present at the close of such taxable year. However, subsequent events may be considered to determine whether the taxpayer actually intended to consummate or has actually consummated the plans for which the earnings and profits were accumulated. In this connection, projected expansion or investment plans shall be reviewed in the light of the facts during each year and as they exist as of the close of the taxable year. If a corporation has justified an accumulation for future needs by plans never consummated, the amount of such an accumulation shall be taken into account in determining the reasonableness of subsequent accumulations.

(c) *Section 303 redemption needs of the business.* (1) The term "section 303 redemption needs" means, with respect to the taxable year of the corporation in which a shareholder of the corporation died or any taxable year thereafter, the amount needed (or reasonably anticipated to be needed) to redeem stock included in the gross estate of such shareholder but not in excess of the amount necessary to effect a distribution to which section 303 applies. For purposes of this paragraph, the term "shareholder" includes an individual in whose gross estate stock of the corporation is includable upon his death for Federal estate tax purposes.

(2) This paragraph applies to a corporation to which section 303(c) would apply if a distribution described therein were made.

(3) If stock included in the gross estate of a decedent is stock of two or more corporations

described in section 303(b)(2)(B), the amount needed by each such corporation for section 303 redemption purposes under this section shall, unless the particular facts and circumstances indicate otherwise, be that amount which bears the same ratio to the amount described in section 303(a) as the fair market value of such corporation's stock included in the gross estate of such decedent bears to the fair market value of all of the stock of such corporations included in the gross estate. For example, facts and circumstances indicating that the allocation prescribed by this subparagraph is not required would include notice given to the corporations by the executor or administrator of the decedent's estate that he intends to request the redemption of stock of only one of such corporations or the redemption of stock of such corporations in a ratio which is unrelated to the respective fair market values of the stock of the corporations included in the decedent's gross estate.

(4) The provisions of this paragraph apply only to taxable years ending after May 26, 1969.

* * *

(e)(1) A determination whether and to what extent an amount is needed (or reasonably anticipated to be needed) for the purpose described in subparagraph (1) of paragraph (c) or (d) of this section is dependent upon the particular circumstances of the case, including the total amount of earnings and profits accumulated in prior years which may be available for such purpose and the existence of a reasonable expectation that a redemption described in paragraph (c) or (d) of this section will in fact be effected. Although paragraph (c) or (d) of this section may apply even though no redemption of stock is in fact effected, the failure to effect such redemption may be taken into account in determining whether the accumulation was needed (or reasonably anticipated to be needed) for a purpose described in paragraph (c) or (d).

(2) In applying subparagraph (1) of paragraph (c) or (d) of this section, the discharge of an obligation incurred to make a redemption shall be treated as the making of the redemption.

(3) In determining whether an accumulation is in excess of the reasonable needs of the business for a particular year, the fact that one of the exceptions specified in paragraph (c) or (d) of this section applies in a subsequent year is not to give rise to an inference that the accumulation would not have been for the reasonable needs of the business in the prior year. Also, no inference is to be drawn from the enactment of section 537(a)(2) and (3) that accumulations in any prior year would not have been for the reasonable needs of the business in the absence of such provisions.

Thus, the reasonableness of accumulations in years prior to a year in which one of the exceptions specified in paragraph (c) or (d) of this section applies is to be determined solely upon the facts and circumstances existing at the times the accumulations occur.

(f) *Product liability loss reserves.* (1) The term "product liability loss reserve" means, with respect to taxable years beginning after September 30, 1979, reasonable amounts accumulated for the payment of reasonably anticipated product liability losses, as defined in section 172(j) and § 1.172-13(b)(1).

(2) For purposes of this paragraph, whether an accumulation for anticipated product liability losses is reasonable in amount and whether such anticipated product liability losses are likely to occur shall be determined in light of all facts and circumstances of the taxpayer making such accumulation. Some of the factors to be considered in determining the reasonableness of the accumulation include the taxpayer's previous product liability experience, the extent of the taxpayer's coverage by commercial product liability insurance, the income tax consequences of the taxpayer's ability to deduct product liability losses and related expenses, and the taxpayer's potential future liability due to defective products in light of the taxpayer's plans to expand the production of products currently being manufactured, provided such plans are specific, definite and feasible. Additionally, a factor to be considered in determining whether the accumulation is reasonable in amount is whether the taxpayer, in accounting for its potential future liability, took into account the reasonably estimated present value of the potential future liability.

(3) Only those accumulations made with respect to products that have been manufactured, leased, or sold shall be considered as accumulations made under this paragraph. Thus, for example, accumulations with respect to a product which has not progressed beyond the development stage are not reasonable accumulations under this paragraph. [Reg. § 1.537-1.]

☐ [*T.D. 6377, 5-12-59. Amended by T.D. 7165, 3-8-72, by T.D. 7678, 2-25-80, and by T.D. 8096, 8-27-86.*]

§ 1.537-2. Grounds for accumulation of earnings and profits.—(a) *In general.* Whether a particular ground or grounds for the accumulation of earnings and profits indicate that the earnings and profits have been accumulated for the reasonable needs of the business or beyond such needs is dependent upon the particular circumstances of the case. Listed below in paragraphs (b) and (c) of this section are some of the grounds which may be used as guides under ordinary circumstances.

(b) *Reasonable accumulation of earnings and profits.* Although the following grounds are not exclusive, one or more of such grounds, if supported by sufficient facts, may indicate that the earnings and profits of a corporation are being accumulated for the reasonable needs of the business provided the general requirements under § § 1.537-1 and 1.537-3 are satisfied:

(1) To provide for bona fide expansion of business or replacement of plant;

(2) To acquire a business enterprise through purchasing stock or assets;

(3) To provide for the retirement of bona fide indebtedness created in connection with the trade or business, such as the establishment of a sinking fund for the purpose of retiring bonds issued by the corporation in accordance with contract obligations incurred on issue;

(4) To provide necessary working capital for the business, such as, for the procurement of inventories;

(5) To provide for investments or loans to suppliers or customers if necessary in order to maintain the business of the corporation; or

(6) To provide for the payment of reasonably anticipated product liability losses, as defined in section 172(j), § 1.172-13(b)(1), and § 1.537-1(f).

(c) *Unreasonable accumulations of earnings and profits.* Although the following purposes are not exclusive, accumulations of earnings and profits to meet any one of such objectives may indicate that the earnings and profits of a corporation are being accumulated beyond the reasonable needs of the business:

(1) Loans to shareholders, or the expenditure of funds of the corporation for the personal benefit of the shareholders;

(2) Loans having no reasonable relation to the conduct of the business made to relatives or friends of shareholders, or to other persons;

(3) Loans to another corporation, the business of which is not that of the taxpayer corporation, if the capital stock of such other corporation is owned, directly or indirectly, by the shareholder or shareholders of the taxpayer corporation and such shareholder or shareholders are in control of both corporations;

(4) Investments in properties, or securities which are unrelated to the activities of the business of the taxpayer corporation; or

(5) Retention of earnings and profits to provide against unrealistic hazards. [Reg. § 1.537-2.]

☐ [*T.D. 6377, 5-12-59. Amended by T.D. 8096, 8-26-86.*]

Reg. § 1.537-2(c)(5)

§ 1.537-3. Business of the corporation.—(a)
The business of a corporation is not merely that which it has previously carried on but includes, in general, any line of business which it may undertake.

(b) If one corporation owns the stock of another corporation and, in effect, operates the other corporation, the business of the latter corporation may be considered in substance, although not in legal form, the business of the first corporation. However, investment by a corporation of its earnings and profits in stock and securities of another corporation is not, of itself, to be regarded as employment of the earnings and profits in its business. Earnings and profits of the first corporation put into the second corporation through the purchase of stock or securities or otherwise, may, if a subsidiary relationship is established, constitute employment of the earnings and profits in its own business. Thus, the business of one corporation may be regarded as including the business of another corporation if such other corporation is a mere instrumentality of the first corporation; that may be established by showing that the first corporation owns at least 80 percent of the voting stock of the second corporation. If the taxpayer's ownership of stock is less than 80 percent in the other corporation, the determination of whether the funds are employed in a business operated by the taxpayer will depend upon the particular circumstances of the case. Moreover, the business of one corporation does not include the business of another corporation if such other corporation is a personal holding company, an investment company, or a corporation not engaged in the active conduct of a trade or business. [Reg. § 1.537-3.]

☐ [*T.D. 6377, 5-12-59.*]

Natural Resources—Deductions

§ 1.611-1. Allowance of deduction for depletion.—(a) *Depletion of mines, oil and gas wells, other natural deposits, and timber*—(1) *In general.* Section 611 provides that there shall be allowed as a deduction in computing taxable income in the case of mines, oil and gas wells, other natural deposits, and timber, a reasonable allowance for depletion. In the case of standing timber, the depletion allowance shall be computed solely upon the adjusted basis of the property. In the case of other exhaustible natural resources the allowance for depletion shall be computed upon either the adjusted depletion basis of the property (see section 612, relating to cost depletion) or upon a percentage of gross income from the property (see section 613, relating to percentage depletion), whichever results in the greater allowance for depletion for any taxable year. In no case will depletion based upon discovery value be allowed.

(2) See § 1.611-5 for methods of depreciation relating to improvements connected with mineral or timber properties.

(3) See paragraph (d) of this section for definition of terms.

(b) *Economic interest.* (1) Annual depletion deductions are allowed only to the owner of an economic interest in mineral deposits or standing timber. An economic interest is possessed in every case in which the taxpayer has acquired by investment any interest in mineral in place or standing timber and secures, by any form of legal relationship, income derived from the extraction of the mineral or severance of the timber, to which he must look for a return of his capital. For an exception in the case of certain mineral production payments, see section 636 and the regulations thereunder. A person who has no capital investment in the mineral deposit or standing timber does not possess an economic interest merely because through a contractual relation he possesses a mere economic or pecuniary advantage derived from production. For example, an agreement between the owner of an economic interest and another entitling the latter to purchase or process the product upon production or entitling the latter to compensation for extraction or cutting does not convey a depletable economic interest. Further, depletion deductions with respect to an economic interest of a corporation are allowed to the corporation and not to its shareholders.

(2) No depletion deduction shall be allowed the owner with respect to any timber, coal, or domestic iron ore that such owner has disposed of under any form of contract by virtue of which he retains an economic interest in such timber, coal, or iron ore, if such disposal is considered a sale of timber, coal, or domestic iron ore under section 631(b) or (c).

(c) *Special rules*—(1) *In general.* For the purpose of the equitable apportionment of depletion among the several owners of economic interests in a mineral deposit or standing timber, if the value of any mineral or timber must be ascertained as of any specific date for the determination of the basis for depletion, the values of such several interests therein may be determined separately, but, when determined as of the same date, shall together never exceed the value at that date of the mineral or timber as a whole.

(2) *Leases.* In the case of a lease, the deduction for depletion under section 611 shall be equitably apportioned between the lessor and lessee. In the case of a lease or other contract providing for the sharing of economic interest in a mineral deposit or standing timber, such deduction shall be computed by each taxpayer by reference to the

adjusted basis of his property determined in accordance with sections 611 and 612, or computed in accordance with section 613, if applicable, and the regulations thereunder.

(3) *Life tenant and remainderman.* In the case of property held by one person for life with remainder to another person, the deduction for depletion under section 611 shall be computed as if the life tenant were the absolute owner of the property so that he will be entitled to the deduction during his life, and thereafter the deduction, if any, shall be allowed to the remainderman.

(4) *Mineral or timber property held in trust.* If a mineral property or timber property is held in trust, the allowable deduction for depletion is to be apportioned between the income beneficiaries and the trustee on the basis of the trust income from such property allocable to each, unless the governing instrument (or local law) requires or permits the trustee to maintain a reserve for depletion in any amount. In the latter case, the deduction is first allocated to the trustee to the extent that income is set aside for a depletion reserve, and any part of the deduction in excess of the income set aside for the reserve shall be apportioned between the income beneficiaries and the trustee on the basis of the trust income (in excess of the income set aside for the reserve) allocable to each. For example:

(i) If under the trust instrument or local law the income of a trust computed without regard to depletion is to be distributed to a named beneficiary, the beneficiary is entitled to the deduction to the exclusion of the trustee.

(ii) If under the trust instrument or local law the income of a trust is to be distributed to a named beneficiary, but the trustee is directed to maintain a reserve for depletion in any amount, the deduction is allowed to the trustee (except to the extent that income set aside for the reserve is less than the allowable deduction). The same result would follow if the trustee sets aside income for a depletion reserve pursuant to discretionary authority to do so in the governing instrument.

No effect shall be given to any allocation of the depletion deduction which gives any beneficiary or the trustee a share of such deduction greater than his pro rata share of the trust income, irrespective of any provisions in the trust instrument, except as otherwise provided in this paragraph when the trust instrument or local law requires or permits the trustee to maintain a reserve for depletion.

(5) *Mineral or timber property held by estate.* In the case of mineral property or timber property held by an estate, the deduction for depletion under section 611 shall be apportioned between the estate and the heirs, legatees, and devisees on the basis of income of the estate from such property which is allocable to each.

(d) *Definitions.* As used in this part, and the regulations thereunder, the term—

(1) "Property" means—(i) in the case of minerals, each separate economic interest owned in each mineral deposit in each separate tract or parcel of land or an aggregation or combination of such mineral interests permitted under section 614(b), (c), (d), or (e); and (ii) in the case of timber, an economic interest in standing timber in each tract or block representing a separate timber account (see paragraph (d) of § 1.611-3). For rules with respect to waste or residue of prior mining, see paragraph (c) of § 1.614-1. When, in the regulations under this part, either the word "mineral" or "timber" precedes the word "property", such adjectives are used only to classify the type of "property" involved. For further explanation of the term "property", see section 614 and the regulations thereunder.

(2) "Fair market value" of a property is that amount which would induce a willing seller to sell and a willing buyer to purchase.

(3) "Mineral enterprise" is the mineral deposit or deposits and improvements, if any, used in mining or in the production of oil and gas and only so much of the surface of the land as is necessary for purposes of mineral extraction. The value of the mineral enterprise is the combined value of its component parts.

(4) "Mineral deposit" refers to minerals in place. When a mineral enterprise is acquired as a unit, the cost of any interest in the mineral deposit or deposits is that proportion of the total cost of the mineral enterprise which the value of the interest in the deposit bears to the value of the entire enterprise at the time of its acquisition.

(5) "Minerals" includes ores of the metals, coal, oil, gas, and all other natural metallic and nonmetallic deposits, except minerals derived from sea water, the air, or from similar inexhaustible sources. It includes but is not limited to all of the minerals and other natural deposits subject to depletion based upon a percentage of gross income from the property under section 613 and the regulations thereunder. [Reg. § 1.611-1.]

☐ [*T.D. 6446, 1-20-60. Amended by T.D. 6841, 7-26-65 and by T.D. 7261, 2-26-73.*]

§ 1.611-2. Rules applicable to mines, oil and gas wells, and other natural deposits.—(a) *Computation of cost depletion of mines, oil and gas wells, and other natural deposits.* (1) The basis upon which cost depletion is to be allowed in respect of any mineral property is the basis provided for in section 612 and the regulations thereunder. After the amount of such basis applicable to the mineral property has been determined for the taxable year, the cost depletion for that year shall be computed by dividing such amount by the number of units of mineral remaining as of the taxable year (see subparagraph (3) of this paragraph), and by multiplying the depletion unit, so determined, by the number of units of mineral sold within the taxable year (see subparagraph (2) of this paragraph). In the selection of a unit of mineral for depletion, preference shall be given to the principal or customary unit or units paid for in the products sold, such as tons of ore, barrels of oil, or thousands of cubic feet of natural gas.

(2) As used in this paragraph the phrase "number of units sold within the taxable year"—

(i) In the case of a taxpayer reporting income on the cash receipts and disbursements method, includes units for which payments were received within the taxable year although produced or sold prior to the taxable year, and excludes units sold but not paid for in the taxable year, and

(ii) In the case of a taxpayer reporting income on the accrual method, shall be determined from the taxpayer's inventories kept in physical quantities and in a manner consistent with his method of inventory accounting under section 471 or 472.

The phrase does not include units with respect to which depletion deductions were allowed or allowable prior to the taxable year.

(3) "The number of units of mineral remaining as of the taxable year" is the number of units of mineral remaining at the end of the period to be recovered from the property (including units recovered but not sold) plus the "number of units sold within the taxable year" as defined in this section.

(4) In the case of a natural gas well where the annual production is not metered and is not capable of being estimated with reasonable accuracy, the taxpayer may compute the cost depletion allowance in respect of such property for the taxable year by multiplying the adjusted basis of the property by a fraction, the numerator of which is equal to the decline in rock pressure during the taxable year and the denominator of which is equal to the expected total decline in rock pressure from the beginning of the taxable year to the economic limit of production. Taxpayers computing depletion by this method must keep accurate records of periodical pressure determinations.

(5) If an aggregation of two or more separate mineral properties is made during a taxable year under section 614, cost depletion for each such property shall be computed separately for that portion of the taxable year ending immediately before the effective date of the aggregation. Cost depletion with respect to the aggregated property shall be computed for that portion of the taxable

year beginning on such effective date. The allowance for cost depletion for the taxable year shall be the sum of such cost depletion computations. For purposes of this paragraph, each such portion of the taxable year shall be considered as a taxable year. Similar rules shall be applied where a separate mineral property is properly removed from an existing aggregation during a taxable year. See section 614 and the regulations thereunder for rules relating to the effective date of an aggregation of mineral interests and for rules relating to the adjusted basis of an aggregation.

(6) The apportionment of the deduction among the several owners of economic interests in the mineral deposit or deposits will be made as provided in paragraph (c) of § 1.611-1.

(b) *Depletion account of mineral property.* (1) Every taxpayer claiming and making a deduction for depletion of mineral property shall keep a separate account in which shall be accurately recorded the cost or other basis provided by section 1012, of such property together with subsequent allowable capital additions to each account and all the other adjustments required by section 1016.

(2) Mineral property accounts shall thereafter be credited annually with amounts of the depletion computed in accordance with section 611 or 613 and the regulations thereunder; or the amounts of the depletion so computed shall be credited to depletion reserve accounts. No further deductions for cost depletion shall be allowed when the sum of the credits for depletion equals the cost or other basis of the property, plus allowable capital additions. However, depletion deductions may be allowable thereafter computed upon a percentage of gross income from the property. See section 613 and the regulations thereunder. In no event shall percentage depletion in excess of cost or other basis of the property be credited to the improvements account or the depreciation reserve account.

(c) *Determination of mineral contents of deposits.* (1) If it is necessary to estimate or determine with respect to any mineral deposit as of any specific date the total recoverable units (tons, pounds, ounces, barrels, thousands of cubic feet, or other measure) of mineral products reasonably known, or on good evidence believed, to have existed in place as of that date, the estimate or determination must be made according to the method current in the industry and in the light of the most accurate and reliable information obtainable. In the selection of a unit of estimate, preference shall be given to the principal unit (or units) paid for in the product marketed. The estimate of the recoverable units of the mineral products in the deposit for the purposes of valuation and depletion shall include as to both quantity and grade:

(i) The ores and minerals "in sight", "blocked out", "developed", or "assured", in the usual or conventional meaning of these terms with respect to the type of the deposits, and

(ii) "Probable" or "prospective" ores or minerals (in the corresponding sense), that is, ores or minerals that are believed to exist on the basis of good evidence although not actually known to occur on the basis of existing development. Such "probable" or "prospective" ores or minerals may be estimated:

(*a*) As to quantity, only in case they are extensions of known deposits or are new bodies or masses whose existence is indicated by geological surveys or other evidence to a high degree of probability, and

(*b*) As to grade, only in accordance with the best indications available as to richness.

(2) If the number of recoverable units of mineral in the deposit has been previously estimated for the prior year or years, and if there has been no known change in the facts upon which the prior estimate was based, the number of recoverable units of mineral in the deposit as of the taxable year will be the number remaining from the prior estimate. However, for any taxable year for which it is ascertained either by the taxpayer or the district director from any source, such as operations or development work prior to the close of the taxable year, that the remaining recoverable mineral units as of the taxable year are materially greater or less than the number remaining from the prior estimate, then the estimate of the remaining recoverable units shall be revised, and the annual cost depletion allowance with respect to the property for the taxable year and for subsequent taxable years will be based upon the revised estimate until a change in the facts requires another revision. Such revised estimate will not, however, change the adjusted basis for depletion.

(d) *Determination of fair market value of mineral properties, and improvements, if any.* (1) If the fair market value of the mineral property and improvements at a specified date is to be determined for the purpose of ascertaining the basis, such value must be determined, subject to approval or revision by the district director, by the owner of such property and improvements in the light of the conditions and circumstances known at that date, regardless of later discoveries or developments or subsequent improvements in methods of extraction and treatment of the mineral product. The district director will give due weight and consideration to any and all factors and evidence having a bearing on the market value, such as cost, actual sales and transfer of similar properties and improvements, bona fide offers, market value of stock or shares, royalties and rentals, valuation for local or State taxation, partnership accountings, records of litigation in which the value of the property and improvements was in question, the amount at which the property and improvements may have been inventoried or appraised in probate or similar proceedings, and disinterested appraisals by approved methods.

(2) If the fair market value must be ascertained as of a certain date, analytical appraisal methods of valuation, such as the present value method will not be used:

(i) If the value of a mineral property and improvements, if any, can be determined upon the basis of cost or comparative values and replacement value of equipment, or

(ii) If the fair market value can reasonably be determined by any other method.

(e) *Determination of the fair market value of mineral property by the present value method.* (1) To determine the fair market value of a mineral property and improvements by the present value method, the essential factors must be determined for each mineral deposit. The essential factors in determining the fair market value of mineral deposits are:

(i) The total quantity of mineral in terms of the principal or customary unit (or units) paid for in the product marketed,

(ii) The quantity of mineral expected to be recovered during each operating period,

(iii) The average quality or grade of the mineral reserves,

(iv) The allocation of the total expected profit to the several processes or operations necessary for the preparation of the mineral for market,

(v) The probable operating life of the deposit in years,

(vi) The development cost,

(vii) The operating cost,

(viii) The total expected profit,

(ix) The rate at which this profit will be obtained, and

(x) The rate of interest commensurate with the risk for the particular deposit.

(2) If the mineral deposit has been sufficiently developed the valuation factors specified in subparagraph (1) of this paragraph may be determined from past operating experience. In the application of factors derived from past experience, full allowance should be made for probable future variations in the rate of exhaustion, quality

Reg. § 1.611-2(e)(2)

or grade of the mineral, percentage of recovery, cost of development, production, interest rate, and selling price of the product marketed during the expected operating life of the mineral deposit. Mineral deposits for which these factors cannot be determined with reasonable accuracy from past operating experience may also be valued by the present value method; but the factors must be deduced from concurrent evidence, such as the general type of the deposit, the characteristics of the district in which it occurs, the habit of the mineral deposits, the intensity of mineralization, the oil-gas ratio, the rate at which additional mineral has been disclosed by exploitation, the stage of the operating life of the deposit, and any other evidence tending to establish a reasonable estimate of the required factors.

(3) Mineral deposits of different grades, locations, and probable dates of extraction should be valued separately. The mineral content of a deposit shall be determined in accordance with paragraph (c) of this section. In estimating the average grade of the developed and prospective mineral, account should be taken of probable increases or decreases as indicated by the operating history. The rate of exhaustion of a mineral deposit should be determined with due regard to the limitations imposed by plant capacity, by the character of the deposit, by the ability to market the mineral product, by labor conditions, and by the operating program in force or reasonably to be expected for future operations. The operating life of a mineral deposit is that number of years necessary for the exhaustion of both the developed and prospective mineral content at the rate determined as above. The operating life of oil and gas wells is also influenced by the natural decline in pressure and flow, and by voluntary or enforced curtailment of production. The operating cost includes all current expense of producing, preparing, and marketing the mineral product sold (due consideration being given to taxes) exclusive of allowable capital additions, as described in §§ 1.612-2 and 1.612-4, and deductions for depreciation and depletion, but including cost of repairs. This cost of repairs is not to be confused with the depreciation deduction by which the cost of improvements is returned to the taxpayer free from tax. In general, no estimates of these factors will be approved by the district director which are not supported by the operating experience of the property or which are derived from different and arbitrarily selected periods.

(4) The value of each mineral deposit is measured by the expected gross income (the number of units of mineral recoverable in marketable form multiplied by the estimated market price per unit) less the estimated operating cost, reduced to a present value as of the date for which the valuation is made at the rate of interest commensurate with the risk for the operating life, and further reduced by the value at that date of the improvements and of the capital additions, if any, necessary to realize the profits. The degree of risk is generally lowest in cases where the factors of valuation are fully supported by the operating record of the mineral enterprise before the date for which the valuation is made. On the other hand, higher risks ordinarily attach to appraisals upon any other basis.

(f) *Revaluation of mineral property not allowed.* No revaluation of a mineral property whose value as of any specific date has been determined and approved will be made or allowed during the continuance of the ownership under which the value was so determined and approved, except in the case of misrepresentation or fraud or gross error as to any facts known on the date as of which the valuation was made. Revaluation on account of misrepresentation or fraud or such gross error will be made only with the written approval of the Commissioner.

* * *

[Reg. § 1.611-2.]

☐ [*T.D.* 6446, 1-20-60. *Amended by T.D.* 6938, 12-6-67 *and by T.D.* 7170, 3-10-72.]

§ 1.612-1. **Basis for allowance of cost depletion.**—(a) *In general.* The basis upon which the deduction for cost depletion under section 611 is to be allowed in respect of any mineral or timber property is the adjusted basis provided in section 1011 for the purpose of determining gain upon the sale or other disposition of such property except as provided in paragraph (b) of this section. The adjusted basis of such property is the cost or other basis determined under section 1012, relating to the basis of property, adjusted as provided in section 1016, relating to adjustments to basis, and the regulations under such sections. In the case of the sale of a part of such property, the unrecovered basis thereof shall be allocated to the part sold and the part retained.

(b) *Special rules.* (1) The basis for cost depletion of mineral or timber property does not include:

(i) Amounts recoverable through depreciation deductions, through deferred expenses, and through deductions other than depletion, and

(ii) The residual value of land and improvements at the end of operations.

In the case of any mineral property the basis for cost depletion does not include amounts representing the cost or value of land for purposes other than mineral production. Furthermore, in the case of certain mineral properties, such basis does not include exploration or development expenditures

Reg. § 1.612-1(a)

which are treated under section 615(b) or 616(b) as deferred expenses to be taken into account as deductions on a ratable basis as the units of minerals benefited thereby are produced and sold.

However, there shall be included in the basis for cost depletion of oil and gas property the amounts of capitalized drilling and development costs which, as provided in § 1.612-4, are recoverable through depletion deductions. In the case of timber property, the basis for cost depletion does not include amounts representing the cost or value of land.

(2) Where a taxpayer elects to treat the cutting of timber as a sale or exchange of such timber, the basis for cost depletion shall be the fair market value of such timber as of the first day of the taxable year in which such timber is cut and such value shall be considered for such taxable year and all subsequent taxable years as the cost of such timber for all purposes for which such cost is a necessary factor. See section 631(a).

(c) *Cross references.* In cases where the valuation, revaluation, or mineral content of deposits is a factor, see paragraphs (c), (d), (e), and (f) of § 1.611-2. In cases where the valuation, revaluation, or quantity of timber is a factor, see paragraphs (e), (f), and (g) of § 1.611-3. For definitions of the terms "property", "fair market value", "mineral enterprise", "mineral deposit", and "minerals", see paragraph (d) of § 1.611-1. For rules with respect to treatment of depletion accounts on taxpayer's books, see paragraph (b) of § 1.611-2 in the case of mineral property, and paragraph (c) of § 1.611-3 in the case of timber property. [Reg. § 1.612-1.]

☐ [*T.D.* 6446, 1-20-60.]

§ 1.612-3. Depletion; treatment of bonus and advanced royalty.—(a) *Bonus.* (1) If a bonus in addition to royalties is received upon the grant of an economic interest in a mineral deposit, or standing timber, there shall be allowed to the payee as a cost depletion deduction in respect of the bonus an amount equal to that proportion of his basis for depletion as provided in section 612 and § 1.612-1 which the amount of the bonus bears to the sum of the bonus and the royalties expected to be received. Such allowance shall be deducted from the payee's basis for depletion and the remainder of the basis is recoverable through depletion deductions as the royalties are thereafter received. (But see paragraph (e) of this section.) For example, a taxpayer leases mineral property to another reserving a one-eighth royalty and in addition receives a bonus of $10,000. Assuming that the taxpayer's basis with respect to the mineral property is $21,000 and that the royalties expected to be received are estimated to

total $20,000, the depletion on the bonus would be $7,000

$$\left(\frac{\$21,000 \ (\text{basis}) \times \$10,000 \ (\text{bonus})}{\$30,000 \ (\text{bonus plus estimated royalties})} \right)$$

The remaining $14,000 of basis will be recovered through depletion as the royalties are received.

(2) If the grant of an economic interest in a mineral deposit or standing timber with respect to which a bonus was received expires, terminates, or is abandoned before there has been any income derived from the extraction of mineral or cutting of timber, the payee shall adjust his capital account by restoring thereto the depletion deduction taken on the bonus and a corresponding amount must be returned as income in the year of such expiration, termination, or abandonment.

(3) In the case of the payor, payment of the bonus constitutes a capital investment made for the acquisition of an economic interest in a mineral deposit or standing timber recoverable through the depletion allowance. See paragraph (c)(5)(ii) of § 1.613-2 in cases in which percentage depletion is used.

(b) *Advanced royalties.* (1) If the owner of an operating interest in a mineral deposit or standing timber is required to pay royalties on a specified number of units of such mineral or timber annually whether or not extracted or cut within the year, and may apply any amounts paid on account of units not extracted or cut within the year against the royalty on the mineral or timber thereafter extracted or cut, the payee shall compute cost depletion on the number of units so paid for in advance of extraction or cutting and shall treat the amount so determined as an allowable deduction for depletion from the gross income of the year in which such payment or payments are made. No deduction for depletion by such payee shall be claimed or allowed in any subsequent year on account of the extraction or cutting in such year of any mineral or timber so paid for in advance and for which deduction has once been made. (But see paragraph (e) of this section.)

(2) If the right to extract minerals or to cut timber against which the advanced royalties may be applied expires, terminates, or is abandoned before all such minerals or timber have been extracted or cut, the payee shall adjust his capital account by restoring thereto the depletion deductions made in prior years on account of any units of mineral or timber paid for in advance but not extracted or cut, and a corresponding amount must be returned as income for the year of such expiration, termination or abandonment. (But see paragraph (e) of this section.)

(3) The payor shall treat the advanced royalties paid or accrued in connection with mineral

Reg. § 1.612-3(b)(3)

property as deductions from gross income for the year the mineral product, in respect of which the advanced royalties were paid or accrued, is sold. For purposes of the preceding sentence, in the case of mineral sold before production the mineral product is considered to be sold when the mineral is produced (*i.e.*, when a mineral product first exists). However, in the case of advanced mineral royalties paid or accrued in connection with mineral property as a result of a minimum royalty provision, the payor, at his option, may instead treat the advanced royalties as deductions from gross income for the year in which the advanced royalties are paid or accrued. See section 446 (relating to general rule for methods of accounting) and the regulations thereunder. For purposes of this paragraph, a minimum royalty provision requires that a substantially uniform amount of royalties be paid at least annually either over the life of the lease or for a period of at least 20 years, in the absence of mineral production requiring payment of aggregate royalties in a greater amount. For purposes of the preceding sentence, in the case of a lease which is subject to renewal or extension, the period for which it can be renewed or extended shall be treated as part of the term of the original lease. For special rules applicable when the payor is a sublessor of coal or domestic iron ore, see paragraph (b)(3) of § 1.631-3. Every taxpayer who pays or accrues advanced royalties resulting from a minimum royalty provision must make an election as to the treatment of all such advanced royalties in his return for the first taxable year ending after December 31, 1939, in which the advanced royalties are paid or accrued. The taxpayer's treatment of the advanced royalties for the first year shall be deemed to be the exercise of the election. Accordingly, a failure to deduct the advanced royalties for that year will constitute an election to have all the advanced royalties treated as deductions for the year of the sale of the mineral product in respect of which the advanced royalties are paid or accrued. See section 7807(b)(2). For additional rules relating to elections in the case of partners and partnerships, see section 703(b) and the regulations thereunder. The provisions of this subparagraph do not allow as deductions from gross income amounts disallowed as deductions under other provisions of the Code, such as section 461 (relating to general rule for taxable year of deduction), section 465 (relating to deductions limited to amount at risk in case of certain activities), or section 704(d) (relating to limitation on allowance to partners of partnership losses).

(4) The application of subparagraphs (2) and (3) of this paragraph may be illustrated by the following examples:

Example (1). B leased certain mineral lands from A under a lease in which A reserved a royalty of 10 cents a ton on minerals mined and sold by B. The lease also provided that B had to pay an annual minimum royalty of $10,000 representing the amount due on 100,000 tons of the particular mineral whether or not B mined and sold that amount. It was further provided that, if B did not mine and sell 100,000 tons in any year, he could mine and sell in any subsequent year the amount of mineral on which he had paid the royalty without the payment of any additional royalty. However, this right of recoupment was limited to minerals mined and sold in any later year in excess of the 100,000 tons represented by the $10,000 minimum royalty required to be paid for that later year. Assume that in 1956 B paid A the minimum royalty of $10,000, but mined and sold only 60,000 tons of the mineral and that in 1957 he abandoned the lease without any further production. Since the $10,000 represents royalties on 100,000 tons of mineral and only 60,000 tons were mined and sold, A must restore in 1957 to his capital account the depletion deductions taken in 1956 on $4,000 on account of the 40,000 tons paid for in advance but not mined and sold, and must also return the corresponding amount as income in 1957.

Example (2). Assume that B, under the lease in example (1), paid the $10,000 minimum royalty and mined no minerals in 1956 but that in 1957 B mined and sold 200,000 tons of mineral. If this is B's first such expenditure, B has an option, for the purpose of computing taxable income under section 63, to deduct in 1956 the $10,000 paid in that year although no mineral was mined, or to take the deduction in 1957 when the mineral, for which the $10,000 was paid in 1956, was mined and sold. (For treatment under percentage depletion, see example in paragraph (c)(5)(iii) of § 1.613-2.)

(c) *Delay rental.* (1) A delay rental is an amount paid for the privilege of deferring development of the property and which could have been avoided by abandonment of the lease, or by commencement of development operations, or by obtaining production.

(2) Since a delay rental is in the nature of rent it is ordinary income to the payee and not subject to depletion. The payor may at his election deduct such amount as an expense, or under section 266 and the regulations thereunder, charge it to depletable capital account.

(d) *Percentage depletion deduction with respect to bonus and advanced royalty.* In lieu of the allowance based on cost depletion computed under paragraphs (a) and (b) of this section, the payees referred to therein may be allowed a depletion

Reg. § 1.612-3(b)(4)

deduction in respect of any bonus or advanced royalty for the taxable year in an amount computed on the basis of the percentage of gross income from the property as provided in section 613 and the regulations thereunder. However, for special rules applicable to certain bonuses and advanced royalties received in connection with oil or gas properties, see paragraph (j) of § 1.613A-3.

(e) *Cross reference.* In the case of bonuses and advanced royalties received in connection with a contract of disposal of timber covered by section 631(b) or coal or iron ore covered by section 631(c), see that section and the regulations thereunder. [Reg. § 1.612-3.]

□ [*T.D. 6446, 1-20-60. Amended by T.D. 6841, 7-26-65; by T.D. 7523, 12-14-77 and T.D. 8348, 5-10-91.*]

§ 1.612-4. Charges to capital and to expense in case of oil and gas wells.—(a) *Option with respect to intangible drilling and development costs.* In accordance with the provisions of section 263(c), intangible drilling and development costs incurred by an operator (one who holds a working or operating interest in any tract or parcel of land either as a fee owner or under a lease or any other form of contract granting working or operating rights) in the development of oil and gas properties may at his option be chargeable to capital or to expense. This option applies to all expenditures made by an operator for wages, fuel, repairs, hauling, supplies, etc., incident to and necessary for the drilling of wells and the preparation of wells for the production of oil or gas. Such expenditures have for convenience been termed intangible drilling and development costs. They include the cost to operators of any drilling or development work (excluding amounts payable only out of production or gross or net proceeds from production, if such amounts are depletable income to the recipient, and amounts properly allocable to cost of depreciable property) done for them by contractors under any form of contract, including turnkey contracts. Examples of items to which this option applies are, all amounts paid for labor, fuel, repairs, hauling, and supplies, or any of them, which are used—

(1) In the drilling, shooting, and cleaning of wells,

(2) In such clearing of ground, draining, road making, surveying, and geological works as are necessary in preparation for the drilling of wells, and

(3) In the construction of such derricks, tanks, pipelines, and other physical structures as are necessary for the drilling of wells and the preparation of wells for the production of oil or gas.

In general, this option applies only to expenditures for those drilling and developing items which in themselves do not have a salvage value. For the purpose of this option, labor, fuel, repairs, hauling, supplies, etc., are not considered as having a salvage value, even though used in connection with the installation of physical property which has a salvage value. Included in this option are all costs of drilling and development undertaken (directly or through a contract) by an operator of an oil and gas property whether incurred by him prior or subsequent to the formal grant or assignment to him of operating rights (a leasehold interest, or other form of operating rights, or working interest); except that in any case where any drilling or development project is undertaken for the grant or assignment of a fraction of the operating rights, only that part of the costs thereof which is attributable to such fractional interest is within this option. In the excepted cases, costs of the project undertaken, including depreciable equipment furnished, to the extent allocable to fractions of the operating rights held by others, must be capitalized as the depletable capital cost of the fractional interest thus acquired.

(b) *Recovery of optional items, if capitalized.* (1) Items returnable through depletion: If the taxpayer charges such expenditures as fall within the option to capital account, the amounts so capitalized and not deducted as a loss are returnable through depletion insofar as they are not represented by physical property. For the purposes of this section the expenditures for clearing ground, draining, road making, surveying, geological work, excavation, grading, and the drilling, shooting, and cleaning of wells, are considered not to be represented by physical property, and when charged to capital account are returnable through depletion.

(2) Items returnable through depreciation: If the taxpayer charges such expenditures as fall within the option to capital account, the amounts so capitalized and not deducted as a loss are returnable through depreciation insofar as they are represented by physical property. Such expenditures are amounts paid for wages, fuel, repairs, hauling, supplies, etc., used in the installation of casing and equipment and in the construction on the property of derricks and other physical structures.

(3) In the case of capitalized intangible drilling and development costs incurred under a contract, such costs shall be allocated between the foregoing classes of items specified in subparagraphs (1) and (2) for the purpose of determining the depletion and depreciation allowances.

Reg. § 1.612-4(b)(3)

(4) Option with respect to cost of nonproductive wells: If the operator has elected to capitalize intangible drilling and development costs, then an additional option is accorded with respect to intangible drilling and development costs incurred in drilling a nonproductive well. Such costs incurred in drilling a nonproductive well may be deducted by the taxpayer as an ordinary loss provided a proper election is made in the return for the first taxable year beginning after December 31, 1942, in which such a nonproductive well is completed. Such election with respect to intangible drilling and development costs of nonproductive wells is a new election, and, when made, shall be binding for all subsequent years. Any taxpayer who incurs optional drilling and development costs in drilling a nonproductive well must make a clear statement of election under this option in the return for the first taxable year beginning after December 31, 1942, in which such nonproductive well is completed. The absence of a clear indication in such return of an election to deduct as ordinary losses intangible drilling and development costs of nonproductive wells shall be deemed to be an election to recover such costs through depletion to the extent that they are not represented by physical property, and through depreciation to the extent that they are represented by physical property.

(c) *Nonoptional items distinguished.* (1) Capital items: The option with respect to intangible drilling and development costs does not apply to expenditures by which the taxpayer acquires tangible property ordinarily considered as having a salvage value. Examples of such items are the costs of the actual materials in those structures which are constructed in the wells and on the property, and the cost of drilling tools, pipe, casing, tubing, tanks, engines, boilers, machines, etc. The option does not apply to any expenditure for wages, fuel, repairs, hauling, supplies, etc., in connection with equipment, facilities, or structures, not incident to or necessary for the drilling of wells, such as structures for storing or treating oil or gas. These are capital items and are returnable through depreciation.

(2) Expense items: Expenditures which must be charged off as expense, regardless of the option provided by this section, are those for labor, fuel, repairs, hauling, supplies, etc., in connection with the operation of the wells and of other facilities on the property for the production of oil or gas.

(d) *Manner of making election.* The option granted in paragraph (a) of this section to charge intangible drilling and development costs to expense may be exercised by claiming intangible drilling and development costs as a deduction on the taxpayer's return for the first taxable year in which the taxpayer pays or incurs such costs; no formal statement is necessary. If the taxpayer fails to deduct such costs as expenses in such return, he shall be deemed to have elected to recover such costs through depletion to the extent that they are not represented by physical property, and through depreciation to the extent that they are represented by physical property.

* * *

[Reg. § 1.612-4.]

☐ [*T.D.* 6836, 7-14-65.]

Estates, Trusts, and Beneficiaries

§ 1.641(c)-1. Electing small business trust.— (a) *In general.* An electing small business trust (ESBT) within the meaning of section 1361(e) is treated as two separate trusts for purposes of chapter 1 of the Internal Revenue Code. The portion of an ESBT that consists of stock in one or more S corporations is treated as one trust. The portion of an ESBT that consists of all the other assets in the trust is treated as a separate trust. The grantor or another person may be treated as the owner of all or a portion of either or both such trusts under subpart E, part I, subchapter J, chapter 1 of the Internal Revenue Code. The ESBT is treated as a single trust for administrative purposes, such as having one taxpayer identification number and filing one tax return. See § 1.1361-1(m).

(b) *Definitions*—(1) *Grantor portion.* The grantor portion of an ESBT is the portion of the trust that is treated as owned by the grantor or another person under subpart E.

(2) *S portion.* The S portion of an ESBT is the portion of the trust that consists of S corporation stock and that is not treated as owned by the grantor or another person under subpart E.

(3) *Non-S portion.* The non-S portion of an ESBT is the portion of the trust that consists of all assets other than S corporation stock and that is not treated as owned by the grantor or another person under subpart E.

(c) *Taxation of grantor portion.* The grantor or another person who is treated as the owner of a portion of the ESBT includes in computing taxable income items of income, deductions, and credits against tax attributable to that portion of the ESBT under section 671.

(d) *Taxation of S portion*—(1) *In general.* The taxable income of the S portion is determined by taking into account only the items of income, loss, deduction, or credit specified in paragraphs (d)(2), (3), and (4) of this section, to the extent not attributable to the grantor portion.

(2) *Section 1366 amounts*—(i) *In general.* The S portion takes into account the items of income, loss, deduction, or credit that are taken into account by an S corporation shareholder pursuant to section 1366 and the regulations thereunder. Rules otherwise applicable to trusts apply in determining the extent to which any loss, deduction, or credit may be taken into account in determining the taxable income of the S portion. See § 1.1361-1(m)(3)(iv) for allocation of those items in the taxable year of the S corporation in which the trust is an ESBT for part of the year and an eligible shareholder under section 1361(a)(2)(A)(i) through (iv) for the rest of the year.

(ii) *Special rule for charitable contributions.* If a deduction described in paragraph (d)(2)(i) of this section is attributable to an amount of the S corporation's gross income that is paid by the S corporation for a charitable purpose specified in section 170(c) (without regard to section 170(c)(2)(A)), the contribution will be deemed to be paid by the S portion pursuant to the terms of the trust's governing instrument within the meaning of section 642(c)(1). The limitations of section 681, regarding unrelated business income, apply in determining whether the contribution is deductible in computing the taxable income of the S portion.

(iii) *Multiple S corporations.* If an ESBT owns stock in more than one S corporation, items of income, loss, deduction, or credit from all the S corporations are aggregated for purposes of determining the S portion's taxable income.

(3) *Gains and losses on disposition of S stock*—(i) *In general.* The S portion takes into account any gain or loss from the disposition of S corporation stock. No deduction is allowed under section 1211(b)(1) and (2) for capital losses that exceed capital gains.

(ii) *Installment method.* If income from the sale or disposition of stock in an S corporation is reported by the trust on the installment method, the income recognized under this method is taken into account by the S portion. See paragraph (g)(3) of this section for the treatment of interest on the installment obligation. See § 1.1361-1(m)(5)(ii) regarding treatment of a trust as an ESBT upon the sale of all S corporation stock using the installment method.

(iii) *Distributions in excess of basis.* Gain recognized under section 1368(b)(2) from distributions in excess of the ESBT's basis in its S corporation stock is taken into account by the S portion.

(4) *State and local income taxes and administrative expenses*—(i) *In general.* State and local income taxes and administrative expenses directly related to the S portion and those allocated to that portion in accordance with paragraph (h) are taken into account by the S portion.

(ii) *Special rule for certain interest.* Interest paid by the trust on money borrowed by the trust to purchase stock in an S corporation is allocated to the S portion but is not a deductible administrative expense for purposes of determining the taxable income of the S portion.

(e) *Tax rates and exemption of S portion*—(1) *Income tax rate.* Except for capital gains, the highest marginal trust rate provided in section 1(e) is applied to the taxable income of the S portion. See section 1(h) for the rates that apply to the S portion's net capital gain.

(2) *Alternative minimum tax exemption.* The exemption amount of the S portion under section 55(d) is zero.

(f) *Adjustments to basis of stock in the S portion under section 1367.* The basis of S corporation stock in the S portion must be adjusted in accordance with section 1367 and the regulations thereunder. If the ESBT owns stock in more than one S corporation, the adjustments to the basis in the S corporation stock of each S corporation must be determined separately with respect to each S corporation. Accordingly, items of income, loss, deduction, or credit of an S corporation that are taken into account by the ESBT under section 1366 can only result in an adjustment to the basis of the stock of that S corporation and cannot affect the basis in the stock of the other S corporations held by the ESBT.

(g) *Taxation of non-S portion*—(1) *In general.* The taxable income of the non-S portion is determined by taking into account all items of income, deduction, and credit to the extent not taken into account by either the grantor portion or the S portion. The items attributable to the non-S portion are taxed under subparts A through D of part I, subchapter J, chapter 1 of the Internal Revenue Code. The non-S portion may consist of more than one share pursuant to section 663(c).

(2) *Dividend income under section 1368(c)(2).* Any dividend income within the meaning of section 1368(c)(2) is includible in the gross income of the non-S portion.

(3) *Interest on installment obligations.* If income from the sale or disposition of stock in an S corporation is reported by the trust on the installment method, the interest on the installment obligation is includible in the gross income of the non-S portion. See paragraph (d)(3)(ii) of this section for the treatment of income from such a sale or disposition.

(4) *Charitable deduction.* For purposes of applying section 642(c)(1) to payments made by the trust for a charitable purpose, the amount of gross

Reg. § 1.641(c)-1(g)(4)

income of the trust is limited to the gross income of the non-S portion. See paragraph (d)(2)(ii) of this section for special rules concerning charitable contributions paid by the S corporation that are deemed to be paid by the S portion.

(h) *Allocation of state and local income taxes and administration expenses.* Whenever state and local income taxes or administration expenses relate to more than one portion of an ESBT, they must be allocated between or among the portions to which they relate. These items may be allocated in any manner that is reasonable in light of all the circumstances, including the terms of the governing instrument, applicable local law, and the practice of the trustee with respect to the trust if it is reasonable and consistent. The taxes and expenses apportioned to each portion of the ESBT are taken into account by that portion.

(i) *Treatment of distributions from the trust.* Distributions to beneficiaries from the S portion or the non-S portion, including distributions of the S corporation stock, are deductible under section 651 or 661 in determining the taxable income of the non-S portion, and are includible in the gross income of the beneficiaries under section 652 or 662. However, the amount of the deduction or inclusion cannot exceed the amount of the distributable net income of the non-S portion. Items of income, loss, deduction, or credit taken into account by the grantor portion or the S portion are excluded for purposes of determining the distributable net income of the non-S portion of the trust.

(j) *Termination or revocation of ESBT election.* If the ESBT election of the trust terminates pursuant to § 1.1361-1(m)(5) or the ESBT election is revoked pursuant to § 1.1361-1(m)(6), the rules contained in this section are thereafter not applicable to the trust. If, upon termination or revocation, the S portion has a net operating loss under section 172; a capital loss carryover under section 1212; or deductions in excess of gross income; then any such loss, carryover, or excess deductions shall be allowed as a deduction, in accordance with the regulations under section 642(h), to the trust, or to the beneficiaries succeeding to the property of the trust if the entire trust terminates.

* * *

[Reg. § 1.641(c)-1.]

☐ [*T.D.* 8994, 5-13-2002.]

Income in Respect of Decedents

§ 1.691(a)-1. Income in respect of a decedent.—(a) *Scope of section 691.* In general, the regulations under section 691 cover: (1) The provisions requiring that amounts which are not includible in gross income for the decedent's last taxable year or for a prior taxable year be included in the gross income of the estate or persons receiving such income to the extent that such amounts constitute "income in respect of a decedent"; (2) the taxable effect of a transfer of the right to such income; (3) the treatment of certain deductions and credit in respect of a decedent which are not allowable to the decedent for the taxable period ending with his death or for a prior taxable year; (4) the allowance to a recipient of income in respect of a decedent of a deduction for estate taxes attributable to the inclusion of the value of the right to such income in the decedent's estate; (5) special provisions with respect to installment obligations acquired from a decedent and with respect to the allowance of a deduction for estate taxes to a surviving annuitant under a joint and survivor annuity contract; and (6) special provisions relating to installment obligations transmitted at death when prior law applied to the transmission.

(b) *General definition.* In general, the term "income in respect of a decedent" refers to those amounts to which a decedent was entitled as gross income but which were not properly includible in computing his taxable income for the taxable year ending with the date of his death or for a previous taxable year under the method of accounting employed by the decedent. See the regulations under section 451. Thus, the term includes—

(1) All accrued income of a decedent who reported his income by use of the cash receipts and disbursements method;

(2) Income accrued solely by reason of the decedent's death in case of a decedent who reports his income by use of an accrual method of accounting; and

(3) Income to which the decedent had a contingent claim at the time of his death.

See sections 736 and 753 and the regulations thereunder for "income in respect of a decedent" in the case of a deceased partner.

(c) *Prior decedent.* The term "income in respect of a decedent" also includes the amount of all items of gross income in respect of a prior decedent, if (1) the right to receive such amount was acquired by the decedent by reason of the death of the prior decedent or by bequest, devise, or inheritance from the prior decedent and if (2) the amount of gross income in respect of the prior decedent was not properly includible in computing the decedent's taxable income for the taxable year ending with the date of his death or for a previous taxable year. See example (2) of paragraph (b) of § 1.691(a)-2.

Reg. § 1.691(a)-1(a)

(d) *Items excluded from gross income*. Section 691 applies only to the amount of items of gross income in respect of a decedent, and items which are excluded from gross income under subtitle A of the Code are not within the provisions of section 691.

(e) *Cross reference*. For items deemed to be income in respect of a decedent for purposes of the deduction for estate taxes provided by section 691(c), see paragraph (c) of § 1.691(c)-1. [Reg. § 1.691(a)-1.]

☐ [*T.D.* 6257, 10-7-57. *Amended by T.D.* 6808, 3-15-65.]

§ 1.691(a)-2. Inclusion in gross income by recipients.—(a) Under section 691(a)(1), income in respect of a decedent shall be included in the gross income, for the taxable year when received, of—

(1) The estate of the decedent, if the right to receive the amount is acquired by the decedent's estate from the decedent;

(2) The person who, by reason of the death of the decedent, acquires the right to receive the amount, if the right to receive the amount is not acquired by the decedent's estate from the decedent; or

(3) The person who acquires from the decedent the right to receive the amount by bequest, devise, or inheritance, if the amount is received after a distribution by the decedent's estate of such right.

These amounts are included in the income of the estate or of such persons when received by them whether or not they report income by use of the cash receipts and disbursements method.

(b) The application of paragraph (a) of this section may be illustrated by the following examples, in each of which it is assumed that the decedent kept his books by use of the cash receipts and disbursements method:

Example (1). The decedent was entitled at the date of his death to a large salary payment to be made in equal annual installments over five years. His estate, after collecting two installments, distributed the right to the remaining installment payments to the residuary legatee of the estate. The estate must include in its gross income the two installments received by it, and the legatee must include in his gross income each of the three installments received by him.

Example (2). A widow acquired, by bequest from her husband, the right to receive renewal commissions on life insurance sold by him in his lifetime, which commissions were payable over a period of years. The widow died before having received all of such commissions, and her son inherited the right to receive the rest of the commissions. The commissions received by the widow were includible in her gross income. The commissions received by the son were not includible in the widow's gross income but must be included in the gross income of the son.

Example (3). The decedent owned a Series E United States savings bond, with his wife as co-owner or beneficiary, but died before the payment of such bond. The entire amount of interest accruing on the bond and not includible in income by the decedent, nor just the amount accruing after the death of the decedent, would be treated as income to his wife when the bond is paid.

Example (4). A, prior to his death, acquired 10,000 shares of the capital stock of the X Corporation at a cost of $100 per share. During his lifetime, A had entered into an agreement with X Corporation whereby X Corporation agreed to purchase and the decedent agreed that his executor would sell the 10,000 shares of X Corporation stock owned by him at the book value of the stock at the date of A's death. Upon A's death, the shares are sold by A's executor for $500 a share pursuant to the agreement. Since the sale of stock is consummated after A's death, there is no income in respect of a decedent with respect to the appreciation in value of A's stock to the date of his death. If, in this example, A had in fact sold the stock during his lifetime but payment had not been received before his death, any gain on the sale would constitute income in respect of a decedent when the proceeds were received.

Example (5). (1) A owned and operated an apple orchard. During his lifetime, A sold and delivered 1,000 bushels of apples to X, a canning factory, but did not receive payment before his death. A also entered into negotiations to sell 3,000 bushels of apples to Y, a canning factory, but did not complete the sale before his death. After A's death, the executor received payment from X. He also completed the sale to Y and transferred to Y 1,200 bushels of apples on hand at A's death and harvested and transferred an additional 1,800 bushels. The gain from the sale of apples by A to X constitutes income in respect of a decedent when received. On the other hand, the gain from the sale of apples by the executor to Y does not.

(2) Assume that, instead of the transaction entered into with Y, A had disposed of the 1,200 bushels of harvested apples by delivering them to Z, a cooperative association, for processing and sale. Each year the association commingles the fruit received from all of its members into a pool and assigns to each member a percentage interest in the pool based on the fruit delivered by him. After the fruit is processed and the products are sold, the association distributes the net proceeds

Reg. § 1.691(a)-2(b)

from the pool to its members in proportion to their interests in the pool. After A's death, the association made distributions to the executor with respect to A's share of the proceeds from the pool in which A had an interest. Under such circumstances, the proceeds from the disposition of the 1,200 bushels of apples constitute income in respect of a decedent. [Reg. § 1.691(a)-2.]

☐ [*T.D. 6257, 10-7-57.*]

§ 1.691(a)-3. Character of gross income.—(a) The right to receive an amount of income in respect of a decedent shall be treated in the hands of the estate, or by the person entitled to receive such amount by bequest, devise, or inheritance from the decedent or by reason of his death, as if it had been acquired in the transaction by which the decedent (or a prior decedent) acquired such right, and shall be considered as having the same character it would have had if the decedent (or a prior decedent) had lived and received such amount. The provisions of section 1014(a), relating to the basis of property acquired from a decedent, do not apply to these amounts in the hands of the estate and such persons. See section 1014(c).

(b) The application of paragraph (a) of this section may be illustrated by the following:

(1) If the income would have been capital gain to the decedent, if he had lived and had received it, from the sale of property held for more than 1 year (6 months for taxable years beginning before 1977; 9 months for taxable years beginning in 1977), the income, when received, shall be treated in the hands of the estate or of such person as capital gain from the sale of the property, held for more than 1 year (6 months for taxable years beginning before 1977; 9 months for taxable years beginning in 1977), in the same manner as if such person had held the property for the period the decedent held it, and had made the sale.

(2) If the income is interest on United States obligations which were owned by the decedent, such income shall be treated as interest on United States obligations in the hands of the person receiving it, for the purpose of determining the credit provided by section 35, as if such person had owned the obligations with respect to which such interest is paid.

(3) If the amounts received would be subject to special treatment under part I (section 1301 and following), subchapter Q, chapter 1 of the Code, relating to income attributable to several taxable years, as in effect for taxable years beginning before January 1, 1964, if the decedent had lived and included such amounts in his gross income, such sections apply with respect to the recipient of the income.

(4) The provisions of sections 632 and 1347, relating to the tax attributable to the sale of certain oil or gas property and to certain claims against the United States, apply to any amount included in gross income, the right to which was obtained by the decedent by a sale or claim within the provisions of those sections. [Reg. § 1.691(a)-3.]

☐ [*T.D. 6257, 10-7-57. Amended by T.D. 6885, 6-1-66 and T.D. 7728, 10-31-80.*]

§ 1.691(a)-4. Transfer of right to income in respect of a decedent.—(a) Section 691(a)(2) provides the rules governing the treatment of income in respect of a decedent (or a prior decedent) in the event a right to receive such income is transferred by the estate or person entitled thereto by bequest, devise, or inheritance, or by reason of the death of the decedent. In general, the transferor must include in his gross income for the taxable period in which the transfer occurs the amount of the consideration, if any, received for the right or the fair market value of the right at the time of the transfer, whichever is greater. Thus, upon a sale of such right by the estate or person entitled to receive it, the fair market value of the right or the amount received upon the sale, whichever is greater, is included in the gross income of the vendor. Similarly, if such right is disposed of by gift, the fair market value of the right at the time of the gift must be included in the gross income of the donor. In the case of a satisfaction of an installment obligation at other than face value, which is likewise considered a transfer under section 691(a)(2), see § 1.691(a)-5.

(b) If the estate of a decedent or any person transmits the right to income in respect of a decedent to another who would be required by section 691(a)(1) to include such income when received in his gross income, only the transferee will include such income when received in his gross income. In this situation, a transfer within the meaning of section 691(a)(2) has not occurred. This paragraph may be illustrated by the following:

(1) If a person entitled to income in respect of a decedent dies before receiving such income, only his estate or other person entitled to such income by bequest, devise, or inheritance from the latter decedent, or by reason of the death of the latter decedent, must include such amount in gross income when received.

(2) If a right to income in respect of a decedent is transferred by an estate to a specific or residuary legatee, only the specific or residuary legatee must include such income in gross income when received.

(3) If a trust to which is bequeathed a right of a decedent to certain payments of income ter-

minates and transfers the right to a beneficiary, only the beneficiary must include such income in gross income when received. If the transferee described in subparagraphs (1), (2), and (3) of this paragraph transfers his right to receive the amounts in the manner described in paragraph (a) of this section, the principles contained in paragraph (a) are applied to such transfer. On the other hand, if the transferee transmits his right in the manner described in this paragraph, the principles of this paragraph are again applied to such transfer. [Reg. § 1.691(a)-4.]

☐ [*T.D.* 6257, 10-7-57.]

§ 1.691(a)-5. **Installment obligations acquired from decedent.**—(a) Section 691(a)(4) has reference to an installment obligation which remains uncollected by a decedent (or a prior decedent) and which was originally acquired in a transaction the income from which was properly reportable by the decedent on the installment method under section 453. Under the provisions of section 691(a)(4), an amount equal to the excess of the face value of the obligation over its basis in the hands of the decedent (determined under section 453(d)(2) and the regulations thereunder) shall be considered an amount of income in respect of a decedent and shall be treated as such. The decedent's estate (or the person entitled to receive such income by bequest or inheritance from the decedent or by reason of the decedent's death) shall include in its gross income when received the same proportion of any payment in satisfaction of such obligations as would be returnable as income by the decedent if he had lived and received such payment. No gain on account of the transmission of such obligations by the decedent's death is required to be reported as income in the return of the decedent for the year of his death. See § 1.691(e)-1 for special provisions relating to the filing of an election to have the provisions of section 691(a)(4) apply in the case of installment obligations in respect of which section 44(d) of the Internal Revenue Code of 1939 (or corresponding provisions of prior law) would have applied but for the filing of a bond referred to therein.

(b) If an installment obligation described in paragraph (a) of this section is transferred within the meaning of section 691(a)(2) and paragraph (a) of § 1.691(a)-4, the entire installment obligation transferred shall be considered a right to income in respect of a decedent but the amount includible in the gross income of the transferor shall be reduced by an amount equal to the basis of the obligation in the hands of the decedent (determined under section 453(d)(2) and the regulations thereunder) adjusted, however, to take into account the receipt of any installment payments after the decedent's death and before such

transfer. Thus, the amount includible in the gross income of the transferor shall be the fair market value of such obligation at the time of the transfer or the consideration received for the transfer of the installment obligation, whichever is greater, reduced by the basis of the obligation as described in the preceding sentence. For purposes of this paragraph, the term "transfer" in section 691(a)(2) and paragraph (a) of § 1.691(a)-4, includes the satisfaction of an installment obligation at other than face value.

(c) The application of this section may be illustrated by the following example:

Example. An heir of a decedent is entitled to collect an installment obligation with a face value of $100, a fair market value of $80, and a basis in the hands of the decedent of $60. If the heir collects the obligation at face value, the excess of the amount collected over the basis is considered income in respect of a decedent and includible in the gross income of the heir under section 691(a)(1). In this case, the amount includible would be $40 ($100 less $60). If the heir collects the obligation at $90, an amount other than face value, the entire obligation is considered a right to receive income in respect of a decedent but the amount ordinarily required to be included in the heir's gross income under section 691(a)(2) (namely, the consideration received in satisfaction of the installment obligation or its fair market value, whichever is greater) shall be reduced by the amount of the basis of the obligation in the hands of the decedent. In this case, the amount includible would be $30 ($90 less $60). [Reg. § 1.691(a)-5.]

☐ [*T.D.* 6257, 10-7-57. *Amended by T.D.* 6808, 3-15-65.]

§ 1.691(b)-1. **Allowance of deductions and credit in respect of decedents.**—(a) Under section 691(b), the expenses, interest, and taxes described in sections 162, 163, 164, and 212 for which the decedent (or a prior decedent) was liable, which were not properly allowable as a deduction in his last taxable year or any prior taxable year, are allowed when paid—

(1) As a deduction by the estate; or

(2) If the estate was not liable to pay such obligation, as a deduction by the person who by bequest, devise, or inheritance from the decedent or by reason of the death of the decedent acquires, subject to such obligation, an interest in property of the decedent (or the prior decedent).

Similar treatment is given to the foreign tax credit provided by section 33. For the purposes of subparagraph (2) of this paragraph, the right to receive an amount of gross income in respect of a decedent is considered property of the decedent; on the other hand, it is not necessary for a person, otherwise within the provisions of subparagraph (2) of this paragraph, to receive the right to any income in respect of a decedent. Thus, an heir who receives a right to income in respect of a decedent (by reason of the death of the decedent) subject to an income tax imposed by a foreign country during the decedent's life, which tax must be satisfied out of such income, is entitled to the credit provided by section 33 when he pays the tax. If a decedent who reported income by use of the cash receipts and disbursements method owned real property on which accrued taxes had become a lien, and if such property passed directly to the heir of the decedent in a jurisdiction in which real property does not become a part of a decedent's estate, the heir, upon paying such taxes, may take the same deduction under section 164 that would be allowed to the decedent if, while alive, he had made such payment.

(b) The deduction for percentage depletion is allowable only to the person (described in section 691(a)(1)) who receives the income in respect of the decedent to which the deduction relates, whether or not such person receives the property from which such income is derived. Thus, an heir who (by reason of the decedent's death) receives income derived from sales of units of mineral by the decedent (who reported income by use of the cash receipts and disbursements method) shall be allowed the deduction for percentage depletion, computed on the gross income from such number of units as if the heir had the same economic interest in the property as the decedent. Such heir need not also receive any interest in the mineral property other than such income. If the decedent did not compute his deduction for depletion on the basis of percentage depletion, any deduction for depletion to which the decedent was entitled at the date of his death would be allowable in computing his taxable income for his last taxable year, and there can be no deduction in respect of the decedent by any other person for such depletion. [Reg. § 1.691(b)-1.]

☐ [T.D. 6257, 10-7-57.]

§ 1.691(c)-1. Deduction for estate tax attributable to income in respect of a decedent.—(a) *In general.* A person who is required to include in gross income for any taxable year an amount of income in respect of a decedent may deduct for the same taxable year that portion of the estate tax imposed upon the decedent's estate which is attributable to the inclusion in the decedent's estate of the right to receive such amount. The deduction is determined as follows:

(1) Ascertain the net value in the decedent's estate of the items which are included under sec-

tion 691 in computing gross income. This is the excess of the value included in the gross estate on account of the items of gross income in respect of the decedent (see § 1.691(a)-1 and paragraph (c) of this section) over the deductions from the gross estate for claims which represent the deductions and credit in respect of the decedent (see § 1.691(b)-1). But see section 691(d) and paragraph (b) of § 1.691(d)-1 for computation of the special value of a survivor's annuity to be used in computing the net value for estate tax purposes in cases involving joint and survivor annuities.

(2) Ascertain the portion of the estate tax attributable to the inclusion in the gross estate of such net value. This is the excess of the estate tax over the estate tax computed without including such net value in the gross estate. In computing the estate tax without including such net value in the gross estate, any estate tax deduction (such as the marital deduction) which may be based upon the gross estate shall be recomputed so as to take into account the exclusion of such net value from the gross estate. See example (2), paragraph (e) of § 1.691(d)-1.

For purposes of this section, the term "estate tax" means the tax imposed under section 2001 or 2101 (or the corresponding provisions of the Internal Revenue Code of 1939), reduced by the credits against such tax. Each person including in gross income an amount of income in respect of a decedent may deduct as his share of the portion of the estate tax (computed under subparagraph (2) of this paragraph) an amount which bears the same ratio to such portion as the value in the gross estate of the right to the income included by such person in gross income (or the amount included in gross income if lower) bears to the value in the gross estate of all the items of gross income in respect of the decedent.

(b) *Prior decedent.* If a person is required to include in gross income an amount of income in respect of a prior decedent, such person may deduct for the same taxable year that portion of the estate tax imposed upon the prior decedent's estate which is attributable to the inclusion in the prior decedent's estate of the value of the right to receive such amount. This deduction is computed in the same manner as provided in paragraph (a) of this section and is in addition to the deduction for estate tax imposed upon the decedent's estate which is attributable to the inclusion in the decedent's estate of the right to receive such amount.

* * *

[Reg. § 1.691(c)-1.]

☐ [T.D. 6257, 10-7-57. *Amended by T.D. 6887, 6-23-66.*]

Partners and Partnerships—Determination of Tax Liability

§ 1.701-1. Partners, not partnership, subject to tax.—Partners are liable for income tax only in their separate capacities. Partnerships as such are not subject to the income tax imposed by subtitle A but are required to make returns of income under the provisions of section 6031 and the regulations thereunder. For definition of the terms "partner" and "partnership", see sections 761 and 7701(a)(2), and the regulations thereunder. For provisions relating to the election of certain partnerships to be taxed as domestic corporations, see section 1361 and the regulations thereunder. [Reg. § 1.701-1.]

☐ [*T.D.* 6175, 5-23-56.]

§ 1.701-2. Anti-abuse rule.—(a) *Intent of subchapter K.* Subchapter K is intended to permit taxpayers to conduct joint business (including investment) activities through a flexible economic arrangement without incurring an entity-level tax. Implicit in the intent of subchapter K are the following requirements—

(1) The partnership must be bona fide and each partnership transaction or series of related transactions (individually or collectively, the transaction) must be entered into for a substantial business purpose.

(2) The form of each partnership transaction must be respected under substance over form principles.

(3) Except as otherwise provided in this paragraph (a)(3), the tax consequences under subchapter K to each partner of partnership operations and of transactions between the partner and the partnership must accurately reflect the partners' economic agreement and clearly reflect the partner's income (collectively, *proper reflection of income*). However, certain provisions of subchapter K and the regulations thereunder were adopted to promote administrative convenience and other policy objectives, with the recognition that the application of those provisions to a transaction could, in some circumstances, produce tax results that do not properly reflect income. Thus, the proper reflection of income requirement of this paragraph (a)(3) is treated as satisfied with respect to a transaction that satisfies paragraphs (a)(1) and (2) of this section to the extent that the application of such a provision to the transaction and the ultimate tax results, taking into account all the relevant facts and circumstances, are clearly contemplated by that provision. See, for example, paragraph (d) *Example 6* of this section (relating to the value-equals-basis rule in § 1.704-1(b)(2)(iii)(*c*)), paragraph (d) *Example 9* of this section (relating to the election under section 754 to adjust basis in partnership property), and paragraph (d) *Examples 10 and 11* of this section (relating to the basis in property distributed by a partnership under section 732). See also, for example, § § 1.704-3(e)(1) and 1.752-2(e)(4) (providing certain de minimis exceptions).

(b) *Application of subchapter K rules.* The provisions of subchapter K and the regulations thereunder must be applied in a manner that is consistent with the intent of subchapter K as set forth in paragraph (a) of this section (*intent of subchapter K*). Accordingly, if a partnership is formed or availed of in connection with a transaction a principal purpose of which is to reduce substantially the present value of the partners' aggregate federal tax liability in a manner that is inconsistent with the intent of subchapter K, the Commissioner can recast the transaction for federal tax purposes, as appropriate to achieve tax results that are consistent with the intent of subchapter K, in light of the applicable statutory and regulatory provisions and the pertinent facts and circumstances. Thus, even though the transaction may fall within the literal words of a particular statutory or regulatory provision, the Commissioner can determine, based on the particular facts and circumstances, that to achieve tax results that are consistent with the intent of subchapter K—

(1) The purported partnership should be disregarded in whole or in part, and the partnership's assets and activities should be considered, in whole or in part, to be owned and conducted, respectively, by one or more of its purported partners;

(2) One or more of the purported partners of the partnership should not be treated as a partner;

(3) The methods of accounting used by the partnership or a partner should be adjusted to reflect clearly the partnership's or the partner's income;

(4) The partnership's items of income, gain, loss, deduction, or credit should be reallocated; or

(5) The claimed tax treatment should otherwise be adjusted or modified.

(c) *Facts and circumstances analysis; factors.* Whether a partnership was formed or availed of with a principal purpose to reduce substantially the present value of the partners' aggregate federal tax liability in a manner inconsistent with the intent of subchapter K is determined based on all of the facts and circumstances, including a comparison of the purported business purpose for a transaction and the claimed tax benefits resulting from the transaction. The factors set forth below may be indicative, but do not necessarily establish, that a partnership was used in such a manner. These factors are illustrative only, and

Reg. § 1.701-2(c)

therefore may not be the only factors taken into account in making the determination under this section. Moreover, the weight given to any factor (whether specified in this paragraph or otherwise) depends on all the facts and circumstances. The presence or absence of any factor described in this paragraph does not create a presumption that a partnership was (or was not) used in such a manner. Factors include:

(1) The present value of the partners' aggregate federal tax liability is substantially less than had the partners owned the partnership's assets and conducted the partnership's activities directly;

(2) The present value of the partners' aggregate federal tax liability is substantially less than would be the case if purportedly separate transactions that are designed to achieve a particular end result are integrated and treated as steps in a single transaction. For example, this analysis may indicate that it was contemplated that a partner who was necessary to achieve the intended tax results and whose interest in the partnership was liquidated or disposed of (in whole or in part) would be a partner only temporarily in order to provide the claimed tax benefits to the remaining partners;

(3) One or more partners who are necessary to achieve the claimed tax results either have a nominal interest in the partnership, are substantially protected from any risk of loss from the partnership's activities (through distribution preferences, indemnity or loss guaranty agreements, or other arrangements), or have little or no participation in the profits from the partnership's activities other than a preferred return that is in the nature of a payment for the use of capital;

(4) Substantially all of the partners (measured by number or interests in the partnership) are related (directly or indirectly) to one another;

(5) Partnership items are allocated in compliance with the literal language of §§ 1.704-1 and 1.704-2 but with results that are inconsistent with the purpose of section 704(b) and those regulations. In this regard, particular scrutiny will be paid to partnerships in which income or gain is specially allocated to one or more partners that may be legally or effectively exempt from federal taxation (for example, a foreign person, an exempt organization, an insolvent taxpayer, or a taxpayer with unused federal tax attributes such as net operating losses, capital losses, or foreign tax credits);

(6) The benefits and burdens of ownership of property nominally contributed to the partnership are in substantial part retained (directly or indirectly) by the contributing partner (or a related party); or

(7) The benefits and burdens of ownership of partnership property are in substantial part shifted (directly or indirectly) to the distributee partner before or after the property is actually distributed to the distributee partner (or a related party).

(d) *Examples.* The following examples illustrate the principles of paragraphs (a), (b), and (c) of this section. The examples set forth below do not delineate the boundaries of either permissible or impermissible types of transactions. Further, the addition of any facts or circumstances that are not specifically set forth in an example (or the deletion of any facts or circumstances) may alter the outcome of the transaction described in the example. Unless otherwise indicated, parties to the transactions are not related to one another.

Example 1. Choice of entity; avoidance of entity-level tax; use of partnership consistent with the intent of subchapter K. (i) A and B form limited partnership PRS to conduct a bona fide business. A, the corporate general partner, has a 1% partnership interest. B, the individual limited partner, has a 99% interest. PRS is properly classified as a partnership under §§ 301.7701-2 and 301.7701-3. A and B chose limited partnership form as a means to provide B with limited liability without subjecting the income from the business operations to an entity-level tax.

(ii) Subchapter K is intended to permit taxpayers to conduct joint business activity through a flexible economic arrangement without incurring an entity-level tax. See paragraph (a) of this section. Although B has retained, indirectly, substantially all of the benefits and burdens of ownership of the money or property B contributed to PRS (see paragraph (c)(6) of this section), the decision to organize and conduct business through PRS under these circumstances is consistent with this intent. In addition, on these facts, the requirements of paragraphs (a)(1), (2), and (3) of this section have been satisfied. The Commissioner therefore cannot invoke paragraph (b) of this section to recast the transaction.

Example 2. Choice of entity; avoidance of subchapter S shareholder requirements; use of partnership consistent with the intent of subchapter K. (i) A and B form partnership PRS to conduct a bona fide business. A is a corporation that has elected to be treated as an S corporation under subchapter S. B is a nonresident alien. PRS is properly classified as a partnership under §§ 301.7701-2 and 301.7701-3. Because section 1361(b) prohibits B from being a shareholder in A, A and B chose partnership form, rather than admit B as a shareholder in A, as a means to retain the benefits of subchapter S treatment for A and its shareholders.

Reg. § 1.701-2(c)(1)

(ii) Subchapter K is intended to permit taxpayers to conduct joint business activity through a flexible economic arrangement without incurring an entity-level tax. See paragraph (a) of this section. The decision to organize and conduct business through PRS is consistent with this intent. In addition, on these facts, the requirements of paragraphs (a)(1), (2), and (3) of this section have been satisfied. Although it may be argued that the form of the partnership transaction should not be respected because it does not reflect its substance (inasmuch as application of the substance over form doctrine arguably could result in B being treated as a shareholder of A, thereby invalidating A's subchapter S election), the facts indicate otherwise. The shareholders of A are subject to tax on their pro rata shares of A's income (see section 1361 et. seq.), and B is subject to tax on B's distributive share of partnership income (see sections 871 and 875). Thus, the form in which this arrangement is cast accurately reflects its substance as a separate partnership and S corporation. The Commissioner therefore cannot invoke paragraph (b) of this section to recast the transaction.

Example 3. Choice of entity; avoidance of more restrictive foreign tax credit limitation; use of partnership consistent with the intent of subchapter K. (i) X, a domestic corporation, and Y, a foreign corporation, form partnership PRS under the laws of foreign Country A to conduct a bona fide joint business. X and Y each owns a 50% interest in PRS. PRS is properly classified as a partnership under §§ 301.7701-2 and 301.7701-3. PRS pays income taxes to Country A. X and Y chose partnership form to enable X to qualify for a direct foreign tax credit under section 901, with look-through treatment under § 1.904-5(h)(1). Conversely, if PRS were a foreign corporation for U.S. tax purposes, X would be entitled only to indirect foreign tax credits under section 902 with respect to dividend distributions from PRS. The look-through rules, however, would not apply, and pursuant to section 904(d)(1)(E) and § 1.904-4(g), the dividends and associated taxes would be subject to a separate foreign tax credit limitation for dividends from PRS, a noncontrolled section 902 corporation.

(ii) Subchapter K is intended to permit taxpayers to conduct joint business activity through a flexible economic arrangement without incurring an entity-level tax. See paragraph (a) of this section. The decision to organize and conduct business through PRS in order to take advantage of the look-through rules for foreign tax credit purposes, thereby maximizing X's use of its proper share of foreign taxes paid by PRS, is consistent with this intent. In addition, on these facts, the requirements of paragraphs (a)(1), (2), and (3) of

this section have been satisfied. The Commissioner therefore cannot invoke paragraph (b) of this section to recast the transaction.

Example 4. Choice of entity; avoidance of gain recognition under sections 351(e) and 357(c); use of partnership consistent with the intent of subchapter K. (i) X, ABC, and DEF form limited partnership PRS to conduct a bona fide real estate management business. PRS is properly classified as a partnership under §§ 301.7701-2 and 301.7701-3. X, the general partner, is a newly formed corporation that elects to be treated as a real estate investment trust as defined in section 856. X offers its stock to the public and contributes substantially all of the proceeds from the public offering to PRS. ABC and DEF, the limited partners, are existing partnerships with substantial real estate holdings. ABC and DEF contribute all of their real property assets to PRS, subject to liabilities that exceed their respective aggregate bases in the real property contributed, and terminate under section 708(b)(1)(A). In addition, some of the former partners of ABC and DEF each have the right, beginning two years after the formation of PRS, to require the redemption of their limited partnership interests in PRS in exchange for cash or X stock (at X's option) equal to the fair market value of their respective interests in PRS at the time of the redemption. These partners are not compelled, as a legal or practical matter, to exercise their exchange rights at any time. X, ABC, and DEF chose to form a partnership rather than have ABC and DEF invest directly in X to allow ABC and DEF to avoid recognition of gain under sections 351(e) and 357(c). Because PRS would not be treated as an investment company within the meaning of section 351(e) if PRS were incorporated (so long as it did not elect under section 856), section 721(a) applies to the contribution of the real property to PRS. See section 721(b).

(ii) Subchapter K is intended to permit taxpayers to conduct joint business activity through a flexible economic arrangement without incurring an entity-level tax. See paragraph (a) of this section. The decision to organize and conduct business through PRS, thereby avoiding the tax consequences that would have resulted from contributing the existing partnerships' real estate assets to X (by applying the rules of sections 721, 731, and 752 in lieu of the rules of sections 351(e) and 357(c)), is consistent with this intent. In addition, on these facts, the requirements of paragraphs (a)(1), (2), and (3) of this section have been satisfied. Although it may be argued that the form of the transaction should not be respected because it does not reflect its substance (inasmuch as the present value of the partners' aggregate federal tax liability is substantially less than would be the case if the transaction were integrated and treated as a contribution of the encumbered assets by ABC and DEF directly to X, see paragraph (c)(2) of this section), the facts indicate otherwise. For example, the right of some of the former ABC and DEF partners after two years to exchange their PRS interests for cash or X stock (at X's option) equal to the fair market value of their PRS interest at that time would not require that right to be considered as exercised prior to its actual exercise. Moreover, X may make other real estate investments and other business decisions, including the decision to raise additional capital for those purposes. Thus, although it may be likely that some or all of the partners with the right to do so will, at some point, exercise their exchange rights, and thereby receive either cash or X stock, the form of the transaction as a separate partnership and real estate investment trust is respected under substance over form principles (see paragraph (a)(2) of this section). The Commissioner therefore cannot invoke paragraph (b) of this section to recast the transaction.

Example 5. Special allocations; dividends received deductions; use of partnership consistent with the intent of subchapter K. (i) Corporations X and Y contribute equal amounts to PRS, a bona fide partnership formed to make joint investments. PRS pays $100x for a share of common stock of Z, an unrelated corporation, which has historically paid an annual dividend of $6x. PRS specially allocates the dividend income on the Z stock to X to the extent of the London Inter-Bank Offered Rate (LIBOR) on the record date, applied to X's contribution of $50x, and allocates the remainder of the dividend income to Y. All other items of partnership income and loss are allocated equally between X and Y. The allocations under the partnership agreement have substantial economic effect within the meaning of § 1.704-1(b)(2). In addition to avoiding an entity-level tax, a principal purpose for the formation of the partnership was to invest in the Z common stock and to allocate the dividend income from the stock to provide X with a floating-rate return based on LIBOR, while permitting X and Y to claim the dividends received deduction under section 243 on the dividends allocated to each of them.

(ii) Subchapter K is intended to permit taxpayers to conduct joint business activity through a flexible economic arrangement without incurring an entity-level tax. See paragraph (a) of this section. The decision to organize and conduct business through PRS is consistent with this intent. In addition, on these facts, the requirements of paragraphs (a)(1), (2), and (3) of this section have been satisfied. Section 704(b) and § 1.704-1(b)(2) permit income realized by the partnership to be

allocated validly to the partners separate from the partners' respective ownership of the capital to which the allocations relate, provided that the allocations satisfy both the literal requirements of the statute and regulations and the purpose of those provisions (see paragraph (c)(5) of this section). Section 704(e)(2) is not applicable to the facts of this example (otherwise, the allocations would be required to be proportionate to the partners' ownership of contributed capital). The Commissioner therefore cannot invoke paragraph (b) of this section to recast the transaction.

Example 6. Special allocations; nonrecourse financing; low-income housing credit; use of partnership consistent with the intent of subchapter K. (i) A and B, high-bracket taxpayers, and X, a corporation with net operating loss carryforwards, form general partnership PRS to own and operate a building that qualifies for the low-income housing credit provided by section 42. The project is financed with both cash contributions from the partners and nonrecourse indebtedness. The partnership agreement provides for special allocations of income and deductions, including the allocation of all depreciation deductions attributable to the building to A and B equally in a manner that is reasonably consistent with allocations that have substantial economic effect of some other significant partnership item attributable to the building. The section 42 credits are allocated to A and B in accordance with the allocation of depreciation deductions. PRS's allocations comply with all applicable regulations, including the requirements of §§ 1.704-1(b)(2)(ii) (pertaining to economic effect) and 1.704-2(e) (requirements for allocations of nonrecourse deductions). The nonrecourse indebtedness is validly allocated to the partners under the rules of § 1.752-3, thereby increasing the basis of the partners' respective partnership interests. The basis increase created by the nonrecourse indebtedness enables A and B to deduct their distributive share of losses from the partnership (subject to all other applicable limitations under the Internal Revenue Code) against their nonpartnership income and to apply the credits against their tax liability.

(ii) At a time when the depreciation deductions attributable to the building are not treated as nonrecourse deductions under § 1.704-2(c) (because there is no net increase in partnership minimum gain during the year), the special allocation of depreciation deductions to A and B has substantial economic effect because of the value-equals-basis safe harbor contained in § 1.704-1(b)(2)(iii)(*c*) and the fact that A and B would bear the economic burden of any decline in the value of the building (to the extent of the partnership's investment in the building), notwithstanding that A and B believe it is unlikely

Reg. § 1.701-2(d)

that the building will decline in value (and, accordingly, they anticipate significant timing benefits through the special allocation). Moreover, in later years, when the depreciation deductions attributable to the building are treated as nonrecourse deductions under § 1.704-2(c), the special allocation of depreciation deductions to A and B is considered to be consistent with the partners' interests in the partnership under § 1.704-2(e).

(iii) Subchapter K is intended to permit taxpayers to conduct joint business activity through a flexible economic arrangement without incurring an entity-level tax. See paragraph (a) of this section. The decision to organize and conduct business through PRS is consistent with this intent. In addition, on these facts, the requirements of paragraphs (a)(1), (2), and (3) of this section have been satisfied. Section 704(b), § 1.704-1(b)(2), and § 1.704-2(e) allow partnership items of income, gain, loss, deduction, and credit to be allocated validly to the partners separate from the partners' respective ownership of the capital to which the allocations relate, provided that the allocations satisfy both the literal requirements of the statute and regulations and the purpose of those provisions (see paragraph (c)(5) of this section). Moreover, the application of the value-equals-basis safe harbor and the provisions of § 1.704-2(e) with respect to the allocations to A and B, and the tax results of the application of those provisions, taking into account all the facts and circumstances, are clearly contemplated. Accordingly, even if the allocations would not otherwise be considered to satisfy the proper reflection of income standard in paragraph (a)(3) of this section, that requirement will be treated as satisfied under these facts. Thus, even though the partners' aggregate federal tax liability may be substantially less than had the partners owned the partnership's assets directly (due to X's inability to use its allocable share of the partnership's losses and credits) (see paragraph (c)(1) of this section), the transaction is not inconsistent with the intent of subchapter K. The Commissioner therefore cannot invoke paragraph (b) of this section to recast the transaction.

Example 7. Partner with nominal interest; temporary partner; use of partnership not consistent with the intent of subchapter K. (i) Pursuant to a plan a principal purpose of which is to generate artificial losses and thereby shelter from federal taxation a substantial amount of income, X (a foreign corporation), Y (a domestic corporation), and Z (a promoter) form partnership PRS by contributing $9,000x$, $990x$, and $10x$, respectively, for proportionate interests (90.0%, 9.9%, and 0.1%, respectively) in the capital and profits of PRS. PRS purchases offshore equipment for $10,000x$ and validly leases the equipment off-

shore for a term representing most of its projected useful life. Shortly thereafter, PRS sells its rights to receive income under the lease to a third party for $9,000x$, and allocates the resulting $9,000x$ of income $8,100x$ to X, $891x$ to Y, and $9x$ to Z. PRS thereafter makes a distribution of $9,000x$ to X in complete liquidation of its interest. Under § 1.704-1(b)(2)(iv)(f), PRS restates the partners' capital accounts immediately before making the liquidating distribution to X to reflect its assets consisting of the offshore equipment worth $1,000x$ and $9,000x$ in cash. Thus, because the capital accounts immediately before the distribution reflect assets of $19,000x$ (that is, the initial capital contributions of $10,000x$ plus the $9,000x$ of income realized from the sale of the lease), PRS allocates a $9,000x$ book loss among the partners (for capital account purposes only), resulting in restated capital accounts for X, Y, and Z of $9,000x$, $990x$, and $10x$, respectively. Thereafter, PRS purchases real property by borrowing the $8,000x$ purchase price on a recourse basis, which increases Y's and Z's bases in their respective partnership interests from $1,881x$ and $19x$, to $9,801x$ and $99x$, respectively (reflecting Y's and Z's adjusted interests in the partnership of 99% and 1%, respectively). PRS subsequently sells the offshore equipment, subject to the lease, for $1,000x$ and allocates the $9,000x$ tax loss $8,910x$ to Y and $90x$ to Z. Y's and Z's bases in their partnership interests are therefore reduced to $891x$ and $9x$, respectively.

(ii) On these facts, any purported business purpose for the transaction is insignificant in comparison to the tax benefits that would result if the transaction were respected for federal tax purposes (see paragraph (c) of this section). Accordingly, the transaction lacks a substantial business purpose (see paragraph (a)(1) of this section). In addition, factors (1), (2), (3), and (5) of paragraph (c) of this section indicate that PRS was used with a principal purpose to reduce substantially the partners' tax liability in a manner inconsistent with the intent of subchapter K. On these facts, PRS is not bona fide (see paragraph (a)(1) of this section), and the transaction is not respected under applicable substance over form principles (see paragraph (a)(2) of this section) and does not properly reflect the income of Y (see paragraph (a)(3) of this section). Thus, PRS has been formed and availed of with a principal purpose of reducing substantially the present value of the partners' aggregate federal tax liability in a manner inconsistent with the intent of subchapter K. Therefore (in addition to possibly challenging the transaction under judicial principles or the validity of the allocations under § 1.704-1(b)(2) (see paragraph (h) of this section)), the Commissioner

Reg. § 1.701-2(d)

can recast the transaction as appropriate under paragraph (b) of this section.

Example 8. Plan to duplicate losses through absence of section 754 election; use of partnership not consistent with the intent of subchapter K. (i) A owns land with a basis of $100x and a fair market value of $60x. A would like to sell the land to B. A and B devise a plan a principal purpose of which is to permit the duplication, for a substantial period of time, of the tax benefit of A's built-in loss in the land. To effect this plan, A, C (A's brother), and W (C's wife) form partnership PRS, to which A contributes the land, and C and W each contribute $30x. All partnership items are shared in proportion to the partners' respective contributions to PRS. PRS invests the cash in an investment asset (that is not a marketable security within the meaning of section 731(c)). PRS also leases the land to B under a three-year lease pursuant to which B has the option to purchase the land from PRS upon the expiration of the lease for an amount equal to its fair market value at that time. All lease proceeds received are immediately distributed to the partners. In year 3, at a time when the values of the partnership's assets have not materially changed, PRS agrees with A to liquidate A's interest in exchange for the investment asset held by PRS. Under section 732(b), A's basis in the asset distributed equals $100x, A's basis in A's partnership interest immediately before the distribution. Shortly thereafter, A sells the investment asset to X, an unrelated party, recognizing a $40x loss.

(ii) PRS does not make an election under section 754. Accordingly, PRS's basis in the land contributed by A remains $100x. At the end of year 3, pursuant to the lease option, PRS sells the land to B for $60x (its fair market value). Thus, PRS recognizes a $40x loss on the sale, which is allocated equally between C and W. C's and W's bases in their partnership interests are reduced to $10x each pursuant to section 705. Their respective interests are worth $30x each. Thus, upon liquidation of PRS (or their interests therein), each of C and W will recognize $20x of gain. However, PRS's continued existence defers recognition of that gain indefinitely. Thus, if this arrangement is respected, C and W duplicate for their benefit A's built-in loss in the land prior to its contribution to PRS.

(iii) On these facts, any purported business purpose for the transaction is insignificant in comparison to the tax benefits that would result if the transaction were respected for federal tax purposes (see paragraph (c) of this section). Accordingly, the transaction lacks a substantial business purpose (see paragraph (a)(1) of this section). In addition, factors (1), (2), and (4) of paragraph (c) of this section indicate that PRS was used with

a principal purpose to reduce substantially the partners' tax liability in a manner inconsistent with the intent of subchapter K. On these facts, PRS is not bona fide (see paragraph (a)(1) of this section), and the transaction is not respected under applicable substance over form principles (see paragraph (a)(2) of this section). Further, the tax consequences to the partners do not properly reflect the partners' income; and Congress did not contemplate application of section 754 to partnerships such as PRS, which was formed for a principal purpose of producing a double tax benefit from a single economic loss (see paragraph (a)(3) of this section). Thus, PRS has been formed and availed of with a principal purpose of reducing substantially the present value of the partners' aggregate federal tax liability in a manner inconsistent with the intent of subchapter K. Therefore (in addition to possibly challenging the transaction under judicial principles or other statutory authorities, such as the substance over form doctrine or the disguised sale rules under section 707 (see paragraph (h) of this section)), the Commissioner can recast the transaction as appropriate under paragraph (b) of this section.

Example 9. Absence of section 754 election; use of partnership consistent with the intent of subchapter K. (i) PRS is a bona fide partnership formed to engage in investment activities with contributions of cash from each partner. Several years after joining PRS, A, a partner with a capital account balance and basis in its partnership interest of $100x, wishes to withdraw from PRS. The partnership agreement entitles A to receive the balance of A's capital account in cash or securities owned by PRS at the time of withdrawal, as mutually agreed to by A and the managing general partner, P. P and A agree to distribute to A $100x worth of non-marketable securities (see section 731(c)) in which PRS has an aggregate basis of $20x. Upon distribution, A's aggregate basis in the securities is $100x under section 732(b). PRS does not make an election to adjust the basis in its remaining assets under section 754. Thus, PRS's basis in its remaining assets is unaffected by the distribution. In contrast, if a section 754 election had been in effect for the year of the distribution, under these facts section 734(b) would have required PRS to adjust the basis in its remaining assets downward by the amount of the untaxed appreciation in the distributed property, thus reflecting that gain in PRS's retained assets. In selecting the assets to be distributed, A and P had a principal purpose to take advantage of the facts that (i) A's basis in the securities will be determined by reference to A's basis in its partnership interest under section 732(b), and (ii) because PRS will not make an election under section 754, the remaining partners

Reg. § 1.701-2(d)

of PRS will likely enjoy a federal tax timing advantage (i.e., from the $80x of additional basis in its assets that would have been eliminated if the section 754 election had been made) that is inconsistent with proper reflection of income under paragraph (a)(3) of this section.

(ii) Subchapter K is intended to permit taxpayers to conduct joint business activity through a flexible economic arrangement without incurring an entity-level tax. See paragraph (a) of this section. The decision to organize and conduct business through PRS is consistent with this intent. In addition, on these facts, the requirements of paragraphs (a)(1) and (2) of this section have been satisfied. The validity of the tax treatment of this transaction is therefore dependent upon whether the transaction satisfies (or is treated as satisfying) the proper reflection of income standard under paragraph (a)(3) of this section. A's basis in the distributed securities is properly determined under section 732(b). The benefit to the remaining partners is a result of PRS not having made an election under section 754. Subchapter K is generally intended to produce tax consequences that achieve proper reflection of income. However, paragraph (a)(3) of this section provides that if the application of a provision of subchapter K produces tax results that do not properly reflect income, but application of that provision to the transaction and the ultimate tax results, taking into account all the relevant facts and circumstances, are clearly contemplated by that provision (and the transaction satisfies the requirements of paragraphs (a)(1) and (2) of this section), then the application of that provision to the transaction will be treated as satisfying the proper reflection of income standard.

(iii) In general, the adjustments that would be made if an election under section 754 were in effect are necessary to minimize distortions between the partners' bases in their partnership interests and the partnership's basis in its assets following, for example, a distribution to a partner. The electivity of section 754 is intended to provide administrative convenience for bona fide partnerships that are engaged in transactions for a substantial business purpose, by providing those partnerships the option of not adjusting their bases in their remaining assets following a distribution to a partner. Congress clearly recognized that if the section 754 election were not made, basis distortions may result. Taking into account all the facts and circumstances of the transaction, the electivity of section 754 in the context of the distribution from PRS to A, and the ultimate tax consequences that follow from the failure to make the election with respect to the transaction, are clearly contemplated by section 754. Thus, the tax consequences of this transaction will be

treated as satisfying the proper reflection of income standard under paragraph (a)(3) of this section. The Commissioner therefore cannot invoke paragraph (b) of this section to recast the transaction.

Example 10. Basis adjustments under section 732; use of partnership consistent with the intent of subchapter K. (i) A, B, and C are partners in partnership PRS, which has for several years been engaged in substantial bona fide business activities. For valid business reasons, the partners agree that A's interest in PRS, which has a value and basis of $100x, will be liquidated with the following assets of PRS: a nondepreciable asset with a value of $60x and a basis to PRS of $40x, and related equipment with two years of cost recovery remaining and a value and basis to PRS of $40x. Neither asset is described in section 751 and the transaction is not described in section 732(d). Under section 732(b) and (c), A's $100x basis in A's partnership interest will be allocated between the nondepreciable asset and the equipment received in the liquidating distribution in proportion to PRS's bases in those assets, or $50x to the nondepreciable asset and $50x to the equipment. Thus, A will have a $10x built-in gain in the nondepreciable asset ($60x value less $50x basis) and a $10x built-in loss in the equipment ($50x basis less $40x value), which it expects to recover rapidly through cost recovery deductions. In selecting the assets to be distributed to A, the partners had a principal purpose to take advantage of the fact that A's basis in the assets will be determined by reference to A's basis in A's partnership interest, thus, in effect, shifting a portion of A's basis from the nondepreciable asset to the equipment, which in turn would allow A to recover that portion of its basis more rapidly. This shift provides a federal tax timing advantage to A, with no offsetting detriment to B or C.

(ii) Subchapter K is intended to permit taxpayers to conduct joint business activity through a flexible economic arrangement without incurring an entity-level tax. See paragraph (a) of this section. The decision to organize and conduct business through PRS is consistent with this intent. In addition, on these facts, the requirements of paragraphs (a)(1) and (2) of this section have been satisfied. The validity of the tax treatment of this transaction is therefore dependent upon whether the transaction satisfies (or is treated as satisfying) the proper reflection of income standard under paragraph (a)(3) of this section. Subchapter K is generally intended to produce tax consequences that achieve proper reflection of income. However, paragraph (a)(3) of this section provides that if the application of a provision of subchapter K produces tax results that do not properly reflect income, but the application of that provision to the transaction and the ultimate tax results, taking into account all the relevant facts and circumstances, are clearly contemplated by that provision (and the transaction satisfies the requirements of paragraphs (a)(1) and (2) of this section), then the application of that provision to the transaction will be treated as satisfying the proper reflection of income standard.

(iii) A's basis in the assets distributed to it was determined under section 732(b) and (c). The transaction does not properly reflect A's income due to the basis distortions caused by the distribution and the shifting of basis from a nondepreciable to a depreciable asset. However, the basis rules under section 732, which in some situations can produce tax results that are inconsistent with the proper reflection of income standard (see paragraph (a)(3) of this section), are intended to provide simplifying administrative rules for bona fide partnerships that are engaged in transactions with a substantial business purpose. Taking into account all the facts and circumstances of the transaction, the application of the basis rules under section 732 to the distribution from PRS to A, and the ultimate tax consequences of the application of that provision of subchapter K, are clearly contemplated. Thus, the application of section 732 to this transaction will be treated as satisfying the proper reflection of income standard under paragraph (a)(3) of this section. The Commissioner therefore cannot invoke paragraph (b) of this section to recast the transaction.

Example 11. Basis adjustments under section 732; plan or arrangement to distort basis allocations artificially; use of partnership not consistent with the intent of subchapter K. (i) Partnership PRS has for several years been engaged in the development and management of commercial real estate projects. X, an unrelated party, desires to acquire undeveloped land owned by PRS, which has a value of $95x and a basis of $5x. X expects to hold the land indefinitely after its acquisition. Pursuant to a plan a principal purpose of which is to permit X to acquire and hold the land but nevertheless to recover for tax purposes a substantial portion of the purchase price for the land, X contributes $100x to PRS for an interest therein. Subsequently (at a time when the value of the partnership's assets have not materially changed), PRS distributes to X in liquidation of its interest in PRS the land and another asset with a value and basis to PRS of $5x. The second asset is an insignificant part of the economic transaction but is important to achieve the desired tax results. Under section 732(b) and (c), X's $100x basis in its partnership interest is allocated between the assets distributed to it in proportion to their bases to PRS, or $50x each. Thereafter, X plans to sell the second asset for its value of $5x, recognizing a

loss of $45x. In this manner, X will, in effect, recover a substantial portion of the purchase price of the land almost immediately. In selecting the assets to be distributed to X, the partners had a principal purpose to take advantage of the fact that X's basis in the assets will be determined under section 732(b) and (c), thus, in effect, shifting a portion of X's basis economically allocable to the land that X intends to retain to an inconsequential asset that X intends to dispose of quickly. This shift provides a federal tax timing advantage to X, with no offsetting detriment to any of PRS's other partners.

(ii) Although section 732 recognizes that basis distortions can occur in certain situations, which may produce tax results that do not satisfy the proper reflection of income standard of paragraph (a)(3) of this section, the provision is intended only to provide ancillary, simplifying tax results for bona fide partnership transactions that are engaged in for substantial business purposes. Section 732 is not intended to serve as the basis for plans or arrangements in which inconsequential or immaterial assets are included in the distribution with a principal purpose of obtaining substantially favorable tax results by virtue of the statute's simplifying rules. The transaction does not properly reflect X's income due to the basis distortions caused by the distribution that result in shifting a significant portion of X's basis to this inconsequential asset. Moreover, the proper reflection of income standard contained in paragraph (a)(3) of this section is not treated as satisfied, because, taking into account all the facts and circumstances, the application of section 732 to this arrangement, and the ultimate tax consequences that would thereby result, were not clearly contemplated by that provision of subchapter K. In addition, by using a partnership (if respected), the partners' aggregate federal tax liability would be substantially less than had they owned the partnership's assets directly (see paragraph (c)(1) of this section). On these facts, PRS has been formed and availed of with a principal purpose to reduce the taxpayers' aggregate federal tax liability in a manner that is inconsistent with the intent of subchapter K. Therefore (in addition to possibly challenging the transaction under applicable judicial principles and statutory authorities, such as the disguised sale rules under section 707, see paragraph (h) of this section), the Commissioner can recast the transaction as appropriate under paragraph (b) of this section.

(e) *Abuse of entity treatment.*

(1) *General rule.* The Commissioner can treat a partnership as an aggregate of its partners in whole or in part as appropriate to carry out the purpose of any provision of the Internal Revenue Code or the regulations promulgated thereunder.

(2) *Clearly contemplated entity treatment.* Paragraph (e)(1) of this section does not apply to the extent that—

(i) A provision of the Internal Revenue Code or the regulations promulgated thereunder prescribes the treatment of a partnership as an entity, in whole or in part, and

(ii) That treatment and the ultimate tax results, taking into account all the relevant facts and circumstances, are clearly contemplated by that provision.

* * *

(h) *Scope and application.* This section applies solely with respect to taxes under subtitle A of the Internal Revenue Code, and for purposes of this section, any reference to a federal tax is limited to any tax imposed under subtitle A of the Internal Revenue Code.

* * *

[Reg. § 1.701-2.]

☐ [*T.D.* 8588, 12-29-94. *Amended by T.D.* 8592, 4-12-95.]

§ 1.702-1. Income and credits of partner.— (a) *General rule.* Each partner is required to take into account separately in his return his distributive share, whether or not distributed, of each class or item of partnership income, gain, loss, deduction, or credit described in subparagraphs (1) through (9) of this paragraph. (For the taxable year in which a partner includes his distributive share of partnership taxable income, see section 706(a) and § 1.706-1(a). Such distributive share shall be determined as provided in section 704 and § 1.704-1.) Accordingly, in determining his income tax:

(1) Each partner shall take into account, as part of his gains and losses from sales or exchanges of capital assets held for not more than 1 year (6 months for taxable years beginning before 1977; 9 months for taxable years beginning in 1977), his distributive share of the combined net amount of such gains and losses of the partnership.

(2) Each partner shall take into account, as part of his gains and losses from sales or exchanges of capital assets held for more than 1 year (6 months for taxable years beginning before 1977; 9 months for taxable years beginning in 1977), his distributive share of the combined net amount of such gains and losses of the partnership.

(3) Each partner shall take into account, as part of his gains and losses from sales or exchanges of property described in section 1231 (relating to property used in the trade or business and involuntary conversions), his distributive share of the combined net amount of such gains

and losses of the partnership. The partnership shall not combine such items with items set forth in subparagraph (1) or (2) of this paragraph.

(4) Each partner shall take into account, as part of the charitable contributions paid by him, his distributive share of each class of charitable contributions paid by the partnership within the partnership's taxable year. Section 170 determines the extent to which such amount may be allowed as a deduction to the partner. For the definition of the term "charitable contribution", see section 170(c).

(5) Each partner shall take into account, as part of the dividends received by him from domestic corporations, his distributive share of dividends received by the partnership, with respect to which the partner is entitled to a credit under section 34 (for dividends received on or before December 31, 1964), an exclusion under section 116, or a deduction under part VIII, subchapter B, chapter 1 of the Code.

(6) Each partner shall take into account, as part of his taxes described in section 901 which have been paid or accrued to foreign countries or to possessions of the United States, his distributive share of such taxes which have been paid or accrued by the partnership, according to its method of treating such taxes. A partner may elect to treat his total amount of such taxes, including his distributive share of such taxes of the partnership, as a deduction under section 164 or as a credit under section 901, the subject to the provisions of sections 901 through 905.

(7) Each partner shall take into account, as part of the partially tax-exempt interest received by him on obligations of the United States or on obligations of instrumentalities of the United States, as described in section 35 or section 242, his distributive share of such partially tax-exempt interest received by the partnership. However, if the partnership elects to amortize premiums on bonds as provided in section 171, the amount received on such obligations by the partnership shall be reduced by the amortizable bond premium applicable to such obligations as provided in section 171(a)(3).

(8)(i) Each partner shall take into account separately, as part of any class of income, gain, loss, deduction, or credit, his distributive share of the following items: recoveries of bad debts, prior taxes, and delinquency amounts (section 111); gains and losses from wagering transactions (section 165(d)); soil and water conservation expenditures (section 175); nonbusiness expenses as described in section 212; medical, dental, etc., expenses (section 213); expenses for care of certain dependents (section 214); alimony, etc., payments (section 215); amounts representing taxes and in-

Reg. § 1.702-1(a)(8)

terest paid to cooperative housing corporations (section 216); intangible drilling and developments costs (section 263(c)); pre-1970 exploration expenditures (section 615); certain mining exploration expenditures (section 617); income, gain, or loss to the partnership under section 751(b); and any items of income, gain, loss, deduction, or credit subject to a special allocation under the partnership agreement which differs from the allocation of partnership taxable income or loss generally.

(ii) Each partner must also take into account separately the partner's distributive share of any partnership item which, if separately taken into account by any partner, would result in an income tax liability for that partner, or for any other person, different from that which would result if that partner did not take the item into account separately. Thus, if any partner is a controlled foreign corporation, as defined in section 957, items of income that would be gross subpart F income if separately taken into account by the controlled foreign corporation must be separately stated for all partners. Under section 911(a), if any partner is a bona fide resident of a foreign country who may exclude from gross income the part of the partner's distributive share which qualifies as earned income, as defined in section 911(b), the earned income of the partnership for all partners must be separately stated. Similarly, all relevant items of income or deduction of the partnership must be separately stated for all partners in determining the applicability of section 183 (relating to activities not engaged in for profit) and the recomputation of tax thereunder for any partner. This paragraph (a)(8)(ii) applies to taxable years beginning on or after July 23, 2002.

(iii) Each partner shall aggregate the amount of his separate deductions or exclusions and his distributive share of partnership deductions or exclusions separately stated in determining the amount allowable to him of any deduction or exclusion under subtitle A of the Code as to which a limitation is imposed. For example, partner A has individual domestic exploration expenditures of $300,000. He is also a member of the AB partnership which in 1971, in its first year of operation has foreign exploration expenditures of $400,000. A's distributable share of this item is $200,000. However, the total amount of his distributable share that A can deduct as exploration expenditures under section 617(a) is limited to $100,000 in view of the limitation provided in section 617(h). Therefore, the excess of $100,000 ($200,000 minus $100,000) is not deductible by A.

(9) Each partner shall also take into account separately his distributive share of the taxable income or loss of the partnership, exclusive of

items requiring separate computations under subparagraphs (1) through (8) of this paragraph. For limitation on allowance of a partner's distributive share of partnership losses, see section 704(d) and paragraph (d) of § 1.704-1.

(b) *Character of items constituting distributive share.* The character in the hands of a partner of any item of income, gain, loss, deduction, or credit described in section 702(a)(1) through (8) shall be determined as if such item were realized directly from the source from which realized by the partnership or incurred in the same manner as incurred by the partnership. For example, a partner's distributive share of gain from the sale of depreciable property used in the trade or business of the partnership shall be considered as gain from the sale of such depreciable property in the hands of the partner. Similarly, a partner's distributive share of partnership "hobby losses" (section 270) or his distributive share of partnership charitable contributions to organizations qualifying under section 170(b)(1)(A) retains such character in the hands of the partner.

(c) *Gross income of a partner*—(1) Where it is necessary to determine the amount or character of the gross income of a partner, his gross income shall include the partner's distributive share of the gross income of the partnership, that is, the amount of gross income of the partnership from which was derived the partner's distributive share of partnership taxable income or loss (including items described in section 702(a)(1) through (8)). For example, a partner is required to include his distributive share of partnership gross income:

(i) In computing his gross income for the purpose of determining the necessity of filing a return (section 6012(a));

(ii) In determining the application of the provisions permitting the spreading of income for services rendered over a 36-month period (section 1301, as in effect for taxable years beginning before January 1, 1964);

(iii) In computing the amount of gross income received from sources within possessions of the United States (section 931);

(iv) In determining a partner's "gross income from farming" (sections 175 and 6073); and

(v) In determining whether the de minimis or full inclusion rules of section 954(b)(3) apply.

(2) In determining the applicability of the 6-year period of limitation on assessment and collection provided in section 6501(e) (relating to omission of more than 25 percent of gross income), a partner's gross income includes his distributive share of partnership gross income (as described in section 6501(e)(1)(A)(i)). In this respect, the amount of partnership gross income from which

was derived the partner's distributive share of any item of partnership income, gain, loss, deduction, or credit (as included or disclosed in the partner's return) is considered as an amount of gross income stated in the partner's return for the purposes of section 6501(e). For example, A, who is entitled to one-fourth of the profits of the ABCD partnership, which has $10,000 gross income and $2,000 taxable income, reports only $300 as his distributive share of partnership profits. A should have shown $500 as his distributive share of profits, which amount was derived from $2,500 of partnership gross income. However, since A included only $300 on his return without explaining in the return the difference of $200, he is regarded as having stated in his return only $1,500 ($300/$500 of $2,500) as gross income from the partnership.

(d) *Partners in community property States.* If separate returns are made by a husband and wife domiciled in a community property State, and only one spouse is a member of the partnership, the part of his or her distributive share of any item or items listed in paragraph (a)(1) through (9) of this section which is community property, or which is derived from community property, should be reported by the husband and wife in equal proportions.

* * *

[Reg. § 1.702-1.]

☐ [*T.D.* 6175, 5-23-56. *Amended by T.D.* 6605, 8-14-62; *T.D.* 6777, 12-15-64; *T.D.* 6885, 6-1-66; *T.D.* 7192, 6-29-72; *T.D.* 7564, 9-11-78; *T.D.* 7728, 10-31-80; *T.D.* 8247, 4-5-89; *T.D.* 8348, 5-10-91 *and T.D.* 9008, 7-22-2002.]

§ 1.702-2. Net operating loss deduction of partner.—For the purpose of determining a net operating loss deduction under section 172, a partner shall take into account his distributive share of items of income, gain, loss, deduction, or credit of the partnership. The character of any such item shall be determined as if such item were realized directly from the source from which realized by the partnership, or incurred in the same manner as incurred by the partnership. See section 702(b) and paragraph (b) of § 1.702-1. To the extent necessary to determine the allowance under section 172(d)(4) of the nonbusiness deductions of a partner (arising from both partnership and nonpartnership sources), the partner shall separately take into account his distributive share of the deductions of the partnership which are not attributable to a trade or business and combine such amount with his nonbusiness deductions from nonpartnership sources. Such partner shall also separately take into account his distributive share of the gross income of the partnership not derived from a trade or business and combine

such amount with his nonbusiness income from nonpartnership sources. See section 172 and the regulations thereunder. [Reg. § 1.702-2.]

☐ [*T.D.* 6175, 5-23-56.]

§ 1.703-1. Partnership computations.—(a) *Income and deductions*—(1) The taxable income of a partnership shall be computed in the same manner as the taxable income of an individual, except as otherwise provided in this section. A partnership is required to state separately in its return the items described in section 702(a)(1) through (7) and, in addition, to attach to its return a statement setting forth separately those items described in section 702(a)(8) which the partner is required to take into account separately in determining his income tax. See paragraph (a)(8) of § 1.702-1. The partnership is further required to compute and to state separately in its return:

(i) As taxable income under section 702(a)(9), the total of all other items of gross income (not separately stated) over the total of all other allowable deductions (not separately stated), or

(ii) As loss under section 702(a)(9), the total of all other allowable deductions (not separately stated) over the total of all other items of gross income (not separately stated).

The taxable income or loss so computed shall be accounted for by the partners in accordance with their partnership agreement.

(2) The partnership is not allowed the following deductions:

(i) The standard deduction provided in section 141.

(ii) The deduction for personal exemptions provided in section 151.

(iii) The deduction provided in section 164(a) for taxes, described in section 901, paid or accrued to foreign countries or possessions of the United States. Each partner's distributive share of such taxes shall be accounted for separately by him as provided in section 702(a)(6).

(iv) The deduction for charitable contributions provided in section 170. Each partner is considered as having paid within his taxable year his distributive share of any contribution or gift, payment of which was actually made by the partnership within its taxable year ending within or with the partner's taxable year. This item shall be accounted for separately by the partners as provided in section 702(a)(4). See also paragraph (b) of § 1.702-1.

(v) The net operating loss deduction provided in section 172. See § 1.702-2.

(vi) The additional itemized deductions for individuals provided in Part VII of Subchapter B,

Chapter 1 of the Code, as follows: expenses for production of income (section 212); medical, dental, etc., expenses (section 213); Expenses for care of certain dependents (section 214); alimony, etc., payments (section 215); and amounts representing taxes and interest paid to cooperative housing corporation (section 216). However, see paragraph (a)(8) of § 1.702-1.

(vii) The deduction for depletion under section 611 with respect to domestic oil or gas which is produced after December 31, 1974, and to which gross income from the property is attributable after such year.

(viii) The deduction for capital gains provided by section 1202 and the deduction for capital loss carryover provided by section 1212.

(b) *Elections of the partnership*—(1) *General rule.* Any elections (other than those described in subparagraph (2) of this paragraph) affecting the computation of income derived from a partnership shall be made by the partnership. For example, elections of methods of accounting, of computing depreciation, of treating soil and water conservation expenditures, and the option to deduct as expenses intangible drilling and development costs, shall be made by the partnership and not by the partners separately. All partnership elections are applicable to all partners equally, but any election made by a partnership shall not apply to any partner's nonpartnership interests.

(2) *Exceptions*—(i) Each partner shall add his distributive share of taxes described in section 901 paid or accrued by the partnership to foreign countries or possessions of the United States (according to its method of treating such taxes) to any such taxes paid or accrued by him (according to his method of treating such taxes), and may elect to use the total amount either as a credit against tax or as a deduction from income.

(ii) Each partner shall add his distributive share of expenses described in section 615 or section 617 paid or accrued by the partnership to any such expenses paid or accrued by him and shall treat the total amount according to his method of treating such expenses, notwithstanding the treatment of the expenses by the partnership.

(iii) Each partner who is a nonresident alien individual or a foreign corporation shall add his distributive share of income derived by the partnership from real property located in the United States, as described in section 871(d)(1) or 882(d)(1), to any such income derived by him and may elect under § 1.871-10 to treat all such income as income which is effectively connected for the taxable year with the conduct of a trade or business in the United States. [Reg. § 1.703-1.]

□ [*T.D.* 6175, 5-23-56. *Amended by T.D.* 7192, 6-29-72, *T.D.* 7332, 12-20-74 *and T.D.* 8348, 5-10-91.]

§ 1.704-1. Partner's distributive share.—(a) *Effect of partnership agreement.* A partner's distributive share of any item or class of items of income, gain, loss, deduction, or credit of the partnership shall be determined by the partnership agreement, unless otherwise provided by section 704 and paragraphs (b) through (e) of this section. For definition of partnership agreement see section 761(c).

(b) *Determination of partner's distributive share*—(0) *Cross-references.*

(1) *In general*—(i) *Basic principles.* Under section 704(b) if a partnership agreement does not provide for the allocation of income, gain, loss, deduction, or credit (or item thereof) to a partner, or if the partnership agreement provides for the allocation of income, gain, loss, deduction, or credit (or item thereof) to a partner but such allocation does not have substantial economic effect, then the partner's distributive share of such income, gain, loss, deduction, or credit (or item thereof) shall be determined in accordance with such partner's interest in the partnership (taking into account all facts and circumstances). If the partnership agreement provides for the allocation of income, gain, loss, deduction, or credit (or item thereof) to a partner, there are three ways in which such allocation will be respected under section 704(b) and this paragraph. First, the allocation can have substantial economic effect in accordance with paragraph (b)(2) of this section. Second, taking into account all facts and circumstances, the allocation can be in accordance with the partner's interest in the partnership. See paragraph (b)(3) of this section. Third, the allocation can be deemed to be in accordance with the partner's interest in the partnership pursuant to one of the special rules contained in paragraph (b)(4) of this section and § 1.704-2. To the extent an allocation under the partnership agreement of income, gain, loss, deduction, or credit (or item thereof) to a partner does not have substantial economic effect, is not in accordance with the partner's interest in the partnership, and is not deemed to be in accordance with the partner's interest in the partnership, such income, gain, loss, deduction, or credit (or item thereof) will be reallocated in accordance with the partner's interest in the partnership (determined under paragraph (b)(3) of this section).

* * *

(iii) *Effect of other sections.* The determination of a partner's distributive share of income, gain, loss, deduction, or credit (or item thereof) under section 704(b) and this paragraph is not conclusive as to the tax treatment of a partner with respect to such distributive share. For example, an allocation of loss or deduction to a partner that is respected under section 704(b) and this paragraph may not be deductible by such partner if the partner lacks the requisite motive for economic gain (see, *e.g., Goldstein v. Commissioner,* 364 F.2d 734 (2d Cir. 1966)), or may be disallowed for that taxable year (and held in suspense) if the limitations of section 465 or section 704(d) are applicable. Similarly, an allocation that is respected under section 704(b) and this paragraph nevertheless may be reallocated under other provisions, such as section 482, section 704(e)(2), section 706(d) (and related assignment of income principles), and paragraph (b)(2)(ii) of § 1.751-1. If a partnership has a section 754 election in effect, a partner's distributive share of partnership income, gain, loss, or deduction may be affected as provided in § 1.743-1 (see paragraph (b)(2)(iv)(m)(2) of this section). A deduction that appears to be a nonrecourse deduction deemed to be in accordance with the partners' interests in the partnership may not be such because purported nonrecourse liabilities of the partnership in fact constitute equity rather than debt. The examples in paragraph (b)(5) of this section concern the validity of allocations under section 704(b) and this paragraph and, except as noted, do not address the effect of other sections or limitations on such allocations.

(iv) *Other possible tax consequences.* Allocations that are respected under section 704(b) and this paragraph may give rise to other tax consequences, such as those resulting from the application of section 61, section 83, section 751, section 2501, paragraph (f) of § 1.46-3, § 1.47-6, paragraph (b)(1) of § 1.721-1 (and related principles), and paragraph (e) of § 1.752-1. The examples in paragraph (b)(5) of this section concern the validity of allocations under section 704(b) and this paragraph and, except as noted, do not address other tax consequences that may result from such allocations.

(v) *Purported allocations.* Section 704(b) and this paragraph do not apply to a purported allocation if it is made to a person who is not a partner of the partnership (see section 7701(a)(2) and paragraph (d) of § 301.7701-3) or to a person who is not receiving the purported allocation in his capacity as a partner (see section 707(a) and paragraph (a) of § 1.707-1).

(vi) *Section 704(c) determinations.* Section 704(c) and § 1.704-3 generally require that if property is contributed by a partner to a partnership, the partners' distributive shares of income, gain, loss, and deduction, as computed for tax purposes, with respect to the property are determined so as to take account of the variation between the adjusted tax basis and fair market value of the property. Although section 704(b) does not directly determine the partners' distributive shares of tax items governed by section 704(c), the partners' distributive shares of tax items may be determined under section 704(c) and § 1.704-3 (depending on the allocation method chosen by the partnership under § 1.704-3) with reference to the partners' distributive shares of the corresponding book items, as determined under section 704(b) and this paragraph. (See paragraphs (b)(2)(iv)(*d*) and (b)(4)(i) of this section.) See § 1.704-3 for methods of making allocations under section 704(c), and § 1.704-3(d)(2) for a special rule in determining the amount of book items if the remedial allocation method is chosen by the partnership. See also paragraph (b)(5) *Example (13)* (i) of this section.

(vii) *Bottom line allocations.* Section 704(b) and this paragraph are applicable to allocations of income, gain, loss, deduction, and credit, allocations of specific items of income, gain, loss, deduction, and credit, and allocations of partnerhip net or"bottom line" taxable income and loss. An allocation to a partner of a share of partnership net or "bottom line" taxable income or loss shall be treated as an allocation to such

partner of the same share of each item of income, gain, loss, and deduction that is taken into account in computing such net or "bottom line" taxable income or loss. See example (15)(i) of paragraph (b)(5) of this section.

(2) *Substantial economic effect*—(i) *Two-part analysis.* The determination of whether an allocation of income, gain, loss, or deduction (or item thereof) to a partner has substantial economic effect involves a two-part analysis that is made as of the end of the partnership taxable year to which the allocation relates. First, the allocation must have economic effect (within the meaning of paragraph (b)(2)(ii) of this section). Second, the economic efect of the allocation must be substantial (within the meaning of paragraph (b)(2)(iii) of this section).

(ii) *Economic effect*—(*a*) *Fundamental principles.* In order for an allocation to have economic effect, it must be consistent with the underlying economic arrangement of the partners. This means that in the event there is an economic benefit or economic burden that corresponds to an allocation, the partner to whom the allocation is made must receive such economic benefit or bear such economic burden.

(*b*) *Three requirements.* Based on the principles contained in paragraph (b)(2)(ii)(*a*) of this section, and except as otherwise provided in this paragraph, an allocation of income, gain, loss, or deduction (or item thereof) to a partner will have economic effect if, and only if, throughout the full term of the partnership, the partnership agreement provides—

(*1*) For the determination and maintenance of the partners' capital accounts in accordance with the rules of paragraph (b)(2)(iv) of this section,

(*2*) Upon liquidation of the partnership (or any partner's interest in the partnership), liquidating distributions are required in all cases to be made in accordance with the positive capital account balances of the partners, as determined after taking into account all capital account adjustments for the partnership taxable year during which such liquidation occurs (other than those made pursuant to this requirement (*2*) and requirement (*3*) of this paragraph (b)(2)(ii)(*b*)), by the end of such taxable year (or, if later, within 90 days after the date of such liquidation), and

(*3*) If such partner has a deficit balance in his capital account following the liquidation of his interest in the partnership, as determined after taking into account all capital account adjustments for the partnership taxable year during which such liquidation occurs (other than those made pursuant to this requirement (*3*)), he is unconditionally obligated to restore the amount of such deficit balance to the partnership by the end of such taxable year (or, if later, within 90 days after the date of such liquidation), which amount shall, upon liquidation of the partnership, be paid to creditors of the partnership or distributed to other partners in accordance with their positive capital account balances (in accordance with requirement (2) of this paragraph (b)(2)(ii)(b)).

Requirements (2) and (3) of this paragraph (b)(2)(ii)(b) are not violated if all or part of the partnership interest of one or more partners is purchased (other than in connection with the liquidation of the partnership) by the partnership or by one or more partners (or one or more persons related, within the meaning of section 267(b) (without modification by section 267(e)(1)) or section 707(b)(1), to a partner) pursuant to an agreement negotiated at arm's length by persons who at the time such agreement is entered into have materially adverse interests and if a principal purpose of such purchase and sale is not to avoid the principles of the second sentence of paragraph (b)(2)(ii)(a) of this section. In addition, requirement (2) of this paragraph (b)(2)(ii)(b) is not violated if, upon the liquidation of the partnership, the capital accounts of the partners are increased or decreased pursuant to paragraph (b)(2)(iv)(f) of this section as of the date of such liquidation and the partnership makes liquidating distributions within the time set out in that requirement (2) in the ratios of the partners' positive capital accounts, except that it does not distribute (A) reserves reasonably required to provide for liabilities (contingent or otherwise) of the partnership and (B) installment obligations owed to the partnership, so long as such withheld amounts are distributed as soon as practicable and in the ratios of the partners' positive capital account balances. For purposes of the preceding sentence, a partnership taxable year shall be determined without regard to section 706 (c)(2)(A). See examples (1)(i) and (ii), (4)(i), (8)(i), and (16)(i) of paragraph (b)(5) of this section.

(c) *Obligation to restore deficit.* If a partner is not expressly obligated to restore the deficit balance in his capital account, such partner nevertheless will be treated as obligated to restore the deficit balance in his capital account (in accordance with requirement (3) of paragraph (b)(2)(ii)(b) of this section) to the extent of—

(1) The outstanding principal balance of any promissory note (of which such partner is the maker) contributed to the partnership by such partner (other than a promissory note that is readily tradable on an established securities market), and

(2) The amount of any unconditional obligation of such partner (whether imposed by the partnership agreement or by State or local law) to make subsequent contributions to the partnership (other than pursuant to a promissory note of which such partner is the maker),

provided that such note or obligation is required to be satisfied at a time no later than the end of the partnership taxable year in which such partner's interest is liquidated (or, if later, within 90 days after the date of such liquidation). If a promissory note referred to in the previous sentence is negotiable, a partner will be considered required to satisfy such note within the time period specified in such sentence if the partnership agreement provides that, in lieu of actual satisfaction, the partnership will retain such note and such partner will contribute to the partnership the excess, if any, of the outstanding principal balance of such note over its fair market value at the time of liquidation. See paragraph (b)(2)(iv)(d)(2) of this section. See examples (1)(ix) and (x) of paragraph (b)(5) of this section. A partner in no event will be considered obligated to restore the deficit balance in his capital account to the partnership (in accordance with requirement (3) of paragraph (b)(2)(ii)(b) of this section) to the extent such partner's obligation is not legally enforceable, or the facts and circumstances otherwise indicate a plan to avoid or circumvent such obligation. See paragraphs (b)(2)(ii)(f), (b)(2)(ii)(h), and (b)(4)(vi) of this section for other rules regarding such obligation. For purposes of this paragraph (b)(2), if a partner contributes a promissory note to the partnership during a partnership taxable year beginning after December 29, 1988, and the maker of such note is a person related to such partner (within the meaning of § 1.752-1T(h), but without regard to subdivision (4) of that section), then such promissory note shall be treated as a promissory note of which such partner is the maker.

(d) *Alternate test for economic effect.* If—

(1) Requirements (1) and (2) of paragraph (b)(2)(ii)(b) of this section are satisfied, and

(2) The partner to whom an allocation is made is not obligated to restore the deficit balance in his capital account to the partnership (in accordance with requirement (3) of paragraph (b)(2)(ii)(b) of this section), or is obligated to restore only a limited dollar amount of such deficit balance, and

(3) The partnership agreement contains a "qualified income offset,"

such allocation will be considered to have economic effect under this paragraph (b)(2)(ii)(d) to the extent such allocation does not cause or increase a deficit balance in such partner's capital account (in excess of any limited dollar amount of such deficit balance that such partner is obligated to restore) as of the end of the partnership taxable year to which such allocation relates. In determining the extent to which the previous sentence is satisfied, such partner's capital account also shall be reduced for—

(4) Adjustments that, as of the end of such year, reasonably are expected to be made to such partner's capital account under paragraph (b)(2)(iv)(*k*) of this section for depletion allowances with respect to oil and gas properties of the partnership, and

(5) Allocations of loss and deduction that, as of the end of such year, reasonably are expected to be made to such partner pursuant to section 704(e)(2), section 706(d), and paragraph (b)(2)(ii) of § 1.751-1, and

(6) Distributions that, as of the end of such year, reasonably are expected to be made to such partner to the extent they exceed offsetting increases to such partner's capital account that reasonably are expected to occur during (or prior to) the partnership taxable years in which such distributions reasonably are expected to be made (other than increases pursuant to a minimum gain chargeback under paragraph (b)(4)(iv)(*e*) of this section or under § 1.704-2(f); however, increases to a partner's capital account pursuant to a minimum gain chargeback requirement are taken into account as an offset to distributions of nonrecourse liability proceeds that are reasonably expected to be made and that are allocable to an increase in partnership minimum gain).

For purposes of determining the amount of expected distributions and expected capital account increases described in (6) above, the rule set out in paragraph (b)(2)(iii)(*c*) of this section concerning the presumed value of partnership property shall apply. The partnership agreement contains a "qualified income offset" if, and only if, it provides that a partner who unexpectedly receives an adjustment, allocation, or distribution described in (4), (5), or (6) above, will be allocated items of income and gain (consisting of a pro rata portion of each item of partnership income, including gross income, and gain for such year) in an amount and manner sufficient to eliminate such deficit balance as quickly as possible. Allocations of items of income and gain made pursuant to the immediately preceding sentence shall be deemed to be made in accordance with the partners' interests in the partnership if requirements (1) and (2) of paragraph (b)(2)(ii)(*b*) of this section are satisfied. See examples (1)(iii), (iv), (v), (vi), (viii), (ix), and (x), (15), and (16)(ii) of paragraph (b)(5) of this section.

(*e*) *Partial economic effect.* If only a portion of an allocation made to a partner with respect to a partnership taxable year has economic effect, both the portion that has economic effect and the portion that is reallocated shall consist of a proportionate share of all items that made up the allocation to such partner for such year. See examples (15)(ii) and (iii) of paragraph (b)(5) of this section.

(*f*) *Reduction of obligation to restore.* If requirements (1) and (2) of paragraph (b)(2)(ii)(*b*) of this section are satisfied, a partner's obligation to restore the deficit balance in his capital account (or any limited dollar amount thereof) to the partnership may be eliminated or reduced as of the end of a partnership taxable year without affecting the validity of prior allocations (see paragraph (b)(4)(vi) of this section) to the extent the deficit balance (if any) in such partner's capital account, after reduction for the items described in (4), (5), and (6) of paragraph (b)(2)(ii)(*d*) of this section, will not exceed the partner's remaining obligation (if any) to restore the deficit balance in his capital account. See example (l)(viii) of paragraph (b)(5) of this section.

(*g*) *Liquidation defined.* For purposes of this paragraph, a liquidation of a partner's interest in the partnership occurs upon the earlier of (*1*) the date upon which there is a liquidation of the partnership, or (*2*) the date upon which there is a liquidation of the partner's interest in the partnership under paragraph (d) of § 1.761-1. For purposes of this paragraph, the liquidation of a partnership occurs upon the earlier of (*3*) the date upon which the partnership is terminated under section 708(b)(1), or (*4*) the date upon which the partnership ceases to be a going concern (even though it may continue in existence for the purpose of winding up its affairs, paying its debts, and distributing any remaining balance to its partners). Requirements (*2*) and (*3*) of paragraph (b)(2)(ii)(*b*) of this section will be considered unsatisfied if the liquidation of a partner's interest in the partnership is delayed after its primary business activities have been terminated (for example, by continuing to engage in a relatively minor amount of business activity, if such actions themselves do not cause the partnership to terminate pursuant to section 708(b)(1)) for a principal purpose of deferring any distribution pursuant to requirement (*2*) of paragraph (b)(2)(ii)(*b*) of this section or deferring any partner's obligation under requirement (*3*) of paragraph (b)(2)(ii)(*b*) of this section.

(*h*) *Partnership agreement defined.* For purposes of this paragraph, the partnership agreement includes all agreements among the partners, or between one or more partners and the partnership, concerning affairs of the partnership and responsibilities of partners, whether oral or written, and whether or not embodied in a document referred to by the partners as the partnership agreement. Thus, in determining whether distributions are required in all cases to be made in accordance with the partners' positive capital account balances (requirement (2) of paragraph (b)(2)(ii)(b) of this section), and in determining the extent to which a partner is obligated to restore a deficit balance in his capital account (requirement (3) of paragraph (b)(2)(ii)(b) of this section), all arrangements among partners, or between one or more partners and the partnership relating to the partnership, direct and indirect, including puts, options, and other buy-sell agreements, and any other "stop-loss" arrangement, are considered to be part of the partnership agreement. (Thus, for example, if one partner who assumes a liability of the partnership is indemnified by another partner for a portion of such liability, the indemnifying partner (depending upon the particular facts) may be viewed as in effect having a partial deficit makeup obligation as a result of such indemnity agreement.) In addition, the partnership agreement includes provisions of Federal, State, or local law that govern the affairs of the partnership or are considered under such law to be a part of the partnership agreement (see the last sentence of paragraph (c) of § 1.761-1). For purposes of this paragraph (b)(2)(ii)(h), an agreement with a partner or a partnership shall include an agreement with a person related, within the meaning of section 267(b) (without modification by section 267(e)(1)) or section 707(b)(1), to such partner or partnership. For purposes of the preceding sentence, sections 267(b) and 707(b)(1) shall be applied for partnership taxable years beginning after December 29, 1988, by (1) substituting "80 percent or more" for "more than 50 percent" each place it appears in such sections, (2) excluding brothers and sisters from the members of a person's family, and (3) disregarding section 267(f)(1)(A).

(i) *Economic effect equivalence.* Allocations made to a partner that do not otherwise have economic effect under this paragraph (b)(2)(ii) shall nevertheless be deemed to have economic effect, provided that as of the end of each partnership taxable year a liquidation of the partnership at the end of such year or at the end of any future year would produce the same economic results to the partners as would occur if requirements (1), (2), and (3) of paragraph (b)(2)(ii)(b) of this section had been satisfied, regardless of the economic performance of the partnership. See examples (4)(ii) and (iii) of paragraph (b)(5) of this section.

(iii) *Substantiality*—(a) *General rules.* Except as otherwise provided in this paragraph (b)(2)(iii), the economic effect of an allocation (or allocations) is substantial if there is a reasonable possibility that the allocation (or allocations) will affect substantially the dollar amounts to be received by the partners from the partnership, independent of tax consequences. Notwithstanding the preceding sentence, the economic effect of an allocation (or allocations) is not substantial if, at the time the allocation becomes part of the partnership agreement, (1) the after-tax economic consequences of at least one partner may, in present value terms, be enhanced compared to such consequences if the allocation (or allocations) were not contained in the partnership agreement, and (2) there is a strong likelihood that the after-tax economic consequences of no partner will, in present value terms, be substantially diminished compared to such consequences if the allocation (or allocations) were not contained in the partnership agreement. In determining the after-tax economic benefit or detriment to a partner, tax consequences that result from the interaction of the allocation with such partner's tax attributes that are unrelated to the partnership will be taken into account. See examples (5) and (9) of paragraph (b)(5) of this section. The economic effect of an allocation is not substantial in the two situations described in paragraphs (b)(2)(iii)(b) and (c) of this section. However, even if an allocation is not described therein, its economic effect may be insubstantial under the general rules stated in this paragraph (b)(2)(iii)(a). References in this paragraph (b)(2)(iii) to allocations includes capital account adjustments made pursuant to paragraph (b)(2)(iv)(k) of this section.

(b) *Shifting tax consequences.* The economic effect of an allocation (or allocations) in a partnership taxable year is not substantial if, at the time the allocation (or allocations) becomes part of the partnership agreement, there is a strong likelihood that—

(1) The net increases and decreases that will be recorded in the partners' respective capital accounts for such taxable year will not differ substantially from the net increases and decreases that would be recorded in such partners' respective capital accounts for such year if the allocations were not contained in the partnership agreement, and

(2) The total tax liability of the partners (for their respective taxable years in which the allocations will be taken into account) will be less than if the allocations were not contained in the partnership agreement (taking into account tax consequences that result from the interaction of the allocation (or allocations) with partner tax attributes that are unrelated to the partnership).

Reg. § 1.704-1(b)(2)

If, at the end of a partnership taxable year to which an allocation (or allocations) relates, the net increases and decreases that are recorded in the partners' respective capital accounts do not differ substantially from the net increases and decreases that would have been recorded in such partners' respective capital accounts had the allocation (or allocations) not been contained in the partnership agreement, and the total tax liability of the partners is (as described in (2) above) less than it would have been had the allocation (or allocations) not been contained in the partnership agreement, it will be presumed that, at the time the allocation (or allocations) became part of such partnership agreement, there was a strong likelihood that these results would occur. This presumption may be overcome by a showing of facts and circumstances that prove otherwise. See examples (6), (7)(ii) and (iii), and (10)(ii) of paragraph (b)(5) of this section.

(c) *Transitory allocations.* If a partnership agreement provides for the possibility that one or more allocations (the "original allocation(s)") will be largely offset by one or more other allocations (the "offsetting allocations(s)"), and, at the time the allocations become part of the partnership agreement, there is a strong likelihood that—

(1) The net increases and decreases that will be recorded in the partners' respective capital accounts for the taxable years to which the allocations relate will not differ substantially from the net increases and decreases that would be recorded in such partners' respective capital accounts for such years if the original allocation(s) and offsetting allocation(s) were not contained in the partnership agreement, and

(2) The total tax liability of the partners (for their respective taxable years in which the allocations will be taken into account) will be less than if the allocations were not contained in the partnership agreement (taking into account tax consequences that result from the interaction of the allocation (or allocations) with partner tax attributes that are unrelated to the partnership)

the economic effect of the original allocation(s) and offsetting allocation(s) will not be substantial. If, at the end of a partnership taxable year to which an offsetting allocation(s) relates, the net increases and decreases recorded in the partners' respective capital accounts do not differ substantially from the net increases and decreases that would have been recorded in such partners' respective capital accounts had the original allocation(s) and the offsetting allocation(s) not been contained in the partnership agreement, and the total tax liability of the partners is (as described in (2) above) less than it would have been had

such allocations not been contained in the partnership agreement, it will be presumed that, at the time the allocations became part of the partnership agreement, there was a strong likelihood that these results would occur. This presumption may be overcome by a showing of facts and circumstances that prove otherwise. See examples (1)(xi), (2), (3), (7), (8)(ii), and (17) of paragraph (b)(5) of this section. Notwithstanding the foregoing, the original allocation(s) and the offsetting allocation(s) will not be insubstantial (under this paragraph (b)(2)(iii)(c)) and, for purposes of paragraph (b)(2)(iii)(a), it will be presumed that there is a reasonable possibility that the allocations will affect substantially the dollar amounts to be received by the partners from the partnership if, at the time the allocations become part of the partnership agreement, there is a strong likelihood that the offsetting allocation(s) will not, in large part, be made within five years after the original allocation(s) is made (determined on a first-in, first-out basis). See example (2) of paragraph (b)(5) of this section. For purposes of applying the provisions of this paragraph (b)(2)(iii) (and paragraphs (b)(2)(ii)(d)(6) and (b)(3)(iii) of this section), the adjusted tax basis of partnership property (or, if partnership property is properly reflected on the books of the partnership at a book value that differs from its adjusted tax basis, the book value of such property) will be presumed to be the fair market value of such property, and adjustments to the adjusted tax basis (or book value) of such property will be presumed to be matched by corresponding changes in such property's fair market value. Thus, there cannot be a strong likelihood that the economic effect of an allocation (or allocations) will be largely offset by an allocation (or allocations) of gain or loss from the disposition of partnership property. See examples (1)(vi) and (xi) of paragraph (b)(5) of this section.

(iv) *Maintenance of capital accounts—(a) In general.* The economic effect test described in paragraph (b)(2)(ii) of this section requires an examination of the capital accounts of the partners of a partnership, as maintained under the partnership agreement. Except as otherwise provided in paragraph (b)(2)(ii)(i) of this section, an allocation of income, gain, loss, or deduction will not have economic effect under paragraph (b)(2)(ii) of this section, and will not be deemed to be in accordance with a partner's interest in the partnership under paragraph (b)(4) of this section, unless the capital accounts of the partners are determined and maintained throughout the full term of the partnership in accordance with the capital accounting rules of this paragraph (b)(2) (iv).

(*b*) *Basic rules*. Except as otherwise provided in this paragraph (b)(2)(iv), the partners' capital accounts will be considered to be determined and maintained in accordance with the rules of this paragraph (b)(2)(iv) if, and only if, each partner's capital account is increased by (*1*) the amount of money contributed by him to the partnership, (*2*) the fair market value of property contributed by him to the partnership (net of liabilities secured by such contributed property that the partnership is considered to assume or take subject to under section 752), and (*3*) allocations to him of partnership income and gain (or items thereof), including income and gain exempt from tax and income and gain described in paragraph (b)(2)(iv)(*g*) of this section, but excluding income and gain described in paragraph (b)(4)(i) of this section; and is decreased by (*4*) the amount of money distributed to him by the partnership, (*5*) the fair market value of property distributed to him by the partnership (net of liabilities secured by such distributed property that such partner is considered to assume or take subject to under section 752), (*6*) allocations to him of expenditures of the partnership described in section 705(a)(2)(B), and (*7*) allocations of partnership loss and deduction (or item thereof), including loss and deduction described in paragraph (b)(2)(iv)(*g*) of this section, but excluding items described in (*6*) above and loss or deduction described in paragraphs (b)(4)(i) or (b)(4)(iii) of this section; and is otherwise adjusted in accordance with the additional rules set forth in this paragraph (b)(2)(iv). For purposes of this paragraph, a partner who has more than one interest in a partnership shall have a single capital account that reflects all such interests, regardless of the class of interests owned by such partner (*e.g.*, general or limited) and regardless of the time or manner in which such interests were acquired.

(*c*) *Treatment of liabilities*. For purposes of this paragraph (b)(2)(iv), (*1*) money contributed by a partner to a partnership includes the amount of any partnership liabilities that are assumed by such partner (other than liabilities described in paragraph (b)(2)(iv)(*b*)(*5*) of this section that are assumed by a distributee partner) but does not include increases in such partner's share of partnership liabilities (see section 752(a)), and (*2*) money distributed to a partner by a partnership includes the amount of such partner's individual liabilities that are assumed by the partnership (other than liabilities described in paragraph (b)(2)(iv)(*b*)(*2*) of this section that are assumed by the partnership) but does not include decreases in such partner's share of partnership liabilities (see section 752(b)). For purposes of this paragraph (b)(2)(iv)(*c*), liabilities are considered assumed only to the extent the assuming party is

thereby subjected to personal liability with respect to such obligation, the obligee is aware of the assumption and can directly enforce the assuming party's obligation, and, as between the assuming party and the party from whom the liability is assumed, the assuming party is ultimately liable.

(*d*) *Contributed property—*(*1*) *In general*. The basic capital accounting rules contained in paragraph (b)(2)(iv)(*b*) of this section require that a partner's capital account be increased by the fair market value of property contributed to the partnership by such partner on the date of contribution. See *Example 13*(i) of paragraph (b)(5) of this section. Consistent with section 752(c), section 7701(g) does not apply in determining such fair market value.

(*2*) *Contribution of promissory notes.* Notwithstanding the general rule of paragraph (b)(2)(iv)(*b*)(*2*) of this section, except as provided in this paragraph (b)(2)(iv)(*d*)(*2*), if a promissory note is contributed to a partnership by a partner who is the maker of such note, such partner's capital account will be increased with respect to such note only when there is a taxable disposition of such note by the partnership or when the partner makes principal payments on such note. See example (1)(ix) of paragraph (b)(5) of this section. The first sentence of this paragraph (b)(2)(iv)(*d*)(*2*) shall not apply if the note referred to therein is readily tradable on an established securities market. See also paragraph (b)(2)(ii)(*c*) of this section. Furthermore, a partner whose interest is liquidated will be considered as satisfying his obligation to restore the deficit balance in his capital account to the extent of (*i*) the fair market value, at the time of contribution, of any negotiable promissory note (of which such partner is the maker) that such partner contributes to the partnership on or after the date his interest is liquidated and within the time specified in paragraph (b)(2)(ii)(*b*)(*3*) of this section, and (*ii*) the fair market value, at the time of liquidation, of the unsatisfied portion of any negotiable promissory note (of which such partner is the maker) that such partner previously contributed to the partnership. For purposes of the preceding sentence, the fair market value of a note will be no less than the outstanding principal balance of such note, provided that such note bears interest at a rate no less than the applicable federal rate at the time of valuation.

(*3*) *Section 704(c) considerations.* Section 704(c) and § 1.704-3 govern the determination of the partners' distributive shares of income, gain, loss, and deduction, as computed for tax purposes, with respect to property contributed to a partnership (see paragraph (b)(1)(vi) of this section). In cases where section 704(c) and

Reg. § 1.704-1(b)(2)

§ 1.704-3 apply to partnership property, the capital accounts of the partners will not be considered to be determined and maintained in accordance with the rules of this paragraph (b)(2)(iv) unless the partnership agreement requires that the partners' capital accounts be adjusted in accordance with paragraph (b)(2)(iv)(g) of this section for allocations to them of income, gain, loss, and deduction (including depreciation, depletion, amortization, or other cost recovery) as computed for book purposes, with respect to the property. See, however, § 1.704-3(d)(2) for a special rule in determining the amount of book items if the partnership chooses the remedial allocation method. See also *Example (13)* (i) of paragraph (b)(5) of this section. Capital accounts are not adjusted to reflect allocations under section 704(c) and § 1.704-3 (e.g., tax allocations of precontribution gain or loss).

(e) *Distributed property—(1) In general.* The basic capital accounting rules contained in paragraph (b)(2)(iv)(b) of this section require that a partner's capital account be decreased by the fair market value of property distributed by the partnership (without regard to section 7701(g)) to such partner (whether in connection with a liquidation or otherwise). To satisfy this requirement, the capital accounts of the partners first must be adjusted to reflect the manner in which the unrealized income, gain, loss, and deduction inherent in such property (that has not been reflected in the capital accounts previously) would be allocated among the partners if there were a taxable disposition of such property for the fair market value of such property (taking section 7701(g) into account) on the date of distribution. See example (14)(v) of paragraph (b)(5) of this section.

(2) *Distribution of promissory notes.* Notwithstanding the general rule of paragraph (b)(2)(iv)(b)(5), except as provided in this paragraph (b)(2)(iv)(e)(2), if a promissory note is distributed to a partner by a partnership that is the maker of such note, such partner's capital account will be decreased with respect to such note only when there is a taxable disposition of such note by the partner or when the partnership makes principal payments on the note. The previous sentence shall not apply if a note distributed to a partner by a partnership who is the maker of such note is readily tradable on an established securities market. Furthermore, the capital account of a partner whose interest in a partnership is liquidated will be reduced to the extent of (i) the fair market value, at the time of distribution, of any negotiable promissory note (of which such partnership is the maker) that such partnership distributes to the partner on or after the date such partner's interest is liquidated and within the time speci-

fied in paragraph (b)(2)(ii)(b)(2) of this section, and (ii) the fair market value, at the time of liquidation, of the unsatisfied portion of any negotiable promissory note (of which such partnership is the maker) that such partnership previously distributed to the partner. For purposes of the preceding sentence, the fair market value of a note will be no less than the outstanding principal balance of such note, provided that such note bears interest at a rate no less than the applicable federal rate at the time of valuation.

(f) *Revaluations of property.* A partnership agreement may, upon the occurrence of certain events, increase or decrease the capital accounts of the partners to reflect a revaluation of partnership property (including intangible assets such as goodwill) on the partnership's books. Capital accounts so adjusted will not be considered to be determined and maintained in accordance with the rules of this paragraph (b)(2)(iv) unless—

(1) The adjustments are based on the fair market value of partnership property (taking section 7701(g) into account) on the date of adjustment, and

(2) The adjustments reflect the manner in which the unrealized income, gain, loss, or deduction inherent in such property (that has not been reflected in the capital accounts previously) would be allocated among the partners if there were a taxable disposition of such property for such fair market value on that date, and

(3) The partnership agreement requires that the partners' capital accounts be adjusted in accordance with paragraph (b)(2)(iv)(g) of this section for allocations to them of depreciation, depletion, amortization, and gain or loss, as computed for book purposes, with respect to such property, and

(4) The partnership agreement requires that the partners' distributive shares of depreciation, depletion, amortization, and gain or loss, as computed for tax purposes, with respect to such property be determined so as to take account of the variation between the adjusted tax basis and book value of such property in the same manner as under section 704(c) (see paragraph (b)(4)(i) of this section), and

(5) The adjustments are made principally for a substantial non-tax business purpose—

(i) In connection with a contribution of money or other property (other than a *de minimis* amount) to the partnership by a new or existing partner as consideration for an interest in the partnership, or

(ii) In connection with the liquidation of the partnership or a distribution of money or other property (other than a *de minimis* amount) by the partnership to a retiring or continuing partner as consideration for an interest in the partnership, or

(*iii*) Under generally accepted industry accounting practices, provided substantially all of the partnership's property (excluding money) consists of stock, securities, commodities, options, warrants, futures, or similar instruments that are readily tradable on an established securities market.

See examples (14) and (18) of paragraph (b)(5) of this section. If the capital accounts of the partners are not adjusted to reflect the fair market value of partnership property when an interest in the partnership is acquired from or relinquished to the partnership, paragraphs (b)(1)(iii) and (b)(1)(iv) of this section should be consulted regarding the potential tax consequences that may arise if the principles of section 704(c) are not applied to determine the partners' distributive shares of depreciation, depletion, amortization, and gain or loss, as computed for tax purposes, with respect to such property.

(*g*) *Adjustments to reflect book value—* (*1*) *In general.* Under paragraphs (b)(2)(iv)(*d*) and (b)(2)(iv)(*f*) of this section, property may be properly reflected on the books of the partnership at a book value that differs from the adjusted tax basis of such property. In these circumstances, paragraphs (b)(2)(iv)(*d*)(3) and (b)(2)(iv)(*f*)(3) of this section provide that the capital accounts of the partners will not be considered to be determined and maintained in accordance with the rules of this paragraph (b)(2)(iv) unless the partnership agreement requires the partners' capital accounts to be adjusted in accordance with this paragraph (b)(2)(iv)(*g*) for allocations to them of depreciation, depletion, amortization, and gain or loss, as computed for book purposes, with respect to such property. In determining whether the economic effect of an allocation of book items is substantial, consideration will be given to the effect of such allocation on the determination of the partners' distributive shares of corresponding tax items under section 704(c) and paragraph (b)(4)(i) of this section. See example (17) of paragraph (b)(5) of this section. If an allocation of book items under the partnership agreement does not have substantial economic effect (as determined under paragraphs (b)(2)(ii) and (b)(2)(iii) of this section), or is not otherwise respected under this paragraph, such items will be reallocated in accordance with the partners' interests in the partnership, and such reallocation will be the basis upon which the partners' distributive shares of the corresponding tax items are determined under section 704(c) and paragraph (b)(4)(i) of this section. See examples (13), (14), and (18) of paragraph (b)(5) of this section.

(*2*) *Payables and receivables.* References in this paragraph (b)(2)(iv) and paragraph (b)(4)(i) of this section to book and tax depreciation, depletion, amortization, and gain or loss with respect to property that has an adjusted tax basis that differs from book value include, under analogous rules and principles, the unrealized income or deduction with respect to accounts receivable, accounts payable, and other accrued but unpaid items.

(*3*) *Determining amount of book items.* The partners' capital accounts will not be considered adjusted in accordance with this paragraph (b)(2)(iv)(*g*) unless the amount of book depreciation, depletion, or amortization for a period with respect to an item of partnership property is the amount that bears the same relationship to the book value of such property as the depreciation (or cost recovery deduction), depletion, or amortization computed for tax purposes with respect to such property for such period bears to the adjusted tax basis of such property. If such property has a zero adjusted tax basis, the book depreciation, depletion, or amortization may be determined under any reasonable method selected by the partnership.

(*h*) *Determinations of fair market value.* For purposes of this paragraph (b)(2)(iv), the fair market value assigned to property contributed to a partnership, property distributed by a partnership, or property otherwise revalued by a partnership, will be regarded as correct, provided that (*1*) such value is reasonably agreed to among the partners in arm's-length negotiations, and (*2*) the partners have sufficiently adverse interests. If, however, these conditions are not satisfied and the value assigned to such property is overstated or understated (by more than an insignificant amount), the capital accounts of the partners will not be considered to be determined and maintained in accordance with the rules of this paragraph (b)(2)(iv). Valuation of property contributed to the partnership, distributed by the partnership, or otherwise revalued by the partnership shall be on a property-by-property basis, except to the extent the regulations under section 704(c) permit otherwise.

(*i*) *Section 705(a)(2)(B) expenditures—* (*1*) *In general.* The basic capital accounting rules contained in paragraph (b)(2)(iv)(*b*) of this section require that a partner's capital account be decreased by allocations made to such partner of expenditures described in section 705(a)(2)(B). See example (11) of paragraph (b)(5) of this section. If an allocation of these expenditures under the partnership agreement does not have substantial economic effect (as determined under paragraphs (b)(2)(ii) and (b)(2)(iii) of this section), or is not otherwise respected under this paragraph, such expenditures will be reallocated in accordance with the partners' interest in the partnership.

(*2*) *Expenses described in section 709.* Except for amounts with respect to which an election is properly made under section 709(b), amounts paid or incurred to organize a partnership or to promote the sale of (or to sell) an interest in such a partnership shall, solely for purposes of this paragraph, be treated as section 705(a)(2)(B) expenditures, and upon liquidation of the partnership no further capital account adjustments will be made in respect thereof.

(*3*) *Disallowed losses.* If a deduction for a loss incurred in connection with the sale or exchange of partnership property is disallowed to the partnership under section 267(a)(1) or section 707(b), that deduction shall, solely for purposes of this paragraph, be treated as a section 705(a)(2)(B) expenditure.

(*j*) *Basis adjustments to section 38 property.* The capital accounts of the partners will not be considered to be determined and maintained in accordance with the rules of this paragraph (b)(2)(iv) unless such capital accounts are adjusted by the partners' shares of any upward or downward basis adjustments allocated to them under this paragraph (b)(2)(iv)(*j*). When there is a reduction in the adjusted tax basis of partnership section 38 property under section 48(q)(1) or section 48(q)(3), section 48(q)(6) provides for an equivalent downward adjustment to the aggregate basis of partnership interests (and no additional adjustment is made under section 705(a)(2)(B)). These downward basis adjustments shall be shared among the partners in the same proportion as the adjusted tax basis or cost of (or the qualified investment in) such section 38 property is allocated among the partners under paragraph (f) of § 1.46-3 (or paragraph (a)(4)(iv) of § 1.48-8). Conversely, when there is an increase in the adjusted tax basis of partnership section 38 property under section 48(q)(2), section 48(q)(6) provides for an equivalent upward adjustment to the aggregate basis or partnership interests. These upward adjustments shall be allocated among the partners in the same proportion as the investment tax credit from such property is recaptured by the partners under § 1.47-6.

(*k*) *Depletion of oil and gas properties*— (*1*) *In general.* The capital accounts of the partners will not be considered to be determined and maintained in accordance with the rules of this paragraph (b)(2)(iv) unless such capital accounts are adjusted for depletion and gain or loss with respect to the oil or gas properties of the partnership in accordance with this paragraph (b)(2)(iv)(*k*).

(*2*) *Simulated depletion.* Except as provided in paragraph (b)(2)(iv)(*k*)(*3*) of this section, a partnership shall, solely for purposes of maintaining capital accounts under this paragraph, compute simulated depletion allowances with respect to its oil and gas properties at the partnership level. These allowances shall be computed on each depletable oil or gas property of the partnership by using either the cost depletion method or the percentage depletion method (computed in accordance with section 613 at the rates specified in section 613A(c)(5) without regard to the limitations of section 613A, which theoretically could apply to any partner) for each partnership taxable year that the property is owned by the partnership and subject to depletion. The choice between the simulated cost depletion method and the simulated percentage depletion method shall be made on a property-by-property basis in the first partnership taxable year beginning after April 30, 1986, for which it is relevant for the property, and shall be binding for all partnership taxable years during which the oil or gas property is held by the partnership. The partnership shall make downward adjustments to the capital accounts of the partners for the simulated depletion allowance with respect to each oil or gas property of the partnership, in the same proportion as such partners (or their predecessors in interest) were properly allocated the adjusted tax basis of each such property. The aggregate capital account adjustments for simulated percentage depletion allowances with respect to an oil or gas property of the partnership shall not exceed the aggregate adjusted tax basis allocated to the partners with respect to such property. Upon the taxable disposition of an oil or gas property by a partnership, such partnership's simulated gain or loss shall be determined by subtracting its simulated adjusted basis in such property from the amount realized upon such disposition. (The partnership's simulated adjusted basis in an oil or gas property is determined in the same manner as adjusted tax basis except that simulated depletion allowances are taken into account instead of actual depletion allowances.) The capital accounts of the partners shall be adjusted upward by the amount of any simulated gain in proportion to such partners' allocable shares of the portion of the total amount realized from the disposition of such property that exceeds the partnership's simulated adjusted basis in such property. The capital accounts of such partners shall be adjusted downward by the amount of any simulated loss in proportion to such partners' allocable shares of the total amount realized from the disposition of such property that represents recovery of the partnership's simulated adjusted basis in such property. See section 613A(c)(7)(D) and the regu-

Reg. § 1.704-1(b)(2)

lations thereunder and paragraph (b)(4)(v) of this section. See example (19)(iv) of paragraph (b)(5) of this section.

(3) *Actual depletion.* Pursuant to section 613A(c)(7)(D) and the regulations thereunder, the depletion allowance under section 611 with respect to the oil and gas properties of a partnership is computed separately by the partners. Accordingly, in lieu of adjusting the partners' capital accounts as provided in paragraph (b)(2)(iv)(k)(2) of this section, the partnership may make downward adjustments to the capital account of each partner equal to such partner's depletion allowance with respect to each oil or gas property of the partnership (for the partner's taxable year that ends with or within the partnership's taxable year). The aggregate adjustments to the capital account of a partner for depletion allowances with respect to an oil or gas property of the partnership shall not exceed the adjusted tax basis allocated to such partner with respect to such property. Upon the taxable disposition of an oil or gas property by a partnership, the capital account of each partner shall be adjusted upward by the amount of any excess of such partner's allocable share of the total amount realized from the disposition of such property over such partner's remaining adjusted tax basis in such property. If there is no such excess, the capital account of such partner shall be adjusted downward by the amount of any excess of such partner's remaining adjusted tax basis in such property over such partner's allocable share of the total amount realized from the disposition thereof. See section 613A(c)(7)(4)(D) and the regulations thereunder and paragraph (b)(4)(v) of this section.

(4) *Effect of book values.* If an oil or gas property of the partnership is, under paragraphs (b)(2)(iv)(d) or (b)(2)(iv)(f) of this section, properly reflected on the books of the partnership at a book value that differs from the adjusted tax basis of such property, the rules contained in this paragraph (b)(2)(iv)(k) and paragraph (b)(4)(v) of this section shall be applied with reference to such book value. A revaluation of a partnership oil or gas property under paragraph (b)(2)(iv)(f) of this section may give rise to a reallocation of the adjusted tax basis of such property, or a change in the partners' relative shares of simulated depletion from such property, only to the extent permitted by section 613A(c)(7)(D) and the regulations thereunder.

(1) *Transfers of partnership interests.* The capital accounts of the partners will not be considered to be determined and maintained in accordance with the rules of this paragraph (b)(2)(iv) unless, upon the transfer of all or a part of an interest in the partnership, the capital account of the transferor that is attributable to the transferred interest carries over to the transferee partner. (See paragraph (b)(2)(iv)(m) of this section for rules concerning the effect of a section 754 election on the capital accounts of the partners.) If the transfer of an interest in a partnership causes a termination of the partnership under section 708(b)(1)(B), the capital account of the transferee partner and the capital accounts of the other partners of the terminated partnership carry over to the new partnership that is formed as a result of the termination of the partnership under § 1.708-1(b)(1)(iv). Moreover, the deemed contribution of assets and liabilities by the terminated partnership to a new partnership and the deemed liquidation of the terminated partnership that occur under § 1.708-1(b)(1)(iv) are disregarded for purposes of paragraph (b)(2)(iv) of this section. See Example 13 of paragraph (b)(5) of this section and the example in § 1.708-1(b)(1)(iv). The previous three sentences apply to terminations of partnerships under section 708(b)(1)(B) occurring on or after May 9, 1997; however, the sentences may be applied to terminations occurring on or after May 9, 1996, provided that the partnership and its partners apply the sentences to the termination in a consistent manner.

(m) *Section 754 elections—(1) In general.* The capital accounts of the partners will not be considered to be determined and maintained in accordance with the rules of this paragraph (b)(2)(iv) unless, upon adjustment to the adjusted tax basis of partnership property under section 732, 734, or 743, the capital accounts of the partners are adjusted as provided in this paragraph (b)(2)(iv)(m).

(2) *Section 743 adjustments.* In the case of a transfer of all or a part of an interest in a partnership that has a section 754 election in effect for the partnership taxable year in which such transfer occurs, adjustments to the adjusted tax basis of partnership property under section 743 shall not be reflected in the capital account of the transferee partner or on the books of the partnership, and subsequent capital account adjustments for distributions (see paragraph (b)(2)(iv)(e)(1) of this section) and for depreciation, depletion, amortization, and gain or loss with respect to such property will disregard the effect of such basis adjustment. The preceding sentence shall not apply to the extent such basis adjustment is allocated to the common basis of partnership property under paragraph (b)(1) of § 1.734-2; in these cases, such basis adjustment shall, except as provided in paragraph (b)(2)(iv)(m)(5) of this section, give rise to adjustments to the capital accounts of the partners in accordance with their interests in the partnership under paragraph

Reg. § 1.704-1(b)(2)

(b)(3) of this section. See examples (13)(iii) and (iv) of paragraph (b)(5) of this section.

(3) *Section 732 adjustments.* In the case of a transfer of all or a part of an interest in a partnership that does not have a section 754 election in effect for the partnership taxable year in which such transfer occurs, adjustments to the adjusted tax basis of partnership property under section 732(d) will be treated in the capital accounts of the partners in the same manner as section 743 basis adjustments are treated under paragraph (b)(2)(iv)(*m*)(*2*) of this section.

(4) *Section 734 adjustments.* Except as provided in paragraph (b)(2)(iv)(*m*)(*5*) of this section, in the case of a distribution of property in liquidation of a partner's interest in the partnership by a partnership that has a section 754 election in effect for the partnership taxable year in which the distribution occurs, the partner who receives the distribution that gives rise to the adjustment to the adjusted tax basis of partnership property under section 734 shall have a corresponding adjustment made to his capital account. If such distribution is made other than in liquidation of a partner's interest in the partnership, however, except as provided in paragraph (b)(2)(iv)(*m*)(*5*) of this section, the capital accounts of the partners shall be adjusted by the amount of the adjustment to the adjusted tax basis of partnership property under section 734, and such capital account adjustment shall be shared among the partners in the manner in which the unrealized income and gain that is displaced by such adjustment would have been shared if the property whose basis is adjusted were sold immediately prior to such adjustment for its recomputed adjusted tax basis.

(5) *Limitations on adjustments.* Adjustments may be made to the capital account of a partner (or his successor in interest) in respect of basis adjustments to partnership property under sections 732, 734, and 743 only to the extent that such basis adjustments (i) are permitted to be made to one or more items of partnership property under section 755, and (ii) result in an increase or a decrease in the amount at which such property is carried on the partnership's balance sheet, as computed for book purposes. For example, if the book value of partnership property exceeds the adjusted tax basis of such property, a basis adjustment to such property may be reflected in a partner's capital account only to the extent such adjustment exceeds the difference between the book value of such property and the adjusted tax basis of such property prior to such adjustment.

(*n*) *Partnership level characterization.* Except as otherwise provided in paragraph (b)(2)(iv)(*k*) of this section, the capital accounts of the partners will not be considered to be determined and maintained in accordance with the rules of this paragraph (b)(2)(iv) unless adjustments to such capital accounts in respect of partnership income, gain, loss, deduction, and section 705(a)(2)(B) expenditures (or item thereof) are made with reference to the Federal tax treatment of such items (and in the case of book items, with reference to the Federal tax treatment of the corresponding tax items) at the partnership level, without regard to any requisite or elective tax treatment of such items at the partner level (for example, under section 58(i)). However, a partnership that incurs mining exploration expenditures will determine the Federal tax treatment of income, gain, loss, and deduction with respect to the property to which such expenditures relate at the partnership level only after first taking into account the elections made by its partners under section 617 and section 703(b)(4).

(*o*) *Guaranteed payments.* Guaranteed payments to a partner under section 707(c) cause the capital account of the recipient partner to be adjusted only to the extent of such partner's distributive share of any partnership deduction, loss, or other downward capital account adjustment resulting from such payment.

(*p*) *Minor discrepancies.* Discrepancies between the balances in the respective capital accounts of the partners and the balances that would be in such respective capital accounts if they had been determined and maintained in accordance with this paragraph (b)(2)(iv) will not adversely affect the validity of an allocation, provided that such discrepancies are minor and are attributable to good faith error by the partnership.

(*q*) *Adjustments where guidance is lacking.* If the rules of this paragraph (b)(2)(iv) fail to provide guidance on how adjustments to the capital accounts of the partners should be made to reflect particular adjustments to partnership capital on the books of the partnership, such capital accounts will not be considered to be determined and maintained in accordance with those rules unless such capital account adjustments are made in a manner that (*1*) maintains equality between the aggregate governing capital accounts of the partners and the amount of partnership capital reflected on the partnership's balance sheet, as computed for book purposes, (*2*) is consistent with the underlying economic arrangement of the partners, and (*3*) is based, wherever practicable, on Federal tax accounting principles.

(*r*) *Restatement of capital accounts.* With respect to partnerships that began operating in a taxable year beginning before May 1, 1986,

Reg. § 1.704-1(b)(2)

the capital accounts of the partners of which have not been determined and maintained in accordance with the rules of this paragraph (b)(2)(iv) since inception, such capital accounts shall not be considered to be determined and maintained in accordance with the rules of this paragraph (b)(2)(iv) for taxable years beginning after April 30, 1986, unless either—

(1) such capital accounts are adjusted, effective for the first partnership taxable year beginning after April 30, 1986, to reflect the fair market value of partnership property as of the first day of such taxable year, and in connection with such adjustment, the rules contained in paragraph (b)(2)(iv)(f)(2), (3), and (4) of this section are satisfied, or

(2) the differences between the balance in each partner's capital account and the balance that would be in such partner's capital account if capital accounts had been determined and maintained in accordance with this paragraph (b)(2)(iv) throughout the full term of the partnership are not significant (for example, such differences are solely attributable to a failure to provide for treatment of section 709 expenses in accordance with the rules of paragraph (b)(2)(iv)(i)(2) of this section or to a failure to follow the rules in paragraph (b)(2)(iv)(m) of this section), and capital accounts are adjusted to bring them into conformity with the rules of this paragraph (b)(2)(iv) no later than the end of the first partnership taxable year beginning after April 30, 1986.

With respect to a partnership that began operating in a taxable year beginning before May 1, 1986, modifications to the partnership agreement adopted on or before November 1, 1988, to make the capital account adjustments required to comply with this paragraph, and otherwise to satisfy the requirements of this paragraph, will be treated as if such modifications were included in the partnership agreement before the end of the first partnership taxable year beginning after April 30, 1986. However, compliance with the previous sentences will have no bearing on the validity of allocations that relate to partnership taxable years beginning before May 1, 1986.

(3) *Partner's interest in the partnership*—(i) *In general.* References in section 704(b) and this paragraph to a partner's interest in the partnership, or to the partners' interests in the partnership, signify the manner in which the partners have agreed to share the economic benefit or burden (if any) corresponding to the income, gain, loss, deduction, or credit (or item thereof) that is allocated.

Except with respect to partnership items that cannot have economic effect (such as nonrecourse deductions of the partnership), this sharing arrangement may or may not correspond to the overall economic arrangement of the partners. (For example, in the case of an unexpected downward adjustment to the capital account of a partner who does not have a deficit makeup obligation that causes such partner to have a negative capital account, it may be necessary to allocate a disproportionate amount of gross income of the partnership to such partner for such year so as to bring that partner's capital account back up to zero.) Thus, a partner who has a 50 percent overall interest in the partnership may have a 90 percent interest in a particular item of income or deduction. The determination of a partner's interest in a partnership shall be made by taking into account all facts and circumstances relating to the economic arrangement of the partners. All partners' interests in the partnership are presumed to be equal (determined on a per capita basis). However, this presumption may be rebutted by the taxpayer or the Internal Revenue Service by establishing facts and circumstances that show that the partners' interests in the partnership are otherwise.

(ii) *Factors considered.* In determining a partner's interest in the partnership, the following factors are among those that will be considered:

(a) The partners' relative contributions to the partnership,

(b) The interests of the partners in economic profits and losses (if different than that in taxable income or loss),

(c) The interests of the partners in cash flow and other non-liquidating distributions, and

(d) The rights of the partners to distributions of capital upon liquidation.

The provisions of this subparagraph (b)(3) are illustrated by examples (1)(i) and (ii), (4)(i), (5)(i) and (ii), (6), (7)(i), (ii), and (iv), (8), (10)(ii), (16)(i), and (19)(iii) of paragraph (b)(5) of this section. See paragraph (b)(4)(i) of this section concerning rules for determining the partners' interests in the partnership with respect to certain tax items.

(iii) *Certain determinations.* If—

(a) Requirements (1) and (2) of paragraph (b)(2)(ii)(b) of this section are satisfied, and

(b) All or a portion of an allocation of income, gain, loss, or deduction made to a partner for a partnership taxable year does not have economic effect under paragraph (b)(2)(ii) of this section,

the partners' interests in the partnership with respect to the portion of the allocation that lacks economic effect will be determined by comparing the manner in which distributions (and contributions) would be made if all partnership property were sold at book value and the partnership were liquidated immediately following the end of the taxable year to which the allocation relates with the manner in which distributions (and contributions) would be made if all partnership property were sold at book value and the partnership were liquidated immediately following the end of the prior taxable year, and adjusting the result for the items described in (4), (5), and (6) of paragraph (b)(2)(ii)(d) of this section. A determination made under this paragraph (b)(3)(iii) will have no force if the economic effect of valid allocations made in the same manner is insubstantial under paragraph (b)(2)(iii) of this section. See examples (1)(iv), (v), and (vi), and (15)(ii) and (iii) of paragraph (b)(5) of this section.

(4) *Special rules*—(i) *Allocations to reflect revaluations.* If partnership property is, under paragraphs (b)(2)(iv)(d) or (b)(2)(iv)(f) of this section, properly reflected in the capital accounts of the partners and on the books of the partnership at a book value that differs from the adjusted tax basis of such property, then depreciation, depletion, amortization, and gain or loss, as computed for book purposes, with respect to such property will be greater or less than the depreciation, depletion, amortization, and gain or loss, as computed for tax purposes, with respect to such property. In these cases the capital accounts of the partners are required to be adjusted solely for allocations of the book items to such partners (see paragraph (b)(2)(iv)(g) of this section), and the partners' shares of the corresponding tax items are not independently reflected by further adjustments to the partners' capital accounts. Thus, separate allocations of these tax items cannot have economic effect under paragraph (b)(2)(ii)(b)(1) of this section, and the partners' distributive shares of such tax items must (unless governed by section 704(c)) be determined in accordance with the partners' interests in the partnership. These tax items must be shared among the partners in a manner that takes account of the variation between the adjusted tax basis of such property and its book value in the same manner as variations between the adjusted tax basis and fair market value of property contributed to the partnership are taken into account in determining the partners' shares of tax items under section 704(c). See examples (14) and (18) of paragraph (b)(5) of this section.

(ii) *Credits.* Allocations of tax credits and tax credit recapture are not reflected by adjustments to the partners' capital accounts (except to the extent that adjustments to the adjusted tax basis of partnership section 38 property in respect of tax credits and tax credit recapture give rise to capital account adjustments under paragraph (b)(2)(iv)(j) of this section). Thus, such allocations cannot have economic effect under paragraph (b)(2)(ii)(b)(1) of this section, and the tax credits and tax credit recapture must be allocated in accordance with the partners' interests in the partnership as of the time the tax credit or credit recapture arises. With respect to the investment tax credit provided by section 38, allocations of cost or qualified investment made in accordance with paragraph (f) of § 1.46-3 and paragraph (a)(4)(iv) of § 1.48-8 shall be deemed to be made in accordance with the partners' interests in the partnership. With respect to other tax credits, if a partnership expenditure (whether or not deductible) that gives rise to a tax credit in a partnership taxable year also gives rise to valid allocations of partnership loss or deduction (or other downward capital account adjustments) for such year, then the partners' interests in the partnership with respect to such credit (or the cost giving rise thereto) shall be in the same proportion as such partners' respective distributive shares of such loss or deduction (and adjustments). See example (11) of paragraph (b)(5) of this section. Identical principles shall apply in determining the partners' interests in the partnership with respect to tax credits that arise from receipts of the partnership (whether or not taxable).

(iii) *Excess percentage depletion.* To the extent the percentage depletion in respect of an item of depletable property of the partnership exceeds the adjusted tax basis of such property, allocations of such excess percentage depletion are not reflected by adjustments to the partners' capital accounts. Thus, such allocations cannot have economic effect under paragraph (b)(2)(ii)(b)(1) of this section, and such excess percentage depletion must be allocated in accordance with the partners' interests in the partnership. The partners' interests in the partnership for a partnership taxable year with respect to such excess percentage depletion shall be in the same proportion as such partners' respective distributive shares of gross income from the depletable property (as determined under section 613(c)) for such year. See example (12) of paragraph (b)(5) of this section. See paragraphs (b)(2)(iv)(k) and (b)(4)(v) of this section for special rules concerning oil and gas properties of the partnership.

* * *

(5) *Examples.* The operation of the rules in this paragraph is illustrated by the following examples:

Example (1). (i) A and B form a general partnership with cash contributions of $40,000 each, which cash is used to purchase depreciable personal property at a cost of $80,000. The partnership elects under section 48(q)(4) to reduce the amount of investment tax credit in lieu of adjusting the tax basis of such property. The partnership agreement provides that A and B will have equal shares of taxable income and loss (computed without regard to cost recovery deductions) and cash flow and that all cost recovery deductions on the property will be allocated to A. The agreement further provides that the partners' capital accounts will be determined and maintained in accordance with paragraph (b)(2)(iv) of this section, but that upon liquidation of the partnership, distributions will be made equally between the partners (regardless of capital account balances) and no partner will be required to restore the deficit balance in his capital account for distribution to partners with positive capital accounts balances. In the partnership's first taxable year, it recognizes operating income equal to its operating expenses and has an additional $20,000 cost recovery deduction, which is allocated entirely to A. That A and B will be entitled to equal distributions on liquidation, even though A is allocated the entire $20,000 cost recovery deduction, indicates A will not bear the full risk of the economic loss corresponding to such deduction if such loss occurs. Under paragraph (b)(2)(ii) of this section, the allocation lacks economic effect and will be disregarded. The partners made equal contributions to the partnership, share equally in other taxable income and loss and in cash flow, and will share equally in liquidation proceeds, indicating that their actual economic arrangement is to bear the risk imposed by the potential decrease in the value of the property equally. Thus, under paragraph (b)(3) of this section the partners' interests in the partnership are equal, and the cost recovery deduction will be reallocated equally between A and B.

(ii) Assume the same facts as in (i) except that the partnership agreement provides that liquidation proceeds will be distributed in accordance with capital account balances if the partnership is liquidated during the first five years of its existence but that liquidation proceeds will be distributed equally if the partnership is liquidated thereafter. Since the partnership agreement does not provide for the requirement contained in paragraph (b)(2)(ii)(*b*)(*2*) of this section to be satisfied throughout the term of the partnership, the partnership allocations do not have economic effect. Even if the partnership agreement provided for the requirement contained in paragraph (b)(2)(ii)(*b*)(*2*) to be satisfied throughout the term of the partnership, such allocations would not have economic effect unless the requirement contained in paragraph (b)(2)(ii)(*b*)(*3*) of this section or the alternate economic effect test contained in paragraph (b)(2)(ii)(*d*) of this section were satisfied.

(iii) Assume the same facts as in (i) except that distributions in liquidation of the partnership (or any partner's interest) are to be made in accordance with the partners' positive capital account balances throughout the term of the partnership (as set forth in paragraph (b)(2)(ii)(*b*)(*2*) of this section). Assume further that the partnership agreement contains a qualified income offset (as defined in paragraph (b)(2)(ii)(*d*) of this section) and that, as of the end of each partnership taxable year, the items described in paragraphs (b)(2)(ii)(*d*)(*4*), (*5*), and (*6*) of this section are not reasonably expected to cause or increase a deficit balance in A's capital account.

	A	B
Capital account upon formation	$40,000	$40,000
Less: year 1 cost recovery deduction	(20,000)	0
Capital account at end of year 1	$20,000	$40,000

Under the alternate economic effect test contained in paragraph (b)(2)(ii)(*d*) of this section, the allocation of the $20,000 cost recovery deduction to A has economic effect.

(iv) Assume the same facts as in (iii) and that in the partnership's second taxable year it recognizes operating income equal to its operating expenses and has a $25,000 cost recovery deduction which, under the partnership agreement, is allocated entirely to A.

	A	B
Capital account at beginning of year 2	$20,000	$40,000
Less: year 2 cost recovery deduction	(25,000)	0
Capital account at end of year 2	$(5,000)	$40,000

The allocation of the $25,000 cost recovery deduction to A satisfies the alternate economic effect test contained in paragraph (b)(2)(ii)(*d*) of this section only to the extent of $20,000. Therefore, only $20,000 of such allocation has economic effect, and the remaining $5,000 must be reallocated in accordance with the partners' interests in the partnership. Under the partnership agreement, if the property were sold immediately following the end of the partnership's second taxable

Reg. § 1.704-1(b)(5)

year for $35,000 (its adjusted tax basis), the $35,000 would be distributed to B. Thus, B, and not A, bears the economic burden corresponding to $5,000 of the $25,000 cost recovery deduction allocated to A. Under paragraph (b)(3)(iii) of this section, $5,000 of such cost recovery deduction will be reallocated to B.

(v) Assume the same facts as in (iv) except that the cost recovery deduction for the partnership's second taxable year is $20,000 instead of

$25,000. The allocation of such cost recovery deduction to A has economic effect under the alternate economic effect test contained in paragraph (b)(2)(ii)(d) of this section. Assume further that the property is sold for $35,000 immediately following the end of the partnership's second taxable year, resulting in a $5,000 taxable loss ($40,000 adjusted tax basis less $35,000 sales price), and the partnership is liquidated.

	A	B
Capital account at beginning of year 2	$20,000	$40,000
Less: year 2 cost recovery deduction	(20,000)	0
Capital account at end of year 2	0	$40,000
Less: loss on sale	(2,500)	(2,500)
Capital account before liquidation	$(2,500)	$37,500

Under the partnership agreement the $35,000 sales proceeds are distributed to B. Since B bears the entire economic burden corresponding to the $5,000 taxable loss from the sale of the property, the allocation of $2,500 of such loss to A does not have economic effect and must be reallocated in accordance with the partners' interests in the partnership. Under paragraph (b)(3)(iii) of this section, such $2,500 loss will be reallocated to B.

(vi) Assume the same facts as in (iv) except that the cost recovery deduction for the partnership's second taxable year is $20,000 instead of $25,000, and that as of the end of the partnership's second taxable year it is reasonably expected that during its third taxable year the partnership will (1) have operating income equal to its operating expenses (but will have no cost recovery deductions), (2) borrow $10,000 (recourse) and distribute such amount $5,000 to A and $5,000 to B, and (3) thereafter sell the part-

nership property, repay the $10,000 liability, and liquidate. In determining the extent to which the alternate economic effect test contained in paragraph (b)(2)(ii)(d) of this section is satisfied as of the end of the partnership's second taxable year, the fair market value of partnership property is presumed to be equal to its adjusted tax basis (in accordance with paragraph (b)(2)(iii)(c) of this section). Thus, it is presumed that the selling price of such property during the partnership's third taxable year will be its $40,000 adjusted tax basis. Accordingly, there can be no reasonable expectation that there will be increases to A's capital account in the partnership's third taxable year that will offset the expected $5,000 distribution to A. Therefore, the distribution of the loan proceeds must be taken into account in determining to what extent the alternate economic effect test contained in paragraph (b)(2)(ii)(d) is satisfied.

	A	B
Capital account at beginning of year 2	$20,000	$40,000
Less: expected future distribution	(5,000)	(5,000)
Less: year 2 cost recovery deduction	(20,000)	(0)
Hypothetical capital account at end of year 2	$(5,000)	$35,000

Upon sale of the partnership property, the $40,000 presumed sales proceeds would be used to repay the $10,000 liability, and the remaining $30,000 would be distributed to B. Under these circumstances the allocation of the $20,000 cost recovery deduction to A in the partnership's second taxable year satisfies the alternate economic effect test contained in paragraph (b)(2)(ii)(d) of this section only to the extent of $15,000. Under paragraph (b)(3)(iii) of this section, the remaining $5,000 of such deduction will be reallocated to B. The results in this example would be the same even if the partnership agreement also provided that any gain (whether ordinary income or capital gain) upon the sale of the property would be allocated to A to the extent of the prior allocations

of cost recovery deductions to him, and, at end of the partnership's second taxable year, the partners were confident that the gain on the sale of the property in the partnership's third taxable year would be sufficient to offset the expected $5,000 distribution to A.

(vii) Assume the same facts as in (iv) except that the partnership agreement also provides that any partner with a deficit balance in his capital account following the liquidation of his interest must restore that deficit to the partnership (as set forth in paragraph (b)(2)(ii)(b)(3) of this section). Thus, if the property were sold for $35,000 immediately after the end of the partnership's second taxable year, the $35,000 would be distributed to B, A would contribute $5,000 (the deficit balance in his capital account) to the partnership, and that $5,000 would be distributed to B. The allocation of the entire $25,000 cost recovery deduction to A in the partnership's second taxable year has economic effect.

(viii) Assume the same facts as in (vii) except that A's obligation to restore the deficit balance in his capital account is limited to a maximum of $5,000. The allocation of the $25,000 cost recovery deduction to A in the partnership's second taxable year has economic effect under the alternate economic effect test contained in paragraph (b)(2)(ii)(d) of this section. At the end of such year, A makes an additional $5,000 contribution to the partnership (thereby eliminating the $5,000 deficit balance in his capital account). Under paragraph (b)(2)(ii)(f) of this section, A's obligation to restore up to $5,000 of the deficit balance in his capital account may be eliminated after he contributes the additional $5,000 without affecting the validity of prior allocations.

(ix) Assume the same facts as in (iv) except that upon formation of the partnership A also contributes to the partnership his negotiable promissory note with a $5,000 principal balance. The note unconditionally obligates A to pay an additional $5,000 to the partnership at the earlier of (a) the beginning of the partnership's fourth taxable year, or (b) the end of the partnership taxable year in which A's interest is liquidated. Under paragraph (b)(2)(ii)(c) of this section, A is considered obligated to restore up to $5,000 of the deficit balance in his capital account to the partnership. Accordingly, under the alternate economic effect test contained in paragraph (b)(2)(ii)(d) of this section, the allocation of the $25,000 cost recovery deduction to A in the partnership's second taxable year has economic effect. The results in this example would be the same if (1) the note A contributed to the partnership were payable only at the end of the partnership's fourth taxable year (so that A would not be required to satisfy the note upon liquidation of his interest in the partnership), and (2) the partnership agreement provided that upon liquidation of A's interest, the partnership would retain A's note, and A would contribute to the partnership the excess of the outstanding principal balance of the note over its then fair market value.

(x) Assume the same facts as in (ix) except that A's obligation to contribute an additional $5,000 to the partnership is not evidenced by a promissory note. Instead, the partnership agreement imposes upon A the obligation to make an additional $5,000 contribution to the partnership at the earlier of (a) the beginning of the partnership's fourth taxable year, or (b) the end of the partnership taxable year in which A's interest is liquidated. Under paragraph (b)(2)(ii)(c) of this

section, as a result of A's deferred contribution requirement, A is considered obligated to restore up to $5,000 of the deficit balance in his capital account to the partnership. Accordingly, under the alternate economic effect test contained in paragraph (b)(2)(ii)(d) of this section, the allocation of the $25,000 cost recovery deduction to A in the partnership's second taxable year has economic effect.

(xi) Assume the same facts as in (vii) except that the partnership agreement also provides that any gain (whether ordinary income or capital gain) upon the sale of the property will be allocated to A to the extent of the prior allocations to A of cost recovery deductions from such property, and additional gain will be allocated equally between A and B. At the time the allocations of cost recovery deductions were made to A, the partners believed there would be gain on the sale of the property in an amount sufficient to offset the allocations of cost recovery deductions to A. Nevertheless, the existence of the gain chargeback provision will not cause the economic effect of the allocations to be insubstantial under paragraph (b)(2)(iii)(c) of this section, since in testing whether the economic effect of such allocations is substantial, the recovery property is presumed to decrease in value by the amount of such deductions.

Example (2). C and D form a general partnership solely to acquire and lease machinery that is 5-year recovery property under section 168. Each contributes $100,000, and the partnership obtains an $800,000 recourse loan to purchase the machinery. The partnership elects under section 48(q)(4) to reduce the amount of investment tax credit in lieu of adjusting the tax basis of such machinery. The partnership, C, and D have calendar taxable years. The partnership agreement provides that the partners' capital accounts will be determined and maintained in accordance with paragraph (b)(2)(iv) of this section, distributions in liquidation of the partnership (or any partner's interest) will be made in accordance with the partners' positive capital account balances, and any partner with a deficit balance in his capital account following the liquidation of his interest must restore that deficit to the partnership (as set forth in paragraphs (b)(2)(ii)(b)(2) and (3) of this section). The partnership agreement further provides that (a) partnership net taxable loss will be allocated 90 percent to C and 10 percent to D until such time as there is partnership net taxable income, and thereafter C will be allocated 90 percent of such taxable income until he has been allocated partnership net taxable income equal to the partnership net taxable loss previously allocated to him, (b) all further partnership net taxable income or loss will be allocated equally

Reg. § 1.704-1(b)(5)

between C and D, and (c) distributions of operating cash flow will be made equally between C and D. The partnership enters into a 12-year lease with a financially secure corporation under which the partnership expects to have a net taxable loss in each of its first 5 partnership taxable years due to cost recovery deductions with respect to the machinery and net taxable income in each of its following 7 partnership taxable years, in part due to the absence of such cost recovery deductions. There is a strong likelihood that the partnership's net taxable loss in partnership taxable years 1 through 5 will be $100,000, $90,000, $80,000, $70,000, and $60,000, respectively, and the partnership's net taxable income in partnership taxable years 6 through 12 will be $40,000, $50,000, $60,000, $70,000, $80,000, $90,000, and $100,000, respectively. Even though there is a strong likelihood that the allocations of net taxable loss in years 1 through 5 will be largely offset by other allocations in partnership taxable years 6 through 12, and even if it is assumed that the total tax liability of the partners in years 1 through 12 will be less than if the allocations had not been provided in the partnership agreement, the economic effect of the allocations will not be insubstantial under paragraph (b)(2)(iii)(c) of this section. This is because at the time such allocations became part of the partnership agreement, there was a strong likelihood that the allocations of net taxable loss in years 1 through 5 would not be largely offset by allocations of income within 5 years (determined on a first-in, first-out basis). The year 1 allocation will not be offset until years 6, 7, and 8, the year 2 allocation will not be offset until years 8 and 9, the year 3 allocation will not be offset until years 9 and 10, the year 4 allocation will not be offset until years 10 and 11, and the year 5 allocation will not be offset until years 11 and 12.

Example (3). E and F enter into a partnership agreement to develop and market experimental electronic devices. E contributes $2,500 cash and agrees to devote his full-time services to the partnership. F contributes $100,000 cash and agrees to obtain a loan for the partnership for any additional capital needs. The partnership agreement provides that all deductions for research and experimental expenditures and interest on partnership loans are to be allocated to F. In addition, F will be allocated 90 percent, and E 10 percent, of partnership taxable income or loss, computed net of the deductions for such research and experimental expenditures and interest, until F has received allocations of such taxable income equal to the sum of such research and experimental expenditures, such interest expense, and his share of such taxable loss. Thereafter, E and F will share all taxable income and loss equally. Operating

cash flow will be distributed equally between E and F. The partnership agreement also provides that E's and F's capital accounts will be determined and maintained in accordance with paragraph (b)(2)(iv) of this section, distributions in liquidation of the partnership (or any partner's interest) will be made in accordance with the partners' positive capital account balances, and any partner with a deficit balance in his capital account following the liquidation of his interest must restore that deficit to the partnership (as set forth in paragraphs (b)(2)(ii)(b)(*2*) and (*3*) of this section). These allocations have economic effect. In addition, in view of the nature of the partnership's activities, there is not a strong likelihood at the time the allocations become part of the partnership agreement that the economic effect of the allocations to F of deductions for research and experimental expenditures and interest on partnership loans will be largely offset by allocations to F of partnership net taxable income. The economic effect of the allocations is substantial.

Example (4). (i) G and H contribute $75,000 and $25,000, respectively, in forming a general partnership. The partnership agreement provides that all income, gain, loss, and deduction will be allocated equally between the partners, that the partners' capital accounts will be determined and maintained in accordance with paragraph (b)(2)(iv) of this section, but that all partnership distributions will, regardless of capital account balances, be made 75 percent to G and 25 percent to H. Following the liquidation of the partnership, neither partner is required to restore the deficit balance in his capital account to the partnership for distribution to partners with positive capital account balances. The allocations in the partnership agreement do not have economic effect. Since contributions were made in a 75/25 ratio and the partnership agreement indicates that all economic profits and losses of the partnership are to be shared in a 75/25 ratio, under paragraph (b)(3) of this section, partnership income, gain, loss, and deduction will be reallocated 75 percent to G and 25 percent to H.

(ii) Assume the same facts as in (i) except that the partnership maintains no capital accounts and the partnership agreement provides that all income, gain, loss, deduction, and credit will be allocated 75 percent to G and 25 percent to H. G and H are ultimately liable (under a State law right of contribution) for 75 percent and 25 percent, respectively, of any debts of the partnership. Although the allocations do not satisfy the requirements of paragraph (b)(2)(ii)(b) of this section, the allocations have economic effect under the economic effect equivalence test of paragraph (b)(2)(ii)(*i*) of this section.

Reg. § 1.704-1(b)(5)

(iii) Assume the same facts as in (i) except that the partnership agreement provides that any partner with a deficit balance in his capital account must restore that deficit to the partnership (as set forth in paragraph (b)(2)(ii)(*b*)(*2*) of this section). Although the allocations do not satisfy the requirements of paragraph (b)(2)(ii)(*b*) of this section, the allocations have economic effect under the economic effect equivalence test of paragraph (b)(2)(ii)(*i*) of this section.

Example (5). (i) Individuals I and J are the only partners of an investment partnership. The partnership owns corporate stocks, corporate debt instruments, and tax-exempt debt instruments. Over the next several years, I expects to be in the 50 percent marginal tax bracket, and J expects to be in the 15 percent marginal tax bracket. There is a strong likelihood that in each of the next several years the partnership will realize between $450 and $550 of tax-exempt interest and between $450 and $550 of a combination of taxable interest and dividends from its investments. I and J made equal capital contributions to the partnership, and they have agreed to share equally in gains and losses from the sale of the partnership's investment securities. I and J agree, however, that rather than share interest and dividends of the partnership equally, they will allocate the partnership's tax-exempt interest 80 percent to I and 20 percent to J and will distribute cash derived from interest received on the tax-exempt bonds in the same percentages. In addition, they agree to allocate 100 percent of the partnership's taxable interest and dividends to J and to distribute cash derived from interest and dividends received on the corporate stocks and debt instruments 100 percent to J. The partnership agreement further provides that the partners' capital accounts will be determined and maintained in accordance with paragraph (b)(2)(iv) of this section, distributions in liquidation of the partnership (or any partner's interest) will be made in accordance with the partner's positive capital account balances, and any partner with a deficit balance in his capital account following the liquidation of his interest must restore that deficit to the partnership (as set forth in paragraphs (b)(2)(ii)(*b*)(*2*) and (*3*) of this section). The allocation of taxable interest and dividends and tax-exempt interest has economic effect, but that economic effect is not substantial under the general rules set forth in paragraph (b)(2)(iii) of this section. Without the allocation I would be allocated between $225 and $275 of tax-exempt interest and between $225 and $275 of a combination of taxable interest and dividends, which (net of Federal income taxes he would owe on such income) would give I between $337.50 and $412.50 after tax. With the allocation, however, I will be allo-

cated between $360 and $440 of tax-exempt interest and no taxable interest and dividends, which (net of Federal income taxes) will give I between $360 and $440 after tax. Thus, at the time the allocations became part of the partnership agreement, I is expected to enhance his after-tax economic consequences as a result of the allocations. On the other hand, there is a strong likelihood that neither I nor J will substantially diminish his after-tax economic consequences as a result of the allocations. Under the combination of likely investment outcomes least favorable for J, the partnership would realize $550 of tax-exempt interest and $450 of taxable interest and dividends, giving J $492.50 after tax (which is more than the $466.25 after tax J would have received if each of such amounts had been allocated equally between the partners). Under the combination of likely investment outcomes least favorable for I, the partnership would realize $450 of tax-exempt interest and $550 of taxable interest and dividends, giving I $360 after tax (which is not substantially less than the $362.50 he would have received if each of such amounts had been allocated equally between the partners). Accordingly, the allocations in the partnership agreement must be reallocated in accordance with the partners' interests in the partnership under paragraph (b)(3) of this section.

(ii) Assume the same facts as in (i). In addition, assume that in the first partnership taxable year in which the allocation arrangement described in (i) applies, the partnership realizes $450 of tax-exempt interest and $550 of taxable interest and dividends, so that, pursuant to the partnership agreement, I's capital account is credited with $360 (80 percent of the tax-exempt interest), and J's capital account is credited with $640 (20 percent of the tax-exempt interest and 100 percent of the taxable interest and dividends). The allocations of tax-exempt interest and taxable interest and dividends (which do not have substantial economic effect for the reasons stated in (i)) will be disregarded and will be reallocated. Since under the partnership agreement I will receive 36 percent (360/1,000) and J will receive 64 percent (640/1,000) of the partnership's total investment income in such year, under paragraph (b)(3) of this section the partnership's tax-exempt interest and taxable interest and dividends each will be reallocated 36 percent to I and 64 percent to J.

Example (6). K and L are equal partners in a general partnership formed to acquire and operate property described in section 1231(b). The partnership, K, and L have calendar taxable years. The partnership agreement provides that the partners' capital accounts will be determined and maintained in accordance with paragraph

Reg. § 1.704-1(b)(5)

(b)(2)(iv) of this section, that distributions in liquidation of the partnership (or any partner's interest) will be made in accordance with the partners' positive capital account balances, and that any partner with a deficit balance in his capital account following the liquidation of his interest must restore that deficit to the partnership (as set forth in paragraphs (b)(2)(ii)(*b*) and (*3*) of this section). For a taxable year in which the partnership expects to incur a loss on the sale of a portion of such property, the partnership agreement is amended (at the beginning of the taxable year) to allocate such loss to K, who expects to have no gains from the sale of depreciable property described in section 1231(b) in that taxable year, and to allocate an equivalent amount of partnership loss and deduction for that year of a different character to L, who expects to have such gains. Any partnership loss and deduction in excess of these allocations will be allocated equally between K and L. The amendment is effective only for that taxable year. At the time the partnership agreement is amended, there is a strong likelihood that the partnership will incur deduction or loss in the taxable year other than loss from the sale of property described in section 1231(b) in an amount that will substantially equal or exceed the expected amount of the section 1231(b) loss. The allocations in such taxable year have economic effect. However, the economic effect of the allocations is insubstantial under the test described in paragraph (b)(2)(iii)(*b*) of this section because there is a stong likelihood, at the time the allocations become part of the partnership agreement, that the net increases and decreases to K's and L's capital accounts will be the same at the end of the taxable year to which they apply with such allocations in effect as they would have been in the absence of such allocations, and that the total taxes of K and L for such year will be reduced as a result of such allocations. If in fact the partnership incurs deduction or loss, other than loss from the sale of property described in section 1231(b), in an amount at least equal to the section 1231(b) loss, the loss and deduction in such taxable year will be reallocated equally between K and L under paragraph (b)(3) of this section. If not, the loss from the sale of property described in section 1231(b) and the items of deduction and other loss realized in such year will be reallocated between K and L in proportion to the net decreases in their capital accounts due to the allocation of such items under the partnership agreement.

Example (7). (i) M and N are partners in the MN general partnership, which is engaged in an active business. Income, gain, loss, and deduction from MN's business is allocated equally between M and N. The partnership, M, and N have calendar taxable years. Under the partnership agreement the partners' capital accounts will be determined and maintained in accordance with paragraph (b)(2)(iv) of this section, distributions in liquidation of the partnership (or any partner's interest) will be made in accordance with the partners' positive capital account balances, and any partner with a deficit balance in his capital account following the liquidation of his interest must restore that deficit to the partnership (as set forth in paragraphs (b)(2)(ii)(*b*)(*2*) and (*3*) of this section). In order to enhance the credit standing of the partnership, the partners contribute surplus funds to the partnership, which the partners agree to invest in equal dollar amounts of tax-exempt bonds and corporate stock for the partnership's first 3 taxable years. M is expected to be in a higher marginal tax bracket than N during those 3 years. At the time the decision to make these investments is made, it is agreed that, during the 3-year period of the investment, M will be allocated 90 percent and N 10 percent of the interest income from the tax-exempt bonds as well as any gain or loss from the sale thereof, and that M will be allocated 10 percent and N 90 percent of the dividend income from the corporate stock as well as any gain or loss from the sale thereof. At the time the allocations concerning the investments become part of the partnership agreement, there is not a strong likelihood that the gain or loss from the sale of the stock will be substantially equal to the gain or loss from the sale of the tax-exempt bonds, but there is a strong likelihood that the tax-exempt interest and the taxable dividends realized from these investments during the 3-year period will not differ substantially. These allocations have economic effect, and the economic effect of the allocations of the gain or loss on the sale of the tax-exempt bonds and corporate stock is substantial. The economic effect of the allocations of the tax-exempt interest and the taxable dividends, however, is not substantial under the test described in paragraph (b)(2)(iii)(*c*) of this section because there is a strong likelihood, at the time the allocations become part of the partnership agreement, that at the end of the 3-year period to which such allocations relate, the net increases and decreases to M's and N's capital accounts will be the same with such allocations as they would have been in the absence of such allocations, and that the total taxes of M and N for the taxable years to which such allocations relate will be reduced as a result of such allocations. If in fact the amounts of tax-exempt interest and taxable dividends earned by the partnership during the 3-year period are equal, the tax-exempt interest and taxable dividends will be reallocated to the partners in equal shares under paragraph (b)(3) of this section. If not, the tax-exempt interest and taxable dividends will be reallocated between M and N in proportion to the net increases in their capital accounts during such 3-year period due to the allocation of such items under the partnership agreement.

(ii) Assume the same facts as in (i) except that gain or loss from the sale of the tax-exempt bonds and corporate stock will be allocated equally between M and N and the partnership agreement provides that the 90/10 allocation arrangement with respect to the investment income applies only to the first $10,000 of interest income from the tax-exempt bonds and the first $10,000 of dividend income from the corporate stock, and only to the first taxable year of the partnership. There is a strong likelihood at the time the 90/10 allocation of the investment income became part of the partnership agreement that in the first taxable year of the partnership, the partnership will earn more than $10,000 of tax-exempt interest and more than $10,000 of taxable dividends. The allocations of tax-exempt interest and taxable dividends provided in the partnership agreement have economic effect, but under the test contained in paragraph (b)(2)(iii)(b) of this section, such economic effect is not substantial for the same reasons stated in (i) (but applied to the 1 taxable year, rather than to a 3-year period). If in fact the partnership realizes at least $10,000 of tax-exempt interest and at least $10,000 of taxable dividends in such year, the allocations of such interest income and dividend income will be reallocated equally between M and N under paragraph (b)(3) of this section. If not, the tax-exempt interest and taxable dividends will be reallocated between M and N in proportion to the net increases in their capital accounts due to the allocations of such items under the partnership agreement.

(iii) Assume the same facts as in (ii) except that at the time the 90/10 allocation of investment income becomes part of the partnership agreement, there is not a strong likelihood that (1) the partnership will earn $10,000 or more of tax-exempt interest and $10,000 or more of taxable dividends in the partnership's first taxable year, and (2) the amount of tax-exempt interest and taxable dividends earned during such year will be substantially the same. Under these facts the economic effect of the allocations generally will be substantial. (Additional facts may exist in certain cases, however, so that the allocation is insubstantial under the second sentence of paragraph (b)(2)(iii). See example (5) above.)

* * *

Example (12). (i) W and X form a general partnership for the purpose of mining iron ore. W makes an initial contribution of $75,000, and X makes an initial contribution of $25,000. The partnership agreement provides that non-liquidating distributions will be made 75 percent to W and 25 percent to X, and that all items of income, gain, loss, and deduction will be allocated 75 percent to W and 25 percent to X, except that all percentage depletion deductions will be allocated to W. The agreement further provides that the partners' capital accounts will be determined and maintained in accordance with paragraph (b)(2)(iv) of this section, distributions in liquidation of the partnership (or any partner's interest) will be made in accordance with the partners' positive capital account balances, and any partner with a deficit balance in his capital account following the liquidation of his interest must restore such deficit to the partnership (as set forth in paragraphs (b)(2)(ii)(b)(2) and (3) of this section). Assume that the adjusted tax basis of the partnership's only depletable iron ore property is $1,000 and that the percentage depletion deduction for the taxable year with respect to such property is $1,500. The allocation of partnership income, gain, loss, and deduction (excluding the percentage depletion deduction) as well as the allocation of $1,000 of the percentage depletion deduction have substantial economic effect. The allocation to W of the remaining $500 of the percentage depletion deduction, representing the excess of percentage depletion over adjusted tax basis of the iron ore property, cannot have economic effect since such amount cannot properly be reflected in the partners' capital accounts. Furthermore, the allocation to W of that $500 excess percentage depletion deduction is not in accordance with the special partners' interests in the partnership rule contained in paragraph (b)(4)(iii) of this section, under which such $500 excess depletion deduction (and all further percentage depletion deductions from the mine) will be reallocated 75 percent to W and 25 percent to X.

(ii) Assume the same facts as in (i) except that the partnership agreement provides that all percentage depletion deductions of the partnership will be allocated 75 percent to W and 25 percent to X. Once again, the allocation of partnership income, gain, loss, and deduction (excluding the percentage depletion deduction) as well as the allocation of $1,000 of the percentage depletion deduction have substantial economic effect. Furthermore, since the $500 portion of the percentage depletion deduction that exceeds the adjusted basis of such iron ore property is allocated in the same manner as valid allocations of the gross income from such property during the taxable year (*i.e.,* 75 percent to W and 25 percent to X), the allocation of the $500 excess percentage depletion contained in the partnership agreement is in accordance with the special partners' interests in the partnership rule contained in paragraph (b)(4)(iii) of this section.

Example (13). (i) Y and Z form a brokerage general partnership for the purpose of investing and trading in marketable securities. Y contributes cash of $10,000, and Z contributes securities of P corporation, which have an adjusted basis of $3,000 and a fair market value of $10,000. The partnership would not be an investment company under section 351(e) if it were incorporated. The partnership agreement provides that the partners' capital accounts will be determined and maintained in accordance with paragraph (b)(2)(iv) of this section, distributions in liquidation of the partnership (or any partner's interest) will be made in accordance with the partners' positive capital account balances, and any partner with a deficit balance in his capital account following the liquidation of his interest must restore that deficit to the partnership (as set forth in paragraphs (b)(2)(ii)(b)(2) and (3) of this section). The partnership uses the interim closing of the books method for purposes of section 706. The initial capital accounts of Y and Z are fixed at $10,000 each. The agreement further provides that all partnership distributions, income, gain, loss, deduction, and credit will be shared equally between Y and Z, except that the taxable gain attributable to the precontribution appreciation in the value of the securities of P corporation will be allocated to Z in accordance with section 704(c). During the partnership's first taxable year, it sells the securities of P corporation for $12,000, resulting in a $2,000 book gain ($12,000 less $10,000 book value) and a $9,000 taxable gain ($12,000 less $3,000 adjusted tax basis). The partnership has no other income, gain, loss, or deductions for the taxable year. The gain from the sale of the securities is allocated as follows:

	Y Tax	Y Book	Z Tax	Z Book
Capital account upon formation	$10,000	$10,000	$3,000	$10,000
Plus: gain	1,000	1,000	8,000	1,000
Capital account at end of year 1	$11,000	$11,000	$11,000	$11,000

The allocation of the $2,000 book gain, $1,000 each to Y and Z, has substantial economic effect. Furthermore, under section 704(c) the partners' distributive shares of the $9,000 taxable gain are $1,000 to Y and $8,000 to Z.

(ii) Assume the same facts as in (i) and that at the beginning of the partnership's second taxable year, it invests its $22,000 of cash in securities of G Corp. The G Corp. securities increase in value to $40,000, at which time Y sells 50 percent of his partnership interest (*i.e.*, a 25 percent interest in the partnership) to LK for $10,000. The partnership does not have a section 754 election in effect for the partnership taxable year during which such sale occurs. In accordance with paragraph (b)(2)(iv)(*l*) of this section, the partnership agreement provides that LK inherits 50 percent of Y's $11,000 capital account balance. Thus, following the sale, LK and Y each have a capital account of $5,500, and Z's capital account remains at $11,000. Prior to the end of the partnership's second taxable year, the securities are sold for their $40,000 fair market value, resulting in an $18,000 taxable gain ($40,000 less $22,000 adjusted tax basis). The partnership has no other income, gain, loss, or deduction in such taxable year. Under the partnership agreement the $18,000 taxable gain is allocated as follows:

	Y	Z	LK
Capital account before sale of securities	$5,500	$11,000	$5,500
Plus: gain	4,500	9,000	4,500
Capital account at end of year 2	$10,000	$20,000	$10,000

The allocation of the $18,000 taxable gain has substantial economic effect.

(iii) Assume the same facts as in (ii) except that the partnership has a section 754 election in effect for the partnership taxable year during which Y sells 50 percent of his interest to LK. Accordingly, under § 1.743-1 there is a $4,500 basis increase to the G Corp. securities with respect to LK. Notwithstanding this basis adjustment, as a result of the sale of the G Corp. securities, LK's capital account is, as in (ii), increased by $4,500. The fact that LK recognizes no taxable gain from such sale (due to his $4,500 section 743 basis adjustment) is irrelevant for capital accounting purposes since, in accordance with paragraph (b)(2)(iv)(*m*)(2) of this section, that basis adjustment is disregarded in the maintenance and computation of the partners' capital accounts.

(iv) Assume the same facts as in (iii) except that immediately following Y's sale of 50 percent of this interest to LK, the G Corp. securi-

Reg. § 1.704-1(b)(5)

ties decrease in value to $32,000 and are sold. The $10,000 taxable gain ($32,000 less $22,000 adjusted tax basis) is allocated as follows:

	Y	Z	LK
Capital account before sale of securities	$5,500	$11,000	$5,500
Plus: gain	2,500	5,000	2,500
Capital account at end of the year 2	$8,000	$16,000	$8,000

The fact that LK recognizes a $2,000 taxable loss from the sale of the G Corp. securities (due to his $4,500 section 743 basis adjustment) is irrelevant for capital accounting purposes since, in accordance with paragraph (b)(2)(iv)(*m*)(*2*) of this section, that basis adjustment is disregarded in the maintenance and computation of the partners' capital accounts.

(v) Assume the same facts as in (ii) except that Y sells 100 percent of his partnership interest (*i.e.,* a 50 percent interest in the partnership) to LK for $20,000. Under section 708(b)(1)(B) the partnership terminates. Under paragraph (b)(1)(iv) of § 1.708-1, there is a constructive liquidation of the partnership. Immediately preceding the constructive liquidation, the capital accounts of Z and LK equal $11,000 each (LK having inherited Y s $11,000 capital account) and the book value of the G Corp. securities is $22,000 (original purchase price of securities). Under paragraph (b)(2)(iv)(*l*) of this section, the deemed contribution of assets and liabilities by the terminated partnership to the new partnership and the deemed liquidation of the terminated partnership that occur under § 1.708-1(b)(1)(iv) in connection with the constructive liquidation of the terminated partnership are disregarded in the maintenance and computation of the partners' capital accounts. As a result, the capital accounts of Z and LK in the new partnership equal $11,000 each (their capital accounts in the terminated partnership immediately prior to the termination), and the book value of the G Corp. securities remains $22,000 (its book value immediately prior to the termination). This *Example 13*(v) applies to terminations of partnerships under section 708(b)(1)(B) occurring on or after May 9, 1997; however, this *Example 13*(v) may be applied to terminations occurring on or after May 9, 1996, provided that the partnership and its partners apply this *Example 13*(v) to the termination in a consistent manner.

Example (14). (i) MC and RW form a general partnership to which each contributes $10,000. The $20,000 is invested in securities of Ventureco (which are not readily tradable on an established securities market). In each of the partnership's taxable years, it recognizes operating income equal to its operating deductions (excluding gain or loss from the sale of securities). The partnership agreement provides that the partners' capital accounts will be determined and maintained in accordance with paragraph (b)(2)(iv) of this section, distributions in liquidation of the partnership (or any partner's interest) will be made in accordance with the partners' positive capital account balances, and any partner with a deficit balance in his capital account following the liquidation of his interest must restore that deficit to the partnership (as set forth in paragraphs (b)(2)(ii)(*b*)(*2*) and (*3*) of this section). The partnership uses the interim closing of the books method for purposes of section 706. Assume that the Ventureco securities subsequently appreciate in value to $50,000. At that time SK makes a $25,000 cash contribution to the partnership (thereby acquiring a one-third interest in the partnership), and the $25,000 is placed in a bank account. Upon SK's admission to the partnership, the capital accounts of MC and RW (which were $10,000 each prior to SK's admission) are, in accordance with paragraph (b)(2)(iv)(*f*) of this section, adjusted upward (to $25,000 each) to reflect their shares of the unrealized appreciation in the Ventureco securities that occurred before SK was admitted to the partnership. Immediately after SK's admission to the partnership, the securities are sold for their $50,000 fair market value, resulting in taxable gain of $30,000 ($50,000 less $20,000 adjusted tax basis) and no book gain or loss. An allocation of the $30,000 taxable gain cannot have economic effect since it cannot properly be reflected in the partners' book capital accounts. Under paragraph (b)(2)(iv)(*f*) of this section and the special partners' interests in the partnership rule contained in paragraph (b)(4)(i) of this section, unless the partnership agreement provides that the $30,000 taxable gain will, in accordance with section 704(c) principles, be shared $15,000 to MC and $15,000 to RW, the partners' capital accounts will not be considered maintained in accordance with paragraph (b)(2)(iv) of this section.

Reg. § 1.704-1(b)(5)

	MC		RW		SK	
	Tax	Book	Tax	Book	Tax	Book
Capital account following SK's admission	$10,000	$25,000	$10,000	$25,000	$25,000	$25,000
Plus: gain	15,000	0	15,000	0	0	0
Capital account following sale	$25,000	$25,000	$25,000	$25,000	$25,000	$25,000

(ii) Assume the same facts as (i), except that after SK's admission to the partnership, the Ventureco securities appreciate in value to $74,000 and are sold, resulting in taxable gain of $54,000 ($74,000 less $20,000 adjusted tax basis) and book gain of $24,000 ($74,000 less $50,000 book value). Under the partnership agreement the $24,000 book gain (the appreciation in value occurring after SK became a partner) is allocated equally among MC, RW, and SK, and such allocations have substantial economic effect. An allocation of the $54,000 taxable gain cannot have economic effect since it cannot properly be reflected in the partners' book capital accounts. Under paragraph (b)(2)(iv)(f) of this section and the special partners' interests in the partnership rule contained in paragraph (b)(4)(i) of this section, unless the partnership agreement provides that the taxable gain will, in accordance with section 704(c) principles, be shared $23,000 to MC, $23,000 to RW, and $8,000 to SK, the partners' capital accounts will not be considered maintained in accordance with paragraph (b)(2)(iv) of this section.

	MC		RW		SK	
	Tax	Book	Tax	Book	Tax	Book
Capital account following SK's admission	$10,000	$25,000	$10,000	$25,000	$25,000	$25,000
Plus: gain	23,000	8,000	23,000	8,000	8,000	8,000
Capital account following sale	$33,000	$33,000	$33,000	$33,000	$33,000	$33,000

(iii) Assume the same facts as (i) except that after SK's admission to the partnership, the Ventureco securities depreciate in value to $44,000 and are sold, resulting in taxable gain of $24,000 ($44,000 less $20,000 adjusted tax basis) and a book loss of $6,000 ($50,000 book value less $44,000). Under the partnership agreement the $6,000 book loss is allocated equally among MC, RW, and SK, and such allocations have substantial economic effect. An allocation of the $24,000 taxable gain cannot have economic effect since it cannot properly be reflected in the partners' book capital accounts. Under paragraph (b)(2)(iv)(f) of this section and the special partners' interests in the partnership rule contained in paragraph (b)(4)(i) of this section, unless the partnership agreement provides that the $24,000 taxable gain will, in accordance with section 704(c) principles, be shared equally between MC and RW, the partners' capital accounts will not be considered maintained in accordance with paragraph (b)(2)(iv) of this section.

	MC		RW		SK	
	Tax	Book	Tax	Book	Tax	Book
Capital account following SK's admission	$10,000	$25,000	$10,000	$25,000	$25,000	$25,000
Plus: gain	12,000	0	12,000	0	0	0
Less: loss	0	(2,000)	0	(2,000)	0	(2,000)
Capital account following sale	$22,000	$23,000	$22,000	$23,000	$25,000	$23,000

That SK bears an economic loss of $2,000 without a corresponding taxable loss is attributable entirely to the "ceiling rule." See paragraph (c)(2) of § 1.704-1.

(iv) Assume the same facts as in (ii) except that upon the admission of SK the capital accounts of MC and RW are not each adjusted upward from $10,000 to $25,000 to reflect the appreciation in the partnership's securities that occurred before SK was admitted to the partnership. Rather, upon SK's admission to the partnership, the partnership agreement is amended to provide that the first $30,000 of taxable gain upon the sale of such securities will be allocated equally between MC and RW, and that all other income, gain, loss, and deduction will be allocated equally between MC, RW, and SK. When the securities are sold for $74,000, the $54,000 of taxable gain is so allocated. These allocations of taxable gain have substantial economic effect. (If the agreement instead provides for all taxable gain (including the $30,000 taxable gain attributable to the appreciation in the securities prior to SK's admission to the partnership) to be allocated equally between MC, RW, and SK, the partners should consider whether, and to what extent, the provisions of paragraphs (b)(1)(iii) and (iv) of this section are applicable.)

(v) Assume the same facts as in (iv) except that instead of selling the securities, the partnership makes a distribution of the securities (which have a fair market value of $74,000). Assume the distribution does not give rise to a transaction described in section 707(a)(2)(B). In accordance with paragraph (b)(2)(iv)(e) of this section, the partners' capital accounts are adjusted immediately prior to the distribution to reflect how taxa-

ble gain ($54,000) would have been allocated had the securities been sold for their $74,000 fair market value, and capital account adjustments in respect of the distribution of the securities are made with reference to the $74,000 "booked-up" fair market value.

	MC	RW	SK
Capital account before adjustment	$10,000	$10,000	$25,000
Deemed sale adjustment	23,000	23,000	8,000
Less: distribution	(24,667)	(24,667)	(24,667)
Capital account after distribution	$ 8,333	$ 8,333	$ 8,333

(vi) Assume the same facts as in (i) except that the partnership does not sell the Ventureco securities. During the next 3 years the fair market value of the Ventureco securities remains at $50,000, and the partnership engages in no other investment activities. Thus, at the end of that period the balance sheet of the partnership and the partners' capital accounts are the same as they were at the beginning of such period. At the end of the 3 years, MC's interest in the partnership is liquidated for the $25,000 cash held by the

partnership. Assume the distribution does not give rise to a transaction described in section 707(a)(2)(B). Assume further that the partnership has a section 754 election in effect for the taxable year during which such liquidation occurs. Under sections 734(b) and 755 the partnership increases the basis of the Ventureco securities by the $15,000 basis adjustment (the excess of $25,000 over the $10,000 adjusted tax basis of MC's partnership interest).

	MC		RW		SK	
	Tax	Book	Tax	Book	Tax	Book
Capital account before distribution	$10,000	$25,000	$10,000	$25,000	$25,000	$25,000
Plus: basis adjustment	15,000	0	0	0	0	0
Less: distribution	(25,000)	(25,000)	0	0	0	0
Capital account, account after liquidation	0	0	$10,000	$25,000	$25,000	$25,000

(vii) Assume the same facts as in (vi) except that the partnership has no section 754 election in effect for the taxable year during which such liquidation occurs.

	MC		RW		SK	
	Tax	Book	Tax	Book	Tax	Book
Capital account before distribution	$10,000	$25,000	$10,000	$25,000	$25,000	$25,000
Less: distribution	25,000	(25,000)	0	0	0	0
Capital account after liquidation	($15,000)	0	$10,000	$25,000	$25,000	$25,000

Following the liquidation of MC's interest in the partnership, the Ventureco securities are sold for their $50,000 fair market value, resulting in no book gain or loss but a $30,000 taxable gain. An allocation of this $30,000 taxable gain cannot have economic effect since it cannot properly be reflected in the partners' book capital accounts. Under paragraph (b)(2)(iv)(f) of this section and the special partners' interests in the partnership rule contained in paragraph (b)(4)(i) of this section, unless the partnership agreement provides that $15,000 of such taxable gain will, in accordance with section 704(c) principles, be included in RW's distributive share, the partners' capital accounts will not be considered maintained in accordance with paragraph (b)(2)(iv) of this section. The remaining $15,000 of such gain will, under paragraph (b)(3) of this section, be shared equally between RW and SK.

Example (15). (i) JB and DK form a limited partnership for the purpose of purchasing residential real estate to lease. JB, the limited partner, contributes $13,500, and DK, the general partner, contributes $1,500. The partnership, which uses the cash receipts and disbursements method of accounting, purchases a building for $100,000 (on leased land), incurring a recourse mortgage of $85,000 that requires the payment of interest only for a period of 3 years. The partnership agreement provides that partnership net taxable income and loss will be allocated 90 percent to JB and 10 percent to DK, the partners' capital accounts will be determined and maintained in accordance with paragraph (b)(2)(iv) of this section, distributions in liquidation of the partnership (or any partner's interest) will be made in accordance with the partners' positive capital account balances (as set forth in paragraph (b)(2)(ii)(b)(2) of this section), and JB is not required to restore any deficit balance in his capital account, but DK is so required. The partnership agreement contains a qualified income offset (as defined in paragraph (b)(2)(ii)(*d*) of this section). As of the end of each of the partnership's first 3 taxable years, the items described in paragraphs (b)(2)(ii)(*d*)(*4*), (*5*), and (*6*) of this section are not reasonably expected to cause or increase a deficit balance in JB's

capital account. In the partnership's first taxable year, it has rental income of $10,000, operating expenses of $2,000, interest expense of $8,000, and cost recovery deductions of $12,000. Under the partnership agreement JB and DK are allocated $10,800 and $1,200, respectively, of the $12,000 net taxable loss incurred in the partnership's first taxable year.

	JB	DK
Capital account upon formation	$13,500	$1,500
Less: year 1 net loss	(10,800)	(1,200)
Capital account at end of year 1	$ 2,700	$ 300

The alternate economic effect test contained in paragraph (b)(2)(ii)(*d*) of this section is satisfied as of the end of the partnership's first taxable year. Thus, the allocation made in the partnership's first taxable year has economic effect.

(ii) Assume the same facts as in (i) and that in the partnership's second taxable year it

again has rental income of $10,000, operating expenses of $2,000, interest expense of $8,000, and cost recovery deductions of $12,000. Under the partnership agreement JB and DK are allocated $10,800 and $1,200, respectively, of the $12,000 net taxable loss incurred in the partnership's second taxable year.

	JB	DK
Capital account at beginning of year 1	$ 2,700	$ 300
Less: year 2 net loss	(10,800)	(1,200)
Capital account at end of year 2	$(8,100)	$ (900)

Only $2,700 of the $10,800 net taxable loss allocated to JB satisfies the alternate economic effect test contained in paragraph (b)(2)(ii)(*d*) of this section as of the end of the partnership's second taxable year. The allocation of such $2,700 net taxable loss to JB (consisting of $2,250 of rental income, $450 of operating expenses, $1,800 of interest expense, and $2,700 of cost recovery deductions) has economic effect. The remaining $8,100 of net taxable loss allocated by the partnership agreement to JB must be reallocated in accordance with the partners' interests in the partnership. Under paragraph (b)(3)(iii) of this section, the determination of the partners' interests in the remaining $8,100 net taxable loss is made by comparing how distributions (and contributions) would be made if the partnership sold its property at its adjusted tax basis and liquidated immediately following the end of the partnership's first taxable year with the results of such a sale and liquidation immediately following the end of the partnership's second taxable year. If the partnership's real property were sold for its $88,000 adjusted tax basis and the partnership were liquidated immediately following the end of the partnership's first taxable year, the $88,000 sales proceeds would be used to repay the $85,000 note, and there would be $3,000 remaining in the partnership, which would be used to make liquidating distributions to DK and JB of $300 and $2,700, respectively. If such property were sold for its $76,000 adjusted tax basis and the partnership were liquidated immediately following the end of the partnership's second taxable year, DK

would be required to contribute $9,000 to the partnership in order for the partnership to repay the $85,000 note, and there would be no assets remaining in the partnership to distribute. A comparison of these outcomes indicates that JB bore $2,700 and DK $9,300 of the economic burden that corresponds to the $12,000 net taxable loss. Thus, in addition to the $1,200 net taxable loss allocated to DK under the partnership agreement, $8,100 of net taxable loss will be reallocated to DK under paragraph (b)(3)(iii) of this section. Similarly, for subsequent taxable years, absent an increase in JB's capital account, all net taxable loss allocated to JB under the partnership agreement will be reallocated to DK.

(iii) Assume the same facts as in (ii) and that in the partnership's third taxable year there is rental income of $35,000, operating expenses of $2,000, interest expense of $8,000, the cost recovery deductions of $10,000. The capital accounts of the partners maintained on the books of the partnership do not take into account the reallocation to DK of the $8,100 net taxable loss in the partnership's second taxable year. Thus, an allocation of the $15,000 net taxable income $13,500 to JB and $1,500 to DK (as dictated by the partnership agreement and as reflected in the capital accounts of the partners) does not have economic effect. The partners' interests in the partnership with respect to such $15,000 taxable gain again is made in the manner described in paragraph (b)(3)(iii) of this section. If the partnership's real property were sold for its $76,000 adjusted tax basis and the partnership were liquidated imme-

Reg. § 1.704-1(b)(5)

diately following the end of the partnership's second taxable year, DK would be required to contribute $9,000 to the partnership in order for the partnership to repay the $85,000 note, and there would be no assets remaining to distribute. If such property were sold for its $66,000 adjusted tax basis and the partnership were liquidated immediately following the end of the partnership's third taxable year, the $91,000 ($66,000 sales proceeds plus $25,000 cash on hand) would be used to repay the $85,000 note and there would be $6,000 remaining in the partnership, which would be used to make liquidating distributions to DK and JB of $600 and $5,400, respectively. Accordingly, under paragraph (b)(3)(iii) of this section the $15,000 net taxable income in the partnership's third taxable year will be reallocated $9,600 to DK (minus $9,000 at end of the second taxable year to positive $600 at end of the third taxable year) and $5,400 to JB (zero at end of the second taxable year to positive $5,400 at end of the third taxable year).

Example (16). (i) KG and WN form a limited partnership for the purpose of investing in improved real estate. KG, the general partner, contributes $10,000 to the partnership, and WN, the limited partner, contributes $990,000 to the partnership. The $1,000,000 is used to purchase an apartment building on leased land. The partnership agreement provides that (1) the partners' capital accounts will be determined and maintained in accordance with paragraph (b)(2)(iv) of this section; (2) cash will be distributed first to WN until such time as he has received the amount of his original capital contribution ($990,000), next to KG until such time as he has received the amount of his original capital contribution ($10,000), and thereafter equally between WN and KG; (3) partnership net taxable income will be allocated 99 percent to WN and 1 percent to KG until the cumulative net taxable income allocated for all taxable years is equal to the cumulative net taxable loss previously allocated to the partners, and thereafter equally between WN and KG; (4) partnership net taxable loss will be allocated 99 percent to WN and 1 percent to KG, unless net taxable income has previously been allocated equally between WN and KG, in which case such net taxable loss first will be allocated equally until the cumulative net taxable loss allocated for all taxable years is equal to the cumulative net taxable income previously allocated to the partners; and (5) upon liquidation, WN is not required to restore any deficit balance in his capital account, but KG is so required. Since distributions in liquidation are not required to be made in accordance with the partners' positive capital account balances, and since WN is not required, upon the liquidation of his interest,

to restore the deficit balance in his capital account to the partnership, the allocations provided by the partnership agreement do not have economic effect and will be reallocated in accordance with the partners' interests in the partnership under paragraph (b)(3) of this section.

(ii) Assume the same facts as in (i) except that the partnership agreement further provides that distributions in liquidation of the partnership (or any partner's interest) are to be made in accordance with the partners' positive capital account balances (as set forth in paragraph (b)(2)(ii)(*b*)(*2*) of this section). Assume further that the partnership agreement contains a qualified income offset (as defined in paragraph (b)(2)(ii)(*d*) of this section) and that, as of the end of each partnership taxable year, the items described in paragraphs (b)(2)(iii)(*d*)(*4*), (*5*), and (*6*) of this section are not reasonably expected to cause or increase a deficit balance in WN's capital account. The allocations provided by the partnership agreement have economic effect.

Example (17). FG and RP form a partnership with FG contributing cash of $100 and RP contributing property, with 2 years of cost recovery deductions remaining, that has an adjusted tax basis of $80 and a fair market value of $100. The partnership, FG, and RP have calendar taxable years. The partnership agreement provides that the partners' capital accounts will be determined and maintained in accordance with paragraph (b)(2)(iv) of this section, liquidation proceeds will be made in accordance with capital account balances, and each partner is liable to restore the deficit balance in his capital account to the partnership upon liquidation of his interest (as set forth in paragraphs (b)(2)(ii)(*b*)(*2*) and (*3*) of this section). FG expects to be in a substantially higher tax bracket than RP in the partnership's first taxable year. In the partnership's second taxable year, and in subsequent taxable years, it is expected that both will be in approximately equivalent tax brackets. The partnership agreement allocates all items equally except that all $50 of book depreciation is allocated to FG in the partnership's first taxable year and all $50 of book depreciation is allocated to RP in the partnership's second taxable year. If the allocation to FG of all book depreciation in the partnership's first taxable year is respected, FG would be entitled under section 704(c) to the entire cost recovery deduction ($40) for such year. Likewise, if the allocation to RP of all the book depreciation in the partnership's second taxable year is respected, RP would be entitled under section 704(c) to the entire cost recovery deduction ($40) for such year. The allocation of book depreciation to FG and RP in the partnership's first 2 taxable years has economic effect within the meaning of paragraph (b)(2)(ii) of this section. However, the economic effect of these allocations is not substantial under the test described in paragraph (b)(2)(iii)(*c*) of this section since there is a strong likelihood at the time such allocations became part of the partnership agreement that at the end of the 2-year period to which such allocations relate, the net increases and decreases to FG's and RP's capital accounts will be the same with such allocations as they would have been in the absence of such allocation, and the total tax liability of FG and RP for the taxable years to which the section 704(c) determinations relate would be reduced as a result of the allocations of book depreciation. As a result the allocations of book depreciation in the partnership agreement will be disregarded. FG and RP will be allocated such book depreciation in accordance with the partners' interests in the partnership under paragraph (b)(3) of this section. Under these facts the book depreciation deductions will be reallocated equally between the partners, and section 704(c) will be applied with reference to such reallocation of book depreciation.

Example (18). (i) WM and JL form a general partnership by each contributing $300,000 thereto. The partnership uses the $600,000 to purchase an item of tangible personal property, which it leases out. The partnership elects under section 48(q)(4) to reduce the amount of investment tax credit in lieu of adjusting the tax basis of such property. The partnership agreement provides that (1) the partners' capital account will be determined and maintained in accordance with paragraph (b)(2)(iv) of this section, (2) distributions in liquidation of the partnership (or any partner's interest) will be made in accordance with the partners' positive capital account balances (as set forth in paragraph (b)(2)(ii)(*b*)(*2*) of this section), (3) any partner with a deficit balance in his capital account following the liquidation of his interest must restore that deficit to the partnership (as set forth in paragraph (b)(2)(ii)(*b*)(*3*) of this section), (4) all income, gain, loss, and deduction of the partnership will be allocated equally between the partners, and (5) all non-liquidating distributions of the partnership will be made equally between the partners. Assume that in each of the partnership's taxable years, it recognizes operating income equal to its operating deductions (excluding cost recovery and depreciation deductions and gain or loss on the sale of its property). During its first 2 taxable years, the partnership has an additional $200,000 cost recovery deduction in each year. Pursuant to the partnership agreement these items are allocated equally between WM and JL.

	WM	JL
Capital account upon formation	$300,000	$300,000
Less: net loss for years 1 and 2	(200,000)	(200,000)
Capital account at end of year 2	$100,000	$100,000

The allocations made in the partnership's first 2 taxable years have substantial economic effect.

(ii) Assume the same facts as in (i) and that MK is admitted to the partnership at the beginning of the partnership's third taxable year. At the time of his admission, the fair market value of the partnership property is $600,000. MK contributes $300,000 to the partnership in exchange for an equal one-third interest in the partnership, and, as permitted under paragraph (b)(2)(iv)(*g*), the capital accounts of WM and JL are adjusted upward to $300,000 each to reflect the fair market value of partnership property. In addition, the partnership agreement is modified to provide that depreciation and gain or loss, as computed for tax purposes, with respect to the partnership property that appreciated prior to MK's admission will be shared among the partners in a manner that takes account of the variation between such property's $200,000 adjusted tax basis and its $600,000 book value in accordance with paragraph (b)(2)(iv)(*f*) and the special rule contained in paragraph (b)(4)(i) of this section. Depreciation and gain or loss, as computed for book purposes, with respect to such property will be allocated equally among the partners and, in accordance with paragraph (b)(2)(iv)(*g*) of this section, will be reflected in the partners' capital accounts, as will all other partnership income, gain, loss, and deduction. Since the requirements of (b)(2)(iv)(*g*) of this section are satisfied, the capital accounts of the partners (as adjusted) continue to be maintained in accordance with paragraph (b)(2)(iv) of this section.

(iii) Assume the same facts as in (ii) and that immediately after MK's admission to the partnership, the partnership property is sold for $600,000, resulting in a taxable gain of $400,000 ($600,000 less $200,000 adjusted tax basis) and no book gain or loss, and the partnership is liquidated. An allocation of the $400,000 taxable gain cannot have economic effect because such gain cannot properly be reflected in the partners' book capital accounts. Consistent with the special partners' interests in the partnership rule contained in paragraph (b)(4)(i) of this section, the partnership agreement provides that the $400,000 taxable gain will, in accordance with section 704(c) principles, be shared equally between WM and JL.

Reg. § 1.704-1(b)(5)

	WM		JL		MK	
	Tax	Book	Tax	Book	Tax	Book
Capital account at beginning of year 3	$100,000	$300,000	$100,000	$300,000	$300,000	$300,000
Plus: gain	200,000	0	200,000	0	0	0
Capital account before liquidation	$300,000	$300,000	$300,000	$300,000	$300,000	$300,000

The $900,000 of partnership cash ($600,000 sales proceeds plus $300,000 contributed by MK) is distributed equally among WM, JL, and MK in accordance with their adjusted positive capital account balances, each of which is $300,000.

(iv) Assume the same facts as in (iii) except that prior to liquidation the property appre-ciates and is sold for $900,000, resulting in a taxable gain of $700,000 ($900,000 less $200,000 adjusted tax basis) and a book gain of $300,000 ($900,000 less $600,000 book value). Under the partnership agreement the $300,000 of book gain is allocated equally among the partners, and such allocation has substantial economic effect.

	WM		JL		MK	
	Tax	Book	Tax	Book	Tax	Book
Capital account at beginning of year 3	$100,000	$300,000	$100,000	$300,000	$300,000	$300,000
Plus: gain	300,000	100,000	300,000	100,000	100,000	100,000
Capital account before liquidation	$400,000	$400,000	$400,000	$400,000	$400,000	$400,000

Consistent with the special partners' interests in the partnership rule contained in paragraph (b)(4)(i) of this section, the partnership agreement provides that the $700,000 taxable gain is, in accordance with section 704(c) principles, shared $300,000 to JL, $300,000 to WM, and $100,000 to MK. This ensures that (1) WM and JL share equally the $400,000 taxable gain that is attributable to appreciation in the property that occurred prior to MK's admission to the partnership in the same manner as it was reflected in their capital accounts upon MK's admission, and

(2) WM, JL, and MK share equally the additional $300,000 taxable gain in the same manner as they shared the $300,000 book gain.

(v) Assume the same facts as in (ii) except that shortly after MK's admission the property depreciates and is sold for $450,000, resulting in a taxable gain of $250,000 ($450,000 less $200,000 adjusted tax basis) and a book loss of $150,000 (450,000 less $600,000 book value). Under the partnership agreement these items are allocated as follows:

	WM		JL		MK	
	Tax	Book	Tax	Book	Tax	Book
Capital account at beginning of year 3	$100,000	$300,000	$100,000	$300,000	$300,000	$300,000
Plus: gain	125,000	0	125,000	0	0	0
Less: loss	0	(50,000)	0	(50,000)	0	(50,000)
Capital account before liquidation	$225,000	$250,000	$225,000	$250,000	$300,000	$250,000

The $150,000 book loss is allocated equally among the partners, and such allocation has substantial economic effect. Consistent with the special partners' interests in the partnership rule contained in paragraph (b)(4)(i) of this section, the partnership agreement provides that the $250,000 taxable gain is, in accordance with section 704(c) principles, shared equally between WM and JL. The fact that MK bears an economic loss of $50,000 without a corresponding taxable loss is attributable entirely to the "ceiling rule." See paragraph (c)(2) of § 1.704-1.

(vi) Assume the same facts as in (ii) except that the property depreciates and is sold for $170,000, resulting in a $30,000 taxable loss ($200,000 adjusted tax basis less $170,000) and a book loss of $430,000 ($600,000 book value less $170,000). The book loss of $430,000 is allocated equally among the partners ($143,333 each) and has substantial economic effect. Consistent with the special partners' interests in the partnership rule contained in paragraph (b)(4)(i) of this section, the partnership agreement provides that the entire $30,000 taxable loss is, in accordance with section 704(c) principles, included in MK's distributive share.

Reg. § 1.704-1(b)(5)

	WM		JL		MK	
	Tax	Book	Tax	Book	Tax	Book
Capital account at beginning of year 3	$100,000	$300,000	$100,000	$300,000	$300,000	$300,000
Less: loss	0	(143,333)	0	(143,333)	(30,000)	(143,333)
Capital account before liquidation	$100,000	$156,667	$100,000	$156,667	$270,000	$156,667

(vii) Assume the same facts as in (ii) and that during the partnership's third taxable year, the partnership has an additional $100,000 cost recovery deduction and $300,000 book depreciation deduction attributable to the property purchased by the partnership in its first taxable year. The $300,000 book depreciation deduction is allocated equally among the partners, and that allocation has substantial economic effect. Consistent with the special partners' interests in the partnership rule contained in paragraph (b)(4)(i) of this section, the partnership agreement provides that the $100,000 cost recovery deduction for the partnership's third taxable year is, in accordance with section 704(c) principles, included in MK's distributive share. This is because under these facts those principles require MK to include the cost recovery deduction for such property in his distributive share up to the amount of the book depreciation deduction for such property properly allocated to him.

	WM		JL		MK	
	Tax	Book	Tax	Book	Tax	Book
Capital account at beginning of year 3	$100,000	$300,000	$100,000	$300,000	$300,000	$300,000
Less: recovery/depreciation deduction for year 3	0	(100,000)	0	(100,000)	(100,000)	(100,000)
Capital account at the end of year 3	$100,000	$200,000	$100,000	$200,000	$200,000	$200,000

(viii) Assume the same facts as in (vii) except that upon MK's admission the partnership property has an adjusted tax basis of $220,000 (instead of $200,000), and thus the cost recovery deduction for the partnership's third taxable year is $110,000. Assume further that upon MK's admission WM and JL have adjusted capital account balances of $110,000 and $100,000, respectively. Consistent with the special partners' interests in the partnership rule contained in paragraph (b)(4)(i) of this section, the partnership agreement provides that the excess $10,000 cost recovery deduction ($110,000 less $100,000 included in MK's distributive share) is, in accordance with section 704(c) principles, shared equally between WM and JL and is so included in their respective distributive shares for the partnership's third taxable year.

(ix) Assume the same facts as in (vii) except that upon MK's admission the partnership agreement is amended to allocate the first $400,000 of book depreciation and loss on partnership property equally between WM and JL and the last $200,000 of such book depreciation and loss to MK. Assume such allocations have substantial economic effect. Pursuant to this amendment the $300,000 book depreciation deduction in the partnership's third taxable year is allocated equally between WM and JL. Consistent with the special partners' interests in the partnership rule contained in paragraph (b)(4)(i) of this section, the partnership agreement provides that the $100,000 cost recovery deduction is, in accordance with section 704(c) principles, shared equally between WM and JL. In the partnership's fourth taxable year, it has a $60,000 cost recovery deduction and a $180,000 book depreciation deduction. Under the amendment described above, the $180,000 book depreciation deduction is allocated $50,000 to WM, $50,000 to JL, and $80,000 to MK. Consistent with the special partners' interests in the partnership rule contained in paragraph (b)(4)(i) of this section, the partnership agreement provides that the $60,000 cost recovery deduction is, in accordance with section 704(c) principles, included entirely in MK's distributive share.

	WM		JL		MK	
	Tax	Book	Tax	Book	Tax	Book
Capital account at beginning of year 3	$100,000	$300,000	$100,000	$300,000	$300,000	$300,000
Less: (a) recovery/depreciation deduction for year 3	(50,000)	(150,000)	(50,000)	(150,000)	0	0
(b) recovery/depreciation deduction for year 4	0	(50,000)	0	(50,000)	(60,000)	(80,000)
Capital account at end of year 4	$ 50,000	$100,000	$ 50,000	$100,000	$240,000	$220,000

Reg. § 1.704-1(b)(5)

(x) Assume the same facts as in (vii) and that at the beginning of the partnership's third taxable year, the partnership purchases a second item of tangible personal property for $300,000 and elects under section 48(q)(4) to reduce the amount of investment tax credit in lieu of adjusting the tax basis of such property. The partnership agreement is amended to allocate the first $150,000 of cost recovery deductions and loss from such property to WM and the next $150,000 of cost recovery deductions and loss from such property equally between JL and MK. Thus, in the partnership's third taxable year it has, in addition to the items specified in (vii), a cost recovery and book depreciation deduction of $100,000 attributable to the newly acquired property, which is allocated entirely to WM. As in (vii), the allocation of the $300,000 book depreciation attributable to the property purchased in the partnership's first taxable year equally among the partners has substantial economic effect, and consistent with the special partners' interests in the partnership rule contained in paragraph (b)(4)(i) of this section, the partnership agreement properly provides for the entire $100,000 cost recovery deduction attributable to such property to be included in MK's distributive share. Furthermore, the allocation to WM of the $100,000 cost recovery deduction attributable to the property purchased in the partnership's third taxable year has substantial economic effect.

	WM		JL		MK	
	Tax	Book	Tax	Book	Tax	Book
Capital account at beginning of year 3	$100,000	$300,000	$100,000	$300,000	$300,000	$300,000
Less: (a) recovery/depreciation deduction for property bought in year 1	0	(100,000)	0	(100,000)	(100,000)	(100,000)
(b) recovery/depreciation deduction for property bought in year 3	(100,000)	(100,000)	0	0	0	0
Capital account at end of year 3	0	$100,000	$100,000	$200,000	$200,000	$200,000

(xi) Assume the same facts as in (x) and that at the beginning of the partnership's fourth taxable year, the properties purchased in the partnership's first and third taxable years are disposed of for $90,000 and $180,000, respectively, and the partnership is liquidated. With respect to the property purchased in the first taxable year, there is a book loss of $210,000 ($300,000 book value less $90,000) and a taxable loss of $10,000 ($100,000 adjusted tax basis less $90,000). The book loss is allocated equally among the partners, and such allocation has substantial economic effect. Consistent with the special partners' interests in the partnership rule contained in paragraph (b)(4)(i) of this section, the partnership agreement provides that the taxable loss of $10,000 will, in accordance with section 704(c) principles, be included entirely in MK's distributive share. With respect to the property purchased in the partnership's third taxable year, there is a book and taxable loss of $20,000. Pursuant to the partnership agreement this loss is allocated entirely to WM, and such allocation has substantial economic effect.

	WM		JL		MK	
	Tax	Book	Tax	Book	Tax	Book
Capital account at beginning of year 4	0	$100,000	$100,000	$200,000	$200,000	$200,000
Less: (a) loss on property bought in year 1	0	(70,000)	0	(70,000)	(10,000)	(70,000)
(b) loss on property bought in year 3	(20,000)	(20,000)	0	0	0	0
Capital account before liquidation	($20,000)	$10,000	$100,000	$130,000	$190,000	$130,000

Partnership liquidation proceeds ($270,000) are properly distributed in accordance with the partners' adjusted positive book capital account balances ($10,000 to WM, $130,000 to JL and $130,000 to MK).

(xii) Assume the same facts as in (x) and that in the partnership's fourth taxable year it has a cost recovery deduction of $60,000 and book depreciation deduction of $180,000 attributable to the property purchased in the partnership's first taxable year, and a cost recovery and book depreciation deduction of $100,000 attributable to the property purchased in the partnership's third taxable year. The $180,000 book depreciation deduction attributable to the property purchased in the partnership's first taxable year is allocated equally among the partners, and such allocation has substantial economic effect. Consistent with the special partners' interests in the partnership rule contained in paragraph (b)(4)(i) of this section, the partnership agreement provides that the $60,000 cost recovery deduction attributable to the property purchased in the first taxable year is, in accordance with section 704(c) principles, included entirely in MK's distributive share. Furthermore, the $100,000 cost recovery deduction attributable to the property purchased in the third taxable year is allocated $50,000 to WM, $25,000 to JL, and $25,000 to MK, and such allocation has substantial economic effect.

	WM		JL		MK	
	Tax	Book	Tax	Book	Tax	Book
Capital account at beginning of year 4	—0—	$100,000	$100,000	$200,000	$200,000	$200,000
Less: (a) recovery/depreciation deduction for property bought in year 1	—0—	(60,000)	—0—	(60,000)	(60,000)	(60,000)
(b) recovery/depreciation deduction for property bought in year 3	(50,000)	(50,000)	(25,000)	(25,000)	(25,000)	(25,000)
Capital account at end of year 4	($50,000)	($ 10,000)	$75,000	$115,000	$115,000	$115,000

At the end of the partnership's fourth taxable year the adjusted tax bases of the partnership properties acquired in its first and third taxable years are $40,000 and $100,000, respectively. If the properties are disposed of at the beginning of the partnership's fifth taxable year for their adjusted tax bases, there would be no taxable gain or loss, a book loss of $80,000 on the property purchased in the partnership's first taxable year ($120,000 book value less $40,000), and cash available for distribution of $140,000.

	WM		JL		MK	
	Tax	Book	Tax	Book	Tax	Book
Capital account at beginning of year 5	($50,000)	($10,000)	$75,000	$115,000	$115,000	$115,000
Less: loss	—0—	(26,667)	—0—	(26,667)	—0—	(26,667)
Capital account before liquidation	($50,000)	($36,667)	$75,000	$88,333	$115,000	$ 88,333

If the partnership is then liquidated, the $140,000 of cash on hand plus the $36,667 balance that WM would be required to contribute to the partnership (the deficit balance in his book capital account) would be distributed equally between JL and MK in accordance with their adjusted positive book capital account balances.

(xiii) Assume the same facts as in (i). Any tax preferences under section 57(a)(12) attributable to the partnership's cost recovery deductions in the first 2 taxable years will be taken into account equally by WM and JL. If the partnership agreement instead provides that the partnership's cost recovery deductions in its first 2 taxable years are allocated 25 percent to WM and 75 percent to JL (and such allocations have substantial economic effect), the tax preferences attributable to such cost recovery deductions would be taken into account 25 percent by WM and 75 percent by JL. The conclusion in the previous sentence is unchanged even if the partnership's operating expenses (exclusive of cost recovery and depreciation deductions) exceed its operating income in each of the partnership's first 2 taxable years, the resulting net loss is allocated entirely to WM, and the cost recovery deductions are allocated 25 percent to WM and 75 percent to JL (provided such allocations have substantial economic effect). If the partnership agreement instead provides that all income, gain, loss, and deduction (including cost recovery and depreciation deductions) are allocated equally between JL and WM, the tax preferences attributable to the cost recovery deductions would be taken into account equally by JL and WM. In this case, if the partnership has a $100,000 cost recovery deduction in its first taxable year and an additional net loss of $100,000 in its first taxable year (i.e., its operating expenses exceed its operating income by $100,000) and purports to categorize JL's $100,000 distributive share of partnership loss as being attributable to the cost recovery deduction and WM's $100,000 distributive share of partnership loss as being attributable to the net loss, the economic effect of such allocations is not substantial, and each partner will be allocated one-half of all partnership income, gain, loss, and deduction and will take into account one-half of the tax preferences attributable to the cost recovery deductions.

Example (19). (i) DG and JC form a general partnership for the purpose of drilling oil wells.

DG contributes an oil lease, which has a fair market value and adjusted tax basis of $100,000. JC contributes $100,000 in cash, which is used to finance the drilling operations. The partnership agreement provides that DG is credited with a capital account of $100,000, and JC is credited with a capital account of $100,000. The agreement further provides that the partners' capital accounts will be determined and maintained in accordance with paragraph (b)(2)(iv) of this section, distributions in liquidation of the partnership (or any partner's interest) will be made in accordance with the partners' positive capital account balances, and any partner with a deficit balance in his capital account following the liquidation of his interest must restore such deficit to the partnership (as set forth in paragraphs (b)(2)(ii)(b)(2) and (3) of this section). The partnership chooses to adjust capital accounts on a simulated cost depletion basis and elects under section 48(q)(4) to reduce the amount of investment tax credit in lieu of adjusting the basis of its section 38 property. The agreement further provides that (1) all additional cash requirements of the partnership will be borne equally by DG and JC, (2) the deductions attributable to the property (including money) contributed by each partner will be allocated to such partner, (3) all other income, gain, loss, and deductions (and item thereof) will be allocated equally between DG and JC, and (4) all cash from operations will be distributed equally between DG and JC. In the partnership's first taxable year $80,000 of partnership intangible drilling cost deductions and $20,000 of cost recovery deductions on partnership equipment are allocated to JC, and the $100,000 basis of the lease is, for purposes of the depletion allowance under sections 611 and 613A(c)(7)(D), allocated to DG. The allocations of income, gain, loss, and deduction provided in the partnership agreement have substantial economic effect. Furthermore, since the allocation of the entire basis of the lease to DG will not result in capital account adjustments (under paragraph (b)(2)(iv)(k) of this section) the economic effect of which is insubstantial, and since all other partnership allocations are recognized under this paragraph, the allocation of the $100,000 adjusted basis of the lease to DG is, under paragraph (b)(4)(v) of this section, recognized as being in accordance with the partners' interests in partnership capital for purposes of section 613A(c)(7)(D).

(ii) Assume the same facts as in (i) except that the partnership agreement provides that (1) all additional cash requirements of the partnership for additional expenses will be funded by additional contributions from JC, (2) all cash from operations will first be distributed to JC until the excess of such cash distributions over the amount of such additional expenses equals his initial $100,000 contribution, (3) all deductions attributable to such additional operating expenses will be allocated to JC, and (4) all income will be allocated to JC until the aggregate amount of income allocated to him equals the amount of partnership operating expenses funded by his initial $100,000 contribution plus the amount of additional operating expenses paid from contributions made solely by him. The allocations of income, gain, loss, and deduction provided in the partnership agreement have economic effect. In addition, the economic effect of the allocations provided in the agreement is substantial. Because the partnership's drilling activities are sufficiently speculative, there is not a strong likelihood at the time the disproportionate allocations of loss and deduction to JC are provided for by the partnership agreement that the economic effect of such allocations will be largely offset by allocations of income. In addition, since the allocation of the entire basis of the lease to DG will not result in capital account adjustments (under paragraph (b)(2)(iv)(k) of this section), the economic effect of which is insubstantial, and since all other partnership allocations are recognized under this paragraph, the allocation of the adjusted basis of the lease to DG is, under paragraph (b)(4)(v) of this section, recognized as being in accordance with the partners' interests in partnership capital under section 613A(c)(7)(D).

(iii) Assume the same facts as in (i) except that all distributions, including those made upon liquidation of the partnership, will be made equally between DG and JC, and no partner is obligated to restore the deficit balance in his capital account to the partnership following the liquidation of his interest for distribution to partners with positive capital account balances. Since liquidation proceeds will be distributed equally between DG and JC irrespective of their capital account balances, and since no partner is required to restore the deficit balance in his capital account to the partnership upon liquidation (in accordance with paragraph (b)(2)(ii)(b)(3) of this section), the allocations of income, gain, loss, and deduction provided in the partnership agreement do not have economic effect and must be reallocated in accordance with the partners' interests in the partnership under paragraph (b)(3) of this section. Under these facts all partnership income, gain, loss, and deduction (and item thereof) will be reallocated equally between JC and DG. Furthermore, the allocation of the $100,000 adjusted tax basis of the lease to DG is not, under paragraph (b)(4)(v) of this section, deemed to be in accordance with the partners' interests in partnership capital under section 613A(c)(7)(D), and such basis must be reallocated in accordance with

Reg. § 1.704-1(b)(5)

the partners' interests in partnership capital or income as determined under section 613A(c)(7)(D). The results in this example would be the same if JC's initial cash contribution were $1,000,000 (instead of $100,000), but in such case the partners should consider whether, and to what extent, the provisions of paragraph (b)(1) of § 1.721-1, and principles related thereto, may be applicable.

(iv) Assume the same facts as in (i) and that for the partnership's first taxable year the simulated depletion deduction with respect to the lease is $10,000. Since DG properly was allocated the entire depletable basis of the lease (such allocation having been recognized as being in accordance with DG's interest in partnership capital with respect to such lease), under paragraph (b)(2)(iv)(*k*)(*1*) of this section the partnership's $10,000 simulated depletion deduction is allocated to DG and will reduce his capital account accordingly. If (prior to any additional simulated depletion deductions) the lease is sold for $100,000, paragraph (b)(4)(v) of this section requires that the first $90,000 (*i.e.*, the partnership's simulated adjusted basis in the lease) out of the $100,000 amount realized on such sale be allocated to DG (but does not directly affect his capital account). The partnersip agreement allocates the remaining $10,000 amount realized equally between JC and DG (but such allocation does not directly affect their capital accounts). This allocation of the $10,000 portion of amount realized that exceeds the partnership's simulated adjusted basis in the lease will be treated as being in accordance with the partners' allocable shares of such amount realized under section 613A(c)(7)(D) because such allocation will not result in capital account adjustments (under paragraph (b)(2)(iv)(*k*) of this section) the economic effect of which is insubstantial, and all other partnership allocations are recognized under this paragraph. Under paragraph (b)(2)(iv)(*k*) of this section, the partners' capital accounts are adjusted upward by the partnership's simulated gain of $10,000 ($100,000 sales price less $90,000 simulated adjusted basis) in proportion to such partners' allocable shares of the $10,000 portion of the total amount realized that exceeds the partnership's $90,000 simulated adjusted basis ($5,000 to JC and $5,000 to DG). If the lease is sold for $50,000, under paragraph (b)(4)(v) of this section the entire $50,000 amount realized on the sale of the lease will be allocated to DG (but will not directly affect his capital account). Under paragraph (b)(2)(iv)(*k*) of this section the partners' capital accounts will be adjusted downward by the partnership's $40,000 simulated loss ($50,000 sales price less $90,000 simulated adjusted basis) in proportion to the partners' alloca-

ble shares of the total amount realized from the property that represents recovery of the partnership's simulated adjusted basis therein. Accordingly, DG's capital account will be reduced by such $40,000.

(c) *Contributed property; cross-reference.* See § 1.704-3 for methods of making allocations that take into account precontribution appreciation or diminution in value of property contributed by a partner to a partnership.

(d) *Limitation on allowance of losses.*

(1) A partner's distributive share of partnership loss will be allowed only to the extent of the adjusted basis (before reduction by current year's losses) of such partner's interest in the partnership at the end of the partnership taxable year in which such loss occurred. A partner's share of loss in excess of his adjusted basis at the end of the partnership taxable year will not be allowed for that year. However, any loss so disallowed shall be allowed as a deduction at the end of the first succeeding partnership taxable year, and subsequent partnership taxable years, to the extent that the partner's adjusted basis for his partnership interest at the end of any such year exceeds zero (before reduction by such loss for such year).

(2) In computing the adjusted basis of a partner's interest for the purpose of ascertaining the extent to which a partner's distributive share of partnership loss shall be allowed as a deduction for the taxable year, the basis shall first be increased under section 705(a)(1) and decreased under section 705(a)(2), except for losses of the taxable year and losses previously disallowed. If the partner's distributive share of the aggregate of items of loss specified in section 702(a)(1), (2), (3), (8), and (9) exceeds the basis of the partner's interest computed under the preceding sentence, the limitation on losses under section 704(d) must be allocated to his distributive share of each such loss. This allocation shall be determined by taking the proportion that each loss bears to the total of all such losses. For purposes of the preceding sentence, the total losses for the taxable year shall be the sum of his distributive share of losses for the current year and his losses disallowed and carried forward from prior years.

(3) For the treatment of certain liabilities of the partner or partnership, see section 752 and § 1.752-1.

(4) The provisions of this paragraph may be illustrated by the following examples:

Example (1). At the end of the partnership taxable year 1955, partnership AB has a loss of $20,000. Partner A's distributive share of this loss is $10,000. At the end [of] such year, A's adjusted basis for his interest in the partnership (not taking into account his distributive share of the loss)

Reg. § 1.704-1(c)

is $6,000. Under section 704(d), A's distributive share of partnership loss is allowed to him (in his taxable year within or with which the partnership taxable year ends) only to the extent of his adjusted basis of $6,000. The $6,000 loss allowed for 1955 decreases the adjusted basis of A's interest to zero. Assume that, at the end of partnership taxable year 1956, A's share of partnership income has increased the adjusted basis of A's interest in the partnership to $3,000 (not taking into account the $4,000 loss disallowed in 1955). Of the $4,000 loss disallowed for the partnership taxable year 1955, $3,000 is allowed A for the partnership taxable year 1956, thus again decreasing the adjusted basis of his interest to zero. If, at the end of partnership taxable year 1957, A has an adjusted basis of his interest of at least $1,000 (not taking into account the disallowed loss of $1,000), he will be allowed the $1,000 loss previously disallowed.

Example (2). At the end of partnership taxable year 1955, partnership CD has a loss of $20,000. Partner C's distributive share of this loss is $10,000. The adjusted basis of his interest in the partnership (not taking into account his distributive share of such loss) is $6,000. Therefore, $4,000 of the loss is disallowed. At the end of partnership taxable year 1956, the partnership has no taxable income or loss, but owes $8,000 to a bank for money borrowed. Since C's share of this liability is $4,000, the basis of his partnership interest is increased from zero to $4,000. (See sections 752 and 722, and §§ 1.752-1 and 1.722-1.) C is allowed the $4,000 loss, disallowed for the preceding year under section 704(d), for his taxable year within or with which partnership taxable year 1956 ends.

Example (3). At the end of partnership taxable year 1955, partner C has the following distributive share of partnership items described in section 702(a); long-term capital loss, $4,000; short-term capital loss, $2,000; income as described in section 702(a)(9), $4,000. Partner C's adjusted basis for his partnership interest at the end of 1955, before adjustment for any of the above items, is $1,000. As adjusted under section 705(a)(1)(A), C's basis is increased from $1,000 to $5,000 at the end of the year. C's total distributive share of partnership loss is $6,000. Since without regard to losses, C has a basis of only $5,000, C is allowed only $5,000/$6,000 of each loss, that is, $3,333 of his long-term capital loss, and $1,667 of his short-term capital loss. C must carry forward to succeeding taxable years $667 as a long-term capital loss and $333 as a short-term capital loss.

(e) *Family partnerships*—(1) *In general*—(i) *Introduction.* The production of income by a partnership is attributable to the capital or services, or both, contributed by the partners. The provi-

sions of subchapter K, chapter 1 of the Code, are to be read in the light of their relationship to section 61, which requires, inter alia, that income be taxed to the person who earns it through his own labor and skill and the utilization of his own capital.

(ii) *Recognition of donee as partner.* With respect to partnerships in which capital is a material income-producing factor, section 704(e)(1) provides that a person shall be recognized as a partner for income tax purposes if he owns a capital interest in such a partnership whether or not such interest is derived by purchase or gift from any other person. If a capital interest in a partnership in which capital is a material income-producing factor is created by gift, section 704(e)(2) provides that the distributive share of the donee under the partnership agreement shall be includible in his gross income, except to the extent that such distributive share is determined without allowance of reasonable compensation for services rendered to the partnership by the donor, and except to the extent that the portion of such distributive share attributable to donated capital is proportionately greater than the share of the donor attributable to the donor's capital. For rules of allocation in such cases, see subparagraph (3) of this paragraph.

(iii) *Requirement of complete transfer to donee.* A donee or purchaser of a capital interest in a partnership is not recognized as a partner under the principles of section 704(e)(1) unless such interest is acquired in a bona fide transaction, not a mere sham for tax avoidance or evasion purposes, and the donee or purchaser is the real owner of such interest. To be recognized, a transfer must vest dominion and control of the partnership interest in the transferee. The existence of such dominion and control in the donee is to be determined from all the facts and circumstances. A transfer is not recognized if the transferor retains such incidents of ownership that the transferee has not acquired full and complete ownership of the partnership interest. Transactions between members of a family will be closely scrutinized, and the circumstances, not only at the time of the purported transfer but also during the periods preceding and following it, will be taken into consideration in determining the bona fides or lack of bona fides of the purported gift or sale. A partnership may be recognized for income purposes as to some partners but not as to others.

(iv) *Capital as a material income-producing factor.* For purposes of section 704(e)(1), the determination as to whether capital is a material income-producing factor must be made by reference to all the facts of each case. Capital is a material income-producing factor if a substantial portion of the gross income of the business is attributable to the employment of capital in the business conducted by the partnership. In general, capital is not a material income-producing factor where the income of the business consists principally of fees, commissions, or other compensation for personal services performed by members or employees of the partnership. On the other hand, capital is ordinarily a material income-producing factor if the operation of the business requires substantial inventories or a substantial investment in plant, machinery, or other equipment.

(v) *Capital interest in a partnership.* For purposes of section 704(e), a capital interest in a partnership means an interest in the assets of the partnership, which is distributable to the owner of the capital interest upon his withdrawal from the partnership or upon liquidation of the partnership. The mere right to participate in the earnings and profits of a partnership is not a capital interest in the partnership.

(2) *Basic tests as to ownership*—(i) *In general.* Whether an alleged partner who is a donee of a capital interest in a partnership is the real owner of such capital interest, and whether the donee has dominion and control over such interest, must be ascertained from all the facts and circumstances of the particular case. Isolated facts are not determinative; the reality of the donee's ownership is to be determined in the light of the transaction as a whole. The execution of legally sufficient and irrevocable deeds or other instruments of gift under State law is a factor to be taken into account but is not determinative of ownership by the donee for the purposes of section 704(e). The reality of the transfer and of the donee's ownership of the property attributed to him are to be ascertained from the conduct of the parties with respect to the alleged gift and not by any mechanical or formal test. Some of the more important factors to be considered in determining whether the donee has acquired ownership of the capital interest in a partnership are indicated in subdivisions (ii) to (x), inclusive, of this subparagraph.

(ii) *Retained controls.* The donor may have retained such controls of the interest which he has purported to transfer to the donee that the donor should be treated as remaining the substantial owner of the interest. Controls of particular significance include, for example, the following:

(*a*) Retention of control of the distribution of amounts of income or restrictions on the distributions of amounts of income (other than amounts retained in the partnership annually with the consent of the partners, including the donee partner, for the reasonable needs of the business). If there is a partnership agreement providing for a managing partner or partners, then amounts of income may be retained in the partnership without the acquiescence of all the partners if such amounts are retained for the reasonable needs of the business.

(*b*) Limitation of the right of the donee to liquidate or sell his interest in the partnership at his discretion without financial detriment.

(*c*) Retention of control of assets essential to the business (for example, through retention of assets leased to the alleged partnership).

(*d*) Retention of management powers inconsistent with normal relationships among partners. Retention by the donor of control of business management or of voting control, such as is common in ordinary business relationships, is not by itself to be considered as inconsistent with normal relationships among partners, provided the donee is free to liquidate his interest at his discretion without financial detriment. The donee shall not be considered free to liquidate his interest unless, considering all the facts, it is evident that the donee is independent of the donor and has such maturity and understanding of his rights as to be capable of deciding to exercise, and capable of exercising, his right to withdraw his capital interest from the partnership. The existence of some of the indicated controls, though amounting to less than substantial ownership retained by the donor, may be considered along with other facts and circumstances as tending to show the lack of reality of the partnership interest of the donee.

(iii) *Indirect controls.* Controls inconsistent with ownership by the donee may be exercised indirectly as well as directly, for example, through a separate business organization, estate, trust, individual, or other partnership. Where such indirect controls exist, the reality of the donee's interest will be determined as if such controls were exercisable directly.

(iv) *Participation in management.* Substantial participation by the donee in the control and management of the business (including participation in the major policy decisions affecting the business) is strong evidence of a donee partner's exercise of dominion and control over his interest. Such participation presupposes sufficient maturity and experience on the part of the donee to deal with the business problems of the partnership.

(v) *Income distributions.* The actual distribution to a donee partner of the entire amount or a major portion of his distributive share of the business income for the sole benefit and use of the donee is substantial evidence of the reality of the donee's interest, provided the donor has not retained controls inconsistent with real ownership by the donee. Amounts distributed are not consid-

Reg. § 1.704-1(e)(2)

ered to be used for the donee's sole benefit if, for example, they are deposited, loaned, or invested in such manner that the donor controls or can control the use or enjoyment of such funds.

(vi) *Conduct of partnership business.* In determining the reality of the donee's ownership of a capital interest in a partnership, consideration shall be given to whether the donee is actually treated as a partner in the operation of the business. Whether or not the donee has been held out publicly as a partner in the conduct of the business, in relations with customers, or with creditors or other sources of financing, is of primary significance. Other factors of significance in this connection include:

(*a*) Compliance with local partnership, fictitious names, and business registration statutes.

(*b*) Control of business bank accounts.

(*c*) Recognition of the donee's rights in distributions of partnership property and profits.

(*d*) Recognition of the donee's interest in insurance policies, leases, and other business contracts and in litigation affecting business.

(*e*) The existence of written agreements, records, or memoranda, contemporaneous with the taxable year or years concerned, establishing the nature of the partnership agreement and the rights and liabilities of the respective partners.

(*f*) Filing of partnership tax returns as required by law.

However, despite formal compliance with the above factors, other circumstances may indicate that the donor has retained substantial ownership of the interest purportedly transferred to the donee.

(vii) *Trustees as partners.* A trustee may be recognized as a partner for income tax purposes under the principles relating to family partnerships generally as applied to the particular facts of the trust-partnership arrangement. A trustee who is unrelated to and independent of the grantor, and who participates as a partner and receives distribution of the income distributable to the trust, will ordinarily be recognized as the legal owner of the partnership interest which he holds in trust unless the grantor has retained controls inconsistent with such ownership. However, if the grantor is the trustee, or if the trustee is amenable to the will of the grantor, the provisions of the trust instrument (particularly as to whether the trustee is subject to the responsibilities of a fiduciary), the provisions of the partnership agreement, and the conduct of the parties must all be taken into account in determining whether the trustee in a fiduciary capacity has become the real owner of the partnership interest.

Where the grantor (or person amenable to his will) is the trustee, the trust may be recognized as a partner only if the grantor (or such other person) in his participation in the affairs of the partnership actively represents and protects the interests of the beneficiaries in accordance with the obligations of a fiduciary and does not subordinate such interests to the interests of the grantor. Furthermore, if the grantor (or person amenable to his will) is the trustee, the following factors will be given particular consideration:

(*a*) Whether the trust is recognized as a partner in business dealings with customers and creditors, and

(*b*) Whether, if any amount of the partnership income is not properly retained for the reasonable needs of the business, the trust's share of such amount is distributed to the trust annually and paid to the beneficiaries or reinvested with regard solely to the interests of the beneficiaries.

(viii) *Interests (not held in trust) of minor children.* Except where a minor child is shown to be competent to manage his own property and participate in the partnership activities in accordance with his interest in the property, a minor child generally will not be recognized as a member of a partnership unless control of the property is exercised by another person as fiduciary for the sole benefit of the child, and unless there is such judicial supervision of the conduct of the fiduciary as is required by law. The use of the child's property or income for support for which a parent is legally responsible will be considered a use for the parent's benefit. "Judicial supervision of the conduct of the fiduciary" includes filing of such accountings and reports as are required by law of the fiduciary who participates in the affairs of the partnership on behalf of the minor. A minor child will be considered as competent to manage his own property if he actually has sufficient maturity and experience to be treated by disinterested persons as competent to enter business dealings and otherwise to conduct his affairs on a basis of equality with adult persons, notwithstanding legal disabilities of the minor under State law.

(ix) *Donees as limited partners.* The recognition of a donee's interest in a limited partnership will depend, as in the case of other donated interests, on whether the transfer of property is real and on whether the donee has acquired dominion and control over the interest purportedly transferred to him. To be recognized for Federal income tax purposes, a limited partnership must be organized and conducted in accordance with the requirements of the applicable State limited-partnership law. The absence of services and participation in management by a donee in a limited

Reg. § 1.704-1(e)(2)

partnership is immaterial if the limited partnership meets all the other requirements prescribed in this paragraph. If the limited partner's right to transfer or liquidate his interest is subject to substantial restrictions (for example, where the interest of the limited partner is not assignable in a real sense or where such interest may be required to be left in the business for a long term of years), or if the general partner retains any other control which substantially limits any of the rights which would ordinarily be exercisable by unrelated limited partners in normal business relationships, such restrictions on the right to transfer or liquidate, or retention of other control, will be considered strong evidence as to the lack of reality of ownership by the donee.

(x) *Motive.* If the reality of the transfer of interest is satisfactorily established, the motives for the transaction are generally immaterial. However, the presence or absence of a tax-avoidance motive is one of many factors to be considered in determining the reality of the ownership of a capital interest acquired by gift.

(3) *Allocation of family partnership income*—(i) *In general.* (a) Where a capital interest in a partnership in which capital is a material income-producing factor is created by gift, the donee's distributive share shall be includible in his gross income, except to the extent that such share is determined without allowance of reasonable compensation for services rendered to the partnership by the donor, and except to the extent that the portion of such distributive share attributable to donated capital is proportionately greater than the distributive share attributable to the donor's capital. For the purpose of section 704, a capital interest in a partnership purchased by one member of a family from another shall be considered to be created by gift from the seller, and the fair market value of the purchased interest shall be considered to be donated capital. The "family" of any individual, for the purpose of the preceding sentence, shall include only his spouse, ancestors, and lineal descendants, and any trust for the primary benefit of such persons.

(b) To the extent that the partnership agreement does not allocate the partnership income in accordance with subdivision (a) of this subdivision, the distributive shares of the partnership income of the donor and donee shall be reallocated by making a reasonable allowance for the services of the donor and by attributing the balance of such income (other than a reasonable allowance for the services, if any, rendered by the donee) to the partnership capital of the donor and donee. The portion of income, if any, thus attributable to partnership capital for the taxable year shall be allocated between the donor and donee in accordance with their respective interests in partnership capital.

(c) In determining a reasonable allowance for services rendered by the partners, consideration shall be given to all the facts and circumstances of the business, including the fact that some of the partners may have greater managerial responsibility than others. There shall also be considered the amount that would ordinarily be paid in order to obtain comparable services from a person not having an interest in the partnership.

(d) The distributive share of partnership income, as determined under subdivision (b) of this subdivision, of a partner who rendered services to the partnership before entering the Armed Forces of the United States shall not be diminished because of absence due to military service. Such distributive share shall be adjusted to reflect increases or decreases in the capital interest of the absent partner. However, the partners may by agreement allocate a smaller share to the absent partner due to his absence.

(ii) *Special rules.* (a) The provisions of subdivision (i) of this subparagraph, relating to allocation of family partnership income, are applicable where the interest in the partnership is created by gift, indirectly or directly. Where the partnership interest is created indirectly, the term "donor" may include persons other than the nominal transferor. This rule may be illustrated by the following examples:

Example (1). A father gives property to his son who shortly thereafter conveys the property to a partnership consisting of the father and the son. The partnership interest of the son may be considered created by gift and the father may be considered the donor of the son's partnership interest.

Example (2). A father, the owner of a business conducted as a sole proprietorship, transfers the business to a partnership consisting of his wife and himself. The wife subsequently conveys her interest to their son. In such case, the father, as well as the mother, may be considered the donor of the son's partnership interest.

Example (3). A father makes a gift to his son of stock in the family corporation. The corporation is subsequently liquidated. The son later contributes the property received in the liquidation of the corporation to a partnership consisting of his father and himself. In such case, for purposes of section 704, the son's partnership interest may be considered created by gift and the father may be considered the donor of his son's partnership interest.

(b) The allocation rules set forth in section 704(e) and subdivision (i) of this subpara-

Reg. § 1.704-1(e)(3)

graph apply in any case in which the transfer or creation of the partnership interest has any of the substantial characteristics of a gift. Thus, allocation may be required where transfer of a partnership interest is made between members of a family (including collaterals) under a purported purchase agreement, if the characteristics of a gift are ascertained from the terms of the purchase agreement, the terms of any loan or credit arrangements made to finance the purchase, or from other relevant data.

(*c*) In the case of a limited partnership, for the purpose of the allocation provisions of subdivision (i) of this subparagraph, consideration shall be given to the fact that a general partner, unlike a limited partner, risks his credit in the partnership business.

(4) *Purchased interest* —(i) *In general.* If a purported purchase of a capital interest in a partnership does not meet the requirements of subdivision (ii) of this subparagraph, the ownership by the transferee of such capital interest will be recognized only if it qualifies under the requirements applicable to a transfer of a partnership interest by gifts. In a case not qualifying under subdivision (ii) of this subparagraph, if payment of any part of the purchase price is made out of partnership earnings, the transaction may be regarded in the same light as a purported gift subject to deferred enjoyment of income. Such a transaction may be lacking in reality either as a gift or as a bona fide purchase.

(ii) *Tests as to reality of purchased interests.* A purchase of a capital interest in a partnership, either directly or by means of a loan or credit extended by a member of the family, will be recognized as bona fide if:

(*a*) It can be shown that the purchase has the usual characteristics of an arm's-length transaction, considering all relevant factors, including the terms of the purchase agreement (as to price, due date of payment, rate of interest, and security, if any) and the terms of any loan or credit arrangement collateral to the purchase agreement; the credit standing of the purchaser (apart from relationship to the seller) and the capacity of the purchaser to incur a legally binding obligation; or

(*b*) It can be shown, in the absence of characteristics of an arm's-length transaction, that the purchase was genuinely intended to promote the success of the business by securing participation of the purchaser in the business or by adding his credit to that of the other participants.

However, if the alleged purchase price or loan has not been paid or the obligation otherwise discharged, the factors indicated in (*a*) and (*b*) of this subdivision shall be taken into account only

as an aid in determining whether a bona fide purchase or loan obligation existed. [Reg. § 1.704-1.]

☐ [*T.D.* 6175, 5-23-56. *Amended by T.D.* 6771, 11-19-64; *T.D.* 8065, 12-24-85; *T.D.* 8099, 9-8-86; *T.D.* 8237, 12-29-88; *T.D.* 8385, 12-26-91; *T.D.* 8500, 12-21-93; *T.D.* 8585, 12-27-94 *and T.D.* 8717, 5-8-97.]

§ 1.704-2. Allocations attributable to nonrecourse liabilities.—* * *

(b) *General principles and definitions*—(1) *Definition of and allocations of nonrecourse deductions.* Allocations of losses, deductions, or section 705(a)(2)(B) expenditures attributable to partnership nonrecourse liabilities ("nonrecourse deductions") cannot have economic effect because the creditor alone bears any economic burden that corresponds to those allocations. Thus, nonrecourse deductions must be allocated in accordance with the partners' interests in the partnership. Paragraph (e) of this section provides a test that deems allocations of nonrecourse deductions to be in accordance with the partners' interests in the partnership. If that test is not satisfied, the partners' distributive shares of nonrecourse deductions are determined under § 1.704-1(b)(3), according to the partners' overall economic interests in the partnership. See also paragraph (i) of this section for special rules regarding the allocation of deductions attributable to nonrecourse liabilities for which a partner bears the economic risk of loss (as described in paragraph (b)(4) of this section).

(2) *Definition of and allocations pursuant to a minimum gain chargeback.* To the extent a nonrecourse liability exceeds the adjusted tax basis of the partnership property it encumbers, a disposition of that property will generate gain that at least equals that excess ("partnership minimum gain"). An increase in partnership minimum gain is created by a decrease in the adjusted tax basis of property encumbered by a nonrecourse liability below the amount of that liability and by a partnership nonrecourse borrowing that exceeds the adjusted tax basis of the property encumbered by the borrowing. Partnership minimum gain decreases as reductions occur in the amount by which the nonrecourse liability exceeds the adjusted tax basis of the property encumbered by the liability. Allocations of gain attributable to a decrease in partnership minimum gain (a "minimum gain chargeback," as required under paragraph (f) of this section) cannot have economic effect because the gain merely offsets nonrecourse deductions previously claimed by the partnership. Thus, to avoid impairing the economic effect of other allocations, allocations pursuant to a minimum gain chargeback must be made to the partners that either were allocated nonrecourse

Reg. § 1.704-2(b)(2)

deductions or received distributions of proceeds attributable to a nonrecourse borrowing. Paragraph (e) of this section provides a test that, if met, deems allocations of partnership income pursuant to a minimum gain chargeback to be in accordance with the partners' interests in the partnership. If property encumbered by a nonrecourse liability is reflected on the partnership's books at a value that differs from its adjusted tax basis, paragraph (d)(3) of this section provides that minimum gain is determined with reference to the property's book basis. See also paragraph (i)(4) of this section for special rules regarding the minimum gain chargeback requirement for partner nonrecourse debt.

(3) *Definition of nonrecourse liability.* "Nonrecourse liability" means a nonrecourse liability as defined in § 1.752-1(a)(2).

(4) *Definition of partner nonrecourse debt.* "Partner nonrecourse debt" or "partner nonrecourse liability" means any partnership liability to the extent the liability is nonrecourse for purposes of § 1.1001-2, and a partner or related person (within the meaning of § 1.752-4(b)) bears the economic risk of loss under § 1.752-2 because, for example, the partner or related person is the creditor or a guarantor.

(c) *Amount of nonrecourse deductions.* The amount of nonrecourse deductions for a partnership taxable year equals the net increase in partnership minimum gain during the year (determined under paragraph (d) of this section), reduced (but not below zero) by the aggregate distributions made during the year of proceeds of a nonrecourse liability that are allocable to an increase in partnership minimum gain (determined under paragraph (h) of this section). See paragraph (m), *Examples* (1)(i) and (vi), (2), and (3) of this section. However, increases in partnership minimum gain resulting from conversions, refinancings, or other changes to a debt instrument (as described in paragraph (g)(3)) do not generate nonrecourse deductions. Generally, nonrecourse deductions consist first of certain depreciation or cost recovery deductions and then, if necessary, a pro rata portion of other partnership losses, deductions, and section 705(a)(2)(B) expenditures for that year, excess nonrecourse deductions are carried over. See paragraphs (j)(1)(ii) and (iii) of this section for more specific ordering rules. See also paragraph (m), *Example* (1)(vi) of this section.

(d) *Partnership minimum gain*—(1) *Amount of partnership minimum gain.* The amount of partnership minimum gain is determined by first computing for each partnership nonrecourse liability any gain the partnership would realize if it disposed of the property subject to that liability for

no consideration other than full satisfaction of the liability, and then aggregating the separately computed gains. The amount of partnership minimum gain includes minimum gain arising from a conversion, refinancing, or other change to a debt instrument, as described in paragraph (g)(3) of this section, only to the extent a partner is allocated a share of that minimum gain. For any partnership taxable year, the net increase or decrease in partnership minimum gain is determined by comparing the partnership minimum gain on the last day of the immediately preceding taxable year with the partnership minimum gain on the last day of the current taxable year. See paragraph (m), *Examples* (l)(i) and (iv), (2), and (3) of this section.

(2) *Property subject to more than one liability.* (i) *In general.* If property is subject to more than one liability, only the portion of the property's adjusted tax basis that is allocated to a nonrecourse liability under paragraph (d)(2)(ii) of this section is used to compute minimum gain with respect to that liability.

(ii) *Allocating liabilities.* If property is subject to two or more liabilities of equal priority, the property's adjusted tax basis is allocated among the liabilities in proportion to their outstanding balances. If property is subject to two or more liabilities of unequal priority, the adjusted tax basis is allocated first to the liability of the highest priority to the extent of its outstanding balance and then to each liability in descending order of priority to the extent of its outstanding balance, until fully allocated. See paragraph (m), *Example* (1)(v) and (vii) of this section.

(3) *Partnership minimum gain if there is a book/tax disparity.* If partnership property subject to one or more nonrecourse liabilities is, under § 1.704-1(b)(2)(iv)(*d*), (*f*), or (*r*), reflected on the partnership's books at a value that differs from its adjusted tax basis, the determinations under this section are made with reference to the property's book value. See section 704(c) and § 1.704-1(b)(4)(i) for principles that govern the treatment of a partner's share of minimum gain that is eliminated by the revaluation. See also paragraph (m), *Example* (3) of this section.

(4) *Special rule for year of revaluation.* If the partners' capital accounts are increased pursuant to § 1.704-1(b)(2)(iv)(*d*), (*f*), or (*r*) to reflect a revaluation of partnership property subject to a nonrecourse liability, the net increase or decrease in partnership minimum gain for the partnership taxable year of the revaluation is determined by:

(i) First calculating the net decrease or increase in partnership minimum gain using the current year's book values and the prior year's partnership minimum gain amount; and

(ii) Then adding back any decrease in minimum gain arising solely from the revaluation.

See paragraph (m), *Example* (3)(iii) of this section. If the partners' capital accounts are decreased to reflect a revaluation, the net increases or decreases in partnership minimum gain are determined in the same manner as in the year before the revaluation, but by using book values rather than adjusted tax bases. See section 7701(g) and § 1.704-1(b)(2)(iv)(*f*)(*1*) (property being revalued cannot be booked down below the amount of any nonrecourse liability to which the property is subject).

(e) *Requirements to be satisfied.* Allocations of nonrecourse deductions are deemed to be in accordance with the partners' interests in the partnership only if—

(1) Throughout the full term of the partnership requirements (*1*) and (*2*) of § 1.704-1(b)(2)(ii)(*b*) are satisfied (*i.e.*, capital accounts are maintained in accordance with § 1.704-1(b)(2)(iv) and liquidating distributions are required to be made in accordance with positive capital account balances), and requirement (*3*) of either § 1.704-1(b)(2)(ii)(*b*) or § 1.704-1(b)(2)(ii)(*d*) is satisfied (*i.e.*, partners with deficit capital accounts have an unconditional deficit restoration obligation or agree to a qualified income offset);

(2) Beginning in the first taxable year of the partnership in which there are nonrecourse deductions and thereafter throughout the full term of the partnership, the partnership agreement provides for allocations of nonrecourse deductions in a manner that is reasonably consistent with allocations that have substantial economic effect of some other significant partnership item attributable to the property securing the nonrecourse liabilities;

(3) Beginning in the first taxable year of the partnership that it has nonrecourse deductions or makes a distribution of proceeds of a nonrecourse liability that are allocable to an increase in partnership minimum gain, and thereafter throughout the full term of the partnership, the partnership agreement contains a provision that complies with the minimum gain chargeback requirement of paragraph (f) of this section; and

(4) All other material allocations and capital account adjustments under the partnership agreement are recognized under § 1.704-1(b) (without regard to whether allocations of adjusted tax basis and amount realized under section 613A(c)(7)(D) are recognized under § 1.704-1(b)(4)(v)).

(f) *Minimum gain chargeback requirement—* (1) *In general.* If there is a net decrease in partnership minimum gain for a partnership taxable year, the minimum gain chargeback requirement

applies and each partner must be allocated items of partnership income and gain for that year equal to that partner's share of the net decrease in partnership minimum gain (within the meaning of paragraph (g)(2)).

(2) *Exception for certain conversions and refinancings.* A partner is not subject to the minimum gain chargeback requirement to the extent the partner's share of the net decrease in partnership minimum gain is caused by a guarantee, refinancing, or other change in the debt instrument causing it to become partially or wholly recourse debt or partner nonrecourse debt, and the partner bears the economic risk of loss (within the meaning of § 1.752-2) for the newly guaranteed, refinanced, or otherwise changed liability.

(3) *Exception for certain capital contributions.* A partner is not subject to the minimum gain chargeback requirement to the extent the partner contributes capital to the partnership that is used to repay the nonrecourse liability or is used to increase the basis of the property subject to nonrecourse liability, and the partner's share of the net decrease in partnership minimum gain results from the repayment or the increase to the property's basis. See paragraph (m), *Example* (1)(iv) of this section.

(4) *Waiver for certain income allocations that fail to meet minimum gain chargeback requirement if minimum gain chargeback distorts economic arrangement.* In any taxable year that a partnership has a net decrease in partnership minimum gain, if the minimum gain chargeback requirement would cause a distortion in the economic arrangement among the partners and it is not expected that the partnership will have sufficient other income to correct that distortion, the Commissioner has the discretion, if requested by the partnership, to waive the minimum gain chargeback requirement. The following facts must be demonstrated in order for a request for a waiver to be considered:

(i) The partners have made capital contributions or received net income allocations that have restored the previous nonrecourse deductions and the distributions attributable to proceeds of a nonrecourse liability; and

(ii) The minimum gain chargeback requirement would distort the partners' economic arrangement as reflected in the partnership agreement and as evidenced over the term of the partnership by the partnership's allocations and distributions and the partners' contributions.

(5) *Additional exceptions.* The Commissioner may, by revenue ruling, provide additional exceptions to the minimum gain chargeback requirement.

Reg. § 1.704-2(f)(5)

(6) *Partnership items subject to the minimum gain chargeback requirement.* Any minimum gain chargeback required for a partnership taxable year consists first of certain gains recognized from the disposition of partnership property subject to one or more partnership nonrecourse liabilities and then if necessary consists of a pro rata portion of the partnership's other items of income and gain for that year. If the amount of the minimum gain chargeback requirement exceeds the partnership's income and gains for the taxable year, the excess carries over. See paragraphs (j)(2)(i) and (iii) of this section for more specific ordering rules.

(7) *Examples.* The following examples illustrate the provisions in § 1.704-2(f).

Example 1. Partnership AB consists of two partners, limited partner A and general partner B. Partner A contributes $90 and partner B contributes $10 to the partnership. The partnership agreement has a minimum gain chargeback provision and provides that, except as otherwise required by section 704(c), all losses will be allocated 90 percent to A and 10 percent to B; and

that all income will be allocated first to restore previous losses and thereafter 50 percent to A and 50 percent to B. Distributions are made first to return initial capital to the partners and then 50 percent to A and 50 percent to B. Final distributions are made in accordance with capital account balances. The partnership borrows $200 on a nonrecourse basis from an unrelated third party and purchases an asset for $300. The partnership's only tax item for each of the first three years is $100 of depreciation on the asset. A's and B's shares of minimum gain (under paragraph (g) of this section) and deficit capital account balances are $180 and $20 respectively at the end of the third year. In the fourth year, the partnership earns $400 of net operating income and allocates the first $300 to restore the previous losses (*i.e.*, $270 to A and $30 to B); the last $100 is allocated $50 each. The partnership distributes $200 of the available cash that same year; the first $100 is distributed $90 to A and $10 to B to return their capital contributions; the last $100 is distributed $50 each to reflect their ratio for sharing profits.

	A	B
Capital account on formation	$90	$10
Less: net loss in years 1-3	($270)	($30)
Capital account at end of year 3	($180)	($20)
Allocation of operating income to restore nonrecourse deductions	$180	$20
Allocation of operating income to restore capital contributions	$90	$10
Allocation of operating income to reflect profits	$50	$50
Capital accounts after allocation of operating income	$140	$60
Distribution reflecting capital contribution	($90)	($10)
Distribution in profit-sharing ratio	($50)	($50)
Capital accounts following distribution	($0)	($0)

In the fifth year, the partnership sells the property for $300 and realizes $300 of gain. $200 of the proceeds are used to pay the nonrecourse lender. The partnership has $300 to distribute, and the partners expect to share that equally. Absent a waiver under paragraph (f)(4) of this section, the minimum gain chargeback would require the partnership to allocate the first $200 of the gain $180 to A and $20 to B, which would distort their economic arrangement. This allocation, together with the allocation of the $100 profit $50 to each partner, would result in A having a positive capital account balance of $230 and B having a positive capital account balance of $70. The allocation of income in year 4 in effect anticipated the minimum gain chargeback that did not occur until year 5. Assuming the partnership would not have sufficient other income to correct the distortion that would otherwise result, the partnership may request that the Commissioner exercise his or her discretion to waive the minimum gain chargeback requirement and recognize allocations that would allow A and B to

share equally the gain on the sale of the property. These allocations would bring the partners' capital accounts to $150 each, allowing them to share the last $300 equally. The Commissioner may, in his or her discretion, permit this allocation pursuant to paragraph (f)(4) of this section because the minimum gain chargeback would distort the partners' economic arrangement over the term of the partnership as reflected in the partnership agreement and as evidenced by the partners' contributions and the partnership's allocations and distributions.

Example 2. A and B form a partnership, contribute $25 each to the partnership's capital, and agree to share all losses and profits 50 percent each. Neither partner has an unconditional deficit restoration obligation and all the requirements in paragraph (e) of this section are met. The partnership obtains a nonrecourse loan from an unrelated third party of $100 and purchases two assets, stock for $50 and depreciable property for $100. The nonrecourse loan is secured by the partnership's depreciable property. The partnership generates $20 of depreciation in each of the first five years as its only tax item. These deductions are properly treated as nonrecourse deductions and the allocation of these deductions 50 percent to A and 50 percent to B is deemed to be in accordance with the partners' interests in the partnership. At the end of year five, A and B each have a $25 deficit capital account and a $50 share of partnership minimum gain. In the beginning of year six, (at the lender's request), A guarantees the entire nonrecourse liability. Pursuant to paragraph (d)(1) of this section, the partnership has a net decrease in minimum gain of $100 and under paragraph (g)(2) of this section, A's and B's shares of that net decrease are $50 each. Under paragraph (f)(1) of this section (the minimum gain chargeback requirement), B is subject to a $50 minimum gain chargeback. Because the partnership has no gross income in year six, the entire $50 carries over as a minimum gain chargeback requirement to succeeding taxable years until there is enough income to cover the minimum gain chargeback requirement. Under the exception to the minimum gain chargeback in paragraph (f)(2) of this section, A is not subject to a minimum gain chargeback for A's $50 share of the net decrease because A bears the economic risk of loss for the liability. Instead, A's share of partner nonrecourse debt minimum gain is $50 pursuant to paragraph (i)(3) of this section. In year seven, the partnership earns $100 of net operating income and uses the money to repay the entire $100 nonrecourse debt (that A has guaranteed). Under paragraph (i)(3) of this section, the partnership has a net decrease in partner nonrecourse debt minimum gain of $50. B must be allocated $50 of the operating income pursuant to the carried over minimum gain chargeback requirement; pursuant to paragraph (i)(4) of this section, the other $50 of operating income must be allocated to A as a partner nonrecourse debt minimum gain chargeback.

(g) *Shares of partnership minimum gain*—(1) *Partner's share of partnership minimum gain.* Except as increased in paragraph (g)(3) of this section, a partner's share of partnership minimum gain at the end of any partnership taxable year equals:

(i) the sum of nonrecourse deductions allocated to that partner (and to that partner's predecessors in interest) up to that time and the distributions made to that partner (and to that partner's predecessors' in interest) up to that time of proceeds of a nonrecourse liability allocable to an increase in partnership minimum gain (see paragraph (h)(1) of this section); minus

(ii) the sum of that partner's (and that partner's predecessors' in interest) aggregate share of the net decreases in partnership mini-

mum gain plus their aggregate share of decreases resulting from revaluations of partnership property subject to one or more partnership nonrecourse liabilities.

For purposes of § 1.704-1(b)(2)(ii)(*d*) a partner's share of partnership minimum gain is added to the limited dollar amount, if any, of the deficit balance in the partner's capital account that the partner is obligated to restore. See paragraph (m), *Examples* (1)(i) and (3)(i) of this section.

(2) *Partner's share of the net decrease in partnership minimum gain.* A partner's share of the net decrease in partnership minimum gain is the amount of the total net decrease multiplied by the partner's percentage share of the partnership's minimum gain at the end of the immediately preceding taxable year. A partner's share of any decrease in partnership minimum gain resulting from a revaluation of partnership property equals the increase in the partner's capital account attributable to the revaluation to the extent the reduction in minimum gain is caused by the revaluation. See paragraph (m), *Example* (3)(ii) of this section.

(3) *Conversions of recourse or partner nonrecourse debt into nonrecourse debt.* A partner's share of partnership minimum gain is increased to the extent provided in this paragraph (g)(3) if a refinancing, the lapse of a guarantee, or other change to a debt instrument causes a recourse or partner nonrecourse liability to become partially or wholly nonrecourse. If a recourse liability becomes a nonrecourse liability, a partner has a share of the partnership's minimum gain that results from the conversion equal to the partner's deficit capital account (determined under § 1.704-1(b)(2)(iv)) to the extent the partner no longer bears the economic burden for the entire deficit capital account as a result of the conversion. For purposes of the preceding sentence, the determination of the extent to which a partner bears the economic burden for a deficit capital account is made by determining the consequences to the partner in the case of a complete liquidation of the partnership immediately after the conversion applying the rules described in § 1.704-1(b)(2)(iii)(*c*) that deem the value of partnership property to equal its basis, taking into account section 7701(g) in the case of property that secures nonrecourse indebtedness. If a partner nonrecourse debt becomes a nonrecourse liability, the partner's share of partnership minimum gain is increased to the extent the partner is not subject to the minimum gain chargeback requirement under paragraph (i)(4) of this section.

(h) *Distribution of nonrecourse liability proceeds allocable to an increase in partnership minimum gain*—(1) *In general.* If during its taxable

Reg. § 1.704-2(h)

year a partnership makes a distribution to the partners allocable to the proceeds of a nonrecourse liability, the distribution is allocable to an increase in partnership minimum gain to the extent the increase results from encumbering partnership property with aggregate nonrecourse liabilities that exceed the property's adjusted tax basis. See paragraph (m), *Example* (1)(vi) of this section. If the net increase in partnership minimum gain for a partnership taxable year is allocable to more than one nonrecourse liability, the net increase is allocated among the liabilities in proportion to the amount each liability contributed to the increase in minimum gain.

(2) *Distribution allocable to nonrecourse liability proceeds.* A partnership nay use any reasonable method to determine whether a distribution by the partnership to one or more partners is allocable to proceeds of a nonrecourse liability. The rules prescribed under § 1.163-8T for allocating debt proceeds among expenditures (applying those rules to the partnership as if it were an individual) constitute a reasonable method for determining whether the nonrecourse liability proceeds are distributed to the partners and the partners to whom the proceeds are distributed.

(3) *Option when there is an obligation to restore.* A partnership may treat any distribution to a partner of the proceeds of a nonrecourse liability (that would otherwise be allocable to an increase in partnership minimum gain) as a distribution that is not allocable to an increase in partnership minimum gain to the extent the distribution does not cause or increase a deficit balance in the partner's capital account that exceeds the amount the partner is otherwise obligated to restore (within the meaning of § 1.704-1(b)(2)(ii)(*c*)) as of the end of the partnership taxable year in which the distribution occurs.

(4) *Carryover to immediately succeeding taxable year.* The carryover rule of this paragraph applies if the net increase in partnership minimum gain for a partnership taxable year that is allocable to a nonrecourse liability under paragraph (h)(2) of this section exceeds the distributions allocable to the proceeds of the liability ("excess allocable amount"), and all or part of the net increase in partnership minimum gain for the year is carried over as an increase in partnership minimum gain for the immediately succeeding taxable year (pursuant to paragraph (j)(1)(iii) of this section). If the carryover rule of this paragraph applies, the excess allocable amount (or the amount carried over under paragraph (j)(1)(iii) of this section, if less) is treated in the succeeding taxable year as an increase in partnership minimum gain that arose in that year as a result of incurring the nonrecourse liability to which the excess allocable amount is attributable. See para-

graph (m), *Example* (1)(vi) of this section. If for a partnership taxable year there is an excess allocable amount with respect to more than one partnership nonrecourse liability, the excess allocable amount is allocated to each liability in proportion to the amount each liability contributed to the increase in minimum gain.

(i) *Partnership nonrecourse liabilities where a partner bears the economic risk of loss—(1) In general.* Partnership losses, deductions, or section 705(a)(2)(B) expenditures that are attributable to a particular partner nonrecourse liability ("partner nonrecourse deductions," as defined in paragraph (i)(2) of this section) must be allocated to the partner that bears the economic risk of loss for the liability. If more than one partner bears the economic risk of loss for a partner nonrecourse liability, any partner nonrecourse deductions attributable to that liability must be allocated among the partners according to the ratio in which they bear the economic risk of loss. If partners bear the economic risk of loss for different portions of a liability, each portion is treated as a separate partner nonrecourse liability.

(2) *Definition of and determination of partner nonrecourse deductions.* For any partnership taxable year, the amount of partner nonrecourse deductions with respect to a partner nonrecourse debt equals the net increase during the year in minimum gain attributable to the partner nonrecourse debt ("partner nonrecourse debt minimum gain"), reduced (but not below zero) by proceeds of the liability distributed during the year to the partner bearing the economic risk of loss for the liability that are both attributable to the liability and allocable to an increase in the partner nonrecourse debt minimum gain. See paragraph (m), *Example* (1)(viii) and (ix) of this section. The determination of which partnership items constitute the partner nonrecourse deductions with respect to a partner nonrecourse debt must be made in a manner consistent with the provisions of paragraphs (c) and (j)(1)(i) and (iii) of this section.

(3) *Determination of partner nonrecourse debt minimum gain.* For any partnership taxable year, the determination of partner nonrecourse debt minimum gain and the net increase or decrease in partner nonrecourse debt minimum gain must be made in a manner consistent with the provisions of paragraphs (d) and (g)(3) of this section.

(4) *Chargeback of partner nonrecourse debt minimum gain.* If during a partnership taxable year there is a net decrease in partner nonrecourse debt minimum gain, any partner with a share of that partner nonrecourse debt minimum gain (determined under paragraph (i)(5) of this

section) as of the beginning of the year must be allocated items of income and gain for the year (and, if necessary, for succeeding years) equal to that partner's share of the net decrease in the partner nonrecourse debt minimum gain. A partner's share of the net decrease in partner nonrecourse debt minimum gain is determined in a manner consistent with the provisions of paragraph (g)(2) of this section. A partner is not subject to this minimum gain chargeback, however, to the extent the net decrease in partner nonrecourse debt minimum gain arises because the liability ceases to be partner nonrecourse debt due to a conversion, refinancing, or other change in the debt instrument that causes it to become partially or wholly a nonrecourse liability. The amount that would otherwise be subject to the partner nonrecourse debt minimum gain chargeback is added to the partner's share of partnership minimum gain under paragraph (g)(3) of this section. In addition, rules consistent with the provisions of paragraphs (f)(2), (3), (4), and (5) of this section apply with respect to partner nonrecourse debt in appropriate circumstances. The determination of which items of partnership income and gain must be allocated pursuant to this paragraph (i)(4) is made in a manner that is consistent with the provisions of paragraph (f)(6) of this section. See paragraph (j)(2)(ii) and (iii) of this section for more specific rules.

(5) *Partner's share of partner nonrecourse debt minimum gain.* A partner's share of partner nonrecourse debt minimum gain at the end of any partnership taxable year is determined in a manner consistent with the provisions of paragraphs (g)(1) and (g)(3) of this section with respect to each particular partner nonrecourse debt for which the partner bears the economic risk of loss. For purposes of § 1.704-1(b)(2)(ii)(*d*), a partner's share of partner nonrecourse debt minimum gain is added to the limited dollar amount, if any, of the deficit balance in the partner's capital account that the partner is obligated to restore, and the partner is not otherwise considered to have a deficit restoration obligation as a result of bearing the economic risk of loss for any partner nonrecourse debt. See paragraph (m), *Example* (1)(viii) of this section.

(6) *Distribution of partner nonrecourse debt proceeds allocable to an increase in partner nonrecourse debt minimum gain.* Rules consistent with the provisions of paragraph (h) of this section apply to distributions of the proceeds of partner nonrecourse debt.

(j) *Ordering Rules.* For purposes of this section, the following ordering rules apply to partnership items. Notwithstanding any other provision in this section and § 1.704-1, allocations of partner nonrecourse deductions, nonrecourse deductions, and minimum gain chargebacks are made before any other allocations.

(1) *Treatment of partnership losses and deductions.* (i) *Partner nonrecourse deductions.* Partnership losses, deductions, and section 705(a)(2)(B) expenditures are treated as partner nonrecourse deductions in the amount determined under paragraph (i)(2) of this section (determining partner nonrecourse deductions) in the following order:

(A) First, depreciation or cost recovery deductions with respect to property that is subject to partner nonrecourse debt;

(B) Then, if necessary, a pro rata portion of the partnership's other deductions, losses, and section 705(a)(2)(B) items.

Depreciation or cost recovery deductions with respect to property that is subject to a partnership nonrecourse liability is first treated as a partnership nonrecourse deduction and any excess is treated as a partner nonrecourse deduction under this paragraph (j)(1)(i).

(ii) *Partnership nonrecourse deductions.* Partnership losses, deductions, and section 705(a)(2)(B) expenditures are treated as partnership nonrecourse deductions in the amount determined under paragraph (c) of this section (determining nonrecourse deductions) in the following order:

(A) First, depreciation or cost recovery deductions with respect to property that is subject to partnership nonrecourse liabilities;

(B) Then, if necessary, a pro rata portion of the partnership's other deductions, losses, and section 705(a)(2)(B) items.

Depreciation or cost recovery deductions with respect to property that is subject to partner nonrecourse debt is first treated as a partner nonrecourse deduction and any excess is treated as a partnership nonrecourse deduction under this paragraph (j)(1)(ii). Any other item that is treated as a partner nonrecourse deduction will in no event be treated as a partnership nonrecourse deduction.

(iii) *Carryover to succeeding taxable year.* If the amount of partner nonrecourse deductions or nonrecourse deductions exceeds the partnership's losses, deductions, and section 705(a)(2)(B) expenditures for the taxable year (determined under paragraphs (j)(1)(i) and (ii) of this section), the excess is treated as an increase in partner nonrecourse debt minimum gain or partnership minimum gain in the immediately succeeding partnership taxable year. See paragraph (m), *Example* (1)(vi) of this section.

Reg. § 1.704-2(j)(1)

(2) *Treatment of partnership income and gains.* (i) *Minimum gain chargeback.* Items of partnership income and gain equal to the minimum gain chargeback requirement (determined under paragraph (f) of this section) are allocated as a minimum gain chargeback in the following order:

(A) First, gain from the disposition of property subject to partnership nonrecourse liabilities;

(B) Then, if necessary, a pro rata portion of the partnership's other items of income and gain for that year. Gain from the disposition of property subject to partner nonrecourse debt is allocated to satisfy a minimum gain chargeback requirement for partnership nonrecourse debt only to the extent not allocated under paragraph (j)(2)(ii) of this section.

(ii) *Chargeback attributable to decrease in partner nonrecourse debt minimum gain.* Items of partnership income and gain equal to the partner nonrecourse debt minimum gain chargeback (determined under paragraph (i)(4) of this section) are allocated to satisfy a partner nonrecourse debt minimum gain chargeback in the following order:

(A) First, gain from the disposition of property subject to partner nonrecourse debt;

(B) Then, if necessary, a pro rata portion of the partnership's other items of income and gain for that year. Gain from the disposition of property subject to a partnership nonrecourse liability is allocated to satisfy a partner nonrecourse debt minimum gain chargeback only to the extent not allocated under paragraph (j)(2)(i) of this section. An item of partnership income and gain that is allocated to satisfy a minimum gain chargeback under paragraph (f) of this section is not allocated to satisfy a minimum gain chargeback under paragraph (i)(4).

(iii) *Carryover to succeeding taxable year.* If a minimum gain chargeback requirement (determined under paragraphs (f) and (i)(4) of this section) exceeds the partnership's income and gains for the taxable year, the excess is treated as a minimum gain chargeback requirement in the immediately succeeding partnership taxable years until fully charged back.

(k) *Tiered partnerships.* For purposes of this section, the following rules determine the effect on partnership minimum gain when a partnership ("upper-tier partnership") is a partner in another partnership ("lower-tier partnership").

(1) *Increase in upper-tier partnership's minimum gain.* The sum of the nonrecourse deductions that the lower-tier partnership allocates to the upper-tier partnership for any taxable year of the upper-tier partnership, and the distributions made during that taxable year from the lower-tier partnership to the upper-tier partnership of proceeds of nonrecourse debt that are allocable to an increase in the lower-tier partnership's minimum gain, is treated as an increase in the upper-tier partnership's minimum gain.

(2) *Decrease in upper-tier partnership's minimum gain.* The upper-tier partnership's share for its taxable year of the lower-tier partnership's net decrease in its minimum gain is treated as a decrease in the upper-tier partnership's minimum gain for that taxable year.

(3) *Nonrecourse debt proceeds distributed from the lower-tier partnership to the upper-tier partnership.* All distributions from the lower-tier partnership to the upper-tier partnership during the upper-tier partnership's taxable year of proceeds of a nonrecourse liability allocable to an increase in the lower-tier partnership's minimum gain are treated as proceeds of a nonrecourse liability of the upper-tier partnership. The increase in the upper-tier partnership's minimum gain (under paragraph (k)(1) of this section) attributable to the receipt of those distributions is, for purposes of paragraph (h) of this section, treated as an increase in the upper-tier partnership's minimum gain arising from encumbering property of the upper-tier partnership with a nonrecourse liability of the upper-tier partnership.

(4) *Nonrecourse deductions of lower-tier partnership treated as depreciation by upper-tier partnership.* For purposes of paragraph (c) of this section, all nonrecourse deductions allocated by the lower-tier partnership to the upper-tier partnership for the upper-tier partnership's taxable year are treated as depreciation or cost recovery deductions with respect to property owned by the upper-tier partnership and subject to a nonrecourse liability of the upper-tier partnership with respect to which minimum gain increased during the year by the amount of the nonrecourse deductions.

* * *

(m) *Examples.* The principles of this section are illustrated by the following examples:

Example 1. Nonrecourse deductions and partnership minimum gain. For *Example* 1, unless otherwise provided, the following facts are assumed. LP, the limited partner, and GP, the general partner, form a limited partnership to acquire and operate a commercial office building. LP contributes $180,000, and GP contributes $20,000. The partnership obtains an $800,000 nonrecourse loan and purchases the building (on leased land) for $1,000,000. The nonrecourse loan is secured only by the building, and no principal payments are due for 5 years. The partnership agreement provides that GP will be required to restore any deficit balance in GP's capital account following the liquidation of GP's interest (as set forth in § 1.704-1(b)(2)(ii)(*b*)(*3*)), and LP will not be required to restore any deficit balance in LP's capital account following the liquidation of LP's interest. The partnership agreement contains the following provisions required by paragraph (e) of this section: a qualified income offset (as defined in § 1.704-1(b)(2)(ii)(*d*)); a minimum gain chargeback (in accordance with paragraph (f) of this section); a provision that the partners' capital accounts will be determined and maintained in accordance with § 1.704-1(b)(2)(ii)(*b*)(*1*); and a provision that distributions will be made in accordance with partners' positive capital account balances (as set forth in § 1.704-1(b)(2)(ii)(*b*)(*2*)). In addition, as of the end of each partnership taxable year discussed herein, the items described in § 1.704-1(b)(2)(ii)(*d*)(*4*), (*5*), and (*6*) are not reasonably expected to cause or increase a deficit balance in LP's capital account. The partnership agreement provides that, except as otherwise required by its qualified income offset and mini-mum gain chargeback provisions, all partnership items will be allocated 90 percent to LP and 10 percent to GP until the first time when the partnership has recognized items of income and gain that exceed the items of loss and deduction it has recognized over its life, and all further partnership items will be allocated equally between LP and GP. Finally, the partnership agreement provides that all distributions, other than distributions in liquidation of the partnership or of a partner's interest in the partnership, will be made 90 percent to LP and 10 percent to GP until a total of $200,000 has been distributed, and thereafter all the distributions will be made equally to LP and GP. In each of the partnership's first 2 taxable years, it generates rental income of $95,000, operating expenses (including land lease payments) of $10,000, interest expense of $80,000, and a depreciation deduction of $90,000, resulting in a net taxable loss of $85,000 in each of those years. The allocations of these losses 90 percent to LP and 10 percent to GP have substantial economic effect.

	LP	GP
Capital account on formation	$180,000	$20,000
Less: net loss in years 1 and 2	(153,000)	(17,000)
Capital account at end of year 2	$27,000	$3,000

In the partnership's third taxable year, it again generates rental income of $95,000, operating expenses of $10,000, interest expense of $80,000, and a depreciation deduction of $90,000, resulting in a net taxable loss of $85,000. The partnership makes no distributions.

(i) *Calculation of nonrecourse deductions and partnership minimum gain.* If the partnership were to dispose of the building in full satisfaction of the nonrecourse liability at the end of the third year, it would realize $70,000 of gain ($800,000 amount realized less $730,000 adjusted tax basis). Because the amount of partnership minimum gain at the end of the third year (and the net increase in partnership minimum gain during the year) is $70,000, there are partnership nonrecourse deductions for that year of $70,000, consisting of depreciation deductions allowable with respect to the building of $70,000. Pursuant to the partnership agreement, all partnership items comprising the net taxable loss of $85,000, including the $70,000 nonrecourse deduction, are allocated 90 percent to LP and 10 percent to GP. The allocation of these items, other than the nonrecourse deductions, has substantial economic effect.

	LP	GP
Capital account at end of year 2	$27,000	$3,000
Less: net loss in year 3 (without nonrecourse deductions)	(13,500)	(1,500)
Less: nonrecourse deductions in year 3	(63,000)	(7,000)
Capital account at end of year 3	($49,500)	($5,500)

The allocation of the $70,000 nonrecourse deduction satisfies requirement (2) of paragraph (e) of this section because it is consistent with allocations having substantial economic effect of other significant partnership items attributable to the building. Because the remaining requirements of paragraph (e) of this section are satisfied, the allocation of nonrecourse deductions is deemed to be in accordance with the partners' interests in the partnership. At the end of the partnership's third taxable year, LP's and GP's shares of partnership minimum gain are $63,000 and $7,000, respectively. Therefore, pursuant to paragraph (g)(1) of this section, LP is treated as obligated to restore a deficit capital account balance of $63,000, so that in the succeeding year LP could be allocated up to an additional $13,500 of partnership deductions, losses, and section 705(a)(2)(B) items that are not nonrecourse deductions. Even though this allocation would increase a deficit capital account balance, it would be considered to have economic effect under the alternate economic effect test contained in § 1.704-1(b)(2)(ii)(*d*). If the partnership were to

Reg. § 1.704-2(m)

dispose of the building in full satisfaction of the nonrecourse liability at the beginning of the partnership's fourth taxable year (and had no other economic activity in that year), the partnership minimum gain would be decreased from $70,000 to zero, and the minimum gain chargeback would require that LP and GP be allocated $63,000 and $7,000, respectively, of the gain from that disposition.

(ii) *Illustration of reasonable consistency requirement.* Assume instead that the partnership

	LP	GP
Capital account on formation................................	$180,000	$20,000
Less: net loss years 1 and 2..............................	(153,000)	(17,000)
Less: net loss in year 3 (without nonrecourse deductions)	(13,500)	(1,500)
Less: nonrecourse deductions in year 3	(35,000)	(35,000)
Capital account at end of year 3	($21,500)	($33,500)

The allocation of the $70,000 nonrecourse deduction equally between LP and GP satisfies requirement (2) of paragraph (e) of this section because the allocation is consistent with allocations, which will have substantial economic effect, of other significant partnership items attributable to the building. Because the remaining requirements of paragraph (e) of this section are satisfied, the allocation of nonrecourse deductions is deemed to be in accordance with the partners' interests in the partnership. The allocation of the nonrecourse deductions 75 percent to LP and 25 percent to GP (or in any other ratio between 90 percent to LP/10 percent to GP and 50 percent to LP/50 percent to GP) also would satisfy requirement (2) of paragraph (e) of this section.

(iii) *Allocation of nonrecourse deductions that fails reasonable consistency requirement.* Assume instead that the partnership agreement provides that LP will be allocated 99 percent, and GP 1 percent, of all nonrecourse deductions of the partnership. Allocating nonrecourse deductions this way does not satisfy requirement (2) of paragraph (e) of this section because the allocations are not reasonably consistent with allocations, having substantial economic effect, of any other significant partnership item attributable to the building. Therefore, the allocation of nonrecourse deductions will be disregarded, and the nonrecourse deductions of the partnership will be reallocated according to the partners' overall economic

agreement provides that all nonrecourse deductions of the partnership will be allocated equally between LP and GP. Furthermore, at the time the partnership agreement is entered into, there is a reasonable likelihood that over the partnership's life it will realize amounts of income and gain significantly in excess of amounts of loss and deduction (other than nonrecourse deductions). The equal allocation of excess income and gain has substantial economic effect.

interests in the partnership, determined under § 1.704-1(b)(3)(ii).

(iv) *Capital contribution to pay down nonrecourse debt.* At the beginning of the partnership's fourth taxable year, LP contributes $144,000 and GP contributes $16,000 of additional capital to the partnership, which the partnership immediately uses to reduce the amount of its nonrecourse liability from $800,000 to $640,000. In addition, in the partnership's fourth taxable year, it generates rental income of $95,000, operating expenses of $10,000, interest expense of $64,000 (consistent with the debt reduction), and a depreciation deduction of $90,000, resulting in a net taxable loss of $69,000. If the partnership were to dispose of the building in full satisfaction of the nonrecourse liability at the end of that year, it would realize no gain ($640,000 amount realized less $640,000 adjusted tax basis). Therefore, the amount of partnership minimum gain at the end of the year is zero, which represents a net decrease in partnership minimum gain of $70,000 during the year. LP's and GP's shares of this net decrease are $63,000 and $7,000 respectively, so that at the end of the partnership's fourth taxable year, LP's and GP's shares of partnership minimum gain are zero. Although there has been a net decrease in partnership minimum gain, pursuant to paragraph (f)(3) of this section LP and GP are not subject to a minimum gain chargeback.

	LP	GP
Capital account at end of year 3................................	($49,500)	($5,500)
Plus: contribution	144,000	16,000
Less: net loss in year 4....................................	(62,100)	(6,900)
Capital account at end of year 4............................	$32,400	$3,600
Minimum gain chargeback carryforward........................	$ 0	$ 0

(v) *Loans of unequal priority.* Assume instead that the building acquired by the partnership is secured by a $700,000 nonrecourse loan and a $100,000 recourse loan, subordinate in priority to

the nonrecourse loan. Under paragraph (d)(2) of this section, $700,000 of the adjusted basis of the building at the end of the partnership's third taxable year is allocated to the nonrecourse liabil-

Reg. § 1.704-2(m)

ity (with the remaining $30,000 allocated to the recourse liability) so that if the partnership disposed of the building in full satisfaction of the nonrecourse liability at the end of that year, it would realize no gain ($700,000 amount realized less $700,000 adjusted tax basis). Therefore, there is no minimum gain (or increase in minimum gain) at the end of the partnership's third taxable year. If, however, the $700,000 nonrecourse loan were subordinate in priority to the $100,000 recourse loan, under paragraph (d)(2) of this section, the first $100,000 of adjusted tax basis in the building would be allocated to the recourse liability leaving only $630,000 of the adjusted basis of the building to be allocated to the $700,000 nonrecourse loan. In that case, the balance of the $700,000 nonrecourse liability would exceed the adjusted tax basis of the building by $70,000, so that there would be $70,000 of minimum gain (and a $70,000 increase in partnership minimum gain) in the partnership's third taxable year.

(vi) *Nonrecourse borrowing; distribution of proceeds in subsequent year.* The partnership obtains an additional nonrecourse loan of $200,000 at the end of its fourth taxable year, secured by a second mortgage on the building, and distributes $180,000 of this cash to its partners at the beginning of its fifth taxable year. In addition, in its fourth and fifth taxable years, the partnership again generates rental income of $95,000, operating expenses of $10,000, interest expense of $80,000 ($100,000 in the fifth taxable year reflecting the interest paid on both liabilities), and a depreciation deduction of $90,000, resulting in a net taxable loss of $85,000 ($105,000 in the fifth taxable year reflecting the interest paid on both

liabilities). The partnership has distributed its $5,000 of operating cash flow in each year ($95,000 of rental income less $10,000 of operating expense and $80,000 of interest expense) to LP and GP at the end of each year. If the partnership were to dispose of the building in full satisfaction of both nonrecourse liabilities at the end of its fourth taxable year, the partnership would realize $360,000 of gain ($1,000,000 amount realized less $640,000 adjusted tax basis). Thus, the net increase in partnership minimum gain during the partnership's fourth taxable year is $290,000 ($360,000 of minimum gain at the end of the fourth year less $70,000 of minimum gain at the end of the third year). Because the partnership did not distribute any of the proceeds of the loan it obtained in its fourth year during that year, the potential amount of partnership nonrecourse deductions for that year is $290,000. Under paragraph (c) of this section, if the partnership had distributed the proceeds of that loan to its partners at the end of its fourth year, the partnership's nonrecourse deductions for that year would have been reduced by the amount of that distribution because the proceeds of that loan are allocable to an increase in partnership minimum gain under paragraph (h)(1) of this section. Because the nonrecourse deductions of $290,000 for the partnership's fourth taxable year exceed its total deductions for that year, all $180,000 of the partnership's deductions for that year are treated as nonrecourse deductions, and the $110,000 excess nonrecourse deductions are treated as an increase in partnership minimum gain in the partnership's fifth taxable year under paragraph (c) of this section.

	LP	GP
Capital account at end of year 3 (including cash flow distributions)	($63,000)	($7,000)
Plus: rental income in year 4	85,500	9,500
Less: nonrecourse deductions in year 4	(162,000)	(18,000)
Less: cash flow distributions in year 4	(4,500)	(500)
Capital account at end of year 4	($144,000)	($16,000)

At the end of the partnership's fourth taxable year, LP's and GP's shares of partnership minimum gain are $225,000 and $25,000, respectively (because the $110,000 excess of nonrecourse deductions is carried forward to the next year). If the partnership were to dispose of the building in full satisfaction of the nonrecourse liabilities at the end of its fifth taxable year, the partnership would realize $450,000 of gain ($1,000,000 amount realized less $550,000 adjusted tax basis). Therefore, the net increase in partnership minimum gain during the partnership's fifth taxable year is $200,000 ($110,000 deemed increase plus the $90,000 by which minimum gain at the end of the fifth year exceeds minimum gain at the end of the fourth year ($450,000 less $360,000)). At the

beginning of its fifth year, the partnership distributes $180,000 of the loan proceeds (retaining $20,000 to pay the additional interest expense). Under paragraph (h) of this section, the first $110,000 of this distribution (an amount equal to the deemed increase in partnership minimum gain for the year) is considered allocable to an increase in partnership minimum gain for the year. As a result, the amount of nonrecourse deductions for the partnership's fifth taxable year is $90,000 ($200,000 net increase in minimum gain less $110,000 distribution of nonrecourse liability proceeds allocable to an increase in partnership minimum gain), and the nonrecourse deductions consist solely of the $90,000 depreciation deduction allowable with respect to the building. As a

Reg. § 1.704-2(m)

result of the distributions during the partnership's fifth taxable year, the total distributions to the partners over the partnership's life equal $205,000. Therefore, the last $5,000 distributed to the partners during the fifth year will be divided equally between them under the partnership agreement. Thus, out of the $185,000 total distribution during the partnership's fifth taxable year, the first $180,000 is distributed 90 percent to LP and 10 percent to GP, and the last $5,000 is divided equally between them.

	LP	GP
Capital account at end of year 4	($144,000)	($16,000)
Less: net loss in year 5 (without nonrecourse deductions)	(13,500)	(1,500)
Less: nonrecourse deductions in year 5	(81,000)	(9,000)
Less: distribution of loan proceeds	(162,000)	(18,000)
Less: cash flow distribution in year 5	(2,500)	(2,500)
Capital account at end of year 5	($403,000)	($47,000)

At the end of the partnership's fifth taxable year, LP's share of partnership minimum gain is $405,000 ($225,000 share of minimum gain at the end of the fourth year plus $81,000 of nonrecourse deductions for the fifth year and a $99,000 distribution of nonrecourse liability proceeds that are allocable to an increase in minimum gain) and GP's share of partnership minimum gain is $45,000 ($25,000 share of minimum gain at the end of the fourth year plus $9,000 of nonrecourse deductions for the fifth year and an $11,000 distribution of nonrecourse liability proceeds that are allocable to an increase in minimum gain).

(vii) *Partner guarantee of nonrecourse debt.* LP and GP personally guarantee the "first" $100,000 of the $800,000 nonrecourse loan (i.e., only if the building is worth less than $100,000 will they be called upon to make up any deficiency). Under paragraph (d)(2) of this section, only $630,000 of the adjusted tax basis of the building is allocated to the $700,000 nonrecourse portion of the loan because the collateral will be applied first to satisfy the $100,000 guaranteed portion, making it superior in priority to the remainder of the loan. On the other hand, if LP and GP were to guarantee the "last" $100,000 (*i.e.,* if the building is worth less than $800,000, they will be called upon to make up the deficiency up to $100,000), $700,000 of the adjusted tax basis of the building would be allocated to the $700,000 nonrecourse portion of the loan because the guaranteed portion would be inferior in priority to it.

(viii) *Partner nonrecourse debt.* Assume instead that the $800,000 loan is made by LP, the limited partner. Under paragraph (b)(4) of this section, the $800,000 obligation does not constitute a nonrecourse liability of the partnership for purposes of this section because LP, a partner, bears the economic risk of loss for that loan within the meaning of § 1.752-2. Instead, the $800,000 loan constitutes a partner nonrecourse debt under paragraph (b)(4) of this section. In the partnership's third taxable year, partnership minimum gain would have increased by $70,000 if the debt were a nonrecourse liability of the partnership. Thus, under paragraph (i)(3) of this section, there is a net increase of $70,000 in the minimum gain attributable to the $800,000 partner nonrecourse debt for the partnership's third taxable year, and $70,000 of the $90,000 depreciation deduction from the building for the partnership's third taxable year constitutes a partner nonrecourse deduction with respect to the debt. See paragraph (i)(4) of this section. Under paragraph (i)(2) of this section, this partner nonrecourse deduction must be allocated to LP, the partner that bears the economic risk of loss for that liability.

(ix) *Nonrecourse debt and partner nonrecourse debt of differing priorities.* As in Example 1 (viii) of this paragraph (m), the $800,000 loan is made to the partnership by LP, the limited partner, but the loan is a purchase money loan that "wraps around" a $700,000 underlying nonrecourse note (also secured by the building) issued by LP to an unrelated person in connection with LP's acquisition of the building. Under these circumstances, LP bears the economic risk of loss with respect to only $100,000 of the liability within the meaning of § 1.752-2. See § 1.752-2(f) (*Example* 6). Therefore, for purposes of paragraph (d) of this section, the $800,000 liability is treated as a $700,000 nonrecourse liability of the partnership and a $100,000 partner nonrecourse debt (inferior in priority to the $700,000 liability) of the partnership for which LP bears the economic risk of loss. Under paragraph (i)(2) of this section, $70,000 of the $90,000 depreciation deduction realized in the partnership's third taxable year constitutes a partner nonrecourse deduction that must be allocated to LP.

Example 2. Netting of increases and decreases in partnership minimum gain. For *Example 2* unless otherwise provided, the following facts are assumed. X and Y form a general partnership to acquire and operate residential real properties. Each partner contributes $150,000 to the partnership. The partnership obtains a $1,500,000 nonrecourse loan and purchases 3 apartment buildings (on leased land) for $720,000 ("Property A"), $540,000 ("Property B"), and $540,000 ("Property C"). The nonrecourse loan is secured only by the 3 buildings, and no principal payments are due for 5 years. In each of the partnership's first 3 taxable years, it generates rental income of $225,000, operating expenses (including land lease payments) of $50,000, interest expense of $175,000, and depreciation deductions on the 3 properties of $150,000 ($60,000 on Property A and $45,000 on each of Property B and Property C), resulting in a net taxable loss of $150,000 in each of those years. The partnership makes no distributions to X or Y.

(i) *Calculation of net increases and decreases in partnership minimum gain.* If the partnership were to dispose of the 3 apartment buildings in full satisfaction of its nonrecourse liability at the end of its third taxable year, it would realize $150,000 of gain ($1,500,000 amount realized less $1,350,000 adjusted tax basis). Because the amount of partnership minimum gain at the end of that year (and the net increase in partnership minimum gain during that year) is $150,000, the amount of partnership nonrecourse deductions for that year is $150,000, consisting of depreciation deductions allowable with respect to the 3 apartment buildings of $150,000. The result would be the same if the partnership obtained 3 separate nonrecourse loans that were "cross-collateralized" (*i.e.*, if each separate loan were secured by all 3 of the apartment buildings).

(ii) *Netting of increases and decreases in partnership minimum gain when there is a disposition.* At the beginning of the partnership's fourth taxable year, the partnership (with the permission of the nonrecourse lender) disposes of Property A for $835,000 and uses a portion of the proceeds to repay $600,000 of the nonrecourse liability (the principal amount attributable to Property A), reducing the balance to $900,000. As a result of the disposition, the partnership realizes gain of $295,000 ($835,000 amount realized less $540,000 adjusted tax basis). If the disposition is viewed in isolation, the partnership has generated minimum gain of $60,000 on the sale of Property A ($600,000 of debt reduction less $540,000 adjusted tax basis). However, during the partnership's fourth taxable year it also generates rental income of $135,000, operating expenses of $30,000, interest expense of $105,000, and depreciation deductions of $90,000 ($45,000 on each remaining building). If the partnership were to dispose of the remaining two buildings in full satisfaction of its nonrecourse liability at the end of the partnership's fourth taxable year, it would realize gain of $180,000 ($900,000 amount realized less $720,000 aggregate adjusted tax basis), which is the amount of partnership minimum gain

at the end of the year. Because the partnership minimum gain increased from $150,000 to $180,000 during the partnership's fourth taxable year, the amount of partnership nonrecourse deductions for that year is $30,000, consisting of a ratable portion of depreciation deductions allowable with respect to the two remaining apartment buildings. No minimum gain chargeback is required for the taxable year, even though the partnership disposed of one of the properties subject to the nonrecourse liability during the year, because there is no net decrease in partnership minimum gain for the year. See paragraph (f)(1) of this section.

Example 3. Nonrecourse deductions and partnership minimum gain before third partner is admitted. For purposes of *Example 3*, unless otherwise provided, the following facts are assumed. Additional facts are given in each of *Examples 3* (ii), (iii), and (iv). A and B form a limited partnership to acquire and lease machinery that is 5-year recovery property. A, the limited partner, and B, the general partner, contribute $100,000 each to the partnership, which obtains an $800,000 nonrecourse loan and purchases the machinery for $1,000,000. The nonrecourse loan is secured only by the machinery. The principal amount of the loan is to be repaid $50,000 per year during each of the partnership's first 5 taxable years, with the remaining $550,000 of unpaid principal due on the first day of the partnership's sixth taxable year. The partnership agreement contains all of the provisions required by paragraph (e) of this section, and, as of the end of each partnership taxable year discussed herein, the items described in § 1.704-1(b)(2)(ii)(*d*)(*4*), (*5*), and (*6*) are not reasonably expected to cause or increase a deficit balance in A's or B's capital account. The partnership agreement provides that, except as otherwise required by its qualified income offset and minimum gain chargeback provisions, all partnership items will be allocated equally between A and B. Finally, the partnership agreement provides that all distributions, other than distributions in liquidation of the partnership or of a partner's interest in the partnership, will be made equally between A and B. In the partnership's first taxable year it generates rental income of $130,000, interest expense of $80,000, and a depreciation deduction of $150,000, resulting in a net taxable loss of $100,000. In addition, the partnership repays $50,000 of the nonrecourse liability, reducing that liability to $750,000. Allocations of these losses equally between A and B have substantial economic effect.

	A	B
Capital account on formation	$100,000	$100,000
Less: net loss in year 1	(50,000)	(50,000)
Capital account at end of year 1	$50,000	$ 50,000

In the partnership's second taxable year, it generates rental income of $130,000, interest expense of $75,000, and a depreciation deduction of $220,000, resulting in a net taxable loss of $165,000. In addition, the partnership repays $50,000 of the nonrecourse liability, reducing that liability to $700,000, and distributes $2,500 of cash to each partner. If the partnership were to dispose of the machinery in full satisfaction of the nonrecourse liability at the end of that year, it would realize $70,000 of gain ($700,000 amount realized less $630,000 adjusted tax basis). Therefore, the amount of partnership minimum gain at the end of that year (and the net increase in partnership minimum gain during the year) is $70,000, and the amount of partnership nonrecourse deductions for the year is $70,000. The partnership nonrecourse deductions for its second taxable year consist of $70,000 of the depreciation deductions allowable with respect to the machinery. Pursuant to the partnership agreement, all partnership items comprising the net taxable loss of $165,000, including the $70,000 nonrecourse deduction, are allocated equally between A and B. The allocation of these items, other than the nonrecourse deductions, has substantial economic effect.

	A	B
Capital account at end of year 1	$ 50,000	$ 50,000
Less: net loss in year 2 (without nonrecourse deductions)	(47,500)	(47,500)
Less: nonrecourse deductions in year 2	(35,000)	(35,000)
Less: distribution	(2,500)	(2,500)
Capital account at end of year 2	($35,000)	($35,000)

(i) *Calculation of nonrecourse deductions and partnership minimum gain.* Because all of the requirements of paragraph (e) of this section are satisfied, the allocation of nonrecourse deductions is deemed to be made in accordance with the partners' interests in the partnership. At the end of the partnership's second taxable year, A's and B's shares of partnership minimum gain are $35,000 each. Therefore, pursuant to paragraph (g)(1) of this section, A and B are treated as obligated to restore deficit balances in their capital accounts of $35,000 each. If the partnership were to dispose of the machinery in full satisfaction of the nonrecourse liability at the beginning of the partnership's third taxable year (and had no other economic activity in that year), the partnership minimum gain would be decreased from $70,000 to zero. A's and B's shares of that net decrease would be $35,000 each. Upon that disposition, the minimum gain chargeback would require that A and B each be allocated $35,000 of that gain before any other allocation is made under section 704(b) with respect to partnership items for the partnership's third taxable year.

(ii) *Nonrecourse deductions and restatement of capital accounts.* (a) *Additional facts.* C is admitted to the partnership at the beginning of the partnership's third taxable year. At the time of C's admission, the fair market value of the machinery is $900,000. C contributes $100,000 to the partnership (the partnership invests $95,000 of this in undeveloped land and holds the other $5,000 in cash) in exchange for an interest in the partnership. In connection with C's admission to the partnership, the partnership's machinery is revalued on the partnership's books to reflect its fair market value of $900,000. Pursuant to § 1.704-1(b)(2)(iv)(*f*), the capital accounts of A and B are adjusted upwards to $100,000 each to reflect the revaluation of the partnership's machinery. This adjustment reflects the manner in which the partnership gain of $270,000 ($900,000 fair market value minus $630,000 adjusted tax basis) would be shared if the machinery were sold for its fair market value immediately prior to C's admission to the partnership.

	A	B
Capital account before C's admission	($ 35,000)	($ 35,000)
Deemed sale adjustment	135,000	135,000
Capital account adjusted for C's admission	$100,000	$100,000

The partnership agreement is modified to provide that, except as otherwise required by its qualified income offset and minimum gain chargeback provisions, partnership income, gain, loss, and deduction, as computed for book purposes, are allocated equally among the partners, and those allocations are reflected in the partners' capital accounts. The partnership agreement also is modified to

Reg. § 1.704-2(m)

provide that depreciation and gain or loss, as computed for tax purposes, with respect to the machinery will be shared among the partners in a manner that takes account of the variation between the property's $630,000 adjusted tax basis and its $900,000 book value, in accordance with § 1.704-1(b)(2)(iv)(f) and the special rule contained in § 1.704-1(b)(4)(i).

(b) *Effect of revaluation.* Because the requirements of § 1.704-1(b)(2)(iv)(g) are satisfied, the capital accounts of the partners (as adjusted) continue to be maintained in accordance with § 1.704-1(b)(2)(iv). If the partnership were to dispose of the machinery in full satisfaction of the nonrecourse liability immediately following the revaluation of the machinery, it would realize no book gain ($700,000 amount realized less $900,000 book value). As a result of the revaluation of the machinery upward by $270,000, under part (i) of paragraph (d)(4) of this section, the partnership minimum gain is reduced from $70,000 immediately prior to the revaluation to zero; but under part (ii) of paragraph (d)(4) of this section, the partnership minimum gain is increased by the $70,000 decrease arising solely from the revaluation. Accordingly, there is no net increase or decrease solely on account of the revaluation, and so no minimum gain chargeback is triggered. All future nonrecourse deductions that occur will be the nonrecourse deductions as calculated for book purposes, and will be charged to all 3 partners in accordance with the partnership agreement. For purposes of determining the partners' shares of minimum gain under paragraph (g) of this section, A's and B's shares of the decrease resulting from the revaluation are $35,000 each. However, as illustrated below, under section 704(c) principles, the tax capital accounts of A and B will eventually be charged $35,000 each, reflecting their 50 percent shares of the decrease in partnership minimum gain that resulted from the revaluation.

(iii) *Allocation of nonrecourse deductions following restatement of capital accounts.* (a) *Additional facts.* During the partnership's third taxable year, the partnership generates rental income of $130,000, interest expense of $70,000, a tax depreciation deduction of $210,000, and a book depreciation deduction (attributable to the machinery) of $300,000. As a result, the partnership has a net taxable loss of $150,000 and a net book loss of $240,000. In addition, the partnership repays $50,000 of the nonrecourse liability (after the date of C's admission), reducing the liability to $650,000, and distributes $5,000 of cash to each partner.

(b) *Allocations.* If the partnership were to dispose of the machinery in full satisfaction of the nonrecourse liability at the end of the year, $50,000 of book gain would result ($650,000 amount realized less $600,000 book basis). Therefore, the amount of partnership minimum gain at the end of the year is $50,000, which represents a net decrease in partnership minimum gain of $20,000 during the year. (This is so even though there would be an increase in partnership minimum gain in the partnership's third taxable year if minimum gain were computed with reference to the adjusted tax basis of the machinery.) Nevertheless, pursuant to paragraph (d)(4) of this section, the amount of nonrecourse deductions of the partnership for its third taxable year is $50,000 (the net increase in partnership minimum gain during the year determined by adding back the $70,000 decrease in partnership minimum gain attributable to the revaluation of the machinery to the $20,000 net decrease in partnership minimum gain during the year). The $50,000 of partnership nonrecourse deductions for the year consist of book depreciation deductions allowable with respect to the machinery of $50,000. Pursuant to the partnership agreement, all partnership items comprising the net book loss of $240,000, including the $50,000 nonrecourse deduction, are allocated equally among the partners. The allocation of these items, other than the nonrecourse deductions, has substantial economic effect. Consistent with the special partners' interests in the partnership rule contained in § 1.704-1(b)(4)(i), the partnership agreement provides that the depreciation deduction for tax purposes of $210,000 for the partnership's third taxable year is, in accordance with section 704(c) principles, shared $55,000 to A, $55,000 to B, and $100,000 to C.

	A		B		C	
	Tax	Book	Tax	Book	Tax	Book
Capital account at beginning of year 3	($35,000)	$100,000	($35,000)	$100,000	$100,000	$100,000
Less: nonrecourse deductions	(9,166)	(16,666)	(9,166)	(16,666)	(16,666)	(16,666)
Less: items other than nonrecourse deductions in year 3	(25,834)	(63,334)	(25,834)	(63,334)	(63,334)	(63,334)
Less: distribution	(5,000)	(5,000)	(5,000)	(5,000)	(5,000)	(5,000)
Capital account at end of year 3	($75,000)	$15,000	($75,000)	$15,000	$15,000	$15,000

Reg. § 1.704-2(m)

Because the requirements of paragraph (e) of this section are satisfied, the allocation of the nonrecourse deduction is deemed to be made in accordance with the partners' interests in the partnership. At the end of the partnership's third taxable year, A's, B's, and C's shares of partnership minimum gain are $16,666 each.

(iv) *Subsequent allocation of nonrecourse deductions following restatement of capital accounts.* (a) *Additional facts.* The partners' capital accounts at the end of the second and third taxable years of the partnership are as stated in *Example 3* (iii) of this paragraph (m). In addition, during the partnership's fourth taxable year the partnership generates rental income of $130,000, interest expense of $65,000, a tax depreciation deduction of $210,000, and a book depreciation deduction (attributable to the machinery) of $300,000. As a result, the partnership has a net taxable loss of $145,000 and a net book loss of $235,000. In addition, the partnership repays $50,000 of the nonrecourse liability, reducing that liability to $600,000, and distributes $5,000 of cash to each partner.

(b) *Allocations.* If the partnership were to dispose of the machinery in full satisfaction of the nonrecourse liability at the end of the fourth year, $300,000 of book gain would result ($600,000 amount realized less $300,000 book value). Therefore, the amount of partnership minimum gain as of the end of the year is $300,000, which represents a net increase in partnership minimum gain during the year of $250,000. Thus, the amount of partnership nonrecourse deductions for that year equals $250,000, consisting of book depreciation deductions of $250,000. Pursuant to the partnership agreement, all partnership items comprising the net book loss of $235,000, including the $250,000 nonrecourse deduction, are allocated equally among the partners. That allocation of all items, other than the nonrecourse deductions, has substantial economic effect. Consistent with the special partners' interests in the partnership rule contained in § 1.704-1(b)(4)(i), the partnership agreement provides that the depreciation deduction for tax purposes of $210,000 in the partnership's fourth taxable year is, in accordance with section 704(c) principles, allocated $55,000 to A, $55,000 to B, and $100,000 to C.

	A Tax	A Book	B Tax	B Book	C Tax	C Book
Capital account at end of year 3 ..	($ 75,000)	$15,000	($ 75,000)	$15,000	$15,000	$15,000
Less: nonrecourse deduction......	(45,833)	(83,333)	(45,833)	(83,333)	(83,333)	(83,333)
Plus: items other than nonrecourse deduction in year 4	12,499	5,000	12,499	5,000	5,000	5,000
Less: distribution	(5,000)	(5,000)	(5,000)	(5,000)	(5,000)	(5,000)
Capital account at end of year 4 ..	($113,334)	($68,333)	($113,333)	($68,333)	($68,333)	($68,333)

The allocation of the $250,000 nonrecourse deduction equally among A, B, and C satisfies requirement (2) of paragraph (e) of this section. Because all of the requirements of paragraph (e) of this section are satisfied, the allocation is deemed to be in accordance with the partners' interests in the partnership. At the end of the partnership's fourth taxable year, A's, B's, and C's shares of partnership minimum gain are $100,000 each.

(v) *Disposition of partnership property following restatement of capital accounts.* (a) *Additional facts.* The partners' capital accounts at the end of the fourth taxable year of the partnership are as stated above in (iv). In addition, at the beginning of the partnership's fifth taxable year it sells the machinery for $650,000 (using $600,000 of the proceeds to repay the nonrecourse liability), resulting in a taxable gain of $440,000 ($650,000 amount realized less $210,000 adjusted tax basis) and a book gain of $350,000 ($650,000 amount realized less $300,000 book basis). The partnership has no other items of income, gain, loss, or deduction for the year.

(b) *Effect of disposition.* As a result of the sale, partnership minimum gain is reduced from $300,000 to zero, reducing A's, B's, and C's shares of partnership minimum gain to zero from $100,000 each. The minimum gain chargeback requires that A, B, and C each be allocated $100,000 of that gain (an amount equal to each partner's share of the net decrease in partnership minimum gain resulting from the sale) before any allocation is made to them under section 704(b) with respect to partnership items for the partnership's fifth taxable year. Thus, the allocation of the first $300,000 of book gain $100,000 to each of the partners is deemed to be in accordance with the partners' interests in the partnership under paragraph (e) of this section. The allocation of the remaining $50,000 of book gain equally among the partners has substantial economic effect. Consistent with the special partners' interests in the partnership rule contained in § 1.704-1(b)(4)(i), the partnership agreement provides that the $440,000 taxable gain is, in accordance with section 704(c) principles, allocated $161,667 to A, $161,667 to B, and $116,666 to C.

Reg. § 1.704-2(m)

	A Tax	A Book	B Tax	B Book	C Tax	C Book
Capital account at end of year 4	($113,334)	($ 68,333)	($113,334)	($ 68,333)	($ 68,333)	($ 68,333)
Plus: minimum gain chargeback	138,573	100,000	138,573	100,000	100,000	100,000
Plus: additional gain	23,094	16,666	23,094	16,666	16,666	16,666
Capital account before liquidation	$ 48,333	$ 48,333	$ 48,333	$ 48,333	$ 48,333	$ 48,333

Example 4. Allocations of increase in partnership minimum gain among partnership properties. For *Example* 4, unless otherwise provided, the following facts are assumed. A partnership owns 4 properties, each of which is subject to a nonrecourse liability of the partnership. During a taxable year of the partnership, the following events take place. First, the partnership generates a depreciation deduction (for both book and tax purposes) with respect to Property W of $10,000 and repays $5,000 of the nonrecourse liability secured only by that property, resulting in an increase in minimum gain with respect to that liability of $5,000. Second, the partnership generates a depreciation deduction (for both book and tax purposes) with respect to Property X of $10,000 and repays none of the nonrecourse liability secured by that property, resulting in an increase in minimum gain with respect to that liability of $10,000. Third, the partnership generates a depreciation deduction (for both book and tax purposes) of $2,000 with respect to Property Y and repays $11,000 of the nonrecourse liability secured only by that property, resulting in a decrease in minimum gain with respect to that liability of $9,000 (although at the end of that year, there remains minimum gain with respect to that liability). Finally, the partnership borrows $5,000 on a nonrecourse basis, giving as the only security for that liability Property Z, a parcel of undeveloped land with an adjusted tax basis (and book value) of $2,000, resulting in a net increase in minimum gain with respect to that liability of $3,000.

(i) *Allocation of increase in partnership minimum gain.* The net increase in partnership minimum gain during that partnership taxable year is $9,000, so that the amount of nonrecourse deductions of the partnership for that taxable year is $9,000. Those nonrecourse deductions consist of $3,000 of depreciation deductions with respect to Property W and $6,000 of depreciation deductions with respect to Property X. See paragraph (c) of this section. The amount of nonrecourse deductions consisting of depreciation deductions is determined as follows. With respect to the nonrecourse liability secured by Property Z, for which there is no depreciation deduction, the amount of depreciation deductions that constitutes nonrecourse deductions is zero. Similarly, with respect to the nonrecourse liability secured by Property Y, for which there is no increase in minimum gain, the amount of depreciation deductions that constitutes nonrecourse deductions is zero. With respect to each of the nonrecourse liabilities secured by Properties W and X, which are secured by property for which there are depreciation deductions and for which there is an increase in minimum gain, the amount of depreciation deductions that constitutes nonrecourse deductions is determined by the following formula:

$$\text{net increase in partnership minimum gain} \times \frac{\text{total depreciation deductions for that taxable year on the specific property securing the nonrecourse liability to the extent gain increased on that liability}}{\text{total depreciation deductions for that taxable year on all properties securing nonrecourse liabilities to the extent of the aggregate increase in minimum gain on all those liabilities}}$$

Thus, for the liability secured by Property W, the amount is $9,000 times $5,000/$15,000, or $3,000. For the liability secured by Property X, the amount is $9,000 times $10,000/$15,000, or $6,000. (If one depreciable property secured two partnership nonrecourse liabilities, the amount of depreciation or book depreciation with respect to that property would be allocated among those liabilities in accordance with the method by which adjusted basis is allocated under paragraph (d)(2) of this section).

(ii) *Alternative allocation of increase in partnership minimum gain among partnership properties.* Assume instead that the loan secured by Property Z is $15,000 (rather than $5,000), resulting in a net increase in minimum gain with respect to that liability of $13,000. Thus, the net increase in partnership minimum gain is $19,000, and the amount of nonrecourse deductions of the partnership for that taxable year is $19,000. Those nonrecourse deductions consist of $5,000 of depreciation deductions with respect to Property

Reg. § 1.704-2(m)

W, $10,000 of depreciation deductions with respect to Property X, and a pro rata portion of the partnership's other items of deduction, loss, and section 705(a)(2)(B) expenditure for that year. The method for computing the amounts of depreciation deductions that constitute nonrecourse deductions is the same as in (i) of this *Example* 4 for the liabilities secured by Properties Y and Z. With respect to each of the nonrecourse liabilities secured by Properties W and X, the amount of depreciation deductions that constitutes nonrecourse deductions equals the total depreciation deductions with respect to the partnership property securing that particular liability to the extent of the increase in minimum gain with respect to that liability. [Reg. § 1.704-2.]

☐ [*T.D.* 8385, 12-26-91.]

§ 1.704-3. Contributed property.—(a) *In general*—(1) *General principles.* The purpose of section 704(c) is to prevent the shifting of tax consequences among partners with respect to precontribution gain or loss. Under section 704(c), a partnership must allocate income, gain, loss, and deduction with respect to property contributed by a partner to the partnership so as to take into account any variation between the adjusted tax basis of the property and its fair market value at the time of contribution. Notwithstanding any other provision of this section, the allocations must be made using a reasonable method that is consistent with the purpose of section 704(c). For this purpose, an allocation method includes the application of all of the rules of this section (e.g., aggregation rules). An allocation method is not necessarily unreasonable merely because another allocation method would result in a higher aggregate tax liability. Paragraphs (b), (c), and (d) of this section describe allocation methods that are generally reasonable. Other methods may be reasonable in appropriate circumstances. Nevertheless, in the absence of specific published guidance, it is not reasonable to use an allocation method in which the basis of property contributed to the partnership is increased (or decreased) to reflect built-in gain (or loss), or a method under which the partnership creates tax allocations of income, gain, loss, or deduction independent of allocations affecting book capital accounts. See § 1.704-3(d). Paragraph (e) of this section contains special rules and exceptions.

(2) *Operating rules.* Except as provided in paragraphs (e)(2) and (e)(3) of this section, section 704(c) and this section apply on a property-by-property basis. Therefore, in determining whether there is a disparity between adjusted tax basis and fair market value, the built-in gains and built-in losses on items of contributed property cannot be aggregated. A partnership may use different methods with respect to different items of contributed property, provided that the partnership and the partners consistently apply a single reasonable method for each item of contributed property and that the overall method or combination of methods are reasonable based on the facts and circumstances and consistent with the purpose of section 704(c). It may be unreasonable to use one method for appreciated property and another method for depreciated property. Similarly, it may be unreasonable to use the traditional method for built-in gain property contributed by a partner with a high marginal tax rate while using curative allocations for built-in gain property contributed by a partner with a low marginal tax rate. A new partnership formed as the result of the termination of a partnership under section 708(b)(1)(B) is not required to use the same method as the terminated partnership with respect to section 704(c) property deemed contributed to the new partnership by the terminated partnership under § 1.7081(b)(1)(iv). The previous sentence applies to terminations of partnerships under section 708(b)(1)(B) occurring on or after May 9, 1997; however, the sentence may be applied to terminations occurring on or after May 9, 1996, provided that the partnership and its partners apply the sentence to the termination in a consistent manner.

(3) *Definitions*—(i) *Section 704(c) property.* Property contributed to a partnership is section 704(c) property if at the time of contribution its book value differs from the contributing partner's adjusted tax basis. For purposes of this section, book value is determined as contemplated by § 1.704-1(b). Therefore, book value is equal to fair market value at the time of contribution and is subsequently adjusted for cost recovery and other events that affect the basis of the property. For a partnership that maintains capital accounts in accordance with § 1.704-1(b)(2)(iv), the book value of property is initially the value used in determining the contributing partner's capital account under § 1.704-1(b)(2)(iv)(*d*), and is appropriately adjusted thereafter (e.g., for book cost recovery under § § 1.704-1(b)(2)(iv)(*g*)(*3*) and 1.704-3(d)(2) and other events that affect the basis of the property). A partnership that does not maintain capital accounts under § 1.704-1(b)(2)(iv) must comply with this section using a book capital account based on the same principles (i.e., a book capital account that reflects the fair market value of property at the time of contribution and that is subsequently adjusted for cost recovery and other events that affect the basis of the property). Property deemed contributed to a new partnership as the result of the termination of a partnership under section 708(b)(1)(B) is treated as section 704(c) property in the hands of the new partnership only to the

Reg. § 1.704-3(a)(1)

extent that the property was section 704(c) property in the hands of the terminated partnership immediately prior to the termination. See § 1.708-1(b)(1)(iv) for an example of the application of this rule. The previous two sentences apply to terminations of partnerships under section 708(b)(1)(B) occurring on or after May 9, 1997; however, the sentences may be applied to terminations occurring on or after May 9, 1996, provided that the partnership and its partners apply the sentences to the termination in a consistent manner.

(ii) *Built-in gain and built-in loss.* The built-in gain on section 704(c) property is the excess of the property's book value over the contributing partner's adjusted tax basis upon contribution. The built-in gain is thereafter reduced by decreases in the difference between the property's book value and adjusted tax basis. The built-in loss on section 704(c) property is the excess of the contributing partner's adjusted tax basis over the property's book value upon contribution. The built-in loss is thereafter reduced by decreases in the difference between the property's adjusted tax basis and book value.

(4) *Accounts payable and other accrued but unpaid items.* Accounts payable and other accrued but unpaid items contributed by a partner using the cash receipts and disbursements method of accounting are treated as section 704(c) property for purposes of applying the rules of this section.

(5) *Other provisions of the Internal Revenue Code.* Section 704(c) and this section apply to a contribution of property to the partnership only if the contribution is governed by section 721, taking into account other provisions of the Internal Revenue Code. For example, to the extent that a transfer of property to a partnership is a sale under section 707, the transfer is not a contribution of property to which section 704(c) applies.

(6) *Other applications of section 704(c) principles*—(i) *Revaluations under section 704(b).* The principles of this section apply to allocations with respect to property for which differences between book value and adjusted tax basis are created when a partnership revalues partnership property pursuant to § 1.704-1(b)(2)(iv)(*f*) (reverse section 704(c) allocations). Partnerships are not required to use the same allocation method for reverse section 704(c) allocations as for contributed property, even if at the time of revaluation the property is already subject to section 704(c) and paragraph (a) of this section. In addition, partnerships are not required to use the same allocation method for reverse section 704(c) allocations each time the partnership revalues its property. A partnership that makes allocations with respect to revalued property must use a reasonable method that is consistent with the purposes of section 704(b) and (c).

(ii) *Basis adjustments.* A partnership making adjustments under § 1.743-1(b) or 1.751-1(a)(2) must account for built-in gain or loss under section 704(c) in accordance with the principles of this section.

(7) *Transfers of a partnership interest.* If a contributing partner transfers a partnership interest, built-in gain or loss must be allocated to the transferee partner as it would have been allocated to the transferor partner. If the contributing partner transfers a portion of the partnership interest, the share of built-in gain or loss proportionate to the interest transferred must be allocated to the transferee partner.

(8) *Disposition of property in nonrecognition transaction.* If a partnership disposes of section 704(c) property in a nonrecognition transaction in which no gain or loss is recognized, the substituted basis property (within the meaning of section 7701(a)(42)) is treated as section 704(c) property with the same amount of built-in gain or loss as the section 704(c) property disposed of by the partnership. If gain or loss is recognized in such a transaction, appropriate adjustments must be made. The allocation method for the substituted basis property must be consistent with the allocation method chosen for the original property. If a partnership transfers an item of section 704(c) property together with other property to a corporation under section 351, in order to preserve that item's built-in gain or loss, the basis in the stock received in exchange for the section 704(c) property is determined as if each item of section 704(c) property had been the only property transferred to the corporation by the partnership.

(9) *Tiered partnerships.* If a partnership contributes section 704(c) property to a second partnership (the lower-tier partnership), or if a partner that has contributed section 704(c) property to a partnership contributes that partnership interest to a second partnership (the upper-tier partnership), the upper-tier partnership must allocate its distributive share of lower-tier partnership items with respect to that section 704(c) property in a manner that takes into account the contributing partner's remaining built-in gain or loss. Allocations made under this paragraph will be considered to be made in a manner that meets the requirements of § 1.704-1(b)(2)(iv)(*q*) (relating to capital account adjustments where guidance is lacking).

(10) *Anti-abuse rule.* An allocation method (or combination of methods) is not reasonable if the contribution of property (or event that results in reverse section 704(c) allocations) and the cor-

responding allocation of tax items with respect to the property are made with a view to shifting the tax consequences of built-in gain or loss among the partners in a manner that substantially reduces the present value of the partners' aggregate tax liability.

(11) *Contributing and noncontributing partners' recapture shares.* For special rules applicable to the allocation of depreciation recapture with respect to property contributed by a partner to a partnership, see §§ 1.1245-1(e)(2) and 1.1250-1(f).

(b) *Traditional method*—(1) *In general.* This paragraph (b) describes the traditional method of making section 704(c) allocations. In general, the traditional method requires that when the partnership has income, gain, loss, or deduction attributable to section 704(c) property, it must make appropriate allocations to the partners to avoid shifting the tax consequences of the built-in gain or loss. Under this rule, if the partnership sells section 704(c) property and recognizes gain or loss, built-in gain or loss on the property is allocated to the contributing partner. If the partnership sells a portion of, or an interest in, section 704(c) property, a proportionate part of the built-in gain or loss is allocated to the contributing partner. For section 704(c) property subject to amortization, depletion, depreciation, or other cost recovery, the allocation of deductions attributable to these items takes into account built-in gain or loss on the property. For example, tax allocations to the noncontributing partners of cost recovery deductions with respect to section 704(c) property generally must, to the extent possible, equal book allocations to those partners. However, the total income, gain, loss, or deduction allocated to the partners for a taxable year with respect to a property cannot exceed the total partnership income, gain, loss, or deduction with respect to that property for the taxable year (the ceiling rule). If a partnership has no property the allocations from which are limited by the ceiling rule, the traditional method is reasonable when used for all contributed property.

(2) *Examples.* The following examples illustrate the principles of the traditional method.

Example 1. Operation of the traditional method—(i) *Calculation of built-in gain on contribution.* A and B form partnership AB and agree that each will be allocated a 50 percent share of all partnership items and that AB will make allocations under section 704(c) using the traditional method under paragraph (b) of this section. A contributes depreciable property with an adjusted tax basis of $4,000 and a book value of $10,000, and B contributes $10,000 cash. Under paragraph (a)(3) of this section, A has built-in gain of $6,000,

the excess of the partnership's book value for the property ($10,000) over A's adjusted tax basis in the property at the time of contribution ($4,000).

(ii) *Allocation of tax depreciation.* The property is depreciated using the straight-line method over a 10-year recovery period. Because the property depreciates at an annual rate of 10 percent, B would have been entitled to a depreciation deduction of $500 per year for both book and tax purposes if the adjusted tax basis of the property equalled its fair market value at the time of contribution. Although each partner is allocated $500 of book depreciation per year, the partnership is allowed a tax depreciation deduction of only $400 per year (10 percent of $4,000). The partnership can allocate only $400 of tax depreciation under the ceiling rule of paragraph (b)(1) of this section, and it must be allocated entirely to B. In AB's first year, the proceeds generated by the equipment exactly equal AB's operating expense. At the end of that year, the book value of the property is $9,000 ($10,000 less the $1,000 book depreciation deduction), and the adjusted tax basis is $3,600 ($4,000 less the $400 tax depreciation deduction). A's built-in gain with respect to the property decreases to $5,400 ($9,000 book value less $3,600 adjusted tax basis). Also, at the end of AB's first year, A has a $9,500 book capital account and a $4,000 tax basis in A's partnership interest. B has a $9,500 book capital account and a $9600 adjusted tax basis in B's partnership interest.

(iii) *Sale of the property.* If AB sells the property at the beginning of AB's second year for $9,000, AB realizes tax gain of $5,400 ($9,000, the amount realized, less the adjusted tax basis of $3,600). Under paragraph (b)(1) of this section, the entire $5,400 gain must be allocated to A because the property A contributed has that much built-in gain remaining. If AB sells the property at the beginning of AB's second year for $10,000, AB realizes tax gain of $6,400 ($10,000, the amount realized, less the adjusted tax basis of $3,600). Under paragraph (b)(1) of this section, only $5,400 of gain must be allocated to A to account for A's built-in gain. The remaining $1,000 of gain is allocated equally between A and B in accordance with the partnership agreement. If AB sells the property for less than the $9,000 book value, AB realizes tax gain of less than $5,400, and the entire gain must be allocated to A.

(iv) *Termination and liquidation of partnership.* If AB sells the property at the beginning of AB's second year for $9,000, and AB engages in no other transactions that year, A will recognize a gain of $5,400, and B will recognize no income or loss. A's adjusted tax basis for A's interest in AB will then be $9,400 ($4,000, A's original tax basis, increased by the gain of $5,400). B's adjusted tax basis for B's interest in AB will be $9,600 ($10,000, B's original tax basis, less the $400 depreciation deduction in he first partnership year). If the partnership then terminates and distributes its assets ($19,000 in cash) to A and B in proportion to their capital account balances, A will recognize a capital gain of $100 ($9,500, the amount distributed to A, less $9,400, the adjusted tax basis of A's interest). B will recognize a capital loss of $100 (the excess of B's adjusted tax basis, $9,600, over the amount received, $9,500).

Example 2. Unreasonable use of the traditional method—(i) *Facts.* C and D form partnership CD and agree that each will be allocated a 50 percent share of all partnership items and that CD will make allocations under section 704(c) using the traditional method under paragraph (b) of this section. C contributes equipment with an adjusted tax basis of $1,000 and a book value of $10,000, with a view to taking advantage of the fact that the equipment has only one year remaining on its cost recovery schedule although its remaining economic life is significantly longer. At the time of contribution, C has a built-in gain of $9,000 and the equipment is section 704(c) property. D contributes $10,000 of cash, which CD uses to buy securities. D has substantial net operating loss carryforwards that D anticipates will otherwise expire unused. Under § 1.704-1(b)(2)(iv)(*g*)(*3*), the partnership must allocate the $10,000 of book depreciation to the partners in the first year of the partnership. Thus, there is $10,000 of book depreciation and $1,000 of tax depreciation in the partnership's first year. CD sells the equipment during the second year for $10,000 and recognizes a $10,000 gain ($10,000, the amount realized, less the adjusted tax basis of $0).

(ii) *Unreasonable use of method*—(A) At the beginning of the second year, both the book value and adjusted tax basis of the equipment are $0. Therefore, there is no remaining built-in gain. The $10,000 gain on the sale of the equipment in the second year is allocated $5,000 each to C and D. The interaction of the partnership's one-year write-off of the entire book value of the equipment and the use of the traditional method results in a shift of $4,000 of the precontribution gain in the equipment from C to D (D's $5,000 share of CD's $10,000 gain, less the $1,000 tax depreciation deduction previously allocated to D).

(B) The traditional method is not reasonable under paragraph (a)(10) of this section because the contribution of property is made, and the traditional method is used, with a view to shifting a significant amount of taxable income to a partner with a low marginal tax rate and away from a partner with a high marginal tax rate.

(C) Under these facts, if the partnership agreement in effect for the year of contribution had provided that tax gain from the sale of the property (if any) would always be allocated first to C to offset the effect of the ceiling rule limitation, the allocation method would not violate the anti-abuse rule of paragraph (a)(10) of this section. See paragraph (c)(3) of this section. Under other facts, (for example, if the partnership holds multiple section 704(c) properties and either uses multiple allocation methods or uses a single allocation method where one or more of the properties are subject to the ceiling rule) the allocation to C may not be reasonable.

(c) *Traditional method with curative allocations*—(1) *In general.* To correct distortions created by the ceiling rule, a partnership using the traditional method under paragraph (b) of this section may make reasonable curative allocations to reduce or eliminate disparities between book and tax items of noncontributing partners. A curative allocation is an allocation of income, gain, loss, or deduction for tax purposes that differs from the partnership's allocation of the corresponding book item. For example, if a noncontributing partner is allocated less tax depreciation than book depreciation with respect to an item of section 704(c) property, the partnership may make a curative allocation to that partner of tax depreciation from another item of partnership property to make up the difference, notwithstanding that the corresponding book depreciation is allocated to the contributing partner. A partnership may limit its curative allocations to allocations of one or more particular tax items (e.g., only depreciation from a specific property or properties) even if the allocation of those available items does not offset fully the effect of the ceiling rule.

(2) *Consistency.* A partnership must be consistent in its application of curative allocations with respect to each item of section 704(c) property from year to year.

(3) *Reasonable curative allocations*—(i) *Amount.* A curative allocation is not reasonable to the extent it exceeds the amount necessary to offset the effect of the ceiling rule for the current taxable year or, in the case of a curative allocation upon disposition of the property, for prior taxable years.

(ii) *Timing.* The period of time over which the curative allocations are made is a factor in determining whether the allocations are reasonable. Notwithstanding paragraph (c)(3)(i) of this section, a partnership may make curative allocations in a taxable year to offset the effect of the ceiling rule for a prior taxable year if those allocations are made over a reasonable period of time, such as over the property's economic life, and are

Reg. § 1.704-3(c)(3)

provided for under the partnership agreement in effect for the year of contribution. See paragraph (c)(4) *Example 3* (ii)(C) of this section.

(iii) *Type*—(A) *In general.* To be reasonable, a curative allocation of income, gain, loss, or deduction must be expected to have substantially the same effect on each partner's tax liability as the tax item limited by the ceiling rule. The expectation must exist at the time the section 704(c) property is obligated to be (or is) contributed to the partnership and the allocation with respect to that property becomes part of the partnership agreement. However, the expectation is tested at the time the allocation with respect to that property is actually made if the partnership agreement is not sufficiently specific as to the precise manner in which allocations are to be made with respect to that property. Under this paragraph (c), if the item limited by the ceiling rule is loss from the sale of property, a curative allocation of gain must be expected to have substantially the same effect as would an allocation to that partner of gain with respect to the sale of the property. If the item limited by the ceiling rule is depreciation or other cost recovery, a curative allocation of income to the contributing partner must be expected to have substantially the same effect as would an allocation to that partner of partnership income with respect to the contributed property. For example, if depreciation deductions with respect to leased equipment contributed by a tax-exempt partner are limited by the ceiling rule, a curative allocation of dividend or interest income to that partner generally is not reasonable, although a curative allocation of depreciation deductions from other leased equipment to the noncontributing partner is reasonable. Similarly, under this rule, if depreciation deductions apportioned to foreign source income in a particular statutory grouping under section 904(d) are limited by the ceiling rule, a curative allocation of income from another statutory grouping to the contributing partner generally is not reasonable, although a curative allocation of income from the same statutory grouping and of the same character is reasonable.

(B) *Exception for allocation from disposition of contributed property.* If cost recovery has been limited by the ceiling rule, the general limitation on character does not apply to income from the disposition of contributed property subject to the ceiling rule, but only if properly provided for in the partnership agreement in effect for the year of contribution or revaluation. For example, if allocations of depreciation deductions to a noncontributing partner have been limited by the ceiling rule, a curative allocation to the contributing partner of gain from the sale of that property, if properly provided for in the partnership agreement, is reasonable for purposes of paragraph (c)(3)(iii)(A) of this section even if not of the same character.

(4) *Examples.* The following examples illustrate the principles of this paragraph (c).

Example 1. Reasonable and unreasonable curative allocations—(i) *Facts.* E and F form partnership EF and agree that each will be allocated a 50 percent share of all partnership items and that EF will make allocations under section 704(c) using the traditional method with curative allocations under paragraph (c) of this section. E contributes equipment with an adjusted tax basis of $4,000 and a book value of $10,000. The equipment has 10 years remaining on its cost recovery schedule and is depreciable using the straight-line method. At the time of contribution, E has a built-in gain of $6,000, and therefore, the equipment is section 704(c) property. F contributes $10,000 of cash, which EF uses to buy inventory for resale. In EF's first year, the revenue generated by the equipment equals EF's operating expenses. The equipment generates $1,000 of book depreciation and $400 of tax depreciation for each of 10 years. At the end of the first year EF sells all the inventory for $10,700, recognizing $700 of income. The partners anticipate that the inventory income will have substantially the same effect on their tax liabilities as income from E's contributed equipment. Under the traditional method of paragraph (b) of this section, E and F would each be allocated $350 of income from the sale of inventory for book and tax purposes and $500 of depreciation for book purposes. The $400 of tax depreciation would all be allocated to F. Thus, at the end of the first year, E and F's book and tax capital accounts would be as follows:

	E		F		
	Book	*Tax*	*Book*	*Tax*	
	$10,000	$4,000	$10,000	$10,000	Initial contribution
	<500>	<0>	<500>	<400>	Depreciation
	350	350	350	350	Sales income
	$ 9,850	$4,350	$ 9,850	$ 9,950	

(ii) *Reasonable curative allocation.* Because the ceiling rule would cause a disparity of $100 between F's book and tax capital accounts, EF may properly allocate to E under paragraph (c) of this section an additional $100 of income from the sale of inventory for tax purposes. This allocation results in capital accounts at the end of EF's first year as follows:

Reg. § 1.704-3(c)(4)

	E		F	
Book	**Tax**	**Book**	**Tax**	
$10,000	$4,000	$10,000	$10,000	Initial contribution
<500>	<0>	<500>	<400>	Depreciation
350	450	350	250	Sales income
$ 9,850	$4,450	$ 9,850	$ 9,850	

(iii) *Unreasonable curative allocation.* (A) The facts are the same as in paragraphs (i) and (ii) of this *Example 1*, except that E and F choose to allocate all the income from the sale of the inventory to E for tax purposes, although they share it equally for book purposes. This allocation results in capital accounts at the end of EF's first year as follows:

	E		F	
Book	**Tax**	**Book**	**Tax**	
$10,000	$4,000	$10,000	$10,000	Initial contribution
<500>	<0>	<500>	<400>	Depreciation
350	700	350	0	Sales income
$ 9,850	$4,700	$ 9,850	$ 9,600	

(B) This curative allocation is not reasonable under paragraph (c)(3)(i) of this section because the allocation exceeds the amount necessary to offset the disparity caused by the ceiling rule.

Example 2. Curative allocations limited to depreciation—(i) *Facts.* G and H form partnership GH and agree that each will be allocated a 50 percent share of all partnership items and that GH will make allocations under section 704(c) using the traditional method with curative allocations under paragraph (c) of this section, but only to the extent that the partnership has sufficient tax depreciation deductions. G contributes property G1, with an adjusted tax basis of $3,000 and a fair market value of $10,000 and H contributes property H1, with an adjusted tax basis of $6,000 and a fair market value of $10,000. Both properties have 5 years remaining on their cost recovery schedules and are depreciable using the straight-line method. At the time of contribution, G1 has a built-in gain of $7,000 and H1 has a built-in gain of $4,000, and therefore, both properties are section 704(c) property. G1 generates $600 of tax depreciation and $2,000 of book depreciation for each of five years. H1 generates $1,200 of tax depreciation and $2,000 of book depreciation for each of 5 years. In addition, the properties each generate $500 of operating income annually. G and H are each allocated $1,000 of book depreciation for each property. Under the traditional method of paragraph (b) of this section, G would be allocated $0 of tax depreciation for G1 and $1,000 for H1, and H would be allocated $600 of tax depreciation for G1 and $200 for H1. Thus, at the end of the first year, G and H's book and tax capital accounts would be as follows:

	G		H	
Book	**Tax**	**Book**	**Tax**	
$10,000	$ 3,000	$10,000	$6,000	Initial contribution
<1,000>	<0>	<1,000>	<600>	G1 depreciation
<1,000>	<1,000>	<1,000>	<200>	H1 depreciation
500	500	500	500	Operating income
$ 8,500	$ 2,500	$ 8,500	$5,700	

(ii) *Curative allocations.* Under the traditional method, G is allocated more depreciation deductions than H, even though H contributed property with a smaller disparity reflected on GH's book and tax capital accounts. GH makes curative allocations to H of an additional $400 of tax depreciation each year, which reduces the disparities between G and H's book and tax capital accounts ratably each year. These allocations are reasonable provided the allocations meet the other requirements of this section. As a result of their agreement, at the end of the first year, G and H's capital accounts are as follows:

	G		H	
Book	**Tax**	**Book**	**Tax**	
$10,000	$3,000	$10,000	$6,000	Initial contribution
<1,000>	<0>	<1,000>	<600>	G1 depreciation
<1,000>	<600>	<1,000>	<600>	H1 depreciation
500	500	500	500	Operating income
$ 8,500	$2,900	$ 8,500	$5,300	

Reg. § 1.704-3(c)(4)

Example 3. Unreasonable use of curative allocations—(i) *Facts.* J and K form partnership JK and agree that each will receive a 50 percent share of all partnership items and that JK will make allocations under section 704(c) using the traditional method with curative allocations under paragraph (c) of this section. J contributes equipment with an adjusted tax basis of $1,000 and a book value of $10,000, with a view to taking advantage of the fact that the equipment has only one year remaining on its cost recovery schedule although it has an estimated remaining economic life of 10 years. J has substantial net operating loss carryforwards that J anticipates will otherwise expire unused. At the time of contribution, J has a built-in gain of $9,000, and therefore, the equipment is section 704(c) property. K contributes $10,000 of cash, which JK uses to buy inventory for resale. In JK's first year, the revenues generated by the equipment exactly equal JK's operating expenses. Under § 1.704-1(b)(2)(iv)(*g*)(*3*), the partnership must allocate the $10,000 of book depreciation to the partners in the first year of the partnership. Thus, there is $10,000 of book depreciation and $1,000 of tax depreciation in the partnership's first year. In addition, at the end of the first year JK sells all of the inventory for $18,000, recognizing $8,000 of income. The partners anticipate that the inventory income will have substantially the same effect on their tax liabilities as income from J's contributed equipment. Under the traditional method of paragraph (b) of this section, J and K's book and tax capital accounts at the end of the first year would be as follows:

	J		K	
Book	Tax	Book	Tax	
$10,000	$1,000	$10,000	$10,000	Initial contribution
<5,000>	<0>	<5,000>	<1,000>	Depreciation
4,000	4,000	4,000	4,000	Sales income
$ 9,000	$5,000	$ 9,000	$13,000	

(ii) *Unreasonable use of method.* (A) The use of curative allocations under these facts to offset immediately the full effect of the ceiling rule would result in the following book and tax capital accounts at the end of JK's first year:

	J		K	
Book	Tax	Book	Tax	
$10,000	$1,000	$10,000	$10,000	Initial contribution
<5,000>	<0>	<5,000>	<1,000>	Depreciation
4,000	8,000	4,000	0	Sales income
$ 9,000	$9,000	$ 9,000	$ 9,000	

(B) This curative allocation is not reasonable under paragraph (a)(10) of this section because the contribution of property is made and the curative allocation method is used with a view to shifting a significant amount of partnership taxable income to a partner with a low marginal tax rate and away from a partner with a high marginal tax rate, within a period of time significantly shorter than the economic life of the property.

(C) The property has only one year remaining on its cost recovery schedule even though its economic life is considerably longer. Under these facts, if the partnership agreement had provided for curative allocations over a reasonable period of time, such as over the property's economic life, rather than over its remaining cost recovery period, the allocations would have been reasonable. See paragraph (c)(3)(ii) of this section. Thus, in this example, JK would make a curative allocation of $400 of sales income to J in the partnership's first year (10 percent of $4,000). J and K's book and tax capital accounts at the end of the first year would be as follows:

	J		K	
Book	Tax	Book	Tax	
$10,000	$1,000	$10,000	$10,000	Initial contribution
<5,000>	<0>	<5,000>	<1,000>	Depreciation
4,000	4,400	4,000	3,600	Sales income
$ 9,000	$5,400	$ 9,000	$12,600	

(d) *Remedial allocation method*—(1) *In general.* A partnership may adopt the remedial allocation method described in this paragraph to eliminate distortions caused by the ceiling rule. A partnership adopting the remedial allocation method eliminates those distortions by creating remedial items and allocating those items to its partners. Under the remedial allocation method, the partnership first determines the amount of book items under paragraph (d)(2) of this section

Reg. § 1.704-3(d)(1)

and the partners' distributive shares of these items under section 704(b). The partnership then allocates the corresponding tax items recognized by the partnership, if any, using the traditional method described in paragraph (b)(1) of this section. If the ceiling rule (as defined in paragraph (b)(1) of this section) causes the book allocation of an item to a noncontributing partner to differ from the tax allocation of the same item to the noncontributing partner, the partnership creates a remedial item of income, gain, loss, or deduction equal to the full amount of the difference and allocates it to the noncontributing partner. The partnership simultaneously creates an offsetting remedial item in an identical amount and allocates it to the contributing partner.

(2) *Determining the amount of book items.* Under the remedial allocation method, a partnership determines the amount of book items attributable to contributed property in the following manner rather than under the rules of § 1.704-1(b)(2)(iv)(g)(3). The portion of the partnership's book basis in the property equal to the adjusted tax basis in the property at the time of contribution is recovered in the same manner as the adjusted tax basis in the property is recovered (generally, over the property's remaining recovery period under section 168(i)(7) or other applicable Internal Revenue Code section). The remainder of the partnership's book basis in the property (the amount by which book basis exceeds adjusted tax basis) is recovered using any recovery period and depreciation (or other cost recovery) method (including first-year conventions) available to the partnership for newly purchased property (of the same type as the contributed property) that is placed in service at the time of contribution.

(3) *Type.* Remedial allocations of income, gain, loss, or deduction to the noncontributing partner have the same tax attributes as the tax item limited by the ceiling rule. The tax attributes of offsetting remedial allocations of income, gain, loss, or deduction to the contributing partner are determined by reference to the item limited by the ceiling rule. Thus, for example, if the ceiling rule limited item is loss from the sale of contributed property, the offsetting remedial allocation to the contributing partner must be gain from the sale of that property. Conversely, if the ceiling rule limited item is gain from the sale of contributed property, the offsetting remedial allocation to the contributing partner must be loss from the sale of that property. If the ceiling rule limited item is depreciation or other cost recovery from the contributed property, the offsetting remedial allocation to the contributing partner must be income of the type produced (directly or indirectly) by that property. Any partner level tax attributes are determined at the partner level.

For example, if the ceiling rule limited item is depreciation from property used in a rental activity, the remedial allocation to the noncontributing partner is depreciation from property used in a rental activity and the offsetting remedial allocation to the contributing partner is ordinary income from that rental activity. Each partner then applies section 469 to the allocations as appropriate.

(4) *Effect of remedial items*—(i) *Effect on partnership.* Remedial items do not affect the partnership's computation of its taxable income under section 703 and do not affect the partnership's adjusted tax basis in partnership property.

(ii) *Effect on partners.* Remedial items are notional tax items created by the partnership solely for tax purposes and do not affect the partners' book capital accounts. Remedial items have the same effect as actual tax items on a partner's tax liability and on the partner's adjusted tax basis in the partnership interest.

(5) *Limitations on use of methods involving remedial allocations*—(i) *Limitation on taxpayers.* In the absence of published guidance, the remedial allocation method described in this paragraph (d) is the only reasonable section 704(c) method permitting the creation of notional tax items.

(ii) *Limitation on Internal Revenue Service.* In exercising its authority under paragraph (a)(10) of this section to make adjustments if a partnership's allocation method is not reasonable, the Internal Revenue Service will not require a partnership to use the remedial allocation method described in this paragraph (d) or any other method involving the creation of notional tax items.

(6) *Adjustments to application of method.* The Commissioner may, by published guidance, prescribe adjustments to the remedial allocation method under this paragraph (d) as necessary or appropriate. This guidance may, for example, prescribe adjustments to the remedial allocation method to prevent the duplication or omission of items of income or deduction or to reflect more clearly the partners' income or the income of a transferee of a partner.

(7) *Examples.* The following examples illustrate the principles of this paragraph (d).

Example 1. Remedial allocation method—(i) *Facts.* On January 1, L and M form partnership LM and agree that each will be allocated a 50 percent share of all partnership items. The partnership agreement provides that LM will make allocations under section 704(c) using the remedial allocation method under this paragraph (d) and that the straight-line method will be used to recover excess book basis. L contributes depreciable property with an adjusted tax basis of $4,000 and a fair market value of $10,000. The property is depreciated using the straight-line method with a 10-year recovery period and has 4 years remaining on its recovery period. M contributes $10,000, which the partnership uses to purchase land. Except for the depreciation deductions, LM's expenses equal its income in each year of the 10 years commencing with the year the partnership is formed.

(ii) *Years 1 through 4.* Under the remedial allocation method of this paragraph (d), LM has book depreciation for each of its first 4 years of $1,600 [$1,000 ($4,000 adjusted tax basis divided by the 4-year remaining recovery period) plus $600 ($6,000 excess of book value over tax basis,

divided by the *new* 10-year recovery period)]. (For the purpose of simplifying the example, the partnership's book depreciation is determined without regard to any first-year depreciation conventions.) Under the partnership agreement, L and M are each allocated 50 percent ($800) of the book depreciation. M is allocated $800 of tax depreciation and L is allocated the remaining $200 of tax depreciation ($1,000 − $800). See paragraph (d)(1) of this section. No remedial allocations are made because the ceiling rule does not result in a book allocation of depreciation to M different from the tax allocation. The allocations result in capital accounts at the end of LM's first 4 years as follows:

	L		M		
	Book	*Tax*	*Book*	*Tax*	
	$10,000	$4,000	$10,000	$10,000	Initial contribution
	<3,200>	<800>	<3,200>	<3,200>	Depreciation
	$ 6,800	$3,200	$ 6,800	$ 6,800	

(iii) *Subsequent years.* (A) For each of years 5 through 10, LM has $600 of book depreciation ($6,000 excess of initial book value over adjusted tax basis divided by the 10-year recovery period that commenced in year 1), but no tax depreciation. Under the partnership agreement, the $600

of book depreciation is allocated equally to L and M. Because of the application of the ceiling rule in year 5, M would be allocated $300 of book depreciation, but no tax depreciation. Thus, at the end of LM's fifth year L's and M's book and tax capital accounts would be as follows:

	L		M		
	Book	*Tax*	*Book*	*Tax*	
	$ 6,800	$3,200	$ 6,800	$ 6,800	End of year 4
	<300>		<300>		Depreciation
	$ 6,500	$3,200	$ 6,500	$ 6,800	

(B) Because the ceiling rule would cause an annual disparity of $300 between M's allocations of book and tax depreciation, LM must make remedial allocations of $300 of tax depreciation deductions to M under the remedial allocation method for each of years 5 through 10. LM must

also make an offsetting remedial allocation to L of $300 of taxable income, which must be of the same type as income produced by the property. At the end of year 5, LM's capital accounts are as follows:

	L		M		
	Book	*Tax*	*Book*	*Tax*	
	$ 6,800	$3,200	$ 6,800	$ 6,800	End of year 4
	<300>		<300>		Depreciation
		300		<300>	Remedial allocations
	$ 6,500	$3,500	$ 6,500	$ 6,500	

(C) At the end of year 10, LM's capital accounts are as follows:

	L		M		
	Book	*Tax*	*Book*	*Tax*	
	$ 6,500	$3,500	$ 6,500	$ 6,500	End of year 5
	<1,500>		<1,500>		Depreciation
		1,500		<1,500>	Remedial allocations
	$ 5,000	$5,000	$ 5,000	$ 5,000	

Example 2. Remedial allocations on sale—(i) *Facts.* N and P form partnership NP and agree that each will be allocated a 50 percent share of all partnership items. The partnership agreement

provides that NP will make allocations under section 704(c) using the remedial allocation method under this paragraph (d). N contributes Blackacre (land) with an adjusted tax basis of

Reg. § 1.704-3(d)(7)

$4,000 and a fair market value of $10,000. Because N has a built-in gain of $6,000, Blackacre is section 704(c) property. P contributes Whiteacre (land) with an adjusted tax basis and fair market value of $10,000. At the end of NP's first year, NP sells Blackacre to Q for $9,000 and recognizes a capital gain of $5,000 ($9,000 amount realized less $4,000 adjusted tax basis) and a book loss of $1,000 ($9,000 amount realized less $10,000 book basis). NP has no other items of income, gain, loss, or deduction. If the ceiling rule were applied, N would be allocated the entire $5,000 of tax gain and N and P would each be allocated $500 of book loss. Thus, at the end of NP's first year N's and P's book and tax capital accounts would be as follows:

	N		P		
	Book	Tax	Book	Tax	
	$10,000	$4,000	$10,000	$10,000	Initial contribution
	<500>	5,000	<500>		Sale of Blackacre
	$ 9,500	$9,000	$ 9,500	$10,000	

(ii) *Remedial allocation.* Because the ceiling rule would cause a disparity of $500 between P's allocation of book and tax loss, NP must make a remedial allocation of $500 of capital loss to P and an offsetting remedial allocation to N of an additional $500 of capital gain. These allocations result in capital accounts at the end of NP's first year as follows:

	N		P		
	Book	Tax	Book	Tax	
	$10,000	$4,000	$10,000	$10,000	Initial contribution
	<500>	5,000	<500>		Sale of Blackacre
		500		<500>	Remedial allocations
	$ 9,500	$9,500	$ 9,500	$ 9,500	

Example 3. Remedial allocation where built-in gain property sold for book and tax loss—(i) Facts. The facts are the same as in Example 2, except that at the end of NP's first year, NP sells Blackacre to Q for $3,000 and recognizes a capital loss of $1,000 ($3,000 amount realized less $4,000 adjusted tax basis) and a book loss of $7,000 ($3,000 amount realized less $10,000 book basis). If the ceiling rule were applied, P would be allocated the entire $1,000 of tax loss and N and P would each be allocated $3,500 of book loss. Thus, at the end of NP's first year, N's and P's book and tax capital accounts would be as follows:

	N		P		
	Book	Tax	Book	Tax	
	$10,000	$4,000	$10,000	$10,000	Initial contribution
	<3,500>	0	<3,500>	<1,000>	Sale of Blackacre
	$ 6,500	$4,000	$ 6,500	$ 9,000	

(ii) *Remedial allocation.* Because the ceiling rule would cause a disparity of $2,500 between P's allocation of book and tax loss on the sale of Blackacre, NP must make a remedial allocation of $2,500 of capital loss to P and an offsetting remedial allocation to N of $2,500 of capital gain. These allocations result in capital accounts at the end of NP's first year as follows:

	N		P		
	Book	Tax	Book	Tax	
	$10,000	$4,000	$10,000	$10,000	Initial contribution
	<3,500>	0	<3,500>	<1,000>	Sale of Blackacre
		<2,500>		<2,500>	Remedial allocations
	$ 6,500	$6,500	$ 6,500	$ 6,500	

(e) *Exceptions and special rules—(1) Small disparities—(i) General rule.* If a partner contributes one or more items of property to a partnership within a single taxable year of the partnership, and the disparity between the book value of the property and the contributing partner's adjusted tax basis in the property is a small disparity, the partnership may—

(A) Use a reasonable section 704(c) method;

(B) Disregard the application of section 704(c) to the property; or

(C) Defer the application of section 704(c) to the property until the disposition of the property.

(ii) *Definition of small disparity.* A disparity between book value and adjusted tax basis is a small disparity if the book value of all properties contributed by one partner during the partnership taxable year does not differ from the adjusted tax

Reg. § 1.704-3(e)(1)

basis by more than 15 percent of the adjusted tax basis, and the total gross disparity does not exceed $20,000.

(2) *Aggregation.* Each of the following types of property may be aggregated for purposes of making allocations under section 704(c) and this section if contributed by one partner during the partnership taxable year.

(i) *Depreciable property.* All property, other than real property, that is included in the same general asset account of the contributing partner and the partnership under section 168.

(ii) *Zero-basis property.* All property with a basis equal to zero, other than real property.

(iii) *Inventory.* For partnerships that do not use a specific identification method of accounting, each item of inventory, other than qualified financial assets (as defined in paragraph (e)(3)(ii) of this section).

(3) *Special aggregation rule for securities partnerships*—(i) *General rule.* For purposes of making reverse section 704(c) allocations, a securities partnership may aggregate gains and losses from qualified financial assets using any reasonable approach that is consistent with the purpose of section 704(c). Notwithstanding paragraphs (a)(2) and (a)(6)(i) of this section, once a partnership adopts an aggregate approach, that partnership must apply the same aggregate approach to all of its qualified financial assets for all taxable years in which the partnership qualifies as a securities partnership. Paragraphs (e)(3)(iv) and (e)(3)(v) of this section describe approaches for aggregating reverse section 704(c) gains and losses that are generally reasonable. Other approaches may be reasonable in appropriate circumstances. See, however, paragraph (a)(10) of this section, which describes the circumstances under which section 704(c) methods, including the aggregate approaches described in this paragraph (e)(3), are not reasonable. A partnership using an aggregate approach must separately account for any built-in gain or loss from contributed property.

(ii) *Qualified financial assets* —(A) *In general.* A qualified financial asset is any personal property (including stock) that is actively traded. Actively traded means actively traded as defined in § 1.1092(d)-1 (defining actively traded property for purposes of the straddle rules).

(B) *Management companies.* For a management company, qualified financial assets also include the following, even if not actively traded: shares of stock in a corporation; notes, bonds, debentures, or other evidences of indebtedness; interest rate, currency, or equity notional principal contracts; evidences of an interest in, or derivative financial instruments in, any security,

currency, or commodity, including any option, forward or futures contract, or short position; or any similar financial instrument.

(C) *Partnership interests.* An interest in a partnership is not a qualified financial asset for purposes of this paragraph (e)(3)(ii). However, for purposes of this paragraph (e)(3), a partnership (upper-tier partnership) that holds an interest in a securities partnership (lower-tier partnership) must take into account the lower-tier partnership's assets and qualified financial assets as follows:

(*1*) In determining whether the upper-tier partnership qualifies as an investment partnership, the upper-tier partnership must treat its proportionate share of the lower-tier securities partnership's assets as assets of the upper-tier partnership; and

(*2*) If the upper-tier partnership adopts an aggregate approach under this paragraph (e)(3), the upper-tier partnership must aggregate the gains and losses from its directly held qualified financial assets with its distributive share of the gains and losses from the qualified financial assets of the lower-tier securities partnership.

(iii) *Securities partnership*—(A) *In general.* A partnership is a securities partnership if the partnership is either a management company or an investment partnership, and the partnership makes all of its book allocations in proportion to the partners' relative book capital accounts (except for reasonable special allocations to a partner that provides management services or investment advisory services to the partnership).

(B) *Definitions*—(*1*) *Management company.* A partnership is a management company if it is registered with the Securities and Exchange Commission as a management company under the Investment Company Act of 1940, as amended (15 U.S.C. 80a).

(*2*) *Investment partnership.* A partnership is an investment partnership if:

(*i*) On the date of each capital account restatement, the partnership holds qualified financial assets that constitute at least 90 percent of the fair market value of the partnership's non-cash assets; and

(*ii*) The partnership reasonably expects, as of the end of the first taxable year in which the partnership adopts an aggregate approach under this paragraph (e)(3) to make revaluations at least annually.

(iv) *Partial netting approach.* This paragraph (e)(3)(iv) describes the partial netting approach of making reverse section 704(c) allocations. See Example 1 of paragraph (e)(3)(ix)

Reg. § 1.704-3(e)(2)

of this section for an illustration of the partial netting approach. To use the partial netting approach, the partnership must establish appropriate accounts for each partner for the purpose of taking into account each partner's share of the book gains and losses and determining each partner's share of the tax gains and losses. Under the partial netting approach, on the date of each capital account restatement, the partnership:

(A) Nets its book gains and book losses from qualified financial assets since the last capital account restatement and allocates the net amount to its partners;

(B) Separately aggregates all tax gains and all tax losses from qualified financial assets since the last capital account restatement; and

(C) Separately allocates the aggregate tax gain and aggregate tax loss to the partners in a manner that reduces the disparity between the book capital account balances and the tax capital account balances (book-tax disparities) of the individual partners.

(v) *Full netting approach.* This paragraph (e)(3)(v) describes the full netting approach of making reverse section 704(c) allocations on an aggregate basis. See Example 2 of paragraph (e)(3)(ix) of this section for an illustration of the full netting approach. To use the full netting approach, the partnership must establish appropriate accounts for each partner for the purpose of taking into account each partner's share of the book gains and losses and determining each partner's share of the tax gains and losses. Under the full netting approach, on the date of each capital account restatement, the partnership:

(A) Nets its book gains and book losses from qualified financial assets since the last capital account restatement and allocates the net amount to its partners;

(B) Nets tax gains and tax losses from qualified financial assets since the last capital account restatement; and

(C) Allocates the net tax gain (or net tax loss) to the partners in a manner that reduces the book-tax disparities of the individual partners.

(vi) *Type of tax gain or loss.* The character and other tax attributes of gain or loss allocated to the partners under this paragraph (e)(3) must:

(A) Preserve the tax attributes of each item of gain or loss realized by the partnership;

(B) Be determined under an approach that is consistently applied; and

(C) Not be determined with a view to reducing substantially the present value of the partners' aggregate tax liability.

(vii) *Disqualified securities partnerships.* A securities partnership that adopts an aggregate approach under this paragraph (e)(3) and subsequently fails to qualify as a securities partnership must make reverse section 704(c) allocations on an asset-by-asset basis after the date of disqualification. The partnership, however, is not required to disaggregate the book gain or book loss from qualified asset revaluations before the date of disqualification when making reverse section 704(c) allocations on or after the date of disqualification.

(viii) *Transitional rule for qualified financial assets revalued after effective date.* A securities partnership revaluing its qualified financial assets pursuant to § 1.704-1(b)(2)(iv)(*f*) on or after the effective date of this section may use any reasonable approach to coordinate with revaluations that occurred prior to the effective date of this section.

(ix) *Examples.* The following examples illustrate the principles of this paragraph (e)(3).

Example 1. Operation of the partial netting approach—(i) Facts. Two regulated investment companies, X and Y, each contribute $150,000 in cash to form PRS, a partnership that registers as a management company. The partnership agreement provides that book items will be allocated in accordance with the partners' relative book capital accounts, that book capital accounts will be adjusted to reflect daily revaluations of property pursuant to § 1.704-1(b)(2)(iv)(*f*)(5)(*iii*), and that reverse section 704(c) allocations will be made using the partial netting approach described in paragraph (e)(3)(iv) of this section. X and Y each have an initial book capital account of $150,000. In addition, the partnership establishes for each of X and Y a revaluation account with a beginning balance of $0. On Day 1, PRS buys Stock 1, Stock 2, and Stock 3 for $100,000 each. On Day 2, Stock 1 increases in value from $100,000 to $102,000, Stock 2 increases in value from $100,000 to $105,000, and Stock 3 declines in value from $100,000 to $98,000. At the end of Day 2, Z, a regulated investment company, joins PRS by contributing $152,500 in cash for a one-third interest in the partnership [$152,500 divided by $300,000 (initial values of stock) + $5,000 (net gain at end of Day 2) + $152,500]. PRS uses this cash to purchase Stock 4. PRS establishes a revaluation account for Z with a $0 beginning balance. As of the close of Day 3, Stock 1 increases in value from $102,000 to $105,000, and Stocks 2, 3, and 4 decrease in value from $105,000 to $102,000, from $98,000 to $96,000, and from $152,500 to $151,500, respectively. At the end of Day 3, PRS sells Stocks 2 and 3.

(ii) Book allocations—Day 2. At the end of Day 2, PRS revalues the partnership's qualified financial assets and increases X's and Y's book

capital accounts by each partner's 50 percent share of the $5,000 ($2,000 + $5,000 − $2,000) net increase in the value of the partnership's assets during Day 2. PRS increases X's and Y's respective revaluation account balances by $2,500 each to reflect the amount by which each part-ner's book capital account increased on Day 2. Z's capital account is not affected because Z did not join PRS until the end of Day 2. At the beginning of Day 3, the partnership's accounts are as follows:

	Stock 1	Stock 2	Stock 3	Stock 4	
	$100,000	$100,000	$100,000	—	Opening Balance
	2,000	5,000	(2,000)	—	Day 2 Adjustment
	$102,000	$105,000	$98,000	$152,500	Total

X

Book	Tax	Revaluation Account	
$150,000	$150,000	$0	Opening Balance
2,500	0	2,500	Day 2 Adjustment
$152,500	$150,000	$2,500	Closing Balance

Y

Book	Tax	Revaluation Account	
$150,000	$150,000	$0	Opening Balance
2,500	0	2,500	Day 2 Adjustment
$152,500	$150,000	$2,500	Closing Balance

Z

Book	Tax	Revaluation Account	
—	—	—	Opening Balance
—	—	—	Day 2 Adjustment
$152,500	$152,500	$0	Closing Balance

(iii) *Book and tax allocations—Day 3.* At the end of Day 3, PRS decreases the book capital accounts of X, Y, and Z by $1,000 to reflect each partner's share of the $3,000 ($3,000 − $3,000 − $2,000 − $1,000) net decrease in the value of the partnership's qualified financial assets. PRS also reduces each partner's revaluation account balance by $1,000. Accordingly, X's and Y's revaluation account balances are reduced to $1,500 each and Z's revaluation account balance is ($1,000). PRS then separately allocates the tax gain from the sale of Stock 2 and the tax loss from the sale of Stock 3. The $2,000 of tax gain recognized on the sale of Stock 2 ($102,000 − $100,000) is allocated among the partners with positive revaluation account balances in accordance with the relative balances of those revaluation accounts. X's and Y's revaluation accounts have equal positive balances; thus, PRS allocates $1,000 of the gain from the sale of Stock 2 to X and $1,000 of that gain to Y. PRS allocates none of the gain from the sale to Z because Z's revaluation account balance is neg-ative. The $4,000 of tax loss recognized from the sale of Stock 3 ($96,000 − $100,000) is allocated first to the partners with negative revaluation account balances to the extent of those balances. Because Z is the only partner with a negative revaluation account balance, the tax loss is allocated first to Z to the extent of Z's ($1,000) balance. The remaining $3,000 of tax loss is allocated among the partners in accordance with their distributive shares of the loss. Accordingly, PRS allocates $1,000 of tax loss from the sale of Stock 3 to each of X and Y. PRS also allocates an additional $1,000 of the tax loss to Z, so that Z's total share of the tax loss from the sale of Stock 3 is $2,000. PRS then reduces each partner's revaluation account balance by the amount of any tax gain allocated to that partner and increases each partner's revaluation account balance by the amount of any tax loss allocated to that partner. At the beginning of Day 4, the partnership's accounts are as follows:

	Stock 1	Stock 2	Stock 3	Stock 4	
	$100,000	$100,000	$100,000	$152,500	Opening Balance
	2,000	5,000	(2,000)	—	Day 2 Adjustment
	3,000	(3,000)	(2,000)	(1,000)	Day 3 Adjustment
	$105,000	$102,000	$96,000	$151,500	Total

Reg. § 1.704-3(e)(3)

X and Y

Book	Tax	Revaluation Account	
$150,000	$150,000	$ 0	Opening Balance
2,500	0	2,500	Day 2 Adjustment
(1,000)	0	(1,000)	Day 3 Adjustment
$151,500	$150,000	$1,500	Total
0	1,000	(1,000)	Gain from Stock 2
0	(1,000)	1,000	Loss from Stock 3
$151,500	$150,000	$1,500	Closing Balance

Z

Book	Tax	Revaluation Account	
$152,500	$152,500	$ 0	Opening Balance
(1,000)	0	(1,000)	Day 3 Adjustment
$151,500	$152,500	($1,000)	Total
0	0	0	Gain from Stock 2
0	(2,000)	2,000	Loss from Stock 3
$151,500	$150,500	$ 1,000	Closing Balance

Example 2. Operation of the full netting approach—(i) *Facts.* The facts are the same as in Example 1, except that the partnership agreement provides that PRS will make reverse section 704(c) allocations using the full netting approach described in paragraph (e)(3)(v) of this section.

(ii) *Book allocations—Days 2 and 3.* PRS allocates its book gains and losses in the manner described in paragraphs (ii) and (iii) of Example 1 (the partial netting approach). Thus, at the end of Day 2, PRS increases the book capital accounts of X and Y by $2,500 to reflect the appreciation in the partnership's assets from the close of Day 1 to the close of Day 2 and records that increase in the revaluation account created for each partner. At the end of Day 3, PRS decreases the book capital accounts of X, Y, and Z by $1,000 to reflect each partner's share of the decline in value of the partnership's assets from Day 2 to Day 3 and reduces each partner's revaluation account by a corresponding amount.

(iii) *Tax allocations—Day 3.* After making the book adjustments described in the previous paragraph, PRS allocates its net tax gain (or net tax loss) from its sales of qualified financial assets during Day 3. To do so, PRS first determines its net tax gain (or net tax loss) recognized from its sales of qualified financial assets for the day. There is a $2,000 net tax loss ($2,000 gain from the sale of Stock 2 less $4,000 loss from the sale of Stock 3) on the sale of PRS's qualified financial assets. Because Z is the only partner with a negative revaluation account balance, the partnership's net tax loss is allocated first to Z to the extent of Z's ($1,000) revaluation account balance. The remaining net tax loss is allocated among the partners in accordance with their distributive shares of loss. Thus, PRS allocates $333.33 of the $2,000 net tax loss to each of X and Y. PRS also allocates an additional $333.33 of the net tax loss to Z, so that the total net tax loss allocation to Z is $1,333.33. PRS then increases each partner's revaluation account balance by the amount of net tax loss allocated to that partner. At the beginning of Day 4, the partnership's accounts are as follows:

Stock 1	Stock 2	Stock 3	Stock 4	
$100,000	$100,000	$100,000	$152,500	Opening Balance
2,000	5,000	(2,000)	—	Day 2 Adjustment
3,000	(3,000)	(2,000)	(1,000)	Day 3 Adjustment
$105,000	$102,000	$ 96,000	$151,500	Total

X and Y

Book	Tax	Revaluation Account	
$150,000	$150,000	$ 0	Opening Balance
2,500	0	2,500	Day 2 Adjustment
(1,000)	0	(1,000)	Day 3 Adjustment
$151,500	$150,000	$1,500	Total
0	(333)	(333)	Net Tax Loss-Stocks 2 & 3
$151,500	$149,667	$1,833	Closing Balance

Reg. § 1.704-3(e)(3)

Z

Book	Tax	Revaluation Account	
$152,500	$152,500	$ 0	Opening Balance
(1,000)	0	(1,000)	Day 3 Adjustment
$151,500	$152,500	($1,000)	Total
0	(1,333)	1,333	Net Tax Loss-Stocks 2 & 3
$151,500	$151,167	$ 333	Closing Balance

(4) *Aggregation as permitted by the Commissioner.* The Commissioner may, by published guidance or by letter ruling, permit:

(i) Aggregation of properties other than those described in paragraphs (e)(2) and (e)(3) of this section;

(ii) Partnerships and partners not described in paragraph (e)(3) of this section to aggregate gain and loss from qualified financial assets; and

(iii) Aggregation of qualified financial assets for purposes of making section 704(c) allocations in the same manner as that described in paragraph (e)(3) of this section.

(f) *Effective date.* With the exception of paragraph (a)(11) of this section, this section applies to properties contributed to a partnership and to restatements pursuant to § 1.704-1(b)(2)(iv)(*f*) on or after December 21, 1993. Paragraph (a)(11) of this section applies to properties contributed by a partner to a partnership on or after August 20, 1997. However, partnerships may rely on paragraph (a)(11) of this section for properties contributed before August 20, 1997, and disposed of on or after August 20, 1997. [Reg. § 1.704-3.]

☐ [*T.D. 8500, 12-21-93. Amended by T.D. 8585, 12-27-94; T.D. 8717, 5-8-97 and T.D. 8730, 8-19-97.*]

§ 1.704-4. Distribution of contributed property.—(a) *Determination of gain and loss*—(1) *In general.* A partner that contributes section 704(c) property to a partnership must recognize gain or loss under section 704(c)(1)(B) and this section on the distribution of such property to another partner within five years of its contribution to the partnership in an amount equal to the gain or loss that would have been allocated to such partner under section 704(c)(1)(A) and § 1.704-3 if the distributed property had been sold by the partnership to the distributee partner for its fair market value at the time of the distribution. See § 1.704-3(a)(3)(i) for a definition of section 704(c) property.

(2) *Transactions to which section 704(c)(1)(B) applies.* Section 704(c)(1)(B) and this section apply only to the extent that a distribution by a partnership is a distribution to a partner acting in the capacity of a partner within the meaning of section 731.

(3) *Fair market value of property.* The fair market value of the distributed section 704(c) property is the price at which the property would change hands between a willing buyer and a willing seller at the time of the distribution, neither being under any compulsion to buy or sell and both having reasonable knowledge of the relevant facts. The fair market value that a partnership assigns to distributed section 704(c) property will be regarded as correct, provided that the value is reasonably agreed to among the partners in an arm's-length negotiation and the partners have sufficiently adverse interests.

(4) *Determination of five-year period*—(i) *General rule.* The five-year period specified in paragraph (a)(1) of this section begins on and includes the date of contribution.

(ii) *Section 708(b)(1)(B) terminations.* A termination of the partnership under section 708(b)(1)(B) does not begin a new five-year period for each partner with respect to the built-in gain and built-in loss property that the terminated partnership is deemed to contribute to the new partnership under § 1.7081(b)(1)(iv). See § 1.704-3(a)(3)(ii) for the definitions of built-in gain and built-in loss on section 704(c) property. This paragraph (a)(4)(ii) applies to terminations of partnerships under section 708(b)(1)(B) occurring on or after May 9, 1997; however, this paragraph (a)(4)(ii) may be applied to terminations occurring on or after May 9, 1996, provided that the partnership and its partners apply this paragraph (a)(4)(ii) to the termination in a consistent manner.

(5) *Examples.* The following examples illustrate the rules of this paragraph (a). Unless otherwise specified, partnership income equals partnership expenses (other than depreciation deductions for contributed property) for each year of the partnership, the fair market value of partnership property does not change, all distributions by the partnership are subject to section 704(c)(1)(B), and all partners are unrelated.

Example 1. Recognition of gain. (i) On January 1, 1995, A, B, and C form partnership ABC as equal partners. A contributes $10,000 cash and Property A, nondepreciable real property with a fair market value of $10,000 and an adjusted tax basis of $4,000. Thus, there is a built-in gain of $6,000 on Property A at the time of contribution.

B contributes $10,000 cash and Property B, nondepreciable real property with a fair market value and adjusted tax basis of $10,000. C contributes $20,000 cash.

(ii) On December 31, 1998, Property A and Property B are distributed to C in complete liquidation of C's interest in the partnership.

(iii) A would have recognized $6,000 of gain under section 704(c)(1)(A) and § 1.704-3 on the sale of Property A at the time of the distribution ($10,000 fair market value less $4,000 adjusted tax basis). As a result, A must recognize $6,000 of gain on the distribution of Property A to C. B would not have recognized any gain or loss under section 704(c)(1)(A) and § 1.704-3 on the sale of Property B at the time of distribution because Property B was not section 704(c) property. As a result, B does not recognize any gain or loss on the distribution of Property B.

Example 2. Effect of post-contribution depreciation deductions. (i) On January 1, 1995, A, B, and C form partnership ABC as equal partners. A contributes Property A, depreciable property with a fair market value of $30,000 and an adjusted tax basis of $20,000. Therefore, there is a built-in gain of $10,000 on Property A. B and C each contribute $30,000 cash. ABC uses the traditional method of making section 704(c) allocations described in § 1.704-3(b) with respect to Property A.

(ii) Property A is depreciated using the straight-line method over its remaining 10-year recovery period. The partnership has book depreciation of $3,000 per year (10 percent of the $30,000 book basis), and each partner is allocated $1,000 of book depreciation per year (one-third of the total annual book depreciation of $3,000). The partnership has a tax depreciation deduction of $2,000 per year (10 percent of the $20,000 tax basis in Property A). This $2,000 tax depreciation deduction is allocated equally between B and C, the noncontributing partners with respect to Property A.

(iii) At the end of the third year, the book value of Property A is $21,000 ($30,000 initial book value less $9,000 aggregate book depreciation) and the adjusted tax basis is $14,000 ($20,000 initial tax basis less $6,000 aggregate tax depreciation). A's remaining section 704(c)(1)(A) built-in gain with respect to Property A is $7,000 ($21,000 book value less $14,000 adjusted tax basis).

(iv) On December 31, 1997, Property A is distributed to B in complete liquidation of B's interest in the partnership. If Property A had been sold for its fair market value at the time of the distribution, A would have recognized $7,000 of gain under section 704(c)(1)(A) and

§ 1.704-3(b). Therefore, A recognizes $7,000 of gain on the distribution of Property A to B.

Example 3. Effect of remedial method. (i) On January 1, 1995, A, B, and C form partnership ABC as equal partners. A contributes Property A1, nondepreciable real property with a fair market value of $10,000 and an adjusted tax basis of $5,000, and Property A2, nondepreciable real property with a fair market value and adjusted tax basis of $10,000. B and C each contribute $20,000 cash. ABC uses the remedial method of making section 704(c) allocations described in § 1.704-3(d) with respect to Property A1.

(ii) On December 31, 1998, when the fair market value of Property A1 has decreased to $7,000, Property A1 is distributed to C in a current distribution. If Property A1 had been sold by the partnership at the time of the distribution, ABC would have recognized the $2,000 of remaining built-in gain under section 704(c)(1)(A) on the sale (fair market value of $7,000 less $5,000 adjusted tax basis). All of this gain would have been allocated to A. ABC would also have recognized a book loss of $3,000 ($10,000 original book value less $7,000 current fair market value of the property). Book loss in the amount of $2,000 would have been allocated equally between B and C. Under the remedial method, $2,000 of tax loss would also have been allocated equally to B and C to match their share of the book loss. As a result, $2,000 of gain would also have been allocated to A as an offsetting remedial allocation. A would have recognized $4,000 of total gain under section 704(c)(1)(A) on the sale of Property A1 ($2,000 of section 704(c) recognized gain plus $2,000 remedial gain). Therefore, A recognizes $4,000 of gain on the distribution of Property A1 to C under this section.

(b) *Character of gain or loss*—(1) *General rule.* Gain or loss recognized by the contributing partner under section 704(c)(1)(B) and this section has the same character as the gain or loss that would have resulted if the distributed property had been sold by the partnership to the distributee partner at the time of the distribution.

(2) *Example.* The following example illustrates the rule of this paragraph (b). Unless otherwise specified, partnership income equals partnership expenses (other than depreciation deductions for contributed property) for each year of the partnership, the fair market value of partnership property does not change, all distributions by the partnership are subject to section 704(c)(1)(B), and all partners are unrelated.

Example. Character of gain. (i) On January 1, 1995, A and B form partnership AB. A contributes $10,000 and Property A, nondepreciable real property with a fair market value of $10,000 and an adjusted tax basis of $4,000, in exchange for a 25 percent interest in partnership capital and profits. B contributes $60,000 cash for a 75 percent interest in partnership capital and profits.

(ii) On December 31, 1998, Property A is distributed to B in a current distribution. Property A is used in a trade or business of B.

(iii) A would have recognized $6,000 of gain under section 704(c)(1)(A) on a sale of Property A at the time of the distribution (the difference between the fair market value ($10,000) and the adjusted tax basis ($4,000) of the property at that time). Because Property A is not a capital asset in the hands of Partner B and B holds more than 50 percent of partnership capital and profits, the character of the gain on a sale of Property A to B would have been ordinary income under section 707(b)(2). Therefore, the character of the gain to A on the distribution of Property A to B is ordinary income.

* * *

(d) *Special rules*—(1) *Nonrecognition transactions.* Property received by the partnership in exchange for section 704(c) property in a nonrecognition transaction is treated as the section 704(c) property for purposes of section 704(c)(1)(B) and this section to the extent that the property received is treated as section 704(c) property under § 1.704-3(a)(8). See § 1.7372(d)(3) for a similar rule in the context of section 737.

(2) *Transfers of a partnership interest.* The transferee of all or a portion of the partnership interest of a contributing partner is treated as the contributing partner for purposes of section 704(c)(1)(B) and this section to the extent of the share of built-in gain or loss allocated to the transferee partner. See § 1.704-3(a)(7).

(3) *Distributions of like-kind property.* If section 704(c) property is distributed to a partner other than the contributing partner and like-kind property (within the meaning of section 1031) is distributed to the contributing partner no later than the earlier of (i) 180 days following the date of the distribution to the non-contributing partner, or (ii) the due date (determined with regard to extensions) of the contributing partner's income tax return for the taxable year of the distribution to the noncontributing partner, the amount of gain or loss, if any, that the contributing partner would otherwise have recognized under section 704(c)(1)(B) and this section is reduced by the amount of built-in gain or loss in the distributed like-kind property in the hands of the contributing partner immediately after the distribution. The contributing partner's basis in the distributed like-kind property is determined as if the like-kind property were distributed in an unrelated distribution prior to the distribution of

any other property distributed as part of the same distribution and is determined without regard to the increase in the contributing partner's adjusted tax basis in the partnership interest under section 704(c)(1)(B) and this section. See § 1.707-3 for provisions treating the distribution of the like-kind property to the contributing partner as a disguised sale in certain situations.

(4) *Example.* The following example illustrates the rules of this paragraph (d). Unless otherwise specified, partnership income equals partnership expenses (other than depreciation deductions for contributed property) for each year of the partnership, the fair market value of partnership property does not change, all distributions by the partnership are subject to section 704(c)(1)(B), and all partners are unrelated.

Example. Distribution of like-kind property. (i) On January 1, 1995, A, B, and C form partnership ABC as equal partners. A contributes Property A, nondepreciable real property with a fair market value of $20,000 and an adjusted tax basis of $10,000. B and C each contribute $20,000 cash. The partnership subsequently buys Property X, nondepreciable real property of a like-kind to Property A with a fair market value and adjusted tax basis of $8,000. The fair market value of Property X subsequently increases to $10,000.

(ii) On December 31, 1998, Property A is distributed to B in a current distribution. At the same time, Property X is distributed to A in a current distribution. The distribution of Property X does not result in the contribution of Property A being properly characterized as a disguised sale to the partnership under § 1.707-3. A's basis in Property X is $8,000 under section 732(a)(1). A therefore has $2,000 of built-in gain in Property X ($10,000 fair market value less $8,000 adjusted tax basis).

(iii) A would generally recognize $10,000 of gain under section 704(c)(1)(B) on the distribution of Property A, the difference between the fair market value ($20,000) of the property and its adjusted tax basis ($10,000). This gain is reduced, however, by the amount of the built-in gain of Property X in the hands of A. As a result, A recognizes only $8,000 of gain on the distribution of Property A to B under section 704(c)(1)(B) and this section.

(e) *Basis adjustments*—(1) *Contributing partner's basis in the partnership interest.* The basis of the contributing partner's interest in the partnership is increased by the amount of the gain, or decreased by the amount of the loss, recognized by the partner under section 704(c)(1)(B) and this section. This increase or decrease is taken into account in determining (i) the contributing partner's adjusted tax basis under section 732 for any property distributed to the partner in a distribution that is part of the same distribution as the distribution of the contributed property, other than like-kind property described in paragraph (d)(3) of this section (pertaining to the special rule for distributions of like-kind property), and (ii) the amount of the gain recognized by the contributing partner under section 731 or section 737, if any, on a distribution of money or property to the contributing partner that is part of the same distribution as the distribution of the contributed property. For a determination of basis in a distribution subject to section 737, see § 1.737-3(a).

(2) *Partnership's basis in partnership property.* The partnership's adjusted tax basis in the distributed section 704(c) property is increased or decreased immediately before the distribution by the amount of gain or loss recognized by the contributing partner under section 704(c)(1)(B) and this section. Any increase or decrease in basis is therefore taken into account in determining the distributee partner's adjusted tax basis in the distributed property under section 732. For a determination of basis in a distribution subject to section 737, see § 1.7373(b).

(3) *Section 754 adjustments.* The basis adjustments to partnership property made pursuant to paragraph (e)(2) of this section are not elective and must be made regardless of whether the partnership has an election in effect under section 754. Any adjustments to the bases of partnership property (including the distributed section 704(c) property) under section 734(b) pursuant to a section 754 election must be made after (and must take into account) the adjustments to basis made under paragraph (e)(2) of this section. See § 1.737-3(c)(4) for a similar rule in the context of section 737.

(4) *Example.* The following example illustrates the rules of this paragraph (e). Unless otherwise specified, partnership income equals partnership expenses (other than depreciation deductions for contributed property) for each year of the partnership, the fair market value of partnership property does not change, all distributions by the partnership are subject to section 704(c)(1)(B), and all partners are unrelated.

Example. Basis adjustment. (i) On January 1, 1995, A, B, and C form partnership ABC as equal partners. A contributes $10,000 cash and Property A, nondepreciable real property with a fair market value of $10,000 and an adjusted tax basis of $4,000. B and C each contribute $20,000 cash.

(ii) On December 31, 1998, Property A is distributed to B in a current distribution.

(iii) Under paragraph (a) of this section, A recognizes $6,000 of gain on the distribution of Property A because that is the amount of gain that would have been allocated to A under section 704(c)(1)(A) and § 1.704-3 on a sale of Property A for its fair market value at the time of the distribution (fair market value of Property A ($10,000) less its adjusted tax basis at the time of distribution ($4,000)). The adjusted tax basis of A's partnership interest is increased from $14,000 to $20,000 to reflect this gain. The partnership's adjusted tax basis in Property A is increased from $4,000 to $10,000 immediately prior to its distribution to B. B's adjusted tax basis in Property A is therefore $10,000 under section 732(a)(1).

(f) *Anti-abuse rule*—(1) *In general.* The rules of section 704(c)(1)(B) and this section must be applied in a manner consistent with the purpose of section 704(c)(1)(B). Accordingly, if a principal purpose of a transaction is to achieve a tax result that is inconsistent with the purpose of section 704(c)(1)(B), the Commissioner can recast the transaction for federal tax purposes as appropriate to achieve tax results that are consistent with the purpose of section 704(c)(1)(B) and this section. Whether a tax result is inconsistent with the purpose of section 704(c)(1)(B) and this section must be determined based on all the facts and circumstances. See § 1.7374 for an anti-abuse rule and examples in the context of section 737.

(2) *Examples.* The following examples illustrate the anti-abuse rule of this paragraph (f). The examples set forth below do not delineate the boundaries of either permissible or impermissible types of transactions. Further, the addition of any facts or circumstances that are not specifically set forth in an example (or the deletion of any facts or circumstances) may alter the outcome of the transaction described in the example. Unless otherwise specified, partnership income equals partnership expenses (other than depreciation deductions for contributed property) for each year of the partnership, the fair market value of partnership property does not change, all distributions by the partnership are subject to section 704(c)(1)(B), and all partners are unrelated.

Example 1. Distribution in substance made within five-year period; results inconsistent with the purpose of section 704(c)(1)(B). (i) On January 1, 1995, A, B, and C form partnership ABC as equal partners. A contributes Property A, nondepreciable real property with a fair market value of $10,000 and an adjusted tax basis of $1,000. B and C each contributes $10,000 cash.

(ii) On December 31, 1998, the partners desire to distribute Property A to B in complete liquidation of B's interest in the partnership. If Property A were distributed at that time, how-

Reg. § 1.704-4(f)(2)

ever, A would recognize $9,000 of gain under section 704(c)(1)(B), the difference between the $10,000 fair market value and the $1,000 adjusted tax basis of Property A, because Property A was contributed to the partnership less than five years before December 31, 1998. On becoming aware of this potential gain recognition, and with a principal purpose of avoiding such gain, the partners amend the partnership agreement on December 31, 1998, and take any other steps necessary to provide that substantially all of the economic risks and benefits of Property A are borne by B as of December 31, 1998, and that substantially all of the economic risks and benefits of all other partnership property are borne by A and C. The partnership holds Property A until January 5, 2000, at which time it is distributed to B in complete liquidation of B's interest in the partnership.

(iii) The actual distribution of Property A occurred more than five years after the contribution of the property to the partnership. The steps taken by the partnership on December 31, 1998, however, are the functional equivalent of an actual distribution of Property A to B in complete liquidation of B's interest in the partnership as of that date. Section 704(c)(1)(B) requires recognition of gain when contributed section 704(c) property is in substance distributed to another partner within five years of its contribution to the partnership. Allowing a contributing partner to avoid section 704(c)(1)(B) through arrangements such as those in this *Example 1* that have the effect of a distribution of property within five years of the date of its contribution to the partnership would effectively undermine the purpose of section 704(c)(1)(B) and this section. As a result, the steps taken by the partnership on December 31, 1998, are treated as causing a distribution of Property A to B for purposes of section 704(c)(1)(B) on that date, and A recognizes gain of $9,000 under section 704(c)(1)(B) and this section at that time.

(iv) Alternatively, if on becoming aware of the potential gain recognition to A on a distribution of Property A on December 31, 1998, the partners had instead agreed that B would continue as a partner with no changes to the partnership agreement or to B's economic interest in partnership operations, the distribution of Property A to B on January 5, 2000, would not have been inconsistent with the purpose of section 704(c)(1)(B) and this section. In that situation, Property A would not have been distributed until after the expiration of the five-year period specified in section 704(c)(1)(B) and this section. Deferring the distribution of Property A until the end of the five-year period for a principal purpose of avoiding the recognition of gain under section

704(c)(1)(B) and this section is not inconsistent with the purpose of section 704(c)(1)(B). Therefore, A would not have recognized gain on the distribution of Property A in that case.

Example 2. Suspension of five-year period in manner consistent with the purpose of section 704(c)(1)(B). (i) A, B, and C form partnership ABC on January 1, 1995, to conduct bona fide business activities. A contributes Property A, nondepreciable real property with a fair market value of $10,000 and an adjusted tax basis of $1,000, in exchange for a 49.5 percent interest in partnership capital and profits. B contributes $10,000 in cash for a 49.5 percent interest in partnership capital and profits. C contributes cash for a 1 percent interest in partnership capital and profits. A and B are wholly owned subsidiaries of the same affiliated group and continue to control the management of Property A by virtue of their controlling interests in the partnership. The partnership is formed pursuant to a plan a principal purpose of which is to minimize the period of time that A would have to remain a partner with a potential acquiror of Property A.

(ii) On December 31, 1997, D is admitted as a partner to the partnership in exchange for $10,000 cash.

(iii) On January 5, 2000, Property A is distributed to D in complete liquidation of D's interest in the partnership.

(iv) The distribution of Property A to D occurred more than five years after the contribution of the property to the partnership. On these facts, however, a principal purpose of the transaction was to minimize the period of time that A would have to remain partners with a potential acquiror of Property A, and treating the five-year period of section 704(c)(1)(B) as running during a time when Property A was still effectively owned through the partnership by members of the contributing affiliated group of which A is a member is inconsistent with the purpose of section 704(c)(1)(B). Prior to the admission of D as a partner, the pooling of assets between A and B, on the one hand, and C, on the other hand, although sufficient to constitute ABC as a valid partnership for federal income tax purposes, is not a sufficient pooling of assets for purposes of running the five-year period with respect to the distribution of Property A to D. Allowing a contributing partner to avoid section 704(c)(1)(B) through arrangements such as those in this *Example 2* would have the effect of substantially nullifying the five-year requirement of section 704(c)(1)(B) and this section and elevating the form of the transaction over its substance. As a result, with respect to the distribution of Property A to D, the five-year period of section 704(c)(1)(B) is tolled until the

Reg. § 1.704-4(f)(2)

admission of D as a partner on December 31, 1997. Therefore, the distribution of Property A occurred before the end of the five-year period of section 704(c)(1)(B), and A recognizes gain of $9,000 under section 704(c)(1)(B) on the distribution.

* * *

[Reg. § 1.704-4.]

□ [*T.D. 8642, 12-22-95. Amended by T.D. 8717, 5-8-97.*]

§ 1.705-1. Determination of basis of partner's interest.—(a) *General rule*—(1) Section 705 and this section provide rules for determining the adjusted basis of a partner's interest in a partnership. A partner is required to determine the adjusted basis of his interest in a partnership only when necessary for the determination of his tax liability or that of any other person. The determination of the adjusted basis of a partnership interest is ordinarily made as of the end of a partnership taxable year. Thus, for example, such year-end determination is necessary in ascertaining the extent to which a partner's distributive share of partnership losses may be allowed. See section 704(d). However, where there has been a sale or exchange of all or a part of a partnership interest or a liquidation of a partner's entire interest in a partnership, the adjusted basis of the partner's interest should be determined as of the date of sale or exchange or liquidation. The adjusted basis of a partner's interest in a partnership is determined without regard to any amount shown in the partnership books as the partner's "capital", "equity", or similar account. For example, A contributes property with an adjusted basis to him of $400 (and a value of $1,000) to a partnership. B contributes $1,000 cash. While under their agreement each may have a "capital account" in the partnership of $1,000, the adjusted basis of A's interest is only $400 and B's interest $1,000.

(2) The original basis of a partner's interest in a partnership shall be determined under section 722 (relating to contributions to a partnership) or section 742 (relating to transfers of partnership interests). Such basis shall be increased under section 722 by any further contributions to the partnership and by the sum of the partner's distributive share for the taxable year and prior taxable years of—

(i) Taxable income of the partnership as determined under section 703(a),

(ii) Tax-exempt receipts of the partnership, and

(iii) The excess of the deductions for depletion over the basis of the depletable property, unless the property is an oil or gas property the basis of which has been allocated to partners under section 613A(c)(7)(D).

(3) The basis shall be decreased (but not below zero) by distributions from the partnership as provided in section 733 and by the sum of the partner's distributive share for the taxable year and prior taxable years of—

(i) Partnership losses (including capital losses), and

(ii) Partnership expenditures which are not deductible in computing partnership taxable income or loss and which are not capital expenditures.

(4) The basis shall be decreased (but not below zero) by the amount of the partner's deduction for depletion allowable under section 611 for any partnership oil and gas property to the extent the deduction does not exceed the proportionate share of the adjusted basis of the property allocated to the partner under section 613A(c)(7)(D).

(5) The basis shall be adjusted (but not below zero) to reflect any gain or loss to the partner resulting from a disposition by the partnership of a domestic oil or gas property after December 31, 1974.

(6) For the effect of liabilities in determining the amount of contributions made by a partner to a partnership or the amount of distributions made by a partnership to a partner, see section 752 and § 1.752-1, relating to the treatment of certain liabilities. In determining the basis of a partnership interest on the effective date of subchapter K, chapter 1 of the Code, or any of the sections thereof, the partner's share of partnership liabilities on that date shall be included.

(7) For basis adjustments necessary to coordinate sections 705 and 1032 in certain situations in which a partnership disposes of stock or any position in stock to which section 1032 applies of a corporation that holds a direct or indirect interest in the partnership, see § 1.705-2.

(b) *Alternative rule.* In certain cases, the adjusted basis of a partner's interest in a partnership may be determined by reference to the partner's share of the adjusted basis of partnership property which would be distributable upon termination of the partnership. The alternative rule may be used to determine the adjusted basis of a partner's interest where circumstances are such that the partner cannot practicably apply the general rule set forth in section 705(a) and paragraph (a) of this section, or where, from a consideration of all the facts, it is, in the opinion of the Commissioner, reasonable to conclude that the result produced will not vary substantially from the result obtainable under the general rule. Where the alternative rule is used, adjustments may be necessary in determining the adjusted basis of a partner's interest in a partnership. Adjustments would be required, for example, in order to reflect in a partner's share of the adjusted basis of partnership property any significant discrepancies arising as a result of contributed property, transfers of partnership interest, or distributions of property to the partners. The operation of the alternative rules may be illustrated by the following examples:

Example (1). The ABC partnership, in which A, B, and C are equal partners, owns various properties with a total adjusted basis of $1,500 and has earned and retained an additional $1,500. The total adjusted basis of partnership property is thus $3,000. Each partner's share in the adjusted basis of partnership property is one-third of this amount, or $1,000. Under the alternative rule, this amount represents each partner's adjusted basis for his partnership interest.

Example (2). Assume that partner A in example (1) of this paragraph sells his partnership interest to D for $1,250 at a time when the partnership property with an adjusted basis of $1,500 had appreciated in value to $3,000, and when the partnership also had $750 in cash. The total adjusted basis of all partnership property is $2,250 and the value of such property is $3,750. D's basis for his partnership interest is his cost, $1,250. However, his one-third share of the ad-

justed basis of partnership property is only $750. Therefore, for the purposes of the alternative rule, D has an adjustment of $500 in determining the basis of his interest. This amount represents the difference between the cost of his partnership interest and his share of partnership basis at the time of his purchase. If the partnership subsequently earns and retains an additional $1,500, its property will have an adjusted basis of $3,750. D's adjusted basis for his interest under the alternative rule is $1,750, determined by adding $500, his basis adjustment, to $1,250 (his one-third share of the $3,750 adjusted basis of partnership property). If the partnership distributes $250 to each partner in a current distribution, D's adjusted basis for his interest will be $1,500 ($1,000, his one-third share of the remaining basis of partnership property, $3,000, plus his basis adjustment of $500).

Example (3). Assume the BCD partnership in example (2) of this paragraph continues to operate. In 1960, D proposes to sell his partnership interest and wishes to evaluate the tax consequences of such sale. It is necessary, therefore, to determine the adjusted basis of his interest in the partnership. Assume further that D cannot determine the adjusted basis of his interest under the general rule. The balance sheet of the BCD partnership is as follows:

Assets	Adjusted Basis per Books	Market Value
Cash	$ 3,000	$ 3,000
Receivables	4,000	4,000
Depreciable Property	5,000	5,000
Land held for investment	18,000	30,000
Total	$30,000	$42,000

Liabilities and Capital	Per Books	
Liabilities	$ 6,000	
Capital Accounts: B	4,500	
C	4,500	
D	15,000	
Total	$30,000	

The $15,000 representing the amount of D's capital account does not reflect the $500 basis adjustment arising from D's purchase of his interest. See example (2) of this paragraph. The ad-

justed basis of D's partnership interest determined under the alternative rule is as follows:

D's share of the adjusted basis of partnership property (reduced by the amount of liabilities) at time of proposed sale	$15,000
D's share of partnership liabilities (under the partnership agreement liabilities are shared equally)	2,000
D's basis adjustment from example (2)	500
Adjusted basis of D's interest at the time of proposed sale, as determined under alternative rule	$17,500

[Reg. § 1.705-1.]

☐ [*T.D.* 6175, 5-23-56. *Amended by T.D.* 8437, 9-22-92; *T.D.* 8986, 3-28-2002 *and T.D.* 9049, 3-17-2003.]

Reg. § 1.705-1(b)

§ 1.705-2. **Basis adjustments coordinating sections 705 and 1032.**—(a) *Purpose.* This section coordinates the application of sections 705 and 1032 and is intended to prevent inappropriate increases or decreases in the adjusted basis of a corporate partner's interest in a partnership resulting from the partnership's disposition of the corporate partner's stock. The rules under section 705 generally are intended to preserve equality between the adjusted basis of a partner's interest in a partnership (outside basis) and such partner's share of the adjusted basis in partnership assets (inside basis). However, in situations where a section 754 election was not in effect for the year in which a partner acquired its interest, the partner's inside basis and outside basis may not be equal. Similarly, in situations where a section 754 election was not in effect for the year in which a partnership distributes money or other property to another partner and that partner recognizes gain or loss on the distribution or the basis of the property distributed to that partner is adjusted, the remaining partners' inside basis and outside basis may not be equal. In these situations, gain or loss allocated to the partner upon disposition of the partnership assets that is attributable to the difference between the adjusted basis of the partnership assets absent the section 754 election and the adjusted basis of the partnership assets had a section 754 election been in effect generally will result in an adjustment to the basis of the partner's interest in the partnership under section 705(a). Such gain (or loss) therefore generally will be offset by a corresponding decrease in the gain or increase in the loss (or increase in the gain or decrease in the loss) upon the subsequent disposition by the partner of its interest in the partnership. Where such a difference exists with respect to stock of a corporate partner that is held by the partnership, gain or loss from the disposition of corporate partner stock attributable to the difference is not recognized by the corporate partner under section 1032. To adjust the basis of the corporate partner's interest in the partnership for this unrecognized gain or loss would not be appropriate because it would create an opportunity for the recognition of taxable gain or loss on a subsequent disposition of the partnership interest where no economic gain or loss has been incurred by the corporate partner and no corresponding taxable gain or loss had previously been allocated to the corporate partner by the partnership.

(b) *Single partnership*—(1) *Required adjustments relating to acquisitions of partnership interest*—(i) This paragraph (b)(1) applies in situations where a corporation acquires an interest in a partnership that holds stock in that corporation (or the partnership subsequently acquires stock in that corporation in an exchanged basis transaction), the partnership does not have an election under section 754 in effect for the year in which the corporation acquires the interest, and the partnership later sells or exchanges the stock. In these situations, the increase (or decrease) in the corporation's adjusted basis in its partnership interest resulting from the sale or exchange of the stock equals the amount of gain (or loss) that the corporate partner would have recognized (absent the application of section 1032) if, for the year in which the corporation acquired the interest, a section 754 election had been in effect.

(ii) The provisions of this paragraph (b)(1) are illustrated by the following example:

Example. (i) A, B, and C form equal partnership PRS. Each partner contributes $30,000 in exchange for its partnership interest. PRS has no liabilities. PRS purchases stock in corporation X for $30,000, which appreciates in value to $120,000. PRS also purchases inventory for $60,000, which appreciates in value to $150,000. A sells its interest in PRS to corporation X for $90,000 in a year for which an election under section 754 is not in effect. PRS later sells the X stock for $150,000. PRS realizes a gain of $120,000 on the sale of the X stock. X's share of the gain is $40,000. Under section 1032, X does not recognize its share of the gain.

(ii) Normally, X would be entitled to a $40,000 increase in the basis of its PRS interest for its allocable share of PRS's gain from the sale of the X stock, but a special rule applies in this situation. If a section 754 election had been in effect for the year in which X acquired its interest in PRS, X would have been entitled to a basis adjustment under section 743(b) of $60,000 (the excess of X's basis for the transferred partnership interest over X's share of the adjusted basis to PRS of PRS's property). See § 1.743-1(b). Under § 1.755-1(b), the basis adjustment under section 743(b) would have been allocated $30,000 to the X stock (the amount of the gain that would have been allocated to X from the hypothetical sale of the stock), and $30,000 to the inventory (the amount of the gain that would have been allocated to X from the hypothetical sale of the inventory).

(iii) If a section 754 election had been in effect for the year in which X acquired its interest in PRS, the amount of gain that X would have recognized upon PRS's disposition of X stock (absent the application of section 1032) would be $10,000 (X's share of PRS's gain from the stock sale, $40,000, minus the amount of X's basis adjustment under section 743(b), $30,000). See § 1.743-1(j). Accordingly, the increase in the basis of X's interest in PRS is $10,000.

(2) *Required adjustments relating to distributions*—(i) This paragraph (b)(2) applies in situations where a corporation owns a direct or

indirect interest in a partnership that owns stock in that corporation, the partnership distributes money or other property to another partner and that partner recognizes gain or loss on the distribution or the basis of the property distributed to that partner is adjusted during a year in which the partnership does not have an election under section 754 in effect, and the partnership subsequently sells or exchanges the stock. In these situations, the increase (or decrease) in the corporation's adjusted basis in its partnership interest resulting from the sale or exchange of the stock equals the amount of gain (or loss) that the corporate partner would have recognized (absent the application of section 1032) if, for the year in which the partnership made the distribution, a section 754 election had been in effect.

(ii) The provisions of this paragraph (b)(2) are illustrated by the following example:

Example. (i) A, B, and corporation C form partnership PRS. A and B each contribute $10,000 and C contributes $20,000 in exchange for a partnership interest. PRS has no liabilities. PRS purchases stock in corporation C for $10,000, which appreciates in value to $70,000. PRS distributes $25,000 to A in complete liquidation of A's interest in PRS in a year for which an election under section 754 is not in effect. PRS later sells the C stock for $70,000. PRS realizes a gain of $60,000 on the sale of the C stock. C's share of the gain is $40,000. Under section 1032, C does not recognize its share of the gain.

(ii) Normally, C would be entitled to a $40,000 increase in the basis of its PRS interest for its allocable share of PRS's gain from the sale of the C stock, but a special rule applies in this situation. If a section 754 election had been in effect for the year in which PRS made the distribution to A, PRS would have been entitled to adjust the basis of partnership property under section 734(b)(1)(A) by $15,000 (the amount of gain recognized by A with respect to the distribution to A under section 731(a)(1)). See § 1.734-1(b). Under § 1.755-1(c)(1)(ii), the basis adjustment under section 734(b) would have been allocated to the C stock, increasing its basis to $25,000 (where there is a distribution resulting in an adjustment under section 734(b)(1)(A) to the basis of undistributed partnership property, the adjustment is allocated only to capital gain property).

(iii) If a section 754 election had been in effect for the year in which PRS made the distribution to A, the amount of gain that PRS would have recognized upon PRS's disposition of C stock

would be $45,000 ($70,000 minus $25,000 basis in the C stock), and the amount of gain C would have recognized upon PRS's disposition of the C stock (absent the application of section 1032) would be $30,000 (C's share of PRS's gain of $45,000 from the stock sale). Accordingly, upon PRS's sale of the C stock, the increase in the basis of C's interest in PRS is $30,000.

* * *

(d) *Positions in stock.* For purposes of this section, stock includes any position in stock to which section 1032 applies.

* * *

[Reg. § 1.705-2.]

☐ [*T.D.* 8986, 3-28-2002. *Amended by T.D.* 9049, 3-17-2003.]

§ 1.706-1. Taxable years of partner and partnership.—(a) *Year in which partnership income is includible*—(1) In computing taxable income for a taxable year, a partner is required to include the partner's distributive share of partnership items set forth in section 702 and the regulations thereunder for any partnership taxable year ending within or with the partner's taxable year. A partner must also include in taxable income for a taxable year guaranteed payments under section 707(c) that are deductible by the partnership under its method of accounting in the partnership taxable year ending within or with the partner's taxable year.

(2) The rules of this paragraph (a)(1) may be illustrated by the following example:

Example. Partner A reports income using a calendar year, while the partnership of which A is a member reports its income using a fiscal year ending May 31. The partnership reports its income and deductions under the cash method of accounting. During the partnership taxable year ending May 31, 2002, the partnership makes guaranteed payments of $120,000 to A for services and for the use of capital. Of this amount, $70,000 was paid to A between June 1 and December 31, 2001, and the remaining $50,000 was paid to A between January 1 and May 31, 2002. The entire $120,000 paid to A is includible in A's taxable income for the calendar year 2002 (together with A's distributive share of partnership items set forth in section 702 for the partnership taxable year ending May 31, 2002).

(3) If a partner receives distributions under section 731 or sells or exchanges all or part of a partnership interest, any gain or loss arising therefrom does not constitute partnership income.

(b) *Taxable year*—(1) *Partnership treated as a taxpayer.* The taxable year of a partnership must be determined as though the partnership were a taxpayer.

(2) *Partnership's taxable year*—(i) *Required taxable year.* Except as provided in paragraph (b)(2)(ii) of this section, the taxable year of a partnership must be—

(A) The majority interest taxable year, as defined in section 706(b)(4);

(B) If there is no majority interest taxable year, the taxable year of all of the principal partners of the partnership, as defined in 706(b)(3) (the principal partners' taxable year); or

(C) If there is no majority interest taxable year or principal partners' taxable year, the taxable year that produces the least aggregate deferral of income as determined under paragraph (b)(3) of this section.

(ii) *Exceptions.* A partnership may have a taxable year other than its required taxable year if it makes an election under section 444, elects to use a 52-53-week taxable year that ends with reference to its required taxable year or a taxable year elected under section 444, or establishes a business purpose for such taxable year and obtains approval of the Commissioner under section 442.

(3) *Least aggregate deferral*—(i) *Taxable year that results in the least aggregate deferral of income.* The taxable year that results in the least aggregate deferral of income will be the taxable year of one or more of the partners in the partnership which will result in the least aggregate deferral of income to the partners. The aggregate deferral for a particular year is equal to the sum of the products determined by multiplying the month(s) of deferral for each partner that would be generated by that year and each partner's interest in partnership profits for that year. The partner's taxable year that produces the lowest sum when compared to the other partner's taxable years is the taxable year that results in the least aggregate deferral of income to the partners. If the calculation results in more than one taxable year qualifying as the taxable year with the least aggregate deferral, the partnership may select any one of those taxable years as its taxable year. However, if one of the qualifying taxable years is also the partnership's existing taxable year, the partnership must maintain its existing taxable year. The determination of the taxable year that results in the least aggregate deferral of income generally must be made as of the beginning of the partnership's current taxable year. The director, however, may determine that the first day of the current taxable year is not the appropriate testing day and require the use of some other day or period that will more accurately reflect the ownership of the partnership and thereby the actual aggregate deferral to the partners where the partners engage in a transaction that has as its principal purpose the avoidance of the principles of this section. Thus, for example the preceding sentence would apply where there is a transfer of an interest in the partnership that results in a temporary transfer of that interest principally for purposes of qualifying for a specific taxable year under the principles of this section. For purposes of this section, deferral to each partner is measured in terms of months from the end of the partnership's taxable year forward to the end of the partner's taxable year.

* * *

(4) *Measurement of partner's profits and capital interest*—(i) *In general.* The rules of this paragraph (b)(4) apply in determining the majority interest taxable year, the principal partners' taxable year, and the least aggregate deferral taxable year.

(ii) *Profits interest*—(A) *In general.* For purposes of section 706(b), a partner's interest in partnership profits is generally the partner's percentage share of partnership profits for the current partnership taxable year. If the partnership does not expect to have net income for the current partnership taxable year, then a partner's interest in partnership profits instead must be the partner's percentage share of partnership net income for the first taxable year in which the partnership expects to have net income.

(B) *Percentage share of partnership net income.* The partner's percentage share of partnership net income for a partnership taxable year is the ratio of: the partner's distributive share of partnership net income for the taxable year, to the partnership's net income for the year. If a partner's percentage share of partnership net income for the taxable year depends on the amount or nature of partnership income for that year (due to, for example, preferred returns or special allocations of specific partnership items), then the partnership must make a reasonable estimate of the amount and nature of its income for the taxable year. This estimate must be based on all facts and circumstances known to the partnership as of the first day of the current partnership taxable year. The partnership must then use this estimate in determining the partners' interests in partnership profits for the taxable year.

(C) *Distributive share.* For purposes of this paragraph (b)(4)(ii), a partner's distributive share of partnership net income is determined by taking into account all rules and regulations affecting that determination, including, without

Reg. § 1.706-1(b)(4)

limitation, sections 704(b), (c), and (e), 736, and 743.

(iii) *Capital interest.* Generally, a partner's interest in partnership capital is determined by reference to the assets of the partnership that the partner would be entitled to upon withdrawal from the partnership or upon liquidation of the partnership. If the partnership maintains capital accounts in accordance with § 1.704-1(b)(2)(iv), then for purposes of section 706(b), the partnership may assume that a partner's interest in partnership capital is the ratio of the partner's capital account to all partners' capital accounts as of the first day of the partnership taxable year.

* * *

(c) *Closing of partnership year*—(1) *General rule.* Section 706(c) and this paragraph provide rules governing the closing of partnership years. The closing of a partnership taxable year or a termination of a partnership for Federal income tax purposes is not necessarily governed by the "dissolution", "liquidation", etc., of a partnership under State or local law. The taxable year of a partnership shall not close as the result of the death of a partner, the entry of a new partner, the liquidation of a partner's entire interest in the partnership (as defined in section 761(d)), or the sale or exchange of a partner's interest in the partnership, except in the case of a termination of a partnership and except as provided in subparagraph (2) of this paragraph. In the case of termination, the partnership taxable year closes for all partners as of the date of termination. See section 708(b) and paragraph (b) of § 1.708-1.

(2) *Partner who retires or sells interest in partnership*—(i) *Disposition of entire interest.* A partnership taxable year shall close with respect to a partner who sells or exchanges his entire interest in a partnership, and with respect to a partner whose entire interest is liquidated. However, a partnership taxable year with respect to a partner who dies shall not close prior to the end of such partnership taxable year, or the time when such partner's interest (held by his estate or other successor) is liquidated or sold or exchanged, whichever is earlier. See subparagraph (3) of this paragraph.

(ii) *Inclusions in taxable income.* In the case of a sale, exchange, or liquidation of a partner's entire interest in a partnership, the partner shall include in his taxable income for his taxable year within or with which his membership in the partnership ends, his distributive share of items described in section 702(a), and any guaranteed payments under section 707(c), for his partnership taxable year ending with the date of such sale, exchange, or liquidation. In order to avoid an interim closing of the partnership books, such

partner's distributive share of items described in section 702(a) may, by agreement among the partners, be estimated by taking his pro rata part of the amount of such items he would have included in his taxable income had he remained a partner until the end of the partnership taxable year. The proration may be based on the portion of the taxable year that has elapsed prior to the sale, exchange, or liquidation, or may be determined under any other method that is reasonable. Any partner who is the transferee of such partner's interest shall include in his taxable income, as his distributive share of items described in section 702(a) with respect to the acquired interest, the pro rata part (determined by the method used by the transferor partner) of the amount of such items he would have included had he been a partner from the beginning of the taxable year of the partnership. The application of this subdivision may be illustrated by the following example:

Example. Assume that a partner selling his partnership interest on June 30, 1955, has an adjusted basis for his interest of $5,000 on that date; that his pro rata share of partnership income up to June 30 is $15,000; and that he sells his interest for $20,000. Under the provisions of section 706(c)(2), the partnership year with respect to him closes at the time of the sale. The $15,000 is includible in his income as his distributive share and, under section 705, it increases the basis of his partnership interest to $20,000, which is also the selling price of his interest. Therefore, no gain is realized on the sale of his partnership interest. The purchaser of this partnership interest shall include in his income as his distributive share his pro rata part of partnership income for the remainder of the partnership taxable year.

(3) *Partner who dies.* (i) When a partner dies, the partnership taxable year shall not close with respect to such partner prior to the end of the partnership taxable year. The partnership taxable year shall continue both for the remaining partners and the decedent partner. Where the death of a partner results in the termination of the partnership, the partnership taxable year shall close for all partners on the date of such termination under section 708(b)(1)(A). See also paragraph (b)(1)(i)(*b*) of § 1.708-1 for the continuation of a 2-member partnership under certain circumstances after the death of a partner. However, if the decedent partner's estate or other successor sells or exchanges its entire interest in the partnership, or if its entire interest is liquidated, the partnership taxable year with respect to the estate or other successor in interest shall close on the date of such sale or exchange, or the date of completion of the liquidation.

(ii) The last return of a decedent partner shall include only his share of partnership taxable

Reg. § 1.706-1(c)(1)

income for any partnership taxable year or years ending within or with the last taxable year for such decedent partner (i.e., the year ending with the date of his death). The distributive share of partnership taxable income for a partnership taxable year ending after the decedent's last taxable year is includible in the return of his estate or other successor in interest. If the estate or other successor in interest of a partner continues to share in the profits or losses of the partnership business, the distributive share thereof is includible in the taxable year of the estate or other successor in interest within or with which the taxable year of the partnership ends. See also paragraph (a)(1)(ii) of § 1.736-1. Where the estate or other successor in interest receives distributions, any gain or loss on such distributions is includible in its gross income for its taxable year in which the distribution is made.

(iii) If a partner (or a retiring partner), in accordance with the terms of the partnership agreement, designates a person to succeed to his interest in the partnership after his death, such designated person shall be regarded as a successor in interest of the deceased for purposes of this chapter. Thus, where a partner designates his widow as the successor in interest, her distributive share of income for the taxable year of the partnership ending within or with her taxable year may be included in a joint return in accordance with the provisions of sections 2 and 6013(a)(2) and (3).

(iv) If, under the terms of an agreement existing at the date of death of a partner, a sale or exchange of the decedent partner's interest in the partnership occurs upon that date, then the taxable year of the partnership with respect to such decedent partner shall close upon the date of death. See section 706(c)(2)(A)(i). The sale or exchange of a partnership interest does not, for the purpose of this rule, include any transfer of a partnership interest which occurs at death as a result of inheritance or any testamentary disposition.

(v) To the extent that any part of a distributive share of partnership income of the estate or other successor in interest of a deceased partner is attributable to the decedent for the period ending with the date of his death, such part of the distributive share is income in respect of the decedent under section 691. See section 691 and the regulations thereunder.

(vi) The provisions of this subparagraph may be illustrated by the following examples:

Example (1). B has a taxable year ending December 31 and is a member of partnership ABC, the taxable year of which ends on June 30. B dies on October 31, 1955. His estate (which as a new taxpayer may, under section 441 and the regulations thereunder, adopt any taxable year) adopts a taxable year ending October 31. The return of the decedent for the period January 1 to October 31, 1955, will include only his distributive share of taxable income of the partnership for its taxable year ending June 30, 1955. The distributive share of taxable income of the partnership for its taxable year ending June 30, 1956, arising from the interest of the decedent, will be includible in the return of the estate for its taxable year ending October 31, 1956. That part of the distributive share attributable to the decedent for the period ending with the date of his death (July 1 through October 31, 1955) is income in respect of a decedent under section 691.

Example (2). Assume the same facts as in example (1) of this subdivision, except that, prior to B's death, B and D had agreed that, upon B's death, D would purchase B's interest for $10,000. When B dies on October 31, 1955, the partnership taxable year beginning July 1, 1955, closes with respect to him. Therefore, the return for B's last taxable year (January 1 to October 31, 1955) will include his distributive share of taxable income of the partnership for its taxable year ending June 30, 1955, plus his distributive share of partnership taxable income for the period July 1 to October 31, 1955. See subdivision (iv) of this subparagraph.

Example (3). H is a member of a partnership having a taxable year ending December 31. Both H and his wife W are on a calendar year and file joint returns. H dies on March 31, 1955. Administration of the estate is completed and the estate, including the partnership interest, is distributed to W as legatee on November 30, 1955. Such distribution by the estate is not a sale or exchange of H's partnership interest. No part of the taxable income of the partnership for the taxable year ending December 31, 1955, which is allocable to H, will be included in H's taxable income for his last taxable year (January 1 through March 31, 1955) or in the taxable income of H's estate for the taxable year April 1 through November 30, 1955. The distributive share of partnership taxable income for the full calendar year that is allocable to H will be includible in the taxable income of W for her taxable year ending December 31, 1955, and she may file a joint return under sections 2 and 6013(a)(3). That part of the distributive share attributable to the decedent for the period ending with the date of his death (January 1 through March 31, 1955) is income in respect of the decedent under section 691.

Example (4). M is a member of partnership JKM which operates on a calendar year. M and his wife S file joint returns for calendar years.

In accordance with the partnership agreement, M designated S to succeed to his interest in the partnership upon his death. M, who had withdrawn $10,000 from the partnership before his death, dies on October 20, 1955. S's distributive share of income for the taxable year 1955 is $15,000 ($10,000 of which represents the amount withdrawn by M). S shall include $15,000 in her income, even though M received $10,000 of this amount before his death. S may file a joint return with M for the year 1955 under sections 2 and 6013(a). That part of the $15,000 distributive share attributable to the decedent for the period ending with the date of his death (January 1 through October 20, 1955) is income in respect of a decedent under section 691.

(4) *Disposition of less than entire interest.* If a partner sells or exchanges a part of his interest in a partnership, or if the interest of a partner is reduced, the partnership taxable year shall continue to its normal end. In such case, the partner's distributive share of items which he is required to include in his taxable income under the provisions of section 702(a) shall be determined by taking into account his varying interests in the partnership during the partnership taxable year in which such sale, exchange, or reduction of interest occurred.

(5) *Transfer of interest by gift.* The transfer of a partnership interest by gift does not close the partnership taxable year with respect to the donor. However, the income up to the date of gift attributable to the donor's interest shall be allocated to him under section 704(e)(2).

* * *

[Reg. § 1.706-1.]

☐ [*T.D.* 6175, 5-23-56. *Amended by T.D.* 7286, 9-26-73; *T.D.* 8123, 2-4-87; *T.D.* 8996, 5-16-2002 and *T.D.* 9009, 7-22-2002.]

[*Caution: Reg.* § 1.707-1 *does not reflect changes made by the Tax Reform Act of 1986 lowering the percentage in Section 707(b)(2) from 80% to 50%.*]

§ 1.707-1. **Transactions between partner and partnership**—(a) *Partner not acting in capacity as partner.* A partner who engages in a transaction with a partnership other than in his capacity as a partner shall be treated as if he were not a member of the partnership with respect to such transaction. Such transactions include, for example, loans of money or property by the partnership to the partner or by the partner to the partnership, the sale of property by the partner to the partnership, the purchase of property by the partner from the partnership, and the rendering of services by the partnership to the partner or by the partner to the partnership. Where a partner retains the ownership of property but allows the

partnership to use such separately owned property for partnership purposes (for example, to obtain credit or to secure firm creditors by guaranty, pledge, or other agreement) the transaction is treated as one between a partnership and a partner not acting in his capacity as a partner. However, transfers of money or property by a partner to a partnership as contributions, or transfers of money or property by a partnership to a partner as distributions, are not transactions included within the provisions of this section. In all cases, the substance of the transaction will govern rather than its form. See paragraph (c)(3) of § 1.731-1.

(b) *Certain sales or exchanges of property with respect to controlled partnerships*—(1) *Losses disallowed.* (i) No deduction shall be allowed for a loss on a sale or exchange of property (other than an interest in the partnership), directly or indirectly, between a partnership and a partner who owns, directly or indirectly, more than 50 percent of the capital interest or profits interest in such partnership. A loss on a sale or exchange of property, directly or indirectly, between two partnerships in which the same persons own, directly or indirectly, more than 50 percent of the capital interest or profits interests in each partnership shall not be allowed.

(ii) If a gain is realized upon the subsequent sale or exchange by transferee of property with respect to which a loss was disallowed under the provisions of subdivision (i) of this subparagraph, section 267(d) (relating to amount of gain where loss previously disallowed) shall apply as though the loss were disallowed under section 267(a)(1).

(2) *Gains treated as ordinary income.* Any gain recognized upon the sale or exchange, directly or indirectly, of property which, in the hands of the transferee immediately after the transfer, is property other than a capital asset, as defined in section 1221, shall be ordinary income if the transaction is between a partnership and a partner who owns, directly or indirectly, more than 80 percent of the capital interest or profits interest in the partnership. This rule also applies where such a transaction is between partnerships in which the same persons own, directly or indirectly, more than 80 percent of the capital interests or profits interests in each partnership. The term "property other than a capital asset" includes (but is not limited to) trade accounts receivable, inventory, stock in trade, and depreciable or real property used in the trade or business.

(3) *Ownership of a capital or profits interest.* In determining the extent of the ownership by a partner, as defined in section 761(b), of his capital

interest or profits interest in a partnership, the rules for constructive ownership of stock provided in section 267(c)(1), (2), (4), and (5) shall be applied for the purpose of section 707(b) and this paragraph. Under these rules, ownership of a capital or profits interest in a partnership may be attributed to a person who is not a partner as defined in section 761(b) in order that another partner may be considered the constructive owner of such interest under section 267(c). However, section 707(b)(1)(A) does not apply to a constructive owner of a partnership interest since he is not a partner as defined in section 761(b). For example, where trust T is a partner in the partnership ABT, and AW, A's wife, is the sole beneficiary of the trust, the ownership of a capital and profits interest in the partnership by T will be attributed to AW only for the purpose of further attributing the ownership of such interest to A. See section 267(c)(1) and (5). If A, B, and T are equal partners, then A will be considered as owning more than 50 percent of the capital and profits interest in the partnership, and losses on transactions between him and the partnership will be disallowed by section 707(b)(1)(A). However, a loss sustained by AW on a sale or exchange of property with the partnership would not be disallowed by section 707, but will be disallowed to the extent provided in paragraph (b) of § 1.267(b)-1. See section 267(a) and (b), and the regulations thereunder.

(c) *Guaranteed payments.* Payments made by a partnership to a partner for services or for the use of capital are considered as made to a person who is not a partner, to the extent such payments are determined without regard to the income of the partnership. However, a partner must include such payments as ordinary income for his taxable year within or with which ends the partnership taxable year in which the partnership deducted such payments as paid or accrued under its method of accounting. See section 706(a) and paragraph (a) of § 1.706-1. Guaranteed payments are considered as made to one who is not a member of the partnership, only for the purposes of section 61(a) (relating to gross income) and section 162(a) (relating to trade or business expenses). For a guaranteed payment to be a partnership deduction, it must meet the same tests under section 162(a) as it would if the payment had been made to a person who is not a member of the partnership, and the rules of section 263 (relating to capital expenditures) must be taken into account. This rule does not affect the deductibility to the partnership of a payment described in section 736(a)(2) to a retiring partner or to a deceased partner's successor in interest. Guaranteed payments do not constitute an interest in partnership profits for purposes of sections 706(b)(3), 707(b), and 708(b). For the purposes of other provisions of the internal revenue laws, guaranteed payments are regarded as a partner's distributive share of ordinary income. Thus, a partner who receives guaranteed payments for a period during which he is absent from work because of personal injuries or sickness is not entitled to exclude such payments from his gross income under section 105(d). Similarly, a partner who receives guaranteed payments is not regarded as an employee of the partnership for the purposes of withholding of tax at source, deferred compensation plans, etc. The provisions of this paragraph may be illustrated by the following examples:

Example (1). Under the ABC partnership agreement, partner A is entitled to a fixed annual payment of $10,000 for services, without regard to the income of the partnership. His distributive share is 10 percent. After deducting the guaranteed payment, the partnership has $50,000 ordinary income. A must include $15,000 as ordinary income for his taxable year within or with which the partnership taxable year ends ($10,000 guaranteed payment plus $5,000 distributive share).

Example (2). Partner C in the CD partnership is to receive 30 percent of partnership income as determined before taking into account any guaranteed payments, but not less than $10,000. The income of the partnership is $60,000, and C is entitled to $18,000 (30 percent of $60,000) as his distributive share. No part of this amount is a guaranteed payment. However, if the partnership had income of $20,000 instead of $60,000, $6,000 (30 percent of $20,000) would be partner C's distributive share, and the remaining $4,000 payable to C would be a guaranteed payment.

Example (3). Partner X in the XY partnership is to receive a payment of $10,000 for services, plus 30 percent of the taxable income or loss of the partnership. After deducting the payment of $10,000 to partner X, the XY partnership has a loss of $9,000. Of this amount, $2,700 (30 percent of the loss) is X's distributive share of partnership loss and, subject to section 704(d), is to be taken into account by him in his return. In addition, he must report as ordinary income the guaranteed payment of $10,000 made to him by the partnership.

Example (4). Assume the same facts as in example (3) of this paragraph except that, instead of a $9,000 loss, the partnership has $30,000 in capital gains and no other items of income or deduction except the $10,000 paid X as a guaranteed payment. Since the items of partnership income or loss must be segregated under section 702(a), the partnership has a $10,000 ordinary loss and $30,000 in capital gains. X's 30 percent distributive shares of these amounts are $3,000 ordinary loss and $9,000 capital gain. In addition,

Reg. § 1.707-1(c)

X has received a $10,000 guaranteed payment which is ordinary income to him. [Reg. § 1.707-1.]

☐ [*T.D. 6175, 5-23-56. Amended by T.D. 6312, 9-10-58 and T.D. 7891, 5-3-83.*]

§ 1.707-3. Disguised sales of property to partnership; general rules.—(a) *Treatment of transfers as a sale*—(1) *In general.* Except as otherwise provided in this section, if a transfer of property by a partner to a partnership and one or more transfers of money or other consideration by the partnership to that partner are described in paragraph (b)(1) of this section, the transfers are treated as a sale of property, in whole or in part, to the partnership.

(2) *Definition and timing of sale.* For purposes of § § 1.707-3 through 1.707-5, the use of the term *sale* (or any variation of that word) to refer to a transfer of property by a partner to a partnership and a transfer of consideration by a partnership to a partner means a sale or exchange of that property, in whole or in part, to the partnership by the partner acting in a capacity other than as a member of the partnership, rather than a contribution and distribution to which sections 721 and 731, respectively, apply. A transfer that is treated as a sale under paragraph (a)(1) of this section is treated as a sale for all purposes of the Internal Revenue Code (*e.g.,* sections 453, 483, 1001, 1012, 1031 and 1274). The sale is considered to take place on the date that, under general principles of Federal tax law, the partnership is considered the owner of the property. If the transfer of money or other consideration from the partnership to the partner occurs after the transfer of property to the partnership, the partner and the partnership are treated as if, on the date of the sale, the partnership transferred to the partner an obligation to transfer to the partner money or other consideration.

(3) *Application of disguised sale rules.* If a person purports to transfer property to a partnership in a capacity as a partner, the rules of this section apply for purposes of determining whether the property was transferred in a disguised sale, even if it is determined after the application of the rules of this section that such person is not a partner. If after the application of the rules of this section to a purported transfer of property to a partnership, it is determined that no partnership exists because the property was actually sold, or it is otherwise determined that the contributed property is not owned by the partnership for tax purposes, the transferor of the property is treated as having sold the property to the person (or persons) that acquired ownership of the property for tax purposes.

(4) *Deemed terminations under section 708.* In applying the rules of this section, transfers resulting from a termination of a partnership under section 708(b)(1)(B) are disregarded.

(b) *Transfers treated as a sale*—(1) *In general.* A transfer of property (excluding money or an obligation to contribute money) by a partner to a partnership and a transfer of money or other consideration (including the assumption of or the taking subject to a liability) by the partnership to the partner constitute a sale of property, in whole or in part, by the partner to the partnership only if based on all the facts and circumstances—

(i) The transfer of money or other consideration would not have been made but for the transfer of property; and

(ii) In cases in which the transfers are not made simultaneously, the subsequent transfer is not dependent on the entrepreneurial risks of partnership operations.

(2) *Facts and circumstances.* The determination of whether a transfer of property by a partner to the partnership and a transfer of money or other consideration by the partnership to the partner constitute a sale, in whole or in part, under paragraph (b)(1) of this section is made based on all the facts and circumstances in each case. The weight to be given each of the facts and circumstances will depend on the particular case. Generally, the facts and circumstances existing on the date of the earliest of such transfers are the ones considered in determining whether a sale exists under paragraph (b)(1) of this section. Among the facts and circumstances that may tend to prove the existence of a sale under paragraph (b)(1) of this section are the following:

(i) That the timing and amount of a subsequent transfer are determinable with reasonable certainty at the time of an earlier transfer;

(ii) That the transferor has a legally enforceable right to the subsequent transfer;

(iii) That the partner's right to receive the transfer of money or other consideration is secured in any manner, taking into account the period during which it is secured;

(iv) That any person has made or is legally obligated to make contributions to the partnership in order to permit the partnership to make the transfer of money or other consideration;

(v) That any person has loaned or has agreed to loan the partnership the money or other consideration required to enable the partnership to make the transfer, taking into account whether any such lending obligation is subject to contingencies related to the results of partnership operations;

(vi) That the partnership has incurred or is obligated to incur debt to acquire the money or other consideration necessary to permit it to make

Reg. § 1.707-3(a)(1)

the transfer, taking into account the likelihood that the partnership will be able to incur that debt (considering such factors as whether any person has agreed to guarantee or otherwise assume personal liability for that debt);

(vii) That the partnership holds money or other liquid assets, beyond the reasonable needs of the business, that are expected to be available to make the transfer (taking into account the income that will be earned from those assets);

(viii) That partnership distributions, allocations or control of partnership operations is designed to effect an exchange of the burdens and benefits of ownership of property;

(ix) That the transfer of money or other consideration by the partnership to the partner is disproportionately large in relationship to the partner's general and continuing interest in partnership profits; and

(x) That the partner has no obligation to return or repay the money or other consideration to the partnership, or has such an obligation but it is likely to become due at such a distant point in the future that the present value of that obligation is small in relation to the amount of money or other consideration transferred by the partnership to the partner.

(c) *Transfers made within two years presumed to be a sale*—(1) *In general.* For purposes of this section, if within a two-year period a partner transfers property to a partnership and the partnership transfers money or other consideration to the partner (without regard to the order of the transfers), the transfers are presumed to be a sale of the property to the partnership unless the facts and circumstances clearly establish that the transfers do not constitute a sale.

(2) *Disclosure of transfers made within two years.* Disclosure to the Internal Revenue Service in accordance with § 1.707-8 is required if—

(i) A partner transfers property to a partnership and the partnership transfers money or other consideration to the partner within a two-year period (without regard to the order of the transfers);

(ii) The partner treats the transfers other than as a sale for tax purposes; and

(iii) The transfer of money or other consideration to the partner is not presumed to be a guaranteed payment for capital under § 1.707-4(a)(1)(ii), is not a reasonable preferred return within the meaning of § 1.707-4(a)(3), and is not an operating cash flow distribution within the meaning of § 1.707-4(b)(2).

(d) *Transfers made more than two years apart presumed not to be a sale.* For purposes of this section, if a transfer of money or other considera-

tion to a partner by a partnership and the transfer of property to the partnership by that partner are more than two years apart, the transfers are presumed not to be a sale of the property to the partnership unless the facts and circumstances clearly establish that the transfers constitute a sale.

(e) *Scope.* This section and §§ 1.707-4 through 1.707-9 apply to contributions and distributions of property described in section 707(a)(2)(A) and transfers described in section 707(a)(2)(B) of the Internal Revenue Code.

(f) *Examples.* The following examples illustrate the application of this section.

Example 1. Treatment of simultaneous transfers as a sale. A transfers property X to partnership AB on April 9, 1992, in exchange for an interest in the partnership. At the time of the transfer, property X has a fair market value of $4,000,000 and an adjusted tax basis of $1,200,000. Immediately after the transfer, the partnership transfers $3,000,000 in cash to A. Assume that, under this section, the partnership's transfer of cash to A is treated as part of a sale of property X to the partnership. Because the amount of cash A receives on April 9, 1992, does not equal the fair market value of the property, A is considered to have sold a portion of property X with a value of $3,000,000 to the partnership in exchange for the cash. Accordingly, A must recognize $2,100,000 of gain ($3,000,000 amount realized less $900,000 adjusted tax basis ($1,200,000 multiplied by $3,000,000/$4,000,000)). Assuming A receives no other transfers that are treated as consideration for the sale of the property under this section, A is considered to have contributed to the partnership, in A's capacity as a partner, $1,000,000 of the fair market value of the property with an adjusted tax basis of $300,000.

Example 2. Treatment of transfers at different times as a sale. (i) The facts are the same as in *Example 1*, except that the $3,000,000 is transferred to A one year after A's transfer of property X to the partnership. Assume that under this section the partnership's transfer of cash to A is treated as part of a sale of property X to the partnership. Assume also that the applicable Federal short-term rate for April, 1992, is 10 percent, compounded semiannually.

(ii) Under paragraph (a)(2) of this section, A and the partnership are treated as if, on April 9, 1992, A sold a portion of property X to the partnership in exchange for an obligation to transfer $3,000,000 to A one year later. Section 1274 applies to this obligation because it does not bear interest and is payable more than six months after the date of the sale. As a result, A's amount realized from the receipt of the partnership's obli-

Reg. § 1.707-3(f)

gation will be the imputed principal amount of the partnership's obligation to transfer $3,000,000 to A, which equals $2,721,088 (the present value on April 9, 1992, of a $3,000,000 payment due one year later, determined using a discount rate of 10 percent, compounded semiannually). Therefore, A's amount realized from the receipt of the partnership's obligation is $2,721,088 (without regard to whether the sale is reported under the installment method). A is therefore considered to have sold only $2,721,088 of the fair market value of property X. The remainder of the $3,000,000 payment ($278,912) is characterized in accordance with the provisions of section 1272. Accordingly, A must recognize $1,904,761 of gain ($2,721,088 amount realized less $816,327 adjusted tax basis ($1,200,000 multiplied by $2,721,088/$4,000,000)) on the sale of property X to the partnership. The gain is reportable under the installment method of section 453 if the sale is otherwise eligible. Assuming A receives no other transfers that are treated as consideration for the sale of property under this section, A is considered to have contributed to the partnership, in A's capacity as a partner, $1,278,912 of the fair market value of property X with an adjusted tax basis of $383,673.

Example 3. Operation of presumption for transfers within two years. (i) C transfers undeveloped land to the CD partnership in exchange for an interest in the partnership. The partnership intends to construct a building on the land. At the time the land is transferred to the partnership, it is unencumbered and has an adjusted tax basis of $500,000 and a fair market value of $1,000,000. The partnership agreement provides that upon completing construction of the building the partnership will distribute $900,000 to C.

(ii) If, within two years of C's transfer of land to the partnership, a transfer is made to C pursuant to the provision requiring a distribution upon completion of the building, the transfer is presumed to be, under paragraph (c) of this section, part of a sale of the land to the partnership. C may rebut the presumption that the transfer is part of a sale if the facts and circumstances clearly establish that—

(A) The transfer to C would have been made without regard to C's transfer of land to the partnership; or

(B) The partnership's obligation or ability to make this transfer to C depends, at the time of the transfer to the partnership, on the entrepreneurial risks of partnership operations.

(iii) For example, if the partnership will be able to fund the transfer of cash to C only to the extent that permanent loan proceeds exceed the cost of constructing the building, the fact that excess permanent loan proceeds will be available only if the cost to complete the building is significantly less than the amount projected by a reasonable budget would be evidence that the transfer to C is not part of a sale. Similarly, a condition that limits the amount of the permanent loan to the cost of constructing the building (and thereby limits the partnership's ability to make a transfer to C) unless all or a substantial portion of the building is leased would be evidence that the transfer to C is not part of a sale, if a significant risk exists that the partnership may not be able to lease the building to that extent. Another factor that may prove that the transfer of cash to C is not part of a sale would be that, at the time the land is transferred to the partnership, no lender has committed to make a permanent loan to fund the transfer of cash to C.

(iv) Facts indicating that the transfer of cash to C is not part of a sale, however, may be offset by other factors. An offsetting factor to restrictions on the permanent loan proceeds may be that the permanent loan is to be a recourse loan and certain conditions to the loan are likely to be waived by the lender because of the creditworthiness of the partners or the value of the partnership's other assets. Similarly, the factor that no lender has committed to fund the transfer of cash to C may be offset by facts establishing that the partnership is obligated to attempt to obtain such a loan and that its ability to obtain such a loan is not significantly dependent on the value that will be added by successful completion of the building, or that the partnership reasonably anticipates that it will have (and will utilize) an alternative source to fund the transfer of cash to C if the permanent loan proceeds are inadequate.

Example 4. Operation of presumption for transfers within two years. E is a partner in the equal EF partnership. The partnership owns two parcels of unimproved real property (*parcels 1 and 2*). Parcels 1 and 2 are unencumbered. Parcel 1 has a fair market value of $500,000, and parcel 2 has a fair market value of $1,500,000. E transfers additional unencumbered, unimproved real property (*parcel 3*) with a fair market value of $1,000,000 to the partnership in exchange for an increased interest in partnership profits of $66\frac{2}{3}$ percent. Immediately after this transfer, the partnership sells parcel 1 for $500,000 in a transaction not in the ordinary course of business. The partnership transfers the proceeds of the sale $333,333 to E and $166,667 to F in accordance with their respective partnership interests. The transfer of $333,333 to E is presumed to be, in accordance with paragraph (c) of this section, a sale, in part, of parcel 3 to the partnership. However, the facts of this example clearly establish that $250,000 of the transfer to E is not part of a sale of parcel 3 to

Reg. § 1.707-3(f)

the partnership because E would have been distributed $250,000 from the sale of parcel 1 whether or not E had transferred parcel 3 to the partnership. The transfer to E exceeds by $83,333 ($333,333 minus $250,000) the amount of the distribution that would have been made to E if E had not transferred parcel 3 to the partnership. Therefore, $83,333 of the transfer is presumed to be part of a sale of a portion of parcel 3 to the partnership by E.

Example 5. Operation of presumption for transfers more than two years apart. (i) G transfers undeveloped land to the GH partnership in exchange for an interest in the partnership. At the time the land is transferred to the partnership, it is unencumbered and has an adjusted tax basis of $500,000 and a fair market value of $1,000,000. H contributes $1,000,000 in cash in exchange for an interest in the partnership. Under the partnership agreement, the partnership is obligated to construct a building on the land. The projected construction cost is $5,000,000, which the partnership plans to fund with its $1,000,000 in cash and the proceeds of a construction loan secured by the land and improvements.

(ii) Shortly before G's transfer of the land to the partnership, the partnership secures commitments from lending institutions for construction and permanent financing. To obtain the construction loan, H guarantees completion of the building for a cost of $5,000,000. The partnership is not obligated to reimburse or indemnify H if H must make payment on the completion guarantee. The permanent loan will be funded upon completion of the building, which is expected to occur two years after G's transfer of the land. The amount of the permanent loan is to equal the lesser of $5,000,000 or 80 percent of the appraised value of the improved property at the time the permanent loan is closed. Under the partnership agreement, the partnership is obligated to apply the proceeds of the permanent loan to retire the construction loan and to hold any excess proceeds for transfer to G 25 months after G's transfer of the land to the partnership. The appraised value of the improved property at the time the permanent loan is closed is expected to exceed $5,000,000 only if the partnership is able to lease a substantial portion of the improvements by that time, and there is a significant risk that the partnership will not be able to achieve a satisfactory occupancy level. The partnership completes construction of the building for the projected cost of $5,000,000 approximately two years after G's transfer of the land. Shortly thereafter, the permanent loan is funded in the amount of $5,000,000. At the time of funding the land and building have an appraised value of $7,000,000. The partnership transfers the $1,000,000 excess permanent loan

proceeds to G 25 months after G's transfer of the land to the partnership.

(iii) G's transfer of the land to the partnership and the partnership's transfer of $1,000,000 to G occurred more than two years apart. In accordance with paragraph (d) of this section, those transfers are presumed not to be a sale unless the facts and circumstances clearly establish that the transfers constitute a sale of the property, in whole or part, to the partnership. The transfer of $1,000,000 to G would not have been made but for G's transfer of the land to the partnership. In addition, at the time G transferred the land to the partnership, G had a legally enforceable right to receive a transfer from the partnership at a specified time an amount that equals the excess of the permanent loan proceeds over $4,000,000. In this case, however, there was a significant risk that the appraised value of the property would be insufficient to support a permanent loan in excess of $4,000,000 because of the risk that the partnership would not be able to achieve a sufficient occupancy level. Therefore, the facts of this example indicate that at the time G transferred the land to the partnership the subsequent transfer of $1,000,000 to G depended on the entrepreneurial risks of partnership operations. Accordingly, G's transfer of the land to the partnership is not treated as part of a sale.

Example 6. Rebuttal of presumption for transfers more than two years apart. The facts are the same as in *Example 5*, except that the partnership is able to secure a commitment for a permanent loan in the amount of $5,000,000 without regard to the appraised value of the improved property at the time the permanent loan is funded. Under these facts, at the time that G transferred the land to the partnership the subsequent transfer of $1,000,000 to G was not dependent on the entrepreneurial risks of partnership operations, because during the period before the permanent loan is funded, the permanent lender's obligation to make a loan in the amount necessary to fund the transfer is not subject to contingencies related to the risks of partnership operations, and after the permanent loan is funded, the partnership holds liquid assets sufficient to make the transfer. Therefore, the facts and circumstances clearly establish that G's transfer of the land to the partnership is part of a sale.

Example 7. Operation of presumption for transfers more than two years apart. The facts are the same as in *Example 6*, except that H does not guarantee either that the improvements will be completed or that the cost to the partnership of completing the improvements will not exceed $5,000,000. Under these facts, if there is a significant risk that the improvements will not be completed, G's transfer of the land to the partnership

Reg. § 1.707-3(f)

will not be treated as part of a sale because the lender is not required to make the permanent loan if the improvements are not completed. Similarly, the transfers will not be treated as a sale to the extent that there is a significant risk that the cost of constructing the improvements will exceed $5,000,000, because, in the absence of a guarantee of the cost of the improvements by H, the $5,000,000 proceeds of the permanent loan might not be sufficient to retire the construction loan and fund the transfer to G. In either case, the transfer of cash to G would be dependent on the entrepreneurial risks of partnership operations.

Example 8. Rebuttal of presumption for transfers more than two years apart. (i) On February 1, 1992, I, J, and K form partnership IJK. On formation of the partnership, I transfers an unencumbered office building with a fair market value of $50,000,000 and an adjusted tax basis of $20,000,000 to the partnership, and J and K each transfer United States government securities with a fair market value and an adjusted tax basis of $25,000,000 to the partnership. Substantially all of the rentable space in the office building is leased on a long-term basis. The partnership agreement provides that all items of income, gain, loss, and deduction from the office building are to be allocated 45 percent to J, 45 percent to K, and 10 percent to I. The partnership agreement also provides that all items of income, gain, loss, and deduction from the government securities are to be allocated 90 percent to I, 5 percent to J, and 5 percent to K. The partnership agreement requires that cash flow from the office building and government securities be allocated between partners in the same manner as the items of income, gain, loss, and deduction from those properties are allocated between them. The partnership agreement complies with the requirements of § 1.704-1(b)(2)(ii)(*b*) It is not expected that the partnership will need to resort to the government securities or the cash flow therefrom to operate the office building. At the time the partnership is formed, I, J, and K contemplated that I's interest in the partnership would be liquidated sometime after January 31, 1994, in exchange for a transfer of the government securities and cash (if necessary). On March 1, 1995, the partnership transfers cash and the government securities to I in liquidation of I's interest in the partnership. The cash transferred to I represents the excess of I's share of the appreciation in the office building since the formation of the partnership over J's and K's share of the appreciation in the government securities since they were acquired by the partnership.

(ii) I's transfer of the office building to the partnership and the partnership's transfer of the government securities and cash to I occurred more than two years apart. Therefore, those transfers are presumed not to be a sale unless the facts and circumstances clearly establish that the transfers constitute a sale. Absent I's transfer of the office building to the partnership, I would not have received the government securities from the partnership. The facts (including the amount and nature of partnership assets) indicate that, at the time that I transferred the office building to the partnership, the timing of the transfer of the government securities to I was anticipated and was not dependent on the entrepreneurial risks of partnership operations. Moreover, the facts indicate that the partnership allocations were designed to effect an exchange of the burdens and benefits of ownership of the government securities in anticipation of the transfer of those securities to I and those burdens and benefits were effectively shifted to I on formation of the partnership. Accordingly, the facts and circumstances clearly establish that I sold the office building to the partnership on February 1, 1992, in exchange for the partnership's obligation to transfer the government securities to I and to make certain other cash transfers to I. [Reg. § 1.707-3.]

☐ [*T.D.* 8439, 9-25-92.]

§ 1.707-4. Disguised sales of property to partnership; special rules applicable to guaranteed payments, preferred returns, operating cash flow distributions, and reimbursements of preformation expenditures.—(a) *Guaranteed payments and preferred returns*—(1) *Guaranteed payment not treated as part of a sale*—(i) *In general.* A guaranteed payment for capital made to a partner is not treated as part of a sale of property under § 1.707-3(a) (relating to treatment of transfers as a sale). A party's characterization of a payment as a guaranteed payment for capital will not control in determining whether a payment is, in fact, a guaranteed payment for capital. The term *guaranteed payment for capital* means any payment to a partner by a partnership that is determined without regard to partnership income and is for the use of that partner's capital. *See* section 707(c). For this purpose, one or more payments are not made for the use of a partner's capital if the payments are designed to liquidate all or part of the partner's interest in property contributed to the partnership rather than to provide the partner with a return on an investment in the partnership.

(ii) *Reasonable guaranteed payments.* Notwithstanding the presumption set forth in § 1.707-3(c) (relating) to transfers made within two years of each other), for purposes of section 707(a)(2) and the regulations thereunder a transfer of money to a partner that is characterized by the parties as a guaranteed payment for capital, is determined without regard to the income of the partnership and is reasonable (within the meaning of paragraph (a)(3) of this section) is presumed to be a guaranteed payment for capital unless the facts and circumstances clearly establish that the transfer is not a guaranteed payment for capital and is part of a sale.

(iii) *Unreasonable guaranteed payments.* A transfer of money to a partner that is characterized by the parties as a guaranteed payment for capital but that is not reasonable (within the meaning of paragraph (a)(3) of this section) is presumed not to be a guaranteed payment for capital unless the facts and circumstances clearly establish that the transfer is a guaranteed payment for capital. A transfer that is not a guaranteed payment for capital is subject to the rules of § 1.707-3.

(2) *Presumption regarding reasonable preferred returns.* Notwithstanding the presumption set forth in § 1.707-3(c) (relating to transfers made within two years of each other), a transfer of money to a partner that is characterized by the parties as a preferred return and that is reasonable (within the meaning of paragraph (a)(3) of this section) is presumed not to be part of a sale of property to the partnership unless the facts and circumstances (including the likelihood and expected timing of the subsequent allocation of income or gain to support the preferred return) clearly establish that the transfer is part of a sale. The term *preferred return* means a preferential distribution of partnership cash flow to a partner with respect to capital contributed to the partnership by the partner that will be matched, to the extent available, by an allocation of income or gain.

(3) *Definition of reasonable preferred returns and guaranteed payments*—(i) *In general.* A transfer of money to a partner that is characterized as a preferred return or guaranteed payment for capital is reasonable only to the extent that the transfer is made to the partner pursuant to a written provision of a partnership agreement that provides for payment for the use of capital in a reasonable amount, and only to the extent that the payment is made for the use of capital after the date on which that provision is added to the partnership agreement.

(ii) *Reasonable amount.* A transfer of money that is made to a partner during any partnership taxable year and is characterized as a preferred return or guaranteed payment for capital is reasonable in amount if the sum of any preferred return and any guaranteed payment for capital that is payable for that year does not exceed the amount determined by multiplying either the partner's unreturned capital at the beginning of the year or, at the partner's option, the partner's weighted average capital balance for the year (with either amount appropriately adjusted, taking into account the relevant compounding periods, to reflect any unpaid preferred return or guaranteed payment for capital that is payable to the partner) by the safe harbor interest rate for that year. The safe harbor interest rate for a partnership's taxable year equals 150 percent of the highest applicable Federal rate, at the appropriate compounding period or periods, in effect at any time from the time that the right to the preferred return or guaranteed payment for capital is first established pursuant to a binding, written agreement among the partners through the end of the taxable year. A partner's unreturned capital equals the excess of the aggregate amount of money and the fair market value of other consideration (net of liabilities) contributed by the partner to the partnership over the aggregate amount of money and the fair market value of other consideration (net of liabilities) distributed by the partnership to the partner other than transfers of money that are presumed to be guaranteed payments for capital under paragraph (a)(1)(ii) of this section, transfers of money that are reasonable preferred returns within the meaning of this paragraph (a)(3), and operating cash flow distributions within the meaning of paragraph (b)(2) of this section.

(4) *Examples.* The following examples illustrate the application of paragraph (a) of this section:

Example 1. Transfer presumed to be a guaranteed payment. (i) A transfers property with a fair market value of $100,000 to partnership AB. At the time of A's transfer, the partnership agreement is amended to provide that A is to receive a guaranteed payment for the use of A's capital of 10 percent (compounded annually) of the fair market value of the transferred property in each of the three years following the transfer. The partnership agreement provides that partnership net taxable income and loss will be allocated equally between partners A and B, and that partnership cash flow will be distributed in accordance with the allocation of partnership net taxable income and loss. The partnership would be allowed a deduction in the year paid if the transfers made to A are treated as guaranteed payments under section 707(c). Under the partnership agreement, that deduction would be allocated in the same manner as any other item of partnership deduction. The partnership agreement complies with the requirements of § 1.704-1(b)(2)(ii)(b). The partnership agreement does not provide for the payment of a preferred return and, other than the guaranteed payment to be paid to A, no transfer is expected to be made during the three year period following A's transfer that is not an operating cash flow distribution (within the meaning of paragraph (b)(2) of this section). Assume that the highest applicable Federal rate in effect at the time of A's transfer is eight percent compounded annually.

(ii) The transfer of money to be made to A under the partnership agreement is characterized by the parties as a guaranteed payment for capital and is determined without regard to the income of the partnership. The transfer is also reasonable within the meaning of § 1.707-4(a)(3). The transfer, therefore, is presumed to be a guaranteed payment for capital. The presumption set forth in § 1.707-3(c) (relating to transfers made within two years of each other) thus does not apply to this transfer. The transfer will not be treated as part of a sale of property to the partnership unless the facts and circumstances clearly establish that the transfer is not a guaranteed payment for capital but is part of a sale.

(iii) The presumption that the transfer is a guaranteed payment for capital is not rebutted, because there are no facts indicating that the transfer is not a guaranteed payment for the use of capital.

Example 2. Transfers characterized as guaranteed payments treated as part of a sale. (i) C and D form partnership CD. C transfers property with a fair market value of $100,000 and an adjusted tax basis of $20,000 in exchange for a partnership interest. D is responsible for managing the day-to-day operations of the partnership and makes no capital contribution to the partnership upon its formation. The partnership agreement provides that C is to receive payments characterized as guaranteed payments and determined without regard to partnership income of $8,333 per year for the first four years of partnership operations for the use of C's capital. In addition, the partnership agreement provides that—

(A) Partnership net taxable income and loss will be allocated 75 percent to C and 25 percent to D; and

(B) All partnership cash flow (determined prior to consideration of the guaranteed payment) will be distributed 75 percent to C and 25 percent to D except that guaranteed payments that the partnership is obligated to make to C are payable solely out of D's share of the partnership's cash flow.

(ii) If D's share of the partnership's cash flow is not sufficient to make the guaranteed payment to C, then D is obligated to contribute any shortfall to the partnership, even in the event the partnership is liquidated. Thus, the effect of the guaranteed payment arrangement is that the guaranteed payment to C is funded entirely by D. The partnership agreement complies with the re-

quirements of § 1.704-1(b)(2)(ii)(*b*). Assume that, at the time the partnership is formed, the partnership or D could borrow $25,000 pursuant to a loan requiring equal payments of principal and interest over a four-year term at the current market interest rate of approximately 12 percent (compounded annually). Assume that the highest applicable Federal rate in effect at the time the partnership is formed is 10 percent compounded annually.

(iii) The transfer of money to be made to C under the partnership agreement is characterized by the parties as a guaranteed payment for capital and is determined without regard to the income of the partnership. The transfer is also reasonable within the meaning of § 1.707-4(a)(3). The transfer, therefore, is presumed to be a guaranteed payment for capital. The presumption set forth in § 1.707-3(c) (relating to transfers made within two years of each other) thus does not apply to this transfer. The transfer will not be treated as part of a sale of property to the partnership unless the facts and circumstances clearly establish that the transfer is not a guaranteed payment for capital and is part of a sale.

(iv) For the first four years of partnership operations, the total guaranteed payments made to C under the partnership agreement will equal $33,332. If the characterization of those payments as guaranteed payments for capital within the meaning of section 707(c) were respected, C would be allocated $24,999 of the deductions that would be claimed by the partnership for those payments, thereby leaving the balance in C's capital account approximately $25,000 less than it would have been if the guaranteed payments had not been made. The guaranteed payments thus have the effect of offsetting approximately $25,000 of the credit made to C's capital account for the property transferred to the partnership by C. C's resulting capital account is approximately equivalent to the capital account C would have had if C had only contributed 75 percent of the property to the partnership. Furthermore, the effect of D's funding the guaranteed payment to C (either through reduced distributions of cash flow to D or additional contributions) is that D's capital account is approximately equivalent to the capital account D would have had if D had contributed 25 percent of the property (or contributed cash so that the partnership could purchase the 25 percent). Moreover, a $25,000 loan requiring equal payments of principal and interest over a four-year term at the current market interest rate of 12 percent (compounded annually), would have resulted in annual payments of principal and interest of $8,230.86. Consequently, the guaranteed payments effectively place the partners in the same economic position that they would have been in had D purchased a one-quarter interest in the property from C financed at the current market rate of interest, and then C and D each contributed their share of the property to the partnership. In view of the burden the guaranteed payments place on D's right to transfers of partnership cash flow and D's legal obligation to make contributions to the partnership to the extent necessary to fund the guaranteed payments, D has effectively purchased through the partnership a one-quarter interest in the property from C.

(v) Under these facts, the presumption that the transfers to C are guaranteed payments for capital is rebutted, because the facts and circumstances clearly establish that the transfers are part of a sale and not guaranteed payments for capital. Under § 1.707-3(a), C and the partnership are treated as if C sold a one-quarter interest in the property to the partnership in exchange for a promissory note evidencing the partnership's obligation to make the guaranteed payments.

(b) *Presumption regarding operating cash flow distributions*—(1) *In general.* Notwithstanding the presumption set forth in § 1.707-3(c) (relating to transfers made within two years of each other), an operating cash flow distribution is presumed not to be part of a sale of property to the partnership unless the facts and circumstances clearly establish that the transfer is part of a sale.

(2) *Operating cash flow distributions*—(i) *In general.* One or more transfers of money by the partnership to a partner during a taxable year of the partnership are operating cash flow distributions for purposes of paragraph (b)(1) of this section to the extent that those transfers are not presumed to be guaranteed payments for capital under paragraph (a)(1)(ii) of this section, are not reasonable preferred returns within the meaning of paragraph (a)(3) of this section, are not characterized by the parties as distributions to the partner acting in a capacity other than as a partner, and to the extent they do not exceed the product of the net cash flow of the partnership from operations for the year multiplied by the lesser of the partner's percentage interest in overall partnership profits for that year or the partner's percentage interest in overall partnership profits for the life of the partnership. For purposes of the preceding sentence, the net cash flow of the partnership from operations for a taxable year is an amount equal to the taxable income or loss of the partnership arising in the ordinary course of the partnership's business and investment activities, increased by tax exempt interest, depreciation, amortization, cost recovery allowances and other noncash charges deducted in determining such taxable income and decreased by—

(A) Principal payments made on any partnership indebtedness;

(B) Property replacement or contingency reserves actually established by the partnership;

(C) Capital expenditures when made other than from reserves or from borrowings the proceeds of which are not included in operating cash flow; and

(D) Any other cash expenditures (including preferred returns) not deducted in determining such taxable income or loss.

(ii) *Operating cash flow safe harbor.* For any taxable year, in determining a partner's operating cash flow distributions for the year, the partner may use the partner's smallest percentage interest under the terms of the partnership agreement in any material item of partnership income or gain that may be realized by the partnership in the three-year period beginning with such taxable year. This provision is merely intended to provide taxpayers with a safe harbor and is not intended to preclude a taxpayer from using a different percentage under the rules of paragraph (b)(2)(i) of this section.

(iii) *Tiered partnerships.* In the case of tiered partnerships, the upper-tier partnership must take into account its share of the net cash flow from operations of the lower-tier partnership applying principles similar to those described in paragraph (b)(2)(i) of this section, so that the amount of the upper-tier partnership's operating cash flow distributions is neither overstated nor understated.

(c) *Accumulation of guaranteed payments, preferred returns, and operating cash flow distributions.* Guaranteed payments for capital, preferred returns, and operating cash flow distributions presumed not to be part of a sale under the rules of paragraphs (a) and (b) of this section do not lose the benefit of the presumption by reason of being retained for distribution in a later year.

(d) *Exception for reimbursements of preformation expenditures.* A transfer of money or other consideration by the partnership to a partner is not treated as part of a sale of property by the partner to the partnership under § 1.707-3(a) (relating to treatment of transfers as a sale) to the extent that the transfer to the partner by the partnership is made to reimburse the partner for, and does not exceed the amount of, capital expenditures that—

(1) Are incurred during the two-year period preceding the transfer by the partner to the partnership; and

(2) Are incurred by the partner with respect to—

Reg. § 1.707-4(d)(2)

(i) Partnership organization and syndication costs described in section 709; or

(ii) Property contributed to the partnership by the partner, but only to the extent the reimbursed capital expenditures do not exceed 20 percent of the fair market value of such property at the time of the contribution. However, the 20 percent of fair market value limitation of this paragraph (d)(2)(ii) does not apply if the fair market value of the contributed property does not exceed 120 percent of the partner's adjusted basis in the contributed property at the time of contribution.

(e) *Other exceptions.* The Commissioner may provide by guidance published in the Internal Revenue Bulletin that other payments or transfers to a partner are not treated as part of a sale for purposes of section 707(a)(2) and the regulations thereunder. [Reg. § 1.707-4.]

☐ [*T.D. 8439, 9-25-92.*]

§ 1.707-5. Disguised sales of property to partnership; special rules relating to liabilities.—(a) *Liability assumed or taken subject to by partnership*—(1) *In general.* For purposes of this section and §§ 1.707-3 and 1.707-4, if a partnership assumes or takes property subject to a qualified liability (as defined in paragraph (a)(6) of this section) of a partner, the partnership is treated as transferring consideration to the partner only to the extent provided in paragraph (a)(5) of this section. By contrast, if the partnership assumes or takes property subject to a liability of the partner other than a qualified liability, the partnership is treated as transferring consideration to the partner to the extent that the amount of the liability exceeds the partner's share of that liability immediately after the partnership assumes or takes subject to the liability as provided in paragraphs (a)(2), (3) and (4) of this section.

(2) *Partner's share of liability.* A partner's share of any liability of the partnership is determined under the following rules:

(i) *Recourse liability.* A partner's share of a recourse liability of the partnership equals the partner's share of the liability under the rules of section 752 and the regulations thereunder. A partnership liability is a recourse liability to the extent that the obligation is a recourse liability under § 1.752-1(a)(1) or would be treated as a recourse liability under that section if it were treated as a partnership liability for purposes of that section.

(ii) *Nonrecourse liability.* A partner's share of a nonrecourse liability of the partnership is determined by applying the same percentage used to determine the partner's share of the excess nonrecourse liability under § 1.752-3(a)(3). A

partnership liability is a nonrecourse liability of the partnership to the extent that the obligation is a nonrecourse liability under § 1.752-1(a)(2) or would be a nonrecourse liability of the partnership under § 1.752-1(a)(2) if it were treated as a partnership liability for purposes of that section.

(3) *Reduction of partner's share of liability.* For purposes of this section, a partner's share of a liability, immediately after a partnership assumes or takes subject to the liability, is determined by taking into account a subsequent reduction in the partner's share if—

(i) At the time that the partnership assumes or takes subject to a liability, it is anticipated that the transferring partner's share of the liability will be subsequently reduced; and

(ii) The reduction of the partner's share of the liability is part of a plan that has as one of its principal purposes minimizing the extent to which the assumption of or taking subject to the liability is treated as part of a sale under § 1.707-3.

(4) *Special rule applicable to transfers of encumbered property to a partnership by more than one partner pursuant to a plan.* For purposes of paragraph (a)(1) of this section, if the partnership assumes or takes property or properties subject to the liabilities of more than one partner pursuant to a plan, a partner's share of the liabilities assumed or taken subject to by the partnership pursuant to that plan immediately after the transfers equals the sum of that partner's shares of the liabilities (other than that partner's qualified liabilities, as defined in paragraph (a)(6) of this section) assumed or taken subject to by the partnership pursuant to the plan. This paragraph (a)(4) does not apply to any liability assumed or taken subject to by the partnership with a principal purpose of reducing the extent to which any other liability assumed or taken subject to by the partnership is treated as a transfer of consideration under paragraph (a)(1) of this section.

(5) *Special rule applicable to qualified liabilities.* (i) If a transfer of property by a partner to a partnership is not otherwise treated as part of a sale, the partnership's assumption of or taking subject to a qualified liability in connection with a transfer of property is not treated as part of a sale. If a transfer of property by a partner to the partnership is treated as part of a sale without regard to the partnership's assumption of or taking subject to a qualified liability (as defined in paragraph (a)(6) of this section) in connection with the transfer of property, the partnership's assumption of or taking subject to that liability is treated as a transfer of consideration made pursuant to a sale of such property to the partnership only to the extent of the lesser of—

Reg. § 1.707-5(a)(1)

(A) The amount of consideration that the partnership would be treated as transferring to the partner under paragraph (a)(1) of this section if the liability were not a qualified liability; or

(B) The amount obtained by multiplying the amount of the qualified liability by the partner's net equity percentage with respect to that property.

(ii) A partner's net equity percentage with respect to an item of property equals the percentage determined by dividing—

(A) The aggregate transfers of money or other consideration to the partner by the partnership (other than any transfer described in this paragraph (a)(5)) that are treated as proceeds realized from the sale of the transferred property; by

(B) The excess of the fair market value of the property at the time it is transferred to the partnership over any qualified liability encumbering the property or, in the case of any qualified liability described in paragraph (a)(6)(i)(C) or (D) of this section, that is properly allocable to the property.

(6) *Qualified liability of a partner defined.* A liability assumed or taken subject to by a partnership in connection with a transfer of property to the partnership by a partner is a qualified liability of the partner only to the extent—

(i) The liability is—

(A) A liability that was incurred by the partner more than two years prior to the earlier of the date the partner agrees in writing to transfer the property or the date the partner transfers the property to the partnership and that has encumbered the transferred property throughout that two-year period;

(B) A liability that was not incurred in anticipation of the transfer of the property to a partnership, but that was incurred by the partner within the two-year period prior to the earlier of the date the partner agrees in writing to transfer the property or the date the partner transfers the property to the partnership and that has encumbered the transferred property since it was incurred (see paragraph (a)(7) of this section for further rules regarding a liability incurred within two years of a property transfer or of a written agreement to transfer);

(C) A liability that is allocable under the rules of § 1.163-8T to capital expenditures with respect to the property; or

(D) A liability that was incurred in the ordinary course of the trade or business in which property transferred to the partnership was used or held but only if all the assets related to that trade or business are transferred other than assets that are not material to a continuation of the trade or business; and

(ii) If the liability is a recourse liability, the amount of the liability does not exceed the fair market value of the transferred property (less the amount of any other liabilities that are senior in priority and that either encumber such property or are liabilities described in paragraph (a)(6)(i)(C) or (D) of this section) at the time of the transfer.

(7) *Liability incurred within two years of transfer presumed to be in anticipation of the transfer*—(i) *In general.* For purposes of this section, if within a two-year period a partner incurs a liability (other than a liability described in paragraph (a)(6)(i)(C) or (D) of this section) and transfers property to a partnership or agrees in writing to transfer the property, and in connection with the transfer the partnership assumes or takes the property subject to the liability, the liability is presumed to be incurred in anticipation of the transfer unless the facts and circumstances clearly establish that the liability was not incurred in anticipation of the transfer.

(ii) *Disclosure of transfers of property subject to liabilities incurred within two years of the transfer.* If a partner treats a liability assumed or taken subject to by a partnership as a qualified liability under paragraph (a)(6)(i)(B) of this section, such treatment is to be disclosed to the Internal Revenue Service in accordance with § 1.707-8.

(b) *Treatment of debt-financed transfers of consideration by partnerships*—(1) *In general.* For purposes of § 1.707-3, if a partner transfers property to a partnership, and the partnership incurs a liability and all or a portion of the proceeds of that liability are allocable under § 1.163-8T to a transfer of money or other consideration to the partner made within 90 days of incurring the liability, the transfer of money or other consideration to the partner is taken into account only to the extent that the amount of money or the fair market value of the other consideration transferred exceeds that partner's allocable share of the partnership liability.

(2) *Partner's allocable share of liability*—(i) *In general.* A partner's allocable share of a partnership liability for purposes of paragraph (b)(1) of this section equals the amount obtained by multiplying the partner's share of the liability as described in paragraph (a)(2) of this section by the fraction determined by dividing—

(A) The portion of the liability that is allocable under § 1.163-8T to the money or other property transferred to the partner; by

(B) The total amount of the liability.

Reg. § 1.707-5(b)(2)

(ii) *Debt-financed transfers made pursuant to a plan.*

(A) *In general.* Except as provided in paragraph (b)(2)(iii) of this section, if a partnership transfers to more than one partner pursuant to a plan all or a portion of the proceeds of one or more partnership liabilities, paragraph (b)(1) of this section is applied by treating all of the liabilities incurred pursuant to the plan as one liability, and each partner's allocable share of those liabilities equals the amount obtained by multiplying the sum of the partner's shares of each of the respective liabilities (as defined in paragraph (a)(2) of this section) by the fraction obtained by dividing—

(*1*) The portion of those liabilities that is allocable under § 1.163-8T to the money or other consideration transferred to the partners pursuant to the plan; by

(*2*) The total amount of those liabilities.

(B) *Special rule.* Paragraph (b)(2)(ii)(A) of this section does not apply to any transfer of money or other property to a partner that is made with a principal purpose of reducing the extent to which any transfer is taken into account under paragraph (b)(1) of this section.

(iii) *Reduction of partner's share of liability.* For purposes of paragraph (b)(2) of this section, a partner's share of a liability, immediately after the partnership assumes or takes subject to the liability, is determined by taking into account a subsequent reduction in the partner's share if—

(A) It is anticipated that the partner's share of the liability that is allocable to a transfer of money or other consideration to the partner will be reduced subsequent to the transfer; and

(B) The reduction of the partner's share of the liability is part of a plan that has as one of its principal purposes minimizing the extent to which the partnership's distribution of the proceeds of the borrowing is treated as part of a sale.

(c) *Refinancings.* To the extent that the proceeds of a partner or partnership liability (the *refinancing debt*) are allocable under the rules of § 1.163-8T to payments discharging all or part of any other liability of that partner or of the partnership, as the case may be, the refinancing debt is treated as the other liability for purposes of applying the rules of this section.

(d) *Share of liability where assumption accompanied by transfer of money.* For purposes of §§ 1.707-3 through 1.707-5, if pursuant to a plan a partner pays or contributes money to the partnership and the partnership assumes or takes subject to one or more liabilities (other than qualified liabilities) of the partner, the amount of those liabilities that the partnership is treated as assuming or taking subject to is reduced (but not below zero) by the money transferred.

(e) *Tiered partnerships and other related persons.* If a lower-tier partnership succeeds to a liability of an upper-tier partnership, the liability in the lower-tier partnership retains the characterization as qualified or nonqualified that it had under these rules in the upper-tier partnership. A similar rule applies to other related party transactions involving liabilities to the extent provided by guidance published in the Internal Revenue Bulletin.

(f) *Examples.* The following examples illustrate the application of this section.

Example 1. Partnership's assumption of nonrecourse liability encumbering transferred property. (i) A and B form partnership AB, which will engage in renting office space. A transfers $500,000 in cash to the partnership, and B transfers an office building to the partnership. At the time it is transferred to the partnership, the office building has a fair market value of $1,000,000, an adjusted basis of $400,000, and is encumbered by a $500,000 liability, which B incurred 12 months earlier to finance the acquisition of other property. No facts rebut the presumption that the liability was incurred in anticipation of the transfer of the property to the partnership. Assume that this liability is a nonrecourse liability of the partnership within the meaning of section 752 and the regulations thereunder. The partnership agreement provides that partnership items will be allocated equally between A and B, including excess nonrecourse deductions under § 1.752-3(a)(3). The partnership agreement complies with the requirements of § 1.704-1(b)(2)(ii)(*b*).

(ii) The nonrecourse liability secured by the office building is not a qualified liability within the meaning of paragraph (a)(6) of this section. B would be allocated 50 percent of the excess nonrecourse liability under the partnership agreement. Accordingly, immediately after the partnership's assumption of that liability, B's share of the liability equals $250,000, which is equal to B's 50 percent share of the excess nonrecourse liability of the partnership as determined in accordance with B's share of partnership profits under § 1.752-3(a)(3).

(iii) The partnership's taking subject to the liability encumbering the office building is treated as a transfer of $250,000 of consideration to B (the amount by which the liability ($500,000) exceeds B's share of that liability immediately after taking subject to ($250,000)). B is treated as having sold $250,000 of the fair market value of the office building to the partnership in exchange for the partnership's taking subject to a $250,000

Reg. § 1.707-5(c)

liability. This results in a gain of $150,000 ($250,000 minus ($250,000/$1,000,000 multiplied by $400,000)).

Example 2. Partnership's assumption of recourse liability encumbering transferred property. (i) C transfers property Y to a partnership. At the time of its transfer to the partnership, property Y has a fair market value of $10,000,000 and is subject to an $8,000,000 liability that C incurred, immediately before transferring property Y to the partnership, in order to finance other expenditures. Upon the transfer of property Y to the partnership, the partnership assumed the liability encumbering that property. The partnership assumed this liability solely to acquire property Y. Under section 752 and the regulations thereunder, immediately after the partnership's assumption of the liability encumbering property Y, the liability is a recourse liability of the partnership and C's share of that liability is $7,000,000.

(ii) Under the facts of this example, the liability encumbering property Y is not a qualified liability. Accordingly, the partnership's assumption of the liability results in a transfer of consideration to C in connection with C's transfer of property Y to the partnership in the amount of $1,000,000 (the excess of the liability assumed by the partnership ($8,000,000) over C's share of the liability immediately after the assumption ($7,000,000)). See paragraphs (a)(1) and (2) of this section.

Example 3. Subsequent reduction of transferring partner's share of liability. (i) The facts are the same as in *Example 2*. In addition, property Y is a fully leased office building, the rental income from property Y is sufficient to meet debt service, and the remaining term of the liability is ten years. It is anticipated that, three years after the partnership's assumption of the liability, C's share of the liability under section 752 will be reduced to zero because of a shift in the allocation of partnership losses pursuant to the terms of the partnership agreement. Under the partnership agreement, this shift in the allocation of partnership losses is dependent solely on the passage of time.

(ii) Under paragraph (a)(3) of this section, if the reduction in C's share of the liability was anticipated at the time of C's transfer, and the reduction was part of a plan that has as one of its principal purposes minimizing the extent of sale treatment under § 1.707-3 (*i.e.*, a principal purpose of allocating a large percentage of losses to C in the first three years when losses were not likely to be realized was to minimize the extent to which C's transfer would be treated as part of a sale), C's share of the liability immediately after the

assumption is treated as equal to C's reduced share.

* * *

[Reg. § 1.707-5.]

□ [*T.D. 8439, 9-25-92.*]

§ 1.707-6. Disguised sales of property by partnership to partner; general rules.—(a) *In general.* Rules similar to those provided in § 1.707-3 apply in determining whether a transfer of property by a partnership to a partner and one or more transfers of money or other consideration by that partner to the partnership are treated as a sale of property, in whole or in part, to the partner.

(b) *Special rules relating to liabilities—*(1) *In general.* Rules similar to those provided in § 1.707-5 apply to determine the extent to which an assumption of or taking subject to a liability by a partner, in connection with a transfer of property by a partnership, is considered part of a sale. Accordingly, if a partner assumes or takes property subject to a qualified liability (as defined in paragraph (b)(2) of this section) of a partnership, the partner is treated as transferring consideration to the partnership only to the extent provided in this paragraph (b). If the partner assumes or takes subject to a liability that is not a qualified liability, the amount treated as consideration transferred to the partnership is the amount that the liability assumed or taken subject to by the partner exceeds the partner's share of that liability (determined under the rules of § 1.707-5(a)(2)) immediately before the transfer. Similar to the rules provided in § 1.707-5(a)(4), if more than one partner assumes or takes subject to a liability pursuant to a plan, the amount that is treated as a transfer of consideration by each partner is the amount by which all of the liabilities (other than qualified liabilities) assumed or taken subject to by the partner pursuant to the plan exceed the partner's share of all of those liabilities immediately before the assumption or taking subject to. This paragraph (b)(1) does not apply to any liability assumed or taken subject to by a partner with a principal purpose of reducing the extent to which any other liability assumed or taken subject to by a partner is treated as a transfer of consideration under this paragraph (b).

(2) *Qualified liabilities.* (i) If a transfer of property by a partnership to a partner is not otherwise treated as part of a sale, the partner's assumption of or taking subject to a qualified liability is not treated as part of a sale. If a transfer of property by a partnership to the partner is treated as part of a sale without regard to the partner's assumption of or taking subject to a qualified liability, the partner's assumption of or

taking subject to that liability is treated as a transfer of consideration made pursuant to a sale of such property to the partner only to the extent of the lesser of—

(A) The amount of consideration that the partner would be treated as transferring to the partnership under paragraph (b) of this section if the liability were not a qualified liability; or

(B) The amount obtained by multiplying the amount of the liability at the time of its assumption or taking subject to by the partnership's net equity percentage with respect to that property.

(ii) A partnership's net equity percentage with respect to an item of property encumbered by a qualified liability equals the percentage determined by dividing—

(A) The aggregate transfers to the partnership from the partner (other than any transfer described in this paragraph (b)(2)) that are treated as the proceeds realized from the sale of the transferred property to the partner; by

(B) The excess of the fair market value of the property at the time it is transferred to the partner over any qualified liabilities of the partnership that are assumed or taken subject to by the partner at that time.

(iii) For purposes of this section, the definition of a qualified liability is that provided in § 1.707-5(a)(6) with the following exceptions—

(A) In applying the definition, the qualified liability is one that is originally an obligation of the partnership and is assumed or taken subject to by the partner in connection with a transfer of property to the partner; and

(B) If the liability was incurred by the partnership more than two years prior to the earlier of the date the partnership agrees in writing to transfer the property or the date the partnership transfers the property to the partner, that liability is a qualified liability whether or not it has encumbered the transferred property throughout the two-year period.

(c) *Disclosure rules.* Similar to the rules provided in § § 1.707-3(c)(2) and 1.707-5(a)(7)(ii), a partnership is to disclose to the Internal Revenue Service, in accordance with § 1.707-8, the facts in the following circumstances:

(1) When a partnership transfers property to a partner and the partner transfers money or other consideration to the partnership within a two-year period (without regard to the order of the transfers) and the partnership treats the transfers as other than a sale for tax purposes; and

(2) When a partner assumes or takes subject to a liability of a partnership in connection with a

transfer of property by the partnership to the partner, and the partnership incurred the liability within the two-year period prior to the earlier of the date the partnership agrees in writing to the transfer of property or the date the partnership transfers the property, and the partnership treats the liability as a qualified liability under rules similar to § 1.707-5(a)(6)(i)(B).

(d) *Examples.* The following examples illustrate the rules of this section.

Example 1. Sale of property by partnership to partner. (i) A is a member of a partnership. The partnership transfers property X to A. At the time of the transfer, property X has a fair market value of $1,000,000. One year after the transfer, A transfers $1,100,000 to the partnership. Assume that under the rules of section 1274 the imputed principal amount of an obligation to transfer $1,100,000 one year after the transfer of property X is $1,000,000 on the date of the transfer.

(ii) Since the transfer of $1,100,000 to the partnership by A is made within two years of the transfer of property X to A, under rules similar to those provided in § 1.707-3(c), the transfers are presumed to be a sale unless the facts and circumstances clearly establish otherwise. If no facts exist that would rebut this presumption, on the date that the partnership transfers property X to A, the partnership is treated as having sold property X to A in exchange for A's obligation to transfer $1,100,000 to the partnership one year later.

Example 2. Assumption of liability by partner. (i) B is a member of an existing partnership. The partnership transfers property Y to B. On the date of the transfer, property Y has a fair market value of $1,000,000 and is encumbered by a nonrecourse liability of $600,000. B takes the property subject to the liability. The partnership incurred the nonrecourse liability six months prior to the transfer of property Y to B and used the proceeds to purchase an unrelated asset. Assume that, under rule of § 1.707-5(a)(2)(ii) (which determines a partner's share of a nonrecourse liability), B's share of the nonrecourse liability immediately before the transfer of property Y was $100,000.

(ii) The liability is not allocable under the rules of § 1.163-8T to capital expenditures with respect to the property transferred to B and was not incurred in the ordinary course of the trade or business in which the property transferred to the partner was used or held. Since the partnership incurred the nonrecourse liability within two years of the transfer to B, under rules similar to those provided in § 1.707-5(a)(5), the liability is presumed to be incurred in anticipation of the transfer unless the facts and circumstances clearly establish the contrary. Assuming no facts exist to rebut this presumption, the liability taken subject to by B is not a qualified liability. The partnership is treated as having received, on the date of the transfer of property Y to B, $500,000 ($600,000 liability assumed by B less B's share of the $100,000 liability immediately prior to the transfer) as consideration for the sale of one-half ($500,000/$1,000,000) of property Y to B. The partnership is also treated as having distributed to B, in B's capacity as a partner, the other one-half of property Y. [Reg. § 1.707-6.]

☐ [*T.D.* 8439, 9-25-92.]

§ 1.708-1. Continuation of partnership.—(a) *General rule.* For purposes of subchapter K, chapter 1 of the Code, an existing partnership shall be considered as continuing if it is not terminated.

(b) *Termination*—(1) *General rule.* A partnership shall terminate when the operations of the partnership are discontinued and no part of any business, financial operation, or venture of the partnership continues to be carried on by any of its partners in a partnership. For example, on November 20, 1956, A and B, each of whom is a 20-percent partner in partnership ABC, sell their interests to C, who is a 60-percent partner. Since the business is no longer carried on by any of its partners in a partnership, the ABC partnership is terminated as of November 20, 1956. However, where partners DEF agree on April 30, 1957, to dissolve their partnership, but carry on the business through a winding up period ending September 30, 1957, when all remaining assets, consisting only of cash, are distributed to the partners, the partnership does not terminate because of cessation of business until September 30, 1957.

(i) Upon the death of one partner in a 2-member partnership, the partnership shall not be considered as terminated if the estate or other successor in interest of the deceased partner continues to share in the profits or losses of the partnership business.

(ii) For the continuation of a partnership where payments are being made under section 736 (relating to payments to a retiring partner or a deceased partner's successor in interest), see paragraph (a)(6) of § 1.736-1.

(2) A partnership shall terminate when 50 percent or more of the total interest in partnership capital and profits is sold or exchanged within a period of 12 consecutive months. Such sale or exchange includes a sale or exchange to another member of the partnership. However, a disposition of a partnership interest by gift (including assignment to a successor in interest), bequest, or inheritance, or the liquidation of a partnership interest, is not a sale or exchange for purposes of this subparagraph. Moreover, if the

sale or exchange of an interest in a partnership (upper-tier partnership) that holds an interest in another partnership (lower-tier partnership) results in a termination of the upper-tier partnership, the upper-tier partnership is treated as exchanging its entire interest in the capital and profits of the lower-tier partnership. If the sale or exchange of an interest in an upper-tier partnership does not terminate the upper-tier partnership, the sale or exchange of an interest in the upper-tier partnership is not treated as a sale or exchange of a proportionate share of the upper-tier partnership's interest in the capital and profits of the lower-tier partnership. The previous two sentences apply to terminations of partnerships under section 708(b)(1)(B) occurring on or after May 9, 1997; however, the sentences may be applied to terminations occurring on or after May 9, 1996, provided that the partnership and its partners apply the sentences to the termination in a consistent manner. Furthermore, the contribution of property to a partnership does not constitute such a sale or exchange. See, however, paragraph (c)(3) of § 1.731-1. Fifty percent or more of the total interest in partnership capital and profits means 50 percent or more of the total interest in partnership capital plus 50 percent or more of the total interest in partnership profits. Thus, the sale of a 30-percent interest in partnership capital and a 60-percent interest in partnership profits is not the sale or exchange of 50 percent or more of the total interest in partnership capital and profits. If one or more partners sell or exchange interests aggregating 50 percent or more of the total interest in partnership capital and 50 percent or more of the total interest in partnership profits within a period of 12 consecutive months, such sale or exchange is considered as being within the provisions of this subparagraph. When interests are sold or exchanged on different dates, the percentages to be added are determined as of the date of each sale. For example, with respect to the ABC partnership, the sale by A on May 12, 1956, of a 30-percent interest in capital and profits to D, and the sale by B on March 27, 1957, of a 30-percent interest in capital and profits to E, is a sale of a 50-percent or more interest. Accordingly, the partnership is terminated as of March 27, 1957. However, if, on March 27, 1957, D, instead of B, sold his 30-percent interest in capital and profits to E, there would be no termination since only one 30-percent interest would have been sold or exchanged within a 12-month period.

(3) For purposes of subchapter K, chapter 1 of the Code, a partnership taxable year closes with respect to all partners on the date on which the partnership terminates. See section 706(c)(1) and

paragraph (c)(1) of § 1.706-1. The date of termination is:

(i) For purposes of section 708(b)(1)(A), the date on which the winding up of the partnership affairs is completed.

(ii) For purposes of section 708(b)(1)(B), the date of the sale or exchange of a partnership interest which, of itself or together with sales or exchanges in the preceding 12 months, transfers an interest of 50 percent or more in both partnership capital and profits.

(4) If a partnership is terminated by a sale or exchange of an interest, the following is deemed to occur: The partnership contributes all of its assets and liabilities to a new partnership in exchange for an interest in the new partnership; and, immediately thereafter, the terminated partnership distributes interests in the new partnership to the purchasing partner and the other remaining partners in proportion to their respective interests in the terminated partnership in liquidation of the terminated partnership, either for the continuation of the business by the new partnership or for its dissolution and winding up. In the latter case, the new partnership terminates in accordance with (b)(1) of this section. This paragraph (b)(4) applies to terminations of partnerships under section 708(b)(1)(B) occurring on or after May 9, 1997; however, this paragraph (b)(4) may be applied to terminations occurring on or after May 9, 1996, provided that the partnership and its partners apply this paragraph (b)(4) to the termination in a consistent manner. The provisions of this paragraph (b)(4) are illustrated by the following example:

Example. (i) A and B each contribute $10,000 cash to form AB, a general partnership, as equal partners. AB purchases depreciable Property X for $20,000. Property X increases in value to $30,000, at which time A sells its entire 50 percent interest to C for $15,000 in a transfer that terminates the partnership under section 708(b)(1)(B). At the time of the sale, Property X had an adjusted tax basis of $16,000 and a book value of $16,000 (original $20,000 tax basis and book value reduced by $4,000 of depreciation). In addition, A and B each had a capital account balance of $8,000 (original $10,000 capital account reduced by $2,000 of depreciation allocations with respect to Property X).

(ii) Following the deemed contribution of assets and liabilities by the terminated AB partnership to a new partnership (new AB) and the liquidation of the terminated AB partnership, the adjusted tax basis of Property X in the hands of new AB is $16,000. See Section 723. The book value of Property X in the hands of new partnership AB is also $16,000 (the book value of Prop-

erty X immediately before the termination) and B and C each have a capital account of $8,000 in new AB (the balance of their capital accounts in AB prior to the termination). See § 1.7041(b)(2)(iv)(l) (providing that the deemed contribution and liquidation with regard to the terminated partnership are disregarded in determining the capital accounts of the partners and the books of the new partnership). Additionally, under § 301.6109-1(d)(2)(iii) of this chapter, new AB retains the taxpayer identification number of the terminated AB partnership.

(iii) Property X was not section 704(c) property in the hands of terminated AB and is therefore not treated as section 704(c) property in the hands of new AB, even though Property X is deemed contributed to new AB at a time when the fair market value of Property X ($30,000) was different from its adjusted tax basis ($16,000). See § 1.704-3(a)(3)(i) (providing that property contributed to a new partnership under § 1.708-1(b)(4) is treated as section 704(c) property only to the extent that the property was section 704(c) property in the hands of the terminated partnership immediately prior to the termination).

(5) If a partnership is terminated by a sale or exchange of an interest in the partnership, a section 754 election (including a section 754 election made by the terminated partnership on its final return) that is in effect for the taxable year of the terminated partnership in which the sale occurs, applies with respect to the incoming partner. Therefore, the bases of partnership assets are adjusted pursuant to sections 743 and 755 prior to their deemed contribution to the new partnership. This paragraph (b)(5) applies to terminations of partnerships under section 708(b)(1)(B) occurring on or after May 9, 1997; however, this paragraph (b)(5) may be applied to terminations occurring on or after May 9, 1996, provided that the partnership and its partners apply this paragraph (b)(5) to the termination in a consistent manner.

(c) *Merger or consolidation—(1) General rule.* If two or more partnerships merge or consolidate into one partnership, the resulting partnership shall be considered a continuation of the merging or consolidating partnership the members of which own an interest of more than 50 percent in the capital and profits of the resulting partnership. If the resulting partnership can, under the preceding sentence, be considered a continuation of more than one of the merging or consolidating partnerships, it shall, unless the Commissioner permits otherwise, be considered the continuation solely of that partnership which is credited with the contribution of assets having the greatest fair market value (net of liabilities) to the resulting partnership. Any other merging or consolidating partnerships shall be considered as terminated. If the members of none of the merging or consolidating partnerships have an interest of more than 50 percent in the capital and profits of the resulting partnership, all of the merged or consolidated partnerships are terminated, and a new partnership results.

(2) *Tax returns.* The taxable years of any merging or consolidating partnerships which are considered terminated shall be closed in accordance with the provisions of section 706(c) and the regulations thereunder, and such partnerships shall file their returns for a taxable year ending upon the date of termination, i.e., the date of merger or consolidation. The resulting partnership shall file a return for the taxable year of the merging or consolidating partnership that is considered as continuing. The return shall state that the resulting partnership is a continuation of such merging or consolidating partnership, shall retain the employer identification number (EIN) of the partnership that is continuing, and shall include the names, addresses, and EINs of the other merged or consolidated partnerships. The respective distributive shares of the partners for the periods prior to and including the date of the merger or consolidation and subsequent to the date of merger or consolidation shall be shown as a part of the return.

(3) *Form of a merger or consolidation*—(i) *Assets-over form.* When two or more partnerships merge or consolidate into one partnership under the applicable jurisdictional law without undertaking a form for the merger or consolidation, or undertake a form for the merger or consolidation that is not described in paragraph (c)(3)(ii) of this section, any merged or consolidated partnership that is considered terminated under paragraph (c)(1) of this section is treated as undertaking the assets-over form for Federal income tax purposes. Under the assets-over form, the merged or consolidated partnership that is considered terminated under paragraph (c)(1) of this section contributes all of its assets and liabilities to the resulting partnership in exchange for an interest in the resulting partnership, and immediately thereafter, the terminated partnership distributes interests in the resulting partnership to its partners in liquidation of the terminated partnership.

(ii) *Assets-up form.* Despite the partners' transitory ownership of the terminated partnership's assets, the form of a partnership merger or consolidation will be respected for Federal income tax purposes if the merged or consolidated partnership that is considered terminated under paragraph (c)(1) of this section distributes all of its assets to its partners (in a manner that causes the partners to be treated, under the laws of the applicable jurisdiction, as the owners of such as-

sets) in liquidation of the partners' interests in the terminated partnership, and immediately thereafter, the partners in the terminated partnership contribute the distributed assets to the resulting partnership in exchange for interests in the resulting partnership.

(4) *Sale of an interest in the merging or consolidating partnership.* In a transaction characterized under the assets-over form, a sale of all or part of a partner's interest in the terminated partnership to the resulting partnership that occurs as part of a merger or consolidation under section 708(b)(2)(A), as described in paragraph (c)(3)(i) of this section, will be respected as a sale of a partnership interest if the merger agreement (or another document) specifies that the resulting partnership is purchasing interests from a particular partner in the merging or consolidating partnership and the consideration that is transferred for each interest sold, and if the selling partner in the terminated partnership, either prior to or contemporaneous with the transaction, consents to treat the transaction as a sale of the partnership interest. See section 741 and § 1.741-1 for determining the selling partner's gain or loss on the sale or exchange of the partnership interest.

(5) *Examples.* The following examples illustrate the rules in paragraphs (c)(1) through (4) of this section:

Example 1. Partnership AB, in whose capital and profits A and B each own a 50-percent interest, and partnership CD, in whose capital and profits C and D each own a 50-percent interest, merge on September 30, 1999, and form partnership ABCD. Partners A, B, C, and D are on a calendar year, and partnership AB and partnership CD also are on a calendar year. After the merger, the partners have capital and profits interests as follows: A, 30 percent; B, 30 percent; C, 20 percent; and D, 20 percent. Since A and B together own an interest of more than 50 percent in the capital and profits of partnership ABCD, such partnership shall be considered a continuation of partnership AB and shall continue to file returns on a calendar year basis. Since C and D own an interest of less than 50 percent in the capital and profits of partnership ABCD, the taxable year of partnership CD closes as of September 30, 1999, the date of the merger, and partnership CD is terminated as of that date. Partnership ABCD is required to file a return for the taxable year January 1 to December 31, 1999, indicating thereon that, until September 30, 1999, it was partnership AB. Partnership CD is required to file a return for its final taxable year, January 1 through September 30, 1999.

Example 2. (i) Partnership X, in whose capital and profits A owns a 40-percent interest and B owns a 60-percent interest, and partnership Y, in whose capital and profits B owns a 60-percent interest and C owns a 40-percent interest, merge on September 30, 1999. The fair market value of the partnership X assets (net of liabilities) is $100X, and the fair market value of the partnership Y assets (net of liabilities) is $200X. The merger is accomplished under state law by partnership Y contributing its assets and liabilities to partnership X in exchange for interests in partnership X, with partnership Y then liquidating, distributing interests in partnership X to B and C.

(ii) B, a partner in both partnerships prior to the merger, owns a greater than 50-percent interest in the resulting partnership following the merger. Accordingly, because the fair market value of partnership Y's assets (net of liabilities) was greater than that of partnership X's, under paragraph (c)(1) of this section, partnership X will be considered to terminate in the merger. As a result, even though, for state law purposes, the transaction was undertaken with partnership Y contributing its assets and liabilities to partnership X and distributing interests in partnership X to its partners, pursuant to paragraph (c)(3)(i) of this section, for Federal income tax purposes, the transaction will be treated as if partnership X contributed its assets to partnership Y in exchange for interests in partnership Y and then liquidated, distributing interests in partnership Y to A and B.

Example 3. (i) The facts are the same as in *Example 2*, except that partnership X is engaged in a trade or business and has, as one of its assets, goodwill. In addition, the merger is accomplished under state law by having partnership X convey an undivided 40-percent interest in each of its assets to A and an undivided 60-percent interest in each of its assets to B, with A and B then contributing their interests in such assets to partnership Y. Partnership Y also assumes all of the liabilities of partnership X.

(ii) Under paragraph (c)(3)(ii) of this section, the form of the partnership merger will be respected so that partnership X will be treated as following the assets-up form for Federal income tax purposes.

Example 4. (i) Partnership X and partnership Y merge when the partners of partnership X transfer their partnership X interests to partnership Y in exchange for partnership Y interests. Immediately thereafter, partnership X liquidates into partnership Y. The resulting partnership is considered a continuation of partnership Y, and partnership X is considered terminated.

(ii) The partnerships are treated as undertaking the assets-over form described in paragraph (c)(3)(i) of this section because the

partnerships undertook a form that is not the assets-up form described in paragraph (c)(3)(ii) of this section. Accordingly, for Federal income tax purposes, partnership X is deemed to contribute its assets and liabilities to partnership Y in exchange for interests in partnership Y, and, immediately thereafter, partnership X is deemed to have distributed the interests in partnership Y to its partners in liquidation of their interests in partnership X.

Example 5. (i) A, B, and C are partners in partnership X. D, E, and F are partners in Partnership Y. Partnership X and partnership Y merge, and the resulting partnership is considered a continuation of partnership Y. Partnership X is considered terminated. Under state law, partnerships X and Y undertake the assets-over form of paragraph (c)(3)(i) of this section to accomplish the partnership merger. C does not want to become a partner in partnership Y, and partnership X does not have the resources to buy C's interest before the merger. C, partnership X, and partnership Y enter into an agreement specifying that partnership Y will purchase C's interest in partnership X for $150 before the merger, and as part of the agreement, C consents to treat the transaction in a manner that is consistent with the agreement. As part of the merger, partnership X receives from partnership Y $150 that will be distributed to C immediately before the merger, and interests in partnership Y in exchange for partnership X's assets and liabilities.

(ii) Because the merger agreement satisfies the requirements of paragraph (c)(4) of this section and C provides the necessary consent, C will be treated as selling its interest in partnership X to partnership Y for $150 before the merger. See section 741 and § 1.741-1 to determine the amount and character of C's gain or loss on the sale or exchange of its interest in partnership X.

(iii) Because the merger agreement satisfies the requirements of paragraph (c)(4) of this section, partnership Y is considered to have purchased C's interest in partnership X for $150 immediately before the merger. See § 1.704-1(b)(2)(iv)(*l*) for determining partnership Y's capital account in partnership X. Partnership Y's adjusted basis of its interest in partnership X is determined under section 742 and § 1.742-1. To the extent any built-in gain or loss on section 704(c) property in partnership X would have been allocated to C (including any allocations with respect to property revaluations under section 704(b) (reverse section 704(c) allocations)), see section 704 and § 1.704-3(a)(7) for determining the built-in gain or loss or reverse section 704(c) allocations apportionable to partnership Y. Similarly, after the merger is completed, the built-in gain or loss and reverse section 704(c) allocations attributable to C's interest are apportioned to D, E, and F under section 704(c) and § 1.704-3(a)(7).

(iv) Under paragraph (c)(3)(i) of this section, partnership X contributes its assets and liabilities attributable to the interests of A and B to partnership Y in exchange for interests in partnership Y; and, immediately thereafter, partnership X distributes the interests in partnership Y to A and B in liquidation of their interests in partnership X. At the same time, partnership X distributes assets to partnership Y in liquidation of partnership Y's interest in partnership X. Partnership Y's bases in the distributed assets are determined under section 732(b).

(6) *Prescribed form not followed in certain circumstances*—(i) If any transactions described in paragraph (c)(3) or (4) of this section are part of a larger series of transactions, and the substance of the larger series of transactions is inconsistent with following the form prescribed in such paragraph, the Commissioner may disregard such form, and may recast the larger series of transactions in accordance with their substance.

(ii) *Example.* The following example illustrates the rules in paragraph (c)(6) of this section:

Example. A, B, and C are equal partners in partnership ABC. ABC holds no section 704(c) property. D and E are equal partners in partnership DE. B and C want to exchange their interests in ABC for all of the interests in DE. However, rather than exchanging partnership interests, DE merges with ABC by undertaking the assets-up form described in paragraph (c)(3)(ii) of this section, with D and E receiving title to the DE assets and then contributing the assets to ABC in exchange for interests in ABC. As part of a prearranged transaction, the assets acquired from DE are contributed to a new partnership, and the interests in the new partnership are distributed to B and C in complete liquidation of their interests in ABC. The merger and division in this example represent a series of transactions that in substance are an exchange of interests in ABC for interests in DE. Even though paragraph (c)(3)(ii) of this section provides that the form of a merger will be respected for Federal income tax purposes if the steps prescribed under the assets-up form are followed, and paragraph (d)(3)(i) of this section provides a form that will be followed for Federal income tax purposes in the case of partnership divisions, these forms will not be respected for Federal income tax purposes under these facts, and the transactions will be recast in accordance with their substance as a taxable exchange of interests in ABC for interests in DE.

(7) *Effective date.* This paragraph (c) is applicable to partnership mergers occurring on or after January 4, 2001. However, a partnership may apply paragraph (c) of this section to partnership mergers occurring on or after January 11, 2000.

(d) *Division of a partnership*—(1) *General rule.* Upon the division of a partnership into two or more partnerships, any resulting partnership (as defined in paragraph (d)(4)(iv) of this section) or resulting partnerships shall be considered a continuation of the prior partnership (as defined in paragraph (d)(4)(ii) of this section) if the members of the resulting partnership or partnerships had an interest of more than 50 percent in the capital and profits of the prior partnership. Any other resulting partnership will not be considered a continuation of the prior partnership but will be considered a new partnership. If the members of none of the resulting partnerships owned an interest of more than 50 percent in the capital and profits of the prior partnership, none of the resulting partnerships will be considered a continuation of the prior partnership, and the prior partnership will be considered to have terminated. Where members of a partnership which has been divided into two or more partnerships do not become members of a resulting partnership which is considered a continuation of the prior partnership, such members' interests shall be considered liquidated as of the date of the division.

(2) *Tax consequences*—(i) *Tax returns.* The resulting partnership that is treated as the divided partnership (as defined in paragraph (d)(4)(i) of this section) shall file a return for the taxable year of the partnership that has been divided and retain the employer identification number (EIN) of the prior partnership. The return shall include the names, addresses, and EINs of all resulting partnerships that are regarded as continuing. The return shall also state that the partnership is a continuation of the prior partnership and shall set forth separately the respective distributive shares of the partners for the periods prior to and including the date of the division and subsequent to the date of division. All other resulting partnerships that are regarded as continuing and new partnerships shall file separate returns for the taxable year beginning on the day after the date of the division with new EINs for each partnership. The return for a resulting partnership that is regarded as continuing and that is not the divided partnership shall include the name, address, and EIN of the prior partnership.

(ii) *Elections.* All resulting partnerships that are regarded as continuing are subject to preexisting elections that were made by the prior partnership. A subsequent election that is made by a resulting partnership does not affect the other resulting partnerships.

Reg. § 1.708-1(d)(2)

(3) *Form of a division*—(i) *Assets-over form.* When a partnership divides into two or more partnerships under applicable jurisdictional law without undertaking a form for the division, or undertakes a form that is not described in paragraph (d)(3)(ii) of this section, the transaction will be characterized under the assets-over form for Federal income tax purposes.

(A) *Assets-over form where at least one resulting partnership is a continuation of the prior partnership.* In a division under the assets-over form where at least one resulting partnership is a continuation of the prior partnership, the divided partnership (as defined in paragraph (d)(4)(i) of this section) contributes certain assets and liabilities to a recipient partnership (as defined in paragraph (d)(4)(iii) of this section) or recipient partnerships in exchange for interests in such recipient partnership or partnerships; and, immediately thereafter, the divided partnership distributes the interests in such recipient partnership or partnerships to some or all of its partners in partial or complete liquidation of the partners' interests in the divided partnership.

(B) *Assets-over form where none of the resulting partnerships is a continuation of the prior partnership.* In a division under the assets-over form where none of the resulting partnerships is a continuation of the prior partnership, the prior partnership will be treated as contributing all of its assets and liabilities to new resulting partnerships in exchange for interests in the resulting partnerships; and, immediately thereafter, the prior partnership will be treated as liquidating by distributing the interests in the new resulting partnerships to the prior partnership's partners.

(ii) *Assets-up form*—(A) *Assets-up form where the partnership distributing assets is a continuation of the prior partnership.* Despite the partners' transitory ownership of some of the prior partnership's assets, the form of a partnership division will be respected for Federal income tax purposes if the divided partnership (which, pursuant to § 1.708-1(d)(4)(i), must be a continuing partnership) distributes certain assets (in a manner that causes the partners to be treated, under the laws of the applicable jurisdiction, as the owners of such assets) to some or all of its partners in partial or complete liquidation of the partners' interests in the divided partnership, and immediately thereafter, such partners contribute the distributed assets to a recipient partnership or partnerships in exchange for interests in such recipient partnership or partnerships. In order for such form to be respected for transfers to a particular recipient partnership, all assets held by the prior partnership that are transferred to the recipient partnership must be distributed to, and

then contributed by, the partners of the recipient partnership.

(B) *Assets-up form where none of the resulting partnerships are a continuation of the prior partnership.* If none of the resulting partnerships are a continuation of the prior partnership, then despite the partners' transitory ownership of some or all of the prior partnership's assets, the form of a partnership division will be respected for Federal income tax purposes if the prior partnership distributes certain assets (in a manner that causes the partners to be treated, under the laws of the applicable jurisdiction, as the owners of such assets) to some or all of its partners in partial or complete liquidation of the partners' interests in the prior partnership, and immediately thereafter, such partners contribute the distributed assets to a resulting partnership or partnerships in exchange for interests in such resulting partnership or partnerships. In order for such form to be respected for transfers to a particular resulting partnership, all assets held by the prior partnership that are transferred to the resulting partnership must be distributed to, and then contributed by, the partners of the resulting partnership. If the prior partnership does not liquidate under the applicable jurisdictional law, then with respect to the assets and liabilities that, in form, are not transferred to a new resulting partnership, the prior partnership will be treated as transferring these assets and liabilities to a new resulting partnership under the assets-over form described in paragraph (d)(3)(i)(B) of this section.

(4) *Definitions*—(i) *Divided partnership.* For purposes of paragraph (d) of this section, the divided partnership is the continuing partnership which is treated, for Federal income tax purposes, as transferring the assets and liabilities to the recipient partnership or partnerships, either directly (under the assets-over form) or indirectly (under the assets-up form). If the resulting partnership that, in form, transferred the assets and liabilities in connection with the division is a continuation of the prior partnership, then such resulting partnership will be treated as the divided partnership. If a partnership divides into two or more partnerships and only one of the resulting partnerships is a continuation of the prior partnership, then the resulting partnership that is a continuation of the prior partnership will be treated as the divided partnership. If a partnership divides into two or more partnerships without undertaking a form for the division that is recognized under paragraph (d)(3) of this section, or if the resulting partnership that had, in form, transferred assets and liabilities is not considered a continuation of the prior partnership, and more than one resulting partnership is considered a continuation of the prior partnership, the

continuing resulting partnership with the assets having the greatest fair market value (net of liabilities) will be treated as the divided partnership.

(ii) *Prior partnership.* For purposes of paragraph (d) of this section, the prior partnership is the partnership subject to division that exists under applicable jurisdictional law before the division.

(iii) *Recipient partnership.* For purposes of paragraph (d) of this section, a recipient partnership is a partnership that is treated as receiving, for Federal income tax purposes, assets and liabilities from a divided partnership, either directly (under the assets-over form) or indirectly (under the assets-up form).

(iv) *Resulting partnership.* For purposes of paragraph (d) of this section, a resulting partnership is a partnership resulting from the division that exists under applicable jurisdictional law after the division and that has at least two partners who were partners in the prior partnership. For example, where a prior partnership divides into two partnerships, both partnerships existing after the division are resulting partnerships.

(5) *Examples.* The following examples illustrate the rules in paragraphs (d)(1), (2), (3), and (4) of this section:

Example 1. Partnership ABCD is in the real estate and insurance businesses. A owns a 40-percent interest, and B, C, and D each owns a 20-percent interest, in the capital and profits of the partnership. The partnership and the partners report their income on a calendar year. On November 1, 1999, they separate the real estate and insurance businesses and form two partnerships. Partnership AB takes over the real estate business, and partnership CD takes over the insurance business. Because members of resulting partnership AB owned more than a 50-percent interest in the capital and profits of partnership ABCD (A, 40 percent, and B, 20 percent), partnership AB shall be considered a continuation of partnership ABCD. Partnership AB is required to file a return for the taxable year January 1 to December 31, 1999, indicating thereon that until November 1, 1999, it was partnership ABCD. Partnership CD is considered a new partnership formed at the beginning of the day on November 2, 1999, and is required to file a return for the taxable year it adopts pursuant to section 706(b) and the applicable regulations.

Example 2. (i) Partnership ABCD owns properties W, X, Y, and Z, and divides into partnership AB and partnership CD. Under paragraph (d)(1) of this section, partnership AB is considered a continuation of partnership ABCD and partnership CD is considered a new partnership. Partnership ABCD distributes property Y to C and titles property Y in C's name. Partnership ABCD distributes property Z to D and titles property Z in D's name. C and D then contribute properties Y and Z, respectively, to partnership CD in exchange for interests in partnership CD. Properties W and X remain in partnership AB.

(ii) Under paragraph (d)(3)(ii) of this section, partnership ABCD will be treated as following the assets-up form for Federal income tax purposes.

Example 3. (i) The facts are the same as in *Example 2*, except partnership ABCD distributes property Y to C and titles property Y in C's name. C then contributes property Y to partnership CD. Simultaneously, partnership ABCD contributes property Z to partnership CD in exchange for an interest in partnership CD. Immediately thereafter, partnership ABCD distributes the interest in partnership CD to D in liquidation of D's interest in partnership ABCD.

(ii) Under paragraph (d)(3)(i) of this section, because partnership ABCD did not undertake the assets-up form with respect to all of the assets transferred to partnership CD, partnership ABCD will be treated as undertaking the assets-over form in transferring the assets to partnership CD. Accordingly, for Federal income tax purposes, partnership ABCD is deemed to contribute property Y and property Z to partnership CD in exchange for interests in partnership CD, and immediately thereafter, partnership ABCD is deemed to distribute the interests in partnership CD to partner C and partner D in liquidation of their interests in partnership ABCD.

Example 4. (i) Partnership ABCD owns three parcels of property: property X, with a value of $500; property Y, with a value of $300; and property Z, with a value of $200. A and B each own a 40-percent interest in the capital and profits of partnership ABCD, and C and D each own a 10 percent interest in the capital and profits of partnership ABCD. On November 1, 1999, partnership ABCD divides into three partnerships (AB1, AB2, and CD) by contributing property X to a newly formed partnership (AB1) and distributing all interests in such partnership to A and B as equal partners, and by contributing property Z to a newly formed partnership (CD) and distributing all interests in such partnership to C and D as equal partners in exchange for all of their interests in partnership ABCD. While partnership ABCD does not transfer property Y, C and D cease to be partners in the partnership. Accordingly, after the division, the partnership holding property Y is referred to as partnership AB2.

(ii) Partnerships AB1 and AB2 both are considered a continuation of partnership ABCD, while partnership CD is considered a new partner-

Reg. § 1.708-1(d)(5)

ship formed at the beginning of the day on November 2, 1999. Under paragraph (d)(3)(i)(A) of this section, partnership ABCD will be treated as following the assets-over form, with partnership ABCD contributing property X to partnership AB1 and property Z to partnership CD, and distributing the interests in such partnerships to the designated partners.

Example 5. (i) The facts are the same as in *Example 4*, except that partnership ABCD divides into three partnerships by operation of state law, without undertaking a form.

(ii) Under the last sentence of paragraph (d)(4)(i) of this section, partnership AB1 will be treated as the resulting partnership that is the divided partnership. Under paragraph (d)(3)(i)(A) of this section, partnership ABCD will be treated as following the assets-over form, with partnership ABCD contributing property Y to partnership AB2 and property Z to partnership CD, and distributing the interests in such partnerships to the designated partners.

Example 6. (i) The facts are the same as in *Example 4*, except that partnership ABCD divides into three partnerships by contributing property X to newly-formed partnership AB1 and property Y to newly-formed partnership AB2 and distributing all interests in each partnership to A and B in exchange for all of their interests in partnership ABCD.

(ii) Because resulting partnership CD is not a continuation of the prior partnership (partnership ABCD), partnership CD cannot be treated, for Federal income tax purposes, as the partnership that transferred assets (i.e., the divided partnership), but instead must be treated as a recipient partnership. Under the last sentence of paragraph (d)(4)(i) of this section, partnership AB1 will be treated as the resulting partnership that is the divided partnership. Under paragraph (d)(3)(i)(A) of this section, partnership ABCD will be treated as following the assets-over form, with partnership ABCD contributing property Y to partnership AB2 and property Z to partnership CD, and distributing the interests in such partnerships to the designated partners.

Example 7. (i) Partnership ABCDE owns Blackacre, Whiteacre, and Redacre, and divides into partnership AB, partnership CD, and partnership DE. Under paragraph (d)(1) of this section, partnership ABCDE is considered terminated (and, hence, none of the resulting partnerships are a continuation of the prior partnership) because none of the members of the new partnerships (partnership AB, partnership CD, and partnership DE) owned an interest of more than 50 percent in the capital and profits of partnership ABCDE.

(ii) Partnership ABCDE distributes Blackacre to A and B and titles Blackacre in the names of A and B. A and B then contribute Blackacre to partnership AB in exchange for interests in partnership AB. Partnership ABCDE will be treated as following the assets-up form described in paragraph (d)(3)(ii)(B) of this section for Federal income tax purposes.

(iii) Partnership ABCDE distributes Whiteacre to C and D and titles Whiteacre in the names of C and D. C and D then contribute Whiteacre to partnership CD in exchange for interests in partnership CD. Partnership ABCDE will be treated as following the assets-up form described in paragraph (d)(3)(ii)(B) of this section for Federal income tax purposes.

(iv) Partnership ABCDE does not liquidate under state law so that, in form, the assets in new partnership DE are not considered to have been transferred under state law. Partnership ABCDE will be treated as undertaking the assets-over form described in paragraph (d)(3)(i)(B) of this section for Federal income tax purposes with respect to the assets of partnership DE. Thus, partnership ABCDE will be treated as contributing Redacre to partnership DE in exchange for interests in partnership DE; and, immediately thereafter, partnership ABCDE will be treated as distributing interests in partnership DE to D and E in liquidation of their interests in partnership ABCDE. Partnership ABCDE then terminates.

(6) *Prescribed form not followed in certain circumstances.* If any transactions described in paragraph (d)(3) of this section are part of a larger series of transactions, and the substance of the larger series of transactions is inconsistent with following the form prescribed in such paragraph, the Commissioner may disregard such form, and may recast the larger series of transactions in accordance with their substance.

(7) *Effective date.* This paragraph (d) is applicable to partnership divisions occurring on or after January 4, 2001. However, a partnership may apply paragraph (d) of this section to partnership divisions occurring on or after January 11, 2000. [Reg. § 1.708-1.]

□ [*T.D.* 6175, 5-23-56. *Amended by T.D.* 8717, 5-8-97 *and T.D.* 8925, 1-3-2001 (*corrected* 9-9-2002).]

§ 1.709-1. Treatment of organization and syndication costs.—(a) *General rule.* Except as provided in paragraph (b) of this section, no deduction shall be allowed under chapter 1 of the Code to a partnership or to any partner for any amounts paid or incurred, directly or indirectly, in partnership taxable years beginning after December 31, 1975, to organize a partnership, or to promote the sale of, or to sell, an interest in the partnership.

(b) *Amortization of organization expenses*—(1) Under section 709(b) of the Code, a partnership may elect to treat its organizational expenses (as defined in section 709(b)(2) and in § 1.709-2(a)) paid or incurred in partnership taxable years beginning after December 31, 1976, as deferred expenses. If a partnership elects to amortize organizational expenses, it must select a period of not less than 60 months, over which the partnership will amortize all such expenses on a straight line basis. This period must begin with the month in which the partnership begins business (as determined under § 1.709-2(c)). However, in the case of a partnership on the cash receipts and disbursements method of accounting, no deduction shall be allowed for a taxable year with respect to any such expenses that have not been paid by the end of that taxable year. Portions of such expenses which would have been deductible under section 709(b) in a prior taxable year if the expenses had been paid are deductible in the year of payment. The election is irrevocable and the period selected by the partnership in making its election may not be subsequently changed.

(2) If there is a winding up and complete liquidation of the partnership prior to the end of the amortization period, the unamortized amount of organizational expenses is a partnership deduction in its final taxable year to the extent provided under section 165 (relating to losses). However, there is no partnership deduction with respect to its capitalized syndication expenses.

(c) *Time and manner of making election.* The election to amortize organizational expenses provided by section 709(b) shall be made by attaching a statement to the partnership's return of income for the taxable year in which the partnership begins business. The statement shall set forth a description of each organizational expense incurred (whether or not paid) with the amount of the expense, the date each expense was incurred, the month in which the partnership began business, and the number of months (not less than 60) over which the expenses are to be amortized. A taxpayer on the cash receipts and disbursements method of accounting shall also indicate the amount paid before the end of the taxable year with respect to each such expense. Expenses less than $10 need not be separately listed, provided the total amount of these expenses is listed with the dates on which the first and last of such expenses were incurred, and, in the case of a taxpayer on the cash receipts and disbursements method of accounting, the aggregate amount of such expenses that was paid by the end of the taxable year is stated. In the case of a partnership which begins business in a taxable year that ends

after March 31, 1983, the original return and statement must be filed (and the election made) not later than the date prescribed by law for filing the return (including any extensions of time) for that taxable year. Once an election has been made, an amended return (or returns) and statement (or statements) may be filed to include any organizational expenses not included in the partnership's original return and statement. [Reg. § 1.709-1.]

☐ *[T.D. 7891, 5-3-83.]*

§ 1.709-2. **Definitions.**—(a) *Organizational expenses.* Section 709(b)(2) of the Internal Revenue Code defines organizational expenses as expenses which:

(1) Are incident to the creation of the partnership;

(2) Are chargeable to capital account; and

(3) Are of a character which, if expended incident to the creation of a partnership having an ascertainable life, would (but for section 709(a)) be amortized over such life.

An expenditure which fails to meet one or more of these three tests does not qualify as an organizational expense for purposes of section 709(b) and this section. To satisfy the statutory requirement described in paragraph (a)(1) of this section, the expense must be incurred during the period beginning at a point which is a reasonable time before the partnership begins business and ending with the date prescribed by law for filing the partnership return (determined without regard to any extensions of time) for the taxable year the partnership begins business. In addition, the expenses must be for creation of the partnership and not for operation or starting operation of the partnership trade or business. To satisfy the statutory requirement described in paragraph (a)(3) of this section, the expense must be for an item of a nature normally expected to benefit the partnership throughout the entire life of the partnership. The following are examples of organizational expenses within the meaning of section 709 and this section: Legal fees for services incident to the organization of the partnership, such as negotiation and preparation of a partnership agreement; accounting fees for services incident to the organization of the partnership; and filing fees. The following are examples of expenses that are not organizational expenses within the meaning of section 709 and this section (regardless of how the partnership characterizes them): Expenses connected with acquiring assets for the partnership or transferring assets to the partnership; expenses connected with the admission or removal of partners other than at the time the partnership is first organized; expenses connected with a contract relating to the operation of the partnership trade or business

Reg. § 1.709-2(a)(3)

(even where the contract is between the partnership and one of its members); and syndication expenses.

(b) *Syndication expenses.* Syndication expenses are expenses connected with the issuing and marketing of interests in the partnership. Examples of syndication expenses are brokerage fees; registration fees; legal fees of the underwriter or placement agent and the issuer (the general partner or the partnership) for securities advice and for advice pertaining to the adequacy of tax disclosures in the prospectus or placement memorandum for securities law purposes; accounting fees for preparation of representations to be included in the offering materials; and printing costs of the prospectus, placement memorandum, and other selling and promotional material. These expenses are not subject to the election under section 709(b) and must be capitalized.

(c) *Beginning business.* The determination of the date a partnership begins business for purposes of section 709 presents a question of fact that must be determined in each case in light of all the circumstances of the particular case. Ordinarily, a partnership begins business when it starts the business operation for which it was organized. The mere signing of a partnership agreement is not alone sufficient to show the beginning of business. If the activities of the partnership have advanced to the extent necessary to establish the nature of its business operations, it will be deemed to have begun business. Accordingly, the acquisition of operating assets which are necessary to the type of business contemplated may constitute beginning business for these purposes. The term "operating assets", as used herein, means assets that are in a state of readiness to be placed in service within a reasonable period following their acquisition. [Reg. § 1.709-2.]

☐ [*T.D.* 7891, 5-3-83.]

Contributions, Distributions and Transfers

§ 1.721-1. Nonrecognition of gain or loss on contribution.—(a) No gain or loss shall be recognized either to the partnership or to any of its partners upon a contribution of property, including installment obligations, to the partnership in exchange for a partnership interest. This rule applies whether the contribution is made to a partnership in the process of formation or to a partnership which is already formed and operating. Section 721 shall not apply to a transaction between a partnership and a partner not acting in his capacity as a partner since such a transaction is governed by section 707. Rather than contributing property to a partnership, a partner may sell property to the partnership or may retain the ownership of property and allow the partnership to use it. In all cases, the substance of the transaction will govern, rather than its form. See paragraph (c)(3) of § 1.731-1. Thus, if the transfer of property by the partner to the partnership results in the receipt by the partner of money or other consideration, including a promissory obligation fixed in amount and time for payment, the transaction will be treated as a sale or exchange under section 707 rather than as a contribution under section 721. For the rules governing the treatment of liabilities to which contributed property is subject, see section 752 and § 1.752-1.

(b)(1) Normally, under local law, each partner is entitled to be repaid his contributions of money or other property to the partnership (at the value placed upon such property by the partnership at the time of the contribution) whether made at the formation of the partnership or subsequent thereto. To the extent that any of the partners gives up any part of his right to be repaid his contributions (as distinguished from a share in partnership profits) in favor of another partner as compensation for services (or in satisfaction of an obligation), section 721 does not apply. The value of an interest in such partnership capital so transferred to a partner as compensation for services constitutes income to the partner under section 61. The amount of such income is the fair market value of the interest in capital so transferred, either at the time the transfer is made for past services, or at the time the services have been rendered where the transfer is conditioned on the completion of the transferee's future services. The time when such income is realized depends on all the facts and circumstances, including any substantial restrictions or conditions on the compensated partner's right to withdraw or otherwise dispose of such interest. To the extent that an interest in capital representing compensation for services rendered by the decedent prior to his death is transferred after his death to the decedent's successor in interest, the fair market value of such interest is income in respect of a decedent under section 691.

(2) To the extent that the value of such interest is: (i) compensation for services rendered to the partnership, it is a guaranteed payment for services under section 707(c); (ii) compensation for services rendered to a partner, it is not deductible by the partnership, but is deductible only be such partner to the extent allowable under this chapter.

(c) *Underwritings of partnership interests*—(1) *In general.* For the purpose of section 721, if a person acquires a partnership interest from an underwriter in exchange for cash in a qualified underwriting transaction, the person who acquires the partnership interest is treated as transferring cash directly to the partnership in exchange for the partnership interest and the underwriter is disregarded. A qualified underwriting transaction is a transaction in which a partnership issues partnership interests for cash in an underwriting in which either the underwriter is an agent of the partnership or the underwriter's ownership of the partnership interests is transitory.

(2) *Effective date.* This paragraph (c) is effective for qualified underwriting transactions occurring on or after May 1, 1996. [Reg. § 1.721-1.]

☐ [*T.D.* 6175, 5-23-56. *Amended by T.D.* 8665, 4-30-96.]

§ 1.722-1. Basis of contributing partner's interest.—The basis to a partner of a partnership interest acquired by a contribution of property, including money, to the partnership shall be the amount of money contributed plus the adjusted basis at the time of contribution of any property contributed. If the acquisition of an interest in partnership capital results in taxable income to a partner, such income shall constitute an addition to the basis of the partner's interest. See paragraph (b) of § 1.721-1. If the contributed property is subject to indebtedness or if liabilities of the partner are assumed by the partnership, the basis of the contributing partner's interest shall be reduced by the portion of the indebtedness assumed by the other partners, since the partnership's assumption of his indebtedness is treated as a distribution of money to the partner. Conversely, the assumption by the other partners of a portion of the contributor's indebtedness is treated as a contribution of money by them. See section 752 and § 1.752-1. The provisions of this section may be illustrated by the following examples:

Example (1). A acquired a 20-percent interest in a partnership by contributing property. At the time of A's contribution, the property had a fair market value of $10,000, an adjusted basis to A of $4,000, and was subject to a mortgage of $2,000. Payment of the mortgage was assumed by the partnership. The basis of A's interest in the partnership is $2,400, computed as follows:

Adjusted basis to A of property contributed	$4,000
Less portion of mortgage assumed by other partners which must be treated as a distribution (80 percent of $2,000).	1,600
Basis of A's interest	2,400

Example (2). If, in example (1) of this section, the property contributed by A was subject to a mortgage of $6,000, the basis of A's interest would be zero, computed as follows:

Adjusted basis to A of property contributed	$4,000
Less portion of mortgage assumed by other partners which must be treated as a distribution (80 percent of $6,000)	4,800
	(800)

Since A's basis cannot be less than zero, the $800 in excess of basis, which is considered as a distribution of money under section 752(b), is treated as capital gain from the sale or exchange of a partnership interest. See section 731(a). [Reg. § 1.722-1.]

☐ [*T.D.* 6175, 5-23-56.]

§ 1.723-1. Basis of property contributed to partnership.—The basis to the partnership of property contributed to it by a partner is the adjusted basis of such property to the contributing partner at the time of the contribution. Since such property has the same basis in the hands of the partnership as it had in the hands of the contributing partner, the holding period of such property for the partnership includes the period during which it was held by the partner. See section 1223(2). For elective adjustments to the basis of partnership property arising from distributions or transfers of partnership interests, see sections 732(d), 734(b), and 743(b). [Reg. § 1.723-1.]

☐ [*T.D.* 6175, 5-23-56.]

§ 1.731-1. Extent of recognition of gain or loss on distribution—(a) *Recognition of gain or loss to partner*—(1) *Recognition of gain*—(i) Where money is distributed by a partnership to a partner, no gain shall be recognized to the partner except to the extent that the amount of money distributed exceeds the adjusted basis of the partner's interest in the partnership immediately before the distribution. This rule is applicable both to current distributions (i. e., distributions other than in liquidation of an entire interest) and to distributions in liquidation of a partner's entire interest in a partnership. Thus, if a partner with a basis for his interest of $10,000 receives a distribution of cash of $8,000 and property with a fair market value of $3,000, no gain is recognized to him. If $11,000 cash were distributed, gain would be recognized to the extent of $1,000. No gain shall be recognized to a distributee partner with respect to a distribution of property (other than money) until he sells or otherwise disposes of such property, except to the extent otherwise provided by section 736 (relating to payments to a retiring partner or a deceased partner's successor in interest) and section 751 (relating to unrealized receivables and inventory items). See section 731(c) and paragraph (c) of this section.

(ii) For the purposes of sections 731 and 705, advances or drawings of money or property against a partner's distributive share of income shall be treated as current distributions made on the last day of the partnership taxable year with respect to such partner.

(2) *Recognition of loss.* Loss is recognized to a partner only upon liquidation of his entire interest in the partnership, and only if the property distributed to him consists solely of money, unrealized receivables (as defined in section 751(c)), and inventory items (as defined in section 751(d)(2)). The term "liquidation of a partner's interest", as defined in section 761(d), is the termination of the partner's entire interest in the partnership by means of a distribution or a series of distributions. Loss is recognized to the distributee partner in such cases to the extent of the excess of the adjusted basis of such partner's interest in the partnership at the time of the distribution over the sum of—

(i) Any money distributed to him, and

(ii) The basis to the distributee, as determined under section 732, of any unrealized receivables and inventory items that are distributed to him. If the partner whose interest is liquidated receives any property other than money, unrealized receivables, or inventory items, then no loss will be recognized. Application of the provisions of this subparagraph may be illustrated by the following examples:

Example (1). Partner A has a partnership interest in partnership ABC with an adjusted basis to him of $10,000. He retires from the partnership and receives, as a distribution in liquidation of his entire interest, his share of partnership property. This share is $5,000 cash and inventory with a basis to him (under section 732) of $3,000. Partner A realizes a capital loss of $2,000, which is recognized under section 731(a)(2).

Example (2). Partner B has a partnership interest in partnership BCD with an adjusted basis to him of $10,000. He retires from the partnership and receives, as a distribution in liquidation of his entire interest, his share of partnership property. This share is $4,000 cash, real property (used in the trade or business) with an adjusted basis to the partnership of $2,000, and unrealized receivables having a basis to him (under section 732) of $3,000. No loss will be recognized to B on the transaction because he received property other than money, unrealized receivables, and inventory items. As determined under section 732, the basis to B for the real property received is $3,000.

(3) *Character of gain or loss.* Gain or loss recognized under section 731(a) on a distribution is considered gain or loss from the sale or exchange of the partnership interest of the distributee partner, that is, capital gain or loss.

(b) *Gain or loss recognized by partnership.* A distribution of property (including money) by a partnership to a partner does not result in recognized gain or loss to the partnership under section 731. However, recognized gain or loss may result to the partnership from certain distributions which, under section 751(b), must be treated as a sale or exchange of property between the distributee partner and the partnership.

(c) *Exceptions*—(1) Section 731 does not apply to the extent otherwise provided by—

(i) Section 736 (relating to payments to a retiring partner or to a deceased partner's successor in interest), and

(ii) Section 751 (relating to unrealized receivables and inventory items). For example, payments under section 736(a), which are considered as a distributive share or guaranteed payment, are taxable as such under that section.

(2) The receipt by a partner from the partnership of money or property under an obligation to repay the amount of such money or to return such property does not constitute a distribution subject to section 731 but is a loan governed by section 707(a). To the extent that such an obligation is canceled, the obligor partner will be considered to have received a distribution of money or property at the time of cancellation.

(3) If there is a contribution of property to a partnership and within a short period:

(i) Before or after such contribution other property is distributed to the contributing partner and the contributed property is retained by the partnership, or

(ii) After such contribution the contributed property is distributed to another partner,

such distribution may not fall within the scope of section 731. Section 731 does not apply to a distribution of property, if, in fact, the distribution was made in order to effect an exchange of property between two or more of the partners or between the partnership and a partner. Such a transaction shall be treated as an exchange of property. [Reg. § 1.731-1.]

☐ [*T.D.* 6175, 5-23-56.]

§ 1.731-2. Partnership distributions of marketable securities.—(a) *Marketable securities treated as money.* Except as otherwise provided in section 731(c) and this section, for purposes of sections 731(a)(1) and 737, the term *money* includes marketable securities and such securities are taken into account at their fair market value as of the date of the distribution.

(b) *Reduction of amount treated as money*—(1) *Aggregation of securities.* For purposes of section 731(c)(3)(B) and this paragraph (b), all marketable securities held by a partnership are treated as marketable securities of the same class and issuer as the distributed security.

(2) *Amount of reduction.* The amount of the distribution of marketable securities that is treated as a distribution of money under section 731(c) and paragraph (a) of this section is reduced (but not below zero) by the excess, if any, of—

(i) The distributee partner's distributive share of the net gain, if any, which would be recognized if all the marketable securities held by the partnership were sold (immediately before the transaction to which the distribution relates) by the partnership for fair market value; over

(ii) The distributee partner's distributive share of the net gain, if any, which is attributable to the marketable securities held by the partnership immediately after the transaction, determined by using the same fair market value as used under paragraph (b)(2)(i) of this section.

(3) *Distributee partner's share of net gain.* For purposes of section 731(c)(3)(B) and paragraph (b)(2) of this section, a partner's distributive share of net gain is determined—

(i) By taking into account any basis adjustments under section 743(b) with respect to that partner;

(ii) Without taking into account any special allocations adopted with a principal purpose of avoiding the effect of section 731(c) and this section; and

(iii) Without taking into account any gain or loss attributable to a distributed security to which paragraph (d)(1) of this section applies.

(c) *Marketable securities*—(1) *In general.* For purposes of section 731(c) and this section, the term *marketable securities* is defined in section 731(c)(2).

(2) *Actively traded.* For purposes of section 731(c) and this section, a financial instrument is actively traded (and thus is a marketable security) if it is of a type that is, as of the date of distribution, actively traded within the meaning of section 1092(d)(1). Thus, for example, if *XYZ* common stock is listed on a national securities exchange, particular shares of *XYZ* common stock that are distributed by a partnership are marketable securities even if those particular shares cannot be resold by the distributee partner for a designated period of time.

(3) *Interests in an entity*—(i) *Substantially all.* For purposes of section 731(c)(2)(B)(v) and this section, substantially all of the assets of an entity consist (directly or indirectly) of marketable securities, money, or both only if 90 percent or more of the assets of the entity (by value) at the time of the distribution of an interest in the entity consist (directly or indirectly) of marketable securities, money, or both.

(ii) *Less than substantially all.* For purposes of section 731(c)(2)(B)(vi) and this section, an interest in an entity is a marketable security to the extent that the value of the interest is attributable (directly or indirectly) to marketable securities, money, or both, if less than 90 percent but 20 percent or more of the assets of the entity (by value) at the time of the distribution of an interest in the entity consist (directly or indirectly) of marketable securities, money, or both.

(4) *Value of assets.* For purposes of section 731(c) and this section, the value of the assets of an entity is determined without regard to any debt that may encumber or otherwise be allocable to those assets, other than debt that is incurred to acquire an asset with a principal purpose of avoiding or reducing the effect of section 731(c) and this section.

(d) *Exceptions*—(1) *In general.* Except as otherwise provided in paragraph (d)(2) of this section, section 731(c) and this section do not apply to the distribution of a marketable security if—

(i) The security was contributed to the partnership by the distributee partner;

(ii) The security was acquired by the partnership in a nonrecognition transaction, and the following conditions are satisfied—

(A) The value of any marketable securities and money exchanged by the partnership in the nonrecognition transaction is less than 20 percent of the value of all the assets exchanged by the partnership in the nonrecognition transaction; and

(B) The partnership distributed the security within five years of either the date the security was acquired by the partnership or, if later, the date the security became marketable; or

(iii) The security was not a marketable security on the date acquired by the partnership, and the following conditions are satisfied—

(A) The entity that issued the security had no outstanding marketable securities at the time the security was acquired by the partnership;

(B) The security was held by the partnership for at least six months before the date the security became marketable; and

(C) The partnership distributed the security within five years of the date the security became marketable.

Reg. § 1.731-2(d)(1)

(2) *Anti-stuffing rule.* Paragraph (d)(1) of this section does not apply to the extent that 20 percent or more of the value of the distributed security is attributable to marketable securities or money contributed (directly or indirectly) by the partnership to the entity to which the distributed security relates after the security was acquired by the partnership (other than marketable securities contributed by the partnership that were originally contributed to the partnership by the distributee partner). For purposes of this paragraph (d)(2), money contributed by the distributing partnership does not include any money deemed contributed by the partnership as a result of section 752.

(3) *Successor security.* Section 731(c) and this section apply to the distribution of a marketable security acquired by the partnership in a nonrecognition transaction in exchange for a security the distribution of which immediately prior to the exchange would have been excepted under this paragraph (d) only to the extent that section 731(c) and this section otherwise would have applied to the exchanged security.

(e) *Investment partnerships*—(1) *In general.* Section 731(c) and this section do not apply to the distribution of marketable securities by an investment partnership (as defined in section 731(c)(3)(C)(i)) to an eligible partner (as defined in section 731(c)(3)(C)(iii)).

(2) *Eligible partner*—(i) *Contributed services.* For purposes of section 731(c)(3)(C)(iii) and this section, a partner is not treated as a partner other than an eligible partner solely because the partner contributed services to the partnership.

(ii) *Contributed partnership interests.* For purposes of determining whether a partner is an eligible partner under section 731(c)(3)(C), if the partner has contributed to the investment partnership an interest in another partnership that meets the requirements of paragraph (e)(4)(i) of this section after the contribution, the contributed interest is treated as property specified in section 731(c)(3)(C)(i).ship is not treated as engaged in a trade or business by reason of—

(i) Any activity undertaken as an investor, trader, or dealer in any asset described in section 731(c)(3)(C)(i), including the receipt of commitment fees, break-up fees, guarantee fees, director's fees, or similar fees that are customary in and incidental to any activities of the partnership as an investor, trader, or dealer in such assets;

(ii) Reasonable and customary management services (including the receipt of reasonable and customary fees in exchange for such management services) provided to an investment partnership (within the meaning of section 731(c)(3)(C)(i)) in which the partnership holds a partnership interest; or

(iii) Reasonable and customary services provided by the partnership in assisting the formation, capitalization, expansion, or offering of interests in a corporation (or other entity) in which the partnership holds or acquires a significant equity interest (including the provision of advice or consulting services, bridge loans, guarantees of obligations, or service on a company's board of directors), provided that the anticipated receipt of compensation for the services, if any, does not represent a significant purpose for the partnership's investment in the entity and is incidental to the investment in the entity.

(4) *Partnership tiers.* For purposes of section 731(c)(3)(C)(iv) and this section, a partnership (upper-tier partnership) is not treated as engaged in a trade or business engaged in by, or as holding (instead of a partnership interest) a proportionate share of the assets of, a partnership (lower-tier partnership) in which the partnership holds a partnership interest if—

(i) The upper-tier partnership does not actively and substantially participate in the management of the lower-tier partnership; and

(ii) The interest held by the upper-tier partnership is less than 20 percent of the total profits and capital interests in the lower-tier partnership.

(f) *Basis rules*—(1) *Partner's basis*—(i) *Partner's basis in distributed securities.* The distributee partner's basis in distributed marketable securities with respect to which gain is recognized by reason of section 731(c) and this section is the basis of the security determined under section 732, increased by the amount of such gain. Any increase in the basis of the marketable securities attributable to gain recognized by reason of section 731(c) and this section is allocated to marketable securities in proportion to their respective amounts of unrealized appreciation in the hands of the partner before such increase.

(ii) *Partner's basis in partnership interest.* The basis of the distributee partner's interest in the partnership is determined under section 733 as if no gain were recognized by the partner on the distribution by reason of section 731(c) and this section.

(2) *Basis of partnership property.* No adjustment is made to the basis of partnership property under section 734 as a result of any gain recognized by a partner, or any step-up in the basis in the distributed marketable securities in the hands of the distributee partner, by reason of section 731(c) and this section.

(g) *Coordination with other sections*—(1) *Sections 704(c)(1)(B) and 737*—(i) *In general.* If a distribution results in the application of sections 731(c) and one or both of sections 704(c)(1)(B) and 737, the effect of the distribution is determined by applying section 704(c)(1)(B) first, section 731(c) second, and finally section 737.

(ii) *Section 704(c)(1)(B).* The basis of the distributee partner's interest in the partnership for purposes of determining the amount of gain, if any, recognized by reason of section 731(c) (and for determining the basis of the marketable securities in the hands of the distributee partner) includes the increase or decrease, if any, in the partner's basis that occurs under section 704(c)(1)(B)(iii) as a result of a distribution to another partner of property contributed by the distributee partner in a distribution that is part of the same distribution as the marketable securities.

(iii) *Section 737*—(A) *Marketable securities as other property.* A distribution of marketable securities is treated as a distribution of property other than money for purposes of section 737 to the extent that the marketable securities are not treated as money under section 731(c). In addition, marketable securities contributed to the partnership are treated as property other than money in determining the contributing partner's net precontribution gain under section 737(b).

(B) *Basis increase under section 737.* The basis of the distributee partner's interest in the partnership for purposes of determining the amount of gain, if any, recognized by reason of section 731(c) (and for determining the basis of the marketable securities in the hands of the distributee partner) does not include the increase, if any, in the partner's basis that occurs under section 737(c)(1) as a result of a distribution of property to the distributee partner in a distribution that is part of the same distribution as the marketable securities.

(2) *Section 708(b)(1)(B).* If a partnership termination occurs under section 708(b)(1)(B), the successor partnership will be treated as if there had been no termination for purposes of section 731(c) and this section. Accordingly, a section 708(b)(1)(B) termination will not affect whether a partnership qualifies for any of the exceptions in paragraphs (d) and (e) of this section. In addition, a deemed distribution that may occur as a result of a section 708(b)(1)(B) termination will not be subject to section 731(c) and this section.

(h) *Anti-abuse rule.* The provisions of section 731(c) and this section must be applied in a manner consistent with the purpose of section 731(c) and the substance of the transaction. Accordingly, if a principal purpose of a transaction is to achieve a tax result that is inconsistent with the purpose of section 731(c) and this section, the Commissioner can recast the transaction for Federal tax purposes as appropriate to achieve tax results that are consistent with the purpose of section 731(c) and this section. Whether a tax result is inconsistent with the purpose of section 731(c) and this section must be determined based on all the facts and circumstances. For example, under the provisions of this paragraph (h)—

(1) A change in partnership allocations or distribution rights with respect to marketable securities may be treated as a distribution of the marketable securities subject to section 731(c) if the change in allocations or distribution rights is, in substance, a distribution of the securities;

(2) A distribution of substantially all of the assets of the partnership other than marketable securities and money to some partners may also be treated as a distribution of marketable securities to the remaining partners if the distribution of the other property and the withdrawal of the other partners is, in substance, equivalent to a distribution of the securities to the remaining partners; and

(3) The distribution of multiple properties to one or more partners at different times may also be treated as part of a single distribution if the distributions are part of a single plan of distribution.

(i) [Reserved]

(j) *Examples.* The following examples illustrate the rules of this section. Unless otherwise specified, all securities held by a partnership are marketable securities within the meaning of section 731(c); the partnership holds no marketable securities other than the securities described in the example; all distributions by the partnership are subject to section 731(a) and are not subject to sections 704(c)(1)(B), 707(a)(2)(B), 751(b), or 737; and no securities are eligible for an exception to section 731(c). The examples read as follows:

Example 1. Recognition of gain. (i) A and B form partnership AB as equal partners. A contributes property with a fair market value of $1,000 and an adjusted tax basis of $250. B contributes $1,000 cash. AB subsequently purchases Security X for $500 and immediately distributes the security to A in a current distribution. The basis in A's interest in the partnership at the time of distribution is $250.

(ii) The distribution of Security X is treated as a distribution of money in an amount equal to the fair market value of Security X on the date of distribution ($500). (The amount of the distribution that is treated as money is not reduced under section 731(c)(3)(B) and paragraph (b) of this section because, if Security X had been sold imme-

Reg. § 1.731-2(j)

diately before the distribution, there would have been no gain recognized by *AB* and *A*'s distributive share of the gain would therefore have been zero.) As a result, *A* recognizes $250 of gain under section 731(a)(1) on the distribution ($500 distribution of money less $250 adjusted tax basis in *A*'s partnership interest).

	Value	Basis	Gain (Loss)
Security *X*	100	70	30
Security *Y*	100	80	20
Security *Z*	100	110	(10)

(ii) If *AB* had sold the securities for fair market value immediately before the distribution to *A*, the partnership would have recognized $40 of net gain ($30 gain on Security *X* plus $20 gain on Security *Y* minus $10 loss on Security *Z*). *A*'s distributive share of this gain would have been $20 (one-half of $40 net gain). If *AB* had sold the remaining securities immediately after the distribution of Security *X* to *A*, the partnership would have $10 of net gain ($20 of gain on Security *Y* minus $10 loss on Security *Z*). *A*'s distributive share of this gain would have been $5 (one-half of $10 net gain). As a result, the distribution resulted in a decrease of $15 in *A*'s distributive share of the net gain in *AB*'s securities ($20 net gain before distribution minus $5 net gain after distribution).

(iii) Under paragraph (b) of this section, the amount of the distribution of Security *X* that is treated as a distribution of money is reduced by $15. The distribution of Security *X* is therefore treated as a distribution of $85 of money to *A* ($100 fair market value of Security *X* minus $15 reduction).

* * *

(k) *Effective date.* This section applies to distributions made on or after December 26, 1996. However, taxpayers may apply the rules of this section to distributions made after December 8, 1994, and before December 26, 1996. [Reg. § 1.731-2.]

☐ [*T.D.* 8707, 12-24-96.]

§ 1.732-1. Basis of distributed property other than money—(a) *Distributions other than in liquidation of a partner's interest.* The basis of property (other than money) received by a partner in a distribution from a partnership, other than in liquidation of his entire interest, shall be its adjusted basis to the partnership immediately before such distribution. However, the basis of the property to the partner shall not exceed the adjusted basis of the partner's interest in the partnership, reduced by the amount of any money distributed to him in the same transaction. The provisions of this paragraph may be illustrated by the following examples:

Example 2. Reduction in amount treated as money—in general. (i) *A* and *B* form partnership *AB* as equal partners. *AB* subsequently distributes Security *X* to *A* in a current distribution. Immediately before the distribution, *AB* held securities with the following fair market values, adjusted tax bases, and unrecognized gain or loss:

Example (1). Partner A, with an adjusted basis of $15,000 for his partnership interest, receives in a current distribution property having an adjusted basis of $10,000 to the partnership immediately before the distribution, and $2,000 cash. The basis of the property in A's hands will be $10,000. Under sections 733 and 705, the basis of A's partnership interest will be reduced by the distribution to $3,000 ($15,000, less $2,000 cash, less $10,000, the basis of the distributed property to A).

Example (2). Partner R has an adjusted basis of $10,000 for his partnership interest. He receives a current distribution of $4,000 cash and property with an adjusted basis to the partnership of $8,000. The basis of the distributed property to partner R is limited to $6,000 ($10,000, the adjusted basis of his interest, reduced by $4,000, the cash distributed).

(b) *Distribution in liquidation.* Where a partnership distributes property (other than money) in liquidation of a partner's entire interest in the partnership, the basis of such property to the partner shall be an amount equal to the adjusted basis of his interest in the partnership reduced by the amount of any money distributed to him in the same transaction. Application of this rule may be illustrated by the following example:

Example. Partner B, with a partnership interest having an adjusted basis to him of $12,000, retires from the partnership and receives cash of $2,000, and real property with an adjusted basis to the partnership of $6,000 and a fair market value of $14,000. The basis of the real property to B is $10,000 (B's basis for his partnership interest, $12,000, reduced by $2,000, the cash distributed).

(c) *Allocation of basis among properties distributed to a partner*—(1) *General rule*—(i) *Unrealized receivables and inventory items.* The basis to be allocated to properties distributed to a partner under section 732(a)(2) or (b) is allocated first to any unrealized receivables (as defined in section 751(c)) and inventory items (as defined in section 751(d)(2)) in an amount equal to the adjusted basis of each such property to the partnership immediately before the distribution. If the basis to be allocated is less than the sum of the adjusted bases to the partnership of the distributed unrealized receivables and inventory items, the adjusted basis of the distributed property must be decreased in the manner provided in paragraph (c)(2)(i) of this section.

(ii) *Other distributed property*. Any basis not allocated to unrealized receivables or inventory items under paragraph (c)(1)(i) of this section is allocated to any other property distributed to the partner in the same transaction by assigning to each distributed property an amount equal to the adjusted basis of the property to the partnership immediately before the distribution. However, if the sum of the adjusted bases to the partnership of such other distributed property does not equal the basis to be allocated among the distributed property, any increase or decrease required to make the amounts equal is allocated among the distributed property as provided in paragraph (c)(2) of this section.

(2) *Adjustment to basis allocation*—(i) *Decrease in basis*. Any decrease to the basis of distributed property required under paragraph (c)(1) of this section is allocated first to distributed property with unrealized depreciation in proportion to each property's respective amount of unrealized depreciation before any decrease (but only to the extent of each property's unrealized depreciation). If the required decrease exceeds the amount of unrealized depreciation in the distributed property, the excess is allocated to the distributed property in proportion to the adjusted bases of the distributed property, as adjusted pursuant to the immediately preceding sentence.

(ii) *Increase in basis*. Any increase to the basis of distributed property required under paragraph (c)(1)(ii) of this section is allocated first to distributed property (other than unrealized receivables and inventory items) with unrealized appreciation in proportion to each property's respective amount of unrealized appreciation before any increase (but only to the extent of each property's unrealized appreciation). If the required increase exceeds the amount of unrealized appreciation in the distributed property, the excess is allocated to the distributed property (other than unrealized receivables or inventory items) in proportion to the fair market value of the distributed property.

(3) *Unrealized receivables and inventory items*. If the basis to be allocated upon a distribution in liquidation of the partner's entire interest in the partnership is greater than the adjusted basis to the partnership of the unrealized receivables and inventory items distributed to the partner, and if there is no other property distributed to which the excess can be allocated, the distributed partner sustains a capital loss under section

731(a)(2) to the extent of the unallocated basis of the partnership interest.

(4) *Examples*. The provisions of this paragraph (c) are illustrated by the following examples:

Example 1. A is a one-fourth partner in partnership PRS and has an adjusted basis in its partnership interest of $650. PRS distributes inventory items and Assets X and Y to A in liquidation of A's entire partnership interest. The distributed inventory items have a basis to the partnership of $100 and a fair market value of $200. Asset X has an adjusted basis to the partnership of $50 and a fair market value of $400. Asset Y has an adjusted basis to the partnership and a fair market value of $100. Neither Asset X nor Asset Y consists of inventory items or unrealized receivables. Under this paragraph (c), A's basis in its partnership interest is allocated first to the inventory items in an amount equal to their adjusted basis to the partnership. A, therefore, has an adjusted basis in the inventory items of $100. The remaining basis, $550, is allocated to the distributed property first in an amount equal to the property's adjusted basis to the partnership. Thus, Asset X is allocated $50 and Asset Y is allocated $100. Asset X is then allocated $350, the amount of unrealized appreciation in Asset X. Finally, the remaining basis, $50, is allocated to Assets X and Y in proportion to their fair market values: $40 to Asset X (400/500 × $50), and $10 to Asset Y (100/500 × $50). Therefore, after the distribution, A has an adjusted basis of $440 in Asset X and $110 in Asset Y.

Example 2. B is a one-fourth partner in partnership PRS and has an adjusted basis in its partnership interest of $200. PRS distributes Asset X and Asset Y to B in liquidation of its entire partnership interest. Asset X has an adjusted basis to the partnership and fair market value of $150. Asset Y has an adjusted basis to the partnership of $150 and a fair market value of $50. Neither of the assets consists of inventory items or unrealized receivables. Under this paragraph (c), B's basis is first assigned to the distributed property to the extent of the partnership's basis in each distributed property. Thus, Asset X and Asset Y are each assigned $150. Because the aggregate adjusted basis of the distributed property, $300, exceeds the basis to be allocated, $200, a decrease of $100 in the basis of the distributed property is required. Assets X and Y have unrealized depreciation of zero and $100, respectively. Thus, the entire decrease is allocated to Asset Y. After the distribution, B has an adjusted basis of $150 in Asset X and $50 in Asset Y.

Example 3. C, a partner in partnership PRS, receives a distribution in liquidation of its entire partnership interest of $6,000 cash, inventory items having an adjusted basis to the partnership of $6,000, and real property having an adjusted basis to the partnership of $4,000. C's basis in its partnership interest is $9,000. The cash distribution reduces C's basis to $3,000, which is allocated entirely to the inventory items. The real property has a zero basis in C's hands. The partnership bases not carried over to C for the distributed properties are lost unless an election under section 754 is in effect requiring the partnership to adjust the bases of remaining partnership properties under section 734(b).

Example 4. Assume the same facts as in *Example 3* of this paragraph except C receives a distribution in liquidation of its entire partnership interest of $1,000 cash and inventory items having a basis to the partnership of $6,000. The cash distribution reduces C's basis to $8,000, which can be allocated only to the extent of $6,000 to the inventory items. The remaining $2,000 basis, not allocable to the distributed property, constitutes a capital loss to partner C under section 731(a)(2). If the election under section 754 is in effect, see section 734(b) for adjustment of the basis of undistributed partnership property.

(5) *Effective date.* This paragraph (c) applies to distributions of property from a partnership that occur on or after December 15, 1999.

(d) *Special partnership basis to transferee under section 732(d).*—(1)(i) A transfer of a partnership interest occurs upon a sale or exchange of an interest or upon the death of a partner. Section 732(d) provides a special rule for the determination of the basis of property distributed to a transferee partner who acquired any part of his partnership interest in a transfer with respect to which the election under section 754 (relating to the optional adjustment to basis of partnership property) was not in effect.

(ii) Where an election under section 754 is in effect, see section 743(b) and §§ 1.743-1 and 1.732-2.

(iii) If a transferee partner receives a distribution of property (other than money) from the partnership within 2 years after he acquired his interest or part thereof in the partnership by a transfer with respect to which the election under section 754 was not in effect, he may elect to treat as the adjusted partnership basis of such property the adjusted basis such property would have if the adjustment provided in section 743(b) were in effect.

(iv) If an election under section 732(d) is made upon a distribution of property to a transferee partner, the amount of the adjustment with respect to the transferee partner is not diminished by any depletion or depreciation on that portion

of the basis of partnership property which arises from the special basis adjustment under section 732(d), since depletion or depreciation on such portion for the period prior to distribution is allowed or allowable only if the optional adjustment under section 743(b) is in effect.

(v) If property is distributed to a transferee partner who elects under section 732(d), and if such property is not the same property which would have had a special basis adjustment, then such special basis adjustment shall apply to any like property received in the distribution, provided that the transferee, in exchange for the property distributed, has relinquished his interest in the property with respect to which he would have had a special basis adjustment. This rule applies whether the property in which the transferee has relinquished his interest is retained or disposed of by the partnership. (For a shift of transferee's basis adjustment under section 743(b) to like property, see § 1.743-1(g).)

(vi) The provisions of this paragraph (d)(1) may be illustrated by the following example:

Example. (i) Transferee partner, T, purchased a one-fourth interest in partnership PRS for $17,000. At the time T purchased the partnership interest, the election under section 754 was not in effect and the partnership inventory had a basis to the partnership of $14,000 and a fair market value of $16,000. T's purchase price reflected $500 of this difference. Thus, $4,000 of the $17,000 paid by T for the partnership interest was attributable to T's share of partnership inventory with a basis of $3,500. Within 2 years after T acquired the partnership interest, T retired from the partnership and received in liquidation of its entire partnership interest the following property:

Assets

	Adjusted Basis to PRS	Fair Market Value
Cash	$1,500	$1,500
Inventory	$3,500	$4,000
Asset X	$2,000	$4,000
Asset Y	$4,000	$5,000

(ii) The fair market value of the inventory received by T was one-fourth of the fair market value of all partnership inventory and was T's share of such property. It is immaterial whether the inventory T received was on hand when T acquired the interest. In accordance with T's election under section 732(d), the amount of T's share of partnership basis that is attributable to partnership inventory is increased by $500 (one-fourth of the $2,000 difference between the fair market value of the property, $16,000, and its $14,000 basis to the partnership at the time T purchased its interest). This adjustment under section 732(d) applies only for purposes of distributions to T, and not for purposes of partnership depreciation, depletion, or gain or loss on disposition. Thus, the amount to be allocated among the properties received by T in the liquidating distribution is $15,500 ($17,000, T's basis for the partnership interest, reduced by the amount of cash received, $1,500). This amount is allocated as follows: The basis of the inventory items received is $4,000, consisting of the $3,500 common partnership basis, plus the basis adjustment of $500 which T would have had under section 743(b). The remaining basis of $11,500 ($15,500 minus $4,000) is allocated among the remaining property distributed to T by assigning to each property the adjusted basis to the partnership of such property and adjusting that basis by any required increase or decrease. Thus, the adjusted basis to T of Asset X is $5,111 ($2,000, the adjusted basis of Asset X to the partnership, plus $2,000, the amount of unrealized appreciation in Asset X, plus $1,111 ($4,000/$9,000 multiplied by $2,500)). Similarly, the adjusted basis of Asset Y to T is $6,389 ($4,000, the adjusted basis of Asset Y to the partnership, plus $1,000, the amount of unrealized appreciation in Asset Y, plus, $1,389 ($5,000/$9,000 multiplied by $2,500)).

(2) A transferee partner who wishes to elect under section 732(d) shall make the election with his tax return—

(i) For the year of the distribution, if the distribution includes any property subject to the allowance for depreciation, depletion, or amortization, or

(ii) For any taxable year no later than the first taxable year in which the basis of any of the distributed property is pertinent in determining his income tax, if the distribution does not include any such property subject to the allowance for depreciation, depletion or amortization.

(3) A taxpayer making an election under section 732(d) shall submit with the return in which the election is made a schedule setting forth the following:

(i) That under section 732(d) he elects to adjust the basis of property received in a distribution; and

(ii) The computation of the special basis adjustment for the property distributed and the properties to which the adjustment has been allocated. For rules of allocation, see section 755.

(4) A partner who acquired any part of his partnership interest in a transfer to which the election provided in section 754 was not in effect, is required to apply the special basis rule contained in section 732(d) to a distribution to him, whether or not made within 2 years after the

transfer, if at the time of his acquisition of the transferred interest—

(i) The fair market value of all partnership property (other than money) exceeded 110 percent of its adjusted basis to the partnership,

(ii) An allocation of basis under section 732(c) upon a liquidation of his interest immediately after the transfer of the interest would have resulted in a shift of basis from property not subject to an allowance for depreciation, depletion, or amortization, to property subject to such an allowance, and

(iii) A basis adjustment under section 743(b) would change the basis to the transferee partner of the property actually distributed.

(5) *Required statements.* If a transferee partner notifies a partnership that it plans to make the election under section 732(d) under paragraph (d)(3) of this section, or if a partnership makes a distribution to which paragraph (d)(4) of this section applies, the partnership must provide the transferee with such information as is necessary for the transferee properly to compute the transferee's basis adjustments under section 732(d).

(e) *Exception.* When a partnership distributes unrealized receivables (as defined in section 751(c)) or substantially appreciated inventory items (as defined in section 751(d)) in exchange for any part of a partner's interest in other partnership property (including money), or, conversely, partnership property (including money) other than unrealized receivables or substantially appreciated inventory items in exchange for any part of a partner's interest in the partnership's unrealized receivables or substantially appreciated inventory items, the distribution will be treated as a sale or exchange of property under the provisions of section 751(b). In such case, section 732 (including subsection (d) thereof) applies in determining the partner's basis of the property which he is treated as having sold to or exchanged with the partnership (as constituted after the distribution). The partner is considered as having received such property in a current distribution and, immediately thereafter, as having sold or exchanged it. See section 751(b) and paragraph (b) of § 1.751-1. However, section 732 does not apply in determining the basis of that part of property actually distributed to a partner which is treated as received by him in a sale or exchange under section 751(b). Consequently, the basis of such property shall be its cost to the partner. [Reg. § 1.732-1.]

☐ [*T.D.* 6175, 5-23-56. *Amended by T.D.* 8847, 12-14-99.]

§ 1.732-2. Special partnership basis of distributed property—(a) *Adjustments under section 734(b).* In the case of a distribution of property to a partner, the partnership bases of the distributed properties shall reflect any increases or decreases to the basis of partnership property which have been made previously under section 734(b) (relating to the optional adjustment to basis of undistributed partnership property) in connection with previous distributions.

(b) *Adjustments under section 743(b).* In the case of a distribution of property to a partner who acquired any part of his interest in a transfer as to which an election under section 754 was in effect, then, for the purposes of section 732 (other than subsection (d) thereof), the adjusted partnership bases of the distributed property shall take into account, in addition to any adjustments under section 734(b), the transferee's special basis adjustment for the distributed property under section 743(b). The application of this paragraph may be illustrated by the following example:

Example. Partner D acquired his interest in partnership ABD from a a previous partner. Since the partnership had made an election under section 754, a special basis adjustment with respect to D is applicable to the basis of partnership property in accordance with section 743(b). One of the assets of the partnership at the time D acquired his interest was property X, which is later distributed to D in a current distribution. Property X has an adjusted basis to the partnership of $1,000 and with respect to D it has a special basis adjustment of $500. Therefore, for purposes of section 732(a)(1), the adjusted basis of such property to the partnership with respect to D immediately before its distribution is $1,500. However, if property X is distributed to partner A, a nontransferee partner, its adjusted basis to the partnership for purposes of section 732(a)(1) is only $1,000. In such case, D's $500 special basis adjustment may shift over to other property. See § 1.743-1(g).

(c) *Adjustments to basis of distributed inventory and unrealized receivables.* Under section 732, the basis to be allocated to distributed properties shall be allocated first to any unrealized receivables and inventory items. If the distributee partner is a transferee of a partnership interest and has a special basis adjustment for unrealized receivables or inventory items under either section 743(b) or section 732(d), then the partnership adjusted basis immediately prior to distribution of any unrealized receivables or inventory items distributed to such partner shall be determined as follows: If the distributee partner receives his entire share of the fair market value of the inventory items or unrealized receivables of the partnership, the adjusted basis of such distributed property to the partnership, for the purposes of section 732, shall take into account the entire amount of any special basis adjustment which the

distributee partner may have for such assets. If the distributee partner receives less than his entire share of the fair market value of partnership inventory items or unrealized receivables, then, for purposes of section 732, the adjusted basis of such distributed property to the partnership shall take into account the same proportion of the distributee's special basis adjustment for unrealized receivables or inventory items as the value of such items distributed to him bears to his entire share of the total value of all such items of the partnership. The provisions of this paragraph may be illustrated by the following example:

Example. Partner C acquired his 40-percent interest in partnership AC from a previous partner. Since the partnership had made an election under section 754, C has a special basis adjustment to partnership property under section 743(b). C retires from the partnership when the adjusted basis of his partnership interest is $3,000. He receives from the partnership in liquidation of his entire interest, $1,000 cash, certain capital assets, depreciable property, and certain inventory items and unrealized receivables. C has a special basis adjustment of $800 with respect to partnership inventory items and of $200 with respect to unrealized receivables. The common partnership basis for the inventory items distributed to him is $500 and for the unrealized receivables is zero. If the value of inventory items and the unrealized receivables distributed to C in [is] his 40-percent share of the total value of all partnership inventory items and unrealized receivables, then, for purposes of section 732, the adjusted basis of such property in C's hands will be $1,300 for the inventory items ($500 plus $800) and $200 for the unrealized receivables (zero plus $200). The remaining basis of $500, which constitutes the basis of the capital assets and depreciable property distributed to C, is determined as follows: $3,000 (total basis) less $1,000 cash, or $2,000 (the amount to be allocated to the basis of all distributed property), less $1,500 ($800 and $200 special basis adjustments, plus $500 common partnership basis, the amount allocated to inventory items and unrealized receivables). However, if the value of the inventory items and unrealized receivables distributed to C consisted of only 20 percent of the total fair market value of such property (i.e., only one-half of C's 40-percent share), then only one-half of C's special basis adjustment of $800 for partnership inventory items and $200 for unrealized receivables would be taken into account. In that case, the basis of the inventory items in C's hands would be $650 ($250, the common partnership basis for inventory items distributed to him, plus $400, one-half of C's special basis adjustment for inventory items). The basis of the unrealized re-

Reg. § 1.732-2(b)

ceivables in C's hands would be $100 (zero plus $100, one-half of C's special basis adjustment for unrealized receivables). [Reg. § 1.732-2.]

☐ [*T.D.* 6175, 5-23-56. *Amended by T.D.* 8847, 12-14-99.]

§ 1.733-1. Basis of distributee partner's interest.—In the case of a distribution by a partnership to a partner other than in liquidation of a partner's entire interest, the adjusted basis to such partner of his interest in the partnership shall be reduced (but not below zero) by the amount of any money distributed to such partner and by the amount of the basis to him of distributed property other than money as determined under section 732 and §§ 1.732-1 and 1.732-2. [Reg. § 1.733-1].

☐ [*T.D.* 6175, 5-23-56.]

§ 1.734-1. Optional adjustment to basis of undistributed partnership property.—(a) *General rule.* A partnership shall not adjust the basis of partnership property as the result of a distribution of property to a partner, unless the election provided in section 754 (relating to optional adjustment to basis of partnership property) is in effect.

(b) *Method of adjustment* —(1) *Increase in basis.* Where an election under section 754 is in effect and a distribution of partnership property is made whether or not in liquidation of the partner's entire interest in the partnership, the adjusted basis of the remaining partnership assets shall be increased by—

(i) The amount of any gain recognized under section 731(a)(1) to the distributee partner, or [and]*

(ii) The excess of the adjusted basis to the partnership immediately before the distribution of any property distributed (including adjustments under section 743(b) or section 732(d) when applied) over the basis under section 732 (including such special basis adjustments) of such property to the distributee partner.

The provisions of this subparagraph may be illustrated by the following examples:

Example (1). Partner A has a basis of $10,000 for his one-third interest in partnership ABC. The partnership has no liabilities and has assets consisting of cash of $11,000 and property with a partnership basis of $19,000 and a value of $22,000. A receives $11,000 in cash in liquidation of his entire interest in the partnership. He has a gain of $1,000 under section 731(a)(1). If the election under section 754 is in effect, the partnership basis for the property becomes $20,000 ($19,000 plus $1,000).

Example (2). Partner D has a basis of $10,000 for his one-third interest in partnership DEF. The partnership balance sheet before the distribution shows the following:

Assets	Adjusted Basis	Value
Cash	$ 4,000	$ 4,000
Property X	11,000	11,000
Property Y	15,000	18,000
Totals	30,000	33,000

Liabilities and Capital		
Liabilities	$ 0	$ 0
Capital: D	10,000	11,000
E	10,000	11,000
F	10,000	11,000
Totals	30,000	33,000

In liquidation of his entire interest in the partnership, D received property X with a partnership basis of $11,000. D's basis for property X is $10,000 under section 732(b). Where the election under section 754 is in effect, the excess of $1,000 (the partnership basis before the distribution less D's basis for property X after distribution) is added to the basis of property Y. The basis of property Y becomes $16,000 ($15,000 plus $1,000). If the distribution is made to a transferee partner who elects under section 732(d), see § 1.734-2.

(2) *Decrease in basis.* Where the election provided in section 754 is in effect and a distribution is made in liquidation of a partner's entire interest, the partnership shall decrease the adjusted basis of the remaining partnership property by—

(i) The amount of loss, if any, recognized under section 731(a)(2) to the distributee partner, or [and]**

(ii) The excess of the basis of the distributed property to the distributee, as determined under section 732 (including adjustments under section 743(b) or section 732(d) when applied) over the adjusted basis of such property to the partnership (including such special basis adjustments) immediately before such distribution.

The provisions of this subparagraph may be illustrated by the following examples:

Example (1). Partner G has a basis of $11,000 for his one-third interest in partnership GHI. Partnership assets consist of cash of $10,000 and property with a basis of $23,000 and a value of $20,000. There are no partnership liabilities. In liquidation of his entire interest in the partnership, G receives $10,000 in cash. He has a loss of $1,000 under section 731(a)(2). If the election under section 754 is in effect, the partnership basis for the property becomes $22,000 ($23,000 less $1,000).

---

* As it appears in Code Sec. 734(b)(1)(A).

** As it appears in Code Sec. 734(b)(2)(A).

Example (2). Partner J has a basis of $11,000 for his one-third interest in partnership JKL. The partnership balance sheet before the distribution shows the following:

Assets	Adjusted Basis	Value
Cash	$ 5,000	$ 5,000
Property X	10,000	10,000
Property Y	18,000	15,000
Total	33,000	30,000

Liabilities and Capital		
Liabilities	$ 0	$ 0
Capital: J	11,000	10,000
K	11,000	10,000
L	11,000	10,000
Total	33,000	30,000

In liquidation of his entire interest in the partnership, J receives property X with a partnership basis of $10,000. J's basis for property X under section 732(b) is $11,000. Where the election under section 754 is in effect, the excess of $1,000 ($11,000 basis of property X to J, the distributee, less its $10,000 adjusted basis to the partnership immediately before the distribution) decreases the basis of property Y in the partnership. Thus, the basis of property Y becomes $17,000 ($18,000 less $1,000). If the distribution is made to a transferee partner who elects under section 732(d), see § 1.734-2.

(c) *Allocation of basis.* For allocation among the partnership properties of basis adjustments under section 734(b) and paragraph (b) of this section, see section 755 and § 1.755-1.

(d) *Returns.* A partnership which must adjust the bases of partnership properties under section 734 shall attach a statement to the partnership return for the year of the distribution setting forth the computation of the adjustment and the partnership properties to which the adjustment has been allocated.

(e) *Recovery of adjustments to basis of partnership property*—(1) *Increases in basis.* For purposes of section 168, if the basis of a partnership's recovery property is increased as a result of the distribution of property to a partner, then the increased portion of the basis must be taken into account as if it were newly-purchased recovery property placed in service when the distribution occurs. Consequently, any applicable recovery period and method may be used to determine the recovery allowance with respect to the increased portion of the basis. However, no change is made for purposes of determining the recovery allowance under section 168 for the portion of the basis for which there is no increase.

(2) *Decreases in basis.* For purposes of section 168, if the basis of a partnership's recovery property is decreased as a result of the distribution of property to a partner, then the decrease in

basis must be accounted for over the remaining recovery period of the property beginning with the recovery period in which the basis is decreased.

(3) *Effective date.* This paragraph (e) applies to distributions of property from a partnership that occur on or after December 15, 1999. [Reg. § 1.734-1.]

☐ [*T.D.* 6175, 5-23-56. *Amended by T.D.* 8847, 12-14-99.]

§ 1.734-2. Adjustment after distribution to transferee partner.—(a) In the case of a distribution of property by the partnership to a partner who has obtained all or part of his partnership interest by transfer, the adjustments to basis provided in section 743(b) and section 732(d) shall be taken into account in applying the rules under section 734(b). For determining the adjusted basis of distributed property to the partnership immediately before the distribution where there has been a prior transfer of a partnership interest with respect to which the election provided in section 754 or section 732(d) is in effect, see §§ 1.732-1 and 1.732-2.

(b)(1) If a transferee partner, in liquidation of his entire partnership interest, receives a distribution of property (including money) with respect to which he has no special basis adjustment, in exchange for his interest in property with respect to which he has a special basis adjustment, and does not utilize his entire special basis adjustment in determining the basis of the distributed property to him under section 732, the unused special basis adjustment of the distributee shall be applied as an adjustment to the partnership basis of the property retained by the partnership and as to which the distributee did not use his special basis adjustment. The provisions of this subparagraph may be illustrated by the following example:

Example. Upon the death of his father, partner S acquires by inheritance a half-interest in partnership ACS. Partners A and C each have a one-quarter interest. The assets of the partnership consist of $10,000 cash and land used in farming worth $10,000 with a basis of $1,000 to the partnership. Since the partnership had made the election under section 754 at the time of the transfer, partner S has a special basis adjustment of $4,500 under section 743(b) with respect to his undivided half-interest in the real estate. The basis of S's partnership interest, in accordance with section 742, is $10,000. S retires from the partnership and receives $10,000 in cash in exchange for his entire interest. Since S has received no part of the real estate, his special basis adjustment of $4,500 will be allocated to the real estate, the remaining partnership property, and will increase its basis to the partnership to $5,500.

Reg. § 1.734-2(a)

(2) The provisions of this paragraph do not apply to the extent that certain distributions are treated as sales or exchanges under section 751(b) (relating to unrealized receivables and substantially appreciated inventory items). See section 751(b) and paragraph (b) of § 1.751-1. [Reg. § 1.734-2.]

☐ [*T.D.* 6175, 5-23-56.]

§ 1.735-1. Character of gain or loss on disposition of distributed property.—(a) *Sale or exchange of distributed property*—(1) *Unrealized receivables.* Any gain realized or loss sustained by a partner on a sale or exchange or other disposition of unrealized receivables (as defined in paragraph (c)(1) of § 1.751-1) received by him in a distribution from a partnership shall be considered gain or loss from the sale or exchange of property other than a capital asset.

(2) *Inventory items.* Any gain realized or loss sustained by a partner on a sale or exchange of inventory items (as defined in section 751(d)(2)) received in a distribution from a partnership shall be considered gain or loss from the sale or exchange of property other than a capital asset if such inventory items are sold or exchanged within 5 years from the date of the distribution by the partnership. The character of any gain or loss from a sale or exchange by the distributee partner of such inventory items after 5 years from the date of distribution shall be determined as of the date of such sale or exchange by reference to the character of the assets in his hands at that date (inventory items, capital assets, property used in a trade or business, etc.).

(b) *Holding period for distributed property.* A partner's holding period for property distributed to him by a partnership shall include the period such property was held by the partnership. The provisions of this paragraph do not apply for the purpose of determining the 5-year period described in section 735(a)(2) and paragraph (a)(2) of this section. If the property has been contributed to the partnership by a partner, then the period that the property was held by such partner shall also be included. See section 1223(2). For a partnership's holding period for contributed property, see § 1.723-1.

(c) *Effective date.* Section 735(a) applies to any property distributed by a partnership to a partner after March 9, 1954. See section 771(b)(2) and paragraph (b)(2) of § 1.771-1. However, see section 771(c). [Reg. § 1.735-1.]

☐ [*T.D.* 6175, 5-23-56. *Amended by T.D.* 6832, 7-6-65.]

[Caution: Reg. § 1.736-1 does not reflect changes made in Section 736(b) by the Revenue Reconciliation Act of 1993.]

§ 1.736-1. Payments to a retiring partner or a deceased partner's successor in interest.—(a) *Payments considered as distributive share or guaranteed payment.* (1) (i) Section 736 and this section apply only to payments made to a retiring partner or to a deceased partner's successor in interest in liquidation of such partner's entire interest in the partnership. See section 761(d). Section 736 and this section do not apply if the estate or other successor in interest of a deceased partner continues as a partner in its own right under local law. Section 736 and this section apply only to payments made by the partnership and not to transactions between the partners. Thus, a sale by partner A to partner B of his entire one-fourth interest in partnership ABCD would not come within the scope of section 736.

(ii) A partner retires when he ceases to be a partner under local law. However, for the purposes of subchapter K, chapter 1 of the Code, a retired partner or a deceased partner's successor will be treated as a partner until his interest in the partnership has been completely liquidated.

(2) When payments (including assumption of liabilities treated as a distribution of money under section 752) are made to a withdrawing partner, that is, a retiring partner or the estate or other successor in interest of a deceased partner, the amounts paid may represent several items. In part, they may represent the fair market value at the time of his death or retirement of the withdrawing partner's interest in all the assets of the partnership (including inventory) unreduced by partnership liabilities. Also, part of such payments may be attributable to his interest in unrealized receivables and part to an arrangement among the partners in the nature of mutual insurance. When a partnership makes such payments, whether or not related to partnership income, to retire the withdrawing partner's entire interest in the partnership, the payments must be allocated between (i) payments for the value of his interest in assets, except unrealized receivables and, under some circumstances, good will (section 736(b)), and (ii) other payments (section 736(a)). The amounts paid for his interest in assets are treated in the same manner as a distribution in complete liquidation under sections 731, 732, and where applicable, 751. See paragraph (b)(4)(ii) of § 1.751-1. The remaining partners are allowed no deduction for these payments since they represent either a distribution or a purchase of the withdrawing partner's capital interest by the partnership (composed of the remaining partners).

Reg. § 1.736-1(a)(2)

(3) Under section 736(a), the portion of the payments made to a withdrawing partner for his share of unrealized receivables, good will (in the absence of an agreement to the contrary), or otherwise not in exchange for his interest in assets under the rules contained in paragraph (b) of this section will be considered either—

(i) A distributive share of partnership income, if the amount of payment is determined with regard to income of the partnership; or

(ii) A guaranteed payment under section 707(c), if the amount of the payment is determined without regard to income of the partnership.

(4) Payments, to the extent considered as a distributive share of partnership income under section 736(a)(1), are taken into account under section 702 in the income of the withdrawing partner and thus reduce the amount of the distributive shares of the remaining partners. Payments, to the extent considered as guaranteed payments under section 736(a)(2), are deductible by the partnership under section 162(a) and are taxable as ordinary income to the recipient under section 61(a). See section 707(c).

(5) The amount of any payments under section 736(a) shall be included in the income of the recipient for his taxable year with or within which ends the partnership taxable year for which the payment is a distributive share, or in which the partnership is entitled to deduct such amount as a guaranteed payment. On the other hand, payments under section 736(b) shall be taken into account by the recipient for his taxable year in which such payments are made. See paragraph (b)(4) of this section.

(6) A retiring partner or a deceased partner's successor in interest receiving payments under section 736 is regarded as a partner until the entire interest of the retiring or deceased partner is liquidated. Therefore, if one of the members of a 2-man partnership retires under a plan whereby he is to receive payments under section 736, the partnership will not be considered terminated, nor will the partnership year close with respect to either partner, until the retiring partner's entire interest is liquidated, since the retiring partner continues to hold a partnership interest in the partnership until that time. Similarly, if a partner in a 2-man partnership dies, and his estate or other successor in interest receives payments under section 736, the partnership shall not be considered to have terminated upon the death of the partner but shall terminate as to both partners only when the entire interest of the decedent is liquidated. See section 708(b).

(b) *Payments for interest in partnership.* (1) Payments made in liquidation of the entire interest of a retiring partner or deceased partner shall, to the extent made in exchange for such partner's interest in partnership property (except for unrealized receivables and good will as provided in subparagraphs (2) and (3) of this paragraph), be considered as a distribution by the partnership (and not as a distributive share or guaranteed payment under section 736(a)). Generally, the valuation placed by the partners upon a partner's interest in partnership property in an arm's length agreement will be regarded as correct. If such valuation reflects only the partner's net interest in the property (i.e., total assets less liabilities), it must be adjusted so that both the value of the partner's interest in property and the basis for his interest take into account the partner's share of partnership liabilities. Gain or loss with respect to distributions under section 736(b) and this paragraph will be recognized to the distributee to the extent provided in section 731 and, where applicable, section 751.

(2) Payments made to a retiring partner or to the successor in interest of a deceased partner for his interest in unrealized receivables of the partnership in excess of their partnership basis, including any special basis adjustment for them to which such partner is entitled, shall not be considered as made in exchange for such partner's interest in partnership property. Such payments shall be treated as payments under section 736(a) and paragraph (a) of this section. For definition of unrealized receivables, see section 751(c).

(3) For the purposes of section 736(b) and this paragraph, payments made to a retiring partner or to a successor in interest of a deceased partner in exchange for the interest of such partner in partnership property shall not include any amount paid for the partner's share of good will of the partnership in excess of its partnership basis, including any special basis adjustments for it to which such partner is entitled, except to the extent that the partnership agreement provides for a reasonable payment with respect to such good will. Such payments shall be considered as payments under section 736(a). To the extent that the partnership agreement provides for a reasonable payment with respect to good will, such payments shall be treated under section 736(b) and this paragraph. Generally, the valuation placed upon good will be an arm's length agreement of the partners, whether specific in amount or determined by a formula, shall be regarded as correct.

(4) Payments made to a retiring partner or to a successor in interest of a deceased partner for his interest in inventory shall be considered as made in exchange for such partner's interest in partnership property for the purposes of section 736(b) and this paragraph. However, payments for an interest in substantially appreciated inven-

Reg. § 1.736-1(a)(3)

tory items, as defined in section 751(d), are subject to the rules provided in section 751(b) and paragraph (b) of § 1.751-1. The partnership basis in inventory items as to a deceased partner's successor in interest does not change because of the death of the partner unless the partnership has elected the optional basis adjustment under section 754. But see paragraph (b)(3)(iii) of § 1.751-1.

(5) Where payments made under section 736 are received during the taxable year, the recipient must segregate that portion of each such payment which is determined to be in exchange for the partner's interest in partnership property and treated as a distribution under section 736(b) from that portion treated as a distributive share or guaranteed payment under section 736(a). Such allocation shall be made as follows—

(i) If a fixed amount (whether or not supplemented by any additional amounts) is to be received over a fixed number of years, the portion of each payment to be treated as a distribution under section 736(b) for the taxable year shall bear the same ratio to the total fixed agreed payments for such year (as distinguished from the amount actually received) as the total fixed agreed payments under section 736(b) bear to the total fixed agreed payments under sections 736(a) and (b). The balance, if any, of such amount received in the same taxable year shall be treated as a distributive share or a guaranteed payment under section 736(a)(1) or (2). However, if the total amount received in any one year is less than the amount considered as a distribution under section 736(b) for that year, then any unapplied portion shall be added to the portion of the payments for the following year or years which are to be treated as a distribution under section 736(b). For example, retiring partner W who is entitled to an annual payment of $6,000 for 10 years for his interest in partnership property, receives only $3,500 in 1955. In 1956, he receives $10,000. Of this amount, $8,500 ($6,000 plus $2,500 from 1955) is treated as a distribution under section 736(b) for 1956; $1,500, as a payment under section 736(a).

(ii) If the retiring partner or deceased partner's successor in interest receives payments which are not fixed in amount, such payments shall first be treated as payments in exchange for his interest in partnership property under section 736(b) to the extent of the value of that interest and, thereafter, as payments under section 736(a).

(iii) In lieu of the rules provided in subdivisions (i) and (ii) of this subparagraph, the allocation of each annual payment between section 736(a) and (b) may be made in any manner to

which all the remaining partners and the withdrawing partner or his successor in interest agree, provided that the total amount allocated to property under section 736(b) does not exceed the fair market value of such property at the date of death or retirement.

(6) Except to the extent section 751(b) applies, the amount of any gain or loss with respect to payments under section 736(b) for a retiring or deceased partner's interest in property for each year of payment shall be determined under section 731. However, where the total of section 736(b) payments is a fixed sum, a retiring partner or a deceased partner's successor in interest may elect (in his tax return for the first taxable year for which he receives such payments), to report and to measure the amount of any gain or loss by the difference between—

(i) The amount treated as a distribution under section 736(b) in that year, and

(ii) The portion of the adjusted basis of the partner for his partnership interest attributable to such distribution (i.e., the amount which bears the same proportion to the partner's total adjusted basis for his partnership interest as the amount distributed under section 736(b) in that year bears to the total amount to be distributed under section 736(b)).

A recipient who elects under this subparagraph shall attach a statement to his tax return for the first taxable year for which he receives such payments, indicating his election and showing the computation of the gain included in gross income.

(7) The provisions of this paragraph may be illustrated by the following examples:

Example (1). Partnership ABC is a personal service partnership and its balance sheet is as follows:

Assets

	Adjusted basis per books	Market value
Cash	$13,000	$13,000
Unrealized receivables	0	30,000
Capital and sec. 1231 assets	20,000	23,000
Total	$33,000	$66,000

Liabilities and Capital

	Per books	Value
Liabilities	$ 3,000	$ 3,000
Capital:		
A	10,000	21,000
B	10,000	21,000
C	10,000	21,000
Total	$33,000	$66,000

Partner A retires from the partnership in accordance with an agreement whereby his share of

Reg. § 1.736-1(b)(7)

liabilities ($1,000) is assumed. In addition he is to receive $9,000 in the year of retirement plus $10,000 in each of the two succeeding years. Thus, the total that A receives for his partnership interest is $30,000 ($29,000 in cash and $1,000 in liabilities assumed). Under the agreement terminating A's interest, the value of A's interest in section 736(b) partnership property is $12,000 (one-third of $36,000, the sum of $13,000 cash and $23,000, the fair market value of capital and section 1231 assets). A's share in unrealized receivables is not included in his interest in partnership property described in section 736(b). Since the basis of A's interest is $11,000 ($10,000 plus $1,000, his share of partnership liabilities), he will realize a capital gain of $1,000 ($12,000 minus $11,000) from the disposition of his interest in partnership property. The remaining $18,000 ($30,000 minus $12,000) will constitute payments under section 736(a)(2) which are taxable to A as guaranteed payments under section 707(c). The payment for the first year is $10,000, consisting of $9,000 in cash, plus $1,000 in liability assumed (section 752(b)). Thus, unless the partners agree otherwise under subparagraph (5)(iii) of this paragraph, each annual payment of $10,000 will be allocated as follows: $6,000 (18,000/30,000 of $10,000) is a section 736(a)(2) payment and $4,000 (12,000/30,000 of $10,000) is a payment for an interest in section 736(b) partnership property. (The Partnership may deduct the $6,000 guaranteed payment made to A in each of the 3 years.) The gain on the payments for partnership property will be determined under section 731, as provided in subparagraph (6) of this paragraph. A will treat only $4,000 of each payment as a distribution in a series in liquidation of his entire interest and, under section 731, will have a capital gain of $1,000 when the last payment is made. However, if A so elects, as provided in subparagraph (6) of this paragraph, he may treat such gain as follows: Of each $4,000 payment attributable to A's interest in partnership property, $333 is capital gain (one-third of the total capital gain of $1,000), and $3,667 is a return of capital.

Example (2). Assume the same facts as in example (1) of this subparagraph except that the agreement between the partners provides for payments to A for 3 years of a percentage of annual income instead of a fixed amount. Unless the partners agree otherwise under subparagraph (5)(iii) of this paragraph, all payments received by A up to $12,000 shall be treated under section 736(b) as payments for A's interest in partnership property. His gain of $1,000 will be taxed only after he has received his full basis under section 731. Since the payments are not fixed in amount, the election provided in subparagraph (6) of this paragraph is not available. Any payments in excess of $12,000 shall be treated as a distributive

share of partnership income to A under section 736(a)(1).

Example (3). Assume the same facts as in example (1) of this subparagraph except that the partnership agreement provides that the payment for A's interest in partnership property shall include payment for his interest in the good will of the partnership. At the time of A's retirement, the partners determine the value of partnership good will to be $9,000. The value of A's interest in partnership property described in section 736(b) is thus $15,000 (one-third of $45,000, the sum of $13,000 cash, plus $23,000, the value of capital and section 1231 assets, plus $9,000 good will). From the disposition of his interest in partnership property, A will realize a capital gain of $4,000 ($15,000, minus $11,000, the basis of his interest). The remaining $15,000 ($30,000 minus $15,000) will constitute payments under section 736(a)(2) which are taxable to A as guaranteed payments under section 707(c).

Example (4). Assume the same facts as in example (1) of this subparagraph except that the capital and section 1231 assets consist of an item of section 1245 property (as defined in section 1245(a)(3)). Assume further that under paragraph (c)(4) of § 1.751-1 the section 1245 property is an unrealized receivable to the extent of $2,000. Therefore, the value of A's interest in section 736(b) partnership property is only $11,333 (one-third of $34,000, the sum of $13,000 cash and $21,000, the fair market value of section 1245 property to the extent not an unrealized receivable). From the disposition of his interest in partnership property, A will realize a capital gain of $333 ($11,333 minus $11,000, the basis of his interest). The remaining $18,667 ($30,000 minus $11,333) will constitute payments under section 736(a)(2) which are taxable to A as guaranteed payments under section 707(c).

(c) *Cross reference.* See section 753 for treatment of payments under section 736(a) as income in respect of a decedent under section 691. [Reg. § 1.736-1.]

☐ [*T.D.* 6175, 5-23-56. *Amended by T.D.* 6832, 7-6-65.]

§ 1.737-1. Recognition of precontribution gain.—(a) *Determination of gain*—(1) *In general.* A partner that receives a distribution of property (other than money) must recognize gain under section 737 and this section in an amount equal to the lesser of the excess distribution (as defined in paragraph (b) of this section) or the partner's net precontribution gain (as defined in paragraph (c) of this section). Gain recognized under section 737 and this section is in addition to any gain recognized under section 731.

(2) *Transactions to which section 737 applies.* Section 737 and this section apply only to the extent that a distribution by a partnership is

a distribution to a partner acting in the capacity of a partner within the meaning of section 731, except that section 737 and this section do not apply to the extent that section 751(b) applies to the distribution.

(b) *Excess distribution*—(1) *Definition*. The excess distribution is the amount (if any) by which the fair market value of the distributed property (other than money) exceeds the distributee partner's adjusted tax basis in the partner's partnership interest.

(2) *Fair market value of property*. The fair market value of the distributed property is the price at which the property would change hands between a willing buyer and a willing seller at the time of the distribution, neither being under any compulsion to buy or sell and both having reasonable knowledge of the relevant facts. The fair market value that a partnership assigns to distributed property will be regarded as correct, provided that the value is reasonably agreed to among the partners in an arm's-length negotiation and the partners have sufficiently adverse interests.

(3) *Distributee partner's adjusted tax basis*—(i) *General rule*. In determining the amount of the excess distribution, the distributee partner's adjusted tax basis in the partnership interest includes any basis adjustment resulting from the distribution that is subject to section 737 (for example, adjustments required under section 752) and from any other distribution or transaction that is part of the same distribution, except for—

(A) The increase required under section 737(c)(1) for the gain recognized by the partner under section 737; and

(B) The decrease required under section 733(2) for any property distributed to the partner other than property previously contributed to the partnership by the distributee partner. See § 1.704-4(e)(1) for a rule in the context of section 704(c)(1)(B). See also § 1.737-3(b)(2) for a special rule for determining a partner's adjusted tax basis in distributed property previously contributed by the partner to the partnership.

(ii) *Advances or drawings*. The distributee partner's adjusted tax basis in the partnership interest is determined as of the last day of the partnership's taxable year if the distribution to which section 737 applies is properly characterized as an advance or drawing against the partner's distributive share of income. See § 1.731-1(a)(1)(ii).

(c) *Net precontribution gain*—(1) *General rule*. The distributee partner's net precontribution gain is the net gain (if any) that would have been recognized by the distributee partner under section 704(c)(1)(B) and § 1.704-4 if all property

that had been contributed to the partnership by the distributee partner within five years of the distribution and is held by the partnership immediately before the distribution had been distributed by the partnership to another partner other than a partner who owns, directly or indirectly, more than 50 percent of the capital or profits interest in the partnership. See § 1.704-4 for provisions determining a contributing partner's gain or loss under section 704(c)(1)(B) on an actual distribution of contributed section 704(c) property to another partner.

(2) *Special rules*—(i) *Property contributed on or before October 3, 1989*. Property contributed to the partnership on or before October 3, 1989, is not taken into account in determining a partner's net precontribution gain. See § 1.704-4(c)(1) for a similar rule in the context of section 704(c)(1)(B).

(ii) *Section 734(b)(1)(A) adjustments*. For distributions to a distributee partner of money by a partnership with a section 754 election in effect that are part of the same distribution as the distribution of property subject to section 737, for purposes of paragraph (a) and (c)(1) of this section the distributee partner's net precontribution gain is reduced by the basis adjustments (if any) made to section 704(c) property contributed by the distributee partner under section 734(b)(1)(A). See § 1.737-3(c)(4) for rules regarding basis adjustments for partnerships with a section 754 election in effect.

(iii) *Transfers of a partnership interest*. The transferee of all or a portion of a contributing partner's partnership interest succeeds to the transferor's net precontribution gain, if any, in an amount proportionate to the interest transferred. See § 1.704-3(a)(7) and § 1.704-4(d)(2) for similar provisions in the context of section 704(c)(1)(A) and section 704(c)(1)(B).

(iv) *Section 704(c)(1)(B) gain recognized in related distribution*. A distributee partner's net precontribution gain is determined after taking into account any gain or loss recognized by the partner under section 704(c)(1)(B) and § 1.704-4 (or that would have been recognized by the partner except for the like-kind exception in section 704(c)(2) and § 1.704-4(d)(3)) on an actual distribution to another partner of section 704(c) property contributed by the distributee partner that is part of the same distribution as the distribution to the distributee partner.

(v) *Section 704(c)(2) disregarded*. A distributee partner's net precontribution gain is determined without regard to the provisions of section 704(c)(2) and § 1.704-4(d)(3) in situations in which the property contributed by the distributee partner is not actually distributed to another partner in a distribution related to the section 737 distribution.

(d) *Character of gain.* The character of the gain recognized by the distributee partner under section 737 and this section is determined by, and is proportionate to, the character of the partner's net precontribution gain. For this purpose, all gains and losses on section 704(c) property taken into account in determining the partner's net precontribution gain are netted according to their character. Character is determined at the partnership level for this purpose, and any character with a net negative amount is disregarded. The character of the partner's gain under section 737 is the same as, and in proportion to, any character with a net positive amount. Character for this purpose is determined as if the section 704(c) property had been sold by the partnership to an unrelated third party at the time of the distribution and includes any item that would have been taken into account separately by the contributing partner under section 702(a) and § 1.702-1(a).

(e) *Examples.* The following examples illustrate the provisions of this section. Unless otherwise specified, partnership income equals partnership expenses (other than depreciation deductions for contributed property) for each year of the partnership, the fair market value of partnership property does not change, all distributions by the partnership are subject to section 737, and all partners are unrelated.

Example 1. Calculation of excess distribution and net precontribution gain. (i) On January 1, 1995, A, B, and C form partnership ABC as equal partners. A contributes Property A, depreciable real property with a fair market value of $30,000 and an adjusted tax basis of $20,000. B contributes Property B, nondepreciable real property with a fair market value and adjusted tax basis of $30,000. C contributes $30,000 cash.

(ii) Property A has 10 years remaining on its cost recovery schedule and is depreciated using the straight-line method. The partnership uses the traditional method for allocating items under section 704(c) described in § 1.704-3(b)(1) for Property A. The partnership has book depreciation of $3,000 per year (10 percent of the $30,000 book basis in Property A) and each partner is allocated $1,000 of book depreciation per year (one-third of the total annual book depreciation of $3,000). The partnership also has tax depreciation of $2,000 per year (10 percent of the $20,000 adjusted tax basis in Property A). This $2,000 tax depreciation is allocated equally between B and C, the noncontributing partners with respect to Property A.

(iii) At the end of 1997, the book value of Property A is $21,000 ($30,000 initial book value less $9,000 aggregate book depreciation) and its adjusted tax basis is $14,000 ($20,000 initial tax basis less $6,000 aggregate tax depreciation).

(iv) On December 31, 1997, Property B is distributed to A in complete liquidation of A's partnership interest. The adjusted tax basis of A's partnership interest at that time is $20,000. The amount of the excess distribution is $10,000, the difference between the fair market value of the distributed Property B ($30,000) and A's adjusted tax basis in A's partnership interest ($20,000). A's net precontribution gain is $7,000, the difference between the book value of Property A ($21,000) and its adjusted tax basis at the time of the distribution ($14,000). A recognizes gain of $7,000 on the distribution, the lesser of the excess distribution and the net precontribution gain.

Example 2. Determination of distributee partner's basis. (i) On January 1, 1995, A, B, and C form general partnership ABC as equal partners. A contributes Property A, nondepreciable real property with a fair market value of $10,000 and an adjusted tax basis of $4,000. B and C each contributes $10,000 cash.

(ii) The partnership purchases Property B, nondepreciable real property with a fair market value of $9,000, subject to a $9,000 nonrecourse liability. This nonrecourse liability is allocated equally among the partners under section 752, increasing A's adjusted tax basis in A's partnership interest from $4,000 to $7,000.

(iii) On December 31, 1998, A receives $2,000 cash and Property B, subject to the $9,000 liability, in a current distribution.

(iv) In determining the amount of the excess distribution, the adjusted tax basis of A's partnership interest is adjusted to take into account the distribution of money and the shift in liabilities. A's adjusted tax basis is therefore increased to $11,000 for this purpose ($7,000 initial adjusted tax basis, less $2,000 distribution of money, less $3,000 (decrease in A's share of the $9,000 partnership liability), plus $9,000 (increase in A's individual liabilities)). As a result of this basis adjustment, the adjusted tax basis of A's partnership interest ($11,000) is greater than the fair market value of the distributed property ($9,000) and therefore, there is no excess distribution. A recognizes no gain under section 737.

Example 3. Net precontribution gain reduced for gain recognized under section 704(c)(1)(B). (i) On January 1, 1995, A, B, and C form partnership ABC as equal partners. A contributes Properties A1 and A2, nondepreciable real properties located in the United States each with a fair market value of $10,000 and an adjusted tax basis of $6,000. B contributes Property B, nondepreciable real property located outside the United States, with a fair market value and adjusted tax basis of $20,000. C contributes $20,000 cash.

(ii) On December 31, 1998, Property B is distributed to A in complete liquidation of A's interest and, as part of the same distribution, Property A1 is distributed to B in a current distribution.

(iii) A's net precontribution gain before the distribution is $8,000 ($20,000 fair market value of Properties A1 and A2 less $12,000 adjusted tax basis of such properties). A recognizes $4,000 of gain under section 704(c)(1)(B) and § 1.704-4 on the distribution of Property A1 to B ($10,000 fair market value of Property A1 less $6,000 adjusted tax basis of Property A1). This gain is taken into account in determining A's excess distribution

and net precontribution gain. As a result, A's net precontribution gain is reduced from $8,000 to $4,000, and the adjusted tax basis in A's partnership interest is increased by $4,000 to $16,000.

(iv) A recognizes gain of $4,000 on the receipt of Property B under section 737, an amount equal to the lesser of the excess distribution of $4,000 ($20,000 fair market value of Property B less $16,000 adjusted tax basis of A's interest in the partnership) and A's remaining net precontribution gain of $4,000.

Example 4. Character of gain. (i) On January 1, 1995, A, B, and C form partnership ABC as equal partners. A contributes the following nondepreciable property to the partnership:

	Fair Market Value	Adjusted Tax Basis
Property A1	$30,000	$20,000
Property A2	30,000	38,000
Property A3	10,000	9,000

(ii) The character of gain or loss on Property A1 and Property A2 is long-term, U.S.-source capital gain or loss. The character of gain on Property A3 is long-term, foreign-source capital gain. B contributes Property B, nondepreciable real property with a fair market value and adjusted tax basis of $70,000. C contributes $70,000 cash.

(iii) On December 31, 1998, Property B is distributed to A in complete liquidation of A's interest in the partnership. A recognizes $3,000 of gain under section 737, an amount equal to the excess distribution of $3,000 ($70,000 fair market value of Property B less $67,000 adjusted tax basis in A's partnership interest) and A's net precontribution gain of $3,000 ($70,000 aggregate fair market value of properties contributed by A less $67,000 aggregate adjusted tax basis of such properties).

(iv) In determining the character of A's gain, all gains and losses on property taken into account in determining A's net precontribution gain are netted according to their character and allocated to A's recognized gain under section 737 based on the relative proportions of the net positive amounts. U.S.-source and foreign-source gains must be netted separately because A would have been required to take such gains into account separately under section 702. As a result, A's net precontribution gain of $3,000 consists of $2,000 of net long-term, U.S.-source capital gain ($10,000 gain on Property A1 and $8,000 loss on Property A2) and $1,000 of net long-term, foreign-source capital gain ($1,000 gain on Property A3).

(v) The character of A's gain under paragraph (d) of this section is therefore $2,000 long-term, U.S.-source capital gain ($3,000 gain recognized under section 737 x $2,000 net long-term, U.S.-source capital gain/$3,000 total net precontribution gain) and $1,000 long-term, foreign-source

capital gain ($3,000 gain recognized under section 737 x $1,000 net long-term, foreign-source capital gain/$3,000 total net precontribution gain). [Reg. § 1.737-1.]

☐ [*T.D. 8642, 12-22-95.*]

§ 1.737-2. Exceptions and special rules.—(a) *Section 708(b)(1)(B) terminations.* Section 737 and this section do not apply to the deemed distribution of interests in a new partnership caused by the termination of a partnership under section 708(b)(1)(B). A subsequent distribution of property by the new partnership to a partner of the new partnership that was formerly a partner of the terminated partnership is subject to section 737 to the same extent that a distribution from the terminated partnership would have been subject to section 737. See also § 1.704-4(c)(3) for a similar rule in the context of section 704(c)(1)(B). This paragraph (a) applies to terminations of partnerships under section 708(b)(1)(B) occurring on or after May 9, 1997; however, this paragraph (a) may be applied to terminations occurring on or after May 9, 1996, provided that the partnership and its partners apply this paragraph (a) to the termination in a consistent manner.

(b) *Transfers to another partnership*—(1) *Complete transfer.* Section 737 and this section do not apply to a transfer by a partnership (transferor partnership) of all of its assets and liabilities to a second partnership (transferee partnership) in an exchange described in section 721, followed by a distribution of the interest in the transferee partnership in liquidation of the transferor partnership as part of the same plan or arrangement. See § 1.704-4(c)(4) for a similar rule in the context of section 704(c)(1)(B).

(2) *Certain divisive transactions.* Section 737 and this section do not apply to a transfer by a partnership (transferor partnership) of all of the

Reg. § 1.737-2(b)(2)

section 704(c) property contributed by a partner to a second partnership (transferee partnership) in an exchange described in section 721, followed by a distribution as part of the same plan or arrangement of an interest in the transferee partnership (and no other property) in complete liquidation of the interest of the partner that originally contributed the section 704(c) property to the transferor partnership.

(3) *Subsequent distributions.* A subsequent distribution of property by the transferee partnership to a partner of the transferee partnership that was formerly a partner of the transferor partnership is subject to section 737 to the same extent that a distribution from the transferor partnership would have been subject to section 737.

(c) *Incorporation of a partnership.* Section 737 and this section do not apply to an incorporation of a partnership by any method of incorporation (other than a method involving an actual distribution of partnership property to the partners followed by a contribution of that property to a corporation), provided that the partnership is liquidated as part of the incorporation transaction. See § 1.704-4(c)(5) for a similar rule in the context of section 704(c)(1)(B).

(d) *Distribution of previously contributed property*—(1) *General rule.* Any portion of the distributed property that consists of property previously contributed by the distributee partner (previously contributed property) is not taken into account in determining the amount of the excess distribution or the partner's net precontribution gain. The previous sentence applies on or after May 9, 1997. See § 1.737-3(b)(2) for a special rule for determining the basis of previously contributed property in the hands of a distributee partner who contributed the property to the partnership.

(2) *Limitation for distribution of previously contributed interest in an entity.* An interest in an entity previously contributed to the partnership is not treated as previously contributed property to the extent that the value of the interest is attribu-

table to property contributed to the entity after the interest was contributed to the partnership. The preceding sentence does not apply to the extent that the property contributed to the entity was contributed to the partnership by the partner that also contributed the interest in the entity to the partnership.

(3) *Nonrecognition transactions.* Property received by the partnership in exchange for contributed section 704(c) property in a nonrecognition transaction is treated as the contributed property with regard to the contributing partner for purposes of section 737 to the extent that the property received is treated as section 704(c) property under § 1.704-3(a)(8). See § 1.7044(d)(1) for a similar rule in the context of section 704(c)(1)(B).

(4) *Undivided interests.* The distribution of an undivided interest in property is treated as the distribution of previously contributed property to the extent that the undivided interest does not exceed the undivided interest, if any, contributed by the distributee partner in the same property. See § 1.704-4(c)(6) for the application of section 704(c)(1)(B) in a similar context. The portion of the undivided interest in property retained by the partnership after the distribution, if any, that is treated as contributed by the distributee partner, is reduced to the extent of the undivided interest distributed to the distributee partner.

(e) *Examples.* The following examples illustrate the rules of this section. Unless otherwise specified, partnership income equals partnership expenses (other than depreciation deductions for contributed property) for each year of the partnership, the fair market value of partnership property does not change, all distributions by the partnership are subject to section 737, and all partners are unrelated.

Example 1. Distribution of previously contributed property. (i) On January 1, 1995, A, B, and C form partnership ABC as equal partners. A contributes the following nondepreciable real property to the partnership:

	Fair Market Value	Adjusted Tax Basis
Property A1	$20,000	$10,000
Property A2	10,000	6,000

(ii) A's total net precontribution gain on the contributed property is $14,000 ($10,000 on Property A1 plus $4,000 on Property A2). B contributes $10,000 cash and Property B, nondepreciable real property with a fair market value and adjusted tax basis of $20,000. C contributes $30,000 cash.

(iii) On December 31, 1998, Property A2 and Property B are distributed to A in complete liquidation of A's interest in the partnership. Property A2 was previously contributed by A and is there-

fore not taken into account in determining the amount of the excess distribution or A's net precontribution gain. The adjusted tax basis of Property A2 in the hands of A is also determined under section 732 as if that property were the only property distributed to A.

(iv) As a result of excluding Property A2 from these determinations, the amount of the excess distribution is $10,000 ($20,000 fair market value of distributed Property B less $10,000 adjusted tax basis in A's partnership interest). A's net

Reg. § 1.737-2(b)(3)

precontribution gain is also $10,000 ($14,000 total net precontribution gain less $4,000 gain with respect to previously contributed Property A2). A therefore recognizes $10,000 of gain on the distribution, the lesser of the excess distribution and the net precontribution gain.

Example 2. Distribution of a previously contributed interest in an entity. (i) On January 1, 1995, A, B, and C form partnership ABC as equal partners. A contributes Property A, nondepreciable real property with a fair market value of $10,000 and an adjusted tax basis of $5,000, and all of the stock of Corporation X with a fair market value and adjusted tax basis of $500. B contributes $500 cash and Property B, nondepreciable real property with a fair market value and adjusted tax basis of $10,000. Partner C contributes $10,500 cash. On December 31, 1996, ABC contributes Property B to Corporation X in a nonrecognition transaction under section 351.

(ii) On December 31, 1998, all of the stock of Corporation X is distributed to A in complete liquidation of A's interest in the partnership. The stock is treated as previously contributed property with respect to A only to the extent of the $500 fair market value of the Corporation X stock contributed by A. The fair market value of the distributed stock for purposes of determining the amount of the excess distribution is therefore $10,000 ($10,500 total fair market value of Corporation X stock less $500 portion treated as previously contributed property). The $500 fair market value and adjusted tax basis of the Corporation X stock is also not taken into account in determining the amount of the excess distribution and the net precontribution gain.

(iii) A recognizes $5,000 of gain under section 737, the amount of the excess distribution ($10,000 fair market value of distributed property less $5,000 adjusted tax basis in A's partnership interest) and A's net precontribution gain ($10,000 fair market value of Property A less $5,000 adjusted tax basis in Property A).

Example 3. Distribution of undivided interest in property. (i) On January 1, 1995, A and B form partnership AB as equal partners. A contributes $500 cash and an undivided one-half interest in Property X. B contributes $500 cash and an undivided one-half interest in Property X.

(ii) On December 31, 1998, an undivided one-half interest in Property X is distributed to A in a current distribution. The distribution of the undivided one-half interest in Property X is treated as a distribution of previously contributed property because A contributed an undivided one-half interest in Property X. As a result, A does not recognize any gain under section 737 on the distribution. [Reg. § 1.737-2.]

□ [*T.D.* 8642, 12-22-95. *Amended by T.D.* 8717, 5-8-97.]

§ 1.737-3. Basis adjustments; Recovery rules.—(a) *Distributee partner's adjusted tax basis in the partnership interest.* The distributee partner's adjusted tax basis in the partnership interest is increased by the amount of gain recognized by the distributee partner under section 737 and this section. This increase is not taken into account in determining the amount of gain recognized by the partner under section 737(a)(1) and this section or in determining the amount of gain recognized by the partner under section 731(a) on the distribution of money in the same distribution or any related distribution. See § 1.704-4(e)(1) for a determination of the distributee partner's adjusted tax basis in a distribution subject to section 704(c)(1)(B).

(b) *Distributee partner's adjusted tax basis in distributed property*—(1) *In general.* The distributee partner's adjusted tax basis in the distributed property is determined under section 732(a) or (b) as applicable. The increase in the distributee partner's adjusted tax basis in the partnership interest under paragraph (a) of this section is taken into account in determining the distributee partner's adjusted tax basis in the distributed property other than property previously contributed by the partner. See § 1.704-4(e)(2) for a determination of basis in a distribution subject to section 704(c)(1)(B).

(2) *Previously contributed property.* The distributee partner's adjusted tax basis in distributed property that the partner previously contributed to the partnership is determined as if it were distributed in a separate and independent distribution prior to the distribution that is subject to section 737 and § 1.737-1.

(c) *Partnership's adjusted tax basis in partnership property*—(1) *Increase in basis.* The partnership's adjusted tax basis in eligible property is increased by the amount of gain recognized by the distributee partner under section 737.

(2) *Eligible property.* Eligible property is property that—

(i) Entered into the calculation of the distributee partner's net precontribution gain;

(ii) Has an adjusted tax basis to the partnership less than the property's fair market value at the time of the distribution;

(iii) Would have the same character of gain on a sale by the partnership to an unrelated party as the character of any of the gain recognized by the distributee partner under section 737; and

(iv) Was not distributed to another partner in a distribution subject to section

Reg. § 1.737-3(c)(2)

704(c)(1)(B) and § 1.704-4 that was part of the same distribution as the distribution subject to section 737.

(3) *Method of adjustment.* For the purpose of allocating the basis increase under paragraph (c)(2) of this section among the eligible property, all eligible property of the same character is treated as a single group. Character for this purpose is determined in the same manner as the character of the recognized gain is determined under § 1.737-1(d). The basis increase is allocated among the separate groups of eligible property in proportion to the character of the gain recognized under section 737. The basis increase is then allocated among property within each group in the order in which the property was contributed to the partnership by the partner, starting with the property contributed first, in an amount equal to the difference between the property's fair market value and its adjusted tax basis to the partnership at the time of the distribution. For property that has the same character and was contributed in the same (or a related) transaction, the basis increase is allocated based on the respective amounts of unrealized appreciation in such properties at the time of the distribution.

(4) *Section 754 adjustments.* The basis adjustments to partnership property made pursuant to paragraph (c)(1) of this section are not elective and must be made regardless of whether the partnership has an election in effect under section 754. Any adjustments to the bases of partnership property (including eligible property as defined in paragraph (c)(2) of this section) under section 734(b) pursuant to a section 754 election (other than basis adjustments under section 734(b)(1)(A) described in the following sentence) must be made after (and must take into account) the adjustments to basis made under paragraph (a) and paragraph (c)(1) of this section. Basis adjustments under section 734(b)(1)(A) that are attributable to distributions of money to the distributee partner that are part of the same distribution as the distribution of property subject to section 737 are made before the adjustments to basis under paragraph (a) and paragraph (c)(1) of this section. See § 1.737-1(c)(2)(ii) for the effect, if any, of basis adjustments under section 734(b)(1)(A) on a partner's net precontribution gain. See also § 1.704-4(e)(3) for a similar rule regarding basis adjustments pursuant to a section 754 election in the context of section 704(c)(1)(B).

(d) *Recovery of increase to adjusted tax basis.* Any increase to the adjusted tax basis of partnership property under paragraph (c)(1) of this section is recovered using any applicable recovery period and depreciation (or other cost recovery) method (including first-year conventions) available to the partnership for newly purchased property (of the type adjusted) placed in service at the time of the distribution.

(e) *Examples.* The following examples illustrate the rules of this section. Unless otherwise specified, partnership income equals partnership expenses (other than depreciation deductions for contributed property) for each year of the partnership, the fair market value of partnership property does not change, all distributions by the partnership are subject to section 737, and all partners are unrelated.

Example 1. Partner's basis in distributed property. (i) On January 1, 1995, A, B, and C form partnership ABC as equal partners. A contributes Property A, nondepreciable real property with a fair market value of $10,000 and an adjusted tax basis of $5,000. B contributes Property B, nondepreciable real property with a fair market value and adjusted tax basis of $10,000. C contributes $10,000 cash.

(ii) On December 31, 1998, Property B is distributed to A in complete liquidation of A's interest in the partnership. A recognizes $5,000 of gain under section 737, an amount equal to the excess distribution of $5,000 ($10,000 fair market value of Property B less $5,000 adjusted tax basis in A's partnership interest) and A's net precontribution gain of $5,000 ($10,000 fair market value of Property A less $5,000 adjusted tax basis of such property).

(iii) A's adjusted tax basis in A's partnership interest is increased by the $5,000 of gain recognized under section 737. This increase is taken into account in determining A's basis in the distributed property. Therefore, A's adjusted tax basis in distributed Property B is $10,000 under section 732(b).

Example 2. Partner's basis in distributed property in connection with gain recognized under section 704(c)(1)(B). (i) On January 1, 1995, A, B, and C form partnership ABC as equal partners. A contributes the following nondepreciable real property located in the United States to the partnership:

	Fair Market Value	Adjusted Tax Basis
Property A1	$10,000	$5,000
Property A2	10,000	2,000

(ii) B contributes $10,000 cash and Property B, nondepreciable real property located outside the United States, with a fair market value and adjusted tax basis of $10,000. C contributes $20,000 cash.

Reg. § 1.737-3(c)(3)

(iii) On December 31, 1998, Property B is distributed to A in a current distribution and Property A1 is distributed to B in a current distribution. A recognizes $5,000 of gain under section 704(c)(1)(B) and § 1.704-4 on the distribution of Property A1 to B, the difference between the fair market value of such property ($10,000) and the adjusted tax basis in distributed Property A1 ($5,000). The adjusted tax basis of A's partnership interest is increased by this $5,000 of gain under section 704(c)(1)(B) and § 1.704-4(e)(1).

(iv) The increase in the adjusted tax basis of A's partnership interest is taken into account in determining the amount of the excess distribution. As a result, there is no excess distribution because the fair market value of Property B ($10,000) is

	Fair Market Value	Adjusted Tax Basis
Property A1	$1,000	$ 500
Property A2	4,000	1,500
Property A3	4,000	6,000
Property A4	6,000	4,000

(ii) The character of gain or loss on Properties A1, A2, and A3 is long-term, U.S.-source capital gain or loss. The character of gain on Property A4 is long-term, foreign-source capital gain. B contributes Property B, nondepreciable real property with a fair market value and adjusted tax basis of $15,000. C contributes $15,000 cash.

(iii) On December 31, 1998, Property B is distributed to A in complete liquidation of A's interest in the partnership. A recognizes gain of $3,000 under section 737, an amount equal to the excess distribution of $3,000 ($15,000 fair market value of Property B less $12,000 adjusted tax basis in A's partnership interest) and A's net precontribution gain of $3,000 ($15,000 aggregate fair market value of the property contributed by A less $12,000 aggregate adjusted tax basis of such property).

(iv) $2,000 of A's gain is long-term, foreign-source capital gain ($3,000 total gain under section 737 x $2,000 net long-term, foreign-source capital gain/$3,000 total net precontribution gain). $1,000 of A's gain is long-term, U.S.-source capital gain ($3,000 total gain under section 737 x $1,000 net long-term, U.S.-source capital gain/$3,000 total net precontribution gain).

(v) The partnership must increase the adjusted tax basis of the property contributed by A by $3,000. All property contributed by A is eligible property. Properties A1, A2, and A3 have the same character and are grouped into a single group for purposes of allocating this basis increase. Property A4 is in a separate character group.

(vi) $2,000 of the basis increase must be allocated to long-term, foreign-source capital assets because $2,000 of the gain recognized by A was

less than the adjusted tax basis of A's interest in the partnership at the time of distribution ($12,000). A therefore recognizes no gain under section 737 on the receipt of Property B. A's adjusted tax basis in Property B is $10,000 under section 732(a)(1). The adjusted tax basis of A's partnership interest is reduced from $12,000 to $2,000 under section 733. See *Example 3* of § 1.737-1(e).

Example 3. Partnership's basis in partnership property after a distribution with section 737 gain. (i) On January 31, 1995, A, B, and C form partnership ABC as equal partners. A contributes the following nondepreciable property to the partnership:

long-term, foreign-source capital gain. The adjusted tax basis of Property A4 is therefore increased from $4,000 to $6,000. $1,000 of the increase must be allocated to Properties A1 and A2 because $1,000 of the gain recognized by A is long-term, U.S.-source capital gain. No basis increase is allocated to Property A3 because its fair market value is less than its adjusted tax basis. The $1,000 basis increase is allocated between Properties A1 and A2 based on the unrealized appreciation in each asset before such basis adjustment. As a result, the adjusted tax basis of Property A1 is increased by $167 ($1,000 x $500/$3,000) and the adjusted tax basis of Property A2 is increased by $833 ($1,000 x $2,500/3,000). [Reg. § 1.737-3.]

□ [*T.D.* 8642, 12-22-95.]

§ 1.737-4. Anti-abuse rule.—(a) *In general.* The rules of section 737 and § § 1.737-1, 1.737-2, and 1.737-3 must be applied in a manner consistent with the purpose of section 737. Accordingly, if a principal purpose of a transaction is to achieve a tax result that is inconsistent with the purpose of section 737, the Commissioner can recast the transaction for federal tax purposes as appropriate to achieve tax results that are consistent with the purpose of section 737. Whether a tax result is inconsistent with the purpose of section 737 must be determined based on all the facts and circumstances. See § 1.704-4(f) for an anti-abuse rule and examples in the context of section 704(c)(1)(B). The anti-abuse rule and examples under section 704(c)(1)(B) and § 1.704-4(f) are relevant to section 737 and § § 1.737-1, 1.737-2, and 1.737-3 to the extent that the net precontribution gain for purposes of section 737 is determined by reference to section 704(c)(1)(B).

Reg. § 1.737-4(a)

(b) *Examples.* The following examples illustrate the rules of this section. The examples set forth below do not delineate the boundaries of either permissible or impermissible types of transactions. Further, the addition of any facts or circumstances that are not specifically set forth in an example (or the deletion of any facts or circumstances) may alter the outcome of the transaction described in the example. Unless otherwise specified, partnership income equals partnership expenses (other than depreciation deductions for contributed property) for each year of the partnership, the fair market value of partnership property does not change, all distributions by the partnership are subject to section 737, and all partners are unrelated.

Example 1. Increase in distributee partner's basis by temporary contribution; results inconsistent with the purpose of section 737. (i) On January 1, 1995, A, B, and C form partnership ABC as equal partners. A contributes Property A1, nondepreciable real property with a fair market value of $10,000 and an adjusted tax basis of $1,000. B contributes Property B, nondepreciable real property with a fair market value of $10,000 and an adjusted tax basis of $10,000. C contributes $10,000 cash.

(ii) On January 1, 1999, pursuant to a plan a principal purpose of which is to avoid gain under section 737, A transfers to the partnership Property A2, nondepreciable real property with a fair market value and adjusted tax basis of $9,000. A treats the transfer as a contribution to the partnership pursuant to section 721 and increases the adjusted tax basis of A's partnership interest from $1,000 to $10,000. On January 1, 1999, the partnership agreement is amended and all other necessary steps are taken so that substantially all of the economic risks and benefits of Property A2 are retained by A. On February 1, 1999, Property B is distributed to A in a current distribution. If the contribution of Property A2 is treated as a contribution to the partnership for purposes of section 737, there is no excess distribution because the fair market value of distributed Property B ($10,000) does not exceed the adjusted tax basis of A's interest in the partnership ($10,000), and therefore section 737 does not apply. A's adjusted tax basis in distributed Property B is $10,000 under section 732(a)(1) and the adjusted tax basis of A's partnership interest is reduced to zero under section 733.

(iii) On March 1, 2000, A receives Property A2 from the partnership in complete liquidation of A's interest in the partnership. A recognizes no gain on the distribution of Property A2 because the property was previously contributed property. See § 1.737-2(d).

(iv) Although A has treated the transfer of Property A2 as a contribution to the partnership that increased the adjusted tax basis of A's interest in the partnership, it would be inconsistent with the purpose of section 737 to recognize the transfer as a contribution to the partnership. Section 737 requires recognition of gain when the value of distributed property exceeds the distributee partner's adjusted tax basis in the partnership interest. Section 737 assumes that any contribution or other transaction that affects a partner's adjusted tax basis in the partnership interest is a contribution or transaction in substance and is not engaged in with a principal purpose of avoiding recognition of gain under section 737. Because the transfer of Property A2 to the partnership was not a contribution in substance and was made with a principal purpose of avoiding recognition of gain under section 737, the Commissioner can disregard the contribution of Property A2 for this purpose. As a result, A recognizes gain of $9,000 under section 737 on the receipt of Property B, an amount equal to the lesser of the excess distribution of $9,000 ($10,000 fair market value of distributed Property B less the $1,000 adjusted tax basis of A's partnership interest, determined without regard to the transitory contribution of Property A2) or A's net precontribution gain of $9,000 on Property A1.

Example 2. Increase in distributee partner's basis; section 752 liability shift; results consistent with the purpose of section 737. (i) On January 1, 1995, A and B form general partnership AB as equal partners. A contributes Property A, nondepreciable real property with a fair market value of $10,000 and an adjusted tax basis of $1,000. B contributes Property B, nondepreciable real property with a fair market value and adjusted tax basis of $10,000. The partnership also borrows $10,000 on a recourse basis and purchases Property C. The $10,000 liability is allocated equally between A and B under section 752, thereby increasing the adjusted tax basis in A's partnership interest to $6,000.

(ii) On December 31, 1998, the partners agree that A is to receive Property B in a current distribution. If A were to receive Property B at that time, A would recognize $4,000 of gain under section 737, an amount equal to the lesser of the excess distribution of $4,000 ($10,000 fair market value of Property B less $6,000 adjusted tax basis in A's partnership interest) or A's net precontribution gain of $9,000 ($10,000 fair market value of Property A less $1,000 adjusted tax basis of Property A).

(iii) With a principal purpose of avoiding such gain, A and B agree that A will be solely liable for the repayment of the $10,000 partnership liability and take the steps necessary so that the entire amount of the liability is allocated to A under section 752. The adjusted tax basis in A's partnership interest is thereby increased from $6,000 to $11,000 to reflect A's share of the $5,000 of liability previously allocated to B. As a result of this increase in A's adjusted tax basis, there is no excess distribution because the fair market value of distributed Property B ($10,000) is less than the adjusted tax basis of A's partnership interest. Recognizing A's increased adjusted tax basis as a result of the shift in liabilities is consistent with the purpose of section 737 and this section. Section 737 requires recognition of gain only when the value of the distributed property exceeds the distributee partner's adjusted tax basis in the partnership interest. The $10,000 recourse liability is a bona fide liability of the partnership that was undertaken for a substantial business purpose and A's and B's agreement that A will assume responsibility for repayment of that debt has substance. Therefore, the increase in A's adjusted tax basis in A's interest in the partnership due to the shift in partnership liabilities under section 752 is respected, and A recognizes no gain under section 737. [Reg. § 1.737-4.]

☐ [T.D. 8642, 12-22-95.]

§ 1.741-1. Recognition and character of gain or loss on sale or exchange.—(a) The sale or exchange of an interest in a partnership shall, except to the extent section 751(a) applies, be treated as the sale or exchange of a capital asset, resulting in capital gain or loss measured by the difference between the amount realized and the adjusted basis of the partnership interest, as determined under section 705. For treatment of selling partner's distributive share up to date of sale, see section 706(c)(2). Where the provisions of section 751 require the recognition of ordinary income or loss with respect to a portion of the amount realized from such sale or exchange, the amount realized shall be reduced by the amount attributable under section 751 to unrealized receivables and substantially appreciated inventory items, and the adjusted basis of the transferor partner's interest in the partnership shall be reduced by the portion of such basis attributable to such unrealized receivables and substantially appreciated inventory items. See section 751 and § 1.751-1.

(b) Section 741 shall apply whether the partnership interest is sold to one or more members of the partnership or to one or more persons who are not members of the partnership. Section 741 shall also apply even though the sale of the partnership interest results in a termination of the partnership under section 708(b). Thus, the provisions of section 741 shall be applicable (1) to the transferor partner in a 2-man partnership when he sells his interest to the other partner, and (2) to all the

members of a partnership when they sell their interest to one or more persons outside the partnership.

(c) See section 351 for nonrecognition of gain or loss upon transfer of a partnership interest to a corporation controlled by the transferor.

(d) For rules relating to the treatment of liabilities on the sale or exchange of interests in a partnership see § § 1.752-1 and 1.1001-2.

(e) For rules relating to the capital gain or loss recognized when a partner sells or exchanges an interest in a partnership that holds appreciated collectibles or section 1250 property with section 1250 capital gain, see § 1.1(h)-1. This paragraph (e) applies to transfers of interests in partnerships that occur on or after September 21, 2000.

(f) For rules relating to dividing the holding period of an interest in a partnership, see § 1.1223-3. This paragraph (f) applies to transfers of partnership interests and distributions of property from a partnership that occur on or after September 21, 2000. [Reg. § 1.741-1.]

☐ [T.D. 6175, 5-23-56. Amended by T.D. 7741, 12-11-80 and T.D. 8902, 9-20-2000.]

§ 1.742-1. Basis of transferee partner's interest.—The basis to a transferee partner of an interest in a partnership shall be determined under the general basis rules for property provided by part II (section 1011 and following), subchapter O, chapter 1 of the Code. Thus, the basis of a purchased interest will be its cost. The basis of a partnership interest acquired from a decedent is the fair market value of the interest at the date of his death or at the alternate valuation date, increased by his estate's or other successor's share of partnership liabilities, if any, on that date, and reduced to the extent that such value is attributable to items constituting income in respect of a decedent (see section 753 and paragraph (c)(3)(v) of § 1.706-1 and paragraph (b) of § 1.753-1) under section 691. See section 1014(c). For basis of contributing partner's interest, see section 722. The basis so determined is then subject to the adjustments provided in section 705. [Reg. § 1.742-1.]

☐ [T.D. 6175, 5-23-56.]

§ 1.743-1. Optional adjustment to basis of partnership property.—(a) *Generally.* The basis of partnership property is adjusted as a result of the transfer of an interest in a partnership by sale or exchange or on the death of a partner only if the election provided by section 754 (relating to optional adjustments to the basis of partnership property) is in effect with respect to the partnership. Whether or not the election provided in section 754 is in effect, the basis of partnership property is not adjusted as the result of a contribution of property, including money, to the partnership.

(b) *Determination of adjustment.* In the case of the transfer of an interest in a partnership, either by sale or exchange or as a result of the death of a partner, a partnership that has an election under section 754 in effect—

(1) Increases the adjusted basis of partnership property by the excess of the transferee's basis for the transferred partnership interest over the transferee's share of the adjusted basis to the partnership of the partnership's property; or

(2) Decreases the adjusted basis of partnership property by the excess of the transferee's share of the adjusted basis to the partnership of the partnership's property over the transferee's basis for the transferred partnership interest.

(c) *Determination of transferee's basis in the transferred partnership interest.* In the case of the transfer of a partnership interest by sale or exchange or as a result of the death of a partner, the transferee's basis in the transferred partnership interest is determined under section 742 and § 1.742-1. See also section 752 and §§ 1.752-1 through 1.752-5.

(d) *Determination of transferee's share of the adjusted basis to the partnership of the partnership's property*—(1) *Generally.* A transferee's share of the adjusted basis to the partnership of partnership property is equal to the sum of the transferee's interest as a partner in the partnership's previously taxed capital, plus the transferee's share of partnership liabilities. Generally, a transferee's interest as a partner in the partnership's previously taxed capital is equal to—

(i) The amount of cash that the transferee would receive on a liquidation of the partnership following the hypothetical transaction, as defined in paragraph (d)(2) of this section (to the extent attributable to the acquired partnership interest); increased by

(ii) The amount of tax loss (including any remedial allocations under § 1.704-3(d)), that would be allocated to the transferee from the hypothetical transaction (to the extent attributable to the acquired partnership interest); and decreased by

(iii) The amount of tax gain (including any remedial allocations under § 1.704-3(d)), that would be allocated to the transferee from the hypothetical transaction (to the extent attributable to the acquired partnership interest).

(2) *Hypothetical transaction defined.* For purposes of paragraph (d)(1) of this section, the hypothetical transaction means the disposition by the partnership of all of the partnership's assets, immediately after the transfer of the partnership

interest, in a fully taxable transaction for cash equal to the fair market value of the assets.

(3) *Examples.* The provisions of this paragraph (d) are illustrated by the following examples:

Example 1. (i) A is a member of partnership PRS in which the partners have equal interests in capital and profits. The partnership has made an election under section 754, relating to the optional adjustment to the basis of partnership property. A sells its interest to T for $22,000. The balance sheet of the partnership at the date of sale shows the following:

Assets

	Adjusted Basis	Fair Market Value
Cash	$ 5,000	$ 5,000
Accounts receivable	10,000	10,000
Inventory	20,000	21,000
Depreciable assets......	20,000	40,000
Total	$55,000	$76,000

Liabilities and Capital

	Adjusted Per Books	Fair Market Value
Liabilities	$10,000	$10,000
Capital:		
A	15,000	22,000
B	15,000	22,000
C	15,000	22,000
Total	$55,000	$76,000

(ii) The amount of the basis adjustment under section 743(b) is the difference between the basis of T's interest in the partnership and T's share of the adjusted basis to the partnership of the partnership's property. Under section 742, the basis of T's interest is $25,333 (the cash paid for A's interest, $22,000, plus $3,333, T's share of partnership liabilities). T's interest in the partnership's previously taxed capital is $15,000 ($22,000, the amount of cash T would receive if PRS liquidated immediately after the hypothetical transaction, decreased by $7,000, the amount of tax gain allocated to T from the hypothetical transaction). T's share of the adjusted basis to the partnership of the partnership's property is $18,333 ($15,000 share of previously taxed capital, plus $3,333 share of the partnership's liabilities). The amount of the basis adjustment under section 743(b) to partnership property therefore, is $7,000, the difference between $25,333 and $18,333.

Example 2. A, B, and C form partnership PRS, to which A contributes land (Asset 1) with a fair market value of $1,000 and an adjusted basis to A of $400, and B and C each contribute $1,000 cash. Each partner has $1,000 credited to it on the books of the partnership as its capital contribution. The partners share in profits equally. During the partnership's first taxable year, Asset 1 appreciates in value to $1,300. A sells its one-third interest in the partnership to T for $1,100, when an election under section 754 is in effect. The amount of tax gain that would be allocated to T from the hypothetical transaction is $700 ($600 section 704(c) built-in gain, plus one-third of the additional gain). Thus, T's interest in the partnership's previously taxed capital is $400 ($1,100, the amount of cash T would receive if PRS liquidated immediately after the hypothetical transaction, decreased by $700, T's share of gain from the hypothetical transaction). The amount of T's basis adjustment under section 743(b) to partnership property is $700 (the excess of $1,100, T's cost basis for its interest, over $400, T's share of the adjusted basis to the partnership of partnership property).

(e) *Allocation of basis adjustment.* For the allocation of the basis adjustment under this section among the individual items of partnership property, see section 755 and the regulations thereunder.

(f) *Subsequent transfers.* Where there has been more than one transfer of a partnership interest, a transferee's basis adjustment is determined without regard to any prior transferee's basis adjustment. In the case of a gift of an interest in a partnership, the donor is treated as transferring, and the donee as receiving, that portion of the basis adjustment attributable to the gifted partnership interest. The provisions of this paragraph (f) are illustrated by the following example:

Example. (i) A, B, and C form partnership PRS. A and B each contribute $1,000 cash, and C contributes land with a basis and fair market value of $1,000. When the land has appreciated in value to $1,300, A sells its interest to T1 for $1,100 (one-third of $3,300, the fair market value of the partnership property). An election under section 754 is in effect; therefore, T1 has a basis adjustment under section 743(b) of $100.

(ii) After the land has further appreciated in value to $1,600, T1 sells its interest to T2 for $1,200 (one-third of $3,600, the fair market value of the partnership property). T2 has a basis adjustment under section 743(b) of $200. This amount is determined without regard to any basis adjustment under section 743(b) that T1 may have had in the partnership assets.

(iii) During the following year, T2 makes a gift to T3 of fifty percent of T2's interest in PRS. At the time of the transfer, T2 has a $200 basis adjustment under section 743(b). T2 is treated as transferring $100 of the basis adjustment to T3 with the gift of the partnership interest.

(g) *Distributions*—(1) *Distribution of adjusted property to the transferee*—(i) *Coordination with section 732.* If a partnership distributes property to a transferee and the transferee has a basis adjustment for the property, the basis adjustment is taken into account under section 732. See § 1.732-2(b).

(ii) *Coordination with section 734.* For certain adjustments to the common basis of remaining partnership property after the distribution of adjusted property to a transferee, see § 1.734-2(b).

(2) *Distribution of adjusted property to another partner*—(i) *Coordination with section 732.* If a partner receives a distribution of property with respect to which another partner has a basis adjustment, the distributee does not take the basis adjustment into account under section 732.

(ii) *Reallocation of basis.* A transferee with a basis adjustment in property that is distributed to another partner reallocates the basis adjustment among the remaining items of partnership property under § 1.755-1(c).

(3) *Distributions in complete liquidation of a partner's interest.* If a transferee receives a distribution of property (whether or not the transferee has a basis adjustment in such property) in liquidation of its interest in the partnership, the adjusted basis to the partnership of the distributed property immediately before the distribution includes the transferee's basis adjustment for the property in which the transferee relinquished an interest (either because it remained in the partnership or was distributed to another partner). Any basis adjustment for property in which the transferee is deemed to relinquish its interest is reallocated among the properties distributed to the transferee under § 1.755-1(c).

(4) *Coordination with other provisions.* The rules of sections 704(c)(1)(B), 731, 737, and 751 apply before the rules of this paragraph (g).

(5) *Example.* The provisions of this paragraph (g) are illustrated by the following example:

Example. (i) A, B, and C are equal partners in partnership PRS. Each partner originally contributed $10,000 in cash, and PRS used the contributions to purchase five nondepreciable capital assets. PRS has no liabilities. After five years, PRS's balance sheet appears as follows:

Assets

	Adjusted Basis	Fair Market Value
Asset 1	$10,000	$10,000
Asset 2	4,000	6,000
Asset 3	6,000	6,000
Asset 4	7,000	4,000
Asset 5	3,000	13,000
Total	$30,000	$39,000

Reg. § 1.743-1(g)(5)

Capital

	Adjusted Per Books	Fair Market Value
Partner A	$10,000	$13,000
Partner B	10,000	13,000
Partner C	10,000	13,000
Total	$30,000	$39,000

(ii) A sells its interest to T for $13,000 when PRS has an election in effect under section 754. T receives a basis adjustment under section 743(b) in the partnership property that is equal to $3,000 (the excess of T's basis in the partnership interest, $13,000, over T's share of the adjusted basis to the partnership of partnership property, $10,000). The basis adjustment is allocated under section 755, and the partnership's balance sheet appears as follows:

Assets

	Adjusted Basis	Fair Market Value	Basis Adjustment
Asset 1	$10,000	$10,000	$ 0.00
Asset 2	4,000	6,000	666.67
Asset 3	6,000	6,000	0.00
Asset 4	7,000	4,000	(1,000.00)
Asset 5	3,000	13,000	3,333.33
Total	$30,000	$39,000	$ 3,000.00

Capital

	Adjusted Per Books	Fair Market Value	Special Basis
Partner T	$10,000	$13,000	$3,000
Partner B	10,000	13,000	0
Partner C	10,000	13,000	0
Total	$30,000	$39,000	$3,000

(iii) Assume that PRS distributes Asset 2 to T in partial liquidation of T's interest in the partnership. T has a basis adjustment under section 743(b) of $666.67 in Asset 2. Under paragraph (g)(1)(i) of this section, T takes the basis adjustment into account under section 732. Therefore, T will have a basis in Asset 2 of $4,666.67 following the distribution.

(iv) Assume instead that PRS distributes Asset 5 to C in complete liquidation of C's interest in PRS. T has a basis adjustment under section 743(b) of $3,333.33 in Asset 5. Under paragraph (g)(2)(i) of this section, C does not take T's basis adjustment into account under section 732. Therefore, the partnership's basis for purposes of sections 732 and 734 is $3,000. Under paragraph (g)(2)(ii) of this section, T's $3,333.33 basis adjustment is reallocated among the remaining partnership assets under $1.755-1(c).

(v) Assume instead that PRS distributes Asset 5 to T in complete liquidation of its interest in PRS. Under paragraph (g)(3) of this section, im-

mediately prior to the distribution of Asset 5 to T, PRS must adjust the basis of Asset 5. Therefore, immediately prior to the distribution, PRS's basis in Asset 5 is equal to $6,000, which is the sum of (A) $3,000, PRS's common basis in Asset 5, plus (B) $3,333.33, T's basis adjustment to Asset 5, plus (C) ($333.33), the sum of T's basis adjustments in Assets 2 and 4. For purposes of sections 732 and 734, therefore, PRS will be treated as having a basis in Asset 5 equal to $6,000.

(h) *Contributions of adjusted property*—(1) *Section 721(a) transactions.* If, in a transaction described in section 721(a), a partnership (the upper tier) contributes to another partnership (the lower tier) property with respect to which a basis adjustment has been made, the basis adjustment is treated as contributed to the lower-tier partnership, regardless of whether the lower-tier partnership makes a section 754 election. The lower tier's basis in the contributed assets and the upper tier's basis in the partnership interest received in the transaction are determined with reference to the basis adjustment. However, that portion of the basis of the upper tier's interest in the lower tier attributable to the basis adjustment must be segregated and allocated solely to the transferee partner for whom the basis adjustment was made. Similarly, that portion of the lower tier's basis in its assets attributable to the basis adjustment must be segregated and allocated solely to the upper tier and the transferee. A partner with a basis adjustment in property held by a partnership that terminates under section 708(b)(1)(B) will continue to have the same basis adjustment with respect to property deemed contributed by the terminated partnership to the new partnership under $1.708-1(b)(1)(iv), regardless of whether the new partnership makes a section 754 election.

(2) *Section 351 transactions*—(i) *Basis in transferred property.* A corporation's adjusted tax basis in property transferred to the corporation by a partnership in a transaction described in section 351 is determined with reference to any basis adjustments to the property under section 743(b) (other than any basis adjustment that reduces a partner's gain under paragraph (h)(2)(ii) of this section).

(ii) *Partnership gain.* The amount of gain, if any, recognized by the partnership on a transfer of property by the partnership to a corporation in a transfer described in section 351 is determined without reference to any basis adjustment to the transferred property under section 743(b). The amount of gain, if any, recognized by the partnership on the transfer that is allocated to a partner with a basis adjustment in the transferred property is adjusted to reflect the partner's basis adjustment in the transferred property.

(iii) *Basis in stock.* The partnership's adjusted tax basis in stock received from a corporation in a transfer described in section 351 is determined without reference to the basis adjustment in property transferred to the corporation in the section 351 exchange. A partner with a basis adjustment in property transferred to the corporation, however, has a basis adjustment in the stock received by the partnership in the section 351 exchange in an amount equal to the partner's basis adjustment in the transferred property, reduced by any basis adjustment that reduced the partner's gain under paragraph (h)(2)(ii) of this section.

(iv) *Example.* The following example illustrates the principles of this paragraph (h)(2):

Example. (i) A, B, and C are equal partners in partnership PRS. The partnership's only asset, Asset 1, has an adjusted tax basis of $60 and a fair market value of $120. Asset 1 is a nondepreciable capital asset and is not section 704(c) property. A has a basis in its partnership interest of $40, and a positive section 743(b) adjustment of $20 in Asset 1. In a transaction to which section 351 applies, PRS contributes Asset 1 to X, a corporation, in exchange for $15 in cash and X stock with a fair market value of $105.

(ii) Under paragraph (h)(2)(ii) of this section, PRS realizes $60 of gain on the transfer of Asset 1 to X ($120, its amount realized, minus $60, its adjusted basis), but recognizes only $15 of that gain under section 351(b)(1). Of this amount, $5 is allocated to each partner. A must use $5 of its basis adjustment in Asset 1 to offset A's share of PRS's gain. Under paragraph (h)(2)(iii) of this section, PRS's basis in the stock received from X is $60. However, A has a basis adjustment in the stock received by PRS equal to $15 (its basis adjustment in Asset 1, $20, reduced by the portion of the adjustment which reduced A's gain, $5). Under paragraph (h)(2)(i) of this section, X's basis in Asset 1 equals $90 (PRS's common basis in the asset, $60, plus the gain recognized by PRS under section 351(b)(1), $15, plus A's basis adjustment under section 743(b), $20, less the portion of the adjustment which reduced A's gain, $5).

(i) [Reserved].

(j) *Effect of basis adjustment*—(1) *In general.* The basis adjustment constitutes an adjustment to the basis of partnership property with respect to the transferee only. No adjustment is made to the common basis of partnership property. Thus, for purposes of calculating income, deduction, gain, and loss, the transferee will have a special basis for those partnership properties the bases of which are adjusted under section 743(b) and this section. The adjustment to the basis of partnership property under section 743(b) has no effect on the partnership's computation of any item under section 703.

(2) *Computation of partner's distributive share of partnership items.* The partnership first computes its items of income, deduction, gain, or loss at the partnership level under section 703. The partnership then allocates the partnership items among the partners, including the transferee, in accordance with section 704, and adjusts the partners' capital accounts accordingly. The partnership then adjusts the transferee's distributive share of the items of partnership income, deduction, gain, or loss, in accordance with paragraphs (j)(3) and (4) of this section, to reflect the effects of the transferee's basis adjustment under section 743(b). These adjustments to the transferee's distributive shares must be reflected on Schedules K and K-1 of the partnership's return (Form 1065). These adjustments to the transferee's distributive shares do not affect the transferee's capital account.

(3) *Effect of basis adjustment in determining items of income, gain, or loss*—(i) *In general.* The amount of a transferee's income, gain, or loss from the sale or exchange of a partnership asset in which the transferee has a basis adjustment is equal to the transferee's share of the partnership's gain or loss from the sale of the asset (including any remedial allocations under $1.704-3(d)), minus the amount of the transferee's positive basis adjustment for the partnership asset (determined by taking into account the recovery of the basis adjustment under paragraph (j)(4)(i)(B) of this section) or plus the amount of the transferee's negative basis adjustment for the partnership asset (determined by taking into the account the recovery of the basis adjustment under paragraph (j)(4)(ii)(B) of this section).

(ii) *Examples.* The following examples illustrate the principles of this paragraph (j)(3):

Example 1. A and B form equal partnership PRS. A contributes nondepreciable property with a fair market value of $50 and an adjusted tax basis of $100. PRS will use the traditional allocation method under § 1.704-3(b). B contributes $50 cash. A sells its interest to T for $50. PRS has an election in effect to adjust the basis of partnership property under section 754. T receives a negative $50 basis adjustment under section 743(b) that, under section 755, is allocated to the nondepreciable property. PRS then sells the property for $60. PRS recognizes a book gain of $10 (allocated equally between T and B) and a tax loss of $40. T will receive an allocation of $40 of tax loss under the principles of section 704(c). However, because T has a negative $50 basis adjustment in the nondepreciable property, T rec-

Reg. § 1.743-1(j)(3)

ognizes a $10 gain from the partnership's sale of the property.

Example 2. A and B form equal partnership PRS. A contributes nondepreciable property with a fair market value of $100 and an adjusted tax basis of $50. B contributes $100 cash. PRS will use the traditional allocation method under $1.704-3(b). A sells its interest to T for $100. PRS has an election in effect to adjust the basis of partnership property under section 754. Therefore, T receives a $50 basis adjustment under section 743(b) that, under section 755, is allocated to the nondepreciable property. PRS then sells the nondepreciable property for $90. PRS recognizes a book loss of $10 (allocated equally between T and B) and a tax gain of $40. T will receive an allocation of the entire $40 of tax gain under the principles of section 704(c). However, because T has a $50 basis adjustment in the property, T recognizes a $10 loss from the partnership's sale of the property.

Example 3. A and B form equal partnership PRS. PRS will make allocations under section 704(c) using the remedial allocation method described in $1.704-3(d). A contributes nondepreciable property with a fair market value of $100 and an adjusted tax basis of $150. B contributes $100 cash. A sells its partnership interest to T for $100. PRS has an election in effect to adjust the basis of partnership property under section 754. T receives a negative $50 basis adjustment under section 743(b) that, under section 755, is allocated to the property. The partnership then sells the property for $120. The partnership recognizes a $20 book gain and a $30 tax loss. The book gain will be allocated equally between the partners. The entire $30 tax loss will be allocated to T under the principles of section 704(c). To match its $10 share of book gain, B will be allocated $10 of remedial gain, and T will be allocated an offsetting $10 of remedial loss. T was allocated a total of $40 of tax loss with respect to the property. However, because T has a negative $50 basis adjustment to the property, T recognizes a $10 gain from the partnership's sale of the property.

(4) *Effect of basis adjustment in determining items of deduction*—(i) *Increases*—(A) *Additional deduction.* The amount of any positive basis adjustment that is recovered by the transferee in any year is added to the transferee's distributive share of the partnership's depreciation or amortization deductions for the year. The basis adjustment is adjusted under section 1016(a)(2) to reflect the recovery of the basis adjustment.

(B) *Recovery period*—(*1*) *In general.* Except as provided in paragraph (j)(4)(i)(B)(2) of this section, for purposes of section 168, if the basis of a partnership's recovery property is in-

creased as a result of the transfer of a partnership interest, then the increased portion of the basis is taken into account as if it were newly-purchased recovery property placed in service when the transfer occurs. Consequently, any applicable recovery period and method may be used to determine the recovery allowance with respect to the increased portion of the basis. However, no change is made for purposes of determining the recovery allowance under section 168 for the portion of the basis for which there is no increase.

(*2*) *Remedial allocation method.* If a partnership elects to use the remedial allocation method described in $1.704-3(d) with respect to an item of the partnership's recovery property, then the portion of any increase in the basis of the item of the partnership's recovery property under section 743(b) that is attributable to section 704(c) built-in gain is recovered over the remaining recovery period for the partnership's excess book basis in the property as determined in the final sentence of $1.704-3(d)(2). Any remaining portion of the basis increase is recovered under paragraph (j)(4)(i)(B)(*1*) of this section.

(C) *Examples.* The provisions of this paragraph (j)(4)(i) are illustrated by the following examples:

Example 1. (i) A, B, and C are equal partners in partnership PRS, which owns Asset 1, an item of depreciable property that has a fair market value in excess of its adjusted tax basis. C sells its interest in PRS to T while PRS has an election in effect under section 754. PRS, therefore, increases the basis of Asset 1 with respect to T.

(ii) Assume that in the year following the transfer of the partnership interest to T, T's distributive share of the partnership's common basis depreciation deductions from Asset 1 is $1,000. Also assume that, under paragraph (j)(4)(i)(B) of this section, the amount of the basis adjustment under section 743(b) that T recovers during the year is $500. The total amount of depreciation deductions from Asset 1 reported by T is equal to $1,500.

Example 2. (i) A and B form equal partnership PRS. A contributes property with an adjusted basis of $100,000 and a fair market value of $500,000. B contributes $500,000 cash. When PRS is formed, the property has five years remaining in its recovery period. The partnership's adjusted basis of $100,000 will, therefore, be recovered over the five years remaining in the property's recovery period. PRS elects to use the remedial allocation method under $1.704-3(d) with respect to the property. If PRS had purchased the property at the time of the partnership's formation, the basis of the property would have been recovered over a 10-year period. The $400,000 of section 704(c) built-in gain will, therefore, be amortized under $1.704-3(d) over a 10-year period beginning at the time of the partnership's formation.

(ii)(A) Except for the depreciation deductions, PRS's expenses equal its income in each

year of the first two years commencing with the year the partnership is formed. After two years, A's share of the adjusted basis of partnership property is $120,000, while B's is $440,000:

Capital Accounts

	A		B	
	Book	Tax	Book	Tax
Initial				
Contribution	$500,000	$100,000	$500,000	$500,000
Depreciation				
Year 1	(30,000)		(30,000)	(20,000)
Remedial		10,000		(10,000)
	470,000	110,000	470,000	470,000
Depreciation				
Year 2	(30,000)		(30,000)	(20,000)
Remedial		10,000		(10,000)
	$440,000	$120,000	$440,000	$440,000

(B) A sells its interest in PRS to T for its fair market value of $440,000. A valid election under section 754 is in effect with respect to the sale of the partnership interest. Accordingly, PRS makes an adjustment, pursuant to section 743(b), to increase the basis of partnership property. Under section 743(b), the amount of the basis adjustment is equal to $320,000. Under section 755, the entire basis adjustment is allocated to the property.

(iii) At the time of the transfer, $320,000 of section 704(c) built-in gain from the property was still reflected on the partnership's books, and all of the basis adjustment is attributable to section 704(c) built-in gain. Therefore, the basis adjustment will be recovered over the remaining recovery period for the section 704(c) built-in gain under $1.704-3(d).

(ii) *Decreases*—(A) *Reduced deduction.* The amount of any negative basis adjustment allocated to an item of depreciable or amortizable property that is recovered in any year first decreases the transferee's distributive share of the partnership's depreciation or amortization deductions from that item of property for the year. If the amount of the basis adjustment recovered in any year exceeds the transferee's distributive share of the partnership's depreciation or amortization deductions from the item of property, then the transferee's distributive share of the partnership's depreciation or amortization deductions from other items of partnership property is decreased. The transferee then recognizes ordinary income to the extent of the excess, if any, of the amount of the basis adjustment recovered in any year over the transferee's distributive share of the partnership's depreciation or amortization deductions from all items of property.

(B) *Recovery period.* For purposes of section 168, if the basis of an item of a partnership's recovery property is decreased as the result of the transfer of an interest in the partnership, then the decrease is recovered over the remaining useful life of the item of the partnership's recovery property. The portion of the decrease that is recovered in any year during the recovery period is equal to the product of—

(1) The amount of the decrease to the item's adjusted basis (determined as of the date of the transfer); multiplied by

(2) A fraction, the numerator of which is the portion of the adjusted basis of the item recovered by the partnership in that year, and the denominator of which is the adjusted basis of the item on the date of the transfer (determined prior to any basis adjustments).

(C) *Examples.* The provisions of this paragraph (j)(4)(ii) are illustrated by the following examples:

Example 1. (i) A, B, and C are equal partners in partnership PRS, which owns Asset 2, an item of depreciable property that has a fair market value that is less than its adjusted tax basis. C sells its interest in PRS to T while PRS has an election in effect under section 754. PRS, therefore, decreases the basis of Asset 2 with respect to T.

(ii) Assume that in the year following the transfer of the partnership interest to T, T's distributive share of the partnership's common basis depreciation deductions from Asset 2 is $1,000. Also assume that, under paragraph (j)(4)(ii)(B) of this section, the amount of the basis adjustment under section 743(b) that T recovers during the year is $500. The total amount of

Reg. § 1.743-1(j)(4)

depreciation deductions from Asset 2 reported by T is equal to $500.

Example 2. (i) A and B form equal partnership PRS. A contributes property with an adjusted basis of $100,000 and a fair market value of $50,000. B contributes $50,000 cash. When PRS is formed, the property has five years remaining in its recovery period. The partnership's adjusted basis of $100,000 will, therefore, be recovered over the five years remaining in the property's recovery period. PRS uses the traditional allocation method under § 1.704-3(b) with respect to the property. As a result, B will receive $5,000 of depreciation deductions from the property in each of years 1-5, and A, as the contributing partner, will receive $15,000 of depreciation deductions in each of these years.

(ii) Except for the depreciation deductions, PRS's expenses equal its income in each of the first two years commencing with the year the partnership is formed. After two years, A's share of the adjusted basis of partnership property is $70,000, while B's is $40,000. A sells its interest in PRS to T for its fair market value of $40,000. A valid election under section 754 is in effect with respect to the sale of the partnership interest. Accordingly, PRS makes an adjustment, pursuant to section 743(b), to decrease the basis of partnership property. Under section 743(b), the amount of the adjustment is equal to ($30,000). Under section 755, the entire adjustment is allocated to the property.

(iii) The basis of the property at the time of the transfer of the partnership interest was $60,000. In each of years 3 through 5, the partnership will realize depreciation deductions of $20,000 from the property. Thus, one third of the negative basis adjustment ($10,000) will be recovered in each of years 3 through 5. Consequently, T will be allocated, for tax purposes, depreciation of $15,000 each year from the partnership and will recover $10,000 of its negative basis adjustment. Thus, T's net depreciation deduction from the partnership in each year is $5,000.

Example 3. (i) A, B, and C are equal partners in partnership PRS, which owns Asset 2, an item of depreciable property that has a fair market value that is less than its adjusted tax basis. C sells its interest in PRS to T while PRS has an election in effect under section 754. PRS, therefore, decreases the basis of Asset 2 with respect to T.

(ii) Assume that in the year following the transfer of the partnership interest to T, T's distributive share of the partnership's common basis depreciation deductions from Asset 2 is $500. PRS allocates no other depreciation to T. Also assume that, under paragraph (j)(4)(ii)(B) of

this section, the amount of the negative basis adjustment that T recovers during the year is $1,000. T will report $500 of ordinary income because the amount of the negative basis adjustment recovered during the year exceeds T's distributive share of the partnership's common basis depreciation deductions from Asset 2.

(5) *Depletion.* Where an adjustment is made under section 743(b) to the basis of partnership property subject to depletion, any depletion allowance is determined separately for each partner, including the transferee partner, based on the partner's interest in such property. See § 1.702-1(a)(8). For partnerships that hold oil and gas properties that are depleted at the partner level under section 613A(c)(7)(D), the transferee partner (and not the partnership) must make the basis adjustments, if any, required under section 743(b) with respect to such properties. See § 1.613A-3(e)(6)(iv).

(6) *Example.* The provisions of paragraph (j)(5) of this section are illustrated by the following example:

Example. A, B, and C each contributes $5,000 cash to form partnership PRS, which purchases a coal property for $15,000. A, B, and C have equal interests in capital and profits. C subsequently sells its partnership interest to T for $100,000 when the election under section 754 is in effect. T has a basis adjustment under section 743(b) for the coal property of $95,000 (the difference between T's basis, $100,000, and its share of the basis of partnership property, $5,000). Assume that the depletion allowance computed under the percentage method would be $21,000 for the taxable year so that each partner would be entitled to $7,000 as its share of the deduction for depletion. However, under the cost depletion method, at an assumed rate of 10 percent, the allowance with respect to T's one-third interest which has a basis to him of $100,000 ($5,000, plus its basis adjustment of $95,000) is $10,000, although the cost depletion allowance with respect to the one-third interest of A and B in the coal property, each of which has a basis of $5,000, is only $500. For partners A and B, the percentage depletion is greater than cost depletion and each will deduct $7,000 based on the percentage depletion method. However, as to T, the transferee partner, the cost depletion method results in a greater allowance and T will, therefore, deduct $10,000 based on cost depletion. See section 613(a).

* * *

[Reg. § 1.743-1.]

□ [*T.D.* 6175, 5-23-56. *Amended by T.D.* 8717, 5-8-97 *and T.D.* 8847, 12-14-99 (*corrected* 2-23-2000).]

§ 1.751-1. **Unrealized receivables and inventory items**—(a) *Sale or exchange of interest in a partnership*—(1) *Character of amount realized.* To the extent that money or property received by a partner in exchange for all or part of his partnership interest is attributable to his share of the value of partnership unrealized receivables or substantially appreciated inventory items, the money or fair market value of the property received shall be considered as an amount realized from the sale or exchange of property other than a capital asset. The remainder of the total amount realized on the sale or exchange of the partnership interest is realized from the sale or exchange of a capital asset under section 741. For definition of "unrealized receivables" and "inventory items which have appreciated substantially in value", see section 751(c) and (d). Unrealized receivables and substantially appreciated inventory items are hereafter in this section referred to as "section 751 property". See paragraph (e) of this section.

(2) *Determination of gain or loss.* The income or loss realized by a partner upon the sale or exchange of its [his] interest in section 751 property is the amount of income or loss from section 751 property (including any remedial allocations under § 1.704-3(d)) that would have been allocated to the partner (to the extent attributable to the partnership interest sold or exchanged) if the partnership had sold all of its property in a fully taxable transaction for cash in an amount equal to the fair market value of such property (taking into account section 7701(g)) immediately prior to the partner's transfer of the interest in the partnership. Any gain or loss recognized that is attributable to section 751 property will be ordinary gain or loss. The difference between the amount of capital gain or loss that the partner would realize in the absence of section 751 and the amount of ordinary income or loss determined under this paragraph (a)(2) is the transferor's capital gain or loss on the sale of its partnership interest.

(3) *Statement required.* A partner selling or exchanging any part of an interest in a partnership that has any section 751 property at the time of sale or exchange must submit with its income tax return for the taxable year in which the sale or exchange occurs a statement setting forth separately the following information—

(i) The date of the sale or exchange;

(ii) The amount of any gain or loss attributable to the section 751 property; and

(iii) The amount of any gain or loss attributable to capital gain or loss on the sale of the partnership interest.

(b) *Certain distributions treated as sales or exchanges*—(1) *In general.* (i) Certain distributions to which section 751(b) applies are treated in part as sales or exchanges of property between the partnership and the distributee partner, and not as distributions to which sections 731 through 736 apply. A distribution treated as a sale or exchange under section 751(b) is not subject to the provisions of section 707(b). Section 751(b) applies whether or not the distribution is in liquidation of the distributee partner's entire interest in the partnership. However, section 751(b) applies only to the extent that a partner either receives section 751 property in exchange for his relinquishing any part of his interest in other property, or receives other property in exchange for his relinquishing any part of his interest in section 751 property.

(ii) Section 751(b) does not apply to a distribution to a partner which is not in exchange for his interest in other partnership property. Thus, section 751(b) does not apply to the extent that a distribution consists of the distributee partner's share of section 751 property or his share of other property. Similarly, section 751(b) does not apply to current drawings or to advances against the partner's distributive share, or to a distribution which is, in fact, a gift or payment for services or for the use of capital. In determining whether a partner has received only his share of either section 751 property or of other property, his interest in such property remaining in the partnership immediately after a distribution must be taken into account. For example, the section 751 property in partnership ABC has a fair market value of $100,000 in which partner A has an interest of 30 percent, or $30,000. If A receives $20,000 of section 751 property in a distribution, and continues to have a 30-percent interest in the $80,000 of section 751 property remaining in the partnership after the distribution, only $6,000 ($30,000 minus $24,000 (30 percent of $80,000)) of the section 751 property received by him will be considered to be his share of such property. The remaining $14,000 ($20,000 minus $6,000) received is in excess of his share.

(iii) If a distribution is, in part, a distribution of the distributee partner's share of section 751 property, or of other property (including money) and, in part, a distribution in exchange of such properties, the distribution shall be divided for the purpose of applying section 751(b). The rules of section 751(b) shall first apply to the part of the distribution treated as a sale or exchange of such properties, and then the rules of sections 731 through 736 shall apply to the part of the distribution not treated as a sale or exchange. See paragraph (b)(4)(ii) of this section for treatment of payments under section 736(a).

(2) *Distribution of section 751 property (unrealized receivables or substantially appreciated inventory items).* (i) To the extent that a partner

Reg. § 1.751-1(b)(2)

receives section 751 property in a distribution in exchange for any part of his interest in partnership property (including money) other than section 751 property, the transaction shall be treated as a sale or exchange of such properties between the distributee partner and the partnership (as constituted after the distribution).

(ii) At the time of the distribution, the partnership (as constituted after the distribution) realizes ordinary income or loss on the sale or exchange of the section 751 property. The amount of the income or loss to the partnership will be measured by the difference between the adjusted basis to the partnership of the section 751 property considered as sold to or exchanged with the partner, and the fair market value of the distributee partner's interest in other partnership property which he relinquished in the exchange. In computing the partners' distributive shares of such ordinary income or loss, the income or loss shall be allocated only to partners other than the distributee and separately taken into account under section 702(a)(8).

(iii) At the time of the distribution, the distributee partner realizes gain or loss measured by the difference between his adjusted basis for the property relinquished in the exchange (including any special basis adjustment which he may have) and the fair market value of the section 751 property received by him in exchange for his interest in other property which he has relinquished. The distributee's adjusted basis for the property relinquished is the basis such property would have had under section 732 (including subsection (d) thereof) if the distributee partner had received such property in a current distribution immediately before the actual distribution which is treated wholly or partly as a sale or exchange under section 751(b). The character of the gain or loss to the distributee partner shall be determined by the character of the property in which he relinquished his interest.

(3) *Distribution of partnership property other than section 751 property.* (i) To the extent that a partner receives a distribution of partnership property (including money) other than section 751 property in exchange for any part of his interest in section 751 property of the partnership, the distribution shall be treated as a sale or exchange of such properties between the distributee partner and the partnership (as constituted after the distribution).

(ii) At the time of the distribution, the partnership (as constituted after the distribution) realizes gain or loss on the sale or exchange of the property other than section 751 property. The amount of the gain to the partnership will be measured by the difference between the adjusted

basis to the partnership of the distributed property considered as sold to or exchanged with the partner, and the fair market value of the distributee partner's interest in section 751 property which he relinquished in the exchange. The character of the gain or loss to the partnership is determined by the character of the distributed property treated as sold or exchanged by the partnership. In computing the partners' distributive shares of such gain or loss, the gain or loss shall be allocated only to partners other than the distributee and separately taken into account under section 702(a)(8).

(iii) At the time of the distribution, the distributee partner realizes ordinary income or loss on the sale or exchange of the section 751 property. The amount of the distributee partner's income or loss shall be measured by the difference between his adjusted basis for the section 751 property relinquished in the exchange (including any special basis adjustment which he may have), and the fair market value of other property (including money) received by him in exchange for his interest in the section 751 property which he has relinquished. The distributee partner's adjusted basis for the section 751 property relinquished is the basis such property would have had under section 732 (including subsection (d) thereof) if the distributee partner had received such property in a current distribution immediately before the actual distribution which is treated wholly or partly as a sale or exchange under section 751(b).

(4) *Exceptions.* (i) Section 751(b) does not apply to the distribution to a partner of property which the distributee partner contributed to the partnership. The distribution of such property is governed by the rules set forth in sections 731 through 736, relating to distributions by a partnership.

(ii) Section 751(b) does not apply to payments made to a retiring partner or to a deceased partner's successor in interest to the extent that, under section 736(a), such payments constitute a distributive share of partnership income or guaranteed payments. Payments to a retiring partner or to a deceased partner's successor in interest for his interest in unrealized receivables of the partnership in excess of their partnership basis, including any special basis adjustment for them to which such partner is entitled, constitute payments under section 736(a) and, therefore, are not subject to section 751(b). However, payments under section 736(b) which are considered as made in exchange for an interest in partnership property are subject to section 751(b) to the extent that they involve an exchange of substantially appreciated inventory items for other property. Thus, payments to a retiring partner or to a deceased partner's successor in interest under section 736 must first be divided between payments under section 736(a) and section 736(b).

The section 736(b) payments must then be divided, if there is an exchange of substantially appreciated inventory items for other property, between the payments treated as a sale or exchange under section 751(b) and payments treated as a distribution under sections 731 through 736. See subparagraph (1)(iii) of this paragraph, and section 736 and § 1.736-1.

(5) *Statement required.* A partnership which distributes section 751 property to a partner in exchange for his interest in other partnership property, or which distributes other property in exchange for any part of the partner's interest in section 751 property, shall submit with its return for the year of the distribution a statement showing the computation of any income, gain, or loss to the partnership under the provisions of section 751(b) and this paragraph. The distributee partner shall submit with his return a statement showing the computation of any income, gain, or loss to him. Such statement shall contain information similar to that required under paragraph (a)(3) of this section.

(c) *Unrealized receivables*—(1) The term "unrealized receivables", as used in subchapter K, chapter 1 of the Code, means any rights (contractual or otherwise) to payment for—

(i) Goods delivered or to be delivered (to the extent that such payment would be treated as received for property other than a capital asset), or

(ii) Services rendered or to be rendered, to the extent that income arising from such rights to payment was not previously includible in income under the method of accounting employed by the partnership. Such rights must have arisen under contracts or agreements in existence at the time of sale or distribution, although the partnership may not be able to enforce payment until a later time. For example, the term includes trade accounts receivable of a cash method taxpayer, and rights to payment for work or goods begun but incomplete at the time of the sale or distribution.

(2) The basis for such unrealized receivables shall include all costs or expenses attributable thereto paid or accrued but not previously taken into account under the partnership method of accounting.

(3) In determining the amount of the sale price attributable to such unrealized receivables, or their value in a distribution treated as a sale or exchange, full account shall be taken not only of the estimated cost of completing performance of the contract or agreement, but also of the time

between the sale or distribution and the time of payment.

(4)(i) With respect to any taxable year of a partnership ending after September 12, 1966 (but only in respect of expenditures paid or incurred after that date), the term *unrealized receivables*, for purposes of this section and sections 731, 736, 741, and 751, also includes potential gain from mining property defined in section 617(f)(2). With respect to each item of partnership mining property so defined, the potential gain is the amount that would be treated as gain to which section 617(d)(1) would apply if (at the time of the transaction described in section 731, 736, 741, or 751, as the case may be) the item were sold by the partnership at its fair market value.

(ii) With respect to sales, exchanges, or other dispositions after December 31, 1975, in any taxable year of a partnership ending after that date, the term *unrealized receivables*, for purposes of this section and sections 731, 736, 741, and 751, also includes potential gain from stock in a DISC as described in section 992(a). With respect to stock in such a DISC, the potential gain is the amount that would be treated as gain to which section 995(c) would apply if (at the time of the transaction described in section 731, 736, 741, or 751, as the case may be) the stock were sold by the partnership at its fair market value.

(iii) With respect to any taxable year of a partnership beginning after December 31, 1962, the term *unrealized receivables*, for purposes of this section and sections 731, 736, 741, and 751, also includes potential gain from section 1245 property. With respect to each item of partnership section 1245 property (as defined in section 1245(a)(3)), potential gain from section 1245 property is the amount that would be treated as gain to which section 1245(a)(1) would apply if (at the time of the transaction described in section 731, 736, 741, or 751, as the case may be) the item of section 1245 property were sold by the partnership at its fair market value. See § 1.1245-1(e)(1). For example, if a partnership would recognize under section 1245(a)(1) gain of $600 upon a sale of one item of section 1245 property and gain of $300 upon a sale of its only other item of such property, the potential section 1245 income of the partnership would be $900.

(iv) With respect to transfers after October 9, 1975, and to sales, exchanges, and distributions taking place after that date, the term *unrealized receivables*, for purposes of this section and sections 731, 736, 741, and 751, also includes potential gain from stock in certain foreign corporations as described in section 1248. With respect to stock in such a foreign corporation, the potential gain is the amount that would be treated as gain to which section 1248(a) would apply if (at the time of the transaction described in section 731, 736, 741, or 751, as the case may be) the stock were sold by the partnership at its fair market value.

(v) With respect to any taxable year of a partnership ending after December 31, 1963, the term *unrealized receivables*, for purposes of this section and sections 731, 736, 741, and 751, also includes potential gain from section 1250 property. With respect to each item of partnership section 1250 property (as defined in section 1250(c)), potential gain from section 1250 property is the amount that would be treated as gain to which section 1250(a) would apply if (at the time of the transaction described in section 731, 736, 741, or 751, as the case may be) the item of section 1250 property were sold by the partnership at its fair market value. See § 1.1250-1(f)(1).

(vi) With respect to any taxable year of a partnership beginning after December 31, 1969, the term *unrealized receivables*, for purposes of this section and sections 731, 736, 741, and 751, also includes potential gain from farm recapture property as defined in section 1251(e)(1) (as in effect before enactment of the Tax Reform Act of 1984). With respect to each item of partnership farm recapture property so defined, the potential gain is the amount which would be treated as gain to which section 1251(c) (as in effect before enactment of the Tax Reform Act of 1984) would apply if (at the time of the transaction described in section 731, 736, 741, or 751, as the case may be) the item were sold by the partnership at its fair market value.

(vii) With respect to any taxable year of a partnership beginning after December 31, 1969, the term *unrealized receivables*, for purposes of this section and sections 731, 736, 741, and 751, also includes potential gain from farm land as defined in section 1252(a)(2). With respect to each item of partnership farm land so defined, the potential gain is the amount that would be treated as gain to which section 1252(a)(1) would apply if (at the time of the transaction described in section 731, 736, 741, or 751, as the case may be) the item were sold by the partnership at its fair market value.

(viii) With respect to transactions which occur after December 31, 1976, in any taxable year of a partnership ending after that date, the term *unrealized receivables*, for purposes of this section and sections 731, 736, 741, and 751, also includes potential gain from franchises, trademarks, or trade names referred to in section 1253(a). With respect to each such item so referred to in section 1253(a), the potential gain is the amount that would be treated as gain to

which section 1253(a) would apply if (at the time of the transaction described in section 731, 736, 741, or 751, as the case may be) the items were sold by the partnership at its fair market value.

(ix) With respect to any taxable year of a partnership ending after December 31, 1975, the term *unrealized receivables*, for purposes of this section and sections 731, 736, 741, and 751, also includes potential gain under section 1254(a) from natural resource recapture property as defined in § 1.1254-1(b)(2). With respect to each separate partnership natural resource recapture property so described, the potential gain is the amount that would be treated as gain to which section 1254(a) would apply if (at the time of the transaction described in section 731, 736, 741, or 751, as the case may be) the property were sold by the partnership at its fair market value.

(5) For purposes of subtitle A of the Internal Revenue Code, the basis of any potential gain described in paragraph (c)(4) of this section is zero.

(6)(i) If (at the time of any transaction referred to in paragraph (c)(4) of this section) a partnership holds property described in paragraph (c)(4) of this section and if—

(A) A partner had a special basis adjustment under section 743(b) in respect of the property;

(B) The basis under section 732 of the property if distributed to the partner would reflect a special basis adjustment under section 732(d); or

(C) On the date a partner acquired a partnership interest by way of a sale or exchange (or upon the death of another partner) the partnership owned the property and an election under section 754 was in effect with respect to the partnership, the partner's share of any potential gain described in paragraph (c)(4) of this section is determined under paragraph (c)(6)(ii) of this section.

(ii) The partner's share of the potential gain described in paragraph (c)(4) of this section in respect of the property to which this paragraph (c)(6)(ii) applies is that amount of gain that the partner would recognize under section 617(d)(1), 995(c), 1245(a), 1248(a), 1250(a), 1251(c) (as in effect before the Tax Reform Act of 1984), 1252(a), 1253(a), or 1254(a) (as the case may be) upon a sale of the property by the partnership, except that, for purposes of this paragraph (c)(6) the partner's share of such gain is determined in a manner that is consistent with the manner in which the partner's share of partnership property is determined; and the amount of a potential special basis adjustment under section 732(d) is treated as if it were the amount of a special basis adjustment under section 743(b). For example, in determining, for purposes of this paragraph (c)(6), the amount of gain that a partner would recognize under section 1245 upon a sale of partnership property, the items allocated under § 1.1245-1(e)(3)(ii) are allocated to the partner in the same manner as the partner's share of partnership property is determined. See § 1.1250-1(f) for rules similar to those contained in § 1.1245-1(e)(3)(ii).

(d) *Inventory items which have substantially appreciated in value*—(1) *Substantial appreciation.* Partnership inventory items shall be considered to have appreciated substantially in value if, at the time of the sale or distribution, the total fair market value of all the inventory items of the partnership exceeds 120 percent of the aggregate adjusted basis for such property in the hands of the partnership (without regard to any special basis adjustment of any partner) and, in addition, exceeds 10 percent of the fair market value of all partnership property other than money. The terms "inventory items which have appreciated substantially in value" or "substantially appreciated inventory items" refer to the aggregate of all partnership inventory items. These terms do not refer to specific partnership inventory items or to specific groups of such items. For example, any distribution of inventory items by a partnership the inventory items of which as a whole are substantially appreciated in value shall be a distribution of substantially appreciated inventory items for the purposes of section 751(b), even though the specific inventory items distributed may not be appreciated in value. Similarly, if the aggregate of partnership inventory items are not substantially appreciated in value, a distribution of specific inventory items, the value of which is more than 120 percent of their adjusted basis, will not constitute a distribution of substantially appreciated inventory items. For the purpose of this paragraph, the "fair market value" of inventory items has the same meaning as "market" value in the regulations under section 471, relating to general rule for inventories.

(2) *Inventory items.* The term "inventory items" as used in subchapter K, chapter 1 of the Code, includes the following types of property:

(i) Stock in trade of the partnership, or other property of a kind which would properly be included in the inventory of the partnership if on hand at the close of the taxable year, or property held by the partnership primarily for sale to customers in the ordinary course of its trade or business. See section 1221(1).

(ii) Any other property of the partnership which, on sale or exchange by the partnership, would be considered property other than a capital asset and other than property described in section 1231. Thus, accounts receivable acquired in the ordinary course of business for services or from the sale of stock in trade constitute inventory items (see section 1221(4)), as do any unrealized receivables.

(iii) Any other property retained by the partnership which, if held by the partner selling his partnership interest or receiving a distribution described in section 751(b), would be considered property described in subdivisions (i) or (ii) of this subparagraph. Property actually distributed to the partner does not come within the provisions of section 751(d)(2)(C) and this subdivision.

(e) *Section 751 property and other property.* For the purposes of this section, "section 751 property" means unrealized receivables or substantially appreciated inventory items, and "other property" means all property (including money) except section 751 property.

* * *

(g) *Examples.* Application of the provisions of section 751 may be illustrated by the following examples:

Example 1. (i)(A) A and B are equal partners in personal service partnership PRS. B transfers its interest in PRS to T for $15,000 when PRS's balance sheet (reflecting a cash receipts and disbursements method of accounting) is as follows:

Assets

	Adjusted Basis	Fair Market Value
Cash	$ 3,000	$ 3,000
Loans Receivable	10,000	10,000
Capital Assets	7,000	5,000
Unrealized Receivables	0	14,000
Total	20,000	32,000

Liabilities and Capital

	Adjusted Per Books	Fair Market Value
Liabilities	$ 2,000	$ 2,000
Capital:		
A	9,000	15,000
B	9,000	15,000
Total	20,000	32,000

(B) None of the assets owned by PRS is section 704(c) property, and the capital assets are nondepreciable. The total amount realized by B is $16,000, consisting of the cash received, $15,000, plus $1,000, B's share of the partnership liabilities assumed by T. See section 752. B's undivided half-interest in the partnership property includes a half-interest in the partnership's unrealized receivables items. B's basis for its partnership interest is $10,000 ($9,000, plus $1,000, B's share of

Reg. § 1.751-1(g)

partnership liabilities). If section 751(a) did not apply to the sale, B would recognize $6,000 of capital gain from the sale of the interest in PRS. However, section 751(a) does apply to the sale.

(ii) If PRS sold all of its section 751 property in a fully taxable transaction immediately prior to the transfer of B's partnership interest to T, B would have been allocated $7,000 of ordinary income from the sale of PRS's unrealized receivables. Therefore, B will recognize $7,000 of ordinary income with respect to the unrealized receivables. The difference between the amount of capital gain or loss that the partner would realize in the absence of section 751 ($6,000) and the amount of ordinary income or loss determined under paragraph (a)(2) of this section ($7,000) is the transferor's capital gain or loss on the sale of its partnership interest. In this case, B will recognize a $1,000 capital loss.

Example (2). (a) Facts. Partnership ABC makes a distribution to partner C in liquidation of his entire one-third interest in the partnership. At the time of the distribution, the balance sheet of the partnership, which uses the accrual method of accounting, is as follows:

Assets

	Adjusted basis per books	Market value
Cash	$15,000	$ 15,000
Accounts receivable . .	9,000	9,000
Inventory	21,000	30,000
Depreciable property .	42,000	48,000
Land	9,000	9,000
Total	96,000	111,000

Liabilities and Capital

	Per books	Value
Current liabilities	$15,000	$ 15,000
Mortgage payable	21,000	21,000
Capital:		
A	20,000	25,000
B	20,000	25,000
C	20,000	25,000
Total	96,000	111,000

The distribution received by C consists of $10,000 cash and depreciable property with a fair market value of $15,000 and an adjusted basis to the partnership of $15,000.

(b) *Presence of section 751 property.* The partnership has no unrealized receivables, but the dual test provided in section 751(d)(1) must be applied to determine whether the inventory items of the partnership, in the aggregate, have appreciated substantially in value. The fair market value of all partnership inventory items, $39,000 (inventory $30,000, and accounts receivable $9,000), exceeds 120 percent of the $30,000 adjusted basis of such items to the partnership. The fair market value of the inventory items, $39,000, also ex-

ceeds 10 percent of the fair market value of all partnership property other than money (10 percent of $96,000 or $9,600). Therefore, the partnership inventory items have substantially appreciated in value.

(c) *The properties exchanged.* Since C's entire partnership interest is to be liquidated, the provisions of section 736 are applicable. No part of the payment, however, is considered as a distributive share or as a guaranteed payment under section 736(a) because the entire payment is made for C's interest in partnership property. Therefore, the entire payment is for an interest in partnership property under section 736(b), and, to the extent applicable, subject to the rules of section 751. In the distribution, C received his share of cash ($5,000) and $15,000 in depreciable property ($1,000 less than his $16,000 share). In addition, he received other partnership property ($5,000 cash and $12,000 liabilities assumed, treated as money distributed under section 752(b)) in exchange for his interest in accounts receivable ($3,000), inventory ($10,000), land ($3,000), and the balance of his interest in depreciable property ($1,000). Section 751(b) applies only to the extent of the exchange of other property for section 751 property (i.e., inventory items, which include trade accounts receivable). The section 751 property exchanged has a fair market value of $13,000 ($3,000 in accounts receivable and $10,000 in inventory). Thus, $13,000 of the total amount C received is considered as received for the sale of section 751 property.

(d) *Distributee partner's tax consequences.* C's tax consequences on the distribution are as follows:

(1) *The section 751(b) sale or exchange.* C's share of the inventory items is treated as if he received them in a current distribution, and his basis for such items is $10,000 ($7,000 for inventory and $3,000 for accounts receivable) as determined under paragraph (b)(3)(iii) of this section. Then C is considered as having sold his share of inventory items to the partnership for $13,000. Thus, on the sale of his share of inventory items, C realizes $3,000 of ordinary income.

(2) *The part of the distribution not under section 751(b).* Section 751(b) does not apply to the balance of the distribution. Before the distribution, C's basis for his partnership interest was $32,000 ($20,000 plus $12,000, his share of partnership liabilities). See section 752(a). This basis is reduced by $10,000, the basis attributed to the section 751 property treated as distributed to C and sold by him to the partnership. Thus, C has a basis of $22,000 for the remainder of his partnership interest. The total distribution to C was $37,000 ($22,000 in cash and liabilities assumed,

Reg. § 1.751-1(g)

and $15,000 in depreciable property). Since C received no more than his share of the depreciable property, none of the depreciable property constitutes proceeds of the sale under section 751(b). C did receive more than his share of money. Therefore, the sale proceeds, treated separately in subparagraph (1) of this paragraph of this example, must consist of money and therefore must be deducted from the money distribution. Consequently, in liquidation of the balance of C's interest, he receives depreciable property and $9,000 in money ($22,000 less $13,000). Therefore, no gain or loss is recognized to C on the distribution. Under section 732(b), C's basis for the depreciable property is $13,000 (the remaining basis of this partnership interest, $22,000, reduced by $9,000, the money received in the distribution).

(e) *Partnership's tax consequences.* The tax consequences to the partnership on the distribution are as follows:

(1) *The section 751(b) sale or exchange.* The partnership consisting of the remaining members has no ordinary income on the distribution since it did not give up any section 751 property in the exchange. Of the $22,000 money distributed (in cash and the assumption of C's share of liabilities), $13,000 was paid to acquire C's interest in inventory ($10,000 fair market value) and in accounts receivable ($3,000). Since under section 751(b) the partnership is treated as buying these properties, it has a new cost basis for the inventory and accounts receivable acquired from C. Its basis for C's share of inventory and accounts receivable is $13,000, the amount which the partnership is considered as having paid C in the exchange. Since the partnership is treated as having distributed C's share of inventory and accounts receivable to him, the partnership must decrease its basis for inventory and accounts receivable ($30,000) by $10,000, the basis of C's increase the basis for inventory and accounts receivable by $13,000 to reflect the purchase prices of the items acquired. Thus, the basis of the partnership inventory is increased from $21,000 to $24,000 in the transaction. (Note that the basis of property acquired in a section 751(b) exchange is determined under section 1012 without regard to any elections of the partnership. See § 1.732-1(e).) Further, the partnership realizes no capital gain or loss on the portion of the distribution treated as a sale under section 751(b) since, to acquire C's interest in the inventory and accounts receivable, it gave up money and assumed C's share of liabilities.

(2) *The part of the distribution not under section 751(b).* In the remainder of the distribution to C which was not in exchange for C's interest in section 751 property, C received only other property as follows: $15,000 in depreciable property (with a basis to the partnership of $15,000) and $9,000 in money ($22,000 less $13,000 treated under subparagraph (1) of this paragraph of this example). Since this part of the distribution is not an exchange of section 751 property for other property, section 751(b) does not apply. Instead, the provisions which apply are sections 731 through 736, relating to distributions by a partnership. No gain or loss is recognized to the partnership on the distribution. (See section 731(b).) Further, the partnership makes no adjustment to the basis of remaining depreciable property unless an election under section 754 is in effect. (See section 734(a).) Thus, the basis of the depreciable property before the distribution, $42,000, is reduced by the basis of the depreciable property distributed, $15,000, leaving a basis for the depreciable property in the partnership of $27,000. However, if an election under section 754 is in effect, the partnership must make the adjustment required under section 734(b) as follows: Since the adjusted basis of the distributed property to the partnership had been $15,000, and is only $13,000 in C's hands (see paragraph (d)(2) of this example), the partnership will increase the basis of the depreciable property remaining in the partnership by $2,000 (the excess of the adjusted basis to the partnership of the distributed depreciable property immediately before the distribution over its basis to the distributee). Whether or not an election under section 754 is in effect, the basis for each of the remaining partner's partnership interests will be $38,000 ($20,000 original contribution, plus $12,000, each partner's original share of the liabilities, plus $6,000, the share of C's liabilities each assumed).

(f) *Partnership trial balance.* A trial balance of the AB partnership after the distribution in liquidation of C's entire interest would reflect the results set forth in the schedule below. Column I shows the amounts to be reflected in the records if an election is in effect under section 754 with respect to an optional adjustment under section 734(b) to the basis of undistributed partnership property. Column II shows the amounts to be reflected in the records where an election under section 754 is not in effect. Note that in column II, the total bases for the partnership assets do not equal the total of the bases for the partnership interests.

Reg. § 1.751-1(g)

	I Sec. 754, Election in effect		II Sec. 754, Election not in effect	
	Basis	Fair market value	Basis	Fair market value
Cash	$ 5,000	$ 5,000	$ 5,000	$ 5,000
Accounts receivable	9,000	9,000	9,000	9,000
Inventory	24,000	30,000	24,000	30,000
Depreciable property	29,000	33,000	27,000	33,000
Land	9,000	9,000	9,000	9,000
	76,000	86,000	74,000	86,000
Current liabilities	15,000	15,000	15,000	15,000
Mortgage	21,000	21,000	21,000	21,000
Capital: A	20,000	25,000	20,000	25,000
B	20,000	25,000	20,000	25,000
	76,000	86,000	76,000	86,000

Example (3). (a) *Facts.* Assume that the distribution to partner C in example (2) of this paragraph in liquidation of his entire interest in partnership ABC consists of $5,000 in cash and $20,000 worth of partnership inventory with a basis of $14,000.

(b) *Presence of section 751 property.* For the same reason as stated in paragraph (b) of that example, the partnership inventory items have substantially appreciated in value.

(c) *The properties exchanged.* In the distribution, C received his share of cash ($5,000) and his share of appreciated inventory items ($13,000). In addition, he received appreciated inventory with a fair market value of $7,000 (and with an adjusted basis to the partnership of $4,900) and $12,000 in money (liabilities assumed). C has relinquished his interest in $16,000 of depreciable property and $3,000 of land. Although C relinquished his interest in $3,000 of accounts receivable, such accounts receivable are inventory items and, therefore, that exchange was not an exchange of section 751 property for other property. Section 751(b) applies only to the extent of the exchange of other property for section 751 property (i.e., depreciable property or land for inventory items). Assume that the partners agree that the $7,000 of inventory in excess of C's share was received by him in exchange for $7,000 of depreciable property.

(d) *Distributee partner's tax consequences.* C's tax consequence on the distributions are as follows:

(1) *The section 751(b) sale or exchange.* C is treated as if he had received his 7/16ths share of the depreciable property in a current distribution. His basis for that share is $6,125 (42,000/48,000 of $7,000), as determined under paragraph (b)(2)(iii) of this section. Then C is considered as having sold his 7/16ths share of depreciable property to the partnership for $7,000, realizing a gain of $875.

(2) *The part of the distribution not under section 751(b).* Section 751(b) does not apply to the balance of the distribution. Before the distribution, C's basis for his partnership interest was $32,000 ($20,000, plus $12,000, his share of partnership liabilities). See section 752(a). This basis is reduced by $6,125, the basis of property treated as distributed to C and sold by him to the partnership. Thus, C will have a basis of $25,875 for the remainder of his partnership interest. Of the $37,000 total distribution to C, $30,000 ($17,000 in money, including liabilities assumed, and $13,000 in inventory) is not within section 751(b). Under section 732(b), C's basis for the inventory with a fair market value of $13,000 (which had an adjusted basis to the partnership of $9,100) is limited to $8,875, the amount of the remaining basis for his partnership interest, $25,875, reduced by $17,000, the money received. Thus, C's total aggregate basis for the inventory received is $15,875 ($7,000 plus $8,875), and not its $14,000 basis in the hands of the partnership.

(e) *Partnership's tax consequences.* The tax consequences to the partnership on the distribution are as follows:

(1) *The section 751(b) sale or exchange.* The partnership consisting of the remaining members has $2,100 of ordinary income on the sale of the $7,000 of inventory which had a basis to the partnership of $4,900 (21,000/30,000 of $7,000). This $7,000 of inventory was paid to acquire 7/16ths of C's interest in the depreciable property. Since, under section 751(b), the partnership is treated as buying this property from C, it has a new cost basis for such property. Its basis for the depreciable property is $42,875 ($42,000 less $6,125, the basis of the 7/16ths share considered as distributed to C, plus $7,000, the partnership purchase price for this share).

(2) *The part of the distribution not under section 751(b).* In the remainder of the distribution to C which was not a sale or exchange of section 751 property for other property, the partnership realizes no gain or loss. See section 731(b).

Reg. § 1.751-1(g)

Further, under section 734(a), the partnership makes no adjustment to the basis of the accounts receivable or the 9/16ths interest in depreciable property which C relinquished. However, if an election under section 754 is in effect, the partnership must make the adjustment required under section 734(b) since the adjusted basis to the partnership of the inventory distributed had been $9,100, and C's basis for such inventory after distribution is only $8,875. The basis of the inventory remaining in the partnership must be increased by $225. Whether or not an election under section 754 is in effect, the basis for each of the remaining partnership interests will be $39,050 ($20,000 original contribution, plus $12,000, each partner's original share of the liabilities, plus $6,000, the share of C's liabilities now assumed, plus $1,050, each partner's share of ordinary income realized by the partnership upon that part of the distribution treated as a sale or exchange).

Example (4). (a) *Facts.* Assume the same facts as in example (3) of this paragraph, except that the partners did not identify the property which C relinquished in exchange for the $7,000 of inventory which he received in excess of his share.

(b) *Presence of section 751 property.* For the same reasons stated in paragraph (b) of example (2) of this paragraph, the partnership inventory items have substantially appreciated in value.

(c) *The properties exchanged.* The analysis stated in paragraph (c) of example (3) of this paragraph is the same in this example, except that, in the absence of a specific agreement among the partners as to the properties exchanged, C will be presumed to have sold to the partnership a proportionate amount of each property in which he relinquished an interest. Thus, in the absence of an agreement, C has received $7,000 of inventory in exchange for his release of 7/19ths of the depreciable property and 7/19ths of the land. ($7,000, fair market value of property released, over $19,000, the sum of the fair market values of C's interest in the land and C's interest in the depreciable property.)

(d) *Distributee partner's tax consequences.* C's tax consequences on the distribution are as follows:

(1) *The section 751(b) sale or exchange.* C is treated as if he had received his 7/19ths shares of the depreciable property and land in a current distribution. His basis for those shares is $6,263 (51,000/57,000 of $7,000, their fair market value), as determined under paragraph (b)(2)(iii) of this section. Then C is considered as having sold his 7/19ths shares of depreciable property and land to the partnership for $7,000, realizing a gain of $737.

(2) *The part of the distribution not under section 751(b).* Section 751(b) does not apply to

the balance of the distribution. Before the distribution C's basis for his partnership interest was $32,000 ($20,000 plus $12,000, his share of partnership liabilities). See section 752(a). This basis is reduced by $6,263, the bases of C's shares of depreciable property and land treated as distributed to him and sold by him to the partnership. Thus, C will have a basis of $25,737 for the remainder of his partnership interest. Of the total $37,000 distributed to C, $30,000 ($17,000 in money, including liabilities assumed, and $13,000 in inventory) is not within section 751(b). Under section 732(b), C's basis for the inventory (with a fair market value of $13,000 and an adjusted basis to the partnership of $9,100) is limited to $8,737, the amount of the remaining basis for his partnership interest ($25,737 less $17,000, money received). Thus, C's total aggregate basis for the inventory he received is $15,737 ($7,000 plus $8,737), and not the $14,000 basis it had in the hands of the partnership.

(e) *Partnership's tax consequences.* The tax consequences to the partnership on the distribution are as follows:

(1) *The section 751(b) sale or exchange.* The partnership consisting of the remaining members has $2,100 of ordinary income on the sale of $7,000 of inventory which had a basis to the partnership of $4,900 (21,000/30,000 of $7,000). This $7,000 of inventory was paid to acquire 7/19ths of C's interest in the depreciable property and land. Since, under section 751(b), the partnership is treated as buying this property from C, it has a new cost basis for such property. The bases of the depreciable property and land would be $42,737 and $9,000, respectively. The basis for the depreciable property is computed as follows: The common partnership basis of $42,000 is reduced by the $5,158 basis (42,000/48,000 of $5,895) for C's 7/19ths interest constructively distributed, and increased by $5,895 (16,000/19,000 of $7,000), the part of the purchase price allocated to the depreciable property. The basis of the land would be computed in the same way. The $9,000 original partnership basis is reduced by $1,105 basis (9,000/9,000 of $1,105) of the land constructively distributed to C, and increased by $1,105 (3,000/19,000 of $7,000), the portion of the purchase price allocated to the land.

(2) *The part of the distribution not under section 751(b).* In the remainder of the distribution to C which was not a sale or exchange of section 751 property for other property, the partnership realizes no gain or loss. See section 731(b). Further, under section 734(a), the partnership makes no adjustment to the basis of the accounts receivable or the 12/19ths interests in depreciable property and land which C relinquished. How-

Reg. § 1.751-1(g)

ever, if an election under section 754 is in effect, the partnership must make the adjustment required under section 734(b) since the adjusted basis to the partnership of the inventory distributed had been $9,100 and C's basis for such inventory after the distribution is only $8,737. The basis of the inventory remaining in the partnership must be increased by the difference of $363. Whether or not an election under section 754 is in effect, the basis for each of the remaining partnership interests will be $39,050 ($20,000 original contribution plus $12,000, each partner's original share of the liabilities, plus $6,000, the share of C's liabilities assumed, plus $1,050, each partner's share of ordinary income realized by the partnership upon the part of the distribution treated as a sale or exchange).

Example (5). (a) *Facts.* Assume that partner C in example (2) of this paragraph agrees to reduce his interest in capital and profits from ⅓ to ⅕ for a current distribution consisting of $5,000 in cash, and $7,500 of accounts receivable with a basis to the partnership of $7,500. At the same time, the total liabilities of the partnership are not reduced. Therefore, after the distribution, C's share of the partnership liabilities has been reduced by $4,800 from $12,000 (⅓ of $36,000) to $7,200 (⅕ of $36,000).

(b) *Presence of section 751 property.* For the same reasons as stated in paragraph (b) of example (2) of this paragraph, the partnership inventory items have substantially appreciated in value.

(c) *The properties exchanged.* C's interest in the fair market value of the partnership properties before and after the distribution can be illustrated by the following table:

| | C's interest Fair Market Value | | C received | | |
Item	One-third before	One-fifth after	Distribution of share	In excess of share	C relinquished
Cash	$ 5,000	$ 2,000	$3,000	$ 2,000	......
Liabilities assumed	(12,000)	(7,200)	.....	$ 4,800	......
Inventory items:					
Accounts receivable	$ 3,000	$ 300	$2,700	$ 4,800	
Inventory	10,000	6,000	.....	......	$ 4,000
Depreciable property	16,000	9,600	.....	......	6,400
Land	3,000	1,800	.....	......	1,200
Total	$25,000	$12,500	$5,700	$11,600	$11,600

Although C relinquished his interest in $4,000 of inventory and received $4,800 of accounts receivable, both items constitute section 751 property and C has received only $800 of accounts receivable for $800 worth of depreciable property or for an $800 undivided interest in land. In the absence of an agreement identifying the properties exchanged, it is presumed C received $800 for proportionate shares of his interests in both depreciable property and land. To the extent that inventory was exchanged for accounts receivable, or to the extent cash was distributed for the release of C's interest in the balance of the depreciable property and land, the transaction does not fall within section 751(b) and is a current distribution under section 732(a). Thus, the remaining $6,700 of accounts receivable are received in a current distribution.

(d) *Distributee partner's tax consequences.* C's tax consequences on the distribution are as follows:

(1) *The Section 751(b) sale or exchange.* Assuming that the partners paid $800 worth of accounts receivable for $800 worth of depreciable property, C is treated as if he received the depreciable property in a current distribution, and his basis for the $800 worth of depreciable property is $700 (42,000/48,000 of $800, its fair market value), as determined under paragraph (b)(2)(iii) of this section. Then C is considered as having sold his $800 share of depreciable property to the partnership for $800. On the sale of the depreciable property, C realizes a gain of $100. If, on the other hand, the partners had agreed that C exchanged an $800 interest in the land for $800 worth of accounts receivable, C would realize no gain or loss, because under paragraph (b)(2)(iii) of this section his basis for the land sold would be $800. In the absence of an agreement, the basis for the depreciable property and land (which C is considered as having received in a current distribution and then sold back to the partnership) would be $716 (51,000/57,000 of $800). In that case, on the sale of the balance of the $800 share of depreciable property and land, C would realize $84 of gain ($800 less $716).

(2) *The part of the distribution not under section 751(b).* Section 751(b) does not apply to the balance of the distribution. Under section 731, C does not realize either gain or loss on the balance of the distribution. The adjustments to the basis of C's interest are illustrated in the following table:

Reg. § 1.751-1(g)

	If accounts receivable received for depreciable property	If accounts receivable received for land	If there is no agreement
Original basis for C's interest	$32,000	$32,000	$32,000
Less basis of property distributed prior to sec. 751(b) sale or exchange	− 700	− 800	− 716
	31,300	31,200	31,284
Less money received in distribution	−9,800	−9,800	−9,800
	21,500	21,400	21,484
Less basis of property received in a current distribution under sec. 732	−6,700	−6,700	−6,700
Resulting basis for C's interest	14,800	14,700	14,784

C's basis for the $7,500 worth of accounts receivable which he received in the distribution will be $7,500, composed of $800 for the portion purchased in the section 751(b) exchange, plus $6,700, the basis carried over under section 732(a) for the portion received in the current distribution.

(e) *Partnership's tax consequences.* The tax consequences to the partnership on the distribution are as follows:

(1) *The section 751(b) sale or exchange.* The partnership realizes no gain or loss in the section 751 sale or exchange because it had a basis of $800 for the accounts receivable for which it received $800 worth of other property. If the partnership agreed to purchase $800 worth of depreciable property, the partnership basis of depreciable property becomes $42,100 ($42,000 less $700 basis of property constructively distributed to C, plus $800, price of property purchased). If the partnership purchased land with the accounts receivable, there would be no change in the basis of the land to the partnership because the basis of land distributed was equal to its purchase price. If there were no agreement, the basis of the depreciable property and land would be $51,084 (depreciable property, $42,084 and land, $9,000). The basis for the depreciable property is computed as follows: The common partnership basis of $42,000 is reduced by the $590 basis (42,000/48,000 of $674) for C's $674 interest constructively distributed, and increased by $674 (6,400/7,600 of $800), the part of the purchase price allocated to the depreciable property. The basis of the land would be computed in the same way. The $9,000 original partnership basis is reduced by $126 basis (9,000/9,000 of $126) of the land constructively distributed to C, and increased by $126 (1,200/7,600 of $800), the portion of the purchase price allocated to the land.

(2) *The part of the distribution not under section 751(b).* The partnership will realize no gain or loss in the balance of the distribution under section 731. Since the property in C's hands after the distribution will have the same basis it had in the partnership, the basis of partnership property remaining in the partnership after the distribution will not be adjusted (whether or not an election under 754 is in effect).

Example (6). (a) *Facts.* Partnership ABC distributes to partner C, in liquidation of his entire one-third interest in the partnership, a machine which is section 1245 property with a recomputed basis (as defined in section 1245(a)(2)) of $18,000. At the time of the distribution, the balance sheet of the partnership is as follows:

Assets	Adjusted basis per books	Market value
Cash	$ 3,000	$ 3,000
Machine (section 1245 property)	9,000	15,000
Land	18,000	27,000
Total	$30,000	$45,000

Liabilities and Capital	Per books	Value
Liabilities	$ 0	$ 0
Capital:		
A	10,000	15,000
B	10,000	15,000
C	10,000	15,000
Total	$30,000	$45,000

Reg. § 1.751-1(g)

(b) *Presence of section 751 property.* The section 1245 property is an unrealized receivable of the partnership to the extent of the potential section 1245 income in respect of the property. Since the fair market value of the property ($15,000) is lower than its recomputed basis ($18,000), the excess of the fair market value over its adjusted basis ($9,000), or $6,000, is the potential section 1245 income of the partnership in respect of the property. The partnership has no other section 751 property.

(c) *The properties exchanged.* In the distribution C received his share of section 751 property (potential section 1245 income of $2,000, i.e., 1/3 of $6,000) and his share of section 1245 property (other than potential section 1245 income) with a fair market value of $3,000, i.e., 1/3 of ($15,000 minus $6,000), and an adjusted basis of $3,000, i.e., 1/3 of $9,000. In addition he received $4,000 of section 751 property (consisting of $4,000 ($6,000 minus $2,000) of potential section 1245 income) and section 1245 property (other than potential section 1245 income) with a fair market value of $6,000 ($9,000 minus $3,000) and an adjusted basis of $6,000 ($9,000 minus $3,000). C relinquished his interest in $1,000 of cash and $9,000 of land. Assume that the partners agree that the $4,000 of section 751 property in excess of C's share was received by him in exchange for $4,000 of land.

(d) *Distributee partner's tax consequences.* C's tax consequences on the distributions are as follows:

(1) *The section 751(b) sale or exchange.* C is treated as if he received in a current distribution 4/9ths of his share of the land with a basis of $2,667 (18,000/27,000 × $4,000). Then C is considered as having sold his 4/9ths share of the land to the partnership for $4,000, realizing a gain of $1,333. C's basis for the remainder of his partnership interest after the current distribution is $7,333, i.e., the basis of his partnership interest before the current distribution ($10,000) minus the basis of the land treated as distributed to him ($2,667).

(2) *The part of the distribution not under section 751(b).* Of the $15,000 total distribution to C, $11,000 ($2,000 of potential section 1245 income and $9,000 section 1245 property other than potential section 1245 income) is not within section 751(b). Under section 732(b) and (c), C's basis for his share of potential section 1245 income is zero (see paragraph (c)(5) of this section) and his basis for $9,000 of section 1245 property (other than potential section 1245 income) is $7,333, i.e., the amount of the remaining basis for his partnership interest ($7,333) reduced by the basis for his share of potential section 1245 income (zero). Thus C's

total aggregate basis for the section 1245 property (fair market value of $15,000) distributed to him is $11,333 ($4,000 plus $7,333). For an illustration of the computation of his recomputed basis for the section 1245 property immediately after the distribution, see example (2) of paragraph (f)(3) of § 1.1245-4.

(e) *Partnership's tax consequences.* The tax consequences to the partnership on the distribution are as follows:

(1) *The section 751(b) sale or exchange.* Upon the sale of $4,000 potential section 1245 income, with a basis of zero, for 4/9ths of C's interest in the land, the partnership consisting of the remaining members has $4,000 ordinary income under sections 751(b) and 1245(a)(1). See section 1245(b)(3) and (6)(A). The partnership's new basis for the land is $19,333, i.e., $18,000, less the basis of the 4/9ths share considered as distributed to C ($2,667), plus the partnership purchase price for this share ($4,000).

(2) *The part of the distribution not under section 751(b).* The analysis under this subparagraph should be made in accordance with the principles illustrated in paragraph (e)(2) of examples (3), (4), and (5) of this paragraph. [Reg. § 1.751-1.]

□ [*T.D. 6175, 5-23-56. Amended by T.D. 6832, 7-6-65, T.D. 7084, 1-7-71; T.D. 8586, 1-9-95 and T.D. 8847, 12-14-99.*]

§ 1.752-1. Treatment of partnership liabilities.—(a) *Definitions.* For purposes of section 752, the following definitions apply:

(1) *Recourse liability defined.* A partnership liability is a recourse liability to the extent that any partner or related person bears the economic risk of loss for that liability under § 1.752-2.

(2) *Nonrecourse liability defined.* A partnership liability is a nonrecourse liability to the extent that no partner or related person bears the economic risk of loss for that liability under § 1.752-2.

(3) *Related person.* Related person means a person having a relationship to a partner that is described in § 1.752-4(b).

(b) *Increase in partner's share of liabilities.* Any increase in a partner's share of partnership liabilities, or any increase in a partner's individual liabilities by reason of the partner's assumption of partnership liabilities, is treated as a contribution of money by that partner to the partnership.

(c) *Decrease in partner's share of liabilities.* Any decrease in a partner's share of partnership liabilities, or any decrease in a partner's individual liabilities by reason of the partnership's assumption of the individual liabilities of the partner, is treated as a distribution of money by the partnership to that partner.

(d) *Assumption of liability.* Except as otherwise provided in paragraph (e) of this section, a person is considered to assume a liability only to the extent that:

(1) The assuming person is personally obligated to pay the liability; and

(2) If a partner or related person assumes a partnership liability, the person to whom the liability is owed knows of the assumption and can directly enforce the partner's or related person's obligation for the liability, and no other partner or person that is a related person to another partner would bear the economic risk of loss for the liability immediately after the assumption.

(e) *Property subject to a liability.* If property is contributed by a partner to the partnership or distributed by the partnership to a partner and the property is subject to a liability of the transferor, the transferee is treated as having assumed the liability, to the extent that the amount of the liability does not exceed the fair market value of the property at the time of the contribution or distribution.

(f) *Netting of increases and decreases in liabilities resulting from same transaction.* If, as a result of a single transaction, a partner incurs both an increase in the partner's share of the partnership liabilities (or the partner's individual liabilities) and a decrease in the partner's share of the partnership liabilities (or the partner's individual liabilities), only the net decrease is treated as a distribution from the partnership and only the net increase is treated as a contribution of money to the partnership. Generally, the contribution to or distribution from a partnership of property subject to a liability or the termination of the partnership under section 708(b) will require that increases and decreases in liabilities associated with the transaction be netted to determine if a partner will be deemed to have made a contribution or received a distribution as a result of the transaction. When two or more partnerships merge or consolidate under section 708(b)(2)(A), as described in § 1.708-1(c)(3)(i), increases and decreases in partnership liabilities associated with the merger or consolidation are netted by the partners in the terminating partnership and the resulting partnership to determine the effect of the merger under section 752.

(g) *Example.* The following example illustrates the principles of paragraphs (b), (c), (e), and (f) of this section.

Example 1. Property contributed subject to a liability; netting of increase and decrease in partner's share of liability. B contributes property with an adjusted basis of $1,000 to a general partnership in exchange for a one-third interest in the partnership. At the time of the contribution, the partnership does not have any liabilities outstanding and the property is subject to a recourse debt of $150 and has a fair market value in excess of $150. After the contribution, B remains personally liable to the creditor and none of the other partners bears any of the economic risk of loss for the liability under state law or otherwise. Under paragraph (e) of this section, the partnership is treated as having assumed the $150 liability. As a result, B's individual liabilities decrease by $150. At the same time, however, B's share of liabilities of the partnership increases by $150. Only the net increase or decrease in B's share of the liabilities of the partnership and B's individual liabilities is taken into account in applying section 752. Because there is no net change, B is not treated as having contributed money to the partnership or as having received a distribution of money from the partnership under paragraph (b) or (c) of this section. Therefore B's basis for B's partnership interest is $1,000 (B's basis for the contributed property).

Example 2. Merger or consolidation of partnerships holding property encumbered by liabilities. (i) B owns a 70 percent interest in partnership T. Partnership T's sole asset is property X, which is encumbered by a $900 liability. Partnership T's adjusted basis in property X is $600, and the value of property X is $1,000. B's adjusted basis in its partnership T interest is $420. B also owns a 20 percent interest in partnership S. Partnership S's sole asset is property Y, which is encumbered by a $100 liability. Partnership S's adjusted basis in property Y is $200, the value of property Y is $1,000, and B's adjusted basis in its partnership S interest is $40.

(ii) Partnership T and partnership S merge under section 708(b)(2)(A). Under section 708(b)(2)(A) and § 1.708-1(c)(1), partnership T is considered terminated and the resulting partnership is considered a continuation of partnership S. Partnerships T and S undertake the form described in § 1.708-1(c)(3)(i) for the partnership merger. Under § 1.708-1(c)(3)(i), partnership T contributes property X and its $900 liability to partnership S in exchange for an interest in partnership S. Immediately thereafter, partnership T distributes the interests in partnership S to its partners in liquidation of their interests in partnership T. B owns a 25 percent interest in partnership S after partnership T distributes the interests in partnership S to B.

(iii) Under paragraph (f) of this section, B nets the increases and decreases in its share of partnership liabilities associated with the merger of partnership T and partnership S. Before the merger, B's share of partnership liabilities was $650 (B had a $630 share of partnership liabilities in partnership T and a $20 share of partnership liabili-

Reg. § 1.752-1(g)

ties in partnership S immediately before the merger). B's share of S's partnership liabilities after the merger is $250 (25 percent of S's total partnership liabilities of $1,000). Accordingly, B has a $400 net decrease in its share of S's partnership liabilities. Thus, B is treated as receiving a $400 distribution from partnership S under section 752(b). Because B's adjusted basis in its partnership S interest before the deemed distribution under section 752(b) is $460 ($420 + $40), B will not recognize gain under section 731. After the merger, B's adjusted basis in its partnership S interest is $60.

(h) *Sale or exchange of a partnership interest.* If a partnership interest is sold or exchanged, the reduction in the transferor partner's share of partnership liabilities is treated as an amount realized under section 1001 and the regulations thereunder. For example, if a partner sells an interest in a partnership for $750 cash and transfers to the purchaser the partner's share of partnership liabilities in the amount of $250, the seller realizes $1,000 on the transaction.

(i) *Bifurcation of partnership liabilities.* If one or more partners bears the economic risk of loss as to part, but not all, of a partnership liability represented by a single contractual obligation, that liability is treated as two or more separate liabilities for purposes of section 752. The portion of the liability as to which one or more partners bear the economic risk of loss is a recourse liability and the remainder of the liability, if any, is a nonrecourse liability. [Reg. § 1.752-1.]

☐ [*T.D. 8380, 12-20-91. Amended by T.D. 8925, 1-3-2001.*]

§ 1.752-2. **Partner's share of recourse liabilities.**—(a) *In general.* A partner's share of a recourse partnership liability equals the portion of that liability, if any, for which the partner or related person bears the economic risk of loss. The determination of the extent to which a partner bears the economic risk of loss for a partnership liability is made under the rules in paragraphs (b) through (j) of this section.

(b) *Obligation to make a payment.*

(1) *In general.* Except as otherwise provided in this section, a partner bears the economic risk of loss for a partnership liability to the extent that, if the partnership constructively liquidated, the partner or related person would be obligated to make a payment to any person (or a contribution to the partnership) because that liability becomes due and payable and the partner or related person would not be entitled to reimbursement from another partner or person that is a related person to another partner. Upon a constructive liquidation, all of the following events are deemed to occur simultaneously:

(i) All of the partnership's liabilities become payable in full;

(ii) With the exception of property contributed to secure a partnership liability (see § 1.752-2(h)(2)), all of the partnership's assets, including cash, have a value of zero;

(iii) The partnership disposes of all of its property in a fully taxable transaction for no consideration (except relief from liabilities for which the creditor's right to repayment is limited solely to one or more assets of the partnership);

(iv) All items of income, gain, loss, or deduction are allocated among the partners; and

(v) The partnership liquidates.

(2) *Treatment upon deemed disposition.* For purposes of paragraph (b)(1) of this section, gain or loss on the deemed disposition of the partnership's assets is computed in accordance with the following:

(i) If the creditor's right to repayment of a partnership liability is limited solely to one or more assets of the partnership, gain or loss is recognized in an amount equal to the difference between the amount of the liability that is extinguished by the deemed disposition and the tax basis (or book value to the extent section 704(c) or § 1.704-1(b)(4)(i) applies) in those assets.

(ii) A loss is recognized equal to the remaining tax basis (or book value to the extent section 704(c) or § 1.704-1(b)(4)(i) applies) of all of the partnership's assets not taken into account in paragraph (b)(2)(i) of this section.

(3) *Obligations recognized.* The determination of the extent to which a partner or related person has an obligation to make a payment under paragraph (b)(1) of this section is based on the facts and circumstances at the time of the determination. All statutory and contractual obligations relating to the partnership liability are taken into account for purposes of applying this section, including:

(i) Contractual obligations outside the partnership agreement such as guarantees, indemnifications, reimbursement agreements, and other obligations running directly to creditors or to other partners, or to the partnership;

(ii) Obligations to the partnership that are imposed by the partnership agreement, including the obligation to make a capital contribution and to restore a deficit capital account upon liquidation of the partnership; and

(iii) Payment obligations (whether in the form of direct remittances to another partner or a contribution to the partnership) imposed by state law, including the governing state partnership statute.

To the extent that the obligation of a partner to make a payment with respect to a partnership liability is not recognized under this paragraph (b)(3), paragraph (b) of this section is applied as if the obligation did not exist.

(4) *Contingent obligations.* A payment obligation is disregarded if, taking into account all the facts and circumstances, the obligation is subject to contingencies that make it unlikely that the obligation will ever be discharged. If a payment obligation would arise at a future time after the occurrence of an event that is not determinable with reasonable certainty, the obligation is ignored until the event occurs.

(5) *Reimbursement rights.* A partner's or related person's obligation to make a payment with respect to a partnership liability is reduced to the extent that the partner or related person is entitled to reimbursement from another partner or a person who is a related person to another partner.

(6) *Deemed satisfaction of obligation.* For purposes of determining the extent to which a partner or related person has a payment obligation and the economic risk of loss, it is assumed that all partners and related persons who have obligations to make payments actually perform those obligations, irrespective of their actual net worth, unless the facts and circumstances indicate a plan to circumvent or avoid the obligation. See § 1.752-2(j).

(c) *Partner or related person as lender—*(1) *In general.* A partner bears the economic risk of loss for a partnership liability to the extent that the partner or a related person makes (or acquires an interest in) a nonrecourse loan to the partnership and the economic risk of loss for the liability is not borne by another partner.

(2) *Wrapped debt.* If a partnership liability is owed to a partner or related person and that liability includes (*i.e.,* is "wrapped" around) a nonrecourse obligation encumbering partnership property that is owed to another person, the partnership liability will be treated as two separate liabilities. The portion of the partnership liability corresponding to the wrapped debt is treated as a liability owed to another person.

(d) *De minimis exceptions—*(1) *Partner as lender.* The general rule contained in paragraph (c)(1) of this section does not apply if a partner or related person whose interest (directly or indirectly through one or more partnerships including the interest of any related person) in each item of partnership income, gain, loss, deduction, or credit for every taxable year that the partner is a partner in the partnership is 10 percent or less, makes a loan to the partnership which constitutes qualified nonrecourse financing within the mean-

ing of section 465(b)(6) (determined without regard to the type of activity financed).

(2) *Partner as guarantor.* The general rule contained in paragraph (b)(1) of this section does not apply if a partner or related person whose interest (directly or indirectly through one or more partnerships including the interest of any related person) in each item of partnership income, gain, loss, deduction, or credit for every taxable year that the partner is a partner in the partnership is 10 percent or less, guarantees a loan that would otherwise be a nonrecourse loan of the partnership and which would constitute qualified nonrecourse financing within the meaning of section 465(b)(6) (without regard to the type of activity financed) if the guarantor had made the loan to the partnership.

(e) *Special rule for nonrecourse liability with interest guaranteed by a partner—*(1) *In general.* For purposes of this section, if one or more partners or related persons have guaranteed the payment of more than 25 percent of the total interest that will accrue on a partnership nonrecourse liability over its remaining term, and it is reasonable to expect that the guarantor will be required to pay substantially all of the guaranteed future interest if the partnership fails to do so, then the liability is treated as two separate partnership liabilities. If this rule applies, the partner or related person that has guaranteed the payment of interest is treated as bearing the economic risk of loss for the partnership liability to the extent of the present value of the guaranteed future interest payments. The remainder of the stated principal amount of the partnership liability constitutes a nonrecourse liability. Generally, in applying this rule, it is reasonable to expect that the guarantor will be required to pay substantially all of the guaranteed future interest if, upon a default in payment by the partnership, the lender can enforce the interest guaranty without foreclosing on the property and thereby extinguishing the underlying debt. The guarantee of interest rule continues to apply even after the point at which the amount of guaranteed interest that will accrue is less than 25 percent of the total interest that will accrue on the liability.

(2) *Computation of present value.* The present value of the guaranteed future interest payments is computed using a discount rate equal to either the interest rate stated in the loan documents, or if interest is imputed under either section 483 or section 1274, the applicable federal rate, compounded semi-annually. The computation takes into account any payment of interest that the partner or related person may be required to make only to the extent that the interest will accrue economically (determined in accordance with section 446 and the regulations there-

under) after the date of the interest guarantee. If the loan document contains a variable rate of interest that is an interest rate based on current values of an objective interest index, the present value is computed on the assumption that the interest determined under the objective interest index on the date of the computation will remain constant over the term of the loan. The term "objective interest index" has the meaning given to it in section 1275 and the regulations thereunder (relating to variable rate debt instruments). Examples of an objective interest index include the prime rate of a designated financial institution, LIBOR (London Interbank Offered Rate), and the applicable federal rate under section 1274(d).

(3) *Safe harbor.* The general rule contained in paragraph (e)(1) of this section does not apply to a partnership nonrecourse liability if the guarantee of interest by the partner or related person is for a period not in excess of the lesser of five years or one-third of the term of the liability.

(4) *De minimis exception.* The general rule contained in paragraph (e)(1) of this section does not apply if a partner or related person whose interest (directly or indirectly through one or more partnerships including the interest of any related person) in each item of partnership income, gain, loss, deduction, or credit for every taxable year that the partner is a partner in the partnership is 10 percent or less, guarantees the interest on a loan to that partnership which con-

stitutes qualified nonrecourse financing within the meaning of section 465(b)(6) (determined without regard to the type of activity financed). An allocation of interest to the extent paid by the guarantor is not treated as a partnership item of deduction or loss subject to the 10 percent or less rule.

(f) *Examples.* The following examples illustrate the principles of paragraphs (a) through (e) of this section.

Example 1. Determining when a partner bears the economic risk of loss. A and B form a general partnership with each contributing $100 in cash. The partnership purchases an office building on leased land for $1,000 from an unrelated seller, paying $200 in cash and executing a note to the seller for the balance of $800. The note is a general obligation of the partnership, *i.e.,* no partner has been relieved from personal liability. The partnership agreement provides that all items are allocated equally except that tax losses are specially allocated 90% to A and 10% to B and that capital accounts will be maintained in accordance with the regulations under section 704(b), including a deficit capital account restoration obligation on liquidation. In a constructive liquidation, the $800 liability becomes due and payable. All of the partnership's assets, including the building, are deemed to be worthless. The building is deemed sold for a value of zero. Capital accounts are adjusted to reflect the loss on the hypothetical disposition, as follows:

	A	B
Initial contribution	$100	$100
Loss on hypothetical sale	(900)	(100)
	($800)	$–0–

Other than the partners' obligation to fund negative capital accounts on liquidation, there are no other contractual or statutory payment obligations existing between the partners, the partnership and the lender. Therefore, $800 of the partnership liability is classified as a recourse liability because one or more partners bears the economic risk of loss for non-payment. B has no share of the $800 liability since the constructive liquidation produces no payment obligation for B. A's share of the partnership liability is $800 because A would have an obligation in that amount to make a contribution to the partnership.

Example 2. Recourse liability; deficit restoration obligation. C and D each contribute $500 in cash to the capital of a new general partnership,

CD. CD purchases property from an unrelated seller for $1,000 in cash and a $9,000 mortgage note. The note is a general obligation of the partnership, *i.e.,* no partner has been relieved from personal liability. The partnership agreement provides that profits and losses are to be divided 40% to C and 60% to D. C and D are required to make up any deficit in their capital accounts. In a constructive liquidation, all partnership assets are deemed to become worthless and all partnership liabilities become due and payable in full. The partnership is deemed to dispose of all its assets in a fully taxable transaction for no consideration. Capital accounts are adjusted to reflect the loss on the hypothetical disposition, as follows:

	C	D
Initial contribution	$ 500	$ 500
Loss on hypothetical sale	(4,000)	(6,000)
	($3,500)	($5,500)

Reg. § 1.752-2(e)(3)

C's capital account reflects a deficit that C would have to make up of $3,500 and D's capital account reflects a deficit that D would have to make up of $5,500. Therefore, the $9,000 mortgage note is a recourse liability because one or more partners bears the economic risk of loss for the liability. C's share of the recourse liability is $3,500 and D's share is $5,500.

Example 3. Guarantee by limited partner; partner deemed to satisfy obligation. E and F form a limited partnership. E, the general partner, contributes $2,000 and F, the limited partner, contributes $8,000 in cash to the partnership. The partnership agreement allocates losses 20% to E and 80% to F until F's capital account is reduced to zero, after which all losses are allocated to E. The partnership purchases depreciable property for $25,000 using its $10,000 cash and a $15,000 recourse loan from a bank. F guarantees payment of the $15,000 loan to the extent the loan remains unpaid after the bank has exhausted its remedies against the partnership. In a constructive liquidation, the $15,000 liability becomes due and payable. All of the partnership's assets, including the depreciable property, are deemed to be worthless. The depreciable property is deemed sold for a value of zero. Capital accounts are adjusted to reflect the loss on the hypothetical disposition, as follows:

	E	F
Initial contribution	$ 2,000	$ 8,000
Loss on hypothetical sale	(17,000)	(8,000)
	($15,000)	–0–

E, as a general partner, would be obligated by operation of law to make a net contribution to the partnership of $15,000. Because E is assumed to satisfy that obligation, it is also assumed that F would not have to satisfy F's guarantee. The $15,000 mortgage is treated as a recourse liability because one or more partners bear the economic risk of loss. E's share of the liability is $15,000, and F's share is zero. This would be so even if E's net worth at the time of the determination is less than $15,000, unless the facts and circumstances indicate a plan to circumvent or avoid E's obligation to contribute to the partnership.

Example 4. Partner guarantee with right of subrogation. G, a limited partner in the GH partnership, guarantees a portion of a partnership liability. The liability is a general obligation of the partnership, *i.e.,* no partner has been relieved from personal liability. If under state law G is subrogated to the rights of the lender, G would have the right to recover the amount G paid to the recourse lender from the general partner. Therefore, G does not bear the economic risk of loss for the partnership liability.

Example 5. Bifurcation of partnership liability; guarantee of part of nonrecourse liability. A partnership borrows $10,000, secured by a mortgage on real property. The mortgage note contains an exoneration clause which provides that in the event of default, the holder's only remedy is to foreclose on the property. The holder may not look to any other partnership asset or to any partner to pay the liability. However, to induce the lender to make the loan, a partner guarantees payment of $200 of the loan principal. The exoneration clause does not apply to the partner's guarantee. If the partner paid pursuant to the guarantee, the partner would be subrogated to the rights of the lender with respect to $200 of the mortgage debt, but the partner is not otherwise entitled to reimbursement from the partnership or any partner. For purposes of section 752, $200 of the $10,000 mortgage liability is treated as a recourse liability of the partnership and $9,800 is treated as a nonrecourse liability of the partnership. The partner's share of the recourse liability of the partnership is $200.

Example 6. Wrapped debt. I, an individual, purchases real estate from an unrelated seller for $10,000, paying $1,000 in cash and giving a $9,000 purchase mortgage note on which I has no personal liability and as to which the seller can look only to the property for satisfaction. At a time when the property is worth $15,000, I sells the property to a partnership in which I is a general partner. The partnership pays for the property with a partnership purchase money mortgage note of $15,000 on which neither the partnership nor any partner (or person related to a partner) has personal liability. The $15,000 mortgage note is a wrapped debt that includes the $9,000 obligation to the original seller. The liability is a recourse liability to the extent of $6,000 because I is the creditor with respect to the loan and I bears the economic risk of loss for $6,000. I's share of the recourse liability is $6,000. The remaining $9,000 is treated as a partnership nonrecourse liability that is owed to the unrelated seller.

Example 7. Guarantee of interest by partner treated as part recourse and part nonrecourse. On January 1, 1992, a partnership obtains a $4,000,000 loan secured by a shopping center owned by the partnership. Neither the partnership nor any partner has any personal liability under the loan documents for repayment of the

Reg. § 1.752-2(f)

stated principal amount. Interest accrues at a 15 percent annual rate and is payable on December 31 of each year. The principal is payable in a lump sum on December 31, 2006. A partner guarantees payment of 50 percent of each interest payment required by the loan. The guarantee can be enforced without first foreclosing on the property. When the partnership obtains the loan, the present value (discounted at 15 percent, compounded annually) of the future interest payments is $3,508,422, and of the future principal payment is $491,578. If tested on that date, the loan would be treated as a partnership liability of $1,754,211 ($3,508,422 × .5) for which the guaranteeing partner bears the economic risk of loss and a partnership nonrecourse liability of $2,245,789 ($1,754,211 + $491,578).

Example 8. Contingent obligation not recognized. J and K form a general partnership with cash contributions of $2,500 each. J and K share partnership profits and losses equally. The partnership purchases an apartment building for its $5,000 of cash and a $20,000 nonrecourse loan from a commercial bank. The nonrecourse loan is secured by a mortgage on the building. The loan documents provide that the partnership will be liable for the outstanding balance of the loan on a recourse basis to the extent of any decrease in the value of the apartment building resulting from the partnership's failure properly to maintain the property. There are no facts that establish with reasonable certainty the existence of any liability on the part of the partnership (and its partners) for damages resulting from the partnership's failure properly to maintain the building. Therefore, no partner bears the economic risk of loss, and the liability constitutes a nonrecourse liability. Under § 1.752-3, J and K share this nonrecourse liability equally because they share all profits and losses equally.

(g) *Time-value-of-money considerations*—(1) *In general.* The extent to which a partner or related person bears the economic risk of loss is determined by taking into account any delay in the time when a payment or contribution obligation with respect to a partnership liability is to be satisfied. If a payment obligation with respect to a partnership liability is not required to be satisfied within a reasonable time after the liability becomes due and payable, or if the obligation to make a contribution to the partnership is not required to be satisfied before the later of—

(i) The end of the year in which the partner's interest is liquidated, or

(ii) 90 days after the liquidation,

the obligation is recognized only to the extent of the value of the obligation.

(2) *Valuation of an obligation.* The value of a payment or contribution obligation that is not required to be satisfied within the time period specified in paragraph (g)(1) of this section equals the entire principal balance of the obligation only if the obligation bears interest equal to or greater than the applicable federal rate under section 1274(d) at the time of valuation, commencing on—

(i) In the case of a payment obligation, the date that the partnership liability to a creditor or other person to whom the obligation relates becomes due and payable, or

(ii) In the case of a contribution obligation, the date of the liquidation of the partner's interest in the partnership.

If the obligation does not bear interest at a rate at least equal to the applicable federal rate at the time of valuation, the value of the obligation is discounted to the present value of all payments due from the partner or related person (*i.e.*, the imputed principal amount computed under section 1274(b)). For purposes of making this present value determination, the partnership is deemed to have constructively liquidated as of the date on which the payment obligation is valued and the payment obligation is assumed to be a debt instrument subject to the rules of section 1274 (*i.e.*, the debt instrument is treated as if it were issued for property at the time of the valuation).

(3) *Satisfaction of obligation with partner's promissory note.* An obligation is not satisfied by the transfer to the obligee of a promissory note by a partner or related person unless the note is readily tradeable on an established securities market.

(4) *Example.* The following example illustrates the principle of paragraph (g) of this section.

Example. Value of obligation not required to be satisfied within specified time period. A, the general partner, and B, the limited partner, each contributes $10,000 to partnership AB. AB purchases property from an unrelated seller for $20,000 in cash and a $70,000 recourse purchase money note. The partnership agreement provides that profits and losses are to be divided equally. A and B are required to make up any deficit in their capital accounts. While A is required to restore any deficit balance in A's capital account within 90 days after the date of liquidation of the partnership, B is not required to restore any deficit for two years following the date of liquidation. The deficit in B's capital account will not bear interest during that two-year period. In a constructive liquidation, all partnership assets are deemed to become worthless and all partnership liabilities become due and payable in full. The partnership

Reg. § 1.752-2(g)(1)

is deemed to dispose of all its assets in a fully taxable transaction for no consideration. Capital accounts are adjusted to reflect the loss on the hypothetical disposition, as follows:

	A	B
Initial contribution	$10,000	$10,000
Loss on hypothetical sale	(45,000)	(45,000)
	($35,000)	($35,000)

A's and B's capital accounts each reflect deficits of $35,000. B's obligation to make a contribution pursuant to B's deficit restoration obligation is recognized only to the extent of the fair market value of that obligation at the time of the constructive liquidation because B is not required to satisfy that obligation by the later of the end of the partnership taxable year in which B's interest is liquidated or within 90 days after the date of the liquidation. Because B's obligation does not bear interest, the fair market value is deemed to equal the imputed principal amount under section 1274(b). Under section 1274(b), the imputed principal amount of a debt instrument equals the present value of all payments due under the debt instrument. Assume the applicable federal rate with respect to B's obligation is 10 percent compounded semiannually. Using this discount rate, the present value of the $35,000 payment that B would be required to make two years after the constructive liquidation to restore the deficit balance in B's capital account equals $28,795. To the extent that B's deficit restoration obligation is not recognized, it is assumed that B's obligation does not exist. Therefore, A, as the sole general partner, would be obligated by operation of law to contribute an additional $6,205 of capital to the partnership. Accordingly, under paragraph (g) of this section, B bears the economic risk of loss for $28,795 and A bears the economic risk of loss for $41,205 ($35,000 + $6,205).

(h) *Partner providing property as security for partnership liability*—(1) *Direct pledge.* A partner is considered to bear the economic risk of loss for a partnership liability to the extent of the value of any of the partner's or related person's separate property (other than a direct or indirect interest in the partnership) that is pledged as security for the partnership liability.

(2) *Indirect pledge.* A partner is considered to bear the economic risk of loss for a partnership liability to the extent of the value of any property that the partner contributes to the partnership solely for the purpose of securing a partnership liability. Contributed property is not treated as contributed solely for the purpose of securing a partnership liability unless substantially all of the items of income, gain, loss, and deduction attributable to the contributed property are allocated to the contributing partner, and this allocation is generally greater than the partner's share of other significant items of partnership income, gain, loss, or deduction.

(3) *Valuation.* The extent to which a partner bears the economic risk of loss as a result of a direct pledge described in paragraph (h)(1) of this section or an indirect pledge described in paragraph (h)(2) of this section is limited to the fair market value of the property at the time of the pledge or contribution.

(4) *Partner's promissory note.* For purposes of paragraph (h)(2) of this section, a promissory note of the partner or related person that is contributed to the partnership shall not be taken into account unless the note is readily tradeable on an established securities market.

(i) *Treatment of recourse liabilities in tiered partnerships.* If a partnership (the "upper-tier partnership") owns (directly or indirectly through one or more partnerships) an interest in another partnership (the "lower-tier partnership"), the liabilities of the lower-tier partnership are allocated to the upper-tier partnership in an amount equal to the sum of the following—

(1) The amount of the economic risk of loss that the upper-tier partnership bears with respect to the liabilities; and

(2) Any other amount of the liabilities with respect to which partners of the upper-tier partnership bear the economic risk of loss.

(j) *Anti-abuse rules*—(1) *In general.* An obligation of a partner or related person to make a payment may be disregarded or treated as an obligation of another person for purposes of this section if facts and circumstances indicate that a principal purpose of the arrangement between the parties is to eliminate the partner's economic risk of loss with respect to that obligation or create the appearance of the partner or related person bearing the economic risk of loss when, in fact, the substance of the arrangement is otherwise. Circumstances with respect to which a payment obligation may be disregarded include, but are not limited to, the situations described in paragraphs (j)(2) and (j)(3) of this section.

(2) *Arrangements tantamount to a guarantee.* Irrespective of the form of a contractual obligation, a partner is considered to bear the economic risk of loss with respect to a partnership liability, or a portion thereof, to the extent that:

Reg. § 1.752-2(j)(2)

(i) The partner or related person undertakes one or more contractual obligations so that the partnership may obtain a loan;

(ii) The contractual obligations of the partner or related person eliminate substantially all the risk to the lender that the partnership will not satisfy its obligations under the loan; and

(iii) One of the principal purposes of using the contractual obligations is to attempt to permit partners (other than those who are directly or indirectly liable for the obligation) to include a portion of the loan in the basis of their partnership interests.

The partners are considered to bear the economic risk of loss for the liability in accordance with their relative economic burdens for the liability pursuant to the contractual obligations. For example, a lease between a partner and a partnership which is not on commercially reasonable terms may be tantamount to a guarantee by the partner of a partnership liability.

(3) *Plan to circumvent or avoid the obligation.* An obligation of a partner to make a payment is not recognized if the facts and circumstances evidence a plan to circumvent or avoid the obligation.

(4) *Example.* The following example illustrates the principle of paragraph (j)(3) of this section.

Example. Plan to circumvent or avoid obligation. A and B form a general partnership. A, a corporation, contributes $20,000 and B contributes $80,000 to the partnership. A is obligated to restore any deficit in its partnership capital account. The partnership agreement allocates losses 20% to A and 80% to B until B's capital account is reduced to zero, after which all losses are allocated to A. The partnership purchases depreciable property for $250,000 using its $100,000 cash and a $150,000 recourse loan from a bank. B guarantees payment of the $150,000 loan to the extent the loan remains unpaid after the bank has exhausted its remedies against the partnership. A is a subsidiary, formed by a parent of a consolidated group, with capital limited to $20,000 to allow the consolidated group to enjoy the tax losses generated by the property while at the same time limiting its monetary exposure for such losses. These facts, when considered together with B's guarantee, indicate a plan to circumvent or avoid A's obligation to contribute to the partnership. The rules of section 752 must be applied as if A's obligation to contribute did not exist. Accordingly, the $150,000 liability is a recourse liability that is allocated entirely to B. [Reg. § 1.752-2.]

☐ [*T.D.* 8380, 12-20-91.]

Reg. § 1.752-3(a)(1)

§ 1.752-3. Partner's share of nonrecourse liabilities.—(a) *In general.* A partner's share of the nonrecourse liabilities of a partnership equals the sum of paragraphs (a)(1) through (a)(3) of this section as follows—

(1) The partner's share of partnership minimum gain determined in accordance with the rules of section 704(b) and the regulations thereunder;

(2) The amount of any taxable gain that would be allocated to the partner under section 704(c) (or in the same manner as section 704(c) in connection with a revaluation of partnership property) if the partnership disposed of (in a taxable transaction) all partnership property subject to one or more nonrecourse liabilities of the partnership in full satisfaction of the liabilities and for no other consideration; and

(3) The partner's share of the excess nonrecourse liabilities (those not allocated under paragraphs (a)(1) and (a)(2) of this section) of the partnership as determined in accordance with the partner's share of partnership profits. The partner's interest in partnership profits is determined by taking into account all facts and circumstances relating to the economic arrangement of the partners. The partnership agreement may specify the partners' interests in partnership profits for purposes of allocating excess nonrecourse liabilities provided the interests so specified are reasonably consistent with allocations (that have substantial economic effect under the section 704(b) regulations) of some other significant item of partnership income or gain. Alternatively, excess nonrecourse liabilities may be allocated among the partners in accordance with the manner in which it is reasonably expected that the deductions attributable to those nonrecourse liabilities will be allocated. Additionally, the partnership may first allocate an excess nonrecourse liability to a partner up to the amount of built-in gain that is allocable to the partner on section 704(c) property (as defined under § 1.704-3(a)(3)(ii)) or property for which reverse section 704(c) allocations are applicable (as described in § 1.704-3(a)(6)(i)) where such property is subject to the nonrecourse liability to the extent that such built-in gain exceeds the gain described in paragraph (a)(2) of this section with respect to such property. This additional method does not apply for purposes of § 1.707-5(a)(2)(ii). To the extent that a partnership uses this additional method and the entire amount of the excess nonrecourse liability is not allocated to the contributing partner, the partnership must allocate the remaining amount of the excess nonrecourse liability under one of the other methods in this paragraph (a)(3). Excess nonrecourse liabilities are not required to be allocated under the same method each year.

(b) *Allocation of a single nonrecourse liability among multiple properties*—(1) *In general.* For purposes of determining the amount of taxable gain under paragraph (a)(2) of this section, if a partnership holds multiple properties subject to a single nonrecourse liability, the partnership may allocate the liability among the multiple properties under any reasonable method. A method is not reasonable if it allocates to any item of property an amount of the liability that, when combined with any other liabilities allocated to the property, is in excess of the fair market value of the property at the time the liability is incurred. The portion of the nonrecourse liability allocated to each item of partnership property is then treated as a separate loan under paragraph (a)(2) of this section. In general, a partnership may not change the method of allocating a single nonrecourse liability under this paragraph (b) while any portion of the liability is outstanding. However, if one or more of the multiple properties subject to the liability is no longer subject to the liability, the portion of the liability allocated to that property must be reallocated among the properties still subject to the liability so that the amount of the liability allocated to any property does not exceed the fair market value of such property at the time of reallocation.

(2) *Reductions in principal.* For purposes of this paragraph (b), when the outstanding principal of a partnership liability is reduced, the reduction of outstanding principal is allocated among the multiple properties in the same proportion that the partnership liability originally was allocated to the properties under paragraph (b)(1) of this section.

(c) *Examples.* The following examples illustrate the principles of this section:

Example 1. Partner's share of nonrecourse liabilities. The AB partnership purchases depreciable property for a $1,000 purchase money note that is a nonrecourse liability under the rules of this section. Assume that this is the only nonrecourse liability of the partnership, and that no principal payments are due on the purchase money note for a year. The partnership agreement provides that all items of income, gain, loss, and deduction are allocated equally. Immediately after purchasing the depreciable property, the partners share the nonrecourse liability equally because they have equal interests in partnership profits. A and B are each treated as if they contributed $500 to the partnership to reflect each partner's increase in his or her share of partnership liabilities (from $0 to $500). The minimum gain with respect to an item of partnership property subject to a nonrecourse liability equals the amount of gain that would be recognized if the partnership disposed of the property in full satisfaction of the nonrecourse liability and for no other consideration. Therefore, if the partnership claims a depreciation deduction of $200 for the depreciable property for the year it acquires that property, partnership minimum gain for the year will increase by $200 (the excess of the $1,000 nonrecourse liability over the $800 adjusted tax basis of the property). See section 704(b) and the regulations thereunder. A and B each have a $100 share of partnership minimum gain at the end of that year because the depreciation deduction is treated as a nonrecourse deduction. See section 704(b) and the regulations thereunder. Accordingly, at the end of that year, A and B are allocated $100 each of the nonrecourse liability to match their shares of partnership minimum gain. The remaining $800 of the nonrecourse liability will be allocated equally between A and B ($400 each).

Example 2. Excess nonrecourse liabilities allocated consistently with reasonably expected deductions. The facts are the same as in *Example 1* except that the partnership agreement provides that depreciation deductions will be allocated to A. The partners agree to allocate excess nonrecourse liabilities in accordance with the manner in which it is reasonably expected that the deductions attributable to those nonrecourse liabilities will be allocated. Assuming that the allocation of all of the depreciation deductions to A is valid under section 704(b), immediately after purchasing the depreciable property, A's share of the nonrecourse liability is $1,000. Accordingly, A is treated as if A contributed $1,000 to the partnership.

Example 3. Allocation of liability among multiple properties. (i) A and B are equal partners in a partnership (PRS). A contributes $70 of cash in exchange for a 50-percent interest in PRS. B contributes two items of property, X and Y, in exchange for a 50-percent interest in PRS. Property X has a fair market value (and book value) of $70 and an adjusted basis of $40, and is subject to a nonrecourse liability of $50. Property Y has a fair market value (and book value) of $120, an adjusted basis of $40, and is subject to a nonrecourse liability of $70. Immediately after the initial contributions, PRS refinances the two separate liabilities with a single $120 nonrecourse liability. All of the built-in gain attributable to Property X ($30) and Property Y ($80) is section 704(c) gain allocable to B.

(ii) The amount of the nonrecourse liability ($120) is less than the total book value of all of the properties that are subject to such liability ($70+$120=$190), so there is no partnership minimum gain. § 1.704-2(d). Accordingly, no portion of the liability is allocated pursuant to paragraph (a)(1) of this section.

(iii) Pursuant to paragraph (b)(1) of this section, PRS decides to allocate the nonrecourse liability evenly between the Properties X and Y. Accordingly, each of Properties X and Y are treated as being subject to a separate $60 nonrecourse liability for purposes of applying paragraph (a)(2) of this section. Under paragraph (a)(2) of this section, B will be allocated $20 of the liability for each of Properties X and Y (in each case, $60 liability minus $40 adjusted basis). As a result, a portion of the liability is allocated pursuant to paragraph (a)(2) of this section as follows:

Partner	Property	Tier 1	Tier 2
A	X	$0	$ 0
	Y	$0	$ 0
B............	X	$0	$20
	Y	$0	$20

(iv) PRS has $80 of excess nonrecourse liability that it may allocate in any manner consistent with paragraph (a)(3) of this section. PRS determines to allocate the $80 of excess nonrecourse liabilities to the partners up to their share of the remaining section 704(c) gain on the properties, with any remaining amount of liabilities being allocated equally to A and B consistent with their equal interests in partnership profits. B has $70 of remaining section 704(c) gain ($10 on Property X and $60 on Property Y), and thus will be allocated $70 of the liability in accordance with this gain. The remaining $10 is divided equally between A and B. Accordingly, the overall allocation of the $120 nonrecourse liability is as follows:

Partner	Tier 1	Tier 2	Tier 3	Total
A	$0	$ 0	$ 5	$ 5
B	$0	$40	$75	$115

[Reg. § 1.752-3.]

☐ [*T.D. 8380, 12-20-91. Amended by T.D. 8906, 10-30-2000.*]

§ 1.752-4. Special rules.—(a) *Tiered partnerships.* An upper-tier partnership's share of the liabilities of a lower-tier partnership (other than any liability of the lower-tier partnership that is owed to the upper-tier partnership) is treated as a liability of the upper-tier partnership for purposes of applying section 752 and the regulations thereunder to the partners of the upper-tier partnership.

(b) *Related person definition.*—(1) *In general.* A person is related to a partner if the person and the partner bear a relationship to each other that is specified in sections 267(b) or 707(b)(1), subject to the following modifications:

(i) Substitute "80 percent or more" for "more than 50 percent" each place it appears in those sections;

(ii) A person's family is determined by excluding brothers and sisters; and

(iii) Disregard sections 267(e)(1) and 267(f)(1)(A).

(2) *Person related to more than one partner*—(i) *In general.* If, in applying the related person rules in paragraph (b)(1) of this section, a person is related to more than one partner, paragraph (b)(1) of this section is applied by treating the person as related only to the partner with whom there is the highest percentage of related ownership. If two or more partners have the same percentage of related ownership and no other partner has a greater percentage, the liability is allocated equally among the partners having the equal percentages of related ownership.

(ii) *Natural persons.* For purposes of determining the percentage of related ownership between a person and a partner, natural persons who are related by virtue of being members of the same family are treated as having a percentage relationship of 100 percent with respect to each other.

(iii) *Related partner exception.* Notwithstanding paragraph (b)(1) of this section (which defines related person), persons owning interests directly or indirectly in the same partnership are not treated as related persons for purposes of determining the economic risk of loss borne by each of them for the liabilities of the partnership. This paragraph (iii) does not apply when determining a partner's interest under the de minimis rules in § 1.752-2(d) and (e).

(iv) *Special rule where entity structured to avoid related person status*—(A) *In general.* If—

(*1*) A partnership liability is owed to or guaranteed by another entity that is a partnership, an S corporation, a C corporation, or a trust;

(*2*) A partner or related person owns (directly or indirectly) a 20 percent or more ownership interest in the other entity; and

(*3*) A principal purpose of having the other entity act as a lender or guarantor of the liability was to avoid the determination that the partner that owns the interest bears the economic risk of loss for federal income tax purposes for all or part of the liability;

then the partner is treated as holding the other entity's interest as a creditor or guarantor to the extent of the partner's or related person's ownership interest in the entity.

(B) *Ownership interest.* For purposes of paragraph (b)(2)(iv)(A) of this section, a person's ownership interest in:

(*1*) A partnership equals the partner's highest percentage interest in any item of partnership loss or deduction for any taxable year;

Reg. § 1.752-4(a)

(*2*) An S corporation equals the percentage of the outstanding stock in the S corporation owned by the shareholder;

(*3*) A C corporation equals the percentage of the fair market value of the issued and outstanding stock owned by the shareholder; and

(*4*) A trust equals the percentage of the actuarial interests owned by the beneficial owner of the trust.

(C) *Example. Entity structured to avoid related person status.* A, B, and C form a general partnership, ABC. A, B, and C are equal partners, each contributing $1,000 to the partnership. A and B want to loan money to ABC and have the loan treated as nonrecourse for purposes of section 752. A and B form partnership AB to which each contributes $50,000. A and B share losses equally in partnership AB. Partnership AB loans partnership ABC $100,000 on a nonrecourse basis secured by the property ABC buys with the loan. Under these facts and circumstances, A and B bear the economic risk of loss with respect to the partnership liability equally based on their percentage interest in losses of partnership AB.

(c) *Limitation.* The amount of an indebtedness is taken into account only once, even though a partner (in addition to the partner's liability for the indebtedness as a partner) may be separately liable therefor in a capacity other than as a partner.

(d) *Time of determination.* A partner's share of partnership liabilities must be determined whenever the determination is necessary in order to determine the tax liability of the partner or any other person. See § 1.705-1(a) for rules regarding when the adjusted basis of a partner's interest in the partnership must be determined. [Reg. § 1.752-4.]

☐ [*T.D.* 8380, 12-20-91.]

§ 1.753-1. Partner receiving income in respect of decedent.—(a) *Income in respect of a decedent under section 736(a).* All payments coming within the provisions of section 736(a) made by a partnership to the estate or other successor in interest of a deceased partner are considered income in respect of the decedent under section 691. The estate or other successor in interest of a deceased partner shall be considered to have received income in respect of a decedent to the extent that amounts are paid by a third person in exchange for rights to future payments from the partnership under section 736(a). When a partner who is receiving payments under section 736(a) dies, section 753 applies to any remaining payments under section 736(a) made to his estate or other successor in interest.

(b) *Other income in respect of a decedent.* When a partner dies, the entire portion of the distributive share which is attributable to the period ending with the date of his death and which is taxable to his estate or other successor constitutes income in respect of a decedent under section 691. This rule applies even though that part of the distributive share for the period before death which the decedent withdrew is not included in the value of the decedent's partnership interest for estate tax purposes. See paragraph (c)(3) of § 1.706-1.

* * *

[Reg. § 1.753-1.]

☐ [*T.D.* 6175, 5-23-56.]

§ 1.754-1. Time and manner of making election to adjust basis of partnership property.— (a) *In general.* A partnership may adjust the basis of partnership property under sections 734(b) and 743(b) if it files an election in accordance with the rules set forth in paragraph (b) of this section. An election may not be filed to make the adjustments provided in either section 734(b) or section 743(b) alone, but such an election must apply to both sections. An election made under the provisions of this section shall apply to all property distributions and transfers of partnership interests taking place in the partnership taxable year for which the election is made and in all subsequent partnership taxable years unless the election is revoked pursuant to paragraph (c) of this section.

(b) *Time and method of making election.* (1) An election under section 754 and this section to adjust the basis of partnership property under sections 734(b) and 743(b), with respect to a distribution of property to a partner or a transfer of an interest in a partnership, shall be made in a written statement filed with the partnership return for the taxable year during which the distribution or transfer occurs. For the election to be valid, the return must be filed not later than the time prescribed by paragraph (e) of § 1.6031-1 (including extensions thereof) for filing the return for such taxable year (or before August 23, 1956, whichever is later). Notwithstanding the preceding two sentences, if a valid election has been made under section 754 and this section for a preceding taxable year and not revoked pursuant to paragraph (c) of this section, a new election is not required to be made. The statement required by this subparagraph shall (i) set forth the name and address of the partnership making the election, (ii) be signed by any one of the partners, and (iii) contain a declaration that the partnership elects under section 754 to apply the provisions of section 734(b) and section 743(b). For rules regarding extensions of time for filing elections, see § 1.9100-1.

Reg. § 1.754-1(b)

(2) The principles of this paragraph may be illustrated by the following example:

Example. A, a U.S. citizen, is a member of partnership ABC, which has not previously made an election under section 754 to adjust the basis of partnership property. The partnership and the partners use the calendar year as the taxable year. A sells his interest in the partnership to D on January 1, 1971. The partnership may elect under section 754 and this section to adjust the basis of partnership property under sections 734(b) and 743(b). Unless an extension of time to make the election is obtained under the provisions of § 1.9100-1, the election must be made in a written statement filed with the partnership return for 1971 and must contain the information specified in subparagraph (1) of this paragraph. Such return must be filed by April 17, 1972 (unless an extension of time for filing the return is obtained). The election will apply to all distributions of property to a partner and transfers of an interest in the partnership occurring in 1971 and subsequent years, unless revoked pursuant to paragraph (c) of this section.

(c) *Revocation of election*—(1) *In general.* A partnership having an election in effect under this section may revoke such election with the approval of the district director for the internal revenue district in which the partnership return is required to be filed. A partnership which wishes to revoke such an election shall file with the district director for the internal revenue district in which the partnership return is required to be filed an application setting forth the grounds on which the revocation is desired. The application shall be filed not later than 30 days after the close of the partnership taxable year with respect to which revocation is intended to take effect and shall be signed by any one of the partners. Examples of situations which may be considered sufficient reason for approving an application for revocation include a change in the nature of the partnership business, a substantial increase in the assets of the partnership, a change in the character of partnership assets, or an increased frequency of retirements or shifts of partnership interests, so that an increased administrative burden would result to the partnership from the election. However, no application for revocation of an election shall be approved when the purpose of the revocation is primarily to avoid stepping down the basis of partnership assets upon a transfer or distribution.

(2) *Revocations effective on December 15, 1999.* Notwithstanding paragraph (c)(1) of this section, any partnership having an election in effect under this section for its taxable year that includes December 15, 1999, may revoke such election effective for transfers or distributions occurring on or after December 15, 1999, by attaching a statement to the partnership's return for such year. For the revocation to be valid, the statement must be filed not later than the time prescribed by § 1.6031(a)-1(e) (including extensions thereof) for filing the return for such taxable year, and must set forth the name and address of the partnership revoking the election, be signed by any one of the partners who is authorized to sign the partnership's federal income tax return, and contain a declaration that the partnership revokes its election under section 754 to apply the provisions of section 734(b) and 743(b). In addition, the following statement must be prominently displayed in capital letters on the first page of the partnership's return for such year: "RETURN FILED PURSUANT TO § 1.754-1(c)(2)." [Reg. § 1.754-1.]

☐ [*T.D.* 6175, 5-23-56. *Amended by T.D.* 7208, 10-2-72 *and T.D.* 8847, 12-14-99 (*corrected* 2-23-2000).]

§ 1.755-1. Rules for allocation of basis.—(a) *Generally.* A partnership that has an election in effect under section 754 must adjust the basis of partnership property under the provisions of section 734(b) and section 743(b) pursuant to the provisions of this section. The basis adjustment is first allocated between the two classes of property described in section 755(b). These classes of property consist of capital assets and section 1231(b) property (capital gain property), and any other property of the partnership (ordinary income property). For purposes of this section, properties and potential gain treated as unrealized receivables under section 751(c) and the regulations thereunder shall be treated as separate assets that are ordinary income property. The portion of the basis adjustment allocated to each class is then allocated among the items within the class. Adjustments under section 743(b) are allocated under paragraph (b) of this section. Adjustments under section 734(b) are allocated under paragraph (c) of this section.

(b) *Adjustments under section 743(b)*—(1) *Generally*—(i) For exchanges in which the transferee's basis in the interest is determined in whole or in part by reference to the transferor's basis in the interest, paragraph (b)(5) of this section shall apply. For all other transfers which result in a basis adjustment under section 743(b), paragraphs (b)(2) through (b)(4) of this section shall apply. Except as provided in paragraph (b)(5) of this section, the portion of the basis adjustment allocated to one class of property may be an increase while the portion allocated to the other class is a decrease. This would be the case even though the total amount of the basis adjustment is zero. Except as provided in paragraph (b)(5) of this section, the portion of the basis adjustment allocated to one item of property within a class may be an increase while the portion allocated to another is a decrease. This would be the case even though the basis adjustment allocated to the class is zero.

(ii) *Hypothetical transaction.* For purposes of paragraphs (b)(2) through (b)(4) of this section, the allocation of the basis adjustment under section 743(b) between the classes of property and among the items of property within each class are made based on the allocations of income, gain, or loss (including remedial allocations under § 1.704-3(d)) that the transferee partner would receive (to the extent attributable to the acquired partnership interest) if, immediately after the transfer of the partnership interest, all of the partnership's property were disposed of in a fully taxable transaction for cash in an amount equal to the fair market value of such property (the hypothetical transaction).

(2) *Allocations between classes of property*— (i) *In general.* The amount of the basis adjustment allocated to the class of ordinary income property is equal to the total amount of income, gain, or loss (including any remedial allocations under § 1.704-3(d)) that would be allocated to the transferee (to the extent attributable to the acquired partnership interest) from the sale of all ordinary income property in the hypothetical transaction. The amount of the basis adjustment to capital gain property is equal to—

(A) The total amount of the basis adjustment under section 743(b); less

(B) The amount of the basis adjustment allocated to ordinary income property under the preceding sentence; provided, however, that in no event may the amount of any decrease in basis allocated to capital gain property exceed the partnership's basis (or in the case of property subject to the remedial allocation method, the transferee's share of any remedial loss under § 1.704-3(d) from the hypothetical transaction) in capital gain property. In the event that a decrease in basis allocated to capital gain property would otherwise exceed the partnership's basis in capital gain property, the excess must be applied to reduce the basis of ordinary income property.

(ii) *Examples.* The provisions of this paragraph (b)(2) are illustrated by the following examples:

Example 1. (i) A and B form equal partnership PRS. A contributes $50,000 and Asset 1, a nondepreciable capital asset with a fair market value of $50,000 and an adjusted tax basis of $25,000. B contributes $100,000. PRS uses the cash to purchase Assets 2, 3, and 4. After a year, A sells its interest in PRS to T for $120,000. At the time of the transfer, A's share of the partnership's basis in partnership assets is $75,000. Therefore, T receives a $45,000 basis adjustment.

(ii) Immediately after the transfer of the partnership interest to T, the adjusted basis and fair market value of PRS's assets are as follows:

Assets

	Adjusted Basis	Fair Market Value
Capital Gain Property:		
Asset 1	$ 25,000	$ 75,000
Asset 2	100,000	117,500
Ordinary Income Property:		
Asset 3	$ 40,000	$ 45,000
Asset 4	10,000	2,500
Total	$175,000	$240,000

(iii) If PRS sold all of its assets in a fully taxable transaction at fair market value immediately after the transfer of the partnership interest to T, the total amount of capital gain that would be allocated to T is equal to $46,250 ($25,000 section 704(c) built-in gain from Asset 1, plus fifty percent of the $42,500 appreciation in capital gain property). T would also be allocated a $1,250 ordinary loss from the sale of the ordinary income property.

(iv) The amount of the basis adjustment that is allocated to ordinary income property is equal to ($1,250) (the amount of the loss allocated to T from the hypothetical sale of the ordinary income property).

(v) The amount of the basis adjustment that is allocated to capital gain property is equal to $46,250 (the amount of the basis adjustment, $45,000, less ($1,250), the amount of loss allocated to T from the hypothetical sale of the ordinary income property).

Example 2. (i) A and B form equal partnership PRS. A and B each contribute $1,000 cash which the partnership uses to purchase Assets 1, 2, 3, and 4. After a year, A sells its partnership interest to T for $1,000. T's basis adjustment under section 743(b) is zero.

(ii) Immediately after the transfer of the partnership interest to T, the adjusted basis and fair market value of PRS's assets are as follows:

Assets

	Adjusted Basis	Fair Market Value
Capital Gain Property:		
Asset 1	$ 500	$ 750
Asset 2	500	500
Ordinary Income Property:		
Asset 3	$ 500	$ 250
Asset 4	500	500
Total	$2,000	$2,000

Reg. § 1.755-1(b)(2)

(iii) If, immediately after the transfer of the partnership interest to T, PRS sold all of its assets in a fully taxable transaction at fair market value, T would be allocated a loss of $125 from the sale of the ordinary income property. Thus, the amount of the basis adjustment to ordinary income property is ($125). The amount of the basis adjustment to capital gain property is $125 (zero, the amount of the basis adjustment under section 743(b), less ($125), the amount of the basis adjustment allocated to ordinary income property).

(3) *Allocation within the class*—(i) *Ordinary income property*. The amount of the basis adjustment to each item of property within the class of ordinary income property is equal to—

(A) The amount of income, gain, or loss (including any remedial allocations under § 1.704-3(d)) that would be allocated to the transferee (to the extent attributable to the acquired partnership interest) from the hypothetical sale of the item; reduced by

(B) The product of—

(*1*) Any decrease to the amount of the basis adjustment to ordinary income property required pursuant to the last sentence of paragraph (b)(2)(i) of this section; multiplied by

(*2*) A fraction, the numerator of which is the fair market value of the item of property to the partnership and the denominator of which is the total fair market value of all of the partnership's items of ordinary income property.

(ii) *Capital gain property*. The amount of the basis adjustment to each item of property within the class of capital gain property is equal to—

(A) The amount of income, gain, or loss (including any remedial allocations under § 1.704-3(d)) that would be allocated to the transferee (to the extent attributable to the acquired partnership interest) from the hypothetical sale of the item; minus

(B) The product of—

(*1*) The total amount of gain or loss (including any remedial allocations under § 1.704-3(d)) that would be allocated to the transferee (to the extent attributable to the acquired partnership interest) from the hypothetical sale of all items of capital gain property, minus the amount of the positive basis adjustment to all items of capital gain property or plus the amount of the negative basis adjustment to capital gain property; multiplied by

(*2*) A fraction, the numerator of which is the fair market value of the item of property to the partnership, and the denominator of which is the fair market value of all of the partnership's items of capital gain property.

(iii) *Examples*. The provisions of this paragraph (b)(3) are illustrated by the following examples:

Example 1. (i) Assume the same facts as Example 1 in paragraph (b)(2)(ii) of this section. Of the $45,000 basis adjustment, $46,250 was allocated to capital gain property. The amount allocated to ordinary income property was ($1,250).

(ii) Asset 1 is a capital gain asset, and T would be allocated $37,500 from the sale of Asset 1 in the hypothetical transaction. Therefore, the amount of the adjustment to Asset 1 is $37,500.

(iii) Asset 2 is a capital gain asset, and T would be allocated $8,750 from the sale of Asset 2 in the hypothetical transaction. Therefore, the amount of the adjustment to Asset 2 is $8,750.

(iv) Asset 3 is ordinary income property, and T would be allocated $2,500 from the sale of Asset 3 in the hypothetical transaction. Therefore, the amount of the adjustment to Asset 3 is $2,500.

(v) Asset 4 is ordinary income property, and T would be allocated ($3,750) from the sale of Asset 4 in the hypothetical transaction. Therefore, the amount of the adjustment to Asset 4 is ($3,750).

Example 2. (i) Assume the same facts as Example 1 in paragraph (b)(2)(ii) of this section, except that A sold its interest in PRS to T for $110,000 rather than $120,000. T, therefore, receives a basis adjustment under section 743(b) of $35,000. Of the $35,000 basis adjustment, ($1,250) is allocated to ordinary income property, and $36,250 is allocated to capital gain property.

(ii) Asset 3 is ordinary income property, and T would be allocated $2,500 from the sale of Asset 3 in the hypothetical transaction. Therefore, the amount of the adjustment to Asset 3 is $2,500.

(iii) Asset 4 is ordinary income property, and T would be allocated ($3,750) from the sale of Asset 4 in the hypothetical transaction. Therefore, the amount of the adjustment to Asset 4 is ($3,750).

(iv) Asset 1 is a capital gain asset, and T would be allocated $37,500 from the sale of Asset 1 in the hypothetical transaction. Asset 2 is a capital gain asset, and T would be allocated $8,750 from the sale of Asset 2 in the hypothetical transaction. The total amount of gain that would be allocated to T from the sale of the capital gain assets in the hypothetical transaction is $46,250, which exceeds the amount of the basis adjustment allocated to capital gain property by $10,000. The amount of the adjustment to Asset 1 is $33,604 ($37,500 minus $3,896 ($10,000 × $75,000/192,500)). The amount of the basis adjustment to Asset 2 is $2,646 ($8,750 minus $6,104 ($10,000 × $117,500/192,500)).

Reg. § 1.755-1(b)(3)

(4) *Income in respect of a decedent*—(i) *In general*. Where a partnership interest is transferred as a result of the death of a partner, under section 1014(c) the transferee's basis in its partnership interest is not adjusted for that portion of the interest, if any, which is attributable to items representing income in respect of a decedent under section 691. See § 1.742-1. Accordingly, if a partnership interest is transferred as a result of the death of a partner, and the partnership holds assets representing income in respect of a decedent, no part of the basis adjustment under section 743(b) is allocated to these assets. See § 1.743-1(b).

(ii) The provisions of this paragraph (b)(4) are illustrated by the following example:

Example. (i) A and B are equal partners in personal service partnership PRS. As a result of B's death, B's partnership interest is transferred to T when PRS's balance sheet (reflecting a cash receipts and disbursements method of accounting) is as follows:

Assets

	Adjusted Basis	Fair Market Value
Capital Asset	$2,000	$ 5,000
Unrealized Receivables . .	0	15,000
Total	2,000	20,000

Liabilities and Capital

	Adjusted Per Books	Fair Market Value
Capital:		
A	1,000	10,000
B	1,000	10,000
Total	2,000	20,000

(ii) None of the assets owned by PRS is section 704(c) property, and the capital asset is nondepreciable. The fair market value of T's partnership interest on the applicable date of valuation set forth in section 1014 is $10,000. Of this amount, $2,500 is attributable to T's share of the partnership's capital asset, and $7,500 is attributable to T's 50% share of the partnership's unrealized receivables. The partnership's unrealized receivables represent income in respect of a decedent. Accordingly, under section 1014(c), T's basis in its partnership interest is not adjusted for that portion of the interest which is attributable to the unrealized receivables. Therefore, T's basis in its partnership interest is $2,500.

(iii) At the time of the transfer, B's share of the partnership's basis in partnership assets is $1,000. Accordingly, T receives a $1,500 basis adjustment under section 743(b). Under this paragraph (b)(4), the entire basis adjustment is allocated to the partnership's capital asset.

(5) *Transferred basis exchanges*—(i) *In general*. This paragraph (b)(5) applies to basis adjustments under section 743(b) which result from exchanges in which the transferee's basis in the interest is determined in whole or in part by reference to the transferor's basis in the interest. For example, this paragraph applies if a partnership interest is contributed to a corporation in a transaction to which section 351 applies or to a partnership in a transaction to which section 721(a) applies.

(ii) *Allocations between classes of property*. If the total amount of the basis adjustment under section 743(b) is zero, then no adjustment to the basis of partnership property will be made under this paragraph (b)(5). If there is an increase in basis to be allocated to partnership assets, such increase must be allocated to capital gain property or ordinary income property, respectively, only if the total amount of gain or loss (including any remedial allocations under § 1.704-3(d)) that would be allocated to the transferee (to the extent attributable to the acquired partnership interest) from the hypothetical sale of all such property would result in a net gain or net income, as the case may be, to the transferee. Where, under the preceding sentence, an increase in basis may be allocated to both capital gain assets and ordinary income assets, the increase shall be allocated to each class in proportion to the net gain or net income, respectively, which would be allocated to the transferee from the sale of all assets in each class. If there is a decrease in basis to be allocated to partnership assets, such decrease must be allocated to capital gain property or ordinary income property, respectively, only if the total amount of gain or loss (including any remedial allocations under § 1.704-3(d)) that would be allocated to the transferee (to the extent attributable to the acquired partnership interest) from the hypothetical sale of all such property would result in a net loss to the transferee. Where, under the preceding sentence, a decrease in basis may be allocated to both capital gain assets and ordinary income assets, the decrease shall be allocated to each class in proportion to the net loss which would be allocated to the transferee from the sale of all assets in each class.

(iii) *Allocations within the classes*—(A) *Increases*. If there is an increase in basis to be allocated within a class, the increase must be allocated first to properties with unrealized appreciation in proportion to the transferee's share of the respective amounts of unrealized appreciation before such increase (but only to the extent of the transferee's share of each property's unrealized appreciation). Any remaining increase must be allocated among the properties within the class in proportion to the transferee's share of the

Reg. § 1.755-1(b)(5)

amount that would be realized by the partnership upon the hypothetical sale of each asset in the class.

(B) *Decreases.* If there is a decrease in basis to be allocated within a class, the decrease must be allocated first to properties with unrealized depreciation in proportion to the transferee's shares of the respective amounts of unrealized depreciation before such decrease (but only to the extent of the transferee's share of each property's unrealized depreciation). Any remaining decrease must be allocated among the properties within the class in proportion to the transferee's shares of their adjusted bases (as adjusted under the preceding sentence).

(C) *Limitation in decrease of basis.* Where, as the result of a transaction to which this paragraph (b)(5) applies, a decrease in basis must be allocated to capital gain assets, ordinary income assets, or both, and the amount of the decrease otherwise allocable to a particular class exceeds the transferee's share of the adjusted basis to the partnership of all depreciated assets in that class, the transferee's negative basis adjustment is limited to the transferee's share of the partnership's adjusted basis in all depreciated assets in that class.

(D) *Carryover adjustment.* Where a transferee's negative basis adjustment under section 743(b) cannot be allocated to any asset, because the adjustment exceeds the transferee's share of the adjusted basis to the partnership of all depreciated assets in a particular class, the adjustment is made when the partnership subsequently acquires property of a like character to which an adjustment can be made.

(iv) *Examples.* The provisions of this paragraph (b)(5) are illustrated by the following examples:

Example 1. A is a member of partnership LTP, which has made an election under section 754. The three partners in LTP have equal interests in capital and profits. Solely in exchange for a partnership interest in UTP, A contributes its interest in LTP to UTP in a transaction described in section 721. At the time of the transfer, A's basis in its partnership interest ($5,000) equals its share of inside basis (also $5,000). Under section 723, UTP's basis in its interest in LTP is $5,000. LTP's only two assets on the date of contribution are inventory with a basis of $5,000 and a fair market value of $7,500, and a nondepreciable capital asset with a basis of $10,000 and a fair market value of $7,500. The amount of the basis adjustment under section 743(b) to partnership property is $0 ($5,000, UTP's basis in its interest in LTP, minus $5,000, UTP's share of LTP's basis in partnership assets). Because UTP acquired its interest in LTP in a transferred basis exchange,

and the total amount of the basis adjustment under section 743(b) is zero, UTP receives no special basis adjustments under section 743(b) with respect to the partnership property of LTP.

Example 2. (i) A purchases a partnership interest in LTP at a time when an election under section 754 is not in effect. The three partners in LTP have equal interests in capital and profits. During a later year for which LTP has an election under section 754 in effect, and in a transaction that is unrelated to A's purchase of the LTP interest, A contributes its interest in LTP to UTP in a transaction described in section 721 (solely in exchange for a partnership interest in UTP). At the time of the transfer, A's adjusted basis in its interest in LTP is $20,433. Under section 721, A recognizes no gain or loss as a result of the contribution of its partnership interest to UTP. Under section 723, UTP's basis in its partnership interest in LTP is $20,433. The balance sheet of LTP on the date of the contribution shows the following:

Assets

	Adjusted Basis	Fair Market Value
Cash	$ 5,000	$ 5,000
Accounts receivable	10,000	10,000
Inventory	20,000	21,000
Nondepreciable capital asset	20,000	40,000
Total	$55,000	$76,000

Liabilities and Capital

	Adjusted Per Books	Fair Market Value
Liabilities	$10,000	$10,000
Capital:		
A	15,000	22,000
B	15,000	22,000
C	15,000	22,000
Total	$55,000	$76,000

(ii) The amount of the basis adjustment under section 743(b) is the difference between the basis of UTP's interest in LTP and UTP's share of the adjusted basis to LTP of partnership property. UTP's interest in the previously taxed capital of LTP is $15,000 ($22,000, the amount of cash UTP would receive if LTP liquidated immediately after the hypothetical transaction, decreased by $7,000, the amount of tax gain allocated to UTP from the hypothetical transaction). UTP's share of the adjusted basis to LTP of partnership property is $18,333 ($15,000 share of previously taxed capital, plus $3,333 share of LTP's liabilities). The amount of the basis adjustment under section 743(b) to partnership property therefore, is $2,100 ($20,433 minus $18,333).

Reg. § 1.755-1(b)(5)

(iii) The total amount of gain that would be allocated to UTP from the hypothetical sale of capital gain property is $6,666.67 (one-third of the excess of the fair market value of LTP's nondepreciable capital asset, $40,000, over its basis, $20,000). The total amount of gain that would be allocated to UTP from the hypothetical sale of ordinary income property is $333.33 (one-third of the excess of the fair market value of LTP's inventory, $21,000, over its basis, $20,000). Under paragraph (b)(5), LTP must allocate $2,000 ($6,666.67 divided by $7,000 times $2,100) of UTP's basis adjustment to the nondepreciable capital asset. LTP must allocate $100 ($333.33 divided by $7,000 times $2,100) of UTP's basis adjustment to the inventory.

(c) *Adjustments under section 734(b)*—(1) *Allocations between classes of property*—(i) *General rule.* Where there is a distribution of partnership property resulting in an adjustment to the basis of undistributed partnership property under section 734(b)(1)(B) or (b)(2)(B), the adjustment must be allocated to remaining partnership property of a character similar to that of the distributed property with respect to which the adjustment arose. Thus, when the partnership's adjusted basis of distributed capital gain property immediately prior to distribution exceeds the basis of the property to the distributee partner (as determined under section 732), the basis of the undistributed capital gain property remaining in the partnership is increased by an amount equal to the excess. Conversely, when the basis to the distributee partner (as determined under section 732) of distributed capital gain property exceeds the partnership's adjusted basis of such property immediately prior to the distribution, the basis of the undistributed capital gain property remaining in the partnership is decreased by an amount equal to such excess. Similarly, where there is a distribution of ordinary income property, and the basis of the property to the distributee partner (as determined under section 732) is not the same as the partnership's adjusted basis of the property immediately prior to distribution, the adjustment is made only to undistributed property of the same class remaining in the partnership.

(ii) *Special rule.* Where there is a distribution resulting in an adjustment under section 734(b)(1)(A) or (b)(2)(A) to the basis of undistributed partnership property, the adjustment is allocated only to capital gain property.

(2) *Allocations within the classes*—(i) *Increases.* If there is an increase in basis to be allocated within a class, the increase must be allocated first to properties with unrealized appreciation in proportion to their respective amounts of unrealized appreciation before such increase (but only to the extent of each property's unrealized appreciation). Any remaining increase must be allocated among the properties within the class in proportion to their fair market values.

(ii) *Decreases.* If there is a decrease in basis to be allocated within a class, the decrease must be allocated first to properties with unrealized depreciation in proportion to their respective amounts of unrealized depreciation before such decrease (but only to the extent of each property's unrealized depreciation). Any remaining decrease must be allocated among the properties within the class in proportion to their adjusted bases (as adjusted under the preceding sentence).

(3) *Limitation in decrease of basis.* Where a decrease in the basis of partnership assets is required under section 734(b)(2) and the amount of the decrease exceeds the adjusted basis to the partnership of property of the required character, the basis of such property is reduced to zero (but not below zero).

(4) *Carryover adjustment.* Where, in the case of a distribution, an increase or a decrease in the basis of undistributed property cannot be made because the partnership owns no property of the character required to be adjusted, or because the basis of all the property of a like character has been reduced to zero, the adjustment is made when the partnership subsequently acquires property of a like character to which an adjustment can be made.

(5) *Example.* The following example illustrates this paragraph (c):

Example. (i) A, B, and C form equal partnership PRS. A contributes $50,000 and Asset 1, capital gain property with a fair market value of $50,000 and an adjusted tax basis of $25,000. B and C each contributes $100,000. PRS uses the cash to purchase Assets 2, 3, 4, 5, and 6. Assets 4, 5, and 6 are the only assets held by the partnership which are subject to section 751. The partnership has an election in effect under section 754. After seven years, the adjusted basis and fair market value of PRS's assets are as follows:

Assets

	Adjusted Basis	Fair Market Value
Capital Gain Property:		
Asset 1	$ 25,000	$ 75,000
Asset 2	100,000	117,500
Asset 3	50,000	60,000
Ordinary Income Property:		
Asset 4	$ 40,000	$ 45,000
Asset 5	50,000	60,000
Asset 6	10,000	2,500
Total	$275,000	$360,000

(ii) *Allocation between classes.* Assume that PRS distributes Assets 3 and 5 to A in complete

Reg. § 1.755-1(c)(5)

liquidation of A's interest in the partnership. A's basis in the partnership interest was $75,000. The partnership's basis in Assets 3 and 5 was $50,000 each. A's $75,000 basis in its partnership interest is allocated between Assets 3 and 5 under sections 732(b) and (c). A will, therefore, have a basis of $25,000 in Asset 3 (capital gain property), and a basis of $50,000 in Asset 5 (section 751 property). The distribution results in a $25,000 increase in the basis of capital gain property. There is no change in the basis of ordinary income property.

(iii) *Allocation within class.* The amount of the basis increase to capital gain property is $25,000 and must be allocated among the remaining capital gain assets in proportion to the difference between the fair market value and basis of each. The fair market value of Asset 1 exceeds its basis by $50,000. The fair market value of Asset 2 exceeds its basis by $17,500. Therefore, the basis of Asset 1 will be increased by $18,519 ($25,000, multiplied by $50,000, divided by $67,500), and the basis of Asset 2 will be increased by $6,481 ($25,000 multiplied by $17,500, divided by $67,500).

(d) *Effective date.* This section applies to transfers of partnership interests and distributions of property from a partnership that occur on or after December 15, 1999. [Reg. § 1.755-1.]

☐ [*T.D. 6175, 5-23-56. Amended by T.D. 8847, 12-14-99 (corrected 2-23-2000).*]

Proposed Regulation

§ 1.755-2. Coordination of sections 755 and 1060.—(a) *Coordination with section 1060*—(1) *In general.* If there is a basis adjustment to which this section applies, the partnership must determine the fair market value of each item of partnership property under the residual method, as described in paragraph (b) of this section, and the rules of § 1.755-1 must be applied using the values so determined.

(2) *Application of this section.* This section applies to any basis adjustment made under section 743(b) (relating to certain transfers of interests in a partnership) or section 732(d) or section 734(b) (relating to certain partnership distributions).

(b) *Residual method*—(1) *In general*—(i) *Five classes*—(A) Except as provided in paragraph (b)(3) of this section, partnership gross value (as defined in paragraph (c) of this section) is allocated among five asset classes in the following order—

(*1*) Among cash and general deposit accounts (including savings and checking accounts) other than certificates of deposit held in banks, savings and loan associations, and other depository institutions (referred to hereafter as cash);

(*2*) Among partnership assets other than cash, capital assets, section 1231(b) property, and section 197 intangibles (referred to hereafter as ordinary income property);

(*3*) Among capital assets and section 1231(b) property other than section 197 intangibles;

(*4*) Among section 197 intangibles other than goodwill and going concern value; and

(*5*) To goodwill and going concern value (referred to hereafter as goodwill).

(B) In determining the values to be assigned to each class, properties or potential gain treated as unrealized receivables under the flush language in section 751(c) are not counted as assets in the second class. For example, any portion of goodwill that would result in ordinary income under section 1245 if the goodwill were sold would be included in the residual class for goodwill.

(ii) *Impaired classes.* If the value assigned to a class is less than the sum of the fair market values (determined under paragraph (b)(2)(i) of this section) of the assets in that class, then the assigned value generally must be allocated among the individual assets in proportion to such fair market values. However, in the third, fourth, and fifth classes, values must be assigned first to properties or potential gain treated as unrealized receivables under the flush language in section 751(c), if any, in proportion to the income that would be recognized if the underlying assets were sold for their fair market values (determined under paragraph (b)(2)(i) of this section), but only to the extent of the income attributable to the unrealized receivables. Any remaining value in each class will be allocated among the remaining portions of the assets in that class in proportion to the fair market values of such portions (determined under paragraph (b)(2)(i) of this section).

(2) *Special rules.* For purposes of this section:

(i) Except as otherwise provided in this section, the fair market value of each item of partnership property (other than goodwill) shall be determined on the basis of all the facts and circumstances, taking into account section 7701(g).

(ii) If goodwill could not under any circumstances attach to the assets of a partnership, then the value of goodwill is zero. This might occur, for example, if a partnership's only asset is a vacant parcel of real estate that does not produce current income.

(iii)(A) The value assigned to an asset (other than goodwill) shall not exceed the fair market value (determined under paragraph (b)(2)(i)) of that asset on the date of the relevant transfer, unless—

(*1*) Partnership gross value (as defined in paragraph (c) of this section) exceeds the aggregate value of the partnership's individual assets; and

(*2*) Goodwill could not under any circumstances attach to the assets.

(B) If both of these conditions are satisfied, the excess must be allocated among all partnership assets other than cash in proportion to such fair market values.

(3) *Special situations.* In certain circumstances, such as where book income or loss with respect to particular partnership properties is allocated differently among partners, partnership gross value may vary depending on the value of particular partnership assets. In these special situations, the fair market value of each item of partnership property (other than goodwill) first shall be determined on the basis of all the facts and circumstances, taking into account section 7701(g). Such value then shall be assigned within the first four asset classes under the residual method described in paragraph (b)(1) of this section in a manner that is consistent with the ordering rule used in paragraph (b)(1) of this section (together with the special rules in paragraph (b)(2) of this section) so that the amount of the liquidating distribution described in paragraph (c)(1) of this section would equal the transferee's basis in the transferred partnership interest. If the value so determined for the assets in the first four asset classes is not sufficient to cause the appropriate liquidating distribution, then, so long as goodwill may attach to the assets of the partnership, the fair market value of goodwill shall be presumed to equal an amount that if assigned to goodwill would cause the appropriate liquidating distribution.

(c) *Partnership gross value*—(1) *Basis adjustments under section 743(b) and section 732(d)*—(i) *In general.* In the case of a basis adjustment under section 743(b) or 732(d), partnership gross value generally is equal to the amount that, if assigned to all partnership property, would result in a liquidating distribution to the partner equal to the transferee's basis in the transferred partnership interest immediately following the relevant transfer (reduced by the amount, if any, of such basis that is attributable to partnership liabilities) pursuant to the hypothetical transaction (as defined in paragraph (c)(3) of this section). Solely for the purpose of determining partnership gross value under the preceding sentence, where a partnership interest is transferred as a result of the death of a partner, the transferee's basis in its

partnership interest is determined without regard to section 1014(c), and is deemed to be adjusted for that portion of the interest, if any, which is attributable to items representing income in respect of a decedent under section 691.

(ii) *Transferred basis transactions.* [Reserved]

(2) *Basis adjustments under section 734(b).* [Reserved]

(3) *Hypothetical transaction.* For purposes of this paragraph (c), the hypothetical transaction means the disposition by the partnership of all partnership property in a fully taxable transaction for cash, followed by the payment of all partnership liabilities (within the meaning of section 752 and the regulations thereunder), and the distribution of all remaining proceeds to the partners.

(d) *Required statements.* See § 1.743-1(k)(2) for provisions requiring the transferee of a partnership interest to provide information to the partnership relating to the transfer of an interest in the partnership. See § 1.743-1(k)(1) for a provision requiring the partnership to attach a statement to the partnership return showing the computation of a basis adjustment under section 743(b) and the partnership properties to which the adjustment is allocated under section 755. See § 1.732-1(d)(3) for a provision requiring a transferee partner to attach a, statement to its return showing the computation of a basis adjustment under section 732(d) and the partnership properties to which the adjustment is allocated under section 755. See § 1.732-1(d)(5) for a provision requiring the partnership to provide information to a transferee partner reporting a basis adjustment under section 732(d).

(e) *Examples.* The provisions of this section are illustrated by the following examples, which assume that the partnerships have an election in effect under section 754 at the time of the transfer. Except as provided, no partnership asset (other than inventory) is property described in section 751(a). The examples are as follows:

Example 1. (i) A is the sole general partner in ABC, a limited partnership. ABC has goodwill and three other assets with fair market values (determined under paragraph (b)(2)(i) of this section) as follows: inventory worth $1,000,000, a building (a capital asset) worth $2,000,000, and section 197 intangibles (other than goodwill) worth $800,000. ABC has one liability of $1,000,000, for which A bears the entire risk of loss under section 752 and the regulations thereunder. Each partner has a one-third interest in partnership capital and profits. D purchases A's partnership interest for $1,000,000.

(ii) D's basis in the transferred partnership interest (reduced by the amount of such basis that is attributable to partnership liabilities) is $1,000,000 ($2,000,000 − $1,000,000). Under paragraph (c) of this section, partnership gross value is $4,000,000 (the amount that, if assigned to all partnership property, would result in a liquidating distribution to D equal to $1,000,000).

(iii) Under paragraph (b) of this section, partnership gross value is allocated first to the inventory ($1,000,000), then to the building ($2,000,000), and third to section 197 intangibles $800,000. The partnership must allocate the remainder of partnership gross value, $200,000, to goodwill ($4,000,000 − $3,800,000). D's section 743(b) adjustment must be allocated under § 1.755-1 using these fair market value calculations for the partnership's assets.

Example 2. (i) D is the sole general partner in DEF, a limited partnership. DEF has goodwill and three other assets with fair market values (determined under paragraph (b)(2)(i) of this section) as follows: inventory worth $1,000,000, a building (a capital asset) worth $2,000,000, and equipment (section 1231(b) property) worth $750,000. DEF has one liability of $1,000,000, for which D bears the entire risk of loss under section 752 and the regulations thereunder. Each partner has a one-third interest in partnership capital and profits. If the equipment were sold for $750,000, $250,000 would be depreciation recapture treated as an unrealized receivable under the flush language in section 751(c). G purchases E's limited partnership interest for $750,000.

(ii) Under paragraph (c) of this section, partnership gross value is $3,250,000 (the amount that, if assigned to all partnership property, would result in a liquidating distribution to G equal to $750,000).

(iii) Under paragraph (b) of this section, partnership gross value is allocated first to inventory ($1,000,000), and then to the class containing capital assets and section 1231(b) property ($2,250,000). Within that class, value must be assigned first to the $250,000 ordinary gain portion of the equipment (properties or potential gain treated as unrealized receivables under the flush language in section 751(c)). The remaining value in the class ($2,250,000 minus $250,000, which is $2,000,000) must be allocated among the remaining portions of the assets in that class in proportion to the fair market values of such portions (determined under paragraph (b)(2)(i) of this section). The remaining portion of the building is $2,000,000. The remaining portion of the

equipment is $500,000 ($750,000, its fair market value, minus $250,000, the section 751(c) portion). Thus, the remaining portion of the building will be allocated $1,600,000 ($2,000,000 multiplied by $2,000,000/$2,500,000) and the remaining portion of the equipment will be allocated $400,000 ($2,000,000 multiplied by $500,000/$2,500,000). Nothing is allocated to goodwill. G's section 743(b) adjustment must be allocated under § 1.755-1 using these fair market value calculations for the partnership's assets.

Example 3. (i) G and H are partners in partnership GH. GH has goodwill and three other assets with fair market values (determined under paragraph (b)(2)(i) of this section) as follows: inventory worth $1,000,000 and two buildings (capital assets), each worth $500,000. GH has no liabilities. The GH partnership agreement provides that the partners will allocate all income, gain, loss, and deductions equally, except with respect to depreciation, loss, and gain from the buildings. With respect to the buildings, depreciation and loss are allocated two-thirds to G and one-third to H. Gain from the disposition of the buildings is charged back two-thirds to G and one-third to H to the extent of accrued depreciation, and then is allocated equally between G and H. G transfers one-half of its interest in GH to I for $450,000. At the time of the transfer, the book value of the inventory is $900,000, the book value of each building is $300,000, and $150,000 of book depreciation has accrued with respect to each building. The capital account attributable to the partnership interest purchased by I from G is equal to $350,000. H's capital account is equal to $800,000, and the capital account attributable to G's retained partnership interest is equal to $350,000.

(ii) Because gain with respect to the inventory and buildings are shared in different ratios as between H, and G and I, a partnership gross value cannot be determined without assuming values for the individual assets of the partnership. Accordingly, the rule for special situations in paragraph (b)(3) of this section must be used to compute the value of the partnership's assets.

(iii) Applying paragraph (b)(2)(i) of this section, the fair market value of the inventory is $1,000,000 and the fair market value of each building is $500,000. These values would result in a liquidating distribution to I under paragraph (c)(1) of this section equal to $500,000, determined as follows. The book gain from the sale of the inventory would equal $100,000 ($1,000,000 − $900,000) and the book gain from the sale of each building would equal $200,000 ($500,000 − $300,000). Book gain from the inventory equal to $25,000 ($100,000 × 1/4) and book gain from each building equal to $62,500 (($150,000 × 1/3)

Reg. § 1.755-2(e)

+ ($50,000 × 1/4)) would be allocated to I. The sum of this book gain ($25,000 + $62,500 + $62,500 = $150,000) and I's capital account inherited from G ($350,000) would equal $500,000.

(iv) Because I's basis in the transferred partnership interest is only $450,000, under paragraph (b)(2)(ii) of this section, the value with respect to the buildings must be reduced in proportion to the fair market values of such assets to an amount that would cause a liquidating distribution to I equal to $450,000. This calculation is accomplished as follows. In order for I to receive a liquidating distribution of $450,000, the book gain attributable to the buildings that is allocated to I must equal $75,000 ($350,000 inherited capital account + $25,000 book gain from inventory + $75,000 book gain from buildings). Each building has the same book value and fair market value, and the allocations with respect to each building are the same as between G, H, and I. Accordingly, I's share of book gain should be allocated equally between the two buildings, $37,500 to each. In order for I to be allocated $37,500 of book gain with respect to each building, the total amount of book gain with respect to each building would have to be $112,500 ($112,500 × 1/3 = $37,500). Adding this book gain to the current book value of each building results in a value for each building of $412,500 ($300,000 + $112,500). Nothing is allocated to goodwill. I's section 743(b) adjustment must be allocated under § 1.755-1 using these fair market value calculations for the partnership's assets.

Example 4. The facts are the same as *Example 3*, except that I purchases one-half of G's partnership interest for $550,000. Because the fair market value of the partnership's assets (as determined under paragraph (b)(2)(i) of this section) in the first four asset classes under the residual method is not sufficient to cause a liquidating distribution to I equal to its basis in the purchased interest (i.e., $550,000), the additional value necessary to cause such a distribution must be allocated to goodwill. Accordingly, under paragraph (b)(3) of this section, the value of the partnership's assets is as follows: inventory $1,000,000, each building $500,000, and goodwill $200,000. I's section 743(b) adjustment must be allocated under § 1.755-1 using these fair market value calculations for the partnership's assets.

(f) *Effective date.* This section applies to any basis adjustment resulting from any distribution of partnership property or transfer of a partnership interest that occurs on or after the date final regulations are published in the Federal Register. [Reg. § 1.755-2.]

[Proposed 4-5-2000.]

Definitions

§ 1.761-1. **Terms defined.**—(a) *Partnership.* The term *partnership* means a partnership as determined under § § 301.7701-1, 301.7701-2, and 301.7701-3 of this chapter.

(b) *Partner.* The term "partner" means a member of a partnership.

(c) *Partnership agreement.* For the purposes of subchapter K, a partnership agreement includes the original agreement and any modifications thereof agreed to by all the partners or adopted in any other manner provided by the partnership agreement. Such agreement or modifications can be oral or written. A partnership agreement may be modified with respect to a particular taxable year subsequent to the close of such taxable year, but not later than the date (not including any extension of time) prescribed by law for the filing of the partnership return. As to any matter on which the partnership agreement, or any modification thereof, is silent, the provisions of local law shall be considered to constitute a part of the agreement.

(d) *Liquidation of partner's interest.* The term "liquidation of a partner's interest" means the termination of a partner's entire interest in a partnership by means of a distribution, or a series of distributions, to the partner by the partnership. A series of distributions will come within the meaning of this term whether they are made in one year or in more than one year. Where a partner's interest is to be liquidated by a series of distributions, the interest will not be considered as liquidated until the final distribution has been made. For the basis of property distributed in one liquidating distribution, or in a series of distributions in liquidation, see section 732(b). A distribution which is not in liquidation of a partner's entire interest, as defined in this paragraph, is a current distribution. Current distributions, therefore, include distributions in partial liquidation of a partner's interest, and distributions of the partner's distributive share. See paragraph (a)(1)(ii) of § 1.731-1.

(e) *Distribution of partnership interest.* For purposes of section 708(b)(1)(B) and § 1.708-1(b)(1)(iv), the deemed distribution of an interest in a new partnership by a partnership that terminates under section 708(b)(1)(B) is not a sale or exchange of an interest in the new partnership. However, the deemed distribution of an interest in a new partnership by a partnership that terminates under section 708(b)(1)(B) is treated as an exchange of the interest in the new partnership for purposes of section 743. This paragraph (e) applies to terminations of partnerships under section 708(b)(1)(B) occurring on or after

May 9, 1997; however, this paragraph (e) may be applied to terminations occurring on or after May 9, 1996, provided that the partnership and its partners apply this paragraph (e) to the termination in a consistent manner. [Reg. § 1.761-1.]

☐ [*T.D. 6175, 5-23-56. Amended by T.D. 6198, 8-15-56; T.D. 7012, 5-14-69; T.D. 7208, 10-2-72; T.D. 8697, 12-17-96 and T.D. 8717, 5-8-97.*]

§ 1.761-2. Exclusion of certain unincorporated organizations from the application of all or part of subchapter K of chapter 1 of the Internal Revenue Code.—(a) *Exclusion of eligible unincorporated organizations*—(1) *In general.* Under conditions set forth in this section, an unincorporated organization described in subparagraph (2) or (3) of this paragraph may be excluded from the application of all or a part of the provisions of subchapter K of chapter 1 of the Code. Such organization must be availed of (i) for investment purposes only and not for the active conduct of a business, or (ii) for the joint production, extraction or use of property, but not for the purpose of selling services or property produced or extracted. The members of such organization must be able to compute their income without the necessity of computing partnership taxable income. Any syndicate, group, pool, or joint venture which is classifiable as an association, or any group operating under an agreement which creates an organization classifiable as an association, does not fall within these provisions.

(2) *Investing partnership.* Where the participants in the joint purchase, retention, sale, or exchange of investment property—

(i) Own the property as coowners,

(ii) Reserve the right separately to take or dispose of their shares of any property acquired or retained, and

(iii) Do not actively conduct business or irrevocably authorize some person or persons acting in a representative capacity to purchase, sell, or exchange such investment property, although each separate participant may delegate authority to purchase, sell, or exchange his share of any such investment property for the time being for his account, but not for a period of more than a year, then

such group may be excluded from the application of the provisions of subchapter K under the rules set forth in paragraph (b) of this section.

(3) *Operating agreements.* Where the participants in the joint production, extraction, or use of property—

(i) Own the property as coowners, either in fee or under lease or other form of contract granting exclusive operating rights, and

(ii) Reserve the right separately to take in kind or dispose of their shares of any property produced, extracted, or used, and

(iii) Do not jointly sell services or the property produced or extracted, although each separate participant may delegate authority to sell his share of the property produced or extracted for the time being for his account, but not for a period of time in excess of the minimum needs of the industry, and in no event for more than one year, then

such group may be excluded from the application of the provisions of subchapter K under the rules set forth in paragraph (b) of this section. However, the preceding sentence does not apply to any unincorporated organization one of whose principal purposes is cycling, manufacturing, or processing for persons who are not members of the organization. * * *

* * *

(c) *Partial exclusion from subchapter K.* An unincorporated organization which wishes to be excluded from only certain sections of subchapter K must submit to the Commissioner, no later than 90 days after the beginning of the first taxable year for which partial exclusion is desired, a request for permission to be excluded from certain provisions of subchapter K. The request shall set forth the sections of subchapter K from which exclusion is sought and shall state that such organization qualifies under subparagraphs (1) and either (2) or (3) of paragraph (a) of this section, and that the members of the organization elect to be excluded to the extent indicated. Such exclusion shall be effective only upon approval of the election by the Commissioner and subject to the conditions he may impose.

* * *

(e) *Cross reference.* For requirements with respect to the filing of a return on Form 1065 by a partnership, see § 1.6031-1. [Reg. § 1.761-2.]

☐ [*T.D. 7208, 10-2-72. Amended by T.D. 8578, 12-22-94.*]

Determination and Recognition of Gain or Loss

§ 1.1001-1. Computation of gain or loss.—(a) *General Rule.* Except as otherwise provided in subtitle A of the Code, the gain or loss realized from the conversion of property into cash, or from the exchange of property for other property differing materially either in kind or in extent, is treated as income or as loss sustained. The amount realized from a sale or other disposition of property is the sum of any money received plus the fair market value of any property (other than money) received. The fair market value of property is a question of fact, but only in rare and extraordinary cases will property be considered to have no fair market value. The general method of computing such gain or loss is prescribed by section 1001(a) through (d) which contemplates that from the amount realized upon the sale or exchange there shall be withdrawn a sum sufficient to restore the adjusted basis prescribed by section 1011 and the regulations thereunder (i.e., the cost or other basis adjusted for receipts, expenditures, losses, allowances, and other items chargeable against and applicable to such cost or other basis). The amount which remains after the adjusted basis has been restored to the taxpayer constitutes the realized gain. If the amount realized upon the sale or exchange is insufficient to restore to the taxpayer the adjusted basis of the property, a loss is sustained to the extent of the difference between such adjusted basis and the amount realized. The basis may be different depending upon whether gain or loss is being computed. For example, see section 1015(a) and the regulations thereunder. Section 1001(e) and paragraph (f) of this section prescribe the method of computing gain or loss upon the sale or other disposition of a term interest in property the adjusted basis (or a portion) of which is determined pursuant, or by reference, to section 1014 (relating to the basis of property acquired from a decedent) or section 1015 (relating to the basis of property acquired by gift or by a transfer in trust).

(b) *Real estate taxes as amounts received.* (1) Section 1001(b) and section 1012 state rules applicable in making an adjustment upon a sale of real property with respect to the real property taxes apportioned between seller and purchaser under section 164(d). Thus, if the seller pays (or agrees to pay) real property taxes attributable to the real property tax year in which the sale occurs, he shall not take into account, in determining the amount realized from the sale under section 1001(b), any amount received as reimbursement for taxes which are treated under section 164(d) as imposed upon the purchaser. Similarly, in computing the cost of the property under section 1012, the purchaser shall not take into account any amount paid to the seller as reimbursement for real property taxes which are treated under section 164(d) as imposed upon the purchaser. These rules apply whether or not the contract of sale calls for the purchaser to reimburse the seller for such real property taxes paid or to be paid by the seller.

(2) On the other hand, if the purchaser pays (or is to pay) an amount representing real property taxes which are treated under section 164(d) as imposed upon the seller, that amount shall be taken into account both in determining the amount realized from the sale under section 1001(b) and in computing the cost of the property

under section 1012. It is immaterial whether or not the contract of sale specifies that the sale price has been reduced by, or is in any way intended to reflect, the taxes allocable to the seller. See also paragraph (b) of § 1.1012-1.

(3) Subparagraph (1) of this paragraph shall not apply to a seller who, in a taxable year prior to the taxable year of sale, pays an amount representing real property taxes which are treated under section 164(d) as imposed on the purchaser, if such seller has elected to capitalize such amount in accordance with section 266 and the regulations thereunder (relating to election to capitalize certain carrying charges and taxes).

(4) The application of this paragraph may be illustrated by the following examples:

Example (1). Assume that the contract price on the sale of a parcel of real estate is $50,000 and that real property taxes thereon in the amount of $1,000 for the real property tax year in which occurred the date of sale were previously paid by the seller. Assume further that $750 of the taxes are treated under section 164(d) as imposed upon the purchaser and that he reimburses the seller in that amount in addition to the contract price. The amount realized by the seller is $50,000. Similarly, $50,000 is the purchaser's cost. If, in this example, the purchaser made no payment other than the contract price of $50,000, the amount realized by the seller would be $49,250, since the sales price would be deemed to include $750 paid to the seller in reimbursement for real property taxes imposed upon the purchaser. Similarly, $49,250 would be the purchaser's cost.

Example (2). Assume that the purchaser in example (1) above, paid all of the real property taxes. Assume further that $250 of the taxes are treated under section 164(d) as imposed upon the seller. The amount realized by the seller is $50,250. Similarly, $50,250 is the purchaser's cost, regardless of the taxable year in which the purchaser makes actual payment of the taxes.

Example (3). Assume that the seller described in the first part of example (1), above, paid the real property taxes of $1,000 in the taxable year prior to the taxable year of sale and elected under section 266 to capitalize the $1,000 of taxes. In such a case, the amount realized is $50,750. Moreover, regardless of whether the seller elected to capitalize the real property taxes, the purchaser in that case could elect under section 266 to capitalize the $750 of taxes treated under section 164(d) as imposed upon him, in which case his adjusted basis would be $50,750 (cost of $50,000 plus capitalized taxes of $570 [$750]).

(c) *Other rules.* (1) Even though property is not sold or otherwise disposed of, gain is realized if the

Reg. § 1.1001-1(c)

sum of all the amounts received which are required by section 1016 and other applicable provisions of subtitle A of the Code to be applied against the basis of the property exceeds such basis. Except as otherwise provided in section 301(c)(3)(B) with respect to distributions out of increase in value of property accrued prior to March 1, 1913, such gain is includible in gross income under section 61 as "income from whatever source derived". On the other hand, a loss is not ordinarily sustained prior to the sale or other disposition of the property, for the reason that until such sale or other disposition occurs there remains the possibility that the taxpayer may recover or recoup the adjusted basis of the property. Until some identifiable event fixes the actual sustaining of a loss and the amount thereof, it is not taken into account.

(2) The provisions of subparagraph (1) of this paragraph may be illustrated by the following example:

Example. A, an individual on a calendar year basis, purchased certain shares of stock subsequent to February 28, 1913, for $10,000. On January 1, 1954, A's adjusted basis for the stock had been reduced to $1,000 by reason of receipts and distributions described in sections 1016(a)(1) and 1016(a)(4). He received in 1954 a further distribution of $5,000, being a distribution covered by section 1016(a)(4), other than a distribution out of increase of value of property accrued prior to March 1, 1913. This distribution applied against the adjusted basis as required by section 1016(a)(4) exceeds that basis by $4,000. The $4,000 excess is a gain realized by A in 1954 and is includible in gross income in his return for that calendar year. In computing gain from the stock, as in adjusting basis, no distinction is made between items of receipts or distributions described in section 1016. If A sells the stock in 1955 for $5,000, he realizes in 1955 a gain of $5,000, since the adjusted basis of the stock for the purpose of computing gain or loss from the sale is zero.

(d) *Installment sales.* In the case of property sold on the installment plan, special rules for the taxation of the gain are prescribed in section 453.

(e) *Transfers in part a sale and in part a gift.* (1) Where a transfer of property is in part a sale and in part a gift, the transferor has a gain to the extent that the amount realized by him exceeds his adjusted basis in the property. However, no loss is sustained on such a transfer if the amount realized is less than the adjusted basis. For determination of basis of the property in the hands of the transferee, see § 1.1015-4. For the allocation of the adjusted basis of property in the case of a bargain sale to a charitable organization, see § 1.1011-2.

(2) *Examples.* The provisions of subparagraph (1) may be illustrated by the following examples:

Example (1). A transfers property to his son for $60,000. Such property in the hands of A has an adjusted basis of $30,000 (and a fair market value of $90,000). A's gain is $30,000, the excess of $60,000, the amount realized, over the adjusted basis, $30,000. He has made a gift of $30,000, the excess of $90,000, the fair market value, over the amount realized, $60,000.

Example (2). A transfers property to his son for $30,000. Such property in the hands of A has an adjusted basis of $60,000 (and a fair market value of $90,000). A has no gain or loss, and has made a gift of $60,000, the excess of $90,000, the fair market value, over the amount realized, $30,000.

Example (3). A transfers property to his son for $30,000. Such property in A's hands has an adjusted basis of $30,000 (and a fair market value of $60,000). A has no gain and has made a gift of $30,000, the excess of $60,000, the fair market value, over the amount realized, $30,000.

Example (4). A transfers property to his son for $30,000. Such property in A's hands has an adjusted basis of $90,000 (and a fair market value of $60,000). A has sustained no loss, and has made a gift of $30,000, the excess of $60,000, the fair market value, over the amount realized, $30,000.

(f) *Sale or other disposition of a term interest in property*—(1) *General rule.* Except as otherwise provided in subparagraph (3) of this paragraph, for purposes of determining gain or loss from the sale or other disposition after October 9, 1969, of a term interest in property (as defined in subparagraph (2) of this paragraph), a taxpayer shall not take into account that portion of the adjusted basis of such interest which is determined pursuant, or by reference, to section 1014 (relating to the basis of property acquired from a decedent) or section 1015 (relating to the basis of property acquired by gift or by a transfer in trust) to the extent that such adjusted basis is a portion of the adjusted uniform basis of the entire property (as defined in § 1.1014-5). Where a term interest in property is transferred to a corporation in connection with a transaction to which section 351 applies and the adjusted basis of the term interest (i) is determined pursuant to section 1014 or 1015 and (ii) is also a portion of the adjusted uniform basis of the entire property, a subsequent sale or other disposition of such term interest by the corporation will be subject to the provisions of section 1001(e) and this paragraph to the extent that the basis of the term interest so sold or otherwise disposed of is determined by reference to its basis in the hands of the transferor as

Reg. § 1.1001-1(c)(2)

provided by section 362(a). See subparagraph (2) of this paragraph for rules relating to the characterization of stock received by the transferor of a term interest in property in connection with a transaction to which section 351 applies. That portion of the adjusted uniform basis of the entire property which is assignable to such interest at the time of its sale or other disposition shall be determined under the rules provided in § 1.1014-5. Thus, gain or loss realized from a sale or other disposition of a term interest in property shall be determined by comparing the amount of the proceeds of such sale with that part of the adjusted basis of such interest which is not a portion of the adjusted uniform basis of the entire property.

(2) *Term interest defined.* For purposes of section 1001(e) and this paragraph, a "term interest in property" means—

(i) A life interest in property,

(ii) An interest in property for a term of years, or

(iii) An income interest in a trust.

Generally subdivisions (i), (ii), and (iii) refer to an interest, present or future, in the income from property or the right to use property which will terminate or fail on the lapse of time, on the occurrence of an event or contingency, or on the failure of an event or contingency to occur. Such divisions do not refer to remainder or reversionary interests in the property itself or other interests in the property which will ripen into ownership of the entire property upon termination or failure of a preceding term interest. A "term interest in property" also includes any property received upon a sale or other disposition of a life interest in property, an interest in property for a term of years, or an income interest in a trust by the original holder of such interest, but only to the extent that the adjusted basis of the property received is determined by reference to the adjusted basis of the term interest so transferred.

(3) *Exception.* Paragraph (1) of section 1001(e) and subparagraph (1) of this paragraph shall not apply to a sale or other disposition of a term interest in property as a part of a single transaction in which the entire interest in the property is transferred to a third person or to two or more other persons, including persons who acquire such entire interest as joint tenants, tenants by the entirety, or tenants in common. See § 1.1014-5 for computation of gain or loss upon such a sale or other disposition where the property has been acquired from a decedent or by gift or transfer in trust.

(4) *Illustrations.* For examples illustrating the application of this paragraph, see paragraph (c) of § 1.1014-5.

(g) *Debt instruments issued in exchange for property*—(1) *In general.* If a debt instrument is issued in exchange for property, the amount realized attributable to the debt instrument is the issue price of the debt instrument as determined under § 1.1273-2 or § 1.1274-2; whichever is applicable. If, however, the issue price of the debt instrument is determined under section 1273(b)(4), the amount realized attributable to the debt instrument is its stated principal amount reduced by any unstated interest (as determined under section 483).

* * *

[Reg. § 1.1001-1.]

☐ [*T.D.* 6265, 11-6-57. *Amended by T.D.* 7142, 9-23-71; *T.D.* 7207, 10-3-72; *T.D.* 7213, 10-17-72; *T.D.* 8517, 1-27-94 *and T.D.* 8674, 6-11-96.]

§ 1.1001-2. Discharge of liabilities.—(a) *Inclusion in amount realized.*—(1) *In general.* Except as provided in paragraph (a)(2) and (3) of this section, the amount realized from a sale or other disposition of property includes the amount of liabilities from which the transferor is discharged as a result of the sale or disposition.

(2) *Discharge of indebtedness.* The amount realized on a sale or other disposition of property that secures a recourse liability does not include amounts that are (or would be if realized and recognized) income from the discharge of indebtedness under section 61(a)(12). For situations where amounts arising from the discharge of indebtedness are not realized and recognized, see section 108 and § 1.61-12(b)(1).

(3) *Liability incurred on acquisition.* In the case of a liability incurred by reason of the acquisition of the property, this section does not apply to the extent that such liability was not taken into account in determining the transferor's basis for such property.

(4) *Special rules.* For purposes of this section—

(i) The sale or other disposition of property that secures a nonrecourse liability discharges the transferor from the liability;

(ii) The sale or other disposition of property that secures a recourse liability discharges the transferor from the liability if another person agrees to pay the liability (whether or not the transferor is in fact released from liability);

(iii) A disposition of property includes a gift of the property or a transfer of the property in satisfaction of liabilities to which it is subject;

(iv) Contributions and distributions of property between a partner and a partnership are not sales or other dispositions of property; and

(v) The liabilities from which a transferor is discharged as a result of the sale or disposition

Reg. § 1.1001-2(a)(4)

of a partnership interest include the transferor's share of the liabilities of the partnership.

(b) *Effect of fair market value of security.* The fair market value of the security at the time of sale or disposition is not relevant for purposes of determining under paragraph (a) of this section the amount of liabilities from which the taxpayer is discharged or treated as discharged. Thus, the fact that the fair market value of the property is less than the amount of the liabilities it secures does not prevent the full amount of those liabilities from being treated as money received from the sale or other disposition of the property. However, see paragraph (a)(2) of this section for a rule relating to certain income from discharge of indebtedness.

(c) *Examples.* The provisions of this section may be illustrated by the following examples. In each example assume the taxpayer uses the cash receipts and disbursements method of accounting, makes a return on the basis of the calendar year, and sells or disposes of all property which is security for a given liability.

Example (1). In 1976 A purchases an asset for $10,000. A pays the seller $1,000 in cash and signs a note payable to the seller for $9,000. A is personally liable for repayment with the seller having full recourse in the event of default. In addition, the asset which was purchased is pledged as security. During the years 1976 and 1977, A takes depreciation deductions on the asset in the amount of $3,100. During this same time period A reduces the outstanding principal on the note to $7,600. At the beginning of 1978 A sells the asset. The buyer pays A $1,600 in cash and assumes personal liability for the $7,600 outstanding liability. A becomes secondarily liable for repayment of the liability. A's amount realized is $9,200 ($1,600 + $7,600). Since A's adjusted basis in the asset is $6,900 ($10,000 − $3,100) A realizes a gain of $2,300 ($9,200 − $6,900).

Example (2). Assume the same facts as in example (1) except that A is not personally liable on the $9,000 note given to the seller and in the event of default the seller's only recourse is to the asset. In addition, on the sale of the asset by A, the purchaser takes the asset subject to the liability. Nevertheless, A's amount realized is $9,200 and A's gain realized is $2,300 on the sale.

Example (3). In 1975 L becomes a limited partner in partnership GL. L contributes $10,000 in cash to GL and L's distributive share of partnership income and loss is 10 percent. L is not entitled to receive any guaranteed payments. In 1978 M purchases L's entire interest in partnership GL. At the time of the sale L's adjusted basis in the partnership interest is $20,000. At that time L's proportionate share of liabilities, of

which no partner has assumed personal liability, is $15,000. M pays $10,000 in cash for L's interest in the partnership. Under section 752(d) and this section, L's share of partnership liabilities, $15,000, is treated as money received. Accordingly, L's amount realized on the sale of the partnership interest is $25,000 ($10,000 + $15,000). L's gain realized on the sale is $5,000 ($25,000 − $20,000).

Example (4). In 1976 B becomes a limited partner in partnership BG. In 1978 B contributes B's entire interest in BG to a charitable organization described in section 170(c). At the time of the contribution all of the partnership liabilities are liabilities for which neither B nor G has assumed any personal liability and B's proportionate share of which is $9,000. The charitable organization does not pay any cash or other property to B, but takes the partnership interest subject to the $9,000 of liabilities. Assume that the contribution is treated as a bargain sale to a charitable organization and that under section 1011 (b) $3,000 is determined to be the portion of B's basis in the partnership interest allocable to the sale. Under section 752(d) and this section, the $9,000 of liabilities is treated by B as money received, thereby making B's amount realized $9,000. B's gain realized is $6,000 ($9,000 − $3,000).

Example (5). In 1975 C, an individual, creates T, an irrevocable trust. Due to certain powers expressly retained by C, T is a "grantor trust" for purposes of subpart E of part 1 of subchapter J of the Code and therefore C is treated as the owner of the entire trust. T purchases an interest in P, a partnership. C, as owner of T, deducts the distributive share of partnership losses attributable to the partnership interest held by T. In 1978, when the adjusted basis of the partnership interest held by T is $1,200, C renounces the powers previously and expressly retained that initially resulted in T being classified as a grantor trust. Consequently, T ceases to be a grantor trust and C is no longer considered to be the owner of the trust. At the time of the renunciation all of J's liabilities are liabilities on which none of the partners have assumed any personal liability and the proportionate share of which of the interest held by T is $11,000. Since prior to the renunciation C was the owner of the entire trust, C was considered the owner of all the trust property for Federal income tax purposes, including the partnership interest. Since C was considered to be the owner of the partnership interest, C not T, was considered to be the partner in P during the time T was a "grantor trust." However, at the time C renounced the powers that gave rise to T's classification as a grantor trust, T no longer qualified as a grantor trust with the result that C was no longer considered to be the owner of the trust and

Reg. § 1.1001-2(b)

trust property for Federal income tax purposes. Consequently, at that time, C is considered to have transferred ownership of the interest in P to T, now a separate taxable entity, independent of its grantor C. On the transfer, C's share of partnership liabilities ($11,000) is treated as money received. Accordingly, C's amount realized is $11,000 and C's gain realized is $9,800 ($11,000 − $1,200).

Example (6). In 1977 D purchases an asset for $7,500. D pays the seller $1,500 in cash and signs a note payable to the seller for $6,000. D is not personally liable for repayment but pledges as security the newly purchased asset. In the event of default, the seller's only recourse is to the asset. During the years 1977 and 1978 D takes depreciation deductions on the asset totaling $4,200 thereby reducing D's basis in the asset to $3,300 ($7,500 − $4,200). In 1979 D transfers the asset to a trust which is not a "grantor trust" for purposes of subpart E of part 1 of subchapter J of the Code. Therefore D is not treated as the owner of the trust. The trust takes the asset subject to the liability and in addition pays D $750 in cash. Prior to the transfer D had reduced the amount outstanding on the liability to $4,700. D's amount realized on the transfer is $5,450 ($4,700 + $750). Since D's adjusted basis is $3,300, D's gain realized is $2,150 ($5,450 − $3,300).

Example (7). In 1974 E purchases a herd of cattle for breeding purposes. The purchase price is $20,000 consisting of $1,000 cash and a $19,000 note. E is not personally liable for repayment of the liability and the seller's only recourse in the event of default is to the herd of cattle. In 1977 E transfers the herd back to the original seller thereby satisfying the indebtedness pursuant to a provision in the original sales agreement. At the time of the transfer the fair market value of the herd is $15,000 and the remaining principal balance on the note is $19,000. At the time E's adjusted basis in the herd is $16,500 due to a deductible loss incurred when a portion of the herd died as a result of a disease. As a result of the indebtedness being satisfied, E's amount realized is $19,000 notwithstanding the fact that the fair market value of the herd was less than $19,000. E's realized gain is $2,500 ($19,000 − $16,500).

Example (8). In 1980, F transfers to a creditor an asset with a fair market value of $6,000 and the creditor discharges $7,500 of indebtedness for which F is personally liable. The amount realized on the disposition of the asset is its fair market value ($6,000). In addition, F has income from the discharge of indebtedness of $1,500 ($7,500 − $6,000). [Reg. § 1.1001-2.]

☐ [*T.D.* 7741, 12-11-80.]

§ 1.1002-1. Sales or exchanges.—(a) *General rule.* The general rule with respect to gain or loss realized upon the sale or exchange of property as determined under section 1001 is that the entire amount of such gain or loss is recognized except in cases where specific provisions of subtitle A of the Code provide otherwise.

(b) *Strict construction of exceptions from general rule.* The exceptions from the general rule requiring the recognition of all gains and losses, like other exceptions from a rule of taxation of general and uniform application, are strictly construed and do not extend either beyond the words or the underlying assumptions and purposes of the exception. Nonrecognition is accorded by the Code only if the exchange is one which satisfies both (1) the specific description in the Code of an excepted exchange, and (2) the underlying purpose for which such exchange is excepted from the general rule. The exchange must be germane to, and a necessary incident of, the investment or enterprise in hand. The relationship of the exchange to the venture or enterprise is always material, and the surrounding facts and circumstances must be shown. As elsewhere, the taxpayer claiming the benefit of the exception must show himself within the exception.

(c) *Certain exceptions to general rule.* Exceptions to the general rule are made, for example, by sections 351(a), 354, 361(a), 371(a)(1), 371(b)(1), 721, 1031, 1035 and 1036. These sections describe certain specific exchanges of property in which at the time of the exchange particular differences exist between the property parted with and the property acquired, but such differences are more formal than substantial. As to these, the Code provides that such differences shall not be deemed controlling, and that gain or loss shall not be recognized at the time of the exchange. The underlying assumption of these exceptions is that the new property is substantially a continuation of the old investment still unliquidated; and, in the case of reorganizations, that the new enterprise, the new corporate structure, and the new property are substantially continuations of the old still unliquidated.

(d) *Exchange.* Ordinarily, to constitute an exchange, the transaction must be a reciprocal transfer of property, as distinguished from a transfer of property for a money consideration only. [Reg. § 1.1002-1.]

☐ [*T.D.* 6265, 11-6-57.]

Basis Rules of General Application

§ 1.1011-1. **Adjusted basis.**—The adjusted basis for determining the gain or loss from the sale or other disposition of property is the cost or other basis prescribed in section 1012 or other applicable provisions of subtitle A of the Code, adjusted to the extent provided in sections 1016, 1017, and 1018 or as otherwise specifically provided for under applicable provisions of internal revenue laws. [Reg. § 1.1011-1.]

☐ [*T.D.* 6265, 11-6-57.]

§ 1.1011-2. **Bargain sale to a charitable organization.**—(a) *In general.* (1) If for the taxable year a charitable contributions deduction is allowable under section 170 by reason of a sale or exchange of property, the taxpayer's adjusted basis of such property for purposes of determining gain from such sale or exchange must be computed as provided in section 1011(b) and paragraph (b) of this section. If after applying the provisions of section 170 for the taxable year, including the percentage limitations of section 170(b), no deduction is allowable under that section by reason of the sale or exchange of the property, section 1011(b) does not apply and the adjusted basis of the property is not required to be apportioned pursuant to paragraph (b) of this section. In such case the entire adjusted basis of the property is to be taken into account in determining gain from the sale or exchange, as provided in § 1.1011-1(e). In ascertaining whether or not a charitable contributions deduction is allowable under section 170 for the taxable year for such purposes, that section is to be applied without regard to this section and the amount by which the contributed portion of the property must be reduced under section 170(e)(1) is the amount determined by taking into account the amount of gain which would have been ordinary income or long-term capital gain if the contributed portion of the property had been sold by the donor at its fair market value at the time of the sale or exchange.

(2) If in the taxable year there is a sale or exchange of property which gives rise to a charitable contribution which is carried over under section 170(b)(1)(D)(ii) or section 170(d) to a subsequent taxable year or is postponed under section 170(a)(3) to a subsequent taxable year, section 1011(b) and paragraph (b) of this section must be applied for purposes of apportioning the adjusted basis of the property for the year of the sale or exchange, whether or not such contribution is allowable as a deduction under section 170 in such subsequent year.

(3) If property is transferred subject to an indebtedness, the amount of the indebtedness must be treated as an amount realized for purposes of determining whether there is a sale or exchange to which section 1011(b) and this section apply, even though the transferee does not agree to assume or pay the indebtedness.

(4)(i) Section 1011(b) and this section apply where property is sold or exchanged in return for an obligation to pay an annuity and a charitable contributions deduction is allowable under section 170 by reason of such sale or exchange.

(ii) If in such case the annuity received in exchange for the property is nonassignable, or is assignable but only to the charitable organization to which the property is sold or exchanged, and if the transferor is the only annuitant or the transferor and a designated survivor annuitant or annuitants are the only annuitants, any gain on such exchange is to be reported as provided in example (8) in paragraph (c) of this section. In determining the period over which gain may be reported as provided in such example, the life expectancy of the survivor annuitant may not be taken into account. The fact that the transferor may retain the right to revoke the survivor's annuity or relinquish his own right to the annuity will not be considered, for purposes of this subdivision, to make the annuity assignable to someone other than the charitable organization. Gain on an exchange of the type described in this subdivision pursuant to an agreement which is entered into after December 19, 1969, and before May 3, 1971, may be reported as provided in example (8) in paragraph (c) of this section, even though the annuity is assignable.

(iii) In the case of an annuity to which subdivision (ii) of this subparagraph applies, the gain unreported by the transferor with respect to annuity payments not yet due when the following events occur is not required to be included in gross income of any person where—

(*a*) The transferor dies before the entire amount of gain has been reported and there is no surviving annuitant, or

(*b*) The transferor relinquishes the annuity to the charitable organization. If the transferor dies before the entire amount of gain on a two-life annuity has been reported, the unreported gain is required to be reported by the surviving annuitant or annuitants with respect to the annuity payments received by them.

(b) *Apportionment of adjusted basis.* For purposes of determining gain on a sale or exchange to which this paragraph applies, the adjusted basis of the property which is sold or exchanged shall be that portion of the adjusted basis of the entire property which bears the same ratio to the adjusted basis as the amount realized bears to the fair market value of the entire property. The amount of such gain which shall be treated as ordinary income (or long-term capital gain) shall be that amount which bears the same ratio to the ordinary income (or long-term capital gain) which would have been recognized if the entire property had been sold by the donor at its fair market value at the time of the sale or exchange as the amount realized on the sale or exchange bears to the fair market value of the entire property at such time. The terms "ordinary income" and "long-term capital gain", as used in this section, have the same meaning as they have in paragraph (a) of § 1.170A-4. For determining the portion of the adjusted basis, ordinary income, and long-term capital gain allocated to the contributed portion of the property for purposes of applying section 170(e)(1) and paragraph (a) of § 1.170A-4 to the contributed portion of the property, and for determining the donee's basis in such contributed portion, see paragraph (c)(2) and (4) of § 1.170A-4. For determining the holding period of such contributed portion, see section 1223(2) and the regulations thereunder.

(c) *Illustrations.* The application of this section may be illustrated by the following examples, which are supplemented by other examples in paragraph (d) of § 1.170A-4:

Example (1). In 1970, a calendar-year individual taxpayer, sells to a church for $4,000 stock held for more than 6 months which has an adjusted basis of $4,000 and a fair market value of $10,000. A's contribution base for 1970, as defined in section 170(b)(1)(F), is $100,000, and during that year he makes no other charitable contributions. Thus, A makes a charitable contribution to the church of $6,000 ($10,000 value − $4,000 amount realized). Without regard to this section, A is allowed a deduction under section 170 of $6,000 for his charitable contribution to the church, since there is no reduction under section 170(e)(1) with respect to the long-term capital gain. Accordingly, under paragraph (b) of this section the adjusted basis for determining gain on the bargain sale is $1,600 ($4,000 adjusted basis × $4,000 amount realized/$10,000 value of property). A has recognized long-term capital gain of $2,400 ($4,000 amount realized − $1,600 adjusted basis) on the bargain sale.

Example (2). The facts are the same as in Example (1) except that A also makes a charitable contribution in 1970 of $50,000 cash to the church. By reason of section 170(b)(1)(A), the deduction allowed under section 170 for 1970 is $50,000 for the amount of cash contributed to the church; however, the $6,000 contribution of property is carried over to 1971 under section 170(d). Under paragraphs (a)(2) and (b) of this section the adjusted basis for determining gain for 1970 on the bargain sale in that year is $1,600 ($4,000

× $4,000/$10,000). A has a recognized long-term capital gain for 1970 of $2,400 ($4,000 − $1,600) on the sale.

* * *

[Reg. § 1.1011-2.]

☐ [*T.D.* 7207, 10-3-72. *Amended by T.D.* 7741, 12-11-80, *T.D.* 8176, 2-24-88 *and T.D.* 8540, 6-9-94.]

§ 1.1012-1. Basis of property.—(a) *General rule.* In general, the basis of property is the cost thereof. The cost is the amount paid for such property in cash or other property. This general rule is subject to exceptions stated in subchapter O (relating to gain or loss on the disposition of property), subchapter C (relating to corporate distributions and adjustments), subchapter K (relating to partners and partnerships), and subchapter P (relating to capital gains and losses), chapter 1 of the Code.

(b) *Real estate taxes as part of cost.* In computing the cost of real property, the purchaser shall not take into account any amount paid to the seller as reimbursement for real property taxes which are treated under section 164(d) as imposed upon the purchaser. This rule applies whether or not the contract of sale calls for the purchaser to reimburse the seller for such real estate taxes paid or to be paid by the seller. On the other hand, where the purchaser pays (or assumes liability for) real estate taxes which are treated under section 164(d) as imposed upon the seller, such taxes shall be considered part of the cost of the property. It is immaterial whether or not the contract of sale specifies that the sale price has been reduced by, or is in any way intended to reflect, real estate taxes allocable to the seller under section 164(d). For illustrations of the application of the paragraph, see paragraph (b) of § 1.1001-1.

(c) *Sale of stock* —(1) *In general.* If shares of stock in a corporation are sold or transferred by a taxpayer who purchased or acquired lots of stock on different dates or at different prices, and the lot from which the stock was sold or transferred cannot be adequately identified, the stock sold or transferred shall be charged against the earliest of such lots purchased or acquired in order to determine the cost or other basis of such stock and in order to determine the holding period of such stock for purposes of subchapter P chapter 1 of the Code. If, on the other hand, the lot from which the stock is sold or transferred can be adequately identified, the rule stated in the preceding sentence is not applicable. As to what constitutes "adequate identification," see subparagraphs (2), (3), and (4) of this paragraph.

(2) *Identification of stock.* An adequate identification is made if it is shown that certificates representing shares of stock from a lot which was

purchased or acquired on a certain date or for a certain price were delivered to the taxpayer's transferee. Except as otherwise provided in subparagraph (3) or (4) of this paragraph, such stock certificates delivered to the transferee constitute the stock sold or transferred by the taxpayer. Thus, unless the requirements of subparagraph (3) or (4) of this paragraph are met, the stock sold or transferred is charged to the lot to which the certificates delivered to the transferee belong, whether or not the taxpayer intends, or instructs his broker or other agent, to sell or transfer stock from a lot purchased or acquired on a different date or for a different price.

(3) *Identification on confirmation document.* (i) Where the stock is left in the custody of a broker or other agent, an adequate identification is made if—

(*a*) At the time of the sale or transfer, the taxpayer specifies to such broker or other agent having custody of the stock the particular stock to be sold or transferred, and

(*b*) Within a reasonable time thereafter, confirmation of such specification is set forth in a written document from such broker or other agent.

Stock identified pursuant to this subdivision is the stock sold or transferred by the taxpayer, even though stock certificates from a different lot are delivered to the taxpayer's transferee.

(ii) Where a single stock certificate represents stock from different lots, where such certificate is held by the taxpayer rather than his broker or other agent, and where the taxpayer sells a part of the stock represented by such certificate through a broker or other agent, an adequate identification is made if—

(*a*) At the time of the delivery of the certificate to the broker or other agent, the taxpayer specifies to such broker or other agent the particular stock to be sold or transferred, and

(*b*) Within a reasonable time thereafter, confirmation of such specification is set forth in a written document from such broker or agent.

Where part of stock represented by a single certificate is sold or transferred directly by the taxpayer to the purchaser or transferee instead of through a broker or other agent, an adequate identification is made if the taxpayer maintains a written record of the particular stock which he intended to sell or transfer.

(4) *Stock held by a trustee, executor, or administrator.* Where stock is held by a trustee or by an executor or administrator of an estate (and not left in the custody of a broker or other agent) an adequate identification is made if at the time of a sale, transfer, or distribution, the trustee, executor, or administrator—

(i) Specifies in writing in the books and records of the trust or estate the particular stock to be sold, transferred, or distributed, and

(ii) In the case of a distribution, also furnishes the distributee with a written document setting forth the particular stock distributed to him. Stock identified pursuant to this subparagraph is the stock sold, transferred, or distributed by the trust or estate, even though stock certificates from a different lot are delivered to the purchaser, transferee, or distributee.

(5) *Subsequent sales.* If stock identified under subparagraph (3) or (4) of this paragraph as belonging to a particular lot is sold, transferred, or distributed, the stock so identified shall be deemed to have been sold, transferred, or distributed, and such sale, transfer, or distribution will be taken into consideration in identifying the taxpayer's remaining stock for purposes of subsequent sales, transfers, or distributions.

(6) *Bonds.* The provisions of subparagraphs (1) through (5) of this paragraph shall apply to the sale or transfer of bonds after July 13, 1965.

* * *

(g) *Debt instruments issued in exchange for property*—(1) *In general.* For purposes of paragraph (a) of this section, if a debt instrument is issued in exchange for property, the cost of the property that is attributable to the debt instrument is the issue price of the debt instrument as determined under § 1.1273-2 or § 1.1274-2, whichever is applicable. If, however, the issue price of the debt instrument is determined under section 1273(b)(4), the cost of the property attributable to the debt instrument is its stated principal amount reduced by any unstated interest (as determined under section 483).

* * *

[Reg. § 1.1012-1.]

☐ [*T.D.* 6265, 11-6-57. *Amended by T.D.* 6311, 9-10-58; *T.D.* 6837, 7-12-65; *T.D.* 6887, 6-23-66; *T.D.* 6934, 11-13-67; *T.D.* 6984, 12-23-68; *T.D.* 7015, 6-19-69; *T.D.* 7081, 12-30-70; *T.D.* 7129, 7-6-71; *T.D.* 7154, 12-27-71; *T.D.* 7213, 10-17-72; *T.D.* 7568, 10-11-78; *T.D.* 7728, 10-31-80; *T.D.* 8517, 1-27-94 *and T.D.* 8674, 6-11-96.]

Proposed Amendment to Regulation

§ 1.1012-2. **Certain sales or exchanges between related parties.**—(a) *In general.* In the case of a sale or exchange of property in which the relationship between the seller and the buyer is such that the sale or exchange is not necessarily an arm's-length transaction, the transaction shall be examined to determine whether the value of the consideration provided by the buyer is greater than or less than the value of the property. If the value of the consideration exceeds the value of the property, this excess shall not be treated as relating to the sale or exchange and will be recharacterized according to the relationship between the parties. If the value of the property exceeds the value of the consideration, this excess generally shall be treated as transferred from the seller to the buyer based on the relationship between the parties and not as transferred in exchange for the debt instrument. The preceding sentence shall not apply to any transaction that would be characterized as in part a gift and in part a sale under § 1.170A-4(c)(2) and § 1.1011-2(b) or under § 1.1015-4.

(b) *Value.* In applying this section to any sale or exchange where all or a part of the consideration furnished by the buyer consists of one or more debt instruments issued by the buyer to the seller, then, for purposes of this section—

(1) The value of any such debt instrument to which section 1274 applies or which has adequate stated interest within the meaning of section 1274(c)(2) or § 1.483-2 shall be its issue price;

(2) The value of any such debt instrument issued under a contract to which section 483 applies shall be the amount described in § 1.483-3(a)(2)(i); and

(3) In determining whether the value of the consideration furnished by the buyer exceeds the value of the property, the value of the property shall be determined by reference to the price that an unrelated buyer (having the same creditworthiness as the actual buyer) would be willing to pay for the property in an arm's-length transaction if seller financing (taken into account at its issue price) were offered on the same terms as those offered to the actual buyer.

(c) *Examples.* The provisions of this section may be illustrated by the following examples:

Example (1). (i) On January 1, 1986, Corporation X sells nonpublicly traded property to A, the sole shareholder of X. In consideration for the sale, A makes a down payment of $200,000 and issues a debt instrument calling for a single payment of $1,000,000 due in five years. No interest is provided for in the debt instrument. Because A is the sole shareholder of X, the transaction must be examined to determine whether the value of the property exceeds the value of the consideration furnished by A. For this purpose, the value of the property is its fair market value (determined without regard to any seller financing).

(ii) Assume that the fair market value of the property is $900,000 and that the issue price of the debt instrument under § 1.1274-4 is $643,928. Thus, the value of the consideration furnished by A is $843,928 (the sum of $200,000 (the portion of the consideration attributable to the down payment) and $643,928 (the portion of the consideration attributable to the debt instrument)). Since the value of the property ($900,000) exceeds the value of the consideration ($843,928), X Corporation is treated as having made a distribution to shareholder A to which section 301 applies. The amount of the distribution is $56,072 (the difference between $900,000 and $843,928). The basis of the property in the hands of A is $900,000 ($843,928 (consideration actually furnished by A) increased by $56,072 (the amount of the section 301 distribution)).

Example (2). The facts are the same as in Example (1) except that the fair market value of the property is $800,000. X is not treated as having made a section 301 distribution to A and A's basis in the property is $800,000. The transaction need not be examined for excessive consideration since a sale from a corporation to a shareholder ordinarily would not be used to disguise a contribution to capital from the shareholder to the corporation.

Example (3). (i) C sells nonpublicly traded property to his employer D for $300,000 in cash and D's debt instrument having a face amount of $1,000,000, payable in 5 years with interest payable semiannually at a rate of 9 percent. Because D is C's employer, the transaction must be examined to determine if a portion of the amount designated as consideration for the property is in fact disguised compensation.

(ii) Assume that the fair market value of the property (assuming no seller financing), is $1,000,000 and that the issue price of D's debt instrument is $1,000,000. Assume further that a buyer unrelated to D and having the same creditworthiness as C would be willing to pay $1,200,000 for the property if allowed to pay $300,000 in cash and $900,000 in the form of a 5-year debt instrument calling for semiannual payments of interest at a rate of 9 percent. The value of the consideration furnished by D is $1,300,000 (cash of $300,000 plus a debt instrument having an issue price of $1,000,000). Since this amount exceeds the value of the property by $100,000, only $200,000 of the $300,000 transferred from D to C is treated as consideration furnished for the property. The remaining $100,000 is treated as compensation. D's basis in the property is $1,200,000 (cash consideration of $200,000 plus a debt instrument with an issue price of $1,000,000).

Example (4). The facts are the same as in Example (3) except that the property could be sold to the unrelated buyer for $1,400,000 (assuming a down payment of $300,000 and 5-year seller

Reg. § 1.1012-2(c)

financing at 9 percent for the balance of the purchase price). Because the value of the consideration furnished by D ($1,300,000) does not exceed the value of the property ($1,400,000), D is not treated as having paid compensation to C. D's basis in the property is $1,300,000. The transaction need not be examined for insufficient consideration since employees ordinarily do not make bargain sales to their employers. [Reg. § 1.1012-2.]

[Proposed 4-8-86.]

§ 1.1014-1. **Basis of property acquired from a decedent.**—(a) *General rule.* The purpose of section 1014 is, in general, to provide a basis for property acquired from a decedent which is equal to the value placed upon such property for purposes of the Federal estate tax. Accordingly, the general rule is that the basis of property acquired from a decedent is the fair market value of such property at the date of the decedent's death, or, if the decedent's executor so elects, at the alternate valuation date prescribed in section 2032, or in section 811(j) of the Internal Revenue Code of 1939. Property acquired from a decedent includes, principally, property acquired by bequest, devise, or inheritance, and, in the case of decedents dying after December 31, 1953, property required to be included in determining the value of the decedent's gross estate under any provision of the Internal Revenue Code of 1954 or the Internal Revenue Code of 1939. The general rule governing basis of property acquired from a decedent, as well as other rules prescribed elsewhere in this section, shall have no application if the property is sold, exchanged, or otherwise disposed of before the decedent's death by the person who acquired the property from the decedent. For general rules on the applicable valuation date where the executor of a decedent's estate elects under section 2032, or under section 811(j) of the Internal Revenue Code of 1939, to value the decedent's gross estate at the alternate valuation date prescribed in such sections, see paragraph (e) of § 1.1014-3.

(b) *Scope and application.* With certain limitations, the general rule described in paragraph (a) of this section is applicable to the classes of property described in paragraphs (a) and (b) of § 1.1014-2, including stock in a DISC or former DISC. In the case of stock in a DISC or former DISC, the provisions of this section and §§ 1.1014-2 through 1.1014-8 are applicable, except as provided in § 1.1014-9. Special basis rules with respect to the basis of certain other property acquired from a decedent are set forth in paragraph (c) of § 1.1014-2. These special rules concern certain stock or securities of a foreign personal holding company and the surviving spouse's one-half share of community property

held with a decedent dying after October 21, 1942, and on or before December 31, 1947. In this section and §§ 1.1014-2 to 1.1014-6, inclusive, whenever the words "property acquired from a decedent" are used, they shall also mean "property passed from a decedent", and the phrase "person who acquired it from the decedent" shall include the "person to whom it passed from the decedent."

(c) *Property to which section 1014 does not apply.* Section 1014 shall have no application to the following classes of property:

(1) Property which constitutes a right to receive an item of income in respect of a decedent under section 691; and

(2) Restricted stock options described in section 421 which the employee has not exercised at death if the employee died before January 1, 1957. In the case of employees dying after December 31, 1956, see paragraph (d)(4) of § 1.421-5. In the case of employees dying in a taxable year ending after December 31, 1963, see paragraph (c)(4) of § 1.421-9 with respect to an option described in part II of subchapter D. [Reg. § 1.1014-1.]

☐ [*T.D.* 6265, 11-6-57. *Amended by T.D.* 6527, 1-18-61, *T.D.* 6887, 6-23-66 *and T.D.* 7283, 8-2-73.]

§ 1.1014-2. **Property acquired from a decedent.**—(a) *In general.* The following property, except where otherwise indicated, is considered to have been acquired from a decedent and the basis thereof is determined in accordance with the general rule in § 1.1014-1:

(1) Without regard to the date of the decedent's death, property acquired by bequest, devise, or inheritance, or by the decedent's estate from the decedent, whether the property was acquired under the decedent's will or under the law governing the descent and distribution of the property of decedents. However, see paragraph (c)(1) of this section if the property was acquired by bequest or inheritance from a decedent dying after August 26, 1937, and if such property consists of stock or securities of a foreign personal holding company.

(2) Without regard to the date of the decedent's death, property transferred by the decedent during his lifetime in trust to pay the income for life to or on the order or direction of the decedent, with the right reserved to the decedent at all times before his death to revoke the trust.

(3) In the case of decedents dying after December 31, 1951, property transferred by the decedent during his lifetime in trust to pay the income for life to or on the order or direction of the decedent with the right reserved to the dece-

dent at all times before his death to make any change in the enjoyment thereof through the exercise of a power to alter, amend, or terminate the trust.

(4) Without regard to the date of the decedent's death, property passing without full and adequate consideration under a general power of appointment exercised by the decedent by will. (See section 2041(b) for definition of general power of appointment.)

(5) In the case of decedents dying after December 31, 1947, property which represents the surviving spouse's one-half share of community property held by the decedent and the surviving spouse under the community property laws of any State, Territory, or possession of the United States or any foreign country, if at least one-half of the whole of the community interest in that property was includible in determining the value of the decedent's gross estate under part III, chapter 11 of the Internal Revenue Code of 1954 (relating to the estate tax) or section 811 of the Internal Revenue Code of 1939. It is not necessary for the application of this subparagraph that an estate tax return be required to be filed for the estate of the decedent or that an estate tax be payable.

* * *

(b) *Property acquired from a decedent dying after December 31, 1953* —(1) *In general.* In addition to the property described in paragraph (a) of this section, and except as otherwise provided in subparagraph (3) of this paragraph, in the case of a decedent dying after December 31, 1953, property shall also be considered to have been acquired from the decedent to the extent that both of the following conditions are met: (i) the property was acquired from the decedent by reason of death, form of ownership, or other conditions (including property acquired through the exercise or non-exercise of a power of appointment), and (ii) the property is includible in the decedent's gross estate under the provisions of the Internal Revenue Code of 1954, or the Internal Revenue Code of 1939, because of such acquisition. The basis of such property in the hands of the person who acquired it from the decedent shall be determined in accordance with the general rule in § 1.1014-1. See, however, § 1.1014-6 for special adjustments if such property is acquired before the death of the decedent. See also subparagraph (3) of this paragraph for a description of property not within the scope of this paragraph.

(2) *Rules for the application of subparagraph (1) of this paragraph.* Except as provided in subparagraph (3) of this paragraph, this paragraph generally includes all property acquired from a decedent, which is includible in the gross estate of

the decedent if the decedent died after December 31, 1953. It is not necessary for the application of this paragraph that an estate tax return be required to be filed for the estate of the decedent or that an estate tax be payable. Property acquired prior to the death of a decedent which is includible in the decedent's gross estate, such as property transferred by a decedent in contemplation of death, and property held by a taxpayer and the decedent as joint tenants or as tenants by the entireties is within the scope of this paragraph. Also, this paragraph includes property acquired through the exercise or non-exercise of a power of appointment where such property is includible in the decedent's gross estate. It does not include property not includible in the decedent's gross estate such as property not situated in the United States acquired from a nonresident who is not a citizen of the United States.

(3) *Exceptions to application of this paragraph.* The rules of this paragraph are not applicable to the following property:

(i) Annuities described in section 72;

(ii) Stock or securities of a foreign personal holding company as described in section 1014(b)(5) (see paragraph (c)(1) of this section);

(iii) Property described in any paragraph other than paragraph (9) of section 1014(b). See paragraphs (a) and (c) of this section.

In illustration of subdivision (ii), assume that A acquired by gift stock of a character described in paragraph (c)(1) of this section from a donor and upon the death of the donor the stock was includible in the donor's estate as being a gift in contemplation of death. A's basis in the stock would not be determined by reference to its fair market value at the donor's death under the general rule in section 1014(a). Furthermore, the special basis rules prescribed in paragraph (c)(1) are not applicable to such property acquired by gift in contemplation of death. It will be necessary to refer to the rules in section 1015(a) to determine the basis.

* * *

[Reg. § 1.1014-2.]

☐ [*T.D.* 6265, 11-6-57.]

§ 1.1014-4. Uniformity of basis; adjustment to basis.—(a) *In general.* (1) The basis of property acquired from a decedent, as determined under section 1014(a), is uniform in the hands of every person having possession or enjoyment of the property at any time under the will or other instrument or under the laws of descent and distribution. The principle of uniform basis means that the basis of the property (to which proper adjustments must, of course, be made) will be the same, or uniform, whether the property is possessed or enjoyed by the executor or administrator, the heir, the legatee or devisee, or the trustee or beneficiary of a trust created by a will or an inter vivos trust. In determining the amount allowed or allowable to a taxpayer in computing taxable income as deductions for depreciation or depletion under section 1016(a)(2), the uniform basis of the property shall at all times be used and adjusted. The sale, exchange, or other disposition by a life tenant or remainderman of his interest in property will, for purposes of this section, have no effect upon the uniform basis of the property in the hands of those who acquired it from the decedent. Thus, gain or loss on sale of trust assets by the trustee will be determined without regard to the prior sale of any interest in the property. Moreover, any adjustment for depreciation shall be made to the uniform basis of the property without regard to such prior sale, exchange, or other disposition.

(2) Under the law governing wills and the distribution of the property of decedents, all titles to property acquired by bequest, devise, or inheritance relate back to the death of the decedent, even though the interest of the person taking the title was, at the date of death of the decedent, legal, equitable, vested, contingent, general, specific, residual, conditional, executory, or otherwise. Accordingly, there is a common acquisition date for all titles to property acquired from a decedent within the meaning of section 1014, and, for this reason, a common or uniform basis for all such interests. For example, if distribution of personal property left by a decedent is not made until one year after his death, the basis of such property in the hands of the legatee is its fair market value at the time when the decedent died, and not when the legatee actually received the property. If the bequest is of the residue to trustees in trust, and the executors do not distribute the residue to such trustees until five years after the death of the decedent, the basis of each piece of property left by the decedent and thus received, in the hands of the trustees, is its fair market value at the time when the decedent dies. If the bequest is to trustees in trust to pay to A during his lifetime the income of the property bequeathed, and after his death to distribute such property to the survivors of a class, and upon A's death the property is distributed to the taxpayer as the sole survivor, the basis of such property, in the hands of the taxpayer, is its fair market value at the time when the decedent died. The purpose of the Code in prescribing a general uniform basis rule for property acquired from a decedent is, on the one hand, to tax the gain, in respect of such property, to him who realizes it (without regard to the circumstance that at the death of the decedent it may have been quite uncertain whether the taxpayer would take or gain anything); and,

on the other hand, not to recognize as gain any element of value resulting solely from the circumstance that the possession or enjoyment of the taxpayer was postponed. Such postponement may be, for example, until the administration of the decedent's estate is completed, until the period of the possession or enjoyment of another has terminated, or until an uncertain event has happened. It is the increase or decrease in the value of property reflected in a sale or other disposition which is recognized as the measure of gain or loss.

(3) The principles stated in subparagraphs (1) and (2) of this paragraph do not apply to property transferred by an executor, administrator or trustee, to an heir, legatee, devisee or beneficiary under circumstances such that the transfer constitutes a sale or exchange. In such a case, gain or loss must be recognized by the transferor to the extent required by the revenue laws, and the transferee acquires a basis equal to the fair market value of the property on the date of the transfer. Thus, for example, if the trustee of a trust created by will transfers to a beneficiary, in satisfaction of a specific bequest of $10,000, securities which had a fair market value of $9,000 on the date of the decedent's death (the applicable valuation date) and $10,000 on the date of the transfer, the trust realizes a taxable gain of $1,000 and the basis of the securities in the hands of the beneficiary would be $10,000. As a further example, if the executor of an estate transfers to a trust property worth $200,000, which had a fair market value of $175,000 on the date of the decedent's death (the applicable valuation date), in satisfaction of the decedent's bequest in trust for the benefit of his wife of cash or securities to be selected by the executor in an amount sufficient to utilize the marital deduction to the maximum extent authorized by law (after taking into consideration any other property qualifying for the marital deduction), capital gain in the amount of $25,000 would be realized by the estate and the basis of the property in the hands of the trustees would be $200,000. If, on the other hand, the decedent bequeathed a fraction of his residuary estate to a trust for the benefit of his wife, which fraction will not change regardless of any fluctuations in value of property in the decedent's estate after his death, no gain or loss would be realized by the estate upon transfer of property to the trust, and the basis of the property in the hands of the trustee would be its fair market value on the date of the decedent's death or on the alternate valuation date.

(b) *Multiple interests.* Where more than one person has an interest in property acquired from a decedent, the basis of such property shall be determined and adjusted without regard to the multiple interests. The basis for computing gain or loss on the sale of any one of such multiple interests shall be determined under § 1.1014-5. Thus, the deductions for depreciation and for depletion allowed or allowable, under sections 167 and 611, to a legal life tenant as if the life tenant were the absolute owner of the property, constitute an adjustment to the basis of the property not only in the hands of the life tenant, but also in the hands of the remainderman and every other person to whom the same uniform basis is applicable. Similarly, the deductions allowed or allowable under sections 167 and 611, both to the trustee and to the trust beneficiaries, constitute an adjustment to the basis of the property not only in the hands of the trustee, but also in the hands of the trust beneficiaries and every other person to whom the uniform basis is applicable. See, however, section 262. Similarly, adjustments in respect of capital expenditures or losses, tax-free distributions, or other distributions applicable in reduction of basis, or other items for which the basis is adjustable are made without regard to which one of the persons to whom the same uniform basis is applicable makes the capital expenditures or sustains the capital losses, or to whom the tax-free or other distributions are made, or to whom the deductions are allowed or allowable. See § 1.1014-6 for adjustments in respect of property acquired from a decedent prior to his death.

(c) *Records.* The executor or other legal representative of the decedent, the fiduciary of a trust under a will, the life tenant and every other person to whom a uniform basis under this section is applicable, shall maintain records showing in detail all deductions, distributions, or other items for which adjustment to basis is required to be made by sections 1016 and 1017, and shall furnish to the district director such information with respect to those adjustments as he may require. [Reg. § 1.1014-4.]

☐ [*T.D.* 6265, 11-6-57.]

§ 1.1014-5. Gain or loss.—(a) *Sale or other disposition of a life interest, remainder interest, or other interest in property acquired from a decedent.* (1) Except as provided in paragraph (b) of this section with respect to the sale or other disposition after October 9, 1969, of a term interest in property, gain or loss from a sale or other disposition of a life interest, remainder interest, or other interest in property acquired from a decedent is determined by comparing the amount of the proceeds with the amount of that part of the adjusted uniform basis which is assignable to the interest so transferred. The adjusted uniform basis is the uniform basis of the entire property adjusted to the date of sale or other disposition of any such interest as required by sections 1016 and 1017. The uniform basis is the unadjusted basis of the entire property determined immediately after the

decedent's death under the applicable sections of part II of subchapter O of chapter 1 of the Code.

(2) Except as provided in paragraph (b) of this section, the proper measure of gain or loss resulting from a sale or other disposition of an interest in property acquired from a decedent is so much of the increase or decrease in the value of the entire property as is reflected in such sale or other disposition. Hence, in ascertaining the basis of a life interest, remainder interest, or other interest which has been so transferred, the uniform basis rule contemplates that proper adjustments will be made to reflect the change in relative value of the interests on account of the passage of time.

(3) The factors set forth in the tables contained in § 20.2031-7 or, for certain prior periods, § 20.2031-7A of Part 20 of this chapter (Estate Tax Regulations) shall be used in the manner provided therein in determining the basis of the life interest, the remainder interest, or the term certain interest in the property on the date such interest is sold. The basis of the life interest, the remainder interest, or the term certain interest is computed by multiplying the uniform basis (adjusted to the time of the sale) by the appropriate factor. In the case of the sale of a life interest or a remainder interest, the factor used is the factor (adjusted where appropriate) which appears in the life interest or the remainder interest column of the table opposite the age (on the date of the sale) of the person at whose death the life interest will terminate. In the case of the sale of a term certain interest, the factor used is the factor (adjusted where appropriate) which appears in the term certain column of the table opposite the number of years remaining (on the date of sale) before the term certain interest will terminate.

(b) *Sale or other disposition of certain term interests.* In determining gain or loss from the sale or other disposition after October 9, 1969, of a term interest in property (as defined in paragraph (f)(2) of § 1.1001-1) the adjusted basis of which is determined pursuant, or by reference, to section 1014 (relating to the basis of property acquired from a decedent) or section 1015 (relating to the basis of property acquired by gift or by a transfer in trust), that part of the adjusted uniform basis assignable under the rules of paragraph (a) of this section to the interest sold or otherwise disposed of shall be disregarded to the extent and in the manner provided by section 1001(e) and paragraph (f) of § 1.1001-1.

* * *

[Reg. § 1.1014-5.]

☐ [*T.D.* 6265, 11-6-57. *Amended by T.D.* 7142, 9-23-71 *and T.D.* 8540, 6-9-94.]

§ 1.1015-1. Basis of property acquired by gift after December 31, 1920.—(a) *General rule.* (1) In the case of property acquired by gift after December 31, 1920 (whether by a transfer in trust or otherwise), the basis of the property for the purpose of determining gain is the same as it would be in the hands of the donor or the last preceding owner by whom it was not acquired by gift. The same rule applies in determining loss unless the basis (adjusted for the period prior to the date of gift in accordance with sections 1016 and 1017) is greater than the fair market value of the property at the time of the gift. In such case, the basis for determining loss is the fair market value at the time of the gift.

(2) The provisions of subparagraph (1) of this paragraph may be illustrated by the following example.

Example. A acquires by gift income-producing property which has an adjusted basis of $100,000 at the date of gift. The fair market value of the property at the date of gift is $90,000. A later sells the property for $95,000. In such case there is neither gain nor loss. The basis for determining loss is $90,000; therefore, there is no loss. Furthermore, there is no gain, since the basis for determining gain is $100,000.

(3) If the facts necessary to determine the basis of property in the hands of the donor or the last preceding owner by whom it was not acquired by gift are unknown to the donee, the district director shall, if possible, obtain such facts from such donor or last preceding owner, or any other person cognizant thereof. If the district director finds it impossible to obtain such facts, the basis in the hands of such donor or last preceding owner shall be the fair market value of such property as found by the district director as of the date or approximate date at which, according to the best information the district director is able to obtain, such property was acquired by such donor or last preceding owner. See paragraph (e) of this section for rules relating to fair market value.

(b) *Uniform basis; proportionate parts of.* Property acquired by gift has a single or uniform basis although more than one person may acquire an interest in such property. The uniform basis of the property remains fixed subject to proper adjustment for items under sections 1016 and 1017. However, the value of the proportionate parts of the uniform basis represented, for instance, by the respective interests of the life tenant and remainderman are adjustable to reflect the change in the relative values of such interest on account of the lapse of time. The portion of the basis attributable to an interest at the time of its sale or other disposition shall be determined under the rule provided in § 1.1014-5. In determining gain or loss from the sale or other disposition after October 9, 1969, of a term interest in property (as defined in § 1.1001-1(f)(2)) the adjusted basis of which is determined pursuant to, or by reference to section 1015, that part of the adjusted uniform basis assignable under the rules of § 1.1014-5(a) to the interest sold or otherwise disposed of shall be disregarded to the extent and in the manner provided by section 1001(e) and § 1.1001-1(f).

(c) *Time of acquisition.* The date that the donee acquires an interest in property by gift is when the donor relinquishes dominion over the property and not necessarily when title to the property is acquired by the donee. Thus, the date that the donee acquires an interest in property by gift where he is a successor in interest, such as in the case of a remainderman of a life estate or a beneficiary of the distribution of the corpus of a trust, is the date such interests are created by the donor and not the date the property is actually acquired.

(d) *Property acquired by gift from a decedent dying after December 31, 1953.* If an interest in property was acquired by the taxpayer by gift from a donor dying after December 31, 1953, under conditions which require the inclusion of the property in the donor's gross estate for estate tax purposes, and the property had not been sold, exchanged, or otherwise disposed of by the taxpayer before the donor's death, see the rules prescribed in section 1014 and the regulations thereunder.

(e) *Fair market value.* For the purposes of this section, the value of property as appraised for the purpose of the Federal gift tax, or, if the gift is not subject to such tax, its value as appraised for the purpose of a State gift tax, shall be deemed to be the fair market value of the property at the time of the gift.

(f) *Reinvestments by fiduciary.* If the property is an investment by the fiduciary under the terms of the gift (as, for example, in the case of a sale by the fiduciary of property transferred under the terms of the gift, and the reinvestment of the proceeds), the cost or other basis to the fiduciary is taken in lieu of the basis specified in paragraph (a) of this section.

(g) *Records.* To insure a fair and adequate determination of the proper basis under section 1015, persons making or receiving gifts of property should preserve and keep accessible a record of the facts necessary to determine the cost of the property and, if pertinent, its fair market value as of March 1, 1913, or its fair market value as of the date of the gift. [Reg. § 1.1015-1.]

☐ [*T.D. 6265, 11-6-57. Amended by T.D. 6693, 12-2-63 and T.D. 7142, 9-23-71.*]

§ 1.1015-2. **Transfer of property in trust after December 31, 1920.**—(a) *General rule.* (1) In the case of property acquired after December 31, 1920, by transfer in trust (other than by a transfer in trust by a gift, bequest, or devise) the basis of property so acquired is the same as it would be in the hands of the grantor increased in the amount of gain or decreased in the amount of loss recognized to the grantor upon such transfer under the law applicable to the year in which the transfer was made. If the taxpayer acquired the property by a transfer in trust, this basis applies whether the property be in the hands of the trustee, or the beneficiary, and whether acquired prior to the termination of the trust and distribution of the property, or thereafter.

(2) The principles stated in paragraph (b) of § 1.1015-1 concerning the uniform basis are applicable in determining the basis of property where more than one person acquires an interest in property by transfer in trust after December 31, 1920.

(b) *Reinvestment by fiduciary.* If the property is an investment made by the fiduciary (as, for example, in the case of a sale by the fiduciary of property transferred by the grantor, and the reinvestment of the proceeds), the cost or other basis to the fiduciary is taken in lieu of the basis specified in paragraph (a) of this section. [Reg. § 1.1015-2.]

☐ [*T.D. 6265, 11-6-57.*]

§ 1.1015-4. **Transfers in part a gift and in part a sale.**—(a) *General rule.* Where a transfer of property is in part a sale and in part a gift, the unadjusted basis of the property in the hands of the transferee is the sum of—

(1) Whichever of the following is the greater:

(i) The amount paid by the transferee for the property, or

(ii) The transferor's adjusted basis for the property at the time of the transfer, and

(2) The amount of increase, if any, in basis authorized by section 1015(d) for gift tax paid (see § 1.1015-5).

For determining loss, the unadjusted basis of the property in the hands of the transferee shall not be greater than the fair market value of the property at the time of such transfer. For determination of gain or loss of the transferor, see § 1.1001-1(e) and § 1.1011-2. For special rule where there has been a charitable contribution of less than a taxpayer's entire interest in property, see section 170(e)(2) and § 1.170A-4(c).

(b) *Examples.* The rule of paragraph (a) of this section is illustrated by the following examples:

Example (1). If A transfers property to his son for $30,000, and such property at the time of the transfer has an adjusted basis of $30,000 in A's hands (and a fair market value of $60,000), the unadjusted basis of the property in the hands of the son is $30,000.

Example (2). If A transfers property to his son for $60,000, and such property at the time of transfer had an adjusted basis of $30,000 in A's hands (and a fair market value of $90,000), the unadjusted basis of such property in the hands of the son is $60,000.

Example (3). If A transfers property to his son for $30,000, and such property at the time of transfer has an adjusted basis in A's hands of $60,000 (and a fair market value of $90,000), the unadjusted basis of such property in the hands of the son is $60,000.

Example (4). If A transfers property to his son for $30,000 and such property at the time of transfer has an adjusted basis of $90,000 in A's hands (and a fair market value of $60,000), the unadjusted basis of the property in the hands of the son is $90,000. However, since the adjusted basis of the property in A's hands at the time of the transfer was greater than the fair market value at that time, for the purpose of determining any loss on a later sale or other disposition of the property by the son its unadjusted basis in his hands is $60,000. [Reg. § 1.1015-4.]

☐ [*T.D. 6265, 11-6-57. Amended by T.D. 6693,* 12-2-63, *and T.D. 7207, 10-3-72.*]

§ 1.1016-1. **Adjustments to basis; scope of section.**—Section 1016 and § § 1.1016-2 to 1016-10, inclusive, contain the rules relating to the adjustments to be made to the basis of property to determine the adjusted basis as defined in section 1011. However, if the property was acquired from a decedent before his death, see § 1.1014-6 for adjustments on account of certain deductions allowed the taxpayer for the period between the date of acquisition of the property and the date of death of the decedent. If an election has been made under the Retirement-Straight Line Adjustment Act of 1958 (26 U.S.C. 1016 note), see § 1.9001-1 for special rules for determining adjusted basis in the case of a taxpayer who has changed from the retirement to the straight-line method of computing depreciation allowances. [Reg. § 1.1016-1.]

☐ [*T.D. 6265, 11-6-57. Amended by T.D. 6418,* 10-9-59.]

§ 1.1016-2. **Items properly chargeable to capital account.**—(a) The cost or other basis shall be properly adjusted for any expenditure, receipt, loss, or other item, properly chargeable to capital account, including the cost of improvements and betterments made to the property. No adjustment shall be made in respect of any item which, under any applicable provision of law or regulation, is treated as an item not properly

Reg. § 1.1016-2(a)

chargeable to capital account but is allowable as a deduction in computing net or taxable income for the taxable year. For example, in the case of oil and gas wells no adjustment may be made in respect of any intangible drilling and development expense allowable as a deduction in computing net or taxable income. See the regulations under section 263(c).

(b) The application of the foregoing provisions may be illustrated by the following example:

Example. A, who makes his returns on the calendar year basis, purchased property in 1941 for $10,000. He subsequently expended $6,000 for improvements. Disregarding, for the purpose of this example, the adjustments required for depreciation, the adjusted basis of the property is $16,000. If A sells the property in 1954 for $20,000, the amount of his gain will be $4,000.

(c) Adjustment to basis shall be made for carrying charges such as taxes and interest, with respect to property (whether real or personal, improved or unimproved, and whether productive or unproductive), which the taxpayer elects to treat as chargeable to capital account under section 266, rather than as an allowable deduction. The term "taxes" for this purpose includes duties and excise taxes but does not include income taxes.

(d) Expenditures described in section 173 to establish, maintain, or increase the circulation of a newspaper, magazine, or other periodical are chargeable to capital account only in accordance with and in the manner provided in the regulations under section 173. [Reg. § 1.1016-2.]

☐ [*T.D.* 6265, 11-6-57.]

§ 1.1016-3. Exhaustion, wear and tear, obsolescence, amortization, and depletion for periods since February 28, 1913.—(a) *In general* — (1) *Adjustment where deduction is claimed.* (i) For taxable periods beginning on or after January 1, 1952, the cost or other basis of property shall be decreased for exhaustion, wear and tear, obsolescence, amortization, and depletion by the greater of the following two amounts: (a) the amount allowed as deductions in computing taxable income, to the extent resulting in a reduction of the taxpayer's income taxes, or (b) the amount allowable for the years involved. See paragraph (b) of this section. Where the taxpayer makes an appropriate election the above rule is applicable for periods since February 28, 1913, and before January 1, 1952. See paragraph (d) of this section. For rule for such periods where no election is made, see paragraph (c) of this section.

(ii) The determination of the amount properly allowable for exhaustion, wear and tear, obsolescence, amortization, and depletion shall be made on the basis of facts reasonably known to

exist at the end of the taxable year. A taxpayer is not permitted to take advantage in a later year of his prior failure to take any such allowance or his taking an allowance plainly inadequate under the known facts in prior years. In the case of depreciation, if in prior years the taxpayer has consistently taken proper deductions under one method, the amount allowable for such prior years shall not be increased even though a greater amount would have been allowable under another proper method. For rules governing losses on retirement of depreciable property, including rules for determining basis, see § 1.167(a)-8. This subdivision may be illustrated by the following example:

Example. An asset was purchased January 1, 1950, at a cost of $10,000. The useful life of the asset is 10 years. It has no salvage value. Depreciation was deducted and allowed for 1950 to 1954 as follows:

1950	$ 500
1951	.....
1952	1,000
1953	1,000
1954	1,000
Total amount allowed	$3,500

The correct reserve as of December 31, 1954, is computed as follows:

Dec. 31:	
1950 ($10,000 ÷ 10)	$1,000
1951 ($9,000 ÷ 9)	1,000
1952 ($8,000 ÷ 8)	1,000
1953 ($7,000 ÷ 7)	1,000
1954 ($6,000 ÷ 6)	1,000
Reserve Dec. 31, 1954	$5,000

Depreciation for 1955 is computed as follows:

Cost.........................	$10,000
Reserve as of December 31, 1954	5,000
Unrecovered cost	5,000
Depreciation allowable for 1955 ($5,000 ÷ 5)	1,000

(2) *Adjustment for amount allowable where no depreciation deduction claimed.* (i) If the taxpayer has not taken a depreciation deduction either in the taxable year or for any prior taxable year, adjustments to basis of the property for depreciation allowable shall be determined by using the straight-line method of depreciation. (See § 1.1016-4 for adjustments in the case of persons exempt from income taxation.)

(ii) For taxable years beginning after December 31, 1953, and ending after August 16, 1954, if the taxpayer with respect to any property has taken a deduction for depreciation properly under one of the methods provided in section 167(b) for one or more years but has omitted the deduction in other years, the adjustment to basis for the depreciation allowable in such a case will be the deduction under the method which was used by the taxpayer with respect to that property. Thus, if A acquired property in 1954 on which he properly computed his depreciation deduction under the method described in section 167(b)(2) (the declining-balance method) for the first year of its useful life but did not take a deduction in the second and third year of the asset's life, the adjustment to basis for depreciation allowable for the second and third year will be likewise computed under the declining-balance method.

* * *

[Reg. § 1.1016-3.]

☐ [*T.D.* 6265, 11-6-57.]

Proposed Amendment to Regulation

§ 1.1016-3. Exhaustion, wear and tear, obsolescence, amortization, and depletion for periods since February 28, 1913.—(a) *In general.*
* * *

(3) *Adjustment for amount allowable where no cost recovery deduction claimed under section 168.* (i) Except as provided in subdivision (iii) of this subparagraph (3), if the taxpayer has not taken a deduction under section 168 (hereinafter referred to as ACRS deduction) either in the taxable year or for any prior taxable year, the adjustments to basis of the property for the ACRS deduction allowable shall be determined by using the recovery method described in section 168(b)(1) or (2) or, where applicable, section 168(f)(2)(A) or (B).

(ii) If the taxpayer with respect to any recovery property has properly taken an ACRS deduction under one of the methods provided in section 168 for one or more years but has omitted the deduction in other years, the adjustment to basis for the ACRS deduction allowable in such a case will be the deduction under the method which was used by the taxpayer with respect to that property. Thus, for example, A acquired property in 1981 for which he properly elected to compute his ACRS deduction by use of one of the optional straight line percentages described in section 168(b)(3) for the first recovery year but did not take a deduction in the second and third years of the asset's recovery period. The adjustment to basis for the ACRS deduction allowable for the second and third recovery years will be computed using the optional straight line percentages which were elected.

(iii) If the taxpayer has made an election under § 1.168-5(e)(5) (relating to special election rules for foreign taxpayers) to use an optional straight line percentage with respect to recovery property, the adjustments to basis of the property

for the ACRS deduction allowable shall be determined pursuant to that election.

(iv) The provisions of subdivision (iii) of this subparagraph (3) may be illustrated by the following example:

Example. In 1981, Corporation F (a calendar year taxpayer) purchases for $100,000 and places in service in a foreign country 5-year recovery property which has a present class life of 7.5 years. F is not subject to United States income tax, other than under section 881, and is not required to compute earnings and profits under section 964. On January 1, 1983, F begins engaging in a trade or business in the United States (making it subject to tax under section 882), and uses the property in the United States in connection with that trade or business. Under § 1.168-5(e)(5)(ii), F may elect to use the optional recovery percentages with respect to the property placed in service in 1981 by submitting the requisite information on its income tax return for the taxable year beginning in 1983. That election will apply with respect to such property from the taxable year in which it is placed in service. Thus, if F elects the optional recovery percentages based on a 12-year recovery period under § 1.168-2(g)(3), the allowable ACRS deductions for 1981 and 1982 would be $4,000 (*i.e.,* .04 × $100,000) and $9,000 (*i.e.,* .09 × $100,000), respectively, and F's adjusted basis in the property on January 1, 1983, would be $87,000 (*i.e.,* $100,000 − $13,000). For the deduction allowable to F with respect to the property in 1983, see § 1.168-2(j)(4)(i) and (j)(6) (relating to change in status).

* * *

[Reg. § 1.1016-3.]

[Proposed 2-16-84.]

§ 1.1016-10. Substituted basis.—(a) Whenever it appears that the basis of property in the hands of the taxpayer is a substituted basis, as defined in section 1016(b), the adjustments indicated in §§ 1.1016-1 to 1.1016-6, inclusive, shall be made after first making in respect of such substituted basis proper adjustments of a similar nature in respect of the period during which the property was held by the transferor, donor, or grantor, or during which the other property was held by the person for whom the basis is to be determined. In addition, whenever it appears that the basis of property in the hands of the taxpayer is a substituted basis, as defined in section 1016(b)(1), the adjustments indicated in §§ 1.1016-7 to 1.1016-9, inclusive, and in section 1017 shall also be made, whenever necessary, after first making in respect of such substituted basis a proper adjustment of a similar nature in respect of the period during which the property was held by the transferor,

Reg. § 1.1016-10(a)

donor, or grantor. Similar rules shall also be applied in the case of a series of substituted bases.

(b) The application of this section may be illustrated by the following example:

Example. A, who makes his returns upon the calendar year basis, in 1935 purchased the X Building and subsequently gave it to his son B. B exchanged the X Building for the Y Building in a tax-free exchange, and then gave the Y Building to his wife C. C, in determining the gain from the sale or disposition of the Y Building in 1954, is required to reduce the basis of the building by deductions for depreciation which were successively allowed (but not less than the amount allowable) to A and B upon the X Building and to B upon the Y Building, in addition to the deductions for depreciation allowed (but not less than the amount allowable) to herself during her ownership of the Y Building. [Reg. § 1.1016-10.]

☐ [*T.D.* 6265, 11-6-57.]

§ 1.1017-1. Basis reductions following a discharge of indebtedness.—(a) *General rule for section 108(b)(2)(E).* This paragraph (a) applies to basis reductions under section 108(b)(2)(E) that are required by section 108(a)(1)(A) or (B) because the taxpayer excluded discharge of indebtedness (COD income) from gross income. A taxpayer must reduce in the following order, to the extent of the excluded COD income (but not below zero), the adjusted bases of property held on the first day of the taxable year following the taxable year that the taxpayer excluded COD income from gross income (in proportion to adjusted basis)—

(1) Real property used in a trade or business or held for investment, other than real property described in section 1221(1), that secured the discharged indebtedness immediately before the discharge;

(2) Personal property used in a trade or business or held for investment, other than inventory, accounts receivable, and notes receivable, that secured the discharged indebtedness immediately before the discharge;

(3) Remaining property used in a trade or business or held for investment, other than inventory, accounts receivable, notes receivable, and real property described in section 1221(1);

(4) Inventory, accounts receivable, notes receivable, and real property described in section 1221(1); and

(5) Property not used in a trade or business nor held for investment.

(b) *Operating rules*—(1) *Prior tax-attribute reduction.* The amount of excluded COD income applied to reduce basis does not include any COD income applied to reduce tax attributes under sections 108(b)(2)(A) through (D) and, if applicable, section 108(b)(5). For example, if a taxpayer excludes $100 of COD income from gross income under section 108(a) and reduces tax attributes by $40 under sections 108(b)(2)(A) through (D), the taxpayer is required to reduce the adjusted bases of property by $60 ($100 − $40) under section 108(b)(2)(E).

(2) *Multiple discharged indebtednesses.* If a taxpayer has COD income attributable to more than one discharged indebtedness resulting in the reduction of tax attributes under sections 108(b)(2)(A) through (D) and, if applicable, section 108(b)(5), paragraph (b)(1) of this section must be applied by allocating the tax-attribute reductions among the indebtednesses in proportion to the amount of COD income attributable to each discharged indebtedness. For example, if a taxpayer excludes $20 of COD income attributable to secured indebtedness A and excludes $80 of COD income attributable to unsecured indebtedness B (a total exclusion of $100), and if the taxpayer reduces tax attributes by $40 under sections 108(b)(2)(A) through (D), the taxpayer must reduce the amount of COD income attributable to secured indebtedness A to $12 ($20 − ($20 / $100 × $40)) and must reduce the amount of COD income attributable to unsecured indebtedness B to $48 ($80 − ($80 / $100 × $40)).

(3) *Limitation on basis reductions under section 108(b)(2)(E) in bankruptcy or insolvency.* If COD income arises from a discharge of indebtedness in a title 11 case or while the taxpayer is insolvent, the amount of any basis reduction under section 108(b)(2)(E) shall not exceed the excess of—

(i) The aggregate of the adjusted bases of property and the amount of money held by the taxpayer immediately after the discharge; over

(ii) The aggregate of the liabilities of the taxpayer immediately after the discharge.

(c) *Modification of ordering rules for basis reductions under sections 108(b)(5) and 108(c)*—(1) *In general.* The ordering rules prescribed in paragraph (a) of this section apply, with appropriate modifications, to basis reductions under sections 108(b)(5) and (c). Thus, a taxpayer that elects to reduce basis under section 108(b)(5) may, to the extent that the election applies, reduce only the adjusted basis of property described in paragraphs (a)(1), (2), and (3) of this section and, if an election is made under paragraph (f) of this section, paragraph (a)(4) of this section. Within paragraphs (a)(1),(2), (3) and (4) of this section, such a taxpayer may reduce only the adjusted bases of depreciable property. A taxpayer that elects to apply section 108(c) may reduce only the adjusted basis of property described in paragraphs (a)(1) and (3) of this section and, within paragraphs (a)(1) and (3) of this section, may reduce only the adjusted bases of depreciable real property. Furthermore, for basis reductions under section 108(c), a taxpayer must reduce the adjusted basis of the qualifying real property to the extent of the discharged qualified real property business indebtedness before reducing the adjusted bases of other depreciable real property. The term *qualifying real property* means real property with respect to which the indebtedness is qualified real property business indebtedness within the meaning of section 108(c)(3). See paragraphs (f) and (g) of this section for elections relating to section 1221(1) property and partnership interests.

(2) *Partial basis reductions under section 108(b)(5).* If the amount of basis reductions under section 108(b)(5) is less than the amount of the COD income excluded from gross income under section 108(a), the taxpayer must reduce the balance of its tax attributes, including any remaining adjusted bases of depreciable and other property, by following the ordering rules under section 108(b)(2). For example, if a taxpayer excludes $100 of COD income from gross income under section 108(a) and elects to reduce the adjusted bases of depreciable property by $10 under section 108(b)(5), the taxpayer must reduce its remaining tax attributes by $90, starting with net operating losses under section 108(b)(2).

(3) *Modification of fresh start rule for prior basis reductions under section 108(b)(5).* After reducing the adjusted bases of depreciable property under section 108(b)(5), a taxpayer must compute the limitation on basis reductions under section 1017(b)(2) using the aggregate of the remaining adjusted bases of property. For example, if, immediately after the discharge of indebtedness in a title 11 case, a taxpayer's adjusted bases of property is $100 and its undischarged indebtedness is $70, and if the taxpayer elects to reduce the adjusted bases of depreciable property by $10 under section 108(b)(5), section 1017(b)(2) limits any further basis reductions under section 108(b)(2)(E) to $20 (($100 − $10) − $70).

(d) *Changes in security.* If any property is added or eliminated as security for an indebtedness during the one-year period preceding the discharge of that indebtedness, such addition or elimination shall be disregarded where a principal purpose of the change is to affect the taxpayer's basis reductions under section 1017.

(e) *Depreciable property.* For purposes of this section, the term *depreciable property* means any property of a character subject to the allowance for depreciation or amortization, but only if the basis reduction would reduce the amount of depre-

ciation or amortization which otherwise would be allowable for the period immediately following such reduction. Thus, for example, a lessor cannot reduce the basis of leased property where the lessee's obligation in respect of the property will restore to the lessor the loss due to depreciation during the term of the lease, since the lessor cannot take depreciation in respect of such property.

* * *

[Reg. § 1.1017-1.]

☐ [*T.D.* 6158, 1-6-56. *Amended by T.D.* 8787, 10-21-98 *and T.D.* 8847, 12-14-99.]

§ 1.1019-1. Property on which lessee had made improvements.—In any case in which a lessee of real property has erected buildings or made other improvements upon the leased property and the lease is terminated by forfeiture or otherwise resulting in the realization by such lessor of income which, were it not for the provisions of section 109, would be includible in gross income of the lessor, the amount so excluded from gross income shall not be taken into account in determining the basis or the adjusted basis of such property or any portion thereof in the hands of the lessor. If, however, in any taxable year beginning before January 1, 1942, there has been included in the gross income of the lessor an amount representing any part of the value of such property attributable to such buildings or improvements, the basis of each portion of such property shall be properly adjusted for the amount so included in gross income. For example, A leased in 1930 to B for a period of 25 years unimproved real property and in accordance with the terms of the lease B erected a building on the property. It was estimated that upon expiration of the lease the building would have a depreciated value of $50,000, which value the lessor elected to report (beginning in 1931) as income over the term of the lease. This method of reporting was used until 1942. In 1952 B forfeits the lease. The amount of $22,000 reported as income by A during the years 1931 to 1941, inclusive, shall be added to the basis of the property represented by the improvements in the hands of A. If in such case A did not report during the period of the lease any income attributable to the value of the building erected by the lessee and the lease was forfeited in 1940 when the building was worth $75,000, such amount, having been included in gross income under the law applicable to that year, is added to the basis of the property represented by the improvements in the hands of A. As to treatment of such property for the purposes of capital gains and losses, see subchapter P (sections 1201 and following), chapter 1 of the Code. [Reg. § 1.1019-1.]

☐ [*T.D.* 6265, 11-6-57.]

Reg. § 1.1019-1

Common Nontaxable Exchanges

§ 1.1031(a)-1. Property held for productive use in trade or business or for investment.— (a) *In general*—(1) *Exchanges of property solely for property of a like kind.* Section 1031(a)(1) provides an exception from the general rule requiring the recognition of gain or loss upon the sale or exchange of property. Under section 1031(a)(1), no gain or loss is recognized if property held for productive use in a trade or business or for investment is exchanged solely for property of a like kind to be held either for productive use in a trade or business or for investment. Under section 1031(a)(1), property held for productive use in trade or business may be exchanged for property held for investment. Similarly, under section 1031(a)(1), property held for investment may be exchanged for property held for productive use in a trade or business. However, section 1031(a)(2) provides that section 1031(a)(1) does not apply to any exchange of—

(i) Stock in trade or other property held primarily for sale;

(ii) Stocks, bonds, or notes;

(iii) Other securities or evidences of indebtedness or interest;

(iv) Interests in a partnership;

(v) Certificates of trust or beneficial interests; or

(vi) Choses in action.

Section 1031(a)(1) does not apply to any exchange of interests in a partnership regardless of whether the interests exchanged are general or limited partnership interests or are interests in the same partnership or in different partnerships. An interest in a partnership that has in effect a valid election under section 761(a) to be excluded from the application of all of subchapter K is treated as an interest in each of the assets of the partnership and not as an interest in a partnership for purposes of section 1031(a)(2)(D) and paragraph (a)(1)(iv) of this section. An exchange of an interest in such a partnership does not qualify for nonrecognition of gain or loss under section 1031 with respect to any asset of the partnership that is described in section 1031(a)(2) or to the extent the exchange of assets of the partnership does not otherwise satisfy the requirements of section 1031(a).

(2) *Exchanges of property not solely for property of a like kind.* A transfer is not within the provisions of section 1031(a) if, as part of the consideration, the taxpayer receives money or property which does not meet the requirements of section 1031(a), but the transfer, if otherwise qualified, will be within the provisions of either section 1031(b) or (c). Similarly, a transfer is not

within the provisions of section 1031(a) if, as part of the consideration, the other party to the exchange assumes a liability of the taxpayer (or acquires property from the taxpayer that is subject to a liability), but the transfer, if otherwise qualified, will be within the provisions of either section 1031(b) or (c). A transfer of property meeting the requirements of section 1031(a) may be within the provisions of section 1031(a) even though the taxpayer transfers in addition property not meeting the requirements of section 1031(a) or money. However, the nonrecognition treatment provided by section 1031(a) does not apply to the property transferred which does not meet the requirements of section 1031(a).

(b) *Definition of "like kind."* As used in section 1031(a), the words "like kind" have reference to the nature or character of the property and not to its grade or quality. One kind or class of property may not, under that section, be exchanged for property of a different kind or class. The fact that any real estate involved is improved or unimproved is not material, for that fact relates only to the grade or quality of the property and not to its kind or class. Unproductive real estate held by one other than a dealer for future use or future realization of the increment in value is held for investment and not primarily for sale. For additional rules for exchanges of personal property, see § 1.1031(a)-2.

(c) *Examples of exchanges of property of a "like kind."* No gain or loss is recognized if (1) a taxpayer exchanges property held for productive use in his trade or business, together with cash, for other property of like kind for the same use, such as a truck for a new truck or a passenger automobile for a new passenger automobile to be used for a like purpose; or (2) a taxpayer who is not a dealer in real estate exchanges city real estate for a ranch or farm, or exchanges a leasehold of a fee with 30 years or more to run for real estate, or exchanges improved real estate for unimproved real estate; or (3) a taxpayer exchanges investment property and cash for investment property of a like kind.

(d) *Examples of exchanges not solely in kind.* Gain or loss is recognized if, for instance, a taxpayer exchanges (1) Treasury bonds maturing March 15, 1958, for Treasury bonds maturing December 15, 1968, unless section 1037(a) (or so much of section 1031 as relates to section 1037(a)) applies to such exchange, or (2) a real estate mortgage for consolidated farm loan bonds.

(e) *Effective date relating to exchanges of partnership interests.* The provisions of paragraph (a)(1) of this section relating to exchanges of partnership interests apply to transfers of property

Reg. § 1.1031(a)-1(a)(1)

made by taxpayers on or after April 25, 1991. [Reg. § 1.1031(a)-1.]

☐ [*T.D.* 6210, 11-6-56. *Amended by T.D.* 6935, 11-16-67; *T.D.* 8343, 4-11-91 *and T.D.* 8346, 4-25-91.]

§ 1.1031(a)-2. Additional rules for exchanges of personal property.—(a) *Introduction.* Section 1.1031(a)-1(b) provides that the nonrecognition rules of section 1031 do not apply to an exchange of one kind or class of property for property of a different kind or class. This section contains additional rules for determining whether personal property has been exchanged for property of a like kind or like class. Personal properties of a like class are considered to be of a "like kind" for purposes of section 1031. In addition, an exchange of properties of a like kind may qualify under section 1031 regardless of whether the properties are also of a like class. In determining whether exchanged properties are of a like kind, no inference is to be drawn from the fact that the properties are not of a like class. Under paragraph (b) of this section, depreciable tangible personal properties are of a like class if they are either within the same General Asset Class (as defined in paragraph (b)(2) of this section) or within the same Product Class (as defined in paragraph (b)(3) of this section). Paragraph (c) of this section provides rules for exchanges of intangible personal property and nondepreciable personal property.

(b) *Depreciable tangible personal property*—(1) *General rule.* Depreciable tangible personal property is exchanged for property of a "like kind" under section 1031 if the property is exchanged for property of a like kind or like class. Depreciable tangible personal property is of a like class to other depreciable tangible personal property if the exchanged properties are either within the same General Asset Class or within the same Product Class. A single property may not be classified within more than one General Asset Class or within more than one Product Class. In addition, property classified within any General Asset Class may not be classified within a Product Class. A property's General Asset Class or Product Class is determined as of the date of the exchange.

(2) *General Asset Classes.* Except as provided in paragraphs (b)(4) and (b)(5) of this section, property within a General Asset Class consists of depreciable tangible personal property described in one of asset classes 00.11 through 00.28 and 00.4 of Rev. Proc. 87-56, 1987-2 C.B. 674. These General Asset Classes describe types of depreciable tangible personal property that frequently are used in many businesses. The General Asset Classes are as follows:

(i) Office furniture, fixtures, and equipment (asset class 00.11),

(ii) Information systems (computers and peripheral equipment) (asset class 00.12),

(iii) Data handling equipment, except computers (asset class 00.13),

(iv) Airplanes (airframes and engines), except those used in commercial or contract carrying of passengers or freight, and all helicopters (airframes and engines) (asset class 00.21),

(v) Automobiles, taxis (asset class 00.22),

(vi) Buses (asset class 00.23),

(vii) Light general purpose trucks (asset class 00.241),

(viii) Heavy general purpose trucks (asset class 00.242),

(ix) Railroad cars and locomotives, except those owned by railroad transportation companies (asset class 00.25),

(x) Tractor units for use over-the-road (asset class 00.26),

(xi) Trailers and trailer-mounted containers (asset class 00.27),

(xii) Vessels, barges, tugs, and similar water-transportation equipment, except those used in marine construction (asset class 00.28), and

(xiii) Industrial steam and electric generation and/or distribution systems (asset class 00.4).

(3) *Product Classes.* Except as provided in paragraphs (b)(4) and (b)(5) of this section, property within a Product Class consists of depreciable tangible personal property that is listed in a 4-digit product class within Division D of the Standard Industrial Classification codes, set forth in Executive Office of the President, Office of Management and Budget, *Standard Industrial Classification Manual* (1987) ("*SIC Manual*"). Copies of the *SIC Manual* may be obtained from the National Technical Information Service, an agency of the U.S. Department of Commerce. Division D of the *SIC Manual* contains a listing of manufactured products and equipment. For this purpose, any 4-digit product class ending in a "9" (*i.e.,* a miscellaneous category) will not be considered a Product Class. If a property is listed in more than one product class, the property is treated as listed in any one of those product classes. A property's 4-digit product classification is referred to as the property's "SIC Code."

(4) *Modifications of Rev. Proc. 87-56 and SIC Manual.* The asset classes of Rev. Proc. 87-56 and the product classes of the *SIC Manual* may be updated or otherwise modified from time to time. In the event Rev. Proc. 87-56 is modified, the General Asset Classes will follow the modification, and the modification will be effective for exchanges occurring on or after the date the modifi-

cation is published in the Internal Revenue Bulletin, unless otherwise provided. Similarly, in the event the *SIC Manual* is modified, the Product Classes will follow the modification, and the modification will be effective for exchanges occurring on or after the effective date of the modification. However, taxpayers may rely on the unmodified *SIC Manual* for exchanges occurring during the one-year period following the effective date of the modification. The *SIC Manual* generally is modified every five years, in years ending in a 2 or 7 (e.g., 1987 and 1992). The effective date of the modified *SIC Manual* is announced in the Federal Register and generally is January 1 of the year the *SIC Manual* is modified.

(5) *Modified classification through published guidance.* The Commissioner may, by guidance published in the Internal Revenue Bulletin, supplement the guidance provided in this section relating to classification of properties. For example, the Commissioner may determine not to follow, in whole or in part, any modification of Rev. Proc. 87-56 or the *SIC Manual.* The Commissioner may also determine that two types of property that are listed in separate product classes each ending in a "9" are of a like class, or that a type of property that has a SIC Code is of a like class to a type of property that does not have a SIC Code.

(6) *No inference outside of Section 1031.* The rules provided in this section concerning the use of Rev. Proc. 87-56 and the *SIC Manual* are limited to exchanges under section 1031. No inference is intended with respect to the classification of property for other purposes, such as depreciation.

(7) *Examples.* The application of this paragraph (b) may be illustrated by the following examples:

Example 1. Taxpayer A transfers a personal computer (asset class 00.12) to B in exchange for a printer (asset class 00.12). With respect to A, the properties exchanged are within the same General Asset Class and therefore are of a like class.

Example 2. Taxpayer C transfers an airplane (asset class 00.21) to D in exchange for a heavy general purpose truck (asset class 00.242). The properties exchanged are not of a like class because they are within different General Asset Classes. Because each of the properties is within a General Asset Class, the properties may not be classified within a Product Class. The airplane and heavy general purpose truck are also not of a like kind. Therefore, the exchange does not qualify for nonrecognition of gain or loss under section 1031.

Example 3. Taxpayer E transfers a grader to F in exchange for a scraper. Neither property is within any of the General Asset Classes, and both properties are within the same Product Class (SIC Code 3533). With respect to E, therefore, the properties exchanged are of a like class.

Example 4. Taxpayer G transfers a personal computer (asset class 00.12), an airplane (asset class 00.21) and a sanding machine (SIC Code 3553), to H in exchange for a printer (asset class 00.12), a heavy general purpose truck (asset class 00.242) and a lathe (SIC Code 3553). The personal computer and the printer are of a like class because they are within the same General Asset Class; the sanding machine and the lathe are of a like class because neither property is within any of the General Asset Classes and they are within the same Product Class. The airplane and the heavy general purpose truck are neither within the same General Asset Class nor within the same Product Class, and are not of a like kind.

(c) *Intangible personal property and nondepreciable personal property*—(1) *General rule.* An exchange of intangible personal property or nondepreciable personal property qualifies for nonrecognition of gain or loss under section 1031 only if the exchanged properties are of a like kind. No like classes are provided for these properties. Whether intangible personal property is of a like kind to other intangible personal property generally depends on the nature or character of the rights involved (*e.g.,* a patent or a copyright) and also on the nature or character of the underlying property to which the intangible personal property relates.

(2) *Goodwill and going concern value.* The goodwill or going concern value of a business is not of a like kind to the goodwill or going concern value of another business.

(3) *Examples.* The application of this paragraph (c) may be illustrated by the following examples:

Example (1). Taxpayer K exchanges a copyright on a novel for a copyright on a different novel. The properties exchanged are of a like kind.

Example (2). Taxpayer J exchanges a copyright on a novel for a copyright on a song. The properties exchanged are not of a like kind.

(d) *Effective date.* Section 1.1031(a)-2 is effective for exchanges occurring on or after April 11, 1991. [Reg. § 1.1031(a)-2.]

☐ [*T.D.* 8343, 4-11-91.]

§ 1.1031(b)-1. Receipt of other property or money in tax-free exchange.—(a) If the taxpayer receives other property (in addition to property permitted to be received without recognition of gain) or money—

(1) In an exchange described in section 1031(a) of property held for investment or productive use in trade or business for property of

Reg. § 1.1031(b)-1(a)(1)

like kind to be held either for productive use or for investment,

(2) In an exchange described in section 1035(a) of insurance policies or annuity contracts,

(3) In an exchange described in section 1036(a) of common stock for common stock, or preferred stock for preferred stock, in the same corporation and not in connection with a corporate reorganization, or

(4) In an exchange described in section 1037(a) of obligations of the United States, issued under the Second Liberty Bond Act (31 U.S.C. 774(2)), solely for other obligations issued under such Act,

the gain, if any, to the taxpayer will be recognized under section 1031(b) in an amount not in excess of the sum of the money and the fair market value of the other property, but the loss, if any, to the taxpayer from such an exchange will not be recognized under section 1031(c) to any extent.

(b) The application of this section may be illustrated by the following examples:

Example (1). A, who is not a dealer in real estate, in 1954 exchanges real estate held for investment, which he purchased in 1940 for $5,000, for other real estate (to be held for productive use in trade or business) which has a fair market value of $6,000, and $2,000 in cash. The gain from the transaction is $3,000, but is recognized only to the extent of the cash received of $2,000.

Example (2). (a) B, who uses the cash receipts and disbursements method of accounting and the calendar year as his taxable year, has never elected under section 454(a) to include in gross income currently the annual increase in the redemption price of non-interest-bearing obligations issued at a discount. In 1943, for $750 each, B purchased four $1,000 series E United States savings bonds bearing an issue date of March 1, 1943.

(b) On October 1, 1963, the redemption value of each such bond was $1,396, and the total redemption value of the four bonds was $5,584. On that date B submitted the four $1,000 series E bonds to the United States in a transaction in which one of such $1,000 bonds was reissued by issuing four $100 series E United States savings bonds bearing an issue date of March 1, 1943, and by considering six $100 series E bonds bearing an issue date of March 1, 1943, to have been issued. The redemption value of each such $100 series E bond was $139.60 on October 1, 1963. Then, as part of the transaction, the six $100 series E bonds so considered to have been issued and the three $1,000 series E bonds were exchanged, in an exchange qualifying under section 1037(a), for five $1,000 series H United States savings bonds plus $25.60 in cash.

(c) The gain realized on the exchange qualifying under section 1037(a) is $2,325.60, determined as follows:

Amount realized:		
Par value of five series H bonds		$5,000.00
Cash received		25.60
Total realized		5,025.60
Less: Adjusted basis of series E bonds surrendered in the exchange:		
Three $1,000 series E bonds	$2,250	
Six $100 series E bonds at $75 each	450	2,700.00
Gain realized		$2,325.60

(d) Pursuant to section 1031(b), only $25.60 (the money received) of the total gain of $2,325.60 realized on the exchange is recognized at the time of exchange and must be included in B's gross income for 1963. The $2,300 balance of the gain ($2,325.60 less $25.60) must be included in B's gross income for the taxable year in which the series H bonds are redeemed or disposed of, or reach final maturity, whichever is earlier, as provided in paragraph (c) of § 1.454-1.

(e) The gain on the four $100 series E bonds, determined by using $75 as a basis for each such bond, must be included in B's gross income for the taxable year in which such bonds are redeemed or disposed of, or reach final maturity, whichever is earlier.

Example (3). (a) The facts are the same as in example (2), except that, as part of the transaction, the $1,000 series E bond is reissued by considering ten $100 series E bonds bearing an issue date of March 1, 1943, to have been issued. Six of the $100 series E bonds so considered to have been issued are surrendered to the United States as part of the exchange qualifying under section 1037(a) and the other four are immediately redeemed.

(b) Pursuant to section 1031(b), only $25.60 (the money received) of the total gain of $2,325.60 realized on the exchange qualifying under section 1037(a) is recognized at the time of the exchange and must be included in B's gross income for 1963. The $2,300 balance of the gain ($2,325.60 less $25.60) realized on such exchange

Reg. § 1.1031(b)-1(b)

must be included in B's gross income for the taxable year in which the series H bonds are redeemed or disposed of, or reach final maturity, whichever is earlier, as provided in paragraph (c) of § 1.454-1.

(c) The redemption on October 1, 1963, of the four $100 series E bonds considered to have been issued at such time results in gain of $258.40, which is then recognized and must be included in B's gross income for 1963. This gain of $258.40 is the difference between the $558.40 redemption value of such bonds on the date of the exchange and the $300 (4 × $75) paid for such series E bonds in 1943.

Example (4). On November 1, 1963, C purchased for $91 a marketable United States bond which was originally issued at its par value of $100 under the Second Liberty Bond Act. On February 1, 1964, in an exchange qualifying under section 1037(a), C surrendered the bond to the United States for another marketable United States bond, which then had a fair market value of $92, and $1.85 in cash, $0.85 of which was interest. The $0.85 interest received is includible in gross income for the taxable year of the exchange, but the $2 gain ($93 less $91) realized on the exchange is recognized for such year under section 1031(b) to the extent of $1 (the money received). Under section 1031(d), C's basis in the bond received in exchange is $91 (his basis of $91 in the bond surrendered, reduced by the $1 money received and increased by the $1 gain recognized).

(c) Consideration received in the form of an assumption of liabilities (or a transfer subject to a liability) is to be treated as "other property or money" for the purposes of section 1031(b). Where, on an exchange described in section 1031(b), each party to the exchange either assumes a liability of the other party or acquires property subject to a liability, then, in determining the amount of "other property or money" for purposes of section 1031(b), consideration given in the form of an assumption of liabilities (or a receipt of property subject to a liability) shall be offset against consideration received in the form of an assumption of liabilities (or a transfer subject to a liability). See § 1.1031(d)-2, examples (1) and (2). [Reg. § 1.1031(b)-1.]

☐ [*T.D.* 6210, 11-6-56. *Amended by T.D.* 6935, 11-16-67.]

§ 1.1031(b)-2. Safe harbor for qualified intermediaries.—(a) In the case of simultaneous transfers of like-kind properties involving a qualified intermediary (as defined in § 1.1031(k)-1(g)(4)(iii)), the qualified intermediary is not considered the agent of the taxpayer for purposes of section 1031(a). In such a case, the transfer and receipt of property by the taxpayer is treated as an exchange.

(b) In the case of simultaneous exchanges of like-kind properties involving a qualified intermediary (as defined in § 1.1031(k)-1(g)(4)(iii)), the receipt by the taxpayer of an evidence of indebtedness of the transferee of the qualified intermediary is treated as the receipt of an evidence of indebtedness of the person acquiring property from the taxpayer for purposes of section 453 and § 15a.453-1(b)(3)(i) of this chapter.

(c) Paragraph (a) of this section applies to transfers of property made by taxpayers on or after June 10, 1991.

(d) Paragraph (b) of this section applies to transfers of property made by taxpayers on or after April 20, 1994. A taxpayer may choose to apply paragraph (b) of this section to transfers of property made on or after June 10, 1991. [Reg. § 1.1031(b)-2.]

☐ [*T.D.* 8346, 4-25-91. *Amended by T.D.* 8535, 4-19-94.]

§ 1.1031(c)-1. Nonrecognition of loss.—Section 1031(c) provides that a loss shall not be recognized from an exchange of property described in section 1031(a), 1035(a), 1036(a), or 1037(a) where there is received in the exchange other property or money in addition to property permitted to be received without recognition of gain or loss. See example (4) of paragraph (a)(3) of § 1.1037-1 for an illustration of the application of this section in the case of an exchange of United States obligations described in section 1037(a). [Reg. § 1.1031(c)-1.]

☐ [*T.D.* 6210, 11-6-56. *Amended by T.D.* 6935, 11-16-67.]

§ 1.1031(d)-1. Property acquired upon a tax-free exchange.—(a) If, in an exchange of property solely of the type described in section 1031, section 1035(a), section 1036(a), or section 1037(a), no part of the gain or loss was recognized under the law applicable to the year in which the exchange was made, the basis of the property acquired is the same as the basis of the property transferred by the taxpayer with proper adjustments to the date of the exchange. If additional consideration is given by the taxpayer in the exchange, the basis of the property acquired shall be the same as the property transferred increased by the amount of additional consideration given (see section 1016 and the regulations thereunder).

(b) If, in an exchange of properties of the type indicated in section 1031, section 1035(a), section 1036(a), or section 1037(a), gain to the taxpayer was recognized under the provisions of section 1031(b) or a similar provision of a prior revenue law, on account of the receipt of money in the transaction, the basis of the property acquired is the basis of the property transferred (adjusted to the date of the exchange), decreased by the amount of money received and increased by the amount of gain recognized on the exchange. The application of this paragraph may be illustrated by the following example:

Example. A, an individual in the moving and storage business, in 1954 transfers one of his moving trucks with an adjusted basis in his hands of $2,500 to B in exchange for a truck (to be used in A's business) with a fair market value of $2,400 and $200 in cash. A realizes a gain of $100 upon the exchange, all of which is recognized under section 1031(b). The basis of the truck acquired by A is determined as follows:

Adjusted basis of A's former truck	$2,500
Less: Amount of money received	200
Difference	2,300
Plus: Amount of gain recognized	100
Basis of truck acquired by A	$2,400

(c) If, upon an exchange of properties of the type described in section 1031, section 1035(a), section 1036(a), or section 1037(a), the taxpayer received other property (not permitted to be received without the recognition of gain) and gain from the transaction was recognized as required under section 1031(b), or a similar provision of a prior revenue law, the basis (adjusted to the date of the exchange) of the property transferred by the taxpayer, decreased by the amount of any money received and increased by the amount of gain recognized, must be allocated to and is the basis of the properties (other than money) received on the exchange. For the purpose of the allocation of the basis of the properties received, there must be assigned to such other property an amount equivalent to its fair market value at the date of the exchange. The application of this paragraph may be illustrated by the following example:

Example. A, who is not a dealer in real estate, in 1954 transfers real estate held for investment which he purchased in 1940 for $10,000 in exchange for other real estate (to be held for investment) which has a fair market value of $9,000, an automobile which has a fair market value of $2,000, and $1,500 in cash. A realizes a gain of $2,500, all of which is recognized under section 1031(b). The basis of the property received in exchange is the basis of the real estate A transfers ($10,000) decreased by the amount of money received ($1,500) and increased in the amount of gain that was recognized ($2,500), which results in a basis for the property received of $11,000. This basis of $11,000 is allocated between the automobile and the real estate received by A, the basis of the automobile being its fair market value at the date of the exchange, $2,000, and the basis of the real estate received being the remainder, $9,000.

(d) Section 1031(c) and, with respect to section 1031 and section 1036(a), similar provisions of prior revenue laws provide that no loss may be recognized on an exchange of properties of a type described in section 1031, section 1035(a), section 1036(a), or section 1037(a), although the taxpayer receives other property or money from the transaction. However, the basis of the property or properties (other than money) received by the taxpayer is the basis (adjusted to the date of the exchange) of the property transferred, decreased by the amount of money received. This basis must be allocated to the properties received, and for this purpose there must be allocated to such other property an amount of such basis equivalent to its fair market value at the date of the exchange.

(e) If, upon an exchange of properties of the type described in section 1031, section 1035(a), section 1036(a), or section 1037(a), the taxpayer also exchanged other property (not permitted to be transferred without the recognition of gain or loss) and gain or loss from the transaction is recognized under section 1002 or a similar provision of a prior revenue law, the basis of the property acquired is the total basis of the properties transferred (adjusted to the date of the exchange) increased by the amount of gain and decreased by the amount of loss recognized on the other property. For purposes of this rule, the taxpayer is deemed to have received in exchange for such other property an amount equal to its fair market value on the date of the exchange. The application of this paragraph may be illustrated by the following example:

Example. A exchanges real estate held for investment plus stock for real estate to be held for investment. The real estate transferred has an adjusted basis of $10,000 and a fair market value of $11,000. The stock transferred has an adjusted basis of $4,000 and a fair market value of $2,000. The real estate acquired has a fair market value of $13,000. A is deemed to have received a $2,000 portion of the acquired real estate in exchange for the stock, since $2,000 is the fair market value of the stock at the time of the exchange. A $2,000 loss is recognized under section 1002 on the exchange of the stock for real estate. No gain or loss is recognized on the exchange of the real estate since the property received is of the type permitted to be received without recognition of gain or loss. The basis of the real estate acquired by A is determined as follows:

Adjusted basis of real estate transferred .	$10,000
Adjusted basis of stock transferred	4,000
	14,000
Less:	
Loss recognized on transfer of stock.....	2,000
Basis of real estate acquired upon the exchange	12,000

[Reg. § 1.1031(d)-1.]

☐ [*T.D. 6210, 11-6-56. Amended by T.D. 6453, 2-16-60 and T.D. 6935, 11-16-67.*]

§ 1.1031(d)-2. Treatment of assumption of liabilities.—For the purposes of section 1031(d), the amount of any liabilities of the taxpayer assumed by the other party to the exchange (or of any liabilities to which the property exchanged by the taxpayer is subject) is to be treated as money received by the taxpayer upon the exchange, whether or not the assumption resulted in a recognition of gain or loss to the taxpayer under the law applicable to the year in which the exchange was made. The application of this section may be illustrated by the following examples:

Example (1). B, an individual, owns an apartment house which has an adjusted basis in his hands of $500,000, but which is subject to a mortgage of $150,000. On September 1, 1954, he transfers the apartment house to C, receiving in exchange therefor $50,000 in cash and another apartment house with a fair market value on that date of $600,000. The transfer to C is made subject to the $150,000 mortgage. B realizes a gain of $300,000 on the exchange, computed as follows:

Value of property received..........		$600,000
Cash		50,000
Liabilities subject to which old property was transferred.................		150,000
Total consideration received		800,000
Less: Adjusted basis of property transferred		500,000
Gain realized		300,000

Under section 1031(b), $200,000 of the $300,000 gain is recognized. The basis of the apartment house acquired by B upon the exchange is $500,000, computed as follows:

Adjusted basis of property transferred.....................		$500,000
Less: Amount of money received:		
Cash	$ 50,000	
Amount of liabilities subject to which property was transferred	150,000	
		200,000
Difference		300,000
Plus: Amount of gain recognized upon the exchange...................		200,000
Basis of property acquired upon the exchange...............		$500,000

Example (2). (a) D, an individual, owns an apartment house. On December 1, 1955, the apartment house owned by D has an adjusted basis in his hands of $100,000, a fair market value of $220,000, but is subject to a mortgage of $80,000. E, an individual, also owns an apartment house. On December 1, 1955, the apartment house owned by E has an adjusted basis of $175,000, a fair market value of $250,000, but is subject to a mortgage of $150,000. On December 1, 1955, D transfers his apartment house to E, receiving in exchange therefor $40,000 in cash and the apartment house owned by E. Each apartment house is transferred subject to the mortgage on it.

(b) D realizes a gain of $120,000 on the exchange, computed as follows:

Value of property received		$250,000
Cash.............................		40,000
Liabilities subject to which old property was transferred..................		80,000
Total consideration received		370,000
Less: Adjusted basis of property transferred ...	$100,000	
Liabilities to which new property is subject	150,000	$250,000
Gain realized		$120,000

For purposes of section 1031(b), the amount of "other property or money" received by D is $40,000. (Consideration received by D in the form of a transfer subject to a liability of $80,000 is offset by consideration given in the form of a receipt of property subject to a $150,000 liability. Thus, only the consideration received in the form of cash, $40,000, is treated as "other property or money" for purposes of section 1031(b).) Accordingly, under section 1031(b), $40,000 of the $120,000 gain is recognized. The basis of the apartment house acquired by D is $170,000, computed as follows:

Adjusted basis of property transferred......................		$100,000
Liabilities to which new property is subject		150,000
Total		$250,000
Less: Amount of money received:		
Cash	$40,000	
Amount of liabilities subject to which property was transferred	80,000	
		$120,000
Difference		$130,000
Plus: Amount of gain recognized upon the exchange...................		40,000
Basis of property acquired upon the exchange...................		$170,000

(c) E realizes a gain of $75,000 on the exchange, computed as follows:

Reg. § 1.1031(d)-2

Value of property received..........	$220,000
Liabilities subject to which old property was transferred.................	$150,000
Total consideration received	370,000
Less: Adjusted basis of property transferred $175,000	
Cash................. 40,000	
Liabilities to which new property is subject ... 80,000	
	$295,000
Gain realized.................	$ 75,000

For purposes of section 1031(b), the amount of "other property or money" received by E is $30,000. (Consideration received by E in the form of a transfer subject to a liability of $150,000 is offset by consideration given in the form of a receipt of property subject to an $80,000 liability and by the $40,000 cash paid by E. Although consideration received in the form of cash or other property is not offset by consideration given in the form of an assumption of liabilities or a receipt of property subject to a liability, consideration given in the form of cash or other property is offset against consideration received in the form of an assumption of liabilities or a transfer of property subject to a liability.) Accordingly, under section 1031(b), $30,000 of the $75,000 gain is recognized. The basis of the apartment house acquired by E is $175,000, computed as follows:

Adjusted basis of property transferred .	$175,000
Cash......................	40,000
Liabilities to which new property is subject	80,000
Total	295,000
Less: Amount of money received: Amount of liabilities subject to which property was transferred .	$150,000
	150,000
Difference	$145,000
Plus: Amount of gain recognized upon the exchange	30,000
Basis of property acquired upon the exchange	$175,000

[Reg. § 1.1031(d)-2.]

☐ [*T.D.* 6210, 11-6-56.]

§ 1.1031(k)-1. Treatment of deferred exchanges.—(a) *Overview.* This section provides rules for the application of section 1031 and the regulations thereunder in the case of a "deferred exchange." For purposes of section 1031 and this section, a deferred exchange is defined as an exchange in which, pursuant to an agreement, the taxpayer transfers property held for productive use in a trade or business or for investment (the "relinquished property") and subsequently receives property to be held either for productive use in a trade or business or for investment (the "replacement property"). In the case of a deferred exchange, if the requirements set forth in paragraphs (b), (c), and (d) of this section (relating to identification and receipt of replacement property) are not satisfied, the replacement property received by the taxpayer will be treated as property which is not of a like kind to the relinquished property. In order to constitute a deferred exchange, the transaction must be an exchange (i.e., a transfer of property for property, as distinguished from a transfer of property for money). For example, a sale of property followed by a purchase of property of a like kind does not qualify for nonrecognition of gain or loss under section 1031 regardless of whether the identification and receipt requirements of section 1031(a)(3) and paragraphs (b), (c), and (d) of this section are satisfied. The transfer of relinquished property in a deferred exchange is not within the provisions of section 1031(a) if, as part of the consideration, the taxpayer receives money or property which does not meet the requirements of section 1031(a), but the transfer, if otherwise qualified, will be within the provisions of either section 1031(b) or (c). See § 1.1031(a)-1(a)(2). In addition, in the case of a transfer of relinquished property in a deferred exchange, gain or loss may be recognized if the taxpayer actually or constructively receives money or property which does not meet the requirements of section 1031(a) before the taxpayer actually receives like-kind replacement property. If the taxpayer actually or constructively receives money or property which does not meet the requirements of section 1031(a) in the full amount of the consideration for the relinquished property, the transaction will constitute a sale, and not a deferred exchange, even though the taxpayer may ultimately receive like-kind replacement property. For purposes of this section, property which does not meet the requirements of section 1031(a)(whether by being described in section 1031(a)(2) or otherwise) is referred to as "other property." For rules regarding actual and constructive receipt, and safe harbors therefrom, see paragraphs (f) and (g), respectively, of this section. For rules regarding the determination of gain or loss recognized and the basis of property received in a deferred exchange, see paragraph (j) of this section.

(b) *Identification and receipt requirements*— (1) *In general.* In the case of a deferred exchange, any replacement property received by the taxpayer will be treated as property which is not of a like kind to the relinquished property if—

(i) The replacement property is not "identified" before the end of the "identification period," or

(ii) The identified replacement property is not received before the end of the "exchange period."

(2) *Identification period and exchange period.* (i) The identification period begins on the date the taxpayer transfers the relinquished property and ends at midnight on the 45th day thereafter.

(ii) The exchange period begins on the date the taxpayer transfers the relinquished property and ends at midnight on the earlier of the 180th day thereafter or the due date (including extensions) for the taxpayer's return of the tax imposed by chapter 1 of subtitle A of the Code for the taxable year in which the transfer of the relinquished property occurs.

(iii) If, as part of the same deferred exchange, the taxpayer transfers more than one relinquished property and the relinquished properties are transferred on different dates, the identification period and the exchange period are determined by reference to the earliest date on which any of the properties are transferred.

(iv) For purposes of this paragraph (b)(2), property is transferred when the property is disposed of within the meaning of section 1001(a).

(3) *Example.* This paragraph (b) may be illustrated by the following example.

Example. (i) M is a corporation that files its Federal income tax return on a calendar year basis. M and C enter into an agreement for an exchange of property that requires M to transfer property X to C. Under the agreement, M is to identify like-kind replacement property which C is required to purchase and to transfer to M. M transfers property X to C on November 16, 1992.

(ii) The identification period ends at midnight on December 31, 1992, the day which is 45 days after the date of transfer of property X. The exchange period ends at midnight on March 15, 1993, the due date for M's Federal income tax return for the taxable year in which M transferred property X. However, if M is allowed the automatic six-month extension for filing its tax return, the exchange period ends at midnight on May 15, 1993, the day which is 180 days after the date of transfer of property X.

(c) *Identification of replacement property before the end of the identification period*—(1) *In general.* For purposes of paragraph (b)(1)(i) of this section (relating to the identification requirement), replacement property is identified before the end of the identification period only if the requirements of this paragraph (c) are satisfied with respect to the replacement property. However, any replacement property that is received by the taxpayer before the end of the identification period will in all events be treated as identified before the end of the identification period.

(2) *Manner of identifying replacement property.* Replacement property is identified only if it is designated as replacement property in a written document signed by the taxpayer and hand delivered, mailed, telecopied, or otherwise sent before the end of the identification period to either—

(i) The person obligated to transfer the replacement property to the taxpayer (regardless of whether that person is a disqualified person as defined in paragraph (k) of this section); or

(ii) Any other person involved in the exchange other than the taxpayer or a disqualified person (as defined in paragraph (k) of this section).

Examples of persons involved in the exchange include any of the parties to the exchange, an intermediary, an escrow agent, and a title company. An identification of replacement property made in a written agreement for the exchange of properties signed by all parties thereto before the end of the identification period will be treated as satisfying the requirements of this paragraph (c)(2).

(3) *Description of replacement property.* Replacement property is identified only if it is unambiguously described in the written document or agreement. Real property generally is unambiguously described if it is described by a legal description, street address, or distinguishable name (e.g., the Mayfair Apartment Building). Personal property generally is unambiguously described if it is described by a specific description of the particular type of property. For example, a truck generally is unambiguously described if it is described by a specific make, model, and year.

(4) *Alternative and multiple properties.* (i) The taxpayer may identify more than one replacement property. Regardless of the number of relinquished properties transferred by the taxpayer as part of the same deferred exchange, the maximum number of replacement properties that the taxpayer may identify is—

(A) Three properties without regard to the fair market values of the properties (the "3-property rule"), or

(B) Any number of properties as long as their aggregate fair market value as of the end of the identification period does not exceed 200 percent of the aggregate fair market value of all the relinquished properties as of the date the relinquished properties were transferred by the taxpayer (the "200-percent rule").

(ii) If, as of the end of the identification period, the taxpayer has identified more properties as replacement properties than permitted by paragraph (c)(4)(i) of this section, the taxpayer is treated as if no replacement property had been identified. The preceding sentence will not apply, however, and an identification satisfying the requirements of paragraph (c)(4)(i) of this section will be considered made, with respect to—

(A) Any replacement property received by the taxpayer before the end of the identification period, and

(B) Any replacement property identified before the end of the identification period and received before the end of the exchange period, but only if the taxpayer receives before the end of the exchange period identified replacement property the fair market value of which is at least 95 percent of the aggregate fair market value of all identified replacement properties (the "95-percent rule").

For this purpose, the fair market value of each identified replacement property is determined as of the earlier of the date the property is received by the taxpayer or the last day of the exchange period.

(iii) For purposes of applying the 3-property rule, the 200-percent rule, and the 95-percent rule, all identifications of replacement property, other than identifications of replacement property that have been revoked in the manner provided in paragraph (c)(6) of this section, are taken into account. For example, if, in a deferred exchange, B transfers property X with a fair market value of $100,000 to C and B receives like-kind property Y with a fair market value of $50,000 before the end of the identification period, under paragraph (c)(1) of this section, property Y is treated as identified by reason of being received before the end of the identification period. Thus, under paragraph (c)(4)(i) of this section, B may identify either two additional replacement properties of any fair market value or any number of additional replacement properties as long as the aggregate fair market value of the additional replacement properties does not exceed $150,000.

(5) *Incidental property disregarded.* (i) Solely for purposes of applying this paragraph (c), property that is incidental to a larger item of property is not treated as property that is separate from the larger item of property. Property is incidental to a larger item of property if—

(A) In standard commercial transactions, the property is typically transferred together with the larger item of property, and

(B) The aggregate fair market value of all of the incidental property does not exceed 15 percent of the aggregate fair market value of the larger item of property.

(ii) This paragraph (c)(5) may be illustrated by the following examples.

Example 1. For purposes of paragraph (c) of this section, a spare tire and tool kit will not be treated as separate property from a truck with a fair market value of $10,000, if the aggregate fair market value of the spare tire and tool kit does not exceed $1,500. For purposes of the 3-property rule, the truck, spare tire, and tool kit are treated as 1 property. Moreover, for purposes of paragraph (c)(3) of this section (relating to the description of replacement property), the truck, spare tire, and tool kit are all considered to be unambiguously described if the make, model, and year of the truck are specified, even if no reference is made to the spare tire and tool kit.

Example 2. For purposes of paragraph (c) of this section, furniture, laundry machines, and other miscellaneous items of personal property will not be treated as separate property from an apartment building with a fair market value of $1,000,000 if the aggregate fair market value of the furniture, laundry machines, and other personal property does not exceed $150,000. For purposes of the 3-property rule, the apartment building, furniture, laundry machines, and other personal property are treated as 1 property. Moreover, for purposes of paragraph (c)(3) of this section (relating to the description of replacement property), the apartment building, furniture, laundry machines, and other personal property are all considered to be unambiguously described if the legal description, street address, or distinguishable name of the apartment building is specified, even if no reference is made to the furniture, laundry machines, and other personal property.

(6) *Revocation of identification.* An identification of replacement property may be revoked at any time before the end of the identification period. An identification of replacement property is revoked only if the revocation is made in a written document signed by the taxpayer and hand delivered, mailed, telecopied, or otherwise sent before the end of the identification period to the person to whom the identification of the replacement property was sent. An identification of replacement property that is made in a written agreement for the exchange of properties is treated as revoked only if the revocation is made in a written amendment to the agreement or in a written document signed by the taxpayer and hand delivered, mailed, telecopied, or otherwise sent before the end of the identification period to all of the parties to the agreement.

(7) *Examples.* This paragraph (c) may be illustrated by the following examples. Unless otherwise provided in an example, the following facts are assumed: B, a calendar year taxpayer, and C agree to enter into a deferred exchange. Pursuant to their agreement, B transfers real property X to C on May 17, 1991. Real property X, which has

been held by B for investment, is unencumbered and has a fair market value on May 17, 1991, of $100,000. On or before July 1, 1991 (the end of the identification period), B is to identify replacement property that is of a like kind to real property X. On or before November 13, 1991 (the end of the exchange period), C is required to purchase the property identified by B and to transfer that property to B. To the extent the fair market value of the replacement property transferred to B is greater or less than the fair market value of real property X, either B or C, as applicable, will make up the difference by paying cash to the other party after the date the replacement property is received by B. No replacement property is identified in the agreement. When subsequently identified, the replacement property is described by legal description and is of a like kind to real property X (determined without regard to section 1031(a)(3) and this section). B intends to hold the replacement property received for investment.

Example 1. (i) On July 2, 1991, B identifies real property E as replacement property by designating real property E as replacement property in a written document signed by B and personally delivered to C.

(ii) Because the identification was made after the end of the identification period, pursuant to paragraph (b)(1)(i) of this section (relating to the identification requirement), real property E is treated as property which is not of a like kind to real property X.

Example 2. (i) C is a corporation of which 20 percent of the outstanding stock is owned by B. On July 1, 1991, B identifies real property F as replacement property by designating real property F as replacement property in a written document signed by B and mailed to C.

(ii) Because C is the person obligated to transfer the replacement property to B, real property F is identified before the end of the identification period. The fact that C is a "disqualified person" as defined in paragraph (k) of this section does not change this result.

(iii) Real property F would also have been treated as identified before the end of the identification period if, instead of sending the identification to C, B had designated real property F as replacement property in a written agreement for the exchange of properties signed by all parties thereto on or before July 1, 1991.

Example 3. (i) On June 3, 1991, B identifies the replacement property as "unimproved land located in Hood County with a fair market value not to exceed $100,000." The designation is made in a written document signed by B and personally delivered to C. On July 8, 1991, B and C agree

that real property G is the property described in the June 3, 1991 document.

(ii) Because real property G was not unambiguously described before the end of the identification period, no replacement property is identified before the end of the identification period.

Example 4. (i) On June 28, 1991, B identifies real properties H, J, and K as replacement properties by designating these properties as replacement properties in a written document signed by B and personally delivered to C. The written document provides that by August 1, 1991, B will orally inform C which of the identified properties C is to transfer to B. As of July 1, 1991, the fair market values of real properties H, J, and K are $75,000, $100,000, and $125,000, respectively.

(ii) Because B did not identify more than three properties as replacement properties, the requirements of the 3-property rule are satisfied, and real properties H, J, and K are all identified before the end of the identification period.

Example 5. (i) On May 17, 1991, B identifies real properties L, M, N, and P as replacement properties by designating these properties as replacement properties in a written document signed by B and personally delivered to C. The written document provides that by July 2, 1991, B will orally inform C which of the identified properties C is to transfer to B. As of July 1, 1991, the fair market values of real properties L, M, N, and P are $30,000, $40,000, $50,000, and $60,000, respectively.

(ii) Although B identified more than three properties as replacement properties, the aggregate fair market value of the identified properties as of the end of the identification period ($180,000) did not exceed 200 percent of the aggregate fair market value of real property X (200% × $100,000 = $200,000). Therefore, the requirements of the 200-percent rule are satisfied, and real properties L, M, N, and P are all identified before the end of the identification period.

Example 6. (i) On June 21, 1991, B identifies real properties Q, R, and S as replacement properties by designating these properties as replacement properties in a written document signed by B and mailed to C. On June 24, 1991, B identifies real properties T and U as replacement properties in a written document signed by B and mailed to C. On June 28, 1991, B revokes the identification of real properties Q and R in a written document signed by B and personally delivered to C.

(ii) B has revoked the identification of real properties Q and R in the manner provided by paragraph (c)(6) of this section. Identifications of replacement property that have been revoked in the manner provided by paragraph (c)(6) of this

Reg. § 1.1031(k)-1(c)(7)

section are not taken into account for purposes of applying the 3-property rule. Thus, as of June 28, 1991, B has identified only replacement properties S, T, and U for purposes of the 3-property rule. Because B did not identify more than three properties as replacement properties for purposes of the 3-property rule, the requirements of that rule are satisfied, and real properties S, T, and U are all identified before the end of the identification period.

Example 7. (i) On May 20, 1991, B identifies real properties V and W as replacement properties by designating these properties as replacement properties in a written document signed by B and personally delivered to C. On June 4, 1991, B identifies real properties Y and Z as replacement properties in the same manner. On June 5, 1991, B telephones C and orally revokes the identification of real properties V and W. As of July 1, 1991, the fair market values of real properties V, W, Y, and Z are $50,000, $70,000, $90,000, and $100,000, respectively. On July 31, 1991, C purchases real property Y and Z and transfers them to B.

(ii) Pursuant to paragraph (c)(6) of this section (relating to revocation of identification), the oral revocation of the identification of real properties V and W is invalid. Thus, the identification of real properties V and W is taken into account for purposes of determining whether the requirements of paragraph (c)(4) of this section (relating to the identification of alternative and multiple properties) are satisfied. Because B identified more than three properties and the aggregate fair market value of the identified properties as of the end of the identification period ($310,000) exceeds 200 percent of the fair market value of real property X (200% × $100,000 = $200,000), the requirements of paragraph (c)(4) of this section are not satisfied, and B is treated as if B did not identify any replacement property.

(d) *Receipt of identified replacement property*—(1) *In general.* For purposes of paragraph (b)(1)(ii) of this section (relating to the receipt requirement), the identified replacement property is received before the end of the exchange period only if the requirements of this paragraph (d) are satisfied with respect to the replacement property. In the case of a deferred exchange, the identified replacement property is received before the end of the exchange period if—

(i) The taxpayer receives the replacement property before the end of the exchange period, and

(ii) The replacement property received is substantially the same property as identified.

If the taxpayer has identified more than one replacement property, section 1031(a)(3)(B) and

this paragraph (d) are applied separately to each replacement property.

(2) *Examples.* This paragraph (d) may be illustrated by the following examples. The following facts are assumed: B, a calendar year taxpayer, and C agree to enter into a deferred exchange. Pursuant to their agreement, B transfers real property X to C on May 17, 1991. Real property X, which has been held by B for investment, is unencumbered and has a fair market value on May 17, 1991, of $100,000. On or before July 1, 1991 (the end of the identification period), B is to identify replacement property that is of a like kind to real property X. On or before November 13, 1991 (the end of the exchange period), C is required to purchase the property identified by B and to transfer that property to B. To the extent the fair market value of the replacement property transferred to B is greater or less than the fair market value of real property X, either B or C, as applicable, will make up the difference by paying cash to the other party after the date the replacement property is received by B. The replacement property is identified in a manner that satisfies paragraph (c) of this section (relating to identification of replacement property) and is of a like kind to real property X (determined without regard to section 1031(a)(3) and this section). B intends to hold any replacement property received for investment.

Example 1. (i) In the agreement, B identifies real properties J, K, and L as replacement properties. The agreement provides that by July 26, 1991, B will orally inform C which of the properties C is to transfer to B.

(ii) As of July 1, 1991, the fair market values of real properties J, K, and L are $75,000, $100,000, and $125,000, respectively. On July 26, 1991, B instructs C to acquire real property K. On October 31, 1991, C purchases real property K for $100,000 and transfers the property to B.

(iii) Because real property K was identified before the end of the identification period and was received before the end of the exchange period, the identification and receipt requirements of section 1031(a)(3) and this section are satisfied with respect to real property K.

Example 2. (i) In the agreement, B identifies real property P as replacement property. Real property P consists of two acres of unimproved land. On October 15, 1991, the owner of real property P erects a fence on the property. On November 1, 1991, C purchases real property P and transfers it to B.

(ii) The erection of the fence on real property P subsequent to its identification did not alter the basic nature or character of real property P as unimproved land. B is considered to have received substantially the same property as identified.

Example 3. (i) In the agreement, B identifies real property Q as replacement property. Real property Q consists of a barn on two acres of land and has a fair market value of $250,000 ($187,500 for the barn and underlying land and $87,500 for the remaining land). As of July 26, 1991, real property Q remains unchanged and has a fair market value of $250,000. On that date, at B's direction, C purchases the barn and underlying land for $187,500 and transfers it to B, and B pays $87,500 to C.

(ii) The barn and underlying land differ in basic nature or character from real property Q as a whole. B is not considered to have received substantially the same property as identified.

Example 4. (i) In the agreement, B identifies real property R as replacement property. Real property R consists of two acres of unimproved land and has a fair market value of $250,000. As of October 3, 1991, real property R remains unimproved and has a fair market value of $250,000. On that date, at B's direction, C purchases 1½ acres of real property R for $187,500 and transfers it to B, and B pays $87,500 to C.

(ii) The portion of real property R that B received does not differ from the basic nature or character of real property R as a whole. Moreover, the fair market value of the portion of real property R that B received ($187,500) is 75 percent of the fair market value of real property R as of the date of receipt. Accordingly, B is considered to have received substantially the same property as identified.

(e) *Special rules for identification and receipt of replacement property to be produced*—(1) *In general.* A transfer of relinquished property in a deferred exchange will not fail to qualify for nonrecognition of gain or loss under section 1031 merely because the replacement property is not in existence or is being produced at the time the property is identified as replacement property. For purposes of this paragraph (e), the terms "produced" and "production" have the same meanings as provided in section 263A(g)(1) and the regulations thereunder.

(2) *Identification of replacement property to be produced.* (i) In the case of replacement property that is to be produced, the replacement property must be identified as provided in paragraph (c) of this section (relating to identification of replacement property). For example, if the identified replacement property consists of improved real property where the improvements are to be constructed, the description of the replacement property satisfies the requirements of paragraph (c)(3) of this section (relating to description of

replacement property) if a legal description is provided for the underlying land and as much detail is provided regarding construction of the improvements as is practicable at the time the identification is made.

(ii) For purposes of paragraphs (c)(4)(i)(B) and (c)(5) of this section (relating to the 200-percent rule and incidental property), the fair market value of replacement property that is to be produced is its estimated fair market value as of the date it is expected to be received by the taxpayer.

(3) *Receipt of replacement property to be produced.* (i) For purposes of paragraph (d)(1)(ii) of this section (relating to receipt of the identified replacement property), in determining whether the replacement property received by the taxpayer is substantially the same property as identified where the identified replacement property is property to be produced, variations due to usual or typical production changes are not taken into account. However, if substantial changes are made in the property to be produced, the replacement property received will not be considered to be substantially the same property as identified.

(ii) If the identified replacement property is personal property to be produced, the replacement property received will not be considered to be substantially the same property as identified unless production of the replacement property received is completed on or before the date the property is received by the taxpayer.

(iii) If the identified replacement property is real property to be produced and the production of the property is not completed on or before the date the taxpayer receives the property, the property received will be considered to be substantially the same property as identified only if, had production been completed on or before the date the taxpayer receives the replacement property, the property received would have been considered to be substantially the same property as identified. Even so, the property received is considered to be substantially the same property as identified only to the extent the property received constitutes real property under local law.

(4) *Additional rules.* The transfer of relinquished property is not within the provisions of section 1031(a) if the relinquished property is transferred in exchange for services (including production services). Thus, any additional production occurring with respect to the replacement property after the property is received by the taxpayer will not be treated as the receipt of property of a like kind.

(5) *Example.* This paragraph (e) may be illustrated by the following example.

Example. (i) B, a calendar year taxpayer, and C agree to enter into a deferred exchange. Pursuant to their agreement, B transfers improved real property X and personal property Y to C on May 17, 1991. On or before November 13, 1991 (the end of the exchange period), C is required to transfer to B real property M, on which C is constructing improvements, and personal property N, which C is producing. C is obligated to complete the improvements and production regardless of when properties M and N are transferred to B. Properties M and N are identified in a manner that satisfies paragraphs (c)(relating to identification of replacement property) and (e)(2) of this section. In addition, properties M and N are of a like kind, respectively, to real property X and personal property Y (determined without regard to section 1031(a)(3) and this section). On November 13, 1991, when construction of the improvements to property M is 20 percent completed and the production of property N is 90 percent completed, C transfers to B property M and property N. If construction of the improvements had been completed, property M would have been considered to be substantially the same property as identified. Under local law, property M constitutes real property to the extent of the underlying land and the 20 percent of the construction that is completed

(ii) Because property N is personal property to be produced and production of property N is not completed before the date the property is received by B, property N is not considered to be substantially the same property as identified and is treated as property which is not of a like kind to property Y.

(iii) Property M is considered to be substantially the same property as identified to the extent of the underlying land and the 20 percent of the construction that is completed when property M is received by B. However, any additional construction performed by C with respect to property M after November 13, 1991, is not treated as the receipt of property of a like kind.

(f) *Receipt of money or other property*—(1) *In general.* A transfer of relinquished property in a deferred exchange is not within the provisions of section 1031(a) if, as part of the consideration, the taxpayer receives money or other property. However, such a transfer, if otherwise qualified, will be within the provisions of either section 1031(b) or (c). See § 1.1031(a)-1(a)(2). In addition, in the case of a transfer of relinquished property in a deferred exchange, gain or loss may be recognized if the taxpayer actually or constructively receives money or other property before the taxpayer actually receives like-kind replacement property. If the taxpayer actually or constructively receives money or other property in the full amount of the

consideration for the relinquished property before the taxpayer actually receives like-kind replacement property, the transaction will constitute a sale and not a deferred exchange, even though the taxpayer may ultimately receive like-kind replacement property.

(2) *Actual and constructive receipt.* Except as provided in paragraph (g) of this section (relating to safe harbors), for purposes of section 1031 and this section, the determination of whether (or the extent to which) the taxpayer is in actual or constructive receipt of money or other property before the taxpayer actually receives like-kind replacement property is made under the general rules concerning actual and constructive receipt and without regard to the taxpayer's method of accounting. The taxpayer is in actual receipt of money or property at the time the taxpayer actually receives the money or property or receives the economic benefit of the money or property. The taxpayer is in constructive receipt of money or property at the time the money or property is credited to the taxpayer's account, set apart for the taxpayer, or otherwise made available so that the taxpayer may draw upon it at any time or so that the taxpayer can draw upon it if notice of intention to draw is given. Although the taxpayer is not in constructive receipt of money or property if the taxpayer's control of its receipt is subject to substantial limitations or restrictions, the taxpayer is in constructive receipt of the money or property at the time the limitations or restrictions lapse, expire, or are waived. In addition, actual or constructive receipt of money or property by an agent of the taxpayer (determined without regard to paragraph (k) of this section) is actual or constructive receipt by the taxpayer.

(3) *Example.* This paragraph (f) may be illustrated by the following example.

Example. (i) B, a calendar year taxpayer, and C agree to enter into a deferred exchange. Pursuant to the agreement, on May 17, 1991, B transfers real property X to C. Real property X, which has been held by B for investment, is unencumbered and has a fair market value on May 17, 1991, of $100,000. On or before July 1, 1991 (the end of the identification period), B is to identify replacement property that is of a like kind to real property X. On or before November 13, 1991 (the end of the exchange period), C is required to purchase the property identified by B and to transfer that property to B. At any time after May 17, 1991, and before C has purchased the replacement property, B has the right, upon notice, to demand that C pay $100,000 in lieu of acquiring and transferring the replacement property. Pursuant to the agreement, B identifies replacement property, and C purchases the replacement property and transfers it to B.

Reg. § 1.1031(k)-1(f)(2)

(ii) Under the agreement, B has the unrestricted right to demand the payment of $100,000 as of May 17, 1991. B is therefore in constructive receipt of $100,000 on that date. Because B is in constructive receipt of money in the full amount of the consideration for the relinquished property before B actually receives the like-kind replacement property, the transaction constitutes a sale, and the transfer of real property X does not qualify for nonrecognition of gain or loss under section 1031. B is treated as if B received the $100,000 in consideration for the sale of real property X and then purchased the like-kind replacement property.

(iii) If B's right to demand payment of the $100,000 were subject to a substantial limitation or restriction (e.g., the agreement provided that B had no right to demand payment before November 14, 1991 (the end of the exchange period)), then, for purposes of this section, B would not be in actual or constructive receipt of the money unless (or until) the limitation or restriction lapsed, expired, or was waived.

(g) *Safe harbors*—(1) *In general.* Paragraphs (g)(2) through (g)(5) of this section set forth four safe harbors the use of which will result in a determination that the taxpayer is not in actual or constructive receipt of money or other property for purposes of section 1031 and this section. More than one safe harbor can be used in the same deferred exchange, but the terms and conditions of each must be separately satisfied. For purposes of the safe harbor rules, the term "taxpayer" does not include a person or entity utilized in a safe harbor (e.g., a qualified intermediary). See paragraph (g)(8), *Example 3(v),* of this section.

(2) *Security or guarantee arrangements.* (i) In the case of a deferred exchange, the determination of whether the taxpayer is in actual or constructive receipt of money or other property before the taxpayer actually receives like-kind replacement property will be made without regard to the fact that the obligation of the taxpayer's transferee to transfer the replacement property to the taxpayer is or may be secured or guaranteed by one or more of the following—

(A) A mortgage, deed of trust, or other security interest in property (other than cash or a cash equivalent),

(B) A standby letter of credit which satisfies all of the requirements of § 15A.453-1(b)(3)(iii) and which may not be drawn upon in the absence of a default of the transferee's obligation to transfer like-kind replacement property to the taxpayer, or

(C) A guarantee of a third party.

(ii) Paragraph (g)(2)(i) of this section ceases to apply at the time the taxpayer has an immediate ability or unrestricted right to receive money or other property pursuant to the security or guarantee arrangement.

(3) *Qualified escrow accounts and qualified trusts.* (i) In the case of a deferred exchange, the determination of whether the taxpayer is in actual or constructive receipt of money or other property before the taxpayer actually receives like-kind replacement property will be made without regard to the fact that the obligation of the taxpayer's transferee to transfer the replacement property to the taxpayer is or may be secured by cash or a cash equivalent if the cash or cash equivalent is held in a qualified escrow account or in a qualified trust.

(ii) A qualified escrow account is an escrow account wherein—

(A) The escrow holder is not the taxpayer or a disqualified person (as defined in paragraph (k) of this section), and

(B) The escrow agreement expressly limits the taxpayer's rights to receive, pledge, borrow, or otherwise obtain the benefits of the cash or cash equivalent held in the escrow account as provided in paragraph (g)(6) of this section.

(iii) A qualified trust is a trust wherein—

(A) The trustee is not the taxpayer or a disqualified person (as defined in paragraph (k) of this section, except that for this purpose the relationship between the taxpayer and the trustee created by the qualified trust will not be considered a relationship under section 267(b)), and

(B) The trust agreement expressly limits the taxpayer's rights to receive, pledge, borrow, or otherwise obtain the benefits of the cash or cash equivalent held by the trustee as provided in paragraph (g)(6) of this section.

(iv) Paragraph (g)(3)(i) of this section ceases to apply at the time the taxpayer has an immediate ability or unrestricted right to receive, pledge, borrow, or otherwise obtain the benefits of the cash or cash equivalent held in the qualified escrow account or qualified trust. Rights conferred upon the taxpayer under state law to terminate or dismiss the escrow holder of a qualified escrow account or the trustee of a qualified trust are disregarded for this purpose.

(v) A taxpayer may receive money or other property directly from a party to the exchange, but not from a qualified escrow account or a qualified trust, without affecting the application of paragraph (g)(3)(i) of this section.

(4) *Qualified intermediaries.* (i) In the case of a taxpayer's transfer of relinquished property involving a qualified intermediary, the qualified intermediary is not considered the agent of the taxpayer for purposes of section 1031(a). In such

Reg. § 1.1031(k)-1(g)(1)

a case, the taxpayer's transfer of relinquished property and subsequent receipt of like-kind replacement property is treated as an exchange, and the determination of whether the taxpayer is in actual or constructive receipt of money or other property before the taxpayer actually receives like-kind replacement property is made as if the qualified intermediary is not the agent of the taxpayer.

(ii) Paragraph (g)(4)(i) of this section applies only if the agreement between the taxpayer and the qualified intermediary expressly limits the taxpayer's rights to receive, pledge, borrow, or otherwise obtain the benefits of money or other property held by the qualified intermediary as provided in paragraph (g)(6) of this section.

(iii) A qualified intermediary is a person who—

(A) Is not the taxpayer or a disqualified person (as defined in paragraph (k) of this section), and

(B) Enters into a written agreement with the taxpayer (the "exchange agreement") and, as required by the exchange agreement, acquires the relinquished property from the taxpayer, transfers the relinquished property, acquires the replacement property, and transfers the replacement property to the taxpayer.

(iv) Regardless of whether an intermediary acquires and transfers property under general tax principals [principles], solely for purposes of paragraph (g)(4)(iii)(B) of this section—

(A) An intermediary is treated as acquiring and transferring property if the intermediary acquires and transfers legal title to that property,

(B) An intermediary is treated as acquiring and transferring the relinquished property if the intermediary (either on its own behalf or as the agent of any party to the transaction) enters into an agreement with a person other than the taxpayer for the transfer of the relinquished property to that person and, pursuant to that agreement, the relinquised property is transferred to that person, and

(C) An intermediary is treated as acquiring and transferring replacement property if the intermediary (either on its own behalf or as the agent of any party to the transaction) enters into an agreement with the owner of the replacement property for the transfer of that property and, pursuant to that agreement, the replacement property is transferred to the taxpayer.

(v) Solely for purposes of paragraphs (g)(4)(iii) and (g)(4)(iv) of this section, an intermediary is treated as entering into an agreement if the rights of a party to the agreement are assigned to the intermediary and all parties to that agreement are notified in writing of the assignment on or before the date of the relevant transfer of property. For example, if a taxpayer enters into an agreement for the transfer of relinquished property and thereafter assigns its rights in that agreement to an intermediary and all parties to that agreement are notified in writing of the assignment on or before the date of the transfer of the relinquished property, the intermediary is treated as entering into that agreement. If the relinquished property is transferred pursuant to that agreement, the intermediary is treated as having acquired and transferred the relinquished property.

(vi) Paragraph (g)(4)(i) of this section ceases to apply at the time the taxpayer has an immediate ability or unrestricted right to receive, pledge, borrow, or otherwise obtain the benefits of money or other property held by the qualified intermediary. Rights conferred upon the taxpayer under state law to terminate or dismiss the qualified intermediary are disregarded for this purpose.

(vii) A taxpayer may receive money or other property directly from a party to the transaction other than the qualified intermediary without affecting the application of paragraph (g)(4)(i) of this section.

(5) *Interest and growth factors.* In the case of a deferred exchange, the determination of whether the taxpayer is in actual or constructive receipt of money or other property before the taxpayer actually receives the like-kind replacement property will be made without regard to the fact that the taxpayer is or may be entitled to receive any interest or growth factor with respect to the deferred exchange. The preceding sentence applies only if the agreement pursuant to which the taxpayer is or may be entitled to the interest or growth factor expressly limits the taxpayer's rights to receive the interest or growth factor as provided in paragraph (g)(6) of this section. For additional rules concerning interest or growth factors, see paragraph (h) of this section.

(6) *Additional restrictions on safe harbors under paragraphs (g)(3) through (g)(5).* (i) An agreement limits a taxpayer's rights as provided in this paragraph (g)(6) only if the agreement provides that the taxpayer has no rights, except as provided in paragraphs (g)(6)(ii) and (g)(6)(iii) of this section, to receive, pledge, borrow, or otherwise obtain the benefits of money or other property before the end of the exchange period.

(ii) The agreement may provide that if the taxpayer has not identified replacement property by the end of the identification period, the taxpayer may have rights to receive, pledge, borrow,

Reg. § 1.1031(k)-1(g)(6)

or otherwise obtain the benefits of money or other property at any time after the end of the identification period.

(iii) The agreement may provide that if the taxpayer has identified replacement property, the taxpayer may have rights to receive, pledge, borrow, or otherwise obtain the benefits of money or other property upon or after—

(A) The receipt by the taxpayer of all of the replacement property to which the taxpayer is entitled under the exchange agreement, or

(B) The occurrence after the end of the identification period of a material and substantial contingency that—

(1) Relates to the deferred exchange,

(2) Is provided for in writing, and

(3) Is beyond the control of the taxpayer and of any disqualified person (as defined in paragraph (k) of this section), other than the person obligated to transfer the replacement property to the taxpayer.

(7) *Items disregarded in applying safe harbors under paragraphs (g)(3) through (g)(5).* In determining whether a safe harbor under paragraphs (g)(3) through (g)(5) of this section ceases to apply and whether the taxpayer's rights to receive, pledge, borrow, or otherwise obtain the benefits of money or other property are expressly limited as provided in paragraph (g)(6) of this section, the taxpayer's receipt of or right to receive any of the following items will be disregarded—

(i) Items that a seller may receive as a consequence of the disposition of property and that are not included in the amount realized from the disposition of property (e.g., prorated rents), and

(ii) Transactional items that relate to the disposition of the relinquished property or to the acquisition of the replacement property and appear under local standards in the typical closing statement as the responsibility of a buyer or seller (e.g., commissions, prorated taxes, recording or transfer taxes, and title company fees).

* * *

(m) *Definition of fair market value.* For purposes of this section, the fair market value of property means the fair market value of the property without regard to any liabilities secured by the property.

(n) *No inference with respect to actual or constructive receipt rules outside of section 1031.* The rules provided in this section relating to actual or constructive receipt are intended to be rules for determining whether there is actual or constructive receipt in the case of a deferred exchange. No inference is intended regarding the application of these rules for purposes of determining whether actual or constructive receipt exists for any other purpose.

* * *

[Reg. § 1.1031(k)-1.]

☐ [*T.D.* 8346, 4-25-91. *Amended by T.D.* 8535, 4-19-94 *and T.D.* 8982, 1-31-2002.]

§ 1.1032-1. Disposition by a corporation of its own capital stock.—(a) The disposition by a corporation of shares of its own stock (including treasury stock) for money or other property does not give rise to taxable gain or deductible loss to the corporation regardless of the nature of the transaction or the facts and circumstances involved. For example, the receipt by a corporation of the subscription price of shares of its stock upon their original issuance gives rise to neither taxable gain nor deductible loss, whether the subscription or issue price be equal to, in excess of, or less than, the par or stated value of such stock. Also, the exchange or sale by a corporation of its own shares for money or other property does not result in taxable gain or deductible loss, even though the corporation deals in such shares as it might in the shares of another corporation. A transfer by a corporation of shares of its own stock (including treasury stock) as compensation for services is considered, for purposes of section 1032(a), as a disposition by the corporation of such shares for money or other property.

(b) Section 1032(a) does not apply to the acquisition by a corporation of shares of its own stock except where the corporation acquires such shares in exchange for shares of its own stock (including treasury stock). See paragraph (e) of § 1.311-1, relating to treatment of acquisition of a corporation's own stock. Section 1032(a) also does not relate to the tax treatment of the recipient of a corporation's stock.

(c) Where a corporation acquires shares of its own stock in exchange for shares of its own stock (including treasury stock) the transaction may qualify not only under section 1032(a), but also under section 368(a)(1)(E)(recapitalization) or section 305(a) (distribution of stock and stock rights).

(d) For basis of property acquired by a corporation in connection with a transaction to which section 351 applies or in connection with a reorganization, see section 362. For basis of property acquired by a corporation in a transaction to which section 1032 applies but which does not qualify under any other nonrecognition provision, see section 1012. [Reg. § 1.1032-1.]

☐ [*T.D.* 6210, 11-6-56.]

§ 1.1032-2. Disposition by a corporation of stock of a controlling corporation in certain triangular reorganizations.—(a) *Scope.* This section provides rules for certain triangular reorganizations described in § 1.358-6(b) when the acquiring corporation (*S*) acquires property or stock of another corporation (*T*) in exchange for stock of the corporation (*P*) in control of S.

(b) *General nonrecognition of gain or loss.* For purposes of § 1.1032-1(a), in the case of a forward triangular merger, a triangular C reorganization, or a triangular B reorganization (as described in § 1.358-6(b)), *P* stock provided by *P* to *S*, or directly to *T* or *T*'s shareholders on behalf of *S*, pursuant to the plan of reorganization is treated as a disposition by *P* of shares of its own stock for *T*'s assets or stock, as applicable. For rules governing the use of *P* stock in a reverse triangular merger, see section 361.

(c) *Treatment of S. S* must recognize gain or loss on its exchange of *P* stock as consideration in a forward triangular merger, a triangular C reorganization, or a triangular B reorganization (as described in § 1.358-6(b)), if *S* did not receive the *P* stock from *P* pursuant to the plan of reorganization. See § 1.358-6(d) for the effect on *P*'s basis in its *S* or *T* stock, as applicable. For rules governing *S*'s use of *P* stock in a reverse triangular merger, see section 361.

(d) *Examples.* The rules of this section are illustrated by the following examples. For purposes of these examples, *P*, *S*, and *T* are domestic corporations, P and *S* do not file consolidated returns *P* owns all of the only class of *S* stock, the *P* stock exchanged in the transaction satisfies the requirements of the applicable reorganization provisions, and the facts set forth the only corporate activity.

Example 1. Forward triangular merger solely for P stock. (a) *Facts. T* has assets with an aggregate basis of $60 and fair market value of $100 and no liabilities. Pursuant to a plan, *P* forms *S* by transferring $100 of *P* stock to *S* and *T* merges into *S*. In the merger, the *T* shareholders receive, in exchange for their *T* stock, the *P* stock that *P* transferred to S. The transaction is a reorganization to which sections 368(a)(1)(A) and (a)(2)(D) apply.

(b) *No gain or loss recognized on the use of P stock.* Under paragraph (b) of this section, the *P* stock provided by *P* pursuant to the plan of reorganization is treated for purposes of § 1.1032-1 (a) as disposed of by *P* for the *T* assets acquired by *S* in the merger. Consequently, neither *P* nor *S* has taxable gain or deductible loss on the exchange.

Example 2. Forward triangular merger solely for P stock provided in part by S. (a) *Facts. T* has assets with an aggregate basis of $60 and fair market value of $100 and no liabilities. *S* is an operating company with substantial assets that has been in existence for several years. *S* also owns *P* stock with a $20 adjusted basis and $30 fair market value. *S* acquired the *P* stock in an unrelated transaction several years before the reorganization. Pursuant to a plan, *P* transfers additional *P* stock worth $70 to *S* and *T* merges into *S*. In the merger, the *T* shareholders receive $100 of *P* stock ($70 of *P* stock provided by *P* to *S* as part of the plan and $30 of *P* stock held by *S* previously). The transaction is a reorganization to which sections 368(a)(1)(A) and (a)(2)(D) apply.

(b) *Gain or loss recognized by S on the use of its P stock.* Under paragraph (b) of this section, the $70 of *P* stock provided by *P* pursuant to the plan of reorganization is treated as disposed of by *P* for the *T* assets acquired by *S* in the merger. Consequently, neither *P* nor *S* has taxable gain or deductible loss on the exchange of those shares. Under paragraph (c) of this section, however, *S* recognizes $10 of gain on the exchange of its *P* stock in the reorganization because *S* did not receive the *P* stock from *P* pursuant to the plan of reorganization. See § 1.358-6(d) for the effect on *P*'s basis in its *S* stock.

* * *

[Reg. § 1.1032-2.]

☐ [*T.D.* 8648, 12-20-95. *Amended by T.D.* 8883, 5-11-2000.]

§ 1.1032-3. Disposition of stock or stock options in certain transactions not qualifying under any other nonrecognition provision.—(a) *Scope.* This section provides rules for certain transactions in which a corporation or a partnership (the acquiring entity) acquires money or other property (as defined in § 1.1032-1) in exchange, in whole or in part, for stock of a corporation (the issuing corporation).

(b) *Nonrecognition of gain or loss*—(1) *General rule.* In a transaction to which this section applies; no gain or loss is recognized on the disposition of the issuing corporation's stock by the acquiring entity. The transaction is treated as if, immediately before the acquiring entity disposes of the stock of the issuing corporation, the acquiring entity purchased the issuing corporation's stock from the issuing corporation for fair market value with cash contributed to the acquiring entity by the issuing corporation (or, if necessary, through intermediate corporations or partnerships). For rules that may apply in determining the issuing corporation's adjustment to basis in the acquiring entity (or, if necessary, in determining the adjustment to basis in intermediate entities), see sections 358, 722, and the regulations thereunder.

Reg. § 1.1032-3(b)(1)

(2) *Special rule for actual payment for stock of the issuing corporation.* If the issuing corporation receives money or other property in payment for its stock, the amount of cash deemed contributed under paragraph (b)(1) of this section is the difference between the fair market value of the issuing corporation stock and the amount of money or the fair market value of other property that the issuing corporation receives as payment.

(c) *Applicability.* The rules of this section apply only if, pursuant to a plan to acquire money or other property—

(1) The acquiring entity acquires stock of the issuing corporation directly or indirectly from the issuing corporation in a transaction in which, but for this section, the basis of the stock of the issuing corporation in the hands of the acquiring entity would be determined, in whole or in part, with respect to the issuing corporation's basis in the issuing corporation's stock under section 362(a) or 723 (provided that, in the case of an indirect acquisition by the acquiring entity, the transfers of issuing corporation stock through intermediate entities occur immediately after one another);

(2) The acquiring entity immediately transfers the stock of the issuing corporation to acquire money or other property (from a person other than an entity from which the stock was directly or indirectly acquired);

(3) The party receiving stock of the issuing corporation in the exchange specified in paragraph (c)(2) of this section from the acquiring entity does not receive a substituted basis in the stock of the issuing corporation within the meaning of section 7701(a)(42); and

(4) The issuing corporation stock is not exchanged for stock of the issuing corporation.

(d) *Stock options.* The rules of this section shall apply to an option issued by a corporation to buy or sell its own stock in the same manner as the rules of this section apply to the stock of an issuing corporation.

(e) *Examples.* The following examples illustrate the application of this section:

Example 1. (i) X, a corporation, owns all of the stock of Y corporation. Y reaches an agreement with C, an individual, to acquire a truck from C in exchange for 10 shares of X stock with a fair market value of $100. To effectuate Y's agreement with C, X transfers to Y the X stock in a transaction in which, but for this section, the basis of the X stock in the hands of Y would be determined with respect to X's basis in the X stock under section 362(a). Y immediately transfers the X stock to C to acquire the truck.

(ii) In this *Example 1*, no gain or loss is recognized on the disposition of the X stock by Y. Immediately before Y's disposition of the X stock, Y is treated as purchasing the X stock from X for $100 of cash contributed to Y by X. Under section 358, X's basis in its Y stock is increased by $100.

Example 2. (i) Assume the same facts as *Example 1*, except that, rather than X stock, X transfers an option with a fair market value of $100 to purchase X stock.

(ii) In this *Example 2*, no gain or loss is recognized on the disposition of the X stock option by Y. Immediately before Y's disposition of the X stock option, Y is treated as purchasing the X stock option from X for $100 of cash contributed to Y by X. Under section 358, X's basis in its Y stock is increased by $100.

Example 3. (i) X, a corporation, owns all of the outstanding stock of Y corporation. Y is a partner in partnership Z. Z reaches an agreement with C, an individual, to acquire a truck from C in exchange for 10 shares of X stock with a fair market value of $100. To effectuate Z's agreement with C, X transfers to Y the X stock in a transaction in which, but for this section, the basis of the X stock in the hands of Y would be determined with respect to X's basis in the X stock under section 362(a). Y immediately transfers the X stock to Z in a transaction in which, but for this section, the basis of the X stock in the hands of Z would be determined under section 723. Z immediately transfers the X stock to C to acquire the truck.

(ii) In this *Example 3*, no gain or loss is recognized on the disposition of the X stock by Z. Immediately before Z's disposition of the X stock, Z is treated as purchasing the X stock from X for $100 of cash indirectly contributed to Z by X through an intermediate corporation, Y. Under section 722, Y's basis in its Z partnership interest is increased by $100, and, under section 358, X's basis in its Y stock is increased by $100.

Example 4. (i) X, a corporation, owns all of the outstanding stock of Y corporation. B, an individual, is an employee of Y. Pursuant to an agreement between X and Y to compensate B for services provided to Y, X transfers to B 10 shares of X stock with a fair market value of $100. Under § 1.83-6(d), but for this section, the transfer of X stock by X to the would be treated as a contribution of the X stock by X to the capital of Y, and immediately thereafter, a transfer of the X stock by Y to B. But for this section, the basis of the X stock in the hands of Y would be determined with respect to X's basis in the X stock under section 362(a).

(ii) In this *Example 4*, no gain or loss is recognized on the deemed disposition of the X stock by Y. Immediately before Y's deemed disposition of the X stock, Y is treated as purchasing the X stock from X for $100 of cash contributed to Y by X. Under section 358, X's basis in its Y stock is increased by $100.

Example 5. (i) X, a corporation, owns all of the outstanding stock of Y corporation. B, an individual, is an employee of Y. To compensate B for services provided to Y, B is offered the opportunity to purchase 10 shares of X stock with a fair market value of $100 at a reduced price of $80. B transfers $80 and Y transfers $10 to X as partial payment for the X stock.

(ii) In this *Example 5*, no gain or loss is recognized on the deemed disposition of the X stock by Y. Immediately before Y's deemed disposition of the X stock, Y is treated as purchasing the X stock from X for $100, $80 of which Y is deemed to have received from B, $10 of which originated with Y, and $10 of which is deemed to have been contributed to Y by X. Under section 358, X's basis in its Y stock is increased by $10.

Example 6. (i) X, a corporation, owns stock of Y. To compensate Y's employee, B, for services provided to Y, X issues 10 shares of X stock to B, subject to a substantial risk of forfeiture. B does not have an election under section 83(b) in effect with respect to the X stock. X retains the only reversionary interest in the X stock in the event that B forfeits the right to the stock. Several years after X's transfer of the X shares, the stock vests. At the time the stock vests, the 10 shares of X stock have a fair market value of $100. Under § 1.83-6(d), but for this section, the transfer of the X stock by X to B would be treated, at the time the stock vests, as a contribution of the X stock by X to the capital of Y, and immediately thereafter, a disposition of the X stock by Y to B. The basis of the X stock in the hands of Y, but for this section, would be determined with respect to X's basis in the X stock under section 362(a).

(ii) In this *Example 6*, no gain or loss is recognized on the deemed disposition of X stock by Y when the stock vests Immediately before Y's deemed disposition of the X stock, Y is treated as purchasing X's stock from X for $100 of cash contributed to Y by X. Under section 358, X's basis in its Y stock is increased by $100.

Example 7. (i) Assume the same facts as in *Example 6*, except that Y (rather than X) retains a reversionary interest in the X stock in the event that B forfeits the right to the stock. Several years after X's transfer of the X shares, the stock vests.

(ii) In this *Example 7*, this section does not apply to Y's deemed disposition of the X shares because Y is not deemed to have transferred the X stock to B immediately after receiving the stock from X. For the tax consequences to Y on the deemed disposition of the X stock, see § 1.83-6(b).

Example 8. (i) X, a corporation, owns all of the outstanding stock of Y corporation. In Year 1, X issues to Y's employee, B, a nonstatutory stock option to purchase 10 shares of X stock as compensation for services provided to Y. The option is exercisable against X and does not have a readily ascertainable fair market value (determined under § 1.83-7(b)) at the time the option is granted. In Year 2, B exercises the option by paying X the strike price of $80 for the X stock, which then has a fair market value of $100.

(ii) In this *Example 8*, because, under section 83(e)(3), section 83(a) does not apply to the grant of the option, paragraph (d) of this section also does not apply to the grant of the option. Section 83 and § 1.1032-3 apply in Year 2 when the option is exercised; thus, no gain or loss is recognized on the deemed disposition of X stock by Y in Year 2. Immediately before Y's deemed disposition of the X stock in Year 2, Y is treated as purchasing the X stock from X for $100, $80 of which Y is deemed to have received from B and the remaining $20 of which is deemed to have been contributed to Y by X. Under section 358, X's basis in its Y stock is increased by $20.

Example 9. (i) A, an individual, owns a majority of the stock of X. X owns stock of Y constituting control of Y within the meaning of section 368(c). A transfers 10 shares of its X stock to B, a key employee of Y. The fair market value of the 10 shares on the date of transfer was $100.

(ii) In this *Example 9*, A is treated as making a nondeductible contribution of the 10 shares of X to the capital of X, and no gain or loss is recognized by A as a result of this transfer. See *Commissioner v. Fink*, 483 U.S. 89 (1987). A must allocate his basis in the transferred shares to his remaining shares of X stock. No gain or loss is recognized on the deemed disposition of the X stock by Y. Immediately before Y's disposition of the X stock, Y is treated as purchasing the X stock from X for $100 of cash contributed to Y by X. Under section 358, X's basis in its Y stock is increased by $100.

Example 10. (i) In Year 1, X, a corporation, forms a trust which will be used to satisfy deferred compensation obligations owed by Y, X's wholly owned subsidiary, to Y's employees. X funds the trust with X stock, which would revert to X upon termination of the trust, subject to the employees' rights to be paid the deferred compensation due to them. The creditors of X can reach all the trust assets upon the insolvency of X. Similarly, Y's creditors can reach all the trust assets upon the insolvency of Y. In Year 5, the trust transfers X stock to the employees of Y in satisfaction of the deferred compensation obligation.

Reg. § 1.1032-3(e)

(ii) In this *Example 10*, *X* is considered to be the grantor of the trust, and, under section 677, *X* is also the owner of the trust. Any income earned by the trust would be reflected on *X*'s income tax return. *Y* is not considered a grantor or owner of the trust corpus at the time *X* transfers *X* stock to the trust. In Year 5, when employees of *Y* receive *X* stock in satisfaction of the deferred compensation obligation, no gain or loss is recognized on the deemed disposition of the *X* stock by *Y*. Immediately before *Y*'s deemed disposition of the *X* stock, *Y* is treated as purchasing the *X* stock from *X* for fair market value using cash contributed to *Y* by *X*. Under section 358, *X*'s basis in its *Y* stock increases by the amount of cash deemed contributed.

(f) *Effective date.* This section applies to transfers of stock or stock options of the issuing corporation occurring on or after May 16, 2000. [Reg. § 1.1032-3.]

☐ [*T.D.* 8883, 5-11-2000 (*corrected* 6-14-2000).]

§ 1.1033(a)-1. Involuntary conversion; nonrecognition of gain.—(a) *In general.* Section 1033 applies to cases where property is compulsorily or involuntarily converted. An "involuntary conversion" may be the result of the destruction of property in whole or in part, the theft of property, the seizure of property, the requisition or condemnation of property, or the threat or imminence of requisition or condemnation of property. An "involuntary conversion" may be a conversion into similar property or into money or into dissimilar property. Section 1033 provides that, under certain specified circumstances, any gain which is realized from an involuntary conversion shall not be recognized. In cases where property is converted into other property similar or related in service or use to the converted property, no gain shall be recognized regardless of when the disposition of the converted property occurred and regardless of whether or not the taxpayer elects to have the gain not recognized. In other types of involuntary conversion cases, however, the proceeds arising from the disposition of the converted property must (within the time limits specified) be reinvested in similar property in order to avoid recognition of any gain realized. Section 1033 applies only with respect to gains; losses from involuntary conversions are recognized or not recognized without regard to this section.

(b) *Special rules.* For rules relating to the application of section 1033 to involuntary conversions of a principal residence with respect to which an election has been made under section 121 (relating to gain from sale or exchange of residence of individual who has attained age 65), see paragraph (g) of § 1.121-5. For rules applicable to involuntary conversions of a principal residence occurring before January 1, 1951, see § 1.1033(a)-3. For rules applicable to involuntary conversions of a principal residence occurring after December 31, 1950, and before January 1, 1954, see paragraph (h)(1) of § 1.1034-1. For rules applicable to involuntary conversions of a personal residence occurring after December 31, 1953, see § 1.1033(a)-3. For special rules relating to the election to have section 1034 apply to certain involuntary conversions of a principal residence occurring after December 31, 1957, see paragraph (h) (2) of § 1.1034-1. For special rules relating to certain involuntary conversions of real property held either for productive use in trade or business or for investment and occurring after December 31, 1957, see § 1.1033(g)-1. See also special rules applicable to involuntary conversions of property sold pursuant to reclamation laws, livestock destroyed by disease, and livestock sold on account of drought provided in § § 1.1033(c)-1, 1.1033(d)-1, and 1.1033(e)-1, respectively. For rules relating to basis of property acquired through involuntary conversions, see § 1.1033(b)-1. For determination of the period for which the taxpayer has held property acquired as a result of certain involuntary conversions, see section 1223 and regulations issued thereunder. For treatment of gains from involuntary conversions as capital gains in certain cases, see section 1231(a) and regulations issued thereunder. For portion of war loss recoveries treated as gain on involuntary conversion, see section 1332(b)(3) and regulations issued thereunder. [Reg. § 1.1033(a)-1.]

☐ [*T.D.* 6222, 1-9-57. *Amended by T.D.* 6338, 12-11-58, *T.D.* 6453, 2-6-60, *T.D.* 6856, 10-19-65, *T.D.* 7625, 5-29-79 *and T.D.* 7758, 1-16-81.]

§ 1.1033(a)-2. Involuntary conversion into similar property, into money or into dissimilar property.—(a) *In general.* The term "disposition of the converted property" means the destruction, theft, seizure, requisition, or condemnation of the converted property, or the sale or exchange of such property under threat or imminence of requisition or condemnation.

(b) *Conversion into similar property.* If property (as a result of its destruction in whole or in part, theft, seizure, or requisition or condemnation or threat or imminence thereof) is compulsorily or involuntarily converted only into property similar or related in service or use to the property so converted, no gain shall be recognized. Such nonrecognition of gain is mandatory.

(c) *Conversion into money or into dissimilar property.* (1) If property (as a result of its destruction in whole or in part, theft, seizure, or requisition or condemnation or threat or imminence thereof) is compulsorily or involuntarily converted into money or into property not similar or related in service or use to the converted property, the gain, if any, shall be recognized, at the election of the taxpayer, only to the extent that the amount realized upon such conversion exceeds the cost of other property purchased by the taxpayer which is similar or related in service or use to the property so converted, or the cost of stock of a corporation owning such other property which is purchased by the taxpayer in the acquisition of control of such corporation, if the taxpayer purchased such other property, or such stock, for the purpose of replacing the property so converted and during the period specified in subparagraph (3) of this paragraph. For the purposes of section 1033 the term "control" means the ownership of stock possessing at least 80 percent of the total combined voting power of all classes of stock entitled to vote and at least 80 percent of the total number of shares of all other classes of stock of the corporation.

(2) All of the details in connection with an involuntary conversion of property at a gain (including those relating to the replacement of the converted property, or a decision not to replace, or the expiration of the period for replacement) shall be reported in the return for the taxable year or years in which any of such gain is realized. An election to have such gain recognized only to the extent provided in subparagraph (1) of this paragraph shall be made by including such gain in gross income for such year or years only to such extent. If, at the time of filing such a return, the period within which the converted property must be replaced has expired, or if such an election is not desired, the gain should be included in gross income for such year or years in the regular manner. A failure to so include such gain in gross income in the regular manner shall be deemed to be an election by the taxpayer to have such gain recognized only to the extent provided in subparagraph (1) of this paragraph even though the details in connection with the conversion are not reported in such return. If, after having made an election under section 1033(a)(2), the converted property is not replaced within the required period of time, or replacement is made at a cost lower than was anticipated at the time of the election, or a decision is made not to replace, the tax liability for the year or years for which the election was made shall be recomputed. Such recomputation should be in the form of an "amended return". If a decision is made to make an election under section 1033(a)(2) after the fil-

ing of the return and the payment of the tax for the year or years in which any of the gain on an involuntary conversion is realized and before the expiration of the period within which the converted property must be replaced, a claim for credit or refund for such year or years should be filed. If the replacement of the converted property occurs in a year or years in which none of the gain on the conversion is realized, all of the details in connection with such replacement shall be reported in the return for such year or years.

(3) The period referred to in subparagraphs (1) and (2) of this paragraph is the period of time commencing with the date of the disposition of the converted property, or the date of the beginning of the threat or imminence of requisition or condemnation of the converted property, whichever is earlier, and ending two years (or, in the case of a disposition occurring before December 31, 1969, one year) after the close of the first taxable year in which any part of the gain upon the conversion is realized, or at the close of such later date as may be designated pursuant to an application of the taxpayer. Such application shall be made prior to the expiration of two years (or, in the case of a disposition occurring before December 31, 1969, one year) after the close of the first taxable year in which any part of the gain from the conversion is realized, unless the taxpayer can show to the satisfaction of the district director—

(i) reasonable cause for not having filed the application within the required period of time, and

(ii) the filing of such application was made within a reasonable time after the expiration of the required period of time.

See section 1033(g)(4) and § 1.1033(g)-1 for the circumstances under which, in the case of the conversion of real property held either for productive use in trade or business or for investment, the 2-year period referred to in this paragraph (c)(3) shall be extended to 3 years.

The application shall contain all of the details in connection with the involuntary conversion. Such application shall be made to the district director for the internal revenue district in which the return is filed for the first taxable year in which any of the gain from the involuntary conversion is realized. No extension of time shall be granted pursuant to such application unless the taxpayer can show reasonable cause for not being able to replace the converted property within the required period of time.

(4) Property or stock purchased before the disposition of the converted property shall be considered to have been purchased for the purpose of replacing the converted property only if such

property or stock is held by the taxpayer on the date of the disposition of the converted property. Property or stock shall be considered to have been purchased only if, but for the provisions of section 1033(b), the unadjusted basis of such property or stock would be its cost to the taxpayer within the meaning of section 1012. If the taxpayer's unadjusted basis of the replacement property would be determined, in the absence of section 1033(b), under any of the exceptions referred to in section 1012, the unadjusted basis of the property would not be its cost within the meaning of section 1012. For example, if property similar or related in service or use to the converted property is acquired by gift and its basis is determined under section 1015, such property will not qualify as a replacement for the converted property.

(5) If a taxpayer makes an election under section 1033(a)(2), any deficiency, for any taxable year in which any part of the gain upon the conversion is realized, which is attributable to such gain may be assessed at any time before the expiration of three years from the date the district director with whom the return for such year has been filed is notified by the taxpayer of the replacement of the converted property or of an intention not to replace, or of a failure to replace, within the required period, notwithstanding the provisions of section 6212(c) or the provisions of any other law or rule of law which would otherwise prevent such assessment. If replacement has been made, such notification shall contain all of the details in connection with such replacement. Such notification should be made in the return for the taxable year or years in which the replacement occurs, or the intention not to replace is formed, or the period for replacement expires, if this return is filed with such district director. If this return is not filed with such district director, then such notification shall be made to such district director at the time of filing this return. If the taxpayer so desires, he may, in either event, also notify such district director before the filing of such return.

(6) If a taxpayer makes an election under section 1033(a)(2) and the replacement property or stock was purchased before the beginning of the last taxable year in which any part of the gain upon the conversion is realized, any deficiency, for any taxable year ending before such last taxable year, which is attributable to such election may be assessed at any time before the expiration of the period within which a deficiency for such last taxable year may be assessed, notwithstanding the provisions of section 6212(c) or 6501 or the provisions of any law or rule of law which would otherwise prevent such assessment.

(7) If the taxpayer makes an election under section 1033(a)(2), the gain upon the conversion

shall be recognized to the extent that the amount realized upon such conversion exceeds the cost of the replacement property or stock, regardless of whether such amount is realized in one or more taxable years.

(8) The proceeds of a use and occupancy insurance contract, which by its terms insured against actual loss sustained of net profits in the business, are not proceeds of an involuntary conversion but are income in the same manner that the profits for which they are substituted would have been.

(9) There is no investment in property similar in character and devoted to a similar use if—

(i) The proceeds of unimproved real estate, taken upon condemnation proceedings, are invested in improved real estate.

(ii) The proceeds of conversion of real property are applied in reduction of indebtedness previously incurred in the purchase of a leasehold.

(iii) The owner of a requisitioned tug uses the proceeds to buy barges.

(10) If, in a condemnation proceeding, the Government retains out of the award sufficient funds to satisfy special assessments levied against the remaining portion of the plot or parcel of real estate affected for benefits accruing in connection with the condemnation, the amount so retained shall be deducted from the gross award in determining the amount of the net award.

(11) If, in a condemnation proceeding, the Government retains out of the award sufficient funds to satisfy liens (other than liens due to special assessments levied against the remaining portion of the plot or parcel of real estate affected for benefits accruing in connection with the condemnation) and mortgages against the property, and itself pays the same, the amount so retained shall not be deducted from the gross award in determining the amount of the net award. If, in a condemnation proceeding, the Government makes an award to a mortgagee to satisfy a mortgage on the condemned property, the amount of such award shall be considered as a part of the "amount realized" upon the conversion regardless of whether or not the taxpayer was personally liable for the mortgage debt. Thus, if a taxpayer has acquired property worth $100,000 subject to a $50,000 mortgage (regardless of whether or not he was personally liable for the mortgage debt) and, in a condemnation proceeding, the Government awards the taxpayer $60,000 and awards the mortgagee $50,000 in satisfaction of the mortgage, the entire $110,000 is considered to be the "amount realized" by the taxpayer.

(12) An amount expended for replacement of an asset, in excess of the recovery for loss, repre-

Reg. § 1.1033(a)-2(c)(5)

sents a capital expenditure and is not a deductible loss for income tax purposes. [Reg. § 1.1033(a)-2.]

☐ [*T.D. 6222, 1-9-57. Amended by T.D. 6679, 9-30-63, T.D. 7075, 11-23-70, T.D. 7625, 5-29-79 and T.D. 7758, 1-16-81.*]

§ 1.1033(b)-1. Basis of property acquired as a result of an involuntary conversion.—(a) The provisions of the first sentence of section 1033(b) may be illustrated by the following example:

Example. A's vessel which has an adjusted basis of $100,000 is destroyed in 1950 and A receives in 1951 insurance in the amount of $200,000. If A invests $150,000 in a new vessel, taxable gain to the extent of $50,000 would be recognized. The basis of the new vessel is $100,000; that is, the adjusted basis of the old vessel ($100,000) minus the money received by the taxpayer which was not expended in the acquisition of the new vessel ($50,000) plus the amount of gain recognized upon the conversion ($50,000). If any amount in excess of the proceeds of the conversion is expended in the acquisition of the new property, such amount may be added to the basis otherwise determined.

(b) The provisions of the last sentence of section 1033(b) may be illustrated by the following example:

Example. A taxpayer realizes $22,000 from the involuntary conversion of his barn in 1955; the adjusted basis of the barn to him was $10,000, and he spent in the same year $20,000 for a new barn which resulted in the nonrecognition of $10,000 of the $12,000 gain on the conversion. The basis of the new barn to the taxpayer would be $10,000—the cost of the new barn ($20,000) less the amount of the gain not recognized on the conversion ($10,000). The basis of the new barn would not be a substituted basis in the hands of the taxpayer within the meaning of section 1016(b)(2). If the replacement of the converted barn had been made by the purchase of two smaller barns which, together, were similar or related in service or use to the converted barn and which cost $8,000 and $12,000, respectively, then the basis of the two barns would be $4,000 and $6,000, respectively, the total basis of the purchased property ($10,000) allocated in proportion to their respective costs (8,000/20,000 of $10,000 or $4,000; and 12,000/20,000 of $10,000, or $6,000). [Reg. § 1.1033(b)-1.]

☐ [*T.D. 6222, 1-9-57. Amended by T.D. 7625, 5-29-79.*]

§ 1.1036-1. Stock for stock of the same corporation.—(a) Section 1036 permits the exchange, without the recognition of gain or loss, of common stock for common stock, or of preferred stock for preferred stock, in the same corporation. Section 1036 applies even though voting stock is exchanged for nonvoting stock or nonvoting stock is exchanged for voting stock. It is not limited to an exchange between two individual stockholders; it includes a transaction between a stockholder and the corporation. However, a transaction between a stockholder and the corporation may qualify not only under section 1036(a), but also under section 368(a)(1)(E) (recapitalization) or section 305(a) (distribution of stock and stock rights). The provisions of section 1036(a) do not apply if stock is exchanged for bonds, or preferred stock is exchanged for common stock, or common stock is exchanged for preferred stock, or common stock in one corporation is exchanged for common stock in another corporation. See paragraph (1) of § 1.301-1 for certain transactions treated as distributions under section 301. See paragraph (e)(5) of § 1.368-2 for certain transactions which result in deemed distributions under section 305(c) to which sections 305(b)(4) and 301 apply.

(b) For rules relating to recognition of gain or loss where an exchange is not wholly in kind, see subsections (b) and (c) of section 1031. For rules relating to the basis of property acquired in an exchange described in paragraph (a) of this section, see subsection (d) of section 1031.

(c) A transfer is not within the provisions of section 1036(a) if as part of the consideration the other party to the exchange assumes a liability of the taxpayer (or if the property transferred is subject to a liability), but the transfer, if otherwise qualified, will be within the provisions of section 1031(b).

(d) *Nonqualified preferred stock.* See § 1.356-7(a) for the applicability of the definition of nonqualified preferred stock in section 351(g)(2) for stock issued prior to June 9, 1997, and for stock issued in transactions occurring after June 8, 1997, that are described in section 1014(f)(2) of the Taxpayer Relief Act of 1997, Public Law 105-34 (111 Stat. 788, 921). [Reg. § 1.1036-1.]

☐ [*T.D. 6210, 11-6-56. Amended by T.D. 7281, 7-11-73 and T.D. 8904, 9-29-2000.*]

§ 1.1041-1T. Treatment of transfer of property between spouses or incident to divorce (temporary).—

Q-1. How is the transfer of property between spouses treated under section 1041?

A-1. Generally, no gain or loss is recognized on a transfer of property from an individual to (or in trust for the benefit of) a spouse or, if the transfer is incident to a divorce, a former spouse. The following questions and answers describe more fully the scope, tax consequences and other rules which apply to transfers of property under section 1041.

Reg. § 1.1041-1T

(a) *Scope of section 1041 in general.*

Q-2. Does section 1041 apply only to transfers of property incident to divorce?

A-2. No. Section 1041 is not limited to transfers of property incident to divorce. Section 1041 applies to any transfer of property between spouses regardless of whether the transfer is a gift or is a sale or exchange between spouses acting at arm's length (including a transfer in exchange for the relinquishment of property or marital rights or an exchange otherwise governed by another nonrecognition provision of the Code). A divorce or legal separation need not be contemplated between the spouses at the time of the transfer nor must a divorce or legal separation ever occur.

Example (1). A and B are married and file a joint return. A is the sole owner of a condominium unit. A sale or gift of the condominium from A to B is a transfer which is subject to the rules of section 1041.

Example (2). A and B are married and file separate returns. A is the owner of an independent sole proprietorship, X Company. In the ordinary course of business, X Company makes a sale of property to B. This sale is a transfer of property between spouses and is subject to the rules of section 1041.

Example (3). Assume the same facts as in example (2), except that X Company is a corporation wholly owned by A. This sale is not a sale between spouses subject to the rules of section 1041. However, in appropriate circumstances, general tax principles, including the step-transaction doctrine, may be applicable in recharacterizing the transaction.

Q-3. Do the rules of section 1041 apply to a transfer between spouses if the transferee spouse is a nonresident alien?

A-3. No. Gain or loss (if any) is recognized (assuming no other nonrecognition provision applies) at the time of a transfer of property if the property is transferred to a spouse who is a nonresident alien.

Q-4. What kinds of transfers are governed by section 1041?

A-4. Only transfers of property (whether real or personal, tangible or intangible) are governed by section 1041. Transfers of services are not subject to the rules of section 1041.

Q-5. Must the property transferred to a former spouse have been owned by the transferor spouse during the marriage?

A-5. No. A transfer of property acquired after the marriage ceases may be governed by section 1041.

(b) *Transfer incident to the divorce.*

Q-6. What is a transfer of property "incident to the divorce"?

A-6. A transfer of property is "incident to the divorce" in either of the following 2 circumstances—

(1) the transfer occurs not more than one year after the date on which the marriage ceases, or

(2) the transfer is related to the cessation of the marriage.

Thus, a transfer of property occurring not more than one year after the date on which the marriage ceases need not be related to the cessation of the marriage to qualify for section 1041 treatment. (See A-7 for transfers occurring more than one year after the cessation of the marriage.)

Q-7. When is a transfer of property "related to the cessation of the marriage"?

A-7. A transfer of property is treated as related to the cessation of the marriage if the transfer is pursuant to a divorce or separation instrument, as defined in section 71(b)(2), and the transfer occurs not more than 6 years after the date on which the marriage ceases. A divorce or separation instrument includes a modification or amendment to such decree or instrument. Any transfer not pursuant to a divorce or separation instrument and any transfer occurring more than 6 years after the cessation of the marriage is presumed to be not related to the cessation of the marriage. This presumption may be rebutted only by showing that the transfer was made to effect the division of property owned by the former spouses at the time of the cessation of the marriage. For example, the presumption may be rebutted by showing that (a) the transfer was not made within the one- and six-year periods described above because of factors which hampered an earlier transfer of the property, such as legal or business impediments to transfer or disputes concerning the value of the property owned at the time of the cessation of the marriage, and (b) the transfer is effected promptly after the impediment to transfer is removed.

Q-8. Do annulments and the cessations of marriages that are void *ab initio* due to violations of state law constitute divorces for purposes of section 1041?

A-8. Yes.

(c) *Transfers on behalf of a spouse.*

Q-9. May transfers of property to third parties on behalf of a spouse (or former spouse) qualify under section 1041?

A-9. Yes. There are three situations in which a transfer of property to a third party on behalf of a spouse (or former spouse) will qualify under section 1041, provided all other requirements of the section are satisfied. The first situation is where

Reg. § 1.1041-1T(a)

the transfer to the third party is required by a divorce or separation instrument. The second situation is where the transfer to the third party is pursuant to the written request of the other spouse (or former spouse). The third situation is where the transferor receives from the other spouse (or former spouse) a written consent or ratification of the transfer to the third party. Such consent or ratification must state that the parties intend the transfer to be treated as a transfer to the nontransferring spouse (or former spouse) subject to the rules of section 1041 and must be received by the transferor prior to the date of filing of the transferor's first return of tax for the taxable year in which the transfer was made. In the three situations described above, the transfer of property will be treated as made directly to the nontransferring spouse (or former spouse) and the nontransferring spouse will be treated as immediately transferring the property to the third party. The deemed transfer from the nontransferring spouse (or former spouse) to the third party is not a transaction that qualifies for nonrecognition of gain under section 1041. This A-9 shall not apply to transfers to which § 1.1041-2 applies.

(d) *Tax consequences of transfers subject to section 1041.*

Q-10. How is the transferor of property under section 1041 treated for income tax purposes?

A-10. The transferor of property under section 1041 recognizes no gain or loss on the transfer even if the transfer was in exchange for the release of marital rights or other consideration. This rule applies regardless of whether the transfer is of property separately owned by the transferor or is a division (equal or unequal) of community property. Thus, the result under section 1041 differs from the result in *United States v. Davis*, 370 U.S. 65 (1962).

Q-11. How is the transferee of property under section 1041 treated for income tax purposes?

A-11. The transferee of property under section 1041 recognizes no gain or loss upon receipt of the transferred property. In all cases, the basis of the transferred property in the hands of the transferee is the adjusted basis of such property in the hands of the transferor immediately before the transfer. Even if the transfer is a bona fide sale, the transferee does not acquire a basis in the transferred property equal to the transferee's cost (the fair market value). This carryover basis rule applies whether the adjusted basis of the transferred property is less than, equal to, or greater than its fair market value at the time of transfer (or the value of any consideration provided by the transferee) and applies for purposes of determining loss as well as gain upon the subsequent dispo-

sition of the property by the transferee. Thus, this rule is different from the rule applied in section 1015(a) for determining the basis of property acquired by gift.

Q-12. Do the rules described in A-10 and A-11 apply even if the transferred property is subject to liabilities which exceed the adjusted basis of the property?

A-12. Yes. For example, assume A owns property having a fair market value of $10,000 and an adjusted basis of $1,000. In contemplation of making a transfer of this property incident to a divorce from B, A borrows $5,000 from a bank, using the property as security for the borrowing. A then transfers the property to B and B assumes, or takes the property subject to, the liability to pay the $5,000 debt. Under section 1041, A recognizes no gain or loss upon the transfer of the property, and the adjusted basis of the property in the hands of B is $1,000.

Q-13. Will a transfer under section 1041 result in a recapture of investment tax credits with respect to the property transferred?

A-13. In general, no. Property transferred under section 1041 will not be treated as being disposed of by, or ceasing to be section 38 property with respect to, the transferor. However, the transferee will be subject to investment tax credit recapture if, upon or after transfer, the property is disposed of by, or ceases to be section 38 property with respect to, the transferee. For example, as part of a divorce property settlement, B receives a car from A that has been used in A's business for two years and for which an investment tax credit was taken by A. No part of A's business is transferred to B and B's use of the car is solely personal. B is subject to recapture of the investment tax credit previously taken by A.

* * *

(g) *Property settlements—time and manner of making the elections under section 1041.*

Q-18. How do spouses (or former spouses) elect to have section 1041 apply to transfers after December 31, 1983, or to transfers after July 18, 1984 under instruments in effect on or before July 18, 1984?

A-18. In order to make an election under section 1041 for property transfers after December 31, 1983, or property transfers under instruments that were in effect on or before July 18, 1984, both spouses (or former spouses) must elect the application of the rules of section 1041 by attaching to the transferor's first filed income tax return for the taxable year in which the first transfer occurs, a statement signed by both spouses (or former spouses) which includes each spouse's social security number and is in substantially the form set forth at the end of this answer.

Reg. § 1.1041-1T(g)

In addition, the transferor must attach a copy of such statement to his or her return for each subsequent taxable year in which a transfer is made that is governed by the transitional election. A copy of the signed statement must be kept by both parties.

* * *

[Temporary Reg. § 1.1041-1T.]

☐ [*T.D. 7973, 8-30-84. Amended by T.D. 9035, 1-10-2003.*]

§ 1.1041-2. Redemptions of stock.—(a) *In general*—(1) *Redemptions of stock not resulting in constructive distributions.* Notwithstanding Q&A-9 of § 1.1041-1T(c), if a corporation redeems stock owned by a spouse or former spouse (transferor spouse), and the transferor spouse's receipt of property in respect of such redeemed stock is not treated, under applicable tax law, as resulting in a constructive distribution to the other spouse or former spouse (nontransferor spouse), then the form of the stock redemption shall be respected for Federal income tax purposes. Therefore, the transferor spouse will be treated as having received a distribution from the corporation in redemption of stock.

(2) *Redemptions of stock resulting in constructive distributions.* Notwithstanding Q&A-9 of § 1.1041-1T(c), if a corporation redeems stock owned by a transferor spouse, and the transferor spouse's receipt of property in respect of such redeemed stock is treated, under applicable tax law, as resulting in a constructive distribution to the nontransferor spouse, then the redeemed stock shall be deemed first to be transferred by the transferor spouse to the nontransferor spouse and then to be transferred by the nontransferor spouse to the redeeming corporation. Any property actually received by the transferor spouse from the redeeming corporation in respect of the redeemed stock shall be deemed first to be transferred by the corporation to the nontransferor spouse in redemption of such spouse's stock and then to be transferred by the nontransferor spouse to the transferor spouse.

(b) *Tax consequences*—(1) *Transfers described in paragraph (a)(1) of this section.* Section 1041 will not apply to any of the transfers described in paragraph (a)(1) of this section. See section 302 for rules relating to the tax consequences of certain redemptions; redemptions characterized as distributions under section 302(d) will be subject to section 301 if received from a Subchapter C corporation or section 1368 if received from a Subchapter S corporation.

(2) *Transfers described in paragraph (a)(2) of this section.* The tax consequences of each deemed transfer described in paragraph (a)(2) of this section are determined under applicable provisions of the Internal Revenue Code as if the spouses had actually made such transfers. Accordingly, section 1041 applies to any deemed transfer of the stock and redemption proceeds between the transferor spouse and the nontransferor spouse, provided the requirements of section 1041 are otherwise satisfied with respect to such deemed transfer. Section 1041, however, will not apply to any deemed transfer of stock by the nontransferor spouse to the redeeming corporation in exchange for the redemption proceeds. See section 302 for rules relating to the tax consequences of certain redemptions; redemptions characterized as distributions under section 302(d) will be subject to section 301 if received from a Subchapter C corporation or section 1368 if received from a Subchapter S corporation.

(c) *Special rules in case of agreements between spouses or former spouses*—(1) *Transferor spouse taxable.* Notwithstanding applicable tax law, a transferor spouse's receipt of property in respect of the redeemed stock shall be treated as a distribution to the transferor spouse in redemption of such stock for purposes of paragraph (a)(1) of this section, and shall not be treated as resulting in a constructive distribution to the nontransferor spouse for purposes of paragraph (a)(2) of this section, if a divorce or separation instrument, or a valid written agreement between the transferor spouse and the nontransferor spouse, expressly provides that—

(i) Both spouses or former spouses intend for the redemption to be treated, for Federal income tax purposes, as a redemption distribution to the transferor spouse; and

(ii) Such instrument or agreement supersedes any other instrument or agreement concerning the purchase, sale, redemption, or other disposition of the stock that is the subject of the redemption.

(2) *Nontransferor spouse taxable.* Notwithstanding applicable tax law, a transferor spouse's receipt of property in respect of the redeemed stock shall be treated as resulting in a constructive distribution to the nontransferor spouse for purposes of paragraph (a)(2) of this section, and shall not be treated as a distribution to the transferor spouse in redemption of such stock for purposes of paragraph (a)(1) of this section, if a divorce or separation instrument, or a valid written agreement between the transferor spouse and the nontransferor spouse, expressly provides that—

(i) Both spouses or former spouses intend for the redemption to be treated, for Federal income tax purposes, as resulting in a constructive distribution to the nontransferor spouse; and

(ii) Such instrument or agreement supersedes any other instrument or agreement concerning the purchase, sale, redemption, or other disposition of the stock that is the subject of the redemption.

(3) *Execution of agreements.* For purposes of this paragraph (c), a divorce or separation instrument must be effective, or a valid written agreement must be executed by both spouses or former spouses, prior to the date on which the transferor spouse (in the case of paragraph (c)(1) of this section) or the nontransferor spouse (in the case of paragraph (c)(2) of this section) files such spouse's first timely filed Federal income tax return for the year that includes the date of the stock redemption, but no later than the date such return is due (including extensions).

* * *

[Reg. § 1.1041-2.]

☐ [*T.D.* 9035, 1-10-2003.]

Special Rules

§ 1.1059(e)-1. Non-pro rata redemptions.—(a) *In general.* Section 1059(d)(6) (exception where stock held during entire existence of corporation) and section 1059(e)(2) (qualifying dividends) do not apply to any distribution treated as an extraordinary dividend under section 1059(e)(1). For example, if a redemption of stock is not pro rata as to all shareholders, any amount treated as a dividend under section 301 is treated as an extraordinary dividend regardless of whether the dividend is a qualifying dividend.

(b) *Reorganizations.* For purposes of section 1059(e)(1), any exchange under section 356 is treated as a redemption and, to the extent any amount is treated as a dividend under section 356(a)(2), it is treated as a dividend under section 301.

(c) *Effective date.* This section applies to distributions announced (within the meaning of section 1059(d)(5)) on or after June 17, 1996. [Reg. § 1.1059(e)-1.]

☐ [*T.D.* 8724, 7-15-97.]

§ 1.1060-1. Special allocation rules for certain asset acquisitions.—(a) *Scope*—(1) *In general.* This section prescribes rules relating to the requirements of section 1060, which, in the case of an applicable asset acquisition, requires the transferor (the seller) and the transferee (the purchaser) each to allocate the consideration paid or received in the transaction among the assets transferred in the same manner as amounts are allocated under section 338(b)(5) (relating to the allocation of adjusted grossed-up basis among the assets of the target corporation when a section 338 election is made). In the case of an applicable asset acquisition described in paragraph (b)(1) of this section, sellers and purchasers must allocate the consideration under the residual method as described in §§ 1.338-6 and 1.338-7 in order to determine, respectively, the amount realized from, and the basis in, each of the transferred assets. For rules relating to distributions of partnership property or transfers of partnership interests which are subject to section 1060(d), see § 1.755-2T.

* * *

(b) *Applicable asset acquisition*—(1) *In general.* An applicable asset acquisition is any transfer, whether direct or indirect, of a group of assets if the assets transferred constitute a trade or business in the hands of either the seller or the purchaser and, except as provided in paragraph (b)(8) of this section, the purchaser's basis in the transferred assets is determined wholly by reference to the purchaser's consideration.

(2) *Assets constituting a trade or business*—(i) *In general.* For purposes of this section, a group of assets constitutes a trade or business if—

(A) The use of such assets would constitute an active trade or business under section 355; or

(B) Its character is such that goodwill or going concern value could under any circumstances attach to such group.

(ii) *Goodwill or going concern value.* Goodwill is the value of a trade or business attributable to the expectancy of continued customer patronage. This expectancy may be due to the name or reputation of a trade or business or any other factor. Going concern value is the additional value that attaches to property because of its existence as an integral part of an ongoing business activity. Going concern value includes the value attributable to the ability of a trade or business (or a part of a trade or business) to continue functioning or generating income without interruption notwithstanding a change in ownership. It also includes the value that is attributable to the immediate use or availability of an acquired trade or business, such as, for example, the use of the revenues or net earnings that otherwise would not be received during any period if the acquired trade or business were not available or operational.

(iii) *Factors indicating goodwill or going concern value.* In making the determination in this paragraph (b)(2), all the facts and circumstances surrounding the transaction are taken into

Reg. § 1.1060-1(b)(2)

account. Whether sufficient consideration is available to allocate to goodwill or going concern value after the residual method is applied is not relevant in determining whether goodwill or going concern value could attach to a group of assets. Factors to be considered include—

(A) The presence of any intangible assets (whether or not those assets are section 197 intangibles), provided, however, that the transfer of such an asset in the absence of other assets will not be a trade or business for purposes of section 1060;

(B) The existence of an excess of the total consideration over the aggregate book value of the tangible and intangible assets purchased (other than goodwill and going concern value) as shown in the financial accounting books and records of the purchaser; and

(C) Related transactions, including lease agreements, licenses, or other similar agreements between the purchaser and seller (or managers, directors, owners, or employees of the seller) in connection with the transfer.

(3) *Examples.* The following examples illustrate paragraphs (b)(1) and (2) of this section:

Example 1. S is a high grade machine shop that manufactures microwave connectors in limited quantities. It is a successful company with a reputation within the industry and among its customers for manufacturing unique, high quality products. Its tangible assets consist primarily of ordinary machinery for working metal and plating. It has no secret formulas or patented drawings of value. P is a company that designs, manufactures, and markets electronic components. It wants to establish an immediate presence in the microwave industry, an area in which it previously has not been engaged. P is acquiring assets of a number of smaller companies and hopes that these assets will collectively allow it to offer a broad product mix. P acquires the assets of S in order to augment its product mix and to promote its presence in the microwave industry. P will not use the assets acquired from S to manufacture microwave connectors. The assets transferred are assets that constitute a trade or business in the hands of the seller. Thus, P's purchase of S's assets is an applicable asset acquisition. The fact that P will not use the assets acquired from S to continue the business of S does not affect this conclusion.

Example 2. S, a sole proprietor who operates a car wash, both leases the building housing the car wash and sells all of the car wash equipment to P. S's use of the building and the car wash equipment constitute a trade or business. P begins operating a car wash in the building it leases from S. Because the assets transferred together with the asset leased are assets which constitute a trade or business, P's purchase of S's assets is an applicable asset acquisition.

Example 3. S, a corporation, owns a retail store business in State X and conducts activities in connection with that business enterprise that meet the active trade or business requirement of section 355. P is a minority shareholder of S. S distributes to P all the assets of S used in S's retail business in State X in complete redemption of P's stock in S held by P. The distribution of S's assets in redemption of P's stock is treated as a sale or exchange under sections 302(a) and 302(b)(3), and P's basis in the assets distributed to it is determined wholly by reference to the consideration paid, the S stock. Thus, S's distribution of assets constituting a trade or business to P is an applicable asset acquisition.

Example 4. S is a manufacturing company with an internal financial bookkeeping department. P is in the business of providing a financial bookkeeping service on a contract basis. As part of an agreement for P to begin providing financial bookkeeping services to S, P agrees to buy all of the assets associated with S's internal bookkeeping operations and provide employment to any of S's bookkeeping department employees who choose to accept a position with P. In addition to selling P the assets associated with its bookkeeping operation, S will enter into a long term contract with P for bookkeeping services. Because assets transferred from S to P, along with the related contract for bookkeeping services, are a trade or business in the hands of P, the sale of the bookkeeping assets from S to P is an applicable asset acquisition.

(4) *Asymmetrical transfers of assets.* A purchaser is subject to section 1060 if—

(i) Under general principles of tax law, the seller is not treated as transferring the same assets as the purchaser is treated as acquiring;

(ii) The assets acquired by the purchaser constitute a trade or business; and

(iii) Except as provided in paragraph (b)(8) of this section, the purchaser's basis in the transferred assets is determined wholly by reference to the purchaser's consideration.

(5) *Related transactions.* Whether the assets transferred constitute a trade or business is determined by aggregating all transfers from the seller to the purchaser in a series of related transactions. Except as provided in paragraph (b)(8) of this section, all assets transferred from the seller to the purchaser in a series of related transactions are included in the group of assets among which the consideration paid or received in such series is allocated under the residual method. The principles of § 1.338-1(c) are also applied in determin-

ing which assets are included in the group of assets among which the consideration paid or received is allocated under the residual method.

(6) *More than a single trade or business.* If the assets transferred from a seller to a purchaser include more than one trade or business, then, in applying this section, all of the assets transferred (whether or not transferred in one transaction or a series of related transactions and whether or not part of a trade or business) are treated as a single trade or business.

(7) *Covenant entered into by the seller.* If, in connection with an applicable asset acquisition, the seller enters into a covenant (e.g., a covenant not to compete) with the purchaser, that covenant is treated as an asset transferred as part of a trade or business.

(8) *Partial non-recognition exchanges.* A transfer may constitute an applicable asset acquisition notwithstanding the fact that no gain or loss is recognized with respect to a portion of the group of assets transferred. All of the assets transferred, including the non-recognition assets, are taken into account in determining whether the group of assets constitutes a trade or business. The allocation of consideration under paragraph (c) of this section is done without taking into account either the non-recognition assets or the amount of money or other property that is treated as transferred in exchange for the non-recognition assets (together, the non-recognition exchange property). The basis in and gain or loss recognized with respect to the non-recognition exchange property are determined under such rules as would otherwise apply to an exchange of such property. The amount of the money and other property treated as exchanged for non-recognition assets is the amount by which the fair market value of the non-recognition assets transferred by one party exceeds the fair market value of the non-recognition assets transferred by the other (to the extent of the money and the fair market value of property transferred in the exchange). The money and other property that are treated as transferred in exchange for the non-recognition assets (and which are not included among the assets to which section 1060 applies) are considered to come from the following assets in the following order: first from Class I assets, then from Class II assets, then from Class III assets, then from Class IV assets, then from Class V assets, then from Class VI assets, and then from Class VII assets. For this purpose, liabilities assumed (or to which a non-recognition exchange property is subject) are treated as Class I assets. See *Example 1* in paragraph (d) of this section for an example of the application of section 1060 to a single transaction which is, in part, a non-recognition exchange.

(c) *Allocation of consideration among assets under the residual method*—(1) *Consideration.* The seller's consideration is the amount, in the aggregate, realized from selling the assets in the applicable asset acquisition under section 1001(b). The purchaser's consideration is the amount, in the aggregate, of its cost of purchasing the assets in the applicable asset acquisition that is properly taken into account in basis.

(2) *Allocation of consideration among assets.* For purposes of determining the seller's amount realized for each of the assets sold in an applicable asset acquisition, the seller allocates consideration to all the assets sold by using the residual method under §§ 1.338-6 and 1.338-7, substituting consideration for ADSP. For purposes of determining the purchaser's basis in each of the assets purchased in an applicable asset acquisition, the purchaser allocates consideration to all the assets purchased by using the residual method under §§ 1.338-6 and 1.338-7, substituting consideration for AGUB. In allocating consideration, the rules set forth in paragraphs (c)(3) and (4) of this section apply in addition to the rules in §§ 1.338-6 and 1.338-7.

(3) *Certain costs.* The seller and purchaser each adjusts the amount allocated to an individual asset to take into account the specific identifiable costs incurred in transferring that asset in connection with the applicable asset acquisition (e.g., real estate transfer costs or security interest perfection costs). Costs so allocated increase, or decrease, as appropriate, the total consideration that is allocated under the residual method. No adjustment is made to the amount allocated to an individual asset for general costs associated with the applicable asset acquisition as a whole or with groups of assets included therein (e.g., non-specific appraisal fees or accounting fees). These latter amounts are taken into account only indirectly through their effect on the total consideration to be allocated.

(4) *Effect of agreement between parties.* If, in connection with an applicable asset acquisition, the seller and purchaser agree in writing as to the allocation of any amount of consideration to, or as to the fair market value of, any of the assets, such agreement is binding on them to the extent provided in this paragraph (c)(4). Nothing in this paragraph (c)(4) restricts the Commissioner's authority to challenge the allocations or values arrived at in an allocation agreement. This paragraph (c)(4) does not apply if the parties are able to refute the allocation or valuation under the standards set forth in *Commissioner v. Danielson,* 378 F.2d 771 (3d Cir.), *cert. denied,* 389 U.S. 858 (1967) (a party wishing to challenge the tax consequences of an agreement as construed by the Commissioner must offer proof that, in an action

Reg. § 1.1060-1(c)(4)

between the parties to the agreement, would be admissible to alter that construction or show its unenforceability because of mistake, undue influence, fraud, duress, etc.).

(d) *Examples.* The following examples illustrate this section:

Example 1. (i) On January 1, 2001, A transfers assets X, Y, and Z to B in exchange for assets D, E, and F plus $1,000 cash.

(ii) Assume the exchange of assets constitutes an exchange of like-kind property to which section

By A	
Asset	*Fair Market Value*
X	$ 400
Y	400
Z	200
Total	$1,000

(iv) Under paragraph (b)(8) of this section, for purposes of allocating consideration under paragraph (c) of this section, the like-kind assets exchanged and any money or other property that are treated as transferred in exchange for the like-kind property are excluded from the application of section 1060.

(v) Since assets X, Y, and Z are like-kind property, they are excluded from the application of the section 1060 allocation rules.

(vi) Since assets D, E, and F are like-kind property, they are excluded from the application of the section 1060 allocation rules. Thus, the allocation rules of section 1060 do not apply in determining B's gain or loss with respect to the disposition of assets D, E, and F, and the allocation rules of section 1060 and paragraph (c) of this section are not applied to determine A's bases of assets D, E, and F. In addition, $900 of the $1,000 cash B gave to A for A's like-kind assets (X, Y, and Z) is treated as transferred in exchange for the like-kind property in order to equalize the fair market values of the like-kind assets. Therefore, $900 of the cash is excluded from the application of the section 1060 allocation rules.

(vii) $100 of the cash is allocated under section 1060 and paragraph (c) of this section.

1031 applies. Assume also that goodwill or going concern value could under any circumstances attach to each of the DEF and XYZ groups of assets and, therefore, each group constitutes a trade or business under section 1060.

(iii) Assume the fair market values of the assets and the amount of money transferred are as follows:

By B	
Asset	*Fair Market Value*
D	$ 40
E	30
F	30
Cash (amount)	1,000
Total	$1,100

(viii) A received $100 that must be allocated under section 1060 and paragraph (c) of this section. Since A transferred no Class I, II, III, IV, V, or VI assets to which section 1060 applies, in determining its amount realized for the part of the exchange to which section 1031 does not apply, the $100 is allocated to Class VII assets (goodwill and going concern value).

(ix) B gave A $100 that must be allocated under section 1060 and paragraph (c) of this section. Since B received from A no Class I, II, III, IV, V, or VI assets to which section 1060 applies, the $100 consideration is allocated by B to Class VII assets (goodwill and going concern value).

Example 2. (i) On January 1, 2001, S, a sole proprietor, sells to P, a corporation, a group of assets that constitutes a trade or business under paragraph (b)(2) of this section. S, who plans to retire immediately, also executes in P's favor a covenant not to compete. P pays S $3,000 in cash and assumes $1,000 in liabilities. Thus, the total consideration is $4,000.

(ii) On the purchase date, P and S also execute a separate agreement that states that the fair market values of the Class II, Class III, Class V, and Class VI assets S sold to P are as follows:

Asset Class	*Asset*	*Fair Market Value*
II	Actively traded securities	$ 500
	Total Class II	500
III	Accounts receivable	200
	Total Class III	200
V	Furniture and fixtures	800
	Building	800

Reg. § 1.1060-1(d)

	Land	200
	Equipment	400
	Total Class V	2,200
VI	Covenant not to compete	900
	Total Class VI	900

(iii) P and S each allocate the consideration in the transaction among the assets transferred under paragraph (c) of this section in accordance with the agreed upon fair market values of the assets, so that $500 is allocated to Class II assets, $200 is allocated to the Class III asset, $2,200 is allocated to Class V assets, $900 is allocated to Class VI assets, and $200 ($4,000 total consideration less $3,800 allocated to assets in Classes II, III, V, and VI) is allocated to the Class VII assets (goodwill and going concern value).

(iv) In connection with the examination of P's return, the Commissioner, in determining the fair market values of the assets transferred, may disregard the parties' agreement. Assume that the Commissioner correctly determines that the fair market value of the covenant not to compete was $500. Since the allocation of consideration among Class II, III, V, and VI assets results in allocation up to the fair market value limitation, the $600 of unallocated consideration resulting from the Commissioner's redetermination of the value of the covenant not to compete is allocated to Class VII assets (goodwill and going concern value).

(e) *Reporting requirements*—(1) *Applicable asset acquisitions*—(i) *In general.* Unless otherwise excluded from this requirement by the Commissioner, the seller and the purchaser in an applicable asset acquisition each must report information concerning the amount of consideration in the transaction and its allocation among the assets transferred. They also must report information concerning subsequent adjustments to consideration.

(ii) *Time and manner of reporting*—(A) *In general.* The seller and the purchaser each must file asset acquisition statements on Form 8594, "Asset Allocation Statement," with their income tax returns or returns of income for the taxable year that includes the first date assets are sold pursuant to an applicable asset acquisition. This reporting requirement applies to all asset acquisitions described in this section. For reporting requirements relating to asset acquisitions occurring before March 16, 2001, as described in paragraph (a)(2) of this section, see the temporary regulations under section 1060 in effect prior to March 16, 2001 (see 26 CFR part 1 revised April 1, 2000).

(B) *Additional reporting requirement.* When an increase or decrease in consideration is taken into account after the close of the first taxable year that includes the first date assets are sold in an applicable asset acquisition, the seller and the purchaser each must file a supplemental asset acquisition statement on Form 8594 with the income tax return or return of income for the taxable year in which the increase (or decrease) is properly taken into account.

(2) *Transfers of interests in partnerships.* For reporting requirements relating to the transfer of a partnership interest, see § 1.755-2T(c). [Reg. § 1.1060-1.]

☐ [*T.D.* 8940, 2-12-2001.]

Wash Sales; Straddles

§ 1.1091-1. Losses from wash sales of stock or securities.—(a) A taxpayer cannot deduct any loss claimed to have been sustained from the sale or other disposition of stock or securities if, within a period beginning 30 days before the date of such sale or disposition and ending 30 days after such date (referred to in this section as the 61-day period), he has acquired (by purchase or by an exchange upon which the entire amount of gain or loss was recognized by law), or has entered into a contract or option so to acquire, substantially identical stock or securities. However, this prohibition does not apply (1) in the case of a taxpayer, not a corporation, if the sale or other disposition of stock or securities is made in connection with the taxpayer's trade or business, or (2) in the case of a corporation, a dealer in stock or securities, if the sale or other disposition of stock or securities is made in the ordinary course of its business as such dealer.

(b) Where more than one loss is claimed to have been sustained within the taxable year from the sale or other disposition of stock or securities, the provisions of this section shall be applied to the losses in the order in which the stock or securities the disposition of which resulted in the respective losses were disposed of (beginning with the earliest disposition). If the order of disposition of stock or securities disposed of at a loss on the same day cannot be determined, the stock or securities will be considered to have been disposed of in the order in which they were originally acquired (beginning with the earliest acquisition).

(c) Where the amount of stock or securities acquired within the 61-day period is less than the amount of stock or securities sold or otherwise disposed of, then the particular shares of stock or securities the loss from the sale or other disposition of which is not deductible shall be those with which the stock or securities acquired are matched in accordance with the following rule: The stock or securities acquired will be matched in accordance with the order of their acquisition (beginning with the earliest acquisition) with an equal number of the shares of stock or securities sold or otherwise disposed of.

(d) Where the amount of stock or securities acquired within the 61-day period is not less than the amount of stock or securities sold or otherwise disposed of, then the particular shares of stock or securities the acquisition of which resulted in the nondeductibility of the loss shall be those with which the stock or securities disposed of are matched in accordance with the following rule: The stock or securities sold or otherwise disposed of will be matched with an equal number of the shares of stock or securities acquired in accordance with the order of acquisition (beginning with the earliest acquisition) of the stock or securities acquired.

(e) The acquisition of any share of stock or any security which results in the nondeductibility of a loss under the provisions of this section shall be disregarded in determining the deductibility of any other loss.

(f) The word "acquired" as used in this section means acquired by purchase or by an exchange upon which the entire amount of gain or loss was recognized by law, and comprehends cases where the taxpayer has entered into a contract or option within the 61-day period to acquire by purchase or by such an exchange.

(g) For purposes of determining under this section the 61-day period applicable to a short sale of stock or securities, the principles of paragraph (a) of § 1.1233-1 for determining the consummation of a short sale shall generally apply except that the date of entering into the short sale shall be deemed to be the date of sale if, on the date of entering into the short sale, the taxpayer owns (or on or before such date has entered into a contract or option to acquire) stock or securities identical to those sold short and subsequently delivers such stock or securities to close the short sale.

(h) The following examples illustrate the application of this section:

Example (1). A, whose taxable year is the calendar year, on December 1, 1954, purchased 100 shares of common stock in the M Company for $10,000 and on December 15, 1954, purchased 100 additional shares for $9,000. On January 3, 1955, he sold the 100 shares purchased on December 1, 1954, for $9,000. Because of the provisions of section 1091, no loss from the sale is allowable as a deduction.

Example (2). A, whose taxable year is the calendar year, on September 21, 1954, purchased 100 shares of the common stock of the M Company for $5,000. On December 21, 1954, he purchased 50 shares of substantially identical stock for $2,750, and on December 27, 1954, he purchased 25 additional shares of such stock for $1,125. On January 3, 1955, he sold for $4,000 the 100 shares purchased on September 21, 1954. There is an indicated loss of $1,000 on the sale of the 100 shares. Since, within the 61-day period, A purchased 75 shares of substantially identical stock, the loss on the sale of 75 of the shares ($3,750 − $3,000, or $750) is not allowable as a deduction because of the provisions of section 1091. The loss on the sale of the remaining 25 shares ($1,250 − $1,000, or $250) is deductible subject to the limitations provided in sections 267 and 1211. The basis of the 50 shares purchased December 21, 1954, the acquisition of which resulted in the nondeductibility of the loss ($500) sustained on 50 of the 100 shares sold on January 3, 1955, is $2,500 (the cost of 50 of the shares sold on January 3, 1955) + $750 (the difference between the purchase price ($2,750) of 50 of the shares acquired on December 21, 1954, and the selling price ($2,000) of the 50 shares sold on January 3, 1955, or $3,250). Similarly, the basis of the 25 shares purchased on December 27, 1954, the acquisition of which resulted in the nondeductibility of the loss ($250) sustained on 25 of the shares sold on January 3, 1955, is $1,250 + $125, or $1,375. See § 1.1091-2.

Example (3). A, whose taxable year is the calendar year, on September 15, 1954, purchased 100 shares of the stock of the M Company for $5,000. He sold these shares on February 1, 1956, for $4,000. On each of the four days from February 15, 1956, to February 18, 1956, inclusive, he purchased 50 shares of substantially identical stock for $2,000. There is an indicated loss of $1,000 from the sale of the 100 shares on February 1, 1956, but, since within the 61-day period A purchased not less than 100 shares of substantially identical stock, the loss is not deductible. The particular shares of stock the purchase of which resulted in the nondeductibility of the loss are the first 100 shares purchased within such period, that is, the 50 shares purchased on February 15, 1956, and the 50 shares purchased on February 16, 1956. In determining the period for which the 50 shares purchased on February 15, 1956, and the 50 shares purchased on February 16, 1956, were held, there is to be included the period for which the 100 shares purchased on September 15, 1954, and sold on February 1, 1956, were held. [Reg. § 1.1091-1.]

☐ [*T.D.* 6178, 6-1-56. *Amended by T.D.* 6926, 8-8-67.]

Reg. § 1.1091-1(d)

§ 1.1091-2. Basis of stock or securities acquired in "wash sales".—(a) *In general.* The application of section 1091(d) may be illustrated by the following examples:

Example (1). A purchased a share of common stock of the X Corporation for $100 in 1935, which he sold January 15, 1955, for $80. On February 1, 1955, he purchased a share of common stock of the same corporation for $90. No loss from the sale is recognized under section 1091. The basis of the new share is $110; that is, the basis of the old share ($100) increased by $10, the excess of the price at which the new share was acquired ($90) over the price at which the old share was sold ($80).

Example (2). A purchased a share of common stock of the Y Corporation for $100 in 1935, which he sold January 15, 1955, for $80. On February 1, 1955, he purchased a share of common stock of the same corporation for $70. No loss from the sale is recognized under section 1091. The basis of the new share is $90; that is, the basis of the old share ($100) decreased by $10, the excess of the price at which the old share was sold ($80) over the price at which the new share was acquired ($70).

(b) *Special rule.* For a special rule as to the adjustment to basis required under section 1091(d) in the case of wash sales involving certain regulated investment company stock for which there is an average basis, see paragraph (e)(3)(iii)(*c*) and (*d*) of § 1.1012-1. [Reg. § 1.1091-2.]

☐ [*T.D.* 6178, 6-1-56. *Amended by T.D.* 7129, 7-6-71.]

General Rules for Determining Capital Gains and Losses

§ 1.1221-1. Meaning of terms.—(a) The term "capital assets" includes all classes of property not specifically excluded by section 1221. In determining whether property is a "capital asset", the period for which held is immaterial.

(b) Property used in the trade or business of a taxpayer of a character which is subject to the allowance for depreciation provided in section 167 and real property used in the trade or business of a taxpayer is excluded from the term "capital assets". Gains and losses from the sale or exchange of such property are not treated as gains and losses from the sale or exchange of capital assets, except to the extent provided in section 1231. See § 1.1231-1. Property held for the production of income, but not used in a trade or business of the taxpayer, is not excluded from the term "capital assets" even though depreciation may have been allowed with respect to such property under section 23(1) of the Internal Revenue Code of 1939 before its amendment by section 121(c) of the Revenue Act of 1942 (56 Stat. 819). However, gain or loss upon the sale or exchange of land held by a taxpayer primarily for sale to customers in the ordinary course of his business, as in the case of a dealer in real estate, is not subject to the provisions of subchapter P (section 1201 and following), chapter 1 of the Code.

(c)(1) A copyright, a literary, musical, or artistic composition, and similar property are excluded from the term "capital assets" if held by a taxpayer whose personal efforts created such property, or if held by a taxpayer in whose hands the basis of such property is determined, for purposes of determining gain from a sale or exchange, in whole or in part by reference to the basis of such property in the hands of a taxpayer whose personal efforts created such property. For purposes of this subparagraph, the phrase "similar property" includes, for example, such property as a theatrical production, a radio program, a newspaper cartoon strip, or any other property eligible for copyright protection (whether under statute or common law), but does not include a patent or an invention, or a design which may be protected only under the patent law and not under the copyright law.

(2) In the case of sales and other dispositions occurring after July 25, 1969, a letter, a memorandum, or similar property is excluded from the term "capital asset" if held by (i) a taxpayer whose personal efforts created such property, (ii) a taxpayer for whom such property was prepared or produced, or (iii) a taxpayer in whose hands the basis of such property is determined, for purposes of determining gain from a sale or exchange, in whole or in part by reference to the basis of such property in the hands of a taxpayer described in subdivision (i) or (ii) of this subparagraph. In the case of a collection of letters, memorandums, or similar property held by a person who is a taxpayer described in subdivision (i), (ii), or (iii) of this subparagraph as to some of such letters, memorandums, or similar property but not as to others, this subparagraph shall apply only to those letters, memorandums, or similar property as to which such person is a taxpayer described in such subdivision. For purposes of this subparagraph, the phrase "similar property" includes, for example, such property as a draft of a speech, a manuscript, a research paper, an oral recording of any type, a transcript of an oral recording, a transcript of an oral interview or of dictation, a personal or business diary, a log or journal, a corporate archive, including a corporate charter, office correspondence, a financial record, a drawing, a photograph, or a dispatch. A letter, memorandum, or property similar to a letter or

Reg. § 1.1221-1(c)(2)

memorandum, addressed to a taxpayer shall be considered as prepared or produced for him. This subparagraph does not apply to property, such as a corporate archive, office correspondence, or a financial record, sold or disposed of as part of a going business if such property has no significant value separate and apart from its relation to and use in such business; it also does not apply to any property to which subparagraph (1) of this paragraph applies (i.e., property to which section 1221(3) applied before its amendment by section 514(a) of the Tax Reform Act of 1969 (83 Stat. 643).

(3) For purposes of this paragraph, in general property is created in whole or in part by the personal efforts of a taxpayer if such taxpayer performs literary, theatrical, musical, artistic, or other creative or productive work which affirmatively contributes to the creation of the property, or if such taxpayer directs and guides others in the performance of such work. A taxpayer, such as corporate executive, who merely has administrative control of writers, actors, artists, or personnel and who does not substantially engage in the direction and guidance of such persons in the performance of their work, does not create property by his personal efforts. However, for purposes of subparagraph (2) of this paragraph, a letter or memorandum, or property similar to a letter or memorandum, which is prepared by personnel who are under the administrative control of a taxpayer, such as a corporate executive, shall be deemed to have been prepared or produced for him whether or not such letter, memorandum, or similar property is reviewed by him.

(4) For the application of section 1231 to the sale or exchange of property to which this paragraph applies, see § 1.1231-1. For the application of section 170 to the charitable contribution of property to which this paragraph applies, see section 170(e) and the regulations thereunder.

(d) Section 1221(4) excludes from the definition of "capital asset" accounts or notes receivable acquired in the ordinary course of trade or business for services rendered or from the sale of stock in trade or inventory or property held for sale to customers in the ordinary course of trade or business. Thus, if a taxpayer acquires a note receivable for services rendered, reports the fair market value of the note as income, and later sells the note for less than the amount previously reported, the loss is an ordinary loss. On the other hand, if the taxpayer later sells the note for more than the amount originally reported, the excess is treated as ordinary income.

(e) Obligations of the United States or any of its possessions, or of a State or Territory, or any political subdivision thereof, or of the District of Columbia, issued on or after March 1, 1941, on a discount basis and payable without interest at a fixed maturity date not exceeding one year from the date of issue, are excluded from the term "capital assets." An obligation may be issued on a discount basis even though the price paid exceeds the face amount. Thus, although the Second Liberty Bond Act (31 U.S.C. 754) provides that United States Treasury bills shall be issued on a discount basis, the issuing price paid for a particular bill may, by reason of competitive bidding, actually exceed the face amount of the bill. Since the obligations of the type described in this paragraph are excluded from the term "capital assets", gains or losses from the sale or exchange of such obligations are not subject to the limitations provided in such subchapter P. It is, therefore, not necessary for a taxpayer (other than a life insurance company taxable under part I (section 801 and following), subchapter L, chapter 1 of the Code, as amended by the Life Insurance Company Tax Act of 1955 (70 Stat. 36), and, in the case of taxable years beginning before January 1, 1955, subject to taxation only on interest, dividends, and rents) to segregate the original discount accrued and the gain or loss realized upon the sale or other disposition of any such obligation. See section 454(b) with respect to the original discount accrued. The provisions of this paragraph may be illustrated by the following examples:

Example (1). A (not a life insurance company) buys a $100,000, 90-day Treasury bill upon issuance for $99,998. As of the close of the forty-fifth day of the life of such bill, he sells it to B (not a life insurance company) for $99,999.50. The entire net gain to A of $1.50 may be taken into account as a single item of income, without allocating $1 to interest and $0.50 to gain. If B holds the bill until maturity his net gain of $0.50 may similarly be taken into account as a single item of income, without allocating $1 to interest and $0.50 to loss.

Example (2). The facts in this example are the same as in example (1) except that the selling price to B is $99,998.50. The net gain to A of $0.50 may be taken into account without allocating $1 to interest and $0.50 to loss, and, similarly, if B holds the bill until maturity his entire net gain of $1.50 may be taken into account as a single item of income without allocating $1 to interest and $0.50 to gain. [Reg. § 1.1221-1.]

☐ [*T.D. 6243, 7-23-57. Amended by T.D. 7369, 7-15-75.*]

§ 1.1221-2. Hedging transactions.—(a) *Treatment of hedging transactions—*(1) *In general.* This section governs the treatment of hedging transactions under section 1221(a)(7). Except as provided in paragraph (g)(2) of this section, the term capital asset does not include property that is part of a hedging transaction (as defined in paragraph (b) of this section).

(2) *Short sales and options.* This section also governs the character of gain or loss from a short sale or option that is part of a hedging transaction. Except as provided in paragraph (g)(2) of this section, gain or loss on a short sale or option that is part of a hedging transaction (as defined in paragraph (b) of this section) is ordinary income or loss.

(3) *Exclusivity.* If a transaction is not a hedging transaction as defined in paragraph (b) of this section, gain or loss from the transaction is not made ordinary on the grounds that property involved in the transaction is a surrogate for a noncapital asset, that the transaction serves as insurance against a business risk, that the transaction serves a hedging function, or that the transaction serves a similar function or purpose.

(4) *Coordination with section 988.* This section does not apply to determine the character of gain or loss realized on a section 988 transaction as defined in section 988(c)(1) or realized with respect to any qualified fund as defined in section 988(c)(1)(E)(iii).

(b) *Hedging transaction defined.* Section 1221(b)(2)(A) provides that a hedging transaction is any transaction that a taxpayer enters into in the normal course of the taxpayer's trade or business primarily—

(1) To manage risk of price changes or currency fluctuations with respect to ordinary property (as defined in paragraph (c)(2) of this section) that is held or to be held by the taxpayer;

(2) To manage risk of interest rate or price changes or currency fluctuations with respect to borrowings made or to be made, or ordinary obligations incurred or to be incurred, by the taxpayer; or

(3) To manage such other risks as the Secretary may prescribe in regulations (see paragraph (d)(6) of this section).

(c) *General rules*—(1) *Normal course.* Solely for purposes of paragraph (b) of this section, if a transaction is entered into in furtherance of a taxpayer's trade or business, the transaction is entered into in the normal course of the taxpayer's trade or business. This rule includes managing risks relating to the expansion of an existing business or the acquisition of a new trade or business.

(2) *Ordinary property and obligations.* Property is ordinary property to a taxpayer only if a sale or exchange of the property by the taxpayer could not produce capital gain or loss under any circumstances. Thus, for example, property used in a trade or business within the meaning of

section 1231(b) (determined without regard to the holding period specified in that section) is not ordinary property. An obligation is an ordinary obligation if performance or termination of the obligation by the taxpayer could not produce capital gain or loss. For purposes of this paragraph (c)(2), the term termination has the same meaning as it does in section 1234A.

(3) *Hedging an aggregate risk.* The term hedging transaction includes a transaction that manages an aggregate risk of interest rate changes, price changes, and/or currency fluctuations only if all of the risk, or all but a de minimis amount of the risk, is with respect to ordinary property, ordinary obligations, or borrowings.

(4) *Managing risk*—(i) *In general.* Whether a transaction manages a taxpayer's risk is determined based on all of the facts and circumstances surrounding the taxpayer's business and the transaction. Whether a transaction manages a taxpayer's risk may be determined on a business unit by business unit basis (for example by treating particular groups of activities, including the assets and liabilities attributable to those activities, as separate business units), provided that the business unit is within a single entity or consolidated return group that adopts the single-entity approach. A taxpayer's hedging strategies and policies as reflected in the taxpayer's minutes or other records are evidence of whether particular transactions were entered into primarily to manage the taxpayer's risk.

(ii) *Limitation of risk management transactions to those specifically described.* Except as otherwise determined by published guidance or by private letter ruling, a transaction that is not treated as a hedging transaction under paragraph (d) does not manage risk. Moreover, a transaction undertaken for speculative purposes will not be treated as a hedging transaction.

* * *

[Reg. § 1.1221-2.]

☐ [*T.D.* 8555, 7-13-94. *Amended by T.D.* 8653, 1-5-96 *and T.D.* 8985, 3-15-2002.]

§ 1.1222-1. Other terms relating to capital gains and losses.—(a) The phrase "short-term" applies to the category of gains and losses arising from the sale or exchange of capital assets held for 1 year (6 months for taxable years beginning before 1977; 9 months for taxable years beginning in 1977) or less; the phrase "long-term" to the category of gains and losses arising from the sale or exchange of capital assets held for more than 1 year (6 months for taxable years beginning before 1977; 9 months for taxable years beginning in 1977). The fact that some part of a loss from the sale or exchange of a capital asset may be finally disallowed because of the operation of section

Reg. § 1.1222-1(a)

1211 does not mean that such loss is not "taken into account in computing taxable income" within the meaning of that phrase as used in sections 1222(2) and 1222(4).

(b)(1) In the definition of "net short-term capital gain", as provided in section 1222(5), the amounts brought forward to the taxable year under section 1212 (other than section 1212 (b)(1)(B)) are short-term capital losses for such taxable year.

(2) In the definition of "net long-term capital gain", as provided in section 1222(7), the amounts brought forward to the taxable year under section 1212(b)(1)(B) are long-term capital losses for such taxable year.

(c) Gains and losses from the sale or exchange of capital assets held for not more than 1 year (6 months for taxable years beginning before 1977; 9 months for taxable years beginning in 1977) (described as short-term capital gains and short-term capital losses) shall be segregated from gains and losses arising from the sale or exchange of such assets held for more than 1 year (6 months for taxable years beginning before 1977; 9 months for taxable years beginning in 1977) (described as long-term capital gains and long-term capital losses).

(d)(1) The term "capital gain net income" (net capital gain for taxable years beginning before January 1, 1977) means the excess of the gains from sales or exchanges of capital assets over the losses from sales or exchanges of capital assets, which losses include any amounts carried to the taxable year pursuant to section 1212(a) or section 1212(b).

(2) Notwithstanding subparagraph (1) of this paragraph, in the case of a taxpayer other than a corporation for taxable years beginning before January 1, 1964, the term "net capital gain" means the excess of (i) the sum of the gains from sales or exchanges of capital assets, plus the taxable income (computed without regard to gains and losses from sales or exchanges of capital assets and without regard to the deductions provided by section 151, relating to personal exemptions, or any deductions in lieu thereof) of the taxpayer or $1,000, whichever is smaller, over (ii) the losses from sales or exchanges of capital assets, which losses include amounts carried to the taxable year by such taxpayer under paragraph (a)(1) of § 1.1212-1. Thus, in the case of estates and trusts for taxable years beginning before January 1, 1964, taxable income for the purposes of this paragraph shall be computed without regard to gains and losses from sales or exchanges of capital assets and without regard to the deductions allowed by section 642(b) to estates and trusts in lieu of personal exemptions. The term "net capital gain" is not applicable in the case of a taxpayer other than a corporation for taxable years beginning after December 31, 1963, and before January 1, 1970. In the case of a taxpayer whose tax liability is computed under section 3 for taxable years beginning before January 1, 1964, the term "taxable income", for purposes of this paragraph, shall be read as "adjusted gross income".

(e) The term "net capital loss" means the excess of the losses from sales or exchanges of capital assets over the sum allowed under section 1211. However, in the case of a corporation, amounts which are short-term capital losses under § 1.1212-1(a) are excluded in determining such "net capital loss".

(f) See section 165(g) and section 166(e), under which losses from worthless stocks, bonds, and other securities (if they constitute capital assets) are required to be treated as losses under subchapter P (section 1201 and following), chapter 1 of the Code, from the sale or exchange of capital assets, even though such securities are not actually sold or exchanged. See also section 1231 and § 1.1231-1 for the determination of whether or not gains and losses from the involuntary conversion of capital assets and from the sale, exchange, or involuntary conversion of certain property used in the trade or business shall be treated as gains and losses from the sale or exchange of capital assets. See also section 1236 and § 1.1236-1 for the determination of whether or not gains from the sale or exchange of securities by a dealer in securities shall be treated as capital gains, or whether losses from such sales or exchanges shall be treated as ordinary losses.

(g) In the case of nonresident alien individuals not engaged in trade or business within the United States, see section 871 and the regulations thereunder for the determination of the net amount of capital gains subject to tax.

(h) The term "net capital gain" ("net section 1201 gain" for taxable years beginning before January 1, 1977) means the excess of the net long-term capital gain for the taxable year over the net short-term capital loss for such year. [Reg. § 1.1222-1.]

☐ [T.D. 6243, 7-23-57. Amended by T.D. 6828, 6-16-65; T.D. 6867, 12-6-65; T.D. 7301, 1-3-74; T.D. 7337, 12-26-74 and T.D. 7728, 10-31-80.]

§ 1.1223-1. Determination of period for which capital assets are held.—(a) The holding period of property received in an exchange by a taxpayer includes the period for which the property which he exchanged was held by him, if the property received has the same basis in whole or in part for determining gain or loss in the hands of the taxpayer as the property exchanged. However, this rule shall apply, in the case of exchanges after March 1, 1954, only if the property exchanged was at the time of the exchange a capital asset in the hands of the taxpayer or property used in his trade or business as defined in section 1231(b). For the purposes of this paragraph the term "exchange" includes the following transactions: (1) An involuntary conversion described in section 1033, and (2) a distribution to which section 355 (or so much of section 356 as relates to section 355) applies. Thus, if property acquired as the result of a compulsory or involuntary conversion of other property of the taxpayer has under section 1033(c) the same basis in whole or in part in the hands of the taxpayer as the property so converted, its acquisition is treated as an exchange and the holding period of the newly acquired property shall include the period during which the converted property was held by the taxpayer. Thus, also, where stock of a controlled corporation is received by a taxpayer pursuant to a distribution to which section 355 (or so much of section 356 as relates to section 355) applies, the distribution is treated as an exchange and the period for which the taxpayer has held the stock of the controlled corporation shall include the period for which he held the stock of the distributing corporation with respect to which such distribution was made.

(b) The holding period of property in the hands of a taxpayer shall include the period during which the property was held by any other person, if such property has the same basis in whole or in part in the hands of the taxpayer for determining gain or loss from a sale or exchange as it would have in the hands of such other person. For example, the period for which property acquired by gift after December 31, 1920, was held by the donor must be included in determining the period for which the property was held by the taxpayer if, under the provisions of section 1015, such property has, for the purpose of determining gain or loss from the sale or exchange, the same basis in the hands of the taxpayer as it would have in the hands of the donor.

(c) In determining the period for which the taxpayer has held stock or securities received upon a distribution where no gain was recognized to the distributee under section 1081(c) (or under section 112(g) of the Revenue Act of 1928 (45 Stat. 818) or the Revenue Act of 1932 (47 Stat. 197)), there shall be included the period for which he held the stock or securities in the distributing corporation before the receipt of the stock or securities on such distribution.

(d) If the acquisition of stock or securities resulted in the nondeductibility (under section 1091, relating to wash sales) of the loss from the sale or other disposition of substantially identical stock or securities, the holding period of the newly acquired securities shall include the period for which the taxpayer held the securities with respect to which the loss was not allowable.

(e) The period for which the taxpayer has held stock, or stock subscription rights, received on a distribution shall be determined as though the stock dividend, or stock right, as the case may be, were the stock in respect of which the dividend was issued if the basis for determining gain or loss upon the sale or other disposition of such stock dividend or stock right is determined under section 307. If the basis of stock received by a taxpayer pursuant to a spin-off is determined under so much of section 1052(c) as refers to section 113(a)(23) of the Internal Revenue Code of 1939, and such stock is sold or otherwise disposed of in a taxable year which is subject to the Internal Revenue Code of 1954, the period for which the taxpayer has held the stock received in such spin-off shall include the period for which he held the stock of the distributing corporation with respect to which such distribution was made.

(f) The period for which the taxpayer has held stock or securities issued to him by a corporation pursuant to the exercise by him of rights to acquire such stock or securities from the corporation will, in every case and whether or not the receipt of taxable gain was recognized in connection with the distribution of the rights, begin with and include the day upon which the rights to acquire such stock or securities were exercised. A taxpayer will be deemed to have exercised rights received from a corporation to acquire stock or securities therein where there is an expression of assent to the terms of such rights made by the taxpayer in the manner requested or authorized by the corporation.

(g) The period for which the taxpayer has held a residence, the acquisition of which resulted under the provisions of section 1034 in the nonrecognition of any part of the gain realized on the sale or exchange of another residence, shall include the period for which such other residence had been held as of the date of such sale or exchange. See § 1.1034-1. For purposes of this paragraph, the term "sale or exchange" includes an involuntary conversion occurring after December 31, 1950, and before January 1, 1954.

(h) If a taxpayer accepts delivery of a commodity in satisfaction of a commodity futures contracts, the holding period of the commodity shall include the period for which the taxpayer held the commodity futures contract, if such futures contract was a capital asset in his hands.

(i) If shares of stock in a corporation are sold from lots purchased at different dates or at different prices and the identity of the lots cannot be determined, the rules prescribed by the regula-

Reg. § 1.1223-1(i)

tions under section 1012 for determining the cost or other basis of such stocks so sold or transferred shall also apply for the purpose of determining the holding period of such stock.

(j) In the case of a person acquiring property, or to whom property passed, from a decedent (within the meaning of section 1014(b)) dying after December 31, 1970, such person shall be considered to have held the property for more than 6 months if the property—

(1) Has a basis in the hands of such person which is determined in whole or in part under section 1014, and

(2) Is sold or otherwise disposed of by such person within 6 months after the decedent's death.

The provisions of this paragraph apply to sales of such property included in the decedent's gross estate for the purposes of the estate tax by the executor or administrator of the estate and to sales of such property by other persons who have acquired property from the decedent. The provisions of this paragraph may also be applicable to cases involving joint tenancies, community property, and properties transferred in contemplation of death. Thus, if a surviving joint tenant, who acquired property by right of survivorship, sells or otherwise disposes of such property within 1 year (6 months for taxable years beginning before 1977; 9 months for taxable years beginning in 1977) after the date of the decedent's death, and the basis of the property in his hands is determined in whole or in part under section 1014, the property shall be considered to have been held by the surviving joint tenant for more than 1 year (6 months for taxable years beginning before 1977; 9 months for taxable years beginning in 1977). Similarly, a surviving spouse's share of community property shall be considered to have been held by her for more than 1 year (6 months for taxable years beginning before 1977; 9 months for taxable years beginning in 1977) if it is sold or otherwise disposed of within 1 year (6 months for taxable years beginning before 1977; 9 months for taxable years beginning in 1977) after the date of the decedent's death, regardless of when the property was actually acquired by the marital community. For the purposes of this paragraph, it is immaterial that the sale or other disposition produces gain or loss. If property is considered to have been held for more than 1 year (6 months for taxable years beginning before 1977; 9 months for taxable years beginning in 1977) by reason of this paragraph, it also is considered to have been held for that period for purposes of section 1231 (if that section is otherwise applicable).

(k) Any reference in section 1223 or this section to another provision of the Internal Revenue Code

of 1954 is, where applicable, to be deemed a reference to the corresponding provision of the Internal Revenue Code of 1939, or prior internal revenue laws. The provisions of prior internal revenue laws here intended are the sections referred to in the sections of the 1939 Code which correspond to the sections of the Internal Revenue Code of 1954 referred to in section 1223. Thus, the sections corresponding to section 1081(c) are section 371(c) of the Revenue Act of 1938 (52 Stat. 553) and section 371(c) of the Internal Revenue Code of 1939. The sections corresponding to section 1091 are section 118 of each of the following: The Revenue Acts of 1928 (45 Stat. 826), 1932 (47 Stat. 208), 1934 (48 Stat. 715), 1936 (49 Stat. 1692), and 1938 (52 Stat. 503), and the Internal Revenue Code of 1939. [Reg. § 1.1223-1.]

☐ [T.D. 6243, 7-23-57. Amended by T.D. 7238, 12-28-72 and T.D. 7728, 10-31-80.]

§ 1.1223-3. Rules relating to the holding periods of partnership interests.—(a) *In general.* A partner shall not have a divided holding period in an interest in a partnership unless—

(1) The partner acquired portions of an interest at different times; or

(2) The partner acquired portions of the partnership interest in exchange for property transferred at the same time but resulting in different holding periods (e.g., section 1223).

(b) *Accounting for holding periods of an interest in a partnership*—(1) *General rule.* The portion of a partnership interest to which a holding period relates shall be determined by reference to a fraction, the numerator of which is the fair market value of the portion of the partnership interest received in the transaction to which the holding period relates, and the denominator of which is the fair market value of the entire partnership interest (determined immediately after the transaction).

(2) *Special rule.* For purposes of applying paragraph (b)(1) of this section to determine the holding period of a partnership interest (or portion thereof) that is sold or exchanged (or with respect to which gain or loss is recognized upon a distribution under section 731), if a partner makes one or more contributions of cash to the partnership and receives one or more distributions of cash from the partnership during the one-year period ending on the date of the sale or exchange (or distribution with respect to which gain or loss is recognized under section 731), the partner may reduce the cash contributions made during the year by cash distributions received on a last-in-first-out basis, treating all cash distributions as if they were received immediately before the sale or exchange (or at the time of the distribution with

respect to which gain or loss is recognized under section 731).

(3) *Deemed contributions and distributions.* For purposes of paragraphs (b)(1) and (2) of this section, deemed contributions of cash under section 752(a) and deemed distributions of cash under section 752(b) shall be disregarded to the same extent that such amounts are disregarded under § 1.704-1(b)(2)(iv)(c).

(4) *Adjustment with respect to contributed section 751 assets.* For purposes of applying paragraph (b)(1) of this section to determine the holding period of a partnership interest (or portion thereof) that is sold or exchanged, if a partner receives a portion of the partnership interest in exchange for property described in section 751(c) or (d) (section 751 assets) within the one-year period ending on the date of the sale or exchange of all or a portion of the partner's interest in the partnership, and the partner recognizes ordinary income or loss on account of such a section 751 asset in a fully taxable transaction (either as a result of the sale of all or part of the partner's interest in the partnership or the sale by the partnership of the section 751 asset), the contribution of the section 751 asset during the one-year period shall be disregarded. However, if, in the absence of this paragraph, a partner would not be treated as having held any portion of the interest for more than one year (e.g., because the partner's only contributions to the partnership are contributions of section 751 assets or section 751 assets and cash within the prior one-year period), this adjustment is not available.

(5) *Exception.* The Commissioner may prescribe by guidance published in the Internal Revenue Bulletin (see § 601.601(d)(2) of this chapter) a rule disregarding certain cash contributions (including contributions of a de minimis amount of cash) in applying paragraph (b)(1) of this section to determine the holding period of a partnership interest (or portion thereof) that is sold or exchanged.

(c) *Sale or exchange of all or a portion of an interest in a partnership*—(1) *Sale or exchange of entire interest in a partnership.* If a partner sells or exchanges the partner's entire interest in a partnership, any capital gain or loss recognized shall be divided between long-term and short-term capital gain or loss in the same proportions as the holding period of the interest in the partnership is divided between the portion of the interest held for more than one year and the portion of the interest held for one year or less.

(2) *Sale or exchange of a portion of an interest in a partnership*—(i) *Certain publicly traded partnerships.* A selling partner in a publicly traded partnership (as defined under section 7704(b)) may use the actual holding period of the portion of a partnership interest transferred if—

(A) The ownership interest is divided into identifiable units with ascertainable holding periods;

(B) The selling partner can identify the portion of the partnership interest transferred; and

(C) The selling partner elects to use the identification method for all sales or exchanges of interests in the partnership after September 21, 2000. The selling partner makes the election referred to in this paragraph (c)(2)(i)(C) by using the actual holding period of the portion of the partner's interest in the partnership first transferred after September 21, 2000 in reporting the transaction for federal income tax purposes.

(ii) *Other partnerships.* If a partner has a divided holding period in a partnership interest, and paragraph (c)(2)(i) of this section does not apply, then the holding period of the transferred interest shall be divided between long-term and short-term capital gain or loss in the same proportions as the long-term and short-term capital gain or loss that the transferor partner would realize if the entire interest in the partnership were transferred in a fully taxable transaction immediately before the actual transfer.

(d) *Distributions*—(1) *In general.* Except as provided in paragraph (b)(2) of this section, a partner's holding period in a partnership interest is not affected by distributions from the partnership.

(2) *Character of capital gain or loss recognized as a result of a distribution from a partnership.* If a partner is required to recognize capital gain or loss as a result of a distribution from a partnership, then the capital gain or loss recognized shall be divided between long-term and short-term capital gain or loss in the same proportions as the long-term and short-term capital gain or loss that the distributee partner would realize if such partner's entire interest in the partnership were transferred in a fully taxable transaction immediately before the distribution.

(e) *Section 751(c) assets.* For purposes of this section, properties and potential gain treated as unrealized receivables under section 751(c) shall be treated as separate assets that are not capital assets as defined in section 1221 or property described in section 1231.

(f) *Examples.* The provisions of this section are illustrated by the following examples:

Example 1. Division of holding period—contribution of money and a capital asset. (i) *A* contributes $5,000 of cash and a nondepreciable capital asset *A* has held for two years to a partnership

(*PRS*) for a 50 percent interest in *PRS*. *A*'s basis in the capital asset is $5,000, and the fair market value of the asset is $10,000. After the exchange, *A*'s basis in *A*'s interest in *PRS* is $10,000, and the fair market value of the interest is $15,000. *A* received one-third of the interest in *PRS* for a cash payment of $5,000 ($5,000/$15,000). Therefore, *A*'s holding period in one-third of the interest received (attributable to the contribution of money to the partnership) begins on the day after the contribution. *A* received two-thirds of the interest in *PRS* in exchange for the capital asset ($10,000/$15,000). Accordingly, pursuant to section 1223(1), *A* has a two-year holding period in two-thirds of the interest received in *PRS*.

(ii) Six months later, when *A*'s basis in *PRS* is $12,000 (due to a $2,000 allocation of partnership income to *A*), *A* sells the interest in *PRS* for $17,000. Assuming *PRS* holds no inventory or unrealized receivables (as defined under section 751(c)) and no collectibles or section 1250 property, *A* will realize $5,000 of capital gain. As determined above, one-third of *A*'s interest in *PRS* has a holding period of one year or less, and two-thirds of *A*'s interest in *PRS* has a holding period equal to two years and six months. Therefore, one-third of the capital gain will be short-term capital gain, and two-thirds of the capital gain will be long-term capital gain.

Example 2. Division of holding period—contribution of section 751 asset and a capital asset. *A* contributes inventory with a basis of $2,000 and a fair market value of $6,000 and a capital asset which *A* has held for more than one year with a basis of $4,000 and a fair market value of $6,000, and *B* contributes cash of $12,000 to form a partnership (*AB*). As a result of the contribution, one-half of *A*'s interest in *AB* is treated as having been held for more than one year under section 1223(1). Six months later. *A* transfers one-half of *A*'s interest in *AB* to *C* for $6,000, realizing a gain of $3,000. If *AB* were to sell all of its section 751 property in a fully taxable transaction immediately before *A*'s transfer of the partnership interest, *A* would be allocated $4,000 of ordinary income on account of the inventory. Accordingly, *A* will recognize $2,000 of ordinary income and $1,000 of capital gain ($3,000 − $2,000) on account of the transfer to *C*. Because *A* recognizes ordinary income on account of the inventory that was contributed to *AB* within the one year period ending on the date of the sale, the inventory will be disregarded in determining the holding period of *A*'s interest in *AB*. All of the capital gain will be long-term.

Example 3. Netting of cash contributions and distributions. (i) On January 1, 2000, *A* holds a 50 percent interest in the capital and profits of a partnership (*PS*). The value of *A*'s *PS* interest is

$900, and *A*'s holding period in the entire interest is long-term. On January 2, 2000, when the value of *A*'s *PS* interest is still $900, *A* contributes $100 to *PS*. On June 1, 2000, *A* receives a distribution of $40 cash from the partnership. On September 1, 2000, when the value of *A*'s interest in *PS* is $1,350, *A* contributes an additional $230 cash to *PS*, and on October 1, 2000, *A* receives another $40 cash distribution from *PS*. *A* sells *A*'s entire partnership interest on November 1, 2000, for $1,600. *A*'s adjusted basis in the *PS* interest at the time of the sale is $1,000.

(ii) For purposes of netting cash contributions and distributions in determining the holding period of *A*'s interest in *PS*, *A* is treated as having received a distribution of $80 on November 1, 2000. Applying that distribution on a last-in-first-out basis to reduce prior contributions during the year, the contribution made on September 1, 2000, is reduced to $150 ($230 − $80). The holding period then is determined as follows: Immediately after the contribution of $100 on January 2, 2000, *A*'s holding period in *A*'s *PS* interest is 90 percent long-term ($900 ÷ ($900 + $100)) and 10 percent short-term ($100 ÷ ($900 + $100)). The contribution of $150 on September 1, 2000, causes 10 percent of *A*'s partnership interest ($150 ÷ ($1,350 + $150)) to have a short-term holding period. Accordingly, immediately after the contribution on September 1, 2000, *A*'s holding period in *A*'s *PS* interest is 81 percent long-term (.90 × .90) and 19 percent short-term ((.10 × .90) + .10). Accordingly, $486 ($600 × .81) of the gain from *A*'s sale of the *PS* interest is long-term capital gain, and $114 ($600 × .19) is short-term capital gain.

Example 4. Division of holding period when capital account is increased by contribution. *A*, *B*, *C*, and *D* are equal partners in a partnership (*PRS*), and the fair market value of a 25 percent interest in *PRS* is $100. *A*, *B*, *C*, and *D* each contribute an additional $100 to partnership capital, thereby increasing the fair market value of each partner's interest to $200. As a result of the contribution, each partner has a new holding period in the portion of the partner's interest in *PRS* that is attributable to the contribution. That portion equals 50 percent ($100 ÷ $200) of each partners interest in *PRS*.

Example 5. Sale or exchange of a portion of an interest in a partnership. (i) *A*, *B*, and *C* form an equal partnership (*PRS*). In connection with the formation, *A* contributes $5,000 in cash and a capital asset (capital asset 1) with a fair market value of $5,000 and a basis of $2,000; *B* contributes $7,000 in cash and a capital asset (capital asset 2) with a fair market value of $3,000 and a basis of $3,000; and *C* contributes $10,000 in cash. At the time of the contribution, *A* had held

Reg. § 1.1223-3(f)

the contributed property for two years. Six months later, when *A*'s basis in *PRS* is $7,000, *A* transfers one-half of *A*'s interest in *PRS* to *T* for $7,000 at a time when *PRS*'s balance sheet (reflecting a cash receipts and disbursements method of accounting) is as follows:

	ASSETS	
	Adjusted Basis	Market Value
Cash	$22,000	$22,000
Unrealized Receivables	0	6,000
Capital Asset 1	2,000	5,000
Capital Asset 2	3,000	9,000
Capital Assets	5,000	14,000
Total	$27,000	$42,000

(ii) Although at the time of the transfer *A* has not held *A*'s interest in *PRS* for more than one year, 50 percent of the fair market value of *A*'s interest in *PRS* was received in exchange for a capital asset with a long-term holding period. Therefore, 50 percent of *A*'s interest in *PRS* has a long-term holding period.

(iii) If *PRS* were to sell all of its section 751 property in a fully taxable transaction immediately before *A*'s transfer of the partnership interest, *A* would be allocated $2,000 of ordinary income. One-half of that amount ($1,000) is attributable to the portion of *A*'s interest in *PRS* transferred to *T*. Accordingly, *A* will recognize $1,000 ordinary income and $2,500 ($3,500 – $1,000) of capital gain on account of the transfer to *T* of one-half of *A*'s interest in *PRS*. Fifty percent ($1,250) of that gain is long-term capital gain and 50 percent ($1,250) is short-term capital gain.

Example 6. Sale of units of interests in a partnership. A publicly traded partnership (*PRS*) has ownership interests that are segregated into identifiable units of interest. *A* owns 10 limited partnership units in *PRS* for which *A* paid $10,000 on January 1, 1999. On August 1, 2000, *A* purchases five additional units for $10,000. At the time of purchase, the fair market value of each unit has increased to $2,000. *A*'s holding period for one-third ($10,000/$30,000) of the interest in *PRS* begins on the day after the purchase of the five additional units. Less than one year later, *A* sells five units of ownership in *PRS* for $11,000. At the time, *A*'s basis in the 15 units *PRS* is $20,000, and *A*'s capital gain on the sale of 5 units is $4,333 (amount realized of $11,000 – one-third of the adjusted basis or $6,667). For purposes of determining the holding period, *A* can designate the specific units of *PRS* sold. If *A* properly identifies the five units sold as five of the ten units for which A has a long-term holding period and elects to use the identification method for all subsequent sales or exchanges of interests in the partnership by using the actual holding period in reporting the transaction on *A*'s federal income tax return, the capital gain realized will be long-term capital gain.

Example 7. Disproportionate distribution. In 1997, *A* and *B* each contribute cash of $50,000 to form and become equal partners in a partnership (*PRS*). More than one year later, *A* receives a distribution worth $22,000 from *PRS*, which reduces *A*'s interest in *PRS* to 36 percent. After the distribution, *B* owns 64 percent of *PRS*. The holding periods of *A* and *B* in their interests in *PRS* are not affected by the distribution.

Example 8. Gain or loss as a result of a distribution—(i) On January 1, 1996, *A* contributes property with a basis of $10 and a fair market value of $10,000 in exchange for an interest in a partnership (*ABC*). On September 30, 2000, when *A*'s interest in *ABC* is worth $12,000 (and the basis of *A*'s partnership interest is still $10), *A* contributes $12,000 cash in exchange for an additional interest in *ABC*. *A* is allocated a loss equal to $10,000 by *ABC* for the taxable year ending December 31, 2000, thereby reducing the basis of *A*'s partnership interest to $2,010. On February 1, 2001, *ABC* makes a cash distribution to *A* of $10,000. *ABC* holds no inventory or unrealized receivables. (Assume that *A* is allocated no gain or loss for the taxable year ending December 31, 2001, so that the basis of *A*'s partnership interest does not increase or decrease as a result of such allocations.)

(ii) The netting rule contained in paragraph (b)(2) of this section provides that, in determining the holding period of *A*'s interest in *ABC*, the cash contribution made on September 30, 2000, must be reduced by the distribution made on February 1, 2001. Accordingly, for purposes of determining the holding period of *A*'s interest in *ABC*, *A* is treated as having made a cash contribution of $2,000 ($12,000 – $10,000) to *ABC* on September 30, 2000. *A*'s holding period in one-seventh of *A*'s interest in *ABC* ($2,000 cash contributed over the $14,000 value of the entire interest (determined as if only $2,000 were contributed rather than $12,000)) begins on the day after the cash contribution. *A* recognizes $7,990 of capital gain as a result of the distribution. See section 731(a)(1). One-seventh of the capital gain recog-

Reg. § 1.1223-3(f)

nized as a result of the distribution is short-term capital gain, and six-sevenths of the capital gain is long-term capital gain. After the distribution, *A*'s basis in the interest in *PRS* is $0, and the holding period for the interest in *PRS* continues to be divided in the same proportions as before the distribution.

(g) *Effective date.* This section applies to transfers of partnership interests and distributions of property from a partnership that occur on or after September 21, 2000. [Reg. § 1.1223-3.]

☐ [*T.D.* 8902, 9-20-2000.]

Special Rules for Determining Capital Gains and Losses

§ 1.1231-1. **Gains and losses from the sale or exchange of certain property used in the trade or business.**—(a) *In general.* Section 1231 provides that, subject to the provisions of paragraph (e) of this section, a taxpayer's gains and losses from the disposition (including involuntary conversion) of assets described in that section as "property used in the trade or business" and from the involuntary conversion of capital assets held for more than 1 year (6 months for taxable years beginning before 1977; 9 months for taxable years beginning in 1977) shall be treated as long-term capital gains and losses if the total gains exceed the total losses. If the total gains do not exceed the total losses, all such gains and losses are treated as ordinary gains and losses. Therefore, if the taxpayer has no gains subject to section 1231, a recognized loss from the condemnation (or from a sale or exchange under threat of condemnation) of even a capital asset held for more than 1 year (6 months for taxable years beginning before 1977; 9 months for taxable years beginning in 1977) is an ordinary loss. Capital assets subject to section 1231 treatment include only capital assets involuntarily converted. The noncapital assets subject to section 1231 treatment are (1) depreciable business property and business real property held for more than 1 year (6 months for taxable years beginning before 1977; 9 months for taxable years beginning in 1977), other than stock in trade and certain copyrights and artistic property and, in the case of sales and other dispositions occurring after July 25, 1969, other than a letter, memorandum, or property similar to a letter or memorandum; (2) timber, coal, and iron ore which do not otherwise meet the requirements of section 1231 but with respect to which section 631 applies; and (3) certain livestock and unharvested crops. See paragraph (c) of this section.

(b) *Treatment of gains and losses.* For the purpose of applying section 1231, a taxpayer must aggregate his recognized gains and losses from—

(1) The sale, exchange, or involuntary conversion of property used in the trade or business (as defined in section 1231(b)), and

(2) The involuntary conversion (but not sale or exchange) of capital assets held for more than 1 year (6 months for taxable years beginning before 1977; 9 months for taxable years beginning in 1977).

If the gains to which section 1231 applies exceed the losses to which the section applies, the gains and losses are treated as long-term capital gains and losses and are subject to the provisions of parts I and II (section 1201 and following), subchapter P, chapter 1, of the Code, relating to capital gains and losses. If the gains to which section 1231 applies do not exceed the losses to which the section applies, the gains and losses are treated as ordinary gains and losses. Therefore, in the latter case, a loss from the involuntary conversion of a capital asset held for more than 1 year (6 months for taxable years beginning before 1977; 9 months for taxable years beginning in 1977) is treated as an ordinary loss and is not subject to the limitation on capital losses in section 1211. The phrase "involuntary conversion" is defined in paragraph (e) of this section.

(c) *Transactions to which section applies.* Section 1231 applies to recognized gains and losses from the following:

(1) The sale, exchange, or involuntary conversion of property held for more than 1 year (6 months for taxable years beginning before 1977; 9 months for taxable years beginning in 1977) and used in the taxpayer's trade or business, which is either real property or is of a character subject to the allowance for depreciation under section 167 (even though fully depreciated), and which is not—

(i) Property of a kind which would properly be includible in the inventory of the taxpayer if on hand at the close of the taxable year, or property held by the taxpayer primarily for sale to customers in the ordinary course of business;

(ii) A copyright, a literary, musical, or artistic composition, or similar property, or (in the case of sales and other dispositions occurring after July 25, 1969) a letter, memorandum, or property similar to a letter or memorandum, held by a taxpayer described in section 1221(3); or

(iii) Livestock held for draft, breeding, dairy, or sporting purposes, except to the extent included under subparagraph (4) of this paragraph, or poultry.

(2) The involuntary conversion of capital assets held for more than 1 year (6 months for taxable years beginning before 1977; 9 months for taxable years beginning in 1977).

Reg. § 1.1231-1(a)

(3) The cutting or disposal of timber, or the disposal of coal or iron ore, to the extent considered arising from a sale or exchange by reason of the provisions of section 631 and the regulations thereunder.

(4) The sale, exchange, or involuntary conversion of livestock if the requirements of § 1.1231-2 are met.

(5) The sale, exchange, or involuntary conversion of unharvested crops on land which is (i) used in the taxpayer's trade or business and held for more than 1 year (6 months for taxable years beginning before 1977; 9 months for taxable years beginning in 1977), and (ii) sold or exchanged at the same time and to the same person. See paragraph (f) of this section. For purposes of section 1231, the phrase "property used in the trade or business" means property described in this paragraph (other than property described in subparagraph (2) of this paragraph). Notwithstanding any of the provisions of this paragraph, section 1231(a) does not apply to gains and losses under the circumstances described in paragraph (e)(2) or (3) of this section.

(d) *Extent to which gains and losses are taken into account.* All gains and losses to which section 1231 applies must be taken into account in determining whether and to what extent the gains exceed the losses. For the purpose of this computation, the provisions of section 1211 limiting the deduction of capital losses do not apply, and no losses are excluded by that section. With that exception, gains are included in the computations under section 1231 only to the extent that they are taken into account in computing gross income, and losses are included only to the extent that they are taken into account in computing taxable income. The following are examples of gains and losses not included in the computations under section 1231:

(1) Losses of a personal nature which are not deductible by reason of section 165(c) or (d), such as losses from the sale of property held for personal use;

(2) Losses which are not deductible under section 267 (relating to losses with respect to transactions between related taxpayers) or section 1091 (relating to losses from wash sales);

(3) Gain on the sale of property (to which section 1231 applies) reported for any taxable year on the installment method under section 453, except to the extent the gain is to be reported under section 453 for the taxable year; and

(4) Gains and losses which are not recognized under section 1002, such as those to which sections 1031 through 1036, relating to common nontaxable exchanges, apply.

(e) *Involuntary conversion*—(1) *General rule.* For purposes of section 1231, the terms "compulsory or involuntary conversion" and "involuntary conversion" of property mean the conversion of property into money or other property as a result of complete or partial destruction, theft or seizure, or an exercise of the power of requisition or condemnation, or the threat of imminence thereof. Losses upon the complete or partial destruction, theft, seizure, requisition, or condemnation of property are treated as losses upon an involuntary conversion whether or not there is a conversion of the property into other property or money and whether or not the property is uninsured, partially insured, or totally insured. For example, if a capital asset held for more than 1 year (6 months for taxable years beginning before 1977; 9 months for taxable years beginning in 1977), with an adjusted basis of $400, but not held for the production of income, is stolen, and the loss which is sustained in the taxable year 1956 is not compensated for by insurance or otherwise, section 1231 applies to the $400 loss. For certain exceptions to this subparagraph, see subparagraphs (2) and (3) of this paragraph.

(2) *Certain uninsured losses.* Notwithstanding the provisions of subparagraph (1) of this paragraph, losses sustained during a taxable year beginning after December 31, 1957, and before January 1, 1970, with respect to both property used in the trade or business and any capital asset held for more than 6 months and held for the production of income, which losses arise from fire, storm, shipwreck, or other casualty, or from theft, and which are not compensated for by insurance in any amount, are not losses to which section 1231(a) applies. Such losses shall not be taken into account in applying the provisions of this section.

(3) *Exclusion of gains and losses from certain involuntary conversions.* Notwithstanding the provisions of subparagraph (1) of this paragraph, if for any taxable year beginning after December 31, 1969, the recognized losses from the involuntary conversion as a result of fire, storm, shipwreck, or other casualty, or from theft, of any property used in the trade or business or of any capital asset held for more than 1 year (6 months for taxable years beginning before 1977; 9 months for taxable years beginning in 1977) exceed the recognized gains from the involuntary conversion of any such property as a result of fire, storm, shipwreck, or other casualty, or from theft, such gains and losses are not gains and losses to which section 1231 applies and shall not be taken into account in applying the provisions of this section. The net loss, in effect, will be treated as an ordinary loss. This subparagraph shall apply whether such property is uninsured, partially insured, or totally insured and, in the case of a

Reg. § 1.1231-1(e)(3)

capital asset held for more than 1 year (6 months for taxable years beginning before 1977; 9 months for taxable years beginning in 1977), whether the property is property used in the trade or business, property held for the production of income, or a personal asset.

(f) *Unharvested crops.*—Section 1231 does not apply to a sale, exchange or involuntary conversion of an unharvested crop if the taxpayer retains any right or option to reacquire the land the crop is on, directly or indirectly (other than a right customarily incident to a mortgage or other security transaction). The length of time for which the crop, as distinguished from the land, is held is immaterial. A leasehold or estate for years is not "land" for the purpose of section 1231.

(g) *Examples.* The provisions of this section may be illustrated by the following examples:

Example (1). A, an individual, makes his income tax return on the calendar year basis. A's recognized gains and losses for 1957 of the kind described in section 1231 are as follows:

	Gains	Losses
1. Gain on sale of machinery, used in the business and subject to an allowance for depreciation, held for more than 6 months	$4,000	
2. Gain reported in 1957 (under sec. 453) on installment sale in 1956 of factory premises used in the business (including building and land, each held for more than 6 months)	6,000	
3. Gain reported in 1957 (under sec. 453) on installment sale in 1957 of land held for more than 6 months, used in the business as a storage lot for trucks	2,000	
4. Gain on proceeds from requisition by Government of boat, held for more than 6 months, used in the business and subject to an allowance for depreciation	500	
5. Loss upon the destruction by fire of warehouse, held for more than 6 months and used in the business (excess of adjusted basis of warehouse over compensation by insurance, etc.)		$3,000
6. Loss upon theft of unregistered bearer bonds, held for more than 6 months		5,000
7. Loss in storm of pleasure yacht, purchased in 1950 for $1,800 and having a fair market value of $1,000 at the time of the storm		1,000
8. Total gains	$12,500	
9. Total losses		$9,000
10. Excess of gains over losses	$3,500	

Since the aggregate of the recognized gains ($12,500) exceeds the aggregate of the recognized losses ($9,000), such gains and losses are treated under section 1231 as gains and losses from the sale or exchange of capital assets held for more than six months. For any taxable year ending after December 31, 1957, and before January 1, 1970, the $5,000 loss upon theft of bonds (item 6) would not be taken into account under section 1231. See paragraph (e)(2) of this section.

Example (2). If in example (1), A also had a loss of $4,000 from the sale under threat of condemnation of a capital asset acquired for profit and held for more than six months, then the gains ($12,500) would not exceed the losses ($9,000 plus $4,000 or $13,000). Neither the loss on that sale nor any of the other items set forth in example (1) would then be treated as gains and losses from the sale or exchange of capital assets, but all of such items would be treated as ordinary gains and losses. Likewise, if A had no other gain or loss, the $4,000 loss would be treated as an ordinary loss.

Example (3). A's yacht, used for pleasure and acquired for that use in 1945 at a cost of $25,000, was requisitioned by the Government in 1957 for $15,000. A sustained no loss deductible under section 165(c) and since no loss with respect to the requisition is recognizable, the loss will not be included in the computations under section 1231.

Example (4). A, an individual, makes his income tax return on a calendar year basis. During 1970 trees on A's residential property which were planted in 1950 after the purchase of such property were destroyed by fire. The loss, which was in the amount of $2,000 after applying section 165(c)(3), was not compensated for by insurance or otherwise. During the same year A also recognized a $1,500 gain from insurance proceeds compensating him for the theft sustained in 1970 of a diamond brooch purchased in 1960 for personal use. A has no other gains or losses for 1970 from the involuntary conversion of property. Since the recognized losses exceed the recognized gains from the involuntary conversion for 1970 as a result of fire, storm, shipwreck, or other casualty, or from theft, of any property used in the trade or business or of any capital asset held for more than 6 months, neither the gain nor loss is included in making the computations under section 1231.

Example (5). The facts are the same as in example (4), except that A also recognized a gain of $1,000 from insurance proceeds compensating him for the total destruction by fire of a truck, held for more than 6 months, used in A's business and subject to an allowance for depreciation. A has no other gains or losses for 1970 from the involuntary conversion of property. Since the recognized losses ($2,000) do not exceed the recognized gains ($2,500) from the involuntary

Reg. § 1.1231-1(f)

conversion for 1970 as a result of fire, storm, shipwreck, or other casualty, or from theft, of any property used in the trade or business or of any capital asset held for more than 6 months, such gains and losses are included in making the computations under section 1231. Thus, if A has no other gains or losses for 1970 to which section 1231 applies, the gains and losses from these in-

voluntary conversions are treated under section 1231 as gains and losses from the sale or exchange of capital assets held for more than 6 months.

Example (6). The facts are the same as in example (5) except that A also has the following recognized gains and losses for 1970 to which section 1231 applies:

	Gains	Losses
Gain on sale of machinery, used in the business and subject to an allowance for depreciation, held for more than 6 months	$ 4,000	
Gain reported in 1970 (under sec. 453) on installment sale in 1969 of factory premises used in the business (including building and land, each held for more than 6 months)	6,000	
Gain reported in 1970 (under sec. 453) on installment sale in 1970 of land held for more than 6 months, used in the business as a storage lot for trucks	2,000	
Loss upon the sale in 1970 of warehouse, used in the business and subject to an allowance for depreciation, held for more than 6 months		$5,000
Total gains	12,000	
Total losses		5,000

Since the aggregate of the recognized gains ($14,500) exceeds the aggregate of the recognized losses ($7,000), such gains and losses are treated under section 1231 as gains and losses from the sale or exchange of capital assets held for more than 6 months.

Example (7). B, an individual, makes his income tax return on the calendar year basis. During 1970 furniture used in his business and held for more than 6 months was destroyed by fire. The recognized loss, after compensation by insurance, was $2,000. During the same year B recognized a $1,000 gain upon the sale of a parcel of real estate used in his business and held for more than 6 months, and a $6,000 loss upon the sale of stock held for more than 6 months. B has no other gains or losses for 1970 from the involuntary conversion, or the sale or exchange of, property. The $6,000 loss upon the sale of stock is not a loss to which section 1231 applies since the stock is not property used in the trade or business, as defined in section 1231(b). The $2,000 loss upon the destruction of the furniture is not a loss to which section 1231 applies since the recognized losses ($2,000) exceed the recognized gains ($0) from the involuntary conversion for 1970 as a result of fire, storm, shipwreck, or other casualty, or from theft, of any property used in the trade or business or of any capital asset held for more than 6 months. Accordingly, the $1,000 gain upon the sale of real estate is considered to be gain from the sale or exchange of a capital asset held for more than 6 months since the gains ($1,000) to which section 1231 applies exceed the losses ($0) to which such section applies.

Example (8). The facts are the same as in example (7) except that B also recognized a gain of $4,000 from insurance proceeds compensating

him for the total destruction by fire of a freighter, held for more than 6 months, used in B's business and subject to an allowance for depreciation. Since the recognized losses ($2,000) do not exceed the recognized gains ($4,000) from the involuntary conversion for 1970 as a result of fire, storm, shipwreck, or other casualty, or from theft, of any property used in the trade or business or of any capital asset held for more than 6 months, such gains and losses are included in making the computations under section 1231. Since the aggregate of the recognized gains to which section 1231 applies ($5,000) exceeds the aggregate of the recognized losses to which such section applies ($2,000), such gains and losses are treated under section 1231 as gains and losses from the sale or exchange of capital assets held for more than 6 months. The $6,000 loss upon the sale of stock is not taken into account in making such computation since it is not a loss to which section 1231 applies. [Reg. § 1.1231-1.]

☐ [T.D. 6253, 9-25-57. *Amended by T.D.* 6394, 7-1-59; *T.D.* 6841, 7-26-65; *T.D.* 7141, 9-21-71; *T.D.* 7369, 7-15-75; *T.D.* 7728, 10-31-80 *and T.D.* 7829, 8-31-82.]

§ **1.1231-2. Livestock held for draft, breeding, dairy, or sporting purposes.**—(a) (1) In the case of cattle, horses, or other livestock acquired by the taxpayer after December 31, 1969, section 1231 applies to the sale, exchange, or involuntary conversion of such cattle, horses, or other livestock, regardless of age, held by the taxpayer for draft, breeding, dairy, or sporting purposes, and held by him—

(i) For 24 months or more from the date of acquisition in the case of cattle or horses, or

(ii) For 12 months or more from the date of acquisition in the case of such other livestock.

(2) In the case of livestock (including cattle or horses) acquired by the taxpayer on or before December 31, 1969, section 1231 applies to the sale, exchange, or involuntary conversion of such livestock, regardless of age, held by the taxpayer for draft, breeding, or dairy purposes, and held by him for 12 months or more from the date of acquisition.

(3) For the purposes of section 1231, the term "livestock" is given a broad, rather than a narrow, interpretation and includes cattle, hogs, horses, mules, donkeys, sheep, goats, fur-bearing animals, and other mammals. However, it does not include poultry, chickens, turkeys, pigeons, geese, other birds, fish, frogs, reptiles, etc.

(b)(1) Whether or not livestock is held by the taxpayer for draft, breeding, dairy, or sporting purposes depends upon all of the facts and circumstances in each case. The purpose for which the animal is held is ordinarily shown by the taxpayer's actual use of the animal. However, a draft, breeding, dairy, or sporting purpose may be present if an animal is disposed of within a reasonable time after its intended use for such purpose is prevented or made undesirable by reason of accident, disease, drought, unfitness of the animal for such purpose, or a similar factual circumstance. Under certain circumstances, an animal held for ultimate sale to customers in the ordinary course of the taxpayer's trade or business may be considered as held for draft, breeding, dairy, or sporting purposes. However, an animal is not held by the taxpayer for draft, breeding, dairy, or sporting purposes merely because it is suitable for such purposes or merely because it is held by the taxpayer for sale to other persons for use by them for such purposes. Furthermore, an animal held by the taxpayer for other purposes is not considered as held for draft, breeding, dairy, or sporting purposes merely because of a negligible use of the animal for such purposes or merely because of the use of the animal for such purposes as an ordinary or necessary incident to the other purposes for which the animal is held. See paragraph (c) of this section for the rules to be used in determining when horses are held for racing purposes and, therefore, are considered as held for sporting purposes.

(2) The application of this paragraph is illustrated by the following examples:

Example (1). An animal intended by the taxpayer for use by him for breeding purposes is discovered to be sterile or unfit for the breeding purposes for which it was held, and is disposed of within a reasonable time thereafter. This animal is considered as held for breeding purposes.

Example (2). The taxpayer retires from the breeding or dairy business and sells his entire herd, including young animals which would have been used by him for breeding or dairy purposes if he had remained in business. These young animals are considered as held for breeding or dairy purposes. The same would be true with respect to young animals which would have been used by the taxpayer for breeding or dairy purposes but which are sold by him in reduction of his breeding or dairy herd, because of, for example, drought.

Example (3). A taxpayer in the business of raising hogs for slaughter customarily breeds sows to obtain a single litter to be raised by him for sale, and sells these brood sows after obtaining the litter. Even though these brood sows are held for ultimate sale to customers in the ordinary course of the taxpayer's trade or business, they are considered as held for breeding purposes.

Example (4). A taxpayer in the business of raising horses for sale to others for use by them as draft horses uses them for draft purposes on his own farm in order to train them. This use is an ordinary or necessary incident to the purpose of selling the animals, and, accordingly, these horses are not considered as held for draft purposes.

Example (5). The taxpayer is in the business of raising registered cattle for sale to others for use by them as breeding cattle. It is the business practice of this particular taxpayer to breed the offspring of his herd which he is holding for sale to others prior to sale in order to establish their fitness for sale as registered breeding cattle. In such case, the taxpayer's breeding of such offspring is an ordinary and necessary incident to his holding them for the purpose of selling them as bred heifers or proven bulls and does not demonstrate that the taxpayer is holding them for breeding purposes. However, those cattle held by the taxpayer as additions or replacements to his own breeding herd to produce calves are considered to be held for breeding purposes, even though they may not actually have produced calves.

Example (6). A taxpayer, engaged in the business of buying cattle and fattening them for slaughter, purchased cows with calf. The calves were born while the cows were held by the taxpayer. These cows are not considered as held for breeding purposes.

(c)(1) For purposes of paragraph (b) of this section, a horse held for racing purposes shall be considered as held for sporting purposes. Whether a horse is held for racing purposes shall be determined in accordance with the following rules:

(i) A horse which has actually been raced at a public race track shall, except in rare and unusual circumstances, be considered as held for racing purposes.

Reg. § 1.1231-2(a)(2)

(ii) A horse which has not been raced at a public track shall be considered as held for racing purposes if it has been trained to race and other facts and circumstances in the particular case also indicate that the horse was held for this purpose. For example, assume that the taxpayer maintains a written training record on all horses he keeps in training status, which shows that a particular horse does not meet objective standards (including, but not limited to, such considerations as failure to achieve predetermined standards of performance during training, or the existence of a physical or other defect) established by the taxpayer for determining the fitness and quality of horses to be retained in his racing stable. Under such circumstances, if the taxpayer disposes of the horse within a reasonable time after he determined that it did not meet his objective standards for retention, the horse shall be considered as held for racing purposes.

(iii) A horse which has neither been raced at a public track nor trained for racing shall not, except in rare and unusual circumstances, be considered as held for racing purposes.

(2) This paragraph may be illustrated by the following examples:

Example (1). The taxpayer breeds, raises, and trains horses for the purpose of racing. Every year he culls some horses from his racing stable. In 1971, the taxpayer decided that in order to prevent his racing stable from getting too large to be effectively operated he must cull six horses from it. All six of the horses culled by the taxpayer had been raced at public tracks in 1970. Under subparagraph (1)(i) of this paragraph, all these horses are considered as held for racing purposes.

Example (2). Assume the same facts as in example (1). Assume further that the taxpayer decided to cull four more horses from his racing stable in 1971. All these horses had been trained to race but had not been raced at public tracks. The taxpayer culled these four horses because the training log which the taxpayer maintains on all the horses he trains showed these horses to be unfit to remain in his racing stable. Horse A was culled because it developed shin splints during training. Horses B and C were culled because of poor temperament. B bolted every time a rider tried to mount it, and C became extremely nervous when it was placed in the starting gate. Horse D was culled because it did not qualify for retention under one of the objective standards the taxpayer had established for determining which horses to retain since it was unable to run a specified distance in a minimum time. These four horses were disposed of within a reasonable time after the taxpayer determined that they were

unfit to remain in his stable. Under subparagraph (1)(ii) of this paragraph, all these horses are considered as held for racing purposes. [Reg. § 1.1231-2.]

☐ [*T.D.* 6253, 9-25-57. *Amended by T.D.* 7141, 9-21-71.]

§ 1.1244(a)-1. Loss on small business stock treated as ordinary loss.—(a) *In general.* Subject to certain conditions and limitations, section 1244 provides that a loss on the sale or exchange (including a transaction treated as a sale or exchange, such as worthlessness) of "section 1244 stock" which would otherwise be treated as loss from the sale or exchange of a capital asset shall be treated as a loss from the sale or exchange of an asset which is not a capital asset (referred to in this section and § § 1.1244(b)-1 to 1.1244(e)-1, inclusive, as an "ordinary loss"). Such a loss shall be allowed as a deduction from gross income in arriving at adjusted gross income. The requirements that must be satisfied in order that stock may be considered section 1244 stock are described in § § 1.1244(c)-1 and 1.1244(c)-2. These requirements relate to the stock itself and the corporation issuing such stock. In addition, the taxpayer who claims an ordinary loss deduction pursuant to section 1244 must satisfy the requirements of paragraph (b) of this section.

(b) *Taxpayers entitled to ordinary loss.* The allowance of an ordinary loss deduction for a loss on section 1244 stock is permitted only to the following two classes of taxpayers:

(1) An individual sustaining the loss to whom the stock was issued by a small business corporation, or

(2) An individual who is a partner in a partnership at the time the partnership acquired the stock in an issuance from a small business corporation and whose distributive share of partnership items reflects the loss sustained by the partnership. The ordinary loss deduction is limited to the lesser of the partner's distributive share at the time of the issuance of the stock or the partner's distributive share at the time the loss is sustained. In order to claim a deduction under section 1244 the individual, or the partnership, sustaining the loss must have continuously held the stock from the date of issuance. A corporation, trust, or estate is not entitled to ordinary loss treatment under section 1244 regardless of how the stock was acquired. An individual who acquires stock from a shareholder by purchase, gift, devise, or in any other manner is not entitled to an ordinary loss under section 1244 with respect to this stock. Thus, ordinary loss treatment is not available to a partner to whom the stock is distributed by the partnership. Stock acquired through an investment banking firm, or other person, participating

Reg. § 1.1244(a)-1(b)(2)

in the sale of an issue may qualify for ordinary loss treatment only if the stock is not first issued to the firm or person. Thus, for example, if the firm acts as a selling agent for the issuing corporation the stock may qualify. On the other hand, stock purchased by an investment firm and subsequently resold does not qualify as section 1244 stock in the hands of the person acquiring the stock from the firm.

(c) *Examples.* The provisions of paragraph (b) of this section may be illustrated by the following examples:

Example (1). A and B, both individuals, and C, a trust, are equal partners in a partnership to which a small business corporation issues section 1244 stock. The partnership sells the stock at a loss. A's and B's distributive share of the loss may be treated as an ordinary loss pursuant to section 1244, but C's distributive share of the loss may not be so treated.

Example (2). The facts are the same as in example (1) except that the section 1244 stock is distributed by the partnership to partner A and he subsequently sells the stock at a loss. Section 1244 is not applicable to the loss since A did not acquire the stock by issuance from the small business corporation. [Reg. § 1.1244(a)-1.]

☐ [*T.D.* 6495, 10-7-60. *Amended by T.D.* 7779, 6-1-81.]

§ 1.1244(b)-1. Annual limitation.—(a) *In general.* Subsection (b) of section 1244 imposes a limitation on the aggregate amount of loss that for any taxable year may be treated as an ordinary loss by a taxpayer by reason of that section. In the case of a partnership, the limitation is determined separately as to each partner. Any amount of loss in excess of the applicable limitation is treated as loss from the sale or exchange of a capital asset.

(b) *Amount of loss*—(1) *Taxable years beginning after December 31, 1978.* For any taxable year beginning after December 31, 1978, the maximum amount that may be treated as an ordinary loss under section 1244 is—

(i) $50,000, or

(ii) $100,000, if a husband and wife file a joint return under section 6013.

These limitations on the maximum amount of ordinary loss apply whether the loss or losses are sustained on pre-November 1978 stock (as defined in § 1.1244(c)-1(a)(1)), post-November 1978 stock (as defined in § 1.1244(c)-1(a)(2)), or on any combination of pre-November 1978 stock and post-November 1978 stock. The limitation referred to in (ii) applies to a joint return whether the loss or losses are sustained by one or both spouses.

* * *

[Reg. § 1.1244(b)-1.]

Reg. § 1.1244(b)-1(a)

☐ [*T.D.* 6495, 10-7-60. *Amended by T.D.* 7779, 6-1-81.]

§ 1.1244(c)-1. Section 1244 stock defined.—(a) *In general.* For purposes of § § 1.1244(a)-1 to 1.1244(e)-1, inclusive—

(1) The term "pre-November 1978 stock" means stock issued after June 30, 1958, and on or before November 6, 1978.

(2) The term "post-November 1978 stock" means stock issued after November 6, 1978.

In order that stock may qualify as section 1244 stock, the requirements described in paragraphs (b) through (e) of this section must be satisfied. In addition, the requirements of paragraph (f) of this section must be satisfied in the case of pre-November 1978 stock. Whether these requirements have been met is determined at the time the stock is issued, except for the requirement in paragraph (e) of this section. Whether the requirement in paragraph (e) of this section, relating to gross receipts of the corporation, has been satisfied is determined at the time a loss is sustained. Therefore, at the time of issuance it cannot be said with certainty that stock will qualify for the benefits of section 1244.

(b) *Common stock.* Only common stock, either voting or nonvoting, in a domestic corporation may qualify as section 1244 stock. For purposes of section 1244, neither securities of the corporation convertible into common stock nor common stock convertible into other securities of the corporation are treated as common stock. An increase in the basis of outstanding stock as a result of a contribution to capital is not treated as an issuance of stock under section 1244. For definition of domestic corporation, see section 7701(a)(4) and the regulations under that section.

(c) *Small business corporation.* At the time the stock is issued (or, in the case of pre-November 1978 stock, at the time of adoption of the plan described in paragraph (f)(1) of this section) the corporation must be a "small business corporation". See § 1.1244(c)-2 for the definition of a small business corporation.

(d) *Issued for money or other property.* (1) The stock must be issued to the taxpayer for money or other property transferred by the taxpayer to the corporation. However, stock issued in exchange for stock or securities, including stock or securities of the issuing corporation, cannot qualify as section 1244 stock, except as provided in § 1.1244(d)-3, relating to certain cases where stock is issued in exchange for section 1244 stock. Stock issued for services rendered or to be rendered to, or for the benefit of, the issuing corporation does not qualify as section 1244 stock. Stock issued in consideration for cancellation of indebtedness of the corporation shall be considered issued in exchange for money or other property unless such indebtedness is evidenced by a security, or arises out of the performance of personal services.

(2) The following examples illustrate situations where stock fails to qualify as section 1244 stock as a result of the rules in subparagraph (1) of this paragraph:

Example (1). A taxpayer owns stock of Corporation X issued to him prior to July 1, 1958. Under a plan adopted in 1977, he exchanges his stock for a new issuance of stock of Corporation X. The stock received by the taxpayer in the exchange may not qualify as section 1244 stock even if the corporation has adopted a valid plan and is a small business corporation.

Example (2). A taxpayer owns stock in Corporation X. Corporation X merges into Corporation Y. In exchange for his stock, Corporation Y issues shares of its stock to the taxpayer. The stock in Corporation Y does not qualify as section 1244 stock even if the stock exchanged by the taxpayer did qualify.

Example (3). Corporation X transfers part of its business assets to Corporation Y, a new corporation, and all of the stock of Corporation Y is issued directly to the shareholders of Corporation X. Since the Corporation Y stock was not issued to the shareholders for a transfer by them of money or other property, none of the Corporation Y stock in the hands of the shareholders can qualify.

(e) *Gross receipts.* (1)(i)(*a*) Except as provided in subparagraph (2) of this paragraph, stock will not qualify under section 1244 if 50 percent or more of the gross receipts of the corporation, for the period consisting of the five most recent taxable years of the corporation ending before the date the loss on such stock is sustained by the shareholders is derived from royalties, rents, dividends, interest, annuities, and sales or exchanges of stock or securities. If the corporation has not been in existence for five taxable years ending before such date, the percentage test referred to in the preceding sentence applies to the period of the taxable years ending before such date during which the corporation has been in existence; and if the loss is sustained during the first taxable year of the corporation such test applies to the period beginning with the first day of such taxable year and ending on the day before the loss is sustained. The test under this paragraph shall be made on the basis of total gross receipts, except that gross receipts from the sales or exchanges of stock or securities shall be taken into account only to the extent of gains therefrom. The term "gross receipts" as used in section 1244(c)(1)(C) is not synonymous with "gross income". Gross receipts means the total amount received or accrued under the method of accounting used by the corporation in computing its taxable income. Thus, the total amount of receipts is not reduced by returns and allowances, cost, or deductions. For example, gross receipts will include the total amount received or accrued during the corporation's taxable year from the sale or exchange (including a sale or exchange to which section 337 applies) of any kind of property, from investments, and for services rendered by the corporation. However, gross receipts does not include amounts received in nontaxable sales or exchanges (other than those to which section 337 applies), except to the extent that gain is recognized by the corporation, nor does that term include amounts received as a loan, as repayment of a loan, as a contribution to capital, or on the issuance by the corporation of its own stock.

(b) The meaning of the term "gross receipts" as used in section 1244(c)(1)(C) may be further illustrated by the following examples:

Example (1). A corporation on the accrual method sells property (other than stock or securities) and receives payment partly in money and partly in the form of a note payable at a future time. The amount of the money and the face amount of the note would be considered gross receipts in the taxable year of the sale and would not be reduced by the adjusted basis of the property, the costs of sale, or any other amount.

Example (2). A corporation has a long-term contract as defined in paragraph (a) of § 1.451-3 with respect to which it reports income according to the percentage-of-completion method as described in paragraph (b)(1) of § 1.451-3. The portion of the gross contract price which corresponds to the percentage of the entire contract which has been completed during the taxable year shall be included in gross receipts for such year.

Example (3). A corporation which regularly sells personal property on the installment plan elects to report its taxable income from the sale of property (other than stock or securities) on the installment method in accordance with section 453. The installment payments actually received in a given taxable year of the corporation shall be included in gross receipts for such year.

(ii) The term "royalties" as used in subdivision (i) of this subparagraph means all royalties, including mineral, oil, and gas royalties (whether or not the aggregate amount of such royalties constitutes 50 percent or more of the gross income of the corporation for the taxable year), and amounts received for the privilege of using patents, copyrights, secret processes and formulas, good will, trademarks, trade brands, franchises, and other like property. The term "royalties" does not include amounts received upon the disposal of

Reg. § 1.1244(c)-1(e)

timber, coal, or domestic iron ore with a retained economic interest to which the special rules of section 631(b) and (c) apply or amounts received from the transfer of patent rights to which section 1235 applies. For the definition of "mineral, oil, or gas royalties," see paragraph (b)(11)(ii) and (iii) of § 1.543-1. For purposes of this subdivision, the gross amount of royalties shall not be reduced by any part of the cost of the rights under which they are received or by any amount allowable as a deduction in computing taxable income.

(iii) The term "rents" as used in subdivision (i) of this subparagraph means amounts received for the use of, or right to use, property (whether real or personal) of the corporation, whether or not such amounts constitute 50 percent or more of the gross income of the corporation for the taxable year. The term "rents" does not include payments for the use or occupancy of rooms or other space where significant services are also rendered to the occupant, such as for the use or occupancy of rooms or other quarters in hotels, boarding houses, or apartment houses furnishing hotel services, or in tourist homes, motor courts, or motels. Generally, services are considered rendered to the occupant if they are primarily for his convenience and are other than those usually or customarily rendered in connection with the rental of rooms or other space for occupancy only. The supplying of maid service, for example, constitutes such services; whereas the furnishing of heat and light, the cleaning of public entrances, exits, stairways, and lobbies, the collection of trash, etc., are not considered as services rendered to the occupant. Payments for the use or occupancy of entire private residences or living quarters in duplex or multiple housing units, of offices in an office building, etc., are generally "rents" under section 1244(c)(1)(C). Payments for the parking of automobiles ordinarily do not constitute rents. Payments for the warehousing of goods or for the use of personal property do no constitute rents if significant services are rendered in connection with such payments.

(iv) The term "dividends" as used in subdivision (i) of this subparagraph includes dividends as defined in section 316, amounts required to be included in gross income under section 551 (relating to foreign personal holding company income taxed to United States shareholders), and consent dividends determined as provided in section 565.

(v) The term "interest" as used in subdivision (i) of this subparagraph means any amounts received for the use of money (including tax-exempt interest).

(vi) The term "annuities" as used in subdivision (i) of this subparagraph means the entire amount received as an annuity under an annuity, endowment, or life insurance contract, regardless of whether only part of such amount would be includible in gross income under section 72.

(vii) For purposes of subdivision (i) of this subparagraph, gross receipts from the sales or exchanges of stock or securities are taken into account only to the extent of gains therefrom. Thus, the gross receipts from the sale of a particular share of stock will be the excess of the amount realized over the adjusted basis of such share. If the adjusted basis should equal or exceed the amount realized on the sale or exchange of a certain share of stock, bond, etc., there would be no gross receipts resulting from the sale of such security. Losses on sales or exchanges of stock or securities do not offset gains on the sales or exchanges of other stock or securities for purposes of computing gross receipts from such sales or exchanges. Gross receipts from the sale or exchange of stocks and securities include gains received from such sales or exchanges by a corporation even though such corporation is a regular dealer in stocks and securities. For the meaning of the term "stocks or securities," see paragraph (b)(5)(i) of § 1.543-1.

(2) The requirement of subparagraph (1) of this paragraph need not be satisfied if for the applicable period the aggregate amount of deductions allowed to the corporation exceeds the aggregate amount of its gross income. But for this purpose the deductions allowed by section 172, relating to the net operating loss deduction, and by sections 242, 243, 244, and 245, relating to certain special deductions for corporations, shall not be taken into account. Notwithstanding the provisions of this subparagraph and of subparagraph (1) of this paragraph, pursuant to the specific delegation of authority granted in section 1244(e) to prescribe such regulations as may be necessary to carry out the purposes of section 1244, ordinary loss treatment will not be available with respect to stock of a corporation which is not largely an operating company within the five most recent taxable years (or such lesser period as the corporation is in existence) ending before the date of the loss. Thus, for example, assume that a person who is not a dealer in real estate forms a corporation which issues stock to him which meets all the formal requirements of section 1244 stock. The corporation then acquires a piece of unimproved real estate which it holds as an investment. The property declines in value and the stockholder sells his stock at a loss. The loss does not qualify for ordinary loss treatment under section 1244 but must be treated as a capital loss.

(3) In applying subparagraphs (1) and (2) of this paragraph to a successor corporation in a reorganization described in section 368(a)(1)(F),

Reg. § 1.1244(c)-1(e)(2)

such corporation shall be treated as the same corporation as its predecessor. See paragraph (d)(2) of § 1.1244(d)-3.

* * *

[Reg. § 1.1244(c)-1.]

☐ *[T.D. 6495, 10-7-60 and T.D. 6508, 12-1-60. Amended by T.D. 6637, 2-25-63, T.D. 6841, 7-26-65, and T.D. 7779, 6-1-81.]*

§ 1.1244(c)-2. Small business corporation defined.—(a) *In general.* A corporation is treated as a small business corporation if it is a domestic corporation that satisfies the requirements described in paragraph (b) or (c) of this section. The requirements of paragraph (b) of this section apply if a loss is sustained on post-November 1978 stock. The requirements of paragraph (c) of this section apply if a loss is sustained on pre-November 1978 stock. If losses are sustained on both pre-November 1978 stock and post-November 1978 stock in the same taxable year, the requirements of paragraph (b) of this section are applied to the corporation at the time of the issuance of the stock (as required by paragraph (b) in the case of a loss on post-November 1978 stock) in order to determine whether the loss on post-November 1978 stock qualifies as a section 1244 loss, and the requirements of paragraph (c) of this section are applied to the corporation at the time of the adoption of the plan (as required by paragraph (c) in the case of a loss on pre-November 1978 stock) in order to determine whether the loss on pre-November 1978 stock qualifies as a section 1244 loss. For definition of domestic corporation, see section 7701(a)(4) and the regulations under that section.

(b) *Post-November 1978 stock* —(1) *Amount received by corporation for stock.* Capital receipts of a small business corporation may not exceed $1,000,000. For purposes of this paragraph the term "capital receipts" means the aggregate dollar amount received by the corporation for its stock, as a contribution to capital, and as paid-in surplus. If the $1,000,000 limitation is exceeded, the rules of subparagraph (2) of this paragraph (b) apply. In making these determinations, (i) property is taken into account at its adjusted basis to the corporation (for determining gain) as of the date received by the corporation, and (ii) this aggregate amount is reduced by the amount of any liability to which the property was subject and by the amount of any liability assumed by the corporation at the time the property was received. Capital receipts are not reduced by distributions to shareholders, even though the distributions may be capital distributions.

(2) *Requirement of designation in event $1,000,000 limitation exceeded.* (i) If capital receipts exceed $1,000,000, the corporation shall designate as section 1244 stock certain shares of post-November 1978 common stock issued for money or other property in the transitional year. For purposes of this paragraph, the term "transitional year" means the first taxable year in which capital receipts exceed $1,000,000 and in which the corporation issues stock. This designation shall be made in accordance with the rules of subdivision (iii) of this paragraph (b)(2). The amount received for designated stock shall not exceed $1,000,000, less amounts received—

(A) In exchange for stock in years prior to the transitional year;

(B) As contributions to capital in years prior to the transitional year; and

(C) As paid-in surplus in years prior to the transitional year.

(ii) Post-November 1978 common stock issued for money or other property before the transitional year qualifies as section 1244 stock without affirmative designation by the corporation. Post-November 1978 common stock issued after the transitional year does not qualify as section 1244 stock.

(iii) The corporation shall make the designation required by subdivision (i) of this paragraph (b)(2) not later than the 15th day of the third month following the close of the transitional year. However, in the case of post-November 1978 common stock issued on or before June 2, 1981 the corporation shall make the required designation by August 3, 1981 or by the 15th day of the 3rd month following the close of the transitional year, whichever is later. The designation shall be made by entering the numbers of the qualifying share certificates on the corporation's records. If the shares do not bear serial numbers or other identifying numbers or letters, or are not represented by share certificates, the corporation shall make an alternative designation in writing at the time of issuance, or, in the case of post-November 1978 common stock issued on or before June 2, 1981 by August 3, 1981. This alternative designation may be made in any manner sufficient to identify the shares qualifying for section 1244 treatment. If the corporation fails to make a designation by share certificate number or an alternative written designation as described, the rules of subparagraph (3) of this paragraph (b) apply.

(3) *Allocation of section 1244 benefit in event corporation fails to designate qualifying shares.* If a corporation issues post-November 1978 stock in the transitional year and fails to designate certain shares of post-November 1978 common stock as section 1244 stock in accordance with the rules of subparagraph (2) of this paragraph (b), the following rules apply:

Reg. § 1.1244(c)-2(b)(3)

(i) Section 1244 treatment is extended to losses sustained on post-November 1978 common stock issued for money or other property in taxable years before the transitional year and is withheld from losses sustained on post-November 1978 stock issued in taxable years after the transitional year.

(ii) Post-1958 capital received before the transitional year is subtracted from $1,000,000.

(iii) Subject to the annual limitation described in § 1.1244(b)-1, an ordinary loss on post-November 1978 common stock issued for money or other property in the transitional year is allowed in an amount which bears the same ratio to the total loss sustained by the individual as—

(A) The amount described in § 1.1244(c)-2(b)(3)(ii) bears to

(B) The total amount of money and other property received by the corporation in exchange for stock, as a contribution to capital, and as paid-in surplus in the transitional year.

(4) *Examples.* The provisions of this paragraph (b) may be illustrated by the following examples:

Example (1). On December 1, 1978, Corporation W, a newly-formed corporation, issues 10,000 shares of common stock at $125 a share for an amount (determined under subparagraph (1) of this paragraph (b)) of money and other property totaling $1,250,000. The board of directors specifies that 8,000 shares are section 1244 stock and records the certificate numbers of the qualifying shares in its minutes. Because Corporation W issued post-November 1978 common stock in exchange for money and other property exceeding $1,000,000, but has designated shares of stock as section 1244 stock and the designated shares were issued in exchange for money and other property not exceeding $1,000,000 (8,000 shares × $125 price per share = $1,000,000), the 8,000 designated shares qualify as section 1244 stock.

Example (2). Corporation X comes into existence on June 1, 1979. On June 10, 1979, Corporation X issues 2,500 shares of common stock at $250 per share to shareholder A and 2,500 shares of common stock at $250 per share to shareholder B. By written agreement dated September 1, 1981, shareholder A and shareholder B determine that 1,500 of shareholder A's shares and all of shareholder B's shares will be treated as section 1244 stock. Although shareholder A's 1,500 shares and shareholder B's 2,500 shares were issued for money and other property not exceeding $1,000,000 (4,000 shares × $250 price per share = $1,000,000), these 4,000 shares do not qualify as section 1244 stock under the rules of subparagraph (2) of this paragraph (b) for three reasons: The agreement of September 1, 1979, (i) did not

identify which 1,500 of shareholder A's 2,500 shares were intended to qualify for section 1244 treatment, (ii) was made by the shareholders and not by Corporation X, and (iii) was made later than the 15th day of the third month following the close of the transitional year. However, certain of the shares issued by Corporation X may qualify as section 1244 stock under the rules of subparagraph (3) of this paragraph (b). See example (4).

* * *

[Reg. § 1.1244(c)-2.]

☐ [*T.D.* 6495, 10-7-60. *Amended by T.D.* 7779, 6-1-81 *and T.D.* 7837, 9-28-82.]

§ 1.1245-1. General rule for treatment of gain from dispositions of certain depreciable property.—(a) *General.* (1) In general, section 1245(a)(1) provides that, upon a disposition of an item of section 1245 property, the amount by which the lower of (i) the "recomputed basis" of the property, or (ii) the amount realized on a sale, exchange, or involuntary conversion (or the fair market value of the property on any other disposition), exceeds the adjusted basis of the property shall be treated as gain from the sale or exchange of property which is neither a capital asset nor property described in section 1231 (that is, shall be recognized as ordinary income). The amount of such gain shall be determined separately for each item of section 1245 property. In general, the term "recomputed basis" means the adjusted basis of property plus all adjustments reflected in such adjusted basis on account of depreciation allowed or allowable for all periods after December 31, 1961. See section 1245(a)(2) and § 1.1245-2. Generally, the ordinary income treatment applies even though in the absence of section 1245 no gain would be recognized under the Code. For example, if a corporation distributes section 1245 property as a dividend, gain may be recognized as ordinary income to the corporation even though, in the absence of section 1245, section 311(a) would preclude any recognition of gain to the corporation. For the definition of "section 1245 property," see section 1245(a)(3) and § 1.1245-3. For exceptions and limitations to the application of section 1245(a)(1), see section 1245(b) and § 1.1245-4.

(2) Section 1245(a)(1) applies to dispositions of section 1245 property in taxable years beginning after December 31, 1962, except that—

(i) In respect of section 1245 property which is an elevator or escalator, section 1245(a)(1) applies to dispositions after December 31, 1963, and

(ii) In respect of section 1245 property which is livestock (described in subparagraph (4) of § 1.1245-3(a)), section 1245(a)(1) applies to dispositions made in taxable years beginning after December 31, 1969, and

(iii) [reserved].

(3) For purposes of this section and §§ 1.1245-2 through 1.1245-6, the term "disposition" includes a sale in a sale-and-leaseback transaction and a transfer upon the foreclosure of a security interest, but such term does not include a mere transfer of title to a creditor upon creation of a security interest or to a debtor upon termination of a security interest. Thus, for example, a disposition occurs upon a sale of property pursuant to a conditional sales contract even though the seller retains legal title to the property for purposes of security but a disposition does not occur when the seller ulitmately gives up his security interest following payment by the purchaser.

(4) For purposes of applying section 1245, the facts and circumstances of each disposition shall be considered in determining what is the appropriate item of section 1245 property. A taxpayer may treat any number of units of section 1245 property in any particular depreciation account (as defined in § 1.167(a)-7) as one time of section 1245 property as long as it is reasonably clear, from the best estimates obtainable on the basis of all the facts and circumstances, that the amount of gain to which section 1245(a)(1) applies is not less than the total of the gain under section 1245(a)(1) which would be computed separately for each unit. Thus, for example, if 50 units of section 1245 property X, 25 units of section 1245 property Y, and other property are accounted for in one depreciation account, and if each such unit is sold at a gain in one transaction in which the total gain realized on the sale exceeds the sum of the adjustments reflected in the adjusted basis (as defined in paragraph (a)(2) of § 1.1245-2) of each such unit on account of depreciation allowed or allowable for periods after December 31, 1961, all 75 units may be treated as one item of section 1245 property. If, however, 5 such units of section 1245 property Y were sold at a loss, then only 70 of such units (50 of X plus the 20 of Y sold at a gain) may be treated as one item of section 1245 property.

(5) In case of a sale, exchange, or involuntary conversion of section 1245 and nonsection 1245 property in one transaction, the total amount realized upon the disposition shall be allocated between the section 1245 property and the nonsection 1245 property in proportion to their respective fair market values. In general, if a buyer and seller have adverse interests as to the allocation of the amount realized between the section 1245 property and the nonsection 1245 property, any arm's length agreement between the buyer and the seller will establish the allocation. In the absence of such an agreement, the allocation shall be made by taking into account the appropriate facts and circumstances. Some of the facts and circumstances which shall be taken into account to the extent appropriate include, but are not limited to, a comparison between the section 1245 property and all the property disposed of in such transaction of (i) the original cost and reproduction cost of construction, erection, or production, (ii) the remaining economic useful life, (iii) state of obsolescence, and (iv) anticipated expenditures to maintain, renovate, or to modernize.

(b) *Sale, exchange, or involuntary conversion.* (1) In the case of a sale, exchange, or involuntary conversion of section 1245 property, the gain to which section 1245(a)(1) applies is the amount by which (i) the lower of the amount realized upon the disposition of the property or the recomputed basis of the property, exceeds (ii) the adjusted basis of the property.

(2) The provisions of this paragraph may be illustrated by the following examples:

Example (1). On January 1, 1964, Brown purchases section 1245 property for use in his manufacturing business. The property has a basis for depreciation of $3,300. After taking depreciation deductions of $1,300 (the amount allowable), Brown realizes after selling expenses the amount of $2,900 upon sale of the property on January 1, 1969. Brown's gain is $900 ($2,900 amount realized minus $2,000 adjusted basis). Since the amount realized upon disposition of the property ($2,900) is lower than its recomputed basis ($3,300, i.e., $2,000 adjusted basis plus $1,300 in depreciation deductions), the entire gain is treated as ordinary income under section 1245(a)(1) and not as gain from the sale or exchange of property described in section 1231.

Example (2). Assume the same facts as in example (1) except that Brown exchanges the section 1245 property for land which has a fair market value of $3,700, thereby realizing a gain of $1,700 ($3,700 amount realized minus $2,000 adjusted basis). Since the recomputed basis of the property ($3,300) is lower than the amount realized upon its disposition ($3,700), the excess of recomputed basis over adjusted basis, or $1,300, is treated as ordinary income under section 1245(a)(1). The remaining $400 of the gain may be treated as gain from the sale or exchange of property described in section 1231.

(c) *Other dispositions.* (1) In the case of a disposition of section 1245 property other than by way of a sale, exchange, or involuntary conversion, the gain to which section 1245(a)(1) applies is the amount by which (i) the lower of the fair market value of the property on the date of disposition or the recomputed basis of the property, exceeds (ii) the adjusted basis of the property. If property is transferred by a corporation to a shareholder for an amount less than its fair market value in a sale or exchange, for purposes of applying section 1245 such transfer shall be treated as a disposition other than by way of a sale, exchange, or involuntary conversion.

(2) The provisions of this paragraph may be illustrated by the following examples:

Example (1). X Corporation distributes section 1245 property to its shareholders as a dividend. The property has an adjusted basis of $2,000 to the corporation, a recomputed basis of $3,300, and a fair market value of $3,100. Since the fair market value of the property ($3,100) is lower than its recomputed basis ($3,300), the excess of fair market value over adjusted basis, or $1,100, is treated under section 1245(a)(1) as ordinary income to the corporation even though, in the absence of section 1245, section 311(a) would preclude recognition of gain to the corporation.

Example (2). Assume the same facts as in example (1) except that X Corporation distributes the section 1245 property to its shareholders in complete liquidation of the corporation. Assume further that section 1245(b)(3) does not apply and that the fair market value of the property is $3,800 at the time of the distribution. Since the recomputed basis of the property ($3,300) is lower than its fair market value ($3,800), the excess of recomputed basis over adjusted basis, or $1,300, is treated under section 1245(a)(1) as ordinary income to the corporation even though, in the absence of section 1245, section 336 would preclude recognition of gain to the corporation.

(d) *Losses.* Section 1245(a)(1) does not apply to losses. Thus, section 1245(a)(1) does not apply if a loss is realized upon a sale, exchange, or involuntary conversion of property, all of which is considered section 1245 property, nor does the section apply to a disposition of such property other than by way of sale, exchange, or involuntary conversion if at the time of the disposition the fair market value of such property is not greater than its adjusted basis.

(e) *Treatment of partnership and partners.* (1) The manner of determining the amount of gain recognized under section 1245(a)(1) to a partnership may be illustrated by the following example:

Example. A partnership sells for $63 section 1245 property which has an adjusted basis to the partnership of $30 and a recomputed basis to the partnership of $60. The partnership recognizes under section 1245(a)(1) gain of $30, i.e., the lower of the amount realized ($63) or recomputed basis ($60), minus adjusted basis ($30). This result would not be changed if one or more partners had, in respect of the property, a special basis

adjustment described in section 743(b) or had taken depreciation deductions in respect of such special basis adjustment.

(2)(i) Unless paragraph (e)(3) of this section applies, a partner's distributive share of gain recognized under section 1245(a)(1) by the partnership is equal to the lesser of the partner's share of total gain from the disposition of the property (gain limitation) or the partner's share of depreciation or amortization with respect to the property (as determined under paragraph (e)(2)(ii) of this section). Any gain recognized under section 1245(a)(1) by the partnership that is not allocated under the first sentence of this paragraph (e)(2)(i) (excess depreciation recapture) is allocated among the partners whose shares of total gain from the disposition of the property exceed their shares of depreciation or amortization with respect to the property. Excess depreciation recapture is allocated among those partners in proportion to their relative shares of the total gain (including gain recognized under section 1245(a)(1)) from the disposition of the property that is allocated to the partners who are not subject to the gain limitation. See *Example 2* of paragraph (e)(2)(iii) of this section.

(ii)(A) Subject to the adjustments described in paragraphs (e)(2)(ii)(B) and (e)(2)(ii)(C) of this section, a partner's share of depreciation or amortization with respect to property equals the total amount of allowed or allowable depreciation or amortization previously allocated to that partner with respect to the property.

(B) If a partner transfers a partnership interest, a share of depreciation or amortization must be allocated to the transferee partner as it would have been allocated to the transferor partner. If the partner transfers a portion of the partnership interest, a share of depreciation or amortization proportionate to the interest transferred must be allocated to the transferee partner.

(C)(*1*) A partner's share of depreciation or amortization with respect to property contributed by the partner includes the amount of depreciation or amortization allowed or allowable to the partner for the period before the property is contributed.

(*2*) A partner's share of depreciation or amortization with respect to property contributed by a partner is adjusted to account for any curative allocations. (See § 1.704-3(c) for a description of the traditional method with curative allocations.) The contributing partner's share of depreciation or amortization with respect to the contributed property is decreased (but not below zero) by the amount of any curative allocation of ordinary income to the contributing partner with respect to that property and by the amount of any curative allocation of deduction or loss (other than capital loss) to the noncontributing partners with respect to that property. A noncontributing partner's share of depreciation or amortization with respect to the contributed property is increased by the noncontributing partner's share of any curative allocation of ordinary income to the contributing partner with respect to that property and by the amount of any curative allocation of deduction or loss (other than capital loss) to the noncontributing partner with respect to that property. The partners' shares of depreciation or amortization with respect to property from which curative allocations of depreciation or amortization are taken is determined without regard to those curative allocations. See *Example* 3(iii) of paragraph (e)(2)(iii) of this section.

(*3*) A partner's share of depreciation or amortization with respect to property contributed by a partner is adjusted to account for any remedial allocations. (See § 1.704-3(d) for a description of the remedial allocation method.) The contributing partner's share of depreciation or amortization with respect to the contributed property is decreased (but not below zero) by the amount of any remedial allocation of income to the contributing partner with respect to that property. A noncontributing partner's share of depreciation or amortization with respect to the contributed property is increased by the amount of any remedial allocation of depreciation or amortization to the noncontributing partner with respect to that property. See *Example* 3(iv) of paragraph (e)(2)(iii) of this section.

(*4*) If, under paragraphs (e)(2)(ii)(C)(*2*) and (e)(2)(ii)(C)(*3*) of this section, the partners' shares of depreciation or amortization with respect to a contributed property exceed the adjustments reflected in the adjusted basis of the property under § 1.1245-2(a) at the partnership level, then the partnership's gain recognized under section 1245(a)(1) with respect to that property is allocated among the partners in proportion to their relative shares of depreciation or amortization (subject to any gain limitation that might apply).

(*5*) This paragraph (e)(2)(ii)(C) also applies in determining a partner's share of depreciation or amortization with respect to property for which differences between book value and adjusted tax basis are created when a partnership revalues partnership property pursuant to § 1.704-1(b)(2)(iv)(*f*).

(iii) *Examples.* The application of this paragraph (e)(2) may be illustrated by the following examples:

Example 1. Recapture allocations. (i) *Facts.* A and B each contribute $5,000 cash to form AB, a general partnership. The partnership agreement provides that depreciation deductions will be allocated 90 percent to A and 10 percent to B, and, on the sale of depreciable property, A will first be allocated gain to the extent necessary to equalize A's and B's capital accounts. Any remaining gain will be allocated 50 percent to A and 50 percent to B. In its first year of operations, AB purchases depreciable equipment for $5,000. AB depreciates the equipment over its 5-year recovery period and elects to use the straight-line method. In its first year of operations, AB's operating income equals its expenses (other than depreciation). (To simplify this example, AB's depreciation deductions are determined without regard to any first-year depreciation conventions.)

(ii) *Year 1.* In its first year of operations, AB has $1,000 of depreciation from the partnership equipment. In accordance with the partnership agreement, AB allocates 90 percent ($900) of the depreciation to A and 10 percent ($100) of the depreciation to B. At the end of the year, AB sells the equipment for $5,200, recognizing $1,200 of gain ($5,200 amount realized less $4,000 adjusted tax basis). In accordance with the partnership agreement, the first $800 of gain is allocated to A to equalize the partners' capital accounts, and the remaining $400 of gain is allocated $200 to A and $200 to B.

(iii) *Recapture allocations.* $1,000 of the gain from the sale of the equipment is treated as section 1245(a)(1) gain. Under paragraph (e)(2)(i) of this section, each partner's share of the section 1245(a)(1) gain is equal to the lesser of the partner's share of total gain recognized on the sale of the equipment or the partner's share of total depreciation with respect to the equipment. Thus, A's share of the section 1245(a)(1) gain is $900 (the lesser of A's share of the total gain ($1,000) and A's share of depreciation ($900)). B's share of the section 1245(a)(1) gain is $100 (the lesser of B's share of the total gain ($200) and B's share of depreciation ($100)). Accordingly, $900 of the $1,000 of total gain allocated to A is treated as ordinary income and $100 of the $200 of total gain allocated to B is treated as ordinary income.

Example 2. Recapture allocation subject to gain limitation. (i) *Facts.* A, B, and C form general partnership ABC. The partnership agreement provides that depreciation deductions will be allocated equally among the partners, but that gain from the sale of depreciable property will be allocated 75 percent to A and 25 percent to B. ABC purchases depreciable personal property for $300 and subsequently allocates $100 of depreciation deductions each to A, B, and C, reducing the adjusted tax basis of the property to $0. ABC then sells the property for $440. ABC allocates $330 of the gain to A (75 percent of $440) and allocates $110 of the gain to B (25 percent of $440). No gain is allocated to C.

(ii) *Application of gain limitation.* Each partner's share of depreciation with respect to the property is $100. C's share of the total gain from the disposition of the property, however, is $0. As a result, under the gain limitation provision in paragraph (e)(2)(i) of this section, C's share of section 1245(a)(1) gain is limited to $0.

(iii) *Excess depreciation recapture.* Under paragraph (e)(2)(i) of this section, the $100 of section 1245(a)(1) gain that cannot be allocated to C under the gain limitation provision (excess depreciation recapture) is allocated to A and B (the partners not subject to the gain limitation at the time of the allocation) in proportion to their relative shares of total gain from the disposition of the property. A's relative share of the total gain allocated to A and B is 75 percent ($330 of $440 total gain). B's relative share of the total gain allocated to A and B is 25 percent ($110 of $440 total gain). However, under the gain limitation provision of paragraph (e)(2)(i) of this section, B cannot be allocated 25 percent of the excess depreciation recapture ($25) because that would result in a total allocation of $125 of depreciation recapture to B (a $100 allocation equal to B's share of depreciation plus a $25 allocation of excess depreciation recapture), which is in excess of B's share of the total gain from the disposition of the property ($110). Therefore, only $10 of excess depreciation recapture is allocated to B and the remaining $90 of excess depreciation recapture is allocated to A. A is not subject to the gain limitation because A's share of the total gain ($330) still exceeds A's share of section 1245(a)(1) gain ($190). Accordingly, all $110 of the total gain allocated to B is treated as ordinary income ($100 share of depreciation allocated to B plus $10 of excess depreciation recapture) and $190 of the total gain allocated to A is treated as ordinary income ($100 share of depreciation allocated to A plus $90 of excess depreciation recapture).

Example 3. Determination of partners' shares of depreciation with respect to contributed property. (i) *Facts.* C and D form partnership CD as equal partners. C contributes depreciable personal property C1 with an adjusted tax basis of $800 and a fair market value of $2,800. Prior to the contribution, C claimed $200 of depreciation from C1. At the time of the contribution, C1 is depreciable under the straight-line method and has four years remaining on its 5-year recovery period. D contributes $2,800 cash, which CD uses to purchase depreciable personal property D1, which is depreciable over seven years under the straight-line method. (To simplify the example, all depreciation is determined without regard to any first-year depreciation conventions.)

(ii) *Traditional method.* C1 generates $700 of book depreciation (1/4 of $2,800 book value) and $200 of tax depreciation (1/4 of $800 adjusted tax basis) each year. C and D will each be allocated $350 of book depreciation from C1 in year 1. Under the traditional method of making section 704(c) allocations, D will be allocated the entire $200 of tax depreciation from C1 in year 1. D1 generates $400 of book and tax depreciation each year (1/7 of $2,800 book value and adjusted tax basis). C and D will each be allocated $200 of book and tax depreciation from D1 in year 1. As a result, after the first year of partnership operations, C's share of depreciation with respect to C1 is $200 (the depreciation taken by C prior to contribution) and D's share of depreciation with respect to C1 is $200 (the amount of tax depreciation allocated to D). C and D each have a $200 share of depreciation with respect to D1. At the end of four years, C's share of depreciation with respect to C1 will be $200 (the depreciation taken by C prior to contribution) and D's share of depreciation with respect to C1 will be $800 (four years of $200 depreciation per year). At the end of four years, C and D will each have an $800 share of depreciation with respect to D1 (four years of $200 depreciation per year).

(iii) *Effect of curative allocations.* (A) *Year 1.* If the partnership elects to make curative allocations under § 1.704-3(c) using depreciation from D1, the results will be the same as under the traditional method, except that $150 of the $200 of tax depreciation from D1 that would be allocated to C under the traditional method will be allocated to D as additional depreciation with respect to C1. As a result, after the first year of partnership operations, C's share of depreciation with respect to C1 will be reduced to $50 (the total depreciation taken by C prior to contribution ($200) decreased by the amount of the curative allocation to D ($150)). D's share of depreciation with respect to C1 will be $350 (the depreciation allocated to D under the traditional method ($200) increased by the amount of the curative allocation to D ($150)). C and D will each have a $200 share of depreciation with respect to D1.

(B) *Year 4.* At the end of four years, C's share of depreciation with respect to C1 will be reduced to $0 (the total depreciation taken by C prior to contribution ($200) decreased, but not below zero, by the amount of the curative allocations to D ($600)), and D's share of depreciation with respect to C1 will be $1,400 (the total depreciation allocated to D under the traditional method ($800) increased by the amount of the curative allocations to D ($600)). However, CD's section 1245(a)(1) gain with respect to C1 will not be more than $1,000 (CD's tax depreciation ($800) plus C's tax depreciation prior to contribution ($200)). Under paragraph (e)(2)(ii)(C)(4) of this section, because the partners' shares of depreciation with respect to C1 exceed the adjustments reflected in the property's adjusted basis, CD's section 1245(a)(1) gain will be allocated in proportion to the partners' relative shares of depreciation with respect to C1. Because C's share of depreciation with respect to C1 is $0, and D's share of depreciation with respect to C1 is $1,400, all of CD's $1,000 of section 1245(a)(1) gain will be allocated to D. At the end of four years, C and D will each have an $800 share of depreciation with respect to D1 (four years of $200 depreciation per year).

(iv) *Effect of remedial allocations.* (A) *Year 1.* If the partnership elects to make remedial allocations under § 1.704-3(d), there will be $600 of book depreciation from C1 in year 1. (Under the remedial allocation method, the amount by which C1's book basis ($2,800) exceeds its tax basis ($800) is depreciated over a 5-year life, rather than a 4-year life.) C and D will each be allocated one-half ($300) of the total book depreciation. As under the traditional method, D will be allocated all $200 of tax depreciation from C1. Because the ceiling rule would cause a disparity of $100 between D's book and tax allocations of depreciation, D will also receive a $100 remedial allocation of depreciation with respect to C1, and C will receive a $100 remedial allocation of income with respect to C1. As a result, after the first year of partnership operations, D's share of depreciation with respect to C1 is $300 (the depreciation allocated to D under the traditional method ($200) increased by the amount of the remedial allocation ($100)). C's share of depreciation with respect to C1 is $100 (the total depreciation taken by C prior to contribution ($200) decreased by the amount of the remedial allocation of income ($100)). C and D will each have a $200 share of depreciation with respect to D1.

(B) *Year 5.* At the end of five years, C's share of depreciation with respect to C1 will be $0 (the total depreciation taken by C prior to contribution ($200) decreased, but not below zero, by the total amount of the remedial allocations of income to C ($600)). D's share of depreciation with respect to C1 will be $1,400 (the total depreciation allocated to D under the traditional method ($800) increased by the total amount of the remedial allocations of depreciation to D ($600)). However, CD's section 1245(a)(1) gain with respect to C1 will not be more than $1,000 (CD's tax depreciation ($800) plus C's tax depreciation prior to contribution ($200)). Under paragraph (e)(2)(ii)(C)(4) of this section, because the

partners' shares of depreciation with respect to C1 exceed the adjustments reflected in the property's adjusted basis, CD's section 1245(a)(1) gain will be allocated in proportion to the partners' relative shares of depreciation with respect to C1. Because C's share of depreciation with respect to C1 is $0, and D's share of depreciation with respect to C1 is $1,400, all of CD's $1,000 of section 1245(a)(1) gain will be allocated to D. At the end of five years, C and D will each have a $1,000 share of depreciation with respect to D1 (five years of $200 depreciation per year).

(iv) *Effective date.* This paragraph (e)(2) is effective for properties acquired by a partnership on or after August 20, 1997. However, partnerships may rely on this paragraph (e)(2) for properties acquired before August 20, 1997, and disposed of on or after August 20, 1997.

(3)(i) If (a) a partner had a special basis adjustment under section 743(b) in respect of section 1245 property, or (b) on the date he acquired his partnership interest by way of a sale or exchange (or upon death of another partner) the partnership owned section 1245 property and an election under section 754 (relating to optional adjustment to basis of partnership property) was in effect with respect to the partnership, then the amount of gain recognized under section 1245(a)(1) by him upon a disposition by the partnership of such property shall be determined under this subparagraph.

(ii) There shall be allocated to such partner, in the same proportion as the partnership's total gain is allocated to him as his distributive share under section 704, a portion of (a) the common partnership adjusted basis for the property, and (b) the amount realized by the partnership upon the disposition, or, if nothing is realized, the fair market value of the property. There shall also be allocated to him, in the same proportion as the partnership's gain recognized under section 1245(a)(1) is allocated under subparagraph (2) of this paragraph as his distributive share of such gain, a portion of "the adjustments reflected in the adjusted basis" (as defined in paragraph (a)(2) of § 1.1245-2) of such property. If on the date he acquired his partnership interest by way of a sale or exchange the partnership owned such property and an election under section 754 was in effect, then for purposes of the preceding sentence the amount of the adjustments reflected in the adjusted basis of such property on such date shall be deemed to be zero. For special rules relating to the amount of adjustments reflected in the adjusted basis of property after partnership transactions, see paragraph (c)(6) of § 1.1245-2.

(iii) The partner's adjusted basis in respect of the property shall be deemed to be (a) the

Reg. § 1.1245-1(e)(3)

portion of the partnership's adjusted basis for the property allocated to the partner under subdivision (ii) of this subparagraph, (*b*) increased by the amount of any special basis adjustment described in section 743(b)(1) (or decreased by the amount of any special basis adjustment described in section 743(b)(2)) which the partner may have in respect of the property on the date the partnership disposed of the property.

(iv) The partner's recomputed basis in respect of the property shall be deemed to be (*a*) the sum of the partner's adjusted basis for the property, as determined in subdivision (iii) of this subparagraph, plus the amount of "the adjustments reflected in the adjusted basis" (as defined in paragraph (a)(2) of § 1.1245-2) for the property allocated to the partner under subdivision (ii) of this subparagraph, (*b*) increased by the amount by which any special basis adjustment described in section 743(b)(1) (or decreased by the amount by which any special basis adjustment described in section 743(b)(2)) in respect of the property was reduced, but only to the extent such amount was applied to adjust the amount of the deductions allowed or allowable to the partner for depreciation or amortization of section 1245 property attributable to periods referred to in paragraph (a)(2) of § 1.1245-2. The terms "allowed or allowable," "depreciation or amortization," and "attributable to periods" shall have the meanings assigned to those terms in paragraph (a) of § 1.1245-2.

(4) The application of subparagraph (3) of this paragraph may be illustrated by the following example:

Example. A, B, and C each hold a one-third interest in calendar year partnership ABC. On December 31, 1962, the firm holds section 1245 property which has an adjusted basis of $30,000 and a recomputed basis of $33,000. Depreciation deductions in respect of the property for 1962 were $3,000. On January 1, 1963, when D purchases C's partnership interest, the election under section 754 is in effect and a $5,000 special basis adjustment is made in respect of D to his one-third share of the common partnership adjusted basis for the property. For 1963 and 1964 the partnership deducts $6,000 as depreciation in respect of the property, thereby reducing its adjusted basis to $24,000, and D deducts $2,800, *i.e.*, his distributive share of partnership depreciation ($2,000) plus depreciation in respect of his special basis adjustment ($800). On March 15, 1965, the partnership sells the property for $48,000. Since the partnership's recomputed basis for the property ($33,000, i.e., $24,000 adjusted basis plus $9,000 in depreciation deductions) is lower than the amount realized upon the sale ($48,000), the excess of recomputed basis over adjusted basis, or $9,000, is treated as partnership gain under section 1245(a)(1). D's distributive share of such gain is $3,000 (1/3 of $9,000). However, the amount of gain recognized by D under section 1245(a)(1) is only $2,800, determined as follows:

(1) Adjusted basis:	
D's portion of partnership adjusted basis (1/3 of $24,000)	$ 8,000
D's special basis adjustment as of December 31, 1964 ($5,000 minus $800)	4,200
D's adjusted basis	$12,200
(2) Recomputed basis:	
D's adjusted basis	$12,200
D's portion of partnership depreciation for 1963 and 1964, *i.e.*, for periods after he acquired his partnership interest (1/3 of $6,000) .	2,000
Depreciation for 1963 and 1964 in respect of D's special basis adjustment	800
D's recomputed basis	$15,000
(3) D's portion of amount realized by partnership (1/3 of $48,000)	$16,000
(4) Gain recognized to D under section 1245(a)(1), *i.e.*, the lower of (2) or (3), minus (1)	$ 2,800

[Reg. § 1.1245-1.]

☐ [*T.D. 6832, 7-6-65. Amended by T.D. 7084, 1-7-71; T.D. 7141, 9-21-71 and T.D. 8730, 8-19-97.*]

§ 1.1245-2. Definition of recomputed basis.—(a) *General rule*—(1) *Recomputed basis defined.* The term "recomputed basis" means, with respect to any property, an amount equal to the sum of—

(i) The adjusted basis of the property, as defined in section 1011, plus

(ii) The amount of the adjustments reflected in the adjusted basis.

(2) *Definition of adjustments reflected in adjusted basis.* The term "adjustments reflected in the adjusted basis" means—

(i) with respect to any property other than property described in subdivision (ii), (iii), or (iv) of this subparagraph, the amount of the adjustments attributable to periods after December 31, 1961,

(ii) with respect to an elevator or escalator, the amount of the adjustments attributable to periods after June 30, 1963,

(iii) with respect to livestock (described in subparagraph (4) of § 1.1245-3(a)), the amount of the adjustments attributable to periods after December 31, 1969, or

(iv) [reserved]

which are reflected in the adjusted basis of such property on account of deductions allowed or allowable for depreciation or amortization (within the meaning of subparagraph (3) of this paragraph). For cases where the taxpayer can establish that the amount allowed for any period was less than the amount allowable, see subparagraph (7) of this paragraph. For determination of adjusted basis of property in a multiple asset account, see paragraph (c)(3) of § 1.167(a)-8.

(3) *Meaning of "depreciation or amortization."* (i) For purposes of subparagraph (2) of this paragraph, the term "depreciation or amortization" includes allowances (and amounts treated as allowances) for depreciation (or amortization in lieu thereof), and deductions for amortization of emergency facilities under section 168. Thus, for example, such term includes a reasonable allowance for exhaustion, wear and tear (including a reasonable allowance for obsolescence) under section 167, an expense allowance (additional first-year depreciation allowance for property placed in service before January 1, 1981) under section 179, an expenditure treated as an amount allowed under section 167 by reason of the application of section 182(d)(2)(B) (relating to expenditures by farmers for clearing land), and a deduction for depreciation of improvements under section 611 (relating to depletion). For further examples, the term "depreciation or amortization" includes periodic deductions referred to in § 1.162-11 in respect of a specified sum paid for the acquisition of a leasehold and in respect of the cost to a lessee of improvements on property of which he is the lessee. However, such term does not include deductions for the periodic payment of rent.

(ii) The provisions of this subparagraph may be illustrated by the following example:

Example. On January 1, 1966, Smith purchases for $1,000, and places in service, an item of property described in section 1245(a)(3)(A). Smith deducts an additional first-year allowance for depreciation under section 179 of $200. Accordingly, the basis of the property for purposes of depreciation is $800 on January 1, 1966. Between that date and January 1, 1974, Smith deducts $640 in depreciation (the amount

allowable) with respect to the property, thereby reducing its adjusted basis to $160. Since this adjusted basis reflects deductions for depreciation and amortization (within the meaning of this subparagraph) amounting to $840 ($200 plus $640), the recomputed basis of the property is $1,000 ($160 plus $840).

(4) *Adjustments of other taxpayers or in respect of other property.* (i) For purposes of subparagraph (2) of this paragraph, the adjustments reflected in adjusted basis on account of depreciation or amortization which must be taken into account in determining recomputed basis are not limited to those adjustments on account of depreciation or amortization with respect to the property disposed of, nor are such adjustments limited to those on account of depreciation or amortization allowed or allowable to the taxpayer disposing of such property. Except as provided in subparagraph (7) of this paragraph, all such adjustments are taken into account, whether the deductions were allowed or allowable in respect of the same or other property and whether to the taxpayer or to any other person. For manner of determining the amount of adjustments reflected in the adjusted basis of property immediately after certain dispositions, see paragraph (c) of this section.

(ii) The provisions of this subparagraph may be illustrated by the following example:

Example. On January 1, 1966, Jones purchases machine X for use in his trade or business. The machine, which is section 1245 property, has a basis for depreciation of $10,000. After taking depreciation deductions of $2,000 (the amount allowable), Jones transfers the machine to his son as a gift on January 1, 1968. Since the exception for gifts in section 1245(b)(1) applies, Jones does not recognize gain under section 1245(a)(1). The son's adjusted basis for the machine is $8,000. On January 1, 1969, after taking a depreciation deduction of $1,000 (the amount allowable), the son exchanges machine X for machine Y in a like kind exchange described in section 1031. Since the exception for like kind exchanges in section 1245(b)(4) applies, the son does not recognize gain under section 1245(a)(1). The son's adjusted basis for machine Y is $7,000. In 1969, the son takes a depreciation deduction of $1,000 (the amount allowable) in respect of machine Y. The son sells machine Y on June 30, 1970. No depreciation was allowed or allowable for 1970, the year of the sale. The recomputed basis of machine Y on June 30, 1970, is determined in the following manner:

Reg. § 1.1245-2(a)(4)

Adjusted basis	$ 6,000
Adjustments reflected in the adjusted basis:	
Depreciation deducted by Jones for 1966 and 1967 on machine X $2,000	
Depreciation deducted by son for 1968 on machine X $1,000	
Depreciation deducted by son for 1969 on machine Y $1,000	
Total adjustments reflected in the adjusted basis	$ 4,000
Recomputed basis	$10,000

(5) *Adjustments reflected in adjusted basis of property described in section 1245(a)(3)(B).* For purposes of subparagraph (2) of this paragraph, the adjustments reflected in the adjusted basis of property described in section 1245(a)(3)(B), on account of depreciation or amortization which must be taken into account in determining recomputed basis, may include deductions attributable to periods during which the property is not used as an integral part of an activity, or does not constitute a facility, specified in section 1245(a)(3)(B)(i) or (ii). Thus, for example, if depreciation deductions taken with respect to such property after December 31, 1961, amount to $10,000 (the amount allowable), of which $6,000 is attributable to periods during which the property is used as an integral part of a specified activity or constitutes a specified facility, then the entire $10,000 of depreciation deductions are adjustments reflected in the adjusted basis for purposes of determining recomputed basis. Moreover, if the property was never so used but was acquired in a transaction to which section 1245(b)(4) (relating to like kind exchanges and involuntaray conversions) applies, and if by reason of the application of paragraph (d)(3) of § 1.1245-4 the property is considered as section 1245 property described in section 1245(a)(3)(B), then the entire $10,000 of depreciation deductions would also be adjustments reflected in the adjusted basis for purposes of determining recomputed basis.

* * *

(7) *Depreciation or amortization allowed or allowable.* For purposes of determining recomputed basis, generally all adjustments (for periods after Dec. 31, 1961, or, in the case of property described in subparagraph (2)(ii), (iii), or (iv) of this paragraph, for periods after the applicable date, 1969, as the case may be) attributable to allowed or allowable depreciation or amortization must be taken into account. See section 1016(a)(2) and the regulations thereunder for the meaning of "allowed" and "allowable". However, if a taxpayer can establish by adequate records or other sufficient evidence that the amount allowed for depreciation or amortization for any period was less than the amount allowable for such period, the amount to be taken into account for such period shall be the amount allowed. No adjustment is to be made on account of the tax imposed by section 56 (relating to the minimum tax for tax preferences). See paragraph (b) of this section (relating to records to be kept and information to be filed). For example, assume that in the year 1967 it becomes necessary to determine the recomputed basis of property, the $500 adjusted basis of which reflects adjustments of $1,000 with respect to depreciation deductions allowable for periods after December 31, 1961. If the taxpayer can establish by adequate records or other sufficient evidence that he had been allowed deductions amounting to $800 for the period, then in determining recomputed basis the amount added to adjusted basis with respect to the $1,000 adjustments to basis for the period will be only $800.

* * *

[Reg. § 1.1245-2.]

☐ [*T.D. 6832, 7-6-65. Amended by T.D. 7084, 1-7-71; T.D. 7141, 9-21-71; T.D. 7564, 9-11-78; and T.D. 8121, 1-5-87.*]

§ 1.1245-3. Definition of section 1245 property.—(a) *In general*—(1) The term "section 1245 property" means any property (other than livestock excluded by the effective date limitation in subparagraph (4) of this paragraph) which is or has been property of a character subject to the allowance for depreciation provided in section 167 and which is either—

(i) Personal property (within the meaning of paragraph (b) of this section),

(ii) Property described in section 1245(a)(3)(B) (see paragraph (c) of this section), or

(iii) An elevator or an escalator within the meaning of subparagraph (C) of section 48(a)(1) (relating to the definition of "section 38 property" for purposes of the investment credit), but without regard to the limitations in such subparagraph (C).

(2) If property is section 1245 property under a subdivision of subparagraph (1) of this paragraph, a leasehold of such property is also section 1245 property under such subdivision. Thus, for example, if A owns personal property which is section 1245 property under subparagraph (1)(i) of this paragraph, and if A leases the personal property to B, B's leasehold is also section 1245 property under such provision. For a further example, if C owns and leases to D for a single lump-sum payment of $100,000 property consisting of land and a fully equipped factory building thereon, and if 40 percent of the fair

Reg. § 1.1245-3(a)(1)

market value of such property is properly allocable to section 1245 property, then 40 percent of D's leasehold is also section 1245 property. A leasehold of land is not section 1245 property.

(3) Even though property may not be of a character subject to the allowance for depreciation in the hands of the taxpayer, such property may nevertheless be section 1245 property if the taxpayer's basis for the property is determined by reference to its basis in the hands of a prior owner of the property and such property was of a character subject to the allowance for depreciation in the hands of such prior owner, or if the taxpayer's basis for the property is determined by reference to the basis of other property which in the hands of the taxpayer was property of a character subject to the allowance for depreciation. Thus, for example, if a father uses an automobile in his trade or business during a period after December 31, 1961, and then gives the automobile to his son as a gift for the son's personal use, the automobile is section 1245 property in the hands of the son.

(4) Section 1245 property includes livestock, but only with respect to taxable years beginning after December 31, 1969. For purposes of section 1245, the term "livestock" includes horses, cattle, hogs, sheep, goats, and mink and other furbearing animals, irrespective of the use to which they are put or the purpose for which they are held.

(b) *Personal property defined.* The term "personal property" means—

(1) Tangible personal property (as defined in paragraph (c) of § 1.48-1, relating to the definition of "section 38 property" for purposes of the investment credit), and

(2) Intangible personal property.

(c) *Property described in section 1245(a)(3)(B)*—(1) The term "property described in section 1245(a)(3)(B)" means tangible property of the requisite depreciable character other than personal property (and other than a building and its structural components), but only if there are adjustments reflected in the adjusted basis of the property (within the meaning of paragraph (a)(2) of § 1.1245-2) for a period during which such property (or other property)—

(i) Was used as an integral part of manufacturing, production, or extraction, or as an integral part of furnishing transportation, communications, electrical energy, gas, water, or sewage disposal services by a person engaged in a trade or business of furnishing any such service, or

(ii) Constituted a research or storage facility used in connection with any of the foregoing activities.

Thus, even though during the period immediately preceding its disposition the property is not used

as an integral part of an activity specified in subdivision (i) of this subparagraph and does not constitute a facility specified in subdivision (ii) of this subparagraph, such property is nevertheless property described in section 1245(a)(3)(B) if, for example, there are no adjustments reflected in the adjusted basis of the property for a period during which the property was used as an integral part of manufacturing by the taxpayer or another taxpayer, or for a period during which other property (which was involuntarily converted into, or exchanged in a like kind exchange for, the property) was so used by the taxpayer or another taxpayer. For rules applicable to involuntary conversions and like kind exchanges, see paragraph (d)(3) of § 1.1245-4.

(2) The language used in subparagraph (1)(i) and (ii) of this paragraph shall have the same meaning as when used in paragraph (a) of § 1.48-1, and the terms "building" and "structural components" shall have the meanings assigned to those terms in paragraph (e) of § 1.48-1. [Reg. § 1.1245-3.]

□ [*T.D. 6832, 7-6-65. Amended by T.D. 7141, 9-21-71.*]

§ 1.1245-4. Exceptions and limitations.—(a) *Exception for gifts.*—(1) *General rule.* Section 1245(b)(1) provides that no gain shall be recognized under section 1245(a)(1) upon a disposition by gift. For purposes of this paragraph, the term "gift" means, except to the extent that subparagraph (3) of this paragraph applies, a transfer of property which, in the hands of the transferee, has a basis determined under the provisions of section 1015(a) or (d) (relating to basis of property acquired by gifts). For reduction in amount of charitable contribution in case of a gift of section 1245 property, see section 170(e) and the regulations thereunder.

* * *

(b) *Exception for transfers at death*—(1) *General rule.* Section 1245(b)(2) provides that, except as provided in section 691 (relating to income in respect of a decedent), no gain shall be recognized under section 1245(a)(1) upon a transfer at death. For purposes of this paragraph, the term "transfer at death" means a transfer of property which, in the hands of the transferee, has a basis determined under the provisions of section 1014(a) (relating to basis of property acquired from a decedent) because of the death of the transferor. For recomputed basis of property acquired in a transfer at death, see paragraph (c)(1)(iv) of § 1.1245-2.

* * *

(c) *Limitation for certain tax-free transactions*—(1) *Limitation on amount of gain.* Section

1245(b)(3) provides that upon a transfer of property described in subparagraph (2) of this paragraph, the amount of gain taken into account by the transferor under section 1245(a)(1) shall not exceed the amount of gain recognized to the transferor on the transfer (determined without regard to section 1245). For purposes of this subparagraph, in case of a transfer of both section 1245 property and non-section 1245 property in one transaction, the amount realized from the disposition of the section 1245 property (as determined under paragraph (a)(5) of § 1.1245-1) shall be deemed to consist of that portion of the fair market value of each property acquired which bears the same ratio to the fair market value of such acquired property as the amount realized from the disposition of the section 1245 property bears to the total amount realized. The preceding sentence shall be applied solely for purposes of computing the portion of the total gain (determined without regard to section 1245) which shall be recognized as ordinary income under section 1245(a)(1). For determination of the recomputed basis of the section 1245 property in the hands of the transferee, see paragraph (c)(2) of § 1.1245-2. Section 1245(b)(3) does not apply to a disposition of property to an organization (other than a cooperative described in section 521) which is exempt from the tax imposed by chapter 1 of the Code.

(2) *Transfers covered.* The transfers referred to in subparagraph (1) of this paragraph are transfers of property which the basis of the property in the hands of the transferee is determined by reference to its basis in the hands of the transferor by reason of the application of any of the following provisions:

(i) Section 332 (relating to distributions in complete liquidation of an 80-percent-or-more controlled subsidiary corporation). See subparagraph (3) of this paragraph.

(ii) Section 351 (relating to transfer to a corporation controlled by transferor).

(iii) Section 361 (relating to exchanges pursuant to certain corporate reorganizations).

(iv) Section 371(a) (relating to exchanges pursuant to certain receivership and bankruptcy proceedings).

(v) Section 374(a) (relating to exchanges pursuant to certain railroad reorganizations).

(vi) Section 721 (relating to transfers to a partnership in exchange for a partnership interest).

(vii) Section 731 (relating to distributions by a partnership to a partner). For special carryover basis rule, see section 1245(b)(6)(A) and paragraph (f)(1) of this section.

* * *

(d) *Limitation for like kind exchanges and involuntary conversions*—(1) *General rule.* Section 1245(b)(4) provides that if property is disposed of and gain (determined without regard to section 1245) is not recognized in whole or in part under section 1031 (relating to like kind exchanges) or section 1033 (relating to involuntary conversions), then the amount of gain taken into account by the transferor under section 1245(a)(1) shall not exceed the sum of—

(i) The amount of gain recognized on such disposition (determined without regard to section 1245), plus

(ii) The fair market value of property acquired which is not section 1245 property and which is not taken into account under subdivision (i) of this subparagraph (that is, the fair market value of non-section 1245 property acquired which is qualifying property under section 1031 or 1033, as the case may be).

* * *

[Reg. § 1.1245-4.]

☐ *[T.D. 6832, 7-6-65. Amended by T.D. 7084, 1-7-71, T.D. 7207, 10-3-72, T.D. 7728, 10-31-80 and T.D. 7927, 12-15-83.]*

§ 1.1245-5. **Adjustments to basis.**—In order to reflect gain recognized under section 1245(a)(1), the following adjustments to the basis of property shall be made:

(a) *Property acquired in like kind exchange or involuntary conversion*—(1) If property is acquired in a transaction to which section 1245(b)(4) applies, its basis shall be determined under the rules of section 1031(d) or 1033(c).

(2) The provisions of this paragraph may be illustrated by the following example:

Example. Jones exchanges property A, which is section 1245 property with an adjusted basis of $10,000, for property B, which has a fair market value of $9,000, and property C, which has a fair market value of $3,500, in a like kind exchange as to which no gain would be recognized under section 1031(a). Upon the exchange $2,500 gain is recognized under section 1245(a)(1), since property C is not section 1245 property. See section 1245(b)(4). Under the rules of section 1031(d), the basis of the properties received in the exchange is $12,500 (i.e., the basis of property transferred, $10,000, plus the amount of gain recognized, $2,500), of which the amount allocated to property C is $3,500 (the fair market value thereof), and the residue, $9,000, is allocated to property B.

* * *

[Reg. § 1.1245-5.]

☐ *[T.D. 6832, 7-6-65.]*

§ 1.1245-6. Relation of section 1245 to other sections.—(a) *General.* The provisions of section 1245 apply notwithstanding any other provision of subtitle A of the Code. Thus, unless an exception or limitation under section 1245 (b) applies, gain under section 1245(a)(1) is recognized notwithstanding any contrary nonrecognition provision or income characterizing provision. For example, since section 1245 overrides section 1231 (relating to property used in the trade or business), the gain recognized under section 1245(a)(1) upon a disposition will be treated as ordinary income and only the remaining gain, if any, from the disposition may be considered as gain from the sale or exchange of a capital asset if section 1231 is applicable. See example (2) of paragraph (b)(2) of § 1.1245-1. For effect of section 1245 on basis provisions of the Code, see § 1.1245-5.

(b) *Nonrecognition sections overridden.* The nonrecognition provisions of subtitle A of the Code which section 1245 overrides include, but are not limited to, sections 267(d), 311(a), 336, 337, 501(a), 512(b)(5), and 1039. See section 1245(b) for the extent to which section 1245(a)(1) overrides sections 332, 351, 361, 371(a), 374(a), 721, 731, 1031, 1033, 1071, and 1081(b)(1) and (d)(1)(A). For limitation on amount of adjustments reflected in adjusted basis of property disposed of by an organization exempt from income taxes (within the meaning of section 501(a)), see paragraph (a)(8) of § 1.1245-2.

(c) *Normal retirement of asset in multiple asset account.* Section 1245(a)(1) does not require recognition of gain upon normal retirements of section 1245 property in a multiple asset account as long as the taxpayer's method of accounting, as described in paragraph (e)(2) of § 1.167(a)-8 (relating to accounting treatment of asset retirements), does not require recognition of such gain.

(d) *Installment method*—(1) Gain from a disposition to which section 1245(a)(1) applies may be reported under the installment method if such method is otherwise available under section 453 of the Code. In such case, the income (other than interest) on each installment payment shall be deemed to consist of gain to which section 1245(a)(1) applies until all such gain has been reported, and the remaining portion (if any) of such income shall be deemed to consist of gain to which section 1245(a)(1) does not apply. For treatment of amounts as interest on certain deferred payments, see section 483.

(2) The provisions of this paragraph may be illustrated by the following example:

Example. Jones contracts to sell an item of section 1245 property for $10,000 to be paid in 10 equal payments of $1,000 each, plus a sufficient amount of interest so that section 483 does not apply. He properly elects under section 453 to report under the installment method gain of $2,000 to which section 1245(a)(1) applies and gain of $1,000 to which section 1231 applies. Accordingly, $300 of each of the first 6 installment payments and $200 of the seventh installment payment is ordinary income under section 1245(a)(1), and $100 of the seventh installment payment and $300 of each of the last 3 installment payments is gain under section 1231.

(e) *Exempt income.* The fact that section 1245 provides for recognition of gain as ordinary income does not change into taxable income any income which is exempt under section 115 (relating to income of states, etc.), 892 (relating to income of foreign governments), or 894 (relating to income exempt under treaties).

(f) *Treatment of gain not recognized under section 1245.* Section 1245 does not prevent gain which is not recognized under section 1245 from being considered as gain under another provision of the Code, such as, for example, section 311(c) (relating to liability in excess of basis), section 341(f) (relating to collapsible corporations), section 357(c) (relating to liabilities in excess of basis), section 1238 (relating to amortization in excess of depreciation), or section 1239 (relating to gain from sale of depreciable property between certain related persons). Thus, for example, if section 1245 property, which has an adjusted basis of $1,000 and a recomputed basis of $1,500, is sold for $1,750 in a transaction to which section 1239 applies, $500 of the gain would be recognized under section 1245(a)(1) and the remaining $250 of the gain would be treated as ordinary income under section 1239. [Reg. § 1.1245-6.]

☐ [*T.D. 6832, 7-6-65. Amended by T.D. 7084, 1-7-71 and T.D. 7400, 2-3-76.*]

Special Rules for Bonds & Other Debt Instruments

§ 1.1272-1. Current inclusion of OID in income.—(a) *Overview*—(1) *In general.* Under section 1272(a)(1), a holder of a debt instrument includes accrued OID in gross income (as interest), regardless of the holder's regular method of accounting. A holder includes qualified stated interest (as defined in § 1.1273-1(c)) in income under the holder's regular method of accounting. See §§ 1.446-2 and 1.451-1.

(2) *Debt instruments not subject to OID inclusion rules.* Sections 1272(a)(2) and 1272(c) list exceptions to the general inclusion rule of section 1272(a)(1). For purposes of section 1272(a)(2)(E) (relating to certain loans between natural persons), a loan does not include a stripped bond or

stripped coupon within the meaning of section 1286(e), and the rule in section 1272(a)(2)(E)(iii), which treats a husband and wife as 1 person, does not apply to loans made between a husband and wife.

(b) *Accrual of OID*—(1) *Constant yield method.* Except as provided in paragraphs (b)(2) and (b)(3) of this section, the amount of OID includible in the income of a holder of a debt instrument for any taxable year is determined using the constant yield method as described under this paragraph (b)(1).

(i) *Step one: Determine the debt instrument's yield to maturity.* The yield to maturity or yield of a debt instrument is the discount rate that, when used in computing the present value of all principal and interest payments to be made under the debt instrument, produces an amount equal to the issue price of the debt instrument. The yield must be constant over the term of the debt instrument and, when expressed as a percentage, must be calculated to at least two decimal places. See paragraph (c) of this section for rules relating to the yield of certain debt instruments subject to contingencies.

(ii) *Step two: Determine the accrual periods.* An accrual period is an interval of time over which the accrual of OID is measured. Accrual periods may be of any length and may vary in length over the term of the debt instrument, provided that each accrual period is no longer than 1 year and each scheduled payment of principal or interest occurs either on the final day of an accrual period or on the first day of an accrual period. In general, the computation of OID is simplest if accrual periods correspond to the intervals between payment dates provided by the terms of the debt instrument. In computing the length of accrual periods, any reasonable counting convention may be used (e.g., 30 days per month/360 days per year).

(iii) *Step three: Determine the OID allocable to each accrual period.* Except as provided in paragraph (b)(4) of this section, the OID allocable to an accrual period equals the product of the adjusted issue price of the debt instrument (as defined in § 1.1275-1(b)) at the beginning of the accrual period and the yield of the debt instrument, less the amount of any qualified stated interest allocable to the accrual period. In performing this calculation, the yield must be stated appropriately taking into account the length of the particular accrual period. *Example 1* in paragraph (j) of this section provides a formula for converting a yield based upon an accrual period of one length to an equivalent yield based upon an accrual period of a different length.

(iv) *Step four: Determine the daily portions of OID.* The daily portions of OID are determined by allocating to each day in an accrual period the ratable portion of the OID allocable to the accrual period. The holder of the debt instrument includes in income the daily portions of OID for each day during the taxable year on which the holder held the debt instrument.

(2) *Exceptions.* Paragraph (b)(1) of this section does not apply to—

(i) A debt instrument to which section 1272(a)(6) applies (certain interests in or mortgages held by a REMIC, and certain other debt instruments with payments subject to acceleration);

(ii) A debt instrument that provides for contingent payments, other than a debt instrument described in paragraph (c) or (d) of this section or except as provided in § 1.1275-4; or

(iii) A variable rate debt instrument to which § 1.1275-5 applies, except as provided in § 1.1275-5.

(3) *Modifications.* The amount of OID includible in income by a holder under paragraph (b)(1) of this section is adjusted if—

(i) The holder purchased the debt instrument at a premium or an acquisition premium (within the meaning of § 1.1272-2); or

(ii) The holder made an election for the debt instrument under § 1.1272-3 to treat all interest as OID.

(4) *Special rules for determining the OID allocable to an accrual period.* The following rules apply to determine the OID allocable to an accrual period under paragraph (b)(1)(iii) of this section.

(i) *Unpaid qualified stated interest allocable to an accrual period.* In determining the OID allocable to an accrual period, if an interval between payments of qualified stated interest contains more than 1 accrual period—

(A) The amount of qualified stated interest payable at the end of the interval (including any qualified stated interest that is payable on the first day of the accrual period immediately following the interval) is allocated on a pro rata basis to each accrual period in the interval; and

(B) The adjusted issue price at the beginning of each accrual period in the interval must be increased by the amount of any qualified stated interest that has accrued prior to the first day of the accrual period but that is not payable until the end of the interval. See *Example 2* of paragraph (j) of this section for an example illustrating the rules in this paragraph (b)(4)(i).

(ii) *Final accrual period.* The OID allocable to the final accrual period is the difference

Reg. § 1.1272-1(b)(1)

between the amount payable at maturity (other than a payment of qualified stated interest) and the adjusted issue price at the beginning of the final accrual period.

(iii) *Initial short accrual period.* If all accrual periods are of equal length, except for either an initial shorter accrual period or an initial and a final shorter accrual period, the amount of OID allocable to the initial accrual period may be computed using any reasonable method. See *Example 3* in paragraph (j) of this section.

(iv) *Payment on first day of an accrual period.* The adjusted issue price at the beginning of an accrual period is reduced by the amount of any payment (other than a payment of qualified stated interest) that is made on the first day of the accrual period.

* * *

(g) *Basis adjustment.* The basis of a debt instrument in the hands of the holder is increased by the amount of OID included in the holder's gross income and decreased by the amount of any payment from the issuer to the holder under the debt instrument other than a payment of qualified stated interest. See, however, § 1.1275-2(f) for rules regarding basis adjustments on a pro rata prepayment.

* * *

[Reg. § 1.1272-1.]

☐ [*T.D.* 8517, 1-27-94. Amended by T.D. 8674, 6-11-96.]

§ 1.1272-2. Treatment of debt instruments purchased at a premium.—(a) *In general.* Under section 1272(c)(1), if a holder purchases a debt instrument at a premium, the holder does not include any OID in gross income. Under section 1272(a)(7), if a holder purchases a debt instrument at an acquisition premium, the holder reduces the amount of OID includible in gross income by the fraction determined under paragraph (b)(4) of this section.

(b) *Definitions and special rules*—(1) *Purchase.* For purposes of section 1272 and this section, purchase means any acquisition of a debt instrument, including the acquisition of a newly issued debt instrument in a debt-for-debt exchange or the acquisition of a debt instrument from a donor.

(2) *Premium.* A debt instrument is purchased at a premium if its adjusted basis, immediately after its purchase by the holder (including a purchase at original issue), exceeds the sum of all amounts payable on the instrument after the purchase date other than payments of qualified stated interest (as defined in § 1.1273-1(c)).

(3) *Acquisition premium.* A debt instrument is purchased at an acquisition premium if its

adjusted basis, immediately after its purchase (including a purchase at original issue), is—

(i) Less than or equal to the sum of all amounts payable on the instrument after the purchase date other than payments of qualified stated interest (as defined in § 1.1273-1(c)); and

(ii) Greater than the instrument's adjusted issue price (as defined in § 1.1275-1(b)).

(4) *Acquisition premium fraction.* In applying section 1272(a)(7), the cost of a debt instrument is its adjusted basis immediately after its acquisition by the purchaser. Thus, the numerator of the fraction determined under section 1272(a)(7)(B) is the excess of the adjusted basis of the debt instrument immediately after its acquisition by the purchaser over the adjusted issue price of the debt instrument. The denominator of the fraction determined under section 1272(a)(7)(B) is the excess of the sum of all amounts payable on the debt instrument after the purchase date, other than payments of qualified stated interest, over the instrument's adjusted issue price.

(5) *Election to accrue discount on a constant yield basis.* Rather than applying the acquisition premium fraction, a holder of a debt instrument purchased at an acquisition premium may elect under § 1.1272-3 to compute OID accruals by treating the purchase as a purchase at original issuance and applying the mechanics of the constant yield method.

(6) *Special rules for determining basis*—(i) *Debt instruments acquired in exchange for other property.* For purposes of section 1272(a)(7), section 1272(c)(1), and this section, if a debt instrument is acquired in an exchange for other property (other than in a reorganization defined in section 368) and the basis of the debt instrument is determined, in whole or in part, by reference to the basis of the other property, the basis of the debt instrument may not exceed its fair market value immediately after the exchange. For example, if a debt instrument is distributed by a partnership to a partner in a liquidating distribution and the partner's basis in the debt instrument would otherwise be determined under section 732, the partner's basis in the debt instrument may not exceed its fair market value for purposes of this section.

(ii) *Acquisition by gift.* For purposes of this section, a donee's adjusted basis in a debt instrument is the donee's basis for determining gain under section 1015(a).

(c) *Examples.* The following examples illustrate the rules of this section.

Example 1. Debt instrument purchased at an acquisition premium—(i) *Facts.* On July 1, 1994, A purchased at original issue, for $500, a debt instrument issued by Corporation X. The debt instrument matures on July 1, 1999, and calls for a single payment at maturity of $1,000. Under section 1273(a), the debt instrument has a stated redemption price at maturity of $1,000 and, thus, OID of $500. On July 1, 1996, when the debt instrument's adjusted issue price is $659.75, A sells the debt instrument to B for $750 in cash.

(ii) *Acquisition premium fraction.* Because the cost to B of the debt instrument is less than the amount payable on the debt instrument after the purchase date, but is greater than the debt instrument's adjusted issue price, B has paid an acquisition premium for the debt instrument. Accordingly, the daily portion of OID for any day that B holds the debt instrument is reduced by a fraction, the numerator of which is $90.25 (the excess of the cost of the debt instrument over its adjusted issue price) and the denominator of which is $340.25 (the excess of the sum of all payments after the purchase date over its adjusted issue price).

* * *

[Reg. § 1.1272-2.]

☐ [T.D. 8517, 1-27-94.]

§ 1.1273-1. Definition of OID.—(a) *In general.* Section 1273(a)(1) defines OID as the excess of a debt instrument's stated redemption price at maturity over its issue price. Section 1.1273-2 defines issue price, and paragraph (b) of this section defines stated redemption price at maturity. Paragraph (d) of this section provides rules for de minimis amounts of OID. Although the total amount of OID for a debt instrument may be indeterminate, § 1.1272-1(d) provides a rule to determine OID accruals on certain debt instruments that provide for a fixed yield. See *Example 10* in § 1.1272-1(j).

(b) *Stated redemption price at maturity.* A debt instrument's stated redemption price at maturity is the sum of all payments provided by the debt instrument other than qualified stated interest payments. If the payment schedule of a debt instrument is determined under § 1.1272-1(c) (relating to certain debt instruments subject to contingencies), that payment schedule is used to determine the instrument's stated redemption price at maturity.

(c) *Qualified stated interest*—(1) *Definition*—(i) *In general.* Qualified stated interest is stated interest that is unconditionally payable in cash or in property (other than debt instruments of the issuer), or that will be constructively received under section 451, at least annually at a single fixed rate (within the meaning of paragraph (c)(1)(iii) of this section).

(ii) *Unconditionally payable.* Interest is unconditionally payable only if reasonable legal remedies exist to compel timely payment or the debt instrument otherwise provides terms and conditions that make the likelihood of late payment (other than a late payment that occurs within a reasonable grace period) or nonpayment a remote contingency (within the meaning of § 1.1275-2(h)). For purposes of the preceding sentence, remedies or other terms and conditions are not taken into account if the lending transaction does not reflect arm's length dealing and the holder does not intend to enforce the remedies or other terms and conditions. For purposes of determining whether interest is unconditionally payable, the possibility of nonpayment due to default, insolvency, or similar circumstances, or due to the exercise of a conversion option described in § 1.1272-1(e) is ignored. This paragraph (c)(1)(ii) applies to debt instruments issued on or after August 13, 1996.

(iii) *Single fixed rate*—(A) *In general.* Interest is payable at a single fixed rate only if the rate appropriately takes into account the length of the interval between payments. Thus, if the interval between payments varies during the term of the debt instrument, the value of the fixed rate on which a payment is based generally must be adjusted to reflect a compounding assumption that is consistent with the length of the interval preceding the payment. See *Example 1* in paragraph (f) of this section.

(B) *Special rule for certain first and final payment intervals.* Notwithstanding paragraph (c)(1)(iii)(A) of this section, if a debt instrument provides for payment intervals that are equal in length throughout the term of the instrument, except that the first or final payment interval differs in length from the other payment intervals, the first or final interest payment is considered to be made at a fixed rate if the value of the rate on which the payment is based is adjusted in any reasonable manner to take into account the length of the interval. See *Example 2* of paragraph (f) of this section. The rule in this paragraph (c)(1)(iii)(B) also applies if the lengths of both the first and final payment intervals differ from the length of the other payment intervals.

(2) *Debt instruments subject to contingencies.* The determination of whether a debt instrument described in § 1.1272-1(c) (a debt instrument providing for an alternative payment schedule (or schedules) upon the occurrence of one or more contingencies) provides for qualified stated interest is made by analyzing each alternative payment schedule (including the stated payment schedule) as if it were the debt instrument's sole payment schedule. Under this analysis, the debt instrument provides for qualified stated in-

terest to the extent of the lowest fixed rate at which qualified stated interest would be payable under any payment schedule. See *Example 4* of paragraph (f) of this section.

(3) *Variable rate debt instrument.* In the case of a variable rate debt instrument, qualified stated interest is determined under § 1.1275-5(e).

(4) *Stated interest in excess of qualified stated interest.* To the extent that stated interest payable under a debt instrument exceeds qualified stated interest, the excess is included in the debt instrument's stated redemption price at maturity.

(5) *Short-term obligations.* In the case of a debt instrument with a term that is not more than 1 year from the date of issue, no payments of interest are treated as qualified stated interest payments.

(d) *De minimis OID*—(1) *In general.* If the amount of OID with respect to a debt instrument is less than the de minimis amount, the amount of OID is treated as zero, and all stated interest (including stated interest that would otherwise be characterized as OID) is treated as qualified stated interest.

(2) *De minimis amount.* The de minimis amount is an amount equal to 0.0025 multiplied by the product of the stated redemption price at maturity and the number of complete years to maturity from the issue date.

(3) *Installment obligations.* In the case of an installment obligation (as defined in paragraph (e)(1) of this section), paragraph (d)(2) of this section is applied by substituting for the number of complete years to maturity the weighted average maturity (as defined in paragraph (e)(3) of this section). Alternatively, in the case of a debt instrument that provides for payments of principal no more rapidly than self-amortizing installment obligation (as defined in paragraph (e)(2) of this section), the de minimis amount defined in paragraph (d)(2) of this section may be calculated by substituting 0.00167 for 0.0025.

(4) *Special rule for interest holidays, teaser rates, and other interest shortfalls*—(i) *In general.* This paragraph (d)(4) provides a special rule to determine whether a debt instrument with a teaser rate (or rates), an interest holiday, or any other interest shortfall has de minimis OID. This rule applies if—

(A) The amount of OID on the debt instrument is more than the de minimis amount as otherwise determined under paragraph (d) of this section; and

(B) All stated interest provided for in the debt instrument would be qualified stated interest under paragraph (c) of this section except

that for 1 or more accrual periods the interest rate is below the rate applicable for the remainder of the instrument's term (e.g., if as a result of an interest holiday, none of the stated interest is qualified stated interest).

(ii) *Redetermination of OID for purposes of the de minimis test.* For purposes of determining whether a debt instrument described in paragraph (d)(4)(i) of this section has de minimis OID, the instrument's stated redemption price at maturity is treated as equal to the instrument's issue price plus the greater of the amount of foregone interest or the excess (if any) of the instrument's stated principal amount over its issue price. The amount of foregone interest is the amount of additional stated interest that would be required to be payable on the debt instrument during the period of the teaser rate, holiday, or shortfall so that all stated interest would be qualified stated interest under paragraph (c) of this section. See *Example 5* and *Example 6* of paragraph (f) of this section. In addition, for purposes of computing the de minimis amount of OID the weighted average maturity of the debt instrument is determined by treating all stated interest payments as qualified stated interest payments.

(5) *Treatment of de minimis OID by holders*—(i) *Allocation of de minimis OID to principal payments.* The holder of a debt instrument includes any de minimis OID (other than de minimis OID treated as qualified stated interest under paragraph (d)(1) of this section, such as de minimis OID attributable to a teaser rate or interest holiday) in income as stated principal payments are made. The amount includible in income with respect to each principal payment equals the product of the total amount of de minimis OID on the debt instrument and a fraction, the numerator of which is the amount of the principal payment made, and the denominator of which is the stated principal amount of the instrument.

(ii) *Character of de minimis OID*—(A) *De minimis OID treated as gain recognized on retirement.* Any amount of de minimis OID includible in income under this paragraph (d)(5) is treated as gain recognized on retirement of the debt instrument. See section 1271 to determine whether a retirement is treated as an exchange of the debt instrument.

(B) *Treatment of de minimis OID on sale or exchange.* Any gain attributable to de minimis OID that is recognized on the sale or exchange of a debt instrument is capital gain if the debt instrument is a capital asset in the hands of the seller.

(iii) *Treatment of subsequent holders.* If a subsequent holder purchases a debt instrument issued with de minimis OID at a premium (as defined in § 1.1272-2(b)(2)), the subsequent holder does not include the de minimis OID in income. Otherwise, a subsequent holder includes any discount in income under the market discount rules (sections 1276 through 1278) rather than under the rules of this paragraph (d)(5).

(iv) *Cross-reference.* See § 1.1272-3 for an election by a holder to treat de minimis OID as OID.

(e) *Definitions*—(1) *Installment obligation.* An installment obligation is a debt instrument that provides for the payment of any amount other than qualified stated interest before maturity.

(2) *Self-amortizing installment obligation.* A self-amortizing installment obligation is an obligation that provides for equal payments composed of principal and qualified stated interest that are unconditionally payable at least annually during the entire term of the debt instrument with no additional payment required at maturity.

(3) *Weighted average maturity.* The weighted average maturity of a debt instrument is the sum of the following amounts determined for each payment under the instrument (other than a payment of qualified stated interest)—

(i) The number of complete years from the issue date until the payment is made, multiplied by

(ii) A fraction, the numerator of which is the amount of the payment and the denominator of which is the debt instrument's stated redemption price at maturity.

(f) *Examples.* The following examples illustrate the rules of this section.

Example 1. Qualified stated interest—(i) *Facts.* On January 1, 1995, A purchases at original issue for $100,000, a debt instrument that matures on January 1, 1999, and has a stated principal amount of $100,000, payable at maturity. The debt instrument provides for interest payments of $8,000 on January 1, 1996, and January 1, 1997, and quarterly interest payments of $1,942.65, beginning on April 1, 1997.

(ii) *Amount of qualified stated interest.* The annual payments of $8,000 and the quarterly payments of $1,942.65 are payable at a single fixed rate because 8 percent, compounded annually, is equivalent to 7.77 percent, compounded quarterly. Consequently, all stated interest payments under the debt instrument are qualified stated interest payments.

Example 2. Qualified stated interest with short initial payment interval. On October 1, 1994, A purchases at original issue, for $100,000, a debt instrument that matures on January 1, 1998, and has a stated principal amount of $100,000, payable at maturity. The debt instrument provides for

an interest payment of $2,000 on January 1, 1995, and interest payments of $8,000 on January 1, 1996, January 1, 1997, and January 1, 1998. Under paragraph (c)(1)(iii)(B) of this section, all stated interest payments on the debt instrument are computed at a single fixed rate and are qualified stated interest payments.

Example 3. Stated interest in excess of qualified stated interest—(i) *Facts.* On January 1, 1995, B purchases at original issue, for $100,000, C corporation's 5-year debt instrument. The debt instrument provides for a principal payment of $100,000, payable at maturity, and calls for annual interest payments of $10,000 for the first 3 years and annual interest payments of $10,600 for the last 2 years.

(ii) *Payments in excess of qualified stated interest.* All of the first three interest payments and $10,000 of each of the last two interest payments are qualified stated interest payments within the meaning of paragraph (c)(1) of this section. Under paragraph (c)(4) of this section, the remaining $600 of each of the last two interest payments is included in the stated redemption price at maturity, so that the stated redemption price at maturity is $101,200. Pursuant to paragraph (e)(3) of this section, the weighted average maturity of the debt instrument is 4.994 years [(4 years × $600/$101,200) + (5 years × $100,600/$101,200)]. The de minimis amount, or one-fourth of 1 percent of the stated redemption price at maturity multiplied by the weighted average maturity, is $1,263.50. Because the actual amount of discount, $1,200, is less than the de minimis amount, the instrument is treated as having no OID, and, under paragraph (d)(1) of this section, all of the interest payments are treated as qualified stated interest payments.

* * *

[Reg. § 1.1273-1.]

☐ [*T.D.* 8517, 1-27-94. Amended by *T.D.* 8674, 6-11-96.]

§ 1.1273-2. Determination of issue price and issue date.—(a) *Debt instruments issued for money*—(1) *Issue price.* If a substantial amount of the debt instruments in an issue is issued for money, the issue price of each debt instrument in the issue is the first price at which a substantial amount of the debt instruments is sold for money. Thus, if an issue consists of a single debt instrument that is issued for money, the issue price of the debt instrument is the amount paid for the instrument. For example, in the case of a debt instrument evidencing a loan to a natural person, the issue price of the instrument is the amount loaned. See § 1.1275-2(d) for rules regarding Treasury securities. For purposes of this paragraph (a), money includes functional currency and, in

Reg. § 1.1273-2(a)(1)

certain circumstances, nonfunctional currency. See § 1.988-2(b)(2) for circumstances when nonfunctional currency is treated as money rather than as property.

(2) *Issue date.* The issue date of an issue described in paragraph (a)(1) of this section is the first settlement date or closing date, whichever is applicable, on which a substantial amount of the debt instruments in the issue is sold for money.

(b) *Publicly traded debt instruments issued for property.*—(1) *Issue price.* If a substantial amount of the debt instruments in an issue is traded on an established market (within the meaning of paragraph (f) of this section) and the issue is not described in paragraph (a)(1) of this section, the issue price of each debt instrument in the issue is the fair market value of the debt instrument, determined as of the issue date (as defined in paragraph (b)(2) of this section).

(2) *Issue date.* The issue date of an issue described in paragraph (b)(1) of this section is the first date on which a substantial amount of the traded debt instruments in the issue is issued.

(c) *Debt instruments issued for publicly traded property*—(1) *Issue price.* If a substantial amount of the debt instrument in an issue is issued for property that is traded on an established market (within the meaning of paragraph (f) of this section) and the issue is not described in paragraph (a)(1) or (b)(1) of this section, the issue price of each debt instrument in the issue is the fair market value of the property, determined as of the issue date (as defined in paragraph (c)(2) of this section). For purposes of the preceding sentence, property means a debt instrument, stock, security, contract, commodity, or nonfunctional currency. But see § 1.988-2(b)(2) for circumstances when nonfunctional currency is treated as money rather than as property.

(2) *Issue date.* The issue date of an issue described in paragraph (c)(1) of this section is the first date on which a substantial amount of the debt instruments in the issue is issued for traded property.

(d) *Other debt instruments*—(1) *Issue price.* If an issue of debt instruments is not described in paragraph (a)(1), (b)(1), or (c)(1) of this section, the issue price of each debt instrument in the issue is determined as if the debt instrument were a separate issue. If the issue price of a debt instrument that is treated as a separate issue under the preceding sentence is not determined under paragraph (a)(1), (b)(1), or (c)(1) of this section, and if section 1274 applies to the debt instrument, the issue price of the instrument is determined under section 1274. Otherwise, the issue price of the debt instrument is its stated redemption price at maturity under section

1273(b)(4). See section 1274(c) and § 1.1274-1 to determine if section 1274 applies to a debt instrument.

(2) *Issue date.* The issue date of an issue described in paragraph (d)(1) of this section is the date on which the debt instrument is issued for money or in a sale or exchange.

(e) *Special rule for certain sales to bond houses, brokers, or similar persons.* For purposes of determining the issue price and issue date of a debt instrument under this section, sales to bond houses, brokers, or similar persons or organizations acting in the capacity of underwriters, placement agents, or wholesalers are ignored.

(f) *Traded on an established market (publicly traded)*—(1) *In general.* Property (including a debt instrument described in paragraph (b)(1) of this section) is traded on an established market for purposes of this section if, at any time during the 60-day period ending 30 days after the issue date, the property is described in paragraph (f)(2), (f)(3), (f)(4), or (f)(5) of this section.

(2) *Exchange listed property.* Property is described in this paragraph (f)(2) if it is listed on—

(i) A national securities exchange registered under section 6 of the Securities Exchange Act of 1934 (15 U.S.C. 78f);

(ii) An interdealer quotation system sponsored by a national securities association registered under section 15A of the Securities Exchange Act of 1934 (15 U.S.C. 78o-3); or

(iii) The International Stock Exchange of the United Kingdom and the Republic of Ireland, Limited, the Frankfurt Stock Exchange, the Tokyo Stock Exchange, or any other foreign exchange or board of trade that is designated by the Commissioner in the Internal Revenue Bulletin (see § 601.601(d)(2)(ii) of this chapter).

(3) *Market traded property.* Property is described in this paragraph (f)(3) if it is property of a kind that is traded either on a board of trade designated as a contract market by the Commodities Futures Trading Commission or on an interbank market.

(4) *Property appearing on a quotation medium.* Property is described in this paragraph (f)(4) if it appears on a system of general circulation (including a computer listing disseminated to subscribing brokers, dealers, or traders) that provides a reasonable basis to determine fair market value by disseminating either recent price quotations (including rates, yields, or other pricing information) of one or more identified brokers, dealers, or traders or actual prices (including rates, yields, or other pricing information) of recent sales transactions (a quotation medium). A quotation medium does not include a directory or

Reg. § 1.1273-2(f)(4)

listing of brokers, dealers, or traders for specific securities, such as yellow sheets, that provides neither price quotations nor actual prices of recent sales transactions.

(5) *Readily quotable debt instruments*—(i) *In general.* A debt instrument is described in this paragraph (f)(5) if price quotations are readily available from dealers, brokers, or traders.

(ii) *Safe harbors.* A debt instrument is not considered to be described in paragraph (f)(5)(i) of this section if—

(A) No other outstanding debt instrument of the issuer (or of any person who gurantees the debt instrument) is described in paragraph (f)(2), (f)(3), or (f)(4) of this section (other traded debt);

(B) The original stated principal amount of the issue that includes the debt instrument does not exceed $25 million;

(C) The conditions and covenants relating to the issuer's performance with respect to the debt instrument are materially less restrictive than the conditions and covenants included in all of the issuer's other traded debt (e.g., the debt instrument is subject to an economically significant subordination provision whereas the issuer's other traded debt is senior); or

(D) The maturity date of the debt instrument is more than 3 years after the latest maturity date of the issuer's other traded debt.

(6) *Effect of certain temporary restrictions on trading.* If there is any temporary restriction on trading a purpose of which is to avoid the characterization of the property as one that is traded on an established market for Federal income tax purposes, then the property is treated as traded on an established market. For purposes of the preceding sentence, a temporary restriction on trading need not be imposed by the issuer.

(7) *Convertible debt instruments.* A debt instrument is not treated as traded on an established market solely because the debt instrument is convertible into property that is so traded.

* * *

(k) *Below-market loans subject to section 7872(b).* The issue price of a below-market loan subject to section 7872(b) (a term loan other than a gift loan) is the issue price determined under this section, reduced by the excess amount determined under section 7872(b)(1).

(l) [Reserved]

* * *

[Reg. § 1.1273-2.]

☐ [*T.D. 8517, 1-27-94.*]

§ 1.1274-1. Debt instruments to which section 1274 applies.—(a) *In general.* Subject to the

exceptions and limitations in paragraph (b) of this section, section 1274 and this section apply to any debt instrument issued in consideration for the sale or exchange of property. For purposes of section 1274, property includes debt instruments and investment units, but does not include money, services, or the right to use property. For the treatment of certain obligations given in exchange for services or the use of property, see sections 404 and 467. For purposes of this paragraph (a), money includes functional currency and, in certain circumstances, nonfunctional currency. See § 1.988-2(b)(2) for circumstances when nonfunctional currency is treated as money rather than as property.

(b) *Exceptions*—(1) *Debt instrument with adequate stated interest and no OID.* Section 1274 does not apply to a debt instrument if—

(i) All interest payable on the instrument is qualified stated interest;

(ii) The stated rate of interest is at least equal to the test rate of interest (as defined in § 1.1274-4);

(iii) The debt instrument is not issued in a potentially abusive situation (as defined in § 1.1274-3); and

(iv) No payment from the buyer-borrower to the seller-lender designated as points or interest is made at the time of issuance of the debt instrument.

(2) *Exceptions under sections 1274(c)(1)(B), 1274(c)(3), 1274A(c), and 1275(b)(1)*—(i) *In general.* Sections 1274(c)(1)(B), 1274(c)(3), 1274A(c), and 1275(b)(1) describe certain transactions to which section 1274 does not apply. This paragraph (b)(2) provides certain rules to be used in applying those exceptions.

(ii) *Special rules for certain exceptions under section 1274(c)(3)*—(A) *Determination of sales price for certain sales of farms.* For purposes of section 1274(c)(3)(A), the determination as to whether the sales price cannot exceed $1,000,000 is made without regard to any other exception to, or limitation on, the applicability of section 1274 (e.g., without regard to the special rules regarding sales of principal residences and land transfers between related persons). In addition, the sales price is determined without regard to section 1274 and without regard to any stated interest. The sales price includes the amount of any liability included in the amount realized from the sale or exchange. See § 1.1001-2.

(B) *Sales involving total payments of $250,000 or less.* Under section 1274(c)(3)(C), the determination of the amount of payments due under all debt instruments and the amount of other consideration to be received is made as of the date of the sale or exchange or, if earlier, the contract date. If the precise amount due under any debt instrument or the precise amount of any other consideration to be received cannot be determined as of that date, section 1274(c)(3)(C) applies only if it can be determined that the maximum of the aggregate amount of payments due under the debt instruments and other consideration to be received cannot exceed $250,000. For purposes of section 1274(c)(3)(C), if a liability is assumed or property is taken subject to a liability, the aggregate amount of payments due includes the outstanding principal balance or adjusted issue price (in the case of an obligation originally issued at a discount) of the obligation.

(C) *Coordination with section 1273 and § 1.1273-2.* In accordance with section 1274(c)(3)(D), section 1274 and this section do not apply if the issue price of a debt instrument issued in consideration for the sale or exchange of property is determined under paragraph (a)(1), (b)(1), or (c)(1) of § 1.1273-2.

(3) *Other exceptions to section 1274*—(i) *Holders of certain below-market instruments.* Section 1274 does not apply to any holder of a debt instrument that is issued in consideration for the sale or exchange of personal use property (within the meaning of section 1275(b)(3)) in the hands of the issuer and that evidences a below-market loan described in section 7872(c)(1).

(ii) *Transactions involving certain demand loans.* Section 1274 does not apply to any debt instrument that evidences a demand loan that is a below-market loan described in section 7872(c)(1).

(iii) *Certain transfers subject to section 1041.* Section 1274 does not apply to any debt instrument issued in consideration for a transfer of property subject to section 1041 (relating to transfers of property between spouses or incident to divorce).

(c) *Examples.* The following examples illustrate the rules of this section.

Example 1. Single stated rate paid semiannually. A debt instrument issued in consideration for the sale of nonpublicly traded property in a transaction that is not a potentially abusive situation calls for the payment of a principal amount of $1,000,000 at the end of a 10-year term and 20 semiannual interest payments of $60,000. Assume that the test rate of interest is 12 percent, compounded semiannually. The debt instrument is not subject to section 1274 because it provides for interest equal to the test rate and all interest payable on the instrument is qualified stated interest.

Example 2. Sale of farm for debt instrument with contingent interest—(i) *Facts.* On July 1, 1995, A, an individual, sells to B land used as a

farm within the meaning of section 6420(c)(2). As partial consideration for the sale, B issues a debt instrument calling for a single $500,000 payment due in 10 years unless profits from the land in each of the 10 years preceding maturity of the debt instrument exceed a specified amount, in which case B is to make a payment of $1,200,000. The debt instrument does not provide for interest.

(ii) *Total payments may exceed $1,000,000.* Even though the total payments ultimately payable under the contract may be less than $1,000,000, at the time of the sale or exchange it cannot be determined that the sales price cannot exceed $1,000,000. Thus, the sale of the land used as a farm is not an excepted transaction described in section 1274(c)(3)(A).

Example 3. Sale between related parties subject to section 483(e)—(i) *Facts.* On July 1, 1995, A, an individual, sells land (not used as a farm within the meaning of section 6420(c)(2)) to A's child B for $650,000. In consideration for the sale, B issues a 10-year debt instrument to A that calls for a payment of $650,000. No other consideration is given. The debt instrument does not provide for interest.

(ii) *Treatment of debt instrument.* For purposes of section 483(e), the $650,000 debt instrument is treated as two separate debt instruments: a $500,000 debt instrument and a $150,000 debt instrument. The $500,000 debt instrument is subject to section 483(e), and accordingly is covered by the exception from section 1274 described in section 1274(c)(3)(F). Because the amount of the payments due as consideration for the sale exceeds $250,000, however, the $150,000 debt instrument is subject to section 1274.

[Reg. § 1.1274-1.]

☐ [*T.D.* 8517, 1-27-94.]

§ 1.1274-2. Issue price of debt instruments to which section 1274 applies.—(a) *In general.* If section 1274 applies to a debt instrument, section 1274 and this section determine the issue price of the debt instrument. For rules relating to the determination of the amount and timing of OID to be included in income, see section 1272 and the regulations thereunder.

(b) *Issue price*—(1) *Debt instruments that provide for adequate stated interest; stated principal amount.* The issue price of a debt instrument that provides for adequate stated interest is the stated principal amount of the debt instrument. For purposes of section 1274, the stated principal amount of a debt instrument is the aggregate amount of all payments due under the debt instrument, excluding any amount of stated interest. Under § 1.1273-2(g)(2)(ii), however, the stated principal amount of a debt instrument is reduced by any payment from the buyer-borrower to the seller-

Reg. § 1.1274-2(b)(1)

lender that is designated as interest or points. See *Example 2* of § 1.1273-2(g)(5).

(2) *Debt instruments that do not provide for adequate stated interest; imputed principal amount.* The issue price of a debt instrument that does not provide for adequate stated interest is the imputed principal amount of the debt instrument.

(3) *Debt instruments issued in a potentially abusive situation; fair market value.* Notwithstanding paragraphs (b)(1) and (b)(2) of this section, in the case of a debt instrument issued in a potentially abusive situation (as defined in § 1.1274-3), the issue price of the debt instrument is the fair market value of the property received in exchange for the debt instrument, reduced by the fair market value of any consideration other than the debt instrument issued in consideration for the sale or exchange.

(c) *Determination of whether a debt instrument provides for adequate stated interest*—(1) *In general.* A debt instrument provides for adequate stated interest if its stated principal amount is less than or equal to its imputed principal amount. Imputed principal amount means the sum of the present values, as of the issue date, of all payments, including payments of stated interest, due under the debt instrument (determined by using a discount rate equal to the test rate of interest as determined under § 1.1274-4). If a debt instrument has a single fixed rate of interest that is paid or compounded at least annually, and that rate is equal to or greater than the test rate, the debt instrument has adequate stated interest.

(2) *Determination of present value.* The present value of a payment is determined by discounting the payment from the date it becomes due to the date of the sale or exchange at the test rate of interest. To determine present value, a compounding period must be selected, and the test rate must be based on the same compounding period.

* * *

[Reg. § 1.1274-2.]

☐ *[T.D. 8517, 1-27-94. Amended by T.D. 8674, 6-11-96.]*

§ 1.1274-4. **Test rate.**—(a) *Determination of test rate of interest*—(1) *In general*—(i) *Test rate is the 3-month rate.* Except as provided in paragraph (a)(2) of this section, the test rate of interest for a debt instrument issued in consideration for the sale or exchange of property is the 3-month rate.

(ii) *The 3-month rate.* Except as provided in paragraph (a)(1)(iii) of this section, the 3-month rate is the lower of—

(A) The lowest applicable Federal rate (based on the appropriate compounding period) in effect during the 3-month period ending with the first month in which there is a binding written contract that substantially sets forth the terms under which the sale or exchange is ultimately consummated; or

(B) The lowest applicable Federal rate (based on the appropriate compounding period) in effect during the 3-month period ending with the month in which the sale or exchange occurs.

(iii) *Special rule if there is no binding written contract.* If there is no binding written contract that substantially sets forth the terms under which the sale or exchange is ultimately consummated, the 3-month rate is the lowest applicable Federal rate (based on the appropriate compounding period) in effect during the 3-month period ending with the month in which the sale or exchange occurs.

(2) *Test rate for certain debt instruments*— (i) *Sale-leaseback transactions.* Under section 1274(e) (relating to certain sale-leaseback transactions), the test rate is 110 percent of the 3-month rate determined under paragraph (a)(1) of this section. For purposes of section 1274(e)(3), related party means a person related to the transferor within the meaning of section 267(b) or 707(b)(1).

(ii) *Qualified debt instrument.* Under section 1274A(a), the test rate for a qualified debt instrument is no greater than 9 percent, compounded semiannually, or an equivalent rate based on an appropriate compounding period.

(iii) *Alternative test rate for short-term obligations*—(A) *Requirements.* This paragraph (a)(2)(iii)(A) provides an alternative test rate under section 1274(d)(1)(D) for a debt instrument with a maturity of 1 year or less. This alternative test rate applies, however, only if the debt instrument provides for adequate stated interest using the alternative test rate, the issuer provides on the face of the debt instrument that the instrument qualifies as having adequate stated interest under section 1274(d)(1)(D), and the issuer and holder treat or agree to treat the instrument as having adequate stated interest.

(B) *Alternative test rate.* For purposes of paragraph (a)(2)(iii)(A), the alternative test rate is the market yield on U.S. Treasury bills with the same maturity date as the debt instrument. If the same maturity date is not available, the market yield on U.S. Treasury bills that mature in the same week or month as the debt instrument is used. The alternative test rate is determined as of the date on which there is a binding written contract that substantially sets forth the terms under which the sale or exchange is ultimately consummated or as of the date of the sale or exchange, whichever date results in a lower rate. If there is no binding written contract, however, the alternative test rate is determined as of the date of the sale or exchange.

(b) *Applicable Federal rate.* Except as otherwise provided in this section, the applicable Federal rate for a debt instrument is based on the term of the instrument (i.e., short-term, mid-term, or long-term). See section 1274(d)(1). The Internal Revenue Service publishes the applicable Federal rates for each month in the Internal Revenue Bulletin (see § 601.601(d)(2)(ii) of this chapter). The applicable Federal rates are based on the yield to maturity of outstanding marketable obligations of the United States of similar maturities during the one month period ending on the 14th day of the month preceding the month for which the rates are applicable.

(c) *Special rules to determine the term of a debt instrument for purposes of determining the applicable Federal rate*—(1) *Installment obligation.* If a debt instrument is an installment obligation (as defined in § 1.1273-1(e)(1)), the term of the instrument is the instrument's weighted average maturity (as defined in § 1.1273-1(e)(3)).

(2) *Certain variable rate debt instruments*—(i) *In general.* Except as otherwise provided in paragraph (c)(2)(ii) of this section, if a variable rate debt instrument (as defined in § 1.1275-5(a)) provides for stated interest at a qualified floating rate (or rates), the term of the instrument is determined by reference to the longest interval between interest adjustment dates, or, if the variable rate debt instrument provides for a fixed rate, the interval between the issue date and the last day on which the fixed rate applies, if this interval is longer.

(ii) *Restrictions on adjustments.* If, due to significant restrictions on variations in a qualified floating rate or the use of certain formulae pursuant to § 1.1275-5(b)(2) (e.g., 15 percent of 1-year LIBOR, plus 800 basis points), the rate in substance resembles a fixed rate, the applicable Federal rate is determined by reference to the term of the debt instrument.

(3) *Counting of either the issue date or the maturity date.* The term of a debt instrument includes either the issue date or the maturity date, but not both dates.

(4) *Certain debt instruments that provide for principal payments uncertain as to time.* If a debt instrument provides for principal payments that are fixed in total amount but uncertain as to time, the term of the instrument is determined by reference to the latest possible date on which a principal payment can be made or, in the case of an installment obligation, by reference to the longest

weighted average maturity under any possible payment schedule.

(e) *Examples.* The following examples illustrate the rules of this section.

Example 1. Variable rate debt instrument that limits the amount of increase and decrease in the rate—(i) *Facts.* On July 1, 1996, A sells nonpublicly traded property to B in return for a 5-year debt instrument that provides for interest to be paid on July 1 of each year, beginning on July 1, 1997, based on the prime rate of a local bank on that date. However, the interest rate cannot increase or decrease from one year to the next by more than .25 percentage points (25 basis points).

(ii) *Significant restriction.* The debt instrument is a variable rate debt instrument (as defined in § 1.1275-5) that provides for stated interest at a qualified floating rate. Assume that based on all the facts and circumstances, the restriction is a significant restriction on the variations in the rate of interest. Under paragraph (c)(2)(ii) of this section, the applicable Federal rate is determined by reference to the term of the debt instrument, and the applicable Federal rate is the Federal mid-term rate.

Example 2. Installment obligation—(i) *Facts.* On January 1, 1996, A sells nonpublicly traded property to B in exchange for a debt instrument that calls for a payment of $500,000 on January 1, 2001, and a payment of $1,000,000 on January 1, 2006. The debt instrument does not provide for any stated interest.

(ii) *Determination of term.* The debt instrument is an installment obligation. Under paragraph (c)(1) of this section, the term of the debt instrument is its weighted average maturity (as defined in § 1.1273-1(e)(3)). The debt instrument's weighted average maturity is 8.33 years, which is the sum of (A) the ratio of the first payment to total payments (500,000/1,500,000), multiplied by the number of complete years from the issue date until the payment is due (5 years), and (B) the ratio of the second payment to total payments (1,000,000/1,500,000), multiplied by the number of complete years from the issue date until the second payment is due (10 years).

(iii) *Applicable Federal rate.* Based on the calculation in paragraph (ii) of this example, the term of the debt instrument is treated as 8.33 years. Consequently, the applicable Federal rate is the Federal mid-term rate.

[Reg. § 1.1274-4.]

☐ [*T.D. 8517, 1-27-94.*]

§ 1.1274A-1. Special rules for certain transactions where stated principal amount does not exceed $2,800,000.—(a) *In general.* Section 1274A allows the use of a lower test rate for purposes of sections 483 and 1274 in the case of a qualified debt instrument (as defined in section 1274A(b)) and, if elected by the borrower and the lender, the use of the cash receipts and disbursements method of accounting for interest on a cash method debt instrument (as defined in section 1274A(c)(2)). This section provides special rules for qualified debt instruments and cash method debt instruments.

(b) *Rules for both qualified and cash method debt instruments*—(1) *Sale-leaseback transactions.* A debt instrument issued in a sale-leaseback transaction (within the meaning of section 1274(e)) cannot be either a qualified debt instrument or a cash method debt instrument.

(2) *Debt instruments calling for contingent payments.* A debt instrument that provides for contingent payments cannot be a qualified debt instrument unless it can be determined at the time of the sale or exchange that the maximum stated principal amount due under the debt instrument cannot exceed the amount specified in section 1274A(b). Similarly, a debt instrument that provides for contingent payments cannot be a cash method debt instrument unless it can be determined at the time of the sale or exchange that the maximum stated principal amount due under the debt instrument cannot exceed the amount specified in section 1274A(c)(2)(A).

(3) *Aggregation of transactions*—(i) *General rule.* The aggregation rules of section 1274A(d)(1) are applied using a facts and circumstances test.

(ii) *Examples.* The following examples illustrate the application of section 1274A(d)(1) and paragraph (b)(3)(i) of this section.

Example 1. Aggregation of two sales to a single person. In two transactions evidenced by separate sales agreements, A sells undivided half interests in Blackacre to B. The sales are pursuant to a plan for the sale of a 100 percent interest in Blackacre to B. These sales or exchanges are part of a series of related transactions and, thus, are treated as a single sale for purposes of section 1274A.

Example 2. Aggregation of two purchases by unrelated individuals. Pursuant to a plan, unrelated individuals X and Y purchase undivided half interests in Blackacre from A and subsequently contribute these interests to a partnership in exchange for equal interests in the partnership. These purchases are treated as part of the same transaction and, thus, are treated as a single sale for purposes of section 1274A.

Example 3. Aggregation of sales made pursuant to a tender offer. Fifteen unrelated individuals own all of the stock of X Corporation. Y Corporation makes a tender offer to these 15 shareholders. The terms offered to each share-

holder are identical. Shareholders holding a majority of the shares of X Corporation elect to tender their shares pursuant to Y Corporation's offer. These sales are part of the same transaction and, thus, are treated as a single sale for purposes of section 1274A.

Example 4. No aggregation for separate sales of similar property to unrelated persons. Pursuant to a newspaper advertisement, X Corporation offers for sale similar condominiums in a single building. The prices of the units vary due to a variety of factors, but the financing terms offered by X Corporation to all buyers are identical. The units are purchased by unrelated buyers who decided whether to purchase units in the building at the price and on the terms offered by X Corporation, without regard to the actions of other buyers. Because each buyer acts individually, the sales are not part of the same transaction or a series of related transactions and, thus, are treated as separate sales.

(4) *Inflation adjustment of dollar amounts.* Under section 1274A(d)(2), the dollar amounts specified in sections 1274A(b) and 1274A(c)(2)(A) are adjusted for inflation. The dollar amounts, adjusted for inflation, are published in the Internal Revenue Bulletin (see § 601.601(d)(2)(ii) of this chapter).

(c) *Rules for cash method debt instruments*—(1) *Time and manner of making cash method election.* The borrower and lender make the election described in section 1274A(c)(2)(D) by jointly signing a statement that includes the names, addresses, and taxpayer identification numbers of the borrower and lender, a clear indication that an election is being made under section 1274A(c)(2), and a declaration that debt instrument with respect to which the election is being made fulfills the requirements of a cash method debt instrument. Both the borrower and the lender must sign this statement not later than the earlier of the last day (including extensions) for filing the Federal income tax return of the borrower or lender for the taxable year in which the debt instrument is issued. The borrower and lender should attach this signed statement (or a copy thereof) to their timely filed Federal income tax returns.

(2) *Successors of electing parties.* Except as othewise provided in this paragraph (c)(2), the cash method election under section 1274A(c) applies to any successor of the electing lender or borrower. Thus, for any period after the transfer of a cash method debt instrument, the successor takes into account the interest (including unstated interest) on the instrument under the cash receipts and disbursements method of accounting. Nevertheless, if the lender (or any successor

thereof) transfers the cash method debt instrument to a taxpayer who uses an accrual method of accounting, section 1272 rather than section 1274A(c) applies to the successor of the lender with respect to the debt instrument for any period after the date of the transfer. The borrower (or any successor thereof), however, remains on the cash receipts and disbursements method of accounting with respect to the cash method debt instrument.

(3) *Modified debt instrument.* In the case of a debt instrument issued in a debt-for-debt exchange that qualifies as an exchange under section 1001, the debt instrument is eligible for the election to be a cash method debt instrument if the other prerequisites to making the election in section 1274A(c) are met. However, if a principal purpose of the modification is to defer interest income or deductions through the use of the election, then the debt instrument is not eligible for the election.

(4) *Debt incurred or continued to purchase or carry a cash method debt instrument.* If a debt instrument is incurred or continued to purchase or carry a cash method debt instrument, rules similar to those under section 1277 apply to determine the timing of the interest deductions for the debt instrument. For purposes of the preceding sentence, rules similar to those under section 265(a)(2) apply to determine whether a debt instrument is incurred or continued to purchase or carry a cash method debt instrument. [Reg. § 1.1274A-1.]

☐ [*T.D. 8517, 1-27-94.*]

§ 1.1275-1. Definitions.—(a) *Applicability.* The definitions contained in this section apply for purposes of sections 163(e) and 1271 through 1275 and the regulations therunder.

(b) *Adjusted issue price*—(1) *In general.* The adjusted issue price of a debt instrument at the beginning of the first accrual period is the issue price. Thereafter, the adjusted issue price of the debt instrument is the issue price of the debt instrument—

(i) Increased by the amount of OID previously includible in the gross income of any holder (determined without regard to section 1272(a)(7) and section 1272(c)(1)); and

(ii) Decreased by the amount of any payment previously made on the debt instrument other than a payment of qualified stated interest. See § 1.1275-2(f) for rules regarding adjustments to adjusted issue price on a pro rata prepayment.

(2) *Bond issuance premium.* If a debt instrument is issued with bond issuance premium (as defined in § 1.163-13(c)), for purposes of determining the issuer's adjusted issue price, the ad-

justed issue price determined under paragraph (b)(1) of this section is also decreased by the amount of bond issuance premium previously allocable under § 1.163-13(d)(3).

(3) *Adjusted issue price for subsequent holders.* for purposes of calculating OID accruals, acquisition premium, or market discount, a holder (other than a purchaser at original issuance) determines adjusted issue price in any manner consistent with the regulations under sections 1271 through 1275.

(c) *OID.* OID means original issue discount (as defined in section 1273(a) and § 1.1273-1).

(d) *Debt instrument.* Except as provided in section 1275(a)(1)(B) (relating to certain annuity contracts; see paragraph (j) of this section), debt instrument means any instrument or contractual arrangement that constitutes indebtedness under general principles of Federal income tax law (including, for example, a certificate of deposit or a loan). Nothing in the regulations under sections 163(e), 483, and 1271 through 1275, however, shall influence whether an instrument constitutes indebtedness for Federal income tax purposes.

(e) *Tax-exempt obligations.* For purposes of section 1275(a)(3)(B), exempt from tax means exempt from Federal income tax.

(f) *Issue*—(1) *Debt instruments issued on or after March 13, 2001.* Except as provided in paragraph (f)(3) of this section, two or more debt instruments are part of the same issue if the debt instruments—

(i) Have the same credit and payment terms;

(ii) Are issued either pursuant to a common plan or as part of a single transaction or a series of related transactions;

(iii) Are issued within a period of thirteen days beginning with the date on which the first debt instrument that would be part of the issue is issued to a person other than a bond house, broker, or similar person or organization acting in the capacity of an underwriter, placement agent, or wholesaler; and

(iv) Are issued on or after March 13, 2001.

(2) *Debt instruments issued before March 13, 2001.* Except as provided in paragraph (f)(3) of this section, two or more debt instruments are part of the same issue if the debt instruments—

(i) Have the same credit and payment terms;

(ii) Are sold reasonably close in time either pursuant to a common plan or as part of a single transaction or a series of related transactions; and

(iii) Are issued on or after April 4, 1994, and before March 13, 2001.

Reg. § 1.1275-1(f)(2)

(3) *Transition rule.* If the issue date of any of the debt instruments that would be part of the same issue (determined as if each debt instrument were part of a separate issue) is on or after March 13, 2001, then the definition of the term *issue* in paragraph (f)(1) of this section applies rather than the definition in paragraph (f)(2) of this section to determine if the debt instruments are part of the same issue.

(4) *Cross-references for reopening and aggregation rules.* See § 1.1275-2(d) and (k) for rules that treat debt instruments issued in certain reopenings as part of an issue of original (outstanding) debt instruments. See § 1.1275-2(c) for rules that treat two or more debt instruments as a single debt instrument.

(g) *Debt instruments issued by a natural person.* If an entity is a primary obligor under a debt instrument, the debt instrument is considered to be issued by the entity and not by a natural person even if a natural person is a co-maker and is jointly liable for the debt instrument's repayment. A debt instrument issued by a partnership is considered to be issued by the partnership as an entity even if the partnership is composed entirely of natural persons.

(h) *Publicly offered debt instrument.* A debt instrument is publicly offered if it is part of an issue of debt instruments the initial offering of which—

(1) Is registered with the Securities and Exchange Commission; or

(2) Would be required to be registered under the Securities Act of 1933 (15 U.S.C. 77a et seq.) but for an exemption from registration—

(i) Under section 3 of the Securities Act of 1933 (relating to exempted securities);

(ii) Under any law (other than the Securities Act of 1933) because of the identity of the issuer or the nature of the security; or

(iii) Because the issue is intended for distribution to persons who are not United States persons.

(i) [Reserved]

* * *

[Reg. § 1.1275-1.]

☐ [*T.D.* 8517, 1-27-94. *Amended by T.D.* 8746, 12-30-97; *T.D.* 8754, 1-7-98; *T.D.* 8934, 1-11-2001 *and T.D.* 8993, 5-6-2002.]

S Corporations and Their Shareholders

§ **1.1361-1. S corporation defined.**—(a) *In general.* For purposes of this title, with respect to any taxable year—(1) The term *S corporation* means a small business corporation (as defined in paragraph (b) of this section) for which an election under section 1362(a) is in effect for that taxable year.

(2) The term *C corporation* means a corporation that is not an S corporation for that taxable year.

(b) *Small business corporation defined*—(1) *In general.* For purposes of subchapter S, chapter 1 of the Code and the regulations thereunder, the term *small business corporation* means a domestic corporation that is not an ineligible corporation (as defined in section 1361(b)(2)) and that does not have—

(i) More than 75 shareholders (35 for taxable years beginning before January 1, 1997);

(ii) As a shareholder, a person (other than an estate and other than certain trusts described in section 1361(c)(2)) who is not an individual;

(iii) A nonresident alien as a shareholder; or

(iv) More than one class of stock.

(2) *Estate in bankruptcy.* The term *estate,* for purposes of this paragraph, includes the estate of an individual in a case under title 11 of the United States Code.

(3) *Treatment of restricted stock.* For purposes of subchapter S, stock that is issued in connection with the performance of services (within the meaning of § 1.83-3(f)) and that is substantially nonvested (within the meaning of § 1.83-3(b)) is not treated as outstanding stock of the corporation, and the holder of that stock is not treated as a shareholder solely by reason of holding the stock, unless the holder makes an election with respect to the stock under section 83(b). In the event of such an election, the stock is treated as outstanding stock of the corporation, and the holder of the stock is treated as a shareholder for purposes of subchapter S. See paragraphs (l)(1) and (3) of this section for rules for determining whether substantially nonvested stock with respect to which an election under section 83(b) has been made is treated as a second class of stock.

(4) *Treatment of deferred compensation plans.* For purposes of subchapter S, an instrument, obligation, or arrangement is not outstanding stock if it—

(i) Does not convey the right to vote;

(ii) Is an unfunded and unsecured promise to pay money or property in the future;

(iii) Is issued to an individual who is an employee in connection with the performance of services for the corporation or to an individual who is an independent contractor in connection with the performance of services for the corporation (and is not excessive by reference to the services performed); and

      (iv) Is issued pursuant to a plan with respect to which the employee or independent contractor is not taxed currently on income.

A deferred compensation plan that has a current payment feature (*e.g.*, payment of dividend equivalent amounts that are taxed currently as compensation) is not for that reason excluded from this paragraph (b)(4).

      (5) *Treatment of straight debt.* For purposes of subchapter S, an instrument or obligation that satisfies the definition of straight debt in paragraph (l)(5) of this section is not treated as outstanding stock.

* * *

      (c) *Domestic corporation.* For purposes of paragraph (b) of this section, the term *domestic corporation* means a domestic corporation as defined in § 301.7701-5 of this chapter, and the term *corporation* includes an entity that is classified as an association taxable as a corporation under § 301.7701-2 of this chapter.

      (d) *Ineligible corporation*—(1) *General rule.* Except as otherwise provided in this paragraph (d), the term *ineligible corporation* means a corporation that is—

      (i) For taxable years beginning on or after January 1, 1997, a financial institution that uses the reserve method of accounting for bad debts described in section 585 (for taxable years beginning prior to January 1, 1997, a financial institution to which section 585 applies (or would apply but for section 585(c)) or to which section 593 applies);

      (ii) An insurance company subject to tax under subchapter

      (iii) A corporation to which an election under section 936 applies; or

      (iv) A DISC or former DISC.

      (2) *Exceptions.* See the special rules and exceptions provided in sections 6(c)(2), (3) and (4) of Pub. L. 97-354 that are applicable for certain casualty insurance companies and qualified oil corporations.

      (e) *Number of shareholders*—(1) *General rule.* A corporation does not qualify as a small business corporation if it has more than 75 shareholders (35 for taxable years beginning prior to January 1, 1997). Ordinarily, the person who would have to include in gross income dividends distributed with respect to the stock of the corporation (if the corporation were a C corporation) is considered to be the shareholder of the corporation. For example, if stock (owned other than by a husband and wife) is owned by tenants in common or joint tenants, each tenant in common or joint tenant is

generally considered to be a shareholder of the corporation. (For special rules relating to stock owned by husband and wife, see paragraph (e)(2) of this section; for special rules relating to restricted stock, see paragraphs (b)(3) and (6) of this section.) The person for whom stock of a corporation is held by a nominee, guardian, custodian, or an agent is considered to be the shareholder of the corporation for purposes of this paragraph (e) and paragraphs (f) and (g) of this section. For example, a partnership may be a nominee of S corporation stock for a person who qualifies as a shareholder of an S corporation. However, if the partnership is the beneficial owner of the stock, then the partnership is the shareholder, and the corporation does not qualify as a small business corporation. In addition, in the case of stock held for a minor under a uniform gifts to minors or similar statute, the minor and not the custodian is the shareholder. For purposes of this paragraph (e) and paragraphs (f) and (g) of this section, if stock is held by a decedent's estate, the estate (and not the beneficiaries of the estate) is considered to be the shareholder; however, if stock is held by a subpart E trust (which includes voting trusts), the deemed owner is considered to be the shareholder.

      (2) *Special rules relating to stock owned by husband and wife.* For purposes of paragraph (e)(1) of this section, stock owned by a husband and wife (or by either or both of their estates) is treated as if owned by one shareholder, regardless of the form in which they own the stock. For example, if husband and wife are owners of a subpart E trust, they will be treated as one individual. Both husband and wife must be U.S. citizens or residents, and a decedent spouse's estate must not be a foreign estate as defined in section 7701(a)(31). The treatment described in this paragraph (e)(2) will cease upon dissolution of the marriage for any reason other than death.

      (f) *Shareholder must be an individual or estate.* Except as otherwise provided in paragraph (e)(1) (relating to nominees and paragraph (h) (relating to certain trusts) of this section, a corporation in which any shareholder is a corporation, partnership, or trust does not qualify as a small business corporation.

      (g) *Nonresident alien shareholder*—(1) *General rule.* (i) A corporation having a shareholder who is a nonresident alien as defined in section 7701(b)(1)(B) does not qualify as a small business corporation. If a U.S. shareholder's spouse is a nonresident alien who has a current ownership interest (as opposed, for example, to a survivorship interest) in the stock of the corporation by reason of any applicable law, such as a state community property law or a foreign country's law, the corporation does not qualify as a small

Reg. § 1.1361-1(g)(1)

business corporation from the time the nonresident alien spouse acquires the interest in the stock. If a corporation's S election is inadvertently terminated as a result of a nonresident alien spouse being considered a shareholder, the corporation may request relief under section 1362(f).

(ii) The following examples illustrate this paragraph (g)(1)(i):

Example 1. In 1990, W, a U.S. citizen, married H, a citizen of a foreign country. At all times H is a nonresident alien under section 7701(b)(1)(B). Under the foreign country's law, all property acquired by a husband and wife during the existence of the marriage is community property and owned jointly by the husband and wife. In 1996 while residing in the foreign country, W formed X, a U.S. corporation, and X simultaneously filed an election to be an S corporation. X issued all of its outstanding stock in W's name. Under the foreign country's law, X's stock became the community property of and jointly owned by H and W. Thus, X does not meet the definition of a small business corporation and therefore could not file a valid S election because H, a nonresident alien, has a current interest in the stock.

Example 2. Assume the same facts as *Example 1,* except that in 1991, W and H filed a section 6013(g) election allowing them to file a joint U.S. tax return and causing H to be treated as a U.S. resident for purposes of chapters 1, 5, and 24 of the Internal Revenue Code. The section 6013(g) election applies to the taxable year for which made and to all subsequent taxable years until terminated. Because H is treated as a U.S. resident under section 6013(g), X does meet the definition of a small business corporation. Thus, the election filed by X to be an S corporation is valid.

(2) *Special rule for dual residents.* [Reserved]

(h) *Special rules relating to trusts—*(1) *General rule.* In general, a trust is not a permitted small business corporation shareholder. However, except as provided in paragraph (h)(2) of this section, the following trusts are permitted shareholders:

(i) *Qualified subpart E trust.* A trust all of which is treated (under subpart E, part I, subchapter J, chapter 1) as owned by an individual (whether or not the grantor) who is a citizen or resident of the United States (a qualified subpart E trust). This requirement applies only during the period that the trust holds S corporation stock.

(ii) *Subpart E trust ceasing to be a qualified subpart E trust after the death of deemed owner.* A trust which was a qualified subpart E trust immediately before the death of the deemed owner and which continues in existence after the death of the deemed owner, but only for the 60-day period beginning on the day of the deemed

owner's death. However, if a trust is described in the preceding sentence and the entire corpus of the trust is includible in the gross estate of the deemed owner, the trust is a permitted shareholder for the 2-year period beginning on the day of the deemed owner's death. A trust is considered to continue in existence if the trust continues to hold the stock of the S corporation during the period of administration of the decedent's estate or if, after the period of administration, the trust continues to hold the stock pursuant to the terms of the will or the trust agreement. See § 1.641(b)-3 for rules concerning the termination of estates and trusts for federal income tax purposes. If the trust consists of community property, and the decedent's community property interest in the trust is includible in the decedent's gross estate under chapter 11 (section 2001 and following, relating to estate tax), then the entire corpus of the trust will be deemed includible in the decedent's gross estate. Further, for the purpose of determining whether the entire corpus of the trust is includible in the gross estate of the deemed owner, if the decedent's spouse was treated as an owner of a portion of the trust under subpart E immediately before the decedent's death, the surviving spouse's portion is disregarded.

(iii) *Electing qualified subchapter S trusts.* A qualified subchapter S trust (QSST) that has a section 1361(d)(2) election in effect (an electing QSST). See paragraph (j) of this section for rules concerning QSSTs including the manner for making the section 1361(d)(2) election.

(iv) *Testamentary trusts.* A trust (other than a qualified subpart E trust or an electing QSST) to which S corporation stock is transferred pursuant to the terms of a will, but only for the 60-day period beginning on the day the stock is transferred to the trust.

(v) *Qualified voting trusts.* A trust created primarily to exercise the voting power of S corporation stock transferred to it. To qualify as a voting trust for purposes of this section (a qualified voting trust), the beneficial owners must be treated as the owners of their respective portions of the trust under subpart E and the trust must have been created pursuant to a written trust agreement entered into by the shareholders, that—

(A) Delegates to one or more trustees the right to vote;

(B) Requires all distributions with respect to the stock of the corporation held by the trust to be paid to, or on behalf of, the beneficial owners of that stock;

(C) Requires title and possession of that stock to be delivered to those beneficial owners upon termination of the trust; and

Reg. § 1.1361-1(g)(2)

(D) Terminates, under its terms or by state law, on or before a specific date or event.

(vi) *Electing small business trusts.* An electing small business trust (ESBT) under section 1361(e). See paragraph (m) of this section for rules concerning ESBTs including the manner of making the election to be an ESBT under section 1361(e)(3).

(2) *Foreign trust.* For purposes of paragraph (h)(1) of this section, in any case where stock is held by a foreign trust as defined in section 7701(a)(31), the trust is considered to be the shareholder and is an ineligible shareholder. Thus, even if a foreign trust qualifies as a subpart E trust (e.g., a qualified voting trust), any corporation in which the trust holds stock does not qualify as a small business corporation.

(3) *Determination of shareholders*—(i) *General rule.* For purposes of paragraph (b) of this section (qualification as a small business corporation), and, except as provided in paragraph (h)(3)(ii) of this section, for purposes of sections 1366 (relating to the pass-through of items of income, loss, deduction, or credit), 1367 (relating to adjustments to basis of shareholder's stock), and 1368 (relating to distributions), the shareholder of S corporation stock held by a trust that is a permitted shareholder under paragraph (h)(1) of this section is determined as follows:

(A) If stock is held by a qualified subpart E trust, the deemed owner of the trust is treated as the shareholder.

(B) If stock is held by a trust defined in paragraph (h)(1)(ii) of this section, the estate of the deemed owner is generally treated as the shareholder as of the day of the deemed owner's death. However, if stock is held by such a trust in a community property state, the decedent's estate is the shareholder only of the portion of the trust included in the decedent's gross estate (and the surviving spouse continues to be the shareholder of the portion of the trust owned by that spouse under the applicable state's community property law). The estate ordinarily will cease to be treated as the shareholder upon the earlier of the transfer of the stock by the trust or the expiration of the 60-day period (or, if applicable, the 2-year period) beginning on the day of the deemed owner's death. If the trust qualifies and becomes an electing QSST, the beneficiary and not the estate is treated as the shareholder as of the effective date of the QSST election, and the rules provided in paragraph (j)(7) of this section apply.

(C) If stock is held by an electing QSST, see paragraph (j)(7) of this section for the rules on who is treated as the shareholder.

(D) If stock is transferred to a testamentary trust (other than a qualified subpart E trust

or an electing QSST), the estate of the testator is treated as the shareholder until the earlier of the transfer of that stock by the trust or the expiration of the 60-day period beginning on the day that the stock is transferred to the trust.

(E) If stock is held by a qualified voting trust, each beneficial owner of the stock, as determined under subpart E, is treated as a shareholder with respect to the owner's proportionate share of the stock held by the trust.

(F) If S corporation stock is held by an ESBT, each potential current beneficiary is treated as a shareholder. However, if for any period there is no potential current beneficiary of the ESBT, the ESBT is treated as the shareholder during such period. See paragraph (m)(4) of this section for the definition of potential current beneficiary.

(ii) *Exceptions.* See § 1.641(c)-1 for the rules for the taxation of an ESBT. Solely for purposes of section 1366, 1367, and 1368 the shareholder of S corporation stock held by a trust is determined as follows—

(A) If stock is held by a trust (as defined in paragraph (h)(1)(ii) of this section) that does not qualify as a QSST, the trust is treated as the shareholder. If the trust continues to own the stock after the expiration of the 60-day period (or, if applicable, the 2-year period), the corporation's S election will terminate unless the trust is otherwise a permitted shareholder. If the trust is a QSST described in section 1361(d) and the income beneficiary of the trust makes a timely QSST election, the beneficiary and not the trust is treated as the shareholder from the effective date of the QSST election; and

(B) If stock is transferred to a testamentary trust described in paragraph (h)(1)(iii) of this section (other than a qualified subpart E trust or a trust that has a QSST election in effect), the trust is treated as the shareholder. If the trust continues to own the stock after the expiration of the 60-day period, the corporation's S election will terminate unless the trust otherwise qualifies as a permitted shareholder.

(i) [Reserved]

(j) *Qualified subchapter S trust*—(1) *Definition.* A qualified subchapter S trust (QSST) is a trust (whether intervivos or testamentary), other than a foreign trust described in section 7701(a)(31), that satisfies the following requirements:

(i) All of the income (within the meaning of § 1.643(b)-1) of the trust is distributed (or is required to be distributed) currently to one individual who is a citizen or resident of the United States. For purposes of the preceding sentence, unless otherwise provided under local law (including pertinent provisions of the governing instrument that are effective under local law), income of the trust includes distributions to the trust from the S corporation for the taxable year in question, but does not include the trust's pro rata share of the S corporation's items of income, loss, deduction, or credit determined under section 1366. See § § 1.651(a)-2(a) and 1.663(b)-1(a) for rules relating to the determination of whether all of the income of a trust is distributed (or is required to be distributed) currently. If under the terms of the trust income is not required to be distributed currently, the trustee may elect under section 663(b) to consider a distribution made in the first 65 days of a taxable year as made on the last day of the preceding taxable year. See section 663(b) and § 1.663(b)-2 for rules on the time and manner for making the election. The income distribution requirement must be satisfied for the taxable year of the trust or for that part of the trust's taxable year during which it holds S corporation stock.

(ii) The terms of the trust must require that—

(A) During the life of the current income beneficiary, there will be only one income beneficiary of the trust;

(B) Any corpus distributed during the life of the current income beneficiary may be distributed only to that income beneficiary;

(C) The current income beneficiary's income interest in the trust will terminate on the earlier of that income beneficiary's death or the termination of the trust; and

(D) Upon termination of the trust during the life of the current income beneficiary, the trust will distribute all of its assets to that income beneficiary.

(iii) The terms of the trust must satisfy the requirements of paragraph (j)(1)(ii) of this section from the date the QSST election is made or from the effective date of the QSST election, whichever is earlier, throughout the entire period that the current income beneficiary and any successor income beneficiary is the income beneficiary of the trust. If the terms of the trust do not preclude the possibility that any of the requirements stated in paragraph (j)(1)(ii) of this section will not be met, the trust will not qualify as a QSST. For example, if the terms of the trust are silent with respect to corpus distributions, and distributions of corpus to a person other than the current income beneficiary are permitted under local law during the life of the current income beneficiary, then the terms of the trust do not preclude the possibility that corpus may be distributed to a person other than

the current income beneficiary and, therefore, the trust is not a QSST.

(2) *Special rules*—(i) If a husband and wife are income beneficiaries of the same trust, the husband and wife file a joint return, and each is a U.S. citizen or resident, the husband and wife are treated as one beneficiary for purposes of paragraph (j) of this section. If a husband and wife are treated by the preceding sentence as one beneficiary, any action required by this section to be taken by an income beneficiary requires joinder of both of them. For example, each spouse must sign the QSST election, continue to be a U.S. citizen or resident, and continue to file joint returns for the entire period that the QSST election is in effect.

(ii) (A) *Terms of the trust and applicable local law.* The determination of whether the terms of a trust meet all of the requirements under paragraph (j)(1)(ii) of this section depends upon the terms of the trust instrument and the applicable local law. For example, a trust whose governing instrument provides that A is the sole income beneficiary of the trust is, nevertheless, considered to have two income beneficiaries if, under the applicable local law, A and B are considered to be the income beneficiaries of the trust.

(B) *Legal obligation to support.* If under local law a distribution to the income beneficiary is in satisfaction of the grantor's legal obligation of support to that income beneficiary, the trust will not qualify as a QSST as of the date of distribution because, under section 677(b), if income is distributed, the grantor will be treated as the owner of the ordinary income portion of the trust or, if trust corpus is distributed, the grantor will be treated as a beneficiary under section 662. See § 1.677(b)-1 for rules on the treatment of trusts for support and § 1.662(a)-4 for rules concerning amounts used in discharge of a legal obligation.

(C) *Example.* The following example illustrates the rules of paragraph (j)(2)(ii)(B) of this section:

Example. F creates a trust for the benefit of F's minor child, G. Under the terms of the trust, all income is payable to G until the trust terminates on the earlier of G's attaining age 35 or G's death. Upon the termination of the trust, all corpus must be distributed to G or G's estate. The trust includes all of the provisions prescribed by section 1361(d)(3)(A) and paragraph (j)(1)(ii) of this section, but does not preclude the trustee from making income distributions to G that will be in satisfaction of F's legal obligation to support G. Under the applicable local law, distributions of trust income to G will satisfy F's legal obligation to support G. If the trustee distributes income to G in satisfaction of F's legal obligation to support

Reg. § 1.1361-1(j)(2)

G, the trust will not qualify as a QSST because F will be treated as the owner of the ordinary income portion of the trust. Further, the trust will not be a qualified subpart E trust because the trust will be subject to tax on the income allocable to corpus.

(iii) If, under the terms of the trust, a person (including the income beneficiary) has a special power to appoint, during the life of the income beneficiary, trust income or corpus to any person other than the current income beneficiary, the trust will not qualify as a QSST. However, if the power of appointment results in the grantor being treated as the owner of the entire trust under the rules of subpart E, the trust may be a permitted shareholder under section 1361(c)(2)(A)(i) and paragraph (h)(1)(i) of this section.

(iv) If the terms of a trust or local law do not preclude the current income beneficiary from transferring the beneficiary's interest in the trust or do not preclude a person other than the current income beneficiary named in the trust instrument from being treated as a beneficiary of the trust under § 1.643(c)-1, the trust will still qualify as a QSST. However, if the income beneficiary transfers or assigns the income interest or a portion of the income interest to another, the trust may no longer qualify as a QSST, depending on the facts and circumstances, because any transferee of the current income beneficiary's income interest and any person treated as a beneficiary under § 1.643(c)-1 will be treated as a current income beneficiary for purposes of paragraph (j)(1)(ii) of this section and the trust may no longer meet the QSST requirements.

(v) If the terms of the trust do not preclude a person other than the current income beneficiary named in the trust instrument from being awarded an interest in the trust by the order of a court, the trust will qualify as a QSST assuming the trust meets the requirements of paragraphs (j)(1)(i) and (ii) of this section. However, if as a result of such court order, the trust no longer meets the QSST requirements, the trust no longer qualifies as a QSST and the corporation's S election will terminate.

(vi) A trust may qualify as a QSST even though a person other than the current income beneficiary is treated under subpart E as the owner of a part or all of that portion of a trust which does not consist of the S corporation stock, provided the entire trust meets the QSST requirements stated in paragraphs (j)(1)(i) and (ii) of this section.

(3) *Separate and independent shares of a trust.* For purposes of sections 1361(c) and (d), a substantially separate and independent share of a trust, within the meaning of section 663(c) and the regulations thereunder, is treated as a separate trust. For a separate share which holds S corporation stock to qualify as a QSST, the terms of the trust applicable to that separate share must meet the QSST requirements stated in paragraphs (j)(1)(i) and (ii) of this section.

(4) *Qualified terminable interest property trust.* If property, including S corporation stock, or stock of a corporation that intends to make an S election, is transferred to a trust and an election is made to treat all or a portion of the transferred property as qualified terminable interest property (QTIP) under section 2056(b)(7), the income beneficiary may make the QSST election if the trust meets the requirements set out in paragraphs (j)(1)(i) and (ii) of this section. However, if property is transferred to a QTIP trust under section 2523(f), the income beneficiary may not make a QSST election even if the trust meets the requirements set forth in paragraph (j)(1)(ii) of this section because the grantor would be treated as the owner of the income portion of the trust under section 677. In addition, if property is transferred to a QTIP trust under section 2523(f), the trust does not qualify as a permitted shareholder under section 1361(c)(2)(A)(i) and paragraph (h)(1)(i) of this section (a qualified subpart E trust), unless under the terms of the QTIP trust, the grantor is treated as the owner of the entire trust under sections 671 to 677. If the grantor ceases to be the income beneficiary's spouse, the trust may qualify as a QSST if it otherwise satisfies the requirements under paragraphs (j)(1)(i) and (ii) of this section.

(5) *Ceasing to meet the QSST requirements.* If a QSST for which an election under section 1361(d)(2) has been made (as described in paragraph (j) (6) of this section) ceases to meet any of the requirements specified in paragraph (j)(1)(ii) of this section, the provisions of this paragraph (j) will cease to apply as of the first day on which that requirement ceases to be met. If such a trust ceases to meet the income distribution requirement specified in paragraph (j)(1)(i) of this section, but continues to meet all of the requirements in paragraph (j)(1)(ii) of this section, the provisions of this paragraph (j) will cease to apply as of the first day of the first taxable year beginning after the first taxable year for which the trust ceased to meet the income distribution requirement of paragraph (j)(1)(i) of this section. If a corporation's S election is inadvertently terminated as a result of a trust ceasing to meet the QSST requirements, the corporation may request relief under section 1362(f).

(6) *Qualified subchapter S trust election*—(i) *In general.* This paragraph (j)(6) applies to the election provided in section 1361(d)(2) (the QSST

election) to treat a QSST (as defined in paragraph (j)(1) of this section) as a trust described in section 1361(c)(2)(A)(i), and thus a permitted shareholder. This election must be made separately with respect to each corporation whose stock is held by the trust. The QSST election does not itself constitute an election as to the status of the corporation; the corporation must make the election provided by section 1362(a) to be an S corporation. Until the effective date of a corporation's S election, the beneficiary is not treated as the owner of the stock of the corporation for purposes of section 678. Any action required by this paragraph (j) to be taken by a person who is under a legal disability by reason of age may be taken by that person's guardian or other legal representative, or if there be none, by that person's natural or adoptive parent.

* * *

(7) *Treatment as shareholder.* (i) The income beneficiary who makes the QSST election and is treated (for purposes of section 678(a)) as the owner of that portion of the trust that consists of S corporation stock is treated as the shareholder for purposes of sections 1361(b)(1), 1366, 1367, and 1368.

(ii) If, upon the death of an income beneficiary, the trust continues in existence, continues to hold S corporation stock but no longer satisfies the QSST requirements, and is not a qualified subpart E trust, then, solely for purposes of section 1361(b)(1), as of the date of the income beneficiary's death, the estate of that income beneficiary is treated as the shareholder of the S corporation with respect to which the income beneficiary made the QSST election. The estate ordinarily will cease to be treated as the shareholder for purposes of section 1361(b)(1) upon the earlier of the transfer of that stock by the trust or the expiration of the 60-day period beginning on the day of the income beneficiary's death. However, if the entire corpus of the trust is includible in the gross estate of that income beneficiary, the estate will cease to be treated as the shareholder for purposes of section 1361(b)(1) upon the earlier of the transfer of that stock by the trust or the expiration of the 2-year period beginning on the day of the income beneficiary's death. For the purpose of determining whether the entire trust corpus is includible in the gross estate of the income beneficiary, any community property interest in the trust held by the income beneficiary's spouse which arises by reason of applicable U.S. state law is disregarded. During the period that the estate is treated as the shareholder for purposes of section 1361(b)(1), the trust is treated as the shareholder for purposes of sections 1366, 1367, and 1368. If, after the 60-day.period, or the

2-year period, if applicable, the trust continues to hold S corporation stock, the corporation's S election terminates. If the termination is inadvertent, the corporation may request relief under section 1362(f).

(8) *Coordination with grantor trust rules.* If a valid QSST election is made, the income beneficiary is treated as the owner, for purposes of section 678(a), of that portion of the trust that consists of the stock of the S corporation for which the QSST election was made. However, solely for purposes of applying the preceding sentence to a QSST, an income beneficiary who is a deemed section 678 owner only by reason of section 1361(d)(1) will not be treated as the owner of the S corporation stock in determining and attributing the federal income tax consequences of a disposition of the stock by the QSST. For example, if the disposition is a sale, the QSST election terminates as to the stock sold and any gain or loss recognized on the sale will be that of the trust, not the income beneficiary. Similarly, if a QSST distributes its S corporation stock to the income beneficiary, the QSST election terminates as to the distributed stock and the consequences of the distribution are determined by reference to the status of the trust apart from the income beneficiary's terminating ownership status under sections 678 and 1361(d)(1). The portions of the trust other than the portion consisting of S corporation stock are subject to subparts A through D of subchapter J of chapter 1, except as otherwise required by subpart E of the Internal Revenue Code.

(9) *Successive income beneficiary.* (i) If the income beneficiary of a QSST who made a QSST election dies, each successive income beneficiary of that trust is treated as consenting to the election unless a successive income beneficiary affirmatively refuses to consent to the election. For this purpose, the term *successive income beneficiary* includes a beneficiary of a trust whose interest is a separate share within the meaning of section 663(c), but does not include any beneficiary of a trust that is created upon the death of the income beneficiary of the QSST and which is a new trust under local law.

(ii) The application of this paragraph (j)(9) is illustrated by the following examples:

Example 1. Shares of stock in Corporation X, an S corporation, are held by Trust A, a QSST for which a QSST election was made. B is the sole income beneficiary of Trust A. On B's death, under the terms of Trust A, J and K become the current income beneficiaries of Trust A. J and K each hold a separate and independent share of Trust A within the meaning of section 663(c). J and K are successive income beneficiaries of Trust

A, and they are treated as consenting to B's QSST election.

Example 2. Assume the same facts as in *Example 1,* except that on B's death, under the terms of Trust A and local law, Trust A terminates and the principal is to be divided equally and held in newly created Trust B and Trust C. The sole income beneficiaries of Trust B and Trust C are J and K, respectively. Because Trust A terminated, J and K are not successive income beneficiaries of Trust A. J and K must make QSST elections for their respective trusts to qualify as QSSTs, if they qualify. The result is the same whether or not the trustee of Trusts B and C is the same as the trustee of trust A.

(10) *Affirmative refusal to consent—(i) Required statement.* A successive income beneficiary of a QSST must make an affirmative refusal to consent by signing and filing with the service center where the corporation files its income tax return a statement that—

(A) Contains the name, address, and taxpayer identification number of the successive income beneficiary, the trust, and the corporation for which the election was made;

(B) Identifies the refusal as an affirmative refusal to consent under section 1361(d)(2); and

(C) Sets forth the date on which the successive income beneficiary became the income beneficiary.

(ii) *Filing date and effectiveness.* The affirmative refusal to consent must be filed within 15 days and 2 months after the date on which the successive income beneficiary becomes the income beneficiary. The affirmative refusal to consent will be effective as of the date on which the successive income beneficiary becomes the current income beneficiary.

(11) *Revocation of QSST election.* A QSST election may be revoked only with the consent of the Commissioner. The Commissioner will not grant a revocation when one of its purposes is the avoidance of federal income taxes or when the taxable year is closed. The application for consent to revoke the election must be submitted to the Internal Revenue Service in the form of a letter ruling request under the appropriate revenue procedure. The application must be signed by the current income beneficiary and must—

(i) Contain the name, address, and taxpayer identification number of the current income beneficiary, the trust, and the corporation with respect to which the QSST election was made;

(ii) Identify the election being revoked as an election made under section 1361(d)(2); and

(iii) Explain why the current income beneficiary seeks to revoke the QSST election and indicate that the beneficiary understands the consequences of the revocation.

(12) *Converting a QSST to an ESBT.* For a trust that seeks to convert from a QSST to an ESBT, the consent of the Commissioner is hereby granted to revoke the QSST election as of the effective date of the ESBT election, if all the following requirements are met:

(i) The trust meets all of the requirements to be an ESBT under paragraph (m)(1) of this section except for the requirement under paragraph (m)(1)(iv)(A) of this section that the trust not have a QSST election in effect.

(ii) The trustee and the current income beneficiary of the trust sign the ESBT election. The ESBT election must be filed with the service center where the S corporation files its income tax return. This ESBT election must state at the top of the document "ATTENTION ENTITY CONTROL—CONVERSION OF A QSST TO AN ESBT PURSUANT TO SECTION 1.1361-1(j)" and include all information otherwise required for an ESBT election under paragraph (m)(2) of this section. A separate election must be made with respect to the stock of each S corporation held by the trust.

(iii) The trust has not converted from an ESBT to a QSST within the 36-month period preceding the effective date of the new ESBT election.

(iv) The date on which the ESBT election is to be effective cannot be more than 15 days and two months prior to the date on which the election is filed and cannot be more than 12 months after the date on which the election is filed. If an election specifies an effective date more than 15 days and two months prior to the date on which the election is filed, it will be effective on the day that is 15 days and two months prior to the date on which it is filed. If an election specifies an effective date more than 12 months after the date on which the election is filed, it will be effective on the day that is 12 months after the date it is filed.

(k)(1) *Examples.* The provisions of paragraphs (h) and (j) of this section are illustrated by the following examples in which it is assumed that all noncorporate persons are citizens or residents of the United States:

Example 1. (i) *Terms of the trust.* In 1996, A and A's spouse, B, created an intervivos trust and each funded the trust with separately owned stock of an S corporation. Under the terms of the trust, A and B designated themselves as the income beneficiaries and each, individually, retained the power to amend or revoke the trust with respect to the trust assets attributable to their respective trust contributions. Upon A's death, the trust is to be divided into two separate parts; one part attributable to the assets A contributed to the trust and one part attributable to B's contributions. Before the trust is divided, and during the administration of A's estate, all trust income is payable to B. The part of the trust attributable to B's contributions is to continue in trust under the terms of which B is designated as the sole income beneficiary and retains the power to amend or revoke the trust. The part attributable to A's contributions is to be divided into two separate trusts both of which have B as the sole income beneficiary for life. One trust, the *Credit Shelter Trust,* is to be funded with an amount that can pass free of estate tax by reason of A's available estate tax unified credit. The terms of the Credit Shelter Trust meet the requirements of section 1361(d)(3) as a QSST. The balance of the property passes to a Marital Trust, the terms of which satisfy the requirements of section 1361(d)(3) as a QSST and section 2056(b)(7) as QTIP. The appropriate fiduciary under § 20.2056(b)-7(b)(3) is directed to make an election under section 2056(b)(7).

(ii) *Results after deemed owner's death.* On February 3, 1997, A dies and the portion of the trust assets attributable to A's contributions including the S stock contributed by A, is includible in A's gross estate under sections 2036 and 2038. During the administration of A's estate, the trust holds the S corporation stock. Under section 1361(c)(2)(B)(ii), A's estate is treated as the shareholder of the S corporation stock that was included in A's gross estate for purposes of section 1361(b)(1); however, for purposes of sections 1366, 1367, and 1368, the trust is treated as the shareholder. B's part of the trust continues to be a qualified subpart E trust of which B is the owner under sections 676 and 677. B, therefore, continues to be treated as the shareholder of the S corporation stock in that portion of the trust. On May 13, 1997, during the continuing administration of A's estate, the trust is divided into separate trusts in accordance with the terms of the trust instrument. The S corporation stock that was included in A's gross estate is distributed to the Marital Trust and to the Credit Shelter Trust. A's estate will cease to be treated as the shareholder of the S corporation under section 1361(c)(2)(B)(ii) on May 13, 1997 (the date on which the S corporation stock was transferred to the trusts). B, as the income beneficiary of the Marital Trust and the Credit Shelter Trust, must make the QSST election for each trust by July 28, 1997 (the end of the 16-day-and-2-month period beginning on the date the estate ceases to be

treated as a shareholder) to have the trusts become permitted shareholders of the S corporation.

Example 2. (i) *Qualified subpart E trust as shareholder.* In 1997, A, an individual established a trust and transferred to the trust A's shares of stock of Corporation M, an S corporation. A has the power to revoke the entire trust. The terms of the trust require that all income be paid to B and otherwise meet the requirements of a QSST under section 1361(d)(3). The trust will continue in existence after A's death. The trust is a qualified subpart E trust described in section 1361(c)(2)(A)(i) during A's life, and A (not the trust) is treated as the shareholder for purposes of sections 1361(b)(1), 1366, 1367, and 1368.

(ii) *Trust ceasing to be a qualified subpart E trust on deemed owner's death.* Assume the same facts as paragraph (i) of this *Example 2,* except that A dies without having exercised A's power to revoke. Upon A's death, the trust ceases to be a qualified subpart E trust described in section 1361(c)(2)(A)(i). A's estate (and not the trust) is treated as the shareholder for purposes of section 1361(b)(1). Because the entire corpus of the trust is includible in A's gross estate under section 2038, A's estate will cease to be treated as the shareholder for purposes of section 1361(b)(1) upon the earlier of the transfer of the Corporation M stock by the trust (other than to A's estate), the expiration of the 2-year period beginning on the day of A's death, or the effective date of a QSST election if the trust qualifies as a QSST. However, until that time, because the trust continues in existence after A's death and will receive any distributions with respect to the stock it holds, the trust is treated as the shareholder for purposes of sections 1366, 1367, and 1368. After the 2-year period, if no QSST election is made, the corporation ceases to be an S corporation, but the trust continues as the shareholder of a C corporation.

(iii) *Trust continuing to be a qualified subpart E trust on deemed owner's death.* Assume the same facts as paragraph (ii) of this *Example 2,* except that the terms of the trust also provide that if A does not exercise the power to revoke before A's death, B will have the sole power to withdraw all trust property at any time after A's death. The trust continues to qualify as a qualified subpart E trust after A's death because, upon A's death, B is deemed to be the owner of the entire trust under section 678. Because the trust does not cease to be a qualified subpart E trust upon A's death, B (and not A's estate) is treated as the shareholder for purposes of sections 1361(b)(1), 1366, 1367, and 1368. Since the trust qualifies as a QSST, B may make a protective QSST election under paragraph (j) (6) (iv) of this section.

Reg. § 1.1361-1(k)

Example 3. 60-day rule under section 1361(c)(2)(A)(ii) and (iii). F owns stock of Corporation P, an S corporation. In addition, F is the deemed owner of a qualified subpart E trust that holds stock in Corporation 0, an S corporation. F dies on July 1, 1996. The trust continues in existence after F's death but is no longer a qualified subpart E trust. The entire corpus of the trust is not includible in F's gross estate. On August 1, 1996, F's shares of stock in Corporation P are transferred to the trust pursuant to the terms of F's will. Because the stock of Corporation P was not held by the trust when F died, section 1361(c)(2)(A)(ii) does not apply with respect to that stock. Under section 1361(c)(2)(A)(iii), the last day on which F's estate could be treated as a permitted shareholder of Corporation P is September 29, 1996 (that is, the last day of the 60-day period that begins on the date of the transfer from the estate to the trust). With respect to the shares of stock in Corporation 0 held by the trust at the time of F's death, section 1361(c)(2)(A)(ii) applies and the last day on which F's estate could be treated as a permitted shareholder of Corporation 0 is August 29, 1996 (that is, the last day of the 60-day period that begins on the date of F's death).

Example 4. (i) *QSST when terms do not require current distribution of income.* Corporation Q, a calender year corporation, makes an election to be an S corporation effective for calendar year 1996. On July 1, 1996, G, a shareholder of Corporation Q, transfers G's shares of Corporation Q stock to a trust with H as its current income beneficiary. The terms of the trust otherwise satisfy the QSST requirements, but authorize the trustee in its discretion to accumulate or distribute the trust income. However, the trust, which uses the calendar year as its taxable year, initially satisfies the income distribution requirement because the trustee is currently distributing all of the income. On August 1, 1996, H makes a QSST election with respect to Corporation Q that is effective as of July 1, 1996. Accordingly, as of July 1, 1996, the trust is a QSST and H is treated as the shareholder for purposes of sections 1361(b)(1), 1366, 1367, and 1368.

(ii) *QSST when trust income is not distributed currently.* Assume the same facts as in paragraph (i) of this *Example 4,* except that, for the taxable year ending on December 31, 1997, the trustee accumulates some trust income. The trust ceases to be a QSST on January 1, 1998, because the trust failed to distribute all of its income for the taxable year ending December 31, 1997. Thus, Corporation Q ceases to be an S corporation as of January 1, 1998, because the trust is not a permitted shareholder.

(iii) *QSST when a person other than the current income beneficiary may receive trust corpus.* Assume the same facts as in paragraph (i) of this *Example 4,* except that H dies on November 1, 1996. Under the terms of the trust, after H's death, L is the income beneficiary of the trust and the trustee is authorized to distribute trust corpus to L as well as to J. The trust ceases to be a QSST as of November 1, 1996, because corpus distributions may be made to someone other than L, the current (successive) income beneficiary. Under section 1361(c)(2)(A)(ii), H's estate (and not the trust) is considered to be the shareholder for purposes of section 1361(b)(1) for the 60-day period beginning on November 1, 1996. However, because the trust continues in existence after H's death and will receive any distributions from the corporation, the trust (and not H's estate) is treated as the shareholder for purposes of sections 1366, 1367, and 1368, during that 60-day period. After the 60day period, the S election terminates and the trust continues as a shareholder of a C corporation. If the termination is inadvertent, Corporation Q may request relief under section 1362(f). However, the S election would not terminate if the trustee distributed all Corporation Q shares to L, J, or both before December 30, 1996, (the last day of the 60-day period) assuming that neither L nor J becomes the 36th shareholder of Corporation Q as a result of the distribution.

Example 5. QSST when current income beneficiary assigns the income interest to a person not named in the trust. On January 1, 1996, stock of Corporation R, a calendar year S corporation, is transferred to a trust that satisfies all of the requirements to be a QSST. Neither the terms of the trust nor local law preclude the current income beneficiary, K, from assigning K's income interest in the trust. K files a timely QSST election that is effective January 1, 1996. On July 1, 1996, K assigns the income interest in the trust to N. Under applicable state law, the trustee is bound as a result of the assignment to distribute the trust income to N. Thus, the QSST will cease to qualify as a QSST under section 1361(d)(3)(A)(iii) because N's interest will terminate on K's death (rather than on N's death). Accordingly, as of the date of the assignment, the trust ceases to be a QSST and Corporation R ceases to be an S corporation.

Example 6. QSST when terms fail to provide for distribution of trust assets upon termination during life of current income beneficiary. A contributes S corporation stock to a trust the terms of which provide for one income beneficiary, annual distributions of income, discretionary invasion of corpus only for the benefit of the income beneficiary, and termination of the trust only upon the death of the current income beneficiary. Since the trust can terminate only upon the death of the income beneficiary, the governing instrument fails to provide for any distribution of trust assets during the income beneficiary's life. The governing instrument's silence on this point does not disqualify the trust under section 1361(d)(3)(A)(ii) or (iv).

* * *

(l) *Classes of stock*—(1) *General rule.* A corporation that has more than one class of stock does not qualify as a small business corporation. Except as provided in paragraph (l)(4) of this section (relating to instruments, obligations, or arrangements treated as a second class of stock), a corporation is treated as having only one class of stock if all outstanding shares of stock of the corporation confer identical rights to distribution and liquidation proceeds. Differences in voting rights among shares of stock of a corporation are disregarded in determining whether a corporation has more than one class of stock. Thus, if all shares of stock of an S corporation have identical rights to distribution and liquidation proceeds, the corporation may have voting and nonvoting common stock, a class of stock that may vote only on certain issues, irrevocable proxy agreements, or groups of shares that differ with respect to rights to elect members of the board of directors.

(2) *Determination of whether stock confers identical rights to distribution and liquidation proceeds*—(i) *In general.* The determination of whether all outstanding shares of stock confer identical rights to distribution and liquidation proceeds is made based on the corporate charter, articles of incorporation, bylaws, applicable state law, and binding agreements relating to distribution and liquidation proceeds (collectively, the governing provisions). A commercial contractual agreement, such as a lease, employment agreement, or loan agreement, is not a binding agreement relating to distribution and liquidation proceeds and thus is not a governing provision unless a principal purpose of the agreement is to circumvent the one class of stock requirement of section 1361(b)(1)(D) and this paragraph (l). Although a corporation is not treated as having more than one class of stock so long as the governing provisions provide for identical distribution and liquidation rights, any distributions (including actual, constructive, or deemed distributions) that differ in timing or amount are to be given appropriate tax effect in accordance with the facts and circumstances.

(ii) *State law requirements for payment and withholding of income tax.* State laws may require a corporation to pay or withhold state income taxes on behalf of some or all of the corporation's shareholders. Such laws are disregarded in determining whether all outstanding shares of stock of the corporation confer identical rights to distribution and liquidation proceeds, within the meaning of paragraph (l)(1) of this section, provided that, when the constructive distributions resulting from the payment or withholding of taxes by the corporation are taken into account, the outstanding shares confer identical rights to distribution and liquidation proceeds. A difference in timing between the constructive distributions and the actual distributions to the other shareholders does not cause the corporation to be treated as having more than one class of stock.

(iii) *Buy-sell and redemption agreements*—(A) *In general.* Buy-sell agreements among shareholders, agreements restricting the transferability of stock, and redemption agreements are disregarded in determining whether a corporation's outstanding shares of stock confer identical distribution and liquidation rights unless—

(*1*) A principal purpose of the agreement is to circumvent the one class of stock requirement of section 1361(b)(1)(D) and this paragraph (1), and

(*2*) The agreement establishes a purchase price that, at the time the agreement is entered into, is significantly in excess of or below the fair market value of the stock.

Agreements that provide for the purchase or redemption of stock at book value or at a price between fair market value and book value are not considered to establish a price that is significantly in excess of or below the fair market value of the stock and, thus, are disregarded in determining whether the outstanding shares of stock confer identical rights. For purposes of this paragraph (l)(2)(iii)(A), a good faith determination of fair market value will be respected unless it can be shown that the value was substantially in error and the determination of the value was not performed with reasonable diligence. Although an agreement may be disregarded in determining whether shares of stock confer identical distribution and liquidation rights, payments pursuant to the agreement may have income or transfer tax consequences.

(B) *Exception for certain agreements.* Bona fide agreements to redeem or purchase stock at the time of death, divorce, disability, or termination of employment are disregarded in determining whether a corporation's shares of stock confer identical rights. In addition, if stock that is substantially nonvested (within the meaning of § 1.83-3(b)) is treated as outstanding under these regulations, the forfeiture provisions that cause the stock to be substantially nonvested are disregarded. Furthermore, the Commissioner may provide by Revenue Ruling or other published guidance that other types of bona fide agreements to redeem or purchase stock are disregarded.

(C) *Safe harbors for determinations of book value.* A determination of book value will be respected if—

(*1*) The book value is determined in accordance with Generally Accepted Accounting Principles (including permitted optional adjustments); or

(*2*) The book value is used for any substantial nontax purpose.

(iv) *Distributions that take into account varying interests in stock during a taxable year.* A governing provision does not, within the meaning of paragraph (l)(2)(i) of this section, alter the rights to liquidation and distribution proceeds conferred by an S corporation's stock merely because the governing provision provides that, as a result of a change in stock ownership, distributions in a taxable year are to be made on the basis of the shareholders' varying interests in the S corporation's income in the current or immediately preceding taxable year. If distributions pursuant to the provision are not made within a reasonable time after the close of the taxable year in which the varying interests occur, the distributions may be recharacterized depending on the facts and circumstances, but will not result in a second class of stock.

(v) *Special rule for section 338(h)(10) elections.* If the shareholders of an S corporation sell their stock in a transaction for which an election is made under section 338(h)(10) and § 1.338(h)(10)-1, the receipt of varying amounts per share by the shareholders will not cause the S corporation to have more than one class of stock, provided that the varying amounts are determined in arm's length negotiations with the purchaser.

(vi) *Examples.* The application of paragraph (l)(2) of this section may be illustrated by the following examples. In each of the examples, the S corporation requirements of section 1361 are satisfied except as otherwise stated, the corporation has in effect an S election under section 1362, and the corporation has only the shareholders described.

Example 1. Determination of whether stock confers identical rights to distribution and liquidation proceeds. (i) The law of State A requires that permission be obtained from the State Commissioner of Corporations before stock may be issued by a corporation. The Commissioner grants permission to S, a corporation, to issue its stock subject to the restriction that any person who is issued stock in exchange for property, and not cash, must waive all rights to receive distribu-

tions until the shareholders who contributed cash for stock have received distributions in the amount of their cash contributions.

(ii) The condition imposed by the Commissioner pursuant to state law alters the rights to distribution and liquidation proceeds conferred by the outstanding stock of S so that those rights are not identical. Accordingly, under paragraph (l)(2)(i) of this section, S is treated as having more than one class of stock and does not qualify as a small business corporation.

Example 2. Distributions that differ in timing. (i) S, a corporation, has two equal shareholders, A and B. Under S's bylaws, A and B are entitled to equal distributions. S distributes $50,000 to A in the current year, but does not distribute $50,000 to B until one year later. The circumstances indicate that the difference in timing did not occur by reason of a binding agreement relating to distribution or liquidation proceeds.

(ii) Under paragraph (l)(2)(i) of this section, the difference in timing of the distributions to A and B does not cause S to be treated as having more than one class of stock. However, section 7872 or other recharacterization principles may apply to determine the appropriate tax consequences.

Example 3. Treatment of excessive compensation. (i) S, a corporation, has two equal shareholders, C and D, who are each employed by S and have binding employment agreements with S. The compensation paid by S to C under C's employment agreement is reasonable. The compensation paid by S to D under D's employment agreement, however, is found to be excessive. The facts and circumstances do not reflect that a principal purpose of D's employment agreement is to circumvent the one class of stock requirement of section 1361(b)(1)(D) and this paragraph (l).

(ii) Under paragraph (l)(2)(i) of this section, the employment agreements are not governing provisions. Accordingly, S is not treated as having more than one class of stock by reason of the employment agreements, even though S is not allowed a deduction for the excessive compensation paid to D.

Example 4. Agreement to pay fringe benefits. (i) S, a corporation, is required under binding agreements to pay accident and health insurance premiums on behalf of certain of its employees who are also shareholders. Different premium amounts are paid by S for each employee-shareholder. The facts and circumstances do not reflect that a principal purpose of the agreements is to circumvent the one class of stock requirement of section 1361(b)(1)(D) and this paragraph (1).

Reg. § 1.1361-1(l)(2)

(ii) Under paragraph (l)(2)(i) of this section, the agreements are not governing provisions. Accordingly, S is not treated as having more than one class of stock by reason of the agreements. In addition, S is not treated as having more than one class of stock by reason of the payment of fringe benefits.

* * *

Example 8. Redemption agreements. (i) F, G, and H are shareholders of S, a corporation. F is also an employee of S. By agreement, S is to redeem F's shares on the termination of F's employment.

(ii) On these facts, under paragraph (l)(2)(iii)(B) of this section, the agreement is disregarded in determining whether all outstanding shares of S's stock confer identical rights to distribution and liquidation proceeds.

Example 9. Analysis of redemption agreements. (i) J, K, and L are shareholders of S, a corporation. L is also an employee of S. L's shares were not issued to L in connection with the performance of services. By agreement, S is to redeem L's shares for an amount significantly below their fair market value on the termination of L's employment or if S's sales fall below certain levels.

(ii) Under paragraph (l)(2)(iii)(B) of this section, the portion of the agreement providing for redemption of L's stock on termination of employment is disregarded. Under paragraph (l)(2)(iii)(A), the portion of the agreement providing for redemption of L's stock if S's sales fall below certain levels is disregarded unless a principal purpose of that portion of the agreement is to circumvent the one class of stock requirement of section 1361(b)(1)(D) and this paragraph (l).

(3) *Stock taken into account.* Except as provided in paragraphs (b)(3), (4), and (5) of this section (relating to restricted stock, deferred compensation plans, and straight debt), in determining whether all outstanding shares of stock confer identical rights to distribution and liquidation proceeds, all outstanding shares of stock of a corporation are taken into account. For example, substantially nonvested stock with respect to which an election under section 83(b) has been made is taken into account in determining whether a corporation has a second class of stock, and such stock is not treated as a second class of stock if the stock confers rights to distribution and liquidation proceeds that are identical, within the meaning of paragraph (l)(1) of this section, to the rights conferred by the other outstanding shares of stock.

(4) *Other instruments, obligations, or arrangements treated as a second class of stock*—(i) *In general.* Instruments, obligations, or arrange-ments are not treated as a second class of stock for purposes of this paragraph (l) unless they are described in paragraphs (l)(4)(ii) or (iii) of this section. However, in no event are instruments, obligations, or arrangements described in paragraph (b)(4) of this section (relating to deferred compensation plans), paragraphs (l)(4)(iii)(B) and (C) of this section (relating to the exceptions and safe harbor for options), paragraph (l)(4)(ii)(B) of this section (relating to the safe harbors for certain short-term unwritten advances and proportionally-held debt), or paragraph (l)(5) of this section (relating to the safe harbor for straight debt), treated as a second class of stock for purposes of this paragraph (l).

(ii) *Instruments, obligations, or arrangements treated as equity under general principles*—(A) *In general.* Except as provided in paragraph (l)(4)(i) of this section, any instrument, obligation, or arrangement issued by a corporation (other than outstanding shares of stock described in paragraph (l)(3) of this section), regardless of whether designated as debt, is treated as a second class of stock of the corporation—

(*1*) If the instrument, obligation, or arrangement constitutes equity or otherwise results in the holder being treated as the owner of stock under general principles of Federal tax law; and

(*2*) A principal purpose of issuing or entering into the instrument, obligation, or arrangement is to circumvent the rights to distribution or liquidation proceeds conferred by the outstanding shares of stock or to circumvent the limitation on eligible shareholders contained in paragraph (b)(1) of this section.

(B) *Safe harbor for certain short-term unwritten advances and proportionately held obligations*—(*1*) *Short-term unwritten advances.* Unwritten advances from a shareholder that do not exceed $10,000 in the aggregate at any time during the taxable year of the corporation, are treated as debt by the parties, and are expected to be repaid within a reasonable time are not treated as a second class of stock for that taxable year, even if the advances are considered equity under general principles of Federal tax law. The failure of an unwritten advance to meet this safe harbor will not result in a second class of stock unless the advance is considered equity under paragraph (l)(4)(ii)(A)(*1*) of this section and a principal purpose of the advance is to circumvent the rights of the outstanding shares of stock or the limitation on eligible shareholders under paragraph (l)(4)(ii)(A)(*2*) of this section.

(*2*) *Proportionately-held obligations.* Obligations of the same class that are considered equity under general principles of Federal tax law, but are owned solely by the owners of, and in the same proportion as, the outstanding stock of the corporation, are not treated as a second class of stock. Furthermore, an obligation or obligations owned by the sole shareholder of a corporation are always held proportionately to the corporation's outstanding stock. The obligations that are considered equity that do not meet this safe harbor will not result in a second class of stock unless a principal purpose of the obligations is to circumvent the rights of the outstanding shares of stock or the limitation on eligible shareholders under paragraph (l)(4)(ii)(A)(2) of this section.

(iii) *Certain call options, warrants or similar instruments*—(A) *In general.* Except as otherwise provided in this paragraph (l)(4)(iii), a call option, warrant, or similar instrument (collectively, call option) issued by a corporation is treated as a second class of stock of the corporation if, taking into account all the facts and circumstances, the call option is substantially certain to be exercised (by the holder or a potential transferee) and has a strike price substantially below the fair market value of the underlying stock on the date that the call option is issued, transferred by a person who is an eligible shareholder under paragraph (b)(1) of this section to a person who is not an eligible shareholder under paragraph (b)(1) of this section, or materially modified. For purposes of this paragraph (l)(4)(iii), if an option is issued in connection with a loan and the time period in which the option can be exercised is extended in connection with (and consistent with) a modification of the terms of the loan, the extension of the time period in which the option may be exercised is not considered a material modification. In addition, a call option does not have a strike price substantially below fair market value if the price at the time of exercise cannot, pursuant to the terms of the instrument, be substantially below the fair market value of the underlying stock at the time of exercise.

(B) *Certain exceptions*—(1) A call option is not treated as a second class of stock for purposes of this paragraph (l) if it is issued to a person that is actively and regularly engaged in the business of lending and issued in connection with a commercially reasonable loan to the corporation. This paragraph (l)(4)(iii)(B)(1) continues to apply if the call option is transferred with the loan (or if a portion of the call option is transferred with a corresponding portion of the loan). However, if the call option is transferred without a corresponding portion of the loan, this paragraph (l)(4)(iii)(B)(1) ceases to apply. Upon that transfer, the call option is tested under paragraph (l)(4)(iii)(A) (notwithstanding anything in that paragraph to the contrary) if, but for this para-

graph, the call option would have been treated as a second class of stock on the date it was issued.

(2) A call option that is issued to an individual who is either an employee or an independent contractor in connection with the performance of services for the corporation or a related corporation (and that is not excessive by reference to the services performed) is not treated as a second class of stock for purposes of this paragraph (l) if—

(*i*) The call option is nontransferable within the meaning of § 1.83-3(d); and

(*ii*) The call option does not have a readily ascertainable fair market value as defined in § 1.83-7(b) at the time the option is issued.

If the call option becomes transferable, this paragraph (l)(4)(iii)(B)(2) ceases to apply. Solely for purposes of this paragraph (l)(4)(iii)(B)(2), a corporation is related to the issuing corporation if more than 50 percent of the total voting power and total value of its stock is owned by the issuing corporation.

(3) The Commissioner may provide other exceptions by Revenue Ruling or other published guidance.

(C) *Safe harbor for certain options.* A call option is not treated as a second class of stock if, on the date the call option is issued, transferred by a person who is an eligible shareholder under paragraph (b)(1) of this section to a person who is not an eligible shareholder under paragraph (b)(1) of this section, or materially modified, the strike price of the call option is at least 90 percent of the fair market value of the underlying stock on that date. For purposes of this paragraph (l)(4)(iii)(C), a good faith determination of fair market value by the corporation will be respected unless it can be shown that the value was substantially in error and the determination of the value was not performed with reasonable diligence to obtain a fair value. Failure of an option to meet this safe harbor will not necessarily result in the option being treated as a second class of stock.

(iv) *Convertible debt.* A convertible debt instrument is considered a second class of stock if—

(A) It would be treated as a second class of stock under paragraph (l)(4)(ii) of this section (relating to instruments, obligations, or arrangements treated as equity under general principles); or

(B) It embodies rights equivalent to those of a call option that would be treated as a second class of stock under paragraph (l)(4)(iii) of this section (relating to certain call options, warrants, and similar instruments).

Reg. § 1.1361-1(l)(4)

(v) *Examples.* The application of this paragraph (l)(4) may be illustrated by the following examples. In each of the examples, the S corporation requirements of section 1361 are satisfied except as otherwise stated, the corporation has in effect an S election under section 1362, and the corporation has only the shareholders described.

Example 1. Transfer of call option by eligible shareholder to ineligible shareholder. (i) S, a corporation, has 10 shareholders. S issues call options to A, B, and C, individuals who are U.S. residents. A, B, and C are not shareholders, employees, or independent contractors of S. The options have a strike price of $40 and are issued on a date when the fair market value of S stock is also $40. A year later, P, a partnership, purchases A's option. On the date of transfer, the fair market value of S stock is $80.

(ii) On the date the call option is issued, its strike price is not substantially below the fair market value of the S stock. Under paragraph (l)(4)(iii)(A) of this section, whether a call option is a second class of stock must be redetermined if the call option is transferred by a person who is an eligible shareholder under paragraph (b)(1) of this section to a person who is not an eligible shareholder under paragraph (b)(1) of this section. In this case, A is an eligible shareholder of S under paragraph (b)(1) of this section, but P is not. Accordingly, the option is retested on the date it is transferred to D.

(iii) Because on the date the call option is transferred to P its strike price is 50% of the fair market value, the strike price is substantially below the fair market value of the S stock. Accordingly, the call option is treated as a second class of stock as of the date it is transferred to P if, at that time, it is determined that the option is substantially certain to be exercised. The determination of whether the option is substantially certain to be exercised is made on the basis of all the facts and circumstances.

Example 2. Call option issued in connection with the performance of services. (i) E is a bona fide employee of S, a corporation. S issues to E a call option in connection with E's performance of services. At the time the call option is issued, it is not transferable and does not have a readily ascertainable fair market value. However, the call option becomes transferable before it is exercised by E.

(ii) While the option is not transferable, under paragraph (l)(4)(iii)(B)(*2*) of this section, it is not treated as a second class of stock, regardless of its strike price. When the option becomes transferable, that paragraph ceases to apply, and the general rule of paragraph (l)(4)(iii)(A) of this section applies. Accordingly, if the option is materially modified or is transferred to a person who is not an eligible shareholder under paragraph (b)(1) of this section, and on the date of such modification or transfer, the option is substantially certain to be exercised and has a strike price substantially below the fair market value of the underlying stock, the option is treated as a second class of stock.

(iii) If E left S's employment before the option became transferable, the exception provided by paragraph (l)(4)(iii)(B)(*2*) would continue to apply until the option became transferable.

(5) *Straight debt safe harbor—*(i) *In general.* Notwithstanding paragraph (l)(4) of this section, straight debt is not treated as a second class of stock. For purposes of section 1361(c)(5) and this section, the term straight debt means a written unconditional obligation, regardless of whether embodied in a formal note, to pay a sum certain on demand, or on a specified due date, which—

(A) Does not provide for an interest rate or payment dates that are contingent on profits, the borrower's discretion, the payment of dividends with respect to common stock, or similar factors;

(B) Is not convertible (directly or indirectly) into stock or any other equity interest of the S corporation; and

(C) Is held by an individual (other than a nonresident alien), an estate, or a trust described in section 1361(c)(2).

(ii) *Subordination.* The fact that an obligation is subordinated to other debt of the corporation does not prevent the obligation from qualifying as straight debt.

(iii) *Modification or transfer.* An obligation that originally qualifies as straight debt ceases to so qualify if the obligation—

(A) Is materially modified so that it no longer satisfies the definition of straight debt; or

(B) Is transferred to a third party who is not an eligible shareholder under paragraph (b)(1) of this section.

(iv) *Treatment of straight debt for other purposes.* An obligation of an S corporation that satisfies the definition of straight debt in paragraph (l)(5)(i) of this section is not treated as a second class of stock even if it is considered equity under general principles of Federal tax law. Such an obligation is generally treated as debt and when so treated is subject to the applicable rules governing indebtedness for other purposes of the Code. Accordingly, interest paid or accrued with respect to a straight debt obligation is generally treated as interest by the corporation and the recipient and does not constitute a distribution to which section 1368 applies. However, if a straight debt obligation bears a rate of interest that is unreasonably high, an appropriate portion of the interest may be recharacterized and treated as a payment that is not interest. Such a recharacterization does not result in a second class of stock.

(v) *Treatment of C corporation debt upon conversion to S status.* If a C corporation has outstanding an obligation that satisfies the definition of straight debt in paragraph (l)(5)(i) of this section, but that is considered equity under general principles of Federal tax law, the obligation is not treated as a second class of stock for purposes of this section if the C corporation converts to S status. In addition, the conversion from C corporation status to S corporation status is not treated as an exchange of debt for stock with respect to such an instrument.

(6) *Inadvertent terminations.* See section 1362(f) and the regulations thereunder for rules relating to inadvertent terminations in cases where the one class of stock requirement has been inadvertently breached.

* * *

(m) *Electing small business trust (ESBT)*—(1) *Definition*—(i) *General rule.* An electing small business trust (ESBT) means any trust if it meets the following requirements: the trust does not have as a beneficiary any person other than an individual, an estate, an organization described in section 170(c)(2) through (5), or an organization described in section 170(c)(1) that holds a contingent interest in such trust and is not a potential current beneficiary; no interest in the trust has been acquired by purchase; and the trustee of the trust makes a timely ESBT election for the trust.

(ii) *Qualified beneficiaries*—(A) *In general.* For purposes of this section, a beneficiary includes a person who has a present, remainder, or reversionary interest in the trust.

(B) *Distributee trusts.* A distributee trust is the beneficiary of the ESBT only if the distributee trust is an organization described in section 170(c)(2) or (3). In all other situations, any person who has a beneficial interest in a distributee trust is a beneficiary of the ESBT. A distributee trust is a trust that receives or may receive a distribution from an ESBT, whether the rights to receive the distribution are fixed or contingent, or immediate or deferred.

(C) *Powers of appointment.* A person in whose favor a power of appointment could be exercised is not a beneficiary of an ESBT until the holder of the power of appointment actually exercises the power in favor of such person.

(D) *Nonresident aliens.* A nonresident alien as defined in section 7701(b)(1)(B) is an eligible beneficiary of an ESBT. However, see paragraph (m)(4)(i) and (m)(5)(iii) of this section if the nonresident alien is a potential current beneficiary of the ESBT (which would result in an ineligible shareholder and termination of the S corporation election).

(iii) *Interests acquired by purchase.* A trust does not qualify as an ESBT if any interest in the trust has been acquired by purchase. Generally, if a person acquires an interest in the trust and thereby becomes a beneficiary of the trust as defined in paragraph (m)(1)(ii)(A), and any portion of the basis in the acquired interest in the trust is determined under section 1012, such interest has been acquired by purchase. This includes a net gift of a beneficial interest in the trust, in which the person acquiring the beneficial interest pays the gift tax. The trust itself may acquire S corporation stock or other property by purchase or in a part-gift, part-sale transaction.

(iv) *Ineligible trusts.* An ESBT does not include—

(A) Any qualified subchapter S trust (as defined in section 1361(d)(3)) if an election under section 1361(d)(2) applies with respect to any corporation the stock of which is held by the trust;

(B) Any trust exempt from tax or not subject to tax under subtitle A; or

(C) Any charitable remainder annuity trust or charitable remainder unitrust (as defined in section 664(d)).

(2) *ESBT election*—(i) *In general.* The trustee of the trust must make the ESBT election by signing and filing, with the service center where the S corporation files its income tax return, a statement that meets the requirements of paragraph (m)(2)(ii) of this section. If there is more than one trustee, the trustee or trustees with authority to legally bind the trust must sign the election statement. If any one of several trustees can legally bind the trust, only one trustee needs to sign the election statement. Generally, only one ESBT election is made for the trust, regardless of the number of S corporations whose stock is held by the ESBT. However, if the ESBT holds stock in multiple S corporations that file in different service centers, the ESBT election must be filed with all the relevant service centers where the corporations file their income tax returns. This requirement applies only at the time of the initial ESBT election; if the ESBT later acquires stock in an S corporation which files its income tax return at a different service center, a new ESBT election is not required.

* * *

(3) *Effect of ESBT election*—(i) *General rule.* If a trust makes a valid ESBT election, the

trust will be treated as an ESBT for purposes of chapter 1 of the Internal Revenue Code as of the effective date of the ESBT election.

(ii) *Employer Identification Number.* An ESBT has only one employer identification number (EIN). If an existing trust makes an ESBT election, the trust continues to use the EIN it currently uses.

(iii) *Taxable year.* If an ESBT election is effective on a day other than the first day of the trust's taxable year, the ESBT election does not cause the trust's taxable year to close. The termination of the ESBT election (including a termination caused by a conversion of the ESBT to a QSST) other than on the last day of the trust's taxable year also does not cause the trust's taxable year to close. In either case, the trust files one tax return for the taxable year.

(iv) *Allocation of S corporation items.* If, during the taxable year of an S corporation, a trust is an ESBT for part of the year and an eligible shareholder under section 1361(c)(2)(A)(i) through (iv) for the rest of the year, the S corporation items are allocated between the two types of trusts under section 1377(a). See § 1.1377-1(a)(2)(iii).

(v) *Estimated taxes.* If an ESBT election is effective on a day other than the first day of the trust's taxable year, the trust is considered one trust for purposes of estimated taxes under section 6654.

(4) *Potential current beneficiaries*—(i) *In general.* For purposes of determining whether a corporation is a small business corporation within the meaning of section 1361(b)(1), each potential current beneficiary of an ESBT generally is treated as a shareholder of the corporation. Subject to the provisions of this paragraph (m)(4), a potential current beneficiary generally is, with respect to any period, any person who at any time during such period is entitled to, or in the discretion of any person may receive, a distribution from the principal or income of the trust. A person is treated as a shareholder of the S corporation at any moment in time when that person is entitled to, or in the discretion of any person may, receive a distribution of principal or income of the trust. No person is treated as a potential current beneficiary solely because that person holds any future interest in the trust.

(ii) *Grantor trusts.* If all or a portion of an ESBT is treated as owned by a person under subpart E, part I, subchapter J, chapter 1 of the Internal Revenue Code, such owner is a potential current beneficiary in addition to persons described in paragraph (m)(4)(i) of this section.

(iii) *Special rule for dispositions of stock.* Notwithstanding the provisions of paragraph

(m)(4)(i) of this section, if a trust disposes of all of its S corporation stock, any person who first met the definition of a potential current beneficiary during the 60-day period ending on the date of such disposition is not a potential current beneficiary and thus is not a shareholder of that corporation.

(iv) *Distributee trusts*—(A) *In general.* This paragraph (m)(4)(iv) contains the rules for determining who are the potential current beneficiaries of an ESBT if a distributee trust becomes entitled to, or at the discretion of any person, may receive a distribution from principal or income of an ESBT. A distributee trust does not include a trust that is not currently in existence. For this purpose, a trust is not currently in existence if the trust has no assets and no items of income, loss, deduction, or credit. Thus, if a trust instrument provides for a trust to be funded at some future time, the future trust is not currently a distributee trust.

(B) If the distributee trust is not a trust described in section 1361(c)(2)(A), then the distributee trust is the potential current beneficiary of the ESBT and the corporation's S corporation election terminates.

(C) If the distributee trust is a trust described in section 1361(c)(2)(A), the persons who would be its potential current beneficiaries (as defined in paragraphs (m)(4)(i) and (ii) of this section) if the distributee trust were an ESBT are treated as the potential current beneficiaries of the ESBT. Notwithstanding the preceding sentence, however, if the distributee trust is a trust described in section 1361(c)(2)(A)(ii) or (iii), the estate described in section 1361(c)(2)(B)(ii) or (iii) is treated as the potential current beneficiary of the ESBT for the 2-year period during which such trust would be permitted as a shareholder.

(D) For the purposes of paragraph (m)(4)(iv)(C) of this section, a trust will be deemed to be described in section 1361(c)(2)(A) if such trust would qualify for a QSST election under section 1361(d) or an ESBT election under section 1361(e) if it owned S corporation stock.

(v) *Contingent distributions.* A person who is entitled to receive a distribution only after a specified time or upon the occurrence of a specified event (such as the death of the holder of a power of appointment) is not a potential current beneficiary until such time or the occurrence of such event.

(vi) *Currently exercisable powers of appointment*—(A) *In general.* A person to whom a distribution is or may be made during a period pursuant to a power of appointment is a potential current beneficiary. Thus, if any person has a lifetime power of appointment that would permit

Reg. § 1.1361-1(m)(4)

distributions from the trust to be made to more than 75 persons, the corporation's S corporation election will terminate because the number of potential current beneficiaries will exceed the 75-shareholder limit of section 1361(b)(1)(A). Also, the S corporation election will terminate if the currently exercisable power of appointment allows distributions to be made to an ineligible shareholder as defined in section 1361(b)(1)(B) and (C).

(B) *Waiver or release.* If the holder of a power of appointment permanently releases the power in a manner that is valid under applicable local law, the persons that would be potential current beneficiaries solely because of the power will not be potential current beneficiaries after the effective date of the release. An attempt to temporarily waive, release, or limit a currently exercisable power of appointment will be ignored in determining who are potential current beneficiaries of the trust.

(vii) *Number of shareholders.* Each potential current beneficiary of the ESBT, as defined in paragraphs (m)(4)(i) through (vi) of this section, is counted as a shareholder of any S corporation whose stock is owned by the ESBT. During any period in which the ESBT has no potential current beneficiaries, the ESBT is counted as the shareholder. A person is counted as only one shareholder of an S corporation even though that person may be treated as a shareholder of the S corporation by direct ownership and through one or more eligible trusts described in section 1361(c)(2)(A). Thus, for example, if a person owns stock in an S corporation and is a potential current beneficiary of an ESBT that owns stock in the same S corporation, that person is counted as one shareholder of the S corporation. Similarly, if a husband owns stock in an S corporation and his wife is a potential current beneficiary of an ESBT that owns stock in the same S corporation, the husband and wife will be counted as one shareholder of the S corporation.

(viii) *Miscellaneous.* Payments made by an ESBT to a third party on behalf of a beneficiary are considered to be payments made directly to the beneficiary. The right of a beneficiary to assign the beneficiary's interest to a third party does not result in the third party being a potential current beneficiary until that interest is actually assigned.

(5) *ESBT terminations—(i) Ceasing to meet ESBT requirements.* A trust ceases to be an ESBT on the first day the trust fails to meet the definition of an ESBT under section 1361(e). The last day the trust is treated as an ESBT is the day before the date on which the trust fails to meet the definition of an ESBT.

(ii) *Disposition of S stock.* In general, a trust ceases to be an ESBT on the first day following the day the trust disposes of all S corporation stock. However, if the trust is using the installment method to report income from the sale or disposition of its stock in an S corporation, the trust ceases to be an ESBT on the day following the earlier of the day the last installment payment is received by the trust or the day the trust disposes of the installment obligation.

(iii) *Potential current beneficiaries that are ineligible shareholders.* If a potential current beneficiary of an ESBT is not an eligible shareholder of a small business corporation within the meaning of section 1361(b)(1), the S corporation election terminates. For example, the S corporation election will terminate if a nonresident alien becomes a potential current beneficiary of an ESBT. Such a potential current beneficiary is treated as an ineligible shareholder beginning on the day such person becomes a potential current beneficiary, and the S corporation election terminates on that date. However, see the special rule of paragraph (m)(4)(iii) of this section. If the S corporation election terminates, relief may be available under section 1362(f).

(6) *Revocation of ESBT election.* An ESBT election may be revoked only with the consent of the Commissioner. The application for consent to revoke the election must be submitted to the Internal Revenue Service in the form of a letter ruling request under the appropriate revenue procedure.

(7) *Converting an ESBT to a QSST.* For a trust that seeks to convert from an ESBT to a QSST, the consent of the Commissioner is hereby granted to revoke the ESBT election as of the effective date of the QSST election, if all the following requirements are met:

(i) The trust meets all of the requirements to be a QSST under section 1361(d).

(ii) The trustee and the current income beneficiary of the trust sign the QSST election. The QSST election must be filed with the service center where the S corporation files its income tax return. This QSST election must state at the top of the document "ATTENTION ENTITY CONTROL—CONVERSION OF AN ESBT TO A QSST PURSUANT TO SECTION 1.1361-1(m)" and include all information otherwise required for a QSST election under § 1.1361-1(j)(6). A separate QSST election must be made with respect to the stock of each S corporation held by the trust.

(iii) The trust has not converted from a QSST to an ESBT within the 36-month period preceding the effective date of the new QSST election.

Reg. § 1.1361-1(m)(7)

(iv) The date on which the QSST election is to be effective cannot be more than 15 days and two months prior to the date on which the election is filed and cannot be more than 12 months after the date on which the election is filed. If an election specifies an effective date more than 15 days and two months prior to the date on which the election is filed, it will be effective on the day that is 15 days and two months prior to the date on which it is filed. If an election specifies an effective date more than 12 months after the date on which the election is filed, it will be effective on the day that is 12 months after the date it is filed.

* * *

[Reg. § 1.1361-1.]

☐ [*T.D.* 8419, 5-28-92. *Amended by T.D.* 8600, 7-20-95; *T.D.* 8869, 1-20-2000; *T.D.* 8940, 2-12-2001 *and T.D.* 8994, 5-13-2002.]

§ 1.1361-2. Definitions relating to S corporation subsidiaries.—(a) *In general.* The term *qualified subchapter S subsidiary* (QSub) means any domestic corporation that is not an ineligible corporation (as defined in section 1361(b)(2) and the regulations thereunder), if—

(1) 100 percent of the stock of such corporation is held by an S corporation; and

(2) The S corporation properly elects to treat the subsidiary as a QSub under § 1.1361-3.

(b) *Stock treated as held by S corporation.* For purposes of satisfying the 100 percent stock ownership requirement in section 1361(b)(3)(B)(i) and paragraph (a)(1) of this section—

(1) Stock of a corporation is treated as held by an S corporation if the S corporation is the owner of that stock for Federal income tax purposes; and

(2) Any outstanding instruments, obligations, or arrangements of the corporation which would not be considered stock for purposes of section 1361(b)(1)(D) if the corporation were an S corporation are not treated as outstanding stock of the QSub.

(c) *Straight debt safe harbor.* Section 1.1361-1(1)(5)(iv) and (v) apply to an obligation of a corporation for which a QSub election is made if that obligation would satisfy the definition of straight debt in § 1.1361-1(1)(5) if issued by the S corporation.

(d) *Examples.* The following examples illustrate the application of this section:

Example 1. X, an S corporation, owns 100 percent of Y, a corporation for which a valid QSub election is in effect for the taxable year. Y owns 100 percent of Z, a corporation otherwise eligible for QSub status. X may elect to treat Z as a QSub under section 1361(b)(3)(B)(ii).

Example 2. Assume the same facts as in *Example 1,* except that Y is a business entity that is disregarded as an entity separate from its owner under § 301.7701-2(c)(2) of this chapter. X may elect to treat Z as a QSub.

Example 3. Assume the same facts as in *Example 1,* except that Y owns 50 percent of Z, and X owns the other 50 percent. X may elect to treat Z as a QSub.

Example 4. Assume the same facts as in *Example 1,* except that Y is a C corporation. Although Y is a domestic corporation that is otherwise eligible to be a QSub, no QSub election has been made for Y. Thus, X is not treated as holding the stock of Z. Consequently, X may not elect to treat Z as a QSub.

Example 5. Individuals A and B own 100 percent of the stock of corporation X, an S corporation, and, except for C's interest (described below), X owns 100 percent of corporation Y, a C corporation. Individual C holds an instrument issued by Y that is considered to be equity under general principles of tax law but would satisfy the definition of straight debt under § 1.1361-1(1)(5) if Y were an S corporation. In determining whether X owns 100 percent of Y for purposes of making the QSub election, the instrument held by C is not considered outstanding stock. In addition, under § 1.1361-1(1)(5)(v), the QSub election is not treated as an exchange of debt for stock with respect to such instrument, and § 1.1361-1(1)(5)(iv) applies to determine the tax treatment of payments on the instrument while Y's QSub election is in effect.

[Reg. § 1.1361-2.]

☐ [*T.D.* 8869, 1-20-2000.]

§ 1.1361-3. QSub election.—(a) *Time and manner of making election*—(1) *In general.* The corporation for which the QSub election is made must meet all the requirements of section 1361(b)(3)(B) at the time the election is made and for all periods for which the election is to be effective.

(2) *Manner of making election.* Except as provided in section 1361(b)(3)(D) and § 1.1361-5(c) (five-year prohibition on reelection), an S corporation may elect to treat an eligible subsidiary as a QSub by filing a completed form to be prescribed by the IRS. The election form must be signed by a person authorized to sign the S corporation's return required to be filed under section 6037. Unless the election form provides otherwise, the election must be submitted to the service center where the subsidiary filed its most recent tax return (if applicable), and, if an S corporation forms a subsidiary and makes a valid QSub election (effective upon the date of the subsidiary's formation) for the subsidiary, the

election should be submitted to the service center where the S corporation filed its most recent return.

(3) *Time of making election.* A QSub election may be made by the S corporation parent at any time during the taxable year.

(4) *Effective date of election.* A QSub election will be effective on the date specified on the election form or on the date the election form is filed if no date is specified. The effective date specified on the form cannot be more than two months and 15 days prior to the date of filing and cannot be more than 12 months after the date of filing. For this purpose, the definition of the term *month* found in § 1.1362-6(a)(2)(ii)(C) applies. If an election form specifies an effective date more than two months and 15 days prior to the date on which the election form is filed, it will be effective two months and 15 days prior to the date it is filed. If an election form specifies an effective date more than 12 months after the date on which the election is filed, it will be effective 12 months after the date it is filed.

(5) *Example.* The following example illustrates the application of paragraph (a)(4) of this section:

Example. X has been a calendar year S corporation engaged in a trade or business for several years. X acquires the stock of Y, a calendar year C corporation, on April 1, 2002. On August 10, 2002, X makes an election to treat Y as a QSub. Unless otherwise specified on the election form, the election will be effective as of August 10, 2002. If specified on the election form, the election may be effective on some other date that is not more than two months and 15 days prior to August 10, 2002, and not more than 12 months after August 10, 2002.

(6) *Extension of time for making a QSub election.* An extension of time to make a QSub election may be available under the procedures applicable under § § 301.9100-1 and 301.9100-3 of this chapter.

(b) *Revocation of QSub election*—(1) *Manner of revoking QSub election.* An S corporation may revoke a QSub election under section 1361 by filing a statement with the service center where the S corporation's most recent tax return was properly filed. The revocation statement must include the names, addresses, and taxpayer identification numbers of both the parent S corporation and the QSub, if any. The statement must be signed by a person authorized to sign the S corporation's return required to be filed under section 6037.

(2) *Effective date of revocation.* The revocation of a QSub election is effective on the date specified on the revocation statement or on the

date the revocation statement is filed if no date is specified. The effective date specified on the revocation statement cannot be more than two months and 15 days prior to the date on which the revocation statement is filed and cannot be more than 12 months after the date on which the revocation statement is filed. If a revocation statement specifies an effective date more than two months and 15 days prior to the date on which the statement is filed, it will be effective two months and 15 days prior to the date it is filed. If a revocation statement specifies an effective date more than 12 months after the date on which the statement is filed, it will be effective 12 months after the date it is filed.

(3) *Revocation after termination.* A revocation may not be made after the occurrence of an event that renders the subsidiary ineligible for QSub status under section 1361(b)(3)(B).

(4) *Revocation before QSub election effective.* For purposes of Section 1361(b)(3)(D) and § 1.1361-5(c) (five-year prohibition on re-election), a revocation effective on the first day the QSub election was to be effective will not be treated as a termination of a QSub election. [Reg. § 1.1361-3.]

☐ [*T.D.* 8869, 1-20-2000.]

§ 1.1361-4. Effect of QSub election.—(a) *Separate existence ignored*—(1) *In general.* Except as otherwise provided in paragraph (a)(3) of this section, for Federal tax purposes—

(i) A corporation which is a QSub shall not be treated as a separate corporation; and

(ii) All assets, liabilities, and items of income, deduction, and credit of a QSub shall be treated as assets, liabilities, and items of income, deduction, and credit of the S corporation.

(2) *Liquidation of subsidiary*—(i) *In general.* If an S corporation makes a valid QSub election with respect to a subsidiary, the subsidiary is deemed to have liquidated into the S corporation. Except as provided in paragraph (a)(5) of this section, the tax treatment of the liquidation or of a larger transaction that includes the liquidation will be determined under the Internal Revenue Code and general principles of tax law, including the step transaction doctrine. Thus, for example, if an S corporation forms a subsidiary and makes a valid QSub election (effective upon the date of the subsidiary's formation) for the subsidiary, the transfer of assets to the subsidiary and the deemed liquidation are disregarded, and the corporation will be deemed to be a QSub from its inception.

(ii) *Examples.* The following examples illustrate the application of this paragraph (a)(2)(i) of this section:

Reg. § 1.1361-4(a)(2)

Example 1. Corporation X acquires all of the outstanding stock of solvent corporation Y from an unrelated individual for cash and short-term notes. Thereafter, as part of the same plan, X immediately makes an S election and a QSub election for Y. Because X acquired all of the stock of Y in a qualified stock purchase within the meaning of section 338(d)(3), the liquidation described in paragraph (a)(2) of this section is respected as an independent step separate from the stock acquisition, and the tax consequences of the liquidation are determined under sections 332 and 337.

Example 2. Corporation X, pursuant to a plan, acquires all of the outstanding stock of corporation Y from the shareholders of Y solely in exchange for 10 percent of the voting stock of X. Prior to the transaction, Y and its shareholders are unrelated to X. Thereafter, as part of the same plan, X immediately makes an S election and a QSub election for Y. The transaction is a reorganization described in section 368(a)(1)(C), assuming the other conditions for reorganization treatment (e.g., continuity of business enterprise) are satisfied.

Example 3. After the expiration of the transition period provided in paragraph (a)(5)(i) of this section, individual A, pursuant to a plan, contributes all of the outstanding stock of Y to his wholly owned S corporation, X, and immediately causes X to make a QSub election for Y. The transaction is a reorganization under section 368(a)(1)(D), assuming the other conditions for reorganization treatment (e.g., continuity of business enterprise) are satisfied. If the sum of the amount of liabilities of Y treated as assumed by X exceeds the total of the adjusted basis of the property of Y, then section 357(c) applies and such excess is considered as gain from the sale or exchange of a capital asset or of property which is not a capital asset, as the case may be.

(iii) *Adoption of plan of liquidation.* For purposes of satisfying the requirement of adoption of a plan of liquidation under section 332, unless a formal plan of liquidation that contemplates the QSub election is adopted on an earlier date, the making of the QSub election is considered to be the adoption of a plan of liquidation immediately before the deemed liquidation described in paragraph (a)(2)(i) of this section.

(iv) *Example.* The following example illustrates the application of paragraph (a)(2)(iii) of this section:

Example. Corporation X owns 75 percent of a solvent corporation Y, and individual A owns the remaining 25 percent of Y. As part of a plan to make a QSub election for Y, X causes Y to redeem A's 25 percent interest on June 1 for cash

and makes a QSub election for Y effective on June 3. The making of the QSub election is considered to be the adoption of a plan of liquidation immediately before the deemed liquidation. The deemed liquidation satisfies the requirements of section 332.

(v) *Stock ownership requirements of section 332.* The deemed exercise of an option under § 1.1504-4 and any instruments, obligations, or arrangements that are not considered stock under § 1.1361-2(b)(2) are disregarded in determining if the stock ownership requirements of section 332(b) are met with respect to the deemed liquidation provided in paragraph (a)(2)(i) of this section.

* * *

(4) *Treatment of stock of QSub.* Except for purposes of section 1361(b)(3)(B)(i) and § 1.1361-2(a)(1), the stock of a QSub shall be disregarded for all Federal tax purposes.

* * *

(b) *Timing of the liquidation*—(1) *In general.* Except as otherwise provided in paragraph (b)(3) or (4) of this section, the liquidation described in paragraph (a)(2) of this section occurs at the close of the day before the Qsub election is effective. Thus, for example, if a C corporation elects to be treated as an S corporation and makes a QSub election (effective the same date as the S election) with respect to a subsidiary, the liquidation occurs immediately before the S election becomes effective, while the S electing parent is still a C corporation.

(2) *Application to elections in tiered situations.* When QSub elections for a tiered group of subsidiaries are effective on the same date, the S corporation may specify the order of the liquidations. If no order is specified, the liquidations that are deemed to occur as a result of the QSub elections will be treated as occurring first for the lowest tier entity and proceed successively upward until all of the liquidations under paragraph (a)(2) of this section have occurred. For example, S, an S corporation, owns 100 percent of C, the common parent of an affiliated group of corporations that includes X and Y. C owns all of the stock of X and X owns all of the stock of Y. S elects under § 1.1361-3 to treat C, X and Y as QSubs effective on the same date. If no order is specified for the elections, the following liquidations are deemed to occur as a result of the elections, with each successive liquidation occuring on the same day immediately after the preceding liquidation: Y is treated as liquidating into X, then X is treated as liquidating into C, and finally C is treated as liquidating into S.

Reg. § 1.1361-4(a)(4)

(3) *Acquisitions*—(i) *In general*. If an S corporation does not own 100 percent of the stock of the subsidiary on the day before the QSub election is effective, the liquidation described in paragraph (a)(2) of this section occurs immediately after the time at which the S corporation first owns 100 percent of the stock.

(ii) *Special rules for acquired S corporations*. Except as provided in paragraph (b)(4) of this section, if a corporation (Y) for which an election under section 1362(a) was in effect is acquired, and a QSub election is made effective on the day Y is acquired, Y is deemed to liquidate into the S corporation at the beginning of the day the termination of its S election is effective. As a result, if corporation X acquires Y, an S corporation, and makes an S election for itself and a QSub election for Y effective on the day of acquisition, Y liquidates into X at the beginning of the day when X's S election is effective, and there is no period between the termination of Y's S election and the deemed liquidation of Y during which Y is a C corporation. Y's taxable year ends for all Federal income tax purposes at the close of the preceding day. Furthermore, if Y owns Z, a corporation for which a QSub election was in effect prior to the acquisition of Y by X, and X makes QSub elections for Y and Z, effective on the day of acquisition, the transfer of assets to Z and the deemed liquidation of Z are disregarded. See §§ 1.1361-4(a)(2) and 1.1361-5(b)(1)(i).

(4) *Coordination with section 338 election*. An S corporation that makes a qualified stock purchase of a target may make an election under section 338 with respect to the acquisition if it meets the requirements for the election, and may make a QSub election with respect to the target. If an S corporation makes an election under section 338 with respect to a subsidiary acquired in a qualified stock purchase, a QSub election made with respect to that subsidiary is not effective before the day after the acquisition date (within the meaning of section 338(h)(2)). If the QSub election is effective on the day after the acquisition date, the liquidation under paragraph (a)(2) of this section occurs immediately after the deemed asset purchase by the new target corporation under section 338. If an S corporation makes an election under section 338 (without a section 338(h)(10) election) with respect to a target, the target must file a final return as a C corporation reflecting the deemed sale. See § 1.338-10(a). If the target was an S corporation on the day before the acquisition date, the final return as a C corporation must reflect the activities of the target for the acquisition date, including the deemed sale. See § 1.338-10(a)(3).

(c) *Carryover of disallowed losses and deductions*. If an S corporation (S1) acquires the stock of another S corporation (S2), and S1 makes a QSub election with respect to S2 effective on the day of the acquisition, see § 1.1366-2(c)(1) for provisions relating to the carryover of losses and deductions with respect to a former shareholder of S2 that may be available to that shareholder as a shareholder of S1.

* * *

[Reg. § 1.1361-4.]

☐ [*T.D.* 8869, 1-20-2000 (*corrected* 3-27-2000). *Amended by T.D.* 8940, 2-12-2001.]

§ 1.1361-5. Termination of QSub election.— (a) *In general*—(1) *Effective date*. The termination of a QSub election is effective—

(i) On the effective date contained in the revocation statement if a QSub election is revoked under § 91.1361-3(b);

(ii) At the close of the last day of the parent's last taxable year as an S corporation if the parent's S election terminates under § 1.1362-2; or

(iii) At the close of the day on which an event (other than an event described in paragraph (a)(1)(ii) of this section) occurs that renders the subsidiary ineligible for QSub status under section 1361(b)(3)(B).

(2) *Information to be provided upon termination of QSub election by failure to qualify as a Qsub*. If a QSub election terminates because an event renders the subsidiary ineligible for QSub status, the S corporation must attach to its return for the taxable year in which the termination occurs a notification that a QSub election has terminated, the date of the termination, and the names, addresses, and employer identification numbers of both the parent corporation and the QSub.

(3) *QSub joins a consolidated group*. If a QSub election terminates because the S corporation becomes a member of a consolidated group (and no election under section 338(g) is made) the principles of § 1.1502-76(b)(1)(ii)(A)(2) (relating to a special rule for S corporations that join a consolidated group) apply to any QSub of the S corporation that also becomes a member of the consolidated group at the same time as the S corporation. See *Example 4* of paragraph (a)(4) of this section.

* * *

(b) *Effect of termination of QSub election*—(1) *Formation of new corporation*—(i) *In general*. If a QSub election terminates under paragraph (a) of this section, the former QSub is treated as a new corporation acquiring all of its assets (and assuming all of its liabilities) immediately before the termination from the S corporation parent in exchange for stock of the new corporation. The tax

Reg. § 1.1361-5(b)(1)

treatment of this transaction or of a larger transaction that includes this transaction will be determined under the Internal Revenue Code and general principles of tax law, including the step transaction doctrine. For purposes of determining the application of section 351 with respect to this transaction, instruments, obligations, or other arrangements that are not treated as stock of the QSub under § 1.1361-2(b) are disregarded in determining control for purposes of section 368(c) even if they are equity under general principles of tax law.

(ii) *Termination for tiered QSubs.* If QSub elections terminate for tiered QSubs on the same day, the formation of any higher tier subsidiary precedes the formation of its lower tier subsidiary. See *Example 6* in paragraph (b)(3) of this section.

(2) *Carryover of disallowed losses and deductions.* If a QSub terminates because the S corporation distributes the QSub stock to some or all of the S corporation's shareholders in a transaction to which section 368(a)(1)(D) applies by reason of section 355 (or so much of section 356 as relates to section 355), see § 1.1366-2(c)(2) for provisions relating to the carryover of disallowed losses and deductions that may be available.

* * *

(c) *Election after QSub termination*—(1) *In general.* Absent the Commissioner's consent, and except as provided in paragraph (c)(2) of this section, a corporation whose QSub election has terminated under paragraph (a) of this section (or a successor corporation as defined in paragraph (b) of this section) may not make an S election under section 1362 or have a QSub election under section 1361(b)(3)(B)(ii) made with respect to it for five taxable years (as described in section 1361(b)(3)(D)). The Commissioner may permit an S election by the corporation or a new QSub election with respect to the corporation before the five-year period expires. The corporation requesting consent to make the election has the burden of establishing that, under the relevant facts and circumstances, the Commissioner should consent to a new election.

(2) *Exception.* In the case of S and QSub elections effective after December 31, 1996, if a corporation,'s QSub election terminates, the corporation may, without requesting the Commissioner's consent, make an S election or have a QSub election made with respect to it before the expiration of the five-year period described in section 1361(b)(3)(D) and paragraph (c)(1) of this section, provided that—

(i) Immediately following the termination, the corporation (or its successor corporation) is otherwise eligible to make an S election or have a QSub election made for it; and

(ii) The relevant election is made effective immediately following the termination of the QSub election.

(3) *Examples.* The following examples illustrate the application of this paragraph (c):

Example 1. Termination upon distribution of QSub stock to shareholders of parent. X, an S corporation, owns Y, a QSub. X distributes all of its Y stock to X's shareholders. The distribution terminates the QSub election because Y no longer satisfies the requirements of a QSub. Assuming Y is otherwise eligible to be treated as an S corporation, Y's shareholders may elect to treat Y as an S corporation effective on the date of the stock distribution without requesting the Commissioner's consent.

Example 2. Sale of 100 percent of QSub stock. X, an S corporation, owns Y, a QSub. X sells 100 percent of the stock of Y to Z, an unrelated S corporation. Z may elect to treat Y as a QSub effective on the date of purchase without requesting the Commissioner's consent.

[Reg. § 1.1361-5.]

☐ [*T.D.* 8869, 1-20-2000 (*corrected* 10-23-2002).]

§ 1.1362-1. Election to be an S corporation.—(a) *In general.* Except as provided in § 1.1362-5, a small business corporation as defined in section 1361 may elect to be an S corporation under section 1362(a). An election may be made only with the consent of all of the shareholders of the corporation at the time of the election. See § 1.1362-6(a) for rules concerning the time and manner of making this election.

(b) *Years for which election is effective.* An election under section 1362(a) is effective for the entire taxable year of the corporation for which it is made and for all succeeding taxable years of the corporation, until the election is terminated. [Reg. § 1.1362-1.]

☐ [*T.D.* 8449, 11-24-92.]

§ 1.1362-2. Termination of election.—(a) *Termination by revocation*—(1) *In general.* An election made under section 1362(a) is terminated if the corporation revokes the election for any taxable year of the corporation for which the election is effective, including the first taxable year. A revocation may be made only with the consent of shareholders who, at the time the revocation is made, hold more than one-half of the number of issued and outstanding shares of stock (including non-voting stock) of the corporation. See § 1.1362-6(a) for rules concerning the time and manner of revoking an election made under section 1362(a).

(2) *When effective*—(i) *In general.* Except as provided in paragraph (a)(2)(ii) of this section, a

revocation made during the taxable year and before the 16th day of the third month of the taxable year is effective on the first day of the taxable year and a revocation made after the 15th day of the third month of the taxable year is effective for the following taxable year. If a corporation makes an election to be an S corporation that is to be effective beginning with the next taxable year and revokes its election on or before the first day of the next taxable year, the corporation is deemed to have revoked its election on the first day of the next taxable year.

(ii) *Revocations specifying a prospective revocation date.* If a corporation specifies a date for revocation and the date is expressed in terms of a stated day, month, and year that is on or after the date the revocation is filed, the revocation is effective on and after the date so specified.

(3) *Effect on taxable year of corporation.* In the case of a corporation that revokes its election to be an S corporation effective on the first day of the first taxable year for which its election is to be effective, any statement made with the election regarding a change in the corporation's taxable year has no effect.

(4) *Rescission of a revocation.* A corporation may rescind a revocation made under paragraph (a)(2) of this section at any time before the revocation becomes effective. A rescission may be made only with the consent of each person who consented to the revocation and by each person who became a shareholder of the corporation within the period beginning on the first day after the date the revocation was made and ending on the date on which the rescission is made. See § 1.1362-6(a) for rules concerning the time and manner of rescinding a revocation.

(b) *Termination by reason of corporation ceasing to be a small business corporation*—(1) *In general.* If a corporation ceases to be a small business corporation, as defined in section 1361(b), at any time on or after the first day of the first taxable year for which its election under section 1362(a) is effective, the election terminates. In the event of a termination under this paragraph (b)(1), the corporation should attach to its return for the taxable year in which the termination occurs a notification that a termination has occurred and the date of the termination.

(2) *When effective.* If an election terminates because of a specific event that causes the corporation to fail to meet the definition of a small business corporation, the termination is effective as of the date on which the event occurs. If a corporation makes an election to be an S corporation that is effective beginning with the following taxable year and is not a small business corporation on the first day of that following taxable

year, the election is treated as having terminated on that first day. If a corporation is a small business corporation on the first day of the taxable year for which its election is effective, its election does not terminate even if the corporation was not a small business corporation during all or part of the period beginning after the date the election was made and ending before the first day of the taxable year for which the election is effective.

(3) *Effect on taxable year of corporation.* In the case of a corporation that fails to meet the definition of a small business corporation on the first day of the first taxable year for which its election to be an S corporation is to be effective, any statement made with the election regarding a change in the corporation's taxable year has no effect.

(c) *Termination by reason of excess passive investment income*—(1) *In general.* A corporation's election under section 1362(a) terminates if the corporation has subchapter C earnings and profits at the close of each of three consecutive taxable years and, for each of those taxable years, has passive investment income in excess of 25 percent of gross receipts. See section 1375 for the tax imposed on excess passive investment income.

(2) *When effective.* A termination under this paragraph (c) is effective on the first day of the first taxable year beginning after the third consecutive year in which the S corporation had excess passive investment income.

(3) *Subchapter C earnings and profits.* For purposes of this paragraph (c), *subchapter C earnings and profits* of a corporation are the earnings and profits of any corporation, including the S corporation or an acquired or predecessor corporation, for any period with respect to which an election under section 1362(a) (or under section 1372 of prior law) was not in effect. The subchapter C earnings and profits of an S corporation are modified as required by section 1371(c).

(4) *Gross receipts*—(i) *In general.* For purposes of this paragraph (c), *gross receipts* generally means the total amount received or accrued under the method of accounting used by the corporation in computing its taxable income and is not reduced by returns and allowances, cost of goods sold, or deductions.

(ii) *Special rules for sales of capital assets, stock and securities*—(A) *Sales of capital assets.* For purposes of this paragraph (c), gross receipts from the sales or exchanges of capital assets (as defined in section 1221), other than stock and securities, are taken into account only to the extent of capital gain net income (as defined in section 1222).

Reg. § 1.1362-2(c)(4)

(B) *Sales of stock or securities—(1) In general.* For purposes of this paragraph (c), gross receipts from the sales or exchanges of stock or securities are taken into account only to the extent of gains therefrom. In addition, for purposes of computing gross receipts from sales or exchanges of stock or securities, losses do not offset gains.

(2) *Treatment of certain liquidations.* Gross receipts from the sales or exchanges of stock or securities do not include amounts described in section 1362(d)(3)(D)(iv), relating to the treatment of certain liquidations. For purposes of section 1362(d)(3)(D)(iv), stock of the liquidating corporation owned by an S corporation shareholder is not treated as owned by the S corporation.

(3) *Definition of stock or securities.* For purposes of this paragraph (c), *stock or securities* includes shares or certificates of stock, stock rights or warrants, or an interest in any corporation (including any joint stock company, insurance company, association, or other organization classified as a corporation under section 7701); an interest as a limited partner in a partnership; certificates of interest or participation in any profit-sharing agreement, or in any oil, gas, or other mineral property, or lease; collateral trust certificates; voting trust certificates; bonds; debentures; certificates of indebtedness; notes; car trust certificates; bills of exchange; or obligations issued by or on behalf of a State, Territory, or political subdivision thereof.

(4) *General partner interests—(i) In general.* Except as provided in paragraph (c)(4)(ii)(B)(4)(ii) of this section, if an S corporation disposes of a general partner interest, the gain on the disposition is treated as gain from the sale of stock or securities to the extent of the amount the S corporation would have received as a distributive share of gain from the sale of stock or securities held by the partnership if all of the stock and securities held by the partnership had been sold by the partnership at fair market value at the time the S corporation disposes of the general partner interest. In applying this rule, the S corporation's distributive share of gain from the sale of stock or securities held by the partnership is not reduced to reflect any loss that would be recognized from the sale of stock or securities held by the partnership. In the case of tiered partnerships, the rules of this section apply by looking through each tier.

(ii) *Exception.* An S corporation that disposes of a general partner interest may treat the disposition, for purposes of this paragraph (c), in the same manner as the disposition of an interest as a limited partner.

(iii) *Other exclusions from gross receipts.* For purposes of this paragraph (c), gross receipts do not include—

(A) Amounts received in nontaxable sales or exchanges except to the extent that gain is recognized by the corporation on the sale or exchange; or

(B) Amounts received as a loan, as a repayment of a loan, as a contribution to capital, or on the issuance by the corporation of its own stock.

(5) *Passive investment income—(i) In general.* In general, *passive investment income* means gross receipts (as defined in paragraph (c)(4) of this section) derived from royalties, rents, dividends, interest, annuities, and gains from the sales or exchanges of stock or securities.

(ii) *Definitions.* For purposes of this paragraph (c)(5), the following definitions apply:

(A) *Royalties—(1) In general. Royalties* means all royalties, including mineral, oil, and gas royalties, and amounts received for the privilege of using patents, copyrights, secret processes and formulas, good will, trademarks, tradebrands, franchises, and other like property. The gross amount of royalties is not reduced by any part of the cost of the rights under which the royalties are received or by any amount allowable as a deduction in computing taxable income.

(2) *Royalties derived in the ordinary course of a trade or business. Royalties* does not include royalties derived in the ordinary course of a trade or business of franchising or licensing property. Royalties received by a corporation are derived in the ordinary course of a trade or business of franchising or licensing property only if, based on all the facts and circumstances, the corporation—

(i) Created the property; or

(ii) Performed significant services or incurred substantial costs with respect to the development or marketing of the property.

(3) *Copyright, mineral, oil and gas, and active business computer software royalties. Royalties* does not include copyright royalties, nor mineral, oil and gas royalties if the income from those royalties would not be treated as personal holding company income under sections 543(a)(3) and (a)(4) if the corporation were a C corporation; amounts received upon disposal of timber, coal, or domestic iron ore with respect to which the special rules of sections 631(b) and (c) apply; and active business computer software royalties as defined under section 543(d) (without regard to paragraph (d)(5) of section 543).

(B) *Rents—(1) In general. Rents* means amounts received for the use of, or right to use,

Reg. § 1.1362-2(c)(5)

property (whether real or personal) of the corporation.

(2) *Rents derived in the active trade or business of renting property.* Rents does not include rents derived in the active trade or business of renting property. Rents received by a corporation are derived in an active trade or business of renting property only if, based on all the facts and circumstances, the corporation provides significant services or incurs substantial costs in the rental business. Generally, significant services are not rendered and substantial costs are not incurred in connection with net leases. Whether significant services are performed or substantial costs are incurred in the rental business is determined based upon all the facts and circumstances including, but not limited to, the number of persons employed to provide the services and the types and amounts of costs and expenses incurred (other than depreciation).

(3) *Produced film rents.* Rents does not include produced film rents as defined under section 543(a)(5).

(4) *Income from leasing self-produced tangible property.* Rents does not include compensation, however designated, for the use of, or right to use, any real or tangible personal property developed, manufactured, or produced by the taxpayer, if during the taxable year the taxpayer is engaged in substantial development, manufacturing, or production of real or tangible personal property of the same type.

(C) *Dividends. Dividends* includes dividends as defined in section 316, amounts to be included in gross income under section 551 (relating to foreign personal holding company income taxed to U.S. shareholders), and consent dividends as provided in section 565. See paragraphs (c)(5)(iii)(B) and (C) of this section for special rules for the treatment of certain dividends and certain payments to a patron of a cooperative. See § 1.1362-8 for special rules regarding the treatment of dividends received by an S corporation from a C corporation in which the S corporation holds stock meeting the requirements of section 1504(a)(2).

(D) *Interest—(1) In general. Interest* means any amount received for the use of money (including tax-exempt interest and amounts treated as interest under section 483, 1272, 1274, or 7872). See paragraph (c)(5)(iii)(B) of this section for a special rule for the treatment of interest derived in certain businesses.

(2) *Interest on obligations acquired in the ordinary course of a trade or business.* Interest does not include interest on any obligation acquired from the sale of property described in section 1221(1) or the performance of services

in the ordinary course of a trade or business of selling the property or performing the services.

(E) *Annuities. Annuities* means the entire amount received as an annuity under an annuity, endowment, or life insurance contract, if any part of the amount would be includible in gross income under section 72.

(F) *Gross receipts from the sale of stock or securities.* Gross receipts from the sales or exchanges of stock or securities, as described in paragraph (c)(4)(ii)(B) of this section, are passive investment income to the extent of gains therefrom. See paragraph (c)(5)(iii)(B) of this section for a special rule for the treatment of gains derived in certain businesses.

(G) *Identified income. Passive investment income* does not include income identified by the Commissioner by regulations, revenue ruling, or revenue procedure as income derived in the ordinary course of a trade or business for purposes of this section.

(iii) *Special rules.* For purposes of this paragraph (c)(5), the following special rules apply:

(A) *Options or commodities dealers.* In the case of an options dealer or commodities dealer, *passive investment income* does not include any gain or loss (in the normal course of the taxpayer's activity of dealing in or trading section 1256 contracts) from any section 1256 contract or property related to the contract. *Options dealer, commodities dealer,* and *section 1256 contract* have the same meaning as in section 1362(d)(3)(E)(ii).

(B) *Treatment of certain lending, financing and other businesses—(1) In general.* Passive investment income does not include gross receipts that are directly derived in the ordinary course of a trade or business of—

(*i*) Lending or financing;

(*ii*) Dealing in property;

(*iii*) Purchasing or discounting accounts receivable, notes, or installment obligations; or

(*iv*) Servicing mortgages.

(2) *Directly derived.* For purposes of this paragraph (c)(5)(iii)(B), gross receipts directly derived in the ordinary course of business includes gain (as well as interest income) with respect to loans originated in a lending business, or interest income (as well as gain) from debt obligations of a dealer in such obligations. However, interest earned from the investment of idle funds in short-term securities does not constitute gross receipts directly derived in the ordinary course of business. Similarly, a dealer's income or gain from an item of property is not directly derived in the ordinary course of its trade or

Reg. § 1.1362-2(c)(5)

business if the dealer held the property for investment at any time before the income or gain is
recognized.

(C) *Payment to a patron of a cooperative. Passive investment income* does not include
amounts included in the gross income of a patron
of a cooperative (within the meaning of section
1381(a), without regard to paragraph (2)(A) or
(C) of section 1381(a)) by reason of any payment
or allocation to the patron based on patronage
occurring in the case of a trade or business of the
patron.

(6) *Examples.* The principles of paragraphs
(c)(4) and (c)(5) of this section are illustrated by
the following examples. Unless otherwise provided
in an example, *S* is an S corporation with subchapter C earnings and profits, and *S*'s gross receipts from operations are gross receipts not
derived from royalties, rents, dividends, interest,
annuities, or gains from the sales or exchanges of
stock or securities. *S* is a calendar year taxpayer
and its first taxable year as an S corporation is
1993.

*Example 1. Sales of capital assets, stock and
securities.* (i) *S* uses an accrual method of accounting and sells:

(1) a depreciable asset, held for more than 6
months, which is used in the corporation's
business;

(2) a capital asset (other than stock or securities) for a gain;

(3) a capital asset (other than stock or securities) for a loss; and

(4) securities.

S receives payment for each asset partly in money
and partly in the form of a note payable at a
future time, and elects not to report the sales on
the installment method.

(ii) The amount of money and the face
amount (or issue price if different) of the note
received for the business asset are considered
gross receipts in the taxable year of sale and are
not reduced by the adjusted basis of the property,
costs of sale, or any other amount. With respect to
the sales of the capital assets, gross receipts include the cash down payment and face amount (or
issue price if different) of any notes, but only to
the extent of *S*'s capital gain net income. In the
case of the sale of the securities, gross receipts
include the cash down payment and face amount
(or issue price if different) of the notes, but only to
the extent of gain on the sale. In determining
gross receipts from sales of securities, losses are
not netted against gains.

*Example 2. Long-term contract reported on
percentage-of-completion method. S* has a long-
term contract as defined in § 1.460-1(b)(1) with

respect to which it reports income according to
the percentage-of-completion method as described
in § 1.460-4(b). The portion of the gross contract
price which corresponds to the percentage of the
entire contract which has been completed during
the taxable year is included in *S*'s gross receipts
for the year.

*Example 3. Income reported on installment
sale method.* For its 1993 taxable year, *S* sells
personal property on the installment plan and
elects to report its taxable income from the sale of
the property (other than property qualifying as a
capital asset or stock or securities) on the installment method in accordance with section 453. The
installment payment actually received in a given
taxable year of *S* is included in gross receipts for
the year.

Example 4. Partnership interests. In 1993, *S*
and two of its shareholders contribute cash to
form a general partnership, *PRS. S* receives a 50
percent interest in the capital and profits of *PRS.
S* formed *PRS* to indirectly invest in marketable
stocks and securities. The only assets of *PRS* are
the stock and securities, and certain real and
tangible personal property. In 1994, *S* needs cash
in its business and sells its partnership interest at
a gain rather than having *PRS* sell the marketable stock or securities that have appreciated.
Under paragraph (c)(4)(ii)(B)(*4*) of this section,
the gain on *S*'s disposition of its interest in *PRS* is
treated as gain from the sale or exchange of stock
or securities to the extent of the amount the
distributive share of gain *S* would have received
from the sale of stock or securities held by *PRS* if
PRS has sold all of its stock or securities at fair
market value at the time *S* disposed of its interest
in *PRS*.

*Example 5. Royalties derived in ordinary
course of trade or business.* (i) In 1993, *S* has gross
receipts of $75,000. Of this amount, $5,000 is
from royalty payments with respect to Trademark A, $8,000 is from royalty payments with
respect to Trademark B, and $62,000 is gross
receipts from operations. *S* created Trademark A,
but *S* did not create Trademark B or perform
significant services or incur substantial costs with
respect to the development or marketing of
Trademark B.

(ii) Because *S* created Trademark A, the royalty payments with respect to Trademark A are
derived in the ordinary course of *S*'s business and
are not included within the definition of *royalties*
for purposes of determining *S*'s passive investment income. However, the royalty payments
with respect to Trademark B are included within
the definition of *royalties* for purposes of determining *S*'s passive investment income. See paragraph (c)(5)(ii)(A) of this section. *S*'s passive

Reg. § 1.1362-2(c)(6)

investment income for the year is $8,000, and S's passive investment income percentage for the taxable year is 10.67% ($8,000/$75,000). This does not exceed 25 percent of S's gross receipts and consequently the three-year period described in section 1362(d)(3) does not begin to run.

Example 6. Dividends; gain on sale of stock derived in the ordinary course of trade or business. (i) In 1993, S receives dividends of $10,000 on stock of corporations P and O, recognizes a gain of $25,000 on sale of the P stock, and recognizes a loss of $12,000 on sale of the O stock. S held the P and O stock for investment, rather than for sale in the ordinary course of a trade or business. S has gross receipts from operations and from gain on the sale of stock in the ordinary course of its trade or business of $110,000.

(ii) S's gross receipts are calculated as follows:

$110,000	Gross receipts from operations and from gain on the sale of stock in the ordinary course of a trade or business
10,000	Gross dividend receipts
25,000	Gain on sale of P stock (Loss on O stock not taken into account)
$145,000	Total gross receipts

(iii) S's passive investment income is determined as follows:

$10,000	Gross dividend receipts
25,000	Gain on sale of P stock (Loss on O stock not taken into account)
$35,000	Total passive investment income

(iv) S's passive investment income percentage for its first year as an S corporation is 24.1% ($35,000/$145,000). This does not exceed 25 percent of S's gross receipts and consequently the three-year period described in section 1362(d)(3) does not begin to run.

Example 7. Interest on accounts receivable; netting of gain on sale of real property investments. (i) In 1993, S receives $6,000 of interest on accounts receivable arising from S's sales of inventory property. S also receives dividends with respect to stock held for investment of $1,500. In addition, S sells two parcels of real property (Property J and Property K) that S had purchased and held for investment. S sells Property J, in which S has a basis of $5,000, for $10,000 (a gain of $5,000). S sells Property K, in which S has a basis of $12,000, for $9,000 (a loss of $3,000). S has gross receipts from operations of $90,000.

(ii) S's gross receipts are calculated as follows:

$90,000	Gross receipts from operations
6,000	Gross interest receipts
1,500	Gross dividend receipts
2,000	Net gain on sale of real property investments
$99,500	Total gross receipts

(iii) Under paragraph (c)(5)(ii)(D) of this section, S's gross interest receipts are not passive investment income. In addition, gain on the sale of real property ($2,000) is not passive investment income. S's passive investment income includes only the $1,500 of gross dividend receipts. Accordingly, S's passive investment income percentage for its first year as an S corporation is 1.51% ($1,500/$99,500). This does not exceed 25 percent of S's gross receipts and consequently the three-year period described in section 1362(d)(3) does not begin to run.

Example 8. Interest received in the ordinary course of a lending business. (i) In 1993, S has gross receipts of $100,000 from loans and investments made in the ordinary course of S's mortgage banking business. This includes, for example, mortgage servicing fees, interest earned on mortgages prior to sale of the mortgages, and gain on sale of mortgages. In addition, S receives, from the investment of idle funds in short-term securities, $15,000 of gross interest income and $5,000 of gain.

(ii) S's gross receipts are calculated as follows:

$100,000	Gross receipts from operations
15,000	Gross interest receipts
5,000	Gain on sale of securities
$120,000	Total gross receipts

Reg. § 1.1362-2(c)(6)

(iii) *S*'s passive investment income is determined as follows:

$15,000	Gross interest receipts
5,000	Gain on sale of securities
$20,000	Total passive investment income

(iv) *S*'s passive investment income percentage for its first year as an S corporation is 16.67% ($20,000/$120,000). This does not exceed 25 percent of *S*'s gross receipts and consequently the three-year period described in section 1362(d)(3) does not begin to run. [Reg. § 1.1362-2.]

☐ [*T.D.* 8449, 11-24-92. *Amended by T.D.* 8869, 1-20-2000 *and T.D.* 8995, 5-14-2002.]

§ 1.1362-3. Treatment of S termination year.—(a) *In general.* If an S election terminates under section 1362(d) on a date other than the first day of a taxable year of the corporation, the corporation's taxable year in which the termination occurs is an S termination year. The portion of the S termination year ending at the close of the day prior to the termination is treated as a short taxable year for which the corporation is an S corporation (the *S short year*). The portion of the S termination year beginning on the day the termination is effective is treated as a short taxable year for which the corporation is a C corporation (the *C short year*). Except as provided in paragraphs (b) and (c)(1) of this section, the corporation allocates income or loss for the entire year on a pro rata basis as described in section 1362(e)(2). To the extent that income or loss is not allocated on a pro rata basis under this section, items of income, gain, loss, deduction, and credit are assigned to each short taxable year on the basis of the corporation's normal method of accounting as determined under section 446. See, however, § 1.1502-76(b)(1)(ii)(A)(*2*) for special rules for an S election that terminates under section 1362(d) immediately before the S corporation becomes a member of a consolidated group (within the meaning of § 1.1502-1(h)).

(b) *Allocations other than pro rata*—(1) *Elections under section 1362(e)(3).* The pro rata allocation rules of section 1362(e)(2) do not apply if the corporation elects to allocate its S termination year income on the basis of its normal tax accounting method. This election may be made only with the consent of each person who is a shareholder in the corporation at any time during the S short year and of each person who is a shareholder in the corporation on the first day of the C short year. See § 1.1362-6(a) for rules concerning the time and manner of making this election.

(2) *Purchase of stock treated as an asset purchase.* The pro rata allocation rules of section 1362(e)(2) do not apply with respect to any item resulting from the application of section 338.

(3) *50 percent change in ownership during S termination year.* The pro rata allocation rules of section 1362(e)(2) do not apply if at any time during the S termination year, as a result of sales or exchanges of stock in the corporation during that year, there is a change in ownership of 50 percent or more of the issued and outstanding shares of stock of the corporation. If stock has already been sold or exchanged during the S termination year, subsequent sales or exchanges of that stock are not taken into account for purposes of this paragraph (b)(3).

(c) *Special rules*—(1) *S corporation that is a partner in a partnership.* For purposes of section 706(c) only, the termination of the election of an S corporation that is a partner in a partnership during any portion of the S short year under § 1.1362-2(a) or (b), is treated as a sale or exchange of the corporation's entire interest in the partnership on the last day of the S short year, if—

(i) The pro rata allocation rules do not apply to the corporation; and

(ii) Any taxable year of the partnership ends with or within the C short year.

(2) *Tax for the C short year.* The taxable income for the C short year is determined on an annualized basis as described in section 1362(e)(5).

(3) *Each short year treated as taxable year.* Except as otherwise provided in paragraph (c)(4) of this section, the S and C short years are treated as two separate years for purposes of all provisions of the Internal Revenue Code.

(4) *Year for carryover purposes.* The S and C short years are treated as one year for purposes of determining the number of taxable years to which any item may be carried back or forward by the corporation.

(5) *Due date for S short year return.* The date by which the return for the S short year must be filed is the same as the date by which the return for the C short year must be filed (including extensions).

(6) *Year in which income from S short year is includible.* A shareholder must include in taxable income the shareholder's pro rata share of the items described in section 1366(a) for the S short year for the taxable year with or within which the S termination year ends.

Reg. § 1.1362-3(a)

(d) *Examples.* The provisions of this section are illustrated by the following examples:

Example 1. S termination year not created. (i) On January 1, 1993, the first day of its taxable year, a subchapter C corporation had three eligible shareholders. During 1993, the corporation properly elected to be treated as an S corporation effective January 1, 1994, the first day of the succeeding taxable year. Subsequently, a transfer of some of the stock in the corporation was made to an ineligible shareholder. The ineligible shareholder still holds the stock on January 1, 1994.

(ii) The corporation fails to meet the definition of a small business corporation on January 1, 1994, and its election is treated as having terminated on that date. See § 1.1362-2(b)(2) for the termination rules. Because the corporation ceases to be a small business corporation on the first day of a taxable year, an S termination year is not created. In addition, if the corporation in the future meets the definition of a small business corporation and desires to elect to be treated as an S corporation, the corporation is automatically granted consent to reelect before the expiration of the 5-year waiting period. See § 1.1362-5 for special rules concerning automatic consent to reelect.

Example 2. More than 50 percent change in ownership during S short year. A, an individual, owns all 100 outstanding shares of stock of S, a calendar year S corporation. On January 31, 1993, A sells 60 shares of S stock to B, an individual. On June 1, 1993, A sells 5 shares of S stock to PRS, a partnership. S ceases to be a small business corporation on June 1, 1993, and pursuant to section 1362(d)(2), its election terminates on that date. Because there was a more than 50 percent change in ownership of the issued and outstanding shares of S stock, S must assign the items of income, loss, deduction, or credit for the S termination year to the two short taxable years on the basis of S's normal method of accounting under the rules of paragraph (b)(3) of this section.

Example 3. More than 50 percent change in ownership during C short year. A, an individual, owns all 100 outstanding shares of stock of S, a calendar year S corporation. On June 1, 1993, A sells 5 shares of S stock to PRS, a partnership. S ceases to be a small business corporation on that date and pursuant to section 1362(d)(3), its election terminates on that date. On July 1, 1993, A sells 60 shares of S stock to B, an individual. Since there was a more than 50 percent change in ownership of the issued and outstanding shares of S stock during the S termination year, S must assign the items of income, loss, deduction, or credit for the S termination year to the two short taxable years on the basis of S's normal method of

accounting under the rules of paragraph (b)(3) of this section.

Example 4. Stock acquired other than by sale or exchange. C and D are shareholders in S, a calendar year S corporation. Each owns 50 percent of the issued and outstanding shares of the corporation on December 31, 1993. On March 1, 1994, C makes a gift of his entire shareholder interest to T, a trust not permitted as a shareholder under section 1361(c)(2). S ceases to be a small business corporation on March 1, 1994, and pursuant to section 1362(d)(2), its S corporation election terminates effective on that date. As a result of the gift, T owns 50 percent of S's issued and outstanding stock. However, because T acquired the stock by gift from C rather than by sale or exchange, there has not been a more than 50 percent change in ownership by sale or exchange of S that would cause the rules of paragraph (b)(3) of this section to apply. [Reg. § 1.1362-3.]

☐ [*T.D. 8449, 11-24-92. Amended by T.D. 8842, 11-9-99.*]

§ 1.1362-4. Inadvertent terminations.—(a) *In general.* A corporation is treated as continuing to be an S corporation during the period specified by the Commissioner if—

(1) The corporation made a valid election under section 1362(a) and the election terminated;

(2) The Commissioner determines that the termination was inadvertent;

(3) Steps were taken by the corporation to return to small business corporation status within a reasonable period after discovery of the terminating event; and

(4) The corporation and shareholders agree to adjustments that the Commissioner may require for the period.

(b) *Inadvertent termination.* For purposes of paragraph (a) of this section, the determination of whether a termination was inadvertent is made by the Commissioner. The corporation has the burden of establishing that under the relevant facts and circumstances the Commissioner should determine that the termination was inadvertent. The fact that the terminating event was not reasonably within the control of the corporation and was not part of a plan to terminate the election, or the fact that the event took place without the knowledge of the corporation, notwithstanding its due diligence to safeguard itself against such an event, tends to establish that the termination was inadvertent.

(c) *Corporation's request for determination of an inadvertent termination.* A corporation that believes its election was terminated inadvertently may request a determination of inadvertent termination from the Commissioner. The request is made in the form of a ruling request and should set forth all relevant facts pertaining to the event including, but not limited to, the facts described in paragraph (b) of this section, the date of the corporation's election under section 1362(a), a detailed explanation of the event causing termination, when and how the event was discovered, and the steps taken to return the corporation to small business corporation status.

(d) *Adjustments.* The Commissioner may require any adjustments that are appropriate. In general, the adjustments required should be consistent with the treatment of the corporation as an S corporation during the period specified by the Commissioner. In the case of a transfer of stock to an ineligible shareholder that causes an inadvertent termination under section 1362(f), the Commissioner may require the ineligible shareholder to be treated as a shareholder of an S corporation during the period the ineligible shareholder actually held stock in the corporation. Moreover, the Commissioner may require protective adjustments that prevent any loss of revenue due to a transfer of stock to an ineligible shareholder (*e.g.*, a transfer to a nonresident alien).

(e) *Corporation and shareholder consents.* The corporation and all persons who were shareholders of the corporation at any time during the period specified by the Commissioner must consent to any adjustments that the Commissioner may require. Each consent should be in the form of a statement agreeing to make the adjustments. The statement must be signed by the shareholder (in the case of shareholder consent) or a person authorized to sign the return required by section 6037 (in the case of corporate consent). See § 1.1362-6(b)(2) for persons required to sign consents. A shareholder's consent statement should include the name, address, and taxpayer identification numbers of the corporation and shareholder, the number of shares of stock owned by the shareholder, and the dates on which the shareholder owned any stock. The corporate consent statement should include the name, address, and taxpayer identification numbers of the corporation and each shareholder.

(f) *Status of corporation.* The status of the corporation after the terminating event and before the determination of inadvertence is determined by the Commissioner. Inadvertent termination relief may be granted retroactive for all years for which the terminating event was effective, in which case the corporation is treated as if its election had not terminated. Alternatively, relief may be granted only for the period in which the corporation again became eligible for subchapter S treatment, in which case the corporation is treated as a C corporation during the period for which the corporation was not eligible to be an S corporation. [Reg. § 1.1362-4.]

☐ [*T.D.* 8449, 11-24-92.]

§ 1.1362-5. Election after termination.—(a) *In general.* Absent the Commissioner's consent, an S corporation whose election has terminated (or a successor corporation) may not make a new election under section 1362(a) for five taxable years as described in section 1362(g). However, the Commissioner may permit the corporation to make a new election before the 5-year period expires. The corporation has the burden of establishing that under the relevant facts and circumstances, the Commissioner should consent to a new election. The fact that more than 50 percent of the stock in the corporation is owned by persons who did not own any stock in the corporation on the date of the termination tends to establish that consent should be granted. In the absence of this fact, consent ordinarily is denied unless the corporation shows that the event causing termination was not reasonably within the control of the corporation or shareholders having a substantial interest in the corporation and was not part of a plan on the part of the corporation or of such shareholders to terminate the election.

(b) *Successor corporation.* A corporation is a *successor corporation* to a corporation whose election under section 1362 has been terminated if—

(1) 50 percent or more of the stock of the corporation (the new corporation) is owned, directly or indirectly, by the same persons who, on the date of the termination, owned 50 percent or more of the stock of the corporation whose election terminated (the old corporation); and

(2) Either the new corporation acquires a substantial portion of the assets of the old corporation, or a substantial portion of the assets of the new corporation were assets of the old corporation.

(c) *Automatic consent after certain terminations.* A corporation may, without requesting the Commissioner's consent, make a new election under section 1362(a) before the 5-year period described in section 1362(g) expires if the termination occurred because the corporation—

(1) Revoked its election effective on the first day of the first taxable year for which its election was to be effective (see § 1.1362-2(a)(2)); or

(2) Failed to meet the definition of a small business corporation on the first day of the first taxable year for which its election was to be effective (see § 1.1362-2(b)(2)). [Reg. § 1.1362-5.]

☐ [*T.D.* 8449, 11-24-92.]

§ 1.1362-6. Elections and consents.—(a) *Time and manner of making elections*—(1) *In general.* An election statement made under this section must identify the election being made, set forth the name, address, and taxpayer identification number of the corporation, and be signed by a person authorized to sign the return required to be filed under section 6037.

Reg. § 1.1362-5(a)

(2) *Election to be an S corporation*—(i) *Manner of making election.* A small business corporation makes an election under section 1362(a) to be an S corporation by filing a completed Form 2553. The election form must be filed with the service center designated in the instructions applicable to Form 2553. The election is not valid unless all shareholders of the corporation at the time of the election consent to the election in the manner provided in paragraph (b) of this section. However, once a valid election is made, new shareholders need not consent to that election.

(ii) *Time of making election*—(A) *In general.* The election described in paragraph (a)(2)(i) of this section may be made by a small business corporation at any time during the taxable year that immediately precedes the taxable year for which the election is to be effective, or during the taxable year for which the election is to be effective provided that the election is made before the 16th day of the third month of the year. If a corporation makes an election for a taxable year, and the election meets all the requirements of this section but is made during the period beginning after the 15th day of the third month of the taxable year, the election is treated as being made for the following taxable year provided that the corporation meets all the requirements of section 1361(b) at the time the election is made. For taxable years of 2½ months or less, an election made before the 16th day of the third month after the first day of the taxable year is treated as made during that year.

(B) *Elections made during the first 2½ months treated as made for the following taxable year.* A timely election made by a small business corporation during the taxable year for which it is intended to be effective is nonetheless treated as made for the following taxable year if—

(*1*) The corporation is not a small business corporation during the entire portion of the taxable year which occurs before the date the election is made; or

(*2*) Any person who held stock in the corporation at any time during the portion of the taxable year which occurs before the time the election is made, and who does not hold stock at the time the election is made, does not consent to the election.

(C) *Definition of month and beginning of the taxable year. Month* means a period commencing on the same numerical day of any calendar month as the day of the calendar month on which the taxable year began and ending with the close of the day preceding the numerically corresponding day of the succeeding calendar month or, if there is no corresponding day, with the close of the last day of the succeeding calendar month.

In addition, the taxable year of a new corporation begins on the date that the corporation has shareholders, acquires assets, or begins doing business, whichever is the first to occur. The existence of incorporators does not necessarily begin the taxable year of a new corporation.

(iii) *Examples.* The provisions of this section are illustrated by the following examples:

Example 1. Effective election; no prior taxable year. A calendar year small business corporation begins its first taxable year on January 7, 1993. To be an S corporation beginning with its first taxable year, the corporation must make the election set forth in this section during the period that begins January 7, 1993, and ends before March 22, 1993. Because the corporation had no taxable year immediately preceding the taxable year for which the election is to be effective, an election made earlier than January 7, 1993, will not be valid.

Example 2. Effective election; taxable year less than 2½ months. A calendar year small business corporation begins its first taxable year on November 8, 1993. To be an S corporation beginning with its first taxable year, the corporation must make the election set forth in this section during the period that begins November 8, 1993, and ends before January 23, 1994.

Example 3. Election effective for the following taxable year; ineligible shareholder. On January 1, 1993, two individuals and a partnership own all of the stock of a calendar year subchapter C corporation. On January 31, 1993, the partnership dissolved and distributed its shares in the corporation to its five partners, all individuals. On February 28, 1993, the seven shareholders of the corporation consented to the corporation's election of subchapter S status. The corporation files a properly completed Form 2553 on March 2, 1993. The corporation is not eligible to be a subchapter S corporation for the 1993 taxable year because during the period of the taxable year prior to the election it had an ineligible shareholder. However, under paragraph (a)(2)(ii)(B) of this section, the election is treated as made for the corporation's 1994 taxable year.

(3) *Revocation of S election*—(i) *Manner of revoking election.* To revoke an election, the corporation files a statement that the corporation revokes the election made under section 1362(a). The statement must be filed with the service center where the election was properly filed. The revocation statement must include the number of shares of stock (including non-voting stock) issued and outstanding at the time the revocation is made. A revocation may be made only with the consent of shareholders who, at the time the revocation is made, hold more than one-half of the

Reg. § 1.1362-6(a)(3)

number of issued and outstanding shares of stock (including non-voting stock) of the corporation. Each shareholder who consents to the revocation must consent in the manner required under paragraph (b) of this section. In addition, each consent should indicate the number of issued and outstanding shares of stock (including non-voting stock) held by each shareholder at the time of the revocation.

(ii) *Time of revoking election.* For rules concerning when a revocation is effective, see § 1.1362-2(a)(2).

(iii) *Examples.* The principles of this paragraph (a)(3) are illustrated by the following examples:

Example 1. Revocation; consent of shareholders owning more than one-half of issued and outstanding shares. A calendar year S corporation has issued and outstanding 40,000 shares of class A voting common stock and 20,000 shares of class B non-voting common stock. The corporation wishes to revoke its election of subchapter S status. Shareholders owning 11,000 shares of class A stock sign revocation consents. Shareholders owning 20,000 shares of class B stock sign revocation consents. The corporation has obtained the required shareholder consent to revoke its subchapter S election because shareholders owning more than one-half of the total number of issued and outstanding shares of stock of the corporation consented to the revocation.

Example 2. Effective prospective revocation. In June 1993, a calendar year S corporation determines that it will revoke its subchapter S election effective August 1, 1993. To do so it must file its revocation statement with consents attached on or before August 1, 1993, and the statement must indicate that the revocation is intended to be effective August 1, 1993.

(4) *Rescission of a revocation*—(i) *Manner of rescinding a revocation.* To rescind a revocation, the corporation files a statement that the corporation rescinds the revocation made under section 1362(d)(1). The statement must be filed with the service center where the revocation was properly filed. A rescission may be made only with the consent (in the manner required under paragraph (b)(1) of this section) of each person who consented to the revocation and of each person who became a shareholder of the corporation within the period beginning on the first day after the date the revocation was made and ending on the date on which the rescission is made.

(ii) *Time of rescinding a revocation.* If the rescission statement is filed before the revocation becomes effective and is filed with proper service center, the rescission is effective on the date it is so filed.

(5) *Election not to apply pro rata allocation.* To elect not to apply the pro rata allocation rules to an S termination year, a corporation files a statement that it elects under section 1362(e)(3) not to apply the rules provided in section 1362(e)(2). In addition to meeting the requirements of paragraph (a)(1) of this section, the statement must set forth the cause of the termination and the date thereof. The statement must be filed with the corporation's return for the C short year. This election may be made only with the consent of all persons who are shareholders of the corporation at any time during the S short year and all persons who are shareholders of the corporation on the first day of the C short year (in the manner required under paragraph (b)(1) of this section).

(b) *Shareholders' consents*—(1) *Manner of consents in general.* A shareholder's consent required under paragraph (a) of this section must be in the form of a written statement that sets forth the name, address, and taxpayer identification number of the shareholder, the number of shares of stock owned by the shareholder, the date (or dates) on which the stock was acquired, the date on which the shareholder's taxable year ends, the name of the S corporation, the corporation's taxpayer identification number, and the election to which the shareholder consents. The statement must be signed by the shareholder under penalties of perjury. Except as provided in paragraph (b)(3)(iii) of this section, the election of the corporation is not valid if any required consent is not filed in accordance with the rules contained in this paragraph (b). The consent statement should be attached to the corporation's election statement.

(2) *Persons required to consent.* The following rules apply in determining persons required to consent:

(i) *Community interest in stock.* When stock of the corporation is owned by husband and wife as community property (or the income from the stock is community property), or is owned by tenants in common, joint tenants, or tenants by the entirety, each person having a community interest in the stock or income therefrom and each tenant in common, joint tenant and tenant by the entirety must consent to the election.

(ii) *Minor.* The consent of a minor must be made by the minor or by the legal representative of the minor (or by a natural or an adoptive parent of the minor if no legal representative has been appointed).

(iii) *Estate.* The consent of an estate must be made by an executor or administrator thereof, or by any other fiduciary appointed by testamen-

Reg. § 1.1362-6(a)(4)

tary instrument or appointed by the court having jurisdiction over the administration of the estate.

(iv) *Trusts.* In the case of a trust described in section 1361(c)(2)(A) (including a trust treated under section 1361(d)(1)(A) as a trust described in section 1361(c)(2)(A)(i) and excepting an electing small business trust described in section 1361(c)(2)(A)(v) (ESBT)), only the person treated as the shareholder for purposes of section 1361(b)(1) must consent to the election. When stock of the corporation is held by a trust, both husband and wife must consent to any election if the husband and wife have a community interest in the trust property. See paragraph (b)(2)(i) of this section for rules concerning community interests in S corporation stock. In the case of an ESBT, the trustee and the owner of any portion of the trust that consists of the stock in one or more S corporations under subpart E, part I, subchapter J, chapter 1 of the Internal Revenue Code must consent to the S corporation election. If there is more than one trustee, the trustee or trustees with authority to legally bind the trust must consent to the S corporation election.

(3) *Special rules for consent of shareholder to election to be an S corporation*—(i) *In general.* The consent of a shareholder to an election by a small business corporation under section 1362(a) may be made on Form 2553 or on a separate statement in the manner described in paragraph (b)(1) of this section. In addition, the separate statement must set forth the name, address, and taxpayer identification number of the corporation. A shareholder's consent is binding and may not be withdrawn after a valid election is made by the corporation. Each person who is a shareholder (including any person who is treated as a shareholder under section 1361(c)(2)(B)) at the time the election is made) must consent to the election. If the election is made before the 16th day of the third month of the taxable year and is intended to be effective for that year, each person who was a shareholder (including any person who was treated as a shareholder under section 1361(c)(2)(B)) at any time during the portion of that year which occurs before the time the election is made, and who is not a shareholder at the time the election is made, must also consent to the election. If the election is to be effective for the following taxable year, no consent need be filed by any shareholder who is not a shareholder on the date of the election. Any person who is considered to be a shareholder under applicable state law solely by virtue of his or her status as an incorporator is not treated as a shareholder for purposes of this paragraph (b)(3)(i).

(ii) *Examples.* The principles of this section are illustrated by the following examples:

Example 1. Effective election; shareholder consents. On January 1, 1993, the first day of its taxable year, a subchapter C corporation had 15 shareholders. On January 30, 1993, two of the C corporation's shareholders, *A* and *B,* both individuals, sold their shares in the corporation to *P, Q,* and *R,* all individuals. On March 1, 1993, the corporation filed its election to be an S corporation for the 1993 taxable year. The election will be effective (assuming the other requirements of section 1361(b) are met) provided that all of the shareholders as of March 1, 1993, as well as former shareholders *A* and *B,* consent to the election.

Example 2. Consent of new shareholder unnecessary. On January 1, 1993, three individuals own all of the stock of a calendar year subchapter C corporation. On April 15, 1993, the corporation, in accordance with paragraph (a)(2) of this section, files a properly completed Form 2553. The corporation anticipates that the election will be effective beginning January 1, 1994, the first day of the succeeding taxable year. On October 1, 1993, the three shareholders collectively sell 75% of their shares in the corporation to another individual. On January 1, 1994, the corporation's shareholders are the three original individuals and the new shareholder. Because the election was valid and binding when made, it is not necessary for the new shareholder to consent to the election. The corporation's subchapter S election is effective on January 1, 1994 (assuming the other requirements of section 1361(b) are met).

(iii) *Extension of time for filing consents to an election*—(A) *In general.* An election that is timely filed for any taxable year and that would be valid except for the failure of any shareholder to file a timely consent is not invalid if consents are filed as required under paragraph (b)(3)(iii)(B) of this section and it is shown to the satisfaction of the district director or director of the service center with which the corporation files its income tax return that—

(*1*) There was reasonable cause for the failure to file the consent;

(*2*) The request for the extension of time to file a consent is made within a reasonable time under the circumstances; and

(*3*) The interests of the Government will not be jeopardized by treating the election as valid.

(B) *Required consents.* Consents must be filed within the extended period of time as may be granted by the Internal Revenue Service, by all persons who—

(*1*) Were shareholders of the corporation at any time during the period beginning as of the date of the invalid election and ending on the date on which an extension of time is granted in accordance with this paragraph (b)(3)(iii); and

(*2*) Have not previously consented to the election. [Reg. § 1.1362-6.]

☐ [*T.D.* 8449, 11-24-92. *Amended by T.D.* 8994, 5-13-2002.]

§ 1.1362-8. Dividends received from affiliated subsidiaries.—(a) *In general.* For purposes of section 1362(d)(3), if an S corporation holds stock in a C corporation meeting the requirements of section 1504(a)(2), the term *passive investment income* does not include dividends from the C corporation to the extent those dividends are attributable to the earnings and profits of the C corporation derived from the active conduct of a trade or business (active earnings and profits). For purposes of applying section 1362(d)(3), earnings and profits of a C corporation are active earnings and profits to the extent that the earnings and profits are derived from activities that would not produce passive investment income (as defined in section 1362(d)(3)) if the C corporation were an S corporation.

* * *

[Reg. § 1.1362-8.]

☐ [*T.D.* 8869, 1-20-2000 (*corrected* 3-27-2000).]

§ 1.1363-1. Effect of election on corporation.—(a) *Exemption of corporation from income tax*—(1) *In general.* Except as provided in this paragraph (a), a small business corporation that makes a valid election under section 1362(a) is exempt from the taxes imposed by chapter 1 of the Internal Revenue Code with respect to taxable years of the corporation for which the election is in effect.

(2) *Corporate level taxes.* An S corporation is not exempt from the tax imposed by section 1374 (relating to the tax imposed on certain built-in gains), or section 1375 (relating to the tax on excess passive investment income). See also section 1363(d) (relating to the recapture of LIFO benefits) for the rules regarding the payment by an S corporation of LIFO recapture amounts.

(b) *Computation of corporate taxable income.* The taxable income of an S corporation is computed as described in section 1363(b).

(c) *Elections of the S corporation*—(1) *In general.* Any elections (other than those described in paragraph (c)(2) of this section) affecting the computation of items derived from an S corporation are made by the corporation. For example, elections of methods of accounting, of computing depreciation, of treating soil and water conservation expenditures, and the option to deduct as expenses intangible drilling and development costs, are made by the corporation and not by the

shareholders separately. All corporate elections are applicable to all shareholders.

(2) *Exceptions.* (i) Each shareholder's pro rata share of expenses described in section 617 paid or accrued by the S corporation is treated according to the shareholder's method of treating those expenses, notwithstanding the treatment of the expenses by the corporation.

(ii) Each shareholder may elect to amortize that shareholder's pro rata share of any qualified expenditure described in section 59(e) paid or accrued by the S corporation.

(iii) Each shareholder's pro rata share of taxes described in section 901 paid or accrued by the S corporation to foreign countries or possessions of the United States (according to its method of treating those taxes) is treated according to the shareholder's method of treating those taxes, and each shareholder may elect to use the total amount either as a credit against tax or as a deduction from income.

* * *

[Reg. § 1.1363-1.]

☐ [*T.D.* 8449, 11-24-92.]

§ 1.1366-1. Shareholder's share of items of an S corporation.—(a) *Determination of shareholder's tax liability*—(1) *In general.* An S corporation must report, and a shareholder is required to take into account in the shareholder's return, the shareholder's pro rata share, whether or not distributed, of the S corporation's items of income, loss, deduction, or credit described in paragraphs (a)(2), (3), and (4) of this section. A shareholder's pro rata share is determined in accordance with the provisions of section 1377(a) and the regulations thereunder. The shareholder takes these items into account in determining the shareholder's taxable income and tax liability for the shareholder's taxable year with or within which the taxable year of the corporation ends. If the shareholder dies (or if the shareholder is an estate or trust and the estate or trust terminates) before the end of the taxable year of the corporation, the shareholder's pro rata share of these items is taken into account on the shareholder's final return. For the limitation on allowance of a shareholder's pro rata share of S corporation losses or deductions, see section 1366(d) and § 1.1366-2.

(2) *Separately stated items of income, loss, deduction, or credit.* Each shareholder must take into account separately the shareholder's pro rata share of any item of income (including tax-exempt income), loss, deduction, or credit of the S corporation that if separately taken into account by any shareholder could affect the shareholder's tax liability for that taxable year differently than if the shareholder did not take the item into account

Reg. § 1.1362-8(a)

separately. The separately stated items of the S corporation include, but are not limited to, the following items—

(i) The corporation's combined net amount of gains and losses from sales or exchanges of capital assets grouped by applicable holding periods, by applicable rate of tax under section 1(h), and by any other classification that may be relevant in determining the shareholder's tax liability;

(ii) The corporation's combined net amount of gains and losses from sales or exchanges of property described in section 1231 (relating to property used in the trade or business and involuntary conversions), grouped by applicable holding periods, by applicable rate of tax under section 1(h), and by any other classification that may be relevant in determining the shareholder's tax liability;

(iii) Charitable contributions, grouped by the percentage limitations of section 170(b), paid by the corporation within the taxable year of the corporation;

(iv) The taxes described in section 901 that have been paid (or accrued) by the corporation to foreign countries or to possessions of the United States;

(v) Each of the corporation's separate items involved in the determination of credits against tax allowable under part IV of subchapter A (section 21 and following) of the Internal Revenue Code, except for any credit allowed under section 34 (relating to certain uses of gasoline and special fuels);

(vi) Each of the corporation's separate items of gains and losses from wagering transactions (section 165(d)); soil and water conservation expenditures (section 175); deduction under an election to expense certain depreciable business expenses (section 179); medical, dental, etc., expenses (section 213); the additional itemized deductions for individuals provided in part VII of subchapter B (section 212 and following) of the Internal Revenue Code; and any other itemized deductions for which the limitations on itemized deductions under sections 67 or 68 applies;

(vii) Any of the corporation's items of portfolio income or loss, and expenses related thereto, as defined in the regulations under section 469;

(viii) The corporation's tax-exempt income. For purposes of subchapter S, tax-exempt income is income that is permanently excludible from gross income in all circumstances in which the applicable provision of the Internal Revenue Code applies. For example, income that is excludible from gross income under section 101 (certain death benefits) or section 103 (interest on state and local bonds) is tax-exempt income, while income that is excludible from gross income under section 108 (income from discharge of indebtedness) or section 109 (improvements by lessee on lessor's property) is not tax-exempt income;

(ix) The corporation's adjustments described in sections 56 and 58, and items of tax preference described in section 57; and

(x) Any item identified in guidance (including forms and instructions) issued by the Commissioner as an item required to be separately stated under this paragraph (a)(2).

(3) *Nonseparately computed income or loss.* Each shareholder must take into account separately the shareholder's pro rata share of the nonseparately computed income or loss of the S corporation. For this purpose, nonseparately computed income or loss means the corporation's gross income less the deductions allowed to the corporation under chapter 1 of the Internal Revenue Code, determined by excluding any item requiring separate computation under paragraph (a)(2) of this section.

(4) *Separate activities requirement.* An S corporation must report, and each shareholder must take into account in the shareholder's return, the shareholder's pro rata share of an S corporation's items of income, loss, deduction, or credit described in paragraphs (a)(2) and (3) of this section for each of the corporation's activities as defined in section 469 and the regulations thereunder.

(5) *Aggregation of deductions or exclusions for purposes of limitations—(i) In general.* A shareholder aggregates the shareholder's separate deductions or exclusions with the shareholder's pro rata share of the S corporation's separately stated deductions or exclusions in determining the amount of any deduction or exclusion allowable to the shareholder under subtitle A of the Internal Revenue Code as to which a limitation is imposed.

(ii) *Example.* The provisions of paragraph (a)(5)(i) of this section are illustrated by the following example:

Example. In 1999, Corporation M, a calendar year S corporation, purchases and places in service section 179 property costing $10,000. Corporation M elects to expense the entire cost of the property. Shareholder A owns 50 percent of the stock of Corporation M. Shareholder A's pro rata share of this item after Corporation M applies the section 179(b) limitations is $5,000. Because the aggregate amount of Shareholder A's pro rata share and separately acquired section 179 expense may not exceed $19,000 (the aggregate maximum cost that may be taken into account under section 179(a) for the applicable taxable year), Shareholder A may elect to expense up to $14,000 of separately acquired section 179 property that is purchased and placed in service in 1999, subject to the limitations of section 179(b).

(b) *Character of items constituting pro rata share*—(1) *In general.* Except as provided in paragraph (b)(2) or (3) of this section, the character of any item of income, loss, deduction, or credit described in section 1366(a)(1)(A) or (B) and paragraph (a) of this section is determined for the S corporation and retains that character in the hands of the shareholder. For example, if an S corporation has capital gain on the sale or exchange of a capital asset, a shareholder's pro rata share of that gain will also be characterized as a capital gain regardless of whether the shareholder is otherwise a dealer in that type of property. Similarly, if an S corporation engages in an activity that is not for profit (as defined in section 183), a shareholder's pro rata share of the S corporation's deductions will be characterized as not for profit. Also, if an S corporation makes a charitable contribution to an organization qualifying under section 170(b)(1)(A), a shareholder's pro rata share of the S corporation's charitable contribution will be characterized as made to an organization qualifying under section 170 (b)(1)(A).

(2) *Exception for contribution of noncapital gain property.* If an S corporation is formed or availed of by any shareholder or group of shareholders for a principal purpose of selling or exchanging contributed property that in the hands of the shareholder or shareholders would not have produced capital gain if sold or exchanged by the shareholder or shareholders, then the gain on the sale or exchange of the property recognized by the corporation is not treated as a capital gain.

(3) *Exception for contribution of capital loss property.* If an S corporation is formed or availed of by any shareholder or group of shareholders for a principal purpose of selling or exchanging contributed property that in the hands of the shareholder or shareholders would have produced capital loss if sold or exchanged by the shareholder or shareholders, then the loss on the sale or exchange of the property recognized by the corporation is treated as a capital loss to the extent that, immediately before the contribution, the adjusted basis of the property in the hands of the shareholder or shareholders exceeded the fair market value of the property.

(c) *Gross income of a shareholder*—(1) *In general.* Where it is necessary to determine the amount or character of the gross income of a shareholder, the shareholder's gross income includes the shareholder's pro rata share of the gross income of the S corporation. The shareholder's pro rata share of the gross income of the S corporation is the amount of gross income of the corporation used in deriving the shareholder's pro rata share

of S corporation taxable income or loss (including items described in section 1366(a)(1)(A) or (B) and paragraph (a) of this section). For example, a shareholder is required to include the shareholder's pro rata share of S corporation gross income in computing the shareholder's gross income for the purposes of determining the necessity of filing a return (section 6012(a)) and the shareholder's gross income derived from farming (sections 175 and 6654(i)).

(2) *Gross income for substantial omission of items*—(i) *In general.* For purposes of determining the applicability of the 6-year period of limitation on assessment and collection provided in section 6501(e) (relating to omission of more than 25 percent of gross income), a shareholder's gross income includes the shareholder's pro rata share of S corporation gross income (as described in section 6501(e)(1)(A)(i)). In this respect, the amount of S corporation gross income used in deriving the shareholder's pro rata share of any item of S corporation income, loss, deduction, or credit (as included or disclosed in the shareholder's return) is considered as an amount of gross income stated in the shareholder's return for purposes of section 6501(e).

(ii) *Example.* The following example illustrates the provisions of paragraph (c)(2)(i) of this section:

Example. Shareholder A, an individual, owns 25 percent of the stock of Corporation N, an S corporation that has $10,000 gross income and $2,000 taxable income. A reports only $300 as A's pro rata share of N's taxable income. A should have reported $500 as A's pro rata share of taxable income, derived from A's pro rata share, $2,500, of N's gross income. Because A's return included only $300 without a disclosure meeting the requirements of section 6501(e)(1)(A)(ii) describing the difference of $200, A is regarded as having reported on the return only $1,500 ($300/$500 of $2,500) as gross income from N.

(d) *Shareholders holding stock subject to community property laws.* If a shareholder holds S corporation stock that is community property, then the shareholder's pro rata share of any item or items listed in paragraphs (a)(2), (3), and (4) of this section with respect to that stock is reported by the husband and wife in accordance with community property rules.

(e) *Net operating loss deduction of shareholder of S corporation.* For purposes of determining a net operating loss deduction under section 172, a shareholder of an S corporation must take into account the shareholder's pro rata share of items of income, loss, deduction, or credit of the corporation. See section 1366(b) and paragraph (b) of this section for rules on determining the character of the items. In determining under section 172(d)(4) the nonbusiness deductions allowable to a shareholder of an S corporation (arising from both corporation sources and any other sources), the shareholder separately takes into account the shareholder's pro rata share of the deductions of the corporation that are not attributable to a trade or business and combines this amount with the shareholder's nonbusiness deductions from any other sources. The shareholder also separately takes into account the shareholder's pro rata share of the gross income of the corporation not derived from a trade or business and combines this amount with the shareholder's nonbusiness income from all other sources. See section 172 and the regulations thereunder.

(f) *Cross-reference.* For rules relating to the consistent tax treatment of subchapter S items, see section 6037(c). [Reg. § 1.1366-1.]

☐ [*T.D.* 8852, 12-21-99.]

§ 1.1366-2. Limitations on deduction of pass-through items of an S corporation to its shareholders.—(a) *In general*—(1) *Limitation on losses and deductions.* The aggregate amount of losses and deductions taken into account by a shareholder under § 1.1366-1(a)(2), (3), and (4) for any taxable year of an S corporation cannot exceed the sum of—

(i) The adjusted basis of the shareholder's stock in the corporation (as determined under paragraph (a)(3)(i) of this section); and

(ii) The adjusted basis of any indebtedness of the corporation to the shareholder (as determined under paragraph (a)(3)(ii) of this section).

(2) *Carryover of disallowance.* A shareholder's aggregate amount of losses and deductions for a taxable year in excess of the sum of the adjusted basis of the shareholder's stock in an S corporation and of any indebtedness of the S corporation to the shareholder is not allowed for the taxable year. However, any disallowed loss or deduction retains its character and is treated as incurred by the corporation in the corporation's first succeeding taxable year, and subsequent taxable years, with respect to the shareholder. For rules on determining the adjusted bases of stock of an S corporation and indebtedness of the corporation to the shareholder, see paragraphs (a)(3)(i) and (ii) of this section.

(3) *Basis limitation amount*—(i) *Stock portion.* A shareholder generally determines the adjusted basis of stock for purposes of paragraphs (a)(1)(i) and (2) of this section (limiting losses and deductions) by taking into account only increases in basis under section 1367(a)(1) for the taxable year and decreases in basis under section 1367(a)(2)(A), (D) and (E) (relating to distributions, noncapital, nondeductible expenses, and

certain oil and gas depletion deductions) for the taxable year. In so determining this loss limitation amount, the shareholder disregards decreases in basis under section 1367(a)(2)(B) and (C) (for losses and deductions, including losses and deductions previously disallowed) for the taxable year., However, if the shareholder has in effect for the taxable year an election under § 1.1367-1(g) to decrease basis by items of loss and deduction prior to decreasing basis by noncapital, nondeductible expenses and certain oil and gas depletion deductions, the shareholder also disregards decreases in basis under section 1367(a)(2)(D) and (E). This basis limitation amount for stock is determined at the time prescribed under § 1.1367-1(d)(1) for adjustments to the basis of stock.

(ii) *Indebtedness portion.* A shareholder determines the shareholder's adjusted basis in indebtedness of the corporation for purposes of paragraphs (a)(1)(ii) and (2) of this section (limiting losses and deductions) without regard to any adjustment under section 1367(b)(2)(A) for the taxable year. This basis limitation amount for indebtedness is determined at the time prescribed under § 1.1367-2(d)(1) for adjustments to the basis of indebtedness.

(4) *Limitation on losses and deductions allocated to each item.* If a shareholder's pro rata share of the aggregate amount of losses and deductions specified in § 1.1366-1(a)(2), (3), and (4) exceeds the sum of the adjusted basis of the shareholder's stock in the corporation (determined in accordance with paragraph (a)(3)(i) of this section) and the adjusted basis of any indebtedness of the corporation to the shareholder (determined in accordance with paragraph (a)(3)(ii) of this section), then the limitation on losses and deductions under section 1366(d)(1) must be allocated among the shareholder's pro rata share of each loss or deduction. The amount of the limitation allocated to any loss or deduction is an amount that bears the same ratio to the amount of the limitation as the loss or deduction bears to the total of the losses and deductions. For this purpose, the total of losses and deductions for the taxable year is the sum of the shareholder's pro rata share of losses and deductions for the taxable year, and the losses and deductions disallowed and carried forward from prior years pursuant to section 1366(d)(2).

(5) *Nontransferability of losses and deductions.* Any loss or deduction disallowed under paragraph (a)(1) of this section is personal to the shareholder and cannot in any manner be transferred to another person. If a shareholder transfers some but not all of the shareholder's stock in the corporation, the amount of any disallowed loss or deduction under this section is not reduced and the transferee does not acquire any portion of the disallowed loss or deduction. If a shareholder

transfers all of the shareholder's stock in the corporation, any disallowed loss or deduction is permanently disallowed.

(6) *Basis of stock acquired by gift.* For purposes of section 1366(d)(1)(A) and paragraphs (a)(1)(i) and (2) of this section, the basis of stock in a corporation acquired by gift is the basis of the stock that is used for purposes of determining loss under section 1015(a).

(b) *Special rules for carryover of disallowed losses and deductions to post-termination transition period described in section 1377(b)*—(1) *In general.* If, for the last taxable year of a corporation for which it was an S corporation, a loss or deduction was disallowed to a shareholder by reason of the limitation in paragraph (a) of this section, the loss or deduction is treated under section 1366(d)(3) as incurred by that shareholder on the last day of any post-termination transition period (within the meaning of section 1377(b)).

(2) *Limitation on losses and deductions.* The aggregate amount of losses and deductions taken into account by a shareholder under paragraph (b)(1) of this section cannot exceed the adjusted basis of the shareholder's stock in the corporation determined at the close of the last day of the post-termination transition period. For this purpose, the adjusted basis of a shareholder's stock in the corporation is determined at the close of the last day of the post-termination transition period without regard to any reduction required under paragraph (b)(4) of this section. If a shareholder disposes of a share of stock prior to the close of the last day of the post-termination transition period, the adjusted basis of that share is its basis as of the close of the day of disposition. Any losses and deductions in excess of a shareholder's adjusted stock basis are permanently disallowed. For purposes of section 1366(d)(3)(B) and this paragraph (b)(2), the basis of stock in a corporation acquired by gift is the basis of the stock that is used for purposes of determining loss under section 1015(a).

(3) *Limitation on losses and deductions allocated to each item.* If the aggregate amount of losses and deductions treated as incurred by the shareholder under paragraph (b)(1) of this section exceeds the adjusted basis of the shareholder's stock determined under paragraph (b)(2) of this section, the limitation on losses and deductions under section 1366(d)(3)(B) must be allocated among each loss or deduction. The amount of the limitation allocated to each loss or deduction is an amount that bears the same ratio to the amount of the limitation as the amount of each loss or deduction bears to the total of all the losses and deductions.

(4) *Adjustment to the basis of stock.* The shareholder's basis in the stock of the corporation is reduced by the amount allowed as a deduction by reason of this paragraph (b). For rules regarding adjustments to the basis of a shareholder's stock in an S corporation, see § 1.1367-1.

(c) *Carryover of disallowed losses and deductions in the case of liquidations, reorganizations, and divisions*—(1) *Liquidations and reorganizations.* If a corporation acquires the assets of an S corporation in a transaction to which section 381(a) applies, any loss or deduction disallowed under paragraph (a) of this section with respect to a shareholder of the distributor or transferor S corporation is available to that shareholder as a shareholder of the acquiring corporation. Thus, where the acquiring corporation is an S corporation, a loss or deduction of a shareholder of the distributor or transferor S corporation disallowed prior to or during the taxable year of the transaction is treated as incurred by the acquiring S corporation with respect to that shareholder if the shareholder is a shareholder of the acquiring S corporation after the transaction. Where the acquiring corporation is a C corporation, a post-termination transition period arises the day after the last day that an S corporation was in existence and the rules provided in paragraph (b) of this section apply with respect to any shareholder of the acquired S corporation that is also a shareholder of the acquiring C corporation after the transaction. See the special rules under section 1377 for the availability of the post-termination transition period if the acquiring corporation is a C corporation.

(2) *Corporate separations to which section 368(a)(1)(D) applies.* If an S corporation transfers a portion of its assets constituting an active trade or business to another corporation in a transaction to which section 368(a)(1)(D) applies, and immediately thereafter the stock and securities of the controlled corporation are distributed in a distribution or exchange to which section 355 (or so much of section 356 as relates to section 355) applies, any loss or deduction disallowed under paragraph (a) of this section with respect to a shareholder of the distributing S corporation immediately before the transaction is allocated between the distributing corporation and the controlled corporation with respect to the shareholder. Such allocation shall be made according to any reasonable method, including a method based on the relative fair market value of the shareholder's stock in the distributing and controlled corporations immediately after the distribution, a method based on the relative adjusted basis of the assets in the distributing and controlled corporations immediately after the distribution, or, in the case of losses and deductions clearly attributable

to either the distributing or controlled corporation, any method that allocates such losses and deductions accordingly. [Reg. § 1.1366-2.]

☐ *[T.D. 8247, 4-4-89. Amended by T.D. 8852, 12-21-99.]*

§ 1.1366-3. Treatment of family groups.—(a) *In general.* Under section 1366(e), if an individual, who is a member of the family of one or more shareholders of an S corporation, renders services for, or furnishes capital to, the corporation without receiving reasonable compensation, the Commissioner shall prescribe adjustments to those items taken into account by the individual and the shareholders as may be necessary to reflect the value of the services rendered or capital furnished. For these purposes, in determining the reasonable value for services rendered, or capital furnished, to the corporation, consideration will be given to all the facts and circumstances, including the amount that ordinarily would be paid in order to obtain comparable services or capital from a person (other than a member of the family) who is not a shareholder in the corporation. In addition, for purposes of section 1366(e), if a member of the family of one or more shareholders of the S corporation holds an interest in a passthrough entity (e.g., a partnership, S corporation, trust, or estate), that performs services for, or furnishes capital to, the S corporation without receiving reasonable compensation, the Commissioner shall prescribe adjustments to the passthrough entity and the corporation as may be necessary to reflect the value of the services rendered or capital furnished. For purposes of section 1366(e), the term *family* of any shareholder includes only the shareholder's spouse, ancestors, lineal descendants, and any trust for the primary benefit of any of these persons.

(b) *Examples.* The provisions of this section may be illustrated by the following examples:

Example 1. The stock of an S corporation is owned 50 percent by F and 50 percent by T, the minor son of F. For the taxable year, the corporation has items of taxable income equal to $70,000. Compensation of $10,000 is paid by the corporation to F for services rendered during the taxable year, and no compensation is paid to T, who rendered no services. Based on all the relevant facts and circumstances, reasonable compensation for the services rendered by F would be $30,000. In the discretion of the Internal Revenue Service, up to an additional $20,000 of the $70,000 of the corporation's taxable income, for tax purposes, may be allocated to F as compensation for services rendered. If the Internal Revenue Service allocates $20,000 of the corporation's taxable income to F as compensation for services, taxable income of the corporation would be reduced by

$20,000 to $50,000, of which F and T each would be allocated $25,000. F would have $30,000 of total compensation paid by the corporation for services rendered.

Example 2. The stock of an S corporation is owned by A and B. For the taxable year, the corporation has paid compensation to a partnership that rendered services to the corporation during the taxable year. The spouse of A is a partner in that partnership. Consequently, if based on all the relevant facts and circumstances the partnership did not receive reasonable compensation for the services rendered to the corporation, the Internal Revenue Service, in its discretion, may make adjustments to those items taken into account by the partnership and the corporation as may be necessary to reflect the value of the services rendered.

[Reg. § 1.1366-3.]

☐ *[T.D. 8852, 12-21-99.]*

§ 1.1366-4. Special rules limiting the passthrough of certain items of an S corporation to its shareholders.—(a) *Passthrough inapplicable to section 34 credit.* Section 1.1366-1(a) does not apply to any credit allowable under section 34 (relating to certain uses of gasoline and special fuels).

(b) *Reduction in passthrough for tax imposed on built-in gains.* For purposes of § 1.1366-1(a), if for any taxable year of the S corporation a tax is imposed on the corporation under section 1374, the amount of the tax imposed is treated as a loss sustained by the S corporation during the taxable year. The character of the deemed loss is determined by allocating the loss proportionately among the net recognized built-in gains giving rise to the tax and attributing the character of each net recognized built-in gain to the allocable portion of the loss.

(c) *Reduction in passthrough for tax imposed on excess net passive income.* For purposes of § 1.1366-1(a), if for any taxable year of the S corporation a tax is imposed on the corporation under section 1375, each item of passive investment income shall be reduced by an amount that bears the same ratio to the amount of the tax as the net amount of the item bears to the total net passive investment income for that taxable year. [Reg. § 1.1366-4.]

☐ *[T.D. 8852, 12-21-99 (corrected 3-8-2000).]*

§ 1.1367-1. Adjustments to basis of shareholder's stock in an S corporation.—(a) *In general*—(1) *Adjustments under section 1367.* This section provides rules relating to adjustments required by section 1367 to the basis of a shareholder's stock in an S corporation. Paragraph (b) of this section provides rules concerning increases in the basis of a shareholder's stock, and paragraph (c) of this section provides rules concerning decreases in the basis of a shareholder's stock.

(2) *Applicability of other Internal Revenue Code provisions.* In addition to the adjustments required by section 1367 and this section, the basis of stock is determined or adjusted under other applicable provisions of the Internal Revenue Code.

(b) *Increase in basis of stock*—(1) *In general.* Except as provided in § 1.1367-2(c) (relating to restoration of basis of indebtedness to the shareholder), the basis of a shareholder's stock in an S corporation is increased by the sum of the items described in section 1367(a)(1). The increase in basis described in section 1367(a)(1)(C) for the excess of the deduction for depletion over the basis of the property subject to depletion does not include the depletion deduction attributable to oil or gas property. See section 613(A)(c)(11).

(2) *Amount of increase in basis of individual shares.* The basis of a shareholder's share of stock is increased by an amount equal to the shareholder's pro rata portion of the items described in section 1367(a)(1) that is attributable to that share, determined on a per share, per day basis in accordance with section 1377(a).

(c) *Decrease in basis of stock*—(1) *In general.* The basis of a shareholder's stock in an S corporation is decreased (but not below zero) by the sum of the items described in section 1367(a)(2).

(2) *Noncapital, nondeductible expenses.* For purposes of section 1367(a)(2)(D), expenses of the corporation not deductible in computing its taxable income and not properly chargeable to a capital account (*noncapital, nondeductible expenses*) are only those items for which no loss or deduction is allowable and do not include items the deduction for which is deferred to a later taxable year. Examples of noncapital, nondeductible expenses include (but are not limited to) the following: illegal bribes, kickbacks, and other payments not deductible under section 162(c); fines and penalties not deductible under section 162(f); expenses and interest relating to tax-exempt income under section 265; losses for which the deduction is disallowed under section 267(a)(1); the portion of meals and entertainment expenses disallowed under section 274; and the two-thirds portion of treble damages paid for violating antitrust laws not deductible under section 162.

(3) *Amount of decrease in basis of individual shares.* The basis of a shareholder's share of stock is decreased by an amount equal to the shareholder's pro rata portion of the passthrough items and distributions described in section 1367(a)(2) attributable to that share, determined on a per share, per day basis in accordance with section

1377(a). If the amount attributable to a share exceeds its basis, the excess is applied to reduce (but not below zero) the remaining bases of all other shares of stock in the corporation owned by the shareholder in proportion to the remaining basis of each of those shares.

(d) *Time at which adjustments to basis of stock are effective*—(1) *In general.* The adjustments described in section 1367(a) to the basis of a shareholder's stock are determined as of the close of the corporation's taxable year, and the adjustments generally are effective as of that date. However, if a shareholder disposes of stock during the corporation's taxable year, the adjustments with respect to that stock are effective immediately prior to the disposition.

(2) *Adjustment for nontaxable item.* An adjustment for a nontaxable item is determined for the taxable year in which the item would have been includible or deductible under the corporation's method of accounting for federal income tax purposes if the item had been subject to federal income taxation.

(3) *Effect of election under section 1377(a)(2) or § 1.1368-1(g)(2).* If an election under section 1377(a)(2) (to terminate the year in the case of the termination of a shareholder's interest) or under § 1.1368-1(g)(2) (to terminate the year in the case of a qualifying disposition) is made with respect to the taxable year of a corporation, this paragraph (d) applies as if the taxable year consisted of separate taxable years, the first of which ends at the close of the day on which either the shareholder's interest is terminated or a qualifying disposition occurs, whichever the case may be.

(e) *Ordering rules for taxable years beginning before January 1, 1997.* For any taxable year of a corporation beginning before January 1, 1997, except as provided in paragraph (g) of this section, the adjustments required by section 1367(a) are made in the following order—

(1) Any increase in basis attributable to the income items described in section 1367(a)(1)(A) and (B) and the excess of the deductions for depletion described in section 1367(a)(1)(C);

(2) Any decrease in basis attributable to noncapital, nondeductible expenses described in section 1367(a)(2)(D) and the oil and gas depletion deduction described in section 1367(a)(2)(E);

(3) Any decrease in basis attributable to items of loss or deduction described in section 1367(a)(2)(B) and (C); and

(4) Any decrease in basis attributable to a distribution by the corporation described in section 1367(a)(2)(A).

(f) *Ordering rules for taxable years beginning on or after August 18, 1998.* For any taxable year of a corporation beginning on or after August 18, 1998, except as provided in paragraph (g) of this section, the adjustments required by section 1367(a) are made in the following order—

(1) Any increase in basis attributable to the income items described in section 1367(a)(1)(A) and (B), and the excess of the deductions for depletion described in section 1367(a)(1)(C);

(2) Any decrease in basis attributable to a distribution by the corporation described in section 1367(a)(2)(A);

(3) Any decrease in basis attributable to noncapital, nondeductible expenses described in section 1367(a)(2)(D), and the oil and gas depletion deduction described in section 1367(a)(2)(E); and

(4) Any decrease in basis attributable to items of loss or deduction described in section 1367(a)(2)(B) and (C).

(g) *Elective ordering rule.* A shareholder may elect to decrease basis under paragraph (e)(3) or (f)(4) of this section, whichever applies, prior to decreasing basis under paragraph (e)(2) or (f)(3) of this section, whichever applies. If a shareholder makes this election, any amount described in paragraph (e)(2) or (f)(3) of this section, whichever applies, that is in excess of the shareholder's basis in stock and indebtedness is treated, solely for purposes of this section, as an amount described in paragraph (e)(2) or (f)(3) of this section, whichever applies, in the succeeding taxable year. A shareholder makes the election under this paragraph by attaching a statement to the shareholder's timely filed original or amended return that states that the shareholder agrees to the carryover rule of the preceding sentence. Once a shareholder makes an election under this paragraph with respect to an S corporation, the shareholder must continue to use the rules of this paragraph for that S corporation in future taxable years unless the shareholder receives the permission of the Commissioner.

(h) *Examples.* The following examples illustrate the principles of § 1.1367-1. In each example, the corporation is a calendar year S corporation:

Example 1. Adjustments to basis of stock for taxable years beginning before January 1, 1997. (i) On December 31, 1994, A owns a block of 50 shares of stock with an adjusted basis per share of $6 in Corporation S. On December 31, 1994, A purchases for $400 an additional block of 50 shares of stock with an adjusted basis of $8 per share. Thus, A holds 100 shares of stock for each day of the 1995 taxable year. For S's 1995 taxable year, A's pro rata share of the amount of the items described in section 1367(a)(1)(A) (relating to increases in basis of stock) is $300, and A's pro rata share of the amount of the items described in section 1367(a)(2)(B) and (D) (relating to decreases in basis of stock) is $500. S makes a distribution to A in the amount of $100 during 1995.

(ii) Pursuant to the ordering rules of paragraph (e) of this section, A increases the basis of each share of stock by $3 ($300 ÷ 100 shares) and decreases the basis of each share of stock by $5 ($500 ÷ 100 shares). Then A reduces the basis of each share by $1 ($100 ÷ 100 shares) for the distribution. Thus, on January 1, 1996, A has a basis of $3 per share in his original block of 50 shares ($6 + $3 − $5 − $1) and a basis of $5 per share in the second block of 50 shares ($8 + $3 − $5 − $1).

Example 2. Adjustments to basis of stock for taxable years beginning on or after August 18, 1998. (i) On December 31, 2001, A owns a block of 50 shares of stock with an adjusted basis per share of $6 in Corporation S. On December 31, 2001, A purchases for $400 an additional block of 50 shares of stock with an adjusted basis of $8 per share. Thus, A holds 100 shares of stock for each day of the 2002 taxable year. For S's 2002 taxable year, A's pro rata share of the amount of items described in section 1367(a)(1)(A) (relating to increases in basis of stock) is $300, A's pro rata share of the amount of the items described in section 1367(a)(2)(B) (relating to decreases in basis of stock attributable to items of loss and deduction) is $300, and A's pro rata share of the amount of the items described in section 1367(a)(2)(D) (relating to decreases in basis of stock attributable to noncapital, nondeductible expenses) is $200. S makes a distribution to A in the amount of $100 during 2002.

(ii) Pursuant to the ordering rules of paragraph (f) of this section, A first increases the basis of each share of stock by $3 ($300/100 shares) and then decreases the basis of each share by $1 ($100/100 shares) for the distribution. A next decreases the basis of each share by $2 ($200/100 shares) for the noncapital, nondeductible expenses and then decreases the basis of each share by $3 ($300/100 shares) for the items of loss. Thus, on January 1, 2003, A has a basis of $3 per share in the original block of 50 shares ($6 + $3 − $1 − $2 − $3) and a basis of $5 per share in the second block of 100 shares ($8 + $3 − $1 − $2 − $3).

Example 3. Adjustments attributable to basis of individual shares of stock. (i) On December 31, 1993, B owns one share of S corporation's 10 outstanding shares of stock. The basis of B's share is $30. On July 2, 1994, B purchases from another shareholder two shares for $25 each. During 1994, S corporation has no income or deductions but incurs a loss of $365. Under section 1377(a)(1)(A) and paragraph (c)(3) of this section, the amount of the loss assigned to each day of S's taxable year is $1.00 ($365/365 days). For each day, $.10 is allocated to each outstanding share ($1.00 amount of loss assigned to each day/10 shares).

(ii) B owned one share for 365 days and, therefore, reduces the basis of that share by the amount of loss attributable to it, *i.e.*, $36.50 ($.10 × 365 days). B owned two shares for 182 days and, therefore, reduces the basis of each of those shares by the amount of the loss attributable to each, *i.e.*, $18.20 ($.10 × 182 days).

(iii) The bases of the shares are decreased as follows:

Share	Original Basis	Decrease	Adjusted Basis	Excess Basis Reduction
No. 1	$30.00	$36.50	$ 0	$6.50
No. 2	25.00	18.20	6.80	0
No. 3	25.00	18.20	6.80	0
Total remaining basis			13.60	

(iv) Because the decrease in basis attributable to share No. 1 exceeds the basis of share No. 1 by $6.50 ($36.50 − $30.00), the excess is applied to reduce the bases of shares No. 2 and No. 3 in proportion to their remaining bases. Therefore, the bases of share No. 2 and share No. 3 are each decreased by an additional $3.25 ($6.50 × $6.80/$13.60). After this decrease, Share No. 1 has a basis of zero, Share No. 2 has a basis of $3.55, and Share No. 3 has a basis of $3.55.

Example 4. Effects of section 1377(a)(2) election and distribution on basis of stock for taxable years beginning before January 1, 1997. (i) On January 1, 1994, individuals B and C each own 50 of the 100 shares of issued and outstanding stock of Corporation S. B's adjusted basis in each share of stock is $120, and C's is $80. On June 30, 1994, S distributes $6,000 to B and $6,000 to C. On June 30, 1994, B sells all of her S stock for $10,000 to D. S elects under section 1377(a)(2) to treat its 1994 taxable year as consisting of two taxable years, the first of which ends at the close of June 30, the date on which B terminates her interest in S.

(ii) For the period January 1, 1994, through June 30, 1994, S has nonseparately computed income of $6,000 and a separately stated deduction item of $4,000. Therefore, on June 30, 1994, B and C, pursuant to the ordering rules of paragraph (e) of this section, increase the basis of each share by $60 ($6,000/100 shares) and decrease the basis of each share by $40 ($4,000/100 shares). Then B and C reduce the basis of each share by $120 ($12,000/100 shares) for the distribution.

(iii) The basis of B's stock is reduced from $120 to $20 per share ($120 + $60 − $40 − $120). The basis of C's stock is reduced from $80 to $0 per share ($80 + $60 − $40 − $120). See section 1368 and § 1.1368-1(c) and (d) for rules relating to the tax treatment of the distributions.

(iv) Pursuant to paragraph (d)(3) of this section, the net reduction in the basis of B's shares of the S stock required by section 1367 and this section is effective immediately prior to B's sale of her stock. Thus, B's basis for determining gain or loss on the sale of the S stock is $20 per share, and B has a gain on the sale of $180 ($200 − $20) per share.

Example 5. Effects of section 1377(a)(2) election and distribution on basis of stock for taxable years beginning on or after August 18, 1998. (i) The facts are the same as in *Example 4*, except that all of the events occur in 2001 rather than in 1994 and except as follows: On June 30, 2001, B sells 25 shares of her stock for $5,000 to D and 25 shares back to Corporation S for $5,000. Under section 1377(a)(2)(B) and § 1.1377-1(b)(2), B, C, and D are affected shareholders because B has transferred shares to Corporations S and D. Pursuant to section 1377(a)(2)(A) and § 1.1377-1(b)(1), B, C, and D, the affected shareholders, and Corporation S agree to treat the taxable year 2001 as if it consisted of two separate taxable years for all affected shareholders for the purposes set forth in § 1.1377-1(b)(3)(i).

(ii) On June 30, 2001, B and C, pursuant to the ordering rules of paragraph (f)(1) of this section, increase the basis of each share by $60 ($6,000/100 shares) for the nonseparately computed income. Then B and C reduce the basis of each share by $120 ($12,000/100 shares) for the distribution. Finally, B and C decrease the basis of each share by $40 ($4,000/100 shares) for the separately stated deduction item.

(iii) The basis of the stock of B is reduced from $120 to $20 per share ($120 + $60 − $120 − $40). Prior to accounting for the separately stated deduction item, the basis of the stock of C is reduced from $80 to $20 ($80 + $60 − $120). Finally, because the period from January 1 through June 30, 2001 is treated under § 1.1377-1(b)(3)(i) as a separate taxable year for purposes of making adjustments to the basis of stock, under section 1366(d) and § 1.1366-2(a)(2), C may deduct only $20 per share of the remaining $40 of the separately stated deduction item, and the basis of the stock of C is reduced from $20 per share to $0 per share. Under section 1366 and § 1.1366-2(a)(2), C's remaining separately stated

Reg. § 1.1367-1(h)

deduction item of $20 per share is treated as having been incurred in the first succeeding taxable year of Corporation S, which, for this purpose, begins on July 1, 2001.]

(i) [Reserved]

(j) *Adjustments for items of income in respect of a decedent.* The basis determined under section 1014 of any stock in an S corporation is reduced by the portion of the value of the stock that is attributable to items constituting income in respect of a decedent. For the determination of items realized by an S corporation constituting income in respect of a decedent, see sections 1367(b)(4)(A) and 691 and applicable regulations thereunder. For the determination of the allowance of a deduction for the amount of estate tax attributable to income in respect of a decedent, see section 691(c) and applicable regulations thereunder. [Reg. § 1.1367-1.]

☐ [*T.D. 8508, 12-30-93. Amended by T.D. 8852, 12-21-99 (corrected 3-8-2000).*]

§ 1.1367-2. Adjustments to basis of indebtedness to shareholder.—(a) *In general.* This section provides rules relating to adjustments required by subchapter S to the basis of indebtedness of an S corporation to a shareholder. For purposes of this section, shareholder advances not evidenced by separate written instruments and repayments on the advances (*open account debt*) are treated as a single indebtedness. The basis of indebtedness of the S corporation to a shareholder is reduced as provided in paragraph (b) of this section and restored as provided in paragraph (c) of this section.

(b) *Reduction in basis of indebtedness*—(1) *General rule.* If, after making the adjustments required by section 1367(a)(1) for any taxable year of the S corporation, the amounts specified in section 1367(a)(2)(B), (C), (D), and (E) (relating to losses, deductions, noncapital, nondeductible expenses, and certain oil and gas depletion deductions) exceed the basis of a shareholder's stock in the corporation, the excess is applied to reduce (but not below zero) the basis of any indebtedness of the S corporation to the shareholder held by the shareholder at the close of the corporation's taxable year. Any such indebtedness that has been satisfied by the corporation, or disposed of or forgiven by the shareholder, during the taxable year, is not held by the shareholder at the close of that year and is not subject to basis reduction.

(2) *Termination of shareholder's interest in corporation during taxable year.* If a shareholder terminates his or her interest in the corporation during the taxable year, the rules of this paragraph (b) are applied with respect to any indebtedness of the S corporation held by the shareholder immediately prior to the termination of the shareholder's interest in the corporation.

(3) *Multiple indebtedness.* If a shareholder holds more than one indebtedness at the close of the corporation's taxable year or, if applicable, immediately prior to the termination of the shareholder's interest in the corporation, the reduction in basis is applied to each indebtedness in the same proportion that the basis of each indebtedness bears to the aggregate bases of the indebtedness to the shareholder.

(c) *Restoration of basis*—(1) *General rule.* If, for any taxable year of an S corporation beginning after December 31, 1982, there has been a reduction in the basis of an indebtedness of the S corporation to a shareholder under section 1367(b)(2)(A), any *net increase* in any subsequent taxable year of the corporation is applied to restore that reduction. For purposes of this section, *net increase* with respect to a shareholder means the amount by which the shareholder's pro rata share of the items described in section 1367(a)(1) (relating to income items and excess deduction for depletion) exceed the items described in section 1367(a)(2) (relating to losses, deductions, noncapital, nondeductible expenses, certain oil and gas depletion deductions, and certain distributions) for the taxable year. These restoration rules apply only to indebtedness held by a shareholder as of the beginning of the taxable year in which the net increase arises. The reduction in basis of indebtedness must be restored before any net increase is applied to restore the basis of a shareholder's stock in an S corporation. In no event may the shareholder's basis of indebtedness be restored above the adjusted basis of the indebtedness under section 1016(a), excluding any adjustments under section 1016(a)(17) for prior taxable years, determined as of the beginning of the taxable year in which the net increase arises.

(2) *Multiple indebtedness.* If a shareholder holds more than one indebtedness as of the beginning of a corporation's taxable year, any net increase is applied first to restore the reduction of basis in any indebtedness repaid (in whole or in part) in that taxable year to the extent necessary to offset any gain that would otherwise be realized on the repayment. Any remaining net increase is applied to restore each outstanding indebtedness in proportion to the amount that the basis of each outstanding indebtedness has been reduced under section 1367(b)(2)(A) and paragraph (b) of this section and not restored under section 1367(b)(2)(B) and this paragraph (c).

(d) *Time at which adjustments to basis of indebtedness are effective*—(1) *In general.* The amounts of the adjustments to basis of indebtedness provided in section 1367(b)(2) and this sec-

Reg. § 1.1367-2(d)(1)

tion are determined as of the close of the corporation's taxable year, and the adjustments are generally effective as of the close of the corporation's taxable year. However, if the shareholder is not a shareholder in the corporation at that time, these adjustments are effective immediately before the shareholder terminates his or her interest in the corporation. If a debt is disposed of or repaid in whole or in part before the close of the taxable year, the basis of that indebtedness is restored under paragraph (c) of this section, effective immediately before the disposition or the first repayment on the debt during the taxable year.

(2) *Effect of election under section 1377(a)(2) or § 1.1368-1(g)(2).* If an election is made under section 1377(a)(2) (to terminate the year in the case of the termination of a shareholder's interest) or under § 1.1368-1(g)(2) (to terminate the year in the case of a qualifying disposition), this paragraph (d) applies as if the taxable year consisted of separate taxable years, the first of which ends at the close of the day on which the shareholder either terminates his or her interest in the corporation or disposes of a substantial amount of stock, whichever the case may be.

(e) *Examples.* The following examples illustrate the principles of § 1.1367-2. In each example, the corporation is a calendar year S corporation. The lending transactions described in the examples do not result in foregone interest (within the meaning of section 7872(e)(2)), original issue discount (within the meaning of section 1273), or total unstated interest (within the meaning of section 483(b)).

Example 1. Reduction in basis of indebtedness. (i) A has been the sole shareholder in Corporation S since 1992. In 1993, A loans S $1,000 (Debt No.

1), which is evidenced by a ten-year promissory note in the face amount of $1,000. In 1996, A loans S $5,000 (Debt No. 2), which is evidenced by a demand promissory note. On December 31, 1996, the basis of A's stock is zero; the basis of Debt No. 1 has been reduced under paragraph (b) of this section to $0; and the basis of Debt No. 2 has been reduced to $1,000. On January 1, 1997, A loans S $4,000 (Debt No. 3), which is evidenced by a demand promissory note. For S's 1997 taxable year, the sum of the amounts specified in section 1367(a)(1) (in this case, nonseparately computed income and the excess deduction for depletion) is $6,000, and the sum of the amounts specified in section 1367(a)(2)(B), (D) and (E) (in this case, items of separately stated deductions and losses, noncapital, nondeductible expenses, and certain oil and gas depletion deductions—there is no nonseparately computed loss) is $10,000. Corporation S makes no payments to A on any of the loans during 1997.

(ii) The $4,000 excess of loss and deduction items is applied to reduce the basis of each indebtedness in proportion to the basis of that indebtedness over the aggregate bases of the indebtedness to the shareholder (determined immediately before any adjustment under section 1367(b)(2)(A) and paragraph (b) of this section is effective for the taxable year). Thus, the basis of Debt No. 2 is reduced in an amount equal to $800 ($4,000 (excess) × $1,000 (basis of Debt No. 2)/ $5,000 (total basis of all debt)). Similarly, the basis in Debt No. 3 is reduced in an amount equal to $3,200 ($4,000 × $4,000/$5,000). Accordingly, on December 31, 1997, A's basis in his stock is zero and his bases in the three debts are as follows:

Debt	1/1/96 Basis	12/31/96 Reduction	1/1/97 Basis	12/31/97 Reduction	1/1/98 Basis
No. 1	$1,000	$1,000	$ 0	$ 0	$ 0
No. 2	5,000	4,000	1,000	800	200
No. 3				4,000	3,200	800

Example 2. Restoration of basis of indebtedness. (i) The facts are the same as in *Example 1.* On July 1, 1998, S completely repays Debt No. 3, and, for S's 1998 taxable year, the net increase (within the meaning of paragraph (c) of this section) with respect to A equals $4,500.

(ii) The net increase is applied first to restore the bases in the debts held on January 1, 1998, before any of the net increase is applied to increase A's basis in his shares of S stock. The net increase is applied to restore first the reduction of basis in indebtedness repaid in 1998. Any remaining net increase is applied to restore the bases of the outstanding debts in proportion to the amount that each of these outstanding debts have been

reduced previously under paragraph (b) of this section and have not been restored. As of December 31, 1998, the total reduction in A's debts held on January 1, 1998 equals $9,000. Thus, the basis of Debt No. 3 is restored by $3,200 (the amount of the previous reduction) to $4,000. A's basis in Debt No. 3 is treated as restored immediately before that debt is repaid. Accordingly, A does not realize any gain on the repayment. The remaining net increase of $1,300 ($4,500 − $3,200) is applied to restore the bases of Debt No. 1 and Debt No. 2. As of December 31, 1998, the total reduction in these outstanding debts is $5,800 ($9,000 − $3,200). The basis of Debt No. 1 is restored in an amount equal to $224 ($1,300 ×

Reg. § 1.1367-2(d)(2)

$1,000/$5,800). Similarly, the basis in Debt No. 2 is restored in an amount equal to $1,076 ($1,300 × $4,800/$5,800). On December 31, 1998, A's

basis in his S stock is zero and his bases in the two remaining debts are as follows:

Original Basis	Amount Reduced	1/1/98 Basis	Amount Restored	12/31/98 Basis
$1,000	$1,000	$ 0	$ 224	$ 224
5,000	4,800	200	1,076	1,276

Example 3. Full restoration of basis in indebtedness when debt is repaid in part during the taxable year. (i) C has been a shareholder in Corporation S since 1992. In 1997, C loans S $1,000. S issues its note to C in the amount of $1,000, of which $950 is payable on March 1, 1998, and $50 is payable on March 1, 1999. On December 31, 1997, C's basis in all her shares of S stock is zero and her basis in the note has been reduced under paragraph (b) of this section to $900. For 1998, the net increase (within the meaning of paragraph (c) of this section) with respect to C is $300.

(ii) Because C's basis of indebtedness was reduced in a prior taxable year under § 1.1367-2(b), the net increase for 1998 is applied to restore this reduction. The restored basis cannot exceed the adjusted basis of the debt as of the beginning of the first day of 1998, excluding prior adjustments under section 1367, or $1,000. Therefore, $100 of the $300 net increase is applied to restore the basis of the debt from $900 to $1,000 effective immediately before the repayment on March 1, 1998. The remaining net increase of $200 increases C's basis in her stock.

Example 4. Determination of net increase— distribution in excess of increase in basis. (i) D has been the sole shareholder in Corporation S since 1990. On January 1, 1996, D loans S $10,000 in return for a note from S in the amount of $10,000 of which $5,000 is payable on each of January 1, 2000, and January 1, 2001. On December 31, 1997, the basis of D's shares of S stock is zero, and his basis in the note has been reduced under paragraph (b) of this section to $8,000. During 1998, the sum of the items under section 1367(a)(1) (relating to increases in basis of stock) with respect to D equals $10,000 (in this case, nonseparately computed income), and the sum of the items under section 1367(a)(2)(B), (C), (D), and (E) (relating to decreases in basis of stock) with respect to D equals $0. During 1998, S also makes distributions to D totaling $11,000. This distribution is an item that reduces basis of stock under section 1367(a)(2)(A) and must be taken into account for purposes of determining whether there is a net increase for the taxable year. Thus, for 1998, there is no net increase with respect to D because the amount of the items provided in section 1367(a)(1) do not exceed the amount of the items provided in section 1367(a)(2).

(ii) Because there is no net increase with respect to D for 1998, none of the 1997 reduction in D's basis in the indebtedness is restored. The $10,000 increase in basis under section 1367(a)(1) is applied to increase D's basis in his S stock. Under section 1367(a)(2)(A), the $11,000 distribution with respect to D's stock reduces D's basis in his shares of S stock to $0. See section 1368 and § 1.1368-1(c) and (d) for the tax treatment of the $1,000 distribution in excess of D's basis.

Example 5. Distributions less than increase in basis. (i) The facts are the same as in *Example 4,* except that in 1998 S makes distributions to D totaling $8,000. On these facts, for 1998, there is a net increase with respect to D of $2,000 (the amount by which the items provided in section 1367(a)(1) exceed the amount of the items provided in section 1367(a)(2)).

(ii) Because there is a net increase of $2,000 with respect to D for 1998, $2,000 of the $10,000 increase in basis under section 1367(a)(1) is first applied to restore D's basis in the indebtedness to $10,000 ($8,000 + $2,000). Accordingly, on December 31, 1998, D has a basis in his shares of S stock of $0 ($0 + $8,000 (increase in basis remaining after restoring basis in indebtedness) − $8,000 (distribution)) and a basis in the note of $10,000. [Reg. § 1.1367-2.]

☐ [*T.D.* 8508, 12-30-93.]

§ 1.1368-1. Distributions by S corporations.—(a) *In general.* This section provides rules for distributions made by an S corporation with respect to its stock which, but for section 1368(a) and this section, would be subject to section 301(c) and other rules of the Internal Revenue Code that characterize a distribution as a dividend.

(b) *Date distribution made.* For purposes of section 1368, a distribution is taken into account on the date the corporation makes the distribution, regardless of when the distribution is treated as received by the shareholder.

(c) *S corporation with no earnings and profits.* A distribution made by an S corporation that has no accumulated earnings and profits as of the end of the taxable year of the S corporation in which the distribution is made is treated in the manner provided in section 1368(b).

(d) *S corporation with earnings and profits*—(1) *General treatment of distribution.* Except as provided in paragraph (d)(2) of this section, a distribution made with respect to its stock by an S corporation that has accumulated earnings and profits as of the end of the taxable year of the S corporation in which the distribution is made is treated in the manner provided in section 1368(c). See section 316 and § 1.316-2 for provisions relating to the allocation of earnings and profits among distributions.

(2) *Previously taxed income.* This paragraph (d)(2) applies to distributions by a corporation that has both accumulated earnings and profits and previously taxed income (within the meaning of section 1375(d)(2), as in effect prior to its amendment by the Subchapter S Revision Act of 1982, and the regulations thereunder) with respect to one or more shareholders. In the case of such a distribution, that portion remaining after the application of section 1368(c)(1) (relating to distributions from the accumulated adjustments account (AAA) as defined in § 1.1368-2(a)) is treated in the manner provided in section 1368(b) (relating to S corporations without earnings and profits) to the extent that portion is a distribution of money and does not exceed the shareholder's net share immediately before the distribution of the corporation's previously taxed income. The AAA and the earnings and profits of the corporation are not decreased by that portion of the distribution. Any distribution remaining after the application of this paragraph (d)(2) is treated in the manner provided in section 1368(c)(2) and (3).

(e) *Certain adjustments taken into account—* (1) *Taxable years beginning before January 1, 1997.* For any taxable year of the corporation beginning before January 1, 1997, paragraphs (c) and (d) of this section are applied only after taking into account—

(i) The adjustments to the basis of the shares of a shareholder's stock described in section 1367 (without regard to section 1367(a)(2)(A) (relating to decreases attributable to distributions not includible in income)) for the S corporation's taxable year; and

(ii) The adjustments to the AAA required by section 1368(e)(1)(A) (but without regard to the adjustments for distributions under § 1.1368-2(a)(3)(iii)) for the S corporation's taxable year.

(2) *Taxable years beginning on or after August 18, 1998.* For any taxable year of the corporation beginning on or after August 18, 1998, paragraphs (c) and (d) of this section are applied only after taking into account—

(i) The adjustments to the basis of the shares of a shareholder's stock described in section

1367(a)(1) (relating to increases in basis of stock) for the S corporation's taxable year; and

(ii) The adjustments to the AAA required by section 1368(e)(1)(A) (but without regard to the adjustments for distributions under § 1.1368-2(a)(3)(iii)) for the S corporation's taxable year. Any net negative adjustment (as defined in section 1368(e)(1)(C)(ii)) for the taxable year shall not be taken into account.

(f) *Elections relating to source of distributions—*(1) *In general.* An S corporation may modify the application of paragraphs (c) and (d) of this section by electing (pursuant to paragraph (f)(5) of this section)—

(i) To distribute earnings and profits first as described in paragraph (f)(2) of this section;

(ii) To make a deemed dividend as described in paragraph (f)(3) of this section; or

(iii) To forego previously taxed income as described in paragraph (f)(4) of this section.

(2) *Election to distribute earnings and profits first—*(i) *In general.* An S corporation with accumulated earnings and profits may elect under this paragraph (f)(2) for any taxable year to distribute earnings and profits first as provided in section 1368(e)(3). Except as provided in paragraph (f)(2)(ii) of this section, distributions made by an S corporation making this election are treated as made first from earnings and profits under section 1368(c)(2) and second from the AAA under section 1368(c)(1). Any remaining portion of the distribution is treated in the manner provided in section 1368(b). This election is effective for all distributions made during the year for which the election is made.

(ii) *Previously taxed income.* If a corporation to which paragraph (d)(2) of this section (relating to corporations with previously taxed income) applies makes the election provided in this paragraph (f)(2) for the taxable year, and does not make the election to forego previously taxed income under paragraph (f)(4) of this section, distributions by the S corporation during the taxable year are treated as made first, from previously taxed income under paragraph (d)(2) of this section; second, from earnings and profits under section 1368(c)(2); and third, from the AAA under section 1368(c)(1). Any portion of a distribution remaining after the previously taxed income, earnings and profits, and the AAA are exhausted is treated in the manner provided in section 1368(b).

(iii) *Corporation with subchapter C and subchapter S earnings and profits.* If an S corporation that makes the election provided in this paragraph (f)(2) has both subchapter C earnings and profits (as defined in section 1362(d)(3)(B)) and subchapter S earnings and profits in a taxable year of the corporation in which the distribution is made, the distribution is treated as made first from subchapter C earnings and profits, and second from subchapter S earnings and profits. *Subchapter S earnings and profits* are earnings and profits accumulated in a taxable year beginning before January 1, 1983 (or in the case of a qualified casualty insurance electing small business corporation or a qualified oil corporation, earnings and profits accumulated in any taxable year), for which an election under subchapter S of chapter 1 of the Internal Revenue Code was in effect.

(3) *Election to make a deemed dividend.* An S corporation may elect under this paragraph (f)(3) to distribute all or part of its subchapter C earnings and profits through a deemed dividend. If an S corporation makes the election provided in this paragraph (f)(3), the S corporation will be considered to have made the election provided in paragraph (f)(2) of this section (relating to the election to distribute earnings and profits first). The amount of the deemed dividend may not exceed the subchapter C earnings and profits of the corporation on the last day of the taxable year, reduced by any actual distributions of subchapter C earnings and profits made during the taxable year. The amount of the deemed dividend is considered, for all purposes of the Internal Revenue Code, as if it were distributed in money to the shareholders in proportion to their stock ownership, received by the shareholders, and immediately contributed by the shareholders to the corporation, all on the last day of the corporation's taxable year.

(4) *Election to forego previously taxed income.* An S corporation may elect to forego distributions of previously taxed income. If such an election is made, paragraph (d)(2) of this section (relating to corporations with previously taxed income) does not apply to any distribution made during the taxable year. Thus, distributions by a corporation that makes the election to forego previously taxed income for a taxable year under this paragraph (f)(4) and does not make the election to distribute earnings and profits first under paragraph (f)(2) of this section are treated in the manner provided in section 1368(c) (relating to distributions by corporations with earnings and profits). Distributions by a corporation that makes both the election to distribute earnings and profits first under paragraph (f)(2) of this section and the election to forego previously taxed income under this paragraph (f)(4), are treated in the manner provided in paragraph (f)(2)(i) of this section.

(5) *Time and manner of making elections—* (i) *For earnings and profits.* If an election is made under paragraph (f)(2) of this section to distribute

earnings and profits first, see section 1368(e)(3) regarding the consent required by shareholders.

(ii) *For previously taxed income and deemed dividends.* If an election is made to forego previously taxed income under paragraph (f)(4) of this section or to make a deemed dividend under paragraph (f)(3) of this section, consent by each "affected shareholder," as defined in section 1368(e)(3)(B), is required.

(iii) *Corporate statement regarding elections.* A corporation makes an election for a taxable year under this paragraph (f) by attaching a statement to a timely filed original or amended return required to be filed under section 6037 for that taxable year. In the statement, the corporation must identify the election it is making under § 1.1368-1(f) and must state that each shareholder consents to the election. An officer of the corporation must sign under penalties of perjury the statement on behalf of the corporation. A statement of election to make a deemed dividend under this paragraph must include the amount of the deemed dividend that is distributed to each shareholder.

(iv) *Irrevocable elections.* The elections under this paragraph (f) are irrevocable and are effective only for the taxable year for which they are made. In applying the preceding sentence to elections under this paragraph (f), an election to terminate the taxable year under section 1377(a)(2) or § 1.1368-1(g)(2) is disregarded.

(g) *Special rule—*(1) *Election to terminate year under § 1.1368-1(g)(2).* If an election is made under paragraph (g)(2) of this section to terminate the year when there is a qualifying disposition, this section applies as if the taxable year consisted of separate taxable years, the first of which ends at the close of the day on which there is a qualifying disposition of stock.

(2) *Election in case of a qualifying disposition—*(i) *In general.* In the case of a qualifying disposition, a corporation may elect under this paragraph (g)(2)(i) to treat the year as if it consisted of separate taxable years, the first of which ends at the close of the day on which the qualifying disposition occurs. A *qualifying disposition* is—

(A) A disposition by a shareholder of 20 percent or more of the outstanding stock of the corporation in one or more transactions during any thirty-day period during the corporation's taxable year;

(B) A redemption treated as an exchange under section 302(a) or section 303(a) of 20 percent or more of the outstanding stock of the corporation from a shareholder in one or more transactions during any thirty-day period during the corporation's taxable year; or

Reg. § 1.1368-1(g)(2)

(C) An issuance of an amount of stock equal to or greater than 25 percent of the previously outstanding stock to one or more new shareholders during any thirty-day period during the corporation's taxable year.

(ii) *Effect of the election.* A corporation making an election under paragraph (g)(2)(i) of this section must treat the taxable year as separate taxable years for purposes of allocating items of income and loss; making adjustments to the AAA, earnings and profits, and basis; and determining the tax effect of distributions under section 1368(b) and (c). An election made under paragraph (g)(2)(i) of this section may be made upon the occurrence of any qualifying disposition. Dispositions of stock that are taken into account as part of a qualifying disposition are not taken into account in determining whether a subsequent qualifying disposition has been made.

(iii) *Time and manner of making election.* A corporation makes an election under paragraph (g)(2)(i) of this section for a taxable year by attaching a statement to a timely filed original or amended return required to be filed under section 6037 for a taxable year (without regard to the election under paragraph (g)(2)(i) of this section). In the statement, the corporation must state that it is electing for the taxable year under § 1.1368-1(g)(2)(i) to treat the taxable year as if it consisted of separate taxable years. The corporation also must set forth facts in the statement relating to the qualifying disposition (e.g., sale, gift, stock issuance, or redemption), and state that each shareholder who held stock in the corporation during the taxable year (without regard to the election under paragraph (g)(2)(i) of this section) consents to this election. An officer of the corporation must sign under penalties of perjury the statement on behalf of the corporation. For purposes of this election, a shareholder of the corporation for the taxable year is a shareholder as described in section 1362(a)(2). A single election statement may be filed for all elections made under paragraph (g)(2)(i) of this section for the taxable year. An election made under paragraph (g)(2)(i) of this section is irrevocable.

(iv) *Coordination with election under section 1377(a)(2).* If the event resulting in a qualifying disposition also results in a termination of a shareholder's entire interest as described in § 1.1377-1(b)(4), the election under this paragraph (g)(2) cannot be made. Rather, the election under section 1377(a)(2) and § 1.1377-1(b) may be made. See § 1.1377-1(b) (concerning the election under section 1377(a)(2)). [Reg. § 1.1368-1.]

☐ [*T.D.* 8508, 12-30-93. *Amended by T.D.* 8696, 12-20-96 *and T.D.* 8852, 12-21-99.]

§ 1.1368-2. Accumulated adjustments account (AAA).—(a) *Accumulated adjustments account*—(1) *In general.* The accumulated adjustments account is an account of the S corporation and is not apportioned among shareholders. The AAA is relevant for all taxable years beginning on or after January 1, 1983, for which the corporation is an S corporation. On the first day of the first year for which the corporation is an S corporation, the balance of the AAA is zero. The AAA is increased in the manner provided in paragraph (a)(2) of this section and is decreased in the manner provided in paragraph (a)(3) of this section. For the adjustments to the AAA in the case of redemptions, liquidations, reorganizations, and corporate separations, see paragraph (d) of this section.

(2) *Increases to the AAA.* The AAA is increased for the taxable year of the corporation by the sum of the following items with respect to the corporation for the taxable year:

(i) The items of income described in section 1366(a)(1)(A) other than income that is exempt from tax;

(ii) Any nonseparately computed income determined under section 1366(a)(1)(B); and

(iii) The excess of the deductions for depletion over the basis of property subject to depletion unless the property is an oil or gas property the basis of which has been allocated to shareholders under section 613A(c)(11).

(3) *Decreases to the AAA*—(i) *In general.* The AAA is decreased for the taxable year of the corporation by the sum of the following items with respect to the corporation for the taxable year—

(A) The items of loss or deduction described in section 1366(a)(1)(A);

(B) Any nonseparately computed loss determined under section 1366(a)(1)(B);

(C) Any expense of the corporation not deductible in computing its taxable income and not properly chargeable to a capital account, other than—

(*1*) Federal taxes attributable to any taxable year in which the corporation was a C corporation; and

(*2*) Expenses related to income that is exempt from tax; and

(D) The sum of the shareholders' deductions for depletion for any oil or gas property held by the corporation described in section 1367(a)(2)(E).

(ii) *Extent of allowable reduction.* The AAA may be decreased under paragraph (a)(3)(i) of this section below zero. The AAA is decreased by noncapital, nondeductible expenses under paragraph (a)(3)(i)(C) of this section even though a

Reg. § 1.1368-2(a)(1)

portion of the noncapital, nondeductible expenses is not taken into account by a shareholder under § 1.1367-1(g) (relating to the elective ordering rule). The AAA is also decreased by the entire amount of any loss or deduction even though a portion of the loss or deduction is not taken into account by a shareholder under section 1366(d)(1) or is otherwise not currently deductible under the Internal Revenue Code. However, in any subsequent taxable year in which the loss, deduction, or noncapital, nondeductible expense is treated as incurred by the corporation with respect to the shareholder under section 1366(d)(2) or § 1.1367-1(g) (or in which the loss or deduction is otherwise allowed to the shareholder), no further adjustment is made to the AAA.

(iii) *Decrease to the AAA for distributions.* The AAA is decreased (but not below zero) by any portion of a distribution to which section 1368(b) or (c)(1) applies.

(4) *Ordering rules for the AAA for taxable years beginning before January 1, 1997.* For any taxable year beginning before January 1, 1997, the adjustments to the AAA are made in the following order—

(i) The AAA is increased under paragraph (a)(2) of this section before it is decreased under paragraph (a)(3) of this section for the taxable year;

(ii) The AAA is decreased under paragraph (a)(3)(i) of this section before it is decreased under paragraph (a)(3) (iii) of this section;

(iii) The AAA is decreased (but not below zero) by any portion of an ordinary distribution to which section 1368(b) or (c)(1) applies; and

(iv) The AAA is adjusted (whether negative or positive) for redemption distributions under paragraph (d)(1) of this section.

(5) *Ordering rules for the AAA for taxable years beginning on or after August 18, 1998.* For any taxable year of the S corporation beginning on or after August 18, 1998, the adjustments to the AAA are made in the following order—

(i) The AAA is increased under paragraph (a)(2) of this section before it is decreased under paragraph (a)(3)(i) of this section for the taxable year;

(ii) The AAA is decreased under paragraph (a)(3)(i) of this section (without taking into account any net negative adjustment (as defined in section 1368(e)(1)(C)(ii)) before it is decreased under paragraph (a)(3)(iii) of this section;

(iii) The AAA is decreased (but not below zero) by any portion of an ordinary distribution to which section 1368(b) or (c)(1) applies;

(iv) The AAA is decreased by any net negative adjustment (as defined in section 1368(e)(1)(C)(ii)); and

(v) The AAA is adjusted (whether negative or positive) for redemption distributions under paragraph (d)(1) of this section.

(b) *Distributions in excess of the AAA*—(1) *In general.* A portion of the AAA (determined under paragraph (b)(2) of this section) is allocated to each of the distributions made for the taxable year if—

(i) An S corporation makes more than one distribution of property with respect to its stock during the taxable year of the corporation (including an S short year as defined under section 1362(e)(1)(A));

(ii) The AAA has a positive balance at the close of the year; and

(iii) The sum of the distributions made during the corporation's taxable year exceeds the balance of the AAA at the close of the year.

(2) *Amount of the AAA allocated to each distribution.* The amount of the AAA allocated to each distribution is determined by multiplying the balance of the AAA at the close of the current taxable year by a fraction, the numerator of which is the amount of the distribution and the denominator of which is the amount of all distributions made during the taxable year. For purposes of this paragraph (b)(2), the term *all distributions made during the taxable year* does not include any distribution treated as from earnings and profits or previously taxed income pursuant to an election made under section 1368(e)(3) and § 1.1368-1(f)(2). See paragraph (d)(1) of this section for rules relating to the adjustments to the AAA for redemptions and distributions in the year of a redemption.

(c) *Distribution of money and loss property*—(1) *In general.* The amount of the AAA allocated to a distribution under this section must be further allocated (under paragraph (c)(2) of this section) if the distribution—

(i) Consists of property the adjusted basis of which exceeds its fair market value on the date of the distribution and money;

(ii) Is a distribution to which § 1.1368-1(d)(1) applies; and

(iii) Exceeds the amount of the corporation's AAA properly allocable to that distribution.

(2) *Allocating the AAA to loss property.* The amount of the AAA allocated to the property other than money is equal to the amount of the AAA allocated to the distribution multiplied by a fraction, the numerator of which is the fair market value of the property other than money on the date of distribution and the denominator of which

is the amount of the distribution. The amount of the AAA allocated to the money is equal to the amount of the AAA allocated to the distribution reduced by the amount of the AAA allocated to the property other than money.

(d) *Adjustment in the case of redemptions, liquidations, reorganizations, and divisions*—(1) *Redemptions*—(i) *General Rule.* In the case of a redemption distribution by an S corporation that is treated as an exchange under section 302(a) or section 303(a) (a *redemption distribution*), the AAA of the corporation is adjusted in an amount equal to the ratable share of the corporation's AAA (whether negative or positive) attributable to the redeemed stock as of the date of the redemption.

(ii) *Special rule for years in which a corporation makes both ordinary and redemption distributions.* In any year in which a corporation makes one or more distributions to which section 1368(a) applies (*ordinary distributions*) and makes one or more redemption distributions, the AAA of the corporation is adjusted first for any ordinary distributions and then for any redemption distributions.

(iii) *Adjustments to earnings and profits.* Earnings and profits are adjusted under section 312 independently of any adjustments made to the AAA.

(2) *Liquidations and reorganizations.* An S corporation acquiring the assets of another S corporation in a transaction to which section 381(a) applies will succeed to and merge its AAA (whether positive or negative) with the AAA (whether positive or negative) of the distributor or transferor S corporation as of the close of the date of distribution or transfer. Thus, the AAA of the acquiring corporation after the transaction is the sum of the AAAs of the corporations prior to the transaction.

(3) *Corporate separations to which section 368(a)(1)(D) applies.* If an S corporation with accumulated earnings and profits transfers a part of its assets constituting an active trade or business to another corporation in a transaction to which section 368(a)(1)(D) applies, and immediately thereafter the stock and securities of the controlled corporation are distributed in a distribution or exchange to which section 355 (or so much of section 356 as relates to section 355) applies, the AAA of the distributing corporation immediately before the transaction is allocated between the distributing corporation and the controlled corporation in a manner similar to the manner in which the earnings and profits of the distributing corporation are allocated under section 312(h). See § 1.312-10(a).

(e) *Election to terminate year under section 1377(a)(2) or § 1.1368-1(g)(2).* If an election is made under section 1377(a)(2) (to terminate the year in the case of termination of a shareholder's interest) or § 1.1368-1(g)(2) (to terminate the year in the case of a qualifying disposition), this section applies as if the taxable year consisted of separate taxable years, the first of which ends at the close of the day on which the shareholder terminated his or her interest in the corporation or makes a substantial disposition of stock, whichever the case may be. [Reg. § 1.1368-2.]

☐ [*T.D. 8508, 12-30-93. Amended by T.D. 8852, 12-21-99 and T.D. 8869, 1-20-2000.*]

§ 1.1368-3. Examples.—The principles of §§ 1.1368-1 and 1.1368-2 are illustrated by the examples below. In each example Corporation S is a calendar year corporation:

Example 1. Distributions by S corporations without C corporation earnings and profits for taxable years beginning before January 1, 1997. (i) Corporation S, an S corporation, has no earnings and profits as of January 1, 1996, the first day of its 1996 taxable year. S's sole shareholder, A, holds 10 shares of S stock with a basis of $1 per share as of that date. On March 1, 1996, S makes a distribution of $38 to A. For S's 1996 taxable year, A's pro rata share of the amount of the items described in section 1367(a)(1) (relating to increases in basis of stock) is $50 and A's pro rata share of the amount of the items described in section 1367(a)(2)(B) through (D) (relating to decreases in basis of stock for items other than distributions) is $26.

(ii) Under section 1368(d)(1) and § 1.1368-1(e)(1), the adjustments to the bases of A's stock in S described in section 1367 are made before the distribution rules of section 1368 are applied. Thus, A's basis per share in the stock is $3.40 ($1 + [($50 − $26) / 10 shares]) before taking into account the distribution. Under section 1367(a)(2)(A), the basis of A's stock is decreased by distributions to A that are not includible in A's income. Under § 1.1367-1(c)(3), the amount of the distribution that is attributable to each share of A's stock is $3.80 ($38 distribution / 10 shares). However, A only has a basis of $3.40 in each share, and basis may not be reduced below zero. Therefore, the basis of each share of his stock is reduced by $3.40 to zero, and the remaining $4.00 of the distribution ([$3.80 − $3.40] × 10 shares) is treated as gain from the sale or exchange of property. As of January 1, 1997, A has a basis of $0 in his shares of S stock.

Example 2. Distributions by S corporations without earnings and profits for taxable years beginning on or after August 18, 1998. (i) Corporation S, an S corporation, has no earnings and profits as of January 1, 2001, the first day of its 2001 taxable year. S's sole shareholder, A, holds 10 shares of S stock with a basis of $1 per share as of that date. On March 1, 2001, S makes a distribution of $38 to A. The balance in Corporation S's AAA is $100. For S's 2001 taxable year, A's pro rata share of the amount of the items described in section 1367(a)(1) (relating to increases in basis of stock) is $50. A's pro rata share of the amount of the items described in sections 1367(a)(2)(B) through (D) (relating to decreases in basis of stock for items other than distributions) is $26, $20 of which is attributable to items described in section 1367(a)(2)(B) and (C) and $6 of which is attributable to items described in section 1367(a)(2)(D) (relating to decreases in basis attributable to noncapital, nondeductible expenses).

(ii) Under section 1368(d)(1) and § 1.1368-1(e)(1) and (2), the adjustments to the basis of A's stock in S described in sections 1367(a)(1) are made before the distribution rules of section 1368 are applied. Thus, A's basis per share in the stock is $6.00 ($1 + [$50/10]) before taking into account the distribution. Under section 1367(a)(2)(A), the basis of A's stock is decreased by distributions to A that are not includible in A's income. Under § 1.1367-1(c)(3), the amount of the distribution that is attributable to each share of A's stock is $3.80 ($38 distribution/10 shares). Thus, A's basis per share in the stock is $2.20 ($6.00 − $3.80), after taking into account the distribution. Under section 1367(a)(2)(D), the basis of each share of A's stock in S after taking into account the distribution, $2.20, is decreased by $.60 ($6 noncapital, nondeductible expenses/10). Thus, A's basis per share after taking into account the nondeductible, noncapital expenses is $1.60. Under section 1367(a)(2)(B) and (C), A's basis per share is further decreased by $2 ($20 items described in section 1367(a)(2)(B) and (C) /10 shares). However, basis may not be reduced below zero. Therefore, the basis of each share of A's stock is reduced to zero. As of January 1, 2002, A has a basis of $0 in his shares of S stock. Pursuant to section 1366(d)(2), the $.40 of loss in excess of A's basis in each of his shares of S stock is treated as incurred by the corporation in the succeeding taxable year with respect to A.

Example 3. Distributions by S corporations with C corporation earnings and profits for taxable years beginning before January 1, 1997. (i) Corporation S properly elects to be an S corporation beginning January 1, 1997, and as of that date has accumulated earnings and profits of $30. B, an individual and sole shareholder of Corporation S, has 10 shares of S stock with a basis of $12 per share. In addition, B lends $30 to S evidenced by a demand note.

(ii) During 1997, S has a nonseparately computed loss of $150. S makes no distributions to B during 1997. Under section 1366(d)(1), B is allowed a loss equal to $150, the amount equal to the sum of B's bases in his shares of stock and his basis in the debt. Under section 1367, the loss reduces B's adjusted basis in his stock and debt to $0. Under § 1.1368-2(a)(3), S's AAA as of December 31, 1997, has a deficit of $150 as a result of S's loss for the year.

(iii) For 1998, S has $220 of separately stated income and distributes $110 to B. The balance in the AAA (negative $150 from 1997) is increased by $220 for S's income for the year and decreased to $0 for the portion of the distribution that is treated as being from the AAA ($70). Under § 1.1367-2(c), B's net increase is $150, determined by reducing the $220 of income by the $70 of the distribution not includible in income by B. Thus, B's basis in the debt is fully restored to $30, and B's basis in S stock (before accounting for the distribution) is increased from zero to $19 per share ([$220 − $30 applied to the debt]/10). Thirty dollars of the distribution is considered a dividend to the extent of S's $30 of earnings and profits, and the remaining $10 of the distribution reduces B's basis in the S stock. Thus, B's basis in the S stock as of December 31, 1998, is $11 per share ($19 − [$70 AAA distribution/10] − [10 distribution treated as a reduction in basis/10]). The balance in the AAA is $0, S's earnings and profits are $0, and B's basis in the loan is $30.

Example 4. Distributions by S corporations with earnings and profits and no net negative adjustment for taxable years beginning on or after August 18, 1998. (i) Corporation S, an S corporation, has accumulated earnings and profits of $1,000 and a balance in the AAA of $2,000 on January 1, 2001. S's sole shareholder B holds 100 shares of stock with a basis of $20 per share as of January 1, 2001. On April 1, 2001, S makes a distribution of $1,500 to B. B's pro rata share of the income earned by S during 2001 is $2,000 and B's pro rata share of S's losses is $1,500. For the taxable year ending December 31, 2001, S does not have a net negative adjustment as defined in section 1368(e)(1)(C). S does not make the election under section 1368(e)(3) and § 1.1368-1(f)(2) to distribute its earnings and profits before its AAA.

(ii) The AAA is increased from $2,000 to $4,000 for the $2,000 of income earned during the 2001 taxable year. The AAA is decreased from $4,000 to $2,500 for the $1,500 of losses. The AAA is decreased from $2,500 to $1,000 for the portion of the distribution ($1,500) to B that does not exceed the AAA.

Reg. § 1.1368-3

(iii) As of December 31, 2001, B's basis in his stock is $10 ($20 + $20 ($2,000 income/100 shares) − $15 ($1,500 distribution/100 shares) − $15 ($1,500 loss/100 shares).

Example 5. Distributions by S corporations with earnings and profits and net negative adjustment for taxable years beginning on or after August 18, 1998. (i) Corporation S, an S corporation, has accumulated earnings and profits of $1,000 and a balance in the AAA of $2,000 on January 1, 2001. S's sole shareholder B holds 100 shares of stock with a basis of $20 per share as of January 1, 2001. On April 1, 2001, S makes a distribution of $2,000 to B. B's pro rata share of the income earned by S during 2001 is $2,000 and B's pro rata share of S's losses is $3,500. For the taxable year ending December 31, 2001, S has a net negative adjustment as defined in section 1368(e)(1)(C). S does not make the election under section 1368(e)(3) and § 1.1368-1(f)(2) to distribute its earnings and profits before its AAA.

(ii) The AAA is increased from $2,000 to $4,000 for the $2,000 of income earned during the 2001 taxable year. Because under section 1368(e)(1)(C)(ii) and § 1.1368-2(a)(ii), the net negative adjustment is not taken into account, the AAA is decreased from $4,000 to $2,000 for the portion of the losses ($2,000) that does not exceed the income earned during the 2001 taxable year. The AAA is reduced from $2,000 to zero for the portion of the distribution to B ($2,000) that does not exceed the AAA. The AAA is decreased from zero to a negative $1,500 for the portion of the $3,500 of loss that exceeds the $2,000 of income earned during the 2001 taxable year.

(iii) Under § 1.1367-1(c)(1), the basis of a shareholder's share in an S corporation stock may not be reduced below zero. Accordingly, as of December 31, 2001, B's basis per share in his stock is zero ($20 + $20 income − $20 distribution − $35 loss). Pursuant to section 1366(d)(2), the $15 of loss in excess of B's basis in each of his shares of S stock is treated as incurred by the corporation in the succeeding taxable year with respect to B.

Example 6. Election in case of disposition of substantial amount of stock. (i) Corporation S, an S corporation, has earnings and profits of $3,000 and a balance in the AAA of $1,000 on January 1, 1997. C, an individual and the sole shareholder of Corporation S, has 100 shares of S stock with a basis of $10 per share. On July 3, 1997, C sells 50 shares of his S stock to D, an individual, for $250. For 1997, S has taxable income of $1,000, of which $500 was earned on or before July 3, 1997, and $500 earned after July 3, 1997. During its 1997 taxable year, S distributes $1,000 to C on February 1 and $1,000 to each of C and D on August 1.

S does not make the election under section 1368(e)(3) and § 1.1368-1(f)(2) to distribute its earnings and profits before its AAA. S makes the election under § 1.1368-1(g)(2) to treat its taxable year as if it consisted of separate taxable years, the first of which ends at the close of July 3, 1997, the date of the qualifying disposition.

(ii) Under section § 1.1368-1(g)(2), for the period ending on July 3, 1997, S's AAA is $500 ($1,000 (AAA as of January 1, 1997) + $500 (income earned from January 1, 1997 through July 3, 1997) − $1,000 (distribution made on February 1, 1997)). C's bases in his shares of stock is decreased to $5 per share ($10 (original basis) + $5 (increase per share for income) − $10 (decrease per share for distribution)).

(iii) The AAA is adjusted at the end of the taxable year for the period July 4 through December 31, 1997. It is increased from $500 (AAA as of the close of July 3, 1997) to $1,000 for the income earned during this period and is decreased by $1,000, the portion of the distribution ($2,000 in total) made to C and D on August 1 that does not exceed the AAA. The $1,000 portion of the distribution that remains after the AAA is reduced to zero is attributable to earnings and profits. Therefore C and D each have a dividend of $500, which does not affect their basis or S's AAA. The earnings and profits account is reduced from $3,000 to $2,000.

(iv) As of December 31, 1997, C and D have bases in their shares of stock of zero ($5 (basis as of July 4) + $5 ($500 income/100 shares) − $10 ($1,000 distribution/100 shares)). C and D each will report $500 as dividend income, which does not affect their basis or S's AAA.

Example 7. Election to distribute earnings and profits first. (i) Corporation S has been a calendar year C corporation since 1975. For 1982, S elects for the first time to be taxed under subchapter S, and during 1982 has $60 of earnings and profits. As of December 31, 1995, S has an AAA of $10 and earnings and profits of $160, consisting of $100 of subchapter C earnings and profits and $60 of subchapter S earnings and profits. For 1996, S has $200 of taxable income and the AAA is increased to $210 (before taking distributions into account). During 1996, S distributes $240 to its shareholders. With its 1996 tax return, S properly elects under section 1368(e)(3) and § 1.1368-1(f)(2) to distribute its earnings and profits before its AAA.

(ii) Because S elected to distribute its earnings and profits before its AAA, the first $100 of the distribution is characterized as a distribution from subchapter C earnings and profits; the next $60 of the distribution is characterized as a distribution from subchapter S earnings and profits.

Reg. § 1.1368-3

Because $160 of the distribution is from earnings and profits, the shareholders of S have a $160 dividend. The remaining $80 of the distribution is a distribution from S's AAA and is treated by the shareholders as a return of capital or gain from the sale or exchange of property, as appropriate, under § 1.1368-1(d)(1). S's AAA, as of December 31, 1996, equals $130 ($210 − $80).

Example 8. Distributions in excess of the AAA. (i) On January 1, 1995, Corporation S has $40 of earnings and profits and a balance in the AAA of $100. S has two shareholders, E and F, each of whom own 50 shares of S's stock. For 1995, S has taxable income of $50, which increases the AAA to $150 as of December 31, 1995 (before taking into account distributions made during 1995). On February 1, 1995, S distributes $60 to each shareholder. On September 1, 1995, S distributes $30 to each shareholder. S does not make the election under section 1368(e)(3) and § 1.1368-1(f)(2) to distribute its earnings and profits before its AAA.

(ii) The sum of the distributions exceed S's AAA. Therefore, under § 1.1368-2(b), a portion of S's $150 balance in the AAA as of December 31, 1995, is allocated to each of the February 1 and September 1 distributions based on the respective sizes of the distributions. Accordingly, S must allocate $100 ($150 (AAA) × ($120 (February 1 distribution) / $180 (the sum of the distributions))) of the AAA to the February 1 distribution, and $50 ($150 × ($60 / $180)) to the September 1 distribution. The portions of the distributions to which the AAA is allocated are treated by the shareholder as a return of capital or gain from the sale or exchange of property, as appropriate. The remainder of the two distributions is treated as a dividend to the extent that it does not exceed S's earnings and profits. E and F must each report $10 of dividend income for the February 1 distribution. For the September 1 distribution, E and F must each report $5 of dividend income.

Example 9. Ordinary and redemption distributions in the same taxable year. (i) On January 1, 1995, Corporation S, an S corporation, has $20 of earnings and profits and a balance in the AAA of $10. S has two shareholders, G and H, each of whom owns 50 shares of S's stock. For 1995, S has taxable income of $16, which increases the AAA to $26 as of December 31, 1995 (before taking into account distributions made during 1995). On February 1, 1995, S distributes $10 to each shareholder. On December 31, 1995, S redeems for $13 all of shareholder G's stock in a redemption that is treated as a sale or exchange under section 302(a).

(ii) The sum of the ordinary distributions does not exceed S's AAA. Therefore, S must reduce the $26 balance in the AAA by $20 for the February 1 ordinary distribution. The portions of the distribu-

tion by which the AAA is reduced are treated by the shareholders as a return of capital or gain from the sale or exchange of property. S must adjust the remaining AAA, $6, in an amount equal to the ratable share of the remaining AAA attributable to the redeemed stock, or $3 (50% × $6).

(iii) S also must adjust the earnings and profits of $20 in an amount equal to the ratable share of the earnings and profits attributable to the redeemed stock. Therefore, S adjusts the earnings and profits by $10 (50% × $20), the ratable share of the earnings and profits attributable to the redeemed stock.

[Reg. § 1.1368-3.]

☐ [*T.D.* 8508, 12-30-93. *Amended by T.D.* 8852, 12-21-99.]

§ 18.1371-1. Election to treat distributions as dividends during certain post-termination transition periods (Temporary).—A corporation may make an election under section 1371(e) (as amended by section 721(o) of the Act) to treat all distributions of money made during the post-termination transition period described in section 1377(b)(1)(A) as coming out of the corporation's earnings and profits (after earnings and profits have been eliminated, the distributions are applied against and reduce the adjusted basis of the stock). The election may be made only with the consent of each shareholder to whom the corporation makes a distribution (whether or not it is a cash distribution) during such post-termination transition period. Any such election shall be made by the corporation by attaching to its income tax return for the C year in which such post-termination transition period ends a statement which clearly indicates that the corporation elects to have section 1371(e)(1) not apply to all distributions made during such post-termination transition period. The election shall not be effective unless such statement is signed by a person authorized to sign the return required to be filed under section 6012 and by each shareholder required to consent to the election. [Temporary Reg. § 18.1371-1.]

☐ [*T.D.* 7976, 9-5-84.]

§ 1.1374-1. General rules and definitions.—(a) *Computation of tax.* The tax imposed on the income of an S corporation by section 1374(a) for any taxable year during the recognition period is computed as follows—

(1) Step One: Determine the net recognized built-in gain of the corporation for the taxable year under section 1374(d)(2) and § 1.1374-2;

(2) Step Two: Reduce the net recognized built-in gain (but not below zero) by any net

Reg. § 1.1374-1(a)(2)

operating loss and capital loss carryforward allowed under section 1374(b)(2) and § 1.1374-5;

(3) Step Three: Compute a tentative tax by applying the rate of tax determined under section 1374(b)(1) for the taxable year to the amount determined under paragraph (a)(2) of this section;

(4) Step Four: Compute the final tax by reducing the tentative tax (but not below zero) by any credit allowed under section 1374(b)(3) and § 1.1374-6.

(b) *Anti-trafficking rules.* If section 382, 383, or 384 would have applied to limit the use of a corporation's recognized built-in loss or section 1374 attributes at the beginning of the first day of the recognition period if the corporation had remained a C corporation, these sections apply to limit their use in determining the S corporation's pre-limitation amount, taxable income limitation, net unrealized built-in gain limitation, deductions against net recognized built-in gain, and credits against the section 1374 tax.

(c) *Section 1374 attributes.* Section 1374 attributes are the loss carryforwards allowed under section 1374(b)(2) as a deduction against net recognized built-in gain and the credit and credit carryforwards allowed under section 1374(b)(3) as a credit against the section 1374 tax.

(d) *Recognition period.* The recognition period is the 10-year (120-month) period beginning on the first day the corporation is an S corporation or the day an S corporation acquires assets in a section 1374(d)(8) transaction. For example, if the first day of the recognition period is July 14, 1996, the last day of the recognition period is July 13, 2006. If the recognition period for certain assets ends during an S corporation's taxable year (for example, because the corporation was on a fiscal year as a C corporation and changed to a calendar year as an S corporation or because an S corporation acquired assets in a section 1374(d)(8) transaction during a taxable year), the S corporation must determine its pre-limitation amount (as defined in § 1.1374-2(a)(1)) for the year as if the corporation's books were closed at the end of the recognition period.

(e) *Predecessor corporation.* For purposes of section 1374(c)(1), if the basis of an asset of the S corporation is determined (in whole or in part) by reference to the basis of the asset (or any other property) in the hands of another corporation, the other corporation is a predecessor corporation of the S corporation. [Reg. § 1.1374-1.]

☐ [T.D. 8579, 12-23-94.]

§ 1.1374-2. Net recognized built-in gain.—(a) *In general.* An S corporation's net recognized built-in gain for any taxable year is the least of—

(1) Its taxable income determined by using all rules applying to C corporations and considering only its recognized built-in gain, recognized built-in loss, and recognized built-in gain carryover (pre-limitation amount);

(2) Its taxable income determined by using all rules applying to C corporations as modified by section 1375(b)(1)(B) (taxable income limitation); and

(3) The amount by which its net unrealized built-in gain exceeds its net recognized built-in gain for all prior taxable years (net unrealized built-in gain limitation).

(b) *Allocation rule.* If an S corporation's pre-limitation amount for any taxable year exceeds its net recognized built-in gain for that year, the S corporation's net recognized built-in gain consists of a ratable portion of each item of income, gain, loss, and deduction included in the pre-limitation amount.

(c) *Recognized built-in gain carryover.* If an S corporation's net recognized built-in gain for any taxable year is equal to its taxable income limitation, the amount by which its pre-limitation amount exceeds its taxable income limitation is a recognized built-in gain carryover included in its pre-limitation amount for the succeeding taxable year. The recognized built-in gain carryover consists of that portion of each item of income, gain, loss, and deduction not included in the S corporation's net recognized built-in gain for the year the carryover arose, as determined under paragraph (b) of this section.

(d) *Accounting methods.* In determining its taxable income for pre-limitation amount and taxable income limitation purposes, a corporation must use the accounting method(s) it uses for tax purposes as an S corporation.

(e) *Example.* The rules of this section are illustrated by the following example.

Example. Net recognized built-in gain. X is a calendar year C corporation that elects to become an S corporation on January 1, 1996. X has a net unrealized built-in gain of $50,000 and no net operating loss or capital loss carryforwards. In 1996, X has a pre-limitation amount of $20,000, consisting of ordinary income of $15,000 and capital gain of $5,000, a taxable income limitation of $9,600, and a net unrealized built-in gain limitation of $50,000. Therefore, X's net recognized built-in gain for 1996 is $9,600, because that is the least of the three amounts described in paragraph (a) of this section. Under paragraph (b) of this section, X's net recognized built-in gain consists of recognized built-in ordinary income of $7,200 [$15,000 × ($9,600/$20,000) = $7,200] and recognized built-in capital gain of $2,400 [$5,000 × ($9,600/$20,000) = $2,400]. Under

Reg. § 1.1374-2(a)(1)

paragraph (c) of this section, X has a recognized built-in gain carryover to 1997 of $10,400 ($20,000 − $9,600 = $10,400), consisting of $7,800 ($15,000 − $7,200 = $7,800) of recognized built-in ordinary income and $2,600 ($5,000 − $2,400 = $2,600) of recognized built-in capital gain.

[Reg. § 1.1374-2.]

[*T.D.* 8579, 12-23-94.]

§ 1.1374-3. Net unrealized built-in gain.—(a) *In general.* An S corporation's net unrealized built-in gain is the total of the following—

(1) The amount that would be the amount realized if, at the beginning of the first day of the recognition period, the corporation had remained a C corporation and had sold all its assets at fair market value to an unrelated party that assumed all its liabilities; decreased by

(2) Any liability of the corporation that would be included in the amount realized on the sale referred to in paragraph (a)(1) of this section, but only if the corporation would be allowed a deduction on payment of the liability; decreased by

(3) The aggregate adjusted bases of the corporation's assets at the time of the sale referred to in paragraph (a)(1) of this section; increased or decreased by

(4) The corporation's section 481 adjustments that would be taken into account on the sale referred to in paragraph (a)(1) of this section; and increased by

(5) Any recognized built-in loss that would not be allowed as a deduction under section 382, 383, or 384 on the sale referred to in paragraph (a)(1) of this section.

(b) *Example.* The rules of this section are illustrated by the following example.

Example. Net unrealized built-in gain. (i) (a) X, a calendar year C corporation using the cash method, elects to become an S corporation on January 1, 1996. On December 31, 1995, X has assets and liabilities as follows:

Assets	FMV	Basis
Factory	$ 500,000	$900,000
Accounts Receivable	300,000	0
Goodwill	250,000	0
Total	$1,050,000	$900,000

Liabilities	Amount	
Mortgage	$ 200,000	
Accounts Payable	100,000	
Total	$ 300,000	

(b) Further, X must include a total of $60,000 in taxable income in 1996, 1997, and 1998 under section 481(a).

(ii) If, on December 31, 1995, X sold all its assets to a third party that assumed all its liabilities, X's amount realized would be $1,050,000 ($750,000 cash received + $300,000 liabilities assumed = $1,050,000). Thus, X's net unrealized built-in gain is determined as follows:

Amount realized	$1,050,000
Deduction allowed	(100,000)
Basis of X's assets	(900,000)
Section 481 adjustments	60,000
Net unrealized built-in gain	$110,000

[Reg. § 1.1374-3.]

□ [*T.D.* 8579, 12-23-94.]

§ 1.1374-4. Recognized built-in gain or loss.—(a) *Sales and exchanges*—(1) *In general.* Section 1374(d)(3) or 1374(d)(4) applies to any gain or loss recognized during the recognition period in a transaction treated as a sale or exchange for federal income tax purposes.

* * *

[Reg. § 1.1374-4.]

□ [*T.D.* 8579, 12-23-94. *Amended by T.D.* 8995, 5-14-2002.]

§ 1.1374-7. Inventory.—(a) *Valuation.* The fair market value of the inventory of an S corporation on the first day of the recognition period equals the amount that a willing buyer would pay a willing seller for the inventory in a purchase of all the S corporation's assets by a buyer that expects to continue to operate the S corporation's business. For purposes of the preceding sentence, the buyer and seller are presumed not to be under any compulsion to buy or sell and to have reasonable knowledge of all relevant facts.

(b) *Identity of dispositions.* The inventory method used by an S corporation for tax purposes must be used to identify whether the inventory it disposes of during the recognition period is inventory it held on the first day of that period. Thus, a corporation using the LIFO method does not dispose of inventory it held on the first day of the recognition period unless the carrying value of its inventory for a taxable year during that period is less than the carrying value of its inventory on the first day of the recognition period (determined using the LIFO method as described in section 472). However, if a corporation changes its method of accounting for inventory (for example, from the FIFO method to the LIFO method or from the LIFO method to the FIFO method) with

Reg. § 1.1374-7(b)

a principal purpose of avoiding the tax imposed under section 1374, it must use its former method to identify its dispositions of inventory. [Reg. § 1.1374-7.]

☐ [*T.D. 8579, 12-23-94.*]

§ 1.1374-8. Section 1374(d)(8) transactions.—(a) *In general.* If any S corporation acquires any asset in a transaction in which the S corporation's basis in the asset is determined (in whole or in part) by reference to a C corporation's basis in the assets (or any other property) (a section 1374(d)(8) transaction), section 1374 applies to the net recognized built-in gain attributable to the assets acquired in any section 1374(d)(8) transaction.

(b) *Separate determination of tax.* For purposes of the tax imposed under section 1374(d)(8), a separate determination of tax is made with respect to the assets the S corporation acquires in one section 1374(d)(8) transaction from the assets the S corporation acquires in another section 1374(d)(8) transaction and from the assets the corporation held when it became an S corporation. Thus, an S corporation's section 1374 attributes when it became an S corporation may only be used to reduce the section 1374 tax imposed on dispositions of assets the S corporation held at that time. Similarly, an S corporation's section 1374 attributes acquired in a section 1374(d)(8) transaction may only be used to reduce a section 1374 tax imposed on dispositions of assets the S corporation acquired in the same transaction. If an S corporation makes QSub elections under section 1361(b)(3) for a tiered group of subsidiaries effective on the same day, see § 1.1361-4(b)(2).

(c) *Taxable income limitation.* For purposes of paragraph (a) of this section, an S corporation's taxable income limitation under § 1.1374-2(a)(2) for any taxable year is allocated between or among each of the S corporation's separate determinations of net recognized built-in gain for that year (determined without regard to the taxable income limitation) based on the ratio of each of those determinations to the sum of all of those determinations.

(d) *Examples.* The rules of this section are illustrated by the following examples.

Example 1. Separate determination of tax. (i) X is a C corporation that elected to become an S corporation effective January 1, 1986 (before section 1374 was amended in the Tax Reform Act of 1986). X has a net operating loss carryforward of $20,000 arising in 1985 when X was a C corporation. On January 1, 1996, Y (an unrelated C corporation) merges into X in a transaction to which section 368(a)(1)(A) applies. Y has no loss carryforwards, credits, or credit carryforwards. The assets X acquired from Y are subject to tax

under section 1374 and have a net unrealized built-in gain of $150,000.

(ii) In 1996, X has a pre-limitation amount of $50,000 on dispositions of assets acquired from Y and a taxable income limitation of $100,000 (because only one group of assets is subject to section 1374, there is no allocation of the taxable income limitation). As a result, X has a net recognized built-in gain on those assets of $50,000. X's $20,000 net operating loss carryforward may not be used as a deduction against its $50,000 net recognized built-in gain on the assets X acquired from Y. Therefore, X has a section 1374 tax of $17,500 ($50,000 × .35 = $17,500, assuming a 35 percent tax rate) for its 1996 taxable year.

Example 2. Allocation of taxable income limitation. (i) Y is a C corporation that elects to become an S corporation effective January 1, 1996. The assets Y holds when it becomes an S corporation have a net unrealized built-in gain of $5,000. Y has no loss carryforwards, credits, or credit carryforwards. On January 1, 1997, Z (an unrelated C corporation) merges into Y in a transaction to which section 368(a)(1)(A) applies. Z has no loss carryforwards, credits, or credit carryforwards. The assets Y acquired from Z are subject to tax under section 1374 and have a net unrealized built-in gain of $80,000.

(ii) In 1997, Y has a pre-limitation amount on the assets it held when it became an S corporation of $15,000, a pre-limitation amount on the assets Y acquired from Z of $15,000, and a taxable income limitation of $10,000. However, because the assets Y held on becoming an S corporation have a net unrealized built-in gain of $5,000, its net recognized built-in gain on those assets is limited to $5,000 before taking into account the taxable income limitation. Y's taxable income limitation of $10,000 is allocated between the assets Y held on becoming an S corporation and the assets Y acquired from Z for purposes of determining the net recognized built-in gain from each pool of assets. Thus, Y's net recognized built-in gain on the assets Y held on becoming an S corporation is $2,500 [$10,000 × ($5,000/$20,000) = $2,500]. Y's net recognized built-in gain on the assets Y acquired from Z is $7,500 [$10,000 × ($15,000/$20,000) = $7,500]. Therefore, Y has a section 1374 tax of $3,500 [($2,500 + $7,500) × .35 = $3,500, assuming a 35 percent tax rate] for its 1997 taxable year.

[Reg. § 1.1374-8.]

☐ [*T.D. 8579, 12-23-94. Amended by T.D. 8869, 1-20-2000.*]

§ 1.1375-1. Tax imposed when passive investment income of corporation having subchapter C earnings and profits exceeds 25 percent of gross receipts.—(a) *General rule.* For taxable years beginning after 1981, section 1375(a) imposes a tax on the income of certain S corporations that have passive investment income. In the case of a taxable year beginning during 1982, an electing small business corporation may elect to have the rules under this section not apply. See the regulations under section 1362 for rules on the election. For purposes of this section, the term "S corporation" shall include an electing small business corporation under prior law. This tax shall apply to an S corporation for a taxable year if the S corporation has—

(1) Subchapter C earnings and profits at the close of such taxable year, and

(2) Gross receipts more than 25 percent of which are passive investment income.

If the S corporation has no subchapter C earnings and profits at the close of the taxable year (because, for example, such earnings and profits were distributed in accordance with section 1368), the tax shall not be imposed even though the S corporation has passive investment income for the taxable year. If the tax is imposed, the tax shall be computed by multiplying the excess net passive income (as defined in paragraph (b) of this section) by the highest rate of tax specified in section 11(b).

(b) *Definitions*—(1) *Excess net passive income*—(i) *In general.* The term "excess net passive income" is defined in section 1375(b)(1), and can be expressed by the following formula:

$$\text{ENPI} = \text{NPI} \times \frac{\text{PII} - (.25 \times \text{GR})}{\text{PII}}$$

Where:
ENPI = excess net passive income
NPI = net passive income
PII = passive investment income
GR = total gross receipts

(ii) *Limitation.* The amount of the excess net passive income for any taxable year shall not exceed the corporation's taxable income for the taxable year (determined in accordance with section 1374(d) and § 1.1374-1(d)).

(2) *Net passive income.* The term "net passive income" means—

(i) Passive investment income, reduced by

(ii) The deductions allowable under chapter 1 of the Internal Revenue Code of 1954 which are directly connected (within the meaning of (b)(3) of this section) with the production of such income (other than deductions allowable under section 172 and part VIII of subchapter B).

(3) *Directly connected*— (i) *In general.* For purposes of paragraph (b)(2)(ii) of this section to be directly connected with the production of income, an item of deduction must have proximate and primary relationship to the income. Expenses, depreciation, and similar items attributable solely to such income qualify for deduction.

(ii) *Allocation of deduction.* If an item of deduction is attributable (within the meaning of paragraph (b)(3)(i) of this section) in part to passive investment income and in part to income other than passive investment income, the deduction shall be allocated between the two types of items on a reasonable basis. The portion of any deduction so allocated to passive investment in-

come shall be treated as proximately and primarily related to such income.

(4) *Other definitions.* The terms "subchapter C earnings and profits," "passive investment income," and "gross receipts" shall have the same meaning given these terms in section 1362(d)(3) and the regulations thereunder.

(c) *Special rules*—(1) *Disallowance of credits.* No credit is allowed under part IV of subchapter A of chapter 1 of the Code (other than section 34) against the tax imposed by section 1375(a) and this section.

(2) *Coordination with section 1374.* If any gain—

(i) Is taken into account in determining passive income for purposes of this section, and

(ii) Is taken into account under section 1374, the amount of such gain taken into account under section 1374(b) and § 1.1374-1(b)(1) and (2) in determining the amount of tax shall be reduced by the portion of the excess net passive income for the taxable year which is attributable (on a pro rata basis) to such gain. For purposes of the preceding sentence, the portion of excess net passive income for the taxable year which is attributable to such capital gain is equal to the amount determined by multiplying the excess net passive income by the following fraction:

$$NCG = E \over NPI$$

Where:

NCG = net capital gain

NPI = net passive income

E = Expense attributable to net capital gain

(d) *Waiver of tax in certain cases*—(1) *In general.* If an S corporation establishes to the satisfaction of the Commissioner that—

(i) It determined in good faith that it had no subchapter C earnings and profits at the close of the taxable year, and

(ii) During a reasonable period of time after it was determined that it did have subchapter C earnings and profits at the close of such taxable year such earnings and profits were distributed,

the Commissioner may waive the tax imposed by section 1375 for such taxable year. The S corporation has the burden of establishing that under the relevant facts and circumstances the Commissioner should waive the tax. For example, if an S corporation establishes that in good faith and using due diligence it determined that it had no subchapter C earnings and profits at the close of a taxable year, but it was later determined on audit that it did have subchapter C earnings and profits at the close of such taxable year, and if the corporation establishes that it distributed such earnings and profits within a reasonable time after the audit, it may be appropriate for the Commissioner to waive the tax on passive income for such taxable year.

(2) *Corporation's request for a waiver.* A request for waiver of the tax imposed by section 1375 shall be made in writing to the district director request and shall contain all relevant facts to establish that the requirements of paragraph (d)(1) of this section are met. Such request shall contain a description of how and on what date the S corporation in good faith and using due diligence determined that it had no subchapter C earnings and profits at the close of the taxable year, a description of how and on what date it was determined that the S corporation had subchapter C earnings and profits at the close of the year and a description (including dates) of any steps taken to distribute such earnings and profits. If the earnings and profits have not yet been distributed, the request shall contain a timetable for distribution and an explanation of why such timetable is reasonable. On the date the waiver is to become effective, all subchapter C earnings and profits must have been distributed.

(e) *Reduction in pass-thru for tax imposed on excess net passive income.* See section 1366(f)(3) for a special rule reducing each item of the corporation's passive investment income for purposes of section 1366(a) if a tax is imposed on the corporation under section 1375.

(f) *Examples.* The following examples illustrate the principles of this section:

Example (1). Assume Corporation M, an S corporation, has for its taxable year total gross receipts of $200,000, passive investment income of $100,000, $60,000 of which is interest income, and expenses directly connected with the production of such interest income in the amount of $10,000. Assume also that at the end of the taxable year Corporation M has subchapter C earnings and profits. Since more than 25 percent of Corporation M's total gross receipts are passive investment income, and since Corporation M has subchapter C earnings and profits at the end of the taxable year, Corporation M will be subject to the tax imposed by section 1375. The amount of excess net passive investment income is $45,000 ($90,000 × ($50,000/$100,000)). Assume that the other $40,000 of passive investment income is attributable to net capital gain and that there are no expenses directly connected with such gain. Under these facts, $20,000 of the excess net passive income is attributable to the net capital gain ($45,000 × ($40,000/$90,000)). Accordingly, the amount of gain taken into account under section 1374(b)(1) and the taxable income of Corporation M under section 1374(b)(2) shall be reduced by $20,000.

Example (2). Assume an S corporation with subchapter C earnings and profits has tax-exempt income of $400, its only passive income, gross receipts of $1,000 and taxable income of $250 and there are no expenses associated with the tax-exempt income. The corporation's excess net passive income for the taxable year would total $150 (400 × ((400 − 250)/400)). This amount is subject to the tax imposed by section 1375, notwithstanding that such amount is otherwise tax-exempt income. [Reg. § 1.1375-1.]

☐ [*T.D. 8104, 9-25-86. Amended by T.D. 8419, 5-28-92.*]

§ 1.1377-1. Pro rata share.—(a) *Computation of pro rata shares*—(1) *In general.* For purposes of subchapter S of chapter 1 of the Internal Revenue Code and this section, each shareholder's pro rata share of any S corporation item described in section 1366(a) for any taxable year is the sum of the amounts determined with respect to the shareholder by assigning an equal portion of the item to each day of the S corporation's taxable year, and then dividing that portion pro rata among the shares outstanding on that day. See paragraph (b) of this section for rules pertaining to the computation of each shareholder's pro rata share when an election is made under section 1377(a)(2) to treat the taxable year of an S corporation as if it consisted of two taxable years in the case of a termination of a shareholder's entire interest in the corporation.

(2) *Special rules*—(i) *Days on which stock has not been issued.* Solely for purposes of determining a shareholder's pro rata share of an item for a taxable year under section 1377(a) and this section, the beneficial owners of the corporation are treated as the shareholders of the corporation for any day on which the corporation has not issued any stock.

(ii) *Determining shareholder for day of stock disposition.* A shareholder who disposes of stock in an S corporation is treated as the shareholder for the day of the disposition. A shareholder who dies is treated as the shareholder for the day of the shareholder's death.

(iii) *Shareholder trust conversions.* If, during the taxable year of an S corporation, a trust that is an eligible shareholder of the S corporation converts from a trust described in section 1361(c)(2)(A)(i), (ii), (iii), or (v) for the first part of the year to a trust described in a different subpart of section 1361(c)(2)(A)(i), (ii), or (v) for the remainder of the year, the trust's share of the S corporation items is allocated between the two types of trusts. The first day that a qualified subchapter S trust (QSST) or an electing small business trust (ESBT) is treated as an S corporation shareholder is the effective date of the QSST or ESBT election. Upon the conversion, the trust is not treated as terminating its entire interest in the S corporation for purposes of paragraph (b) of this section, unless the trust was a trust described in section 1361(c)(2)(A)(ii) or (iii) before the conversion.

(b) *Election to terminate year*—(1) *In general.* If a shareholder's entire interest in an S corporation is terminated during the S corporation's taxable year and the corporation and all affected shareholders agree, the S corporation may elect under section 1377(a)(2) and this paragraph (b) (terminating election) to apply paragraph (a) of this section to the affected shareholders as if the corporation's taxable year consisted of two separate taxable years, the first of which ends at the close of the day on which the shareholder's entire interest in the S corporation is terminated. If the event resulting in the termination of the shareholder's entire interest also constitutes a qualifying disposition as described in § 1.1368-1(g)(2)(i), the election under § 1.1368-1(g)(2) cannot be made. An S corporation may not make a terminating election if the cessation of a shareholder's

interest occurs in a transaction that results in a termination under section 1362(d)(2) of the corporation's election to be an S corporation. (See section 1362(e)(3) for an election to have items assigned to each short taxable year under normal tax accounting rules in the case of a termination of a corporation's election to be an S corporation.) A terminating election is irrevocable and is effective only for the terminating event for which it is made.

(2) *Affected shareholders.* For purposes of the terminating election under section 1377(a)(2) and paragraph (b) of this section, the term *affected shareholders* means the shareholder whose interest is terminated and all shareholders to whom such shareholder has transferred shares during the taxable year. If such shareholder has transferred shares to the corporation, the term *affected shareholders* includes all persons who are shareholders during the taxable year.

(3) *Effect of the terminating election*—(i) *In general.* An S corporation that makes a terminating election for a taxable year must treat the taxable year as separate taxable years for all affected shareholders for purposes of allocating items of income (including tax-exempt income), loss, deduction, and credit; making adjustments to the accumulated adjustments account, earnings and profits, and basis; and determining the tax effect of a distribution. An S corporation that makes a terminating election must assign items of income (including tax-exempt income), loss, deduction, and credit to each deemed separate taxable year using its normal method of accounting as determined under section 446(a).

(ii) *Due date of S corporation return.* A terminating election does not affect the due date of the S corporation's return required to be filed under section 6037(a) for a taxable year (determined without regard to a terminating election).

(iii) *Taxable year of inclusion by shareholder.* A terminating election does not affect the taxable year in which an affected shareholder must take into account the affected shareholder's pro rata share of the S corporation's items of income, loss, deduction, and credit.

(iv) *S corporation that is a partner in a partnership.* A terminating election by an S corporation that is a partner in a partnership is treated as a sale or exchange of the corporation's entire interest in the partnership for purposes of section 706(c) (relating to closing the partnership taxable year), if the taxable year of the partnership ends after the shareholder's interest is terminated and within the taxable year of the S corporation (determined without regard to any terminating election) for which the terminating election is made.

(4) *Determination of whether an S shareholder's entire interest has terminated.* For purposes of the terminating election under section

1377(a)(2) and paragraph (b) of this section, a shareholder's entire interest in an S corporation is terminated on the occurrence of any event through which a shareholder's entire stock ownership in the S corporation ceases, including a sale, exchange, or other disposition of all of the stock held by the shareholder; a gift under section 102(a) of all the shareholder's stock; a spousal transfer under section 1041(a) of all the shareholder's stock; a redemption, as defined in section 317(b), of all the shareholder's stock, regardless of the tax treatment of the redemption under section 302; and the death of the shareholder. A shareholder's entire interest in an S corporation is not terminated if the shareholder retains ownership of any stock (including an interest treated as stock under § 1.1361-1(1)) that would result in the shareholder continuing to be considered a shareholder of the corporation for purposes of section 1362(a)(2). Thus, in determining whether a shareholder's entire interest in an S corporation has been terminated, any interest held by the shareholder as a creditor, employee, director, or in any other non-shareholder capacity is disregarded.

(5) *Time and manner of making a terminating election*—(i) *In general.* An S corporation makes a terminating election by attaching a statement to its timely filed original or amended return required to be filed under section 6037(a) (that is, a Form 1120S) for the taxable year during which a shareholder's entire interest is terminated. A single election statement may be filed by the S corporation for all terminating elections for the taxable year. The election statement must include—

(A) A declaration by the S corporation that it is electing under section 1377(a)(2) and this paragraph to treat the taxable year as if it consisted of two separate taxable years;

(B) Information setting forth when and how the shareholder's entire interest was terminated (for example, a sale or gift);

(C) The signature on behalf of the S corporation of an authorized officer of the corporation under penalties of perjury; and

(D) A statement by the corporation that the corporation and each affected shareholder consent to the S corporation making the terminating election.

(ii) *Affected shareholders required to consent.* For purposes of paragraph (b)(5)(i)(D) of this section, a shareholder of the S corporation for the taxable year is a shareholder as described in section 1362(a)(2). For example, the person who under § 1.1362-6(b)(2) must consent to a corporation's S election in certain special cases is the person who must consent to the terminating election. In addition, an executor or administrator of the estate of a deceased affected shareholder may consent to the terminating election on behalf of the deceased affected shareholder.

(iii) *More than one terminating election.* A shareholder whose entire interest in an S corporation is terminated in an event for which a terminating election was made is not required to consent to a terminating election made with respect to a subsequent termination within the same taxable year unless the shareholder is an affected shareholder with respect to the subsequent termination.

(c) *Examples.* The following examples illustrate the provisions of this section:

Example 1. Shareholder's pro rata share in the case of a partial disposition of stock. (i) On January 6, 1997, X incorporates as a calendar year corporation, issues 100 shares of common stock to each of A and B, and files an election to be an S corporation for its 1997 taxable year. On July 24, 1997, B sells 50 shares of X stock to C. Thus, in 1997, A owned 50 percent of the outstanding shares of X on each day of X's 1997 taxable year, B owned 50 percent on each day from January 6, 1997, to July 24, 1997 (200 days), and 25 percent from July 25, 1997, to December 31, 1997 (160 days), and C owned 25 percent from July 25, 1997, to December 31, 1997 (160 days).

(ii) Because B's entire interest in X is not terminated when B sells 50 shares to C on July 24, 1997, X cannot make a terminating election under section 1377(a)(2) and paragraph (b) of this section for B's sale of 50 shares to C. Although B's sale of 50 shares to C is a qualifying disposition under § 1.1368-1(g)(2)(i), X does not make an election to terminate its taxable year under § 1.1368-1(g)(2). During its 1997 taxable year, X has nonseparately computed income of $720,000.

(iii) For each day in X's 1997 taxable year, A's daily pro rata share of X's nonseparately computed income is $1,000 ($720,000/360 days × 50%). Thus, A's pro rata share of X's nonseparately computed income for 1997 is $360,000 ($1,000 × 360 days). B's daily pro rata share of X's nonseparately computed income is $1,000 ($720,000/360 × 50%) for the first 200 days of X's 1997 taxable year, and $500 ($720,000/360 × 25%) for the following 160 days in 1997. Thus, B's pro rata share of X's nonseparately computed income for 1997 is $280,000 (($1,000 × 200 days) + ($500 × 160 days)). C's daily pro rata share of X's nonseparately computed income is $500 ($720,000/360 × 25%) for 160 days in 1997. Thus, C's pro rata share of X's nonseparately computed income for 1997 is $80,000 ($500 × 160 days).

Example 2. Shareholder's pro rata share when an S corporation makes a terminating election under section 1377(a)(2). (i) On January 6, 1997, X incorporates as a calendar year corporation,

Reg. § 1.1377-1(b)(5)

issues 100 shares of common stock to each of A and B, and files an election to be an S corporation for its 1997 taxable year. On July 24, 1997, B sells B's entire 100 shares of X stock to C. With the consent of B and C, X makes an election under section 1377(a)(2) and paragraph (b) of this section for the termination of B's entire interest arising from B's sale of 100 shares to C. As a result of the election, the pro rata shares of B and C are determined as if X's taxable year consisted of two separate taxable years, the first of which ends on July 24, 1997, the date B's entire interest in X terminates. Because A is not an affected shareholder as defined by section 1377(a)(2)(B) and paragraph (b)(2) of this section, the treatment as separate taxable years does not apply to A.

(ii) During its 1997 taxable year, X has non-separately computed income of $720,000. Under X's normal method of accounting, $200,000 of the $720,000 of nonseparately computed income is allocable to the period of January 6, 1997, through July 24, 1997 (the first deemed taxable year), and the remaining $520,000 is allocable to the period of July 25, 1997, through December 31, 1997 (the second deemed taxable year).

(iii) B's pro rata share of the $200,000 of non-separately computed income for the first deemed taxable year is determined by assigning the $200,000 of nonseparately computed income to each day of the first deemed taxable year ($200,000/200 days = $1,000 per day). Because B held 50% of X's authorized and issued shares on each day of the first deemed taxable year, B's daily pro rata share for each day of the first deemed taxable year is $500 ($1,000 per day × 50%). Thus, B's pro rata share of the $200,000 of nonseparately computed income for the first deemed taxable year is $100,000 ($500 per day x 200 days). B must report this amount for B's taxable year with or within which X's full taxable year ends (December 31, 1997).

(iv) C's pro rata share of the $520,000 of non-separately computed income for the second deemed taxable year is determined by assigning the $520,000 of nonseparately computed income to each day of the second deemed taxable year ($520,000/160 days = $3,250 per day). Because C held 50% of X's authorized and issued shares on each day of the second deemed taxable year, C's daily pro rata shares for each day of the second deemed taxable year is $1,625 ($3,250 per day × 50%). Therefore, C's pro rata share of the $520,000 of nonseparately computed income is $260,000 ($1,625 per day × 160 days). C must report this amount for C's taxable year with or within which X's full taxable year ends (December 31, 1997).

Example 3. Effect of conversion of a qualified subchapter S trust (QSST) to an electing small business trust (ESBT). (i) On January 1, 2003, Trust receives stock of S corporation. Trust's current income beneficiary makes a timely QSST election under section 1361(d)(2), effective January 1, 2003. Subsequently, the trustee and current income beneficiary of Trust elect, pursuant to § 1.1361-1(j)(12), to terminate the QSST election and convert to an ESBT, effective July 1, 2004. The taxable year of S corporation is the calendar year. In 2004, Trust's pro rata share of S corporation's nonseparately computed income is $100,000.

(ii) For purposes of computing the income allocable to the QSST and to the ESBT, Trust is treated as a QSST through June 30, 2004, and Trust is treated as an ESBT beginning July 1, 2004. Pursuant to section 1377(a)(1), the pro rata share of S corporation income allocated to the QSST is $49,727 ($100,000 × 182 days/366 days), and the pro rata share of S corporation income allocated to the ESBT is $50,273 ($100,000 × 184 days/366 days).

[Reg. § 1.1377-1.]

□ [*T.D.* 8696, 12-20-96. *Amended by T.D.* 8994, 5-13-2002.]

§ 1.1377-2. Post-termination transition period.—(a) *In general.* For purposes of subchapter S of chapter 1 of the Internal Revenue Code (Code) and this section, the term *post-termination transition period* means—

(1) The period beginning on the day after the last day of the corporation's last taxable year as an S corporation and ending on the later of—

(i) The day which is 1 year after such last day; or

(ii) The due date for filing the return for the last taxable year as an S corporation (including extensions);

(2) The 120-day period beginning on the date of any determination pursuant to an audit of the taxpayer which follows the termination of the corporation's election and which adjusts a subchapter S item of income, loss, or deduction of the corporation arising during the S period (as defined in section 1368(e)(2)); and

(3) The 120-day period beginning on the date of a determination that the corporation's election under section 1362(a) had terminated for a previous taxable year.

(b) *Special rules for post-termination transition period.* Pursuant to section 1377(b)(1) and paragraph (a)(1) of this section, a post-termination transition period arises the day after the last day that an S corporation was in existence if a C corporation acquires the assets of the S corporation in a transaction to which section 381(a)(2) applies. However, if an S corporation acquires the assets of another S corporation in a transaction to which section 381(a)(2) applies, a post-termination transition period does not arise. (See § 1.1368-2(d)(2) for the treatment of the acquisition of the assets of an S corporation by another S corporation in a transaction to which section 381(a)(2) applies.) The special treatment under section 1371(e)(1) of distributions of money by a corporation with respect to its stock during the post-termination transition period is available only to those shareholders who were shareholders in the S corporation at the time of the termination.

(c) *Determination defined.* For purposes of section 1377(b)(1) and paragraph (a) of this section, the term *determination* means—

(1) A determination as defined in section 1313(a);

(2) A written agreement between the corporation and the Commissioner (including a statement acknowledging that the corporation's election to be an S corporation terminated under section 1362(d)) that the corporation failed to qualify as an S corporation;

(3) For a corporation subject to the audit and assessment provisions of subchapter C of chapter 63 of subtitle A of the Code, the expiration of the period specified in section 6226 for filing a petition for readjustment of a final S corporation administrative adjustment finding that the corporation failed to qualify as an S corporation, provided that no petition was timely filed before the expiration of the period; and

(4) For a corporation not subject to the audit and assessment provisions of subchapter C of chapter 63 of subtitle A of the Code, the expiration of the period for filing a petition under section 6213 for the shareholder's taxable year for which the Commissioner has made a finding that the corporation failed to qualify as an S corporation, provided that no petition was timely filed before the expiration of the period.

(d) *Date a determination becomes effective—* (1) *Determination under section 1313(a).* A determination under paragraph (c)(1) of this section becomes effective on the date prescribed in section 1313 and the regulations thereunder.

(2) *Written agreement.* A determination under paragraph (c)(2) of this section becomes effective when it is signed by the district director having jurisdiction over the corporation (or by another Service official to whom authority to sign the agreement is delegated) and by an officer of the corporation authorized to sign on its behalf. Neither the request for a written agreement nor the terms of the written agreement suspend the running of any statute of limitations.

(3) *Implied agreement.* A determination under paragraph (c)(3) or (4) of this section becomes effective on the day after the date of expiration of the period specified under section 6226 or 6213, respectively. [Reg. § 1.1377-2.]

☐ [*T.D.* 8696, 12-20-96.]

§ 1.1378-1. Taxable year of S corporation.— (a) *In general.* The taxable year of an S corporation must be a permitted year. A permitted year is the required taxable year (i.e., a taxable year ending on December 31), a taxable year elected under section 444, a 52-53-week taxable year ending with reference to the required taxable year or a taxable year elected under section 444, or any other taxable year for which the corporation establishes a business purpose to the satisfaction of the Commissioner under section 442.

(b) *Adoption of taxable year.* An electing S corporation may adopt, in accordance with § 1.441-1(c), its required taxable year, a taxable year elected under section 444, or a 52-53-week taxable year ending with reference to its required taxable year or a taxable year elected under section 444 without the approval of the Commissioner. See § 1.441-1. An electing S corporation that wants to adopt any other taxable year, must establish a business purpose and obtain the approval of the Commissioner under section 442.

(c) *Change in taxable year—*(1) *Approval required.* An S corporation or electing S corporation that wants to change its taxable year must obtain the approval of the Commissioner under section 442 or make an election under section 444. However, an S corporation or electing S corporation may obtain automatic approval for certain changes, including a change to its required taxable year, pursuant to administrative procedures published by the Commissioner.

(2) *Short period tax return.* An S corporation or electing S corporation that changes its taxable year must make its return for a short period in accordance with section 443, but must not annualize the corporation's taxable income.

(d) *Retention of taxable year.* In certain cases, an S corporation or electing S corporation will be required to change its taxable year unless it obtains the approval of the Commissioner under section 442, or makes an election under section 444, to retain its current taxable year. For example, a corporation using a June 30 fiscal year that elects to be an S corporation and, as a result, is required to use the calendar year must obtain the approval of the Commissioner to retain its current fiscal year.

(e) *Procedures for obtaining approval or making a section 444 election—*(1) *In general.* See § 1.442-1(b) for procedures to obtain the approval of the Commissioner (automatically or otherwise) to adopt, change, or retain a taxable year. See §§ 1.444-1T and 1.444-2T for qualifications, and 1.444-3T for procedures, for making an election under section 444.

(2) *Special rules for electing S corporations.* An electing S corporation that wants to adopt, change to, or retain a taxable year other than its required taxable year must request approval of the Commissioner on Form 2553, "Election by a Small Business Corporation," when the election to be an S corporation is filed pursuant to section 1362(b) and § 1.1362-6. See § 1.1362-6(a)(2)(i) for the manner of making an election to be an S corporation. If such corporation receives permis-sion to adopt, change to, or retain a taxable year other than its required taxable year, the election to be an S corporation will be effective. Denial of the request renders the election ineffective unless the corporation agrees that, in the event the request to adopt, change to, or retain a taxable year other than its required taxable year is denied, it will adopt, change to, or retain its required taxable year or, if applicable, make an election under section 444.

(f) *Effective date.* The rules of this section are applicable for taxable years ending on or after May 17, 2002. [Reg. § 1.1378-1.]

☐ [*T.D.* 8996, 5-16-2002.]

Certain Controlled Corporations

§ 1.1563-1. Definition of controlled group of corporations and component members.—(a) *Controlled group of corporations*—(1) *In general.* For purposes of sections 1561 through 1563 and the regulations thereunder, the term "controlled group of corporations" means any group of corpo-rations which is either a "parent-subsidiary con-trolled group" (as defined in subparagraph (2) of this paragraph), a "brother-sister controlled group" (as defined in subparagraph (3) of this paragraph), a "combined group" (as defined in subparagraph (4) of this paragraph), or an "insur-ance group" (as defined in subparagraph (5) of this paragraph). For the exclusion of certain stock for purposes of applying the definitions contained in this paragraph, see section 1563(c) and § 1.1563-2.

(2) *Parent-subsidiary controlled group.* (i) The term "parent-subsidiary controlled group" means one or more chains of corporations con-nected through stock ownership with a common parent corporation if—

(*a*) Stock possessing at least 80 percent of the total combined voting power of all classes of stock entitled to vote or at least 80 percent of the total value of shares of all classes of stock of each of the corporations, except the common parent corporation, is owned (directly and with the appli-cation of paragraph (b)(1) of § 1.1563-3, relating to options) by one or more of the other corpora-tions; and

(*b*) The common parent corporation owns (directly and with the application of para-graph (b)(1) of § 1.1563-3, relating to options) stock possessing at least 80 percent of the total combined voting power of all classes of stock enti-tled to vote or at least 80 percent of the total value of shares of all classes of stock of at least one of the other corporations, excluding, in computing such voting power or value, stock owned directly by such other corporations.

(ii) The definition of a parent-subsidiary controlled group of corporations may be illus-trated by the following examples:

Example (1). P Corporation owns stock possessing 80 percent of the total combined voting power of all classes of stock entitled to vote of S Corporation. P is the common parent of a parent-subsidiary controlled group consisting of member corporations P and S.

Example (2). Assume the same facts as in example (1). Assume further that S owns stock possessing 80 percent of the total value of shares of all classes of stock of T Corporation. P is the common parent of a parent-subsidiary controlled group consisting of member corporations P, S, and T. The result would be the same if P, rather than S, owned the T stock.

Example (3). L Corporation owns 80 per-cent of the only class of stock of M Corporation and M, in turn, owns 40 percent of the only class of stock of O Corporation. L also owns 80 percent of the only class of stock of N Corporation and N, in turn, owns 40 percent of the only class of stock of O. L is the common parent of a parent-subsidi-ary controlled group consisting of member corpo-rations L, M, N, and O.

Example (4). X Corporation owns 75 per-cent of the only class of stock of Y and Z Corpora-tions; Y owns all the remaining stock of Z; and Z owns all the remaining stock of Y. Since intercom-pany stockholdings are excluded (that is, are not treated as outstanding) for purposes of determin-ing whether X owns stock possessing at least 80 percent of the voting power or value of at least one of the other corporations, X is treated as the owner of stock possessing 100 percent of the vot-ing power and value of Y and of Z for purposes of subdivision (i)(*b*) of this subparagraph. Also, stock possessing 100 percent of the voting power and value of Y and Z is owned by the other corporations in the group within the meaning of subdivision (i)(*a*) of this subparagraph. (X and Y together own stock possessing 100 percent of the voting power and value of Z, and X and Z together own stock possessing 100 percent of the voting power and value of Y.) Therefore, X is the common parent of a parent-subsidiary controlled group of corporations consisting of member corporations X, Y, and Z.

(3) *Brother-sister controlled group*—(i) The term "brother-sister controlled group" means two or more corporations if the same five or fewer persons who are individuals, estates, or trusts own (directly and with the application of the rules contained in paragraph (b) of § 1.1563-3), stock possessing—

(*a*) At least 80 percent of the total combined voting power of all classes of stock entitled to vote or at least 80 percent of the total value of shares of all classes of the stock of each corporation; and

(*b*) More than 50 percent of the total combined voting power of all classes of stock entitled to vote or more than 50 percent of the total value of shares of all classes of stock of each corporation, taking into account the stock ownership of each such person only to the extent such stock ownership is identical with respect to each such corporation.

The five or fewer persons whose stock ownership is considered for purposes of the 80 percent requirement must be the same persons whose stock ownership is considered for purposes of the more-than-50 percent requirement.

(ii) The principles of this subparagraph may be illustrated by the following examples:

Example (1). The outstanding stock of corporations P, Q, R, S, and T, which have only one class of stock outstanding is owned by the following unrelated individuals:

CORPORATIONS

Individuals	P	Q	R	S	T	Identical ownership
A	55%	51%	55%	55%	55%	51%.
B	45%	49%	...	...	...	(45% in P & Q).
C	...	...	45%	...	...	
D	...	...	...	45%	...	
E	...	...	...	...	45%	
Total	100%	100%	100%	100%	100%	

Corporations P and Q are members of a brother-sister controlled group of corporations. Although the more-than-50 percent identical ownership requirement is met for all 5 corporations, corporations R, S, and T are not members because at least 80 percent of the stock of each of those corporations is not owned by the same 5 or fewer persons whose stock ownership is considered for purposes of the more-than-50 percent identical ownership requirement.

Example (2). The outstanding stock of corporations U and V, which have only one class of stock outstanding, is owned by the following unrelated individuals:

Individuals	Corporations	
	U (percent)	V (percent)
A	12	12
B	12	12
C	12	12
D	12	12
E	13	13
F	13	13
G	13	13
H	13	13
Total	100	100

Any group of five of the shareholders will own more than 50 percent of the stock in each corporation, in identical holdings. However, U and V are not members of brother-sister controlled group because at least 80 percent of the stock of each corporation is not owned by the same five or fewer persons.

Example (3). Corporations X and Y each have two classes of stock outstanding, voting common and non-voting common. (None of this stock is excluded from the definition of stock under section 1563(c).) Unrelated individuals A and B own the following percentages of the class of stock entitled to vote (voting) and of the total value of shares of all classes of stock (value) in each of corporations X and Y:

Individuals	Corporations	
	X	Y
A	100% voting, 60% value.	75% voting, 60% value.
B	0% voting, 10% value.	25% voting, 10% value.

No other shareholder of X owns (or is considered to own) any stock in Y. X and Y are a brother-sister controlled group of corporations. The group meets the more-than-50 percent owner-

Reg. § 1.1563-1(a)(3)

ship requirements because A and B own more than 50 percent of the total value of shares of all classes of stock of X and Y in identical holdings. (The group also meets the more-than-50 percent ownership requirement because of A's voting stock ownership.) The group meets the 80 percent requirement because A and B own at least 80 percent of the total combined voting power of all classes of stock entitled to vote.

Example (4). Assume the same facts as in example (3) except that the value of the stock owned by A and B is not more than 50 percent of the total value of shares of all classes of stock of each corporation in identical holdings. X and Y are not a brother-sister controlled group of corporations. The group meets the more-than-50 percent ownership requirement because A owns more than 50 percent of the total combined voting power of the voting stock of each corporation. For purposes of the 80 percent requirement, B's voting stock in Y cannot be combined with A's voting stock in Y since B, who does not own any voting stock in X, is not a person whose ownership is considered for purposes of the more-than-50 percent requirement. Because no other shareholder owns stock in both X and Y, these other shareholders' stock ownership is not counted towards meeting either the more-than-50 percent ownership requirement or the 80 percent ownership requirement.

(iii) Paragraph (a)(3) of this section, as amended by T.D. 8179, applies to taxable years ending on or after December 31, 1970. See, however, the transitional rule in paragraph (d) of this section.

(4) *Combined group.* (i) The term "combined group" means any group of three or more corporations, if—

(a) Each such corporation is a member of either a parent-subsidiary controlled group of corporations or a brother-sister controlled group of corporations, and

(b) At least one of such corporations is the common parent of a parent-subsidiary controlled group and also is a member of a brother-sister controlled group.

(ii) The definition of a combined group of corporations may be illustrated by the following examples:

Example (1). Smith, an individual, owns stock possessing 80 percent of the total combined voting power of all classes of the stock of corporations X and Y. Y, in turn, owns stock possessing 80 percent of the total combined voting power of all classes of the stock of corporation Z. Since—

(a) X, Y, and Z are each members of either a parent-subsidiary or brother-sister controlled group of corporations, and

(b) Y is the common parent of a parent-subsidiary controlled group of corporations consisting of Y and Z, and also is a member of a brother-sister controlled group of corporations consisting of X and Y,

X, Y, and Z are members of the same combined group.

Example (2). Assume the same facts as in example (1), and further assume that corporation X owns 80 percent of the total value of shares of all classes of stock of corporation T. X, Y, Z, and T are members of the same combined group.

(5) *Insurance group.* (i) The term "insurance group" means two or more insurance companies subject to taxation under section 802 each of which is a member of a controlled group of corporations described in subparagraph (2), (3), or (4) of this paragraph. Such insurance companies shall be treated as a controlled group of corporations separate from any other corporations which are members of the controlled group described in such subparagraph (2), (3), or (4). For purposes of this section and § 1.1562-5, the common parent of the controlled group described in subparagraph (2) of this paragraph shall be referred to as the common parent of the insurance group.

(ii) The definition of an insurance group may be illustrated by the following example:

Example. Corporation P owns all the stock of corporation I which, in turn, owns all the stock of corporation X. P also owns all the stock of corporation Y which, in turn, owns all the stock of corporation J. I and J are life insurance companies subject to taxation under section 802 of the Code. Since I and J are members of a parent-subsidiary controlled group of corporations, such companies are treated as members of an insurance group separate from the parent-subsidiary controlled group consisting of P, X, and Y. For purposes of this section and § 1.1562-5, P is referred to as the common parent of the insurance group even though P is not a member of such group.

(6) *Voting power of stock.* For purposes of § 1.1562-5, this section and §§ 1.1563-2, and 1.1563-3, in determining whether the stock owned by a person (or persons) possesses a certain percentage of the total combined voting power of all classes of stock entitled to vote of a corporation, consideration will be given to all the facts and circumstances of each case. A share of stock will

Reg. § 1.1563-1(a)(6)

generally be considered as possessing the voting power accorded to such share by the corporate charter, by-laws, or share certificate. On the other hand, if there is any agreement, whether express or implied, that a shareholder will not vote his stock in a corporation, the formal voting rights possessed by his stock may be disregarded in determining the percentage of the total combined voting power possessed by the stock owned by other shareholders in the corporation, if the result is that the corporation becomes a component member of a controlled group of corporations. Moreover, if a shareholder agrees to vote his stock in a corporation in the manner specified by another shareholder in the corporation, the voting rights possessed by the stock owned by the first shareholder may be considered to be possessed by the stock owned by such other shareholder if the result is that the corporation becomes a component member of a controlled group of corporations.

(b) *Component members*—(1) *In general.* For purposes of sections 1561 through 1563 and the regulations thereunder, a corporation is a component member of a controlled group of corporations on a December 31 (and with respect to the taxable year which includes such December 31) if such corporation—

(i) Is a member of such controlled group on such December 31 and is not treated as an excluded member under subparagraph (2) of this paragraph, or

(ii) Is not a member of such controlled group on such December 31 but is treated as an additional member under subparagraph (3) of this paragraph.

(2) *Excluded members.* (i) A corporation, which is a member of a controlled group of corporations on the December 31 included within its taxable year, but was a member of such group for less than one-half of the number of days in such taxable year which precede such December 31, shall be treated as an excluded member of such group on such December 31.

(ii) A corporation which is a member of a controlled group of corporations on any December 31 shall be treated as an excluded member of such group on such date if, for its taxable year including such date, such corporation is—

(*a*) Exempt from taxation under section 501(a) (except a corporation which has unrelated business taxable income for such taxable year which is subject to tax under section 511) or 521,

(*b*) A foreign corporation not subject to taxation under section 882(a) for the taxable year,

(*c*) An electing small business corporation (as defined in section 1371(b)) not subject to the tax imposed by section 1378,

(*d*) A franchised corporation (as defined in section 1563(f)(4) and § 1.1563-4), or

(*e*) An insurance company subject to taxation under section 802 or 821, except that an insurance company taxable under section 802 which (without regard to this subdivision) is a component member of an insurance group described in paragraph (a)(5) of this section shall not be treated as an excluded member of such insurance group.

(iii) A corporation which has a taxable year ending on December 31, 1963, shall be treated as an excluded member of a controlled group on such date.

(3) *Additional members.* A corporation which—

(i) Is not a member of a controlled group of corporations on the December 31 included within its taxable year, and

(ii) Is not described, with respect to such taxable year, in subparagraph (2)(ii) (*a*), (*b*), (*c*), (*d*), or (*e*), or (2) (iii) of this paragraph, shall be treated as an additional member of such group on such December 31 if it was a member of such group for one-half (or more) of the number of days in such taxable year which precede such December 31.

(4) *Examples.* The provisions of the paragraph may be illustrated by the following examples:

Example (1). Brown, an individual, owns all of the stock of corporations W and X on each day of 1964. W and X each uses the calendar year as its taxable year. On January 1, 1964, Brown also owns all of the stock of corporation Y (a fiscal year corporation with a taxable year beginning on July 1, 1964, and ending on June 30, 1965), which stock he sells on October 15, 1964. On December 1, 1964, Brown purchases all the stock of corporation Z (a fiscal year corporation with a taxable year beginning on September 1, 1964, and ending on August 31, 1965). On December 31, 1964, W, X, and Z are members of the same controlled group. However, the component members of the group on such December 31 are W, X, and Y. Under subparagraph (2)(i) of this paragraph, Z is treated as an excluded member of the group on December 31, 1964, since Z was a member of the group for less than one-half of the number of days (29 out of 121 days) during the period beginning on September 1, 1964 (the first day of its taxable year) and ending on December 30, 1964. Under subparagraph (3) of this paragraph, Y is treated as an additional member of the group on December 31, 1964, since Y was a member of the group for at least one-half of the number of days (107 out of 183 days) during the period beginning on

July 1, 1964 (the first day of its taxable year) and ending on December 30, 1964.

Example (2). On January 1, 1964, corporation P owns all the stock of corporation S, which in turn owns all the stock of corporation S-1. On November 1, 1964, P purchases all of the stock of corporation X from the public and sells all of the stock of S to the public. Corporation X owns all the stock of corporation Y during 1964. P, S, S-1, X, and Y file their returns on the basis of the calendar year. On December 31, 1964, P, X, and Y are members of a parent-subsidiary controlled group of corporations; also, corporations S and S-1 are members of a different parent-subsidiary controlled group on such date. However, since X and Y have been members of the parent-subsidiary controlled group of which P is the common parent for less than one-half the number of days during the period January 1 through December 30, 1964, they are not component members of such group on such date. On the other hand, X and Y have been members of a parent-subsidiary controlled group of which X is the common parent for at least one-half the number of days during the period January 1 through December 30, 1964, and therefore they are component members of such group on December 31, 1964. Also since S and S-1 were members of the parent-subsidiary controlled group of which P is the common parent for at least one-half the number of days in the taxable years of each such corporation during the period January 1 through December 30, 1964, P, S, and S-1 are component members of such group on December 31, 1964.

Example (3). Throughout 1964, corporation M owns all the stock of corporation F which, in turn, owns all the stock of corporations L-1, L-2, X, and Y. M is a domestic mutual insurance company subject to taxation under section 821, F is a foreign corporation not engaged in trade or business within the United States, L-1 and L-2 are domestic life insurance companies subject to taxation under section 802, and X and Y are domestic corporations subject to tax under section 11 of the Code. Each corporation uses the calendar year as its taxable year. On December 31, 1964, M, F, L-1, L-2, X, and Y are members of a parent-subsidiary controlled group of corporations. However, under subparagraph (2)(ii) of this paragraph, M, F, L-1, and L-2 are treated as excluded members of the group on December 31, 1964. Thus, on December 31, 1964, the component members of the parent-subsidiary controlled group of which M is the common parent include only X and Y. Furthermore, since subparagraph (2)(ii)(e) of this paragraph does not result in L-1 and L-2 being treated as excluded members of an insurance group, L-1 and L-2 are component

members of an insurance group on December 31, 1964.

(5) *Application of constructive ownership rules.* For purposes of subparagraphs (2)(i) and (3) of this paragraph, it is necessary to determine whether a corporation was a member of a controlled group of corporations for one-half (or more) of the number of days in its taxable year which precede the December 31 falling within such taxable year. Therefore, the constructive ownership rules contained in paragraph (b) of § 1.1563-3 (to the extent applicable in making such determination) must be applied on a day-by-day basis. For example, if P Corporation owns all the stock of X Corporation on each day of 1964, and on December 30, 1964, acquires an option to purchase all the stock of Y Corporation (a calendar-year taxpayer which has been in existence on each day of 1964), the application of paragraph (b)(1) of § 1.1563-3 on a day-by-day basis results in Y being a member of the brother-sister controlled group on only one day of Y's 1964 year which precedes December 31, 1964. Accordingly, since Y is not a member of such group for one-half or more of the number of days in its 1964 year preceding December 31, 1964, Y is treated as an excluded member of such group on December 31, 1964.

(c) *Overlapping groups*—(1) *In general.* If on a December 31 a corporation is a component member of a controlled group of corporations by reason of ownership of stock possessing at least 80 percent of the total value of shares of all classes of stock of the corporation, and if on such December 31 such corporation is also a component member of another controlled group of corporations by reason of ownership of other stock (that is, stock not used to satisfy the at-least-80-percent total value test) possessing at least 80 percent of the total combined voting power of all classes of stock of the corporation entitled to vote, then such corporation shall be treated as a component member only of the controlled group of which it is a component member by reason of the ownership of at least 80 percent of the total value of its shares.

(2) *Brother-sister controlled groups.* (i) If on a December 31, a corporation would, without application of this subparagraph, be a component member of more than one brother-sister controlled group on such date, such corporation shall be treated as a component member of only one such group on such date. Such a corporation may select which group in which it is to be included by filing an election as provided in this subparagraph. The election shall be in the form of a statement designating the group in which the corporation is to be included. The statement shall provide all the information with respect to stock ownership which is reasonably necessary to satisfy the Internal Revenue officer with whom it is filed that the

Reg. § 1.1563-1(c)(2)

corporation would, but for the election, be a component member of more than one controlled group. Once filed, the election is irrevocable and effective until such time that a change in the stock ownership of the corporation results in termination of membership in the controlled group in which such corporation has been included.

(ii) Except as provided in subdivision (iii) of this subparagraph, the statement shall be signed by a person duly authorized to act on behalf of such corporation and shall be filed on or before the due date (including extension of time) for the filing of the income tax return of such corporation for the taxable year. However, in the case of an election with respect to December 31, 1970, the statement shall be considered as timely filed if filed on or before December 15, 1971. In the event no election is filed in accordance with the provisions of this subdivision, then the district director with audit jurisdiction of such corporation's return for the taxable year which includes such December 31 shall determine the group in which such corporation is to be included, and such determination shall be binding for all subsequent years unless the corporation files a valid election with respect to any such subsequent year.

(iii) If more than one corporation would, without application of this subparagraph, be a component member of more than one controlled group, a single statement shall be signed by persons duly authorized to act on behalf of each such corporation. Such statement shall designate the group in which each corporation is to be included. The statement shall be attached to the income tax return of the corporation that, among those corporations which would (without the application of this subparagraph) belong to more than one group, has the taxable year including such December 31 which ends on the earliest date. However, in the case of an election with respect to December 31, 1970, the statement may be filed by December 15, 1971, with the service center director with whom such corporation's return is filed for the taxable year which includes such December 31. In the event no election is filed in accordance with the provisions of this subdivision, then the district director with audit jurisdiction of such corporation's return for the taxable year that includes such December 31 shall determine the group in which each corporation is to be included, and such determination shall be binding for all subsequent years unless the corporations file a valid election with respect to any such subsequent year.

(iv) The provisions of this subparagraph may be illustrated by the following examples (in which it is assumed that all the individuals are unrelated):

Example (1). On each day of 1970 all the outstanding stock of corporations M, N, and P is held in the following manner:

Individuals	Corporations		
	M	N	P
A	55%	40%	5%
B	40%	20%	40%
C	5%	40%	55%

Since the more-than-50-percent stock ownership requirement of section 1563(a)(2)(B) is met with respect to corporations M and N and with respect to corporations N and P, but not with respect to corporations M, N, and P, corporation N would, without the application of this subparagraph, be a component member on December 31, 1970, of overlapping groups consisting of M and N and of N and P. If N does not file an election in accordance with subdivision (ii) of this subparagraph, the district director with audit jurisdiction of N's return will determine the group in which N is to be included.

Example (2). On each day of 1970, all the outstanding stock of corporations S, T, W, X, and Z is held in the following manner:

Individuals	Corporations				
	S	T	W	X	Z
D	52%	52%	52%	52%	52%
E	40%	2%	2%	2%	2%
F	2%	40%	2%	2%	2%
G	2%	2%	40%	2%	2%
H	2%	2%	2%	40%	2%
I	2%	2%	2%	2%	40%

On December 31, 1970, the more-than-50-percent stock ownership requirement of section 1563(a)(2)(B) may be met with regard to any combination of the corporations but all five corporations cannot be included as component members of a single controlled group because the inclusion of all the corporations in a single group would be dependent upon taking into account the stock ownership of more than five persons. Therefore, if the corporations do not file a statement in accordance with subdivision (iii) of this subparagraph, the district director with audit jurisdiction of the return of the corporation whose taxable year ends on the earliest date will determine the group in which each corporation is to be included. The corporations or the district director, as the case may be, may designate that three corporations be included in one group and two corporations in another, or that any four corporations be included in one group and that the remaining corporation not be included in any group.

* * *

[Reg. § 1.1563-1.]

☐ [*T.D.* 6845, 8-4-65. *Amended by T.D.* 6960, 6-24-68, *T.D.* 7181, 4-24-72, *T.D.* 7293, 11-27-73, *and T.D.* 8179, 3-1-88.]

§ 1.1563-2. **Excluded stock.**—(a) *Certain stock excluded.* For purposes of sections 1561 through 1563 and the regulations thereunder, the term "stock" does not include—

(1) Nonvoting stock which is limited and preferred as to dividends, and

(2) Treasury stock.

(b) *Stock treated as excluded stock*—(1) *Parent-subsidiary controlled group.* If a corporation (hereinafter in this paragraph referred to as "parent corporation") owns 50 percent or more of the total combined voting power of all classes of stock entitled to vote or 50 percent or more of the total value of shares of all classes of stock in another corporation (hereinafter in this paragraph referred to as "subsidiary corporation"), the provisions of subparagraph (2) of this paragraph shall apply. For purposes of this subparagraph, stock owned by a corporation means stock owned directly plus stock owned with the application of the constructive ownership rules of paragraph (b)(1) and (4) of § 1.1563-3, relating to options and attribution from corporations. In determining whether the stock owned by a corporation possesses the requisite percentage of the total combined voting power of all classes of stock entitled to vote of another corporation, see paragraph (a)(6) of § 1.1563-1.

(2) *Stock treated as not outstanding.* If the provisions of this subparagraph apply, then for purposes of determining whether the parent corporation or the subsidiary corporation is a member of a parent-subsidiary controlled group of corporations within the meaning of paragraph (a)(2) of § 1.1563-1, the following stock of the subsidiary corporation shall, except as otherwise provided in paragraph (c) of this section, be treated as if it were not outstanding:

(i) *Plan of deferred compensation.* Stock in the subsidiary corporation held by a trust which is part of a plan of deferred compensation for the benefit of the employees of the parent corporation or the subsidiary corporation. The term "plan of deferred compensation" shall have the same meaning such term has in section 406(a)(3) and the regulations thereunder.

(ii) *Principal stockholders and officers.* Stock in the subsidiary corporation owned (directly and with the application of the rules contained in paragraph (b) of § 1.1563-3) by an individual who is a principal stockholder or officer of the parent corporation. A principal stockholder of the parent corporation is an individual who owns (directly and with the application of the rules contained in paragraph (b) of § 1.1563-3) 5 percent or more of the total combined voting power of all classes of stock entitled to vote or 5 percent or more of the total value of shares of all classes of stock of the parent corporation. An officer of the parent corporation includes the president, vice-presidents, general manager, treasurer, secretary, and comptroller of such corporation, and any other person who performs duties corresponding to those normally performed by persons occupying such positions.

(iii) *Employees.* Stock in the subsidiary corporation owned (directly and with the application of the rules contained in paragraph (b) of § 1.1563-3) by an employee of the subsidiary corporation if such stock is subject to conditions which substantially restrict or limit the employee's right (or if the employee constructively owns such stock, the direct owner's right) to dispose of such stock and which run in favor of the parent or subsidiary corporation. In general, any condition which extends, directly or indirectly, to the parent corporation or the subsidiary corporation preferential rights with respect to the acquisition of the employee's (or direct owner's) stock will be considered to be a condition described in the preceding sentence. It is not necessary, in order for a condition to be considered to be in favor of the parent corporation or the subsidiary corporation, that the parent or subsidiary be extended a discriminatory concession with respect to the price of the stock. For example, a condition whereby the parent corporation is given a right of first refusal with respect to any stock of the subsidiary corporation offered by an employee for sale is a condition which substantially restricts or limits the employee's right to dispose of such stock and runs in favor of the parent corporation. Moreover, any legally enforceable condition which prohibits the employee from disposing of his stock without the consent of the parent (or a subsidiary of the parent) will be considered to be a substantial limitation running in favor of the parent corporation.

(iv) *Controlled exempt organization.* Stock in the subsidiary corporation owned (directly and with the application of the rules contained in paragraph (b) of § 1.1563-3) by an organization (other than the parent corporation)—

(*a*) To which section 501 (relating to certain educational and charitable organizations which are exempt from tax) applies, and

(*b*) Which is controlled directly or indirectly by the parent corporation or subsidiary corporation, by an individual, estate, or trust that is a principal stockholder of the parent corporation, by an officer of the parent corporation, or by any combination thereof.

Reg. § 1.1563-2(b)(2)

The terms "principal stockholder of the parent corporation" and "officer of the parent corporation" shall have the same meanings in this subdivision as in subdivision (ii) of this subparagraph. The term "control" as used in this subdivision means control in fact and the determination of whether the control requirement of (b) of this subdivision is met will depend upon all the facts and circumstances of each case, without regard to whether such control is legally enforceable and irrespective of the method by which such control is exercised or exercisable.

(3) *Brother-sister controlled group.* If 5 or fewer persons (hereinafter referred to as common owners) who are individuals, estates, or trusts own (directly and with the application of the rules contained in paragraph (b) of § 1.1563-3) stock possessing 50 percent or more of the total combined voting power of all classes of stock entitled to vote or 50 percent or more of the total value of shares of all classes of stock in a corporation, the provisions of subparagraph (4) of this paragraph shall apply. In determining whether the stock owned by such person or persons possesses the requisite percentage of the total combined voting power of all classes of stock entitled to vote of a corporation, see paragraph (a)(6) of § 1.1563-1.

(4) *Stock treated as not outstanding.* If the provisions of this subparagraph apply, then for purposes of determining whether a corporation is a member of a brother-sister controlled group of corporations within the meaning of paragraph (a)(3) of § 1.1563-1, the following stock of such corporation shall, except as otherwise provided in paragraph (c) of this section, be treated as if it were not outstanding:

(i) *Exempt employees' trust.* Stock in such corporation held by an employees' trust described in section 401(a) which is exempt from tax under section 501(a), if such trust is for the benefit of the employees of such corporation.

(ii) *Employees.* Stock in such corporation owned (directly and with the application of the rules contained in paragraph (b) of § 1.1563-3) by an employee of such corporation if such stock is subject to conditions which run in favor of a common owner of such corporation (or in favor of such corporation) and which substantially restrict or limit the employee's right (or if the employee constructively owns such stock, the record owner's right) to dispose of such stock. The principles of subparagraph (2)(iii) of this paragraph shall apply in determining whether a condition satisfies the requirements of the preceding sentence. Thus, in general, a condition which extends, directly or indirectly, to a common owner or such corporation preferential rights with respect to the acquisition of the employee's (or record owner's) stock will be considered to be a condition which satisfies such requirements. For purposes of this subdivision, if a condition which restricts or limits an employee's right (or record owner's right) to dispose of his stock also applies to the stock in such corporation held by such common owner pursuant to a bona fide reciprocal stock purchase arrangement, such condition shall not be treated as one which restricts or limits the employee's (or record owner's) right to dispose of such stock. An example of a reciprocal stock purchase arrangement is an agreement whereby a common owner and the employee are given a right of first refusal with respect to stock of the employer corporation owned by the other party. If, however, the agreement also provides that the common owner has the right to purchase the stock of the employer corporation owned by the employee in the event that the corporation should discharge the employee for reasonable cause, the purchase arrangement would not be reciprocal within the meaning of this subdivision.

(iii) *Controlled exempt organization.* Stock in such corporation owned (directly and with the application of the rules contained in paragraph (b) of § 1.1563-3) by an organization—

(a) To which section 501(c)(3) (relating to certain educational and charitable organizations which are exempt from tax) applies, and

(b) Which is controlled directly or indirectly by such corporation, by an individual, estate, or trust that is a principal stockholder of such corporation, by an officer of such corporation, or by any combination thereof. The terms "principal stockholder" and "officer" shall have the same meanings in this subdivision as in subparagraph (2)(ii) of this paragraph. The term "control" as used in this subdivision means control in fact and the determination of whether the control requirement of (b) of this subdivision is met will depend upon all the facts and circumstances of each case, without regard to whether such control is legally enforceable and irrespective of the method by which such control is exercised or exercisable.

(5) *Other controlled groups.* The provisions of subparagraphs (1), (2), (3), and (4) of this paragraph shall apply in determining whether a corporation is a member of a combined group (within the meaning of paragraph (a)(4) of § 1.1563-1) or an insurance group (within the meaning of paragraph (a)(5) of § 1.1563-1). For example, under paragraph (a)(4) of § 1.1563-1, in order for a corporation to be a member of a combined group such corporation must be a member of a parent-subsidiary group or a brother-sister group. Accordingly, the excluded stock rules provided by this

paragraph are applicable in determining whether the corporation is a member of such group.

(6) *Meaning of employee.* For purposes of this section, § § 1.1563-3 and 1.1563-4, the term "employee" has the same meaning such term is given in section 3306(i) of the Code (relating to definitions for purposes of the Federal Unemployment Tax Act). Accordingly, the term employee as used in such sections includes an officer of a corporation.

(7) *Examples.* The provisions of this paragraph may be illustrated by the following examples:

Example (1). Corporation P owns 70 of the 100 shares of the only class of stock of corporation S. The remaining shares of S are owned as follows: 4 shares by Jones (the general manager of P), and 26 shares by Smith (who also owns 5 percent of the total combined voting power of the stock of P). P satisfies the 50 percent stock ownership requirement of subparagraph (1) of this paragraph with respect to S. Since Jones is an officer of P and Smith is a principal stockholder of P, under subparagraph (2)(ii) of this paragraph the S stock owned by Jones and Smith is treated as not outstanding for purposes of determining whether P and S are members of a parent-subsidiary controlled group of corporations within the meaning of paragraph (a)(2) of § 1.1563-1. Thus, P is considered to own stock possessing 100 percent (70 ÷ 70) of the total voting power and value of all the S stock. Accordingly, P and S are members of a parent-subsidiary controlled group of corporations.

Example (2). Assume the same facts as in example (1) and further assume that Jones owns 15 shares of the 100 shares of the only class of stock of corporation S-1, and corporation S owns 75 shares of such stock. P satisfies the 50 percent stock ownership requirement of subparagraph (1) of this paragraph with respect to S-1 since P is considered as owning 52.5 percent (70 percent × 75 percent) of the S-1 stock with the application of paragraph (b)(4) of § 1.1563-3. Since Jones is an officer of P, under subparagraph (2)(ii) of this paragraph, the S-1 stock owned by Jones is treated as not outstanding for purposes of determining whether S-1 is a member of the parent-subsidiary controlled group of corporations. Thus, S is considered to own stock possessing 88.2 percent (75 ÷ 85) of the voting power and value of the S-1 stock. Accordingly, P, S, and S-1 are members of a parent-subsidiary controlled group of corporations.

Example (3). Corporation X owns 60 percent of the only class of stock of corporation Y. Davis, the president of Y, owns the remaining 40 percent of the stock of Y. Davis has agreed that if he offers his stock in Y for sale he will first offer the stock to X at a price equal to the fair market value of the stock on the first date the stock is offered for sale. Since Davis is an employee of Y within the meaning of section 3306(i) of the Code, and his stock in Y is subject to a condition which substantially restricts or limits his right to dispose of such stock and runs in favor of X, under subparagraph (2)(iii) of this paragraph such stock is treated as if it were not outstanding for purposes of determining whether X and Y are members of a parent subsidiary controlled group of corporations. Thus, X is considered to own stock possessing 100 percent of the voting power and value of the stock of Y. Accordingly, X and Y are members of a parent-subsidiary controlled group of corporations. The result would be the same if Davis's wife, instead of Davis, owned directly the 40 percent stock interest in Y and such stock was subject to a right of first refusal running in favor of X.

(c) *Exception*—(1) *General.* If stock of a corporation is owned by a person directly or with the application of the rules contained in paragraph (b) of § 1.1563-3 and such ownership results in the corporation being a component member of a controlled group of corporations on a December 31, then the stock shall not be treated as excluded stock under the provisions of paragraph (b) of this section if the result of applying such provisions is that such corporation is not a component member of a controlled group of corporations on such December 31.

(2) *Illustration.* The provisions of this paragraph may be illustrated by the following example:

Example. On each day of 1965, corporation P owns directly 50 of the 100 shares of the only class of stock of corporation S. Jones, an officer of P, owns directly 30 shares of S stock and P has an option to acquire such 30 shares from Jones. The remaining shares of S are owned by unrelated persons. If, pursuant to the provisions of paragraph (b)(2)(ii) of this section, the 30 shares of S stock owned directly by Jones is treated as not outstanding, the result is that P would be treated as owning stock possessing only 71 percent (50 ÷ 70) of the total voting power and value of S stock, and S would not be a component member of a controlled group of corporations on December 31, 1965. However, since P is considered as owning the 30 shares of S stock with the application of paragraph (b)(1) of this section, and such ownership plus the S stock directly owned by P (50 shares) results in S being a component member of a controlled group of corporations on December 31, 1965, the provisions of this paragraph apply. Therefore, the provisions of paragraph (b)(2)(ii) of this section do not apply with respect to the 30

Reg. § 1.1563-2(c)(2)

shares of S stock, and on December 31, 1965, S is a component member of a controlled group of corporations consisting of P and S. [Reg. § 1.1563-2.]

☐ [*T.D. 6845, 8-4-65. Amended by T.D. 7181, 4-24-72.*]

§ 1.1563-3. Rules for determining stock ownership.—(a) *In general.* In determining stock ownership for purposes of §§ 1.1562-5, 1.1563-1, 1.1563-2, and this section, the constructive ownership rules of paragraph (b) of this section apply to the extent such rules are referred to in such sections. The application of such rules shall be subject to the operating rules and special rules contained in paragraphs (c) and (d) of this section.

(b) *Constructive ownership*—(1) *Options.* If a person has an option to acquire any outstanding stock of a corporation, such stock shall be considered as owned by such person. For purposes of this subparagraph, an option to acquire such an option, and each one of a series of such options, shall be considered as an option to acquire such stock. For example, assume Smith owns an option to purchase 100 shares of the outstanding stock of M Corporation. Under this subparagraph, Smith is considered to own such 100 shares. The result would be the same if Smith owned an option to acquire the option (or one of a series of options) to purchase 100 shares of M stock.

(2) *Attribution from partnerships.* (i) Stock owned, directly or indirectly, by or for a partnership shall be considered as owned by any partner having an interest of 5 percent or more in either the capital or profits of the partnership in proportion to his interest in capital or profits, whichever such proportion is the greater.

(ii) The provisions of this subparagraph may be illustrated by the following example:

Example. Green, Jones, and White, unrelated individuals, are partners in the GJW partnership. The partners' interests in the capital and profits of the partnership are as follows:

Partner	Capital	Profits
Green	36%	25%
Jones	60	71
White	4	4

The GJW partnership owns the entire outstanding stock (100 shares) of X Corporation. Under this subparagraph, Green is considered to own the X stock owned by the partnership in proportion to his interest in capital (36 percent) or profits (25 percent), whichever such proportion is the greater. Therefore, Green is considered to own 36 shares of the X stock. However, since Jones has a greater interest in the profits of the partnership,

he is considered to own the X stock in proportion to his interest in such profits. Therefore, Jones is considered to own 71 shares of the X stock. Since White does not have an interest of 5 percent or more in either the capital or profits of the partnership, he is not considered to own any shares of the X stock.

(3) *Attribution from estates or trusts.* (i) Stock owned, directly or indirectly, by or for an estate or trust shall be considered as owned by any beneficiary who has an actuarial interest of 5 percent or more in such stock, to the extent of such actuarial interest. For purposes of this subparagraph, the actuarial interest of each beneficiary shall be determined by assuming the maximum exercise of discretion by the fiduciary in favor of such beneficiary and the maximum use of such stock to satisfy his rights as a beneficiary. A beneficiary of an estate or trust who cannot under any circumstances receive any interest in stock held by the estate or trust, including the proceeds from the disposition thereof, or the income therefrom, does not have an actuarial interest in such stock. Thus, where stock owned by a decedent's estate has been specifically bequeathed to certain beneficiaries and the remainder of the estate is bequeathed to other beneficiaries, the stock is attributable only to the beneficiaries to whom it is specifically bequeathed. Similarly, a remainderman of a trust who cannot under any circumstances receive any interest in the stock of a corporation which is a part of the corpus of the trust (including any accumulated income therefrom or the proceeds from a disposition thereof) does not have an actuarial interest in such stock. However, an income beneficiary of a trust does have an actuarial interest in stock if he has any right to the income from such stock even though under the terms of the trust instrument such stock can never be distributed to him. The factors and methods prescribed in § 20.2031-7 of this chapter (Estate Tax Regulations) [Reg. § 20.2031-7 of this chapter is reproduced at ¶ 2391.05.—CCH.] for use in ascertaining the value of an interest in property for estate tax purposes shall be used for purposes of this subdivision in determining a beneficiary's actuarial interest in stock owned directly or indirectly by or for a trust.

(ii) For the purposes of this subparagraph, property of a decedent shall be considered as owned by his estate if such property is subject to administration by the executor or administrator for the purposes of paying claims against the estate and expenses of administration notwithstanding that, under local law, legal title to such property vests in the decedent's heirs, legatees or devisees immediately upon death. With respect to an estate, the term "beneficiary" includes any

Reg. § 1.1563-3(a)

person entitled to receive property of the decedent pursuant to a will or pursuant to laws of descent and distribution. A person shall no longer be considered a beneficiary of an estate when all the property to which he is entitled has been received by him, when he no longer has a claim against the estate arising out of having been a beneficiary, and when there is only a remote possibility that it will be necessary for the estate to seek the return of property or to seek payment from him by contribution or otherwise to satisfy claims against the estate or expenses of administration. When pursuant to the preceding sentence, a person ceases to be a beneficiary, stock owned by the estate shall not thereafter be considered owned by him.

(iii) Stock owned, directly or indirectly, by or for any portion of a trust of which a person is considered the owner under subpart E, part I, subchapter J of the Code (relating to grantors and others treated as substantial owners) is considered as owned by such person.

(iv) This subparagraph does not apply to stock owned by any employees' trust described in section 401(a) which is exempt from tax under section 501(a).

(4) *Attribution from corporations.* (i) Stock owned, directly or indirectly, by or for a corporation shall be considered as owned by any person who owns (within the meaning of section 1563(d)) 5 percent or more in value of its stock in that proportion which the value of the stock which such person so owns bears to the value of all the stock in such corporation.

(ii) The provisions of this subparagraph may be illustrated by the following example:

Example. Brown, an individual, owns 60 shares of the 100 shares of the only class of outstanding stock of corporation P. Smith, an individual, owns 4 shares of the P stock, and corporation X owns 36 shares of the P stock. Corporation P owns, directly and indirectly, 50 shares of the stock of corporation S. Under this subparagraph, Brown is considered to own 30 shares of the S stock (60/100 × 50), and X is considered to own 18 shares of the S stock (36/100 × 50). Since Smith does not own 5 percent or more in value of the P stock, he is not considered as owning any of the S stock owned by P. If, in this example, Smith's wife had owned directly 1 share of the P stock, Smith (and his wife) would each own 5 shares of the P stock, and therefore Smith (and his wife) would be considered as owning 2.5 shares of the S stock (5/100 × 50).

(5) *Spouse.* (i) Except as provided in subdivision (ii) of this subparagraph, an individual shall be considered to own the stock owned, directly or indirectly, by or for his spouse, other than a spouse who is legally separated from the individual under a decree of divorce, whether interlocutory or final, or a decree of separate maintenance.

(ii) An individual shall not be considered to own stock in a corporation owned, directly or indirectly, by or for his spouse on any day of a taxable year of such corporation, provided that each of the following conditions are satisfied with respect to such taxable year:

(*a*) Such individual does not, at any time during such taxable year, own directly any stock in such corporation.

(*b*) Such individual is not a member of the board of directors or an employee of such corporation and does not participate in the management of such corporation at any time during such taxable year.

(*c*) Not more than 50 percent of such corporation's gross income for such taxable year was derived from royalties, rents, dividends, interest, and annuities.

(*d*) Such stock in such corporation is not, at any time during such taxable year, subject to conditions which substantially restrict or limit the spouse's right to dispose of such stock and which run in favor of the individual or his children who have not attained the age of 21 years. The principles of paragraph (b)(2)(iii) of § 1.1563-2 shall apply in determining whether a condition is a condition described in the preceding sentence.

(iii) For purposes of subdivision (ii)(*c*) of this subparagraph, the gross income of a corporation for a taxable year shall be determined under section 61 and the regulations thereunder. The terms "royalties", "rents", "dividends", "interest", and "annuities" shall have the same meanings such terms are given for purposes of section 1244(c). See paragraph (e)(1)(ii), (iii), (iv), (v), and (vi) of § 1.1244(c)-1.

(6) *Children, grandchildren, parents, and grandparents.* (i) An individual shall be considered to own the stock owned, directly or indirectly, by or for his children who have not attained the age of 21 years, and, if the individual has not attained the age of 21 years, the stock owned, directly or indirectly, by or for his parents.

(ii) If an individual owns (directly, and with the application of the rules of this paragraph but without regard to this subdivision) stock possessing more than 50 percent of the total combined voting power of all classes of stock entitled to vote or more than 50 percent of the total value of shares of all classes of stock in a corporation, then such individual shall be considered to own the stock in such corporation owned, directly or indirectly, by or for his parents, grandparents,

Reg. § 1.1563-3(b)(6)

grandchildren, and children who have attained the age of 21 years. In determining whether the stock owned by an individual possesses the requisite percentage of the total combined voting power of all classes of stock entitled to vote of a corporation, see paragraph (a)(6) of § 1.1563-1.

(iii) For purposes of section 1563, and §§ 1.1563-1 through 1.1563-4, a legally adopted child of an individual shall be treated as a child of such individual by blood.

(iv) The provisions of this subparagraph may be illustrated by the following example:

Example—(a) Facts. Individual F owns directly 40 shares of the 100 shares of the only class of stock of Z Corporation. His son, M (20 years of age), owns directly 30 shares of such stock, and his son, A (30 years of age), owns directly 20 shares of such stock. The remaining 10 shares of the Z stock are owned by an unrelated person.

(b) F's ownership. Individual F owns 40 shares of the Z stock directly and is considered to own the 30 shares of Z stock owned directly by M. Since, for purposes of the more-than-50-percent stock ownership test contained in subdivision (ii) of this subparagraph, F is treated as owning 70 shares or 70 percent of the total voting power and value of the Z stock, he is also considered as owning the 20 shares owned by his adult son, A. Accordingly, F is considered as owning a total of 90 shares of the Z stock.

(c) M's ownership. Minor son, M, owns 30 shares of the Z stock directly, and is considered to own the 40 shares of Z stock owned directly by his father, F. However, M is not considered to own the 20 shares of Z stock owned directly by his brother, A, and constructively by F, because stock constructively owned by F by reason of family attribution is not considered as owned by him for purposes of making another member of his family the constructive owner of such stock. See paragraph (c)(2) of this section. Accordingly, M owns and is considered as owning a total of 70 shares of the Z stock.

(d) A's ownership. Adult son, A, owns 20 shares of the Z stock directly. Since, for purposes of the more-than-50-percent stock ownership test contained in subdivision (ii) of this subparagraph, A is treated as owning only the Z stock which he owns directly, he does not satisfy the condition precedent for the attribution of Z stock from his father. Accordingly, A is treated as owning only the 20 shares of Z stock which he owns directly.

(c) *Operating rules and special rules*—(1) *In general.* Except as provided in subparagraph (2) of this paragraph, stock constructively owned by a person by reason of the application of subparagraph (1), (2), (3), (4), (5), or (6) of paragraph (b) of this section shall, for purposes of applying such subparagraphs, be treated as actually owned by such person.

(2) *Members of family.* Stock constructively owned by an individual by reason of the application of subparagraph (5) or (6) of paragraph (b) of this section shall not be treated as owned by him for purposes of again applying such subparagraphs in order to make another the constructive owner of such stock.

(3) *Precedence of option attribution.* For purposes of this section, if stock may be considered as owned by a person under subparagraph (1) of paragraph (b) of this section (relating to option attribution) and under any other subparagraph of such paragraph, such stock shall be considered as owned by such person under subparagraph (1) of such paragraph.

(4) *Examples.* The provisions of this paragraph may be illustrated by the following examples:

Example (1). A, 30 years of age, has a 90 percent interest in the capital and profits of a partnership. The partnership owns all the outstanding stock of corporation X and X owns 60 shares of the 100 outstanding shares of corporation Y. Under subparagraph (1) of this paragraph, the 60 shares of Y constructively owned by the partnership by reason of subparagraph (4) of paragraph (b) of this section is treated as actually owned by the partnership for purposes of applying subparagraph (2) of paragraph (b) of this section. Therefore, A is considered as owning 54 shares of the Y stock (90 percent of 60 shares).

Example (2). Assume the same facts as in example (1). Assume further that B, who is 20 years of age and the brother of A, directly owns 40 shares of Y stock. Although the stock of Y owned by B is considered as owned by C (the father of A and B) under paragraph (b)(6)(i) of this section, under subparagraph (2) of this paragraph such stock may not be treated as owned by C for purposes of applying paragraph (b)(6)(ii) of this section in order to make A the constructive owner of such stock.

Example (3). Assume the same facts assumed for purposes of example (2), and further assume that C has an option to acquire the 40 shares of Y stock owned by his son, B. The rule contained in subparagraph (2) of this paragraph does not prevent the reattribution of such 40 shares to A because, under subparagraph (3) of this paragraph, C is considered as owning the 40 shares by reason of option attribution and not by reason of family attribution. Therefore, since A satisfies the more-than-50-percent stock ownership test contained in paragraph (b)(6)(ii) of this section with respect to Y, the 40 shares of Y stock construc-

Reg. § 1.1563-3(c)(1)

tively owned by C are reattributed to A, and A is considered as owning a total of 94 shares of Y stock.

* * *

[Reg. § 1.1563-3.]

☐ [*T.D. 6845, 8-4-65. Amended by T.D. 7181, 4-24-72, T.D. 7779, 6-1-81 and T.D. 8179, 3-1-88.*]

Tax Returns or Statements

§ 1.6015-1. Relief from joint and several liability on a joint return.—(a) *In general.*—(1) An individual who qualifies and elects under section 6013 to file a joint Federal income tax return with another individual is jointly and severally liable for the joint Federal income tax liabilities for that year. A spouse or former spouse may be relieved of joint and several liability for Federal income tax for that year under the following three relief provisions:

(i) Innocent spouse relief under § 1.6015-2.

(ii) Allocation of deficiency under § 1.6015-3.

(iii) Equitable relief under § 1.6015-4.

* * *

[Reg. § 1.6015-1.]

☐ [*T.D. 9003, 7-17-2002.*]

§ 1.6015-2. Relief from liability applicable to all qualifying joint filers.—(a) *In general.* A requesting spouse may be relieved of joint and several liability for tax (including additions to tax, penalties, and interest) from an understatement for a taxable year under this section if the requesting spouse elects the application of this section in accordance with § § 1.6015-1(h)(5) and 1.6015-5, and—

(1) A joint return was filed for the taxable year;

(2) On the return there is an understatement attributable to erroneous items of the nonrequesting spouse;

(3) The requesting spouse establishes that in signing the return he or she did not know and had no reason to know of the understatement; and

(4) It is inequitable to hold the requesting spouse liable for the deficiency attributable to the understatement.

(b) *Understatement.* The term *understatement* has the meaning given to such term by section 6662(d)(2)(A) and the regulations thereunder.

(c) *Knowledge or reason to know.* A requesting spouse has knowledge or reason to know of an understatement if he or she actually knew of the understatement, or if a reasonable person in similar circumstances would have known of the understatement. For rules relating to a requesting spouse's actual knowledge, see § 1.6015-3(c)(2). All of the facts and circumstances are considered in determining whether a requesting spouse had reason to know of an understatement. The facts and circumstances that are considered include, but are not limited to, the nature of the erroneous item and the amount of the erroneous item relative to other items; the couple's financial situation; the requesting spouse's educational background and business experience; the extent of the requesting spouse's participation in the activity that resulted in the erroneous item; whether the requesting spouse failed to inquire, at or before the time the return was signed, about items on the return or omitted from the return that a reasonable person would question; and whether the erroneous item represented a departure from a recurring pattern reflected in prior years' returns (e.g., omitted income from an investment regularly reported on prior years' returns).

(d) *Inequity.* All of the facts and circumstances are considered in determining whether it is inequitable to hold a requesting spouse jointly and severally liable for an understatement. One relevant factor for this purpose is whether the requesting spouse significantly benefitted, directly or indirectly, from the understatement. A significant benefit is any benefit in excess of normal support. Evidence of direct or indirect benefit may consist of transfers of property or rights to property, including transfers that may be received several years after the year of the understatement. Thus, for example, if a requesting spouse receives property (including life insurance proceeds) from the nonrequesting spouse that is beyond normal support and traceable to items omitted from gross income that are attributable to the nonrequesting spouse, the requesting spouse will be considered to have received significant benefit from those items. Other factors that may also be taken into account, if the situation warrants, include the fact that the requesting spouse has been deserted by the nonrequesting spouse, the fact that the spouses have been divorced or separated, or that the requesting spouse received benefit on the return from the understatement. For guidance concerning the criteria to be used in determining whether it is inequitable to hold a requesting spouse jointly and severally liable under this section, see Rev. Proc. 2000-15 (2000-1 C.B. 447), or other guidance published by the Treasury and IRS (see § 601.601(d)(2) of this chapter).

* * *

[Reg. § 1.6015-2.]

☐ [*T.D. 9003, 7-17-2002.*]

§ 1.6015-3. Allocation of deficiency for individuals who are no longer married, are legally separated, or are not members of the same household.—(a) *Election to allocate deficiency.* A requesting spouse may elect to allocate a deficiency if, as defined in paragraph (b) of this section, the requesting spouse is divorced, widowed, or legally separated, or has not been a member of the same household as the nonrequesting spouse at any time during the 12-month period ending on the date an election for relief is filed. For purposes of this section, the marital status of a deceased requesting spouse will be determined on the earlier of the date of the election or the date of death in accordance with section 7703(a)(1). Subject to the restrictions of paragraph (c) of this section, an eligible requesting spouse who elects the application of this section in accordance with § § 1.6015-1(h)(5) and 1.6015-5 generally may be relieved of joint and several liability for the portion of any deficiency that is allocated to the nonrequesting spouse pursuant to the allocation methods set forth in paragraph (d) of this section. Relief may be available to both spouses filing the joint return if each spouse is eligible for and elects the application of this section.

(b) *Definitions*—(1) *Divorced.* A determination of whether a requesting spouse is divorced for purposes of this section will be made in accordance with section 7703 and the regulations thereunder. Such determination will be made as of the date the election is filed.

(2) *Legally separated.* A determination of whether a requesting spouse is legally separated for purposes of this section will be made in accordance with section 7703 and the regulations thereunder. Such determination will be made as of the date the election is filed.

(3) *Members of the same household*—(i) *Temporary absences.* A requesting spouse and a nonrequesting spouse are considered members of the same household during either spouse's temporary absences from the household if it is reasonable to assume that the absent spouse will return to the household, and the household or a substantially equivalent household is maintained in anticipation of such return. Examples of temporary absences may include, but are not limited to, absence due to incarceration, illness, business, vacation, military service, or education.

(ii) *Separate dwellings.* A husband and wife who reside in the same dwelling are considered members of the same household. In addition, a husband and wife who reside in two separate dwellings are considered members of the same household if the spouses are not estranged or one spouse is temporarily absent from the other's household within the meaning of paragraph (b)(3)(i) of this section.

* * *

[Reg. § 1.6015-3.]

☐ [*T.D.* 9003, 7-17-2002.]

Information Returns

Proposed Regulation

§ 1.6045-5. Information reporting on payments to attorneys.—(a) *Requirement of reporting*—(1) *In general.* Except as provided in paragraph (c) of this section, every payor engaged in a trade or business who, in the course of that trade or business, makes payments aggregating $600 or more during a calendar year to an attorney in connection with legal services (whether or not the services are performed for the payor) must file an information return for such payments. The information return must be filed on the form and in the manner required by the Commissioner. For the time and place of filing the form, see § 1.6041-6. For definitions of the terms under this section, see paragraph (d) of this section. The requirements of this paragraph (a)(1) apply whether or not—

(i) A portion of a payment is kept by the attorney as compensation for legal services rendered; or

(ii) Other information returns are required with respect to some or all of a payment under other provisions of the Internal Revenue Code and the regulations thereunder.

(2) *Information required.* The information return required under paragraph (a)(1) of this section must include the following information—

(i) The name, address, and taxpayer identification number (TIN) (as defined in section 7701(a)) of the payor;

(ii) The name, address, and TIN of the payee attorney;

(iii) The amount of the payment or payments (as defined in paragraph (d)(5) of this section); and

(iv) Any other information required by the Commissioner.

(3) *Requirement to furnish statement.* A person required to file an information return under paragraph (a)(1) of this section must furnish to the attorney a written statement of the information required to be shown on the return. This requirement may be met by furnishing a copy of the return to the attorney. The written statement must be furnished to the attorney on or before

January 31 of the year following the calendar year in which the payment was made.

(b) *Special rules*—(1) *Joint or multiple payees*—(i) *Check delivered to payee attorney.* If more than one attorney is listed as a payee on a check, an information return must be filed under paragraph (a)(1) of this section with respect to the payee attorney, if any, who received the check.

(ii) *Check delivered to nonpayee or to payee nonattorney.* If one or more than one attorney is listed as a payee on a check and the check is delivered to a person who is not a payee on the check, or to a payee who is not an attorney, an information return must be filed under paragraph (a)(1) of this section with respect to the first-listed payee attorney on the check.

(2) *Attorney required to report payments made to other attorneys.* If, due to the payment of a check, an information return is required to be filed under paragraph (b)(1) of this section, the attorney with respect to whom the information return is required to be filed (tier-one attorney) must file an information return, as required under this section, for any payment that the tier-one attorney makes to other attorneys with respect to that check, regardless of whether the tier-one attorney is a payor under paragraph (d)(3) of this section.

(c) *Exceptions.* Notwithstanding paragraphs (a) and (b) of this section, a return of information is not required under section 6045(f) with respect to the following payments—

(1) Payments of wages or other compensation paid to an attorney by the attorney's employer.

(2) Payments of compensation or profits paid or distributed to its partners by a partnership engaged in providing legal services.

(3) Payments of dividends or corporate earnings and profits paid to its shareholders by a corporation engaged in providing legal services.

(4) Payments made by a person to the extent that the person is required to report with respect to the same payee the payments or portions thereof under section 6041(a) and § 1.6041-1(a) (or would be required to so report the payments or portions thereof but for the dollar amount limitation contained in section 6041(a) and § 1.6041-1(a)).

(5) Payments made to a nonresident alien individual, foreign partnership, or foreign corporation that does not engage in a trade or business in the United States and does not perform any labor or personal services in the United States. For how a payor determines whether a payment is subject to this exception, see § 1.6041-4(a)(1).

(6) Payments made to an attorney in the attorney's capacity as the person responsible for closing a transaction within the meaning of § 1.6045-4(e)(3) for the sale or exchange of any present or future ownership interest in real estate described in § 1.6045-4(b)(2)(i) through (iv).

(d) *Definitions.* The following definitions apply for purposes of this section:

(1) *Attorney* means a person engaged in the practice of law, whether as a sole proprietor, partnership, corporation, or joint venture.

(2) *Legal services* means all services related to, or supportive of, the practice of law performed by, or under the supervision of, an attorney.

(3) *Payor* means a person who makes a payment if that person is an obligor on the payment, or the obligor's insurer or guarantor. For example, a payor includes a person who pays a settlement amount to an attorney of a client who has asserted a tort, contract, violation of law, or workers' compensation claim against that person and the person's insurer if the insurer pays the settlement amount to the attorney.

(4) *Payments to an attorney* in the case of a payment by check means a check on which the attorney is named as a sole, joint, or alternative payee.

(5) *Amount of the payment* in the case of a check means the amount of the check plus the amount required to be withheld from the payment under section 3406(a)(1), because a condition for withholding exists with respect to the attorney for whom an information return is required to be filed under paragraph (a)(1) of this section.

(e) *Attorney to furnish TIN.* A payor that is required to file an information return under this section must solicit a TIN from the attorney at or before the time the payor makes a payment to the attorney. Any attorney must furnish the TIN to the payor, but is not required to certify that the TIN is correct. See, however, paragraph (c)(5) of this section regarding payments to certain foreign attorneys. A payment for which a return of information is required under this section is subject to backup withholding under section 3406 and the regulations thereunder.

* * *

[Reg. § 1.6045-5.]

[Proposed 5-17-2002.]

Accuracy-Related and Fraud Penalties

§ 1.6662-1. Overview of the accuracy-related penalty.—Section 6662 imposes an accuracy-related penalty on any portion of an underpayment of tax required to be shown on a return that is attributable to one or more of the following:

(a) Negligence or disregard of rules or regulations;

(b) Any substantial understatement of income tax;

(c) Any substantial valuation misstatement under chapter 1;

(d) Any substantial overstatement of pension liabilities; or

(e) Any substantial estate or gift tax valuation understatement.

Sections 1.6662-1 through 1.6662-5 address only the first three components of the accuracy-related penalty, *i.e.*, the penalties for negligence or disregard of rules or regulations, substantial understatements of income tax, and substantial (or gross) valuation misstatements under chapter 1. The penalties for disregard of rules or regulations and for a substantial understatement of income tax may be avoided by adequately disclosing certain information as provided in § 1.6662-3(c) and §§ 1.6662-4(e) and (f), respectively. The penalties for negligence and for a substantial (or gross) valuation misstatement under chapter 1 may not be avoided by disclosure. No accuracy-related penalty may be imposed on any portion of an underpayment if there was reasonable cause for, and the taxpayer acted in good faith with respect to, such portion. The reasonable cause and good faith exception to the accuracy-related penalty is set forth in § 1.6664-4. [Reg. § 1.6662-1.]

☐ [*T.D.* 8381, 12-30-91. *Amended by T.D.* 8617, 8-31-95.]

§ 1.6662-2. Accuracy-related penalty.—(a) *In general*. Section 6662(a) imposes an accuracy-related penalty on any portion of an underpayment of tax (as defined in section 6664(a) and § 1.6664-2) required to be shown on a return if such portion is attributable to one or more of the following types of misconduct:

(1) Negligence or disregard of rules or regulations (see § 1.6662-3);

(2) Any substantial understatement of income tax (see § 1.6662-4); or

(3) Any substantial (or gross) valuation misstatement under chapter 1 ("substantial valuation misstatement" or "gross valuation misstatement"), provided the applicable dollar limitation set forth in section 6662(e)(2) is satisfied (see § 1.6662-5).

The accuracy-related penalty applies only in cases in which a return of tax is filed, except that the penalty does not apply in the case of a return prepared by the Secretary under the authority of section 6020(b). The accuracy-related penalty under section 6662 and the penalty under section 6651 for failure to timely file a return of tax may both be imposed on the same portion of an underpayment if a return is filed, but is filed late. The fact that a return is filed late, however, is not taken into account in determining whether an accuracy-related penalty should be imposed. No accuracy-related penalty may be imposed on any portion of an underpayment of tax on which the fraud penalty set forth in section 6663 is imposed.

(b) *Amount of penalty*—(1) *In general*. The amount of the accuracy-related penalty is 20 percent of the portion of an underpayment of tax required to be shown on a return that is attributable to any of the types of misconduct listed in paragraphs (a)(1) through (a)(3) of this section, except as provided in paragraph (b)(2) of this section.

(2) *Increase in penalty for gross valuation misstatement*. In the case of a gross valuation misstatement, as defined in section 6662(h)(2) and § 1.6662-5(e)(2), the amount of the accuracy-related penalty is 40 percent of the portion of an underpayment of tax required to be shown on a return that is attributable to the gross valuation misstatement, provided the applicable dollar limitation set forth in section 6662(e)(2) is satisfied.

(c) *No stacking of accuracy-related penalty components*. The maximum accuracy-related penalty imposed on a portion of an underpayment may not exceed 20 percent of such portion (40 percent of the portion attributable to a gross valuation misstatement), notwithstanding that such portion is attributable to more than one of the types of misconduct described in paragraph (a) of this section. For example, if a portion of an underpayment of tax required to be shown on a return is attributable both to negligence and a substantial understatement of income tax, the maximum accuracy-related penalty is 20 percent of such portion. Similarly, the maximum accuracy-related penalty imposed on any portion of an underpayment that is attributable both to negligence and a gross valuation misstatement is 40 percent of such portion.

* * *

[Reg. § 1.6662-2.]

[*T.D.* 8381, 12-30-91. *Amended by T.D.* 8617, 8-31-95 *and T.D.* 8790, 12-1-98.]

§ 1.6662-3. Negligence or disregard of rules or regulations.—(a) *In general*. If any portion of an underpayment, as defined in section 6664(a) and § 1.6664-2, of any income tax imposed under subtitle A of the Code that is required to be shown on a return is attributable to negligence or disregard of rules or regulations, there is added to the tax an amount equal to 20 percent of such portion. The penalty for disregarding rules or regulations does not apply, however, if the requirements of § 1.6662-3(c)(1) are satisfied and the position in question is adequately disclosed as provided in § 1.6662-3(c)(2), or to the extent that the reasonable cause and good faith exception to this penalty set forth in § 1.6664-4 applies. In addition, if a position with respect to an item is contrary to a revenue ruling or notice (other than a notice of proposed rulemaking) issued by the Internal Revenue Service and published in the Internal Revenue Bulletin, this penalty does not apply if the position has a realistic possibility of being sustained on its merits. See § 1.6694-2(b) of the preparer penalty regulations for a description of the realistic possibility standard.

(b) *Definitions and rules*—(1) *Negligence*. The term "negligence" includes any failure to make a reasonable attempt to comply with the provisions of the internal revenue laws or to exercise ordinary and reasonable care in the preparation of a tax return. "Negligence" also includes any failure by the taxpayer to keep adequate books and records or to substantiate items properly. A return position that has a reasonable basis as defined in paragraph (b)(3) of this section is not attributable to negligence. Negligence is strongly indicated where—

(i) A taxpayer fails to include on an income tax return an amount of income shown on an information return, as defined in section 6724(d)(1);

(ii) A taxpayer fails to make a reasonable attempt to ascertain the correctness of a deduction, credit or exclusion on a return which would seem to a reasonable and prudent person to be "too good to be true" under the circumstances;

(iii) A partner fails to comply with the requirements of section 6222, which requires that a partner treat partnership items on its return in a manner that is consistent with the treatment of such items on the partnership return (or notify the Secretary of the inconsistency); or

(iv) A shareholder fails to comply with the requirements of section 6242, which requires that an S corporation shareholder treat subchapter S items on its return in a manner that is consistent with the treatment of such items on the corporation's return (or notify the Secretary of the inconsistency).

(2) *Disregard of rules or regulations*. The term "disregard" includes any careless, reckless or intentional disregard of rules or regulations. The term "rules or regulations" includes the provisions of the Internal Revenue Code, temporary or final Treasury regulations issued under the Code, and revenue rulings or notices (other than notices of proposed rulemaking) issued by the Internal Revenue Service and published in the Internal Revenue Bulletin. A disregard of rules or regulations is "careless" if the taxpayer does not exercise reasonable diligence to determine the correctness of a return position that is contrary to the rule or regulation. A disregard is "reckless" if the taxpayer makes little or no effort to determine whether a rule or regulation exists, under circumstances which demonstrate a substantial deviation from the standard of conduct that a reasonable person would observe. A disregard is "intentional" if the taxpayer knows of the rule or regulation that is disregarded. Nevertheless, a taxpayer who takes a position contrary to a revenue ruling or a notice has not disregarded the ruling or notice if the contrary position has a realistic possibility of being sustained on its merits.

(3) *Reasonable basis*. Reasonable basis is a relatively high standard of tax reporting, that is, significantly higher than not frivolous or not patently improper. The reasonable basis standard is not satisfied by a return position that is merely arguable or that is merely a colorable claim. If a return position is reasonably based on one or more of the authorities set forth in § 1.6662-4(d)(3)(iii) (taking into account the relevance and persuasiveness of the authorities, and subsequent developments), the return position will generally satisfy the reasonable basis standard even though it may not satisfy the substantial authority standard as defined in § 1.6662-4(d)(2). (See § 1.6662-4(d)(3)(ii) for rules with respect to relevance, persuasiveness, subsequent developments, and use of a well-reasoned construction of an applicable statutory provision for purposes of the substantial understatement penalty.) In addition, the reasonable cause and good faith exception in § 1.6664-4 may provide relief from the penalty for negligence or disregard of rules or regulations, even if a return position does not satisfy the reasonable basis standard.

(c) *Exception for adequate disclosure*—(1) *In general*. No penalty under section 6662(b)(1) may be imposed on any portion of an underpayment that is attributable to a position contrary to a rule or regulation if the position is disclosed in accordance with the rules of paragraph (c)(2) of this section and, in the case of a position contrary to a regulation, the position represents a good faith challenge to the validity of the regulation. This disclosure exception does not apply, however, in the case of a position that does not have a reasonable basis or where the taxpayer fails to keep adequate books and records or to substantiate items properly.

Reg. § 1.6662-3(c)(1)

(2) *Method of disclosure.* Disclosure is adequate for purposes of the penalty for disregarding rules or regulations if made in accordance with the provisions of §§ 1.6662-4(f)(1), (3), (4) and (5), which permit disclosure on a properly completed and filed Form 8275 or 8275-R, as appropriate. In addition, the statutory or regulatory provision or ruling in question must be adequately identified on the Form 8275 or 8275-R, as appropriate. The provisions of § 1.6662-4(f)(2), which permit disclosure in accordance with an annual revenue procedure for purposes of the substantial understatement penalty, do not apply for purposes of this section.

* * *

[Reg. § 1.6662-3.]

☐ [*T.D.* 8381, 12-30-91. *Amended by T.D.* 8617, 8-31-95 *and T.D.* 8790, 12-1-98.]

§ 1.6662-4. Substantial understatement of income tax.—(a) *In general.* If any portion of an underpayment, as defined in section 6664(a) and § 1.6664-2, of any income tax imposed under subtitle A of the Code that is required to be shown on a return is attributable to a substantial understatement of such income tax, there is added to the tax an amount equal to 20 percent of such portion. Except in the case of any item attributable to a tax shelter (as defined in paragraph (g)(2) of this section), an understatement is reduced by the portion of the understatement that is attributable to the tax treatment of an item for which there is substantial authority, or with respect to which there is adequate disclosure. General rules for determining the amount of an understatement are set forth in paragraph (b) of this section and more specific rules in the case of carrybacks and carryovers are set forth in paragraph (c) of this section. The rules for determining when substantial authority exists are set forth in § 1.6662-4(d). The rules for determining when there is adequate disclosure are set forth in § 1.6662-4(e) and (f). This penalty does not apply to the extent that the reasonable cause and good faith exception to this penalty set forth in § 1.6664-4 applies.

(b) *Definitions and computational rules*—(1) *Substantial.* An understatement (as defined in paragraph (b)(2) of this section) is "substantial" if it exceeds the greater of—

(i) 10 percent of the tax required to be shown on the return for the taxable year (as defined in paragraph (b)(3) of this section); or

(ii) $5,000 ($10,000 in the case of a corporation other than an S corporation (as defined in section 1361(a)(1)) or a personal holding company (as defined in section 542)).

(2) *Understatement.* Except as provided in paragraph (c)(2) of this section (relating to special rules for carrybacks), the term "understatement" means the excess of—

(i) The amount of the tax required to be shown on the return for the taxable year (as defined in paragraph (b)(3) of this section), over

(ii) The amount of the tax imposed which is shown on the return for the taxable year (as defined in paragraph (b)(4) of this section), reduced by any rebate (as defined in paragraph (b)(5) of this section).

The definition of understatement also may be expressed as—

$$Understatement = X - (Y - Z)$$

where X = the amount of the tax required to be shown on the return; Y = the amount of the tax imposed which is shown on the return; and Z = any rebate.

(3) *Amount of the tax required to be shown on the return.* The "amount of the tax required to be shown on the return" for the taxable year has the same meaning as the "amount of income tax imposed" as defined in § 1.6664-2(b).

(4) *Amount of the tax imposed which is shown on the return.* The "amount of the tax imposed which is shown on the return" for the taxable year has the same meaning as the "amount shown as the tax by the taxpayer on his return," as defined in § 1.6664-2(c), except that—

(i) There is no reduction for the excess of the amount described in § 1.6664-2(c)(1)(i) over the amount described in § 1.6664-2(c)(1)(ii), and

(ii) The tax liability shown by the taxpayer on his return is recomputed as if the following items had been reported properly:

(A) Items (other than tax shelter items as defined in § 1.6662-4(g)(3)) for which there is substantial authority for the treatment claimed (as provided in § 1.6662-4(d)).

(B) Items (other than tax shelter items as defined in § 1.6662-4(g)(3)) with respect to which there is adequate disclosure (as provided in § 1.6662-4(e) and (f)).

(C) Tax shelter items (as defined in § 1.6662-4(g)(3)) for which there is substantial authority for the treatment claimed (as provided in § 1.6662-4(d)), and with respect to which the taxpayer reasonably believed that the tax treatment of the items was more likely than not the proper tax treatment (as provided in § 1.6662-4(g)(4)).

(5) *Rebate.* The term "rebate" has the meaning set forth in § 1.6664-2(e), except that—

(i) "Amounts not so shown previously assessed (or collected without assessment)" includes only amounts not so shown previously assessed (or collected without assessment) as a deficiency, and

(ii) The amount of the rebate is determined as if any items to which the rebate is attributable that are described in paragraph (b)(4) of this section had received the proper tax treatment.

Reg. § 1.6662-4(a)

(6) *Examples.* The following examples illustrate the provisions of paragraph (b) of this section. These examples do not take into account the reasonable cause exception under § 1.6664-4:

Example 1. In 1990, Individual A, a calendar year taxpayer, files a return for 1989, which shows taxable income of $18,200 and tax liability of $2,734. Subsequent adjustments on audit for 1989 increase taxable income to $51,500 and tax liability to $12,339. There was substantial authority for an item resulting in an adjustment that increases taxable income by $5,300. The item is not a tax shelter item. In computing the amount of the understatement, the amount of tax shown on A's return is determined as if the item for which there was substantial authority had been given the proper tax treatment. Thus, the amount of tax that is treated as shown on A's return is $4,176, i.e., the tax on $23,500 ($18,200 taxable income actually shown on A's return plus $5,300, the amount of the adjustment for which there was substantial authority). The amount of the understatement is $8,163, i.e., $12,339 (the amount of tax required to be shown) less $4,176 (the amount of tax treated as shown on A's return after adjustment for the item for which there was substantial authority). Because the $8,163 understatement exceeds the greater of 10 percent of the tax required to be shown on the return for the year, i.e., $1,234 ($12,339 × .10) or $5,000, A has a substantial understatement of income tax for the year.

Example 2. Individual B, a calendar year taxpayer, files a return for 1990 that fails to include income reported on an information return, Form 1099, that was furnished to B. The Service detects this omission through its document matching program and assesses $3,000 in unreported tax liability. B's return is later examined and as a result of the examination the Service makes an adjustment to B's return of $4,000 in additional tax liability. Assuming there was neither substantial authority nor adequate disclosure with respect to the items adjusted, there is an understatement of $7,000 with respect to B's return. There is also an underpayment of $7,000. (See § 1.6664-2.) The amount of the understatement is not reduced by imposition of a negligence penalty on the $3,000 portion of the underpayment that is attributable to the unreported income. However, if the Service does impose the negligence penalty on this $3,000 portion, the Service may only impose the substantial understatement penalty on the remaining $4,000 portion of the underpayment. (See § 1.6662-2(c), which prohibits stacking of accuracy-related penalty components.)

* * *

(d) *Substantial authority*—(1) *Effect of having substantial authority.* If there is substantial authority for the tax treatment of an item, the item is treated as if it were shown properly on the return for the taxable year in computing the amount of the tax shown on the return. Thus, for purposes of section 6662(d), the tax attributable to the item is not included in the understatement for that year. (For special rules relating to tax shelter items see § 1.6662-4(g).)

(2) *Substantial authority standard.* The substantial authority standard is an objective standard involving an analysis of the law and application of the law to relevant facts. The substantial authority standard is less stringent than the more likely than not standard (the standard that is met when there is a greater than 50-percent likelihood of the position being upheld), but more stringent than the reasonable basis standard as defined in § 1.6662-3(b)(3). The possibility that a return will not be audited or, if audited, that an item will not be raised on audit, is not relevant in determining whether the substantial authority standard (or the reasonable basis standard) is satisfied.

(3) *Determination of whether substantial authority is present*—(i) *Evaluation of authorities.* There is substantial authority for the tax treatment of an item only if the weight of the authorities supporting the treatment is substantial in relation to the weight of authorities supporting contrary treatment. All authorities relevant to the tax treatment of an item, including the authorities contrary to the treatment, are taken into account in determining whether substantial authority exists. The weight of authorities is determined in light of the pertinent facts and circumstances in the manner prescribed by paragraph (d)(3)(ii) of this section. There may be substantial authority for more than one position with respect to the same item. Because the substantial authority standard is an objective standard, the taxpayer's belief that there is substantial authority for the tax treatment of an item is not relevant in determining whether there is substantial authority for that treatment.

(ii) *Nature of analysis.* The weight accorded an authority depends on its relevance and persuasiveness, and the type of document providing the authority. For example, a case or revenue ruling having some facts in common with the tax treatment at issue is not particularly relevant if the authority is materially distinguishable on its facts, or is otherwise inapplicable to the tax treatment at issue. An authority that merely states a conclusion ordinarily is less persuasive than one that reaches its conclusion by cogently relating the applicable law to pertinent facts. The weight of an authority from which information has been

Reg. § 1.6662-4(d)(3)

deleted, such as a private letter ruling, is diminished to the extent that the deleted information may have affected the authority's conclusions. The type of document also must be considered. For example, a revenue ruling is accorded greater weight than a private letter ruling addressing the same issue. An older private letter ruling, technical advice memorandum, general counsel memorandum or action on decision generally must be accorded less weight than a more recent one. Any document described in the preceding sentence that is more than 10 years old generally is accorded very little weight. However, the persuasiveness and relevance of a document, viewed in light of subsequent developments, should be taken into account along with the age of the document. There may be substantial authority for the tax treatment of an item despite the absence of certain types of authority. Thus, a taxpayer may have substantial authority for a position that is supported only by a well-reasoned construction of the applicable statutory provision.

(iii) *Types of authority.* Except in cases described in paragraph (d)(3)(iv) of this section concerning written determinations, only the following are authority for purposes of determining whether there is substantial authority for the tax treatment of an item: applicable provisions of the Internal Revenue Code and other statutory provisions; proposed, temporary and final regulations construing such statutes; revenue rulings and revenue procedures; tax treaties and regulations thereunder, and Treasury Department and other official explanations of such treaties; court cases; congressional intent as reflected in committee reports, joint explanatory statements of managers included in conference committee reports, and floor statements made prior to enactment by one of a bill's managers; General Explanations of tax legislation prepared by the Joint Committee on Taxation (the Blue Book); private letter rulings and technical advice memoranda issued after October 31, 1976; actions on decisions and general counsel memoranda issued after March 12, 1981 (as well as general counsel memoranda published in pre-1955 volumes of the Cumulative Bulletin); Internal Revenue Service information or press releases; and notices, announcements and other administrative pronouncements published by the Service in the Internal Revenue Bulletin. Conclusions reached in treatises, legal periodicals, legal opinions or opinions rendered by tax professionals are not authority. The authorities underlying such expressions of opinion where applicable to the facts of a particular case, however, may give rise to substantial authority for the tax treatment of an item. Notwithstanding the preceding list of authorities, an authority does not continue to be an authority to the extent it is overruled or modi-

fied, implicitly or explicitly, by a body with the power to overrule or modify the earlier authority. In the case of court decisions, for example, a district court opinion on an issue is not an authority if overruled or reversed by the United States Court of Appeals for such district. However, a Tax Court opinion is not considered to be overruled or modified by a court of appeals to which a taxpayer does not have a right of appeal, unless the Tax Court adopts the holding of the court of appeals. Similarly, a private letter ruling is not authority if revoked or if inconsistent with a subsequent proposed regulation, revenue ruling or other administrative pronouncement published in the Internal Revenue Bulletin.

(iv) *Special rules*—(A) *Written determinations.* There is substantial authority for the tax treatment of an item by a taxpayer if the treatment is supported by the conclusion of a ruling or a determination letter (as defined in § 301.6110-2(d) and (e)) issued to the taxpayer, by the conclusion of a technical advice memorandum in which the taxpayer is named, or by an affirmative statement in a revenue agent's report with respect to a prior taxable year of the taxpayer ("written determinations"). The preceding sentence does not apply, however, if—

(*1*) There was a misstatement or omission of a material fact or the facts that subsequently develop are materially different from the facts on which the written determination was based, or

(*2*) The written determination was modified or revoked after the date of issuance by—

(*i*) A notice to the taxpayer to whom the written determination was issued,

(*ii*) The enactment of legislation or ratification of a tax treaty,

(*iii*) A decision of the United States Supreme Court,

(*iv*) The issuance of temporary or final regulations, or

(*v*) The issuance of a revenue ruling, revenue procedure, or other statement published in the Internal Revenue Bulletin.

Except in the case of a written determination that is modified or revoked on account of § 1.6662-4(d)(3)(iv)(A)(*1*), a written determination that is modified or revoked as described in § 1.6662-4(d)(3)(iv)(A)(*2*) ceases to be authority on the date, and to the extent, it is so modified or revoked. See section 6404(f) for rules which require the Secretary to abate a penalty that is attributable to erroneous written advice furnished to a taxpayer by an officer or employee of the Internal Revenue Service.

Reg. § 1.6662-4(d)(3)

(B) *Taxpayer's jurisdiction*. The applicability of court cases to the taxpayer by reason of the taxpayer's residence in a particular jurisdiction is not taken into account in determining whether there is substantial authority for the tax treatment of an item. Notwithstanding the preceding sentence, there is substantial authority for the tax treatment of an item if the treatment is supported by controlling precedent of a United States Court of Appeals to which the taxpayer has a right of appeal with respect to the item.

(C) *When substantial authority determined*. There is substantial authority for the tax treatment of an item if there is substantial authority at the time the return containing the item is filed or there was substantial authority on the last day of the taxable year to which the return relates.

* * *

(e) *Disclosure of certain information*—(1) *Effect of adequate disclosure*. Items for which there is adequate disclosure as provided in this paragraph (e) and in paragraph (f) of this section are treated as if such items were shown properly on the return for the taxable year in computing the amount of the tax shown on the return. Thus, for purposes of section 6662(d), the tax attributable to such items is not included in the understatement for that year.

(2) *Circumstances where disclosure will not have an effect*. The rules of paragraph (e)(1) of this section do not apply where the item or position on the return —

(i) Does not have a reasonable basis (as defined in § 1.6662-3(b)(3));

(ii) Is attributable to a tax shelter (as defined in section 6662(d)(2)(C)(iii) and paragraph (g)(2) of this section); or

(iii) Is not properly substantiated, or the taxpayer failed to keep adequate books and records with respect to the item or position.

(3) *Restriction for corporations*. For purposes of paragraph (e)(2)(i) of this section, a corporation will not be treated as having a reasonable basis for its tax treatment of an item attributable to a multi-party financing transaction entered into after August 5, 1997, if the treatment does not clearly reflect the income of the corporation.

(f) *Method of making adequate disclosure*—(1) *Disclosure statement*. Disclosure is adequate with respect to an item (or group of similar items, such as amounts paid or incurred for supplies by a taxpayer engaged in business) or a position on a return if the disclosure is made on a properly completed form attached to the return or to a qualified amended return (as defined in § 1.6664-2(c)(3)) for the taxable year. In the case of an item or position other than one that is contrary to a regulation, disclosure must be made on Form 8275 (Disclosure Statement); in the case of a position contrary to a regulation, disclosure must be made on Form 8275-R (Regulation Disclosure Statement).

(2) *Disclosure on return*. The Commissioner may by annual revenue procedure (or otherwise) prescribe the circumstances under which disclosure of information on a return (or qualified amended return) in accordance with applicable forms and instructions is adequate. If the revenue procedure does not include an item, disclosure is adequate with respect to that item only if made on a properly completed Form 8275 or 8275-R, as appropriate, attached to the return for the year or to a qualified amended return.

(3) *Recurring item*. Disclosure with respect to a recurring item, such as the basis of recovery property, must be made for each taxable year in which the item is taken into account.

(4) *Carrybacks and carryovers*. Disclosure is adequate with respect to an item which is included in any loss, deduction or credit that is carried to another year only if made in connection with the return (or qualified amended return) for the taxable year in which the carryback or carryover arises (the "loss or credit year"). Disclosure is not also required in connection with the return for the taxable year in which the carryback or carryover is taken into account.

(5) *Pass-through entities*. Disclosure in the case of items attributable to a pass-through entity (pass-through items) is made with respect to the return of the entity, except as provided in this paragraph (f)(5). Thus, disclosure in the case of pass-through items must be made on a Form 8275 or 8275-R, as appropriate, attached to the return (or qualified amended return) of the entity, or on the entity's return in accordance with the revenue procedure described in paragraph (f)(2) of this section, if applicable. A taxpayer (i.e., partner, shareholder, beneficiary, or holder of a residual interest in a REMIC) also may make adequate disclosure with respect to a pass-through item, however, if the taxpayer files a properly completed Form 8275 or 8275-R, as appropriate, in duplicate, one copy attached to the taxpayer's return (or qualified amended return) and the other copy filed with the Internal Revenue Service Center with which the return of the entity is required to be filed. Each Form 8275 or 8275-R, as appropriate, filed by the taxpayer should relate to the pass-through items of only one entity. For purposes of this paragraph (f)(5), a pass-through entity is a partnership, S corporation (as defined in section 1361(a)(1)), estate, trust, regulated investment company (as defined in section 851(a)),

Reg. § 1.6662-4(f)(5)

real estate investment trust (as defined in section 856(a)), or real estate mortgage investment conduit ("REMIC") (as defined in section 860D(a)).

* * *

[Reg. § 1.6662-4.]

☐ [*T.D. 8381, 12-30-91. Amended by T.D. 8617, 8-31-95 and T.D. 8790, 12-1-98.*]

§ 1.6662-5. Substantial and gross valuation misstatements under chapter 1.—(a) *In general*. If any portion of an underpayment, as defined in section 6664(a) and § 1.6664-2, of any income tax imposed under chapter 1 of subtitle A of the Code that is required to be shown on a return is attributable to a substantial valuation misstatement under chapter 1 ("substantial valuation misstatement"), there is added to the tax an amount equal to 20 percent of such portion. Section 6662(h) increases the penalty to 40 percent in the case of a gross valuation misstatement under chapter 1 ("gross valuation misstatement"). No penalty under section 6662(b)(3) is imposed, however, on a portion of an underpayment that is attributable to a substantial or gross valuation misstatement unless the aggregate of all portions of the underpayment attributable to substantial or gross valuation misstatements exceeds the applicable dollar limitation ($5,000 or $10,000), as provided in section 6662(e)(2) and paragraphs (b) and (f)(2) of this section. This penalty also does not apply to the extent that the reasonable cause and good faith exception to this penalty set forth in § 1.6664-4 applies. There is no disclosure exception to this penalty.

(b) *Dollar limitation*. No penalty may be imposed under section 6662(b)(3) for a taxable year unless the portion of the underpayment for that year that is attributable to substantial or gross valuation misstatements exceeds $5,000 ($10,000 in the case of a corporation other than an S corporation (as defined in section 1361(a)(1)) or a personal holding company (as defined in section 542)). This limitation is applied separately to each taxable year for which there is a substantial or gross valuation misstatement.

* * *

(e) *Definitions*—(1) *Substantial valuation misstatement*. There is a substantial valuation misstatement if the value or adjusted basis of any property claimed on a return of tax imposed under chapter 1 is 200 percent or more of the correct amount.

(2) *Gross valuation misstatement*. There is a gross valuation misstatement if the value or adjusted basis of any property claimed on a return of tax imposed under chapter 1 is 400 percent or more of the correct amount.

(3) *Property*. For purposes of this section, the term "property" refers to both tangible and intangible property. Tangible property includes property such as land, buildings, fixtures and inventory. Intangible property includes property such as goodwill, covenants not to compete, leaseholds, patents, contract rights, debts and choses in action.

(f) *Multiple valuation misstatements on a return*—(1) *Determination of whether valuation misstatements are substantial or gross*. The determination of whether there is a substantial or gross valuation misstatement on a return is made on a property-by-property basis. Assume, for example, that property A has a value of 60 but a taxpayer claims a value of 110, and that property B has a value of 40 but the taxpayer claims a value of 100. Because the claimed and correct values are compared on a property-by-property basis, there is a substantial valuation misstatement with respect to property B, but not with respect to property A, even though the claimed values (210) are 200 percent or more of the correct values (100) when compared on an aggregate basis.

(2) *Application of dollar limitation*. For purposes of applying the dollar limitation set forth in section 6662(e)(2), the determination of the portion of an underpayment that is attributable to a substantial or gross valuation misstatement is made by aggregating all portions of the underpayment attributable to substantial or gross valuation misstatements. Assume, for example, that the value claimed for property C on a return is 250 percent of the correct value, and that the value claimed for property D on the return is 400 percent of the correct value. Because the portions of an underpayment that are attributable to a substantial or gross valuation misstatement on a return are aggregated in applying the dollar limitation, the dollar limitation is satisfied if the portion of the underpayment that is attributable to the misstatement of the value of property C, when aggregated with the portion of the underpayment that is attributable to the misstatement of the value of property D, exceeds $5,000 ($10,000 in the case of most corporations).

(g) *Property with a value or adjusted basis of zero*. The value or adjusted basis claimed on a return of any property with a correct value or adjusted basis of zero is considered to be 400 percent or more of the correct amount. There is a gross valuation misstatement with respect to such property, therefore, and the applicable penalty rate is 40 percent.

(h) *Pass-through entities*—(1) *In general*. The determination of whether there is a substantial or gross valuation misstatement in the case of a return of a pass-through entity (as defined in

Reg. § 1.6662-5(a)

§ 1.6662-4(f)(5)) is made at the entity level. However, the dollar limitation ($5,000 or $10,000, as the case may be) is applied at the taxpayer level (*i.e.*, with respect to the return of the shareholder, partner, beneficiary, or holder of a residual interest in a REMIC).

* * *

[Reg. § 1.6662-5.]

☐ [*T.D.* 8381, 12-30-91.]

§ 1.6664-1. Accuracy-related and fraud penalties; definitions and special rules.—(a) *In general.* Section 6664(a) defines the term "underpayment" for purposes of the accuracy-related penalty under section 6662 and the fraud penalty under section 6663. The definition of "underpayment" of income taxes imposed under subtitle A is set forth in § 1.6664-2. Ordering rules for computing the total amount of accuracy-related and fraud penalties imposed with respect to a return are set forth in § 1.6664-3. Section 6664(c) provides a reasonable cause and good faith exception to the accuracy-related penalty. Rules relating to the reasonable cause and good faith exception are set forth in § 1.6664-4.

* * *

[Reg. § 1.6664-1.]

☐ [*T.D.* 8381, 12-30-91. *Amended by T.D.* 8617, 8-31-95.]

§ 1.6664-4. Reasonable cause and good faith exception to section 6662 penalties.—(a) *In general.* No penalty may be imposed under section 6662 with respect to any portion of an underpayment upon a showing by the taxpayer that there was reasonable cause for, and the taxpayer acted in good faith with respect to, such portion. Rules for determining whether the reasonable cause and good faith exception applies are set forth in paragraphs (b) through (g) of this section.

(b) *Facts and circumstances taken into account*—(1) *In general.* The determination of whether a taxpayer acted with reasonable cause and in good faith is made on a case-by-case basis, taking into account all pertinent facts and circumstances. (See paragraph (e) of this section for certain rules relating to a substantial understatement penalty attributable to tax shelter items of corporations.) Generally, the most important factor is the extent of the taxpayer's effort to assess the taxpayer's proper tax liability. Circumstances that may indicate reasonable cause and good faith include an honest misunderstanding of fact or law that is reasonable in light of all of the facts and circumstances, including the experience, knowledge, and education of the taxpayer. An isolated computational or transcriptional error generally is not inconsistent with reasonable cause and good faith. Reliance on an information return or on the advice of a professional tax advisor or an appraiser does not necessarily demonstrate reasonable cause and good faith. Similarly, reasonable cause and good faith is not necessarily indicated by reliance on facts that, unknown to the taxpayer, are incorrect. Reliance on an information return, professional advice, or other facts, however, constitutes reasonable cause and good faith if, under all the circumstances, such reliance was reasonable and the taxpayer acted in good faith. (See paragraph (c) of this section for certain rules relating to reliance on the advice of others.) For example, reliance on erroneous information (such as an error relating to the cost or adjusted basis of property, the date property was placed in service, or the amount of opening or closing inventory) inadvertently included in data compiled by the various divisions of a multidivisional corporation or in financial books and records prepared by those divisions generally indicates reasonable cause and good faith, provided the corporation employed internal controls and procedures, reasonable under the circumstances, that were designed to identify such factual errors. Reasonable cause and good faith ordinarily is not indicated by the mere fact that there is an appraisal of the value of property. Other factors to consider include the methodology and assumptions underlying the appraisal, the appraised value, the relationship between appraised value and purchase price, the circumstances under which the appraisal was obtained, and the appraiser's relationship to the taxpayer or to the activity in which the property is used. (See paragraph (g) of this section for certain rules relating to appraisals for charitable deduction property.) A taxpayer's reliance on erroneous information reported on a Form W-2, Form 1099, or other information return indicates reasonable cause and good faith, provided the taxpayer did not know or have reason to know that the information was incorrect. Generally, a taxpayer knows, or has reason to know, that the information on an information return is incorrect if such information is inconsistent with other information reported or otherwise furnished to the taxpayer, or with the taxpayer's knowledge of the transaction. This knowledge includes, for example, the taxpayer's knowledge of the terms of his employment relationship or of the rate of return on a payor's obligation.

(2) *Examples.* The following examples illustrate this paragraph (b). They do not involve tax shelter items. (See paragraph (e) of this section for certain rules relating to the substantial understatement penalty attributable to the tax shelter items of corporations.)

Example 1. A, an individual calendar year taxpayer, engages B, a professional tax advisor, to give A advice concerning the deductibility of certain state and local taxes. A provides B with full details concerning the taxes at issue. B advises A that the taxes are fully deductible. A, in preparing his own tax return, claims a deduction for the taxes. Absent other facts, and assuming the facts and circumstances surrounding B's advice and A's reliance on such advice satisfy the requirements of paragraph (c) of this section, A is considered to have demonstrated good faith by seeking the advice of a professional tax advisor, and to have shown reasonable cause for any underpayment attributable to the deduction claimed for the taxes. However, if A had sought advice from someone that A knew, or should have known, lacked knowledge in the relevant aspects of Federal tax law, or if other facts demonstrate that A failed to act reasonably or in good faith, A would not be considered to have shown reasonable cause or to have acted in good faith.

* * *

(c) *Reliance on opinion or advice*—(1) *Facts and circumstances; minimum requirements.* All facts and circumstances must be taken into account in determining whether a taxpayer has reasonably relied in good faith on advice (including the opinion of a professional tax advisor) as to the treatment of the taxpayer (or any entity, plan, or arrangement) under Federal tax law. However, in no event will a taxpayer be considered to have reasonably relied in good faith on advice unless the requirements of this paragraph (c)(1) are satisfied. The fact that these requirements are satisfied will not necessarily establish that the taxpayer reasonably relied on the advice (including the opinion of a professional tax advisor) in good faith. For example, reliance may not be reasonable or in good faith if the taxpayer knew, or should have known, that the advisor lacked knowledge in the relevant aspects of Federal tax law.

(i) *All facts and circumstances considered.* The advice must be based upon all pertinent facts and circumstances and the law as it relates to those facts and circumstances. For example, the advice must take into account the taxpayer's purposes (and the relative weight of such purposes) for entering into a transaction and for structuring a transaction in a particular manner. In addition, the requirements of this paragraph (c)(1) are not satisfied if the taxpayer fails to disclose a fact that it knows, or should know, to be relevant to the proper tax treatment of an item.

(ii) *No unreasonable assumptions.* The advice must not be based on unreasonable factual or legal assumptions (including assumptions as to future events) and must not unreasonably rely on the representations, statements, findings, or agreements of the taxpayer or any other person.

For example, the advice must not be based upon a representation or assumption which the taxpayer knows, or has reason to know, is unlikely to be true, such as an inaccurate representation or assumption as to the taxpayer's purposes for entering into a transaction or for structuring a transaction in a particular manner.

(2) *Advice defined.* Advice is any communication, including the opinion of a professional tax advisor, setting forth the analysis or conclusion of a person, other than the taxpayer, provided to (or for the benefit of) the taxpayer and on which the taxpayer relies, directly or indirectly, with respect to the imposition of the section 6662 accuracy-related penalty. Advice does not have to be in any particular form.

(3) *Cross-reference.* For rules applicable to advisors, see e.g., § § 1.6694-1 through 1.6694-3 (regarding preparer penalties), 31 CFR 10.22 (regarding diligence as to accuracy), 31 CFR 10.33 (regarding tax shelter opinions), and 31 CFR 10.34 (regarding standards for advising with respect to tax return positions and for preparing or signing returns).

(d) *Pass-through items.* The determination of whether a taxpayer acted with reasonable cause and in good faith with respect to an underpayment that is related to an item reflected on the return of a pass-through entity is made on the basis of all pertinent facts and circumstances, including the taxpayer's own actions, as well as the actions of the pass-through entity.

(e) *Special rules for substantial understatement penalty attributable to tax shelter items of corporations*—(1) *In general; facts and circumstances.* The determination of whether a corporation acted with reasonable cause and in good faith in its treatment of a tax shelter item (as defined in § 1.6662-4(g)(3)) is based on all pertinent facts and circumstances. Paragraphs (e)(2), (3), and (4) of this section set forth rules that apply, in the case of a penalty attributable to a substantial understatement of income tax (within the meaning of section 6662(d)), in determining whether a corporation acted with reasonable cause and in good faith with respect to a tax shelter item.

(2) *Reasonable cause based on legal justification*—(i) *Minimum requirements.* A corporation's legal justification (as defined in paragraph (e)(2)(ii) of this section) may be taken into account, as appropriate, in establishing that the corporation acted with reasonable cause and in good faith in its treatment of a tax shelter item only if the authority requirement of paragraph (e)(2)(i)(A) of this section and the belief requirement of paragraph (e)(2)(i)(B) of this section are satisfied (the minimum requirements). Thus, a failure to satisfy the minimum requirements will

preclude a finding of reasonable cause and good faith based (in whole or in part) on the corporation's legal justification.

(A) *Authority requirement.* The authority requirement is satisfied only if there is substantial authority (within the meaning of § 1.6662-4(d)) for the tax treatment of the item.

(B) *Belief requirement.* The belief requirement is satisfied only if, based on all facts and circumstances, the corporation reasonably believed, at the time the return was filed, that the tax treatment of the item was more likely than not the proper treatment. For purposes of the preceding sentence, a corporation is considered reasonably to believe that the tax treatment of an item is more likely than not the proper-tax treatment if (without taking into account the possibility that a return will not be audited, that an issue will not be raised on audit, or that an issue will be settled)—

(*1*) The corporation analyzes the pertinent facts and authorities in the manner described in § 1.6662-4(d)(3)(ii), and in reliance upon that analysis, reasonably concludes in good faith that there is a greater than 50-percent likelihood that the tax treatment of the item will be upheld if challenged by the Internal Revenue Service; or

(*2*) The corporation reasonably relies in good faith on the opinion of a professional tax advisor, if the opinion is based on the tax advisor's analysis of the pertinent facts and authorities in the manner described in § 1.6662-4(d)(3)(ii) and unambiguously states that the tax advisor concludes that there is a greater than 50-percent likelihood that the tax treatment of the item will be upheld if challenged by the Internal Revenue Service. (For this purpose, the requirements of paragraph (c) of this section must be met with respect to the opinion of a professional tax advisor.)

(ii) *Legal justification defined.* For purposes of this paragraph (e), *legal justification* includes any justification relating to the treatment or characterization under the Federal tax law of the tax shelter item or of the entity, plan, or arrangement that gave rise to the item. Thus, a taxpayer's belief (whether independently formed or based on the advice of others) as to the merits of the taxpayer's underlying position is a legal justification.

(3) *Minimum requirements not dispositive.* Satisfaction of the minimum requirements of paragraph (e)(2) of this section is an important factor to be considered in determining whether a corporate taxpayer acted with reasonable cause and in good faith, but is not necessarily dispositive. For example, depending on the circumstances, satisfaction of the minimum requirements may not be dispositive if the taxpayer's participation in the tax shelter lacked significant business purpose, if the taxpayer claimed tax benefits that are unreasonable in comparison to the taxpayer's investment in the tax shelter, or if the taxpayer agreed with the organizer or promoter of the tax shelter that the taxpayer would protect the confidentiality of the tax aspects of the structure of the tax shelter.

(f) *Transactions between persons described in section 482 and net section 482 transfer price adjustments.* [Reserved]

(g) *Valuation misstatements of charitable deduction property*—(1) *In general.* There may be reasonable cause and good faith with respect to a portion of an underpayment that is attributable to a substantial (or gross) valuation misstatement of charitable deduction property (as defined in paragraph (g)(2) of this section) only if—

(i) The claimed value of the property was based on a qualified appraisal (as defined in paragraph (g)(2) of this section) by a qualified appraiser (as defined in paragraph (g)(2) of this section); and

(ii) In addition to obtaining a qualified appraisal, the taxpayer made a good faith investigation of the value of the contributed property.

(2) *Definitions.* For purposes of this paragraph (g):

Charitable deduction property means any property (other than money or publicly traded securities, as defined in § 1.170A-13(c)(7)(xi)) contributed by the taxpayer in a contribution for which a deduction was claimed under section 170.

Qualified appraisal means a qualified appraisal as defined in § 1.170A-13(c)(3).

Qualified appraiser means a qualified appraiser as defined in § 1.170A-13(c)(5).

(3) *Special rules.* The rules of this paragraph (g) apply regardless of whether § 1.170A-13 permits a taxpayer to claim a charitable contribution deduction for the property without obtaining a qualified appraisal. The rules of this paragraph (g) apply in addition to the generally applicable rules concerning reasonable cause and good faith. [Reg. § 1.6664-4.]

□ [*T.D.* 8381, 12-30-91. *Amended by T.D.* 8617, 8-31-95 *and T.D.* 8790, 12-1-98.]

Reg. § 1.6664-4(g)(3)

Definitions

§ 301.7701-1. Classification of organizations for federal tax purposes.—(a) *Organizations for federal tax purposes*—(1) *In general.* The Internal Revenue Code prescribes the classification of various organizations for federal tax purposes. Whether an organization is an entity separate from its owners for federal tax purposes is a matter of federal tax law and does not depend on whether the organization is recognized as an entity under local law.

(2) *Certain joint undertakings give rise to entities for federal tax purposes.* A joint venture or other contractual arrangement may create a separate entity for federal tax purposes if the participants carry on a trade, business, financial operation, or venture and divide the profits therefrom. For example, a separate entity exists for federal tax purposes if co-owners of an apartment building lease space and in addition provide services to the occupants either directly or through an agent. Nevertheless, a joint undertaking merely to share expenses does not create a separate entity for federal tax purposes. For example, if two or more persons jointly construct a ditch merely to drain surface water from their properties, they have not created a separate entity for federal tax purposes. Similarly, mere co-ownership of property that is maintained, kept in repair, and rented or leased does not constitute a separate entity for federal tax purposes. For example, if an individual owner, or tenants in common, of farm property lease it to a farmer for a cash rental or a share of the crops, they do not necessarily create a separate entity for federal tax purposes.

(3) *Certain local law entities not recognized.* An entity formed under local law is not always recognized as a separate entity for federal tax purposes. For example, an organization wholly owned by a State is not recognized as a separate entity for federal tax purposes if it is an integral part of the State. Similarly, tribes incorporated under section 17 of the Indian Reorganization Act of 1934, as amended, 25 U.S.C. 477, or under section 3 of the Oklahoma Indian Welfare Act, as amended, 25 U.S.C. 503, are not recognized as separate entities for federal tax purposes.

(4) *Single owner organizations.* Under §§ 301.7701-2 and 301.7701-3, certain organizations that have a single owner can choose to be recognized or disregarded as entities separate from their owners.

(b) *Classification of organizations.* The classification of organizations that are recognized as separate entities is determined under §§ 301.7701-2, 301.7701-3, and 301.7701-4 unless a provision of the Internal Revenue Code (such as section 860A addressing Real Estate Mortgage Investment Conduits (REMICs)) provides for special treatment of that organization. For the classification of organizations as trusts, see § 301.7701-4. That section provides that trusts generally do not have associates or an objective to carry on business for profit. Sections 301.7701-2 and 301.7701-3 provide rules for classifying organizations that are not classified as trusts.

(c) *Qualified cost sharing arrangements.* A qualified cost sharing arrangement that is described in § 1.482-7 of this chapter and any arrangement that is treated by the Commissioner as a qualified cost sharing arrangement under § 1.482-7 of this chapter is not recognized as a separate entity for purposes of the Internal Revenue Code. See § 1.482-7 of this chapter for the proper treatment of qualified cost sharing arrangements.

(d) *Domestic and foreign entities.* For purposes of this section and §§ 301.7701-2 and 301.7701-3, an entity is a domestic entity if it is created or organized in the United States or under the law of the United States or of any State; an entity is foreign if it is not domestic. See sections 7701(a)(4) and (a)(5).

(e) *State.* For purposes of this section and § 301.7701-2, the term *State* includes the District of Columbia.

(f) *Effective date.* The rules of this section are effective as of January 1, 1997. [Reg. § 301.7701-1.]

☐ [*T.D.* 6503, 11-15-80. *Amended by T.D.* 6797, 2-2-65; *T.D.* 7515, 10-17-77 *and T.D.* 8697, 12-17-96.]

§ 301.7701-2. Business entities; definitions.—(a) *Business entities.* For purposes of this section and § 301.7701-3, a *business entity* is any entity recognized for federal tax purposes (including an entity with a single owner that may be disregarded as an entity separate from its owner under § 301.7701-3) that is not properly classified as a trust under § 301.7701-4 or otherwise subject to special treatment under the Internal Revenue Code. A business entity with two or more members is classified for federal tax purposes as either a corporation or a partnership. A business entity with only one owner is classified as a corporation or is disregarded; if the entity is disregarded, its activities are treated in the same manner as a sole proprietorship, branch, or division of the owner.

(b) *Corporations.* For federal tax purposes, the term *corporation* means—

(1) A business entity organized under a Federal or State statute, or under a statute of a federally recognized Indian tribe, if the statute describes or refers to the entity as incorporated or as a corporation, body corporate, or body politic;

(2) An association (as determined under § 301.7701-3);

(3) A business entity organized under a State statute, if the statute describes or refers to the entity as a joint-stock company or joint-stock association;

(4) An insurance company;

(5) A State-chartered business entity conducting banking activities, if any of its deposits are insured under the Federal Deposit Insurance Act, as amended, 12 U.S.C. 1811 et seq., or a similar federal statute;

(6) A business entity wholly owned by a State or any political subdivision thereof, or a business entity wholly owned by a foreign government or any other entity described in § 1.892-2T;

(7) A business entity that is taxable as a corporation under a provision of the Internal Revenue Code other than section 7701(a)(3); and

* * *

(c) *Other business entities.* For federal tax purposes—

(1) The term *partnership* means a business entity that is not a corporation under paragraph (b) of this section and that has at least two members.

(2) *Wholly owned entities*—(i) *In general.* A business entity that has a single owner and is not a corporation under paragraph (b) of this section is disregarded as an entity separate from its owner.

(ii) *Special rule for certain business entities.* If the single owner of a business entity is a bank (as defined in section 581, or, in the case of a foreign bank, as defined in section 585(a)(2)(B) without regard to the second sentence thereof), then the special rules applicable to banks under the Internal Revenue Code will continue to apply to the single owner as if the wholly owned entity were a separate entity. For this purpose, the special rules applicable to banks under the Internal Revenue Code do not include the rules under sections 864(c), 882(c), and 884.

* * *

(e) *Effective date.* Except as otherwise provided in this paragraph (e), the rules of this section apply as of January 1, 1997, except that paragraph (b)(6) applies on or after January 14, 2002, to a business entity wholly owned by a foreign government regardless of any prior entity classification, and paragraph (c)(2)(ii) of this section applies to taxable years beginning after January 12, 2001. The reference to the Finnish, Maltese, and Norwegian entities in paragraph (b)(8)(i) of this section is applicable on November 29, 1999. The reference to the Trinidadian entity

in paragraph (b)(8)(i) of this section applies to entities formed on or after November 29, 1999. Any Maltese or Norwegian entity that becomes an eligible entity as a result of paragraph (b)(8)(i) of this section in effect on November 29, 1999 may elect by February 14, 2000 to be classified for federal tax purposes as an entity other than a corporation retroactive to any period from and including January 1, 1997. Any Finnish entity that becomes an eligible entity as a result of paragraph (b)(8)(i) of this section in effect on November 29, 1999 may elect by February 14, 2000 to be classified for federal tax purposes as an entity other than a corporation retroactive to any period from and including September 1, 1997. [Reg. § 301.7701-2.]

☐ [*T.D.* 6503, 11-15-60. *Amended by T.D.* 6797, 2-2-65; *T.D.* 7515, 10-17-77; *T.D.* 7889, 4-25-83; *T.D.* 8475, 5-13-93; *T.D.* 8697, 12-17-96; *T.D.* 8844, 11-26-99 *and T.D.* 9012, 7-31-2002.]

§ 301.7701-3. Classification of certain business entities.—(a) *In general.* A business entity that is not classified as a corporation under § 301.7701-2(b)(1), (3), (4), (5), (6), (7), or (8) (an *eligible entity*) can elect its classification for federal tax purposes as provided in this section. An eligible entity with at least two members can elect to be classified as either an association (and thus a corporation under § 301.7701-2(b)(2)) or a partnership, and an eligible entity with a single owner can elect to be classified as an association or to be disregarded as an entity separate from its owner. Paragraph (b) of this section provides a default classification for an eligible entity that does not make an election. Thus, elections are necessary only when an eligible entity chooses to be classified initially as other than the default classification or when an eligible entity chooses to change its classification. An entity whose classification is determined under the default classification retains that classification (regardless of any changes in the members' liability that occurs at any time during the time that the entity's classification is relevant as defined in paragraph (d) of this section) until the entity makes an election to change that classification under paragraph (c)(1) of this section. Paragraph (c) of this section provides rules for making express elections. Paragraph (d) of this section provides special rules for foreign eligible entities. Paragraph (e) of this section provides special rules for classifying entities resulting from partnership terminations and divisions under section 708(b). Paragraph (f) of this section sets forth the effective date of this section and a special rule relating to prior periods.

(b) *Classification of eligible entities that do not file an election*—(1) *Domestic eligible entities.* Except as provided in paragraph (b)(3) of this section, unless the entity elects otherwise, a domestic eligible entity is—

(i) A partnership if it has two or more members; or

(ii) Disregarded as an entity separate from its owner if it has a single owner.

* * *

(3) *Existing eligible entities*—(i) *In general.* Unless the entity elects otherwise, an eligible entity in existence prior to the effective date of this section will have the same classification that the entity claimed under §§ 301.7701-1 through 301.7701-3 as in effect on the date prior to the effective date of this section; except that if an eligible entity with a single owner claimed to be a partnership under those regulations, the entity will be disregarded as an entity separate from its owner under this paragraph (b)(3)(i). For special rules regarding the classification of such entities for periods prior to the effective date of this section, see paragraph (f)(2) of this section.

(ii) *Special rules.* For purposes of paragraph (b)(3)(i) of this section, a foreign eligible entity is treated as being in existence prior to the effective date of this section only if the entity's classification was relevant (as defined in paragraph (d) of this section) at any time during the sixty months prior to the effective date of this section. If an entity claimed different classifications prior to the effective date of this section, the entity's classification for purposes of paragraph (b)(3)(i) of this section is the last classification claimed by the entity. If a foreign eligible entity's classification is relevant prior to the effective date of this section, but no federal tax or information return is filed or the federal tax or information return does not indicate the classification of the entity, the entity's classification for the period prior to the effective date of this section is determined under the regulations in effect on the date prior to the effective date of this section.

(c) *Elections*—(1) *Time and place for filing*—(i) *In general.* Except as provided in paragraphs (c)(1)(iv) and (v) of this section, an eligible entity may elect to be classified other than as provided under paragraph (b) of this section, or to change its classification, by filing Form 8832, Entity Classification Election, with the service center designated on Form 8832. An election will not be accepted unless all of the information required by the form and instructions, including the taxpayer identifying number of the entity, is provided on Form 8832. See § 301.6109-1 for rules on applying for and displaying Employer Identification Numbers.

(ii) *Further notification of elections.* An eligible entity required to file a federal tax or information return for the taxable year for which

an election is made under paragraph (c)(1)(i) of this section must attach a copy of its Form 8832 to its federal tax or information return for that year. If the entity is not required to file a return for that year, a copy of its Form 8832 must be attached to the federal income tax or information return of any direct or indirect owner of the entity for the taxable year of the owner that includes the date on which the election was effective. An indirect owner of the entity does not have to attach a copy of the Form 8832 to its return if an entity in which it has an interest is already filing a copy of the Form 8832 with its return. If an entity, or one of its direct or indirect owners, fails to attach a copy of a Form 8832 to its return as directed in this section, an otherwise valid election under paragraph (c)(1)(i) of this section will not be invalidated, but the non-filing party may be subject to penalties, including any applicable penalties if the federal tax or information returns are inconsistent with the entity's election under paragraph (c)(1)(i) of this section.

(iii) *Effective date of election.* An election made under paragraph (c)(1)(i) of this section will be effective on the date specified by the entity on Form 8832 or on the date filed if no such date is specified on the election form. The effective date specified on Form 8832 can not be more than 75 days prior to the date on which the election is filed and can not be more than 12 months after the date on which the election is filed. If an election specifies an effective date more than 75 days prior to the date on which the election is filed, it will be effective 75 days prior to the date it was filed. If an election specifies an effective date more than 12 months from the date on which the election is filed, it will be effective 12 months after the date it was filed. If an election specifies an effective date before January 1, 1997, it will be effective as of January 1, 1997. If a purchasing corporation makes an election under section 338 regarding an acquired subsidiary, an election under paragraph (c)(1)(i) of this section for the acquired subsidiary can be effective no earlier than the day after the acquisition date (within the meaning of section 338(h)(2)).

(iv) *Limitation.* If an eligible entity makes an election under paragraph (c)(1)(i) of this section to change its classification (other than an election made by an existing entity to change its classification as of the effective date of this section), the entity cannot change its classification by election again during the sixty months succeeding the effective date of the election. However, the Commissioner may permit the entity to change its classification by election within the sixty months if more than fifty percent of the ownership interests in the entity as of the effective date of the subsequent election are owned by persons that did not own any interests in the entity on the filing date or on the effective date of the entity's prior election. An election by a newly formed eligible entity that is effective on the date of formation is not considered a change for purposes of this paragraph (c)(1)(iv).

(v) *Deemed elections*—(A) *Exempt organizations.* An eligible entity that has been determined to be, or claims to be, exempt from taxation under section 501(a) is treated as having made an election under this section to be classified as an association. Such election will be effective as of the first day for which exemption is claimed or determined to apply, regardless of when the claim or determination is made, and will remain in effect unless an election is made under paragraph (c)(1)(i) of this section after the date the claim for exempt status is withdrawn or rejected or the date the determination of exempt status is revoked.

(B) *Real estate investment trusts.* An eligible entity that files an election under section 856(c)(1) to be treated as a real estate investment trust is treated as having made an election under this section to be classified as an association. Such election will be effective as of the first day the entity is treated as a real estate investment trust.

(vi) *Examples.* The following examples illustrate the rules of this paragraph (c)(1):

Example 1. On July 1, 1998, X, a domestic corporation, purchases a 10% interest in Y, an eligible entity formed under Country A law in 1990. The entity's classification was not relevant to any person for federal tax or information purposes prior to X's acquisition of an interest in Y. Thus, Y is not considered to be in existence on the effective date of this section for purposes of paragraph (b)(3) of this section. Under the applicable Country A statute, all members of Y have limited liability as defined in paragraph (b)(2)(ii) of this section. Accordingly, Y is classified as an association under paragraph (b)(2)(i)(B) of this section unless it elects under this paragraph (c) to be classified as a partnership. To be classified as a partnership as of July 1, 1998, Y must file a Form 8832 by September 14, 1998. See paragraph (c)(1)(i) of this section. Because an election cannot be effective more than 75 days prior to the date on which it is filed, if Y files its Form 8832 after September 14, 1998, it will be classified as an association from July 1, 1998, until the effective date of the election. In that case, it could not change its classification by election under this paragraph (c) during the sixty months succeeding the effective date of the election.

Example 2. (i) Z is an eligible entity formed under Country B law and is in existence on the effective date of this section within the meaning of paragraph (b)(3) of this section. Prior to the effective date of this section, Z claimed to be classified as an association. Unless Z files an election under this paragraph (c), it will continue to be classified as an association under paragraph (b)(3) of this section.

(ii) Z files a Form 8832 pursuant to this paragraph (c) to be classified as a partnership, effective as of the effective date of this section. Z can file an election to be classified as an association at any time thereafter, but then would not be permitted to change its classification by election during the sixty months succeeding the effective date of that subsequent election.

(2) *Authorized signatures*—(i) *In general.* An election made under paragraph (c)(1)(i) of this section must be signed by—

(A) Each member of the electing entity who is an owner at the time the election is filed; or

(B) Any officer, manager, or member of the electing entity who is authorized (under local law or the entity's organizational documents) to make the election and who represents to having such authorization under penalties of perjury.

(ii) *Retroactive elections.* For purposes of paragraph (c)(2)(i) of this section, if an election under paragraph (c)(1)(i) of this section is to be effective for any period prior to the time that it is filed, each person who was an owner between the date the election is to be effective and the date the election is filed, and who is not an owner at the time the election is filed, must also sign the election.

(iii) *Changes in classification.* For paragraph (c)(2)(i) of this section, if an election under paragraph (c)(1)(i) of this section is made to change the classification of an entity, each person who was an owner on the date that any transactions under paragraph (g) of this section are deemed to occur, and who is not an owner at the time the election is filed, must also sign the election. This paragraph (c)(2)(iii) applies to elections filed on or after November 29, 1999.

* * *

(f) *Changes in number of members of an entity*—(1) *Associations.* The classification of an eligible entity as an association is not affected by any change in the number of members of the entity.

(2) *Partnerships and single member entities.* An eligible entity classified as a partnership becomes disregarded as an entity separate from its owner when the entity's membership is reduced to one member. A single member entity disregarded as an entity separate from its owner is classified as a partnership when the entity has more than one member. If an elective classification change under paragraph (c) of this section is effective at

Reg. § 301.7701-3(f)(2)

the same time as a membership change described in this paragraph (f)(2), the deemed transactions in paragraph (g) of this section resulting from the elective change preempt the transactions that would result from the change in membership.

(3) *Effect on sixty month limitation.* A change in the number of members of an entity does not result in the creation of a new entity for purposes of the sixty month limitation on elections under paragraph (c)(1)(iv) of this section.

(4) *Examples.* The following examples illustrate the application of this paragraph (f):

Example 1. A, a U.S. person, owns a domestic eligible entity that is disregarded as an entity separate from its owner. On January 1, 1998, B, a U.S. person, buys a 50 percent interest in the entity from A. Under this paragraph (f), the entity is classified as a partnership when B acquires an interest in the entity. However, A and B elect to have the entity classified as an association effective on January 1, 1998. Thus, B is treated as buying shares of stock on January 1, 1998. (Under paragraph (c)(1)(iv) of this section, this election is treated as a change in classification so that the entity generally cannot change its classification by election again during the sixty months succeeding the effective date of the election.) Under paragraph (g)(1) of this section, A is treated as contributing the assets and liabilities of the entity to the newly formed association immediately before the close of December 31, 1997. Because A does not retain control of the association as required by section 351, A's contribution will be a taxable event. Therefore, under section 1012, the association will take a fair market value basis in the assets contributed by A, and A will have a fair market value basis in the stock received. A will have no additional gain upon the sale of stock to B, and B will have a cost basis in the stock purchased from A.

Example 2. (i) On April 1, 1998, A and B, U.S. persons, form X, a foreign eligible entity. X is treated as an association under the default provisions of paragraph (b)(2)(i) of this section, and X does not make an election to be classified as a partnership. A subsequently purchases all of B's interest in X.

(ii) Under paragraph (f)(1) of this section, X continues to be classified as an association. X, however, can subsequently elect to be disregarded as an entity separate from A. The sixty month limitation of paragraph (c)(1)(iv) of this section does not prevent X from making an election because X has not made a prior election under paragraph (c)(1)(i) of this section.

Example 3. (i) On April 1, 1998, A and B, U.S. persons, form X, a foreign eligible entity. X is treated as an association under the default provi-

sions of paragraph (b)(2)(i) of this section, and X does not make an election to be classified as a partnership. On January 1, 1999, X elects to be classified as a partnership effective on that date. Under the sixty month limitation of paragraph (c)(1)(iv) of this section, X cannot elect to be classified as an association until January 1, 2004 (i.e., sixty months after the effective date of the election to be classified as a partnership).

(ii) On June 1, 2000, A purchases all of B's interest in X. After A's purchase of B's interest, X can no longer be classified as a partnership because X has only one member. Under paragraph (f)(2) of this section, X is disregarded as an entity separate from A when A becomes the only member of X. X, however, is not treated as a new entity for purposes of paragraph (c)(1)(iv) of this section. As a result, the sixty month limitation of paragraph (c)(1)(iv) of this section continues to apply to X, and X cannot elect to be classified as an association until January 1, 2004 (i.e., sixty months after January 1, 1999, the effective date of the election by X to be classified as a partnership).

(5) *Effective date.* This paragraph (f) applies as of November 29, 1999.

(g) *Elective changes in classification*—(1) *Deemed treatment of elective change*—(i) *Partnership to association.* If an eligible entity classified as a partnership elects under paragraph (c)(1)(i) of this section to be classified as an association, the following is deemed to occur: The partnership contributes all of its assets and liabilities to the association in exchange for stock in the association, and immediately thereafter, the partnership liquidates by distributing the stock of the association to its partners.

(ii) *Association to partnership.* If an eligible entity classified as an association elects under paragraph (c)(1)(i) of this section to be classified as a partnership, the following is deemed to occur: The association distributes all of its assets and liabilities to its shareholders in liquidation of the association, and immediately thereafter, the shareholders contribute all of the distributed assets and liabilities to a newly formed partnership.

(iii) *Association to disregarded entity.* If an eligible entity classified as an association elects under paragraph (c)(1)(i) of this section to be disregarded as an entity separate from its owner, the following is deemed to occur: The association distributes all of its assets and liabilities to its single owner in liquidation of the association.

(iv) *Disregarded entity to an association.* If an eligible entity that is disregarded as an entity separate from its owner elects under paragraph (c)(1)(i) of this section to be classified as an association, the following is deemed to occur: The owner of the eligible entity contributes all of the assets and liabilities of the entity to the association in exchange for stock of the association.

(2) *Effect of elective changes*—(i) *In general.* The tax treatment of a change in the classification of an entity for federal tax purposes by election under paragraph (c)(1)(i) of this section is determined under all relevant provisions of the Internal Revenue Code and general principles of tax law, including the step transaction doctrine.

(ii) *Adoption of plan of liquidation.* For purposes of satisfying the requirement of adoption of a plan of liquidation under section 332, unless a formal plan of liquidation that contemplates the election to be classified as a partnership or to be disregarded as an entity separate from its owner is adopted on an earlier date, the making, by an association, of an election under paragraph (c)(1)(i) of this section to be classified as a partnership or to be disregarded as an entity separate from its owner is considered to be the adoption of a plan of liquidation immediately before the deemed liquidation described in paragraph (g)(1)(ii) or (iii) of this section. This paragraph (g)(2)(ii) applies to elections filed on or after December 17, 2001. Taxpayers may apply this paragraph (g)(2)(ii) retroactively to elections filed before December 17, 2001, if the corporate owner claiming treatment under section 332 and its subsidiary making the election take consistent positions with respect to the federal tax consequences of the election.

(3) *Timing of election*—(i) *In general.* An election under paragraph (c)(1)(i) of this section that changes the classification of an eligible entity for federal tax purposes is treated as occurring at the start of the day for which the election is effective. Any transactions that are deemed to occur under this paragraph (g) as a result of a change in classification are treated as occurring immediately before the close of the day before the election is effective. For example, if an election is made to change the classification of an entity from an association to a partnership effective on January 1, the deemed transactions specified in paragraph (g)(1)(ii) of this section (including the liquidation of the association) are treated as occurring immediately before the close of December 31 and must be reported by the owners of the entity on December 31. Thus, the last day of the association's taxable year will be December 31 and the first day of the partnership's taxable year will be January 1.

(ii) *Coordination with section 338 election.* A purchasing corporation that makes a qualified stock purchase of an eligible entity taxed as a corporation may make an election under section 338 regarding the acquisition if it satisfies the requirements for the election, and may also make an election to change the classification of the target corporation. If a taxpayer makes an election under section 338 regarding its acquisition of another entity taxable as a corporation and makes an election under paragraph (c) of this section for the acquired corporation (effective at the earliest possible date as provided by paragraph (c)(1)(iii) of this section), the transactions under paragraph (g) of this section are deemed to occur immediately after the deemed asset purchase by the new target corporation under section 338.

(iii) *Application to successive elections in tiered situations.* When elections under paragraph (c)(1)(i) of this section for a series of tiered entities are effective on the same date, the eligible entities may specify the order of the elections on Form 8832. If no order is specified for the elections, any transactions that are deemed to occur in this paragraph (g) as a result of the classification change will be treated as occurring first for the highest tier entity's classification change, then for the next highest tier entity's classification change, and so forth down the chain of entities until all the transactions under this paragraph (g) have occurred. For example, Parent, a corporation, wholly owns all of the interest of an eligible entity classified as an association (S1), which wholly owns another eligible entity classified as an association (S2), which wholly owns another eligible entity classified as an association (S3). Elections under paragraph (c)(1)(i) of this section are filed to classify S1, S2, and S3 each as disregarded as an entity separate from its owner effective on the same day. If no order is specified for the elections, the following transactions are deemed to occur under this paragraph (g) as a result of the elections, with each successive transaction occurring on the same day immediately after the preceding transaction: S1 is treated as liquidating into Parent, then S2 is treated as liquidating into Parent, and finally S3 is treated as liquidating into Parent.

(4) *Effective date.* Except as otherwise provided in paragraph (g)(2)(ii) of this section, this paragraph (g) applies to elections that are filed on or after November 29, 1999. Taxpayers may apply this paragraph (g) retroactively to elections filed before November 29, 1999 if all taxpayers affected by the deemed transactions file consistently with this paragraph (g).

(h) *Effective date*—(1) *In general.* Except as otherwise provided in this section, the rules of this section are applicable as of January 1, 1997.

(2) *Prior treatment of existing entities.* In the case of a business entity that is not described in § 301.7701-2(b)(1), (3), (4), (5), (6), or (7), and that was in existence prior to January 1, 1997, the

Reg. § 301.7701-3(h)(2)

entity's claimed classification(s) will be respected for all periods prior to January 1, 1997, if—

(i) The entity had a reasonable basis (within the meaning of section 6662) for its claimed classification;

(ii) The entity and all members of the entity recognized the federal tax consequences of any change in the entity's classification within the sixty months prior to January 1, 1997; and

(iii) Neither the entity nor any member was notified in writing on or before May 8, 1996, that the classification of the entity was under examination (in which case the entity's classification will be determined in the examination). [Reg. § 301.7701-3.]

□ [*T.D.* 6503, 11-15-60. *Amended by T.D.* 8632, 12-19-95; *T.D.* 8697, 12-17-96; *T.D.* 8767, 3-23-98; *T.D.* 8827, 7-12-99 (*corrected* 10-29-99); *T.D.* 8844, 11-26-99 *and T.D.* 8970, 12-14-2001.]

§ 301.7701-4. Trusts.—(a) *Ordinary trusts.* In general, the term "trust" as used in the Internal Revenue Code refers to an arrangement created either by a will or by an inter vivos declaration whereby trustees take title to property for the purpose of protecting or conserving it for the beneficiaries under the ordinary rules applied in chancery or probate courts. Usually the beneficiaries of such a trust do no more than accept the benefits thereof and are not the voluntary planners or creators of the trust arrangement. However, the beneficiaries of such a trust may be the persons who create it and it will be recognized as a trust under the Internal Revenue Code if it was created for the purpose of protecting or conserving the trust property for beneficiaries who stand in the same relation to the trust as they would if the trust had been created by others for them. Generally speaking, an arrangement will be treated as a trust under the Internal Revenue Code if it can be shown that the purpose of the arrangement is to vest in trustees responsibility for the protection and conservation of property for beneficiaries who cannot share in the discharge of this responsibility and, therefore, are not associates in a joint enterprise for the conduct of business for profit.

(b) *Business trusts.* There are other arrangements which are known as trusts because the legal title to property is conveyed to trustees for the benefit of beneficiaries, but which are not classified as trusts for purposes of the Internal Revenue Code because they are not simply arrangements to protect or conserve the property for the beneficiaries. These trusts, which are often known as business or commercial trusts, generally are created by the beneficiaries simply as a device to carry on a profit-making business which normally would have been carried on through business orga-

nizations that are classified as corporations or partnerships under the Internal Revenue Code. However, the fact that the corpus of the trust is not supplied by the beneficiaries is not sufficient reason in itself for classifying the arrangement as an ordinary trust rather than as an association or partnership. The fact that any organization is technically cast in the trust form, by conveying title to property to trustees for the benefit of persons designated as beneficiaries, will not change the real character of the organization if the organization is more properly classified as a business entity under § 301.7701-2.

(c) *Certain investment trusts.*—(1) An "investment" trust will not be classified as a trust if there is a power under the trust agreement to vary the investment of the certificate holders. *See Commissioner v. North American Bond Trust,* 122 F. 2d 545 [41-2 USTC ¶ 9644] (2d Cir. 1941), *cert. denied,* 314 U.S. 701 (1942). An investment trust with a single class of ownership interests, representing undivided beneficial interests in the assets of the trust, will be classified as a trust if there is no power under the trust agreement to vary the investment of the certificate holders. An investment trust with multiple classes of ownership interests ordinarily will be classified as a business entity under § 301.7701-2; however, an investment trust with multiple classes of ownership interests, in which there is no power under the trust agreement to vary the investment of the certificate holders, will be classified as a trust if the trust is formed to facilitate direct investment in the assets of the trust and the existence of multiple classes of ownership interests is incidental to that purpose.

(2) The provisions of paragraph (c)(1) of this section may be illustrated by the following examples:

Example (1): A corporation purchases a portfolio of residential mortgages and transfers the mortgages to a bank under a trust agreement. At the same time, the bank as trustee delivers to the corporation certificates evidencing rights to payments from the pooled mortgages; the corporation sells the certificates to the public. The trustee holds legal title to the mortgages in the pool for the benefit of the certificate holders but has no power to reinvest proceeds attributable to the mortgages in the pool or to vary investments in the pool in any other manner. There are two classes of certificates. Holders of class A certificates are entitled to all payments of mortgage principal, both scheduled and prepaid, until their certificates are retired; holders of class B certificates receive payments of principal only after all class A certificates have been retired. The different rights of the class A and class B certificates serve to shift to the holders of the class A certifi-

Reg. § 301.7701-4(a)

cates, in addition to the earlier scheduled payments of principal, the risk that mortgages in the pool will be prepaid so that the holders of the class B certificates will have "call protection" (freedom from premature termination of their interests on account of prepayments). The trust thus serves to create investment interests with respect to the mortgages held by the trust that differ significantly from direct investment in the mortgages. As a consequence, the existence of multiple classes of trust ownership is not incidental to any purpose of the trust to facilitate direct investment, and, accordingly, the trust is classified as a business entity under § 301.7701-2.

Example (2): Corporation M is the originator of a portfolio of residential mortgages and transfers the mortgages to a bank under a trust agreement. At the same time, the bank as trustee delivers to M certificates evidencing rights to payments from the pooled mortgages. The trustee holds legal title to the mortgages in the pool for the benefit of the certificate holders, but has no power to reinvest proceeds attributable to the mortgages in the pool or to vary investments in the pool in any other manner. There are two classes of certificates. Holders of class C certificates are entitled to receive 90 percent of the payments of principal and interest on the mortgages; class D certificate holders are entitled to receive the other ten percent. The two classes of certificates are identical except that, in the event of a default on the underlying mortgages, the payment rights of class D certificate holders are subordinated to the rights of class C certificate holders. M sells the class C certificates to investors and retains the class D certificates. The trust has multiple classes of ownership interests, given the greater security provided to holders of class C certificates. The interests of certificate holders, however, are substantially equivalent to undivided interests in the pool of mortgages, coupled with a limited recourse guarantee running from M to the holders of class C certificates. In such circumstances, the existence of multiple classes of ownership interests is incidental to the trust's purpose of facilitating direct investment in the assets of the trust. Accordingly, the trust is classified as a trust.

Example (3): A promoter forms a trust in which shareholders of a publicly traded corporation can deposit their stock. For each share of stock deposited with the trust, the participant receives two certificates that are initially attached, but may be separated and traded independently of each other. One certificate represents the right to dividends and the value of the underlying stock up to a specified amount; the other certificate represents the right to appreciation in the stock's value above the specified

amount. The separate certificates represent two different classes of ownership interest in the trust, which effectively separate dividend rights on the stock held by the trust from a portion of the right to appreciation in the value of such stock. The multiple classes of ownership interests are designed to permit investors, by transferring one of the certificates and retaining the other, to fulfill their varying investment objectives of seeking primarily either dividend income or capital appreciation from the stock held by the trust. Given that the trust serves to create investment interests with respect to the stock held by the trust that differ significantly from direct investment in such stock, the trust is not formed to facilitate direct investment in the assets of the trust. Accordingly, the trust is classified as a business entity under § 301.7701-2.

Example (4): Corporation N purchases a portfolio of bonds and transfers the bonds to a bank under a trust agreement. At the same time, the trustee delivers to N certificates evidencing interests in the bonds. These certificates are sold to public investors. Each certificate represents the right to receive a particular payment with respect to a specific bond. Under section 1286, stripped coupons and stripped bonds are treated as separate bonds for federal income tax purposes. Although the interest of each certificate holder is different from that of each other certificate holder, and the trust thus has multiple classes of ownership, the multiple classes simply provide each certificate holder with a direct interest in what is treated under section 1286 as a separate bond. Given the similarity of the interests acquired by the certificate holders to the interests that could be acquired by direct investment, the multiple classes of trust interests merely facilitate direct investment in the assets held by the trust. Accordingly, the trust is classified as a trust.

(d) *Liquidating trusts.* Certain organizations which are commonly known as liquidating trusts are treated as trusts for purposes of the Internal Revenue Code. An organization will be considered a liquidating trust if it is organized for the primary purpose of liquidating and distributing the assets transferred to it, and if its activities are all reasonably necessary to, and consistent with, the accomplishment of that purpose. A liquidating trust is treated as a trust for purposes of the Internal Revenue Code because it is formed with the objective of liquidating particular assets and not as an organization having as its purpose the carrying on of a profit-making business which normally would be conducted through business organizations classified as corporations or partnerships. However, if the liquidation is unreasonably prolonged or if the liquidation purpose becomes so obscured by business activities that the declared purpose of liquidation can be said to be lost or abandoned, the status of the organization will no longer be that of a liquidating trust. Bondholders' protective committees, voting trusts, and other agencies formed to protect the interests of security holders during insolvency, bankruptcy, or corporate reorganization proceedings are analogous to liquidating trusts but if subsequently utilized to further the control or profitable operation of a going business on a permanent continuing basis, they will lose their classification as trusts for purposes of the Internal Revenue Code.

* * *

[Reg. § 301.7701-4.]

☐ [*T.D.* 6503, 11-15-60. *Amended by T.D.* 8080, 3-21-86; *T.D.* 8668, 4-30-96 *and T.D.* 8697, 12-17-96.]

§ 301.7701-6. Definitions; person, fiduciary.—(a) *Person.* The term *person* includes an individual, a corporation, a partnership, a trust or estate, a joint-stock company, an association, or a syndicate, group, pool, joint venture, or other unincorporated organization or group. The term also includes a guardian, committee, trustee, executor, administrator, trustee in bankruptcy, receiver, assignee for the benefit of creditors, conservator, or any person acting in a fiduciary capacity.

(b) *Fiduciary*—(1) *In general.* Fiduciary is a term that applies to persons who occupy positions of peculiar confidence toward others, such as trustees, executors, and administrators. A fiduciary is a person who holds in trust an estate to which another has a beneficial interest, or receives and controls income of another, as in the case of receivers. A committee or guardian of the property of an incompetent person is a fiduciary.

(2) *Fiduciary distinguished from agent.* There may be a fiduciary relationship between an agent and a principal, but the word agent does not denote a fiduciary. An agent having entire charge of property, with authority to effect and execute leases with tenants entirely on his own responsibility and without consulting his principal, merely turning over the net profits from the property periodically to his principal by virtue of authority conferred upon him by a power of attorney, is not a fiduciary within the meaning of the Internal Revenue Code. In cases when no legal trust has been created in the estate controlled by the agent and attorney, the liability to make a return rests with the principal.

(c) *Effective date.* The rules of this section are effective as of January 1, 1997. [Reg. § 301.7701-6.]

☐ [*T.D.* 6503, 11-15-60. *Amended by T.D.* 8697, 12-17-96.]

§ 1.7704-1. Publicly traded partnerships.—(a) *In general*—(1) *Publicly traded partnership.* A domestic or foreign partnership is a publicly traded partnership for purposes of section 7704(b) and this section if—

(i) Interests in the partnership are traded on an established securities market; or

(ii) Interests in the partnership are readily tradable on a secondary market or the substantial equivalent thereof.

(2) *Partnership interest*—(i) *In general.* For purposes of section 7704(b) and this section, an interest in a partnership includes—

(A) Any interest in the capital or profits of the partnership (including the right to partnership distributions); and

(B) Any financial instrument or contract the value of which is determined in whole or in part by reference to the partnership (including the amount of partnership distributions, the value of partnership assets, or the results of partnership operations).

(ii) *Exception for non-convertible debt.* For purposes of section 7704(b) and this section, an interest in a partnership does not include any financial instrument or contract that—

(A) Is treated as debt for federal tax purposes; and

(B) Is not convertible into or exchangeable for an interest in the capital or profits of the partnership and does not provide for a payment of equivalent value.

(iii) *Exception for tiered entities.* For purposes of section 7704(b) and this section, an interest in a partnership or a corporation (including a regulated investment company as defined in section 851 or a real estate investment trust as defined in section 856) that holds an interest in a partnership (lower-tier partnership) is not considered an interest in the lower-tier partnership.

(3) *Definition of transfer.* For purposes of section 7704(b) and this section, a transfer of an interest in a partnership means a transfer in any form, including a redemption by the partnership or the entering into of a financial instrument or contract described in paragraph (a)(2)(i)(B) of this section.

(b) *Established securities market.* For purposes of section 7704(b) and this section, an established securities market includes—

(1) A national securities exchange registered under section 6 of the Securities Exchange Act of 1934 (15 U.S.C. 78f);

(2) A national securities exchange exempt from registration under section 6 of the Securities

Exchange Act of 1934 (15 U.S.C. 78f) because of the limited volume of transactions;

(3) A foreign securities exchange that, under the law of the jurisdiction where it is organized, satisfies regulatory requirements that are analogous to the regulatory requirements under the Securities Exchange Act of 1934 described in paragraph (b)(1) or (2) of this section (such as the London International Financial Futures Exchange; the Marche a Terme International de France; the International Stock Exchange of the United Kingdom and the Republic of Ireland, Limited; the Frankfurt Stock Exchange; and the Tokyo Stock Exchange);

(4) A regional or local exchange; and

(5) An interdealer quotation system that regularly disseminates firm buy or sell quotations by identified brokers or dealers by electronic means or otherwise.

(c) *Readily tradable on a secondary market or the substantial equivalent thereof*—(1) *In general.* For purposes of section 7704(b) and this section, interests in a partnership that are not traded on an established securities market (within the meaning of section 7704(b) and paragraph (b) of this section) are readily tradable on a secondary market or the substantial equivalent thereof if, taking into account all of the facts and circumstances, the partners are readily able to buy, sell, or exchange their partnership interests in a manner that is comparable, economically, to trading on an established securities market.

(2) *Secondary market or the substantial equivalent thereof.* For purposes of paragraph (c)(1) of this section, interests in a partnership are readily tradable on a secondary market or the substantial equivalent thereof if—

(i) Interests in the partnership are regularly quoted by any person, such as a broker or dealer, making a market in the interests;

(ii) Any person regularly makes available to the public (including customers or subscribers) bid or offer quotes with respect to interests in the partnership and stands ready to effect buy or sell transactions at the quoted prices for itself or on behalf of others;

(iii) The holder of an interest in the partnership has a readily available, regular, and ongoing opportunity to sell or exchange the interest through a public means of obtaining or providing information of offers to buy, sell, or exchange interests in the partnership; or

(iv) Prospective buyers and sellers otherwise have the opportunity to buy, sell, or exchange interests in the partnership in a time frame and with the regularity and continuity that

is comparable to that described in the other provisions of this paragraph (c)(2).

(3) *Secondary market safe harbors.* The fact that a transfer of a partnership interest is not within one or more of the safe harbors described in paragraph (e), (f), (g), (h), or (j) of this section is disregarded in determining whether interests in the partnership are readily tradable on a secondary market or the substantial equivalent thereof.

(d) *Involvement of the partnership required.* For purposes of section 7704(b) and this section, interests in a partnership are not traded on an established securities market within the meaning of paragraph (b)(5) of this section and are not readily tradable on a secondary market or the substantial equivalent thereof within the meaning of paragraph (c) of this section (even if interests in the partnership are traded or readily tradable in a manner described in paragraph (b)(5) or (c) of this section) unless—

(1) The partnership participates in the establishment of the market or the inclusion of its interests thereon; or

(2) The partnership recognizes any transfers made on the market by—

(i) Redeeming the transferor partner (in the case of a redemption or repurchase by the partnership); or

(ii) Admitting the transferee as a partner or otherwise recognizing any rights of the transferee, such as a right of the transferee to receive partnership distributions (directly or indirectly) or to acquire an interest in the capital or profits of the partnership.

(e) *Transfers not involving trading*—(1) *In general.* For purposes of section 7704(b) and this section, the following transfers (private transfers) are disregarded in determining whether interests in a partnership are readily tradable on a secondary market or the substantial equivalent thereof—

(i) Transfers in which the basis of the partnership interest in the hands of the transferee is determined, in whole or in part, by reference to its basis in the hands of the transferor or is determined under section 732;

(ii) Transfers at death, including transfers from an estate or testamentary trust;

(iii) Transfers between members of a family (as defined in section 267(c)(4));

(iv) Transfers involving the issuance of interests by (or on behalf of) the partnership in exchange for cash, property, or services;

(v) Transfers involving distributions from a retirement plan qualified under section 401(a) or an individual retirement account;

Reg. § 1.7704-1(e)(1)

(vi) Block transfers (as defined in paragraph (e)(2) of this section);

(vii) Transfers pursuant to a right under a redemption or repurchase agreement (as defined in paragraph (e) (3) of this section) that is exercisable only—

(A) Upon the death, disability, or mental incompetence of the partner; or

(B) Upon the retirement or termination of the performance of services of an individual who actively participated in the management of, or performed services on a full-time basis for, the partnership;

(viii) Transfers pursuant to a closed end redemption plan (as defined in paragraph (e)(4) of this section);

(ix) Transfers by one or more partners of interests representing in the aggregate 50 percent or more of the total interests in partnership capital and profits in one transaction or a series of related transactions; and

(x) Transfers not recognized by the partnership (within the meaning of paragraph (d)(2) of this section).

(2) *Block transfers.* For purposes of paragraph (e)(1)(vi) of this section, a block transfer means the transfer by a partner and any related persons (within the meaning of section 267(b) or 707(b)(1)) in one or more transactions during any 30 calendar day period of partnership interests representing in the aggregate more than 2 percent of the total interests in partnership capital or profits.

(3) *Redemption or repurchase agreement.* For purposes of section 7704(b) and this section, a redemption or repurchase agreement means a plan of redemption or repurchase maintained by a partnership whereby the partners may tender their partnership interests for purchase by the partnership, another partner, or a person related to another partner (within the meaning of section 267(b) or 707(b)(1)).

(4) *Closed end redemption plan.* For purposes of paragraph (e)(1)(viii) of this section, a redemption or repurchase agreement (as defined in paragraph (e)(3) of this section) is a closed end redemption plan only if—

(i) The partnership does not issue any interest after the initial offering (other than the issuance of additional interests prior to August 5, 1988); and

(ii) No partner or person related to any partner (within the meaning of section 267(b) or 707(b)(1)) provides contemporaneous opportunities to acquire interests in similar or related partnerships which represent substantially identical investments.

* * *

[Reg. § 1.7704-1.]

□ [*T.D.* 8629, 11-29-95.]

Provisions Affecting More Than One Subtitle

Proposed Regulations

§ 1.7872-1. Introduction.—(a) *Statement of purpose.* Section 7872 generally treats certain loans in which the interest rate charged is less than the applicable Federal rate as economically equivalent to loans bearing interest at the applicable Federal rate, coupled with a payment by the lender to the borrower sufficient to fund all or part of the payment of interest by the borrower. Such loans are referred to as "below-market loans." See § 1.7872-3 for detailed definitions of below-market loans and the determination of the applicable Federal rate.

Accordingly, section 7872 recharacterizes a below-market loan as two transactions:

(1) An arm's-length transaction in which the lender makes a loan to the borrower in exchange for a note requiring the payment of interest at the applicable Federal rate; and

(2) A transfer of funds by the lender to the borrower ("imputed transfer").

The timing and the characterization of the amount of the imputed transfer by the lender to the borrower are determined in accordance with the substance of the transaction. The timing and the amount of the imputed interest payment (the excess of the amount of interest required to be paid using the applicable Federal rate, *over* the amount of interest required to be paid according to the loan agreement) by the borrower to the lender depend on the character of the imputed transfer by the lender to the borrower and whether the loan is a term loan or a demand loan. If the imputed transfer by the lender is characterized as a gift, the provisions of chapter 12 of the Internal Revenue Code, relating to gift tax, also apply. All imputed transfers under section 7872 (*e.g.,* interest, compensation, gift) are characterized in accordance with the substance of the transaction, and, except as otherwise provided in the regulations under section 7872, are treated as so characterized for all purposes of the Code. For example, for purposes of section 170, an interest-free loan to a charity referred to in section 170 for which interest is imputed under section 7872, is treated as an interest bearing loan coupled with periodic gifts to the charity in the amount of the imputed transfer, for purposes of section 170. In addition, all applicable information and reporting requirements (*e.g.,* reporting on W-2 and Form 1099) must be satisfied.

* * *

[Reg. § 1.7872-1.]

[Proposed 8-20-85.]

§ 1.7872-2. Definition of loan.—(a) *In general*—(1) *"Loan" interpreted broadly.* For purposes of section 7872, the term "loan" includes generally any extension of credit (including, for example, a purchase money mortgage) and any transaction under which the owner of money permits another person to use the money for a period of time after which the money is to be transferred to the owner or applied according to an express or implied agreement with the onwer. The term "loan" is interpreted broadly to implement the anti-abuse intent of the statute. An integrated series of transactions which is the equivalent of a loan is treated as a loan. A payment for property, goods, or services under a contract, however, is not a loan merely because one of the payor's remedies for breach of the contract is recovery of the payment. Similarly, a bona fide prepayment made in a manner consistent with normal commercial practices for services, property, or the use of property, generally, is not a loan; see section 461 and the regulations thereunder for the treatment of certain prepaid expenses and for the special rules of sections 461(h) and (i). However, a taxpayer's characterization of a transaction as a prepayment or as a loan is not conclusive. Transactions will be characterized for tax purposes according to their economic substance, rather than the terms used to describe them. Thus, for example, receipt by a partner from a partnership of money is treated as a loan if it is so characterized under § 1.731-1(c)(2).

* * *

(b) *Examples of transactions treated as loans*—(1) *Refundable deposits*—(i) *In general.* If an amount is treated for Federal tax purposes as a deposit rather than as a prepayment or an advance payment, the amount is treated as a loan for purposes of section 7872.

(ii) *Partially refundable deposits.* If an amount is treated for Federal tax purposes as a deposit rather than as a prepayment or an advance payment and the amount is refundable only for a certain period of time or is only partially refundable, then the deposit is treated as a loan only to the extent that it is refundable and only for the period of time that it is refundable.

(iii) *Exception.* Paragraph (b)(1)(i) does not apply if the deposit is custodial in nature or is held in trust for the benefit of the transferor. The deposit is treated as custodial in nature if the transferee is not entitled to the beneficial enjoyment of the amount deposited including interest thereon (except as security for an obligation of the transferor). Thus, if an amount is placed in escrow to secure a contractual obligation of the transferor, and the escrow agreement provides that all interest earned is paid to the transferor and that the transferee has no rights to or interest in the escrowed amount unless and until the transferor

defaults on the obligation, then, in the absence of any facts which indicate that the transaction was entered into for tax avoidance purposes, the deposit is not a loan.

* * *

[Reg. § 1.7872-2.]

[Proposed 8-20-85.]

§ 1.7872-4. Types of below-market loans.—(a) *In general.* Section 7872 applies only to certain categories of below-market loans. These categories are gift loans, compensation-related loans, corporation-shareholder loans, tax avoidance loans, and certain other loans classified in the regulations under section 7872 as significant tax effect loans (*i.e.,* loans whose interest arrangements have a significant effect on any Federal tax liability of the lender or the borrower).

(b) *Gift loans*—(1) *In general.* The term "gift loan" means any below-market loan in which the foregoing of interest is in the nature of a gift within the meaning of Chapter 12 of the Internal Revenue Code (whether or not the lender is a natural person).

(2) *Cross reference.* See § 1.7872-8 for special rules limiting the application of section 7872 to gift loans. See paragraph (g) of this section for rules with respect to below-market loans which are indirectly gift loans.

(c) *Compensation-related loans*—(1) *In general.* A compensation-related loan is a below-market loan that is made in connection with the performance of services, directly or indirectly, between—

(i) An employer and an employee,

(ii) An independent contractor and a person for whom such independent contractor provides services, or

(iii) A partnership and a partner if the loan is made in consideration for services performed by the partner acting other than in his capacity as a member of the partnership.

The imputed transfer (amount of money treated as transferred) by the lender to the borrower is compensation. For purposes of this section, the term "in connection with the performance of services" has the same meaning as the term has for purposes of section 83. A loan from a qualified pension, profit-sharing, or stock bonus plan to a participant of the plan is not, directly or indirectly, a compensation-related loan.

(2) *Loan in part in exchange for services.* Except as provided in paragraph (d)(2) of this section (relating to a loan from a corporation to an employee who is also a shareholder of the corporation), a loan which is made in part in exchange for services and in part for other reasons is treated as a compensation-related loan for purposes of section 7872(c)(3) only if more than 25 percent of the amount loaned is attributable to the performance of services. If 25 percent or less of the amount

loaned is attributable to the performance of services, the loan is not subject to section 7872 by reason of being a compensation-related loan. The loan may, however, be subject to section 7872 by reason of being a below-market loan characterized other than as a compensation-related loan (*e.g.*, corporation-shareholder loan or tax avoidance loan). If—

(i) a loan is characterized as a "compensation-related" loan under this paragraph (c),

(ii) less than 100 percent of the amount loaned is attributable to the performance of services, and

(iii) the portion of the amount loaned that is not attributable to the performance of services is not subject to section 7872,

then the amounts of imputed transfer (as defined in § 1.7872-1(a)(2)) and imputed interest (as defined in § 1.7872-1(a)) are determined only with respect to that part of the loan which is attributable to services. All of the facts and circumstances surrounding the loan agreement and the relationship between the lender and the borrower are taken into account in determining the portion of the loan made in exchange for services.

(3) *Third-party lender as agent.* A below-market loan by an unrelated third-party lender to an employee is treated as attributable to the performance of services if, taking into account all the facts and circumstances, the transaction is in substance a loan by the employer made with the aid of a third-party lender acting as an agent of the employer. Among the facts and circumstances which indicate whether such a loan has been made is whether the employer bears the risk of default at and immediately after the time the loan is made. The principles of this paragraph (c)(3) also apply with respect to a below-market loan by an unrelated third-party lender to an independent contractor.

(4) *Special rule for continuing care facilities.* Any loan to a continuing care facility will not be treated, in whole or in part, as a compensation-related loan.

(5) *Cross-references.* For a special rule in the case of a below-market loan that could be characterized as both a compensation-related loan and a corporation-shareholder loan, see paragraph (d)(2) of this section. See paragraph (g) of this section for rules with respect to below-market loans which are indirectly compensation-related loans.

(d) *Corporation-shareholder loans—*(1) *In general.* A below-market loan is a corporation-shareholder loan if the loan is made directly or indirectly between a corporation and any shareholder of the corporation. The amount of money treated as transferred by the lender to the borrower is a distribution of money (characterized according to section 301 or, in the case of an S

corporation, section 1368) if the corporation is the lender, or a contribution to capital if the shareholder is the lender.

(2) *Special rule.* A below-market loan—

(i) from a publicly held corporation to an employee of the corporation who is also a shareholder owning directly or indirectly more than 0.5 percent of the total voting power of all classes of stock entitled to vote or more than 0.5 percent of the total value of shares of all other classes of stock or 0.5 percent of the total value of shares of all other classes of stock or 5 percent of the total value of shares of all classes of stock (including voting stock) of the corporation; or

(ii) from a corporation that is not a publicly held corporation to an employee of the corporation who is also a shareholder owning directly or indirectly more than 5 percent of the total voting power of all classes of stock entitled to vote or more than 5 percent of the total number of shares of all other classes of stock or 5 percent of the total value of shares of all classes of stock (including voting stock) of the corporation;

will be presumed to be a corporation-shareholder loan, in the absence of clear and convincing evidence that the loan is made solely in connection with the performance of services. For purposes of determining the percentage of direct and indirect stock ownership, the constructive ownership rules of section 267(c) apply.

(3) *Cross-reference.* See paragraph (g) of this section for rules with respect to below-market loans which are indirectly corporation-shareholder loans.

(e) *Tax avoidance loans—*(1) *In general.* A tax avoidance loan is any below-market loan one of the principal purposes for the interest arrangements of which is the avoidance of Federal tax with respect to either the borrower or the lender, or both. For purposes of this rule, tax avoidance is a principal purpose of the interest arrangements if a principal factor in the decision to structure the transaction as a below-market loan (rather than, for example, as a market interest rate loan and a payment by the lender to the borrower) is to reduce the Federal tax liability of the borrower or the lender or both. The purpose for entering into the transaction (for example, to make a gift or to pay compensation) is irrelevant in determining whether a principal purpose of the interest arrangements of the loan is the avoidance of Federal tax.

(2) *Certain loans incident to sales or exchanges.* If, pursuant to a plan that is incident to a sale or exchange of property, a party who is related (within the meaning of section 168(e)(4)(D)) to the seller—

(i) Makes a below-market loan to the buyer of the property, or

Reg. § 1.7872-4(c)(3)

(ii) Makes a below-market loan to the seller that is assumed by the buyer in connection with the sale or exchange,

then the loan shall be treated as a tax avoidance loan within the meaning of paragraph (e)(1) of this section. There shall be an irrebuttable presumption that such a plan exists if such a loan is made within one year of the sale or exchange.

(3) *Examples.* The provisions of paragraph (e) of this section may be illustrated by the following examples:

Example (1). (i) S and T are each wholly-owned subsidiaries of P. S sells property to an individual, A, for cash of $3,000,000. Three months after the sale, T loans to A $2,000,000 for 10 years at an interest rate of 6%, payable semiannually. On the date the loan is made, the Federal long-term rate is 12%, compounded semiannually.

(ii) The loan from T to A is a tax avoidance loan pursuant to paragraph (e)(2) of this section. The issue price of the debt instrument given in exchange for the loan is $1,311,805, and the total amount of foregone interest is $688,195. On the date the loan is made, A is treated as having received a refund of $688,195 of the purchase price of the property from S, thereby reducing A's basis in the property by this amount. T is treated as having paid a dividend of $688,195 to P, and P is treated as having made a contribution to the capital of S in the same amount.

Example (2). The facts are the same as in example (1), except that T loans the $2,000,000 to S immediately before the sale. A purchases the property for cash of $1,000,000 and assumes S's debt to T. On the date of the sale, the Federal long-term rate is 12%, compounded semiannually. The loan from T to S is a tax-avoidance loan. The issue price of the debt instrument and the amount of foregone interest are the same as in example (1). A's basis in the property is limited to $2,311,805 (see § 1.1274-7(d)). T is treated as having paid a dividend of $688,195 to P, and P is treated as having made a contribution to the capital of S in the same amount.

(f) *Certain below-market loans with significant effect on tax liability ("significant-effect" loans)*—[Reserved].

(g) *Indirect loans*—(1) *In general.* If a below-market loan is made between two persons and, based on all the facts and circumstances, the effect of the loan is to make a gift or a capital contribution or a distribution of money (under section 301 or in the case of an S corporation, section 1368), or to pay compensation to a third person ("indirect participant"), or is otherwise attributable to the relationship of the lender or borrower to the indirect participant, the loan is restructured as two or more successive below-market loans ("deemed loans") for purposes of section 7872, as follows:

(i) A deemed below-market loan made by the named lender to the indirect participant; and

(ii) A deemed below-market loan made by the indirect participant to the borrower.

Section 7872 is applied separately to each deemed loan, and each deemed loan is treated as having the same provisions as the original loan between the lender and the borrower. Thus, for example, if a father makes an interest-free loan to his daughter's corporation, the loan is restructured as a below-market loan from father to daughter (deemed gift loan) and a second below-market loan from daughter to corporation (deemed corporation-shareholder loan). Similarly, if a corporation makes an interest-free loan to another commonly controlled corporation, the loan is restructured as a below-market loan from the lending corporation to the common parent corporation and a second below-market loan from the parent corporation to the borrowing corporation.

(2) *Special rule for intermediaries.* If a lender and a borrower use another person, such as an individual, a trust, a partnership, or a corporation, as an intermediary or middleman in a loan transaction and a purpose for such use is to avoid the application of section 7872(c)(1)(A), (B), or (C), the intermediary will be ignored and the loan will be treated as made directly between the lender and the borrower. Thus, for example, if a father and a son arrange their below-market loan transaction by having the father make a below-market loan to the father's partnership, followed by a second below-market loan (with substantially identical terms and conditions as the first loan) made by the partnership to the son, the two below-market loans will be restructured as one below-market loan from the father to the son. [Reg. § 1.7872-4.]

[Proposed 8-20-85 and 4-8-86.]

§ 1.7872-5T. Exempted loans (temporary).— (a) *In general*—(1) *General rule.* Except as provided in paragraph (a) (2) of this section, notwithstanding any other provision of section 7872 and the regulations thereunder, section 7872 does not apply to the loans listed in paragraph (b) of this section because the interest arrangements do not have a significant effect on the Federal tax liability of the borrower or the lender.

(2) *No exemption for tax avoidance loans.* If a taxpayer structures a transaction to be a loan described in paragraph (b) of this section and one of the principal purposes of so structuring the transaction is the avoidance of Federal tax, then the transaction will be recharacterized as a tax avoidance loan as defined in section 7872(c)(1)(D).

Reg. § 1.7872-5T(a)(2)

(b) *List of exemptions.* Except as provided in paragraph (a) of this section, the following transactions are exempt from section 7872:

(1) Loans which are made available by the lender to the general public on the same terms and conditions and which are consistent with the lender's customary business practice;

(2) Accounts or withdrawable shares with a bank (as defined in section 581), or an institution to which section 591 applies, or a credit union, made in the ordinary course of its business;

(3) Acquisitions of publicly traded debt obligations for an amount equal to the public trading price at the time of acquisition;

(4) Loans made by a life insurance company (as defined in section 816(a)), in the ordinary course of its business, to an insured, under a loan right contained in a life insurance policy and in which the cash surrender values are used as collateral for the loans;

(5) Loans subsidized by the Federal, State (including the District of Columbia), or Municipal government (or any agency or instrumentality thereof), and which are made available under a program of general application to the public;

(6) Employee-relocation loans that meet the requirements of paragraph (c)(1) of this section;

(7) Obligations the interest on which is excluded from gross income under section 103;

(8) Obligations of the United States government;

(9) Gift loans to a charitable organization (described in section 170(c)), but only if at no time during the taxable year will the aggregate outstanding amount of loans by the lender to that organization exceed $250,000. Charitable organizations which are effectively controlled, within the meaning of section 1.482-1(a)(1), by the same person or persons shall be considered one charitable organization for purposes of this limitation.

(10) Loans made to or from a foreign person that meet the requirements of paragraph (c)(2) of this section;

(11) Loans made by a private foundation or other organization described in section 170(c), the primary purpose of which is to accomplish one or more of the purposes described in section 170(c)(2)(B);

(12) Indebtedness subject to section 482, but such indebtedness is exempt from the application of section 7872 only during the interest-free period, if any, determined under § 1.482-2(a)(1)(iii) with respect to intercompany trade receivables described in § 1.482-2(a)(1)(ii)(A)(*ii*). See also § 1.482-2(a)(3);

(13) All money, securities, and property—

(i) Received by a futures commission merchant or registered broker/dealer or by a clearing organization (A) to margin, guarantee or secure contracts for future delivery on or subject to the rules of a qualified board or exchange (as defined in section 1256(g)(7)), or (B) to purchase, margin, guarantee or secure options contracts traded on or subject to the rules of a qualified board or exchange, so long as the amounts so received to purchase, margin, guarantee or secure such contracts for future delivery or such options contracts are reasonably necessary for such purposes and so long as any commissions received by the futures commission merchant, registered broker/dealer, or clearing organization are not reduced for those making deposits of money, and all money accruing to account holders as the result of such futures and options contracts or

(ii) Received by a clearing organization from a member thereof as a required deposit to a clearing fund, guaranty fund, or similar fund maintained by the clearing organization to protect it against defaults by members.

(14) Loans the interest arrangements of which the taxpayer is able to show have no significant effect of any Federal tax liability of the lender or the borrower, as described in paragraph (c)(3) of this section; and

(15) Loans, described in revenue rulings or revenue procedures issued under section 7872(g)(1)(C), if the Commissioner finds that the factors justifying an exemption for such loans are sufficiently similar to the factors justifying the exemptions contained in this section.

(c) *Special rules*—* * *

(3) *Loans without significant tax effect.* Whether a loan will be considered to be a loan the interest arrangements of which have a significant effect on any Federal tax liability of the lender or the borrower will be determined according to all of the facts and circumstances. Among the factors to be considered are—

(i) whether items of income and deduction generated by the loan offset each other;

(ii) the amount of such items;

(iii) the cost to the taxpayer of complying with the provisions of section 7872 if such section were applied; and

(iv) any non-tax reasons for deciding to structure the transaction as a below-market loan rather than a loan with interest at a rate equal to or greater than the applicable Federal rate and a payment by the lender to the borrower. [Temporary Reg. § 1.7872-5T.]

□ [*T.D. 8045, 8-15-85. Amended by T.D. 8093, 7-9-86 and T.D. 8204, 5-20-88.*]

Reg. § 1.7872-5T(b)(1)

INDEX TO CODE

References are to Code Section numbers.

COM

DIV